SOLIDWORKS 2021 for Engineers and Designers

Sham Tickoo
Professor
Purdue University Northwest
Hammond, Indiana, USA

Contributing Authors
Tickoo Institute of Emerging Technologies (TIET)
Gurugram, India

CADCIM Technologies
Indiana, USA

www.bpbonline.com

REPRINT 2023
ISBN: 9789391392598

Limits of Liability and Disclaimer of Warranty

The information contained in this book is the best of Author's & Publisher's knowledge. We are committed to serve students with best of our knowledge and resources. We have taken utmost care and attention while editing and printing of this book but Author and Publisher should not be held responsible for errors, omissions and any other unintentional mistake that might have crept in. However, errors brought to our notice shall be gratefully acknowledged and attended to.

All trademarks referred to in the book are acknowledged as properties of their respective owners. This book is written solely for the benefit and guidance of the students.

Distributors

COMPUTER BOOK CENTRE
12, Shrungar Shopping Centre
M.G. Road
BENGALURU–560001
Ph: 25587923/25584641

DECCAN AGENCIES
4-3-329, Bank Street
HYDERABAD-500195
Ph: 24756967/24756400

MICRO MEDIA
Shop No. 5, Mahendra Chambers
150 DN Rd. Next to Capital Cinema
V.T (C.S.T.) Station
MUMBAI-400001

BPB BOOK CENTRE
376 Old Lajpat Rai Market
DELHI-110006
Ph: 23861747

INFOTECH
G-2, Sidhartha Building, 96 Nehru Place
NEW DELHI-110019
Ph: 26438245

BPB PUBLICATIONS
20, Ansari Road, Darya Ganj
New Delhi-110002
Ph: 23254990/23254991

Published by Manish Jain for BPB Publications, 20 Ansari Road, Darya Ganj New Delhi-110002 and Printed by Manipal Technologies Limited, Manipal

DEDICATION

To teachers, who make it possible to disseminate knowledge to enlighten the young and curious minds of our future generations

To students, who are dedicated to learning new technologies and making the world a better place to live in

SPECIAL RECOGNITION

A special thanks to Mr. Denis Cadu and the ADN team of Autodesk Inc. for their valuable support and professional guidance to procure the software for writing this textbook

THANKS

To employees of CADCIM Technologies and Tickoo Institute of Emerging Technologies for their valuable help

This page is intentionally left blank

Table of Contents

Chapter 2: Drawing Sketches for Solid Models

Chapter 3: Editing and Modifying Sketches

Chapter 4: Adding Relations and Dimensions to Sketches

Chapter 5: Advanced Dimensioning Techniques and Base Feature Options

Chapter 6: Creating Reference Geometries

Chapter 7: Advanced Modeling Tools-I

Chapter 8: Advanced Modeling Tools-II

Chapter 9: Editing Features

Chapter 10: Advanced Modeling Tools-III

Chapter 11: Advanced Modeling Tools-IV

Chapter 12: Assembly Modeling-I

Chapter 13: Assembly Modeling-II

Chapter 14: Working with Drawing Views-I

Chapter 15: Working with Drawing Views-II

Chapter 16: Surface Modeling

Chapter 17: Working with Blocks

Chapter 18: Sheet Metal Design

Chapter 19: Equations, Configurations, and Library Features

PROJECTS AVAILABLE FOR FREE DOWNLOAD

In this textbook, four projects are available for free download. You can download these projects from our website **www.cadcim.com**.

To download these projects, follow the path: *Textbooks > CAD/CAM > SOLIDWORKS > SOLIDWORKS 2021 for Designers > Projects for Free Download* and then select the project name from the **Projects for Free Download** drop-down. Click the **Download** button to download the project in the PDF format.

Note

For additional projects, visit **www.cadcim.com** and follow the path: *Textbooks > CAD/CAM > Parametric Solid Modeling > Parametric Solid Modeling Projects*

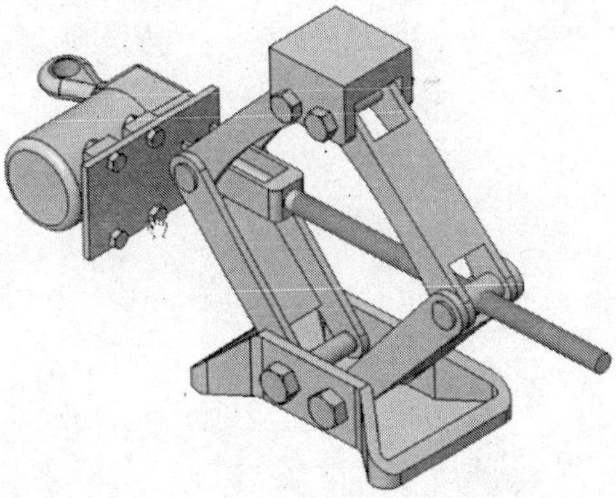

Project 1: *Car Jack Assembly*

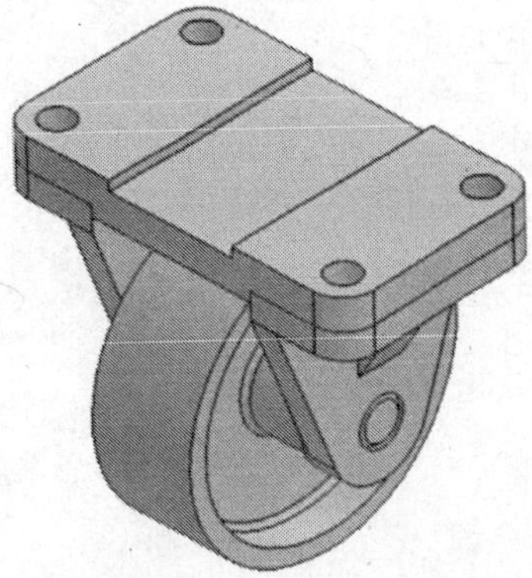

Project 2: *Wheel Assembly*

Project 3: *Angle Clamp Assembly*

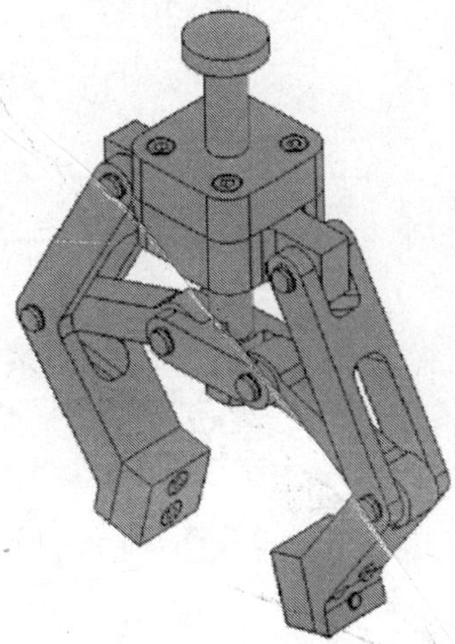

Project 4: *Pneumatic Gripper Assembly*

SOLIDWORKS Certification Exam

Preface

SOLIDWORKS 2021

SOLIDWORKS, originally developed by the SOLIDWORKS Corporation, USA, was acquired by Dassault Systemes, France, in 1997. Dassault Systemes is world's leading developer of product life cycle management (PLM) solutions. It is one of the fastest growing solid modeling software. It is a parametric, feature-based solid modeling tool that not only unites the three-dimensional (3D) parametric features with two-dimensional (2D) tools, but also addresses every design-through-manufacturing needs. SOLIDWORKS 2020 includes a number of customer requested enhancements, substantiating that it is completely tailored to address customers needs. Based mainly on the user feedback, this solid modeling tool is remarkably user-friendly and allows you to be productive from day one.

In SOLIDWORKS, you can easily generate the 2D drawing views of the components. The drawing views that can be generated include detailed, orthographic, isometric, auxiliary, section, and other views. You can use any predefined standard drawing document to generate the drawing views. Besides displaying the model dimensions in the drawing views or adding reference dimensions and other annotations, you can also add the parametric Bill of Materials (BOM) and balloons in the drawing view. If a component in the assembly is replaced, removed, or a new component is assembled, the modification will automatically reflect in the BOM placed in the drawing document. The bidirectional associative nature of this software ensures that any modification made in the model is automatically reflected in the drawing views and any modification made in the dimensions in the drawing views automatically updates the model.

In addition to creating solid models, assembly features, and drawing views, SOLIDWORKS enables you to effectively and easily create complex sheet metal components using a number of tools. Apart from modeling and detailing, you can print your solid models directly through 3D printers. You can also define position, orientation and other parameters of the model for 3D printing in SOLIDWORKS.

SOLIDWORKS 2021 for Engineers and Designers textbook has been written to help the users who are interested in learning 3D design. Real-world mechanical engineering industry examples and tutorials have been used to ensure that the users can relate the knowledge of this textbook with the actual mechanical industry designs. The textbook also includes one chapter on mold designing using SOLIDWORKS as well as four student projects for the students to practice. In addition, the book contains SOLIDWORKS Certification Exam questions as tutorials to acquaint user with certification questions and help them to get certified.

Some of the main features of the textbook are as follows:

- **Tutorial Approach**
  The author has adopted the tutorial point-of-view and the learn-by-doing approach throughout the textbook. This approach guides the users through the process of creating the models in the tutorials.

- **Real-world Mechanical Engineering Projects as Tutorials**
  The author has used the real-world mechanical engineering projects as tutorials in this textbook so that the readers can correlate the tutorials with the real-time models in the mechanical engineering industry.

- **Coverage of Major SOLIDWORKS Modes**
  All major modes of SOLIDWORKS are covered in this textbook. These include the **Part** mode, the **Assembly** mode, and the **Drawing** mode.

- **Tips and Notes**
  Additional information related to various topics is provided to the users in the form of tips and notes.

- **Learning Objectives**
  The first page of every chapter summarizes the topics that are covered in the chapter.

- **Self-Evaluation Test, Review Questions, and Exercises**
  Each chapter ends with Self-Evaluation Test that enables the users to assess their knowledge of the chapter. The answers to Self-Evaluation Test are given at the end of the chapter. Also, the Review Questions and Exercises are given at the end of the chapters and they can be used by the Instructors as test questions and exercises.

- **Heavily Illustrated Text**
  The text in this textbook is heavily illustrated with the help of around 800 line diagrams and 900 screen captures.

Symbols Used in this Textbook

Note

The author has provided additional information to the users about the topic being discussed in the form of Notes.

Tip

Special information on various techniques is provided in the form of Tips that will increase the efficiency of the users.

New

This icon indicates that the command or tool being discussed is new.

Enhanced

This icon indicates that the command or tool being discussed is enhanced.

Formatting Conventions Used in the Textbook

Please refer to the following list for the formatting conventions used in this textbook.

- Names of tools, buttons, options, toolbars, and are written in boldface.
  Example: The **Extrude Boss/Base** tool, the **Mid-Plane** option, the **OK** button, the **Features** toolbar, and so on.

- Names of CommandManager, PropertyManager, rollouts, dialog box, drop-down lists, spinners, selection boxes, areas, edit boxes, check boxes, and radio buttons are written in boldface.
  Example: The **Features CommandManager**, the **Boss-Extrude PropertyManager**, the **Open** dialog box, the **End Condition** drop-down list, the **Depth** spinner, the **Direction of Extrusion** selection box, the **Draft outward** check box, and so on.

- Values entered in edit boxes are written in boldface.
  Example: Enter **5** in the **Radius** edit box.

- Names and paths of the files are written in italics.
  Example: *C:\Documents\SOLIDWORKS\c08\c08_tut01*

Naming Conventions Used in the Textbook

Tool

If you click on an item in a toolbar and a command is invoked to create/edit an object or perform some action, then that item is termed as tool.

For example:
To Create: **Line** tool, **Smart Dimension** tool, **Extruded Boss/Base** tool
To Modify: **Fillet** tool, **Draft** tool, **Trim Surface** tool
Action: **Zoom to Fit** tool, **Pan** tool, **Copy** tool

If you click on an item in a toolbar and a dialog box is invoked wherein you can set the properties to create/edit an object, then that item is also termed as tool, refer to Figure 1.

For example:
To Create: Extruded Boss/Base tool, **Mirror** tool, **Rib** tool
To Modify: Flex tool, **Deform** tool

In this textbook, the path to invoke a tool is given as:

CommandManager:	Features > Extruded Boss/Base
SOLIDWORKS Menus:	Insert > Boss/Base > Extrude
Toolbar:	Features > Extruded Boss/Base

Flyout

A flyout is the one in which a set of tools are grouped together. You can identify a flyout with a down arrow on it. A flyout is given a name based on the types of tools grouped in it. For example, **Line** flyout, **View Settings** flyout, **Fillet** flyout, and so on; refer to Figure 1.

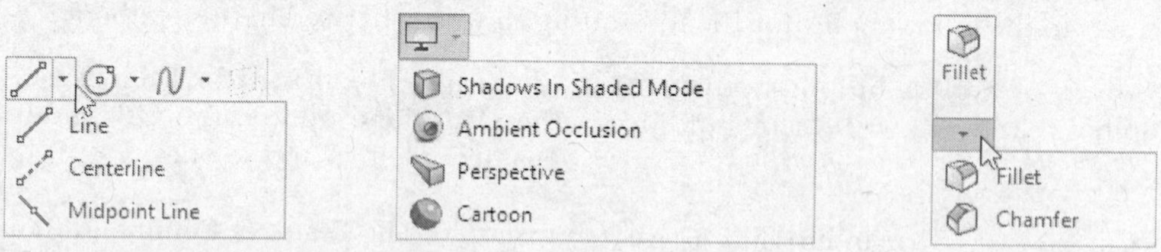

Figure 1 The ***Line, View Settings,*** *and* ***Fillet*** *flyouts*

PropertyManager

The naming conventions for the components in a PropertyManager are mentioned in Figure 2.

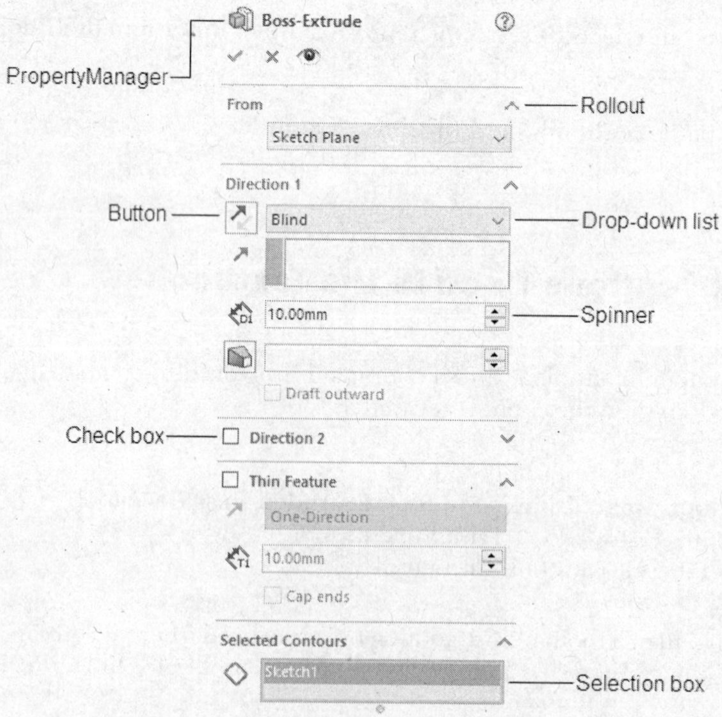

Figure 2 The ***Boss-Extrude PropertyManager***

Button

The items in a dialog box that has a 3D shape like a button is termed as **Button**. For example, **OK** button, **Cancel** button, and so on.

Free Companion Website

It has been our constant endeavor to provide you the best textbooks and services at affordable price. In this endeavor, we have come out with a Free Companion website that will facilitate the process of teaching and learning of SOLIDWORKS 2021. If you purchase this textbook, you will get access to the files on the Companion website.

Following resources are available in this website:

- **Technical Support**
  You can get online technical support by contacting ***techsupport@cadcim.com***.

- **Instructor Guide**
  Solutions to all review questions and exercises in the textbook are provided in the instructor guide to help the faculty members test the skills of the students.

- **Part Files and Input Files**
  The part files and Input files used in illustrations, examples, and exercises are available for free download.

You can access additional learning information by visiting ***https://allaboutcadcam.blogspot.com***.

If you face any problem in accessing these files, please contact the publisher at ***sales@cadcim.com*** or the author at ***Stickoo@pnw.edu*** or ***tickoo525@gmail.com***.

Video Courses

CADCIM offers video courses in CAD, CAE Simulation, BIM, Civil/GIS, and Animation domains on various e-Learning/Video platforms. To enroll for the video courses, please visit the CADCIM website using the link ***https://www.cadcim.com/video-courses***.

Stay Connected

You can now stay connected with us through Facebook and Twitter to get the latest information about our textbooks, videos, and teaching/learning resources. To stay informed of such updates, follow us on Facebook ***(www.facebook.com/cadcim)*** and Twitter (***@cadcimtech***). You can also subscribe to our YouTube channel ***(www.youtube.com/cadcimtech)*** to get the information about our latest video tutorials.

This page is intentionally left blank

Chapter 1

Introduction to SOLIDWORKS 2021

Learning Objectives

After completing this chapter, you will be able to:

- *Understand how to start SOLIDWORKS*
- *Understand the system requirements to run SOLIDWORKS*
- *Understand various modes of SOLIDWORKS*
- *Work with various CommandManagers of SOLIDWORKS*
- *Understand various important terms in SOLIDWORKS*
- *Save files automatically in SOLIDWORKS*
- *Change the color schemes in SOLIDWORKS*

INTRODUCTION TO SOLIDWORKS 2021

Welcome to the world of Computer Aided Design (CAD) with SOLIDWORKS. If you are a new user of this software package, you will be joining hands with thousands of users of this parametric, feature-based, and one of the most user-friendly software packages. If you are familiar with the previous releases of this software, you will be able to upgrade your designing skills with this improved release of SOLIDWORKS.

SOLIDWORKS, developed by the SOLIDWORKS Corporation, USA, is a feature-based, parametric solid-modeling mechanical design and automation software. SOLIDWORKS is the first CAD package to use the Microsoft Windows graphical user interface. The use of the drag and drop (DD) functionality of Windows makes this CAD package extremely easy to learn. The Windows graphic user interface makes it possible for the mechanical design engineers to innovate their ideas and implement them in the form of virtual prototypes or solid models, large assemblies, subassemblies, and detailing and drafting.

SOLIDWORKS is one of the products of SOLIDWORKS Corporation, which is a part of Dassault Systemes. SOLIDWORKS also works as platform software for a number of software. This implies that you can also use other compatible software within the SOLIDWORKS window. There are a number of software provided by the SOLIDWORKS Corporation, which can be used as add-ins with SOLIDWORKS. Some of the software that can be used on SOLIDWORKS's work platform are listed below:

SOLIDWORKS Motion	SOLIDWORKS Routing	ScanTo3D	eDrawings
SOLIDWORKS Simulation	SOLIDWORKS Toolbox	PhotoView 360	CircuitWorks
SOLIDWORKS Plastics	SOLIDWORKS Inspection	TolAnalyst	

As mentioned earlier, SOLIDWORKS is a parametric, feature-based, and easy-to-use mechanical design automation software. It enables you to convert the basic 2D sketch into a solid model by using simple but highly effective modeling tools. It also enables you to create the virtual prototype of a sheet metal component and the flat pattern of the component. This helps you in the complete process planning for designing and creating a press tool. SOLIDWORKS helps you to extract the core and the cavity of a model that has to be molded or cast. With SOLIDWORKS, you can also create complex parametric shapes in the form of surfaces. Some of the important modes of SOLIDWORKS are discussed next.

Part Mode

The **Part** mode of SOLIDWORKS is a feature-based parametric environment in which you can create solid models. In this mode, you are provided with three default planes named as **Front Plane**, **Top Plane**, and **Right Plane**. First, you need to select a sketching plane to create a sketch for the base feature. On selecting a sketching plane, you enter the sketching environment. The sketches for the model are drawn in the sketching environment using easy-to-use tools. After drawing the sketches, you can dimension them and apply the required relations in the same sketching environment. The design intent is captured easily by adding relations and equations and using the design table in the design. You are provided with the standard hole library known as the **Hole Wizard** in the **Part** mode. You can create simple holes, tapped holes, counterbore holes, countersink holes, and so on by using this wizard. The holes can be of any standard such as ISO, ANSI, JIS, and so on. You can also create complicated surfaces by using the surface modeling tools available in the **Part** mode. Annotations such as weld symbols, geometric tolerance, datum references, and surface finish symbols can be added to the model within the **Part** mode. The standard features that are used frequently can be saved as library features and retrieved when needed. The palette feature library of SOLIDWORKS contains a number of standard mechanical parts and features. You can also create the sheet metal components in this mode of SOLIDWORKS by using the related tools. Besides this, you can also analyze the part model for various stresses applied to it in the real physical conditions by using an easy and user-friendly tool called SimulationXpress. It helps you reduce the cost and time in physically testing your design in real testing conditions (destructive tests). You can also analyze the component during modeling in the SOLIDWORKS windows. In addition, you can work with the weld modeling within the **Part** mode of SOLIDWORKS by creating steel structures and adding weld beads. All standard weld types and welding conditions are available for your reference. You can extract the core and the cavity in the **Part** mode by using the mold design tools.

Assembly Mode

In the **Assembly** mode, you can assemble components of the assembly with the help of the required tools. There are two methods of assembling the components:

1. Bottom-up assembly
2. Top-down assembly

In the bottom-up assembly method, the assembly is created by assembling the components created earlier and maintaining their design intent. In the top-down method, the components are created in the assembly mode. You may begin with some ready-made parts and then create other components in the context of the assembly. You can refer to the features of some components of the assembly to drive the dimensions of other components. You can assemble all components of an assembly by using a single tool, the **Mate** tool. While assembling the components of an assembly, you can also animate the assembly by dragging. Besides this, you can also check the working of your assembly. Collision detection is one of the important features in this mode. Using this feature, you can rotate and move components as well as detect the interference and collision between the assembled components. You can see the realistic motion of the assembly by using physical dynamics. Physical simulation is used to simulate the assembly with the effects of motors, springs, and gravity on the assemblies.

Drawing Mode

The **Drawing** mode is used for the documentation of the parts or the assemblies created earlier in the form of drawing views. The procedure for creating drawing views is called drafting. There are two types of drafting done in SOLIDWORKS:

1. Generative drafting
2. Interactive drafting

Generative drafting is a process of generating drawing views of a part or an assembly created earlier. The parametric dimensions and the annotations added to the component in the **Part** mode can be generated in the drawing views. Generative drafting is bidirectionally associative in nature. Automatic BOMs and balloons can be added to an assembly while generating the drawing views of it.

In interactive drafting, you have to create the drawing views by sketching them using normal sketching tools and then add dimensions to them.

SYSTEM REQUIREMENTS

The system requirements to ensure the smooth functioning of SOLIDWORKS on your system are as follows:

- Microsoft Windows 10 (64-bit).
- Intel or AMD Processor with SSE2 support.
- 16 GB RAM minimum.
- Hard disk space 2 GB minimum (5 GB recommended).
- A certified graphics card and driver.
- A word processing program.
- Adobe Acrobat higher than 8.0.7 or any similar program.
- DVD drive and Mouse or any other compatible pointing device.
- Internet Explorer version 8 or higher.

GETTING STARTED WITH SOLIDWORKS

Install SOLIDWORKS 2021 on your system; on doing so, a shortcut icon of SOLIDWORKS 2021 will automatically be created on the desktop. Double-click on this icon; the system will prepare to start SOLIDWORKS and after sometime, the SOLIDWORKS window will be displayed on the screen. On opening SOLIDWORKS for the first time, the **SOLIDWORKS License Agreement** dialog box will be displayed, as shown in Figure 1-1. Choose the **Accept** button in this dialog box; the **SOLIDWORKS 2021** window will open and the **SOLIDWORKS Resources** task pane will be displayed on the right. Also, the **Welcome - SOLIDWORKS** dialog box will be invoked simultaneously, as shown in Figure 1-2. This window can be used to open a new file or an existing file.

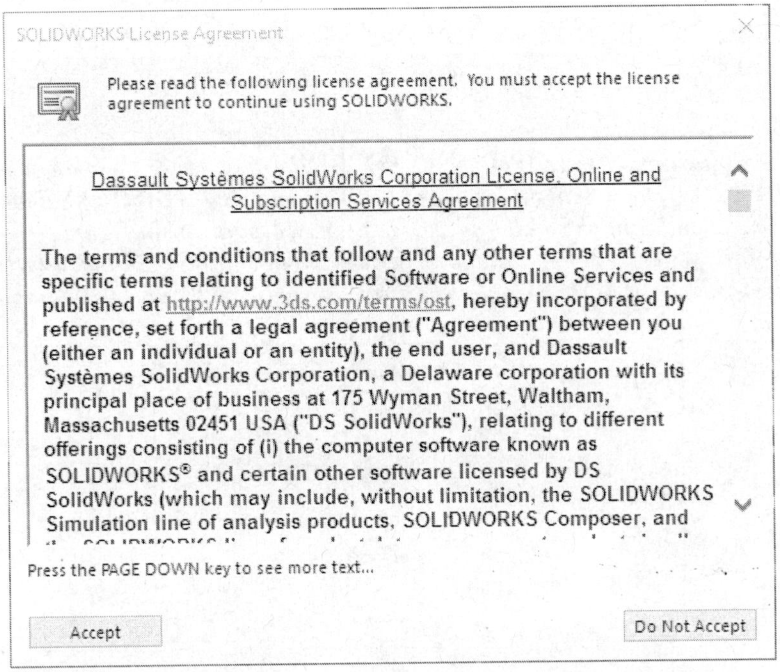

*Figure 1-1 The **SOLIDWORKS License Agreement** dialog box*

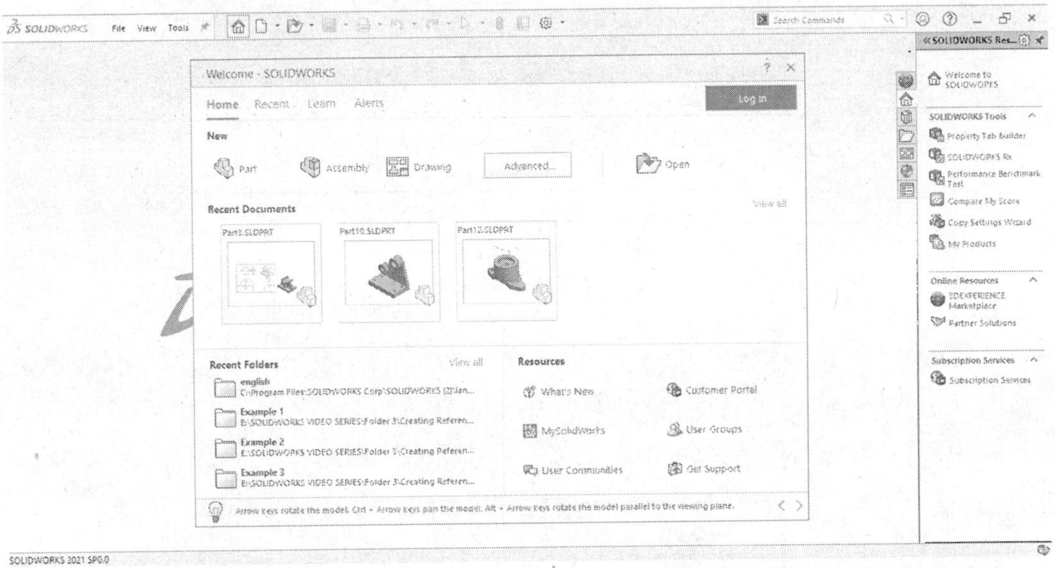

*Figure 1-2 The **SOLIDWORKS 2021** window and the **SOLIDWORKS Resources** task pane*

If the **SOLIDWORKS Resources** task pane is not displayed or expanded, choose the **SOLIDWORKS Resources** button located on the right side of the window to display it. This task pane can be used to open online tutorials and to visit the website of SOLIDWORKS partners. Choose the **Part** button from the **Welcome - SOLIDWORKS** dialog box or the **New** button from the Menu Bar to create a new document. If you start a new document using the **New** button from the Menu Bar then the **New SOLIDWORKS Document** dialog box will be displayed, as shown in Figure 1-3.

Note

If you are starting SOLIDWORKS 2021 for the first time, then on invoking the ***New SOLIDWORKS Document*** *dialog box or the* ***Welcome - SOLIDWORKS*** *dialog box, the* ***Units and Dimension Standard*** *dialog box will be displayed, as shown in Figure 1-4. Using this dialog box, you can specify the default units and dimension standards for SOLIDWORKS. In this book, the unit system used is MMGS (millimeter, gram, second) and the dimension standard used is ISO.*

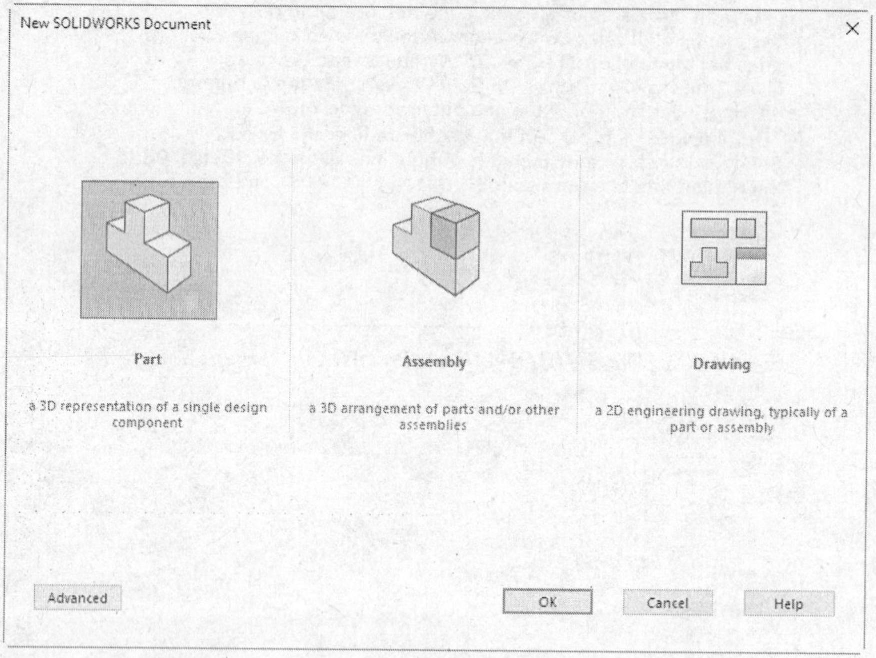

Figure 1-3 *The* ***New SOLIDWORKS Document*** *dialog box*

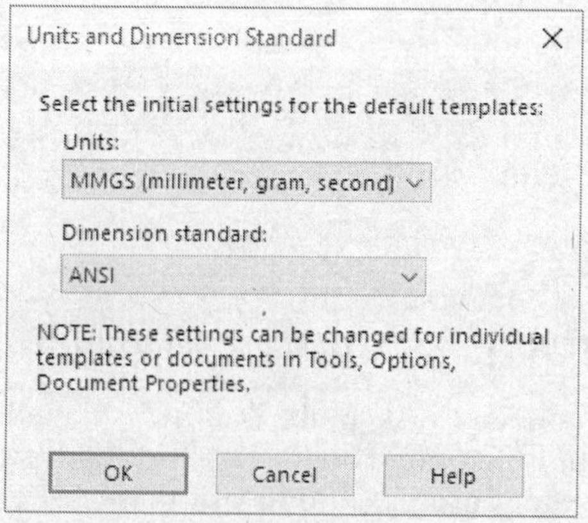

Figure 1-4 *The* ***Units and Dimension Standard*** *dialog box*

Choose the **Part** button to create a part model and then choose the **OK** button from the **New SOLIDWORKS Document** dialog box to enter the **Part** mode of SOLIDWORKS. Hover the cursor over the SOLIDWORKS logo; the SOLIDWORKS Menus will be displayed on the right of the logo. Note that the task pane is automatically closed once you start a new file and click in the drawing area. The initial screen display on starting a new part file of SOLIDWORKS using the **New** button in the Menu Bar is shown in Figure 1-5.

> **Tip**
> *In SOLIDWORKS, the tip of the day is displayed at the bottom of the* ***Welcome - SOLIDWORKS*** *dialog box. You can click on the arrows to view additional tips. These tips help you use SOLIDWORKS efficiently. It is recommended that you view at least 2 or 3 tips every time you start a new session of SOLIDWORKS 2021.*

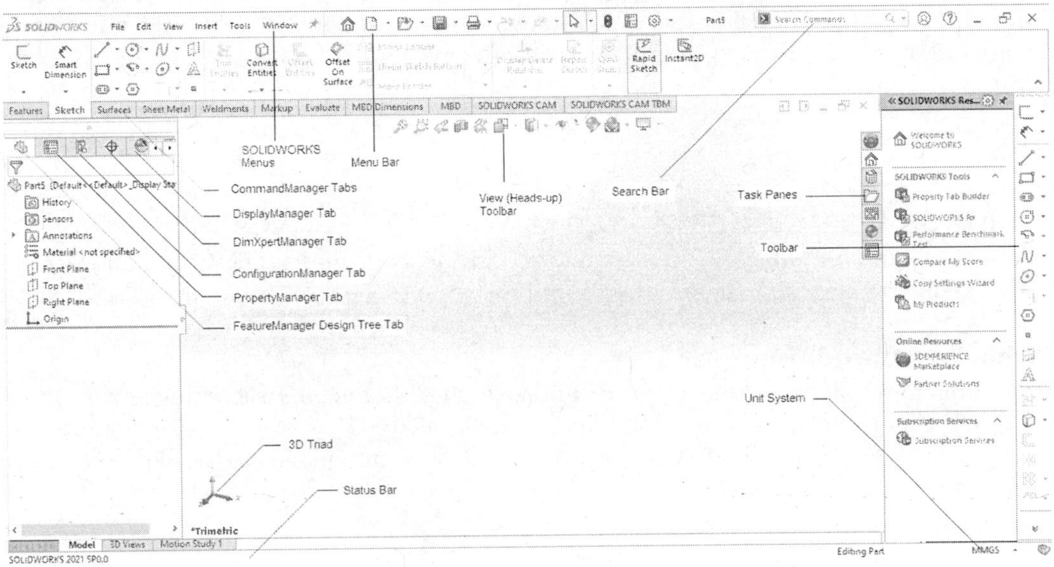

Figure 1-5 *The components of a new part document*

It is evident from the screen that SOLIDWORKS is a very user-friendly solid modeling software. Apart from the default CommandManager shown in Figure 1-5, you can also invoke other CommandManagers. To do so, move the cursor on a CommandManager tab and right-click; a shortcut menu will be displayed. Choose the required CommandManager from the shortcut menu; it will be added. Besides the existing CommandManager, you can also create a new CommandManager.

MENU BAR AND SOLIDWORKS MENUS

In SOLIDWORKS, the display area of the screen has been increased by grouping the tools that have similar functions or purposes. For example, the tools that are in the **Standard** toolbar are also available in the Menu Bar, as shown in Figure 1-6. This toolbar is available above the drawing area. When you move the cursor to the arrow on the right of the SOLIDWORKS logo, the SOLIDWORKS menus will be displayed as shown in Figure 1-7. You can also fix them by choosing the push-pin button.

Figure 1-6 The Menu Bar

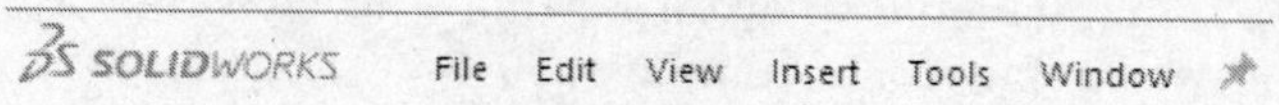

Figure 1-7 The SOLIDWORKS menus

CommandManager

You can invoke a tool in SOLIDWORKS from four locations, CommandManager, SOLIDWORKS menus on top of the screen, toolbar, and shortcut menu. The CommandManagers are docked above the drawing area. While working with CommandManager, you will realize that invoking a tool from the CommandManager is the most convenient method to invoke a tool. Different types of CommandManagers are used for different design environments. These CommandManagers are discussed next.

Part Mode CommandManagers

A number of CommandManagers can be invoked in the **Part** mode. The CommandManagers that are extensively used during the designing process in this environment are described next.

Sketch CommandManager

This CommandManager is used to enter and exit the 2D and 3D sketching environments. The tools available in this CommandManager are used to draw sketches for features. This CommandManager is also used to add relations and smart dimensions to the sketched entities. The **Sketch CommandManager** is shown in Figure 1-8.

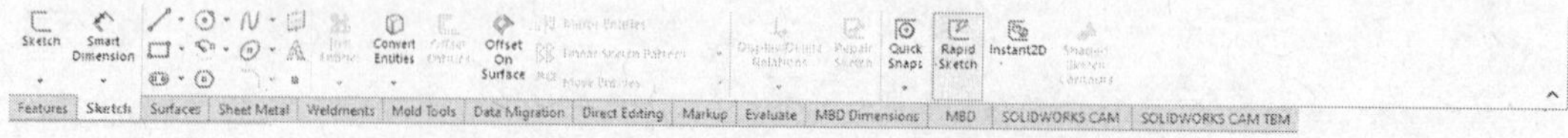

*Figure 1-8 The **Sketch CommandManager***

Tip

You can collapse the CommandManager to show only the tabs until you want to access the tools.

*To collapse the CommandManager, click on the **Collapse CommandManager** button available at the right of the Ribbon, refer to Figure 1-8. In the collapsed view, click a tab to expand the CommandManager and access the tools. In the expanded view, click on the **Pin CommandManager** button to keep the CommandManager expanded.*

Features CommandManager

This is one of the most important CommandManagers provided in the **Part** mode. Once the sketch has been drawn, you need to convert the sketch into a feature by using the modeling tools. This CommandManager contains all the modeling tools that are used for feature-based solid modeling. The **Features CommandManager** is shown in Figure 1-9.

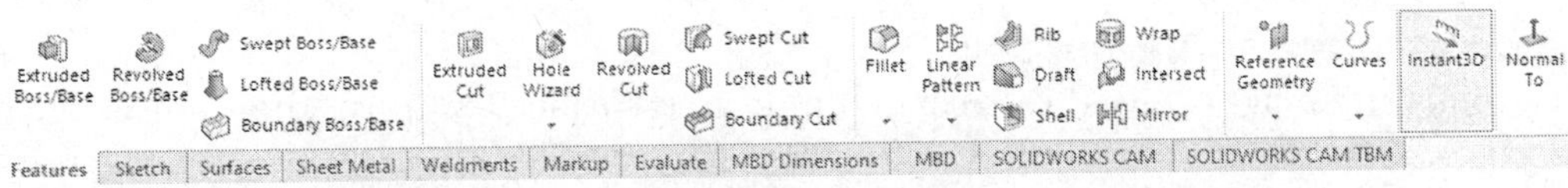

*Figure 1-9 The **Features CommandManager***

MBD Dimensions CommandManager

This CommandManager is used to add dimensions and tolerances to the features of a part. The **MBD Dimensions CommandManager** is shown in Figure 1-10.

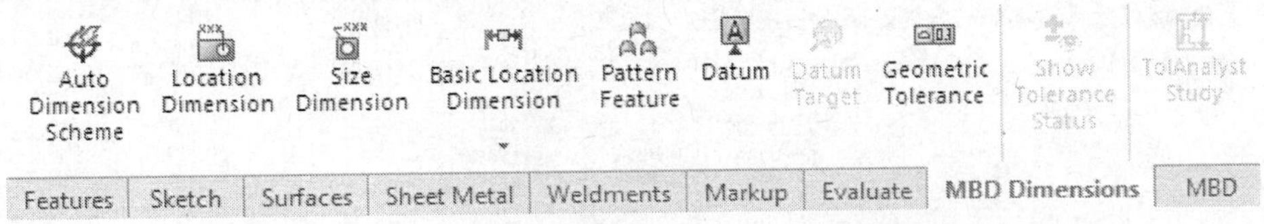

*Figure 1-10 The **MBD Dimensions CommandManager***

Sheet Metal CommandManager

This CommandManager provides you the tools that are used to create the sheet metal parts. In SOLIDWORKS, you can also create sheet metal parts while working in the **Part** mode. This is done with the help of the **Sheet Metal CommandManager** shown in Figure 1-11.

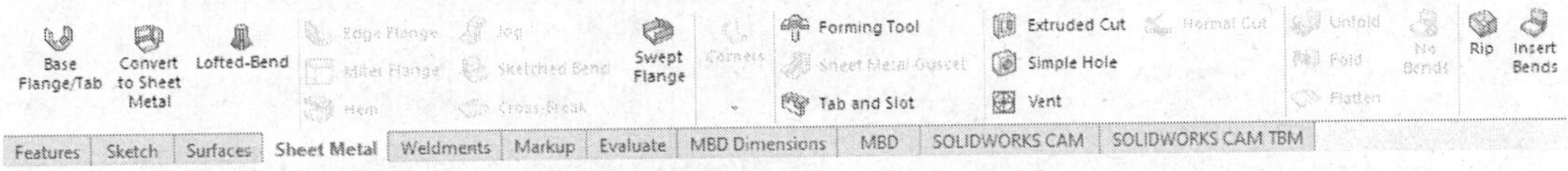

*Figure 1-11 The **Sheet Metal CommandManager***

Mold Tools CommandManager

The tools in this CommandManager are used to design a mold and to extract its core and cavity. The **Mold Tools CommandManager** is shown in Figure 1-12.

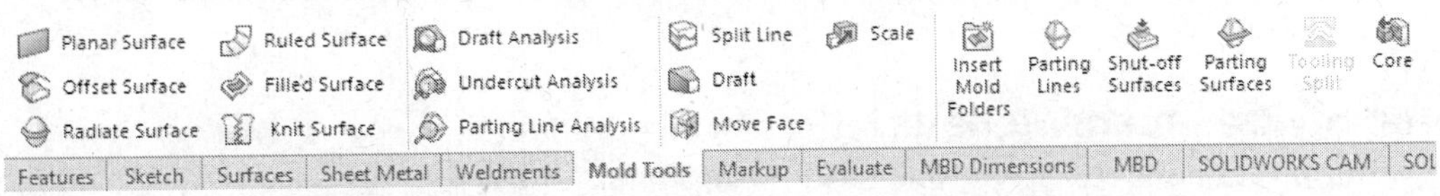

*Figure 1-12 The **Mold Tools CommandManager***

Evaluate CommandManager

This CommandManager is used to measure the distance between two entities, add equations in the design, calculate the mass properties of a solid model, and so on. The **Evaluate CommandManager** is shown in Figure 1-13.

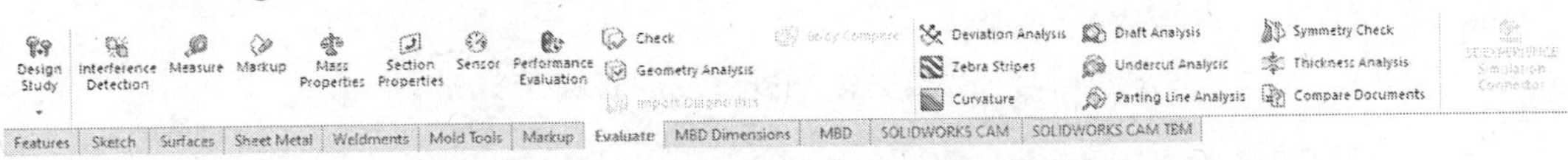

*Figure 1-13 The **Evaluate CommandManager***

Surfaces CommandManager

This CommandManager is used to create complicated surface features. These surface features can be converted into solid features. The **Surfaces CommandManager** is shown in Figure 1-14.

*Figure 1-14 The **Surfaces CommandManager***

Direct Editing CommandManager

This CommandManager consists of tools that are used for editing a feature, refer to Figure 1-15.

*Figure 1-15 The **Direct Editing CommandManager***

Data Migration CommandManager

This CommandManager consist of tools that are used to work with the models created in other packages or in different environments, refer to Figure 1-16.

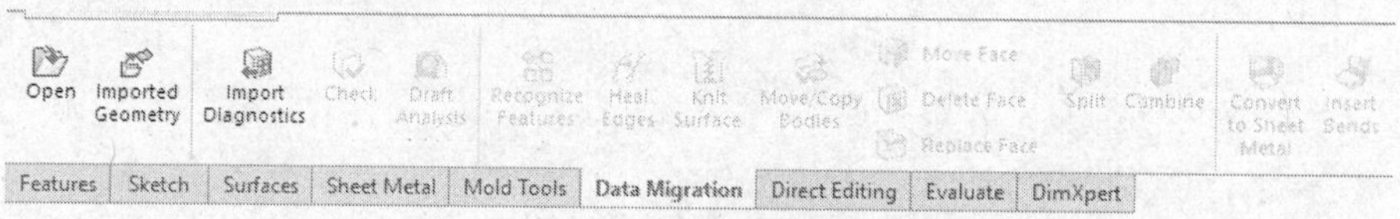

*Figure 1-16 The **Data Migration CommandManager***

Assembly Mode CommandManagers

The CommandManagers in the **Assembly** mode are used to assemble the components, create an explode line sketch, and simulate the assembly. The CommandManagers in the **Assembly** mode are discussed next.

Assembly CommandManager

This CommandManager is used to insert a component and apply various types of mates to the assembly. Mates are the constraints that can be applied to components to restrict their degrees of freedom. You can also move and rotate a component in the assembly, change the hidden and suppression states of the assembly and individual components, edit the component of an assembly, and so on. The **Assembly CommandManager** is shown in Figure 1-17.

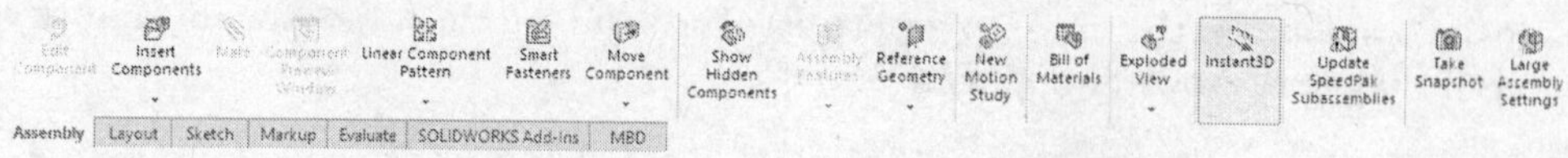

*Figure 1-17 The **Assembly CommandManager***

Layout CommandManager

The tools in this CommandManager are used to create and edit blocks, refer to Figure 1-18.

Figure 1-18 The Layout CommandManager

Drawing Mode CommandManagers

You can invoke a number of CommandManagers in the **Drawing** mode. The CommandManagers that are extensively used during the designing process in this mode are discussed next.

Drawing CommandManager

This CommandManager is used to generate the drawing views of an existing model or an assembly. The views that can be generated using this CommandManager are model view, three standard views, projected view, section view, aligned section view, detail view, crop view, relative view, auxiliary view, and so on. The **Drawing CommandManager** is shown in Figure 1-19.

Figure 1-19 The Drawing CommandManager

Annotation CommandManager

The **Annotation CommandManager** is used to generate the model items and to add notes, balloons, geometric tolerance, surface finish symbols, and so on to the drawing views. The **Annotation CommandManager** is shown in Figure 1-20.

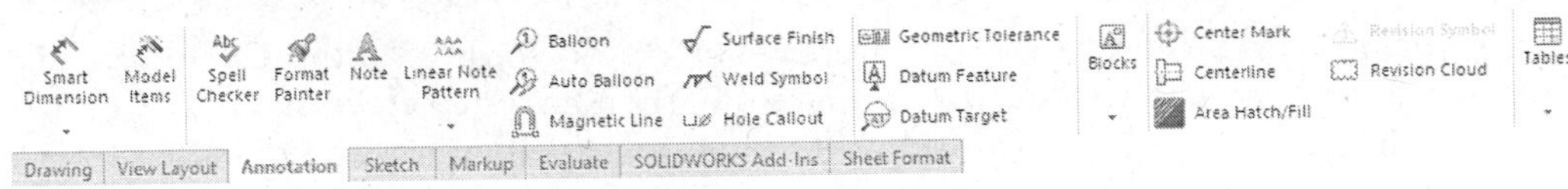

Figure 1-20 The Annotation CommandManager

Customized CommandManager

If you often work on a particular set of tools, you can create a customized CommandManager to cater to your needs. To do so, right-click on a tab in the CommandManager; a shortcut menu will be displayed. Choose the **Customize** option from the shortcut menu; the **Customize** dialog box will be displayed. Also, a new tab will be added to the CommandManager. Click on this tab; a flyout will be displayed with **Empty Tab** as the first option and followed by the list of toolbars. Choose the **Empty Tab** option; another tab named **New Tab** will be added to the CommandManager. Rename the new tab. Next, choose the **Commands** tab from the **Customize** dialog box. Select a category from the **Toolbars** list box; the tools under the selected category will be displayed in the **Buttons** area. Select a tool, press and hold the left mouse button, and drag the tool to the customized CommandManager; the tool will be added to the customized CommandManager. Choose the **OK** button from the **Customize** dialog box.

To add all the tools of a toolbar to the new CommandManager, invoke the **Customize** dialog box and click on the new tab; a flyout will be displayed with **Empty Tab** as the first option followed by the list of toolbars. Choose a toolbar from the flyout; all tools in the toolbar will be added to the **New Tab** and its name will be changed to that of the toolbar.

To delete a customized CommandManager, invoke the **Customize** dialog box as discussed earlier. Next, choose the CommandManager tab to be deleted and right-click; a shortcut menu will be displayed. Choose the **Delete** option from the shortcut menu; the CommandManager will be deleted.

Note

You cannot delete the default CommandManagers.

TOOLBAR

In SOLIDWORKS, you can choose most of the tools from the CommandManager or from the SOLIDWORKS menus. However, if you hide the CommandManager to increase the drawing area, you can use the toolbars to invoke a tool. To display a toolbar, right-click on the CommandManager; the list of toolbars available in SOLIDWORKS will be displayed. Select the required toolbar.

Pop-up Toolbar

A pop-up toolbar will be displayed when you select a feature or an entity and do not move the mouse. Figure 1-21 shows a pop-up toolbar displayed on selecting a feature. Remember that this toolbar will disappear if you move the cursor away from the selected feature or entity.

Figure 1-21 *The pop-up toolbar*

You can switch off the display of the pop-up toolbar. To do so, invoke the **Customize** dialog box. In the **Context toolbar** area of the **Toolbars** tab, the **Show on selection** check box will be selected by default. It means that the display of the pop-up toolbar is on, by default. To turn off the display of the pop-up toolbar, clear this check box and choose the **OK** button.

View (Heads-Up) Toolbar

In SOLIDWORKS, some of the display tools have been grouped together and are displayed in the drawing area in a toolbar, as shown in Figure 1-22. This toolbar is known as **View (Heads-Up)** toolbar.

Figure 1-22 *The* ***View (Heads-Up)*** *toolbar*

Customizing the CommandManagers and Toolbars

In SOLIDWORKS, all buttons are not displayed by default in toolbars or CommandManagers. You need to customize and add buttons to them according to your need and specifications. Follow the procedure given below to customize the CommandManagers and toolbars:

1. Choose **Tools > Customize** from the SOLIDWORKS menus or right-click on a CommandManager and choose the **Customize** option to display the **Customize** dialog box.
2. Choose the **Commands** tab from the **Customize** dialog box.
3. Select a category from the **Toolbars** list box of the **Customize** dialog box; the tools available in the selected category will be displayed in the **Buttons** area.

4. Click on a button in the **Buttons** area; the description of the selected button will be displayed in the **Description** area.
5. Press and hold the left mouse button on a button in the **Buttons** area of the **Customize** dialog box.
6. Drag the mouse to a CommandManager or a toolbar and then release the left mouse button to place the button on that CommandManager or toolbar. Next, choose **OK**.

To remove a tool from the CommandManager or toolbar, invoke the **Customize** dialog box and drag the tool that you need to remove from the CommandManager to the graphics area.

Shortcut Bar

On pressing the S key on the keyboard, some of the tools that can be used in the current mode will be displayed near the cursor. This is called as shortcut bar. To customize the tools in the shortcut bar, right-click on it, and choose the **Customize** option. Then, follow the procedure discussed earlier.

Mouse Gestures

In SOLIDWORKS, when you press the right mouse button and drag the cursor in any direction, a set of tools that are arranged radially will be displayed. This is called as Mouse Gesture. After displaying the tools by using the Mouse Gesture, move the cursor over a particular tool to invoke it. By default, four tools will be displayed in a Mouse Gesture. However, you can customize the Mouse Gesture and display 2, 3, 4, 8 or 12 tools. To customize a Mouse Gesture, invoke the **Customize** dialog box. Next, choose the **Mouse Gestures** tab; the **Mouse Gesture Guide** window will be displayed, showing various tools that are used in different environments, refer to Figure 1-23. Now you can drag and drop the required tools to this window. Next, specify the options in the appropriate field and choose the **OK** button.

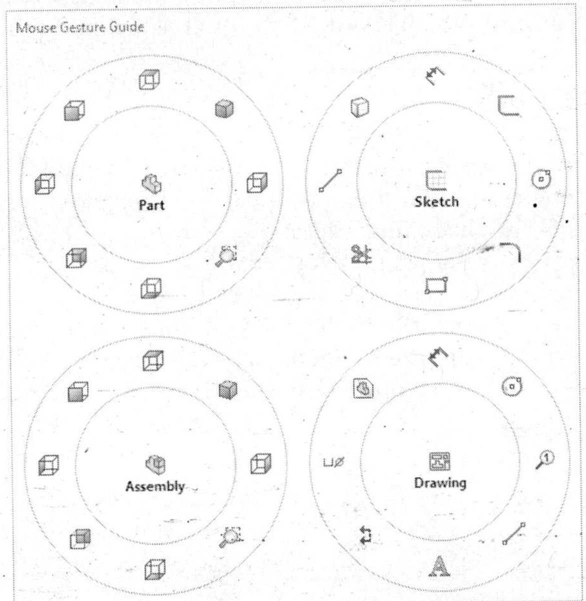

Figure 1-23 *Tools displayed in the* ***Mouse Gesture Guide*** *window in different environments*

Tip

You can display some of the tools by pressing a key on the keyboard. To assign a shortcut key to a tool, invoke the ***Customize*** *toolbar and choose the* ***Keyboard*** *tab. Enter the key in the* ***Shortcut*** *column for the corresponding tool and choose* ***OK****.*

DIMENSIONING STANDARDS AND UNITS

While installing SOLIDWORKS on your system, you can specify the units and dimensioning standards for dimensioning the model. There are various dimensioning standards such as ANSI, ISO, DIN, JIS, BSI, and GOST that can be specified for dimensioning a model and units such as millimeters, centimeters, inches, and so on. This book follows millimeters as the unit for dimensioning and ISO as the dimension standard. Therefore, it is recommended that you install SOLIDWORKS with ISO as the dimensioning standard and millimeter as units.

IMPORTANT TERMS AND THEIR DEFINITIONS

Before you proceed, it is very important to understand the following terms as they have been widely used in this book.

Feature-based Modeling

A feature is defined as the smallest building block that can be modified individually. In SOLIDWORKS, the solid models are created by integrating a number of these building blocks. A model created in SOLIDWORKS is a combination of a number of individual features that are related to one another, directly or indirectly. These features understand their fits and functions properly and therefore can be modified at any time during the design process. If proper design intent is maintained while creating the model, these features automatically adjust their values to any change in their surrounding. This provides greater flexibility to the design.

Parametric Modeling

The parametric nature of a software package is defined as its ability to use the standard properties or parameters in defining the shape and size of a geometry. The main function of this property is to drive the selected geometry to a new size or shape without considering its original dimensions. You can change or modify the shape and size of any feature at any stage of the design process. This property makes the designing process very easy.

For example, consider the design of the body of a pipe housing shown in Figure 1-24. In order to change the design by modifying the diameter of the holes and the number of holes on the front, top, and bottom faces, you need to select the feature and change the diameter and the number of instances in the pattern. The modified design is shown in Figure 1-25.

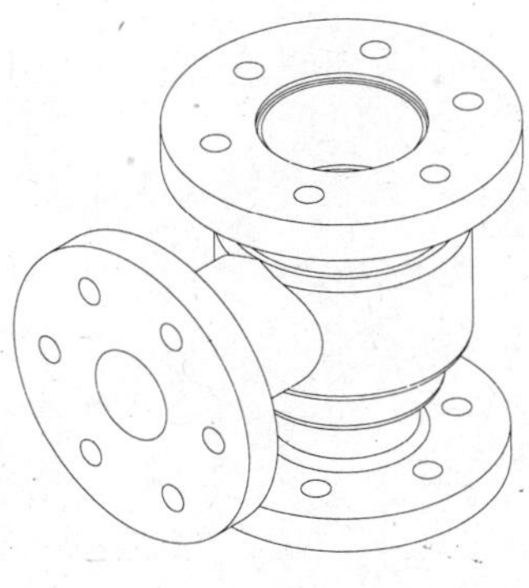

Figure 1-24 *Body of pipe housing*

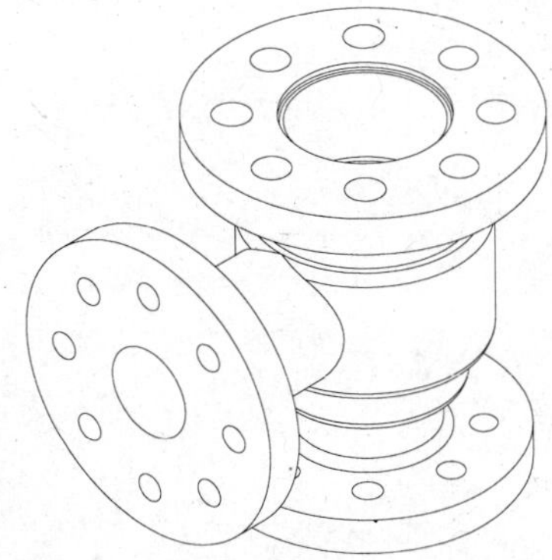

Figure 1-25 *Design after modifications*

Bidirectional Associativity

As mentioned earlier, SOLIDWORKS has different modes such as **Part**, **Assembly**, and **Drawing**. There exists bidirectional associativity among all these modes. This associativity ensures that any modification made in the model in any one of these modes of SOLIDWORKS is automatically reflected in the other modes immediately. For example, if you modify the dimension of a part in the **Part** mode, the change will reflect in the **Assembly** and **Drawing** modes as well. Similarly, if you modify the dimensions of a part in the drawing views generated in the **Drawing** mode, the changes will reflect in the **Part** and **Assembly** modes. Consider the drawing views shown in Figure 1-26 of the body of the pipe housing shown in Figure 1-24. Now, when you modify the model of the body of the pipe housing in the **Part** mode, the changes will reflect in the **Drawing** mode automatically. Figure 1-27 shows the drawing views of the pipe housing after increasing the diameter and the number of holes.

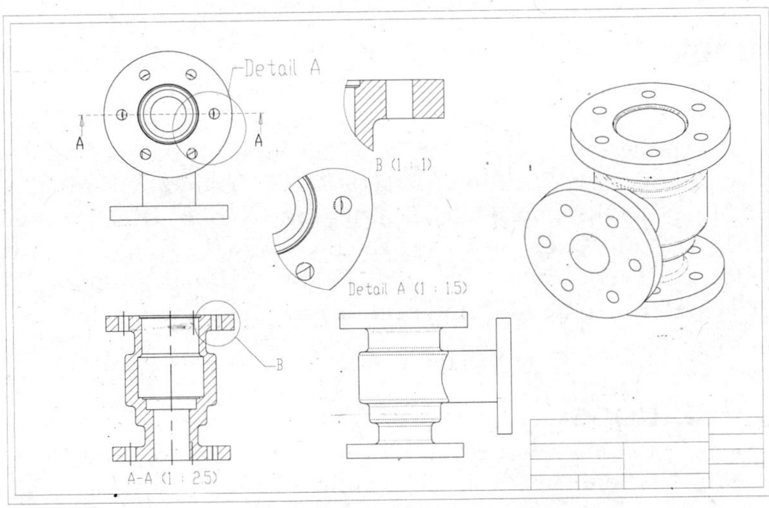

Figure 1-26 *Drawing views of the body part*

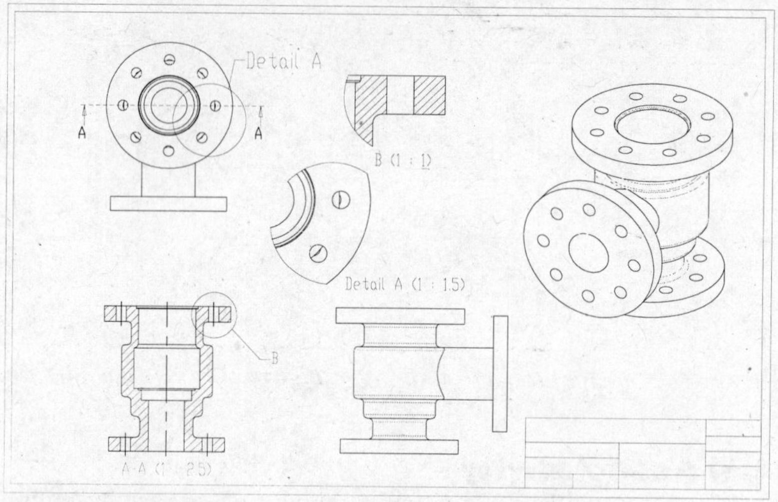

Figure 1-27 Drawing views after modifications

Windows Functionality

SOLIDWORKS is a Windows-based 3D CAD package. It uses Window's graphical user interface and the functionalities such as drag and drop, copy paste, and so on. For example, consider that you have created a hole feature on the front planar surface of a model. Now, to create another hole feature on the top planar surface of the same model, select the hole feature and press CTRL+C (copy) on the keyboard. Next, select the top planar surface of the base feature and press CTRL+V (paste); the copied hole feature will be pasted on the selected face. You can also drag and drop the standard features from the **Design Library** task pane to the face of the model on which the feature is to be added.

SWIFT Technology

SWIFT is the acronym for SOLIDWORKS Intelligent Feature Technology. This technology makes SOLIDWORKS more user-friendly. This technology helps the user think more about the design rather than the tools in the software. Therefore, even the novice users find it very easy to use SOLIDWORKS for their design. The tools that use SWIFT Technology are called as *Xperts*. The different *Xperts* in SOLIDWORKS are **SketchXpert**, **FeatureXpert**, **DimXpert**, **AssemblyXpert**, **FilletXpert**, **DraftXpert**, and **MateXpert**. The **SketchXpert** in the sketching environment is used to resolve the conflicts that arise while applying relations to a sketch. Similarly, the **FeatureXpert** in the Part mode is used when the fillet and draft features fail. You will learn about these tools in the later chapters.

Geometric Relations

Geometric relations are the logical operations that are performed to add a relationship (like tangent or perpendicular) between the sketched entities, planes, axes, edges, or vertices. When adding relations, one entity can be a sketched entity and the other entity can be a sketched entity, or an edge, face, vertex, origin, plane, and so on. There are two methods to create the geometric relations: Automatic Relations and Add Relations.

Automatic Relations

The sketching environment of SOLIDWORKS has been provided with the facility of applying auto relations. This facility ensures that the geometric relations are applied to the sketch automatically while creating it. Automatic relations are also applied in the **Drawing** mode while working with interactive drafting.

Add Relations

Add relations is used to add geometric relations manually to the sketch. The sixteen types of geometric relations that can be manually applied to the sketch are as follows:

Horizontal

This relation forces the selected line segment to become a horizontal line. You can also select two points and force them to be aligned horizontally.

Vertical

This relation forces the selected line segment to become a vertical line. You can also select two points and force them to be aligned vertically.

Collinear

This relation forces the two selected entities to be placed in the same line.

Coradial

This relation is applied to any two selected arcs, two circles, or an arc and a circle to force them to become equi-radius and also to share the same center point.

Perpendicular

This relation is used to make selected line segment perpendicular to another selected segment.

Parallel

This relation is used to make the selected line segment parallel to another selected segment.

Tangent

This relation is used to make the selected line segment, arc, spline, circle, or ellipse tangent to another arc, circle, spline, or ellipse.

Note

In case of splines, relations are applied to their control points.

Concentric

This relation forces two selected arcs, circles, a point and an arc, a point and a circle, or an arc and a circle to share the same center point.

Midpoint

This relation forces a selected point to be placed on the mid point of a selected line.

Intersection

This relation forces a selected point to be placed at the intersection of two selected entities.

Coincident
This relation is used to make two points, a point and a line, or a point and an arc coincident.

Equal
The equal relation forces the two selected lines to become equal in length. This relation is also used to force two arcs, two circles, or an arc and a circle to have equal radii.

Symmetric
The symmetric relation is used to force the selected entities to become symmetrical about a selected center line, so that they remain equidistant from the center line.

Fix
This relation is used to fix the selected entity to a particular location with respect to the coordinate system. The endpoints of the fixed line, arc, spline, or elliptical segment are free to move along the line.

Pierce
This relation forces the sketched point to be coincident to the selected axis, edge, or curve where it pierces the sketch plane. The sketched point in this relation can be the end point of the sketched entity.

Merge
This relation is used to merge two sketched points or end points of entities.

Blocks
A block is a set of entities grouped together to act as a single entity. Blocks are used to create complex mechanisms as sketches and check their functioning before developing them into complex 3D models.

Library Feature
Generally, in a mechanical design, some features are used frequently. In most of the other solid modeling tools, you need to create these features whenever you need them. However, SOLIDWORKS allows you to save these features in a library so that you can retrieve them whenever you want. This saves a lot of designing time and effort of a designer.

Design Table
Design tables are used to create a multi-instance parametric component. For example, some components in your organization may have the same geometry but different dimensions. Instead of creating each component of the same geometry with a different size, you can create one component and then using the design table, create different instances of the component by changing the dimension as per your requirement. You can access all these components in a single part file.

Equations
Equations are the analytical and numerical formulae applied to the dimensions during the sketching of the feature sketch or after sketching the feature sketch. The equations can also be applied to the placed features.

Collision Detection

Collision detection is used to detect interference and collision between the parts of an assembly when the assembly is in motion. While creating the assembly in SOLIDWORKS, you can detect collision between parts by moving and rotating them.

What's Wrong Functionality

While creating a feature of the model or after editing a feature, if the geometry of the feature is not compatible and the system is not able to construct that feature, then the **What's Wrong** functionality is used to detect the possible error that may have occurred while creating the feature.

SimulationXpress

In SOLIDWORKS, you are provided with an analysis tool named as SimulationXpress, which is used to execute the static or stress analysis. In SimulationXpress, you can only execute the linear static analysis. Using the linear static analysis, you can calculate the displacement, strain, and stresses applied on a component with the effect of material, various loading conditions, and restraint conditions applied on a model. A component fails when the stress applied on it reaches beyond a certain permissible limit. The Static Nodal stress plot of the crane hook designed in SOLIDWORKS and analyzed using SimulationXpress is shown in Figure 1-28.

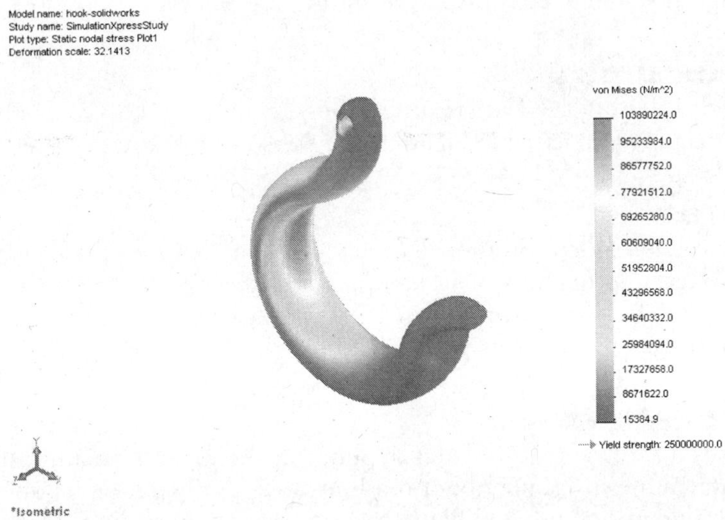

Figure 1-28 *The crane hook analyzed using SimulationXpress*

Physical Dynamics

The Physical Dynamics is used to observe the motion of the assembly. With this option selected, the component dragged in the assembly applies a force to the component that it touches. As a result, the other component moves or rotates within its allowable degrees of freedom.

Physical Simulation

The Physical Simulation is used to simulate the assemblies created in the assembly environment of SOLIDWORKS. You can assign and simulate the effect of different simulation elements such as linear, rotary motors, and gravity to the assemblies. After creating a simulating assembly, you can record and replay the simulation.

Seed Feature

The original feature that is used as the parent feature to create any type of pattern or mirror feature is known as the seed feature. You can edit or modify only a seed feature. You cannot edit the instances of the pattern feature.

FeatureManager Design Tree

The **FeatureManager Design Tree** is one the most important components of SOLIDWORKS screen. It contains information about default planes, materials, lights, and all the features that are added to the model. When you add features to the model using various modeling tools, the same are also displayed in the **FeatureManager Design Tree**. You can easily select and edit the features using the **FeatureManager Design Tree**. When you invoke any tool to create a feature, the **FeatureManager Design Tree** is replaced by the respective PropertyManager. At this stage, the **FeatureManager Design Tree** is displayed in the drawing area.

Absorbed Features

Features that are directly involved in creating other features are known as absorbed features. For example, the sketch of an extruded feature is an absorbed feature of the extruded feature.

Child Features

The features that are dependent on their parent feature and cannot exist without their parent features are known as child features. For example, consider a model with extrude feature and filleted edges. If you delete the extrude feature, the fillet feature will also get deleted because its existence is not possible without its parent feature.

Dependent Features

Dependent features are those features that depend on their parent feature but can still exist without the parent feature with some minor modifications. If the parent feature is deleted, then by specifying other references and modifying the feature, you can retain the dependent features.

AUTO-BACKUP OPTION

SOLIDWORKS also allows you to set the option to save the SOLIDWORKS document automatically after a regular interval of time. While working on a design project, if the system crashes, you may lose the unsaved design data. If the auto-backup option is turned on, your data will be saved automatically after regular intervals. To turn this option on, choose **Tools > Options** from the SOLIDWORKS menus; the **System Options - General** dialog box will be displayed. Select the **Backup/Recover** option from the display area provided on the left of this dialog box. Next, choose the **Save auto-recover information every** check box in the **Auto-recover** area, if it is not chosen by default. On doing so, the spinner and the drop-down list provided on the right of the check box will be enabled. Use the spinner and the drop-down list to set the number of changes or minutes after which the document will be saved automatically. By default, the backup files are saved at the location *X:\Users\<name of your machine>AppData\Local\TempSWBackupDirectory\swxauto* (where *X* is the drive in which you have installed SOLIDWORKS 2021 and the *AppData* folder is a hidden folder). You can also change the path of this location. To change this path, choose the button provided on the right of the edit box; the **Select Folder** dialog box will be displayed. You can specify the location of the folder to save the backup files using this dialog box. If you need to save the backup files in the current folder, select the **Number of backup copies per document** check box and then select the **Save backup files in the same location as the original** radio button. You can set the number of backup files that you need to save using the **Number of backup copies per document** spinner. After setting all options, choose the **OK** button from the **System Options - Backup/Recover** dialog box.

SELECTING HIDDEN ENTITIES

Sometimes, while working on a model, you need to select an entity that is either hidden behind another entity or is not displayed in the current orientation of the view. SOLIDWORKS allows you to select these entities using the **Select Other** option. For example, consider that you need to select the back face of a model, which is not displayed in the current orientation. In such a case, you need to move the cursor over the visible face such that the cursor is also in line with the back face of the model. Now, click on the front face and choose the **Select Other** button from the pop-up toolbar; the cursor changes to the select other cursor and the **Select Other** list box will be displayed. This list box displays all entities that can be selected. The item on which you move the cursor in the list box will be highlighted in the drawing area. You can select the hidden face using this box.

HOT KEYS

SOLIDWORKS is more popularly known for its mouse gesture functionality. However, you can also use the keys of the keyboard to invoke some tools, windows, dialog boxes, and so on. These keys are known as hot keys. Some hot keys along with their functions are given next.

Hot Key	Function
F11	Full screen
S	Invokes the shortcut bar
R	Invokes the recent documents
F	Fits the object in the drawing over the screen
Z	Zooms out
SPACE BAR	Invokes the **Orientation** menu
CTRL+1	Changes the current view to the Front View
CTRL+2	Changes the current view to the Back View

CTRL+3	Changes the current view to the Left View
CTRL+4	Changes the current view to the Right View
CTRL+5	Changes the current view to the Top View
CTRL+6	Changes the current view to the Bottom View
CTRL+7	Changes the current view to the Isometric View
CTRL+8	Changes the current view to the Normal View
CTRL+SHIFT+Z	Changes the current view to the Previous View
CTRL+Arrows	Moves the feature along the arrows direction
SHIFT+Arrows	Rotates the feature along the arrows direction
CTRL+B	Rebuilds the model
CTRL+Z	Invokes the **Undo** tool
CTRL+N	Invokes the **New SOLIDWORKS Document** dialog box
CTRL+O	Invokes the **Open** window
CTRL+S	Saves the document
CTRL+P	Prints the document
CTRL+A	Selects all the parts in the document
CTRL+C	Copies the selected feature
CTRL+V	Pastes the selected feature
CTRL+X	Cuts the selected feature
ALT+F	Opens the **File** menu
ALT+E	Opens the **Edit** menu
ALT+V	Opens the **View** menu
ALT+I	Opens the **Insert** menu
ALT+T	Opens the **Tool** menu

ALT+W	Opens the **Window** menu
ALT+H	Opens the **Help** menu
CTRL+W	Closes the current document

COLOR SCHEME

SOLIDWORKS allows you to use various color schemes as the background color of the screen, color and display style of **FeatureManager Design Tree**, and for displaying the entities on the screen. Note that the color scheme used in this book is neither the default color scheme nor the predefined color scheme. To set the color scheme, choose **Tools > Options** from the SOLIDWORKS menus; the **System Options - General** dialog box will be displayed. Select the **Colors** option from the left of this dialog box; the option related to the color scheme will be displayed in the dialog box and the name of the dialog box will change to **System Options - Colors**. In the list box available in the **Color scheme settings** area, the **Viewport Background** option is available. Select this option and choose the **Edit** button from the preview area on the right. Select white color from the **Color** dialog box and choose the **OK** button. After setting the color scheme, you need to save it so that next time if you need to set this color scheme, you do not need to configure all the settings. You just need to select the name of the saved color scheme from the **Current color scheme** drop-down list. To save the color scheme, choose the **Save As Scheme** button; the **Color Scheme Name** dialog box will be displayed. Enter the name of the color scheme as **SOLIDWORKS 2021** in the edit box in the **Color Scheme Name** dialog box and choose the **OK** button. Now, choose the **OK** button from the **System Options - Colors** dialog box.

Note

In this book, the description of the color has been given considering Window 10 as the operating system.

Self-Evaluation Test

Answer the following questions and then compare them to those given at the end of this chapter:

1. The __________ property ensures that any modification made in a model in any of the modes of SOLIDWORKS is also reflected in the other modes immediately.

2. The __________ relation forces two selected arcs, two circles, a point and an arc, a point and a circle, or an arc and a circle share the same centerpoint.

3. The __________ relation is used to make two points, a point and a line, or a point and an arc coincident.

4. The __________ relation forces two selected lines to become equal in length.

5. The __________ is used to detect interference and collision between the parts of an assembly when the assembly is in motion.

Review Questions

Answer the following questions:

1. __________ are the analytical and numerical formulae applied to the dimensions during or after sketching of the feature sketch.

2. The **Part** mode of SOLIDWORKS is a feature-based parametric environment in which you can create solid models. (T/F)

3. Generative drafting is the process of generating drawing views of a part or an assembly created earlier. (T/F)

4. The tip of the day is displayed at the bottom of the task pane. (T/F)

5. In SOLIDWORKS, solid models are created by integrating a number of building blocks called features. (T/F)

Answers to Self-Evaluation Test

1. Bidirectional associativity, **2.** concentric, **3.** coincident, **4.** equal, **5.** collision detection

Chapter 2

Drawing Sketches for Solid Models

Learning Objectives

After completing this chapter, you will be able to:

- *Understand the sketching environment*
- *Start a new document*
- *Set the document options*
- *Learn the sketcher terms*
- *Use various sketching tools*
- *Use the drawing display tools*
- *Delete sketched entities*

THE SKETCHING ENVIRONMENT

Most of the products designed by using SOLIDWORKS are a combination of sketched, placed, and derived features. The placed and derived features are created without drawing a sketch, but the sketched features require a sketch to be drawn first. Generally, the base feature of any design is a sketched feature and is created using the sketch. Therefore, while creating any design, the first and foremost requirement is to draw a sketch for the base feature. Once you have drawn the sketch, you can convert it into the base feature and then add the other sketched, placed, and derived features to complete the design. In this chapter, you will learn to create the sketch for the base feature using various sketching tools.

In general terms, a sketch is defined as the basic contour for a feature. For example, consider the solid model of a spanner shown in Figure 2-1.

This spanner consists of a base feature, cut feature, mirror feature (cut on the back face), fillets, and an extruded text feature. The base feature of this spanner is shown in Figure 2-2. It is created using a single sketch drawn on the **Front Plane**, refer to Figure 2-3. This sketch is drawn in the sketching environment using various sketching tools. Therefore, to draw the sketch of the base feature, you first need to invoke the sketching environment where you will draw the sketch.

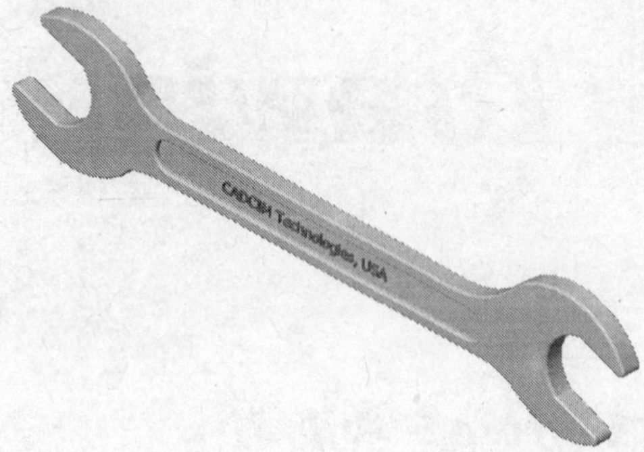

Figure 2-1 *Solid model of a spanner*

Figure 2-2 *Base feature of the spanner*

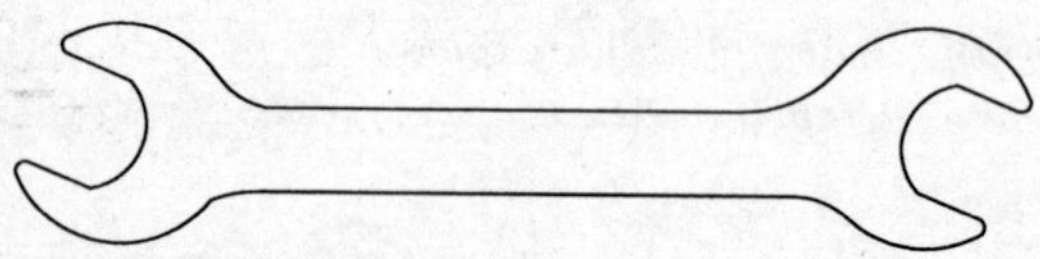

Figure 2-3 *Sketch for the base feature of the spanner*

Note

Once you are familiar with various options of SOLIDWORKS, you can also use a derived feature or a derived part as the base feature.

The sketching environment of SOLIDWORKS can be invoked anytime in the **Part** or **Assembly** mode. You just have to specify that you need to draw the sketch of a feature and then select the plane on which you need to draw the sketch.

STARTING A NEW SESSION OF SOLIDWORKS 2021

Double-click on the **SOLIDWORKS 2021** icon; the **SOLIDWORKS 2021** window will be displayed. If you are starting the SOLIDWORKS application for the first time after installing it, the **SOLIDWORKS License Agreement** dialog box will be displayed. Choose **Accept** from this dialog box; the **SOLIDWORKS** interface window along with the **Welcome - SOLIDWORKS** dialog box will be displayed, as shown in Figure 2-4. Click anywhere in **SOLIDWORKS 2021** window to collapse the **Welcome - SOLIDWORKS** dialog box.

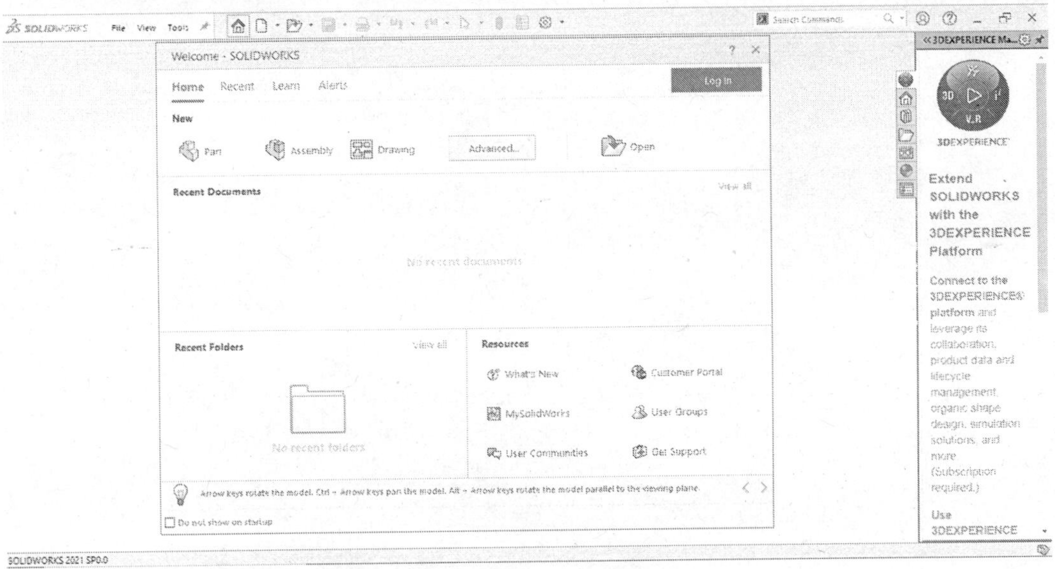

*Figure 2-4 The **SOLIDWORKS** window*

TASK PANES

In SOLIDWORKS, the task panes are displayed on the right of the window. These task panes contain various options that are used to start a new file, open an existing file, browse the related links of SOLIDWORKS, and so on. Various task panes in SOLIDWORKS are shown in Figure 2-5 and are discussed next.

Figure 2-5 Various task panes in SOLIDWORKS

SOLIDWORKS Resources Task Pane

By default, **SOLIDWORKS Resources** task pane is displayed when you start a SOLIDWORKS session. Different rollouts available in this task pane are discussed next.

Welcome to SOLIDWORKS

This option is used to open the **Welcome - SOLIDWORKS** dialog box, refer to Figure 2-6. This dialog box provides a convenient way to open new and saved documents. It also provides access to various folders, SOLIDWORKS resources, and various technical news alerts related to SOLIDWORKS. It appears by default whenever you open a new session of SOLIDWORKS. However, if you select the **Do not show on startup** check box available at the bottom-left corner then from the next time it will not appear by default. There are four tabs available in this dialog box which are discussed next.

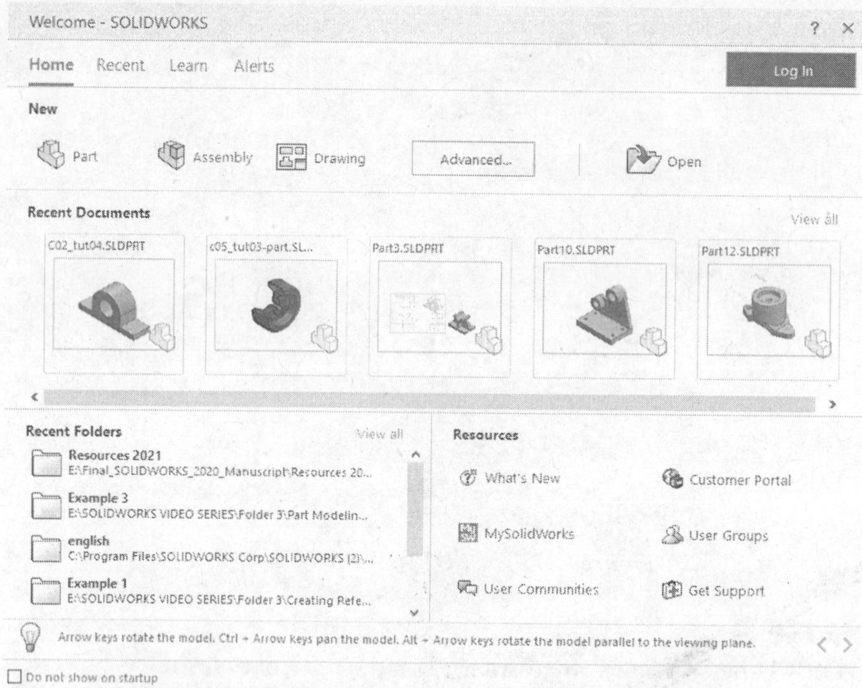

*Figure 2-6 The **Welcome - SOLIDWORKS** dialog box*

Home Tab

The **Home** tab is chosen by default and the options under this tab are used to open new and existing documents. This tab also provides access to recent documents and folders. Various resources like updates in the current version, user groups for discussion, technical support can be accessed using this tab.

Recent Tab

The **Recent** tab lists large number of recent documents and folders as compared to **Home** tab. You can also browse your saved files by using the **Browse** button available at the right in this tab.

Learn Tab

The **Learn** tab provides various resources to learn more about SOLIDWORKS through PDF files and tutorials for practical approach.

Alerts Tab

The **Alert** tab lists various news and alerts regarding SOLIDWORKS.

SOLIDWORKS Tools Rollout

The options in this rollout are used for customizing the tab, diagnosing and troubleshooting SOLIDWORKS, performing system maintenance, checking performance test, saving and restoring the customization settings of SOLIDWORKS, and so on.

Online Resources Rollout

The options in this rollout are used to invoke the discussion forum of SOLIDWORKS, partner solutions, and manufacturing network.

Subscription Services Rollout

The options in this rollout are used to get direct access to the Dassault Systemes partner products website. This partner products website will help you to interact with the design partners and designers for various technical supports and tips.

Design Library Task Pane

The **Design Library** task pane is invoked by choosing the **Design Library** tab from the window. This task pane is used to browse the default **Design Library** and the toolbox components, and also to access the **3D ContentCentral** web site. Note that to access the **3D ContentCentral** website, your computer needs to be connected to the Internet. To access the toolbox components, you need to install **Toolbox** add-in in your computer. To add this add-in, choose **Tools > Add-Ins** from the SOLIDWORKS menus; the **Add-Ins** dialog box will be displayed. Select the **SOLIDWORKS Toolbox Library** check box in this dialog box and then choose OK. The **Toolbox** add-in will be displayed in the **Design Library** task pane.

File Explorer Task Pane

The **File Explorer** task pane is invoked by choosing the **File Explorer** tab from the window. This task pane is used to explore the files and folders that are saved in the hard disk of your computer.

View Palette Task Pane

The **View Palette** task pane is invoked by choosing the **View Palette** tab from the window. This task pane is used to drag and drop the drawing views into a drawing sheet. This is available only when you are in the drafting environment.

Appearances, Scenes, and Decals Task Pane

The **Appearances, Scenes, and Decals** task pane is used to change the appearance of model or display area. On choosing the **Appearances, Scenes, and Decals** tab from the window, you will notice three nodes, **Appearances(color)**, **Scenes**, and **Decals** in the **Appearances, Scenes, and Decals** task pane. The **Appearances(color)** node is used to change the appearance of model, the **Scenes** node is used to change the background of the graphics area, and the **Decals** node is used to apply decals to a model. To assign appearance to the model, expand the desired category node from the **Appearances** node. Next, select a sub-category; different appearances of the selected sub-category will be displayed at the bottom area of the window. Now, drag and drop the required appearance on the model in the graphics area by selecting and holding the left-mouse button; the **Appearance Target** palette will be displayed. Select the required button from this palette to apply the selected appearance. You can change the properties of the appearance added by using the corresponding appearance PropertyManager. You will learn about this PropertyManager in later chapters.

To change the background of the graphics area, expand the **Scenes** node from the **Appearances, Scenes, and Decals** task pane and select a category; the preview of different backgrounds available for the selected category will be displayed. Drag and drop the background in the graphics area; the background of the graphics area will be changed. You can also click the down-arrow next to the **Apply Scene** button in the **View (Heads-Up)** toolbar and select an option from this toolbar to change the background of the drawing area.

Similarly, to apply an image as a decal, expand the **Decals** node and select the **logos** subnode; the default logos will be displayed. Drag and drop the image on the model; the **Decals PropertyManager** will be displayed. Set the properties in this PropertyManager and choose the **OK** button.

Custom Properties Task Pane

The **Custom Properties** task pane is displayed on choosing the **Custom Properties** tab from the window. This task pane is used to view the properties of the files. If you do not have a property template for the files, then you can create it by choosing the **Create now** button from the **Custom Properties** task pane. On choosing this button, the **Property Tab Builder 2021** window will be displayed. Set the properties in this window and save it. Afse saving the properties, you can view them in the **Custom Properties** task pane. To do.alog box **Tools > Options** from the SOLIDWORKS menus; the **System Options - Gen**ptions related will be displayed. Choose the **File Locations** option from this dialog box. Select the **Custom** to the **File Locations** option will be displayed on the right of the dialog, browse the property **Property Files** option from the **Show folders for** drop-down lis **OK** button from the dialog template in the **Folders** area by choosing the **Add** button. Cho **Properties** task pane. box to exit. Now, you can view these properties in the **Cu**

Tip

To expand the task pane at any stag ...ne design cycle, choose any one of the tabs provided on the task pane. Choose the ***Auto*** *...w button to pin the task pane. To collapse the task pane, click anywhere in the draw... area when the* ***Auto Show*** *button is not chosen.*

Note

In asse... ...ies, you can assign properties to multiple parts at the same time.

STARTING A NEW DOCUMENT IN SOLIDWORKS 2021

To start a new document in SOLIDWORKS 2021, select the **Welcome to SOLIDWORKS** option from the **SOLIDWORKS Resources** task pane; the **Welcome - SOLIDWORKS** dialog box will be displayed, as shown in Figure 2-6. You can also invoke this dialog box by choosing the **Welcome to SOLIDWORKS** button from the Menu Bar. The options to start a new document using this dialog box are discussed next.

Part

The **Part** button is available in the **New** area of the **Home** tab in the **Welcome - SOLIDWORKS** dialog box. On choosing this button from the dialog box; the **Part** document will be invoked. In this mode, you can create solid models, surface models, or sheet metal components.

Assembly

Choose the **Assembly** button from the **Welcome - SOLIDWORKS** dialog box to start a new assembly document. In the assembly document, you can assemble the components created in the part documents. You can also create components or new layout in the assembly document.

Drawing

Choose the **Drawing** button from the **Welcome - SOLIDWORKS** dialog box to start a new drawing document. In a drawing document, you can generate or create the drawing views of the parts created in the part documents or the assemblies created in the assembly documents.

You can also start a new document using the **New SOLIDWORKS Document** dialog box. To invoke this dialog box choose the **New** button from the Menu Bar, the **New SOLIDWORKS Document** dialog box will be displayed, as shown in Figure 2-7. Choose the desired button and then the **OK** button to start a new document.

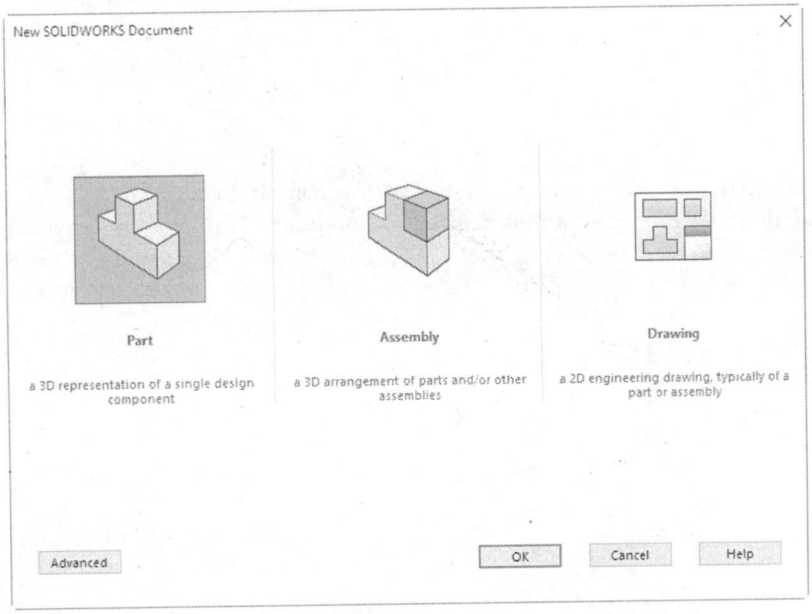

*Figure 2-7 The **New SOLIDWORKS Document** dialog box*

UNDERSTANDING THE SKETCHING ENVIRONMENT

Whenever you start a new part document, by default, you are in the part modeling environment. But you need to start the design by first creating the sketch of the base feature in the sketching environment. To invoke the sketching environment, choose the **Sketch** tab from the **CommandManager**. Next, choose the **Sketch** button from the **Sketch CommandManager** tab. For your convenience, you can add the **Sketch** button to the Menu Bar and invoke the sketching environment using this button. To do so, right-click on any toolbar and choose the **Customize** option from the shortcut menu; the **Customize** dialog box will be displayed. Choose the **Commands** tab and select the **Sketch** option from the **Toolbars** list box; all tools in the sketch categories will be displayed in the **Buttons** area. Press and hold the left mouse button on the **Sketch** button and then drag it to the Menu Bar. Click the **OK** button to exit the **Customize** dialog box. Figure 2-8 shows the **Sketch** button added to the Menu Bar.

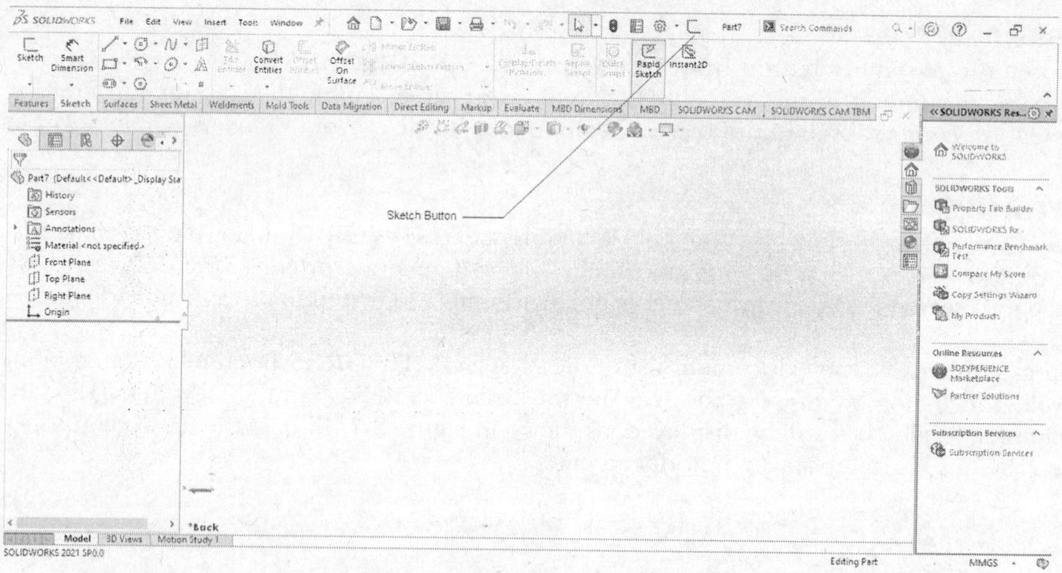

***Figure 2-8** SOLIDWORKS 2021 screen displaying the **Sketch** button in the Menu Bar*

When you choose the **Sketch** button from the Menu Bar or invoke any tool from the **Sketch CommandManager** tab, the **Edit Sketch PropertyManager** is displayed on the left in the drawing area and you are prompted to select the plane on which the sketch will be created. Also, the three default planes (Front Plane, Right Plane, and Top Plane) are temporarily displayed on the screen, as shown in Figure 2-9.

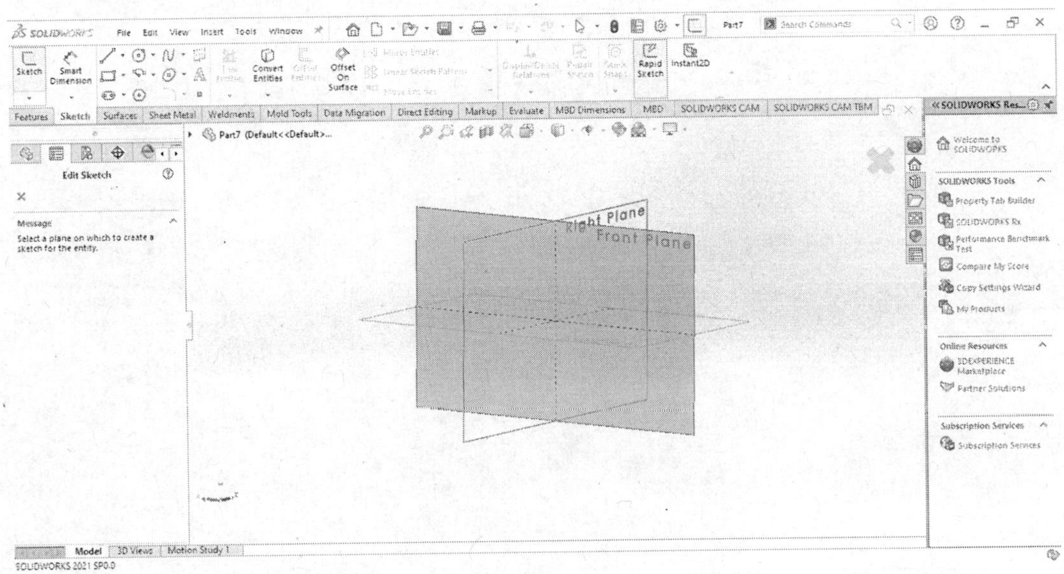

Figure 2-9 *The three default planes displayed on the screen*

You can select a plane to draw the sketch of the base feature depending on the requirement of the design. As soon as you select a plane, the **CommandManager** will display various sketching tools to draw the sketch.

The default screen appearance of a SOLIDWORKS part document in the sketching environment is shown in Figure 2-10.

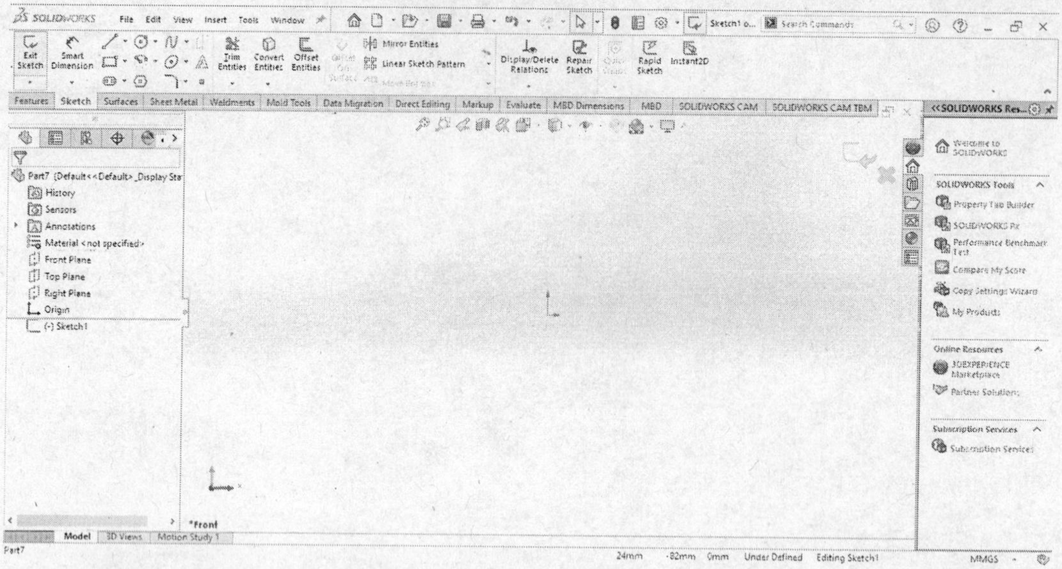

Figure 2-10 Default screen display of a part document in the sketching environment

SETTING THE DOCUMENT OPTIONS

When you install SOLIDWORKS on your computer, you will be prompted to specify the dimensioning standards and units for measuring distances. The settings specified at that time will become the default settings and will be applied on any new SOLIDWORKS document opened thereafter. However, if you want to modify these settings for a particular document, you can do so easily by using the **Document Properties** dialog box. To invoke this dialog box, choose the **Options** button from the Menu Bar; the **System Options - General** dialog box will be displayed, as shown in Figure 2-11. Alternatively, choose **Tools > Options** from the SOLIDWORKS menus to invoke the **System Options - General** dialog box. In this dialog box, choose the **Document Properties** tab; the name of this dialog box will change to the **Document Properties - Drafting Standard** dialog box. The procedure to set the options for the current document using this dialog box is discussed next.

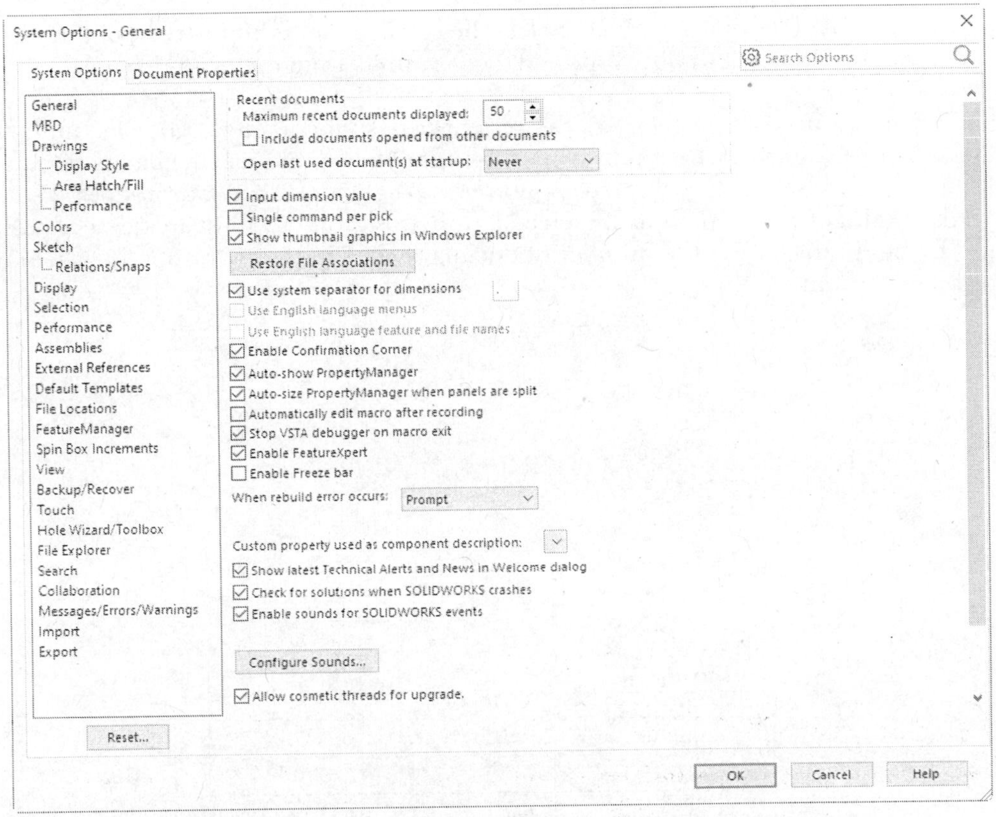

*Figure 2-11 The **System Options - General** dialog box*

Modifying the Drafting Standards

To modify the **Drafting** standards, invoke the **System Options - General** dialog box and then choose the **Document Properties** tab. You will notice that the **Drafting Standard** option is selected by default in the area available on the left of the dialog box to display the drafting options.

The default drafting standard that was selected while installing SOLIDWORKS will be displayed in the drop-down list in the **Overall drafting standard** area. You can select the required drafting standard from this drop-down list. The standards available in this drop-down list are ANSI, ISO, DIN, JIS, BSI, GOST, and GB. You can select any one of these drafting standards for the current document.

Modifying the Linear and Angular Units

To modify the linear and angular units, invoke the **System Options - General** dialog box and then choose the **Document Properties** tab. In this tab, choose the **Units** option from the area available on the left in the dialog box to display the options related to the linear and angular units, refer to Figure 2-12. The default option that was selected for measuring the linear distances while installing SOLIDWORKS will be available in the **Length** field under the **Unit** column. You can set the units for the current document from the options in the **Unit system** area. To specify the units other than the standard unit system in this area, select the **Custom** radio button;. the options in the tabulation will be enabled. Select the cell corresponding to the **Length** and **Unit** parameter; a drop-down list will be displayed. Set the units from the drop-down list.

The units that can be selected for **Length** are angstroms, nanometers, microns, millimeters, centimeters, meters, microinches, mils, inches, feet, and feet & inches. To change the units for angular dimensions, select the cell corresponding to **Angle** and **Unit**; a drop-down list will be displayed. The angular units that can be selected from this drop-down list are degrees, deg/min, deg/min/sec, and radians. Set the number of decimal places in the corresponding field under the **Decimals** column.

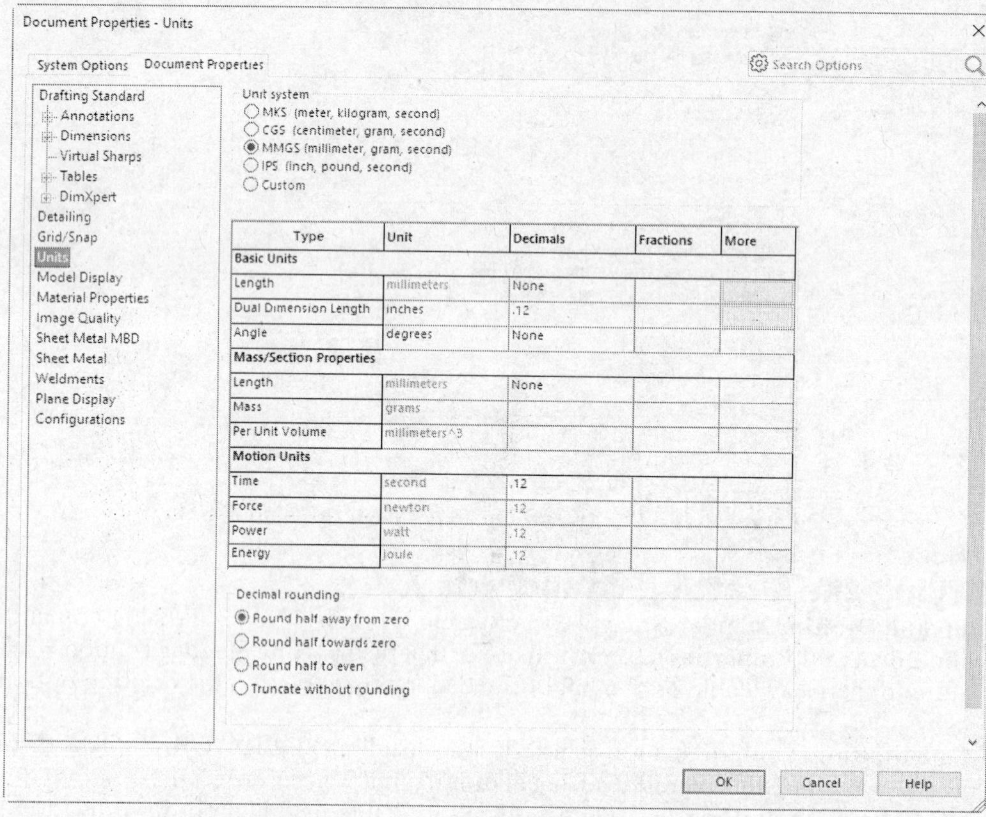

***Figure 2-12** Setting the dimensioning standards*

In SOLIDWORKS, you can also change the unit system for the current document by using the **Unit system** button that is located on the right in the status bar. To change the unit system using this option, click on the **Unit system** button; a flyout will be displayed with a tick mark next to the unit system of the activated document, refer to Figure 2-13. Now, you can select the required unit system for the activated document from this flyout. You can also invoke the **Document Properties - Units** dialog box by choosing the **Edit Document Units** option from this flyout.

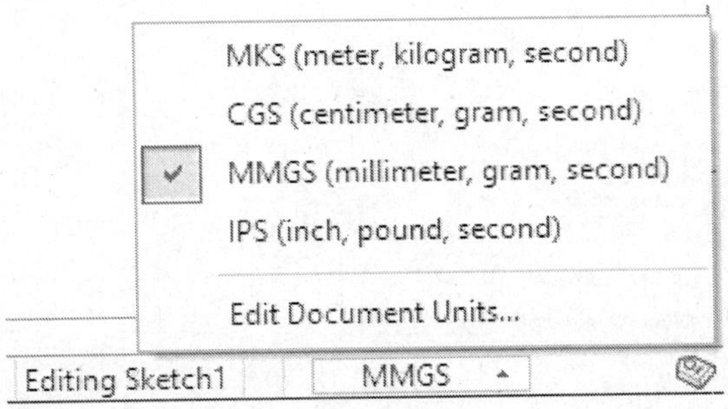

Figure 2-13 *Flyout displayed after choosing the* ***Unit system*** *button*

Modifying the Snap and Grid Settings

In the sketching environment of SOLIDWORKS, you can make the cursor jump through a specified distance while creating the sketch. Therefore, if you draw a sketched entity, its length will change in the specified increment. For example, while drawing a line, if you make the cursor jump through a distance of 10 mm, the length of the line will be incremented by a distance of 10 mm. To modify the snap and grid settings, choose the **Options** button from the Menu Bar to display the **System Options - General** dialog box. To ensure that the cursor jumps through the specified distance, you need to activate the snap option. Select the **Relations/Snaps** sub-option of the **Sketch** option to display the related settings. From the options available on the right, select the **Grid** check box. Next, clear the **Snap only when grid is displayed** check box, if it is selected. If this check box is selected, then the cursor will snap the sketched entities only when the grid is displayed.

Next, choose the **Go To Document Grid Settings** button to invoke the **Document Properties - Grid/Snap** dialog box, refer to Figure 2-14. The distance through which the cursor jumps is dependent on the ratio between the values in the **Major grid spacing** and **Minor-lines per major** spinners available in the **Grid** area. For example, if you want the coordinates to increment by 10 mm, you will have to make the ratio of the major and minor lines to 10. This can be done by setting the value of the **Major grid spacing** spinner to **100** and that of the **Minor-lines per major** spinner to **10**. Similarly, to make the cursor jump through a distance of 5 mm, set the value of the **Major grid spacing** spinner to **50** and that of the **Minor-lines per major** spinner to **10**.

Note

Remember that these grid and snap settings will be applicable for the current documents only. When you open a new document, it will have the default settings that were defined while installing SOLIDWORKS.

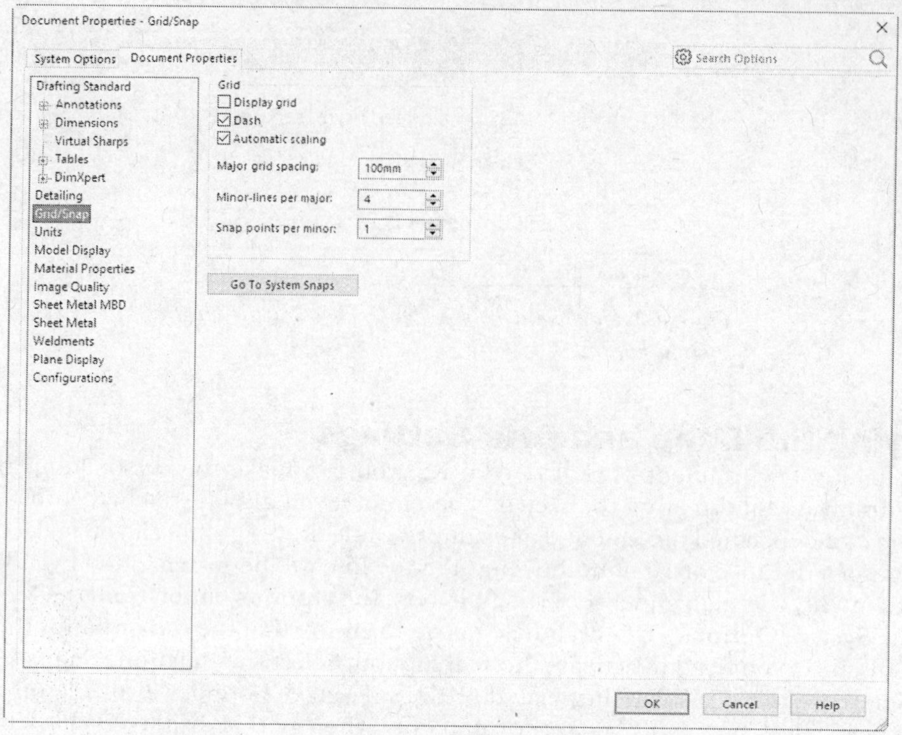

*Figure 2-14 The **Document Properties - Grid/Snap** dialog box*

Tip

*If you want to display the grid in the sketching environment, select the **Display grid** check box from the **Grid** area of the **Document Properties - Grid/Snap** dialog box. Alternatively, choose **Hide/Show Items > View Grid** from the **View (Heads-Up)** toolbar.*

While drawing a sketched entity by snapping through grips, the grips symbol will be displayed below the cursor on the right.

LEARNING SKETCHER TERMS

Before you learn about various sketching tools, it is important to understand some terms that are used in the sketching environment. These tools and terms are discussed next.

Origin

The origin is represented by a blue colored point displayed at the center of the sketching environment screen. By default, there are two arrows at the origin displaying the horizontal and vertical directions of the current sketching plane. The point of intersection of these two axes is the origin point and the coordinates of this point are 0,0. To display or hide the origin, choose **Hide/Show Items > View Origins** from the **View (Heads-Up)** toolbar.

Inferencing Lines

The inferencing lines are the temporary lines that are used to track a particular point on the screen. These lines are the dashed lines and are automatically displayed when you select a sketching tool in the sketching environment. These lines are created from the endpoints or the midpoint of a sketched entity or from the origin. For example, if you want to draw a line from the point where two imaginary lines intersect, you can use the inferencing lines to locate the point and then draw the line from that point. Figure 2-15 shows the use of inferencing lines to locate the point of intersection of two imaginary lines. Figure 2-16 shows the use of inferencing lines to locate the center of a circle. Notice that the inferencing lines are created from the endpoint of the line and from the origin.

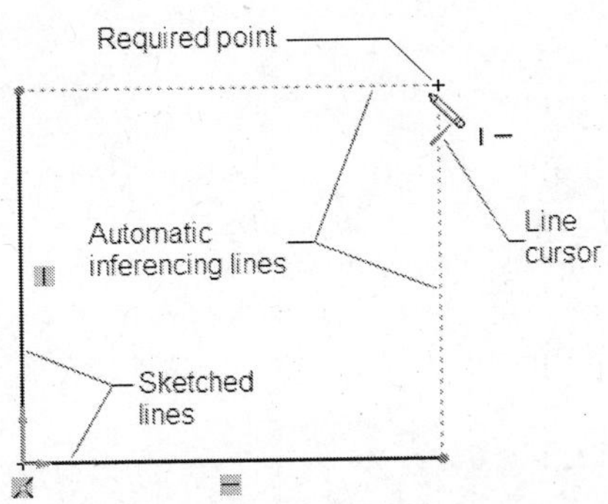

Figure 2-15 Using inferencing lines to locate a point

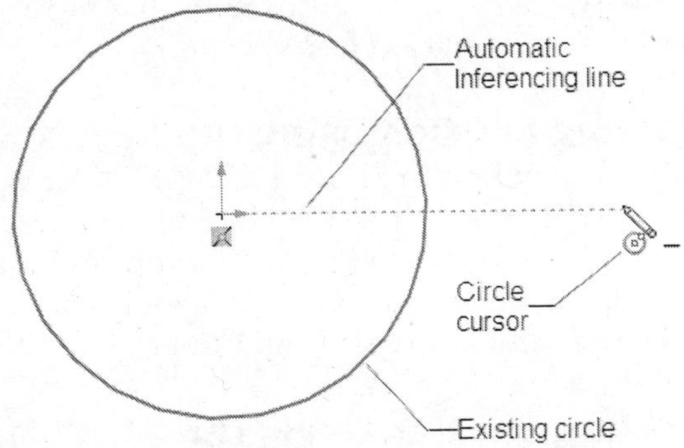

Figure 2-16 Using inferencing lines to locate the center of a circle

Note

The inferencing lines that are displayed on the screen will be either blue or yellow. The blue inferencing lines indicate that the relations are not added to the sketched entity and the yellow inferencing lines indicate that the relations are added to the sketched entity. You will learn about various relations in the later chapters.

Inferencing lines will be displayed only when a sketching tool is active.

Tip

You can disable the inferencing line temporarily by pressing and holding the CTRL key.

Select Tool

SOLIDWORKS menus: Tools > Select

The **Select** tool is used to select a sketched entity or exit any sketching tool that is active. You can select the sketched entities by selecting them one by one using the left mouse button. You can also hold the left mouse button and drag the cursor around the multiple sketched entities to define a box and select the multiple entities. There are two methods of selection, box selection and cross selection. You can also select multiple entities by pressing the SHIFT and CTRL keys. These selection methods are discussed next.

Selecting Entities Using the Box Selection

A box is a window that is created by pressing the left mouse button and dragging the cursor from left to right in the drawing area. The selection box will be displayed by continuous lines. When you create a box, the entities that lie completely inside it will be selected. The selected entities will be displayed in light blue and a pop-up toolbar will be displayed near the cursor.

Selecting Entities Using the Cross Selection

When you press the left mouse button and drag the cursor from right to left in the drawing area, a box of dashed lines is drawn. The entities that lie completely or partially inside this box or the entities that touch the dashed lines of the box will be selected. The selected entities will be displayed in light blue and a pop-up toolbar will be displayed near the cursor. This method of selection is known as cross selection.

Selecting Entities Using the Lasso Selection

Lasso selection is a freehand selection. To make a freehand selection, click-drag the mouse pointer; a continuous loop will be displayed. The entities that lie completely inside the loop will be selected and highlighted. Also, a pop-up toolbar will be displayed near the mouse pointer. Note that you need to change the default selection method for using lasso selection. To do so, choose **Tools > Lasso Selection** from the SOLIDWORKS menus.

Selecting Entities Using the SHIFT and CTRL Keys

You can also use the SHIFT and CTRL keys to manage the selection procedure. To select multiple entities, press and hold the SHIFT key and select the entities. After selecting some entities, if you need to select more entities using the windows or cross selection, press and hold the SHIFT key. Now, create a window or a cross selection; all the entities that touch the crossing or are inside the window will be selected.

If you need to remove a particular entity from a group of selected entities, press the CTRL key and select the entity. You can also invert the current selection using the CTRL key. To do so, select the entities that you do not want to be included in the selection set. Next, press the CTRL key and create a window or a cross selection.

Note

*1. When a sketching tool is active, you can invoke the **Select** tool or press the ESC key to exit the sketching tool. You can also right-click and choose the **Select** option from the shortcut menu to exit the tool.*

2. In SOLIDWORKS, when you select an entity, a pop-up toolbar will be displayed with options to edit the sketch. You will learn about these options in the later chapters.

Invert Selection Tool

SOLIDWORKS menus:	Tools > Invert Selection
Toolbar:	Selection Filter > Invert Selection

The **Invert Selection** tool will be active only when an entity is selected and is used to invert the selection set. This tool is used to remove entities from the current selection set and select all other entities that are not in the current selection set. To invert the selection, select the entities that you do not want to be included in the final selection set and then choose **Tools > Invert Selection** from the SOLIDWORKS menus. You can also invoke the **Invert Selection** tool from the shortcut menu. All entities that were not selected earlier will now be selected and the entities that were in the selection set earlier will now be removed from the selection set.

Now, you are familiar with the important sketching terms. Next, you will learn about the sketching tools available in SOLIDWORKS.

DRAWING LINES

CommandManager:	Sketch > Line flyout > Line
SOLIDWORKS menus:	Tools > Sketch Entities > Line
Toolbar:	Sketch > Line flyout > Line

Lines are one of the basic sketching entities available in SOLIDWORKS. In general terms, a line is defined as the shortest distance between two points. As mentioned earlier, SOLIDWORKS is a parametric solid modeling tool. This property allows you to draw a line of any length and at any angle so that it can be forced to the desired length and angle.

To draw a line in the sketching environment of SOLIDWORKS, invoke the **Line** tool from the **Line** flyout in the **Sketch CommandManager**; the **Insert Line PropertyManager** will be displayed, as shown in Figure 2-17. Alternatively, right-click in the drawing area; a shortcut menu will be displayed with tools and options. Choose the **Line** tool from the shortcut menu to display the **Insert Line PropertyManager**. You will notice that the cursor, which was an arrow, is replaced by the line cursor. You can also invoke the **Line** tool by pressing the L key.

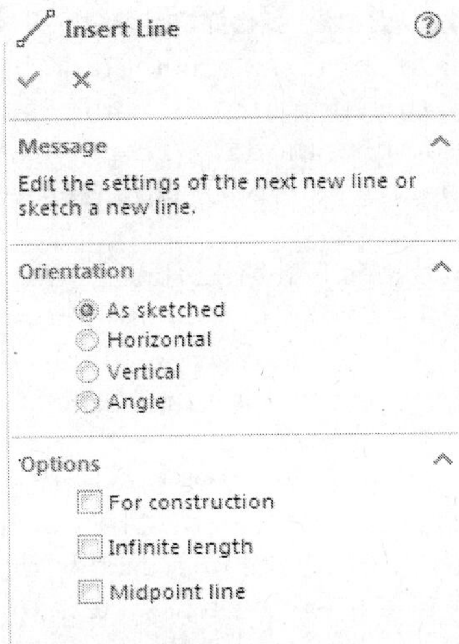

Figure 2-17** Partial view of the **Insert Line PropertyManager

The **Message** rollout of the **Insert Line PropertyManager** informs you to edit the settings of the next line or sketch a new line. The options in this **PropertyManager** can be used to set the orientation and other sketching options to draw a line. All these options are discussed next.

Orientation Rollout

The **Orientation** rollout is used to define the orientation of the line to be drawn. By default, the **As sketched** radio button is selected, so that you can draw the line in any orientation. If you need to draw only horizontal lines, select the **Horizontal** radio button. On selecting this radio button, the **Parameters** rollout will be displayed and you can specify the length of the line in the **Length** spinner provided in this rollout. You will learn more about dimensioning in the later chapters. After specifying the parameters, choose the start point and the endpoint in succession to create the horizontal line.

Similarly, to draw a vertical line, select the **Vertical** radio button, specify the parameters in the **Parameters** rollout, and then choose the start point and the endpoint in succession.

Note

*If the value 0 is set in the **Length** spinner of the **Parameters** rollout, you can draw horizontal/vertical line of any length.*

The **Angle** radio button is selected to draw lines at a specified angle. When you select this radio button, the **Parameters** rollout will be displayed, where you can set the values of the length of the line and the angle or the orientation of the line.

Options Rollout

Select the **For construction** check box available in this rollout to draw a construction line. You will learn more about construction lines later in this chapter. To draw a line of infinite length, select the **Infinite length** check box. Select the **Midpoint line** check box to draw a line by defining its midpoint and one of its endpoints.

On selecting the **As sketched** radio button in the **Orientation** rollout, you can draw lines by using two methods. The first method is to draw continuous lines and the second method is to draw individual lines. Both these methods are discussed next.

Drawing Continuous Lines

This is the default method of drawing lines. In this method, you have to specify the start point and the endpoint of the line using the left mouse button. As soon as you specify the start point of the line, the **Line Properties PropertyManager** will be displayed. The options in the **Line Properties PropertyManager** will not be activated at this stage.

After specifying the start point, move the cursor away from it and specify the endpoint of the line using the left mouse button. A line will be drawn between the two points. You will also notice that the line has filled squares at the two ends. The line will be displayed in light blue color because it is still selected.

Move the cursor away from the endpoint of the line and you will notice that another line is attached to the cursor. The start point of this line is the endpoint of the last line and the length of this line can be increased or decreased by moving the cursor. This line is called a rubber-band line as this line stretches like a rubber-band when you move the cursor. The point that you specify next on the screen will be taken as the endpoint of the new line and a line will be drawn such that the endpoint of the first line is taken as the start point of the new line and the point you specify is taken as the endpoint of the new line. Now, a new rubber-band line is displayed starting from the endpoint of the last line. This is a continuous process and you can draw a chain of as many continuous lines as needed by specifying the points on the screen using the left mouse button.

You can exit the process of drawing continuous line by pressing the ESC key, by double-clicking on the screen, or by invoking the **Select** tool from the Menu Bar. You can also right-click to display the shortcut menu and choose the **End chain (double-click)** or **Select** option to exit the **Line** tool.

Figure 2-18 shows a sketch drawn using continuous lines. You need to draw this sketch from the lower left corner and in this sketch, the horizontal line has to be drawn first. Draw the other lines and to close the loop, move the cursor attached to the last line close to the start point of the first line; you will notice that an orange colored circle will be displayed at the start point. If you specify the endpoint of the line at this stage, the loop will be closed and no rubber-band line will be displayed now. This is because the loop is already closed and you may not need another continuous line now. However, the **Line** tool is still active and you can draw other lines.

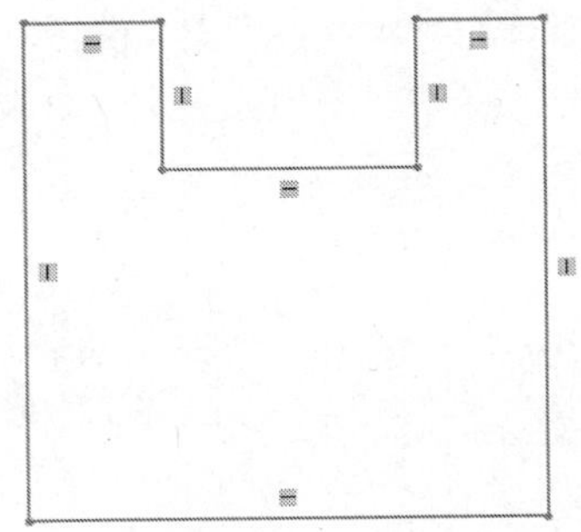

Figure 2-18 Sketch drawn using continuous lines

Note

When you terminate the process of drawing a line by double-clicking on the screen or by choosing ***End chain (double-click)*** *from the shortcut menu, the current chain ends but the* ***Line*** *tool still remains active. As a result, you can draw other lines. However, to exit the* ***Line*** *tool, you can choose the* ***Select*** *option from the shortcut menu or press the ESC key.*

Drawing Individual Lines

This is the second method of drawing lines. This method is used to draw individual lines in which the start point of the new line will not necessarily be the endpoint of the previous line. To draw individual lines, you need to press and hold the left mouse button to specify the start point, and then drag the cursor without releasing the mouse button. Once you have dragged the cursor to the endpoint, release the left mouse button; a line will be drawn between the two points.

To make the sketching process easy in SOLIDWORKS, you are provided with the **PropertyManager**. The **PropertyManager** is a table that will be displayed on the left of the screen as soon as you select a sketched entity. The **PropertyManager** has all parameters related to the sketched entity such as the start point, endpoint, angle, length, and so on. You will notice that as you start dragging the mouse, the **Line Properties PropertyManager** is displayed on the left of the drawing area. All options in the **Line Properties PropertyManager** will be available when you release the left mouse button. Figure 2-19 shows partial view of the **Line Properties PropertyManager**.

Note

The ***Line Properties PropertyManager*** *also displays additional options about relations. You will learn more about relations in the later chapters.*

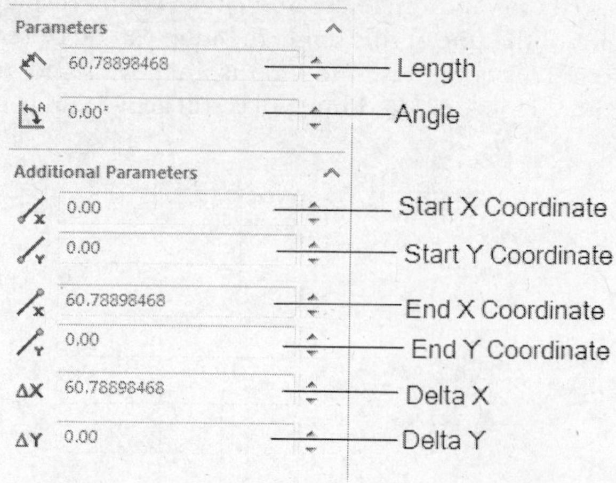

*Figure 2-19 Partial view of the **Line Properties PropertyManager***

After you have drawn the line, modify the parameters in the **Line Properties PropertyManager** to create the line to the desired length and angle. You can also modify the line dynamically by selecting its endpoints and then dragging them.

Line Cursor Parameters

When you draw lines in the sketching environment of SOLIDWORKS, you will notice that a numeric value is displayed above the line cursor, refer to Figure 2-20. This numeric value indicates the length of the line you draw. This value is the same as the one displayed in the **Length** spinner of the **Line Properties PropertyManager**. The only difference is that in the **Line Properties PropertyManager**, the value will be displayed with more precision.

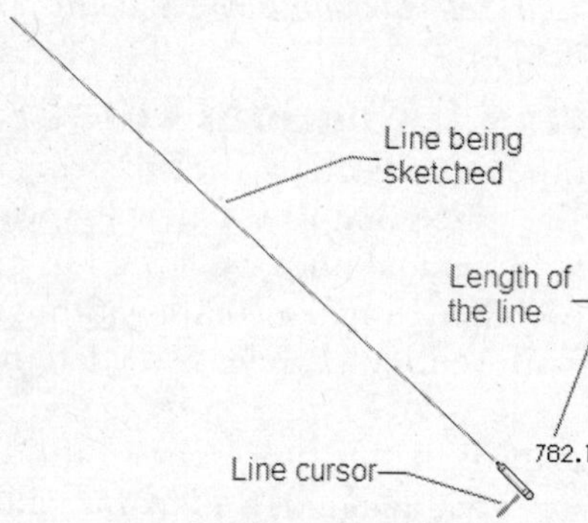

Figure 2-20 The length of the line displayed on the screen while drawing it

The other thing that you will notice while drawing horizontal or vertical line is that two symbols are displayed below the line cursor. These are the symbols of the **Vertical** and **Horizontal** relations. SOLIDWORKS applies these relations automatically to lines. These relations ensure that the lines you draw are vertical or horizontal. Figure 2-21 shows the symbol of the **Vertical** relation on a line and Figure 2-22 shows the symbol of the **Horizontal** relation on a line.

Note

*In addition to the **Horizontal** and **Vertical** relations, you can apply a number of other relations such as **Tangent**, **Concentric**, **Perpendicular**, **Parallel**, and so on. You will learn about all these relations and other options in the **Line Properties PropertyManager** in the later chapters.*

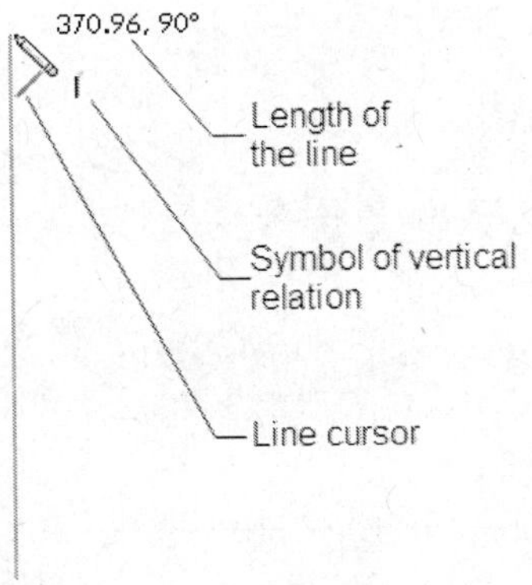

Figure 2-21 Symbol of the ***Vertical*** *relation*

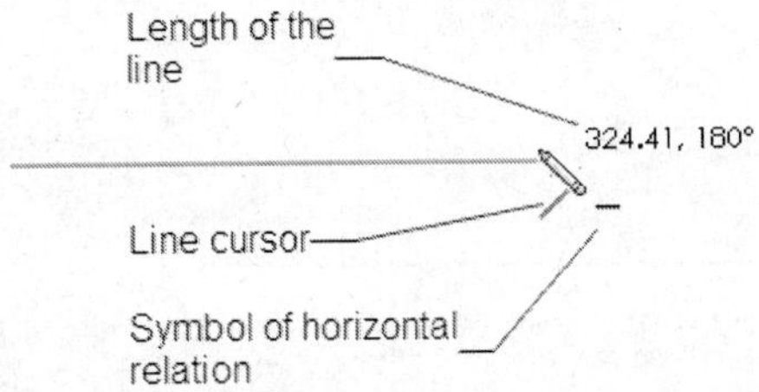

Figure 2-22 Symbol of the ***Horizontal*** *relation*

Drawing Tangent or Normal Arcs Using the Line Tool

SOLIDWORKS allows you to draw tangent or normal arcs originating from the endpoint of the line while drawing continuous lines. Note that these arcs can be drawn only if you have drawn at least one line, arc, or spline. To draw such arcs, draw a line by specifying the start point and the endpoint. Move the cursor away from the endpoint of the last line to display the rubber-band line. Now, when you move the cursor back to the endpoint of the last line, the arc mode will be invoked. The angle and the radius of the arc will be displayed above the arc cursor. You can also invoke the arc mode by right-clicking and choosing the **Switch to arc (A)** option from the shortcut menu or pressing the A key on the keyboard.

To draw a tangent arc, invoke the arc mode by moving the cursor back to the endpoint of the last line. Now, move the cursor through a small distance along the tangent direction of the line; a dotted line will be drawn. Next, move the cursor in the direction in which the arc should be drawn. You will notice that a tangent arc is drawn. Specify the endpoint of the tangent arc using the left mouse button. Figure 2-23 shows an arc tangent to an existing line.

To draw a normal arc, invoke the arc mode. Next, move the cursor through a small distance in the direction normal to the line and then move it in the direction of the endpoint of the arc; the normal arc will be drawn, as shown in Figure 2-24.

As soon as the endpoint of the tangent or the normal arc is defined, the line mode will be invoked again. You can continue drawing lines using the line mode or move the cursor back to the endpoint of the arc to invoke the arc mode.

Note

If the arc mode is invoked by mistake while drawing lines, you can cancel the arc mode and invoke the line mode again by pressing the A key. Alternatively, you can right-click and choose ***Switch to Line (A)*** *from the shortcut menu or move the cursor back to the endpoint and press the left mouse button to invoke the line mode.*

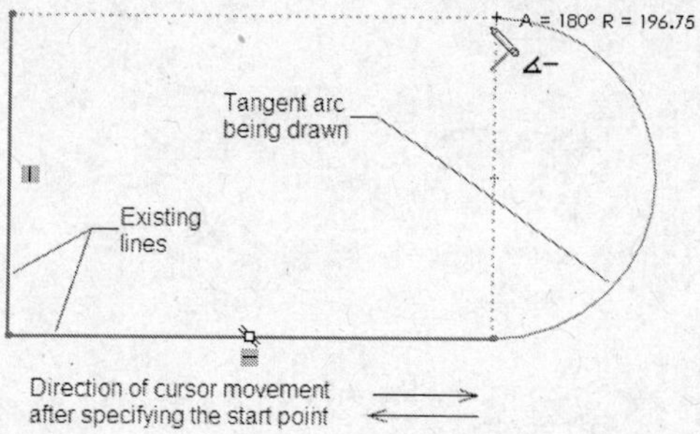

*Figure 2-23 Drawing a tangent arc using the **Line** tool*

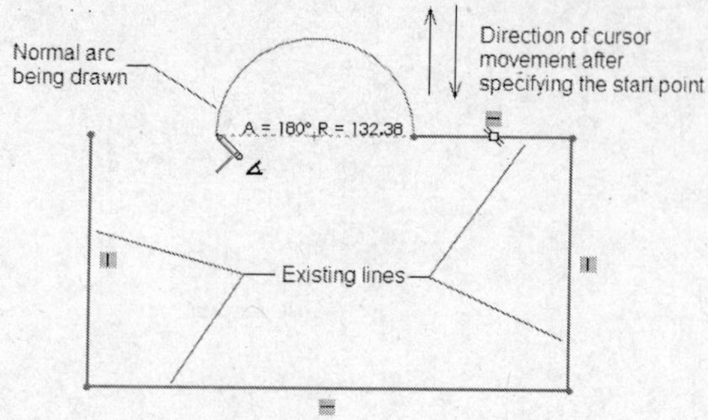

*Figure 2-24 Drawing a normal arc using the **Line** tool*

Tip

*You can flip the tangency of a tangent arc by right-clicking on the arc drawn and then selecting the **Reverse Endpoint Tangent** option from the short-cut menu displayed.*

Drawing Construction Lines or Centerlines

CommandManager:	Sketch > Line flyout > Centerline
SOLIDWORKS menus:	Tools > Sketch Entities > Centerline
Toolbar:	Sketch > Line flyout > Centerline

The construction lines or the centerlines are the ones that are drawn only for the aid of sketching. These lines are not considered while converting the sketches into features. You can draw a construction line similar to the sketched line by using the **Centerline** tool. You will notice that when you draw a construction line, the **For construction** check box in the **Options** rollout of the **Line Properties PropertyManager** is selected. You can also draw a construction line using the **Line** tool. To do so, invoke the **Insert Line PropertyManager** by choosing the **Line** tool, select the **For construction** check box in the **Options** rollout, and draw the line.

Drawing Midpoint Line

CommandManager:	Sketch > Line flyout > Midpoint Line
SOLIDWORKS menus:	Tools > Sketch Entities > Midpoint Line
Toolbar:	Sketch > Line flyout > Midpoint Line

The **Midpoint Line** tool is used to draw a line by specifying its midpoint and end point. To invoke this tool, choose the **Midpoint Line** tool from the **Line** flyout of the **Sketch** toolbar.

Drawing the Lines of Infinite Length

SOLIDWORKS allows you to draw lines of infinite length. Note that these lines can be drawn only if the **Line** or **Centerline** tool is invoked. To draw lines of infinite length, invoke the **Insert Line PropertyManager** and then select the **Infinite length** check box available in the **Options** rollout of this PropertyManager. Next, specify two points in the drawing area; a line of infinite length will be drawn.

To convert a solid infinite length line to a construction infinite length line, you need to select the **For construction** check box in the **Options** rollout of the **Line Properties PropertyManager**. You can also set the angle value for infinite length lines in the **Angle** spinner available in the **Parameters** rollout of this PropertyManager.

Tip

When you select a line, a pop-up toolbar will be displayed. Choose the ***Construction Geometry*** *button from this toolbar to convert the line into a construction line.*

DRAWING CIRCLES

In SOLIDWORKS, there are two methods to draw circles. In the first method, you can specify the center point of a circle and then defining its radius. In the second method, you can draw a circle by defining three points that lie on its periphery. The tools for drawing a circle are grouped together in the **Circle** flyout in the **Sketch CommandManager**. To draw a circle, select the down arrow on the **Circle** tool; a flyout with both the tools will be displayed. Invoke a tool from this flyout; the **Circle PropertyManager** will be displayed, as shown in Figure 2-25. Alternatively, right-click and then choose the **Circle** option from the shortcut menu to display the **Circle PropertyManager**. You can also invoke the **Circle** tool by using the Mouse Gesture. After invoking the **Circle PropertyManager**, select the appropriate method from the **Circle Type** rollout to draw the circle. Both methods to draw the circles are discussed next.

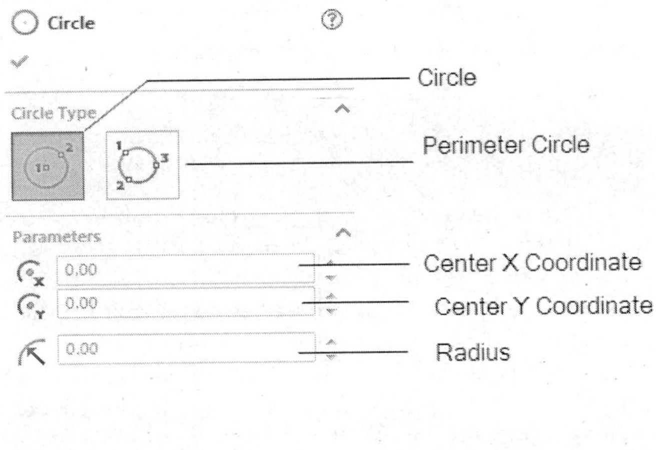

Figure 2-25 *Partial view of the* ***Circle PropertyManager***

Drawing Circles by Defining Their Center Points

CommandManager:	Sketch > Circle flyout > Circle
SOLIDWORKS menus:	Tools > Sketch Entities > Circle
Toolbar:	Sketch > Circle flyout > Circle

When you invoke the **Circle PropertyManager**, the **Circle** button is chosen by default in the **Circle Type** rollout. Also, the arrow cursor is replaced by the circle cursor. Specify the center point of the circle and then move the cursor away from the point to define its radius. The current radius of the circle will be displayed above the circle cursor. This radius will change as you move the cursor. Click on the drawing area away from the center point to define the radius. This radius can be modified by using the **Circle PropertyManager**. Also, the coordinates of the center point of the circle can be modified by using the **Circle PropertyManager**. Figure 2-26 shows a circle being drawn using the **Circle** tool by specifying the center point and dragging the cursor.

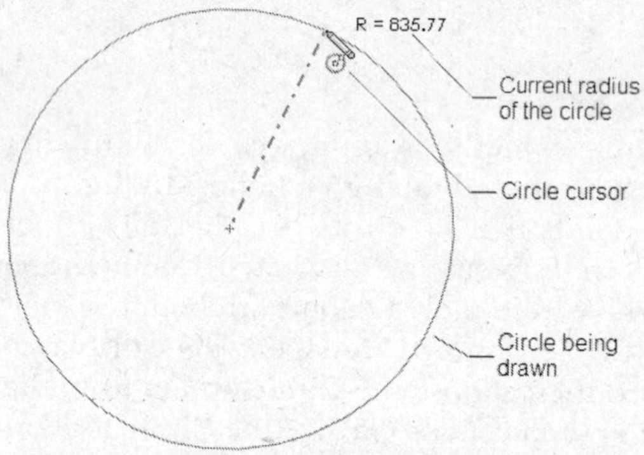

Figure 2-26 Drawing a circle by specifying the center point

Drawing Circles by Defining Three Points

CommandManager:	Sketch > Circle flyout > Perimeter Circle
SOLIDWORKS menus:	Tools > Sketch Entities > Perimeter Circle
Toolbar:	Sketch > Circle flyout > Perimeter Circle

The **Perimeter Circle** tool is used to draw a circle by defining three points that lie on the periphery of a circle. To draw a circle using this method, choose the **Perimeter Circle** tool from the **Circle** flyout. Alternatively, invoke the **Circle PropertyManager** and choose the **Perimeter Circle** button from the **Circle Type** rollout; the select cursor will be replaced by a three-point circle cursor. Specify the first point of the circle in the drawing area. Next, specify the other two points of the circle. The resulting circle will be highlighted in light blue and you can modify the circle by setting its parameters in the **Circle PropertyManager**. Figure 2-27 shows a circle being drawn by specifying three points.

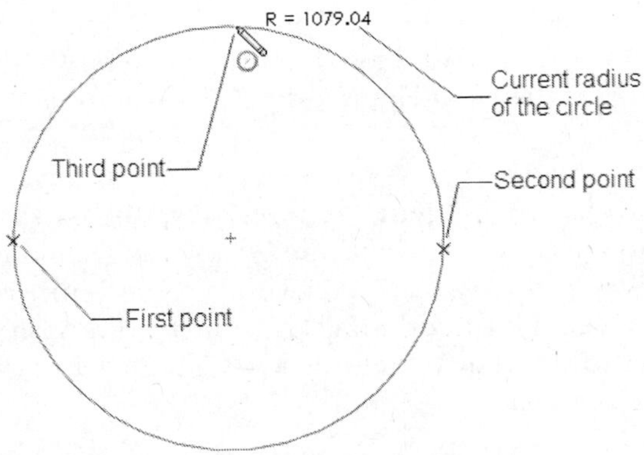

Figure 2-27 Drawing a circle by specifying three points

Drawing Construction Circles

If you want to sketch a construction circle, draw a circle using the **Circle** tool and then select the **For construction** check box in the **Options** rollout of the **Circle PropertyManager**.

Tip

To convert a construction entity back to a sketched entity, invoke the ***Select*** *tool and then select the construction entity; a popup toolbar will be displayed. Deactivate the* ***Construction Geometry*** *button in this toolbar.*

DRAWING ARCS

In SOLIDWORKS, you can draw arcs by using three tools: **Centerpoint Arc**, **Tangent Arc**, and **3 Point Arc**. All these tools are grouped together in the **Arc** flyout in the **Sketch CommandManager**. You can invoke these tools from the flyout displayed on choosing the down arrow on the right of the **Centerpoint Arc** tool. The methods used to create arcs using these tools are discussed next.

Drawing Tangent/Normal Arcs

CommandManager:	Sketch > Arc flyout > Tangent Arc
SOLIDWORKS menus:	Tools > Sketch Entities > Tangent Arc
Toolbar:	Sketch > Arc flyout > Tangent Arc

The tangent arcs are the ones that are drawn tangent to an existing sketched entity. The existing sketched entities include the sketched and construction lines, arcs, and splines. The normal arcs are the ones that are drawn normal to an existing entity. You can draw tangent and normal arcs using the **Tangent Arc** tool.

To draw a tangent arc, invoke the **Tangent Arc** tool; the arrow cursor will be replaced by the tangent arc cursor. Move the arc cursor close to the endpoint of the entity that you want to select as the tangent entity. You will notice that an orange colored dot is displayed at the endpoint. Also, a yellow symbol is displayed with two concentric circles. Now, press the left mouse button once and move the cursor along the tangent direction through a small distance and then move the cursor to size the arc. The arc will start from the endpoint of the tangent entity and its size will change as you move the cursor. Note that the angle and radius of the tangent arc are displayed above the cursor, as shown in Figure 2-28. Click when the radius and angle values are closer to the desired values.

To draw a normal arc, invoke the **Tangent Arc** tool. Move the cursor close to the endpoint of the entity that you want to select as the normal entity; an orange colored dot will be displayed at the endpoint. Also, a yellow symbol is displayed with two concentric circles. Now, press the left mouse button once and move the cursor along the normal direction through a small distance and then move the cursor to size the arc, refer to Figure 2-29. Click when the radius and angle values are closer to the desired values.

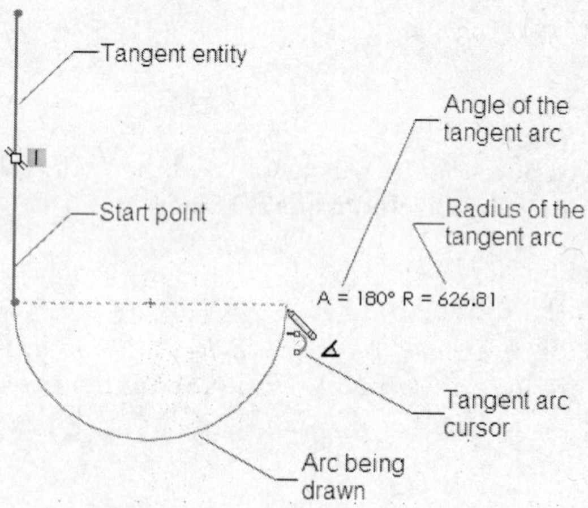

Figure 2-28 Drawing a tangent arc

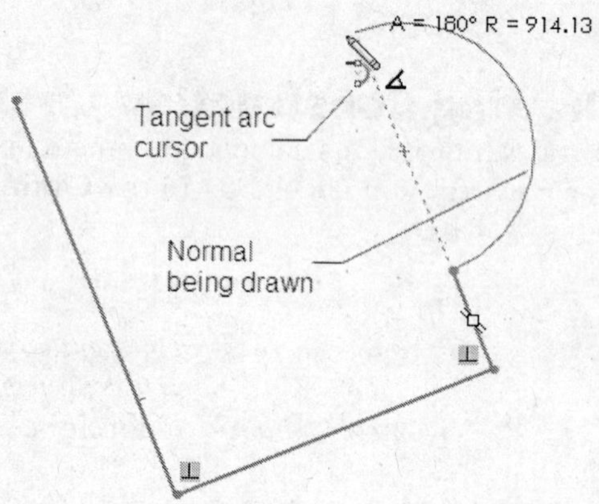

Figure 2-29 Drawing a normal arc

On invoking the **Tangent Arc** tool, the **Arc PropertyManager** will be displayed. However, the options in the **Arc PropertyManager** will not be enabled at this stage. These options will be enabled on selecting the completed tangent or normal arc.

You can draw an arbitrary arc and then modify its value using the **Arc PropertyManager**. Figure 2-30 shows partial view of the **Arc PropertyManager**.

Note

*When you select a tangent entity to draw a tangent arc, the **Tangent** relation is applied between the start point of the arc and the tangent entity. Therefore, if you change the coordinates of the start point of the arc, the tangent entity will also be modified accordingly.*

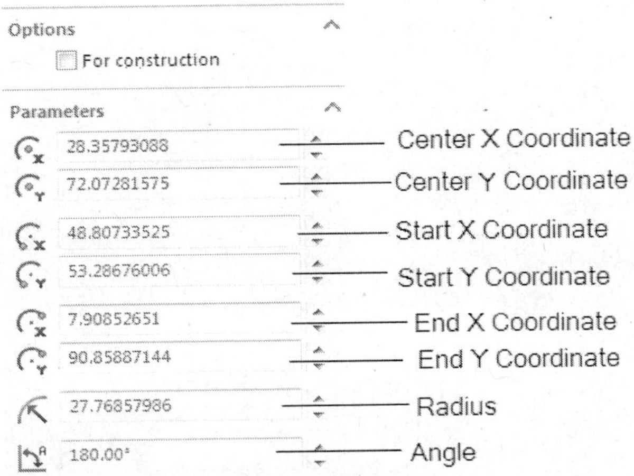

Figure 2-30 Partial view of the ***Arc PropertyManager***

Drawing Centerpoint Arcs

CommandManager:	Sketch > Arc flyout > Centerpoint Arc
SOLIDWORKS menus:	Tools > Sketch Entity > Centerpoint Arc
Toolbar:	Sketch > Arc flyout > Centerpoint Arc

The center point arcs are the ones that are drawn by defining the centerpoint, start point, and endpoint of the arc. When you invoke this tool, the arrow cursor is replaced by the arc cursor.

To draw a center point arc, invoke the **Centerpoint Arc** tool and then move the arc cursor to the point that you want to specify as the center point of the arc. Press the left mouse button once at the location of the center point and then move the cursor to the point from where you want to start the arc. You will notice that a dotted circle is displayed on the screen. The size of this circle will modify as you move the mouse. This circle is drawn for your reference and the center point of this circle lies at the point that you specified as the center of the arc. Press the left mouse button once at the point that you want to select as the start point of the arc. Next, move the cursor to specify the endpoint of the arc. You will notice that the reference circle is no longer displayed and an arc is being drawn with the start point as the point that you specified after specifying the center point. Also, the **Arc PropertyManager**, similar to the one that is shown in the tangent arc, is displayed on the left of the drawing area. Note that the options in the **Arc PropertyManager** will not be available at this stage.

If you move the cursor in the clockwise direction, the resulting arc will be drawn in the clockwise direction. However, if you move the cursor in the counterclockwise direction, the resulting arc will be drawn in the counterclockwise direction. Specify the endpoint of the arc using the left mouse button. Figure 2-31 shows the reference circle displayed when you move the mouse button after specifying the center point of the arc and Figure 2-32 shows the resulting center point arc.

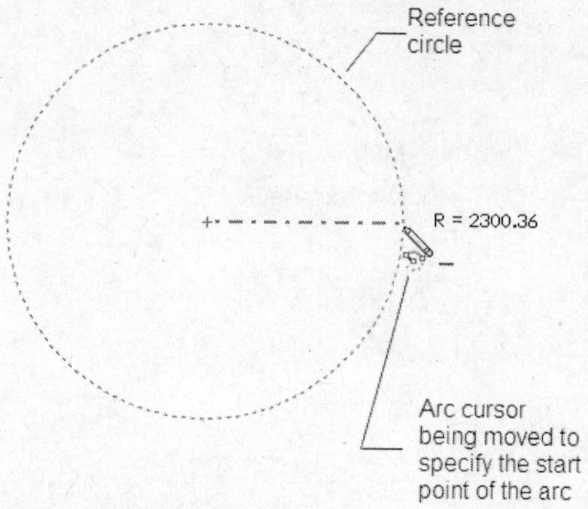

Figure 2-31 Reference circle displayed after specifying the center point of the arc

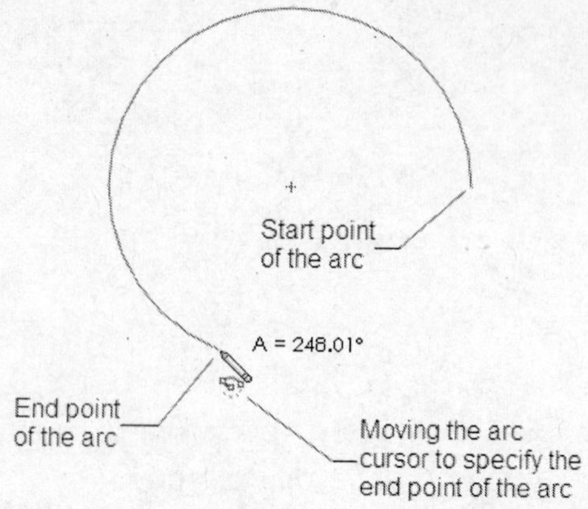

Figure 2-32 The resulting center point arc

Drawing 3 Point Arcs

CommandManager:	Sketch > Arc flyout > 3 Point Arc
SOLIDWORKS menus:	Tools > Sketch Entities > 3 Point Arc
Toolbar:	Sketch > Arc flyout > 3 Point Arc

The three point arcs are the ones that are drawn by defining the start point and the endpoint of the arc, and a point on the circumference or the periphery of the arc. On invoking this tool, the arrow cursor is replaced by the three-point arc cursor.

To draw a 3 point arc, invoke the **3 Point Arc** tool and then move the three-point arc cursor to the point that you want to specify as the start point of the arc. Press the left mouse button once at the location of the start point and then move the cursor to the point that you want to specify as the endpoint of the arc. As soon as you invoke the **3 Point Arc** tool, the **Arc PropertyManager** will be displayed. Note that when you start moving the cursor after specifying the start point, a reference arc will be displayed. However, the options in the **Arc PropertyManager** will not be activated at this stage.

Specify the endpoint of the arc using the left mouse button. You will notice that the reference arc is no longer displayed. Instead, a solid arc is displayed and the cursor is attached to it. As you move the cursor, the arc will also be modified dynamically. Using the left mouse button, specify a point on the screen to create the arc. The last point that you specify will determine the direction and radius of the arc. The options in the **Arc PropertyManager** will be displayed once you draw the arc. You can modify the properties of the arc using the **Arc PropertyManager**. Figure 2-33 shows the reference arc drawn by specifying the start point and endpoint of the arc and Figure 2-34 shows the third point being specified for drawing the arc.

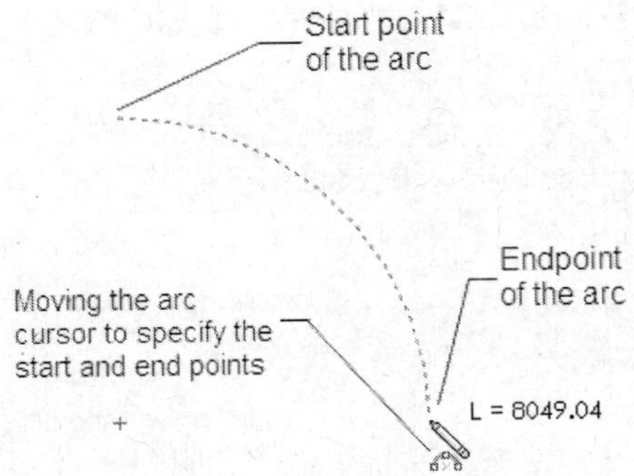

Figure 2-33 *Specifying the start point and endpoint of the arc*

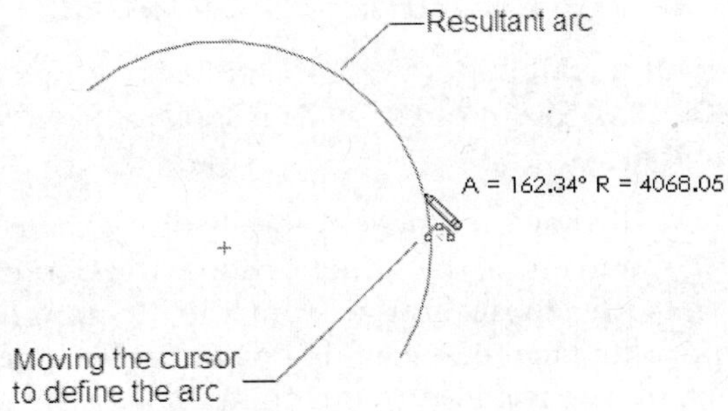

Figure 2-34 *Specifying the third point for drawing the arc*

DRAWING RECTANGLES

In SOLIDWORKS, the tools that are used to draw rectangles are grouped together in the **Rectangle** flyout. On invoking a tool from this flyout, the **Rectangle PropertyManager** will be displayed. Select an appropriate method to draw a rectangle from the **Rectangle Type** rollout. Alternatively, right-click and then choose the **Corner Rectangle** option from the shortcut menu to display the **Rectangle PropertyManager**. You can also invoke this PropertyManager by using the Mouse Gesture. Various methods to create a rectangle are discussed next.

Drawing Rectangles by Specifying Their Corners

CommandManager:	Sketch > Rectangle flyout > Corner Rectangle
SOLIDWORKS menus:	Tools > Sketch Entities > Corner Rectangle
Toolbar:	Sketch > Rectangle flyout > Corner Rectangle

To draw a rectangle by specifying the two diagonally opposite corners, choose the **Corner Rectangle** button from the **Rectangle Type** rollout in the **Rectangle PropertyManager**, if it is not chosen by default. Next, move the cursor to the point that you want to specify as the first corner of the rectangle and then click the left mouse button once to specify the first corner. Now, move the cursor diagonally away from it. You will notice that the length and width of the rectangle are displayed above the rectangle cursor. The length is measured along the X-axis and the width is measured along the Y-axis. Next, specify the other corner of the rectangle using the left mouse button. Figure 2-35 shows a rectangle being drawn by specifying two diagonally opposite corners.

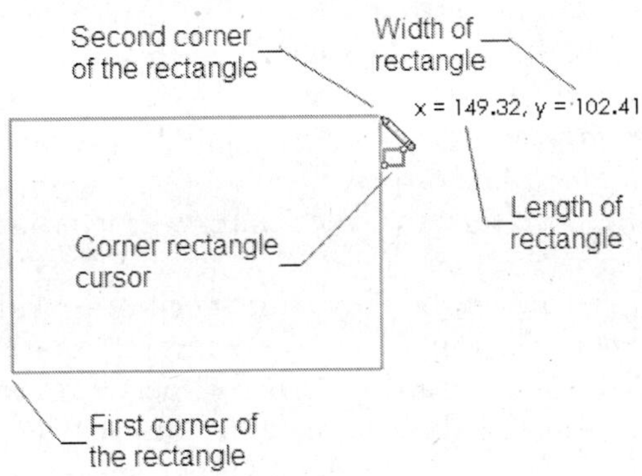

Figure 2-35 *Drawing a rectangle by specifying two diagonally opposite corners*

Drawing Rectangles by Specifying the Center and a Corner

CommandManager:	Sketch > Rectangle flyout > Center Rectangle
SOLIDWORKS menus:	Tools > Sketch Entities > Center Rectangle
Toolbar:	Sketch > Rectangle flyout > Center Rectangle

To draw a rectangle by specifying the center and one of the corners, choose the **Center Rectangle** button from the **Rectangle Type** rollout in the **Rectangle PropertyManager**. Next, move the cursor to the point that you want to specify as the center of the rectangle and click the left mouse button. Then, move the cursor and specify one of the corners of the rectangle using the left mouse button. You will notice that the length and width of the rectangle are displayed above the rectangle cursor. The length is measured along the X-axis and the width is measured along the Y-axis. Figure 2-36 shows a rectangle being drawn by specifying its center and one of the corners.

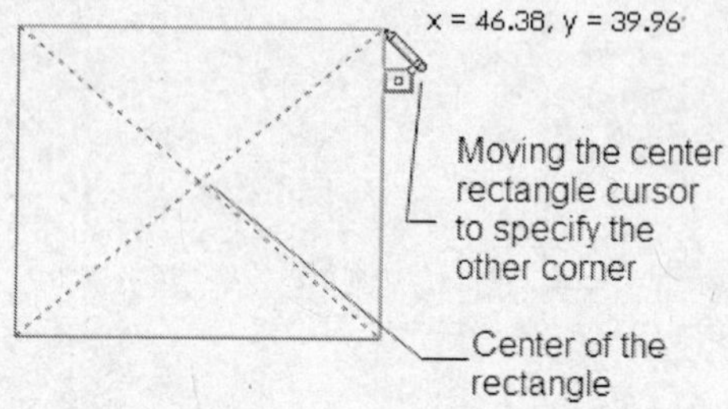

Figure 2-36 *Drawing a rectangle by specifying its center and one of the corners*

Drawing Rectangles at an Angle

CommandManager:	Sketch > Rectangle flyout > 3 Point Corner Rectangle
SOLIDWORKS menus:	Tools > Sketch Entities > 3 Point Corner Rectangle
Toolbar:	Sketch > Rectangle flyout > 3 Point Corner Rectangle

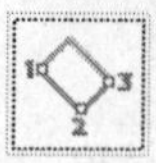

To draw a rectangle at an angle, choose the **3 Point Corner Rectangle** button from the **Rectangle Type** rollout in the **Rectangle PropertyManager**. Move the cursor to the point that you want to specify as the start point of one of the edges of the rectangle. Click the left mouse button at this point and move the cursor to size the edge. You will notice that a reference line is being drawn. Depending on the current position of the cursor, the reference line will be horizontal, vertical, or inclined. The current length of the edge and its angle will be displayed above the rectangle cursor. Specify the second point as the endpoint of the edge such that the reference line is at an angle.

Next, move the cursor to specify the width of the rectangle. You will notice that a reference rectangle is drawn at an angle. Also, irrespective of the current position of the cursor, the width will be specified normal to the first edge, either above or below it. Specify the third point using the left mouse button to define the width of the rectangle, as shown in Figure 2-37; the reference rectangle will be converted into a sketched rectangle.

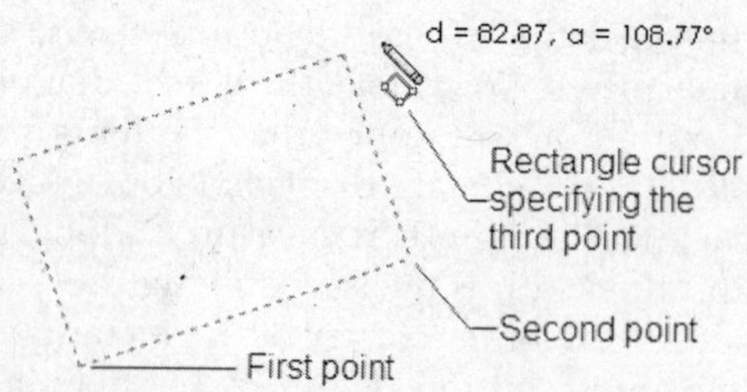

Figure 2-37 *Drawing a rectangle at an angle*

Drawing Centerpoint Rectangles at an Angle

CommandManager:	Sketch > Rectangle flyout > 3 Point Center Rectangle
SOLIDWORKS menus:	Tools > Sketch Entities > 3 Point Center Rectangle
Toolbar:	Sketch > Rectangle flyout > 3 Point Center Rectangle

To draw a centerpoint rectangle at an angle, choose the **3 Point Center Rectangle** button from the **Rectangle Type** rollout in the **Rectangle PropertyManager**. Next, move the cursor to the point that you want to specify as the center point of the rectangle. Click the left mouse button once at this point and move the cursor to a distance that is equal to half the length of the rectangle to be drawn. You will notice that a reference line is being drawn. Depending on the current position of the cursor, the reference line can be horizontal, vertical, or inclined. The current length of the edge and its angle will be displayed above the rectangle cursor. Specify the second point using the left mouse button. Next, specify the third point to define the width of the rectangle.

You can select the **From Corners** or **From Midpoints** radio button from the **Rectangle Type** rollout to add construction lines from corner to corner or from midpoint of the sides of the rectangle respectively, as shown in Figures 2-38 and 2-39.

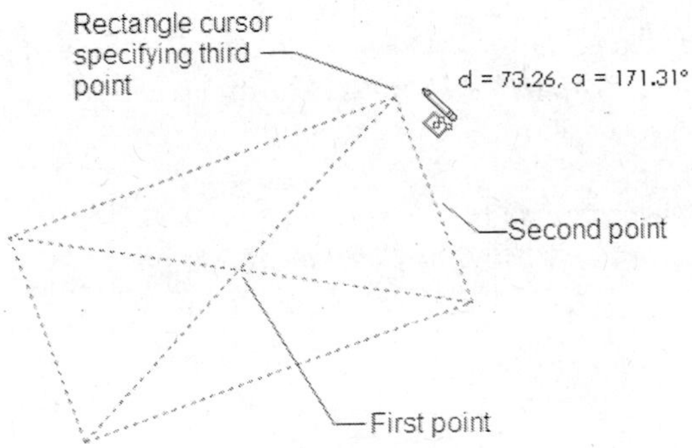

*Figure 2-38 Specifying the third point when the **From Corners** radio button is selected*

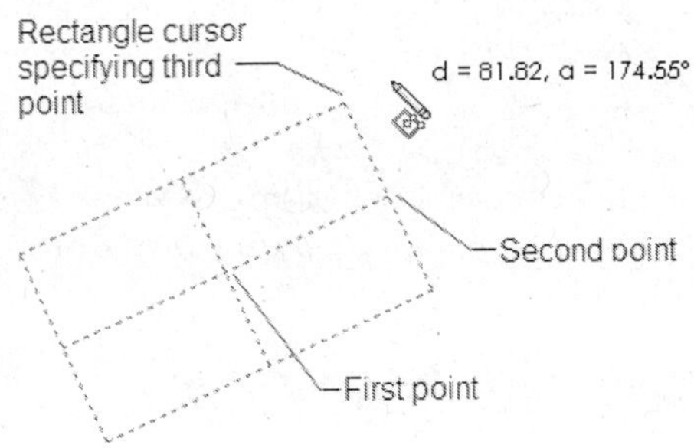

*Figure 2-39 Specifying the third point when the **From Midpoints** radio button is selected*

Drawing Parallelograms

CommandManager:	Sketch > Rectangle flyout > Parallelogram
SOLIDWORKS menus:	Tools > Sketch Entities > Parallelogram
Toolbar:	Sketch > Rectangle flyout > Parallelogram

To draw a parallelogram, choose the **Parallelogram** button from the **Rectangle Type** rollout of the **Rectangle PropertyManager**. Specify two points on the screen to define one edge in the parallelogram. Next, move the mouse to define the width of the parallelogram. As you move the mouse, a reference parallelogram will be drawn. The size and shape of the reference parallelogram will depend on the current location of the cursor.

Specify a point on the screen to define the parallelogram. Figure 2-40 shows the parallelogram cursor specifying the third point to draw a parallelogram.

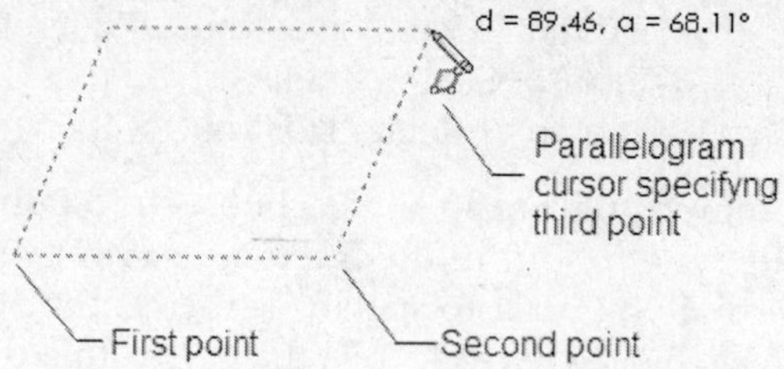

Figure 2-40 Drawing a parallelogram

Note

*In SOLIDWORKS, a rectangle is considered as a combination of four individual lines. Therefore, after drawing the rectangle by using the **Rectangle PropertyManager**. If you select one of the lines of the rectangle, the **Line Properties PropertyManager** will be displayed instead of the **Rectangle PropertyManager**. You can modify the parameters of the selected line using the **Line Properties PropertyManager**.*

*Remember that because the relations are applied to all four corners of the rectangle, on modifying the parameters of one of the lines using the **Line Properties PropertyManager**, the other three lines will also be modified accordingly.*

*You can convert a rectangle into a construction rectangle by selecting all lines together using a window and then selecting the **For construction** check box from the PropertyManager.*

DRAWING POLYGONS

CommandManager:	Sketch > Polygon
SOLIDWORKS menus:	Tools > Sketch Entities > Polygon
Toolbar:	Sketch > Polygon

A polygon is defined as a multisided geometric figure in which length of all the sides and angle between them are same. In SOLIDWORKS, you can draw a polygon with the number of sides ranging from 3 to 40. The dimensions of a polygon are controlled by using the diameter of a construction circle that is inscribed inside the polygon or circumscribed outside the polygon. If the construction circle is inscribed inside the polygon, the diameter of the construction circle will be taken perpendicularly from the edges of the polygon. If the construction circle is circumscribed about the polygon, the diameter of the construction circle will be taken from the vertices of the polygon.

To draw a polygon, invoke the **Polygon** tool; the **Polygon PropertyManager** will be displayed, as shown in Figure 2-41.

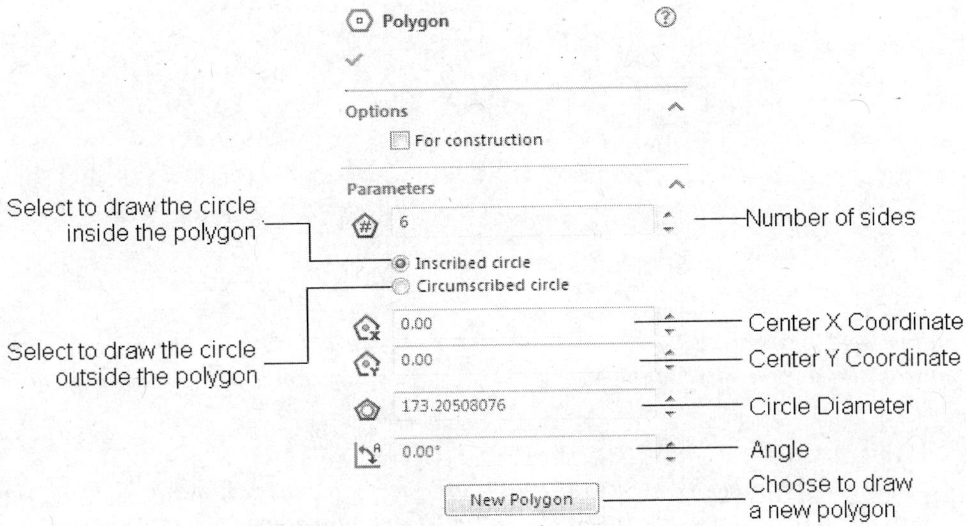

*Figure 2-41 The **Polygon PropertyManager***

Set the parameters such as the number of sides, inscribed or circumscribed circle, and so on in the **Polygon PropertyManager**. You can also modify these parameters after drawing the polygon. When you invoke this tool, the arrow cursor will be replaced by the polygon cursor. Click the left mouse button at the point that you want to specify as the center point of the polygon and then move the cursor to size the polygon. The length of each side and the rotation angle of the polygon will be displayed above the polygon cursor as you drag it. Using the left mouse button, specify a point on the screen after you get the desired length and rotation angle of the polygon. You will notice that based on whether you selected the **Inscribed circle** or the **Circumscribed circle** radio button in the **Polygon PropertyManager**, a construction circle will be drawn inside or outside the polygon. After you have drawn the polygon, you can modify the parameters such as the center point of the polygon, the diameter of the construction circle, the angle of rotation, and so on using the **Polygon PropertyManager**. If you want to draw another polygon, choose the **New Polygon** button provided below the **Angle** spinner in the **Polygon PropertyManager**.

Figure 2-42 shows a six-sided polygon with the construction circle inscribed inside the polygon and Figure 2-43 shows a six-sided polygon with the construction circle circumscribed about the polygon. Note that the reference circle is retained with the polygon. Remember that this circle will not be considered while converting the polygon into a feature.

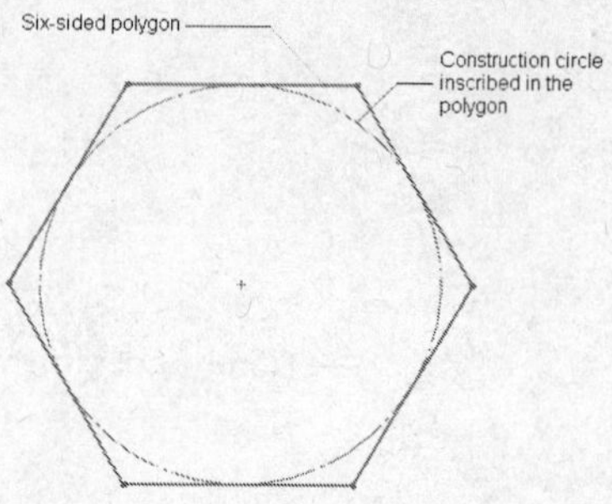

Figure 2-42 *Six-sided polygon with the construction circle inscribed inside it*

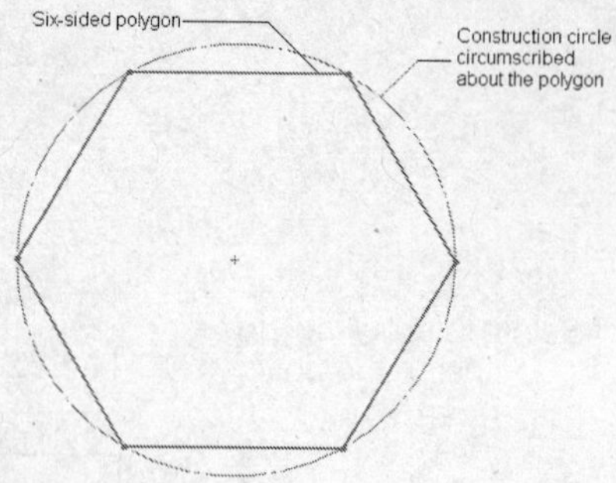

Figure 2-43 *Six-sided polygon with the construction circle circumscribed about it*

Tip

*You can invoke the list of recently used tools by using the shortcut menu. To do so, right-click in the drawing area and choose the **Recent Commands** option from the shortcut menu; a cascading menu will be displayed with the most recently used tools.*

DRAWING SPLINES

CommandManager:	Sketch > Spline flyout > Spline
SOLIDWORKS menus:	Tools > Sketch Entities > Spline
Toolbar:	Sketch > Spline flyout > Spline

To draw a spline, choose the **Spline** tool from the **Sketch CommandManager**. Then, using the left mouse button continuously, specify the points through which the spline will pass. This method of drawing splines is similar to that of drawing continuous lines. After specifying all points of the spline, right-click to invoke the shortcut menu. Now, you can draw a new spline. If you need to exit the **Spline** tool, choose the **Select** option. Figure 2-44 shows a spline drawn with its start point at the origin.

Figure 2-44 *Spline with its start point at the origin*

Note

*When you select a spline using the **Select** tool, handles are displayed on the points. These handles are used to edit a spline. You will learn more about these handles in the later chapters while editing splines. Similar to individual line, you can also create individual spline segments by specifying the start point and then dragging the mouse to specify the endpoint.*

Tip

*After creating a spline, if you select it by using the **Select** tool, the **Spline PropertyManager** will be displayed. Also, the control points will be displayed with a blue filled square. The number of the current control point and its X and Y coordinates will be displayed in the **Parameters** rollout of the **Spline PropertyManager**. You can modify these coordinates to modify the position of the selected control point. A double-sided arrow along with the handle will also be displayed. You will learn more about the handle in later chapters.*

DRAWING SLOTS

In SOLIDWORKS, the tools used to draw slot profile are grouped together in the **Slot** flyout. To draw a slot profile, invoke the **Slot PropertyManager** by choosing the **Slot** button from the **Slot** flyout and select an appropriate method to draw a slot profile from the **Slot Type** rollout. Alternatively, right-click and then choose an option from the shortcut menu to draw a slot profile. Various methods to create a slot profile are discussed next.

Creating a Straight Slot

CommandManager:	Sketch > Slot flyout > Straight Slot
SOLIDWORKS menus:	Tools > Sketch Entities > Straight Slot
Toolbar:	Sketch > Slot flyout > Straight Slot

To create a straight slot, choose the **Straight Slot** button from the **Sketch CommandManager**; the **Slot PropertyManager** will be displayed. Next, move the cursor where you want to specify the first endpoint of the straight slot. Press the left mouse button once at the first endpoint, and then move the cursor and specify the second endpoint of the straight slot; a preview of the slot will be attached to the cursor. Move the cursor and specify the width of the straight slot, as shown in Figure 2-45. The options in the **Slot PropertyManager** will be enabled once you draw the straight slot. You can modify the properties of the straight slot using the options available in the **Slot PropertyManager**.

Creating a Centerpoint Straight Slot

CommandManager:	Sketch > Slot flyout > Centerpoint Straight Slot
SOLIDWORKS menus:	Tools > Sketch Entities > Centerpoint Straight Slot
Toolbar:	Sketch > Slot flyout > Centerpoint Straight Slot

To draw a centerpoint straight slot, choose the **Centerpoint Straight Slot** button from the **Slot** flyout; the **Slot PropertyManager** will be displayed. Specify the center point of the slot by using the left mouse button. Next, move the cursor and specify the endpoint of the slot; a preview of the slot will be attached to the cursor. The options in the **Slot PropertyManager** will not be enabled at this stage. Move the cursor and specify the width of the centerpoint straight slot, as shown in Figure 2-46. The options in the **Slot PropertyManager** will be enabled once you draw the centerpoint straight slot. You can modify the properties of the centerpoint straight slot using the options in the **Slot PropertyManager**.

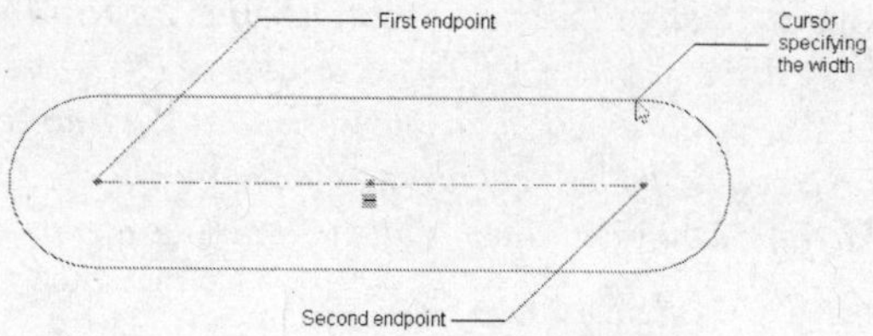

Figure 2-45 Specifying the points to create a straight slot

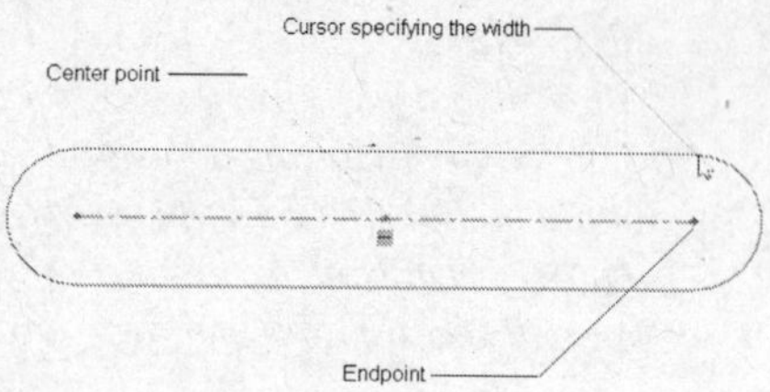

Figure 2-46 Specifying the points to create a centerpoint straight slot

Creating a 3 Point Arc Slot

CommandManager:	Sketch > Slot flyout > 3 Point Arc Slot
SOLIDWORKS menus:	Tools > Sketch Entities > 3 Point Arc Slot
Toolbar:	Sketch > Slot flyout > 3 Point Arc Slot

To create a 3 point arc slot, choose the **3 Point Arc Slot** button from the **Slot** flyout; the **Slot PropertyManager** will be displayed. You need to specify three points in the drawing area to create a 3 point arc slot. Move the cursor to the point where you want to specify the start point of the slot and then specify the start point of the slot by using the left mouse button. Note that as soon as you specify the start point, a reference arc will be attached to the cursor. Move the cursor to the location where you want to specify the second point of the slot and then click to specify the second point of the slot. Next, specify the third point of the slot; a preview of the 3 point arc slot will be attached to the cursor. The options in the **Slot PropertyManager** will not be enabled at this stage. Move the cursor and specify the width of the 3 point arc slot, as shown in Figure 2-47. The options in the **Slot PropertyManager** will be enabled once you draw the 3 point arc slot. You can modify the properties of the 3 point arc slot using the options available in the **Slot PropertyManager**.

Creating a Centerpoint Arc Slot

CommandManager:	Sketch > Slot flyout > Centerpoint Arc Slot
SOLIDWORKS menus:	Tools > Sketch Entities > Centerpoint Arc Slot
Toolbar:	Sketch > Slot flyout > Centerpoint Arc Slot

To create a centerpoint arc slot, choose the **Centerpoint Arc Slot** button from the **Slot** flyout; the **Slot PropertyManager** will be displayed. Specify the center point of the slot; a reference circle will be attached to the cursor. Move the cursor and specify the start point of the slot. Next, specify the endpoint of the slot by using the left mouse button; the preview of the centerpoint arc slot will be attached to the cursor. Next, move the cursor and specify the point to create the centerpoint arc slot, as shown in Figure 2-48.

Tip

*If the **Add dimension** check box is selected while creating slots, the dimensions will be added to them. Also, while creating straight slots, you can specify whether the center to center distance or the overall length of the slot is to be dimensioned.*

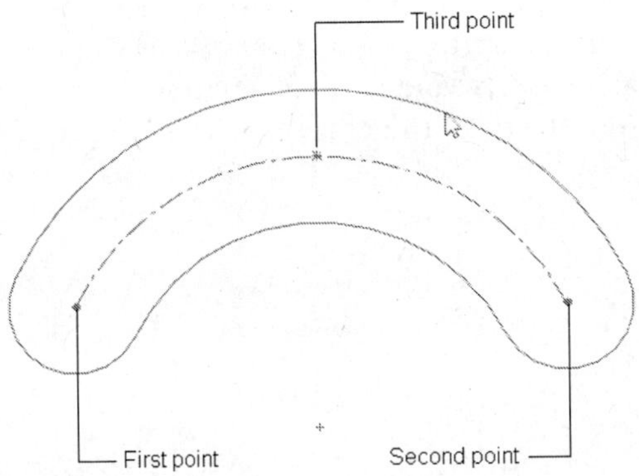

Figure 2-47 Specifying points to create a 3 point arc slot

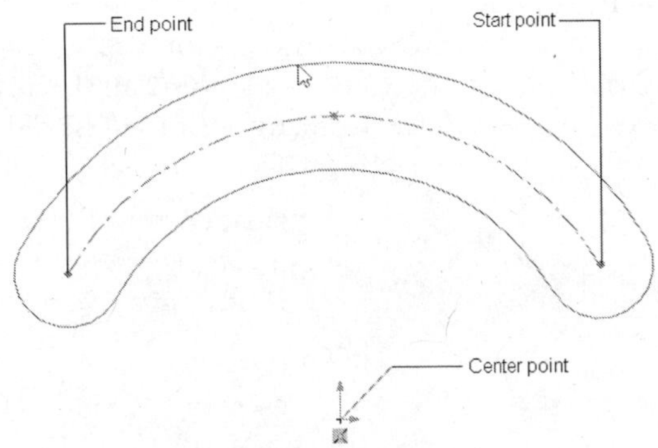

Figure 2-48 Specifying points to create a centerpoint arc slot

PLACING SKETCHED POINTS

CommandManager:	Sketch > Point
SOLIDWORKS menus:	Tools > Sketch Entities > Point
Toolbar:	Sketch > Point

To place a sketched point, choose the **Point** tool from the **Sketch CommandManager** and then specify the point on the screen where you want to place it; the **Point PropertyManager** will be displayed with the X and Y coordinates of the current point. You can change/shift the location of the point by modifying its X and Y coordinates in the **Point PropertyManager**.

DRAWING ELLIPSES

CommandManager:	Sketch > Ellipse flyout > Ellipse
SOLIDWORKS menus:	Tools > Sketch Entities > Ellipse
Toolbar:	Sketch > Ellipse flyout > Ellipse

In SOLIDWORKS, an ellipse is drawn by specifying its centerpoint and two ellipse axes by moving the mouse. To draw an ellipse, choose the **Ellipse** tool from the **Ellipse** flyout in the **Sketch CommandManager**; the arrow cursor will be replaced by the ellipse cursor. Move the cursor to the point that you want to specify as the centerpoint of the ellipse. Click the left mouse button at that point and then move the cursor to specify one of the ellipse axes. You will notice that a reference circle is drawn and two values are displayed above the ellipse cursor. The first value that shows R = * is the radius of the first axis or the major axis that you are defining and the second value that shows r = * is the radius of the other axis or minor axis of the ellipse. While defining the first axis, the second axis is taken equal to the first axis. Therefore, a reference circle is drawn, instead of a reference ellipse, as shown in Figure 2-49.

Specify a point on the screen to define the first axis. Next, move the cursor to size the other ellipse axis. As you move the cursor, the second value above the ellipse cursor that shows r = * and the value in the **Radius 2** spinner in the **Ellipse PropertyManager** will change dynamically. Specify a point in the drawing area to define the second axis of the ellipse, refer to Figure 2-50.

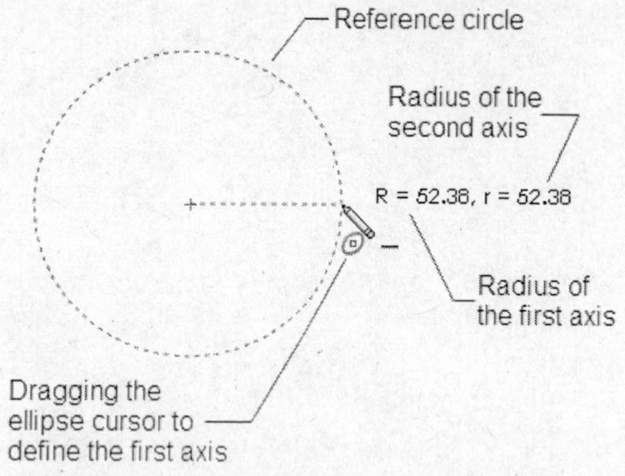

Figure 2-49 Dragging the cursor to define the ellipse axis

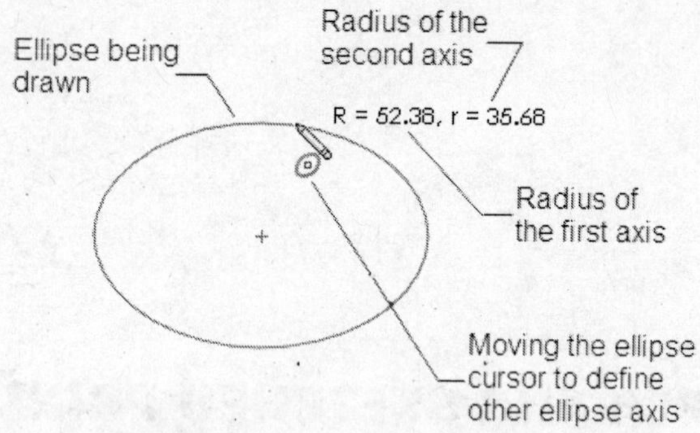

Figure 2-50 Defining the second axis of the ellipse

DRAWING ELLIPTICAL ARCS

CommandManager:	Sketch > Ellipse flyout > Partial Ellipse
SOLIDWORKS menus:	Tools > Sketch Entities > Partial Ellipse
Toolbar:	Sketch > Ellipse flyout > Partial Ellipse

In SOLIDWORKS, the process of drawing an elliptical arc is similar to that of drawing an ellipse. You will follow the same process of defining the ellipse first. The point that you specify on the screen to define the second axis of the ellipse is taken as the start point of the elliptical arc. You can define the endpoint of the elliptical arc by specifying a point on the screen, as shown in Figure 2-51.

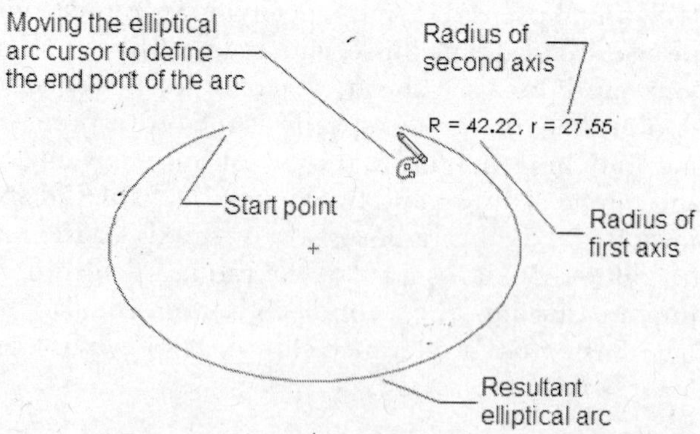

Figure 2-51 Drawing an elliptical arc

After drawing the elliptical arc, you can also modify its parameters in the **Ellipse PropertyManager**, as shown in Figure 2-52.

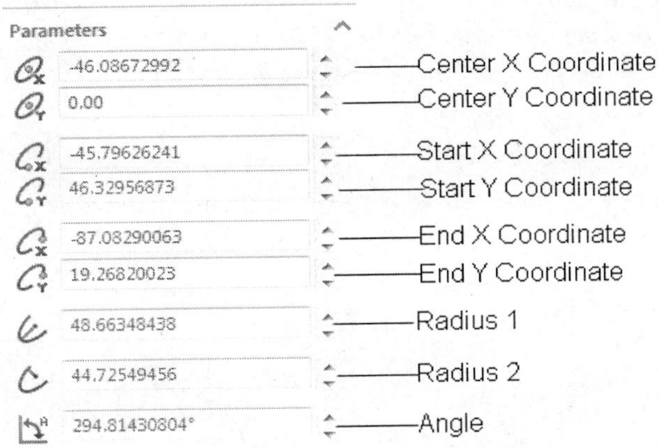

Figure 2-52 Partial view of the ***Ellipse PropertyManager***

Tip
In SOLIDWORKS, when you are in the sketching environment, press the S key to invoke the shortcut bar that contains the tools for sketching.

DRAWING PARABOLIC CURVES

CommandManager:	Sketch > Ellipse flyout > Parabola
SOLIDWORKS menus:	Tools > Sketch Entities > Parabola
Toolbar:	Sketch > Ellipse flyout > Parabola

In SOLIDWORKS, you can draw a parabolic curve by specifying the focus point, apex point, and then two endpoints of the parabolic curve. To draw a parabolic curve, choose the **Parabola** tool from the **Ellipse** flyout; the cursor will be replaced by the parabola cursor. Move the cursor to the point that you want to specify as the focal point of the parabola. Press the left mouse button once at that point. You will notice that a reference parabolic arc is displayed. Then, move the cursor to define the apex point and to size the parabola. As you move the cursor away from the focal point, the parabola will be flattened. After getting the basic shape of the parabolic curve, specify a point by using the left mouse button. This point is taken as the apex of the parabolic curve. Next, specify two points with respect to the reference parabola to define the guide of the parabolic curve, see Figure 2-53.

As you move the mouse after specifying the focal point of the parabola, the **Parabola PropertyManager** will be displayed with the options inactive. These options will be available only after you have drawn the parabola. Figure 2-54 shows partial view of the **Parabola PropertyManager**.

Tip

*To dislodge the task pane, choose the **Auto Show** button and double-click on the gray bar at the top where its name is displayed. Now, you can move it at the desired location. To place it back on its original position, again double-click on the gray bar or choose the **Dock Task Pane** button provided at the top right corner of the task pane.*

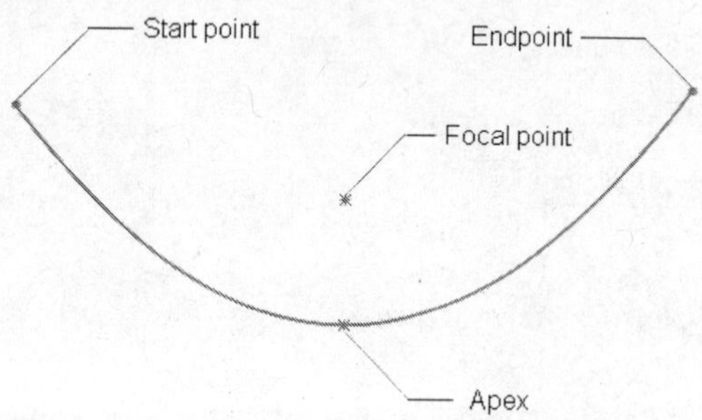

Figure 2-53 Parabola and its parameters

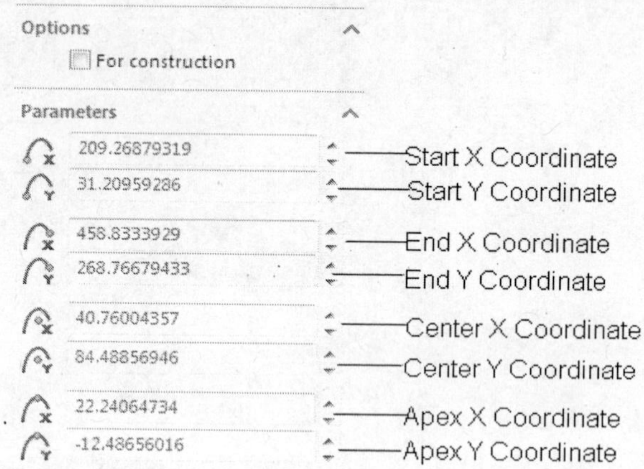

*Figure 2-54 Partial view of the **Parabola PropertyManager***

DRAWING CONIC CURVES

CommandManager:	Sketch > Ellipse flyout > Conic
SOLIDWORKS menus:	Tools > Sketch Entities > Conic
Toolbar:	Sketch > Ellipse flyout > Conic

In SOLIDWORKS, you can draw a conic curve by specifying the endpoints and the Rho value. To create the conic curve, choose **Tools > Sketch Entities > Conic** from the SOLIDWORKS menus; the cursor will be replaced by the conic cursor. Click to specify the first end point of the conic curve and move the cursor away from it; a reference line will get attached to the cursor. Next, click to specify the second endpoint of the conic curve and move the cursor away from it; the preview of the conic curve will get attached to the cursor and will be displayed in yellow color. Additionally, the **Conic PropertyManager** will be displayed with its options inactive. As you move the cursor, the curve will change dynamically with the cursor movement, refer to Figure 2-55. Move the cursor to a distance and click to specify the top vertex of the conic curve to be drawn. A reference line will be generated and the Rho value will be displayed above the cursor. As you move the cursor, the Rho value of the conic curve will be modified accordingly. Click the left mouse button when the required Rho value is displayed above the conic cursor; the conic curve will be created and the options in the **Conic PropertyManager** will be activated, refer to Figure 2-56. You can also modify the parameters of the conic curve drawn by using this PropertyManager.

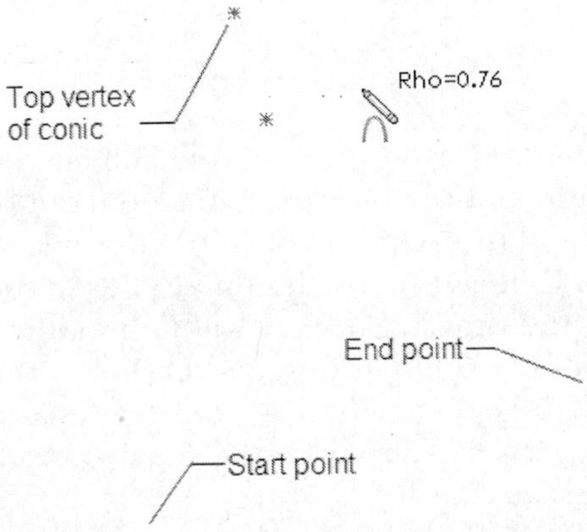

Figure 2-55 Conic and its parameters

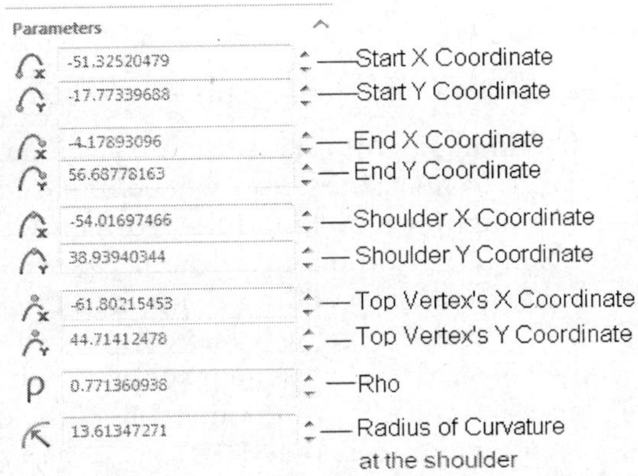

Figure 2-56 Partial view of the ***Conic PropertyManager***

DRAWING DISPLAY TOOLS

The drawing display tools are one of the most important tools provided in any of the solid modeling software. These tools allow you to modify the display of a drawing by zooming or panning it. In SOLIDWORKS, some of these tools are displayed in the drawing area in the **View (Heads-Up)** toolbar. Some of the drawing display tools available in SOLIDWORKS are discussed in this chapter. The remaining tools will be discussed in the later chapters.

Zoom to Fit

View (Heads-Up): Zoom to Fit
SOLIDWORKS menus: View > Modify > Zoom to Fit

The **Zoom to Fit** tool available in the **View (Heads-Up)** toolbar is used to increase or decrease the drawing display area so that all the sketched entities or dimensions are fitted inside the current view. You can also press the F key to invoke this tool. Alternatively, double-click the middle mouse button in the drawing area to invoke this tool.

Zoom to Area

View (Heads-Up): Zoom to Area
SOLIDWORKS menus: View > Modify > Zoom to Area

The **Zoom to Area** tool available in the **View (Heads-Up)** toolbar is used to magnify a specified area so that the part of the drawing inside the magnified area can be viewed in the current window. The area is defined inside a window that is created by dragging the cursor. When you choose this button, the cursor is replaced by a magnifying glass cursor. Press and hold the left mouse button and drag the cursor to specify the opposite corners of the window. The area enclosed inside the window will be magnified.

Zoom In/Out

SOLIDWORKS menus: View > Modify > Zoom In/Out

The **Zoom In/Out** tool is used to dynamically zoom in or out the drawing. When you invoke this tool, the cursor will be replaced by the Zoom In/Out cursor. To zoom out of a drawing, press and hold the left mouse button and drag the cursor in the downward direction. Similarly, to zoom in a drawing, press and hold the left mouse button and drag the cursor in the upward direction. As you drag the cursor, the drawing display will be modified dynamically. After you get the desired view, exit this tool by right-clicking and choosing the **Select** option from the shortcut menu or by pressing the ESC key. If you have a mouse with scroll wheel, then scroll the wheel to zoom in/out of the drawing. You can also press the Z key to zoom out of a drawing and press the SHIFT+Z keys to zoom in the drawing.

Zoom to Selection

SOLIDWORKS menus: View > Modify > Zoom to Selection

The **Zoom to Selection** tool is used to modify the drawing display area such that the selected entity fits inside the current display. After selecting the entity, choose the **Zoom to Selection** tool; the drawing display area will be modified such that the selected entity fits inside the current view. Press and hold the CTRL key while selecting multiple entities. In SOLIDWORKS, if you select an entity, a pop-up toolbar will be displayed in the drawing area and you can invoke the **Zoom to Selection** tool from it.

Pan

View (Heads-Up): Pan (Customize to Add)

The **Pan** tool is used to drag the view in the current display. You can also press the CTRL key and the middle mouse button and then drag the cursor to move the entities.

> **Tip**
> *You can also invoke the **Pan** tool using the CTRL key and the arrow keys on the keyboard. For example, to pan toward the right, press the CTRL key and then press the right arrow key. Similarly, to pan upward, press the CTRL key and then press the up arrow key.*

Previous View

View (Heads-Up): Previous View

The **Previous View** tool is used to display the last view of the model and it can be useful if you have zoomed the model at many levels. You can view the last ten views using this tool. You can invoke this tool from the drawing area or press the CTRL+SHIFT+Z keys.

Redraw

SOLIDWORKS menus: View > Redraw

The **Redraw** tool is used to refresh the screen. Sometimes when you draw a sketched entity, some unwanted elements remain on the screen. To remove these unwanted elements from the screen, use this tool. The screen will be refreshed and all the unwanted elements will be removed. You can invoke this tool by pressing the CTRL+R keys.

Tip

You can also invoke some of the drawing display tools from the shortcut menu. To do so, right-click and choose the ***Zoom/Pan/Rotate*** *option; a cascading menu will be displayed with different display tools.*

SHADED SKETCH CONTOURS

In SOLIDWORKS, you can view all the closed sketch contours and sub-contours in shaded mode by using the **Shaded Sketch Contours** setting. Using this setting, you can resize, move, and apply relations to different entities in a sketch. This setting makes it easier to determine whether the sketch is open or closed. This setting can be turned on by choosing **Tools > Sketch Settings > Shaded Sketch Contours** from the SOLIDWORKS menus. You can also directly extrude a closed contour using this setting. The Extrude feature is discussed in later chapters.

DELETING SKETCHED ENTITIES

You can delete the sketched entities by selecting them using the **Select** tool and then pressing the DELETE key on the keyboard. You can select the entities individually or select more than one entity by defining a window or crossing around the entities. When you select the entities, they turn light blue. Now, press the DELETE key. You can also delete the sketched entities by selecting them and choosing the **Delete** option from the shortcut menu that is displayed on right-clicking.

TUTORIALS

Tutorial 1

In this tutorial, you will draw the basic sketch of the revolved solid model shown in Figure 2-57. The sketch of this model is shown in Figure 2-58. Do not dimension the sketch as the solid model and its dimensions are given for your reference only. **(Expected time: 30 min)**

Figure 2-57 Revolved solid model for Tutorial 1

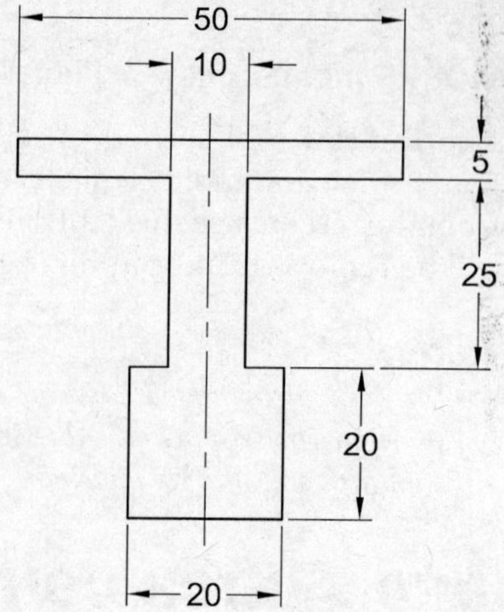

Figure 2-58 Sketch of the revolved solid model

The following steps are required to complete this tutorial:

a. Start a new part document.
b. Invoke the sketching environment.
c. Modify the settings of the snap and grid so that the cursor jumps through a distance of 5 mm.
d. Draw the sketch of the model using the **Line** tool.
e. Save the sketch and then close the document.

Opening a New Part Document

1. Start SolidWorks by double-clicking on the shortcut icon of SOLIDWORKS 2021 available on the desktop of your computer; the SOLIDWORKS 2021 window along with the **Welcome - SOLIDWORKS** dialog box is displayed.

2. Choose the **Part** button available in the **New** area of the **Home** tab in the **Welcome - SOLIDWORKS** dialog box. A new SOLIDWORKS part document is invoked. You can also select the **New** button from the Menu Bar; the **New SOLIDWORKS Document** dialog box is displayed, as shown in Figure 2-59.

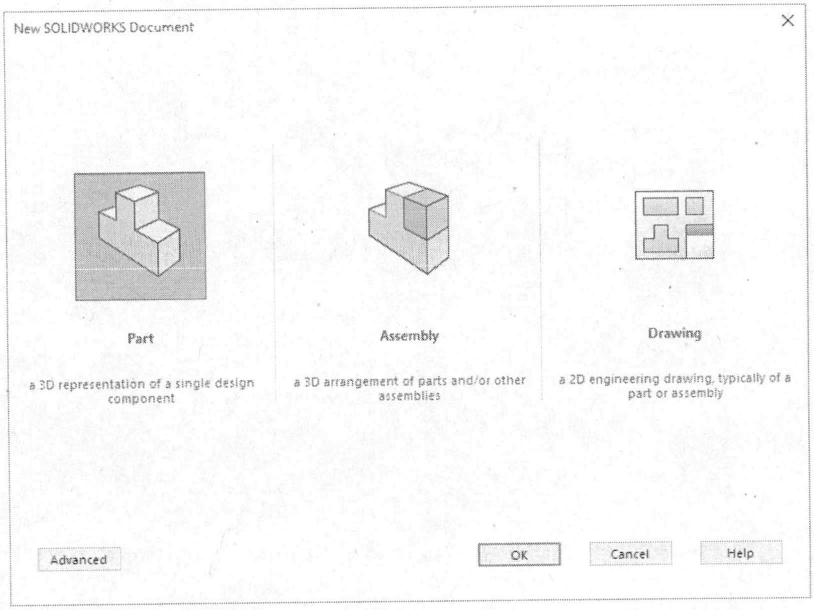

*Figure 2-59 The **New SOLIDWORKS Document** dialog box*

3. In the **New SOLIDWORKS Document** dialog box, the **Part** button is chosen by default. Therefore, choose the **OK** button; a new SOLIDWORKS part document starts.

   You need to invoke the sketching environment to draw the sketch.

4. Choose the **Sketch** tab from the **CommandManager** and then select the **Sketch** tool from the **Sketch CommandManager**; the **Edit Sketch PropertyManager** is displayed and you are prompted to select a plane on which you want to draw the sketch.

5. Select the **Front Plane** from the drawing area; the sketching environment is invoked and the plane gets oriented normal to the view. You will notice that red colored arrows are displayed at the center of the screen indicating that you are in the sketching environment. Also, the confirmation corner with the **Exit Sketch** and **Cancel** options is displayed on the upper right corner in the graphics area. The screen display in the sketching environment of SOLIDWORKS 2021 is shown in Figure 2-60.

Tip

*In SOLIDWORKS 2021, you can set that the orientation of the sketching plane becomes automatically parallel to the screen whenever you start a new sketch or edit an existing sketch. This setting can be toggled by selecting the **Auto-rotate view normal to sketch plane on sketch creation and sketch edit** check box in the **Sketch** area in the **System Options - General** dialog box.*

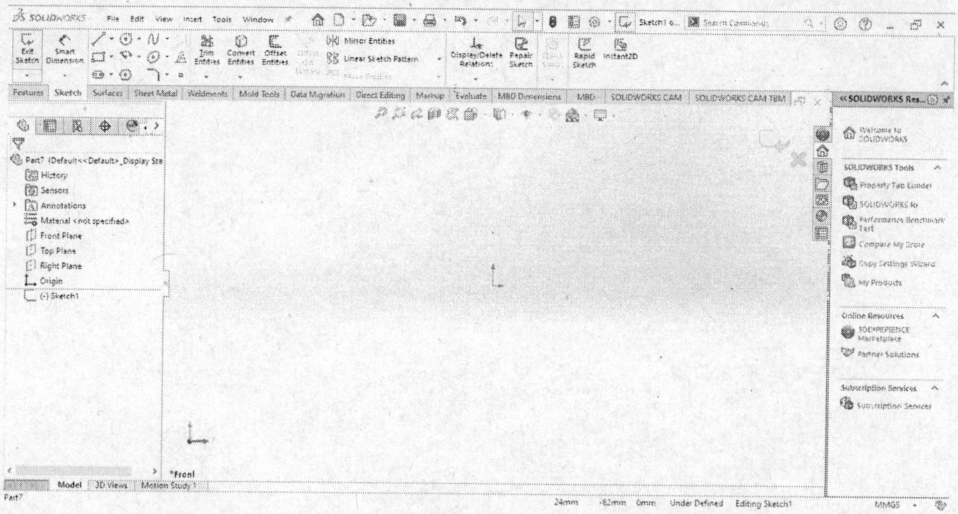

Figure 2-60 Screen display in the sketching environment

Modifying the Snap, Grid, and Dimensioning Unit Settings

It is assumed that while installing SOLIDWORKS, you have selected the **MMGS (millimeters, gram, second)** option for measuring the length. Therefore, the length of an entity will be measured in millimeters in the current file. But, if you have selected some other unit at the time of installation, you need to change the linear and angular unit settings before drawing the sketch. For this tutorial, you need to modify the grid and snap settings so that the cursor jumps through a distance of 5 mm.

1. Choose the **Options** button from the Menu Bar; the **System Options - General** dialog box is displayed.

2. Choose the **Document Properties** tab; the name of the dialog box changes to the **Document Properties - Drafting Standard**.

Note

If you have selected millimeters as the unit of measurement while installing SOLIDWORKS, skip steps 3 and 4 in this section.

3. Select the **Units** option from the area on the left to display the options related to the linear and angular units.

4. Select the **MMGS (millimeter, gram, second)** radio button in the **Unit system** area. Also, select the **degrees** option in the **Unit** column as unit of angle if not selected by default. You can also change the unit system using the **Unit system** button located at the right-side of the status bar.

It is evident from Figure 2-58 that the dimensions in the sketch are multiples of 5. Therefore, you need to modify the grid and snap settings so that the cursor jumps through a distance of 5 mm instead of 10 mm.

5. Select the **Grid/Snap** option from the area on the left to display grid options. Set the value in the **Major grid spacing** spinner to **50** and the value in the **Minor-lines per major** spinner to **10**.

6. Select the **Display grid** check box if it is cleared. Next, choose the **Go To System Snaps** button; the system options related to relations and snaps are displayed.

7. Select the **Grid** check box from the **Sketch snaps** area and clear the **Snap only when grid is displayed** check box. Choose **OK** to exit the dialog box.

   Note that in the sketching environment, the lower right corner of the drawing area displays the information about the status of the sketch and location of the cursor in the X, Y, and Z coordinates. You will use the coordinates displayed to draw the sketch of the model. These coordinates will be modified as you move the cursor around the drawing area. If you move the cursor after initial settings, the coordinates will show an increment of 5 mm instead of the default increment of 10 mm.

Drawing the Sketch

It is evident from Figure 2-58 that the sketch will be drawn using the **Line** tool. Therefore, you need to start drawing the sketch from the lower left corner of the sketch.

1. Choose the **Line** tool from the **Sketch CommandManager**; the arrow cursor is replaced by the line cursor.

2. Move the line cursor to the origin.

3. Left-click at this point and move the cursor horizontally toward the right. You will notice that the symbol of the **Horizontal** relation is displayed below the line cursor and the length and angle of the line are displayed above the line cursor.

4. Left-click again when the length of the line above the line cursor shows 20.

   The first horizontal line is drawn. As you are drawing continuous lines, the endpoint of the line drawn is automatically selected as the start point of the next line.

5. Move the line cursor vertically upward. The symbol of **Vertical** relation is displayed on the right of the line cursor and the length of the line is displayed above the line cursor. Click when the length of the line on the line cursor is displayed as 20.

6. Move the cursor horizontally toward the left and click when the length of the line on the line cursor is displayed as 5.

7. Move the line cursor vertically upward and press the left mouse button when the length of the line on the line cursor is displayed as 25.

8. Move the line cursor horizontally toward the right and click when the length of the line on the line cursor is displayed as 20.

9. Move the line cursor vertically upward and click when the length of the line on the line cursor is displayed as 5.

10. Press F on the keyboard to fit the sketch on the screen.

11. Move the line cursor horizontally toward the left and click when the length of the line on the line cursor is displayed as 50.

12. Move the line cursor vertically downward and click when the length of the line on the line cursor is displayed as 5.

13. Move the line cursor horizontally toward the right and press the left mouse button when the length of the line on the line cursor is displayed as 20.

14. Move the line cursor vertically downward and click when the length of the line on the line cursor is displayed as 25.

15. Move the line cursor horizontally toward the left and click when the length of the line on the line cursor is displayed as 5.

16. Move the line cursor vertically downward to the start point of the first line. Click when an orange circle is displayed; the final sketch for Tutorial 1 is created, as shown in Figure 2-61.

    In this figure, the grid display and **Shaded Sketch Contours** settings are turned off for clarity.

17. Right-click and then choose the **Select** option from the shortcut menu to exit the **Line** tool.

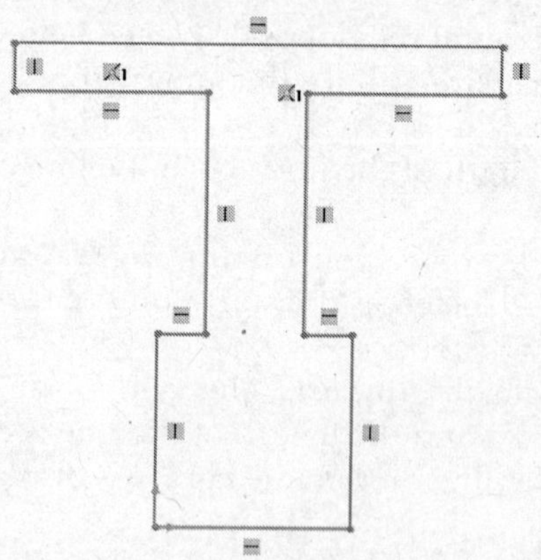

Figure 2-61 *Final sketch for Tutorial 1*

Note

*In Figure 2-61, the display of relations is turned on. To turn off the display of relations, choose the **View Sketch Relations** button from the **Hide/Show Items** flyout in the **View (Head-Up)** toolbar.*

Tip

*To turn off the grid display, right-click in the drawing area to display a shortcut menu. Choose the **Display Grid** button to turn off the grid display. This is a toggle button.*

Saving the Sketch

It is recommended that you create a separate folder for saving the tutorial files of this book. Next, you can save the tutorials of a chapter in the folder of that chapter.

1. Choose the **Save** button from the Menu Bar to invoke the **Save As** dialog box. Create the *SOLIDWORKS* folder inside the *\Documents* folder and then create the *c02* folder inside the *SOLIDWORKS* folder.

2. Enter **c02_tut01** as the name of the document in the **File name** edit box and choose the **Save** button. The document is saved at the location *\Documents\SOLIDWORKS\c02*.

3. Close the document by choosing **File > Close** from the SOLIDWORKS menus.

Tutorial 2

In this tutorial, you will draw the sketch of the solid model shown in Figure 2-62. The sketch of the model is shown in Figure 2-63. Do not dimension the sketch as the solid model and the dimensions are given for your reference only. **(Expected time: 30 min)**

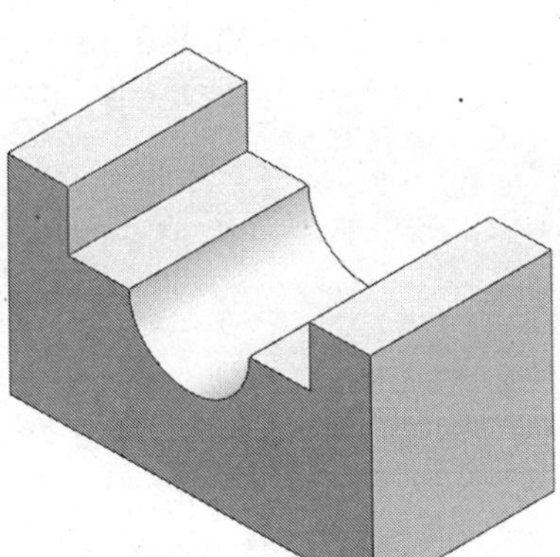

Figure 2-62 Solid model for Tutorial 2

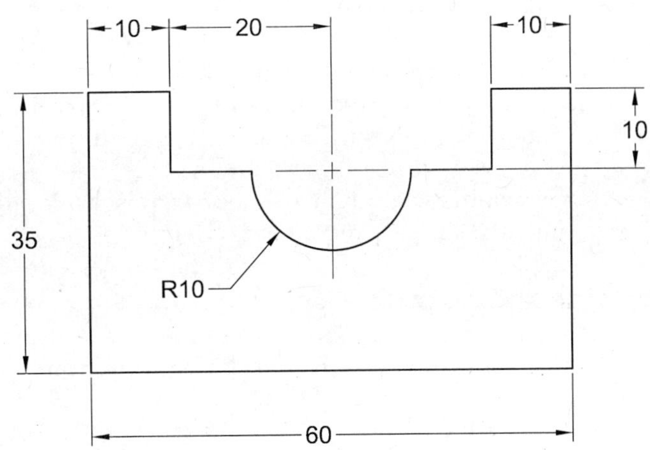

Figure 2-63 Sketch for Tutorial 2

The following steps are required to complete this tutorial:

a. Start SOLIDWORKS and then start a new part document.

b. Invoke the sketching environment.
c. Modify the snap and grid settings so that the cursor jumps through a distance of 5 mm.
d. Draw the sketch using the **Line** tool.
e. Save the sketch and then close the file.

Opening a New File

1. Choose the **New** button from the Menu Bar to invoke the **New SOLIDWORKS Document** dialog box.

Make sure that the **Part** button is chosen in the **New SOLIDWORKS Document** dialog box.

2. Choose the **OK** button from the dialog box.

You need to invoke the sketching environment to draw the sketch of the model first.

3. Choose the **Sketch** tool from the **Sketch CommandManager** and select the **Front Plane** to invoke the sketching environment.

Modifying the Snap, Grid, Dimensioning Unit Settings

It is evident from Figure 2-63 that the dimensions in the sketch are multiples of 5. Therefore, you need to modify the grid and snap settings so that the cursor jumps through a distance of 5 mm.

1. Choose the **Options** button from the Menu Bar to invoke the **System Options - General** dialog box. In this dialog box, choose the **Document Properties** tab.

2. Select the **Grid/Snap** option from the area on the left and select the **Display grid** check box if cleared. Set the value in the **Major grid spacing** spinner to **50** and in the **Minor-lines per major** spinner to **10**.

3. Choose the **Go To System Snaps** button to display the **System Options - Relations/Snaps** dialog box. Make sure that the **Grid** check box is selected in the **System Options - Relations/Snaps** dialog box. Next, choose the **OK** button.

When you move the cursor, the coordinates displayed close to the lower right corner of the drawing area show an increment of 5 mm.

Drawing the Sketch

The sketch will be drawn using the **Line** tool. The arc in the sketch will also be drawn using the same tool. You need to start the drawing from the lower left corner of the sketch.

1. Invoke the **Line** tool by pressing the L key; the arrow cursor is replaced by the line cursor.

2. Move the line cursor to origin.

3. Click at this point and move the cursor horizontally toward the right. Click again when the length of the line above the line cursor displays 60; a horizontal line of 60 mm length is drawn.

4. Move the line cursor vertically upward and click when the length above the line cursor is displayed as 35.

5. Choose the **Zoom to Fit** button from the **View (Heads-Up)** toolbar to fit the sketch into the screen. 

   As mentioned earlier, you can invoke the drawing display tools while some other tools are still active. After modifying the drawing display area, the **Line** tool that was active before invoking the drawing display tool will be restored and you can continue drawing lines using the **Line** tool.

6. Move the line cursor horizontally toward the left and click the left mouse button when the length of the line above the line cursor shows the value 10.

7. Move the line cursor vertically downward and click when the length of the line above the line cursor is displayed as 10.

8. Move the line cursor horizontally toward the left and click when the length of the line above the line cursor is displayed as 10.

   Next, you need to draw an arc normal to the last line using the **Line** tool. It is recommended to use the **Line** tool when you need to draw a sketch that is a combination of lines and arcs. This increases productivity by reducing the time taken in invoking tools for drawing an arc and a line.

9. Move the line cursor away from the endpoint of the last line and then move it back close to the endpoint; the arc mode is invoked.

10. Move the arc cursor vertically downward up to the next grid point.

11. Move the arc cursor toward the left.

    You will notice that a normal arc is being drawn and the angle and radius of the arc are displayed above the line cursor.

12. Move the cursor to the left and click when the angle value on the arc cursor is displayed as 180 and the radius value is displayed as 10; an arc normal to the last line is drawn and the line mode is invoked.

13. Move the line cursor horizontally toward the left and click when the length of the line on the line cursor is displayed as 10.

14. Move the line cursor vertically upward and click when the length of the line on the line cursor is displayed as 10.

15. Move the line cursor horizontally toward the left and click when the length of the line on the line cursor is displayed as 10.

16. Move the line cursor to the start point of the first line and click when an orange circle is displayed.

17. Press the ESC key to exit the **Line** tool.

    This completes the sketch. However, you need to modify the drawing display area such that the sketch fits the screen.

18. Press the F key to modify the drawing display area. The final sketch for Tutorial 2 with the grid display and the **Shaded Sketch Contours** settings turned off is shown in Figure 2-64.

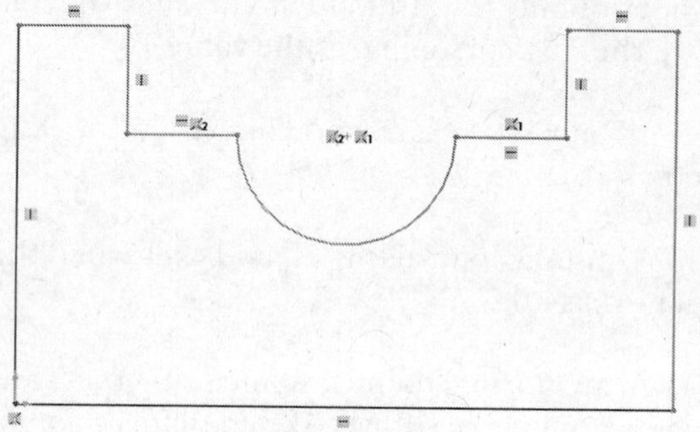

***Figure 2-64** Final sketch for Tutorial 2*

Saving the Sketch

1. Choose the **Save** button from the Menu Bar to invoke the **Save As** dialog box. 

2. Enter **c02_tut02** as the name of the document in the **File name** edit box. Choose the **Save** button and then save the file at the location *\Documents\SOLIDWORKS\c02*.

3. Close the document by choosing **File > Close** from the SOLIDWORKS menus.

Tutorial 3

In this tutorial, you will draw the basic sketch of the model shown in Figure 2-65. The sketch to be drawn is shown in Figure 2-66. Do not dimension the sketch as the solid model and its dimensions are given for your reference only. **(Expected time: 30 min)**

The following steps are required to complete this tutorial:

a. Start SOLIDWORKS and then start a new part file.
b. Invoke the sketching environment.
c. Modify the snap and grid settings so that the cursor jumps through a distance of 5 mm.
d. Draw the outer loop of the sketch using the **Line** tool.
e. Draw the inner circle using the **Circle** tool.
f. Save the sketch and then close the file.

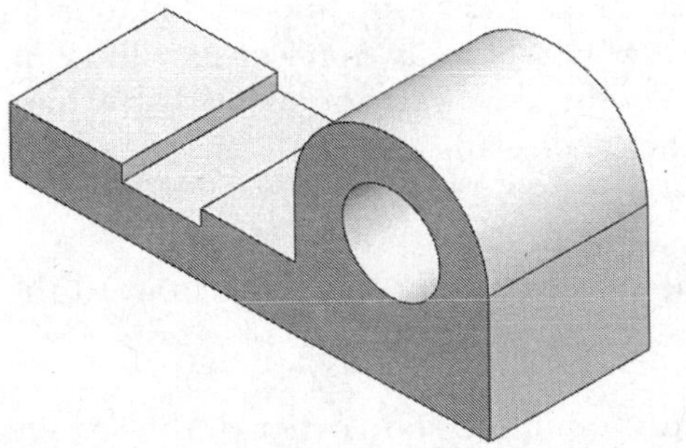

Figure 2-65 Solid model for Tutorial 3

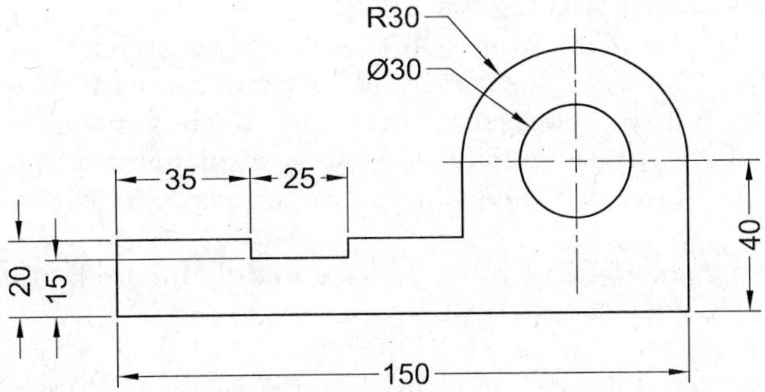

Figure 2-66 Sketch for Tutorial 3

Starting a New File

1. Choose the **New** button from the Menu Bar to invoke the **New SOLIDWORKS Document** dialog box. Make sure the **Part** button is chosen in this dialog box.

2. Choose the **OK** button from the dialog box; a new SOLIDWORKS part document is started.

   To draw the sketch of the model, you need to invoke the sketching environment.

3. Choose the **Sketch** button from the **Sketch CommandManager**; the **Edit Sketch PropertyManager** is displayed.

4. Select **Front Plane** from the drawing area; the sketching environment is invoked. Also, the confirmation corner is displayed with the **Exit Sketch** and **Cancel** options at the upper right corner of the drawing area.

Modifying the Snap, Grid, and Dimensioning Unit Settings

As the dimensions in the sketch are multiples of 5, you need to modify the grid and snap settings so that the cursor jumps through a distance of 5 mm.

1. Choose the **Options** button from the Menu Bar to invoke the **System Options - General** dialog box. Next, choose the **Document Properties** tab from this dialog box.

2. Select the **Grid/Snap** option from the area on the left and select the **Display grid** check box if cleared. Set the value in the **Major grid spacing** spinner to **50** and the value in the **Minor-lines per major** spinner to **10**.

3. Next, choose the **Go To System Snaps** button to invoke the **System Options - Relations/Snaps** dialog box. Make sure that the **Grid** check box is selected in this dialog box and choose **OK** to close the dialog box.

Drawing the Outer Loop

It is evident from Figure 2-66 that the sketch consists of an outer loop and an inner circle. Therefore, this sketch will be drawn using the **Line** and **Circle** tools. You will start drawing from the lower left corner of the sketch. As the length of the lower horizontal line is 150 mm, you need to modify the drawing display area such that the drawing area in the first quadrant is increased. This can be done by using the **Pan** tool.

1. Press the CTRL key and the middle mouse button, and then drag the cursor toward the bottom left corner of the screen.

   You will notice that the origin is also moved toward the bottom left corner of the screen, thus increasing the drawing area in the first quadrant.

2. After dragging the origin close to the lower left corner, release the CTRL key and middle mouse button.

3. Choose the **Line** button from the **Sketch CommandManager**. 

4. Move the line cursor to a location whose coordinates are 0 mm, 0 mm, and 0 mm. Click to specify the start point of the line.

5. Move the cursor horizontally toward the right and click when the length of the line above the line cursor is displayed as 150.

6. Next, move the line cursor vertically upward and click when the length of the line on the line cursor is displayed as 40.

   The next entity to be drawn is a tangent arc. The tangent arc will be drawn by invoking the arc mode using the **Line** tool.

7. Move the line cursor away from the endpoint of the last line and then move it back to the endpoint; the arc mode is invoked and the line cursor is replaced by the arc cursor.

8. Move the arc cursor vertically upward to a small distance and then move it to the left when the dotted line is displayed.

   You will notice that a tangent arc is being drawn. The angle of the tangent arc and its radius are displayed above the arc cursor.

9. Click when the angle value above the arc cursor is displayed as 180 and the radius is displayed as 30 to complete the arc.

   The required tangent arc is drawn. As mentioned earlier, the line mode is automatically invoked after you have drawn the arc by using the **Line** tool.

10. Move the line cursor vertically downward and click when the length of the line on the line cursor is displayed as 20.

11. Move the line cursor horizontally toward the left and click when the length of the line on the line cursor is displayed as 30.

12. Move the line cursor vertically downward and click when the length of the line on the line cursor is displayed as 5.

13. Move the line cursor horizontally toward the left and click when the length of the line on the line cursor is displayed as 25.

14. Move the line cursor vertically upward and click when the length of the line on the line cursor is displayed as 5.

15. Move the line cursor horizontally toward the left and click when the length of the line on the line cursor is displayed as 35.

16. Move the line cursor to the start point of the first line. Click when an orange circle is displayed.

    The length of the line at this point is 20 mm.

17. Right-click and then choose **Select** from the shortcut menu to exit the **Line** tool.

18. Choose the **Zoom to Fit** button from the **View (Heads-Up)** toolbar to fit the sketch into the screen. This completes the outer loop of the sketch. The sketch after drawing the outer loop appears, as shown in Figure 2-67.

Tip
If the arc mode is invoked by mistake while drawing continuous lines, press the A key; the line mode will be invoked again.

Drawing the Circle

The circle in the sketch will be drawn using the **Circle** tool. The centerpoint of the circle will be the centerpoint of the arc, which is represented by a plus sign. The plus sign is automatically drawn when you draw an arc. You can select this centerpoint to draw the circle.

1. Choose the **Circle** button from the **Circle** flyout in the **Sketch CommandManager**; the **Circle PropertyManager** is invoked.

2. Move the circle cursor close to the centerpoint of the arc and click when an orange circle is displayed.

3. Move the cursor toward the left and click when the radius of the circle above the circle cursor shows 15; a circle of 15 mm radius is drawn. This completes the sketch for Tutorial 3.

4. Right-click and then choose the **Select** option from the shortcut menu to exit the **Circle** tool.

The final sketch for Tutorial 3 is shown in Figure 2-67.

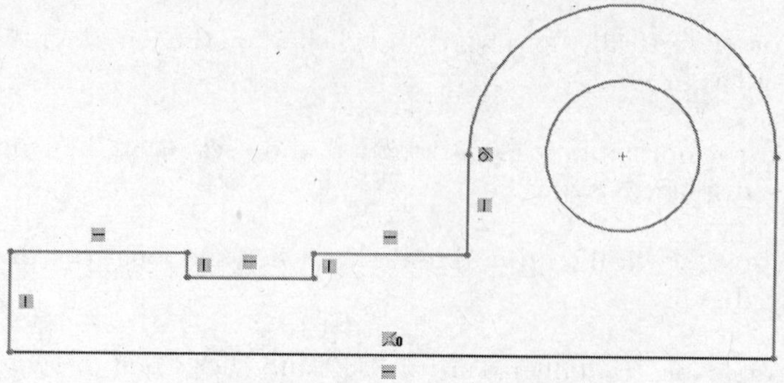

Figure 2-67 *Final sketch for Tutorial 3*

> **Tip**
> *You will notice that the bottom horizontal line in the sketch is black and the remaining lines are blue. In the next chapter, you will learn why some entities in a sketch have different colors.*

Saving the Sketch

1. Choose the **Save** button from the Menu Bar to invoke the **Save As** dialog box.

2. Enter **c02_tut03** as the name of the document in the **File name** edit box. Choose **Save** and save the file at the location *\Documents\SOLIDWORKS\c02*.

3. Close the document by choosing **File > Close** from the SOLIDWORKS menus.

Tutorial 4

In this tutorial, you will draw the sketch of the model shown in Figure 2-68. The sketch of the model is shown in Figure 2-69. Do not dimension the sketch as the solid model and the dimensions are given for your reference only. **(Expected time: 30 min)**

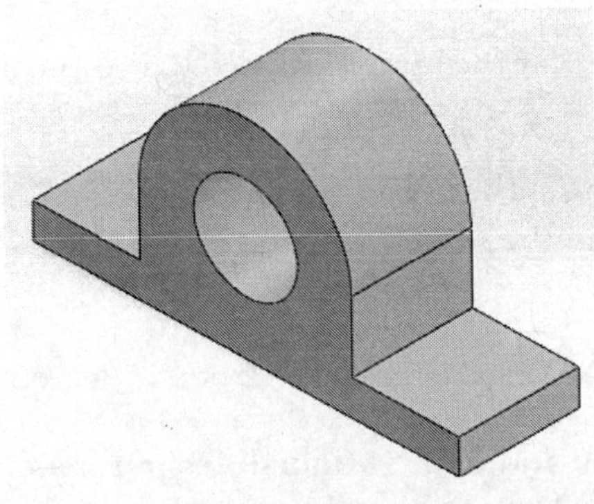

Figure 2-68 Solid model for Tutorial 4

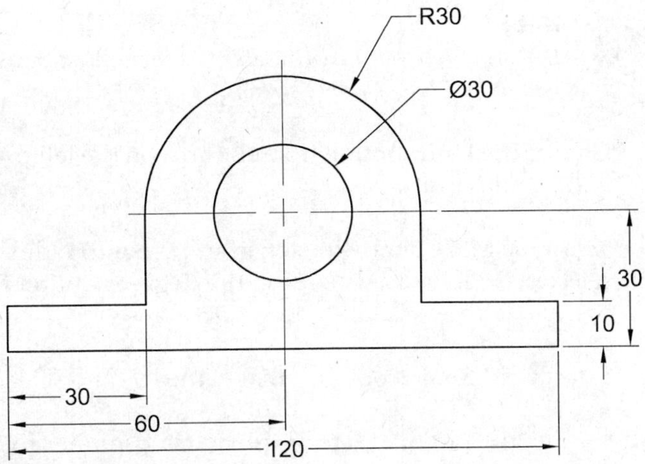

Figure 2-69 Sketch of the model for Tutorial 4

The following steps are required to complete this tutorial:

a. Start SOLIDWORKS and then start a new part document.
b. Invoke the sketching environment.
c. Draw the outer loop of the sketch.
d. Draw the sketch of the inner circle.
e. Save the sketch and then close the document.

Starting a New File

1. Choose the **New** button from the Menu Bar to invoke the **New SOLIDWORKS Document** dialog box. Make sure that the **Part** button is chosen in the this dialog box.

2. Choose the **OK** button from the **New SOLIDWORKS Document** dialog box; a new SOLIDWORKS part document is started. To draw the sketch of the model, you need to invoke the sketching environment.

3. Choose the **Sketch** button from the **Sketch CommandManager**; the **Edit Sketch PropertyManager** is displayed.

4. Select **Front Plane** from the drawing area; the sketching environment is invoked.

Modifying the Unit and Grid Settings

You need to modify the initial settings to change the linear and angular units before drawing the sketch.

1. Choose the **Options** button from the Menu Bar to invoke the **System Options - General** dialog box.

2. Choose the **Document Properties** tab; the dialog box is renamed as **Document Properties - Drafting Standard**.

Note

*If you have selected **Millimeters** as the unit of measurement while installing SOLIDWORKS, skip steps 3 and 4 in the section.*

3. Choose the **Units** option from the area on the left to display the options related to the linear and angular units.

4. Select the **MMGS (millimeter, gram, second)** radio button from the **Unit system** area if not selected by default. Also, select the **degrees** option from the **Angle** area, if it is not selected by default.

5. Select **Grid/Snap** from the area on the left and select the **Display grid** check box if cleared.

6. Set the value in the **Major grid spacing** spinner to **100** and in the **Minor-lines per major** spinner to **10**. Next, choose the **Go To System Snaps** button; the system options related to relations and snaps are displayed.

7. Select the **Grid** check box from the **Sketch snaps** area, if it is cleared. Make sure you clear the **Snap only when grid is displayed** check box if selected. Choose **OK** to exit the dialog box.

Tip

*If grid is displayed on the screen when you invoke the sketching environment for the first time, turn off the grid display by right-clicking in the drawing area; a shortcut menu is displayed. Click the **Display Grid** option in the shortcut menu to turn the grid off.*

Drawing the Outer Loop of the Sketch

The sketch of the model consists of an outer loop that has a circle inside it. You will first draw the outer loop and then the inner circle. The sketch will be drawn by using the **Line** and **Circle** tools.

The outer loop will be drawn using continuous lines and arcs. You will start drawing the sketch from the lower left corner of the sketch.

1. Choose the **Line** button from the **Sketch CommandManager** to invoke the **Line** tool; the arrow cursor is replaced by the line cursor.

2. Move the cursor in the first quadrant close to the origin; the coordinates of the point are displayed close to the lower left corner of the screen.

3. Click where the coordinates are 10 mm, 10 mm, and 0 mm, and then move the cursor horizontally toward right.

4. Click when the length of the line above the line cursor is displayed as 120; a horizontal line is created. Refer to Line 1 in Figure 2-70.

5. Move the line cursor vertically upward. The symbol of the **Vertical** relation is displayed below the line cursor and the length of the line is displayed above the line cursor.

6. Click when the length of the line above the line cursor is displayed as 10; a vertical line is created. Refer to Line 2 in Figure 2-70.

7. Move the line cursor horizontally toward the left. Click when the length of the line above the line cursor is displayed as 30; the next horizontal line of 30 mm length is drawn. Refer to Line 3 in Figure 2-70.

8. Move the line cursor vertically upward and click when the length of the line on the line cursor is displayed as 20. Refer to Line 4 in Figure 2-70.

   The next entity to be drawn is a tangent arc. The tangent arc will be drawn by invoking the arc mode using the **Line** tool.

9. Move the line cursor away from the endpoint of the last line and then move it back to the endpoint; the arc mode is invoked and the line cursor is replaced by the arc cursor.

10. Move the arc cursor vertically upward slightly and then move it to the left when the dotted line is displayed.

    You will notice that a tangent arc is being drawn. The angle of the tangent arc and its radius are displayed above the arc cursor.

11. Click when the angle value above the arc cursor is displayed as 180 and the radius is displayed as 30 to complete the arc.

    The required tangent arc is drawn. As mentioned earlier, the line mode is automatically invoked after you have drawn the arc by using the **Line** tool.

12. Move the line cursor vertically downward and click when the length of the line on the line cursor is displayed as 20. Refer to Line 5 in Figure 2-70.

13. Move the line cursor horizontally toward the left and click when the length of the line on the line cursor is displayed as 30. Refer to Line 6 in Figure 2-70.

14. Move the line cursor vertically downward and click when the length of the line on the line cursor is displayed as 10.

    This completes the sketch of the outer loop. Since the display of the sketch is small, you need to modify the drawing display area such that the sketch fits the screen. The drawing display area is modified by using the **Zoom to Fit** tool.

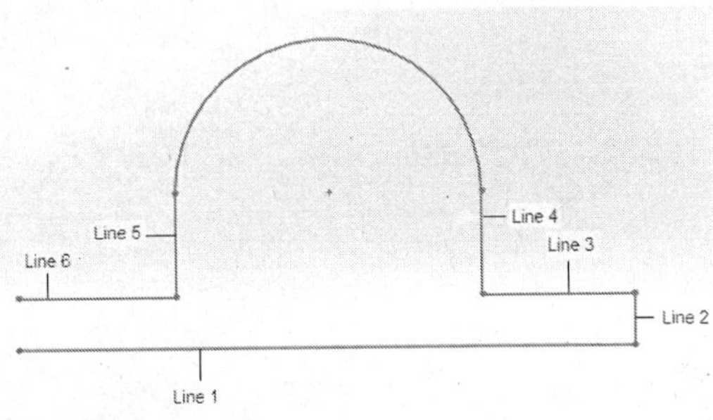

Figure 2-70 *Partial outer loop of the sketch*

15. Choose the **Zoom to Fit** tool from the **View (Heads-Up)** toolbar to fit the current sketch into the screen. The outer loop of the sketch is completed and is shown in Figure 2-71. Note that in this figure, the grid display and the **Shaded Sketch Contours** settings are turned off for better visibility.

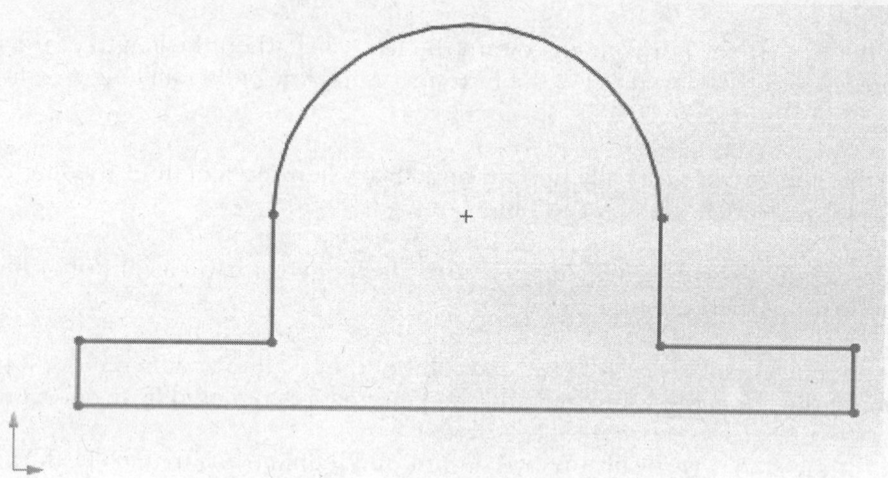

Figure 2-71 Outer loop of the sketch

Drawing Circle

In this section, you will invoke the **Circle** tool by using the Mouse Gesture to draw the inner circle.

1. Press and hold the right mouse button in the drawing area and drag the mouse; a set of tools is displayed. Move the cursor on the **Circle** tool; the **Circle PropertyManager** is displayed. Choose the **Circle** button from the **Circle Type** rollout if not already chosen.

   When you invoke the **Circle** tool, the arrow cursor is replaced by the circle cursor.

2. Move the circle cursor to the center of the outer arc; the center point is highlighted, refer to Figure 2-72.

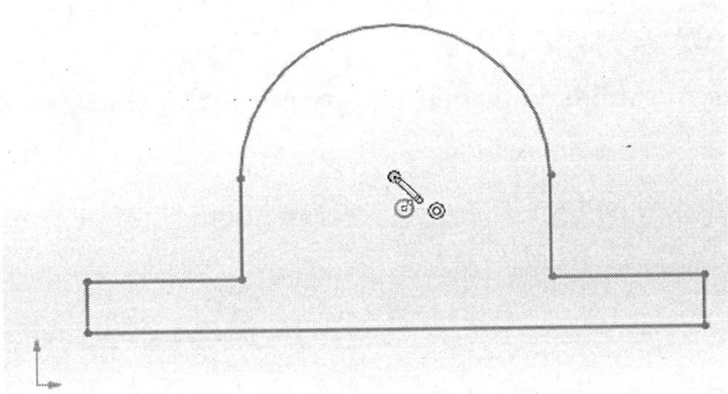

Figure 2-72 Drawing a circle at the center of outer arc

3. Click at the highlighted point. Next, move the circle cursor toward the left to define the circle.

4. Click when the radius of the circle displayed above the circle cursor shows a value 15; a circle is created.

5. The final sketch after drawing a circle inside the outer loop is shown in Figure 2-73.

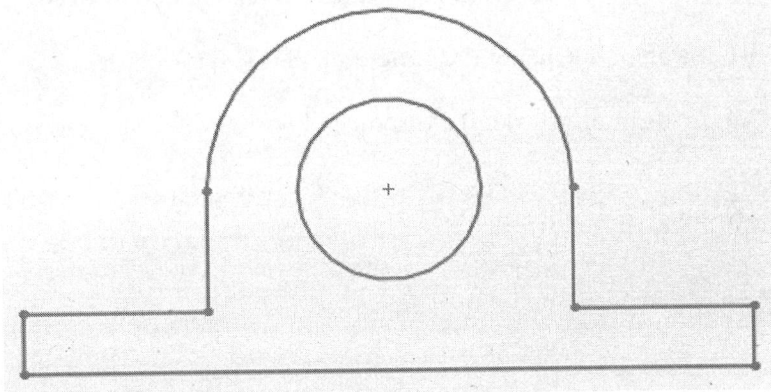

Figure 2-73 Final sketch after drawing the inner circle

6. Right-click in the drawing area and then choose the **Select** option from the shortcut menu displayed to exit the **Circle** tool.

Saving the Sketch

1. Choose the **Save** button from the Menu Bar to invoke the **Save As** dialog box. 

2. Enter **c02_tut04** as the name of the document in the **File name** edit box and choose the **Save** button; the document is saved at the location *\Documents\SOLIDWORKS\c02*.

3. Close the document by choosing **File > Close** from the SOLIDWORKS menus.

Self-Evaluation Test

Answer the following questions and then compare them to those given at the end of this chapter:

1. You can convert a sketched entity into a construction entity by selecting the __________ check box provided in the PropertyManager.
2. To draw a rectangle at an angle, you need to use the __________ tool.
3. __________ are temporary lines that are used to track a particular point on the screen.
4. You can invoke the __________ tool or press the ESC key to exit the currently active sketching tool.
5. When you select a tangent entity to draw a tangent arc, the __________ relation is applied between the start point of the arc and the tangent entity.
6. In SOLIDWORKS, a rectangle is considered as a combination of individual __________.
7. The base feature of any design is a sketched feature and is created by drawing a sketch. (T/F)
8. You can invoke the arc mode using the **Line** tool. (T/F)
9. By default, the cursor jumps through a distance of 5 mm when the grid snap is on. (T/F)
10. If you save a file in the sketching environment and then open it the next time, it will open in the part modeling environment. (T/F)

Review Questions

Answer the following questions:

1. In SOLIDWORKS, a polygon is considered as a combination of which of the following entities?

   (a) Lines (b) Arcs
   (c) Splines (d) None of these

2. Which of the following options is not displayed in the **New SOLIDWORKS Document** dialog box?

   (a) **Part** (b) **Assembly**
   (c) **Drawing** (d) **Sketch**

3. Which of the following entities is not considered while converting a sketch into a feature?

   (a) Sketched circles (b) Sketched lines
   (c) Construction lines (d) None of these

4. Which of the following PropertyManagers is displayed when you select a line of a rectangle?

   (a) **Line Properties PropertyManager** (b) **Line/Rectangle PropertyManager**
   (c) **Rectangle PropertyManager** (d) None of these

5. Which of the following PropertyManagers is displayed while drawing an elliptical arc?

   (a) **Arc PropertyManager** (b) **Ellipse PropertyManager**
   (c) **Elliptical Arc PropertyManager** (d) None of these

6. A three point arc is drawn by defining the start point, the endpoint, and a point on the arc. (T/F)

7. You can delete the sketched entities by right-clicking on them and then choosing the **Delete** option from the shortcut menu. (T/F)

8. The origin is a blue icon that is displayed in the middle of the sketcher screen. (T/F)

9. In SOLIDWORKS, circles are drawn by specifying the centerpoint of the circle and then entering the radius of the circle in the dialog box displayed. (T/F)

10. When you open a new SOLIDWORKS document, it is not maximized in the SOLIDWORKS window. (T/F)

EXERCISES

Exercise 1

Draw the sketch of the model shown in Figure 2-74. The sketch to be drawn is shown in Figure 2-75. Do not dimension the sketch. The solid model and its dimensions are given for your reference only.
(Expected time: 30 min)

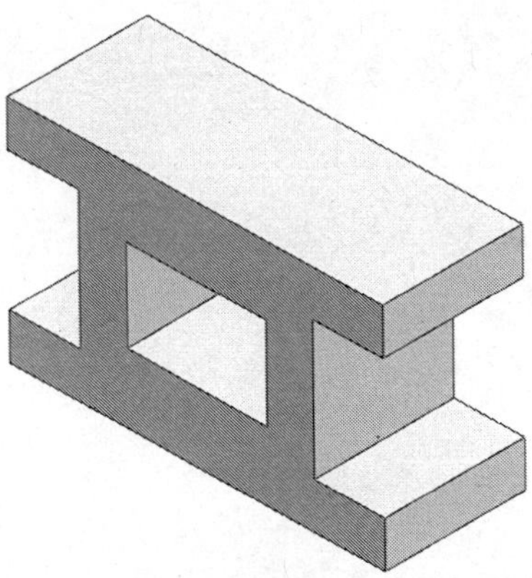

Figure 2-74 *Solid model for Exercise 1*

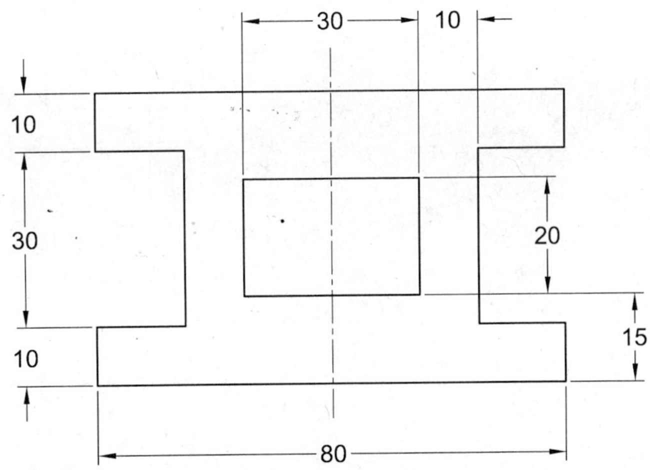

Figure 2-75 *Sketch for Exercise 1*

Exercise 2

Draw the sketch of the model shown in Figure 2-76. The sketch to be drawn is shown in Figure 2-77. Do not dimension the sketch. The solid model and its dimensions are given for your reference only.

(Expected time: 30 min)

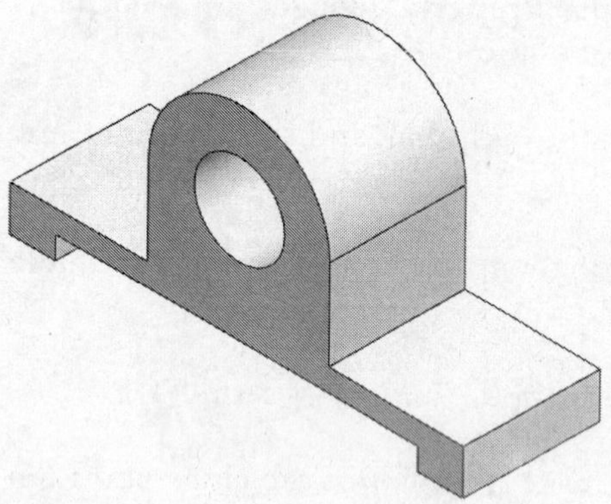

Figure 2-76 Solid model for Exercise 2

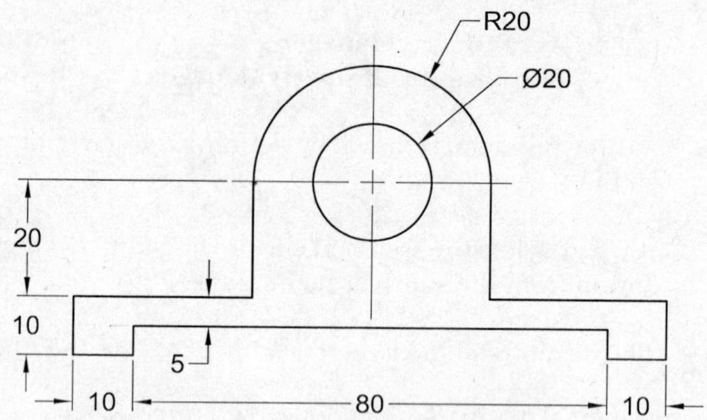

Figure 2-77 Sketch for Exercise 2

Exercise 3

Draw the sketch of the model shown in Figure 2-78. The sketch to be drawn is shown in Figure 2-79. Do not dimension the sketch. The solid model and its dimensions are given for your reference only.

(Expected time: 30 min)

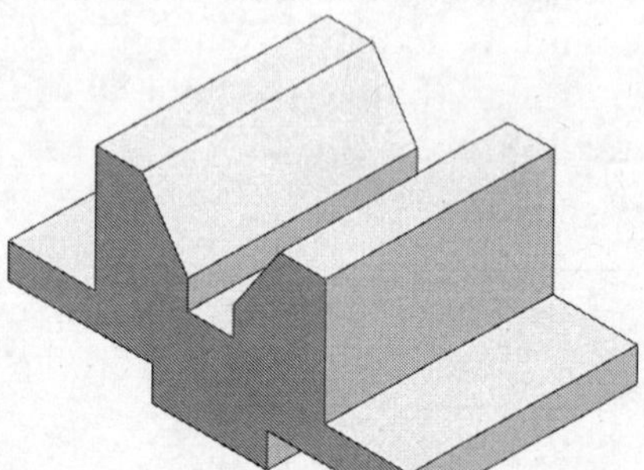

Figure 2-78 Solid model for Exercise 3

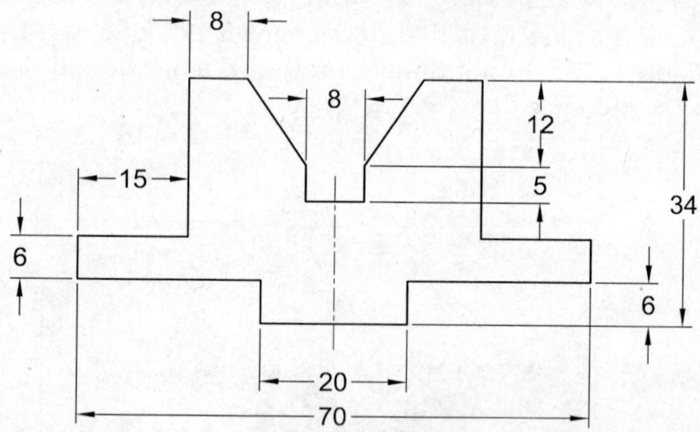

Figure 2-79 Sketch for Exercise 3

Exercise 4

Draw the sketch of the model shown in Figure 2-80. The sketch to be drawn is shown in Figure 2-81. Do not dimension the sketch. The solid model and its dimensions are given for your reference only. **(Expected time: 30 min)**

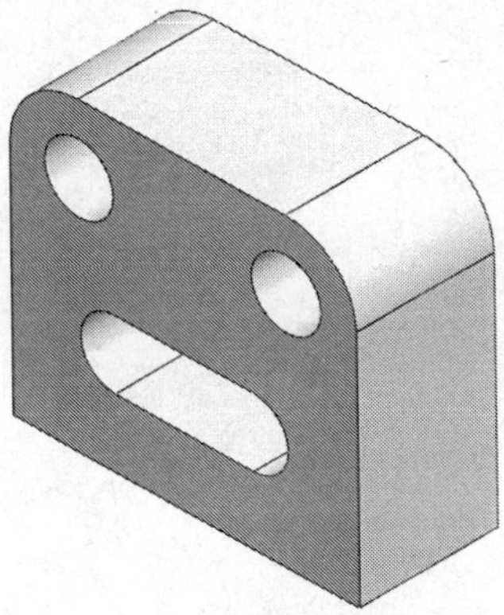

Figure 2-80 Solid model for Exercise 4

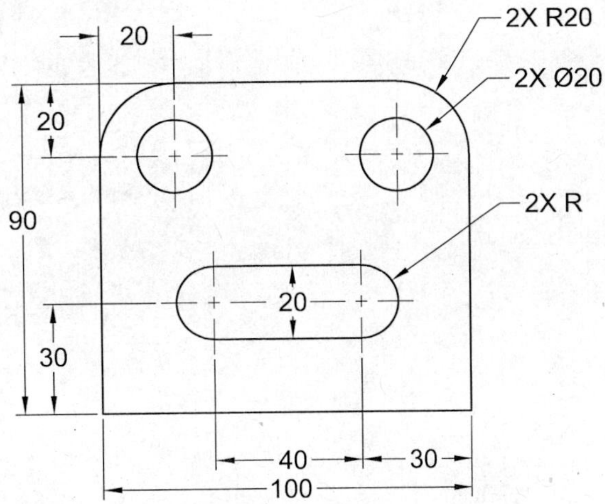

Figure 2-81 Sketch for Exercise 4

Answers to Self-Evaluation Test

1. For construction, **2. 3 Point Corner Rectangle**, **3.** Inferencing lines, **4. Select**, **5.** Tangent, **6.** lines, **7.** T, **8.** T, **9.** F, **10.** F

Chapter 3

Editing and Modifying Sketches

Learning Objectives

After completing this chapter, you will be able to:

- *Edit sketches using various editing tools*
- *Create rectangular patterns of sketched entities*
- *Create circular patterns of sketched entities*
- *Write text in the sketching environment*
- *Modify sketched entities*
- *Modify sketches by dynamically dragging sketched entities*

EDITING SKETCHED ENTITIES

In SOLIDWORKS, there are various tools that can be used to edit the sketched entities. These tools are used to trim, extend, offset, or mirror the sketched entities. You can also perform various other editing operations by using these tools. Various editing operations and the tools used to perform them are discussed next.

Trimming Sketched Entities

CommandManager:	Sketch > Trim Entities flyout > Trim Entities
SOLIDWORKS menus:	Tools > Sketch Tools > Trim
Toolbar:	Sketch > Trim Entities flyout > Trim Entities

The **Trim Entities** tool is used to trim the unwanted entities in a sketch. You can use this tool to trim a line, arc, ellipse, parabola, circle, spline, or centerline intersecting another line, arc, ellipse, parabola, circle, spline, or centerline. You can also extend the sketched entities using the **Trim Entities** tool. To trim an entity, choose the **Trim Entities** button from the **Sketch CommandManager**; the **Trim PropertyManager** will be displayed, as shown in Figure 3-1.

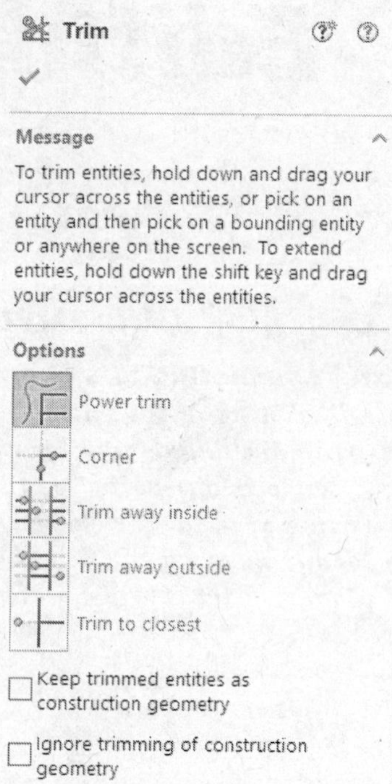

Figure 3-1** The **Trim PropertyManager

The options in this PropertyManager to trim the sketched entities are discussed next.

Message Rollout

The **Message** rollout in this PropertyManager informs you about the procedure of trimming and extending the sketched elements, depending upon the option selected in the **Options** rollout of the **Trim PropertyManager**.

Options Rollout

The **Options** rollout displays all the options that are used to trim the sketched entities. These options are discussed next.

Power trim

When the **Power trim** button is chosen in the **Options** rollout, the **Message** rollout in this PropertyManager will inform you about the procedure of trimming and extending the sketched elements using this option. To trim the unwanted portion of a sketch using this option, press and hold the left mouse button and drag the cursor. You will notice that a gray-colored drag trace line is displayed along the path of the cursor. When you drag the cursor across the unwanted sketched entity, it will be trimmed and a small red-colored box will be displayed in its place. You can continue trimming the entities by dragging the cursor across them. After trimming all the unwanted entities, release the left mouse button.

To extend or shorten an entity dynamically using this tool, click once on the entity and then move the cursor; the entity will extend or shorten dynamically depending upon the direction of movement. Move the cursor up to the level to which the entity has to be extended or shortened. Press the left mouse button to complete the operation.

To extend a line or a curve such that it intersects with other entity, select the first entity and then select the second entity; the first entity will extend and intersect the second entity. While extending, if the first entity cannot intersect the second entity then the first entity will extend up to the apparent intersection point.

Corner

The **Corner** button in the **Options** rollout is used to trim or extend the sketched entities in such a way that the resulting entities form a corner. To trim the unwanted elements using this option, choose the **Corner** button from the **Options** rollout; you will be prompted to select an entity. Select the entity from the geometry area; you will be prompted to select another entity. When you move the cursor over the second entity, the preview of the resulting entity will be displayed in a different color. In the second entity, select the portion to be retained, as shown in Figure 3-2. The selected portions of the entities will be retained and the resulting entities will form a corner, as shown in Figure 3-3.

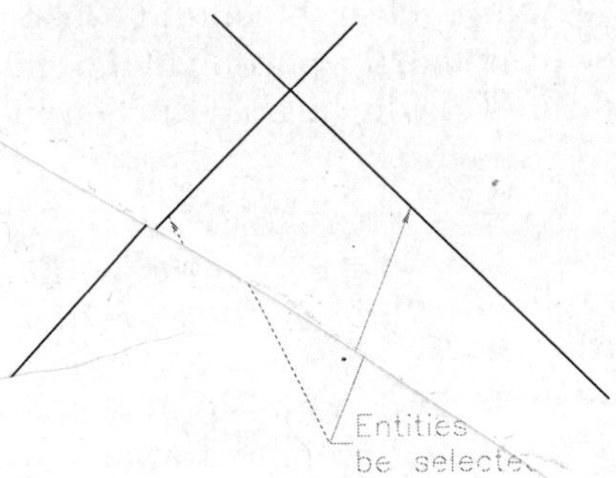

Figure 3-2 Entities to be selected for trimming

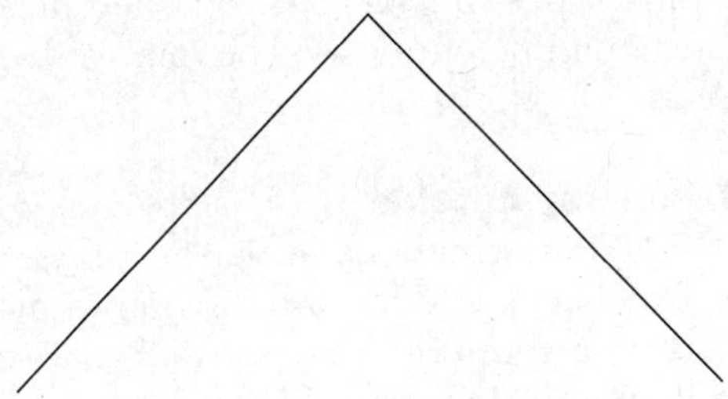

Figure 3-3 Entities after trimming

You can also extend the entities using this tool. To do so, choose the **Corner** button from the **Options** rollout. Select the entities to be extended; the selected entities will be extended to their apparent intersection, refer to Figures 3-4 and 3-5.

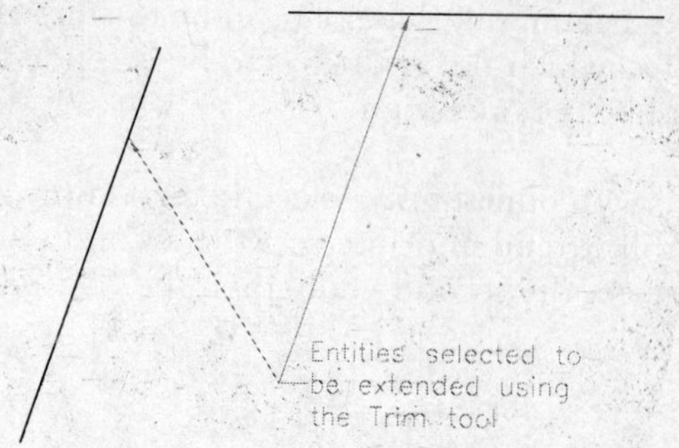

Figure 3-4 Entities selected to extend

Figure 3-5 Sketch after extension

Trim away inside

The **Trim away inside** button in the **Options** rollout is used to trim the portion of a selected entity that lies inside two bounding entities. To trim the sketched entities using this tool, invoke the **Trim PropertyManager** and choose the **Trim away inside** button from the **Options** rollout; the **Message** rollout will be displayed informing you to select the two bounding entities, and then to select the entities to be trimmed. Select the bounding entities from the drawing area, refer to Figure 3-6. Now, select the entities to be trimmed from the drawing area. As you select an entity to be trimmed, the portion of the entity inside the bounding entities will be removed and the portion outside the bounding entities will be retained, refer to Figure 3-6.

Trim away outside

The **Trim away outside** button in the **Options** rollout is used to trim the portion of an entity that extend beyond the bounding entities. To trim the sketched entities using this tool, invoke the **Trim PropertyManager** and choose the **Trim away outside** button from the **Options** rollout; the **Message** rollout will inform you to select two bounding entities, and then to select the entities to be trimmed. Select the bounding entities from the drawing area, refer to Figure 3-7. Now, select the entities to be trimmed from the drawing area. As soon as you select an entity to be trimmed, the portion that lies outside the bounding entities will be removed and the portion lying inside will be retained, refer to Figure 3-7.

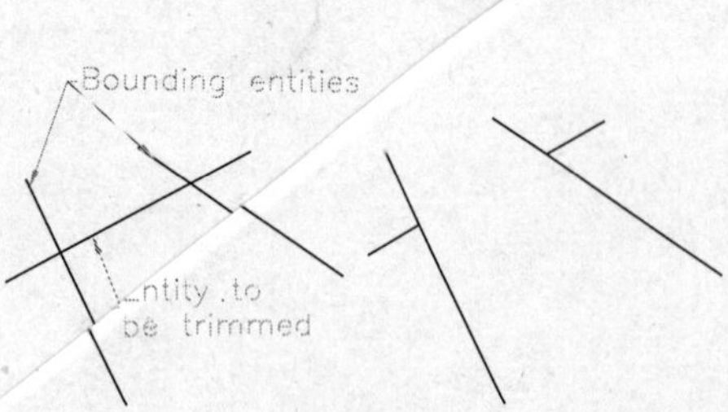

*Figure 3-6 Entity trimmed using the **Trim away inside** button*

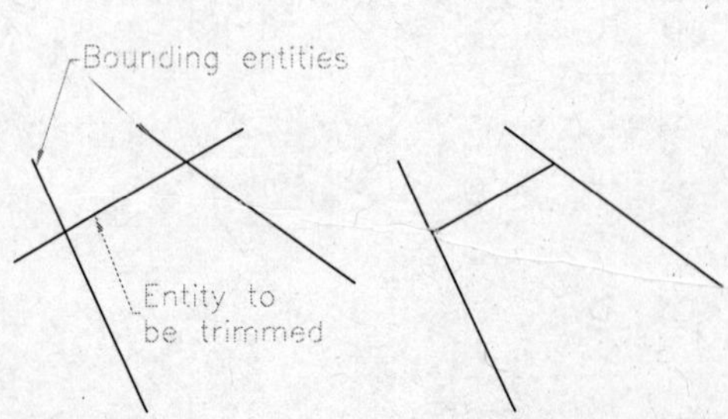

*Figure 3-7 Entity trimmed using the **Trim away outside** button*

Trim to closest

The **Trim to closest** button is used to trim the selected entity to its closest intersection. To trim the entities using this tool, invoke the **Trim PropertyManager** and then choose the **Trim to closest** button from the **Options** rollout; the cursor will be replaced by the trim cursor. Move the trim cursor near the portion of the sketched entity to be removed. The entity or the portion of the entity to be removed will be highlighted. Press the left mouse button to remove the highlighted entity. Figure 3-8 shows the entities to be trimmed and Figure 3-9 shows the sketch after trimming the entities.

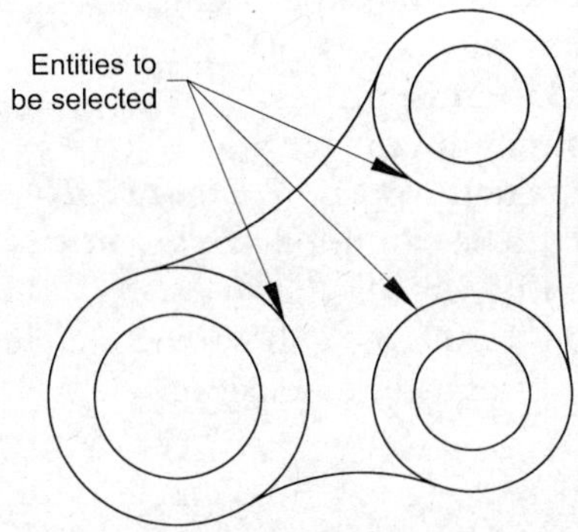

Figure 3-8 Entities to be trimmed

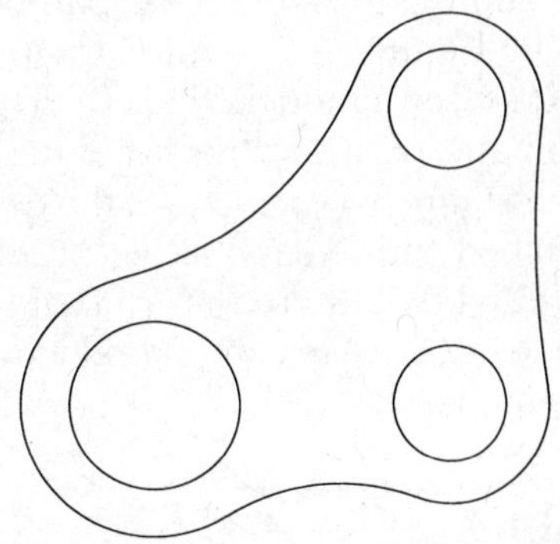

Figure 3-9 Sketch after trimming the entities

You can also use this option to extend the sketched entities. To do so, move the trim cursor to the entity to be extended. When the sketched entity turns orange, press the left mouse button and drag the cursor to the entity up to which it has to be extended. You will notice the preview of the extended entity. Release the left mouse button when the preview of the extended entity appears; the entity will be extended.

Keep trimmed entities as construction geometry

The **Keep trimmed entities as construction geometry** check box if selected converts the trimmed entities into construction geometry.

Ignore trimming of construction geometry

If the **Ignore trimming of construction geometry** check box is selected, it leaves construction geometry unaffected when you trim entities.

Extending Sketched Entities

CommandManager: Sketch > Trim Entities flyout > Extend Entities
SOLIDWORKS menus: Tools > Sketch Tools > Extend
Toolbar: Sketch > Trim Entities flyout > Extend Entities

The **Extend Entities** tool is used to extend the sketched entity to intersect the next available entity. The tool is used to extend a line, arc, ellipse, parabola, circle, spline, or centerline to intersect another line, arc, ellipse, parabola, circle, spline, or centerline. The sketched entity is extended up to its intersection with another sketched entity or a model edge. To do so, choose the **Extend Entities** button from the **Trim Entities** flyout in the **Sketch CommandManager**, as shown in Figure 3-10 and move the extend cursor close to the portion of the sketched entity that is to be extended. The entity to be extended will be highlighted and the preview of the extended entity will also be displayed. Click once to complete the extend operation. Figure 3-11 shows the sketched entities to be extended and Figure 3-12 shows the sketched entities after extension.

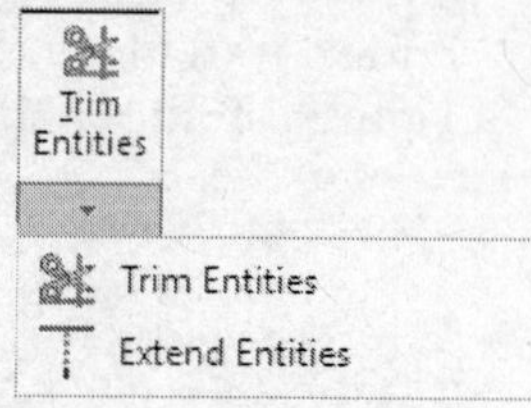

Figure 3-10 *Tools in the **Trim Entities** flyout*

Tip
If the preview of the sketched entity to be extended is shown in the wrong direction, move the extend cursor to a position on the other half of the entity and observe the new preview.

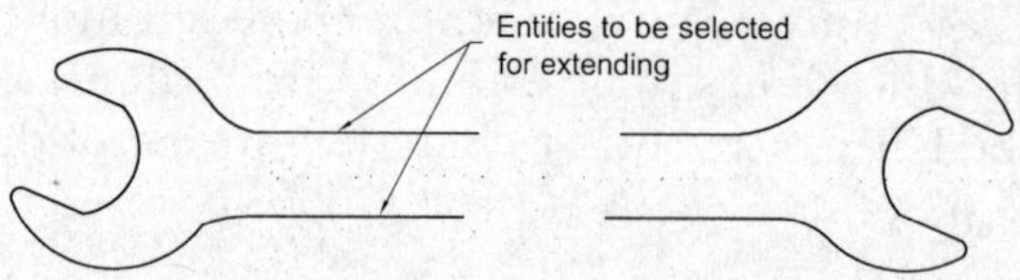

Figure 3-11 *Sketched entities to be extended*

Figure 3-12 *Sketched entities after extension*

Tip
*You can toggle between the **Trim Entities** and **Extend Entities** tools using the shortcut menu that will be displayed on right-clicking when any one of these tools is active.*

Convert Entities

CommandManager: Sketch > Convert Entities flyout > Convert Entities
SOLIDWORKS menus: Tools > Sketch Tools > Convert Entities
Toolbar: Sketch > Convert Entities flyout > Convert Entities

The **Convert Entities** tool is used to generate sketch entities by projecting existing edges of the model on to the current sketching plane. To generate the sketch entities, choose the **Convert Entities** tool from the **Sketch CommandManager**; the **Convert Entities PropertyManager** will be displayed, as shown in Figure 3-13. Select the face/faces or edge/edges of the solid/surface model; the projected curves of the selected entities will be generated on the current sketching plane. Figure 3-14 shows a model with the curves generated by projecting the edges of the model onto the current sketching plane.

The **Select chain** check box is used to select the entire chain of contiguous sketched entities. You can select the **Inner loops one by one** check box to select the required loops. The **Select all inner loops** button available below these check boxes will be activated only when internal loops are present in the selected face of the model. You can choose this button to convert all internal loops into sketched entities.

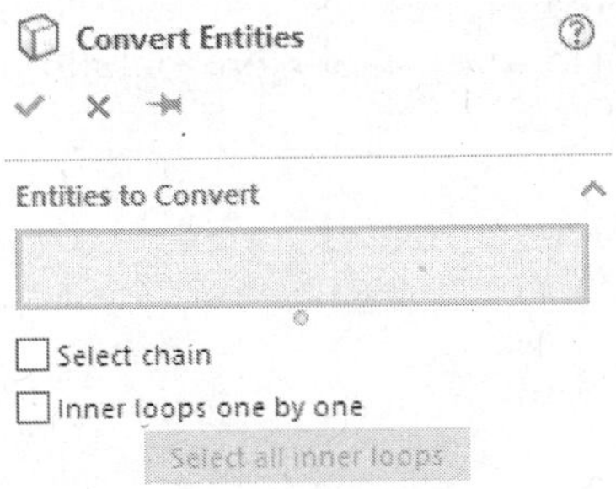

*Figure 3-13 The **Convert Entities** PropertyManager*

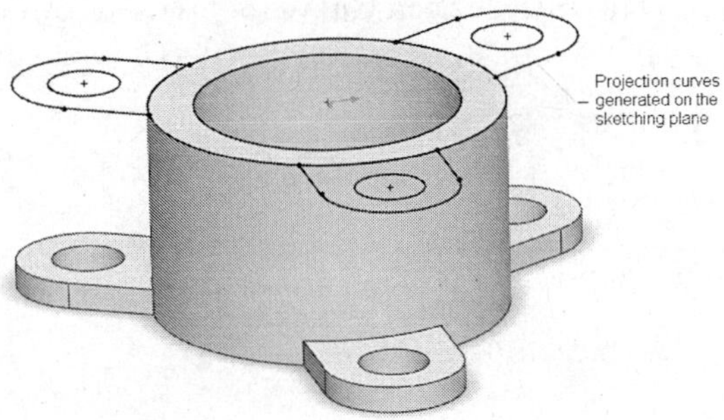

Figure 3-14 The model with its projection curves on the sketching plane

Silhouette Entities

CommandManager: Sketch > Convert Entities flyout > Silhouette Entities
SOLIDWORKS menus: Tools > Sketch Tools > Silhouette Entities
Toolbar: Sketch > Convert Entities flyout > Silhouette Entities

The **Silhouette Entities** tool is used to generate sketch entities of a body on current sketching plane. To generate the sketching entities, choose the **Silhouette Entities** tool from the **Sketch CommandManager**; the **Silhouette Entities PropertyManager** will be displayed, as shown in Figure 3-15. Select the body from the drawing area and then choose the **OK** button. The curves get extracted on the current plane. Figure 3-16 shows a model with the generated curves.

When the **External silhouette** entities check box is selected then the external edge of the body gets extracted. If this check box is clear then the innerloops in the model get extracted.

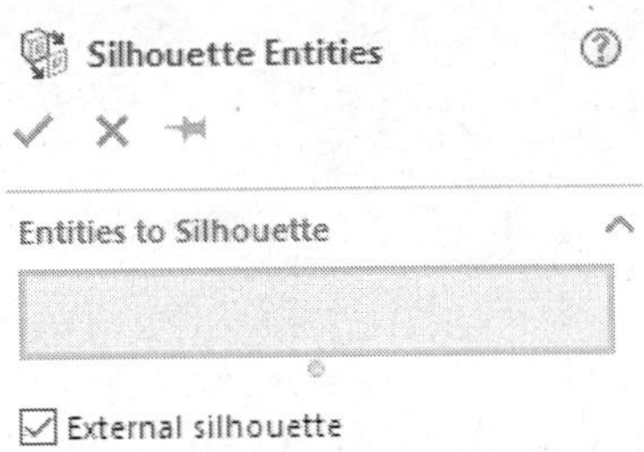

*Figure 3-15 The **Silhoutte Entities PropertyManager***

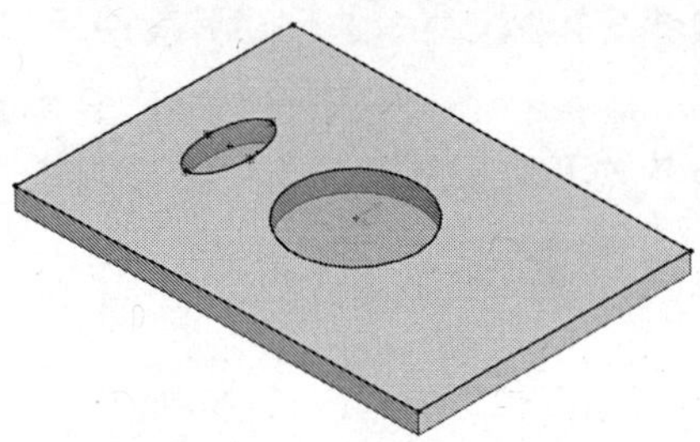

Figure 3-16 The model with Silhouette Entities

Intersection Curves

CommandManager:	Sketch > Convert Entities flyout > Intersection Curve
SOLIDWORKS menus:	Tools > Sketch Tools > Intersection Curve
Toolbar:	Sketch > Convert Entities flyout > Intersection Curve

The **Intersection Curve** tool is used to generate sketch entities or curves at the intersection of two objects. The intersection curves can be generated for the combination of following objects:

1. A plane and a surface/face
2. Two surfaces
3. A surface and a face
4. A plane and a part
5. A surface and a part

To generate the curves at the intersection, choose the **Intersection Curve** tool from the **Convert Entities** flyout in the **Sketch CommandManager**; the **Intersection Curves PropertyManager** will be displayed, as shown in Figure 3-17. Select the intersecting entities from the graphics area. Next, choose the **OK** button from the PropertyManager; the intersection curve will be created at the intersection of the entities selected, refer to Figure 3-18.

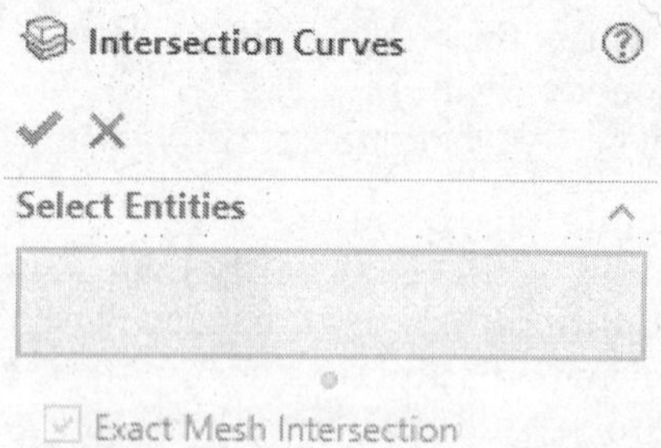

Figure 3-17** The **Intersection Curves PropertyManager

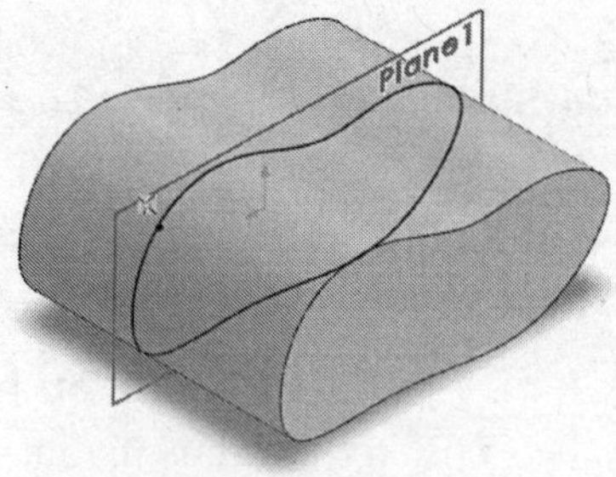

***Figure 3-18** The intersection curve projected on sketching plane*

Filleting Sketched Entities

CommandManager:	Sketch > Sketch Fillet flyout > Sketch Fillet
SOLIDWORKS menus:	Tools > Sketch Tools > Fillet
Toolbar:	Sketch > Sketch Fillet flyout > Sketch Fillet

A fillet creates a tangent arc at the intersection of two sketched entities. It trims or extends the entities to be filleted, depending on the geometry of the sketched entity. You can apply a fillet to two nonparallel lines, two arcs, two splines, an arc and a line, a spline and a line, or a spline and an arc. A fillet between two arcs, or between an arc and a line depends on the compatibility of the geometry to be extended or filleted along the given radius. You can first choose the **Sketch Fillet** tool from the **Sketch CommandManager**, and then select the entities to be filleted or select the vertex formed at the intersection of the two entities to be filleted. Alternatively, you can hold the CTRL key and select the two entities to be filleted and then invoke this tool.

When you invoke the **Sketch Fillet** tool, the **Sketch Fillet PropertyManager** will be displayed, as shown in Figure 3-19. Next, select the entities; the preview of the fillet with default radius will be displayed. You can drag the fillet preview to resize it to the required radius or set the radius in the **Fillet Radius** spinner and press ENTER; a fillet will be created and the **Sketch Fillet PropertyManager** will be displayed even after applying a fillet. This enables you to create multiple fillets in a sketch. The consecutive fillets with the same radius are not dimensioned individually. An automatic equal radii relation is applied to all fillets. However, if you need to dimension each fillet then, select the **Dimension each fillet** check box. If you need to create multiple fillets of same dimension, then it is recommended that this check box should be cleared. If the **Keep constrained corners** check box is selected, the dimension and geometric relations applied to the sketch with respect to the corner to be filleted will not be deleted. Choose the **OK** button to exit the **Sketch Fillet PropertyManager**.

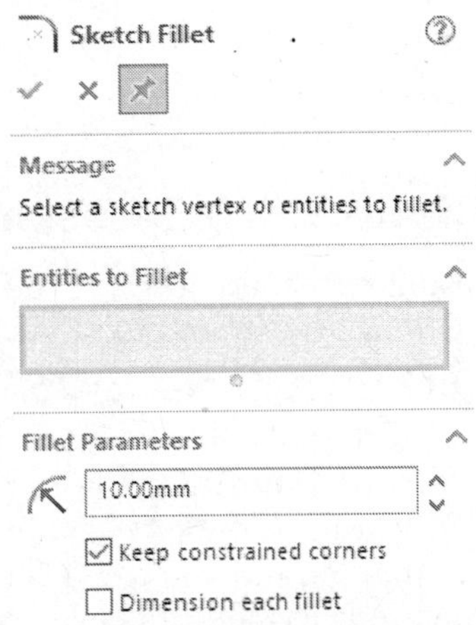

Figure 3-19** The **Sketch Fillet PropertyManager

Figure 3-20 shows the intersecting entities before and after applying the fillet. You can also select the non-intersecting entities for creating a fillet. In this case, the selected entities will be extended to form a fillet, as shown in Figure 3-21.

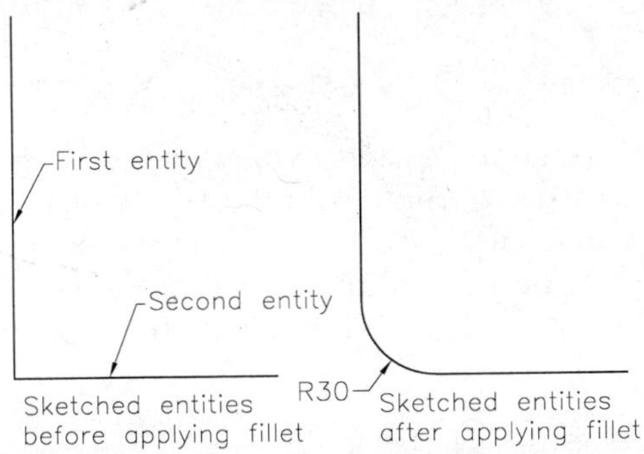

***Figure 3-20** Intersecting entities before and after applying a fillet*

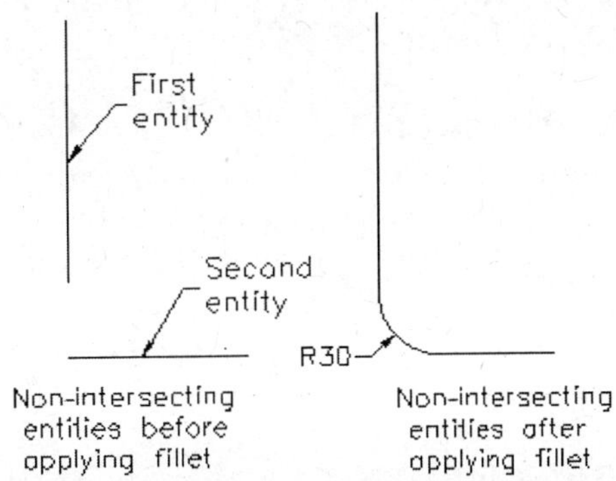

***Figure 3-21** Non-intersecting entities before and after applying a fillet*

Tip

*You can also create a fillet between two entities by drawing a window around them after invoking the **Sketch Fillet** tool. To fillet the entities using this method, invoke the **Sketch Fillet** tool. Set the **Radius** spinner to the required value. Now, drag the cursor to create a window around the two entities to be filleted such that they are enclosed inside the window; preview of the fillet will be displayed. Choose the **OK** button; the fillet will be created.*

Note

The fillet creation between two splines, a spline and a line, and a spline and an arc depends on the compatibility of the spline to be trimmed or extended.

Chamfering Sketched Entities

CommandManager:	Sketch > Sketch Fillet flyout > Sketch Chamfer
SOLIDWORKS menus:	Tools > Sketch Tools > Chamfer
Toolbar:	Sketch > Sketch Fillet flyout > Sketch Chamfer

The **Sketch Chamfer** tool is used to apply a chamfer to the adjacent sketch entities at the point of intersection. A chamfer can be specified by two lengths or an angle and a length from the point of intersection. You can apply a chamfer between two nonparallel lines that may be intersecting or non-intersecting. The creation of a chamfer between two non-intersecting lines depends on the length of the lines and the chamfer distance. To create a chamfer, choose the **Sketch Chamfer** button from the **Sketch Fillet** flyout of the **Sketch CommandManager**; the **Sketch Chamfer PropertyManager** will be displayed, as shown in Figure 3-22. Next, select the two entities to be chamfered. You can also select the two entities before invoking the **Sketch Chamfer** tool. The options in the **Sketch Chamfer PropertyManager** are discussed next.

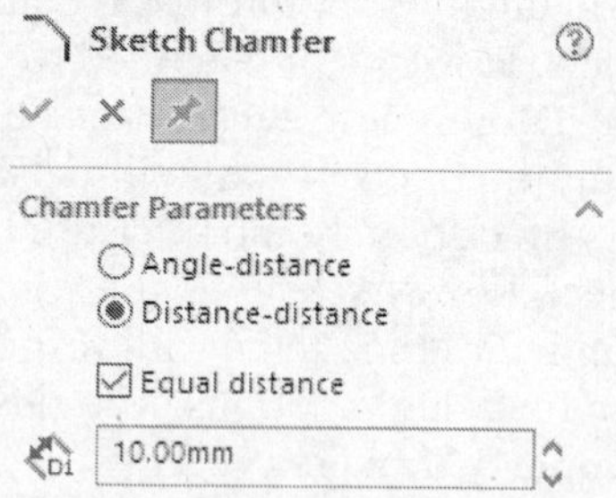

***Figure 3-22** The Sketch Chamfer Property Manager*

Angle-distance

The **Angle-distance** radio button is selected to create a chamfer by specifying the angle and the distance. When you select this radio button, the **Direction 1 Angle** spinner will be displayed below the **Distance 1** spinner. Specify the distance and angle values in the **Distance 1** and **Direction 1 Angle** spinners, respectively. Next, select the two entities to which the chamfer needs to be applied; a chamfer will be created, as shown in Figure 3-23(a). Note that the angle will be measured from the first entity you have selected.

Distance-distance

When you invoke the **Sketch Chamfer PropertyManager**, the **Distance-distance** radio button and the **Equal distance** check box are selected by default. Clear this check box to specify two different distances for creating chamfer, refer to Figure 3-23(b). When you clear this check box, the **Distance 2** spinner will be displayed below the **Distance 1** spinner to set the value of the distance in the second direction. Specify the distance value in both the spinners. Next, select the two entities that need to be chamfered; the chamfer will be created, as shown in Figure 3-23(b). Note that the distance 1 value will be measured along the first entity that you have selected and the distance 2 value will be measured along the second entity.

Equal distance

When you invoke the **Sketch Chamfer PropertyManager**, the **Distance-distance** radio button and the **Equal distance** check box are selected by default. As a result, you can create an equal distance chamfer between the selected entities. Specify the distance value in the **Distance 1** spinner and select the entities; the chamfer will be created, as shown in Figure 3-23(c).

You can also invoke the shortcut menu to choose the options discussed to create a chamfer. Choose the **OK** button from the **PropertyManager** to exit the tool.

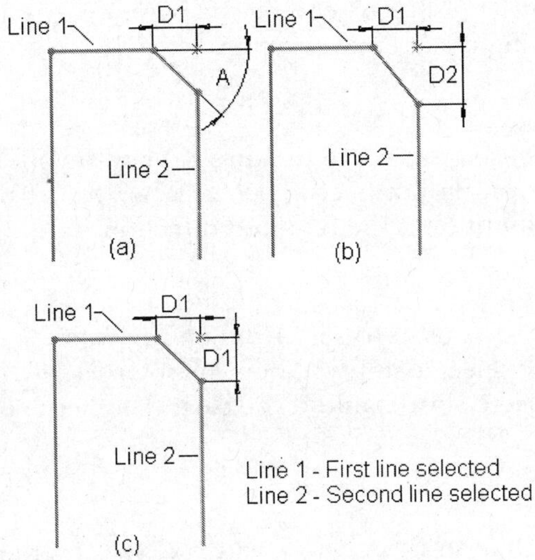

Figure 3-23 Chamfer and its parameters

Offsetting Sketched Entities

CommandManager: Sketch > Offset Entities
SOLIDWORKS menus: Tools > Sketch Tools > Offset Entities
Toolbar: Sketch > Offset Entities

Offsetting is one of the easiest methods to draw parallel lines or concentric arcs and circles. You can select the entire chain of entities as a single entity or select an individual entity to be offset. You can offset the selected sketched entities, edges, loops, and curves. You can also select the parabolic curves, ellipses, and elliptical arcs to be offset. When you choose the **Offset Entities** button from the **Sketch CommandManager**, the **Offset Entities PropertyManager** will be displayed, as shown in Figure 3-24. The options in the **Offset Entities PropertyManager** are discussed next.

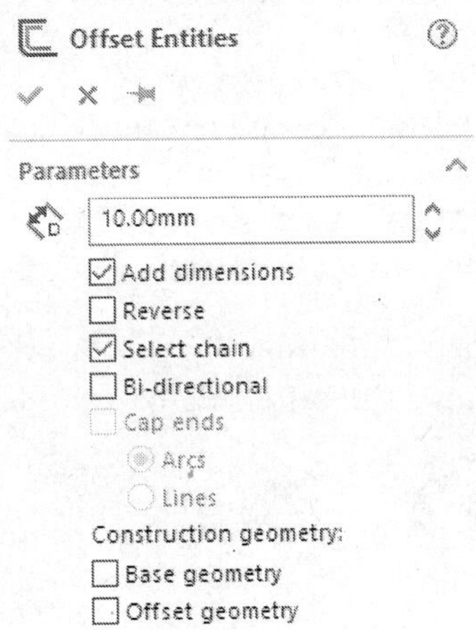

Figure 3-24 The ***Offset Entities PropertyManager***

Offset Distance

The **Offset Distance** spinner is used to set the distance through which the selected entity needs to be offset. You can set the value of the offset distance in this spinner or set the value by dragging the offset entity in the drawing area.

Add dimensions

The **Add dimensions** check box is selected by default in the **Parameters** rollout. Therefore, a dimension showing the offset distance between the parent entity and the resulting offset entity will be displayed on creating offset entities.

Reverse

The **Reverse** check box is used to change the direction of the offset. Note that while offsetting the entities by dragging, you do not need this check box as the direction of the offset can be changed by dragging the entities in the required direction.

Select chain

The **Select chain** check box is used to select the entire chain of continuous sketched entities that are in contact with the selected entity. When you invoke the **Offset Entities** tool, the **Select chain** check box will be selected by default. If you clear this check box, only the selected sketched entity will be offset.

Bi-directional

The **Bi-directional** radio button is used to create an offset of the selected entity in both the directions of the selected entity. If the **Bi-directional** check box is selected, the **Reverse** check box will be deactivated in the **Parameters** rollout.

Cap ends

The **Cap ends** check box will be available only when the sketch to be offset is an open sketch. On selecting this check box, the ends of the bidirectionally offset entities will be closed. You can select the **Arcs** or **Lines** radio button to specify the type of cap to close the ends. Note that if you are offsetting a closed entity in both the directions, this option will not be available.

Base geometry

The **Base geometry** check box is used to convert the parent entity into a construction entity.

Offset geometry

The **Offset geometry** check box is used to convert an offset entity into a construction entity.

Figure 3-25 shows a new chain of entities created by offsetting the chain of entities and Figure 3-26 shows the offsetting of a single entity.

Tip

*While performing any kind of editing operation if you want to clear the current selection set, right-click in the drawing area and choose **Clear Selections** from the shortcut menu displayed.*

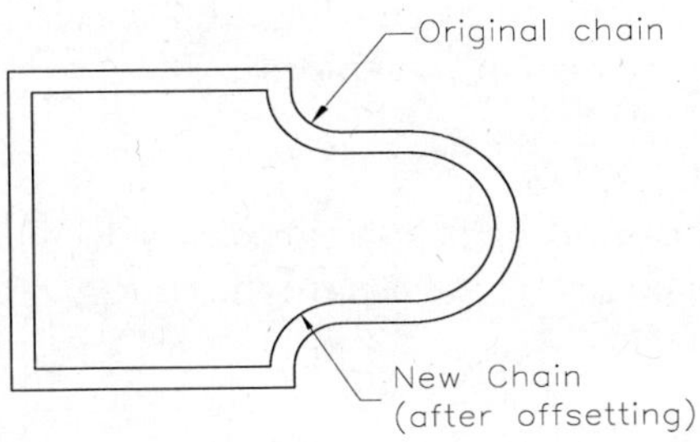

Figure 3-25 Offsetting a chain of entities

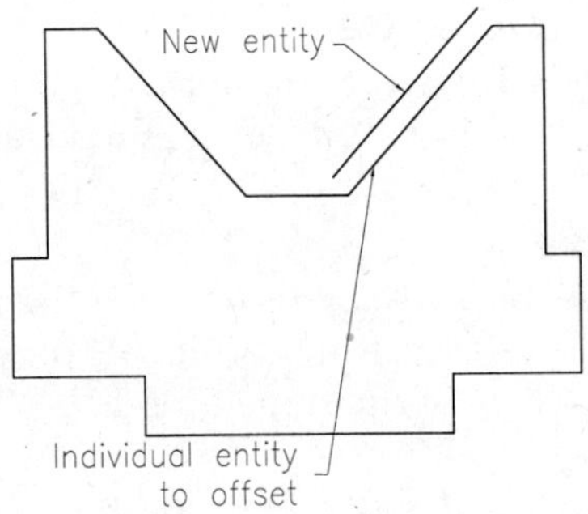

Figure 3-26 Offsetting a single entity

Offsetting Edges or Face of a Model

CommandManager:	Sketch > Offset On Surface
SOLIDWORKS menus:	Tools > Sketch Tools > Offset On Surface
Toolbar:	Sketch > Offset On Surface(Customize to add)

The **Offset On Surface** tool is used to offset edges or faces of a model in a 3D sketch. To offset model edges or faces, choose the **Offset On Surface** tool from the **Sketch CommandManager**; the **Offset On Surface PropertyManager** will be displayed, as shown in Figure 3-27. The options in the **Offset On Surface PropertyManager** are discussed next.

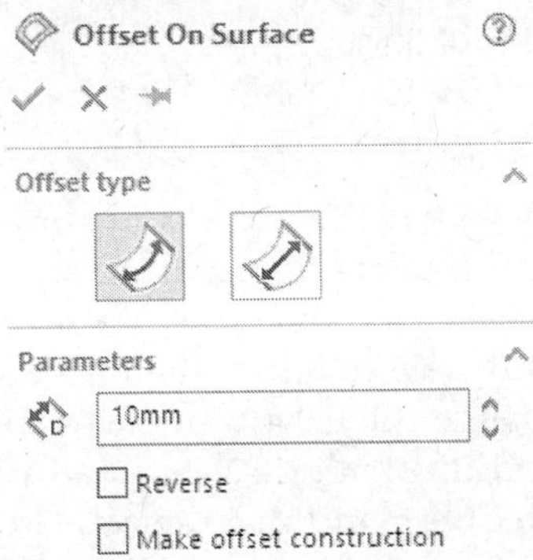

*Figure 3-27 The **Offset On Surface PropertyManager***

Geodesic Offset

This option creates the shortest possible offset distance between the selected edge and the resultant offset entity taking the support curvature of the given surface into account.

Euclidean Offset

This option creates linear offset distance between selected edge and the offset entity. This distance does not include the curvature of the given surface.

Offset Distance

The **Offset Distance** spinner is used to specify the distance through which the selected entity needs to be offset. You can set the value of the offset distance in this spinner.

Reverse

The **Reverse** check box is used to offset an entity to the opposite face of the edge selected. Note that this check box will be available only if the selected edge is connected to the contiguous faces which are part of the same model.

Make offset construction

The **Make offset construction** check box is used to convert the offset entity into construction entity,Figure 3-28 shows the face of a model selected to offset and the offset entity created.

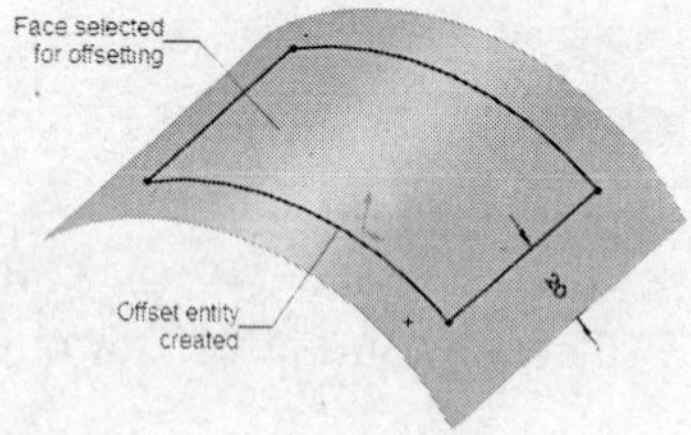

***Figure 3-28** Face selected for offsetting and offset created*

Mirroring Sketched Entities

CommandManager:	Sketch > Mirror Entities
SOLIDWORKS menus:	Tools > Sketch Tools > Mirror
Toolbar:	Sketch > Mirror Entities

The **Mirror Entities** tool is used to create a mirror image of the selected entities. The entities are mirrored about a centerline, face or plane. When you create the mirrored entity, SOLIDWORKS applies the symmetric relation between the sketched entities. If you change the entity, its mirror image will also change. To mirror the existing entities, choose the **Mirror Entities** button from the **Sketch CommandManager**; the **Mirror PropertyManager** will be displayed, as shown in Figure 3-29. Also, you will be prompted to select the entities to be mirrored. Select the entities from the drawing area; the name of the selected entities will be displayed in the **Entities to mirror** selection box. After selecting all entities to be mirrored, click once in the **Mirror about** selection box in the **Mirror PropertyManager**. Alternatively, pause the mouse after selecting an entity; the **Select** symbol will be displayed below the cursor. Right-click when this symbol is displayed; the **Mirror about** selection box will be activated automatically and you will be prompted to select a line, linear model edge, or a planar entity to mirror about. Select a line, centerline, or a planar entity from the drawing area; the preview

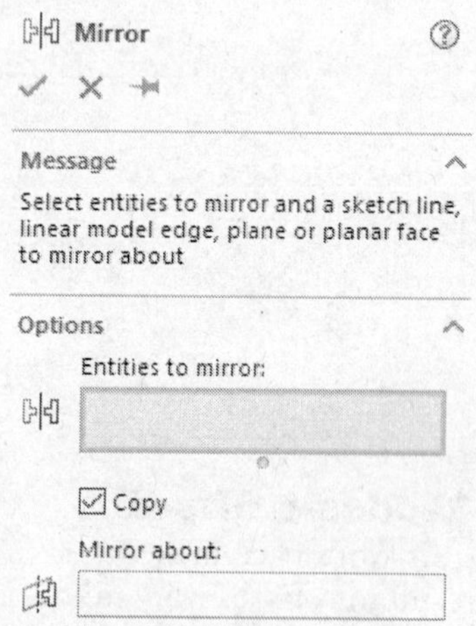

***Figure 3-29** The Mirror PropertyManager*

of the mirrored entities will be displayed. You need to make sure that the **Copy** check box is selected in the **Mirror PropertyManager**. If you clear this **Copy** check box, the parent selected entities will be removed and only the mirror image will be retained when you mirror the sketched entities. Choose the **OK** button from the **Mirror PropertyManager**.

Figure 3-30 shows the sketched entities with the centerline and Figure 3-31 shows the resulting mirror image of the sketched entities.

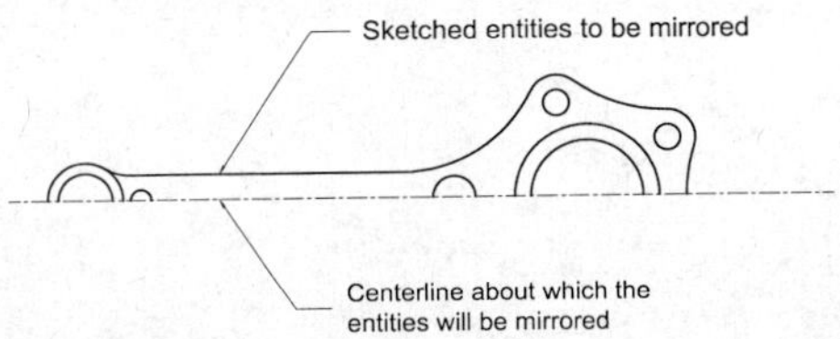

Figure 3-30 *Selecting the sketched entities and the centerline*

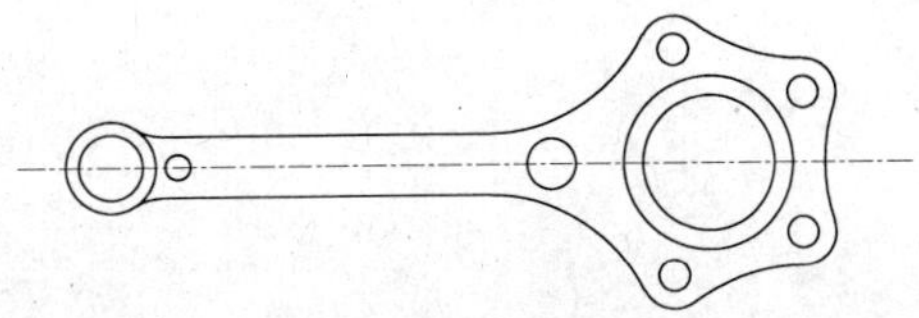

Figure 3-31 *Sketch after mirroring the geometry*

Mirroring Entities Dynamically

CommandManager:	Sketch > Dynamic Mirror Entities	*(Customize to add)*
SOLIDWORKS menus:	Tools > Sketch Tools > Dynamic Mirror	
Toolbar:	Sketch > Dynamic Mirror Entities	*(Customize to add)*

The **Dynamic Mirror Entities** tool is used to mirror the entities dynamically about a symmetry line while sketching. This tool is recommended when you are drawing the symmetric sketches. You need to add this tool to the **Sketch CommandManager** by using the **Customize** dialog box, as discussed earlier. To mirror the entities while sketching, choose the **Dynamic Mirror Entities** button from the **Sketch CommandManager**; the **Mirror PropertyManager** will be displayed, as shown in Figure 3-32. The **Message** rollout in the **Mirror PropertyManager** informs that you need to select a sketch line or a linear model edge to mirror about. Select a line, a centerline, or a model edge from the drawing area that will be used as a symmetry line; the symmetry symbols appear at both the ends of the centerline to indicate that the automatic mirroring is activated, as shown in Figure 3-33.

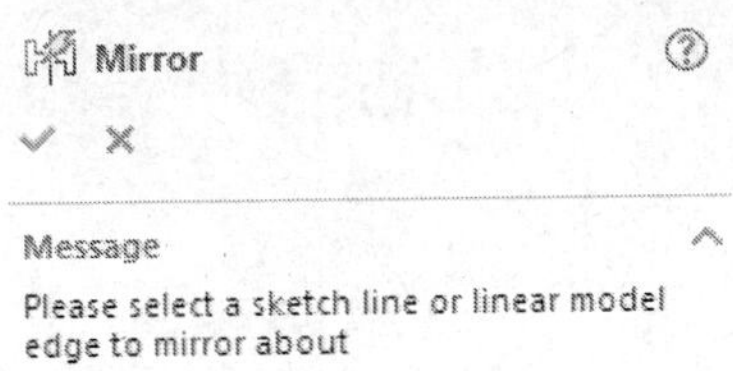

Figure 3-32 *The **Mirror PropertyManager***

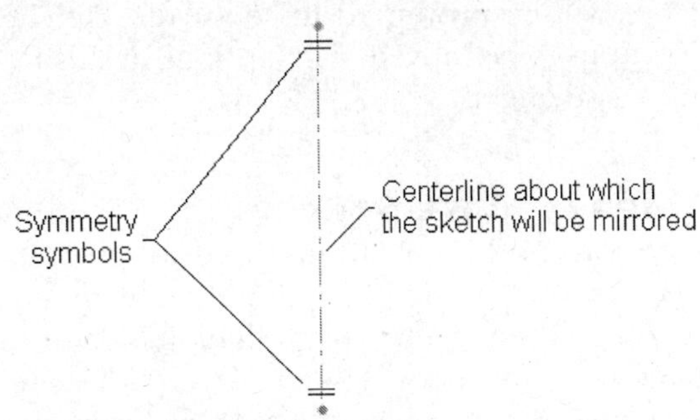

Figure 3-33 *The centerline and the symmetry symbols*

Now, start drawing the sketch. The entity that you draw on one side of the centerline will automatically be created on the other side of the mirror line (centerline). As evident from Figure 3-34, the entities are mirrored automatically while sketching. Figure 3-35 shows the complete sketch with automatic mirroring. After completing the sketch using the automatic mirroring option, you need to choose the **Dynamic Mirror Entities** tool again to exit the tool.

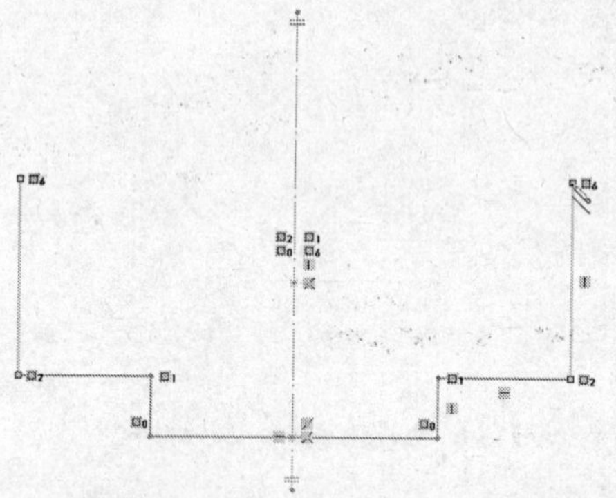

***Figure 3-34** Sketch drawn using the **Dynamic Mirror Entities** tool*

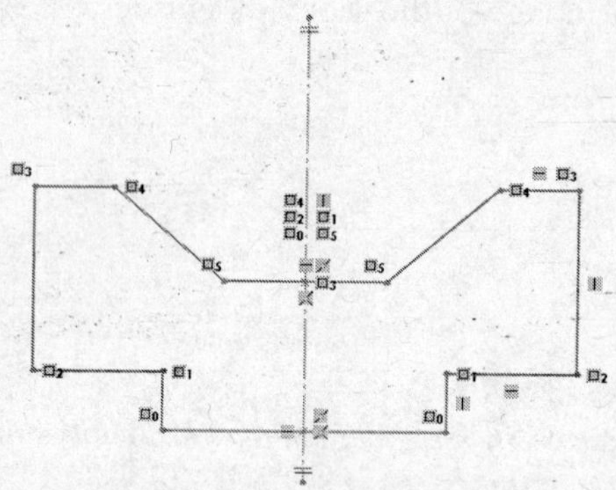

***Figure 3-35** Complete sketch drawn using the **Dynamic Mirror Entities** tool*

Moving Sketched Entities

CommandManager: Sketch > Move Entities flyout > Move Entities
SOLIDWORKS menus: Tools > Sketch Tools > Move
Toolbar: Sketch > Move Entities flyout > Move Entities

The **Move Entities** tool in the **Sketch CommandManager** is used to move an entity from one location to other. To move an entity, invoke this tool from the **Sketch CommandManager** or select the entities, right-click, and then choose the **Move Entities** option from the shortcut menu. Remember that this tool will be available only when at least one sketched entity is drawn. When you invoke this tool, the **Move PropertyManager** will be displayed, as shown in Figure 3-36, and you will be prompted to select the sketched items or the annotations to be moved. The options in this PropertyManager are discussed next.

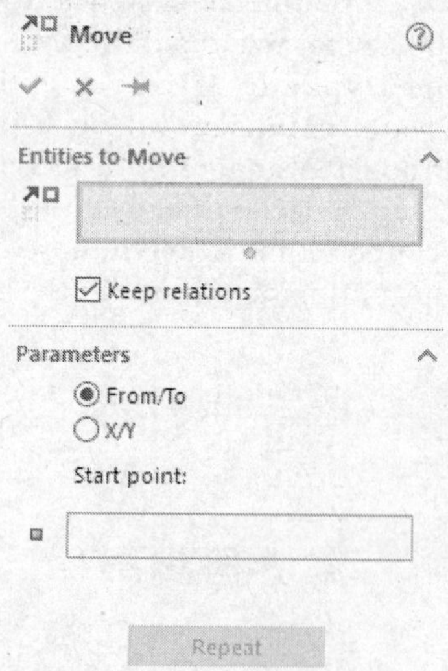

Figure 3-36** The **Move PropertyManager

Entities to Move Rollout

The options in this rollout are used to select the entities to be moved. You will notice that the **Sketch items or annotations** selection box is active in this rollout. The names of the entities selected to be moved will be displayed in this selection box. To remove an entity from the selection set, select it again from the drawing area. Alternatively, you can select its name from the **Sketch items or annotations** selection box and right-click to display the shortcut menu. Choose the **Delete** option from the shortcut menu. If you choose the **Clear Selections** option from the shortcut menu, all the entities in the selection set will be removed. You will notice that by default, the **Keep relations** check box is selected. If you move the sketched entities with this check box cleared, the relations applied to the entities to be moved will be removed. If you select this check box and then move the entities, then the relations applied to the sketched entities are retained even if you move the entities. You will learn more about relations later in this chapter.

Parameters Rollout

The **Parameters** rollout is used to specify the origin and destination positions of the entities selected to move. The options in this rollout are discussed next.

From/To

The **From/To** radio button is selected by default. So, you can move the selected entities from one point to another. To move the selected entities using this option, click once in the **Base point** selection box; you will be prompted to define the base point. Click anywhere in the drawing area to specify the base point; a yellow circle will be displayed where the start point is specified and you will be prompted to define the destination point. Select a point anywhere in the drawing area to place the selected entities.

X/Y

The **X/Y** radio button is selected to move the selected entities by specifying the relative coordinates of X and Y. On selecting this radio button, the **Delta X** and **Delta Y** spinners will be displayed below this radio button. Set the values of the destination coordinates in these spinners with respect to the current location.

Repeat

If the **Repeat** button is chosen, the entities will move further with the incremental distance specified in the **Delta X** and **Delta Y** spinners.

Figure 3-37 shows the selected entities being moved using the **Move Entities** tool. In this figure, the selected rectangle is moved from its selected base point to the new location.

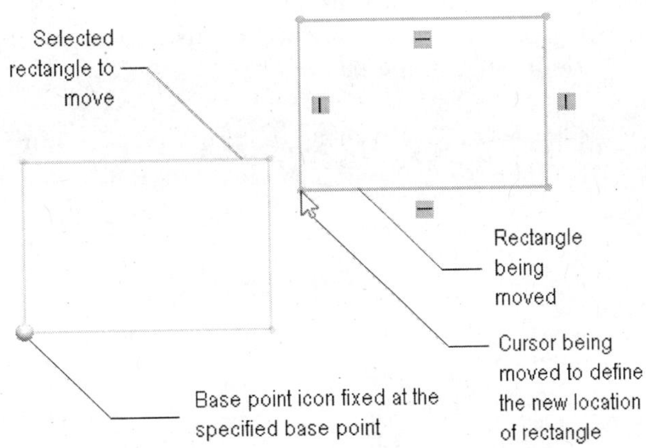

Figure 3-37 *Moving the selected entities*

Rotating Sketched Entities

CommandManager:	Sketch > Move Entities flyout > Rotate Entities
SOLIDWORKS menus:	Tools > Sketch Tools > Rotate
Toolbar:	Sketch > Move Entities flyout > Rotate Entities

To rotate the sketched entities, choose the **Rotate Entities** tool from the **Move Entities** flyout in the **Sketch CommandManager**, as shown in Figure 3-38. On doing so, the **Rotate PropertyManager** will be displayed, as shown in Figure 3-39, and you will be prompted to select the sketched items or annotations. Alternatively, to display this Property Manager, right-click in the drawing area and choose **Rotate Entities** from the shortcut menu displayed.

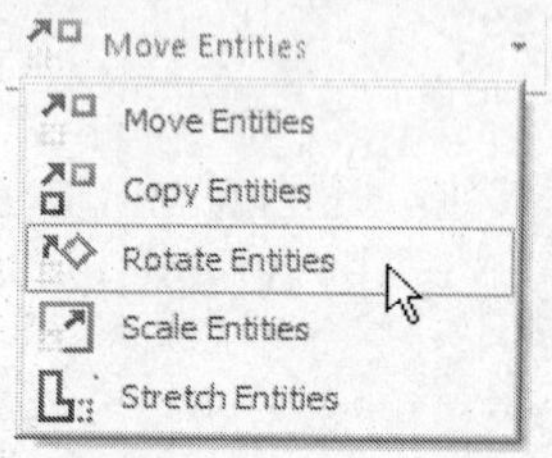

Figure 3-38 Tools in the ***Move Entities*** *flyout*

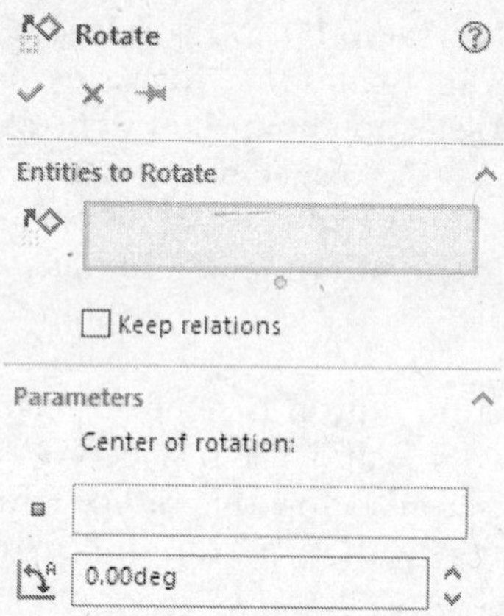

Figure 3-39 The ***Rotate PropertyManager***

Select the entities to be rotated; the names of the selected entities will be displayed in the **Sketch items or annotations** selection box of the **Entities to Rotate** rollout. Next, click in the **Base point** selection box in the **Parameters** rollout; you will be prompted to specify the center point of rotation. As soon as you specify the center point, the **Angle** spinner in the **Parameters** rollout will be highlighted. You can specify the angle of rotation using this spinner. You can also drag the mouse on the screen to define the angle of rotation.

Figure 3-40 shows a rectangle being rotated by dragging the cursor to define the angle of rotation. The lower right vertex of the rectangle is taken as the center point of rotation.

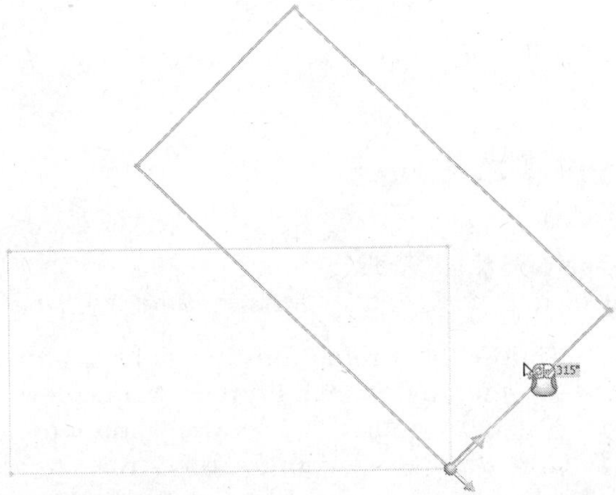

Figure 3-40 Dragging the cursor to rotate the rectangle

Scaling Sketched Entities

CommandManager:	Sketch > Move Entities flyout > Scale Entities
SOLIDWORKS menus:	Tools > Sketch Tools > Scale
Toolbar:	Sketch > Move Entities flyout > Scale Entities

To resize the entities, choose the **Scale Entities** tool from the **Move Entities** flyout in the **Sketch CommandManager**; the **Scale PropertyManager** will be displayed, as shown in Figure 3-41, and you will be prompted to select the sketched items or annotations. You can also invoke this PropertyManager by right clicking in the drawing area to display a shortcut menu and then choosing the **Scale Entities** tool from it.

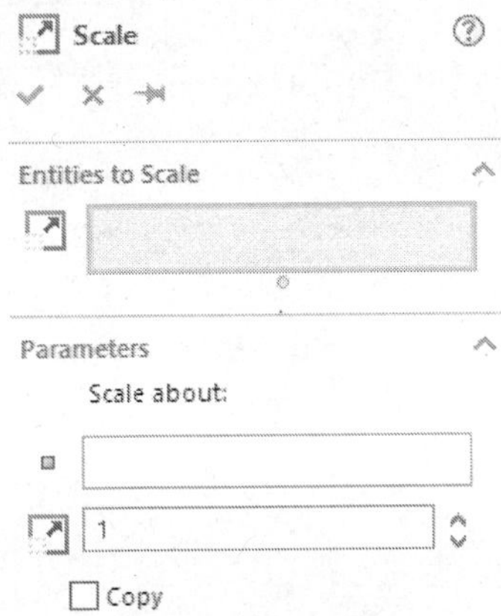

Figure 3-41 The ***Scale PropertyManager***

Select the entities to be resized; the names of the selected entities will be displayed in the **Sketch items or annotations** selection box of the **Entities to Scale** rollout. After selecting the entities to be scaled, right-click; you will be prompted to specify the point about which to scale. Specify the base point in the drawing area by clicking the left mouse button.

After specifying the base point, specify the magnification factor in the **Scale Factor** spinner of the **Parameters** rollout. The entities will be resized based on the value set in this spinner.

If you need to create the copies of the selected entities, select the **Copy** check box. Else, choose the **OK** button from the **Scale PropertyManager**; the selected entities will be resized. If you select the **Copy** check box, the **Number of Copies** spinner will be displayed. Set the number of instances in this spinner and choose the **OK** button from the **Scale PropertyManager**; the entities will be resized and their copies will be created with an incremental scale factor with respect to the original entities selected.

Note

If in a selected set, geometric dimensions are assigned to entities, then those entities will not be modified.

Stretching Sketched Entities

CommandManager:	Sketch > Move Entities flyout > Stretch Entities
SOLIDWORKS menus:	Tools > Sketch Tools > Stretch Entities
Toolbar:	Sketch > Move Entities flyout > Stretch Entities

To stretch the entities, choose the **Stretch Entities** tool from the **Move Entities** flyout in the **Sketch CommandManager**; the **Stretch PropertyManager** will be displayed, as shown in Figure 3-42, and you will be prompted to select the entities to stretch. Select the entities to be stretched by using the cross-window selection method, refer to Figure 3-43; the name of the entities selected will be displayed in the **Entities To Stretch** rollout of the **Stretch PropertyManager**. Click in the **Stretch about** selection box in the **Parameters** rollout and specify a point in the drawing area as the base point, refer to Figure 3-44. Now, move the cursor to the desired location; the selected entities will be stretched to the specified location. Figure 3-45 shows the stretched sketch.

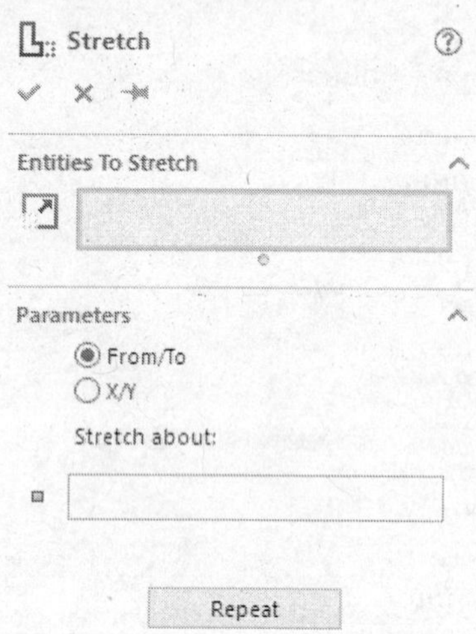

Figure 3-42** The **Stretch PropertyManager

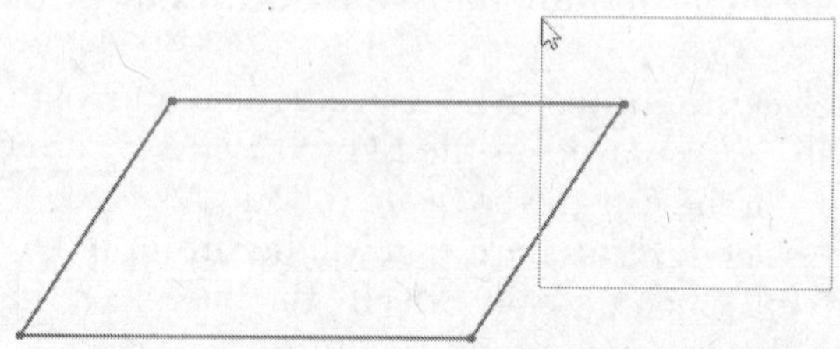

***Figure 3-43** Selecting entities for stretching*

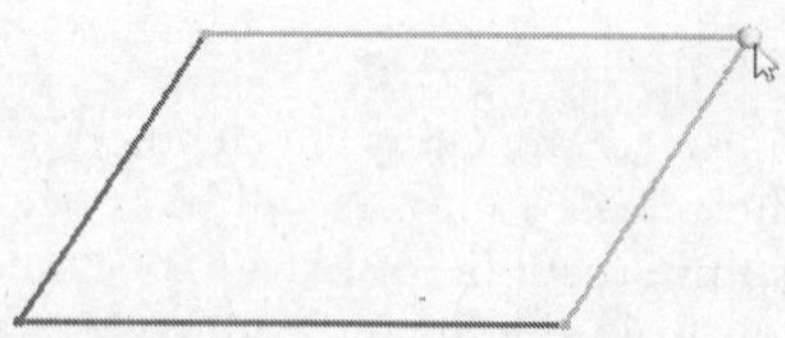

***Figure 3-44** Selecting the corner point for stretching*

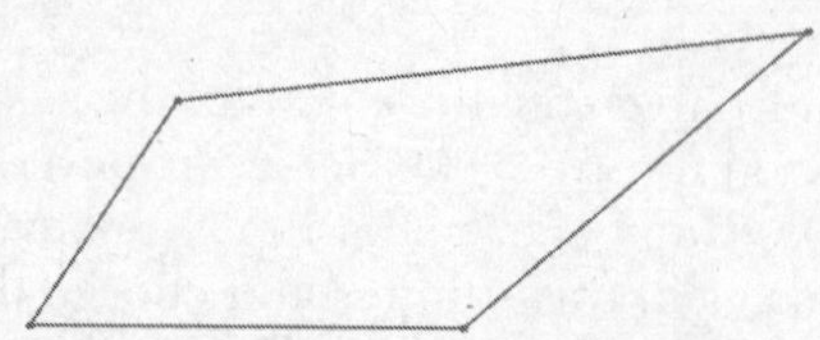

***Figure 3-45** The sketch after stretching*

You can also stretch entities along X and Y axes. To do so, select the **X/Y** radio button from the **Parameters** rollout; the **Parameters** rollout will be modified, as shown in Figure 3-46. Now, set the desired distance values in the **Delta X** and **Delta Y** spinners; dynamic preview of the selected entities to be stretched will be displayed in the drawing area. Once you are done, choose the **OK** button from the PropertyManager.

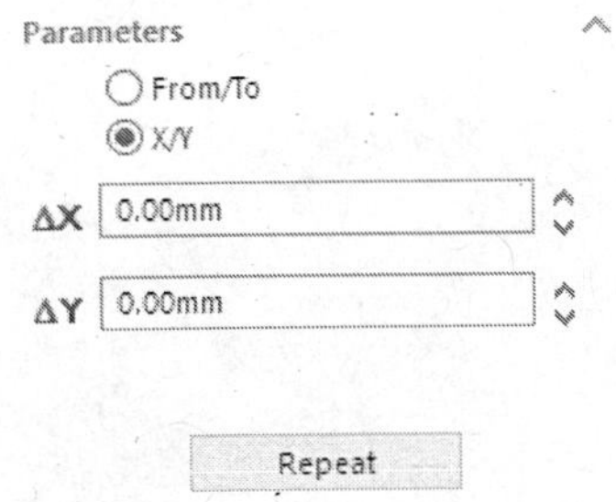

*Figure 3-46 The **Parameters** rollout*

Copying and Pasting Sketched Entities

CommandManager: Sketch > Move Entities flyout > Copy Entities
SOLIDWORKS menus: Tools > Sketch Tools > Copy
Toolbar: Sketch > Move Entities flyout > Copy Entities

The **Copy Entities** tool allows you to copy the selected sketched entity and paste it to other location. Note that if dimensions are also selected along with the entities to be copied, then the dimensions will also be copied along with the sketched entities. To copy and paste the sketched entities, choose the **Copy Entities** tool from the **Move Entities** flyout in the **Sketch CommandManager**; the **Copy PropertyManager** will be displayed, as shown in Figure 3-47.

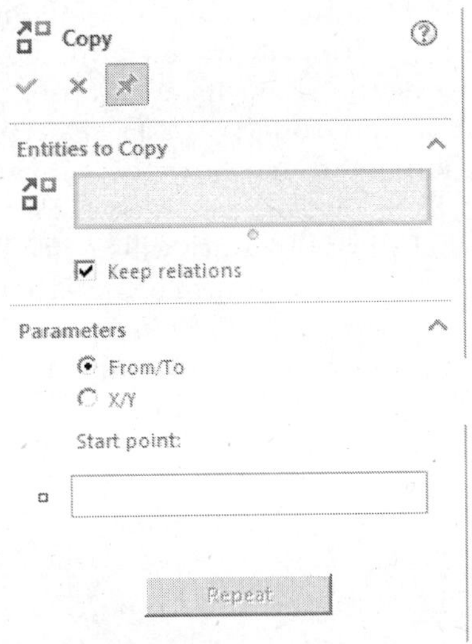

*Figure 3-47 The **Copy** PropertyManager*

Select the entities that you want to copy and then select the **From/To** radio button, if it is not selected by default. Next, click once in the **Base point** selection box and then specify the base point. Now, move the cursor; you will notice that the preview of the entities to be copied will be attached to the cursor. Click at a location in the drawing area to place the copied entities. If you need to create multiple copies, left-click at different locations. Else, right-click to invoke the shortcut menu and then choose the **OK** option from it to exit the tool. On selecting the **X/Y** radio button in the **Parameters** rollout of the **Copy PropertyManager**, you need to specify the X and Y coordinates of the new entities with respect to their current location and choose the **OK** button. Note that on selecting the **X/Y** radio button, you cannot create multiple copies of the selected entities.

CREATING PATTERNS

Sometimes, while creating a base feature, you may need to place the sketched entities in a particular arrangement such as along linear edges or around a circle. Figures 3-48 and 3-49 show the base features with slots. These slots are created with the help of linear and circular patterns of the sketched entities. The tools that are used to create the linear and circular patterns of the sketched entities are discussed next.

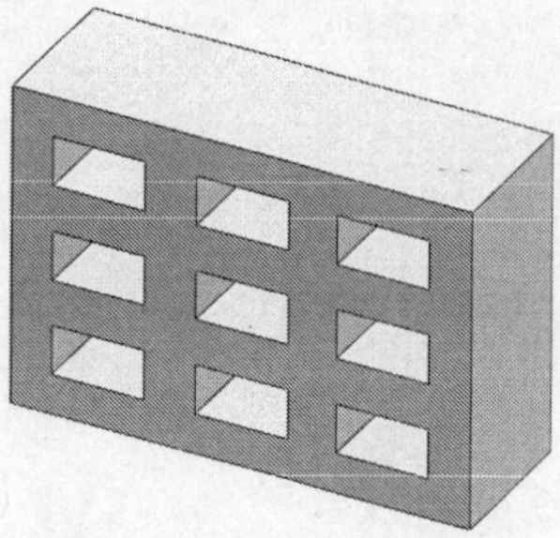

Figure 3-48 *Base feature with slots created along the linear edges*

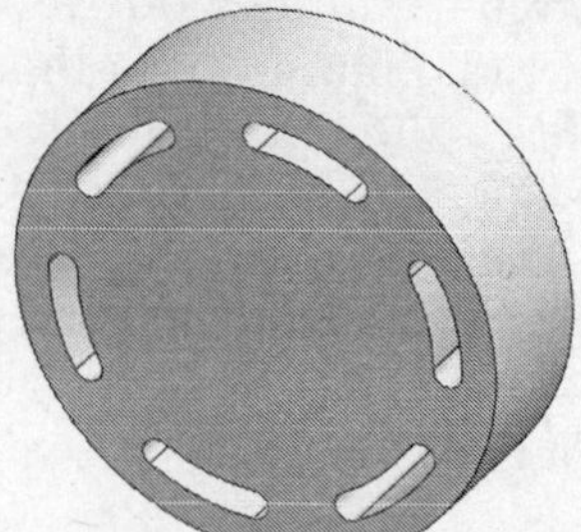

Figure 3-49 *Base feature with slots created in circular pattern*

Creating Linear Sketch Patterns

CommandManager: Sketch > Pattern flyout > Linear Sketch Pattern
SOLIDWORKS menus: Tools > Sketch Tools > Linear Pattern
Toolbar: Sketch > Pattern flyout > Linear Sketch Pattern

In SOLIDWORKS, the linear pattern of the sketched entities is created using the **Linear Sketch Pattern** tool. To create the linear pattern, select the sketched entities from the drawing area. Then, choose the **Linear Sketch Pattern** tool from the **Pattern** flyout in the **Sketch CommandManager**; the **Linear Pattern PropertyManager** will be displayed, as shown in Figure 3-50. Also, the preview of the linear pattern will be displayed in the drawing area and the arrow cursor will be replaced by the linear pattern cursor. Note that if you have not selected the sketched entities to be patterned before invoking this tool, you will have to select them one by one using the linear pattern cursor. The names of the selected entities are displayed in the **Entities to Pattern** rollout. You cannot draw a window to select entities by using the linear pattern cursor.

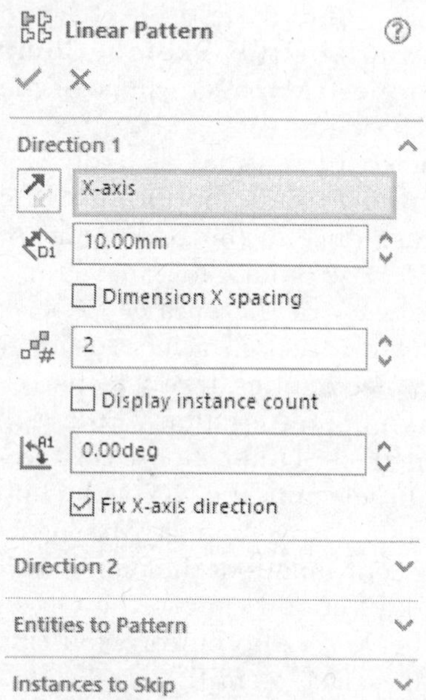

Figure 3-50 *The* ***Linear Pattern PropertyManager***

The options in this PropertyManager are discussed next.

Direction 1 Rollout

The options in the **Direction 1** rollout are used to define the first direction, distance between instances, number of instances, and the angle of pattern direction.

When the **Linear Pattern PropertyManager** is invoked, you will notice that only the options in the **Direction 1** rollout are active. Select the sketched entities to be patterned; a callout will be attached to the direction arrow. The edit boxes in this callout are used to define the number of instances and the distance between the instances to be created. Alternatively, you can define these values in the **Spacing** and **Number of Instances** spinners in the **Direction 1** rollout. You can also define the distance between the instances by dragging the select point provided on the tip of the direction arrow. By default, direction 1 is parallel to the X-axis. If you need to select any existing line or a model edge to define direction 1, click in the selection box in the **Direction 1** rollout and select a line or an edge of the existing feature. Click on the direction arrow or choose the **Reverse Direction** button from this rollout to reverse the pattern direction, if required. The **Angle** spinner is used to define the angle of the direction of the pattern. By default, the direction of the pattern is set to 0-degree. Select the **Fix X-axis direction** check box to constrain the angle of the pattern defined in the **Angle** spinner. If the **Dimension X spacing** check box is selected, the dimension will be attached between the parent instance and the first instance of the pattern. On selecting the **Display instance count** check box, the number of instances will be displayed in the resulting sketch pattern. Select this check box, if you need to create configurations in sketch patterns using the **Design Table**. Creating configurations using the **Design Table** is discussed in the later chapters.

Figure 3-51 shows preview of the linear pattern with instances along direction 1. Figure 3-52 shows a linear pattern at an angle of 30 degrees.

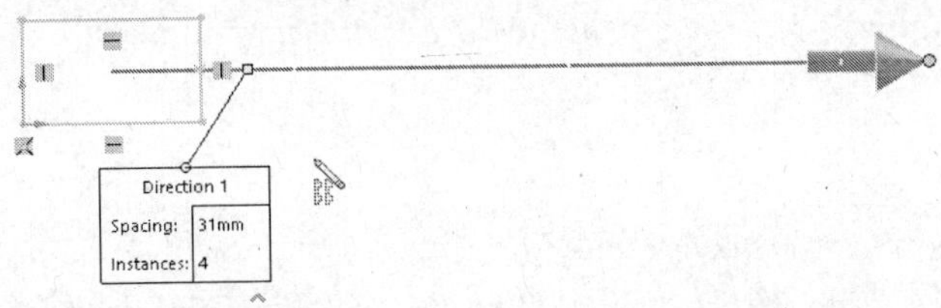

Figure 3-51 Preview of the linear pattern with four instances along direction 1 and one instance along direction 2

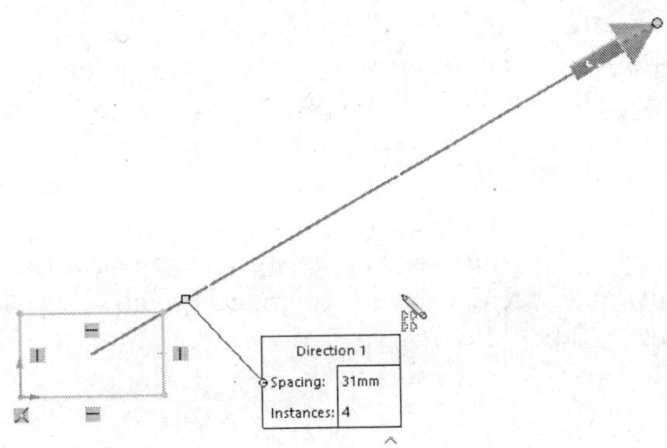

Figure 3-52 Preview of the linear pattern at an angle of 30 degrees along direction 1

Direction 2 Rollout

The options in the **Direction 2** rollout are used to create pattern of the selected entities in the second direction. You will notice that the preview is not displayed in the second direction. This is because the value of the number of instances is set to 1 in the **Number** spinner. This means by default, only one instance will be created in the second direction and that is the parent instance. If you set the value of the number of instances to more than 1, then the options in this rollout will be enabled. All options in this rollout are the same, except the **Dimension angle between axes** check box. Select this check box to apply an angular dimension to the reference direction lines of both directions. Figure 3-53 shows a linear pattern created by specifying instances in both directions.

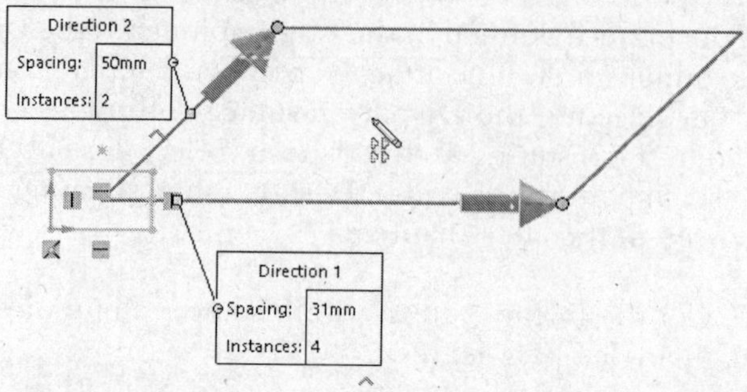

Figure 3-53 *Preview of the linear pattern at an angle of 45 degrees along direction 2*

> **Tip**
> *You can also specify the spacing and angle values dynamically in the preview of the linear pattern. To do so, press the left mouse button on a control point displayed at the end of the arrow in the pattern preview and drag the cursor. After placing the arrow at the desired location, release the left mouse button; the new spacing and angle value will be displayed in the respective spinner.*

Instances to Skip Rollout

The **Instances to Skip** rollout is used to remove some of the instances from the pattern temporarily. By default, this rollout is not invoked. To invoke it, click on the down-arrow on the right side of the rollout. As soon as you activate the selection box in this rollout, pink dots will be displayed at the center of each pattern instance. To remove an instance from a pattern temporarily, move the cursor on the pink dot; a hand symbol will be displayed and its location will be displayed in the tooltip below the hand symbol in the matrix format. Click at the pink dot to remove a particular instance; the display of the instance will be turned off and its location will be displayed in the selection box. Also, the pink dot will change to an orange dot. Similarly, remove as many instances that you do not want to include in the pattern.

To restore the temporarily removed instances, select the orange dot displayed after hiding the instances. Alternatively, you can select the name of the instances from the **Instances to Skip** rollout and then press the DELETE key.

> **Tip**
> *You can also add entities to the current selection set by selecting them using the linear pattern cursor. To remove an entity from the selection set, select the entity from the selection box in the* ***Entities to Pattern*** *rollout, right-click, and then choose* ***Delete*** *from the shortcut menu. As you add or remove instances, the effect can be seen dynamically in the preview of the pattern.*

Creating Circular Sketch Patterns

CommandManager:	Sketch > Pattern flyout > Circular Sketch Pattern
SOLIDWORKS menus:	Tools > Sketch Tools > Circular Pattern
Toolbar:	Sketch > Pattern flyout > Circular Sketch Pattern

In SOLIDWORKS, the circular pattern of the sketched entities is created using the **Circular Sketch Pattern** tool. To create the circular pattern of an entity, select it and then choose the **Circular Sketch Pattern** tool from the **Pattern** flyout in the **Sketch CommandManager**; the **Circular Pattern PropertyManager** will be displayed, as shown in Figure 3-54, and the preview of the circular pattern will be displayed. Also, the arrow cursor will be replaced by the circular pattern cursor and the names of the selected entities will be displayed in the **Entities to Pattern** rollout.

The options in the **Circular Pattern PropertyManager** are discussed next.

Parameters Rollout

The options in the **Parameters** rollout are used to define the centerpoint of the circular pattern, coordinates of the centerpoint of the reference circle, number of instances, angle between the instances or the total angle of pattern, radius of the reference circle, and so on. Figure 3-55 shows the parameters associated with the circular pattern. The options to define all these parameters are discussed next.

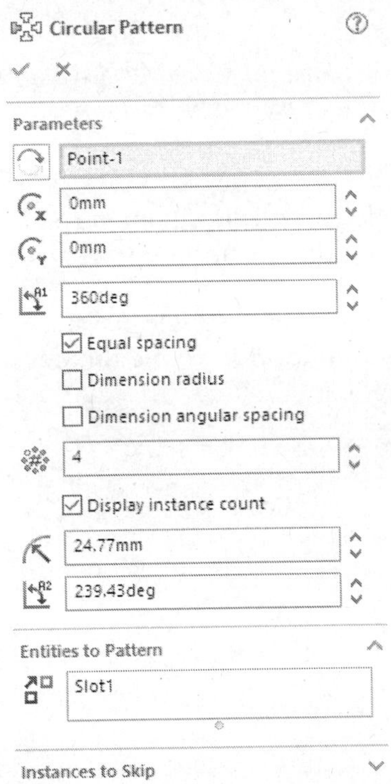

*Figure 3-54 The **Circular Pattern PropertyManager***

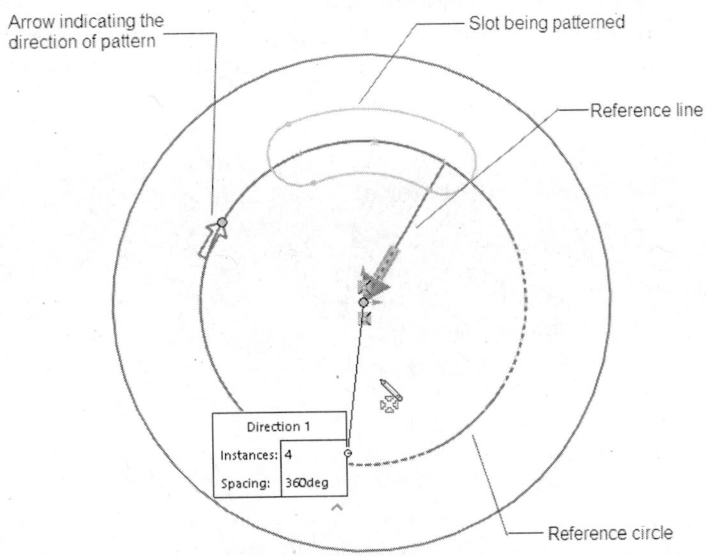

Figure 3-55 Parameters associated with the circular pattern

The **Reverse Direction** button is used to reverse the default direction of the circular pattern. The selection box on the right of this button is used to select the centerpoint of the circular pattern. By default, the origin is selected as the center of the circular pattern. You can modify this location by using the **Center X** and **Center Y** spinners. Alternatively, click once in the selection box and select the point that you want to be the new centerpoint or drag the center point to the new point. You can set the value of the number of instances using the **Number of Instances** spinner. By default, the **Equal spacing** check box is selected and the value of angle in the **Spacing** spinner is set to 360-degree. When this check box is selected, the specified number of instances are equi-spaced radially. If you modify the default value in the **Spacing** spinner, the angle between the instances will be adjusted accordingly. However, if the **Equal spacing** check box is cleared, then you need to specify the incremental angle between the instances using the **Spacing** spinner.

The **Radius** spinner is used to modify the radius of the reference circle around which the circular pattern will be created. The **Arc Angle** spinner provided in this rollout is used to modify the angle between the centerpoint of the original pattern instance and the center of the reference circle.

The **Dimension radius** and **Dimension angular spacing** check boxes are used to display the radius and angle between the pattern instances of the circular pattern. On selecting the **Display instance count** check box, the number of instances will be displayed in the resulting sketch pattern. Select this check box, if you need to create configurations in sketch patterns by using the **Design Table**. Creating configurations using the **Design Table** is discussed in the later chapters.

Note

If you know the location of the centerpoint of the circular pattern then it is recommended to drag the tip of the arrow to the center of the reference circle for defining the center of the circular pattern.

Instances to Skip Rollout

The **Instances to Skip** rollout is used to remove instances temporarily from the pattern. The procedure to skip instances is the same as discussed while creating the linear pattern.

Figure 3-56 shows preview of the circular pattern with a 75-degree incremental angle between two successive instances. Figure 3-57 shows a circular pattern with the angle and spacing dimension values displayed in the pattern.

Tip

You can modify the total angle between instances by pressing the left mouse button on the tip of the direction arrow and then dragging the cursor.

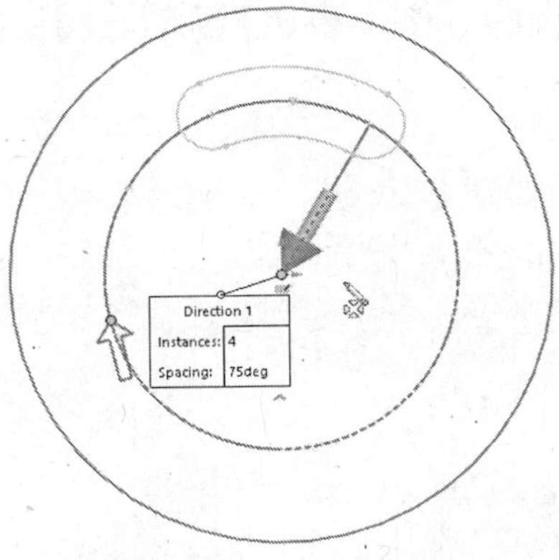

Figure 3-56 *Creating circular pattern by defining incremental angle between individual instances*

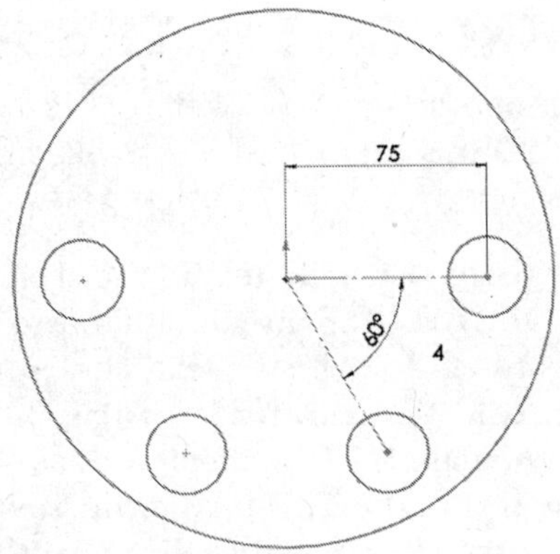

Figure 3-57 *Spacing and angle values placed in circular pattern*

EDITING PATTERNS

You can edit the patterns of the sketched entities by using the shortcut menu that will be displayed when you right-click on any instance of the pattern. Depending on whether you right-click on the instance of the linear or circular pattern, the **Edit Linear Pattern** or **Edit Circular Pattern** option will be available in the shortcut menu. Figure 3-58 shows partial view of the shortcut menu displayed when you right-click on one of the instances of circular pattern.

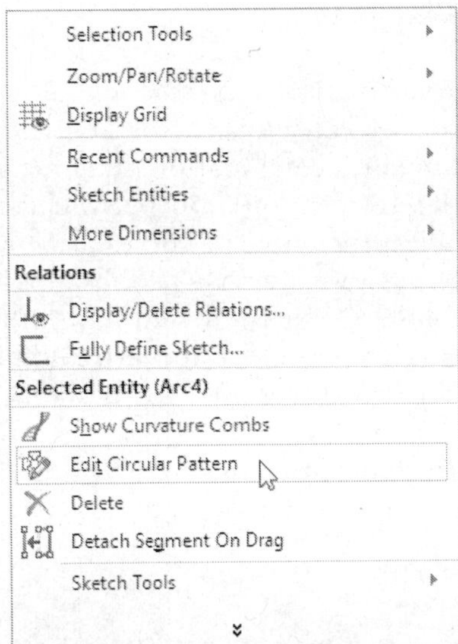

Figure 3-58 *Partial view of the shortcut menu displayed*

Depending on whether you choose the option to edit a linear pattern or a circular pattern, the **Linear Pattern Property Manager** or the **Circular Pattern PropertyManager** will be displayed. Note that only the parameters will be available in these PropertyManagers.

By using the **Circular Pattern PropertyManager**, you can edit the parameters of the patterns. If the distance between the instances or the angular dimension between the instances is displayed, then to change it without invoking a shortcut menu, double-click on the corresponding value; the **Modify** dialog box will be displayed. Enter a new value in the **Modify** dialog box and press ENTER. Similarly, if the number of instances is displayed in the sketch pattern, you can edit it by double-clicking on it and entering a new value in the edit box displayed. Note that if you are changing the number of instances, then the distances between the instances and the angle between the instances will be deleted. However, you can add dimensions using the **Smart Dimension** tool and this procedure is discussed in the later chapters.

WRITING TEXT IN THE SKETCHING ENVIRONMENT

CommandManager:	Sketch > Text
SOLIDWORKS menus:	Tools > Sketch Entities > Text
Toolbar:	Sketch > Text

You can also write text in the sketching environment of SOLIDWORKS and use it later to create extrude or cut features. To write the text, choose the **Text** button from the **Sketch CommandManager**; the **Sketch Text PropertyManager** will be displayed, as shown in Figure 3-59. Enter the text in the **Text** box in the **Text** rollout; the text will start from the sketch origin. To place the text at a specified location, exit the **Sketch Text PropertyManager** after writing the text. You will notice a dot at the start of the text. Drag the text and place at the required location. You can also change the format, font, justification, and so on using the options in the **Text** rollout. Figure 3-60 shows the text created using the **Text** tool.

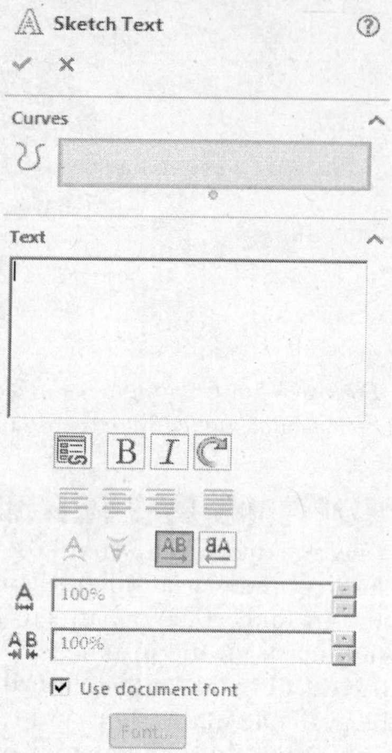

*Figure 3-59 The **Sketch Text PropertyManager***

You can also create the text along a curve. To do so, first you need to create a curve. The curve can be an arc, a spline, a line, or a combination of a line, arc, and spline. Next, choose the **Text** button to invoke the **Sketch Text PropertyManager**. Select the curve or curves along which you need to create the text. Now, enter the text in the **Text** edit box; you will observe that the text is created along the arc. You can use the **Flip Horizontal** and **Flip Vertical** buttons to modify the position of the text. Figure 3-61 shows the text created along an arc.

To change the font size, clear the **Use document font** check box and set the value in the **Width Factor** and **Spacing** spinners. You can also choose the **Font** button to change the font and text size.

***Figure 3-60** Text created using the **Text** tool*

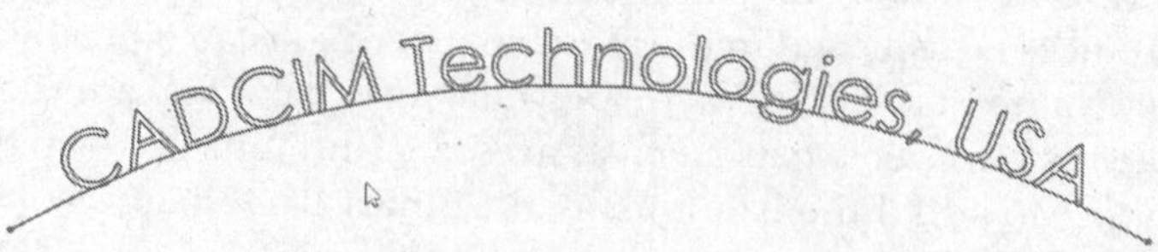

***Figure 3-61** Text created along an arc*

Note
In SOLIDWORKS, you can link the sketch text with the file properties by choosing the ***Link to Property*** *button in the* ***Text*** *rollout.*

Tip
If the text that you write appears reversed, you can draw a line from left to right and then use it as an element to align the text.

MODIFYING SKETCHED ENTITIES

Most of the sketches require modification at some stages of design. Therefore, it is important for a designer to understand the process of modification in SOLIDWORKS. Modification of various sketched entities is discussed next.

Modifying a Sketched Line

You can modify a sketched line by using the **Line Properties PropertyManager**. This PropertyManager is displayed when you select a line using the **Select** tool. Note that if the selected line is a part of a rectangle, polygon, or parallelogram, the entire object will be modified as you modify the line. This is because relations are applied to all lines of a rectangle, polygon, and a parallelogram.

Similarly, you can also modify a centerline using the **Line Properties PropertyManager** which will be displayed when you select the centerline.

Modifying a Sketched Circle

To modify a sketched circle, select it using the **Select** tool; the **Circle PropertyManager** will be displayed with the coordinate values of the centerpoint of the circle and the value of the radius in the **Parameters** rollout. You can modify the values in the respective edit boxes.

Tip
The status of the sketched entity that you select for modification is displayed in the ***Existing Relations*** *rollout of the PropertyManager which is displayed on selecting an entity. For example, if the selected entity is fully defined, it will be displayed in the PropertyManager and if the entity is underdefined, the PropertyManager will display a message that the entity is underdefined.*

Modifying a Sketched Arc

To modify a sketched arc, select it using the **Select** tool; the **Arc PropertyManager** will be displayed with the coordinate values of the centerpoint, start point, and endpoint. The values of the radius and the included angle will also be displayed. You can modify the values in the respective edit boxes.

Modifying a Sketched Polygon

To modify a sketched polygon, right-click on any one edge of the polygon to display the shortcut menu. Choose the **Edit polygon** option from the shortcut menu to display the **Polygon PropertyManager**. You can modify the selected polygon using the options in the **Polygon PropertyManager**.

Note

If you right-click on the reference circle that is automatically drawn when you draw a polygon, the ***Edit polygon*** *option will not be available in the shortcut menu.*

Modifying a Spline

You can perform four types of modification on a spline. The first is the modification of the coordinates of the selected control point. The second modification is by using the Spline Handles. The third type of modification is by using the Control polygons. The fourth type of modification is the addition of a curvature control symbol. These modifications are discussed in detail next.

Modifying a Spline by using the Control Points

To modify the location of the control points of a spline, select the spline; the **Spline PropertyManager** will be displayed. The control points of the spline will be displayed with a square. The number of the current control point and its coordinates will also be displayed in the **Parameters** rollout of the **Spline PropertyManager**, as shown in Figure 3-62. When you set the value in the **Spline Point Number** spinner, the corresponding control point will be selected in the spline. Now, you can modify its coordinates using the **X Coordinate** and **Y Coordinate** spinners. Alternatively, you can select and drag a control point to place it on desired location.

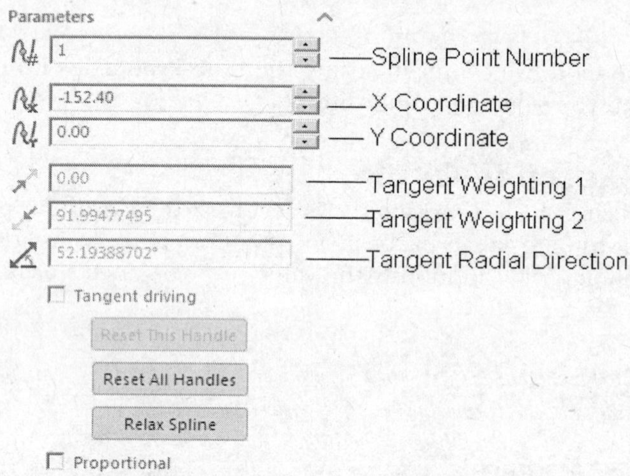

Figure 3-62 The ***Parameters*** *rollout of the* ***Spline PropertyManager***

You can also add more control points to a spline. To do so, choose **Tools > Spline Tools > Insert Spline Point** from the SOLIDWORKS menus. Alternatively, select the spline and right-click to invoke the shortcut menu. In this menu, choose the **Insert Spline Point** option. Now, specify a location on the spline where you need to add the control point; a point and a spline handle will be displayed at the point specified on the spline. The spline handles are discussed in the next section. Similarly, you can add as many control points as needed. After adding the required number of control points, invoke the **Select** tool and select the spline again. You will notice that the boxes of control points are displayed on all points including the newly added points.

Modifying a Spline by using the Spline Handles

A spline handle is a line with diamond handle, arrow, and circular handle on both its endpoints. The spline handles will be displayed when you select a spline using the **Select** tool. The default spline handles will be displayed in gray, which implies that they are not selected. When you move the cursor over a spline handle, it will be highlighted in orange. Additionally, a rotate symbol will be displayed if you move the cursor near the diamond handle. A black colored arrow symbol will be displayed, if you move the cursor near the arrow. If you move the cursor near the circular handle, both the symbols will be displayed, as shown in Figure 3-63.

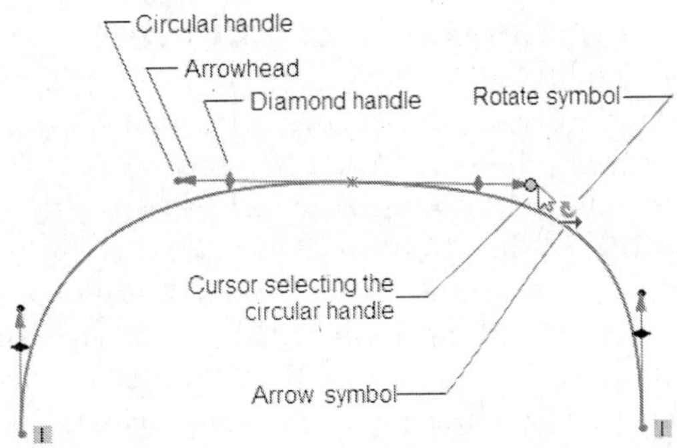

Figure 3-63 The spline and the spline handle

Move the cursor near the diamond handle, arrows, or circular handle; it will be highlighted. On selecting any of these entities, the number of respective control points and their coordinates will be displayed in the **Parameters** rollout. Select and drag the diamond handle to dynamically modify the direction of the tangent. As you drag the diamond handle, the value in the **Tangent Radial Direction** spinner will change dynamically. When you drag the cursor the **Tangent driving** check box is also selected automatically. After modifying the shape of the spline, click anywhere in the drawing area to exit the current selection set. You will notice that the currently modified spline handle is displayed in blue, which implies that the default setting of this spline handle is modified. Select and drag the arrowhead to modify the tangent weighting. As you drag the arrowhead, the value in the **Tangent Weighting** spinner will change dynamically. If you press the ALT key while dragging the arrowhead, the spline will get deformed symmetrically. Similarly, you can edit the spline using the circular handle. In this case, both the symbols will be displayed. So, the values in the **Tangent Radial Direction** and **Tangent Weighting** spinners will change dynamically.

Choose the **Reset This Handle** button to reset the current handle to the original position. Choose the **Reset All Handles** button to reset all handles to the default position. To create a smooth curvature after editing the handles, choose the **Relax Spline** button.

To add more spline handles, select the spline and right-click to invoke the shortcut menu. Choose the **Add Tangency Control** option from the shortcut menu; a spline handle will be attached to the selected spline. Move the cursor to the location where you want to place the spline handle and click on that location. A spline control point will also be added along with the spline handle. You can also apply relations to the spline handles. You will learn more about relations in the later chapters. You can also delete the spline handles by selecting the control point and pressing the DELETE key.

You can also apply dimensions to the spline handles to shape a spline accurately. You will learn more about dimensioning in the later chapters.

Modifying a Spline by using the Control Polygon

To display the control polygon, select a spline and right-click; a shortcut menu will be displayed. Choose the **Display Control Polygon** option; the control polygons will be displayed, as shown in Figure 3-64. When you select a control polygon, the **Spline Polygon PropertyManager** will be displayed. You can also set the location of the control points by using the **X Coordinate** and **Y Coordinate** spinners in the **Spline Polygon PropertyManager**. You can modify the location of a control point by dragging it. To turn off the display of the control polygon, select a spline, invoke the shortcut menu, and choose **Display Control Polygon** again.

Adding the Curvature Control

You can also add a curvature control to a spline to modify its curvature. To add a curvature control, move the cursor over the spline and invoke the shortcut menu. Choose the **Add Curvature Control** option from it; the curvature control will be attached to the selected spline. Move the cursor to the location where you want to place the curvature control symbol and click; the curvature control will be added. Also, a spline handle will be placed at the location where the curvature control symbol is attached tangent to the spline. Now, select and drag the dot symbol at the end of this curvature control symbol. You will notice that the curvature of the spline is modified dynamically as you drag the cursor. After modifying the shape of the spline, release the left mouse button. You can also delete the curvature control symbol by selecting it and pressing the DELETE key.

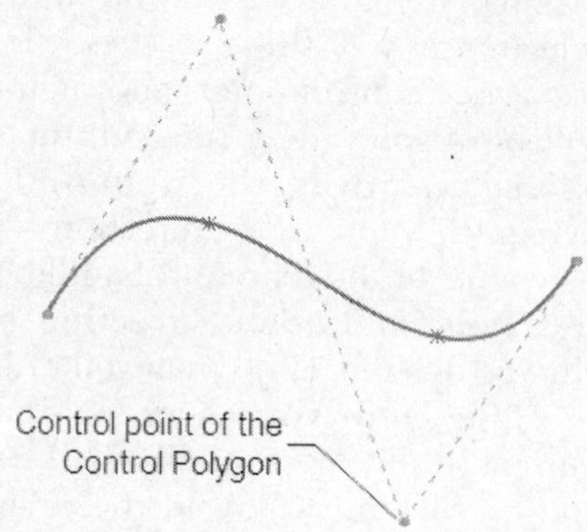

***Figure 3-64** Control point of the control polygon*

Modifying the Coordinates of a Point

To modify the location of a point, select it using the **Select** tool; the **Point PropertyManager** will be displayed. You can modify the coordinates of the sketched point using this PropertyManager.

Modifying an Ellipse or an Elliptical Arc

To modify an ellipse or an elliptical arc, select it using the **Select** tool; the **Ellipse PropertyManager** will be displayed. You can modify the parameters of the ellipse using the options in this PropertyManager.

Modifying a Parabola

To modify a parabola, select the parabola using the **Select** tool; the **Parabola PropertyManager** will be displayed. Modify the parameters of the parabola from this PropertyManager.

Dynamically Modifying and Copying Sketched Entities

In the sketching environment of SOLIDWORKS, you can relocate the sketched entities by dynamically dragging them using the left mouse button. For example, consider a case where you create the sketch of a rectangle and you want to increase the size of the rectangle. You simply have to select any of the lines or vertices of the rectangle and hold the left mouse button to drag the cursor. Drag the sketch according to your requirement and then release the left mouse button; all the segments in the rectangle will be dragged. However, if you choose **Tools > Sketch Settings > Detach Segment on Drag** from the SOLIDWORKS menus and select a line of a rectangle to drag, the line segment will be detached from the rectangle. As this option is not activated by default, the segments of the selected entities are not detached on dragging.

You can also copy the sketched entities dynamically. To do so, select the sketched entity or entities to be copied. Press and hold the CTRL key and then drag the selected entity or entities; preview of the copied entities will be displayed. Release the left mouse button at the location where you want to place the new entities. You can make multiple copies of the selected entities by repeating this procedure.

Splitting Sketched Entities

CommandManager:	Sketch > Split Entities	*(Customize to add)*
SOLIDWORKS menus:	Tools > Sketch Tools > Split Entities	
Toolbar:	Sketch > Split Entities	*(Customize to add)*

The **Split Entities** tool is used to split a sketched entity into two or more entities. To split an entity, invoke the **Split Entities** tool from the **Sketch CommandManager**; the **Split Entities PropertyManager** will be displayed. Move the cursor to a location from where you want to split the sketched entity. When the cursor snaps to the entity, press the left mouse button to add a split point. Next, right-click to display the shortcut menu and then choose the **OK** option from the shortcut menu. Select the sketched entity using the select cursor. You will notice that the sketched entity gets divided in two entities and a split point is added between the two sketched entities. You can add as many split points as you need. Remember that to split a circle, a full ellipse, or a closed spline, you need to split them at least at two points.

You can also delete the split points to convert a split entity into a single entity. To delete a split point, select the split point and press the DELETE key.

Creating Segments in Sketched Entities

CommandManager:	Sketch > Segment	*(Customize to add)*
SOLIDWORKS menus:	Tools > Sketch Tools > Segment	
Toolbar:	Sketch > Segment	*(Customize to add)*

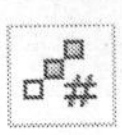

The **Segment** tool is used to create equidistant point and segments in a sketched entity. To create segments in an entity, invoke the **Segment** tool from the **Sketch CommandManager**; the **Segment PropertyManager** will be displayed, as shown in Figure 3-65. Select the sketch entity on which you need to add segments; the selected entity will be displayed in the **Select single entity(Arc, line, circle)** selection box in the **Segment Parameters** rollout. Also, preview of segments points created on the selected sketch entity is displayed. You can change the number of segments points using the edit box provided. Next, select the **Sketch points** radio button if you need to add equidistant point on the sketched entity or else select the **Sketch segments** radio button to split the sketch entity into equal

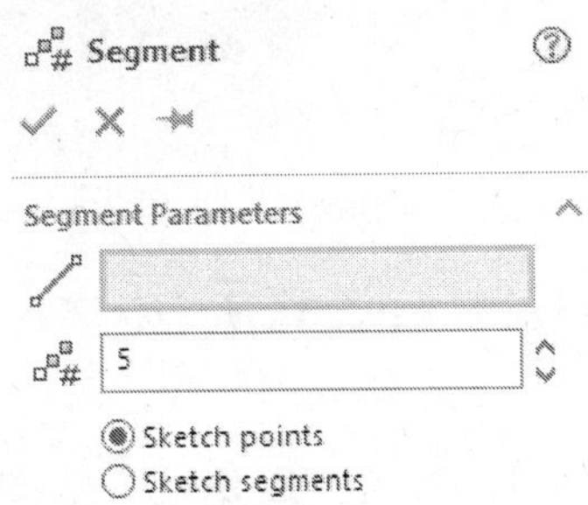

Figure 3-65** The **Segment PropertyManager

segments. Choose the **OK** button from the **Segment PropertyManager**; the segments will be created.

TUTORIALS

Tutorial 1

In this tutorial, you will draw the base sketch of the model shown in Figure 3-66. The sketch of the model is shown in Figure 3-67. You will draw the sketch with a mirror line and a mirror tool. After drawing the sketch, you will modify it by dragging the sketched entities.

(Expected time: 30 min)

The following steps are required to complete this tutorial:

a. Start SOLIDWORKS and then start a new part document.
b. Invoke the sketching environment.
c. Create centerlines and convert one of the centerlines to mirror line using the **Dynamic Mirror Entities** tool.
d. Create the sketch in the third quadrant; the sketch will automatically be mirrored on the other side of the mirror line.
e. Mirror the entire sketch along the second mirror line.
f. Modify the sketch by dragging the sketched entities.

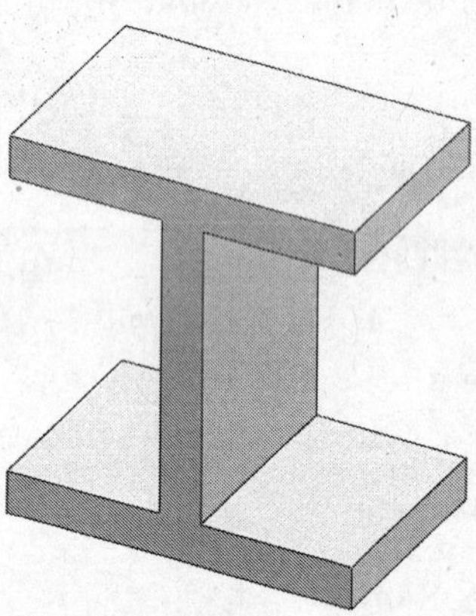

Figure 3-66 *Solid model for Tutorial 1*

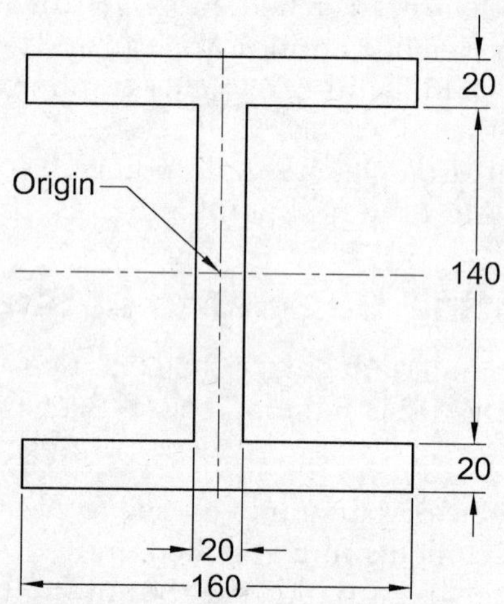

Figure 3-67 *Sketch for Tutorial 1*

Starting SOLIDWORKS and then a New SOLIDWORKS Document

1. Start SOLIDWORKS by double-clicking on the shortcut icon of SOLIDWORKS 2021 on the desktop of your computer; the SOLIDWORKS 2021 window along with the **WELCOME- SOLIDWORKS** dialog box will be displayed.

2. Choose the **Part** button available in the **New** area of the **Home** tab in the **Welcome - SOLIDWORKS** dialog box. A new **SOLIDWORKS** part document starts.

Next, you need to invoke the sketching environment.

3. Choose the **Sketch** tab from the **CommandManager** if not selected by default. Next, choose the **Sketch** button from the **Sketch CommandManager**; the **Edit Sketch PropertyManager** is invoked and you are prompted to select the plane to create the sketch.

4. Select the **Front Plane**; the sketching environment is invoked and the plane is oriented normal to the view.

Modifying the Grid and Snap Settings and the Dimensioning Units

Before drawing the sketch, you need to modify the grid and snap settings to make the cursor jump through a distance of 10 mm.

1. Choose the **Options** button from the Menu Bar; the **System Options - General** dialog box is displayed.

While installing SOLIDWORKS if you have selected a unit other than millimeter to measure the length then you need to select millimeter as the unit for the current drawing by following the next two steps.

2. Choose the **Document Properties** tab and select the **Units** option from the area on the left-side of the **Document Properties - Drafting Standard** dialog box.

3. Next, select the **MMGS (millimeter, gram, second)** radio button in the **Unit system** area and select **degrees** from the drop-down list in the cell corresponding to the **Angle** row and the **Unit** column if not selected by default.

4. Next, click on the **Grid/Snap** option from the area on the left in the dialog box. Set the values **100** and **10** in the **Major grid spacing** spinner and the **Minor-lines per major** spinner, respectively.

On invoking the sketching environment, if the grid is displayed by default, you can turn off its display by clearing the **Display grid** check box in the **Grid** area.

5. Choose the **Go To System Snaps** button and select the **Grid** check box. Next, clear the **Snap only when grid is displayed** check box, if it is selected.

6. After making the necessary settings, choose the **OK** button.

The coordinates displayed close to the lower right corner of the SOLIDWORKS window show an increment of 10 mm when you move the cursor in the drawing area after exiting the dialog box.

Drawing the Centerlines and Converting Them into Mirror Lines

It is recommended that you draw symmetrical sketches about an axis by using any of the mirroring tools. In this tutorial, you will draw the sketch using the **Line**, **Dynamic Mirror**, and **Mirror Entities** tools. However, you can also complete this tutorial by using the **Line** and **Dynamic Mirror** tools.

1. Choose the **Centerline** button from the **Line** flyout available in the **Sketch CommandManager**.

2. Move the line cursor to a location whose coordinates are 0 mm, 100 mm, and 0 mm. You may need to zoom in the drawing to locate that point.

3. Specify the start point of the centerline at this point, move the cursor vertically downward and draw a line of 200 mm length. You may need to zoom and pan the drawing to draw a line of this length.

4. Now, double-click anywhere on the screen to end the current chain or right-click anywhere in the drawing area to invoke the shortcut menu and choose the **End chain** option from it.

5. Move the line cursor to a location whose coordinates are -100 mm, 0 mm, and 0 mm.

6. Specify the start point of the centerline and move the cursor horizontally toward the right to draw a line of 200 mm length. Pan the drawing, if required.

7. Press F to fit the drawing on the screen. Right-click and choose the **Select** option from the shortcut menu; the line cursor is replaced by the select cursor.

8. Select the vertical centerline.

9. Choose **Tools > Sketch Tools > Dynamic Mirror** tool from the SOLIDWORKS menus; the vertical centerline is converted into a mirror line and the dynamic mirror option is activated.

   You can confirm the creation of the mirror line and the activation of the dynamic mirror option by observing the symmetrical symbol displayed on both ends of the centerline.

Drawing the Sketch

Next, you need to draw the sketch of the base feature. You will draw the sketch in the third quadrant and the same sketch will be created automatically on the other side of the mirror line. The symmetrical relation is applied between the parent entity and the mirrored entity.

1. Press the L key on the keyboard; the **Line** tool is invoked.

2. Move the line cursor to a location whose coordinates are 0 mm, -100 mm, and 0 mm.

3. Specify this point as the start point of the line and move the cursor horizontally toward the left.

4. Specify the endpoint of the line when 80 is displayed above the line cursor.

You will notice that as soon as you specify the endpoint of the line, a mirror image is automatically created on the other side of the mirror line. The line drawn as the mirrored entity gets merged with the line drawn on the left. Therefore, the entire line becomes a single entity. Remember that the lines will merge only if one of the endpoints of the line drawn is coincident with the mirror line.

5. Move the cursor vertically upward and click to specify the endpoint of the line when the length of the line above the line cursor shows the value 30.

   You will notice that as soon as you specify the endpoint of the line, a mirror image is created automatically on the other side of the mirror line.

6. Move the line cursor toward the right and click to specify the endpoint of the line when the length of the line above the line cursor shows the value 30; a mirror image is created automatically on the other side of the mirror line.

7. Move the line cursor vertically upward and click to specify the endpoint of the line when the line cursor snaps the horizontal centerline. Exit the **Line** tool. The sketch after drawing the lines is shown in Figure 3-68.

Mirroring the Entire Sketch

After creating one-half of the sketch, you need to mirror the entire sketch about the horizontal centerline. But, first you need to disable automatic mirroring.

1. Right-click and choose **Recent Commands > Dynamic Mirror Entities** from the shortcut menu to disable dynamic mirroring.

2. Use the box selection method to select all the lines sketched earlier and also the horizontal centerline. Make sure you do not select the vertical centerline.

3. Choose the **Mirror Entities** tool from the **Sketch CommandManager**; the entire sketch is mirrored about the horizontal centerline. The sketch after mirroring the sketched entities is shown in Figure 3-69.

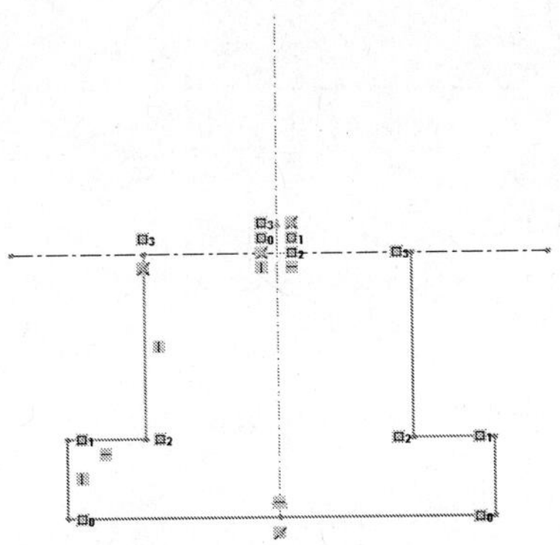

Figure 3-68 *Sketch after drawing the lines*

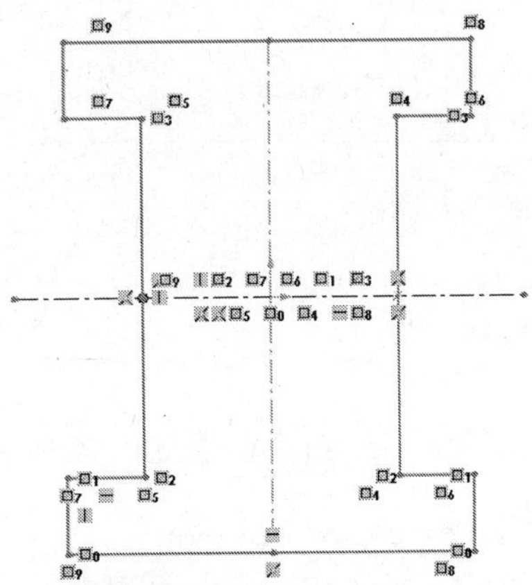

Figure 3-69 *Sketch after mirroring sketched entities*

Modifying the Sketch by Dragging Entities

Next, you need to modify the sketch by dragging. While dragging the entities, you will observe that the corresponding mirrored entity is also being modified.

1. Select the lower right vertical line; the **Line Properties PropertyManager** is displayed on the left of the drawing area. You will notice that the value in the **Length** spinner is 30.
2. As the required length of this line is 20, set the value in the **Length** spinner to **20** in the **Parameters** rollout. You will observe that all the dependent lines are also modified. This is because they are created as mirror images.
3. Choose the **Close Dialog** button or click once in the drawing area.
4. Select the midpoint of the right vertical line that passes through the horizontal centerline; the **Point PropertyManager** is displayed. You will notice that the coordinates of this point are 50,0.
5. Press and hold the left mouse button and drag the point toward the origin; the value in the **X Coordinate** spinner of the **Parameters** rollout changes dynamically.
6. Release the left mouse button when the **X Coordinate** spinner shows the value 10. The final sketch after modifying the sketched entities by dragging them is shown in Figure 3-70.

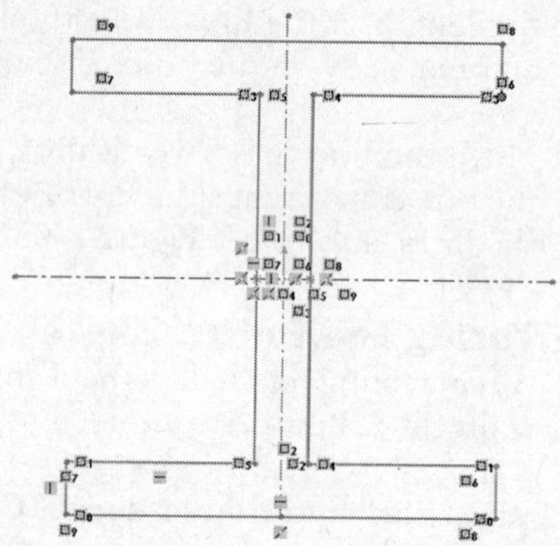

Figure 3-70 Final sketch for Tutorial 1

Saving the Sketch

1. Choose the **Save** button from the Menu Bar to invoke the **Save As** dialog box.
2. Choose the **New folder** button from the **Save As** dialog box. Enter the name of the folder as **c03** and press ENTER. Enter the name of the document as **c03_tut01** in the **File name** edit box and choose the **Save** button.
3. Press CTRL+W to close the file.

Tutorial 2

In this tutorial, you will create the sketch of the model shown in Figure 3-71. The sketch of the model is shown in Figure 3-72. Do not dimension the sketch as the solid model and the dimensions are given for your reference only. **(Expected time: 30 min)**

The following steps are required to complete this tutorial:

a. Start a new part document.
b. Invoke the sketching environment.
c. Create a centerline.

d. Draw and edit the sketch using the **Mirror Entities** and **Trim Entities** tools.
e. Offset the entire sketch.
f. Complete the final editing of the sketch using the **Extend Entities** and **Trim Entities** tools.

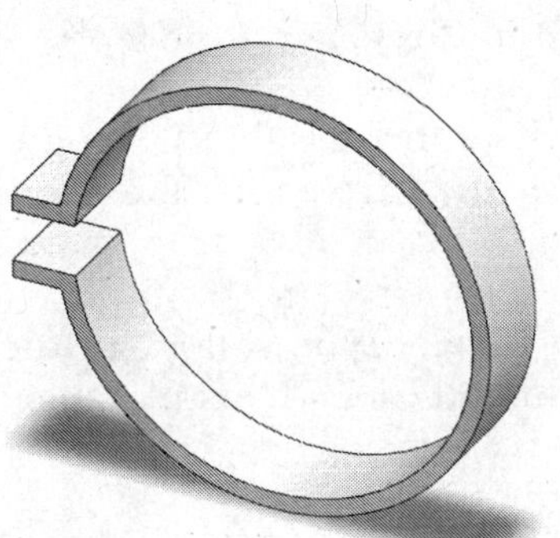

Figure 3-71 Solid model for Tutorial 2

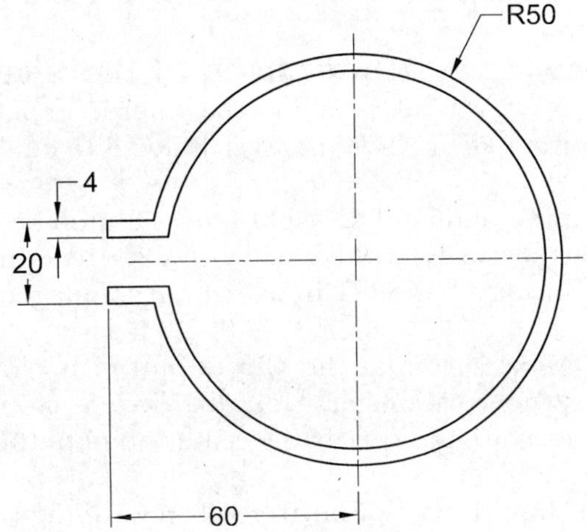

Figure 3-72 Sketch for Tutorial 2

Starting a New Document

1. Choose the **New** button from the Menu Bar to invoke the **New SOLIDWORKS Document** dialog box.

2. The **Part** button is chosen by default in the **New SOLIDWORKS Document** dialog box. Choose the **OK** button.

3. Choose the **Sketch** button from the **Sketch CommandManager** and select **Front Plane** to invoke the sketching environment.

4. Invoke the **Document Properties - Units** dialog box and change the units to **MMGS (millimeter, gram, second)** if it is not selected by default.

5. Invoke the **Document Properties - Grid/Snap** dialog box. Now, set **100** in the **Major grid spacing** spinner and **10** in the **Minor-lines per major** spinner. Choose the **Ok** button.

Drawing the Centerline

Before drawing the sketch, you need to draw a centerline that will act as reference for other sketched entities. This centerline will also be used for mirroring.

1. Choose the **Centerline** button from the **Line** flyout in the **Sketch CommandManager**.

2. Move the cursor to a location whose coordinates are -70 mm, 0 mm, and 0 mm.

3. Specify this point as the start point and move the cursor horizontally toward the right.

4. Specify the endpoint of the centerline by clicking at a location when the value of the length of the centerline above the line cursor is 140.

5. Double-click anywhere.in the drawing area to end the line creation and exit the **Centerline** tool.

Drawing the Outer Loop of the Sketch

Next, you need to draw the outer loop of the sketch using the sketch tools. As it is evident from Figure 3-74, the sketch needs to be drawn using the **Circle** and **Line** tools.

1. Press and hold the right-mouse button and drag the cursor to the right; the mouse gesture is displayed with sketching tools. Move the cursor over the **Circle** tool; the **Circle** tool is invoked and the **Circle PropertyManager** is displayed.

2. Make sure that the **Circle** button is chosen in the **Circle Type** rollout in the **Circle PropertyManager**. Move the circle cursor to the origin and click when an orange circle is displayed to specify the center point of the circle.

3. Move the cursor horizontally toward the right and draw a circle of 100 mm diameter.

4. Choose the **Zoom to Fit** button from the **View (Heads-Up)** toolbar to increase the display of the sketch.

5. Choose the **Line** button from the **Sketch CommandManager** and move the cursor to a location whose coordinates are -60 mm, 10 mm, and 0 mm. Specify the start point of the line at this location.

6. Move the cursor horizontally toward the right and click to specify the endpoint of the line when the line cursor snaps the circle. Exit the **Line** tool.

7. Press and hold the SHIFT key and then using the left mouse button, select the centerline, and the horizontal line created in the last step.

8. Choose the **Mirror Entities** button from the **Sketch CommandManager**; the mirror image of the horizontal line is created on the other side of the centerline.

9. Choose the **Line** button using the mouse gesture, refer to Figure 3-73 and then move the cursor to the left endpoint of the upper horizontal line. Click to specify the start point of the line when the orange circle is displayed.

10. Move the cursor vertically downward. Click in the drawing area when the cursor snaps to the left endpoint of the lower horizontal line. Exit the **Line** tool.

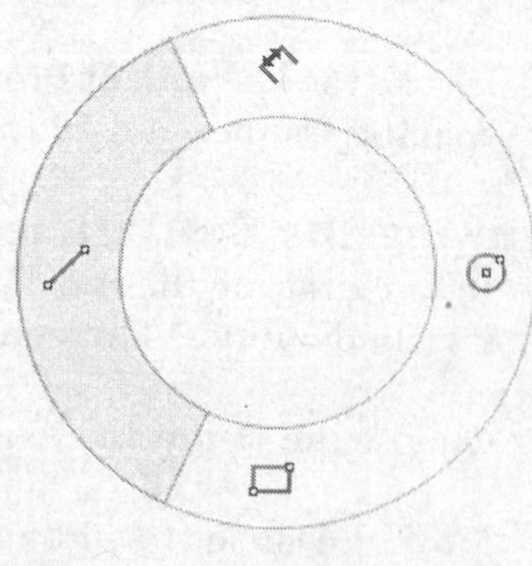

***Figure 3-73** Line button in mouse gesture*

11. Choose the **Trim Entities** button from the **Sketch CommandManager**; the **Trim PropertyManager** is displayed.

12. Choose the **Power trim** button from the PropertyManager. Press and hold the left mouse button and drag the cursor over the portion to be removed. Choose the **Close Dialog** button from the PropertyManager. The sketch after removing the unwanted portion is shown in Figure 3-74.

> **Tip**
> *If you have trimmed the centerline, invoke the shortcut menu and choose the* ***Extend Entities*** *option. Then, move the cursor over one end of the centerline and press the left mouse button to extend the line. Alternatively, perform the undo operation.*

Offsetting the Entities

After drawing the outer loop of the sketch, you need to draw the inner loop. The first step for drawing the inner loop of the sketch is offsetting the entire sketch inward.

1. Choose the **Offset Entities** button from the **Sketch CommandManager**; the **Offset Entities PropertyManager** is displayed on the left in the drawing area.

2. Set the value of the **Offset Distance** spinner to **4**. Select the **Add dimensions** and **Select chain** check boxes, if they are not selected. Select any one entity of the sketch; the entire sketch is selected.

   When you select the sketch, the preview of the offset sketch is displayed in the drawing area. The direction of the offset is outward. However, the direction of the offset should be inward of the sketch. Therefore, you need to flip the direction.

3. Move the cursor inside the sketch and press the left mouse button to offset the sketch inside the original sketch; a dimension with the value 4 is displayed with the sketch.

   The sketch after offsetting the outer loop is shown in Figure 3-75.

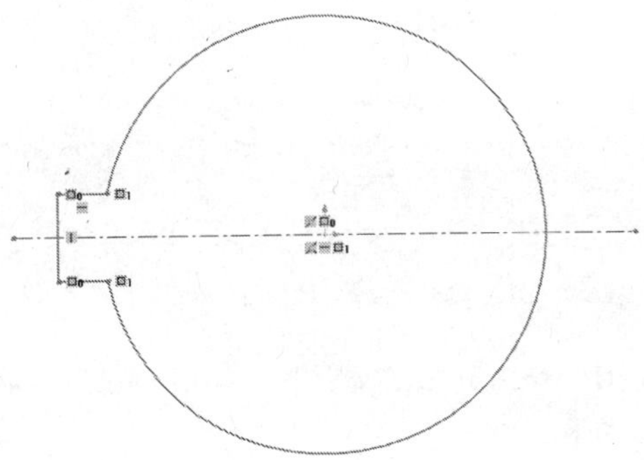

Figure 3-74 The sketch after removing the unwanted portion

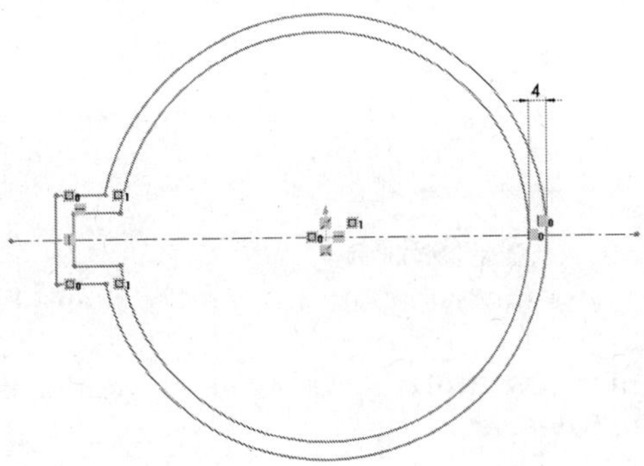

Figure 3-75 Sketch after offsetting the outer loop

Extending and Trimming the Entities

1. Choose the **Extend Entities** button from the **Trim Entities** flyout in the **Sketch CommandManager**; the select cursor is replaced by the extend cursor.

2. Move the cursor close to the left end of the lower horizontal line of the inner loop. You can preview the extended line appearing in orange.

   You need to move the cursor a little toward the left if the preview of the extended line appears on the right.

3. Press the left mouse button to extend the line.

4. Similarly, extend the upper horizontal line of the inner sketch. The sketch after extending the lines is shown in Figure 3-76.

5. Right-click and choose the **Trim Entities** option from the shortcut menu; the extend cursor is replaced by the trim cursor.

6. Trim the unwanted entities as discussed earlier and exit the trim command. The final sketch is shown in Figure 3-77.

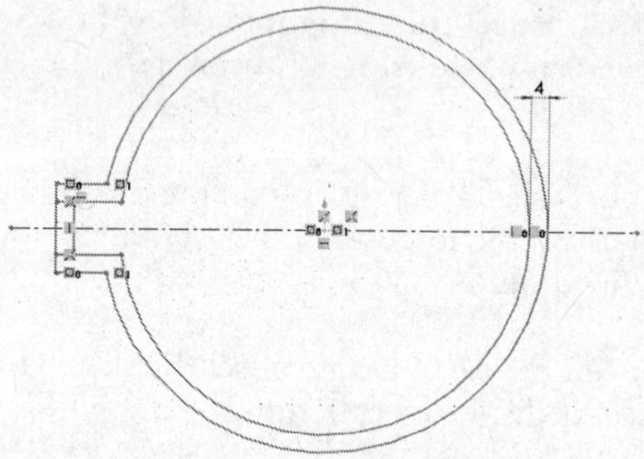

Figure 3-76 *Sketch after extending the lines*

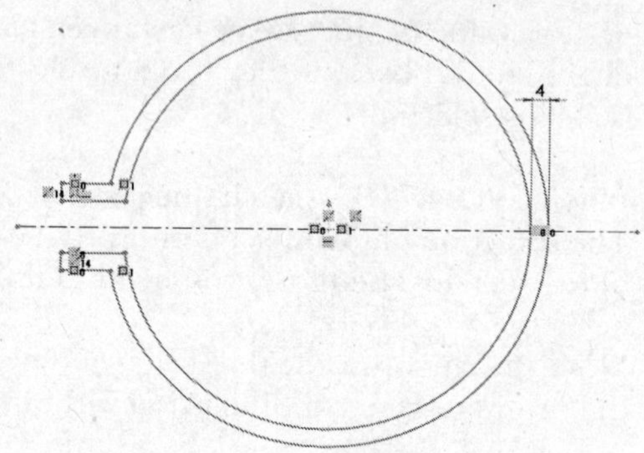

Figure 3-77 *Final sketch for Tutorial 2*

> **Tip**
> *You can turn on/off the display of the relation symbols on the sketched entities by choosing the* ***Hide/Show Items > View Sketch Relations*** *button from the* ***View (Heads-Up)*** *toolbar.*

Saving the Sketch

1. Choose the **Save** button from the Menu Bar to invoke the **Save As** dialog box.

2. Enter **c03_tut02** as the name of the document in the **File name** edit box and then choose the **Save** button.

3. Close the file by choosing **File > Close** from the SOLIDWORKS menus.

Tutorial 3

In this tutorial, you will create the model shown in Figure 3-78. To create this model, you will first create the sketch of the base feature by using the sketch tools. Also, you will modify and edit the sketch using various modifying options. Do not create the center marks and centerlines as they are for your reference only. The dimensions required to create the base sketch for the model are shown in Figure 3-79. The extrusion depth of the model is 20 mm. After creating the model, you will create a new drawing document, generate the views of the model, and place them on a drawing sheet.

(Expected time: 30 min)

Figure 3-78 Solid Model for Tutorial 3

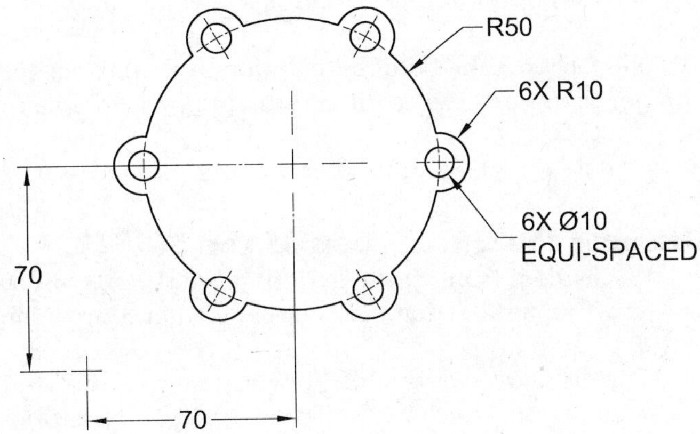

Figure 3-79 Sketch for Tutorial 3

The following steps are required to complete this tutorial:

a. Start a new part document.
b. Invoke the sketching environment.
c. Draw the outer loop of the sketch.
d. Create a circle to define the hole in the outer loop.
e. Use the **Circular Sketch Pattern** tool to create a circular pattern of circles in the outer loop.
f. Invoke the **Extruded Boss/Base** tool and extrude the sketch through a distance of 20 mm.
g. Start a new drawing document, generate the views of the model, and place them on a drawing sheet.

Starting a New Document

1. Choose the **New** button from the Menu Bar to invoke the **New SOLIDWORKS Document** dialog box.

2. In this dialog box, the **Part** button is chosen by default. Choose the **OK** button.

   Next, you need to invoke the sketching environment.

3. Choose the **Sketch** button from the **Sketch CommandManager**; the **Edit Sketch PropertyManager** is invoked and you are prompted to select the plane to create the sketch.

4. Select the **Front Plane** as the sketching plane; the sketching environment is invoked and the plane is oriented normal to the view.

5. Choose the **Options** button from Menu Bar; the **System Option - General** dialog box is displayed.

6. Choose the **Document Properties** tab from this dialog box and select the **Units** option from the area on the left. Set the units to millimeters by selecting the **MMGS (millimeter, gram, second)** option from the **Units system** area.

7. Next, choose the **Grid/Snap** option from the area on the left. Set the value of the **Minor-lines per major** spinner to **20** and the **Major grid spacing** spinner to **100**.

8. Choose the **OK** button after making the necessary settings.

Drawing the Outer Loop of the Sketch

It is evident from Figure 3-79 that the sketch consists of an outer loop and inner cavities. It is recommended that you create the outer loop of the sketch first and then the inner cavities.

The origin of the sketching environment is in the middle of the drawing area and you need to create the sketch in the first quadrant. Therefore, it is recommended that you modify the drawing area by relocating the origin.

1. Press the CTRL key and the middle mouse button and then drag the cursor in such a way that the origin of the sketch is moved near the lower left corner of the drawing area.

2. Press and hold the right mouse button and drag the cursor to the right; the sketching tools are displayed in the mouse gesture. Move the cursor over the **Circle** tool; the **Circle** tool is invoked and the **Circle PropertyManager** is displayed.

3. Make sure that the **Circle** button is chosen in the **Circle Type** rollout of the **Circle PropertyManager**.

4. Move the cursor to a location whose coordinates are 70 mm, 70 mm, and 0 mm.

5. Click to specify the center point of the circle at this location and move the cursor horizontally toward the right. Click when the radius above the circle cursor shows the value **50**.

6. Choose the **Zoom to Area** button from the **View (Heads-Up)** toolbar. Press and hold the left mouse button and drag the cursor to define a window such that the sketched circle and the origin are placed in the window.

7. Release the left mouse button; the display area of the sketch is increased.

8. Invoke the **Circle** tool by using the mouse gesture and move the cursor to the right quadrant of the circle. All the quadrants of the circle are displayed and the right quadrant on which you have placed the cursor is displayed in orange. Also, the symbol of coincident constraint is displayed below the cursor.

9. Specify the center point of the circle at this location and move the cursor horizontally toward the right. When the value of the radius above the circle cursor shows 10, press the left mouse button.

10. Press the S key from the keyboard; a toolbar is displayed. Choose the **Trim Entities** button; the **Trim PropertyManager** is displayed. Next, choose the **Trim to closest** button from this PropertyManager.

11. Trim the sketch such that it looks similar to the one shown in Figure 3-80. Exit the **Trim** tool.

12. Select the trimmed circle of radius **10** mm and choose the **Circular Sketch Pattern** button from the **Pattern** flyout in the **Sketch CommandManager**; the **Circular Pattern PropertyManager** is displayed and a preview of the circular pattern with default setting is displayed in the drawing area.

    On doing this, you will notice that the center of the circular pattern is placed at the origin and an arrow is displayed indicating that the origin is the center of the circular pattern. But, in this sketch, the center of the circular pattern is not at the origin, so you need to modify it. This can be done by setting the coordinates of the point in the **Center X** and **Center Y** spinners in the **Parameters** rollout of this PropertyManager. However, it is recommended that you drag the arrow displayed at the center of the pattern to the required location.

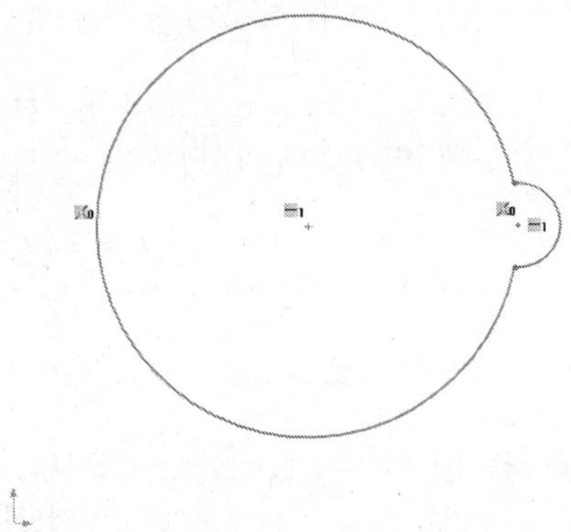

Figure 3-80 *Sketch after trimming the unwanted entities*

13. Move the circular pattern cursor to the control point available at the end of the arrow.

14. Press and hold the left mouse button at the control point and drag it to the center of the 100 mm diameter circle. Release the left mouse button when an orange circle is displayed at the center point of the circle.

    You will notice that both the **Center X** and **Center Y** spinners display the value **70** mm. This is because the center of the 100 mm diameter circle is located at a distance of 70 mm along the X and Y axis directions.

15. Set **6** in the **Number of Instances** spinner.

16. Clear the **Dimension angular spacing** check box if selected.

17. Select the **Display instance count** check box. Accept the remaining default values and choose the **OK** button to create the pattern.

18. Trim the unwanted portion of the 100 mm diameter circle using the **Trim Entities** tool. You need to use the **Trim to closest** button for this trimming.

19. Choose **Close Dialog** from the **Trim PropertyManager** after trimming. The outer loop of the sketch is created, as shown in Figure 3-81.

Sketching the Holes

Next, you need to draw the sketch of the holes. It is evident from Figure 3-79 that you need to create six circles. After drawing the first circle, you need to create the other five circles by creating a circular pattern of the parent circle.

1. Invoke the **Circle** tool by using the mouse gesture.

2. Select the center point of the **10** mm radius arc on the left quadrant of the larger circle as the center point of the new circle.

3. Press and hold the CTRL key and then draw a circle of diameter close to **10**. Make sure you press the CTRL key so that the cursor does not snap to the points or grid.

4. Set **5** in the **Radius** spinner in the **Circle PropertyManager**.

Creating the Circular Pattern of the Holes

1. Choose the **Circular Sketch Pattern** button from the **Pattern** flyout in the **Sketch CommandManager**; the **Circular Pattern PropertyManager** is displayed and the preview of the circular pattern is displayed with an arrow at the center.

2. Move the circular pattern cursor to the control point that is available at the end of the arrow head indicating the center point of the pattern. Press and hold the left mouse button at the control point and drag it to the center of the **100** mm diameter circle. Release the left mouse button when an orange circle is displayed at the center point of the circle.

3. Set **6** in the **Number of Instances** spinner.

4. Clear the **Dimension angular spacing** check box.

5. Select the **Display instance count** check box. Accept the remaining default values and choose the **OK** button to create the pattern.

The final sketch of the model is shown in Figure 3-82. In this figure, all the relations are hidden for clarity.

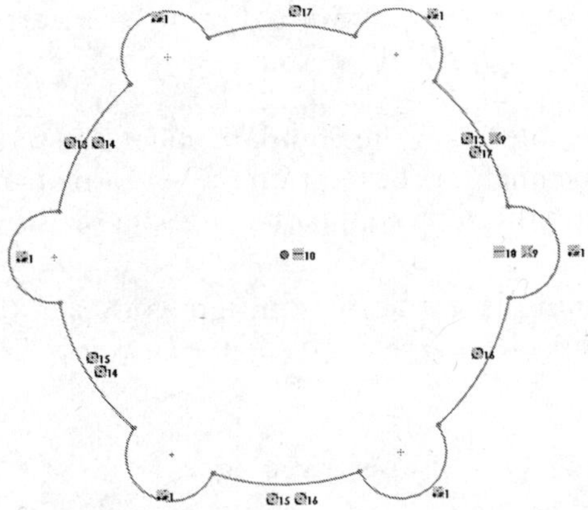

Figure 3-81 Outer loop of the sketch

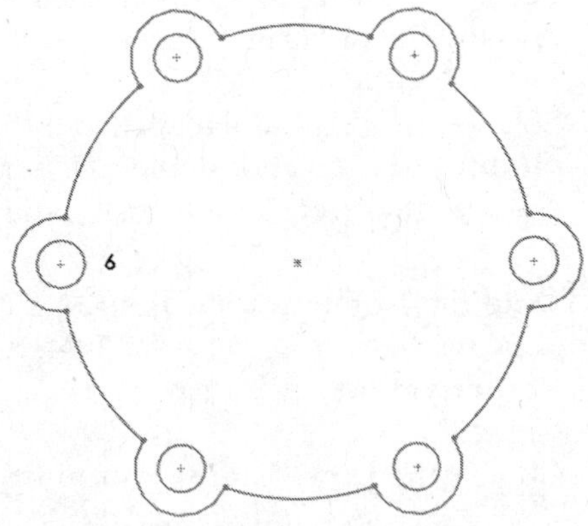

Figure 3-82 Final sketch for Tutorial 3

Extruding the Sketch

Next, you need to invoke the **Extruded Boss/Base** tool and extrude the sketch using the parameters given in the tutorial description.

1. Choose the **Features** tab from the CommandManager to display the **Features CommandManager**. Then, choose the **Extruded Boss/Base** button; the sketch is automatically oriented to the trimetric view and the **Boss-Extrude PropertyManager** is displayed, as shown in Figure 3-83.

   As you are converting the closed sketch into a feature, only the **Direction 1** rollout is displayed in the **Boss-Extrude PropertyManager**. Also, a preview of the feature is displayed in the temporary shaded graphics with the default values.

2. Make sure that the value in the **Depth** spinner is 20. Next, choose the **OK** button to create the feature.

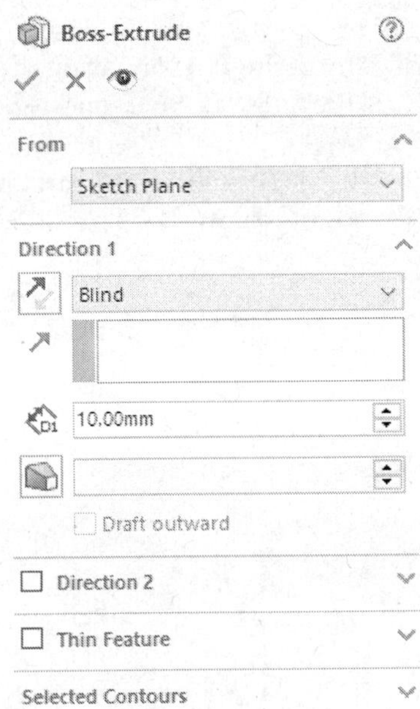

Figure 3-83 The ***Boss-Extrude PropertyManager***

Note

For detailed information on extruding sketches, refer to Chapter 5.

Starting a New Drawing Document and Placing the Views on a Sheet

As mentioned in the tutorial description, you need to start a new drawing document, generate the views of the model, and then place them on a drawing sheet. This is done by using the **Make Drawing from Part** tool.

1. Choose **File > Make Drawing from Part** from the SOLIDWORKS menus; the **New SOLIDWORKS Document** is displayed.

2. Select a drawing template and choose the **OK** button; a new drawing document is started and the **Sheet Format/Size** dialog box is displayed.

3. Select **A (ANSI) Landscape** from the list box available below the **Standard sheet size** radio button and then choose the **OK** button; a new document is started with the set format and size and the **View Palette** task pane is displayed on the right in the drawing window.

3. Drag the Isometric view from the **View Palette** and place it at the top right corner of the drawing sheet, refer to Figure 3-84; the **View Palette** task pane is closed and the **Drawing View PropertyManager** is displayed.

4. Choose the **Close Dialog** button from the **Drawing View PropertyManager**.

Note

*The **Drawing View PropertyManager** will be displayed only if you drag and drop the Isometric view first instead of any plan or elevation views from the **View Palette** task pane.*

5. Choose the **View Palette** tab to invoke the **View Palette** task pane again. Next, drag and drop the **Top** view on the sheet, refer to Figure 3-84; the **Projected View PropertyManager** is displayed and you are prompted to select a location to place the new view.

6. Drag the cursor vertically downward and place the **Front** view of the model, refer to Figure 3-84. Next, choose the **OK** button from the **Projected View PropertyManager**.

7. Invoke the **View Palette** task pane again. Next drag and drop the **Right** view on the sheet, refer to Figure 3-84. Next, choose the **OK** button from the **Projected View PropertyManager**.

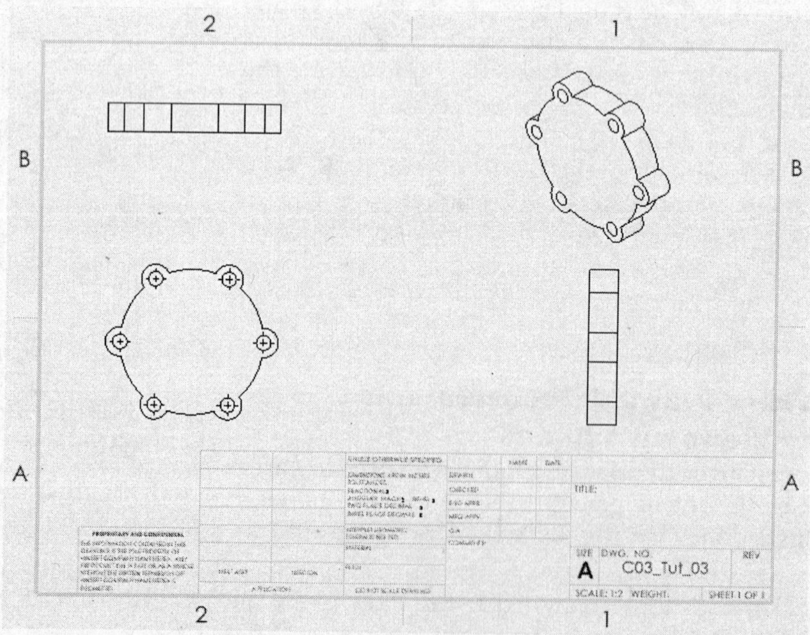

Figure 3-84 *Views placed on the drawing sheet*

Note
For detailed information on creating drawing views, refer to Chapters 14 and 15.

Saving the Sketch

1. Choose the **Save** button from the **Menu Bar** to invoke the **Save As** dialog box.

2. Enter the name of the document as **c03_tut03** in the **File name** edit box and choose the **Save** button.

   The document is saved at the location */Documents/SOLIDWORKS/c03*.

3. Close the file by choosing **File** > **Close** from the SOLIDWORKS menus.

Self-Evaluation Test

Answer the following questions and then compare them to those given at the end of this chapter:

1. The __________ tool is used to create a linear pattern in the sketching environment of SOLIDWORKS.

2. The __________ tool is used to create a circular pattern in the sketching environment of SOLIDWORKS.

3. To modify a sketched circle, select it using the __________ tool.

4. The __________ tool is used to invoke dynamic mirroring.

5. The **Trim Entities** tool is also used to extend the sketched entities. (T/F)

6. In the sketching environment, you can apply fillets to two parallel lines. (T/F)

7. You can apply a fillet to two nonparallel and non-intersecting entities. (T/F)

8. You cannot offset a single entity using the **Offset Entities** tool. (T/F)

9. You can choose **Insert** > **Customize Menu** from the SOLIDWORKS menus to display the **Customize** dialog box. (T/F)

10. The design intent is not captured in the sketch created using the mirror line. (T/F)

Review Questions

Answer the following questions:

1. Which of the following PropertyManagers is displayed when you choose the **Sketch Fillet** button from the **Sketch CommandManager**?

   (a) **Sketch Fillet** (b) **Fillet**
   (c) **Surface Fillet** (d) **Sketching Fillet**

2. Which of the following PropertyManagers is displayed on the left of the drawing area when you choose **Tools** > **Sketch Tools** > **Chamfer** from the SOLIDWORKS menus?

   (a) **Sketch Chamfer** (b) **Sketcher Chamfer**
   (c) **Sketching Chamfer** (d) **Chamfer**

3. Which of the following tools is used to create an automatic mirror line?

   (a) **Dynamic Mirror Entities** (b) **Mirror**
   (c) **Automatic Mirror** (d) None of these

4. Which of the following tools is used to break a sketched entity into two or more entities?

   (a) **Split Entities** (b) **Trim Sketch**
   (c) **Break Curve** (d) **Trim Curve**

5. Which of the following tools is used to create a circular pattern in SOLIDWORKS?

   (a) **Pattern** (b) **Circular Sketch Pattern**
   (c) **Array** (d) None of these

6. You cannot trim a sketched entity using the **Trim Entities** tool. (T/F)

7. The preview of an entity to be extended is displayed in red. (T/F)

8. There are four types of slot tools available in SOLIDWORKS. (T/F)

9. The sketched entities can be mirrored without using a centerline. (T/F)

10. The **Dimension angle between axes** check box in the **Linear Pattern PropertyManager** is used to display the angular dimension between the two directions of a pattern. (T/F)

EXERCISES

Exercise 1

Create the sketch of the model shown in Figure 3-85. The sketch of the model is shown in Figure 3-86. The solid model and dimensions are given for reference only.

(Expected time: 30 min)

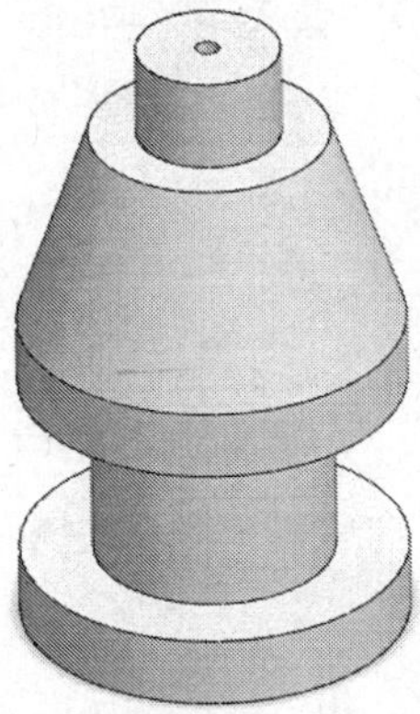

Figure 3-85 Solid model for Exercise 1

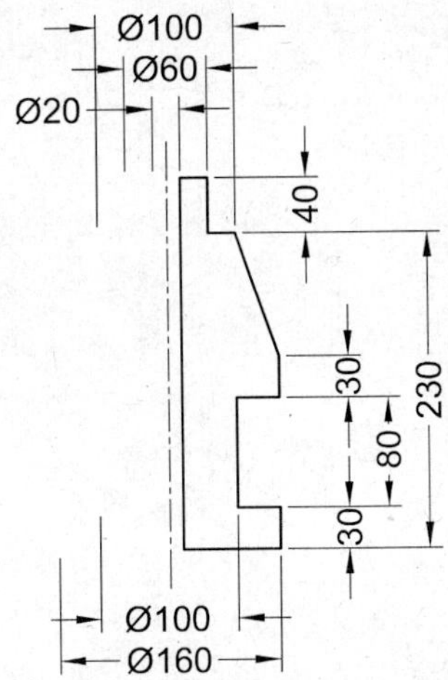

Figure 3-86 Sketch for Exercise 1

Exercise 2

Create the sketch of the model shown in Figure 3-87. The sketch of the model is shown in Figure 3-88. This model is created using a revolved feature. Therefore, you will create the sketch on one side of the centerline. The solid model and dimensions are given for reference only.

(Expected time: 30 min)

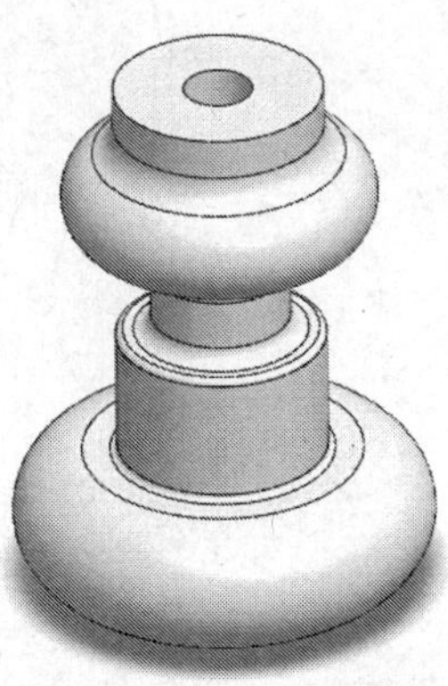

Figure 3-87 Solid model for Exercise 2

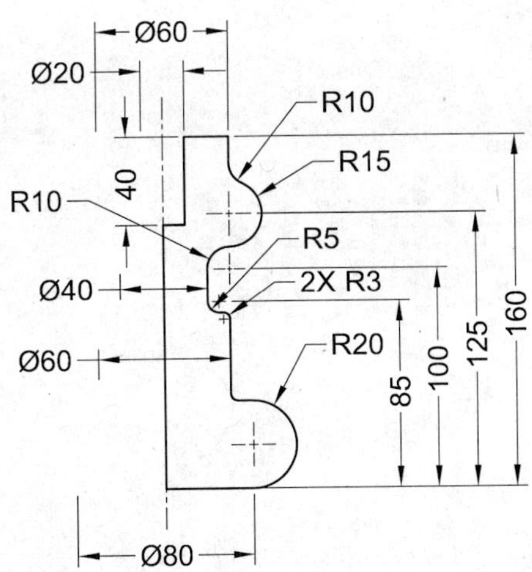

Figure 3-88 Sketch for Exercise 2

Exercise 3

Create the sketch of the model shown in Figure 3-89. The sketch of the model is shown in Figure 3-90. The solid model and its dimensions are given only for reference. Create the sketch on one side and then mirror it on the other side. Make sure you do not use the **Dynamic Mirror** tool to draw this sketch to avoid some relations getting applied to the sketch. These relations interfere while creating fillets.

(Expected time: 30 min)

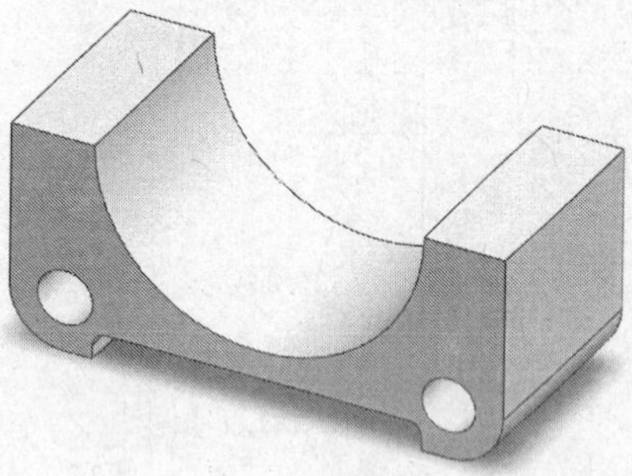

Figure 3-89 Solid model for Exercise 3

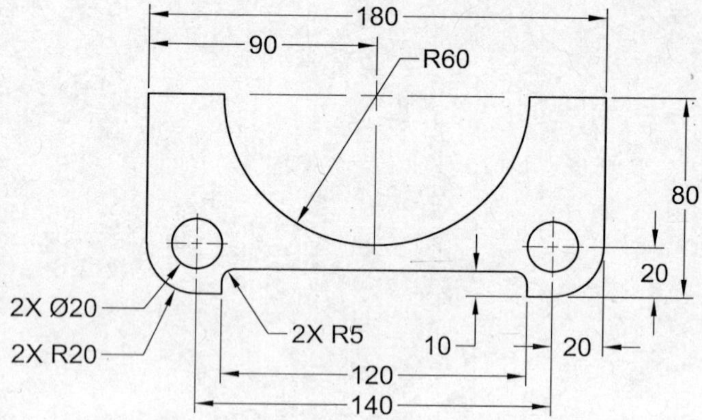

Figure 3-90 Sketch for Exercise 3

Exercise 4

Create the sketch of the model shown in Figure 3-91. The sketch of the model is shown in Figure 3-92. The solid model and dimensions are given only for reference. Create the sketch using the sketching tools and then edit the sketch using the **Circular Pattern** and **Trim** tools.

(Expected time: 30 min)

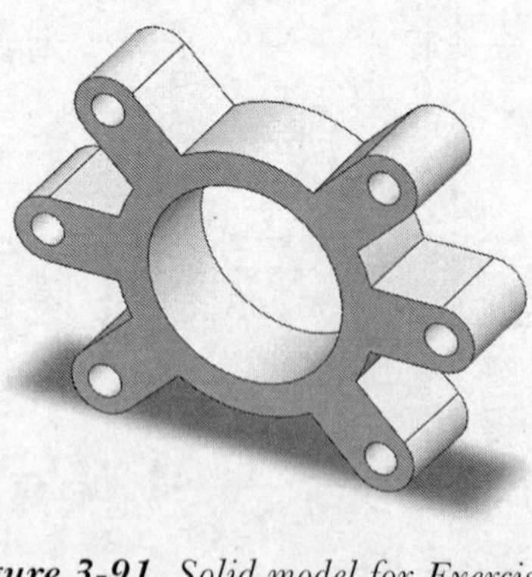

Figure 3-91 Solid model for Exercise 4

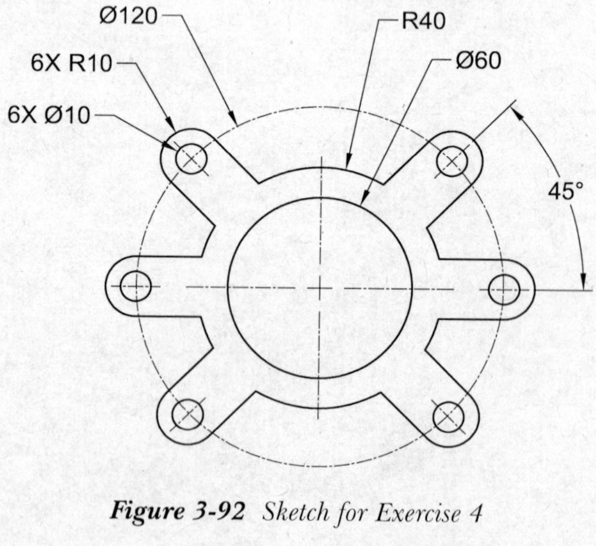

Figure 3-92 Sketch for Exercise 4

Exercise 5

Create the sketch of the model shown in Figure 3-93. The sketch of the model is shown in Figure 3-94. The solid model and dimensions are given only for reference. Create the sketch using the **Offset Entities** tool. Make sure that the **Reverse** check box is selected.

(Expected time: 30 min)

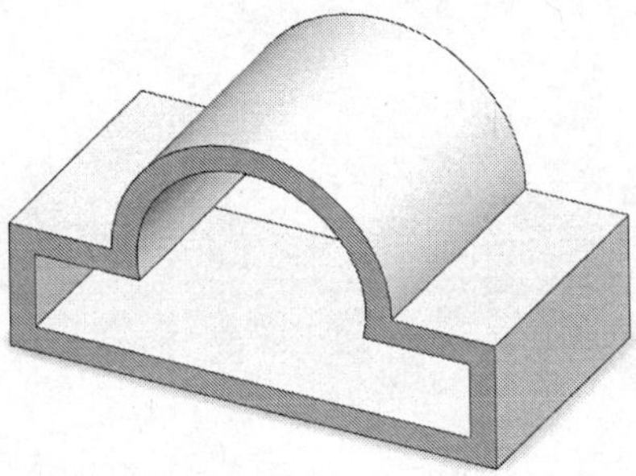

Figure 3-93 Solid model for Exercise 5

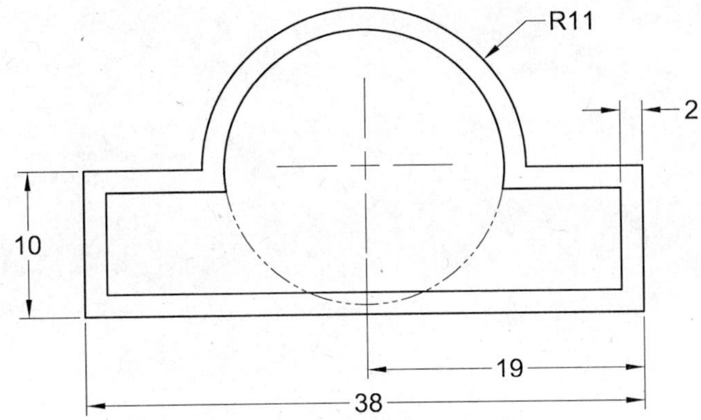

Figure 3-94 Sketch for Exercise 5

Exercise 6

Draw the sketch of the model shown in Figure 3-95. The sketch to be drawn is shown in Figure 3-96. Do not dimension the sketch. The solid model and its dimensions are given for your reference only.

(Expected time: 30 min)

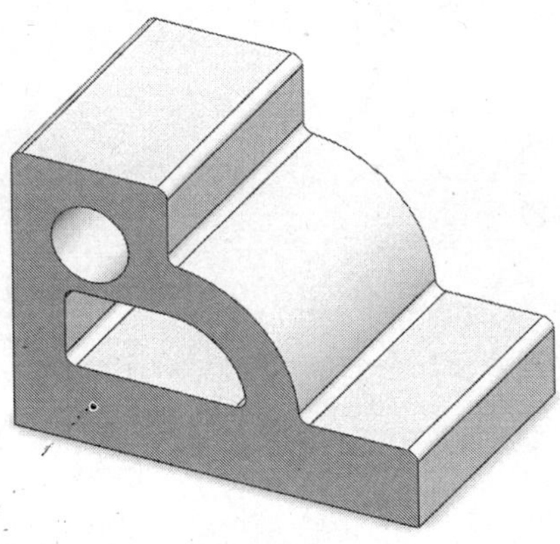

Figure 3-95 Solid model for Exercise 6

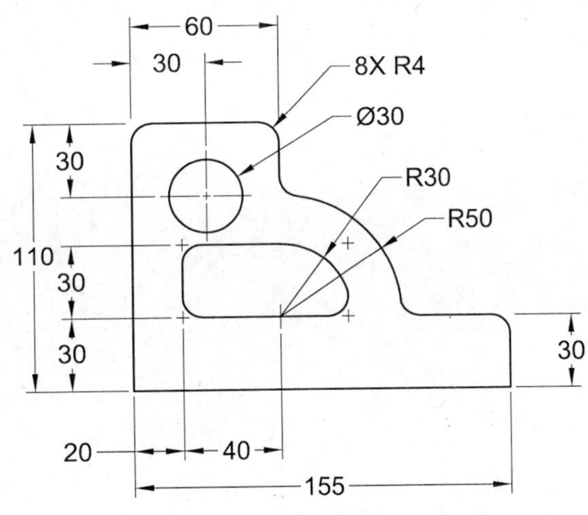

Figure 3-96 Sketch for Exercise 6

Answers to Self-Evaluation Test

1. Linear Sketch Pattern, **2.** Circular Sketch Pattern, **3.** Select, **4.** Dynamic Mirror Entities, **5.** T, **6.** F, **7.** T, **8.** F, **9.** F, **10.** F

Chapter 4

Adding Relations and Dimensions to Sketches

Learning Objectives

After completing this chapter, you will be able to:

- *Add geometric relations to sketches*
- *Dimension sketches*
- *Modify the dimensions of sketches*
- *Understand the concept of fully defined sketches*
- *View and examine the relations applied to sketches*
- *Open an existing file*

APPLYING GEOMETRIC RELATIONS TO SKETCHES

Geometric relations are the logical operations that are performed to add relationships (such as tangent, perpendicular, or parallel) between the sketched entities, planes, axes, edges, or vertices. The relations applied to the sketched entities are used to capture the design intent. Geometric relations constrain the degree of freedom of the sketched entities. You can apply relations to a sketch by using the **Add Relations PropertyManager** and Automatic Relations.

Applying Relations using the Add Relations PropertyManager

CommandManager:	Sketch > Display/Delete Relations flyout > Add Relation
SOLIDWORKS menus:	Tools > Relations > Add
Toolbar:	Sketch > Display/Delete Relations flyout > Add Relation

The **Add Relations PropertyManager** is widely used to apply relations to a sketch in the sketching environment of SOLIDWORKS. To invoke this PropertyManager, choose the **Add Relation** button from the **Display/Delete Relations** flyout in the **Sketch CommandManager**, as shown in Figure 4-1. Alternatively, right-click on an entity in the drawing area and then choose the **Add Relation** option from the **Sketch Tools** cascade menu displayed; the **Add Relations PropertyManager** will be displayed, refer to Figure 4-2. Also, the confirmation corner will be displayed at the top right corner of the drawing area. Different rollouts in the **Add Relations PropertyManager** are discussed next.

***Figure 4-1** Tools in the **Display/Delete Relations** flyout*

Selected Entities Rollout

The **Selected Entities** rollout displays the name of the entities selected to apply relations. The selected entities are displayed in light blue and are added in the area below the **Selected Entities** rollout. You can remove the selected entity from the selection set by selecting the same entity again in the drawing area.

Alternatively, select an entity in the **Selected Entities** rollout and then right-click; a shortcut menu will be displayed. Next, choose the **Delete** option from the shortcut menu to remove the selected entity from the selection set. If you choose the **Clear Selections** option from the shortcut menu, all entities will be removed from the selection set.

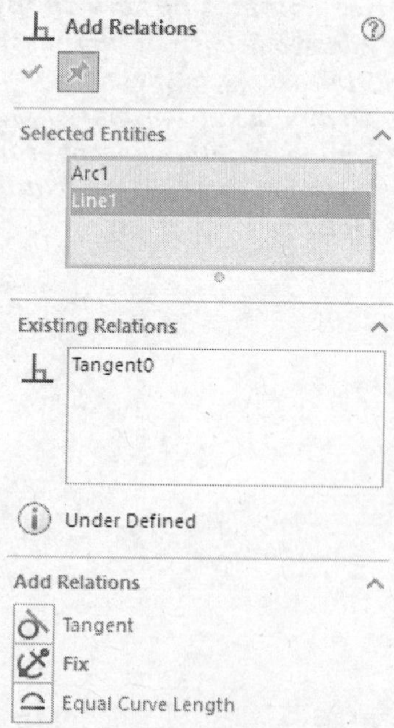

Figure 4-2** The **Add Relations PropertyManager

Existing Relations Rollout

The **Existing Relations** rollout displays the relations that are already applied to the selected sketch entities. It also shows the status of the sketch entities. You can delete the existing relation from this rollout. To do so, select the existing relation from the selection box and right-click to display the shortcut menu. Choose the **Delete** option from this shortcut menu to delete the selected relation. If you choose the **Delete All** option, all relations displayed in the selection box of the **Existing Relations** rollout will be deleted.

> **Tip**
> *You can apply relation to a single entity or between two or more entities. In order to apply relation between two or more entities, at least one entity should be a sketched entity. The other entity or entities can be sketched entities, edges, faces, vertices, origins, plane, or axes. The sketch curves from other sketches that form lines or arcs when projected on a sketch plane can also be included in the relation.*

Add Relations Rollout

The **Add Relations** rollout is used to apply the relations to the selected entity. This rollout contains list of relations that you can apply to a selected entity or entities. The most appropriate relation for the selected entities appears in bold letters.

The relations that can be applied to the sketches using the **Add Relations** rollout are discussed next.

Horizontal

The Horizontal relation forces one or more selected lines or centerlines to become horizontal. You can also force two or more points to become horizontal using the Horizontal relation. A point can be a sketch point, a center point, an endpoint, a control point of a spline, or an external entity such as origin, vertex, axis, or point in an external sketch. To apply this relation, invoke the **Add Relations PropertyManager**. Select the entity or entities to apply the Horizontal relation. Choose the **Horizontal** button from the **Add Relations** rollout in the **Add Relations PropertyManager**. You will notice that the name of the horizontal relation will be displayed in the **Existing Relations** rollout.

Vertical

The Vertical relation forces one or more selected lines or centerlines to become vertical. You can force two or more points to become vertical using the **Vertical** relation. To apply this relation, invoke the **Add Relations PropertyManager** and select the entity or entities to apply the Vertical relation. Choose the **Vertical** button from the **Add Relations** rollout. You will notice that the name of the vertical relation is displayed in the **Existing Relations** rollout.

Collinear

The Collinear relation forces the selected lines to lie on the same line. To apply this relation, invoke the **Add Relations PropertyManager.** Select the lines to apply the Collinear relation. Choose the **Collinear** button from the **Add Relations** rollout.

Perpendicular

The Perpendicular relation forces the selected lines to become perpendicular to each other. To apply this relation, invoke the **Add Relations PropertyManager**. Select two lines and choose the **Perpendicular** button from the **Add Relations** rollout. Figure 4-3 shows two lines before and after applying the **Perpendicular** relation.

Parallel

The Parallel relation forces the selected lines to become parallel to each other. To apply this relation, invoke the **Add Relations PropertyManager**. Select two lines and choose the **Parallel** button from the **Add Relations** rollout. Figure 4-4 shows two lines before and after applying this relation.

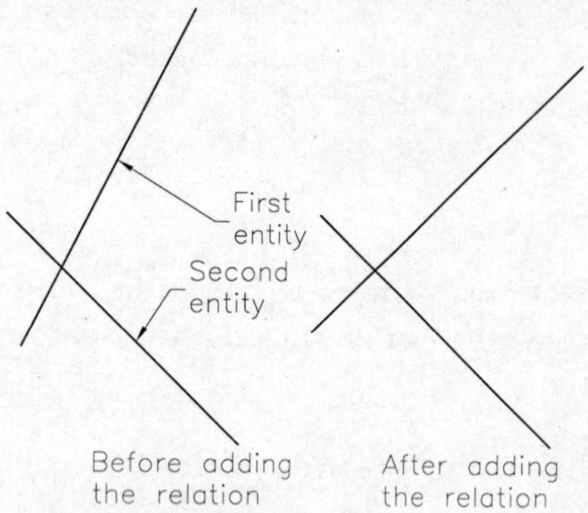

Figure 4-3 *Entities before and after applying the Perpendicular relation*

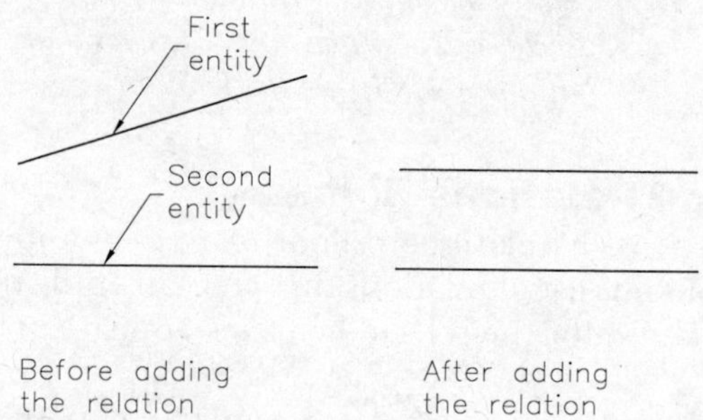

Figure 4-4 *Entities before and after applying the Parallel relation*

ParallelYZ

The ParallelYZ relation forces a line in the three-dimensional (3D) sketch to become parallel to the YZ plane with respect to the selected plane. To apply this relation, invoke the **Add Relations PropertyManager**. Select a line in the 3D sketch and then select a plane. Next, choose the **ParallelYZ** button from the **Add Relations** rollout.

Note

You will learn more about the 3D curves in the later chapters.

ParallelZX

The ParallelZX relation forces a line in the 3D sketch to become parallel to the ZX plane with respect to the selected plane. To apply this relation, invoke the **Add Relations PropertyManager**. Select a line in the 3D sketch and then select a plane. Next, choose the **ParallelZX** button from the **Add Relations** rollout.

Along X

The AlongX relation forces a line in the 3D sketch to become parallel to the X-axis. To apply this relation, invoke the **Add Relations PropertyManager**. Select a line in the 3D sketch and then choose the **Along X** button from the **Add Relations** rollout; the selected line will be oriented along the X axis.

Along Y

The Along Y relation forces a line in the 3D sketch to become parallel to the Y-axis. To apply this relation, invoke the **Add Relations PropertyManager**. Select a line in the 3D sketch and then choose the **Along Y** button from the **Add Relations** rollout; the selected line will be oriented along the Y axis.

Along Z

The AlongZ relation forces a line in the 3D sketch to become parallel to the Z-axis. To apply this relation, invoke the **Add Relations PropertyManager**. Select a line in the 3D sketch and then choose the **Along Z** button from the **Add Relations** rollout; the selected line will be oriented along the Z axis.

Normal

The Normal relation forces a line in the 3D sketch to become normal to the selected plane. To apply this relation, invoke the **Add Relations PropertyManager**. Select a line in the 3D sketch and then select a plane. Next, choose the **Normal** button from the **Add Relations** rollout; the selected line will be oriented normal to the plane.

On Plane

The On Plane relation forces a line in the 3D sketch to become parallel and is placed on the selected plane. To apply this relation, invoke the **Add Relations PropertyManager**. Select a line in the 3D sketch and then select a plane. Next, choose the **On Plane** button from the **Add Relations** rollout; the selected line will be oriented parallel to the selected plane and is placed on it.

Tangent

The Tangent relation forces a selected arc, circle, spline, or ellipse to become tangent to other arc, circle, spline, ellipse, line, or edge. To apply this relation, invoke the **Add Relations PropertyManager**. Select two entities and then choose the **Tangent** button from the **Add Relations** rollout. Figure 4-5 shows a line and a circle before and after applying the Tangent relation. Figure 4-6 shows two arcs before and after applying the Tangent relation.

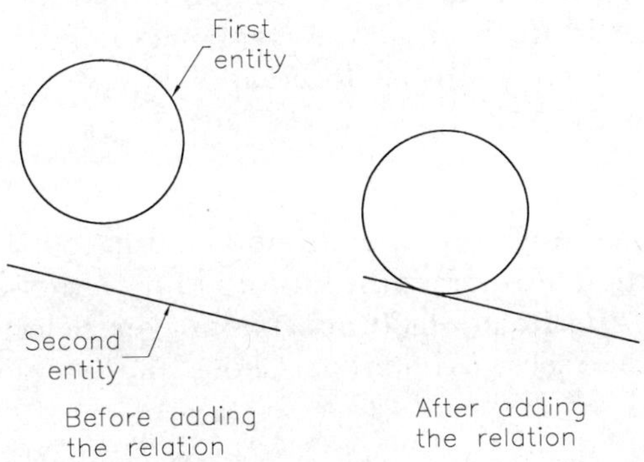

***Figure 4-5** Line and circle before and after applying the Tangent relation*

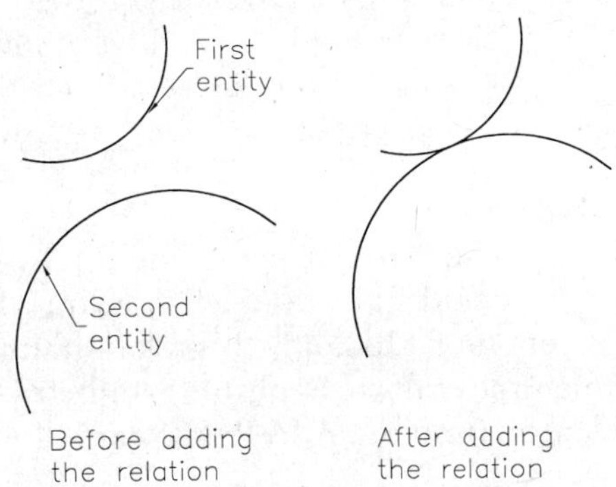

***Figure 4-6** Two arcs before and after applying the Tangent relation*

Coradial

The Coradial relation forces a selected arc or circle to share the same center point and the same radius with other arc or circle. To apply this relation, invoke the **Add Relations PropertyManager**. Next, select more than one circular entities and choose the **Coradial** button from the **Add Relations** rollout; the selected entities will be then merged together and a coradial symbol will be displayed.

Concentric

The Concentric relation forces a selected arc or circle to share the same center point with other arc, circle, point, vertex, or circular edge. To apply this relation, invoke the **Add Relations PropertyManager**. Select the required entity to apply the Concentric relation and then choose the **Concentric** button from the **Add Relations** rollout.

Equal

The Equal relation forces the selected lines to have equal length and the selected arcs, circles, or arc and circle to have equal radii. To apply this relation, invoke the **Add Relations PropertyManager**. Select the required entity to apply the Equal relation and choose the **Equal** button from the **Add Relations** rollout.

Intersection

The Intersection relation forces a selected point to move at the intersection of two selected lines. To apply this relation, invoke the **Add Relations PropertyManager**. Select the required entity to apply the Intersection relation. Choose the **Intersection** button from the **Add Relations** rollout.

Coincident

The Coincident relation forces a selected point to be coincident with a selected line, arc, circle, or ellipse. To apply this relation, invoke the **Add Relations PropertyManager**. Select the required entity to apply the Coincident relation. Choose the **Coincident** button from the **Add Relations** rollout.

Midpoint

The Midpoint relation forces a selected point to move to the midpoint of a selected line. To apply this relation, invoke the **Add Relations PropertyManager**. Select the point and the line to which the midpoint relation has to be applied. Choose the **Midpoint** button from the **Add Relations** rollout.

Symmetric

The Symmetric relation forces two selected lines, arcs, points, and ellipses to remain equidistant from a centerline. This relation also forces the entities to have the same orientation. To apply this relation, invoke the **Add Relations PropertyManager**. Select the required entity to apply the Symmetric relation and select a centerline. Choose the **Symmetric** button from the **Add Relations** rollout.

Fix

The Fix relation forces the selected entity to be fixed at the specified position. If you apply this relation to a line or an arc, its location will be fixed but you can change its size by dragging the endpoints. To apply this relation, invoke the **Add Relations PropertyManager**. Select the required entity and choose the **Fix** button from the **Add Relations** rollout.

Merge

The Merge relation forces two sketch points or endpoints to merge in a single point. To apply this relation, invoke the **Add Relations PropertyManager**. Select the required entities to apply the Merge relation and choose the **Merge** button from the **Add Relations** rollout.

Pierce

The Pierce relation forces a sketch point or an endpoint of an entity to be coincident with the entity drawn at another plane or sketch. To apply this relation, invoke the **Add Relations PropertyManager**. Select the required entities to apply the Pierce relation and choose the **Pierce** button from the **Add Relations** rollout.

Tip

You can also apply the relations using the ***Properties PropertyManager****. This PropertyManager is automatically invoked if you select more than one entity from the drawing area. The possible relations for the selected geometry will be displayed in the* ***Add Relations*** *rollout. Choose the relation you need to apply to the selected geometry.*

Alternatively, select the entity or entities to which you need to apply the relation and do not move the mouse for a while; a pop-up toolbar will be displayed with few relations. Select the relations from the pop-up toolbar. You can also select the entity or entities and right-click to display these relations in a shortcut menu.

Automatic Relations

Automatic relations are applied automatically to a sketch while drawing. For example, you will notice that when you specify the start point of a line and move the cursor horizontally toward the right or left, the horizontal line symbol is displayed below the line cursor. This is the symbol of the Horizontal relation that is applied to the line while drawing. If you move the cursor vertically downward or upward, the vertical line symbol for the Vertical relation will be displayed below the line cursor. If you move the cursor to the intersection of two or more sketched entities, the intersection symbol will appear below the cursor. Similarly, other relations are also applied automatically to the sketch when you draw it.

You can activate the automatic relations option if it is not activated. To do so, choose the **Options** button from the Menu Bar; the **System Options - General** dialog box will be displayed. Select the **Relations/Snaps** option from the area on the left, then select the **Automatic relations** check box from this dialog box, and finally choose the **OK** button. You can also activate or deactivate the Automatic Relations option from the SOLIDWORKS menus. To activate it, choose **Tools > Sketch Settings > Automatic Relations** from the SOLIDWORKS menus. This is a toggle option. So, you can use the same option to deactivate it.

The Horizontal, Vertical, Coincident, Midpoint, Intersection, Tangent, Perpendicular, and Coradial relations can be applied automatically to a sketch while drawing.

Tip

While drawing a sketch, you will observe that two types of inferencing lines are displayed: one in blue and the other in yellow. The yellow inferencing line indicates that a relation has been applied automatically to the sketch whereas the blue inferencing line indicates that no automatic relation has been applied.

DESIGN INTENT

Design Intent is an important concept in Parametric Solid Modeling Design. It means when you create a part, it should be created in such a way that if any change is made in future, the change should propagate throughout the design without affecting the purpose of the design. This is achieved by applying proper constraints. If you are able to capture the design intent of a model, then it will be easy to create and edit a robust solid model. Therefore, some forethought must be put while creating a model.

Consider a simple design of a plate with two holes at a distance of 25mm from the edge. Assume that at the time of initial design, the dimension of the plate needs to be 250mmX150mm. Based on this specification, you need to draw a rectangle with two circles. Now, you can dimension the circles in two ways, dimension each circle separately from the edges or dimension one circle from one of the edges and dimension the other circle with respect to the previous one, as shown in Figures 4-7 and 4-8, and call them as Design 1 and Design 2, respectively. Note that in these figures, the dimensions that are in parenthesis are given for reference only.

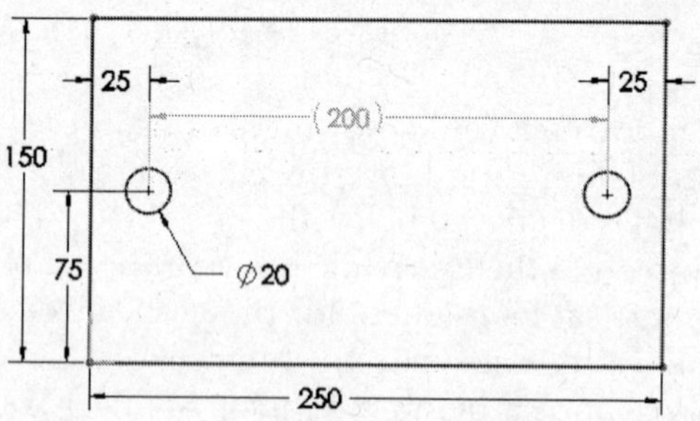

Figure 4-7 *Circles dimensioned from edges*

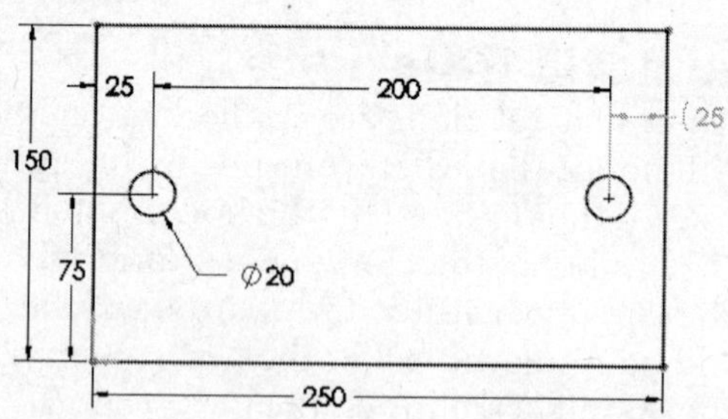

Figure 4-8 *Circle dimensioned with respect to each other*

As mentioned above, the requirement for this design is that the holes need to be placed at the distance of 25mm from the edges. Now assume that the final dimension of the plate is changed to 230mmX150mm. You will find that the Design 1 satisfies the design requirement, whereas the Design 2 does not, refer to Figures 4-9 and 4-10. This shows the importance of dimensioning in a proper way. Therefore, you need to apply both the geometric and dimensional constraints in such a way that design intent is captured.

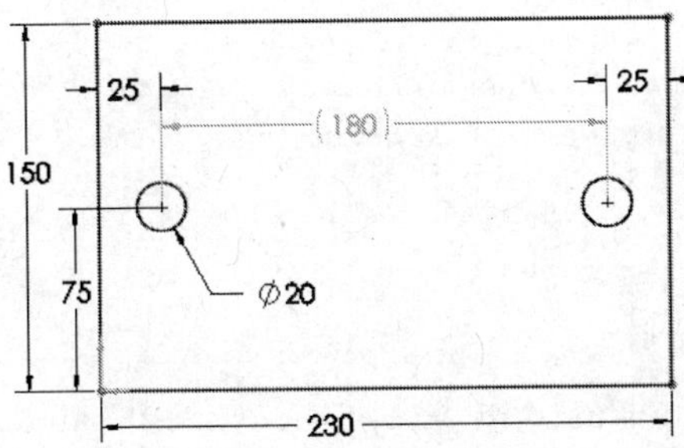

***Figure 4-9** Sketch satisfying the design requirement*

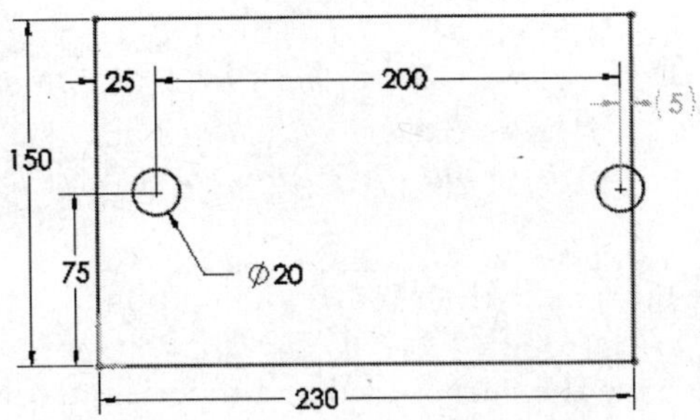

***Figure 4-10** Sketch not satisfying the design requirement*

DIMENSIONING A SKETCH

After drawing sketches and adding relations, the most important step in creating a design is dimensioning. SOLIDWORKS being a parametric software, the entity on dimensioning is driven by the specified value irrespective of the original size. Therefore, when you apply and modify the dimension of an entity, it is forced to change its size in accordance with the specified dimension value.

You can dimension any kind of entity by using the **Smart Dimension** tool, available in the **Sketch CommandManager**. If you use the **Smart Dimension** tool, the type of dimension to be applied will depend on the type of entity selected. For example, if you select a line, then a horizontal, vertical, or aligned dimension will be applied. If you select a circle, a diametric dimension will be applied. Similarly, if you select an arc, a radial dimension will be applied. However, if you want to apply a particular type of dimension, then choose the required tool from the **Smart Dimension** flyout. You can also invoke these tools from the **Dimensions/Relations** toolbar.

As soon as you place dimension, the **Modify** dialog box will be displayed, as shown in Figure 4-11. You can modify the default dimension value by using the spinner or by entering a new value in the edit box available in the **Modify** dialog box. You can also drag the thumbwheel provided below the spinner to the right to increase and to the left to decrease the value.

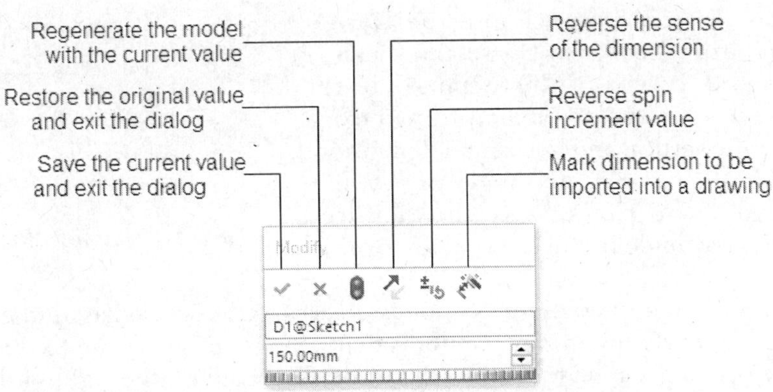

***Figure 4-11** The **Modify** dialog box*

> **Tip**
> *If the **Modify** dialog box is not displayed when you place the dimension, you need to set its preference manually. To do this, invoke the **System Options - General** dialog box and select the **Input dimension value** check box.*

The buttons in the **Modify** dialog box are discussed next.

The **Save the current value and exit the dialog** button is used to accept the current value and exit the dialog box. The **Restore the original value and exit the dialog** button is used to restore the last dimensional value applied to the sketch and exit the dialog box. The **Regenerate the model with the current value** button is used to preview the geometry of the sketch with the modified dimensional value. The **Reverse the sense of the dimension** button is used to flip the dimension value of an entity. This button will be available in the **Modify** dialog box when the selected dimension is a linear dimension. The **Reset spin increment value** button is used to modify the increment value of the spinner. If you choose this button, the **Increment** dialog box will be displayed. Enter a value and press ENTER. This new value will be added to or subtracted from the current value when you click on the spinner arrow. The **Mark dimensions to be imported into a drawing** button is chosen to make sure that the selected dimension is generated as a model annotation in the drawing views. If this button is not chosen, the selected dimension will not be generated in the drafting environment. You can drive a dimension by an equation and also link it to other dimensions using the **Add equation** and **Link value** options in the drop-down list of the **Modify** dialog box. You will learn more about these options in the later chapters.

In SOLIDWORKS, you can also specify numeric input while creating lines, rectangles, circles, and arcs. To do so, choose the **Options** button from the Menu Bar; the **System Options - General** dialog box will be displayed. Select the **Sketch** option from the area on the left of the dialog box; the options related to the sketch will be displayed on the right in the dialog box. Select the **Enable on screen numeric input on entity creation** check box and then choose the **OK** button to apply the changes and close the dialog box. Now, you can specify the numeric input while creating the lines, rectangles, circles, and arcs. For example, choose the **Corner Rectangle** button from the **Sketch CommandManager** and specify the first corner of the rectangle in the drawing area. Next, move the cursor away from the first corner. Note that the vertical and horizontal dimensions will be attached to the reference rectangle, as shown in Figure 4-12. Now, you can specify the required dimensions of the rectangle in the drawing area.

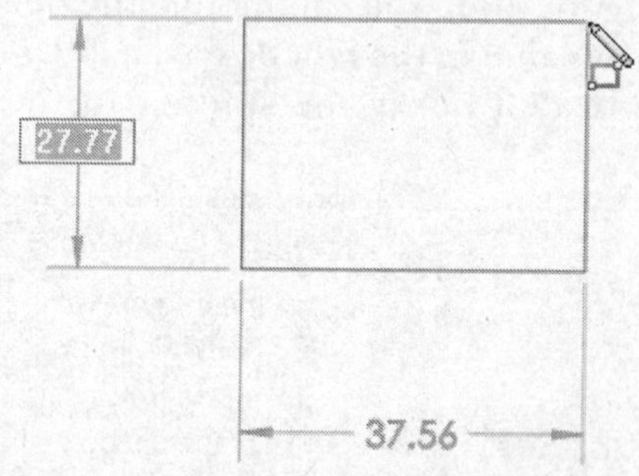

***Figure 4-12** Linear dimensioning of lines*

In SOLIDWORKS, the specified numeric input values can also be used as applied dimensions. To do so, invoke the **System Options- General** dialog box and select the **Sketch** option from the left area; the options related to the sketch will be displayed on the right of the dialog box. Select the **Create Dimensions only when the value is entered** check box and then choose the **OK** button. Now, on entering the numeric input value in the edit box displayed while drawing the sketch, the entered value will be applied as dimension to the sketch.

The types of dimensions that can be applied to the sketches in the sketching environment of SOLIDWORKS are discussed next.

Tip

*You can also enter the arithmetic symbols directly in the edit box of the **Modify** toolbar to calculate the dimension. For example, if you need to enter a dimension after solving a complex arithmetic function such as (220*12.5)-3+150, which is equal to 2897, there is no need to calculate this function using the calculator. Just enter the statement in the edit box and press ENTER; SOLIDWORKS will automatically solve the mathematical expression to get the value of the dimension.*

Horizontal/Vertical Dimensioning

CommandManager: Sketch > Smart Dimension flyout > Horizontal/Vertical Dimension
SOLIDWORKS menus: Tools > Dimensions > Horizontal/Vertical
Toolbar: Sketch > Smart Dimension flyout > Horizontal/Vertical Dimension

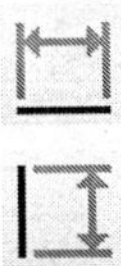

These dimensions are used to define the horizontal or vertical dimension of a selected line or between two points. The points can be the endpoints of lines or arcs, or the center points of circles, arcs, ellipses, or parabolas. You can dimension a vertical or horizontal line by selecting it directly. To invoke these tools, choose the **Horizontal Dimension/Vertical Dimension** button from the **Smart Dimension** flyout in the **Sketch CommandManager**. You can also right-click in the drawing area and choose **More Dimensions > Horizontal/Vertical** from the shortcut menu displayed. When you move the cursor on a line, the line will be highlighted and will turn orange. As soon as you select the line, it will turn light blue and the dimension will be attached to the cursor. Move the cursor and place the dimension at an appropriate place by clicking the left mouse button. The **Modify** dialog box will be displayed with the default value in it. Enter a new value of the dimension in the **Modify** dialog box and press ENTER. Figure 4-13 shows the horizontal and vertical dimensioning of lines.

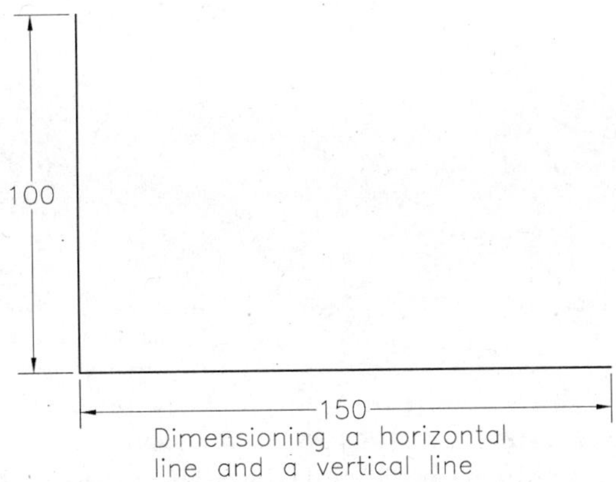

Figure 4-13 *Horizontal and vertical dimensioning of lines*

If the dimension is selected from the drawing area, the **Dimension PropertyManager** will be displayed, as shown in Figure 4-14. The different rollouts in the **Value** tab of the **Dimension PropertyManager** are discussed next.

Style Rollout

The **Style** rollout, as shown in Figure 4-15, is used to create, save, delete, and retrieve the dimension style in the current document. You can also retrieve the dimension styles saved in other documents using this rollout. The options in this rollout are discussed next.

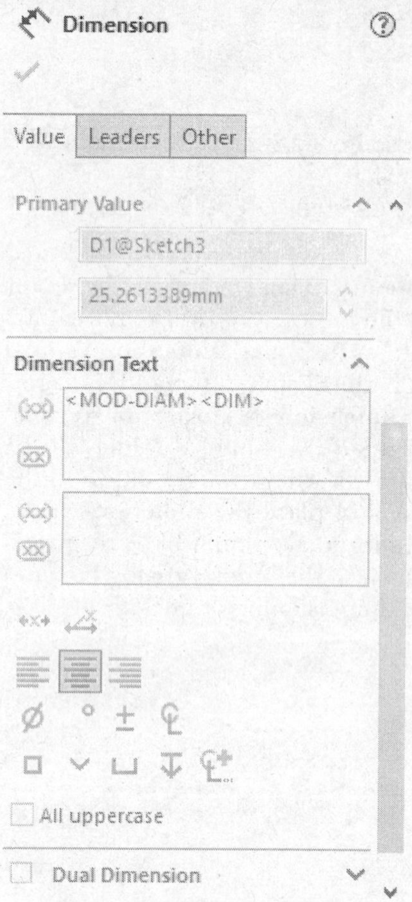

Figure 4-14 The ***Dimension PropertyManager***

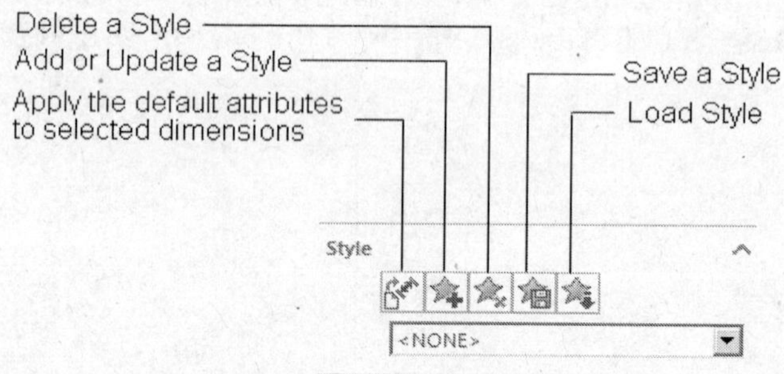

Figure 4-15 The ***Style*** *rollout*

Apply the default attributes to selected dimensions

The **Apply the default attributes to selected dimensions** button is used to apply the default attributes to the selected dimension(s). The attributes include the tolerance, precision, arrow style, dimension text, and so on. This option is generally used when you modify the settings applied to a dimension and then to restore the default settings on that dimension.

Add or Update a Style

The **Add or Update a Style** button is used to add a dimension style to the current document for a selected dimension. After invoking the **Dimension PropertyManager**, set the attributes using various options provided in this PropertyManager. Next, choose the **Add or Update a Style** button; the **Add or Update a Style** dialog box will be displayed, as shown in Figure 4-16. Enter the name of the dimension style in the edit box and press ENTER; the dimension style will be added to the current document.

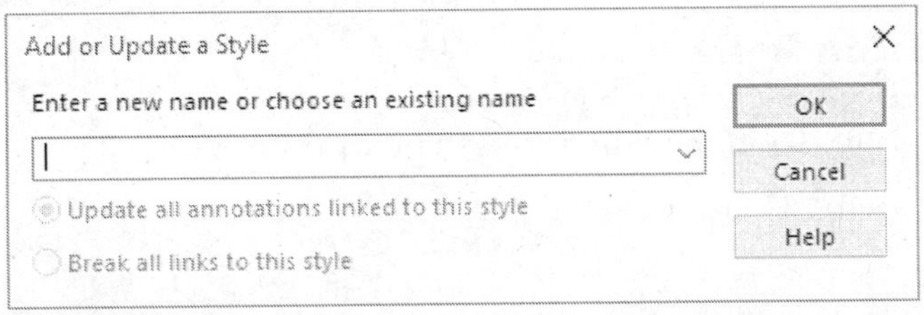

*Figure 4-16 The **Add or Update a Style** dialog box*

You can apply a new dimension style to the selected dimension by selecting a dimension style from the **Set a current Style** drop-down list in the **Style** rollout. You can also update a dimension style. To do so, select the dimension and set the options of the dimension style according to your need. Next, choose the **Add or Update a Style** button to invoke the **Add or Update a Style** dialog box. Select the dimension style to update from the drop-down list in the dialog box; the two radio buttons in this dialog box will be enabled. Select the **Update all annotations linked to this Style** radio button and choose the **OK** button to update all the dimensions linked to the selected **Style**. If you select the **Break all links to this Style** radio button and choose the **OK** button, then the link between the other dimensions having the same style and the selected **Style** will be broken.

Delete a Style

The **Delete a Style** button is used to delete a dimension style. Select a dimension style from the **Set a current Style** drop-down list and then choose the **Delete a Style** button. Note that even after deleting the dimension style, the properties of the dimensions will be the same as those with the deleted style. You can set the properties of a dimension to the default settings using the **Apply the default attributes to selected dimension** button.

Save a Style

The **Save a Style** button is used to save a dimension style so that it can be retrieved in some other document. Select a dimension style from the **Set a current Style** drop-down list and choose the **Save a Style** button; the **Save As** dialog box will be displayed. Browse to the folder in which you want to save the style and enter its name in the **File name** edit box. Choose the **Save** button from the **Save As** dialog box. The style file will be saved with the extension *.sldstl*.

Load Style

The **Load Style** button is used to open a saved style in the current document. The properties of that favorite will be applied to the selected dimension. To load a style, choose the **Load Style** button to invoke the **Open** dialog box. Browse to the folder in which the style is saved.

Now, select the file with the extension *.sldstl* and choose the **Open** button; the **Add or Update a Style** dialog box will be displayed. Choose the **OK** button from this dialog box.

Tip
You can load more than one style by pressing the SHIFT key and selecting the style from the ***Open*** *dialog box. All styles will be displayed in the* ***Set a current Style*** *drop-down list.*

Tolerance/Precision Rollout

The **Tolerance/Precision** rollout shown in Figure 4-17 is used to specify tolerance and precision in dimensions. The options in this rollout are discussed next.

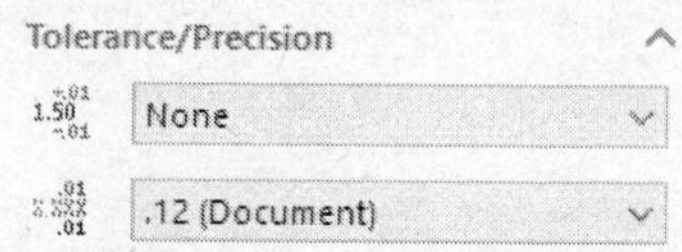

Figure 4-17 *The* ***Tolerance/ Precision*** *rollout*

Tolerance Type

The **Tolerance Type** drop-down list is used to apply tolerance to a dimension. By default, the **None** option is selected. Therefore, no tolerance is applied to the dimensions. The other tolerance types available in this drop-down list are discussed next.

Basic: The basic dimension is the one that is enclosed in a rectangle. To display the basic dimension, select the dimension that you want to display as the basic dimension and then select the **Basic** option from the **Tolerance Type** drop-down list. You will notice that the dimension is enclosed in a rectangle indicating that it is a basic dimension, see Figure 4-18.

Bilateral: The bilateral tolerance provides the maximum and minimum variations in the value of a dimension that is acceptable in a design. To apply the bilateral tolerance, select the dimension and then select the **Bilateral** option from the **Tolerance Type** drop-down list; the **Maximum Variation** and **Minimum Variation** edit boxes will be enabled, where you can enter the maximum and minimum variations for a dimension. Also, the **Show parentheses** check box will be displayed. If you select this check box, the bilateral tolerance will be displayed with parentheses. The dimension with a bilateral tolerance is shown in Figure 4-19.

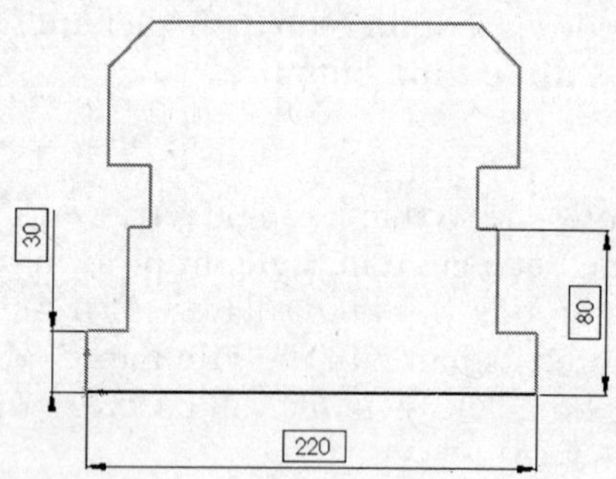

Figure 4-18 *Basic dimensions*

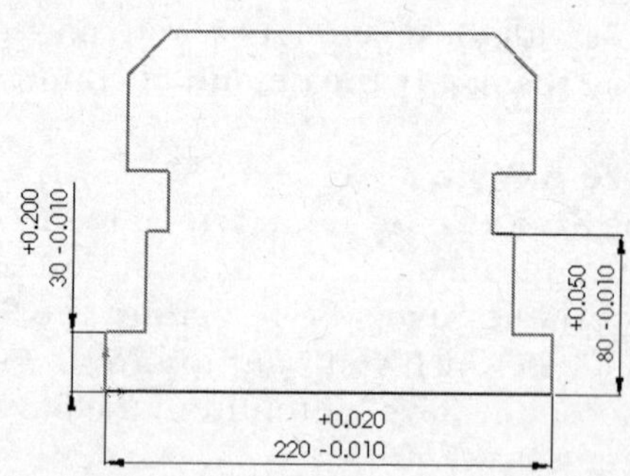

Figure 4-19 *Bilateral tolerance*

Note
The ISO and ANSI standard has been used as the dimension standard for the sketches in this book.

Limit: The maximum and minimum permissible dimensional values of an entity are displayed on selecting the **Limit** option. To apply this tolerance type, select the dimension to be displayed as the limit dimension and select the **Limit** option; the **Maximum Variation** and **Minimum Variation** edit boxes will be enabled. Enter the values of the maximum and minimum variations. The dimension along with the limit tolerance is shown in Figure 4-20.

Symmetric: The symmetric tolerance is displayed with the plus and minus signs. To use this tolerance, first select the dimension and then select the **Symmetric** option; the **Maximum Variation** edit box will be displayed. Enter the value of the tolerance in this edit box. Also, you can select the **Show parentheses** check box to show the tolerance in parentheses. The dimension along with the symmetric tolerance is shown in Figure 4-21.

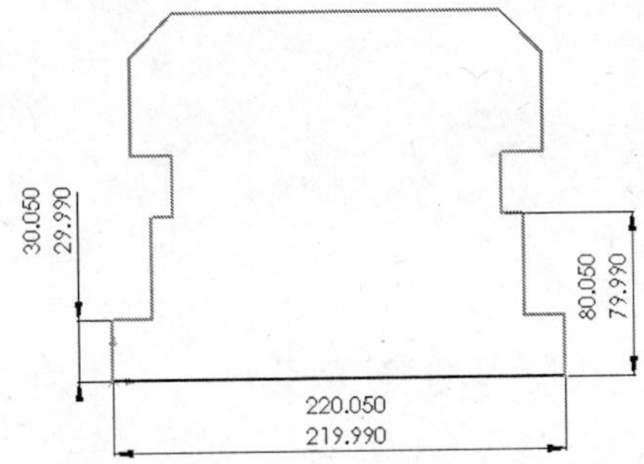

Figure 4-20 *Limit tolerance*

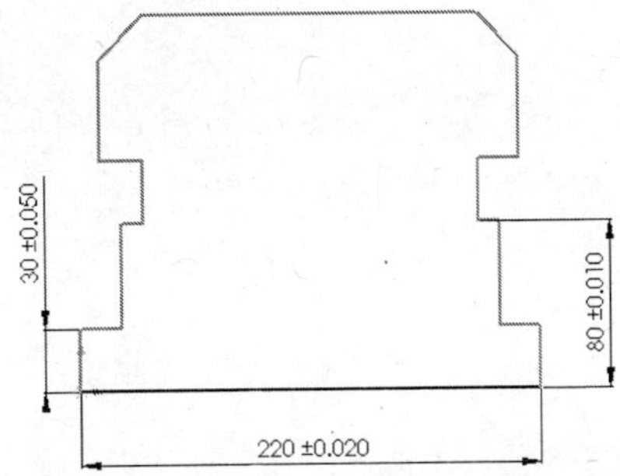

Figure 4-21 *Symmetric tolerance*

MIN: In this dimensional tolerance, the **min.** symbol is added to dimension as suffix. This implies that the dimensional value is the minimum value that is allowed in the design. To display this dimensional tolerance, select a dimension and then the **MIN** option from the **Tolerance Type** drop-down list. The dimension along with the minimum tolerance is shown in Figure 4-22.

MAX: In this dimensional tolerance, the **max.** symbol is added to dimension as suffix. This implies that the dimensional value is the maximum value that is allowed in the design. To display this dimensional tolerance, select a dimension and then the **MAX** option from the **Tolerance Type** drop-down list. The dimension along with the maximum tolerance is shown in Figure 4-23.

Fit: This option is used to apply fit according to the Hole Fit and Shaft Fit systems. The **Tolerance/Precision** rollout with the **Fit** option selected in the **Tolerance Type** drop-down list is shown in Figure 4-24.

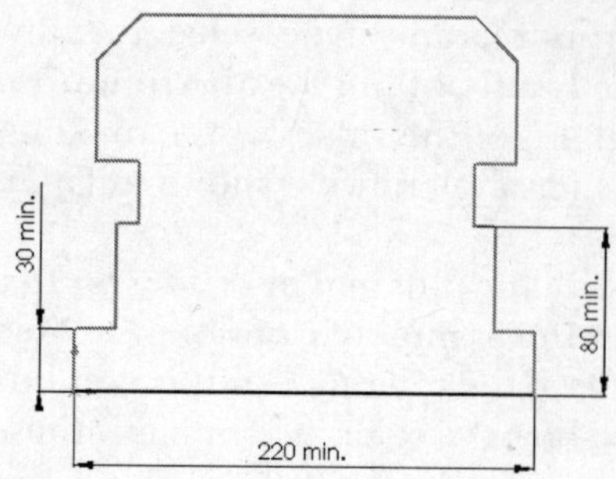

Figure 4-22 Minimum tolerance

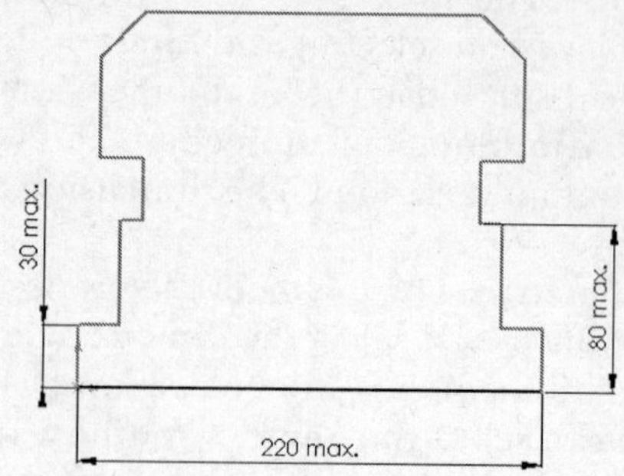

Figure 4-23 Maximum tolerance

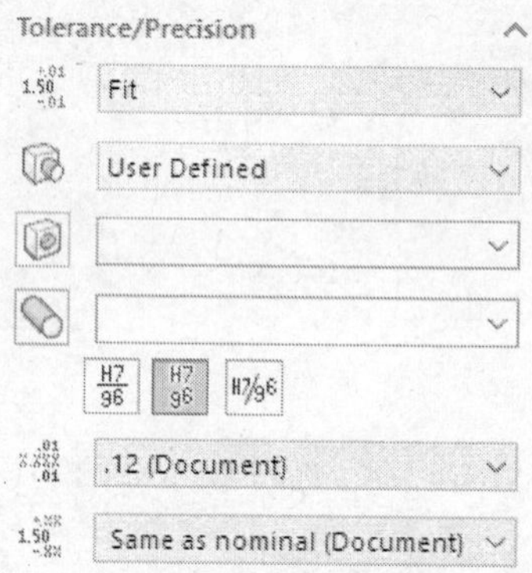

*Figure 4-24 The **Tolerance/Precision** rollout with the **Fit** option selected in the **Tolerance Type** drop-down list*

Select the type of fit from the **Classification** drop-down list. The **Classification** drop-down list is used to define the **User Defined** fit, **Clearance** fit, **Transitional** fit, or **Press** fit. To apply a fit using the Hole Fit system or the Shaft Fit system, select the dimension and then the **Fit** option from the **Tolerance Type** drop-down list. The **Classification, Hole Fit**, and **Shaft Fit** drop-down lists will be displayed below the **Tolerance Type** drop-down list. Select the required fit from the **Classification** drop-down list and select the fit standard from the **Hole Fit** drop-down list or the **Shaft Fit** drop-down list. If you select the **Clearance, Transitional**, or **Press** option from the **Classification** drop-down list and the fit standard from the **Hole Fit** drop-down list, then only the standards matching the selected hole fit will be displayed in the **Shaft Fit** drop-down list and vice versa. However, if you select the **User Defined** option from the **Classification** drop-down list, you can select any standard from the **Hole Fit** and **Shaft Fit** drop-down lists. The **Stacked with line display** button is chosen to display the stacked tolerance with a line. You can also display the tolerance as stacked without a line using the **Stacked without line display** button. If you choose the **Linear display** button, the tolerance will be displayed in the linear form. The dimension along with the hole fit and shaft fit is shown in Figure 4-25.

Fit with tolerance: This option in the **Tolerance Type** drop-down list is used to display tolerance along with the hole fit and shaft fit in a dimension. To apply fit with tolerance, select a dimension, and then select the **Fit with tolerance** option from the **Tolerance Type** drop-down list. Select the type of fit from the **Classification** drop-down list. Next, select the fit standard from the **Hole Fit** or the **Shaft Fit** drop-down list. Tolerance will be displayed with the fit standard only if you select a fit system from the **Hole Fit** or **Shaft Fit** drop-down list. Tolerance will be displayed along with the fit standard in the drawing area. In SOLIDWORKS, tolerance is calculated automatically, depending on the type and standard of the fit selected. The **Show parentheses** check box can be selected to show tolerance in parentheses. The dimension along with the fit and tolerance is shown in Figure 4-26.

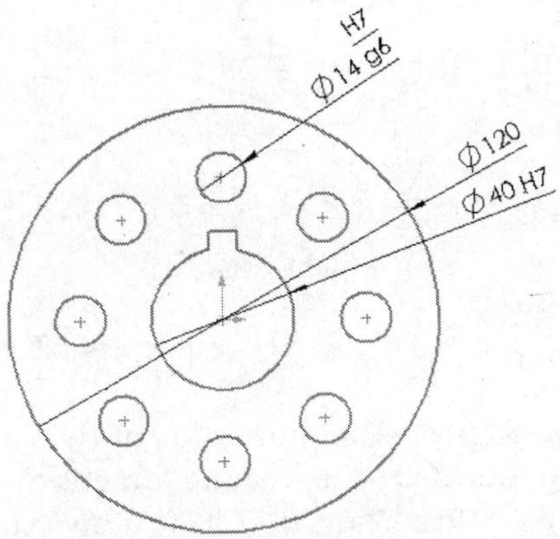

***Figure 4-25** Hole fit and shaft fit*

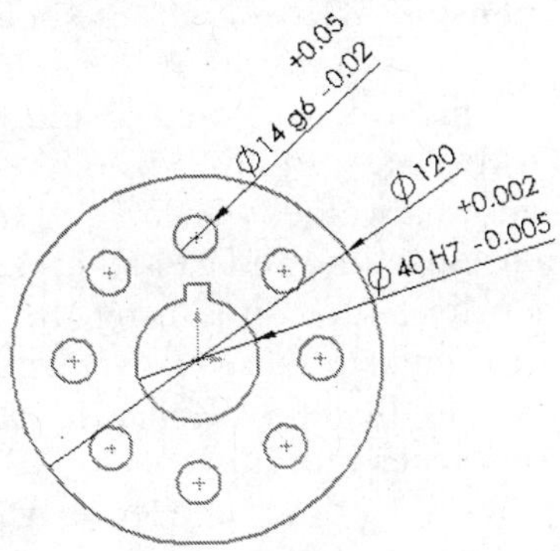

***Figure 4-26** Dimensioning along with the fit and tolerance*

Fit (tolerance only): This option in the **Tolerance Type** drop-down list is used to display the tolerance in a dimension based on the hole fit or shaft fit.

None: This option in the **Tolerance Type** drop-down list is used to display the dimensional value without any tolerance.

Unit Precision

The **Unit Precision** drop-down list is used to specify the precision of the number of places after the decimal for dimensions. By default, the selected precision is two places after the decimal.

Tolerance Precision

The **Tolerance Precision** drop-down list is used to specify the precision of the number of places after the decimal for tolerance. By default, the selected precision is two places after the decimal. This drop-down list will not be available if the **None** option is selected in the **Tolerance Type** drop-down list.

Primary Value Rollout

The **Primary Value** rollout is used to modify the name and value of the dimension. The text box in this rollout is used to change the name of the dimension and the value of the dimension can be changed from the spinner given below the text box.

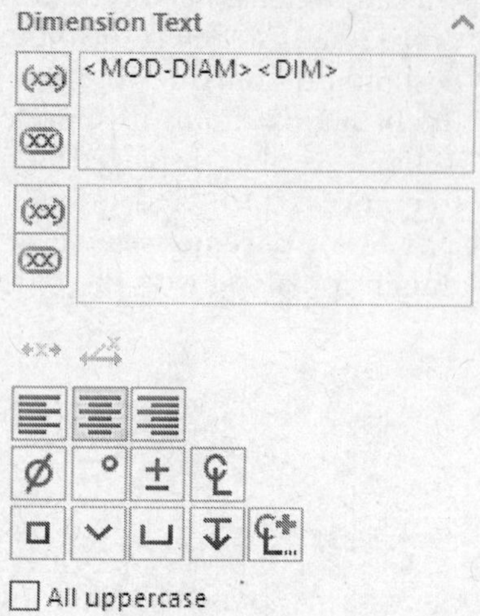

*Figure 4-27 The **Dimension Text** rollout*

Dimension Text Rollout

The **Dimension Text** rollout, as shown in Figure 4-27, is used to add text and symbols to the dimension. The textbox in this rollout is used to add text to dimension. The **<DIM>** text displayed in the text box symbolizes the dimensional value. You can add text before or after the dimension value. You can add text above and below the leader/dimension line using the upper dimension and lower dimension textboxes, respectively. There are two buttons on the left side of each text box. Choose the **Add Parentheses** button to enclose the dimension text in parentheses. Choose the **Center Dimension** button to place the dimension at the center of the dimension line. Choose the **Inspection Dimension** button to enclose the dimension text in an obround shape and this dimension will be checked during inspection. If you need to place the text at a distance from the dimension line, choose the **Offset Text** button and drag the dimension to the required location. Note that you can also choose all four buttons simultaneously for a specified dimension.

This rollout also provides buttons to modify text justification and add symbols such as diameter, degree, plus/minus, centerline, and so on to the dimension text. You can add more symbols by choosing the **More Symbols** button from the **Dimension Text** rollout. On choosing this button, the **Symbol Library** dialog box will be displayed, as shown in Figure 4-28.

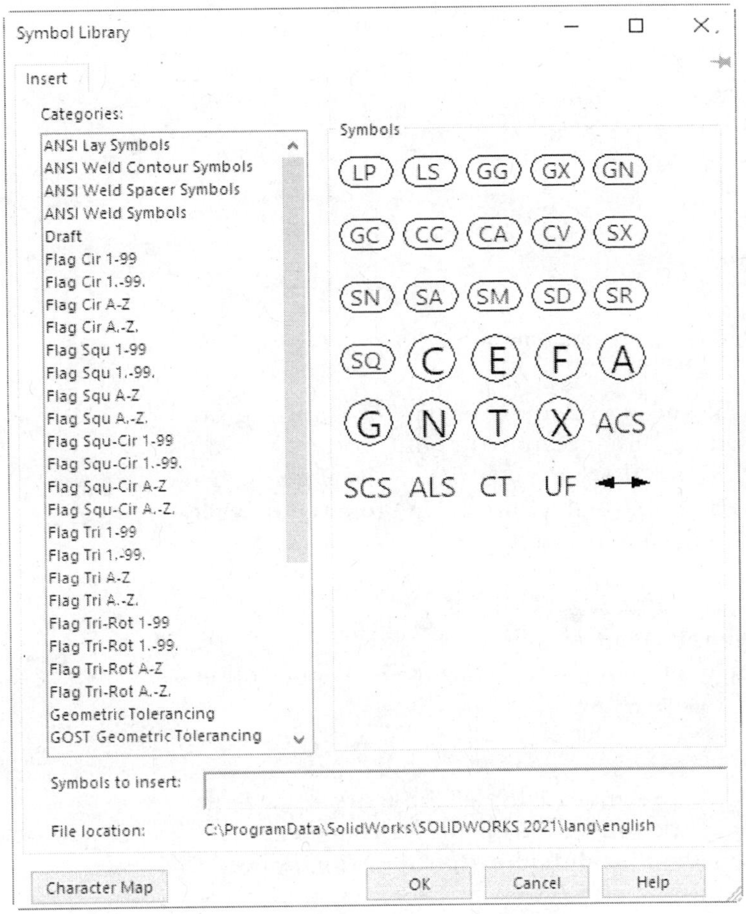

*Figure 4-28 The **Symbol Library** dialog box*

All uppercase Check Box

Select this check box to make the text uppercase.

Dual Dimension Rollout

You need to select the check box in the **Dual Dimension** rollout to enable the options in this rollout, refer to Figure 4-29. The options in this rollout are used to display the alternative dimension value. Note that the alternative dimension value is displayed in square brackets, as shown in Figure 4-30. Select the **Split** check box to split the primary dimension value and alternate dimension value using the leader/dimension line. The other options in this rollout are similar to those discussed in the earlier sections. Note that the alternative unit is set in the **Dual Dimension Length** cell in the **Document Property - Units** dialog box. To invoke this dialog box, choose **Tools > Options** from the SOLIDWORKS menus; the **System Options - General** dialog box will be displayed. Choose the **Document Properties** tab; the name of this dialog box will be changed to the **Document Properties - Drafting Standard** dialog box. In this dialog box, select the **Units** option from the area on the left to display the options for setting units. Note that on selecting the **Units** option, the name of this dialog box will be changed to the **Document Properties - Units** dialog box.

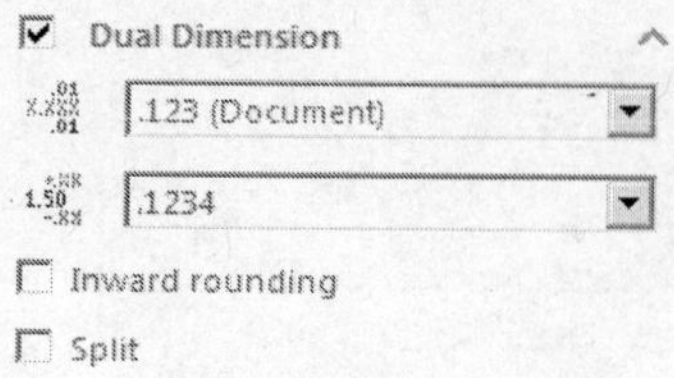

*Figure 4-29 The **Dual Dimension** rollout*

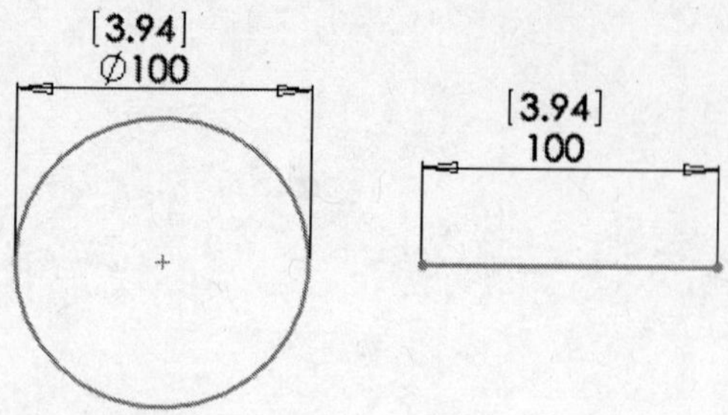

Figure 4-30 Entities with dual dimension

Sometimes, you may need to change the type of arrowheads or place the dimension at a distance from the entity because of space constraint. In SOLIDWORKS, these actions can be performed by choosing the **Leaders** tab in the **Dimension PropertyManager**. The rollouts in this tab are discussed next.

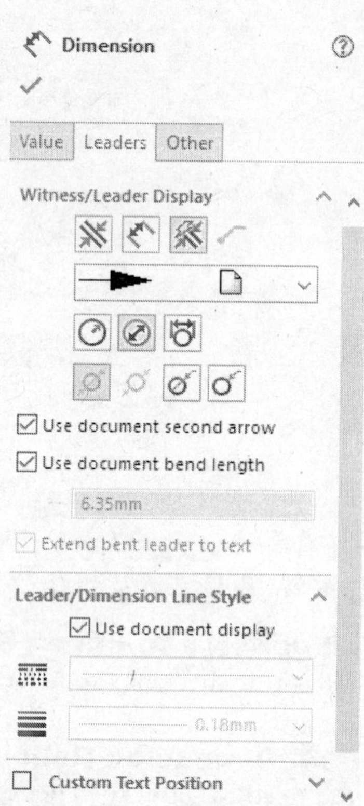

*Figure 4-31 The rollouts in the **Leaders** tab*

Witness/Leader Display Rollout

The **Witness/Leader Display** rollout is used to specify the arrowhead style in dimensions, refer to Figure 4-31. The options in this rollout are discussed next.

Outside

The **Outside** button is used to display the arrows outside the extension line. To do so, select a dimension from the drawing area and choose the **Outside** button from the **Witness/Leader Display** rollout.

Inside

The **Inside** button is used to display the arrows inside the extension line. To do so, select a dimension from the drawing area and choose the **Inside** button. You can also click on the control point displayed on the arrowhead to reverse its direction.

Smart

The **Smart** button is chosen by default and the arrows are displayed inside or outside the extension line, depending on the space available between the extension lines.

Directed Leader

This button is chosen to change the leader style of a dimension created on a surface by using the **DimXpert commands**.

Style

The **Style** drop-down list is used to select the style of the arrowhead. The default arrow style depends on the dimension standard selected. You can select any arrowhead style for a particular dimension or dimension style. To change the arrowhead style, select a dimension from the drawing area and then the arrowhead style from the **Style** drop-down list. Figure 4-32 shows dimensions with different styles of arrowheads.

Use document bend length

To change the length of a leader line after the bend, clear this check box and specify the length in the edit box below the check box. By default, the value specified in the **Document Properties - Dimensions** dialog box will be displayed in the edit box given below this check box. Figure 4-33 shows dimensions with leader lines.

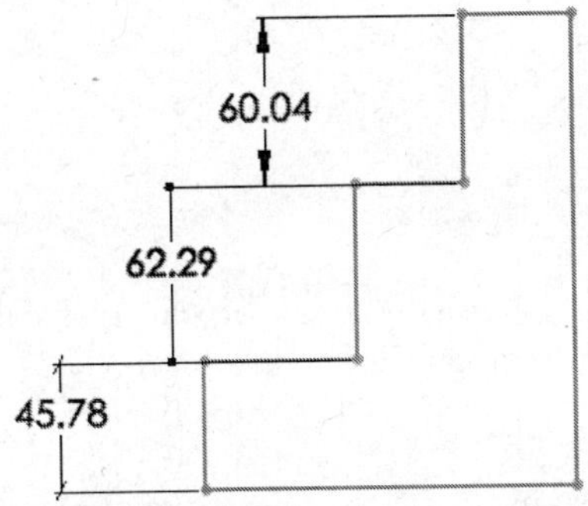

Figure 4-32 Dimensions with different styles of arrowheads

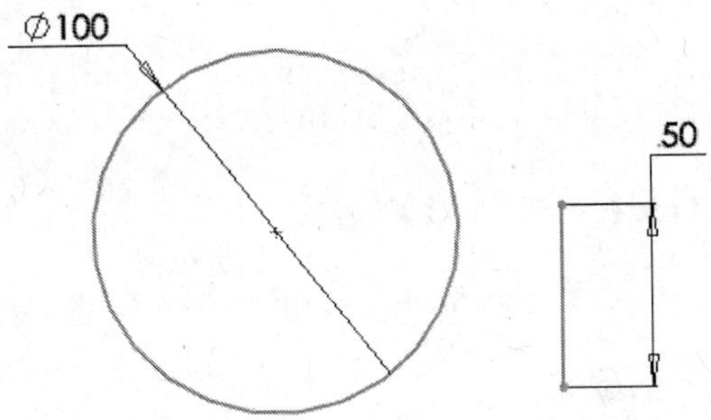

Figure 4-33 Dimensions with leader lines

Leader/Dimension Line Style Rollout

To enable the options in the **Leader/Dimension Line Style** rollout, you need to clear the **Use document display** check box in it. After clearing this check box, the **Leader Style** and **Leader Thickness** drop-down lists will be enabled. The **Leader Style** drop-down list is used to specify the leader style whereas the **Leader Thickness** drop-down list is used to specify the thickness of the leader. You can also select the **Custom Size** option from the **Leader Thickness** drop-down list and specify the thickness of the leader in the **Custom Thickness** edit box available below this drop-down list as per your requirement.

Extension Line Style Rollout

By default, the **Same as leader style** check box is not selected in this rollout. If you select this check box then the leader/dimension line style will be applied to the extension lines of dimension. If you clear the **Same as leader style** check box, then the **Use document display** check box will be activated. To activate the **Extension Line Style** and **Extension Line Thickness** drop-down lists below this check box, you need to clear the **Use document display** check box; otherwise default style will be applied to the extension lines.

Custom Text Position Rollout

The options in this rollout are used to specify the position of the text on a dimension line. Select the check box on the left in the **Custom Text Position** rollout to enable the options in this rollout. The options in this rollout are discussed next.

Solid Leader, Aligned Text

If you choose this button, the dimension line will not be broken. The dimension text will be placed parallely above or left to the dimension line.

Broken Leader, Horizontal Text

On choosing this button, the dimension line will be broken. The dimension text will be placed horizontally and at the center of the dimension line.

Broken Leader, Aligned Text

On choosing this button the dimension line will be broken. The dimension text will be centrally aligned with the dimension line.

In SOLIDWORKS, you can change the units and font of the dimension text by choosing the **Other** tab. The rollouts in this tab are discussed next.

Override Units Rollout

If you need to change the existing units of the dimension, select the check box in this rollout to expand it and select the units from the **Length Units** drop-down list.

Note

*On selecting the units such as **Microinches, Mils, Inches**, and so on, the **Decimal** and **Fractions** radio buttons will be displayed in the **Override Units** rollout. Select the **Decimal** radio button to display the dimensional value in the decimal format. Select the **Fractions** radio button to display the dimensional value in the fractional format. On selecting the **Fractions** radio button, you need to specify the denominator value and select the **Round to nearest fraction** check box to display the value as fractions.*

Text Fonts Rollout

The font style set in the **Document Properties - Annotations** dialog box will be the default font style. To change the font style, clear the **Use document font** check box and change the font style by choosing the **Font** button in the **Text Fonts** rollout.

Options Rollout

If you select the **Read only** check box in this rollout, the dimensional value cannot be changed. If you select the **Driven** check box, the value will be the driven value.

Horizontal/Vertical Dimensioning between Points

As mentioned earlier, you can add a horizontal or vertical dimension between two points. To add any of these dimensions, choose the required button from the **Dimensions/Relations** toolbar or the **Smart Dimension** flyout in the **Sketch CommandManager**. Select the first point and then the second point. Next, specify a point to place the dimension; the **Modify** dialog box will be displayed. Enter a new dimension value in this dialog box and press ENTER. Figure 4-34 shows the horizontal and vertical dimensions between two points. Figure 4-35 shows horizontal and vertical dimensions of an inclined line.

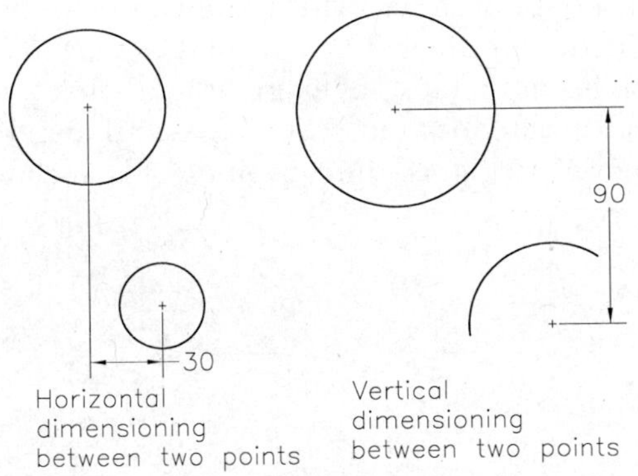

***Figure 4-34** Applying the horizontal and vertical dimensions between two points*

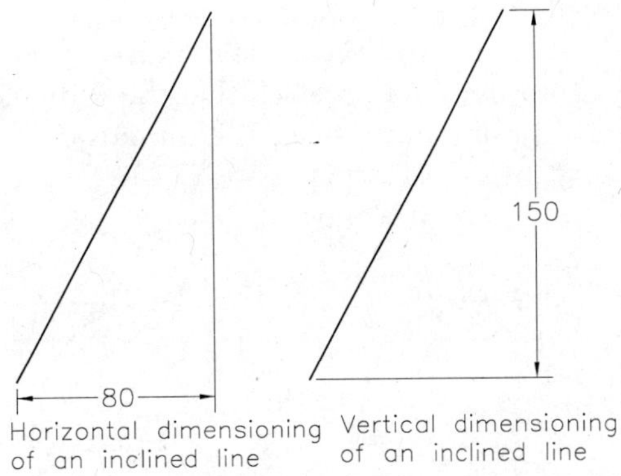

***Figure 4-35** Applying the horizontal and vertical dimensions of an inclined line*

You can also apply the horizontal or vertical (linear) dimensioning to a circle. However, these types of dimensions can only be applied to a circle by using the **Smart Dimension** tool. To apply this type of dimension to a circle, choose the **Smart Dimension** button from the **Sketch CommandManager** and select the circle; the dimension will be attached to the cursor. If you have to apply the vertical dimension, move the cursor to the right or left of the sketch. If you have to apply the horizontal dimension, move the cursor to the top or bottom of the sketch. Use the left mouse button to place the dimension and enter a new value in the **Modify** dialog box. The linear dimensioning of a circle is shown in Figure 4-36.

Aligned Dimensioning

CommandManager:	Sketch > Smart Dimension flyout > Smart Dimension
SOLIDWORKS menus:	Tools > Dimensions > Smart
Toolbar:	Sketch > Smart Dimension flyout > Smart Dimension

Aligned dimensions are used to dimension the lines that are at an angle with respect to the X-axis and the Y-axis. These types of dimensions are used to measure the actual length of the inclined lines. You can directly select an inclined line or two points to apply this dimension. The points that can be used to apply aligned dimensions include the endpoints of a line, arc, parabolic arc, or spline and the center points of arcs, circles, ellipse, or parabolic arc. To apply an aligned dimension to an inclined line, choose the **Smart Dimension** tool from the **Smart Dimension** flyout in the **Sketch CommandManager** and select the line. Next, move the cursor at an angle such that the dimension line is parallel to the inclined line. Place the dimension at an appropriate place and enter a new value in the **Modify** dialog box.

To apply an aligned dimension between two points, choose the **Smart Dimension** button, select the first point, and then select the second point; the dimension will be attached to the cursor. Next, move the cursor such that the dimension line is parallel to the imaginary line that joins the two points. Now, place the dimension at an appropriate location. Enter a new value in the **Modify** dialog box and press ENTER. Figure 4-37 shows the aligned dimensioning of an inclined line and between two points.

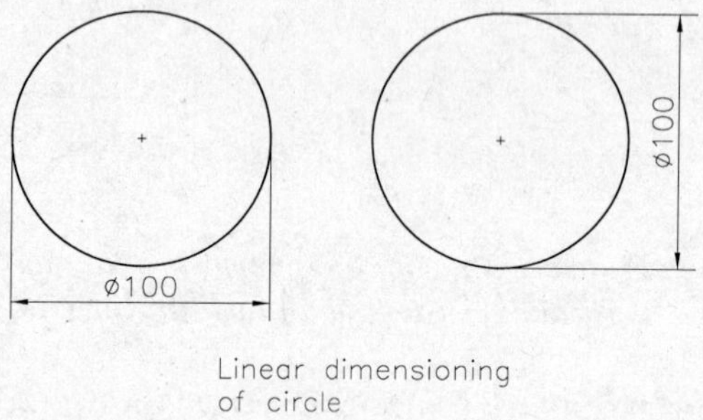

Figure 4-36 *Linear dimensioning of a circle*

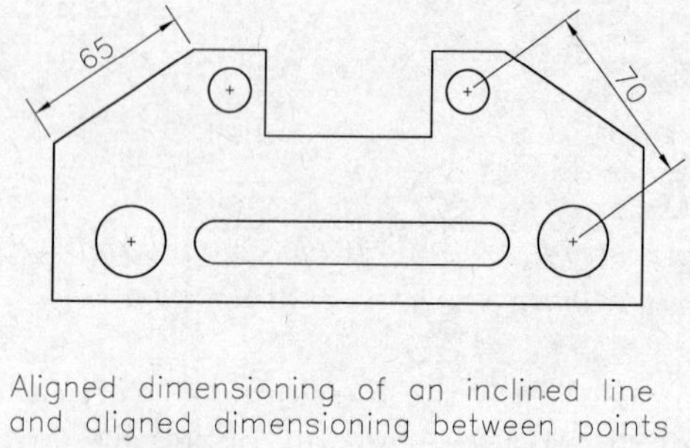

Figure 4-37 *Aligned dimensioning*

Angular Dimensioning

Angular dimensions are used to dimension angles. You can apply angular dimensions between two line segments or between three points of an arc. Various methods of applying angular dimensioning are discussed next.

Angular Dimensioning between Two Line Segments

CommandManager:	Sketch > Smart Dimension flyout > Smart Dimension
SOLIDWORKS menus:	Tools > Dimensions > Smart
Toolbar:	Sketch > Smart Dimension flyout > Smart Dimension

To apply angular dimensions between two lines, choose the **Smart Dimension** tool from the **Smart Dimension** flyout in the **Sketch CommandManager** and select the first line segment; a dimension will be attached to the cursor. Next, select the second line segment; an angular dimension will be attached to the cursor. Place the angular dimension and enter a new value of angular dimension in the **Modify** dialog box. Depending on the location of the placement of a dimension, the interior angle, exterior angle, major angle, or minor angle will be displayed. Therefore, you need to be very careful while placing the angular dimension. Figures 4-38 through 4-41 illustrate various angular dimensions depending on the placement of dimension.

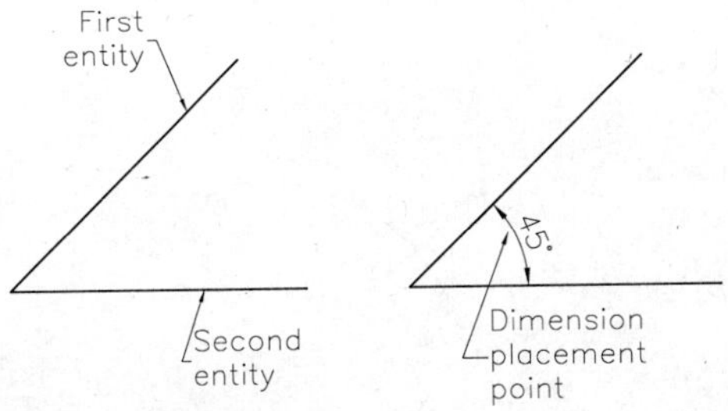

Figure 4-38 Angular dimension displayed according to the dimension placement point

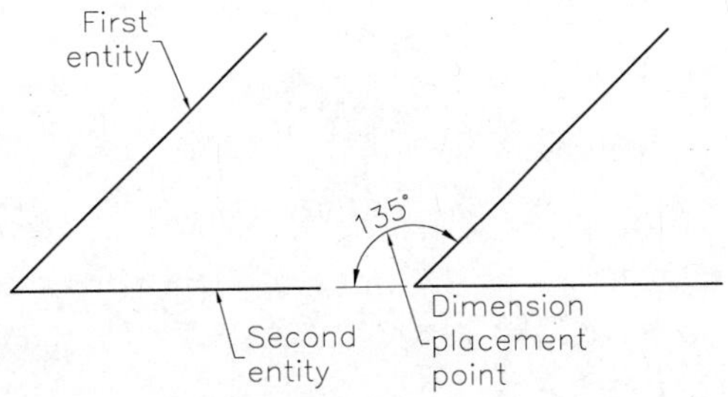

Figure 4-39 Angular dimension displayed according to the dimension placement point

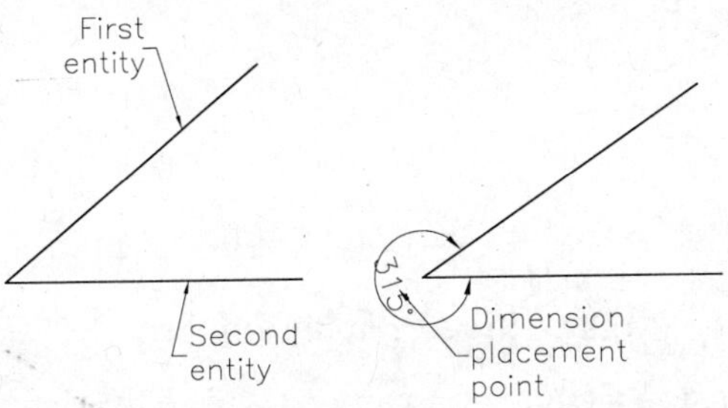

Figure 4-40 Angular dimension displayed according to the dimension placement point

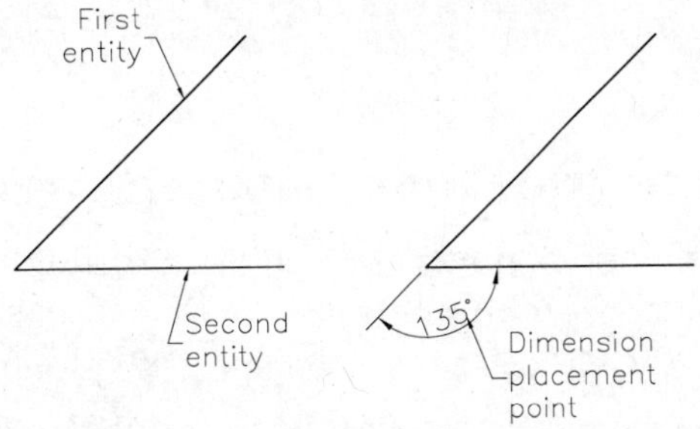

Figure 4-41 Angular dimension displayed according to the dimension placement point

Angular Dimensioning between Three Points

To add angular dimensions between three points, you need to be extremely careful while selecting points. To do so, choose the **Smart Dimension** button from the **Sketch CommandManager**. Next, select the first point by using the left mouse button. This is the angle vertex point. Select the second point; a linear dimension will be attached to the cursor. Next, select the third point; an angular dimension will be attached to the cursor. Place the angular dimension at an appropriate location and enter a new value of angular dimension in the **Modify** dialog box if you need to change the value. Figure 4-42 shows the angular dimensioning between three points.

Angular Dimensioning of an Arc

You can use angular dimensions to dimension an arc. To do so, select the two endpoints and the center point of the arc. Figure 4-43 shows the angular dimensioning of an arc. You can also dimension the circumference value of an arc. To do so, first select the arc and then select its two endpoints; the circumference dimension will be displayed.

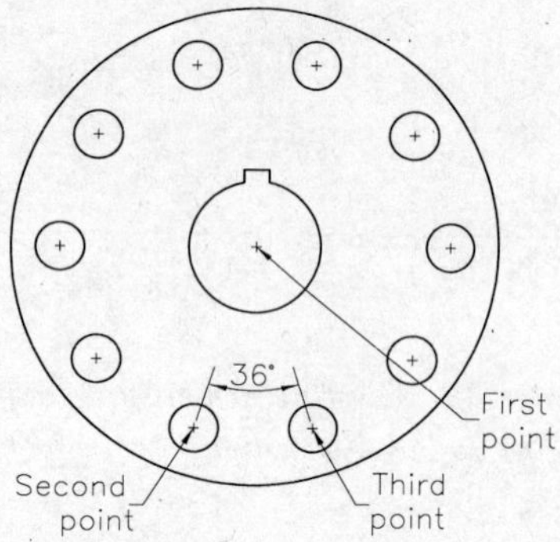

Figure 4-42 Angular dimension specified between three points

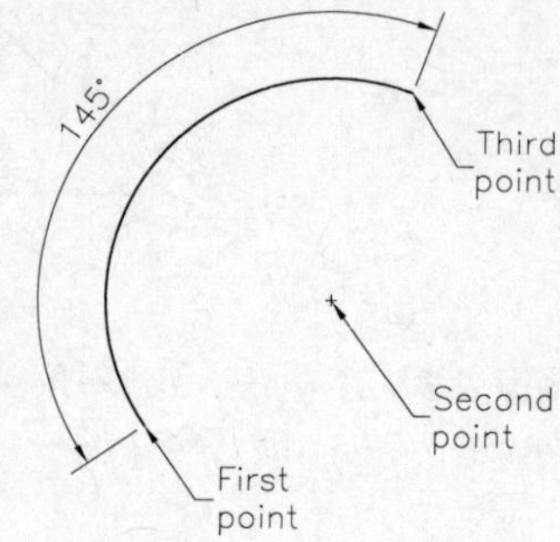

Figure 4-43 Angular dimension displayed on an arc

Diametric Dimensioning

CommandManager:	Sketch > Smart Dimension flyout > Smart Dimension
SOLIDWORKS menus:	Tools > Dimensions > Smart
Toolbar:	Sketch > Smart Dimension flyout > Smart Dimension

Diametric dimensions are applied to dimension a circle or an arc in terms of its diameter. To apply the diametric dimension, choose the **Smart Dimension** button from the **Smart Dimension** flyout in the **Sketch CommandManager**. Select a circle or an arc and place the dimension. In SOLIDWORKS, when you select a circle to dimension, the diametric dimension is applied to it by default. However, when you select an arc, the radial dimension is applied to it. To apply the diametric dimension to an arc, select the dimensional value; the **Dimension PropertyManager** will be displayed. Choose the **Diameter** button in the **Witness/Leader Display** rollout of the **Leaders** tab and choose **OK**. Alternatively, right-click on the dimension; a shortcut menu will be displayed. Choose **Display Options**; a cascading menu will be displayed. Next, choose the **Display As Diameter** option. Figure 4-44 shows a circle and an arc with the diameter dimension.

Radial Dimensioning

CommandManager:	Sketch > Smart Dimension flyout > Smart Dimension
SOLIDWORKS menus:	Tools > Dimensions > Smart
Toolbar:	Sketch > Sketch > Smart Dimension flyout > Smart Dimension

Radial dimensions are applied to dimension a circle or an arc in terms of its radius. As mentioned earlier, by default, the dimension applied to a circle is in the diameter form and the dimension applied to an arc is a radial dimension. To apply a radial dimension to a circle, select the dimensional value; the **Dimension PropertyManager** will be displayed. Choose the **Radius** button from the **Witness/Leader Display** rollout of the **Leaders** tab and choose **OK**. Alternatively, right-click on the dimension; a shortcut menu will be displayed. Choose **Display Options**; a cascading menu will be displayed. Next, choose the **Display As Radius** option. Figure 4-45 displays the radial dimensioning of a circle and an arc.

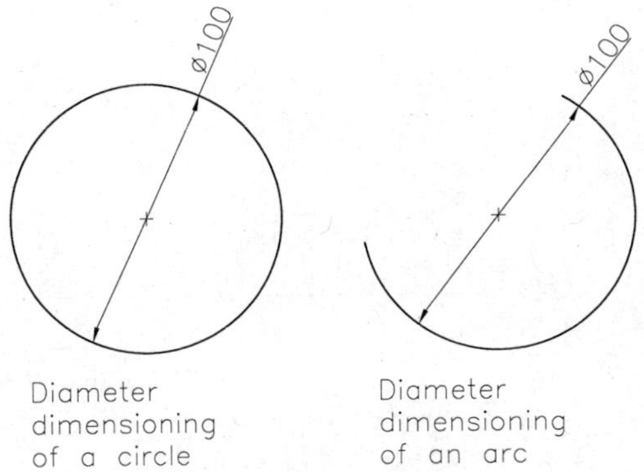

Figure 4-44 *Diametric dimensioning of a circle and an arc*

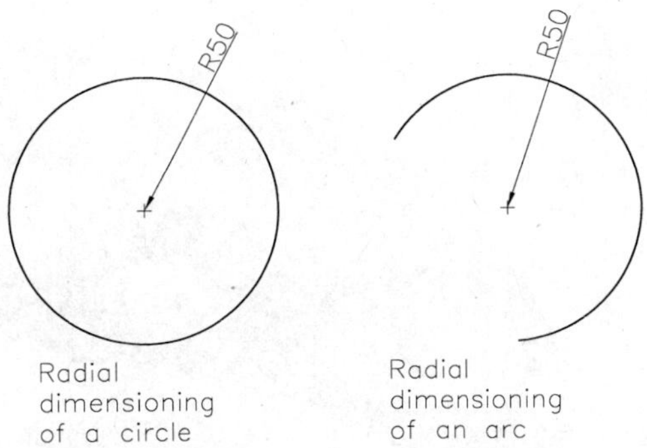

Figure 4-45 *Radial dimensioning of a circle and an arc*

Linear Diametric Dimensioning

CommandManager: Sketch > Smart Dimension flyout > Smart Dimension
SOLIDWORKS menus: Tools > Dimensions > Smart
Toolbar: Sketch > Smart Dimension flyout > Smart Dimension

Linear diametric dimensioning is used to dimension the sketch of a revolved component. An example of a revolved component is shown in Figure 4-46. The sketch for the revolved component is drawn using the sketching tools, as shown in Figure 4-47. If you dimension the sketch of the base feature of the given model using the linear dimensioning method, the same dimensions will be generated in the drawing views. This may be confusing because in the shop floor drawing, you need the diametric dimension of a revolved model. To overcome this problem, it is recommended that you create a linear diametric dimension, as shown in Figure 4-47. To create a linear diametric dimension, choose the **Smart Dimension** tool from the **Smart Dimension** flyout in the **Sketch CommandManager**. Select the entity to be dimensioned and then select the centerline around which the sketch will be revolved. Next, move the cursor to the other side of the centerline; a linear diametric dimension will be displayed. Place the dimension and enter a new value in the **Modify** dialog box.

In SOLIDWORKS, after applying the linear diametric dimensions between the selected entities, the centerline still remains selected. It indicates that there is no need to select the centerline again for applying linear diametric dimensions. You can directly select entities and apply linear diametric dimensions with respect to the selected centerline.

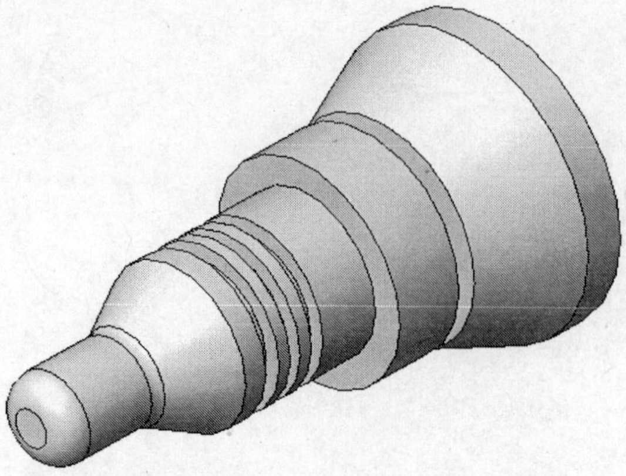

Figure 4-46 A revolved component

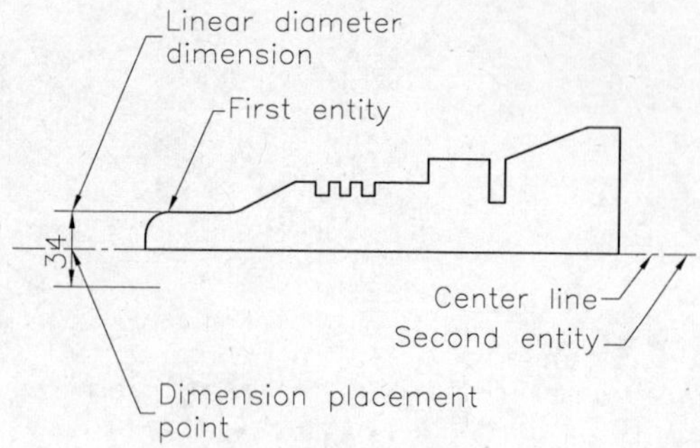

Figure 4-47 Sketch for the revolved feature with linear diametric dimensioning

Ordinate Dimensioning

Ordinate dimensions are used to dimension a sketch with respect to a specified datum. Depending on the requirement of the design, the datum can be an entity in the sketch or the origin. The ordinate dimensions are of two types, horizontal and vertical. The methods of creating these types of ordinate dimensions are discussed next.

Baseline Dimension

CommandManager:	Sketch > Smart Dimension flyout > Baseline Dimension
SOLIDWORKS menus:	Tools > Dimensions > Baseline Dimension
Toolbar:	Dimensions/Relations > Baseline Dimension

Baseline dimensions are used to dimension the distance between selected entity and specified datum. To apply baseline dimension, invoke the **Baseline Dimension** tool. Next select the entities between which you want to apply the baseline dimension; the baseline dimension will be applied. If you want to change the alignment of the dimensions, right-click and choose **Break Alignment** from the shortcut menu displayed.

Chain Dimension

CommandManager:	Sketch > Smart Dimension flyout> Chain Dimension
SOLIDWORKS menus:	Tools > Dimensions > Chain Dimension
Toolbar:	Dimensions/Relations > Chain Dimension

When you create chain dimensions, your first selection defines the starting edge of the chain. Subsequent selections are measured from one selection to the next. To apply the chain dimensions, invoke the **Chain Dimension** tool. Next, select an entity of the chain and then keep on selecting subsequent entities, the dimensions between the consequent entities will be displayed. If you want to change the alignment of the dimensions, right-click and choose **Break Alignment** from the shortcut menu displayed.

Horizontal Ordinate Dimensioning

CommandManager: Sketch > Smart Dimension flyout > Horizontal Ordinate Dimension
SOLIDWORKS menus: Tools > Dimensions > Horizontal Ordinate
Toolbar: Dimensions/Relations > Horizontal Ordinate Dimension

Horizontal ordinate dimensions are used to dimension the horizontal distances of the selected entities from the specified datum, refer to Figure 4-48. Note that when you apply the ordinate dimensions, the **Modify** dialog box will not be displayed to modify dimension values. After placing all ordinate dimensions, you need to exit the ordinate dimensioning tool and then double-click on the dimensions to modify their values.

To apply a horizontal ordinate dimension, choose the **Horizontal Ordinate Dimension** tool from the **Sketch CommandManager**; you will be prompted to select an edge or a vertex. Note that the first entity selected is taken as the datum entity from where the remaining entities will be measured. Select the first entity and place the dimension above or below it. You will notice that the dimension shows value 0. Refer to the dimension of the left vertical line in Figure 4-48.

After placing the first dimension, you will be prompted again to select an edge or a vertex. Select the edge that you need to dimension with respect to the first selected edge as datum. As soon as you select the edge, a horizontal dimension between the datum and the entity will be placed. Similarly, place other dimensions to apply multiple horizontal ordinate dimensions, refer to Figure 4-48.

Vertical Ordinate Dimensioning

CommandManager: Sketch > Smart Dimension flyout> Vertical Ordinate Dimension
SOLIDWORKS menus: Tools > Dimensions > Vertical Ordinate
Toolbar: Dimensions/Relations > Vertical Ordinate Dimension

Vertical ordinate dimensions are used to dimension the vertical distances of the selected entities from the specified datum, see Figure 4-49. To add a vertical ordinate dimension, choose the **Vertical Ordinate Dimension** tool from the **Sketch CommandManager**; you will be prompted to select an edge or a vertex. As mentioned earlier, the first entity that you select is taken as the datum entity from where the remaining entities are measured. Select the first entity and place the dimension on its right or left. You will notice that the dimension shows the value 0. Refer to the dimension of the bottom horizontal line in Figure 4-49. Next, select the edge that you need to dimension with respect to the first selected edge as datum. As soon as you select the edge, a vertical dimension will be placed between the datum and this entity. Similarly, place other dimensions to create multiple vertical ordinate dimensions, refer to Figure 4-49.

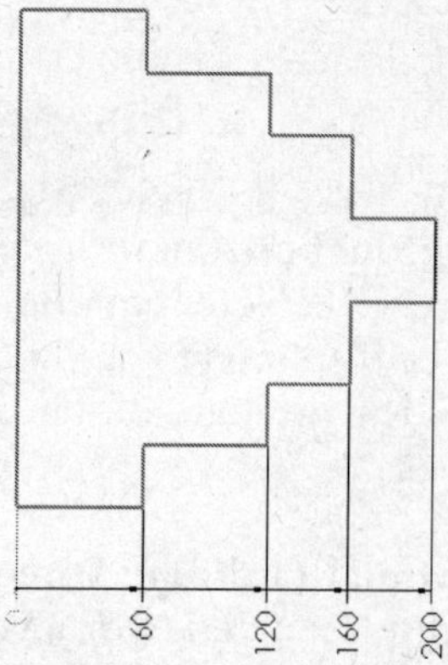

Figure 4-48 Horizontal ordinate dimensions

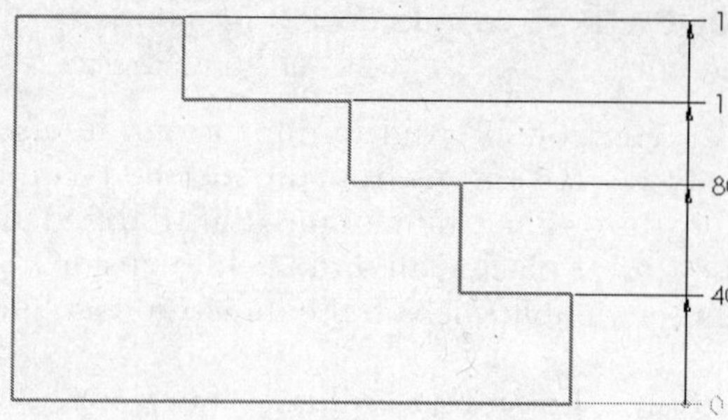

Figure 4-49 Vertical ordinate dimensions

Path Length Dimension

CommandManager: Sketch > Smart Dimension flyout> Path Length Dimension
SOLIDWORKS menus: Tools > Dimensions > Path Length
Toolbar: Dimensions/Relations > Path Length Dimension

The **Path Length Dimension** tool is used to dimension a chain of sketch entities which are joined end-to-end. You can set the dimension as a driving dimension, so that when you drag the entities, the shape of the path changes but its length remains same.

Auto Insert Dimension

The **Auto Insert Dimension** tool is used to add dimensions automatically to the selected sketch entity (or entities). The type of dimension added will depend upon the type of entity selected. To add a dimension select a sketch entity; a pop-up toolbar is displayed. Choose the **Auto Insert Dimension** button from the pop-up toolbar; the **Modify** dialog box is invoked. Enter desired value in the edit box and then choose the **OK** button. If you select a single line then the aligned dimension is added to the selected line, radius dimension to an arc, linear dimension to parallel lines, angular dimension to non-parallel lines, and so on.

CONCEPT OF A FULLY DEFINED SKETCH

It is important for you to understand the concept of fully defined sketches. While creating a model, you first need to draw the sketch of the base feature and then proceed further to create other features. After creating the sketches, you need to add required relations and dimensions to constrain the sketch with respect to the surroundings. After adding required relations and dimensions, the sketch may exist in any of the six states discussed next:

Fully Defined

A fully defined sketch is the one in which all entities of the sketch and their positions are completely defined by the relations or dimensions, or both. In a fully defined sketch, all degrees of freedom of a sketch are constrained. Therefore, the sketched entities cannot move or change their size and location unexpectedly. If a sketch is not fully defined, it can change its size or position at any time during the design because all degrees of freedom are not constrained. All entities in a fully defined sketch are displayed in black.

Overdefined

An overdefined sketch is the one in which some of the dimensions, relations, or both are conflicting or the dimensions or relations have exceeded the required number. An overdefined sketch is displayed in yellow. It is recommended not to proceed further to create the feature with an overdefined sketch. When a sketch is overdefined, you need to delete the extra and conflicting relations or dimensions. An overdefined sketch can be changed to fully defined or underdefined sketch by deleting the conflicting relations or dimensions. You will learn more about deleting the overdefining relations or dimensions later in this chapter.

Underdefined

An underdefined sketch is the one in which some of the dimensions or relations are not defined and the degree of freedom of the sketch is not fully constrained. In these types of sketches, the entities may move or change their size unexpectedly. As a result, the sketched entities of the underdefined sketch are displayed in blue. When you add relations and dimensions, the color of the entities in the sketch changes to black, indicating that the sketch is fully defined. If the entire sketch is displayed in black and only some of the entities are displayed in blue, it means that the entities in blue require some more dimensions or relations.

Tip

1. In SOLIDWORKS, it is not necessary to fully dimension or define the sketches before using them to create features of a model. However, it is recommended that you define the sketches fully before you proceed further to create the feature.

*2. If you always want to use fully defined sketches before proceeding further, you can do so by choosing **Tools > Options** from the SOLIDWORKS menus to display the **System Options - General** dialog box. Select the **Sketch** option from the area on the left. Next, select the **Use fully defined sketches** check box and choose **OK** from this dialog box.*

Note

This chapter onward, you will work with fully defined sketches. Therefore, follow the above mentioned procedure to use the fully defined sketches.

Dangling

In a dangling sketch, the dimensions or relations applied to an entity lose their reference because of deletion of the entity from which they were referenced. These entities are displayed in golden brown. You need to delete the dangling entities, dimensions, or relations that conflict.

No Solution Found

In the no solution found state, the sketch is not solved with the current constraints. Therefore, you need to delete the conflicting dimensions or relations and add other dimensions or relations. In such cases, the sketched entity, dimension, or relation will be displayed in yellow.

Invalid Solution Found

In the invalid solution found state, the sketch is solved but it will result in invalid geometry such as a zero length line, zero radius arc, or self-intersecting spline. The sketch entities in this state are displayed in yellow.

Sketch Dimension or Relation Status

In SOLIDWORKS, while applying the dimensions and relations to the sketches, sometimes you apply the ones that are not compatible with the geometry of the sketched entities or they make the dimensioned entity overdefined. In addition to the fully defined state, the sketch dimensions or relations may have any of the following states:

Dangling Satisfied Overdefining Not Solved Driven

Dangling

A dangling dimension or relation is the one that cannot be resolved because the entity to which it was referenced is deleted. The dangling dimension appears in golden brown.

Satisfied

A satisfied dimension is the one that is completely defined and is displayed in black.

Overdefining

An overdefining dimension or relation overdefines one or more entities in a sketch. This type of dimensioning appears in yellow.

Not Solved

The not solved dimension or relation cannot determine the position of the sketched entities. The not solved dimension appears in yellow.

Driven

In a sketch, the driven dimension's value is driven by other dimensions that solve the sketch. The driven dimension appears in gray.

Tip

*In the sketching environment, the status bar of the SOLIDWORKS window is divided into four areas. The **Sketch Definition** area of the status bar always displays the status, dimension, and relation applied to the sketch. If the sketch is underdefined, the status area will display **Under Defined**; if the sketch is overdefined, the message displayed in the status area will be **Over Defined**; and if the sketch is fully defined, the message displayed in the status area will be **Fully Defined**.*

DELETING OVERDEFINED DIMENSIONS

In SOLIDWORKS, when you add a dimension that overdefines a sketch, the color of the sketch and dimension changes and the **Make Dimension Driven?** message box is displayed, as shown in Figure 4-50. This message box informs you that adding this dimension will overdefine the sketch or the sketch will not be solved. You are also prompted to specify whether you want to add the dimension as a driven dimension. If you select the **Make this dimension driven** radio button and choose **OK**, then the selected dimension will become a driven dimension. The driven dimension is displayed in gray and cannot be modified. Its value depends on the value of the driver dimension. If you change the value of the driver dimension, the value of the driven dimension will be automatically changed.

If you select the **Leave this dimension driving** radio button and choose **OK**, then some of the entities and dimensions in the sketch will be displayed in yellow. Next, you need to delete the relation or dimension that is overdefining the sketch. In SOLIDWORKS, the **Over Defined** button is provided in the status bar, as shown in Figure 4-51.

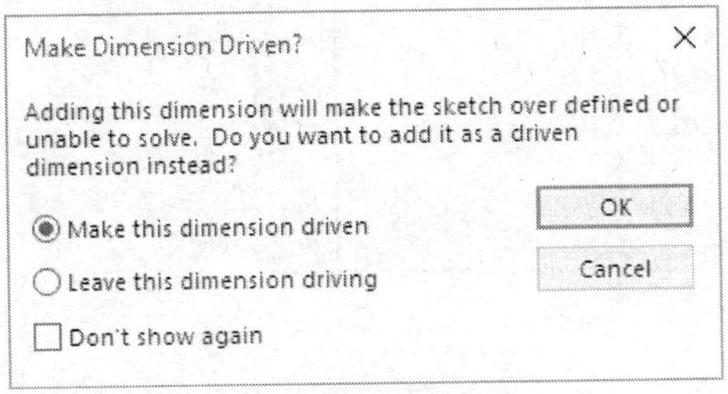

*Figure 4-50 The **Make Dimension Driven?** message box*

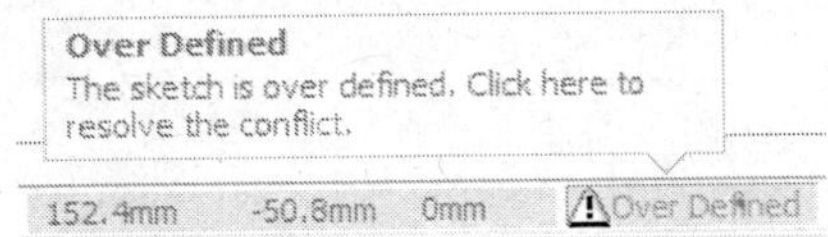

*Figure 4-51 The **Over Defined** button in the status bar*

To resolve the overdefining relations or dimensions, click on the **Over Defined** button displayed in the status bar; the **SketchXpert PropertyManager** will be displayed, as shown in Figure 4-52. In this PropertyManager, you can choose the **Diagnose** button in the **Message** rollout to automatically resolve possible errors or choose the **Manual Repair** button to resolve errors manually. On choosing the **Diagnose** button, various possible solutions will be listed in the **Results** rollout. Also, the conflicting relations will be listed in the **More Information/Options** rollout. Choose the arrows in the **Results** rollout to view various solutions. On choosing the arrows, the additional relation or dimension to be deleted will be displayed with a strike mark. Figure 4-53 shows sketch that is overdefined because of the additional vertical dimension 100. Figure 4-54 shows the additional vertical relation struck out. To remove a particular relation or

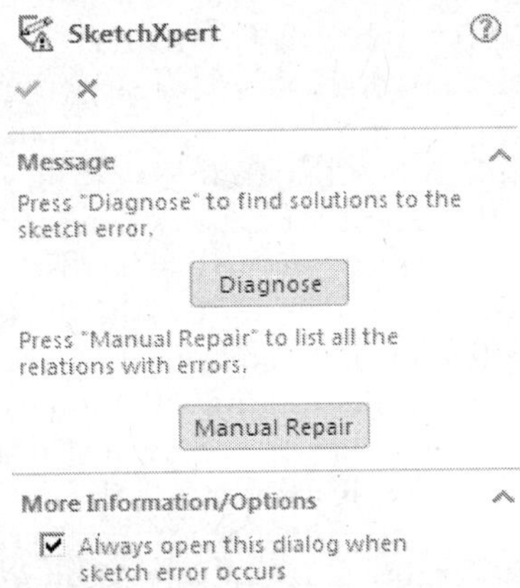

*Figure 4-52 Partial view of the **SketchXpert PropertyManager***

dimension, choose the **Accept** button in the **Results** rollout; the relation or dimension that has been struck out will be removed and the sketch will be fully defined. Also, a message informing that the sketch can now find a valid solution will be displayed in the **SketchXpert PropertyManager**. Choose the **OK** button.

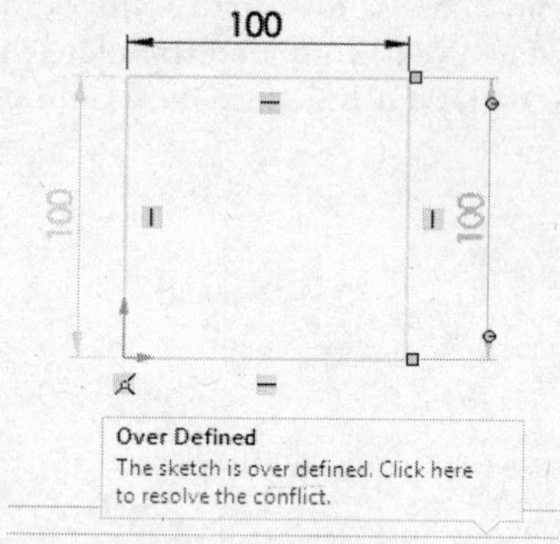

Figure 4-53 *An overdefined sketch*

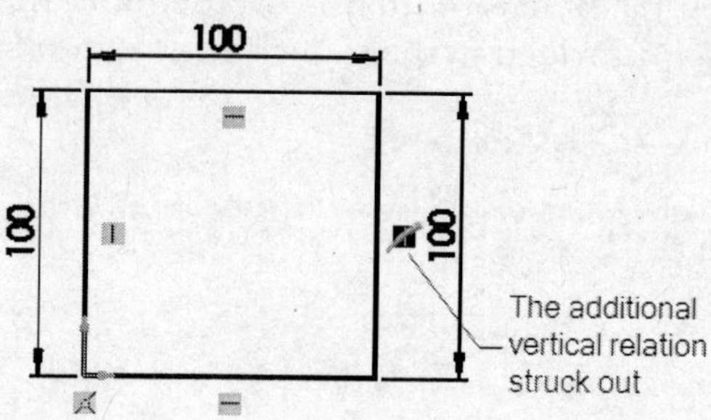

Figure 4-54 *The additional vertical relation struck out*

If you choose the **Manual Repair** button from the **Message** rollout, the relations or dimensions that are responsible for over defining the sketch will be displayed in the **Conflicting Relations/ Dimensions** rollout, as shown in Figure 4-55. Select any of the relations or dimensions responsible for overdefining the sketch and choose the **Delete** button. If the overdefining status of the sketch is removed, then a message stating that the sketch can now find a valid solution will be displayed in green background in the **Message** rollout. If the dimensions or relations deleted are not sufficient to find out a valid solution, the **Conflicting Relations/ Dimensions** rollout will still be displayed. Therefore, you need to delete few more dimensions or relations to remove the overdefining status from the sketch.

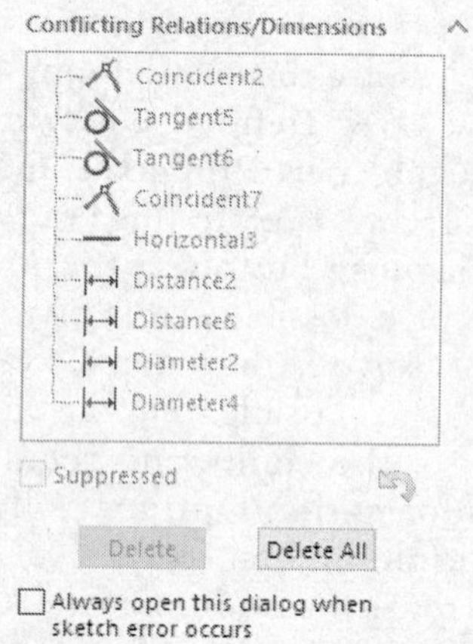

Figure 4-55 *The* ***Conflicting Relations/Dimensions*** *rollout*

You need to delete the relation or dimension displayed in red to make sure that the sketch is no longer overdefined. When the sketch is no longer overdefined, the **Message** rollout in the **SketchXpert PropertyManager** will inform you that **The sketch can now find a valid solution**. Choose **OK** from the **SketchXpert PropertyManager**; the sketch will be displayed in black or blue, depending on the current state of the sketch. Note that if you select the **Always open this dialog when sketch error occurs** check box, the **SketchXpert PropertyManager** will be displayed automatically when a sketch is overdefined.

You can also prevent the sketch from being overdefined by choosing the **Cancel** button from the **Make Dimension Driven?** message box. If you choose **Cancel** from the **Make Dimension Driven?** message box, the **SOLIDWORKS** information dialog box will be displayed with a message that **The sketch is no longer over defined.**

Displaying and Deleting Relations

CommandManager: Sketch > Display/Delete Relations flyout> Display/Delete Relations
SOLIDWORKS menus: Tools > Relations > Display/Delete
Toolbar: Sketch > Display/Delete Relations flyout > Display/Delete Relations

If a sketch is overdefined after adding dimensions and relations, you need to delete some of the overdefining, dangling, or unsolved relations or dimensions. You can view and delete the relations applied to a sketch by using the **Display/Delete Relations PropertyManager**. To invoke this PropertyManager, choose the **Display/Delete Relations** button from the **Sketch CommandManager**. Alternatively, right-click in the drawing area when the sketched entities are selected; a shortcut menu will be displayed. Choose the **Display/Delete Relations** option from it. On doing so, the **Display/Delete Relations PropertyManager** will be displayed, as shown in Figure 4-56. The rollouts in this PropertyManager are discussed next.

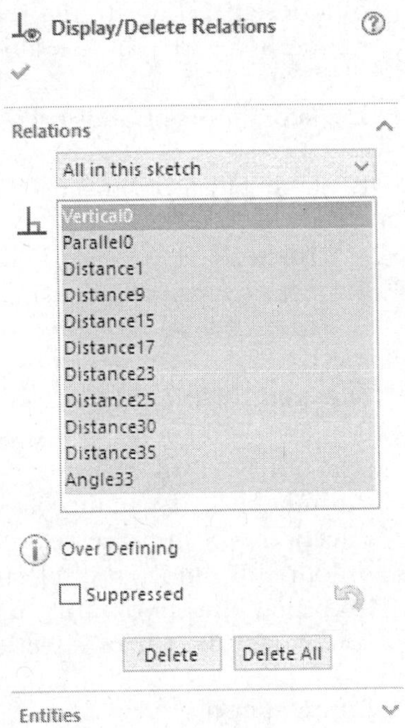

*Figure 4-56 The **Display/Delete Relations PropertyManager***

Relations Rollout

The **Relations** rollout is used to check, delete, and suppress the unwanted and conflicting relations. The status of the sketch or the selected entity is displayed below the **Relations** list in this rollout. The options in this rollout are discussed next.

Filter

The **Filter** drop-down list is used to select the filter to display the relations in this rollout. The options in the **Filter** drop-down list are discussed next.

All in this sketch: This option is used to display all relations applied to a sketch. The first relation displayed in the list will be selected by default and it will appear in a blue background. The status of the selected relations is displayed below the list box in the **Relations** rollout. The overdefined relations are highlighted in yellowish green. If you select a relation highlighted in yellowish green in the **Relations** rollout, the status of the selected relation will be displayed as **Over Defining**. The dangling relation is highlighted in brownish green. When you select the dangling relation, the status of the relation will be displayed as **Dangling** below the **Relations** list. Similarly, the not solved relation will be highlighted in yellow and the driven relation in gray.

Dangling: This option is used to display only the dangling relations applied to the sketch.

Overdefining/Not Solved: This option is used to display only the overdefining and not solved relations. The dangling relations are also not solved relations. Therefore, they will also be displayed in the list box.

External: This option is used to display the relations that have a reference with an entity outside the sketch. This entity can be an edge, vertex, or origin within the same model or it can be an edge, vertex, or origin of different models within an assembly.

Defined In Context: This option is used to display only the relations that are in the context of a design. They are the relations between the sketched entity in one part and an entity in another part. These relations are defined while working with the top-down assemblies.

Locked: This option is used to display only the locked relations.

Broken: This option is used to display only the broken relations.

Note

The Locked and Broken relations are applied while creating a part within the assembly environment. You will learn more about creating parts within an assembly in the later chapters.

Selected Entities. This option is used to display the relations of only the selected set of entities. When you select this option from the **Filter** drop-down list, the **Selected Entities** selection box will be displayed in the **Relations** rollout. When you select an entity to display the relations, the name of the selected entity will be displayed in the **Selected Entities** selection box and the relations applied to this entity will be displayed in the **Relations** rollout. To remove the selected entity from the selection set, select it and then right-click to display the shortcut menu. Next, choose the **Delete** option from the shortcut menu. If you choose the **Clear Selections** option, all entities will be removed from the selection set.

Suppressed

The **Suppressed** check box is selected to suppress the selected relation. When you suppress a relation, it will be displayed in gray in the list box. The status of the suppress relation will be displayed as **Satisfied** or **Driven** in the information area. If you suppress the overdefining dimensions, the **SOLIDWORKS** message box will be displayed with a message that **The sketch is no longer over defined**. Choose the **OK** button from this dialog box.

Delete

The **Delete** button is used to delete the relation selected in the **Relations** rollout.

Delete All

The **Delete All** button is used to delete all relations displayed in the **Relations** rollout.

Undo last relation change

The **Undo last relation change** button is used to undo the action performed by using the **Delete**, **Replace**, or **Suppressed** option earlier. The **Replace** option is discussed later in this chapter.

Entities Rollout

The **Entities** rollout is used to display the entities to which the selected relation is referred. This rollout is also used to display the status of the selected relation and the external reference, if any. By default, the **Entities** rollout is collapsed. You can expand this rollout by clicking on the down arrow displayed on the right of this rollout, refer to Figure 4-57. The options in this rollout are discussed next.

Entities used in the selected relation

The **Entities used in the selected relation** area is used to display the information about the entities used in the selected relation. This area provides the information about the name of the entity, its status, and the place it is defined. This area is divided into three columns, which are discussed next.

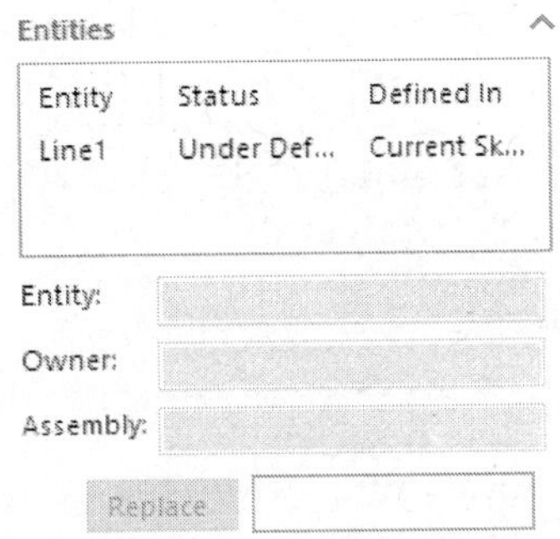

Figure 4-57 The ***Entities*** *rollout*

Entity: The **Entity** column is used to display the entity or entities to which the selected relation is applied.

Status: The **Status** column is used to display the status of the selected entity. The status can be **Fully Defined**, **Dangling**, **Over Defined**, or **Not Solved**.

Defined In: The **Defined In** column is used to display the position of the entity. On the basis of placement, the entity can be defined as **Current Sketch**, **Same Model**, or **External Model** in the **Defined In** column.

The **Current Sketch** option is displayed in the **Defined In** column when the entity is positioned in the same sketch. The **Same Model** option is displayed in the **Defined In** column when the entity to be referenced is placed in the same model but is not a part of the current sketch. The entity can be an edge, vertex, or origin of the same model.

Tip

1. If an entity is dimensioned, you cannot change its dimensions by dragging its keypoints. To change the dimensions of a dimensioned entity by dragging, choose ***Tools > Sketch Settings*** *from the SOLIDWORKS menus and select the* ***Override Dims on Drag/Move*** *option.*

2. By default, the ***Automatic Solve*** *option is selected from the* ***Tools > Sketch Settings*** *menu in the SOLIDWORKS menus. This option helps you solve the relations and dimensions automatically when you drag or modify a sketched entity. If you clear this option and drag an entity, a message box will be displayed informing you that the sketch cannot be dragged because the* ***Automatic Solve*** *mode is off. It will further inform you that to drag the sketch, please turn the* ***Automatic Solve*** *mode on. If you modify the dimension value using the* ***Modify*** *dialog box, the dimension will not be updated automatically, and you have to update the new dimension manually. To update and solve the dimension, you need to choose the* ***Rebuild*** *button from the Menu Bar or press CTRL+B on the keyboard.*

Entity

The **Entity** display box is used to display the name of the entity and the name of the part in which the selected entity is placed. This entity is selected in the **Entity** column of the **Name of External Entities used in the selected relation** area. The selected entity is also highlighted in the drawing area.

Owner
The **Owner** display box is used to display the name of the model in which the entity is placed when the **External Model** option is displayed in the **Defined In** column.

Assembly
The **Assembly** display box is used to display the path of the assembly in which the entity is placed when the **External Model** option is displayed in the **Defined In** column.

Replace
The **Replace** button is used to replace the selected entity from the **Entity** column with some other entity from the drawing area. When you select the entity from the drawing area, the entity will be displayed in the **Entity to replace the one selected above** display box available on the right of the **Replace** button. Choose the **Replace** button to replace the entity. If the sketch is overdefined, a warning message will be displayed. Sometimes after replacing the entity, the status of the entity is changed to not solved or overdefining. In such cases, you need to undo the last operation.

> **Tip**
> *By default, the relations applied to the sketched entities are displayed when you draw them or apply a relation to them. Therefore, sometimes the sketch looks cluttered as all the relations concerned with the sketch are displayed. To turn off the display of these relations, choose* ***Hide/Show Items > View Sketch Relations*** *from the* ***View (Heads-Up)*** *toolbar. As it is a toggle button, you can choose this button again to turn on the display of these relations.*

OPENING AN EXISTING FILE

Menu Bar:	Open
SOLIDWORKS menus:	File > Open

You can open an existing SOLIDWORKS part, assembly, or drawing document by using the **Open** dialog box. You can also use this dialog box to import files from other applications saved in some standard file formats. To invoke this dialog box, choose the **Open** button from the Menu Bar, or press the CTRL+O keys. Figure 4-58 shows the **Open** dialog box. The options in this dialog box are discussed next.

Address Bar
The **Address bar** drop-down list is used to specify the drive or directory in which the file is saved. The location of the file and the folder that you browse is displayed in this drop-down list.

File name
The name of the selected file is displayed in the **File name** edit box. You can also enter the name of the file to open in this edit box.

Type Drop-Down List
The **Type** drop-down list is used to specify the type of file to open. You can use this drop-down list to select a particular type of file such as the part file, assembly file, drawing file, all SOLIDWORKS

files, and so on. You can also define the standard file format in this drop-down list to import the files saved in those file formats.

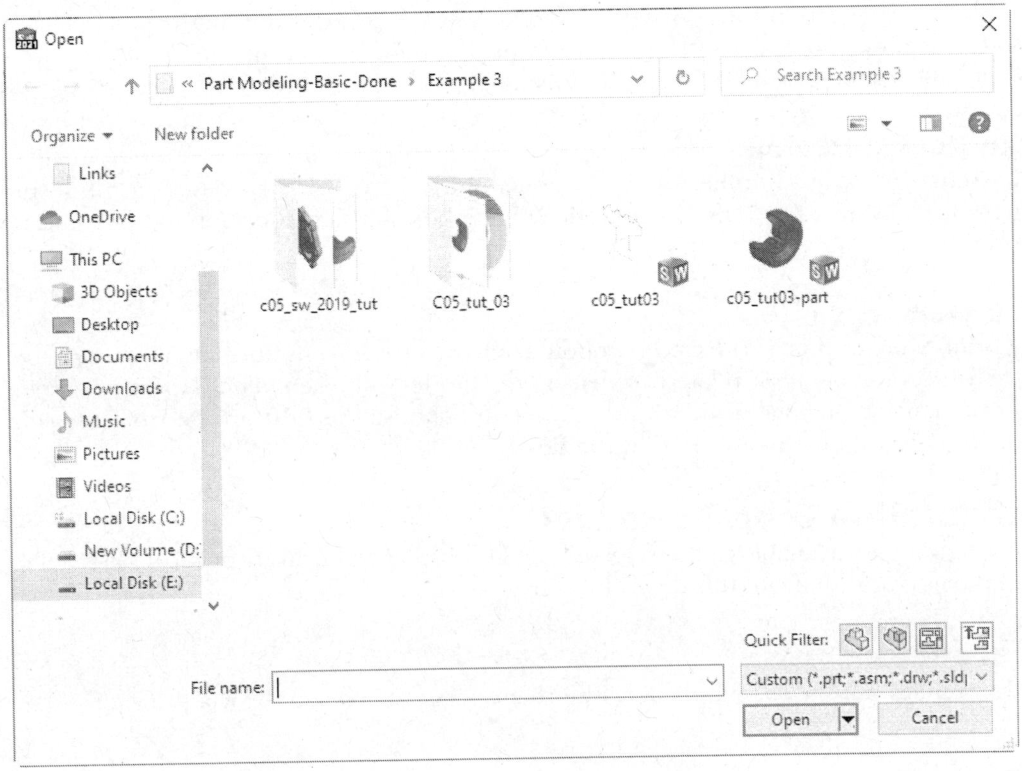

*Figure 4-58 The **Open** dialog box*

Open Read-only

The **Open Read-only** option is selected to open a document as a read-only file. This option is available in the flyout that will be displayed on choosing the down arrow on the right of the **Open** button. If you modify the design in a read-only file, the changes will be saved in a new file, and the original file will not be modified. This option also allows other users to access the document while it is open on your computer.

Mode

The options available in the **Mode** area are used to open various parts and assemblies in different modes. These options are discussed next.

Resolved

The **Resolved** option is used to resolve all the unsolved components.

Lightweight

If a large assembly is opened by selecting this option, the assembly will rebuild faster as less data is evaluated when an operation is performed.

Large Assembly Mode

If an assembly contains number of components more than that is specified in the respective spinner of the **System Options - Assemblies** dialog box, select this option to open the assembly as large assembly. On opening the assembly in this mode, some of the display options are automatically disabled to increase the performance of the assembly.

Large Design Review

If an assembly contains number of components more than that is specified in the respective spinner of the **System Options - Assemblies** dialog box, select this option to open and review the assembly in large assembly mode.

Quick view

The **Quick view** option is selected to open a part in a view-only format. When you open a view-only file, only the tools related to viewing the model will be enabled. However, if you want to edit the part, right-click in the drawing area and choose the **Edit** option from the shortcut menu; all tools will be available to edit the design.

Configuration Drop-Down List

The configurations available in the selected file are displayed in this drop-down list. Select the required configuration from this drop-down list.

References

The **References** button is used to check the references of an assembly or a drawing.

Quick Filter

There are four different buttons in this area that are used for filtering the file types that are frequently used in SOLIDWORKS. These buttons are discussed next.

Filter Parts

The **Filter Parts** button is used to filter the part files that are in the *.sldprt* or *.prt* file format. On choosing this button, the **Type** drop-down list will be set to **part (.prt;*.sldprt)** file format. The files which are in this format will be displayed in the **Document Library** area of the **Open** dialog box.

Filter Assemblies

The **Filter Assemblies** button is used to filter the part files that are in the *.sldasm* or *.asm* file format. On choosing this button, the **Type** drop-down list will be set to **Assembly (.asm;*.sldasm)** file format. The files which are in this format will be displayed in the **Document Library** area of the **Open** dialog box.

Filter Drawings

The **Filter Drawings** button is used to filter the part files that are in the *.slddrw* or *.drw* file format. On choosing this button, the **Type** drop-down list will be set to **Drawing (.drw;*.slddrw)** file format. The files which are in this format will be displayed in the **Document Library** area of the **Open** dialog box.

You can toggle all these three buttons at a time and can filter part, assembly and drawing files. On doing so, the **Type** drop-down list will be customized such that you can have access to all the three types mentioned above.

Filter Top-Level Assemblies

The **Filter Top-Level Assemblies** button is used to filter only custom top-level assemblies files that are in the *.sldasm* file format. On choosing this button, the **Type** drop-down list will be set to the **Custom Top-Level** assemblies and the assemblies that are created in the top-level mode are displayed in the **Document Library** area of the **Open** dialog box.

Display States Drop-Down List

The options in this drop-down list are used to select the required display state of the selected component. If you select the **Do not load hidden components** check box, the components that are in the hidden state will not be displayed. This check box will be available if the entity to be opened is an assembly file. You will learn about display states in the later chapters.

TUTORIALS

Tutorial 1

In this tutorial, you will draw the sketch of the model shown in Figure 4-59. You will draw the sketch using the mirror line and then add the required relations and dimensions to it. The sketch of the model is shown in Figure 4-60. The solid model is given for reference only. **(Expected time: 30 min)**

Figure 4-59 Solid Model for Tutorial 1

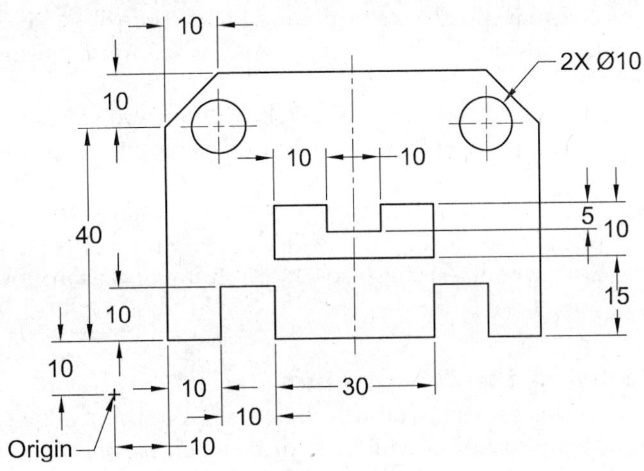

Figure 4-60 Sketch of the model

The following steps are required to complete this tutorial:

a. Start SOLIDWORKS and then start a new part document.
b. Create a mirror line using the **Centerline** and **Dynamic Mirror** tools.
c. Draw the sketch of the model on one side of the mirror line so that it is automatically drawn on the other side.
d. Add relations to the sketch.
e. Add dimensions to the sketch and fully define the sketch.
f. Save the sketch and then close the document.

Starting SOLIDWORKS and a New Part Document

1. Start SOLIDWORKS by double-clicking on the shortcut icon of SOLIDWORKS 2021 available on the desktop of your computer, the SOLIDWORKS 2021 window along with the **WELCOME- SOLIDWORKS** dialog box will be displayed.

2. Choose the **New** button from the Menu Bar; the **New SOLIDWORKS Document** dialog box with the **Part** button chosen is displayed.

3. Choose the **OK** button from the **New SOLIDWORKS Document** dialog box; a new SOLIDWORKS part document is started.

4. Choose the **Sketch** button from the **Sketch CommandManager** and then select the **Front Plane** to invoke the sketching environment.

   In the previous chapters, you used the grid and snap settings to create sketches. From this chapter, you are recommended not to use those settings. By doing so, you can draw sketches at arbitrary locations and then apply dimensions and relations to them.

5. If the grid is displayed, invoke the **System Options - Relations/Snaps** dialog box and then clear the **Grid** check box from the **Sketch snaps** area to hide the grid.

6. Set the unit for measuring linear dimensions to millimeters and the unit for angular dimensions to degree using the **Document Properties - Units** dialog box and choose **OK**. However, if you have selected millimeters as unit while installing SOLIDWORKS, you can skip this step.

Drawing the Mirror Line

In this tutorial, you will draw the sketch of the given model with the help of the **Dynamic Mirror** tool. So, when you draw an entity on one side of the centerline, the same entity will be drawn automatically on its other side. Also, the symmetric relation will be applied to the entities on both sides of the centerline. Therefore, if you modify an entity on one side of the centerline, the same modification will be reflected in the mirrored entity and vice-versa. However, to follow these steps, first you need to draw the centerline to proceed to the next steps.

The origin of the sketching environment is placed at the center of the drawing area and you need to create the sketch in the first quadrant. Therefore, it is recommended that you modify the drawing area such that the area in the first quadrant is increased. This can be done by using the **Pan** tool.

1. Press the CTRL key and the middle mouse button and then drag the cursor toward the bottom left corner of the drawing area.

2. Choose the **Centerline** button from the **Line** flyout in the **Sketch CommandManager**; the **Insert Line PropertyManager** is displayed. 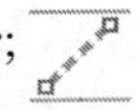

3. Move the line cursor to a location whose coordinates are close to 45 mm, 70 mm, and 0 mm.

4. Click to specify the start point of the centerline and move the line cursor vertically downward to draw a line of length close to 80 mm. As soon as you specify the endpoint of the centerline, a rubber-band line is attached to the line cursor.

5. Right-click and choose the **Select** option from the the shortcut menu to exit the **Centerline** tool.

6. Press the F key; the sketch is zoomed and fits the screen.

7. Select the centerline and choose **Tools > Sketch Tools > Dynamic Mirror** from the SOLIDWORKS menus to convert the centerline into a mirror line.

Drawing the Sketch

You will draw the sketch on the right of the mirror line and the same sketch will automatically be drawn on the other side of the mirror line.

1. Choose the **Line** button from the **Sketch CommandManager**; the arrow cursor is replaced by the line cursor.

2. Move the line cursor close to the lower side of the centerline; the cursor snaps to the mirror line and a coincident symbol is displayed below the cursor.

3. Click to specify the start point of the line at this point and move the cursor horizontally toward the right. Specify the endpoint of the line when its length shows a value close to 15. As soon as you click the left mouse button to specify the endpoint of the line, a line of the same length is drawn automatically on the other side of the mirror line. Figure 4-61 shows the mirrored entity created automatically on the other side of the mirror line. The display of relations in this figure can be turned off by choosing the **View Sketch Relations** button in the **Hide/Show Items** flyout in the **View (Heads-Up)** toolbar.

   Note that the mirrored entity that is automatically created on the left of the mirror line is merged with the line drawn on the right. Therefore, the entire line becomes a single entity. The mirror image of the line will merge with the line that you draw only if one of the endpoints of the line is coincident with the mirror line.

4. Move the cursor vertically upward. Specify the endpoint of the line when the length of the line displays a value close to 10. Figure 4-62 shows the sketch after drawing vertical lines.

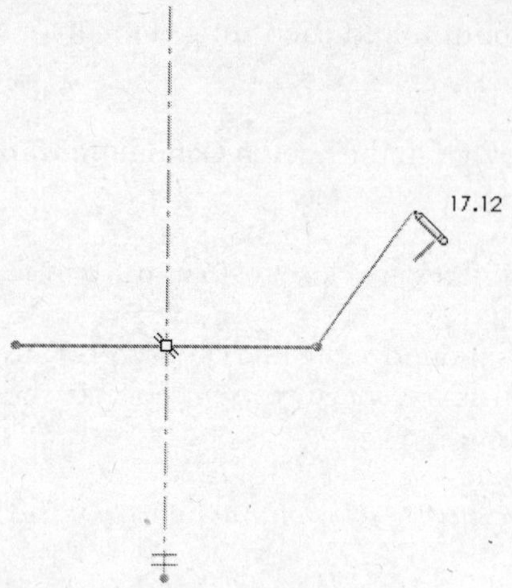

Figure 4-61 *Sketching using automatic mirroring*

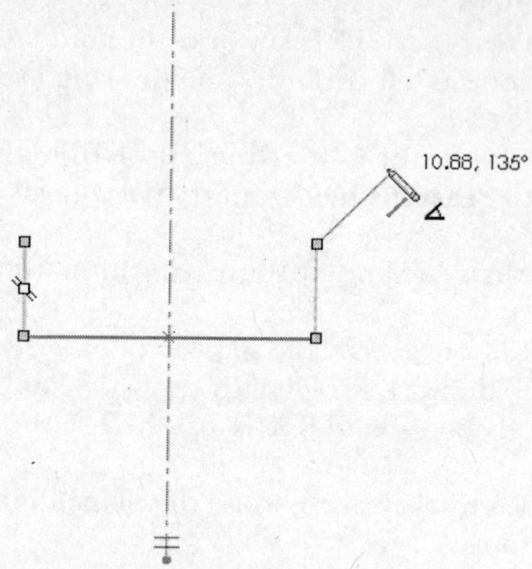

Figure 4-62 *Sketch after drawing vertical lines*

5. Move the line cursor horizontally toward right. Specify the endpoint of the line when the length of the line displays a value close to 10.

6. Move the line cursor vertically downward. Specify the endpoint when the length of the line displays a value close to 10.

7. Move the line cursor horizontally toward right. Specify the endpoint when the length of the line displays a value close to 10.

8. Move the line cursor vertically upward. Specify the endpoint when the length of the line displays a value close to 40.

9. Move the line cursor at an angle close to 135-degree from the horizontal reference and to a length close to 14, specify the endpoint of the line. Figure 4-63 shows the sketch after drawing the inclined line.

10. Move the line cursor horizontally toward left. Specify the endpoint when the cursor snaps to the mirror line and the mirror line is highlighted. Double-click anywhere in the drawing area to end the creation of line. The sketch after completing the outer profile is shown in Figure 4-64.

Next, you will draw the sketch of the inner cavity. To draw the sketch of the inner cavity, you will start with the lower horizontal line.

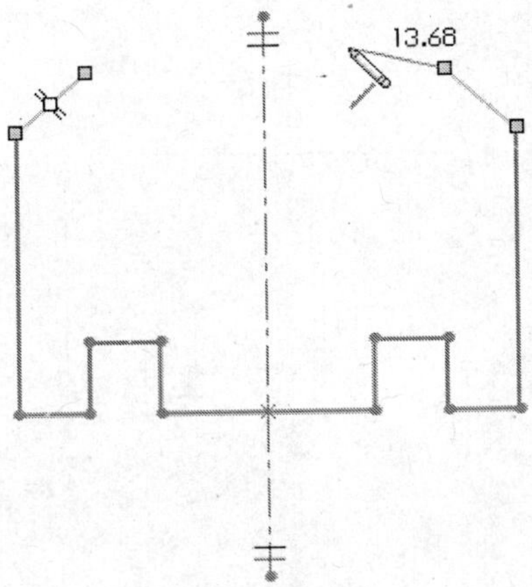

Figure 4-63 Sketch after drawing the inclined line

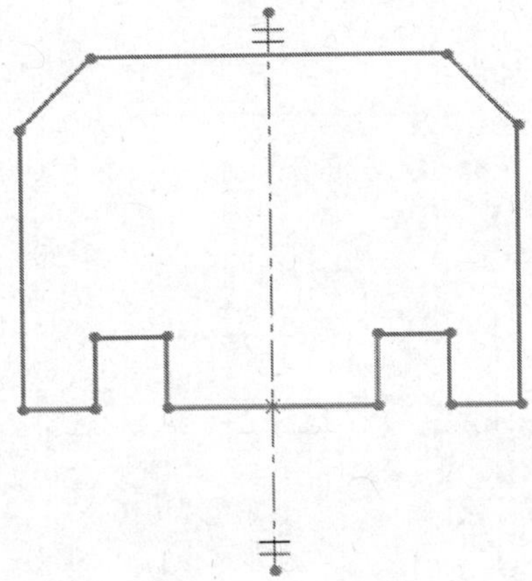

Figure 4-64 Sketch after completing the outer profile of the sketch

11. Specify the start point of the line in the mirror line, refer to Figure 4-65 and move the cursor horizontally toward the right. Specify the endpoint when the length of the line displays a value close to 15.

12. Move the line cursor vertically upward. Specify the endpoint when the length of the line displays a value close to 10.

13. Move the line cursor horizontally toward the left. Specify the endpoint when the length of the line displays a value close to 10.

14. Move the line cursor vertically downward. Specify the endpoint when the length of the line displays a value close to 5.

15. Move the line cursor horizontally toward the left. Specify the endpoint when the line cursor snaps to the mirror line.

16. Right-click to display the shortcut menu and then choose the **Select** option from it to exit the **Line** tool. The sketch after completing the inner cavity is shown in Figure 4-65.

17. Choose the **Circle** button from the **Sketch CommandManager** to invoke the **Circle** tool.

18. Move the circle cursor to the point where the inferencing lines originating from the endpoints of the right inclined line intersects.

19. Specify the center of the circle at this point and move the circle cursor toward the left to define the radius of the circle. Press the left mouse button when the radius of the circle displays a value close to 5 and exit the **Circle** tool.

The circle is automatically mirrored on the other side of the mirror line. The sketch after drawing the circle is shown in Figure 4-66.

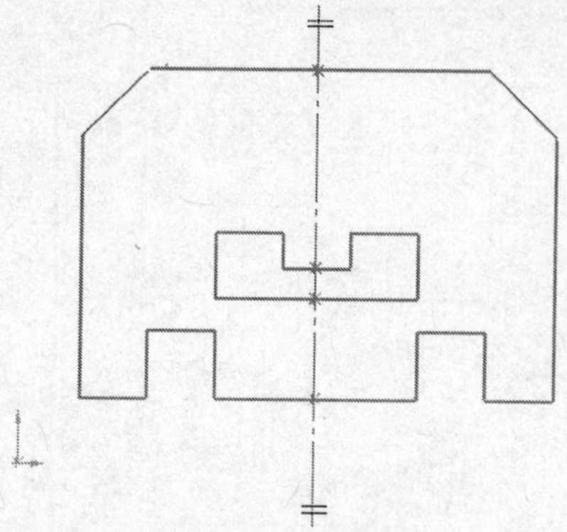

Figure 4-65 Sketch after drawing the inner cavity

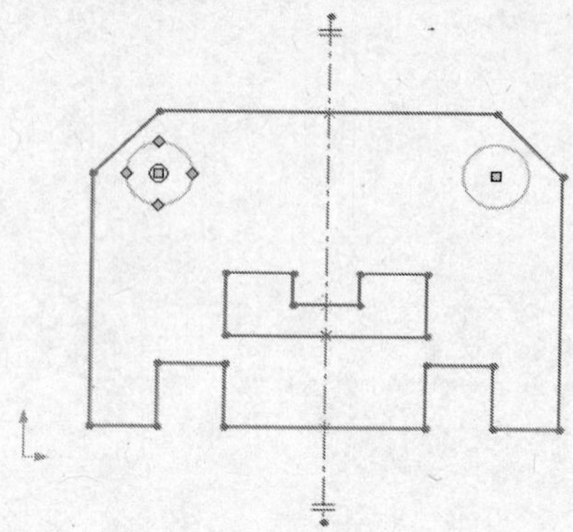

Figure 4-66 Sketch after drawing the circle

20. Exit the **Dynamic Mirror** tool by choosing **Tools > Sketch Tools > Dynamic Mirror** from the SOLIDWORKS menus.

Adding Relations to the Sketch

After drawing the sketch, you need to add relations to it by using the **Add Relations PropertyManager**. Relations are applied to a sketch to constrain its degree of freedom, reduce the number of dimensions in the sketch, and capture the design intent of the sketch.

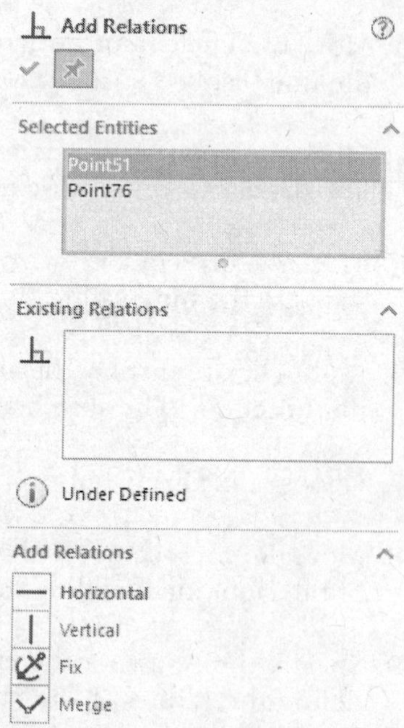

*Figure 4-67 The **Add Relations PropertyManager***

1. As the circles are still selected, press the ESC key to remove the circles created previously from the selection set.

2. Choose the **Add Relation** button from the **Display/Delete Relations** flyout in the **Sketch CommandManager**; the **Add Relations PropertyManager** is displayed. Also, the confirmation corner is displayed at the upper right corner of the drawing area.

3. Select the center point of the circle on the right and then the lower endpoint of the right inclined line. The names of the selected entities are displayed in the **Selected Entities** rollout of the **Add Relations PropertyManager**.

   The relations that can be applied to the two selected entities are displayed in the **Add Relations** rollout of the **Add Relations PropertyManager**, as shown in Figure 4-67. The **Horizontal** option is highlighted suggesting that the horizontal relation is the most appropriate relation for the selected entities.

4. Choose the **Horizontal** button from the **Add Relations** rollout to apply the **Horizontal** relation to the selected entities.

5. Move the cursor to the drawing area and right-click to display the shortcut menu. Choose the **Clear Selections** option from the shortcut menu to remove the selected entities from the selection set.

6. Select the center point of the circle on the right and then the upper endpoint of the right inclined line; the relations that can be applied to the selected entities are displayed and the **Vertical** button is highlighted in the **Add Relations** rollout.

7. Choose the **Vertical** button from the **Add Relations PropertyManager**. Right-click in the drawing area and choose the **Clear Selections** option.

8. Select the entities, as shown in Figure 4-68. Choose the **Equal** button from the **Add Relations** rollout in the **Add Relations PropertyManager**.

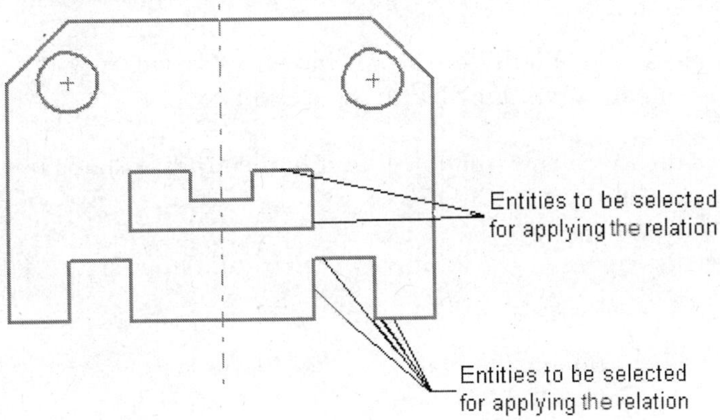

Figure 4-68 *Entities to be selected to apply the Equal relation*

9. Choose the **OK** button from the **Add Relations PropertyManager** or choose **OK** from the confirmation corner to close the PropertyManager. Click anywhere in the drawing area to clear the selected entities.

Applying Dimensions to the Sketch

Next, you will apply dimensions to the sketch and fully define it. As mentioned earlier, the sketched entities are shown in blue indicating that the sketch is underdefined. After required dimensions are applied, the sketched entities will turn black indicating that the sketch is fully defined now.

1. Choose **Options** from the Menu Bar; the **System Options - General** dialog box is displayed. Select the **Input dimension value** check box, if cleared, and then choose **OK** from the **System Options - General** dialog box.

This check box is selected to invoke the **Modify** dialog box. This dialog box is used to enter a new dimension value and modify the sketch as you place the dimension.

2. Choose the **Smart Dimension** tool from the **Smart Dimension** flyout in the **Sketch CommandManager**; the select cursor is replaced by the dimension cursor. You can also right-click in the drawing area and choose the **Smart Dimension** option from the shortcut menu displayed or use the Mouse Gesture to invoke this **Smart Dimension** tool.

3. Move the cursor to the origin and click when an orange circle is displayed.

4. Select the outer left vertical line (Figure 4-69, line 1); a horizontal dimension is attached to the cursor.

5. Place it at a suitable location; the **Modify** dialog box is displayed. Enter **10** in this dialog box and press ENTER.

   Next, you need to apply a vertical dimension between the origin and the left horizontal line.

6. Select the origin and the left most horizontal line (line 2 in Figure 4-69) with the dimension cursor; a vertical dimension is attached to the cursor.

7. Place the vertical dimension at a suitable location; the **Modify** dialog box is displayed. Type **10** in this dialog box and press ENTER.

8. Move the dimension cursor to the lower right horizontal line (Figure 4-69, line 3); the line is highlighted.

9. Select the line; a linear dimension is attached to the cursor.

10. Move the cursor downward and click to place the dimension below the line, refer to Figure 4-70. As you place the dimension, the **Modify** dialog box is displayed.

11. Enter **10** as the value of dimension in this dialog box and press ENTER; the dimension is placed and the length of the line is modified to 10.

12. Select the lower-middle horizontal line (Figure 4-69, line 4) by using the dimension cursor; a dimension is attached to the cursor.

13. Move the cursor downward and click to place the dimension. Enter **30** in the **Modify** dialog box and press ENTER.

14. Select the left vertical line (Figure 4-69, line 1) by using the dimension cursor; a dimension is attached to the cursor.

15. Move the cursor to the left and then click to place the dimension. Enter **40** in the **Modify** dialog box and press ENTER.

16. Select the right inclined line; a dimension is attached to the cursor. Move the cursor vertically upward to apply the horizontal dimension to the selected line. Click to place the dimension at an appropriate place, see Figure 4-70.

17. Enter **10** in the **Modify** dialog box and press ENTER.

18. Again, select the right inclined line; a dimension is attached to the cursor. Move the cursor horizontally toward the right to apply the vertical dimension for the selected line. Click to place the dimension at an appropriate place, see Figure 4-70.

19. Enter **10** in the **Modify** dialog box and press ENTER.

20. Move the cursor to the left circle and when the circle is highlighted, select it; a diametric dimension is attached to the cursor. Next, move the cursor outside the sketch.

21. Place the diametric dimension. Enter **10** in the **Modify** dialog box and press ENTER.

22. Select the lower horizontal line (Figure 4-69, line 5) of the inner cavity sketch; a linear dimension is attached to the cursor. Select the lower right horizontal line (Figure 4-69, line 3) of the outer loop.

    A vertical dimension between the lower horizontal line of the inner cavity sketch and the lower right horizontal line of the outer sketch is attached to the cursor.

23. Move the cursor horizontally toward the right and place the dimension. Enter **15** in the **Modify** dialog box and press ENTER.

24. Select the inner right vertical line (Figure 4-69, line 6) of the inner cavity sketch and place the dimension outside the sketch. Enter **5** in the **Modify** dialog box and press ENTER.

25. Select the upper-middle horizontal line (Figure 4-69, line 11) of the inner cavity sketch and place the dimension above the slot. Enter **10** in the **Modify** dialog box and press ENTER.

Now, all entities are displayed in black. This indicates that the sketch is fully defined. If the sketch is not fully defined, you may need to apply collinear relation between lines 7 and 8, lines 9 and 10, lines 2, 3, and 4. The fully defined sketch after applying all required relations and dimensions is shown in Figure 4-70.

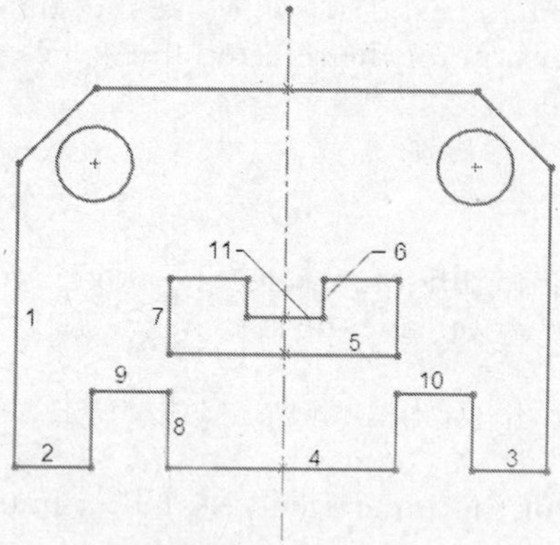

Figure 4-69 The lines to be dimensioned

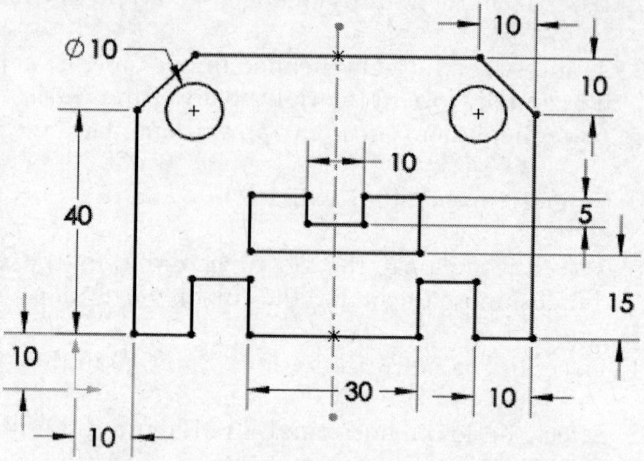

Figure 4-70 Fully defined sketch after applying all the required relations and dimensions

Saving the Sketch

1. Choose the **Save** button from the Menu Bar to invoke the **Save As** dialog box. Browse to the *\Documents\SOLIDWORKS* folder. Choose the **New Folder** button from the **Save As** dialog box. Enter **c04** as the name of the folder and press ENTER.

2. Enter **c04_tut01** as the name of the document in the **File name** edit box and choose the **Save** button. The document will be saved at the location *\Documents\SOLIDWORKS\c04*.

3. Close the document by choosing **File > Close** from the SOLIDWORKS menus.

Tutorial 2

In this tutorial, you will draw the sketch of the revolved model shown in Figure 4-71. The sketch of the feature is shown in Figure 4-72. The solid model is given for your reference only.

(Expected time: 30 min)

The following steps are required to complete this tutorial:

a. Start a new part document and then invoke the sketching environment.
b. Draw a centerline to add the linear diametric dimensions to the sketch of the piston.
c. Create the sketch by using various sketching tools.

d. Offset the required lines by using the **Offset Entities** tool.
e. Draw arcs and trim unwanted entities.
f. Add relations to the sketch.
g. Add dimensions to the sketch to fully define it.

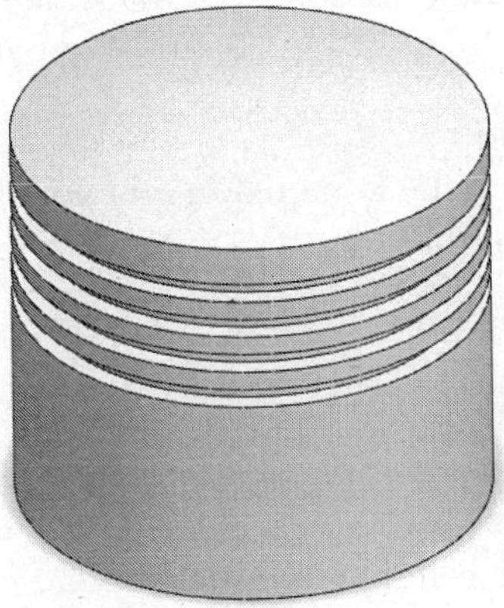

Figure 4-71 *Solid model of the piston*

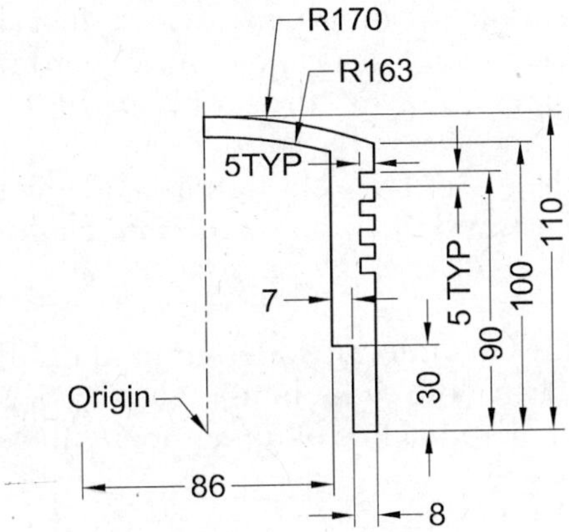

Figure 4-72 *The sketch of the base feature*

Starting a New Part Document

1. Choose the **New** button from the Menu Bar; the **New SOLIDWORKS Document** dialog box with the **Part** button chosen is invoked.

2. Choose the **OK** button; a new SOLIDWORKS part document is started.

3. Choose the **Sketch** button from the **Sketch CommandManager** and select the **Front Plane** to invoke the sketching environment.

4. Invoke the **System Options - General** dialog box and set units for this tutorial.

Drawing the Sketch

To draw the sketch of the revolved model, you need to draw a centerline around which the sketch of the base feature will be revolved. In this tutorial, you will add the dimensions for the entities while drawing the sketch.

1. Invoke the **System Options - General** dialog box and select the **Sketch** option from the left side of the dialog box. The **System Options - Sketch** dialog box will be invoked. In this dialog box, select the **Enable on screen numeric input on entity creation** and **Create dimension only when the value is entered** check boxes and choose the **OK** button to save the settings.

2. Choose the **Centerline** tool from the **Sketch CommandManager**; the **Insert Line PropertyManager** will be displayed. 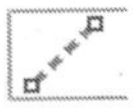

3. Draw a vertical centerline of length 120 starting from the origin. Next, press the ESC key.

   Now, you need to draw the sketch of the piston.

4. Right-click in the drawing area, and then choose the **Line** option from the shortcut menu. Move the cursor to a location whose coordinates are close to 58 mm, 0 mm, and 0 mm. Click at this point to specify the start point of the line.

5. Move the cursor vertically upward and enter **100** mm in the **Dimension** edit box displayed. Right-click and then choose the **End chain** option from the shortcut menu, refer to Line 1 in Figure 4-73.

6. Move the cursor to the lower endpoint of the line drawn earlier. Specify the start point of the line when the endpoint is highlighted. Move the cursor horizontally toward the left and draw a horizontal line of dimension 8 mm, refer to Line 2 in Figure 4-73.

7. Move the line cursor vertically upward and draw a vertical line of dimension 30 mm, refer to Line 3 in Figure 4-73.

8. Move the cursor horizontally toward the left and draw a horizontal line of dimension 7 mm. The sketch after drawing the horizontal line is shown in Figure 4-73.

9. Move the line cursor vertically upward and draw a vertical line of dimension 70 mm.

10. Right-click and then choose the **Select** option from the shortcut menu. Next, choose **3 Point Arc** tool from the **Arc** flyout in the **Sketch CommandManager**. Move the cursor near the upper endpoint of the right vertical line.

11. Specify the first point of the arc when the endpoint is highlighted. Move the cursor horizontally toward left; a reference arc is attached to the cursor. Specify the second point of the arc when the coordinates are close to -58 mm, 100 mm, and 0 mm, refer to Figure 4-74.

12. Move the cursor vertically upward and enter **170** in the **Dimension** edit box, refer to Figure 4-74.

13. Invoke the **Line** tool. Move the line cursor near the outer vertical line on the right and specify the start point of the line such that the start point is on the vertical line and its X and Y coordinates are close to 58, 90.

14. Move the cursor horizontally toward the left and then draw a line of dimension **5** mm. Right-click and then choose the **Select** option to end the creation of the line. The sketch after drawing the horizontal line is shown in Figure 4-74.

15. Choose **Zoom To Fit** from the **View (Heads-Up)** toolbar to fit the sketch into the drawing area.

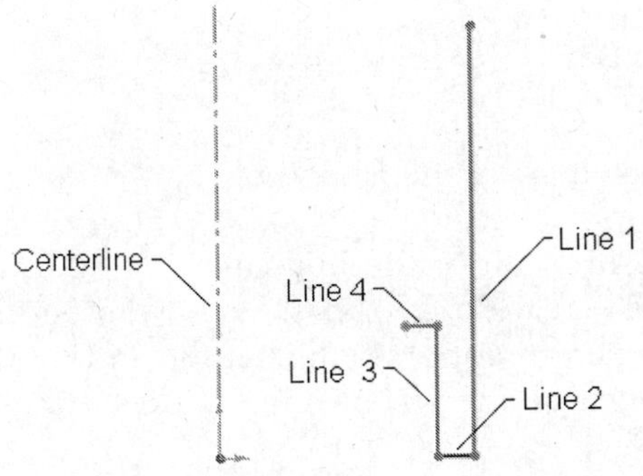

*Figure 4-73 Sketch drawn using the **Line** tool*

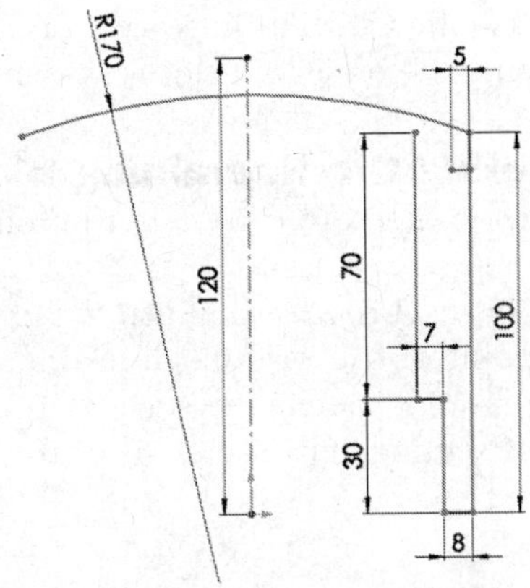

Figure 4-74 Sketch after drawing arc and line

Offsetting Lines

You need to offset the entities created earlier using the **Offset Entities** tool.

1. Select the line of 5 mm length created earlier.

2. Choose the **Offset Entities** button from the **Sketch CommandManager**; the **Offset Entities PropertyManager** is displayed. Also, the confirmation corner is displayed at the upper right corner of the drawing area.

3. Choose the **Keep Visible** button in the **Offset Entities PropertyManager** to pin the PropertyManager.

4. Set the value in the **Offset Distance** spinner to **5**. Next, select the **Reverse** check box to offset the entity in the reverse direction; preview of the entity to be offset is modified in the drawing area.

5. Choose the **OK** button from the **Offset Entities PropertyManager**.

   You will notice that an entity is created at an offset distance of 5 mm from the original entity. Also, a dimension of value 5 mm is applied between the newly created entity and the original entity with value 5. This dimension is the offset distance between the two entities.

6. Select the newly created entity. Move the cursor vertically downward; preview of the entity and the direction of the offset creation are also displayed. Press the left mouse button to offset the selected line.

   Repeat this procedure to offset the entities until you have got eight entities including the original entity.

7. Set the value in the **Offset Distance** spinner to **7** and clear the **Select chain** check box if it is selected. Next, select the upper arc; preview of the offset arc is displayed in the drawing area.

8. Choose the **OK** button twice from the **Offset Entities PropertyManager**. The sketch after creating the offset entities is shown in Figure 4-75.

Completing the Remaining Sketch

Next, you need to complete the remaining sketch using the **Line** tool.

1. Invoke the **Line** tool by using the Mouse Gesture. Move the line cursor close to the left endpoint of the original line that was used to create offset lines. When the endpoint is highlighted, specify the start point. Specify the endpoint of the line at the endpoint of the last offset line. The sketch after drawing the vertical line is shown in Figure 4-76.

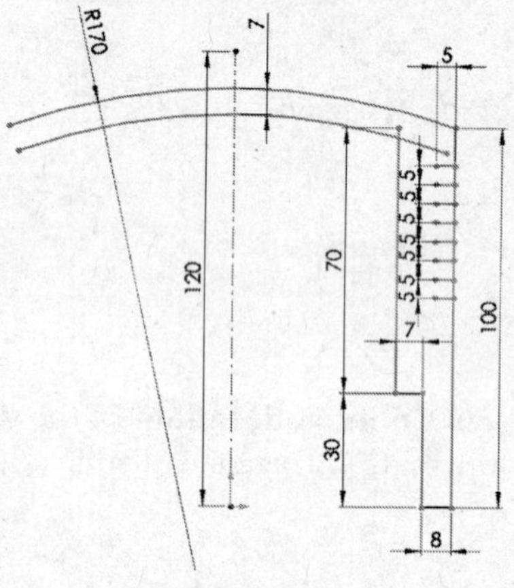

Figure 4-75 Sketch after offsetting the entities

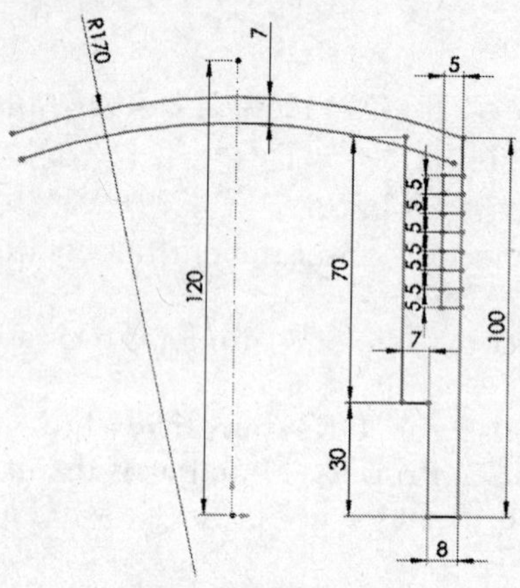

Figure 4-76 Sketch after drawing the vertical line

2. Move the cursor to the intersection point of the upper arc and the centerline. When the cursor snaps to the intersection, draw a vertical line that snaps to the intersection point of the lower arc and the centerline. Next, press the ESC key to exit the tool.

Trimming Unwanted Entities

Next, you need to trim the unwanted entities by using the **Trim Entities** tool.

1. Choose the **Trim Entities** tool from the **Sketch CommandManager**.

2. Choose the **Trim to closest** button from the **Trim PropertyManager** and trim the unwanted entities by using the left mouse button. While trimming the arc or line, if you get a message stating that the trimming will delete the relations, choose **Yes** to trim the entities. The sketch after trimming the unwanted entities is shown in Figure 4-77.

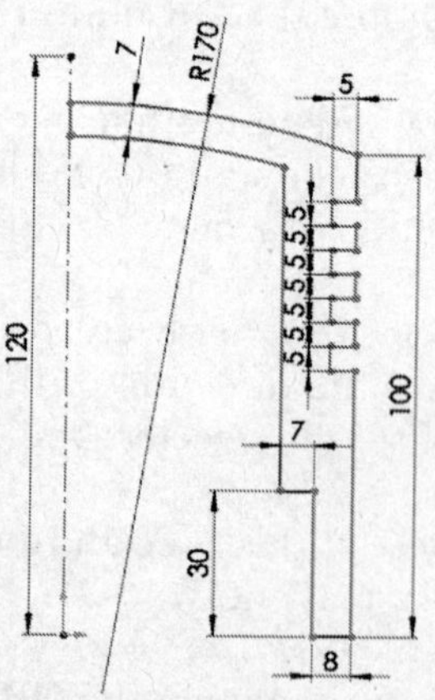

Figure 4-77 Sketch after trimming the unwanted entities

Adding Relations to the Sketch

Next, you will add the required relations to the sketched entities.

1. Right-click and then choose the **Select** option from the shortcut menu. Press and hold the CTRL key and select one of the endpoints of the lower horizontal line and then select the origin. Now, release the CTRL key after the selection; a pop-up toolbar is displayed. Choose the **Make Horizontal** option from the pop-up toolbar to add the Horizontal relation to the selected entities. Click anywhere in the drawing area to clear the selection set.

2. Press and hold the CTRL key and then select the horizontal lines created by offsetting. Release the CTRL key after selecting the lines; a pop-up toolbar is displayed. Choose the **Make Equal** option from it to apply the Equal relation.

3. Zoom out the drawing using the **Zoom In/Out** tool.

Adding Dimensions to the Sketch

After drawing, editing, and applying relations to the sketch, you need to add dimensions to fully define the sketch. Note that as in this tutorial, some dimensions of the sketch entities are applied automatically while drawing, you only need to apply the dimensions of the sketch that were not applied.

1. Select the dimension with value 7 which is placed between the upper arcs, and press the DELETE key to delete this dimension.

   This dimension needs to be deleted because during the design and manufacturing, the dimension between the tangents should be avoided.

2. Invoke the **Smart Dimension** tool by using the Mouse Gesture.

3. Select the inner vertical line and then the centerline, refer to Figure 4-78. Move the cursor to the other side of the centerline and click to place the dimension below the sketch. Next, enter **86** in the **Modify** dialog box and press ENTER.

4. Add the remaining dimensions to fully define the sketch, as shown in Figure 4-79.

5. Select one of the dimensions created after offsetting the entities. Press and hold the left mouse button and drag the cursor toward the right. Then, left-click to place the dimension at an appropriate place.

6. Arrange all the dimensions using the above procedure. The fully defined sketch is shown in Figure 4-79. In this figure, the display of relations is turned off.

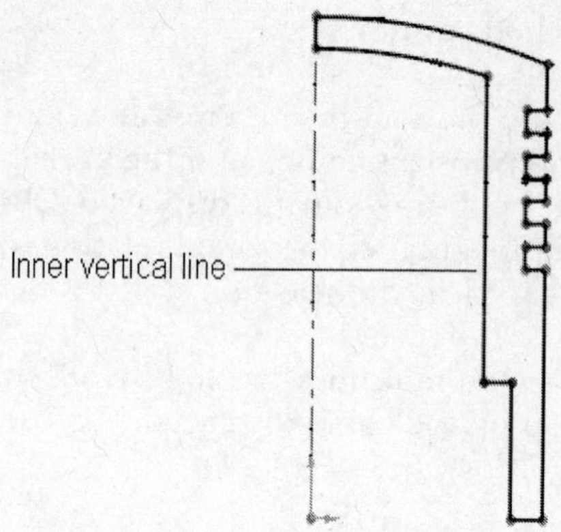

Figure 4-78 Reference to create the dimension

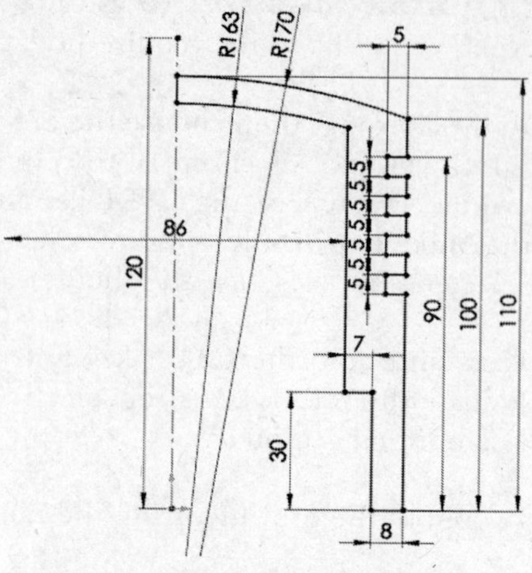

Figure 4-79 Fully defined sketch

Saving the Sketch

1. Choose the **Save** button from the Menu Bar and save the sketch with the name *c04_tut02* at the location *\Documents\SOLIDWORKS\c04*
2. Choose **File > Close** from the SOLIDWORKS menus to close the document.

Tutorial 3

In this tutorial, you will draw the sketch of the model shown in Figure 4-80 and then add required relations and dimensions to it. The sketch is shown in Figure 4-81. The solid model is given for your reference only.

(Expected time: 30 min)

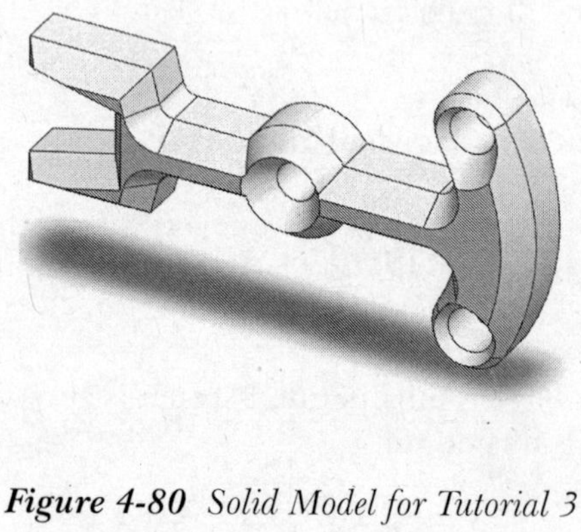

Figure 4-80 Solid Model for Tutorial 3

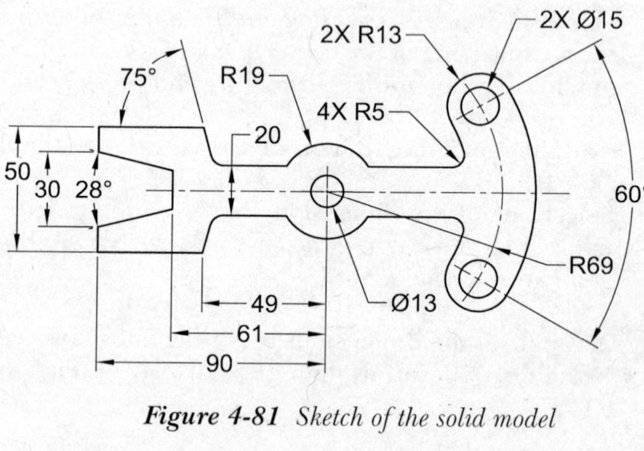

Figure 4-81 Sketch of the solid model

The following steps are required to complete this tutorial:

a. Start a new document file.
b. Create a mirror line.

c. Draw the sketch on one side of the mirror line and add relations to the sketch.
d. Trim arcs and circles and add fillets.
e. Add dimensions to the sketch to fully define it.

Starting a New Document and Invoking the Sketching Environment

1. Choose the **New** button from the Menu Bar; the **New SOLIDWORKS Document** dialog box is invoked with the **Part** button chosen.

2. Choose the **OK** button; a new SOLIDWORKS part document is started.

3. Choose the **Sketch** button from the **Sketch CommandManager** and select **Front Plane** to invoke the sketching environment.

4. Set the units for this tutorial by using the **System Options** dialog box. Also, clear the **Create dimension only when value is entered** check box available in the **System Options - Sketch** dialog box, if selected.

Drawing the Mirror Line

After invoking the sketching environment, you need to draw the sketch of the given model with the help of a mirror line.

1. Increase the display of the drawing area by using the **Zoom In/Out** tool and invoke the **Centerline** tool from the **Sketch CommandManager**.

2. Move the line cursor to a location whose coordinates are close to -102 mm, 0 mm, and 0 mm. You can move it to a point close to this location.

3. Click to specify the start point of the centerline at this point and move the line cursor horizontally toward the right. Specify the endpoint of the centerline when the length of the line shows a value close to 204. Right-click and then choose the **Select** option to exit the **Centerline** tool.

4. Choose the **Zoom to Fit** button from the **View (Heads-Up)** toolbar to fit the sketch into the drawing area.

Drawing the Sketch

You need to draw the profile of the slot using the **Centerpoint Arc Slot** tool.

1. Choose the **Centerpoint Arc Slot** button from the **Straight Slot** flyout; the arrow cursor is replaced by the arc cursor and the **Slot PropertyManager** is displayed.

2. Move the arc cursor close to the origin. Specify the center point of the slot when the cursor snaps to the origin. Next, move the cursor toward right and below the horizontal axis to a location where the radius of the slot is close to 69, refer to Figure 4-82. Click at this point to specify the start point of the slot.

3. Move the arc cursor in the counterclockwise direction. Specify the endpoint of the arc slot when the value of the angle above the arc cursor is close to 60-degree; a reference slot is

attached to the cursor. Specify the point in the drawing area where the value of width of the slot is close to 26 mm, refer to Figure 4-83. Modify the values of the slot in the **Slot PropertyManager** to exact dimensions, refer to Figure 4-81 and then press the ESC key to exit the **Slot PropertyManager**.

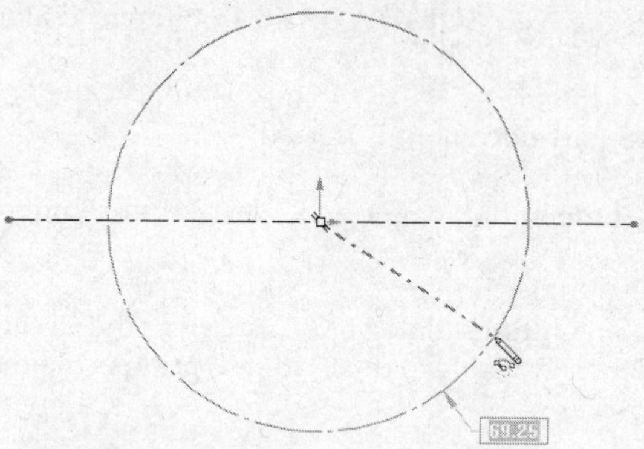

Figure 4-82 *Specifying the start point of the slot*

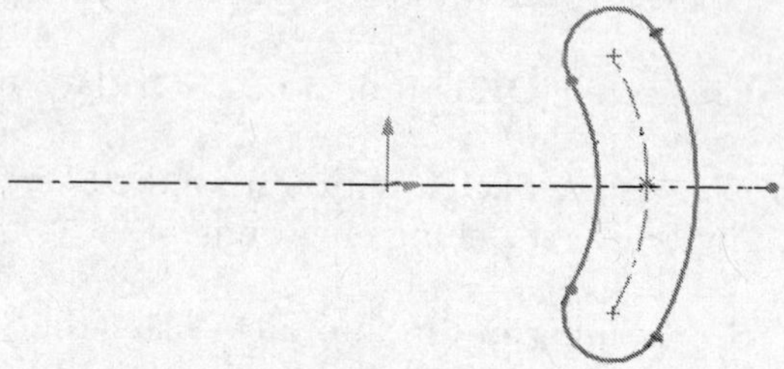

Figure 4-83 *The sketch after drawing the slot*

4. Choose the **Add Relation** button from the **Display/Delete Relations** flyout of the **Sketch PropertyManager**; the **Add Relations PropertyManager** is invoked.

5. Right-click in the drawing area and then choose the **Clear Selections** option from the shortcut menu to clear the selections, if any, from the selection set. Select the centerline and the coordinate point of the slot, as shown in Figure 4-84; the **Coincident** button is highlighted in bold in the **Add Relations** rollout of the **Add Relation PropertyManager**. This indicates that the **Coincident** relation is the most appropriate relation for the selected entities.

6. Choose the **Coincident** button from the **Add Relations PropertyManager**.

7. Choose the **OK** button from the **Add Relations PropertyManager** or choose **OK** from the confirmation corner. The sketch after applying the coincident relation is shown in Figure 4-85.

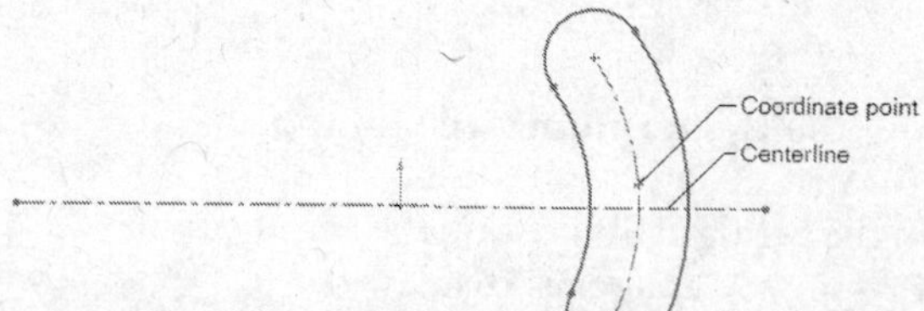

Figure 4-84 *The centerline and the coordinate point to be selected*

Figure 4-85 *The sketch after applying the coincident relation*

Next, you need to make the centerline as the mirror line and draw the sketch on the upper side of the mirror line. On doing so, the same sketch is reflected on the other side of the mirror line.

8. Choose **Tools > Sketch Tools > Dynamic Mirror** from the SOLIDWORKS menus and select the centerline; the centerline is converted into a mirror line.

9. Invoke the **Line** tool from the **Sketch CommandManager** and move the cursor to the point whose coordinates are close to -61, 0, and 0.

10. Click to specify this point as the start point of the line and move the cursor vertically upward and then draw a line of length close to 7.

11. Move the cursor toward left at an angle close to 166 degrees with respect to the horizontal axis in the drawing area. For angle measurement, refer to the **Parameters** rollout of the PropertyManager. Next, specify the endpoint of the line where the length of the line is close to 30; the mirrored entities are created on the other side.

12. Move the cursor vertically upward and specify the endpoint of the vertical line where the length of the line is close to 10.

13. Move the cursor horizontally toward the right and specify the endpoint where the length of the line above the line cursor is close to 42.

14. Move the cursor downward at an angle close to 285 degrees, refer to the **Parameters** rollout of the PropertyManager and specify the endpoint of the line where the length is close to 15.

    The sketch after drawing the inclined line is shown in Figure 4-86.

15. Move the cursor horizontally toward the right and specify the endpoint when the line cursor snaps to the left arc of the slot, as shown in Figure 4-87.

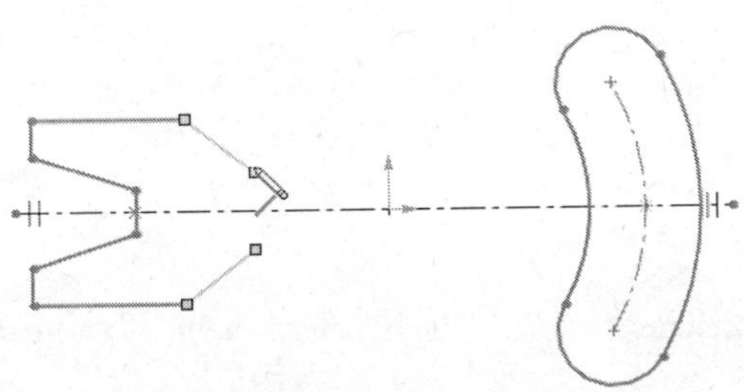

Figure 4-86 Sketch after drawing the inclined line

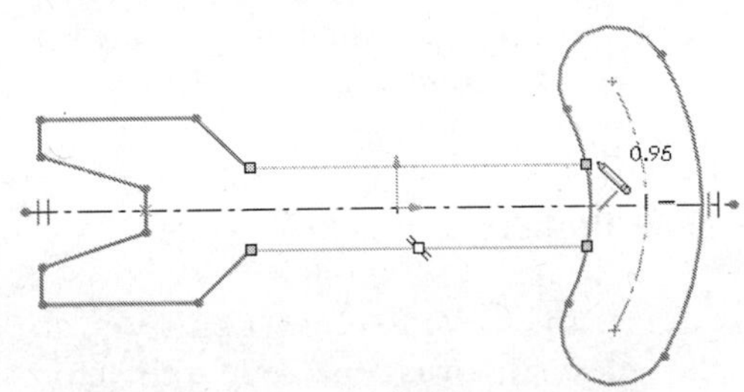

Figure 4-87 The line cursor snapping to the slot arc

16. Press the ESC key to exit the **Insert Line PropertyManager** and then choose the **Circle** button from the **Sketch CommandManager**.

17. Move the cursor to the endpoint of the slot and specify the center point of the circle when the center point is highlighted. Next, move the cursor horizontally toward right. Press the left mouse button when the diameter of the circle in the **Dimension** edit box is about 15. Figure 4-88 shows the sketch after drawing two circles.

18. Right-click and then choose **Recent Commands > Dynamic Mirror Entities** to exit the **Dynamic Mirror** tool.

19. Choose the **Circle** button from the **Sketch CommandManager**.

20. Move the cursor to the origin and when it is highlighted, specify the center point of the circle. Next, move the cursor horizontally toward the right and press the left mouse button when the diameter of the circle in the **Dimension** edit box shows a value close to 13.

21. Move the cursor to the origin and when it is highlighted, specify the center point of the circle. Next, move the cursor horizontally toward the right and press the left mouse button when the diameter of the circle in the **Dimension** edit box displays a value close to 38.

The sketch after drawing the required slot, circles, and lines is shown in Figure 4-89.

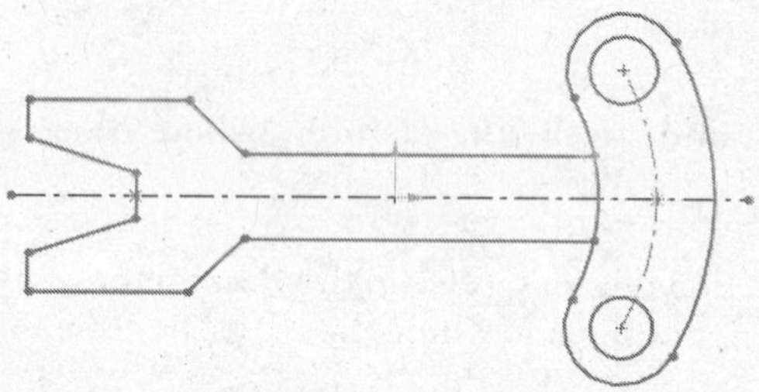

Figure 4-88 *Sketch after drawing two circles*

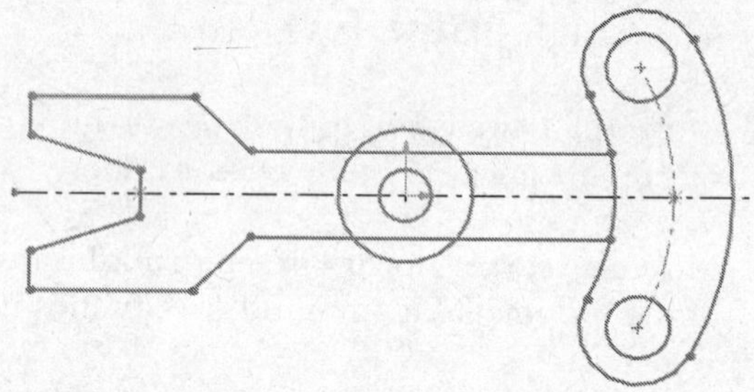

Figure 4-89 *Sketch after drawing slots, circles, and lines*

Trimming Unwanted Entities

After drawing the sketch, you need to trim some of the unwanted sketched entities using the **Trim Entities** tool.

1. Choose the **Trim Entities** button from the **Sketch CommandManager** to display the **Trim PropertyManager**.

2. Choose the **Trim to closest** button from the **Options** rollout, if it is not chosen by default; the select cursor is replaced by the trim cursor.

3. Select the entities to be trimmed, as shown in Figure 4-90; the entities are dynamically trimmed.

Note

While trimming the unwanted sketches of the slot, the ***SOLIDWORKS*** *message box is displayed with the message* ***This trim operation will destroy the slot entity. Do you want to continue?****. Choose the* ***OK*** *button to continue the trimming operation.*

4. As the trim operation destroys the slot entity, apply the tangent and symmetric relations to the slot entity, as shown in Figure 4-91.

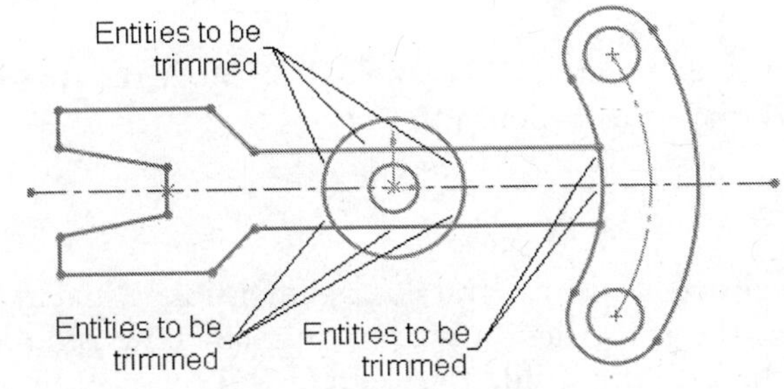

Figure 4-90 The entities to be trimmed

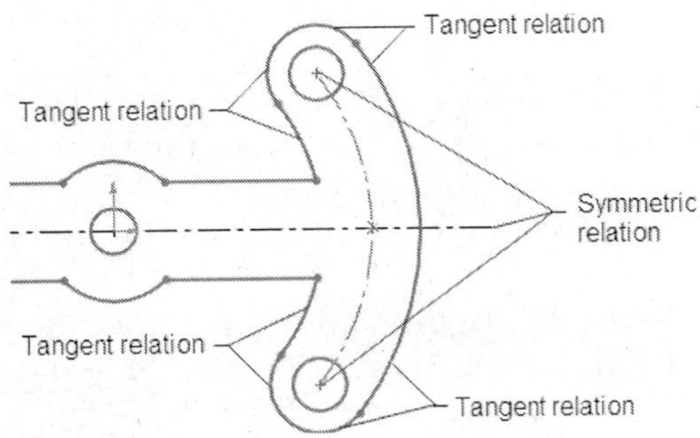

Figure 4-91 Relations to be applied to the slot

Filleting Sketched Entities

Next, you need to fillet the sketched entities. Fillets are generally added to avoid the stress concentration at sharp corners and also for smooth handling.

1. Choose the **Sketch Fillet** button from the **Sketch CommandManager**. Set **5** as the value in the **Fillet Radius** spinner of the **Sketch Fillet PropertyManager**.

2. Select the entities shown in Figure 4-92 to apply fillet.

3. Choose the **OK** button from the **Sketch Fillet PropertyManager** to exit the **Sketch Fillet** tool. The sketch after adding fillets is shown in Figure 4-93.

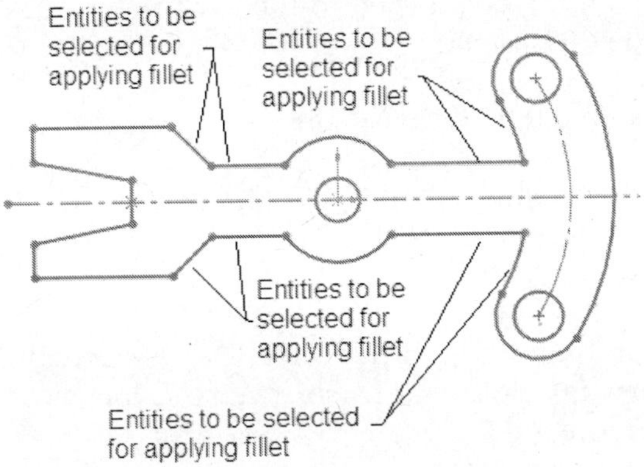

Figure 4-92 Entities to be selected for filleting

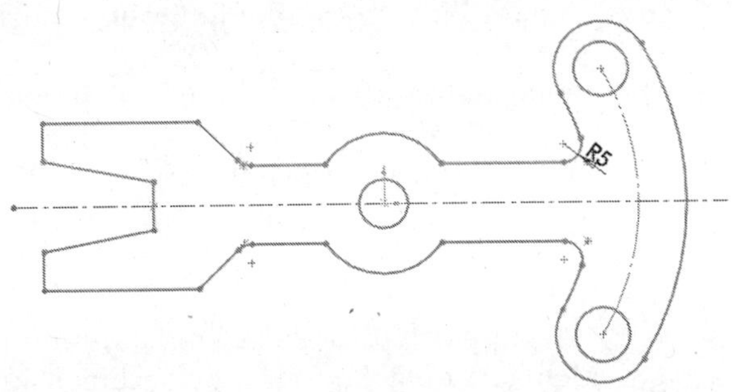

Figure 4-93 The sketch after adding fillets

Adding Dimensions to the Sketch

Next, you will apply dimensions to the sketch and fully define it.

1. Choose the **Smart Dimension** button from the **Sketch CommandManager**; the arrow cursor is replaced by the dimension cursor.

2. Select the construction arc of the slot that is displayed as a construction entity; a radial dimension is attached to the cursor. Move the cursor away from the sketch toward the right and place the dimension.

3. Enter **69** in the **Modify** dialog box and press ENTER.

4. Select the upper arc of the slot; a radial dimension is attached to the cursor. Move the cursor away from the sketch toward the right and place the dimension.

5. Enter **13** in the **Modify** dialog box and press ENTER.

6. Select the origin and the start point of the construction arc of the slot; a dimension is attached to the cursor. Next, select the endpoint of the construction arc; an angular dimension is attached to the cursor. Place the angular dimension outside the sketch.

7. Enter **60** as the value of the angular dimension in the **Modify** dialog box and press ENTER.

8. Select the upper right circle; a diametric dimension is attached to the cursor. Place the dimension outside the sketch.

9. Enter **15** as the value of the diametric dimension in the **Modify** dialog box and press ENTER.

10. Select the upper right horizontal line and the lower right horizontal line that coincides with the trimmed circle, refer to Figure 4-94. A vertical dimension is attached to the cursor. Move the cursor vertically upward and click to place the dimension.

11. Enter **20** in the **Modify** dialog box.

12. Select the circle at the origin; a diametric dimension is attached to the cursor. Move the cursor upward and place the dimension outside the sketch.

13. Enter **13** as the value of the diametric dimension in the **Modify** dialog box.

14. Select the outer trimmed circle and place the radial dimension outside the sketch.

15. Enter **19** as the value of the radial dimension in the **Modify** dialog box.

16. Select the upper left inclined line; a dimension is attached to the cursor. Next, select the upper left horizontal line; an angular dimension is attached to the cursor. Place the dimension above the upper left horizontal line, refer to Figure 4-94.

17. Enter **75** as the value of the angular dimension in the **Modify** dialog box.

18. Select the origin and the lower endpoint of the lower left inclined line. Move the cursor vertically downward and place the dimension. Enter **49** in the **Modify** dialog box and press ENTER.

19. Select the origin and the middle left vertical line, refer to Figure 4-94. Move the cursor vertically downward and place the dimension below the previous dimension.

20. Enter **61** in the **Modify** dialog box and press ENTER.

21. Select the origin and the lower endpoint of the outer left vertical line. Move the cursor vertically downward and place the dimension below the last dimension.

22. Enter **90** in the **Modify** dialog box and press ENTER.

23. Select the upper left inclined line and the lower left inclined line, refer to Figure 4-94; an angular dimension is attached to the cursor. Move the cursor horizontally toward the left and place the dimension.

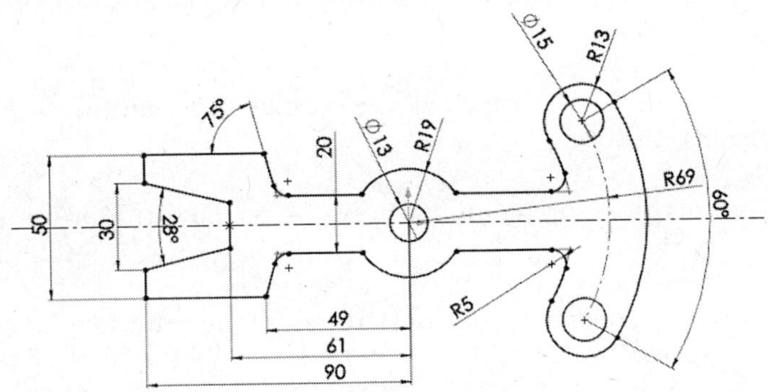

Figure 4-94 Sketch after applying all relations and dimensions

24. Enter **28** as the value of the angular dimension in the **Modify** dialog box.

25. Select the upper left horizontal line and the lower left horizontal line; a linear dimension is attached to the cursor. Move the cursor horizontally toward left and place the dimension.

26. Enter **50** in the **Modify** dialog box.

27. Select the lower endpoint of the upper left vertical line and the upper endpoint of the lower left vertical line; a linear dimension is attached to the cursor. Move the cursor horizontally toward left and left-click to place the dimension.

28. Enter **30** in the **Modify** dialog box.

29. Add remaining dimensions to the sketch and make it a fully defined sketch.

Saving the Sketch

1. Choose the **Save** button from the Menu Bar to invoke the **Save As** dialog box.

2. Browse to the location *\Documents\SOLIDWORKS\c04* and enter **c04_tut03** as the name of the document in the **File name** edit box and choose the **Save** button.

3. Close the document by choosing **File > Close** from the SOLIDWORKS menus.

Self-Evaluation Test

Answer the following questions and then compare them to those given at the end of this chapter:

1. The __________ **PropertyManager** is displayed on invoking the **Dynamic Mirror Entities** tool.

2. The __________ dimension is used to dimension a line that is at an angle with respect to the X-axis or the Y-axis.

3. A __________ sketch is the one in which all the entities and their positions are described by relations, dimensions, or both.

4. The __________ dimensions or relations cannot determine the position of one or more sketched entities.

5. The __________ option is displayed in the **Defined In** column when an entity is defined as placed in the same sketch.

6. Some relations are automatically applied to a sketch while it is being drawn. (T/F)

7. When you choose the **Add Relation** button, the **Apply Relations PropertyManager** is displayed. (T/F)

8. You can modify the arrowhead style of a selected dimension. (T/F)

9. A favorite dimension created in one document cannot be retrieved in another document. (T/F)

10. You can make modifications in the read-only file. (T/F)

Review Questions

Answer the following questions:

1. Which of the following relations forces a selected arc to share the same center point with another arc or point?

   (a) **Concentric** (b) **Coradial**
   (c) **Merge points** (d) **Equal**

2. Which of the following types of sketch status changes the color of entities to red?

   (a) Underdefined (b) Overdefined
   (c) Dangling (d) None of these

3. Which of the following dialog boxes is displayed when you modify a dimension?

   (a) **Modify Dimensional Value** (b) **Insert a value**
   (c) **Modify** (d) None of these

4. Which of the following dialog boxes is displayed when you add an extra dimension to a sketch or add an extra relation that overdefines the sketch?

   (a) **Over defining** (b) **Delete relation**
   (c) **Make Dimension Driven?** (d) **Add Geometric Relations**

5. You can invoke the **Display/Delete Relations PropertyManager** by using the **Display/Delete Relations** button from the __________ **CommandManager**.

6. The linear diametric dimensions are applied to the sketches of __________ features.

7. You can modify a dimension to display the minimum or maximum distance between two circles using the __________ **PropertyManager**.

8. The __________ sketch geometry is constrained by too many dimensions and/or relations.

9. The __________ relation forces two selected lines, arcs, points, or ellipses to remain equidistant from the centerline.

10. In SOLIDWORKS, by default, the dimensioning between two arcs, two circles, or between an arc and a circle is done from the __________.

EXERCISES

Exercise 1

Create the sketch of the model shown in Figure 4-95. Apply the required relations and dimensions to the sketch and fully define it. The sketch is shown in Figure 4-96. The solid model is given for your reference only. **(Expected time: 30 min)**

Figure 4-95 Solid model for Exercise 1

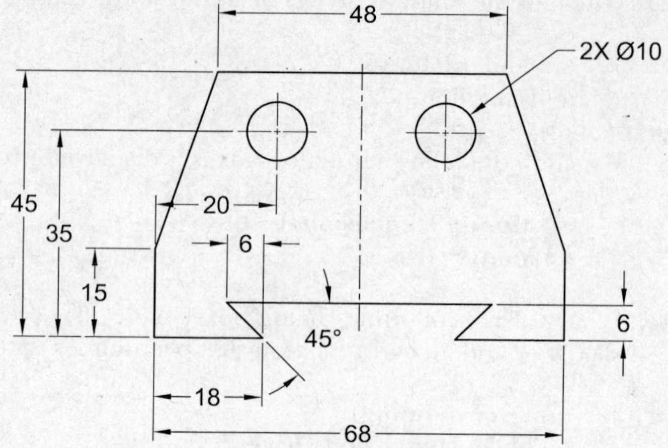

Figure 4-96 Sketch for Exercise 1

Exercise 2

Create the sketch of the model shown in Figure 4-97. Apply the required relations and dimensions to the sketch and fully define it. The sketch is shown in Figure 4-98. The solid model is given for your reference only. **(Expected time: 30 min)**

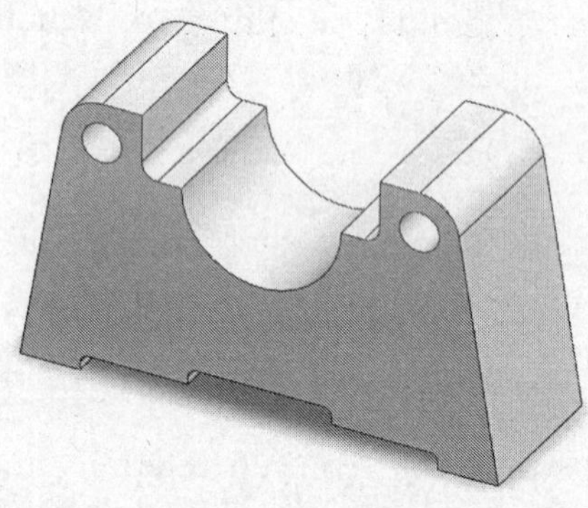

Figure 4-97 Solid model for Exercise 2

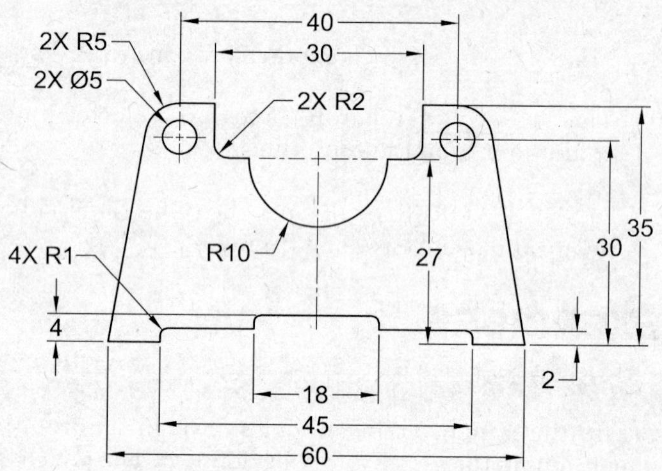

Figure 4-98 Sketch for Exercise 2

Exercise 3

Create the sketch of the model shown in Figure 4-99. Apply the required relations and dimensions to the sketch and fully define it. The sketch is shown in Figure 4-100. The solid model is given for your reference only.
(Expected time: 30 min)

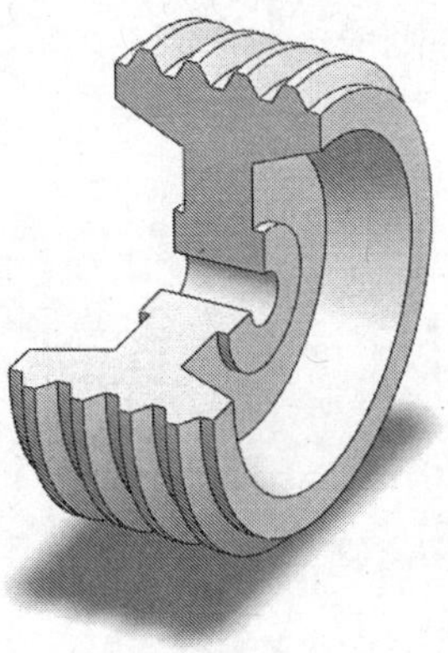

Figure 4-99 Solid model for Exercise 3

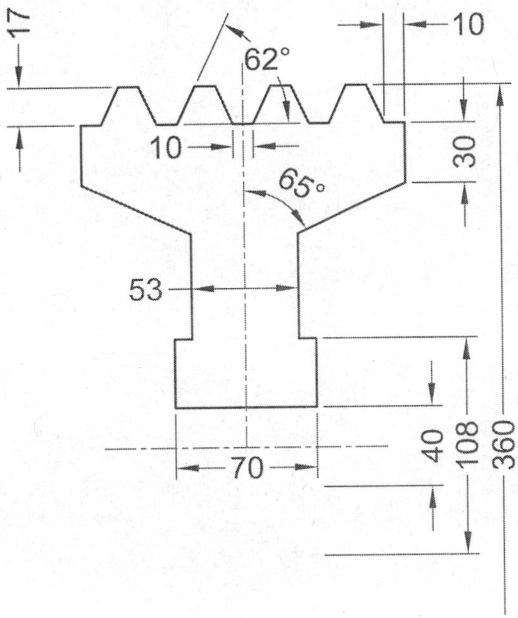

Figure 4-100 Sketch for Exercise 3

Answers to Self-Evaluation Test

1. Mirror, **2.** aligned, **3.** fully defined, **4.** dangling, **5. Current Sketch**, **6.** T, **7.** F, **8.** T, **9.** F, **10.** F

Chapter 5

Advanced Dimensioning Techniques and Base Feature Options

Learning Objectives

After completing this chapter, you will be able to:

- *Fully define a sketch*
- *Dimension the true length of an arc*
- *Measure distances and view section properties*
- *Create solid base extruded features*
- *Create thin base extruded features*
- *Create solid base revolved features*
- *Create thin base revolved features*
- *Dynamically rotate the view of model*
- *Modify the orientation of view*
- *Change the display modes of solid models*
- *Apply materials to models*
- *Change the appearances of models*

ADVANCED DIMENSIONING TECHNIQUES

In this chapter, you will learn about the advanced dimensioning techniques that are used to dimension the sketches. In SOLIDWORKS, you can apply all possible relations and dimensions to a sketch by using a single tool to make it fully defined. The advanced dimensioning techniques are discussed next.

Fully Defining the Sketches

SOLIDWORKS menus:	Tools > Dimensions > Fully Define Sketch
Toolbar:	Dimensions/Relations > Fully Define Sketch

The **Fully Define Sketch** tool is used to apply relations and dimensions to a sketch automatically. To fully define a sketch, draw the sketch using the standard sketching tools.Choose the **Fully Define Sketch** tool from the **Dimensions/Relations** toolbar; the **Fully Define Sketch PropertyManager** will be displayed, refer to Figure 5-1. You can also right-click and choose the **Fully Define Sketch** option from the shortcut menu to display this PropertyManager after selecting the sketch. Various rollouts in this PropertyManager are discussed next.

Entities to Fully Define

The **Entities to Fully Define** rollout is used to specify the entities to which the relations and dimensions need to be applied. The **All entities in sketch** radio button is selected by default. As a result, all the entities drawn in the current sketching environment are selected to apply relations and dimensions. If you need to fully define only the selected entities, select the **Selected entities** radio button; the **Selected Entities to Fully Define** selection box will be displayed in the **Entities to Fully Define** rollout. Select the entities to be dimensioned using the select cursor; the names of the selected entities will be displayed in the **Selected Entities to Fully Define** selection box. If you select one or more entities before invoking the **Fully Define Sketch PropertyManager** and then select the **Selected entities** radio button from the **Entities to Fully Define** rollout, the names of the selected entities will be displayed in the **Selected Entities to Fully Define** selection box. After specifying other parameters, choose the **Calculate** button to calculate and place the required number of relations and dimensions to fully define the sketch.

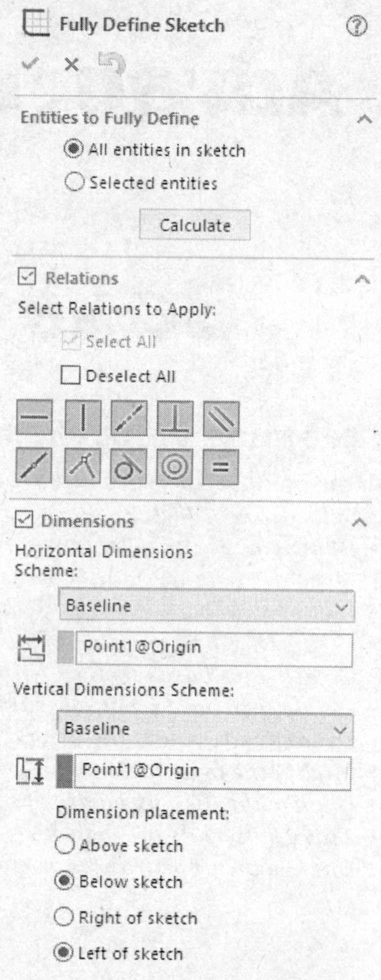

*Figure 5-1 The **Fully Define Sketch PropertyManager***

Relations

The **Relations** rollout displays the buttons for applying various relations. This rollout is expanded by default. If it is not expanded then click on the arrow on the right in the **Relations** rollout; the rollout will expand. All buttons in this rollout are chosen by default. You can disable all the buttons by selecting the **Deselect All** check box from this rollout. You can also choose only those buttons that you want to apply to the sketch from this rollout.

Dimensions

The **Dimensions** rollout is used to specify the type of dimensions to be applied, reference for the dimensions, and the placement of the dimensional value. The options in this rollout are discussed next.

Horizontal Dimensions Scheme and Vertical Dimensions Scheme

The **Horizontal Dimensions Scheme** and **Vertical Dimensions Scheme** drop-down lists in the **Dimensions** rollout are used to specify the dimensioning scheme to be applied to the horizontal and vertical dimensions in the sketch, respectively. The dimensioning schemes in these drop-down lists are discussed next.

Chain: The **Chain** option is used for the relative horizontal/vertical dimensioning of the sketch. When you invoke the **Fully Define Sketch PropertyManager** and select this option, the origin will be selected as the reference entity. This reference entity is used as a datum for generating dimensions. The name of the origin will be displayed in the **Datums - Vertical Model Edge, Model Vertex, Vertical Line or Point** selection box and the reference entity will be displayed in pink in the drawing area. You can also specify a user-defined reference entity after clicking in this selection box.

Note

If tolerances relative to a common datum are required in the part, chain dimensioning should be avoided.

Baseline: The **Baseline** option is used for the absolute vertical/horizontal dimensioning of the sketch. In this dimensioning method, the dimensions are applied to the sketch with respect to the common datum. When you invoke the **Fully Define Sketch PropertyManager**, this option is selected by default. Also, the origin will be selected as the reference entity and will be used as a datum for generating dimensions. The name of the origin will be displayed in the **Datums - Vertical Model Edge, Model Vertex, Vertical Line or Point** selection box. You can also specify a user-defined reference entity.

Ordinate: The **Ordinate** option is used for the ordinate dimensioning of the sketch. When you invoke the **Fully Define Sketch PropertyManager** and select this option, the origin will be selected as the reference entity and will be used as a datum for generating dimensions. The name of the selected reference entity will be displayed in the **Datums - Vertical Model Edge, Model Vertex, Vertical Line or Point** selection box and the reference entity will be displayed in pink in the drawing area. You can also specify a user-defined reference entity.

Dimension placement

The **Dimension placement** area is used to define the position where the generated dimensions will be placed. Four radio buttons are available in this area. The first is the **Above sketch** radio button and if you select this radio button, the horizontal dimensions generated using the **Fully Define Sketch** tool will be placed above the sketch. The **Below sketch** radio button is selected by default and is used to place the horizontal dimensions below the sketch. The **Right of sketch** radio button is selected to place the vertical dimensions on the right of the sketch. The **Left of sketch** radio button is selected to place the vertical dimensions on the left of the sketch. This radio button is selected by default.

After specifying all parameters in the **Fully Define Sketch PropertyManager**, choose the **Calculate** button; the sketch will be fully defined. Next, choose the **OK** button or choose the **OK** icon from the confirmation corner. The relations and dimension with the selected dimension scheme will be applied to the sketch. Figure 5-2 shows the Baseline scheme with the origin as the datum, Figure 5-3 shows the Ordinate scheme with the origin as the datum, and Figure 5-4 shows the Chain scheme with the origin as the datum.

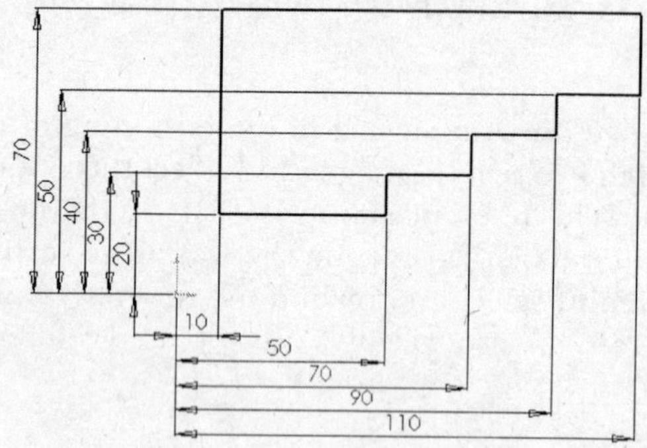

***Figure 5-2** Baseline dimension created using the origin as the reference entity*

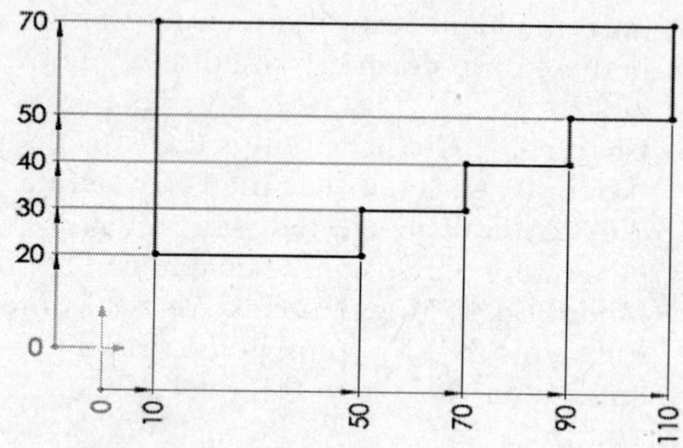

***Figure 5-3** Ordinate dimension created using the origin as the reference entity*

Dimensioning the True Length of an Arc

In SOLIDWORKS, you can also apply the dimension of the true length of an arc which is one of the advantages of the sketching environment of SOLIDWORKS. To apply the dimension of the true length, invoke the **Smart Dimension** tool and select the arc by using the dimension cursor; a radial dimension will be attached to the cursor. Move the cursor to any of the endpoints of the arc. When the cursor snaps the endpoint, click to specify the first endpoint of the arc; a linear dimension will be attached to the cursor. Move the cursor to the second endpoint of the arc and when the cursor snaps the endpoint, select it; a dimension will be attached to the cursor. Move the cursor to an appropriate distance to place the dimension. The dimension of the true length of the arc is shown in Figure 5-5.

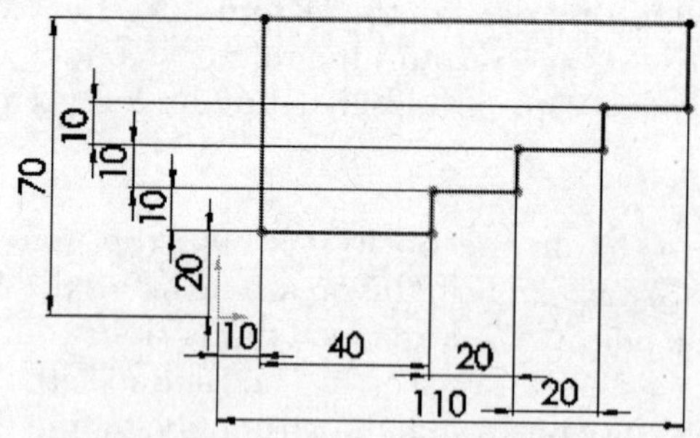

***Figure 5-4** Chain dimension created using the origin as the reference entity*

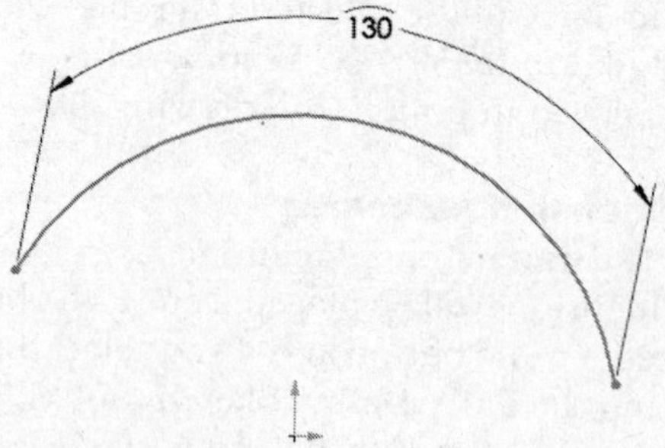

***Figure 5-5** Dimensioning the true length of an arc*

MEASURING DISTANCES AND VIEWING SECTION PROPERTIES

In SOLIDWORKS, you can measure the distance of the entities and view the section properties using various tools that are discussed next.

Measuring Distances

CommandManager:	Evaluate > Measure
SOLIDWORKS menus:	Tools > Evaluate > Measure
Toolbar:	Tools > Measure

The **Measure** tool is used to measure the perimeter, angle, radius, and distance between the lines, points, surfaces, and planes in sketches, 3D models, assemblies, or drawings. To measure an entity, invoke the **Measure** toolbar by choosing the **Measure** tool from the **Evaluate CommandManager**. On doing so, the name of the document in which you are working will be displayed at the top of the **Measure** toolbar, refer to Figure 5-6. Also, the current cursor will be replaced by the measure cursor. Select the entity or entities to be measured using the measure cursor; the result related to the selected element or elements will be displayed in a callout. You can also view this result in the **Measure** toolbar by expanding it. To expand the toolbar, choose the button with the down arrow on the right of the toolbar. You can change the size of the text displayed in the toolbar by clicking on the buttons provided on the right in the expanded toolbar. If you hover the cursor over the numeric value displayed, a copy icon ( ) is displayed. Select this icon to copy the numeric value to the clipboard. The various options in the **Measure** toolbar are discussed next.

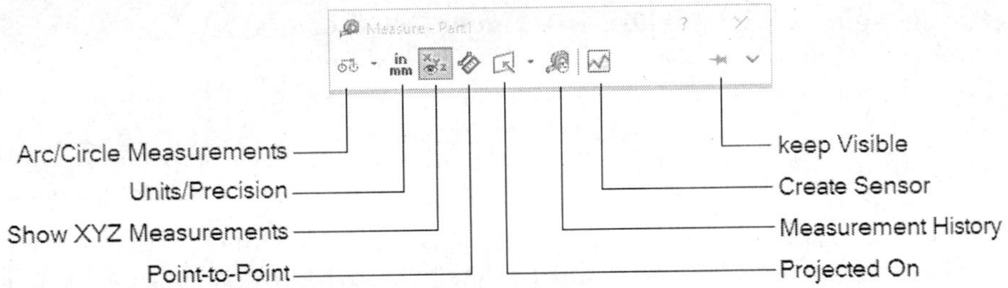

*Figure 5-6 The **Measure** toolbar*

Arc/Circle Measurements

The **Arc/Circle Measurements** button is used to specify the technique of measuring the distance between the selected arcs or circles. When you choose the **Arc/Circle Measurements** button, a flyout will appear. The **Center to Center** option will be chosen by default in this flyout. So, the center-to-center distance will be measured when you select two arcs or circles. If you choose the **Minimum Distance** option from this flyout, the minimum tangential distance between the two selected arcs or circles will be measured. However, if you choose the **Maximum Distance** option from this flyout, the maximum tangential distance between the selected arcs or circles will be measured. If you choose the **Custom Distance** option, you can customize for each selection separately.

Units/Precision

The **Units/Precision** button is used to set the type of units and their precision. Choose this button; the **Measure Units/Precision** dialog box will be displayed, as shown in Figure 5-7. The **Use document settings** radio button is selected by default in this dialog box. The default units and precision of the document are used while measuring the entities. You can also set the type of units and their precision for measuring the entities. To set the type of units and their precision, select the **Use custom settings** radio button from this dialog box. The other options in this dialog box will be displayed, refer to Figure 5-7. These options are discussed next.

Length unit Area

The **Length unit** area is used to set the units and the options of linear measurements of the entities. The **Unit** drop-down list is provided at the top left corner of the **Length unit** area. In this drop-down list, you can select any type of unit such as **Angstroms, Nanometers, Microns, Millimeters, Centimeters, Meters, Microinches, Mils, Inches, Feet**, and **Feet & Inches**. The other options in the **Length unit** area are discussed next.

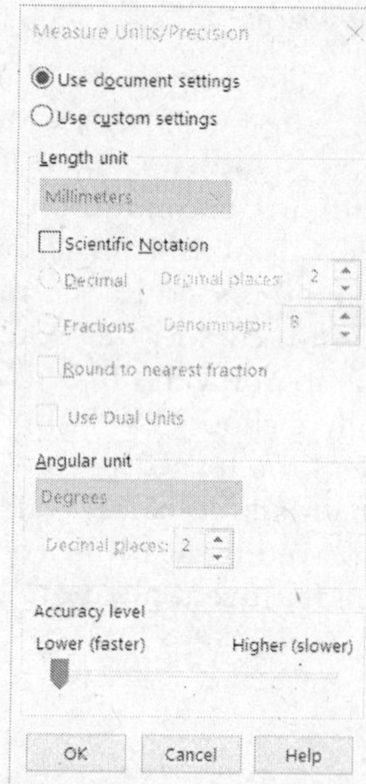

Figure 5-7 The ***Measure Units/Precision*** *dialog box*

Scientific Notation: The **Scientific Notation** check box is selected to display the value in the scientific notation units.

Decimal places: This spinner is used to control the decimal places.

Decimal: The **Decimal** radio button is available only when you select the units as **Microinches, Mils, Inches**, or **Feet and Inches** from the **Unit** drop-down list. Select this radio button to display the dimension in the decimal form. You can also specify the decimal places using the **Decimal places** spinner provided on the right of the **Decimal** radio button.

Fractions: The **Fractions** radio button is available only when you select the units as **Microinches, Mils, Inches**, or **Feet and Inches** from the **Units** drop-down list. This radio button is selected to display the dimension in the fraction form. You can also set the value of the denominator by using the **Denominator** spinner provided on the right of the **Fractions** radio button.

Round to nearest fraction: The **Round to nearest fraction** check box is selected to display the value in fractions by rounding the value to the nearest fraction.

Use Dual Units: Select this check box to display the value in alternate units also. On selecting this check box, the dialog box will expand and the options for the alternate units will be displayed. Specify the units and the corresponding options.

Angular unit Area

The **Angular unit** area is used to set the units for the angular measurement. This area is provided with a drop-down list to specify the angular measurement units such as **Degrees, Deg/Min, Deg/Min/Sec**, and **Radians**. The **Decimal places** spinner is used to specify the decimal places.

Accuracy level

The **Accuracy level** slider is used to increase the accuracy level of measurements.

Show XYZ Measurements

The **Show XYZ measurements** button is activated by default in the **Measure** toolbar, so the dx, dy, and dz values of the selected entities are displayed in the drawing area. If you deactivate this button, only the distance between the selected entities will be displayed.

Point-to-Point

By default, the **Point-to-Point** button is activated in the **Measure** toolbar. As a result, when you select two points or vertices of any entity or model, the distance between the selected points will be displayed.

Projected On

The **Projected On** button is used to specify the location where the selected entity should be projected. You can project the selected entity on the screen or on a specific plane. The system will then calculate the measurement of the true projection. To specify the location, choose the **Projected On** button from the **Measure** toolbar; a callout will be displayed and you can select the location where you need to project the selected entity.

Measurement History

The **Measurement History** button is used to view all the measurements made during the current session of SOLIDWORKS. When you choose this button, the **Measurement History** message box will be displayed showing all measurements.

Create Sensor

The **Create Sensor** button is used to create the measurement sensor for the selected measurement. If the measurement changes then the software gives an alert message.

Keep Visible

The **Keep Visible** button is used to pin the **Measure** toolbar in the graphics area so that you need not invoke it again to measure distances for the current session. You can close the **Measure** toolbar by pressing the **ESC** key if the toolbar is unpinned.

Determining the Section Properties of Closed Sketches

CommandManager:	Evaluate > Section Properties
SOLIDWORKS menus:	Tools > Evaluate > Section Properties
Toolbar:	Tools > Section Properties

The **Section Properties** tool enables you to determine the section properties of the sketch in the sketching environment or of the selected planar face in the **Part** mode or in the **Assembly** mode. Remember that only the section properties of the closed sketches with non-intersecting closed loops can be determined. The section properties include the area, centroid relative to sketch origin, centroid relative to the part origin, moment of inertia, polar moment of inertia, angle between principle axes and sketch axes, and principle moment of inertia.

To calculate section properties, select a sketch or a face and then choose the **Section Properties** button from the **Evaluate CommandManager**; the **Section Properties** dialog box will be displayed, as shown in Figure 5-8.

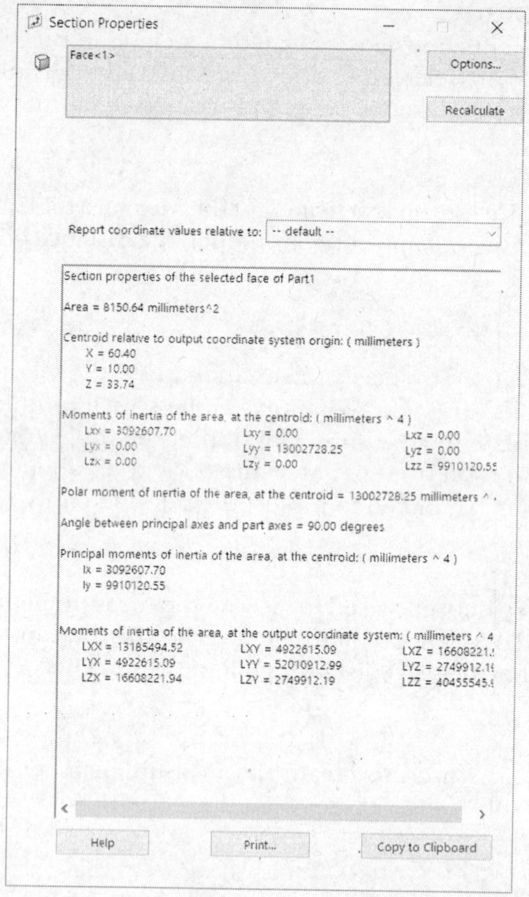

Figure 5-8 The ***Section Properties*** *dialog box*

When you invoke the **Section Properties** dialog box, a 3D triad will be placed at the centroid of the sketch. The section properties of the sketch are displayed in the **Section Properties** dialog box. The **Selected items** display box is used to display the name of the selected planar face or the sketch whose section properties are to be calculated. When you are in the **Part** mode, select a face to calculate the section properties and choose **Recalculate** to display the properties. To calculate the section properties of some other face, remove the previously selected face from the selection set, and then select the new face and choose the **Recalculate** button.

The **Print** button in the **Section Properties** dialog box is used to print the section properties. You can choose the **Copy to Clipboard** button to copy the section properties to the clip board, from where you can copy them to a program such as MS Word. By using the **Options** button in the **Section Properties** dialog box, you can change the unit system, accuracy levels, and material properties of the selected section. The rest of the options in this dialog box are similar to those discussed earlier.

CREATING BASE FEATURES BY EXTRUDING SKETCHES

CommandManager:	Features > Extruded Boss/Base
SOLIDWORKS Menus:	Insert > Boss/Base > Extrude
Toolbar:	Features > Extruded Boss/Base > Extruded Boss/Base

The sketches that you have drawn can be converted into base features by extruding the sketch using the **Extruded Boss/Base** tool from the **Features CommandManager**. After drawing the sketch, choose the **Features** tab from the **CommandManager** to display the **Features CommandManager**. Next, choose the **Extruded Boss/Base** tool from the **Features CommandManager**; the sketching environment will be closed and the part modeling environment will be invoked. Also, the preview of the feature that is created using the default options will be displayed in the trimetric view. The trimetric view gives a better display of the solid feature.

On the basis of the options and the sketch selected for extruding, the resulting feature can be a solid feature or a thin feature. If the sketch is closed, it can be converted into a solid feature or a thin feature. However, if the sketch is open, it will be converted into a thin feature. The solid and thin features are discussed next.

Creating Solid Extruded Features

After you have completed drawing a closed sketch, dimension it to convert it into a fully defined sketch. Next, choose the **Features** tab from the **CommandManager**; the **Features CommandManager** will be displayed. Choose the **Extruded Boss/Base** tool; the **Boss-Extrude PropertyManager** will be displayed, refer to Figure 5-9. Also, you will notice that the view is automatically changed to the trimetric view.

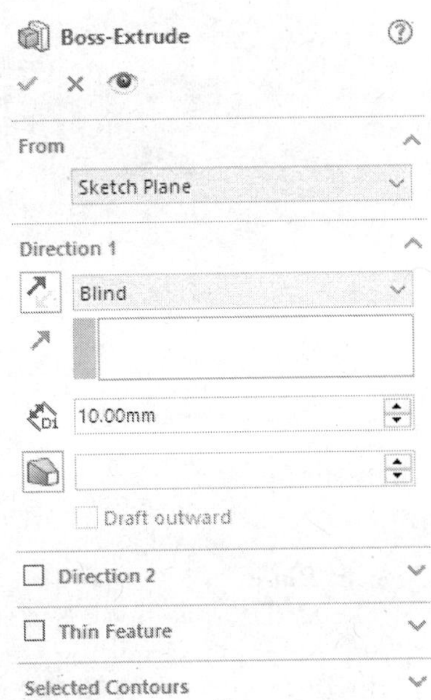

*Figure 5-9 The **Boss-Extrude PropertyManager***

You will also notice that the preview of the base feature is displayed in temporary graphics. Additionally, an arrow will appear in front of the sketch. Note that if the sketch consists of some closed loops inside the outer loop, they will automatically be subtracted from the outer loop while extruding, as shown in Figure 5-10.

The options in the **Boss-Extrude PropertyManager** are discussed next.

Direction 1

The **Direction 1** rollout is used to specify the end condition for extruding the sketch in one direction from the sketch plane. The options in the **Direction 1** rollout list are discussed next.

End Condition

The **End Condition** drop-down list provides options to define the termination of the extruded feature. Note that when you create the first feature, some of the options in this drop-down list will not be used. Also, some additional options will be available later in this drop-down list. Some of the options that will be used to define the termination of the base feature are discussed next.

Blind

The **Blind** option is selected by default and is used to define the termination of the extruded base feature by specifying the depth of extrusion. The depth of the extrusion is specified in the **Depth** spinner. This spinner will be displayed in the **Direction 1** rollout on selecting the **Blind** option. To reverse the extrusion direction, choose the **Reverse Direction** button provided on the left of this drop-down list. Figure 5-10 shows preview of the feature being created by extruding the sketch using this option.

You can also extrude a sketch to a blind depth by dragging the feature dynamically using the mouse. To do so, move the mouse to the arrow displayed in the preview; the move cursor will be displayed and the color of the arrow will also be changed. Left-click once on the arrow; a scale will be displayed, as shown in Figure 5-11. Now, move the cursor to specify the depth of extrusion; the value of the depth of extrusion will change dynamically on this scale as you move the cursor. Left-click again to specify the termination of the extruded feature, the select cursor will be replaced by the mouse cursor. Right-click and choose **OK** to complete the feature creation or choose the **OK** button from the **Boss-Extrude PropertyManager**.

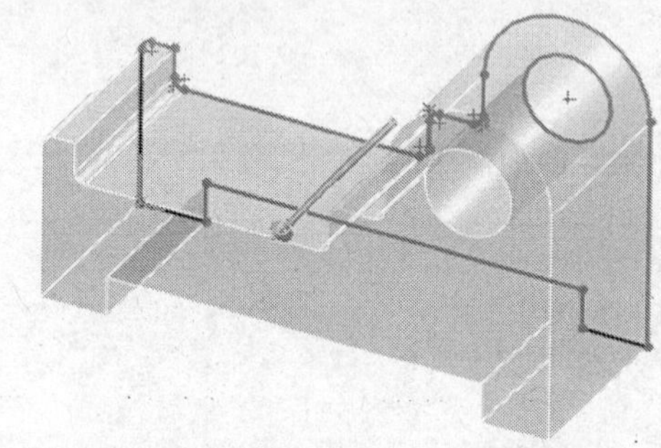

***Figure 5-10** Preview of the feature being extruded using the **Blind** option*

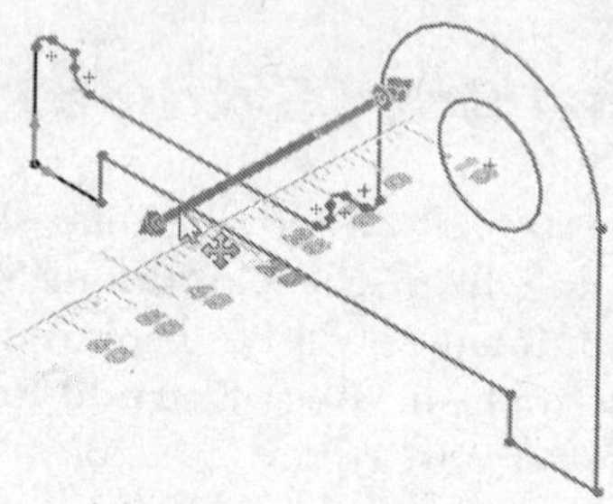

***Figure 5-11** Preview of the feature being extruded by dragging the arrow dynamically*

Tip

You can also choose the termination options using the shortcut menu that is displayed when you right-click in the drawing area.

Mid Plane

The **Mid Plane** option is used to create the base feature by extruding the sketch equally in both the directions of the plane on which the sketch is drawn. For example, if the total depth of the extruded feature is 30 mm, it will be extruded 15 mm toward the front of the sketching plane and 15 mm toward the back. The depth of the feature can be defined in the **Depth** spinner that is displayed below the **Direction of Extrusion** selection box. Figure 5-12 shows preview of the feature being created by extruding the sketch using the **Mid Plane** option.

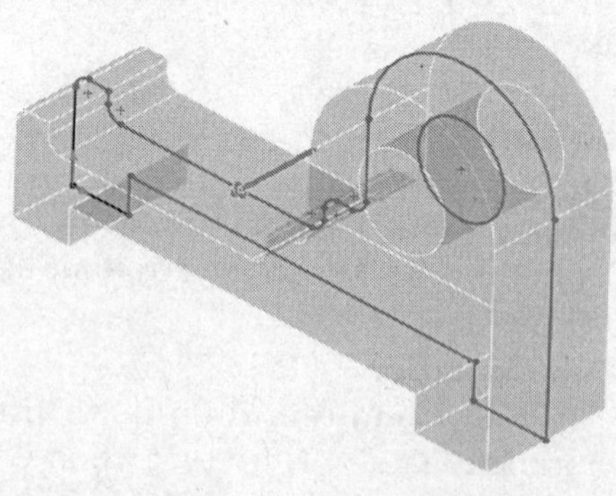

***Figure 5-12** Preview of the feature being extruded using the **Mid Plane** option*

Draft On/Off

The **Draft On/Off** button is used to specify a draft angle while extruding a sketch. Apply a draft angle to taper the resulting feature. This button is not chosen by default. Therefore, the resulting base feature will not have any taper. However, if you want to add a draft angle to the feature, choose this button; the **Draft Angle** spinner and the **Draft outward** check box will be available. You can enter the draft angle for the feature in the **Draft Angle** spinner. By default, the feature will be tapered inward, as shown in Figure 5-13.

If you want to taper the feature outward, select the **Draft outward** check box that is displayed below the **Draft Angle** spinner. The feature created with the outward draft is shown in Figure 5-14.

Note

*The **Direction of Extrusion** area will be discussed in the later chapters.*

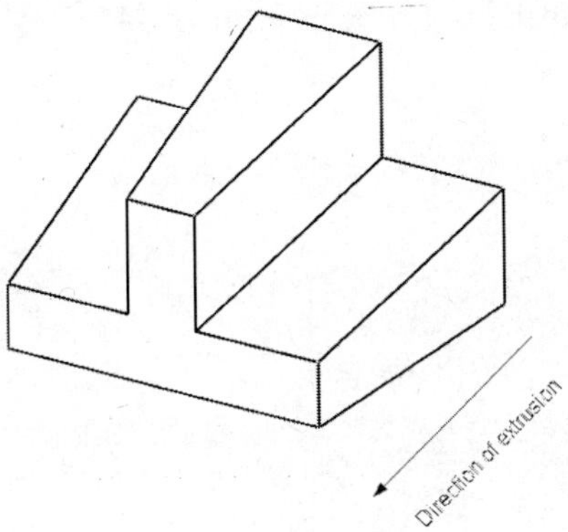

Figure 5-13 Feature created with inward draft

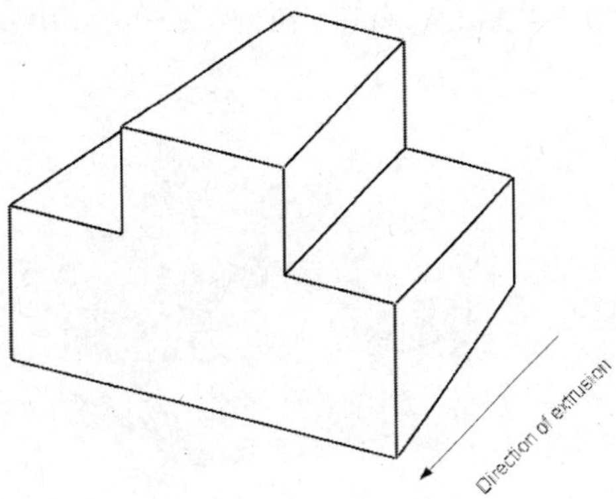

Figure 5-14 Feature created with outward draft

Direction 2

The **Direction 2** rollout is used to extrude a sketch with different values in the second direction of the sketching plane. The **Direction 2** rollout is activated only when you select the **Direction 2** check box. This rollout will not be available, if you select the **Mid Plane** termination type in the **Direction 1** rollout.

The options in this rollout are similar to those in the **Direction 1** rollout. Note that unlike the **Mid Plane** termination option, the depth of extrusion and other parameters in both directions can be different. For example, you can extrude the sketch to a blind depth of 10 mm and an inward draft of 35-degree in front of the sketching plane, and to a blind depth of 15 mm and an outward draft of 0-degree behind the sketching plane, as shown in Figure 5-15.

Figure 5-15 Feature created in two directions with different values

After setting the values for both directions, choose the **OK** button or choose the **OK** icon from the confirmation corner; the feature will be created with defined values.

Note

*You can extrude an underdefined or overdefined sketch. If you extrude an underdefined sketch, a (-) sign will be displayed on the left of the sketch name in the **FeatureManager Design Tree**. Similarly, if you extrude an overdefined sketch, a (+) sign will be displayed on the left of the sketch name in the **FeatureManager Design Tree**. To view these signs, click on the ▸ sign available on the left of **Boss-Extrude1** in the **FeatureManager Design Tree**; the (+/-) sign will be displayed before the sketch name. The **Selected Contours** rollout will be discussed in the later chapters.*

Creating Thin Extruded Features

The thin extruded features can be created using a closed or an open sketch. If the sketch is closed, the thickness will be specified inside or outside the sketch to create a cavity inside the feature, as shown in Figure 5-16. To convert a closed sketch into a thin feature, select the check box in the **Thin Feature** rollout title bar; the rollout will expand, as shown in Figure 5-17.

Figure 5-16 Thin extruded feature created using a closed loop

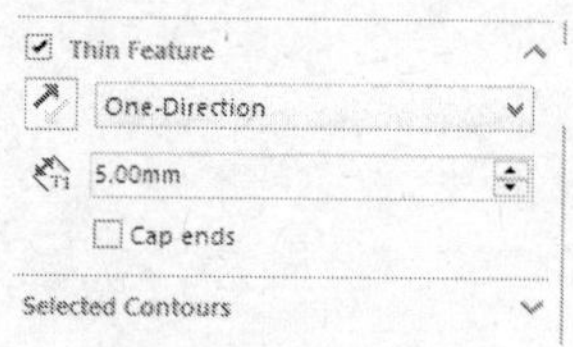

*Figure 5-17 The **Thin Feature** rollout*

The options in the **Thin Feature** rollout of the **Boss-Extrude PropertyManager** are discussed next.

Type

The options provided in the **Type** drop-down list are used to select the method of defining the thickness of the thin feature. These options are discussed next.

One-Direction

The **One-Direction** option is used to add thickness on one side of the sketch. The amount of thickness to be applied can be specified in the **Thickness** spinner provided below the **Type** drop-down list. For the closed sketches, the direction can be inside or outside the sketch. Similarly, for open sketches, the direction can be below or above the sketch. You can reverse the direction of thickness using the **Reverse Direction** button available on the left of the **Type** drop-down list. This button will be available only when you select the **One-Direction** option from this drop-down list.

Mid-Plane

The **Mid-Plane** option is used to add the thickness equally on both sides of the sketch. The value of the thickness of the thin feature can be specified in the **Thickness** spinner provided below this drop-down list.

Two-Direction

The **Two-Direction** option is used to create a thin feature by adding different thicknesses on both sides of a sketch. The thickness values in direction 1 and direction 2 can be specified in the **Direction 1 Thickness** spinner and the **Direction 2 Thickness** spinner, respectively. These spinners will automatically be displayed below the **Type** drop-down list when you select the **Two-Direction** option from this drop-down list.

Cap ends

The **Cap ends** check box will be displayed only when you select a closed sketch for converting into a thin feature. This check box is selected to cap the two open faces of the thin extruded feature. Both the open faces will be capped with a face having specified thickness. When you select this check box, the **Cap Thickness** spinner will be displayed below this check box. The thickness of the end caps can be specified by using this spinner.

If the sketch to be extruded is open, as shown in Figure 5-18, the **Thin Feature** rollout will be invoked automatically on invoking the **Boss-Extrude PropertyManager**. The resulting feature is shown in Figure 5-19.

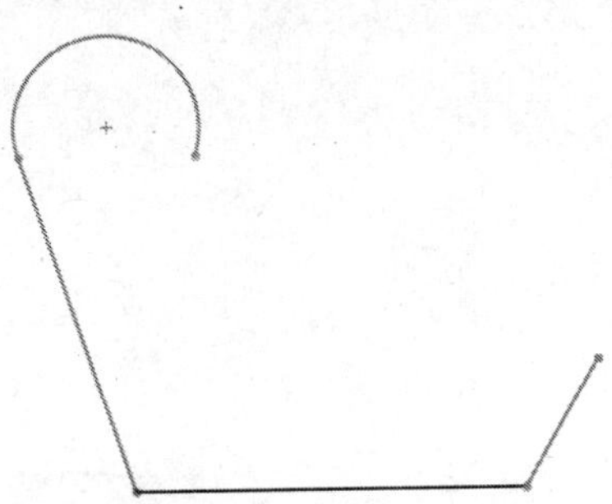

Figure 5-18 *Open sketch to be converted into a thin feature*

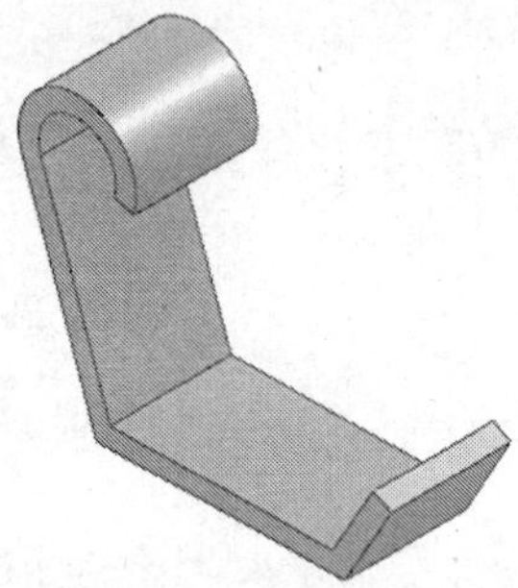

Figure 5-19 *Resulting thin feature*

Auto-fillet corners

The **Auto-fillet corners** check box will be displayed only when you select an open sketch to convert it to a thin feature. If you select this check box, all sharp vertices in the sketch will automatically be filleted during conversion into a thin feature. As a result, the thin feature will have filleted edges. The radius of the fillet can be specified in the **Fillet Radius** spinner, which will be displayed below the **Auto-fillet corners** check box.

Figure 5-20 shows the thin feature created by extruding an open sketch in both directions. Note that a draft angle is applied to the feature while extruding in the front direction and the **Auto-fillet corners** check box is selected while creating this thin feature.

Note

The corners of thin features that can accommodate a given radius will only get filleted.

CREATING BASE FEATURES BY REVOLVING SKETCHES

CommandManager: Features > Revolved Boss/Base
SOLIDWORKS menus: Insert > Boss/Base > Revolve
Toolbar: Features > Extruded Boss/Base > Revolved Boss/Base

You can create the base feature by revolving a sketch about an axis with the help of the **Revolved Boss/Base** tool. This tool is available in the **Features CommandManager**. Choose this tool to revolve the sketch about a revolution axis. The revolution axis could be an axis, an entity of the sketch, or an edge of another feature. Note that whether you use a centerline or an edge to revolve the sketch, the sketch should be drawn on one side of the centerline or the edge.

In SOLIDWORKS, the right-hand thumb rule is followed for determining the direction of revolution. This rule states that if the thumb of your right hand points in the direction of the axis of revolution, the direction of the curled fingers will determine the default direction of revolution, refer to Figure 5-21.

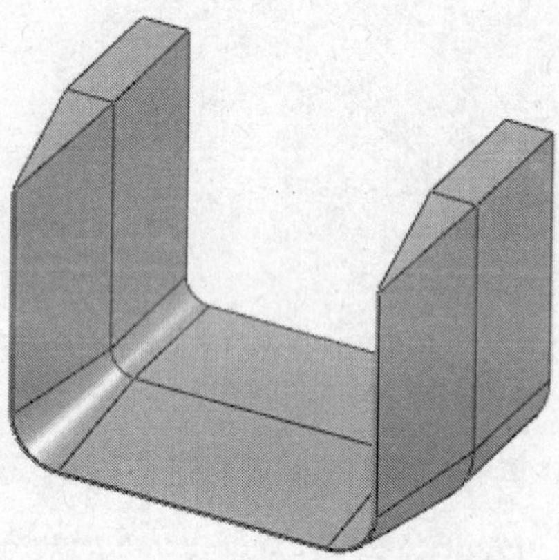

Figure 5-20 *Thin feature created in both directions*

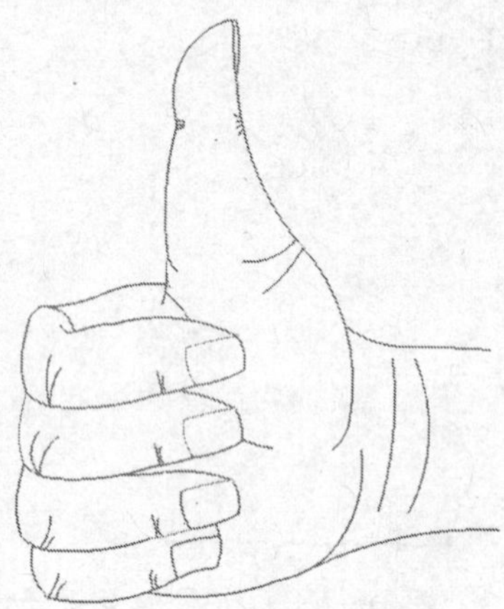

Figure 5-21 *The right-hand thumb rule*

For example, consider a case in which you draw a centerline from bottom to top (direction of thumb in Figure 5-21) in the drawing area. Now, if you use this centerline to create a revolved feature, the default direction of revolution will be along the direction of the curled fingers.

Note

*You can also reverse the direction of revolution using the **Reverse Direction** button in the **Revolve PropertyManager**.*

Invoke the **Revolved Boss/Base** tool after drawing the sketch; the sketching environment is closed and the part modeling environment is invoked. Similar to extruding the sketches, the resulting revolved feature can be a solid feature or a thin feature depending on the sketch and the options selected to be revolved. If the sketch is closed, it can be converted into a solid feature or a thin feature. However, if the sketch is open, it can be converted only into a thin feature. The solid and thin features are discussed next.

Creating Solid Revolved Features

After you have completed drawing a closed sketch, dimension it to convert it into a fully defined sketch. Next, choose the **Features** tab above the **FeatureManager Design Tree**; the **Features CommandManager** will be displayed. Next, choose the **Revolved Boss/Base** button; the **Revolve PropertyManager** will be displayed, as shown in Figure 5-22. Also, the confirmation corner will be displayed and preview of the base feature created using the default options will be displayed in temporary shaded graphics. The direction arrow will also be displayed in gray. If you have not drawn the centerline, you will be prompted to select an axis of revolution. Select an edge or a line as the axis of revolution; preview will be displayed. The options in the **Revolve PropertyManager** are discussed next.

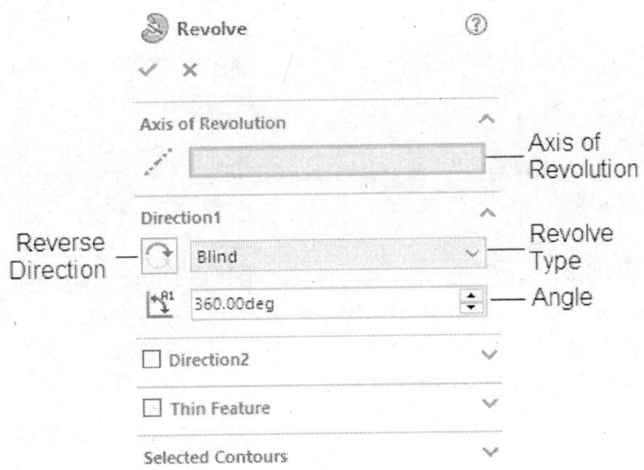

*Figure 5-22 The **Revolve PropertyManager***

Direction1

In SOLIDWORKS, you can specify the end condition for a revolve feature as you did for an extrude feature. The options in the **Direction1** rollout are discussed next.

Revolve Type

The **Revolve Type** drop-down list is used to define the termination of the revolved feature. The options in this drop-down list are similar to those in the **End Condition** drop-down list of the **Extrude PropertyManager**. The only difference being that you need to specify the angle of revolution instead of the extrusion depth.

The **Blind** option is selected by default in this drop-down list and you need to specify the angle of revolution. You can specify the angle of revolution in the **Direction 1 Angle** spinner displayed below this drop-down list. The default value in the **Direction 1 Angle** spinner is **360** degrees. Therefore, if you revolve the sketch using this value, a complete round feature will be created. You can also reverse the direction of revolution of the sketch by choosing the **Reverse Direction** button that is displayed on the left of the **Revolve Type** drop-down list. Figure 5-23 shows the sketch of a piston and Figure 5-24 shows the resulting piston created by revolving the sketch through an angle of 360 degrees. Note that the left vertical edge of the sketch that is vertically in line with the origin is used to revolve the sketch.

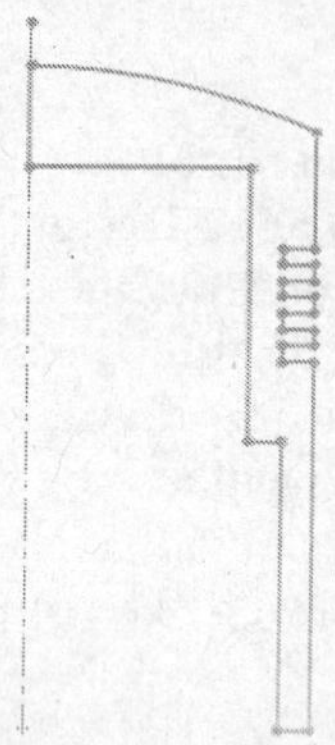

Figure 5-23 Sketch of the piston to be revolved

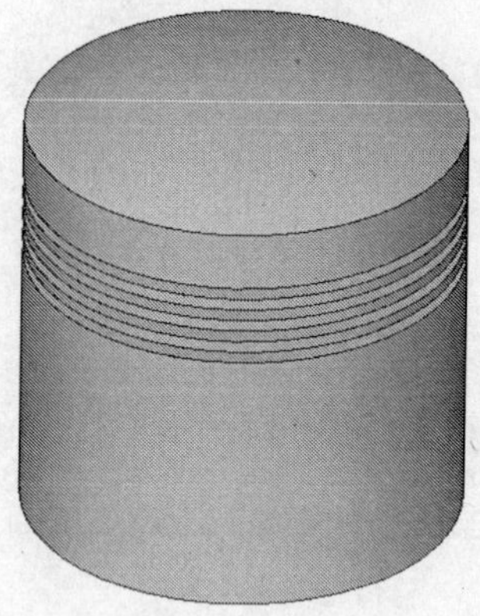

Figure 5-24 Feature created by revolving the sketch through an angle of 360 degrees

Figure 5-25 shows a piston created by revolving the same sketch through an angle of 270 degrees.

If you select the **Mid-Plane** option from the **Revolve Type** drop-down list, the feature will be created by revolving the sketch equally on both sides of the sketch plane. The angle of revolution can be specified in the **Angle** spinner. On selecting this option, the **Reverse Direction** button will not be available.

Direction2

Expand the **Direction2** rollout by selecting the check box on its left. This rollout is used to revolve a sketch with different values in the second direction of the sketching plane. This rollout will not be available, if you select the **Mid Plane** option in the **Revolve Type** drop-down list in the **Direction1** rollout. The options in this rollout are similar to those in the **Direction1** rollout.

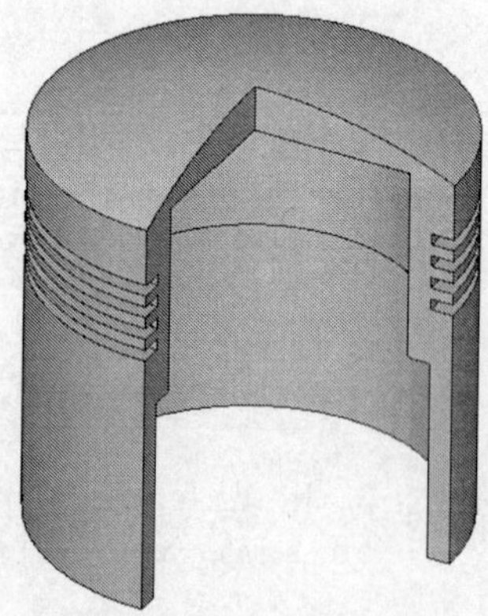

Figure 5-25 Feature created by revolving the sketch through an angle of 270 degrees

Creating Thin Revolved Features

The thin revolved features can be created using the closed or the open sketch. If the sketch is closed, it will be offset inside or outside to create a cavity in the feature, as shown in Figure 5-26. In this figure, the sketch is revolved through an angle of 180 degrees. To convert a closed sketch into a thin feature, select the **Thin Feature** check box from the **Revolve PropertyManager**; the **Thin Feature** rollout will expand, as shown in Figure 5-27. However, if the sketch to be revolved is open and you invoke the **Revolved Boss/Base** tool, the **SOLIDWORKS** information box will be displayed. This information box will inform you that the sketch is currently open and a non-thin revolved feature requires a closed sketch. You will be given an option of automatically closing the sketch. If you choose **Yes** from this information box, a line segment will automatically be drawn between the first and the last segment of the sketch and the **Revolve PropertyManager** will be displayed. However, if you choose **No** from this information box, the **Revolve PropertyManager** will be displayed and the **Thin Feature** rollout will be displayed automatically.

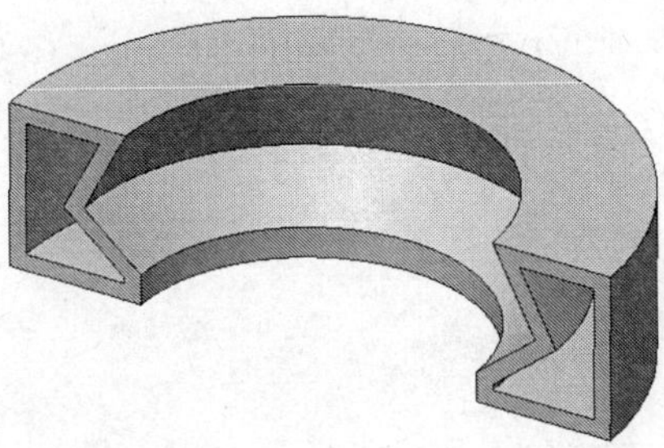

Figure 5-26 *Thin feature created by revolving the sketch through an angle of 180 degrees*

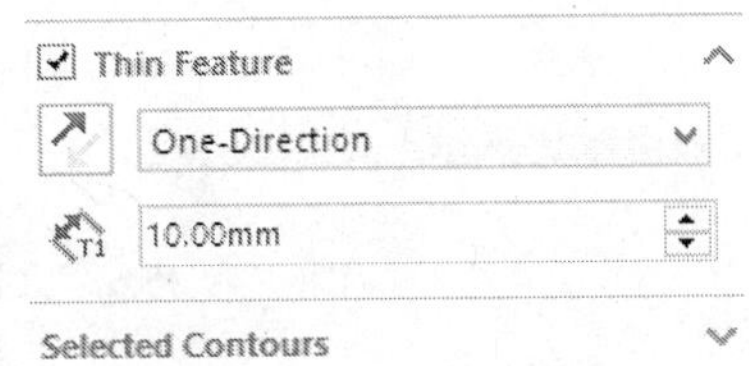

Figure 5-27 *The* ***Thin Feature*** *rollout*

> **Tip**
> 1. *Even though you can revolve a sketch using an edge in the sketch, it is recommended to draw a centerline so that you can create linear diameter dimensions for the revolved features.*
>
> 2. *You can dynamically modify the angle of a revolved feature by dragging the direction arrows.*
>
> 3. *To change the type of revolution, right-click to display a shortcut menu and then choose the required option from it.*

The options in the **Thin Feature** rollout of the **Revolve PropertyManager** are discussed next.

Type

The options in the **Type** drop-down list are used to select a method to specify the thickness of the thin feature. These options are discussed next.

One-Direction

The **One-Direction** option is used to add the thickness on one side of the sketch. The thickness can be specified in the **Direction 1 Thickness** spinner provided below this drop-down list. For the closed sketches, the direction can be inside or outside the sketch. Similarly, for open sketches, the direction can be below or above the sketch. You can reverse the direction of thickness using the **Reverse Direction** button available on the left of this drop-down list. This button will be available only when you select the **One-Direction** option from the **Type** drop-down list.

Mid-Plane

The **Mid-Plane** option is used to add the thickness equally on both sides of the sketch. The value of the thickness of the thin feature can be specified in the **Direction 1 Thickness** spinner provided below the **Type** drop-down list.

Two-Direction

The **Two-Direction** option is used to create a thin feature by adding different thicknesses on both sides of the sketch. The thickness values for direction 1 and direction 2 can be specified in the **Direction 1 Thickness** spinner and the **Direction 2 Thickness** spinner, respectively. These spinners will be displayed below the **Type** drop-down list automatically when you select the **Two-Direction** option from this drop-down list.

If the sketch is open, as shown in Figure 5-28, the resulting feature will be similar to that shown in Figure 5-29.

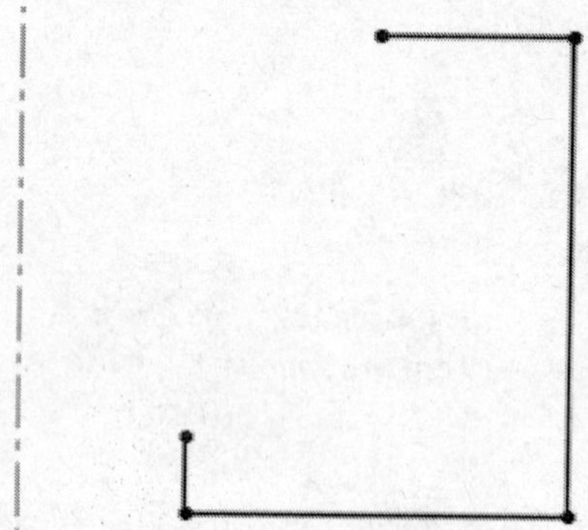

Figure 5-28 The open sketch to be revolved and the centerline as the revolution axis

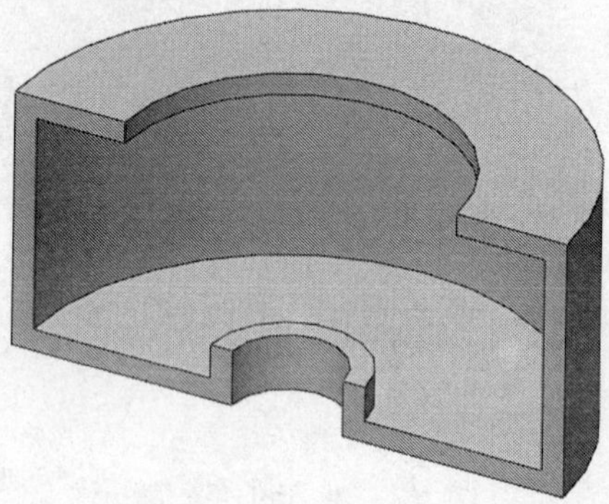

Figure 5-29 Thin feature created by revolving the open sketch through an angle of 180 degrees

Tip

While defining the wall thickness of a thin revolved feature, remember that the wall thickness should be added such that the centerline does not intersect with the sketch. If the centerline intersects with the sketch, the sketch will not get revolved.

DETERMINING THE MASS PROPERTIES OF PARTS

CommandManager:	Evaluate > Mass Properties
SOLIDWORKS menus:	Tools > Evaluate >Mass Properties
Toolbar:	Tools > Mass Properties

The **Mass Properties** tool enables you to determine the mass properties of the part or assembly that is available in the current session. Note that this tool will not be enabled if there is no solid model in the current session. Mass properties include density, mass, volume, surface area, center of mass, principal axes of inertia and principal moments of inertia, and moments of inertia.

To calculate the mass properties of the current model, choose the **Mass Properties** tool from the **Evaluate CommandManager**; the **Mass Properties** dialog box will be displayed with the mass properties of the current model. As soon as you invoke the **Mass Properties** dialog box, a 3D triad will be placed at the center of the model. The other options in this dialog box are same as discussed in the **Section Properties** dialog box.

In SOLIDWORKS, you can also override the properties of the model like mass, center of mass, moment of inertia, principle stresses, and so on. To do so, invoke the **Mass properties** dialog box and choose the **Override Mass Properties** button; the **Override Mass Properties** dialog box will be displayed. By using the options in this dialog box, you can override the mass properties of the selected model.

DYNAMICALLY ROTATING THE VIEW OF A MODEL

In SOLIDWORKS, you can dynamically rotate the view in the 3D space so that the solid models in the current document can be viewed from all directions. This allows you to visually maneuver around the model to view all the features clearly. This tool can be invoked even when you are using some other tool. For example, you can invoke this tool when the **Boss-Extrude PropertyManager** is displayed. You can freely rotate the model in the 3D space or rotate it around a selected vertex, edge, or face. Both methods of rotating the model are discussed next.

Rotating the View Freely in 3D Space

SOLIDWORKS menus:	View > Modify > Rotate
Shortcut Key:	Middle Mouse Button

You can rotate the view freely in the 3D space by using the **Rotate** tool. To invoke this tool, choose **View > Modify > Rotate** from the SOLIDWORKS menus. You can also invoke this tool by choosing the **Rotate View** option from the shortcut menu that will be displayed when you right-click in the drawing area. When you are inside some other tool, right-click and then choose the **Zoom/Pan/Rotate > Rotate View** from the shortcut menu to invoke the **Rotate View** tool. When you invoke this tool, the cursor will be replaced by the rotate view cursor. Now, press and hold the left mouse button and drag the cursor to rotate the view. Figure 5-30 shows the rotated view of the model.

Rotating the View around a Selected Vertex, Edge, or Face

To rotate a view around a vertex, edge, or face, invoke the **Rotate** tool and move the rotate view cursor close to the vertex, edge, or the face around which you want to rotate the view. When it is highlighted, select it using the left mouse button; the rotate view cursor will be displayed, as shown in Figure 5-31. Next, drag the cursor to rotate the view around the selected vertex, edge, or face.

Tip

To resume rotating the view freely after you have rotated it around a selected vertex, edge, or face, click anywhere in the drawing area. Now when you drag the cursor, you will notice that the view is rotated freely in the 3D space. Invoke the ***Select*** *tool to exit the* ***Rotate*** *tool.*

You can also press the middle mouse button and drag the cursor to rotate the model freely in the 3D space.

Figure 5-30 Rotating the view to display the model from different directions

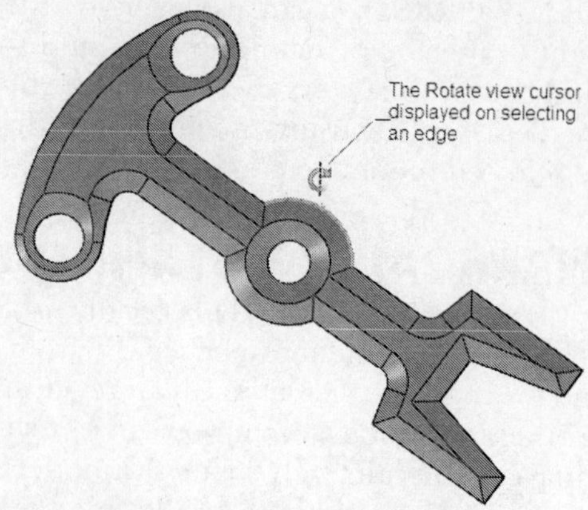

Figure 5-31 The rotate view cursor displayed on selecting an edge

MODIFYING THE VIEW ORIENTATION

In SOLIDWORKS, you can manually change the view orientation using some predefined standard views or user-defined views. To invoke these standard views, choose the **View Orientation** flyout from the **View (Heads-Up)** toolbar; the **View Orientation** flyout will be displayed, as shown in Figure 5-32. Also, the view selector will be displayed around the model, as shown in Figure 5-33.

You can choose the required view from this flyout or view selector and orient the model to standard views. You need to choose the **Normal To** option to reorient the view normal to a viewing direction of the selected face or plane. To do so, select the face normal to which you need to reorient the model and choose the **Normal To** option from this flyout. If you have not selected a face before choosing this option, the view will be oriented to the rotated coordinated system or the XY plane. You can also choose the **Normal To** option from the pop-up toolbar that will be displayed on selecting an entity.

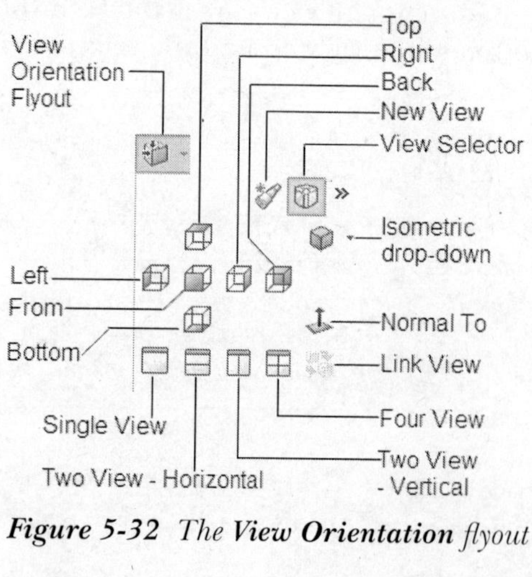

Figure 5-32 The ***View Orientation*** *flyout*

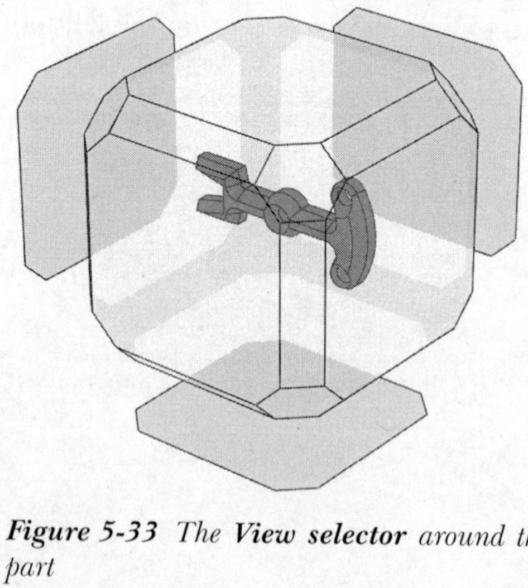

Figure 5-33 The ***View selector*** *around the part*

Alternatively, to orient the model, choose **View > Modify > Orientation** from the SOLIDWORKS menus; the **Orientation** dialog box will be displayed, as shown in Figure 5-34 and a View Selector will be displayed around the model. You can invoke the standard views using the **Orientation** dialog box. This dialog box can also be invoked by choosing **View Orientation** from the shortcut menu or by pressing SPACEBAR on the keyboard.

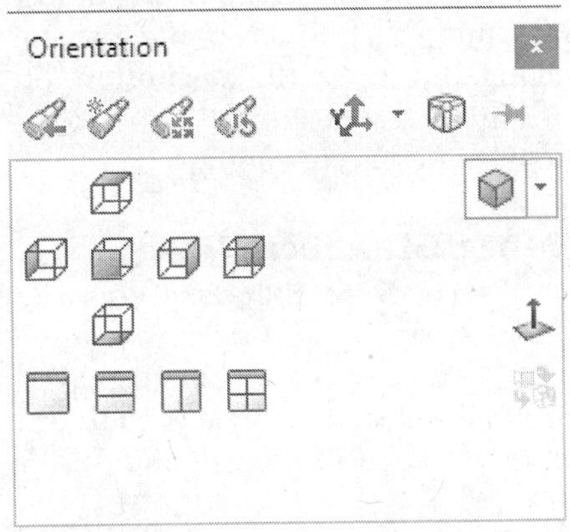

*Figure 5-34 The **Orientation** dialog box*

You can invoke a view by clicking on the buttons available in this dialog box. These buttons are discussed next.

Pin/Unpin the dialog

You will notice that when you select a view or invoke a tool, the **Orientation** dialog box is automatically closed. If you want this dialog box to be retained on the screen, you can pin it at a location by choosing the **Pin/Unpin the dialog** button which is available on the upper right corner on this dialog box. Move the dialog box to the desired location and choose this button; the dialog box will be pinned to that location and will not be closed when you perform any operation.

View Selector

By default, the **View Selector** button is chosen in the **View Orientation** flyout and **Orientation** dialog box. As a result, the selector views will be displayed around the model. These selector views are used to orient the model in the required view easily. On selecting the required view of the model from the view selector, the model will be oriented to the selected view and aligned normal to the graphical window.

Previous View

The **Previous View** button is used to modify the orientation of the model to its previous view. You can also use the keyboard shortcut CTRL+SHIFT+Z to modify the orientation of the view.

New View

The **New View** button is chosen to create a user-defined view and save it in the list of views in the **Orientation** dialog box. Modify the current view using various drawing display tools and the **Rotate View** tool and then choose this button; the **Named View** dialog box will be displayed. Enter the name of the view in the **View name** edit box and then choose the **OK** button. You will notice that a user-defined view is created and it is saved in the list in the **Orientation** dialog box.

Update Standard Views

The **Update Standard Views** button is chosen to modify the orientation of the standard views. For example, when you select the **Top** option from this dialog box, the top view of a model will be displayed. If you want to make this view as the front view, change the current view to the front view. To do so, click on the **Front** option in the **Orientation** dialog box.

Now, choose the **Update Standard Views** button and then click on the **Top** option in the **Orientation** dialog box. On doing so, the **SOLIDWORKS** message box will be displayed informing that if you change the standard view, all other named views in the model will also be changed. Choose the **Yes** button; the views are modified. You will notice that the view that was originally displayed as the top view is now displayed as the front view. Also, all other views will be modified accordingly.

Reset Standard Views

The **Reset Standard Views** button is chosen to reset the standard settings of all standard views in the current drawing. When you choose this button, the **SOLIDWORKS** warning message box will be displayed and you will be prompted to confirm whether you want to reset all the standard views to their default settings or not. If you choose **Yes**, all the standard views will reset to their default settings.

Changing the Orientation Using the Reference Triad

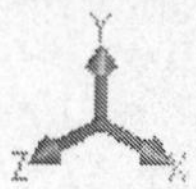

In SOLIDWORKS, you can also change the view orientation using the reference triad available at the lower left corner of the drawing area. To orient the view normal to the screen, you need to select an axis of the reference triad. If you select the Y-axis, the top view will be oriented normal to the screen. Similarly, if you select the X or Z-axis, the right or front view will be oriented normal to the screen. You can also change the current view direction by 180-degree using the reference triad. To do so, select an axis normal to the screen. To rotate the view 90-degree about the selected axis, press and hold the SHIFT key and then select the axis of the reference triad; you will note that the view will be rotated about the selected axis. You can also rotate the view opposite to this direction. To do so, press and hold the CTRL + SHIFT keys and then select the axis.

To rotate the view about the selected axis, press and hold the ALT key and then select the required axis of the reference triad; the part will rotate to the default angle, 15-degree. To rotate the view in the opposite direction, press and hold the ALT+ CTRL keys and then select the axis. In this way, you can rotate the part at an increment of 15-degree. You can also rotate view using different arrow keys. To change this angle value, choose the **Options** button from the Menu Bar; the **System Options - General** dialog box will be displayed. Choose the **View** option from the area on the left of the dialog box to display the options related to the view. Next, set the required angle value in the **Arrow keys** spinner and choose the **OK** button.

RESTORING THE PREVIOUS VIEW

While working on a model, you may need to temporarily change the view of the model to view it from different directions. Once you have finished editing or viewing the model in the current view, choose the **Previous View** button in the **View (Heads-Up)** toolbar to restore the previous view.

DISPLAYING THE DRAWING AREA IN VIEWPORTS

In SOLIDWORKS, you can display the drawing area in multiple viewports. The procedure to do so is discussed next.

Displaying the Drawing Area in Two Horizontal Viewports

SOLIDWORKS menus:	Window > Viewport > Two View - Horizontal
Toolbar:	View (Heads-Up) > View Orientation > Two View - Horizontal

The **Two View - Horizontal** option is used to split the drawing view to display the model in two viewports that are placed horizontally. To do so, choose **View Orientation > Two View - Horizontal** from the **View (Heads-Up)** toolbar; the drawing area will be displayed in two viewports. Figure 5-35 shows the model placed with the top orientation in the upper row and with the front orientation in the lower row. The type of orientation of both the models is displayed at the lower left corner of each viewport.

To switch back to the single viewport, choose **View Orientation > Single View** from the **View (Heads-Up)** toolbar or choose **Window > Viewport > Single View** from the SOLIDWORKS menus.

Displaying the Drawing Area in Two Vertical Viewports

SOLIDWORKS menus:	Window > Viewport > Two View - Vertical
Toolbar:	View (Heads-Up) > View Orientation > Two View - Vertical

The **Two View - Vertical** button is used to split the drawing view to display a model in two viewports that are placed vertically. To display the model in this fashion, choose **View Orientation > Two View - Vertical** from the **View (Heads-Up)** toolbar; the drawing area will be divided into two viewports placed vertically. Figure 5-36 shows the model placed with the front orientation in the left column and with the right orientation in the right column.

Tip
On creating multiple viewports, you will notice that the ***View (Heads-Up)*** *toolbar will be available in the currently active viewport. To activate another viewport, click once in the drawing area of that viewport.*

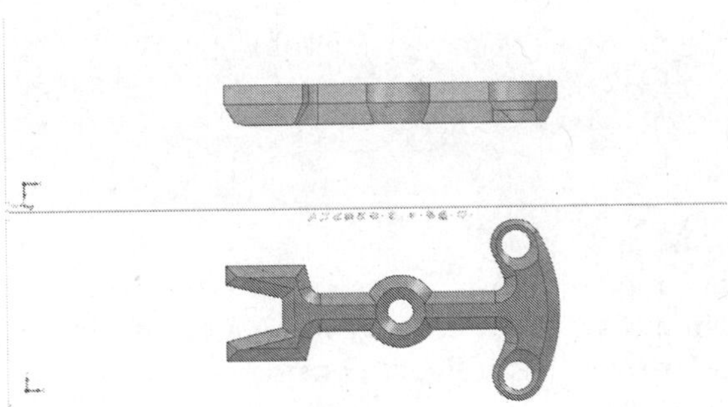

Figure 5-35 *Drawing area divided into two horizontal viewports*

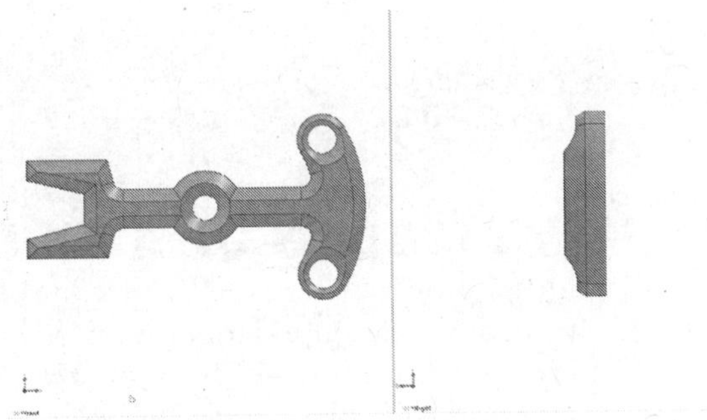

Figure 5-36 *Drawing area divided into two vertical viewports*

Displaying the Drawing Area in Four Viewports

SOLIDWORKS menus: Window > Viewport > Four View
Toolbar: View (Heads-Up) > View Orientation > Four View

The **Four View** option is used to split the drawing view to display a model in four viewports, as shown in Figure 5-37. To display the model in this fashion, choose **View Orientation > Four View** from the **View (Heads-Up)** toolbar; the drawing area will be divided into four viewports. The model is placed in the front, top, left, and trimetric orientations in these four viewports. The type of orientation of all the models is displayed at the lower left corner of each viewport.

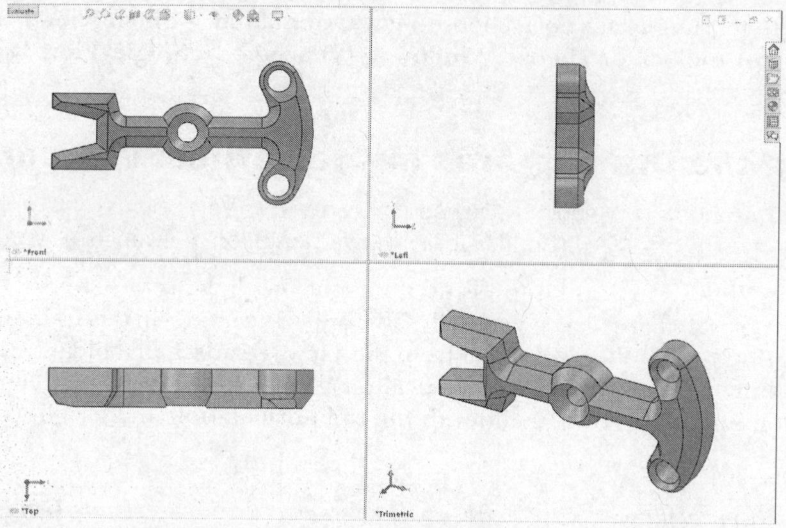

***Figure 5-37** Model displayed in four viewports*

Tip

*Right-click and choose **Link Views** from the shortcut menu to link the viewports. Now, if you pan or zoom one view while multiple viewports are being displayed, the model will pan or zoom accordingly in all the other viewports. Note that this linking is not applicable for the viewport in which the model is displayed in 3D orientation.*

DISPLAY MODES OF A MODEL

SOLIDWORKS provides you with various predefined modes to display model. In SOLIDWORKS, the display modes are grouped together in the **Display Style** flyout. To invoke this flyout, choose the **Display Style** button from the **View (Heads-Up)** toolbar; a flyout consisting of tools that are used for various display modes will be displayed. Choose any of the display modes. These modes are discussed next.

Wireframe

When you choose the **Wireframe** button, all the hidden lines will be displayed along with the visible lines in the model. However, if you set this display mode for complex models, it may become difficult to recognize the visible lines and the hidden lines.

Hidden Lines Visible

When you choose the **Hidden Lines Visible** button, the model will be displayed in the wireframe and the hidden lines in the model will be displayed as dashed lines.

Hidden Lines Removed

When you choose the **Hidden Lines Removed** button, the hidden lines in the model will not be displayed. In such case, only the edges of the faces visible in the current view of the model will be displayed.

Shaded With Edges

The **Shaded With Edges** mode is the default mode in which the model is displayed. In this display mode, the model is shaded and the edges of the visible faces of the model are displayed in the default color applied for visible edges.

Shaded

This display mode is similar to the **Shaded With Edges** mode with the only difference being that in this case the edges of the visible faces are displayed in the same color as of the model.

Tip

Sometimes, when you rotate the view of an assembly or a model having large number of features in the ***Shaded*** *or* ***Hidden Lines Removed*** *shading mode, the regeneration of the model takes a lot of time. This can be avoided by choosing the* ***Draft Quality HLR/HLV*** *button combined with other shading modes. This button is not available by default, therefore, you need to customize a toolbar or a* ***CommandManager****. On choosing this button, you can speed up the regeneration time and easily rotate the view. This is a toggle mode and is turned on when you choose this button.*

ADDITIONAL DISPLAY MODES

In addition to the standard display modes discussed earlier, you can also display a model in the shaded mode, or view a model in the perspective view. The tools for displaying these views are available in the **View (Heads-Up)** toolbar. These tools are discussed next.

Shadows In Shaded Mode

Toolbar: View (Heads-Up) > View Settings flyout > Shadows In Shaded Mode

The **Shadows In Shaded Mode** button is used to display the shadow of a model as if the light is falling on the model from its top in the current viewport. With this option activated, the performance of the system is affected during the dynamic orientation. Remember that the position of the shadow is not changed when you rotate the model in the 3D space. Figure 5-38 shows a T-section in the shadow in the shaded mode.

Perspective

Toolbar: View (Heads-Up) > View Settings flyout > Perspective

You can display the perspective view of a model by choosing **View Settings > Perspective** from the **View (Heads-Up)** toolbar. Figure 5-39 shows the T-section with shadow in the perspective view. You can also modify the settings of the perspective view. To modify the settings, choose **View > Modify > Perspective** from the SOLIDWORKS menus; the **Perspective View PropertyManager** will be displayed. Use the **Object Sizes Away** spinner of this PropertyManager to modify the observer's position. The **Perspective** option in the SOLIDWORKS menus will be enabled only when the model is set to perspective view using the tool in the **View (Heads-Up)** toolbar.

Figure 5-38 Shadow in active shaded mode

Figure 5-39 T-section displayed in perspective view with shadow

ASSIGNING MATERIALS AND TEXTURES TO MODELS

You can assign materials and textures to models. When you apply a material to a model, the physical properties such as density, young's modulus, and so on will be assigned to the model. When you apply a texture to a model or its face, the image of that texture will be applied to the model or its selected face. However, on applying the texture to a model, the physical properties are not applied to it. The method to assign materials and textures is discussed next.

Tip

You can also save a perspective view as a named view. To do this, invoke the perspective view and define the orientation by rotating the view. Press SPACEBAR to invoke the **Orientation** *dialog box. Next, choose the* **New View** *button and specify the name of the view in the* **Named View** *dialog box.*

Assigning Materials to a Model

SOLIDWORKS menus: Edit > Appearance > Material

Whenever you assign a material to a model, all the physical properties of the selected material are also assigned to the model. As a result, when you calculate the mass properties of the model, the calculations will be based on the physical properties of the material applied. To assign a material to a model, choose **Edit > Appearance > Material** from the SOLIDWORKS menus; the **Material** dialog box will be displayed, as shown in Figure 5-40 . You can also right-click on the **Material <not specified>** node in the **FeatureManager Design Tree** and select the **Edit Material** option to invoke the **Material** dialog box.

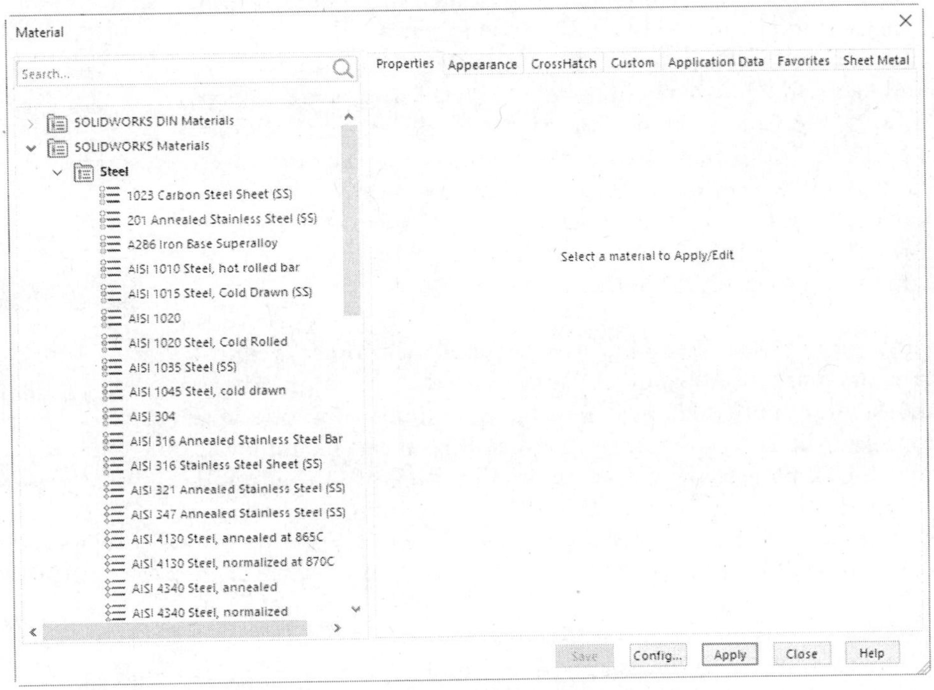

Figure 5-40 The ***Material*** *dialog box*

A number of material families are available in the left area of the dialog box. Click on the sign located on the left of the material family to display all materials under that family. Select the material from that family.

Changing the Appearance of the Model

SOLIDWORKS menus: Edit > Appearance > Appearance
Toolbar: View > Edit Appearance

In SOLIDWORKS, you can change the appearance of a model by assigning color, texture or decals to it. To do so, choose **Edit > Appearance > Appearance** from the SOLIDWORKS menus; the **color PropertyManager** will be displayed, as shown in Figure 5-41. Also, the **Appearances, Scenes, and Decals** task pane will be displayed on the right-side of the drawing area. You can also invoke the **color PropertyManager** using another method. In this method, first you need to select a face; a pop-up toolbar will be displayed. Now, choose the **Appearance** button from this toolbar; a flyout will be displayed with the name of the Face, Feature name, Body, and Part name. Select the feature for which you need to change the color; the **color PropertyManager** will be displayed. In this PropertyManager, the **Selected Geometry** rollout has five buttons on its left; namely, **Select Part**, **Select Faces**, **Select Surfaces**, **Select Bodies**, and **Select Features**. These buttons are used as filters for making a selection to assign the texture or the color to a model. For example, if you want to assign the color to the face of the model, clear the existing selection from the **Selected Entities** area and then choose the **Select Faces** button from the **Selected Geometry** rollout. This allows you to select only a specified face of the model. Select the required face from the model; the name of the selected face will be displayed in the **Selected Entities** area. Next, select a color in the **Color** rollout. You can also set the required color using the **Pick a Color** display area; the selected color will be displayed in the **Color** display area of this rollout. You can also use the **Red Component of Color**, **Green Component of Color**, and **Blue Component of Color** spinners to set the color. The color selected in this rollout will be applied to the selected faces of the entity.

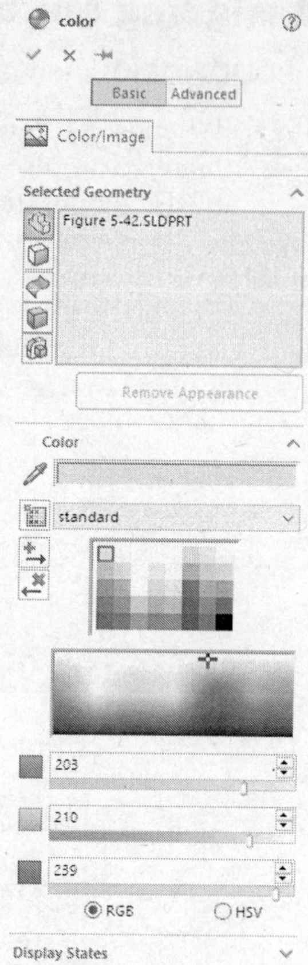

***Figure 5-41** The **color** PropertyManager*

To apply a texture to a face or a part, invoke the **Appearances, Scenes, and Decals** task pane, if it is not already invoked. Next, expand the **Appearances(color)** node. Then, expand the required sub-node and select an option; the corresponding texture will be listed in the lower portion of the task pane. Now, select the required texture from it and then drag and drop on the face of the model; a pop-up toolbar will be displayed. Choose the required option from the pop-up toolbar; the selected texture will be applied.

In SOLIDWORKS, you can add decals to the model. To do so, invoke the **Appearances, Scenes, and Decals** task pane, expand the **Decals** node, and then select the **logos** subnode from it; the available decals will be displayed. Drag and drop the decals on a face; the **Decals PropertyManager** will be displayed. You can change the decal or other properties and choose the **OK** button to apply the decal.

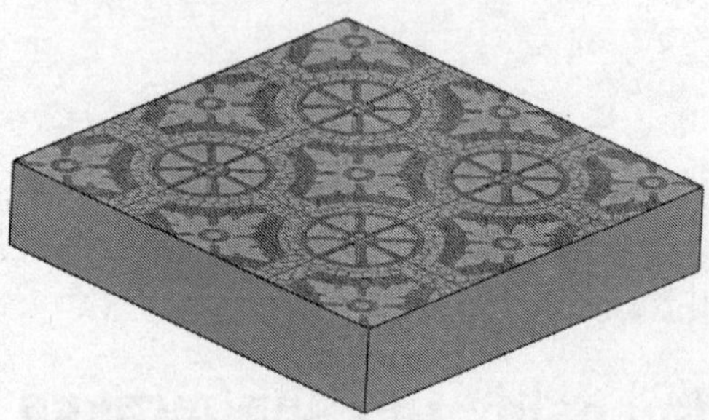

***Figure 5-42** Appearances applied on the top face of the model*

Figure 5-42 shows the model with the texture of **floor tile 1** type applied to its top face. You can apply this texture by choosing **Stone > Architectural > Floor Tile** from the **Appearances/Scenes** task pane.

Editing the Appearances

In SOLIDWORKS, the **DisplayManager** contains the details of the texture, color, and decals applied to a model. To view these details, choose the **DisplayManager** tab; the **DisplayManager** will be displayed with the details of the color and texture applied. Expand the **color** or **texture** node to view the feature to which the color or texture is applied, refer to Figure 5-43. To edit the color or texture of a feature, double-click on the corresponding node; the PropertyManager of the selected entity will be displayed. Change the properties and choose the **OK** button.

If you have not applied any appearance on a model, a message will be displayed, stating that no appearance is assigned. Also, the **Open Appearance Library** button will be available below that message. On choosing this button, the **Appearances, Scenes, and Decals** task pane will be displayed. You can apply the color or texture by using this task pane.

Similarly, to edit the decals applied, choose the **View Decals** button in the **DisplayManager**; the decals applied will be listed. Expand the node to view the feature to which the decal has to be applied. Figure 5-44 shows the logo applied as decals to a face. Double-click on the decal node; the corresponding PropertyManager will be displayed. Change the properties of the decal and choose the **OK** button.

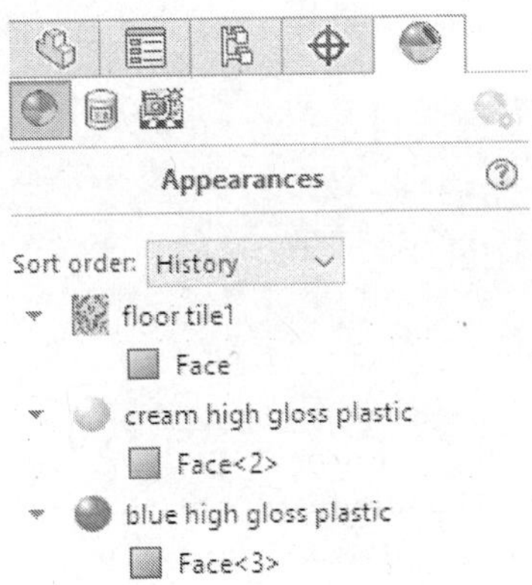

Figure 5-43 The ***DisplayManager*** *displaying the details of the color and texture applied*

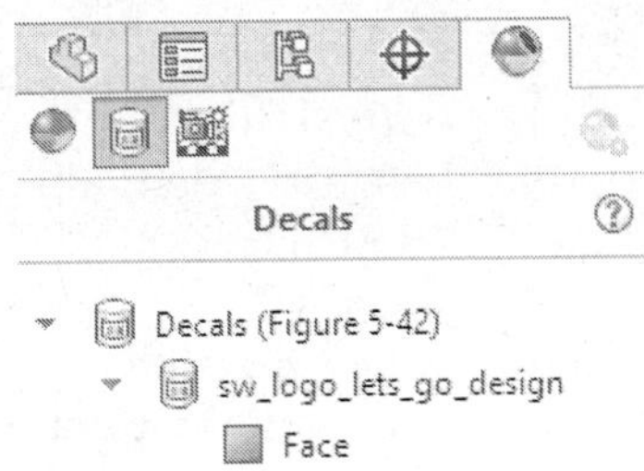

Figure 5-44 The ***DisplayManager*** *displaying the details of the decals applied*

If you have not applied any decals, then a message stating that no decal has been assigned will be displayed and the **Open Decals Library** button will be available below that message box. On choosing this button, the **Appearances, Scenes, and Decals** task pane will be displayed with the default decals. Now, you can apply the desired decal.

You can also edit the appearances of a model without invoking the **DisplayManager**. To do so, select the face where the texture or color is applied; a pop up toolbar will be displayed. Next, choose the **Appearances** button from the toolbar; a flyout will be displayed with the name of the Face, Extrude, Body, and Part. Select the feature for which you need to edit the texture; the corresponding PropertyManager will be displayed. If you do not want to keep a particular appearance, you can remove it by selecting it and then choosing the **Remove Appearance** button available below the **Selected Entities** area of the **Selected Geometry** rollout. Change the parameters and choose the **OK** button.

TUTORIALS

Tutorial 1

In this tutorial, you will open the sketch drawn in Tutorial 3 of Chapter 4. You will then convert that sketch into an extruded model by extruding it along two directions, as shown in Figure 5-45. The parameters for extruding the sketch are given next. **(Expected time: 30 min)**

Direction 1
Depth = 10 mm
Draft angle = 35 degrees
Direction 2
Depth = 15 mm
Draft angle = 0 degree

After creating the model, you will rotate the view using the **Rotate View** tool and then modify the standard views such that the front view of the model becomes the top view. You will then save the model with the current settings. Next, you will create a new drawing document, generate the views of the model, and place them on a drawing sheet.

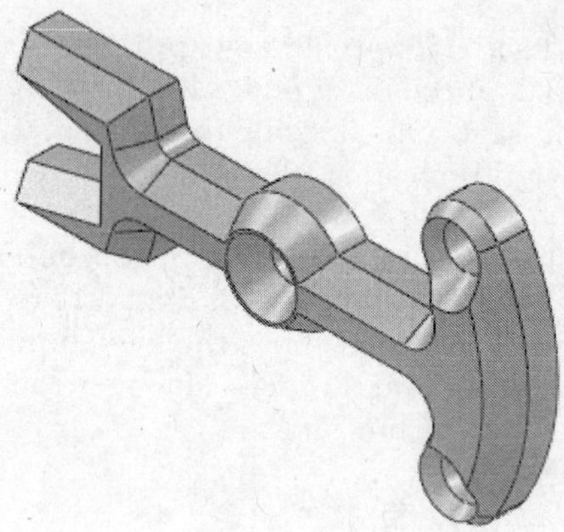

Figure 5-45 *Model for Tutorial 1*

The following steps are required to complete this tutorial:

a. Open Tutorial 3 of Chapter 4.
b. Save this document in the *c05* folder with a new name.
c. Invoke the **Extruded Boss/Base** tool and convert the sketch into a model.
d. Rotate the view by using the **Rotate View** tool to view the model from all directions.
e. Invoke the **Orientation** dialog box and then modify the standard view.
f. Start a new drawing document, generate the views of the model, and place them on a drawing sheet.

Opening Tutorial 3 of Chapter 4

As the required document is saved in the *c04* folder, you need to select this folder and then open the *c04_tut03.sldprt* document.

1. Start SOLIDWORKS by double-clicking on its shortcut icon on the desktop of your computer.

2. Choose the **Open** button from the Menu Bar to display the **Open** dialog box.

3. Browse to the *SOLIDWORKS* folder and select the *c04* folder.

4. Select the *c04_tut03.sldprt* document and then choose the **Open** button.

As the sketch was saved in the sketching environment in Chapter 4, it opens in the sketching environment.

Saving the Document in the c05 Folder

When you open a document from another chapter, it is recommended that to avoid the original document from getting modified, first save the opened document with a new name in the folder of the current chapter.

1. Choose the **Save As** button from the **Save** flyout in the Menu Bar; the **Save As** dialog box is displayed. 

2. Browse to the SOLIDWORKS folder and then create a new folder with the name *c05* by using the **Create New Folder** button. Make the *c05* folder as the current folder by double-clicking on it.

3. Enter **c05_tut01** as the new name of the document in the **File name** edit box and then choose the **Save** button to save the document.

   The document is saved with the new name and gets opened in the drawing area, as shown in Figure 5-46.

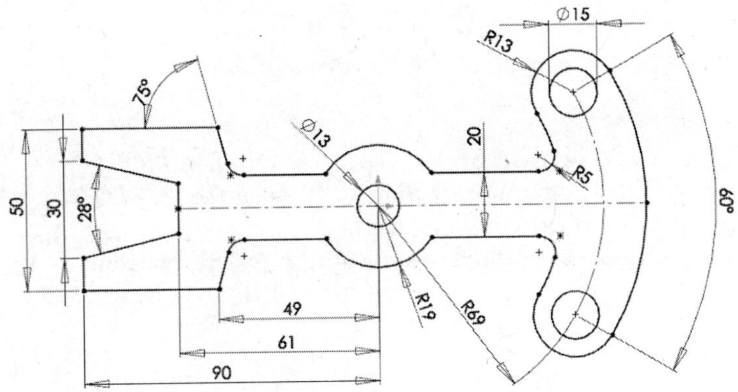

Figure 5-46 *Sketch opened in the drawing area*

Extruding the Sketch

Next, you need to invoke the **Extruded Boss/Base** tool and extrude the sketch using the parameters given in the tutorial description.

1. Choose the **Features** tab from the CommandManager to display the **Features CommandManager**. Then, choose the **Extruded Boss/Base** button; the sketch is automatically oriented to the trimetric view and the **Boss-Extrude PropertyManager** is displayed, as shown in Figure 5-47. 

   As you are converting the closed sketch into a feature, only the **Direction 1** rollout is displayed in the **Boss-Extrude PropertyManager**. Also, a preview of the feature is displayed in the temporary shaded graphics with the default values.

2. Make sure that the value in the **Depth** spinner is 10 and choose the **Draft On/Off** button from the **Direction 1** rollout. Then set **35** in the **Draft Angle** spinner.

These are the settings for direction 1. Next, you need to specify the settings for direction 2.

3. Select the **Direction 2** check box to expand the **Direction 2** rollout.

You will notice that the default values in this rollout are same as you have specified in the **Direction 1** rollout.

4. Choose the **Draft On/Off** button in the **Direction 2** rollout to turn off this option.

This is because you do not require the draft angle in the second direction.

5. Set **15** in the **Depth** spinner as the depth in the second direction.

6. Choose the **OK** button to create the feature or choose **OK** from the confirmation corner.

It is recommended that you change the view to isometric after creating the feature so that you can view it properly.

*Figure 5-47 The **Boss-Extrude** PropertyManager*

7. Choose the **View Orientation** button from the **View (Heads-Up)** toolbar; a flyout is displayed. Choose the **Isometric** button from it. If the origin is displayed, turn off the display of the origin in the model by choosing **Hide/Show Items > View Origins** from the **View (Heads-Up)** toolbar. The isometric view of the resulting solid model is shown in Figure 5-48.

Rotating the View

As mentioned earlier, you can rotate the view to view the model from all directions.

1. Press the middle mouse button and move the cursor; the arrow cursor is replaced by the rotate view cursor.

2. Hold the mouse button and drag the cursor in the drawing area to rotate the view, as shown in Figure 5-49.

You will notice that the model is being displayed from different directions. Remember that when you rotate the view, the model does not rotate but only the camera that is used to view the model rotates around the model.

3. After viewing the model from all directions, press CTRL+7 from the keyboard; the model again gets oriented to the isometric view.

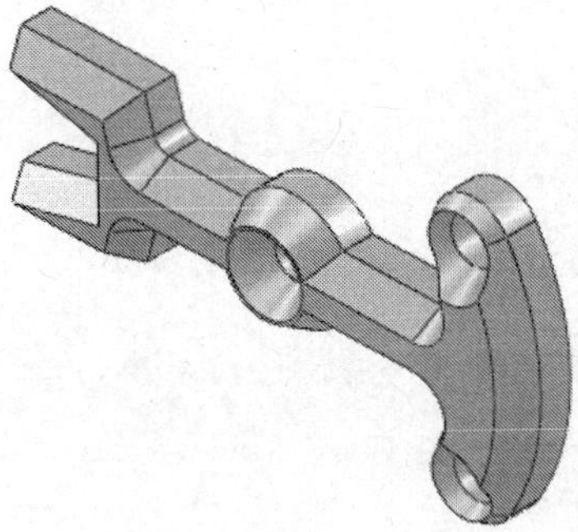

Figure 5-48 *Isometric view of the solid model*

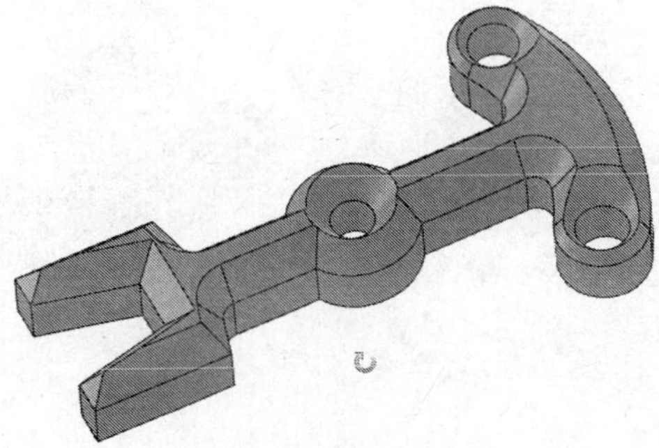

Figure 5-49 *Rotating the view to display the model from different directions*

Modifying Standard Views

As mentioned in the tutorial description, you need to modify the standard views such that the front view of the model becomes the top view. This is done by using the **Orientation** dialog box.

1. Press SPACEBAR on the keyboard; the **Orientation** dialog box is displayed.

2. Drag the **Orientation** dialog box to the top right corner of the drawing area. The **Orientation** dialog box will close automatically if you perform any other operation. Therefore, you need to pin this dialog box.

3. Choose the **Pin/Unpin the dialog** button to pin this dialog box at the top right corner of the drawing area.

4. Click on the **Front** option in the list box of the **Orientation** dialog box; the current view is automatically changed to the front view and the model is now reoriented toward the front.

   Now, you need to modify the standard views such that the front view of the model becomes the top view. Then, you need to save the model with the current settings.

5. Choose the **Update Standard Views** button from the **Orientation** dialog box; the button is activated.

6. Now, choose the **Top** button to update the standard views; the **SOLIDWORKS** warning message box is displayed and you are warned that on modifying the standard views, the orientation of any named view in this document will change.

7. Choose **Yes** from this warning box to modify the standard view.

8. Now, click on the **Isometric** option in the list box of the **Orientation** dialog box. You will notice that the isometric view is modified, refer to Figure 5-50.

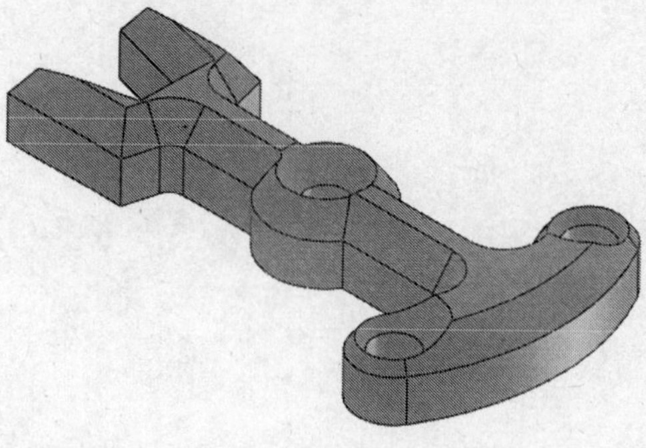

Figure 5-50 The modified isometric view of the model

9. Choose the **Pin/Unpin the dialog** button from the **Orientation** dialog box again and left-click anywhere in the drawing area to close the dialog box.

Starting a New Drawing Document and Placing the Views on a Sheet

As mentioned in the tutorial description, you need to start a new drawing document, generate the views of the model and then place them on a drawing sheet. This is done by using the **Make Drawing from Part** tool.

1. Choose **File > Make Drawing from Part** from the SOLIDWORKS menus; the **New SOLIDWORKS Document** is displayed.

2. Select a drawing template and choose the **OK** button; a new drawing document is started and the **Sheet Format/Size** dialog box is displayed.

3. Select **A (ANSI) Landscape** from the list box available below the **Standard sheet size** radio button and then choose the **OK** button; a new document is started with the set format and size and the **View Palette** task pane is displayed on the right in the drawing window.

3. Drag the Isometric view from the **View Palette** and place it at the top right corner of the drawing sheet, refer to Figure 5-51; the **View Palette** task pane is closed and the **Drawing View PropertyManager** is displayed.

4. Choose the **Close Dialog** button from the **Drawing View PropertyManager**.

Note

*The **Drawing View PropertyManager** will be displayed only if you drag and drop the Isometric view first instead of any plan or elevation views from the **View Palette** task pane.*

5. Click on the **View Palette** tab to invoke the **View Palette** task pane again. Next, drag and drop the **Top** view on the sheet, refer to Figure 5-51; the **Projected View PropertyManager** is displayed and you are prompted to select a location to place the new view.

6. Drag the cursor vertically downward and place the **Front** view of the model, refer to Figure 5-51. Next, choose the **OK** button from the **Projected View PropertyManager**.

7. Invoke the **View Palette** task pane again. Next drag and drop the **Right** view on the sheet, refer to Figure 5-51. Next, choose the **OK** button from the **Projected View PropertyManager**.

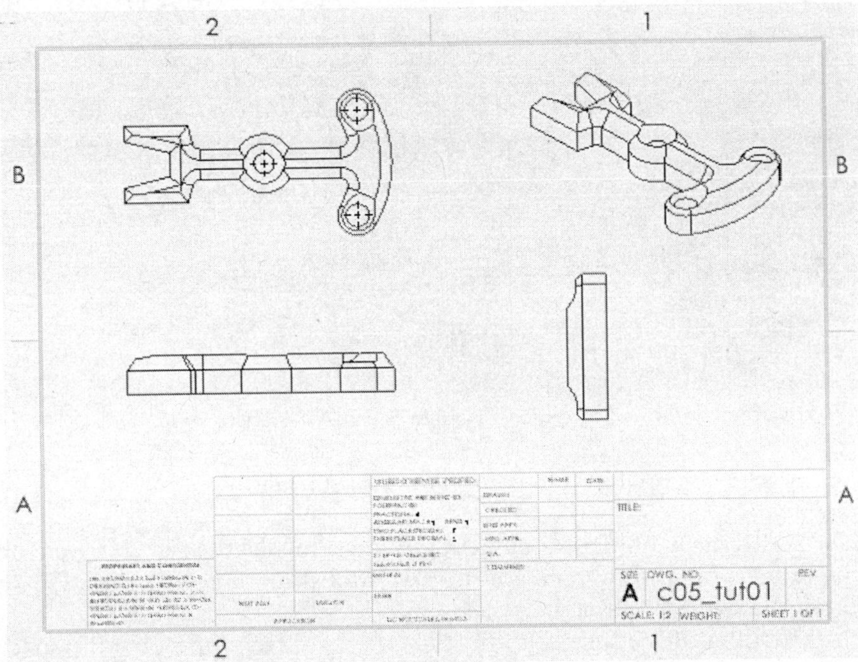

Figure 5-51 *Views placed on the drawing sheet*

Note

For detailed information on creating drawing views, refer to Chapters 14 and 15.

Saving the Model

As the name of the document is specified in the beginning, you need to choose the **Save** button to save the document.

1. Choose the **Save** button from the Menu Bar and save the model at the location *\Documents\SOLIDWORKS\c05*.

2. Choose **File > Close** from the SOLIDWORKS menus to close the document.

Tutorial 2

In this tutorial, you will create the model shown in Figure 5-52. Its dimensions are shown in Figure 5-53. The extrusion depth of the model is 20 mm. After creating the model, add a color of your choice to it and apply a decal as well. **(Expected time: 45 min)**

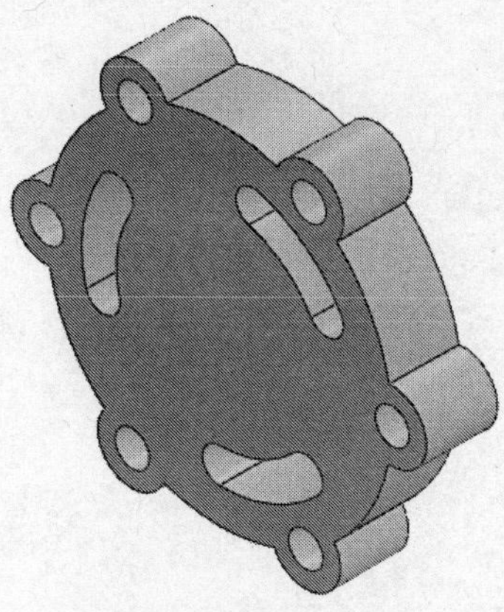

Figure 5-52 Model for Tutorial 2

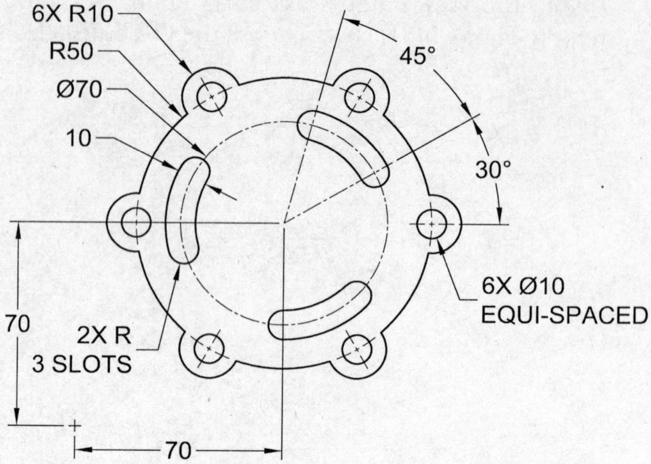

Figure 5-53 Dimensions of the model for Tutorial 2

The following steps are required to complete this tutorial:

a. Start a new SOLIDWORKS part document and then invoke the sketching environment.
b. Create the outer loop and then create the sketch of three inner cavities. Finally, draw six circles inside the outer loop for the holes.
c. Invoke the **Extruded Boss/Base** tool and extrude the sketch through a distance of 20 mm.
d. Rotate the view by using the **Rotate View** tool.
e. Change the current view to isometric view and then save the document.

Starting a New Part Document

1. Choose the **New** button from the Menu Bar and start a new part document using the **New SOLIDWORKS Document** dialog box.

2. Choose the **Sketch** button from the **Sketch CommandManager** and then select the **Front Plane**; the sketching environment is invoked.

Drawing the Outer Loop

This is the same sketch that was created in Tutorial 3 of Chapter 3. In this tutorial, you will create only the outer loop using the steps that were discussed in Chapter 3. It is recommended that you add relations and dimensions to it to make it fully defined.

1. Follow the steps that were discussed in Tutorial 3 of Chapter 3 to create the outer loop.

2. Add dimensions to it to fully define the sketch, as shown in Figure 5-54.

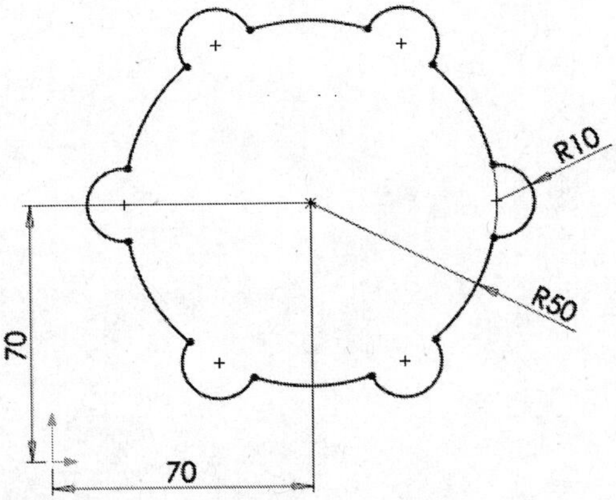

Figure 5-54 Sketch after creating the outer loop

Drawing the Sketch of Inner Cavities

Now, you need to draw the sketch of inner cavities. Draw the sketch of one of the cavities and then add required relations and dimensions to it. Next, you need to create a circular pattern of this cavity. The number of instances in the circular pattern is 3.

1. Choose the **Centerpoint Arc Slot** button from the **Sketch CommandManager**. Next, draw a slot with its center at the center point of the larger arc of diameter 100 mm. Make sure the start point and endpoint of the slot arc are in the first quadrant.

2. Complete the slot and then add dimensions to it, as shown in Figure 5-55. The slot turns black indicating that it is fully defined.

   Next, you need to create a circular pattern of the inner cavity.

3. Select the sketch of the inner cavity and then invoke the **Circular Pattern PropertyManager**.

4. Drag the center of the circular pattern to the center of the circle of diameter 100 mm.

5. Set the value **3** in the **Number of Instances** spinner of the **Parameters** rollout and then choose the **OK** button to create the circular pattern shown in Figure 5-56.

6. Draw a circle of 10 mm diameter which is concentric to the circle of 20 mm diameter and then create a circular pattern of the circle. This completes the sketch of the model. Final sketch of the inner cavity is shown in Figure 5-57.

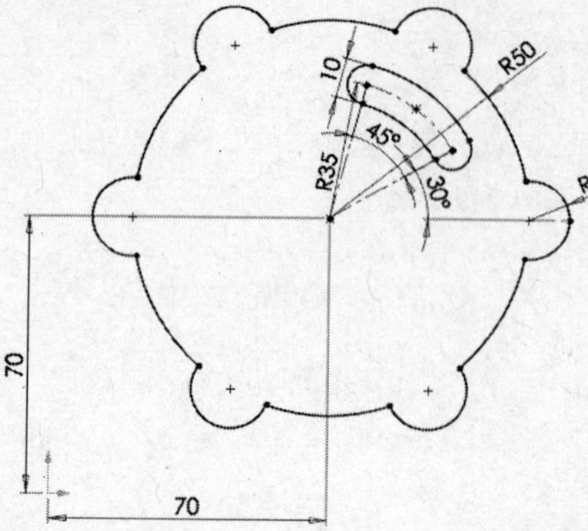

Figure 5-55 Sketch after the first slot is drawn

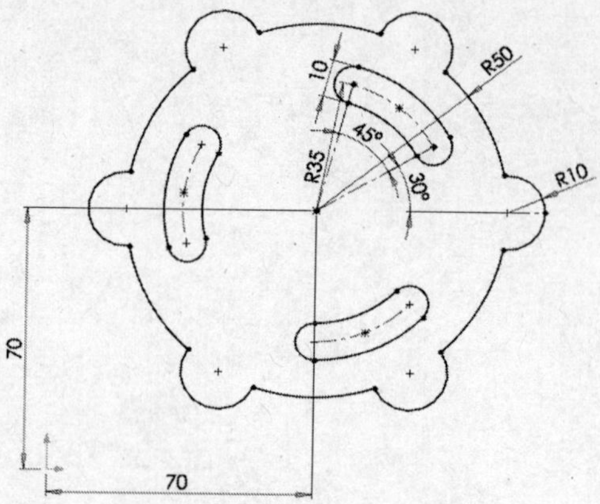

Figure 5-56 Sketch after creating the circular pattern of the inner cavity

Note

*If the status of the sketch drawn shows **Under Defined** in the Status Bar and the circles created by using the circular pattern appear in blue color, you need to drag any of the circles to check its degree of freedom. The moment you drag a circle, the status of the sketch updates to **Fully Defined** and the color of the entities turns black.*

Extruding the Sketch

The next step after creating the sketch is to extrude it. You can extrude the sketch using the **Extruded Boss/Base** tool.

1. Choose the **Features** tab from the CommandManager to display the **Features CommandManager** and then choose the **Extruded Boss/Base** tool.

   The current view is changed to trimetric view and the **Boss-Extrude PropertyManager** is displayed. Also, preview of the model created using the default values is displayed in the drawing area.

2. Set **20** in the **Depth** spinner and then choose the **OK** button to extrude the sketch.

3. Choose **View Settings > Shadows In Shaded Mode** from the **View (Heads-Up)** toolbar to display the model with shadow.

4. Press SPACEBAR and then click on the **Isometric** option in the **Orientation** dialog box to change the current view to the isometric view. The complete model for Tutorial 2 is shown in Figure 5-58.

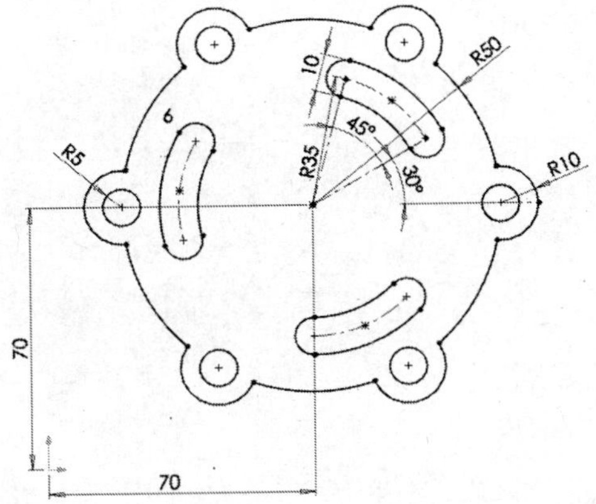

Figure 5-57 Sketch after drawing the inner cavity

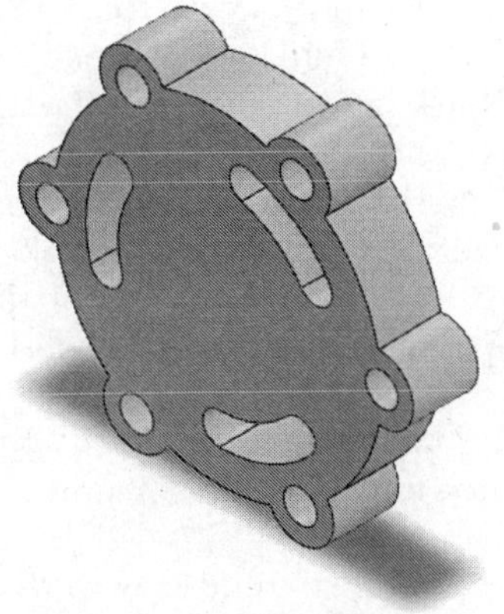

Figure 5-58 Complete model for Tutorial 2

Adding Color to the Front Face

1. Choose the **DisplayManager** tab to view the DisplayManager.

2. Choose the **Open Appearance Library** button; the **Appearances, Scenes, and Decals** task pane is displayed.

3. Select the **Color** thumbnail in the lower portion of the task pane, and drag and drop it on the front face of the model and do not move the cursor; a pop-up toolbar with six options is displayed.

4. Select the **Face (Boss-Extrude-1)** option; a color node is added to the **Appearances** section.

   If the default color set in your system is dull, you may not able to view the color applied. To change the color, you need to edit it.

5. Double-click on the color node in the **DisplayManager**; the front face of the model is highlighted and the **color PropertyManager** is displayed.

6. Select a color of your choice and choose the **OK** button; the new color is applied.

Applying Decal to the Back Face

1. Choose the **View Decals** button from the **DisplayManager**; the **Decals** area is displayed.

2. Choose the **Open Decal Library** button; the **Appearances, Scenes, and Decals** task pane with default decals is displayed.

   Now, you need to place the back face of the model parallel to the screen. Before you start rotating the view of the model, it is recommended that you turn off the display of the shadow.

3. Choose **View Settings > Shadows In Shaded Mode** from the **View (Heads-Up)** toolbar to turn off the display of the shadow.

4. Rotate the model such that the back face of the model is visible. Then, set the view orientation to normal; the back face is set parallel to the screen.

5. Select the **Design with SOLIDWORKS** logo in the lower portion of the task pane. Now, drag and drop it on the back face of the model; the **Decals PropertyManager** is displayed.

6. Scale the decal and place it at the center of the face, as shown in Figure 5-59, and choose the **OK** button.

7. Change the current view to the isometric view using the **Orientation** dialog box.

Figure 5-59 *Decal placed at the center of the face*

Note

1. To remove the color applied, right-click on the color node in the ***DisplayManager*** *and choose the* ***Remove Appearance*** *option from the menu displayed.*

2. On dragging and dropping the ***color*** *thumbnail from the* ***Appearances, Scenes, and Decals*** *task pane to the face of the model, a pop-up toolbar will be displayed with six options. Click on these options one by one to check their effect.*

3. To edit the decal applied, expand the ***Decals*** *node in the* ***DisplayManager****. Next, right-click on the* ***logos*** *subnode and choose the* ***Edit Decal*** *option from the shortcut menu displayed. On doing so, the* ***Decals PropertyManager*** *will be displayed. You can set the properties of decal by choosing the* ***Mapping*** *and* ***Illumination*** *tabs. To change the image, choose the* ***Image*** *tab and specify the location of the new image in the* ***Decal Preview*** *rollout.*

Saving the Model

1. Choose the **Save** button from the Menu Bar and save the model with the name *c05_tut02* at the location given next.

   \Documents\SOLIDWORKS\c05

2. Choose **File > Close** from the SOLIDWORKS menus to close the document.

Tutorial 3

In this tutorial, you will create the model of the shaft shown in Figure 5-60. Its dimensions are shown in Figure 5-61. After creating the model, you will turn on the option to display shadows and also apply Steel material to the model. Additionally, you will determine the mass properties.

(Expected time: 30 min)

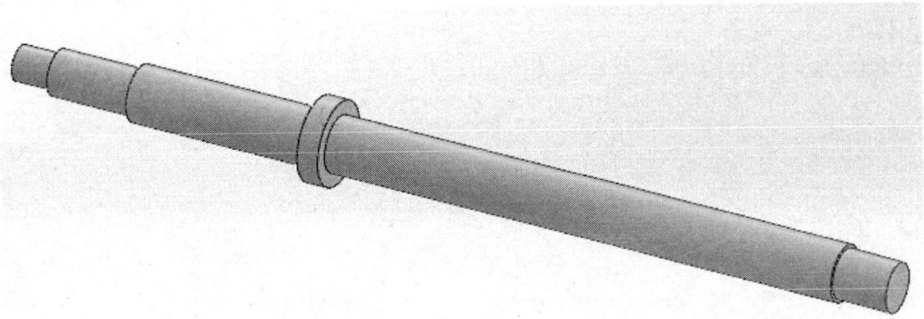

Figure 5-60 Revolved model for Tutorial 3

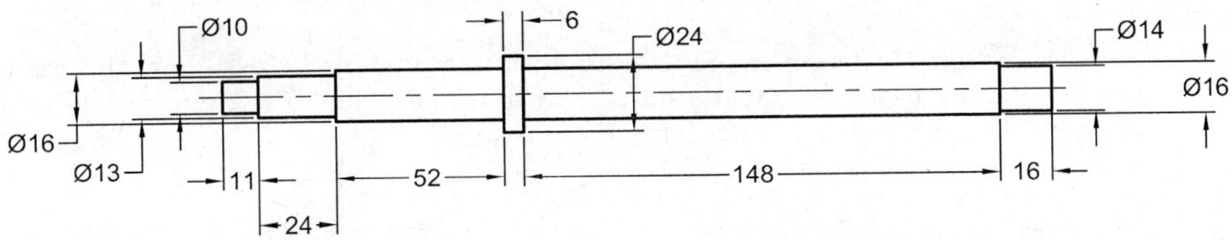

Figure 5-61 Sketch for the revolved model

The following steps are required to complete this tutorial:

a. Start a new SOLIDWORKS part document and then invoke the sketching environment.
b. Create the sketch for the revolve feature.
c. Invoke the **Revolved Boss/Base** tool and revolve the sketch through an angle of 360 degrees.
d. Set the isometric view as the current view and then turn on the option to display shadow in the model.
e. Assign steel material to the model and then check the mass properties.

Opening a New Part Document

1. Start SOLIDWORKS by double-clicking on the shortcut icon of SOLIDWORKS 2021 available on the desktop of your computer; the SOLIDWORKS 2021 window along with the **Welcome - SOLIDWORKS** dialog box is displayed.

2. Choose the **Part** button available in the **New** area of the **Home** tab in the **Welcome - SOLIDWORKS** dialog box; a new SOLIDWORKS part document is invoked.

   You need to invoke the sketching environment to draw the sketch.

3. Choose the **Sketch** tab from the **CommandManager** and then select the **Sketch** tool from the **Sketch CommandManager**; the **Edit Sketch PropertyManager** is displayed and you are prompted to select a plane on which you want to draw the sketch.

   Sketch

4. Select the **Front Plane** from the drawing area; the sketching environment is invoked and the plane gets oriented normal to the view.

Drawing the Sketch

It is evident from Figure 5-61 that the sketch will be drawn using the **Line** tool and for creating the revolve feature, you need to draw only the portion of the sketch that is above the center line.

1. Choose the **Line** tool from the **Sketch CommandManager**; the arrow cursor is replaced by the line cursor.

2. Move the line cursor to the origin, click, and then move the cursor vertically upward. You will notice that the symbol of the Vertical relation is displayed next to the line cursor and the length of the line is displayed above the line cursor.

3. Click when the length of the line above the line cursor shows a value close to 5.

   First vertical line is drawn. As you are drawing continuous lines, the endpoint of the line drawn is automatically selected as the start point of the next line. Continue creating the line segments and create a sketch similar to the one shown in Figure 5-62. The lines in the sketch are labelled for your reference.

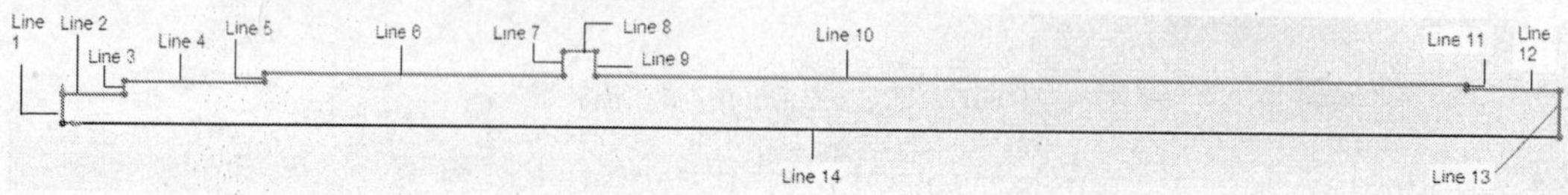

Figure 5-62 *Sketch for the revolved model*

4. Choose the **Smart Dimension** tool from the **Sketch CommandManager** and then select the line labelled 1, refer to Figure 5-62; the **Line Properties PropertyManager** is displayed. Also, a dimension value is attached to the cursor.

5. Click to place the dimension value; the **Modify** dialog box is displayed along with the **Dimension PropertyManager**. Enter **5** in the **Distance** edit box of the **Modify** dialog box and then choose the **Save the current value and exit the dialog** button to exit the **Modify** dialog box. Next, choose the line labelled 2 and make the dimension value equal to 11.

   Similarly, select the other lines and assign dimension values to them, refer to Figure 5-63 for dimension values.

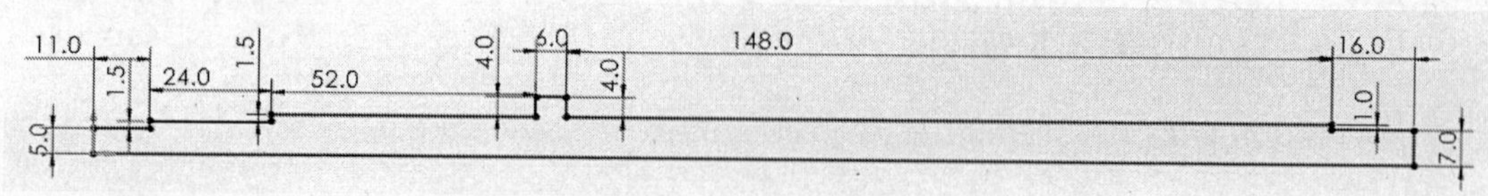

Figure 5-63 *Dimensions of the line segments*

6. After assigning dimension values to all the lines, choose the **Close Dialog** button from the **Dimension PropertyManager** and exit the sketching environment using the **Exit Sketch** button.

Revolving the Sketch

The sketch needs to be revolved using Line 14, refer to Figure 5-62, as the centerline for revolution.

1. Choose the **Features** tab from the **CommandManager** to display the **Features CommandManager**. Now, choose the **Revolved Boss/Base** button; the sketch is automatically oriented in the trimetric view and the **Revolve PropertyManager** is displayed. Also, you are prompted to select the axis of revolution.

2. Select Line 14 as the axis of revolution; the preview of the revolved feature in temporary shaded graphics is displayed in the drawing area. As the preview of the model is not displayed properly in the current view, you need to zoom the drawing.

3. Choose the **Zoom to Fit** button from the **View (Heads-Up)** toolbar or press the F key on the keyboard.

4. In the **Direction1** rollout of the **Revolve PropertyManager**, select the **Blind** option from the **Revolve Type** drop-down list if not selected by default. Next, set the value of the **Direction 1 Angle** spinner to **360** and click anywhere on the screen; the preview of the revolved model is also modified accordingly.

5. Choose the **OK** button; the revolved feature is created, as shown in Figure 5-64.

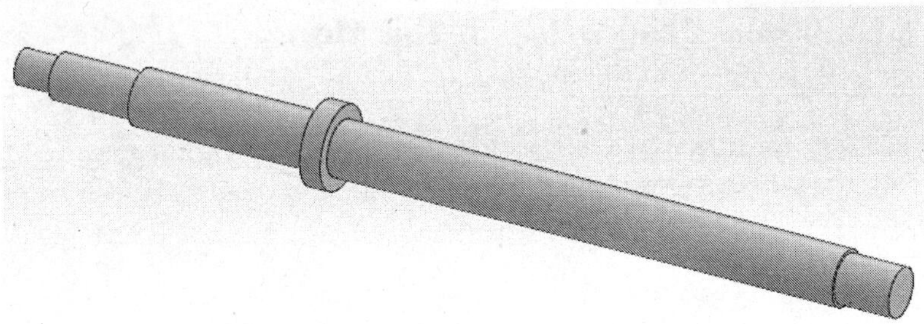

Figure 5-64 *Model created by revolving the sketch*

6. Choose the **View Orientation** button from the **View (Heads-Up)** toolbar; a flyout is displayed. Choose the **Isometric** option from the flyout to display the isometric view of the model.

Displaying the Shadow

As mentioned in the tutorial description, you need to display the shadow of the model if not displayed by default. You can turn on the display of the shadow using the **View (Heads-Up)** toolbar.

1. Choose **View Settings > Shadows In Shaded Mode** from the **View (Heads-Up)** toolbar to display the model with shadow, as shown in Figure 5-65.

Assigning Materials to the Model

Now you need to assign the required material to the model.

1. Right-click on the **Material <not specified>** node in the **FeatureManager Design Tree** and choose the **Edit Material** option; the **Material** dialog box is displayed.

2. In the left area of the dialog box where the list of materials is available, click on the > sign located on the left of the **Steel** option; the tree view expands and materials in this family are displayed.

3. Select the **Alloy Steel** option and then choose the **Apply** button and then the **Close** button to exit the dialog box. The model after assigning the material is shown in Figure 5-66.

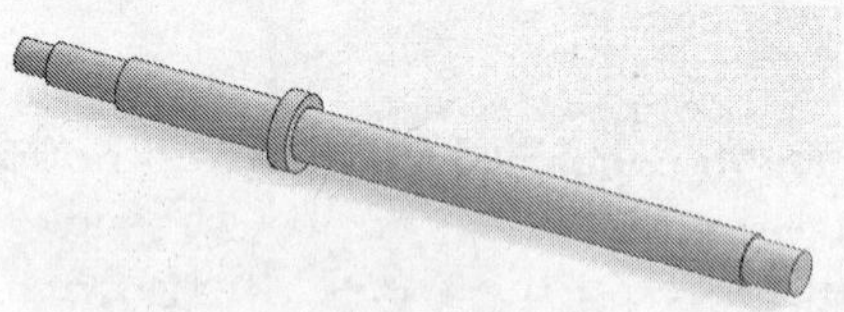

Figure 5-65 *Model with the display of shadow turned on*

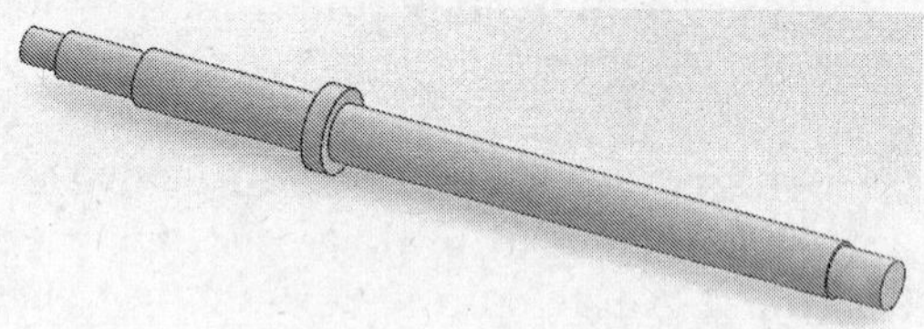

Figure 5-66 *Model after assigning the steel material*

Determining the Mass Properties of the Model

After assigning the material to the model, you need to determine its mass properties.

1. Choose the **Mass Properties** tool from the **Evaluate CommandManager**; the **Mass Properties** dialog box with the mass properties of the current model is displayed, as shown in Figure 5-67.

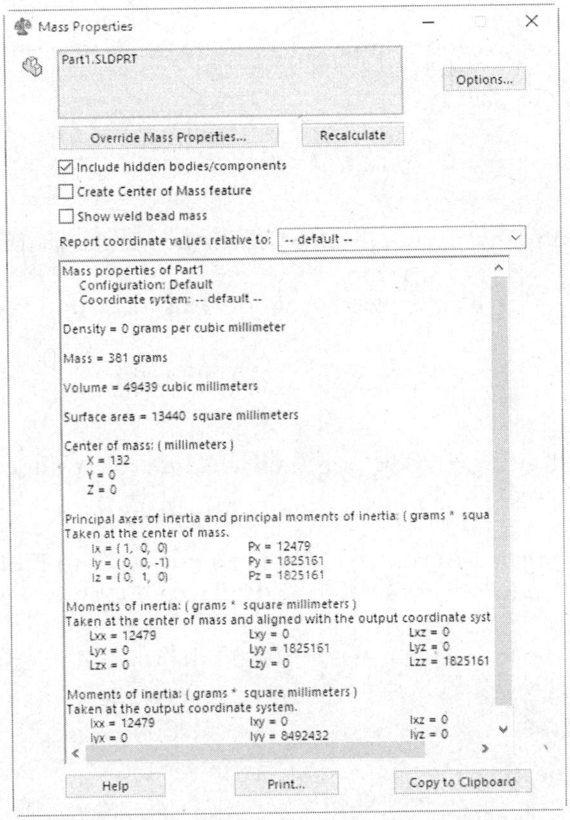

*Figure 5-67 The **Mass Properties** dialog box*

Saving the Model

1. Choose the **Save** button from the Menu Bar to invoke the **Save As** dialog box.

2. Enter **c05_tut03** as the name of the document in the **File name** edit box. Choose the **Save** button and then save the file at the location *\Documents\SOLIDWORKS\c05*.

3. Close the document by choosing **File > Close** from the SOLIDWORKS menus.

Self-Evaluation Test

Answer the following questions and then compare them to those given at the end of this chapter:

1. The __________ tool is used to display the perspective view of a model.

2. The **Cap ends** check box is displayed in the **Boss-Extrude PropertyManager** only when the sketch for the thin base feature is __________.

3. The __________ check box is used to create a feature with different extrude values in both directions of the sketching plane.

4. The __________ check box is used to apply automatic fillets while creating an open sketch thin feature.

5. The __________ button is used to display the shadow in the shaded mode.

6. In SOLIDWORKS, a sketch is revolved using the **Boss-Extrude PropertyManager**. (T/F)

7. You can also specify the depth of extrusion dynamically in the preview of the extruded feature. (T/F)

8. You can invoke the drawing display tools such as **Zoom to Fit** while the preview of a model is displayed on the screen. (T/F)

9. If you rotate the view when the current display mode is set to **Hidden Lines Visible**, the hidden lines in the model are automatically displayed. (T/F)

10. In SOLIDWORKS, the mass properties of the model cannot be overridden. (T/F)

Review Questions

Answer the following questions:

1. Which of the following buttons is used to modify the orientation of the standard views?

   (a) **Update Standard Views** (b) **Reset Standard Views**
   (c) None (d) Both

2. Which of the following buttons is not available in the Display Style of the **View (Heads-up)** toolbar?

   (a) **Hidden Lines Removed** (b) **Hidden Lines Visible**
   (c) **Shaded** (d) **Perspective**

3. Which of the following parameters is not displayed in the preview of the model?

   (a) Depth (b) Draft angle
   (c) None of these (d) Both (a) and (b)

4. In which of the following features an open sketch can be converted?

   (a) Thin feature (b) Solid feature
   (c) Both (a) and (b) (d) None of these

5. In SOLIDWORKS, which of the following tools is used to make a sketch fully defined?

   (a) **Fully Define Sketch** (b) **Smart Dimension**
   (c) None of these (d) Both (a) and (b)

6. You can also invoke the **Rotate View** tool by choosing the **Rotate View** option from the __________ that is displayed when you right-click in the drawing area.

7. When you choose the **Wireframe** button, all __________ lines will be displayed along with the visible lines in the model.

8. The __________ button is used to display the shadow of a model.

9. When you invoke the **Extruded Boss/Base** tool or the **Revolved Boss/Base** tool, the view is automatically changed into a __________.

10. The thin revolved features can be created by using a ________ or an ________ sketch.

EXERCISES

Exercise 1

Create the model shown in Figure 5-68. The sketch of the model is shown in Figure 5-69. Create the sketch and dimension it using the fully defined sketch option. The extrusion depth of the model is 15 mm. After creating the model, rotate the view. **(Expected time: 30 min)**

Figure 5-68 Model for Exercise 1

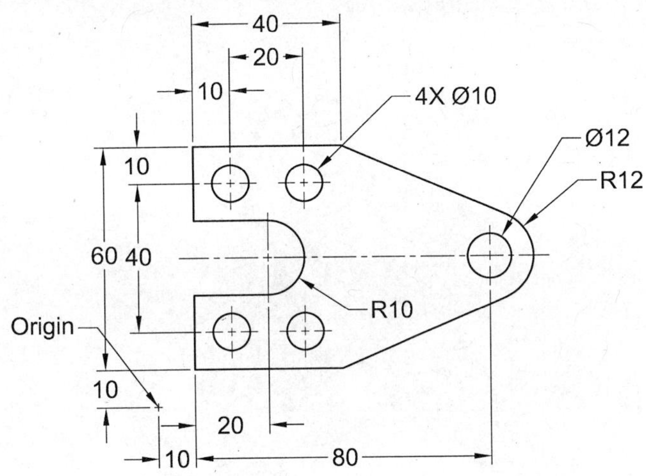

Figure 5-69 Sketch of the model for Exercise 1

Exercise 2

Create the model shown in Figure 5-70. The sketch of the model is shown in Figure 5-71. Create the sketch and dimension it using the fully defined sketch option. The extrusion depth of the model is 25 mm. Modify the standard view such that the current front view of the model is displayed when you invoke the top view. **(Expected time: 30 min)**

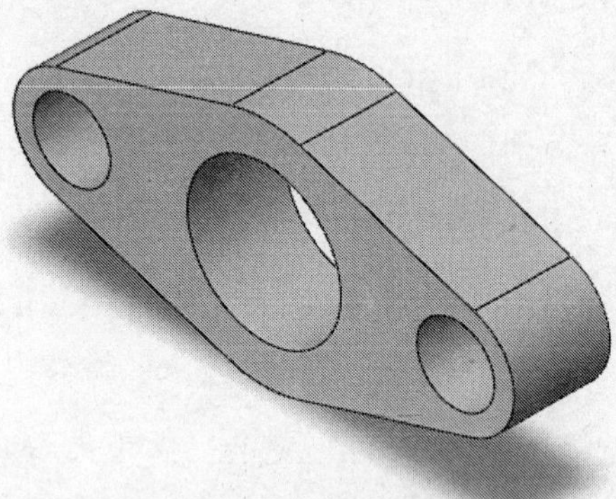

Figure 5-70 *Model for Exercise 2*

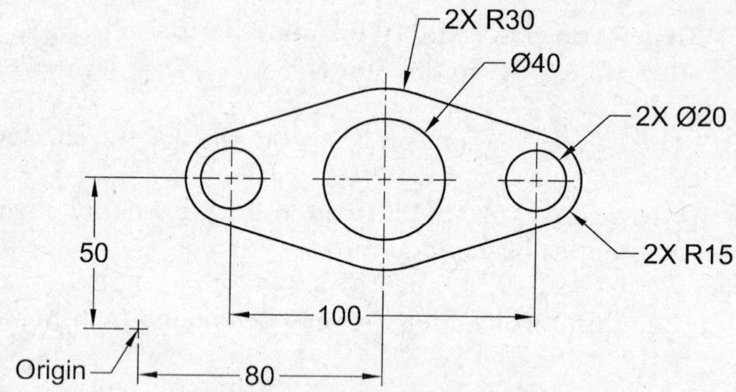

Figure 5-71 *Sketch of the model for Exercise 2*

Exercise 3

Create the model shown in Figure 5-72. The sketch of the model is shown in Figure 5-73. Create the sketch and dimension it using the fully defined sketch option. The Direction 1 angle of the model is 270 degrees. **(Expected time: 30 min)**

Figure 5-72 *Model for Exercise 3*

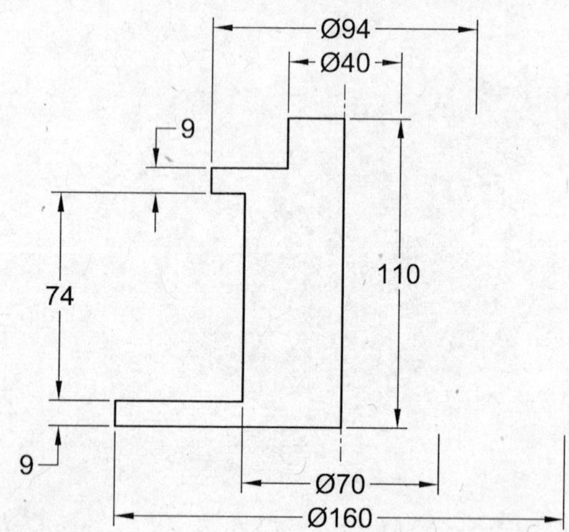

Figure 5-73 *Sketch of the model for Exercise 3*

Answers to Self-Evaluation Test

1. **Perspective**, **2.** closed, **3.** **Direction 2**, **4.** **Auto-fillet corners**, **5.** **Shadows In Shaded Mode**, **6.** F, **7.** T, **8.** T, **9.** T, **10.** F

Chapter 6

Creating Reference Geometries

Learning Objectives

After completing this chapter, you will be able to:

- *Create a reference plane*
- *Create a reference axis*
- *Create reference points*
- *Create a reference coordinate system*
- *Create a model using the advanced Boss/Base options*
- *Create a model using the contour selection technique*
- *Create a cut feature*
- *Create multiple disjoint bodies*

IMPORTANCE OF SKETCHING PLANES

In the earlier chapters, you created basic models by extruding or revolving the sketches. All those models were created on a single sketching plane, the **Front Plane**. But most mechanical designs consist of multiple sketched features, referenced geometries, and placed features. These features are integrated together to complete a model. Most of these features lie on different planes. When you start a new SOLIDWORKS document and try to invoke a sketching plane, you are prompted to select the plane on which you want to draw the sketch. On the basis of design requirements, you can select any plane to create the base feature. To create additional sketched features, you need to select an existing plane or a planar surface, or you need to create a plane that will be used as a sketching plane. For example, consider the model shown in Figure 6-1.

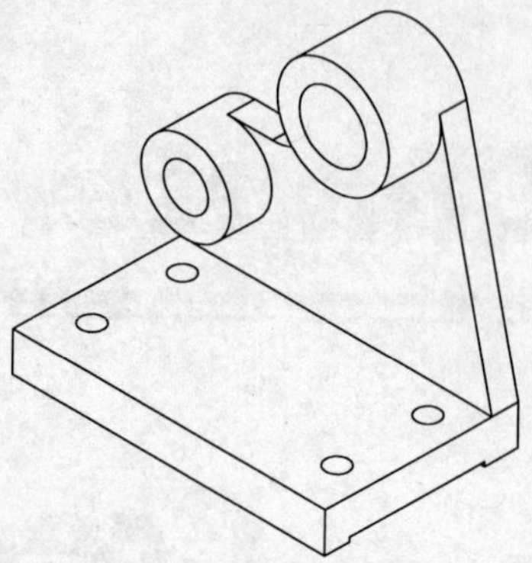

Figure 6-1 *A multifeatured model*

The base feature of this model is shown in Figure 6-2. The sketch for the base feature is drawn on the **Top Plane**. After creating the base feature, you need to create other sketched features, applied features, and referenced features, see Figure 6-3. Boss features and cut features are the sketched features that require sketching planes on which you draw the sketches of the features.

It is evident from Figure 6-3 that the features added to the base feature are not created on the same plane on which the sketch for the base feature is created. Therefore, to draw the sketches of other sketched features, you need to define other sketching planes.

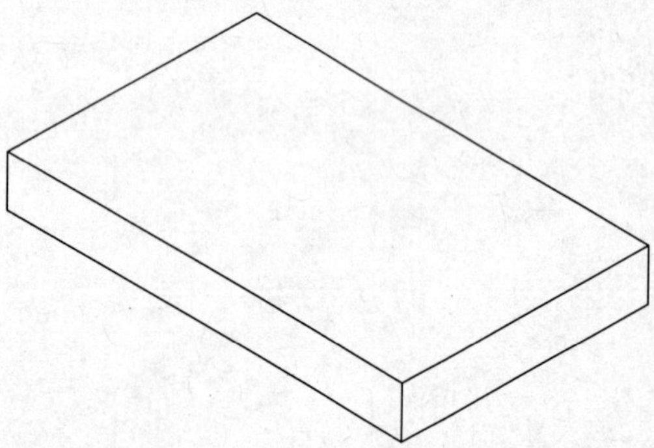

Figure 6-2 *Base feature of the model*

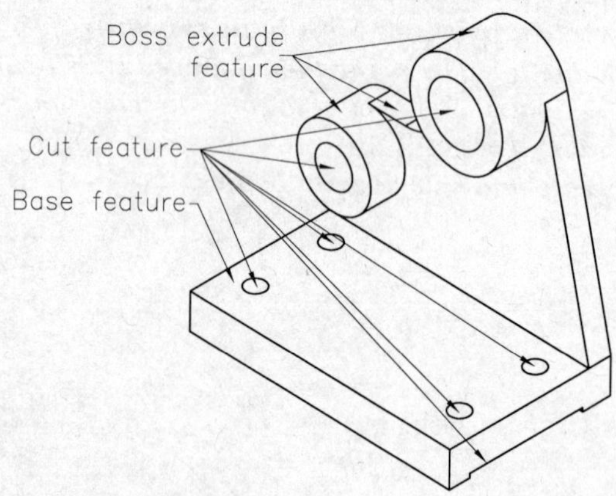

Figure 6-3 *Model after adding other features*

CREATING REFERENCE GEOMETRY

The reference geometry features are those that are available only to assist you in creating models. The reference geometries in SOLIDWORKS include planes, axes, points, and coordinate systems. These reference geometries act as reference for drawing the sketches for the sketched features, defining the sketch plane, and assembling the components. They also act as references for various applied features and sketched features. These features have no mass or volume. You must have a good understanding of these geometries because they are widely used in creating complex models. The tools to create the reference geometries are grouped together in the **Reference Geometry** flyout in the **Features CommandManager**, refer to Figure 6-4. The reference planes and the procedure of creating new planes is discussed next.

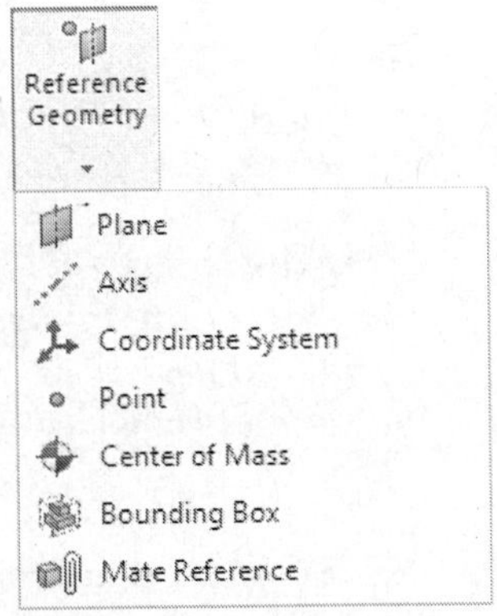

***Figure 6-4** Tools in the **Reference Geometry** flyout*

Reference Planes

Generally, all engineering components or designs are multifeatured models. Also, as discussed earlier, all features of a model are not created on the same plane on which the base feature is created. Therefore, you need to select one of the default planes or create a new plane that will be used as the sketching plane for the second feature. It is clear from the above discussion that you can use the default planes as the sketching plane or you can create a plane that can be used as a sketching plane.

Default Planes

When you start a new SOLIDWORKS part document, SOLIDWORKS provides you with three default planes: **Front Plane**, **Top Plane**, and **Right Plane**.

The orientation of the component depends upon the sketching plane of the base feature. Therefore, it is recommended that you should select the sketching plane carefully to draw the sketch for the base feature. The sketching plane for drawing the sketch of the base feature can be one of the three datum planes provided by default.

The three default planes will automatically be displayed in the drawing area only if the sketching environment is invoked for the first time to create the sketch. These planes will not be displayed when you invoke the sketching environment again to create the sketch for the additional feature. You need to select the required plane manually.

To select a plane for an additional feature, choose the **Sketch** button; the **Edit Sketch PropertyManager** will be displayed. Whenever the PropertyManager is displayed, the **FeatureManager Design Tree** shifts to the drawing area. Click on the ► sign located on the left of the part document name in the **FeatureManager Design Tree**; the tree view will expand and display the names of the planes. You can also press the C key from the keyboard to expand the Design Tree. Select the required plane from the tree view.

Note

*You can also select a plane before choosing the **Sketch** button to invoke the sketching environment. In this case, the **Edit Sketch PropertyManager** will not be displayed and you will not be prompted to select a plane for sketching. The selected plane will automatically be taken as the sketching plane.*

Tip

You can turn on the display of the default planes in the drawing area using the following procedure:

*1. Press and hold the CTRL key, select **Front Plane**, **Top Plane**, and **Right Plane** one-by-one from the **FeatureManager Design Tree**; a pop-up toolbar will be displayed. Choose the **Show** button from the toolbar. Set the view to **Isometric** by using the **Orientation** dialog box; the three default planes will set isometrically.*

*2. The reference planes are not shaded. To turn on the shading of the planes, choose the **Options** button from the **Menu Bar**; the **System Options - General** dialog box will be invoked. Select the **Display** option on the left in this dialog box; the name of the dialog box will change to **System Options - Display**. Select the **Display shaded planes** check box from this dialog box, if it is not selected, and choose the **OK** button.*

*3. When the planes are displayed in the shaded mode, invoke the **Rotate** tool and drag the rotate view cursor to rotate the shaded planes. You will observe that both sides of the plane are displayed in different colors. This is to symbolize the positive and negative sides of the plane. This means that when you create an extruded feature, the depth of extrusion will be assigned to the positive side of the plane by default. When you create a cut feature, the depth of the cut feature will be assigned to the negative direction by default.*

Creating New Planes

CommandManager:	Features > Reference Geometry flyout > Plane
SOLIDWORKS menus:	Insert > Reference Geometry > Plane
Toolbar:	Reference Geometry > Plane

The default planes or the reference planes are used to draw sketches for creating sketched features. These planes are also used for creating placed features such as holes, reference an entity or a feature, and so on. You can also select a planar face of a feature that will be used as the sketching plane. Generally, it is recommended that you should use the planar faces of the features as the sketching planes. However, sometimes you have to create a sketch on a plane that is at some offset distance or at an angle from a reference plane or a planar face. In such a case, you have to create a new reference plane at an offset distance from a plane or a planar face. Consider another case, where you have to define a sketching plane tangent to a cylindrical face of a shaft and this plane will be used as a sketching plane.

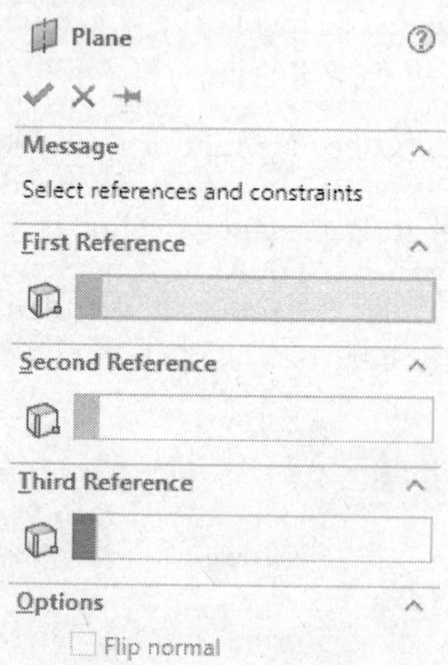

Figure 6-5** Partial view of the **Plane PropertyManager

To create a plane, choose the **Plane** tool from the **Reference Geometry** flyout in the **Features CommandManager**; the **Plane PropertyManager** will be displayed, as shown in Figure 6-5. Also, the confirmation corner will be displayed at the top right corner of the drawing area.

The different methods used to create a new plane using the **Plane PropertyManager** are discussed next.

Creating a Plane at an Offset from an Existing Plane or a Planar Face

To create a plane at an offset distance from a reference plane or a planar face, invoke the **Plane PropertyManager**; the **First Reference** selection box will be selected by default. Select a plane or a planar face as the first reference; some constraints will be displayed in the **First Reference** rollout. The **Offset distance** button will be chosen by default in this rollout. Therefore, the **Offset distance** spinner, the **Flip offset** check box, and the **Number of planes to create** spinner will be enabled in the **First Reference** rollout. Set an offset value in the **Offset distance** spinner; a message **Fully defined** will be displayed in the **Message** rollout. Choose the **OK** button in the **Plane PropertyManager**. You can reverse the direction of plane creation by selecting the **Flip offset** check box. You can create multiple planes by increasing the value in the **Number of planes to create** spinner. In such a case, each plane will be placed at the offset distance specified in the **Offset distance** spinner. Figure 6-6 shows a plane selected to create an offset plane and Figure 6-7 shows the plane created at the required offset.

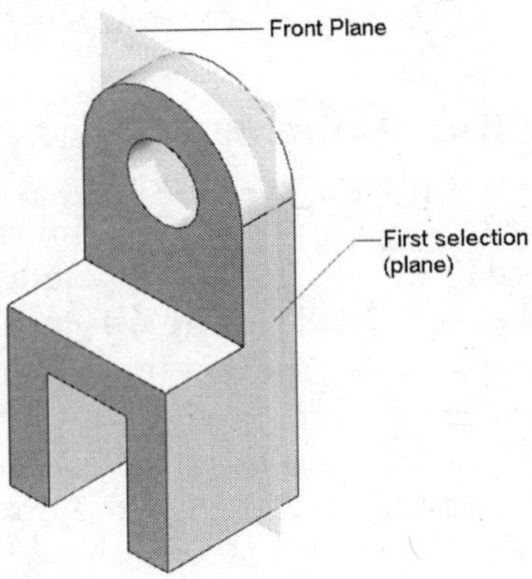

Figure 6-6 *Plane to be selected*

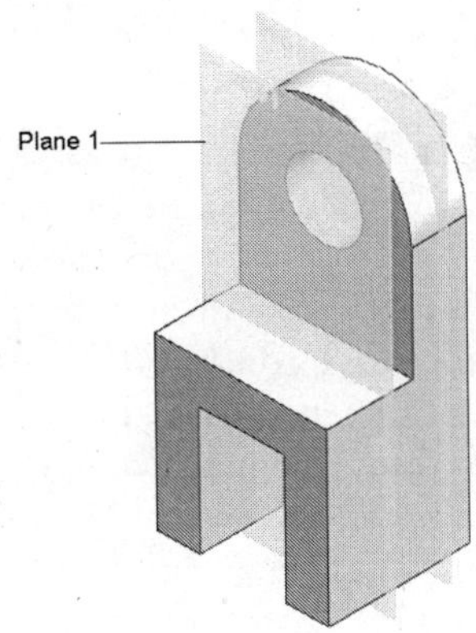

Figure 6-7 *Resulting plane*

Tip

You can also create planes at offset distance by dragging the existing plane dynamically. To do so, select the plane from the drawing area by clicking on its boundary. Press and hold the CTRL key and drag the cursor; the ***Plane PropertyManager*** *will be displayed. Drag the cursor to the required distance and then release the left mouse button. Alternatively, enter an offset distance in the* ***Offset distance*** *spinner. Right-click and choose the* ***OK*** *option or choose the* ***OK*** *button from the* ***Plane PropertyManager****.*

Creating a Plane Parallel to an Existing Plane or a Planar Face and Passing through a Point

You can create a plane parallel to another plane or a planar face and passing through a point. To do so, invoke the **Plane PropertyManager** and select a planar face or an existing plane as the first reference to which the new plane will be parallel. Next, choose the **Parallel** button from the **First Reference** rollout and select a sketched point, an endpoint of an edge, or the midpoint of an edge as the second reference. A preview of the new plane will be displayed passing through this point. Choose the **OK** button. Figure 6-8 shows a planar face and a point selected to create the parallel plane. Figure 6-9 shows the resulting plane.

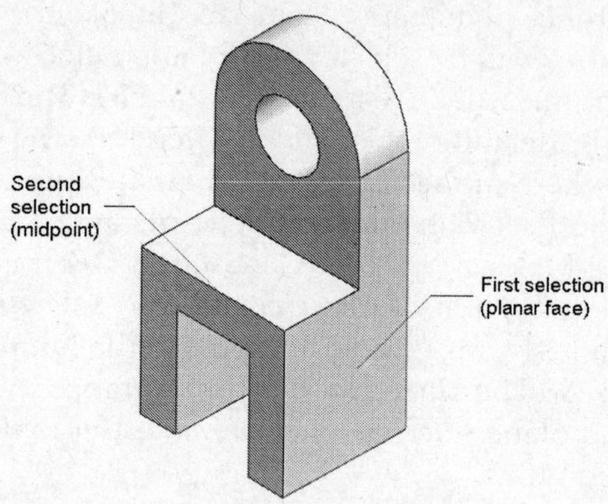

Figure 6-8 *Selecting a planar face and a vertex*

Figure 6-9 *Resulting plane*

Creating a Plane at an Angle to an Existing Plane or a Planar Face

You can also create a plane at an angle to a selected plane or a planar face, and passing through an edge, an axis, or a sketched line. To create a plane at an angle, invoke the **Plane PropertyManager** and select a plane or a planar face. Next, choose the **At angle** button from the **First Reference** rollout; the **Angle** spinner will be enabled. The **Flip offset** check box and the **Number of planes to create** spinner will also appear below the **Angle** spinner in the **First Reference** rollout. Now, select an edge, an axis, or a sketched line through which the plane will pass as the second reference. After selecting the edge or axis, set the angle value in the **Angle** spinner. You can reverse the direction of the plane creation by selecting the **Flip offset** check box. You can also create multiple planes by increasing the value in the **Number of planes to create** spinner. Each plane will be incremented by the angle value specified in the **Angle** spinner. Figure 6-10 shows a planar face and an edge selected. Figure 6-11 shows the resulting plane created at an angle of 45-degree to the selected plane.

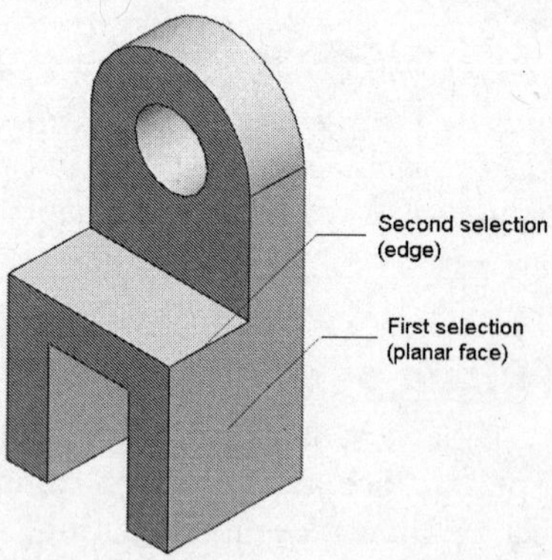

Figure 6-10 *A planar face and an edge selected*

Figure 6-11 *Resulting plane*

Creating a Plane Passing through Lines/Points

You can create a plane that passes through an edge and a point, an axis and a point, or a sketch line and a point. You can also create a plane that passes through three points. These points can be a sketched point or a vertex. To create a plane passing through lines/points, invoke the **Plane PropertyManager** and select an edge or a point as the first reference; some constraints will be displayed in the **First Reference** rollout. Select constraints according to your requirement. Next, select an edge or a point as the second reference and specify constraints; the preview will be displayed in the drawing area and the **Fully defined** message will be displayed in the **Message** rollout. Choose the **OK** button from the **Plane PropertyManager**; a new plane will be created according to the reference selected. Figure 6-12 shows an edge and a vertex to be selected for creating a plane. The resulting plane is displayed in Figure 6-13. To create a plane passing through three points, select three points or three vertices as the first, second, and third references, as shown in Figure 6-14. Choose the **OK** button from the **Plane PropertyManager**; a new plane will be created, as shown in Figure 6-15. Note that if you want to flip the normal vector of the plane then you need to select the **Flip normal** check box in the **Options** rollout.

Note

The color of the resulting plane is changed for better visualization. You can change the color from ***Document Properties -Plane Display*** *dialog box. By default, the color of the resulting plane is blue.*

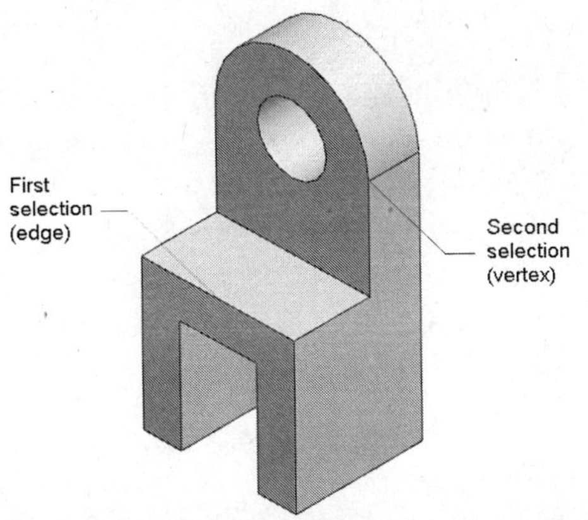

Figure 6-12 *Selecting an edge and a vertex*

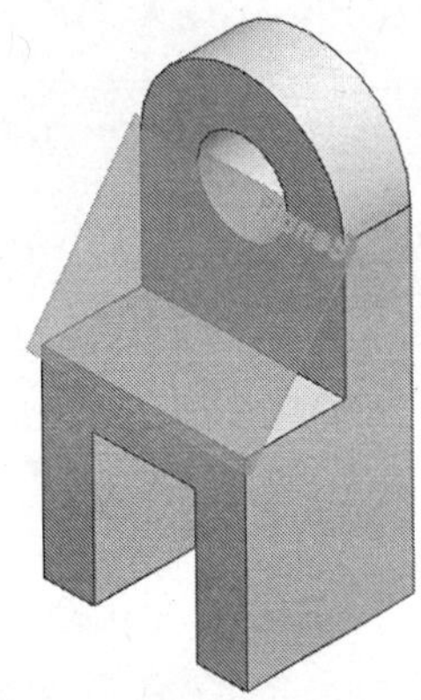

Figure 6-13 *Resulting plane*

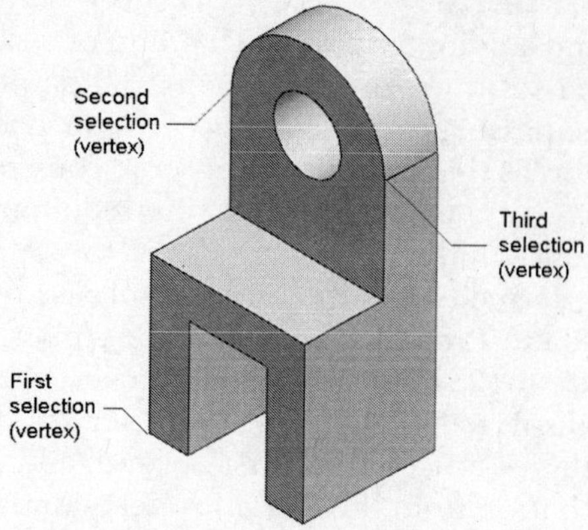

Figure 6-14 *Selecting the vertices*

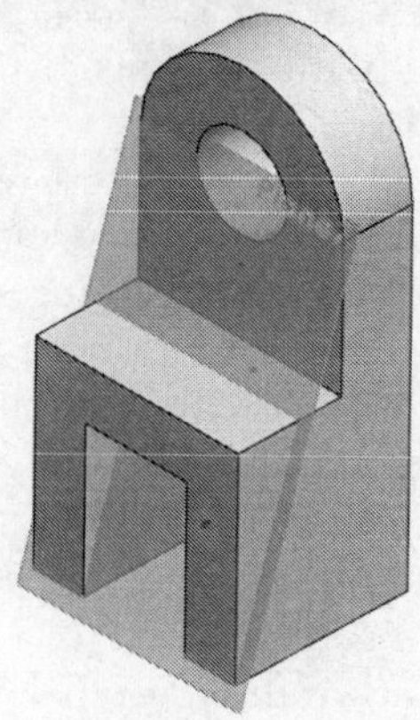

Figure 6-15 *Resulting plane*

Creating a Plane Normal to a Curve

To create a plane normal to a selected curve or an edge of a feature, invoke the **Plane PropertyManager**, and select a curve or an edge and choose the **Perpendicular** button from the **First Reference** rollout; the preview of the plane will be displayed in the drawing area. Next, select an endpoint or any other point on the curve; the preview of the plane will change accordingly. Next, choose the **OK** button to create the plane.

When you choose the **Perpendicular** button from the **First Reference** rollout, the **Set origin on curve** check box will be displayed below this button. Select this check box to set the origin of the plane on the curve. Figure 6-16 shows a curve and a point to create the plane and Figure 6-17 shows the resulting plane created normal to the selected curve.

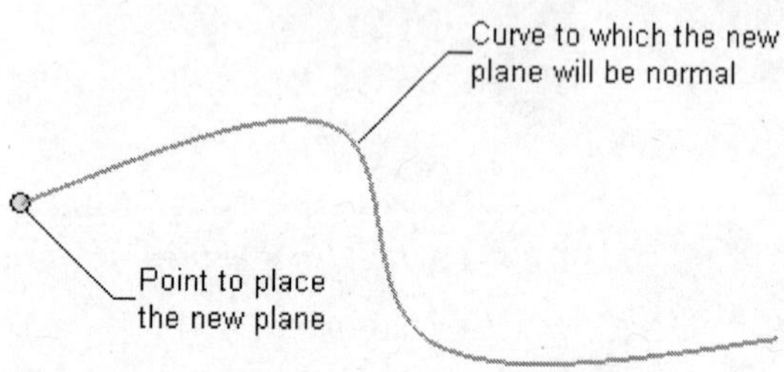

Figure 6-16 *Entities to be selected*

Figure 6-17 *Resulting plane*

Tip

If you select an edge of a model or an existing curve and invoke the sketching environment, a reference plane will automatically be created normal to that edge or curve. Also, it will be selected as the sketching plane.

Creating a Plane on a Non-Planar Surface

To create a plane passing through a point on the non-planar surface, as shown in Figure 6-18, invoke the **Plane PropertyManager** and select a non-planar surface as the first reference; the **Tangent** constraint will be selected by default in the **First Reference** rollout. Next, select a sketched point or a point on the surface as the second reference; preview of the plane will be displayed in the drawing area. You can also select a point that is created on a plane at an offset distance from the selected surface. In such cases, you need to choose the **Project** button from the **Second Reference** rollout. On choosing this button, the **Nearest location on surface** and **Along sketch normal** radio buttons will be displayed. On selecting the **Nearest location on surface** radio button, a plane will be created with the point projected on the nearest surface, refer to Figure 6-19. On selecting the **Along sketch normal** radio button, the point will be projected on the surface along normal to the plane on which the sketch point is located and a plane will be created on that location, refer to Figure 6-19.

Creating a Plane in the Middle of Two Faces/Planes

You can also create a plane in the middle of two faces/planes. The two faces/planes can be parallel or at an angle. To create a plane in the middle of two faces/planes, invoke the **Plane PropertyManager** and choose a face/plane as the first reference. Next, choose the **Mid Plane** constraint from the **First Reference** rollout. Next, select a plane/face as the second reference; the preview of the new plane will be displayed. If the two planes selected are at an angle, then the new plane will bisect them. Figure 6-20 shows the two faces selected and Figure 6-21 shows the resulting new plane.

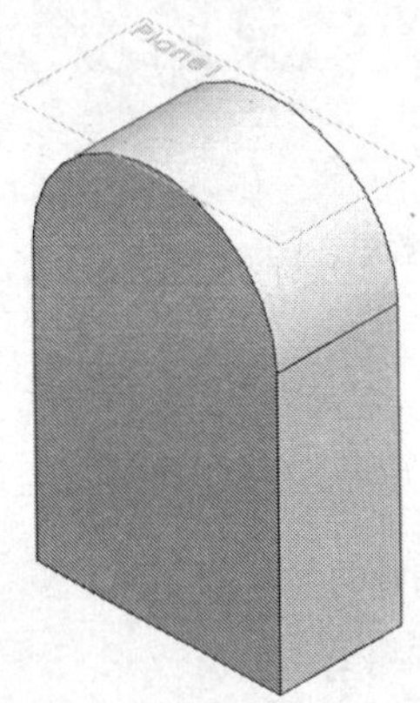

Figure 6-18 *Plane created on the non planar surface*

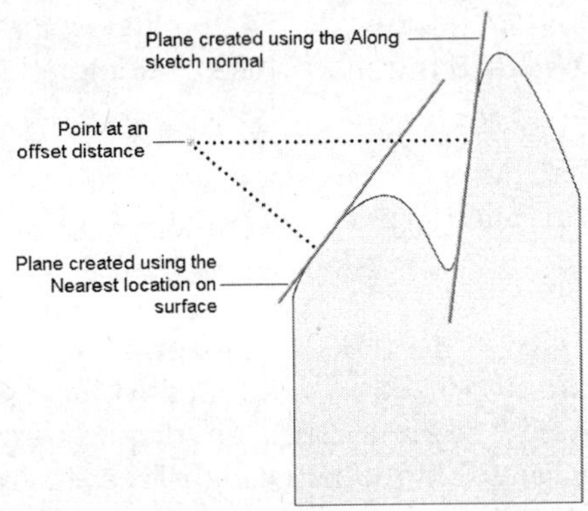

Figure 6-19 *Planes created on non planar surface with point at an offset distance*

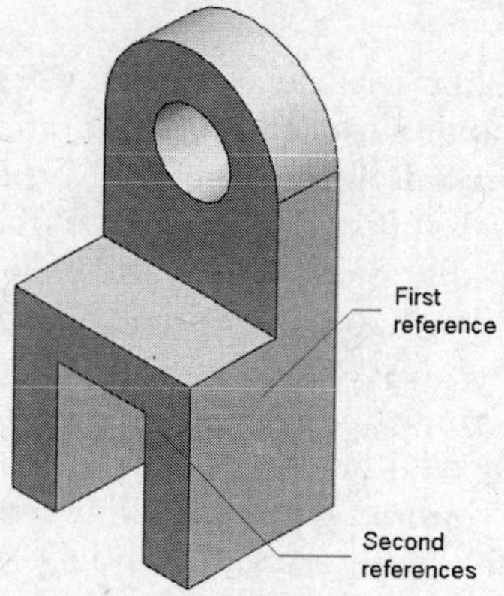

Figure 6-20 References to be selected

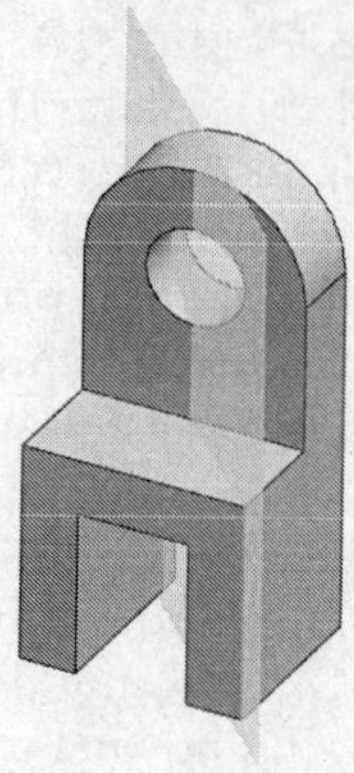

Figure 6-21 Resulting plane

Tip

*In SOLIDWORKS if you choose the **Rapid Sketch** button from the **Sketch CommandManager**, you can draw a sketch for the additional features in an existing plane or face without actually selecting the plane.*

Creating Reference Axis

CommandManager:	Features > Reference Geometry flyout > Axis
SOLIDWORKS menus:	Insert > Reference Geometry > Axis
Toolbar:	Reference Geometry > Axis

The **Axis** tool is used to create a reference axis or a construction axis. These axes are parametric lines passing through a model, feature, or a reference entity. The reference axes are used to create reference planes, coordinate systems, circular patterns, and for applying mates in the assembly. These are also used as reference while sketching or creating features. The reference axes are displayed in the model as well as in the **FeatureManager Design Tree**. To create an axis, choose the **Axis** tool from the **Features CommandManager**; the **Axis PropertyManager** will be displayed, as shown in Figure 6-22.

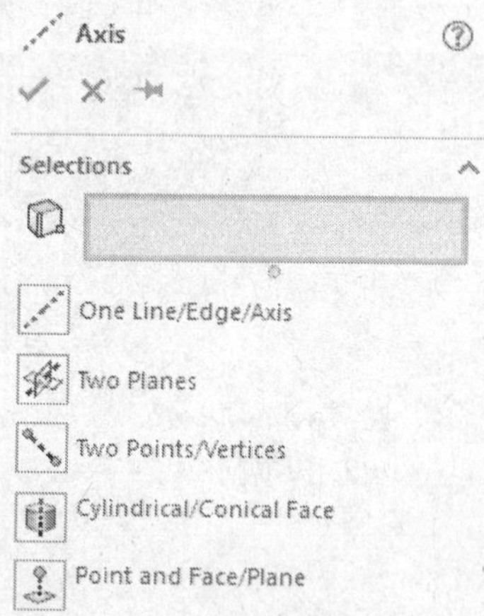

*Figure 6-22 The **Axis PropertyManager***

The usage of options in the **Axis PropertyManager** is discussed next.

Creating a Reference Axis Using One Line/Edge/Axis

The **One Line/Edge/Axis** option is used to create a reference axis by selecting a sketched line or a construction line, an edge, or a temporary axis. To use this option, invoke the **Axis PropertyManager** and choose the **One Line/Edge/Axis** button. Select a sketched line, an edge, or a temporary axis, refer to Figure 6-23; the name of the selected entity will be displayed in the **Reference Entities** selection box and preview of the reference axis will be displayed in the drawing area. Choose the **OK** button to create the reference axis, as shown in Figure 6-24.

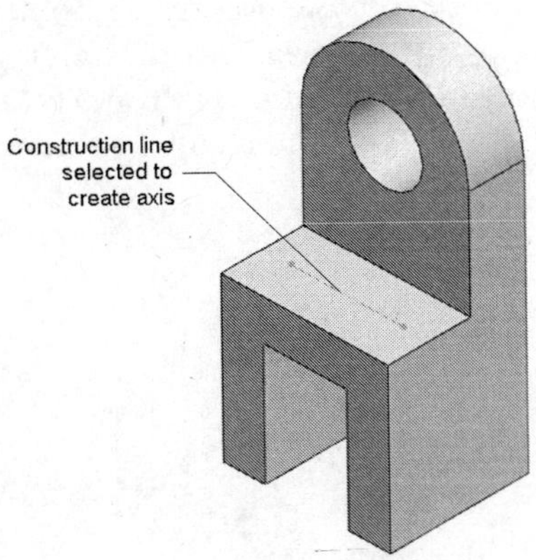

Figure 6-23 Line to be selected

Figure 6-24 Resulting reference axis

Tip

*If the axis is not displayed in the drawing area even after you have created it, choose **Hide/Show Items > View Axes** from the **View (Heads-Up)** toolbar; the axis will be displayed.*

Creating a Reference Axis Using Two Planes

You can use the **Two Planes** option to create a reference axis at the intersection of two planes. To create a reference axis using this option, invoke the **Axis PropertyManager** and then choose the **Two Planes** button. Now, select two planes, two planar faces, or a plane and a planar face that you want to use to create the axis; the preview of the axis will be displayed in the drawing area. Choose the **OK** button from the **Axis PropertyManager**. Figure 6-25 shows the two planes selected and Figure 6-26 shows the resulting reference axis created using the **Two Planes** option.

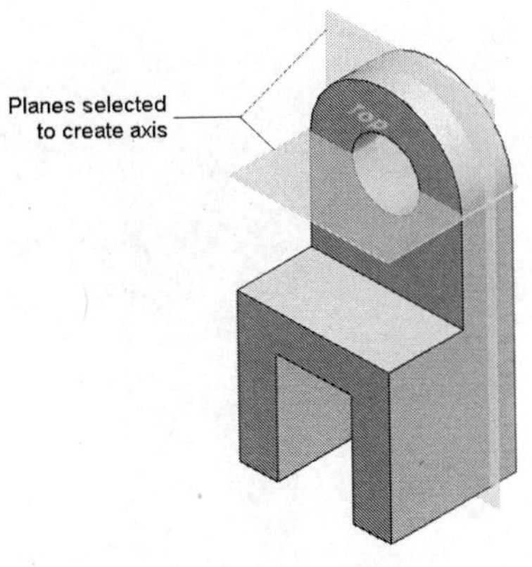

Figure 6-25 Planes to be selected

Figure 6-26 Resulting reference axis

Creating a Reference Axis Using Two Points or Vertices

You can use the **Two Points/Vertices** option to create a reference axis that passes through two points or two vertices. To create a reference axis using this option, invoke the **Axis PropertyManager** and choose the **Two Points/Vertices** button. Now, select two points or two vertices through which you want the reference axis to pass; the preview of the reference axis will be displayed in the drawing area. Choose the **OK** button from the **Axis PropertyManager**. Figure 6-27 shows two vertices to be selected and Figure 6-28 shows the resulting reference axis created using the **Two Points/Vertices** option.

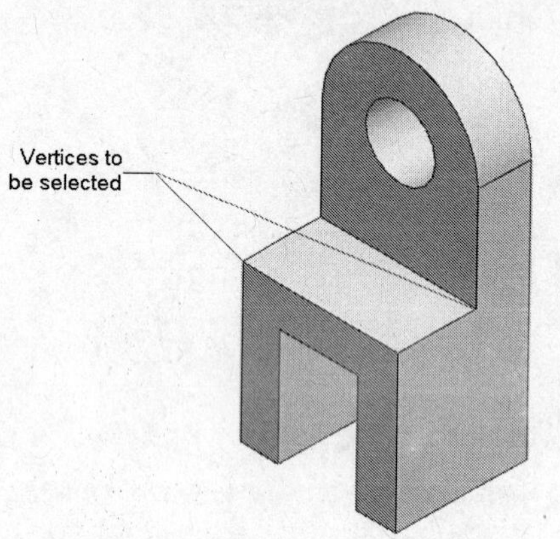

Figure 6-27 *Vertices to be selected*

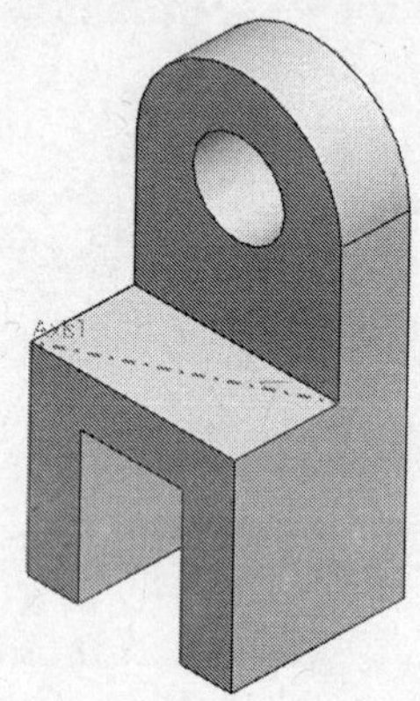

Figure 6-28 *Resulting reference axis*

Creating a Reference Axis Using a Cylindrical or a Conical Face

You can use the **Cylindrical/Conical Face** option to create a reference axis that passes through the center of a cylindrical or a conical face. To create a reference axis using this option, invoke the **Axis PropertyManager** and choose the **Cylindrical/Conical Face** button. Now, select the cylindrical or the conical face through the center of which the axis needs to pass. The preview of the reference axis will be displayed in the drawing area. Choose the **OK** button from the **Axis PropertyManager**. Figure 6-29 shows a cylindrical face selected and Figure 6-30 shows the resulting reference axis created using this option.

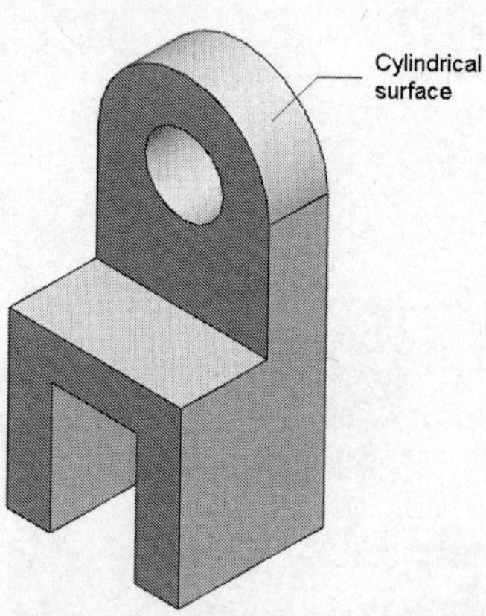

Figure 6-29 *Cylindrical face to be selected*

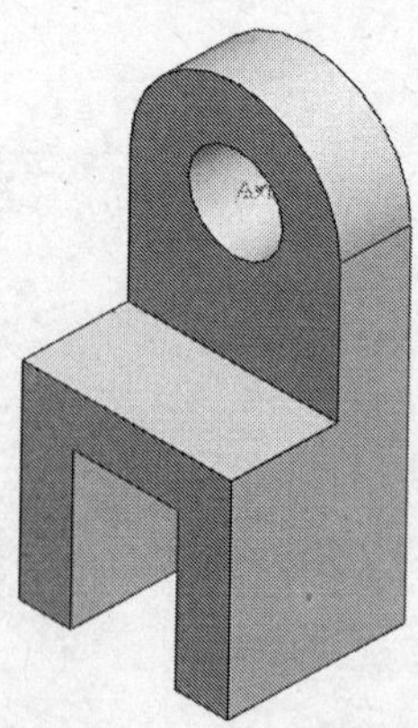

Figure 6-30 *Resulting reference axis*

Creating a Reference Axis on a Face/Plane Passing through a Point

Use the **Point and Face/Plane** option to create a reference axis that passes through a point and is normal to the selected face/plane. If the face to be selected is a non-planar face, the point should be on the face. To create a reference axis using this option, invoke the **Axis PropertyManager**. Choose the **Point and Face/Plane** button from this PropertyManager. Now, select a point, a vertex, or a midpoint and then select a face or a plane; the preview of the axis will be displayed in the drawing area. Choose the **OK** button from the **Axis PropertyManager**. The newly created axis will be normal to the selected face or the selected plane. Figure 6-31 shows the point and the face selected and Figure 6-32 shows the resulting reference axis created using this option.

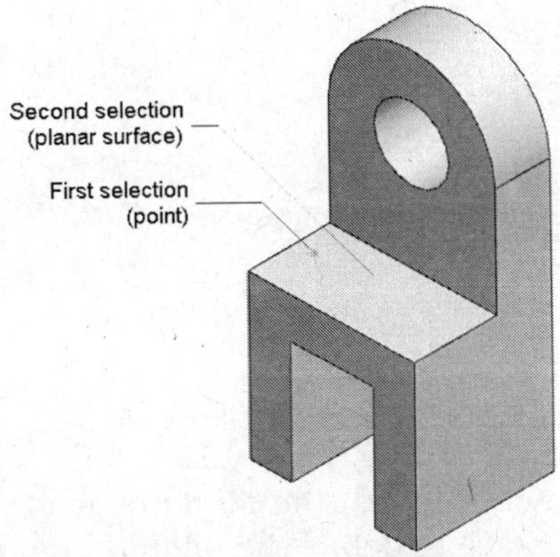

Figure 6-31 *Point and face to be selected*

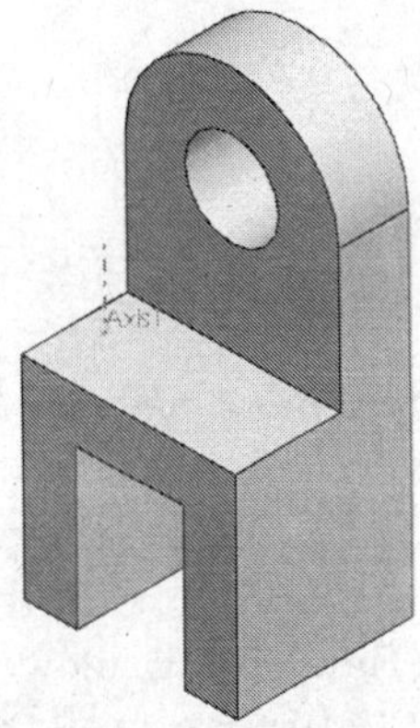

Figure 6-32 *Resulting reference axis*

Creating Reference Points

CommandManager: Features > Reference Geometry flyout > Point
SOLIDWORKS menu: Insert > Reference Geometry > Point
Toolbar: Reference Geometry > Point

Reference points are created to assist you in designing. They work as an aid to create another reference geometry or feature. To create a reference point, choose the **Point** tool from the **Features CommandManager**; the **Point PropertyManager** will be displayed, as shown in Figure 6-33.

There are six options in this PropertyManager for creating reference points. These options are discussed next.

Creating a Reference Point at the Center of an Arc or a Curved Edge

The **Arc Center** option is used to create a reference point at the center of a sketched arc or a curved edge. When you invoke the **Point PropertyManager** and choose the **Arc Center** button, you will be prompted to select an arc or a circular edge to define the reference point. As soon as you select a sketched arc, circle, or a curved edge, the preview of the reference point will be displayed at its center. Choose **OK** to confirm the creation of the reference point. Figure 6-34 shows a curved edge selected to create a reference point and a preview of the resulting reference point.

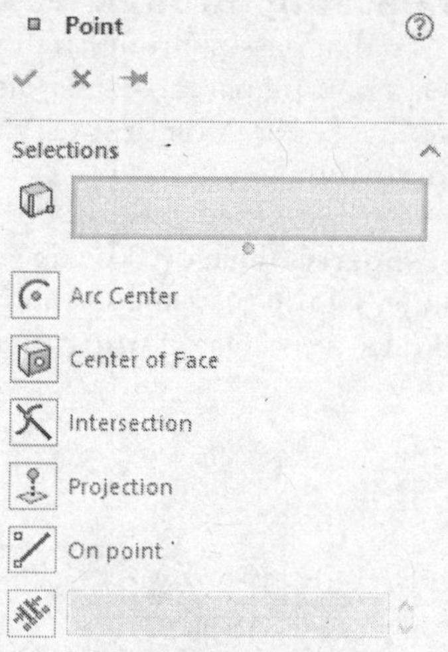

*Figure 6-33 The **Point** PropertyManager*

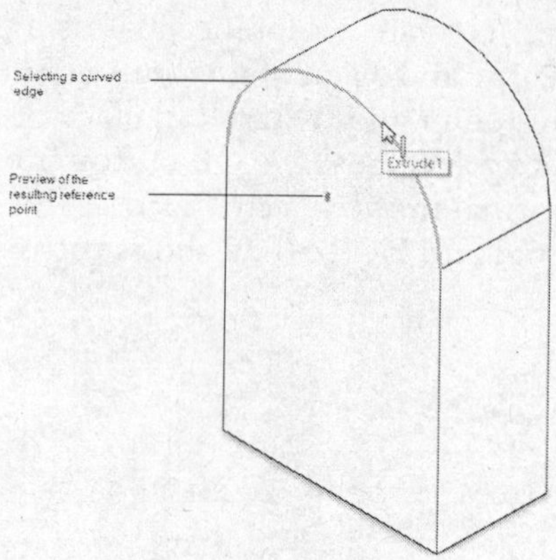

Figure 6-34 Reference point at the center of the selected curved edge

Creating a Reference Point at the Center of a Face

The **Center of Face** option allows you to create a reference point at the center of a face. When you choose this button, you will be prompted to select a face to define the reference point. You can select a plane or a curved face. The resulting point is automatically placed at the point of the center of gravity of the selected face.

Creating a Reference Point at the Intersection of Two Edges, Sketched Segments, or Reference Axes

The **Intersection** option allows you to create a reference point at the intersection of two edges, sketched segments, or reference axes.

Creating a Reference Point by Projecting an Existing Point

The **Projection** option allows you to create a reference point by projecting a point from some other plane to a specified plane. The point that you can project can be a sketched point, endpoints, center points of the sketched entities, or a reference point.

Creating a Reference Point on a Sketched Point

The **On point** option allows you to create a reference point on the sketched point. To create the reference point using this option, choose the **On point** option from the **Point PropertyManager** and then select the sketched point in the drawing area; the name of the selected sketched points will be shown in the **Reference Entities** selection box and then choose the **OK** button to confirm the creation of reference point.

Creating Single Point or Multiple Reference Point along the Distance of a Sketched Curve or an Edge

The **Along curve distance or multiple reference point** option allows you to create single or multiple reference points along the distance of a selected curve. When you choose this button, the **Selections** rollout of the **Point PropertyManager** will expand providing you additional options. These options are discussed next.

Enter the distance/percentage value according to distance

This spinner is used to specify the distance or the percentage value between the individual reference points along the selected curve.

Distance

This radio button is selected to define the distance between the individual points in terms of the distance value. If this radio button is selected, the value entered in the **Enter the distance/percentage value according to distance** spinner will be in terms of linear units of the current document.

Percentage

This radio button is selected to define the gap between the individual points in terms of the percentage of the length of the selected curve. If this radio button is selected, the total length of the selected curve will be taken as 100%. Now, the value entered in the **Enter the distance/percentage value according to distance** spinner will be in terms of the percentage of the selected curve.

Evenly Distribute

This radio button is selected to distribute the specified number of reference points evenly through the length of the selected curve. If this radio button is selected, the **Enter the distance/percentage value according to distance** spinner will not be available.

Enter the number of reference points to be created along the selected entity

This spinner is used to specify the number of reference points to be created. The specified number of reference points will be placed at a gap specified in the **Enter the distance/percentage value according to distance** spinner along the selected curve.

Creating Reference Coordinate Systems

CommandManager:	Features > Reference Geometry flyout > Coordinate System
SOLIDWORKS menu:	Insert > Reference Geometry > Coordinate System
Toolbar:	Reference Geometry > Coordinate System

In SOLIDWORKS, you may need to define some reference coordinate systems other than the default coordinate system for creating features, analyzing the geometry, analyzing the assemblies, and so on. To create a user-defined coordinate system, choose the **Coordinate System** tool from the **Features CommandManager**; the **Coordinate System PropertyManager** will be displayed, as shown in Figure 6-35. Also, a coordinate system will be displayed at the origin of the current document.

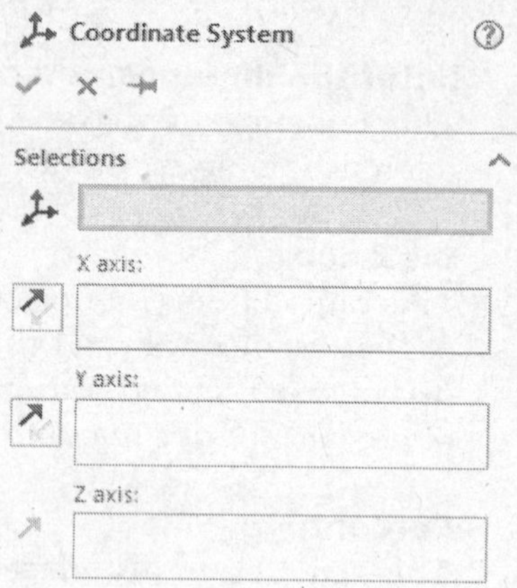

Figure 6-35 The ***Coordinate System PropertyManager***

To create a new coordinate system, you need to select a point that will be selected as the origin for the new coordinate system, and then define the directions of the X and Y, Y and Z, or Z and X axes. On selecting the point for the origin, the preview of the new coordinate system will be displayed. Define the direction of the axis by selecting an edge, point, or reference axes. You need to specify the direction of any two axes. The direction of the third axis will be automatically determined.

You can reverse the directions of the axes by choosing the corresponding buttons available on the right of their respective selection boxes.

Creating Center of Mass

CommandManager:	Features > Reference Geometry flyout > Center of Mass
SOLIDWORKS menu:	Insert > Reference Geometry > Center of Mass
Toolbar:	Reference Geometry > Center of Mass

The **Center of Mass** tool is used to locate a point where the total mass of the part or assembly acts. The entire mass of the body concentrates at this point and it determines the dynamic response of the part or assembly to the external forces and vibrations. While calculating the mass properties of the part or assembly, this point will play a major role. The position of the center of mass point will change if the geometry of the body is changed. To determine the center of mass of the body, choose the **Center of Mass** tool from the **Features CommandManager**; the point where the center of mass is lying will be displayed and the **Center of Mass** node will be added to the **FeatureManager Design Tree** under the **Origin** node.

Tip

You can add a point at the center of mass of a body for your reference. To add a reference point, select the ***Center of Mass*** *node in the* ***FeatureManager Design Tree****; a pop-up toolbar will be displayed. Choose the* ***Center of Mass Reference Point*** *from the pop-up toolbar; a point will be created at the center of mass of the body.*

Creating a Bounding Box

CommandManager:	Features > Reference Geometry flyout > Bounding Box
SOLIDWORKS menu:	Insert > Reference Geometry > Bounding Box
Toolbar:	Reference Geometry > Bounding Box

The **Bounding Box** tool is used to create a box that can completely enclose a body or bodies within a smallest volume. The bounding box is created by using a 3D sketch. It is useful for packaging industries as this tool can help in determining the dimensions required for packaging a product. Also, in manufacturing industries, you can find the stock size required for a product using the length, width, and height of the bounding box. In **SOLIDWORKS 2021,** when you suppress or hide the bounding box feature, it will not rebuild further.

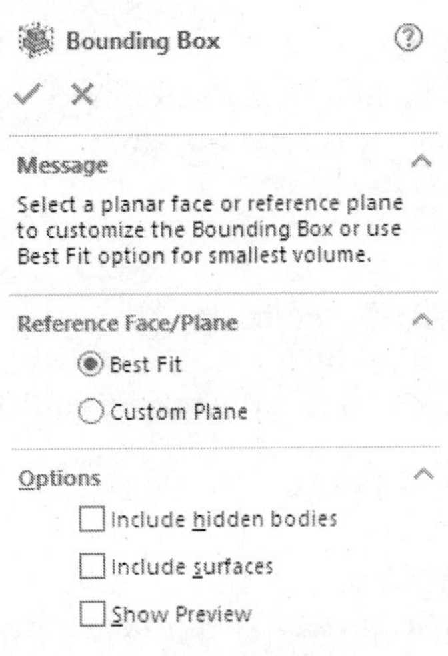

Figure 6-36 The Bounding Box PropertyManager

To create a bounding box, choose the **Bounding Box** tool from the **Features CommandManager**; the **Bounding Box PropertyManager** will be displayed, as shown in Figure 6-36. By default, the **Best Fit** radio button is selected in the **Reference Face/Plane** rollout. It is used to create smallest volume of the bounding box. You can also select the **Custom Plane** radio button to display **Select a planar face or plane** selection box. Select a planar surface or plane using this selection box for the orientation of the bounding box. Select the **Include hidden bodies** check box in the **Options** rollout to include hidden bodies in the bounding box. You can also include surface bodies in the bounding box using the **Include surfaces** check box. To preview the bounding box generated, select the **Show Preview** check box. Choose the **OK** button to close the **Bounding Box PropertyManager**; a 3D sketch will be generated enclosing the bodies. Also, a **Bounding Box** node is added to the **FeatureManager Design Tree**. Figure 6-37 shows a Offset bracket model within a bounding box. You can view the properties of bounding by hovering the cursor over the **Bounding Box** node or by choosing **File > Properties > Configuration Specific** from the SOLIDWORKS menus.

Figure 6-37 Offset Bracket model with a Bounding Box

ADVANCED BOSS/BASE OPTIONS

In the previous chapter, you learned to create the base feature. Some of the options in the **Boss-Extrude PropertyManager** or **Revolved PropertyManager** cannot be used while creating the base feature. In this section, you will learn to use these advanced options.

From

The **Start Condition** drop-down list in the **From** rollout of the **Boss-Extrude PropertyManager** is used to specify the position from where the sketch will start to extrude, refer to Figure 6-38. The options in this rollout are discussed next.

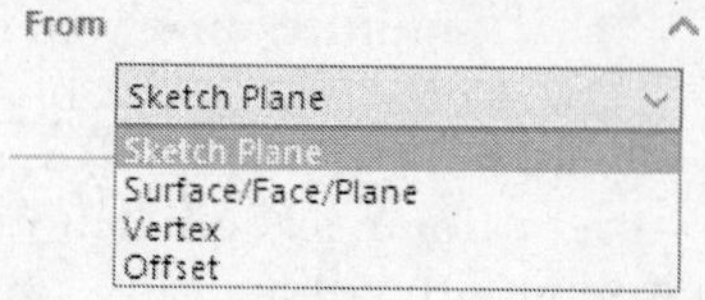

*Figure 6-38 The **From** rollout of the **Boss-Extrude PropertyManager***

Sketch Plane

When you invoke the **Boss-Extrude PropertyManager**, the **Sketch Plane** option will be selected by default in the **Start Condition** drop-down list of the **From** rollout. So, the extrude feature will start from the sketching plane on which the sketch is drawn. This option is mostly used while creating the extrude features.

Surface/Face/Plane

The **Surface/Face/Plane** option is used to start the extrude feature from a selected surface, face, or a plane, instead of the plane on which the sketch is drawn. To do so, invoke the **Boss-Extrude PropertyManager** and select the **Surface/Face/Plane** option from the **Start Condition** drop-down list in the **From** rollout; the **Select A Surface/Face/Plane** selection box will be displayed in the **From** rollout. Select a surface, a face, or a plane from where you need to start the extrude feature, as shown in Figure 6-39. Make sure that the sketch is drawn in such a way that if the surface or the plane on which the sketch is to be projected is curved, then all the entities of the sketch drawn should intersect that surface or plane. However, for a planar surface the sketch need not to be encapsulated by the selected plane. Figure 6-40 shows the resulting extruded feature formed on the selected face up to a specified depth.

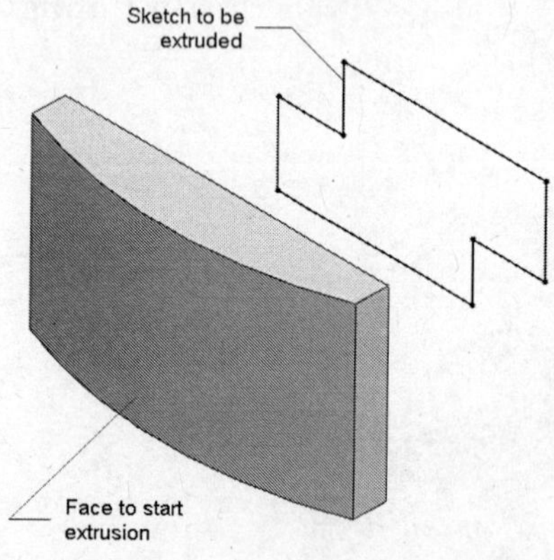

Figure 6-39 Sketch to be extruded and the reference face selected

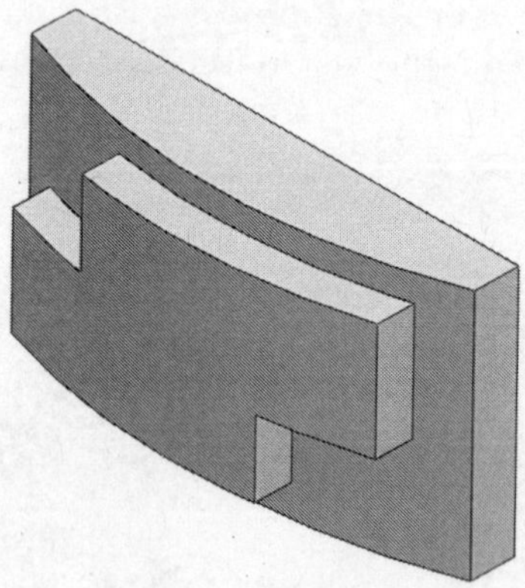

Figure 6-40 Resulting extruded feature

Vertex

The **Vertex** option is used to specify a vertex as a reference for starting the extrude feature. To do so, invoke the **Boss-Extrude PropertyManager** and select the **Vertex** option from the **Start Condition** drop-down list; the **Select A Vertex** selection box will be displayed. Select a vertex on an existing feature or the endpoint of an existing sketch. Figure 6-41 shows the sketch to be extruded and the vertex to be selected as reference to start the extrude feature. Figure 6-42 shows the resulting extruded feature formed on the selected vertex to the defined depth.

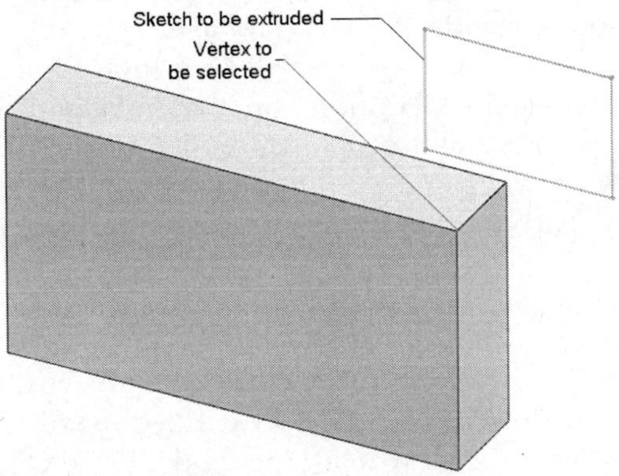

Figure 6-41 Sketch to be extruded and a reference vertex to be selected

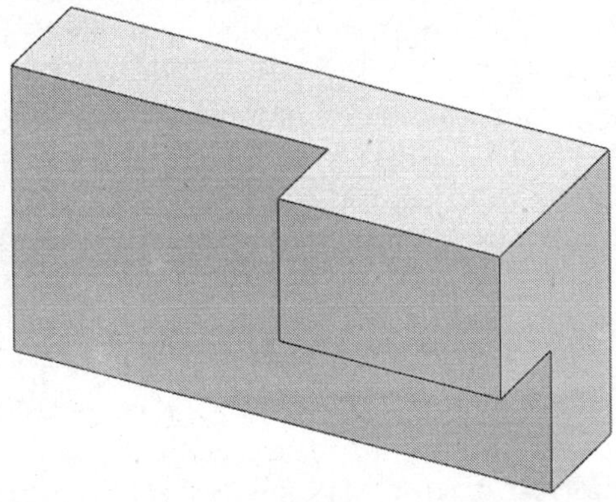

Figure 6-42 Resulting extruded feature

Offset

The **Offset** option is used to start the extrude feature at an offset from the plane on which the sketch is drawn. To do so, select the **Offset** option from the **Start Condition** drop-down list; the **Enter Offset Value** spinner will be displayed. Set the value of the offset in this spinner. Figure 6-43 shows a preview of a sketch drawn on the front plane which is being extruded using the **Offset** option. Figure 6-44 shows the resulting extruded feature at an offset distance from the sketching plane.

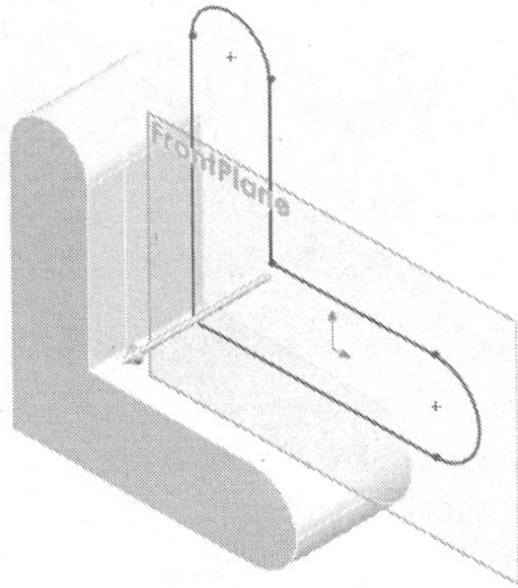

*Figure 6-43 Sketch being extruded using the **Offset** option*

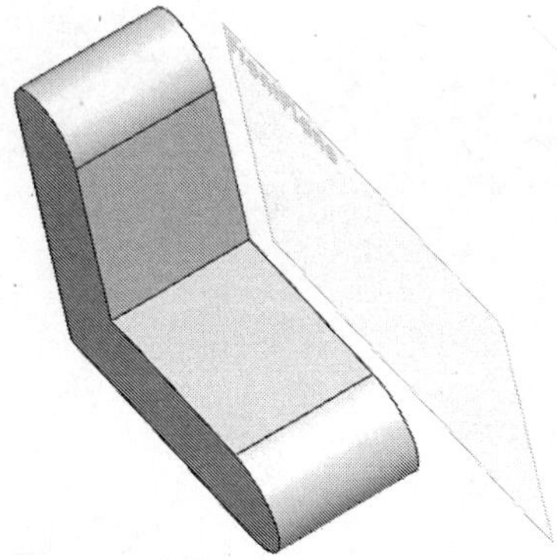

Figure 6-44 Resulting extruded feature

End Condition

The options in the **End Condition** drop-down list in the **Boss-Extrude PropertyManager** and the **Revolve Type** drop-down list in the **Revolve PropertyManager** are discussed next.

Through All

The **Through All** option will be available in the **End Condition** drop-down list only after you create a base feature. After creating a base feature, define a new sketching plane and draw the sketch using the standard sketching tools. Now, choose the **Extruded Boss/Base** button from the **Features CommandManager** to invoke the **Boss-Extrude PropertyManager**. The preview of the extruded feature that will be created using the default settings will be displayed in the temporary graphics in the drawing area. Select the **Through All** option from the **End Condition** drop-down list; the extrude feature will extend from the sketching plane through all the existing geometric entities. You can also reverse the direction of extrusion using the **Reverse Direction** button available on the left of the **End Condition** drop-down list.

When you select the **Through All** option, the sketch will be extruded through all the existing geometries. You will observe that the **Merge result** check box is displayed in the **Boss-Extrude PropertyManager**. This check box is selected by default. Therefore, the newly created extruded feature will merge with the base feature. If you clear this check box, this extruded feature will not merge with the existing base feature, resulting in the creation of another body. The creation of a new body can be confirmed with the display of the **Solid Bodies** folder in the **FeatureManager design tree**. The value of the number of disjoint bodies in the model is displayed in parentheses on the right of the **Solid Bodies** folder. You can click on the ► sign on the left of the **Solid Bodies** folder to expand it. To collapse the folder back, click on the ▾ sign.

Figure 6-45 displays a sketch created on the sketching plane at an offset distance from the right planar face of the model. Figure 6-46 displays the feature created by extruding the sketch using the **Through All** option.

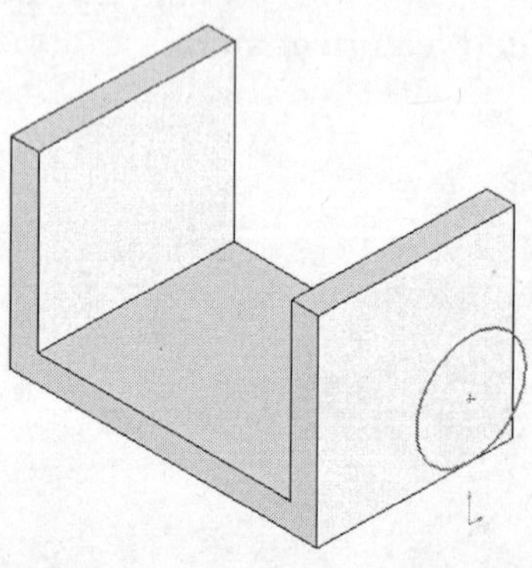

Figure 6-45 *A sketch drawn at an offset distance from the right planar surface*

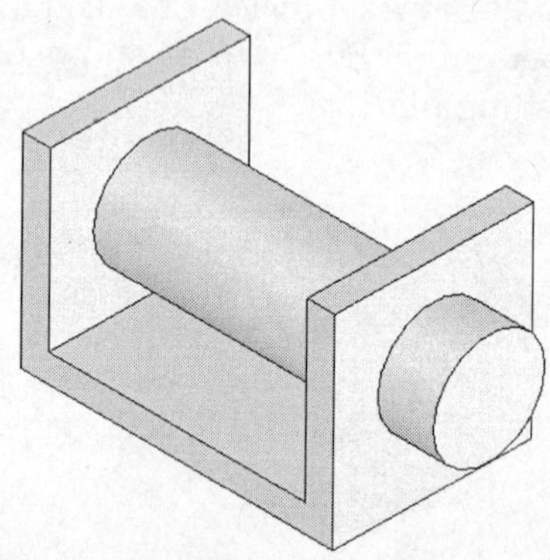

Figure 6-46 *Sketch extruded using the* ***Through All*** *option*

Note

It is recommended that while creating additional features after creating the base feature, you should always select the ***Merge result*** *check box in the* ***Feature PropertyManager****.*

Tip
The feature created from multiple disjoint closed contours results in the creation of disjoint bodies.

Up To Next

The **Up To Next** option is used to extrude the sketch from the sketching plane to the next surface that intersects the feature. After creating the base feature, create a sketch by selecting or creating a sketching plane. Next, invoke the **Boss-Extrude PropertyManager**; a preview of the new feature will be displayed with the default options. Now, select the **Up To Next** option from the **End Condition** drop-down list. You can also reverse the direction of feature creation by choosing the **Reverse Direction** button. The preview of the feature will be modified accordingly and the sketch will be displayed as extruded from the sketching plane to the next surface that completely intersects the feature geometry. Figure 6-47 shows the sketch that will be extruded using the **Up To Next** option and Figure 6-48 shows the resulting feature.

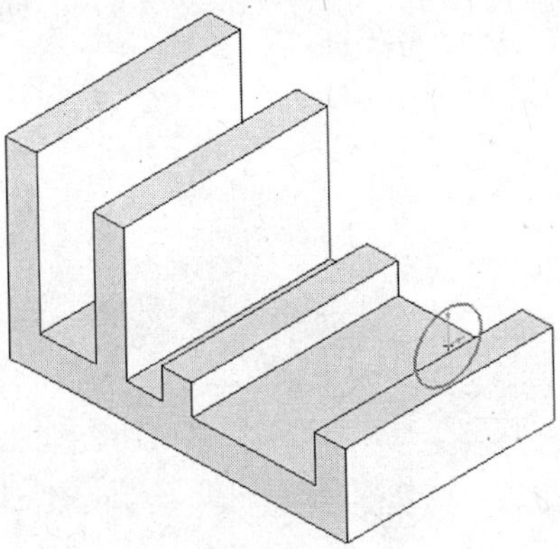

Figure 6-47 *A sketch drawn on the Right Plane for extrusion*

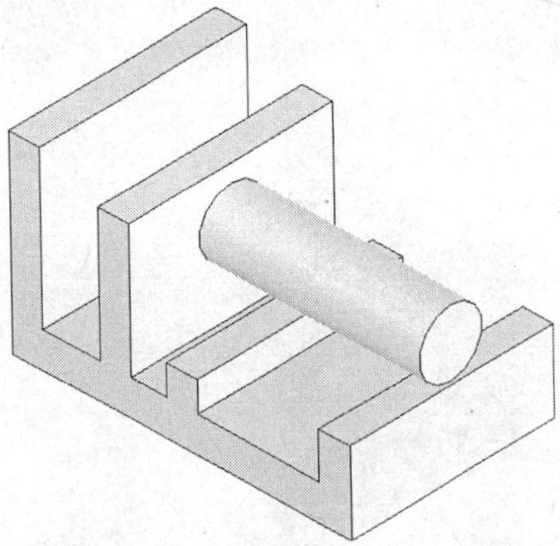

Figure 6-48 *Sketch extruded using the **Up To Next** option*

Up To Vertex

The **Up To Vertex** option is used to define the termination of a feature at a virtual plane that is parallel to the sketching plane and passes through the selected vertex. The vertex can be a point on an edge, a sketched point, or a reference point. In SOLIDWORKS, you can also revolve a sketch up to a vertex. Figure 6-49 shows a sketch drawn on a plane at an offset distance and Figure 6-50 shows the model in which the sketch is extruded up to the selected vertex. Figure 6-51 shows a profile to be revolved and Figure 6-52 shows a preview of the revolved feature when the **Up To Vertex** option is selected.

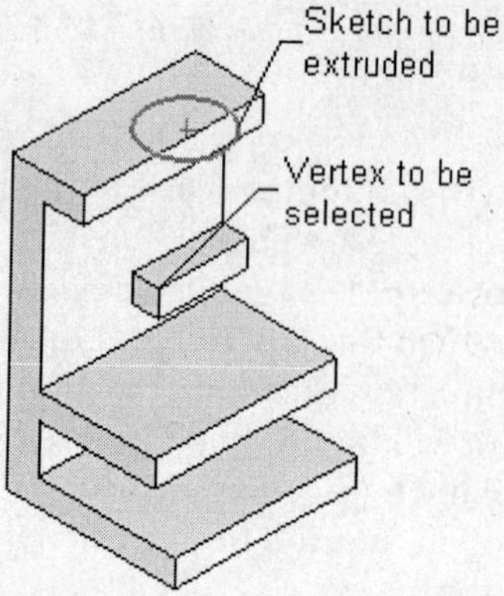

Figure 6-49 Sketch drawn on a plane created at an offset distance and the vertex to be selected

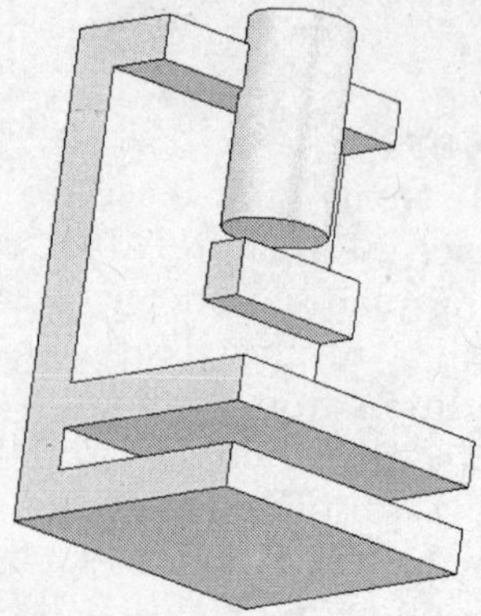

*Figure 6-50 Sketch extruded using the **Up To Vertex** option*

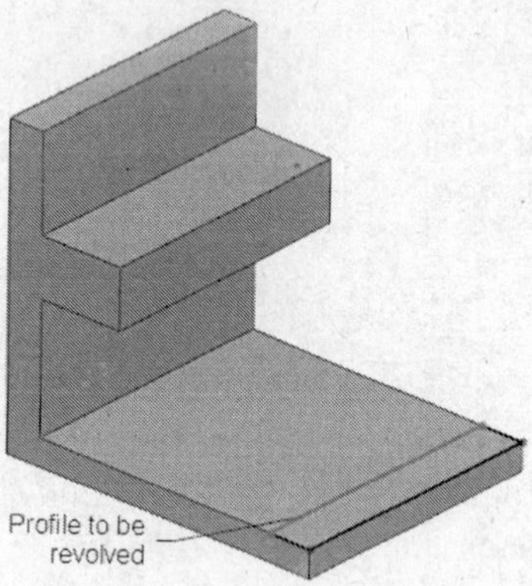

Figure 6-51 Profile to be revolved

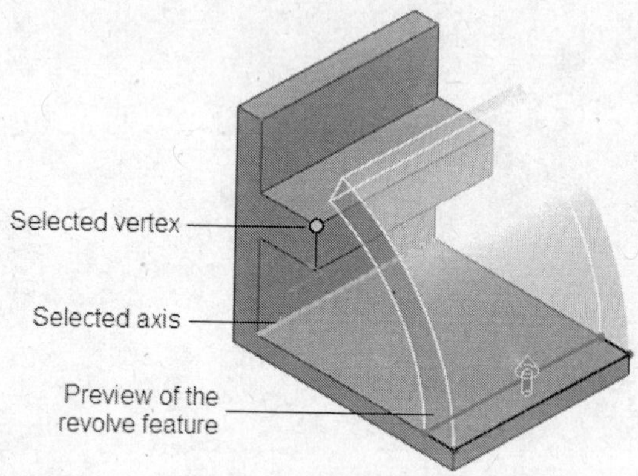

*Figure 6-52 Preview of the revolved feature when **Up To Vertex** is selected*

Up To Surface

The **Up To Surface** option is used to define the termination of a feature up to a selected surface or face. To extrude a sketch up to a surface, invoke the **Boss-Extrude PropertyManager** and then select the **Up To Surface** option from the **End Condition** drop-down list; the **Face/Plane** selection box will be displayed and you will be prompted to select a face or a surface. Select the surface up to which you want to extrude the feature; the feature is extruded. Similarly, to revolve a sketch up to a surface, select the **Up To Surface** option from the **Revolve Type** drop-down list of the **Revolve PropertyManager** and select a face or surface. Figure 6-53 shows the sketch drawn at an offset distance and the surface to be selected. Figure 6-54 shows the resulting feature extruded up to the selected surface. Figure 6-55 shows the profile to be revolved. Figure 6-56 shows preview of the revolved feature when the **Up To Surface** option is selected.

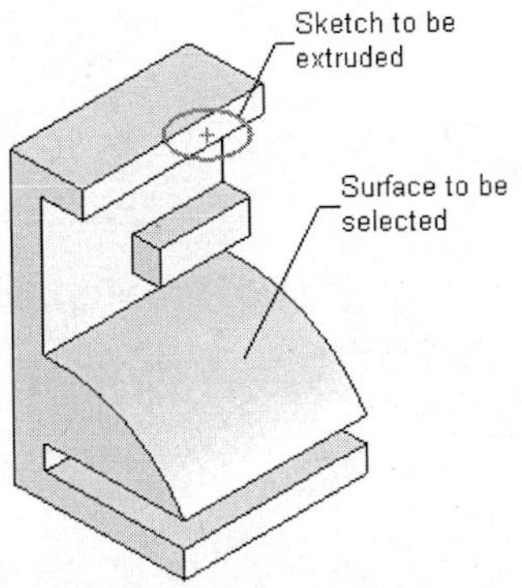

Figure 6-53 Sketch drawn on a plane created at an offset distance and the surface to be selected

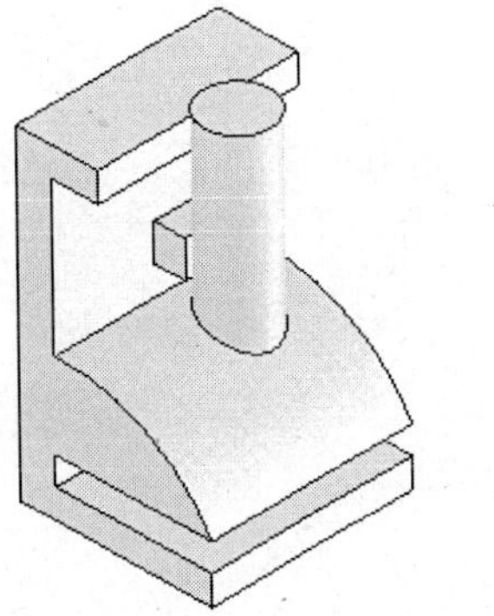

*Figure 6-54 Sketch extruded using the **Up To Surface** option*

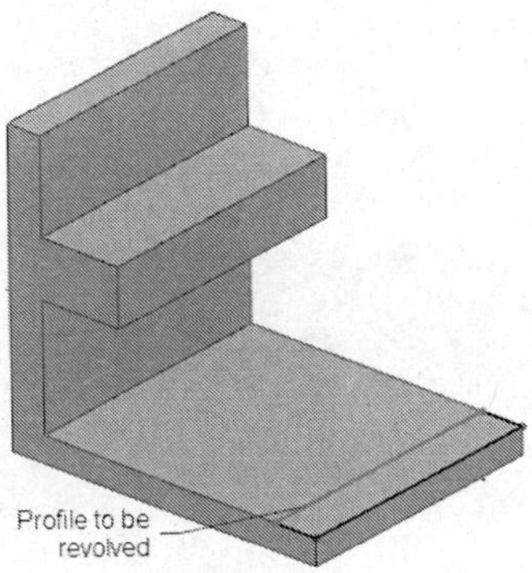

Figure 6-55 Profile to be revolved

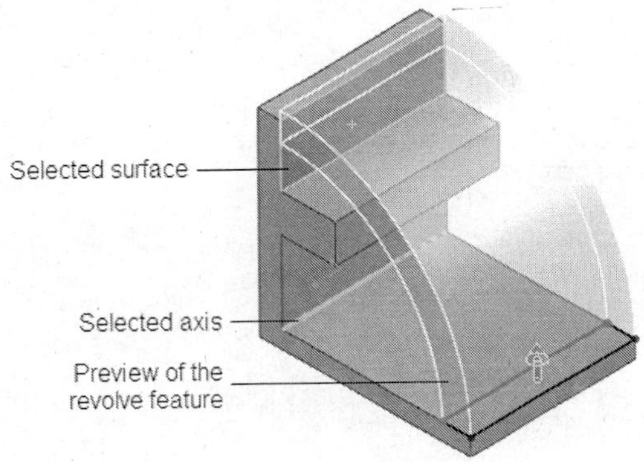

*Figure 6-56 Preview of the revolved feature when the **Up To Surface** option is selected*

Offset From Surface

The **Offset From Surface** option is used to define the termination of a feature on a virtual surface created at an offset distance from the selected surface. To extrude a sketch up to an offset distance from the surface, invoke the **Boss-Extrude PropertyManager** and select the **Offset From Surface** option from the **End Condition** drop-down list; the **Face/Plane** selection box will be displayed along with the **Offset Distance** spinner. Next, select the surface and set the offset distance in the **Offset Distance** spinner. You can reverse the direction of the offset by selecting the **Reverse offset** check box from the **Direction 1** rollout. If the **Translate surface** check box is cleared in the **Direction 1** rollout, the virtual surface created for the termination of the extruded feature will have parallel relation for planar surface and concentric for curved surface. It means that the virtual surface thus created will reflect the true offset of the selected surface. If the **Translate surface** check box is selected, the virtual surface will be translated to the distance provided as the offset distance from the reference surface. It means that a virtual surface will be created to define the termination of the extruded feature, but it will not reflect the true offset of the selected surface. Refer to Figure 6-57 to understand this concept in a better way. Similar to extrusion, you can also revolve a sketch up to an offset distance from a surface.

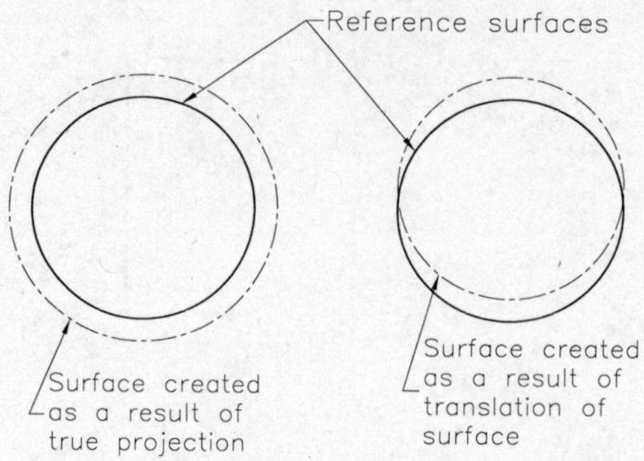

***Figure 6-57** Surfaces created with true projection and translation*

Figure 6-58 shows the front view of the sketch extruded with its termination at an offset distance from the selected cylindrical surface and the **Translate surface** check box cleared. Figure 6-59 shows the front view of the extruded feature with the **Translate surface** check box selected.

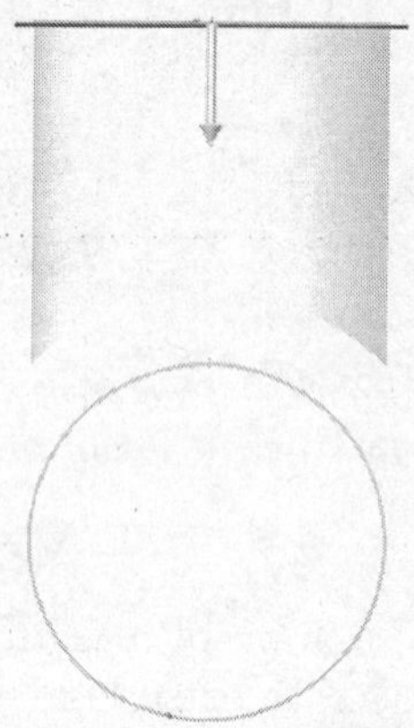

***Figure 6-58** Sketch extruded using the **Offset From Surface** option with the **Translate surface** check box cleared*

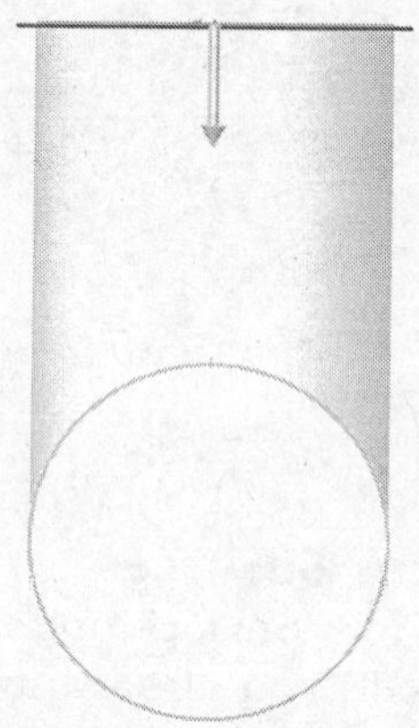

***Figure 6-59** Sketch extruded using the **Offset From Surface** option with the **Translate surface** check box selected*

Up To Body

The **Up To Body** option is used to define the termination of the extruded feature to another body. To create an extruded feature using the **Up To Body** option, invoke the **Boss-Extrude PropertyManager** and select the **Up To Body** option from the **End Condition** drop-down list; the **Solid/Surface Body** selection box will be displayed. Select the body to terminate the feature and choose the **OK** button. Figure 6-60 shows the sketch for the extruded feature and a body up to which the sketch will be extruded. Figure 6-61 shows the resulting feature.

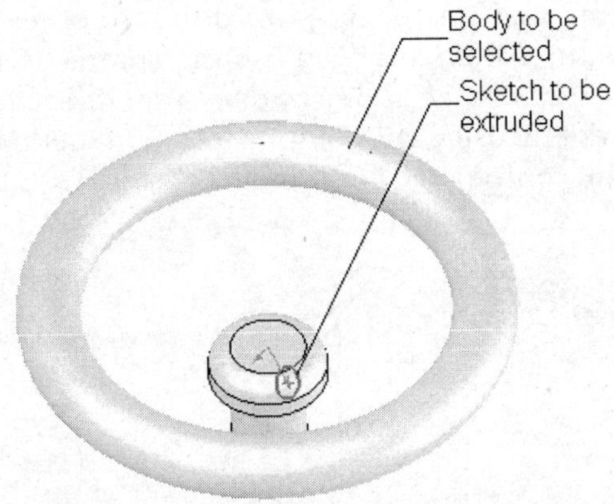

Figure 6-60 *Sketch to be extruded and the body to be selected for the extrude feature*

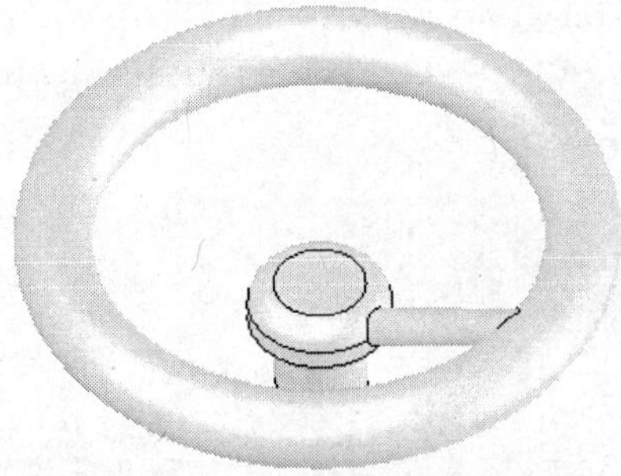

Figure 6-61 *Sketch extruded using the* ***Up To Body*** *option*

Direction of Extrusion

In SOLIDWORKS, you can define the direction of extrusion for the sketches. As mentioned in the previous chapter, the direction of extrusion is generally normal to the sketching plane. You can also define the direction of extrusion using a sketched line, an edge, or a reference axis. Note that the entity you want to use for defining the direction of extrusion should not be drawn on the sketch plane parallel to the plane on which the sketch to be extruded is drawn.

To define the direction of extrusion, click on the **Direction of Extrusion** selection box in the **Direction 1** area of the **Boss-Extrude PropertyManager**. Next, select an edge, a sketched line segment, or an axis. Figure 6-62 shows a sketch drawn on the top face of a rectangular block and a line sketched on the left face of the block to define the direction of extrusion. Figure 6-63 shows the resulting extruded feature.

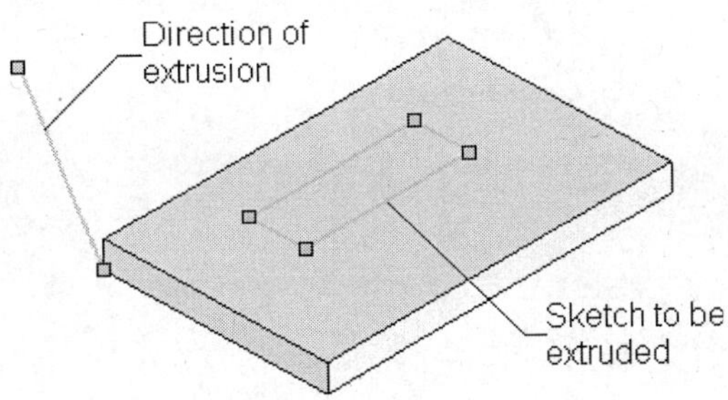

Figure 6-62 *Sketch to be extruded and the direction of extrusion*

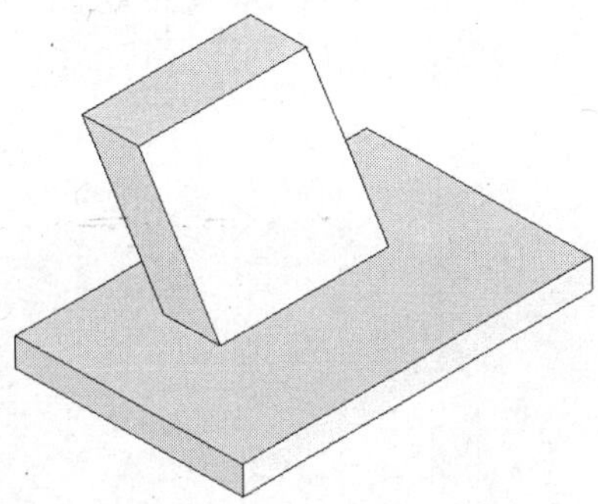

Figure 6-63 *Resulting extruded feature*

MODELING USING THE CONTOUR SELECTION METHOD

Modeling using the contour selection method allows you to use partial sketches for creating the features. You can use this method to create a model from a single sketch that has multiple contours. To understand this concept, consider the multifeatured solid model shown in Figure 6-64. For creating a multifeatured model similar to the one shown in Figure 6-64, ideally you first need to draw the sketch for the base feature and then convert it into the base feature. Next, you need to draw the sketch for the second sketched feature and convert it into feature. In other words, you have to draw separate sketches for each feature. But when you use the contour selection method, you can create the sketch with all contours and select it one by one to create the feature. Figure 6-65 shows the sketch to be drawn for modeling using the contour selection method. The procedure to convert sketch into model using the contour selection method is discussed next.

Figure 6-64 *Multifeatured solid model*

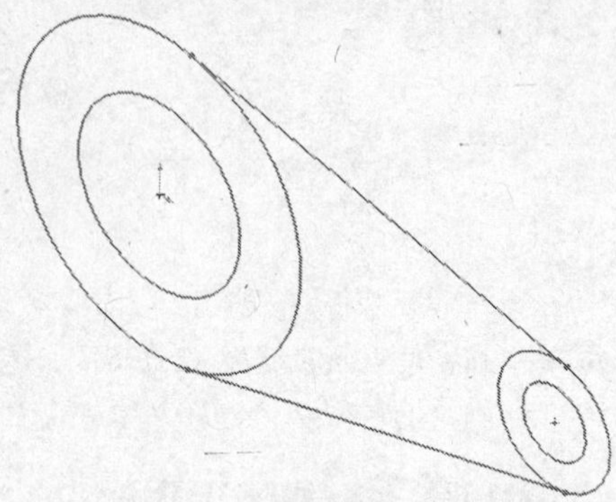

Figure 6-65 *Sketch for creating the model*

After drawing the entire sketch, right-click in the drawing area to invoke the shortcut menu. Make sure you are still in the sketching environment. Choose the **Contour Select Tool** option from the shortcut menu. If this option is not displayed by default in the shortcut menu, you have to select the **Contour Select Tool** check box from the customize menu available in the shortcut menu. When you choose this option, the select cursor will be replaced by a contour selection cursor and the contour selection confirmation corner will be displayed. Click the contour selection cursor between the two circles on the left, the area between the two circles will be selected, as shown in Figure 6-66. Invoke the **Boss-Extrude PropertyManager** and extrude the selected contour using the **Mid Plane** option. Finally, choose the **OK** button from the PropertyManager to exit from it. Figure 6-67 shows the extruded feature created using the **Mid Plane** option.

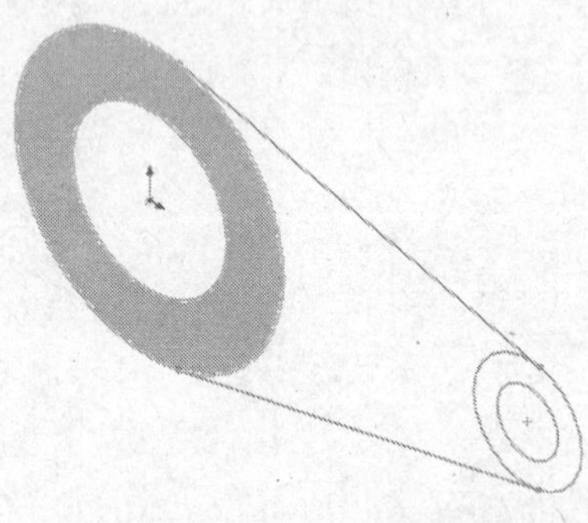

Figure 6-66 *Contour selected for creating the extruded feature*

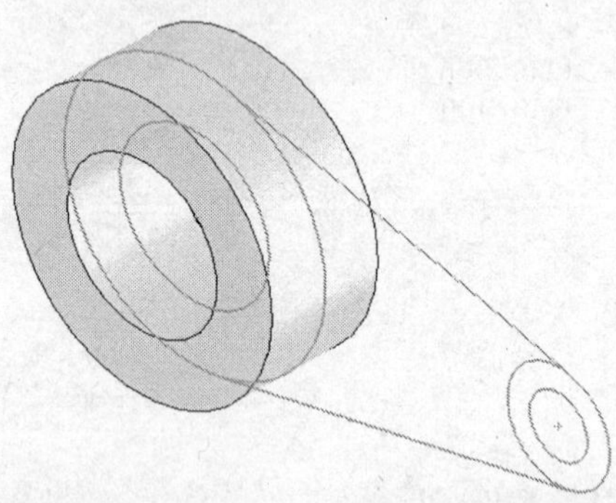

Figure 6-67 *Isometric view of the feature created by extruding the selected contour*

Now, right-click in the drawing area and again choose the **Contour Select Tool** option from the shortcut menu. Select any entity in the sketch using the contour selection cursor and then select the middle contour of the sketch, as shown in Figure 6-68. Invoke the **Boss-Extrude PropertyManager** and extrude the selected contour using the **Mid Plane** option. Again, invoke the **Contour Select Tool** and select an entity in the sketch. Next, specify a point between the two circles on the right and extrude the same using the **Mid Plane** option.

> **Tip**
> *When you move the contour selection cursor in the sketch, the areas where the contour selection is possible are highlighted dynamically.*

After creating the model using this option, you will notice that the sketches are displayed in the model. So, you need to hide them. Click on the sign ▸ located on the left of any of the extruded features to expand the tree view. Select the sketch icon; a pop-up toolbar will be displayed. Choose the **Hide** option. Figure 6-69 shows the model after creating all the features using the contour selection method and after hiding the sketch.

Figure 6-68 *Contour selected for the second feature*

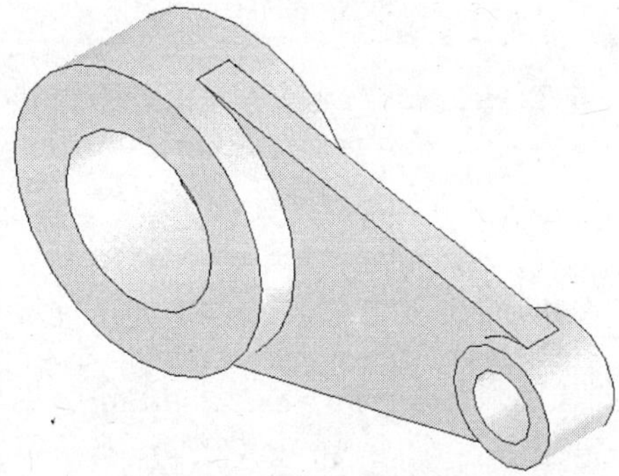

Figure 6-69 *Final model*

In SOLIDWORKS, you can also select the model edges as a part of the contour. For example, consider Figure 6-70. This figure shows a line drawn on the top face of a rectangular block. You can use the edges of the top face that form a contour with the line as the sketch to be extruded, see Figure 6-71. Figure 6-72 shows the resulting extruded feature.

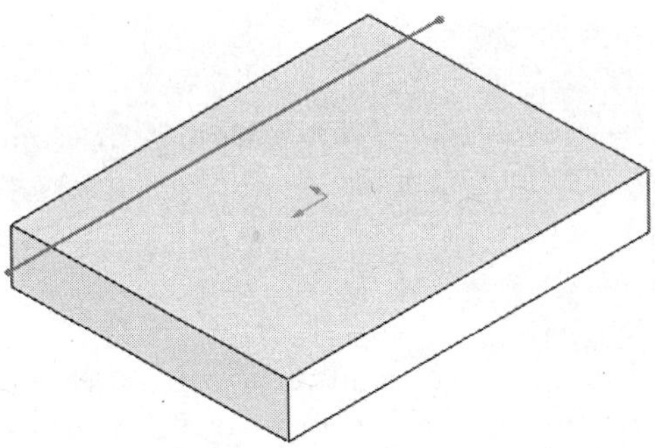

Figure 6-70 *Line drawn on the top face of a rectangular model*

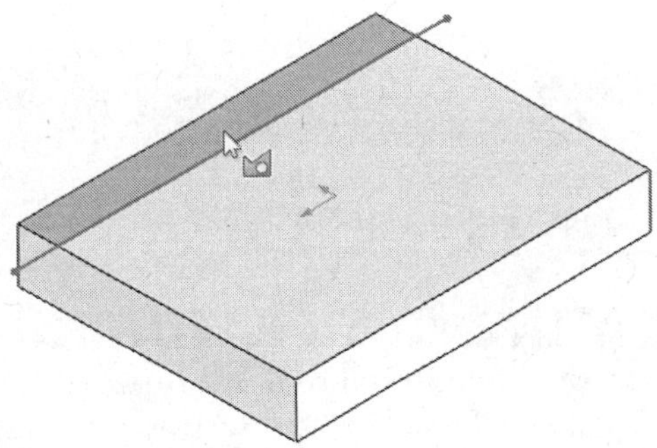

Figure 6-71 *Selecting the contour formed by the line and the edges of the model*

In SOLIDWORKS, you can also create a revolve feature by using the contour selection method. Figure 6-73 shows the revolved feature created using the model edges as a part of the contour.

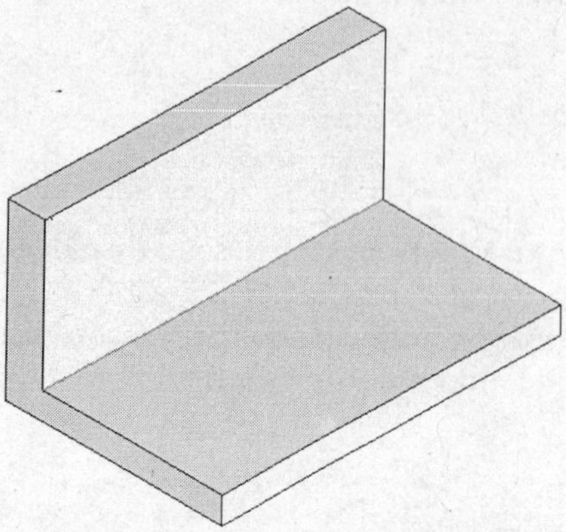

Figure 6-72 Extruded feature created using the edges of the model as a part of the contour

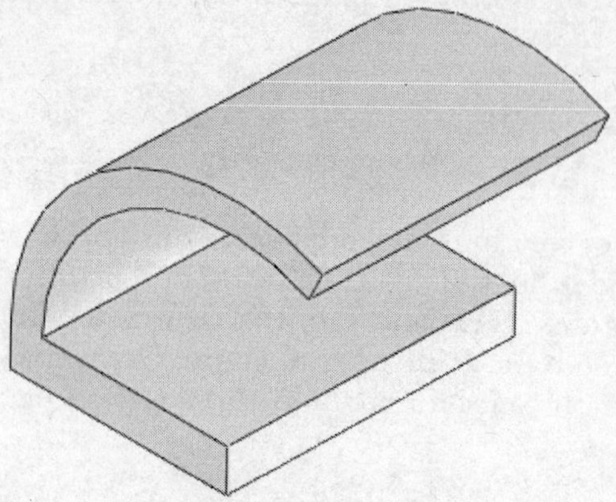

Figure 6-73 Revolved feature created using the edges of the model as a part of the contour

Tip

*When you select a contour using the **Contour Select Tool** option and invoke the **Boss-Extrude PropertyManager**, you will observe that the name of the selected contour is displayed in the selection box of the **Selected Contours** rollout.*

You can select the contours for all the sketched features such as revolve, cut, sweep, loft, and so on.

*You can also select a single sketched entity from a sketch using the **Contour Select Tool** option instead of selecting the contour for creating the sketched features.*

*When you select a closed contour, a pop-up toolbar is displayed from which you can directly invoke the **Extrude Boss/Base** tool.*

Note

*If you click on the ▸ sign to expand the extruded feature in the **FeatureManager Design Tree**, you will notice that instead of showing the icon of a simple sketch, it will show the icon of the contour selected sketch.*

CREATING CUT FEATURES

Cut extrude is a material removal process. You can define a cut feature by extruding a sketch, revolving a sketch, sweeping a section along a path, lofting sections, or by using a surface. You will learn more about sweep, loft, and surface in the later chapters. The cut feature can be created only if a base feature exists. The extruded and revolved cut features are discussed next.

Creating Extruded Cuts

CommandManager:	Features > Extruded Cut
SOLIDWORKS menu:	Insert > Cut > Extrude
Toolbar:	Features > Extruded Cut

To create an extruded cut feature, create a sketch for the cut feature and then choose the **Extruded Cut** button from the **Features CommandManager**; the **Cut-Extrude PropertyManager** will be displayed, as shown in Figure 6-74. Also, preview of the cut feature with default options will be displayed in the drawing area.

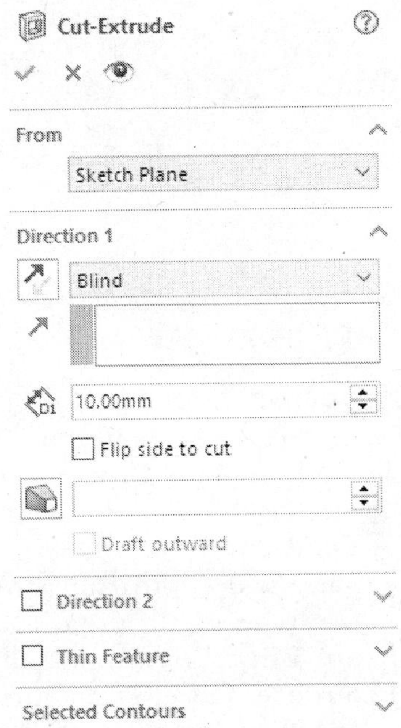

Figure 6-74 The ***Cut-Extrude PropertyManager***

Figure 6-75 shows preview of the cut feature when you invoke the **Cut-Extrude PropertyManager** after creating a sketch. Remember that when you create a cut feature, the current view will not change automatically to a 3D view, you need to change it manually. The material to be removed will be displayed in the temporary graphics. Figure 6-76 shows the model after creating the cut feature.

The options in the **Cut-Extrude PropertyManager** are discussed next.

From

In SOLIDWORKS, you are provided with the options for specifying parameters at the start of the extruded cut. These options are in the **Start Condition** drop-down list of the **From** rollout and are the same as those discussed for the **Extrude Boss/Base** tool.

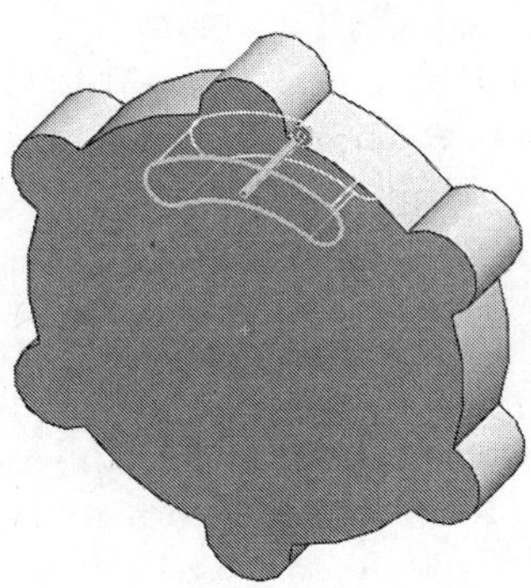

Figure 6-75 *Preview of the cut feature*

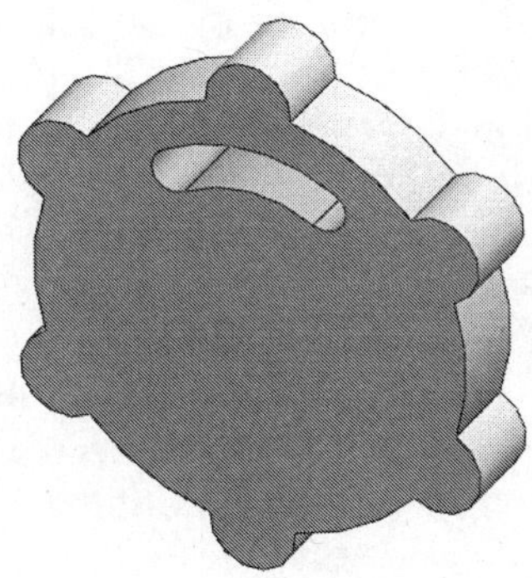

Figure 6-76 *Cut feature added to the model*

Figure 6-77 shows the sketch to be extruded and the curved face selected as the reference face for starting the extrusion. Figure 6-78 shows the resulting extruded cut feature.

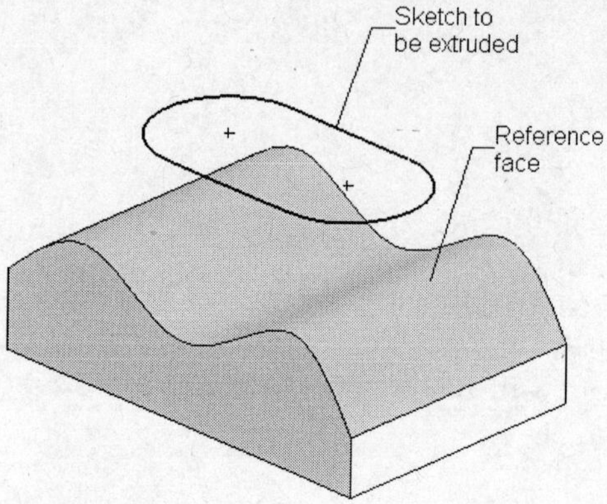

Figure 6-77 *Sketch to be extruded and the reference face*

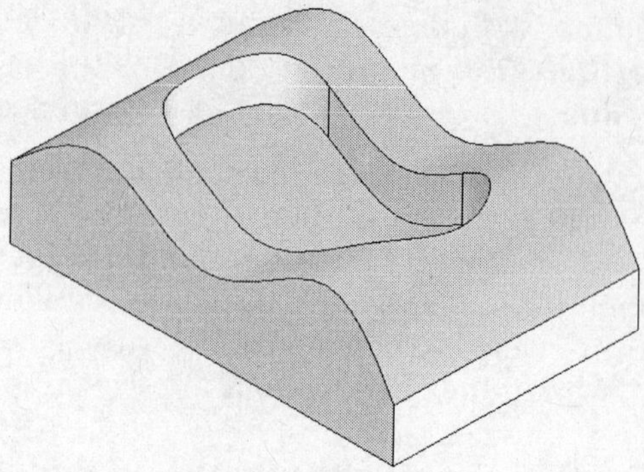

Figure 6-78 *Resulting extruded cut feature*

Direction 1

The **Direction 1** rollout is used to define the termination of the extrusion in the first direction. The options in the **Direction 1** rollout are discussed next.

End Condition

The **End Condition** drop-down list in the **Direction 1** rollout is used to specify the type of termination. The feature termination options in this drop-down list are **Blind**, **Through All**, **Through All - Both**, **Up To Next**, **Up To Vertex**, **Up To Surface, Offset From Surface, Up To Body**, and **Mid Plane**. These options are the same as those discussed for the **Extrude Boss/Base** tool. By default, the **Blind** option is selected in the **End Condition** drop-down list. Therefore, the **Depth** spinner is displayed to specify the depth. If you select the **Through All - Both** option from the drop-down list, then the extruded cut will be created through all the geometries on both sides of the sketching plane. If you choose the **Through All** or the **Up to Next** options, the spinner will not be displayed. The type of spinner or the selection box displayed depends on the option selected from the **End Condition** drop-down list. The **Reverse Direction** button is used to reverse the direction of the feature creation. If you select the **Mid Plane** option from the **End Condition** drop-down list, the **Reverse Direction** button will not be available.

Flip side to cut

The **Flip side to cut** check box is used to define the side from where the material has to be removed with respect to the profile drawn for the cut feature. By default, the **Flip side to cut** check box is cleared. Therefore, the material enclosed by the profile will be removed. If you select this check box, the material left outside the profile will be removed. Figure 6-79 shows a cut feature created with the **Flip side to cut** check box cleared and Figure 6-80 shows a cut feature created with the **Flip side to cut** check box selected.

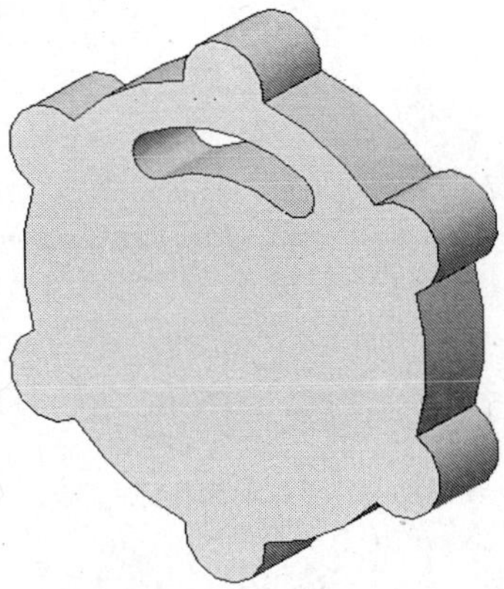

Figure 6-79 Cut feature created with the ***Flip side to cut*** *check box cleared*

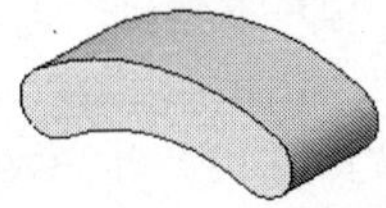

Figure 6-80 Cut feature created with the ***Flip side to cut*** *check box selected*

Tip

You can also flip the direction of cut by clicking on the arrow on the sketch while creating the cut feature. This arrow is available only if you have selected or cleared the ***Flip side to cut*** *check box once.*

Draft On/Off

The **Draft On/Off** button is used to apply the draft angle to the extruded cut feature. The **Draft Angle** spinner on the right of the **Draft On/Off** button is used to set the value of the draft angle. By default, the **Draft outward** check box is cleared. Therefore, the draft is created inward with respect to the direction of feature creation. If you select this check box, the draft added to the cut feature will be created outward with respect to the direction of the feature creation. Figure 6-81 shows the draft added to the cut feature with the **Draft outward** check box cleared and Figure 6-82 shows the draft added to the cut feature with the **Draft outward** check box selected.

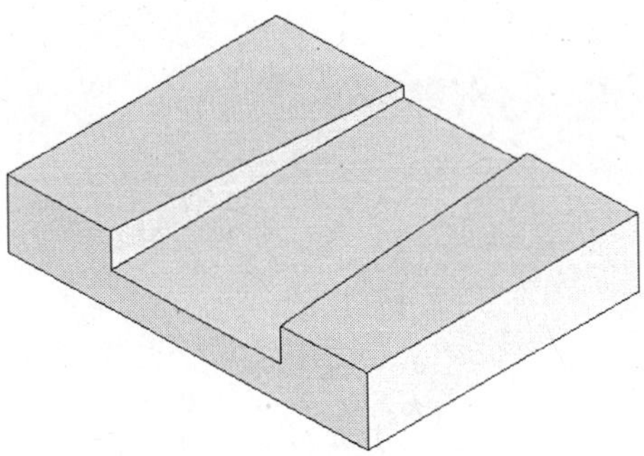

Figure 6-81 Cut feature with the ***Draft outward*** *check box cleared*

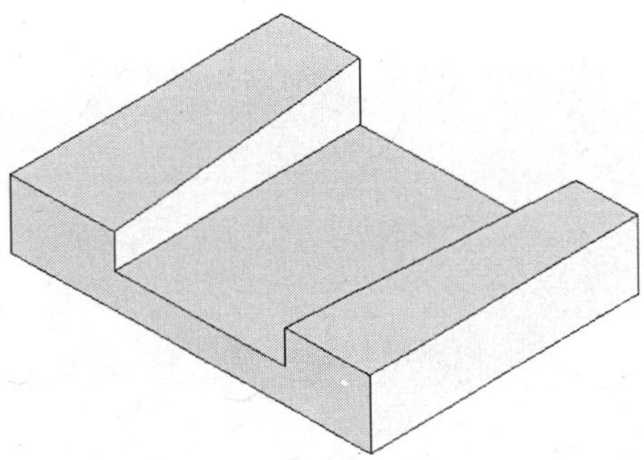

Figure 6-82 Cut feature with the ***Draft outward*** *check box selected*

The **Direction 2** rollout is used to specify the termination of the feature creation in the second direction. The options in the **Direction 2** rollout are the same as those discussed the **Direction 1** rollout.

The **Selected Contours** rollout is used to select specific contours from the current sketch.

> **Tip**
> *The sketch used for the cut feature can be a closed loop or an open sketch. Note that if the sketch is an open sketch, the sketch should completely divide the model into two or more parts and the depth of the cut should not exceed the depth of the target part.*

Thin Feature

The **Thin Feature** rollout is used to create a thin cut feature. When you create a cut feature, you need to apply thickness to the sketch in addition to the end condition. This rollout is used to specify the parameters to create a thin feature. To create a thin cut feature, invoke the **Extruded Cut** tool after creating the sketch and specify the end conditions in the **Direction 1** and **Direction 2** rollouts. Now, select the check box in the **Thin Feature** rollout to activate it. The options in this rollout are the same as those discussed for the thin feature in the **Extruded Boss/Base** tool.

Creating Multiple Bodies in the Cut Feature

While creating a cut feature, sometimes because of geometric conditions, feature termination, or end conditions, the cut feature results in the creation of multiple bodies. Figure 6-83 shows a sketch created on the top planar surface of the base feature to create a cut feature. Figure 6-84 shows the multiple bodies created using the cut feature with the end condition as **Through All**. On choosing the **OK** button from the **Cut-Extrude PropertyManager** with this type of sketch and end condition, the **Bodies to Keep** dialog box will be displayed, as shown in Figure 6-85. This dialog box is used to define the part of the model to be kept, as multiple bodies are created while applying the cut feature.

By default, the **All bodies** radio button is selected in the **Bodies to Keep** dialog box. Therefore, if you choose the **OK** button from this dialog box, all bodies created after the cut feature will remain in the model. If you want the cut feature to consume any of the bodies, select the **Selected bodies** radio button to expand the dialog box, as shown in Figure 6-86.

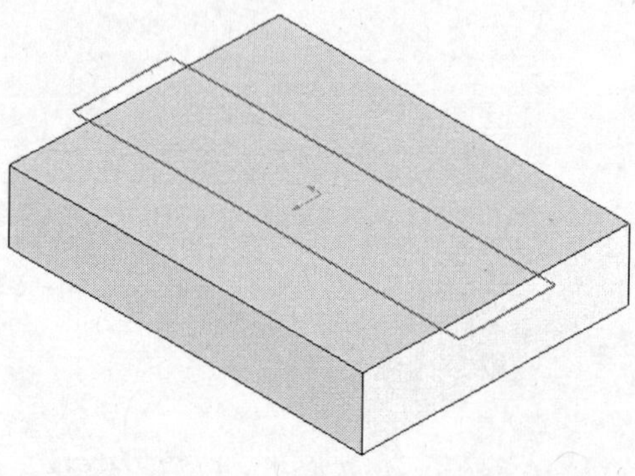

Figure 6-83 *Sketch created for the cut feature*

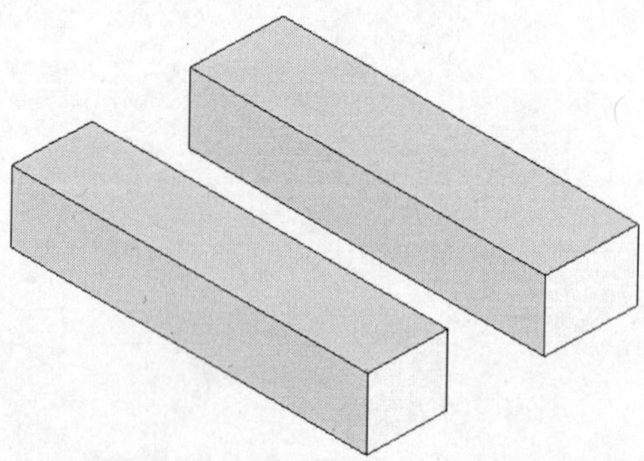

Figure 6-84 *Multiple bodies created using the cut feature*

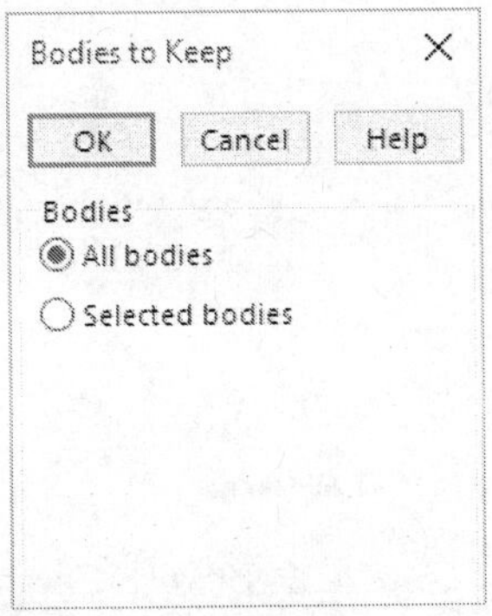

Figure 6-85 The ***Bodies to Keep*** *dialog box*

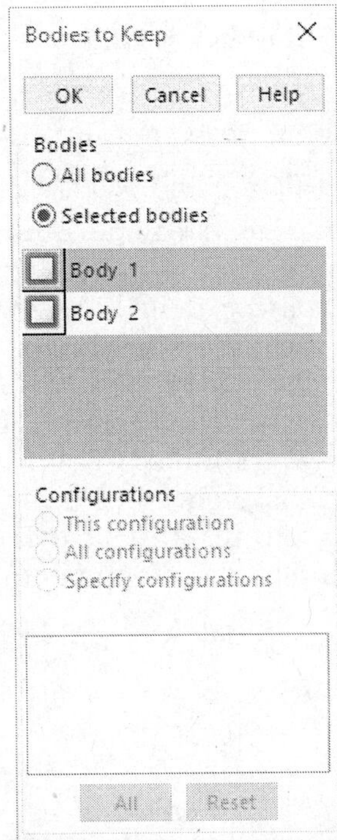

Figure 6-86 The ***Bodies to Keep*** *dialog box with the* ***Selected bodies*** *radio button selected*

You can select the check box provided on the left of the name of the body to specify the body to keep. On selecting a check box, the corresponding body will be displayed in different colors in temporary graphics. Choose the **OK** button from the **Bodies to Keep** dialog box. Figure 6-87 shows a sketch created for the cut feature. Figure 6-88 shows the cut feature created using the **Thin Feature** option and the **All bodies** radio button selected in the **Bodies to Keep** dialog box.

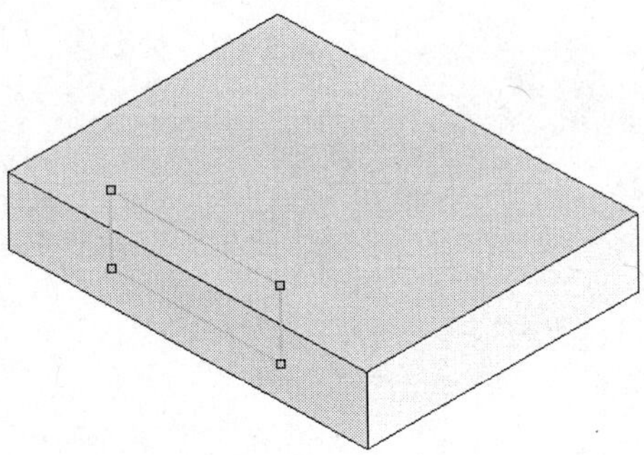

Figure 6-87 Sketch to create a cut feature using the ***Thin Feature*** *option*

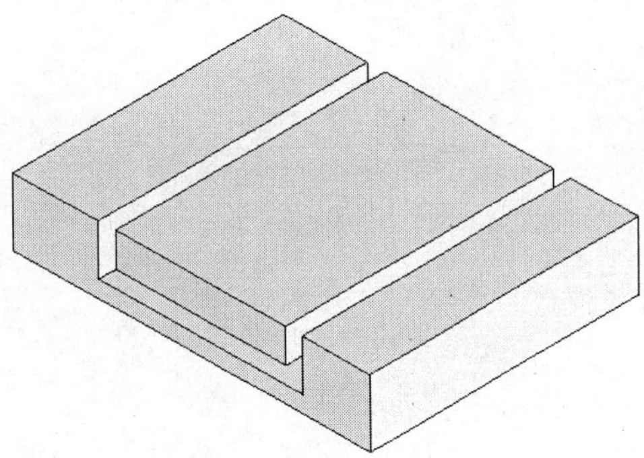

Figure 6-88 A thin cut feature created with all the resulting bodies retained

Note

You will learn about configurations in the later chapters.

Creating Revolved Cuts

CommandManager:	Features > Revolved Cut
SOLIDWORKS menu:	Insert > Cut > Revolve
Toolbar:	Features > Extruded Cut > Revolved Cut

Revolved cuts are used to remove the material by revolving a sketch around a selected axis. Similar to the revolved boss/base feature, you can define the revolution axis using a centerline or using an edge in the sketch. When you invoke the **Revolved Cut** tool, the **Cut-Revolve PropertyManager** will be displayed, as shown in Figure 6-89. The options in this PropertyManager are similar to those discussed earlier. Figure 6-90 shows a sketch for a revolved cut feature and Figure 6-91 shows the resulting cut feature. Note that in Figure 6-91, a texture has been applied to the cut feature.

Figure 6-89** The **Cut-Revolve PropertyManager

Note

*You can also select the tool first and then the plane to create the sketch. On doing so, the feature tool will be activated automatically after you exit the sketching environment and you can define the parameters in their respective rollouts. For example, you can invoke the **Revolved Cut** tool without creating any sketch. In this case, the **Revolve PropertyManager** will be displayed and you will be prompted to select a plane or a planar face to create a sketch or to select a sketch. As soon as you exit the sketching environment after creating the sketch, the **Cut-Revolve PropertyManager** will be displayed automatically.*

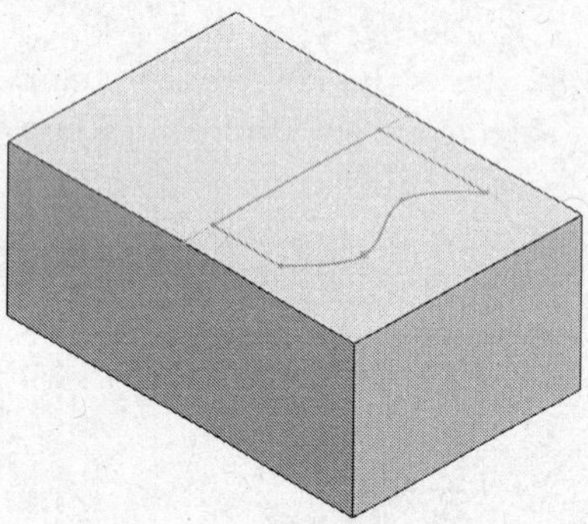

***Figure 6-90** Sketch for the revolved cut feature*

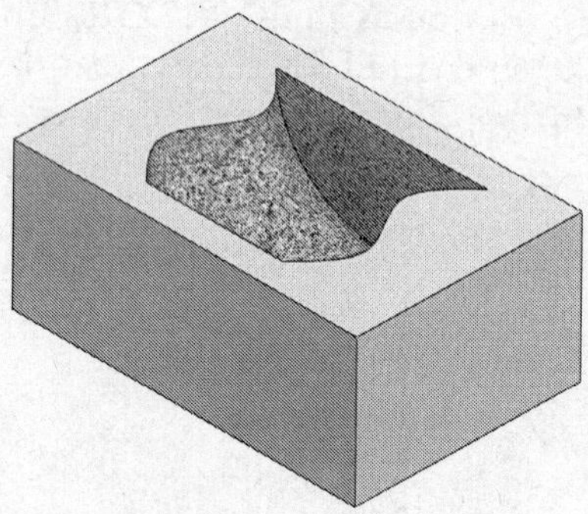

***Figure 6-91** Resulting cut feature with a texture*

CONCEPT OF THE FEATURE SCOPE

As discussed earlier, you can create different disjoint bodies in a single part file in SOLIDWORKS. After creating two or more disjoint bodies, when you create another feature, the **Feature Scope** rollout will be displayed in the **Cut-Revolve PropertyManager**. The **Feature scope** rollout is used with the Extrude boss and cut, Revolve boss and cut, Sweep boss and cut, Loft boss and cut, Boss thicken, Surface cut, and Cavity features.

In the **Feature Scope** rollout, the **Selected bodies** radio button and the **Auto-select** check box are selected by default. With the **Auto-select** check box selected, all disjoint bodies will be selected and they will be affected by the feature creation. If you clear the **Auto-select** check box, a selection box will be invoked. You can select the bodies that you want to be affected by the feature creation. The name of the selected body will be displayed in the selection box. If you select the **All bodies** radio button, all bodies in the part file will be selected and affected by the creation of the feature.

TUTORIALS

Tutorial 1

In this tutorial, you will create the model shown in Figure 6-92. The dimensions of the model are also shown in the same figure. Create the model by extruding the contours of the sketch.

(Expected time: 30 min)

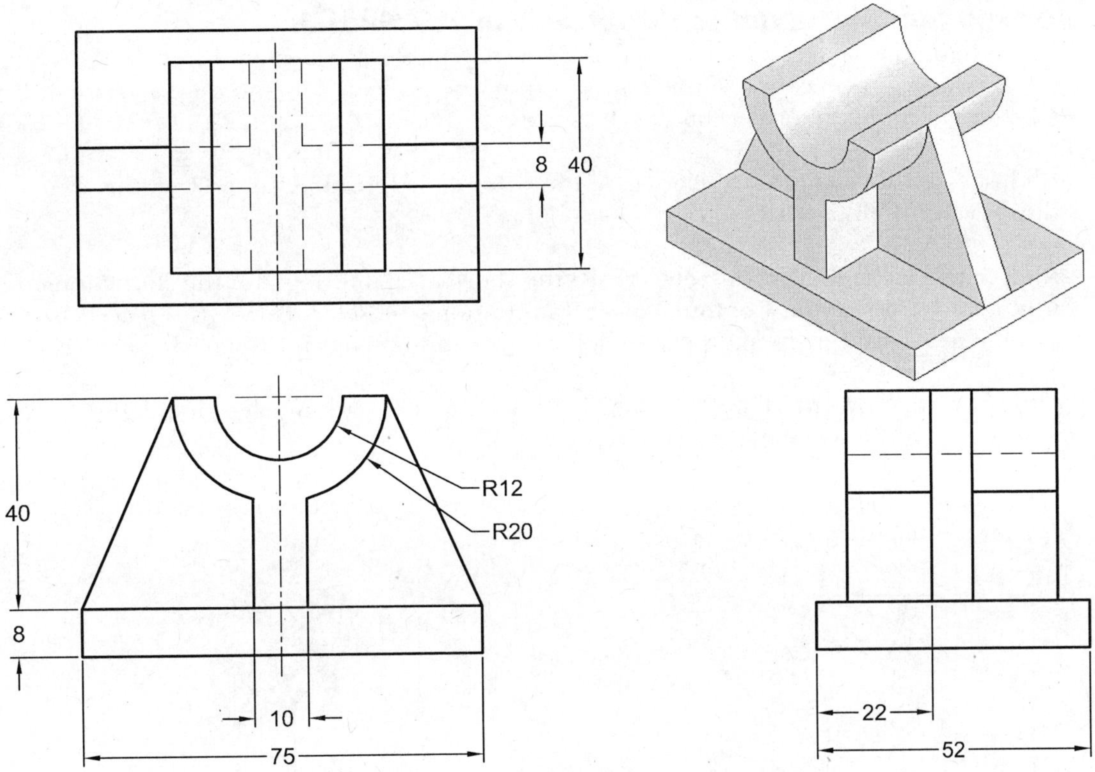

Figure 6-92 *Dimensions and views for Tutorial 1*

It is clear from the above figure that the given model is a multifeatured model. It consists of various extruded features. In conventional methods, you need to create a separate sketch for each sketched feature and then convert it into a feature. But in this tutorial, you will draw the sketch of the front view of the model and extrude it by selecting different contours in it.

The following steps are required to complete this tutorial:

a. Create the sketch on the default plane and apply required relations and dimensions to it.
b. Invoke the **Extrude Boss/Base** tool and extrude the selected contour.
c. Select the second set of contours and extrude them up to the required distance.
d. Select the third set of contours and extrude them up to the required distance.
e. Save and close the document.

Creating the Sketch of the Model

1. Start a new SOLIDWORKS part document using the **New SOLIDWORKS Document** dialog box.

2. Draw the sketch of the front view of the model on the Front Plane. Apply the required relations and dimensions to the sketch, as shown in Figure 6-93. Make sure that you do not exit the sketching environment.

Selecting and Extruding the Contours of the Sketch

In this tutorial, you need to use the contour selection method to create the model. Therefore, you first need to select one of the contours from the given sketch and then extrude it. For a better view, you can orient the sketch to Isometric view.

1. Choose **View Orientation > Isometric** from the **View (Heads-Up)** toolbar; the sketch is displayed in the isometric view.

2. Right-click in the drawing area to invoke the shortcut menu. Expand the shortcut menu, if required. Choose the **Contour Select Tool** option; the select cursor is replaced by the contour selection cursor and the selection confirmation corner is displayed.

3. Move the cursor to the lower rectangle of the sketch; the rectangle is highlighted. This indicates that this rectangle is a closed profile.

4. Click on the highlighted rectangular area; the lower rectangular area is selected as a contour, as shown in Figure 6-94.

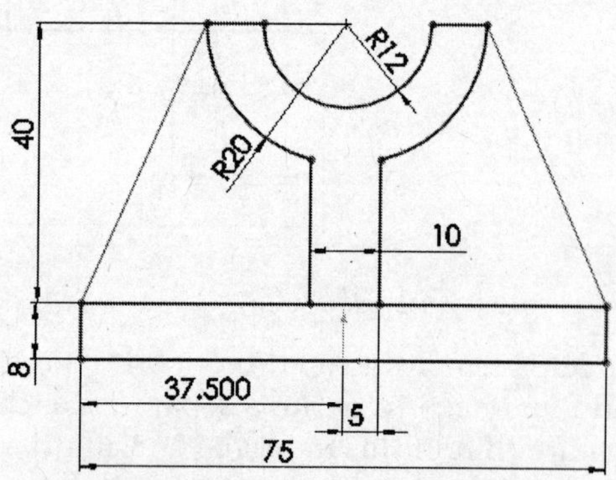

Figure 6-93 Fully defined sketch for creating the model

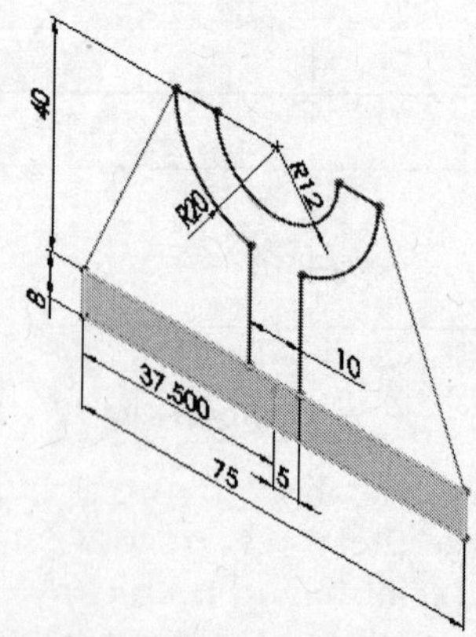

Figure 6-94 Lower rectangle selected as a contour

5. Choose the **Extruded Boss/Base** tool from the **Features CommandManager** or from the pop-up toolbar; the **Boss-Extrude PropertyManager** is invoked and preview of the base feature is displayed in the drawing area in temporary graphics.

   The name of the selected contour is displayed in the selection box of the **Selected Contours** rollout.

6. Right-click in the drawing area and choose the **Mid Plane** option from the shortcut menu; preview of the feature is modified.

7. Set **52** in the **Depth** spinner and choose the **OK** button from the **Boss-Extrude PropertyManager**; the selected contour is extruded, refer to Figure 6-95.

8. Again, right-click in the drawing area and choose the **Contour Select Tool** option from the shortcut menu; the select cursor is replaced by the contour selection cursor.

9. Select an entity of the sketch using the contour selection cursor to invoke the selection mode of the sketch.

10. Select the middle contour of the sketch using the left mouse button; the selected region is highlighted, as shown in Figure 6-96.

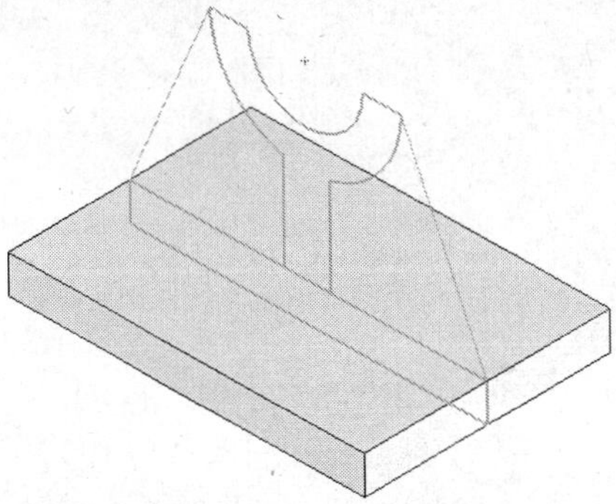

Figure 6-95 *Base feature of the model*

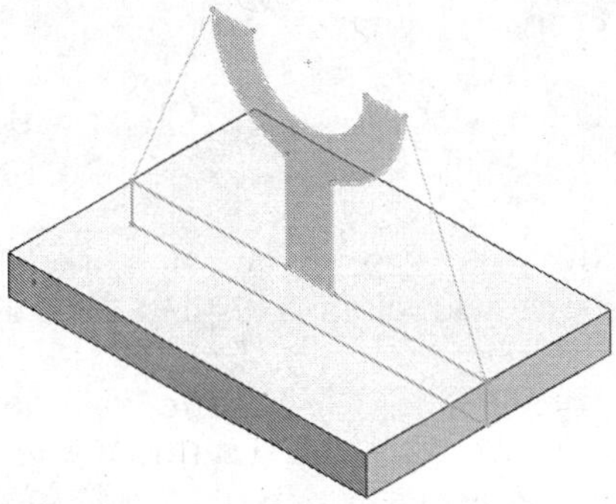

Figure 6-96 *Middle contour selected using the **Contour Select Tool***

11. Invoke the **Extruded Boss/Base** tool. Right-click in the drawing area and choose the **Mid Plane** option from the shortcut menu.

12. Set the value of the **Depth** spinner to **40** and choose the **OK** button from the **Boss-Extrude PropertyManager**. The feature created by extruding the middle contour is shown in Figure 6-97.

13. Choose the **Contour Select Tool** option again and then select a sketched entity. Next, select the contour on the right. Press and hold the CTRL key and then select the contour on the left side, see Figure 6-98.

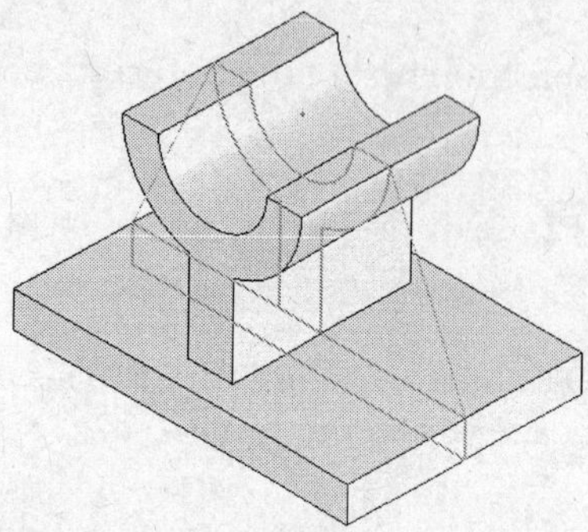

Figure 6-97 *Second feature created by extruding the middle contour*

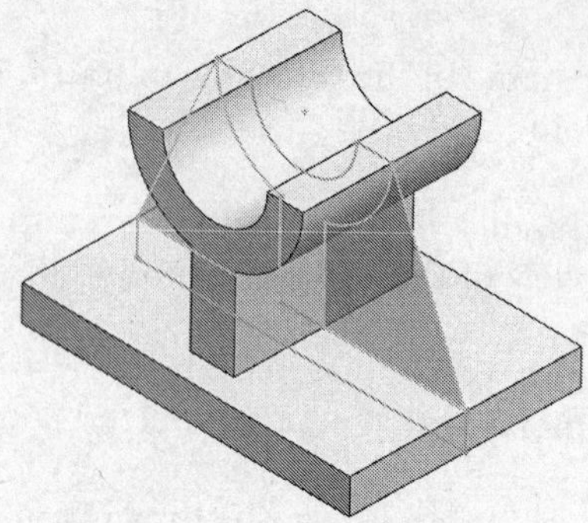

Figure 6-98 *The right and the left contours selected*

14. Invoke the **Extruded Boss/Base** tool. Right-click and choose the **Mid Plane** option from the shortcut menu.

15. Set the value of the **Depth** spinner to **8** and choose the **OK** button from the **Boss-Extrude PropertyManager**.

    The model is completed, but the sketch is still displayed in the model. Therefore, you need to hide the sketch.

16. Move the cursor to any of the sketched entities and when the entity is highlighted, select it; a pop-up toolbar is displayed. Choose the **Hide** button from the pop-up toolbar.

    The isometric view of the final model after turning off the display of the sketch is shown in Figure 6-99. The **FeatureManager Design Tree** displaying various parts of the model is shown in Figure 6-100.

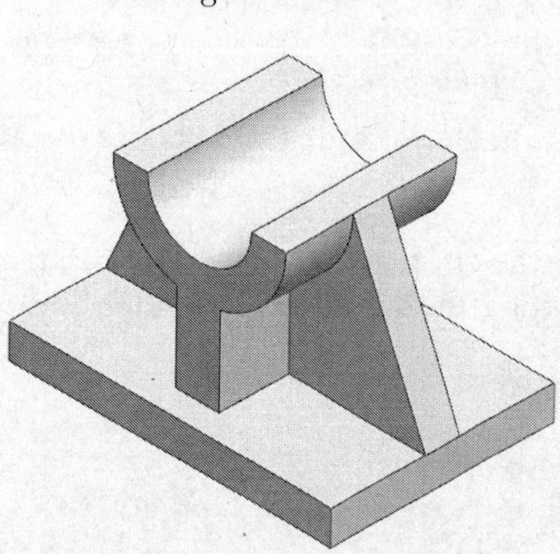

Figure 6-99 *Final solid model*

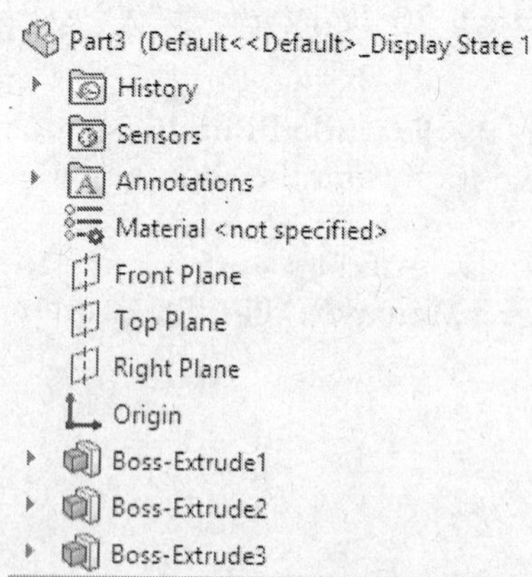

Figure 6-100 *The* ***FeatureManager Design Tree***

Saving the Model

1. Choose the **Save** button from the Menu Bar and save the model with the name *c06_tut01* at the location given below:

   \Documents\SOLIDWORKS\c06

2. Choose **File > Close** from the SOLIDWORKS menus to close the document.

Tutorial 2

In this tutorial, you will create the model shown in Figure 6-101. You will use a combination of the conventional modeling method and the contour selection method to create this model. The views and dimensions of the model are given in the same figure. **(Expected time: 30 min)**

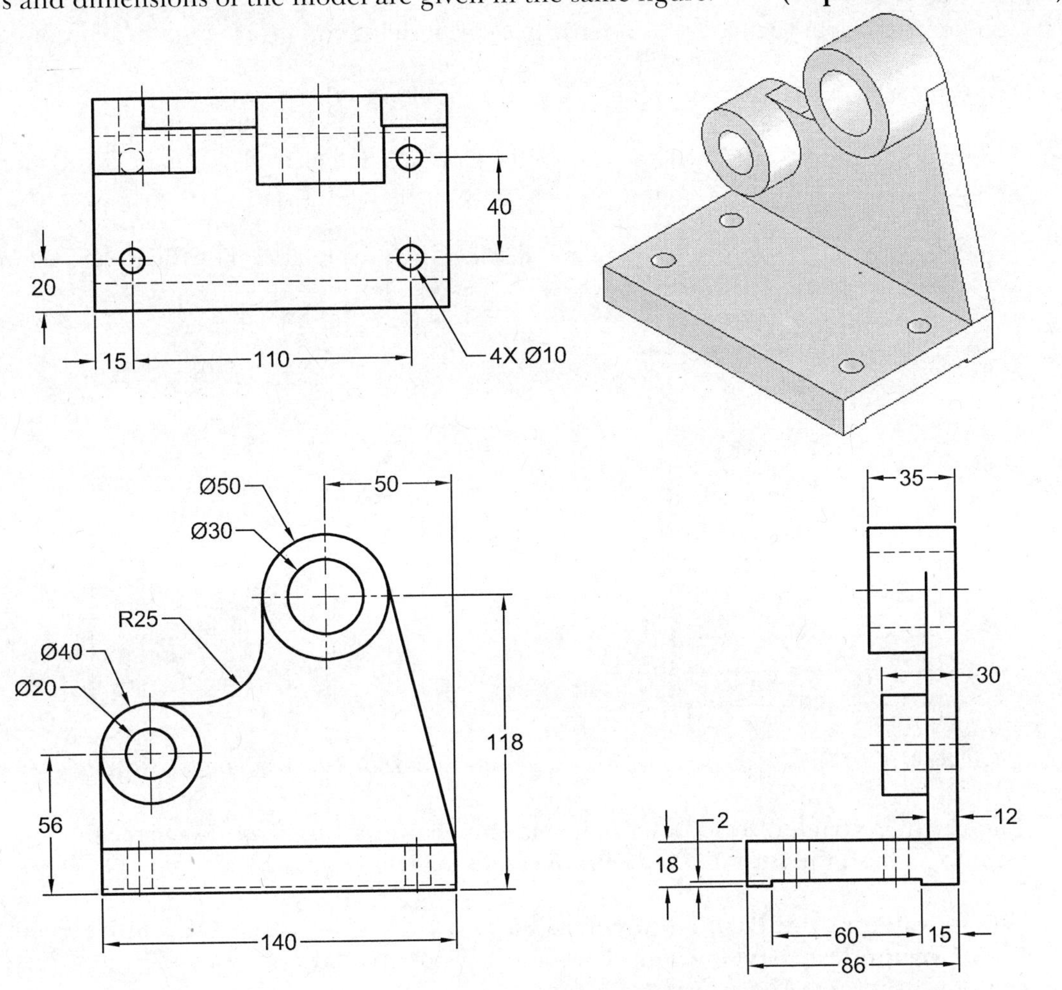

Figure 6-101 Solid model for Tutorial 2

The following steps are required to complete this tutorial:

a. Draw the sketch of the front view of the model.
b. Extrude the selected contours.
c. Add the recess feature to the model by drawing the sketch on the right planar face.
d. Create four holes using the cut feature on the top face of the base feature.
e. Save and close the document.

Drawing the Sketch for the Contour Selection Modeling

1. Start a new SOLIDWORKS part document. Draw the sketch of the front view of the model on the Front Plane using the sketching tools.

2. Apply required relations and dimensions to fully define the sketch, refer to Figure 6-102.

   You need to orient the view to isometric because it helps you in selecting the contours.

3. Press the SPACEBAR key and change the current view to the isometric view.

4. Right-click in the drawing area and choose the **Contour Select Tool** option from the shortcut menu; the select cursor is replaced by the contour selection cursor.

5. Now, by using the contour selection cursor, select the area enclosed by the lower rectangle, as shown in Figure 6-103.

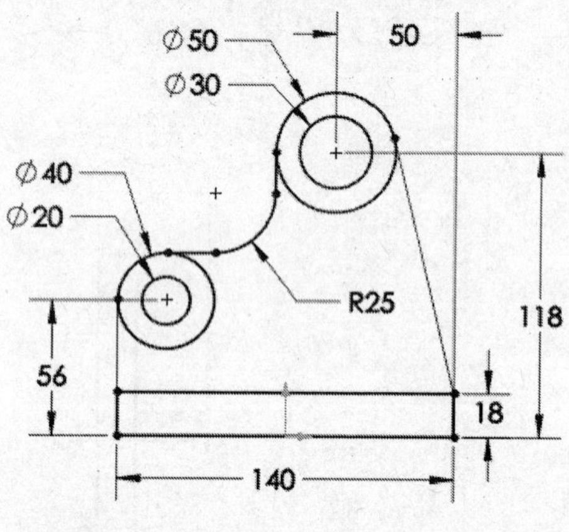

Figure 6-102 *The fully defined sketch*

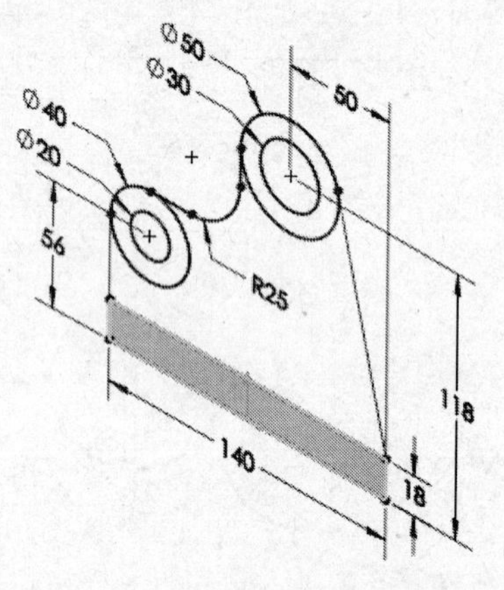

Figure 6-103 *Lower rectangle selected as a contour*

6. Choose the **Extruded Boss/Base** tool from the **Features CommandManager** or from the pop-up toolbar; the **Boss-Extrude PropertyManager** is displayed.

7. Set the value in the **Depth** spinner to **86** and then choose the **OK** button from the **Boss-Extrude PropertyManager**. The base feature created after extruding the selected contour is shown in Figure 6-104.

8. Use the **Contour Select Tool** and **Extruded Boss/Base** tools to create other features and then hide the sketch. For the depth of the extruded features, refer to Figure 6-101. The model created after extruding all contours and hiding the sketch is shown in Figure 6-105.

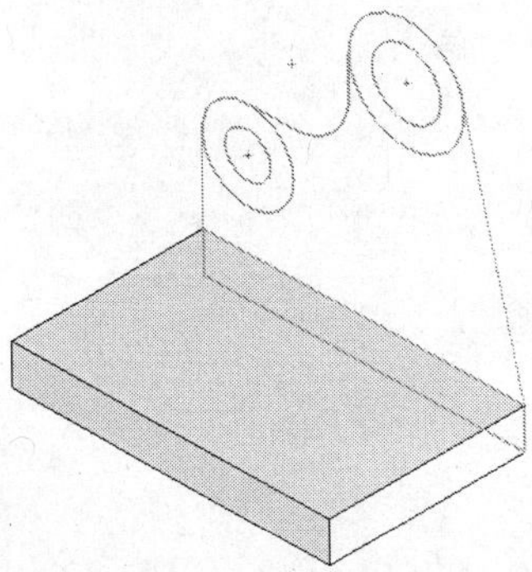

Figure 6-104 *Base feature created after extruding the selected contour*

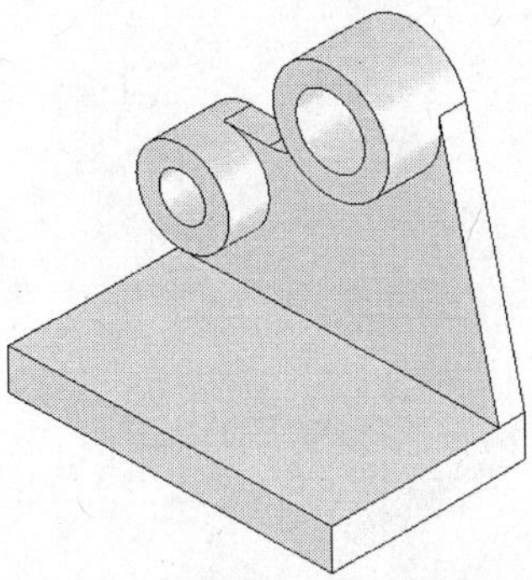

Figure 6-105 *Model created after extruding all contours*

Creating the Recess on the Base of the Model

After creating extruded features, you need to create recess at the base of the model. The recess is created as a cut extrude feature. This cut extrude feature is created by drawing a sketch on the right planar face of the model.

1. Select the right planar face of the base feature as the sketching plane; the selected face is highlighted and a pop-up toolbar is displayed.

2. Choose the **Sketch** option from the pop-up toolbar to invoke the sketching environment.

   Now, you need to orient the view such that the selected face is normal to your eye view.

3. Choose **View Orientation > Normal To** from the **View (Heads-Up)** toolbar to orient the selected plane normal to the view.

4. Draw the sketch for the recess using the sketching tools and apply required relations and dimensions to it. The fully defined sketch for the cut feature is shown in Figure 6-106.

5. Choose the **Extruded Cut** tool from the **Features CommandManager** to invoke the **Cut-Extrude PropertyManager**. Preview of the cut feature is displayed in the drawing area in temporary graphics. 

6. Right-click in the drawing area and choose the **Through All** option from the shortcut menu.

7. Choose **OK** from the **Cut-Extrude PropertyManager** to complete the feature creation. The isometric view of the model after creating the cut feature is shown in Figure 6-107.

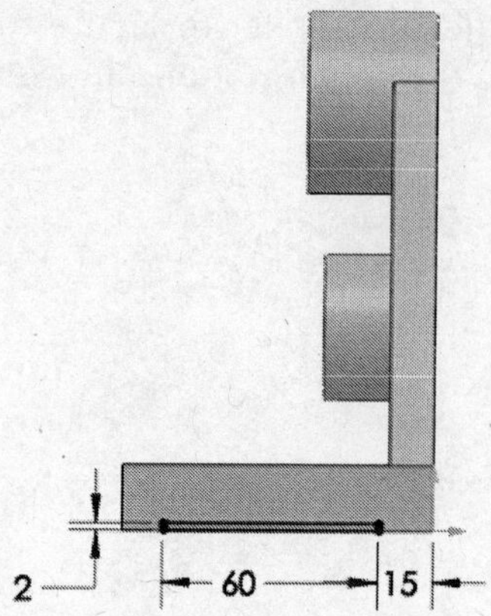

Figure 6-106 Sketch for the cut feature

Figure 6-107 Cut feature added to the model

Creating Holes

Next, you need to create holes at the base of the model. These holes will be created as the extruded cut features. You need to draw the sketch of the hole feature on the top planar face of the base feature of the model. To draw the sketch of holes, you first need to draw a circle and then create the pattern of remaining circles.

1. Select the top planar face of the base feature; a pop-up toolbar is displayed. Choose the **Sketch** tool from the pop-up toolbar.

2. Orient the current view normal to the viewing direction. Draw a circle of 10 mm diameter and pattern it using the **Linear Sketch Pattern** tool. You may need to apply horizontal relations between the center points of the top circles to fully define the sketch. The fully defined sketch is shown in Figure 6-108.

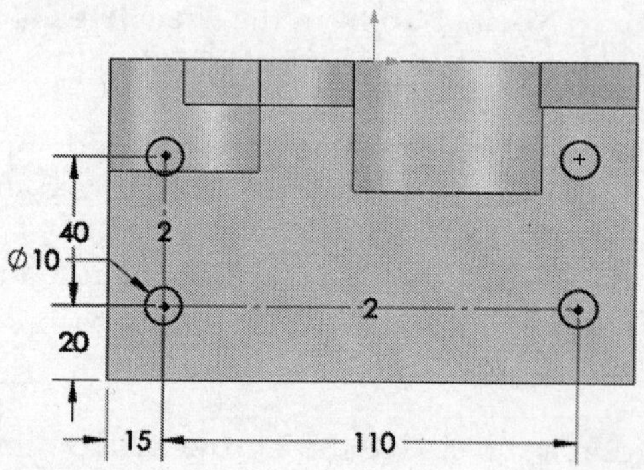

Figure 6-108 Holes sketched for the cut feature

3. Change the current view to the isometric view and then choose the **Extruded Cut** button from the **Features CommandManager** to invoke the **Cut-Extrude PropertyManager**.

4. Right-click in the drawing area and choose the **Through All** option from the shortcut menu. Choose the **OK** button from the **Cut-Extrude PropertyManager**. The isometric view of the final model after hiding the sketch is shown in Figure 6-109. The **FeatureManager Design Tree** displaying various features of the model is shown in Figure 6-110.

Figure 6-109 Final solid model

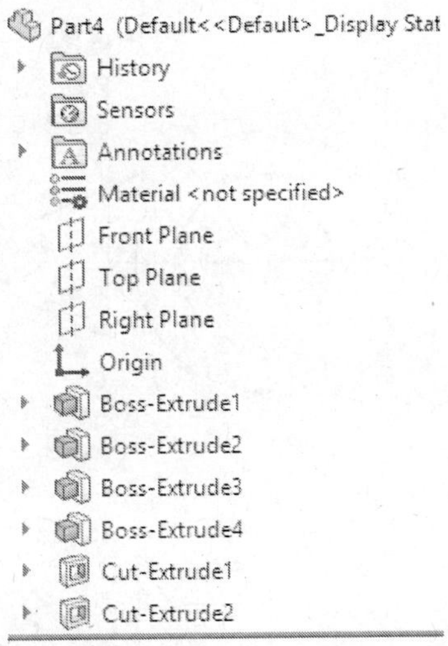

Figure 6-110 *The* ***FeatureManager Design Tree***

Saving the Model

1. Choose the **Save** button from the Menu Bar and save the model with the name *c06_tut02* at the location given below.

   \Documents\SOLIDWORKS\c06

2. Choose **File > Close** from the SOLIDWORKS menus to close the file.

Tutorial 3

In this tutorial, you will create a model whose dimensions are shown in Figure 6-111. The solid model is shown in Figure 6-112. **(Expected time: 30 min)**

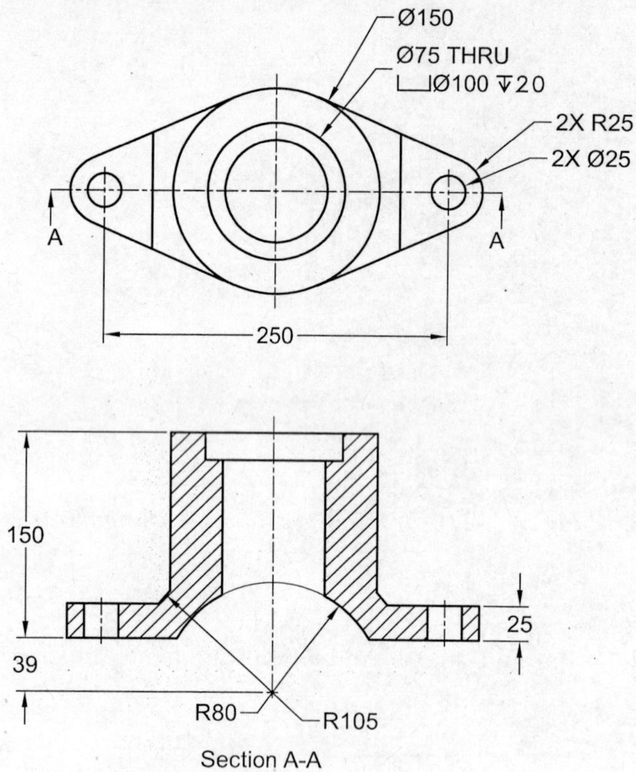

Figure 6-111 Dimensions of the model

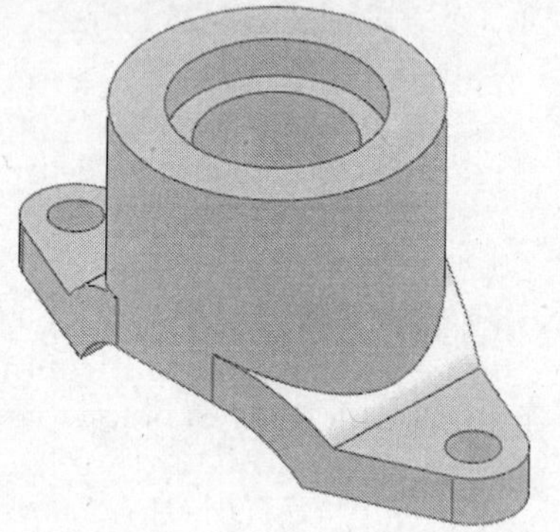

Figure 6-112 Solid model for Tutorial 3

The following steps are required to complete this tutorial:

a. Create the base feature by extruding the sketch drawn on the Front Plane.
b. Extrude the sketch created on the Top Plane to create a cut feature.
c. Create a plane at an offset distance of 150 mm from the Top Plane.
d. Draw a sketch on the newly created plane and extrude it to the selected surface.
e. Create a counterbore hole using the cut revolve option.
f. Create holes using the cut feature.
g. Save and close the document.

Creating the Base Feature

It is evident from the model that its base comprises of a complex geometry. Therefore, you first need to create base feature of the model and then apply cut feature to it to get the desired shape. You need to create the base feature on the Front Plane which is the sketching plane. After drawing the sketch, you need to extrude it using the mid plane option to complete the feature creation.

1. Start a new SOLIDWORKS part document and invoke the **Extruded Boss/Base** tool; you are prompted to select a plane.

2. Select the Front Plane and then draw the sketch of the base feature. Apply required relations and dimensions to the sketch, as shown in Figure 6-113.

3. Exit the sketching environment; the **Boss-Extrude PropertyManager** and preview of the base feature are displayed. Right-click in the drawing area and choose the **Mid Plane** option from the shortcut menu displayed.

4. Set the value of the **Depth** spinner to **150** in the **Boss-Extrude PropertyManager** and then choose the **OK** button from it. The isometric view of the base feature of the model is shown in Figure 6-114.

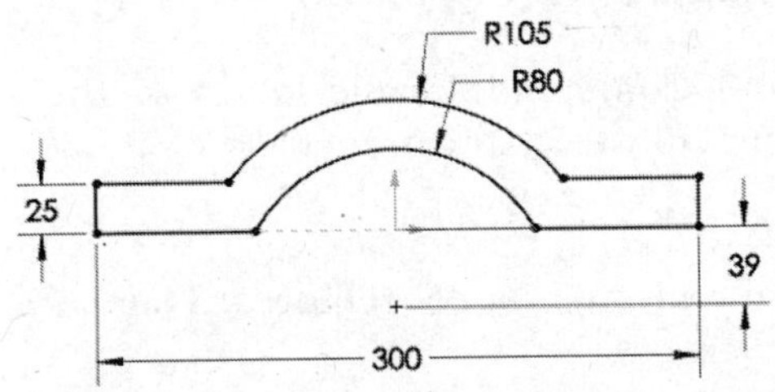

Figure 6-113 *Sketch of the base feature*

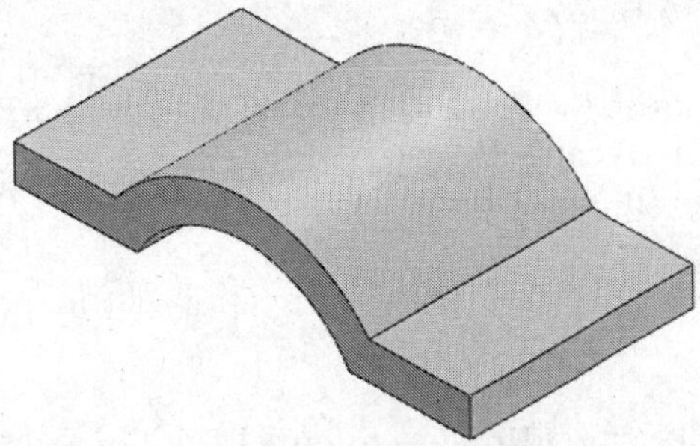

Figure 6-114 *Base feature of the solid model*

Creating the Cut Feature

Now, you need to create a cut feature to get required shape of the base feature. The sketch for this cut feature is created using a reference plane defined tangent to the curved face of the previous feature.

1. Choose the **Plane** tool from the **Reference Geometry** flyout in the **Features CommandManager** to display the **Plane PropertyManager**.

2. Select the upper curved face of the existing feature as the first reference; the **Tangent** button is chosen automatically in the **First Reference** rollout. Now, move the cursor close to the midpoint of the curved edge of the upper curved face as the second reference; the midpoint is highlighted, see Figure 6-115. Select this point; preview of the plane tangent to the curved face and passing through the midpoint of the curved edge is displayed. Choose **OK** to create the reference plane.

3. Draw the sketch for the cut feature using the standard sketching tools and then apply the required relations and dimensions to the sketch, as shown in Figure 6-116.

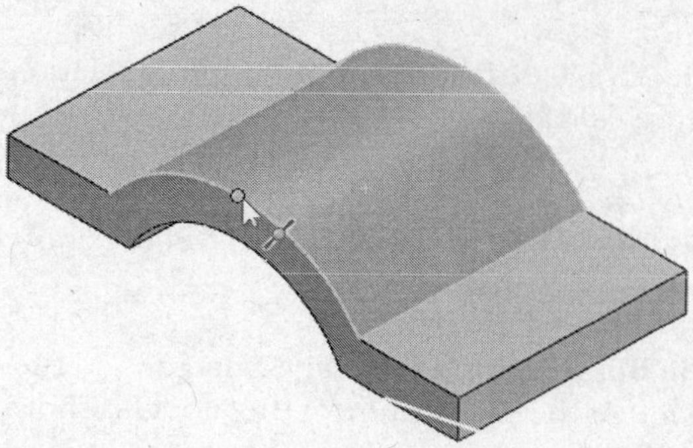

Figure 6-115 Selecting the midpoint to define the tangent plane

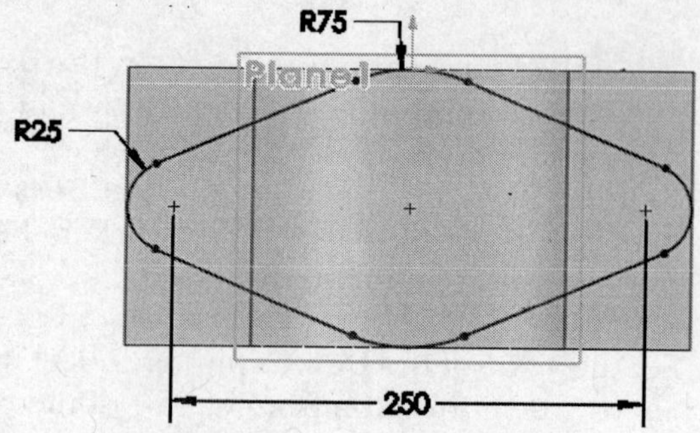

Figure 6-116 Fully dimensioned sketch for the cut feature

4. Choose the **Extruded Cut** tool from the **Features CommandManager** to invoke the **Cut-Extrude PropertyManager**. Change the current view to the isometric view if not set automatically.

   You will notice that the direction of the material removal is not as required. Therefore, you need to flip the direction.

5. Select the **Flip side to cut** check box; the direction of the material removal is reversed in the preview.

6. Right-click in the drawing area and choose the **Through All** option from the shortcut menu, and then choose the **OK** button from the **Cut-Extrude PropertyManager**.

   The reference plane is displayed in the drawing area. Therefore, you need to hide it.

7. Left-click on **Plane1** in the drawing area and choose **Hide** from the pop-up toolbar; the display of the reference plane is turned off. The model after adding the cut feature is shown in Figure 6-117.

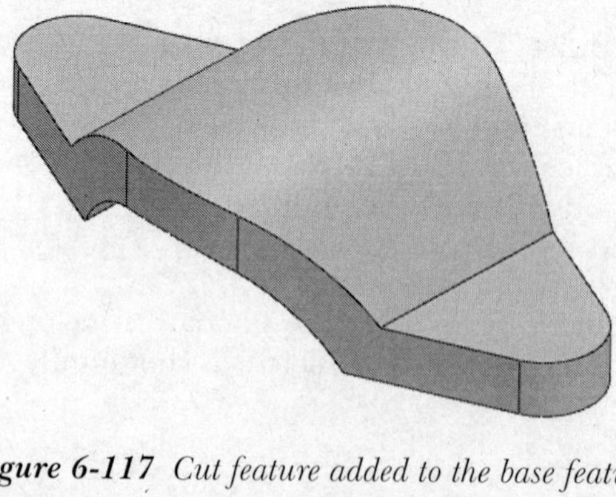

Figure 6-117 Cut feature added to the base feature

Creating a Plane at an Offset Distance for the Extruded Feature

After creating the base of the model, you need to create a plane at an offset distance of 150 mm from the Top Plane. This newly created plane will be used as the sketching plane for the next feature.

1. Choose the **Plane** tool from the **Reference Geometry** flyout in the **Features CommandManager** to display the **Plane PropertyManager**.

2. Click on the ► sign located on the left of the **FeatureManager Design Tree** which is now displayed in the drawing area. The design tree expands and the three default planes are now visible in the design tree.

3. Select the **Top Plane** as the first reference and choose the **Offset distance** button from the **First Reference** rollout if not selected by default; the **Offset distance** spinner, the **Flip offset** check box, and the **Number of planes to create** spinner are displayed in the **Plane PropertyManager**.

4. Set the value in the **Offset distance** spinner to **150** and choose the **OK** button from the **Plane PropertyManager**; the required plane is created.

Creating the Extruded Feature

After creating the plane at an offset distance from the Top Plane, you need to draw the sketch for the next feature.

1. Select the reference plane which you just created if not already selected, and invoke the sketching environment. Set the current view normal to the eye view.

2. Draw the sketch of the circle and apply required relations to the sketch, as shown in Figure 6-118.

3. Change the current view to the isometric view and invoke the **Extruded Boss/Base** tool. You will observe in the preview that the direction of the feature creation is opposite to the required direction. Therefore, you need to change the direction of the feature creation.

4. Choose the **Reverse Direction** button on the left of the **End Condition** drop-down list to reverse the direction of feature creation; preview of the feature changes dynamically.

5. Right-click in the drawing area and choose the **Up To Surface** option from the shortcut menu; you are prompted to select a face or a surface to specify the first direction. Also, the **Face/Plane** selection box is displayed below the **Direction of Extrusion** selection box in the **Direction 1** rollout.

6. Select the upper curved surface of the model using the left mouse button. You will observe in the preview that the feature is extruded up to the selected surface.

7. Choose the **OK** button from the **Boss-Extrude PropertyManager**.

   The plane is displayed in the drawing area. Therefore, you need to turn off its display.

8. Select **Plane2** from the **FeatureManager Design Tree** or from the drawing area and choose the **Hide** option from the pop-up toolbar. The model after creating the extruded feature is shown in Figure 6-119.

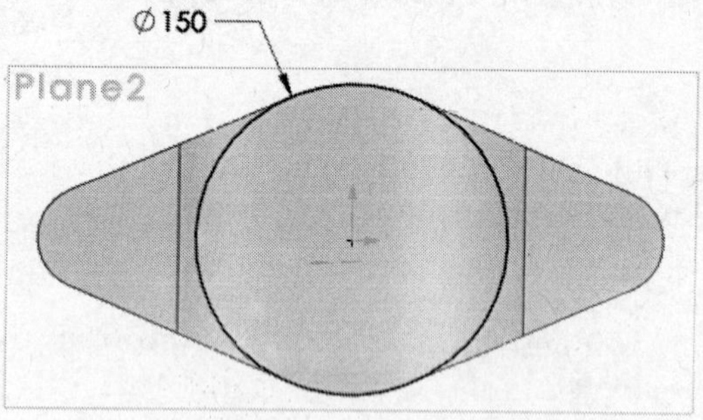

***Figure 6-118** Sketch created on the newly created plane*

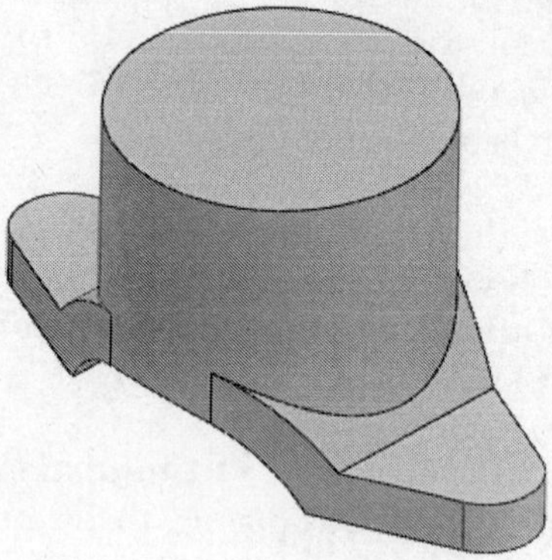

***Figure 6-119** Sketch extruded up to the selected surface*

Creating the Counterbore Hole

Next, you need to create counterbore hole. It will be created as a revolved cut feature by using a sketch drawn on the Front Plane.

1. Invoke the sketching environment by selecting the **Front Plane** as the sketching plane from the **FeatureManager Design Tree**. Next, orient the sketching plane normal to the view.

2. Draw the sketch of the counterbore hole using the standard sketching tools. Add required relations and then add the linear diameter dimensions, as shown in Figure 6-120.

3. Set the current view to the isometric view and then choose the **Revolved Cut** tool from the **Features CommandManager**; the **Cut-Revolve PropertyManager** is displayed.

   Preview of the cut feature is displayed in the drawing area in temporary graphics. The value of the angle in the **Direction 1 Angle** spinner is set to **360** by default. Therefore, you do not need to set the value in the **Direction 1 Angle** spinner.

4. Choose the **OK** button from the **Cut-Revolve PropertyManager**. Figure 6-121 shows the model after creating the revolved cut feature.

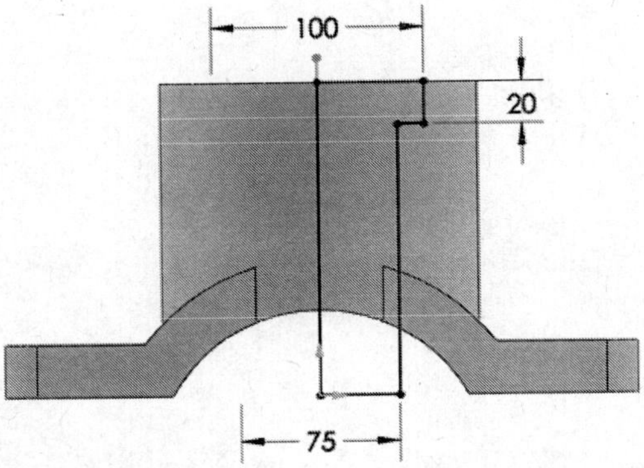

Figure 6-120 *Fully defined sketch for the counterbore hole*

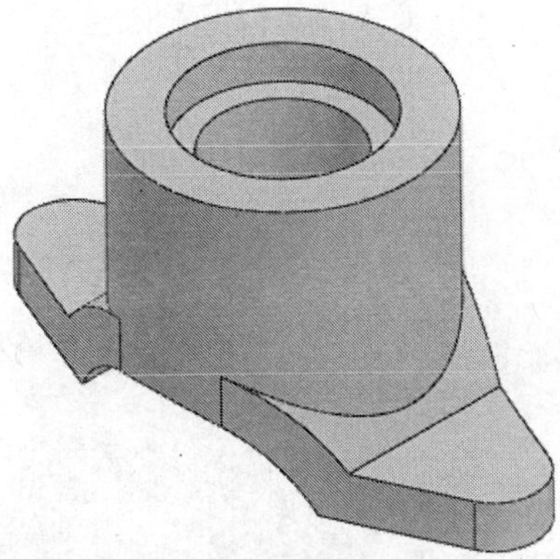

Figure 6-121 *Counterbore hole added using the **Revolved Cut** tool*

Creating Holes

After creating all the features, you need to create holes using the extruded cut feature to complete the model. The sketch for the cut feature is to be drawn by using the top planar surface of the base feature as the sketching plane.

1. Select the top planar surface of the base feature and invoke the sketching environment. Orient the model such that the selected face of the model is oriented normal to the view.

2. Draw the sketch using the standard sketching tools and apply required relations and dimensions to it, as shown in Figure 6-122.

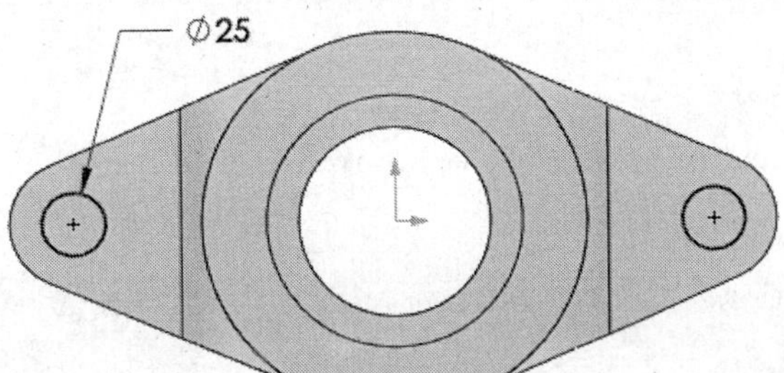

Figure 6-122 *Fully defined sketch for the cut feature*

3. Change the current view to the isometric view. Choose the **Extruded Cut** tool from the **Features CommandManager**; the **Cut-Extrude PropertyManager** is displayed.

4. Right-click and choose the **Through All** option from the shortcut menu and choose the **OK** button from the **Cut-Extrude PropertyManager**. Final model is shown in Figure 6-123. The **FeatureManager Design Tree** displaying various features of the model is shown in Figure 6-124.

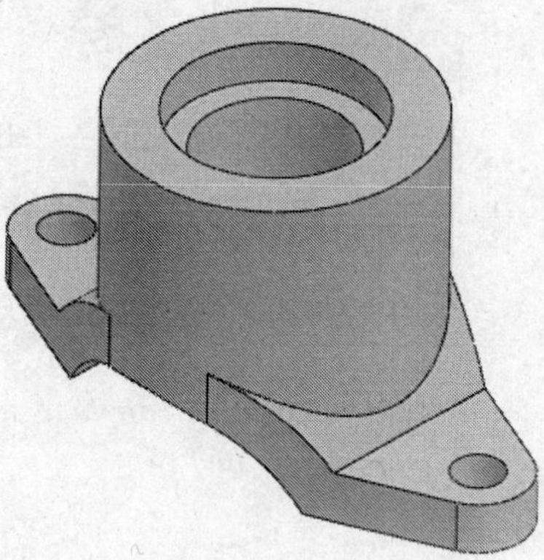

Figure 6-123 *Final model*

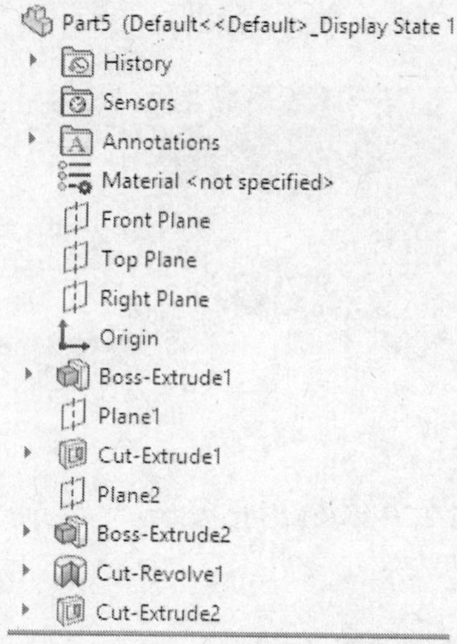

Figure 6-124 *The* ***FeatureManager Design Tree***

Saving the Model

1. Choose the **Save** button from the Menu Bar and save the model with the name *c06_tut03* at the location given next:

   \Documents\SOLIDWORKS\c06

2. Choose **File > Close** from the SOLIDWORKS menus to close the file.

Self-Evaluation Test

Answer the following questions and then compare them to those given at the end of this chapter:

1. The __________ option is used to extrude a sketch such that it intersects next surface.

2. The _________ option in the **End Condition** drop-down list is used to terminate the extruded feature up to another body.

3. The _________ check box is used to merge the newly created body with the parent body.

4. You can use the _________ option to create a reference axis that passes through the center point of a cylindrical or conical surface.

5. If multiple bodies are created while applying the cut feature then you can specify the body to keep in the _________ dialog box.

6. When a new sketchis drawn in the sketching environment, it is drawn on the **Front Plane** which is dafault plane. (T/F)

7. When you start a new SOLIDWORKS part document, SOLIDWORKS provides you with two default planes. (T/F)

8. You can choose the **Plane** button from the **Features CommandManager** to invoke the **Plane PropertyManager**. (T/F)

9. You cannot create a plane at an offset distance by dragging a default plane dynamically. (T/F)

10. When you create a circular feature, a temporary axis is displayed automatically. (T/F)

Review Questions

Answer the following questions:

1. Which of the following check boxes needs to be selected while creating a feature in a single-body modeling?

   (a) **Combine results** (b) **Fix bodies**
   (c) **Merge result** (d) **Union results**

2. Which of the following buttons is used to add a draft angle to a cut feature?

   (a) **Add Draft** (b) **Create Draft**
   (c) **Draft On/Off** (d) None of these

3. Which of the following PropertyManagers is invoked to create a cut feature by extruding a sketch?

   (a) **Extruded Cut** (b) **Cut-Extrude**
   (c) **Extrude-Cut** (d) **Cut**

4. Which of the following options is used to define the termination of feature creation at an offset distance to a selected surface?

   (a) **Distance To Surface** (b) **Normal From Surface**
   (c) **Distance From Surface** (d) **Offset From Surface**

5. Which of the following options is used to define the termination of feature creation upto a selected surface?

   (a) **To Surface** (b) **Selected Surface**
   (c) **Up To Surface** (d) None of these

6. If the __________ check box is cleared, the virtual surface created for the termination of the extruded feature will have a concentric relation with the selected surface.

7. Choose the __________ option from the shortcut menu to select the contours.

8. The __________ option will be available in the **End Condition** drop-down list only after creating a base feature.

9. The __________ check box is used to specify a side from where the material is removed.

10. The __________ check box is used to create an outward draft in a cut feature.

EXERCISES

Exercise 1

Create the solid model shown in Figure 6-125. The dimensions of the model are given in Figure 6-126.
(Expected time: 30 min)

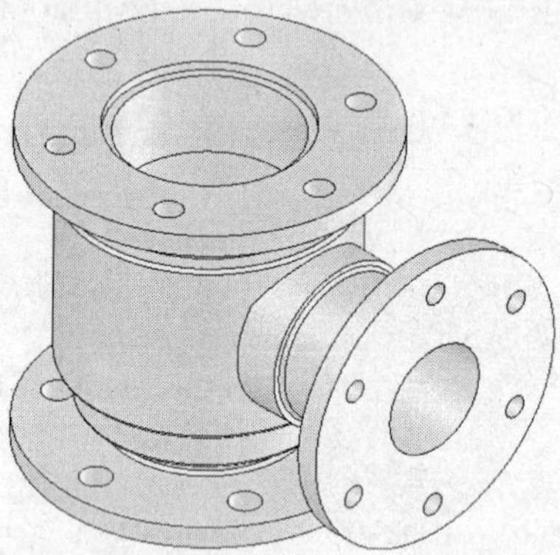

Figure 6-125 *Model for Exercise 1*

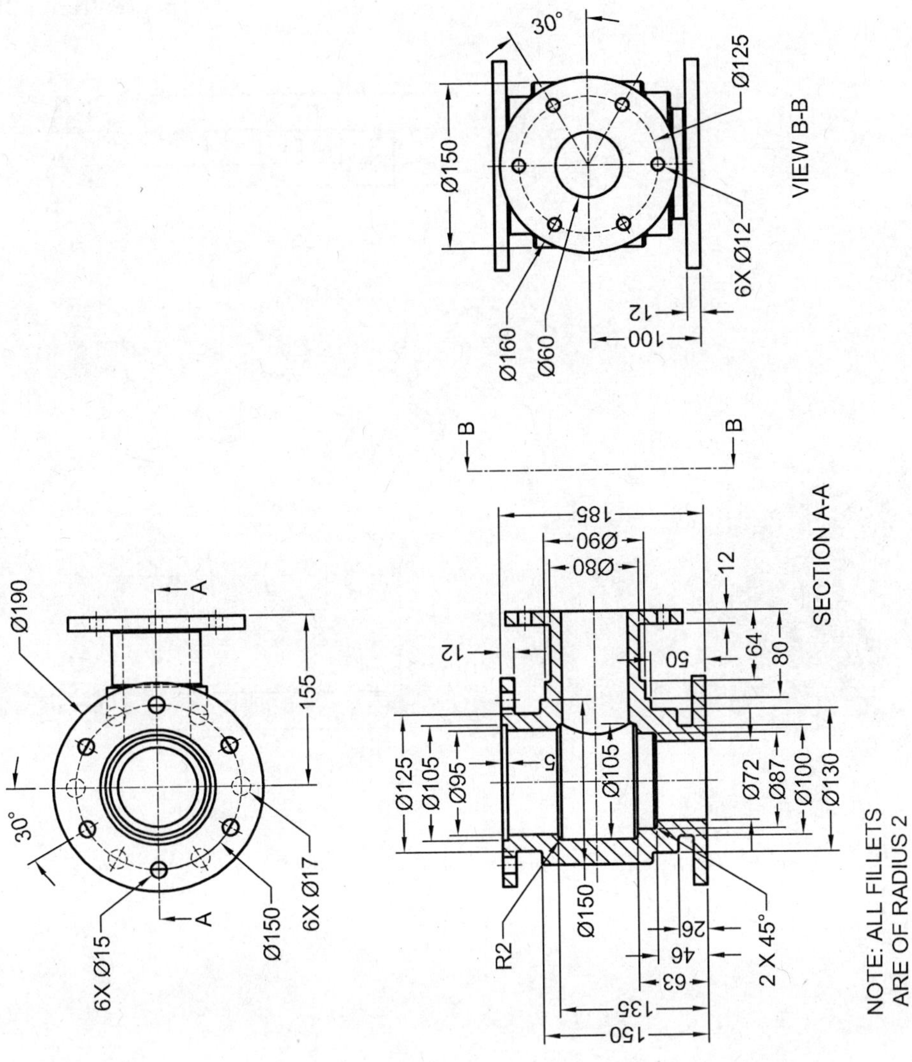

Figure 6-126 *Views and dimensions of the model for Exercise 1*

Exercise 2

Create the model shown in Figure 6-127. The dimensions of the model are given in Figure 6-128. **(Expected time: 30 min)**

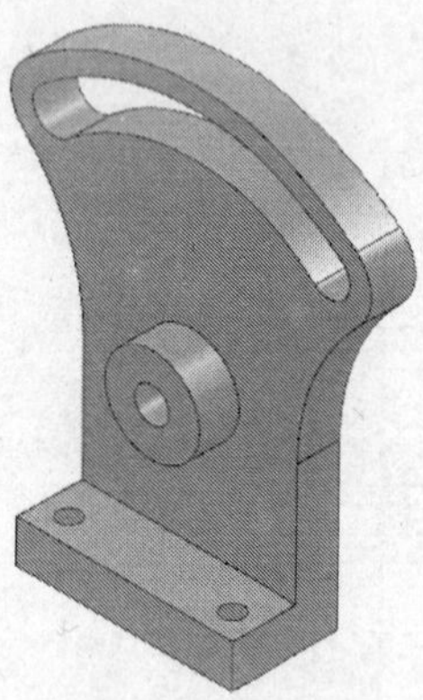

Figure 6-127 Model for Exercise 2

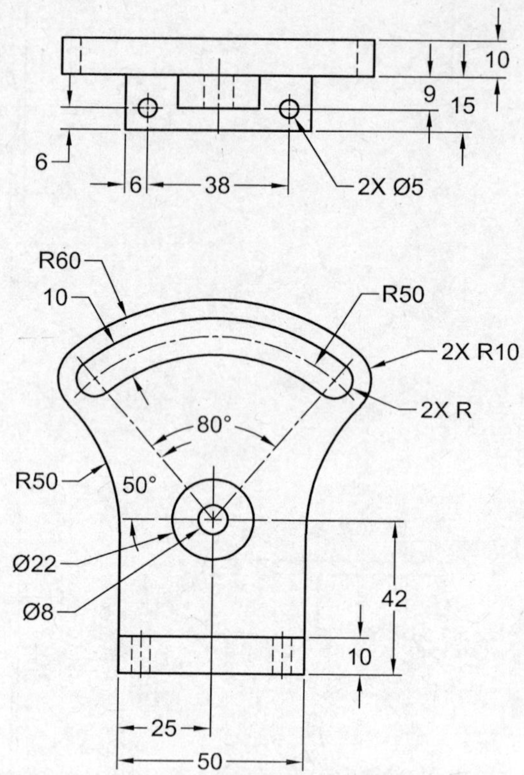

Figure 6-128 Dimensions of the model for Exercise 2

Exercise 3

Create the model shown in Figure 6-129. The dimensions of the model are given in the same figure. **(Expected time: 30 min)**

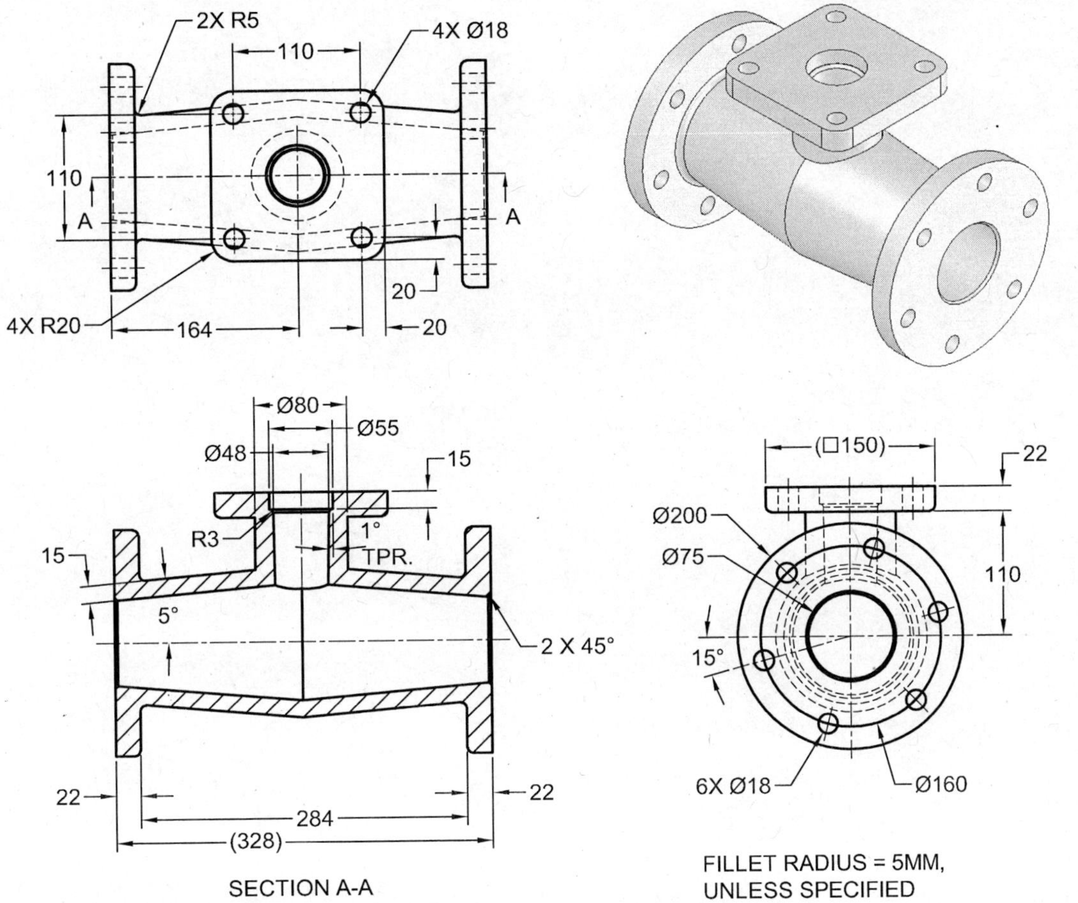

Figure 6-129 The model and its dimensions for Exercise 3

Answers to Self-Evaluation Test

1. **Up To Next**, **2.** **Up To Body**, **3.** **Merge result**, **4.** **Cylindrical/Conical Face**, **5.** **Bodies to Keep**, **6.** F, **7.** F, **8.** T, **9.** F, **10.** F

Chapter 7

Advanced Modeling Tools-I

Learning Objectives

After completing this chapter, you will be able to:

- *Create holes using the Simple Hole option*
- *Create standard holes using the Hole Wizard option*
- *Create standard threads using the Thread option*
- *Apply External Cosmetic Threads*
- *Apply simple and advanced fillets*
- *Understand various selection methods*
- *Chamfer the edges and vertices of a model*
- *Create the shell feature*
- *Create the wrap feature*

ADVANCED MODELING TOOLS

This chapter discusses various advanced modeling tools available in SOLIDWORKS that assist you in creating a better and accurate design by capturing the design intent in a model. In the previous chapters, you have learned to create holes using the **Extruded Cut** tool. In this chapter, you will learn to create holes using the **Simple Hole**, **Hole Wizard**, and **Advanced Holes** options. The hole wizard is used to create standard holes that are defined based on the industrial standards, screw types, and sizes. The **Hole Wizard** tool of SOLIDWORKS is one of the largest standard industrial virtual hole generation tools available in any CAD package. You will also learn about some other advanced modeling tools such as the thread, fillet, chamfer, shell, and wrap.

Creating Simple Holes

CommandManager: Features > Simple Hole *(Customize to add)*
SOLIDWORKS menus: Insert > Features > Simple Hole
Toolbar: Features > Simple Hole *(Customize to add)*

In the previous chapter, you have learned to create holes by extruding a circle using the **Extruded Cut** tool. Now, you will learn how to create a hole feature using the **Simple Hole** tool. If you use this tool, you do not need to draw the sketch of a hole. The holes created using this option act as applied features. To create a hole using this tool, first select the planar face of any solid model on which you want to place the hole feature. Then, choose **Insert > Features > Simple Hole** from the **SOLIDWORKS** menus; the **Hole PropertyManager** will be displayed. If you invoke this tool before selecting a plane, the **Hole PropertyManager** will be displayed prompting you to select a placement plane. Select a plane to place the hole feature; the **Hole PropertyManager** will get modified, as shown in Figure 7-1. Also, a preview of the hole feature will be displayed in the drawing area in temporary graphics with default values, as shown in Figure 7-2.

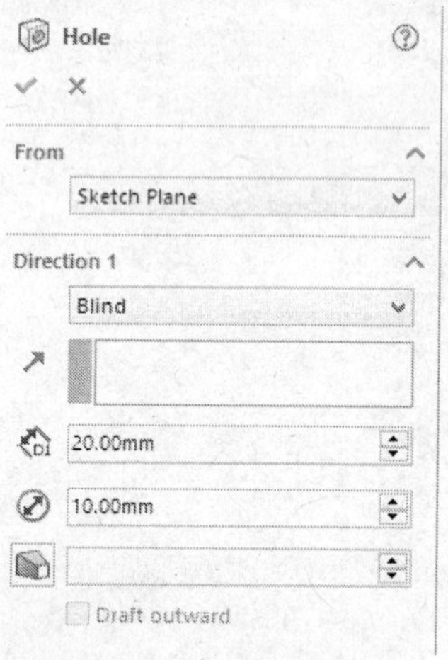

Figure 7-1 The modified Hole PropertyManager

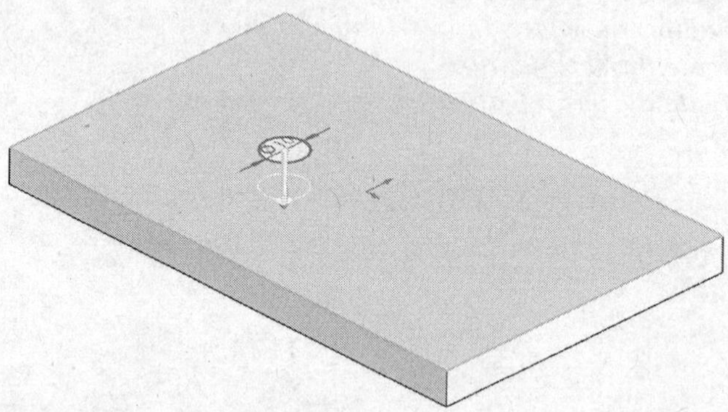

Figure 7-2 Preview of the hole created using the Simple Hole tool

Specify the termination type of the hole feature using the **End Condition** drop-down list and set the value of the hole diameter in the **Hole Diameter** spinner. You can also use the **Direction of Extrusion** selection box to specify the direction of extrusion. If the hole feature to be created is a tapered hole, specify a draft angle using the **Draft On/Off** button and set the value of the draft angle using the **Draft Angle** spinner. The preview of the draft angle is displayed in the drawing area in temporary graphics. After setting all parameters, choose the **OK** button from the **Hole PropertyManager**.

The hole feature created using this option is placed on the selected plane but the placement of the hole is not yet defined. So, select the hole feature from the **FeatureManager Design Tree**; a pop-up toolbar will be displayed. Choose **Edit Sketch** from the pop-up toolbar; the sketching environment will be invoked. Apply relations and dimensions to define the placement of the hole feature on the selected face and exit the sketching environment.

Creating Standard Holes Using the Hole Wizard

CommandManager: Features > Hole Wizard flyout > Hole Wizard
SOLIDWORKS menus: Insert > Features > Hole Wizard
Toolbar: Features > Hole Wizard flyout > Hole Wizard

The **Hole Wizard** tool is used to add standard holes such as the counterbore, countersink, drilled, tapped, legacy holes, and so on. You can also add a user-defined counterbore drill holes, simple holes, simple drilled holes, tapered holes, and so on. You can control all the parameters of the holes including the termination options. You can also modify the holes according to your requirement after placing them. Therefore, you can place the standard parametric holes using this tool. You can select a face or a plane to place the hole even before invoking this tool. The placement face can be a planar face or a curved face. After selecting the placement plane or face, choose the **Hole Wizard** button from the **Hole Wizard** flyout in the **Features CommandManager**; the **Hole Specification PropertyManager** will be displayed, as shown in Figure 7-3.

In SOLIDWORKS, if you preselect a placement plane and invoke the **Hole Specification PropertyManager**, you can directly specify the position of the hole after choosing the **Positions** tab of the PropertyManager. As a result, when you move the cursor on a planar face of the model, the preview of the hole feature is displayed in the graphics area. Specify the placement point; you will be prompted to use the dimensions and other sketch tools to specify the hole center. Now, if you modify the parameters of the hole or change its type, the preview of the hole will also be modified dynamically. The options in the **Hole Specification PropertyManager** are discussed next.

Favorite Rollout

The **Favorite** rollout is used to add the frequently used holes to the favorite list. If you add a hole to the favorite list, you will not have to configure the same settings to add similar types of holes every time. The method of adding a hole setting to the favorite list is same as adding the dimensional settings, as discussed in Chapter 4.

Hole Type Rollout

The **Hole Type** rollout in the **Type** tab of the **Hole Specification PropertyManager** is used to define the type of standard hole to be created. You will notice that the **Counterbore** button is chosen by default. As a result, a counterbore hole will be created. Figure 7-4 shows the buttons in the **Hole Type** rollout. Each button is used to create a specific type of standard hole. In

SOLIDWORKS, you can also create standard slots by using the buttons available in the bottom row of this rollout. The other options in this rollout are discussed next.

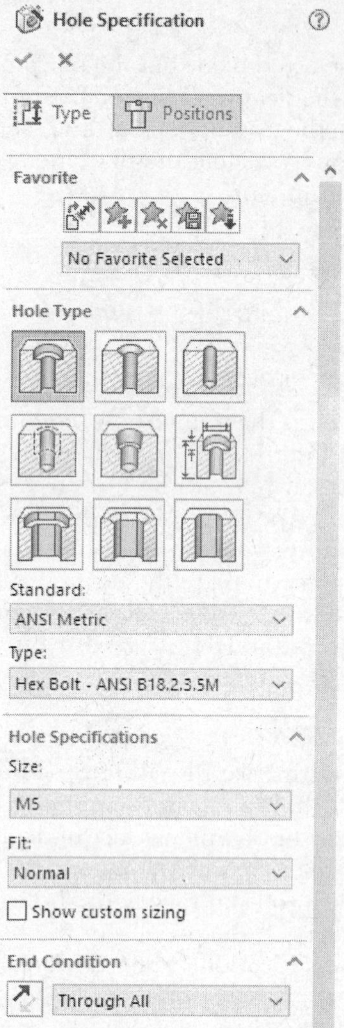

*Figure 7-3 Partial view of the **Hole Specification PropertyManager***

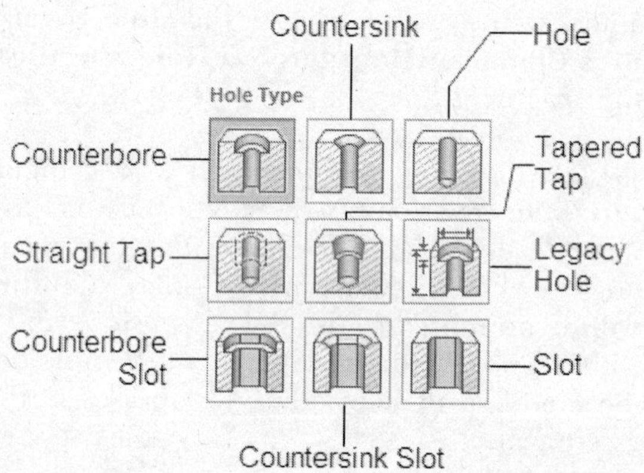

*Figure 7-4 Buttons in the **Hole Type** rollout*

Standard

The **Standard** drop-down list is used to specify the industrial dimensioning standard for creating holes. By default, the **Ansi Metric** standard is selected. Other dimensioning standards available in this drop-down list are **ANSI Inch**, **AS**, **BSI**, **DIN**, **GB**, **IS**, **ISO**, **JIS**, **KS**, **DME**, **HASCO Metric**, **PCS**, **Progressive**, and **Superior.**

Type

The **Type** drop-down list is used to define the type of fastener to be inserted in a hole. The standard holes created using the **Hole Wizard** tool depend on the type and the size of the fastener to be inserted in that hole. You can select the screw type from the **Type** drop-down list. The types of screws and bolts available in this drop-down list depend on the standard selected from the **Standard** drop-down list.

The options in the **Type** drop-down list are displayed based on the hole type selected in the **Hole Type** rollout.

Hole Specifications Rollout

The **Hole Specifications** rollout, refer to Figure 7-5, in the **Type** tab of the **Hole Specification PropertyManager** is used to define the size and fit of the standard hole to be created. The options in this rollout are discussed next.

Size

The **Size** drop-down list is used to define the size of the fastener to be inserted in the hole that is created using the **Hole Wizard** tool. The size of the fasteners in the **Size** drop-down list depends on the standard selected from the **Standard** drop-down list in the **Hole Type** rollout.

Fit

The **Fit** drop-down list is used to specify the type of fit to be applied to a hole. You can apply the **Close**, **Normal**, or **Loose** fit type to a hole.

Show custom sizing

The **Show custom sizing** check box is used to create a user-defined hole feature. On selecting this check box, the parameters to be specified to create a user defined hole feature will be displayed below the check box, as shown in Figure 7-6. If you change the default values of various parameters meant for the standard holes, the corresponding spinners will turn yellow. Also, the **Restore Default Values** button will be displayed in this area. You can choose this button to restore the default values of the standard holes.

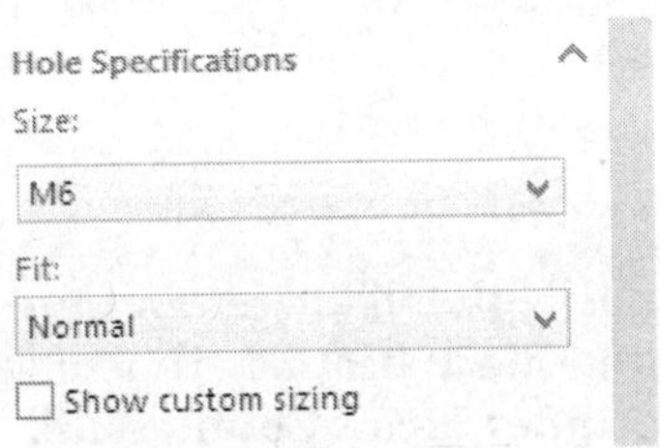

*Figure 7-5 The **Hole Specifications** rollout*

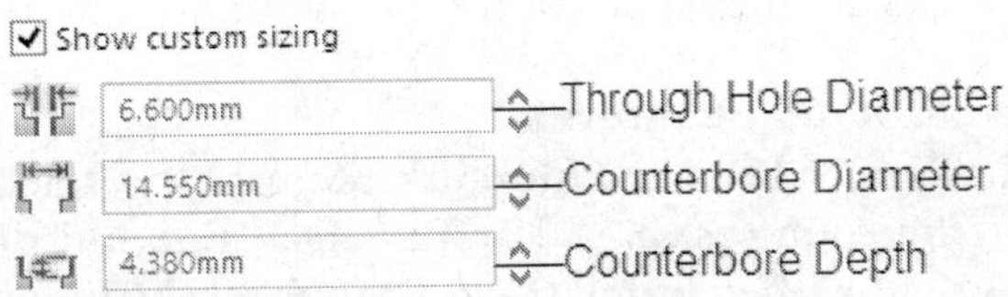

*Figure 7-6 The parameters for the counterbore hole displayed on selecting the **Show custom sizing** check box*

The options used to create the standard holes except the **Legacy Hole**, are the same as those discussed above. If you choose the **Legacy Hole** button from the **Hole Type** rollout of the **PropertyManager**, the preview of the hole will be displayed in the preview area below the **Type** drop-down list. Also, the **Section Dimensions** rollout will be displayed. Select the type of hole that you need to create using the **Type** drop-down list; the preview of the hole feature will be updated automatically. You can set the parameters of the hole by double-clicking on the fields in the **Value** column of the **Section Dimensions** rollout.

End Condition Rollout

The **End Condition** rollout, as shown in Figure 7-7, is used to specify the hole termination options. By default, the **Blind** option is selected in this drop-down list. The hole termination options are similar to the other feature termination options discussed in the earlier chapters. You can also flip the direction of the hole creation using the **Reverse Direction** button.

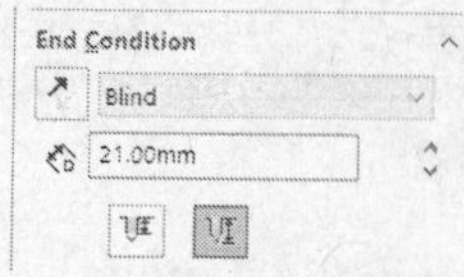

Figure 7-7 The End Condition rollout

If you are creating a tapped hole, the additional options will be displayed to specify the termination conditions for threads.

Options Rollout

The options in the **Options** rollout are used to define some of the additional parameters of the hole. These parameters are optional and are specified only if required. Also, the availability of these options depends upon the hole type selected. Figure 7-8 shows the **Options** rollout with all the check boxes selected. All these options are discussed next.

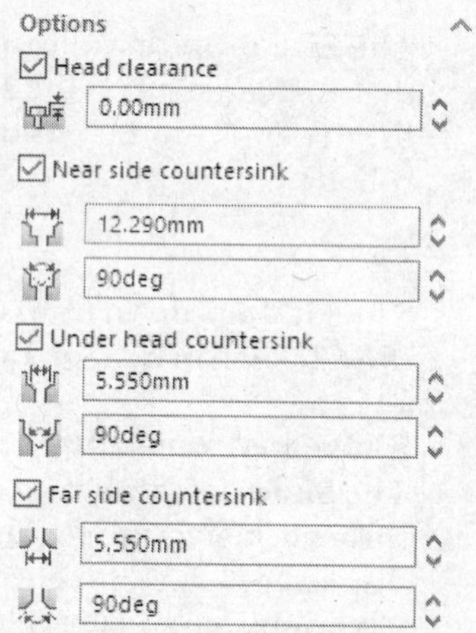

*Figure 7-8 The **Options** rollout*

Head clearance

The **Head clearance** check box is selected to specify the clearance distance between the head of the fastener and the placement plane of the hole feature. If you select this check box, the **Head Clearance** spinner will be displayed. You can set the clearance value in this spinner.

Near side countersink

The **Near side countersink** check box is selected to specify the diameter and the angle for the countersink on the upper face, which is the placement plane of the hole feature. If you select this check box, the **Near Side Countersink Diameter** and **Near Side Countersink Angle** spinners will be displayed. You can set the values of the diameter and angle using their respective spinners.

Under head countersink

The **Under head countersink** check box is selected to specify the diameter and the angle for the countersink to be applied at the end of the counterbore head. If you select this check box, the **Under Head Countersink Diameter** and **Under Head Countersink Angle** spinners will be displayed. You can set the values of the diameter and the angle using the corresponding spinners.

Far side countersink

The **Far side countersink** check box is displayed when you select the **Through All** option in the **End Condition** rollout. This check box is selected to specify the diameter and the angle for the countersink on the bottom face of the hole feature. If you select this check box, the **Far Side Countersink Diameter** and **Far Side Countersink Angle** spinners will be displayed. You can set the values of the diameter and the angle using their respective spinners.

If you create a user-defined hole using the **Legacy Hole** button from the **Hole Type** roll out, the **Options** rollout will not be displayed. If you are creating the **Straight Tap** hole, some additional options will be displayed in the **Options** rollout. These options are discussed next.

Tap drill diameter

You can choose this button to create a hole that has diameter equal to the diameter of the tap drill.

Cosmetic thread

The **Cosmetic thread** button is used to create a hole that is equal to the diameter of the tap drill as well as to display the schematic representation of the thread, as shown in Figure 7-9. On selecting this option, the **With thread callout** check box will be displayed. On selecting this check box, a callout will be attached to the hole feature when you create drawings in the drawing environment.

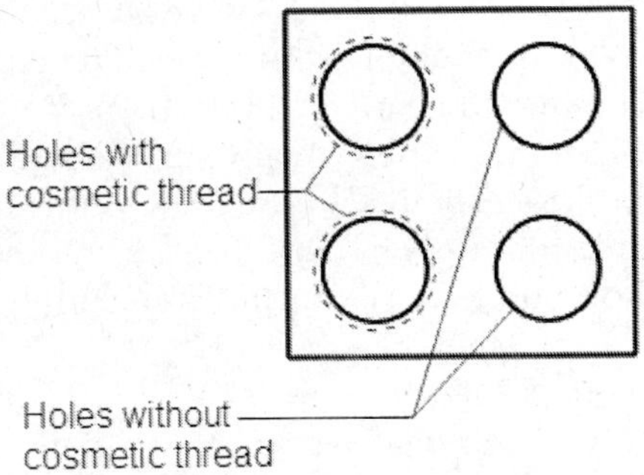

Figure 7-9 The holes with and without cosmetic thread

Remove thread

You can choose this button to create a hole that has diameter equal to the diameter of a thread.

Thread class

The **Thread class** check box is selected to specify the class of the thread. On selecting this check box, the **Thread Class** drop-down list will be displayed. You can select the type of class using this drop-down list.

Tip

By default, the shaded display mode of the cosmetic thread is off. To turn it on, choose the ***Options*** *button from the Menu Bar; the* ***System Options - General*** *dialog box will be displayed. Choose the* ***Document Properties*** *tab and then select the* ***Detailing*** *option on the left. Next, select the* ***Shaded cosmetic threads*** *check box and choose* ***OK****.*

Defining the Position for Placing a Hole

As discussed earlier, in SOLIDWORKS, if you preselect a placement plane and invoke the **Hole Specification PropertyManager**, you can directly specify the position of the hole after choosing the **Positions** tab of the PropertyManager. On doing so, when you move the cursor on a planar face of the model, the preview of the hole feature will be displayed in the graphics area. Specify the placement point; you will be prompted to use the dimensions and other sketch tools to specify the hole center. Also, the preview of the hole feature will be updated dynamically as you define the parameters of the hole feature using the options in the **Type** tab.

After configuring all parameters of the hole feature, you need to define its placement position. To do so, choose the **Positions** tab from the **Hole Specification PropertyManager**; the **Hole Specification PropertyManager** will change into the **Hole Position PropertyManager**, as shown in Figure 7-10. Now, you can specify the location of the holes by using the 2D sketch method or the 3D sketch method. Both these methods are discussed next.

To specify the location of the hole feature using a 2D sketch, you need to choose the **Positions** tab and click on a planar face where you need to place the hole feature; the select cursor will be replaced by the point cursor. Use this cursor to place more holes on coplanar surfaces and use the dimension tool to locate the 2D sketch. Next, choose the **OK** button to complete the feature creation. However, remember that by using this method, you can create holes only on a coplanar surface.

After choosing the **Positions** tab, choose the **3D Sketch** button to locate the holes using the 3D sketch. On doing so, the select cursor will change to the 3D point cursor. Use this cursor to place more holes on any surface and use the dimension tool to locate the hole. Choose the **OK** button to complete the feature creation. Remember that by using this method, you can create holes on multiple surfaces, including non-planar surfaces.

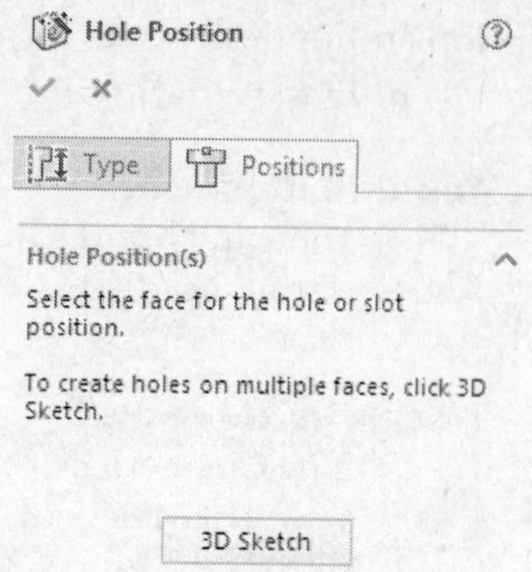

Figure 7-10 *The* ***Hole Position PropertyManager***

Figures 7-11 through 7-14 show models with various types of holes placed using the **Hole Wizard** tool. Figure 7-15 shows a base plate on which various types of holes are created using the **Hole Wizard** tool.

Figure 7-11 *Counterbore holes*

Figure 7-12 *Countersink holes*

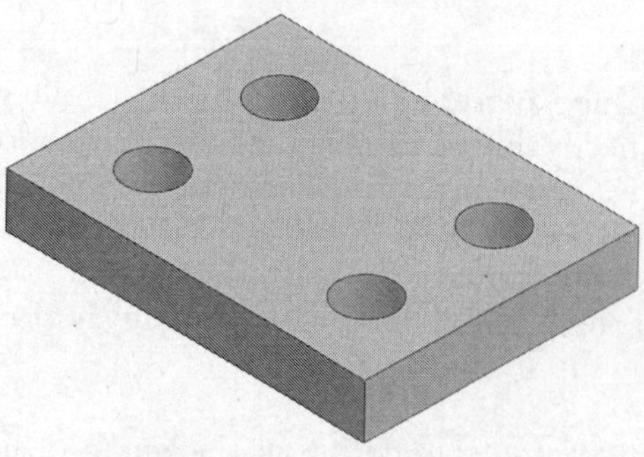

Figure 7-13 *Drilled holes*

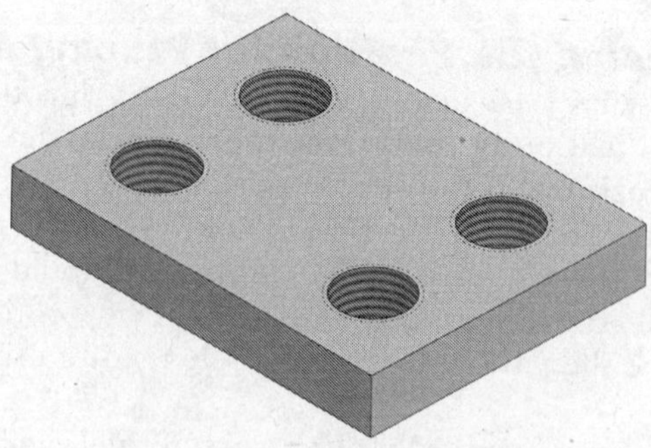

Figure 7-14 *Tapped holes*

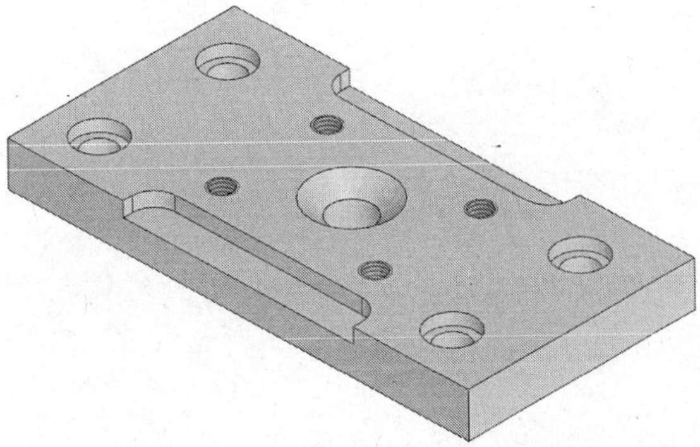

*Figure 7-15 Base plate with holes created using the **Hole Wizard** tool*

Note

*If you create a pattern feature of a tapped hole feature, the thread graphics will not be displayed in the other instances of the pattern, except in the parent instance. Therefore, to add a thread graphic in other pattern instances, select the **Propagate visual properties** check box. You will learn more about patterns in the later chapters.*

Tip

*The hole feature created using the **Hole Wizard** tool consists of two sketches. The first sketch is the sketch of the placement point and the second sketch is the sketch of the profile of the hole feature. As discussed, the placement sketch can be a 2D sketch or 3D sketch. You will learn more about 3D sketches in the later chapters.*

*If a cosmetic thread is added to a tapped hole, the cosmetic thread will also be displayed along with the placement and hole profile sketches. To edit the cosmetic threads, select them from the **FeatureManager Design Tree**; a pop-up toolbar will be displayed. Choose the **Edit Feature** option from the pop-up toolbar; the **Cosmetic Thread PropertyManager** will be displayed.*

You can also view the convention of a thread if the cosmetic thread is added to a tapped hole feature. Orient the model to the top view to observe the thread convention from the top view. Similarly, orient the model to the front, back, or any side view to observe the thread convention from different side views.

Creating Advanced Holes

CommandManager:	Features > Hole Wizard flyout > Advanced Hole
SOLIDWORKS menus:	Insert > Features > Advanced Hole
Toolbar:	Features > Hole Wizard flyout > Advanced Hole

The **Advanced Hole** tool is used to add combination of standard holes such as counterbore, countersink, drilled, straight, and tapered tap from near and side faces of the model. To create an advanced hole feature, choose the **Advanced Hole** tool from the **Hole Wizard** flyout in the **Features CommandManager**; the **Advanced Hole PropertyManager** will be displayed, as shown in Figure 7-16. The options in the **Advanced Hole PropertyManager** are discussed next.

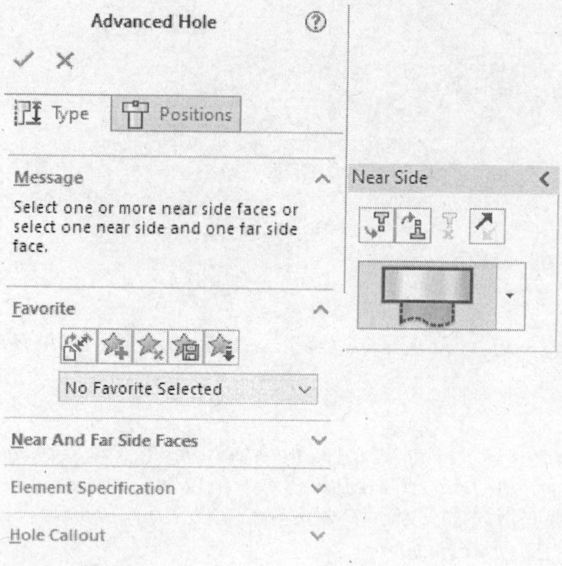

Figure 7-16 Partial view of the ***Advanced Hole PropertyManager***

Element Flyout

The **Element Flyout** is used to select elements and define their order of placement for near and far side faces. To display the **Element Flyout**, click on the arrow provided at the top-right corner of this PropertyManager, refer to Figure 7-16. Initially, it shows the **Near Side** stack in which you can add, change, or reverse the order of hole elements. The **Insert Element Below Active Element** and **Insert Element Above Active Element** buttons in the stack are used to add an element below and above the currently selected element, respectively. The **Delete Active Element** button is used to delete the currently selected element. Note that this button will be active only when you have added two or more hole elements. The **Reverse Stack Direction** button is used to reverse the direction of hole elements and works only for **Near Side** stack. You can select the required hole type from the various holes available in the flyout located in the **Near Side** stack. If you select the **Far Side** check box in the **Near And Far Side Faces** rollout then the **Far Side** stack will also be added to the **Element Flyout**. The buttons and their functions in this stack are similar to those discussed for the **Near Side** stack.

Favorite Rollout

The **Favorite** rollout is used to add frequently used hole settings to the favorite list so as to not configure it again and again. The method of adding a hole setting to the favorite list is the same as adding the dimensional settings discussed in Chapter 4.

Near And Far Side Faces Rollout

The **Near And Far Side Faces** rollout in the **Type** tab of the **Advanced Hole PropertyManager** is used to select the near and far side faces of the model. Initially there is one selection box in this rollout in which you can specify the faces or planes from the near side of the model. As soon as you select a face from the near side, a preview of the hole is displayed on the model. Select the desired type of the hole to start from the near side face of the model. If you need to add more hole elements then use the buttons provided in the **Near Side** stack. The **Far Side** check box in this rollout is used to display the selection box for selecting the far side of the model. When you select this check box, the **Far Side** stack will be added to the **Element Flyout**, refer to Figure 7-17. Also a bar line will appear separating both the stacks. You can also add required hole type and number of elements in the **Far Side** stack as discussed for **Near Side** stack. If you select the **Use baseline dimensions** check box then all the elements of the hole stack are measured from the face selected as near side face. Also, the end condition for each element get sets to **Offset from Surface** automatically.

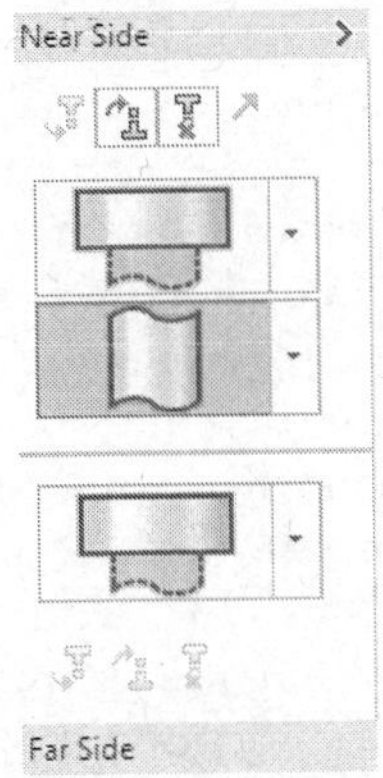

***Figure 7-17** The **Near Side** and **Far Side** stacks*

Element Specification Rollout

The **Element Specification** rollout in the **Type** tab of the **Advanced Hole PropertyManager** is used to define the type of standard hole to be created. The options in this rollout are similar to those discussed in the **Hole Wizard** tool. After selecting the hole element from the **Element Flyout**, their specifications can be changed as required by using various drop-down lists available in this rollout.

Hole Callout Rollout

In SOLIDWORKS, you can edit the callout for an advanced hole using the **Hole Callout** rollout in the **Advanced Hole PropertyManager**. By default, the **Default callout** radio button is selected as result a default callout is generated for the hole. If you select the **Customize callout** radio button then the **Callout String** table gets enable. You can modify the order of the strings by selecting a string and then choosing the **Move Up** or **Move Down** buttons provided below the table. You can also customize a callout string. To do so, double-click on the callout string in the table; the callout variables gets enabled. You can also select the **Callout Variables** button to list all the available callout variables. To restore the changes made, right-click on a callout string and then select the **Restore Default String** option from the shortcut menu displayed.

After defining all the hole parameters, you can directly specify the position of the hole by choosing the **Positions** tab of the PropertyManager. As the near and far side faces are already defined in the **Type** tab; a preview of the hole feature will be displayed in the graphics area on moving the cursor on the near side face of the model. Specify the placement point; you will be prompted to use dimensions and other sketch tools to specify the position of the hole. To skip instances, expand the **Instances To Skip** rollout; pink dots will be displayed at the center of all the instances. Next, move the cursor to the pink dot of the instance to be skipped; the cursor will be replaced by the instance to skip cursor and the position of that instance will be displayed as a tool tip in the form of a matrix below the cursor. Click on the pink dot to skip that instance; the pink dot will be replaced by a white dot and the preview of that instance will disappear from the pattern. Also, the position of the skipped instance in the form of a matrix will be displayed in the **Instances To Skip** selection box of the **Instances To Skip** rollout. You can resume the skipped instances by deleting the name of the instance from the **Instances To Skip** selection box or by selecting the corresponding white dot from the graphics area.

The **Create instances on sketch geometry** check box in the **Sketch Options** rollout is used to place the instances of holes on the sketched geometry. After selecting this check box, if you draw a line then hole instances will be placed on the endpoints of the line. The **Create instances on construction geometry** check box allows you to place instances of hole on the sketch made with construction lines. Figure 7-18 shows the section view of a model with hole created using the **Advanced Hole** tool.

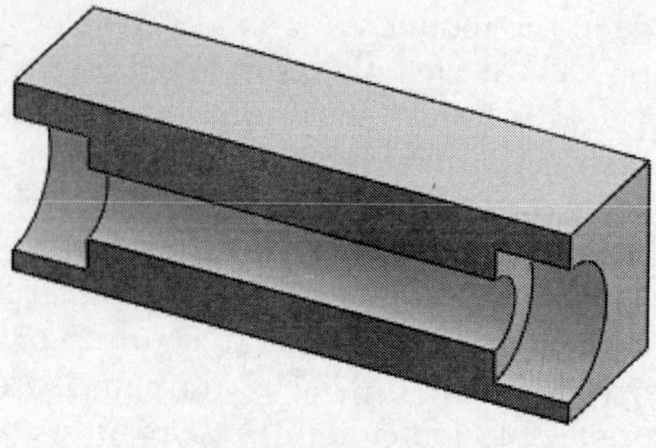

Figure 7-18 *Section view of the model with hole created using the* ***Advanced Hole*** *tool*

Creating Threads

CommandManager: Features > Hole Wizard flyout > Thread
SOLIDWORKS menus: Insert > Features > Thread
Toolbar: Features > Hole Wizard flyout > Thread

The **Thread** tool is used to create helical threads on cylindrical faces. You can also store custom thread profile as a library feature and then use it later as per your requirement. This tool enables you to modify the parameters of the threads even after their creation. Thus, you can create standard parametric threads with this tool. To create threads, choose the **Thread** button from the **Hole Wizard** flyout in the **Features CommandManager**; a message box will appear stating that the thread feature is for nominal use only and not for production use. Click on the **OK** button; the **Thread PropertyManager** will be displayed, as shown in Figure 7-19. Also, you will be prompted to select an edge of the given cylindrical face for thread creation. Select the edge; a preview of the thread feature will be displayed. Choose the **OK** button to create the feature with default settings. The options in the **Thread PropertyManager** are discussed next.

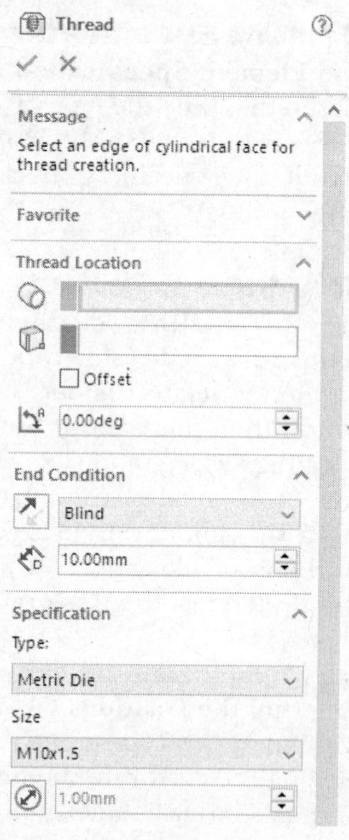

Figure 7-19 *Partial view of the* ***Thread PropertyManager***

Favorite Rollout

The **Favorite** rollout is used to add frequently used thread settings to the favorite list. If you add a thread setting to the favorite list, you will not have to configure that setting to add similar types of threads every time. The method of adding a thread setting to the favorite list is the same as adding the dimensional settings discussed in Chapter 4.

Thread Location Rollout

The **Thread Location** rollout in the **Thread PropertyManager** is used to define the placement location of the thread to be created. The options in this rollout are discussed next.

Edge of Cylinder

The **Edge of Cylinder** selection box is used to specify the cylindrical edge for thread creation.

Optional Start Location

The **Optional Start Location** selection box is used to specify the optional location for the starting point of the threads. To specify the optional location, you can select a vertex/edge/plane/planar surface. Note that the selected entity should be perpendicular to the axis of the thread. Figure 7-20 shows face and edge to be selected and Figure 7-21 shows resultant thread.

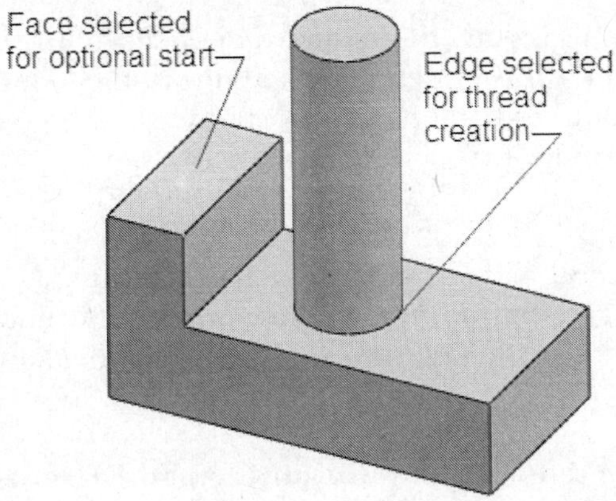

Figure 7-20 Selected face and edge for thread creation

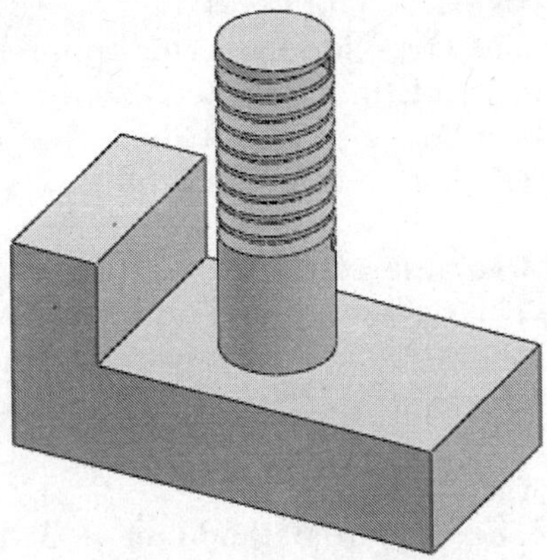

Figure 7-21 Resultant thread

Offset

The **Offset** check box is used to offset the starting point of the thread. When you select the **Offset** check box, the **Offset Distance** spinner appears below it where you can specify the offset distance. You can also reverse the direction of feature (thread) creation by using the **Reverse Direction** button provided on the left of the **Offset Distance** spinner.

Start Angle

The **Start Angle** spinner is used to specify the start angle of the thread.

End Condition Rollout

The **End Condition** rollout of the **Thread PropertyManager** is used to specify the thread termination options. By default, the **Blind** option is selected in the drop-down list of this rollout. The thread termination options in this drop-down list are similar to the feature termination options discussed in earlier chapters, except the **Revolutions** option. The **Revolutions** option is used to terminate the thread by specifying total number of revolutions. When you select this option, the **Revolutions** spinner will appear where you can specify the required number of revolutions for the threads.

Specification Rollout

The **Specification** rollout of the **Thread PropertyManager** is used to define the type and size of the standard thread to be created. The options in this rollout are discussed next.

Type

The **Type** drop-down list is used to specify the type of method to be used for the creation of thread.

Size

The **Size** drop-down list is used to define the size of the thread to be created in the hole or on the shaft using the **Thread** tool. The size for the threads in the **Size** drop-down list depends on the standard selected from the **Type** drop-down list in the **Specification** rollout.

Override Diameter

The **Override Diameter** option is used to modify the standard diameter of the threads. To override the diameter, choose the **Override Diameter** toggle button; the spinner next to this button will be enabled. Set the required diameter in this spinner and then choose the **OK** button from the Confirmation Corner.

Override Pitch

The **Override Pitch** option is used to modify the standard pitch of the threads. To use this option, choose the **Override Pitch** toggle button; the spinner next to this button will be activated. Set the required pitch and choose the **OK** button from the Confirmation Corner.

Thread method

The **Thread method** area provides two radio buttons: **Cut thread** and **Extrude thread**. If you select the **Cut thread** radio button then the thread will be created as a cut feature. If you select the **Extrude thread** radio button then the thread will be created as a extrude feature.

Mirror Profile

The **Mirror Profile** check box is used to mirror the thread profile around an axis. If you select this check box, two radio buttons below it will be available. If you select the **Mirror Horizontally** radio button, the profile will be mirrored about the vertical axis. However, if you select the **Mirror Vertically** radio button, the profile will be mirrored about the horizontal axis.

Rotation Angle

The **Rotation Angle** spinner is used to set the angle of the thread profile.

Locate Profile

The **Locate Profile** button is used to provide enlarged view of the thread profile.

Thread Options Rollout

The two radio buttons in the **Thread Options** rollout of the **Thread PropertyManager** are used to define the orientation of the helix of the thread. If you select the **Right-hand thread** radio button from the **Thread Options** rollout then the thread will follow the right hand thumb rule for thread creation. If you select the **Left-hand thread** radio button then the thread will follow the left hand thumb rule for thread generation. When you select the **Multiple Start** check box, the **Number of Starts** spinner will appear below this check box. This spinner is used to specify the number of thread starts on the model. The **Trim with start face** and **Trim with end face** check boxes are used to align threads with the end faces. Figures 7-22 and 7-23 show threads before and after using the trim options.

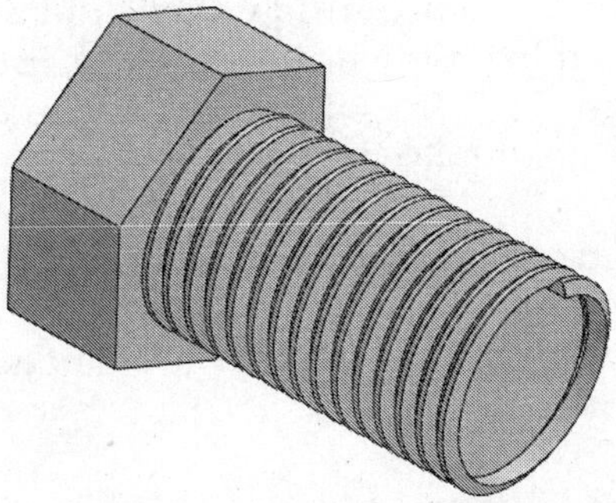

Figure 7-22 *Extrude thread before trim*

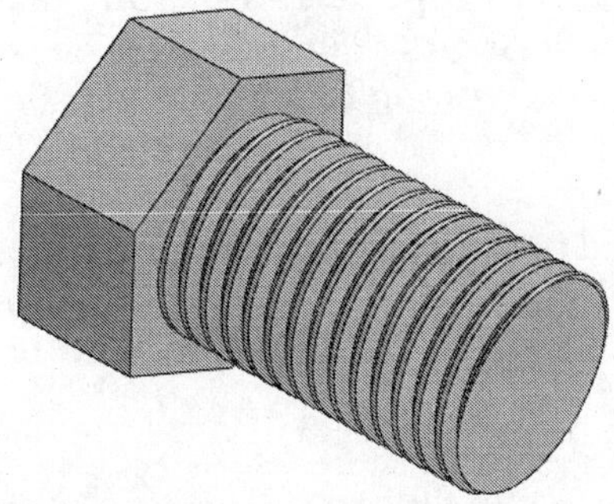

Figure 7-23 *Extrude thread after trim*

Preview Options Rollout

The options in this rollout, except the **Wireframe preview** option, are same as discussed in earlier chapters. When you select **Wireframe preview** option, the preview of the thread feature is displayed in the wireframe mode. Also, the slider below it is activated using which you can increase or decrease the wireframe quality.

Adding External Cosmetic Threads

CommandManager: Features > Cosmetic Thread (*Customize to Add*)
SOLIDWORKS menus: Insert > Annotations > Cosmetic Thread

In SOLIDWORKS, you can also add external cosmetic threads to cylindrical surfaces to give them a realistic look like threads. To do so, you need to invoke the **Cosmetic Thread** tool. This tool is not available by default in the **Features CommandManager**. Therefore, you need to add this tool from the list of the **Annotation** commands given in the **Customize** dialog box.

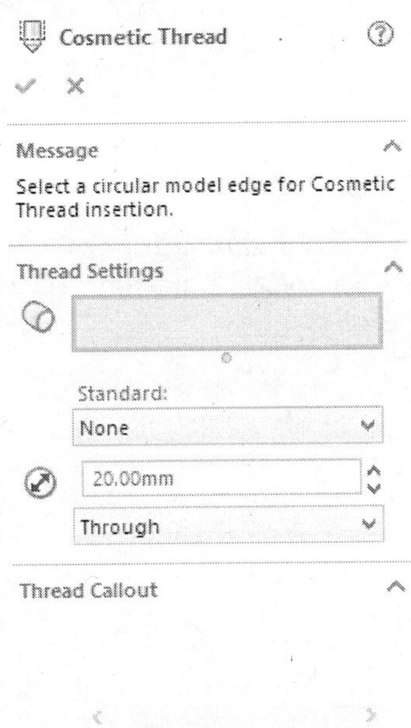

Figure 7-24 *The* ***Cosmetic Thread PropertyManager***

On choosing the **Cosmetic Thread** button; the **Cosmetic Thread PropertyManager** will be displayed, as shown in Figure 7-24. Also, you will be prompted to select the edge and specify the parameters for adding the thread features. Select the circular edge and specify the parameters of the thread in the corresponding **Standard** drop-down lists; the preview of the cosmetic thread to be added will be displayed on the cylindrical surface. On selecting the type of standard from the **Standard** drop-down list, the selected standard thread will be applied based on the diameter of the selected circular edge. You can change the type of threads according to your requirement. Next, specify the end condition and choose the **OK** button; the cosmetic thread will be created, as shown in Figure 7-25. If you want to display the custom thread callout in the drawing environment, enter the description in the edit box available in the **Thread Callout** rollout and choose the **OK** button. However, this edit box will be available only when the **None** option is selected in the **Standard** drop-down list. Note that if the **Shaded cosmetic threads** check box is selected in the **Document Properties - Detailing** dialog box, the cosmetic thread will be displayed in the shaded mode, refer to Figure 7-25. The name of the added cosmetic thread will be listed in the node of the corresponding feature, as shown in Figure 7-26. In SOLIDWORKS, you can select the configuration for which the thread callout has to be displayed.

To edit the cosmetic thread added to a feature, expand the node corresponding to the feature and select the **Cosmetic Thread** sub-option; a pop-up toolbar will be displayed. Choose the **Edit Feature** option from the pop-up toolbar and edit the parameters of the cosmetic thread.

Note

Generally, the creation of threads in a model is avoided as they results in the creation of a complex geometry, which is difficult to understand. Therefore, it is better to add cosmetic threads instead of creating threads to avoid complexity and to get the thread convention in the drawing views.

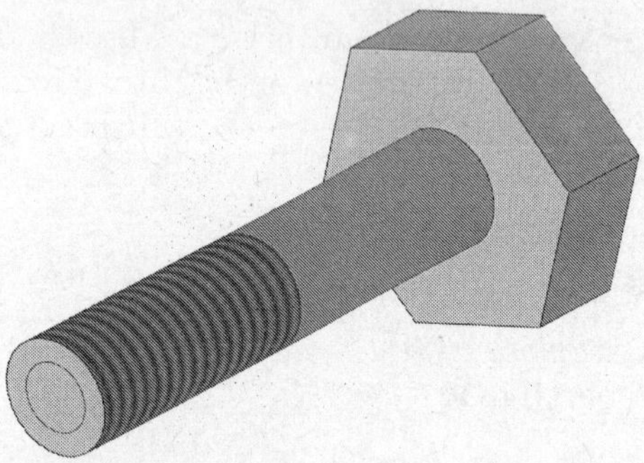

Figure 7-25 *Part with cosmetic thread*

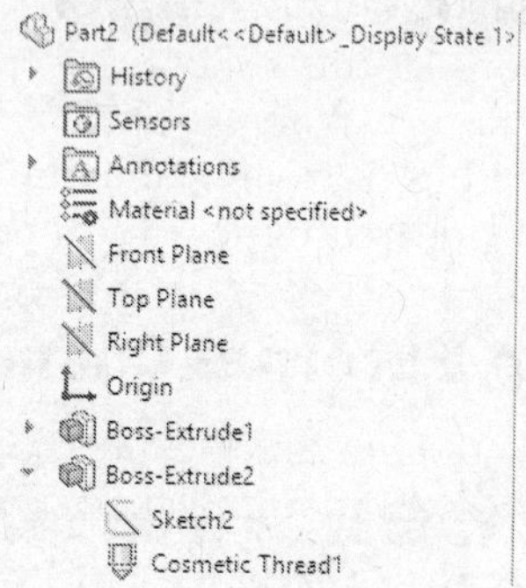

Figure 7-26 *The* ***Cosmetic Thread*** *node in the* ***FeatureManager Design Tree***

Creating Fillets

CommandManager:	Features > Fillet flyout > Fillet
SOLIDWORKS menus:	Insert > Features > Fillet/Round
Toolbar:	Features > Fillet flyout > Fillet

In SOLIDWORKS, you can add fillets to a model as a feature using the **Manual** or **FilletXpert** option. The **Manual** option is used to fillet an internal or external face or the edge of a model. You can preselect the face, edge, or feature to which the fillet has to be added. You can also select the entity to be filleted after invoking the **Fillet** tool. To add a fillet using the **Manual** option, choose the **Fillet** button from the **Fillet** flyout in the **Features CommandManager**. On doing so, the **Fillet PropertyManager** will be displayed. But, if the **FilletXpert PropertyManager** is displayed, then choose the **Manual** button to display the **Fillet PropertyManager**, as shown in Figure 7-27. If the entities to be filleted are preselected, a preview of the fillet feature along with the fillet callout will be displayed in the drawing area. This is because the **Full preview** radio button will be selected by default in the **Fillet PropertyManager**. If the entities are not preselected, you will be prompted to select the edges, faces, features, or loops to add the fillet feature. Use the select cursor to select the entity to be filleted; the preview of the fillet and a callout will be displayed. Figure 7-28 shows a preview of the fillet feature with the fillet callout.

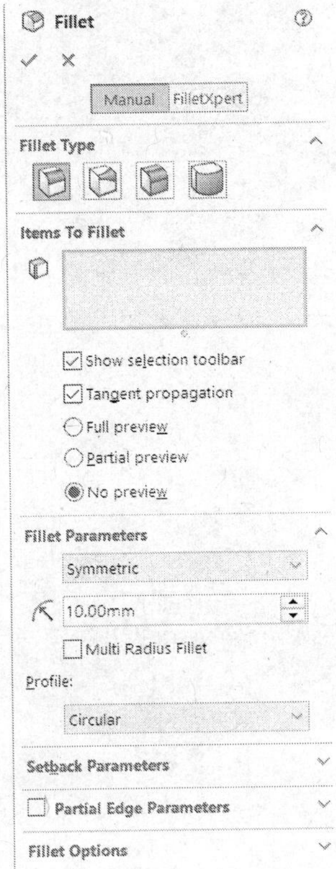

Figure 7-27 *The* ***Fillet PropertyManager***

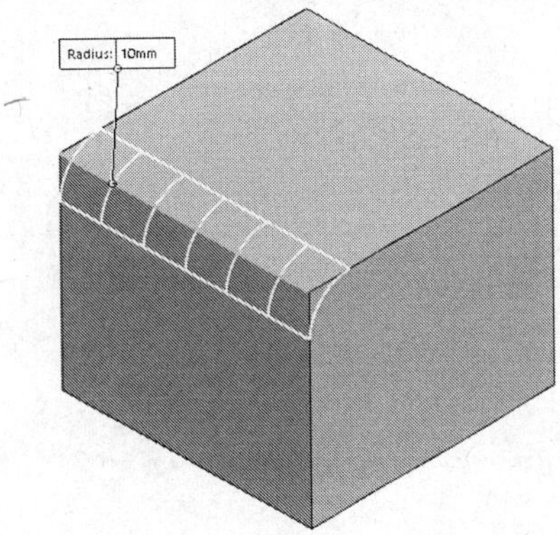

Figure 7-28 *Preview of the fillet feature*

The types of fillets that can be created using the **Fillet** tool are: **Constant Size Fillet**, **Variable Size Fillet**, **Face Fillet**, and **Full Round Fillet**. The methods of creating fillets are discussed next.

Creating Constant Size Fillet

Choose the **Constant Size Fillet** button in the **Fillet Type** rollout of the **Fillet PropertyManager** to create a fillet of a constant radius along the selected entity. The **Symmetric** option is selected by default in the **Fillet Method** drop-down list of the **Fillet Parameters** rollout. You can set the value of the fillet radius in the **Radius** spinner provided in the **Fillet Parameters** rollout or by clicking in the value area of the fillet callout. Enter the value of the radius and press ENTER; the preview of the fillet will be changed dynamically on modifying the value of the radius of the fillet. The entities that you can select to add the fillet feature are faces, edges, features, and loops. The names of the selected entities are displayed in the **Edges, Faces, Features and Loops** selection box. Next, choose the **OK** button from the **Fillet PropertyManager**. Figures 7-29 through 7-34 show the selection of different entities and the resulting fillets.

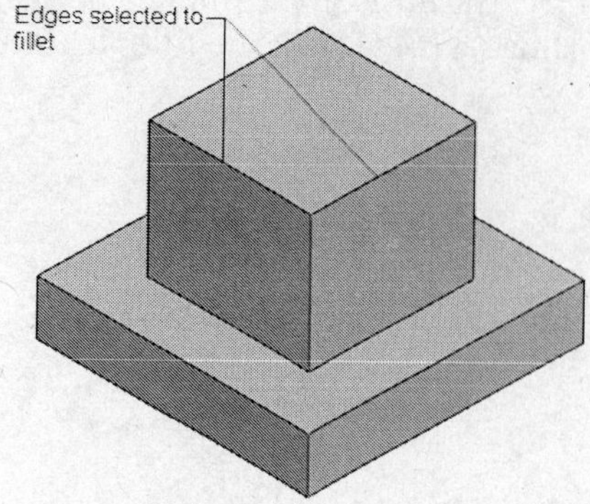

***Figure 7-29** Selecting the edges*

***Figure 7-30** Resulting fillet feature*

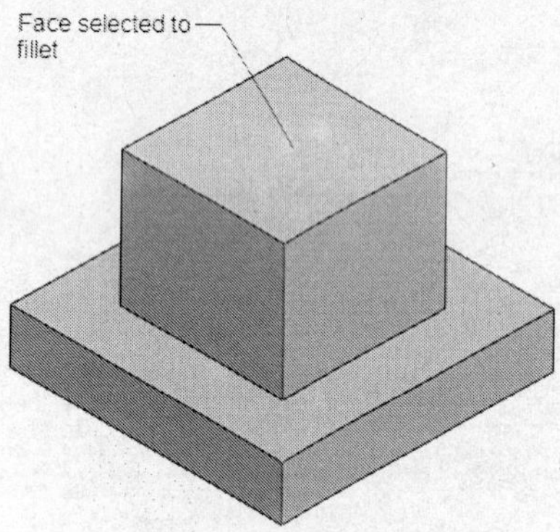

***Figure 7-31** Selecting the face*

***Figure 7-32** Resulting fillet feature*

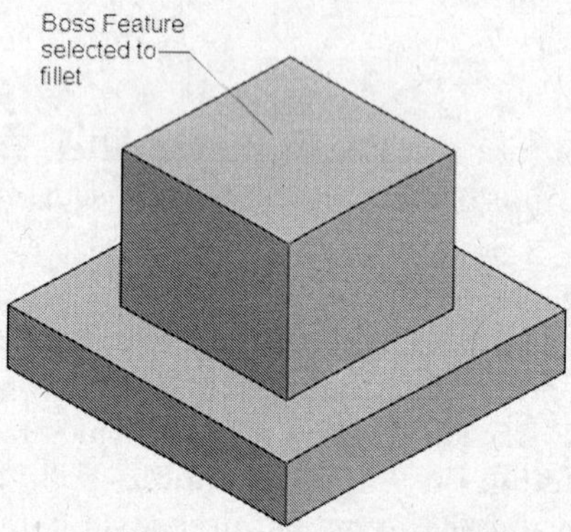

***Figure 7-33** Selecting the feature*

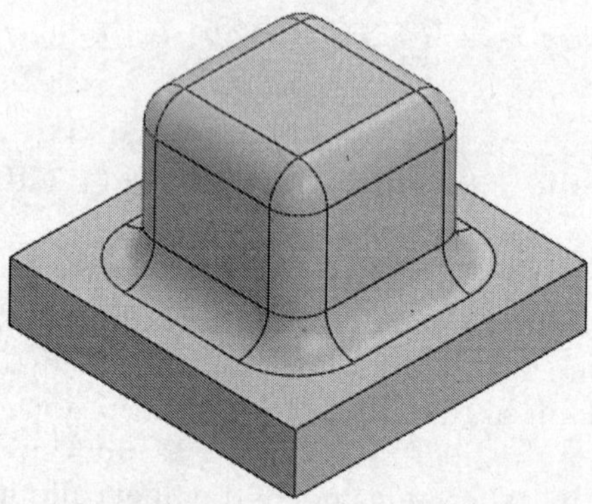

***Figure 7-34** Resulting fillet feature*

If you choose the **Constant Size Fillet** button in the **Fillet PropertyManager**, various options will be displayed in the **Fillet Parameters** rollout, refer to Figure 7-27. These options are discussed next.

Multiple Radius Fillet

The **Multi Radius Fillet** check box in the **Fillet Parameters** rollout of the **Fillet PropertyManager** is selected to specify a fillet of different radii for all selected edges. To create a fillet feature using this option either preselect the edges, faces, or features or select them after invoking the **Fillet PropertyManager**. After invoking the **Fillet** tool, select the **Multi Radius Fillet** check box; a preview of the fillet feature with the default values will be displayed in the drawing area. You will notice that you are provided with different callouts for each selected entity. Figure 7-35 shows a preview of the fillet feature with the **Multi Radius Fillet** check box selected.

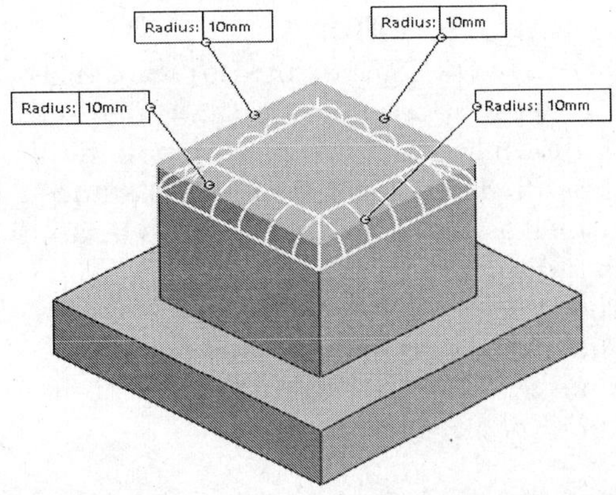

***Figure 7-35** Preview of the fillet feature with the **Multiple Radius Fillet** check box selected*

The names of the selected entities will be displayed in the **Edges, Faces, Features and Loops** selection box. The boundaries of the currently selected entity in the selection box will be highlighted with a thick line. You can set the value for each selected entity by using the **Radius** spinner or by specifying the value of the fillet radius in the radius callout, as shown in Figure 7-36. As you modify the value of the radius, a preview of the fillet feature will be modified dynamically in the drawing area. Figure 7-37 shows the fillet created using the multiple radius fillets.

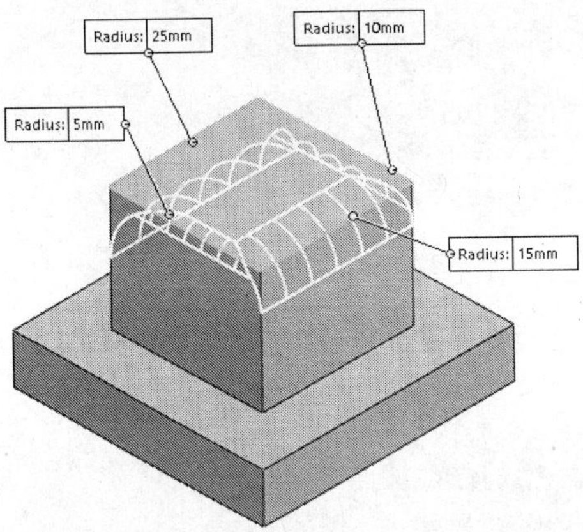

***Figure 7-36** Different radii specified in each radius callout*

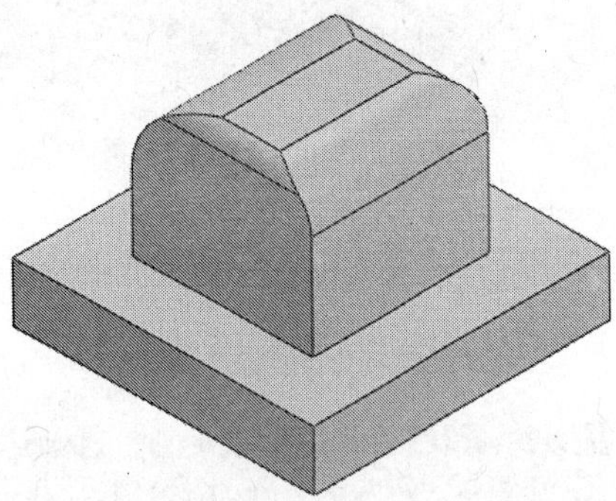

***Figure 7-37** Resulting fillet feature*

In SOLIDWORKS, you can change the profile of the fillet to be created by using the options available in the **Profile** drop-down list of the **Fillet Parameters** rollout. There are four options available in this drop-down list: **Circular**, **Conic Rho**, **Conic Radius**, and **Curvature Continuous**. By default, the **Circular** option is selected in this drop-down list. As a result, the fillet created is of circular profile. If you select the **Conic Rho** option then you need to specify the value of Rho for the conic arc in the edit box displayed below the drop-down list. If the **Conic Radius** option is selected then you need to specify the radius of the conic fillet in the edit box displayed below the drop-down list.

Asymmetric Fillet

In SOLIDWORKS, you can also create an asymmetric fillet. To create an asymmetric fillet, invoke the **Fillet PropertyManager** and then select the **Asymmetric** option from the **Fillet Method** drop-down list of the **Fillet Parameters** rollout. On doing so, the **Fillet Parameters** rollout will be modified and **Distance 1** and **Distance 2** spinners will be displayed. Now, select the edge(s) on which asymmetric fillet needs to be applied; a preview of the asymmetric fillet and a callout with radius values will be displayed, as shown in Figure 7-38. You can change these radius values in the **Distance 1** and **Distance 2** spinners of the **Fillet Parameters** rollout or specify the value of the fillet radius in the radius callout. Next, specify the profile curvature of the fillet using the options available in the **Profile** drop-down list. Figure 7-39 shows the resulting asymmetric fillet created on the selected edges.

Tip

*By default, the **Elliptic** option is selected in the **Profile** drop-down list when creating asymmetric fillet. When you select the **Conic Rho** option from the **Profile** drop-down list, the **Conic Rho** spinner will be displayed. The value of the **Conic Rho** ranges between **0.05** to **0.95**.*

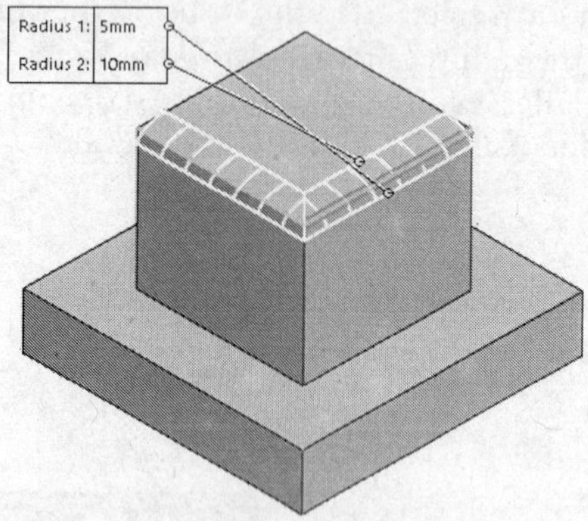

Figure 7-38 *Preview of asymmetric fillet on selected edges*

Figure 7-39 *Resulting asymmetric fillet*

Fillet with and without Tangent Propagation

In SOLIDWORKS, you can add a fillet feature to a model with or without the tangent propagation. When you invoke the **Fillet PropertyManager**, you will notice that the **Tangent propagation** check box is selected by default in the **Items To Fillet** rollout. Therefore, if you select an edge, face, feature, or a loop to fillet, it will automatically select other entities that are tangential to the selected entity. Thus, it will apply the fillet feature to all the entities that are tangential to the selected one. If you clear the **Tangent propagation** check box, the fillet will be applied only to the selected entity. Figure 7-40 shows the existing fillet and the edge to be selected to add a fillet feature. Figures 7-41 and 7-42 show the fillet feature created with the **Tangent propagation** check box cleared and selected, respectively.

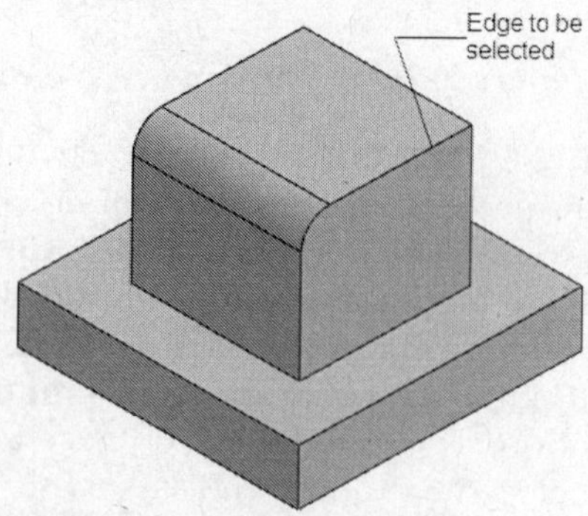

Figure 7-40 *Edge to be selected to apply the fillet feature*

Note

*The **Full preview** radio button in the **Fillet PropertyManager** is used to preview the fillet feature before actually creating it. If you select the **Partial preview** radio button, you can view only partial preview of the fillet feature. If you select a face to add a fillet feature and select the **Partial preview** radio button, you cannot preview the fillet feature created on all the edges adjacent to the selected face. You can preview only the fillet on the single edge of the selected face. Click in the **Items To Fillet** selection box then press the A key to cycle the preview of the fillet feature on the other edges of the selected face. If you select the **No preview** radio button, preview of the fillet feature will not be displayed.*

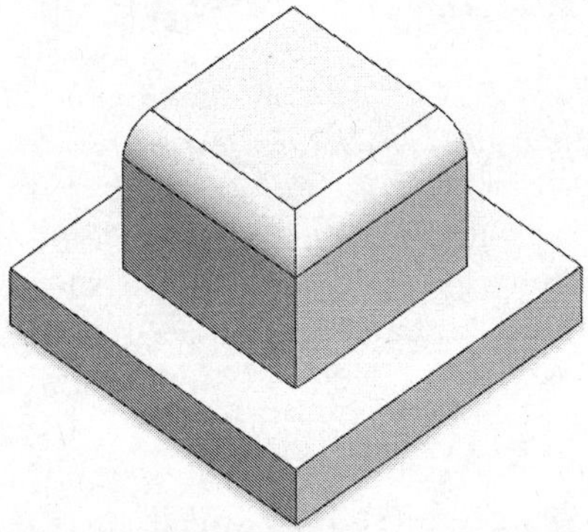

Figure 7-41 *Fillet feature created with the **Tangent propagation** check box cleared*

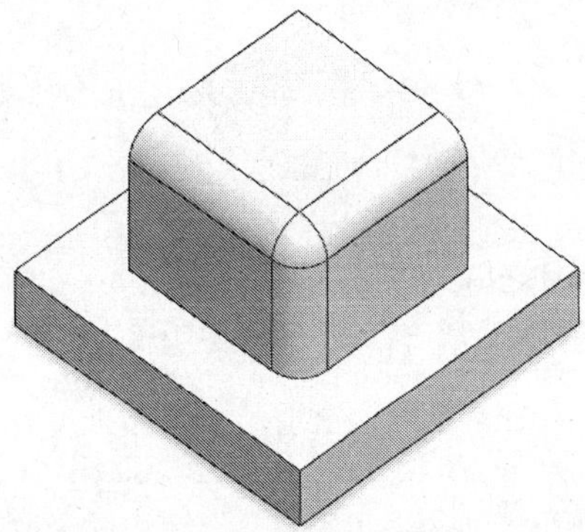

Figure 7-42 *Fillet feature created with the **Tangent propagation** check box selected*

Setback Fillets

A setback fillet is created where three or more edges are merged into a vertex. This type of fillet is used to smoothly blend the transition surfaces generated from the edges to the fillet vertex. This smooth transition is created between all the selected edges and the vertex selected for this type of fillet. To create a setback fillet, invoke the **Fillet PropertyManager** and select three or more edges to apply the fillet. Note that the edges should share the same vertex. The preview of the fillet will be displayed in the drawing area. Now, click on the **Setback Parameters** rollout; the **Setback Parameters** rollout will expand, as shown in Figure 7-43. This rollout is used to specify the setback parameters. Click once in the **Setback Vertices** selection box to invoke the setback vertex selection command. Now, select the vertex where the edges meet. Figure 7-44 shows the edges and the vertex to be selected to assign the setback parameters.

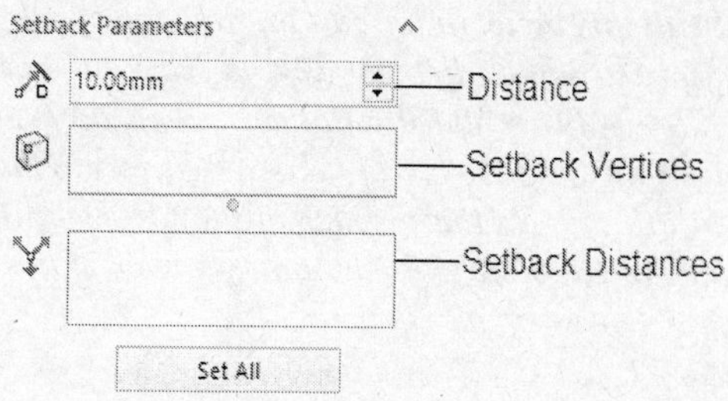

Figure 7-43 *The **Setback Parameters** rollout*

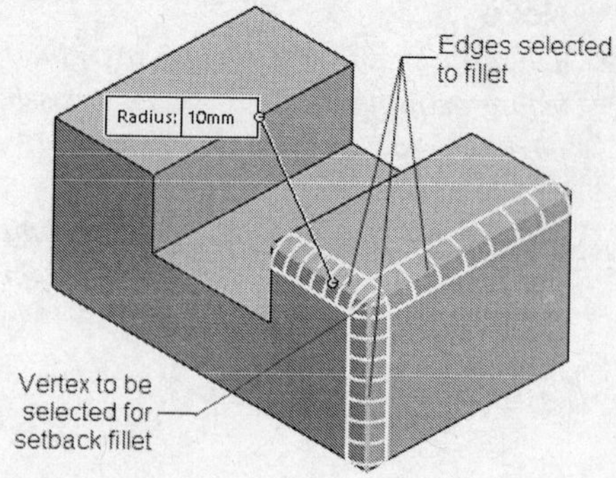

Figure 7-44 *Edges and vertex to be selected to apply the setback fillet feature*

When you select the vertex for the setback fillet, you will notice that the callouts with the unassigned setback distances are displayed in the drawing area. The name of the selected vertex and edges will be displayed in the **Setback Vertices** and **Setback Distances** selection boxes, respectively. Select the name of the edge in **Setback Distances** selection box to assign a setback distance to that edge; a magenta colored arrow will be displayed along that edge. Use the **Distance** spinner to assign a setback distance to the selected edge. Similarly, assign the setback distance to all edges. You can also assign the setback distance directly by specifying the value in the setback callouts displayed in the drawing area. As discussed earlier, the preview of the fillet will be updated automatically when you assign any value. The **Set All** button is used to assign the setback distance displayed in the **Distance** spinner to all selected edges. Figure 7-45 shows the preview of the setback fillet and Figure 7-46 shows a setback fillet on one side of the model and a normal fillet on the other sides of the model.

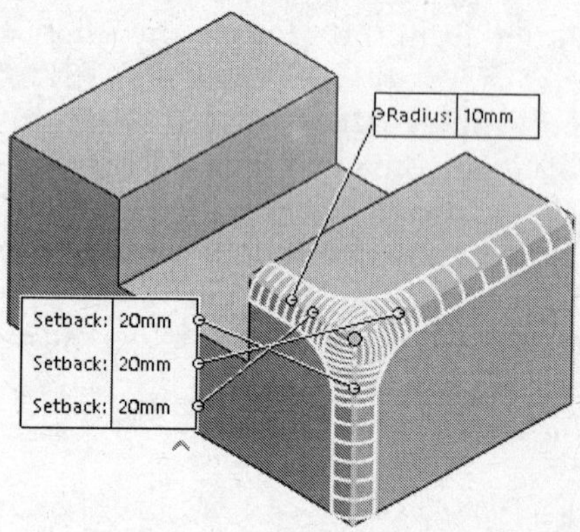

Figure 7-45 *Preview of the setback fillet*

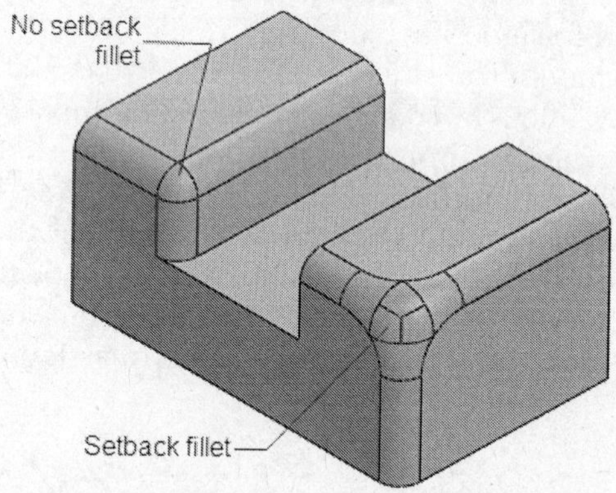

Figure 7-46 *Simple and setback fillet features*

Tip

*You can also drag and drop the fillet features created on one edge to the other. To do so, select the fillet feature from the **FeatureManager Design Tree** or from the drawing area. Then, hold the left mouse button, drag the cursor and release the left mouse button to drop the feature on the required edge or face. You can also copy the fillet feature and paste it on the selected entity.*

Creating Partial Fillets

You can create partial fillets of specified lengths along the model edges. The **Manual** tab of the **Fillet PropertyManager** contain the **Partial Edge Parameters** rollout where you can specify parameters. This option is available only for constant size fillets. To create partial fillet, select the edge as shown in Figure 7-47. Click **Fillet** or choose **Insert > Features > Fillet/Round**. Right-click the edge, refer to Figure 7-47 and choose **Select Tangency**. In the **Fillet PropertyManager** under **Fillet Type**, select **Constant Size Fillet**. Select **Full preview** radio button under **Items To Fillet** rollout. Enter **5** in the **Radius** edit box. Select the **Partial Edge Parameters** check box. In **Start condition** drop down, select **Distance offset** option. Enter **10**mm in the **Offset distance from start point** edit box. In **End condition** drop down, select **Distance offset** option. Enter **20**mm in the **Offset distance from end point** edit box. You can also drag the handles shown in Figure 7-48 to change the value dynamically. Figure 7-49 shows partial fillet applied on the selected edge.

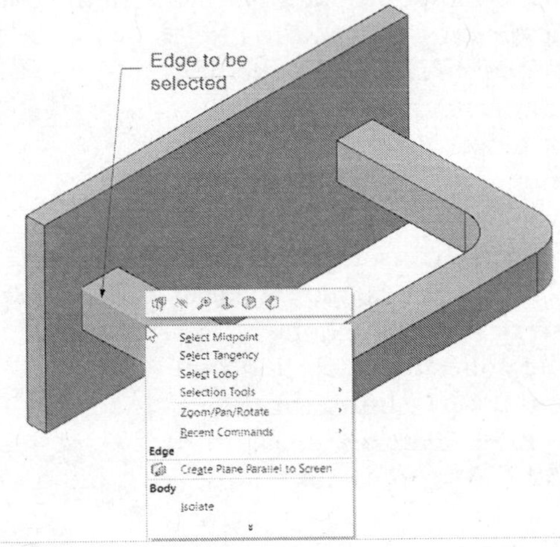

Figure 7-47 *Edge to be selected to apply the fillet feature*

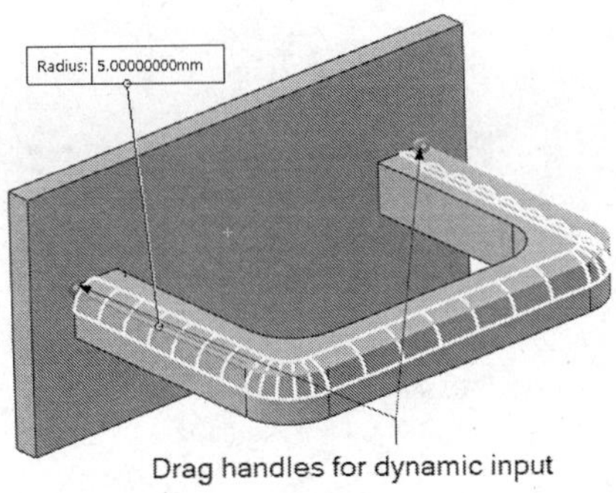

Figure 7-48 *Dynamic drag handles*

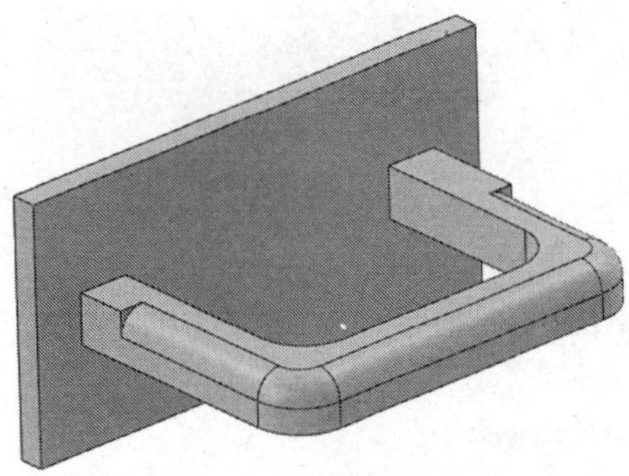

Figure 7-49 *Final model with partial fillet*

Fillet Options

You are also provided with various other fillet options in the **Fillet Options** rollout of the **Fillet PropertyManager**. These options are used to create an accurate and aesthetic design. The fillet options are **Select through faces**, **Keep features**, **Round corners**, **Overflow type**, and **Feature attachment**. These options are discussed next.

Select through faces

This option allows you to select the edges hidden behind the faces of the model.

Keep features

If there are boss or cut features in a model and the fillet created is large enough to consume them, it is recommended that you select the **Keep features** check box in the **Fillet Options** rollout. This check box is selected by default, but you should confirm it before creating any fillet feature. If you clear this check box, the fillet feature will consume the features that obstruct its path. Note that the features that are consumed by the fillet feature are not deleted from the model. They disappear from the model because of some geometric inconsistency. However, if you rollback, suppress, or delete the fillet, the consumed features will reappear. You will learn more about rollback and suppress in the later chapters. Figure 7-50 shows the model and the edge to be selected for applying the fillet. Figure 7-51 shows the fillet feature created with the **Keep features** check box selected and Figure 7-52 shows the fillet feature created with the **Keep features** check box cleared.

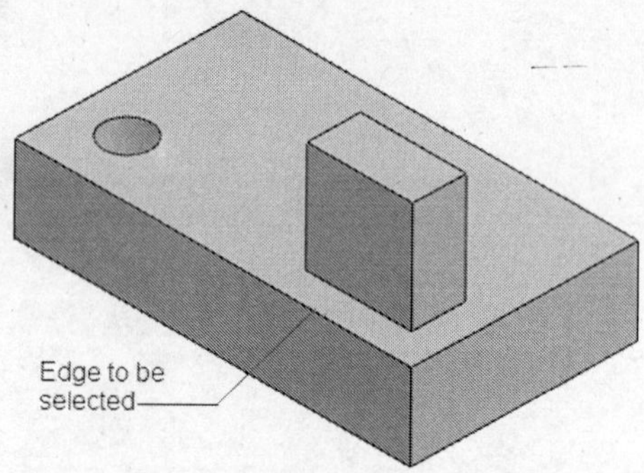

Figure 7-50 *Edge to be selected to apply the fillet feature*

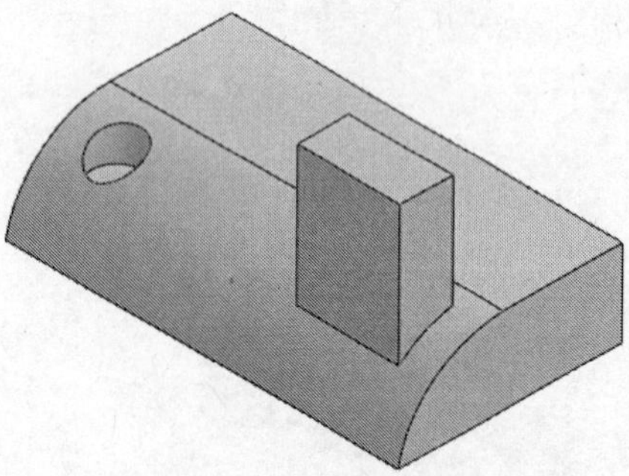

Figure 7-51 *Fillet feature created with the **Keep features** check box selected*

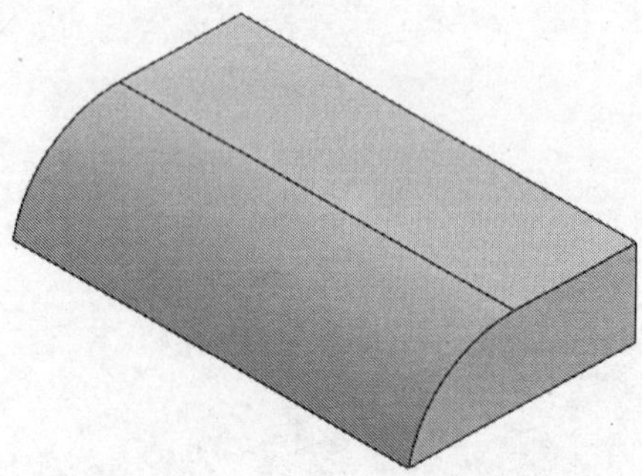

Figure 7-52 *Fillet feature created with the **Keep features** check box cleared*

Round corners

The **Round corners** option is used to round the edges at the corner of the fillet feature. To create a fillet feature with round corners, select the **Round corners** check box from the **Fillet Options** rollout after specifying all parameters of the fillet feature. Figure 7-53 shows a fillet feature created with the **Round corners** check box cleared and Figure 7-54 shows a fillet feature created with the **Round corners** check box selected.

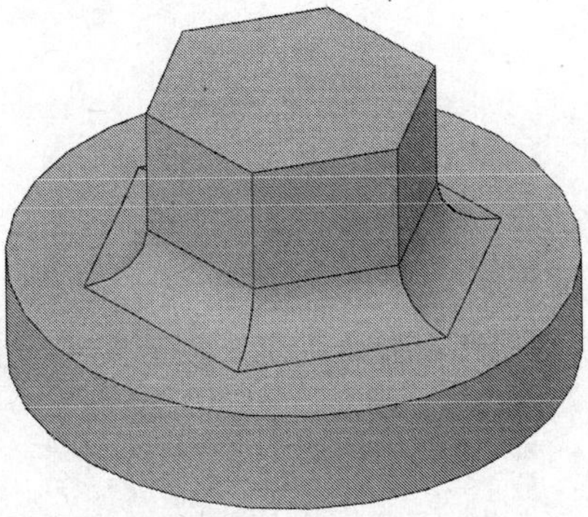

Figure 7-53 *Fillet feature created with the* **Round corners** *check box cleared*

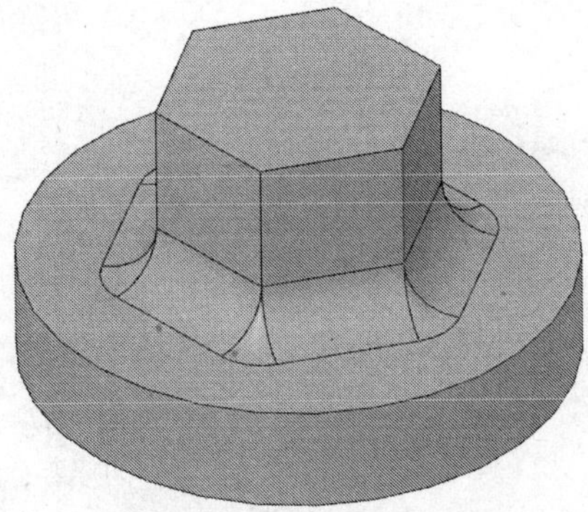

Figure 7-54 *Fillet feature created with the* **Round corners** *check box selected*

Overflow type

The **Overflow type** area is used to specify the physical condition that the fillet feature should adopt when it extends beyond an area. By default, SOLIDWORKS automatically adopts the best possible flow type to accommodate the fillet, depending on the geometric conditions. This is because the **Default** radio button is selected by default in the **Overflow type** area. The options in this area are discussed next.

Default

On selecting the **Default** radio button, SOLIDWORKS calculates the best suitable option for creating a fillet when the fillet feature created extends beyond a specified area.

Keep edge

The **Keep edge** radio button is selected when the fillet feature extends beyond a specified area. Therefore, to accommodate the fillet feature, this option will divide the fillet into multiple surfaces and the adjacent edges will not be disturbed, as shown in Figure 7-55. A dip will be created at the top of the fillet feature.

Keep surface

The **Keep surface** radio button in this area is selected to accommodate the fillet feature by trimming it. This will maintain the smoothness of the rounded fillet surface but it will disturb the adjacent edges. As this option maintains the smooth fillet surface, therefore the fillet will extend to the adjacent surface, as shown in Figure 7-56.

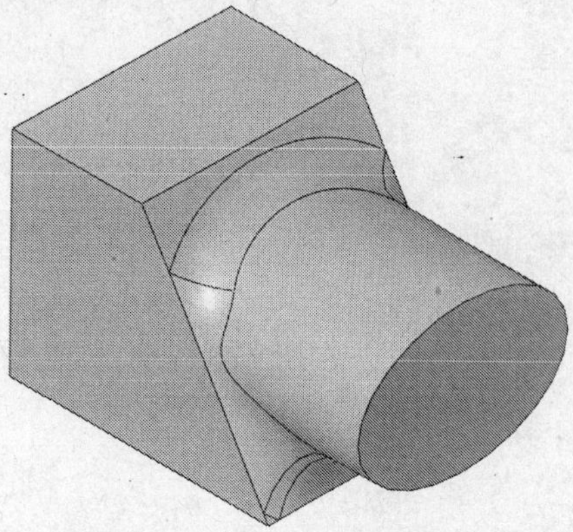

Figure 7-55 Fillet feature created with the ***Keep edge*** *radio button selected*

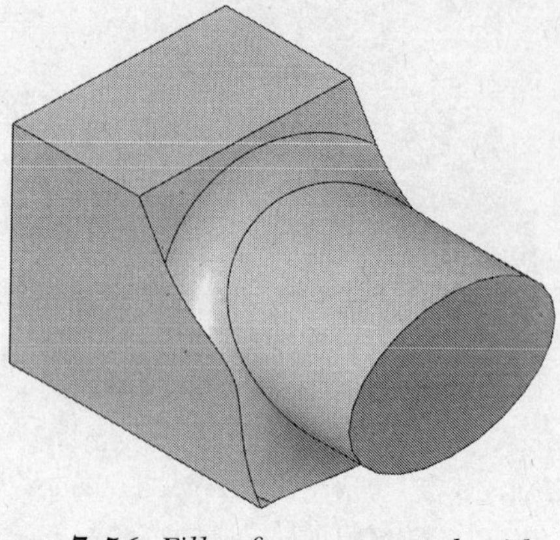

Figure 7-56 Fillet feature created with the ***Keep surface*** *radio button selected*

Feature attachment

The **Feature attachment** area regulates the fillet created at the attaching edges of different features. Note that this option will be available only when you select a whole feature to be filleted. When you select the **Omit attach edges** check box available in this area, the edges attaching the two features will not be filleted, as shown in Figure 7-57. However, to include the attaching edges in the fillet selection, clear the **Omit attach edges** check box; the fillet feature will be created, as shown in Figure 7-58.

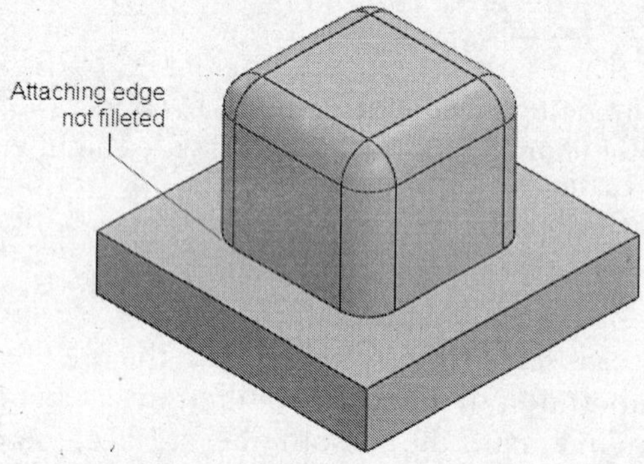

Figure 7-57 Fillet feature created with the ***Omit attach edges*** *check box selected*

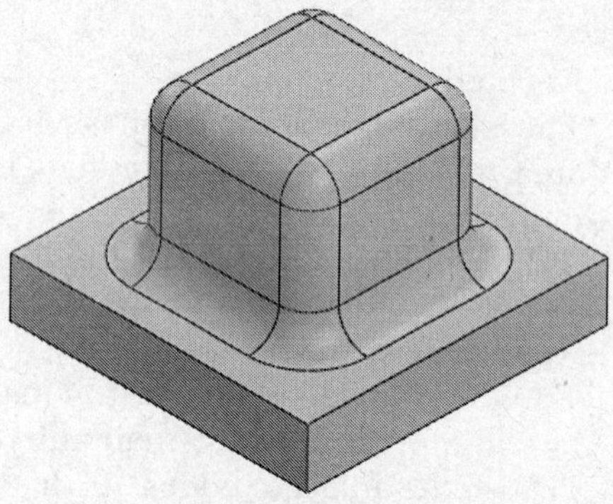

Figure 7-58 Fillet feature created with the ***Omit attach edges*** *check box cleared*

Creating Variable Size Fillet

The variable radius fillet is created by specifying different radii along the length of the selected edge at specified intervals. You can create a smooth or a straight transition between the vertices to which the radii are applied by selecting suitable options. To create a variable radius fillet, invoke the **Fillet PropertyManager**. Next, choose the **Variable Size Fillet** button from the **Fillet Type** rollout; the **Variable Radius Parameters** rollout will be displayed in the **Fillet PropertyManager**, as shown in Figure 7-59. Also, you will be prompted to select the edges to fillet.

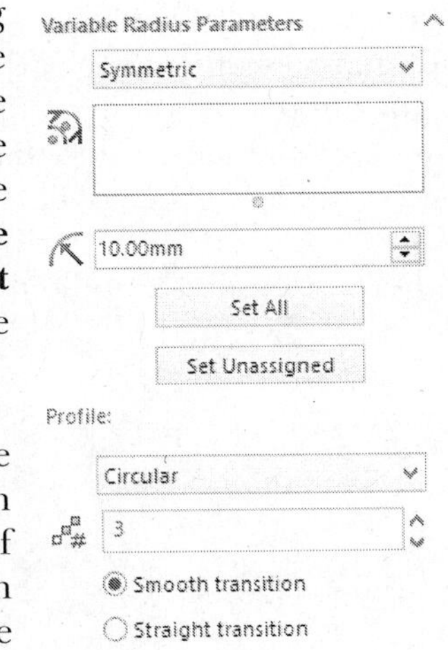

*Figure 7-59 The **Variable Radius Parameters** rollout*

Make sure that the **Edges to Fillet** selection box is activated in the **Items to Fillet** rollout to select the edges. Use the left mouse button to select the edge or the edges that you want to fillet; the name of the selected edge will be displayed in the **Edges to Fillet** selection box. By default no radius will be applied at the start point and the endpoint. Also, the variable radius callouts will be displayed at the vertices of the selected edge, as shown in Figure 7-60.

The names of the vertices on which the callouts are added are listed in the **Attached Radii** display box in the **Variable Radius Parameters** rollout. You will find three red points on the selected edge because by default, the value of the control points in the **Number of Instances** spinner is set to **3**. You can add additional control points using the **Number of Instances** spinner. These control points are also called movable points because you can change their positions. The additional radii are specified on these points on the selected edge.

Use the left mouse button to select the control points available on the selected edge. As you select the control point, the Radius and Position callouts are displayed for each control point, as shown in Figure 7-61. The name of the selected points will also be displayed in the **Attached Radii** display box.

You will notice that the position of the three points is described in terms of percentage. You can modify the position of the points by modifying the value of percentage in the **Position** area of the Radius and Position callout. Following this procedure, you can also modify the placement of the other points.

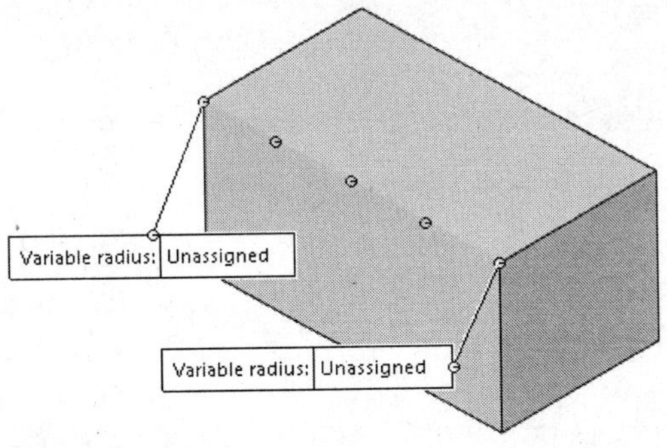

***Figure 7-60** Variable radius callouts displayed on the vertices of the selected edge*

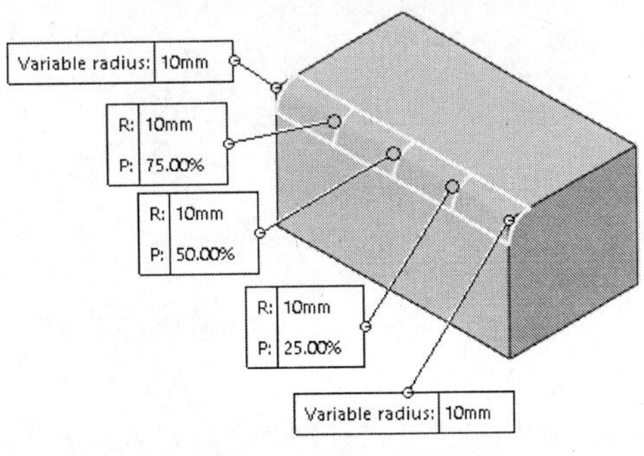

***Figure 7-61** The Radius and Position callouts displayed after selecting the control points*

Use the left mouse button to select the name of the vertex in the **Attached Radii** selection list; the name of the selected item will be highlighted in its respective callout. Use the **Radius** spinner to set the value of the radius for the selected item. You can also specify the value of the radius in the radius area of the callout. Set the value of each radius. The **Set All** button is used to assign the same value that is displayed in the **Radius** spinner to all the points. Figure 7-62 shows preview of the fillet feature with modified positions of the control points and the radius values specified for all points and vertices. Figure 7-63 shows the resulting fillet feature. The other options in this rollout are discussed next.

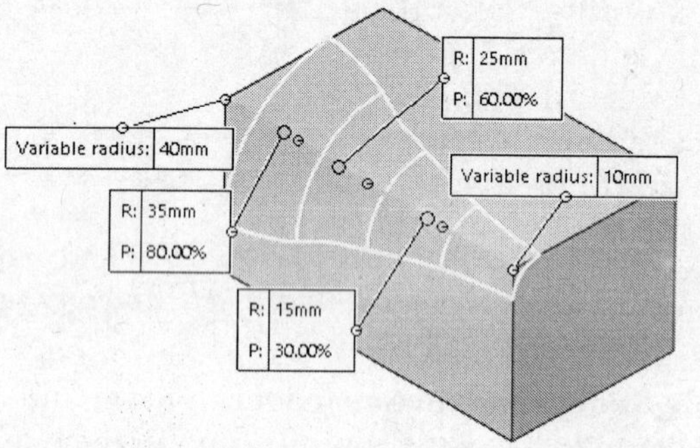

***Figure 7-62** Preview of the variable radius fillet*

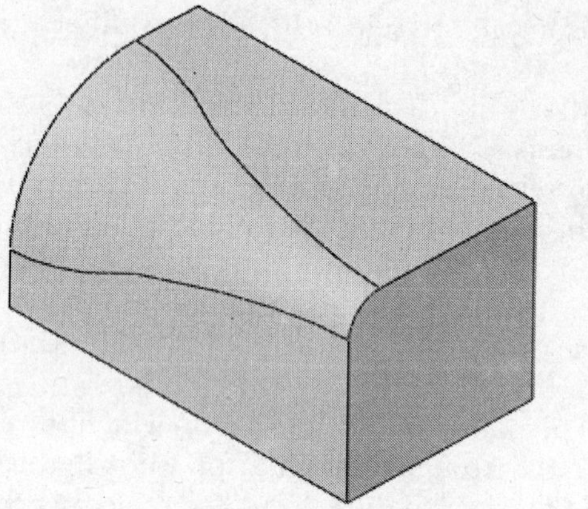

***Figure 7-63** Resulting fillet feature*

Smooth transition

Select this radio button to create a smooth transition by smoothly blending the fillets at the points and vertices on which the radius has been defined, as shown in Figure 7-64.

Straight transition

Select this radio button to create a linear transition by blending the fillets at the points and vertices on which you have defined the radius. In this case, the edge tangency is not maintained between one fillet radius and the adjacent face, as shown in Figure 7-65.

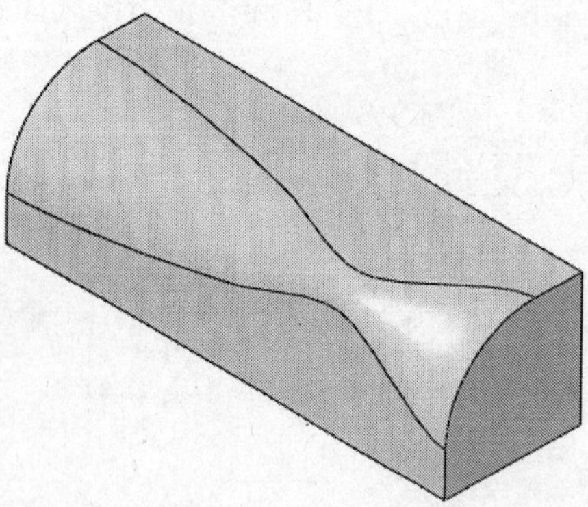

***Figure 7-64** Variable radius fillet with smooth transition*

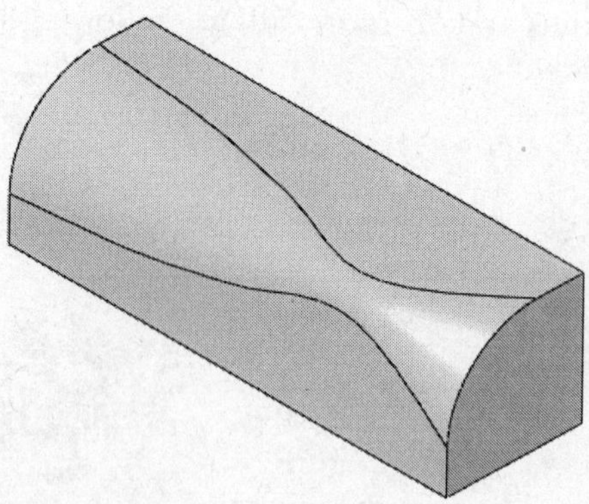

***Figure 7-65** Variable radius fillet with straight transition*

Creating Face Fillet

In SOLIDWORKS, you can add a fillet between two sets of faces. It blends the first set of faces with the second set of faces. It adds or removes the material according to the geometric conditions. It can also remove the faces completely or partially to accommodate the fillet feature. To create a face fillet feature, invoke the **Fillet PropertyManager** and choose the **Face Fillet** button from the **Fillet Type** rollout; the **Items To Fillet** rollout will be modified and the **Face Set 1** and **Face Set 2** selection boxes will be enabled. The **Fillet PropertyManager** with the **Face Fillet** button chosen is shown in Figure 7-66. Also, you will be prompted to select the faces to fillet for face set 1 and face set 2.

Use the left mouse button to select the first set of faces. You can even select more than one face in a set. The name of the selected faces will be displayed in the **Face Set 1** selection box and the selected faces will be highlighted. The Face Set 1 callout with radius will be displayed in the drawing area. Click in the **Face Set 2** selection box to invoke the selection tool and select the second set of faces. The second set of selected faces will be displayed in magenta and the Face Set 2 callout will be displayed in the drawing area. Also, the preview of the face fillet will be displayed in the drawing area. Now, set the value of the radius in the **Radius** spinner. The **Tangent propagation** check box is selected to create the face fillet tangent to the adjacent faces. This check box is selected by default. If you clear this check box, the fillet will not be forced to be tangent to the adjacent faces. Figure 7-67 shows the faces to be selected to apply the face fillet. Figure 7-68 displays the resulting fillet feature with three faces of the slot completely eliminated after applying the fillet.

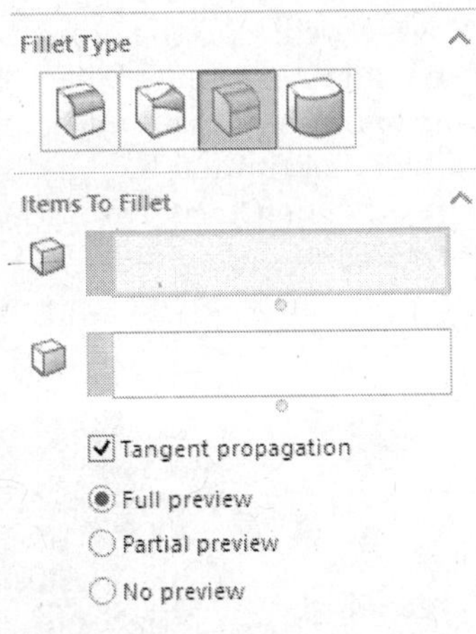

Figure 7-66 Partial view of ***Fillet PropertyManager*** *with the* ***Face Fillet*** *button chosen*

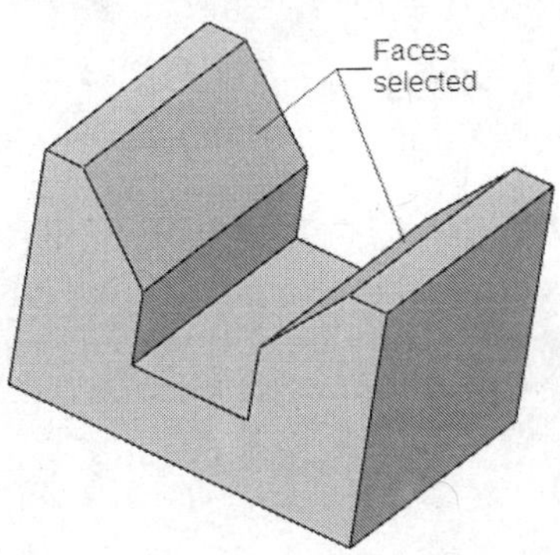

Figure 7-67 Faces to be selected

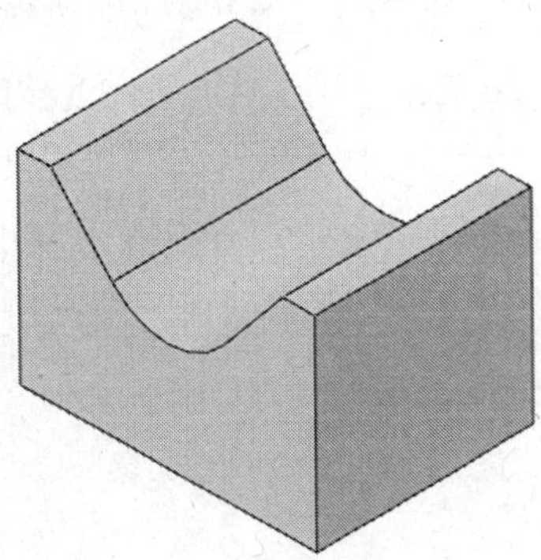

Figure 7-68 Resulting fillet feature

Creating the Face Fillet using the Hold Line

The radius and the shape of the fillet can be controlled by using a hold line. A hold line can be a set of edges, or a split line projected on a face. You will learn more about split lines in the later chapters. To create a face fillet using a hold line, invoke the **Fillet PropertyManager**. On doing so, the selection mode will be activated by default in the **Face Set 1** selection box in the **Items To Fillet** rollout and you will be prompted to select the faces to be filleted. Select the faces for the face set 1; the names of the selected faces will be displayed in the **Face Set 1** selection box and the selected faces will be highlighted. Now, click in the **Face Set 2** selection box to activate the selection mode and select the faces to add in the Face Set 2; the selected faces will be displayed in magenta. Also, the preview of the face fillet with the default settings will be displayed in the drawing area. By default, the **Tangent propagation** check box is selected. Therefore, you do not need to select the tangent faces in both the face sets. Next, select the **Hold Line** option in the **Fillet Method** drop-down list from the **Fillet Parameters** rollout, refer to Figure 7-69.

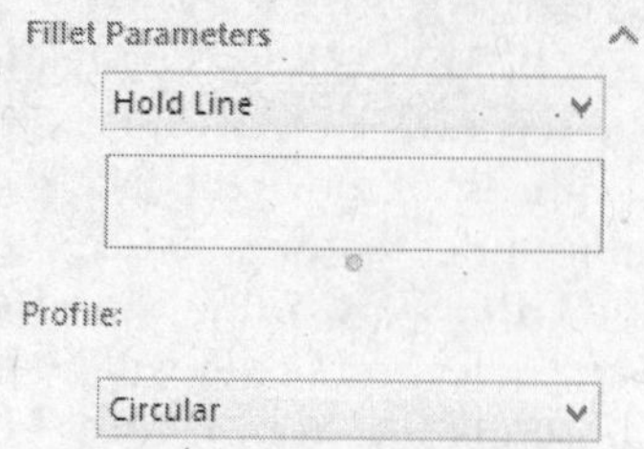

***Figure 7-69** The **Fillet Parameters** rollout*

Now, left-click on the **Hold Line Edges** selection box and select the hold line or lines. The preview of the face fillet will be modified automatically. Note that the **Radius** spinner will not be available in the **Items To Fillet** rollout and the radius of the fillet will be determined by the distance between the hold line and the edges or faces selected to be filleted. The **Circular** option is selected by default in the **Profile** drop-down list. Now, choose the **OK** button from the **Fillet PropertyManager**. Figure 7-70 shows an example in which the faces and the hold line are selected. Figure 7-71 shows the resulting face fillet using the hold line.

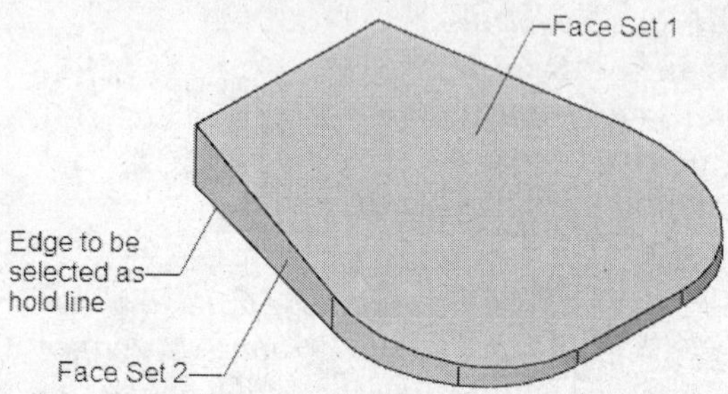

***Figure 7-70** Faces and hold line to be selected*

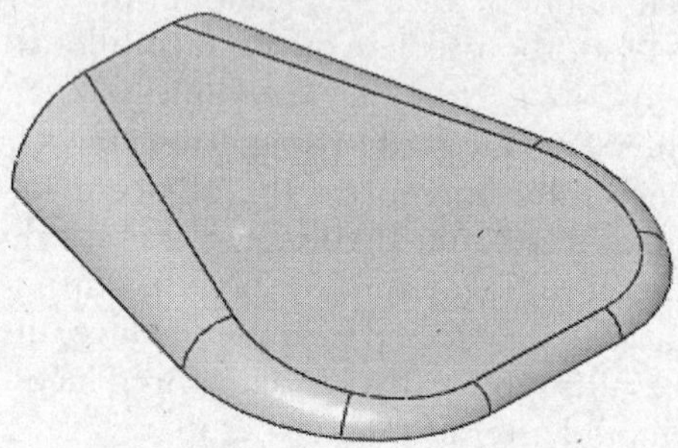

***Figure 7-71** Resulting face fillet*

Curvature Continuous in the Face Fillet with Hold Line

The **Curvature Continuous** option of the **Profile** drop-down list in the **Fillet Property Manager** is selected to apply the face fillet feature with continuous curvature throughout the fillet feature. Note that the curvature continuous fillets are spline based whereas the circular fillets are arc based. Figure 7-72 shows a model in which a face fillet is created on both the pillars using the hold line. On the right pillar, the face fillet is created with the **Circular** option selected and on the left pillar, the face fillet is created with the **Curvature Continuous** option selected.

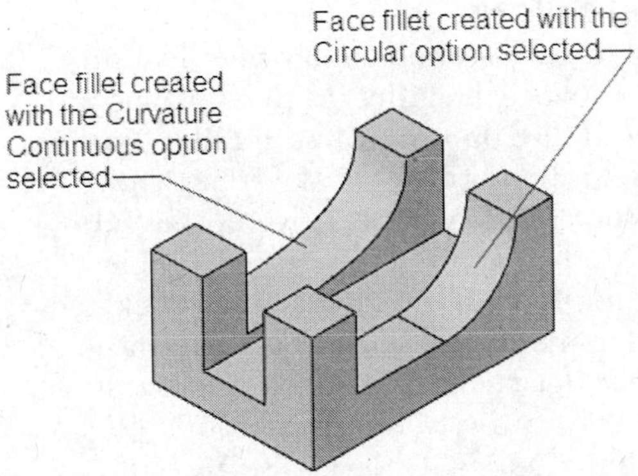

Figure 7-72 Face fillet created with the ***Curvature Continuous*** *and* ***Circular*** *options selected*

Chord Width

Consider a case in which you have applied a face fillet to the faces that are at an angle other than 90 degrees to each other. You will notice that additional material is added to the fillet on the side that forms an acute angle with the other face, refer to Figure 7-73. However, if you select the **Chord Width** option from the **Fillet Method** drop-down list in the **Fillet PropertyManager**, a fillet of constant width will be applied between the selected faces, refer to Figure 7-74.

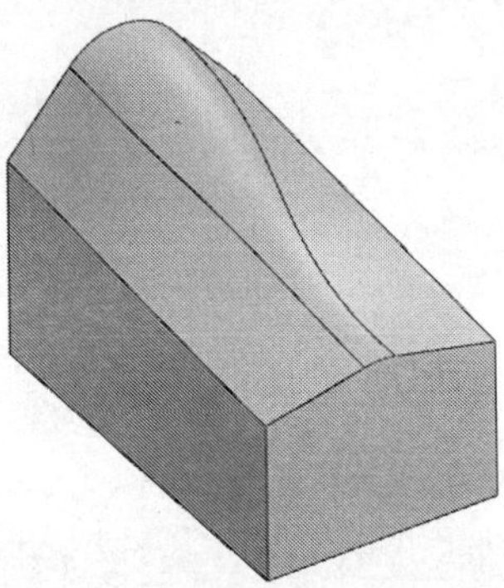

Figure 7-73 Face fillet without the ***Chord Width*** *option selected*

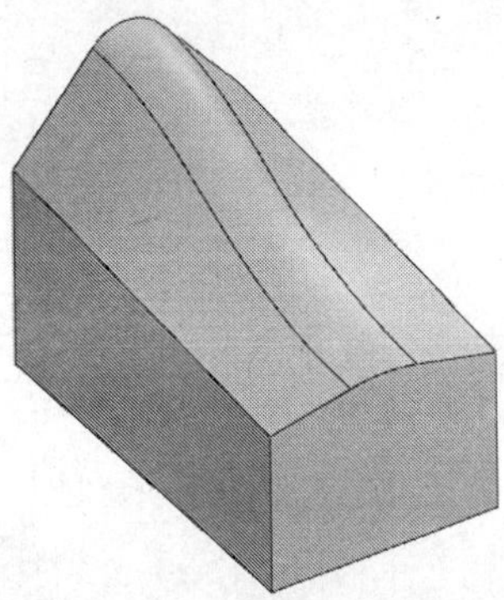

Figure 7-74 Face fillet with the ***Chord Width*** *option selected*

Creating Full Round Fillet

A full round fillet is used to add a semi-circular fillet feature. To create a full round fillet, invoke the **Fillet PropertyManager** and select the **Full Round Fillet** button from the **Fillet Type** rollout; the **Items To Fillet** rollout will be displayed, as shown in Figure 7-75. The selection mode will be active in the **Side Face Set 1** selection box and you will be prompted to select faces. Select the first face for the Side Face Set 1. Now, click in the **Center Face Set** selection box and select the center face. Next, click in the **Side Face Set 2** selection box and select the face for the Side Face Set 2; the preview of the full round fillet will be displayed in the drawing area. Choose the **OK** button from the **Fillet PropertyManager**. Figure 7-76 shows the faces to be selected to create the full round fillet. Note that the third face is the left face which is parallel to the first selected face. Figure 7-77 shows the resulting full round fillet.

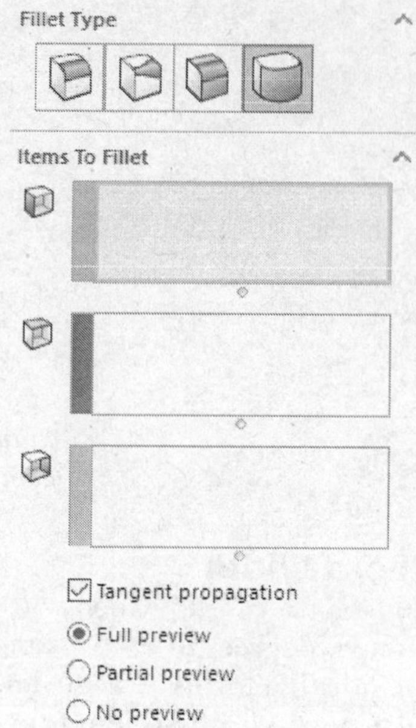

*Figure 7-75 The **Items To Fillet** rollout*

> **Tip**
>
> *You can turn on or off the display of the tangent edges of the model. To do so, choose **Options** from the Menu Bar to display the **System Options - General** dialog box. Select the **Display** option from the left pane and then select the **As visible** or **Removed** radio button from the **Part/Assembly tangent edge display** area.*

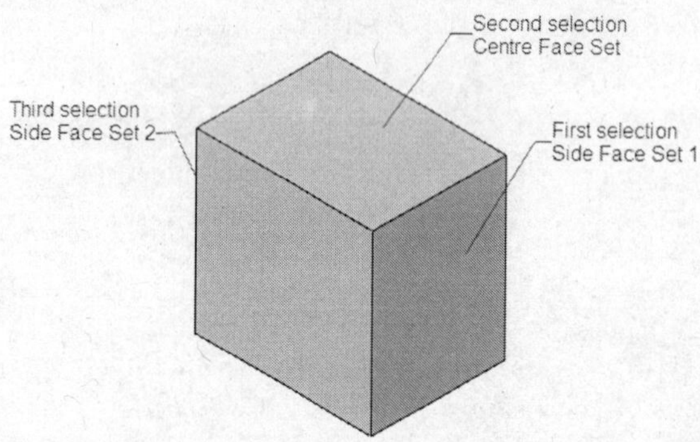

***Figure 7-76** Faces selected to create the full round fillet*

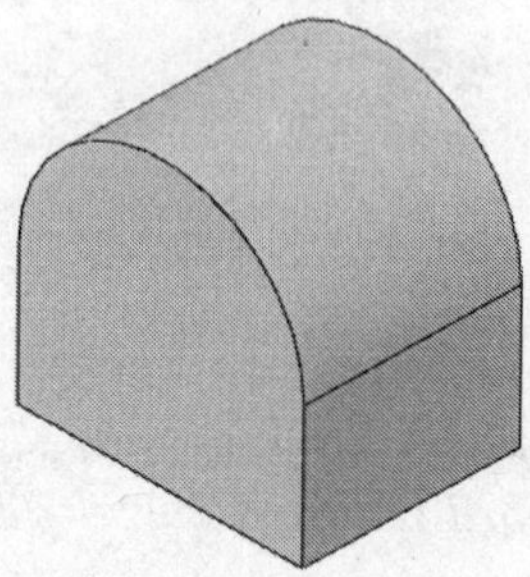

***Figure 7-77** Resulting full round fillet*

Selection Options

You have already learned about the basic and advanced modeling tools. Now, you will learn about some selection options that will increase your productivity and speed of modeling. These options are discussed next.

Select Other

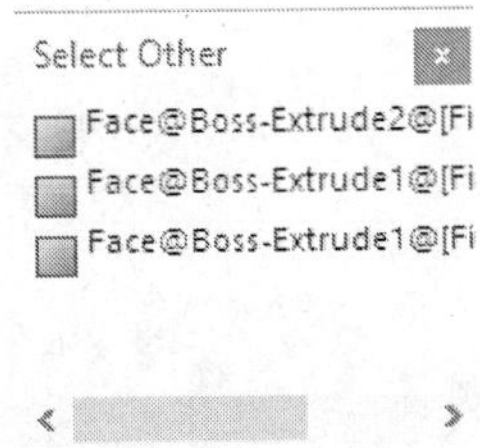

*Figure 7-78 The **Select Other** list box*

The **Select Other** option is the most common tool to cycle through entities for selection. This option is used when the selection is difficult in a multifeatured complex model. Before invoking any other tool, select an entity and do not move the mouse; a pop-up toolbar will be displayed. Choose the **Select Other** option from the pop-up toolbar to display the **Select Other** list box, as shown in Figure 7-78, and the select cursor will be replaced by the select next cursor. The entities that surround the selected entities will be listed in this list box. Also, the entities that are hidden behind the selected entity will be listed in this list box. When you move the cursor on the name of an entity in the **Select Other** list box, the entity will be highlighted in the drawing area. To select an entity using this list box, you need to select the name of the entity in the list box.

If you select a face and invoke the **Select Other** list box, the display of the selected face will be turned off and you can easily select the face that is behind the selected face. The name of the hidden face will be displayed in the **Select Other** list box.

Select Loop

The **Select Loop** option is used to select the loops. You can also cycle through various loops before confirming the selection. This option is useful when you are working on a complex model and you need to select a loop from that model. Select any of the edges of the loop and right-click to invoke the shortcut menu. Choose the **Select Loop** option from the shortcut menu. The loop that is possible by selecting that edge will be highlighted and an arrow will be displayed in yellow. Move the cursor on that arrow and when the arrow is highlighted in orange, left-click to cycle through the loops. Repeat these steps until you select the required loop. Figure 7-79 shows a loop selected using the **Select Loop** option. Figure 7-80 shows the second loop selected when you click on the arrow to cycle through the loops.

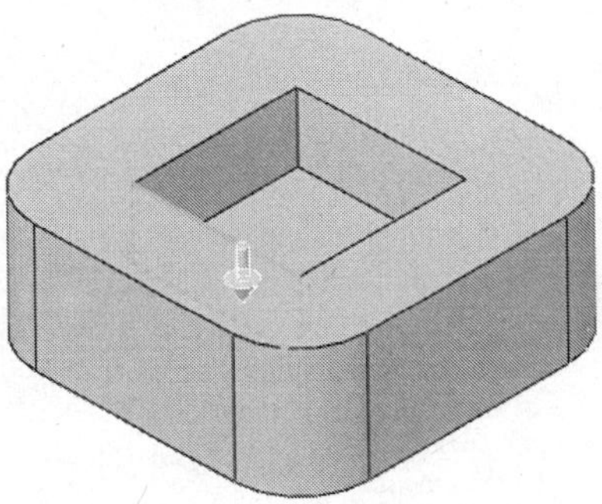

*Figure 7-79 Loop selected using the **Select Loop** option*

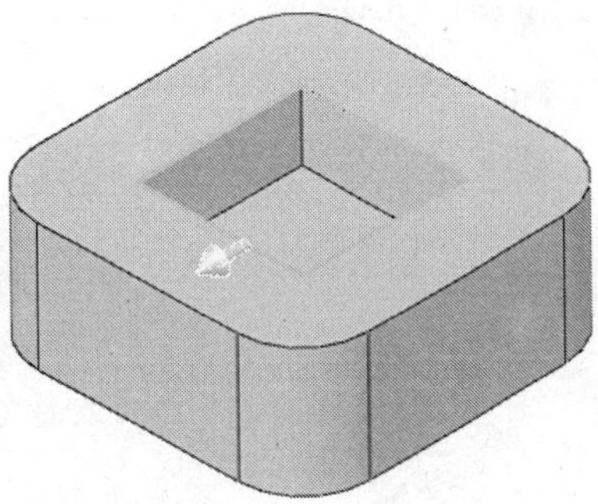

Figure 7-80 Second loop selected while cycling through the loops

Select Partial Loop

This option is used to select the partial loop created by joining two edges. To select a partial loop, select two edges, as shown in Figure 7-81. Invoke the shortcut menu and choose the **Select Partial Loop** option from the shortcut menu. Generally, the selection point on the second edge defines the major or minor partial loop selection. Figure 7-82 shows the resulting partial loop selected.

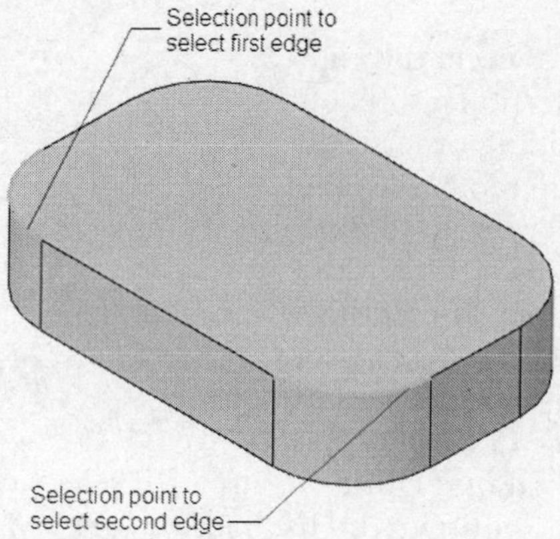

Figure 7-81 Selecting edges to define the partial loop

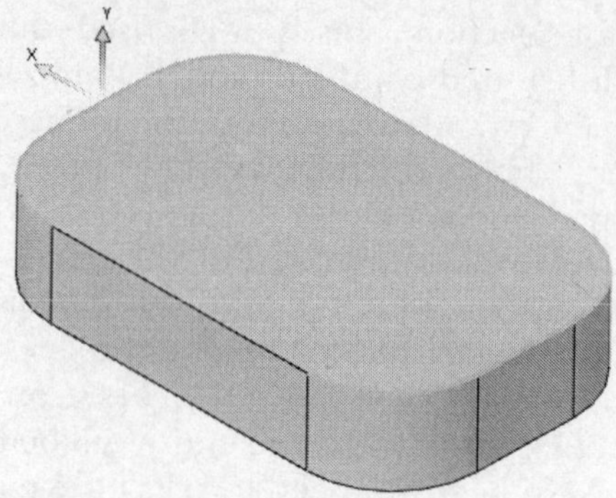

Figure 7-82 Resulting partial loop selected

Select Midpoint

The **Select Midpoint** option is used to select the mid-points of the selected edge without creating a separate point. This option will be available in the shortcut menu only when an edge is selected. To use this option, select an edge using the **Select** tool and then right-click; a shortcut menu will be displayed. Choose the **Select Midpoint** option from the shortcut menu. The mid point of the selected edge will be highlighted in blue.

Select Tangency

The **Select Tangency** option is used to automatically select the edges or the faces that are tangent to the selected face. This option will be available in the shortcut menu only when a face or an edge is tangent to the selected face or edge. To use this option, select any face or edge using the **Select** tool and right-click on it; a shortcut menu will be displayed. Choose the **Select Tangency** option from the shortcut menu.

Tip

*The **Select Midpoint** option in the shortcut menu is generally used in the sketching environment or while creating the 3D sketches. You will learn more about the 3D sketches in the later chapters.*

Creating Fillets Using the FilletXpert

CommandManager: Features > Fillet flyout > Fillet
SOLIDWORKS menus: Insert > Features > Fillet/Round
Toolbar: Features > Fillet flyout > Fillet

The **FilletXpert** tool allows you to create single or multiple fillets, change the existing fillet, and create fillets at corners. To create fillets using the **FilletXpert**, invoke the **Fillet PropertyManager** and then choose the **FilletXpert** button; the **FilletXpert** options will be displayed, as shown in Figure 7-83.

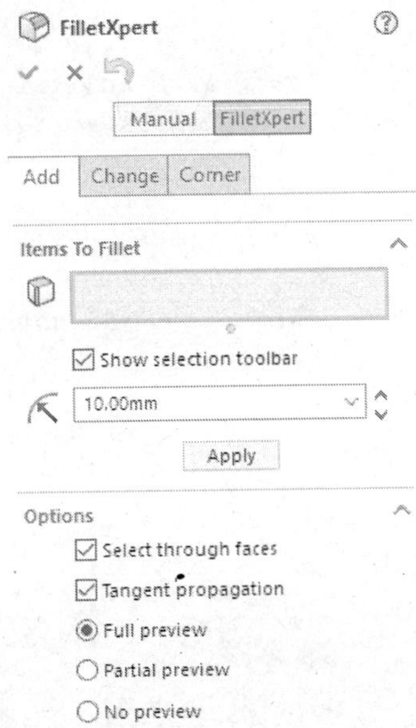

*Figure 7-83 The **FilletXpert** options in the **Fillet Property Manager***

By default, the **Add** tab is chosen in the **FilletXpert**. This tab provides the options to create single or multiple fillets. To create a single fillet, select an edge, specify the fillet radius, and then choose the **OK** button. To create multiple fillets, create a single fillet, and then choose **Apply** from the **Items To Fillet** rollout. Now, add other fillets. Once a fillet is created, it will be listed in the **Existing Fillets** rollout of the **Change** tab of the **FilletXpert PropertyManager**. You can select the existing fillets from the **Existing Fillets** rollout of this tab to resize or remove them.

Choose the **Corner** tab to modify the shape of the fillets that are formed at the intersection of three fillets, as shown in Figure 7-84. Note that the fillet at the corner can be modified only if it is created by the combination of concave and convex shaped fillets. To change the shape of a corner fillet, invoke the **FilletXpert PropertyManager** and then choose the **Corner** tab; the selection box in the **Corner Faces** rollout will be activated and you will be prompted to select the corner fillet to be modified. Select the corner fillet from the model; the **Show Alternatives** button will be available in the **Corner Faces** rollout. Choose this button; the **Select Alternatives** display box, with all possible alternatives will be displayed. Select the required shape from the display box; the shape of the corner fillet will be modified in the model.

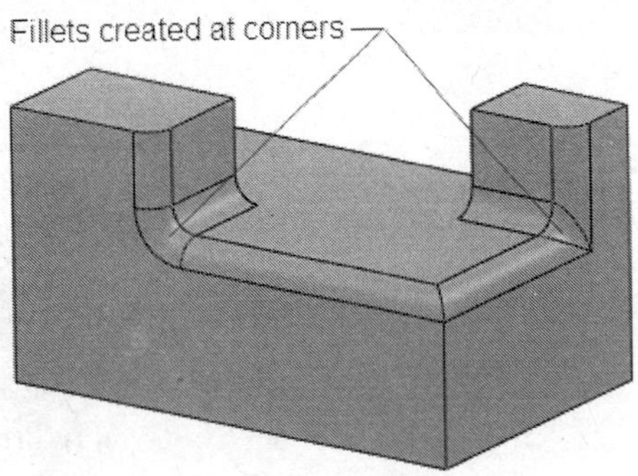

Figure 7-84 Fillets created at the corners

After modifying the shape of a corner fillet, you can copy its shape to the other corner fillets. To do so, select the modified corner fillet; it will be displayed in the selection box in the **Corner Faces** rollout. Next, click on the selection box in the **Copy Targets** rollout. Now, select the corner fillets to be changed; the **Copy to** button will be enabled in the **Copy Targets** rollout. Choose the **Copy to** button; the shape of the selected fillet will be modified. Also, the **Fillet-Corner** node will be added to the **FeatureManager Design Tree**. If the **Enable Highlighting** check box is selected in the **Copy Targets** rollout, the filleted corner to which the selected fillet can be applied will be highlighted in the model. Figure 7-85 shows the fillet to be copied and modified. Figure 7-86 shows the resulting copied fillet.

Tip

*1. If you select an edge and pause when the **Add** tab is chosen in the **FilletXpert PropertyManager**, a selection toolbar will be displayed. Move the cursor on the buttons in this toolbar; the corresponding entities will be highlighted in the model. Click when the required entities are highlighted; the entities will be selected.*

*2. You can turn off the display of selection toolbar, which is displayed on selecting an edge while using the **Fillet** tool. To do so, clear the **Show selection toolbar** check box from the **Fillet PropertyManager**.*

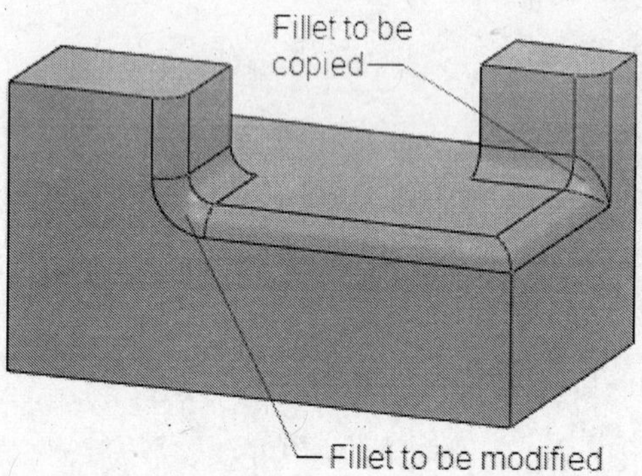

Figure 7-85 *Fillets to be copied and changed*

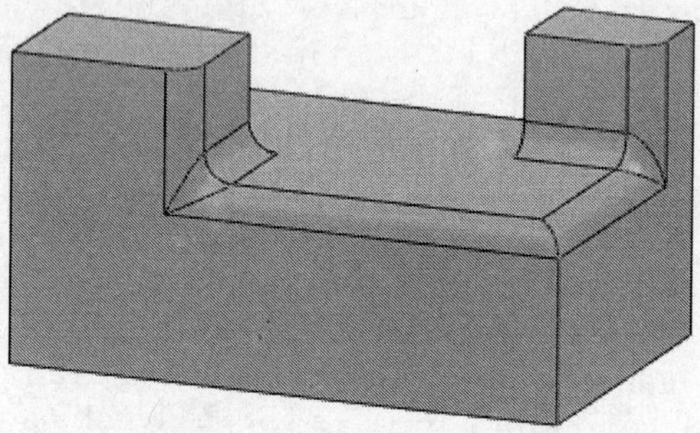

Figure 7-86 *Resulting copied fillet*

Creating Chamfers

CommandManager:	Features > Fillet flyout > Chamfer
SOLIDWORKS menus:	Insert > Features > Chamfer
Toolbar:	Features > Fillet flyout > Chamfer

Chamfering is a process in which the sharp edges are beveled in order to reduce the area of stress concentration. This process also eliminates the undesirable sharp edges and corners. In SOLIDWORKS, a chamfer is created using the **Chamfer** tool. This tool is invoked by choosing the **Chamfer** button from the **Fillet** flyout in the **Features CommandManager**, refer to Figure 7-87. On choosing this button, the **Chamfer PropertyManager** is displayed, as shown in Figure 7-88. Various types of chamfers that can be created using the **Chamfer PropertyManager** are discussed next.

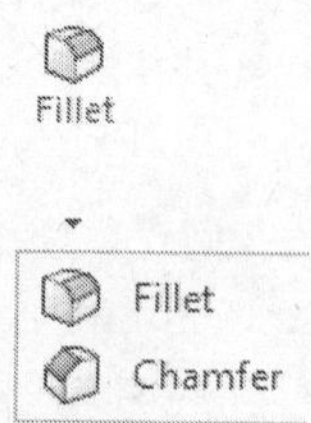

Figure 7-87 *Tools in the **Fillet** flyout*

Creating Edge Chamfer

The chamfers that are applied to the edges are known as the edge chamfer. To create an edge chamfer, invoke the **Chamfer PropertyManager** and then select the edges to be chamfered. On selecting an edge to be chamfered, the preview of the chamfer with a distance and angle callout will be displayed in the drawing area. The name of the selected edge will be displayed in the **Edges, Faces and Loops** selection box. Also, the selected entity will be highlighted and the preview will be displayed. The **Tangent propagation** check box is selected by default. Therefore, the edges tangent to the selected edge are selected automatically. If the **Partial preview** button is chosen by default, then choose the **Full preview** button to display the full preview of the chamfer feature. Figure 7-89 shows the edge to be selected for chamfering and Figure 7-90 shows the full preview of the chamfer feature.

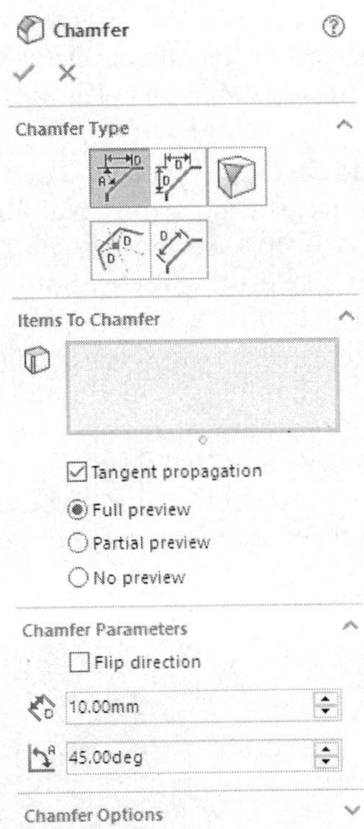

Figure 7-88 The Chamfer PropertyManager

By default, the **Angle Distance** button is selected in the **Chamfer Type** rollout. Therefore, the distance and angle callouts are displayed in the drawing area. You can set the value of the distance and angle using the **Distance** and **Angle** spinners or enter their values directly in the **Distance** and **Angle** callouts. The **Flip direction** check box is used to specify the direction of the distance measurement. You can also flip the direction by clicking on the arrow in the drawing area.

> **Tip**
> *You can also select a face to apply the chamfer feature. If you do so, the chamfer will be applied to all the edges of the selected face.*

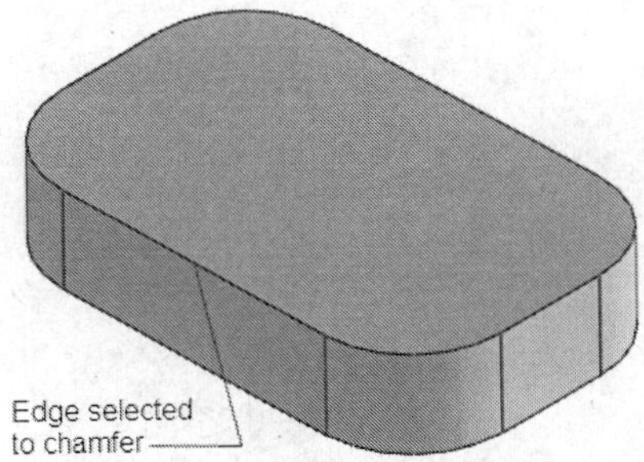

Figure 7-89 *Edge selected to chamfer*

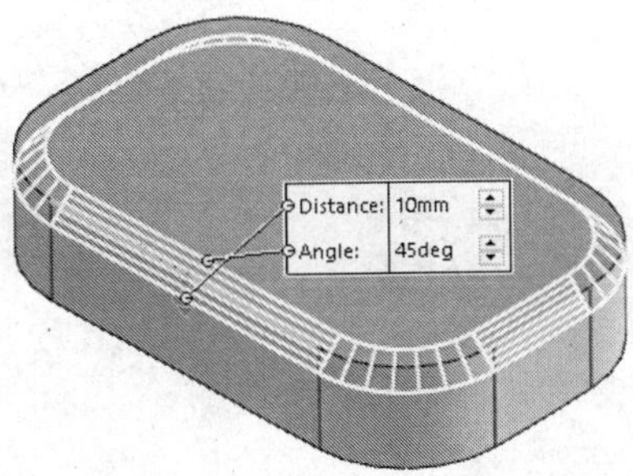

Figure 7-90 *Preview of the chamfer feature*

If you select the **Distance Distance** button from the **Chamfer Type** rollout, the **Flip direction** check box will be replaced by the **Chamfer Method** drop-down list. Also, the **Angle** and **Distance** callouts will be replaced by the **Distance** callout. By default, the **Symmetric** option is selected in this drop-down list. Set the value of the chamfer distance in the **Distance** spinner or specify the value in the callout. If you need to specify the different distance for creating the chamfer, select the **Asymmetric** option in this drop-down list. The **Distance 2** spinner will appear in the **Chamfer Parameters** rollout. Now, you can specify different values in the **Distance 1** and **Distance 2** spinners. After specifying all parameters, choose the **OK** button from the **Chamfer PropertyManager**. Figure 7-91 shows the chamfer created on a base plate.

Creating Vertex Chamfer

You can also use the **Chamfer** tool to add a chamfer to the selected vertex by chopping the selected vertex to a specified distance. To create the vertex chamfer, invoke the **Chamfer PropertyManager** and select the **Vertex** button from the **Chamfer Type** rollout. Select the vertex; the preview of the chamfer will be displayed in the drawing area with the **Distance** callouts. Figure 7-92 shows the vertex to be selected and Figure 7-93 shows preview of the vertex chamfer. Set the value of the chamfer distance along each edge in the **Distance 1**, **Distance 2**, and **Distance 3** spinners. You can also specify the value of the chamfer distance in the distance callouts. If you want to specify an equal distance for all the edges, select the **Equal distance** check box. After specifying all parameters, choose the **OK** button from the **Chamfer PropertyManager**. Figure 7-94 shows the vertex chamfer feature created on the base feature.

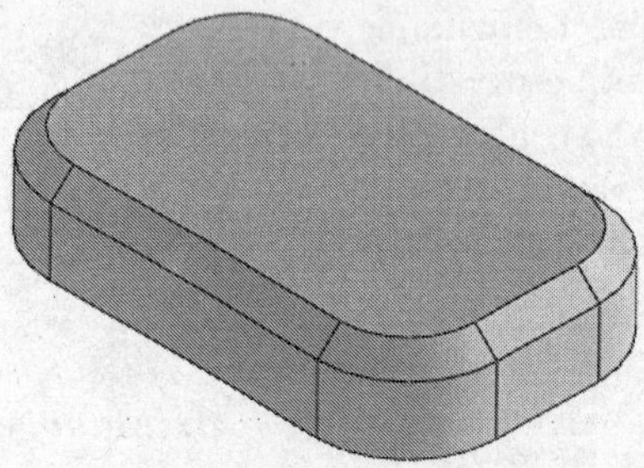

Figure 7-91 *Chamfer created on a base plate*

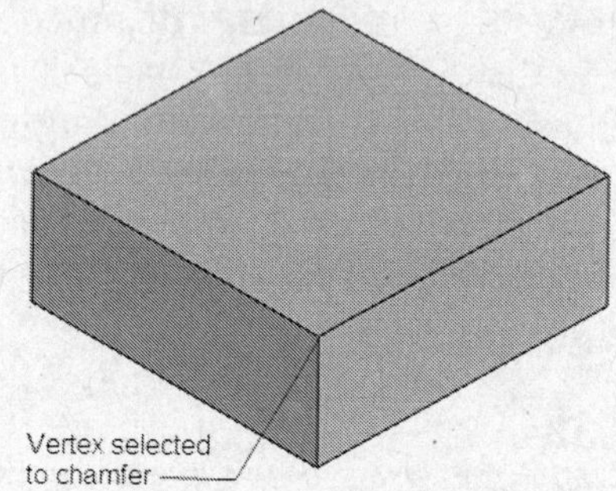

Figure 7-92 *Vertex to be selected*

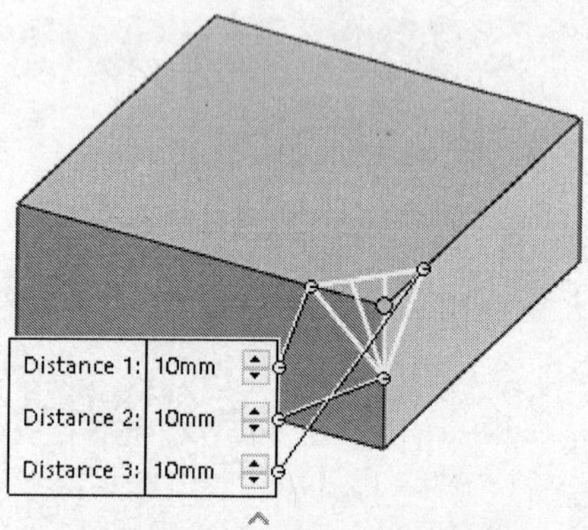

Figure 7-93 *Preview of the vertex chamfer*

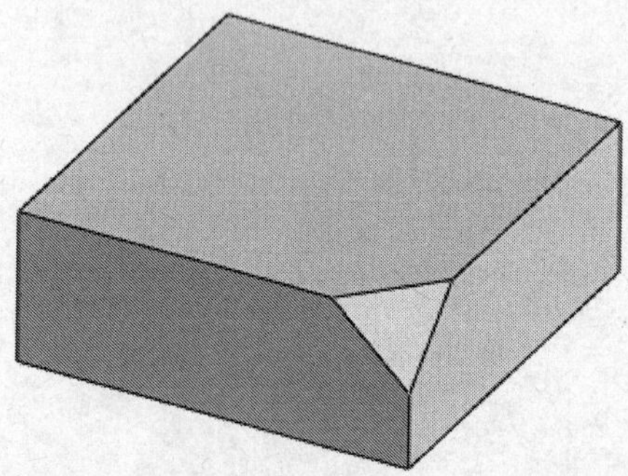

Figure 7-94 *Vertex chamfer created on a base feature*

Chamfer created with and without Keep features Option

If you have boss or cut features in a model and the chamfer created is large enough to consume those features, it is recommended that you select the **Keep features** check box. If this check box is cleared, the chamfer feature will not consume the features that will obstruct its path.

Note that the features that are consumed by the chamfer feature are not deleted from the model. They are removed from the model because of some geometric inconsistency. When you rollback or delete the chamfer, the consumed features will reappear. Figure 7-95 shows the chamfer feature with the **Keep features** check box cleared and Figure 7-96 shows the chamfer feature with the **Keep features** check box selected.

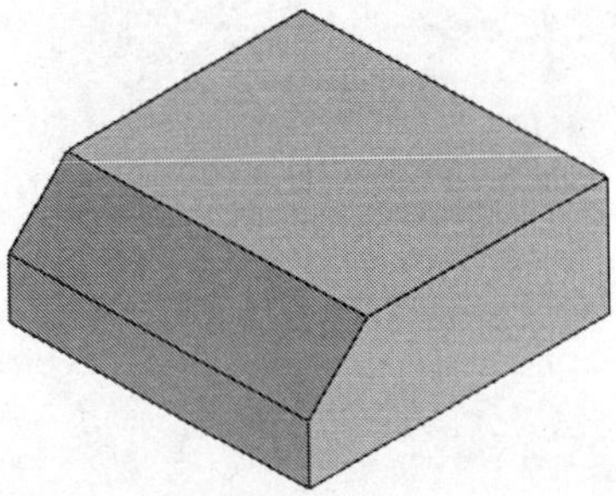

***Figure 7-95** Chamfer feature with the **Keep features** check box cleared*

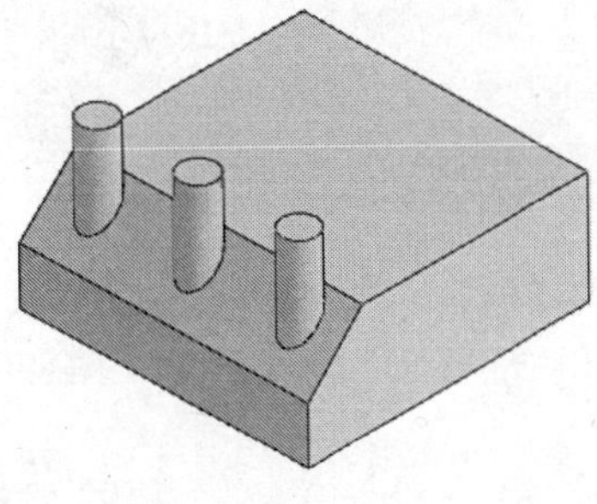

***Figure 7-96** Chamfer feature with the **Keep features** check box selected*

Creating Face Face Chamfer

In SOLIDWORKS, you can add a chamfer between sets of faces. Chamfer blends non-adjacent or non-continuous faces and adds or removes the material according to the geometric conditions. In addition, it can remove the faces completely or partially to accommodate the feature. To create a face face chamfer feature, invoke the **Chamfer PropertyManager** and choose the **Face Face** button from the **Chamfer Type** rollout, refer to Figure 7-97; the **Items To Chamfer** rollout will be modified and the **Face Set 1** and **Face Set 2** selection boxes will be enabled. Also, you will be prompted to select the faces to chamfer for Face Set 1 and Face Set 2. Select the face(s) for the first set. The name of the selected faces will be displayed in the **Face Set 1** selection box. The selected faces will be highlighted, also the Face Set 1 callout with distance will be attached to the selected faces. Click in the **Face Set 2** selection box and select the second set of face(s). The second set of selected faces will be displayed in magenta and the Face Set 2 callout will be attached to the selected face. Also, the preview of the face face chamfer will be displayed in the graphics area. Now, set the value of the distance in the **Offset Distance** spinner. Figure 7-98 shows the faces to be selected to apply the face chamfer. Figure 7-99 displays the resulting chamfer feature with three faces of the slot completely eliminated after applying the chamfer.

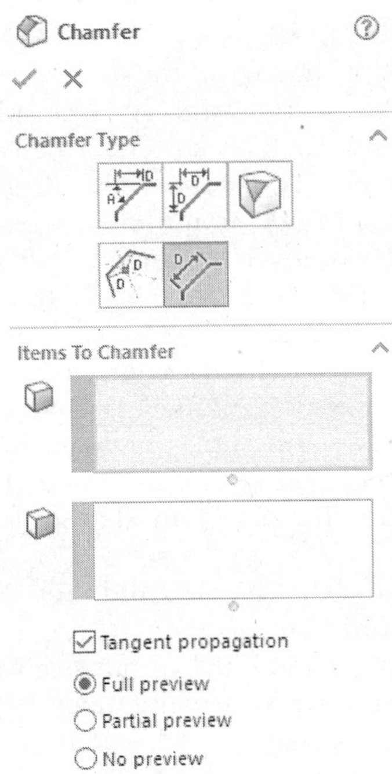

***Figure 7-97** Partial view of **Chamfer PropertyManager** with the **Face Face** button chosen*

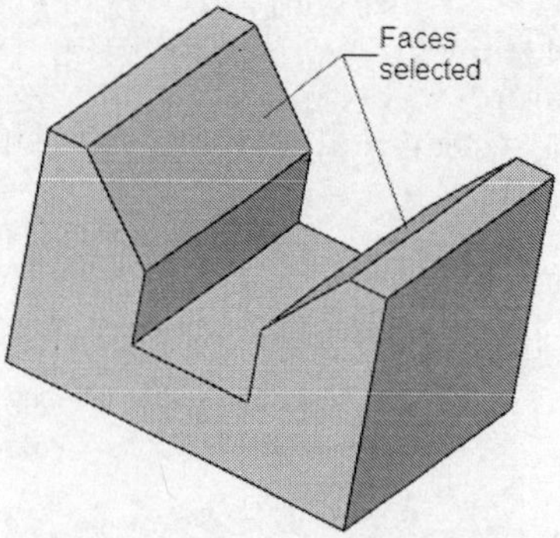

Figure 7-98 Faces to be selected

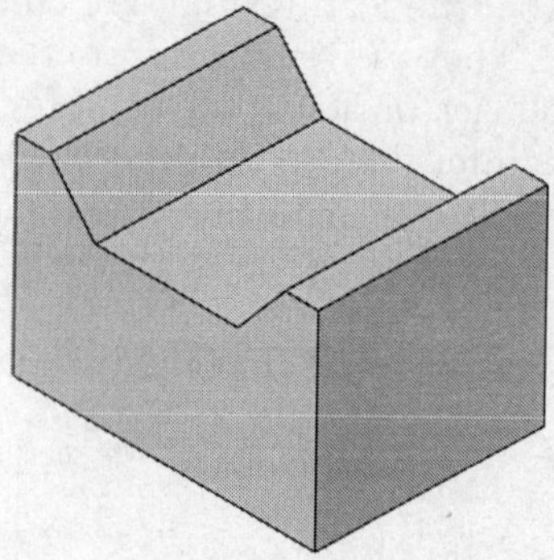

Figure 7-99 Resulting chamfer feature

Tip
In SOLIDWORKS, you can swap a face face chamfer with a face fillet feature. To do so, right-click on the chamfer feature in the ***FeatureManager Design Tree*** *and choose the* ***Convert Chamfer to Fillet*** *option.*

Creating the Face Face Chamfer using the Hold Line

You can control the distance and the shape of the chamfer by defining a hold line. A hold line can be a set of edges or a split line projected on a face. You will learn more about split lines in the later chapters. To create a face face chamfer using a hold line, invoke the **Chamfer PropertyManager**. Next, choose the **Face Face** button; the selection mode will be activated and you will be prompted to select the faces to be chamfered. Also, the **Face Set 1** selection box of the **Items To Chamfer** rollout will be enabled. Select the faces for the face set 1; the names of the selected faces will be displayed in the **Face Set 1** selection box and the selected faces will be highlighted. Now, click in the **Face Set 2** selection box to activate the selection mode and select the faces to add in the face set 2; the selected faces will be displayed in magenta. Also, the preview of the face chamfer with the default settings will be displayed in the drawing area. By default, the **Tangent propagation** check box is selected in the **Chamfer PropertyManager**. Therefore, you do not need to select the tangent faces. Next, select the **Hold Line** option in the **Chamfer Method** drop-down list of the **Chamfer Parameters** rollout, refer to Figure 7-100.

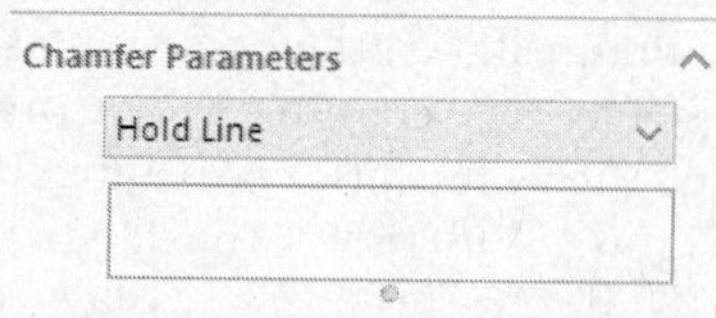

Figure 7-100 The ***Chamfer Parameters*** *rollout*

Now, click on the **Hold Line Edges** selection box and select the hold line or lines; the preview of the face face chamfer will be modified automatically. Note that the **Distance** spinner is not available in the **Items To Chamfer** rollout and the distance of the chamfer will be determined by the distance between the hold line and the edges or faces selected to be chamfered. Now, choose the **OK** button from the **Chamfer PropertyManager**. Figure 7-101 shows an example in which the faces and the hold line are selected. Figure 7-102 shows the resulting face face chamfer using the hold line.

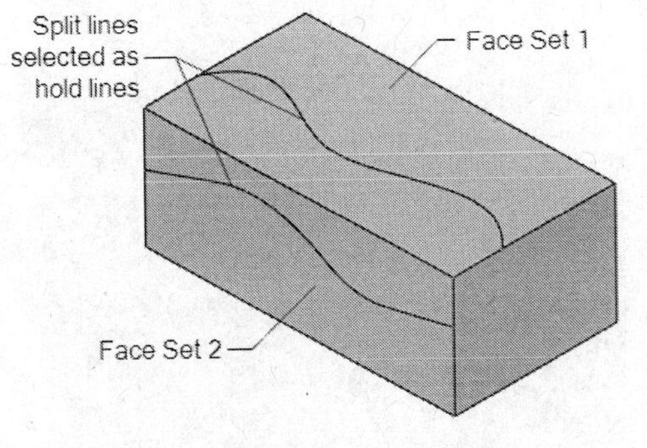

Figure 7-101 Faces and hold lines to be selected

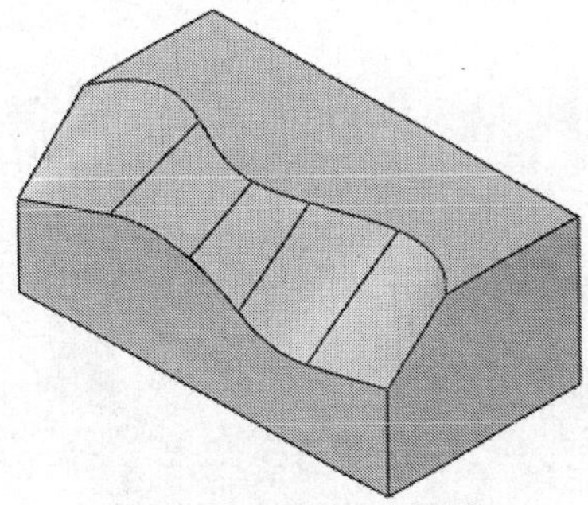

Figure 7-102 Resulting face fillet

Chord Width

Consider a case in which you have applied a face chamfer to the faces that are at an angle other than 90 degrees to each other. You will notice that the additional material is removed from the chamfer on the side that forms an acute angle with the other face, refer to Figure 7-103. However, if you select the **Chord Width** option from the **Chamfer Method** drop-down list in the **Chamfer PropertyManager**, a chamfer of constant width will be applied between the selected faces, refer to Figure 7-104.

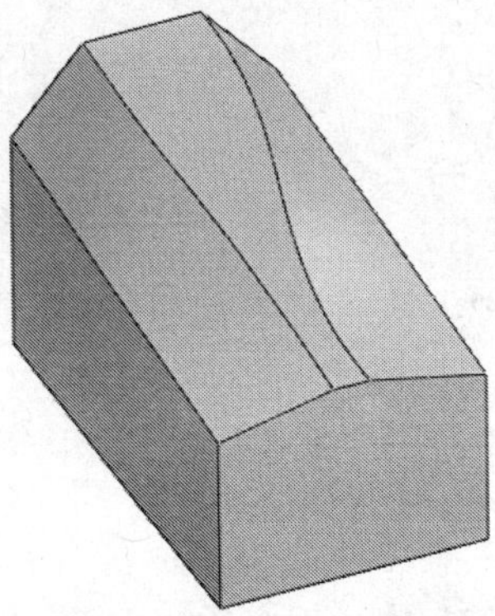

*Figure 7-103 Face chamfer without the **Chord Width** option selected*

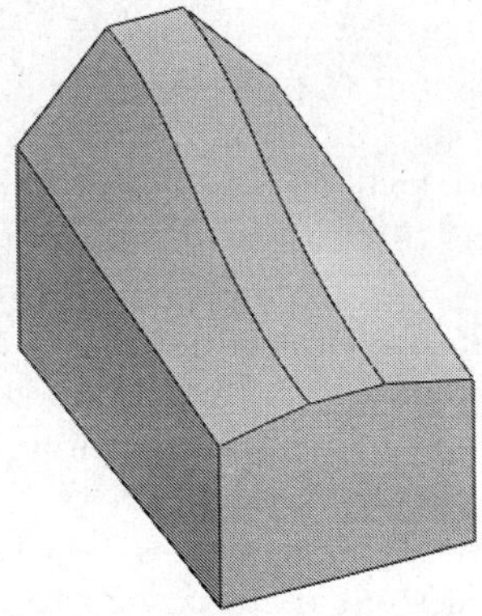

*Figure 7-104 Face chamfer with the **Chord Width** option selected*

Creating the Offset Face Chamfer

To create the face face chamfer, select the edge or edges; a preview of the chamfer feature will be displayed. Next, specify the offset distance value in the **Offset Distance** spinner and then choose the **OK** button. The software calculates the intersection point of the offset faces and then calculates the normal from the intersection point to each face to create the chamfer. Figure 7-105 shows calculation of the chamfer and Figure 7-106 shows the chamfer created. You can also create multi distance chamfer on multiple edges selected using the **Multi Distance Chamfer** check box in the **Chamfers Parameters** rollout. The **Partial Edge Parameters** check box will only be available in **Offset Face** chamfer type. The use of this check box is same as discussed in **Fillet PropertyManager**.

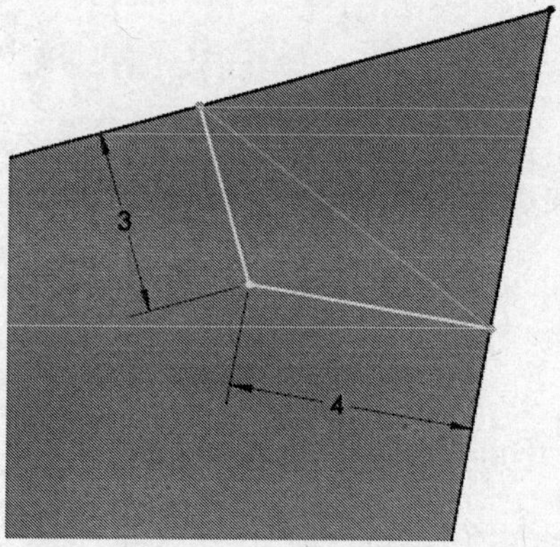

Figure 7-105 *Offset calculation for Chamfer*

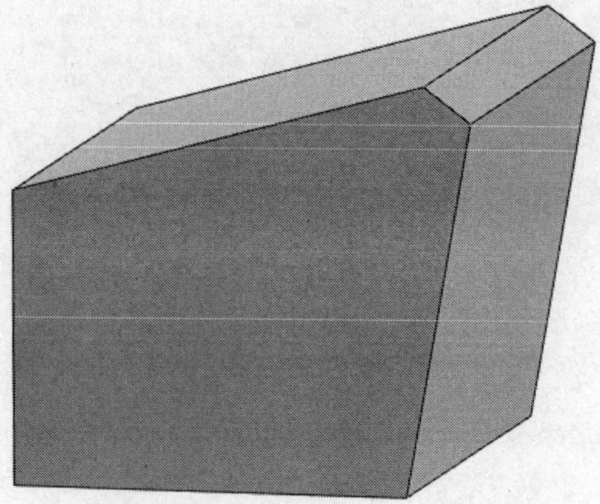

Figure 7-106 *Resulting Offset Face Chamfer*

Creating Shell Features

CommandManager: Features > Shell
SOLIDWORKS menus: Insert > Features > Shell
Toolbar: Features > Shell

Shelling is a process in which the material is scooped out from a model. The resulting model will be a hollow model with walls of a specified thickness and a cavity inside. The selected face or the faces of the model are also removed in this operation. If you do not select a face to be removed, a closed hollow model will be created. You can also specify multiple thicknesses to the walls.

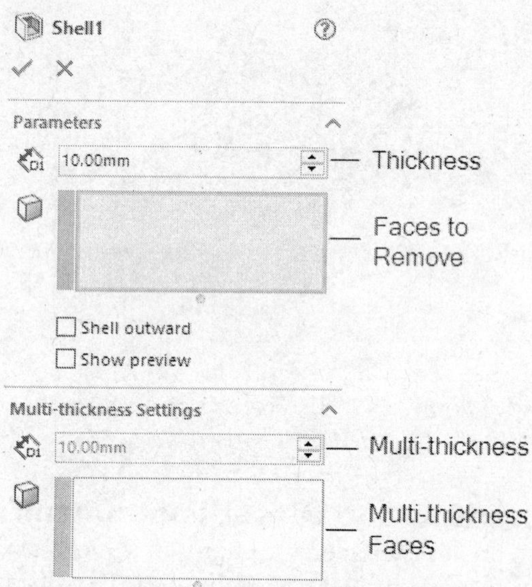

Figure 7-107 *The* ***Shell PropertyManager***

To create a shell feature, invoke the **Shell** tool from the **Features CommandManager**; the **Shell PropertyManager** will be displayed, as shown in Figure 7-107. Also, you will be prompted to select the faces to be removed. Select the face or the faces of the model that you want to remove. The selected faces will be highlighted in blue and their names will be displayed in the **Faces to Remove** selection box. Set the value of the wall thickness in the **Thickness** spinner and choose the **OK** button from the **Shell PropertyManager**. Figure 7-108 shows the face selected to remove and Figure 7-109 shows the resultant shell feature.

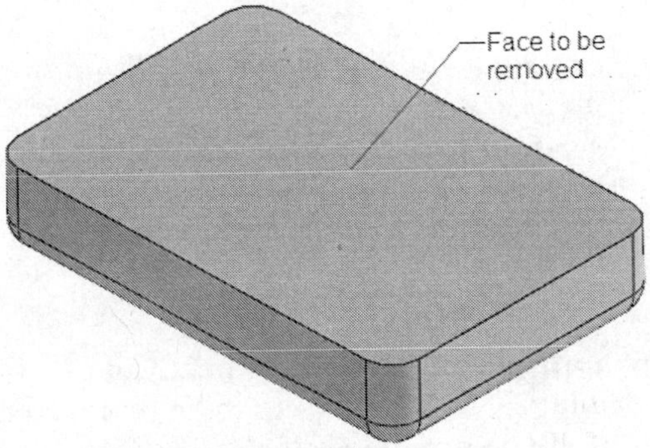

Figure 7-108 Face to be removed

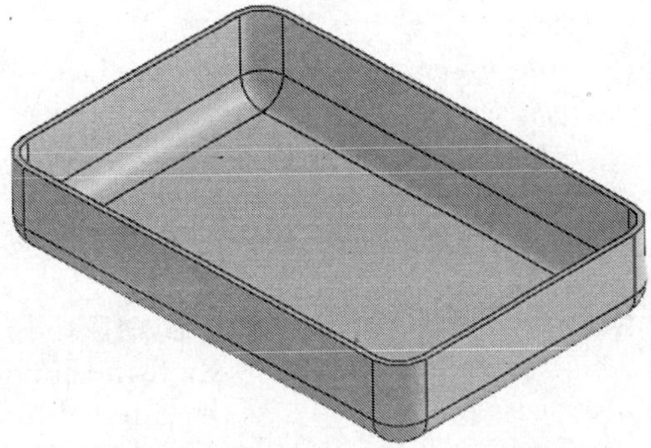

Figure 7-109 Resultant shell feature

If none of the faces are selected to be removed, the resulting model will be hollowed from inside with no face removed. Figure 7-110 shows a model in the **Hidden Lines Visible** mode with a shell feature in which no face is selected to be removed.

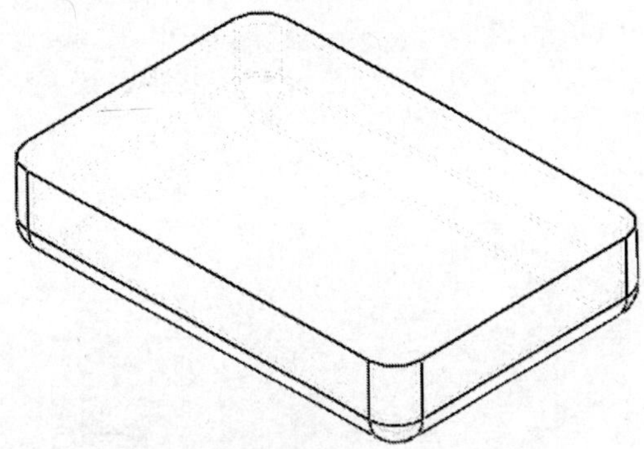

Figure 7-110 Shell feature with no face selected to be removed

Based on the geometric conditions, the quantity of the material to be removed from the shell feature will be decided automatically. Figure 7-111 shows the shell feature whose wall thickness is small for uniform shelling of the entire model. Figure 7-112 shows the shell feature whose wall thickness is large. As a result it cannot accommodate uniform shelling of the entire model. Therefore, the shell feature will not remove the material from the area where the material removal is not possible.

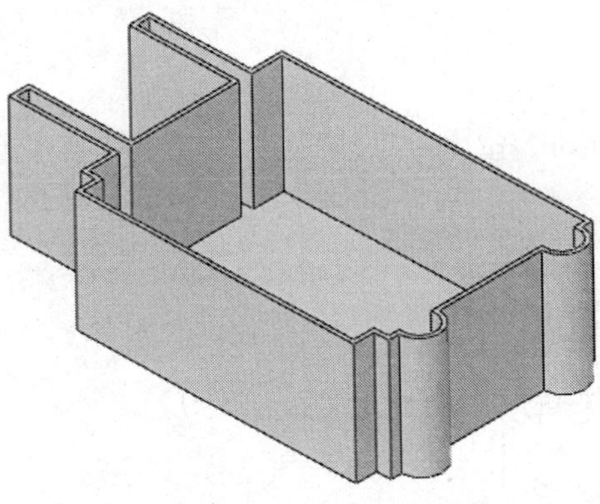

Figure 7-111 Shell feature with small shell thickness

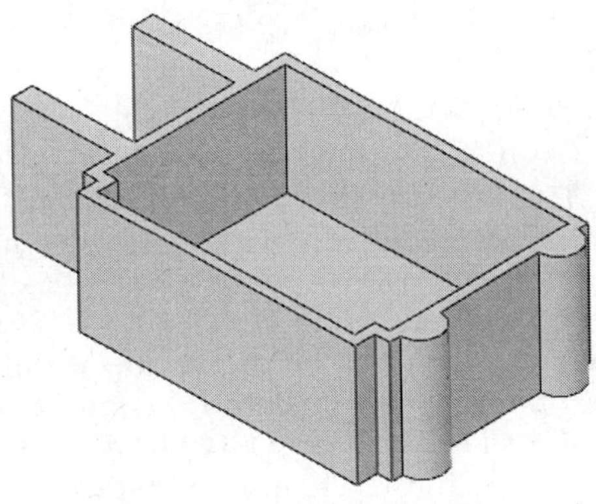

Figure 7-112 Shell feature with larger shell thickness

The **Shell outward** check box is selected to create the shell feature on the outer side of the model. You can also display the preview of the shell feature by selecting the **Show preview** check box from the **Parameters** rollout of the **Shell PropertyManager**.

Note

If the thickness of the shell feature is more than the radius of the fillet feature, the fillet will not be included in the shell feature. Therefore, it results in sharp edges after adding the fillet. The same is true in the case of the chamfer feature. The face selected to be removed in the shell feature can be a planar face or a curved face. But creating a shell by removing a curved face depends on the geometry of the curved face to adopt the specified shell thickness and other geometric conditions.

Creating Multi-thickness Shell

The **Shell** tool can be used to shell the model by applying different thickness values to the selected faces. To do so, invoke the **Shell PropertyManager**, select the faces to be removed and then specify the thickness in the **Thickness** spinner of the **Parameters** rollout. Click once in the **Multi-thickness Faces** selection box to activate the selection mode. Select the faces for which you want to specify different thicknesses. Set the thickness value using the **Multi-thickness(es)** spinner and choose the **OK** button. Note that you can specify different thickness for each face. Figure 7-113 shows the faces selected to create a multi-thickness shell and Figure 7-114 shows the resulting shell feature.

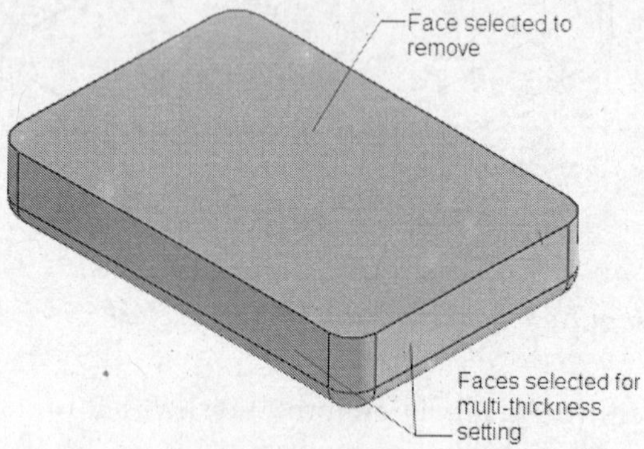

Figure 7-113 *Faces selected to create the multi-thickness shell feature*

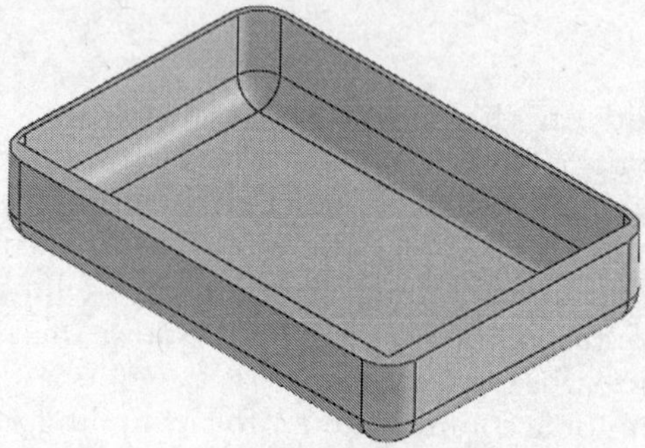

Figure 7-114 *Resulting multi-thickness shell*

Error Diagnostics

While creating the shell feature, specify all parameters in the **Shell PropertyManager** and choose the **OK** button. If the creation of shell feature fails because of geometric inconsistency, the **Error Diagnostics** rollout will be displayed in the **Shell PropertyManager**, as shown in Figure 7-115. Also, the **Rebuild Errors** dialog box will be displayed informing you about the possible errors that can lead to the failure of feature creation. You will learn more about the **Rebuild Errors** dialog box in the later chapters. In the **Error Diagnostics** rollout, you can figure out the possible reasons behind the failure of the shell feature creation.

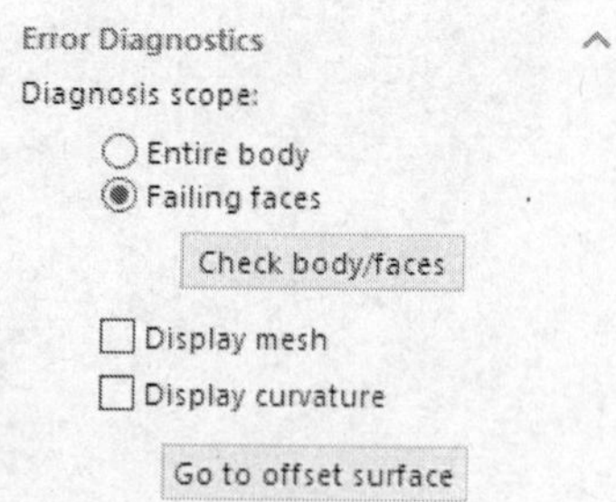

Figure 7-115 *The* ***Error Diagnostics*** *rollout*

The radio buttons in the **Diagnosis scope** area are used to specify whether the diagnosis has to be done on the entire body or only on the faces that have failed while being shelled. The **Check body/faces** button is used to run the diagnostic tool. On choosing this button, the areas of the model that are responsible for the feature creation failure will be highlighted using callouts. The **Display mesh** check box is used to display the surface curvature mesh. The **Display curvature** check box is selected to display the surface curvature. The **Go to offset surface** button is used to open **Offset Surface PropertyManager** where you can offset faces with smaller gaps which sometimes lead to errors.

Creating Wrap Features

CommandManager: Features > Wrap
SOLIDWORKS menus: Insert > Features > Wrap
Toolbar: Features > Wrap *(Customize to add)*

The **Wrap** tool is used to emboss, deboss, or scribe a closed multiloop sketch on a selected planar, curved, or splined face. There are two methods for creating wrap features: Analytical and Spline Surface. For planar or curved surfaces, use Analytical wrap and for spline surfaces, use Spline Surface wrap. For Analytical wrap, the planar or curved face must be tangent to the plane on which the selected sketch is created. Using the Spline Surface method, you cannot create wrap around bodies. You can create a wrap feature on multiple faces. You can also create this type of geometry by extruding the sketch from a selected surface using the **Extruded Boss/Base** or **Extruded Cut** tool. There are two main differences between the emboss and the deboss features created using the **Wrap** tool and those created using the **Extruded Boss/Base** or **Extruded Cut** tool. The first difference is in the method of projection. The projection of the geometry using the **Wrap** tool follows the rule of true length, which means the actual length of the geometry remains the same after projecting it on the surface. The projection of the geometry created using the **From** option of the **Extruded Boss/Base** or **Extruded Cut** tool follows the rule of true projection. Therefore, the original size of the geometry is distorted. The second difference is the direction of the side faces of the geometry. The side faces of the geometry created using the **Wrap** tool are always normal to the reference surface, while those created using the **From** option of the **Extruded Boss/Base** or the **Extruded Cut** tool are normal to the sketching plane or parallel to the direction vector.

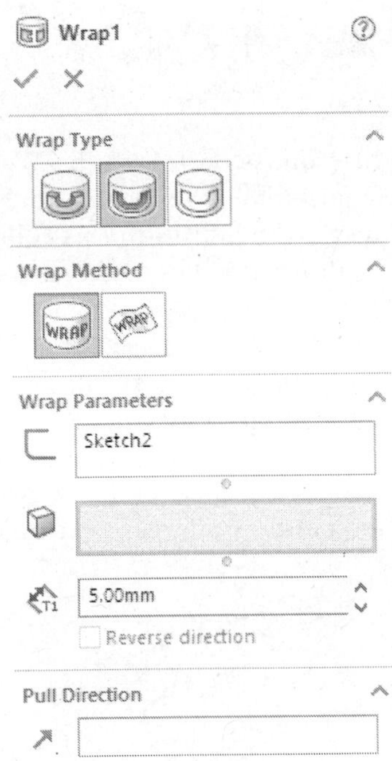

*Figure 7-116 The **Wrap** PropertyManager*

To create a wrap feature, create a closed multiloop or a single loop sketch and then choose the **Wrap** button from the **Features CommandManager**; the **Message PropertyManager** will be displayed and you will be prompted to select a plane or a face on which you need to create a closed counter or select an existing sketch. Select an existing sketch from the **Features CommandManager**; the **Wrap PropertyManager** will be displayed, as shown in Figure 7-116.

You will notice that the **Emboss** button is selected by default in the **Wrap Type** rollout. This button is selected to create an embossed wrap feature. To create a wrap feature, choose the **Analytical** or **Spline Surface** button from the **Wrap Method** rollout based on the surface on which you need to create a wrap feature. Next, select the face on which you need to wrap the sketch. As soon as you select the face, the preview of the wrap feature created will be displayed with the default setting in the drawing area. Set the value of the thickness using the **Thickness** spinner. Choose the **OK** button from the **Wrap PropertyManager**. Figure 7-117 shows the sketch and the face selected to create the wrap feature and Figure 7-118 shows the resulting embossed wrap feature.

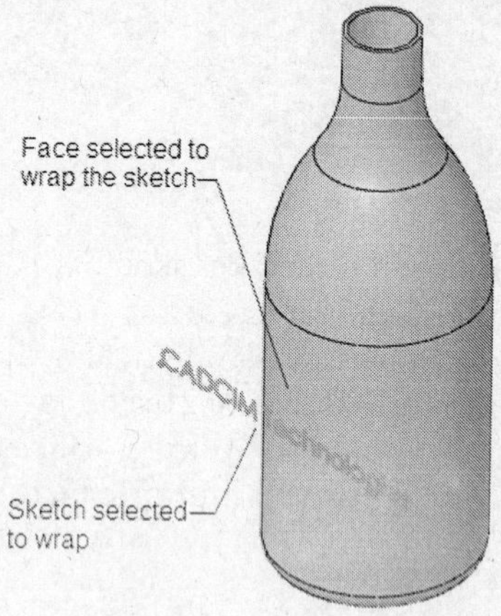

Figure 7-117 Sketch and face selected to create the wrap feature

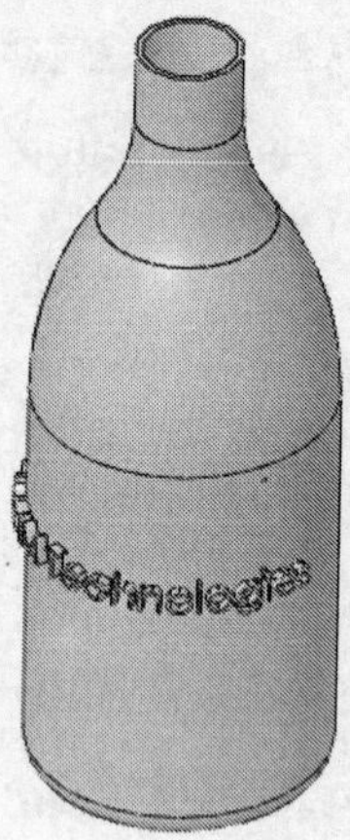

Figure 7-118 Resulting embossed wrap feature

The **Deboss** button in the **Wrap Type** rollout can be used to engrave the sketch on a selected planar, curved, or spline face. Figure 7-119 shows a wrap feature created using the **Deboss** button. The **Scribe** button in this rollout is selected to project the selected sketch on a planar, curved, or spline face. The projected sketch will split the face on which it is projected.

If you need to project the sketch in a direction other than normal, then expand the **Pull Direction** rollout and click once in the selection box. Note that if the **Scribe** button is selected in the **Wrap Type** rollout then the **Pull Direction** rollout will not be available. Next, select a sketched line or a linear edge as the pull direction along which you need to emboss or deboss the sketch. Figure 7-120 shows the wrap feature created using the **Scribe** option. Figure 7-121 shows embossed wrap feature created on a spline surface of the model.

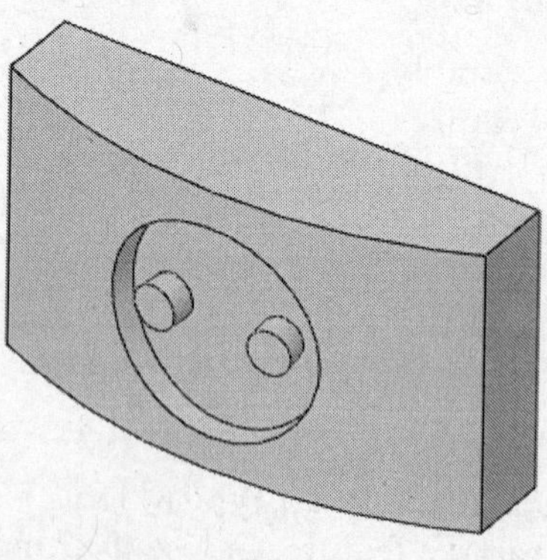

*Figure 7-119 Wrap feature created using the **Deboss** button*

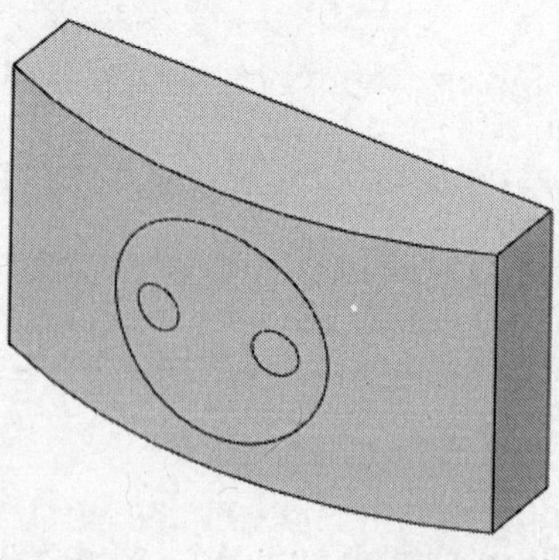

*Figure 7-120 Wrap feature created using the **Scribe** button*

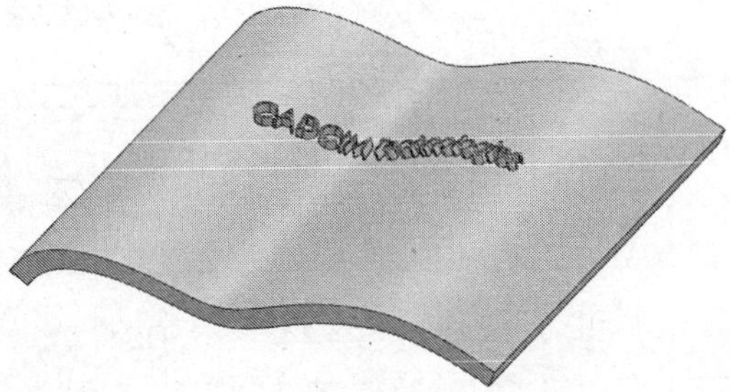

Figure 7-121 Embossed wrap feature created on a spline surface

TUTORIALS

Tutorial 1

In this tutorial, you will create the model of the Plummer Block Casting shown in Figure 7-122. The dimensions of the model are shown in Figure 7-123. **(Expected time: 30 min)**

The following steps are required to complete this tutorial:

a. Create the base feature of the model on the Front Plane.
b. Create the second feature, which is a cut feature on the top planar face of the base feature.
c. Create the rectangular recess as a cut feature at the bottom of the base.
d. Create the square cuts that will act as the recess for the head of the square head bolts.
e. Create the hole feature using the **Hole PropertyManager** and modify the placement of the hole feature.
f. Create the cut feature on the second top planar face of the base feature.
g. Add the fillet feature to the model.
h. Add chamfers to the model.
i. Save the model.

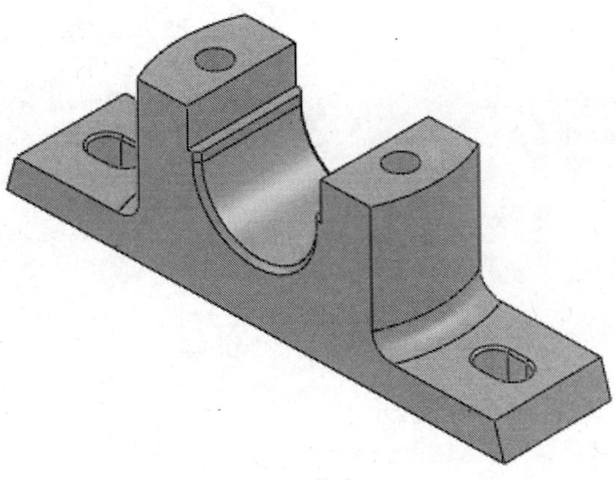

Figure 7-122 Solid model of the Plummer Block Casting

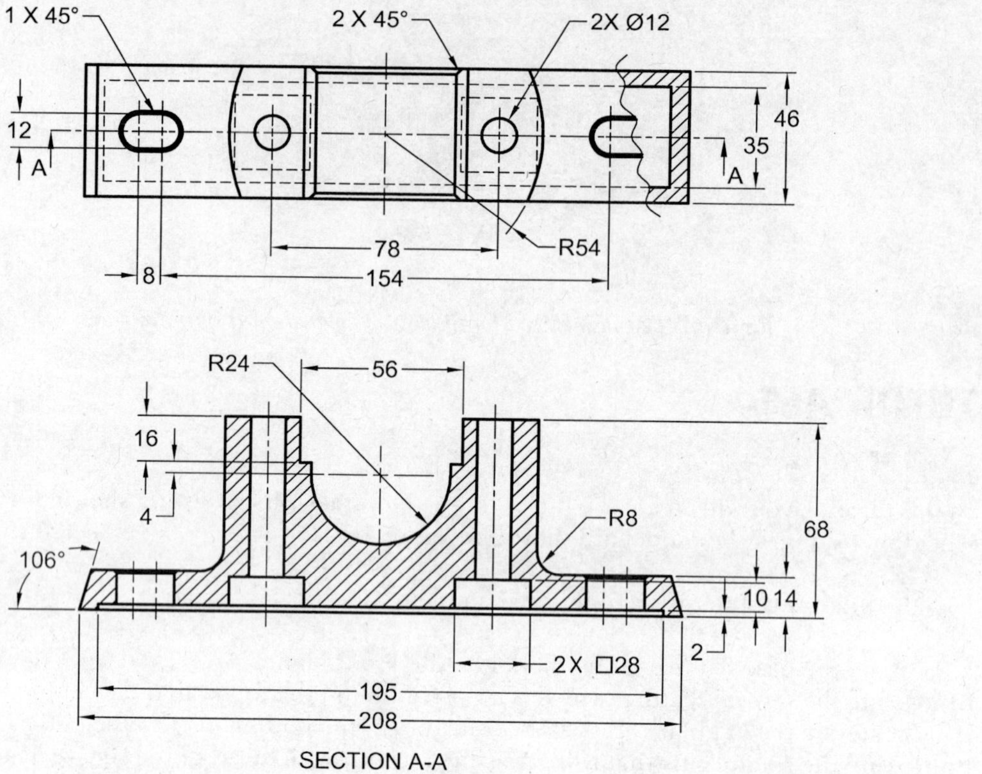

Figure 7-123 Dimensions of the Plummer Block Casting

Creating the Base Feature

1. Start a new SOLIDWORKS part document using the **New SOLIDWORKS Document** dialog box.

2. Invoke the **Extruded Boss/Base** tool and select the **Front Plane** as the sketching plane.

3. Draw the sketch of the front view of the model. Use the **Mirror Entities** tool to capture the design intent of the model.

4. Add required relations and dimensions to fully define the sketch, refer to Figure 7-124.

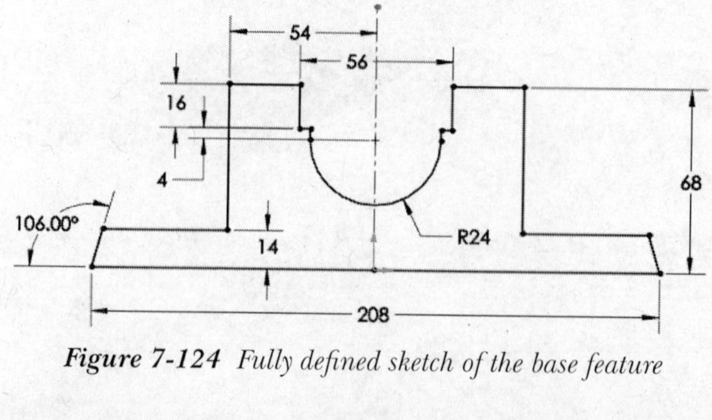

Figure 7-124 Fully defined sketch of the base feature

Note

After adding the dimensions to the sketch, select the radial dimension and add tolerance to them using the ***Dimension PropertyManager****, as discussed in the earlier chapters. Also, change the radial dimension of the arc into the diameter dimension by using the* ***Leaders*** *tab of the* ***Dimension PropertyManager****.*

You need to extrude the sketch to a distance of 46 mm using the **Mid Plane** option so that the parts to be assembled have the default planes at the center of the model.

5. Exit the sketching environment to display the **Boss-Extrude PropertyManager**.
6. Right-click in the drawing area and choose the **Mid Plane** option from the shortcut menu to extrude the sketch symmetrically on both sides of the sketching plane.
7. Set **46** in the **Depth** spinner and choose the **OK** button from the **Boss-Extrude PropertyManager**.
8. Change the view orientation to isometric. The resulting base feature after extruding the sketch to a given depth is shown in Figure 7-125.

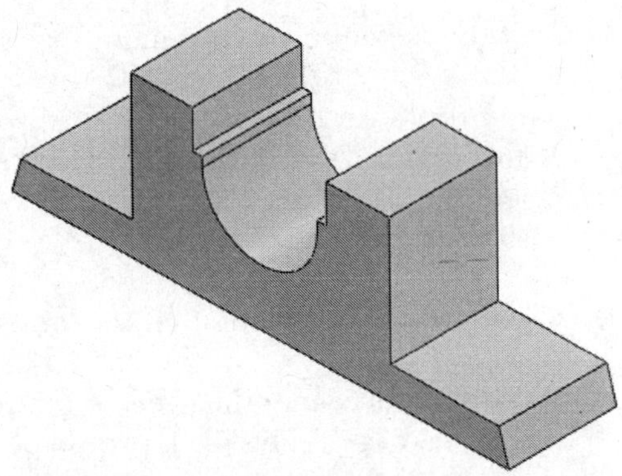

Figure 7-125 *Isometric view of the base feature of the model*

Tip

Sometimes you need to set tolerance for the dimensions of a feature. For example, consider a case where depth of the extruded feature has a tolerance applied to it. In such cases, double-click on the extruded feature in the ***FeatureManager Design Tree*** *or in the drawing area. On doing so, all dimensions applied to the model will be displayed. Double-click on the dimension that reflects the depth of the extruded feature and apply the tolerance using the* ***Dimension PropertyManager****.*

Creating the Second Feature

The second feature of the model is a cut-extrude feature. The sketch of the cut-extrude feature will be drawn on the top planar face of the base feature. This sketch will be extruded up to the specified plane to create the resulting cut feature.

1. Invoke the **Extruded Cut** tool and select the top planar face of the base feature as the sketching plane; the sketching plane orients parallel to screen.
2. Draw the sketch for the cut feature using the sketching tools. Apply required relations to the sketch.

The sketch of the cut-extrude feature is shown in Figure 7-126.

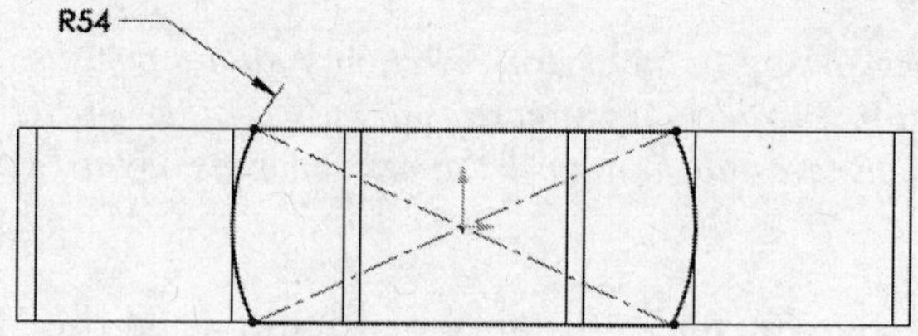

Figure 7-126 Sketch of the second feature

3. Exit the sketching environment to display the **Cut-Extrude PropertyManager**.

   The preview of the cut feature is displayed in the drawing area with default values of the **Blind** option. You need to extrude the cut feature up to the selected surface. Therefore, orient the model in the isometric view so that the feature termination surface can be selected easily in this view.

4. Change the view orientation to isometric.

   You will observe that the preview of the cut feature is inside the model. You need to remove the outer part of the sketch profile by changing the side of the cut feature.

5. Select the **Flip side to cut** check box; the preview of the cut feature is modified dynamically.

6. Right-click in the drawing area and choose **Up To Surface** from the shortcut menu; you are prompted to select a face or a surface to complete the specification of direction 1.

7. Select the surface for feature termination, refer to Figure 7-127. Right-click and choose **OK** from the shortcut menu to exit the tool.

   The model after creating the cut feature is shown in Figure 7-128.

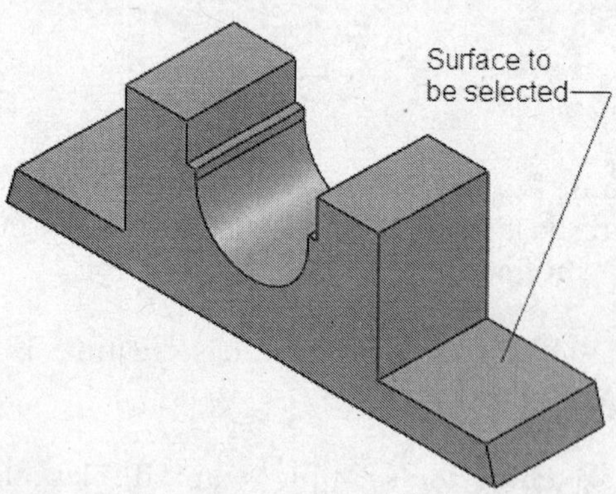

***Figure 7-127** Surface to be selected for the cut feature*

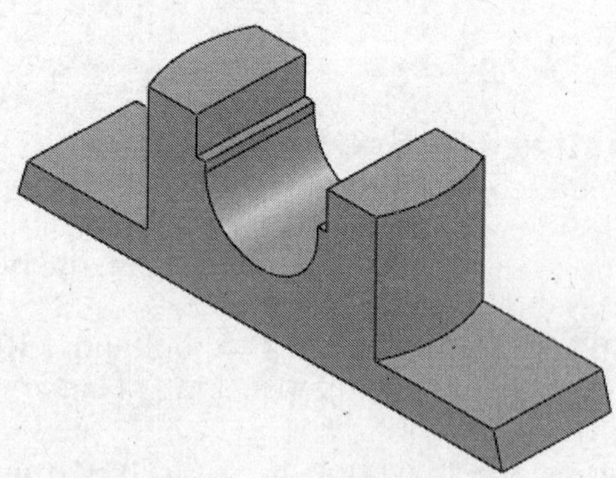

***Figure 7-128** Model after creating the cut feature*

Creating the Rectangular Recess

The third feature is the rectangular recess. This feature will be created by using a rectangular cut feature created on the bottom face of the model.

1. Orient the model using the **Rotate View** tool and select the bottom face of the base feature as the sketching plane.

2. Choose the **Extruded Cut** tool; the sketching environment is invoked.

3. Use standard sketching tools to draw a rectangle of dimension 195 mm x 35 mm as the sketch for the rectangular recess. Apply the required relations and dimensions to the sketch.

4. Exit the sketching environment.

5. Set the value to **2** in the **Depth** spinner and choose **OK** from the **Cut-Extrude PropertyManager**.

Creating the Recess for the Head of the Square-headed Bolt

It is evident from Figure 7-123 that the bolt to be inserted in the part is a square-headed bolt. Therefore, you need to create the recess for the head of this bolt. A square of 28 mm length will be used to create this recess.

1. Rotate the model and select the upper face of the recess created in the previous section as the sketching plane. Invoke the **Extruded Cut** tool; the model orients normal to the sketching plane.

2. Draw a sketch using the sketching tools. The sketch includes two squares of 28 mm length with the distance between their centers as 78 mm, refer to Figure 7-123. Apply the required relations and dimensions to fully define the sketch.

3. Exit the sketching environment and extrude the sketch to a depth of 10 mm. Exit the tool. The rotated model after adding this cut feature is shown in Figure 7-129.

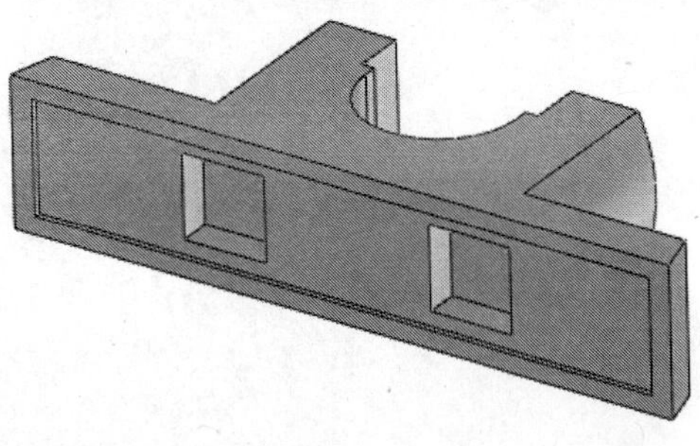

***Figure 7-129** Model after creating recess for the square-headed bolts*

Creating the Hole Features

After creating the recess for the head of the square-headed bolt, you need to create a hole. You can create a hole using the **Hole Wizard** tool. However, for this tutorial, you will create the hole using the **Simple Hole** tool.

1. Select the top planar surface of the base feature as the placement plane for the hole feature.

2. Choose **Insert > Features > Simple Hole** from the SOLIDWORKS menus to invoke the **Hole PropertyManager**; preview of the hole feature with default settings is displayed in the drawing area.

3. Right-click in the drawing area and choose the **Through All** option from the shortcut menu to specify the feature termination.

4. Set **12** in the **Hole Diameter** spinner.

5. Choose the **OK** button from the **Hole PropertyManager**.

6. Select **Hole1** from the **FeatureManager Design Tree**; a pop-up toolbar is displayed.

7. Choose **Edit Sketch** from the pop-up toolbar; the sketching environment is displayed. Apply relations and dimensions (refer to Figure 7-123) to locate the hole feature.

8. Press CTRL+B to rebuild the model.

9. Use the same procedure as discussed above to create the second hole feature on the model. The model after creating both hole features is displayed in Figure 7-130.

10. Create the cut feature on the second top planar face of the base feature. Refer to Figure 7-127 for the surface to be selected and Figure 7-123 for the dimensions of the sketch.

    The model after creating the cut features is shown in Figure 7-131.

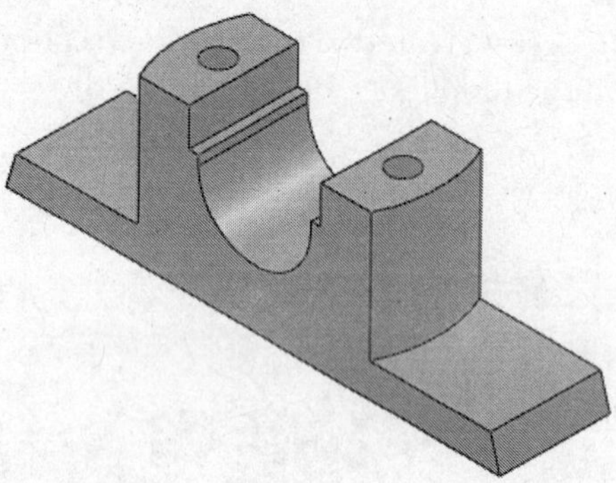

Figure 7-130 *Model after creating the hole features*

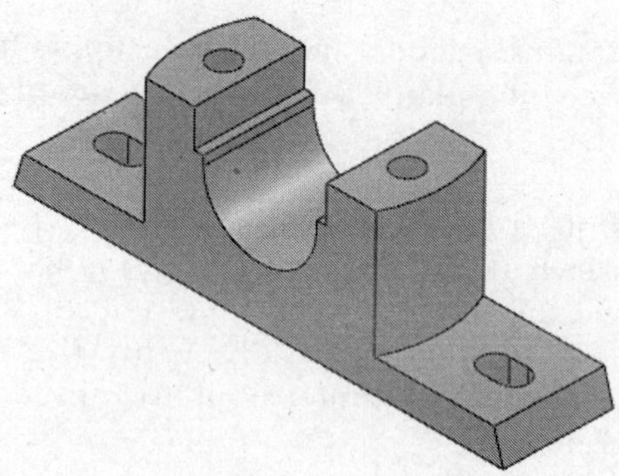

Figure 7-131 *Model after creating the cut features*

Tip

In this tutorial, you will draw the sketch of the slot on one side, mirror it, and then create the cut feature. You can also create a cut feature on one side and then mirror it on the other side. Mirroring a feature will be discussed in the later chapters.

Adding a Fillet to the Model

Now, you need to add the fillet feature to the model.

1. Choose the **Fillet** button from the **Fillet** flyout in the **Features CommandManager** to invoke the **Fillet PropertyManager**. But if the **FilletXpert PropertyManager** is displayed then choose the **Manual** button.

On invoking the **Fillet PropertyManager**, you are prompted to select the edges, faces, features, or loops to be filleted. It is evident from the model that you need to select only the edges to apply the fillet feature.

2. Choose the **Constant Size Fillet** button from the **Fillet PropertyManager** and then select the edges to be filleted, as shown in Figure 7-132.

   As soon as you select the edges, the preview of the fillet feature with default values appears in the drawing area. Also, a radius callout is displayed along the selected edge.

Note
*If the preview of the fillet feature is not displayed in the drawing area, select the **Full Preview** radio button in the **Items To Fillet** rollout of the **Fillet PropertyManager**.*

Now, you need to modify the default radius value of the fillet feature.

3. Set the value to **8** in the **Radius** spinner and choose the **OK** button from the **Fillet PropertyManager**.

   The model after adding the fillet is shown in Figure 7-133.

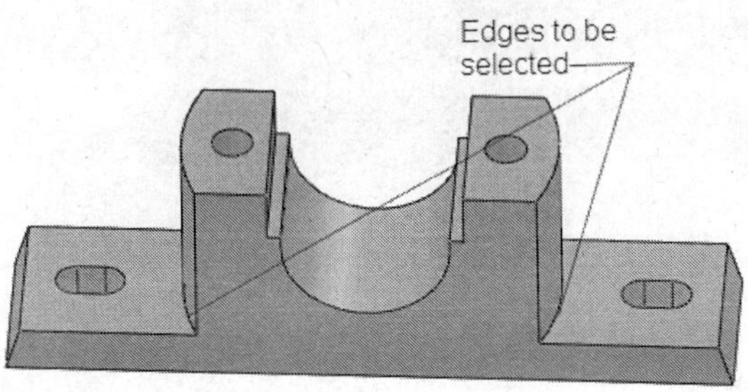

Figure 7-132 Edges to be selected for the fillet feature

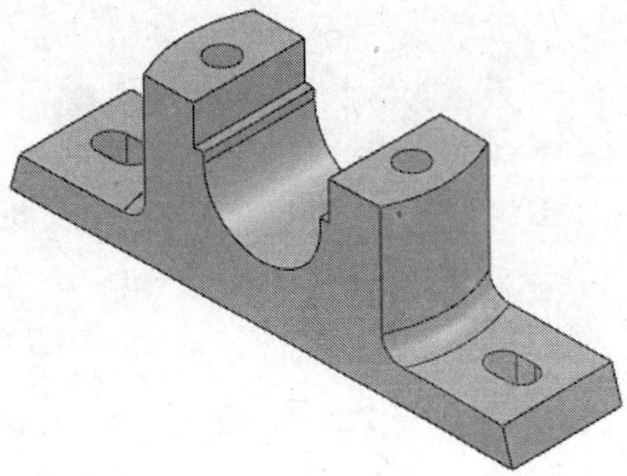

Figure 7-133 Model after adding the fillet

Adding Chamfers to the Model

The next feature that you need to add to this model is a chamfer feature.

1. Choose the **Chamfer** button from the **Fillet** flyout in the **Features CommandManager** to invoke the **Chamfer PropertyManager**.

2. Select the edges of the cut features, as shown in Figure 7-134. On doing so, the edges that are tangent to the selected edges are selected automatically because by default the selection mode of the chamfer feature uses the tangent propagation.

   As soon as you select the edges, the preview of the chamfer feature is displayed in the drawing area with default values. The angle and distance callouts are also displayed. Next, you need to set the chamfer parameters.

You need to create the chamfer by using 1 mm distance and 45 degrees angle. The **Angle Distance** button is selected by default in the **Chamfer Type** rollout. The value of the angle in the **Angle** spinner is set to 45 degrees by default. Therefore, you do not need to modify this value. You need to set only the value of the distance in the **Distance** spinner.

3. Set the value to **1** in the **Distance** spinner and choose the **OK** button from the **Chamfer PropertyManager**. Refer to Figure 7-123 for the parameters of the chamfer feature.

4. Similarly, create the chamfer of dimension 2 X 45° on the base feature, refer to Figure 7-123. The final solid model is shown in Figure 7-135.

Saving the Model

Next, you need to save the document.

1. Choose the **Save** button from the Menu Bar and save the document with the name *c07_tut01* at the location *\Documents\SOLIDWORKS\c07*.

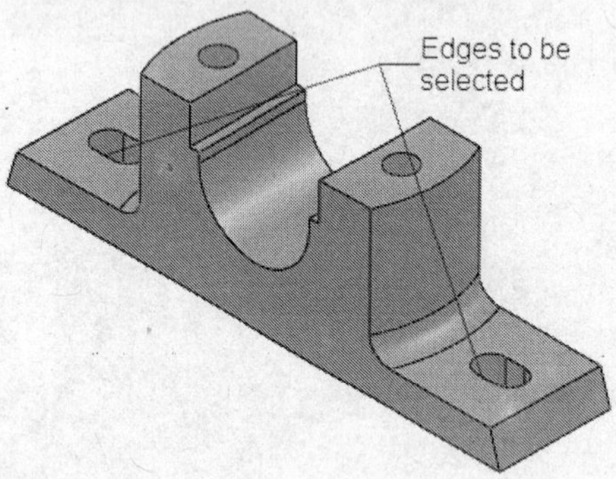

Figure 7-134 *Edges to be selected*

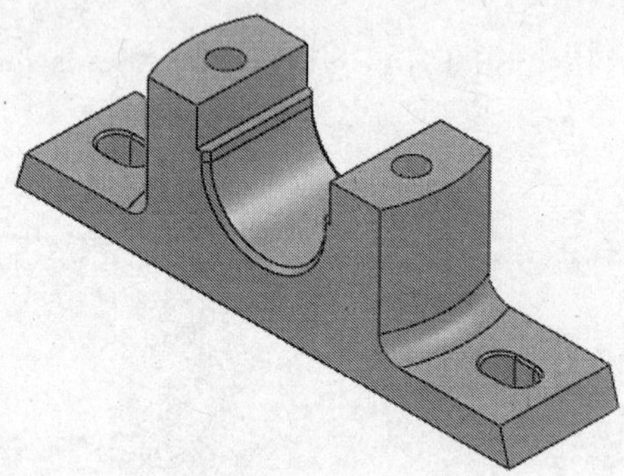

Figure 7-135 *Final solid model*

2. Choose **File > Close** from the SOLIDWORKS menus to close the file.

Tutorial 2

In this tutorial, you will create the model shown in Figure 7-136. For a better understanding, the section view of the model is shown in Figure 7-137. The dimensions of the model are shown in Figure 7-138. **(Expected time: 30 min)**

The following steps are required to complete this tutorial:

a. Create the base feature of the model by extruding a rectangle of 100 mm x 70 mm to a distance of 20 mm.
b. Add a fillet to the base feature.
c. Create the shell feature to create a thin-walled part and remove some of the faces.
d. Create a reference plane at an offset distance from the top planar face of the base feature and extrude the sketch created on the new plane.

e. Use the **Hole Wizard** tool to add the countersink hole to the model.
f. Add a fillet to the extruded feature.
g. Create the lip of the component by extruding the sketch.
h. Save the model.

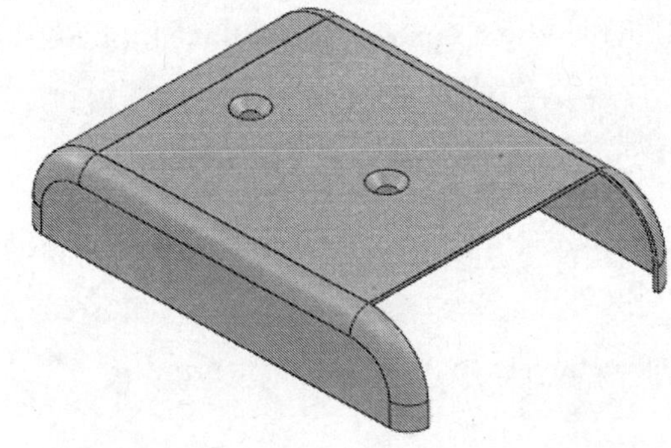

Figure 7-136 *Solid model for Tutorial 2*

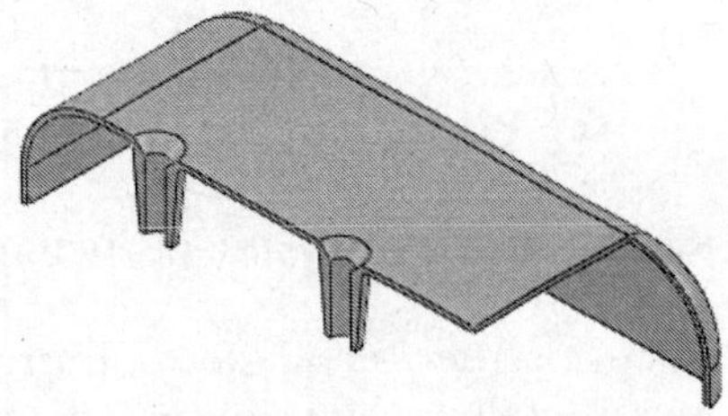

Figure 7-137 *Section view of the model*

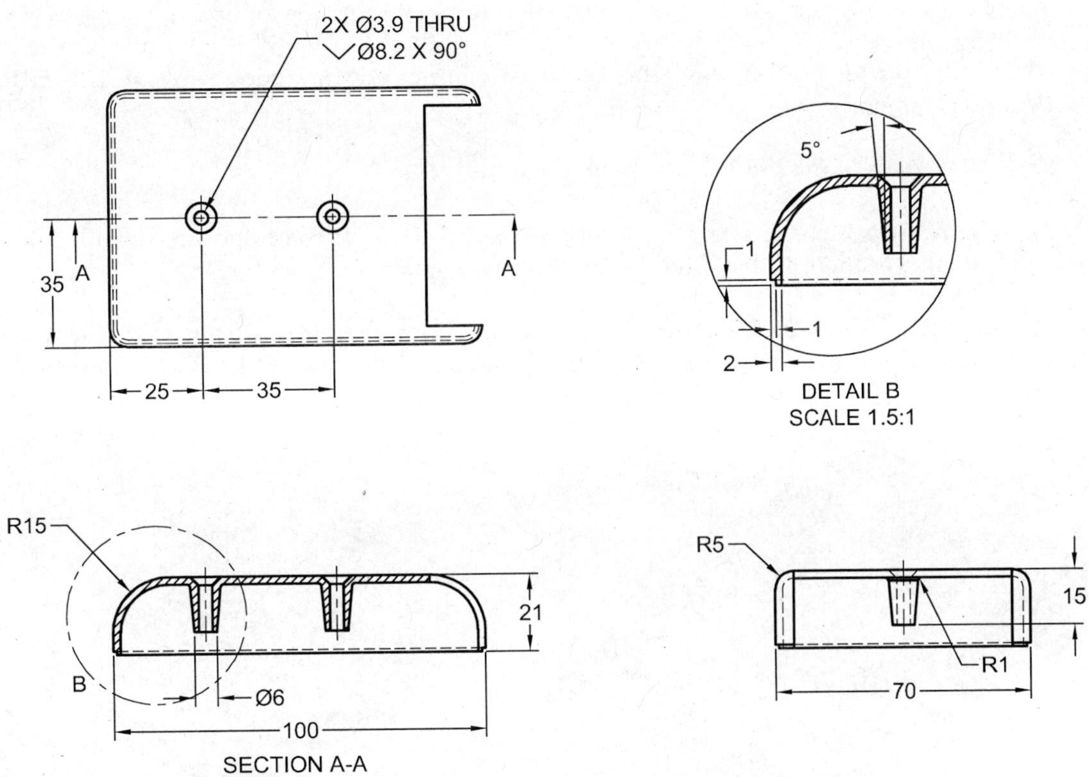

Figure 7-138 *Top view, front section view, and right side view with dimensions*

Creating the Base Feature

The base feature of the model will be created by extruding a rectangle of 100 mm x 70 mm to a distance of 20 mm. It is evident from the model that the sketch of the base feature is created on the Top Plane. Therefore, you need to select the Top Plane as the sketching plane.

1. Start a new SOLIDWORKS part document and invoke the **Extruded Boss/Base** tool. Select the **Top Plane** from the **FeatureManager Design Tree** or from the drawing area.

2. Orient the sketch plane normal to the viewing direction if not oriented by default.

3. By using the **Rectangle** tool, draw a rectangle of size 100 mm x 70 mm. Add the other required dimensions to fully define the sketch.

4. Exit the sketching environment and extrude the rectangle to a depth of 21 mm.

Creating the Fillet Features

After creating the base feature, you need to add fillets to the model. In this model, you need to add three fillet features. Two fillet features will be added at this stage of the design process and the remaining one will be added at the later stage of the design process.

1. Choose the **Fillet** button from the **Features CommandManager** to invoke the **Fillet PropertyManager**.

2. Select the edges of the model, as shown in Figure 7-139.

   As soon as you select the edges of the model, the preview of the fillet with default values and the radius callout is displayed in the drawing area.

3. Set the value in the **Radius** spinner to **15** and choose the **OK** button from the **Fillet PropertyManager**. Figure 7-140 shows the model after adding the first fillet feature.

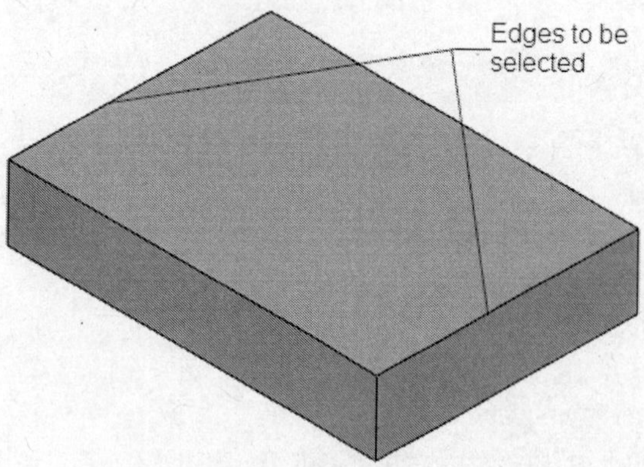

Figure 7-139 Edges to be selected

Figure 7-140 Fillet added to the base feature

Now, you need to add the second fillet feature to the model.

4. Again, invoke the **Fillet PropertyManager** and set the value to **5** in the **Radius** spinner.

5. Select the edges of the model, as shown in Figure 7-141. Right-click and then choose **OK** from the shortcut menu to complete the feature creation. The model after adding the second fillet feature is shown in Figure 7-142.

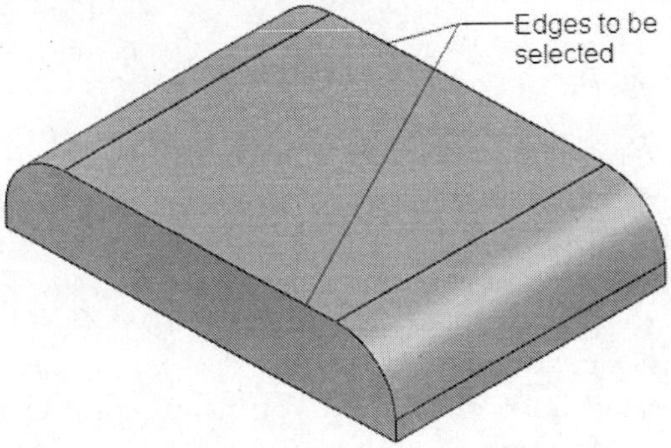

Figure 7-141 Edges to be selected

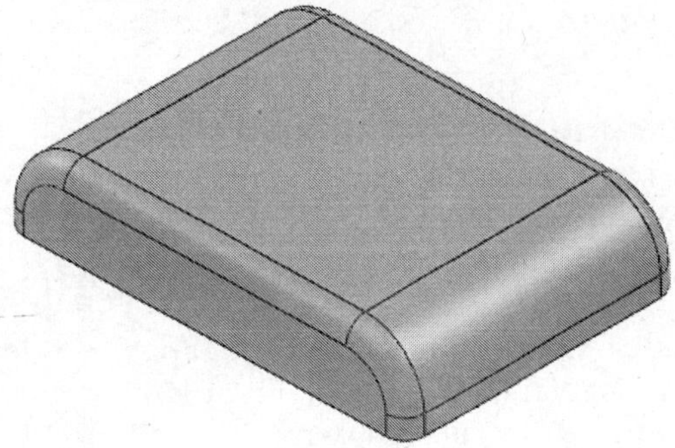

Figure 7-142 Second fillet added to the model

Note

*You can also create two fillets in a single step by selecting the **Multiple radius** check box in the **Fillet PropertyManager** and specifying the appropriate radius.*

Creating the Shell Feature

It is evident from Figures 7-136 and 7-137 that you need to create a thin-walled structure. This will be created using the **Shell** tool. As discussed earlier, the **Shell** tool is used to scoop out material from the model leaving behind a thin-walled hollow part.

1. Choose the **Shell** button from the **Features CommandManager**; the **Shell PropertyManager** is displayed and you are prompted to select the faces to be removed.

2. Rotate the model and select the faces to be removed, as shown in Figure 7-143; the names of the selected faces are displayed in the **Faces to Remove** selection box.

3. Set the value to **2** in the **Thickness** spinner and choose the **OK** button from the **Shell PropertyManager**.

The model after creating the shell feature is shown in Figure 7-144.

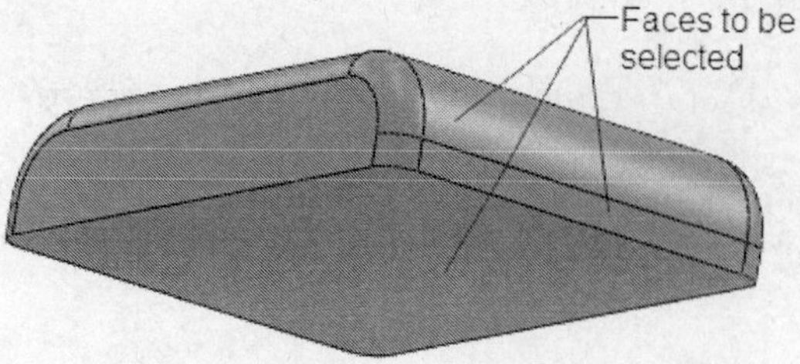

Figure 7-143 Faces selected to be removed

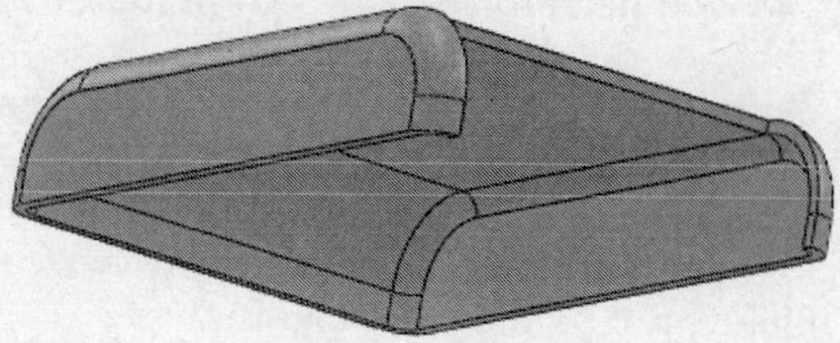

Figure 7-144 Model after creating the shell feature

Creating the Extruded Feature

The next feature that you need to create is an extruded feature. Before creating this feature, you need to create a reference plane at an offset distance from the top planar face of the base feature.

1. Invoke the **Plane PropertyManager**, select the top planar face of the base feature as the first reference, and create a plane at an offset distance of 15 mm. You need to select the **Flip offset** check box from the **Plane PropertyManager** to reverse the direction of plane creation. Choose the **OK** button from the **Plane PropertyManager** to close it.

2. Invoke the **Extruded Boss/Base** tool, select the newly created plane as the sketching plane, and create the sketch using the standard sketching tools. The sketch consists of two circles of 6 mm diameter. For other dimensions, refer to Figure 7-138.

3. Exit the sketching environment and extrude the sketch using the **Up To Next** option and activate the **Draft on/off** button. Next, add an outward draft of 5-degree in the **Draft Angle** edit box. Choose the **OK** button from the **Boss-Extrude PropertyManager** to close it. Also, hide the reference plane.

Figure 7-145 shows the rotated model after creating the extruded feature with draft and hiding the reference plane.

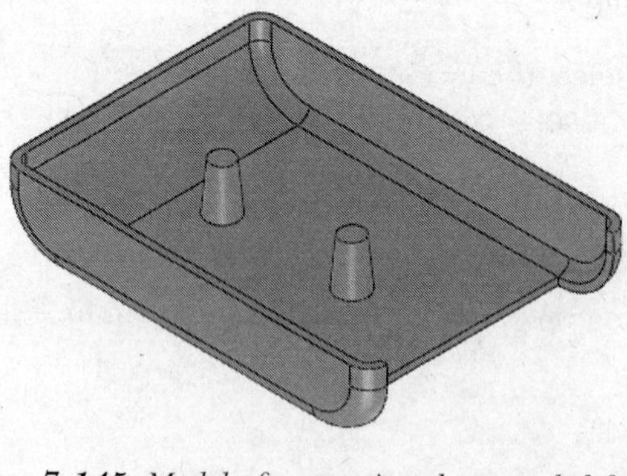

Figure 7-145 Model after creating the extruded feature

Adding the Countersink Hole using the Hole Wizard Tool

The next feature that you need to create is a countersink hole, refer to Figure 7-137. In SOLIDWORKS, you are provided with one of the largest standard hole-generating tools known as **Hole Wizard**. You can use the **Hole Wizard** tool to add standard holes to the model so that the holes can accommodate standard fasteners.

1. Choose the **Hole Wizard** button in **Hole Wizard** flyout from the **Features CommandManager**; the **Hole Specification PropertyManager** is displayed.

2. Choose the **Countersink** button from the **Hole Type** rollout. Now, set the parameters to define the standard hole.
3. Select the **ANSI Metric** option from the **Standard** drop-down list.
4. Select the **Flat Head Screw - ANSI B18.6.7M** option from the **Type** drop-down list.
5. Select the **M3.5** option from the **Size** drop-down list and the **Normal** option from the **Fit** drop-down list in the **Hole Specifications** rollout.
6. Select the **Through All** option from the **End Condition** rollout.
7. Choose the **Positions** tab from the **Hole Specification PropertyManager**; you are prompted to select the face to place the hole.
8. Move the point cursor on the top planar face and select the planar face; the select cursor is replaced by the point cursor. Also, you are prompted to use the dimensions and other sketching tools to position the hole.
9. Specify a point for the placement of the left countersink hole. Similarly, specify one more point for the placement of the right countersink hole.

   If you place the points anywhere in the top planar face, you need to add the required relations and dimensions to define the location of these points. Before doing that, you need to change the model display from **Shaded With Edges** to **Hidden Lines Visible** for a better visibility.

10. Right-click in the drawing area and choose the **Select** option.
11. Choose the **Hidden Lines Visible** button from the **Display Style** flyout in the **View (Heads-Up)** toolbar to display the model with the hidden lines visible.
12. Select the left placement point and right-click to choose the **Add Relation** option from the **Sketch Tools** cascade menu to display the **Add Relations PropertyManager**.
13. Select the upper left hidden circle and choose the **Concentric** button from the **Add Relations** rollout.
14. Right-click in the drawing area and choose **Clear Selections** from the shortcut menu. Select the right placement point and the upper right hidden circle. Choose the **Concentric** button from the **Add Relations** rollout. Now, choose **OK** from the confirmation corner.

15. Choose the **OK** button from the **Hole Position PropertyManager**. Next, choose the **Shaded With Edges** button from the **View** toolbar.

The isometric view of the model after adding the hole feature is shown in Figure 7-146.

Adding a Fillet to the Model

Now, you need to add the fillet to the edges of the extruded feature with the draft that was created earlier.

1. Rotate the model and choose the **Fillet** button; the **Fillet PropertyManager** is displayed.

2. Choose the **FilletXpert** button; the **FilletXpert PropertyManager** is displayed with the **Add** tab chosen by default.

3. Select one of the edges of the draft, as shown in Figure 7-147, and do not move the mouse; a pop-up toolbar is displayed. Remember that if you move the cursor away from the edge after selecting it, the pop-up toolbar will disappear.

Figure 7-146 Model after adding the hole feature using the ***Hole Wizard*** *tool*

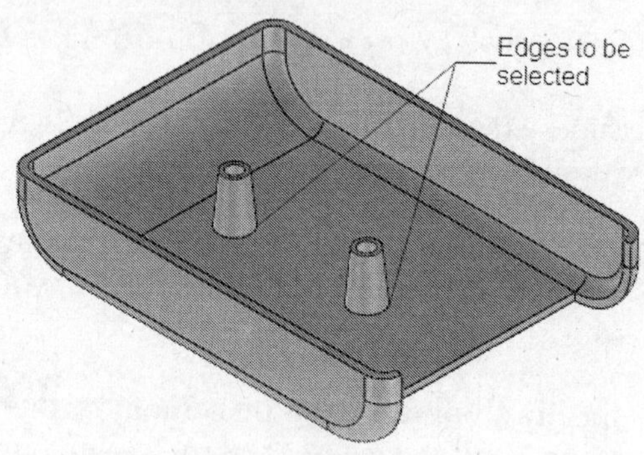

Figure 7-147 Edges to be selected

4. Move the cursor on the **All internal loops of right face, 1 Edge** button in the pop-up toolbar; the edge of the other draft that has to be filleted is highlighted, refer to Figure 7-147.

5. Choose the **All internal loops of right face, 1 Edge** button to select the edge; the name of the edge is displayed in the selection box in the **Items To Fillet** rollout.

6. Set the value of the **Radius** spinner to **1** and choose the **OK** button to end the feature creation. The model after adding the fillet is shown in Figure 7-148.

Adding a Lip to the Model

The last feature that you need to add to the model is a lip. It is created by extruding the open sketch.

1. Invoke the **Extruded Boss/Base** tool and select the bottom face of the base feature as the sketching plane.

2. Right-click on any one of the inner edges of the model on the current sketching plane using the **Select** tool to display a shortcut menu. Now, choose the **Select Tangency** option from the shortcut menu.

   If you need to create a sketch similar to that of an existing entity, it is recommended to convert the existing entity into a sketch by invoking the **Convert Entities** tool.

3. Choose the **Convert Entities** button from the **Sketch CommandManager**; the selected edges are converted into the sketched entities.

4. Exit the sketching environment; the **Boss-Extrude PropertyManager** is displayed and the **Thin Feature** rollout is invoked automatically because you are extruding an open sketch.

5. In the **Direction 1** rollout, set the value to **1** in the **Depth** as well as the **Thickness** spinners of the **Thin Feature** rollout.

6. Choose the **OK** button from the **Boss-Extrude PropertyManager**. The rotated view of the final model is shown in Figure 7-149.

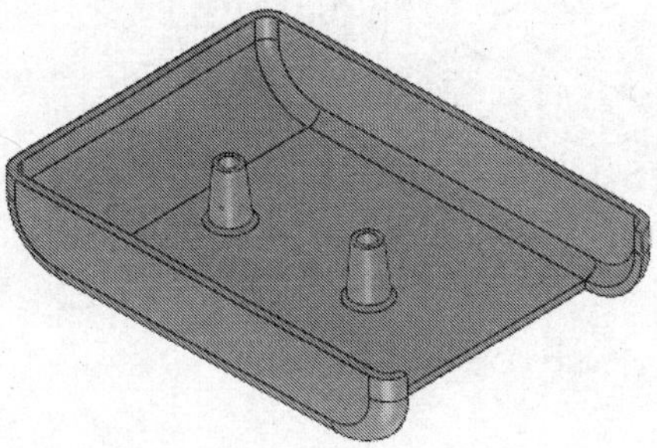

***Figure 7-148** Model after adding the fillet*

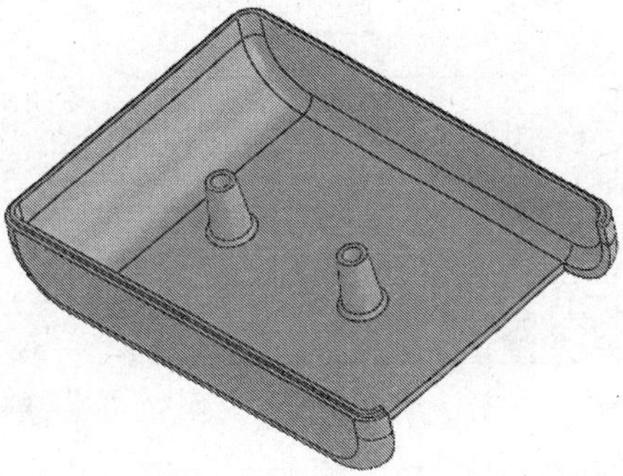

***Figure 7-149** Rotated model displaying maximum features*

Saving the Model

1. Save the part document with the name *c07_tut02* at the following location: *\Documents\SOLIDWORKS\c07*

2. Choose **File > Close** from the SOLIDWORKS menus to close the document.

Tutorial 3

In this tutorial, you will create the model shown in Figure 7-150. For a better understanding, the section view of the model is shown in Figure 7-151. The views and dimensions of the model are shown in Figure 7-152. The model has a uniform shell thickness of 1 mm. You also need to add fillet features of radius 2 mm and 1 mm to the model by using the **FilletXpert** tool. **(Expected time: 45 min)**

Figure 7-150 Solid model for Tutorial 3

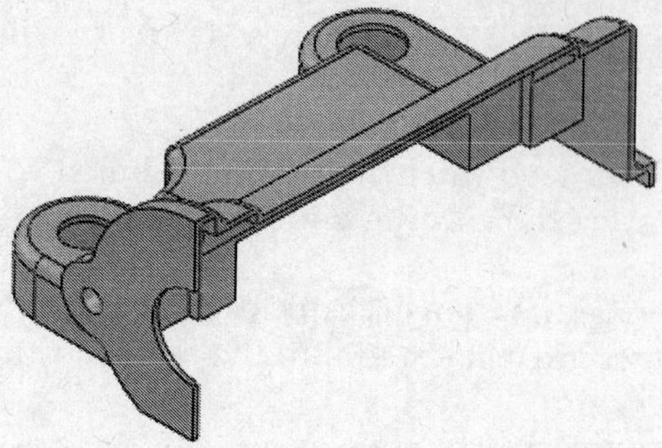

Figure 7-151 Section view of the model

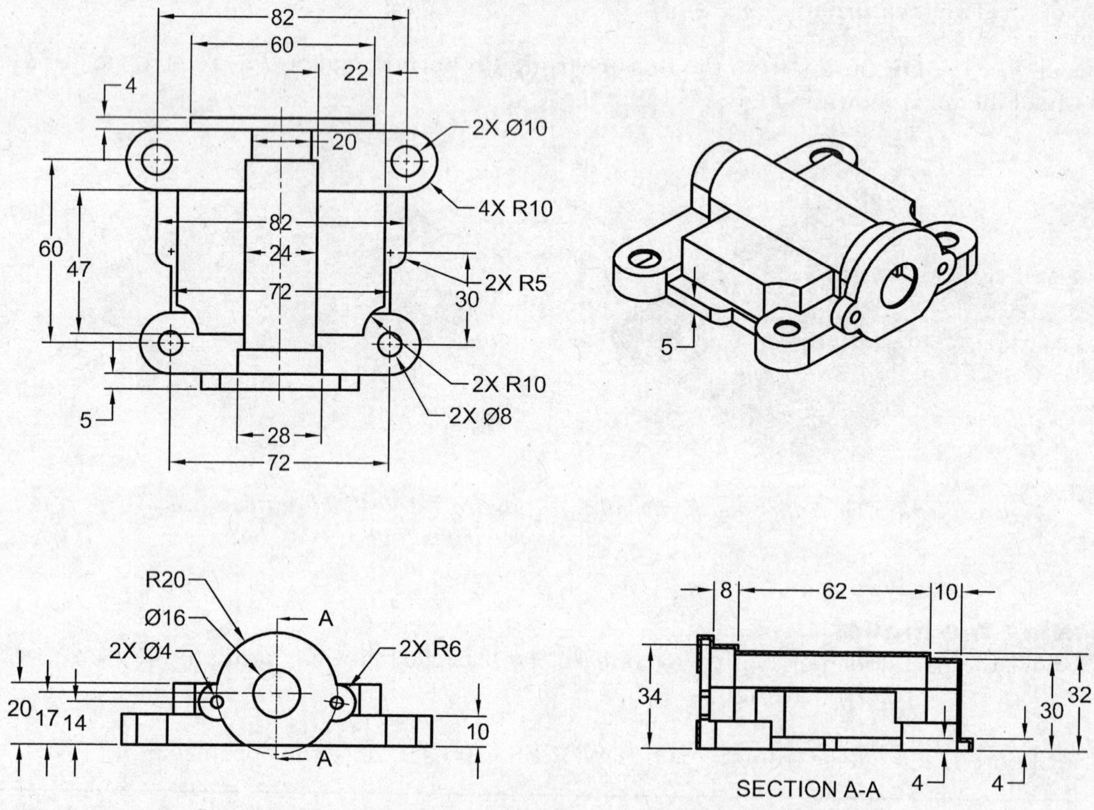

Figure 7-152 *Views and dimensions of the model*

The following steps are required to complete this tutorial:

a. Create the sketch of the model on the default plane and apply the required relations and dimensions to it.
b. Invoke the **Extruded Boss/Base** tool and extrude the selected contour.
c. Select the other set of contours and extrude them to the required distance.
d. Create the full round fillets.

e. Create the next circular extrude feature on the model.
f. Create the extrude feature and its mirror image.
g. Create the shell feature with a wall thickness of 1 mm.
h. Create the cut feature.
i. Create the simple hole feature.
j. Create the fillet features.
k. Save the model.

Creating the Sketch of the Model

1. Start a new SOLIDWORKS part document using the **New SOLIDWORKS Document** dialog box.

2. Draw the sketch of the model on the Top Plane. Apply the required relations and dimensions to the sketch, as shown in Figure 7-153. Do not exit the sketching environment.

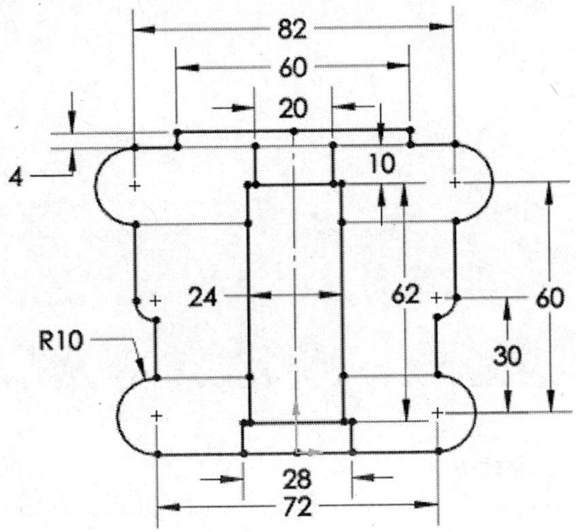

Figure 7-153 The sketch of the model

Selecting and Extruding the Contours of the Sketch

You need to use the contour selection method to create the model. Therefore, you first need to select one of the contours from the given sketch and then extrude it. For a better view, you can also orient the sketch to isometric view.

1. Choose the **Isometric** button from the **View Orientation** flyout in the **View (Heads-Up)** toolbar; the sketch is displayed in the isometric view.

2. Right-click in the drawing area to invoke a shortcut menu. Expand the shortcut menu, if required. Choose the **Contour Select Tool** option from the shortcut menu; the select cursor is replaced by the contour selection cursor and the selection confirmation corner is displayed.

3. Move the cursor over the rectangle having dimensions 60 x 4 and select it; the selected area of the rectangle is highlighted. This indicates that the rectangle is a closed profile.

4. Click on the highlighted rectangular area; the area is selected as a contour, as shown in Figure 7-154.

5. Choose the **Extruded Boss/Base** button from the **Features CommandManager** or from the pop-up toolbar; the **Boss-Extrude PropertyManager** is invoked and the preview of the base feature is displayed in the drawing area.

   Also, the name of the selected contour is displayed in the selection box of the **Selected Contours** rollout.

6. Enter the value **4** mm in the **Depth** spinner and choose the **OK** button; the selected contour is extruded, as shown in Figure 7-155.

7. Similarly, extrude the other contours of the sketch. The final model after extruding the other contours of the sketch is shown in Figure 7-156.

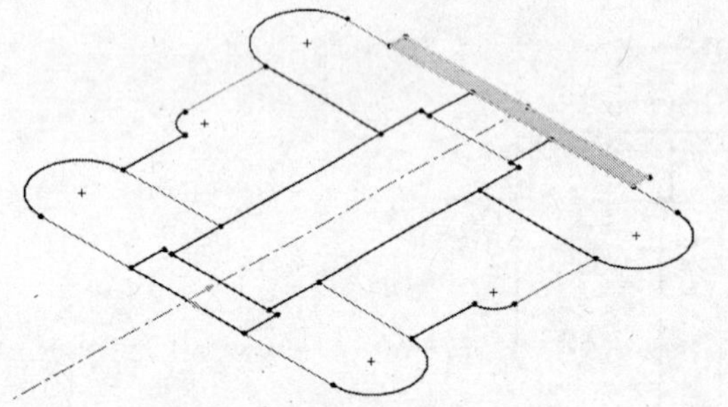

Figure 7-154 The rectangle selected as a contour

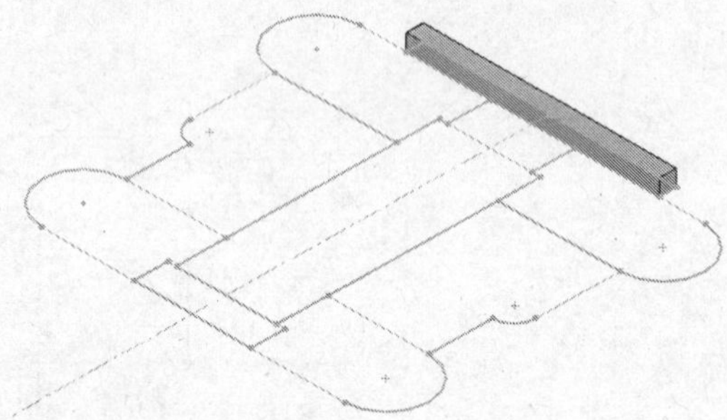

Figure 7-155 The extruded selected rectangle

Creating the Fillet Features

After creating the extrude features, you need to add full round fillets to the model.

1. Choose the **Fillet** button from the **Features CommandManager**; the **Fillet PropertyManager** is displayed. Choose the **Full Round Fillet** button from the **Fillet Type** rollout of the **PropertyManager**.

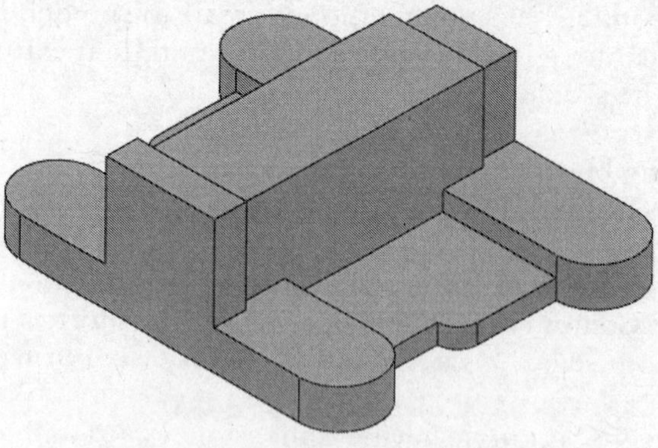

Figure 7-156 The final model after extruding the other contours of the sketch

2. The **Face Set 1** selection box is activated by default in the **Items to Fillet** rollout. Select a face as Face Set 1, refer to Figure 7-157. Next, click on the **Center Face Set** selection box in this rollout to activate it. Now, select the top face of the model, as the Center Face Set, refer to Figure 7-157. Next, activate the **Face Set 2** selection box and select the face, as the Face Set 2, refer to Figure 7-157. The preview of the full round fillet on the selected face sets is displayed in the drawing area with their respective callouts, as shown in Figure 7-158.

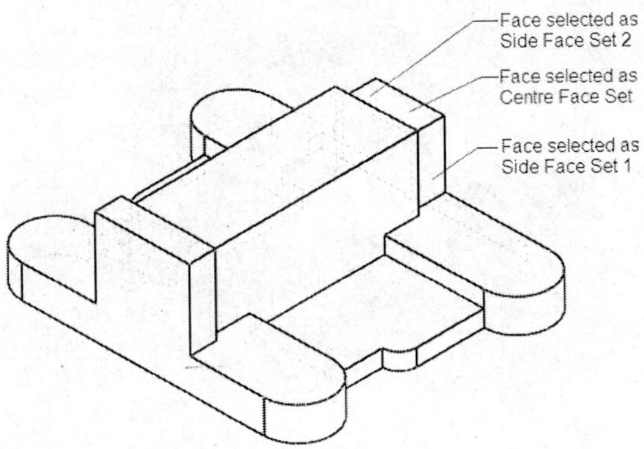

***Figure 7-157** The faces to be selected*

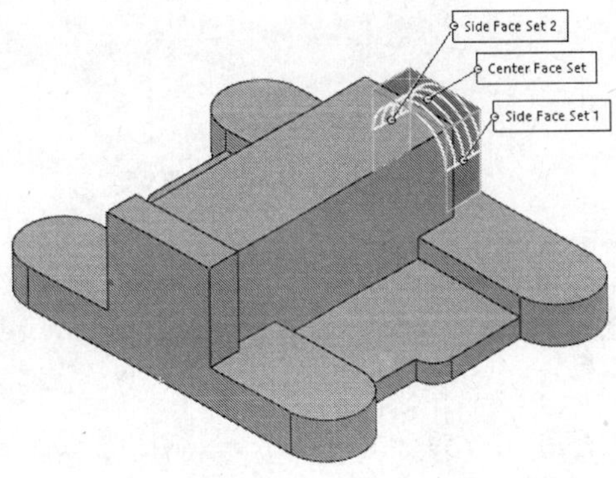

***Figure 7-158** The preview of the full round fillet*

3. Choose the **OK** button from the **PropertyManager** to exit. A rotated view of the model after creating the full round fillet is shown in Figure 7-159.

4. Similarly, create the full round fillets on the other features, as shown in Figure 7-160.

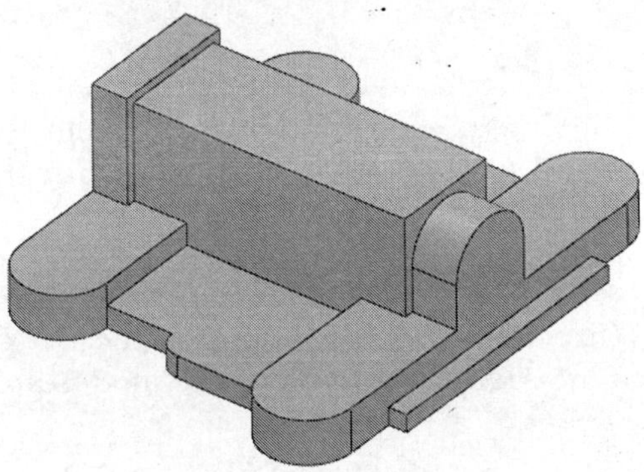

***Figure 7-159** The rotated view after creating the full round fillet*

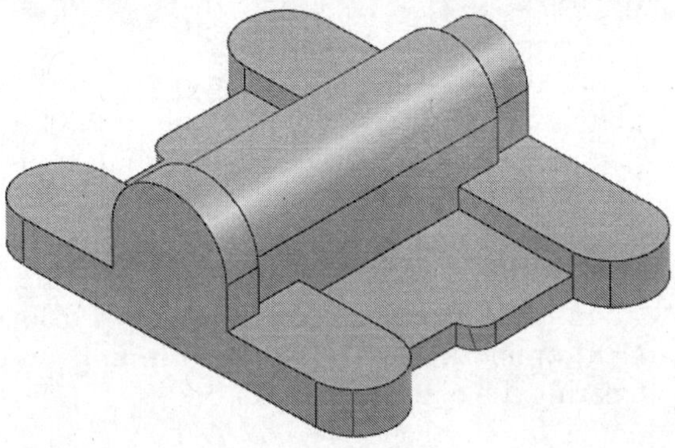

***Figure 7-160** The isometric view after creating other full round fillets*

Creating the Next Circular Extrude Feature

1. Choose the **Extruded Boss/Base** button from the **Features CommandManager**; the **Extrude PropertyManager** is invoked.

2. Select the front planar face of the model as the sketching plane and draw the sketch of the extrude feature, as shown in Figure 7-161.

3. Click on the confirmation corner; the **Boss-Extrude PropertyManager** is displayed. Enter the value **5** in the **Depth** spinner.

4. Choose the **OK** button. The isometric view of the model after creating the circular feature is shown in Figure 7-162.

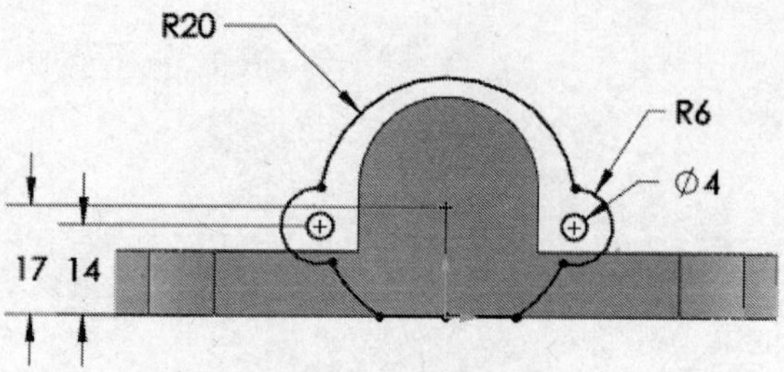

Figure 7-161 *Sketch of the extrude feature*

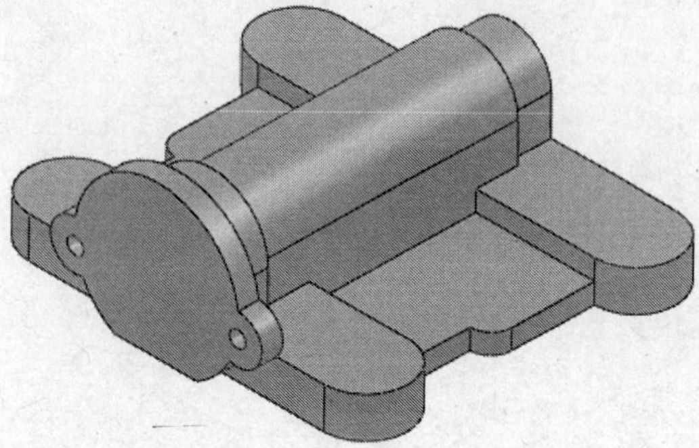

Figure 7-162 *Isometric view after creating the circular feature*

Creating an Extrude Feature and its Mirror Image

To create the next extrude feature, you need to create a reference plane at an offset distance from the top plane. Draw the sketch and extrude it.

1. Invoke the **Plane PropertyManager** and create a plane at an offset distance of 20 mm from the top plane.

2. Invoke the **Extruded Boss/Base** tool and select the newly created plane as the sketching plane. Orient the sketching plane normal to the viewing direction and draw the sketch on one side using the standard sketching tools, as shown in Figure 7-163. Then, mirror the sketch to the other side.

3. Exit from the sketching environment; the **Boss-Extrude PropertyManager** is invoked. Choose the **Reverse Direction** button from the **Direction 1** rollout and select the **Up To Next** option from the **End Condition** drop-down list. Figure 7-164 shows the model after creating the extrude feature.

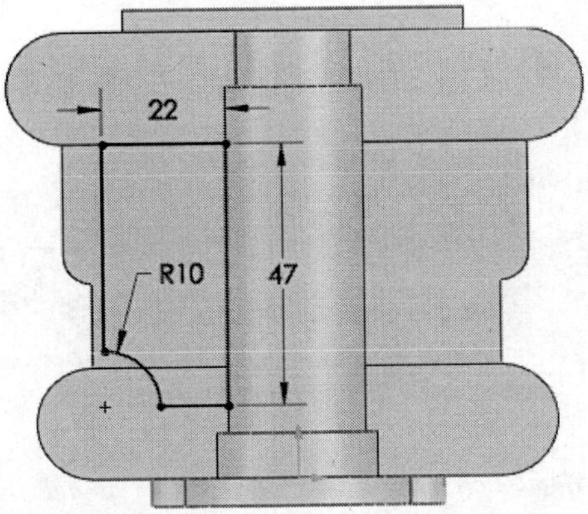

Figure 7-163 Sketch of the extrude feature

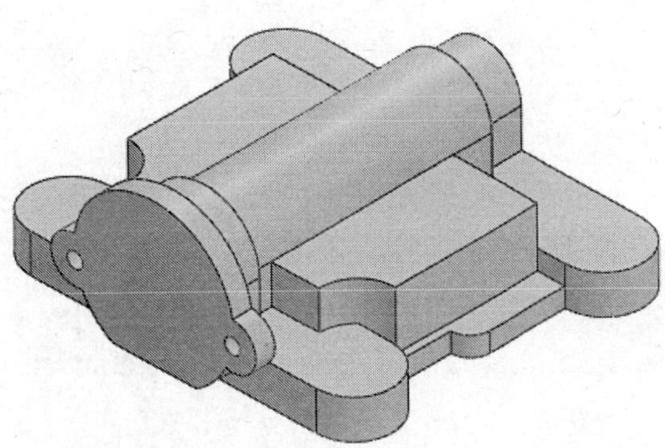

Figure 7-164 Isometric view of the model after creating the extrude feature

Note

*You can also extrude the sketch on one side and mirror the feature to the other side using the **Mirror** tool. You will learn more about the **Mirror** tool in the later chapters.*

Creating the Shell Feature

It is evident from Figures 7-150 and 7-151 that a shell feature is required to create a thin-walled structure.

1. Invoke the **Shell PropertyManager**; you are prompted to select the faces to be removed.
2. Rotate the model and select the bottom planar face of the model; the selected face is displayed in the **Faces to Remove** selection box.
3. Set the value to **1 mm** in the **Thickness** spinner of the **PropertyManager**. Choose the **OK** button to exit.

The rotated view of the model after creating the shell feature is shown in Figure 7-165.

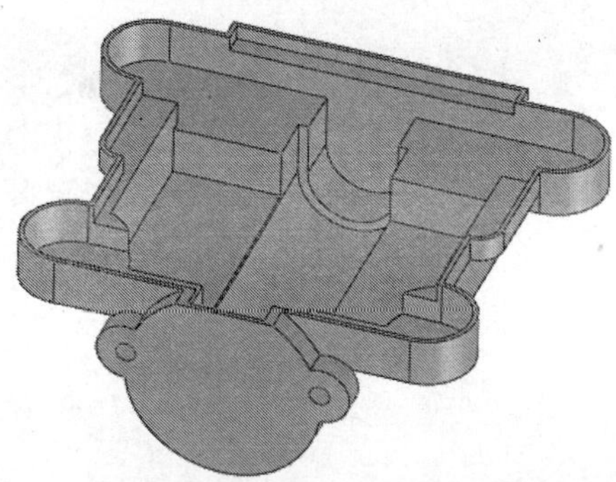

Figure 7-165 Model after creating the shell feature

Creating the Cut Feature

1. Invoke the **Extruded Cut** tool and select the front circular face of the model as the sketching plane.
2. Draw the sketch of the cut feature, as shown in Figure 7-166, and extrude it using the **Up To Next** option. Figure 7-167 shows the isometric view of the model after creating the cut feature.

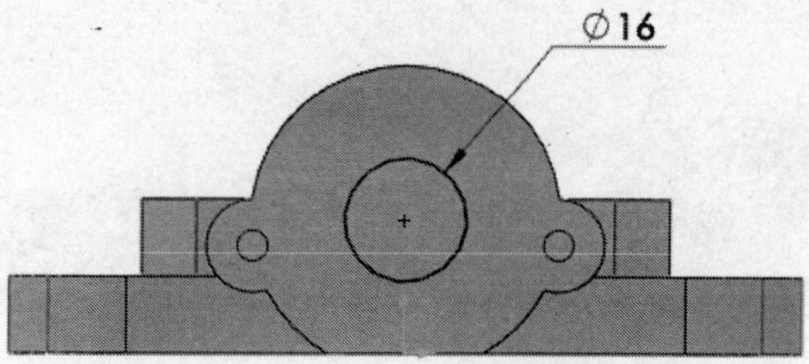

Figure 7-166 Sketch of the cut feature

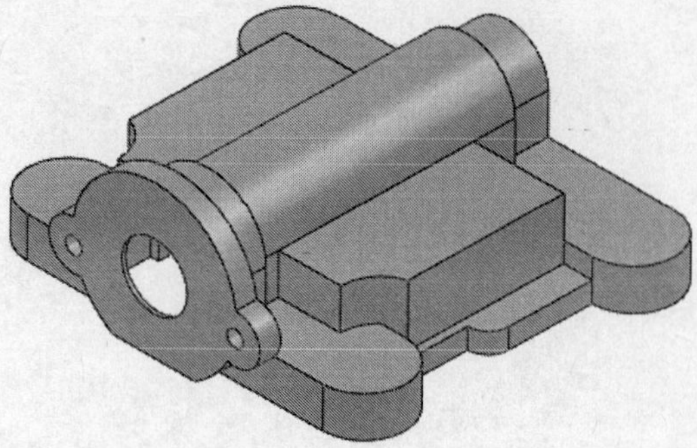

Figure 7-167 Isometric view of the model after creating the cut feature

Creating the Simple Hole Features

1. Choose the **Hole Wizard** button; the **Hole Specification PropertyManager** is invoked.

2. Choose the **Hole** button and create simple holes on the model using this PropertyManager. Figure 7-168 shows the model after creating simple hole features. For dimensions of the holes, you can refer to Figure 7-152.

Figure 7-168 Model after creating simple hole features

Creating the Fillet Features

1. Invoke the **Fillet PropertyManager** and choose the **FilletXpert** button; the **FilletXpert PropertyManager** is displayed.

2. Set the value to **2 mm** in the **Radius** spinner.

3. Rotate the model and select an edge, as shown in Figure 7-169; the selected edge is displayed in the **Edges, Faces, Features and Loops** selection box. As soon as you select the edge, a pop-up toolbar is displayed near the cursor.

4. Choose the **Connected, 137 Edges** button from the pop-up toolbar; all the related edges are displayed in the **Edges, Faces, Features and Loops** selection box.

5. Choose the **Apply** button; the **FeatureXpert** window is displayed and the process of creating the fillet starts. Note that after some time, the **SOLIDWORKS** message box is displayed with the message **FeatureXpert has not resolved all the features in this model**.

   The fillet of radius 2 mm is not created on all the edges related to the selected edge. The edges for which the fillet of radius 2 mm cannot be applied are listed in the **Items to Fillet** rollout. So, you need to reduce the fillet radius.

6. Choose **OK** from the **SOLIDWORKS** message box.

7. Set the value **1 mm** in the **Radius** spinner and choose the **Apply** button. If any edge is still left unfilleted then you need to close the **FilletXpert PropertyManager** and apply fillets manually.

8. Use the manual fillet option and apply the remaining fillets, except on the inner edges and hole features. The isometric view of the resultant model is shown in Figure 7-170.

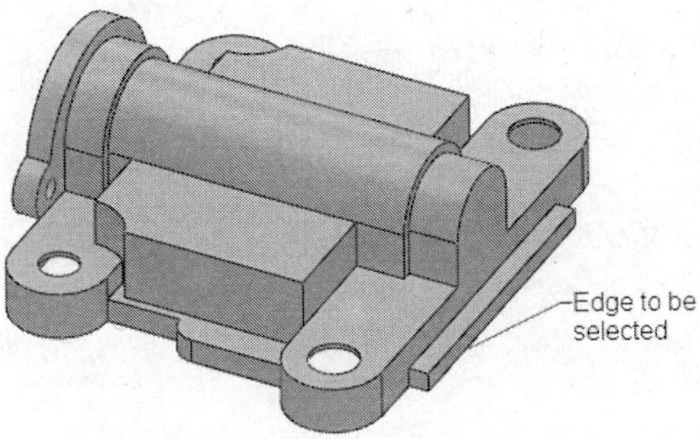

Figure 7-169 The edge to be selected for adding fillet

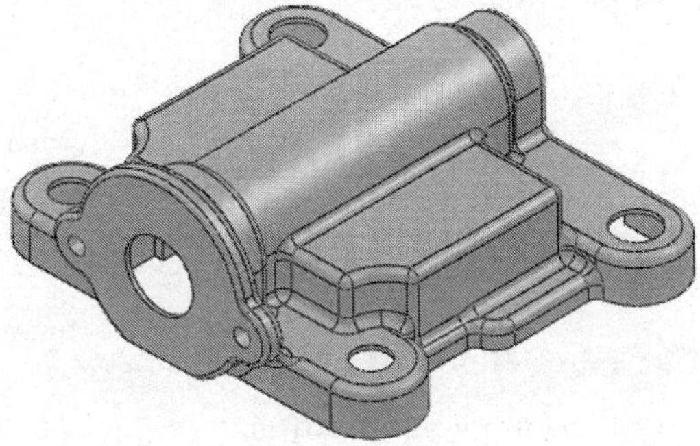

Figure 7-170 The final model

Saving the Model

1. Save the part document with the name *c07_tut03* at the location given next:
   \Documents\SOLIDWORKS\c07

2. Choose **File > Close** from the SOLIDWORKS menus to close the document.

Self-Evaluation Test

Answer the following questions and then compare them to those given at the end of this chapter:

1. The __________ check box is selected to create a shell feature on the outer side of the model.

2. A __________ is created by specifying different radii along the length of the selected edge at specified intervals.

3. The names of the faces to be removed in the shell features are displayed in the __________ selection box.

4. If you want to specify different value for distances while creating a chamfer, select the __________ option from the **Chamfer Method** drop-down list.

5. The __________ option in the **Profile** drop-down list is used to apply the face fillet feature with continuous curvature throughout the fillet feature.

6. You can create counterbore, countersink, and tapped holes using the **Hole PropertyManager**. (T/F)

7. The hole features created using the **Hole Wizard** tool and the **Hole PropertyManager** are not parametric. (T/F)

8. You cannot define a user-defined hole using the **Hole Wizard** tool. (T/F)

9. You cannot preselect the edges or faces for creating a fillet feature. (T/F)

10. In SOLIDWORKS, you can create a multi-thickness shell feature. (T/F)

Review Questions

Answer the following questions:

1. If you preselect the placement surface to create a hole feature using the **Hole Wizard** tool then what type of resultant placement sketch will be created?

   (a) 2D sketch (b) Planar sketch
   (c) Bezier spline (d) 3D sketch

2. Which one of the following options, when selected, does not require a radius to create a fillet feature?

   (a) **Face Fillet with Symmetric** (b) **Constant Size Fillet**
   (c) **Variable Size Fillet** (d) **Full Round Fillet**

3. Which of the following radio buttons in the **Variable Radius Parameters** rollout is used to create a smooth transition while creating a variable radius fillet?

   (a) **Straight transition** (b) **Parametric transition**
   (c) **Smooth transition** (d) **Surface transition**

4. Which of the following model will be created if you do not remove a face while creating the shell feature?

(a) Remains a complete solid model. (b) Thin walled hollow model
(c) Automatically removes one face (d) None of these

5. Which PropertyManager is displayed by default when you choose the **Hole Wizard** button from the **Features CommandManager**?

(a) **Hole** (b) **Hole Definition**
(c) **Hole Wizard** (d) **Hole Specification**

6. The __________ option is used to add standard holes to a model.

7. After specifying all parameters of a hole feature using the **Hole Specification PropertyManager**, the __________ tab is chosen to specify the placement of the hole feature.

8. Invoke the__________ **PropertyManager** to modify the fillets created at corners.

9. The __________ button from the **Hole Specifications** rollout is used to define a standard drilled hole.

10. By default, the __________ button is selected in the **Chamfer PropertyManager**.

EXERCISES

Exercise 1

Create the model shown in Figure 7-171. The views and dimensions of the model are shown in Figure 7-172. **(Expected time: 30 min)**

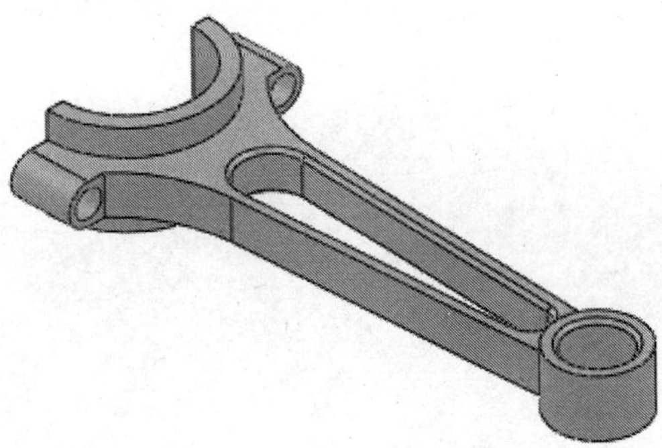

Figure 7-171 *Solid model for Exercise 1*

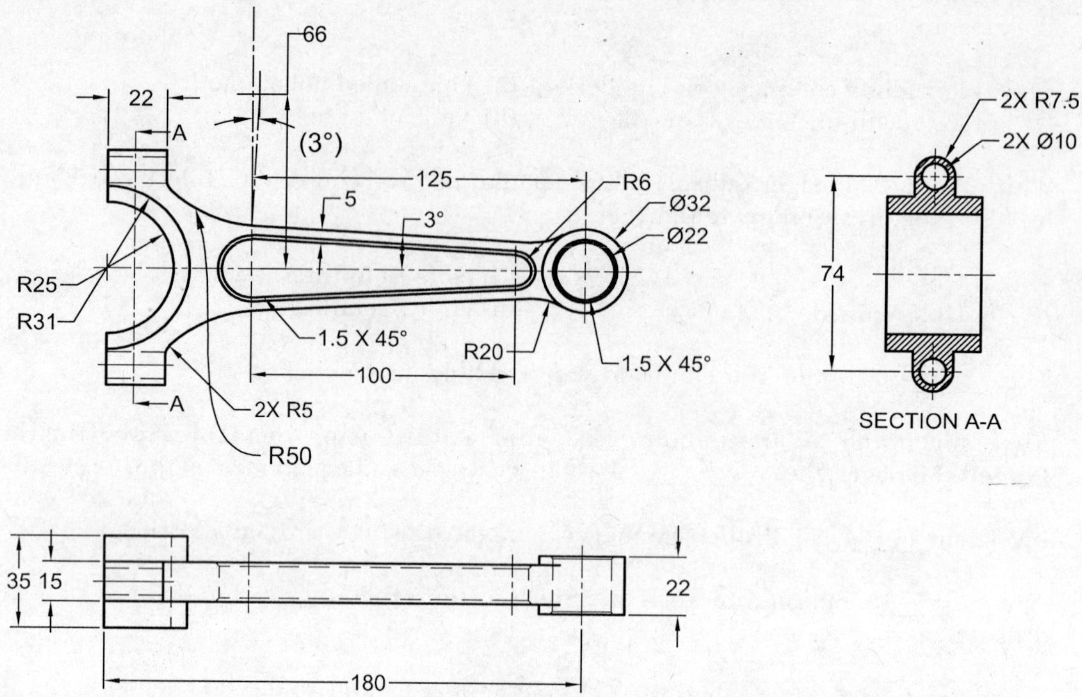

Figure 7-172 Views and dimensions of the model for Exercise 1

Exercise 2

Create the model shown in Figure 7-173. The views and dimensions of the model are shown in Figure 7-174.

(Expected time: 30 min)

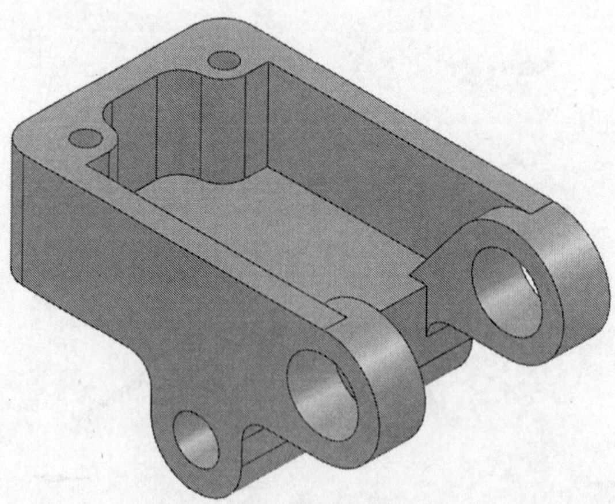

Figure 7-173 Solid model for Exercise 2

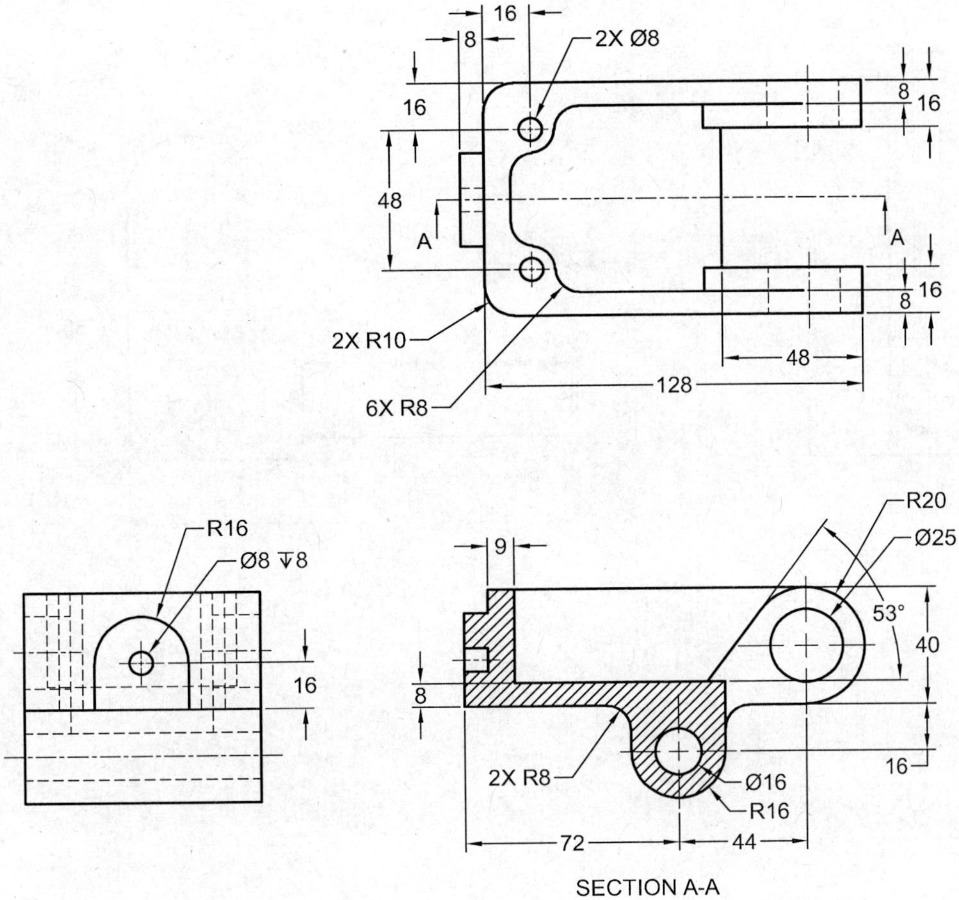

Figure 7-174 *Views and dimensions of the model for Exercise 2*

Exercise 3

Create the model shown in Figure 7-175. The views and dimensions of the model are shown in Figures 7-176. **(Expected time: 30 min)**

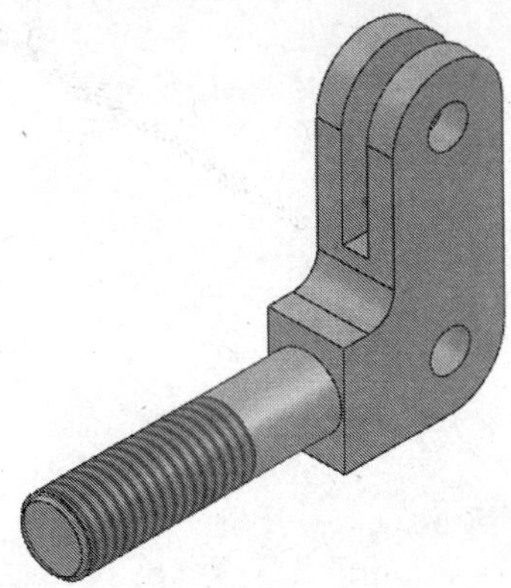

Figure 7-175 *Solid model for Exercise 3*

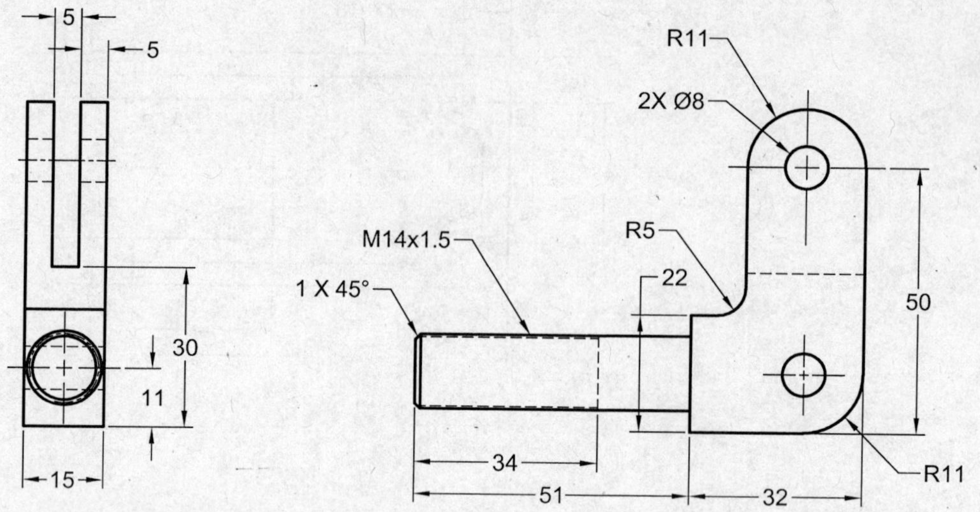

Figure 7-176 Dimensions of the model

Answers to Self-Evaluation Test

1. Shell outward, **2.** variable radius fillet, **3. Faces to Remove**, **4. Asymmetric**, **5. Curvature Continuous**, **6.** F, **7.** F, **8.** F, **9.** F, **10.** T

Chapter 8

Advanced Modeling Tools-II

Learning Objectives

After completing this chapter, you will be able to:

- *Mirror features, faces, and bodies*
- *Create linear patterns*
- *Create circular patterns*
- *Create sketch driven patterns*
- *Create curve driven patterns*
- *Create table driven patterns*
- *Create rib features*
- *Display the section view of a model*
- *Change the display state of a part*

ADVANCED MODELING TOOLS

Some of the advanced modeling tools were discussed in Chapter 7, Advanced Modeling Tools-I. In this chapter, you will learn about some more advanced modeling tools that can be used to capture the design intent of a model. The rest of the advanced modeling tools will be discussed in the later chapters.

Creating Mirror Features

CommandManager:	Features > Linear Pattern flyout > Mirror
SOLIDWORKS menus:	Insert > Pattern/Mirror > Mirror
Toolbar:	Features > Linear Pattern flyout > Mirror

The **Mirror** tool is used to copy or mirror a selected feature, face, or body about a specified mirror plane which can be a reference plane or a planar face. To invoke this tool, choose the **Mirror** button from the **Linear Pattern** flyout in the **Features CommandManager**, refer to Figure 8-1; the **Mirror PropertyManager** will be displayed, as shown in Figure 8-2. You can also invoke the **Mirror PropertyManager** by choosing **Insert > Pattern/Mirror > Mirror** from the SOLIDWORKS menus. On doing so, the confirmation corner is also displayed in the drawing area.

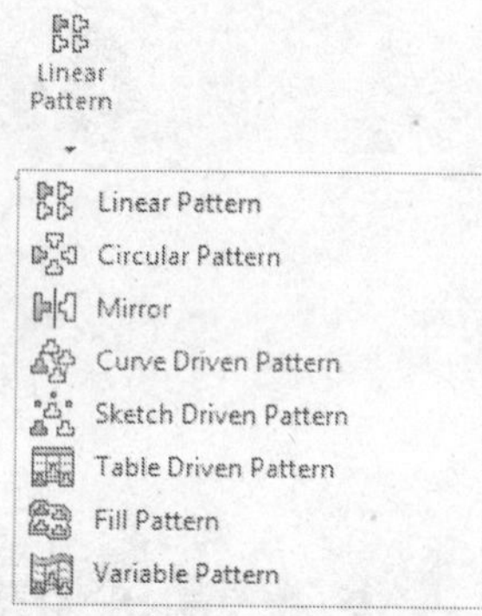

*Figure 8-1 Tools in the **Linear Pattern** flyout*

The options used to mirror features, faces, and bodies are discussed next.

Mirroring Features

You can mirror a selected feature along the specified mirror plane or face by using this feature. To do so, invoke the **Mirror PropertyManager**; you will be prompted to select a plane or a planar face about which the features will be mirrored, followed by the features to be mirrored. Select a plane or a planar face that will act as a mirror plane or mirror face. After selecting the mirror plane or face, the selection box of the **Features to Mirror** rollout will be activated and you will be prompted to select the features to mirror. Select the feature or features from the drawing area or from the **FeatureManager Design Tree** that is displayed in the drawing area. When you select the features to be mirrored, a preview of the mirrored feature will be displayed in the drawing area. After selecting the required features, choose the **OK** button from the **Mirror PropertyManager**. Figure 8-3 shows the mirror plane and the features to be mirrored and Figure 8-4 shows the resulting mirrored features.

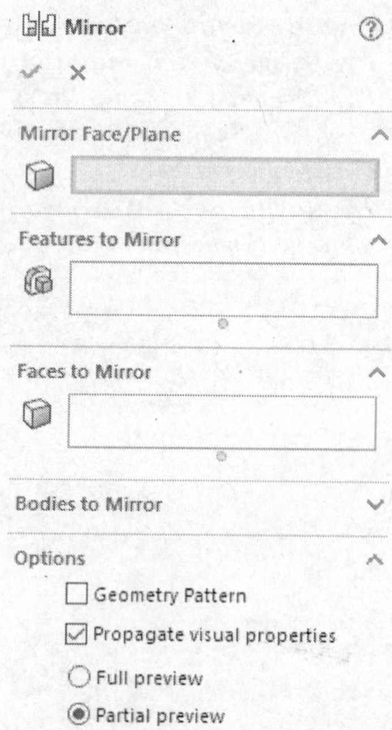

*Figure 8-2 The **Mirror PropertyManager***

Mirroring with and without the Geometric Pattern

When you create a mirror feature, you are provided with the **Geometry Pattern** option. This option is available in the **Options** rollout.

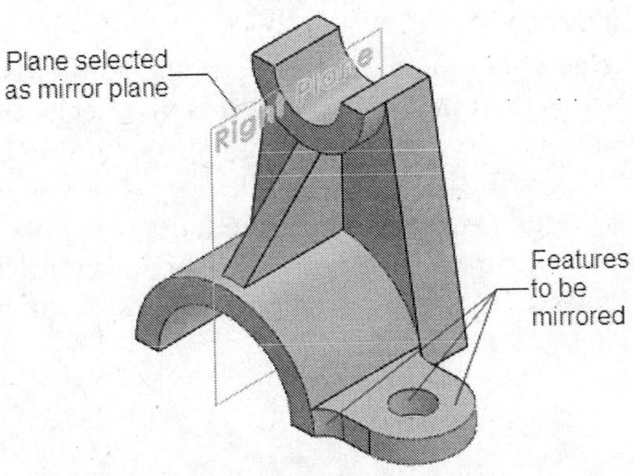

Figure 8-3 Mirror plane and the features to be mirrored

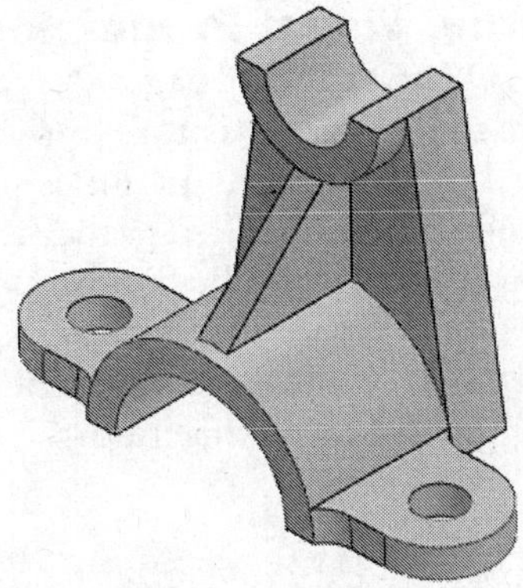

Figure 8-4 The resulting mirrored features

> **Tip**
> *You can also preselect the mirror plane or the mirror face and the features to be mirrored before invoking the **Mirror PropertyManager**.*

By default, the **Geometry Pattern** check box is cleared in this rollout. Therefore, if you mirror a feature that is related to other entity, the same relationship will be applied to the mirrored feature. Consider a case in which an extruded cut is created using the **Offset From Surface** option. If you mirror the cut feature along a plane, the same relationship will be applied to the mirrored cut feature. The mirrored cut feature will be created with the same end condition with which the original feature was terminated. Figure 8-5 shows a hole feature created on the right and mirrored along **Plane 1**, with the **Geometry Pattern** check box cleared.

If you select the **Geometry Pattern** check box, the resulting mirror feature will not depend on the relational references. It will create a replica of the selected geometry, as shown in Figure 8-6. Note that the visual properties will be visible only after you exit this tool.

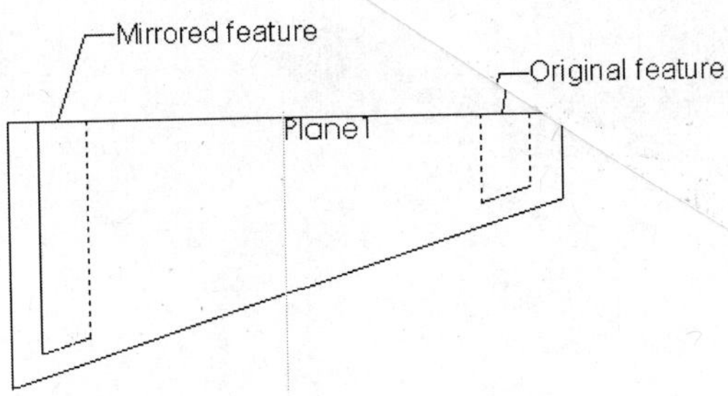

*Figure 8-5 Mirrored feature created with the **Geometry Pattern** check box cleared*

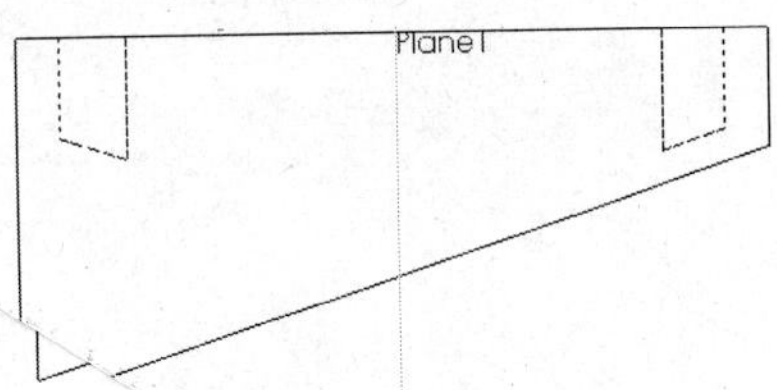

*Figure 8-6 Mirrored feature created with the **Geometry Pattern** check box selected*

Propagating Visual Properties while Mirroring

In SOLIDWORKS, the **Propagate visual properties** check box is used to transfer the visual properties assigned to the feature or the parent body to the mirrored instance. This check box is provided in the **Options** rollout and is selected by default. Note that the visual properties such as the colors and textures applied to the features or the part bodies will be visible only after you exit this tool. If you clear this check box, the color or the texture applied on the faces, features, or the bodies will not be reflected in the resulting mirrored instance. Figure 8-7 shows the mirror feature with the **Propagate visual properties** check box selected and Figure 8-8 shows the mirror feature with this check box cleared.

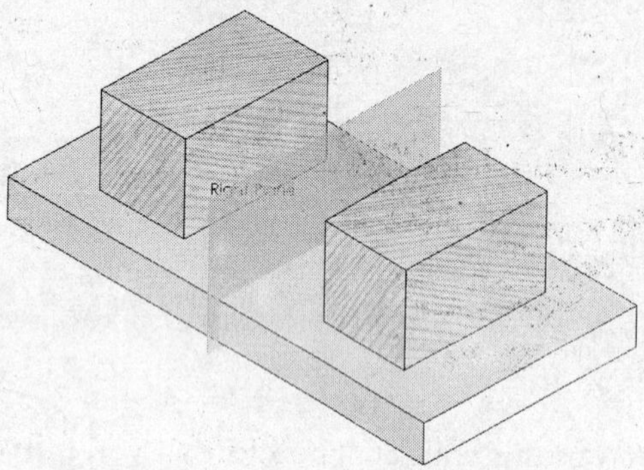

Figure 8-7 *Mirror feature with the* ***Propagate visual properties*** *check box selected*

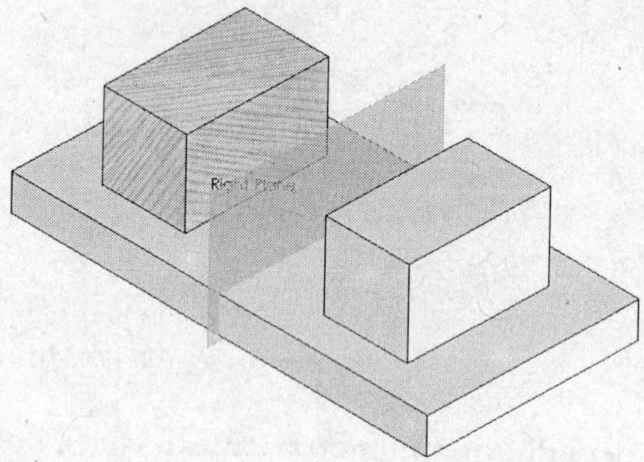

Figure 8-8 *Mirror feature with the* ***Propagate visual properties*** *check box cleared*

Mirroring Faces

In SOLIDWORKS, you can mirror faces about a plane or a face. To use this option, invoke the **Mirror PropertyManager**; you will be prompted to select a plane or a planar face about which the selected faces will be mirrored. Select the planar face or plane. Next, click once in the **Faces to Mirror** selection box to invoke the selection mode and select the faces to be mirrored. The selected faces must form a closed body. Else, the feature creation will not be possible. Choose the **OK** button from the **Mirror PropertyManager** to complete the feature creation. Figure 8-9 shows the faces and mirror plane selected to mirror. Figure 8-10 shows the resulting mirrored feature.

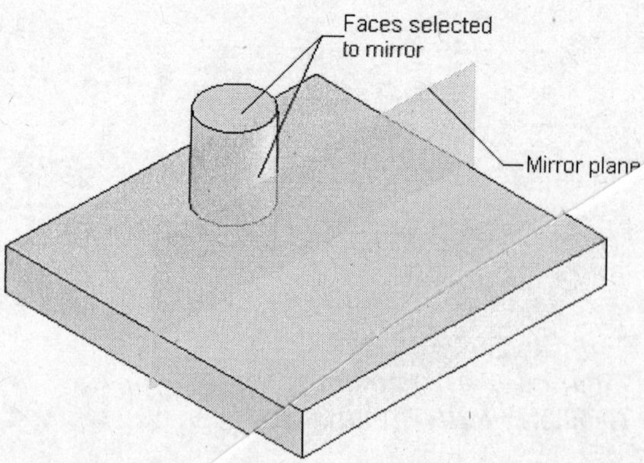

Figure 8-9 *Mirror plane and faces selected to mirror*

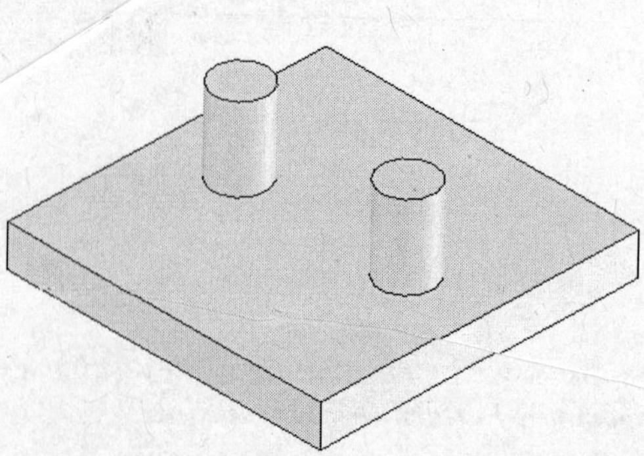

Figure 8-10 *Resulting mirrored feature*

Note

The following are some of the factors that should be considered while creating a mirror feature of the faces along the selected plane or planar face:

1. If replica of the faces is not coincident with the parent part body, SOLIDWORKS will give an error while creating the mirror feature.

2. If replica of the faces exist on faces other than the original face, SOLIDWORKS will give an error while creating the mirror feature.

3. If selected faces form a complex geometry, SOLIDWORKS will give an error while creating the mirror feature.

4. If mirrored faces exist on more than a face, SOLIDWORKS will give an error while creating the mirror feature.

Mirroring Bodies

As discussed in the earlier chapters, SOLIDWORKS supports the multi body environment. Therefore, using the **Mirror** tool, you can also mirror the disjoint bodies. To mirror a body along a plane, invoke the **Mirror PropertyManager** and select a plane or a planar face that will act as a mirror plane. Expand the **Bodies to Mirror** rollout and select the body to be mirrored from the drawing area. Alternatively, you can expand the **FeatureManager design tree** and select the body to be mirrored from the **Solid Bodies** folder; the name of the selected body will be displayed in the **Solid/Surface Bodies to Mirror** selection box. Also, the preview of the mirrored body will be displayed in the drawing area. Choose the **OK** button from the **Mirror PropertyManager**. Figure 8-11 shows the plane and the body to be mirrored. Figure 8-12 shows the resulting mirrored feature.

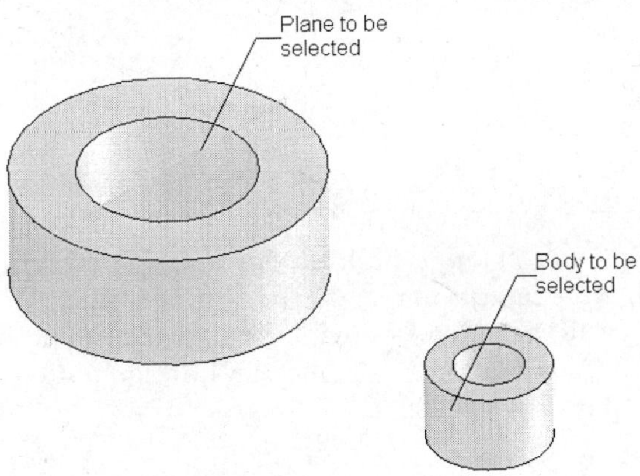

Figure 8-11 *Selecting the mirror plane and body to be mirrored*

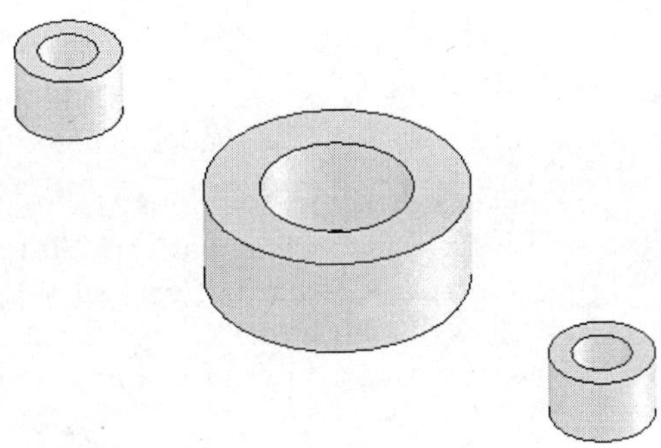

Figure 8-12 *Resulting mirrored feature*

Options Rollout

Figure 8-13 shows the options in the **Options** rollout of the **Mirror PropertyManager**. These options are discussed next.

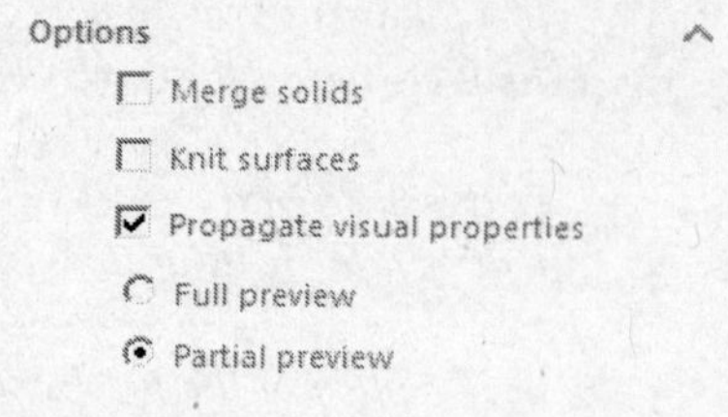

*Figure 8-13 The **Options** rollout*

Merge solids

The **Merge solids** check box is used to merge the mirrored body with the parent body. Consider that you want to mirror a body along a selected plane or a planar face of the same body and the resulting mirrored body is joined to the parent body. In this case, if you select the **Merge solids** check box, the resulting mirrored body will merge with the parent body and will turn into a single body. If the **Merge solids** check box is cleared, the resulting body will join with the parent body, but will not merge with it. Therefore, it will result in two separate bodies.

Knit surfaces

If you mirror a surface body, then select the **Knit surfaces** check box to knit the mirrored and parent bodies together.

Tip

1. As discussed earlier, the design intent is captured easily in the model using the mirror option. Therefore, if you modify the parent feature, face, or body, the same will be reflected in the mirrored feature, face, or body.

*2. If you want to mirror all the features of the model using the **Features to Mirror** option, you need to select all the features. But for using the **Bodies to Mirror** option, you need to select the body from the **Solid Bodies** folder. By selecting the body, all the features will be added to the mirror image.*

Creating Linear Pattern Features

CommandManager:	Features > Linear Pattern flyout > Linear Pattern
SOLIDWORKS Menus:	Insert > Pattern/Mirror > Linear Pattern
Toolbar:	Features > Linear Pattern flyout > Linear Pattern

As discussed in the previous chapters, you can arrange multiple instances of sketched entities in a particular pattern. Similarly, you can also arrange the features, faces, and bodies in a particular pattern. In SOLIDWORKS, you are provided with various types of patterns such as linear patterns, circular patterns, sketch driven patterns, curve driven patterns, table driven patterns, fill patterns, and variable patterns.

In this section, you will learn to create linear patterns. The other types of patterns are discussed later in this chapter.

To create a linear pattern, choose the **Linear Pattern** button from the **Features CommandManager** or choose **Insert > Pattern/Mirror > Linear Pattern** from the SOLIDWORKS menus; the **Linear Pattern PropertyManager** will be invoked and the confirmation corner will be displayed. Partial view of the **Linear Pattern PropertyManager** is shown in Figure 8-14. Various options in the **Linear Pattern PropertyManager** are discussed next.

Linear Pattern in One Direction

When you invoke the **Linear Pattern PropertyManager**, the **Direction 1** rollout, the **Direction 2** rollout, and the **Features and Faces** rollout are expanded by default. Also, you will be prompted to select an edge or an axis for the direction reference and face of the feature to pattern. Select an edge or an axis as the direction reference; the name of the selected reference will be displayed in the **Pattern Direction** selection box of the **Direction 1** rollout. Also, the selected reference will be highlighted and the **Direction 1** callout will be attached to it. The **Direction 1** callout has two edit boxes, one to define the spacing and the other to define the number of instances. Also, the **Reverse Direction** arrow will be displayed along with the selected reference. As soon as you define the first direction, the **Pattern Direction** selection box in the **Direction 2** rollout is activated. Select an edge or an axis as the second direction reference or you can skip by clicking once in the **Features to Pattern** selection box of the **Features and Faces** rollout. Now, select the feature to be patterned; the name of the selected feature will be displayed in the **Features to Pattern** selection box of the **Features and Faces** rollout. You can also select a face of the feature to pattern. To do so, activate the **Faces to Pattern** selection box in the **Features and Faces** rollout and select the required face; the name of the selected face will be displayed in the **Faces to Pattern** selection box. You can also select the bodies that are not intersecting the parent feature. To do so, expand the **Bodies** rollout by selecting the down arrows on its right; the rollout will be expanded. To activate the options in the **Bodies** rollout, you need to select the check box on its left. Next, select the body to be patterned. The name of the selected body will be displayed in the **Solid/Surface Bodies to Pattern** selection box.

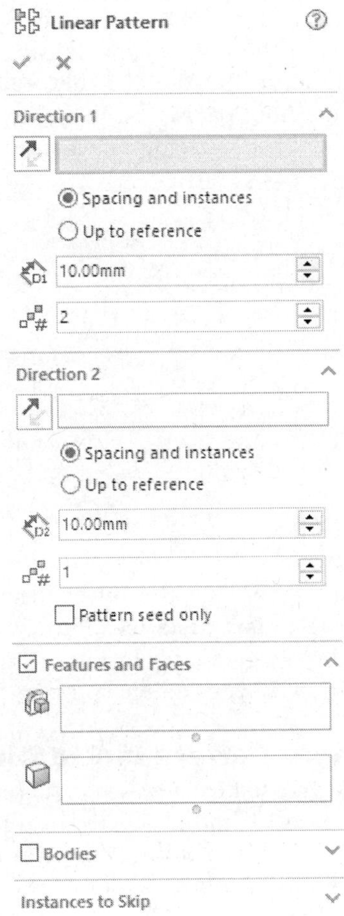

Figure 8-14** Partial view of the **Linear Pattern PropertyManager

A preview of the pattern will be displayed in the drawing area with the default values. By default, the **Spacing and instances** radio button is selected in the **Direction 1** rollout. Set the value of the center to center spacing between the pattern instances in the **Spacing** spinner. Set the value of the number of instances to be patterned in the **Number of Instances** spinner. You can also set these values in the **Direction 1** callout. You can choose the **Reverse Direction** button from the **PropertyManager** or the **Reverse Direction** arrow from the drawing area to reverse the direction of the resulting pattern feature. Figure 8-15 shows the feature and edge selected for directional reference and Figure 8-16 shows the model after the pattern has been created.

You can control the number of instances to be created or spacing between them using the reference geometry such as vertex, edge, surface, or plane. To do so, select the **Up to reference** radio button in the **Direction 1** rollout; the **Direction 1** rollout will be modified. Now, select the required reference geometry from the drawing area; the name of the selected geometry will be displayed in the **Reference Geometry** selection box available below the **Up to reference** radio button. If you choose the **Set Spacing** button located at the bottom of the **Direction 1** rollout and set the value of spacing in the **Spacing** spinner; the number of instances will be calculated automatically. Alternatively, you can choose the **Set Number of Instances** button on the right of the **Set Spacing** button and set the value of instances in the **Number of Instances** spinner; the value of spacing between instances will be calculated automatically.

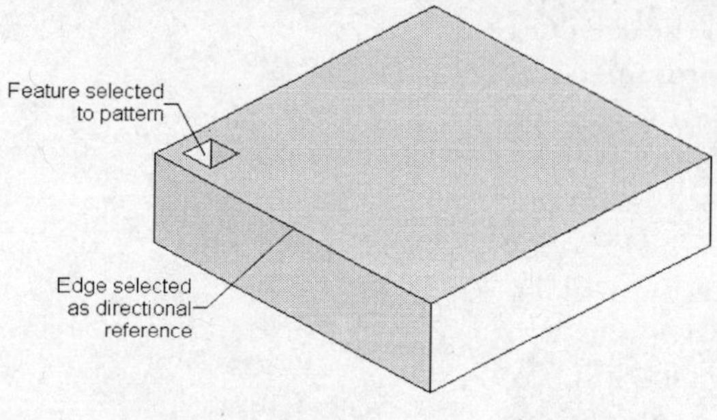

Figure 8-15 *The feature and edge selected for directional reference*

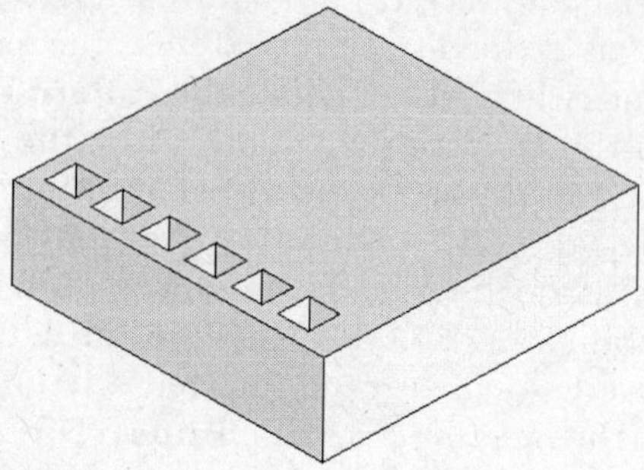

Figure 8-16 *Linear pattern created in one direction*

You can also set the offset distance of the last pattern instance from the reference geometry in the **Offset distance** spinner. Similarly, you can reverse the direction of the offset from the reference geometry by choosing the **Reverse offset direction** button available on the left side of the **Offset distance** spinner.

Linear Pattern in Two Directions

As discussed earlier, you can create a linear pattern of features, faces, and bodies by defining a single direction using the **Direction 1** rollout. You can also define parameters in the **Direction 2** rollout to define the pattern in the second direction. The **Direction 2** rollout is shown in Figure 8-17. If the **Direction 2** rollout is not expanded by default in the **Linear Pattern PropertyManager**, click on the arrow in the **Direction 2** rollout to expand it. When you define the pattern in the second direction, the entire row created by specifying the parameters in the first direction will be patterned in the second direction. To create a pattern by specifying the parameters in both the directions, select the feature to be patterned, and invoke the **Linear Pattern PropertyManager**. Select the first directional reference.

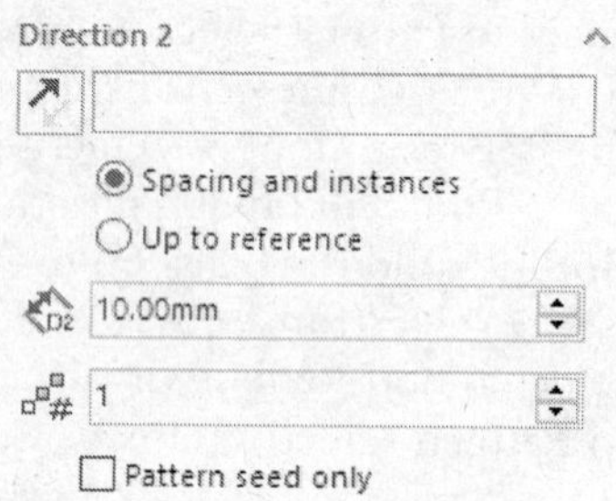

Figure 8-17 *The* ***Direction 2*** *rollout*

Next, specify the parameters in the **Direction 1** rollout. Now, select the second directional reference and specify the parameters in the **Direction 2** rollout. The options in the **Direction 2** rollout are the same as those discussed in the **Direction 1** rollout. Figure 8-18 shows the directional references and feature to be selected. Figure 8-19 shows the linear pattern created using the **Direction 1** and **Direction 2** rollouts.

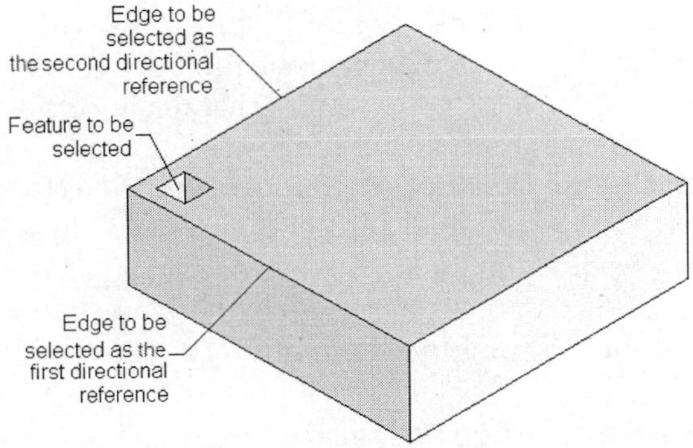

***Figure 8-18** References and feature to be selected*

By default, all rows of the instances created in the first direction are patterned in the second direction also. This is because the **Pattern seed only** check box in the **Direction 2** rollout is cleared. You can select this check box to pattern only the original selected feature (also called seed feature) in the second direction. Figure 8-20 shows the pattern created with the **Pattern seed only** check box selected.

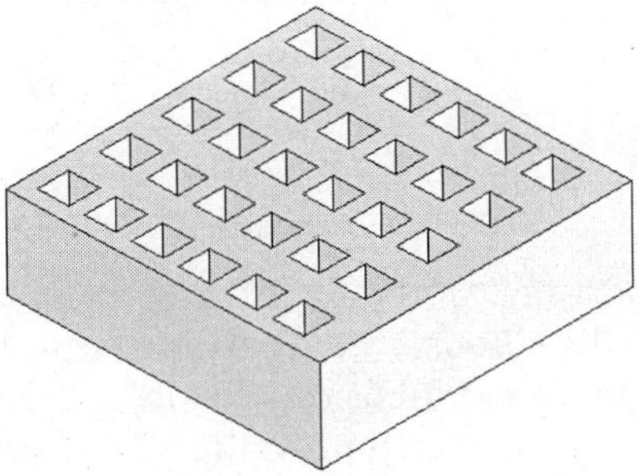

***Figure 8-19** Linear pattern created using the **Direction 1** and **Direction 2** rollouts*

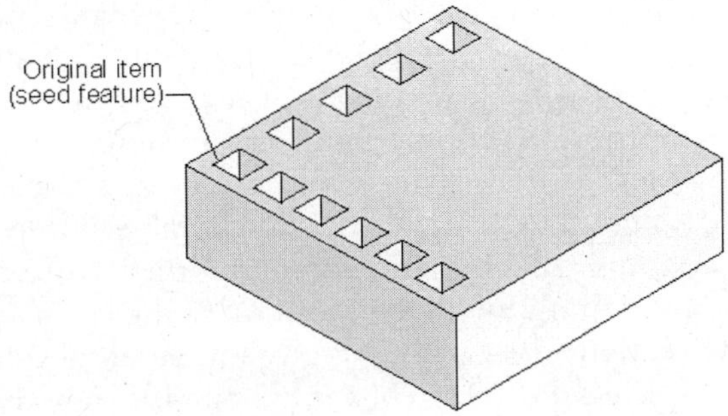

***Figure 8-20** Linear pattern created with the **Pattern seed only** check box selected*

Tip

When you select a feature to be patterned, its dimensions are also displayed in the drawing area. You can also select the dimensions as directional reference.

Instances to Skip

The **Instances to Skip** rollout is used to skip some of the instances from the pattern. These instances are not actually deleted but they disappear from the pattern feature. You can resume these instances at any time of your design cycle. To skip pattern instances, expand the **Instances to Skip** rollout from the **Linear Pattern PropertyManager**; the **Instances to Skip** rollout will be displayed, as shown in Figure 8-21.

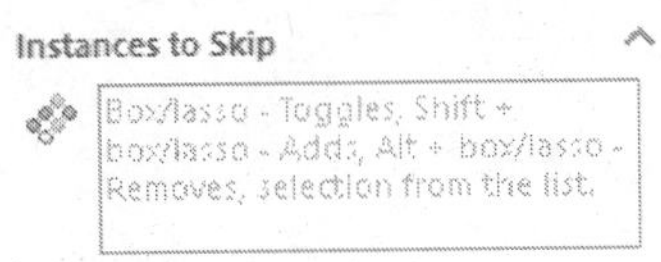

***Figure 8-21** The **Instances to Skip** rollout*

As soon as you expand this rollout, pink dots will be displayed at the center of all pattern instances except the parent instance. Therefore, you cannot skip the parent instance. Next, move the cursor to the pink dot of the instance to be skipped; the cursor will be replaced by the instance to skip cursor and the position of that instance will be displayed, as a tool tip, in the form of a matrix below this cursor. Click on the pink dot to skip that instance; the pink dot will be replaced by an white dot, and the preview of that instance will disappear from the pattern. Also, the position of the skipped instance in the form of a matrix will be displayed in the **Instances to Skip** selection box of the **Instances to Skip** rollout. In SOLIDWORKS, you can select multiple instances to be skipped in one selection. To do so, select the instances to be skipped using box or lasso selection method. Figure 8-22 shows a pattern created with some instances skipped. You can resume the skipped instances by deleting the name of the instance from the **Instances to Skip** selection box or selecting the white dot from the drawing area.

Instances to Vary

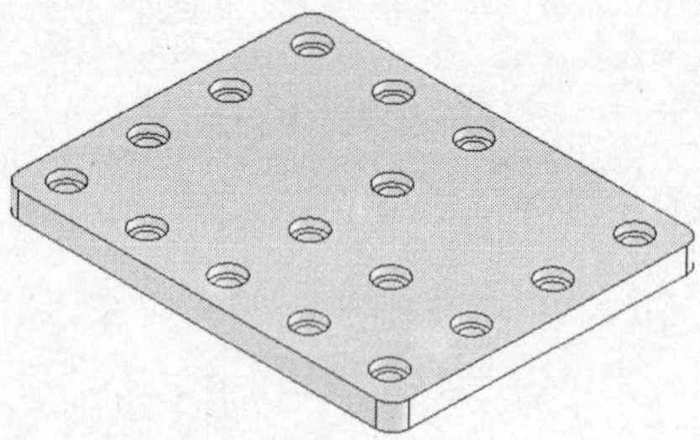

Figure 8-22 Linear pattern created with some instances skipped

The options in the **Instances to Vary** rollout are used to vary the dimensions of some of the instances from the pattern. By default, the options in this rollout are not activated. To make them active, select the check box on the left side of the **Instances to Vary** rollout; the options will be activated, as shown in Figure 8-23. As soon as you expand this rollout, pink dots will be displayed at the center of all pattern instances except the parent instances. Now, set the distance value in the **Direction 1 Spacing Increment** spinner; the last series of the instances that are in direction 1 will be re-arranged based on the distance value entered in the **Direction 1 Spacing Increment** spinner. Note that the value entered in the spinner will be measured from the current position of the last instance. The **Choose Feature dimension to vary in Direction1** area is used to give incremental values to feature dimension. To give incremental values, select dimension of a feature in this area; the table with **Dimension**, **Value**, and **Increment** columns will be displayed. Now, enter the desired values in respective columns. Similarly, specify the distance value in the **Direction 2 Spacing Increment** spinner. Figure 8-24 shows a pattern created with dimension variation and space variation of instances. You can also change the dimension of a single instance in the pattern. To do so, select the pink dot of the instance by left clicking on it; a shortcut menu will be displayed. Choose the **Modify Instance** option from the shortcut menu; the **Instance** callout will be displayed. Specify the dimensional values for the directions in the callout; the selected instance of the pattern will be re-arranged in the graphical window.

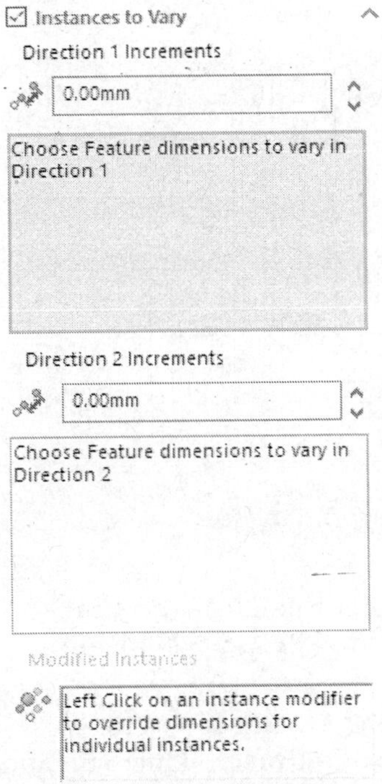

*Figure 8-23 Partial view of the **Instances to Vary** rollout*

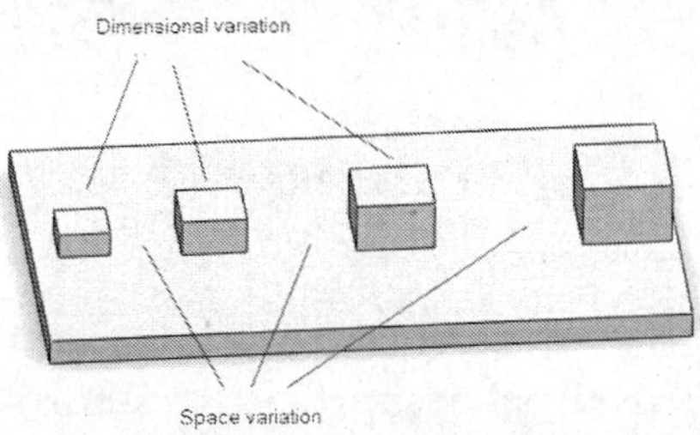

Figure 8-24 Linear pattern created with dimension variation of the instance

Creating Pattern Using a Varying Sketch

The **Vary sketch** option in the **Options** rollout is used in a pattern where the shape and size of each pattern instance is controlled by the relations and dimensions of the sketch of that feature. In this type of pattern, the dimension of the sketch of the feature is selected as the directional reference, which in turn drives the shape and size of the sketch of the feature to be patterned. In Figure 8-25, a cut feature is created on the base feature. Figure 8-26 shows linear pattern created with the **Vary sketch** check box selected. To create this type of pattern, the sketch of the feature to be patterned should be in relation with the geometry along which it will vary. The dimensions of the sketch should be such that it allows the sketch to change its shape and size easily. You should also provide a linear dimension that will drive the entire sketch and will also be the directional reference. Select the feature to be patterned from the **FeatureManager Design Tree** and then invoke the **Linear Pattern PropertyManager**. Next, select the dimension to specify the directional reference and set the value of spacing and the number of instances. In this case, the horizontal dimension that measures 5 will be selected as the dimensional reference. Next, expand the **Options** rollout and select the **Vary sketch** check box; the preview of the pattern will be displayed, if the **Full Preview** radio button is selected. Choose the **OK** button from the **Linear Pattern PropertyManager** to end the feature creation. In this case, the lower edge of the cut feature will be constrained to the bottom face of the model and top edge will vary along the curved edge of the model. Therefore, the pattern instances will be created such that their height varies along with the curved edge of the model. Note that the **Geometry pattern** check box in the **Options** rollout should be cleared.

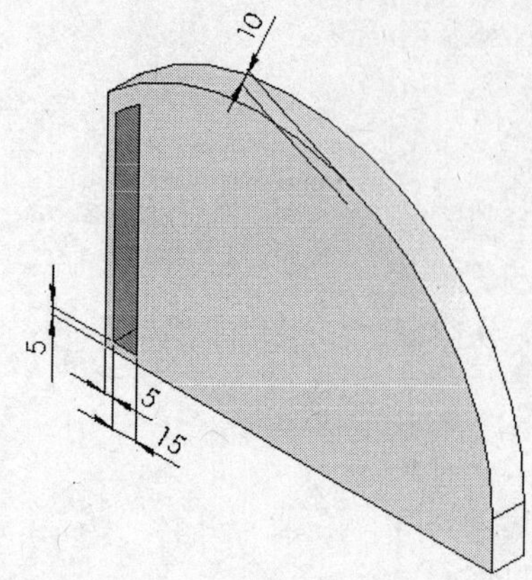

Figure 8-25 Cut feature created on the base feature

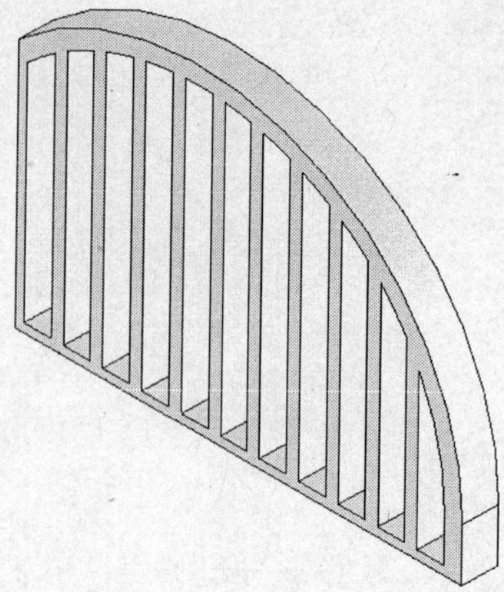

*Figure 8-26 Linear pattern created with the **Vary sketch** check box selected*

The use of the **Geometry pattern** check box in the **Options** rollout of the **Linear Pattern PropertyManager** is same as that discussed earlier in the **Mirror PropertyManager**.

Propagating Visual Properties while Patterning Components

The **Propagate visual properties** check box is provided in the **Options** rollout. This check box is selected by default. The use of this option has already been discussed in the previous section.

Creating Circular Pattern Features

CommandManager:	Features > Linear Pattern flyout > Circular Pattern
SOLIDWORKS menus:	Insert > Pattern/Mirror > Circular Pattern
Toolbar:	Features > Linear Pattern flyout > Circular Pattern

As discussed in the previous chapters, you can arrange sketched entities in a circular pattern using the **Circular Pattern** tool. In this section, you will learn to create the circular pattern of a feature, face, or body by using the **Circular Pattern** tool. To create a circular pattern, select features and choose the **Circular Pattern** button from the **Linear Pattern** flyout or choose **Insert > Pattern/Mirror > Circular Pattern** from the SOLIDWORKS menus; the **CirPattern PropertyManager** will be invoked and the confirmation corner will be displayed. Partial view of the **CirPattern PropertyManager** is shown in Figure 8-27.

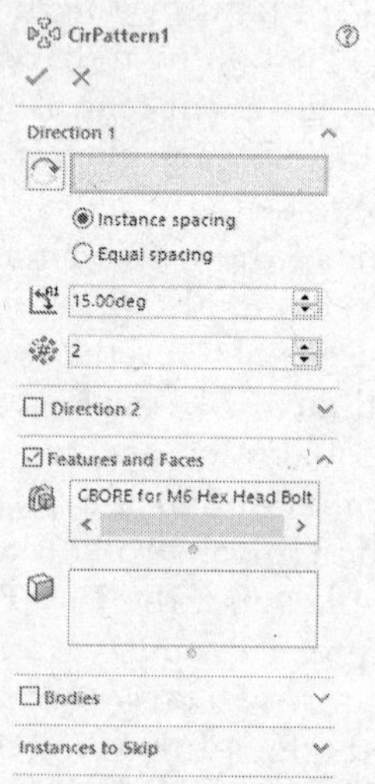

*Figure 8-27 Partial view of the **Circular Pattern PropertyManager***

After invoking the **CirPattern PropertyManager**, you will be prompted to select an edge or an axis for the direction reference, and a face of the feature to be patterned. If you need to create a circular pattern on the circular feature, click in the **Pattern Axis** selection box in the **Direction 1** rollout to enable it and then select the circular edge; the center of the circular feature will be selected as the pattern axis. You can also select an edge, axis, or a sketched line as the pattern axis. The **Direction 1** callout is also displayed with the **Reverse Direction** arrow in the drawing area. By default, the **Instance spacing** check box is selected in the **Direction 1** rollout. As a result, you need to enter the value of the incremental angle between the instances in the **Angle** spinner. If the **Equal spacing** check box is selected, then you need to enter the value of the angle along which all the instances of the pattern will be placed. On doing so, the angular spacing between the instances will be automatically calculated. You can set the number of instances to pattern in the **Number of Instances** spinner.

The **Reverse Direction** button available on the left of the **Pattern Axis** selection box is used to change the direction of rotation. By default, the direction of the pattern creation is counterclockwise. If you choose this button then the resulting pattern will be created in the clockwise direction. You can also change the direction of the pattern creation by clicking on the arrow in the drawing area. Figure 8-28 shows the feature and temporary axis selected. Figure 8-29 shows the resulting pattern feature. In SOLIDWORKS, you can create circular pattern bidirectionally to modify spacing, number of instances, and angle settings for both the directions separately. The **Direction 2** rollout in the **CirPattern PropertyManager** lets you create pattern in the second direction also. To create pattern in the second direction, select the check box available on the left in the **Direction 2** rollout. The options in this rollout are similar to those in the **Direction 1** rollout except the **Symmetric** check box. This check box is cleared by default. On selecting this check box, the settings specified in the **Direction 1** rollout are also applied to the **Direction 2** rollout.

Tip
You can pattern a patterned feature or a mirrored feature. You can also mirror a patterned feature.

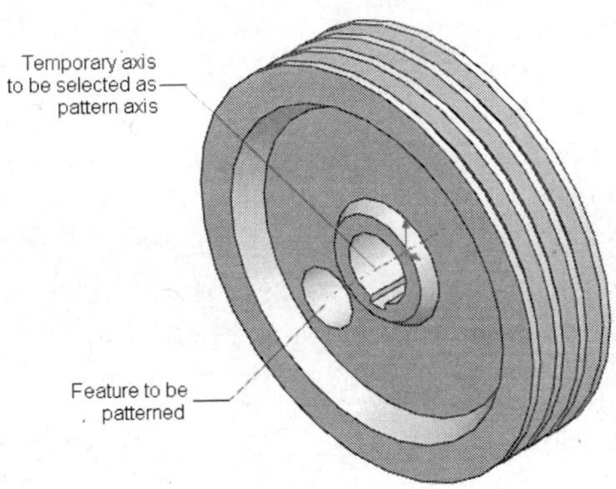

Figure 8-28 The reference to be selected for creating a circular pattern

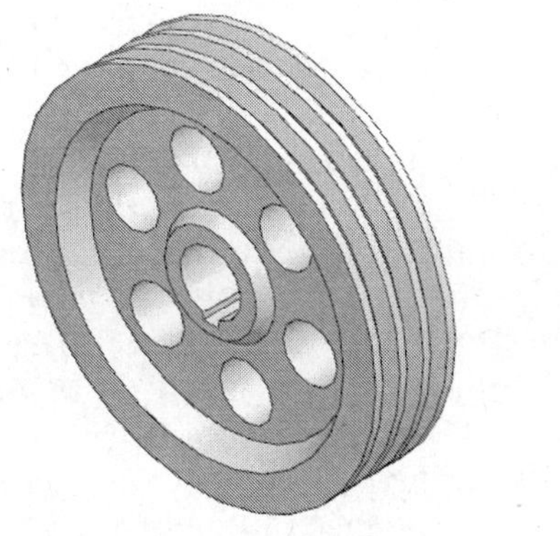

Figure 8-29 The resulting circular pattern

Creating Circular Pattern by Using a Dimensional Reference

You can also create a circular pattern by selecting an angular dimension. To créate a pattern using this option, you need to create an angular dimension in the sketch of the feature that you want to pattern. Next, invoke the **CirPattern PropertyManager** and select the feature to be patterned; the dimensions of the feature to be patterned will be displayed in the drawing area, as shown in Figure 8-30. Click in the **Pattern Axis** selection box in the **Direction 1** rollout to enable it. Then, select the angular dimension and set the value of the total angle and spacing in the **CirPattern PropertyManager**. Figure 8-31 shows the circular pattern created by selecting the angular dimension as the angular reference. You can also create the dimension variations of the instances and skip some of the instances from the pattern. The other options in the **CirPattern PropertyManager** are the same as those discussed earlier for the **Linear Pattern PropertyManager**.

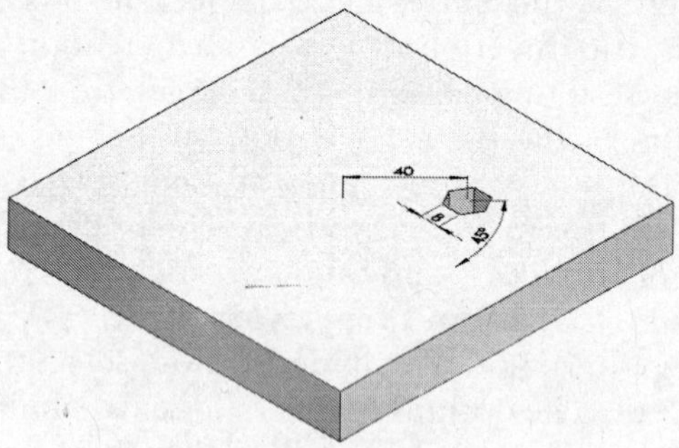

Figure 8-30 *Dimensions displayed after selecting the feature to be patterned*

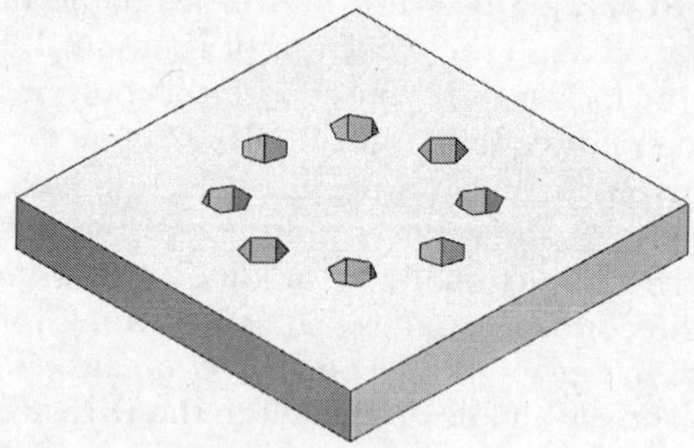

Figure 8-31 *Circular pattern created by selecting the angular dimension as the angular reference*

Creating Sketch Driven Patterns

CommandManager:	Features > Linear Pattern flyout > Sketch Driven Pattern
SOLIDWORKS menus:	Insert > Pattern/Mirror > Sketch Driven Pattern
Toolbar:	Features > Linear Pattern flyout > Sketch Driven Pattern

A sketch driven pattern is created when features, faces, or bodies are to be arranged in a nonuniform manner, which is neither rectangular nor circular. To create a sketch driven pattern, first you need to create an arrangement of the sketch points in a single sketch. This arrangement of sketch points will drive the instances in the pattern feature. After creating the feature to be patterned and placing the points in the sketch, choose the **Sketch Driven Pattern** button from the **Linear Pattern** flyout; the **Sketch Driven Pattern PropertyManager** will be displayed, as shown in Figure 8-32, and you will be prompted to select a sketch for the pattern layout and the face of the feature to be patterned. Select any one of the sketched points from the drawing area or you can also select sketch by expanding the **FeatureManager Design Tree** available in the drawing area; the **Features to Pattern** selection box will be enabled. Select the feature or features to be patterned. Next, choose the **OK** button from the **Sketch Driven Pattern PropertyManager**. Figure 8-33 shows the feature and the sketch point to be selected and Figure 8-34 shows the resulting pattern feature.

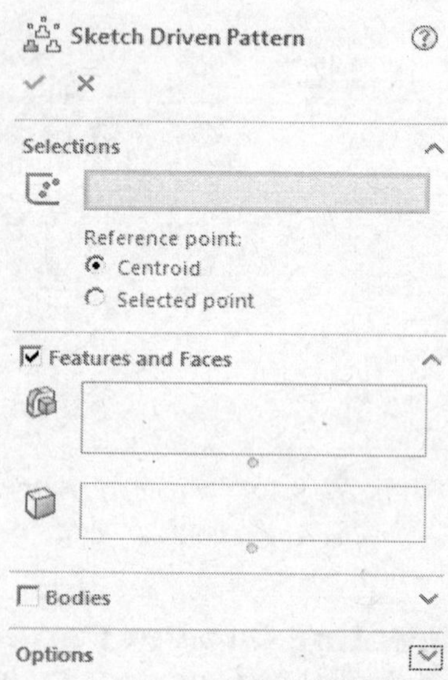

Figure 8-32 *The* ***Sketch Driven Pattern PropertyManager***

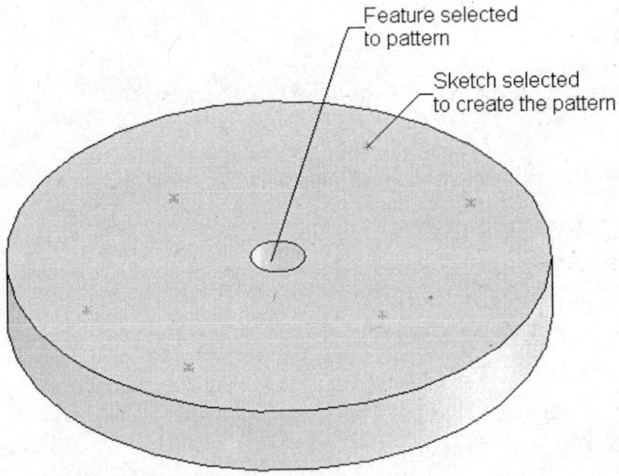

Figure 8-33 The feature and the sketch points to be selected

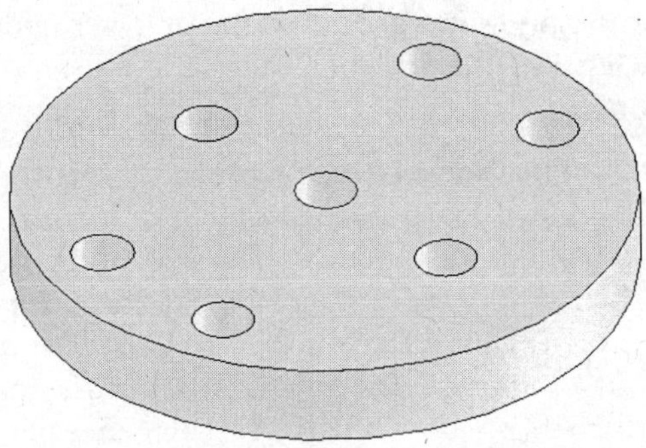

Figure 8-34 The resulting sketch driven pattern feature

The options in the **Sketch Driven Pattern PropertyManager** are discussed next.

Creating Sketch Driven Pattern by Using a Centroid

When you invoke the **Sketch Driven Pattern PropertyManager**, the **Centroid** radio button is selected by default in the **Reference point** area of the **Selections** rollout. Therefore, the pattern will be created such that the centroid of the instances coincides with the sketched points.

Creating Sketch Driven Pattern by Using a Selected Point

If you select the **Selected point** radio button from the **Reference point** area of the **Selections** rollout, the pattern will be created with reference to the selected point. When you select this radio button, the **Reference Vertex** selection box will be displayed. Select a point as a vertex in the original instance; the pattern will be created in such a way that the specified vertex in the resulting instance will coincide with the sketched point.

Creating Curve Driven Patterns

CommandManager:	Features > Linear Pattern flyout > Curve Driven Pattern
SOLIDWORKS menus:	Insert > Pattern/Mirror > Curve Driven Pattern
Toolbar:	Features > Linear Pattern flyout > Curve Driven Pattern

The **Curve Driven Pattern** tool is used to pattern features, faces, or bodies along a selected reference curve. A reference curve can be a sketched entity, an edge, an open profile, or a closed loop. To create a pattern using this option, choose the **Curve Driven Pattern** button from the **Linear Pattern** flyout or choose **Insert > Pattern/Mirror > Curve Driven Pattern** from the SOLIDWORKS menus; the **Curve Driven Pattern PropertyManager** will be displayed, as shown in Figure 8-35.

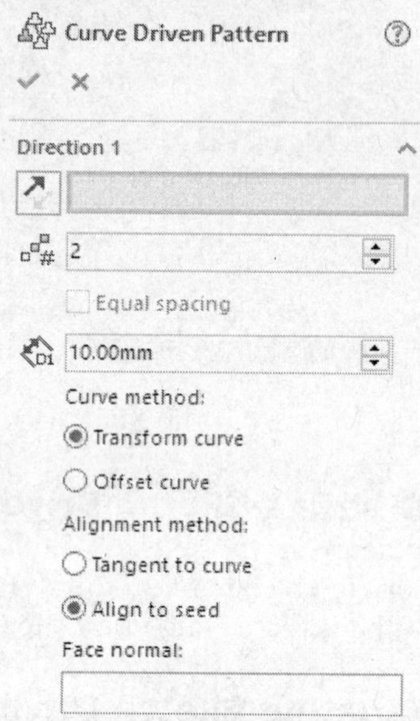

Figure 8-35** Partial view of the **Curve Driven Pattern PropertyManager

On invoking the **Curve Driven Pattern PropertyManager**, you will be prompted to select an edge, a curve, or a sketch segment for pattern layout and select a face of the feature to be patterned. Select the reference curve along which the feature, face, or body is to be patterned. In SOLIDWORKS, you can also select 3D curves or sketches as reference curve. You will learn more about 3D curves and sketches in the later chapters. When you select the reference curve, its name will be displayed in the **Pattern Direction** selection box and the **Direction 1** callout will also be displayed. As discussed earlier, the **Direction 1** callout is divided into two areas. On selecting a curve for the directional reference, the **Features to Pattern** selection box will be activated. Select the feature to be patterned; preview of the pattern will be displayed in the drawing area. Set required parameters in the **Direction 1** callout and choose the **OK** button from the **Curve Driven Pattern PropertyManager**. Figure 8-36 shows the feature and the curve that will be used to create the pattern. Figure 8-37 shows the resulting curve driven pattern feature.

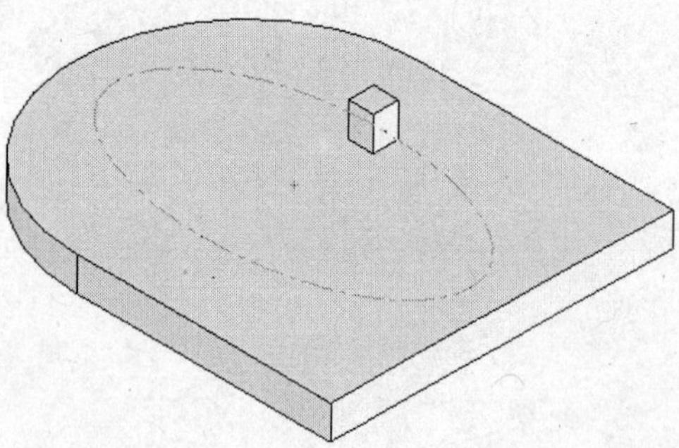

***Figure 8-36** The feature and the curve to be used to create the curve driven pattern feature*

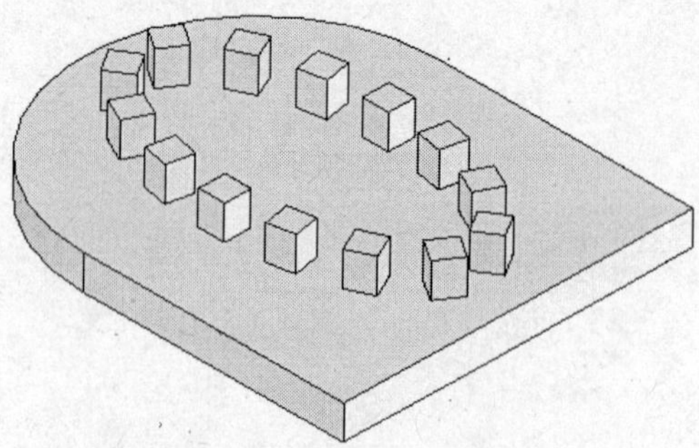

***Figure 8-37** The resulting curve driven pattern feature*

The options available in the **Direction 1** rollout are discussed next.

Equal Spacing

The **Equal spacing** check box is used to accommodate all instances of the pattern along the selected curve. By default, this check box is cleared. Therefore, you have to specify the distance between the instances and the total number of instances to be created along the selected curve. When you select this check box, the **Spacing** spinner will not be available and you have to specify only the total number of instances. The distance between the instances is calculated automatically.

Curve method and Alignment method

The **Curve method** area of the **Direction 1** rollout is used to specify the type of curve method to be followed while creating patterns. The two options available in this area are **Transform curve** and **Offset curve**. If you select the **Transform curve** option then delta X and Y from start point of curve to seed feature is maintained in all instances, whereas in the **Offset curve** option the normal distance from curve to seed feature is maintained. The **Alignment method** area of the **Direction 1** rollout is used to specify the type of alignment method to be applied. The two alignment methods are **Tangent to curve** method and **Align to seed** method. Figure 8-38 shows the curve driven pattern created with the **Transform curve** and **Tangent to curve** radio buttons selected. Figure 8-39 shows the curve driven pattern created with the **Transform curve** and **Align to seed** radio buttons selected.

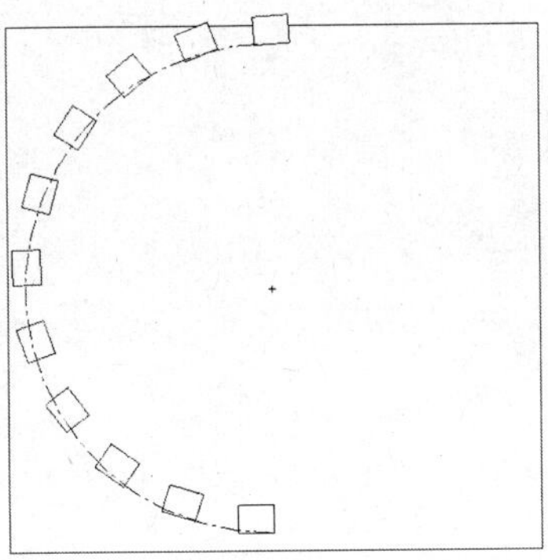

***Figure 8-38** Pattern created with the **Transform curve** and **Tangent to curve** radio buttons selected*

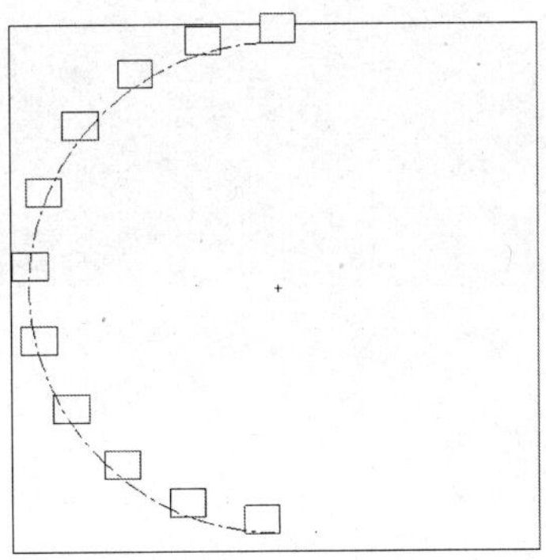

***Figure 8-39** Pattern created with the **Transform curve** and **Align to seed** radio buttons selected*

Figure 8-40 shows the curve driven pattern created with the **Offset curve** and **Tangent to curve** radio buttons selected. Figure 8-41 shows the curve driven pattern created with the **Offset curve** and **Align to seed** radio buttons selected.

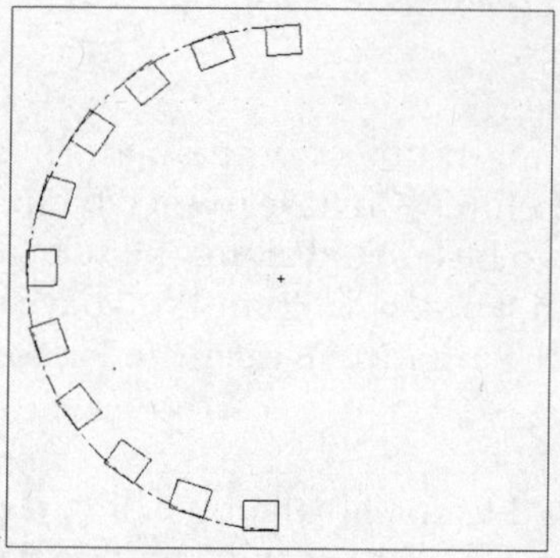

Figure 8-40 Pattern created with the ***Offset curve*** *and* ***Tangent to curve*** *radio buttons selected*

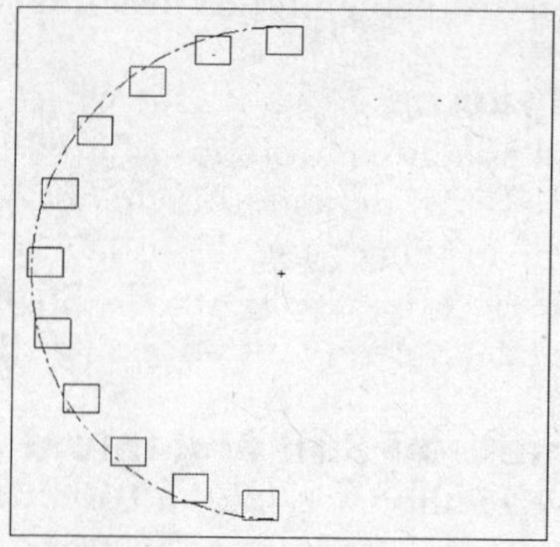

Figure 8-41 Pattern created with the ***Offset curve*** *and* ***Align to seed*** *radio buttons selected*

The other options in the **Curve Driven PropertyManager** are the same as those discussed earlier for the mirror and other pattern features. By selecting the check box in the **Direction 2** rollout, you can also specify the parameters in the second direction. Figure 8-42 shows the curve driven pattern feature created with the pattern defined in the first and second directions.

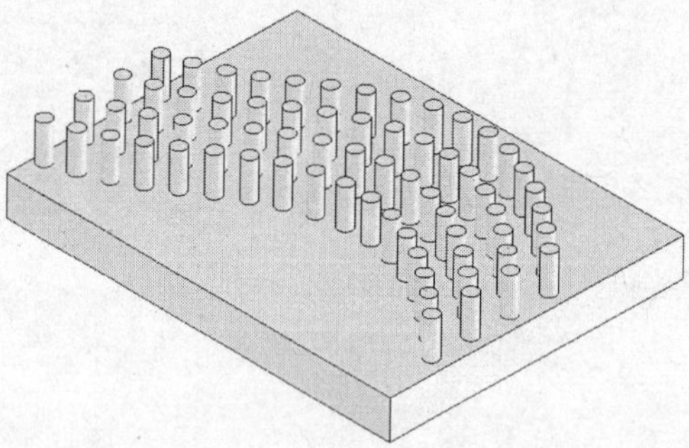

Figure 8-42 A curve driven pattern created by specifying parameters in both the directions

Creating Table Driven Patterns

CommandManager:	Features > Linear Pattern flyout >Table Driven Pattern
SOLIDWORKS menus:	Insert > Pattern/Mirror > Table Driven Pattern
Toolbar:	Features > Linear Pattern flyout > Table Driven Pattern

A table driven pattern is created by specifying the X and Y coordinates of the pattern feature with reference to a coordinate system. The instances of the selected features, faces, or bodies are created at the points specified using the X and Y coordinates. To create this pattern, first you need to create a coordinate system using the **Coordinate System** button from the **Reference Geometry** toolbar. The coordinate system defines the direction along which the selected feature will be patterned. Choose the **Table Driven Pattern** button from the **Linear Pattern** flyout or choose **Insert > Pattern/Mirror > Table Driven Pattern** from the SOLIDWORKS menus; the **Table Driven Pattern** dialog box will be displayed, as shown in Figure 8-43.

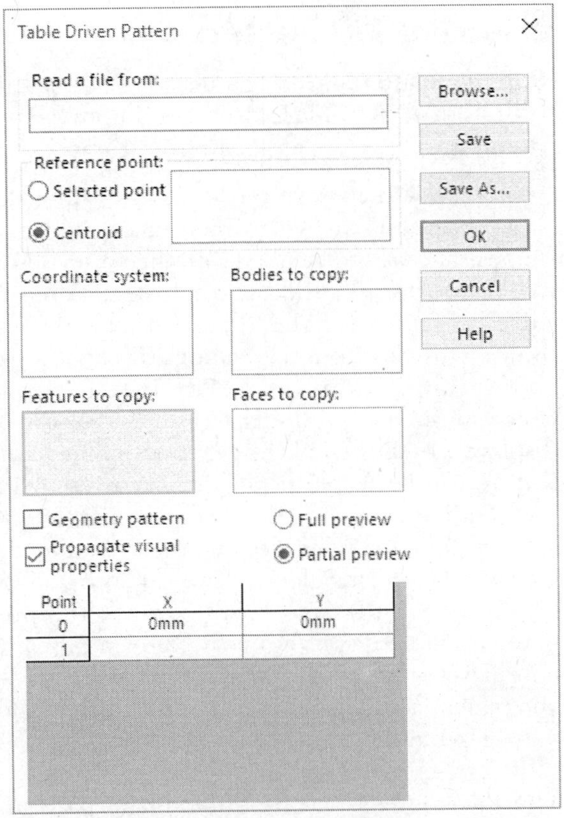

*Figure 8-43 The **Table Driven Pattern** dialog box*

Select the feature to be patterned and the coordinate system from the drawing area or from the **FeatureManager Design Tree**. Also, enter the coordinates in the Coordinate points area of the **Table Driven Pattern** dialog box for creating the instances. As you enter the coordinates, the preview of the pattern will be displayed in the drawing area. After entering all coordinate points, choose the **OK** button from the **Table Driven Pattern** dialog box. Figure 8-44 shows the feature and coordinate system to be selected. Figure 8-45 shows the table driven pattern created after entering the coordinate values in the **Table Driven Pattern** dialog box.

You can save the table driven pattern file by choosing the **Save** button. Choose the **Browse** button to retrieve the already saved file and it will be displayed in the **Read a file from** selection box. You can also write the coordinates in a text file and browse the same file while creating a table driven pattern. The other options in this dialog box are the same as those discussed earlier.

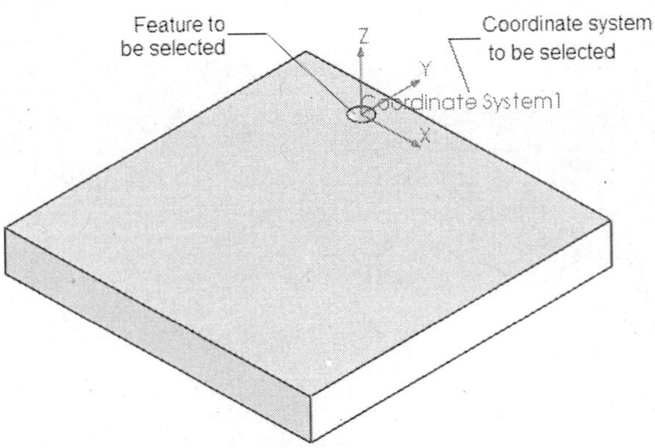

***Figure 8-44** The feature and coordinate system to be selected*

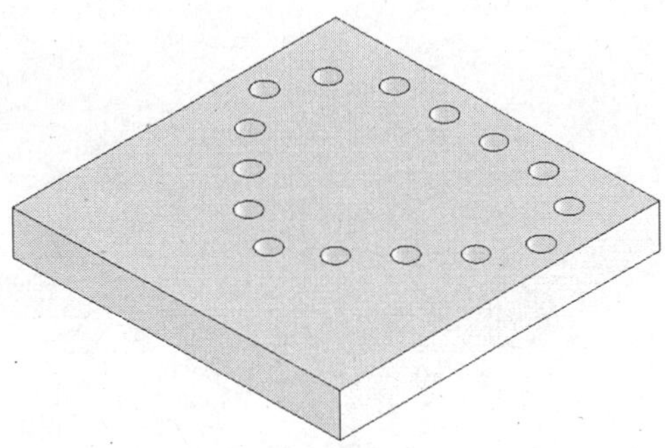

***Figure 8-45** The table driven pattern created after specifying the coordinate points*

Creating Fill Patterns

CommandManager:	Features > Linear Pattern flyout > Fill Pattern
SOLIDWORKS menus:	Insert > Pattern/Mirror > Fill Pattern
Toolbar:	Features > Linear Pattern flyout > Fill Pattern

The **Fill Pattern** tool is used to fill a defined area with the pattern of features, faces, bodies, or predefined shapes. The area to be filled with the pattern of features or holes can be a sketched entity, a face, or a coplanar face. To create a fill pattern, select the feature to be patterned from the drawing area or from the **FeatureManager Design Tree**. Next, choose **Linear Pattern > Fill Pattern** from the **Features CommandManager**; the **Fill Pattern PropertyManager** will be displayed, as shown in Figure 8-46. Also, the name of the selected feature will be displayed in the **Features to Pattern** selection box. Additionally, you will be prompted to select the edge or the axis for direction reference and the face of feature to define the area of fill pattern. Select a sketched entity, a face, or a coplanar face to define the area of fill pattern; the preview of the fill pattern will be displayed in the drawing area. Choose the **OK** button from the PropertyManager. Figure 8-47 shows the feature and planar face to be selected and Figure 8-48 shows the resulting pattern feature.

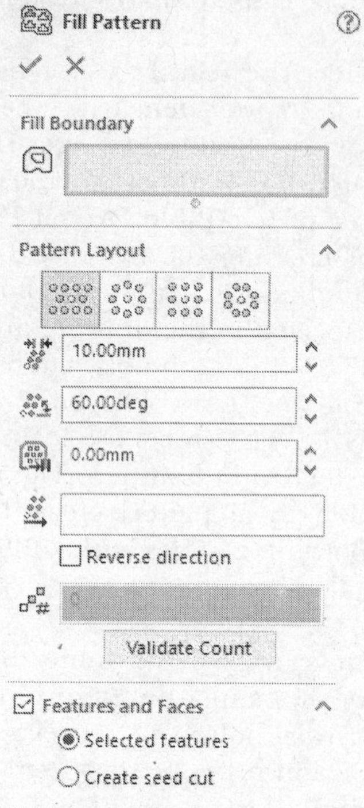

Figure 8-46 Partial view of the Fill Pattern PropertyManager

The procedures to create different fill patterns using the **Fill Pattern PropertyManager** are discussed next.

Creating a Fill Pattern of the Selected Features

When you invoke the **Fill Pattern PropertyManager**, the **Selected features** radio button is selected by default in the **Features and Faces** rollout. Therefore, to create a fill pattern, you only need to select a feature from the graphics area.

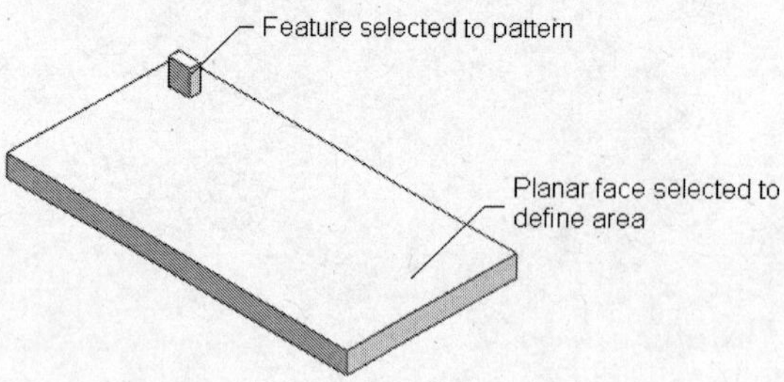

Figure 8-47 *The feature and planar face to be selected*

Figure 8-48 *Resulting pattern feature*

Creating a Fill Pattern of the Predefined Holes

Select the **Create seed cut** radio button from the **Features and Faces** rollout of the **Fill Pattern PropertyManager** to create a pattern of the predefined holes. The available predefined cut shapes are circle, square, diamond, and polygon. On selecting this radio button, the **Circle**, **Square**, **Diamond**, and **Polygon** buttons will be enabled below it. The **Circle** button is chosen by default; therefore a pattern of circular holes will be created with the default settings. Figure 8-49 shows the planar face to be selected and Figure 8-50 shows the fill pattern created by choosing the **Circle** button.

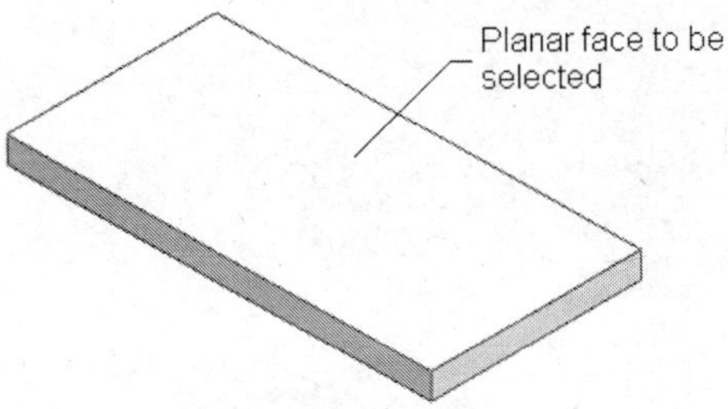

Figure 8-49 *The planar face to be selected*

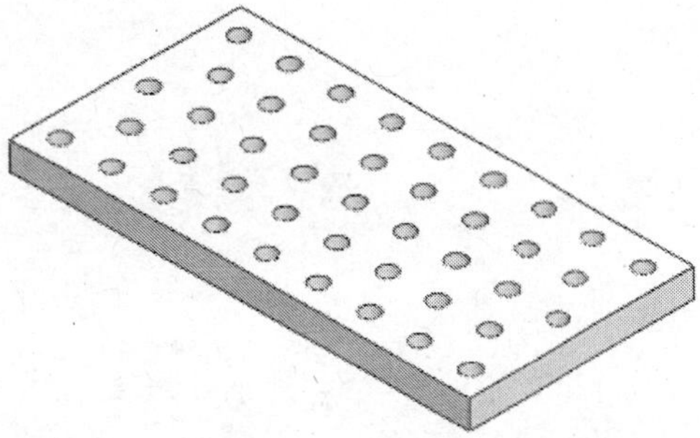

Figure 8-50 *The resultant fill pattern*

Creating a Fill Pattern by Specifying a Vertex or a Sketch Point

The **Vertex or Sketch Point** selection box will be available when the **Create seed cut** radio button is selected in the **Features and Faces** rollout of the PropertyManager. By default, the seed feature is located at the center of the fill boundary and the pattern feature is created around the seed feature. Using this selection box, you can change the location of the seed feature to any vertex or sketched point. The spacing between loops can be controlled using the **Loop Spacing** spinner provided below the **Pattern Layout** buttons. Figure 8-51 shows the fill pattern when the seed feature is at the center of the fill boundary and Figure 8-52 shows the fill pattern when the seed feature is at the right vertex of the fill boundary.

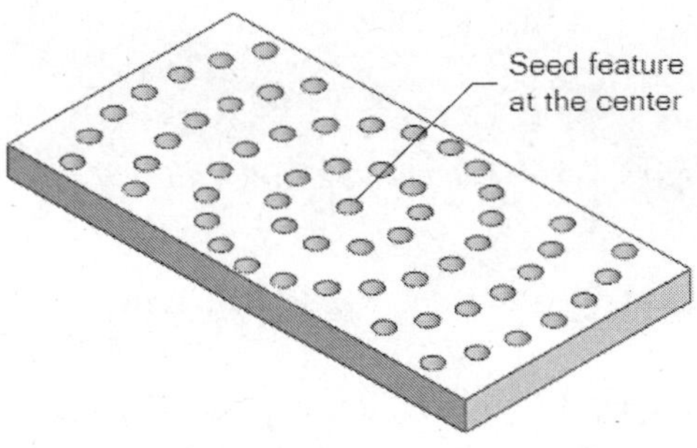

Figure 8-51 *The fill pattern with the seed feature at the center of the fill boundary*

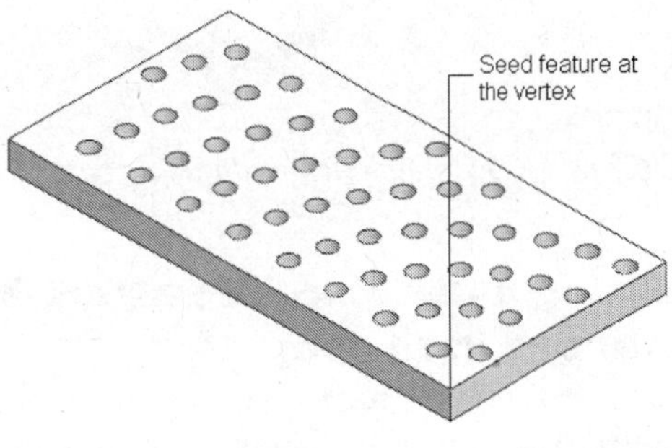

Figure 8-52 *The fill pattern with the seed feature at the right vertex of the fill boundary*

Creating a Fill Pattern of Different Layouts

You can define the layout of instances within the fill boundary using the **Perforation**, **Circular**, **Square**, and **Polygon** buttons available in the **Pattern Layout** rollout of the PropertyManager. The **Perforation** button is chosen by default in this rollout. Using this button, you can create a perforated style pattern. To create a circular shape pattern, choose the **Circular** button from the **Pattern Layout** rollout. Similarly, the **Square** and **Polygon** buttons are used to create square and polygon shape patterns, respectively. Figures 8-53 through 8-56 show different fill patterns created using the buttons available in the **Pattern Layout** rollout when the **Create seed cut** radio button is selected.

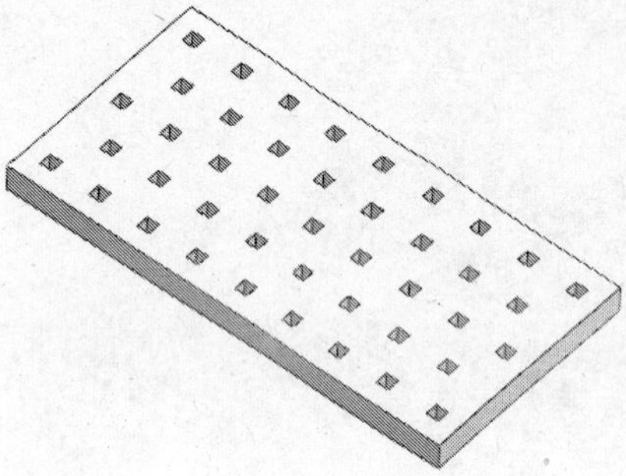

Figure 8-53 *The perforated style fill pattern*

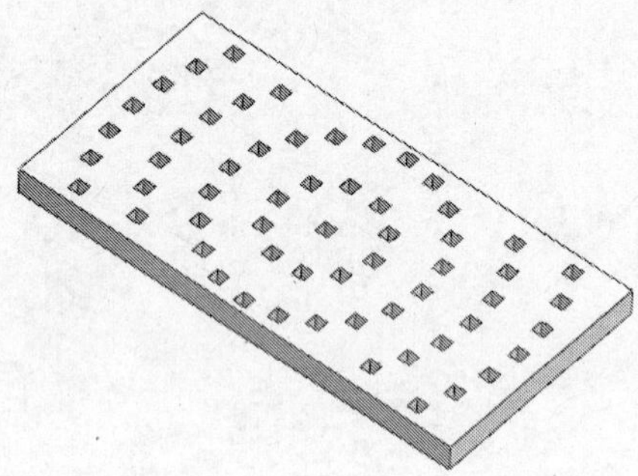

Figure 8-54 *The circular shape fill pattern*

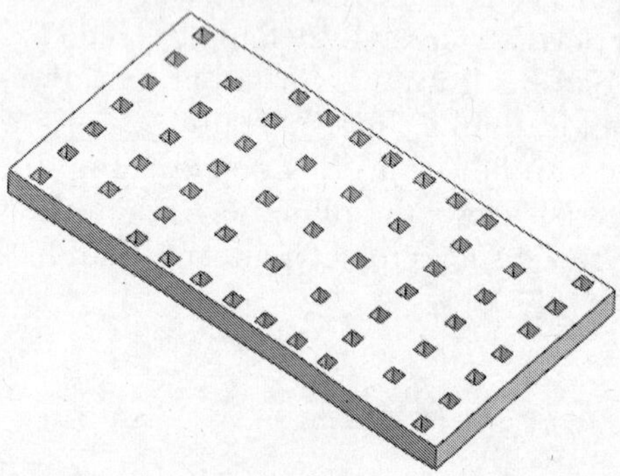

Figure 8-55 *The square shape fill pattern*

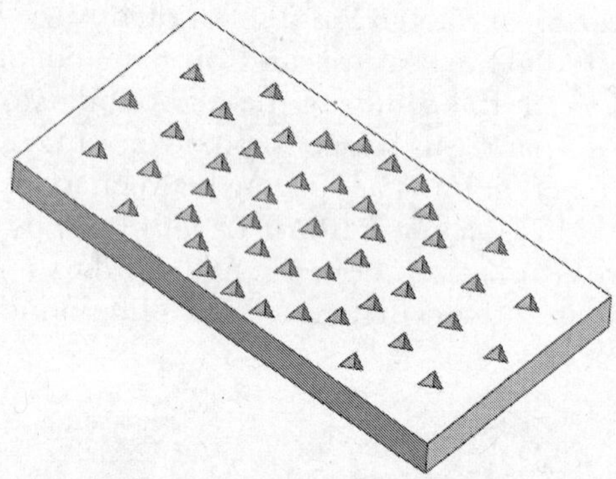

Figure 8-56 *The polygon shape fill pattern*

Creating a Circular Fill Pattern by Specifying Target Spacing and Instances Per Loop

When you choose the **Circular** button from the **Pattern Layout** rollout of the **Fill Pattern PropertyManager**, the **Target spacing** and **Instances per loop** radio buttons will be enabled. By default, the **Target spacing** radio button is selected. Therefore, you need to specify the spacing between the instances using the **Instance Spacing** spinner. On selecting the **Target spacing** radio button, the number of instances will be calculated such that the instances fit evenly. If you select the **Instances per loop** radio button from the **Pattern Layout** rollout, you need to specify the number of instances for each loop of the fill pattern in the **Number of Instances** spinner. Figure 8-57 shows the circular shape fill pattern created when the **Target spacing** radio button is selected. Figure 8-58 shows the circular shape fill pattern created when the **Instances per loop** radio button is selected.

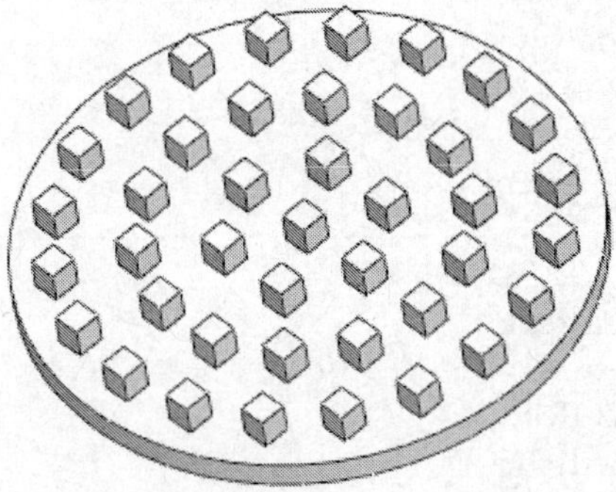

Figure 8-57 Fill pattern created when the ***Target spacing*** *radio button is selected*

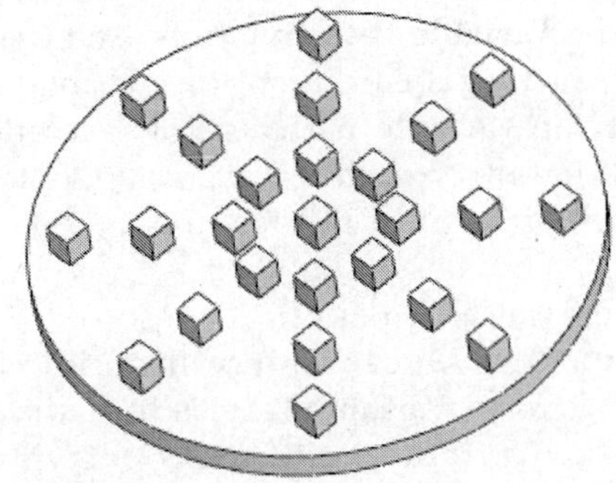

Figure 8-58 Fill pattern created when the ***Instances per loop*** *radio button is selected*

Creating a Square or Polygon Fill Pattern by Specifying Target Spacing and Instances Per Loop

When you choose the **Square** or **Polygon** button from the **Pattern Layout** rollout of the **Fill Pattern PropertyManager**, the **Target spacing** and **Instances per side** radio buttons will be enabled below these buttons. By default, the **Target spacing** radio button is selected. Therefore, you need to specify the spacing between the instances using the **Instance Spacing** spinner. On selecting the **Target spacing** radio button, the number of instances will be calculated such that the instances fit evenly. If you select the **Instances per side** radio button from the **Pattern Layout** rollout, you need to specify the number of instances for each side of the fill pattern in the **Number of Instances** spinner. Figure 8-59 shows the square shape fill pattern created when the **Instances per side** radio button is selected. Figure 8-60 shows the square shape fill pattern created when the **Target spacing** radio button is selected.

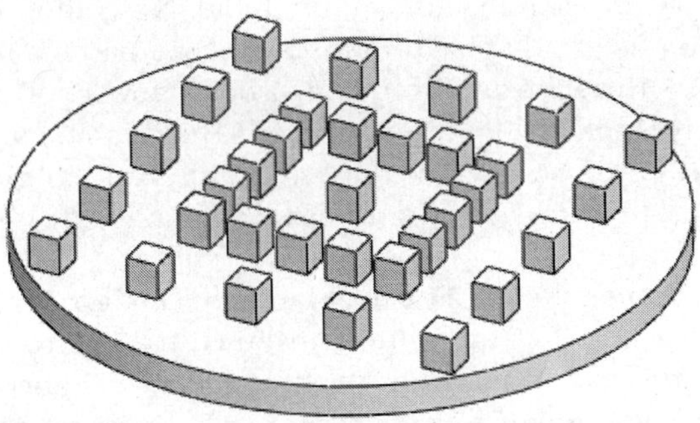

Figure 8-59 Square shape fill pattern created on selecting the ***Instances per side*** *radio button*

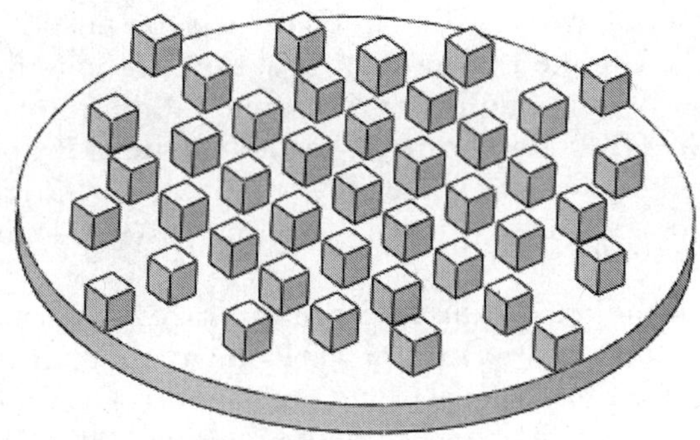

Figure 8-60 Square shape fill pattern created on selecting the ***Target spacing*** *radio button*

Creating Variable Patterns

CommandManager:	Features > Linear Pattern flyout > Variable Pattern
SOLIDWORKS menus:	Insert > Pattern/Mirror > Variable Pattern
Toolbar:	Features > Linear Pattern flyout > Variable Pattern

The **Variable Pattern** tool is used to pattern features by varying their dimensions. Using this tool, you can create variable patterns for Extrude/Cut Extrude, Revolve/Cut Revolve, Sweep/Cut Sweep, Loft/Cut Loft, Fillet, Chamfer, Dome, and Draft features.

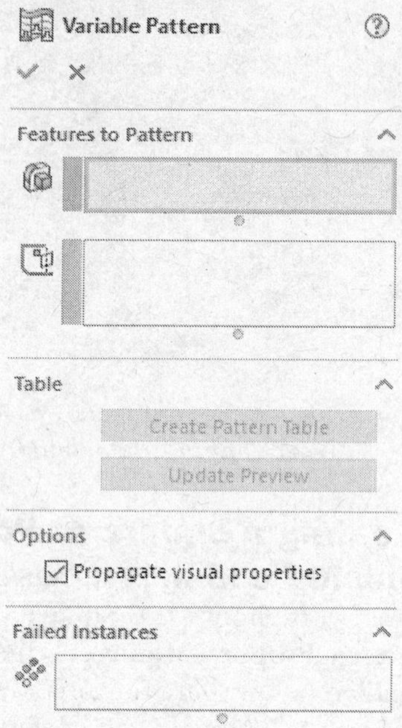

Figure 8-61 The ***Variable Pattern PropertyManager***

To create a variable pattern, choose the **Variable Pattern** button from the **Linear Pattern** flyout or choose **Insert > Pattern/Mirror > Variable Pattern** from the SOLIDWORKS menus; the **Variable Pattern PropertyManager** will be displayed, as shown in Figure 8-61.

Also, you will be prompted to select the feature to be patterned. Now, select the feature from the drawing area; the name of the feature will be displayed in the **Features to Pattern** selection box and all dimensions of the selected feature will be displayed in the drawing area. Also, the **Create Pattern Table** button will be activated in the **Table rollout.** Now, choose this button; the **Pattern Table** dialog box will be displayed with rows and columns of the instances. Also, you will be prompted to select the dimensions from the graphics area to add them to this table. Select the dimensions of the feature that is to be varied from the drawing area; a column for each dimension will be added in the **Pattern Table** dialog box. Now, you need to add more instances in the table. To do so, enter the desired number of instances in the **Number of instances to add** edit box located at the bottom of the **Pattern Table** dialog box and then choose the **Add instances** button. You will notice that desired number of rows will be added in the table. Modify the value of the dimensions which you need to vary for each instance in the table. Now, choose the **Update Preview** button at the bottom of dialog box to display the preview of the pattern in temporary graphics. Choose the **OK** button to exit the **Pattern Table** dialog box. Now, choose the **OK** button from the **Variable Pattern PropertyManager**. Figure 8-62 shows the dimensions to be selected for creating a variable pattern and here you need to vary the radius and angle dimension to create the resulting pattern. Figure 8-63 shows the resulting variable pattern.

All the created instances of the variable pattern appear in the **FeatureManager Design Tree** as the child feature of **VarPattern**. You can right-click on any pattern instance to suppress, unsuppress, or delete it. You can also view and edit each dimension of the selected instance. To do so, double-click on an instance in the **FeatureManager Design tree**; its dimensions will be displayed in the drawing area. Double-click on the required dimension; the **Modify** dialog box will be displayed. Change the value of the selected dimensions in the **Modify** dialog box and then choose the **Save the current value and exit the dialog** button to confirm the change. Choose the **Rebuild** button from the SOLIDWORKS menus to view the changes.

You can also include dimensions used for creating reference geometries such as plane, axis, point and also of 2D or 3D sketch in a pattern table. To do so, click once in the **Reference Geometry to drive seeds** selection box in the **Features to Pattern** rollout and then select the reference geometry; all related dimensions will be displayed. Note that you can select reference geometries only, if you used them in creating feature for pattern.

> **Note**
> *The location of the patterned instance should be such that it does not overlap with the seed feature or else variable pattern will not be created.*

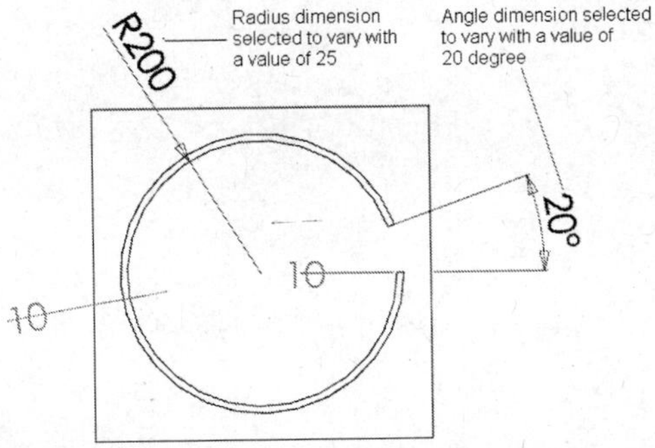

Figure 8-62 The dimensions to be selected for creating a variable pattern

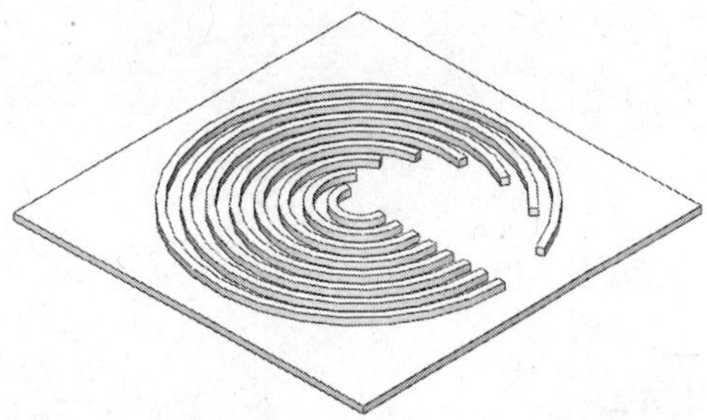

Figure 8-63 The resulting variable pattern

Creating Rib Features

CommandManager:	Features > Rib
SOLIDWORKS menus:	Insert > Features > Rib
Toolbar:	Features > Rib

Ribs are defined as the thin-walled structures that are used to increase the strength of the entire structure of a component so that it does not fail under an increased load. In SOLIDWORKS, the ribs are created using an open sketch as well as a closed sketch. To create a rib feature, draw a sketch and exit the sketching environment. Invoke the **Rib** tool by choosing the **Rib** button from the **Features CommandManager** or by choosing **Insert > Features > Rib** from the SOLIDWORKS menus; the **Rib PropertyManager** will be displayed and you will be prompted to select a plane, a planar face, an edge to sketch the feature, or an existing sketch to be used for the feature. Select the sketch from the drawing area; the **Rib PropertyManager** will be modified, as shown in Figure 8-64, and the preview of the rib feature with the direction arrow and the confirmation corner will be displayed in the drawing area. You can also invoke the **Rib** tool, select a plane, draw a sketch, and then exit the sketching environment to display the **Rib PropertyManager** and the preview of the rib feature.

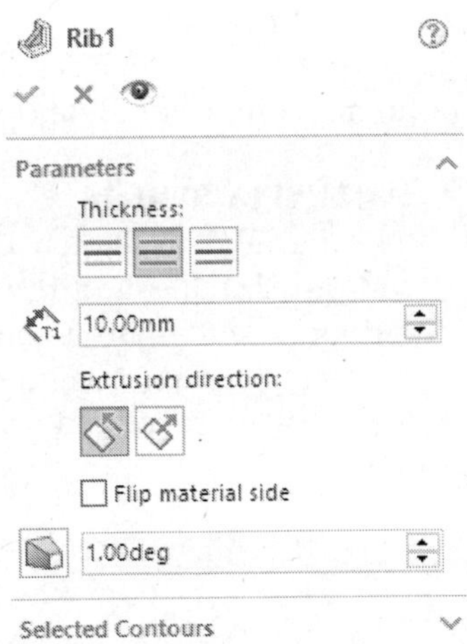

*Figure 8-64 Partial view of the **Rib PropertyManager***

Specify the rib parameters in the **Rib PropertyManager** and view the detailed preview using the **Detailed Preview** button. Figure 8-65 shows the sketch drawn for the rib feature and Figure 8-66 shows the resulting rib feature.

The options in the **Rib PropertyManager** are discussed next.

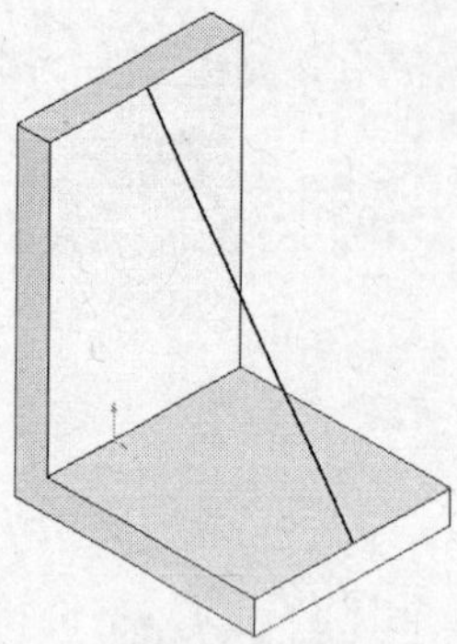

Figure 8-65 *Sketch for the rib feature*

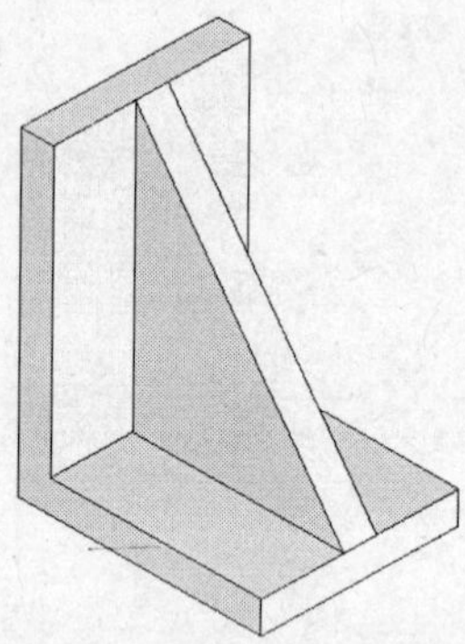

Figure 8-66 *Resulting rib feature*

Thickness

The **Thickness** area in the **Parameters** rollout is used to specify the side of the sketch where the material is to be added and the thickness of the rib feature. The buttons in the **Thickness** area are used to control the side on which you want to add the rib thickness. By default, the **Both Sides** button is chosen. Therefore, the rib is created on both sides of the sketch. You can choose the **First Side, Both Sides** or **Second Side** buttons to create ribs on either sides of the sketch. The **Rib Thickness** spinner in this area is used to specify the rib thickness.

Extrusion direction

The **Extrusion direction** area in the **Parameters** rollout is used to specify the method of extrusion for the closed or the open sketch. When you invoke the **Rib PropertyManager**, the option that is suitable for creating the rib feature will be activated by default, depending on the geometric conditions. The options in this area are discussed next.

Parallel to Sketch

The **Parallel to Sketch** button is used to extrude a sketch in a direction that is parallel to both sketches and the sketching plane. When the sketch created for the rib feature is an open sketch and a continuous single entity, this button is chosen by default in the **Rib PropertyManager**. Figure 8-67 shows an open sketch for creating a rib. Figure 8-68 shows the rib feature created using the **Parallel to Sketch** button.

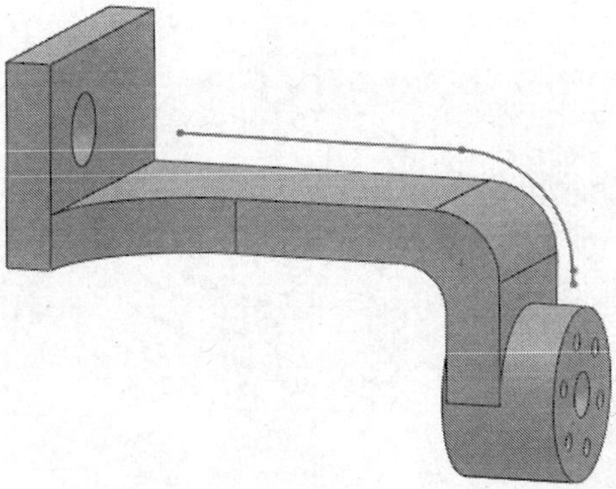

Figure 8-67 An open sketch for the rib feature

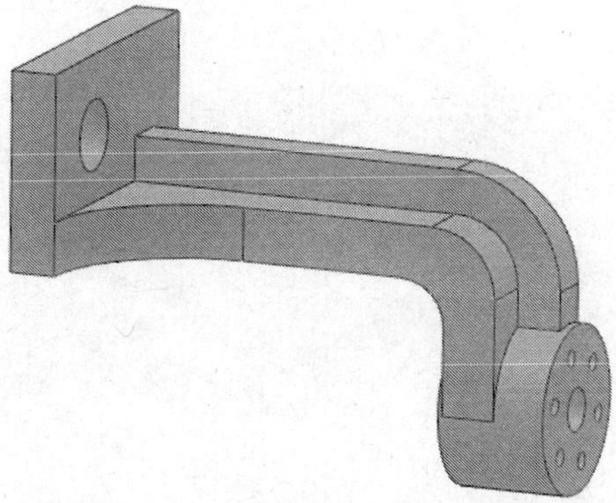

Figure 8-68 The resulting rib feature

Note

You will observe that the endpoints of the sketched lines drawn in Figure 8-67 do not merge with the edges of the model. However, the rib created using this sketch merges with the edges of the model. This is because while creating the sketch for the rib feature, the ends of the rib feature automatically extend to the next surface; you do not need to create a complete sketch.

Normal to Sketch

The **Normal to Sketch** option is used to extrude a sketch in a direction that is normal to both the sketch and the sketching plane. This button is used when the sketch of the rib feature is a closed loop sketch or it consists of multiple sketched entities. The sketch with multiple entities can be a closed loop or an open profile. If you draw a sketch with a closed loop or with multiple sketched entities and invoke the **Rib** tool, the **Normal to Sketch** button will be chosen by default. You can also choose the **Normal to Sketch** button from the **Extrusion direction** area if it is not chosen by default. Figure 8-69 shows multiple sketched entities for the rib feature. Figure 8-70 shows the resulting rib feature.

When you choose the **Normal to Sketch** button, the **Type** area is displayed under the **Draft Angle** spinner. The **Type** area has two radio buttons: **Linear** and **Natural**. These radio buttons are used if the endpoints of the open sketch for the rib are not coincident with the faces of the existing feature. If the **Linear** radio button is selected, the rib will be created by extending the sketch normal to the sketched entity direction and the sketch will extend up to a point where it meets the boundary. On the other hand, if the **Natural** radio button is selected, the rib feature will be created by extending the sketch along the same curvature of the sketched entities.

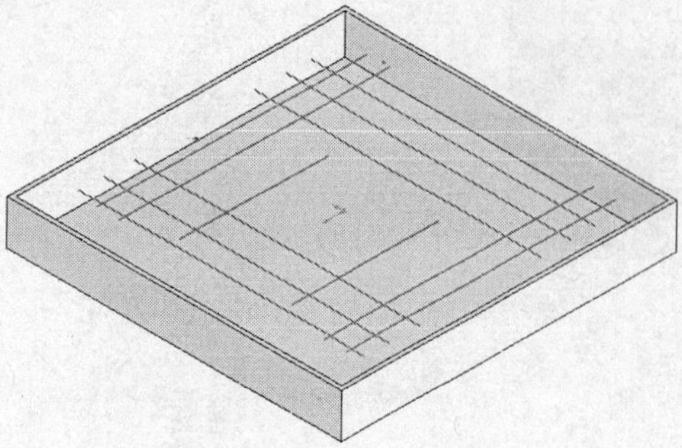

Figure 8-69 Multiple sketch entities for the rib feature

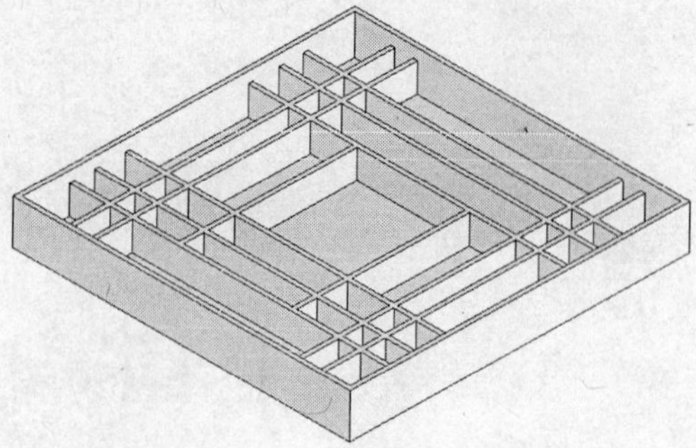

Figure 8-70 The resulting rib feature

For example, consider a sketch that has multiple sketched entities created for the rib feature, as shown in Figure 8-71. Figure 8-72 shows a rib feature created by extending the sketch normal to the arc and the line with the **Linear** radio button selected. Similarly, in Figure 8-73, the feature is created by extending the sketch along the line and arc with the **Natural** radio button selected.

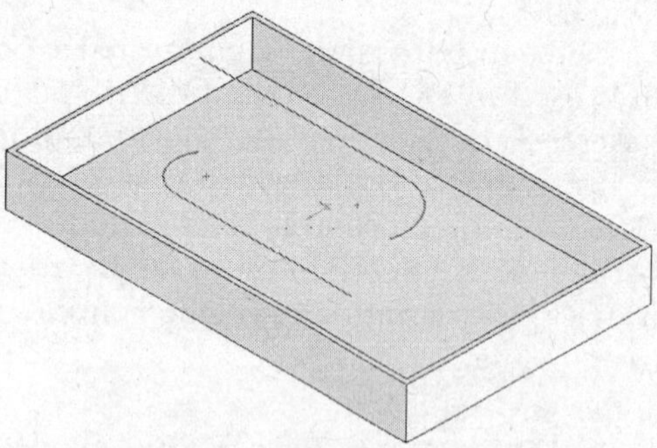

Figure 8-71 Sketch for the rib feature

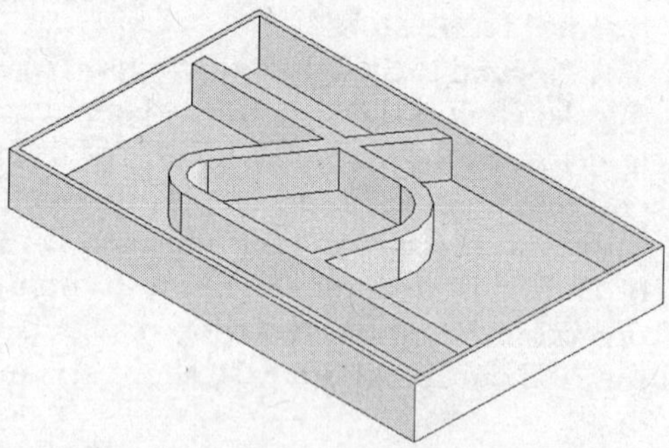

*Figure 8-72 Rib feature created with the **Linear** radio button selected*

Flip material side

The **Flip material side** check box is selected to reverse the direction for adding material, while creating the rib feature. You can also left-click on the arrow displayed in the preview to reverse the direction.

Draft On/Off

The **Draft On/Off** button is used to add taper to the faces of a rib feature. When you choose the **Draft On/Off** button, the **Draft Angle** spinner will become available. If you are creating a rib feature by using multiple sketched entities, you can add only a simple draft to it. Figure 8-74 shows the draft angle added to the rib feature.

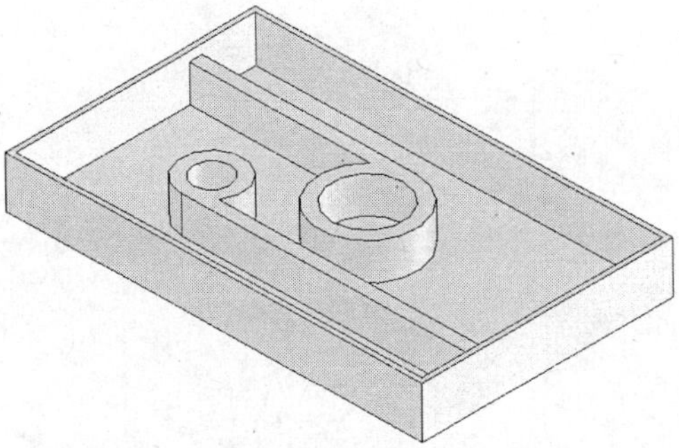

__Figure 8-73__ Rib feature created with the ***Natural*** *radio button selected*

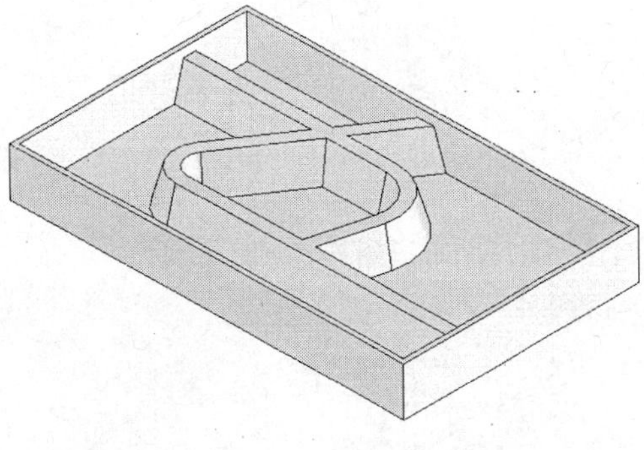

__Figure 8-74__ Draft angle added to the rib feature

By default, the **Draft outward** check box is selected. As a result, draft is added outward. To add the draft inward, you need to clear this check box. If the rib feature to be created consists of single continuous sketch and if you choose the **Draft On/Off** button, the **Next Reference** button will be displayed below the **Draft outward** check box. Also, a reference arrow will be displayed in the drawing area. Choose the **Next Reference** button to cycle through the reference along which you want to add the draft angle.

When you choose the **Draft On/Off** button, the **At sketch plane** and **At wall interface** radio buttons will be displayed below the **Rib Thickness** spinner. The **At sketch plane** radio button is selected by default. Therefore, the rib thickness will be applied on the sketch plane. On selecting the **At wall interface** radio button, the rib thickness will be applied at the point where the rib meets the wall. Figure 8-75 shows the sketch and preview of rib feature and Figure 8-76 shows the resulting rib feature created with the **Draft outward** check box selected.

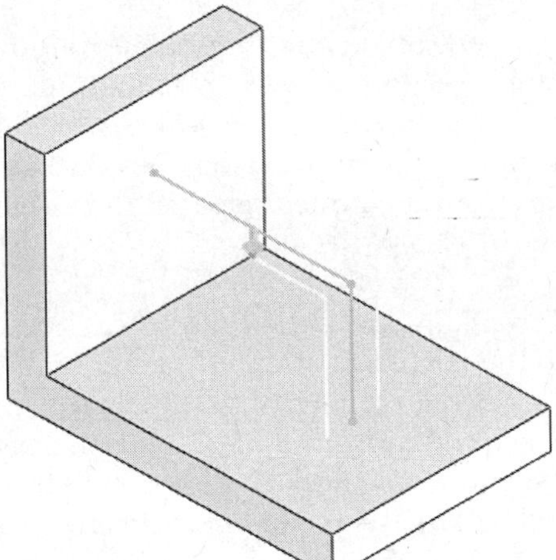

__Figure 8-75__ The sketch and preview of the rib feature

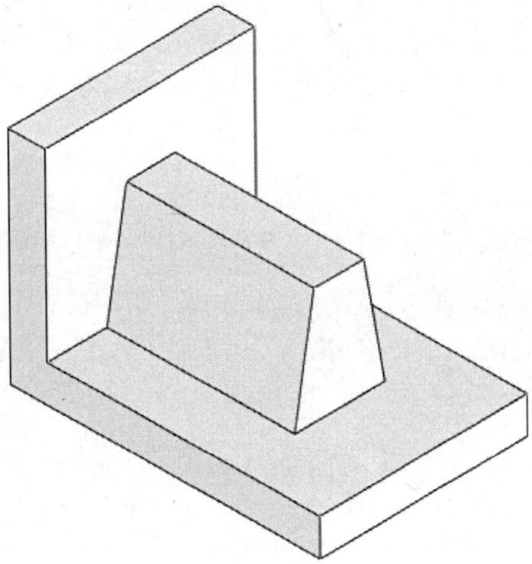

__Figure 8-76__ The rib feature created with the ***Draft outward*** *check box selected*

Figure 8-77 shows the sketch and preview of the rib feature and Figure 8-78 shows the resulting rib feature created with the **Draft outward** check box cleared.

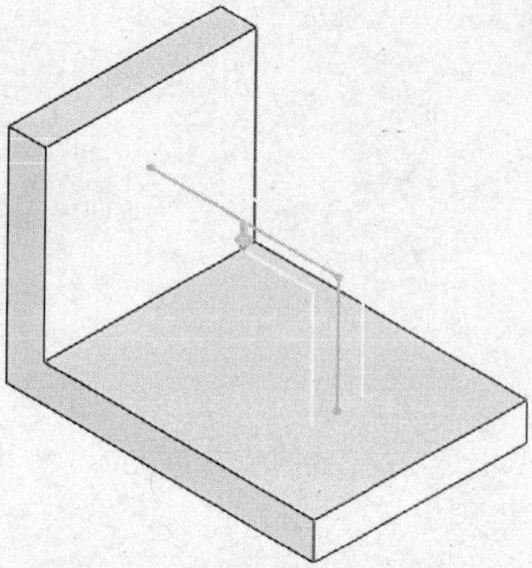

Figure 8-77 The sketch and preview of the rib feature

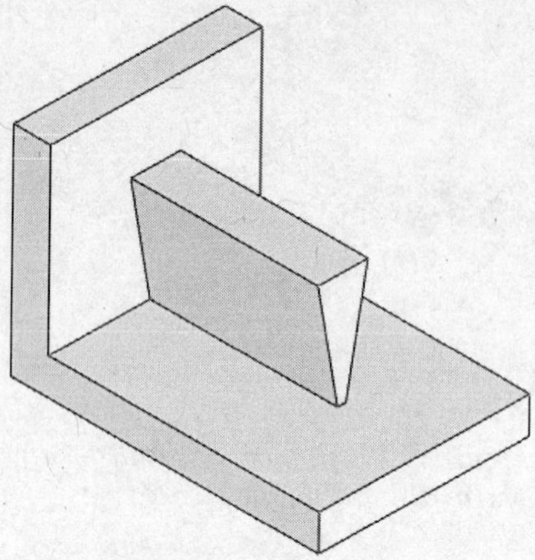

Figure 8-78 Resulting rib feature

Displaying the Section View of a Model

SOLIDWORKS menus: View > Display > Section View
Toolbar: View (Heads-Up) > Section View

The **Section View** tool is used to display the section view of a model by cutting it using a plane or a face. You can also save the section view with a name to generate the section view directly on the drawing sheet in the drawing mode. To display the section view of a model, choose the **Section View** button from the **View (Heads-Up)** toolbar. On invoking this tool, the **Section View PropertyManager** will be displayed, as shown in Figure 8-79.

Expand the **Section Method** rollout, if it is not expanded. By default, the **Planar** radio button is selected in this rollout. As a result, you can create a section view by selecting one, two, or three planes or planar faces. Select the **Zonal** radio button to create a section view by selecting one or more zones. Zones are created by the intersection of the selected planes or faces and the bounding box of the model. You can select the zones from the **Zones selected to be sectioned** selection box available below the **Zonal** radio button.

In the **Section Options** rollout, by default the **Reference plane** radio button is selected. As a result, the offset values will be calculated normal to the currently oriented plane. If you select the **Selected plane** radio button, offset values will be calculated normal to the plane which you have selected in the **Section 1** rollout. The difference in the offset values in both the cases can be observed by the position of the triad. The **Show section cap** check box is selected by default and therefore section cap is displayed in specified color. The **Keep cap color** check box is used to display the color on the section cap after exiting the PropertyManager.

By default, the **Front Plane** is automatically selected in the **Section 1** rollout of the **Section View PropertyManager** and the section view of the model created using the **Front Plane** as the section plane is displayed in the drawing area. If you need to select the Right Plane or Top Plane as the section plane, choose the respective buttons from the **Section 1** rollout. You can also select a face or a user defined plane as the section plane. To do so, clear the reference plane selected in the **Reference Section Plane/Face** selection box and select the face or the plane from the drawing area.

A triad is displayed at the center of the section plane to drag and dynamically adjust the offset distance and angle of the section plane, as shown in Figure 8-80. You can also specify the offset distance using the **Offset Distance** spinner. While modifying the offset distance, you will observe that the preview of the section view gets modified automatically. You can also rotate the section plane along the X-axis and the Y-axis using the **X Rotation** and **Y Rotation** spinners, respectively. Alternatively, you can rotate the section plane dynamically by using the triad.

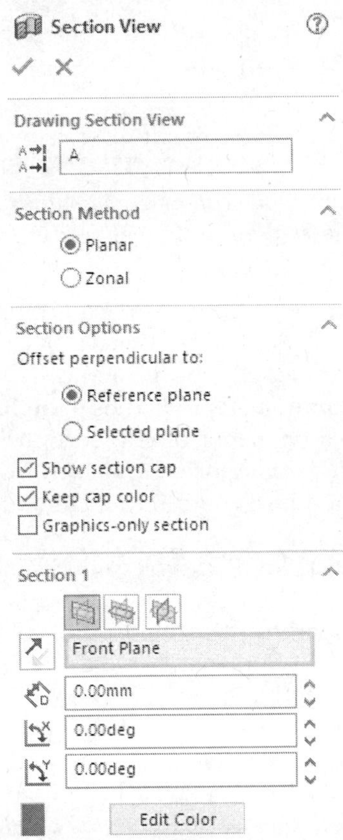

Figure 8-79** Partial view of the **Section View PropertyManager

The **Edit Color** button is used to modify the color of the preview of the section cap. However, the color of the section cap will be displayed only when the **keep cap color** check box is selected in the **Section Options** rollout. When you exit the PropertyManager, the color will not be displayed in the section view.

To create a half section view, you need to activate the **Section 2** rollout by selecting the check box available on the left in this rollout and specify the section plane in it. You can also specify the offset distance and the rotation of the plane in this rollout, as discussed earlier for **Section 1**. After setting all parameters, choose the **OK** button from the **Section View PropertyManager**. Figure 8-81 shows the preview of the model after defining the second section plane.

You can also define the third section plane by using the **Section 3** rollout. This rollout is displayed only if you activate the **Section 2** rollout. You can specify all the parameters as defined earlier in **Section 1** and **Section 2** rollouts.

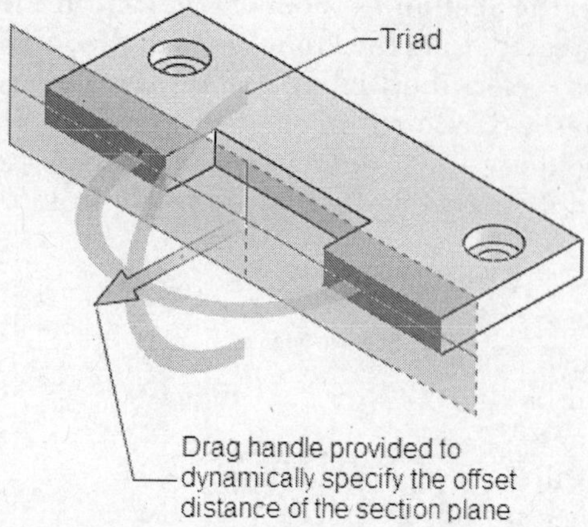

Figure 8-80 Triad for dynamically specifying the offset distance and rotation

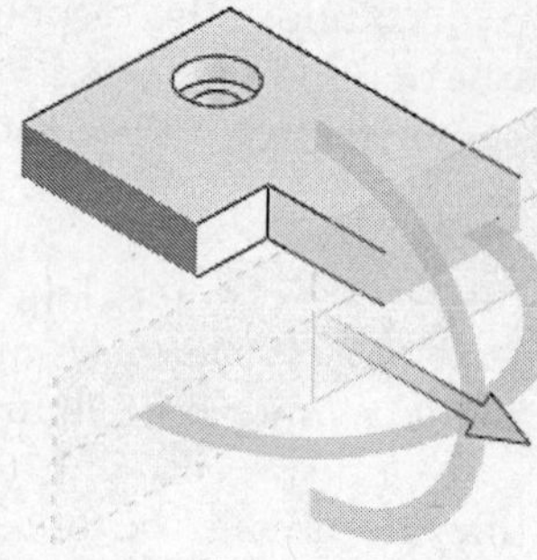

Figure 8-81 Section preview after selecting the second section plane

You can include or exclude one or more bodies in the section view by selecting the required option from the **Section by Body** rollout. To do so, select the check box on the left in the **Section by Body** rollout; all options in this rollout will be activated. Select the bodies and components in the **Components or bodies to include or exclude from the section view** selection box to include or exclude them from the section view. Select the **Exclude selected** radio button to exclude the selected bodies or components from the section view. Alternatively, you can select the **Include selected** radio button to include the bodies or components in the section view.

In SOLIDWORKS, you can view the removed section in the transparent mode so that the whole part or assembly is visible even after activating the section view. To do so, activate the **Transparently Section Bodies** rollout; a message box appears prompting you to switch to zonal sectioning if planar sectioning is set by default. Choose **OK** to close the message box. Then select the body or the component to show it in the transparent mode. The name of the selected body will be displayed in the **Components or bodies to include or exclude from the transparent sectioning** selection box. The **Exclude selected** and **Include selected** radio buttons are same as discussed earlier. The transparency of the section view can be controlled by using the **Section transparency** spinner or the sliding bar beneath. Choose **OK** from the PropertyManager. Figure 8-82 shows model with transparent sectioning.

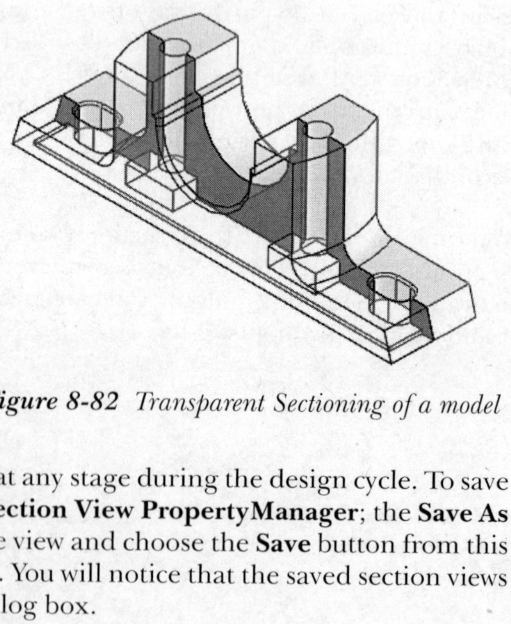

Figure 8-82 Transparent Sectioning of a model

You can save the sectioned view and retrieve it later at any stage during the design cycle. To save a sectioned view, choose the **Save** button from the **Section View PropertyManager**; the **Save As** dialog box will be displayed. Specify the name of the view and choose the **Save** button from this dialog box. Now, invoke the **Orientation** dialog box. You will notice that the saved section views will be listed along with the default views in this dialog box.

Tip

To switch back to the full view mode, you need to choose the ***Section View*** *button from the* ***View (Heads-Up)*** *toolbar. You can also right-click to invoke the shortcut menu and then choose the* ***Section View*** *option from the shortcut menu; you will switch back to the full view mode.*

To modify the section view, invoke the shortcut menu. Choose the ***Section View Properties*** *option from it; the* ***Section View PropertyManager*** *will be displayed and you can modify the section view.*

CHANGING THE DISPLAY STATES

In SOLIDWORKS, you can control the transparency of individual features and display a model in different display states in the part environment also. The name of the default display state is displayed in parenthesis next to the name of the model in the **FeatureManager Design Tree**. To display a model in different display states, first you need to create different display states and then change the display of features for each display state created. To create different display states, choose the **ConfigurationManager** tab available in the Manager Pane; the **ConfigurationManager** along with the default display state **<Default>_Display State 1** will be displayed, as shown in Figure 8-83. Right-click on the default display state in the **Display States** area and choose the **Add Display State** option from the shortcut menu; a new display state, **Display State-2**, will be added. Also, you will notice that the default display state, **<Default>_ Display State 1**, is greyed out. You can rename the newly created display state by using the F2 key. Similarly, you can add multiple display states to a model and rename them.

To change the display of a feature for a particular display state created, double-click on that display state in the **ConfigurationManager**; the name of the selected display state will be displayed in parenthesis next to the name of the model in the design tree. Next, choose the arrow on the top right of the **FeatureManager Design Tree**; the **FeatureManager Design Tree** will expand and the **Display Pane** will be displayed. To change the transparency of a feature, move the cursor over the corresponding area, refer to Figure 8-84, and then click; the transparency of the feature will change.

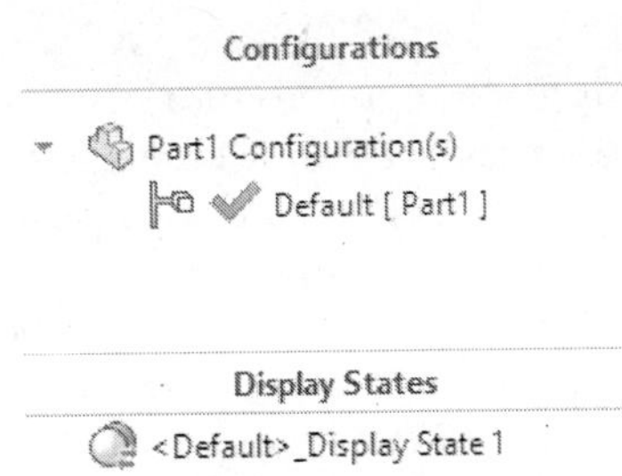

Figure 8-83 *The* ***Configurations Manager*** *with the default display states*

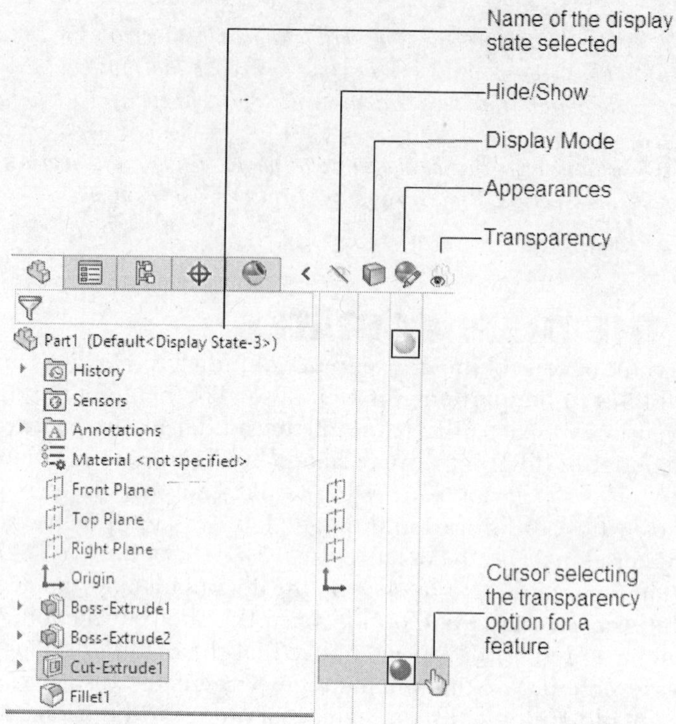

Figure 8-84 Changing the transparency of a feature

Similarly, to change the color of a feature, move the cursor over the corresponding option in the **FeatureManager Design Tree** and then click; a flyout will be displayed. Choose the **Appearance** option from this flyout; the **Appearances, Scenes, and Decals** task pane will be displayed on the right side of the drawing area. Also, the **color PropertyManager** of the default material will be displayed on the left side of the drawing area. Select a color from the **Color** rollout and set the parameters of the color in other rollouts. Expand the **Display States** rollout and specify the display state in which you need to the change the color. Next, choose the **OK** button from the **color PropertyManager**; the selected color will be applied to the feature. Now, double-click on any other display state in the **ConfigurationManager**; you can notice the difference in the display states of the model. In this way, you can change the transparency and the color of a feature and change the display states of a model.

Tip

In SOLIDWORKS, if a model has one display state, you can hide the name of the display state shown in parenthesis in the ***FeatureManager Design Tree****. To do so, right-click on the part name in the design tree and choose* ***Tree Display > Do not show Configuration/Display State Names if only one exists*** *from the shortcut menu displayed.*

TUTORIALS

Tutorial 1

In this tutorial, you will create the model shown in Figure 8-85. The dimensions of the model are shown in same figure. **(Expected time: 30 min)**

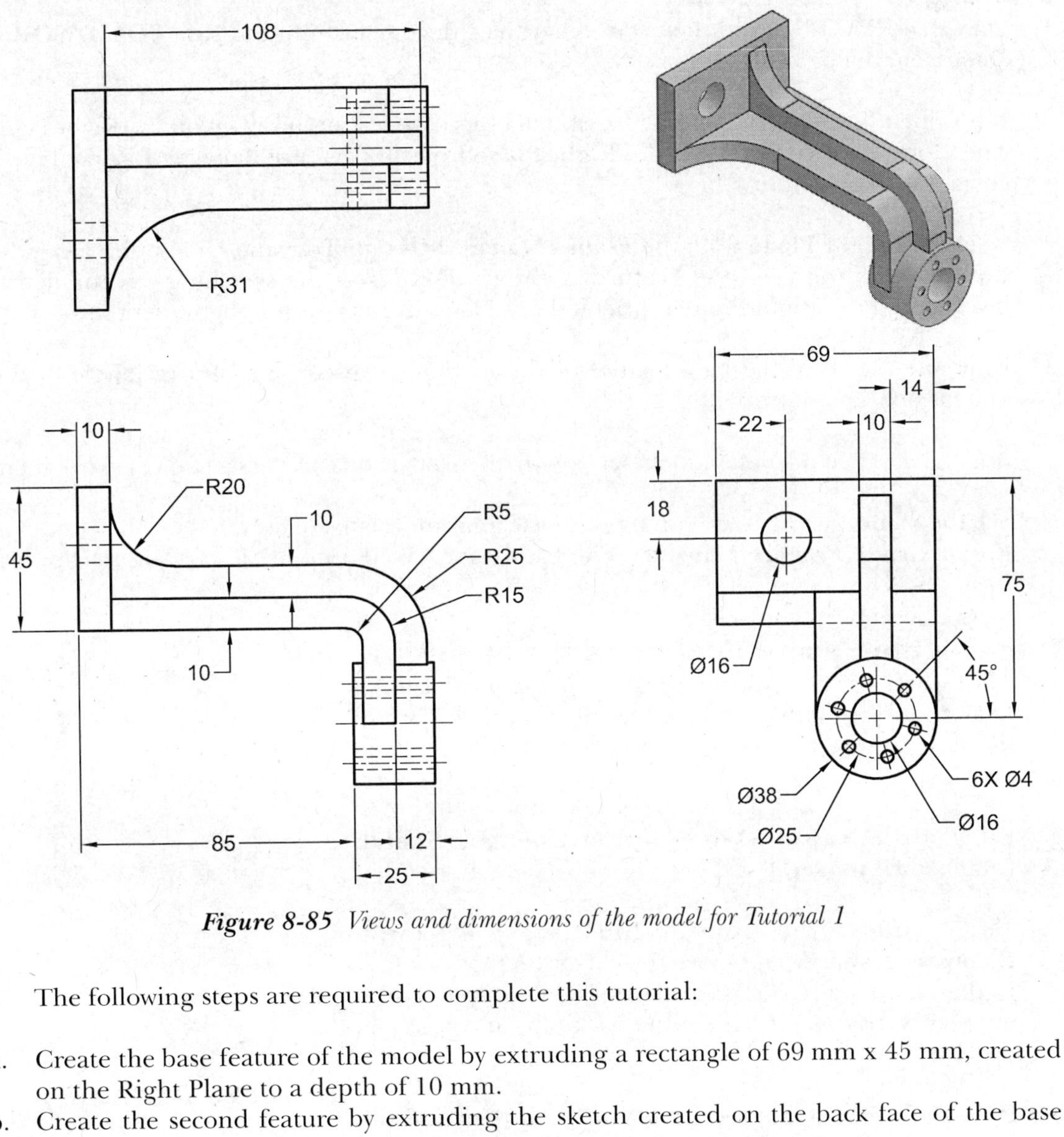

Figure 8-85 *Views and dimensions of the model for Tutorial 1*

The following steps are required to complete this tutorial:

a. Create the base feature of the model by extruding a rectangle of 69 mm x 45 mm, created on the Right Plane to a depth of 10 mm.
b. Create the second feature by extruding the sketch created on the back face of the base feature.
c. Create the third feature by extruding a circle created on the second feature.
d. Create a hole feature placed concentric to the circular feature.

e. Create a hole on the specified Pitch circle, and pattern the hole feature using the circular pattern option.
f. Create a hole feature on the base feature.
g. Create a fillet feature to add the required fillets.
h. Create a rib feature.

Creating the Base Feature

1. Start SOLIDWORKS and then start a new part document from the **New SOLIDWORKS Document** dialog box.

   It is evident from the model that the sketch of its base feature is drawn on the Right Plane. Therefore, you need to select the **Right Plane** from the **FeatureManager Design Tree** to create the base feature.

2. Select the **Right Plane** from the **FeatureManager Design Tree** and choose the **Extruded Boss/Base** button from the **Features CommandManager**; the sketching environment is invoked and the **Right Plane** is oriented normal to the view, if not then orient it.

3. Draw the sketch of the base feature of the model which consists of a rectangle having dimensions 69 mm x 45 mm.

4. Add the required relations and dimensions to the sketch and exit the sketching environment.

5. Set the value of the **Depth** spinner to **10 mm** and choose the **OK** button to exit the **Boss-Extrude PropertyManager**. The base feature of the model is created, as shown in Figure 8-86.

Creating the Second Feature of the Model

The second feature of the model is also an extruded feature. Draw the sketch for the second feature on the back face of the base feature and extrude this sketch upto the given depth.

1. Choose the **Rapid Sketch** button from the **Sketch CommandManager**, if it is not chosen by default.

2. Then, choose the **Line** button from the **Sketch CommandManager** and move the cursor on the back face of the base feature; the sketch plane is displayed in the temporary graphics. Click on the back face to invoke the sketching environment.

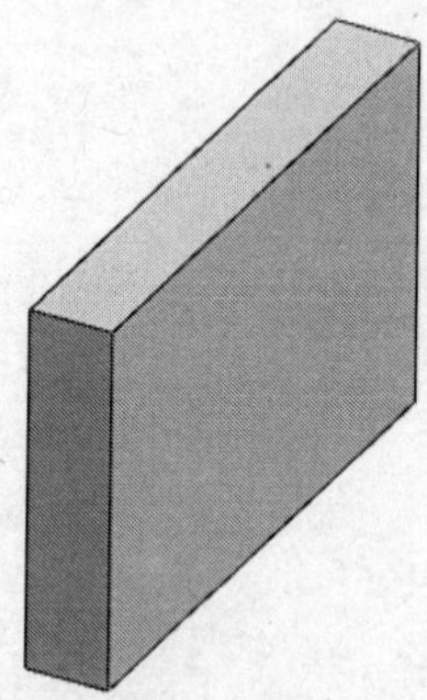

Figure 8-86 *Base feature of the model*

3. Draw the sketch of the second feature, and then add the required relations, as shown in Figure 8-87. Then, exit the sketching environment.

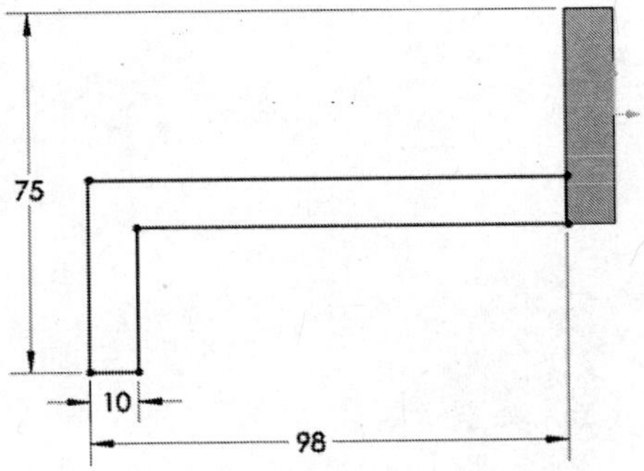

Figure 8-87 Sketch for the second feature

4. Make sure that the sketch is selected and then choose the **Extruded Boss/Base** tool from the **Feature CommandManager** and choose the **Reverse Direction** button in the **Direction 1** rollout from the **Boss-Extrude PropertyManager**.

5. Set the value of the **Depth** spinner to **38** and exit the feature creation.

   The model after creating the second feature is shown in Figure 8-88.

Creating the Third Feature

The third feature of this model is a circular extruded feature. The sketch for this feature will be drawn on the right planar face of the second feature and then extruded on both sides of the sketching plane.

1. Choose the **Circle** tool from the **Sketch CommandManager** and select the right planar face of the second feature. As the **Rapid Sketch** button is already chosen, the sketching environment will be displayed automatically.

2. Draw the sketch using the **Circle** tool and add the required relations and dimensions to it, refer to Figure 8-85.

3. Invoke the **Extruded Boss/Base** tool and set the value of the **Depth** spinner in the **Direction 1** rollout to **12**. Since you need to extrude the sketch in both directions with variable values, activate the **Direction 2** rollout and set the value of the **Depth** spinner in the **Direction 2** rollout to **13**, and end the feature creation. Figure 8-89 shows the model after adding the third feature.

Figure 8-88 Second feature added to the model

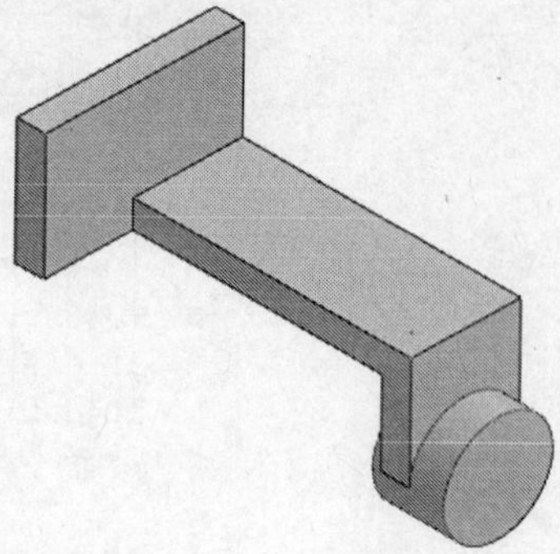

Figure 8-89 Third feature added to the model

Creating the Fourth Feature

The fourth feature of this model is a hole feature. You need to create a hole arbitrarily on the right face of the third feature using the **Simple Hole** tool and position it later.

1. Select the right face of the third feature and choose the **Simple Hole** button from the **Features CommandManager**, or choose **Insert > Features > Simple Hole** from the SOLIDWORKS menu to invoke the **Hole PropertyManager**.

2. Select the **Up To Next** option from the **End Condition** drop-down list and set the value of the **Hole Diameter** spinner to **16**.

3. Choose the **OK** button from the **Hole PropertyManager**; the hole feature is placed arbitrarily on the selected face.

   Now, you need to position the hole feature concentric to the circular feature.

4. Select the hole feature from the **FeatureManager Design Tree**; a pop-up toolbar is displayed.

5. Choose **Edit Sketch** from the pop-up toolbar; the sketching environment is displayed.

6. Apply concentric relation between the circle and the circular edge of the face.

7. Press CTRL+B keys on the keyboard to rebuild the model; the hole feature is positioned.

Creating the Fifth Feature

1. Follow the procedure given in the previous section to create the fifth feature, which is also a hole feature, on the specified Pitch circle, as shown in Figure 8-85. This feature will be created on the right face of the third feature. The hole feature is created using the **Up To Next** option, with the diameter of the hole as 4 mm. Next, define the placement of the feature by adding the required relations and dimensions to it.

Patterning the Hole Feature

After creating the fifth feature, which is a hole feature, you will pattern it using the **Circular Pattern** tool.

1. Choose the **Circular Pattern** button from the **Linear Pattern** flyout; the **CirPattern PropertyManager** is invoked and you are prompted to select the features to pattern.

2. Select the hole feature created in the previous step from the drawing area. Alternatively, expand the **FeatureManager Design Tree** displayed in the drawing area and then select the **Hole2** feature from it.

3. Click on the **Pattern Axis** selection box in the **CirPattern PropertyManager** and select the circular edge of the hole feature created earlier; preview of the circular pattern of the hole feature is displayed.

4. Select the **Equal spacing** check box, if it is not selected, and set the value in the **Number of Instances** spinner to **6**. Also, set the value in the **Angle** spinner to **360**. Choose the **OK** button from the PropertyManager.

Creating the Hole Feature

The next feature to be created is also a hole feature.

1. Create this hole feature by using the same procedure followed to create the fourth feature. This hole feature needs to be placed on the right planar face of the base feature. Therefore, after selecting the right planar face of the base feature, place the hole feature on it.

2. Next, define the placement of the hole feature by adding the required relations and dimensions. Figure 8-90 shows the model after adding all the hole features.

Figure 8-90 *Model after adding all the hole features*

Creating the Fillet Feature

Next, you need to create the fillet feature. It is evident from the model that the fillets to be added to it are of different radii. In SOLIDWORKS, you can specify different radii to the selected edges, faces, or loops individually in a single fillet feature.

1. Choose the **Fillet** button from the **Features CommandManager**; the **Fillet PropertyManager** is displayed. If the **FilletXpert PropertyManager** is displayed, choose the **Manual** button from it to display the **Fillet PropertyManager**.

2. Select the **Multi Radius Fillet** check box from the **Fillet Parameters** rollout in the **Fillet PropertyManager**.

3. Select the edges to be filleted, as shown in Figure 8-91. When the **Multi Radius Fillet** check box is selected, a separate **Radius** callout will be displayed on each selected edge.

4. Modify the values of the radii as required in their respective **Radius** callouts.

5. Choose the **OK** button from the **Fillet PropertyManager**.

The isometric view of the model after adding the fillet feature is shown in Figure 8-92.

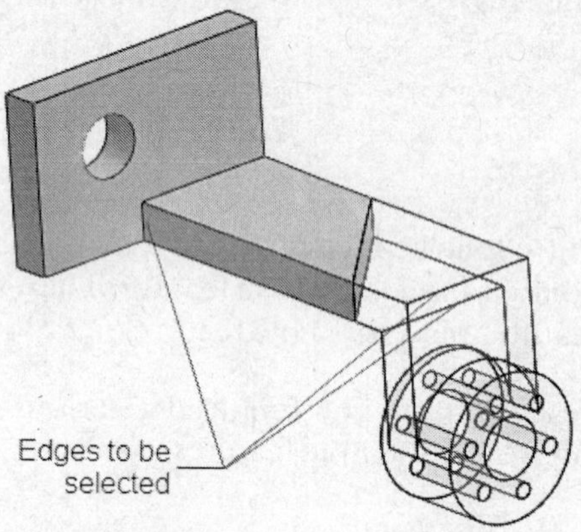

Figure 8-91 *Edges to be filleted*

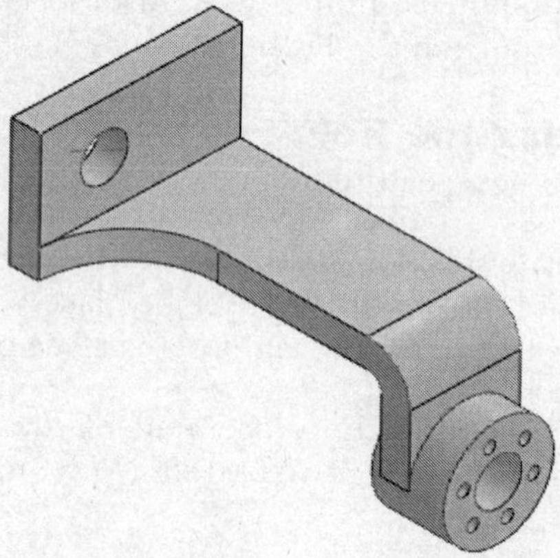

Figure 8-92 *Model after adding the fillet feature*

Creating the Rib Feature

The next feature that you need to create is a rib feature. The sketch of the rib feature needs to be drawn on a sketching plane at an offset distance from the back planar face of the model. Therefore, you first need to create a reference plane at an offset distance from the back planar face of the model.

1. Choose the **Plane** button from the **Reference Geometry** flyout; the **Plane PropertyManager** is invoked.

2. Rotate the model and select its back planar face as the first reference. Select the **Flip offset** check box below the **Offset distance** spinner and set the value in the **Offset distance** spinner to **19**.

3. Choose the **OK** button from the **Plane PropertyManager** to end the feature creation; a new plane is created at an offset distance from the back planar face of the model.

4. Choose the **Rib** button from the **Features CommandManager**.

5. Create a sketch for the rib feature on the newly created plane and add the required relations and dimensions to the sketch, as shown in Figure 8-93.

6. Exit the sketching environment; the **Rib PropertyManager** is displayed.

   Preview of the rib feature is displayed in the drawing area. You will notice that the direction of material addition is displayed by an arrow in the drawing area. The direction of material addition is opposite to the required direction. Therefore, you need to flip its direction. If the direction of material addition is the required one, skip the next step.

7. Select the **Flip material side** check box to flip the direction of the material addition.

   The **Both Sides** button is chosen by default in the **Parameters** rollout and the default value of the rib thickness is **10** which is also the required value. Therefore, you do not need to change it.

8. Choose the **OK** button from the **Rib PropertyManager**. Also, hide the newly created plane.

   The last feature of the model is a fillet feature. Add the fillet feature on the left edge of the rib using the **Fillet** tool. Figure 8-94 shows the isometric view of the final model.

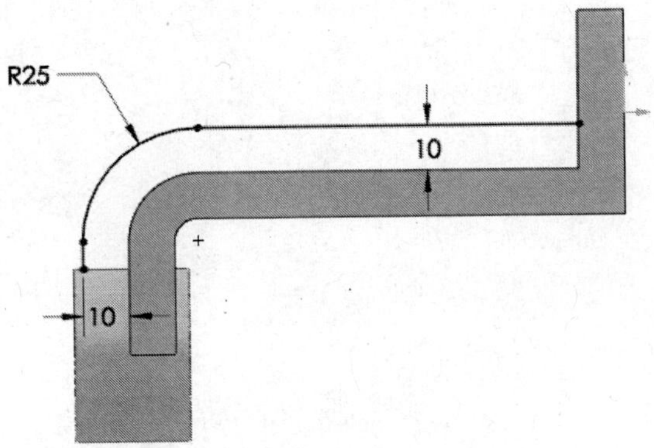

***Figure 8-93** Sketch for the rib feature*

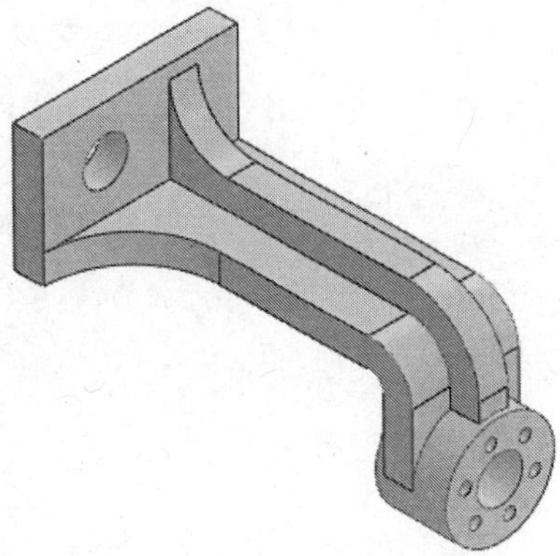

***Figure 8-94** The final solid model*

Saving the Model

1. Create a folder with the name *c08* in the *SOLIDWORKS* folder and choose the **Save** button from the Menu Bar. Save the model with the name *c08_tut01* at the location given below: *\Documents\SOLIDWORKS\c08*

2. Choose **File > Close** from the SOLIDWORKS menus to close the document.

Tutorial 2

In this tutorial, you will create the model of a cover. The dimensions of the model are shown in Figure 8-95. The model is shown in Figure 8-96. **(Expected time: 30 min)**

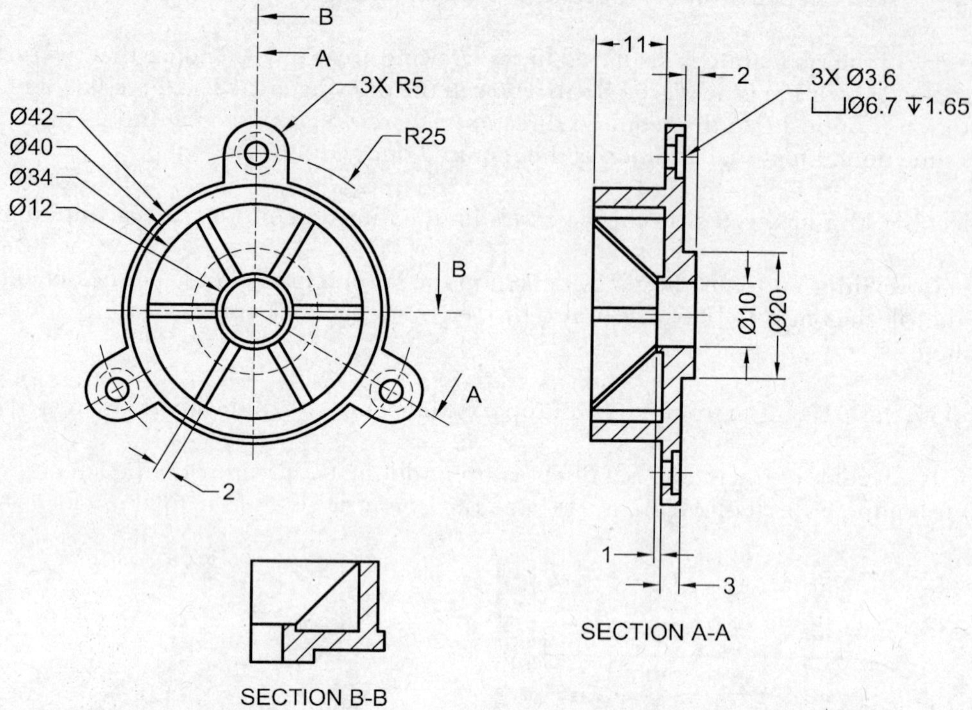

Figure 8-95 *Different views of the model with dimensions*

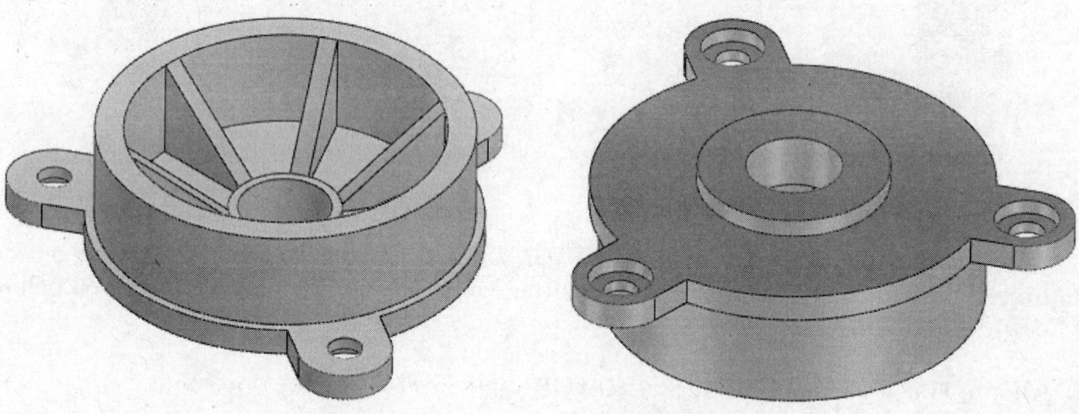

Figure 8-96 *Two different views of the model for Tutorial 2*

The following steps are required to complete this tutorial:

a. Create the base feature of the model by revolving the sketch along the centerline.
b. Create the second feature by extruding the sketch from the sketch plane to the selected surface.
c. Place a counterbore hole feature on the bottom face of the second feature using the **Hole Wizard** tool.

d. Pattern the second and third features along the temporary axis using the **Circular Pattern** tool.
e. Create the rib feature.
f. Pattern the rib feature along a temporary axis using the **Circular Pattern** tool.

Creating the Base Feature

Start a new SOLIDWORKS part document. First, you need to create the base feature of the model by revolving the sketch along the axis of revolution. The axis of revolution will be a centerline and the sketch for the base feature will be drawn on the Right Plane.

1. Invoke the **Revolved Boss/Base** tool and select the **Right Plane** as the sketching plane.

2. Create the sketch for the base feature and add the required relations and dimensions to the sketch, as shown in Figure 8-97.

3. Exit the sketching environment and set the value in the **Direction 1 Angle** spinner as **360**.

4. Choose the **OK** button from the **Revolve PropertyManager**; the base feature is created, as shown in Figure 8-98.

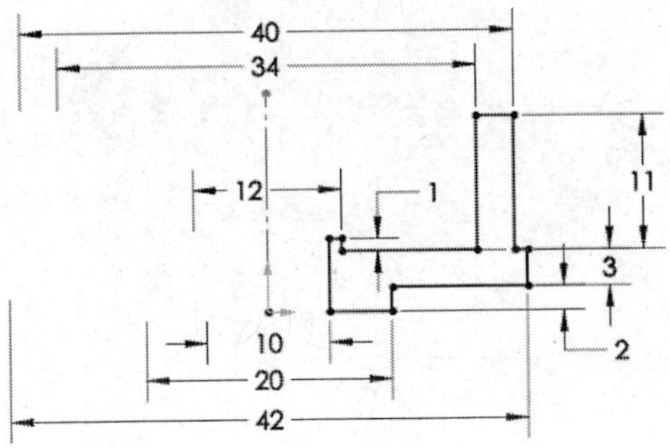

Figure 8-97 *Sketch for the base feature*

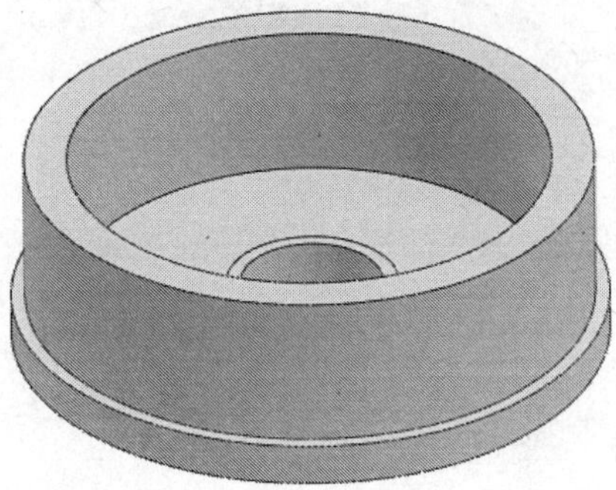

Figure 8-98 *Base feature of the model*

Creating the Second Feature

The second feature needs to be created by extruding the sketch up to the selected surface.

1. Invoke the **Extruded Boss/Base** tool and select the face as the sketching plane, as shown in Figure 8-99.

2. Create the sketch of the second feature and add the required relations and dimensions to it, as shown in Figure 8-100.

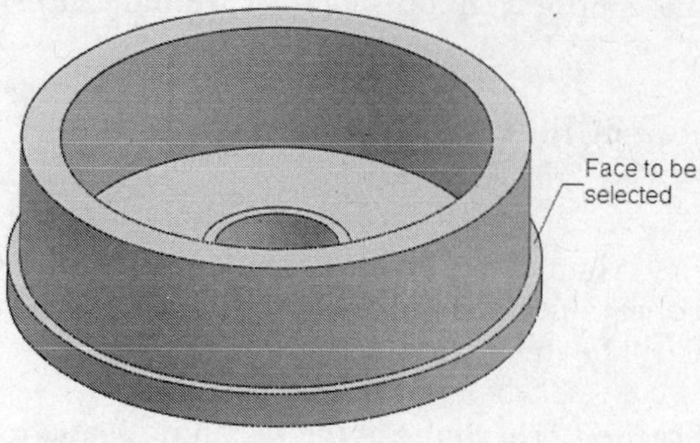

Figure 8-99 Face to be selected

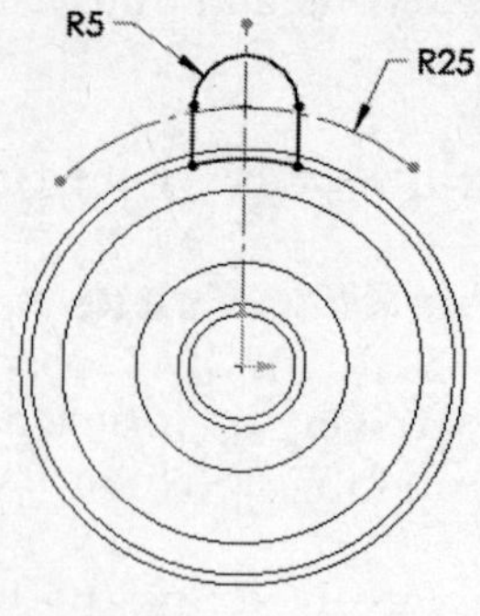

Figure 8-100 Sketch created for the second feature

3. Exit the sketching environment. Use the **Up To Surface** option to extrude the sketch. The surface to be selected is shown in Figure 8-101.

4. Choose the **OK** button from the **Boss-Extrude PropertyManager**; the second feature is created, as shown in Figure 8-102.

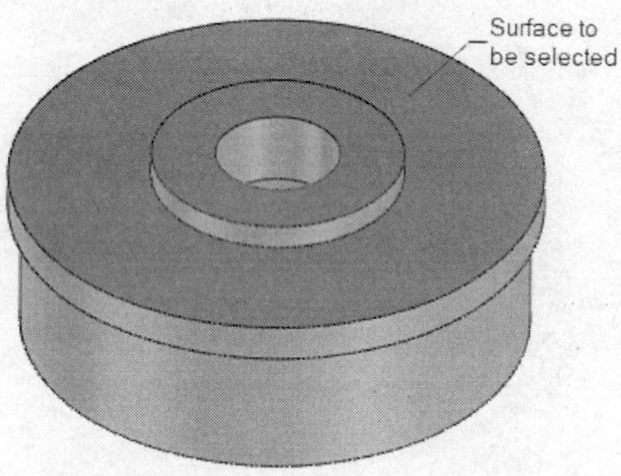

Figure 8-101 Surface to be selected

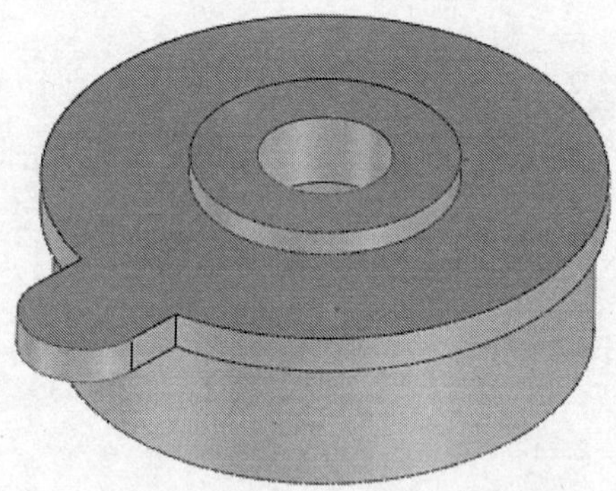

Figure 8-102 Second feature created

Creating the Hole Feature

It is evident from Figure 8-95 that a counterbore hole needs to be added to the model. It can be added by using the **Hole Wizard** tool.

1. Select the bottom face of the second feature as the placement plane for the hole feature and press the **S** key; the **Shortcut** toolbar is displayed.

2. Choose **Hole Wizard** from the **Shortcut** toolbar to invoke the **Hole Specification PropertyManager**.

3. Choose the **Counterbore** button from the **Hole Type** rollout, if it is not chosen by default, and select the **ANSI Metric** option from the **Standard** drop-down list.

4. Select the **Socket Button Head Cap Screw - ANSI B18.3.4M** option from the **Type** drop-down list. Select the **M3** option from the **Size** drop-down list. Select **Through All** in the **End Condition** drop-down list in the **End Condition** rollout.

5. Select the **Show custom sizing** check box to customize the size of the counterbore hole and then enter the following parameters:

   Through Hole Diameter: **3.6 mm** Counterbore Diameter: **6.70 mm**
   Counterbore Depth: **1.65 mm**

6. Choose the **Positions** tab from the **Hole Specification PropertyManager**; you are prompted to use dimensions and other sketching tools to position the center of the holes.

7. Specify the position of the hole and then choose the **Add Relation** button from the **Sketch CommandManager**; the **Add Relations PropertyManager** will be invoked. Now apply the concentric relation between the center point of the hole feature and the circular edge of the second feature. Choose the **OK** button to exit the **Add Relations PropertyManager**.

8. Now, choose the **OK** button from the **Hole Position PropertyManager** to end the feature creation.

Patterning the Features

After creating the second and third features, you need to pattern them using the **Circular Pattern** tool.

1. Choose the **Circular Pattern** button from the **Linear Pattern** flyout; the **CirPattern PropertyManager** is invoked.

2. Select the second and third features from the drawing area or from the **FeatureManager Design Tree** that is displayed in the drawing area.

3. Click on the **Pattern Axis** selection box in the **CirPattern PropertyManager** and select the circular edge of the base feature; preview of the circular pattern of the hole feature is displayed.

4. Set the value in the **Number of Instances** spinner to **3** and make sure the **Equal spacing** check box is selected. Clear the **Geometry pattern** check box from the **Options** rollout, if it is selected.

5. Choose the **OK** button from the **CirPattern PropertyManager**; the features are patterned, as shown in Figure 8-103.

Creating the Rib Feature

The next feature is a rib feature. The sketch for the rib feature will be created on the Front Plane.

1. Choose the **Rib** button from the **Features CommandManager** and select the **Front Plane** from the **FeatureManager Design Tree**; the sketch environment will be invoked.

2. Set the display mode to wireframe and then create the sketch for the rib feature and add the required relations, as shown in Figure 8-104.

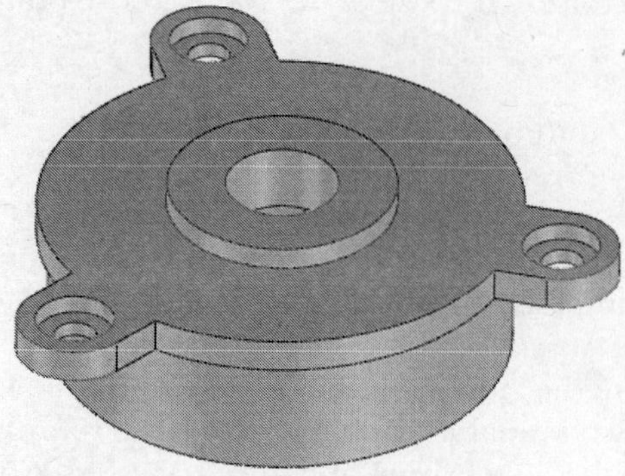

Figure 8-103 Model after patterning the features

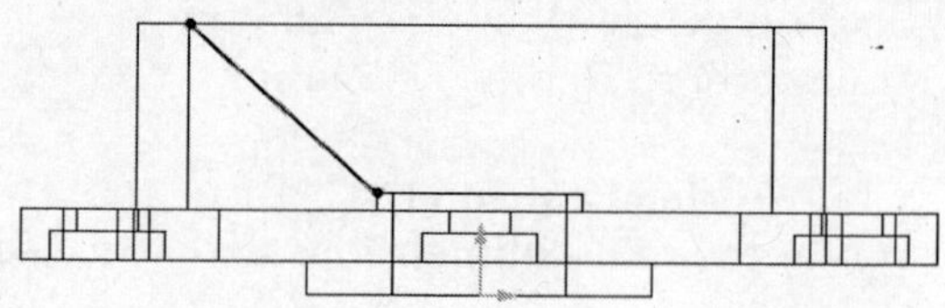

Figure 8-104 Sketch for the rib feature

3. Exit the sketching environment and set the value of the **Rib Thickness** spinner to **2**. Reverse the direction of material, if required, using the **Flip material side** check box. Use the default values for other options and choose the **OK** button from the **Rib PropertyManager**.

4. Change the display mode of the model to shaded with edges.

5. Use the **Circular Pattern** tool to create six instances of the rib feature. The final model after creating all the features is shown in Figure 8-105.

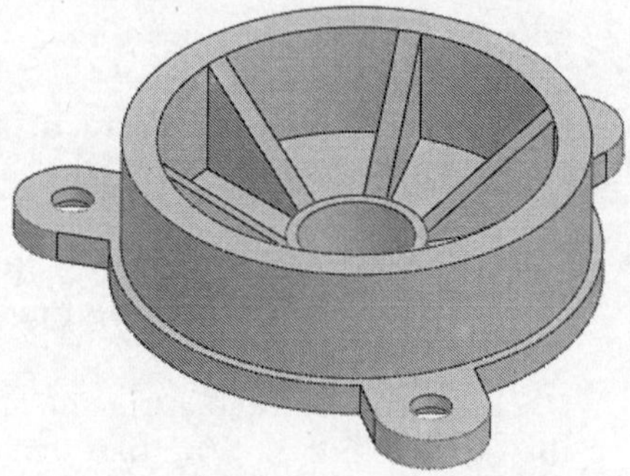

Figure 8-105 Final solid model

Saving the Model

1. Save the model with the name *c08_tut02* at the location given below:

   \Documents\SOLIDWORKS\c08

2. Choose **File > Close** from the SOLIDWORKS menus to close the document.

Tutorial 3

In this tutorial, you will create the cylinder head of a two-stroke automobile engine. The model is shown in Figure 8-106. The dimensions of the model are shown in Figure 8-107. Also, you will create a section view of the model using the **Section View** tool. Then, you will create two display states, one with transparent fins and other with colored fins. **(Expected time: 1 hr)**

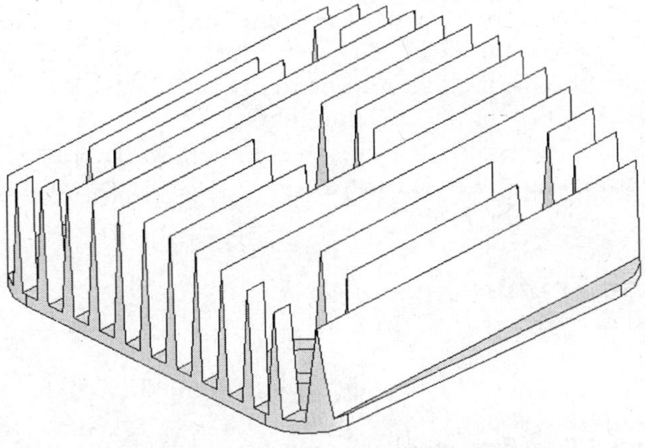

Figure 8-106 Model for Tutorial 3

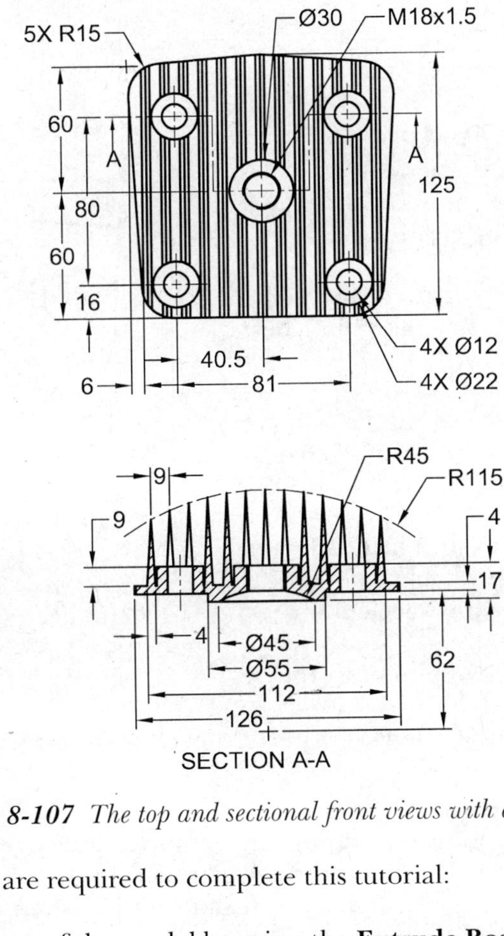

Figure 8-107 The top and sectional front views with dimensions

The following steps are required to complete this tutorial:

a. Create the base feature of the model by using the **Extrude Boss/Base** tool.
b. Add a fillet to the base feature.
c. Create a circular feature at the bottom face of the base feature.

d. Create the revolve cut feature to create the dome of the cylinder head.
e. Create the left fin of the cylinder head by extruding the sketch. The sketch for this feature should be carefully dimensioned and defined,
f. Use the **Vary sketch** option to pattern the fins.
g. Create the other cut and extrude features to complete the model.
h. Create a tap hole by using the hole wizard.
i. Create the section view of the model.

Creating the Base Feature

1. Start a new SOLIDWORKS part document.

   The base feature of the model will be created by extruding the sketch created on the Top Plane.

2. Invoke the **Extruded Boss/Base** tool and select the Top Plane as the sketching plane.

3. Create the sketch for the base feature and add the required relations and dimensions to the sketch, as shown in Figure 8-108.

4. Exit the sketching environment and extrude the sketch upto a depth of 4 mm.

Creating the Second Feature

The second feature of the model is a fillet feature. You need to fillet all vertical edges of the base feature using the given radius.

1. Invoke the **Fillet** tool and choose the **FilletXpert** button to display the **FilletXpert PropertyManager**.

2. Choose one of the vertical edges and do not move the mouse; a pop-up toolbar is displayed.

3. Choose the **Connected to start face, 4 Edges** button from the pop-up toolbar; all vertical edges of the base feature are selected.

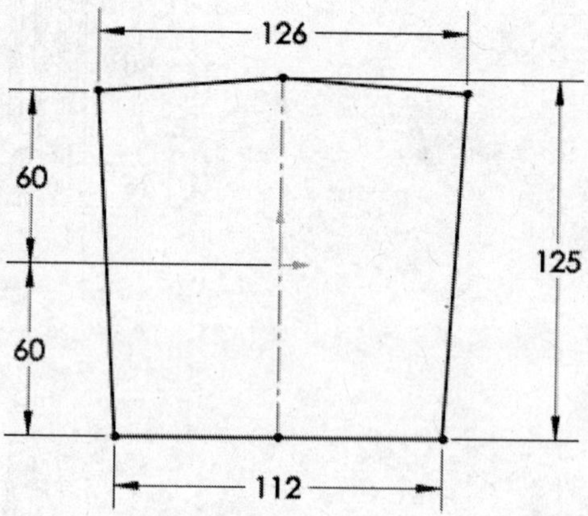

Figure 8-108 Sketch for the base feature

4. Set the value in the **Radius** spinner to **15**.

5. Choose the **OK** button from the **FilletXpert PropertyManager**; the fillets are created.

Creating the Third Feature

After creating the base feature and adding fillets at its vertical edges, you need to create the third feature of the model which is a circular extruded feature. The sketch of the feature will be drawn on the bottom face of the base feature, and it will be extruded upto the given depth.

1. Select the bottom face of the base feature as the sketching plane and press **S** on the keyboard. Invoke the **Extruded Boss/Base** tool from the pop-up toolbar.

2. Create a circle of 55 mm diameter with its center point at the origin.

3. Exit the sketching environment and extrude the sketch to a depth of 4 mm.

Creating the Fourth Feature

The fourth feature is a revolved cut feature whose sketch will be drawn on the Front Plane. After drawing the sketch, apply the required relations and dimensions to it.

1. Invoke the **Revolved Cut** tool and select the **Front Plane** from the **FeatureManager Design Tree**.

2. Draw a sketch for the revolved cut feature and add the required relations and dimensions to it, as shown in Figure 8-109. You need to apply vertical relation between the center point of the arc and the origin to fully define the sketch.

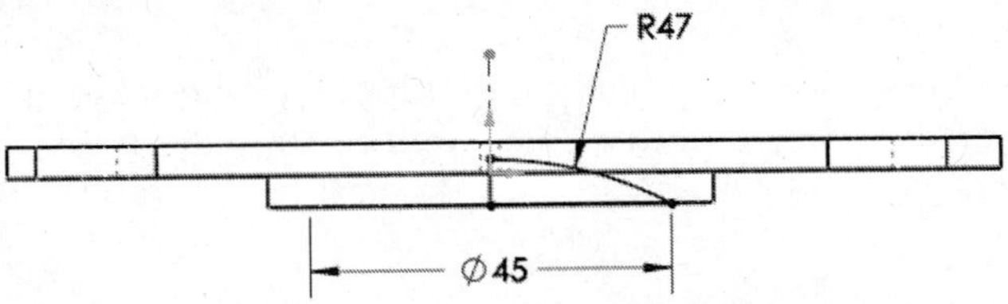

Figure 8-109 Sketch for the revolved cut feature

3. Select the vertical centerline and exit the sketching environment. Make sure that the value in the **Angle** spinner is 360.

4. Choose the **OK** button from the **Cut-Revolve PropertyManager**.

The rotated model after creating the fourth feature is shown in Figure 8-110.

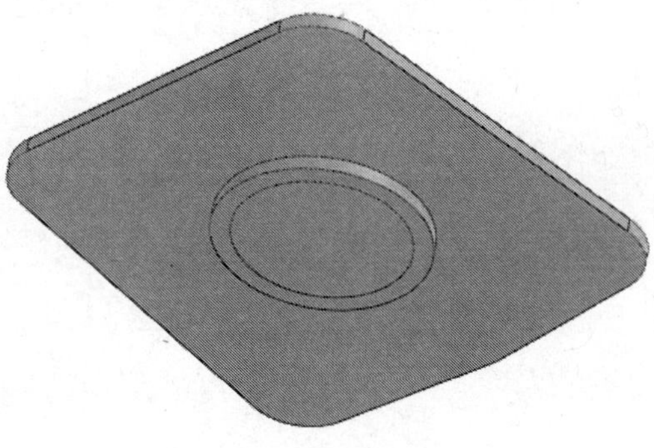

Figure 8-110 Cut revolve feature added to the model

Creating the Fifth Feature

Next, you will create the left fin of the cylinder head. It will be created by extruding a sketch in both directions using the **Mid Plane** option. The sketch of this feature drawn on the Front Plane will be dimensioned and defined such that the length of the fin is driven by the construction arc and the horizontal dimension. The detailed procedure of drawing, dimensioning, and defining the sketch is discussed next.

1. Invoke the **Extruded Boss/Base** tool and select the **Front Plane** from the **FeatureManager Design Tree**.

2. Use the **Line** tool to draw a triangle and then draw a vertical centerline that passes through the upper vertex of the triangle, refer to Figure 8-111.

3. Invoke the **3 Point Arc** tool and draw the arc, refer to Figure 8-111. Select the arc and then select the **For construction** check box from the **Options** rollout of the **Arc PropertyManager**.

4. Invoke the **Add Relations PropertyManager** and add coincident relation between the upper vertex of the triangle and the centerline.

5. Add the midpoint relation between the lower endpoint of the centerline and the horizontal line of the triangle. Make sure that the Coincident relation exists between the upper vertex of the triangle and the centerline. Also, add the vertical relation to the centerline, if it is missing.

6. Add the coincident relation between the upper vertex of the triangle and the arc.

7. Add the required dimensions and relations to fully define the sketch, refer to Figure 8-111.

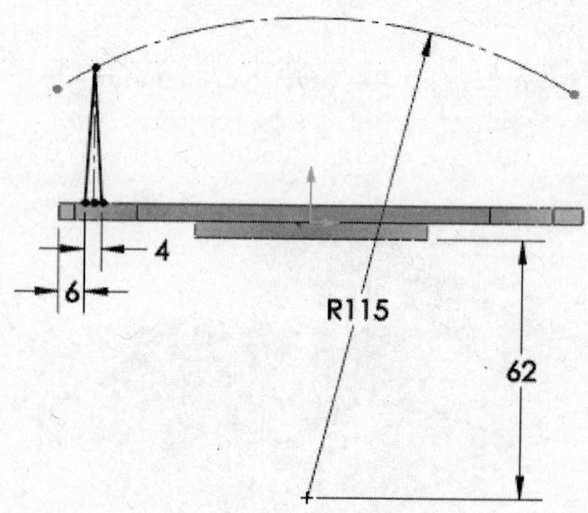

Figure 8-111 *Sketch for the fin of the cylinder head*

8. Exit the sketching environment and extrude the sketch in both directions using the **Mid Plane** option and set the value **130** in the **Depth** spinner. Choose the **OK** button from the PropertyManager. You will notice that the fin extends out of the base feature at both ends. You will learn how to remove the unwanted material of the fin later in this tutorial.

Patterning the Fifth Feature

You will pattern the fin using the **Vary sketch** option from the **Linear Pattern** tool. On choosing the **Vary sketch** option, the geometry of each instance of the pattern will vary according to the driven dimension and the relation added to the sketch of the feature to be patterned.

1. Select the fifth feature, if it is not already selected, and choose the **Linear Pattern** button from the **Features CommandManager** to invoke the **Linear Pattern PropertyManager**; you are prompted to select the directional reference.

2. Select the horizontal dimension with the value 6 as the directional reference from the drawing area.

3. Set the value of the **Spacing** spinner to **9** and set the value of the **Number of Instances** spinner to **13**. Choose the **Reverse Direction** button, if required.

4. Expand the **Options** rollout and clear the **Geometry Pattern** check box if it is selected.

5. Select the **Vary sketch** check box from this rollout. Select the **Full preview** radio button to preview the pattern to be created.

6. Choose the **OK** button from the **Linear Pattern PropertyManager**.

The model after adding the pattern feature is shown in Figure 8-112.

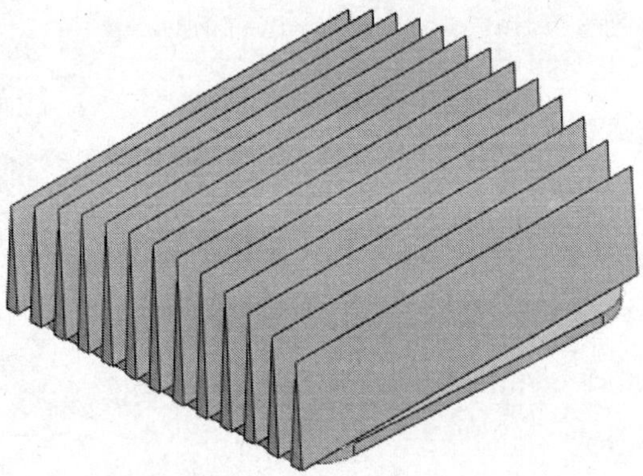

Figure 8-112 *Model after patterning the fin of the cylinder head*

Creating the Cut Feature

The next feature that you will create is a cut feature. Rotate the solid model using the **Rotate** tool. You will observe that the fins of the cylinder head that you patterned in the last feature extend beyond the boundary of the base feature. Therefore, to trim the extended portion of the fins, you need to create a cut feature.

1. Select the top planar face of the base feature as the sketching plane and press **S** on the keyboard. Invoke the **Extruded Cut** tool from the **Shortcut** toolbar.

2. Draw a sketch using the standard sketch tools. The sketch for this feature will be the outer profile of the base feature.

Tip
You can draw the outer profile of the base feature using the ***Convert Entities*** *tool. To do so, select the lower flat face of the base feature and choose the* ***Convert Entities*** *button from the* ***Sketch CommandManager****. You will notice that the sketch similar to the outer boundary of the base feature will be placed on the sketching plane.*

3. Exit the sketching environment and choose the **Reverse Direction** button from the **Direction 1** rollout and select the **Through All** option from the **End Condition** drop-down list.

Since the side from which the material is to be removed is opposite to the required side, you need to flip the direction of material removal.

4. Select the **Flip side to cut** check box from the **Direction 1** rollout and choose the **OK** button from the **Cut-Extrude PropertyManager**.

5. Use the **Extruded Cut** and **Extruded Boss/Base** tools to create the model, as shown in Figure 8-113.

Patterning the Cut, Extrude, and Hole Features

Now, you need to pattern the previously created cut, extrude, and hole features at the lower left corner of the model.

1. Invoke the **Linear Pattern PropertyManager** and select the cut, extrude, and hole features created on the lower left corner of the model.

2. Select the two directional references to pattern the features in both directions and set the distance values between the instances and the number of instances, refer to Figure 8-107.

3. Choose the **OK** button from the **Linear Pattern PropertyManager**.

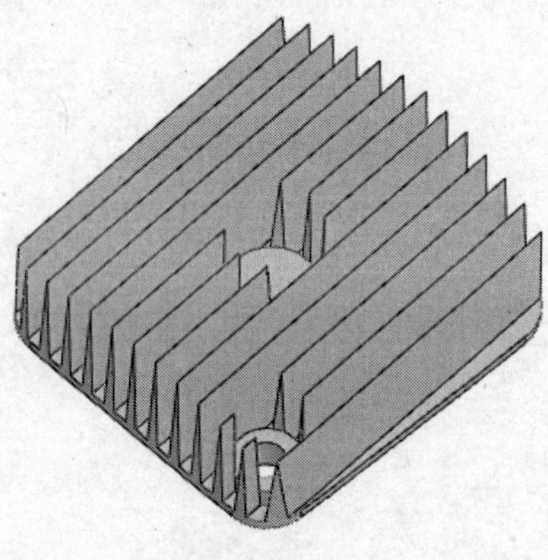

Figure 8-113 Model after adding other extrude and cut features

Creating a Tapped Hole

The last feature of the model is a hole feature. You need to create a tapped hole by using the **Hole Wizard** tool and then specify the location of the hole.

1. Select the top face of the middle circular extrude feature as the plane for the hole feature.

2. Invoke the **Hole Specification PropertyManager** by choosing the **Hole Wizard** button from the **Features CommandManager**. Next, choose the **Straight Tap** button from the **Hole Type** rollout and select **ANSI Metric** from the **Standard** drop-down list.

3. Select the **M18x1.5** option from the **Size** drop-down list to define the size of the tap hole.

4. Select the **Through All** option from the **End Condition** drop-down list in the **End Condition** rollout. Also, select the **Through All** option from the **Thread** drop-down list.

5. Choose the **Cosmetic thread** button from the **Options** rollout. Also, select the **With thread callout** check box.

6. Choose the **Positions** tab from the **Hole Specification PropertyManager** and move the cursor on the top face of the middle circular extrude feature. Next, click on it to specify a point for the location of the tapped hole. This location is not the required position to place the hole. Therefore, you need to relocate the tapped hole concentric with the center circular feature.

7. Invoke the **Add Relations PropertyManager** and add the **Concentric** relation between the center point of the tapped hole and the circular extruded feature of diameter 30 mm. Now, exit the Property manager.

8. Choose the **OK** button from the **Hole Specification PropertyManager** to end the tapped hole feature creation. The final rotated model after creating the hole feature is shown in Figure 8-114.

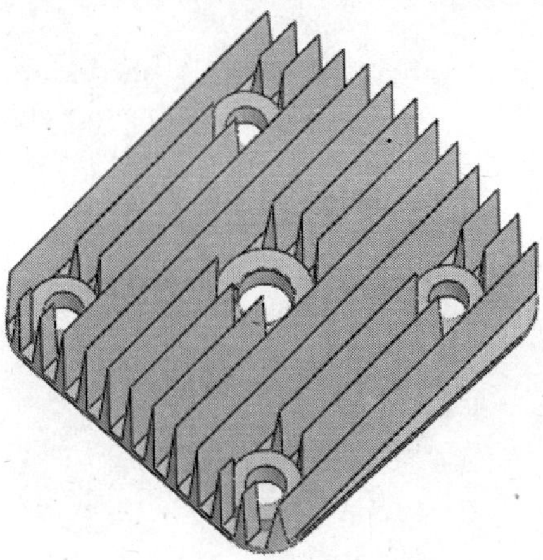

Figure 8-114 *Final solid model*

Tip

If the graphic thread is not displayed in the tapped hole, invoke the ***Document Properties - Detailing*** *dialog box. Select the* ***Shaded cosmetic threads*** *check box in the* ***Display filter*** *area.*

On orienting the model in the top view, you will observe that the thread convention is visible. Similarly, on orienting the model to the front, back, right, or left views, you can view the thread conventions of corresponding views.

You can also hide the cosmetic thread. To do so, move the cursor on the cosmetic thread; the cosmetic thread cursor is displayed. Select the cosmetic thread; a pop-up toolbar is displayed. Choose ***Hide Cosmetic Thread*** *to hide the cosmetic thread.*

Displaying the Section View of the Model

Next, you need to display the section view of the model. The section view of the model will be created using the **Section View PropertyManager**.

1. Orient the model to the isometric view.

2. Choose the **Section View** button from the **View (Heads-Up)** toolbar.

   By default, the **Front Plane** is selected as the section plane in the **Section View PropertyManager**. Preview of the section, by using the **Front Plane** as the section plane, is displayed in the drawing area.

3. Choose the **OK** button from the **Section View PropertyManager** to display the section view of the model. The section view of the model is shown in Figure 8-115.

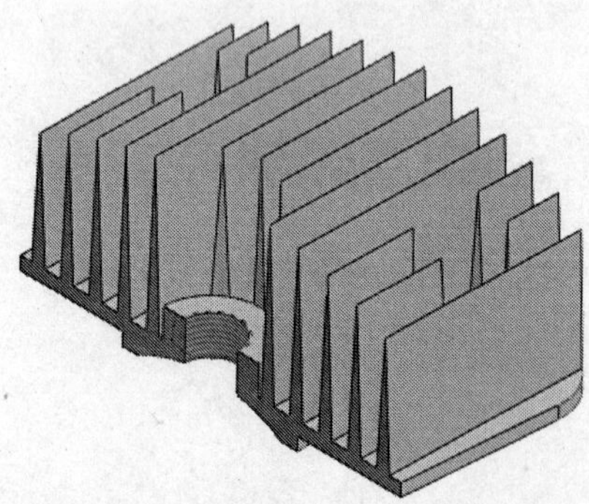

Figure 8-115 *Section view of the model*

4. Choose the **Section View** button again from the **View (Heads-Up)** toolbar to return to the full view mode.

Changing the Display State

To change the display state, you need to create multiple display states and change the transparency and color of the feature.

1. Choose the **ConfigurationManager** button on the top of the **FeatureManager Design Tree**; the **ConfigurationManager** is displayed with the default display state.

2. Left-click once on **<Default>_Display State 1** under the **Display States** area of the **ConfigurationManager** to select it. Next, right-click and then choose the **Add Display State** option from the shortcut menu displayed; a new display state is added.

3. Select the newly added display state, press the F2 key, and rename it as **Transparent Fins**.

4. Similarly, add one more display state and rename it as **Colored Fins**.

5. Make sure that the **Colored Fins** display state is active. Next, choose the **FeatureManager Design Tree** button.

6. Expand the **FeatureManager Design Tree** by clicking on the arrow on its top right corner to display the **Display Pane**.

7. Click once on the boss-extrude feature corresponding to the fin and left-click on the region corresponding to the **Appearances** option in the **Display Pane**; a flyout is displayed.

8. Choose the **Appearances** option from the flyout; the **Appearances, Scenes, and Decals** task pane with a default material is displayed on the right and corresponding **color PropertyManager** is displayed on the left.

9. Select a color of your choice from the **Color** rollout and set the parameters of the color in other rollouts.

10. Expand the **Display States** rollout of the PropertyManager and select the **This display state** radio button. Next, choose the **OK** button from the PropertyManager.

11. Similarly, apply the same color to the fins created by linear pattern.

12. Invoke the **ConfigurationManager** and double-click on the **Transparent Fins** display state. Next, choose the **FeatureManager Design Tree** button.

13. Click once on the boss-extrude feature corresponding to the fin and left-click on the region corresponding to the **Transparent** option in the **Display Pane**; the fin becomes transparent.

14. Similarly, change the fins that are created by linear pattern to transparent.

15. Invoke the **ConfigurationManager** and double-click on each display state to view the model in different display states. Figure 8-116 shows the model in Transparent Fins display state and Figure 8-117 shows the model with Colored Fins display state.

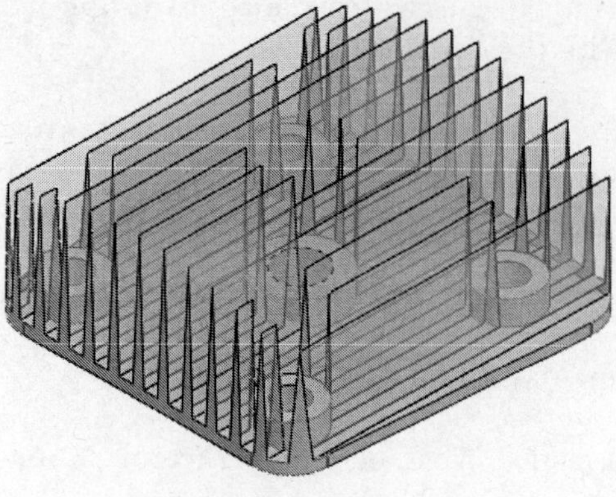

Figure 8-116 Model displayed in Transparent Fins display state

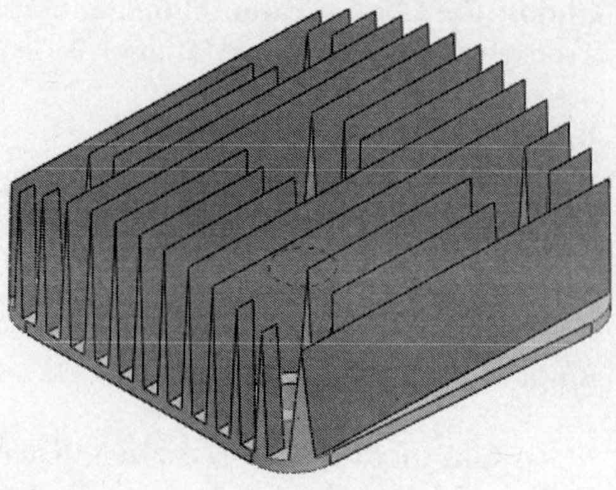

Figure 8-117 Model displayed in Colored Fins display state

Saving the Model

1. Save the model with the name *c08_tut03* at the location given below.

   \Documents\SOLIDWORKS\c08

2. Choose **File > Close** from the SOLIDWORKS menus to close the document.

Self-Evaluation Test

Answer the following questions and then compare them to those given at the end of this chapter:

1. The __________ **PropertyManager** is used to view a section view.
2. A __________ is provided in the drawing area to adjust the offset distance of a section plane dynamically.
3. The __________ option is used to create a pattern by specifying coordinates.
4. The __________ option is used to create a pattern with respect to sketched points.
5. The __________ rollout is used to hide pattern instances.
6. To invoke the **Mirror PropertyManager**, choose **View > Pattern/Mirror > Mirror** from the SOLIDWORKS menus. (T/F)
7. If you modify the parent feature, the same change will not be reflected in the mirrored feature. (T/F)
8. You cannot preselect the mirror plane and the feature to be mirrored before invoking the **Mirror** tool. (T/F)

9. You can mirror a single face using the **Mirror** tool. (T/F)

10. You can pattern a patterned feature. (T/F)

Review Questions

Answer the following questions:

1. Which of the following PropertyManagers is displayed when you choose the **Mirror** button from the **Features CommandManager**?

   (a) **Mirror Feature PropertyManager** (b) **Mirror All PropertyManager**
   (c) **Mirror PropertyManager** (d) **Copy/Mirror PropertyManager**

2. Which of the following options is used to mirror exact geometry of a feature independent of relationships between geometries?

   (a) **Same Mirror** (b) **Geometry Pattern**
   (c) **Geometry Copy** (d) **Copy Geometry**

3. Which of the following patterns is created along the sketched lines, arcs, or splines?

   (a) **Curve Driven Pattern** (b) **Sketch Driven Pattern**
   (c) **Geometry Driven pattern** (d) **Linear Pattern**

4. Which of the following dialog boxes is invoked to create a pattern by specifying coordinate points?

   (a) **Sketch Driven Pattern** (b) **Table Driven Pattern**
   (c) **Mirror** (d) None of these

5. Which of the following planes is selected by default when you invoke the **Section View PropertyManager** to view a section of the model?

   (a) **Right** (b) **Top**
   (c) **Front** (d) **Plane 1**

6. The _________ check box is used to accommodate all instances of a pattern along a selected curve.

7. You need to enter coordinates for creating instances in the _________ area of the **Table Driven Pattern** dialog box.

8. You need to invoke the _________ to create a rib feature.

9. The _________ check box is used to transfer visual properties assigned to the feature or the parent body to the mirrored instance.

EXERCISES

Exercise 1

Create the model shown in Figure 8-118. The views and dimensions of the model are given in the same figure.

(Expected time: 1 hr)

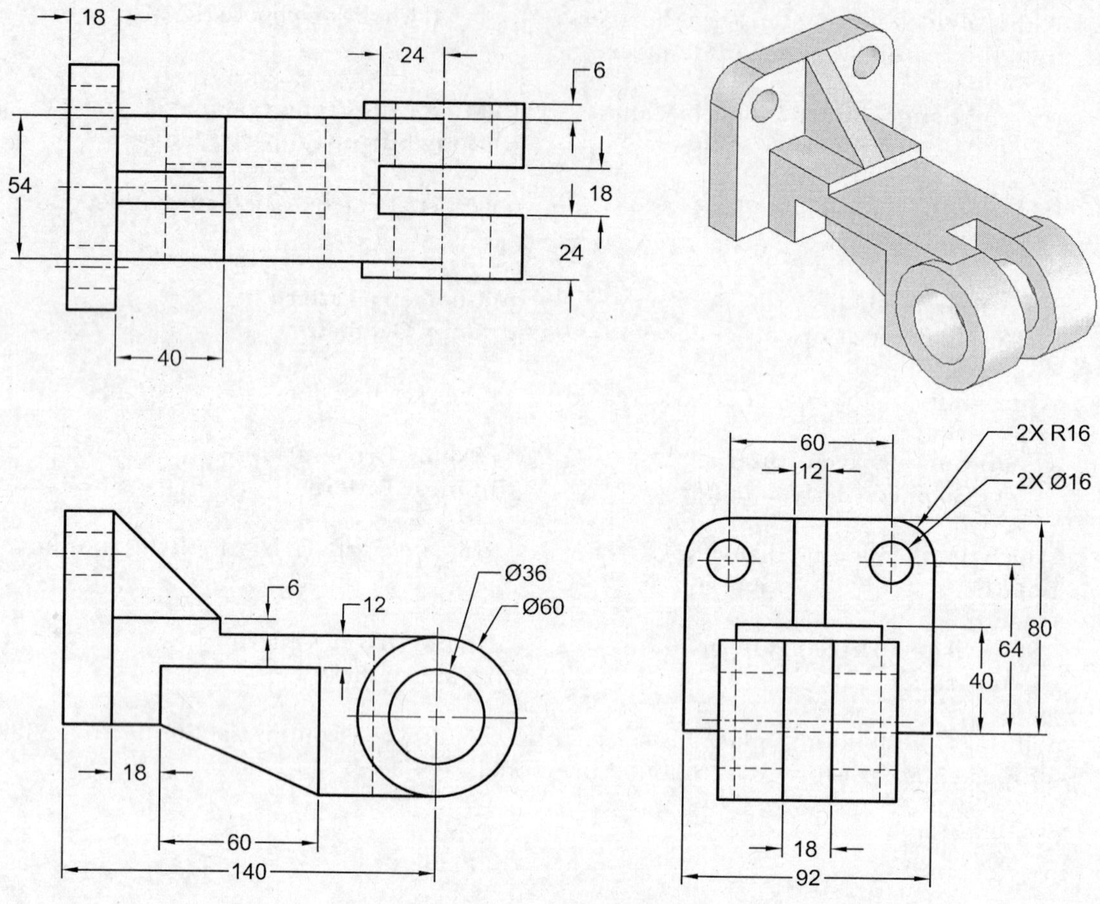

Figure 8-118 Views and dimensions of the model for Exercise 1

Exercise 2

Create the model shown in Figure 8-119. The views and dimensions of the model are given in Figure 8-120.

(Expected time: 1 hr)

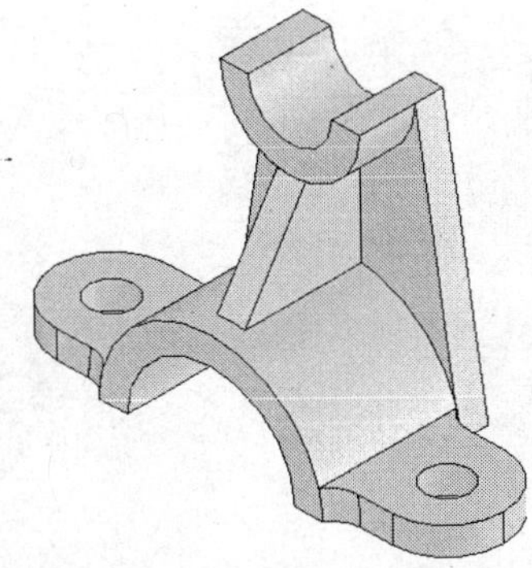

Figure 8-119 Solid model for Exercise 2

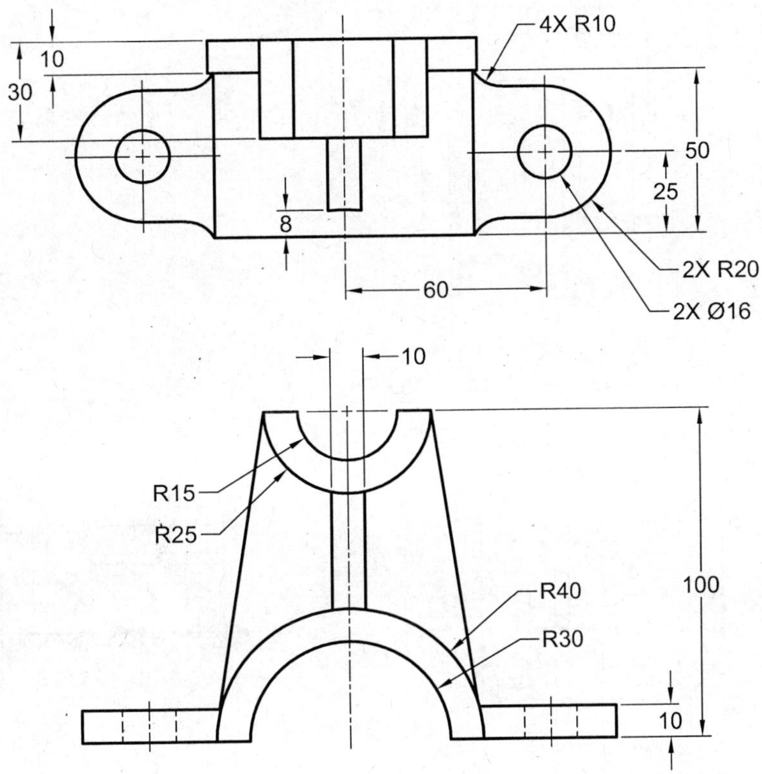

Figure 8-120 Views and dimensions of the model for Exercise 2

Exercise 3

Create the model shown in Figure 8-121. Next, create the section view of the model using the Right Plane. Figure 8-122 shows the section view of the model whose dimensions are given in Figure 8-123. **(Expected time: 45 min)**

Figure 8-121 Solid model for Exercise 3

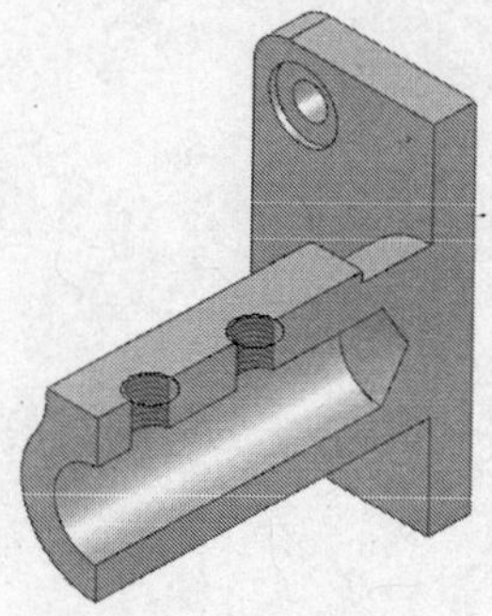

Figure 8-122 Section view of the model

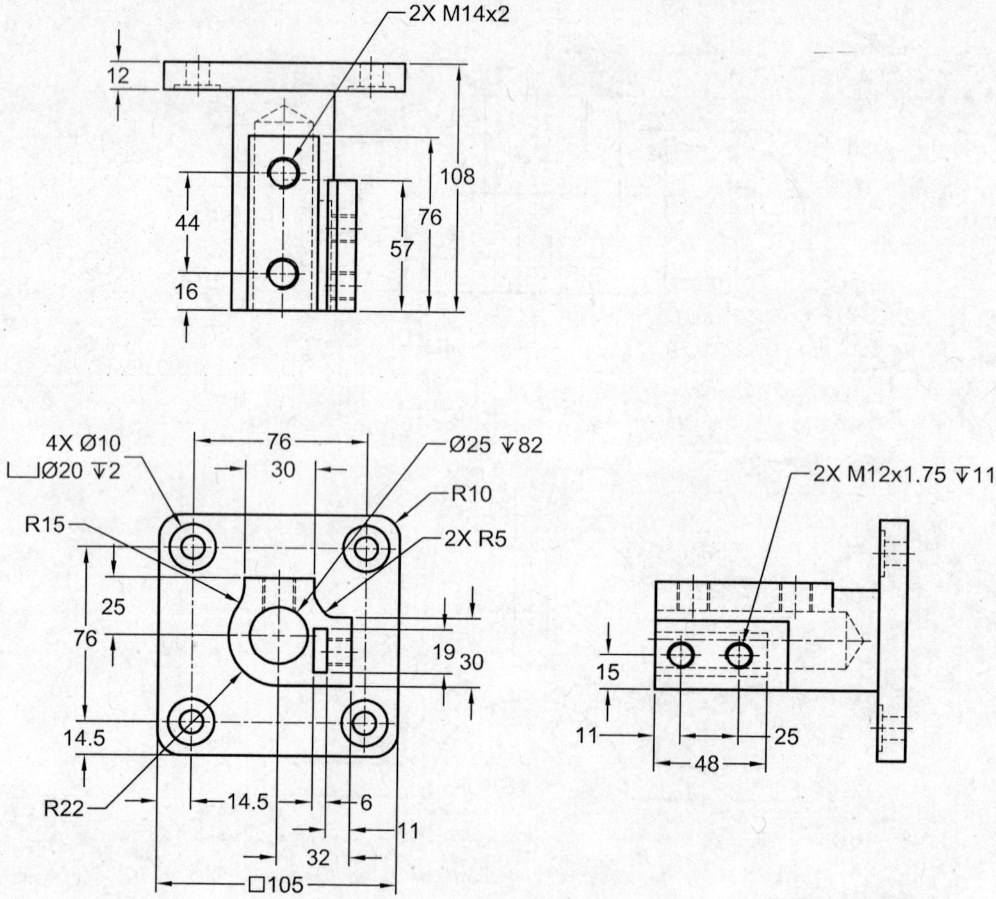

Figure 8-123 Views and dimensions of the model for Exercise 3

Exercise 4

Create the model shown in Figure 8-124. Next, create the section view of the model using the Front Plane. Figure 8-125 shows the section view of the model whose dimensions are given in Figure 8-126. **(Expected time: 45 min)**

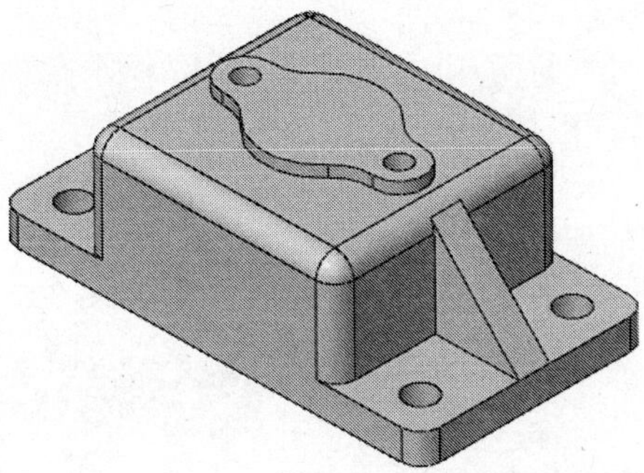

Figure 8-124 *Solid model for Exercise 4*

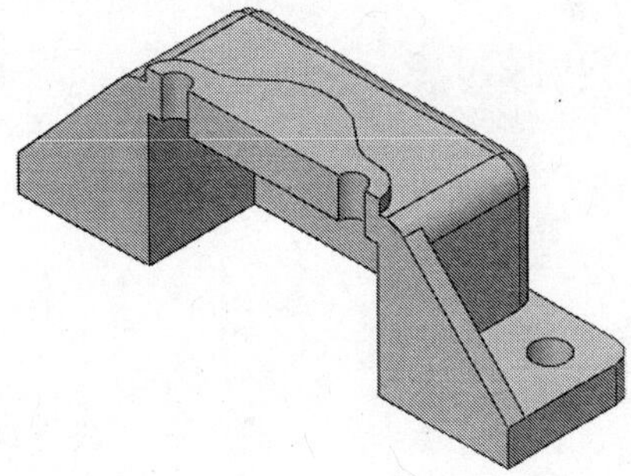

Figure 8-125 *Section view of the model*

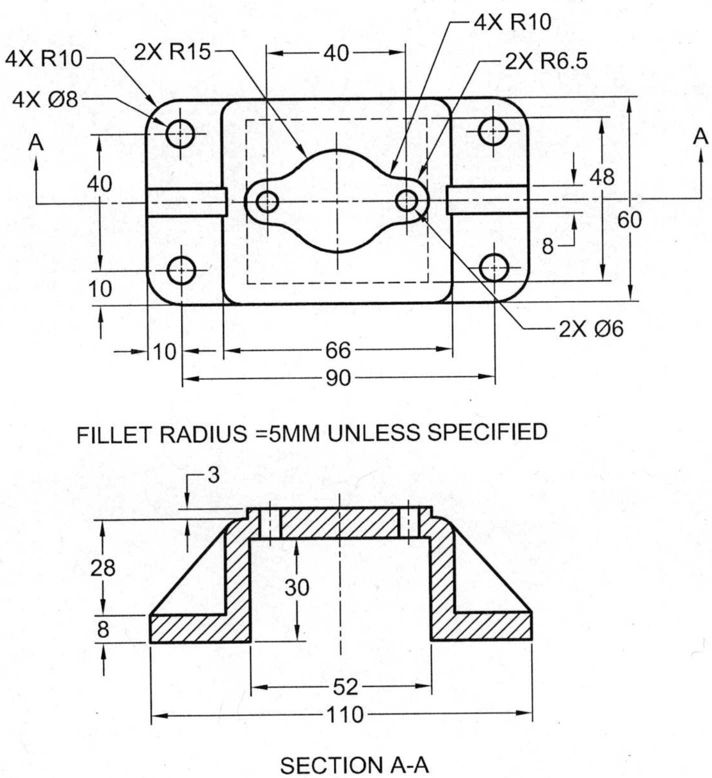

Figure 8-126 *Views and dimensions of the model for Exercise 4*

Answers to Self-Evaluation Test

1. Section View, **2.** drag handle, **3. Table Driven Pattern**, **4. Sketch Driven Pattern**, **5.Instances to Skip**, **6.** F, **7.** F, **8.** F, **9.** F, **10.** T

Chapter 9

Editing Features

Learning Objectives

After completing this chapter, you will be able to:

- *Edit features*
- *Edit the sketch plane of the sketch-based features*
- *Cut, copy, and paste features and sketches*
- *Delete features and bodies*
- *Suppress and unsuppress features*
- *Move or copy bodies*
- *Reorder features*
- *Roll back the model*
- *Rename features*
- *Use the What's Wrong functionality*

EDITING THE FEATURES OF A MODEL

Editing is one of the most important aspects of the product design cycle. Almost all designs require editing during or after their creation. As discussed earlier, SOLIDWORKS is a feature-based parametric software. Therefore, the design created in SOLIDWORKS is a combination of individual features integrated together to form a solid model. All these features can be edited individually.

For example, Figure 9-1 shows a base plate with some drilled holes. To replace the four drilled holes with four counterbore holes, you need to perform an editing operation. For editing the holes, you need to select the hole feature and right-click; a shortcut menu will be displayed. Choose the **Edit Feature** tool from the shortcut menu to invoke the **Hole Specification PropertyManager**. Alternatively, select the hole feature and do not move the mouse; a pop-up toolbar will be displayed. Choose the **Edit Feature** tool from the pop-up toolbar to display the **Hole Specification PropertyManager**. Set new parameters in the **Hole Specification PropertyManager** and end the feature modification; the drilled holes will be automatically replaced by counterbore holes, as shown in Figure 9-2.

Figure 9-1 *Base plate with drilled holes*

Figure 9-2 *Base plate with counterbore holes*

Similarly, you can also edit the reference geometry and the sketches of the sketch-based features. When you modify the reference geometry, the feature created using the reference geometry is also modified. For example, if you create a feature on a plane at some angle and then edit the angle of the plane, the resulting feature will be automatically modified. In SOLIDWORKS, you can perform editing tasks using various methods, which are discussed next.

Editing Using the Edit Feature Tool

In SOLIDWORKS, the **Edit Feature** tool is the most commonly used tool for editing. To edit a feature of the model using this tool, select the feature from the **FeatureManager Design Tree** or from the drawing area. Next, right-click on it to invoke the shortcut menu and choose the **Edit Feature** tool from it, as shown in Figure 9-3; the Property Manager will be invoked depending on the feature selected. Alternatively, select the feature and do not move the mouse; a pop-up toolbar will be displayed. Choose the **Edit Feature** tool from the pop-up toolbar to display the Property Manager. You can modify the parameters of that feature using the Property Manager. The Property Manager has the sequence name of the feature, as shown in Figure 9-4. After editing the parameters, choose the **OK** button to complete the feature creation; the feature will be modified automatically.

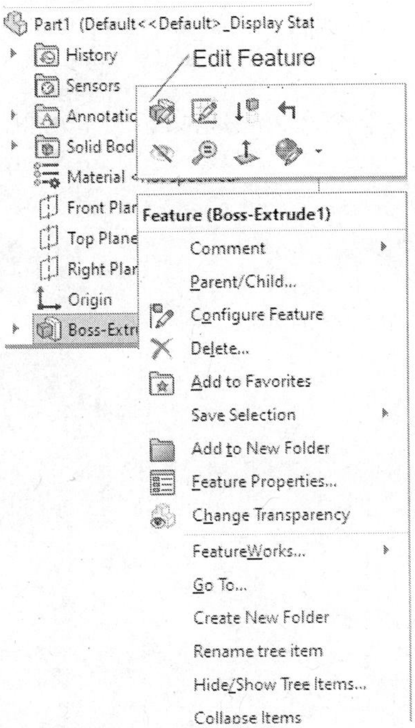

*Figure 9-3 Choosing the **Edit Feature** tool from the shortcut menu*

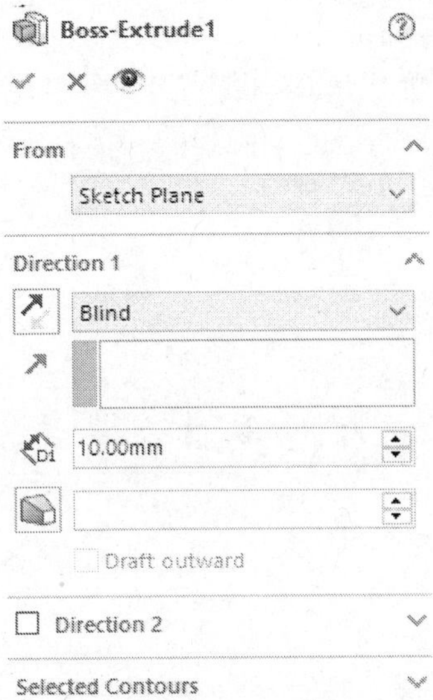

Figure 9-4** Partial view of the **Boss-Extrude Property Manager

Editing Sketches of the Sketch-based Features

In SOLIDWORKS, you can also edit the sketches of the sketch-based features. To do so, select the feature from the **FeatureManager Design Tree** or from the drawing area and right-click on it to invoke the shortcut menu. Choose the **Edit Sketch** tool from it; the sketching environment will be invoked. Alternatively, select the feature and do not move the mouse; a pop-up toolbar will be displayed. Choose the **Edit Sketch** tool from the pop-up toolbar to invoke the sketching environment. Edit the sketch of the sketch based feature using the sketching tools and exit the sketching environment. Choose CTRL+B keys to rebuild the model. You can also choose the **Rebuild** button from the Menu Bar to exit the sketching environment and rebuild the model.

> **Tip**
>
> *You can also use the ▸ sign available on the left of the sketched feature to expand the sketched feature in the **FeatureManager Design Tree**; the sketch icon will be displayed. Select the sketch icon and invoke the pop-up toolbar. Choose the **Edit Sketch** tool from it to invoke the sketching environment and edit the sketch.*

Editing the Sketch Plane Using the Edit Sketch Plane Tool

You can also change the sketch plane of the sketches of the sketch-based features. To do so, expand the sketched feature in the **FeatureManager Design Tree** by clicking on the ▸ sign on its left. Select the sketch icon in the **FeatureManager Design Tree**. , right-click on the feature and choose the **Edit Feature** tool from the shortcut menu displayed, as shown in Figure 9-5. Alternatively, you can choose this tool from the pop-up toolbar as discussed earlier. On choosing this tool, the **Sketch Plane PropertyManager** will be displayed, as shown in Figure 9-6. The name of the current sketch plane will be displayed in the **Sketch Plane/Face** selection box. Now, select any other plane or face as the sketching plane and choose **OK** from the **Sketch Plane PropertyManager**; the sketch plane will be modified.

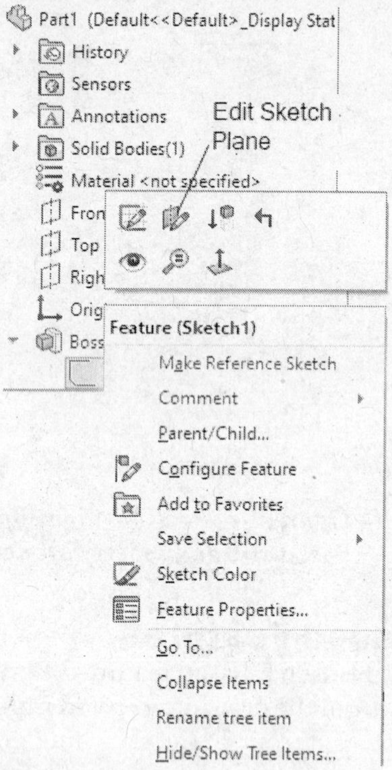

***Figure 9-5** Choosing the **Edit Sketch Plane** tool from the shortcut menu*

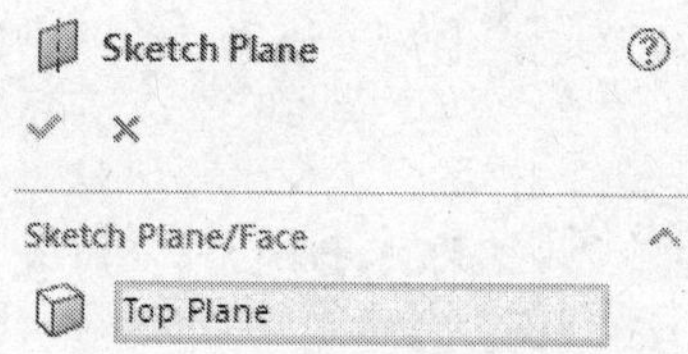

Figure 9-6** The **Sketch Plane PropertyManager

Tip

*While modifying the sketch plane if you select a sketch plane on which the relations and dimensions do not find any reference for being placed, the **What's Wrong** dialog box will be displayed. In such a case, you need to undo the last step, invoke the **Sketch Plane PropertyManager** again, and then select an appropriate plane. You will learn more about the **What's Wrong** dialog box later in this chapter.*

Editing Using the Instant3D Tool

CommandManager:	Features > Instant3D
Toolbar:	Features > Instant3D

In SOLIDWORKS, you can modify the feature and the sketch of the sketched feature dynamically without invoking the sketching environment. To edit a feature or its sketch, choose the **Instant3D** tool from the **Features CommandManager**, if not chosen by default, and select any face of the feature to be modified in the drawing area; the selected face will be highlighted. Also, the handles to resize and relocate the feature will be displayed, as shown in Figure 9-7.

To resize the feature, move the cursor to the resize handle, press and hold the left mouse button at this location and drag the cursor; a scale will be displayed. Drag the cursor further to resize the feature. On doing so, you will notice that the feature is dynamically resized. Release the left mouse button after resizing the feature. Note that while dragging the cursor, if you move the cursor on the scale, the values displayed will be integers and if you move the cursor away from the scale, the values displayed will be rational numbers. Figure 9-8 shows the resize handle being dragged to resize the feature and Figure 9-9 shows the resultant feature.

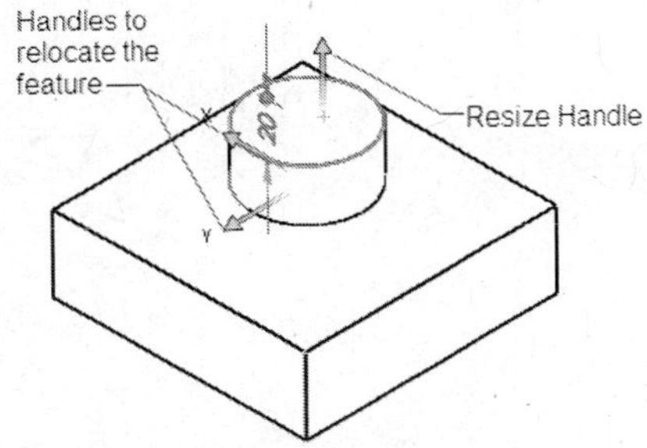

Figure 9-7 *Resize and relocate handles displayed on the selected feature*

To rotate the feature, move the cursor to the white sphere of the handle in the drawing area and right-click; a shortcut menu will be displayed. Choose the **Show Rotate Handle** option; the cursor changes into a rotate cursor and a circular path will be displayed. Select the circular path and then drag the cursor to rotate the feature. You can drag the cursor clockwise or counterclockwise. You can rotate the model at any angle. The feature will be rotated dynamically in the drawing area. Release the left mouse button after rotating the feature to a required angle.

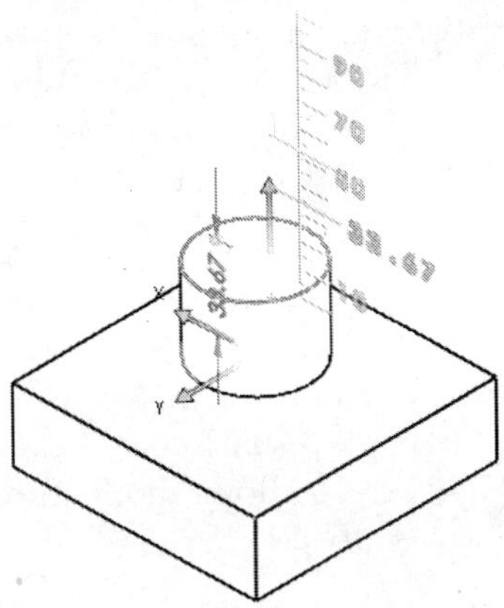

Figure 9-8 *Resize handle being dragged to resize the feature*

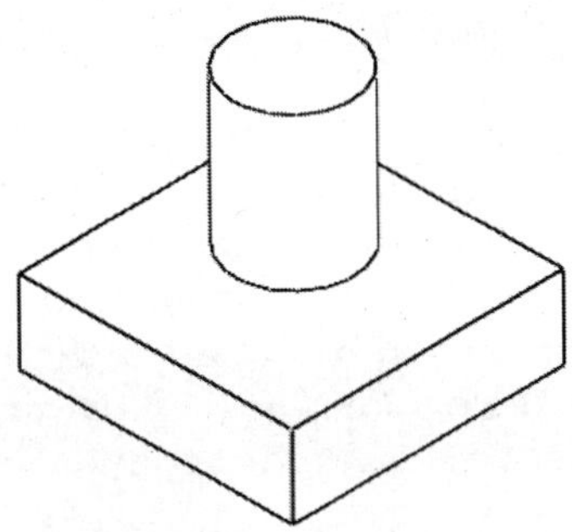

Figure 9-9 *Resultant feature*

While rotating the feature, if the **Move Confirmation** dialog box is displayed, you need to choose either the **Delete** or the **Keep** button based on the geometric and dimensional conditions. Next, click anywhere in the drawing area to exit the rotate handle. Figure 9-10 shows preview of the feature being rotated. Figure 9-11 shows the resultant feature.

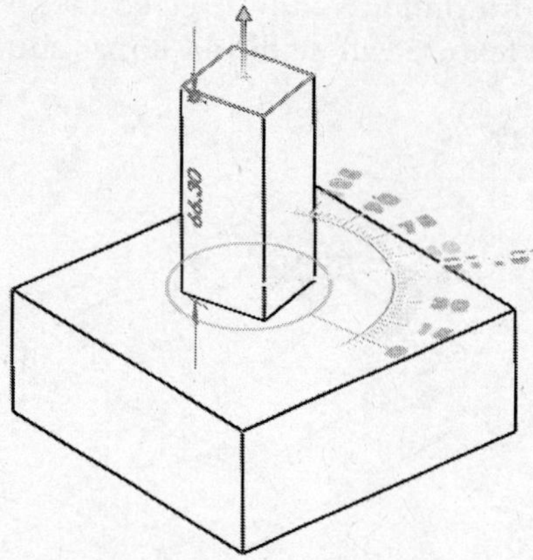

Figure 9-10 Preview of the feature being rotated

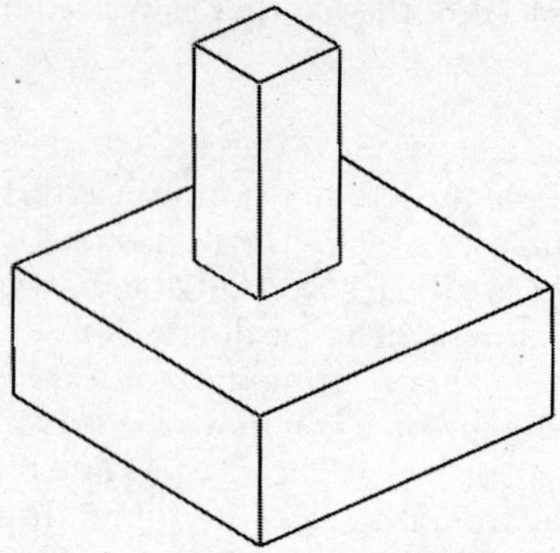

Figure 9-11 Resultant rotated feature

Note

If you rotate the sketched feature whose sketch is fully or partially defined using the relations and dimensions, the **Move Confirmation** *dialog box will be displayed, as shown in Figure 9-12. This dialog box informs you that the external constraints in the feature are being moved and asks whether you want to delete those constraints or keep them by recalculating or dangling them. The relations or the dimensions that do not find the external reference after the placement are made dangling.*

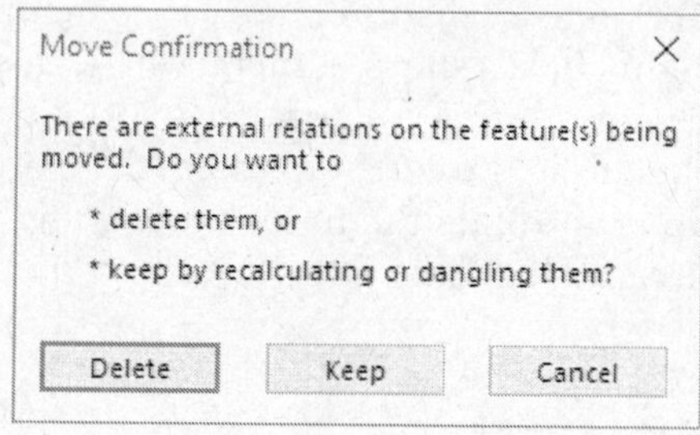

Figure 9-12 The **Move Confirmation** dialog box

You can also change the placement plane or the sketch plane of the feature by choosing the bubble in the relocating handle. To do so, select a face of the feature and move the cursor to the bubble on the relocate handle. Press and hold the left mouse button on the bubble, drag the cursor, and then release the left mouse button on another face. If the feature has some external reference, the **Move Confirmation** dialog box will be displayed. Choose the appropriate button in this dialog box; the feature will be relocated. Figure 9-13 shows the feature being moved to another face. Figure 9-14 shows the feature after being moved.

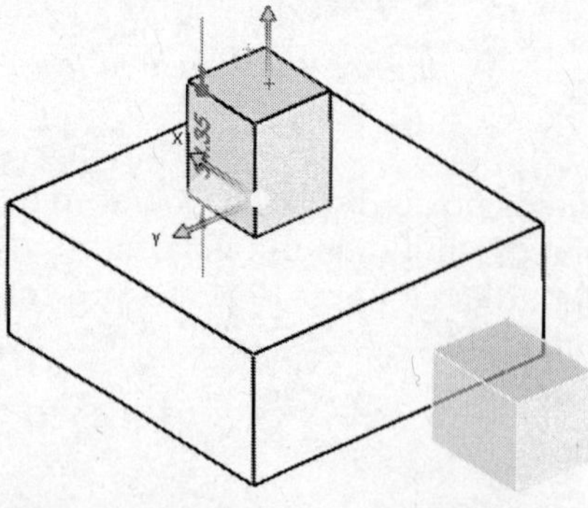

Figure 9-13 The feature being moved

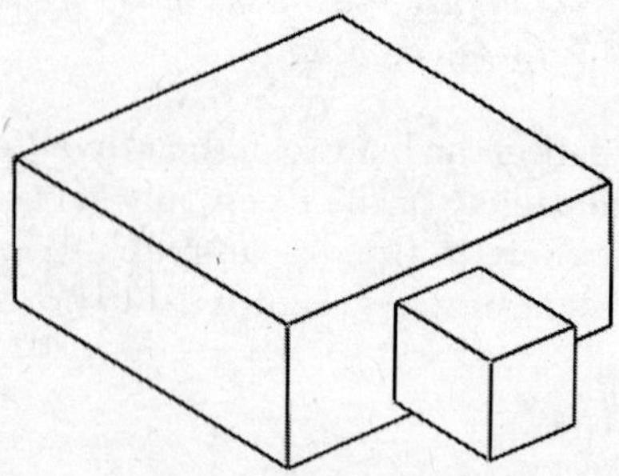

Figure 9-14 Feature after being moved

Tip

In SOLIDWORKS, you can modify the cut feature and the sketch of the cut feature dynamically, as done earlier.

To translate the feature on the same plane, select a face of the feature and move the cursor to the move handle. Press and hold the left mouse button on the arrow and drag the cursor.

You can also view the cross-section of a model without sectioning it. To view the cross-section of a model, select a planar face or a plane and right-click. Choose the **Live Section Plane** option from the shortcut menu; the triad and a section plane parallel to the selected face will be displayed. Also, the **Live Section Planes** folder containing all the live section planes will be added to the **FeatureManager Design Tree**. You can rotate the section plane about the horizontal and vertical axis by selecting corresponding rings of the triad. Press and hold the left mouse button on a selected ring and move the cursor; the section plane will be rotated about the required axis. As a result you will be able to view the cross section of the model at different angles. You can also select the arrow inside the rings and drag the cursor to relocate the live section plane linearly in the direction of the selected arrow. Click anywhere in the drawing area to exit the live section plane. To delete a live section plane, right-click on it in the **FeatureManager Design Tree** or near the edges of the section plane in the drawing area. Next, choose the **Delete** option from the shortcut menu displayed.

You can also edit a feature, reference geometry, or a sketch by selecting the entity either from the **FeatureManager Design Tree** or from the drawing area. To do so, ensure that the **Instant 3D** tool is chosen in the **Features CommandManager** and then left-click on a feature in the **FeatureManager Design Tree** or in the drawing area; all the dimensions of the feature and the sketch used for creating it are displayed. Note that the dimensions of the sketch will be displayed in black and the dimensions of the feature will be displayed in blue. Double-click on the dimension that you need to modify; the **Modify** dialog box will be invoked. Set a new value in the **Modify** dialog box and press the ENTER key or choose the **Save the current value and exit the dialog** button from the dialog box. You will notice that the value of the dimension is modified but the model is not modified with respect to the modified value. Therefore, you need to rebuild the model using the **Rebuild** option. To rebuild the model, choose the **Rebuild** button from the Menu Bar or press CTRL+B.

Editing Features and Sketches by Using the Cut, Copy, and Paste Options

SOLIDWORKS allows you to adapt to the windows functionality of cut, copy, and paste to copy and paste the features and sketches. The method of using this functionality is the same as used in other windows-based applications. To cut a feature, select the feature to be cut, and then choose **Edit > Cut** from the SOLIDWORKS menus or use the shortcut keys, CTRL+X; the **Confirm Delete** dialog box will be displayed. Choose the **Yes** button from this dialog box; the selected feature will be cut, but the sketch will still be displayed in the plane. This is because when you cut the feature, only the selected feature will be deleted from the document. You will learn more about deleting of features later in this chapter.

After you cut a feature, select the placement plane or the placement reference to place the feature. Choose **Edit > Paste** from the SOLIDWORKS menus or use the shortcut keys, CTRL+V. If you cut and paste a feature that has some external reference, the **Copy Confirmation** dialog box will be displayed, as shown in Figure 9-15, prompting you to delete the external constraints or leave them dangling. You need to choose the appropriate button to paste the feature.

If you copy and paste an item, the selected item will remain at its position and its copy will be pasted on the selected reference. To copy an item, select the feature or sketch. Next, choose **Edit > Copy** from the SOLIDWORKS menus, or press CTRL+C. Select the reference where you want to paste the selected item and choose **Edit > Paste** from the SOLIDWORKS menus, or press CTRL+V to paste it. You can paste the selected item any number of times. If you select another item and copy it on the clipboard, the last copied item will be deleted from the memory of the clipboard.

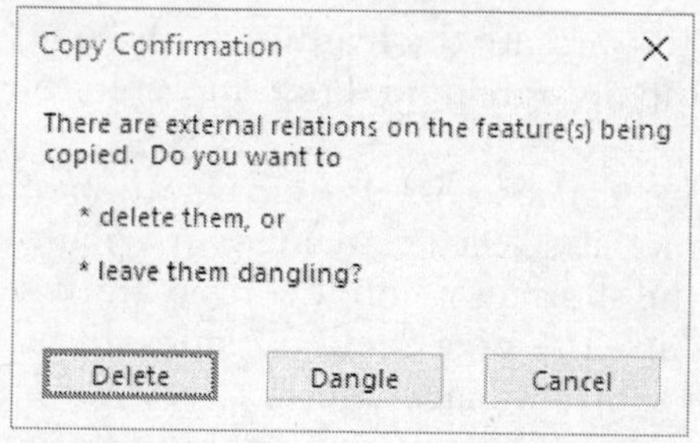

*Figure 9-15 The **Copy Confirmation** dialog box*

Tip

For pasting a sketch based feature, a simple hole, or a hole created using the hole wizard, you have to select a plane or a planar face as the reference. For pasting chamfers and fillets, you have to select an edge, edges, or a face as the reference.

Cutting, Copying, and Pasting Features and Sketches from One Document to Another

You can also cut or copy the features and sketches from one document and paste them in another document. For example, if you need to copy a sketch created in the current document and paste it in a new document, then select the sketch and press CTRL+C to copy the item to the clipboard. Then, create a new document in the **Part** mode and select the plane on which you want to paste the sketch. Press CTRL+V to paste the sketch on the selected plane. Use the same procedure to copy features from one document to the other.

Copying Features using Drag and Drop

SOLIDWORKS also provides you with the drag and drop functionality of Windows to copy and paste an item within the document. Press and hold the CTRL key on the keyboard. Next, select and drag the item from the **FeatureManager Design Tree**. Drag the cursor to a location where you want to paste the item and release the left mouse button. If the item to be pasted is defined using the dimensions or the relations, the **Copy Confirmation** dialog box will be displayed to delete or dangle those constraints. Figure 9-16 shows the feature being dragged and Figure 9-17 shows the resultant pasted feature.

Dragging and Dropping Features from One Document to the Other

You can also drag and drop features as well as sketches from one document to the other. To do so, you should open both the documents in the SOLIDWORKS session. Choose **Windows > Tile Vertically/Tile Horizontally** from the SOLIDWORKS menus; both the documents are displayed at the same time in the SOLIDWORKS window. Select the feature or the sketch in the **Feature Manager Design Tree** in one document, and then drag and place it on the required entity in the other document, as shown in Figure 9-18. Note that you cannot drag and drop the base feature.

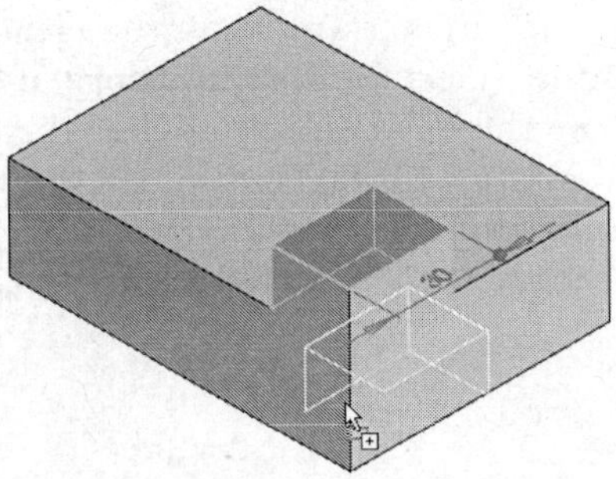

Figure 9-16 Feature being dragged

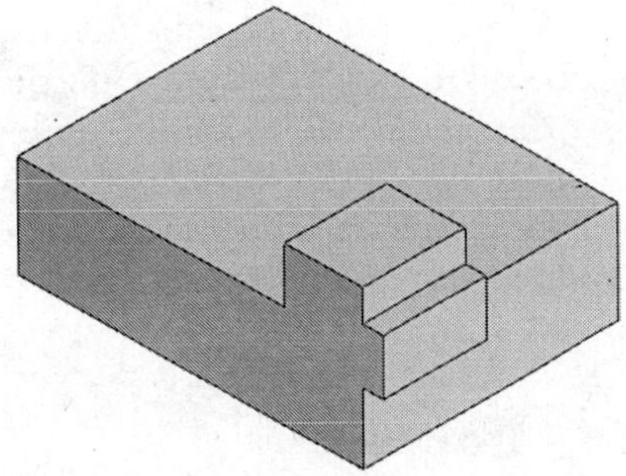

Figure 9-17 Resultant pasted feature

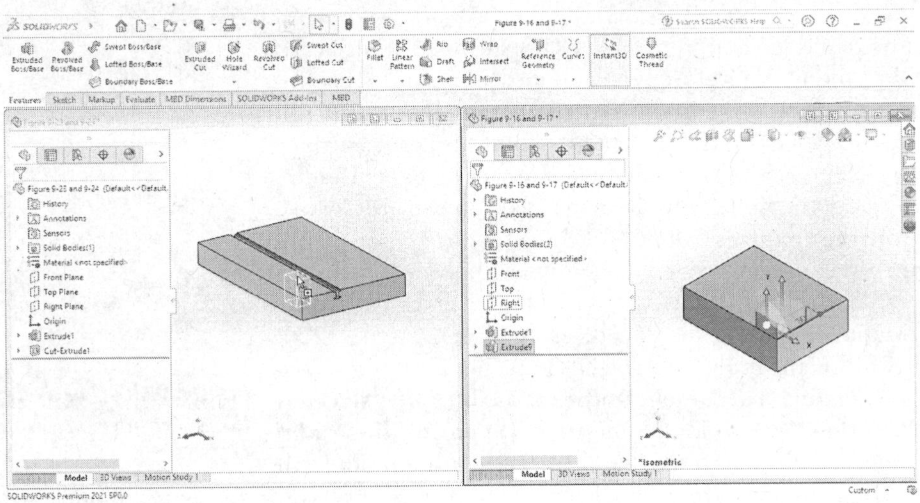

Figure 9-18 Feature being dragged to be pasted in the second document

Deleting Features

You can delete the unwanted features from the model by selecting the feature from the **FeatureManager Design Tree** or from the drawing area. After selecting the feature to be deleted, press the DELETE key on the keyboard, or right-click to invoke the shortcut menu and choose **Delete** from the shortcut menu displayed; the **Confirm Delete** dialog box will be displayed, as shown in Figure 9-19. The features that are dependent on the feature to be deleted are also displayed in the **Confirm Delete** dialog box which informs you that all the dependent features of the parent feature will also be deleted. If the **Delete child features** check box is selected, all the child features related to the parent feature will be also deleted. But if you delete a sketched feature,

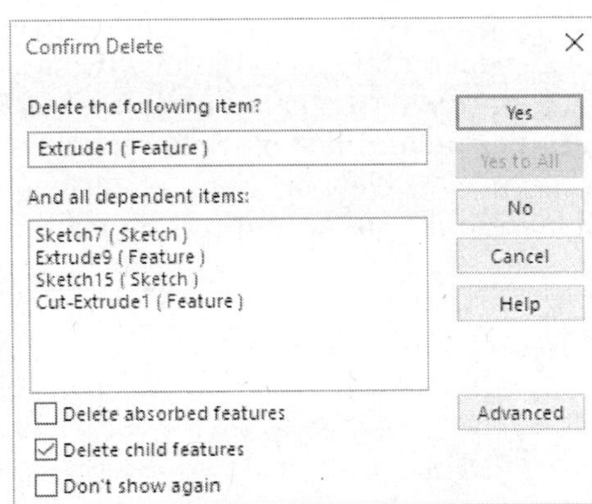

*Figure 9-19 The **Confirm Delete** dialog box*

the sketches related to it will not be deleted. These sketches are known as absorbed features. To delete the absorbed features along with the parent feature, select the **Delete absorbed features** check box from the **Confirm Delete** dialog box. Choose the **Yes** button to delete the selected features; choose the **No** button to cancel the delete operation. You can also delete a selected feature by choosing **Edit > Delete** from the SOLIDWORKS menus. In SOLIDWORKS, you can use the **Confirm Delete** dialog box to delete the child feature of the selected feature by choosing the **Advanced** button.

Deleting Bodies

CommandManager:	Features > Delete/Keep Body	*(Customize to add)*
SOLIDWORKS menus:	Insert > Features > Delete/Keep Body	
Toolbar:	Features > Delete/Keep Body	*(Customize to add)*

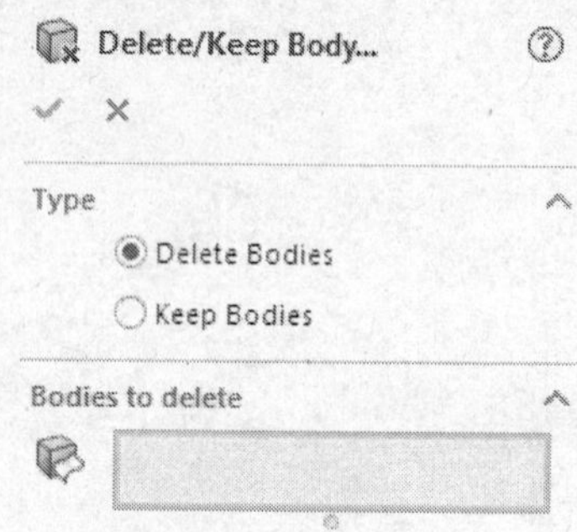

*Figure 9-20 The **Delete/Keep Body PropertyManager***

As discussed earlier, SOLIDWORKS supports multibody environment. Therefore, you can create multiple disjoint bodies in SOLIDWORKS. You can also delete unwanted bodies. The bodies to be deleted can be solid bodies or surface bodies. To delete a body, choose **Insert > Features > Delete/Keep Body** from the SOLIDWORKS menus. You can also invoke this tool from the **Features CommandManager** after customizing the **CommandManager**. When you invoke this tool from the **Features CommandManager**, the **Delete/Keep Body PropertyManager** will be displayed, as shown in Figure 9-20. Also, you will be prompted to select the solid and/or surface bodies to be deleted. The **Delete Bodies** radio button is selected by default in the **Type** rollout. When the **Delete Bodies** radio button is selected, the selected bodies/surfaces of the model will be deleted. But when the **Keep Bodies** radio button is selected in the **Type** rollout, the selected bodies/surfaces will be retained and the remaining portion of the model will be deleted.

Select the body or the bodies from the drawing area or from the **Solid Bodies** folder available in the **FeatureManager Design Tree** which is displayed in the drawing area; the selected body will be displayed in blue and its name will be displayed in the **Solid/Surface Bodies to Delete/Keep** selection box. Choose the **OK** button from the **Delete/Keep Body PropertyManager**; a new feature with the name **Body-Delete/Keep 1** will be added to the **FeatureManager Design Tree**. This item will store the deleted or kept bodies. Therefore, at any point of your design cycle, you can delete or suppress this item to resume the deleted body back in your design. You will learn more about suppressing features later in this chapter.

Tip

*You can also choose the **Delete** option from the shortcut menu. To do so, select the body and right-click. Choose the **Delete/Keep Body** option from the **Body** area of the shortcut menu; the **Delete/Keep Body PropertyManager** will be displayed. Choose the **OK** button from the **Delete/Keep Body PropertyManager** to delete the body.*

Suppressing Features

CommandManager:	Features > Suppress	*(Customize to add)*
SOLIDWORKS menus:	Edit > Suppress > This Configuration	
Toolbar:	Features > Suppress	*(Customize to add)*

Sometimes, you do not want some feature or features to be displayed in the model or in the drawing views. Instead of deleting such features, they can be suppressed. When you suppress a feature, it is neither visible in the model nor in the drawing views. Also, if you create an assembly using that model, the suppressed feature will not be displayed even in the assembly. You can resume such suppressed features anytime by unsuppressing them. When you suppress a feature, the features that are dependent on it are also suppressed. To suppress a feature, select it from the **FeatureManager Design Tree** or from the drawing area. Choose the **Suppress** button from the **Features CommandManager** after customizing it, or right-click and choose the **Suppress** option from the shortcut menu. You can also choose **Suppress** from the pop-up toolbar that will be displayed on selecting a feature. The suppressed feature will be removed from the display of the model and the name of the feature will be displayed in gray in the **FeatureManager Design Tree**.

Unsuppressing the Suppressed Features

CommandManager:	Features > Unsuppress	*(Customize to add)*
SOLIDWORKS menus:	Edit > Unsuppress > This Configuration	
Toolbar:	Features > Unsuppress	*(Customize to add)*

The suppressed features can be unsuppressed using the **Unsuppress** tool. To resume the suppressed feature, select the suppressed feature from the **FeatureManager Design Tree** and choose the **Unsuppress** button. You can also choose this option from the shortcut menu or from the pop-up toolbar after selecting the suppressed feature. Note that when you resume a suppressed feature using this tool, the dependent features remain suppressed. Therefore, you need to unsuppress all the features independently.

Unsuppressing Features with Dependents

CommandManager:	Features > Unsuppress with Dependents	*(Customize to add)*
SOLIDWORKS menus:	Edit > Unsuppress with Dependents > This Configuration	
Toolbar:	Features > Unsuppress with Dependents	*(Customize to add)*

As discussed earlier, when you suppress a feature, the dependent features are also suppressed. You can resume the suppressed feature along with the dependents of the suppressed parent feature in a single-click using the **Unsuppress with Dependents** tool. To do so, select the suppressed feature from the **FeatureManager Design Tree**. Next, choose the **Unsuppress with Dependents** button from the **Features CommandManager**. Note that this tool will be available only after customizing the **Features CommandManager**. You will observe that the dependent suppressed features are also unsuppressed.

Hiding Bodies

While working in the multibody environment, you can also hide the bodies. The hidden body is not displayed in the model, assembly, or in the drawing views. To hide a body, expand the **Solid Bodies** folder in the **FeatureManager Design Tree**, and select the body to be hidden.

Right-click to invoke the shortcut menu and choose the **Hide** option from it. The selected body will disappear from the drawing area. The icon of the hidden body is displayed in wireframe in the **Solid Bodies** folder. To turn on the display of the hidden body, select it from the **Solid Bodies** folder and then choose the **Show** option from the shortcut menu.

Moving and Copying Bodies

CommandManager: Direct Editing > Move/Copy Bodies
SOLIDWORKS menus: Insert > Features > Move/Copy
Toolbar: Features > Move/Copy Bodies *(Customize to add)*

You can move or copy bodies in the multibody environment by using the **Move/Copy Bodies** tool. To do so, choose the **Move/Copy Bodies** tool from the **Direct Editing CommandManager** or choose **Insert > Features > Move/Copy** from the SOLIDWORKS menus; the **Move/Copy Body PropertyManager** will be displayed. By default, it shows the **Mate Settings** rollout. Choose the **Translate/Rotate** button from the **Options** rollout; the **Translate** and **Rotate** rollouts will be displayed, refer to Figure 9-21.

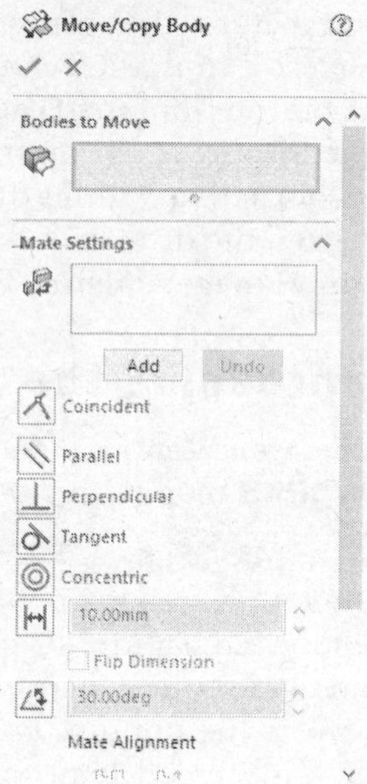

*Figure 9-21 Partial view of **Move/Copy Body PropertyManager***

The **Bodies to Move/Copy** rollout is used to define the body to copy or move. On invoking the **Move/Copy Body PropertyManager**, you will be prompted to select the bodies to move/copy and set the required options. Move the cursor on the body to be selected; the cursor will be replaced by the body selection cursor and the edges of the body will be highlighted. The name of the body will also be displayed in the tooltip. Select the body; it will be highlighted and a 3D triad will be displayed. The name of the body will be displayed in the **Solid and Surface or Graphics Bodies to Move/Copy** selection box. You can also select the body from the **Solid Bodies** folder after expanding the **FeatureManager Design Tree**.

The **Copy** check box is cleared by default. Select the **Copy** check box to create multiple copies of the selected body. When you select this check box, the **Number of Copies** spinner will be displayed below the **Copy** check box. Set the number of copies in this spinner.

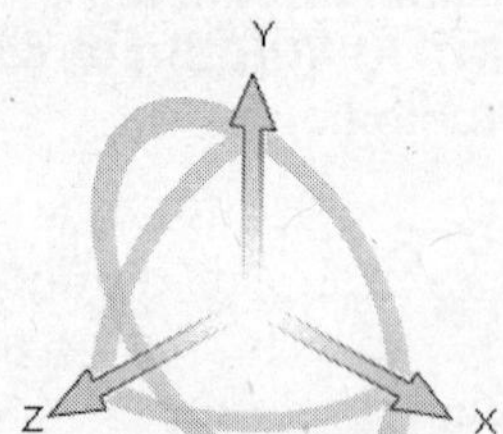

Figure 9-22 3D triad to move and rotate the body

The 3D triad displayed at the centroid of the selected body is used to dynamically rotate or move the body. The three arrows of this triad are the X, Y, and Z axes along which the body can be translated. This triad also has one ring and two wings by which the body can be rotated, see Figure 9-22.

To move a body dynamically, move the cursor close to any one of the arrows of the triad; the arrow will be highlighted and the select cursor will be replaced by the move cursor. Press and hold the left mouse button and drag the cursor to move the body. You can also move the cursor on the plane displayed between two arrows and drag the cursor to move the body in that plane.

To rotate the body, move the cursor over the ring or one of the wings; the ring will be highlighted and the cursor will be replaced by the rotate cursor. Press and hold the left mouse button and drag the cursor to rotate the body. Other rollouts in the **Move/Copy Body PropertyManager** are discussed next.

Translate Rollout

The **Translate** rollout in the **Move/Copy Body PropertyManager** is used to define the translational parameters to move the selected body. Set the value of the destination in the **Delta X**, **Delta Y**, and **Delta Z** spinners. When you set the values, the preview of the moved body will be displayed in temporary graphics in the drawing area. You can also move or copy the selected body with respect to two points. To move or copy a body by specifying two points, select the **Translation Reference (Linear Entity, Coordinate System, or Vertex)** selection box. The selection mode in this area becomes active. Select the vertex from which you want the translation to start. When you select the first vertex as the translation reference, the **Delta X**, **Delta Y**, and **Delta Z** spinners will be replaced by the **To Vertex** selection box. Now, the selection mode in the **To Vertex** selection box will be activated. Select the second translation reference. You will observe the preview of the translated body with respect to the selected points. The placement of the body also depends on the sequence of selection of the vertices. Therefore, you need to be very careful, while selecting the two vertices. Figure 9-23 shows the sequence for the selection of references and Figure 9-24 shows the resultant copied body.

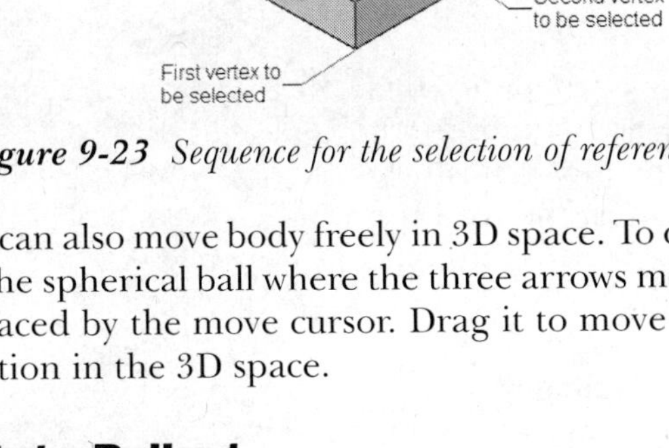

Figure 9-23 *Sequence for the selection of references*

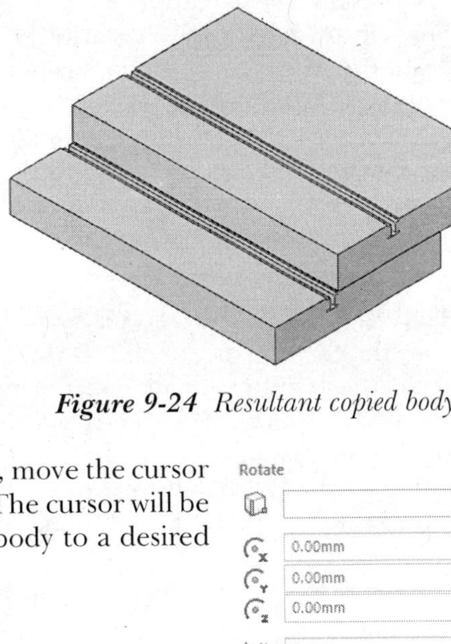

Figure 9-24 *Resultant copied body*

You can also move body freely in 3D space. To do so, move the cursor on the spherical ball where the three arrows meet. The cursor will be replaced by the move cursor. Drag it to move the body to a desired location in the 3D space.

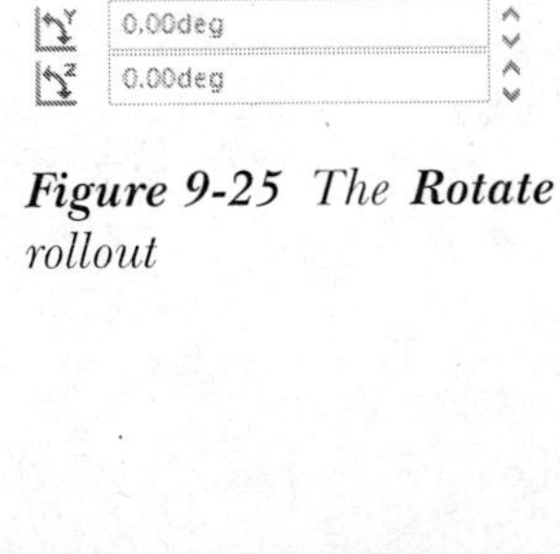

Figure 9-25 *The* ***Rotate*** *rollout*

Rotate Rollout

The **Rotate** rollout in the **Move/Copy Body PropertyManager** is used to define the parameters to rotate the body. To expand this rollout, click once on the arrow provided on the right of this rollout. The expanded **Rotate** rollout is shown in Figure 9-25. A filled square is placed at the origin when you invoke the **Move/Copy Body**

PropertyManager. It is clearly visible, when you hide the origin by choosing **Hide/Show Items > View Origins** from the **View (Heads-Up)** toolbar. It indicates the origin along which the selected body will be rotated. You can adjust the position of this temporary moveable origin using the **X Rotation Origin**, **Y Rotation Origin**, and **Z Rotation Origin** spinners. The **X Rotation Angle** spinner is used to set the value of the angular increment to rotate or copy the body along the X-axis, the **Y Rotation Angle** spinner is used to rotate or copy the body along the Y-axis, and the **Z Rotation Angle** spinner is used to rotate or copy the body along the Z-axis. You can also dynamically rotate the model. To do so, press and hold the left mouse button on the bubble, drag the cursor, and relocate the triad. Now, left-click on a ring and drag the cursor to rotate the model. You can drag the cursor clockwise or counterclockwise. The model will be rotated dynamically in the drawing area. Release the left mouse button after rotating the feature to the required angle.

To rotate or copy the selected body along an edge, click once in the **Rotation Reference (Linear Entity, Coordinate System, or Vertex)** selection box to invoke the selection. Select the edge about which you want to rotate the selected body. When you select an edge, all the other spinners will disappear from the rollout, and the **Angle** spinner will be enabled in the **Rotate** rollout. Set the value of the angular increment in this spinner.

Instead of selecting an edge, you can also select a vertex along which the body will rotate or copy. Next, you need to specify the axis along which you want to rotate it.

Constraints

In SOLIDWORKS, you can apply mates between multiple bodies to place them at an appropriate location. Choose the **Constraints** button from the **Move/Copy Body PropertyManager**; the **Bodies to Move** and the **Mate Settings** rollouts will be displayed, as shown in Figure 9-26. You need to select the body that you want to move. The **Mate Settings** rollout helps you to position the selected body by applying mates. You will learn more about mates in the later chapters.

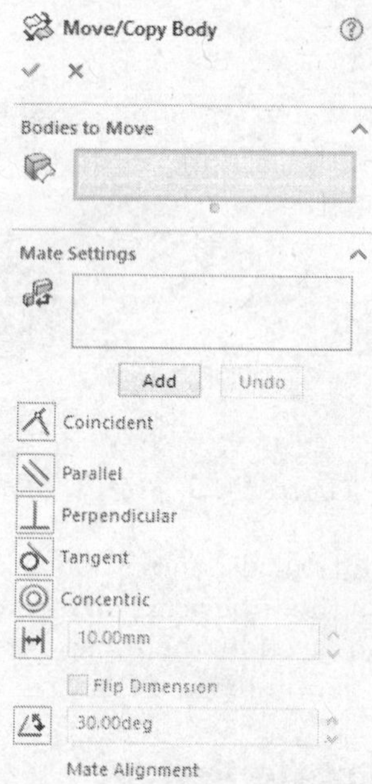

Figure 9-26 *The* ***Property Manager*** *after choosing the* ***Constraints*** *button*

Reordering the Features

Reordering the features is defined as the process of changing the sequence of the features created in the model. Sometimes after creating a model, it may be required to change the order in which its features were created. For reordering the features, the features are dragged and placed before or after other features in the **FeatureManager Design Tree**.

To reorder a feature, select the feature in the **FeatureManager Design Tree** and drag it; a bend arrow pointer will be displayed which suggests that feature dragging is possible. Drop the feature at the required position. If you try to drag and drop the child feature above the parent feature, the reorder error pointer will be displayed and you will not be able to drop the child feature above the parent feature.

Consider a case in which you have created a rectangular block with a pattern of through holes created on its base feature, as shown in Figure 9-27. Now, if you create a shell feature and remove the top face, front face, and right face of the model, it will appear, as shown in Figure 9-28.

Figure 9-27 *Model created with a pattern of through holes on the base feature*

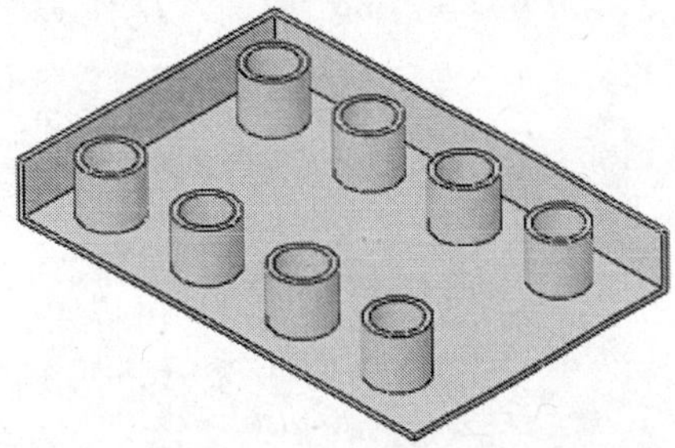

Figure 9-28 *Shell feature added to the model*

But this is not the desired result. Therefore, you need to reorder the shell feature above the holes. Select the shell feature in the **FeatureManager Design Tree** and drag it above the holes; all the features will be automatically adjusted in the new order, as shown in Figure 9-29.

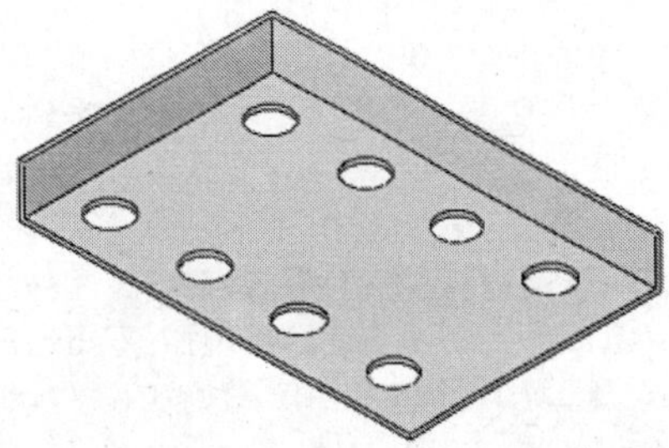

Figure 9-29 *Model after reordering the features*

Rolling Back the Feature

Rolling back a feature is defined as a process in which you rollback the feature to an earlier stage. When you roll back a feature, it will be suppressed and you can add new features to the model in the roll back state. The newly added features are added before the features that are rolled back. While working with a multi featured model, if you want to edit a feature that was created at the starting stage of the design cycle, it is recommended that you rollback the feature up to that stage. This is because after each editing operation, the time of regeneration will be minimized. Rolling back is done by shifting the **Rollback Bar** in the **FeatureManager Design Tree**.

To roll back a feature, press and hold the left mouse button on the **Rollback Bar**; the color of the bar will change and the select cursor will be replaced by a hand pointer, refer to Figure 9-30. Drag the hand pointer to the feature up to the stage you want to roll back, and then release it. To resume the model, drag the **Rollback Bar** to the last feature of the model. You can also roll back the features using the SOLIDWORKS menus. To do so, select the feature up to which you want to roll back the model and choose **Edit > Rollback** from the SOLIDWORKS menus.

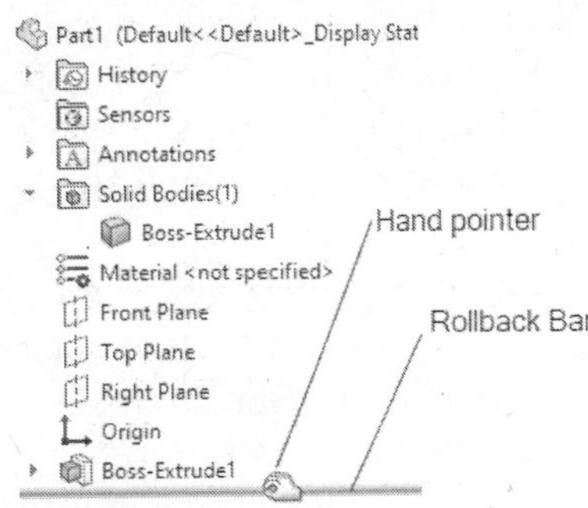

Figure 9-30 *The **Rollback Bar** of the **FeatureManager Design Tree***

Tip

If you want to roll back a feature to the previous step, choose ***Edit > Roll to Previous*** *from the SOLIDWORKS menus. To roll back the entire model to its original position, choose* ***Edit > Roll to End*** *from the SOLIDWORKS menus.*

You can also choose the ***Roll Forward****,* ***Roll to Previous****, or* ***Roll to End*** *option from the shortcut menu invoked by selecting and then right-clicking on the features placed below the* ***Rollback Bar****. These options are used to control the roll forward and roll back of the feature.*

You can also roll back a feature using the keyboard. To do so, select the ***Rollback Bar*** *and press the CTRL+ SHIFT+Up arrow keys to roll forward. Similarly, use the CTRL+ SHIFT+Down arrow keys to roll backward.*

Renaming Features

By default, the naming of the features is done according to the sequence in which they are created. The names of the features are displayed in the **FeatureManager Design Tree**. You can also rename the features according to your convenience by first selecting the feature from the **FeatureManager Design Tree** and then clicking once again on it; a text box will be displayed. Type the name of the feature in it and press ENTER or click anywhere on the screen; the feature will be renamed.

Creating Folders in the FeatureManager Design Tree

You can add folders to the **FeatureManager Design Tree** and add the features displayed in the **FeatureManager Design Tree** to that folder. This is done to reduce the length of the **FeatureManager Design Tree**. Consider a case in which the base of the model consists of more than one feature. You can add a folder named Base Feature, and add all the features used for creating the base part to that folder. To add a folder in the **FeatureManager Design Tree**, select any feature in the **FeatureManager Design Tree**, right-click to invoke the shortcut menu, and then choose the **Create New Folder** option; a new folder will be created above the selected feature. Specify the name of the folder and click anywhere on the screen. Now, you can drag and drop the features to the newly created folder. You can also rename the folder by selecting it and then clicking on it once. Now, enter its name in the edit box and press the ENTER key.

To add the selected feature to a new folder, choose **Add to New Folder** from the shortcut menu; a new folder will be created in the **FeatureManager Design Tree** and the selected feature will be added to the newly created folder. To delete the folder, select it, right-click, and then choose the **Delete** option from the shortcut menu. You can use the options in this shortcut menu to rollback and suppress the features in the selected folder.

What's Wrong Functionality

When you modify a sketch or a feature, sometimes a model may not be rebuilt properly because of the errors resulting from the modification. Therefore, you are provided with the **What's Wrong** dialog box, as shown in Figure 9-31. The possible errors in the feature are displayed in this dialog box along with their detailed description.

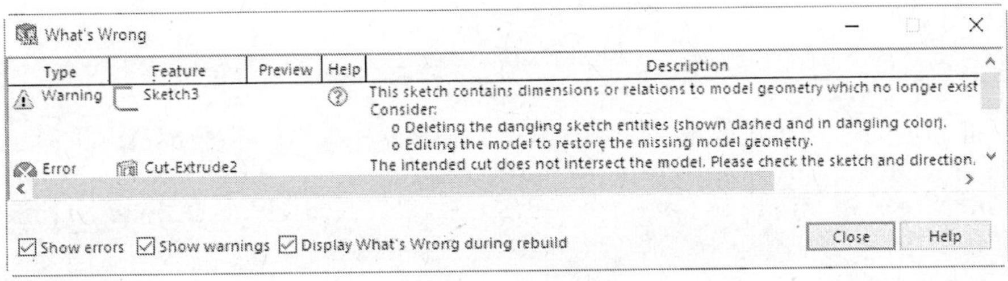

*Figure 9-31 The **What's Wrong** dialog box*

The **Show errors**, **Show warnings**, and **Display What's Wrong during rebuild** check boxes are selected by default; as a result, errors, warning messages, and errors at every rebuild of the model, respectively are displayed in the **What's Wrong** dialog box. After reading the description of the errors from this dialog box, choose the **Close** button to exit it. The errors will also be displayed in the **FeatureManager Design Tree**, refer to Figure 9-32. If there is an error in a model or in an assembly, the down arrow symbol will appear on the left of the name of the model or the assembly in the **FeatureManager Design Tree**. If a feature has an error, then the cross symbol will appear on the left of the feature in the **FeatureManager Design Tree**. If there is an error in the child feature, the error symbol will appear on the left of the parent feature and also on the name of the document in the **FeatureManager Design Tree**. If a warning message appears for a feature, then a triangle with an exclamation mark will appear on the left of that feature in the **FeatureManager Design Tree**.

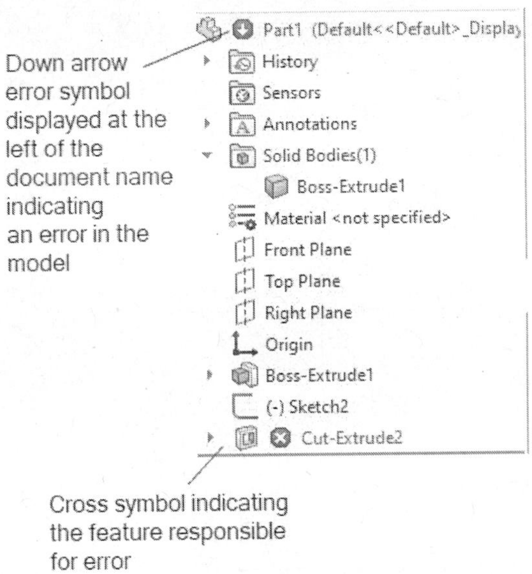

*Figure 9-32 The **FeatureManager Design Tree** with a feature having errors*

TUTORIALS

Tutorial 1

In this tutorial, you will create the model shown in Figure 9-33. After creating some of its features, you will dynamically modify it and then undo the modifications. The views and dimensions of the model are shown in Figure 9-34. **(Expected time: 30 min)**

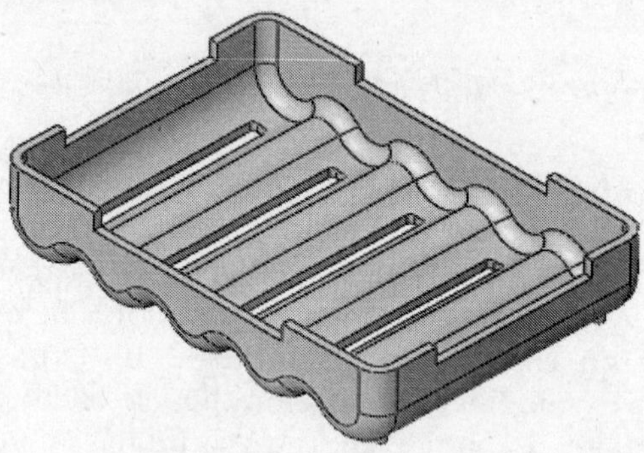

Figure 9-33 *Model for Tutorial 1*

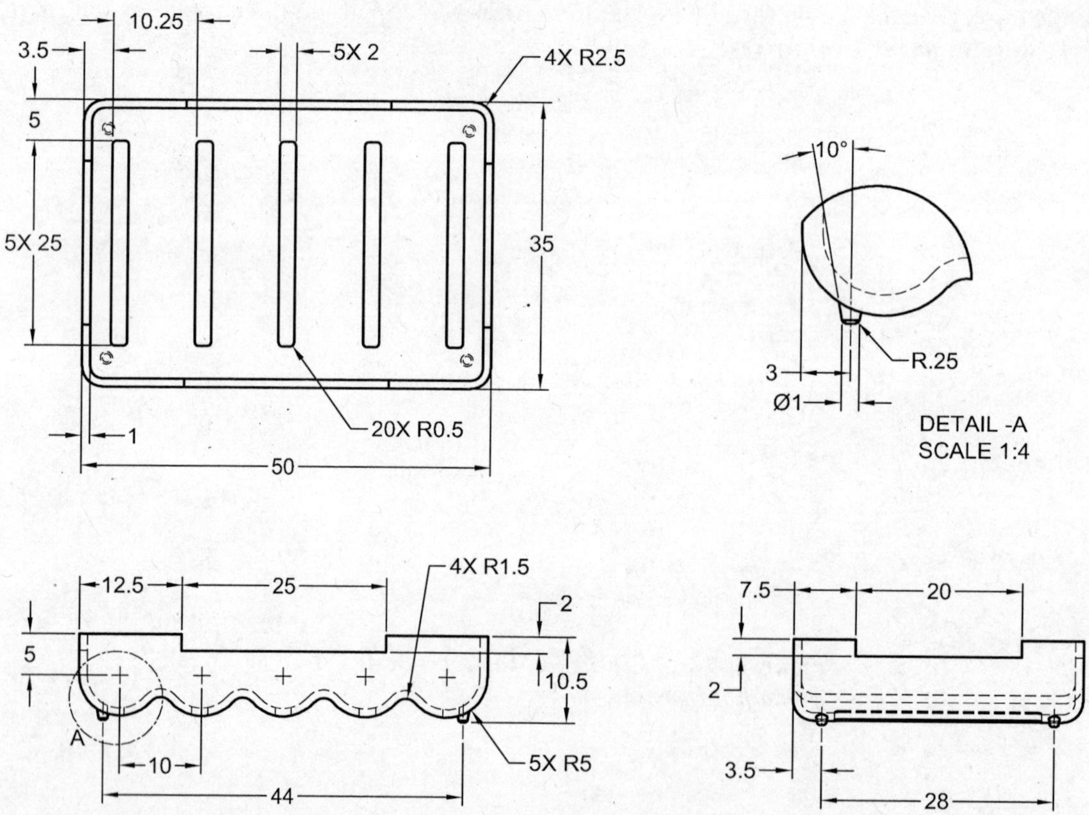

Figure 9-34 *Views and dimensions of the model for Tutorial 1*

The following steps are required to complete this tutorial:

a. Create the base feature of the model by extruding the profile to a given distance.
b. Add fillets to the base feature.
c. Add the shell feature to the model and remove the top face of the base feature.
d. Dynamically modify the model.
e. Create cuts on the sides of the model.
f. Create slots on the lower part of the base and add fillet to the slots feature.
g. Create a plane at an offset distance from the **Top Plane**.
h. Create the standoffs using the **Extrude Boss/Base** and **Fillet** tools, and pattern the standoffs.
i. Save the model.

Creating the Base Feature

For creating the base feature, you need to draw the sketch of the base feature on the Front Plane and then extrude it by using the **Mid Plane** option.

1. Start SOLIDWORKS and open a new part document using the **New SOLIDWORKS Document** dialog box.

2. Invoke the **Extruded Boss/Base** tool and draw the sketch of the base feature on the **Front Plane**. Add required relations and dimensions to the sketch, as shown in Figure 9-35. Exit the sketching environment; the **Boss-Extrude PropertyManager** is invoked.

3. Extrude the sketch to a distance of 35 mm using the **Mid Plane** option.

   The base feature of the model is shown in Figure 9-36.

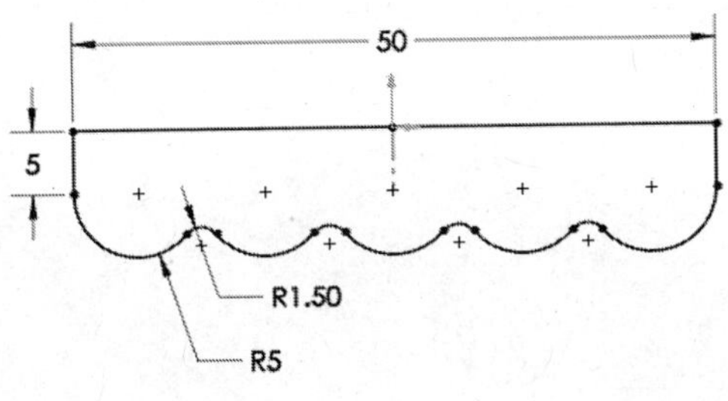

Figure 9-35 Sketch for the base feature

Figure 9-36 Base feature of the model

Adding Fillets to the Base Feature

After creating the base feature, you will fillet its lower edges.

1. Invoke the **Fillet PropertyManager** and then choose the **Constant Size Fillet** button from the **Fillet Type** rollout if not chosen by default.

2. Rotate the model and then select the edges of the base feature, as shown in Figure 9-37.

3. Set **2.5** as the value in the **Radius** spinner in the **Fillet Parameters** rollout and choose the **OK** button from the **Fillet PropertyManager**.

The model after adding fillet to its edges is shown in Figure 9-38.

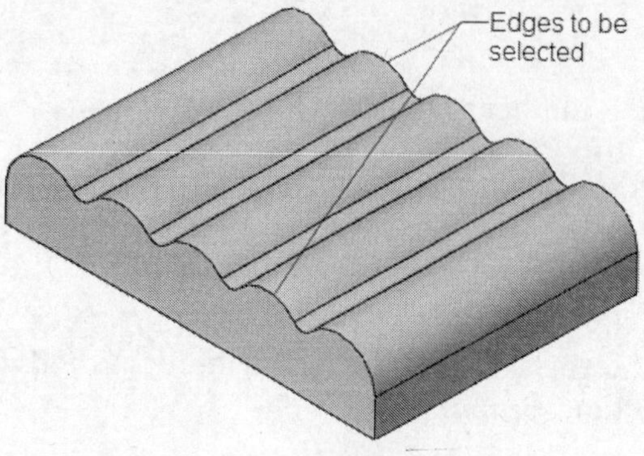

Figure 9-37 *Edges to be selected*

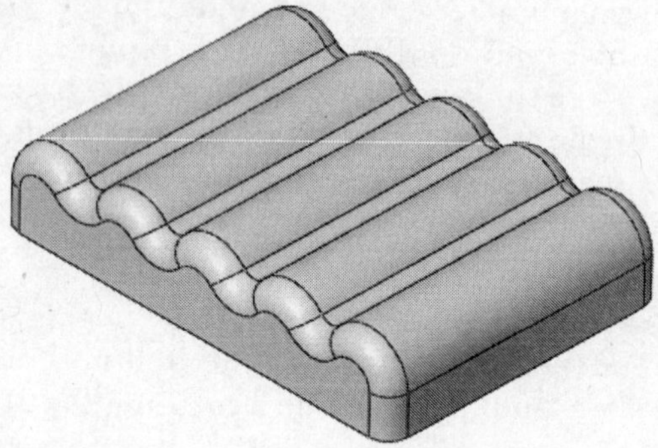

Figure 9-38 *Fillet added to the model*

Adding Shell to the Model

After creating the fillet feature, you need to shell the model using the **Shell** tool.

1. Orient the model in the isometric view and invoke the **Shell PropertyManager**.

2. Select the top planar face of the model, as shown in Figure 9-39.

3. Set the value in the **Thickness** spinner to **1**, and choose the **OK** button from the **Shell PropertyManager**.

The model after adding the shell feature is shown in Figure 9-40.

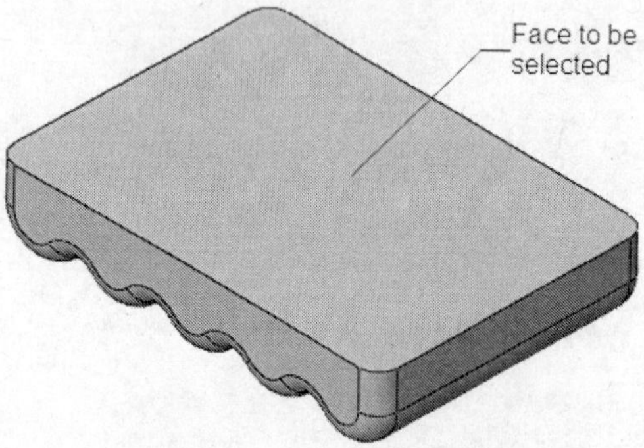

Figure 9-39 *Face to be selected*

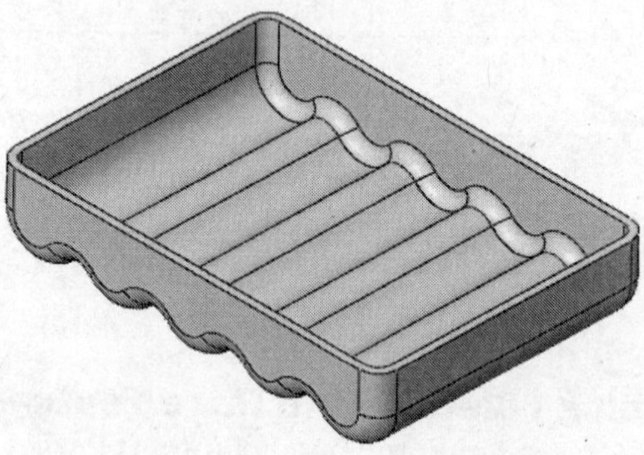

Figure 9-40 *Shell feature added to the model*

Dynamically Editing the Features

After adding the shell feature to the base of the model, you need to edit the features dynamically using the **Instant3D** tool.

1. Choose the **Instant3D** tool from the **Features CommandManager** if not already chosen. 

2. Select the front planar face of the base feature from the drawing area; the selected face is highlighted in blue and an orange colored arrow is displayed.

3. Move the cursor to the orange colored arrow and press and hold the left mouse button; the move cursor is displayed, as shown in Figure 9-41. Drag the cursor to resize the feature.

   A preview of the resized feature and its dimensions are displayed in the drawing area.

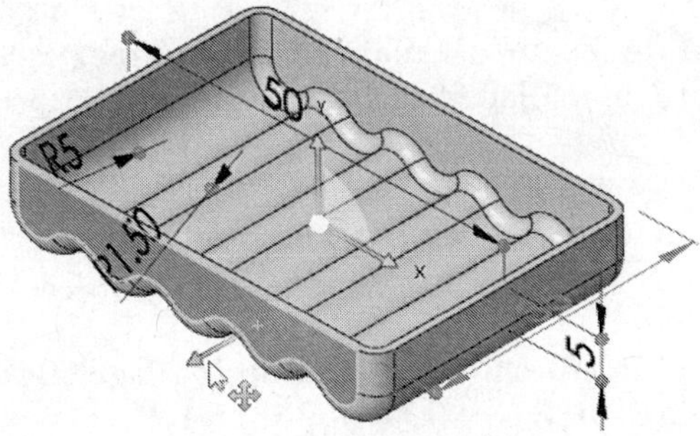

Figure 9-41 *Editing handles for editing the base feature*

   As you drag the cursor, the preview and the dimensions are updated automatically.

4. Release the left mouse button after dragging the cursor to some distance. Figure 9-42 shows preview of the feature while dragging it and Figure 9-43 shows the edited feature.

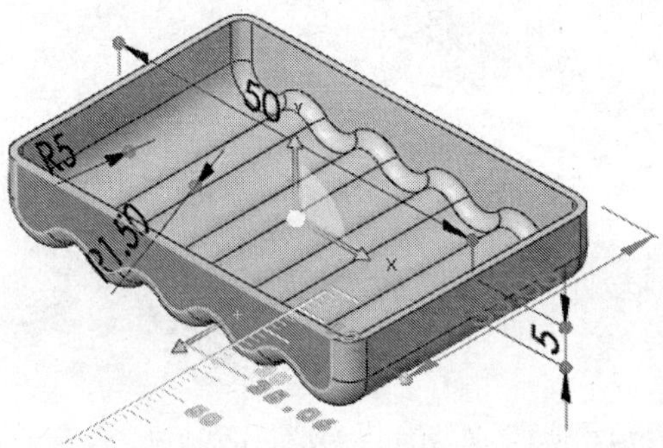

Figure 9-42 *Preview of the feature while dragging*

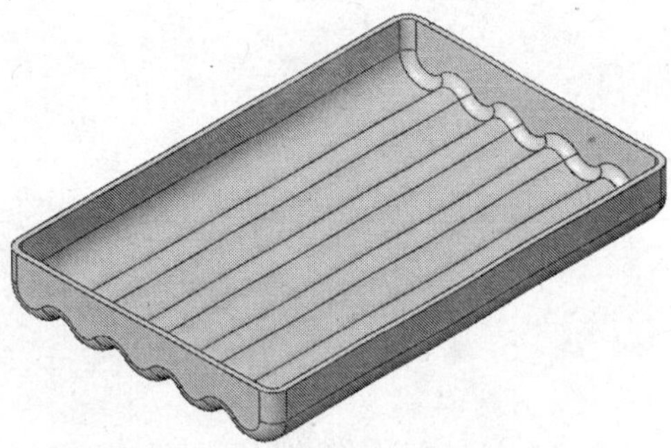

Figure 9-43 *Resultant edited feature*

   After editing the model dynamically by dragging, the depth of its base feature changes. To bring the base feature back to its original size of 35 mm, you need to edit the feature again.

5. Select the base feature from the **FeatureManager Design Tree** or from the drawing area; all the dimensions of the feature are displayed in the drawing area.

6. Double-click on the dimension that is displayed in blue and reflects the depth of the base feature; the selected dimension is displayed in the edit box.

7. Set the value in the **Distance** spinner to **35** and then press the ENTER key.

8. Choose the **Rebuild** button from the Menu Bar or press CTRL+B to rebuild the model.

Creating the Cut Feature

Next, you need to create a cut feature on the front face and copy this cut feature on the right planar face.

1. Invoke the **Extruded Cut** tool and create the cut feature on the front face, as shown in Figure 9-44.

2. Select the cut feature in the **FeatureManager Design Tree**, press and hold the CTRL key, drag the selected feature, and place it on the right planar face; the **Copy Confirmation** dialog box is displayed.

3. Choose the **Delete** button from the dialog box; the cut feature is created on the right planar face.

4. Select the newly created cut feature from the **FeatureManager Design Tree**; a pop-up toolbar is displayed. Choose **Edit Sketch** from the pop-up toolbar.

5. Apply suitable constraints and dimensions to make it a fully-defined sketch.

6. Choose the **Rebuild** button from the Menu Bar or press CTRL+B to rebuild the model. The model after copying the feature is shown in Figure 9-45.

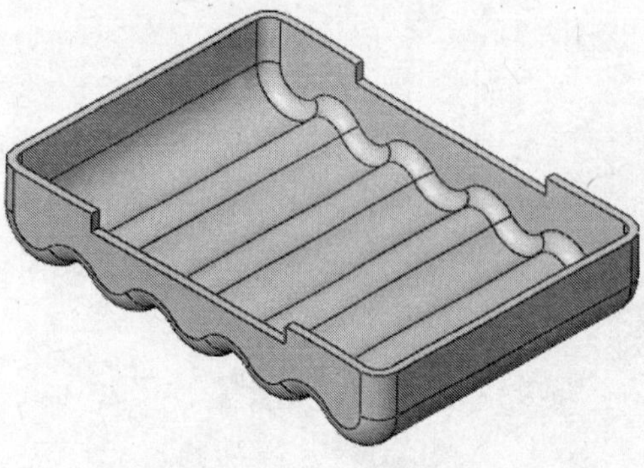

Figure 9-44 *The cut feature created on the front face*

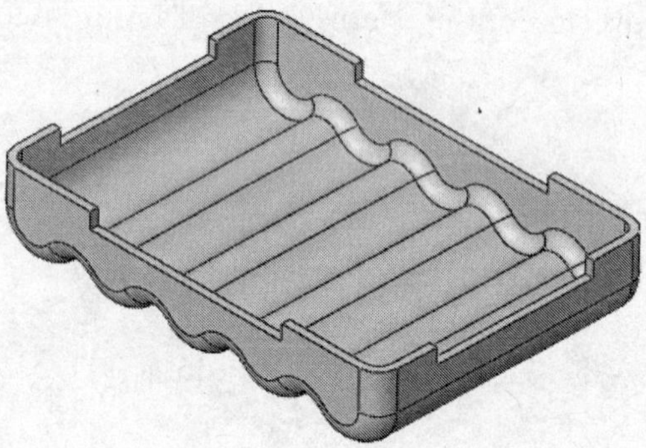

Figure 9-45 *The model after copying the feature*

7. Create slots, add fillet, and pattern the features. The model after creating these features is shown in Figure 9-46.

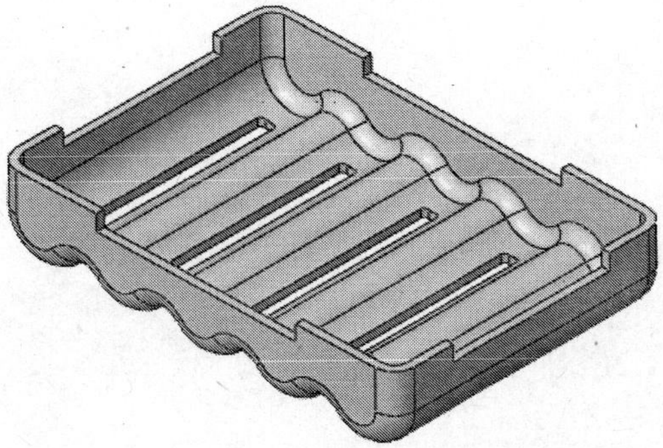

Figure 9-46 Model after creating the features

> **Tip**
> *To create a fillet, invoke the **Fillet** tool and choose the **Add** tab in the **FilletXpert PropertyManager**. Now, choose an edge of the slot; a pop-up toolbar will be displayed. Choose **Connected to start loop, 3 Edges** from the pop-up toolbar to select all the vertical edges of the slot.*

Creating the Standoff

Now, you need to create the standoff for the model. It is created by extruding a sketch drawn on the sketch plane at an offset distance from the Top Plane. You also need to specify a draft angle while creating this feature.

1. Create a reference plane at an offset distance of 10.5 mm from the **Top Plane**. To flip the direction of the reference plane, you need to select the **Flip offset** check box from the **Plane PropertyManager** if required.

2. Select the newly created plane as the sketching plane, draw the sketch of the standoff, and apply required relations and dimensions. The sketch consists of a circle of 1 mm diameter. For other dimensions, refer to Figure 9-34.

3. Extrude the sketch using the **Up To Next** option with an outward draft angle of 10-degree. Hide the newly created plane; the standoffs of the model are created.

4. Rotate the model and add a fillet of radius 0.25 mm to the base of the standoff.

   The rotated and zoomed view of the complete standoff is displayed in Figure 9-47.

5. Pattern the filleted standoff feature using the **Linear Pattern** tool. The isometric view of the final model is shown in Figure 9-48.

Saving the Model

1. Save the model with the name *c09_tut01* at the following location: *\Documents\SOLIDWORKS\c09*

2. Choose **File > Close** from the SOLIDWORKS menus to close the document.

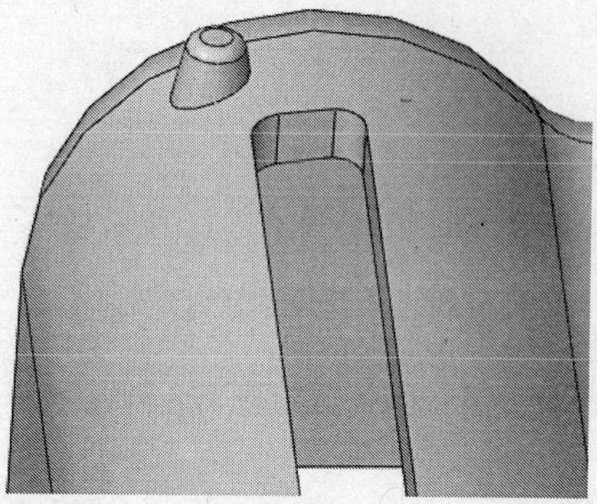

Figure 9-47 *Rotated and zoomed view of the model to show the standoff*

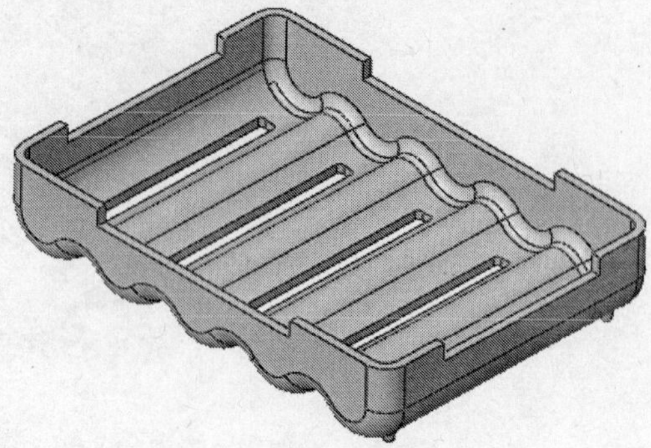

Figure 9-48 *Final model*

Tutorial 2

In this tutorial, you will create the model shown in Figure 9-49. The views and dimensions of the model are shown in the same figure. **(Expected time: 45 min)**

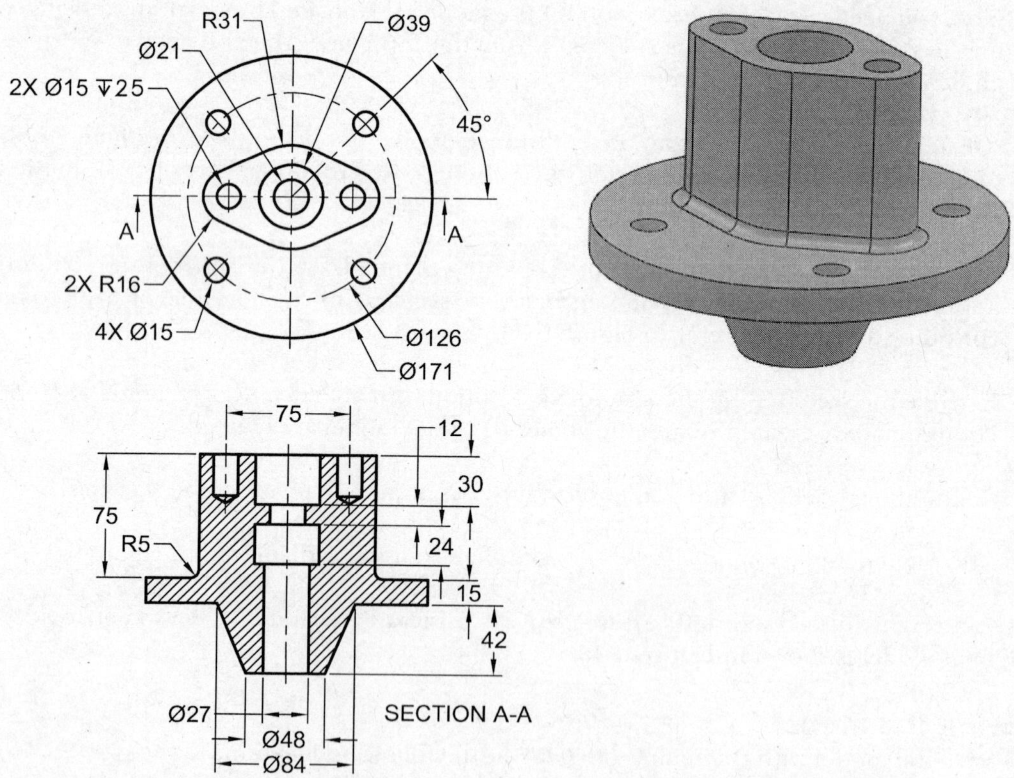

Figure 9-49 *Views and dimensions of the model for Tutorial 2*

The following steps are required to complete this tutorial:

a. Create the base feature of the model by revolving the sketch along its central axis.
b. Draw the sketch of the second feature on the top face of the base feature and extrude it up to a given dimension.
c. Create the revolve cut feature.
d. Create the hole using the **Simple Hole** tool, and then pattern it using the **Circular Pattern** tool.
e. Create a drilled hole feature using the **Hole Wizard** tool.
f. Mirror the hole feature about the **Right Plane**.
g. Apply the fillet.
h. Perform the live sectioning of the model.
i. Save the model.

Creating the Base Feature

First, you need to create the base feature of the model by revolving the sketch created on the **Front Plane**.

1. Start a new SOLIDWORKS Part document using the **New SOLIDWORKS Document** dialog box.

2. Invoke the **Revolved Boss/Base** tool and draw the sketch of the base feature on the **Front Plane**. Add required relations and dimensions to the sketch, as shown in Figure 9-50.

3. Exit the sketching environment.

   You do not need to set any parameters in the **Revolve PropertyManager** because the default value in the **Angle** spinner is 360 degrees as required.

4. Choose the **OK** button from the **Revolve PropertyManager**. The base feature created after revolving the sketch is shown in Figure 9-51.

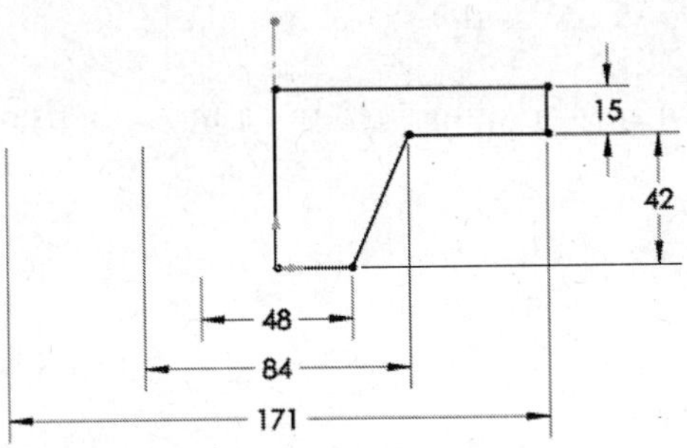

Figure 9-50 *Sketch for the base feature*

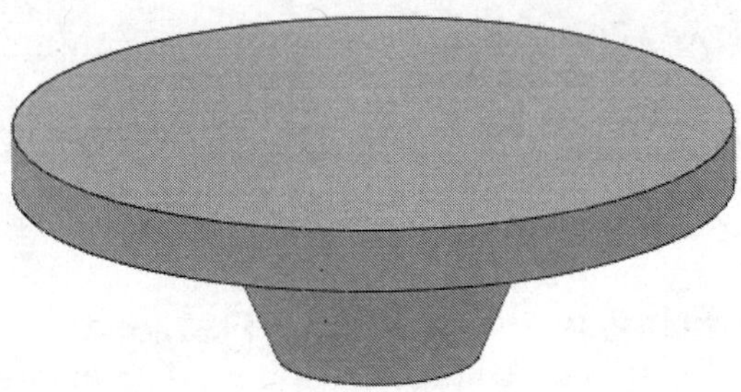

Figure 9-51 *The dimetric view of the base feature*

Creating the Second Feature

The second feature of this model is an extruded feature. It can be created by extruding the sketch created on the top planar face of the base feature.

1. Invoke the **Extruded Boss/Base** tool and select the top planar face of the base feature as the sketching plane.

2. Draw the sketch of the second feature and apply required relations and dimensions to it, as shown in Figure 9-52. Make sure the sketch is symmetric about the centerline.

3. Extrude the sketch upto a distance of 75 mm. The isometric view of the model after creating the second feature is shown in Figure 9-53.

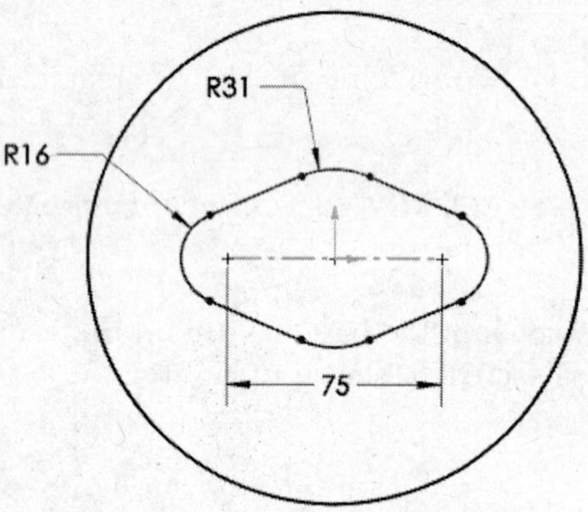

Figure 9-52 *Sketch for the second feature*

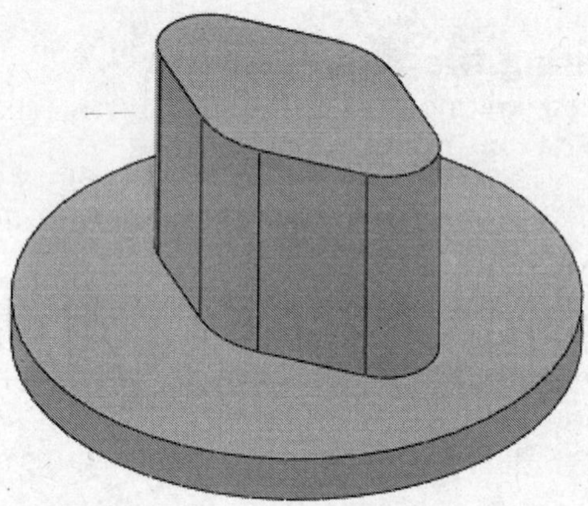

Figure 9-53 *Model after adding the second feature*

Creating the Third Feature

The third feature of the model can be created by revolving a sketch using the cut option. The sketch for this feature will be created on the **Front Plane**.

1. Invoke the **Revolved Cut** tool and select the **Front Plane** as the sketching plane.

2. Draw the sketch of the revolved cut feature, and then apply required relations and dimensions to it, as shown in Figure 9-54.

3. Exit the sketching environment and create a revolved cut feature with a default angle value of 360 degrees.

Creating the Remaining Features

1. Create the remaining features of the model using the **Fillet**, **Simple Hole**, **Mirror**, **Hole Wizard** tools and circular pattern.

The isometric view of the model after creating all the remaining features is displayed in Figure 9-55.

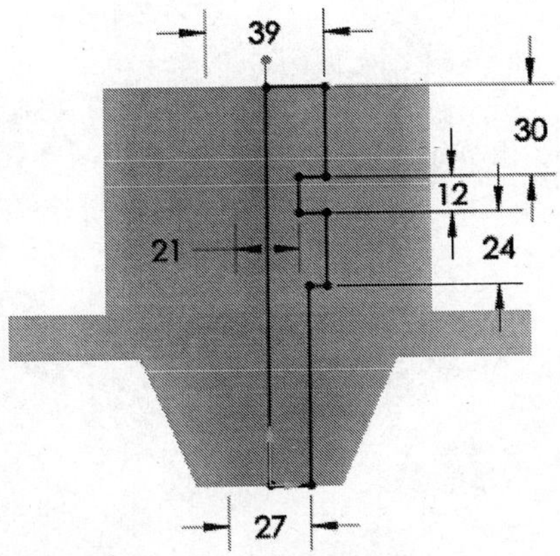

Figure 9-54 Sketch for the revolved cut feature

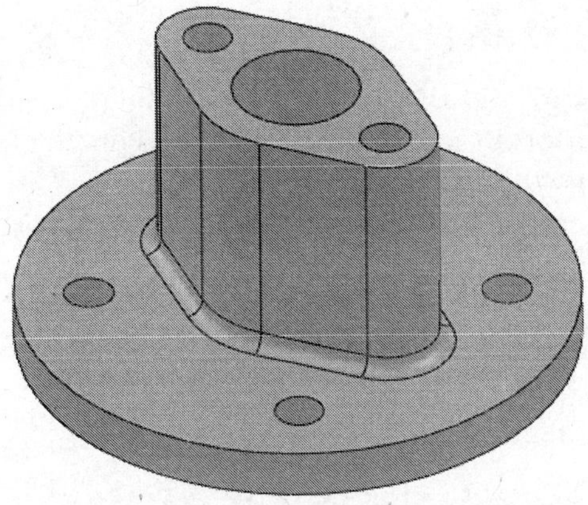

Figure 9-55 Isometric view of the final model

Sectioning the Model

1. Choose the top planar surface of the base feature and right-click; a shortcut menu is displayed.

2. Choose the **Live Section Plane** option from the shortcut menu; a sectioning plane is displayed with one ring and two wings at the center.

3. Right-click and choose the **Fit To Part** option.

4. Move the cursor to the vertical wing, press and hold the left mouse button, and drag the cursor to section the model along the vertical plane. Figure 9-56 shows the live section of the model when the sectioning plane is at an angle of 270 degree.

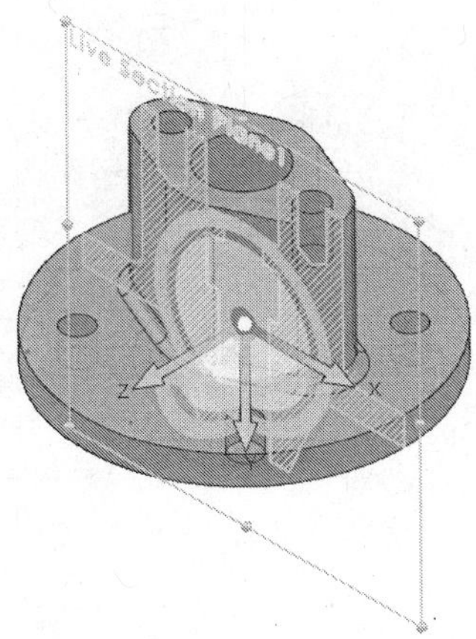

Figure 9-56 Model with the sectioning plane

5. Similarly, you can rotate the sectioning plane using the other wing.

6. Move the cursor near the edges of the section plane in the drawing area and then right-click. Next, choose the **Delete** option from the shortcut menu displayed; the sectioning plane gets removed.

Saving the Model

Now, you need to save the model.

1. Save the model with the name *c09_tut02* at the following location: *\Documents\SOLIDWORKS\c09*

2. Choose **File > Close** from the SOLIDWORKS menus to close the document.

Tutorial 3

In this tutorial, you will create the model shown in Figure 9-57. While creating it, you will also perform some editing operations on it. The views and dimensions of the model are given in the same figure.

(Expected time: 45min)

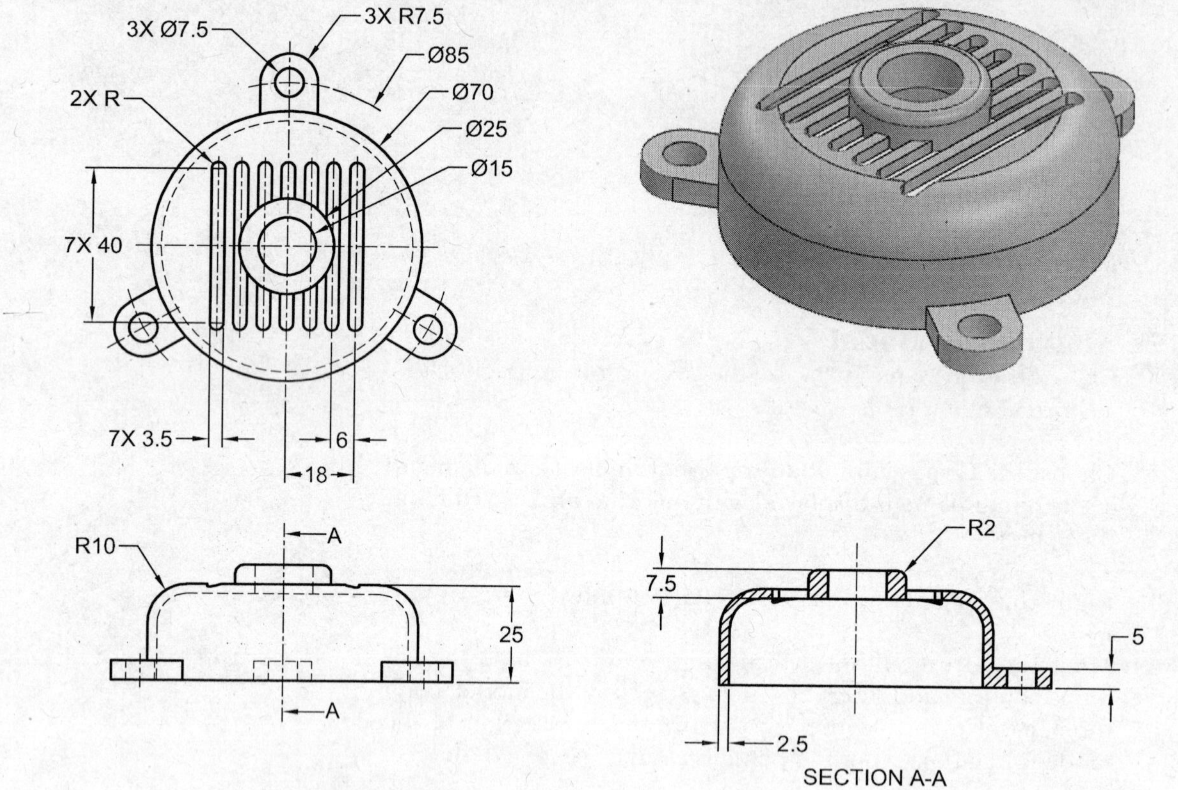

***Figure 9-57** Views and dimensions of the model for Tutorial 3*

The following steps are required to complete this tutorial:

a. Create the base feature of the model by revolving the sketch drawn on the **Front Plane**.
b. Shell the model using the **Shell** tool.
c. Draw the sketch on the **Top Plane** and extrude it to a given distance.
d. Pattern the extrude feature using the **Circular Pattern** tool.
e. Edit the circular pattern.
f. Create the features on the top planar face.
g. Create the slot on the top planar face and pattern it.
h. Unsuppress the suppressed features and create the remaining features of the model.
i. Save the model.

Creating the Base Feature

First, you need to create the base feature of the model by revolving the sketch created on the **Front Plane**.

1. Start a new SOLIDWORKS Part document using the **New SOLIDWORKS Document** dialog box.

2. Invoke the **Revolved Boss/Base** tool and draw the sketch of the base feature on the **Front Plane**. Add required relations and dimensions to it, as shown in Figure 9-58.

3. Exit the sketching environment and create the revolved base feature of the model, as shown in Figure 9-59.

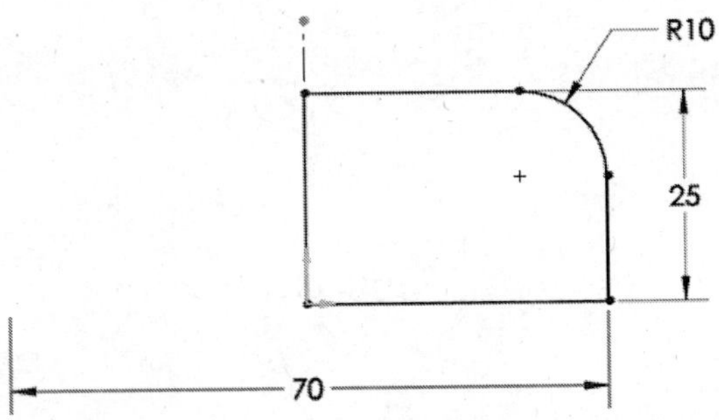

Figure 9-58 Sketch of the base feature

Figure 9-59 Base feature of the model

Shelling the Base Feature

After creating the base feature, you need to shell the model using the **Shell** tool. You also need to remove the bottom face of the base feature leaving behind a thin-walled model.

1. Invoke the **Shell PropertyManager** and set the value in the **Thickness** spinner to **2.5**.

2. Rotate the model and select its bottom face to remove it.

3. Choose the **OK** button from the **Shell PropertyManager**. The rotated view of the model after adding the shell feature is displayed in Figure 9-60.

Creating the Third Feature

After adding the shell feature to the model, you need to create the third feature which is an extruded feature. The sketch for this feature will be drawn on the Top Plane.

1. Invoke the **Extruded Boss/Base** tool and select the **Top Plane** as the sketching plane.

2. Orient the sketching plane normal to the viewing direction by selecting the **Normal To** option from the **Orientation** dialog box if not set by default.

3. Draw the sketch of the third feature and then add required relations and dimensions to it, as shown in Figure 9-61.

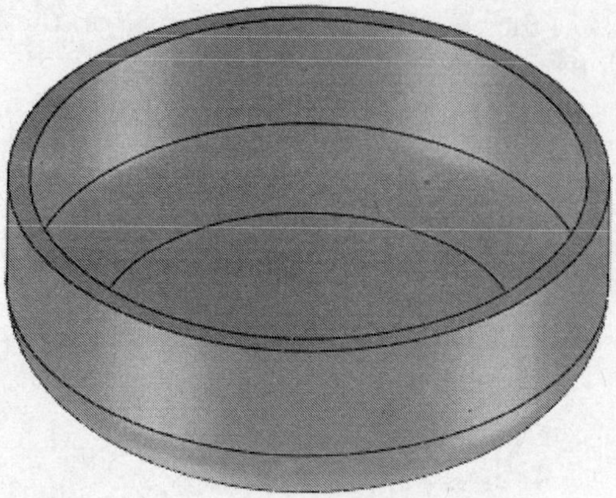

Figure 9-60 Shell feature added to the model

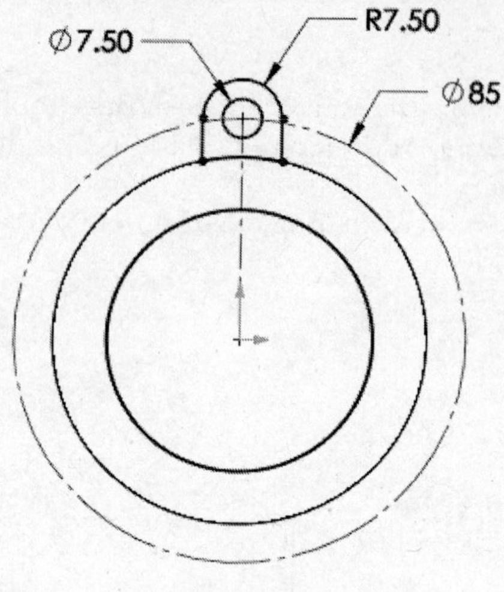

Figure 9-61 Sketch of the third feature

4. Exit the sketching environment and extrude the sketch upto a depth of 5 mm.

Patterning the Third Feature

You need to pattern the third feature after creating it. This feature will be patterned using the **Circular Pattern** tool.

1. Invoke the **CirPattern PropertyManager.**

2. Select the third feature from the drawing area if not selected in the **Features to Pattern** selection box.

3. Left-click once in the **Pattern Axis** selection box and select the circular edge of the base feature; a preview of the pattern feature is displayed.

4. Set the value in the **Number of Instances** spinner to **6** and select the **Equal spacing** check box if not selected.

5. Choose **OK** from the **CirPattern PropertyManager**.

The model after creating the pattern feature is displayed in Figure 9-62.

Editing the Pattern Feature

The number of instances in the pattern created is not the same as required for this model, refer to Figure 9-57. Therefore, you need to skip the instances that are not required.

1. Select **CirPattern1** from the **FeatureManager Design Tree** or any one of the pattern instances other than the parent instance from the drawing area. Right-click and choose the **Edit Feature** option from the shortcut menu; the **CirPattern1 PropertyManager** is displayed.

You will notice that the number of instances in the pattern feature is 6, but the required number of instances is 3. Therefore, you need to edit the number of instances.

2. Expand the **Instances to Skip** rollout; a pink dot is displayed on the patterned features.

3. Move the cursor to the pink dot; the number of the instance is displayed on that pink dot. Left-click on the second, fourth, and sixth instances.

4. Choose the **OK** button from the **CirPattern1 PropertyManager**; the selected instances are suppressed. The model after editing the features is shown in Figure 9-63.

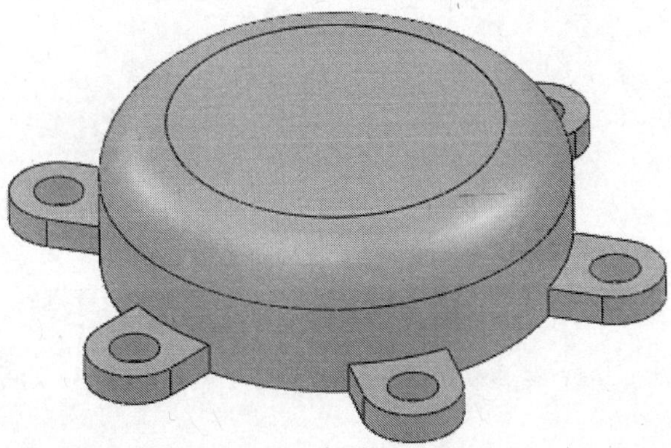

Figure 9-62 *Pattern feature added to the model*

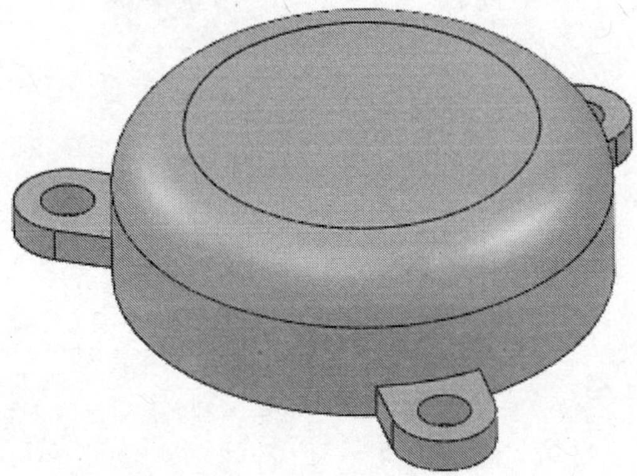

Figure 9-63 *The edited pattern feature*

Suppressing the Features

As discussed earlier, sometimes you may need to suppress some features to reduce the complications in the model. The suppressed features are not actually deleted, but their display is turned off. When you suppress a feature, the child features associated with that feature are also suppressed.

1. Select the **Boss-Extrude1** feature, which is the third feature of the model, from the **FeatureManager Design Tree**; a pop-up toolbar is displayed. Choose **Suppress** from the pop-up toolbar; the extrude feature and its instances will turn gray in the **FeatureManager Design Tree** indicating that these are suppressed.

Note

1. The circular pattern feature is the child feature of the extrude feature. Therefore, on choosing the ***Suppress*** *button, it also gets suppressed and hence both the features are not displayed in the drawing area.*

2. Suppressing some of the patterned instances and the features is done only to make the users understand the usage of these options. You can create this model without performing these steps also.

Creating the Protrusion

The next feature that you need to create is a protrusion on the top(inner) face of the base feature. You need to create this feature using the **Extruded Boss/Base** tool.

1. Invoke the **Extruded Boss/Base** tool and draw the sketch of the feature on the top(inner) face of the base feature. Then, extrude it to a distance of 7.5 mm, as shown in Figure 9-64. Choose the **Reverse Direction** button, if required.

2. Create the remaining features using the **Simple Hole** and **Fillet** tools, as shown in Figure 9-65.

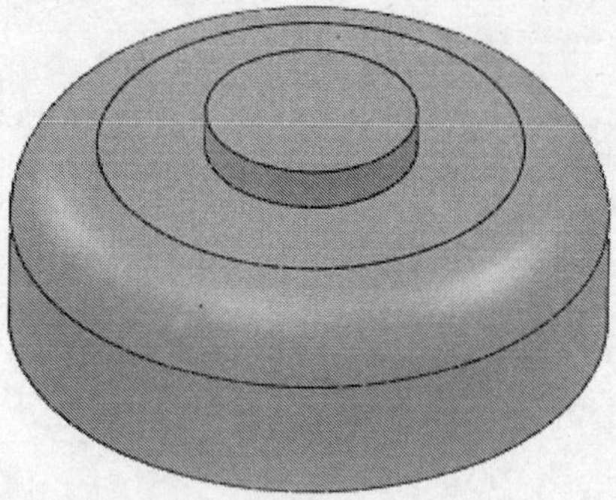

Figure 9-64 *The extrude feature*

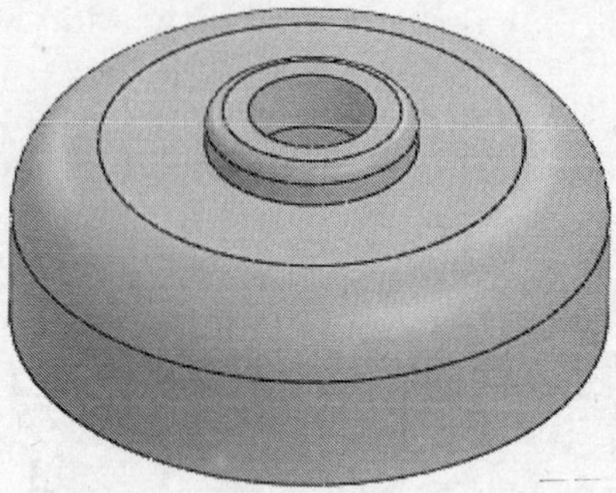

Figure 9-65 *Model after creating other features*

Note

The protrusion should be created after creating the slot. But for the purpose of tutorial, it has been created earlier.

Rollback the Feature

Now, you will rollback this feature and create a slot.

1. Select the **Rollback Bar** and drag it to some distance above the **Boss-Extrude2** feature using the hand pointer; the feature upto the specified distance is rolled-back.

Creating the Slots

Next, you need to create the slots. The sketch for this feature will be drawn on the top planar face of the base feature.

1. Invoke the **Extruded Cut** tool and select the top planar face of the base feature as the sketching plane.

2. Draw the sketch of the cut feature and add required relations and dimensions to the sketch, as shown in Figure 9-66.

3. Exit the sketching environment and specify the end condition as **Through All** from the **Cut-Extrude PropertyManager**.

4. Choose the **OK** button from the **PropertyManager**.

5. Now, using the **Linear Pattern** tool, create a linear pattern of the cut feature. You can select the dimension 18 in the drawing area as the directional reference X, flip the direction if required. The model after creating the linear pattern is shown in Figure 9-67.

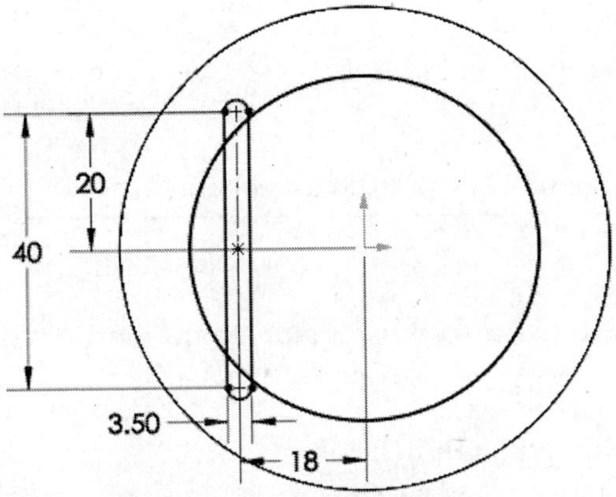

Figure 9-66 Sketch of the slot

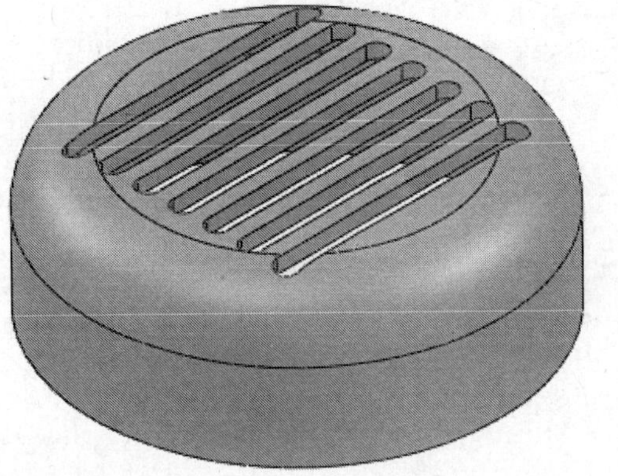

Figure 9-67 Model after patterning the slot

Roll Forward the Feature

1. Select the **CirPattern1** feature from the **FeatureManager Design Tree** and right-click; a shortcut menu is displayed.

2. Choose the **Roll to End** option from the shortcut menu to display all the features that are rolled-back.

Unsuppressing the Features

After completing the model, you need to unsuppress the features that you suppressed earlier.

1. Press and hold the CTRL key and select all the suppressed features from the **FeatureManager Design Tree**.

2. Right-click and choose the **Unsuppress** option from the shortcut menu; the suppressed features are restored in the model. Final model after unsuppressing the features is shown in Figure 9-68.

Note

1. If you select and unsuppress only the parent suppressed feature, the child features will not be unsuppressed. Therefore, you have to select the parent feature as well as the corresponding suppressed child features.

2. To unsuppress the child features along with the parent feature, select the parent feature and then choose ***Edit > Unsuppress with Dependents > This Configuration*** *from the SOLIDWORKS menus; all the features will get unsuppressed. On unsuppressing a child feature, its parent feature will be unsuppressed automatically. You will learn more about the configurations in the later chapters.*

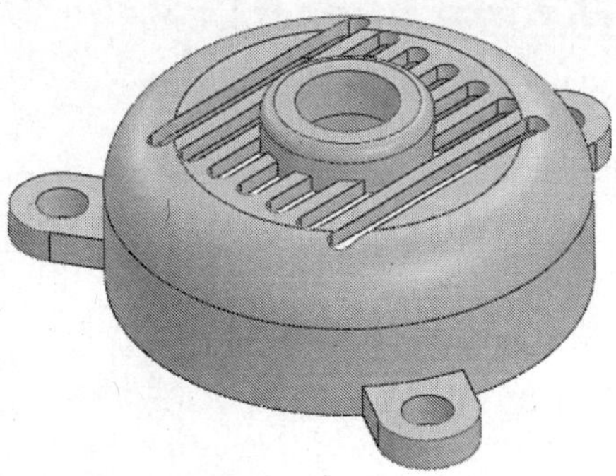

Figure 9-68 The final model

Saving the Model

1. Save the model with the name *c09_tut03* at the following location: *\Documents\SOLIDWORKS\c09*
2. Choose **File > Close** from the SOLIDWORKS menus to close the document.

Self-Evaluation Test

Answer the following questions and then compare them to those given at the end of this chapter:

1. The __________ dialog box is displayed when you edit a dimension.
2. The process of changing the position of a feature in the **FeatureManager Design Tree** is known as __________.
3. To edit a feature or a sketch dynamically, choose the __________ button.
4. The __________ **PropertyManager** is used to move or copy the bodies.
5. The __________ dialog box is displayed when there is an error in a feature.
6. On modifying the reference geometry, the feature created using the reference geometry is also modified. (T/F)
7. The **Edit Feature** option is used to edit the selected feature. (T/F)
8. You cannot rename a feature in the **FeatureManager Design Tree**. (T/F)
9. You can rebuild a model by pressing CTRL+R keys. (T/F)
10. Rebuilding a feature is defined as a process in which you roll back the feature to an earlier stage. (T/F)

Review Questions

Answer the following questions:

1. The __________ **PropertyManager** is invoked to delete a body.
2. You can rotate a body using the __________ **PropertyManager**.
3. The __________ key is used to copy a feature or a sketch.
4. The __________ key is used to cut a feature or a sketch.
5. When the __________ tool is active, preview of the feature is displayed in temporary graphics while editing the sketches.

6. The __________ **PropertyManager** is used to edit the sketch plane of a sketch.

7. To add the selected feature to a new folder, you need to choose **Add to New Folder** from the shortcut menu. (T/F)

8. For reordering the features, select the feature in the **FeatureManager Design Tree** and drag the feature to the required position. (T/F)

9. When you click once on a dimension, the **Modify** dialog box will be displayed. (T/F)

10. If you want to modify a fully or partially defined sketch by dragging, the **Override Dims on Drag/Move** option should be selected. (T/F)

EXERCISES

Exercise 1

Create the model, as shown in Figure 9-69. The other views and dimensions of the model are also given in the same figure. **(Expected time: 45 min)**

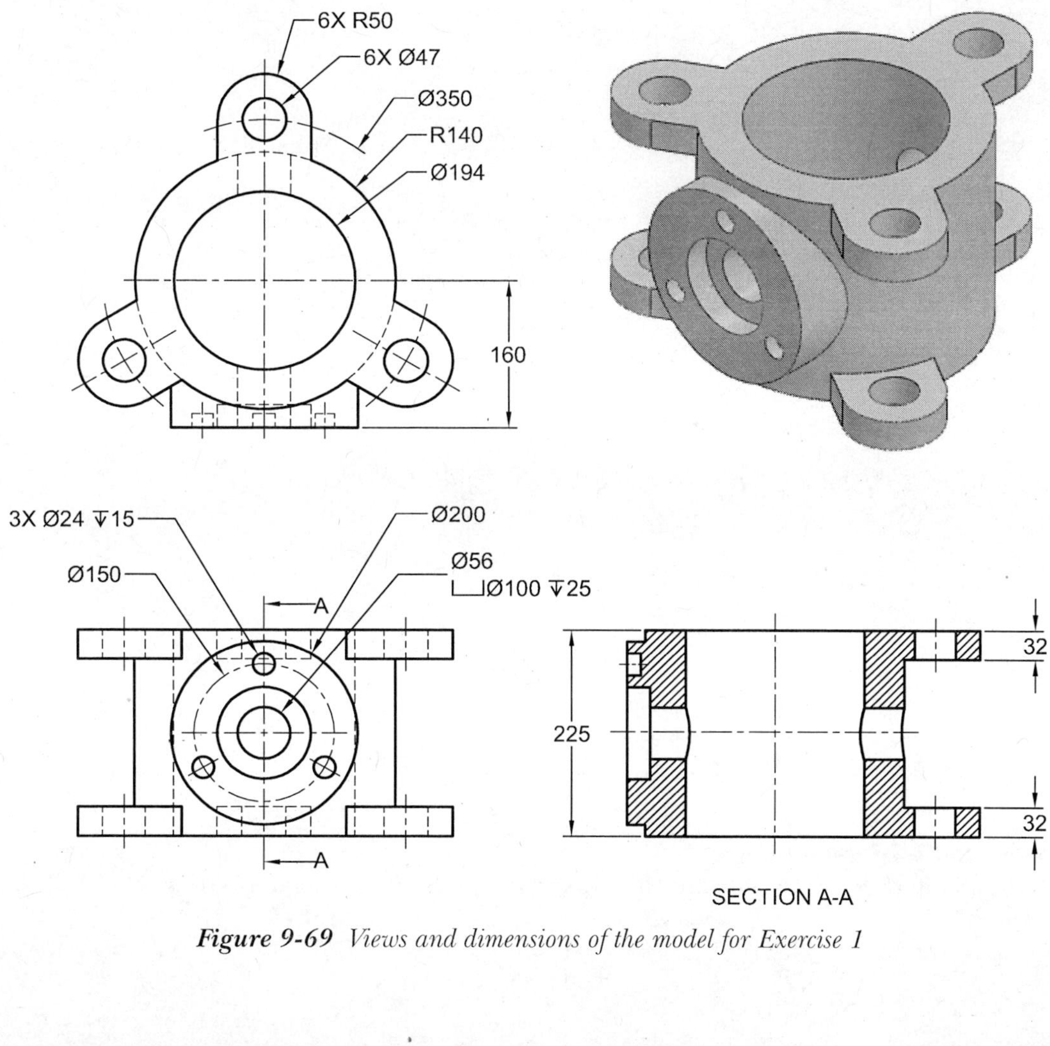

Figure 9-69 *Views and dimensions of the model for Exercise 1*

Exercise 2

Create the model, as shown in Figure 9-70. The views and dimensions of the model are shown in the same figure. **(Expected time: 30 min)**

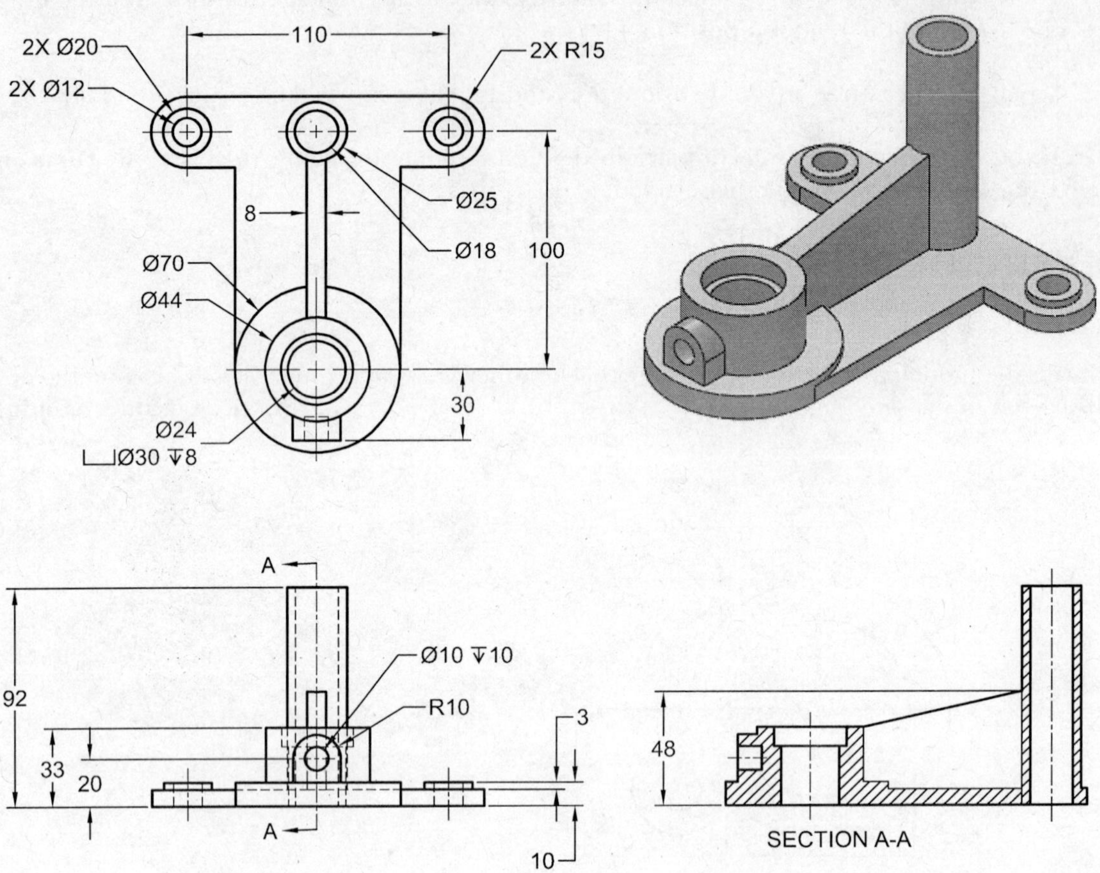

Figure 9-70 *Views and dimensions of the model for Exercise 2*

Answers to Self-Evaluation Test

1. Modify, **2.** Reordering, **3. Instant3D**, **4. Move/Copy Body**, **5. What's Wrong**, **6.** T, **7.** T, **8.** F, **9.** F, **10.** F

Chapter 10

Advanced Modeling Tools-III

Learning Objectives

After completing this chapter, you will be able to:

- *Create sweep features*
- *Create loft features*
- *Create 3D sketches*
- *Edit 3D sketches*
- *Create various types of curves*
- *Extrude 3D sketches*
- *Create draft features using the manual and DraftXpert methods*

ADVANCED MODELING TOOLS

Some of the advanced modeling tools were discussed in the earlier chapters. In this chapter, you will learn about some more advanced modeling tools such as sweep, loft, draft, curves, 3D sketches, and so on.

Creating Sweep Features

CommandManager:	Features > Swept Boss/Base
SOLIDWORKS menus:	Insert > Boss/Base > Sweep
Toolbar:	Features > Extruded Boss/Base > Swept Boss/Base

One of the most important advanced modeling tools is the **Swept Boss/Base** tool. This tool is used to extrude a closed profile along an open or a closed path. Therefore, you need a profile and a path to create a sweep feature. A profile is a section for the sweep feature and a path is the course taken by the profile while creating the sweep feature. The profile has to be a sketch, but the path can be a sketch, curve, or an edge. You will learn more about the procedure to create the curves later in this chapter. Figure 10-1 shows a profile and a path for creating a sweep feature.

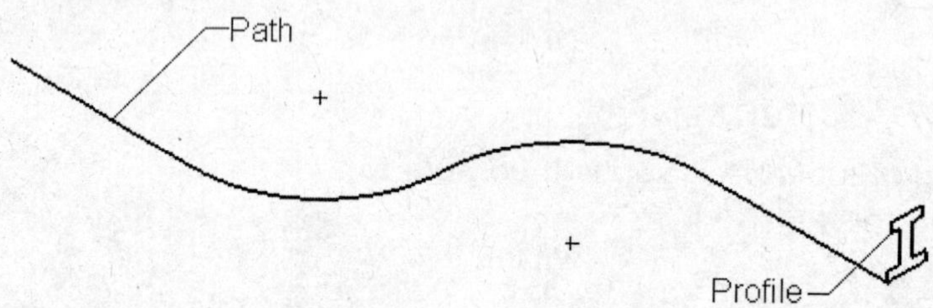

***Figure 10-1** Profile and path to create a sweep feature*

To create a sweep feature, choose the **Swept Boss/Base** button from the **Features** CommandManager; the **Sweep PropertyManager** will be displayed, as shown in Figure 10-2. You can create swept feature using sketch based profile or circular profile. By default, the **Sketch Profile** radio button is selected. As a result, you are prompted to select a sweep profile. Select the sketch drawn as the profile from the drawing area; the sketch will be highlighted and the **Profile** callout will be displayed. Also, you will be prompted to select a path for the sweep feature. Select the sketch or an edge to be used as the path; selection will be highlighted in magenta and the **Path** callout will be displayed. Also, the preview of the sweep feature will be displayed in the drawing area. Choose the **OK** button from the **Sweep PropertyManager** to end the feature creation. Figure 10-3 shows the resulting sweep feature.

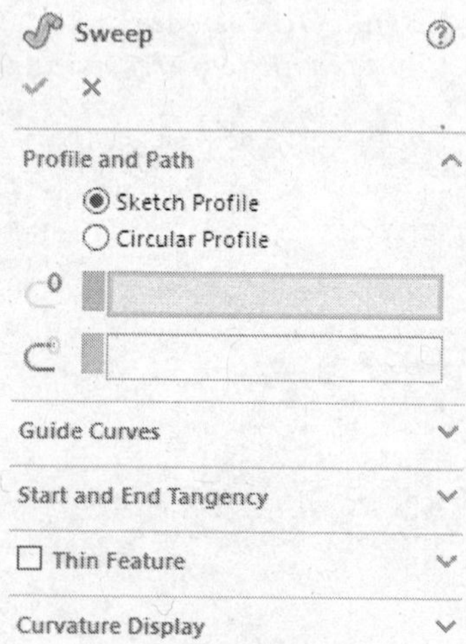

***Figure 10-2** The Sweep PropertyManager*

To create a Sweep feature using the circular profile along a sketch line, edge, or curve directly on a model, you need to choose the **Circular Profile** button from the **Profile and Path** rollout in the **Sweep PropertyManager**. Next, select the sketch or edge as a path along which circular profile is to be created from the drawing area and enter the diameter value in the **Diameter** spinner.

Tip

*You can also use the **Contour Select** tool to select a contour as the section for the sweep feature. To do so, invoke the **Sweep PropertyManager**. Next, right-click in the drawing area and choose **SelectionManager** from the shortcut menu displayed; the **SelectionManager** will be displayed. Choose the **Select Region** button from the **SelectionManager**, select the contour from the drawing area and then choose **OK** from the **SelectionManager**. You can also select multiple contours. If you pin the **SelectionManager**, it will be displayed by default whenever you invoke the **Sweep PropertyManager**. You can also use a shared sketch as the section of the sweep feature.*

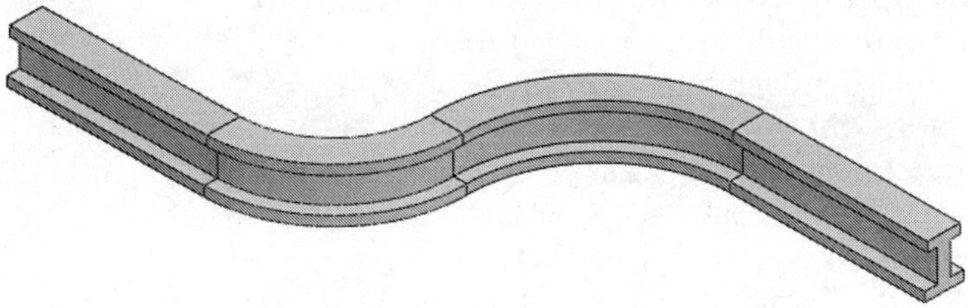

Figure 10-3 *Sweep feature*

It is not necessary that a sketch drawn for the profile of a sweep feature has to intersect the path. However, a plane on which the profile is drawn should lie at one of the endpoints of the path. Figure 10-4 shows the non-intersecting sketches of a profile and a path. Figure 10-5 shows the resulting sweep feature. Figure 10-6 shows the sketch of a profile and a closed path. Note that a plane on which the profile is drawn should intersect the closed path. Figure 10-7 shows the resulting sweep feature.

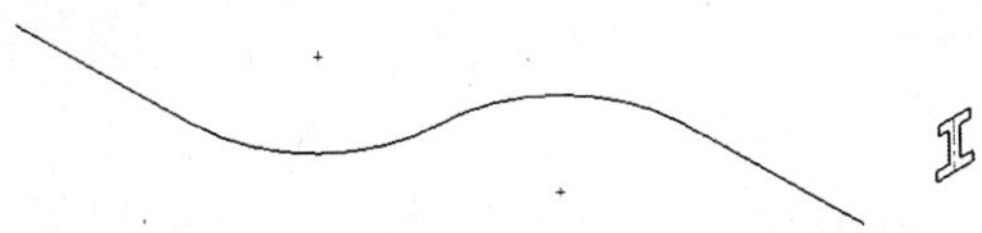

Figure 10-4 *Non-intersecting sketches of a profile and a path*

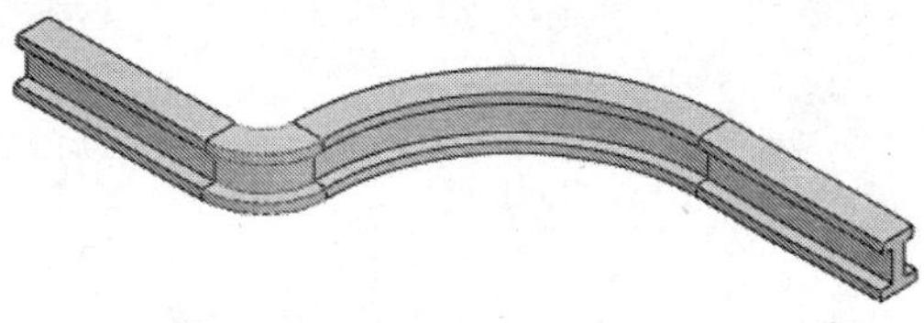

Figure 10-5 *Sweep feature created using a non-intersecting sketch*

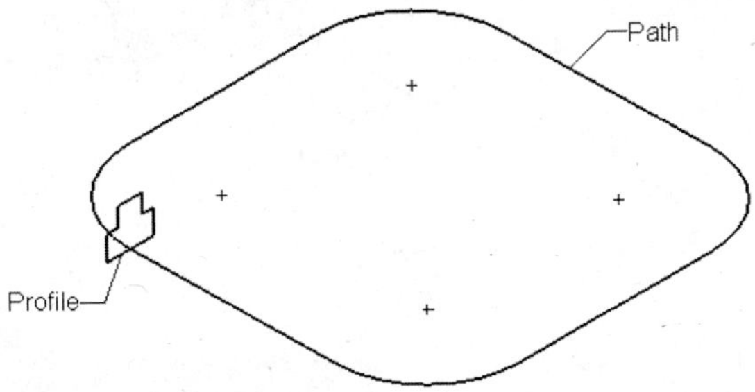

Figure 10-6 *Sketch of a profile and a closed path*

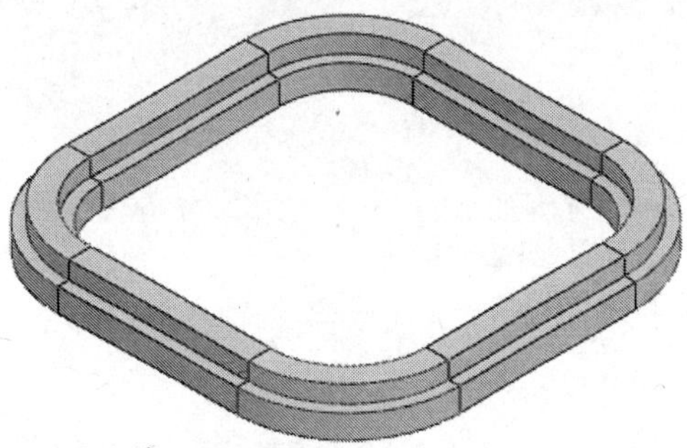

Figure 10-7 *Sweep feature created using a closed profile and a closed path*

The other options available in the **Sweep PropertyManager** to create the advanced sweep features are discussed next.

Creating a Sweep Feature Using the Follow Path and Keep Normal Constant Options

In the **Sweep PropertyManager**, the **Follow Path** option is selected by default in the **Profile Orientation** drop-down list available in the **Options** rollout, as shown in Figure 10-8. While creating a sweep feature using the **Follow Path** option, the section will follow the path to create it. If you select the **Keep Normal Constant** option from the **Profile Orientation** drop-down list, the section will be swept along the path with a normal constraint and will not change its orientation along the sweep path. Therefore, the start and end face of the sweep feature will be parallel. Figure 10-9 shows the sketches of the path and the profile for creating the sweep feature. Figure 10-10 shows the sweep feature created using the **Follow Path** option. Figure 10-11 shows the sweep feature created using the **Keep Normal Constant** option.

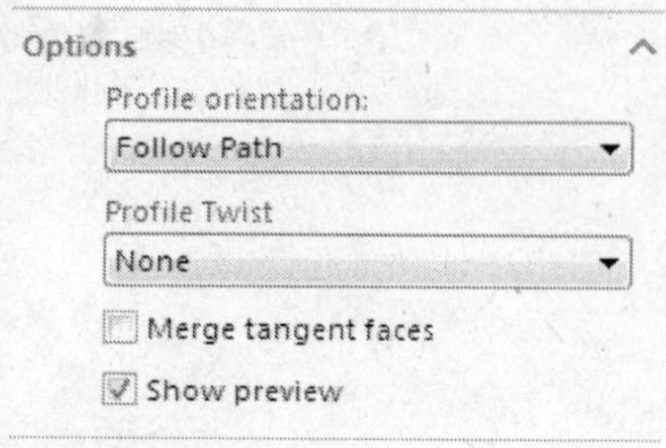

Figure 10-8 *The* ***Options*** *rollout*

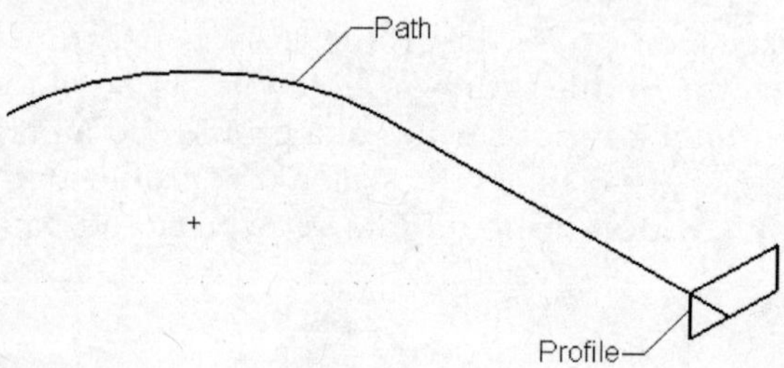

Figure 10-9 *Sketches of the path and the profile for creating the sweep feature*

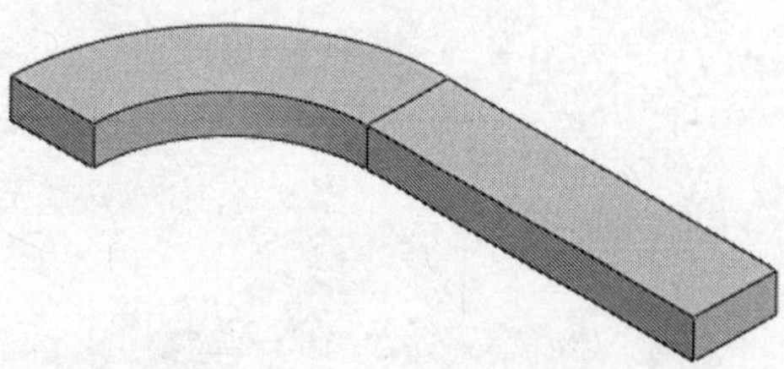

Figure 10-10 *Sweep feature created with the* ***Follow Path*** *option selected from the* ***Profile Orientation*** *drop-down list*

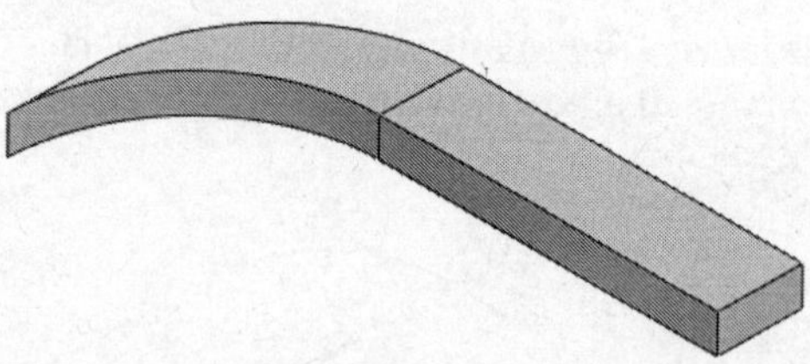

Figure 10-11 *Sweep feature created with the* ***Keep Normal Constant*** *option selected from the* ***Profile Orientation*** *drop-down list*

Creating a Sweep Feature Using Follow Path and Specify Twist Value Options

In the **Sweep PropertyManager**, the **Follow Path** option is selected by default in the **Profile Orientation** drop-down list available in the **Options** rollout, refer to Figure 10-8. As a result, other options like **None, Specify Twist Value, Specify Direction Vector**, and so on are available in the **Profile Twist** drop-down list. When you select the **Specify Twist Value** option from the **Profile Twist** drop-down list, then the **Twist control** drop-down list with the **Direction 1** spinner will be displayed in the **Options** rollout, refer to Figure 10-12. By default, the **Degrees** option is selected in the **Twist control** drop-down list. By keeping this option selected, you need to specify the twist angle in the **Direction 1** spinner. You can reverse the direction of the twist by using the **Reverse Twist Direction** button. You can also specify the twist in terms of radians or revolutions by selecting the **Radians** or **Revolutions** option in the **Twist control** drop-down list. Figure 10-13 shows sweep feature created before specifying twist value and Figure 10-14 shows the sweep feature after specifying twist parameters.

*Figure 10-12 The **Options** rollout*

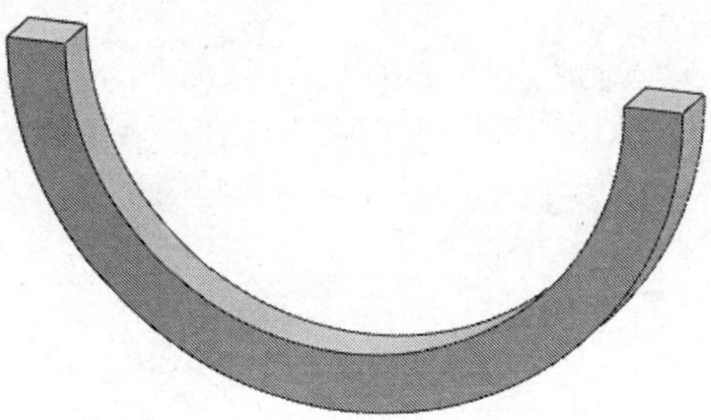

Figure 10-13 Sweep feature created before specifying twist value

Figure 10-14 Sweep feature after specifying twist value

Creating a Sweep Feature Using Follow Path and Specify Direction Vector Options

If you select the **Specify Direction Vector** option, the starting of the sweep feature will be tangent to the virtual normal that has been created from the selected entity. On selecting this option, the **Direction Vector** selection box will also be displayed. You need to select a linear edge, axis, planar face, or plane to specify the direction of sweep in this selection box.

Creating a Sweep Feature Using Follow Path and Tangent to Adjacent Faces

The **Tangent to Adjacent Faces** option is used to sweep the feature tangent to the adjoining faces at the start of the existing geometry.

Creating a Sweep Feature Using Keep Normal Constant and Specify Twist Value Options

You can also apply twist to a swept feature keeping its end face parallel to the profile and the entire transition normal to the sweep path. To apply this type of twist, select the **Keep Normal Constant** option from the **Profile Orientation** drop-down list and the **Specify Twist Value** option from the **Profile Twist** drop-down list and then set the twist parameters. Figure 10-15 shows the twist applied using the **Follow Path** option and Figure 10-16 shows the twist applied using the **Keep Normal Constant** option.

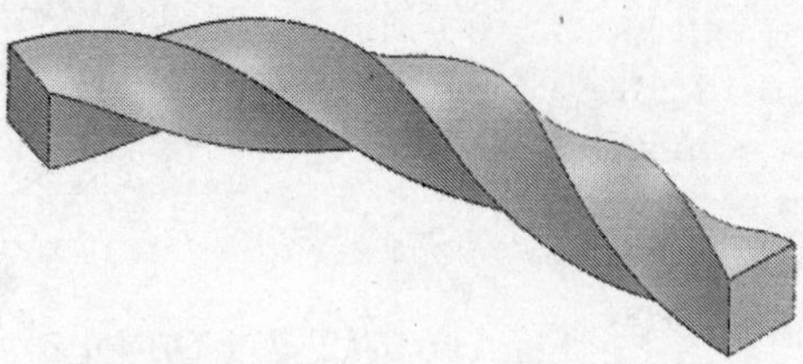

Figure 10-15 *Twist applied using the* ***Follow Path*** *option*

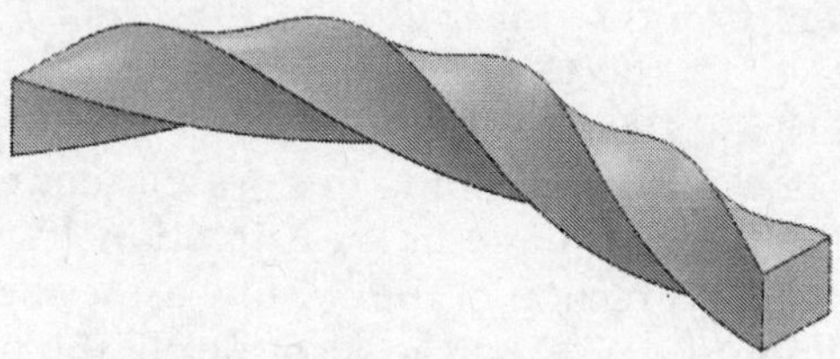

Figure 10-16 *Twist applied using the* ***Keep Normal Constant*** *option*

Tip

On selecting a model edge as the sweep path, the ***Tangent propagation*** *check box is displayed in the* ***Options*** *rollout. If this check box is selected, the edges tangent to the selected edge will be selected automatically as the path of the sweep feature.*

Merge tangent faces

The **Merge tangent faces** check box in the **Options** rollout is used to merge the tangent faces of a profile throughout the sweep feature.

Show preview

The **Show preview** check box in the **Options** rollout is used to display the preview of a sweep feature in the drawing area. This check box is selected by default. If you clear it, the preview of the sweep feature will not be displayed in the drawing area.

Merge result

The **Merge result** check box will be available only when you have at least one feature in the current document and it is selected by default. If you clear this check box, it will result in the creation of the sweep feature as a separate body.

Align with end faces

The **Align with end faces** check box will be available in the **Options** rollout only when at least one feature has already been created in the current document. On selecting this check box, the sweep feature is extended or trimmed to align with the end faces. Figure 10-17 shows the profile and path for creating sweep feature. Figure 10-18 shows the sweep feature created with the **Align with end faces** check box cleared. Figure 10-19 shows the sweep feature created with the **Align with end faces** check box selected.

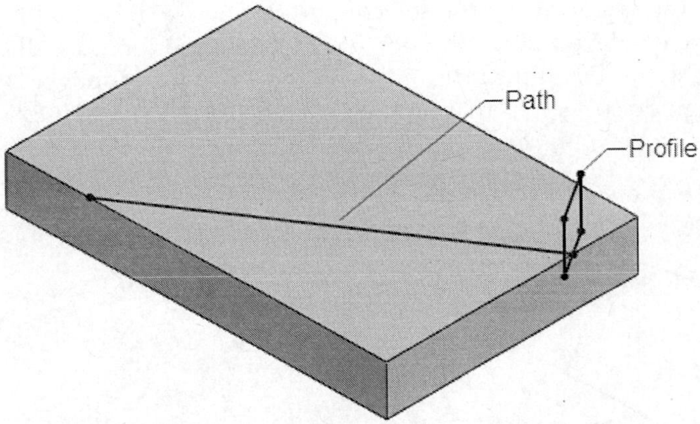

Figure 10-17 Sketches for creating sweep feature

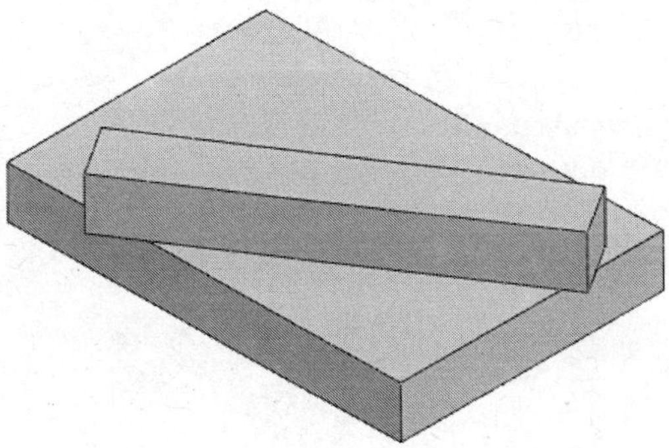

Figure 10-18 Sweep feature created with the ***Align with end faces*** *check box cleared*

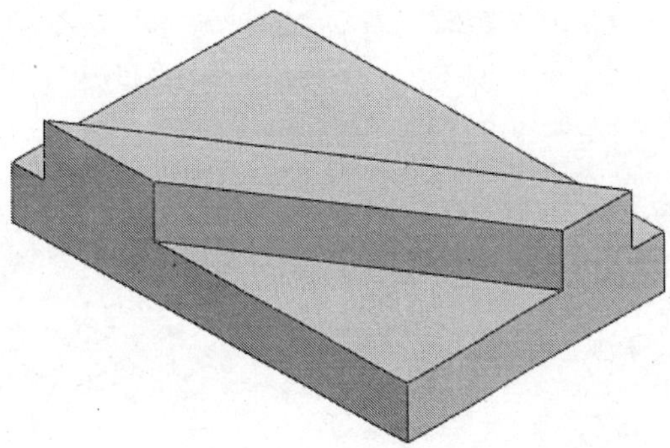

Figure 10-19 Sweep feature created with the ***Align with end faces*** *check box selected*

Note
If the sweep feature does not merge, you need to reduce the size of the profile.

Sweep with Guide Curves

The sweep with guide curves is the most important feature in the advanced modeling tools. In this sweep feature, the section of the sweep profile varies according to the guide curves along the sweep path. To create this type of feature, you need a profile, a path, and the guide curves. After drawing the sketch of the profile, path, and guide curve, apply the coincident relation between the guide curves and the profile. Make sure that the guide curves intersect the profile. Now, invoke the **Sweep PropertyManager**. Select the profile and the path; the preview of the sweep feature will be displayed in the drawing area. Click on the arrow on the right of the **Guide Curves** rollout to expand this rollout. The expanded **Guide Curves** rollout is shown in Figure 10-20.

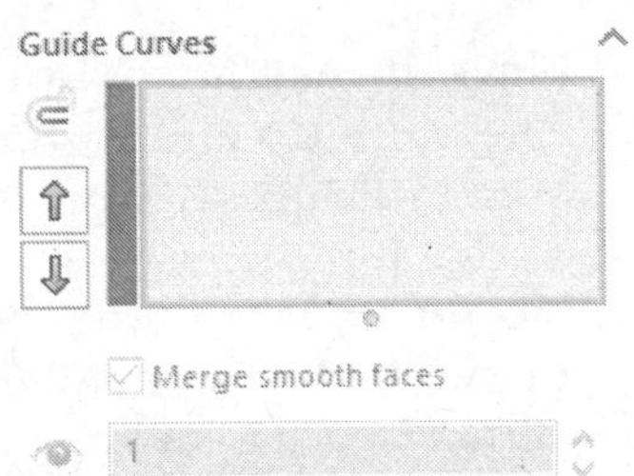

Figure 10-20 The ***Guide Curves*** *rollout*

Select the sketch of the guide curve; the selected guide curve will be highlighted and a **Guide Curve** callout will be displayed. Also, the preview of the sweep feature will be displayed in the drawing area. Choose the **OK** button from the **Sweep PropertyManager**. Figure 10-21 shows the sketch with the guide curve for creating the sweep feature. Figure 10-22 shows the resulting sweep feature.

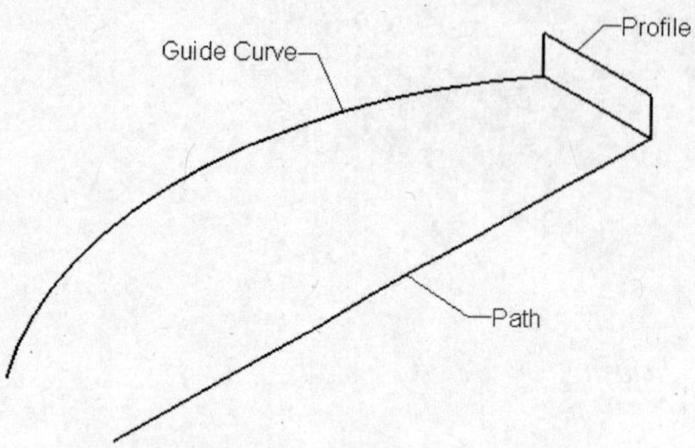

Figure 10-21 *Sketch with the path and guide curve for creating the sweep feature*

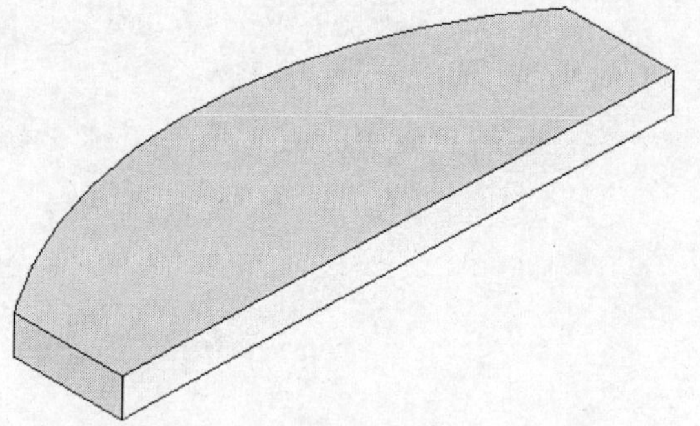

Figure 10-22 *Resulting sweep feature*

In the previous case, the path of the sweep feature was a straight line and the guide curve was an arc. In the next case, an arc will be selected as the path of the sweep feature and a straight line will be selected as the guide curve. Figure 10-23 shows the sketches for creating the sweep feature. Figure 10-24 shows the resulting sweep feature.

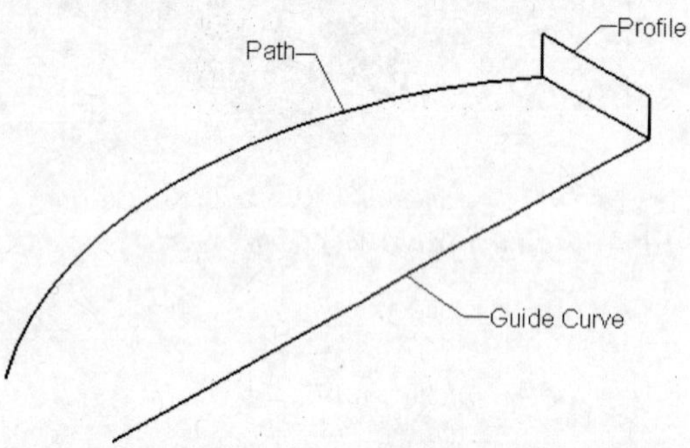

Figure 10-23 *Sketch with the path and the guide curve for creating the sweep feature*

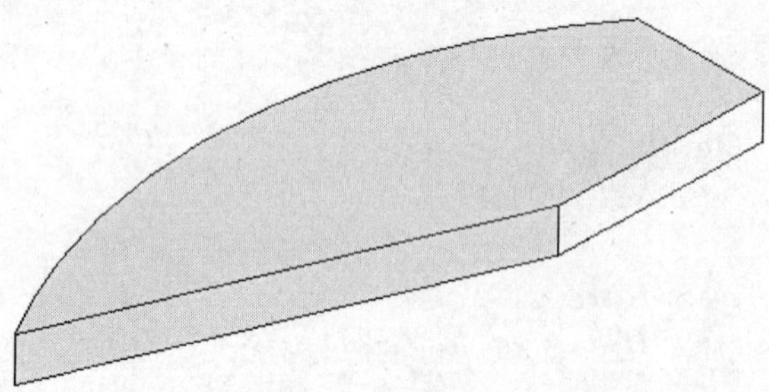

Figure 10-24 *Resulting sweep feature*

Move Up and Move Down

The **Move Up** and **Move Down** buttons on the left of the **Guide Curves** selection box are used to change the sequence of the selected guide curves.

Merge smooth faces

In the **Guide Curves** rollout, the **Merge smooth faces** check box is selected by default. This option is used to merge all smooth faces together, resulting in a smooth sweep feature. After creating the sweep feature when you edit it and clear the **Merge smooth faces** check box, the **SOLIDWORKS** message box will be displayed, as shown in Figure 10-25. This message box warns that the feature you are creating may fail because of the change in the smooth face option. Choose the **Yes** button from this dialog box to accept the change option. If you create a sweep feature with guide curves and this option is cleared, the smooth faces will not merge together in the resulting feature. Therefore, a sweep feature with a noncontinuous curvature surface will be created. Figure 10-26 shows a sweep feature created with the **Merge smooth faces** check box selected. Figure 10-27 shows the same sweep feature with the **Merge smooth faces** check box cleared.

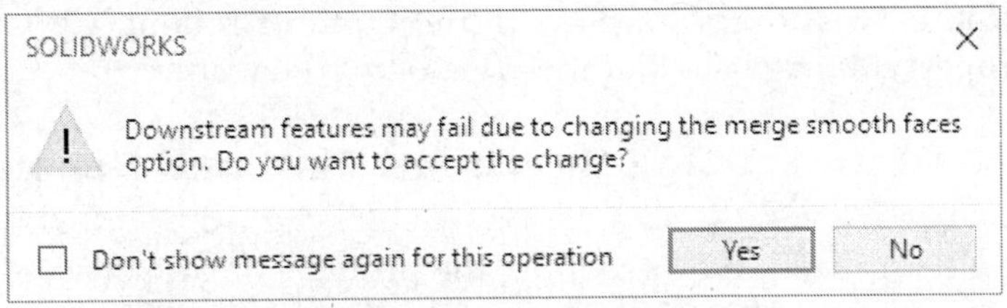

Figure 10-25 The ***SOLIDWORKS*** *message box*

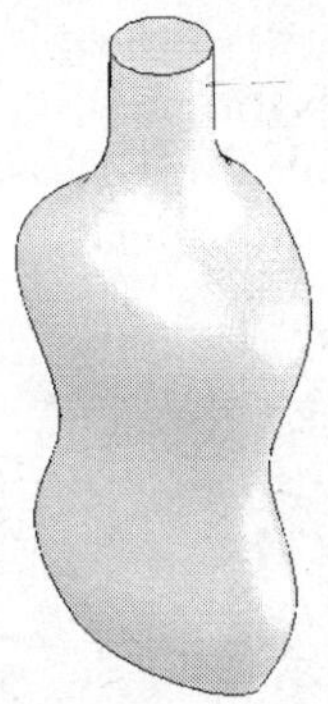

Figure 10-26 Sweep feature created with the ***Merge smooth faces*** *check box selected*

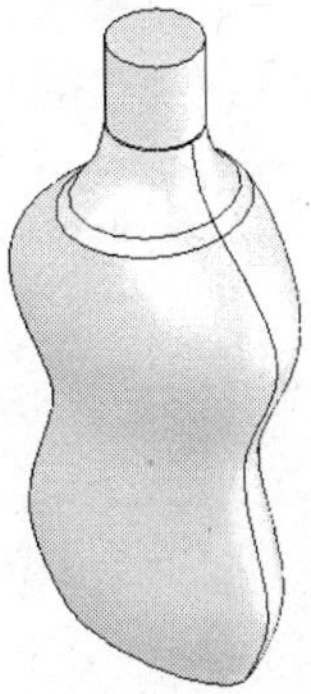

Figure 10-27 Sweep feature created with the ***Merge smooth faces*** *check box cleared*

Note

If you create a sweep feature with the ***Merge smooth faces*** *check box cleared, the resulting feature will be generated faster.*

Show Sections

The **Show Sections** button in the **Guide Curves** rollout is used to display the intermediate sections while creating a sweep feature with the guide curves. To display the intermediate profiles or the sections along the sweep path, choose the **Show Sections** button from the **Guide Curves** rollout; the **Section Number** spinner will be activated. This spinner is used to view the sections of the profile along the sweep path. The maximum value of the spinner goes up to the number of sections that fit inside the sweep feature. Figure 10-28 shows a section displayed using the **Show Sections** option and constrained by the guide curves.

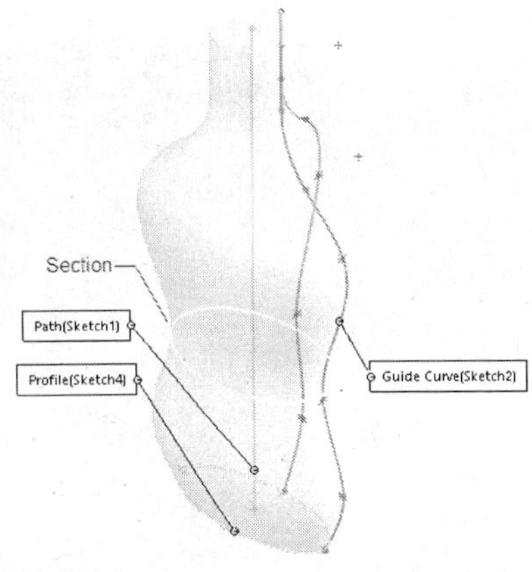

Figure 10-28 Section displayed on selecting the ***Show Sections*** *option*

Creating a Sweep Feature Using the Follow Path and First Guide Curve Option

To create a sweep feature by using the **Follow Path and First Guide Curve** option, invoke the **Sweep PropertyManager** and select the profile, path, and guide curve(s). Select the **Follow Path** option from the **Profile Orientation** drop-down list and the **Follow Path and First Guide Curve** option from the **Profile Twist** drop-down list in the **Options** rollout. Choose the **OK** button from the **Sweep PropertyManager** to end the creation of the feature.

Creating Sweep Feature Using the Follow First and Second Guide Curves Option

You can also create a sweep feature by sweeping the profile along a path and also by following the two guide curves. To create this type of sweep feature, select the **Follow First and Second Guide Curves** option from the **Profile Twist** drop-down list in the **Options** rollout. Choose the **OK** button from the **Sweep PropertyManager** to end the creation of the feature.

Figure 10-29 shows the sketch of the profile, path, and guide curves for creating a sweep feature. Figures 10-30 and 10-31 show the sweep features created by using the **Follow Path and First Guide Curve** and **Follow First and Second Guide Curves** options, respectively.

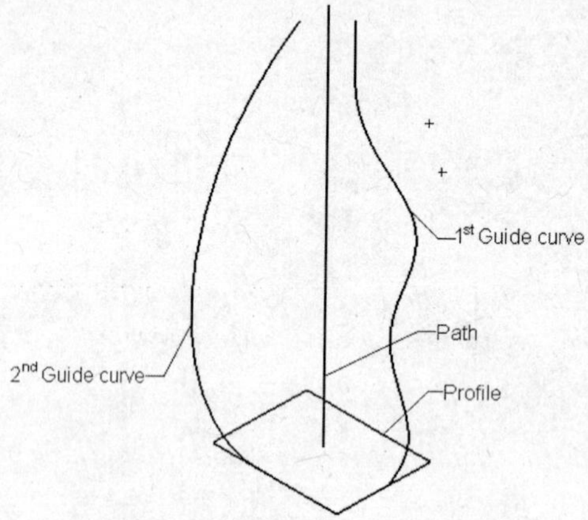

Figure 10-29 *Sketches of the profile, path, and guide curves for creating the sweep feature*

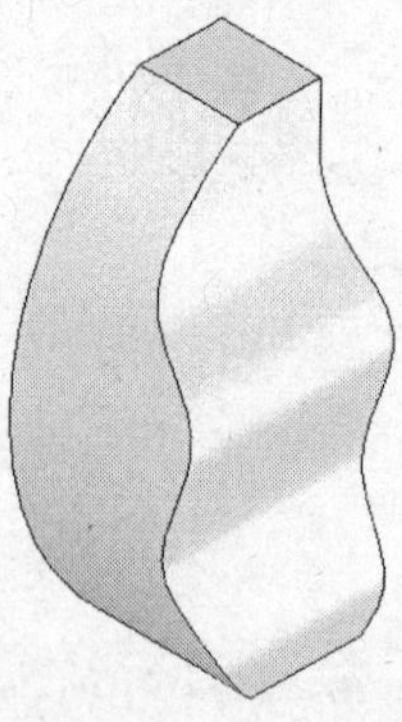

Figure 10-30 *Sweep feature created using the* ***Follow Path and First Guide Curve*** *option*

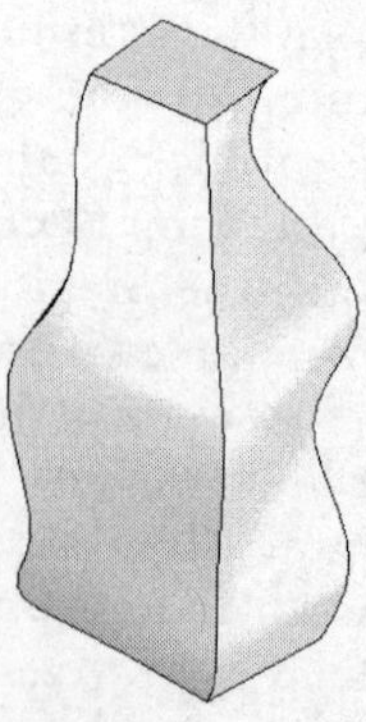

Figure 10-31 *Sweep feature created using the* ***Follow First and Second Guide Curves*** *option*

Start and End Tangency Rollout

The **Start and End Tangency** rollout in the **Sweep PropertyManager** is used to define the tangency conditions at the start and end of a feature. Expand the **Start and End Tangency** rollout, refer to Figure 10-32. Various options in the **Start and End Tangency** rollout are discussed next.

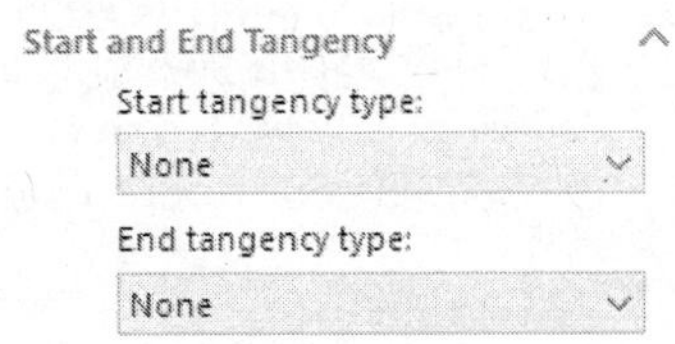

Figure 10-32 The ***Start and End Tangency*** *rollout*

Start tangency type

The **Start tangency type** drop-down list is used to specify the options for defining the tangency at the start of the sweep feature. Various options in this drop-down list are discussed next.

None

The **None** option is selected by default and is used to create a sweep feature without applying any start tangency.

Path Tangent

The **Path Tangent** option is used to maintain the sweep feature tangent normal to the path at the start.

The options in the **End tangency type** drop-down list are same as those discussed above in the **Start tangency type** drop-down list.

Thin Feature Rollout

You can also create a thin sweep feature by specifying the thickness of the sweep feature. To do so, expand the **Thin Feature** rollout by selecting the check box on the top-left in this rollout. The **Thin Feature** rollout is shown in Figure 10-33. The options in this rollout are the same as those discussed in the earlier chapters where extruding and revolving of thin features were discussed. Figure 10-34 shows a thin sweep feature.

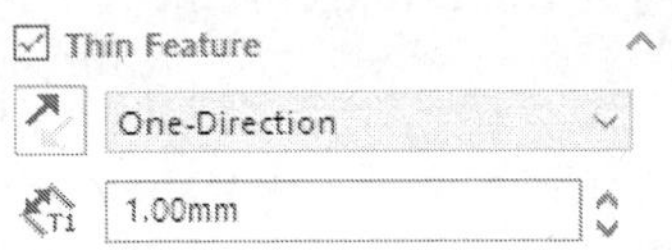

Figure 10-33 The ***Thin Feature*** *rollout*

Curvature Display Rollout

The **Curvature Display** rollout in the **Sweep PropertyManager** is used to display the mesh preview, zebra stripes, and curvature combs of the sweep feature. Expand this rollout to display the options in it, refer to Figure 10-35. The options in this rollout are discussed next.

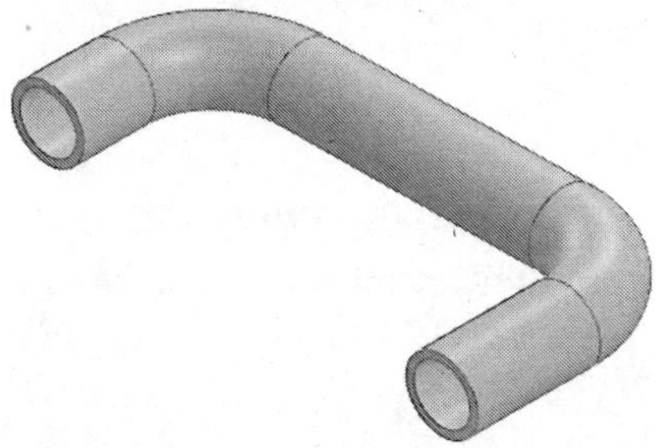

Figure 10-34 Thin sweep feature

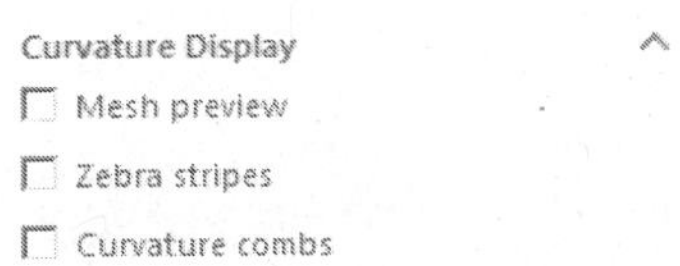

Figure 10-35 The ***Curvature Display*** *rollout*

Mesh preview

Select the **Mesh preview** check box in the **Curvature Display** rollout to display the mesh preview of the sweep feature in the drawing area. When you select this check box, the **Mesh preview density** spinner will be displayed. Using this spinner, you can increase or decrease the number of lines of the mesh.

Zebra stripes

Select the **Zebra stripes** check box in the **Curvature Display** rollout to display the zebra stripes on the surface of the sweep feature. Using the Zebra stripes, you can easily identify surface wrinkles or defects.

Curvature combs

Select the **Curvature combs** check box to visualize the continuity of the curve and also to get a better idea of the quality of the surface of the sweep feature. The **Direction 1** and **Direction 2** check boxes, available below the **Curvature combs** check box in this rollout, are used to toggle the display of curvature combs along the direction 1 and direction 2. You can also adjust the scale and density of curvature combs by using the **Curvature Comb Scale** and **Curvature Comb Density** spinners, respectively.

Creating Cut-Sweep Features

CommandManager:	Features > Swept Cut
SOLIDWORKS menus:	Insert > Cut > Sweep
Toolbar:	Features > Extruded Cut > Swept Cut

You can also remove material from an existing feature or a model by creating a cut-sweep feature. To create a cut-sweep feature, choose the **Swept Cut** button from the **Features CommandManager**; the **Cut-Sweep PropertyManager** will be displayed, as shown in Figure 10-36. In SOLIDWORKS, you can create a cut-sweep feature by sweeping a sketch profile, circular profile or a solid profile along the specified path. If you need to create a cut-sweep feature by using a sketch profile, select the **Sketch Profile** radio button from the **Profile and Path** rollout. The options that will be displayed in the **Cut-Sweep PropertyManager** on selecting the **Sketch Profile** radio button are same as those discussed in the **Sweep PropertyManager** with the only difference that the options in this case are meant for the cut operation. Figure 10-37 shows the profile and the path for creating a cut-sweep feature. Figure 10-38 shows the cut-sweep feature created by selecting the **Sketch Profile** radio button from the **Profile and Path** rollout.

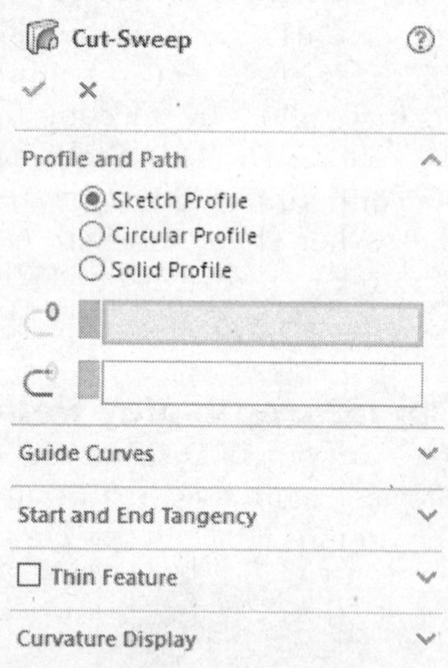

Figure 10-36** The **Cut-Sweep PropertyManager

To create circular Cut-sweep feature, you need to select the **Circular Profile** button from the **Profile and Path** rollout in the **Cut-Sweep PropertyManager**. Next, select the sketch or edge as the path along on which circular profile is to be created in the drawing area and then enter the diameter value in the **Diameter** spinner.

If you need to create a cut-sweep feature by using a disjoint body, select the **Solid Profile** radio button in the **Profile and Path** rollout. Select the solid body from the drawing area as the tool body. Note that the tool body must be convex, should not be merging with the main body, and should consist of revolved feature or extruded cylindrical feature. Next, select the path along which the cut-sweep feature is to be created. Note that the path must be continuous and should begin from a point on or within the tool body. The options in the **Options** rollout are similar to those discussed earlier. Figure 10-39 shows the solid body and the path for creating the cut-sweep feature. Figure 10-40 shows the cut-sweep feature created using the disjoint solid body.

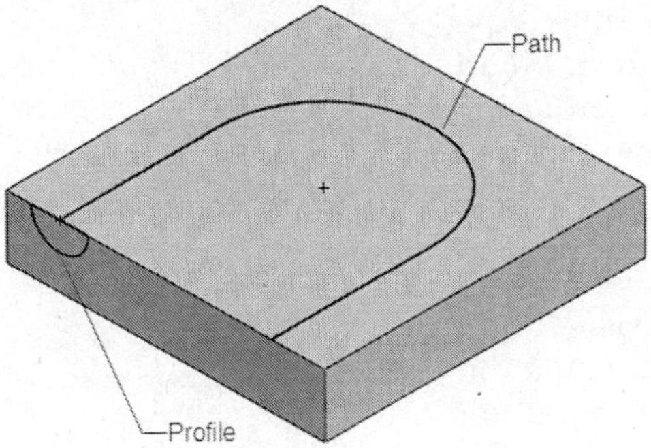

Figure 10-37 *Profile and path for creating the cut-sweep feature*

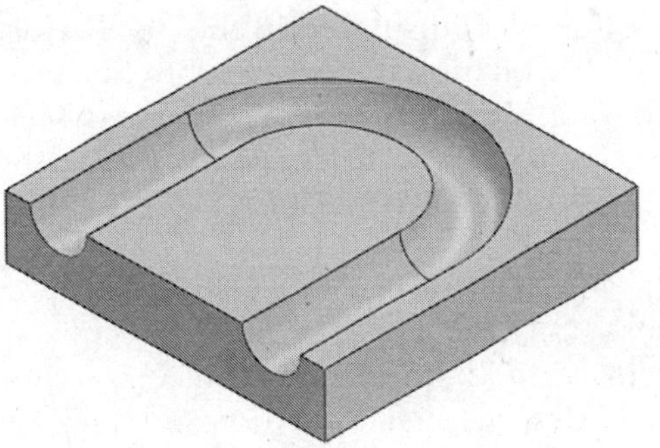

Figure 10-38 *Cut-sweep feature created using a profile and a path*

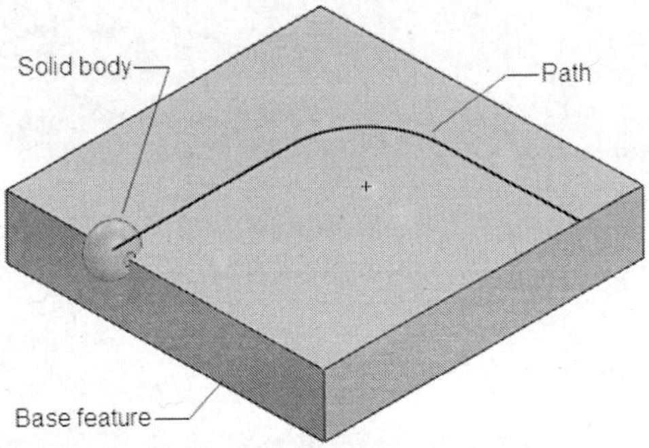

Figure 10-39 *Solid body and the path*

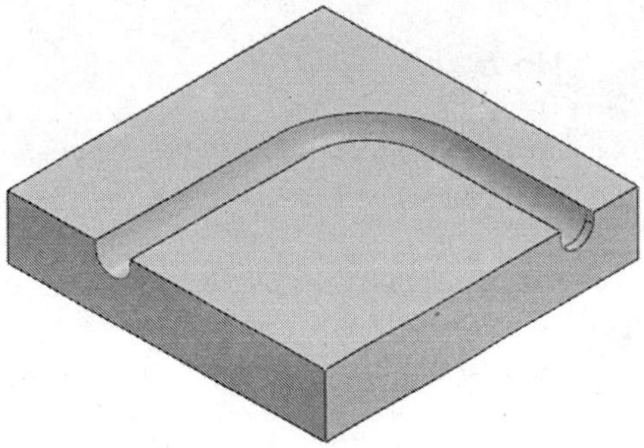

Figure 10-40 *Cut-sweep feature created using a solid body and a path*

Creating Loft Features

CommandManager:	Features > Lofted Boss/Base
SOLIDWORKS menus:	Insert > Boss/Base > Loft
Toolbar:	Features > Extruded Boss/Base > Lofted Boss/Base

 The loft features are created by blending more than one similar or dissimilar sections together to get a free form shape. These similar or dissimilar sections may or may not be parallel to each other. Note that the sections for the solid lofts should be the closed sketches.

To create a loft feature, draw the sketches and invoke the **Loft PropertyManager** by choosing the **Lofted Boss/Base** button from the **Features CommandManager**. The **Loft PropertyManager** is shown in Figure 10-41.

On invoking the **Loft PropertyManager**, you will be prompted to select at least two profiles. Select the profiles from the drawing area; the preview of the loft feature along with a connector will be displayed in it. Choose the **OK** button from the **Loft PropertyManager** to end the creation of the loft feature. Figure 10-42 shows preview of the loft feature along with a connector and Figure 10-43 shows the resulting loft feature. Note that if mesh is displayed in the preview of the loft feature, You can turn off this mesh by right-clicking on the preview and choosing **Mesh Preview > Clear All Meshed Faces** from the shortcut menu. In this textbook, the meshes are removed from all faces for a better display.

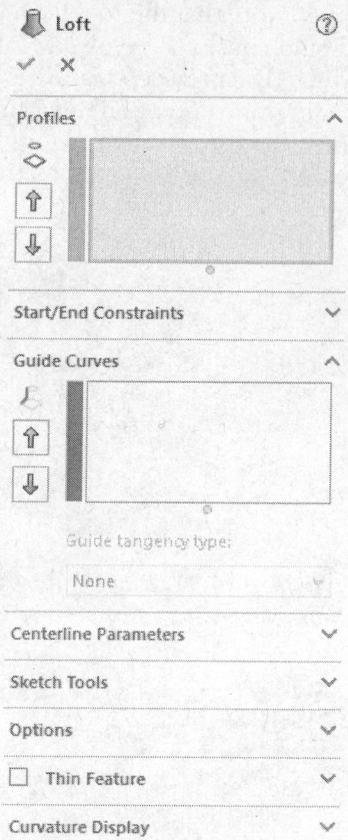

Figure 10-41** The **Loft PropertyManager

The loft feature can be reshaped using the handles of the connector that appear as the filled circle in the preview. To do so, press and hold the left mouse button on a handle, drag the cursor to specify a new location and release the left mouse button to place the connector on it. The process of controlling the loft shape using the connectors is known as Loft Synchronization. Figure 10-44 shows preview of the loft feature after modifying the location of the handle of the connector. Figure 10-45 shows the resulting loft feature.

Note

While creating a loft feature, relocating a connecting point using default connector is known as global twisting. This means if you change the location of one connecting point of the profile, the other connecting points of the profile will automatically change their positions with respect to the modified connecting point.

In global twisting of non-tangent profiles, the handles of the connectors move only from vertex to vertex.

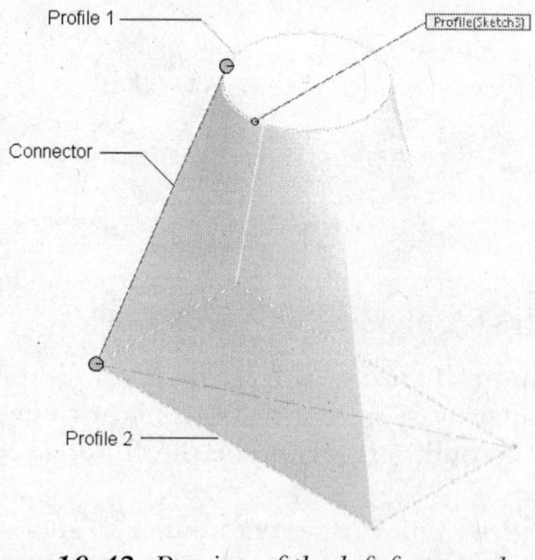

***Figure 10-42** Preview of the loft feature along with a connector*

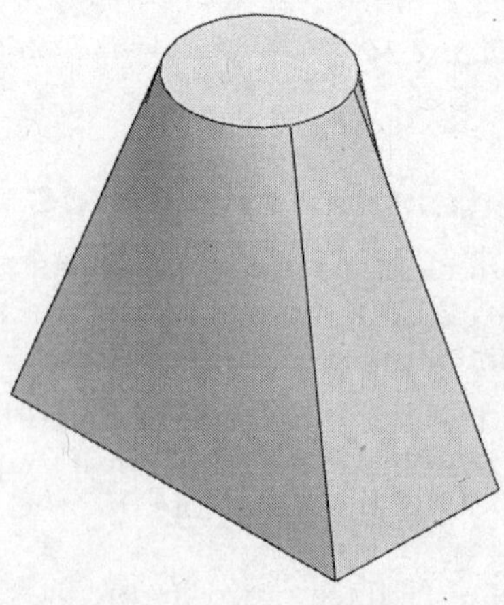

***Figure 10-43** Resulting loft feature*

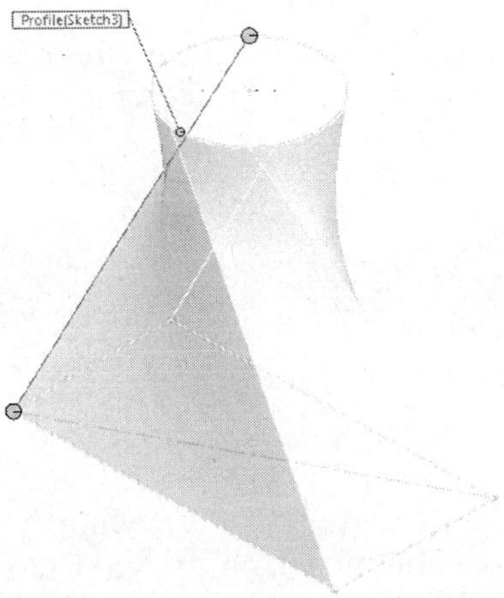

Figure 10-44 Preview of the loft feature after modifying the location of the connector

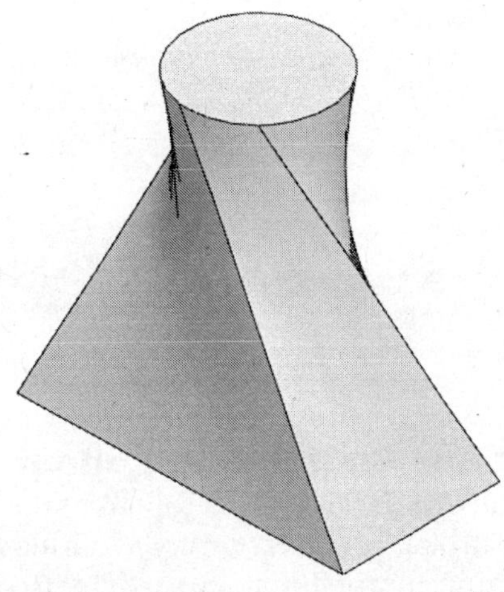

Figure 10-45 Loft feature resulted on modifying the location of the connector

To display all the connectors, right-click in the drawing area and then choose the **Show All Connectors** option from the shortcut menu displayed. The number of connectors displayed using this option depends on the maximum number of vertices in the start or the end loft section. If the start and end loft sections are circular, elliptical, or closed spline sections, then only one controller will be displayed.

You can also add more connectors to manipulate the loft feature. Connectors can be added to the straight profiles or the curved profiles. To add a connector, right-click in the sketch on the location where you need to add the connector to invoke the shortcut menu. Choose the **Add Connector** option from the shortcut menu; a connector will be added to the loft feature. Similarly, you can add more connectors using this option. You can also modify them by dragging their handles. Figure 10-46 shows preview of the loft feature after modifying all additional connectors and Figure 10-47 shows the resulting loft feature.

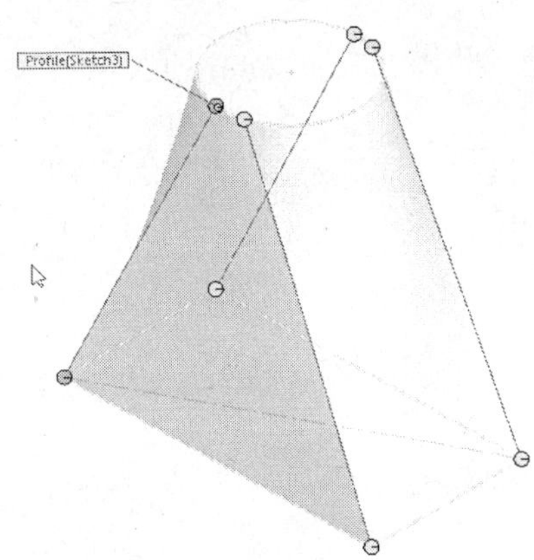

Figure 10-46 Preview after modifying all connectors

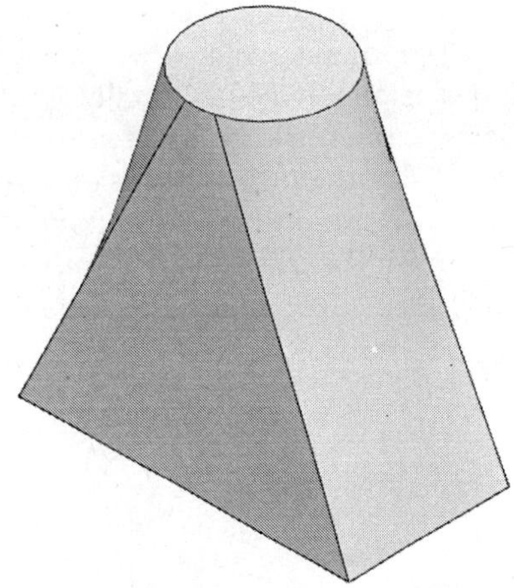

Figure 10-47 Resulting loft feature

Note

Relocating a connecting point using additional connectors is known as local twisting because twisting using one connector does not affect the other connecting points of a profile. Therefore, you can independently modify all the connectors simply by dragging the handles along the profile.

Tip

You can also use the ***Contour Select*** *tool to select a contour that will be used as profile to create the loft feature. You can also use a shared sketch, currently used by some other sketched feature as profile.*

Start/End Constraints Rollout

The **Start/End Constraints** rollout in the **Loft PropertyManager** is used to define the constraints at the start and end sections of a loft feature. You can define the normal, tangency, or continuity constraints for the loft feature. Expand this rollout to define the tangency. By default, the **None** option is selected in the **Start constraint** and **End constraint** drop-down lists. This implies that no constraint is applied to the loft feature. The other options in these drop-down lists are discussed next.

Normal To Profile

The **Normal To Profile** option is used to define the tangency normal to a profile. When you select this option from the **Start constraint** and **End constraint** drop-down lists, an arrow will be displayed at both the start and end sections. Also, some additional options will be displayed in the **Start/End Constraints** rollout, as shown in Figure 10-48. You can set the length of the tangency by dragging the tangency arrows attached to the sections or by setting the values in the **Start Tangent Length** and **End Tangent Length** spinners provided in this rollout. You can also specify a draft angle using the **Draft angle** spinner. You will notice that the **Apply to all** check box is selected by default, which implies that the tangency is applied evenly to all the vertices of the sections. However, on clearing these check boxes, you can apply the values of tangency individually to all the vertices. Figure 10-49 shows preview of the loft feature with the tangency arrows attached to the end sections of the loft feature. Figure 10-50 shows the tangency arrows attached to all vertices of the end sections of the loft feature. Figure 10-51 shows the resulting loft feature after specifying the length of tangent.

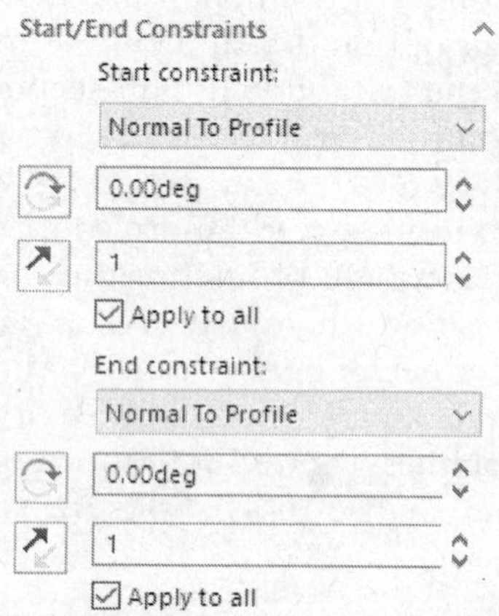

Figure 10-48 The ***Start/End Constraints*** *rollout with the* ***Normal To Profile*** *option selected*

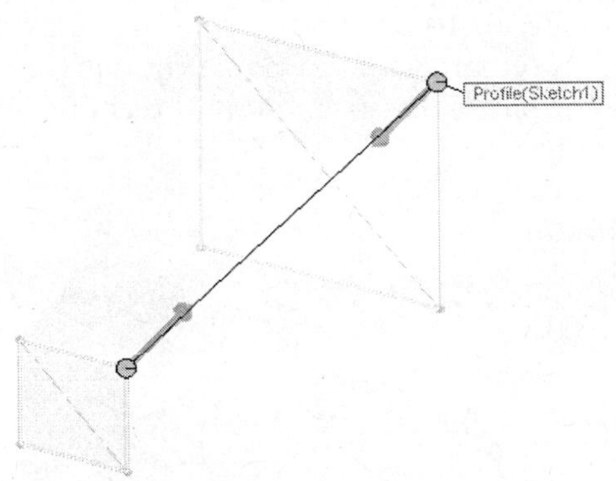

Figure 10-49 *Tangency arrows attached to the end sections*

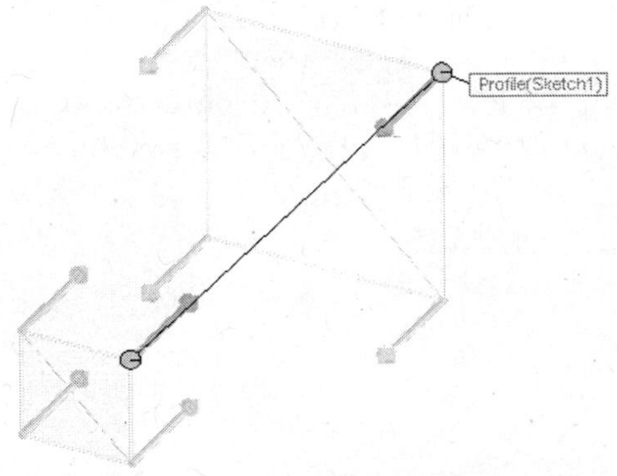

Figure 10-50 *Tangency arrows attached to all vertices*

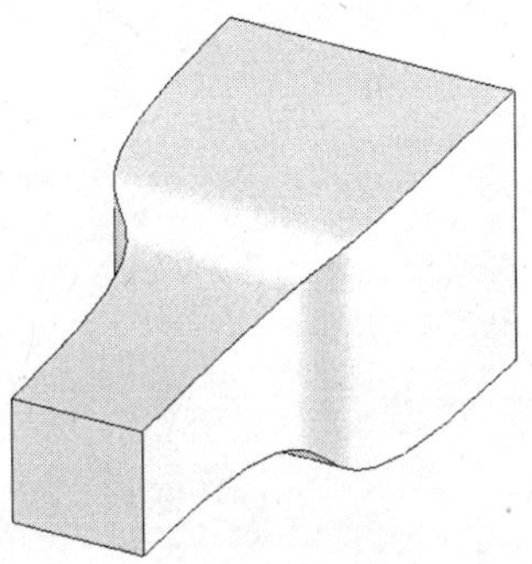

Figure 10-51 *Resulting loft feature*

Tip
*Right-click in the drawing area and invoke the shortcut menu and then choose **Hide All Connectors** to hide all the connectors. The connectors will not be displayed in the preview, but the settings made by them remain in the loft feature. To hide a specific connector, select it and invoke the shortcut menu. Then, choose the **Hide Connector** option.*

*If you choose the **Reset Connectors** option from the shortcut menu, all connectors and the settings related to the connectors will be deleted from the memory of the feature. Also, the default connector will be displayed with default connection points lying between the profiles of the loft feature.*

Direction Vector

The **Direction Vector** option is used to define the tangency at the start and end of the loft feature by defining a direction vector. On selecting this option, you will be provided with the **Direction Vector** selection box and the spinners to define the length of the tangents and the draft angle. You need to select the direction vectors to specify the tangent direction at the start and end of the loft feature. Specify the length of the tangents using the spinners in the **Start/End Constraints** rollout. The **Start/End Constraints** rollout with the **Direction Vector** option selected is shown in Figure 10-52.

Figure 10-53 shows sections for the loft feature. Figure 10-54 shows initial preview of the loft feature. Figure 10-55 shows preview of the loft feature with normal at the start section of the loft feature and Figure 10-56 shows the normal at the start and end sections of the loft feature. Figure 10-57 shows the final loft feature.

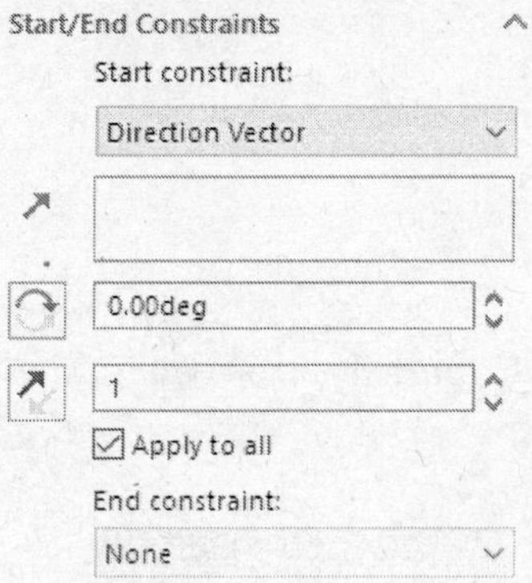

***Figure 10-52** The **Start/End Constraints** rollout with the **Direction Vector** option selected*

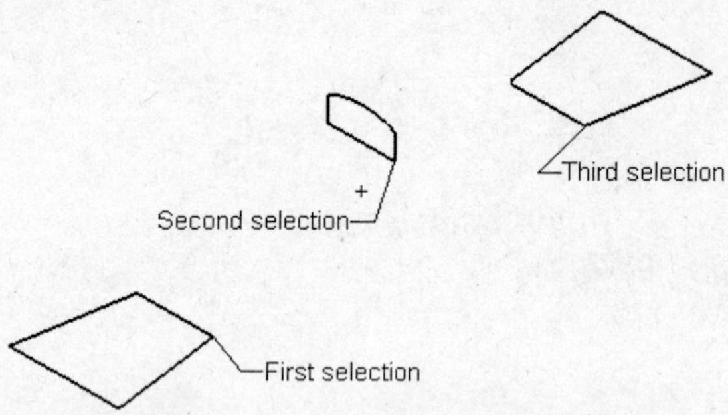

***Figure 10-53** Sections, selection points, and sequence of selection to create the loft feature*

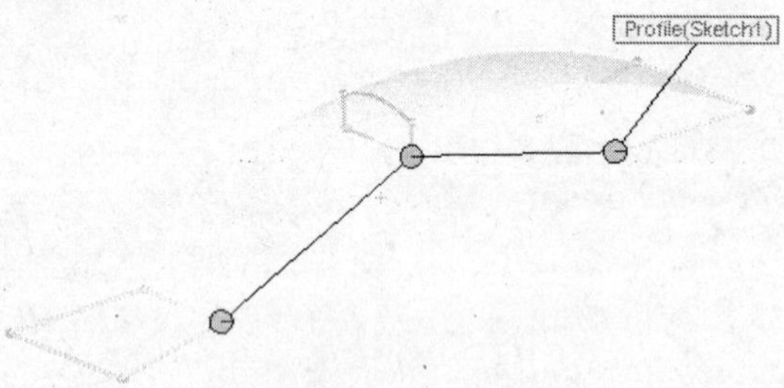

***Figure 10-54** Preview of the loft feature*

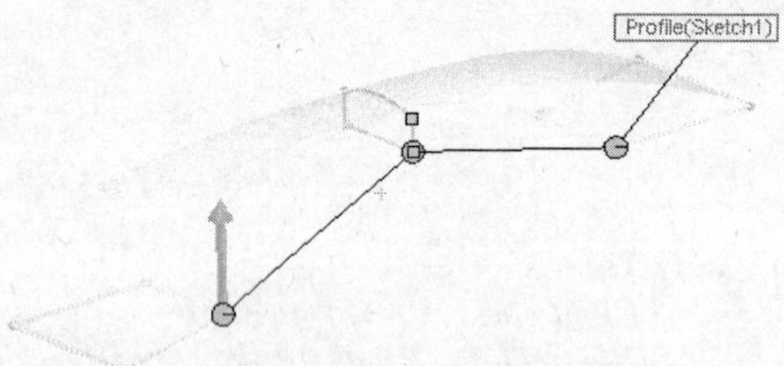

***Figure 10-55** Normal applied to the start section*

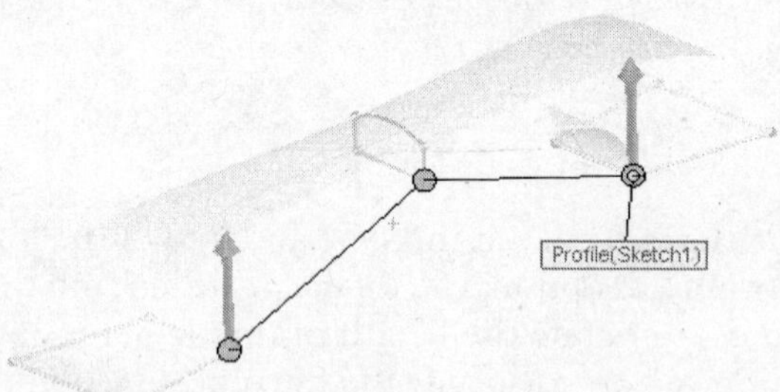

***Figure 10-56** Normal applied at the start and end sections of the loft feature*

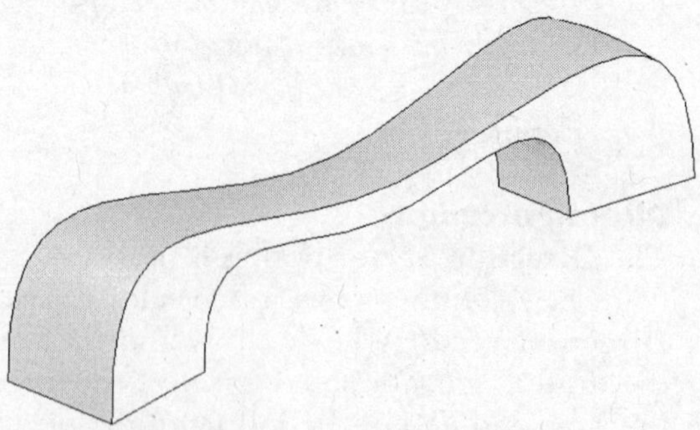

***Figure 10-57** The final loft feature*

Tangency to Face

This option will be available only if the resulting loft feature will lie on an existing feature. If you select this option from the **Start constraint** or **End constraint** drop-down list, the resulting loft feature will maintain tangency along adjacent curved faces. Also, the face along which the tangency is to be maintained will be highlighted. You can also switch between the faces along which you need to maintain the tangency by using the **Next Face** button. The spinners below the **Next Face** button can be used to specify the length of the start and end tangents.

Curvature To Face

This option will be available only if the resulting loft feature lies on an existing feature. If you select the **Curvature To Face** option from the **Start constraint** or **End constraint** drop-down list, the resulting loft feature will maintain curvature along adjacent curved faces. Also, the face along which the curvature is to be maintained will be highlighted. You can also switch between the faces along which you need to maintain the tangency using the **Next Face** button.

Guide Curves Rollout

You can create a loft feature by specifying the guide curves between the profiles to define the path of transition of the loft feature. The sketches drawn for the guide curve must coincide with the sketches that define the loft sections.

Figure 10-58 shows the profiles and the guide curves for creating a loft feature. Figure 10-59 shows the loft feature created using guide curves.

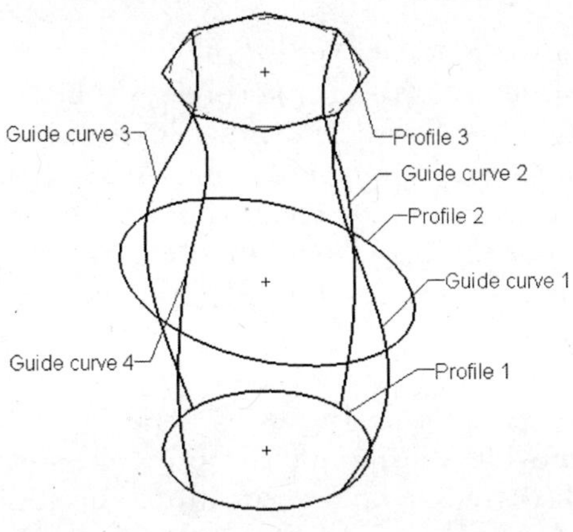

Figure 10-58 *Profiles and guide curves*

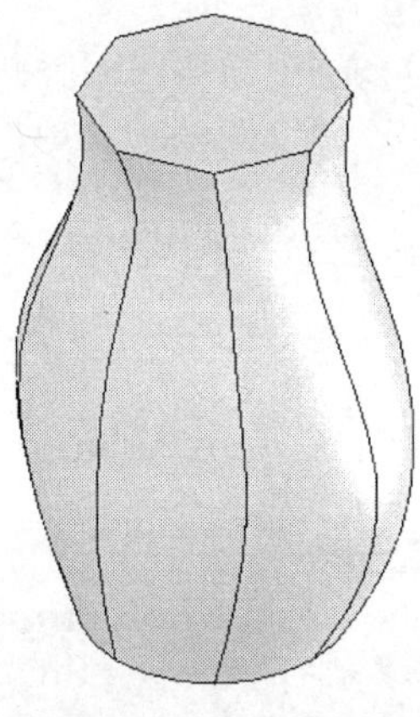

Figure 10-59 *Loft feature created using profiles and guide curve*

Centerline Parameters Rollout

The **Centerline Parameters** rollout is used to create a loft feature by blending two or more than two sections along a specified path. You can specify the centerline and the guide curves of a loft feature created by using the centerline. Note that the path that specifies the transition is called the centerline and the profile that defines the external shape are the guide curves. The options in this rollout are discussed next.

Centerline

On selecting the sketch that defines the centerline for the loft feature, the name of the sketch will be displayed in the **Centerline** selection box.

Number of sections

The **Number of sections** slider bar provided in the **Centerline Parameters** rollout is used to define the number of intermediate sections, which further defines the accuracy and smoothness of the loft feature.

The **Show Sections** button and the **Section Number** spinner in this rollout are used to display the intermediate sections, as discussed earlier. Figure 10-60 shows the sketches of the profiles and the centerline used to create the loft feature. Figure 10-61 shows the resulting loft feature.

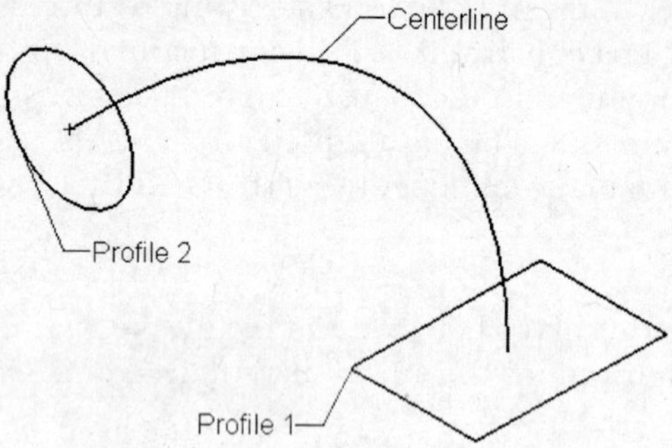

Figure 10-60 *Profiles and centerline*

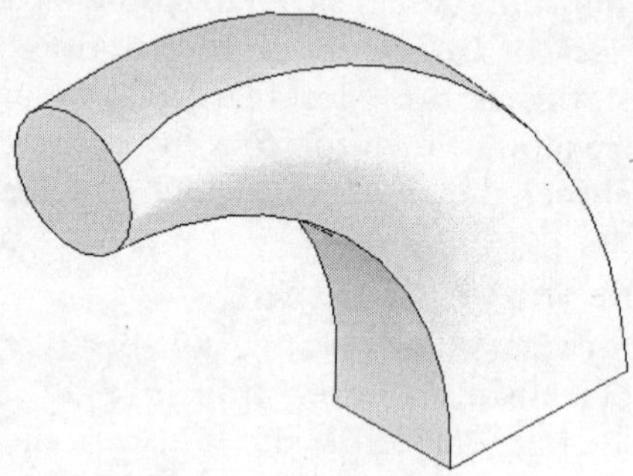

Figure 10-61 *Resulting loft feature*

Sketch Tools

You can also select the 3D sketches as the profile or the guide curves for the loft feature. If you create the loft feature using the 3D sketches, the sketches or the guide curves will be from the same 3D sketch. Therefore, use the **Selection Manager** to select the individual loops as the sketch profiles and create the loft feature. The button in the **Sketch Tools** rollout is used to edit the loft features that are created using the 3D sketch. This button will be enabled only when you edit the loft feature created by using the 3D sketches. While editing, choose the **Drag Sketch** button to drag the 3D sketch. Choose the **Undo sketch drag** button to undo the dragging of the 3D sketch. You will learn more about the 3D sketches later in this chapter.

Options Rollout

The **Options** rollout in the **Loft PropertyManager** provides the options to improve the creation of a loft feature. These options are the same as those discussed in the sweep feature. The additional option in this rollout is discussed next.

Close loft

A closed loft feature is the one in which the start and end sections of the loft features are joined together. The **Close loft** check box is selected to create a closed loft feature. Note that the angle between the start and end sections should be more than 180 degrees to create the closed loft feature and also there should be at least three sections. Figure 10-62 shows a loft feature created with the **Close loft** check box cleared. Figure 10-63 shows a loft feature created with the **Close loft** check box selected.

You can also create a thin loft feature by defining the thin parameters by using the **Thin Feature** rollout. The options in this rollout are the same as those discussed in the earlier chapters. Figure 10-64 shows a thin loft feature created using the options in the **Thin Feature** rollout of the **Loft PropertyManager**.

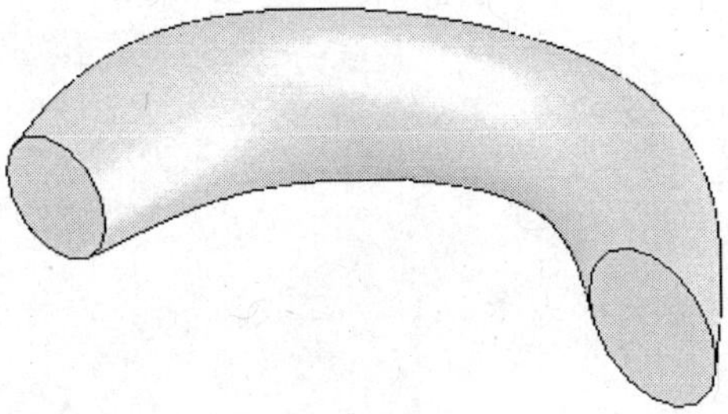

Figure 10-62 *Loft feature created with the* ***Close loft*** *check box cleared*

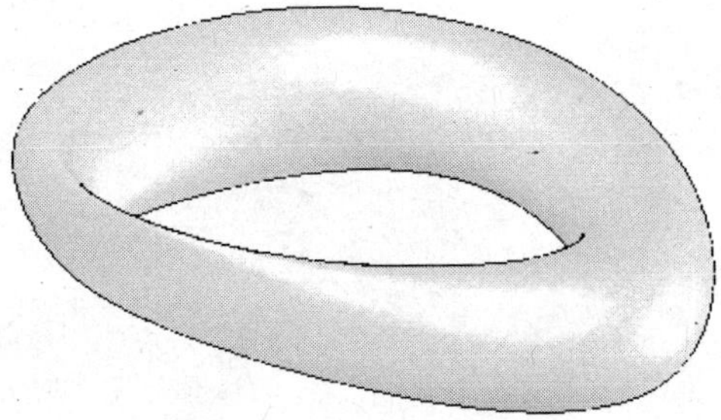

Figure 10-63 *Loft feature created with the* ***Close loft*** *check box selected*

Curvature Display Rollout

The **Curvature Display** rollout in the **Loft PropertyManager** is used to display the mesh preview, zebra stripes, and curvature combs of the sweep feature. The options in this rollout are the same as those discussed for the sweep feature.

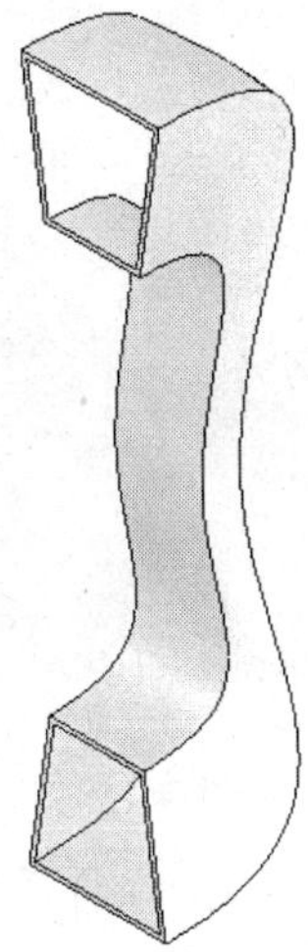

Figure 10-64 *A thin loft feature*

Note

To create a smooth loft feature between a circle and a polygon, it is a good practice to split the circle into a number of arcs. The number of arcs that form the circle should be same as that of the sides of the polygon. Now, if you create the loft feature, the number of connecting points in both the sections will be predefined which results in a smoother loft feature.

Adding a Section to a Loft Feature

After creating a loft feature, you can also add a section to it by selecting one of the side faces of the loft feature and then right-clicking to invoke the shortcut menu. Choose the **Add Loft Section** option from it; the **Add Loft Section PropertyManager** will be displayed. You will be provided with a plane that can be moved or rotated dynamically. To move the plane, place the cursor on the arrows displayed on it, press and hold the left mouse button, and drag the cursor to move the plane. To rotate the plane, select one of its edges and drag the cursor. Set the position of the plane by dynamically moving and rotating it to specify the position to add the sketch. Figures 10-65 and 10-66 show the planes being moved and rotated. After specifying the position of the plane, choose the **OK** button from the **Add Loft Section PropertyManager**. Figure 10-67 shows the section added to the loft feature. This is a closed section created using a spline.

Expand the **Loft1** feature and select the sketch that is added using the **Add Loft Section** tool. Right-click and choose the **Edit Sketch** option from the shortcut menu. Edit the sketch, as shown in Figure 10-68, and rebuild the part. Figure 10-69 shows the modified loft feature.

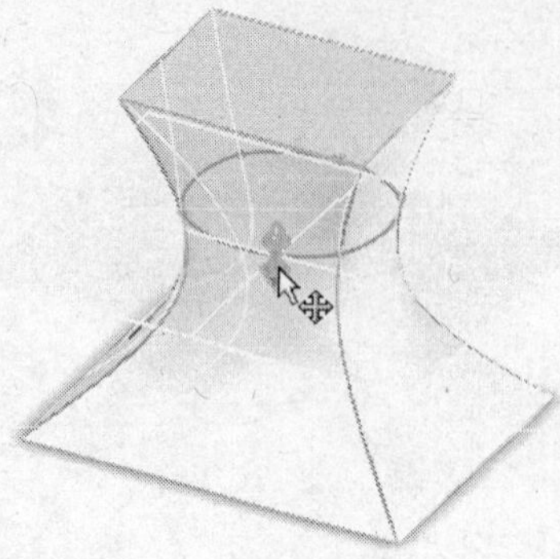

Figure 10-65 *The plane being moved*

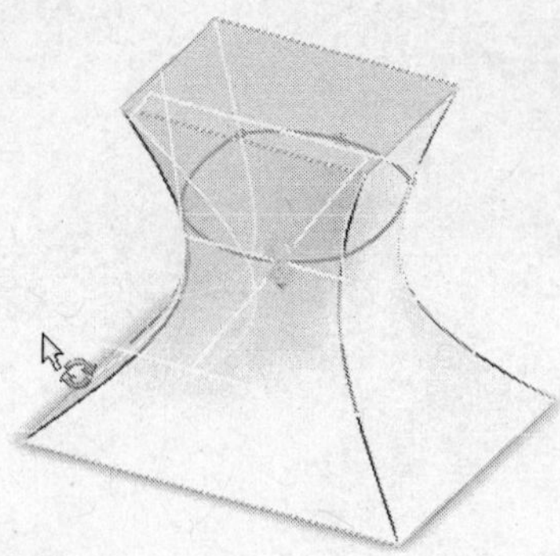

Figure 10-66 *The plane being rotated*

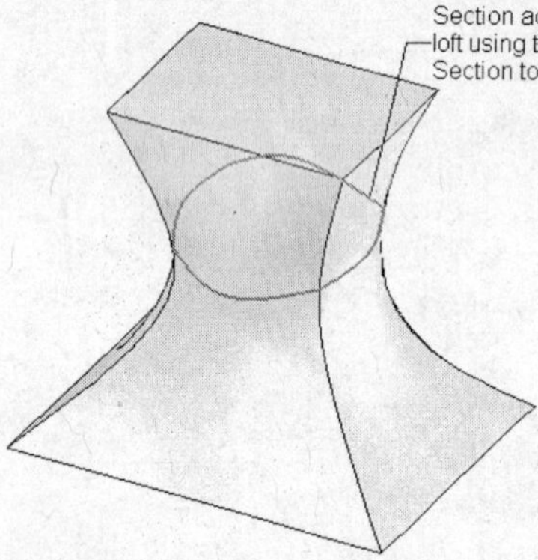

Figure 10-67 *Section added to the loft feature*

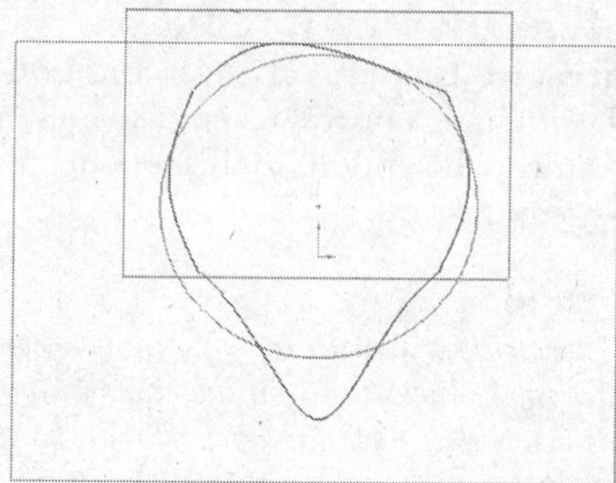

Figure 10-68 *Edited loft section*

Note

You can also display a mesh in the preview of a loft feature. To do so, right-click in the drawing area; a shortcut menu will be invoked. Choose ***Mesh Preview > Mesh All Faces*** *from this menu to display the mesh preview. The mesh preview will only be displayed on the non-planar faces and not on the planar faces. To display a mesh preview on all faces of the loft preview, you need to change the planar faces to non-planar faces by manipulating the connectors.*

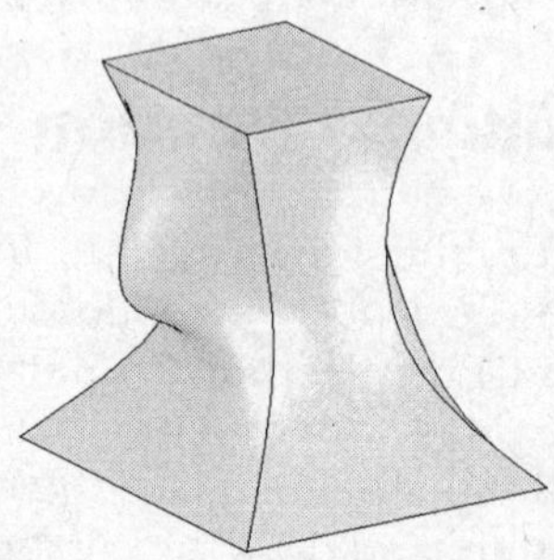

Figure 10-69 *The loft feature after modification*

Creating Lofted Cuts

CommandManager:	Features > Lofted Cut
SOLIDWORKS menus:	Insert > Cut > Loft
Toolbar:	Features > Extruded Cut > Lofted cut

You can remove the material in a part by using the **Cut Loft PropertyManager**. This PropertyManager is invoked by choosing **Insert > Cut > Loft** from the SOLIDWORKS menus and the options in this PropertyManager are the same as discussed in the **Lofted Boss/Base** tool.

Creating 3D Sketches

CommandManager:	Sketch > Sketch > 3D Sketch
SOLIDWORKS menus:	Insert > 3D Sketch
Toolbar:	Sketch > Sketch > 3D Sketch

In the earlier chapters, you have learned to draw 2D sketches in the sketching environment. In this chapter, you will learn to draw 3D sketches. 3D sketches are mostly used to create 3D paths for the sweep features, 3D curves, and so on. Figure 10-70 shows a chair frame created by sweeping a profile along a 3D path.

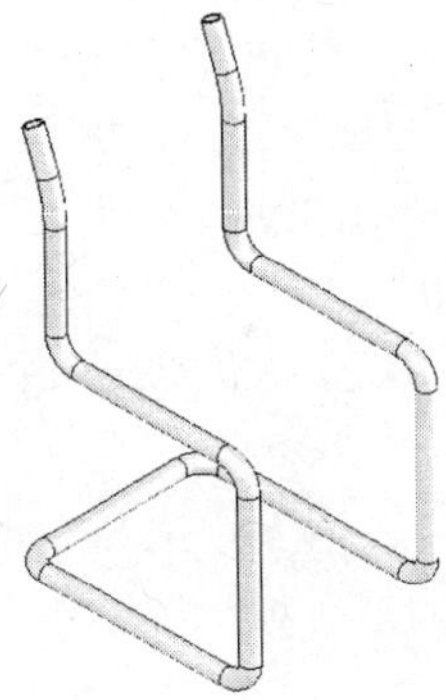

***Figure 10-70** A chair frame created by sweeping a profile along a 3D path*

To draw a 3D sketch, choose the **3D Sketch** button from the **Sketch CommandManager**; the 3D sketching environment will be invoked and the origin will be displayed in red color. You do not need to select a sketching plane to draw a 3D sketch. On invoking the 3D sketching environment, some of the sketching tools are activated in the **Sketch CommandManager**. These tools can be used in the 3D sketching environment and are discussed next.

Line

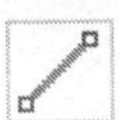

It is better to orient the view to isometric for drawing lines in the 3D sketching environment. Choose the **Line** button from the **Sketch CommandManager**; the **Insert Line PropertyManager** will be displayed. The **As sketched** radio button is selected in the **Orientation** rollout, while the other options are disabled. The select cursor will be replaced by the line cursor with **XY** displayed at its bottom. This implies that by default, the sketch will be drawn in the XY plane. The coordinate system is also displayed in the current plane. You can toggle between the default planes using the TAB key. On doing so, the orientation of the coordinate system also modifies with respect to the current plane. Move the cursor to the location from where you want to start sketching. On specifying the start point of the line, you are provided with a space handle.

You can also toggle the plane after specifying the start point of the line. The coordinate system will also change with respect to the current plane. Move the cursor to specify the endpoint of the line. Its length will be displayed above the line cursor. Specify the endpoint of the line at this location. You will notice that a rubber-band line segment is attached to the cursor. Toggle the plane using the TAB key, if required. Next, move the cursor to draw another line and specify its endpoint at the desired location. Right-click to invoke the shortcut menu and choose the **Select** or **Line** option to exit from the tool. Figures 10-71 through 10-73 show sketching in different planes in the 3D sketching environment. Figure 10-74 shows an example of a 3D sketch.

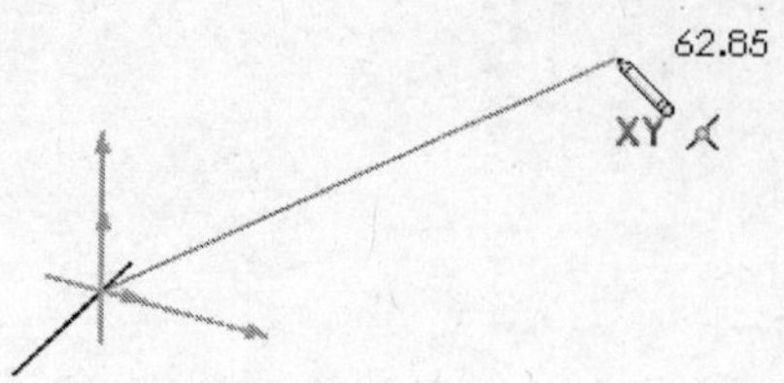

Figure 10-71 *Sketching in the XY plane*

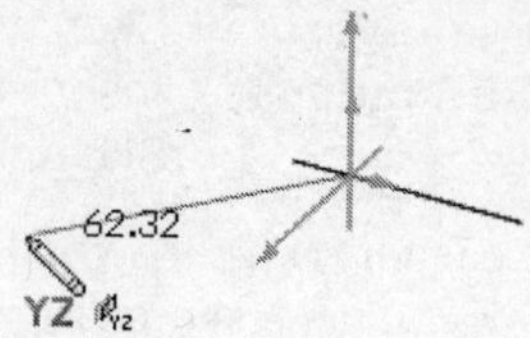

Figure 10-72 *Sketching in the YZ plane*

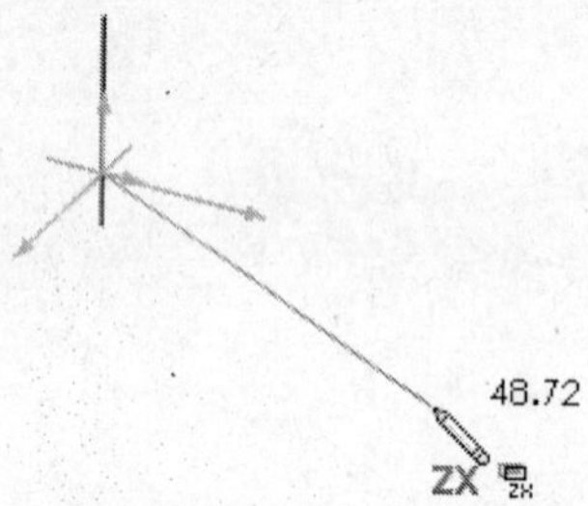

Figure 10-73 *Sketching in the ZX plane*

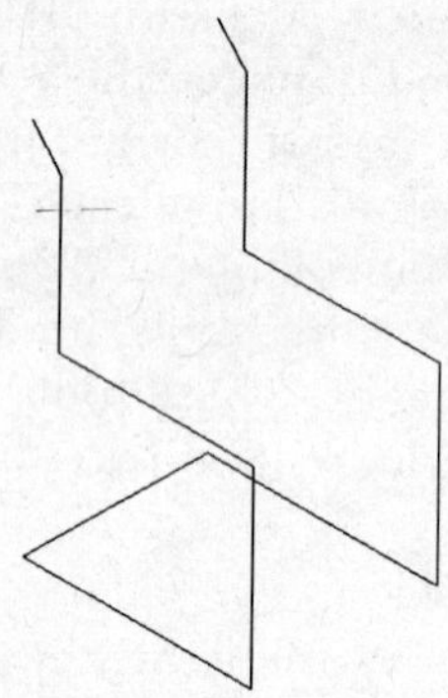

Figure 10-74 *3D sketch created using the* ***Line*** *tool*

Spline

To draw a spline in the 3D sketching environment, choose the **Spline** button from the **Sketch CommandManager**; the select cursor will be replaced by the spline cursor. Move it to the desired location to start the sketch. Specify the start point of the spline; a space handle will be displayed. You can toggle between the default planes using the TAB key. Move the cursor and specify the second point of the spline. Follow the same procedure to continue drawing the spline. To end the spline creation, right-click and choose the **Select** or **Spline** option from the shortcut menu.

Point

Choose the **Point** button from the **Sketch CommandManager**; the select cursor will be replaced by the point cursor. Use the left mouse button to place points.

Centerline

You can also draw centerlines in the 3D sketching environment. To do so, invoke the 3D sketching environment and orient the view to isometric. Choose **Line > Centerline** from the **Sketch CommandManager** to draw a centerline; the select cursor will be replaced by the line cursor. The procedure of drawing the centerline is the same as that discussed for drawing lines in the 2D sketching environment.

The dimensioning of 3D sketches is the same as the dimensioning of 2D sketches.

Creating Grid Systems

In SOLIDWORKS, you can easily draw the profiles of models, such as a book shelf or a multi-story building structure with columns and roofs, by using grid systems and 3D sketches. To create a grid system, choose **Insert > Reference Geometry > Grid System** from the SOLIDWORKS menus; the 3D sketching environment will be invoked and you will be prompted to draw a sketch. Draw the profile that needs to be replicated and exit the 3D sketching environment; the **GridSystem PropertyManager** will be displayed. Figure 10-75 shows the profile drawn and Figure 10-76 shows the **GridSystem PropertyManager**. In this PropertyManager, set the number of levels and the distance between the levels in their respective spinners in the **Level Parameters** rollout; the **Level details** table below the **Default Height** spinner will be updated accordingly. If you want the levels to be spread unevenly, then you can set the height in the **Level details** table.

If you want to connect each level by discontinuous lines, select the **3DSketch Split Lines** check box. If this check box is not selected then the profile in each level will be connected by continuous 3D line. If the **Autonumber Balloons** check box is selected then on editing the sketch, the keypoints or the vertices along the X and Y directions will be numbered and updated automatically.

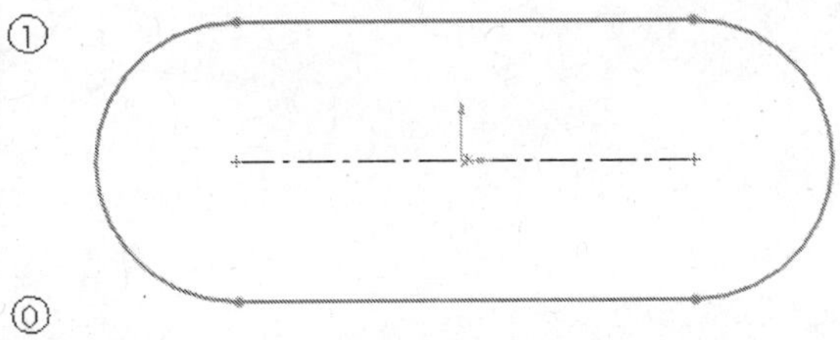

Figure 10-75 *The profile to be replicated*

After setting all the parameters, choose the **OK** button; the grid system will be displayed, as shown in Figure 10-77. If the 3D sketch lines are not displayed automatically, then expand the **Grid System** node in the **FeatureManager Design Tree**. Next, right-click on the **3D Sketch** sub-node and choose the **Show** option; the 3D sketch will be displayed in the grid system, as shown in Figure 10-78.

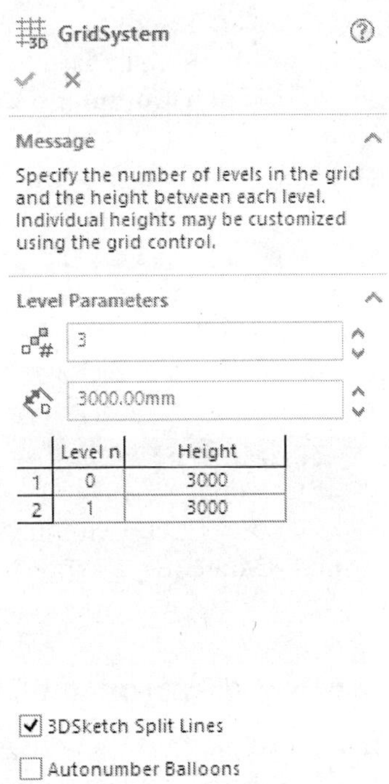

Figure 10-76 *The **Grid System PropertyManager***

To edit the profile, right-click on the **Grid System** node and choose the **Edit Sketch** option; the 3D sketching environment will be invoked. Edit the profile and exit; the grid system will be modified. Figure 10-79 shows the grid system of the modified profile.

On expanding the **Grid System** node, you will notice that the **Surface-Extrude** sub-node is also in the **FeatureManager Design Tree** and the **Surface Bodies** node is created in the **FeatureManager Design Tree**. This is because the grid system displayed is a surface. But, by default, the surface is hidden. To view the surface, expand the **Surface Bodies** node in the **FeatureManager Design Tree**; the names of the grid systems available in the drawing will be listed as sub-nodes. Right-click on a **Grid System** sub-node and choose the **Show** option to view the surface.

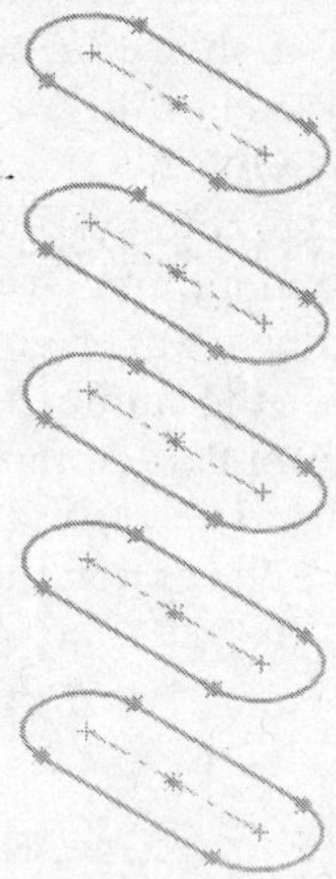

Figure 10-77 The grid system without 3D sketch lines

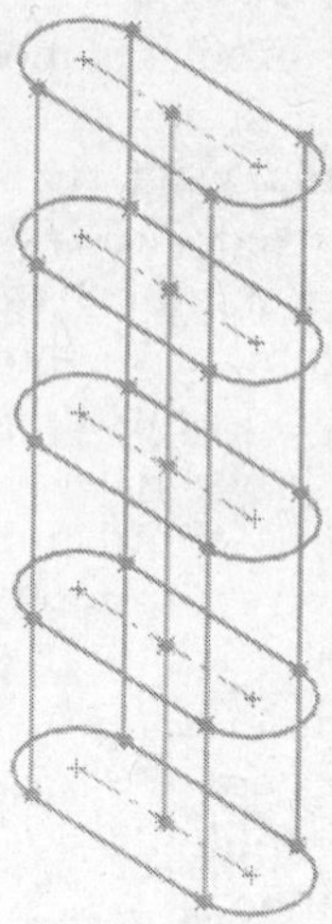

Figure 10-78 The grid system with 3D sketch lines

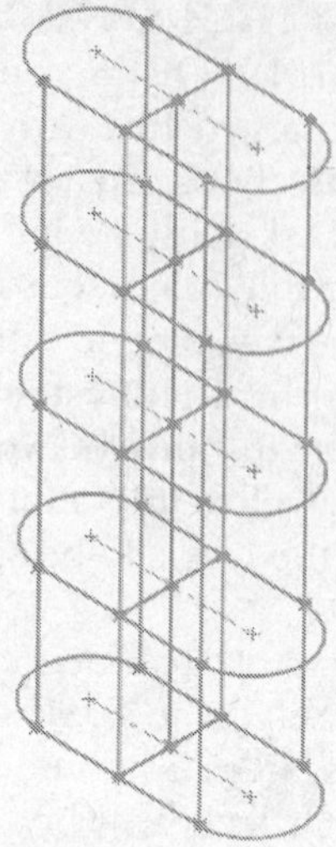

Figure 10-79 The grid system after modifying the profile

Mirroring Sketch Entities in a 3D Sketch

In SOLIDWORKS 2020, you can mirror the sketch entities of a 3D sketch. To do so, start a 3D sketch and then create sketch entities. In the open sketch, choose the **Mirror Entities** button from the **Sketch CommandManager**; the **Mirror PropertyManager** will be displayed. Select the entities from the drawing area and then select a plane or a planar entity from the drawing area as the mirror line; the selected entities will be mirrored.

Editing 3D Sketches

You can edit a 3D sketch using the editing tools such as **Convert Entities**, **Sketch Chamfer**, **Trim Entities**, **Fit Spline**, **Sketch Fillet**, **Extend Entities**, **Construction Geometry**, and **Split Entities**. All these tools have been discussed in the previous chapters.

Creating Curves

In SOLIDWORKS, you can create various types of curves that can be used to create complex shapes. The tools to create such curves are grouped together in the **Curves** flyout of the **Features CommandManager**, as shown in Figure 10-80. The curve types that can be created by using these tools are discussed next.

Creating a Projected Curve

CommandManager:	Features > Curves > Project Curve
SOLIDWORKS menus:	Insert > Curve > Projected
Toolbar:	Curves > Project Curve

The **Project Curve** tool is used to project a closed/open sketched entity on one or more than one planar or curved faces. You can also project a sketched entity on another sketched entity to create a 3D curve. To create a projected curve, draw at least two sketches or a single sketch and at least one feature that do not lie on the same plane. Next, choose the **Project Curve** tool from the **Curves** flyout of the **Features CommandManager**; the **Projected Curve PropertyManager** will be displayed, as shown in Figure 10-81. Also, the confirmation corner will be displayed in the drawing area. The two options to create projected curves are discussed next.

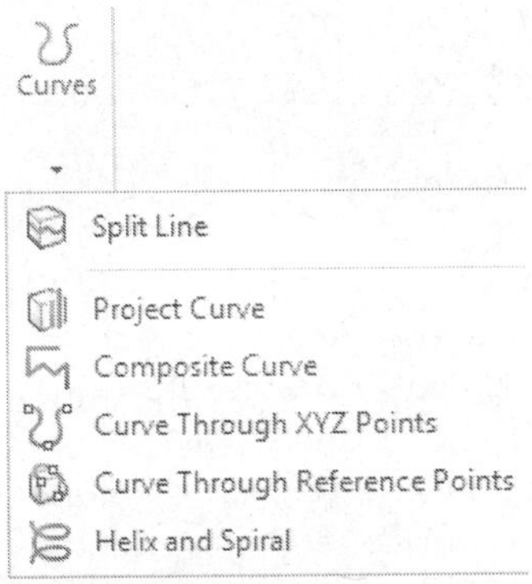

Figure 10-80 Tools in the ***Curves*** *flyout*

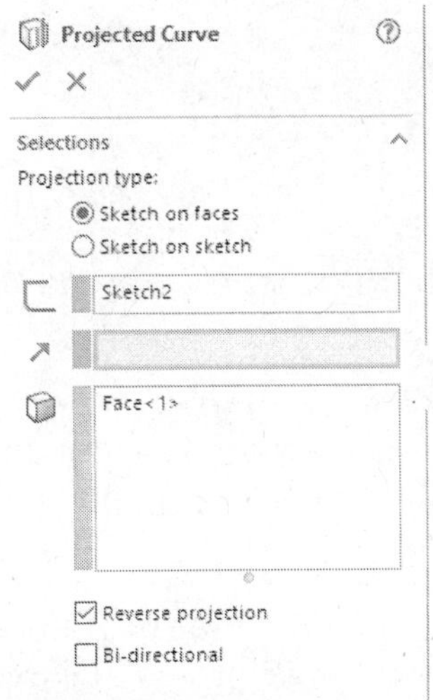

Figure 10-81 The ***Projected Curve PropertyManager***

Sketch on Faces

The **Sketch on faces** radio button in the **Projection type** area is selected by default and is used to project a sketch on a planar or curved faces. The **Projected Curve PropertyManager** with the **Sketch on faces** radio button selected is shown in Figure 10-81. On selecting this option, the **Sketch to Project** and the **Projection Faces** selection boxes will be displayed in the **Selections** rollout. Select the sketch from the drawing area and the face or faces on which you want to project the sketch. The selected sketch will be highlighted in blue and the selected face will be highlighted in magenta. The **Direction of Projection** selection box is used to select the direction of projection as an axis, linear sketch entity, linear edge, plane, or a planar face. This selection box gets available only on choosing the **Sketch on faces** radio button. The arrow provided in the drawing area is used to reverse the direction of the projection. You can also reverse the direction of projection using the **Reverse projection** check box. Choose the **OK** button from the **Projected Curve PropertyManager** or choose **OK** from the confirmation corner. Figure 10-82 shows the sketch to be selected for projection and also the face to be selected on which the sketch will be projected. Figure 10-83 shows the resulting projected curve.

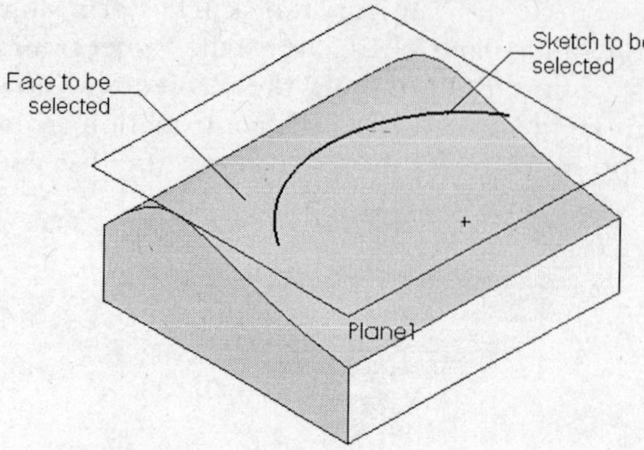

Figure 10-82 Sketch and face to be selected

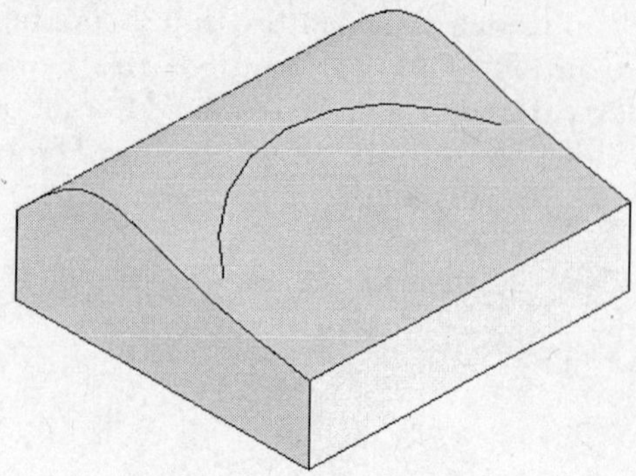

Figure 10-83 Resulting projected curve

Sketch on Sketch

If this radio button is selected in the **Project Curve PropertyManager**, you are prompted to select two sketches to project one over another. Select the two sketches that do not lie on the same plane; their names will be displayed in the **Sketches to Project** selection box. The preview of the projected curve will also be displayed in the drawing area. Choose the **OK** button from the **Projected Curve PropertyManager** or choose **OK** from the confirmation corner to create projected curve. Figure 10-84 shows the two sketches selected to create a projected curve. Figure 10-85 shows preview of the projected curve. Figure 10-86 shows the resulting projected curve.

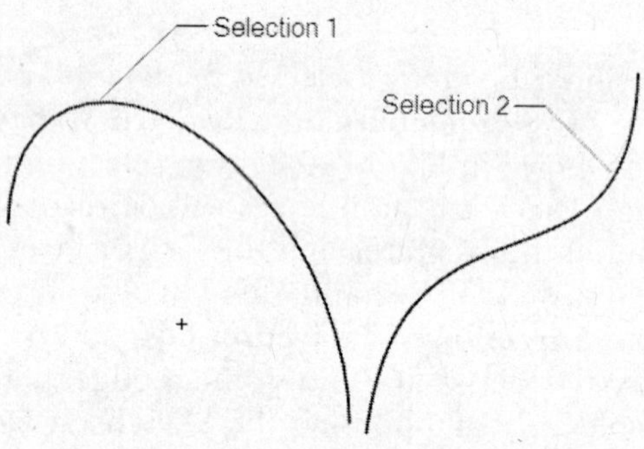

Figure 10-84 Sketches to be selected

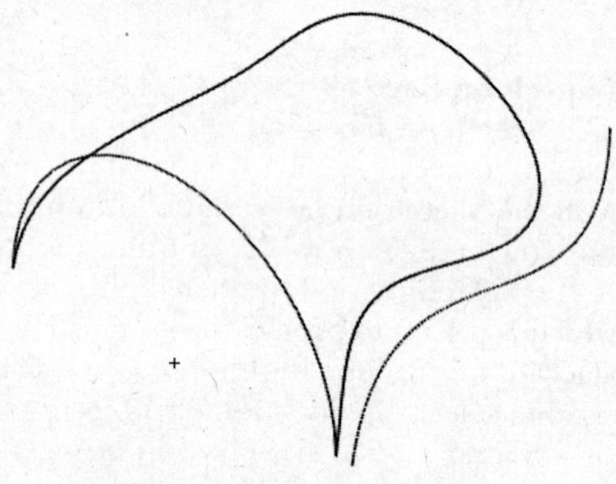

Figure 10-85 Preview of the projected curve

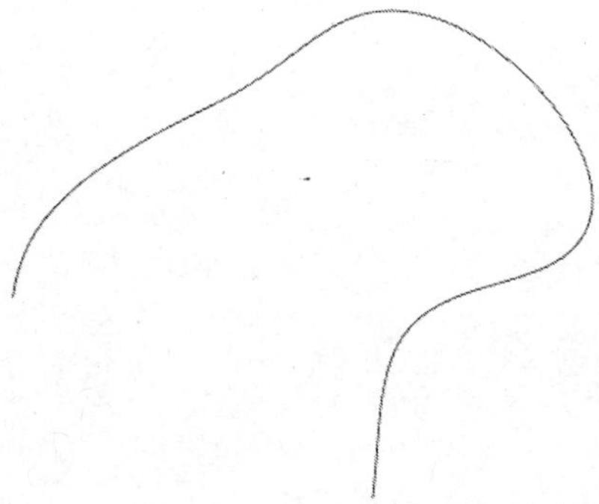

Figure 10-86 Resulting projected curve

Creating Split Lines

CommandManager:	Features > Curves > Split Line
SOLIDWORKS menus:	Insert > Curve > Split Line
Toolbar:	Curves > Split Line

The **Split Line** tool is generally used to project a sketch on a planar or curved face. This sketch in turn splits or divides the single face into two or more faces. To split a face, choose the **Split Line** button from the **Features CommandManager**; the **Split Line PropertyManager** will be displayed, as shown in Figure 10-87. The three options in this PropertyManager are discussed next.

Silhouette

You can split a curved face by creating a silhouette line at the intersection of the projection of direction entity and the curved face. To do so, select the **Silhouette** radio button, if not selected by default, from the **Type of Split** rollout. Next select an edge, line or plane to define the direction of pull; the selected entity will be highlighted. Next, select the curved face; the selected face will be highlighted. Choose the **OK** button from the **Split Line PropertyManager** or choose the **OK** button from the confirmation corner. The curved face will be divided into two or more faces. The **Angle** spinner in the **Selections** rollout is used to define the draft angle for creating the silhouette line. By default, the value in this spinner is set to 0 degree.

Consider a case in which you need to split a circular face using this option. The plane will be selected to define the direction of pull. Figure 10-88 shows the plane and the face to be selected. Figure 10-89 shows the resulting split line created to split the selected face.

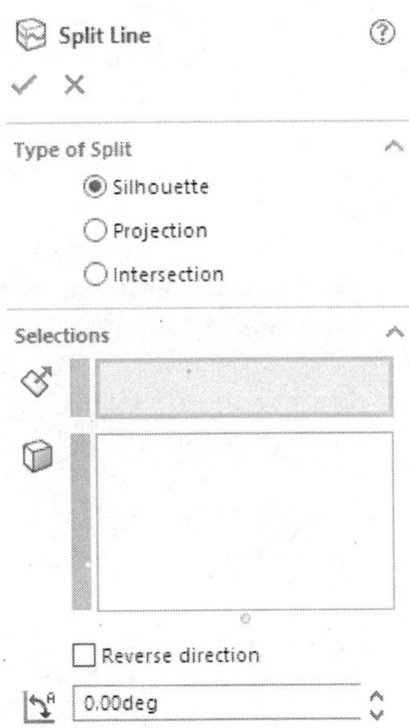

*Figure 10-87 The **Split Line** PropertyManager*

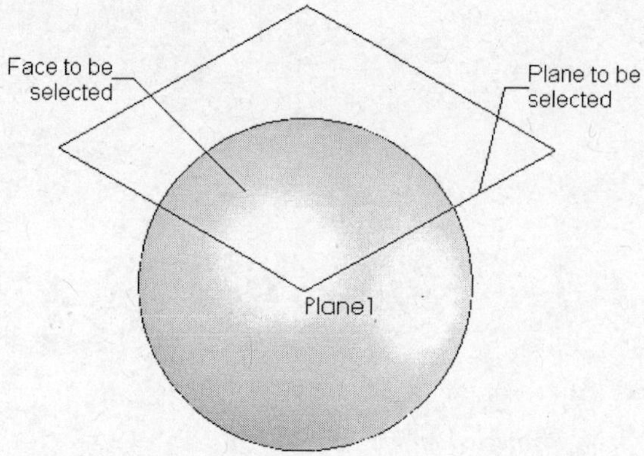

Figure 10-88 *Plane and face to be selected*

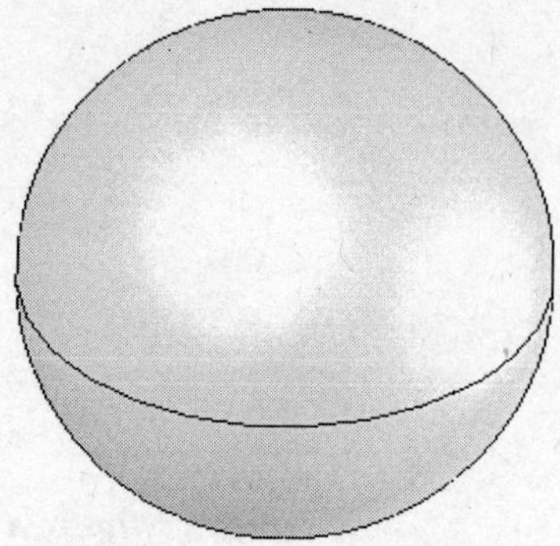

Figure 10-89 *Resulting split line*

Tip

You can also use the ***Contour Select Tool*** *to select contours for creating a projected curve or a split line.*

Projection

You can project a sketched entity onto a planar or curved face to create a split line on it. A split line splits the selected face on which a sketch is projected. The sketch selected can have multiple closed contours or it can be a text. Also, you can project the sketch on multiple bodies. To use this option, select the **Projection** radio button from the **Type of Split** rollout in the **Split Line PropertyManager**, as shown in Figure 10-90. On doing so, you will be prompted to change the type of split, or select the sketch to project, direction, and faces to be split. First select the sketch and then select the face to be split. Choose the **OK** button from the **Split Line PropertyManager**; the selected face will be split into two or more than two faces, depending on the sketch that is used to project it. Figure 10-91 shows the sketch and the face to be selected. Figure 10-92 shows the resulting split line created to split the selected face.

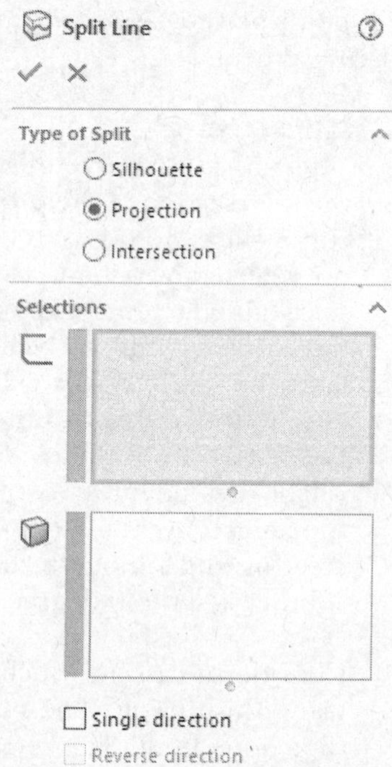

Figure 10-90 *The* ***Split Line PropertyManager*** *with the* ***Projection*** *radio button selected*

The other options in the **Selections** rollout of the **Split Line PropertyManager** are discussed next.

Single direction

If the sketching plane on which a sketch is created lies within the model, the split line will be created on its two sides. Select the **Single direction** check box in the **Selections** rollout to create the split line only in one direction.

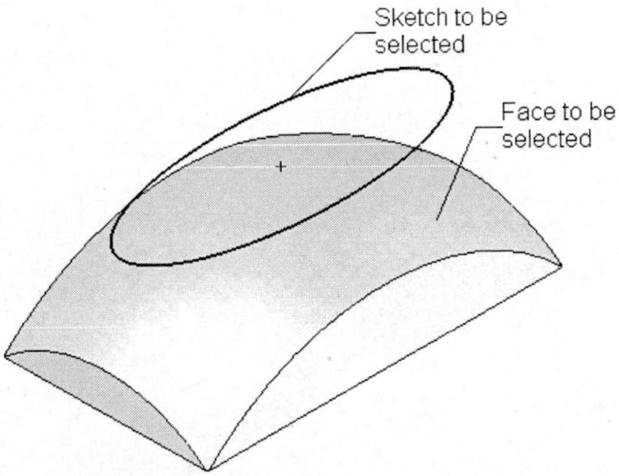

Figure 10-91 Sketch and face to be selected

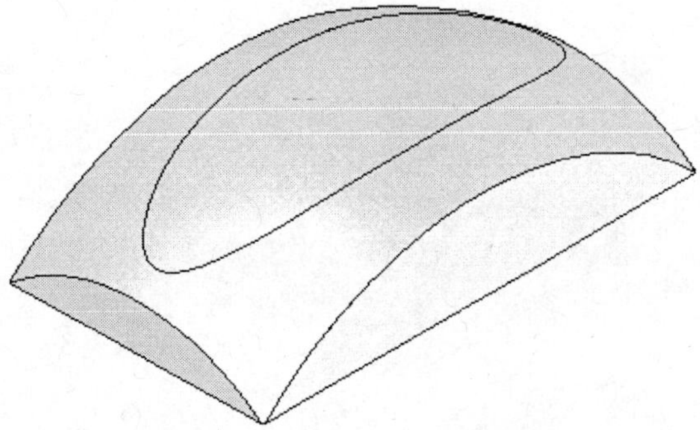

Figure 10-92 Resulting split line

Reverse direction
The **Reverse direction** check box will be activated only if the **Single direction** check box is selected. This option is used to reverse the direction of the split line created. Figure 10-93 shows a split line created on both sides of the model. Figure 10-94 shows the split line created on single side of the model.

Intersection
The **Intersection** radio button is used to split the selected bodies or faces using the tool bodies, faces, or planes. To split the selected body in this way, select the **Intersection** radio button from the **Type of Split** rollout; the **Splitting Bodies/Faces/Planes** selection box will be displayed. Select the bodies, faces, or planes to be used as tool bodies. Next, click in the **Faces/Bodies to Split** selection box and select the bodies to be split.

Figure 10-93 Split line created on both sides

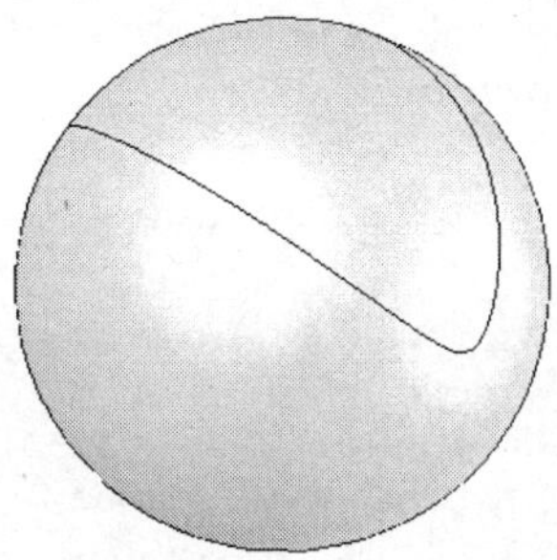

Figure 10-94 Split line created on single side

The **Split all** check box in the **Surface Split Options** rollout is used to split almost all areas of surfaces using the current selection set. You can also select the **Natural** or **Linear** radio button to define the shape of the split. Figure 10-95 shows the plane to be selected as the split tool and also the faces to be split. Figure 10-96 shows the resulting split faces.

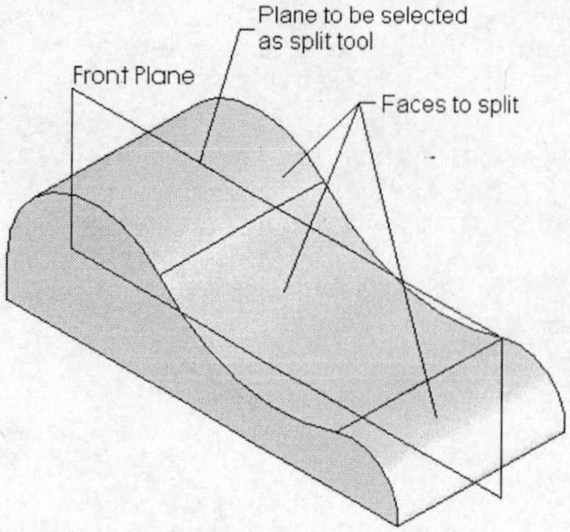

Figure 10-95 Plane and faces to be split

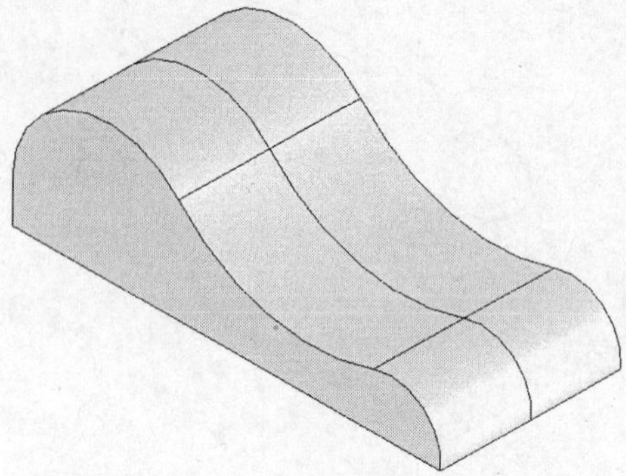

Figure 10-96 Resulting split faces

Creating a Composite Curve

CommandManager:	Features > Curves > Composite Curve
SOLIDWORKS menus:	Insert > Curve > Composite
Toolbar:	Curves > Composite Curve

The **Composite Curve** tool is used to create a curve by combining 2D or 3D curves, sketched entities, and part edges into a single curve. You need to ensure that the selected entities form a continuous chain. A composite curve is mainly used while creating a sweep or loft feature. To create a composite curve, choose the **Composite Curve** button from the Curves flyout in the **Features CommandManager**; the Composite **Curve PropertyManager** will be displayed, as shown in Figure 10-97. On invoking the **Composite Curve PropertyManager**, you will be prompted to select a continuous set of sketches, edges, and/or curves. Select the continuous edges, curves, or sketched entities to create a composite curve. Choose the **OK** button to end its creation.

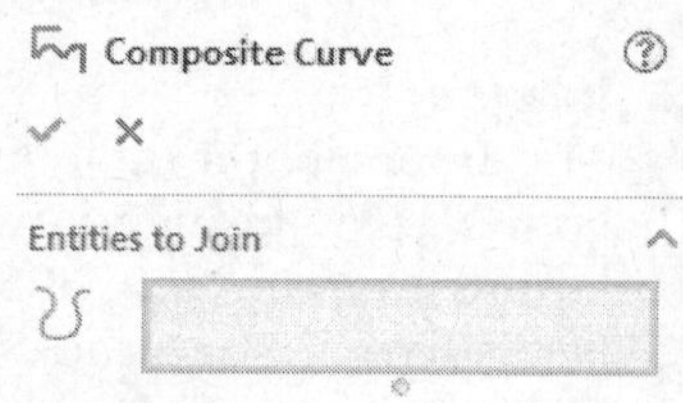

*Figure 10-97 The **Composite Curve PropertyManager***

Creating a Curve Through XYZ Points

CommandManager:	Features > Curves > Curve Through XYZ Points
SOLIDWORKS menus:	Insert > Curve > Curve Through XYZ Points
Toolbar:	Curves > Curve Through XYZ Points

The **Curve Through XYZ Points** tool is used to create a curve by specifying the coordinate points. To create a curve using this tool, choose the **Curve Through XYZ Points** tool from the **Curves** flyout in the **Features CommandManager**; the **Curve File** dialog box will be displayed, as shown in Figure 10-98. Double-click in the cell below the **X** column to enter the X coordinate as the start point of the curve. Similarly, double-click in the **Y** and **Z** cells to enter the respective Y and Z coordinates of the start point of the curve. Double-click in the cell below the first cell to enter the coordinates for the second point to create the curve. Similarly, specify the coordinates of other points of the curve, as shown in Figure 10-99.

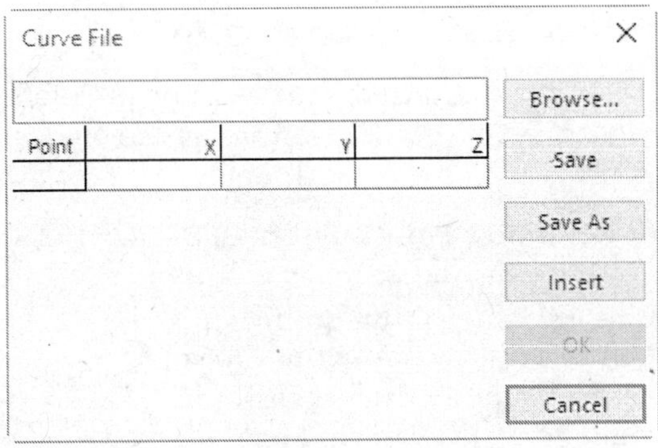

Figure 10-98 *The* ***Curve File*** *dialog box*

When you enter the coordinates of the points, the preview of the curve will be displayed in the drawing area. Choose the **OK** button from the **Curve File** dialog box to complete the feature creation, as shown in Figure 10-100.

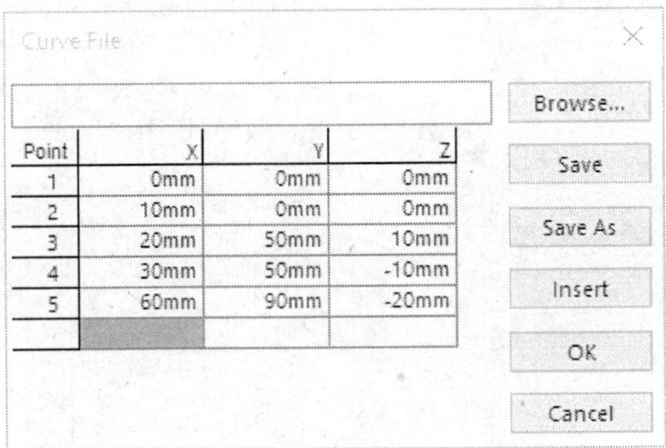

Figure 10-99 *Coordinates entered in the* ***Curve File*** *dialog box*

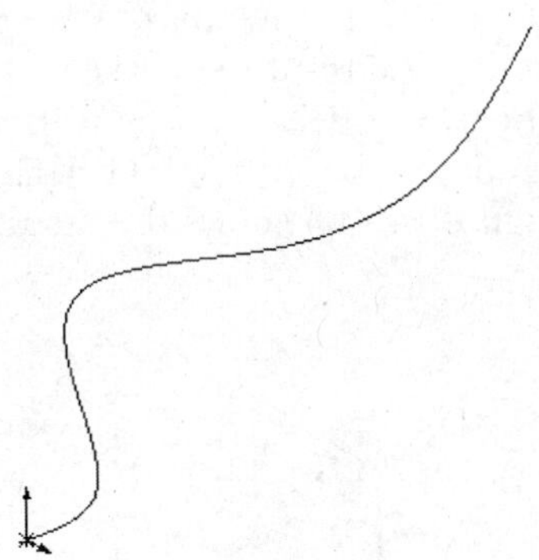

Figure 10-100 *Resulting 3D curve*

You can also save the current set of coordinates using the **Save** button in the **Curve File** dialog box. On choosing this button, the **Save As** dialog box will be displayed. Browse to the folder where you need to save the coordinates, enter the name of the file in the **File name** edit box, and choose the **Save** button. The curve file will be saved with the *.sldcrv* extension. Choose **Save As** to save the current set of coordinates in a file with some other name.

On choosing the **Browse** button, the **Open** dialog box will be displayed. You can browse to the previously saved curve file to specify the coordinate points. You can also write the coordinates in a text (notepad) file and save it. In the **Open** dialog box, select the **Text Files (*.txt)** option from the **Files of type** drop-down list and browse the text file to specify the coordinates.

Tip

To delete a row from the ***Curve File*** *dialog box, select the row and then press the DELETE key; the selected row will be deleted. To insert a new row in the* ***Curve File*** *dialog box, select the row and then choose the* ***Insert*** *button; the new row will be inserted above the selected row.*

Creating a Curve Through Reference Points

CommandManager:	Features > Curves > Curve Through Reference Points
SOLIDWORKS menus:	Insert > Curve > Curve Through Reference Points
Toolbar:	Curves > Curve Through Reference Points

The **Curve Through Reference Points** tool enables you to create a curve by selecting the sketched points, vertices, origin, endpoints, or center points. To create a curve through reference points, choose the **Curve Through Reference Points** tool from the **Curves** flyout in the **Features CommandManager**; the **Curve Through Reference Points PropertyManager** will be displayed, as shown in Figure 10-101.

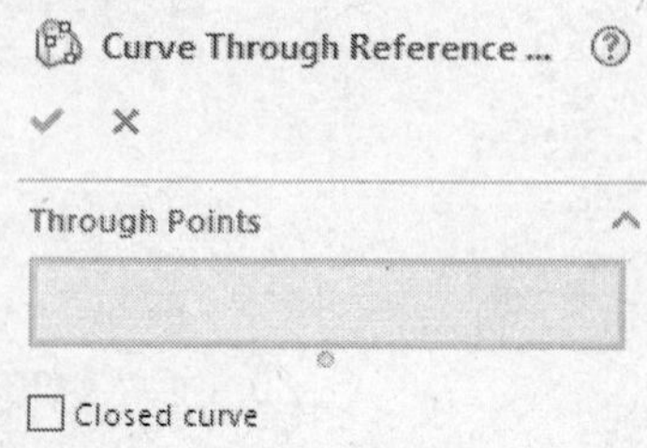

Figure 10-101** The **Curve Through Reference Points PropertyManager

On invoking this tool, you will be prompted to select the vertices to define the through points for the curve. Select the points to define the curve. On specifying the points, the preview of the resulting curve will be displayed in the drawing area. After specifying all the points, choose the **OK** button. You can select the **Closed curve** check box to create a closed curve. Figure 10-102 shows the vertices to be selected to create the curve through the reference points. Figure 10-103 shows the resulting 3D curve.

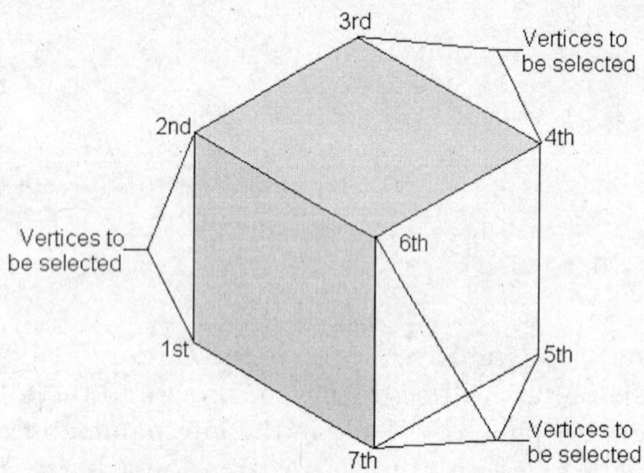

***Figure 10-102** Vertices to be selected*

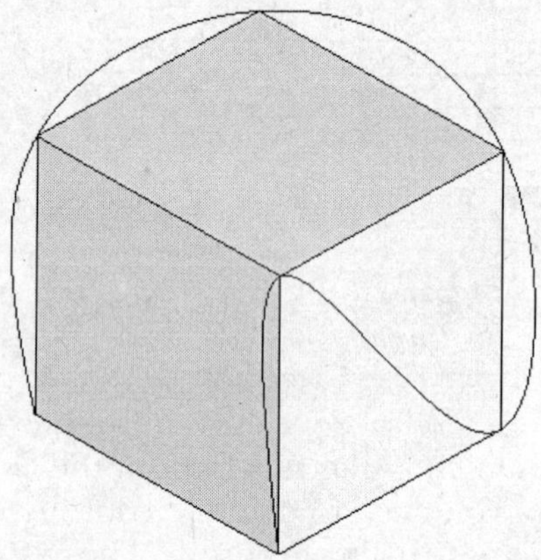

***Figure 10-103** Resulting 3D curve*

Creating a Helical/Spiral Curve

CommandManager:	Features > Curves > Helix and Spiral
SOLIDWORKS menus:	Insert > Curve > Helix/Spiral
Toolbar:	Curves > Helix and Spiral

The **Helix and Spiral** tool is used to create a helical curve or a spiral curve. This curve is generally used as the sweep path to create springs, threads, spiral coils, and so on. Figure 10-104 shows a spring created by sweeping a circular profile along a helical path. Figure 10-105 shows a spiral coil created by sweeping a rectangular profile along a spiral path.

Figure 10-104 *Spring created*

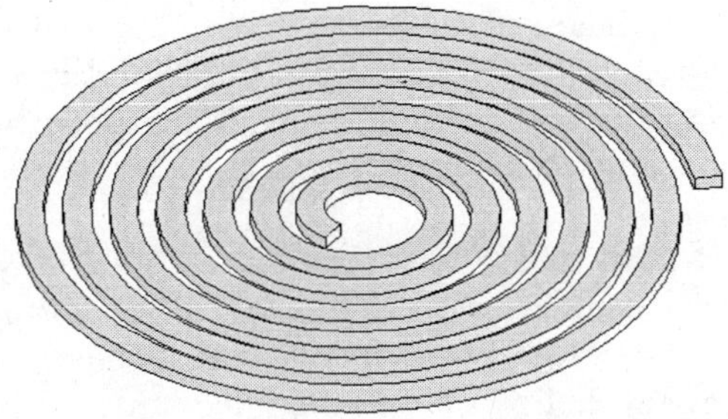

Figure 10-105 *Spiral coil created*

To create a helix, choose the **Helix and Spiral** button from the **Curves** flyout in the **Features CommandManager**; the **Helix/ Spiral PropertyManager** will be displayed. Also, you will be prompted to select a plane, a planar face, or an edge to sketch a circle to define helical cross-section or to select a single circle. The circle will define the diameter of the spring. If you are creating a spiral, the sketch will define the starting diameter of the spiral curve. The **Helix/Spiral PropertyManager** disappears on selecting a plane and the sketching environment is invoked where you can draw the cross-section sketch for the helix or spiral. Exit the sketching environment after drawing the sketch. The **Helix/Spiral PropertyManager** will be displayed again, refer to Figure 10-106.

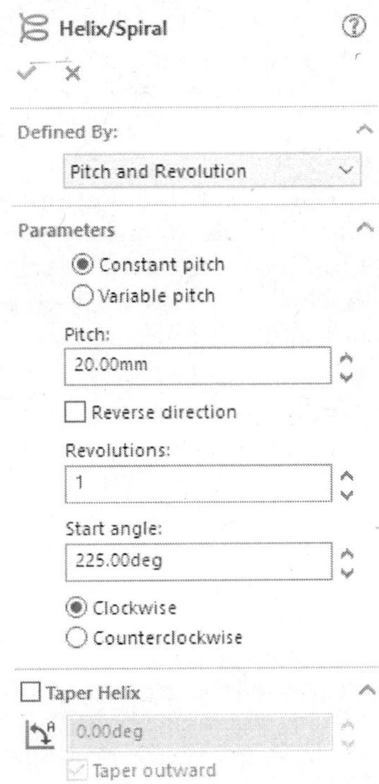

Figure 10-106 *The* ***Helix/Spiral PropertyManager***

When the **Helix/Spiral PropertyManager** is displayed again, set the view to isometric. On doing so, you will notice that two arrows are displayed. One arrow emerges from the center of the circle and it defines the direction of the helix. The second arrow is tangent to the circle and it defines the start point of the helix, either clockwise or counterclockwise. The preview of the helix curve, with the default values, will be displayed in the drawing area. Various methods to specify the parameters of the helical curve are discussed next.

Pitch and Revolution

The **Pitch and Revolution** option in the **Type** drop-down list of the **Defined By** rollout is selected by default and is used to specify the pitch of the helical curve and the number of revolutions. When this option is selected, you can define the value of pitch and the number of revolutions in the **Pitch** spinner and the **Revolutions** spinner in the **Parameters** rollout, respectively. You can also select the **Reverse direction** check box available in the **Parameters** rollout to reverse the direction of the helix creation. You can specify the start angle of the helical curve using the **Start Angle** spinner. The **Clockwise** and **Counterclockwise** radio buttons in this rollout are used to define the direction of rotation of the helix.

Height and Revolution

The **Height and Revolution** option in the **Type** drop-down list is used to define the parameters of the helix curve in the form of total helix height and the number of revolutions. On selecting this option, the **Height** and **Revolutions** spinners will be displayed in the **Parameters** rollout along with the other options where you can specify the required parameters.

Height and Pitch

The **Height and Pitch** option in the **Type** drop-down list is used to define the parameters of the helix curve in terms of height and pitch of the helix. When you select this option, the **Height** and **Pitch** spinners will be displayed in the **Parameters** rollout along with the other the options that can be used to specify the required parameters.

After specifying all parameters to create the helix curve, the preview in the drawing area will be modified automatically. Figure 10-107 shows a helix curve.

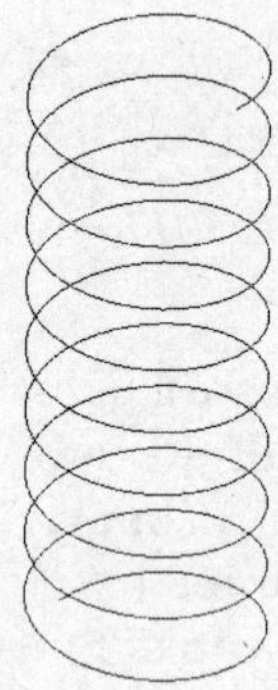

Figure 10-107 *Helix Curve*

If you want to create a helix of varying pitch, select the **Variable pitch** radio button in the **Parameters** rollout and specify the number of revolutions, the diameter, and the pitch in the table displayed in the **Region parameters** area. Also, callouts for specifying the variable pitch helix curve will be displayed in the drawing window. You can specify the values in the callout.

Taper Helix

You can create a tapered helix by using the **Taper Helix** rollout. Select the check box on the left of the **Taper Helix** rollout; the **Taper Angle** spinner and the **Taper outward** check box will be available. Specify the angle between the central axis of the helix and the periphery of the helix using the **Taper Angle** spinner. The **Taper outward** check box is selected to create an outward taper. When you specify the parameters to create a tapered helical curve, the preview of the helical curve will update automatically in the drawing area. Figure 10-108 shows a tapered helical curve. Figure 10-109 shows a tapered helical curve created with the **Taper outward** check box selected.

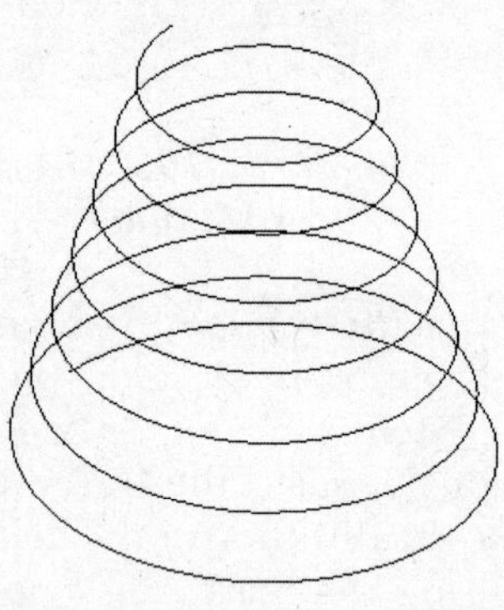

Figure 10-108 *Tapered helical curve*

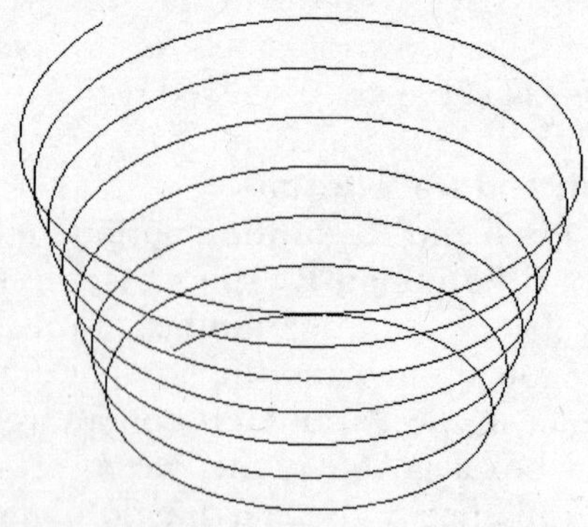

Figure 10-109 *Tapered helical curve with the* ***Taper outward*** *check box selected*

By default, the helical curve is created in the clockwise direction because the **Clockwise** radio button is selected in the **Parameters** rollout of the **Helix/Spiral PropertyManager**. Select the **Counterclockwise** radio button to create a helical curve in the counterclockwise direction. After setting the parameters, choose the **OK** button from the **Helix/Spiral PropertyManager**.

Spiral

The **Spiral** option is used to create a spiral curve. To create a spiral curve, select the **Spiral** option from the **Type** drop-down list in the **Defined By** rollout; the preview of the spiral curve will be displayed in the drawing area. You can define the pitch and the number of revolutions in the **Pitch** and **Revolutions** spinners, respectively. The other options in the **Parameters** rollout are the same as those discussed earlier. After specifying all the required parameters, choose the **OK** button. Figure 10-110 shows a spiral curve.

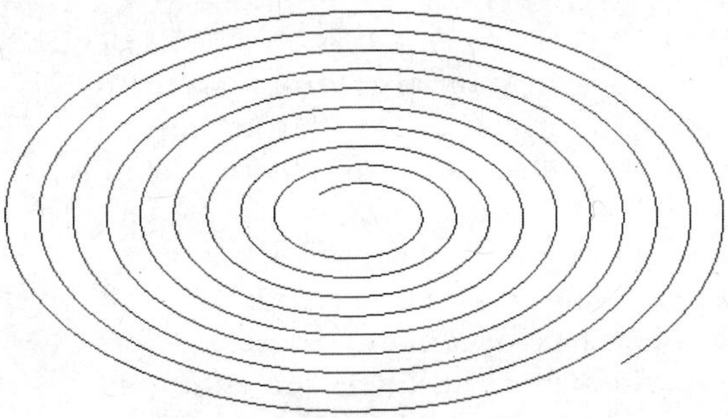

Figure 10-110 *Spiral curve*

Extruding a 3D Sketch

You can also extrude a 3D sketch drawn in the 3D sketching environment. A 3D sketch is always extruded along a direction vector, which can be a line, edge, planar face, or a plane. Invoke the **Boss-Extrude PropertyManager** and select the 3D sketch that you need to extrude. Also, you need to select a direction vector along which the sketch will be extruded. Set the parameters at the start of the extrude feature using the **From** rollout. Now, set the value of the depth of the extrude feature and choose the **OK** button from the **Boss-Extrude PropertyManager**. Figure 10-111 shows a 3D sketch and the direction vector along which it will be extruded. Figure 10-112 shows the resulting extruded feature.

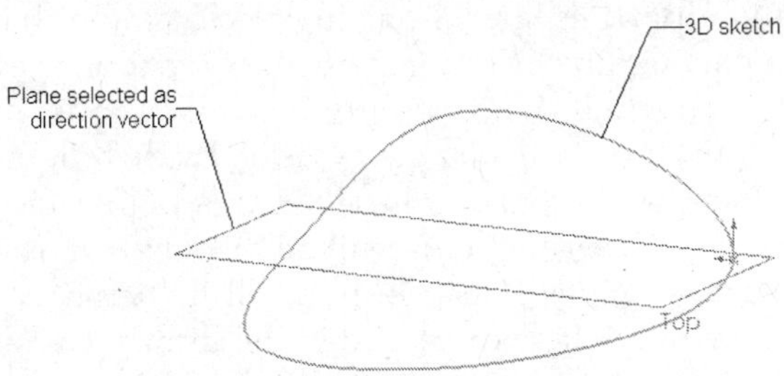

Figure 10-111 *3D sketch and the direction vector*

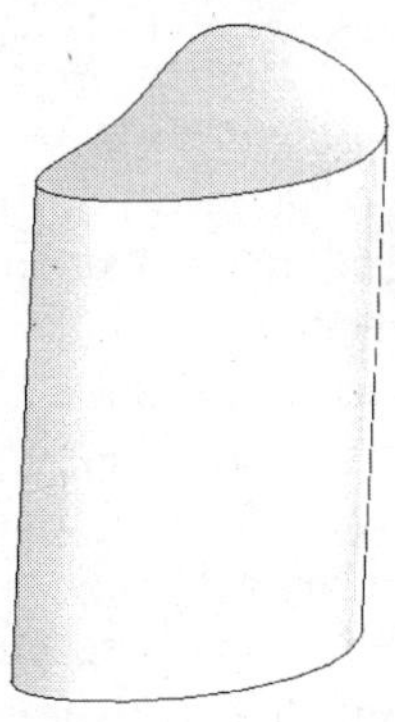

Figure 10-112 *Resulting extruded feature*

Creating Draft Features

CommandManager:	Features > Draft
SOLIDWORKS menus:	Insert > Features > Draft
Toolbar:	Features > Draft

The **Draft** tool is used to add taper to the selected faces of a model. Draft feature is mostly added to the models that are to be molded or cast as it will be easier to remove them from the mold or die. To apply draft, choose the **Draft** button from the **Features CommandManager**; the **Draft PropertyManager** will be displayed, refer to Figure 10-113. In SOLIDWORKS, you can create drafts manually or by using the **DraftXpert**. The process of creating the draft using the manual method is discussed next.

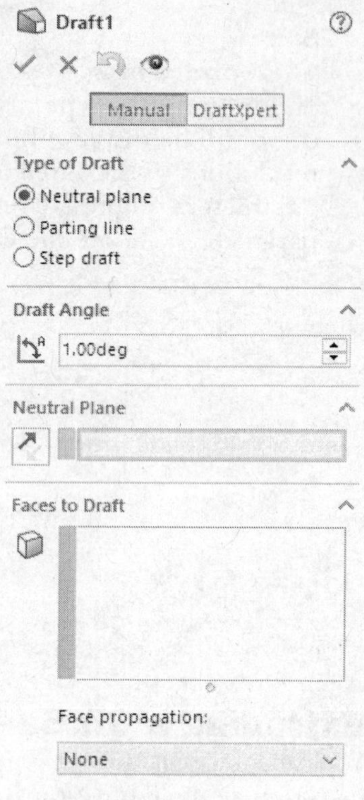

Figure 10-113 The Draft PropertyManager

To create a manual draft, choose the **Manual** tab from the **Draft PropertyManager**, refer to Figure 10-113; you will be prompted to select a neutral plane and faces to add draft. Neutral plane is the plane with respect to which the draft angle is measured. The **Neutral plane** radio button is selected by default in the **Type of Draft** rollout. Select a neutral plane to create the draft feature. You can select a planar face or a plane that acts as the neutral plane. On doing so, the name of the selected entity will appear in the **Neutral Plane** selection box of the **Neutral Plane** rollout. The **Reverse Direction** arrow will also be displayed in the drawing area. After selecting neutral plane the **Faces to Draft** selection box of the **Faces to Draft** rollout will be activated. Select the faces to apply the draft; the selected faces will be displayed with the **Draft Face** callout. Next, set the value of the draft angle in the **Draft Angle** spinner available in the **Draft Angle** rollout. Choose the **OK** button from the **Draft PropertyManager** or choose **OK** from the confirmation corner.

Figure 10-114 shows the neutral face and the faces to be selected to add draft. Figure 10-115 shows the resulting draft feature.

You can draft a portion of the selected faces using a parting line. A parting line is a line that divides the faces of a feature. You need to create a parting line by using the **Split Line** tool or by using the edges of an existing model. To apply a draft using the parting line, invoke the **Draft PropertyManager** and select the **Parting Line** radio button from the **Type of Draft** rollout; you will be prompted to select the pulling direction and the parting line. Select a planar face or a plane that act as a pulling direction; the **Reverse Direction** arrow will be displayed in the drawing area. Also, the selection mode in the **Parting Lines** selection box will be activated. Select the parting lines from the drawing area; the arrows will be displayed in the drawing area. These arrows specify different draft directions for each segment of the parting line. To change the direction of these arrows, select the respective parting line from the **Parting Lines** selection area and then choose the **Other Face** button available below the **Parting Lines** selection box.

Next, specify the angle of the draft in the **Draft Angle** spinner and choose the **OK** button from the **Draft PropertyManager**. Figure 10-116 shows the pulling direction and parting lines to be selected and Figure 10-117 shows the resulting draft feature.

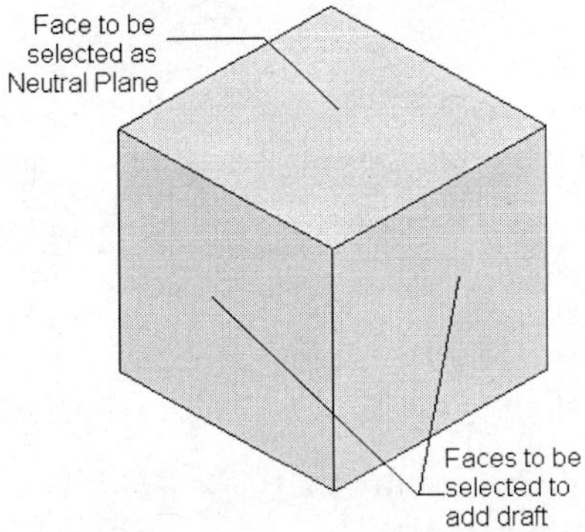

Figure 10-114 *Faces to be selected*

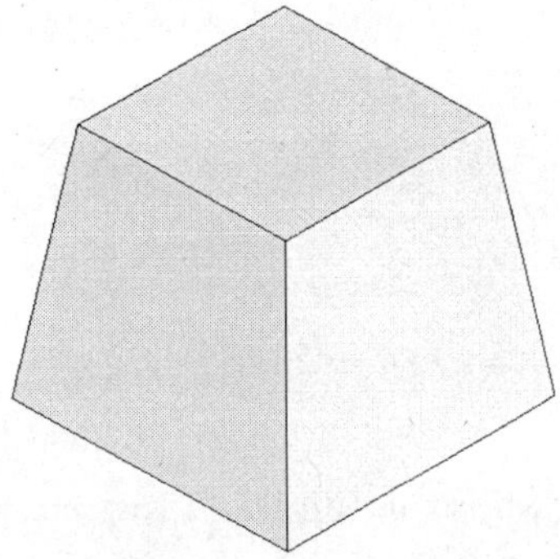

Figure 10-115 *Resulting draft feature*

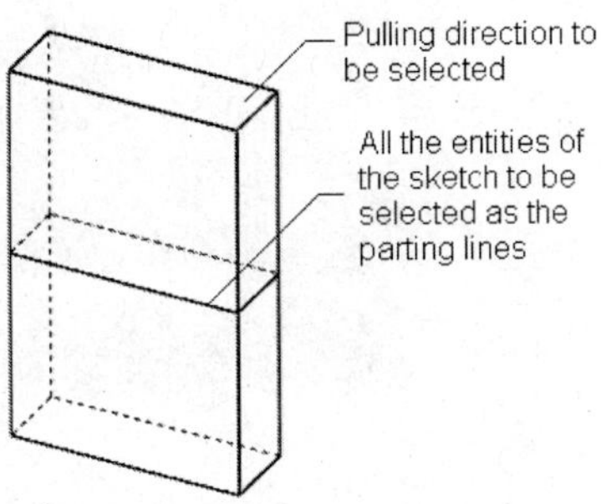

Figure 10-116 *Pulling direction and parting lines to be selected*

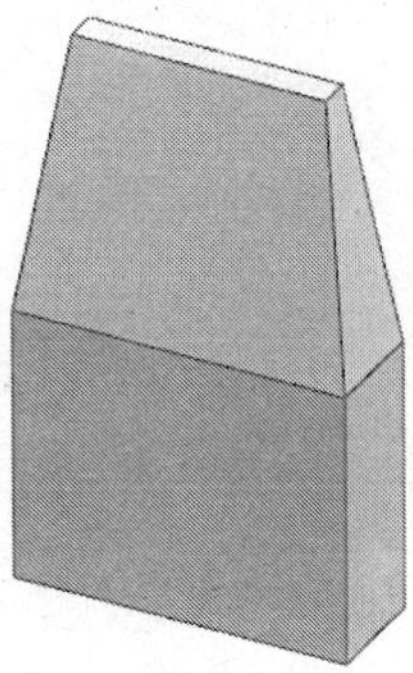

Figure 10-117 *The resulting draft feature*

The **Step draft** radio button in the **Type of Draft** rollout is used to apply step draft. To do so, invoke the **Draft PropertyManager** and then select the **Step draft** radio button; the **Tapered steps** and **Perpendicular steps** radio buttons will be displayed. The **Tapered steps** radio button is selected by default. As a result, the surfaces will be generated in the same manner as the tapered surfaces. On selecting the **Perpendicular steps** radio button, the surfaces will be generated perpendicular to the original faces. Select the pulling direction and then the parting line from the drawing area. Next, specify the draft angle in the **Draft Angle** spinner and choose the **OK** button from the **Draft PropertyManager**. Figure 10-118 shows the pulling direction and the parting lines to be selected. Figures 10-119 and 10-120 show the resulting step draft features on selecting the **Tapered steps** and **Perpendicular steps** radio buttons, respectively.

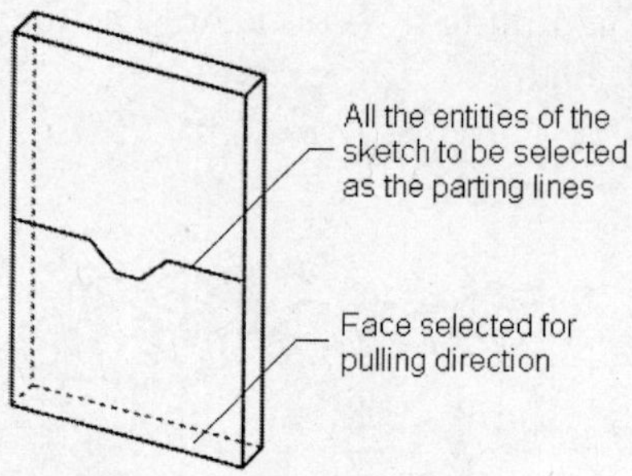

Figure 10-118 Parting lines and pulling direction to be selected

Figure 10-119 The resulting draft feature on selecting the ***Tapered steps*** *radio button*

The other options in the **Draft PropertyManager** are discussed next.

Reverse Direction

The **Reverse Direction** button on the left of the **Neutral Plane** selection box in the **Neutral Plane** rollout is used to reverse the direction of creation of the draft. You can also reverse the direction of the draft creation by selecting the **Reverse Direction** arrow in the drawing area.

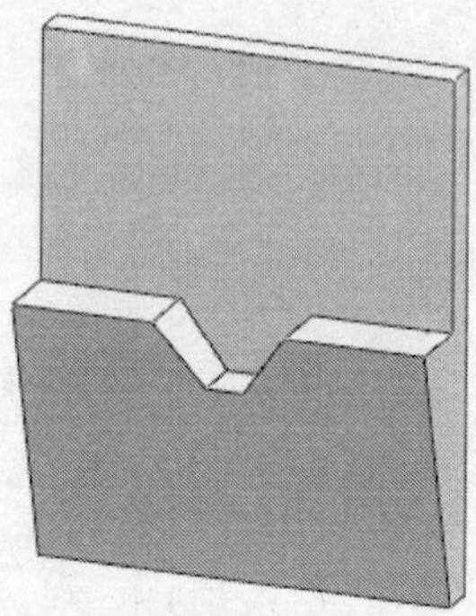

Figure 10-120 The resulting draft feature on selecting the ***Perpendicular steps*** *radio button*

Face Propagation

The options in the **Face Propagation** drop-down list in the **Faces to Draft** rollout are used to extend the draft feature to the other faces. These options are discussed next.

None

The **None** option is selected by default. This option is used when you do not need to apply any type of face propagation.

Along Tangent

The **Along Tangent** option is used to apply the draft to the faces tangent to the selected face.

All Faces

The **All Faces** option is used to apply the draft to all the faces attached to the neutral plane or face.

Inner Faces

This option is used to draft all the faces inside the model such as holes, slots, and so on that are attached to the neutral plane or face.

Outer Faces

This option is used to draft all the outside faces of the model that are attached to the neutral plane or face.

The **DraftXpert** is used to create or modify an existing draft feature. To create the draft using the **DraftXpert**, choose this tab; the **DraftXpert PropertyManager** will be displayed, as shown in Figure 10-121. Also, the **Add** tab will be chosen by default and the related options will be displayed in the **DraftXpert PropertyManager**. Most of the options used to create the draft feature are the same as those discussed in the manual draft. The options in the **Draft Analysis** rollout are different and are discussed next.

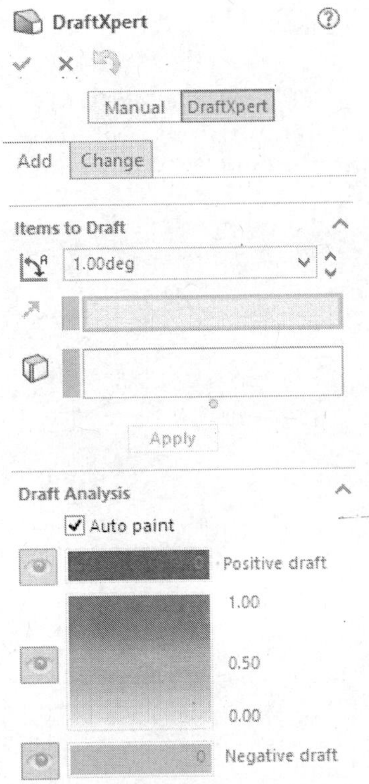

Figure 10-121 The options in the DraftXpert Property Manager

Auto paint

Select the **Auto paint** check box to enable the draft analysis options. These options are discussed next.

Show/hide faces with positive draft

This is the first button below the **Auto paint** check box. If this button is chosen, the faces with the positive draft will be highlighted in the color shown in the color box on the right of this button. Note that the faces will be highlighted only after you select the faces to add the draft and choose the **Apply** button from the **Items to Draft** rollout.

Show/hide faces requiring draft

If this button is chosen, while analyzing the draft, SOLIDWORKS will highlight the faces that require a draft.

Show/hide faces with negative draft

Choose this button to highlight the faces with the negative draft in the color shown in the color box on the right of this button. Note that the faces will be highlighted only after you select the faces to add the draft and choose the **Apply** button from the **Items to Draft** rollout.

To modify or remove an existing draft, choose the **Change** tab and select the draft faces to be changed. If you need to remove the draft, choose the **Remove** button. If you need to change the draft angle, set the new draft angle in the **Draft Angle** spinner and choose the **Change** button; the draft angle will be changed. If there are multiple drafts, you can filter the drafts using the options in the **Existing Drafts** rollout. To do so, select an option from the **Sort list by** drop-down list in this rollout; the items related to the options in the **Sort list by** drop-down list will be listed in the **Filtered face groups** list box. On selecting an item from this list box, the corresponding face, neutral plane, and the draft angle will be displayed in the **Drafts to Change** rollout. Now, you can change or remove the selected draft face. Choose the **OK** button after creating or modifying the feature.

Tip

*After choosing the **Apply** button and selecting the **Auto paint** check box in the **DraftXpert PropertyManager**, if you move the cursor over any face of the model other than the neutral plane, the draft angle of that face will be displayed above the cursor.*

TUTORIALS

Tutorial 1

In this tutorial, you will create the model shown in Figure 10-122. The dimensions of the model are shown in the same figure.

(Expected time: 45 min)

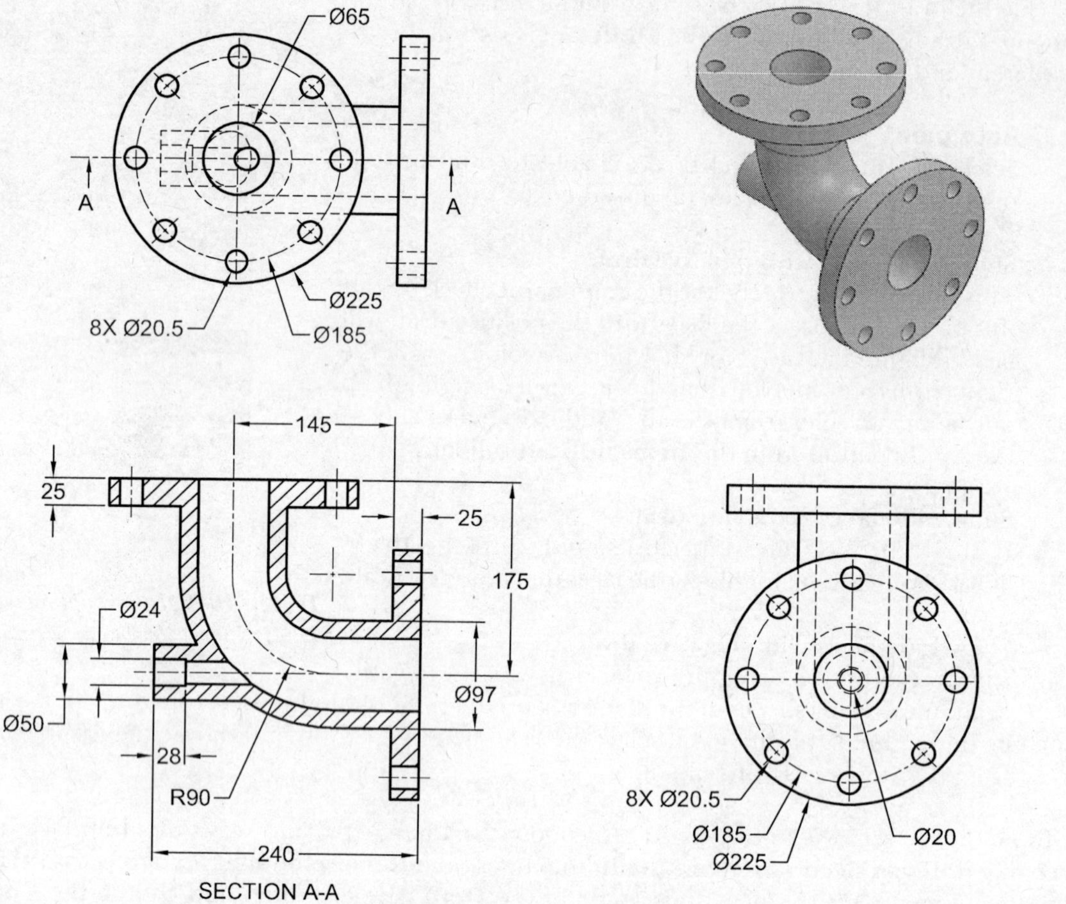

Figure 10-122 *Views and dimensions of the model for Tutorial 1*

The following steps are required to complete this tutorial:

a. The base feature of the model is a sweep feature. First, you need to create a path for the sweep feature on the Front Plane. Next, you need to create a thin circular sweep feature because the base feature of the model is a hollow feature.

b. Create the remaining features.

c. Save the model.

Creating the Path for the Sweep Feature

As discussed earlier, the base feature of the model is a sweep feature. To create the sweep feature, you first need to create its path on the Front Plane.

1. Start a new SOLIDWORKS part document using the **New SOLIDWORKS Document** dialog box.

2. Draw the sketch of the path for the sweep feature on the **Front Plane** and add required relations and dimensions to the sketch, as shown in Figure 10-123. Exit the sketching environment and change the view to isometric, as shown in Figure 10-124.

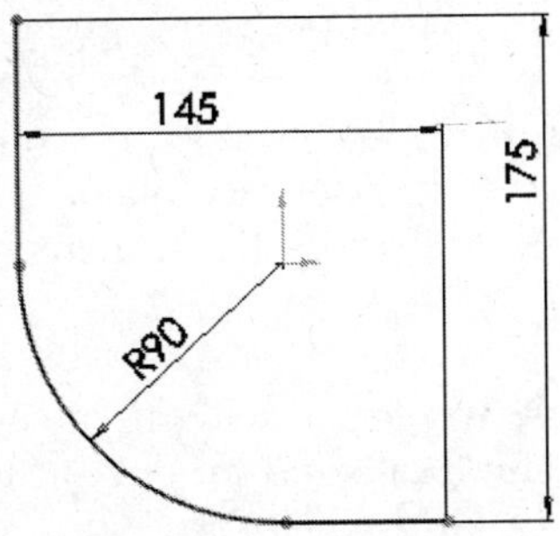

Figure 10-123 *Sketch of the path*

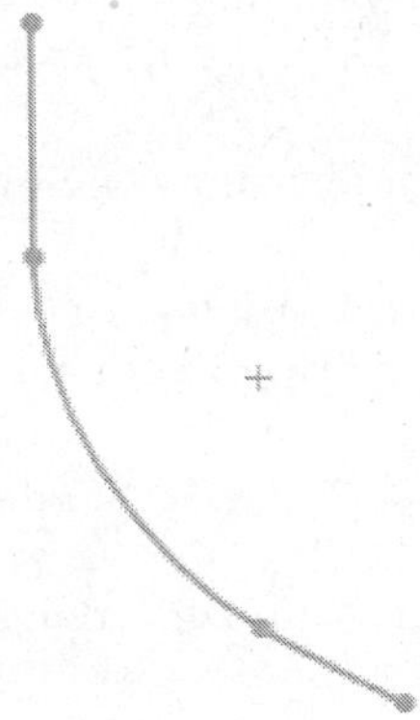

Figure 10-124 *Isometric view of the sketch*

Creating the Sweep Feature

The sweep feature that you need to create is a thin circular sweep feature. You need to use the **Thin Feature** rollout to specify the parameters of the sweep feature.

1. Choose the **Swept Boss/Base** tool from the **Features CommandManager**; the **Sweep PropertyManager** is displayed. 

2. Select the **Circular Profile** radio button from the **Profile and Path** rollout. As a result, the **Path** selection box and the **Diameter** spinner is displayed.

3. Select the path from the drawing area, the name of the sketch will be displayed in the **Path** selection box. Also, set the value of diameter in the **Diameter** spinner to 97.

4. Select the check box on the left of the **Thin Feature** rollout; the **Thin Feature** rollout is invoked.

5. Set the value of thickness in the **Thickness** spinner to **16**.

   Since the direction of thickness addition is opposite to the required direction, therefore you need to reverse the direction.

6. Choose the **Reverse Direction** button from the **Thin Feature** rollout. Choose the **OK** button from the **Sweep PropertyManager** or choose **OK** from the confirmation corner.

The base feature created by sweeping a circular profile along a path is shown in Figure 10-125.

Note
Instead of creating a thin sweep feature, you can also create a solid sweep feature and then add a shell feature to hollow the base feature.

Creating Remaining Features

1. Create the remaining features (flanges) on both ends of the sweep feature using the **Extruded Boss/Base** tool, refer to Figure 10-126.

2. Create the hole using the **Simple Hole** tool and create circular pattern of the hole feature.

3. Create a plane at an offset distance of **240** mm from the right face of the model. Make sure that the **Flip offset** check box is selected while creating reference plane. Then, create the circular feature by extruding it using the **Up To Next** option. For dimensions refer to Figure 10-122.

4. Create the custom-sized counterbore hole using the **Hole Wizard** tool on the extruded feature created in the previous step, refer to Figure 10-122. The final solid model for Tutorial 1 is shown in Figure 10-126.

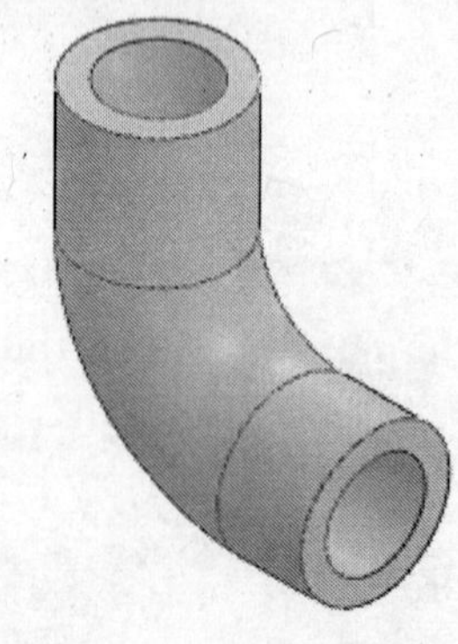

Figure 10-125 *Base feature of the model*

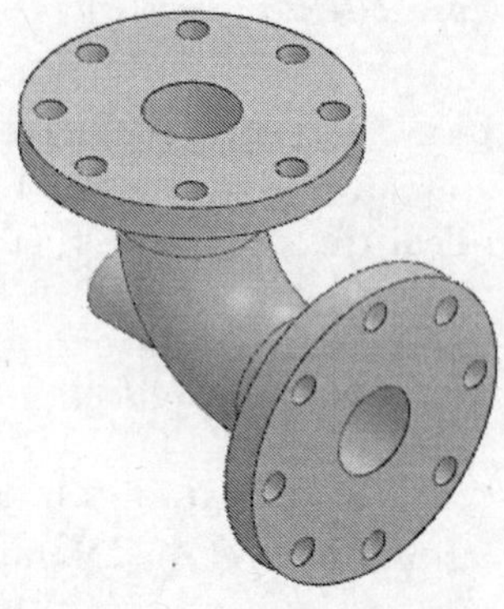

Figure 10-126 *Final model for Tutorial 1*

Saving the Model

1. Save the model with the name *c10_tut01* at the following location:
\Documents\SOLIDWORKS\c10

2. Choose **File > Close** from the SOLIDWORKS menus to close the file.

Tutorial 2

In this tutorial, you will create the chair frame shown in Figure 10-127. The dimensions of the chair frame are also shown in the same figure. **(Expected time: 30 min)**

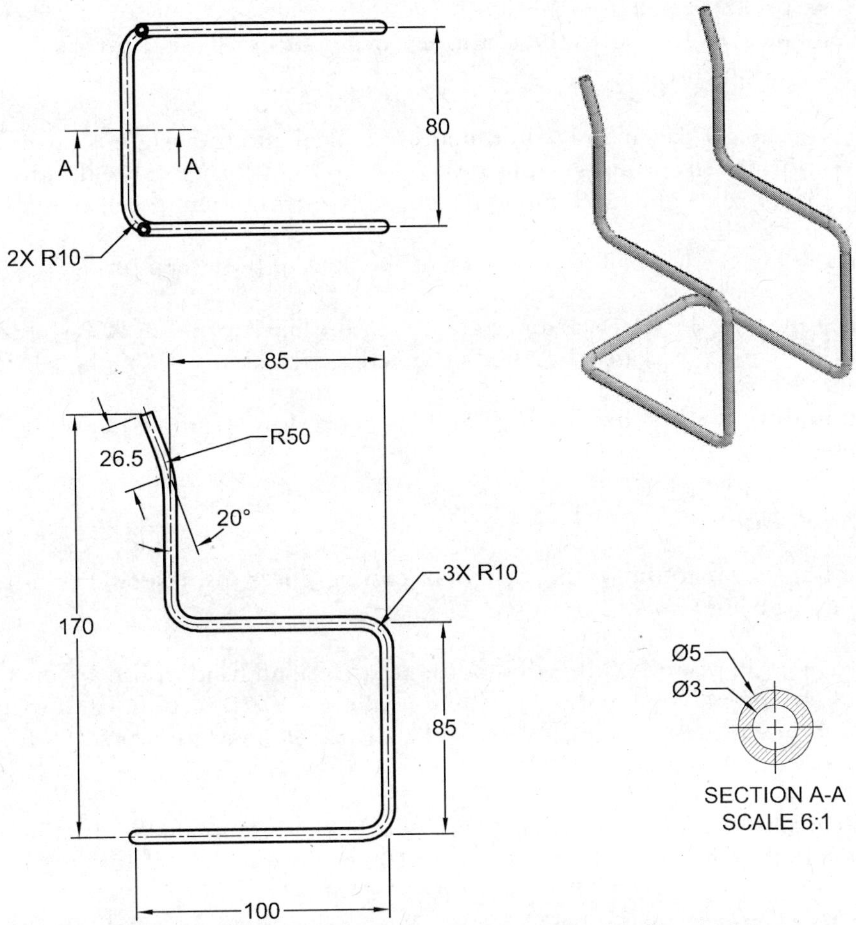

Figure 10-127 Views and dimensions of the model for Tutorial 2

The following steps are required to complete this tutorial:

a. Invoke the 3D sketching environment and then draw the sketch of a 3D path. Create only the left half of the 3D path in the 3D sketching environment.
b. Sweep the profile along the 3D path using the **Thin Feature** option.
c. Mirror the sweep feature using the Front Plane.
d. Save the model.

Creating the Path for the Sweep Feature Using the 3D Sketching Environment

It is evident from Figure 10-127 that the model needs to be created by sweeping a profile along the 3D path. Therefore, you need to create a path for the sweep feature in the 3D sketching environment.

1. Start a new SOLIDWORKS part document.

2. Change the current view to isometric.

3. Choose **Insert > 3D Sketch** from the SOLIDWORKS menus or choose the **3D Sketch** button from the **Sketch** flyout in the **FeatureManager Design Tree** to invoke the 3D sketching environment.

   On doing so, the 3D sketching environment is invoked and the origin is displayed in red. Also, the confirmation corner is displayed on the top right corner of the drawing area. The sketching tools that can be used in the 3D sketching environment are also highlighted.

   You need to draw the left half of the sketch as the path of the sweep profile.

4. Invoke the **Line** tool; the select cursor is replaced by the line cursor. The **XY** symbol displayed below the line cursor indicates that the line will be sketched in the XY plane by default.

   You need to draw the first line in the ZX plane. Therefore, you need to toggle the plane before you start creating the sketch.

5. Press the TAB key twice to switch to the ZX plane.

6. Move the line cursor to the origin. When an orange dot is displayed, click to specify the start point of the line.

7. Move the cursor in positive Z direction of the triad; a small triad with Z appears below the cursor indicating that you are drawing the line along the **Z** direction. Click to specify the endpoint of the line when a value close to **40** is displayed above the cursor; a rubber-band line is attached to the cursor.

8. Move the cursor toward the right along the infinite line indicating the X-axis. Click to specify the endpoint of the line when a value close to **100** is displayed above the cursor.

9. Press the TAB key to switch to the XY plane. Next, move the cursor vertically upward.

10. Specify the endpoint of the line when the value above the cursor is close to **85**.

11. Similarly, draw the remaining part of the sketch, and then add required relations and dimensions to it.

12. Add the Parallel relation between the last line drawn in the 3D sketch and the Front plane. The final sketch is displayed in Figure 10-128.

13. Exit the 3D sketching environment by using the confirmation corner.

Creating the Sweep Feature along the 3D Path

After creating the 3D path for the sweep feature, you need to sweep a circular profile along the 3D path using the **Swept Boss/Base** tool.

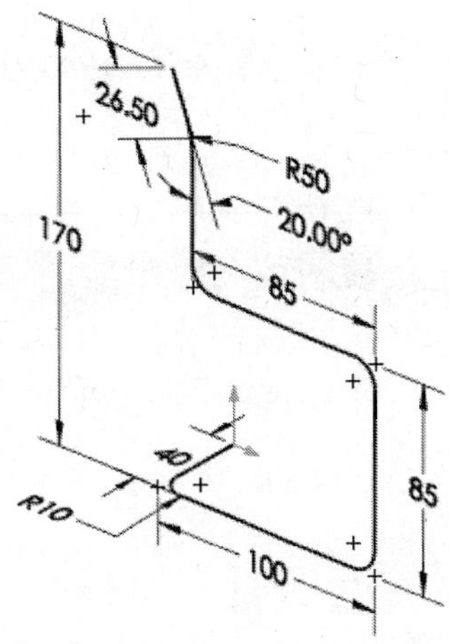

Figure 10-128 *Sketch of the 3D path*

1. Choose the **Swept Boss/Base** button from the **Features CommandManager**; the **Sweep PropertyManager** is displayed.

2. Select the **Circular Profile** radio button from the **Profile and Path** rollout. As a result, the **Path** selection box and the **Diameter** spinner is displayed.

3. Select the path from the drawing area if not selected by default; the name of the path will be displayed in the **Path** selection box. Also set the value of diameter in the **Diameter** spinner to 5.

   As evident from Figure 10-127, frame of the chair is made up of a hollow pipe. Therefore, you need to create a thin sweep feature to create a hollow chair frame.

4. Expand the **Thin Feature** rollout and set the value in the **Thickness** spinner to **1**.

5. Choose the **Reverse Direction** button from the **Thin Features** rollout to reverse the direction of the thin feature creation.

6. Choose the **OK** button from the **Sweep PropertyManager** to end the creation of the feature.

   The model after creating the sweep feature is displayed in Figure 10-129.

7. Mirror the sweep feature about the Front Plane using the **Mirror** tool. The model after mirroring is shown in Figure 10-130.

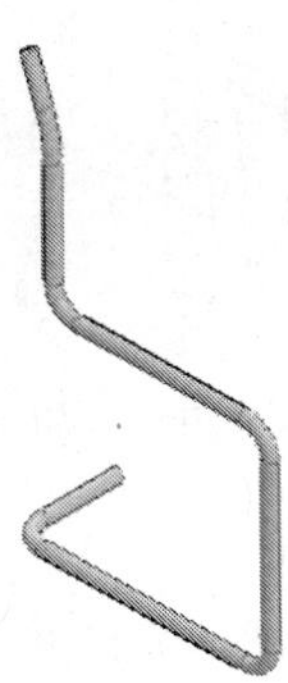

Figure 10-129 *Sweep feature created by sweeping a profile along a 3D path*

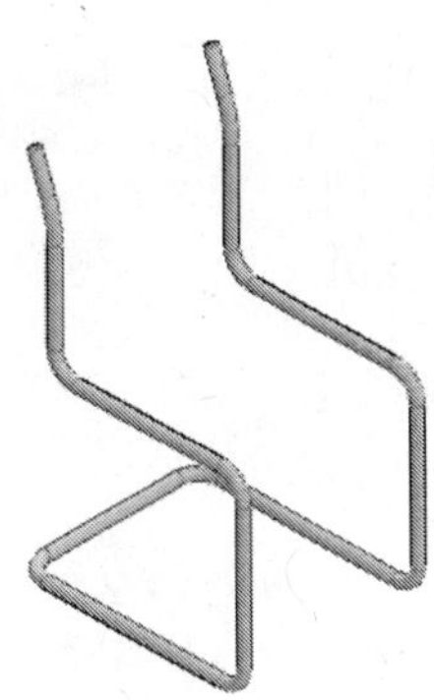

Figure 10-130 *The final model*

Saving the Model

1. Save the model with the name *c10_tut02* at the following location:
\Documents\SOLIDWORKS\c10

2. Close the document.

Tutorial 3

In this tutorial, you will create a spring shown in Figure 10-131. The views and dimensions of the spring are shown in the same figure. **(Expected time: 45 min)**

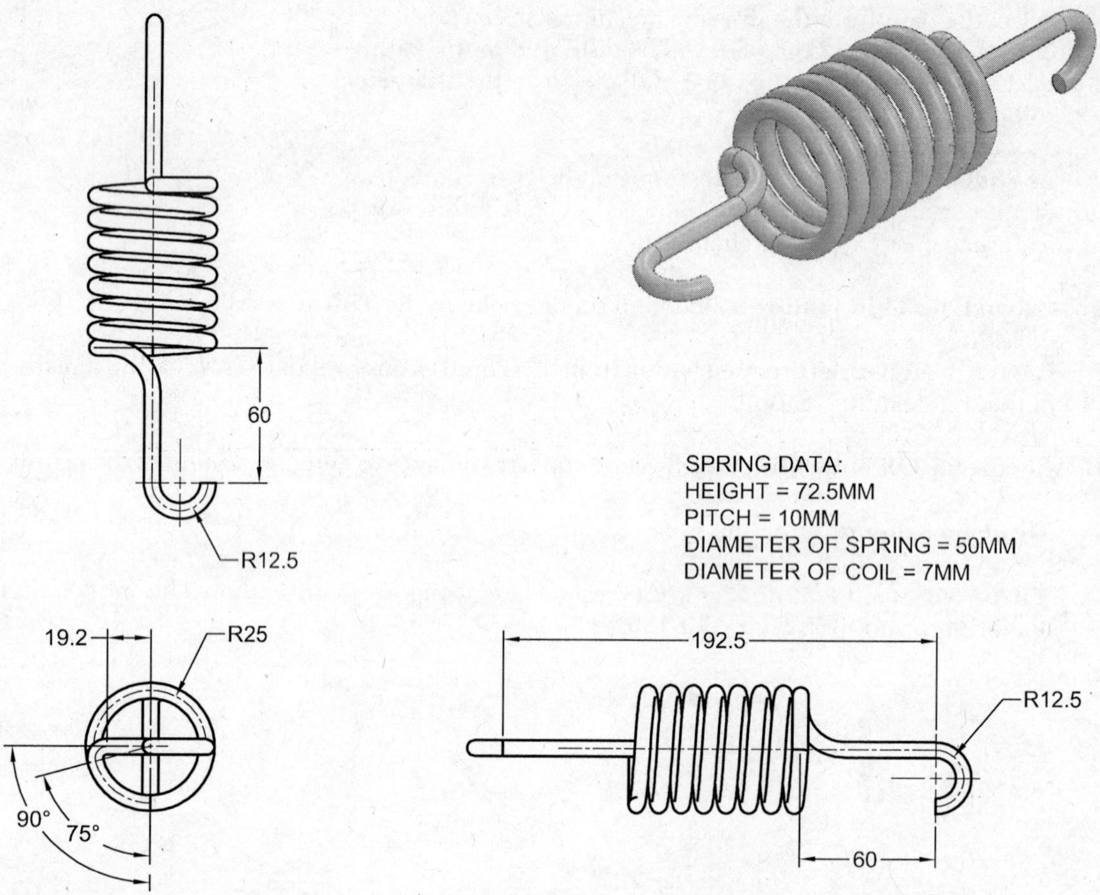

Figure 10-131 *Views and dimensions of the model for Tutorial 3*

The following steps are required to complete this tutorial:

a. Create the helical path of the spring.
b. Create the end clips of the spring.
c. Combine the end clips and the helical curve to create a single curve using the **Composite Curve** option.
d. Create the sweep feature along the curve.

Creating the Helical Curve

To create this model, you need to create a helical curve. For creating a helical curve, you first need to create a circular sketch to define the diameter of the spring.

1. Start a new SOLIDWORKS Part document.

2. Choose the **Helix and Spiral** button from the **Curves** flyout in the **Features CommandManager** and select the **Front Plane** as the sketching plane.

3. Draw a circle of diameter **50** mm. Change its view to isometric and exit the sketching environment; the **Helix/Spiral PropertyManager** is displayed and preview of the helical curve with default values is displayed in the drawing area.

4. Select the **Height and Pitch** option from the **Type** drop-down list in the **Defined By** rollout.

5. Set the value in the **Height** spinner to **72.5** and the value in the **Pitch** spinner to **10**. You will observe that preview of the helical curve is updated automatically when you modify the values in the spinners.

6. Set the value of the **Start angle** spinner to **0** and choose the **OK** button from the **Helix/Spiral PropertyManager**; a helical curve is created, as shown in Figure 10-132.

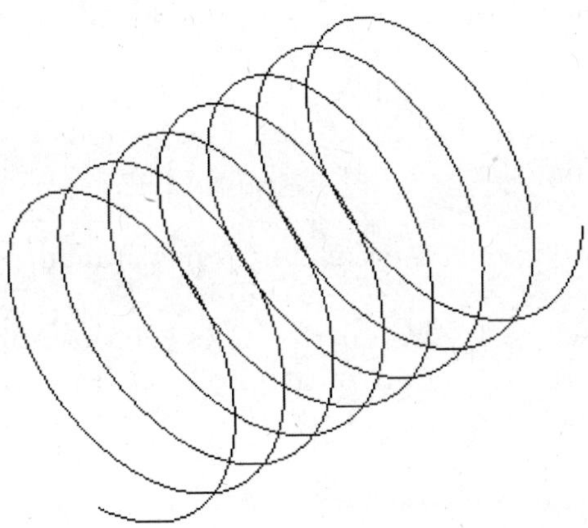

Figure 10-132 *Helical curve*

Drawing the Sketch of the End Clips of the Spring

After creating the helical curve, you need to draw a sketch to define the path of the end clips. There are two end clips in this spring, and each end clip is created by using two sketches. First, you will create the right end-clip and then the left end-clip.

1. Select the **Front Plane** as the sketching plane and invoke the sketching environment.

The first sketch of the right end-clip consists of two arcs. First arc will be drawn using the **Centerpoint Arc** tool and second arc will be drawn using the **3 Point Arc** tool.

2. Choose the **Centerpoint Arc** tool from the **Sketch CommandManager** and specify the centerpoint of the arc at the origin.

3. Move the cursor toward right and click to specify the start point of the arc when a value close to 25 is displayed as the radius of the reference circle.

4. Move the cursor in counterclockwise direction. Specify the endpoint of the arc when the value of the angle above the cursor is close to **75**.

5. Set the view to the front view.

6. Choose the **3 Point Arc** button from the **Arc PropertyManager**. Specify the start point of the arc on the upper endpoint of the previous arc. Create the arc, as shown in Figure 10-133.

7. Add the Pierce relation between the lower endpoint of the first arc and the helical curve. To do so, select the lower end point of the first arc and the helical curve by holding the CTRL key; the **Properties PropertyManager** is displayed. Now, choose the **Pierce** button in the **Add Relations** rollout and then choose the **OK** button in the **Properties PropertyManager**. Add other relations and dimensions to fully define the sketch. The fully defined sketch is shown in Figure 10-133.

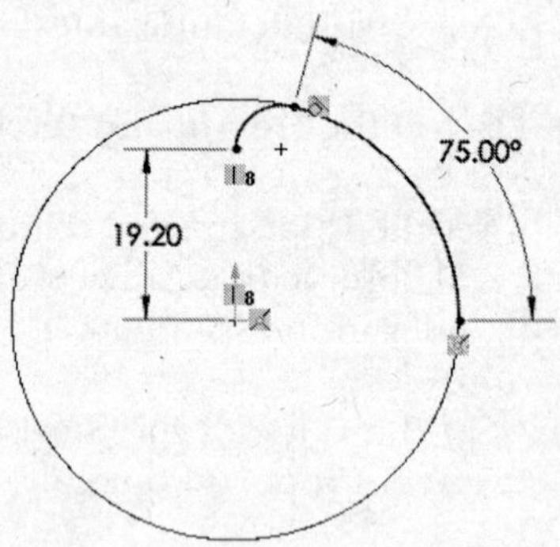

Figure 10-133 *First sketch of the right end-clip*

8. Exit the sketching environment.

After drawing the first sketch of the right end-clip, you need to draw the second sketch of the right end-clip. The second sketch of the right end-clip is drawn on the Right Plane.

9. Select the Right Plane and invoke the sketching environment.

10. Draw the sketch, as shown in Figure 10-134. You need to apply the Coincident relation between the endpoint of the upper arc of the previous sketch and the left endpoint of the left arc of the current sketch.

11. Add the Tangent relation between the left arc of the current sketch and the upper arc of the sketch drawn previously. Add required relations and dimensions to the current sketch. The sketch after applying all the relations and dimensions is shown in Figure 10-134.

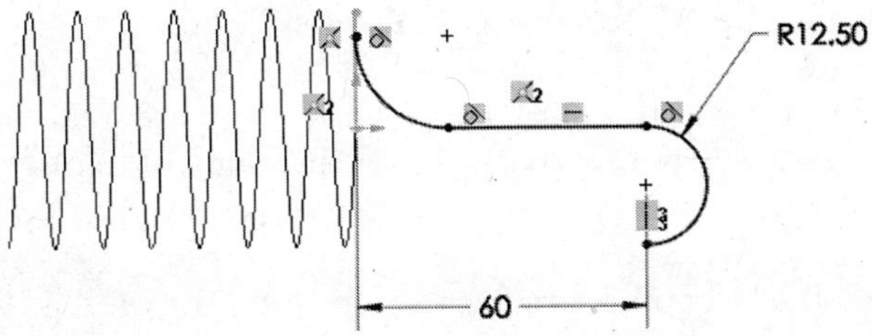

Figure 10-134 Second sketch of the right end-clip

12. Similarly, draw the sketch for the left end-clip. Figure 10-135 shows the path for the spring after creating the helical curve, right end-clip, and the left end-clip.

Creating the Composite Curve

After creating all the required sketches and the helical curve, you need to combine them so that they form a single curve. This is done because the path of the sweep feature has to be a single curve or sketch.

1. Choose the **Composite Curve** button from the **Curves** flyout or choose **Insert > Curve > Composite** from the SOLIDWORKS menus; the **Composite Curve PropertyManager** is displayed with confirmation corner on its top right corner.

2. Select both the end-clips and the helical curve from the drawing area or from the **FeatureManager Design Tree**.

3. Choose the **OK** button from the **Composite Curve PropertyManager** or choose **OK** from the confirmation corner; the composite curve is created, as shown in Figure 10-136.

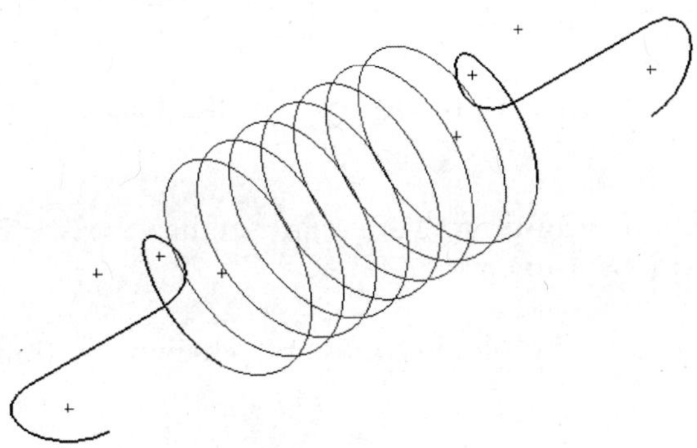

Figure 10-135 Path for the spring

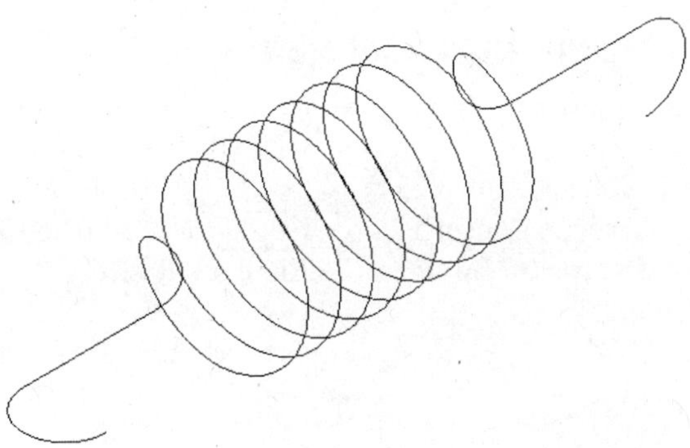

Figure 10-136 Composite curve

Creating the Sweep Feature

You need to create a sweep feature to complete the creation of the spring.

1. Invoke the **Sweep PropertyManager**; you are prompted to select the sweep profile.

2. Select the **Circular Profile** radio button from the **Profile and Path** rollout. As a result, the **Path** selection box and the **Diameter** spinner is displayed.

3. Select the composite curve as the path from the drawing area, the name of the curve will be displayed in the **Path** selection box. Also, set the value of diameter in the **Diameter** spinner to 7.

The spring created after sweeping circular profile along the path is shown in Figure 10-137.

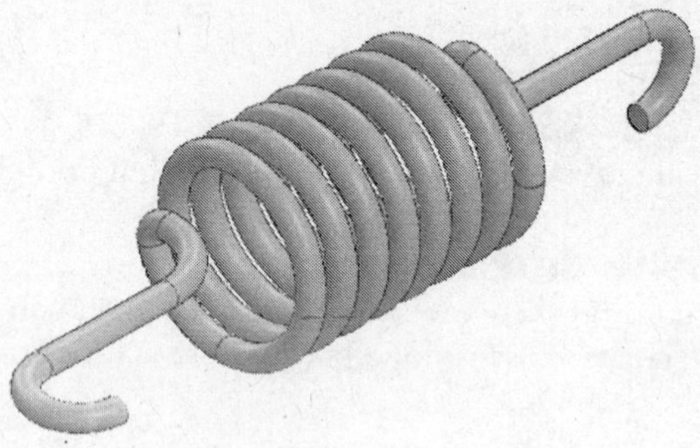

***Figure 10-137** The final model*

Saving the Model

1. Choose the **Save** button from the Menu Bar and save the model with the name *c10_tut03* at the following location:
\Documents\SOLIDWORKS\c10

2. Close the document.

Self-Evaluation Test

Answer the following questions and then compare them to those given at the end of this chapter:

1. You can select the __________ radio button from the **Profile and Path** rollout of the **Cut-Sweep PropertyManager** to create a cut-sweep feature by using a solid body.

2. The __________ option is used to create a single curve by joining continuous chain of existing sketches, edges, or curves.

3. You need to apply the __________ relation between a sketch and a guide curve for sweeping a profile along a path using guide curves.

4. The __________ option is used to create a curve by defining coordinates.

5. The __________ button in the **Guide Curves** rollout is used to display intermediate sections while creating a sweep feature with the guide curves.

6. You need a profile and a path to create a sweep feature. (T/F)

7. At least two sections are required to create a loft feature. (T/F)

8. You cannot sweep a closed profile along a closed path. (T/F)

9. You cannot create a thin sweep feature. (T/F)

10. You can create a loft feature by using open sections. (T/F)

Review Questions

Answer the following questions:

1. Which of the following buttons is used to invoke the 3D sketching environment?

   (a) **2D Sketch** (b) **3D Sketching Environment**
   (c) **3D Sketch** (d) **Sketch**

2. Which of the following rollouts in the **Sweep PropertyManager** is used to define the tangency?

   (a) **Start/End Tangency** (b) **Tangency**
   (c) **Options** (d) None of these

3. Which of the following buttons in the **Features CommandManager** is used to invoke the **Draft PropertyManager**?

   (a) **Draft** (b) **Taper Angle**
   (c) **Draft Feature** (d) **Draft Angle**

4. Which of the following PropertyManagers is used to change an existing draft feature?

   (a) **DraftXpert** (b) **Draft**
   (c) Both a and b (d) None of these

5. Which of the following buttons in the **Guide Curves** rollout is used to display sections while creating the sweep feature with guide curves?

   (a) **Preview Sections** (b) **Show Sections**
   (c) **Sections** (d) **Preview**

6. In the __________ rollout, you can define the tangency at the start and end sections in the sweep feature.

7. The _________ rollout is used to create a thin loft feature.

8. You need to invoke the _________ dialog box to create a spiral curve.

9. The __________ **PropertyManager** is used to project a curve on a surface.

10. The __________ dialog box is used to specify coordinates to create a curve.

EXERCISES

Exercise 1

Create the model of the Upper Housing shown in Figure 10-138. The dimensions of the model are shown in Figure 10-139. **(Expected time: 1 hr)**

Tip

This model is divided into three major parts. The first part is the base and is created by extruding the sketch upto a distance of 80 mm using the ***Mid Plane*** *option.*

The second part of this model is the right portion of the discharge venturi and is created by using the sweep feature. The path of the sweep feature will be created on the Right Plane.

The third part of this model is the left portion of the discharge venturi created using the loft feature. You need to create the first section of the loft feature on the planar face of the sweep feature created earlier. The second section will be created on a plane at an offset distance from the planar face of the sweep feature created earlier. Create a loft feature using the two sections created earlier. The other features needed to complete the model are fillets, hole, circular pattern, and so on.

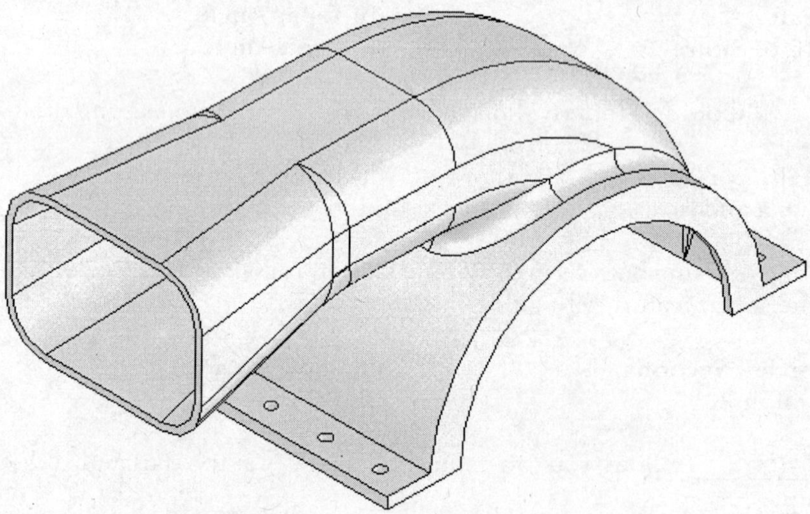

Figure 10-138 *Model of the Upper Housing*

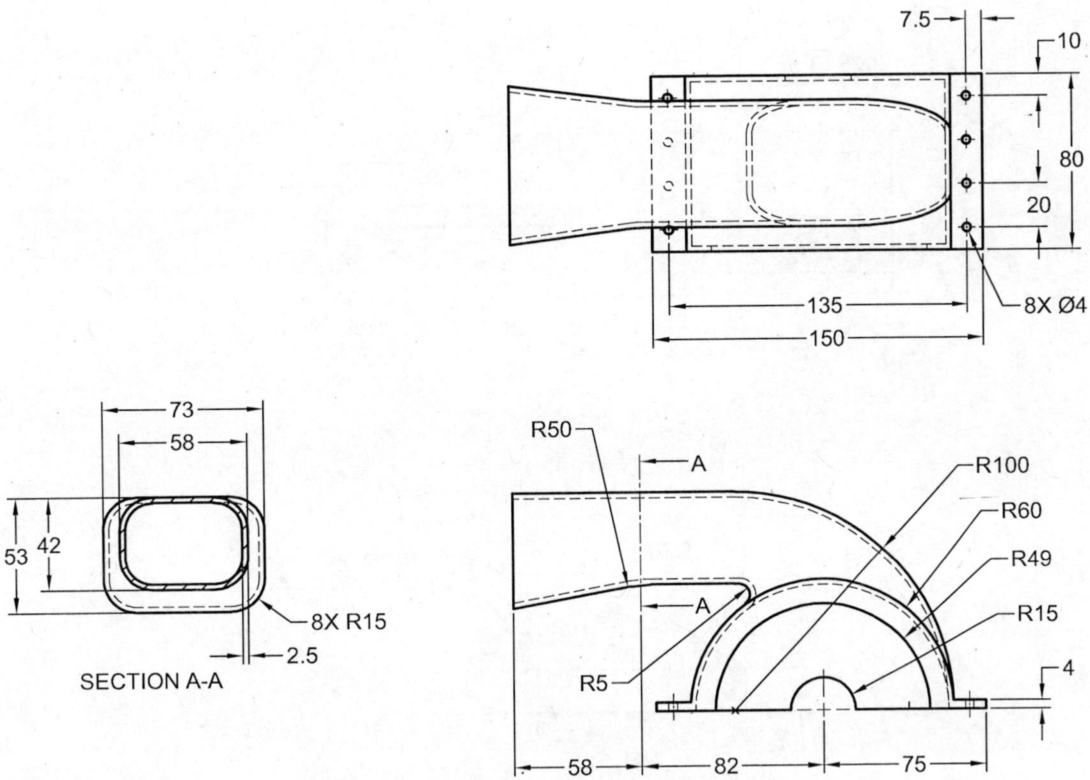

Figure 10-139 Dimensions of the Upper Housing

Exercise 2

Create the model shown in Figure 10-140. The dimensions of the model are shown in Figure 10-141. **(Expected time: 1 hr)**

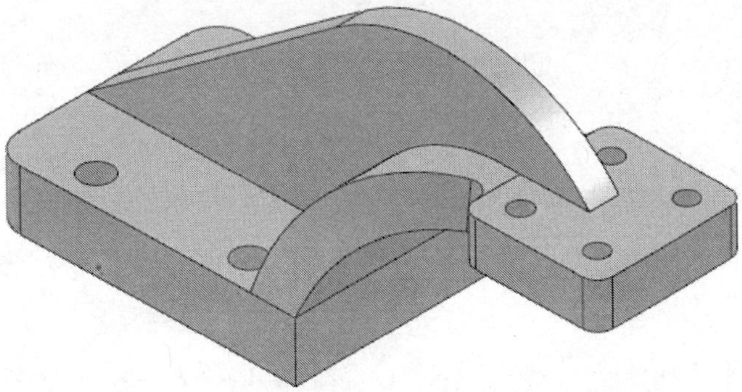

Figure 10-140 Model for Exercise 2

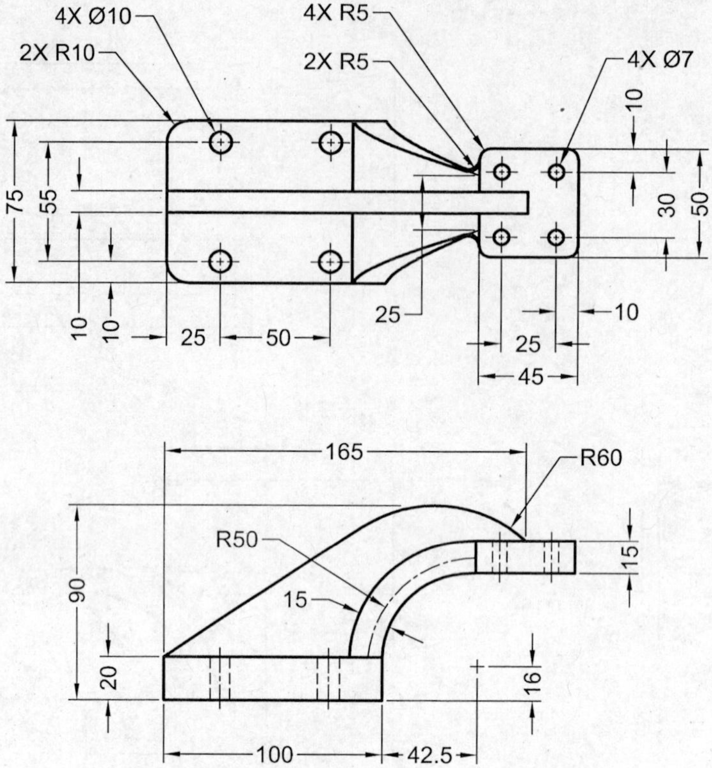

Figure 10-141 Dimensions of the model

Exercise 3

Create the model shown in Figure 10-142. Its rotated view is shown in Figure 10-143. The dimensions of the model are shown in Figure 10-144. **(Expected time: 1 hr)**

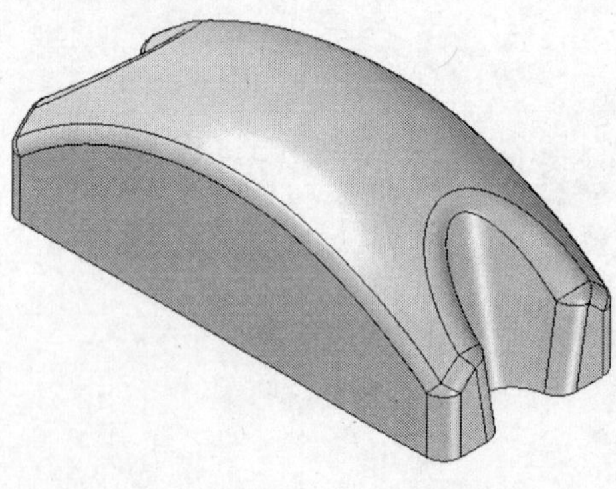

Figure 10-142 Model for Exercise 3

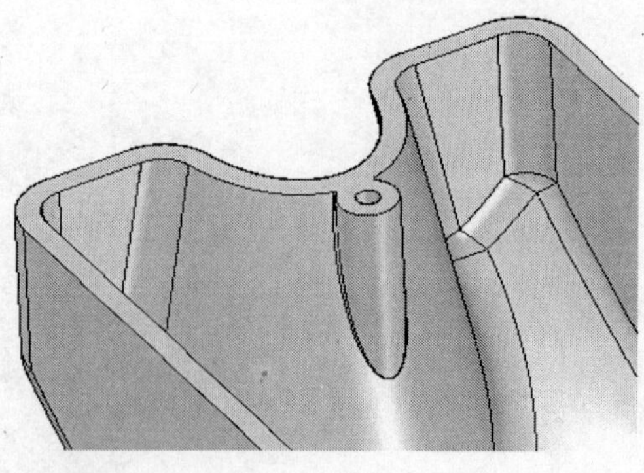

Figure 10-143 Rotated view of the model

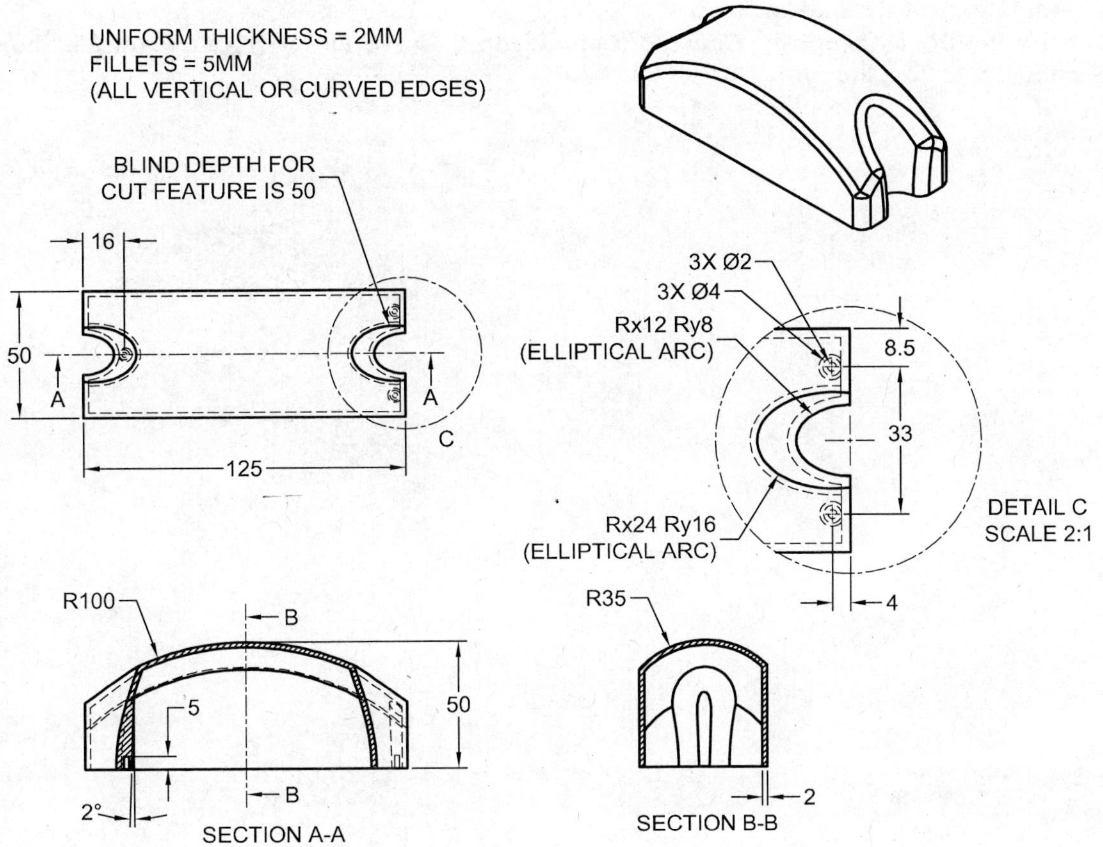

Figure 10-144 Dimensions of the model

Answers to Self-Evaluation Test

1. Solid Profile, **2.** Composite Curve, **3.** Coincident, **4.** Curve Through XYZ Points, **5.** Show Sections, **6.** T, **7.** T, **8.** F, **9.** F, **10.** T

Chapter 11

Advanced Modeling Tools-IV

Learning Objectives

After completing this chapter, you will be able to:

- *Create dome features*
- *Create indent features*
- *Create deform features*
- *Create flex features*
- *Create fastening features*
- *Create freeform features*
- *Dimension a part using DimXpert*

ADVANCED MODELING TOOLS

Some of the advanced modeling tools have already been discussed in Chapters 7, 8, and 10. In this chapter, you will learn about some more advanced modeling tools that can be used to enhance your modeling ability.

Creating Dome Features

CommandManager:	Features > Dome	*(Customize to add)*
SOLIDWORKS menus:	Insert > Features > Dome	
Toolbar:	Features > Dome	*(Customize to add)*

The **Dome** tool is used to create a dome feature on the selected face. Depending on the direction along which a feature is created, a dome can be of convex or concave shape. To create a dome feature, choose the **Dome** button from the **Features CommandManager**, or choose **Insert > Features > Dome** from the SOLIDWORKS menus; the **Dome PropertyManager** will be displayed, as shown in Figure 11-1. Also, you will be prompted to select a face or faces on which you want to add the dome feature. The face to be selected can be a planar or a non-planar face. Select the face on which you need to create the dome feature; the name of the selected face will be displayed in the **Faces to Dome** selection box. Also, the preview of the dome feature, with the default values, will be displayed in the drawing area. Set the height of the dome feature in the **Distance** spinner. You can also move the cursor on the thumbwheel below the **Distance** spinner and drag the cursor to modify its value. If you drag the thumbwheel to the right, the value will increase and if you drag it to the left, the value will decrease. The preview of the dome feature will modify dynamically when you modify the height using the **Distance** spinner. The height of the dome feature is calculated from the centroid of the selected face to the top of the dome feature. After specifying the height of the dome feature, choose the **OK** button from the **Dome PropertyManager**. Figure 11-2 shows the planar face to be selected for the dome feature. Figure 11-3 shows the resulting dome feature.

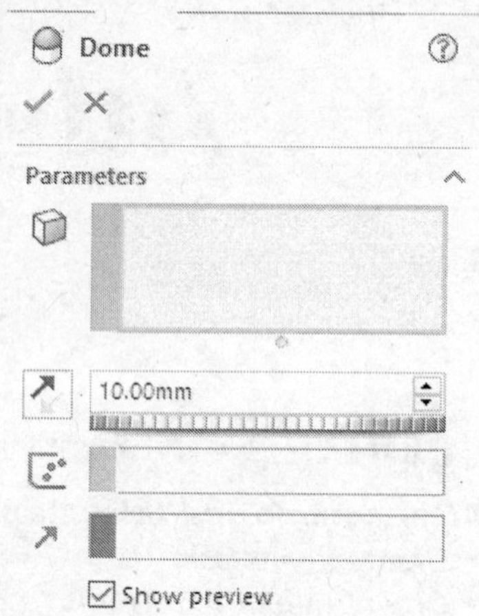

Figure 11-1 *The **Dome** PropertyManager*

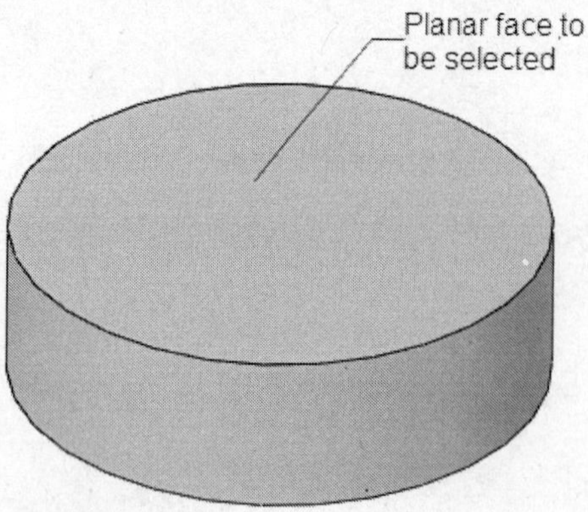

Figure 11-2 *Planar face to be selected*

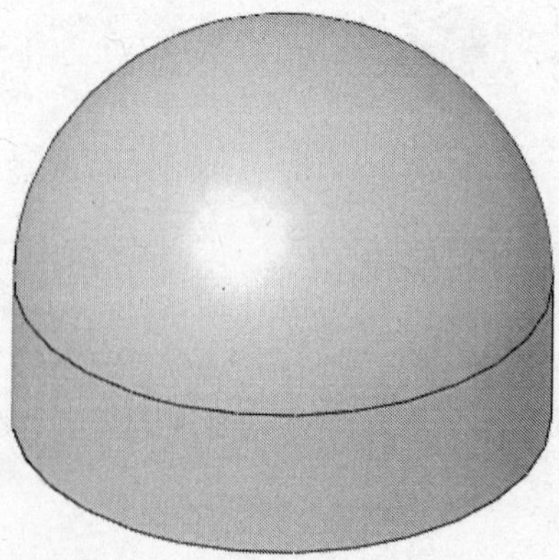

Figure 11-3 *Resulting dome feature*

If the selected planar face belongs to a circular or an elliptical feature, the **Elliptical dome** check box will be displayed in the **Dome PropertyManager**. You can create an elliptical dome feature by selecting this check box. Figure 11-4 shows a circular dome created by selecting a top planar face. Figure 11-5 shows an elliptical dome created by selecting the **Elliptical dome** check box.

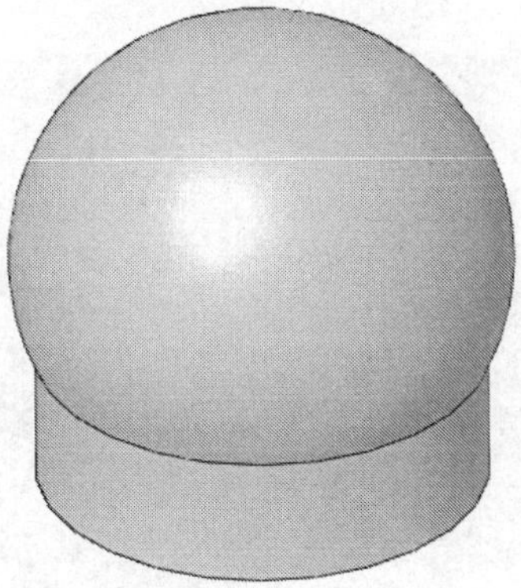

Figure 11-4 Circular dome

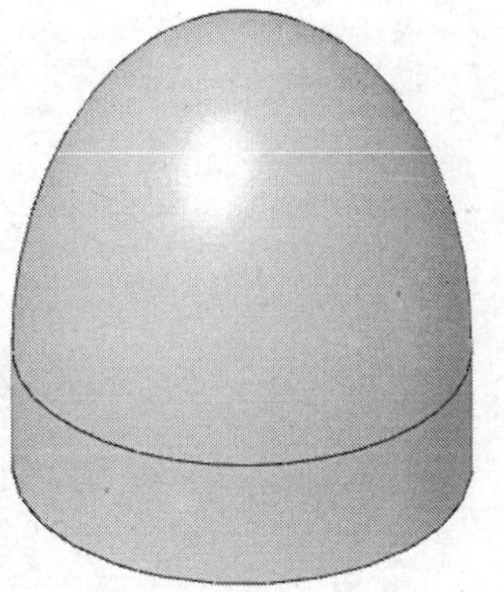

Figure 11-5 Elliptical dome

You can also create a concave shaped dome by removing its material to create a cavity in the form of a dome. To do so, choose the **Reverse Direction** button on the left of the **Distance** spinner; a concave shaped dome will be created, as shown in Figure 11-6. You can also create continuous dome on polygonal models by selecting the **Continuous dome** check box, as shown in Figure 11-7.

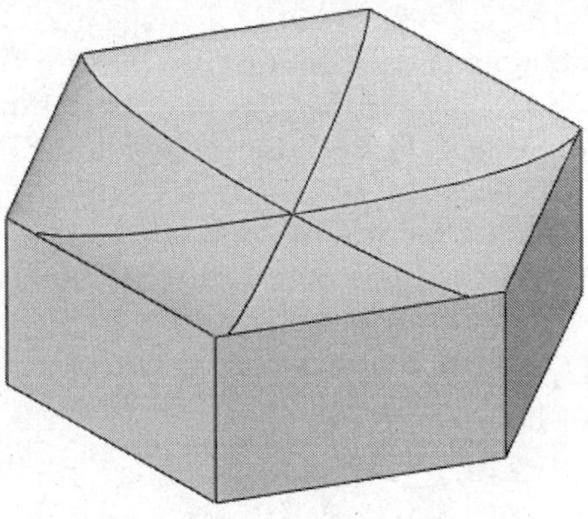

Figure 11-6 Concave dome

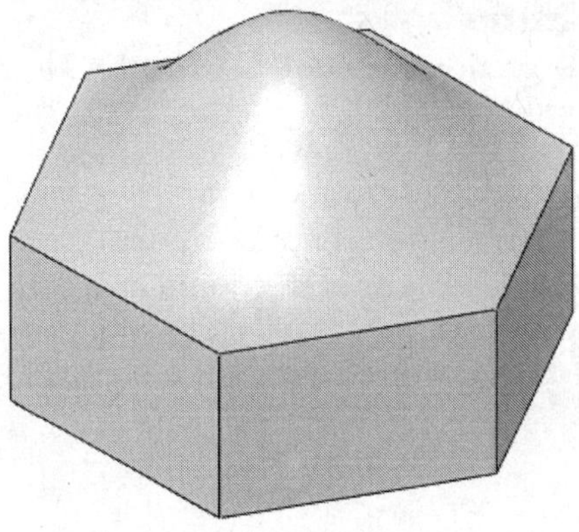

Figure 11-7 Continuous dome

Other options in the **Dome PropertyManager** are discussed next.

Constraint Point or Sketch

The **Constraint Point or Sketch** selection box in the **Dome PropertyManager** is used to constraint the dome creation to a selected reference. The selected reference can be a point, a sketched point, or an endpoint of an entity. To create a dome feature using the **Constraint Point or Sketch** option, invoke the **Dome PropertyManager** and select the face on which you need to add the dome feature. Now, click once in the **Constraint Point or Sketch** selection box and select the constraint point from the drawing area and then choose the **OK** button from the **Dome PropertyManager**. Figure 11-8 shows the face on which you need to add the dome feature and the point to be selected as the constraint point. Figure 11-9 shows the resulting dome feature.

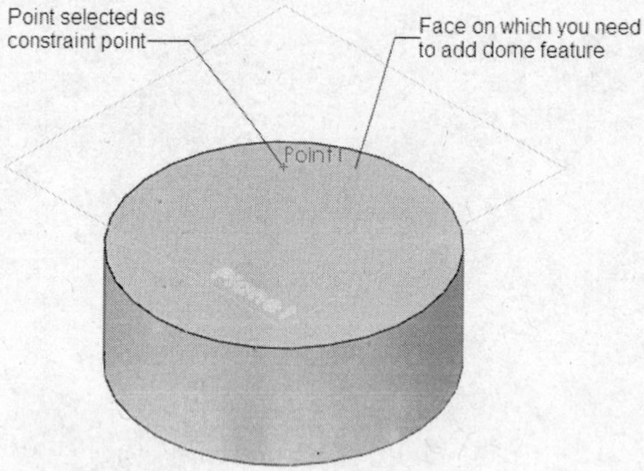

Figure 11-8 Face and the point to be selected

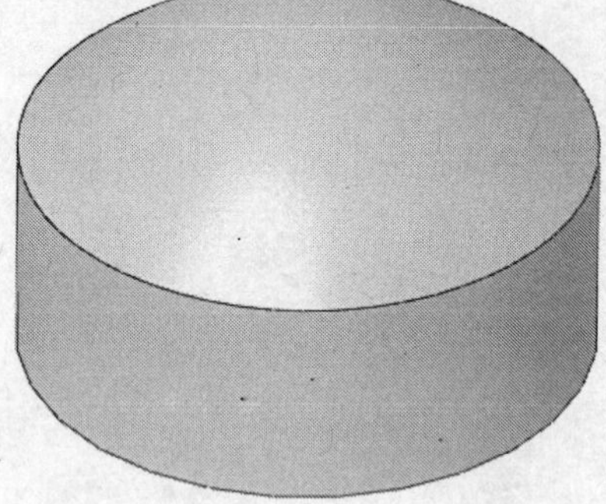

Figure 11-9 Resulting dome feature

Note

The dome feature will be created depending on the height and the position of the constraint point. You can also specify zero distance value for cylindrical and conical models.

Direction

The **Direction** selection box in the **Dome PropertyManager** is used to specify the direction vector along which you need to create the dome feature. To create the dome feature by defining the direction vector, invoke the **Dome PropertyManager**. Select the face on which you need to create the dome feature. Now, click once in the **Direction** selection box and select an edge as the directional reference from the drawing area; the selected edge will be highlighted. Set the value of the height of the dome and choose the **OK** button from the **Dome PropertyManager**. Figure 11-10 shows the face on which you need to add the dome feature and the edge to be selected as the direction vector. Figure 11-11 shows the resulting dome.

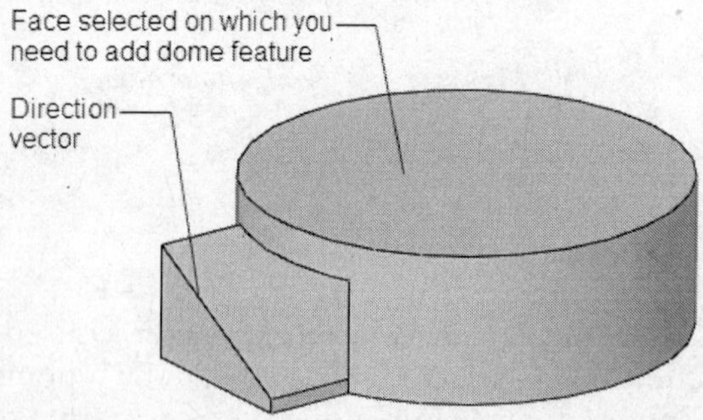

Figure 11-10 Face and direction vector to be selected

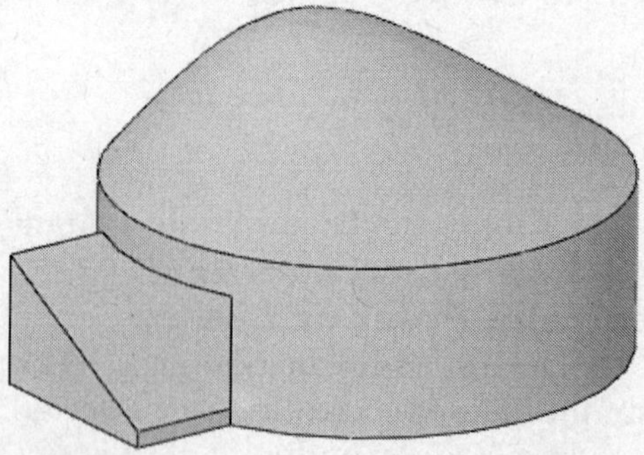

Figure 11-11 Resulting dome feature

Creating Indents

CommandManager:	Features > Indent	*(Customize to add)*
SOLIDWORKS menus:	Insert > Features > Indent	
Toolbar:	Features > Indent	*(Customize to add)*

The **Indent** tool is extremely useful for the packaging industries, industrial designers, and product designers. The **Indent** tool is used in the multibody environment. This tool is used to add or scoop out material from a target body. The body that is used to add or scoop out the material is known as the tool body. Depending on the geometry, the tool is used to add or scoop material from the target body.

To create an indent feature, choose **Insert > Features > Indent** from the SOLIDWORKS menus; the **Indent PropertyManager** will be displayed, as shown in Figure 11-12. The rollouts in this PropertyManager are discussed next.

*Figure 11-12 The **Indent** PropertyManager*

Selections Rollout

The options in the **Selections** rollout are used to select the target body, the tool body, and to set some parameters. These options are discussed next.

Target body

After invoking the **Indent PropertyManager**, you need to select the body that will be deformed using the tool body. This selected body is known as the target body. The name of the selected body is displayed in the **Target body** selection box.

Tool body region

After selecting the target body, you need to select a body that will be used as the tool for deforming the target body. This body is known as the tool body. Select the body that needs to be defined as the tool body; the selected portion of the body will be highlighted and its name will be displayed in the **Tool body region** selection box. Also, you will notice that by default, the **Keep selections** radio button is selected. Therefore, the selected portion of the tool body will be retained and the other portion will be removed. If you select the **Remove selections** radio button, the selected portion of the tool body will be removed and the remaining portion will be retained.

Cut

The **Cut** check box is selected to create a cut in the target body. This cut is defined by the geometry of the tool body.

Parameters Rollout

The **Parameters** rollout is used to specify the values of clearance and thickness in the **Clearance** and **Thickness** spinners, respectively. To understand more about clearance and thickness, refer to Figure 11-13. Note that, on selecting the **Cut** check box from the **Selections** rollout, the **Thickness** spinner gets inactive.

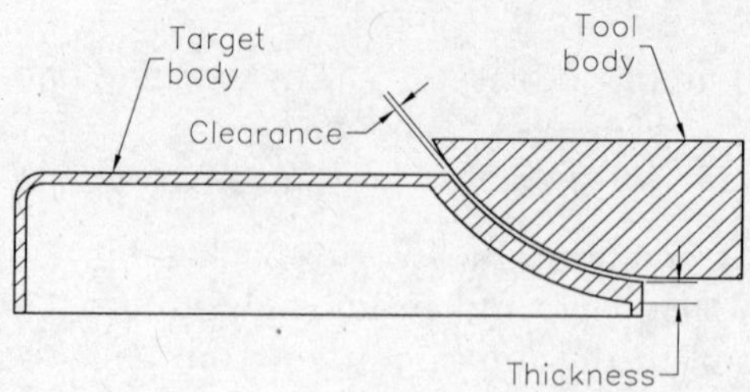

Figure 11-13 The parameters to create an indent feature

Figure 11-14 shows two different bodies with the small rectangular body placed inside the main body. Figure 11-15 shows the target body and the portion of the tool body to be selected. Figure 11-16 shows the resulting body after removing the material by using the **Indent** tool. In this figure, the display of the tool body is turned off. To do so, select the tool body in the **FeatureManager Design Tree** and choose **Hide** from the pop-up toolbar. You will learn more about toggling the display of the bodies in the later chapters. Figure 11-17 shows the resulting body after rotating the view of the model.

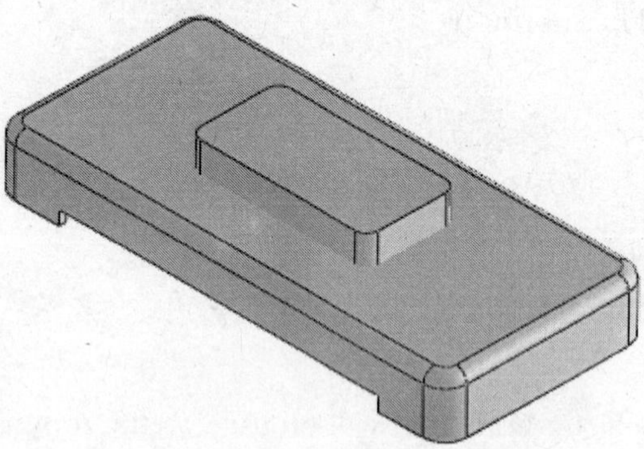

Figure 11-14 Two separate bodies

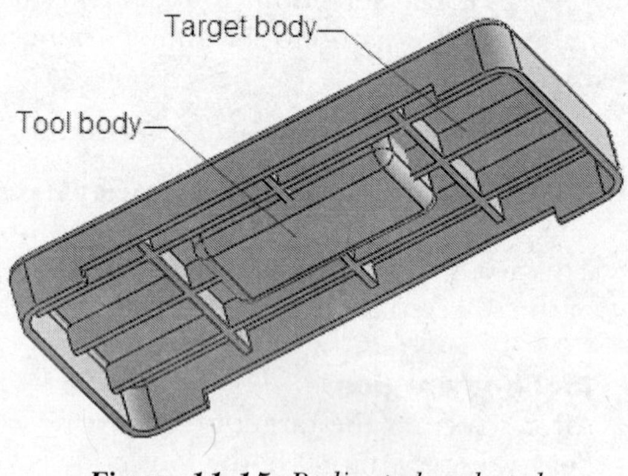

Figure 11-15 Bodies to be selected

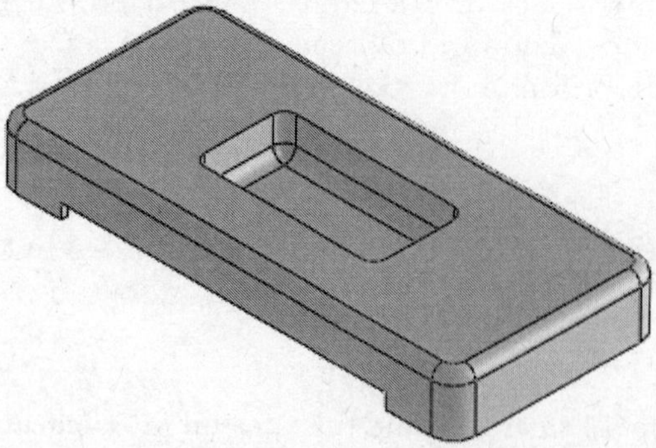

Figure 11-16 Resulting body after removing the material

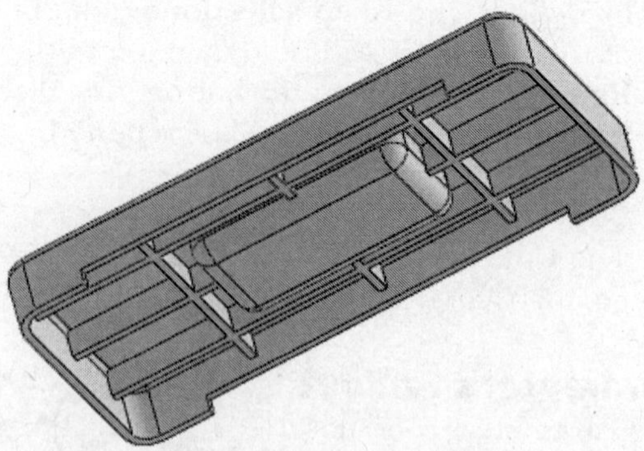

Figure 11-17 Resulting body after rotating its view

Figure 11-18 shows the target body and the tool body to be selected. Figure 11-19 shows the resulting body created using the **Indent** tool with the **Cut** check box selected. The display of the tool body is turned off in this figure.

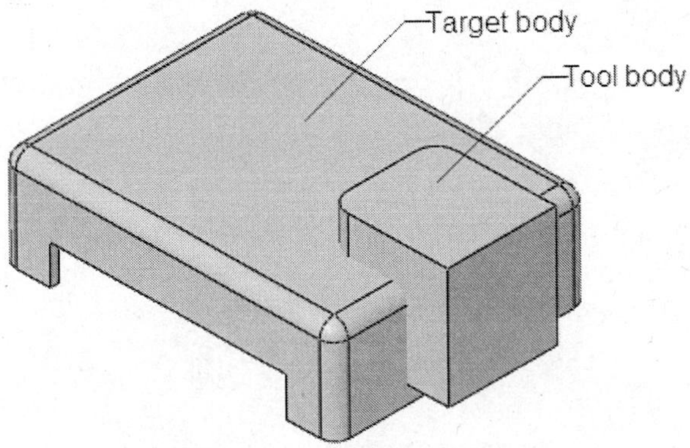

Figure 11-18 Bodies to be selected

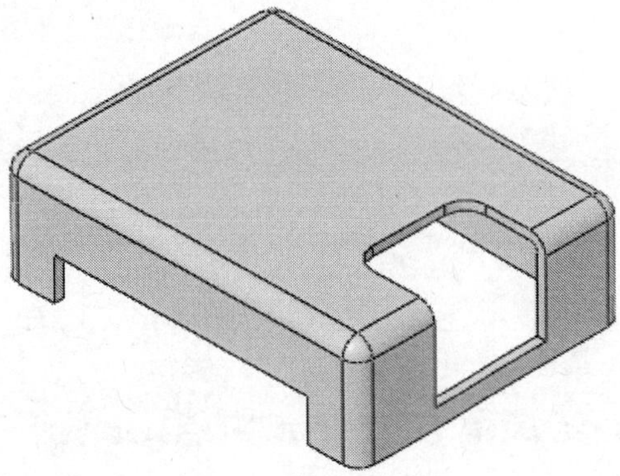

Figure 11-19 *Resulting body created using the* ***Indent*** *tool with the* ***Cut*** *check box selected*

Figure 11-20 shows the eggs created by revolving the sketch and then patterned by using the **Linear Pattern** tool. Figure 11-21 shows the eggs placed on a base plate created as a separate body. In this example, the base plate is selected as the target body and all eggs are selected from the bottom portion as tool bodies. Figure 11-22 shows the egg tray created using the **Indent** tool with the **Remove selections** radio button selected in the **Indent PropertyManager**. In this figure, the display of all the eggs is turned off.

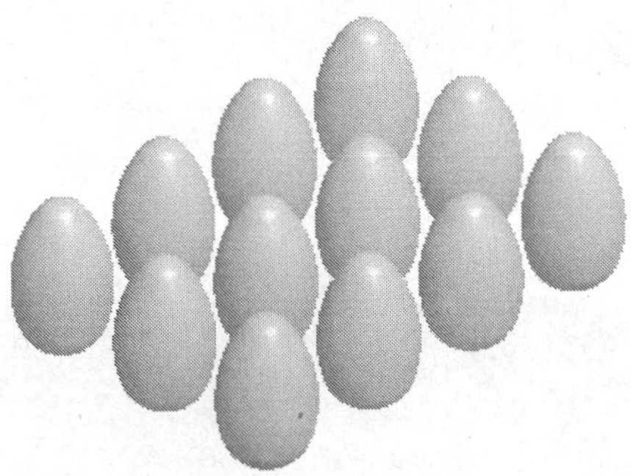

Figure 11-20 *Eggs patterned using the* ***Linear Pattern*** *tool*

Figure 11-21 *Eggs placed on a base plate created as a separate body*

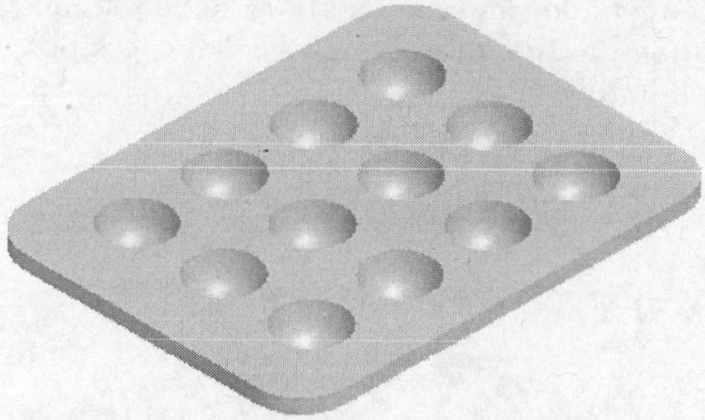

Figure 11-22 Resulting egg tray

Creating Deform Features

CommandManager:	Features > Deform	*(Customize to add)*
SOLIDWORKS menus:	Insert > Features > Deform	
Toolbar:	Features > Deform	*(Customize to add)*

The **Deform** tool is used to create free-style designs by manipulating the shape of the entire model or a particular portion of it. After customizing the **CommandManager**, choose the **Deform** button from the **Features CommandManager**; the **Deform PropertyManager** will be displayed. Its partial view is shown in Figure 11-23. There are three methods to create a deform feature which are discussed next.

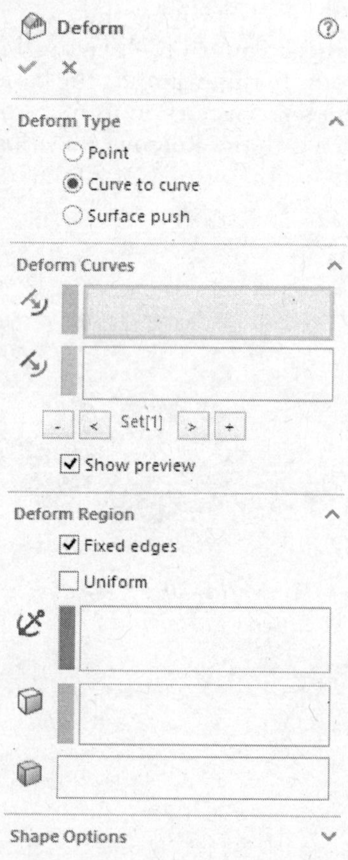

Figure 11-23** Partial view of the **Deform PropertyManager

Creating Deform Features Using the Curve to curve Method

To create a deform feature using the **Curve to curve** method, invoke the **Deform PropertyManager**. Next, select the **Curve to curve** radio button in the **Deform Type** rollout, if it is not selected by default. The options to create the deform feature using this method are discussed next.

Deform Curves Rollout

The **Deform Curves** rollout is used to define the curves that are used to deform the shape of the model. On invoking the **Deform** tool, you will be prompted to select the geometry to define the deformation and the fixed geometry for the deform operation. Select an edge, a chain of edges, or curves to define the initial curve. The initial curve defines the reference from where the deformation will start. Next, you need to select the target curves. Click once in the **Target Curves** selection box and select the target curve that can be a sketch, an edge, or a curve. The profile of the target curve will define the shape of the deform feature.

When you select the initial curve and the target curve, a connector connecting both the curves will be displayed. You can position the connector by using the handles provided by its sides. To define additional connectors, invoke the shortcut menu by right clicking in the drawing area and choose the **Add Connector** option from it.

Deform Region Rollout

The **Deform Region** rollout is used to define the options to deform a specific area of the model. By default, the entire model will be deformed when you specify the initial curves and the target curves. The **Fixed edges** check box is selected by default. As a result, the **Fixed Curves/Edges/Faces** selection box will be activated. Using this selection box, you can select the curves, edges, or faces that you need to keep fixed while creating the deform feature. The **Additional Faces to be Deformed** selection box is used to specify the additional faces that you need to deform. If you clear the **Fixed edges** check box, the **Fixed Curves/Edges/Faces**, and **Additional Faces to be Deformed** selection boxes will not be displayed.

The **Uniform** check box in the **Deform Region** rollout is used to deform the model uniformly. If you clear the **Fixed edges** check box and select the **Uniform** check box from the **Deform Region** rollout, the **Deform Radius** spinner will be displayed. The **Bodies to be Deformed** selection box is used to define the bodies that you need to deform. This option is used in a multibody model.

Note

If you select the ***Uniform*** *check box in the* ***Deform Region*** *rollout, the* ***Weight*** *slider bar in the* ***Shape Options*** *rollout will not be available.*

Shape Options Rollout

The options in this rollout are used to define the intensity of stiffness, the shape accuracy, and the intensity of weight along the fixed reference or moving reference.

Figure 11-24 shows the references to be selected and Figure 11-25 shows a preview of the deform feature. Note that the selection for target curves should be in appropriate manner.

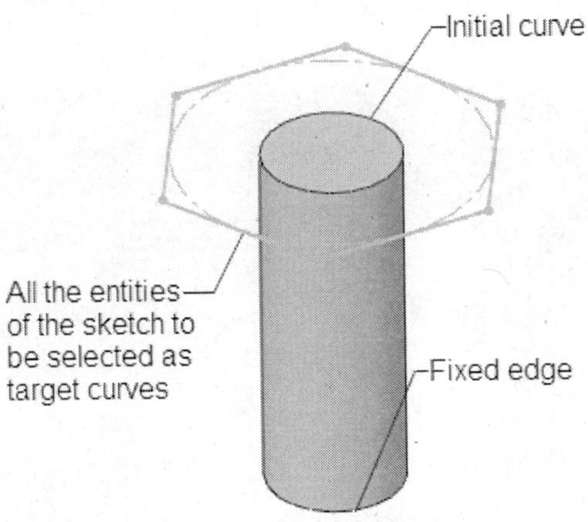

Figure 11-24 References to be selected

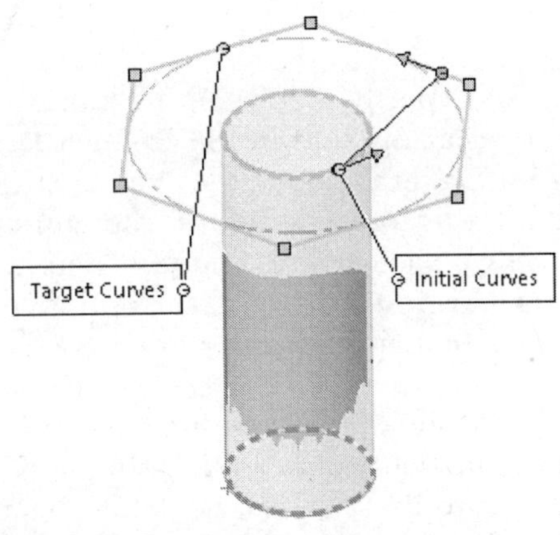

Figure 11-25 Preview of the deform feature

After setting all parameters, choose the **OK** button from the **Deform PropertyManager**. Figure 11-26 shows the resulting deform feature.

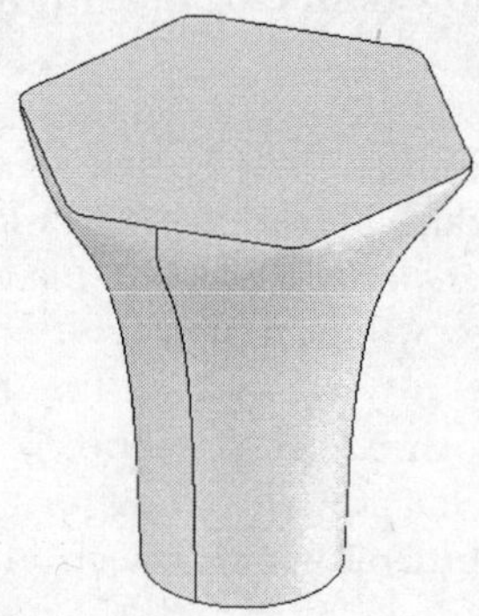

Figure 11-26 Resulting deform feature

Creating the Deform Feature Using the Point Method

To create the deform feature by using the **Point** method, select the **Point** radio button from the **Deform Type** rollout in the **Deform PropertyManager**, refer to Figure 11-27; you will be prompted to select the geometry to define the region, deformation point, and fixed geometry for the deform operation. Select a point on the face of the model, vertex, or edge from where you need to deform the model; the model will be deformed at the selected point as per the default value of the deform distance and deform radius. You can set the value of the deform distance and the deform radius by using the **Deform Distance** and **Deform Radius** spinners from the **Deform Point** and **Deform Region** rollouts, respectively. You can reverse the deform direction of feature by using the **Reverse deform direction** button in the **Deform Point** rollout.

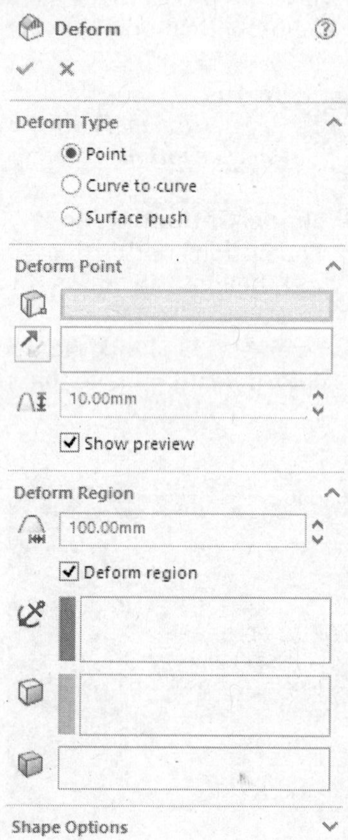

Figure 11-27 Partial view of the Deform PropertyManager

You can also specify a deform direction to create a deform feature by clicking once in the **Deform Direction** selection box and selecting the direction to create the deform feature. By default, this tool will deform the entire model. You can also specify a particular portion for deforming by selecting the **Deform region** check box. The options to specify a region for deformation are the same as discussed earlier.

Figure 11-28 shows the point where you need to select the face of the model. Figure 11-29 shows the resulting deform feature. Figure 11-30 shows the deform feature created with the **Point** radio button and the **Deform region** check box selected. Figure 11-31 shows the deform feature with the **Deform region** check box selected and the front face of the base feature selected as the additional face to be deformed.

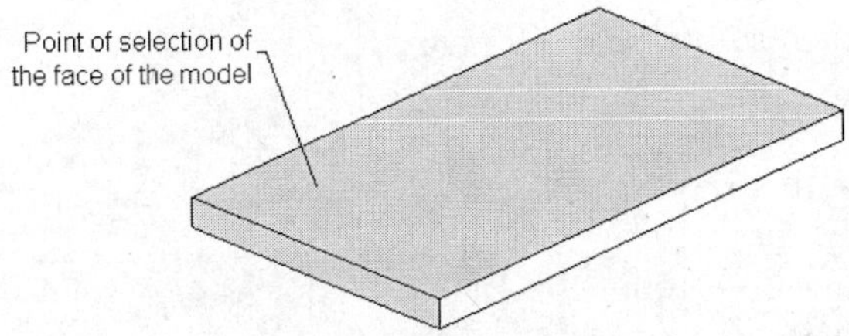

Figure 11-28 References to be selected

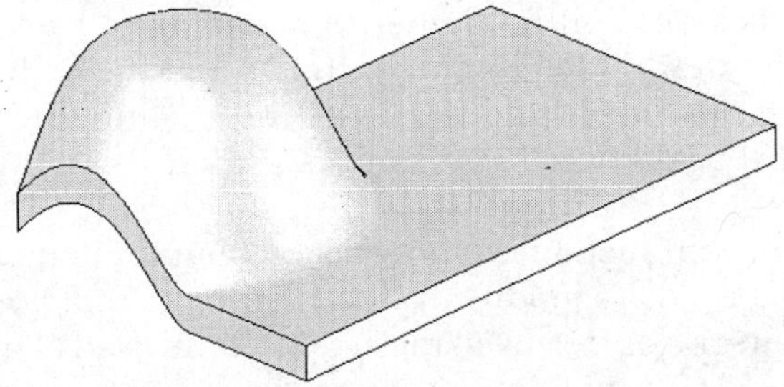

Figure 11-29 Resulting deform feature

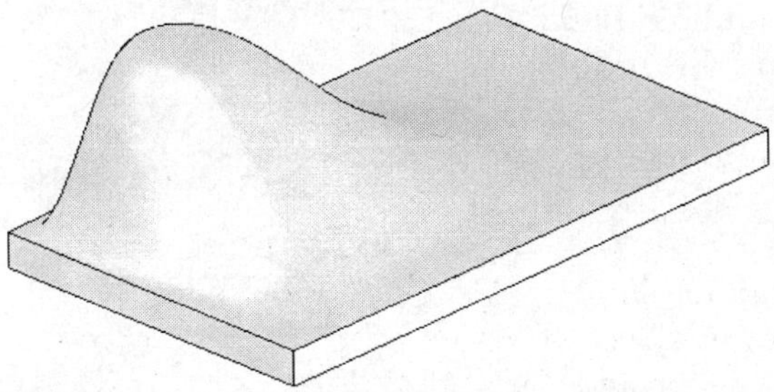

*Figure 11-30 Deform feature with the **Point** radio button and the **Deform region** check box selected*

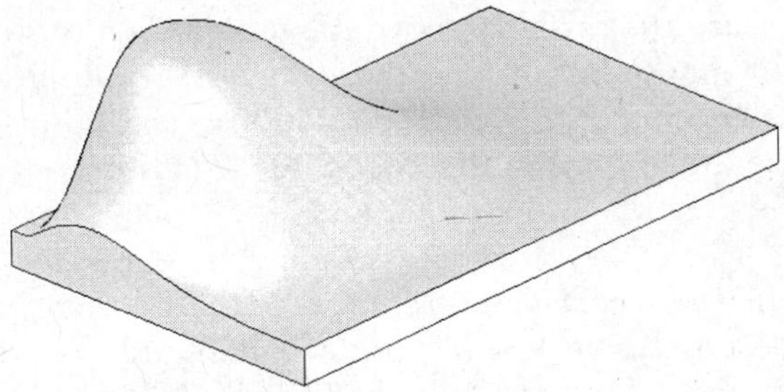

Figure 11-31 Deform feature with front face selected as the additional face to be deformed

You can also define the deform axis for deforming the entire model by specifying it in the **Deform axis** selection box in the **Shape Options** rollout. The other options are the same as discussed earlier.

Creating the Deform Feature Using the Surface Push Method

This option is used to deform the selected body or bodies by pushing the tool bodies inside them. To deform a body using this option, invoke the **Deform PropertyManager** and select the **Surface push** radio button from the **Deform Type** rollout. Partial view of the **Deform PropertyManager** is shown in Figure 11-32.

A 3D triad along with the axes rings will be placed coincident to the part origin. You can use different types of geometries such as ellipse, ellipsoid, polygon, rectangle, and sphere as the tool body using the options in the **Tool Body** drop-down list. You can also select a separately created body as the tool body by selecting the **Select Body** option from the **Tool Body** drop-down list and then selecting the body required as the tool body. You will notice that with each type of default tool body, a callout is displayed. This callout can be used to modify the shape and size of the geometry of the tool body.

Next, you need to select the direction along which you need to push the target body. Click once in the **Push Direction** selection box if it is not selected already and then select an edge, a sketched line, or a face to define the push direction reference. Choose the **Reverse Direction** button to flip the default push direction, if required.

Click once in the **Bodies to be Deformed** selection box in the **Deform Region** rollout and select the body or bodies to be deformed; the preview of the resulting deformed body will be displayed in the drawing area.

You can modify the position of the tool body by using the 3D triad. To modify the location of the tool body, move the cursor close to any of the arrows of the triad along which you need to move or rotate the tool body. On doing so, the cursor will be replaced by the modify cursor. Press and hold the left mouse button and drag the cursor in the direction pointing toward the arrow to move the tool body. Press and hold the left mouse button and drag the cursor along the direction of the ring of the triad to rotate the tool body. You can also use the options in the **Tool Body Position** rollout to modify the position of the tool body.

The **Deform Deviation** spinner in the **Deform Region** rollout is used to define the fillet radius where the tool body intersects the face of the target body. Figure 11-33 shows a deformed feature with a lower value of deviation and Figure 11-34 shows a deformed feature with a higher value of deviation.

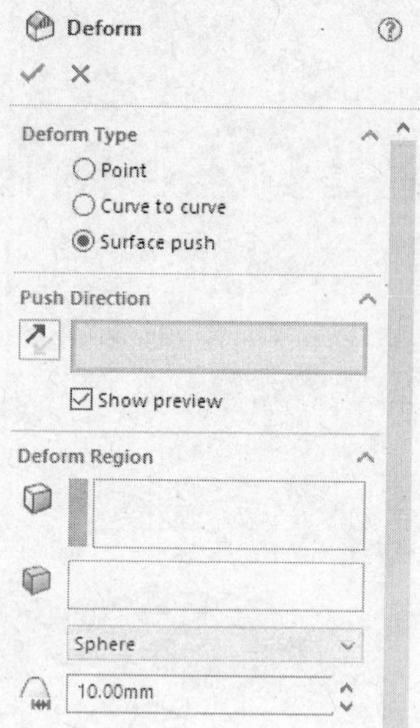

Figure 11-32 *Partial view of the **Deform Property Manager** with the **Surface push** radio button selected*

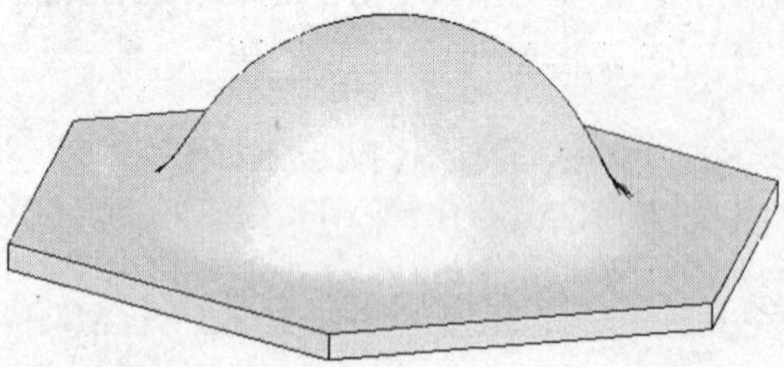

Figure 11-33 *Deform feature with a lower value of deviation*

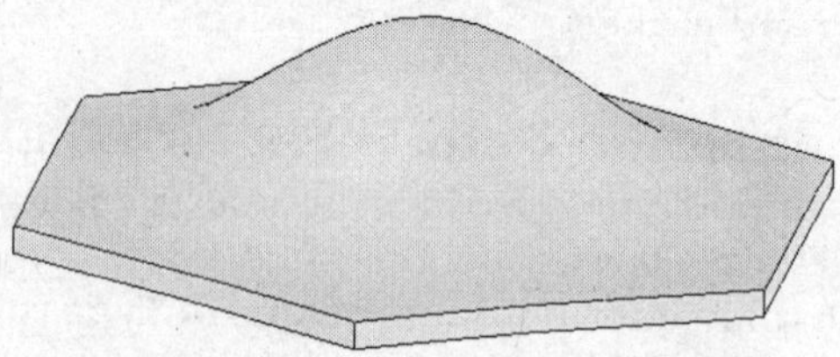

Figure 11-34 *Deform feature with a higher value of deviation*

Creating Flex Features

CommandManager:	Features > Flex	*(Customize to add)*
SOLIDWORKS menus:	Insert > Features > Flex	
Toolbar:	Features > Flex	*(Customize to add)*

The **Flex** tool is used to perform free form bending, twisting, tapering, and stretching of a selected body. The portion of the bodies to be deformed is defined by two planes known as trimming planes. You will learn more about these planes later in this chapter. To deform a body using this tool, choose the **Flex** button from the **Features CommandManager**; the **Flex PropertyManager** will be displayed. Partial view of the **Flex PropertyManager** is shown in Figure 11-35.

The **Bending** radio button is selected by default in the **Flex Input** rollout and you are prompted to select the bodies for flex and set the options. Select the body from the drawing area; the selected body will turn transparent and will be placed between the two trimming planes. Also, the bend axis passing through the selected body will be displayed. The body will be bent along this axis. A 3D triad along with the axes rings will be placed coincident to the part origin. Figure 11-36 shows the selected body along with the trimming planes, 3D triad, axes rings, and the bend axis.

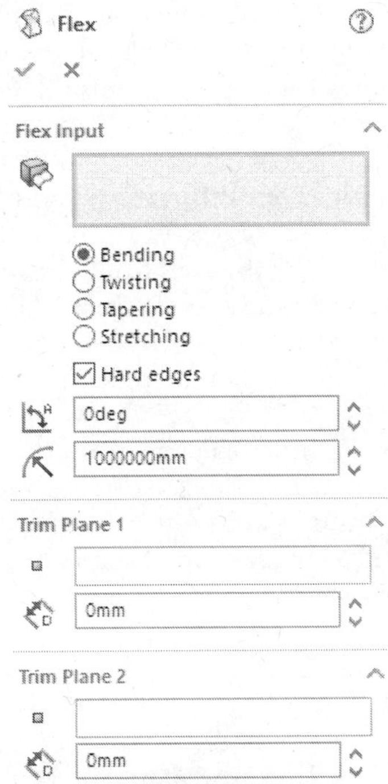

Figure 11-35 *Partial view of the* ***Flex PropertyManager***

You can modify the position and location of the trimming planes and the bend axis using the 3D triad and axes rings. To do so, move the cursor on the triad arrow along which you need to move the bend axis or the ring about which you need to rotate the trimming plane; the select cursor will be replaced by the move or rotate cursor. Press and hold the left mouse button on the arrow to move the location of the bend axis. Figure 11-37 shows the preview of the flex feature after modifying the value of the bend axis and the trimming planes.

You can also modify the location of the 3D triad. To do so, move the cursor to the origin of the triad, press and hold the left mouse button and drag the cursor to change the location of the triad. You can also use the **Triad** rollout to modify the position of the triad, rotation angle of the bend axis, and the trimming planes.

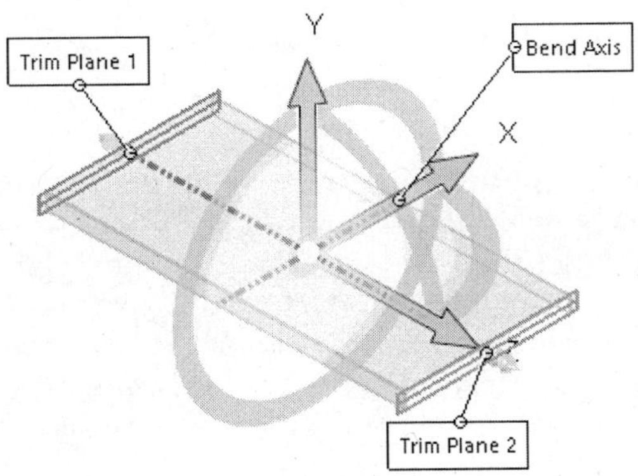

Figure 11-36 *The selected body along with trimming planes, 3D triad, and the bend axis*

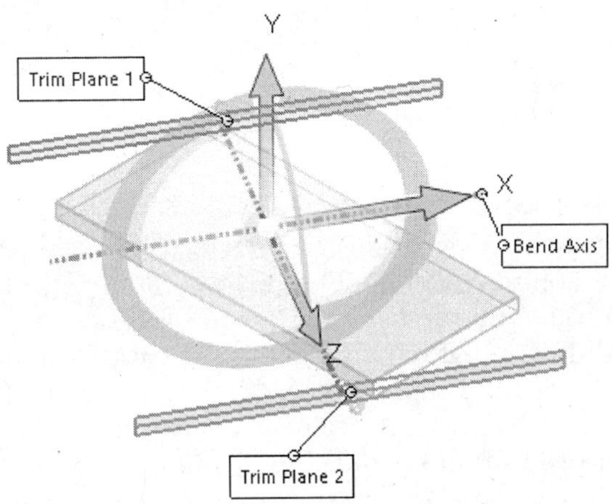

Figure 11-37 *Body after modifying the bend axis and the trimming planes*

As discussed earlier, by default, the 3D triad is placed coincident to the centre of mass of the part. Therefore, the body is deformed about the centre of mass of the part. If you need to fix a face of the body while deforming it, move the cursor to the origin of the triad and press and hold the left mouse button. Drag the cursor and place it on the face that you need to fix. You can also right-click on the sphere of the triad and select **Move to selection** from the shortcut menu and then click the left mouse button when the boundary of the face on which the cursor moves is displayed in red. Note that you can coincide the origin of the triad with an existing geometry such as a vertex, an edge, or a sketched entity.

In the **Flex PropertyManager**, the **Trim Plane 1** and **Trim Plane 2** rollouts are used to specify the offset values for the current trimming planes. You can modify the gap between the trimming planes by dragging them using the arrows attached to them. The **Select a reference entity for Trim Plane 1** and **Select a reference entity for Trim Plane 2** selection boxes are used to select a vertex along which you need to align the trimming planes. The slider bar provided in the **Flex Options** rollout is used to increase the accuracy of the **Flex** tool.

Next, move the cursor on the boundary of any of the trimming planes; the Select cursor will be replaced by the Rotate cursor. Click and drag the cursor to dynamically define the bending angle and the radius of the bend. You can also define them by using the **Angle** and **Radius** spinners, respectively of the **Flex Input** rollout. Figure 11-38 shows the preview of a body being bent and Figure 11-39 shows the body after bending it using the **Flex** tool.

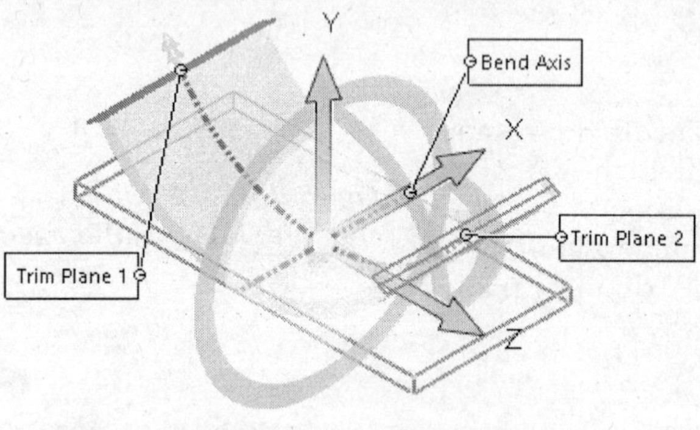

Figure 11-38 Body being bent dynamically

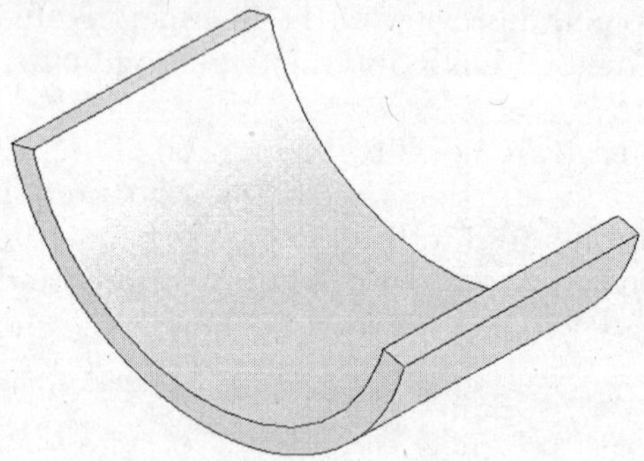

Figure 11-39 Body after bending

Twisting a Body

To twist a body by using the **Flex** tool, invoke the **Flex PropertyManager** and select the **Twisting** radio button from the **Flex Input** rollout. Select the body or bodies that you need to twist; the 3D triad and the trimming planes will be displayed. Set the location of the trimming planes and the triad, if required. Move the cursor on the boundary of any of the trimming planes; the Select cursor will be replaced by the Rotate cursor. Drag the cursor to twist the selected body dynamically, or set the value of the twisting angle in the **Angle** spinner of the **Flex Input** rollout. Figure 11-40 shows the body being twisted with the triad placed coincident to the left face of the body and Figure 11-41 shows the resulting twisted body.

Tip

*While creating a flex feature, you can restore the original shape of the model by right-clicking in the drawing area and then choosing **Reset Flex** from the shortcut menu displayed.*

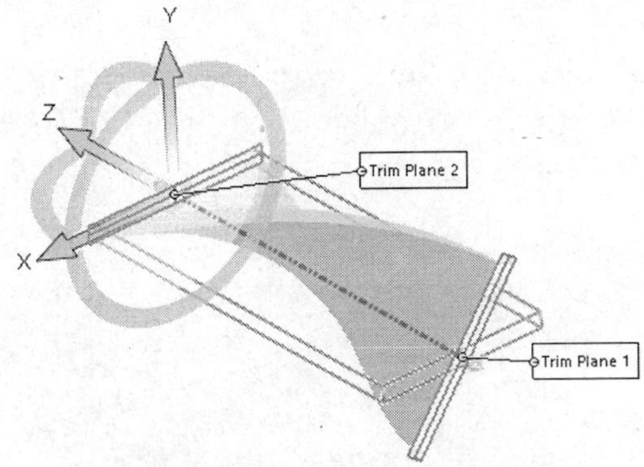

Figure 11-40 The body being twisted

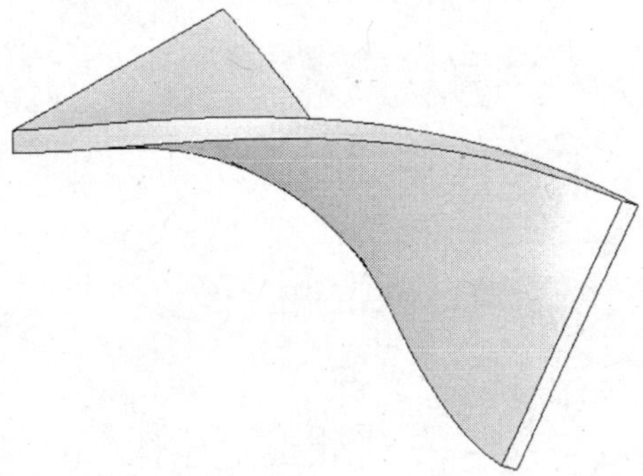

Figure 11-41 Resulting twisted body

Tapering a Body

To taper a body using the **Flex** tool, invoke the **Flex PropertyManager**, and then select the **Tapering** radio button from the **Flex Input** rollout. Next, select the body and set the position of the 3D triad and the trimming planes, if required. Move the cursor close to the boundary of any of the trimming planes; the Select cursor will be replaced by the Rotate cursor. Drag the cursor to specify the taper factor. You can also set the taper factor by using the **Taper factor** spinner in the **Flex Input** rollout. Figure 11-42 shows the body being tapered and Figure 11-43 shows the resulting tapered body.

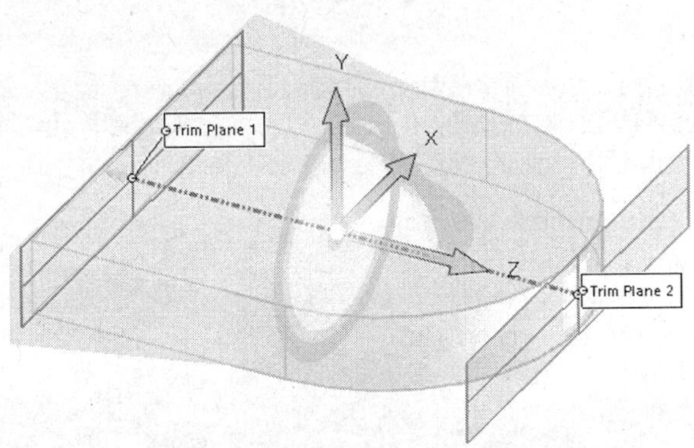

Figure 11-42 The body being tapered

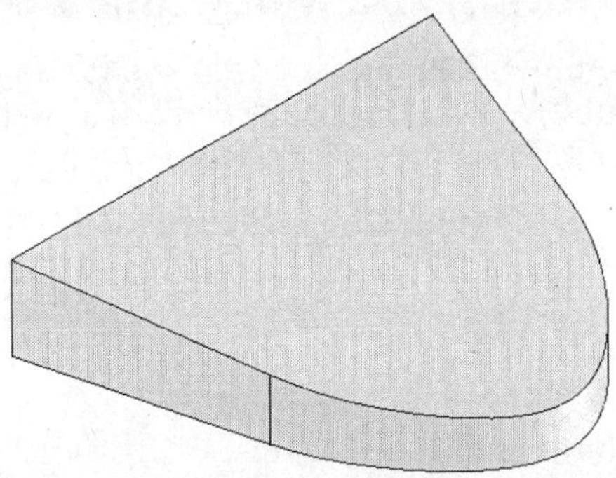

Figure 11-43 Resulting tapered body

Stretching a Body

You can also stretch a selected body by using the **Flex** tool. To do so, invoke the **Flex PropertyManager** and select the **Stretching** radio button from it. Next, select the body and move the cursor on the boundary of any one of the trimming planes; the select cursor will be replaced by the rotate cursor. Drag the cursor to specify the stretching distance. You can also specify it using the **Stretch distance** spinner of the **Flex Input** rollout. Figure 11-44 shows the body being stretched and Figure 11-45 shows the resulting stretched body.

Tip

While creating a flex feature, if the ***Hard edges*** *check box is selected then the faces of the model are divided where trim planes intersect the model. However, on clearing this check box, the faces remain intact.*

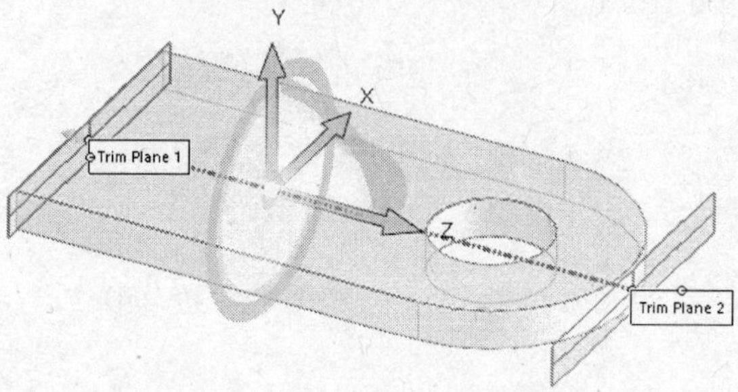

Figure 11-44 *The body being stretched*

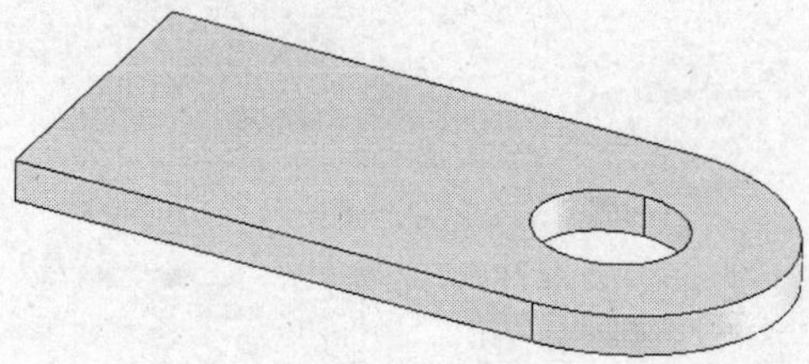

Figure 11-45 *Resulting stretched body*

CREATING FASTENING FEATURES

SOLIDWORKS has a set of tools that are used to design the plastic products. These tools are known as fastening feature tools and are discussed next.

Creating the Mounting Boss

CommandManager: Features > Fastening Feature > Mounting Boss *(Customize to add)*
SOLIDWORKS menus: Insert > Fastening Feature > Mounting Boss
Toolbar: Fastening Feature > Mounting Boss

The **Mounting Boss** tool is used to create mounting boss features that are used in plastic components to accommodate fasteners while assembling the components. Figure 11-46 shows the mounting boss features created on a component. In a mounting boss, the central cylindrical feature is termed as boss and the side features are termed as fins.

Figure 11-46 *Component with the mounting boss*

When you invoke the **Mounting Boss** tool, the **Mounting Boss PropertyManager** will be displayed. The options in this PropertyManager are discussed next.

Position

The options in this rollout of the PropertyManager, as shown in Figure 11-47 are used to specify the location of the mounting boss. When you invoke the **Mounting Boss PropertyManager**, the **Select a face or a 3D point** selection box will be highlighted. The face that you select will be taken as the placement face for the mounting boss and the preview of the mounting boss, created with the default parameters will be displayed. By default, the preview of the mounting boss to be created will be normal to the

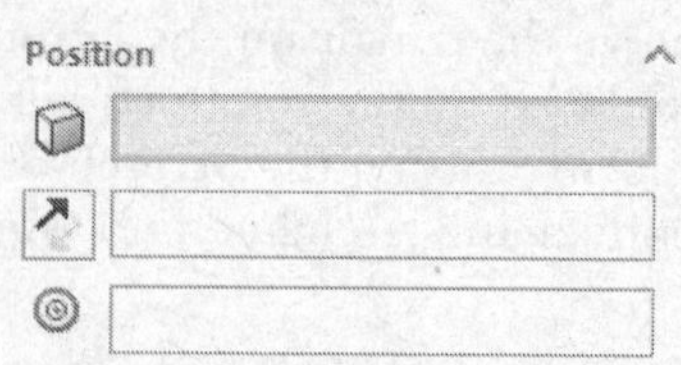

Figure 11-47 *The* ***Position*** *rollout*

placement plane selected. You can change the direction of the mounting boss created. To do so, activate the **Select Direction** selection box and select the reference entity for defining the direction of the mounting boss; the mounting boss will be oriented in that direction. If the mounting boss is placed at a face that has a circular or filleted edge, you can make the center of the mounting boss concentric with the circular edge. To do so, click once in the **Select circular edge to position the mounting boss** selection box and then select the circular edge; the preview of the mounting boss will be repositioned such that it is concentric with the circular edge.

When you specify the location of the mounting boss, a 3D point will be created at that point. After creating the mounting boss, you can edit the 3D point to define its exact location using the dimensions.

Boss Type

The options in this rollout are used to select the type of mounting bosses. By default, the **Hardware Boss** radio button and the **Head** button are chosen in this rollout, as shown in Figure 11-48. As a result, you can create a mounting boss with hole on the top of the boss. If you choose the **Thread** button in this rollout, the option for specifying the dimensions for the thread will be displayed in the **Boss** rollout. Based on the selection type in the **Boss Type** rollout, the options for dimensioning the boss features in the **Boss** rollout and **Fins** rollout will be modified. You can also create a pin type mounting boss by selecting the **Pin Boss** radio button.

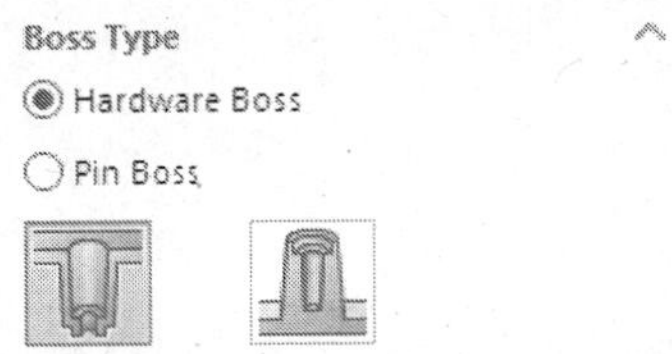

Figure 11-48 The ***Boss Type*** *rollout*

Boss

The options in this rollout are used to specify the dimensions of the cylindrical feature (boss) in the mounting boss, refer to Figure 11-49. You can set the values of the diameter, height, the draft angle of the outer and inner cylindrical face of the boss, diameter and depth of the holes, and so on by using the spinners in this rollout. By default, the **Enter boss height** radio button is selected in this rollout. As a result, you can specify the value of the height. If you select the **Select mating face** radio button, the **Select mating face** selection box will be displayed below this radio button. This selection box allows you to select a mating face that will determine the height of the boss.

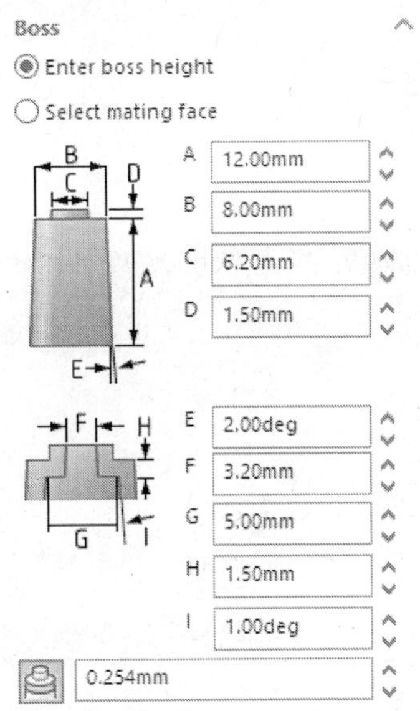

Figure 11-49 The ***Boss*** *rollout*

Fins

The options in this rollout are used to specify the dimensions of the fins in the mounting boss, refer to Figure 11-50. The selection box in this rollout allows you to select a vector to define the orientation of the fins. You can specify the height, width, length, and the draft angle of the fins by using the spinners in this rollout. You can also specify the number of fins by using the **Enter number of fins** spinner in this rollout. Figures 11-51 and 11-52 show the mounting boss with different numbers of fins and with different boss and fins parameters. The options in this rollout will be modified based on the **Mounting Boss** type selected in the **Boss Type** rollout of the **Mounting Boss PropertyManager**. Figure 11-53 shows the mounting boss with a hole and Figure 11-54 shows the mounting boss with a pin.

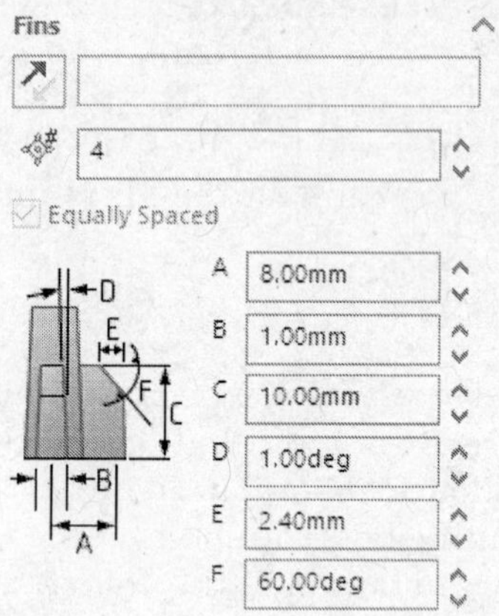

Figure 11-50 *The **Fins** rollout*

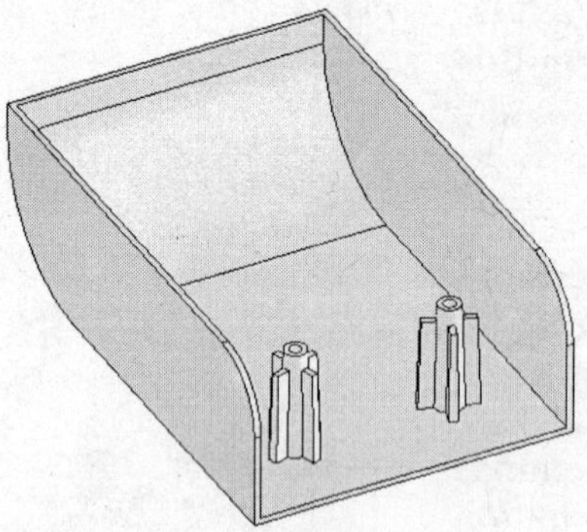

Figure 11-51 *Mounting boss with 4 fins*

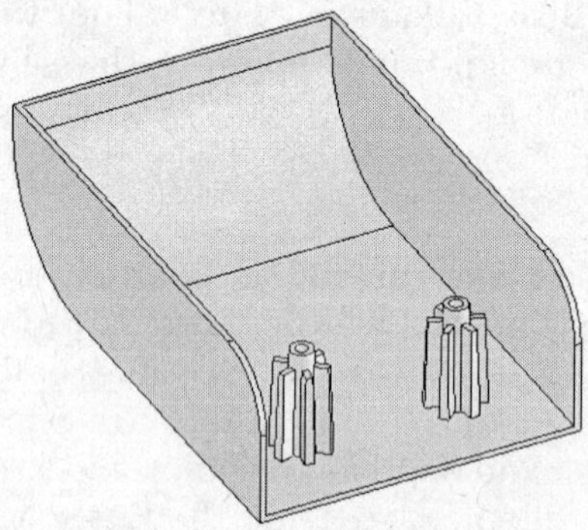

Figure 11-52 *Mounting boss with 6 fins*

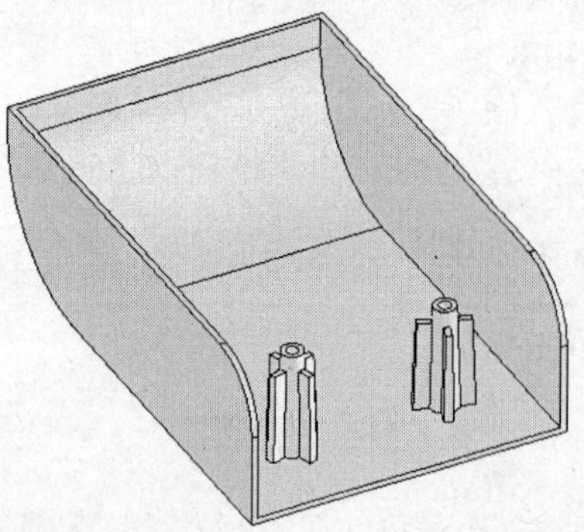

Figure 11-53 *Mounting boss with hole in the boss*

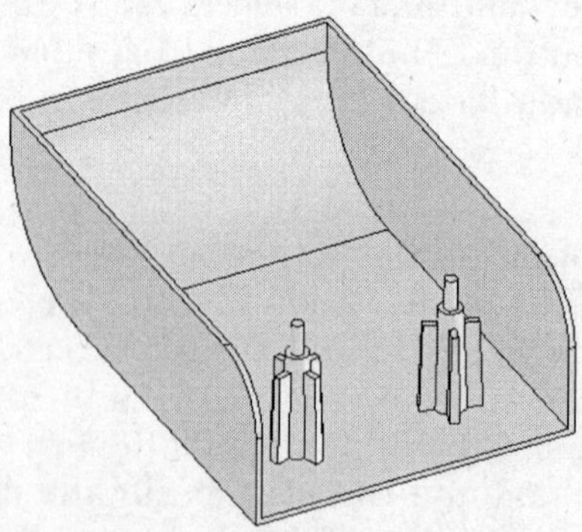

Figure 11-54 *Mounting boss with pin in the boss*

Favorites

The options in this rollout are used to add the frequently used mounting bosses to the favorite list. If you add a mounting boss to the favorite list, you will not have to configure the same settings to add similar types of mounting bosses every time.

Creating Snap Hooks

CommandManager:	Features > Fastening Feature > Snap Hook *(Customize to add)*
SOLIDWORKS menus:	Insert > Fastening Feature > Snap Hook
Toolbar:	Fastening Feature > Snap Hook

The snap hooks are generally created in small plastic boxes to create a push fit type arrangement to close or open a box. Figure 11-55 shows a plastic box with a snap hook. To create a snap hook, choose **Insert > Fastening Feature > Snap Hook** from the SOLIDWORKS menus; the **Snap Hook PropertyManager** will be displayed. The rollouts and the options in this PropertyManager are discussed next.

Snap Hook Selections

The options in this rollout are used to specify the location and orientation of a snap hook, refer to Figure 11-56. These options are discussed next.

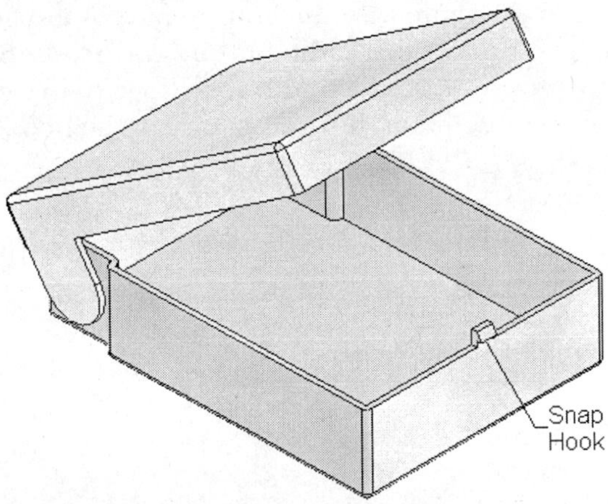

Figure 11-55 Box with a snap hook

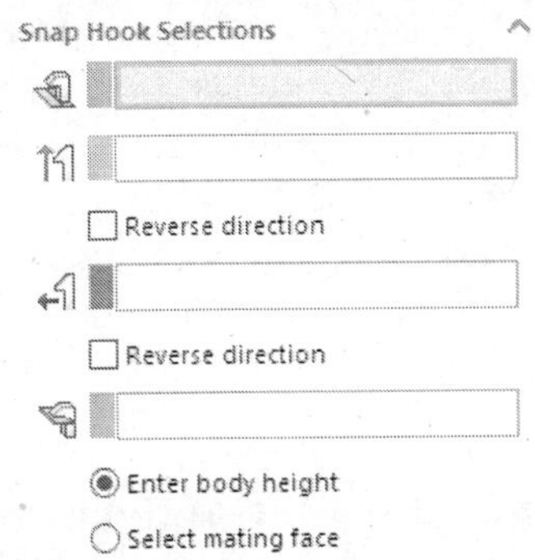

*Figure 11-56 The **Snap Hook Selections** rollout*

Select a position for the location of the hook

This selection box is active by default when you invoke the **Snap Hook PropertyManager**. You can select a face or an edge to define the location of the snap hook. On selecting the location, the preview of the snap hook, created using the default values, will be displayed.

Define the vertical direction of the hook

This selection box is used to define the vertical direction of the hook. You can select a planar face or an edge to define the direction. You can select the **Reverse direction** check box below this selection box to reverse the vertical direction of the hook.

Define the direction of the hook
This selection box is used to define the direction of the hook. You need to select a face to define the direction. The face selected should be parallel to the front face of the body of the snap hook. You can select the **Reverse direction** check box below this selection box to reverse the direction of the hook.

Select a face to mate the body of the hook
This selection box is used to select a face that will mate with the bottom face of the body of the snap hook.

Enter body height
Select this radio button to specify the height of the body of the snap hook. On selecting this radio button, the **Body height** spinner will get enabled in the **Snap Hook Data** rollout and you can specify the height in this spinner.

> **Tip**
> *After placing the snap hook, you can edit its sketch to modify its location on the placement face.*

Select mating face
This radio button is used to select a face that will mate with the bottom face of the hook to define the height of the snap hook. When you select this radio button, the **Select mating face** selection box will be displayed. You can use this selection box to specify the mating face. On doing so, the snap hook will be resized such that the bottom face of the hook mates with the selected face.

Snap Hook Data
The spinners in this rollout are used to specify the parameters of the snap hook, refer to Figure 11-57. As you modify these parameters, you can dynamically view the changes in the snap hook. These spinners are discussed next.

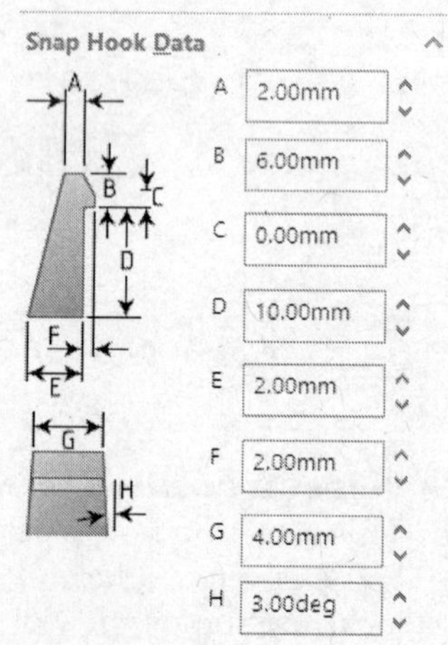

Figure 11-57 The ***Snap Hook Data*** *rollout*

Depth at the top of the hook
This spinner is used to specify the total thickness of the snap hook at its top. Note that the depth at the top should always be equal to or less than that at the bottom. If the depth at the top is less than that at the bottom, the back face of the snap hook will be tapered.

Hook height
This spinner is used to specify the height of the hook.

Hook lip height
This spinner is used to specify the height of the lip of the hook. By default, the value in this spinner is 0. This value should always be less than the height of the hook.

Body height

This spinner is used to specify the height of the body of the snap hook.

Hook overhang

This spinner is used to specify the distance by which the hook overhangs from the front face of the body of the snap hook.

Depth at the base of the hook

This spinner is used to specify total thickness of the snap hook at its base. Note that the base of the hook is the face that is specified in the **Select a position for the location of the hook** selection box in the **Snap Hook Selections** rollout.

Total width

This spinner is used to specify total width of the top edge of the snap hook. Note that the width of the bottom edge of the snap hook is determined by the draft angle, which is also specified using the **Top draft angle** spinner in this rollout.

Top draft angle

This spinner is used to specify draft angle from the top of the hook. This angle will determine the width of the hook at its bottom.

Figure 11-58 shows a snap hook without a lip and Figure 11-59 shows the snap hook with a lip.

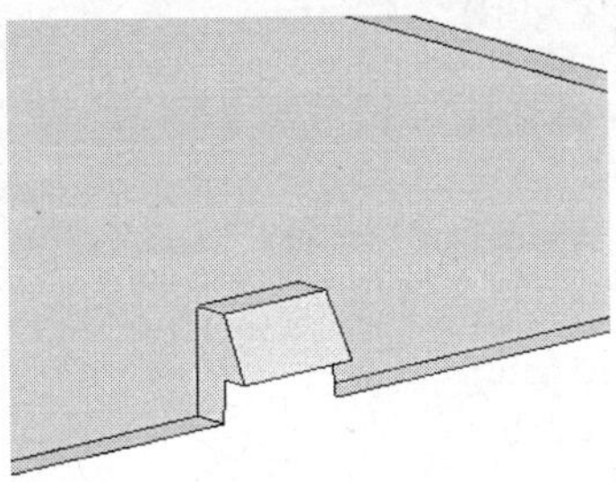

Figure 11-58 *Snap hook without a lip*

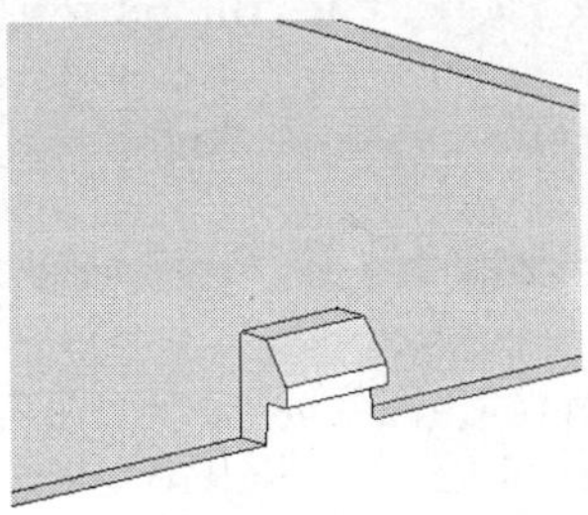

Figure 11-59 *Snap hook with a lip*

Creating Snap Hook Grooves

CommandManager: Features > Fastening Feature > Snap Hook Groove *(Customize to add)*
SOLIDWORKS menus: Insert > Fastening Feature > Snap Hook Groove
Toolbar: Fastening Feature > Snap Hook Groove

The snap hook grooves are the cut features that are created to accommodate a snap hook in order to create a push fit type arrangement to close or open a box. Note that this feature works only in the case of multibody models. This is because you need to take reference from the snap hook created in one of the bodies to create the snap hook groove in the other body. Figure 11-60 shows the cap of a plastic box with the snap hook groove. Note that to create the snap hook groove, the two bodies should be placed such that the snap hook intersects with the body in which you want to create the snap hook groove. In Figure 11-60, the display of the body with the snap hook is turned off to make

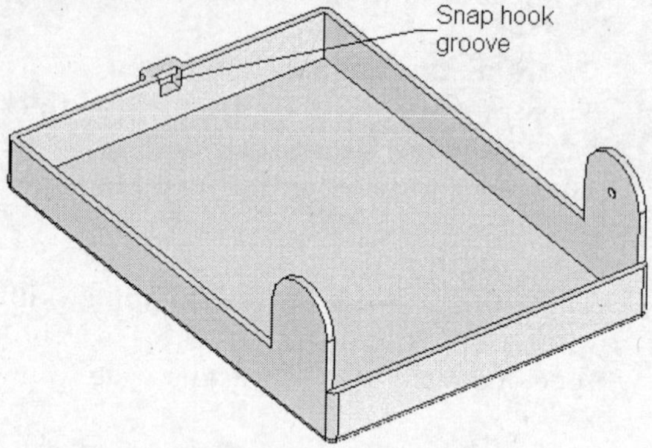

Figure 11-60 Box with a snap hook groove

When you choose the **Snap Hook Groove** tool, the **Snap Hook Groove PropertyManager** will be displayed, as shown in Figure 11-61. You can use the options in the **Feature and Body Selections** rollout of this PropertyManager to create a snap hook groove. The options in this PropertyManager are discussed next.

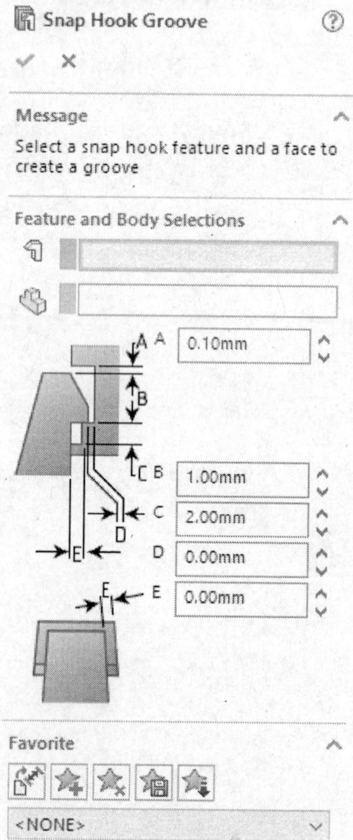

*Figure 11-61 The **Snap Hook Groove PropertyManager***

Select a snap hook feature from the feature tree

This selection box is active by default when you invoke the **Snap Hook Groove** tool and is used to select a snap hook from another body. The resulting groove will be used to accommodate the selected snap hook. Note that the snap hook created prior to snap hook groove must intersect the body in which you need to create the snap hook groove.

Select a body

This selection box is used to select the body in which the snap hook groove will be created.

Offset height from Snap Hook

This spinner is used to specify the offset height between the top face of the snap hook and the top face of the snap hook groove when you insert the hook inside the groove.

Gap Height
This spinner is used to specify the gap height of the snap hook groove.

Groove Clearance
This spinner is used to specify the clearance between the snap hook and the groove.

Gap Distance
This spinner is used to specify the distance between the body of the snap hook and the groove.

Offset width from Snap Hook
This spinner is used to specify the offset width between the side face of the snap hook and the side face of the groove when you insert the hook inside the groove.

Creating Vents

CommandManager:	Features > Fastening Feature > Vent *(Customize to add)*
SOLIDWORKS menus:	Insert > Fastening Feature > Vent
Toolbar:	Fastening Feature > Vent

The **Vent** tool is used to create vents in the existing models. This tool uses a closed sketch as the boundary of the vent and the open or closed sketched segments inside the closed sketch as the ribs and spars of the vent. Figure 11-62 shows a sketch created at an offset plane and the parameters required to create a vent, and Figure 11-63 shows the resulting vent. To invoke this tool, choose **Insert > Fastening Feature > Vent** from the SOLIDWORKS menus; the **Vent PropertyManager** will be displayed. The options in this PropertyManager are discussed next.

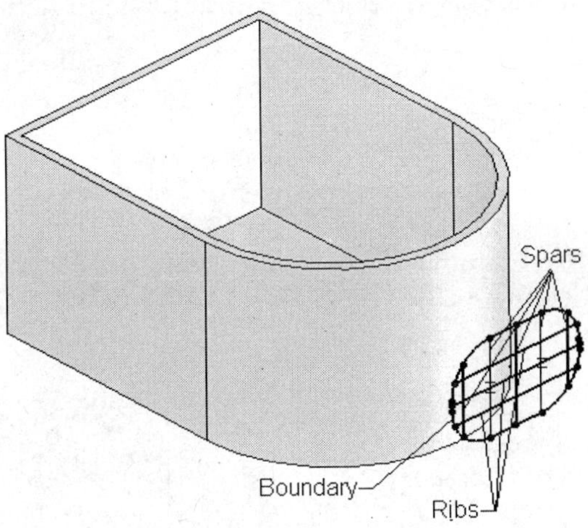

Figure 11-62 *Parameters required to create a vent*

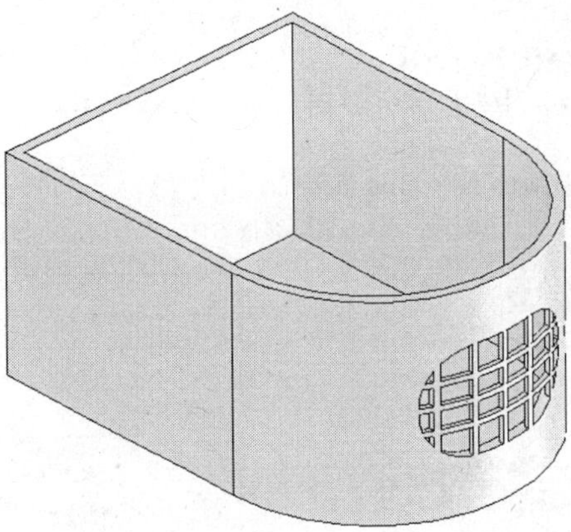

Figure 11-63 *Resulting vent*

Boundary

The selection box in this rollout allows you to select a closed sketch that will act as the boundary of the vent. You need to select the segments of the sketch individually to make sure that the result is a closed loop.

Geometry Properties

The options in this rollout are used to specify the face on which the vent will be created, refer to Figure 11-64. These options are discussed next.

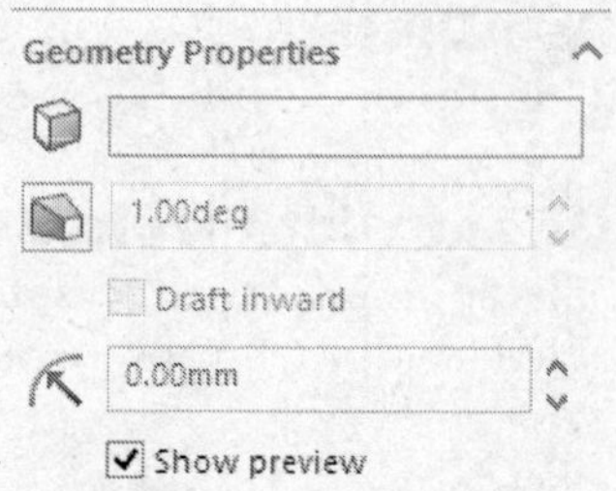

Figure 11-64 *The* ***Geometry Properties*** *rollout*

Select a face on which to place the vent

This selection box is used to specify the face on which you want to create the vent. In Figure 11-65, the non-planar face has been selected as the face to place the vent. After selecting the boundary, select the face; the preview of the vent will be displayed, if the **Show preview** check box is selected.

Draft On/Off

This button is chosen to add a draft angle to the ribs and spars. Note that before adding the draft angle, you need to select the segments to define the ribs and spars. When you choose this button, the **Draft Angle** spinner on the right of this button will be enabled. You can specify the draft angle in this spinner.

Neutral Plane

This selection box is displayed below the **Draft Angle** spinner when you choose the **Draft On/Off** button. Note that this selection box will be available only after you select a curve face for placing the vent. This selection box allows you to select a neutral plane to define the draft angle direction.

Draft inward

This check box is used to reverse the direction of the draft.

Radius for the fillets

This spinner is used to add fillets between the boundaries, ribs, and spars in the vent. Figure 11-65 shows a vent without a fillet and Figure 11-66 shows a vent with fillets.

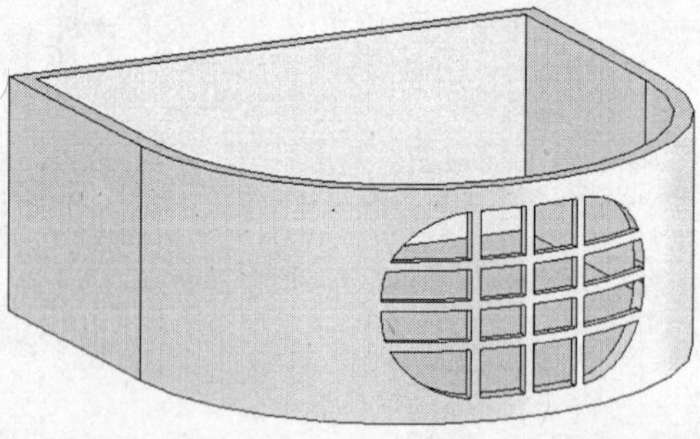

Figure 11-65 *Vent without a fillet*

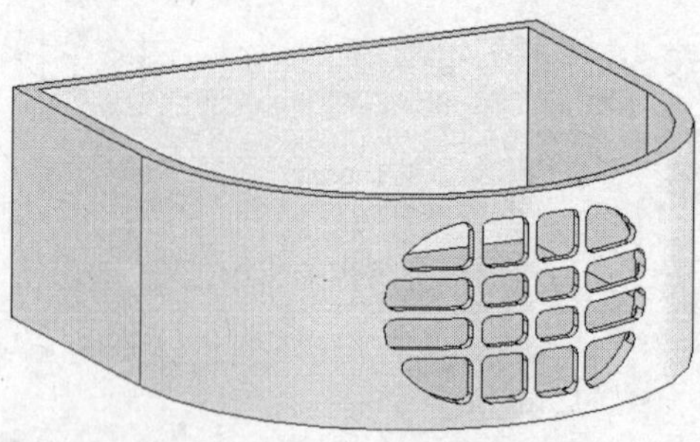

Figure 11-66 *Vent with fillets*

Show preview

If this check box is selected, the preview of the vent will be displayed while it is being created. The changes made in the parameters will also be dynamically reflected in the preview.

Note

*If you have selected the **Show preview** check box and still the preview of the vent is not displayed, this indicates that there is an error in the selections or in the dimensions of the ribs and spars. In that case, you need to modify these values to create the vent.*

Flow Area

This rollout displays the total area of the vent and the unfilled area in the vent. As you increase the number of ribs and spars, the open area in the vent reduces.

Ribs

The options in this rollout are used to specify the segments that define the ribs and the dimensional and offset values of ribs, refer to Figure 11-67. These options are discussed next.

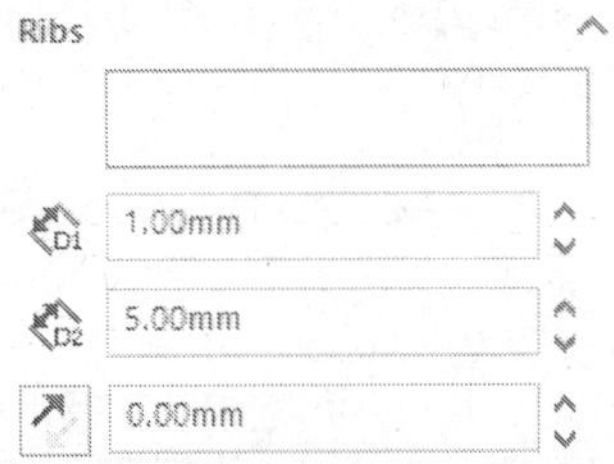

***Figure 11-67** The **Ribs** rollout*

Select 2D sketch segments that represent ribs of the vent

This selection box is used to select the sketch segments that will create ribs in the vent. If you select segments for the ribs after selecting the **Show preview** check box, then you can preview the vent with the ribs.

Enter the depth of the ribs

This spinner is used to specify the depth of the ribs in the vent. Figures 11-68 and 11-69 show the ribs with different depths.

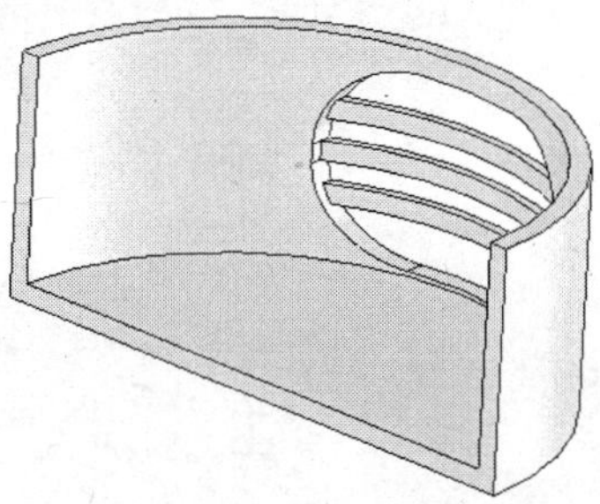

***Figure 11-68** Component with rib depth less than the thickness of the component*

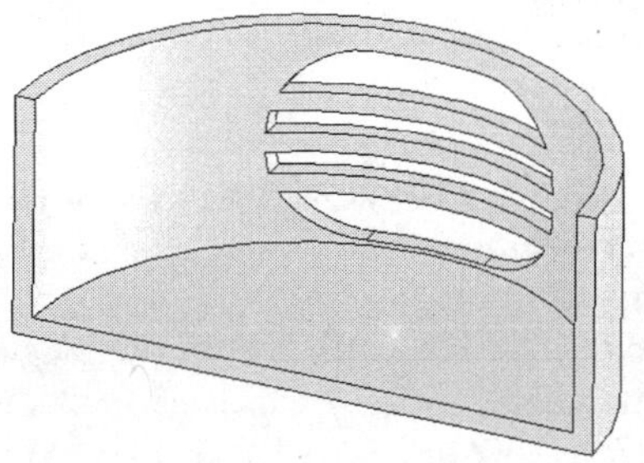

***Figure 11-69** Component with rib depth equal to the thickness of the component*

Enter the width of the ribs

This spinner is used to specify the width of the ribs in the vent.

Enter the offset of the ribs from the surface

This spinner is used to specify the value by which the ribs will be offset from the face on which the vent will be created. Figure 11-70 shows the ribs of a vent created at an offset. You can reverse the offset direction by choosing the **Select Direction** button, as shown in Figure 11-71.

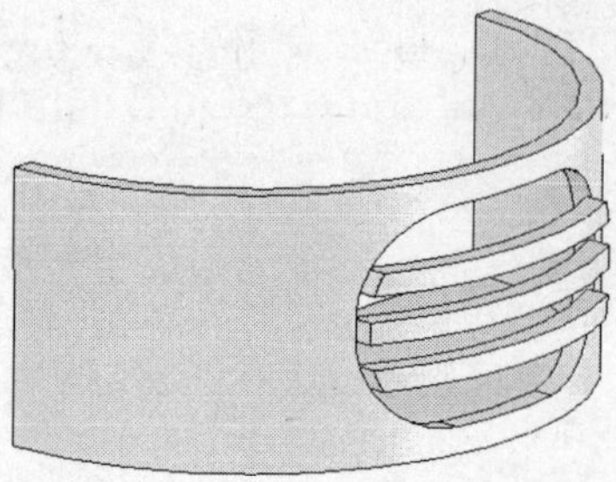

Figure 11-70 Ribs created at an offset

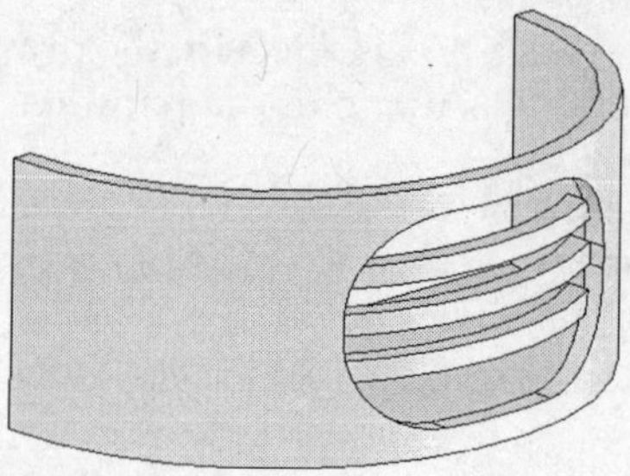

Figure 11-71 Ribs after reversing the offset direction

Spars

The options in this rollout are used to specify the segments that define the spars and the dimensional and offset values of spars, refer to Figure 11-72. These options are discussed next.

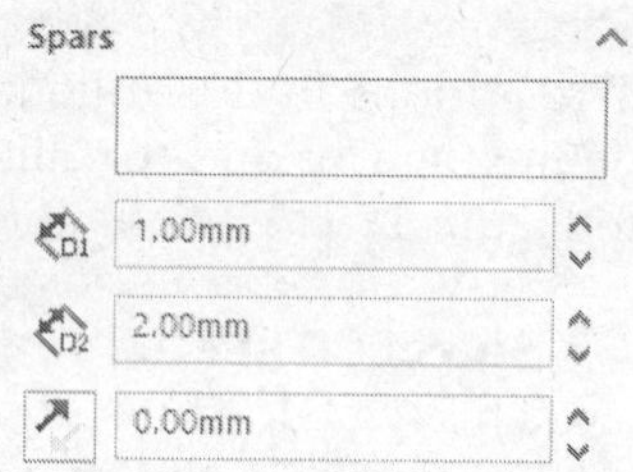

*Figure 11-72 The **Spars** rollout*

Select 2D sketch segments that represent spars of the vent

This selection box is used to select the sketch segments that will create spars in the vent. If you select the segments for the spars after selecting the **Show preview** check box, then you can preview the vent with the spars.

Enter the depth of the spars

This spinner is used to specify the depth of the spars in the vent.

Enter the width of the spars

This spinner is used to specify the width of the spars in the vent.

Enter the offset of the spars from the surface

This spinner is used to specify the value by which the spars will be offset from the face on which the vent will be created. Figure 11-73 shows a model with a vent having ribs and spars. Note that in this model, the spars are created at an offset. You can reverse the offset direction by choosing the **Select Direction** button.

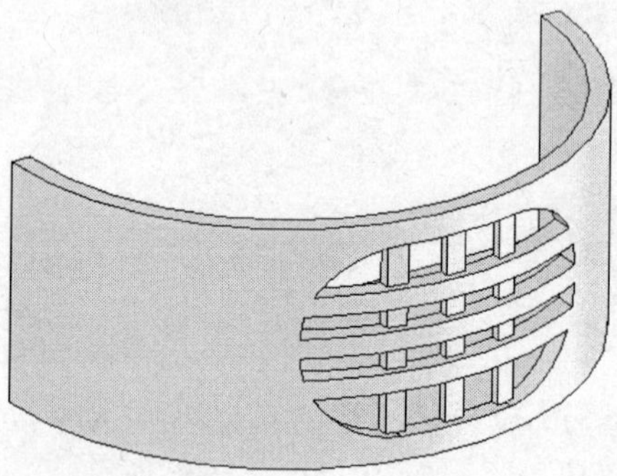

Figure 11-73 Vent with ribs and spars

Fill-In Boundary

The options in this rollout are used to specify a support boundary for the vent. These options are discussed next.

Select 2D sketch segments that form a closed profile to define a support boundary for the vent

This selection box is used to select the sketch segments that will create a filled feature inside the vent. Note that at least one segment of the rib should intersect the closed profile. Figure 11-74 shows the preview of a filled feature created inside the vent using the closed profile shown in the preview.

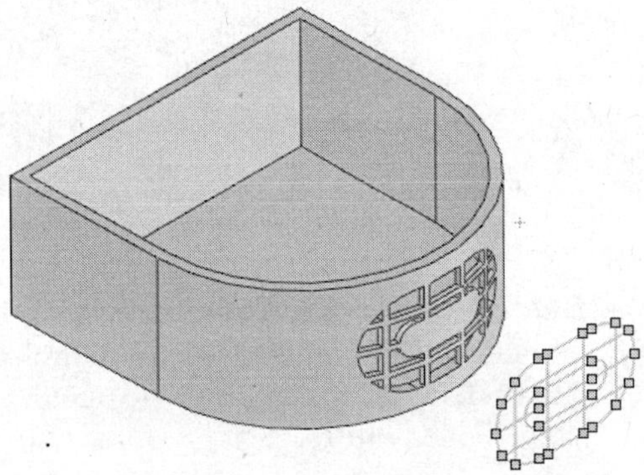

***Figure 11-74** Preview of the filled feature*

Enter the depth of the support area

This spinner is used to specify the depth of the filled area.

Enter the offset of the support area

This spinner is used to specify the offset value for the filled area. You can reverse the offset direction by choosing the **Select Direction** button on the left of this spinner.

Creating a Lip/Groove Feature

CommandManager: Features > Fastening Feature > Lip / Groove *(Customize to add)*
SOLIDWORKS menus: Insert > Fastening Feature > Lip / Groove
Toolbar: Fastening Feature > Lip / Groove

The **Lip/Groove** tool is used to create lip or groove features on a component. These features are mainly used in plastic boxes in which they create a push-fit type arrangement. This arrangement is used for opening and closing of the plastic boxes. In the groove feature, material is removed from a component whereas in the lip feature material is added to the component, see Figure 11-75.

On invoking this tool, the **Lip/Groove PropertyManager** will be displayed. The options in this PropertyManager are discussed next.

Body/Part Selection

The options available in this rollout are used to specify the components to create lip and groove features, refer to Figure 11-76. The options in this rollout are discussed next.

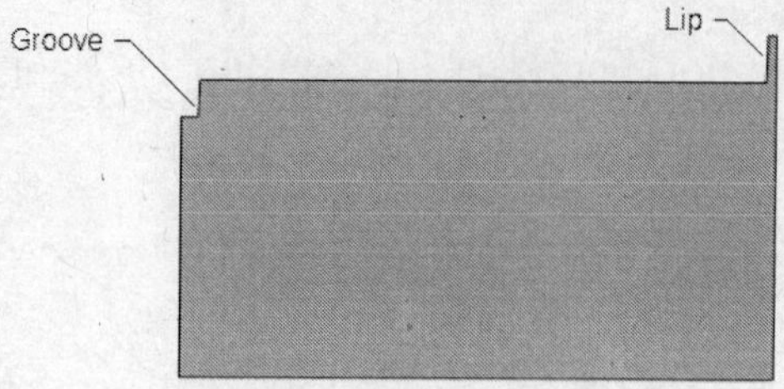

Figure 11-75 Groove and lip features

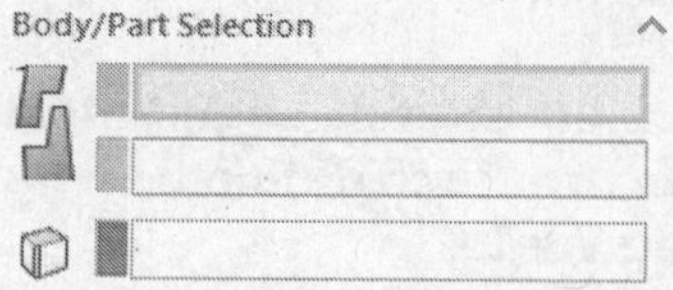

*Figure 11-76 The **Body/Part Selection** rollout*

Select body/component on which to create the groove

This selection box is active by default when you invoke the **Lip/Groove PropertyManager**. This selection box is used to specify the body or component on which you want to create the groove feature.

Select body/component on which to create the lip

This selection box is used to select the body or component on which you want to create the lip feature.

Select a plane, a planar face or a straight edge to define the direction of the lip/groove

This selection box is used to define the direction of the lip/groove. You can select a planar face, plane, or a straight edge to define the direction.

Groove Selection

On selecting the body or component on which you need to create a groove, the **Groove Selection** rollout will be displayed, as shown in Figure 11-77. The options in this rollout are discussed next.

Select faces on which to create the groove

This selection box is used to select the faces on which you want to create the groove.

Select inner or outer edge for groove to remove material

This selection box is used to define the edge along which the material is to be removed from the selected faces.

The **Tangent propagation** check boxes available in this rollout are used to extend the selection to tangent faces. You can specify the groove width, groove draft angle, and groove height in the **Groove Width**, **Groove draft angle**, and **Groove Height** spinners, respectively.

Figure 11-78 shows the direction, face, and edges to be selected for creating a groove feature and Figure 11-79 shows the resultant groove feature.

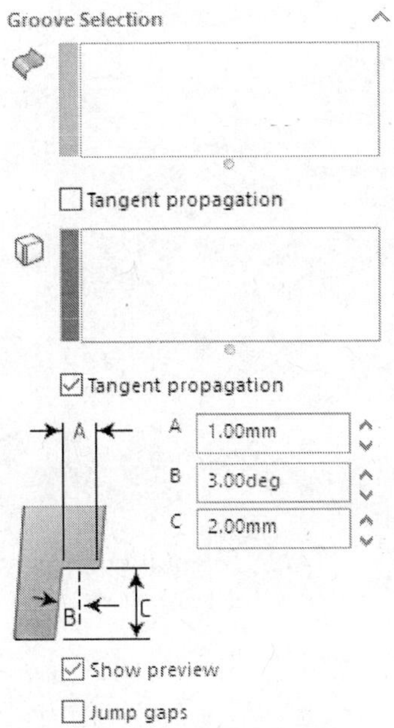

Figure 11-77 The **Groove Selection** rollout

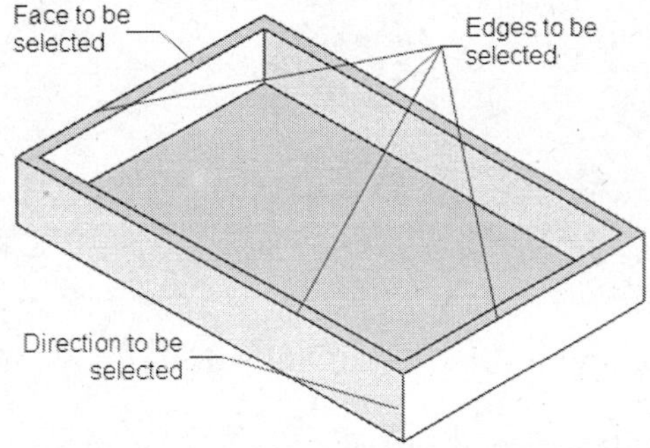

Figure 11-78 *Selecting edges, faces and directions for creating a groove*

On selecting the body or component on which you want to create a lip, the **Lip Selection** rollout will be displayed, as shown in Figure 11-80. The options in this rollout are similar to those discussed in the **Groove Selection** rollout.

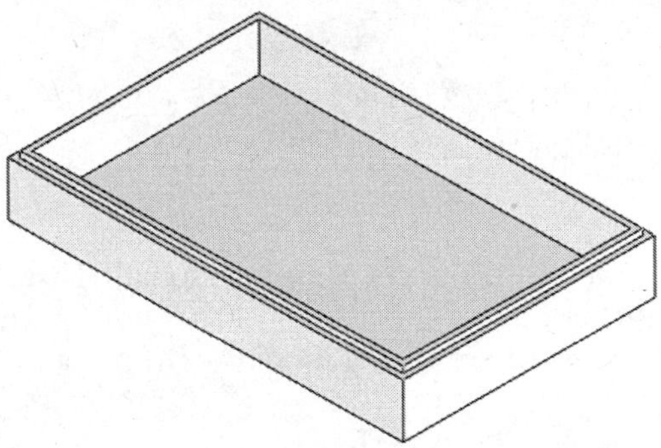

Figure 11-79 *The resultant groove feature*

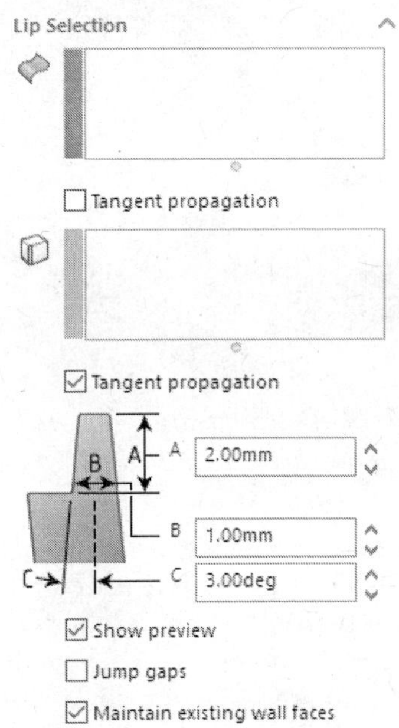

Figure 11-80 The **Lip Selection** rollout

Figure 11-81 shows the direction, face, and edges to be selected for creating a lip feature and Figure 11-82 shows the resultant lip feature.

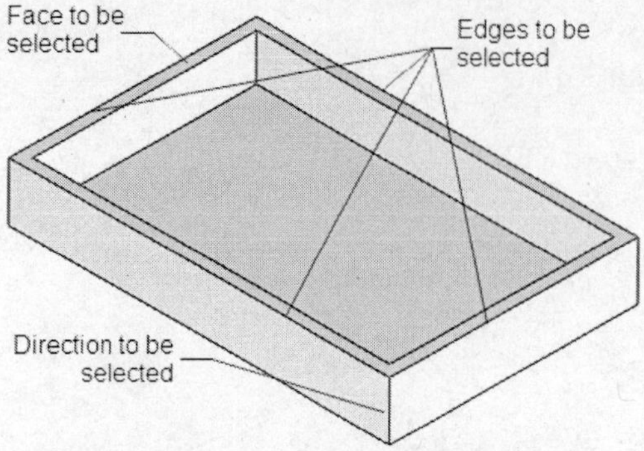

Figure 11-81 *Selection for creating a lip feature*

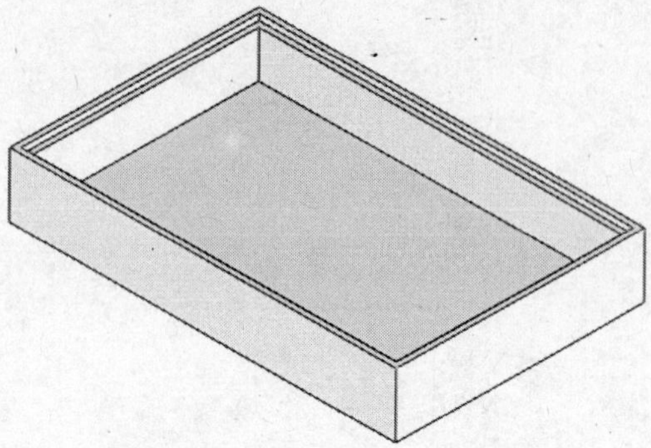

Figure 11-82 *The resultant lip feature*

Some of the options in the **Lip Selection** rollout are discussed next.

Jump gaps

If the model contains ribs or any obstructing feature in the path of the lips, select the **Jump gaps** check box to make the lip run continuously. Figure 11-83 shows the lip created by clearing the **Jump gaps** check box and Figure 11-84 shows the lip created by selecting the **Jump gaps** check box.

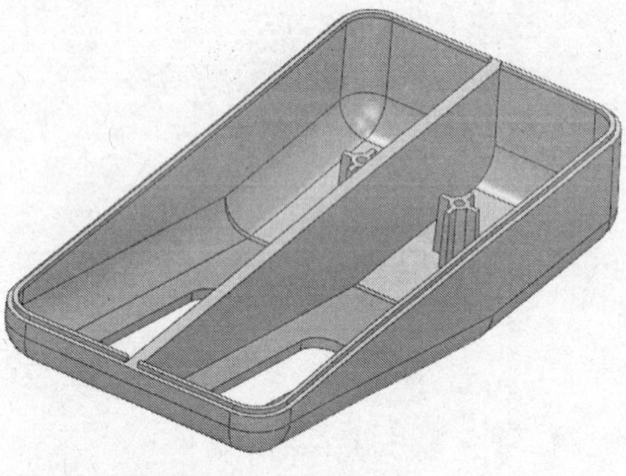

Figure 11-83 *Lip feature created when the* ***Jump gaps*** *check box is cleared*

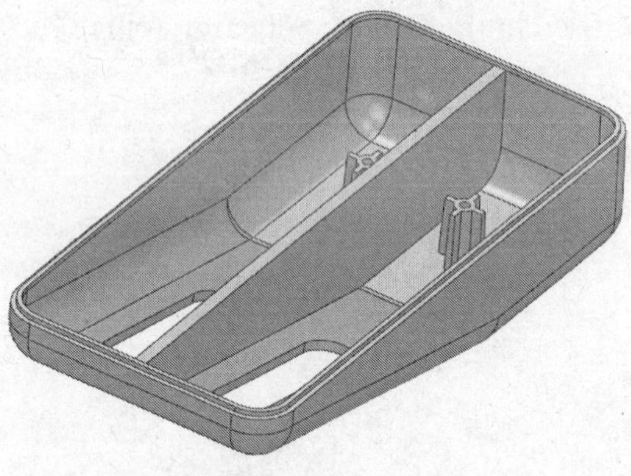

Figure 11-84 *Lip feature created when the* ***Jump gaps*** *check box is selected*

Maintain existing wall faces

While creating a lip feature on an inclined wall, selecting the **Maintain existing wall faces** check box will result in a lip feature that has the same angle as that of the wall, as shown in Figure 11-85. Similarly, if you clear this check box, the resulting lip feature will not maintain the draft angle, as shown in Figure 11-86.

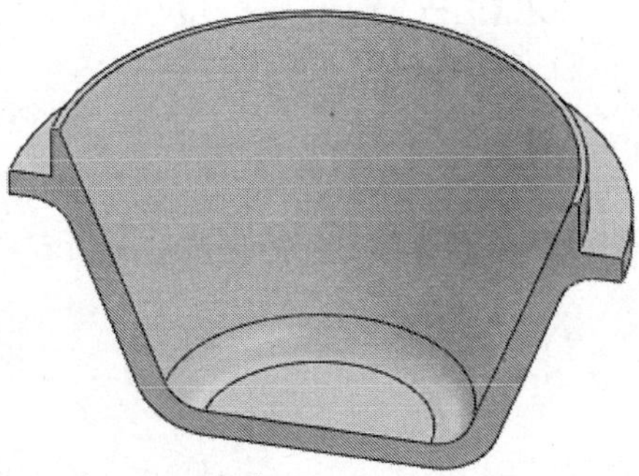

Figure 11-85 Lip feature created when the **Maintain existing wall faces** check box is selected

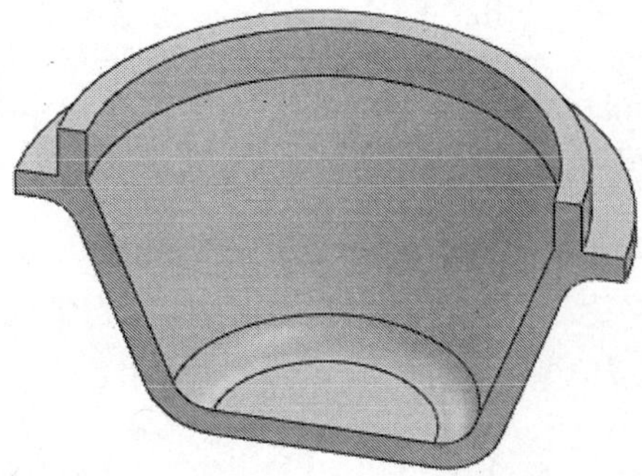

Figure 11-86 Lip feature created when the **Maintain existing wall faces** check box is cleared

CREATING FREEFORM FEATURES

CommandManager:	Features > Freeform	*(Customize to add)*
SOLIDWORKS menus:	Insert > Features > Freeform	
Toolbar:	Features > Freeform	*(Customize to add)*

The **Freeform** tool is used to deform a face to get the required shape. This tool allows you to create the freeform features using the n-sided face of an existing feature. You can select the face of an existing feature and then deform it to any freeform shape. Figure 11-87 shows the model of a tube before deforming its face and Figure 11-88 shows the same tube after deforming its face using the **Freeform** tool.

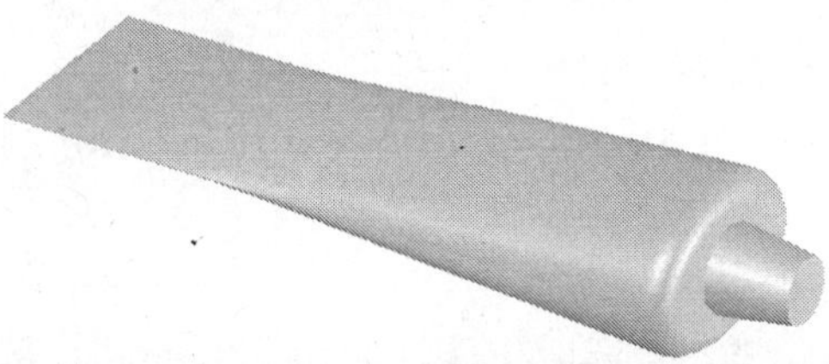

Figure 11-87 Model before deforming the face

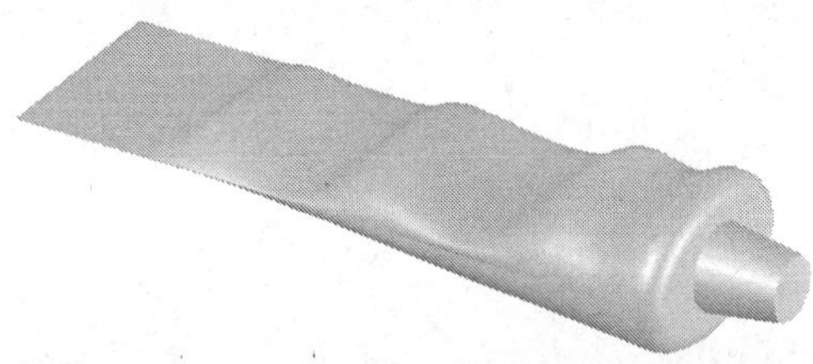

Figure 11-88 Model after deforming the face

To create a freeform feature, perform the following steps:

1. Create the base feature and then invoke the **Freeform** tool; the **Freeform PropertyManager** will be displayed and the **Face to deform** selection box will become active in the **Face Settings** rollout.

2. Select the face that you want to deform; the grid lines mesh will be displayed on the face.

   Next, you need to define a curve and add points to it. These points will be used to hold the curve and deform it. The same deformation will then be applied to the selected faces.

3. Choose the **Add Curves** button from the **Control Curves** rollout in the **Freeform PropertyManager**. Alternatively, you can right-click and choose **Add Curves** from the shortcut menu. Next, move the cursor over the selected face; a preview of the curve, parallel to the direction of one set of mesh grid lines will be displayed.

4. Choose the **Flip Direction (Tab)** button from the **Control Curves** rollout if you want to add curves parallel to the other set of mesh grid lines.

5. Place one or more curves to deform the face, as shown in Figure 11-89.

6. Next, choose the **Add Points** button from the **Control Points** rollout. Alternatively, you can right-click and choose the **Add Points** option from the shortcut menu.

7. Move the cursor on the curve added and then add control points to the curve, as shown in Figure 11-90. Note that more the number of points, more precise the deformation that can be added to the face.

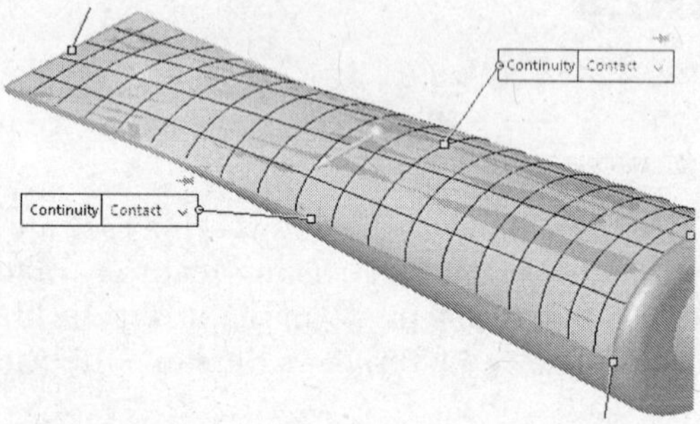

Figure 11-89 *Partial display of the model with a curve being added*

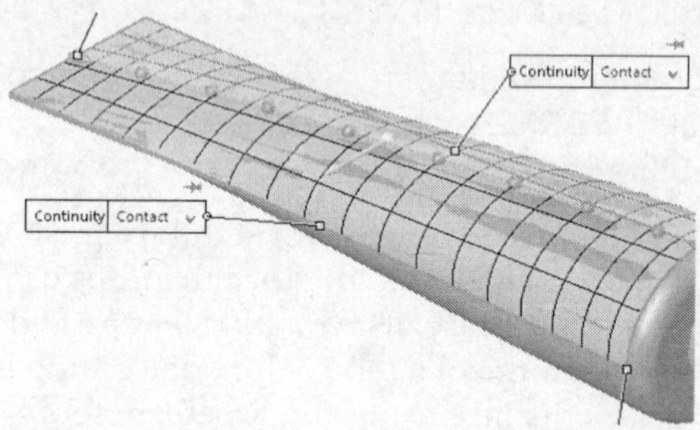

Figure 11-90 *Partial display of the model with points being added*

8. Right-click and choose **Add Points** again from the shortcut menu to clear this option.

9. Move the cursor over any of the points and then drag it; the selected face will be deformed.

10. Similarly, you can drag the other points to deform the face. You can also use the axes of the triad displayed on the selected control point to deform the face. Figure 11-91 shows the points being dragged to deform the face.

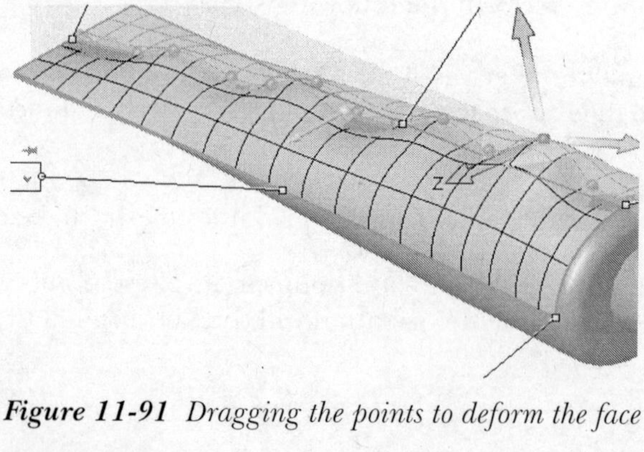

Figure 11-91 *Dragging the points to deform the face*

Whenever you select a face to deform, some callouts will be displayed on it. These callouts control the continuity of the face. After dragging the points and deforming the face, you can select options from these callouts to modify the continuity of the face.

The rollouts and the options in the **Freeform PropertyManager** are discussed next.

Face Settings

The options in this rollout are discussed next.

Face to deform

This selection box is used to select the face to be deformed. It is active by default when you invoke the **Freeform** tool.

Direction 1 symmetry

This check box will be activated only when the face selected to be deformed is symmetric in one direction. If you select this check box, the preview of the symmetry plane will be displayed on the selected face. Now, if you add a curve, a similar curve will be added on the other side of the symmetry plane. Also, the points added to one of the curves will be added automatically to the symmetric curve. You can drag the points on any of the symmetric curves to deform the face.

Direction 2 symmetry

This check box will be activated only when the face selected to be deformed is symmetric in both the directions. If you select this check box, the preview of the symmetry plane in the second direction will be displayed on the selected face. This option works similar to the **Direction 1 symmetry** option.

Control Curves

The options in this rollout are discussed next.

Control type

The options in this area are used to set the type of control to deform the face. The **Through points** radio button is chosen by default. As a result, the points will be added to the curve and you can use these points to deform the face. If you choose the **Control polygon** radio button, polygons will be displayed on all the control points on the curve and you can use these polygons to deform the face.

Add Curves

This button is chosen to add a curve to deform the selected face.

Flip Direction (Tab)

This button is chosen to add the curve in the other direction. You can also press the TAB key to add the curve in the other direction.

Control Points

The options available in this rollout are discussed next.

Add Points

This button is chosen to add points to the control curve. After creating the control curve, choose this button and add the control points. After adding the required control points, choose this button again to start dragging the points.

Snap to geometry

You can also create a sketched curve to match the shape of the deformed face before invoking the **Freeform** tool. If this check box is selected and you drag the control points to the points of the sketched curve, the cursor snaps to the control points of the sketched curve. In this way, you can match the shape of the face with that of the sketched curve. Note that to use this option, the control curve should be added close to the sketched curve. Figure 11-92 shows the control point of the curve being dragged to the control point of a spline curve.

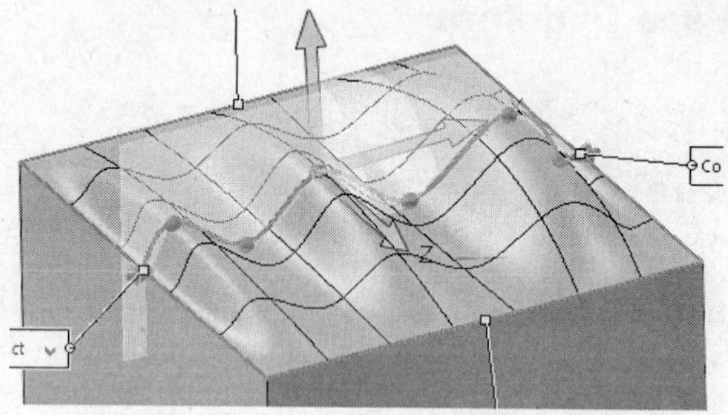

***Figure 11-92** Dragging the point to the control point of a spline curve*

Triad orientation

This area is used to specify whether the triad will be oriented with reference to the current part axes, selected surface, or the control curve. You can select the radio button corresponding to the requirement.

Triad follows selection

Select this check box to move the triad to the selected control point. If this check box is cleared, the triad will remain at its current position, even if you select some other control point on the curve.

Triad X/Y/Z Direction

These spinners will be available in the **Control Points** rollout only when you select a point to drag. These spinners are used to move the selected control point along the X, Y, and Z directions. You can also use the thumbwheel located below these spinners to modify the value.

Display

The options in this rollout are discussed next.

Face transparency

This slider is used to set the transparency of the face selected to be deformed.

Mesh preview

This check box is used to turn on the display of the mesh on the selected surface. If this check box is selected, you can control the density of the mesh by using the slider given below this check box.

Zebra stripes

Select this check box to display the zebra stripes on the selected face. The zebra stripes are used to check the change in the curvature of the face.

Curvature combs

This check box is used to display the curvature combs on the grid lines of the mesh to check the curvature of the face. You can specify the directions, curvature type, scale, and density of the grid curvature combs using the available options.

DIMENSIONING A PART USING MBD DIMENSION

The set of tools in the **MBD Dimensions CommandManager** are used to specify dimensions and tolerances on a part. Practice of using such type of dimensioning is termed as Mode-based definition. This helps in checking the design intent and providing exact information to the production team about the parts without the need of engineering drawings. The tolerances created using the MBD Dimension tools can be further used for tolerance analysis. Note that the dimensions created using the MBD Dimension tools are not parametric in nature. You can create the dimensions on the parts manually or automatically. The **DimXpertManager** keeps a track of the dimensions placed on the model. The tools in the **MBD Dimensions CommandManager** that are used to dimension the part are discussed next.

Specifying the Datum

CommandManager:	MBD Dimensions > Datum
SOLIDWORKS menus:	Tools > MBD Dimension > Datum
Toolbar:	Tools > MBD Dimension > Datum

To dimension a part manually, you need to specify a datum using the **Datum** tool. A datum is specified on a face, as shown in Figure 11-93, so that other features are measured with respect to the datum. To specify a datum, invoke the **Datum** tool from the **MBD Dimensions CommandManager**; the **Datum Feature PropertyManager** will be displayed, as shown in Figure 11-94. Also, a datum feature symbol with default parameters will be attached to the cursor. The options in the **Datum Feature PropertyManager** are discussed next.

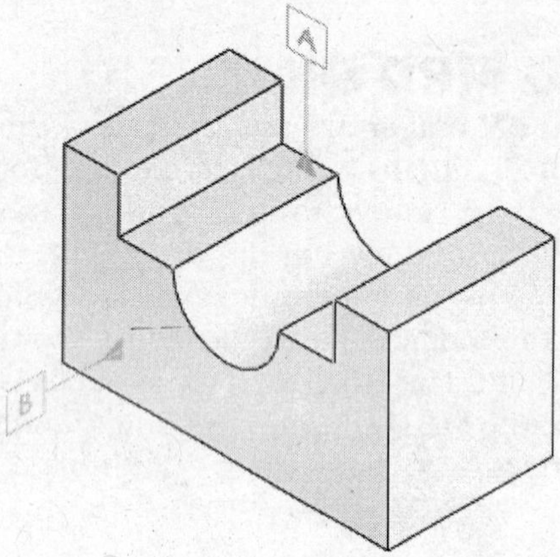

Figure 11-93 Model with datum

Figure 11-94 Partial view of the **Datum Feature PropertyManager**

Style Rollout

The options in the **Style** rollout are used to add the frequently used datum settings to the favorite list. The method of adding the datum settings is same as discussed in Chapter 4.

Label

The **Label** edit box in the **Label Settings** rollout is used to define the label to be used in the datum feature symbol. You can only use the capital alphabets as labels.

Use document style

This check box is selected in the **Leader** rollout to use the datum feature style that is defined in the document to display the datum feature symbol.

Square

The **Square** button will be displayed when you clear the **Use document style** check box. This button is used to place the text of the datum feature inside a square. By default, the text of the datum feature is placed using this option. Therefore, by using the buttons available below the **Square** button, you can set the style of attachment for placing the datum feature such as filled triangle, filled triangle with shoulder, empty triangle, and empty triangle with shoulder.

Round (GB)

The **Round (GB)** button will be displayed when you clear the **Use document style** check box. This button is used to place the text of the datum feature inside a circle. To do so, you first need to clear the **Use document style** check box and then choose the **Round (GB)** button. On doing so, additional buttons will be displayed below the **Round (GB)** button. These buttons are used to set the style of attachment for the datum feature.

After defining all parameters of the datum feature symbol, specify a point on an existing entity in the drawing area. Next, move the cursor to define the length and the placement of the datum feature symbol. As soon as you place a datum feature symbol, another datum feature symbol will be attached to the cursor. Therefore, you can place as many datum feature symbols as you want using the **Datum Feature PropertyManager**. As you place multiple datum feature symbols, the sequence of the names of the datum feature symbols automatically follows the order based on the labels.

Pop-up Toolbar

When you invoke the **Datum** tool from the **MBD Dimensions CommandManager** and select a feature, a pop-up toolbar will be displayed with the possible options that are applicable for that tool, as shown in Figure 11-95. Select an option from this toolbar to filter the features.

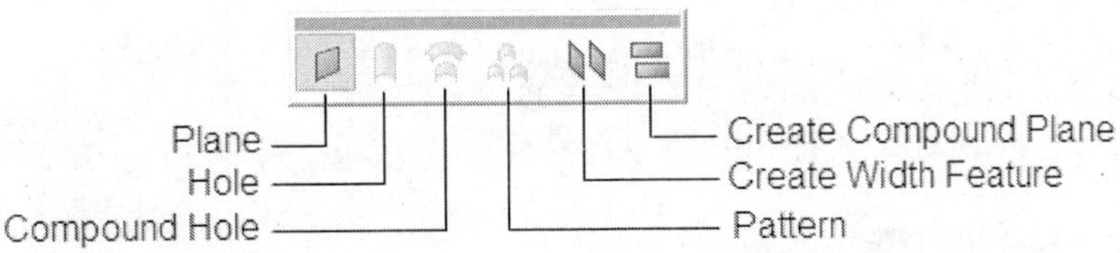

Figure 11-95 The pop-up toolbar displayed on selecting a feature

Some of the options that will be displayed in the pop-up toolbar are discussed next.

Plane

Select this option to select a plane. By default, this option will be selected when you invoke the **Datum** tool and select a face.

Hole

Select this option to specify the circular feature as a hole.

Cylinder

Select this option to specify the circular feature as a cylinder.

Compound Hole

On selecting this option, you will be prompted to select the holes that are coaxial and coradial. Select the holes and choose **OK** from the pop-up toolbar.

Create Compound Plane

On selecting this option, you will be prompted to select the coplanar planes. Select the planes from the drawing area and choose **OK** from the pop-up toolbar.

Pattern

Select this option if you need to select the patterned features as Datum.

Create Width Feature

Select this option to specify the width between the two selected faces as Datum. On selecting this option, you will be prompted to select two parallel faces. Select them from the drawing area and choose **OK** from the pop-up toolbar.

> **Note**
> *The options in the pop-up toolbar depend upon the tool and the feature selected. Therefore, all the options in this toolbar are not discussed here.*

Adding Dimensions

CommandManager:	MBD Dimensions > Size Dimension
SOLIDWORKS menus:	Tools > MBD Dimension > Size Dimension
Toolbar:	Tools > MBD Dimension > Size Dimension

After specifying the datum, you need to add dimensions to the part. You need to add dimensions with respect to the datums to make the feature fully defined. To add a dimension, choose the **Size Dimension** button from the **MBD Dimensions CommandManager**; the select cursor will change into a dimension cursor. Select a face or placed feature; a pop-up toolbar will be displayed. Choose an option from the pop-up toolbar and place the dimension, as shown in Figure 11-96.

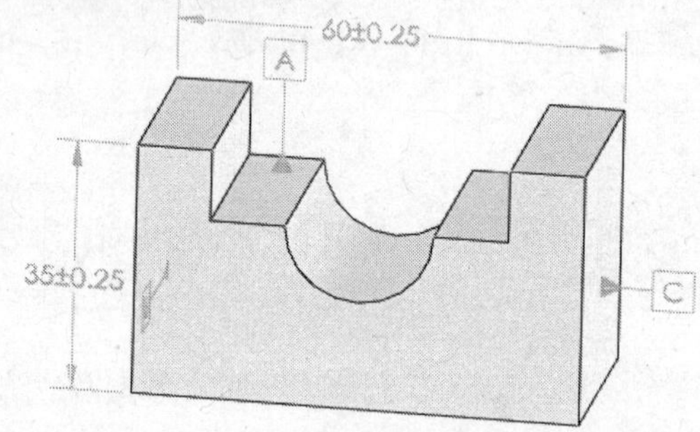

***Figure 11-96** Dimensions placed on a model*

When you add dimension to a feature, you will notice that the name of the feature is displayed in the **DimXpertManager**. The name will be displayed in blue color with a minus sign if the feature is under defined. The name will be displayed in black, if the feature is fully defined and the name will be displayed in red color with a plus sign, if the feature is over defined. You can also choose the **Show Tolerance Status** button to check the status of the feature. If the feature is fully defined, it is displayed in green. An under defined feature is displayed in yellow color and an over defined feature is displayed in red color. Besides adding a dimension to a feature, you can make a feature fully defined by locating it using the **Location Dimension** tool.

As mentioned earlier, these dimensions are not parametric in nature. They are added for the display purpose. However, you can display these dimensions while creating the drawing of the model in the drafting environment.

> **Note**
> *If you do not want a particular dimension to be displayed in the drafting environment, select the dimension, right-click, and clear the **Mark For Drawing** check mark displayed on the left of this option.*

Specifying the Location of a Feature

CommandManager:	MBD Dimensions > Location Dimension
SOLIDWORKS menus:	Tools > MBD Dimension > Location Dimension
Toolbar:	Tools > MBD Dimension > Location Dimension

After adding the dimension, you may need to specify the location of a feature with respect to a datum to make the feature fully defined. To specify the location, choose the **Location Dimension** button from the **MBD Dimensions CommandManager**; the select cursor will be changed into a dimension cursor. Select the feature; a pop-up toolbar will be displayed. Choose an option from the pop-up toolbar, if required, and also select the datum with respect to which the feature has to be located; the dimension will be attached to the cursor. Place the dimension, as shown in Figure 11-97.

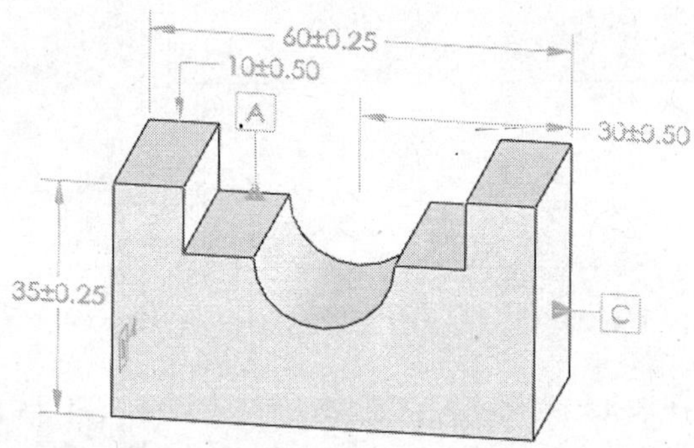

Figure 11-97 *Model with location dimension*

Adding Geometric Tolerance to the Features

Command Manager:	MBD Dimensions > Geometric Tolerance
SOLIDWORKS menus:	Tools > MBD Dimension > Geometric Tolerance
Toolbar:	Tools > MBD Dimension > Geometric Tolerance

In a shop floor drawing, you need to provide various other parameters along with the dimensions and dimensional tolerance. These parameters can be geometric condition, surface profile, material condition, and so on. All these parameters are defined using the **Geometric Tolerance** tool. To add geometric tolerance to features, choose the **Geometric Tolerance** button from the **MBD Dimensions CommandManager**; the **Properties** dialog box will be displayed, as shown in Figure 11-98. Also, the **Geometric Tolerance PropertyManager** will be displayed. You will also observe that a geometric tolerance of default parameter is attached to the cursor.

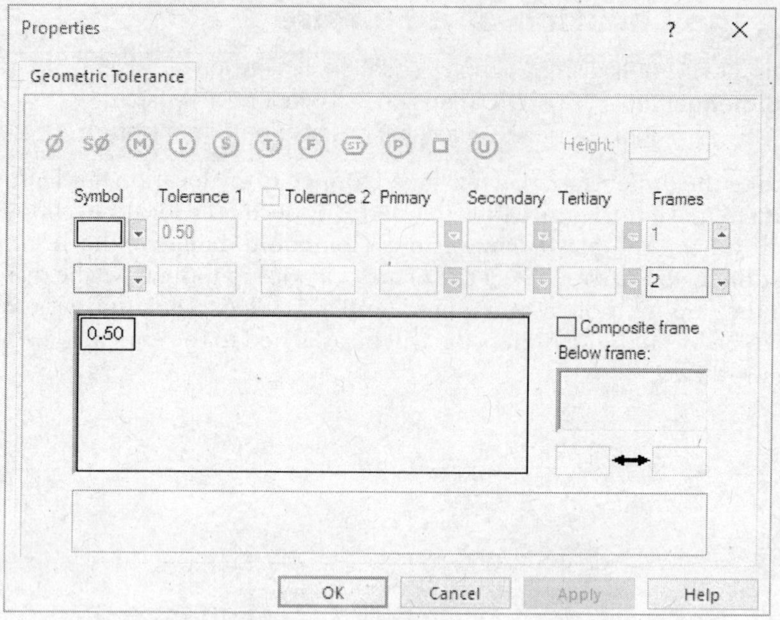

Figure 11-98 The ***Properties*** *dialog box*

The two rows in this dialog box are separate frames. You can add additional frames using the **Frames** spinner provided on the right of the **Tertiary** edit box. The parameters that can be added to these frames are geometric condition symbols, diameter symbol, value of tolerance, material condition, and datum references. The options in the **Properties** dialog box are used to add the geometric tolerances to the drawing views and are discussed next.

Symbol

The **Symbol** edit box is used to define the geometric condition. When you choose the down arrow button on the right of this edit box, the **Symbols** flyout will be displayed, as shown in Figure 11-99. This is used to define the geometric condition in the geometric tolerance. Select the symbol that defines the geometric condition. On selecting a symbol from this flyout, the flyout will disappear and the selected symbol will be displayed in the **Symbol** edit box. Also, the preview of the geometric tolerance will be displayed in the preview area.

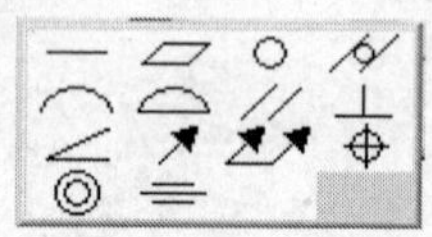

Figure 11-99 The ***Symbols*** *flyout*

Tolerance 1

The **Tolerance 1** edit box is used to specify the tolerance value with respect to the geometric condition that is defined using the **Symbols** flyout. You can use the buttons available above the rows of the frames to add symbols such as diameter, spherical diameter, material conditions, and so on.

Tolerance 2

The use of the **Tolerance 2** edit box is the same as that of **Tolerance 1**. This edit box is used to define the second geometric tolerance, if required.

Primary

The **Primary** edit box is used to specify the characters to define the datum reference that you add to the entities in the drawing view using the **Datum** tool.

Similarly, you can define the **Secondary** datum reference and the **Tertiary** datum reference.

Frames

The **Frames** spinner is used to increase the number of frames for applying more geometric tolerances.

Projected tolerance

The **Projected tolerance** button is available above the frame rows. This button is chosen to define the height of the projected tolerance. When you choose this button, the **Height** edit box will be enabled and you can specify the projected tolerance zone height in this edit box.

Note

*Similar to Projected tolerance, the geometric symbol buttons on the left of the **Height** edit box are used to define geometric conditions for a model.*

Composite frame

The **Composite frame** check box is selected to use a composite frame to add the tolerance. When you select this check box, the tolerance frame will be converted into a composite frame and the preview will be modified accordingly.

Between Two Points

The **Between Two Points** edit boxes are used to apply a geometric tolerance between two points or entities. To do so, specify the points in the edit boxes provided in the **Between Two Points** area.

Collecting Pattern Features

CommandManager:	MBD Dimensions > Pattern Feature
SOLIDWORKS menus:	Tools > MBD Dimension > Pattern Feature
Toolbar:	Tools > MBD Dimension > Pattern Feature

While applying the dimensions and tolerances, it is recommended to collect the patterned features. You can also collect the identical features that are not created using the pattern tool. To collect features, choose the **Pattern Feature** button from the **MBD Dimensions CommandManager**; the **MBD Dimension Pattern/Collection PropertyManager** will be displayed. If you Select the **Linked Patterns** radio button, then the name of the feature as described in the Design Tree will be displayed in the **Features** selection box. If you Select the **Manual Patterns** radio button, then the name of the selected features will be displayed as defined by DimXpert. Select the **Collection** radio button to collect and group the dissimilar features. After selecting the appropriate radio button from the **Create Pattern** rollout and selecting the feature from the drawing area, choose the **OK** button; the features will be collected and displayed in the **DimXpert PropertyManager**.

Tip

If you have generated the dimensions of two features with respect to a datum and both have the same values, you can combine the dimensions. To do so, select the dimensions and right-click to invoke the shortcut menu. Choose the ***Combine Dimension*** *option from the shortcut menu.*

Adding Dimensions Automatically

CommandManager:	MBD Dimensions > Auto Dimension Scheme
SOLIDWORKS menus:	Tools > MBD Dimension > Auto Dimension Scheme
Toolbar:	Tools > MBD Dimension > Auto Dimension Scheme

You can also add dimensions to a part automatically. To add dimensions to a part automatically, choose the **Auto Dimension Scheme** button from the **MBD Dimensions CommandManager**; the **Auto Dimension Scheme PropertyManager** will be displayed, as shown in Figure 11-100. The rollouts and options in this PropertyManager are discussed next.

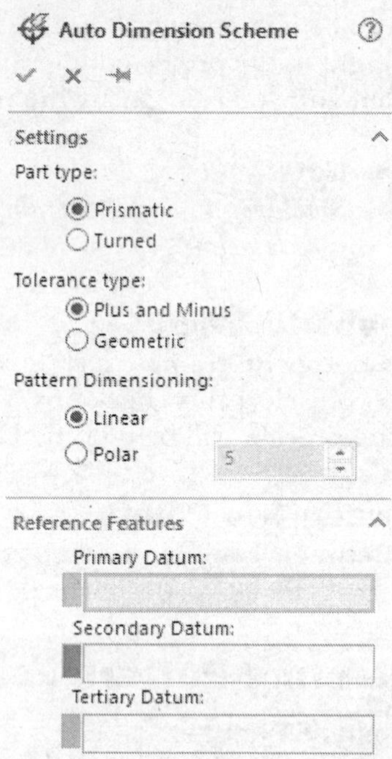

Figure 11-100 *Partial view of the* ***Auto Dimension Scheme PropertyManager***

Settings Rollout

The options in this rollout are selected based on the method used for manufacturing a part and the tolerance type that has to be specified for the part. In SOLIDWORKS, when you use the plus and minus types of tolerances, you can specify the dimension scheme to be used as **Linear** or **Polar**. Polar dimension scheme is used to dimension the axial components. In this case, you need to specify the number of holes to be identified as pattern in the **Minimum number of holes** spinner.

Reference Features Rollout

The options in this rollout are used to specify the datum. You need to specify three non-parallel datums.

Scope Rollout

The options in this rollout are used to specify whether the dimension has to be created for the selected features or the whole part.

Feature Filters Rollout

If you do not want to add dimension to a particular category of features using the **MBD Dimensions** tool, then clear the corresponding check box from this rollout.

Tip

To break the combined dimension, select the combined dimension, right-click and choose the ***Break Combined Dimension*** *option from the shortcut menu.*

TUTORIALS

Tutorial 1

In this tutorial, you will create the plastic cover shown in Figure 11-101. The dimensions of this cover are shown in Figure 11-102. Note that a draft angle of 1-degree has to be applied to the side faces of the cover. The parameters of the mounting boss are: Boss height = **14** mm, Boss diameter = **4.8** mm, Diameter of the boss step = **4** mm, Height of the boss step = **1.5** mm, Draft angle of the main boss = **2**-degree, Diameter of the inside hole = **3** mm, Diameter of the inside counter bore = **4** mm, Depth of the inside counter bore = **2** mm, Draft angle of the inside hole = **1**-degree, Length of fins = **4** mm, Width of fins = **1.5** mm, Height of fins = **12** mm, Draft angle of fins = **1**-degree, Distance for the fin chamfer from the edge of fin = **1.5** mm, Angle for the fin chamfer = **45**-degrees, and Number of Fins = **4**. **(Expected time: 30 min)**

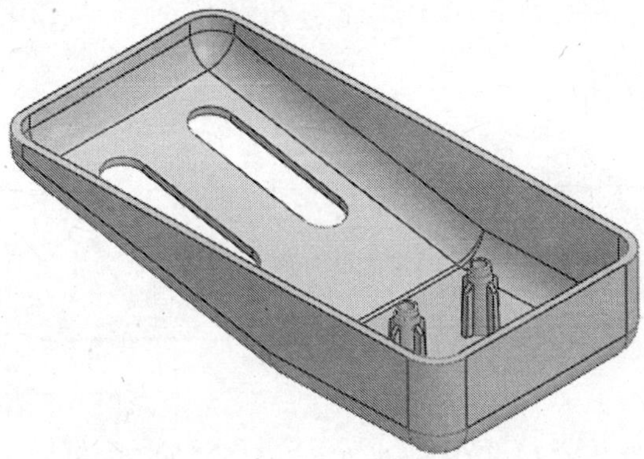

Figure 11-101 *Plastic cover for Tutorial 1*

The following steps are required to complete this tutorial:

a. Create the base feature of the model on the **Front Plane** and extrude it using the **Mid Plane** option.
b. Add the face draft to the side faces of the model and then create the fillets.
c. Create the shell feature by removing the top face.
d. Create the cut feature.
e. Add one of the mounting bosses and then edit its sketch to locate it by using dimensions.
f. Mirror the mounting boss feature on the other side.

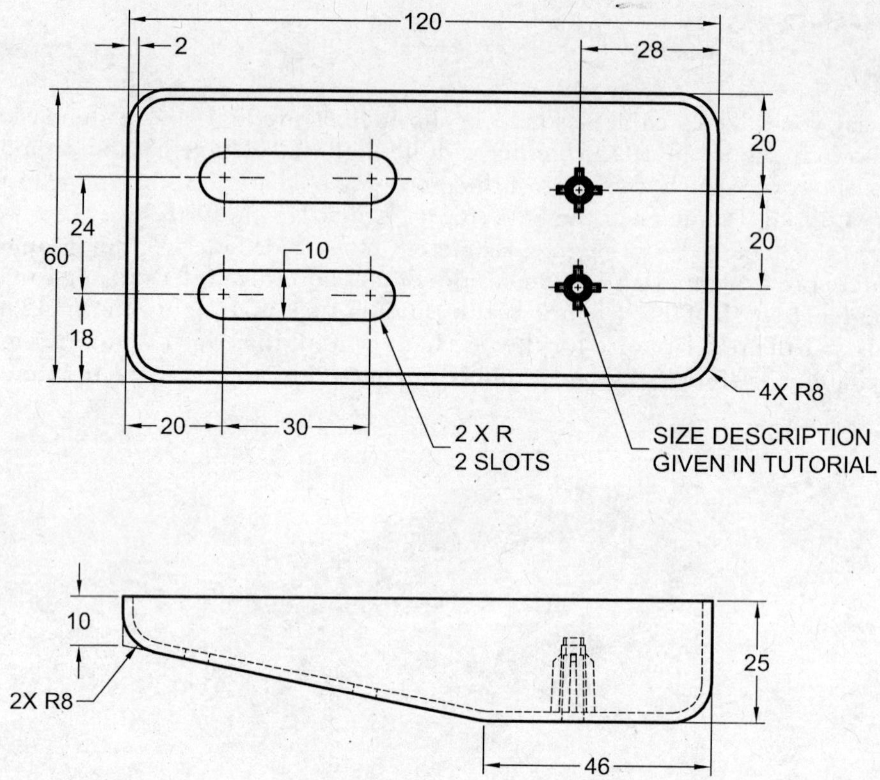

Figure 11-102 Dimensions of the plastic cover

Creating the Base Feature

1. Start SOLIDWORKS and then start a new part file.

2. Create the extruded base feature of the model on the Front Plane using the **Mid Plane** option. The base feature is shown in Figure 11-103.

Adding Draft and Creating Fillets

1. Invoke the **Draft** tool and add a draft of 1-degree to all the four vertical side faces of the model by selecting the top planar face as the neutral face.

2. Add a fillet of **8** mm radius to all the sharp edges of the model excluding those of the top planar face of the base feature, refer to Figure 11-104.

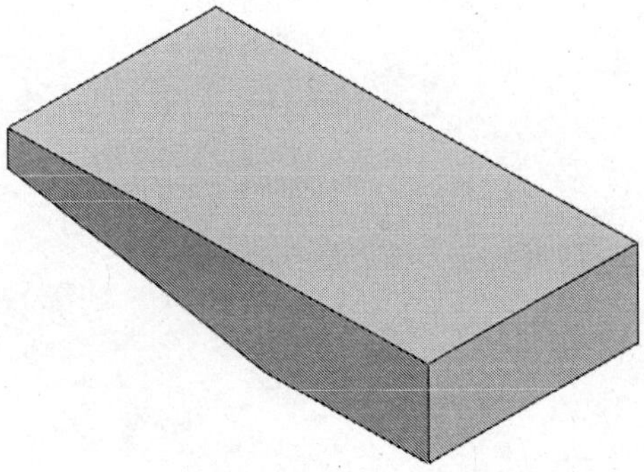

Figure 11-103 *Base feature of the model*

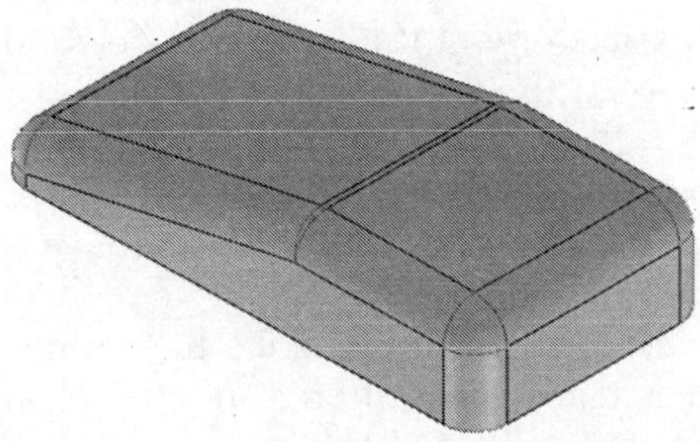

Figure 11-104 *Base feature with draft and fillet*

Creating the Shell and Cut Features

1. Create the shell feature for a wall thickness **2** mm by removing the top planar face of the model, as shown in Figure 11-105.

2. Create the extruded cut feature, as shown in Figure 11-106. For dimensions, refer to Figure 11-102.

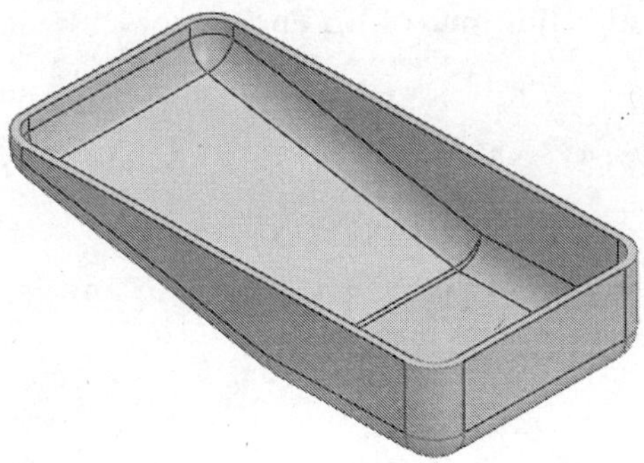

Figure 11-105 *Model after creating the shell*

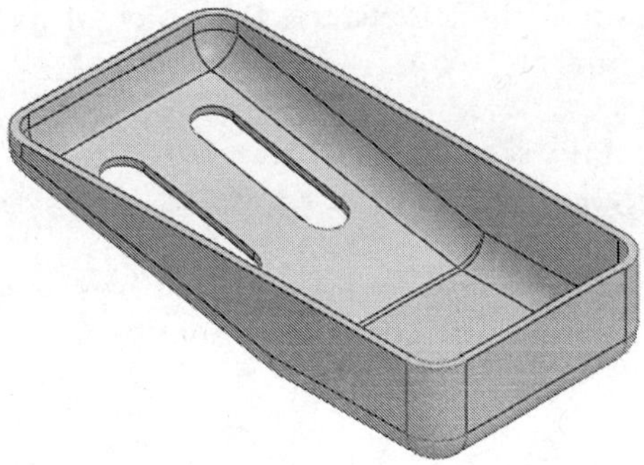

Figure 11-106 *Model after creating the cut feature*

Creating the Mounting Boss

Next, you need to create two mounting bosses. First you need to create only one mounting boss and then mirror it to create another instance. After creating the mounting bosses, you need to edit its sketch to place it at the exact location using the given dimensions.

1. Choose **Insert > Fastening Feature > Mounting Boss** from the SOLIDWORKS menus; the **Mounting Boss PropertyManager** is displayed and the **Select a face or a 3D point** selection box in the **Position** rollout is highlighted in it.

2. Click on the horizontal face close to the top edge as the face to place the mounting boss; a preview of the mounting boss feature is displayed, as shown in Figure 11-107.

3. Modify the mounting boss parameters based on the values given in the tutorial description.

4. Click in the **Select a vector to define orientation of the fins** selection box of the **Fins** rollout and then select one of the bottom horizontal edges to reorient the fins in the mounting boss.

5. Choose the **OK** button from the **Mounting Boss PropertyManager**; the mounting boss is created.

   You will notice that by default, the mounting boss is created at a point where you have selected the plane. So, you need to change the position of the mounting boss and move it to the required location. This is done by editing the sketch of the mounting boss which is automatically created when you create the mounting boss.

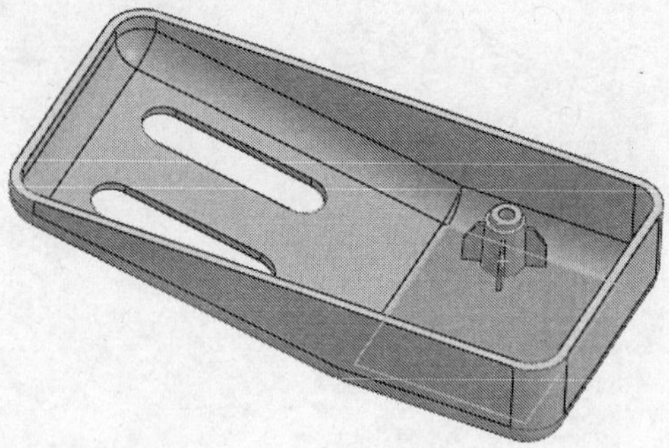

Figure 11-107 *Preview of the mounting boss*

6. Click on the (▸) sign located on the left of the **Mounting Boss** in the **FeatureManager Design Tree** to expand it. Now, right-click on the **3DSketch** and choose **Edit Sketch** from the shortcut menu.

7. Position the 3D Sketch to its actual location using the **Smart Dimension** tool. Refer to Figure 11-102 for dimensions.

8. Exit the sketching environment; the mounting boss is created and gets placed at its proper location, as shown in Figure 11-108.

9. Use the **Mirror** tool to create mirror image of the mounting boss. Select **Front Plane** as the mirroring plane. The final model of the plastic cover is shown in Figure 11-109.

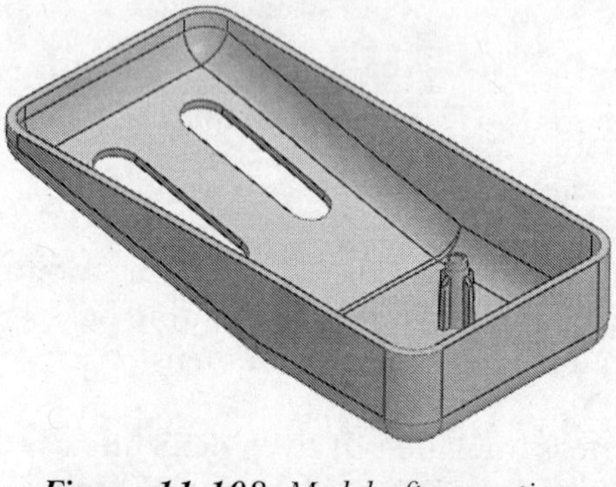

Figure 11-108 *Model after creating and positioning the mounting boss*

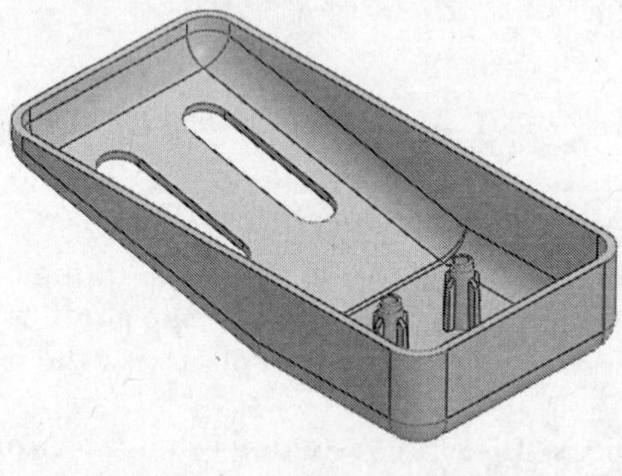

Figure 11-109 *Final model of the plastic cover*

Saving the Model

1. Save the model with the name *c11_tut01* at the following location:

   \Documents\SOLIDWORKS\c11

2. Choose **File > Close** from the SOLIDWORKS menus to close the document.

Tutorial 2

In this tutorial, you will create the plastic cover shown in Figure 11-110. The dimensions of this cover are shown in Figure 11-111. In the lower vent, the vertical lines are ribs and the horizontal lines are spars. The other parameters of this vent are given below:

Depth of ribs = 1 mm, Width of ribs = 2 mm, Depth of spars = 0.5 mm, Width of spars = 2 mm, Offset of spars from surface = 0.5 mm.

(Expected time: 30 min)

Figure 11-110 *Model for Tutorial 2*

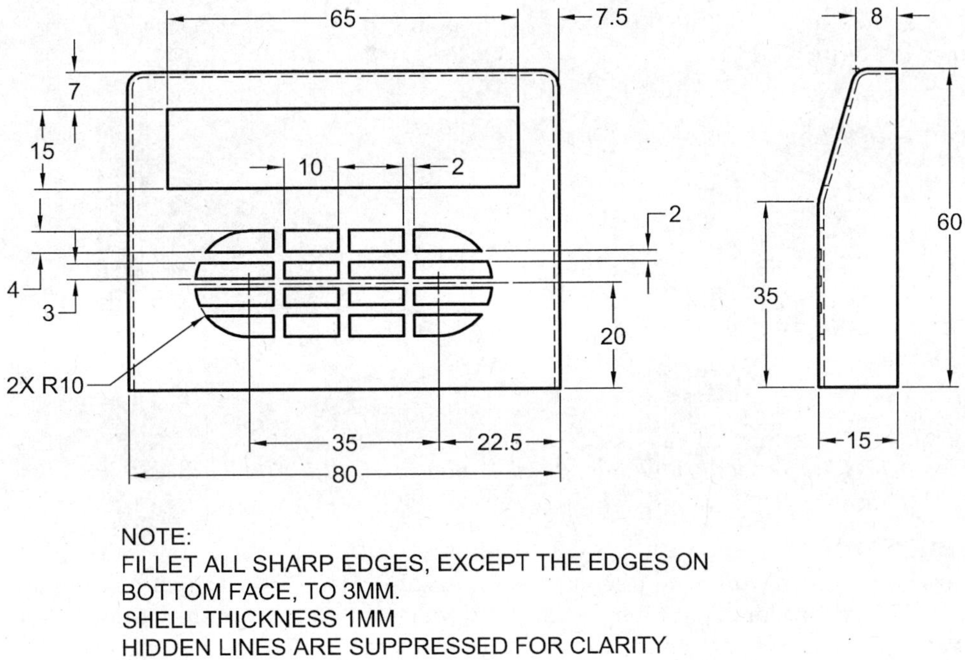

Figure 11-111 *Dimensions of the cover for Tutorial 2*

The following steps are required to complete this tutorial:

a. Create the base feature of the model on the **Right Plane** and extrude it using the **Mid Plane** option.

b. Add the required fillets.
c. Create the shell feature by removing the back and bottom faces.
d. Create the first vent.
e. Create the second vent.
f. Save the model.

Creating the Base Feature

1. Start a new part file using the **New SOLIDWORKS Document** dialog box.

2. Create the base feature of the model using the **Right Plane** as the sketching plane, refer to Figure 11-112.

Figure 11-112 *Base feature of the model*

Adding Fillets

1. Add fillets of radius **3** mm to all the sharp edges of the model, except for the edges on the bottom and back faces. The model after adding the fillets is shown in Figure 11-113.

Creating the Shell Feature

1. Create the shell feature with a shell thickness value of **1** mm. Remove the back face and the bottom face of the model, as shown in Figure 11-114.

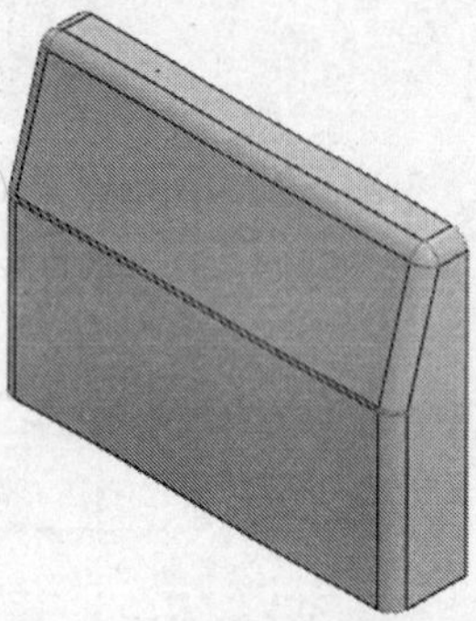

Figure 11-113 *Model after adding fillets*

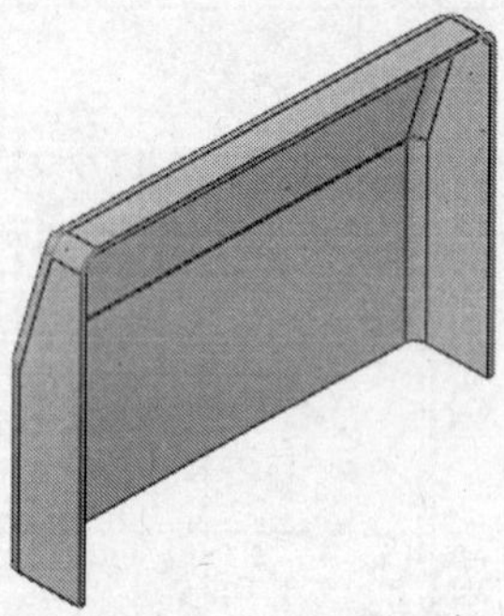

Figure 11-114 *Model after creating the shell feature*

Creating Vents

In the given model, you need to create two vents. The lower vent, which has arcs at the two ends, also has fins and spars. However, the upper vent consists of only the boundary. You will first create the lower vent.

1. Select the front face of the model as the sketching plane and draw the sketch of the vent, as shown in Figure 11-115.

2. Exit the sketching environment and then invoke the **Vent** tool; the **Vent PropertyManager** is displayed and the selection box in the **Boundary** rollout is activated.

3. Select the outer loop as the boundary of the vent. Make sure that the front face of the model is selected as the face on which the vent will be placed.

4. Select the vertical lines as ribs and then set the parameters of the ribs based on the information given in the tutorial statement.

5. Select the horizontal lines as spars and then set the parameters of the spars based on the information given in the tutorial statement. Reverse the direction of spars offset if the preview disappears.

6. Choose **OK** to exit the **Vent PropertyManager**. The model after creating the lower vent is shown in Figure 11-116.

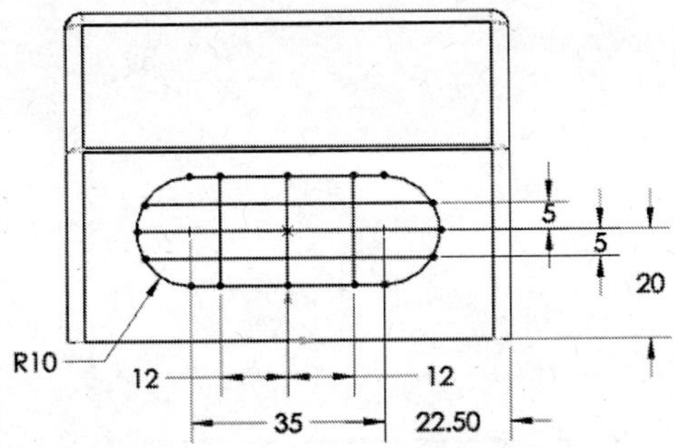

Figure 11-115 *Sketch for the vent*

Figure 11-116 *Model after creating the lower vent*

7. Draw the sketch for the upper vent on the front face of the model, as shown in Figure 11-117.

8. Exit the sketching environment and then invoke the **Vent** tool. Select the sketch as the boundary of the vent to create the vent.

9. Exit the **Vent** tool. The final model after creating the vent is shown in Figure 11-118.

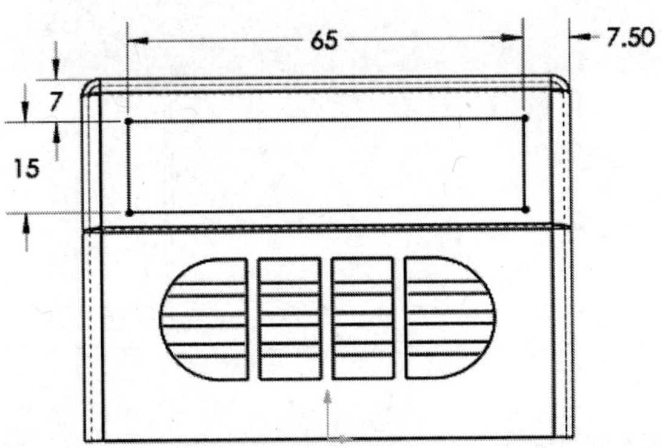

Figure 11-117 *Sketch for the upper vent*

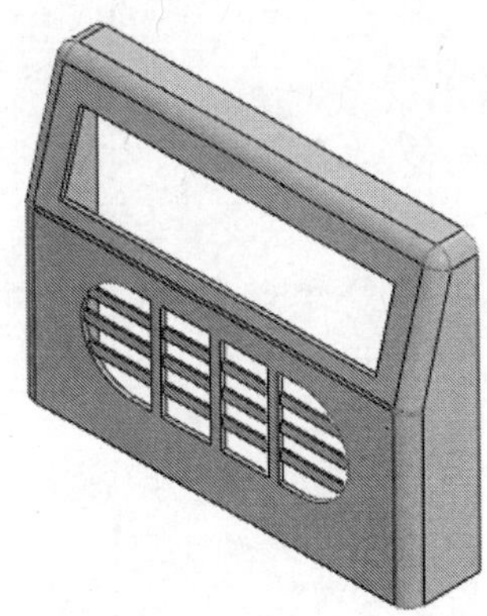

Figure 11-118 *Final model*

Saving the Model

1. Save the model with the name *c11_tut02* at the following location: *\Documents\SOLIDWORKS\c11*

2. Choose **File > Close** from the SOLIDWORKS menus to close the document.

Tutorial 3

In this tutorial, you will create the model of the tube shown in Figure 11-119. The three sections to be used to create the base loft feature and the dimensions are shown in Figure 11-120.

(Expected time: 30 min)

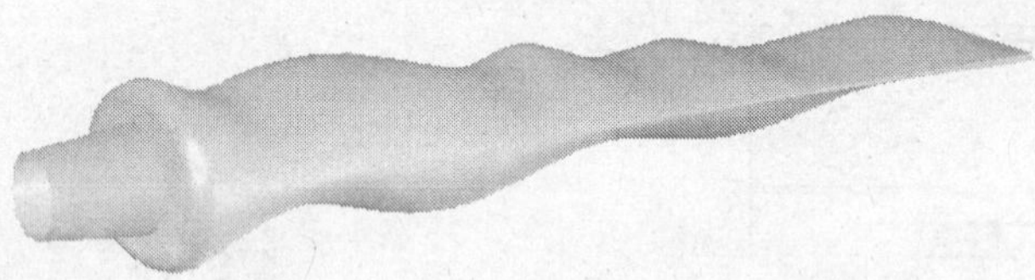

Figure 11-119 *Model for Tutorial 3*

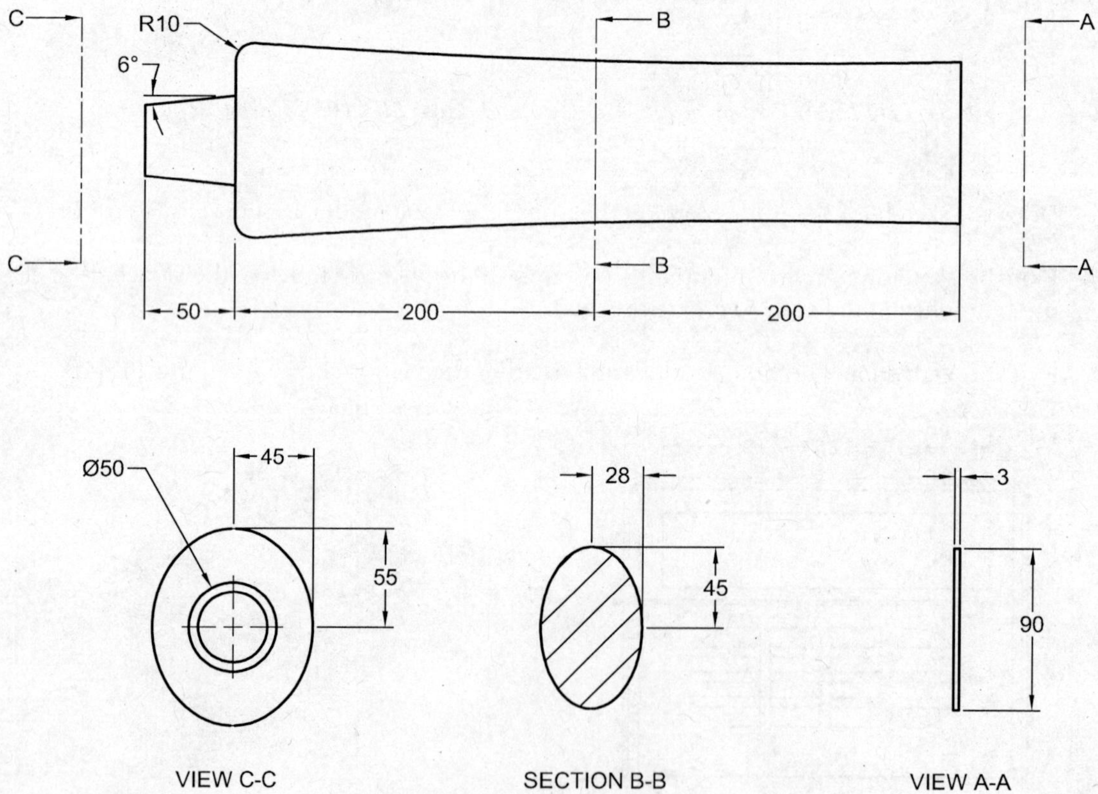

Figure 11-120 *Sections for the base feature*

The following steps are required to complete this tutorial:

a. Create the first section for the base feature of the model on the **Front Plane**.
b. Create a plane at an offset of **200** mm from the **Front Plane** and create the second section on this plane.
c. Create a plane at an offset of **200** mm from the previous plane and create the third section on this plane.
d. Create the loft feature using three sections.
e. Create an extruded feature with a draft on the front face of the base feature.
f. Create the freeform feature on the top and bottom faces of the loft feature.
g. Create the fillet and the shell feature.

Creating the Base Feature

1. Start a new part file and draw section 1 for the loft feature on the **Front Plane**, refer to Figure 11-21.

2. Create a plane at an offset of **200** mm from the **Front Plane** and create the second section on it, refer to Figure 11-21.

3. Create a plane at an offset of **200** mm from the previous plane and create the third section on it, refer to Figure 11-21.

4. Create the loft feature using these three sections, the resultant loft feature is shown in Figure 11-122.

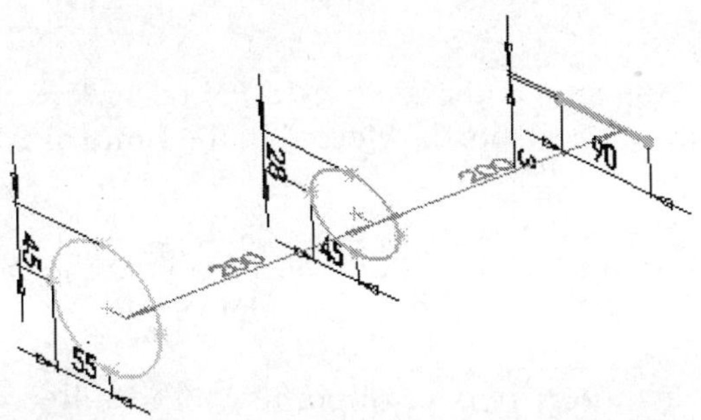

Figure 11-121 *Sections for the loft feature*

Figure 11-122 *The resultant loft feature*

Creating the Extruded Feature

1. Draw a circle of **50** mm diameter at the center on the front face of the base feature and extrude it upto a distance of **50** mm with a draft angle of **6**-degree. The model after creating this feature is shown in Figure 11-123.

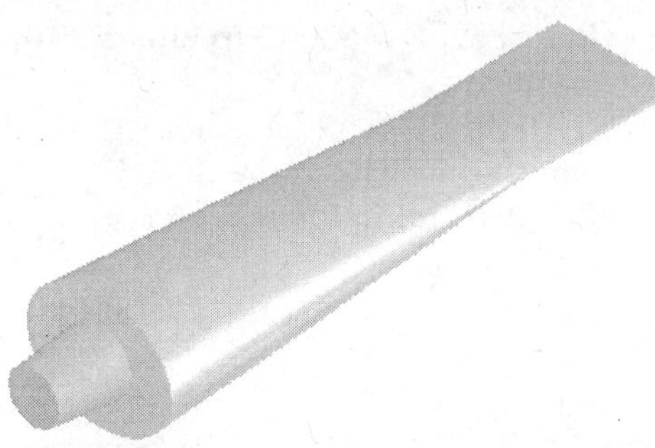

Figure 11-123 *Model after creating the extruded feature*

Creating the Freeform Feature

It is recommended that you draw a spline first and then use it to create the freeform feature by snapping to the control points of the spline.

1. Select the **Right Plane** as the sketching plane and draw a spline, refer to Figure 11-124.

2. Choose **Insert > Features > Freeform** from the SOLIDWORKS menus to invoke the **Freeform PropertyManager**.

3. Select the top face of the loft feature as the face to be deformed; the grid mesh is displayed on the face, as shown in Figure 11-125.

4. Right-click in the drawing area away from the model and choose **Add Curves** from the shortcut menu. Click on the grid mesh to add a curve below the spline curve drawn earlier.

5. Right-click in the drawing area away from the model and choose **Add Points** from the shortcut menu. Add the same number of control points to the curve as in the spline.

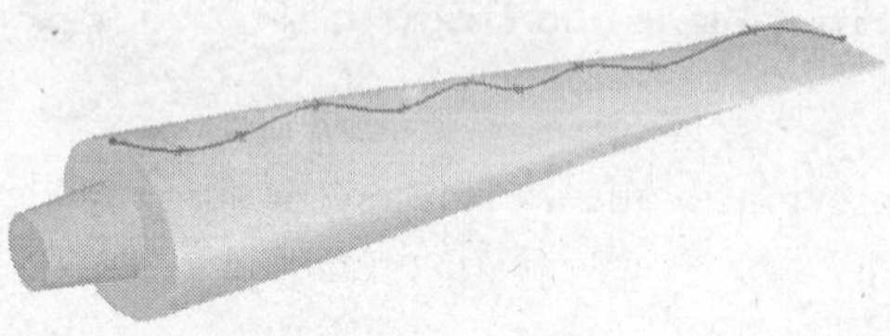

Figure 11-124 Spline drawn to deform the face

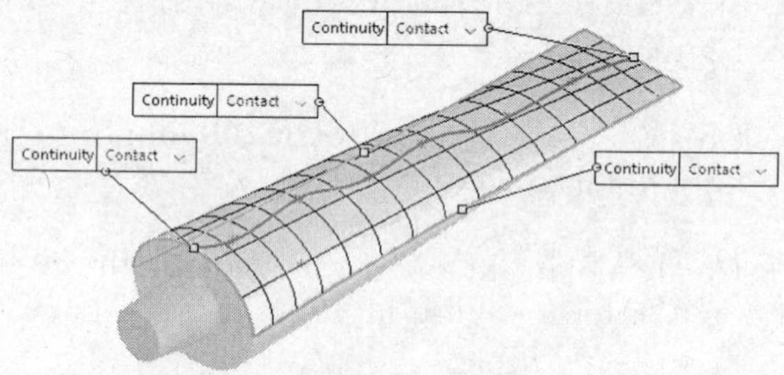

Figure 11-125 The grid mesh displayed on the face

6. Right-click away from the model in the drawing area and choose **Add Points** again to turn off this option. Make sure the **Snap to geometry** check box is selected in the **Control Points** rollout of the **Freeform PropertyManager**.

7. Drag one of the control points to the corresponding control point of the spline; the cursor snaps to the control point of the spline. Also, observe that the face is deformed.

8. Similarly, drag all the control points to their respective control points on the spline. The model after dragging all the control points is shown in Figure 11-126.

9. Choose **OK** from the **Freeform PropertyManager** and then hide the display of the spline.

10. Similarly, deform the other side of the base feature. In this case, you can drag the control points arbitrarily in the 3D space. You do not need to draw the spline for this. The model after deforming the other face is shown in Figure 11-127.

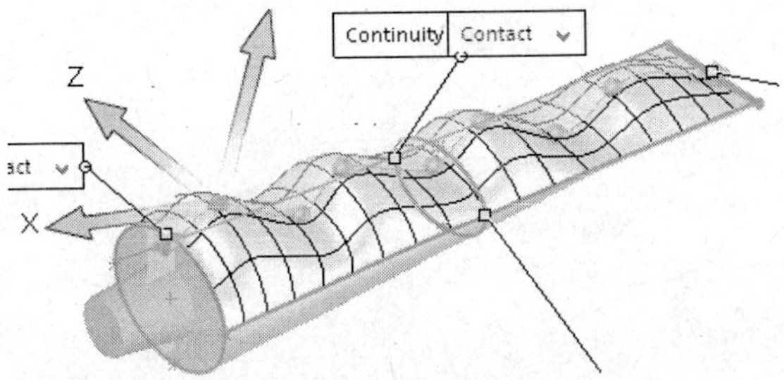

Figure 11-126 Dragging the control points

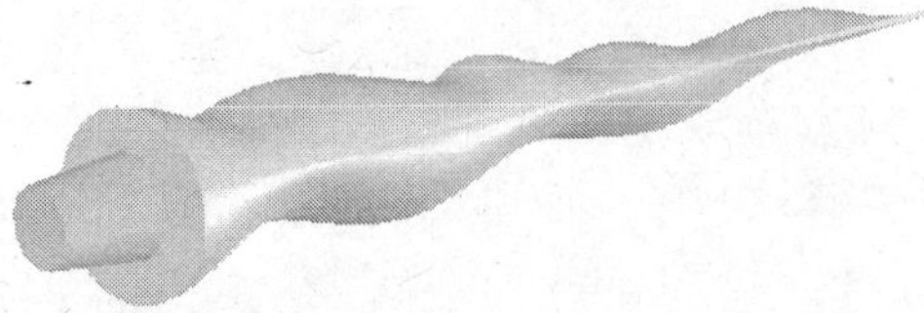

Figure 11-127 Model after deforming the other side of the base feature

Creating the Remaining Features

1. Create a fillet feature of radius **10** mm on the front edge of the base feature.

2. Create a shell feature of thickness **0.25** mm by removing the front face of the extruded feature. The final model of the tube is shown in Figure 11-128.

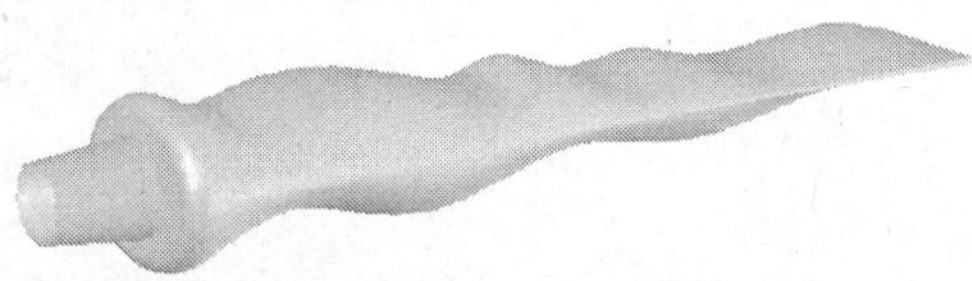

Figure 11-128 Final model of the tube

Saving the Model

1. Save the model with the name *c11_tut03* at the following location: *\Documents\SOLIDWORKS\c11*

2. Choose **File > Close** from the SOLIDWORKS menus to close the document.

Tutorial 4

In this tutorial, you will open the model created in Exercise 1 of Chapter 5. You will apply dimensions to the features using the **MBD Dimension** tool. The model after applying the dimensions is shown in Figure 11-129. **(Expected time: 30 min)**

The following steps are required to complete this tutorial:

a. Open the model created in Exercise 1 of Chapter 5.
b. Save it in a new folder.
c. Specify the datum, add dimensions to the model, and position the features.
d. Save the model.

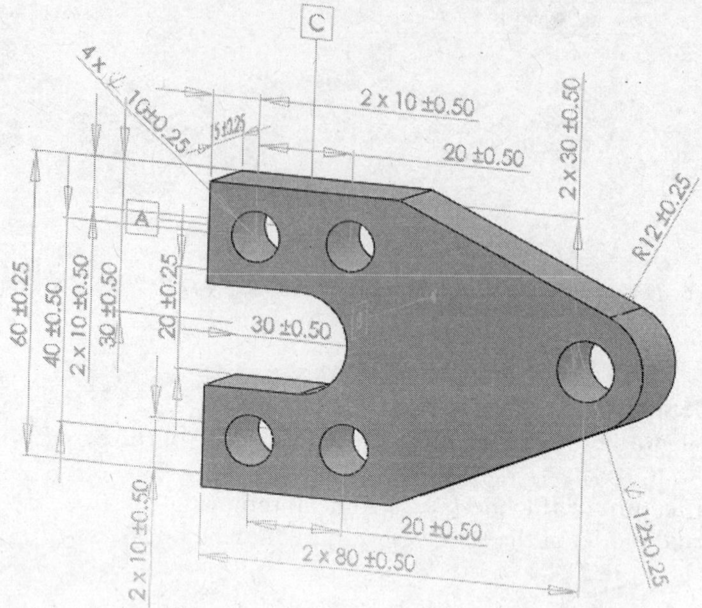

Figure 11-129 Model and its dimensions for Tutorial 4

Opening and Saving the Model Created in Exercise 1 of Chapter 5

1. Choose the **Open** button from the Menu Bar; the **Open** dialog box is displayed. Open the model created in Exercise 1 of Chapter 5.

2. Choose **File > Save As** from the SOLIDWORKS menus and save the model with the name *c11_tut04* in the *c11* folder. The location for saving the model is *Documents\SOLIDWORKS\c11*. The saved model is shown in Figure 11-130.

Specifying the Datum

When you are applying the dimensions manually using the **MBD Dimension** toolbar, you need to specify the datum.

1. Choose the **Datum** button from the **MBD Dimensions CommandManager**; the **Datum Feature PropertyManager** is displayed.

2. Enter **A** in the **Label** edit box.

3. Specify the Datum **A** on one of the left faces; a pop-up toolbar is displayed.

4. Choose the **Create Compound Plane** button from the pop-up toolbar; the pop-up toolbar expands and name of the selected face is displayed in the selection box.

5. Select the other face on the left side; the name of the selected face is displayed in the selection box, refer to Figure 11-131.

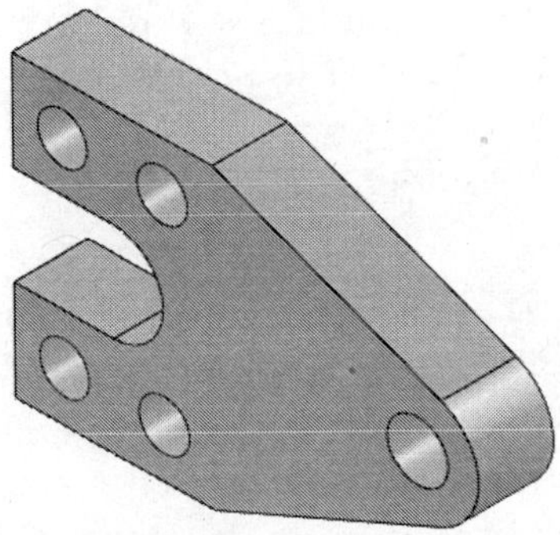

Figure 11-130 The model created in Chapter 5

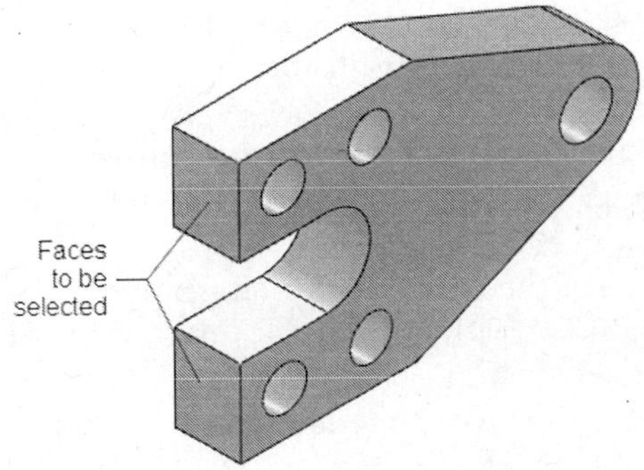

Figure 11-131 Faces to be selected for Datum A

6. Choose **OK** from the pop-up toolbar and place the Datum A at a suitable location, as shown in Figure 11-132.

7. Specify the front face as Datum **B** and the top face as Datum **C**. The model after specifying the datums is shown in Figure 11-133. Next, close the **Datum Feature PropertyManager**.

Figure 11-132 Datum A specified

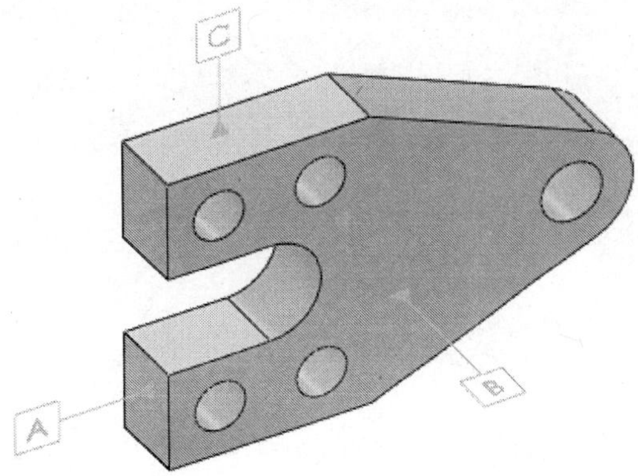

Figure 11-133 All datums specified in the model

Adding Dimensions to Features

Next, you need to add dimensions to the features.

1. Choose the **Size Dimension** button from the **MBD Dimensions CommandManager** and select the top face that is selected for the Datum C; a pop-up toolbar is displayed.

2. Choose the **Create Width Feature** button; the pop-up toolbar expands with the selection box. Note that **Face <1>** is already selected in the selection box.

3. Select the bottom face which is opposite to the Datum C face and choose **OK** from the pop-up toolbar; the dimension value 60 along with the default tolerance is displayed. Place the dimension at a suitable location.

4. As the **Size Dimension** button is still activated, select the front face selected as Datum B; a pop-up toolbar is displayed.

5. Choose the **Create Width Feature** button; the pop-up toolbar expands with the selection box. The **Face <1>** is already selected in the box.

6. Select the back face which is opposite to the Datum B face and choose **OK**; the dimension value 15 with the default tolerance is displayed. Place the dimension at a suitable place.

7. Exit the **Size Dimension** tool, select the dimension value 15, and right-click.

8. Choose **Select Annotation View (*Right)** from the **Selected Entities** area in the shortcut menu; the **Select annotation view** dialog box is displayed as shown in Figure 11-134. Select the ***Right** option from the dialog box, the dimension value gets oriented as shown in Figure 11-135.

The model after adding the two dimensions is shown in Figure 11-135.

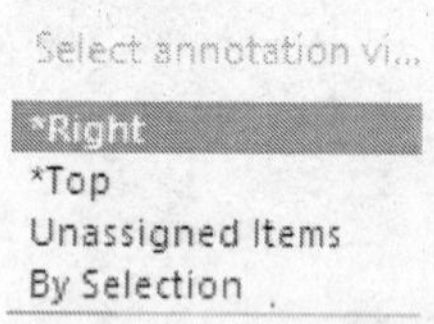

Figure 11-134 *The* ***Selected annotation view*** *dialog box*

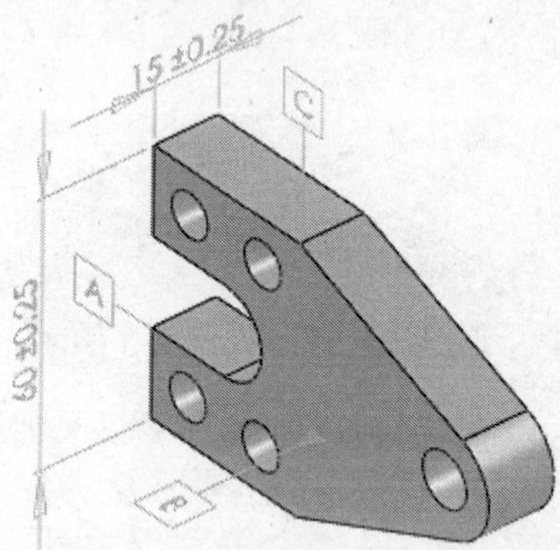

Figure 11-135 *Model after adding two dimensions*

Adding Dimension to the Notch

Next, you will add the dimension to the notch and locate it.

1. Choose the **Size Dimension** button from the **MBD Dimensions CommandManager** and select the curved face in the slot; a pop-up toolbar is displayed.

2. Choose the **Notch** button if it is not selected by default in the pop-up toolbar; the length and width of the notch are displayed attached to the cursor.

3. Place it at a suitable location and choose **OK** from the **DimXpert PropertyManager**.

You will notice that **Notch1** is displayed in the **DimXpertManager** in blue color with a minus sign. This indicates that it is underdefined. You need to locate the notch with respect to a datum to fully define it.

4. Choose the **Location Dimension** button from the **MBD Dimensions CommandManager** and select the cylindrical face of the notch; a pop-up toolbar is displayed with the **Notch** button chosen. 

5. Select the top face which is selected for the Datum C; the dimension is displayed. Place it at a suitable location and choose **OK** from the **DimXpert PropertyManager**; the notch is fully defined.

6. Orient the model to the front view. The notch and its dimensions are shown in Figure 11-136. Note that the other dimensions are suppressed for clarity.

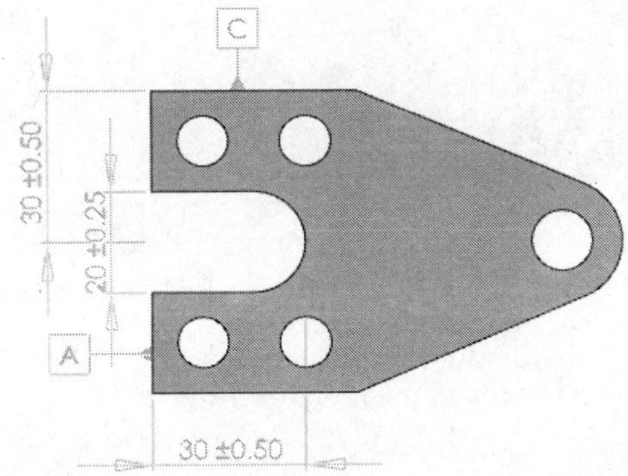

Figure 11-136 *The notch and its dimension*

Adding Dimensions to the Hole and the Curved Surface

Next, you need to add dimensions to the hole and the curved surface on the right side.

1. Choose the **Size Dimension** button from the **MBD Dimensions CommandManager** and select the hole feature of diameter 12 mm; the diameter of the hole feature is displayed.

2. Place the dimension at a suitable location and choose **OK** from the **DimXpert PropertyManager**.

3. Choose the **Location Dimension** button from the **MBD Dimensions CommandManager** and select the hole feature of diameter 12 mm and the face that is selected for the Datum A. Place the horizontal dimension at a suitable location and click anywhere in the drawing area.

4. Now, select the hole feature of diameter 12 mm and the face that is selected for the Datum C. Place the vertical dimension at a suitable location.

5. Similarly, add the three dimensions to the curved face that is concentric to the hole feature. The model after placing all the dimensions is shown in Figure 11-137. Note that the other dimensions are suppressed for clarity.

Next, you will combine the two dimensions that are measured from the same datum.

6. Select the two horizontal dimensions by pressing the CTRL key and then right-click.

7. Choose the **Combine Dimension** option from the shortcut menu; the horizontal dimensions are combined together.

8. Similarly, combine the vertical dimensions. The model after combining the dimensions is shown in Figure 11-138.

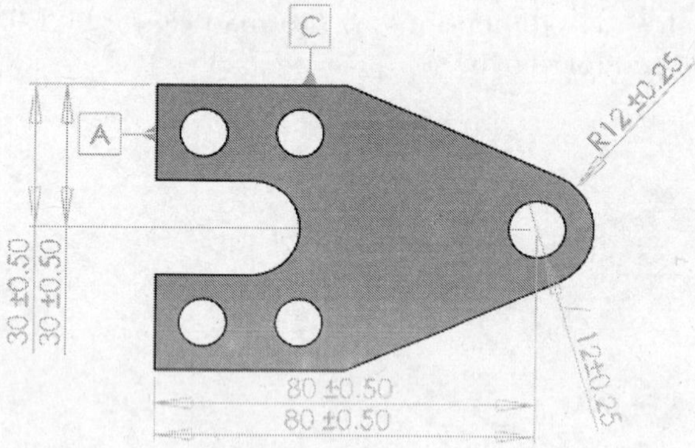

Figure 11-137 Model after placing the horizontal and vertical dimensions

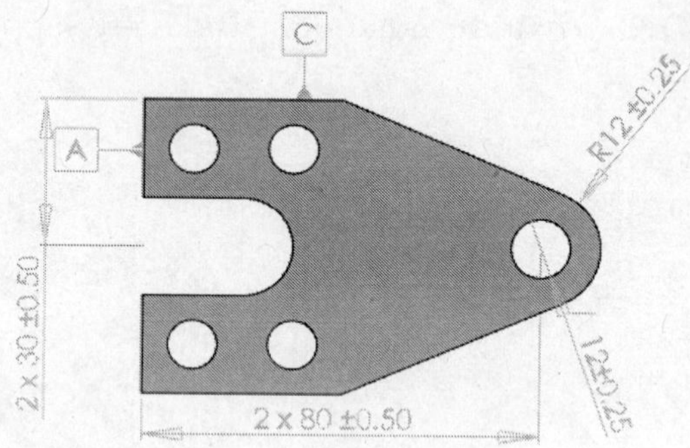

Figure 11-138 Model after combining the dimensions

Adding Dimensions to the Patterned Holes

Next, you need to add the dimension to the hole and the curved surface on the right side.

1. Choose the **Pattern Feature** button from the **MBD Dimensions CommandManager**; the **MBD Dimension Pattern/Collection PropertyManager** is displayed.

2. Select the **Manual Patterns** radio button, if it is not selected by default.

3. Select one of the holes; all the hole features are selected.

4. Choose **OK** from the **MBD Dimension Pattern/Collection PropertyManager**; the Hole **Pattern1** node is created in the **DimXpertManager**.

5. Select the left most hole feature and choose the **Size Dimension** button from the **MBD Dimensions CommandManager**; the dimension of the hole feature is displayed. Place it at a suitable location.

6. Position the hole feature using the **Location Dimension** tool, refer to Figure 11-139.

7. Locate the other hole features with respect to the left most hole, Datum A and Datum C, refer to Figure 11-140.

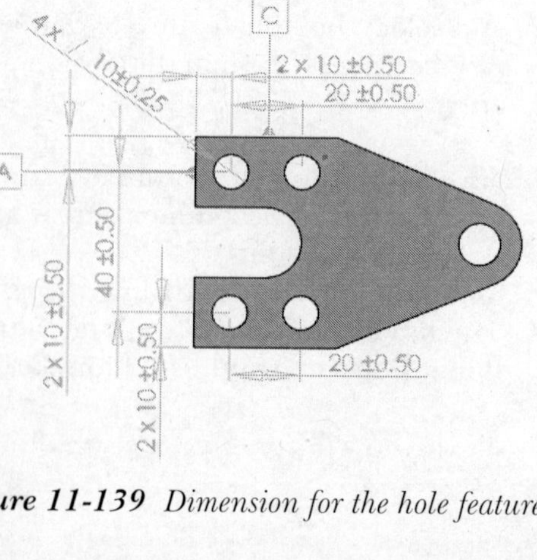

Figure 11-139 Dimension for the hole features

8. Set the view to Dimetric. The dimensions are displayed in the model, as shown in Figure 11-140.

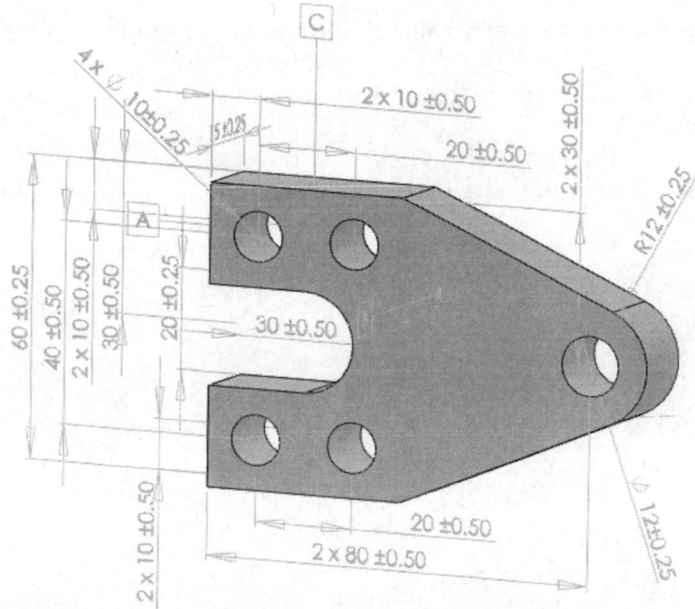

Figure 11-140 Dimensions displayed in the model

Saving the Model

1. Since model name is already specified, Save the changes made in the model.

2. Choose **File > Close** from the SOLIDWORKS menus to close the document.

Self-Evaluation Test

Answer the following questions and then compare them to those given at the end of this chapter:

1. The __________ tool allows you to create vents in a solid model.

2. Using the __________ option, you can deform a selected body or bodies by pushing the tool bodies inside them.

3. __________ are generally created in small plastic boxes to create a push fit type arrangement to close and open the plastic boxes.

4. The __________ check box is selected to create an elliptical dome feature.

5. __________ are the cut features that are created to accommodate a snap hook.

6. A concave dome is the one in which material is removed by creating a cavity in the form of a dome. (T/F)

7. A lip feature is created by removing material from the selected face. (T/F)

8. The **Deform** tool is used to create free-style designs by manipulating the shape of the entire model or a particular portion of it. (T/F)

9. Mounting boss features cannot be used in plastic components to accommodate fasteners. (T/F)

10. The vents may or may not have ribs and spars. (T/F)

Review Questions

Answer the following questions:

1. Which of the following tools is used to perform the freeform bending, twisting, tapering, and stretching of a selected body?

   (a) **Flex** (b) **Indent**
   (c) **Snap Hook** (d) **Vent**

2. Which of the following tools is used to create a feature to accommodate a snap hook?

   (a) **Snap Hook** (b) **Snap Groove**
   (c) **Hook** (d) **Snap Hook Groove**

3. Which of the following options in the **Dome PropertyManager** is used to specify the direction vector for creating the dome feature?

   (a) **Direction** (b) **Side**
   (c) **Tangent** (d) **Push Direction**

4. While using the **Flex** tool, which of the following radio buttons needs to be selected to twist a body?

   (a) **Rotate** (b) **Twist**
   (c) **Move** (d) None of these

5. Which one of the following operations cannot be performed using the **Flex** tool?

   (a) Twisting (b) Stretching
   (c) Tapering (d) Aligning

6. By using the __________ rollout, you can define spars in the vent feature.

7. The __________ tool is used to create lip/groove in a component.

8. The total thickness of a snap hook at its base can be defined using the _________ rollout.

9. The _________ tool is extremely useful for the packaging industry, industrial designers, and product designers.

10. You can modify the position and location of the trimming planes and the bend axis in the **Flex** tool by using the _________.

EXERCISE

Exercise 1

Open the model created in Tutorial 1 of this chapter and then use the **Flex** tool to twist, bend, and stretch it. Figure 11-141 shows the model after twisting the body of the model.

(Expected time: 15 min)

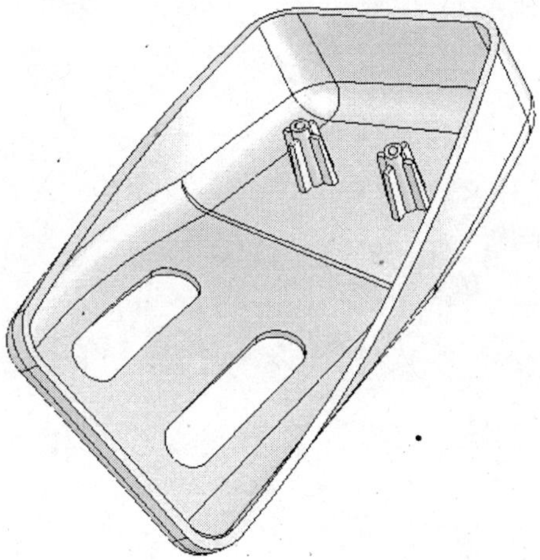

Figure 11-141 *Twisted body of the plastic cover*

Answers to Self-Evaluation Test

1. **Vent**, **2.** **Surface push**, **3.** Snap hooks, **4.** **Elliptical dome**, **5.** Snap hook grooves, **6.** T, **7.** F, **8.** T, **9.** F, **10.** T

Chapter 12

Assembly Modeling-I

Learning Objectives

After completing this chapter, you will be able to:

- *Create bottom-up assemblies*
- *Add mates to assemblies*
- *Create top-down assemblies*
- *Move individual components*
- *Rotate individual components*
- *Visualize the components of assemblies based on their physical properties*

ASSEMBLY MODELING

An assembly design consists of two or more components assembled together at their respective work positions by using parametric relations. In SOLIDWORKS, these relations are called mates. Mates allow you to constrain the degrees of freedom of components at their respective work positions. To start the assembly mode of SOLIDWORKS, invoke the **New SOLIDWORKS Document** dialog box and then choose the **Assembly** button, as shown in Figure 12-1 or from the **Welcome - SOLIDWORKS** dialog box .

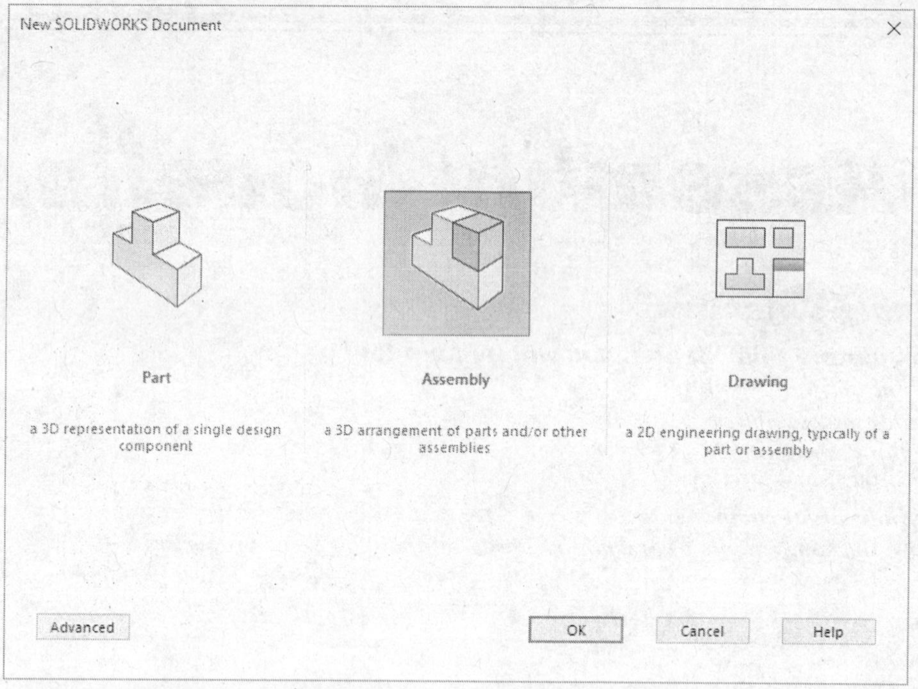

Figure 12-1 *The **New SOLIDWORKS Document** dialog box*

Next, choose the **OK** button to create a new assembly document. On doing so, a new SOLIDWORKS document will open in the **Assembly** mode and the **Begin Assembly PropertyManager** along with the **Open** dialog box will be invoked, as shown in Figure 12-2.

Types of Assembly Design Approach

In SOLIDWORKS, assemblies are created using two types of design approach: bottom-up approach and top-down approach. These approaches are discussed next.

Bottom-up Assembly Design Approach

The bottom-up assembly design approach is the traditional and the most widely preferred approach of assembly design. In this assembly design approach, all components are created as separate part documents, and then they are placed and referenced in the assembly as external components. In this type of approach, components are created in the **Part** mode and saved as the *.sldprt* documents. After creating and saving all components of the assembly, start a new assembly document (*.sldasm*) and insert the components in it using the tools provided in the **Assembly** mode. After inserting the components, assemble them using the assembly mates.

The main advantage of this assembly design approach is that the view of the part is not restricted because there is only a single part in the current file. Therefore, this approach allows you to concentrate on the complex individual features. This approach is preferred while handling large assemblies or assemblies with complex parts.

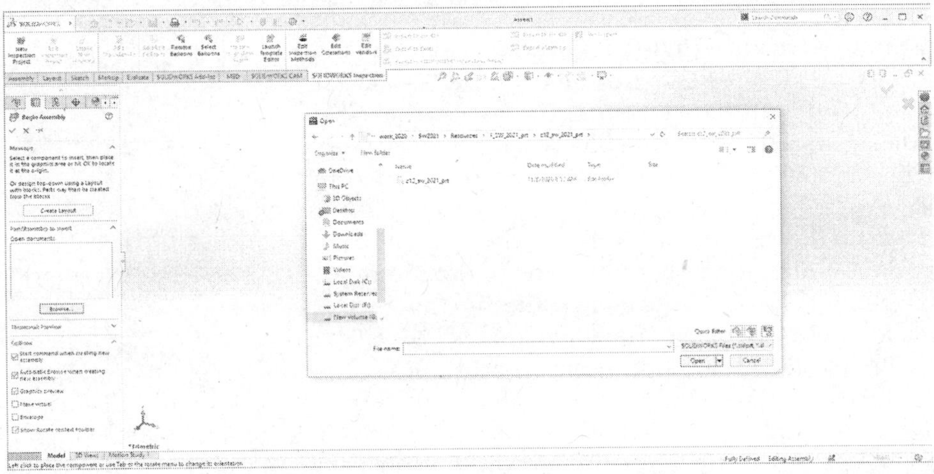

*Figure 12-2 The Assembly mode with the **Begin Assembly PropertyManager***

Top-down Assembly Design Approach

In the top-down assembly design approach, the components are created in the same assembly document and can be saved within the assembly or as separate part files. Therefore, the top-down assembly design approach is entirely different from the bottom-up design approach. In this approach, you will start your work in the assembly document and the geometry of one part will help in defining the geometry of the other.

Note

You can also create an assembly by using a combination of both the bottom-up and top-down assembly approaches.

CREATING BOTTOM-UP ASSEMBLIES

As mentioned earlier, bottom-up assemblies are those in which components are created as separate part documents in the **Part** mode. After creating components, they are inserted into an assembly and then assembled by using assembly mates. To create an assembly by following this approach, you first need to insert components into the assembly. It is recommended to place the first component at the origin of the assembly document. By doing this, the default planes of the assembly and the part will coincide and the component will be in the same orientation as it was in the **Part** mode. When you place the first component in the assembly, that component will become fixed at its placement position. The techniques used to place the components in the assembly file are discussed next.

Placing Components in the Assembly Document

In SOLIDWORKS, there are various options to place components in the assembly. These options are discussed next.

Placing Components Using the PropertyManager

CommandManager:	Assembly > Insert Components flyout > Insert Components
SOLIDWORKS menus:	Insert > Component > Existing Part/Assembly
Toolbar:	Assembly > Insert Components flyout > Insert Components

When you start a new SOLIDWORKS document in the **Assembly** mode, the **Begin Assembly PropertyManager** will be displayed, refer to Figure 12-3. Note that this PropertyManager will be displayed only when you start a new assembly document. The working procedure is provided in the **Message** rollout. As stated earlier, you can select a part or an assembly and then place component in the graphics area or choose the **Create Layout** button to create the top-down assembly. When you choose the **Browse** button in the **Part/Assembly to Insert** rollout, the **Open** dialog box will be displayed. Browse to the location where the component is saved and then select the component and choose the **Open** button. The cursor will be replaced by the component cursor and a graphic preview of the component will be displayed along with the **Rotate context toolbar**, as shown in Figure 12-4. If the **Rotate context toolbar** is not displayed in the drawing area then you can invoke it by selecting the **Show Rotate context toolbar** check box in the **Options** rollout of the **Begin Assembly PropertyManager**. You can rotate the component about the X, Y or Z axis in the drawing area before placing it. To do so, enter the value of angle in the **Angle** spinner and choose the **Rotate component about X**, **Rotate component about Y**, or **Rotate component about Z** option to rotate the component about the X, Y, or Z axis, respectively. You can also rotate the component through 90 degrees by right-clicking in the drawing area and then choosing **Rotate X 90 Deg**, **Rotate Y 90 Deg**, or **Rotate Z 90 Deg** from the shortcut menu displayed. Press **Tab** or **Shift + Tab** keys to rotate the component through 90 degrees or -90 degrees in recently selected direction. You can drag the **Rotate context toolbar** anywhere in the drawing area. Also, the name of the selected component will be displayed in the **Insert Component** selection box of the **Part/Assembly to Insert** rollout and the preview of the part will be displayed in the **Preview** area of the **Thumbnail Preview** rollout. It is recommended to align the origin of the first component with the assembly origin. To place the component origin on the assembly origin, choose the **OK** button from the **Begin Assembly PropertyManager**.

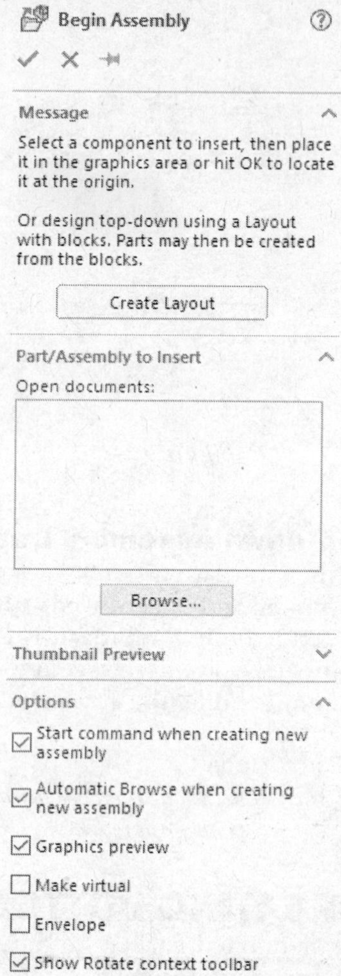

*Figure 12-3 The **Begin Assembly PropertyManager***

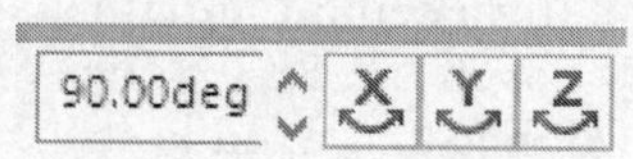

*Figure 12-4 The **Rotate context toolbar***

To place other components in the assembly document, invoke the **Insert Components** tool from the **Assembly CommandManager**; the **Insert Component PropertyManager** will be displayed. Now, choose the **Browse** button; the **Open** dialog box will be displayed if not displayed by default. Select the component from the **Open** dialog box; the cursor will be replaced by the component cursor and a preview of the component will also be displayed in the drawing area. Left-click anywhere in the drawing area to place the component.

If the component to be inserted is opened in another window, then it will be listed in the **Open documents** selection box of the **Begin Assembly PropertyManager** or the **Insert Component PropertyManager**. To insert the component, select it and move the cursor to the drawing area; the component will be attached to the cursor. Left-click to place the component. To preview the selected component, expand the **Thumbnail Preview** rollout.

The **Start command when creating new assembly** check box in the **Options** rollout of the **Begin Assembly PropertyManager** is selected by default. So, the **Begin Assembly PropertyManager** will be invoked automatically when you start a new SOLIDWORKS assembly document. The **Automatic Browse when creating new assembly** check box in the options rollout is used to display the **Open** dialog box just after the **Begin Assembly PropertyManager** is invoked. The **Graphics preview** check box in the **Options** rollout is also selected by default and is used to display the graphic preview of the component selected to be inserted. In the conceptual stage of the design process, you may need to insert a component and carry out various trials in the design. In such cases, select the **Make virtual** check box to insert a component as a virtual component. On selecting this check box, the component will be saved in the assembly file itself. Therefore, if you change the properties of the part in the original file, it will not reflect in the inserted virtual component and vice-versa. To save the virtual component in an external file, right-click on the part, and then choose the **Save Part (in External File)** option from the shortcut menu and specify the location. Similarly, to rename the virtual component, right-click on the component and choose the **Rename Part** option. Then specify the location using the **Save As** dialog box.

In SOLIDWORKS, you can also insert a part as an envelope into the assembly environment. The component inserted as an envelope component will be displayed transparent so that the other components placed inside it can be viewed from outside. To place a component in the assembly environment as an envelope component, select the **Envelope** check box in the **Options** rollout; the part to be inserted in the assembly will be set as a transparent part. Now, click the left mouse button in the graphics area to place the part. You can change the envelope state of the component at any time. To do so, select the part and choose the **Component Properties** option from the pop-up toolbar displayed; the **Component Properties** dialog box will be displayed. Clear the **Envelope** check box in the **Configuration specific properties** area of the **Component Properties** dialog box; the component will be modified in a manner other assembled components are modified. By default, the **Show Rotate context toolbar** check box is selected in the **Options** rollout. As a result, the **Rotate context toolbar** is displayed in the drawing area. To hide the **Rotate context toolbar**, clear the **Show Rotate context toolbar** check box from the **Options** rollout.

Tip

To place multiple components or multiple instances of the same component, choose the ***Keep Visible*** *button at the top of the* ***Begin Assembly PropertyManager*** *and select placement points in the drawing area to place multiple components.*

Starting an Assembly from the Part Document

SOLIDWORKS menus:	File > Make Assembly from Part
Menu Bar:	New flyout > Make Assembly from Part/Assembly

You can also start an assembly document from the part document. If the part document of the base component of the assembly is opened, choose **New > Make Assembly from Part/Assembly** from the Menu Bar or choose **File > Make Assembly from Part** from the SOLIDWORKS menus. If the **New SOLIDWORKS Document** dialog box is invoked, choose the **OK** button from this dialog box; an assembly document will be started and the **Begin Assembly PropertyManager** will be invoked. Choose the **OK** button from this PropertyManager to place the component at the origin.

Placing Components Using the Opened Document Window

Another most widely used method for placing the components in the assembly is the use of currently opened part documents. For example, if the assembly that you need to create consists of three components, open the part document that you want to insert and then start a new assembly document. Close the **Begin Assembly PropertyManager**. Next, choose **Window > Tile Horizontally** or **Tile Vertically** from the SOLIDWORKS menus; all SOLIDWORKS document windows will be tiled horizontally or vertically, depending upon the option chosen.

You need to place the first component in the assembly document at the origin. If the origin is not displayed in the assembly document by default, choose **Visibility off > View Origins** from the **View (Heads-Up)** toolbar. Next, move the cursor on the component in the other window. Press and hold the left mouse button on the component and drag the cursor to the assembly origin in the assembly window, as shown in Figure 12-5. When the coincident symbol appears below the component cursor, release the left mouse button. If the **Mate** pop-up toolbar is displayed, choose the **Add/Finish Mate** button from it to place the component in the assembly. Similarly, place other components in the assembly.

If another existing assembly document is opened, you can also drag and drop the part from that assembly document.

Tip

*You can hide origins, sketch relations, default planes, axes and so on simultaneously by invoking the **Hide All Types** tool from the **View Heads-Ups** toolbar.*

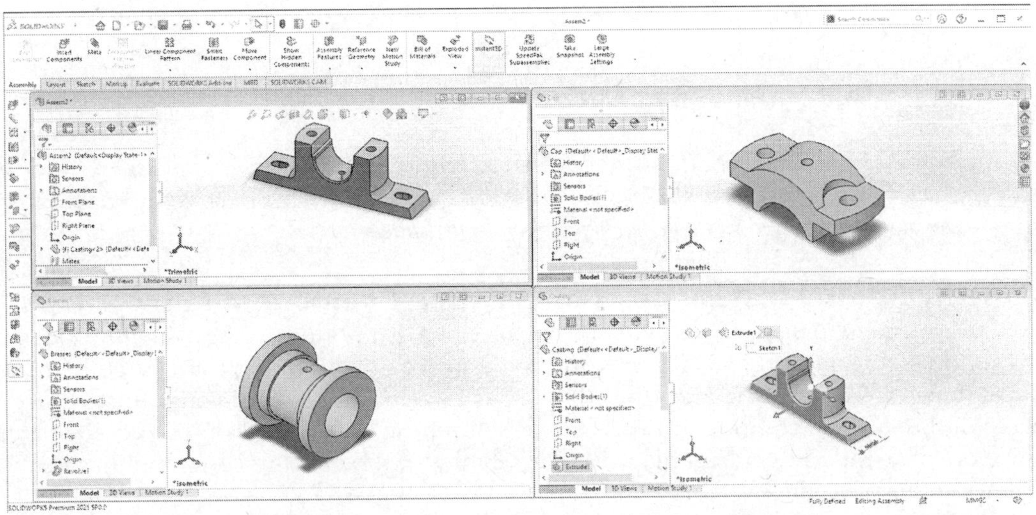

Figure 12-5 Placing a component in the assembly file by dragging it from an existing window

Placing Components Using the File Explorer Task Pane

You can also place components in the assembly document by selecting them from the **File Explorer** task pane. To do so, open the **File Explorer** task pane and browse to the location where part documents are saved. Move the cursor on the icon of the part document in the task pane; a preview of the component will be displayed, refer to Figure 12-6. Press and hold the left mouse button on it and drag the cursor to the assembly document window. Release the left mouse button in the drawing area of the assembly document to place the component.

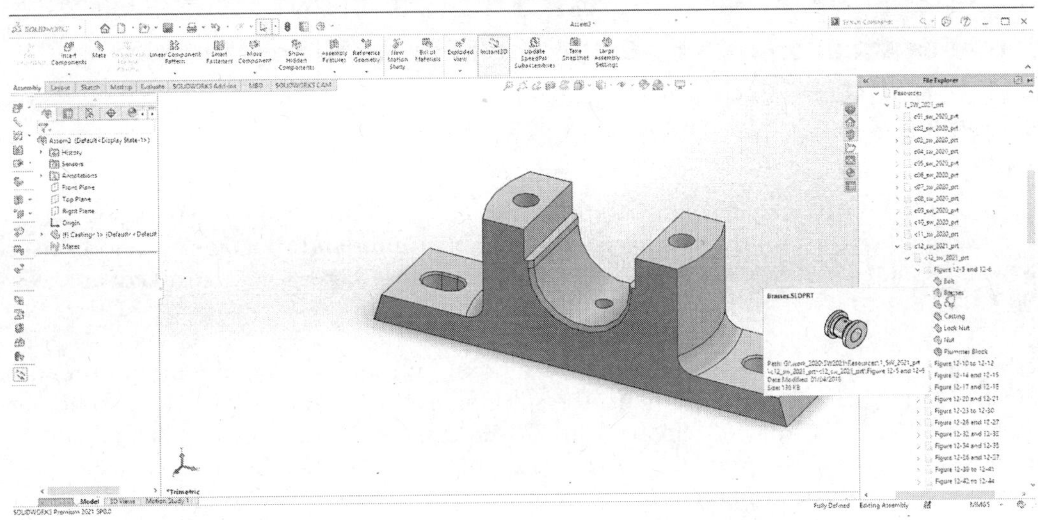

*Figure 12-6 Selecting a part from the **File Explorer** task pane*

Tip

Only the information about the mates is stored in the assembly file. The feature information of parts is stored in individual part files. Therefore, the size of the assembly file is small.

It is recommended that all parts of an assembly should be saved in the folder in which the assembly is saved. If you do not save the parts and the assembly in the same folder, the part may not be displayed in the assembly and will may show errors.

Placing Additional Instances of an Existing Component in the Assembly

Sometimes you need to place more than one instance of a component in the assembly document. To do so, press and hold the CTRL key on the keyboard. Then, select the component in the **FeatureManager Design Tree** and drag the cursor to a location where you want to place the instance of the selected component. Release the left mouse button to drop the new instance of an component. Similarly, you can place as many copies of the existing component as you want by following this procedure.

Assembling Components

After placing the components in the assembly document, you need to assemble them. By assembling the components, you can constrain their degrees of freedom. As mentioned earlier, the components are assembled using mates. Mates help you to precisely place and position the component with respect to the other components and surroundings in the assembly. You can also define the linear and rotatory movements of the component with respect to the other components. Additionally, you can create a dynamic mechanism and check its stability by precisely defining the combination of mates. There are two methods for adding mates to the assembly, by using the **Mate PropertyManager** and by using the **Smart Mates**. Both these methods are discussed next.

Assembling Components by Using the Mate PropertyManager

CommandManager:	Assembly > Mate
SOLIDWORKS menus:	Insert > Mate
Toolbar:	Assembly > Mate

In SOLIDWORKS, mates can be applied using the **Mate PropertyManager**. To apply mates, choose the **Mate** button from the **Assembly CommandManager** or choose **Insert > Mate** from the SOLIDWORKS menus; the **Mate PropertyManager** will be invoked, as shown in Figure 12-7.

Select a planar face, a curved face, an axis, or a point on the first component and then select the entities from the second component; the selected entities will be highlighted. The names of the selected entities will be displayed in the **Entities to Mate** selection box of the **Mate Selections** rollout. Also, the **Mate** pop-up toolbar will be invoked, as shown in Figure 12-8. The most suitable mates to be applied to the current selection set are displayed in the **Mate** pop-up toolbar. Also, in the **Mate Type** rollout in the **Standard** tab of the **Mate PropertyManager**, the most appropriate mate is selected by default. A preview of the assembly using the most appropriate mate is displayed in the drawing area. You can also select other mates from the given list to apply them to the current selection set. If you select a mate other than the default one from the **Mate** pop-up toolbar, the preview of the assembly will be displayed using the newly selected mate. Now, choose the **Add/Finish Mate** button from the **Mate** pop-up toolbar; the **Mate PropertyManager** will still be displayed, and you can add other mates to the assembly.

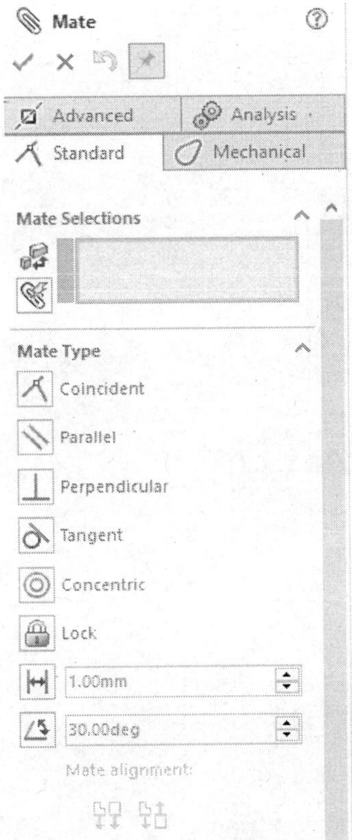

Figure 12-7 Partial view of the ***Mate PropertyManager***

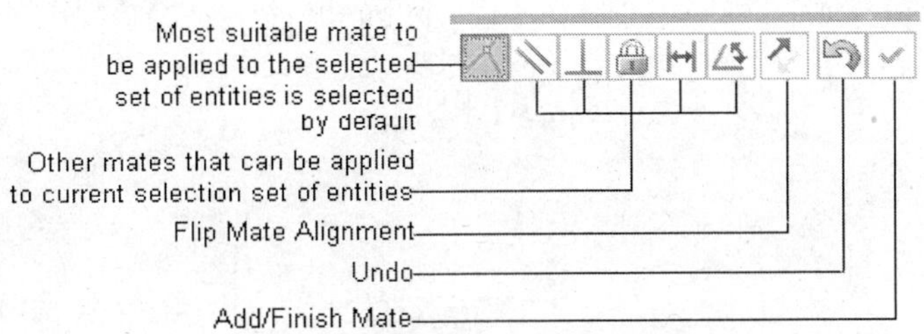

Figure 12-8 The ***Mate*** *pop-up toolbar*

After adding all mates, choose the **OK** button from the **Mate PropertyManager**. Various types of mates that can be applied to components are discussed next.

Coincident

The coincident mate is applied to make two planar faces coplanar. However, you can apply this mate to other entities as well. The details of the geometries on which the coincident mate can be applied are shown in Figure 12-9.

When you choose the **Coincident** button from the **Mate** pop-up toolbar, the preview of the model will be displayed according to the current selection of the mate. Also, depending on the current orientation of the model, the model will be assembled in aligned or anti-aligned direction. You can modify the orientation of the assembled component by choosing the **Aligned** or **Anti-Aligned** buttons from the **Mate Type** rollout in the **Standard** tab. You can also choose the **Flip Mate Alignment** button from the **Mate** pop-up toolbar to modify the mate alignment. Figure 12-10 shows the faces to be selected for applying the coincident mate. Figure 12-11 shows the coincident mate applied with the **Anti-Aligned** button chosen. Figure 12-12 shows the coincident mate applied with the **Aligned** button chosen.

ASSEMBLY MATE COMBINATIONS (USING COINCIDENT MATE)		Second Component									
		Cone	Cylinder	Line	Point	Sphere	Circular/ Arc Edge	Extrusion	Surface	Plane	Cam
First Component	Cylinder	✗	✗	✓	✓	✗	✓	✗	✗	✗	✗
	Sphere	✗	✗	✗	✓	✗	✗	✗	✗	✗	✗
	Cone	✓	✗	✗	✓	✗	✓	✗	✗	✗	✗
	Circular/ Arc Edge	✗	✓	✗	✗	✗	✓	✗	✗	✓	✗
	Line	✗	✓	✓	✓	✗	✗	✗	✗	✓	✗
	Point	✗	✓	✓	✓	✓	✗	✓	✓	✓	✓
	Extrusion	✗	✗	✗	✓	✗	✗	✗	✗	✗	✗
	Surface	✗	✗	✗	✓	✗	✗	✗	✗	✗	✗
	Plane	✗	✗	✓	✓	✗	✓	✗	✗	✓	✗

Figure 12-9 *Combinations for applying the coincident mate*

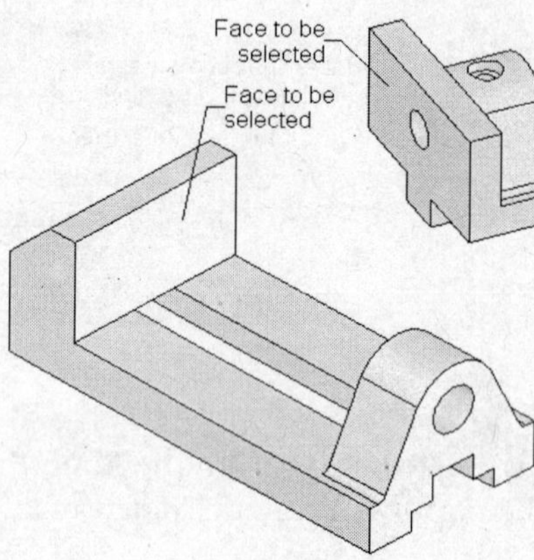

Figure 12-10 *Faces to be selected to for applying the coincident mate*

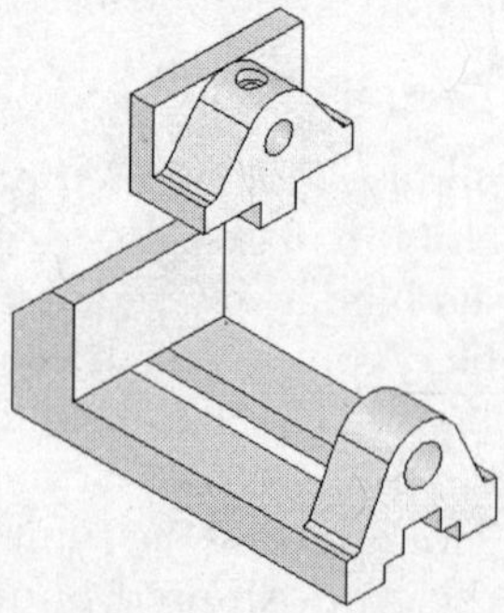

Figure 12-11 *The coincident mate applied with the **Anti-Aligned** button chosen*

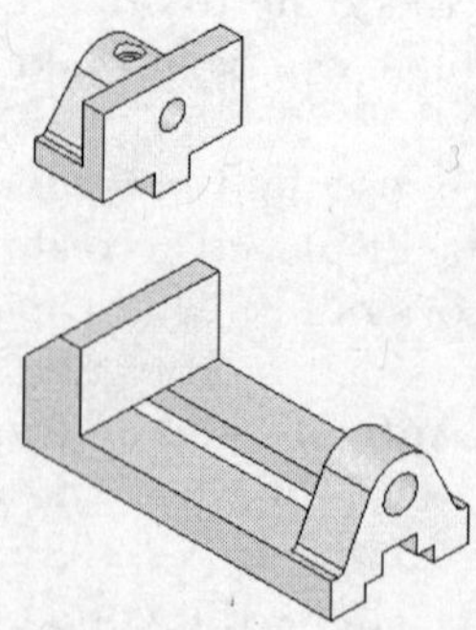

Figure 12-12 *The coincident mate applied with the **Aligned** button chosen*

Parallel

The **Parallel** button in the **Mate** pop-up toolbar is used to apply the parallel mate between two components. To apply the parallel mate, invoke the **Mate PropertyManager** and select two entities from two components. Choose the **Parallel** button from the **Mate** pop-up toolbar to apply the mate. You can also choose the **Aligned** button or the **Anti-Aligned** button. After applying the mate, choose the **Add/Finish Mate** button from the **Mate** pop-up toolbar.

Figure 12-13 shows combinations of components for applying the parallel mate. Figure 12-14 shows the faces to be selected for applying the parallel mate and Figure 12-15 shows the assembly after applying the parallel mate.

ASSEMBLY MATE COMBINATIONS (USING PARALLEL MATE)		Second Component									
		Cylinder	Extrusion	Line	Plane	Sphere	Circular/ Arc Edge	Cone	Surface	Point	Cam
First Component	Cylinder	✓	✓	✓	X	X	X	X	X	X	X
	Extrusion	✓	✓	✓	X	X	X	X	X	X	X
	Line	✓	✓	✓	✓	X	X	X	X	X	X
	Plane	X	X	✓	✓	X	X	X	X	X	X
	Circular/ Arc Edge	X	X	X	X	X	X	X	X	X	X
	Sphere	X	X	X	X	X	X	X	X	X	X
	Cone	✓	✓	✓	X	X	X	✓	X	X	X
	Surface	X	X	X	X	X	X	X	X	X	X

***Figure 12-13** Combinations for applying the parallel mate*

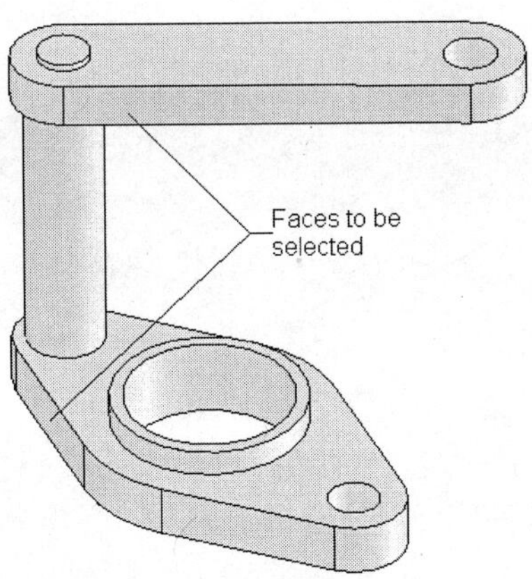

***Figure 12-14** Faces to be selected to apply the parallel mate*

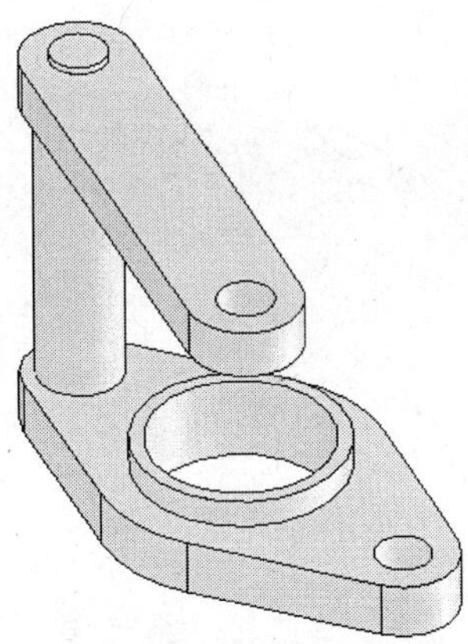

***Figure 12-15** Assembly after applying the parallel mate*

Perpendicular

The **Perpendicular** button in the **Mate Type** rollout in the **Standard** tab is used to apply the perpendicular mate between the two components. Invoke the **Mate PropertyManager** and select two entities from the two components. Choose the **Perpendicular** button from the **Mate** pop-up toolbar. You can also choose the **Aligned** button or the **Anti-Aligned** button. Choose the **Add/Finish Mate** button from the **Mate** pop-up toolbar. Figure 12-16 displays combinations for applying the perpendicular mate. Figure 12-17 shows the entities to be selected for applying the perpendicular mate and Figure 12-18 shows the perpendicular mate applied to the assembly.

ASSEMBLY MATE COMBINATIONS (USING PERPENDICULAR MATE)		Second Component									
		Cylinder	Extrusion	Line	Plane	Sphere	Circular/ Arc Edge	Cone	Surface	Point	Cam
First Component	Cylinder	✓	✓	✓	X	X	X	X	X	X	X
	Extrusion	✓	✓	✓	X	X	X	X	X	X	X
	Line	✓	✓	✓	✓	X	X	X	X	X	X
	Plane	X	X	✓	✓	X	X	X	X	X	X
	Circular/ Arc Edge	X	X	X	X	X	X	X	X	X	X
	Sphere	X	X	X	X	X	X	X	X	X	X
	Cone	✓	✓	✓	X	X	X	✓	X	X	X
	Surface	✓	X	✓	X	X	X	✓	✓	X	X

Figure 12-16 Combinations for applying the perpendicular mate

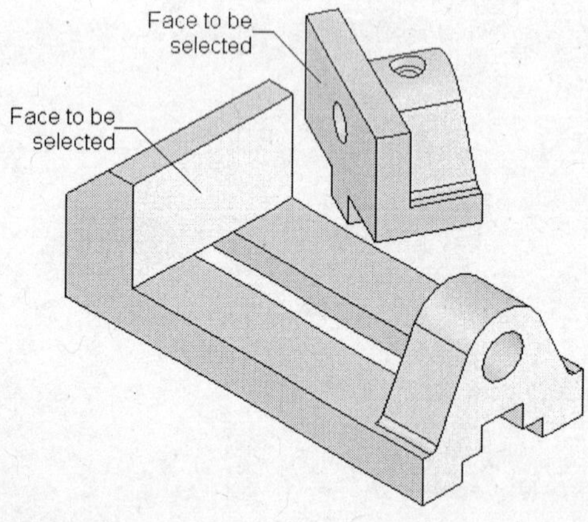

Figure 12-17 *Faces to be selected to apply the perpendicular mate*

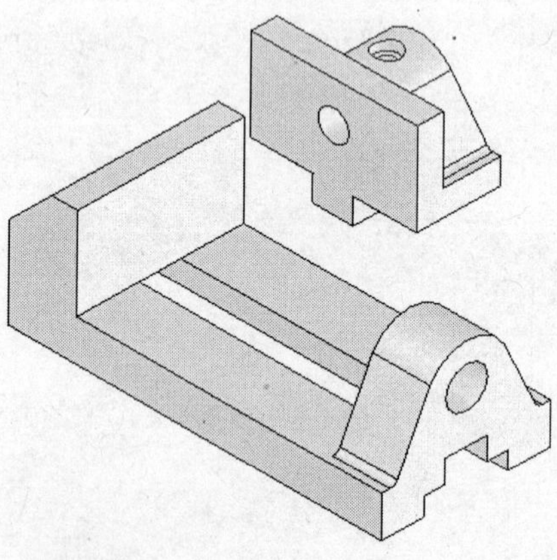

Figure 12-18 *Assembly after applying the perpendicular mate*

Tangent

The **Tangent** button in the **Mate** pop-up toolbar is used to apply the tangent mate between two components. To apply the tangent mate between two components, invoke the **Mate PropertyManager** and select the two components. Choose the **Tangent** button from the **Mate** pop-up toolbar. Figure 12-19 displays the combinations for applying the tangent mate. Figure 12-20 shows the entities to be selected for applying the tangent mate and Figure 12-21 shows the tangent mate applied to the assembly.

ASSEMBLY MATE COMBINATIONS (USING TANGENT MATE)		Second Component								
		Cone	Cylinder	Line	Point	Sphere	Plane	Surface	Cam	Extrusion
First Component	Cylinder	✓	✓	✓	X	✓	✓	✓	✓	✓
	Sphere	✓	✓	✓	X	✓	✓	X	X	X
	Cone	X	X	X	X	✓	✓	X	X	X
	Plane	X	✓	X	X	✓	X	✓	✓	✓
	Line	X	✓	✓	✓	✓	✓	✓	✓	✓
	Extrusion	X	✓	X	X	X	✓	X	X	X
	Surface	X	✓	X	X	X	✓	X	X	X
	Cam	X	X	X	X	X	X	X	X	X

***Figure 12-19** Combinations for applying the tangent mate*

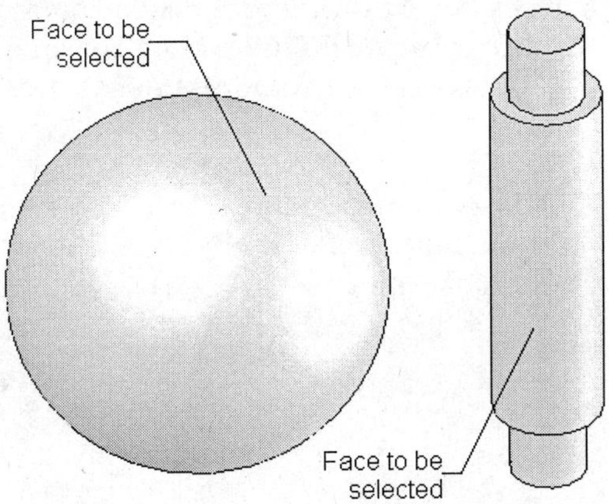

***Figure 12-20** Entities to be selected to apply the tangent mate*

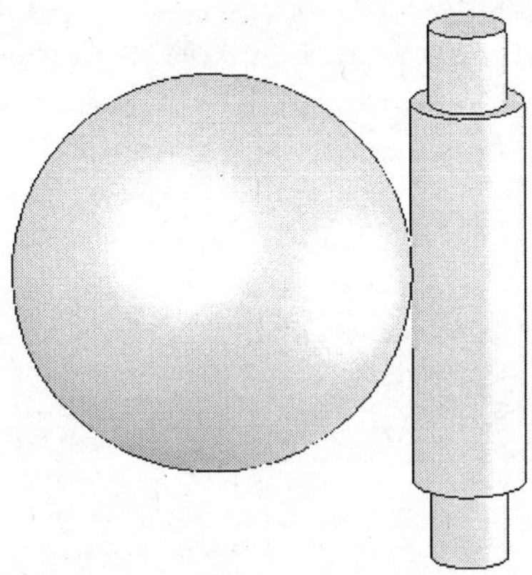

***Figure 12-21** Assembly after applying the tangent mate*

Concentric

The concentric mate is used to align the central axis of one component with that of the other. You need to select the circular faces or circular edges to apply the concentric mate. You can also apply the concentric mate between a point and a circular face or circular edge. Other combinations for applying the concentric mate are displayed in Figure 12-22.

ASSEMBLY MATE COMBINATIONS (USING CONCENTRIC MATE)		Second Component									
		Cone	Cylinder	Line	Point	Sphere	Circular/ Arc Edge	Extrusion	Surface	Plane	Cam
First Component	Cylinder	✓	✓	✓	✓	✓	✓	✗	✗	✗	✗
	Sphere	✗	✓	✓	✓	✓	✗	✗	✗	✗	✗
	Cone	✓	✓	✓	✓	✗	✓	✗	✗	✗	✗
	Circular/ Arc Edge	✗	✓	✓	✗	✗	✓	✗	✗	✗	✗
	Line	✓	✓	✗	✗	✓	✓	✗	✗	✗	✗
	Point	✓	✓	✗	✗	✓	✗	✗	✗	✗	✗
	Extrusion	✗	✗	✗	✗	✗	✗	✗	✗	✗	✗
	Surface	✗	✗	✗	✗	✗	✗	✗	✗	✗	✗
	Plane	✗	✗	✗	✗	✗	✗	✗	✗	✗	✗

Figure 12-22 *Combinations for applying the concentric mate*

To apply the concentric mate, invoke the **Mate PropertyManager**. Select circular faces or edges from two different components; the names of the selected entities will be displayed in the **Entities to Mate** selection box. The **Concentric** button is chosen by default in the **Mate** pop-up toolbar. If this button is not chosen by default, you need to choose this manually. The preview of the models being assembled, after applying this mate, will be displayed in the graphics area. You can choose the **Aligned** or **Anti-Aligned** button on the basis of the design requirement. Also, you can lock the rotation of the concentric component with respect to each other. To do so, select the **Lock rotation** check box below the **Concentric** button in the **Mate Type** rollout in the **Standard** tab. Finally, choose the **Add/Finish Mate** button from the **Mate** pop-up toolbar. The icon under the **Mates** node in **FeatureManager Design Tree** indicates the locked rotation concentric mates.

Figure 12-23 shows the faces to be selected to apply the concentric mate. Figure 12-24 shows the concentric mate applied with the **Aligned** button chosen and Figure 12-25 shows the concentric mate applied with the **Anti-Aligned** button chosen.

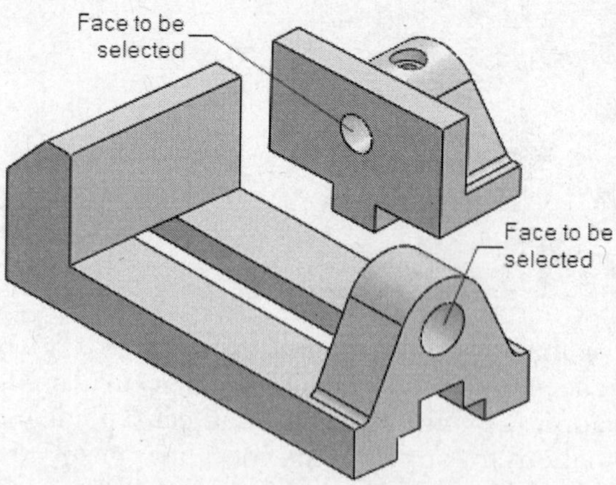

Figure 12-23 *Faces to be selected to apply the concentric mate*

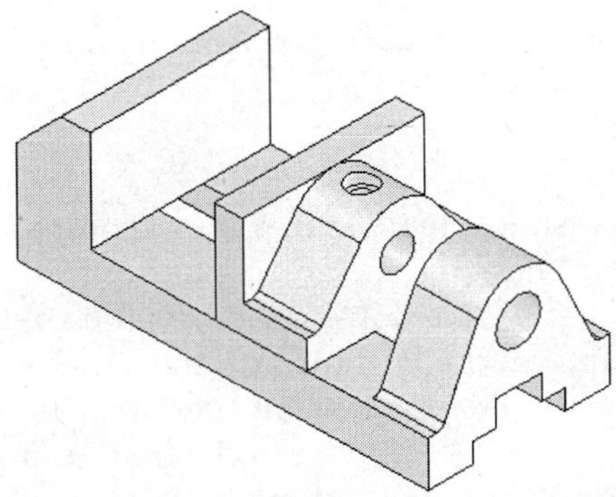

Figure 12-24 *The concentric mate applied with the* ***Aligned*** *button chosen*

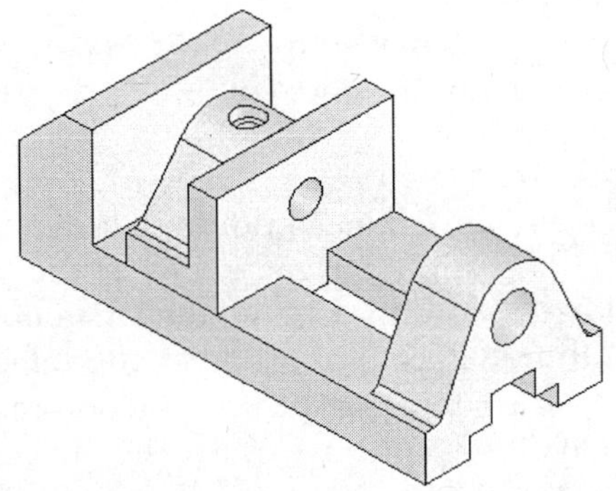

Figure 12-25 *The concentric mate applied with the* ***Anti-Aligned*** *button chosen*

In SOLIDWORKS 2021, you can apply concentric mate between misaligned holes. Refer to plates shown in Figure 12-26, having two holes in each plate. If you apply a concentric mate between one set of holes then there is a deviation in another set of holes. Prior to SOLIDWORKS 2020, if you have applied a concentric mate to the second set of holes then you will have error in the assembly. But in SOLIDWORKS 2020 and 2021, concentric mate is supported in holes that have some deviation in their center points.

Consider the plates shown in Figure 12-26 in which the concentric mate between the first set of holes has caused a deviation in the second set of holes. Now, invoke the **Mate PropertyManager** and select the circular faces or edges of the second set of holes; the **Mate** pop-up toolbar will be displayed. Choose the **Concentric** button from the **Mate PropertyManager** or from the **Mate** pop-up toolbar; the **Misaligned** button appears in the **Mate** pop-up toolbar. Choose this button; various options are displayed under the **Concentric** mate in the **Mate Type** rollout in the **Standard** tab of the **Mate PropertyManager**. Select the **Align Linked mate** option in the **Misalignment** drop-down if you need to add deviation in the current set of holes or select **Align this mate** option if you need to add deviation to the holes that have concentric mate defined earlier. You can also select the **Symmetric** option to distribute the deviation equally in both set of holes, refer to Figure 12-27. The **Maximum deviation** edit box is used to set the maximum value of deviation supported. To modify the default value, clear the **Use Document Property** check box. The **Result** area displays the state of the concentric mates applied. You can also choose the **Remove link between mates** button to delete the misalignment link between the mates. Choose the **OK** button; the mate is applied and a **Misaligned** sub-folder with two concentric mates is added under the **Mates** folder in the **FeatureManager Design Tree**.

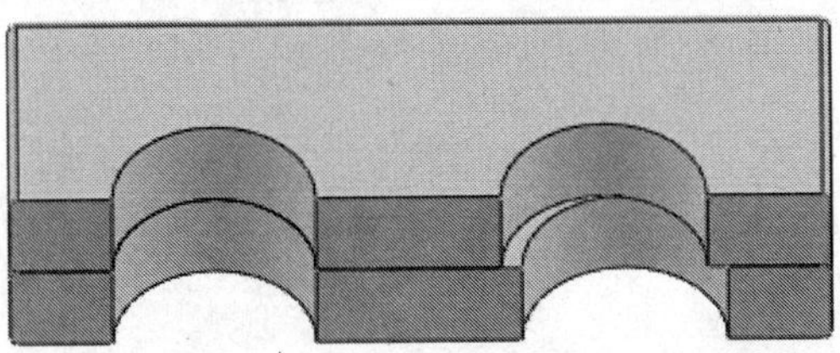

Figure 12-26 *Plates with concentric mate in first set of holes and deviation in another set of holes*

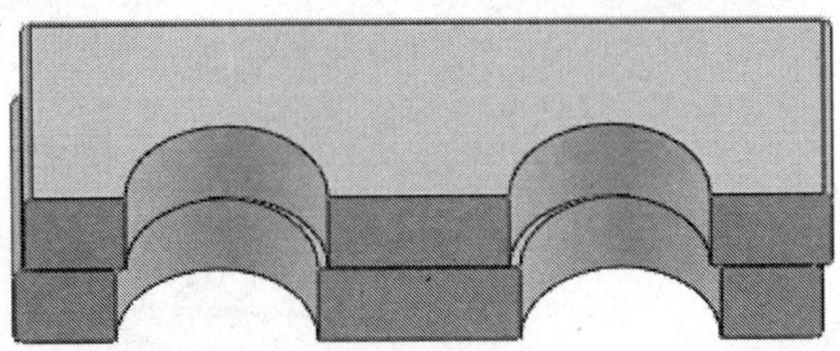

Figure 12-27 *Plates with deviation distributed equally in both set of holes*

Lock

The **Lock** button in the **Mate** pop-up toolbar is used to lock the position and rotation of two or more components with respect to each other.

Distance

The **Distance** button is chosen to apply the distance mate between two components. To apply this mate, invoke the **Mate PropertyManager** and select entities from both the components. Choose the **Distance** button from the **Mate** pop-up toolbar; the **Distance** spinner will be displayed. Set the value of the distance in the **Distance** spinner; the preview of the assembly will be updated automatically. Select the **Flip dimension** check box available below this spinner to reverse the direction of the mate. If needed, you can choose the **Aligned** or **Anti-Aligned** button. Figure 12-28 shows combinations of components to apply the distance mate. Figure 12-29 shows the faces to be selected and Figure 12-30 shows the distance mate applied between two components.

ASSEMBLY MATE COMBINATIONS (USING DISTANCE MATE)		Second Component									
		Cone	Cylinder	Line	Point	Sphere	Plane	Extrusion	Surface	Circular/ Arc Edge	Cam
First Component	Cylinder	✗	✓	✓	✓	✗	✓	✗	✗	✗	✗
	Sphere	✗	✗	✓	✓	✓	✗	✗	✗	✗	✗
	Cone	✓	✗	✗	✗	✗	✗	✗	✗	✗	✗
	Plane	✗	✓	✓	✓	✓	✓	✗	✗	✗	✗
	Line	✗	✓	✓	✓	✓	✓	✗	✗	✗	✗
	Point	✗	✓	✓	✓	✓	✓	✗	✗	✗	✗
	Extrusion	✗	✗	✗	✗	✗	✗	✗	✗	✗	✗
	Surface	✗	✗	✗	✗	✗	✗	✗	✗	✗	✗
	Circular/ Arc Edge	✗	✗	✗	✗	✗	✗	✗	✗	✗	✗

Figure 12-28 Combinations for applying the distance mate

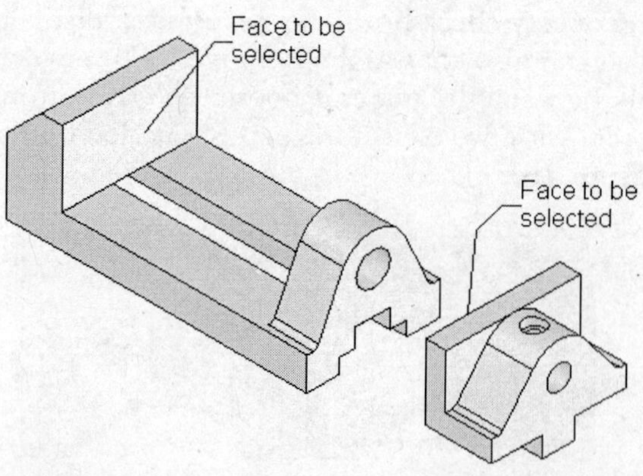

Figure 12-29 Faces to be selected to apply the distance mate

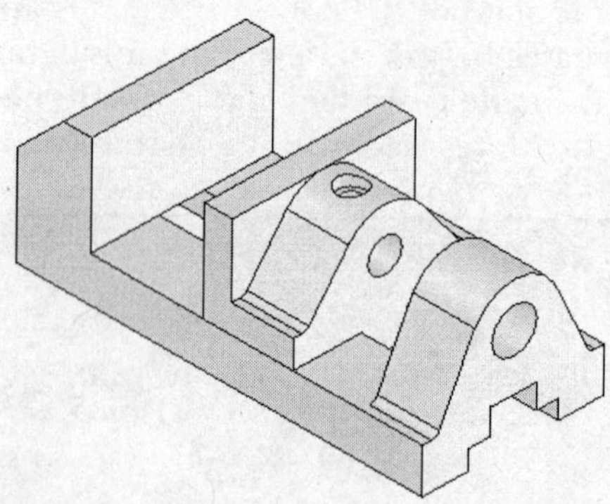

Figure 12-30 The distance mate applied between the selected faces

While applying distance mate in cylindrical components four options are available below the **Distance** spinner or in the **Mate** pop-up toolbar for measurement of the distance. The **Center to Center** option is selected by default, therefore distance is measured between the axes of the cylinders. If the **Minimum Distance** option is selected then cylinders are placed closest to each other. If the **Maximum Distance** option is selected then the distance is measured from the farthest points in the cylinders. By selecting the **Custom Distance** button, various combinations of distance measurement can be applied to the selected entities. Note that these options are available when you add the distance mate between a cylindrical component and a point, vertex, line, an axis, edge, or a plane.

Angle

The **Angle** button is used to apply the angle mate between two components. This mate is used to specify the angular position between the selected planes, planar faces, or edges of the two components. To apply this mate, invoke the **Mate PropertyManager** and select the entities from the two components. Choose the **Angle** button from the **Mate** pop-up toolbar; the preview of the models will be modified according to the default value of the angle. Also, the **Angle** spinner will be invoked and you can set the value of the angle in this spinner. You can also change the angle direction using the **Flip Dimension** button provided on the left of the angle spinner. You can choose the **Aligned** button or the **Anti-Aligned** button on the basis of the design requirement. After adding the mate, choose the **Add/ Finish Mate** button from the **Mate** pop-up toolbar.

Various combinations for applying the angle mate are shown in Figure 12-31.

ASSEMBLY MATE COMBINATIONS (USING ANGLE MATE)		Second Component									
		Cylinder	Extrusion	Line	Plane	Sphere	Circular/ Arc Edge	Cone	Surface	Point	Cam
First Component	Cylinder	✓	✓	✓	✗	✗	✗	✗	✗	✗	✗
	Extrusion	✓	✓	✓	✗	✗	✗	✗	✗	✗	✗
	Line	✓	✓	✓	✗	✗	✗	✗	✗	✗	✗
	Plane	✗	✗	✗	✓	✗	✗	✗	✗	✗	✗
	Sphere	✗	✗	✗	✗	✗	✗	✗	✗	✗	✗
	Circular/ Arc Edge	✗	✗	✗	✗	✗	✗	✗	✗	✗	✗
	Cone	✓	✓	✓	✗	✗	✗	✓	✗	✗	✗
	Point	✗	✗	✗	✗	✗	✗	✗	✗	✗	✗
	Surface	✗	✗	✗	✗	✗	✗	✗	✗	✗	✗

Figure 12-31 *Combinations for applying the angle mate*

Figure 12-32 shows the faces to be selected to apply the angle mate and Figure 12-33 shows the assembly after applying the angle mate with 90 degrees angle value.

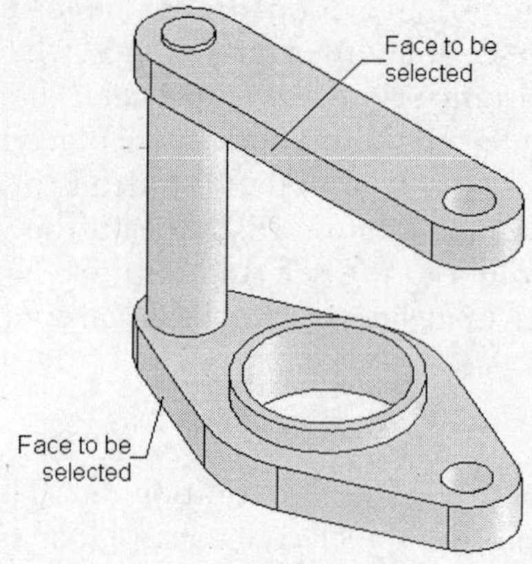

Figure 12-32 Faces to be selected to apply the angle mate

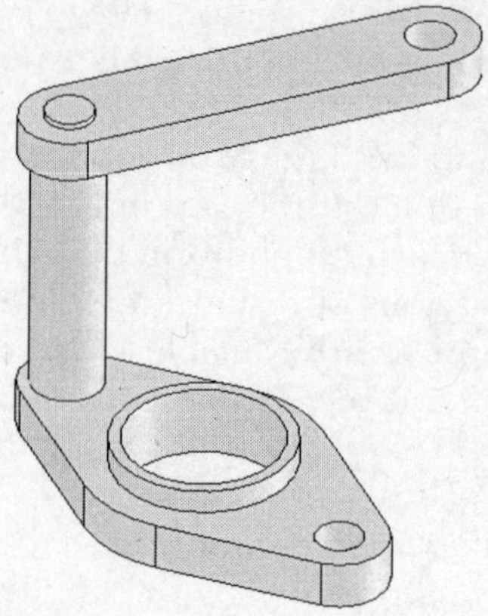

Figure 12-33 Assembly after applying the angle mate

You can define the axis of rotation for the angle mate with the reference entity. If you do not specify the reference entity for the angle mate then there will be two solutions for the angle mate. So to avoid the unexpected result from the angle mate, it is necessary to define the reference entity and make the angle mate more predictable.

To specify a reference entity for an angle mate, it is necessary to constrain the components with either coincident, parallel, or distance mate. To do so, apply the coincident mate between Edge 1 and Edge 2 and between Face 1 and Face 2, as shown in Figure 12-34.

Invoke the **Mate PropertyManager** by choosing the **Mate** button from the **Assembly CommandManager**. Select Face 3 and Face 4 of the component from the drawing area, as shown in Figure 12-34; the name of the faces will be displayed in the **Entities to Mate** selection box of the **Mate Selections** rollout. Now, choose the **Angle** button from the **Mate Type** rollout in the **Standard** tab; the preview of the models will be modified based on the default value set for the angle. Now, choose the **Auto Fill Reference Entity** button from the **Reference entity** area of the **Mate Selections** rollout. The reference entity will be selected automatically. You can also select the reference entity manually from the **Optional Direction Reference** selection box available on the right of the **Auto Fill Reference Entity** button. Now, you can select the placement of the angle by using the dimension selector in the drawing area and then modify its value using the **Angle** spinner in the **Mate Type** rollout in the **Standard** tab. Select any sector of the dimension using the dimension selector, as shown in Figure 12-35. Now, choose the **OK** button from the **Mate PropertyManager** to confirm the change.

Note

*The options in the **Advanced** tab are discussed in the next chapter.*

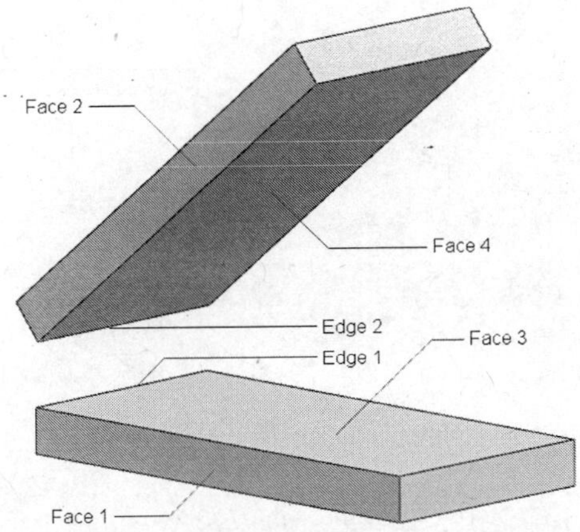

Figure 12-34 *Faces to be selected to apply the angle mate with reference entites*

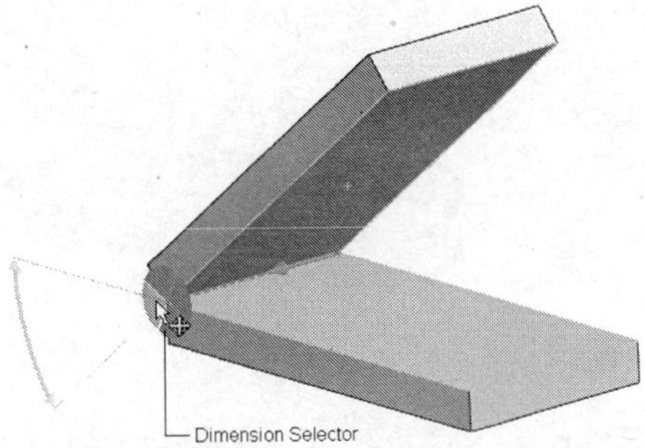

Figure 12-35 *Dimension selector*

Applying Multiple Mates

SOLIDWORKS allows you to apply multiple mates to a common reference. Consider the Base Plate shown in Figure 12-36. There are four bolts to be assembled to the Base Plate. To assemble these bolts, apply the concentric mate between a bolt and the cylindrical face of a hole in the Base Plate. Then, apply the coincident mate to the bottom face of the head of the bolt and the top face of the Base Plate. All these mates will be applied to the four bolts individually. However, if you want to apply a mate to multiple entities and a common reference, you need to use the **Multiple mate mode** option. Thus, you will apply the coincident mate to the bottom face of the head of the bolt and the top face of the Base Plate using this option. To use this option, first apply the concentric mate between the bolt and the cylindrical face of the hole in the Base Plate. Next, choose the **Multiple mate mode** button available at the left of the **Entities to Mate** selection box in the **Mate Selections** rollout; the **Common reference** and **Component references** selection boxes will be displayed. The **Common reference** selection box will be highlighted by default. Therefore, you need to select the common reference. In this case, select the top face of the Base Plate. As you select the common reference (top face), the **Component references** selection box will be highlighted. Next, select the bottom face of the head of one of the bolts; the **Mate** pop-up toolbar will be displayed. Select the required mate type from this toolbar. Similarly, select the faces of other bolts to apply the mate with the common face. You can create a group of resulting mates in the **Multi-Mates** folder in the **FeatureManager Design Tree**. To do so, select the **Create multi-mate folder** check box below the **Component references** selection box. You can change the common reference, mate type, or distance for all mates with a single operation. The **Link dimensions** check box below the **Create multi-mate folder** will be available only when you select the **Distance** or **Angle** mate from the **Mate** pop-up toolbar. When you edit the dimension of any of the component of the group in the **Mate PropertyManager**, the dimensions of all the grouped components in the **Multi-Mates** sub-node will change accordingly. Figure 12-36 shows the top face of the Base Plate selected as the common reference and the four bolts to be assembled. Note that the concentric mate has already been applied between the selected faces. Figure 12-37 shows the assembly after applying the coincident mate to the bottom faces of the heads of all bolts and the top face of the Base Plate.

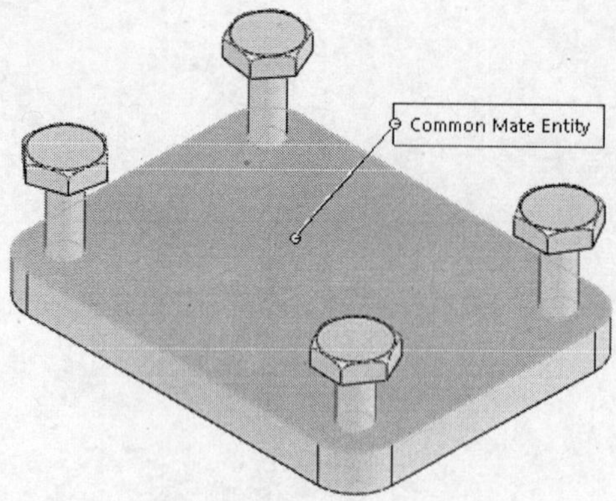

Figure 12-36 Top face of the Base Plate selected as the common reference

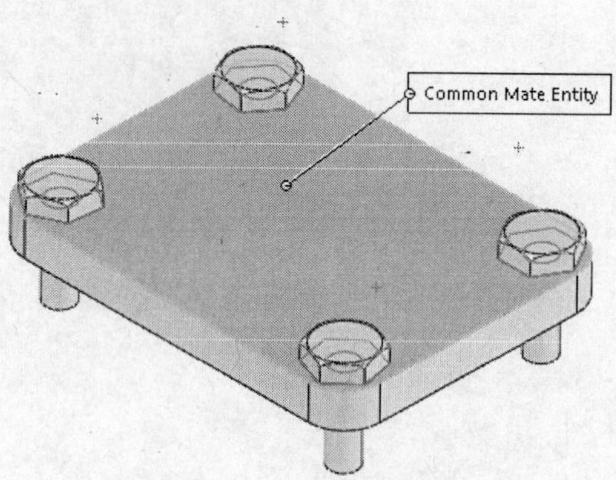

Figure 12-37 Assembly after applying the coincident mate between the bolts and the Base Plate

The remaining options in the **Mate PropertyManager** are discussed next.

Mates

The **Mates** rollout is used to display the mates that are applied between the selected entities.

Options

The **Add to new folder** check box in this rollout is used to add the currently applied mate to a folder. This folder is placed in the **Mates** node in the **FeatureManager Design Tree**. You can also drag and drop other mates from the **Mates** node in the newly created folder. The **Show popup dialog** check box is selected by default. As a result, the **Mate** pop-up toolbar is displayed. The **Show preview** check box is selected by default in this toolbar and is used to display a dynamic preview of the assembly as you apply mates to the components. The **Use for positioning only** check box is used to define the position of the component on applying the mate virtually. If you select this check box, the mate will not be applied. So, this mate will not be displayed in the **Mates** node of the **FeatureManager Design Tree**. By default, the **Make first selection transparent** check box is selected in this rollout and used to make the first selected component transparent.

Tip

When you insert a component in an assembly, it will be displayed in the ***FeatureManager Design Tree****. The naming convention for the first component will be* ***(f) Name of Component <1>****. In this convention,* ***(f)*** *indicates that the component is fixed. You cannot move a fixed component. You will learn more about the fixed and floating components later in this chapter. Next, the name of the component will be displayed. The* ***<1>*** *symbol denotes the serial number of the same component in the entire assembly.*

The ***(-)*** *symbol before the name of the component implies that the component is floating and under-defined. You need to apply the required mates to the component to fully define it. You will learn more about assembly mates later in this chapter. The* ***(+)*** *symbol implies that the component is over-defined. If no symbol appears before the name of the component then the component will be fully defined.*

Assembling Components Using the Smart Mates

CommandManager: Assembly > Move Component
SOLIDWORKS menus: Tools > Component > Move
Toolbar: Assembly > Move Component

Smart Mates is the most attractive feature of the assembly design environment in SOLIDWORKS. Smart Mates technology speeds up the design process in the assembly environment of SOLIDWORKS. To add smart mates to the components, choose the **Move Component** button from the **Assembly CommandManager**; the **Move Component PropertyManager** will be displayed. Next, choose the **SmartMates** button in the **Move** rollout; the **Move Component PropertyManager** will be replaced by the **SmartMates PropertyManager**, as shown in Figure 12-38. Also, the select cursor will be replaced by the move cursor. Next, double-click on an entity of the first component to add a mate; the component will appear transparent and the cursor will be replaced by the smart mates cursor. Press and hold the left mouse button on the selected entity and drag the cursor to the entity with which you want to mate the previously selected entity. The symbol of the constraint that can be applied between the two entities will be displayed below the smart mates cursor. When the symbol of the mate is displayed below the cursor, release the left mouse button; the **Mate** pop-up toolbar will be displayed. Choose the **Add/Finish Mate** button from this toolbar. Figure 12-39 shows the face to be selected to apply a smart mate and Figure 12-40 shows the component being dragged.

***Figure 12-38** Partial view of the SmartMates PropertyManager*

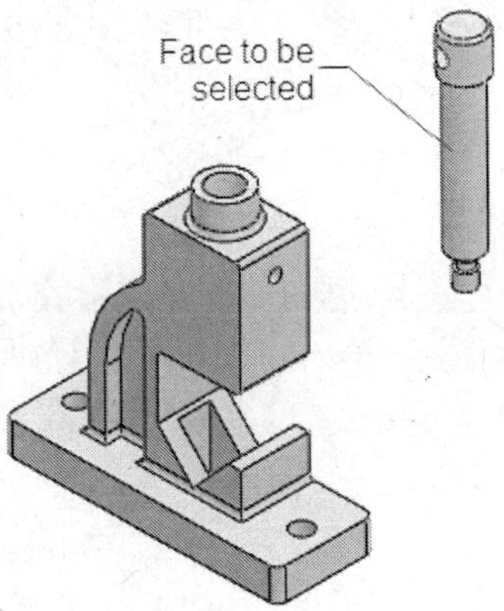

***Figure 12-39** Face to be selected to apply the smart mate*

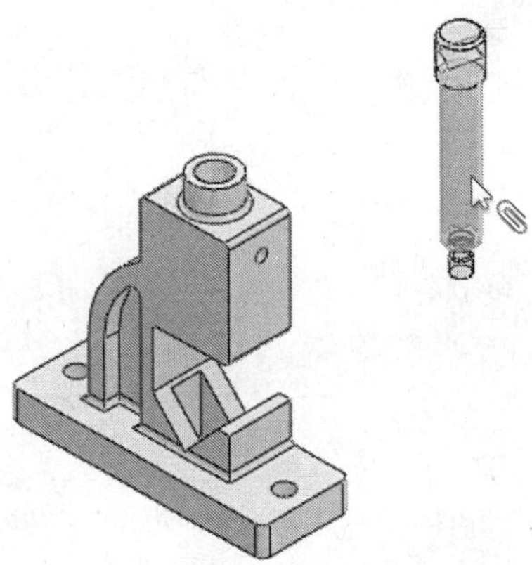

***Figure 12-40** Component being dragged to apply the smart mate*

When the smart mates cursor is placed near the circular face of the other component, the concentric symbol appears below the cursor, as shown in Figure 12-41.

Figure 12-41 *Concentric symbol displayed below the smart mates cursor*

Figure 12-42 shows a planar face selected to apply the smart mate. Figure 12-43 shows the coincident symbol displayed below the cursor and Figure 12-44 shows the assembly after applying the coincident mate by using the **SmartMates** button.

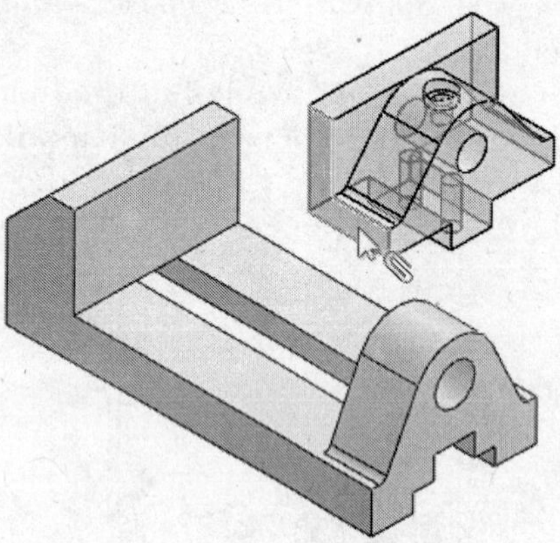

Figure 12-42 *Planar face selected to apply Smart Mate*

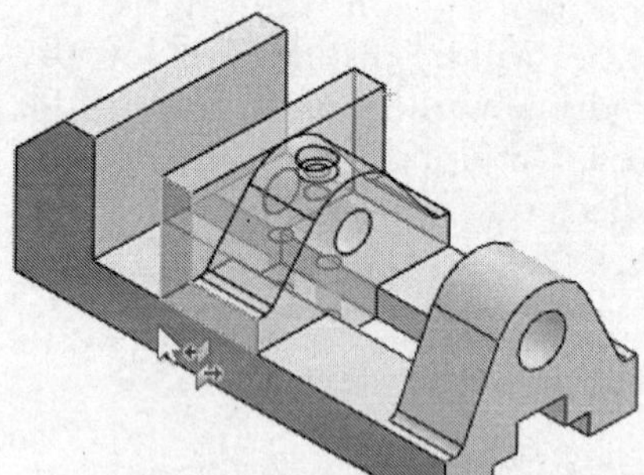

Figure 12-43 *Coincident symbol appears after dragging the component near another planar face*

Tip

You can also add smart mates without dragging the component. To do so, invoke the ***SmartMates*** *tool. Double-click on an entity of the first component; the component will be displayed as transparent. Now, select an entity of the second component; a preview with the most appropriate mate will be displayed and the* ***Mate*** *pop-up toolbar will be invoked.*

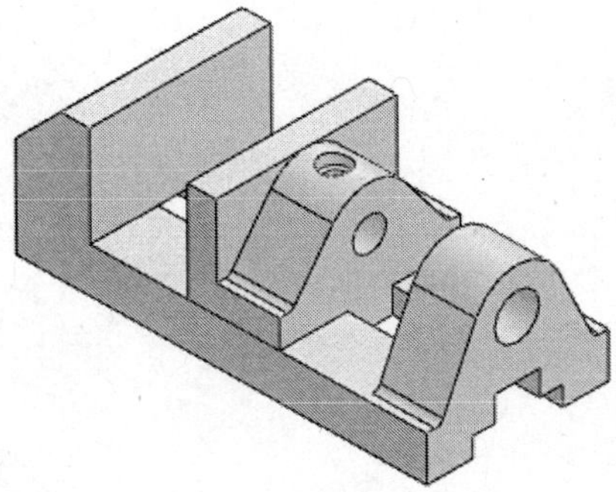

*Figure 12-44 The **Coincident** mate applied to the assembly by using the **SmartMates** tool*

Note

*To apply Smart Mate without invoking the **SmartMates PropertyManager**, press and hold the ALT key and select the first component. Drag the component to the entity of the other component to which you need to apply the mate. On doing so, a symbol of the constraint that can be applied between the selected entities will be displayed below the mates cursor. As you release the left mouse button, the **Mate** pop-up toolbar will be displayed. Choose the **Add/Finish Mate** button from this toolbar.*

When you drag a component for applying a Smart Mate, the selected entity of the first component will snap to the corresponding entity of the second component. You can press the ALT key to exit the snap mode. To enter the snap mode, press the ALT key again.

Geometry-based Mates

In the assembly design environment of SOLIDWORKS, you can also add geometry-based mates. Geometry-based mates are also a type of Smart Mates and are applied while placing a component in the assembly environment. Consider a case in which the first component is already placed in the assembly environment. Now, open the part document of the second component. Choose **Window > Tile Horizontally** or **Tile Vertically** from the SOLIDWORKS menus.

Suppose, you need to insert the revolved feature of the second component into the circular slot of the first component and at the same time align the larger bottom face of the second component with the upper face of the first component. Then, press and hold the left mouse button on the edge of the second component, as shown in Figure 12-45. Drag the cursor to the assembly window near the upper edge of the circular slot of the first component; the second component mated with the first component will be displayed in temporary graphics, as shown in Figure 12-46. The coincident symbol will also be displayed below the smart mates cursor.

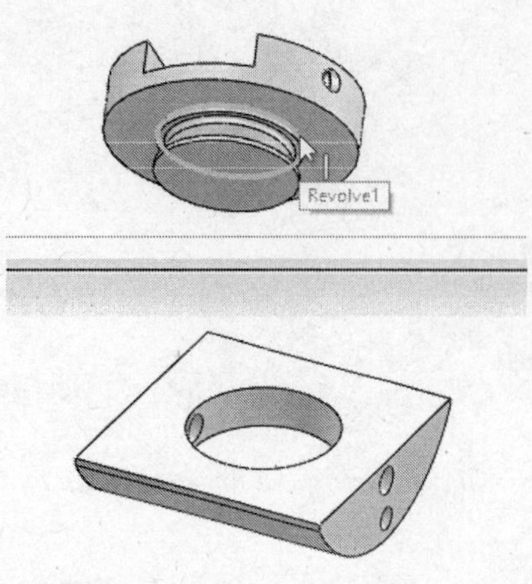

Figure 12-45 Edge of the second component to be selected

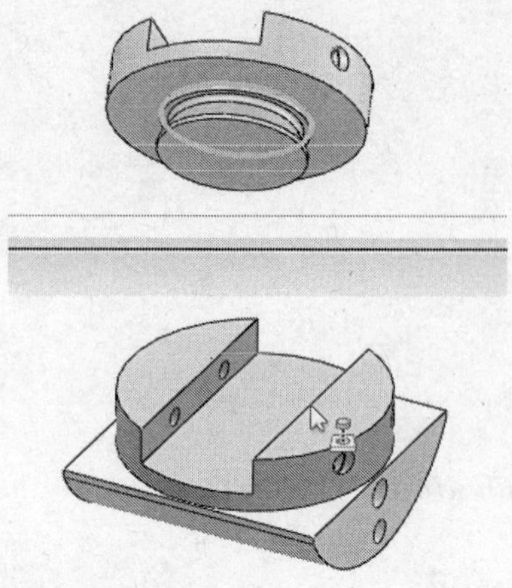

Figure 12-46 Component being dragged into the assembly window for applying the geometry-based mates

You can also toggle the direction of placement of the component. Figure 12-47 shows the direction of placement flipped using the TAB key. To return to the default direction, press the TAB key again. Release the left mouse button to place the component. On expanding the **Mates** option from the **FeatureManager Design Tree**, you will notice that two mates are applied to the assembly: one is the coincident mate and the other is the concentric mate. Figure 12-48 shows the assembly after adding the geometry-based smart mates.

Tip

You can add the geometry-based mates between two linear edges, two planar faces, two vertices, two conical faces, two axes, between an axis and a conical face, and between two circular edges.

Figure 12-47 The placement direction of the component flipped using the TAB key

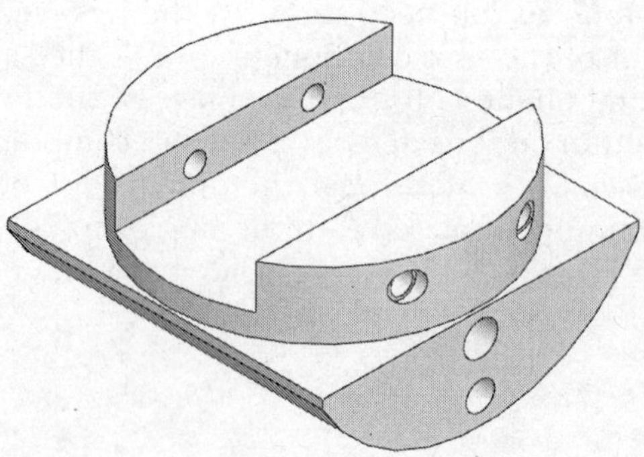

Figure 12-48 Assembly after adding geometry-based mates

Feature-based Mates

In the assembly mode of SOLIDWORKS, you can also add the feature-based mates. For adding feature-based mates, one of the features of the first component must have a circular base or a boss feature and the second component must have a hole or a circular cut feature. The feature can be an extruded or a revolved feature. Also, in the assembly document one of the parts must be placed earlier. Open the part document of the component to be placed and then tile both document windows. In the **FeatureManager Design Tree** of the part document, select the extruded or revolved feature and drag it to the assembly window. Place the cursor at a location where you need to place the component. You can also change the alignment or direction of the placement using the TAB key. Release the left mouse button to drop the component. Figure 12-49 shows the component being dragged by selecting the extruded feature from the **FeatureManager Design Tree** of the part document. Figure 12-50 shows the resultant component assembled using the feature-based mates.

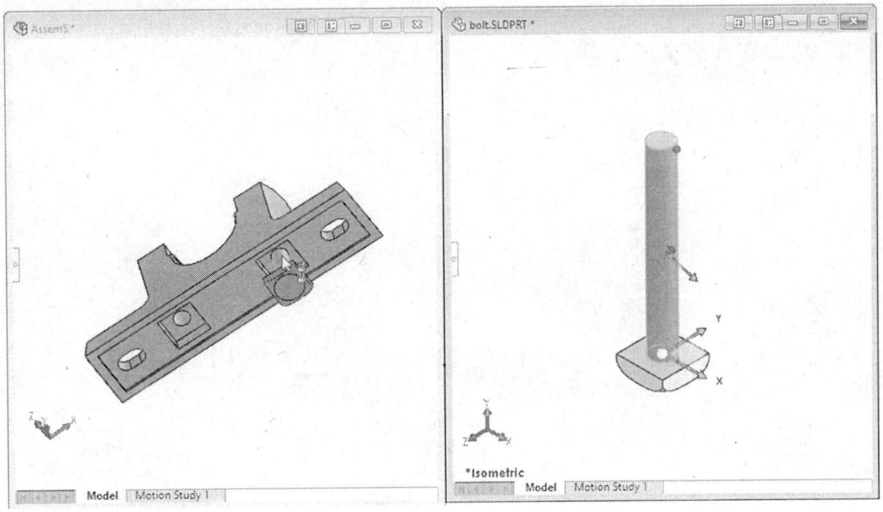

***Figure 12-49** Component being dragged by selecting the extruded feature*

Note

The feature-based mates are applied only to the components that have cylindrical or conical features. If you are adding feature-based mates to a component that has a conical face, the second component also must have a conical face. You cannot apply a feature-based mate to two features if the geometry of one of them is cylindrical and that of the other is conical.

If you are adding feature-based mates by using the features having conical geometry, there must be a planar face adjacent to the conical face of both features.

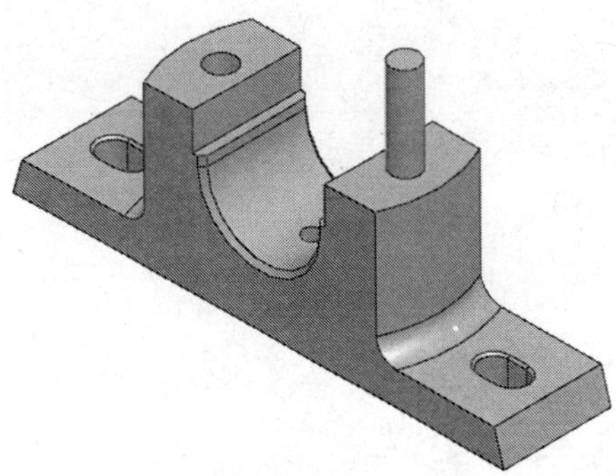

***Figure 12-50** Component assembled using the feature-based mates*

Pattern-based Mates

The pattern-based mates are used to assemble the components that have a circular pattern created on the circular feature. The best example of these components is a flange or a shaft coupling. Note that all components that will be assembled for creating pattern-based mates must have circular pattern on the mating faces. To create pattern-based mates, select the outer edge of the second component and drag it to the circular edge of the first component that is already placed in the assembly document; the preview of the component assembled with the first component will be displayed. Use the TAB key to switch the part with respect to the pattern instances. Release the left mouse button to drop the part. Figure 12-51 shows the component dragged to the assembly document window.

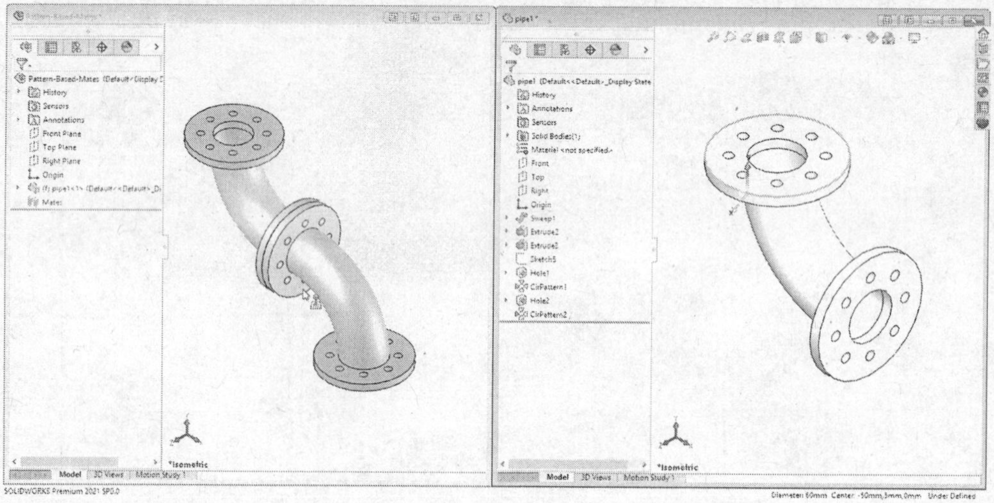

Figure 12-51 *Component dragged to the assembly document window*

Figure 12-52 shows a preview of the component being assembled and Figure 12-53 shows the component assembled using pattern-based mates.

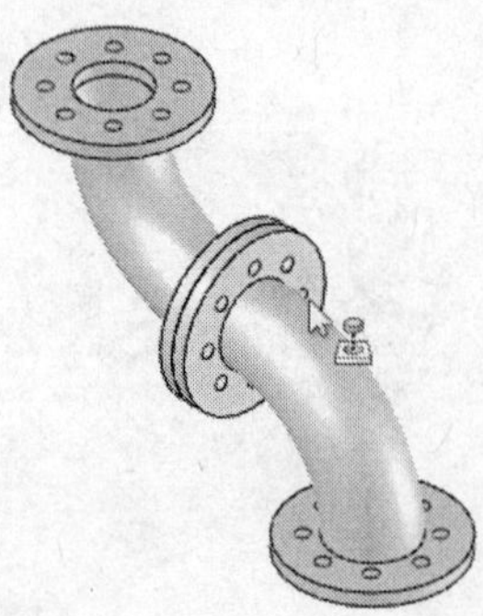

Figure 12-52 *Preview of the component being assembled using* ***pattern-based mates***

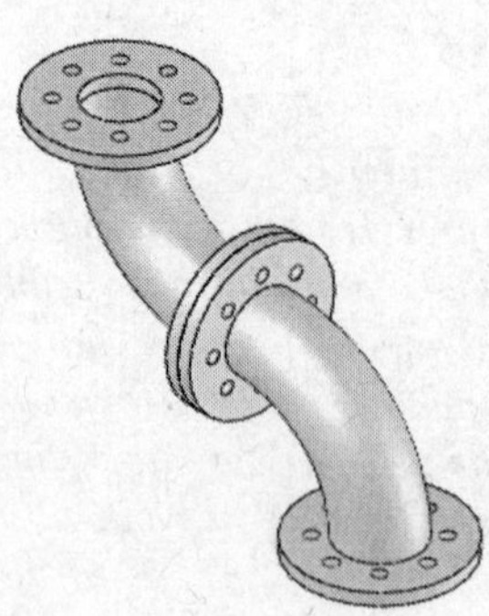

Figure 12-53 *Component assembled using* ***pattern-based mates***

Assembling Components Using the Mate Reference

CommandManager:	Assembly > Reference Geometry flyout > Mate Reference
SOLIDWORKS menus:	Insert > Reference Geometry > Mate Reference
Toolbar:	Assembly > Reference Geometry flyout > Mate Reference

In SOLIDWORKS, you can define mate reference for part in the **Part** or **Assembly** mode. Mate references allow you to define the mating references such as planar surfaces, axes, edges, and so on before assembling a component.

To define mate references, choose the **Mate Reference** button from the **Assembly CommandManager**; the **Mate Reference PropertyManager** will be displayed, as shown in Figure 12-54.

The **Mate Reference Name** text box is used to define the name of the mate reference. The **Primary Reference Entity** rollout is used to define the primary mate reference. The **Mate Reference Type** drop-down list is used to define the type of mate. The **Mate Reference Alignment** drop-down list is used to define the type of alignment. The **Secondary Reference Entity** rollout is used to define the secondary mate reference and the **Tertiary Reference Entity** rollout is used to define the tertiary mate reference.

On adding the mate reference, you will notice that the **MateReferences** folder will be displayed in the **FeatureManager Design Tree**.

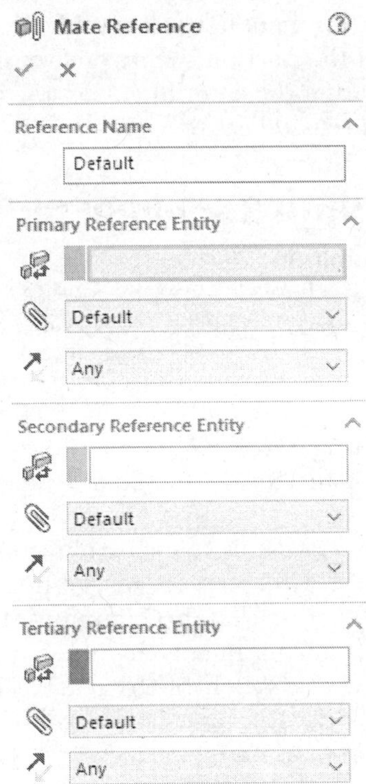

Figure 12-54 *The* ***Mate Reference PropertyManager***

To assemble a component using the mate reference, you need to define the mate references for two components. Also, the names of the mate references should be the same for both the components. After defining the mate references for both the components, place the first component coincident with the origin in the assembly document. Now, drag the second component in the assembly document. You will notice that the second component is aligned according to the references that were defined as mate references. Therefore, you do not need to apply mates in the assembly environment.

Note

As discussed earlier, when you place the first component of an assembly in the bottom-up assembly design approach, it gets fixed automatically. You cannot apply any mates to the fixed component. To add some mates to the fixed component, you first need to float the component. To do so, select the component from the drawing area or from the ***FeatureManager Design Tree****. Right-click to invoke the shortcut menu and choose the* ***Float*** *option.*

By default, the components placed after the first component are floating components. If you need to fix a floating component, select the component and invoke the shortcut menu. Choose the ***Fix*** *option from the shortcut menu.*

CREATING TOP-DOWN ASSEMBLIES

As mentioned earlier, the top-down assemblies are the assemblies in which all the components are created in the same assembly file. However, to create the components, you require an environment in which you can draw the sketches of the sketched features and then convert them into features. In other words, you need a sketching environment and a part modeling environment in the assembly file. In SOLIDWORKS, you can invoke the sketching environment and the part modeling environment in the assembly document itself. The basic procedure for creating the components in the assembly, or the procedure for creating the top-down assembly is discussed next.

Creating Components in the Top-down Assembly

CommandManager:	Assembly > Insert Components flyout > New Part
SOLIDWORKS menus:	Insert > Component > New Part
Toolbar:	Assembly > Insert Components flyout > New Part

Before creating the first component in the top-down assembly approach, you first need to save the assembly document. To do so, choose the **Save** button from the Menu Bar after starting a new assembly document; the **Save As** dialog box will be displayed. Save the assembly file using this dialog box.

Now, choose the **New Part** button from the **Assembly CommandManager**; you will be prompted to select the plane or face to position the new part. To create the base feature, select the default plane; the **Sketch CommandManager** will be displayed with the **Edit Component** button chosen. This means that the part modeling environment is invoked in the assembly document. Draw the sketch of the feature in the current sketching environment and create the feature using the **Features CommandManager**. Choose the **Edit Component** button from the **Features CommandManager** to exit the part modeling environment. The newly created component will have an InPlace mate with the default assembly plane on which it was placed earlier. Therefore, the newly created component is fixed.

Similarly, create the remaining features in the model. Whenever you create a component in a top-down assembly, the component will be fixed using the InPlace mate. To delete this mate, expand the **Mates** node in the **FeatureManager Design Tree** and select the InPlace mate. Then, press the DELETE key; the **Confirm Delete** dialog box will be displayed. Choose the **Yes** button from the dialog box; the InPlace mate will be deleted. Now, this component will be floating and you can move it. You can also assemble this component according to your requirement. You will learn more about the fixed and floating components later in this chapter.

After creating the components in a top-down assembly, you can save them either internally in the assembly or externally. To do so, choose the **Save** button from the Menu Bar; the **Save Modified Documents** dialog box will be displayed. Next, choose the **Save All** button from it; the **Save As** dialog box will be displayed with two radio buttons namely, **Save internally(inside the assembly)** and **Save externally (specify paths)**. Also, you will be prompted to save the parts internally or externally. Select a radio button and choose the **OK** button. It is recommended to save the file externally. So, select the **Save externally (specify paths)** radio button and specify a new folder to save the assembly file and the other referenced file in the same folder.

MOVING INDIVIDUAL COMPONENTS

In SOLIDWORKS, you can move the individual unconstrained components in the assembly document without affecting the position and location of the other components. There are three methods of moving an individual component. Two methods are discussed next and the third method will be discussed later in this chapter.

Moving Individual Components by Dragging

In the assembly environment of SOLIDWORKS, you can move the component placed in an assembly without invoking any tool. To move an individual component, press and hold the left mouse button on the component and drag the cursor to move the component. Release the left mouse button to place the component at the desired location.

Moving Individual Components Using the Move Component Tool

CommandManager:	Assembly > Move Component flyout > Move Component
SOLIDWORKS menus:	Tools > Component > Move
Toolbar:	Assembly > Move Component flyout > Move Component

You can also move an individual component by using the **Move Component** tool. To do so, choose the **Move Component** tool from the **Assembly CommandManager**; the **Move Component PropertyManager** will be displayed with the **Free Drag** option selected by default in the **Move** drop-down list of the **Move** rollout. You will be prompted to select a component and drag it. The select cursor will be replaced by the move cursor. Select the component and drag the cursor to move the component. Release the left mouse button to place the component at the desired location. The other options available in the **Move** drop-down list to move the component are discussed next.

Along Assembly XYZ

The **Along Assembly XYZ** option in the **Move** drop-down list is used to move the component dynamically along the X, Y, and Z axes of the assembly document. Select the **Along Assembly XYZ** option from the **Move** drop-down list; an assembly coordinate system will be displayed in the drawing area and you will be prompted to select a component. Then, drag the cursor parallel to the assembly axis to move the component along that axis. Select the component and drag the cursor to move the component along any one of the assembly axes.

Along Entity

The **Along Entity** option is used to move the component along the direction of the selected entity. On selecting this option, the **Selected item** selection box will be displayed and you will be prompted to select an entity to drag along, and a component to drag. Select an entity to define the direction to move the component; the name of the selected entity will be displayed in the **Selected item** selection box. Now, select the component and drag the cursor to move the component along the defined direction.

By Delta XYZ

The **By Delta XYZ** option in the **Move** drop-down list is used for moving the selected component to a given distance in the specified direction. On selecting this option, the **Delta X**, **Delta Y**, and

Delta Z spinners will be available and you will be prompted to select a component and enter the distance in the PropertyManager. An assembly coordinate system will also be displayed. Select the component to move and specify the distance in the respective direction spinners. Choose the **Apply** button to move the component.

To XYZ Position

The **To XYZ Position** option is used to specify the coordinates of the origin of the part where the component will be placed after moving. When you select this option, the **X Coordinate**, **Y Coordinate**, and **Z Coordinate** spinners will be available and you will be prompted to select a component and enter the X, Y, Z coordinates for the part's origin. An assembly coordinate system will also be displayed. Select the component and enter the respective coordinates of the part origin in the spinners and choose the **Apply** button to place the component.

ROTATING INDIVIDUAL COMPONENTS

In SOLIDWORKS, you can rotate an individual unconstrained component in the assembly document without affecting the position and location of the other components. The **Rotate Component** tool is used to rotate the component. There are three methods of rotating an individual component. Two methods are discussed next and the third method will be discussed later in this chapter.

Rotating Individual Components by Dragging

You can rotate a component placed in an assembly without invoking any tool. To rotate an individual component, select the component, press and hold the right mouse button, and then drag the cursor to rotate the component. Release the right mouse button after attaining the desired orientation of the individual component.

Rotating Individual Components Using the Rotate Component Tool

CommandManager:	Assembly > Move Component flyout > Rotate Component
SOLIDWORKS menus:	Tools > Component > Rotate
Toolbar:	Assembly > Move Component flyout > Rotate Component

You can also rotate an individual component by using the **Rotate Component** tool. To rotate an individual component by using this tool, choose the **Rotate Component** button from the **Move Component** flyout in the **Assembly CommandManager**; the **Rotate Component PropertyManager** will be invoked. You will notice that the **Free Drag** option is selected in the **Rotate** drop-down list in the **Rotate** rollout by default. Therefore, you are prompted to select a component and drag it to rotate. Select the component and drag the cursor to rotate the component. The other options in the **Rotate** drop-down list are discussed next.

About Entity

The **About Entity** option in the **Rotate** drop-down list is used to rotate the component with respect to a selected entity. The selected entity is defined as the rotational axis. When you select this option, the **Selected item** selection box will be displayed and you will be prompted to select an axis to rotate about. Select an edge to define the axis of rotation; the name of the selected entity will be displayed in the **Selected item** selection box. Now, select the component and drag the cursor to rotate the component about the selected axis.

By Delta XYZ

The **By Delta XYZ** option available in the **Rotate** drop-down list is used to rotate the selected component by a given incremental angle along the specified axis. When you select this option, the **Delta X**, **Delta Y**, and **Delta Z** spinners will be available and you will be prompted to select a component and enter the desired rotation in the PropertyManager. Select the component to rotate and set the rotation angle in the respective spinners to specify the direction in which you need to rotate the component. Choose the **Apply** button to rotate the component.

MOVING AND ROTATING INDIVIDUAL COMPONENTS USING THE TRIAD

To move an individual component using the triad, you first need to select the component and then right-click to invoke the shortcut menu. Next, choose the **Move with Triad** option from the shortcut menu; the triad will be displayed on the selected component. You can move or rotate the component by using this triad. The components of the triad are displayed in Figure 12-55.

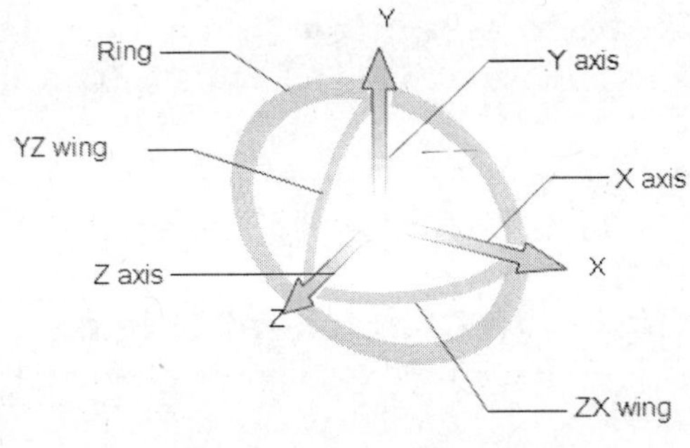

Figure 12-55 *Triad with rings*

To move a component along the X direction, press and hold the left mouse button on the X arm; the select cursor will be replaced by the move cursor. Use the left mouse button to drag the selected component in the X direction. Similarly, you can select the Y or the Z arm and drag the cursor to move the component in the Y or Z direction.

To rotate the component about the X-axis, move the cursor on the YZ wing and drag the cursor; the component will rotate about X-axis.

You can also move a component in the XY plane by selecting the XY wing plane of the triad and dragging the cursor. To move the component in the YZ plane, select the YZ wing plane of the triad and drag the cursor. Similarly, by selecting the ZX wing plane and dragging the cursor, you can move the component in the ZX plane.

If you select the center ball of the triad and invoke the shortcut menu, various options will be available. These options are discussed next.

Show Translate XYZ Box

The **Show Translate XYZ Box** option available in the shortcut menu is used to display the **Translate XYZ** box and is chosen by default. You can use this box to specify the value of the X, Y, and Z coordinates of the destination where you need to place the selected component. Specify the X, Y, and Z coordinates in the respective edit boxes and then choose **OK** from the box. When you move the component by dragging, the values of the X, Y, and Z spinners will change automatically.

Show Translate Delta XYZ Box

The **Show Translate Delta XYZ Box** option available in the shortcut menu is used to display the **Translate Delta XYZ** box. Use this box to specify the incremental value by which you need to move the selected component in the X, Y, or Z direction. Set the incremental value in the **X**, **Y**, or **Z** edit box and then choose **OK** from the box.

Show Rotate Delta XYZ Box

The **Show Rotate Delta XYZ Box** option available in the shortcut menu is used to display the **Rotate Delta XYZ** box. You can use this box to specify the incremental value by which the selected component will rotate in the X, Y, or Z direction. Set the incremental value in the **X**, **Y**, or **Z** edit box and then choose **OK**.

Move to selection

This option is used to relocate the triad and the rings to a selected component or a feature.

Align to

This option is used to align the triad and the rings to a selected component or a feature.

Align with Component Origin

This option is used to align the triad and the rings to the origin of the selected component.

Align with Assembly Origin

This option is used to align the triad and the rings to the origin of the assembly.

Align with selection

This option is used to align the triad and the rings to a selected component or a feature.

ASSEMBLY VISUALIZATION

In SOLIDWORKS, you can display the components of an assembly based on their physical properties. You can also group and display the components in same colors based on a property. To do so, choose **Assembly Visualization** from the **Evaluate CommandManager**; the **Assembly Visualization PropertyManager** will be displayed with a list of all the components in the assembly, as shown in Figure 12-56. You can list the components in the assembly as nested view or as flat view by choosing the **Flat/Nested View** button. Figure 12-56 shows the components of the assembly in nested view. By default, the mass of the components will be listed randomly. To list the mass of the component in the ascending or descending order, click the **Mass** option once. To display other physical properties such as density, volume, and so on, click the side arrow next to the **Mass** option; a flyout will be displayed. Select the appropriate physical properties from the flyout.

To display the components in different colors according to their physical properties, click once on the colored strip; the components will be displayed in different colors. If you need to display the components in more colors with respect to their physical properties then move the cursor to the left of the colored strip and left-click once when the **Add slider** tooltip is displayed; the **Color** dialog box will be displayed. Select a color and choose the **OK** button; a new slider will be added. Now, drag the new slider to new location; some of the components will be displayed based on their color specified by the new slider.

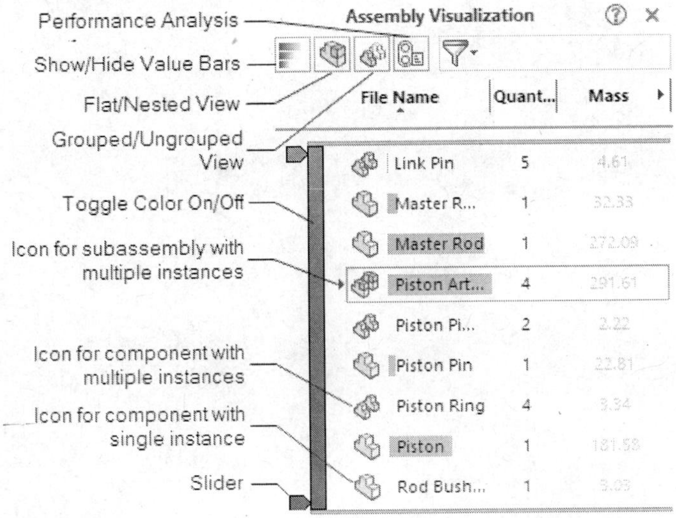

*Figure 12-56 The **Assembly Visualization PropertyManager***

To add more columns to **Assembly Visualization PropertyManager**, right-click on the title of a column and then choose the **Add Column** option from the shortcut menu displayed; a new column will be added. To view a property column and its values for different parts in the **Assembly Visualization PropertyManager**, click the side arrow on the title of the column and choose the required option from the flyout displayed. You can also sort components according to their performance by using various options such as graphics triangles, open time and rebuild time. These options are displayed on choosing the **Add Column** button.

To change the color of the slider, right-click on it and choose the **Change Color** option; the **Color** dialog box will be displayed. Select a color and choose the **OK** button; a new color will be applied to the slider and the components will be displayed depending upon the newly specified color.

TUTORIALS

Tutorial 1

In this tutorial, you will create all components of a Bench Vice assembly and then assemble them. The Bench Vice assembly is shown in Figure 12-57. The dimensions of various components of the assembly are given in Figure 12-58 through 12-62. **(Expected time: 2 hr 45 min)**

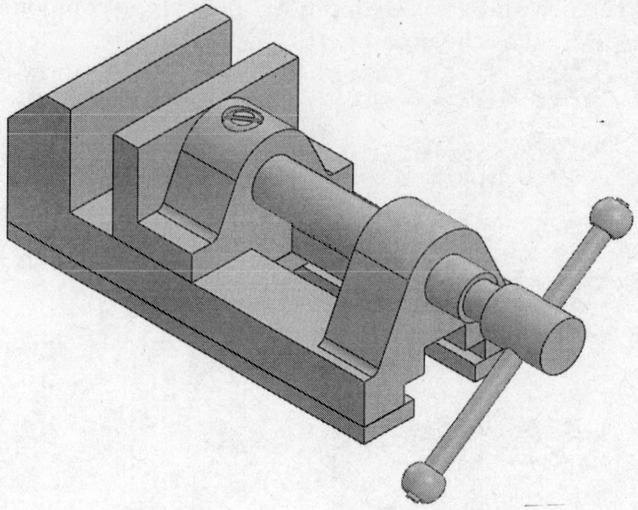

Figure 12-57 Bench Vice assembly

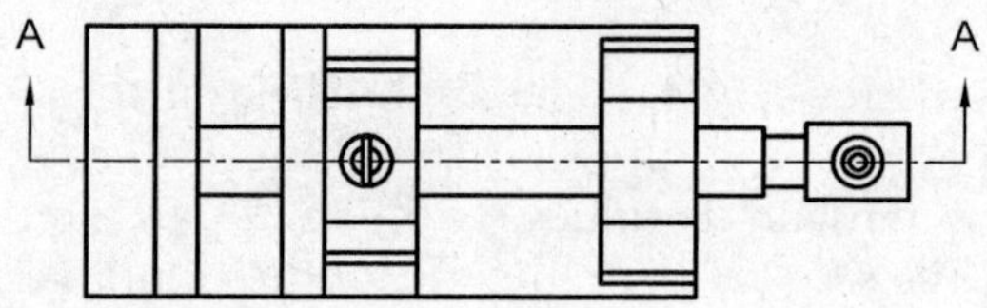

ITEM NO.	PART NO.	DESCRIPTION	QTY.
1	Vice Body		1
2	Vice Jaw		1
3	Jaw Screw		1
4	Clamping Plate		1
5	Base Plate		2
6	Screw Bar		1
7	Bar Globes		2
8	Oval Fillister		1
9	Set Screw1		4
10	Set Screw2		2

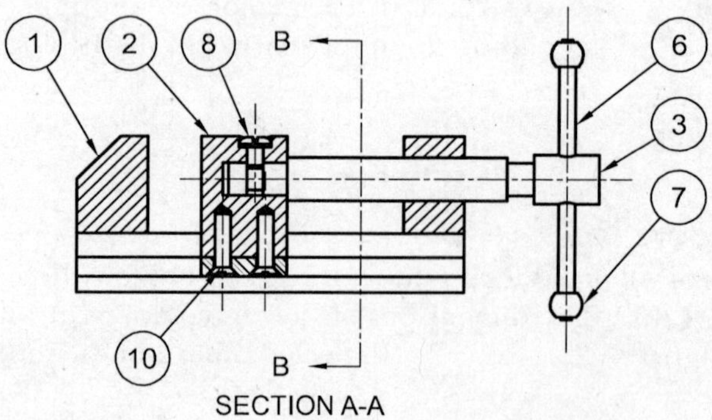

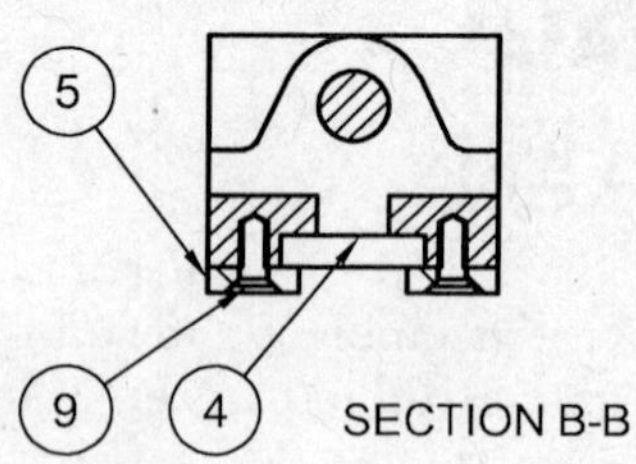

Figure 12-58 Bench Vice assembly

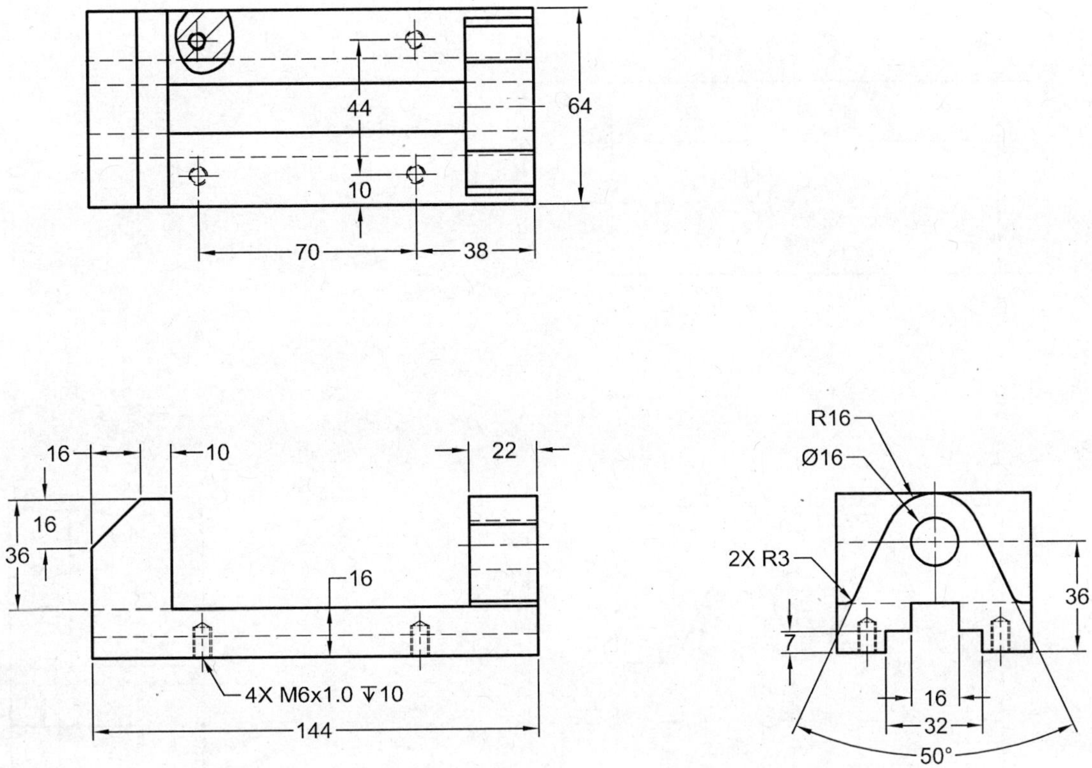

Figure 12-59 Orthographic views and dimensions of the Vice Body

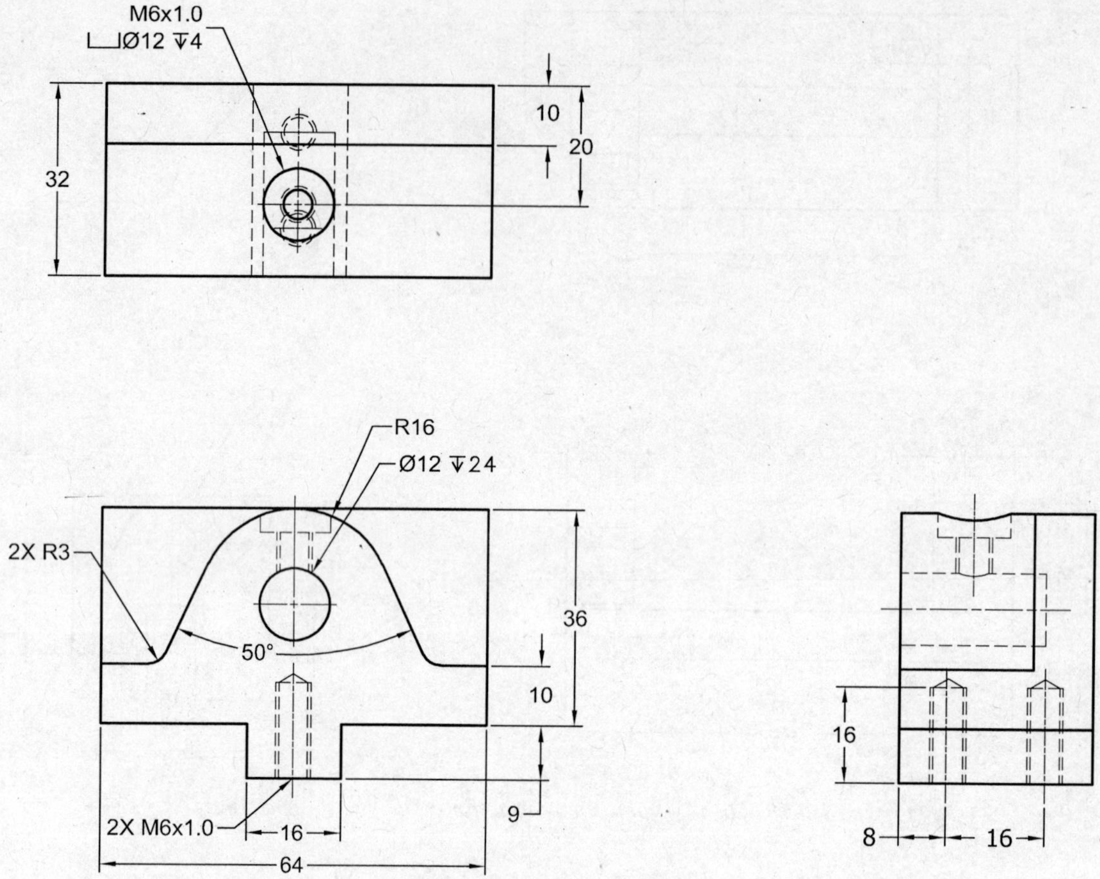

Figure 12-60 *Orthographic views and dimensions of the Vice Jaw*

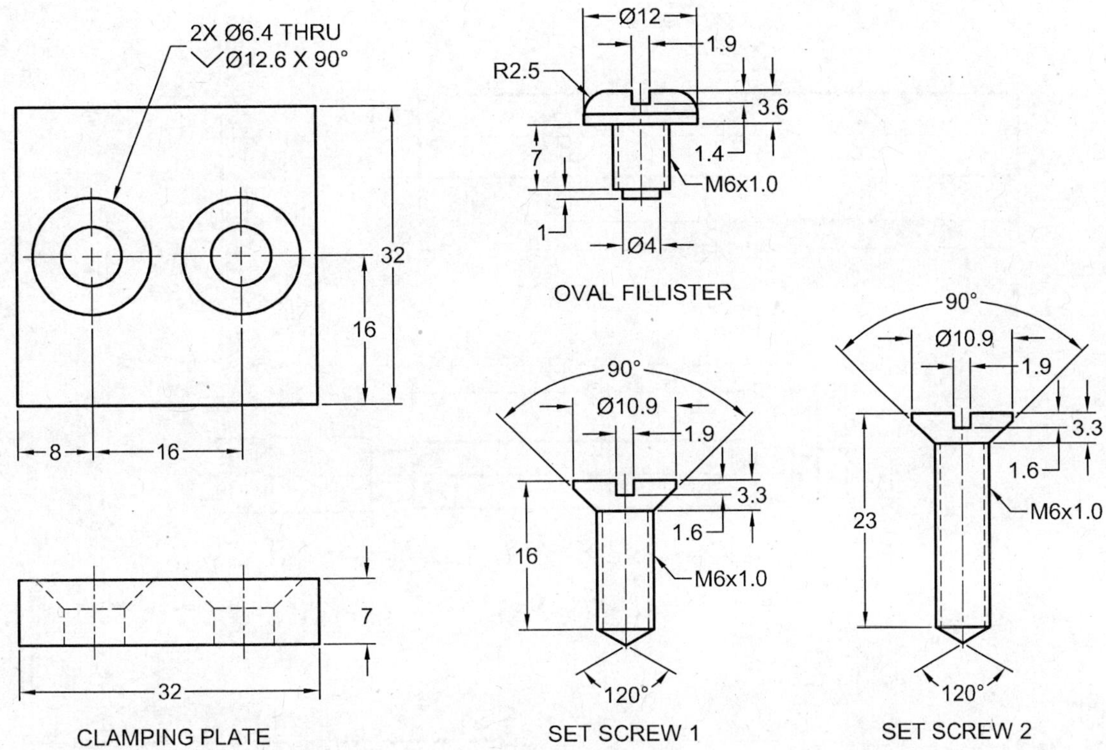

Figure 12-61 *Orthographic views and dimensions of various components of the Bench Vice assembly*

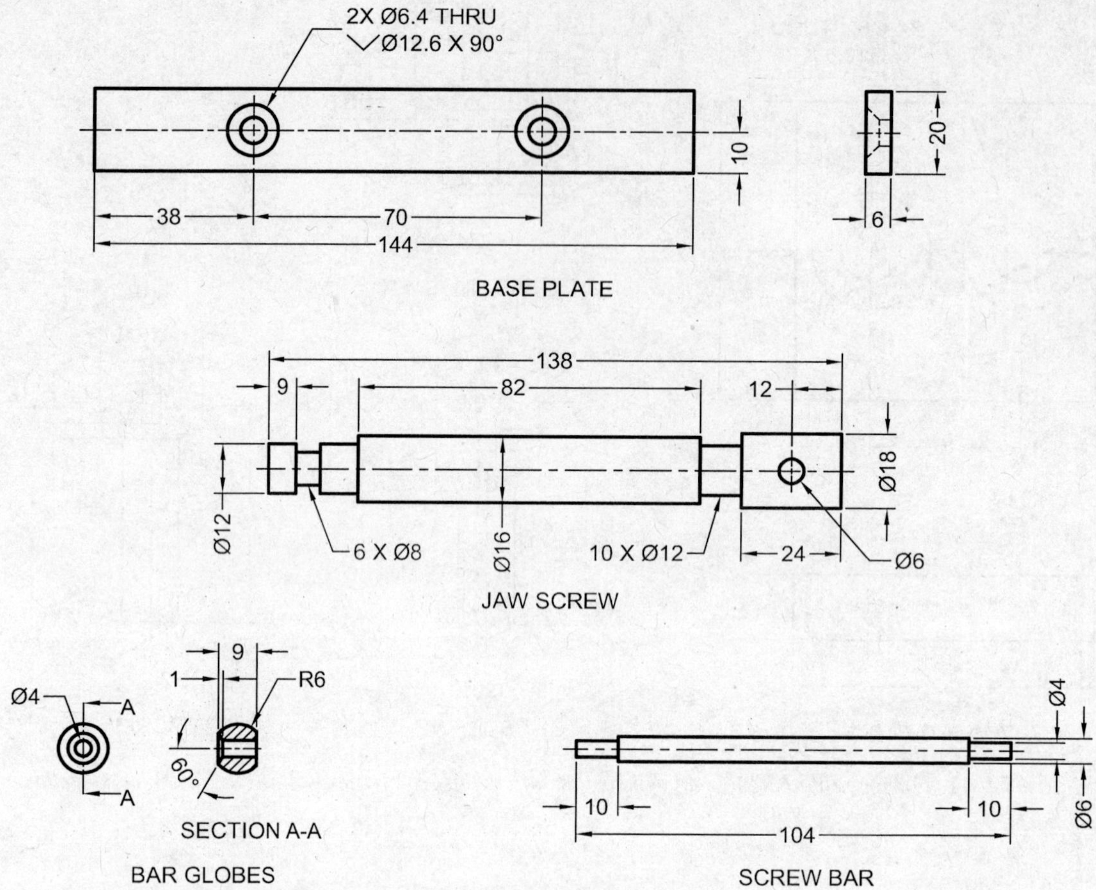

Figure 12-62 Orthographic views and dimensions of various components of the Bench Vice assembly

The following steps are required to complete this tutorial:

a. Create all components as individual part documents and save them at the location *\Documents\SOLIDWORKS\c12\Bench Vice*.
b. Open the Vice Body and Vice Jaw part documents and define mate references in both the part documents.
c. Create a new assembly document and open all part documents. Place the first component, which is the Vice Body. Next, drag and drop the Vice Jaw in the assembly document. It will automatically be assembled with the Vice Jaw because mate references have already been defined in both the part documents.
d. Drag and drop the Jaw Screw in the assembly document and apply mates.
e. Apply mates for constraining the required degrees of freedom.
f. Assemble the Clamping Plate.
g. Assemble the Oval Fillister and Set Screws by using the feature-based mates.
h. Similarly, assemble other components.
i. Save the assembly.

Creating Components

1. Create all the components of the Bench Vice assembly as separate part documents. Specify the names of the documents, as shown in Figures 12-58 through 12-62. Save the files at the location *\Documents\SOLIDWORKS\c12\Bench Vice*. Make sure that *Bench Vice* is your current folder.

Creating Mate References

In this tutorial, you will assemble the first two components of the assembly by using mate references. For assembling components using mate references, first you need to create mate references. To do so, you need to open the part documents in which the mate references will be added.

1. Choose the **Open** button from the Menu Bar; the **Open** dialog box will be displayed. Browse to the location of *Bench Vice* folder.

2. Double-click on the Vice Body; the Vice Body part document is opened in the SOLIDWORKS window.

3. Choose the **Mate Reference** tool from the **Reference Geometry** flyout in the **Features CommandManager**; the **Mate Reference PropertyManager** is invoked. Also, the **Primary Reference Entity** selection box becomes active.

4. Select the planar face of the model as the primary reference, refer to Figure 12-63; the selected planar face is highlighted and the **Secondary Reference Entity** selection box becomes active.

5. Select the **Coincident** option from the **Mate Reference Type** drop-down list in the **Primary Reference Entity** rollout.

6. As the **Secondary Reference Entity** selection box is active, select the planar face of the model as the secondary reference, refer to Figure 12-63; the selected face is highlighted and the **Tertiary Reference Entity** selection box becomes active.

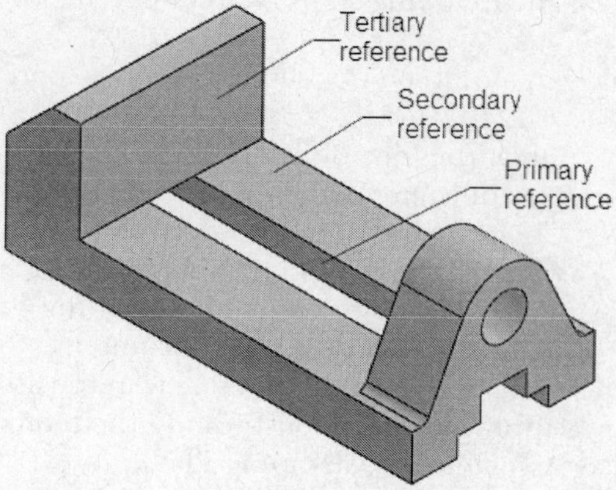

Figure 12-63 *Faces to be selected as mate references*

7. Select the **Coincident** option from the **Mate Reference Type** drop-down list in the **Secondary Reference Entity** rollout.

8. Select the planar face of the model as the tertiary reference, as shown in Figure 12-63; the selected face is highlighted.

9. Select the **Parallel** option from the **Mate Reference Type** drop-down list in the **Tertiary Reference Entity** rollout.

10. Enter **Vice Mate Reference** as the name of the mate reference in the **Mate Reference Name** edit box available in the **Reference Name** rollout.

11. Choose the **OK** button from the **Mate Reference PropertyManager**.

12. Open the Vice Jaw part document.

13. Create the mate reference in the Vice Jaw part document. The faces to be selected as references are shown in Figure 12-64. For the Vice Jaw part, enter **Vice Mate Reference** as the name of the mate reference in the **Mate Reference Name** edit box.

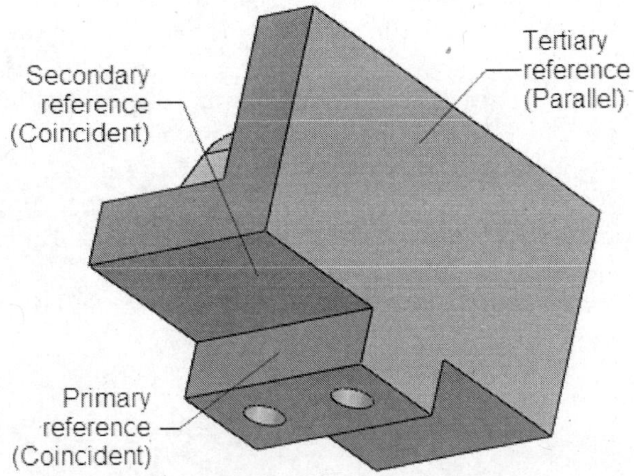

Figure 12-64 *Faces to be selected as mate references*

14. Close all the part documents except *Vice Body.sldprt* and *Vice Jaw.sldprt* if they are opened.

Assembling the First Two Components of the Assembly

After creating mate references in the part documents, you need to assemble the components. To do so, you need to start a new SOLIDWORKS assembly document.

1. Start a new SOLIDWORKS assembly document; the **Begin Assembly PropertyManager** is invoked automatically and the names of the opened components are displayed in the **Open documents** selection box.

2. Select the Vice Body from the **Open documents** selection box; a preview of the Vice Body is displayed along with the component cursor.

   It is recommended to place the first component of the assembly at the assembly origin.

3. Choose the **OK** button from the **Begin Assembly PropertyManager**; the first component is placed coincident to the origin.

4. Change the current view to isometric.

   Next, you need to place the second component in the assembly. As mentioned earlier, the second component of the assembly, which is the Vice Jaw, is assembled with the Vice Body by using mate references.

5. Choose the **Insert Components** button from the **Assembly CommandManager**; the **Insert Component PropertyManager** is invoked and the names of the components opened in other windows are displayed in the **Open documents** selection box.

6. Select the Vice Jaw from the **Open documents** selection box; a preview of the Vice Jaw is displayed in the drawing area.

When you move the cursor close to the Vice Body in the assembly document, a preview of the Vice Jaw after applying mates with the Vice Body is displayed in the assembly document.

7. Place the component at the required location. The mates specified in the mate references are applied between the Vice Jaw and the Vice Body automatically.

   Figure 12-65 shows the second component placed in the assembly document and Figure 12-66 shows the isometric view of the Vice Jaw assembled with the Vice Body.

8. Before proceeding further, close the part document windows of all the parts that are placed in the assembly document.

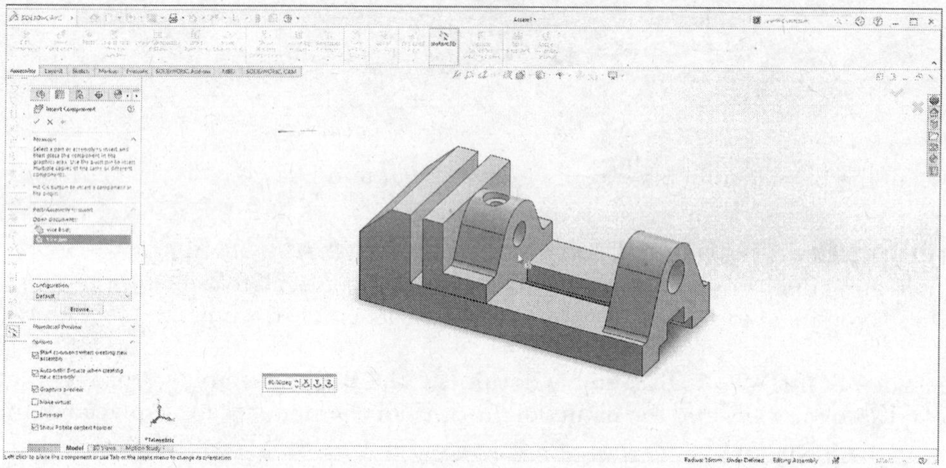

Figure 12-65 *The second component placed in the assembly document*

Figure 12-66 *Vice Jaw assembled with the Vice Body*

> **Tip**
> *The mates defined in the mate references are applied to the components when the components are placed in the assembly. You can view the mates applied to both the components by expanding the* ***Mates*** *node from the* ***FeatureManager Design Tree*** *of the assembly document.*

Assembling the Jaw Screw

Next, you need to place the Jaw Screw in the assembly document.

1. Choose the **Insert Components** button from the **Assembly CommandManager**.

2. Choose the **Browse** button in the **Part/Assembly to Insert** rollout if the **Open** dialog box is not displayed by default.

3. Double-click on the Jaw Screw to open its part document; a preview of the Jaw Screw is displayed in the drawing area.

4. Click anywhere in the drawing area to place the Jaw Screw, as shown in Figure 12-67.

   Next, you need to add assembly mates to assemble the components placed in the assembly.

5. Press and hold the ALT key and select the face of the Jaw Screw, refer to Figure 12-68.

6. Drag the Jaw Screw to the hole in the Vice Body, as shown in Figure 12-69; the Jaw Screw appears transparent and the select cursor is replaced by the smart mates cursor. Also, a symbol of the concentric mate is displayed below the cursor.

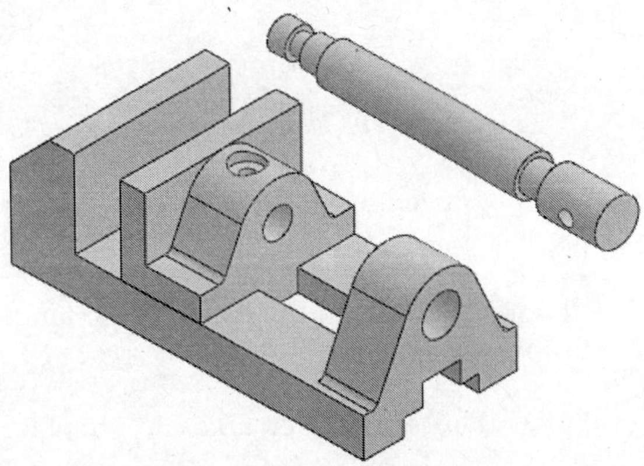

Figure 12-67 *Jaw Screw placed in the assembly*

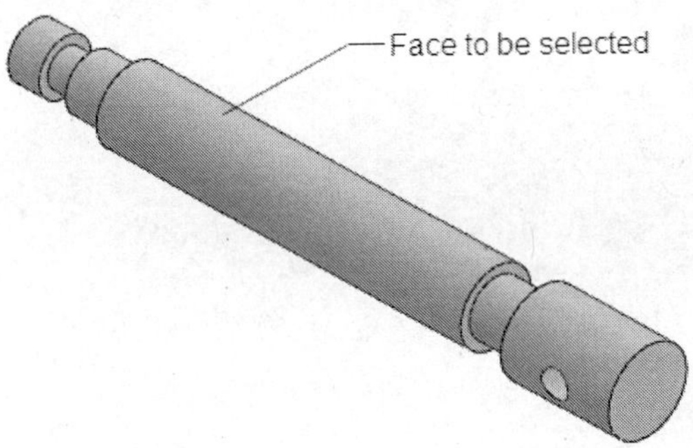

Figure 12-68 *Face to be selected*

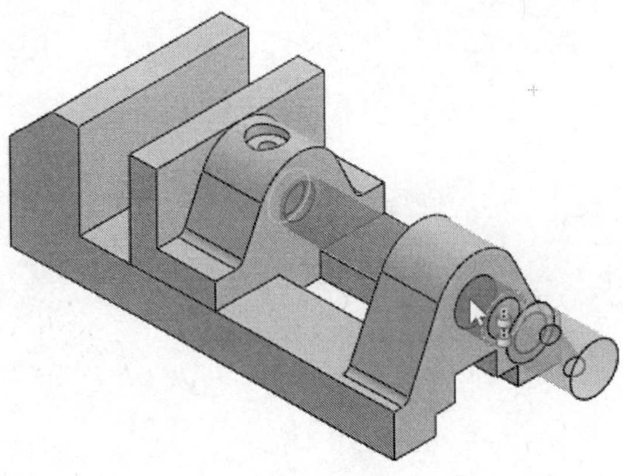

Figure 12-69 *Jaw Screw being dragged*

7. Release the left mouse button and the ALT key at this location; the **Mate** pop-up toolbar is displayed with the **Concentric** button chosen by default indicating that the concentric mate is the most appropriate mate to be applied. Choose the **Add/Finish Mate** button from the **Mate** pop-up toolbar. Figure 12-70 shows the Jaw Screw assembled in the Vice Body.

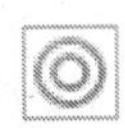

Figure 12-70 The concentric mate applied between the Jaw Screw and the Vice Body

Next, you need to apply the coincident mate between the planar faces of the Jaw Screw and the Vice Jaw.

8. Choose the **Mate** button from the **Assembly CommandManager** to invoke the **Mate PropertyManager**. 

9. Rotate the assembly view and select the face of the Vice Jaw, as shown in Figure 12-71. Next, select the face of the Jaw Screw, as shown in Figure 12-72.

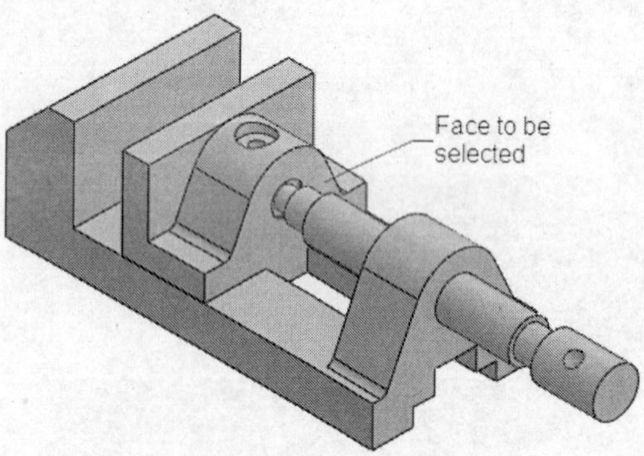

Figure 12-71 *Face of the Vice Jaw to be selected*

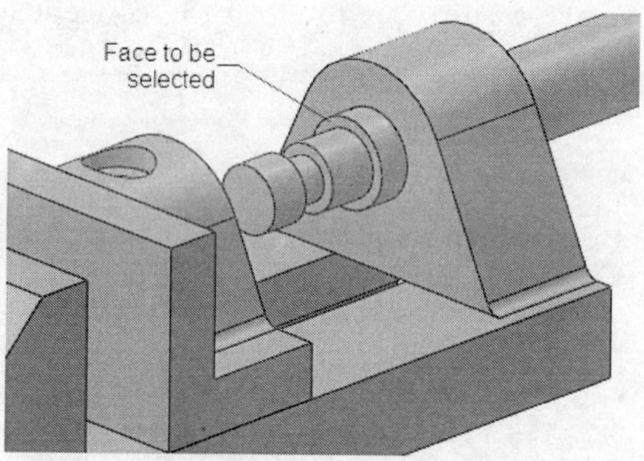

Figure 12-72 *Face of the Jaw Screw to be selected*

As soon as you select the faces, the **Mate** pop-up toolbar is invoked with the **Coincident** button chosen and a preview of the assembly with the coincident mate is displayed in the drawing area. 

10. Choose the **Add/Finish Mate** button from the **Mate** pop-up toolbar. The assembly after adding the coincident mate is displayed in Figure 12-73.

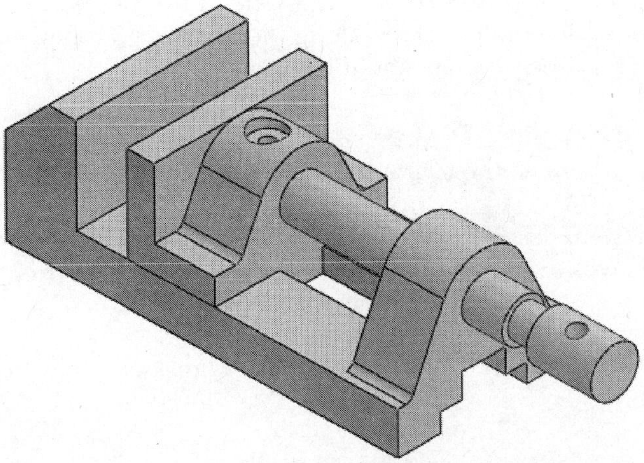

Figure 12-73 Assembly after applying the coincident mate to the Jaw Screw

Next, you need to apply the distance mate to the Vice Body and the Vice Jaw. Make sure you apply the distance mate with maximum and minimum limits so that the Vice Jaw can slide over the Vice Body between these limits. You can do so by using the distance mate.

11. Select the two faces, one of the Vice Body and the other of the Vice Jaw, refer to Figures 12-74 and 12-75.

    As soon as you select the faces, the **Mate** pop-up toolbar is invoked with the **Coincident** button chosen and a preview of the assembly with the coincident mate is displayed in the drawing area.

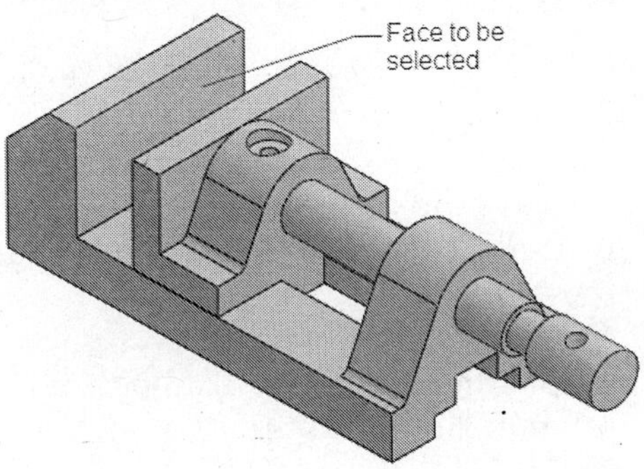

Figure 12-74 *Face of the Vice Body to be selected*

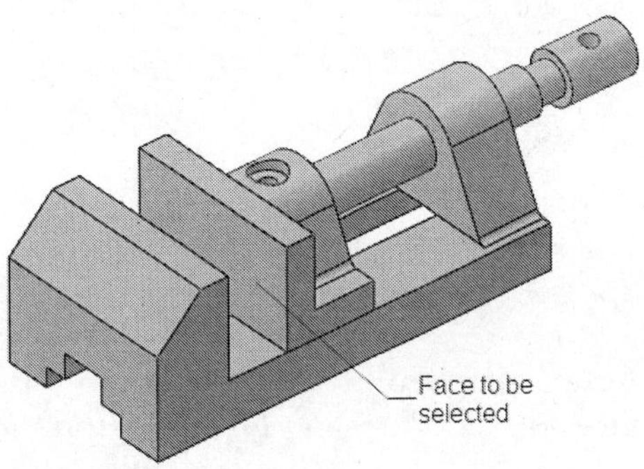

Figure 12-75 *Face of the Vice Jaw to be selected*

12. Next, expand the **Mate Types** rollout in the **Advanced** tab and then choose the **Distance** button from it; the **Maximum Value** and **Minimum Value** edit boxes become available.

13. Enter **60** and **0** in the **Maximum Value** and **Minimum Value** edit boxes, respectively. Next, choose the **OK** button twice from the PropertyManager.

    You will learn more about the advanced mates in the next chapter.

To view the effect after the distance mate is applied with the specified limits, drag the Jaw Screw. You will notice that the Jaw Screw along with the Vice Jaw moves between these limits. Also, the Jaw Screw is free to rotate about its own axis.

Assembling the Clamping Plate

Next, you need to assemble the Clamping Plate with the assembly.

1. Invoke the **Insert Component PropertyManager** and choose the **Browse** button if the **Open** dialog box is not invoked by default. Open the Clamping Plate and place it in the drawing area.

2. Rotate the assembly such that the bottom face of the assembly is displayed, as shown in Figure 12-76.

3. Select the Clamping Plate by using the right mouse button and drag the cursor to rotate it. Figure 12-77 shows the rotated Clamping Plate.

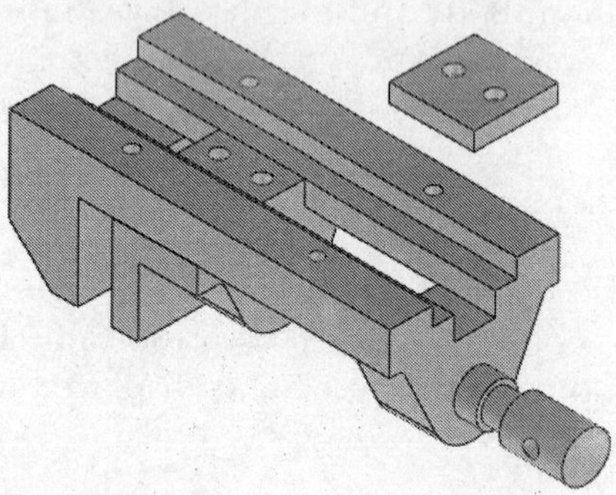

Figure 12-76 *Rotated assembly showing the bottom face*

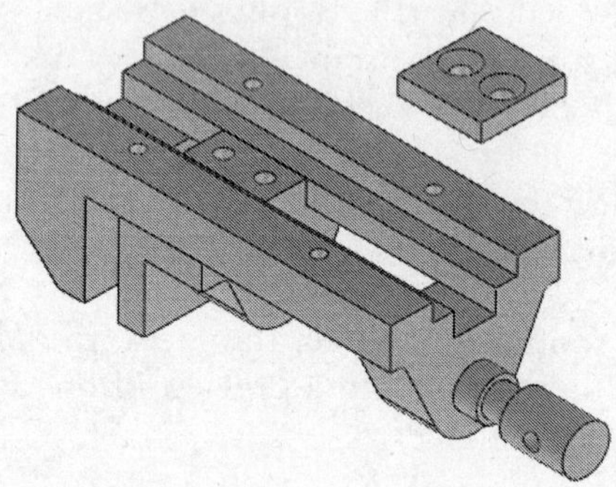

Figure 12-77 *Rotated Clamping Plate*

4. Apply the concentric mate between two cylindrical faces of the Clamping Plate and the two holes of the Vice Jaw, refer to Figure 12-78. You may need to move the Clamping Plate after applying the first mate.

5. Rotate the Clamping Plate by dragging it. Next, apply the coincident mate between the faces of the Clamping Plate and the Vice Jaw, as shown in Figure 12-79.

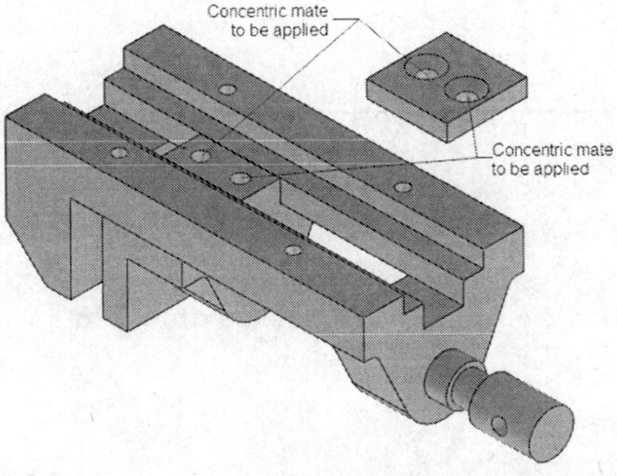

Figure 12-78 *Faces to be selected to apply mate*

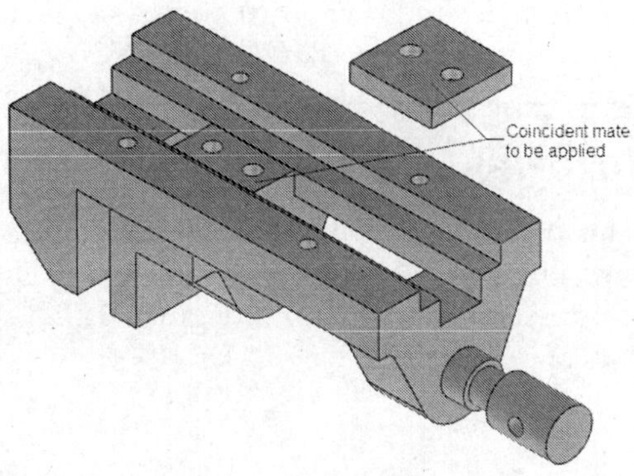

Figure 12-79 *Faces to be selected to apply mate*

Tip

*Whenever you invoke the **Insert Component PropertyManager**, the **Open** dialog box is also invoked simultaneously. However, this dialog box will only appear when there is no other SOLIDWORKS open document.*

Assembling the Remaining Components

After assembling the Clamping Plate, you need to assemble the Screw Bar, Base Plates, Bar Globes, Oval Fillister, Set Screw 1, and Set Screw 2.

1. Follow the same procedure for assembling the Screw Bar, Base Plates, Bar Globes, Oval Fillister, Set Screw 1, and Set Screw 2 with the assembly. Make sure that you specify the required mating references on all parts for assembling them using the Mate References. The assembly after assembling all these components is shown in Figure 12-80. The rotated view of the assembly after assembling the Set Screw 1 and Set Screw 2 is shown in Figure 12-81.

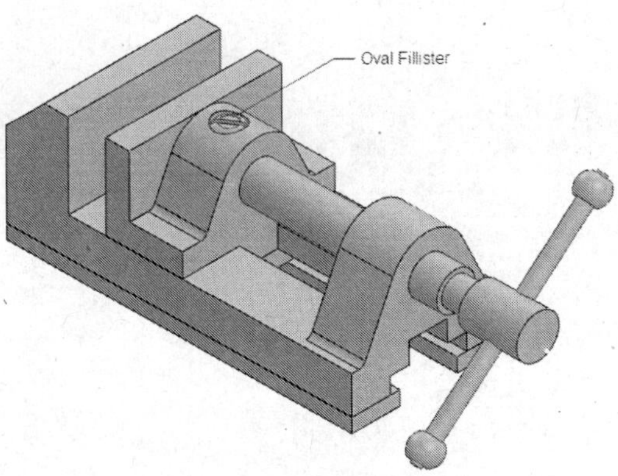

Figure 12-80 *Assembly after assembling the remaining parts*

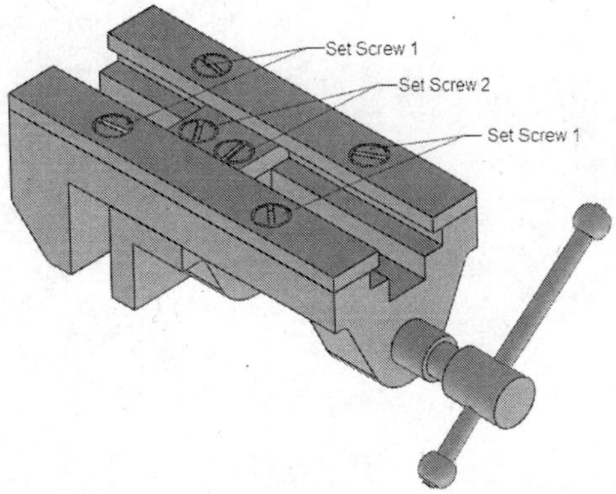

Figure 12-81 *Rotated view of the final assembly*

2. Choose the **Save** button to save the assembly with the name *Bench Vice* at the location *\Documents\SOLIDWORKS\c12\Bench Vice.*

Tutorial 2

In this tutorial, you will create all the components of the Pipe Vice assembly and then assemble them. The Pipe Vice assembly is shown in Figure 12-82. The dimensions of various components of this assembly are given in Figures 12-83 through 12-85. **(Expected time: 2 hr 45 min)**

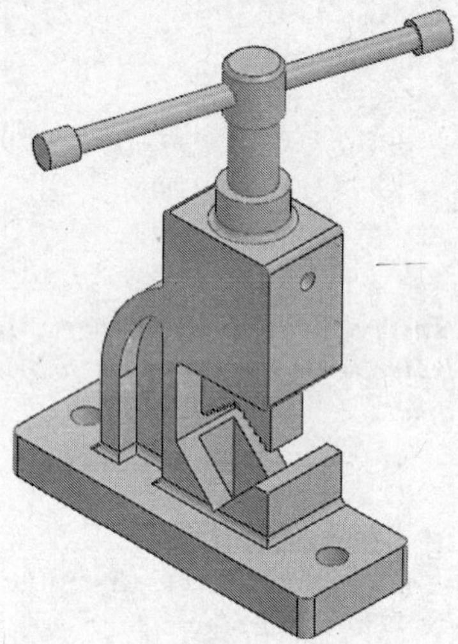

Figure 12-82 *Pipe Vice assembly*

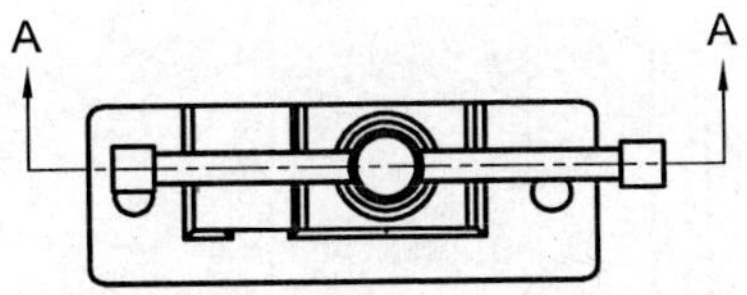

ITEM NO.	PART NO.	DESCRIPTION	QTY.
1	Base		1
2	Moveable Jaw		1
3	Screw		1
4	Handle		1
5	Handle Stop		2

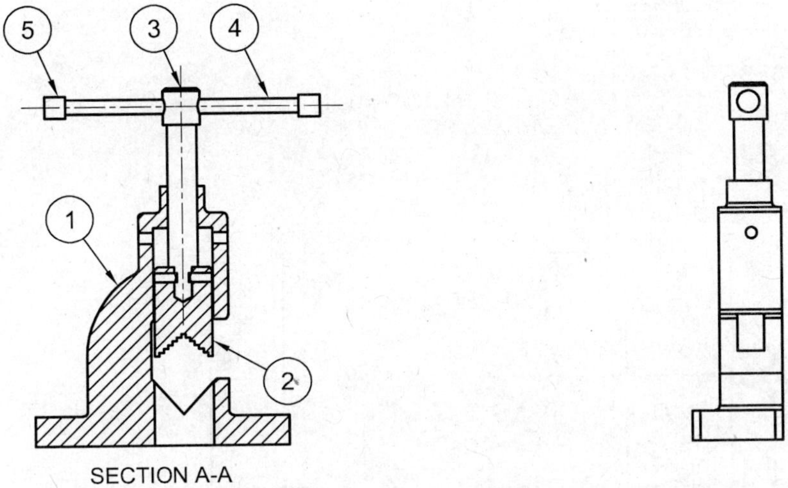

Figure 12-83 *Pipe Vice assembly*

You will create all components of the Pipe Vice assembly as separate part documents. After creating the parts, you will assemble them in the assembly document. In this tutorial, you need to use the bottom-up approach for creating the assembly.

The following steps are required to complete this tutorial:

a. Create all the components as separate part documents and then save them. The part documents will be saved at *\Documents\SOLIDWORKS\c12\Pipe Vice*.
b. Place the Base at the origin of the assembly.
c. Place the Moveable Jaw and the Screw in the assembly. Apply mates between the Moveable Jaw and the Screw.
d. Assemble the Screw with the Base.
e. Place other components in the assembly and apply mates to the assembly.

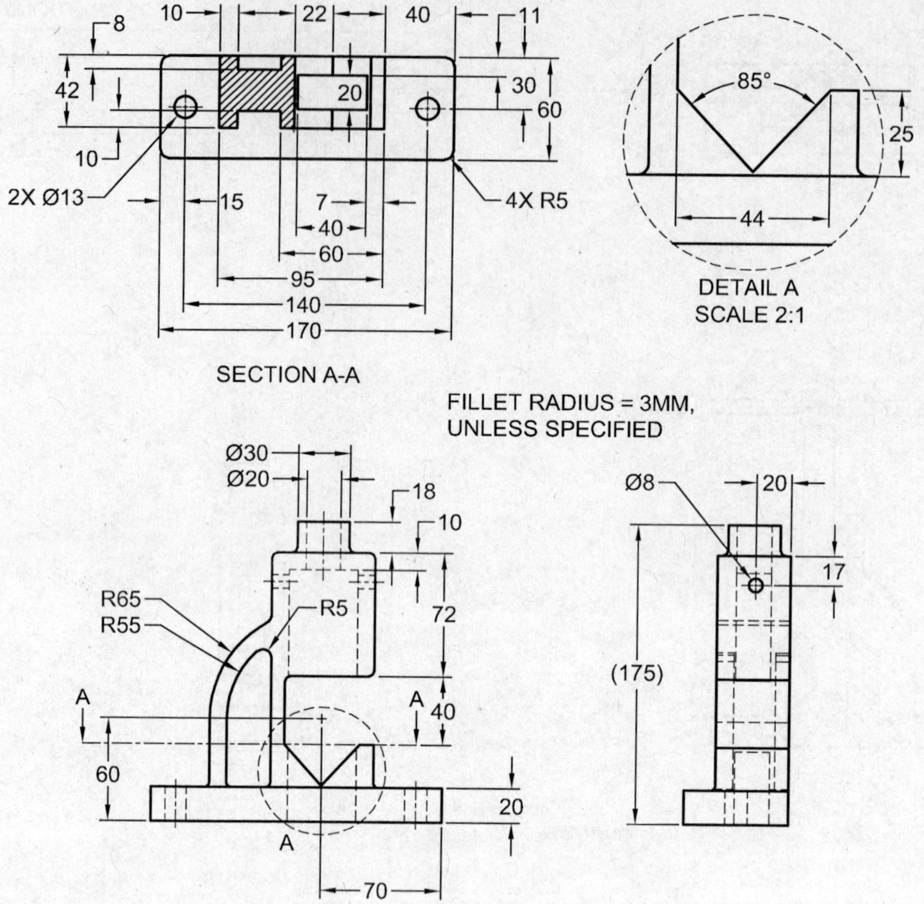

Figure 12-84 *Views and dimensions of the Base*

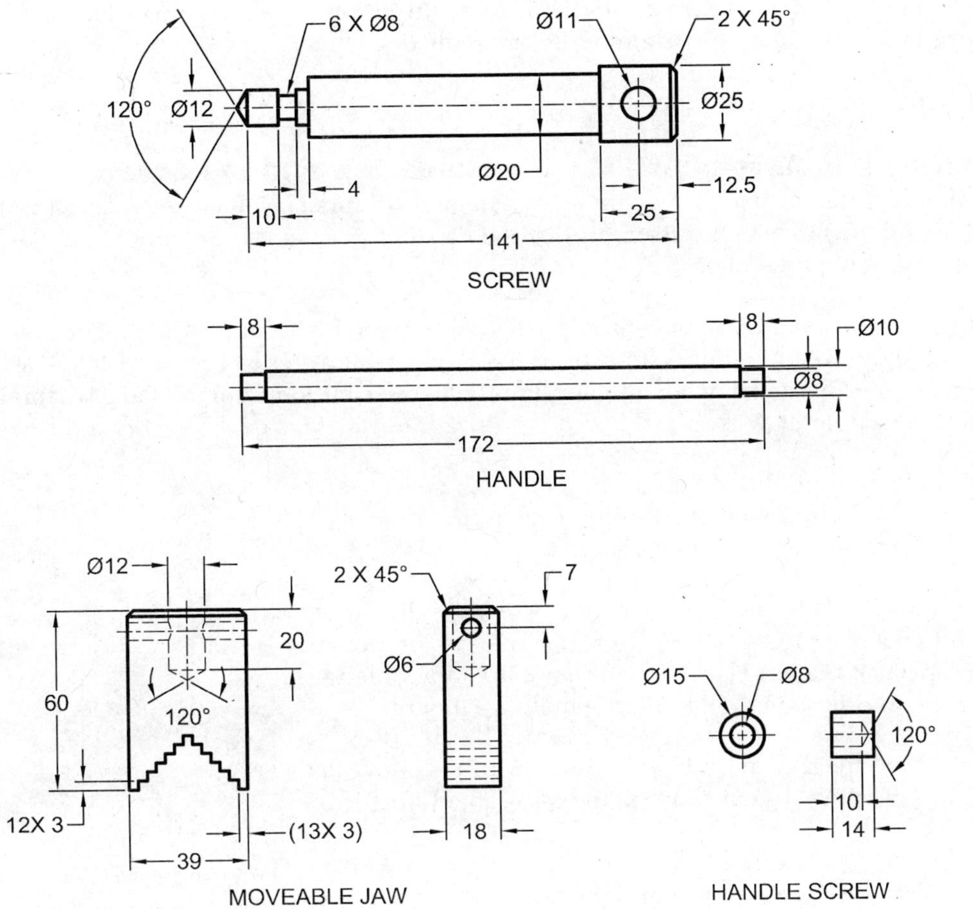

Figure 12-85 *Views and dimensions of the Screw, Handle, Moveable Jaw, and Handle Screw*

Creating Components

1. Create all the components of the Pipe Vice assembly as separate part documents. Specify the names of the files, as shown in Figures 12-83 to 12-85. Save the documents at the location *\Documents\SOLIDWORKS\c12\Pipe Vice*.

Inserting the First Component into the Assembly

After creating all the components of the Pipe Vice assembly, you need to start a new SOLIDWORKS assembly document.

1. Start a new SOLIDWORKS assembly document; the **Begin Assembly PropertyManager** is displayed by default.

2. Choose the **Browse** button from the **Part/Assembly to Insert** rollout to display the **Open** dialog box if not displayed by default. Open the **Pipe Vice** folder and double-click on the Base.

3. Choose the **OK** button from the **Begin Assembly PropertyManager** to place the Base part origin coincident at the origin of the assembly document.

4. Change the view orientation to isometric.

Inserting and Assembling the Moveable Jaw and the Screw

After placing the first component in the assembly document, you need to place the Moveable Jaw and the Screw in the assembly document. After placing these components, you need to apply the required mates.

1. Choose the **Insert Components** button from the **Assembly CommandManager**. Then, choose the **Keep Visible** button from the PropertyManager to keep it visible. Next, invoke the **Open** dialog box by choosing the **Browse** button from the **Part/Assembly to Insert** rollout.

2. Double-click on the Moveable Jaw. Place the component anywhere in the assembly document such that it does not interfere with the existing component.

3. Similarly, place the Screw in the assembly document and choose the **OK** button from the **Insert Component PropertyManager**. Figure 12-86 shows the Moveable Jaw, Screw, and Base placed in the assembly document.

   First, you need to assemble the Screw with the Moveable Jaw. Therefore, you need to fix the Moveable Jaw.

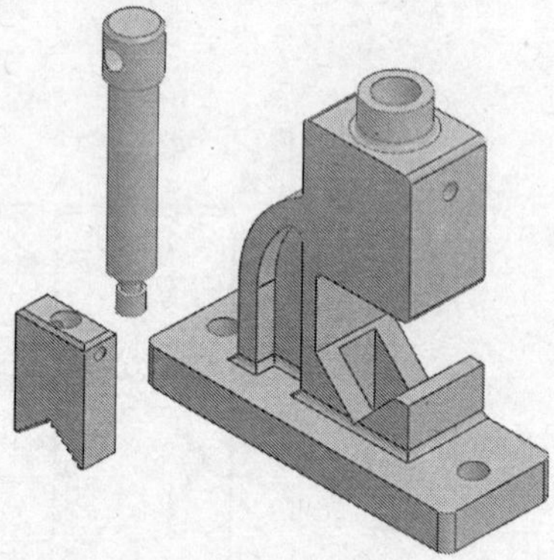

***Figure 12-86** The Moveable Jaw, Screw, and Base placed in the assembly document*

4. Select the Moveable Jaw from the drawing area or from the **FeatureManager Design Tree**. Right-click to invoke the shortcut menu.

5. Choose the **Fix** option from the shortcut menu; the Moveable Jaw becomes fixed and you cannot move or rotate it.

6. Invoke the **Move Component PropertyManager** and choose the **SmartMates** button from the **Move** rollout. Double-click on the lowermost cylindrical face of the Screw; the Screw appears transparent.

7. Drag the cursor to the hole located at the top of the Moveable Jaw. Release the left mouse button as soon as the concentric symbol is displayed below the cursor. Next, choose the **Add/Finish Mate** button from the **Mate** pop-up toolbar.

8. Select the Screw and move it up so that it is not inside the Moveable Jaw.

9. Right-click in the drawing area and then choose **Clear Selections** from the shortcut menu to clear the current selection.

10. Rotate the assembly and double-click on the lower flat face of the Screw; the Screw appears transparent.

11. Rotate the model again and select the top planar face of the Moveable Jaw. The coincident mate is applied between the two selected faces. Choose the **Add/Finish Mate** button from the **Mate** pop-up toolbar.

12. Choose the **OK** button from the **SmartMates PropertyManager**. Figure 12-87 shows the Screw after applying mates.

Next, you need to assemble the Screw and the Moveable Jaw with the Base.

13. Select the Moveable Jaw and right click on it; a shortcut menu will be displayed. Choose the **Float** option from this shortcut menu. Now, you can move the Moveable Jaw and the Screw assembled to it.

14. Press the ALT key, select the cylindrical face of the Screw and move the screw toward the hole created on the top face of the Base to add the concentric mate.

15. Invoke the **Mate PropertyManager** and then select the front planar face of the Moveable Jaw and the front planar face of the Base.

16. Choose the **Parallel** button from the **Mate** pop-up toolbar and then choose the **Add/Finish Mate** button to add the **Parallel** mate between the selected faces.

17. Next, select the faces, as shown in Figure 12-88.

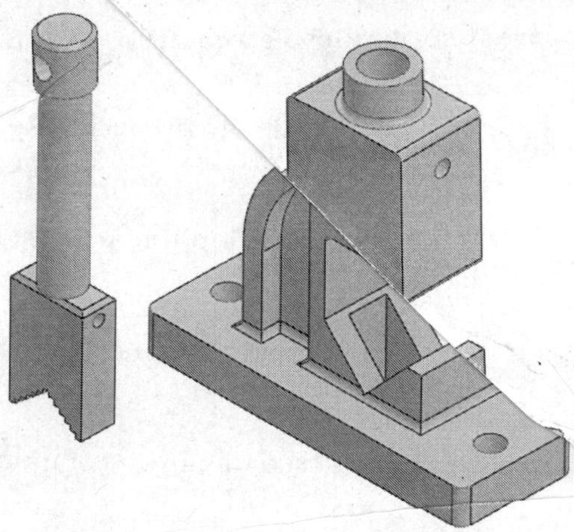

Figure 12-87 The Screw assembled with the Moveable Jaw

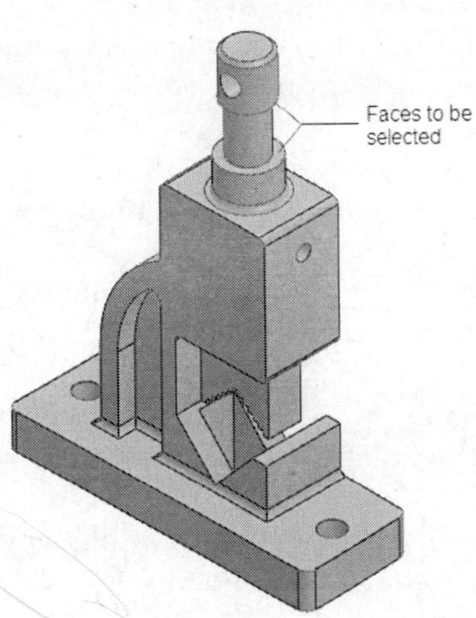

Figure 12-88 Faces to be selected

18. Expand the **Mate Types** rollout in the **Advanced** tab and then choose the **Distance** button from it; the **Maximum Value** and **Minimum Value** edit boxes become available.

19. Enter **65** and **5** in the **Maximum Value** and **Minimum Value** edit boxes respectively. Next, choose **OK** from the **Mate PropertyManager**.

You will learn more about the advanced mates in the next chapter.

20. Similarly, assemble the other components of the Pipe Vice assembly. Figure 12-89 shows the final Pipe Vice assembly.

Figure 12-89 Final Pipe Vice assembly

21. Choose the **Save** button to save the assembly document at the location *\Documents\SOLIDWORKS\c12\Pipe Vice*.

Self-Evaluation Test

Answer the following questions and then compare them to those given at the end of this chapter:

1. Choose the _________ button from the **Assembly CommandManager** to invoke the **Rotate Component PropertyManager**.

2. The _________ option available in the **Rotate** drop-down list is used to rotate a selected component by an incremental angle about the specified axis.

3. The _________ mate is generally used to align the central axis of one component with that of the other.

4. The _________ option available in the **Move** drop-down list is used to move a component along the direction of a selected entity.

5. Pattern-based mates are used to assemble the components that have a circular pattern created. (T/F)

6. The bottom-up assembly design approach is a traditional and widely preferred approach used for creating an assembly design. (T/F)

7. In the top-down assembly design approach, all the components are created in the same assembly document. (T/F)

8. The coincident mate is generally applied to make two planar faces coplanar. (T/F)

9. The most suitable mates that can be applied to the current selection set are displayed in the **Mate Selections** rollout of the **Mate PropertyManager**. (T/F)

10. Feature-based mates can be applied to the components that have cylindrical or conical features. (T/F)

Review Questions

Answer the following questions:

1. Which of the following methods is the most widely used method for adding mates to the components in an assembly?

   (a) **Smart Mates** (b) **Mate PropertyManager**
   (c) By dragging from part document (d) None of these

2. Which of the following buttons is used to make the **Mate PropertyManager** available after applying a mate to the selected entities?

   (a) **Help** (b) **OK**
   (c) **Keep Visible** (d) **Cancel**

3. Which of the following options in the **Rotate** drop-down list is used to rotate a component with respect to a selected entity?

   (a) **About Entity** (b) **Selected Edge**
   (c) **Reference Entity** (d) **Along Entity**

4. Which of the following options is used to specify the coordinates of the origin of the part where the component will be placed after it has been moved?

   (a) **To XYZ Position** (b) **Reference Position**
   (c) **Along Entity** (d) **Along Assembly XYZ**

5. The names of the selected entities are displayed in the __________ selection box of the **Mate PropertyManager**.

6. Choose __________ from the Menu Bar to place a component in an assembly document.

7. Select the __________ option from the **Move** drop-down list to move a component dynamically along the X, Y, or Z axis of an assembly document.

8. The __________ button available in the **Mate Type** rollout in the **Standard** tab is used to make two selected entities normal to each other.

9. While moving a component by using the **Move with Triad** tool, choose the __________ option to relocate the triad and its rings to a selected component or a feature.

10. If you are adding feature-based mates by using the features that have a conical geometry then there must be a __________ face adjacent to the conical face of both the features.

EXERCISES

Exercise 1

Create the Plummer Block assembly, as shown in Figure 12-90. The views and dimensions of various components of the assembly are shown in Figures 12-91 through 12-94.

(Expected time: 1 hr)

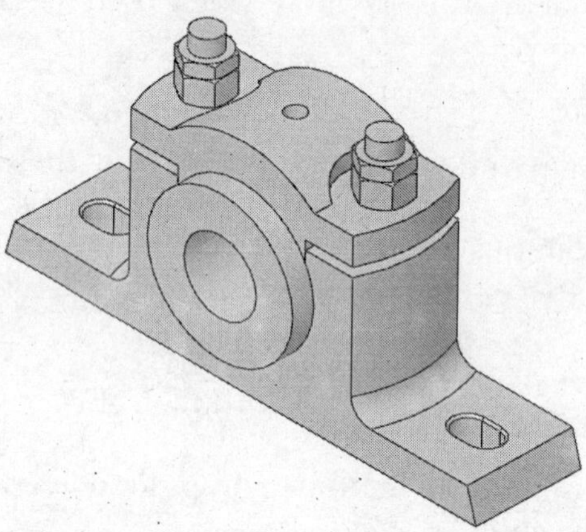

Figure 12-90 Plummer Block assembly

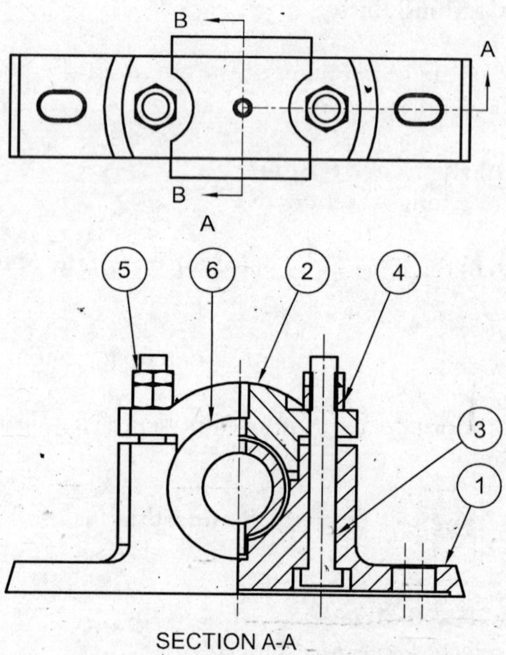

ITEM NO.	PART NO.	DESCRIPTION	QTY.
1	Casting		1
2	Cap		1
3	Bolt		2
4	Nut		2
5	Lock Nut		2
6	Brasses		1

Figure 12-91 Plummer Block assembly

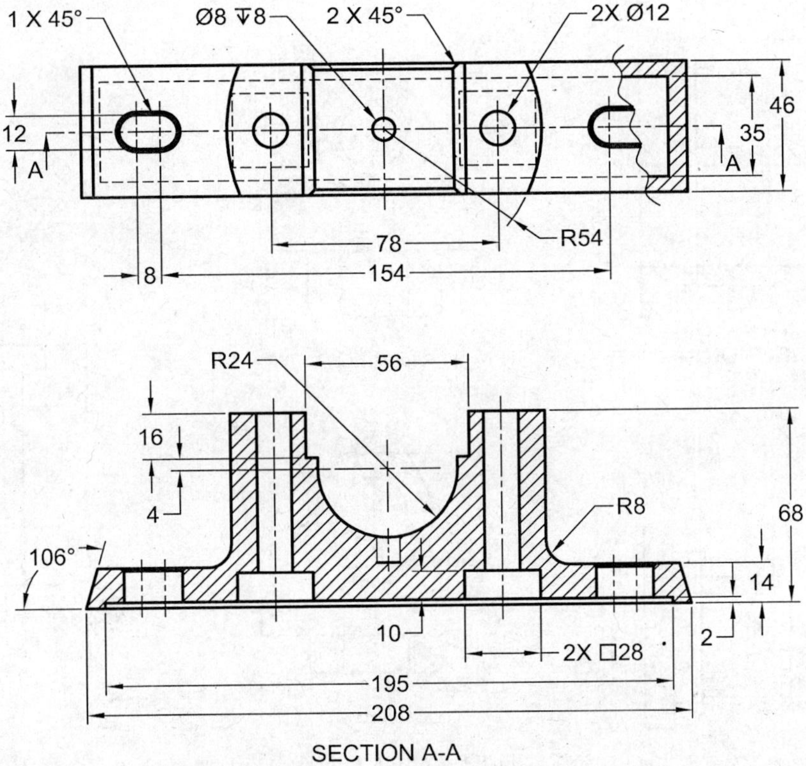

Figure 12-92 Views and dimensions of the Casting

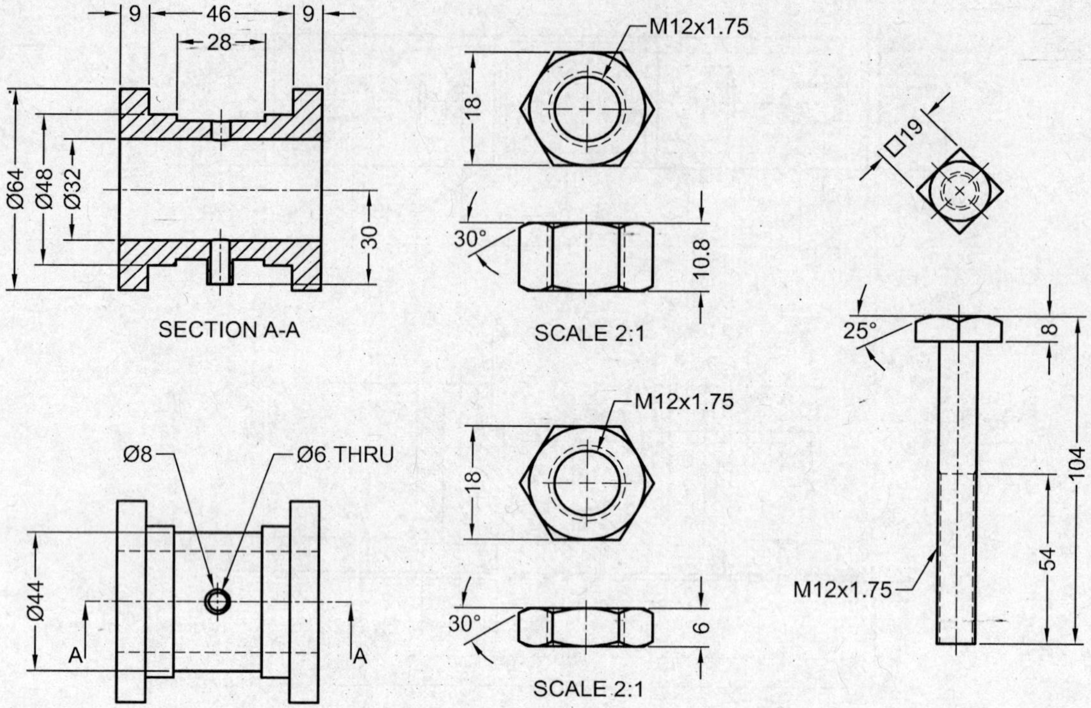

Figure 12-93 *Views and dimensions of the Brasses, Nut, Lock Nut, and Bolt*

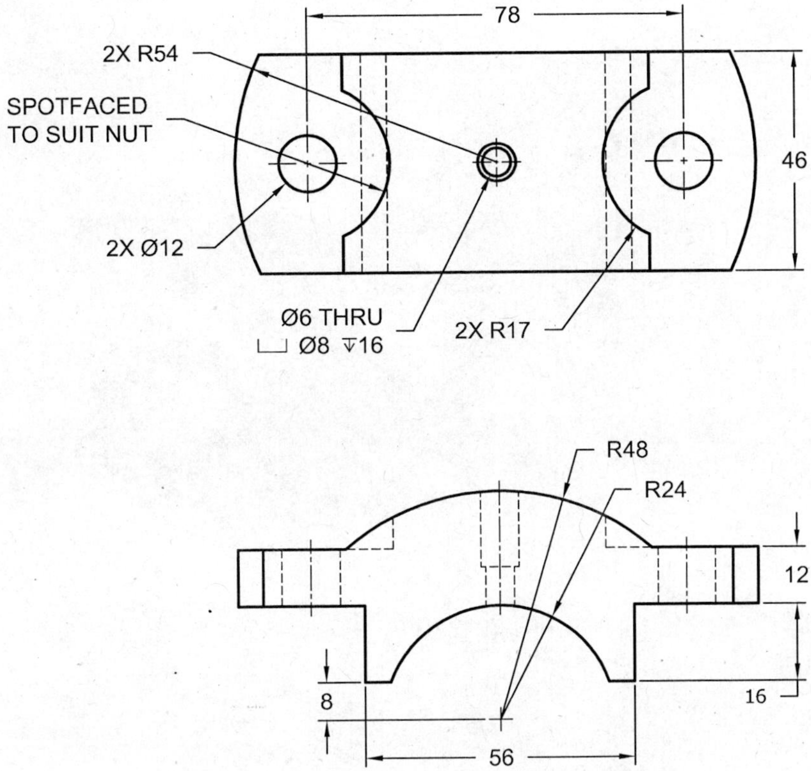

Figure 12-94 Views and dimensions of the Cap

Exercise 2

Create all the components of the Blower assembly and assemble them. The Blower assembly is shown in Figure 12-95. The exploded view of the assembly is given in Figure 12-96 for reference. The views and dimensions of various components of this assembly are given in Figures 12-97 through 12-103. Note all dimensions are in centimeters. **(Expected time: 1 hr)**

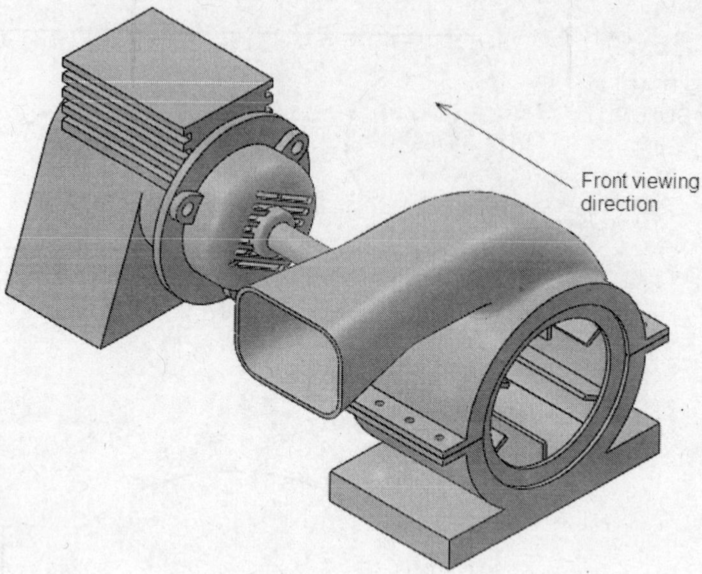

Figure 12-95 Blower assembly

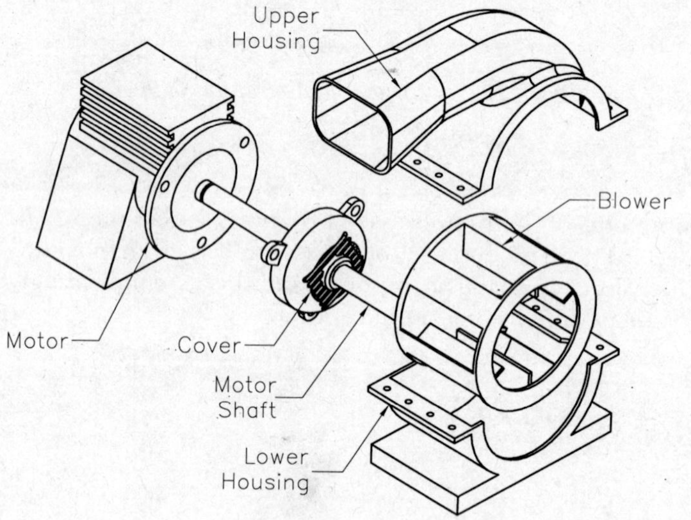

Figure 12-96 Exploded view of the Blower assembly

ITEM NO.	PART NO.	DESCRIPTION	QTY.
1	Lower Housing		1
2	Blower		1
3	Upper Housing		1
4	Motor Shaft		1
5	Cover		1
6	Motor		1

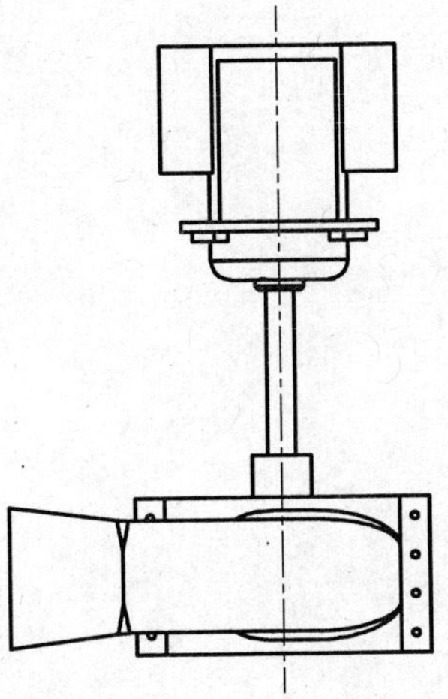

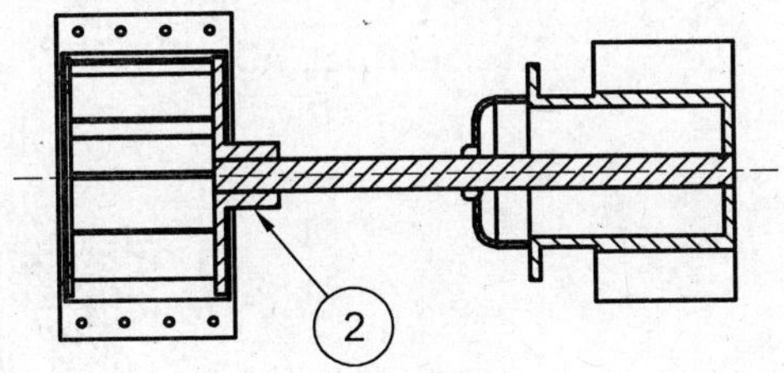

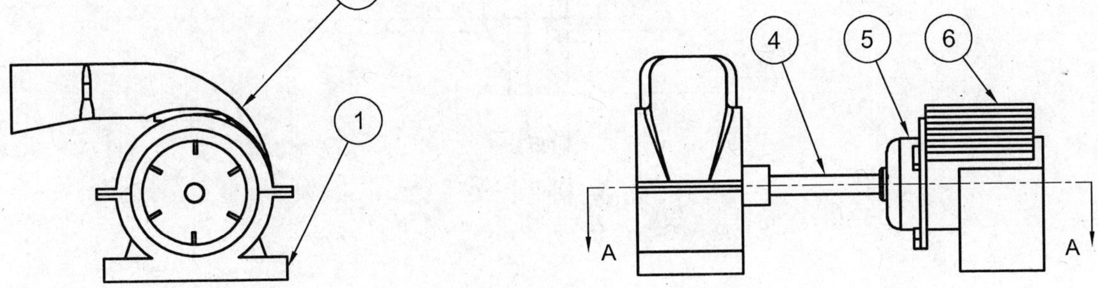

Figure 12-97 *Blower assembly*

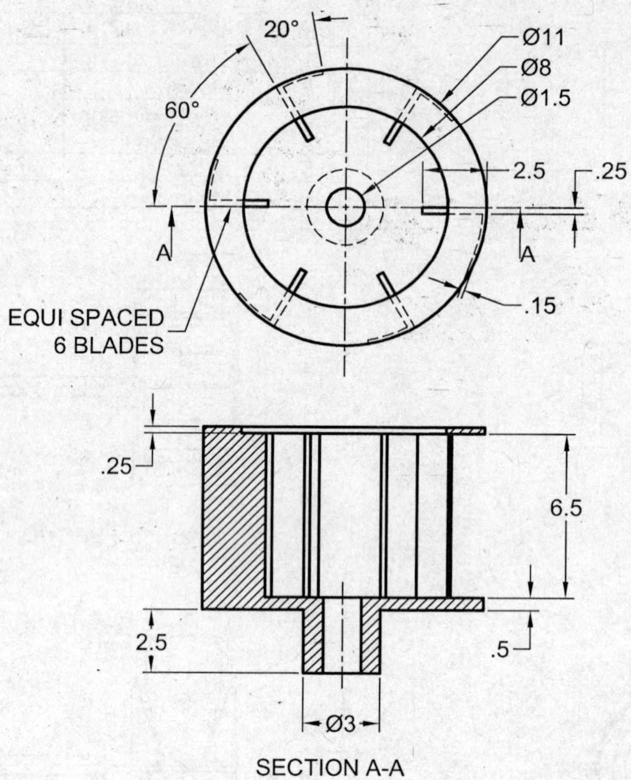

Figure 12-98 Dimensions of the Blower

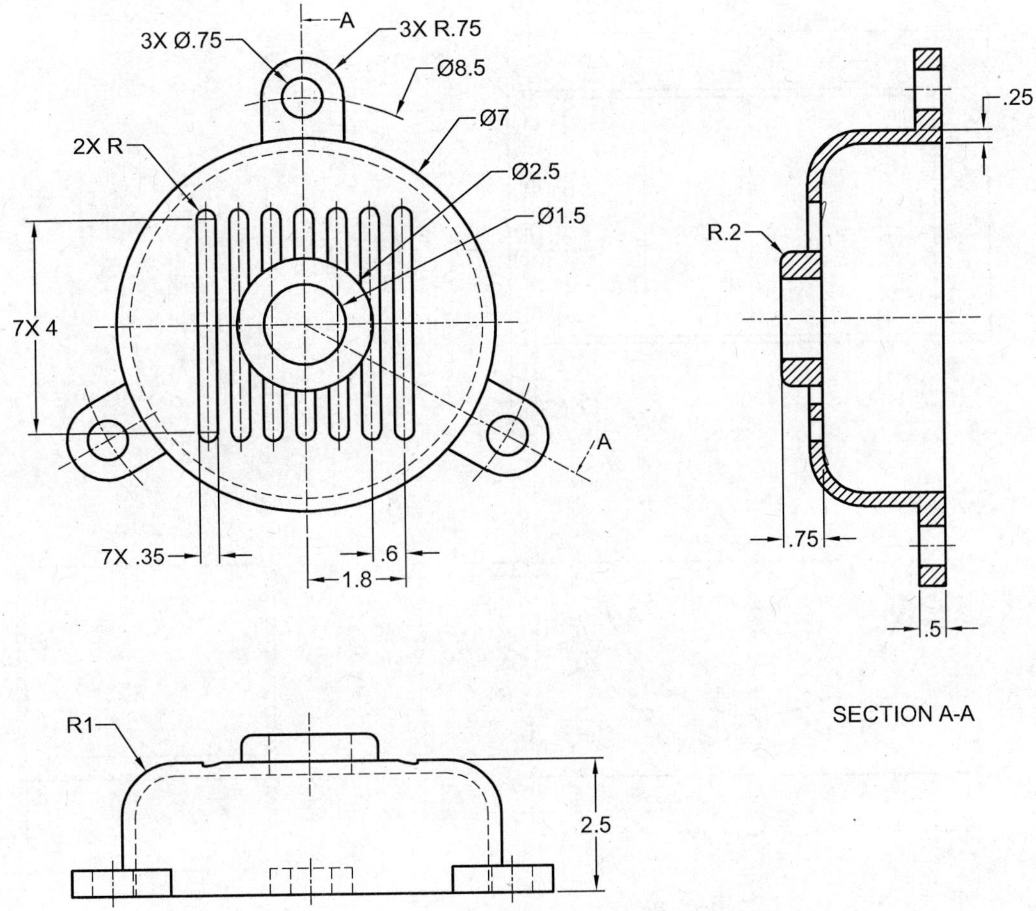

Figure 12-99 Dimensions of the Cover

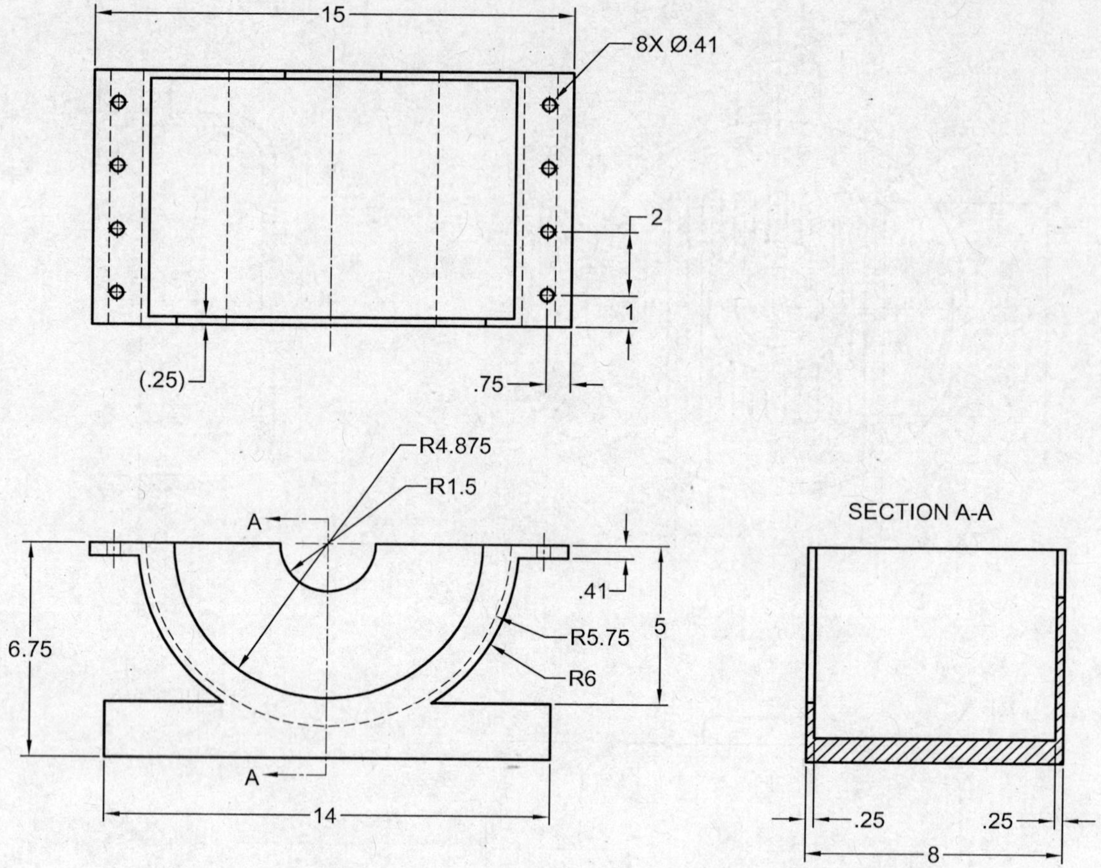

Figure 12-100 Dimensions of the Lower Housing

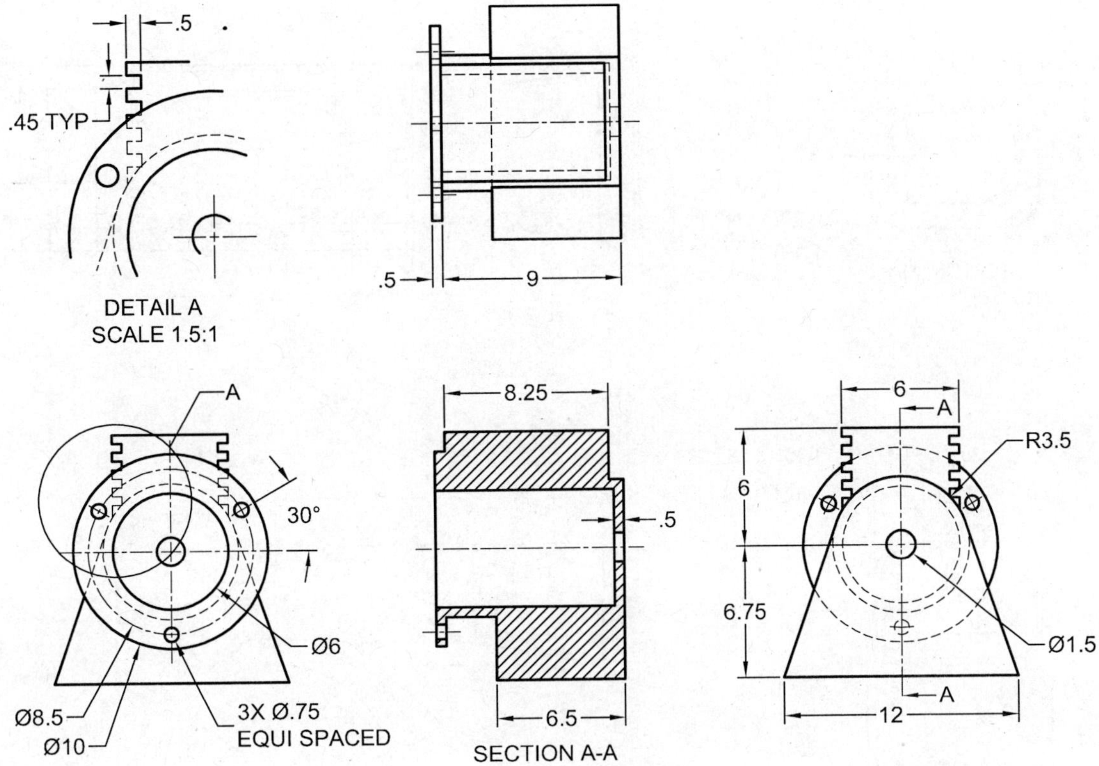

Figure 12-101 Dimensions of the Motor

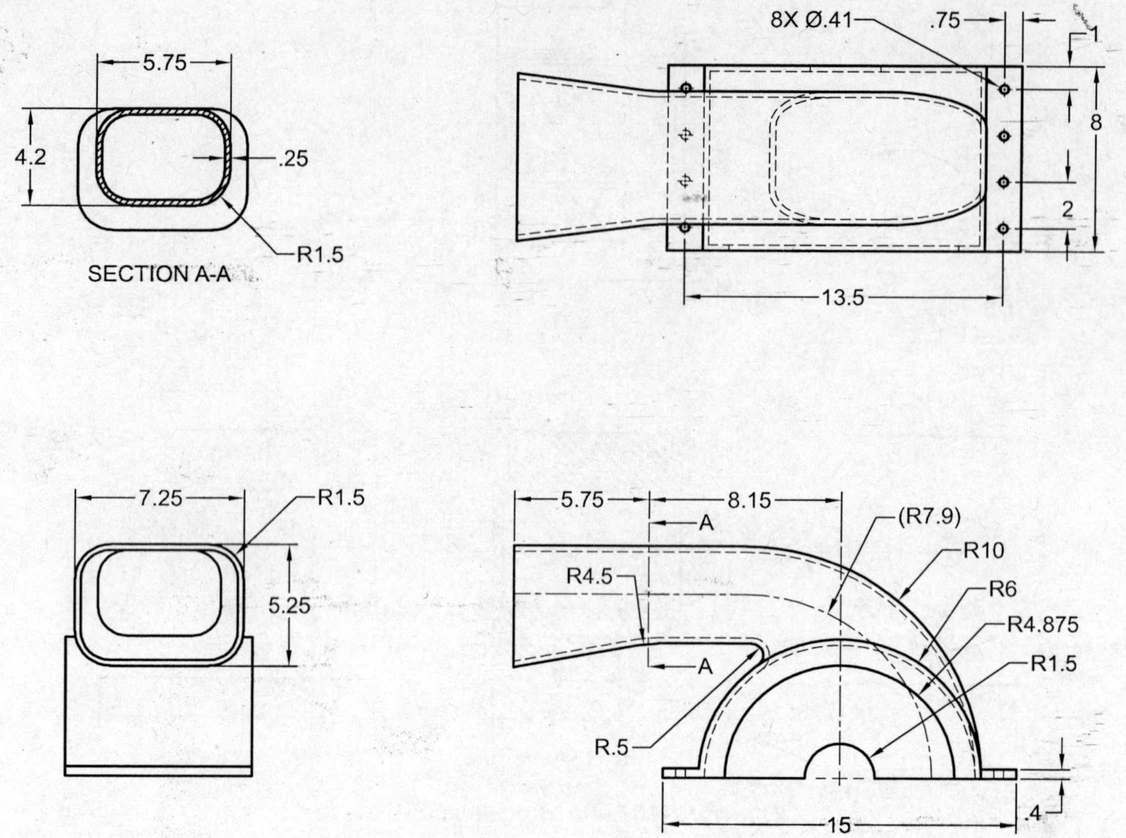

Figure 12-102 Dimensions of the Upper Housing

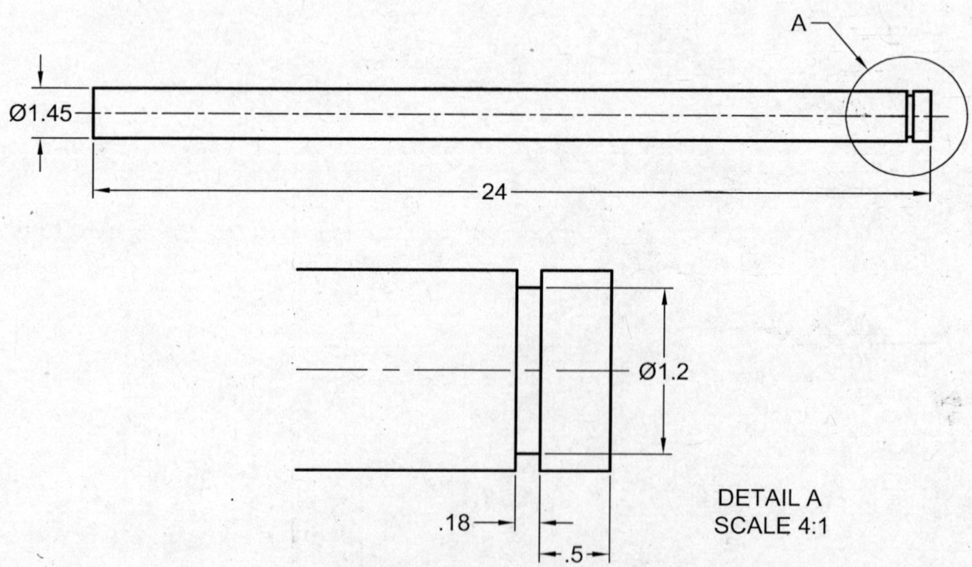

Figure 12-103 Dimensions of the Motorshaft

Exercise 3

Create all the components of the Anti Vibration Mount assembly and assemble them. Its assembly is shown in Figure 12-104. The views and dimensions of various components of this assembly are given in Figures 12-105 through 12-110. Note that all dimensions are in mm.

(Expected time: 1 hr)

Figure 12-104 *Anti Vibration Mount*

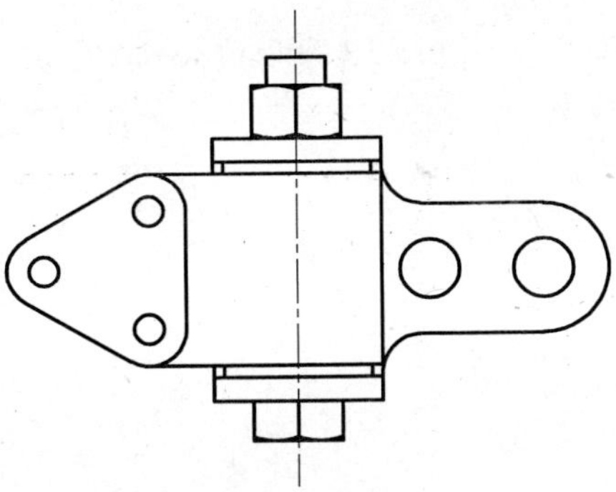

ITEM NO.	PART NO.	DESCRIPTION	QTY.
1	Yoke Plate		1
2	Body		1
3	Bushing Rubber		2
4	Hex Bolt		1
5	Nut		1

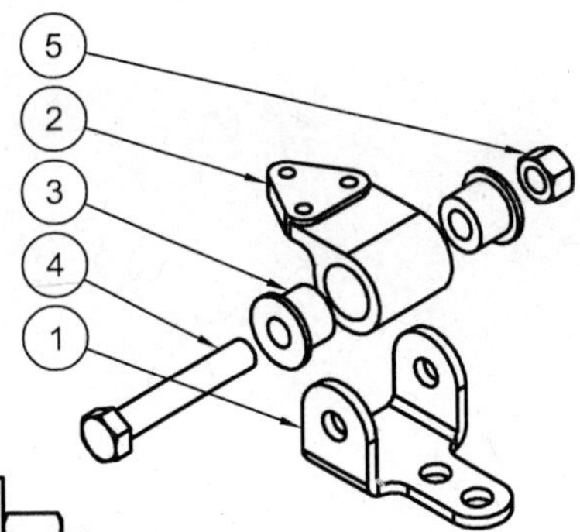

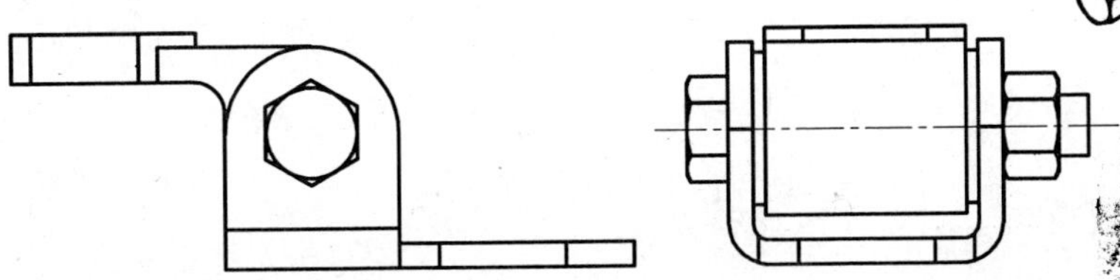

Figure 12-105 *Anti Vibration Mount*

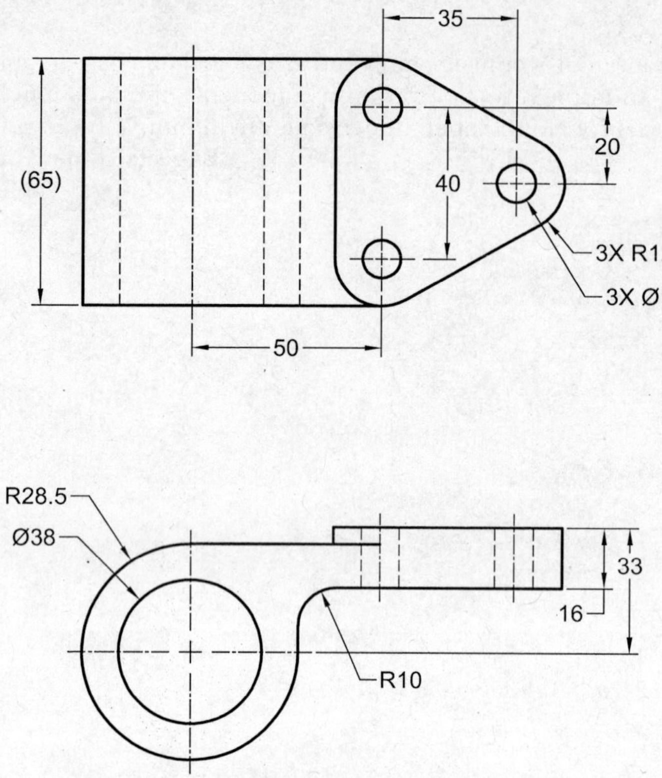

Figure 12-106 *Top and front views of Body*

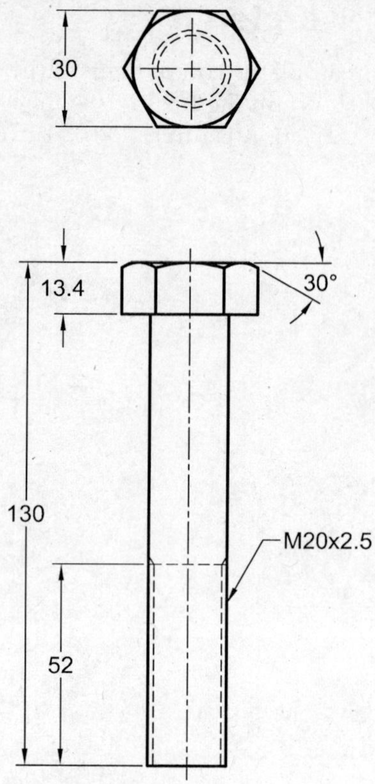

Figure 12-107 *Top and front views of Hex Bolt*

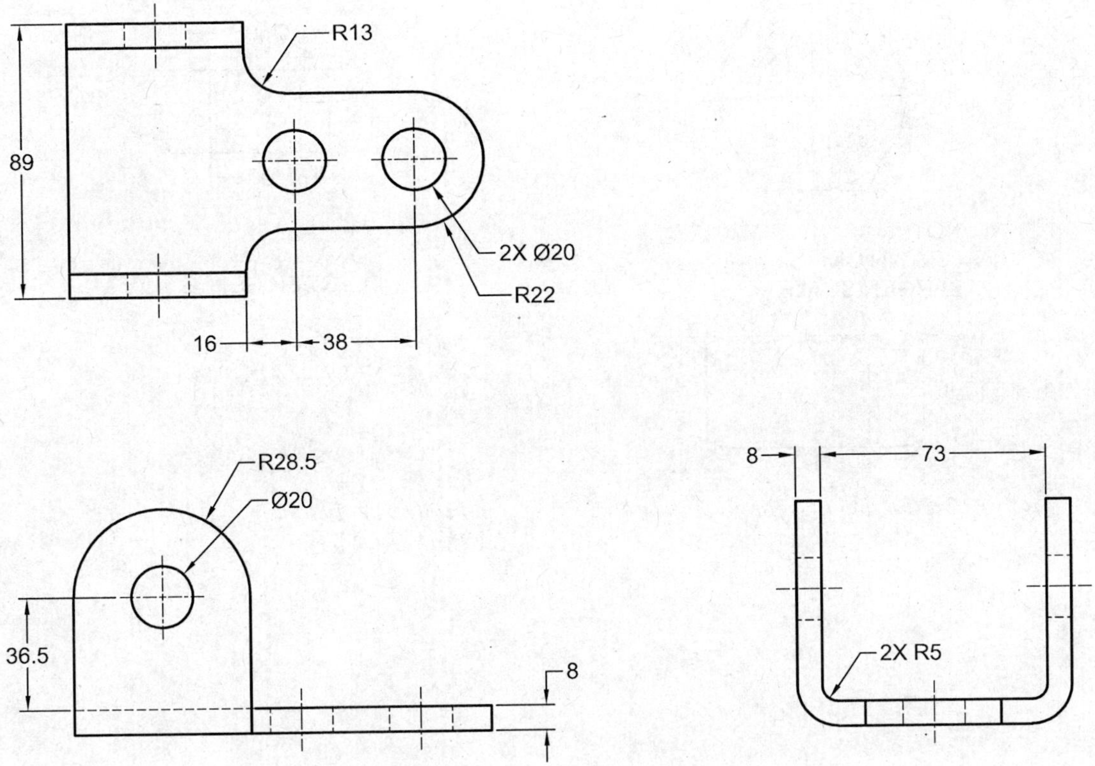

Figure 12-108 Top, front, and side views of Yoke plate

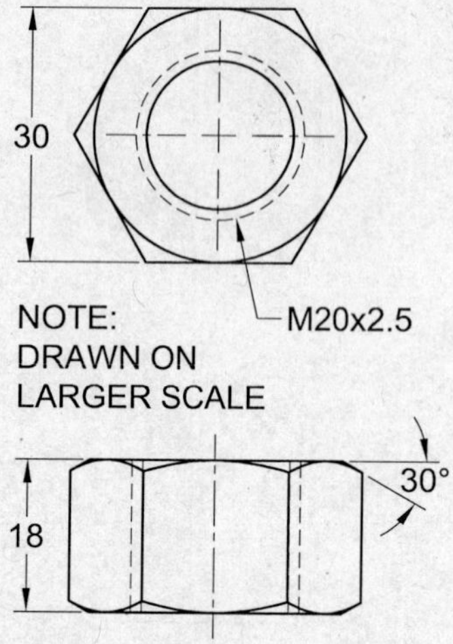

Figure 12-109 Top and front views of Nut

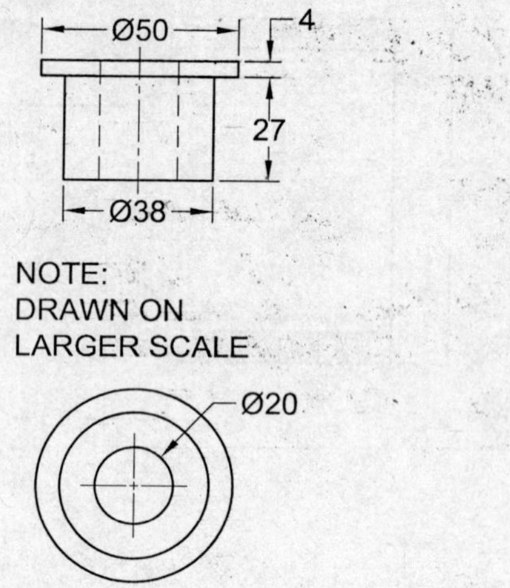

Figure 12-110 Top and front views of Bushing Rubber

Answers to Self-Evaluation Test

1. Rotate Component, **2.** By Delta XYZ, **3.** Coincident, **4.** Along Entity, **5.** T, **6.** T, **7.** T, **8.** T, **9.** F, **10.** T

Chapter 13

Assembly Modeling-II

Learning Objectives

After completing this chapter, you will be able to:

- *Apply advanced mates*
- *Create subassemblies*
- *Delete components and subassemblies*
- *Edit assembly mates*
- *Edit components and subassemblies*
- *Replace components in assemblies*
- *Create the patterns of components in an assembly*
- *Create mirrored components*
- *Hide and suppress components in assemblies*
- *Change the transparency condition of an assembly*
- *Check the interference in an assembly*
- *Create assemblies for a mechanism*
- *Detect collision while the assembly is in motion*
- *Create the exploded state of an assembly*

ADVANCED ASSEMBLY MATES

In the previous chapter, you learned to place the components in an assembly document and also to apply the assembly mates to them. On applying all possible mates to the components, they will be fully defined and they cannot be moved. But in actual practice, you may need to create assemblies in which some of the parts such as gears, pulleys, and so on need to be moved. In SOLIDWORKS, this can be achieved by applying advanced mates. In this chapter, you will learn to apply the advanced mates such as Profile Center, Symmetric, Width, Path Mate, Distance, and Angle to components. These mates are available in the **Mate Types** rollout in the **Advanced** tab, refer to Figure 13-1, of the **Mate PropertyManager** and are discussed next.

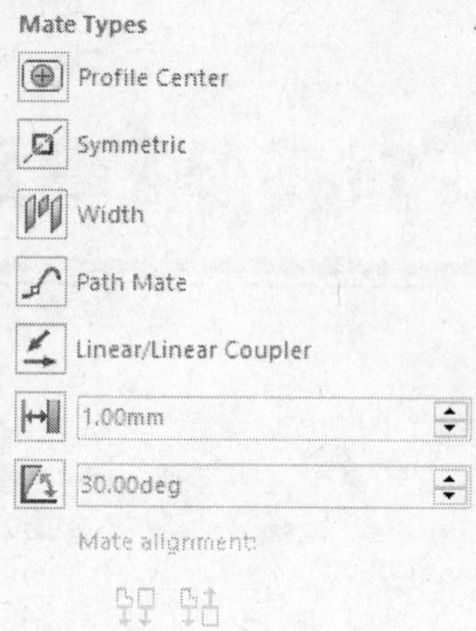

Figure 13-1 *The **Mate Types** rollout*

Applying the Profile Center Mate

The Profile Center mate is used to automatically center align the components having profiles such as rectangles, squares, and circles. To apply this mate, choose the **Profile Center** button from the **Mate Types** rollout in the **Advanced** tab and then select the entities to mate, as shown in Figure 13-2; both the components will automatically align to the common center of the components, as shown in Figure 13-3. Also, name of the selected entities will be displayed in the **Entities to Mate** selection box. If you want to maintain a gap between the mating faces, specify the offset value in the **Offset Distance** spinner available in the **Mate Types** rollout. Also, you can lock the rotational movement of the components by selecting the **Lock rotation** check box available in the **Mate Types** rollout. Choose the **OK** button from the **ProfileCenter PropertyManager**; the Profile Center mate will be applied.

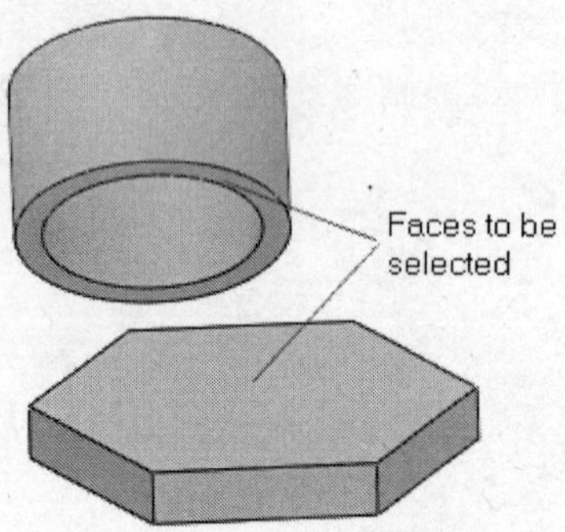

Figure 13-2 *Faces to be selected for applying the Profile Center mate*

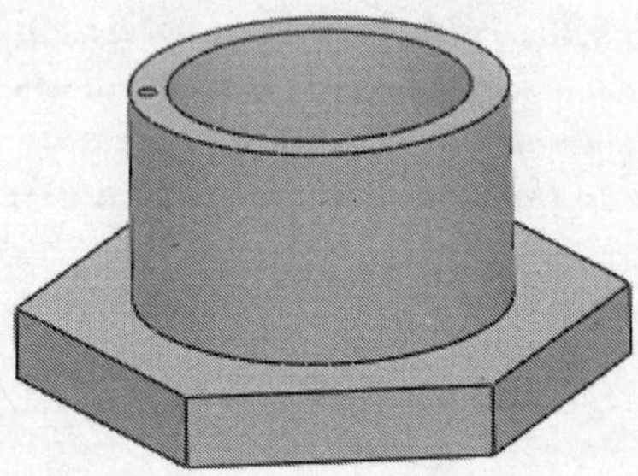

Figure 13-3 *Preview of the assembly with the Profile Centre mate applied*

Note

*The **Lock rotation** check box will be available only when at least one of the mating components is cylindrical.*

Applying the Symmetric Mate

The Symmetric mate is applied to create a symmetric relation between two components. To apply this mate, choose the **Symmetric** button from the **Mate Types** rollout; the **Symmetry Plane** selection box will be displayed in the **Mate Selections** rollout. Select a plane or a planar face that will act as the symmetry plane; the **Symmetry Plane** callout will be attached to the selected plane. Next, you need to select two similar entities from the two components to which you need to apply the Symmetric mate. The two similar entities can be two edges, two vertices, two planar faces, and so on. As soon as the symmetry plane is selected, the **Entities to Mate** selection box will be activated. Select the entities, as shown in Figure 13-4. Choose the **OK** button from the **Mate PropertyManager**; the Symmetric mate will be applied, as shown in Figure 13-5. After applying the Symmetric mate, if you modify the location of one component, the other will also be relocated accordingly.

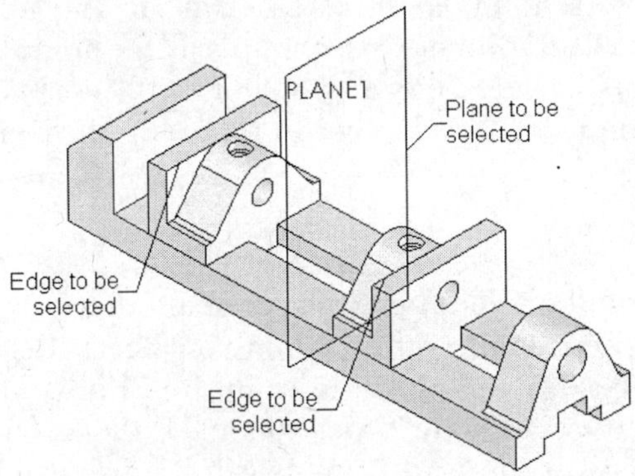

Figure 13-4 Entities and the plane to be selected to apply the Symmetric mate

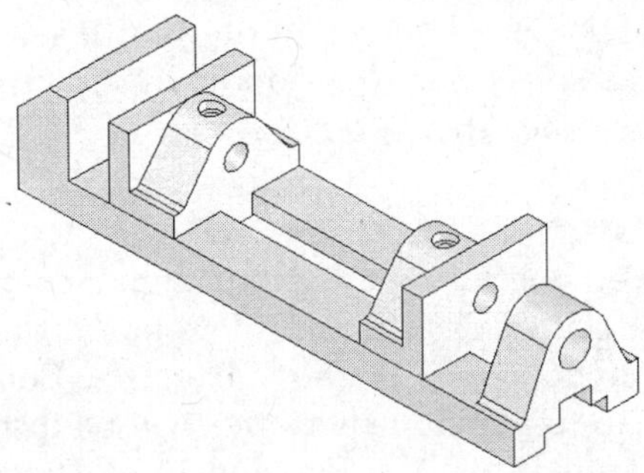

Figure 13-5 Assembly after applying the Symmetric mate

Applying the Width Mate

The Width mate is used to align a component between the two faces of another component. The faces between which you want to align another component should be planar faces. However, the component to be aligned may contain a nonplanar face. To apply this mate, choose the **Width** button from the **Mate Types** rollout in the **Mate PropertyManager**; the **Width selections** and **Tab selections** selection boxes will be displayed in the **Mate Selections** rollout. Also, the **Constraint** drop-down list with the **Centered** option selected by default will be displayed in the **Mate Types** rollout, as shown in Figure 13-6. The options in the **Constraint** drop-down list are used to define the type of Width mate to be applied to the components. These options are discussed next.

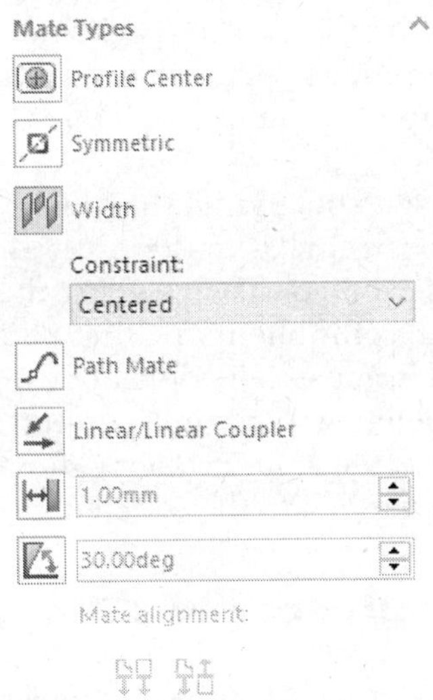

*Figure 13-6 The **Constraint** drop-down list with the **Centered** option selected*

Centered

The **Centered** option is used to align a component at an equal distance between the two faces of another component.

Free

The **Free** option is used to align a component between the two faces of another component and allows to move freely between the faces.

Dimension

The **Dimension** option is used to align a component between two faces of another component at a specified distance or angle. When you select the **Dimension** option from the **Constraint** drop-down list of the **Mate Types** rollout, the **Distance from the End** or **Percentage of Angle from the End** spinner and the **Flip dimension** check box will be displayed in the **Mate Types** rollout. If the mating faces are parallel then the **Distance from the End** spinner will be displayed and if the mating faces are at an angle then the **Percentage of Angle from the End** spinner will be displayed. The **Distance from the End** spinner is used to specify the distance between one of the faces specified in the **Width selections** selection box and another in the **Tab selections** selection box. The **Percentage of Angle from the End** spinner is used to specify the angle between one of the face assigned in the **Width selections** selection box and one of the faces specified in the **Tab selections** selection box. The **Flip dimension** check box is used to flip the dimension between the other two faces.

Percent

The **Percent** option is used to align a component between the two faces of another component at a specified distance or angle based on the percentage value. When you select this option, the **Percentage of Distance from the End** or **Percentage of Angle from the End** spinner and the **Flip dimension** check box will be displayed in the **Mate Types** rollout. If the mating faces are parallel then the **Percentage of Distance from the End** spinner will be displayed and if the mating faces are at an angle then the **Percentage of Angle from the End** spinner will be displayed. The **Percentage of Distance from the End** spinner is used to specify the percentage distance between one of the faces specified in the **Width selections** selection box and one of the faces specified in the **Tab selections** selection box. The **Percentage of Angle from the End** spinner is used to specify the percentage angle between one of the faces specified in the **Width selections** selection box and one of the faces specified in the **Tab selections** selection box. The **Flip dimension** check box is used to flip the dimension between the other two faces.

After specifying the desired constraint from the **Constraint** drop-down list and related options of the selected constraint, select the corresponding faces of the components in the **Width Reference** and **Tab Reference** selection boxes of the **Mate Selections** rollout, as shown in Figure 13-7. Choose the **OK** button from the **Mate PropertyManager**; the Width mate will be applied to the selected faces.

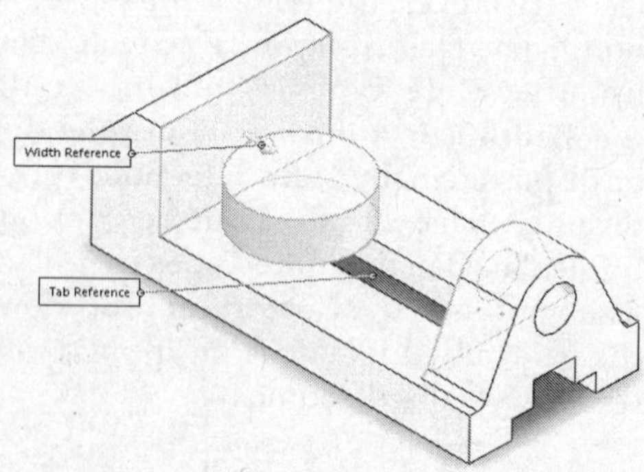

***Figure 13-7** Selecting the faces for the width and tab references*

Applying the Path Mate

The Path Mate is used to apply a mate such that the part moves along a path. To apply this mate, choose the **Path Mate** button in the **Mate Types** rollout of the **Advanced** tab; the **Path Constraint**, **Pitch/Yaw Control**, and **Roll Control** drop-down lists will be displayed in the **Mate Types** rollout. In addition, the **Components Vertex** and **Path Selection** selection boxes will be displayed in the **Mate Selections** rollout with the **Components Vertex** selected by default. Select the vertex of the component that travels along the path. After the vertex is defined, the **Path Selection** selection box becomes active. Select the contiguous curves, edges, or sketch entities as path. The **SelectionManager** button available in the **Mate Selections** rollout is used to facilitate the selection. Select the required options from the **Path Constraint**, **Pitch/Yaw Control**, and **Roll Control** drop-down lists in the **Mate Types** rollout and then choose the **OK** button. The options in these drop-down lists are discussed next.

Path Constraint Drop-down List

The options in the **Path Constraint** drop-down list are discussed next.

Free

This option allows you to drag the component freely along the selected path.

Distance Along Path

This option is used to constrain the vertex of the component that travels along the path to a specified distance. Specify the distance using the **Distance from the End** spinner available below this drop-down list.

Percent Along Path

This option is used to constrain the vertex of the component that travels along the path to a specified distance. The distance is specified as a percentage along the path. Specify the percentage using the **Percentage of Distance from the End** spinner available below this drop-down list.

Pitch/Yaw Control Drop-down List

The options in the **Pitch/Yaw Control** drop-down list are discussed next.

Free

On selecting this option, the Pitch/Yaw of the component that travels along the path will not be constrained.

Follow Path

This option allows one of the axes of the component to be tangent along the path.

Roll Control Drop-down List

The options in this drop-down list are discussed next.

Free

On selecting this option, the roll of the component that travels along the path will not be constrained.

Up Vector

This option allows you to constrain one of the axes of the component to align with the vector. You can select the linear edge or planar face to define the vector.

Applying the Distance Mate

The Distance mate is used to create a to and fro motion between components. To apply this mate, choose the **Distance** button from the **Mate Types** rollout; the **Distance**, **Maximum Value**, and **Minimum Value** spinners will be displayed. Select the two faces between which you need to apply the **Distance** mate. The maximum distance by which the two selected faces can be moved apart is specified in the **Distance** spinner; this value will be displayed in both the **Maximum Value** and **Minimum Value** spinners. However, if you want the selected faces to be moved in a to and fro motion, specify the minimum distance in the **Minimum Value** spinner. Choose the **OK** button twice. On moving one of the components, you will notice that it can be moved to and fro between the specified distance.

Applying the Angle Mate

The Angle mate is applied to create a swinging motion between components. To apply this mate, choose the **Angle** button from the **Mate Types** rollout; the **Angle**, **Maximum Value**, and **Minimum Value** spinners will be displayed. Select the two faces between which you need to apply the **Angle** mate. The maximum angle by which one of the selected faces has to be moved will be specified in the **Angle** spinner. This value will be displayed in both the **Maximum Value** and **Minimum Value** spinners. The minimum angle between the selected faces is specified in the **Minimum Value** spinner. Choose the **OK** button twice. Now, if you move the floating component, it will swing.

Applying the Linear/Linear Coupler Mate

The Linear/Linear Coupler mate is applied to create linear motion between components. To apply this mate, choose the **Linear/Linear Coupler** button from the **Mate Types** rollout; the **Entity to Mate**, **Reference Component for Mate Entity1**, **Entity to Mate**, and **Reference Component for Mate Entity2** selection boxes will be enabled. Select faces or edges of components between which you need to apply this mate. Note that the selected faces or edges should be linear. Now specify ratio values in the **Ratio** area and choose the **OK** button twice; the linear mate is created between components. You will notice that on moving one component, the other moves linear to it.

MECHANICAL MATES

In SOLIDWORKS, the mates that are applied to create mechanical drives and joints are grouped in the **Mechanical Mates** tab. These mates are discussed next.

Applying the Cam Mate

This mate is used to establish Cam follower relation between two components. You can add a Cam mate between a face formed by closed and continuous extruded faces from a single profile and a face of the follower. The face of the follower could be cylindrical, planar, or a vertex. To apply the Cam mate, you need to select a chain of continuous tangent faces that will act as a surface of the Cam. Next, select a curved face, a planar face, or a vertex from the follower that will remain in contact with the selected chain of tangent faces. To apply the Cam mate, expand the **Mate Type** rollout in the **Mate PropertyManager** if it is not expanded. Next, choose the **Cam** button from this rollout; the **Cam Path** and **Cam Follower** selection boxes will be displayed in the **Mate Selections** rollout. Select the chain of continuous faces that will act as the Cam path; the selected faces will be highlighted and displayed in the **Cam Path** selection box. As soon as the Cam path is defined, the **Cam Follower** selection box is selected. Select the face from the second component that will act as the surface of the follower; the **Cam Follower** callout will be attached to the selected face. Remember that the follower will touch the surface of the Cam. Choose the **OK** button twice. On rotating the Cam, you will observe that the follower is moving in the linear motion following the Cam surface. Figure 13-8 shows the faces to be selected and Figure 13-9 shows preview of the assembly after applying the Cam mate.

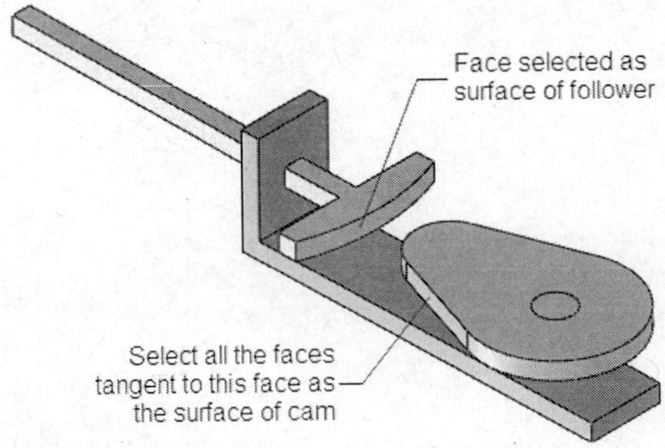

Figure 13-8 Faces selected to apply the Cam mate

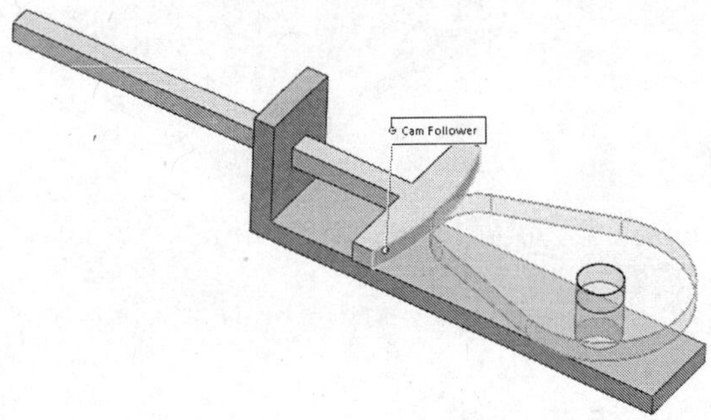

Figure 13-9 Preview of the assembly after applying the Cam mate

Note

For a better understanding of this mate, make sure that the front faces of the Cam and follower are coplanar. Also,ensure that proper degree of freedom is applied to components of Cam and follower assembly.

Applying the Slot Mate

This mate is used to establish a slot follower relation between two components such as bolt having cylindrical face and a component having slot feature. Note that after applying the slot mate, the component having cylindrical feature will be constrained within the boundary of the slot feature of the other component. To apply the **Slot** mate, expand the **Mate Type** rollout in the **Mate PropertyManager** if it is not expanded. Choose the **Slot** button from this rollout; the **Entities to Mate** selection box and the **Constraint** drop-down list will be displayed in the **Mate Selections** rollout. The **Free** option is selected by default in the **Constraint** drop-down list. Select a slot face and then select an axis, cylindrical face or another slot face to apply the **Slot** mate. You can constrain the position of the entity in the slot by using the options available in the **Constraint** drop-down list. Choose the **OK** button to apply the mate. Figure 13-10 shows the faces to be selected and Figure 13-11 shows preview of the assembly after applying the Slot mate. In this mate, the cylindrical component is free to move in the slot. The remaining options in the **Constraint** drop-down list are discussed next.

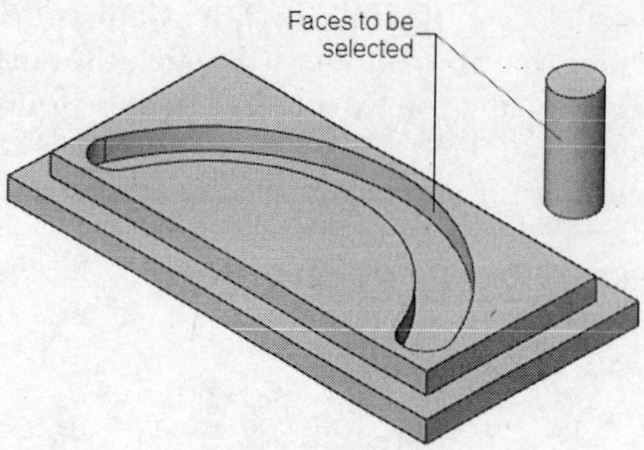

***Figure 13-10** Faces selected to apply the Slot mate*

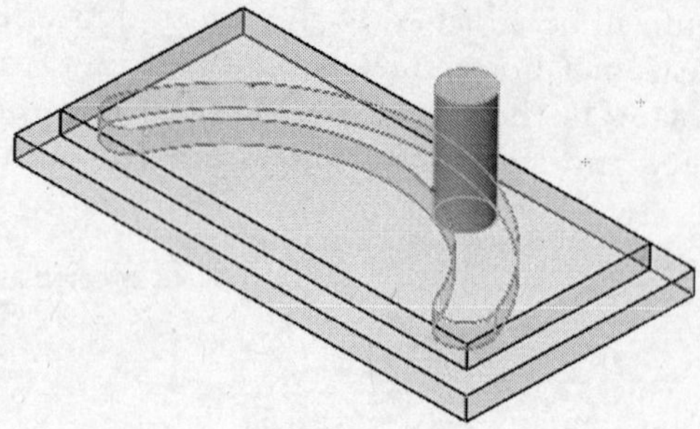

***Figure 13-11** Preview of the assembly with the Slot mate*

Center in Slot

If you select the **Center in Slot** option from the **Constraint** drop-down list, the cylindrical component will get fixed at the center of the slot.

Distance Along Slot

The **Distance Along Slot** option is used to align the cylindrical component by specifying distance in the **Distance from the End** spinner of the **Mate Type** rollout.

Percent Along Slot

The **Percent Along Slot** option works similar to the **Distance Along Slot** option. However, the distance in this case is specified as the percentage of the slot distance in the **Percentage of Distance from the End** spinner of the **Mate Type** rollout.

Applying the Hinge Mate

The Hinge mate is applied to create a swinging motion between two parts about an axis. To apply this mate between two components, expand the **Mate Type** rollout in the **Mate PropertyManager** if it is not expanded and choose the **Hinge** button from this rollout; two selection boxes will be displayed in the **Mate Selections** rollout, **Concentric Selections** and **Coincident Selections**. The **Concentric Selections** selection box is selected by default. Next, select the two circular faces that are to be concentric, as shown in Figure 13-12; the names of the selected faces will be displayed in the **Concentric Selections** selection box. Also, the **Coincident Selections** selection box will get selected. Now, select the planar faces on which you need to apply the coincident relation, as shown in Figure 13-13. The names of the selected faces will be displayed in the **Coincident Selections** selection box. If you need to swing the selected components within a specific angle, then select the **Specify angle limits** check box; the **Angle**, **Maximum Value**, and **Minimum Value** spinners with the **Angle Selections** selection box will be displayed in the **Mate Selections** rollout.

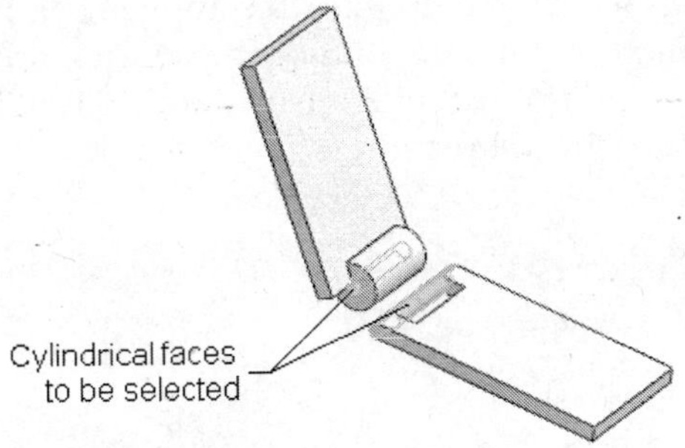

Figure 13-12 Faces to be selected to apply the Concentric relation

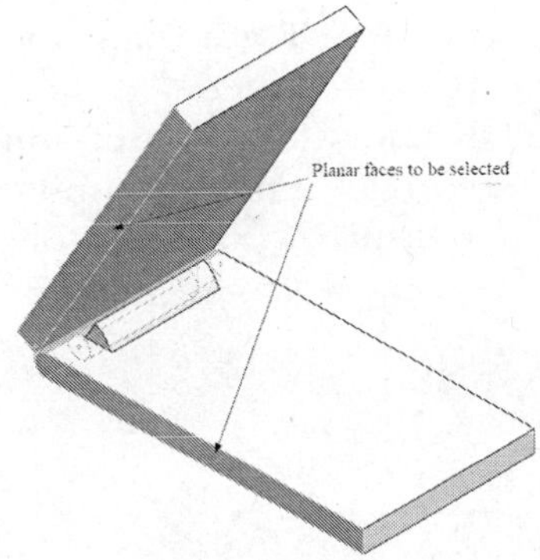

Figure 13-13 Faces to be selected to apply the Coincident relation

Select the two planar faces that can be rotated, as shown in Figure 13-14. Set the maximum and minimum angular limits in the corresponding spinners. The maximum angle by which the two selected faces can be rotated apart is specified in the **Angle** spinner and this value will be displayed in the **Maximum Value** spinner. The minimum angle between the selected faces is specified in the **Minimum Value** spinner. Choose the **OK** button twice. Figure 13-15 shows the resulting assembly after applying the Hinge mate. Now, if you drag the floating component, it will swing about the rotation axis.

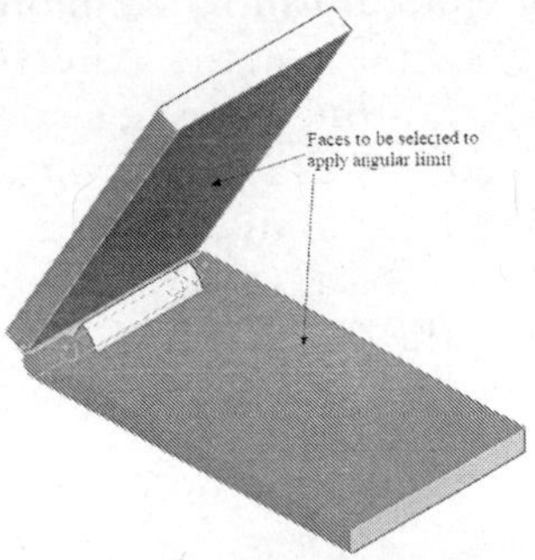

Figure 13-14 Faces to be selected to apply the angular rotation

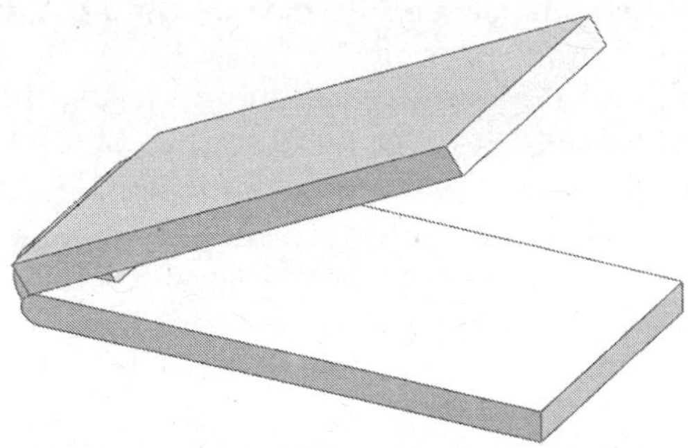

Figure 13-15 The resultant assembly after applying the Hinge mate

Applying the Gear Mate

The Gear mate allows you to rotate two components such as gears with respect to each other about a selected axis. You can also define a specific gear ratio between the selected components. To apply this mate between two components, expand the **Mate Type** rollout in the **Mate PropertyManager** if it is not expanded. Choose the **Gear** button from the **Mate Type** rollout; the **Ratio** edit boxes and the **Reverse** check box will be displayed. You need to select the references about which the two components will be rotated. These references can be cylindrical faces, conical faces, axes, circular edges, or linear edges. Select the required references, as shown in Figure 13-16; the names of selected references will be displayed in the **Entities to Mate** selection box. The **Teeth/Diameter** callouts will also be attached to the selected references, as shown in Figure 13-17. You can set the ratio of rotation by using the **Ratio** edit boxes or by using the **Teeth/Diameter** callouts. The **Reverse** check box is selected to change the direction of rotation of one component with respect to the other. After applying the mate, choose the **OK** button twice. After applying this mate, rotate any one of the components and you will observe that the other component rotates as per the specified gear ratio. Generally, this mate is used to display the rotation of gears in a particular direction.

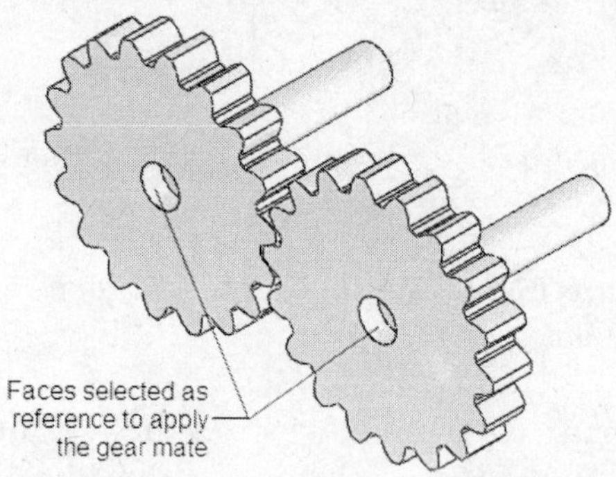

Figure 13-16 *Faces to be selected to apply the Gear mate*

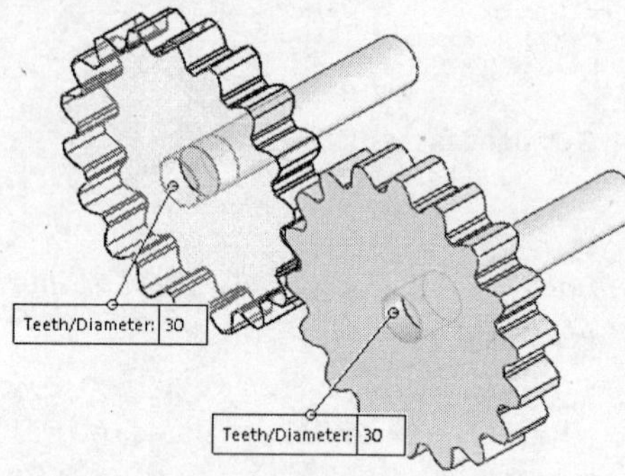

Figure 13-17 *The* ***Teeth/Diameter*** *callouts attached to the selected faces*

Applying the Rack Pinion Mate

The Rack Pinion mate allows you to create a rack and pinion relationship between two components. As a result, the rack undergoes translation motion and the pinion undergoes rotational motion. To apply this mate, choose the **Rack Pinion** button in the **Mate Type** rollout; the **Rack** and **Pinion/Gear** selection boxes will be displayed in the **Mate Selections** rollout. Select the linear edge of the rack and then select the circular edge of the pinion; the Rack Pinion mate will be applied to the two components. Select the **Pinion pitch diameter** radio button if you need to specify the circumference of the pinion as the distance travelled by the rack. Select the **Rack travel/revolution** radio button if you need to specify the distance travelled by the rack in per revolution of the pinion. You can select the **Reverse** check box to change the direction of movement of the components relative to each other.

Applying the Screw Mate

The Screw mate allows you to create a mate for the threaded features. If you rotate the head of the male part after applying this mate, the male part will advance over the female part. To apply this mate, choose the **Screw** button from the **Mate Type** rollout; the **Entities to Mate** selection box in the **Mate Selections** rollout will be displayed. Also, two radio buttons will appear in the **Mate Type** rollout. Select the mating surfaces of male and female parts; the selected surfaces will be highlighted and added to the **Entities to Mate** selection box. Select the **Revolutions/mm** radio button, if you need to specify the number of revolutions required by the male part to advance 1 mm over the female part. Specify the number of revolutions in the edit box. Select the **Distance/revolution** radio button if you need to specify the distance by which the male part needs to advance in one revolution. Then, specify the distance to be advanced in the edit box and choose **OK** twice. By default, the left hand thread (counterclockwise direction) will be applied. Select the **Reverse** check box to change the direction of thread to the right hand thread.

Applying the Universal Joint Mate

The Universal Joint Mate allows you to create a mate for the shafts whose axes are nonlinear. This joint allows rotation of the input shaft about its axis which drives the output shaft to rotate about its axis. To apply this mate, choose the **Universal Joint** button from the **Mate Type** rollout; the **Entities to Mate** selection box and the **Define Joint point** check box will be displayed in the **Mate Selections** rollout. Now, select the two components and the joining point, and then choose the **OK** button twice. The mate is applied to the components, rotate any one of the shafts and you will observe that the other shaft rotates accordingly. This type of mate is generally used to display the rotation of automobiles axle shafts.

CREATING SUB-ASSEMBLIES

In the previous chapter, you learned to place the individual parts in the assembly document and apply the assembly mates to them to create an assembly. However, this method will not be effective if you create a large assembly like assembling a machine tool, car, and so on. In such cases, you need to create the assemblies of smaller units. These are known as sub-assemblies. Then, you need to assemble the parts and the subassemblies to create the main assembly. Different methods to create the subassemblies in the main assembly are discussed next.

Bottom-up Sub-assembly Design Approach

In the bottom-up sub-assembly design approach, the subassemblies are created separately and then saved as an individual assembly file. To place a sub-assembly in the main assembly, open the main assembly document and invoke the **Insert Component PropertyManager**; the **Open** dialog box will be displayed. Select **SOLIDWORKS Assembly (*.asm;*.sldasm)** from the **Files of type** drop-down list; all assemblies saved in the current location will be displayed. Select the required sub-assembly and choose the **Open** button from the **Open** dialog box. Click once in the drawing area to place the sub-assembly. Now, assemble the sub-assembly with the parts in the main assembly using the assembly mates. You can also place an assembly in the other assembly by using the drag and drop method that was discussed in the previous chapter. In this case, the assembly that was dragged and dropped will be a sub-assembly. Figure 13-18 shows the sub-assembly of a piston and an articulated rod. Figure 13-19 shows the main assembly of the piston and the master rod.

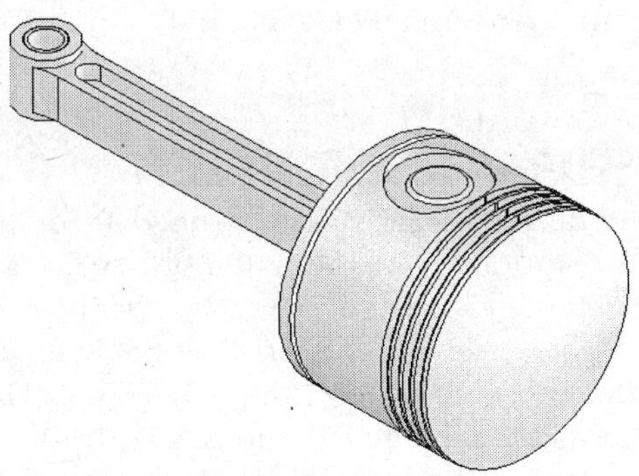

Figure 13-18 *The sub-assembly*

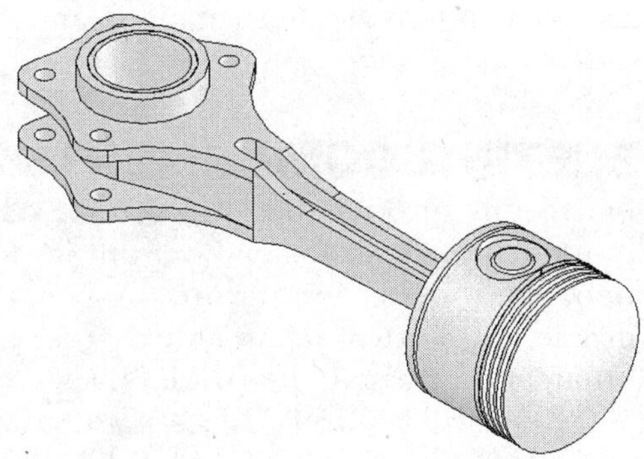

Figure 13-19 *The main assembly*

Top-down Sub-assembly Design Approach

The top-down sub-assembly design approach is the most flexible sub-assembly design approach. In this approach, you need to create a new sub-assembly in the main assembly document.

The approach is generally used in the conceptual design or while managing a large assembly. To create a new sub-assembly in the assembly document, choose the **New Assembly** button from the **Insert Components** flyout in the **Assembly CommandManager**; a new assembly node with the default name will be added to the **FeatureManager Design Tree**. Note that the new sub-assembly will be added as a virtual component. To open this sub-assembly, select it from the **FeatureManager Design Tree** and choose **Open Subassembly** from the pop-up toolbar; the sub-assembly document will be opened. Create the sub-assembly and switch to the main assembly. Press CTRL+TAB keys to cycle through the documents opened. Choose the **Save** button to save the assembly; the **Save Modified Documents** dialog box will be displayed stating that the models referenced in this document are modified and they will be saved when the document is saved. Choose the **Save All** button from this dialog box to save all components.

As the new sub-assembly is added as a virtual component, you need to save it in an internal or external file. As soon as you choose the **Save All** button from the **Save Modified Documents** dialog box; the **Save As** dialog box will be displayed. Select the required radio button from this dialog box to save the sub-assembly. You can also right-click on the name of the sub-assembly and choose the **Save Assembly (in External File)** option from the shortcut menu; the **Save As** dialog box will be displayed. Specify the path and choose the **OK** button. Alternatively, open the sub-assembly and choose the **Save As** button; the **SOLIDWORKS** message box will be displayed stating that this file is referenced in other documents as a virtual component. Choose the **OK** button from this message box; the **Save As** dialog box will be displayed. Specify the path and choose the **Save** button; the components will be saved as an external file.

Inserting a New Sub-assembly

You can also create a sub-assembly by grouping the parts in the existing assembly. To do so, select the components, right-click on a component in the **FeatureManager Design Tree**, and choose the **Form New Subassembly** option from the shortcut menu; a new sub-assembly node will be displayed in the **FeatureManager Design Tree**. You need to expand the shortcut menu, if the option is not displayed by default. You can also select a component and choose **Insert > Component > Assembly from [Selected] Components** from the SOLIDWORKS menus to insert a sub-assembly. Note that the new sub-assembly will be added as a virtual component. You need to invoke the shortcut menu and save the components in an external file as discussed in the previous topic.

DELETING COMPONENTS AND SUB-ASSEMBLIES

After creating an assembly, at a certain stage of your design cycle, you may need to delete a component or a sub-assembly from it. To delete a component of the assembly, select the component from the drawing area or from the **FeatureManager Design Tree**. Next, right-click to invoke the shortcut menu and choose the **Delete** option. You can also delete the selected component by pressing the DELETE key. When you delete a component, the **SOLIDWORKS** message box will be displayed stating that whether you want to delete the sub-assembly or the selected components only. Choose the required option from the message box; the **Confirm Delete** dialog box will be displayed. The name of the component and the items dependent on it will be displayed in this dialog box. Choose the **Yes** button from the **Confirm Delete** dialog box.

To delete a sub-assembly, select it from the **FeatureManager Design Tree** and press the DELETE key; the **Confirm Delete** dialog box will be displayed. Choose the **YES** button from it. Note that on deleting the sub-assembly, all the components of the sub-assembly are also deleted.

EDITING ASSEMBLY MATES

After creating the assembly or during the process of assembling the components, you may need to edit the assembly mates. The editing operations that can be performed include modifying the type of the assembly mate or angle and offset values, changing the component to which the mate was applied, and so on. To edit the mates in an assembly, you first need to expand the **Mates** node at the end of the **FeatureManager Design Tree**. Next, select the mate that you need to modify; a pop-up toolbar will be displayed. Choose the **Edit Feature** option from the pop-up toolbar; the respective **Mate PropertyManager** will be displayed with the **Standard** tab chosen. The name of the **Mate PropertyManager** will depend on the name and sequence of the mate applied. Figure 13-20 shows partial view of the **Mate PropertyManager** to edit the **Concentric** mate. You can edit the entities to mate, type of mate, value of offset, value of angle, and so on by using this PropertyManager.

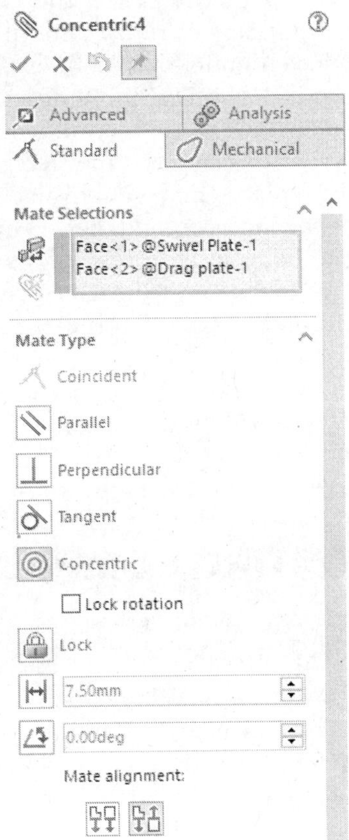

*Figure 13-20 Partial view of the **Mate PropertyManager** to edit the **Concentric** mate*

Note that to edit the mates in a sub-assembly, expand the **Mates** sub-assembly node, choose the mate to be changed, and select the **Edit Feature** option from the pop-up toolbar that will be displayed; the corresponding **Mate PropertyManager** will be displayed. Choose the **OK** button after editing the mate and then choose the **OK** button to close the **Mate PropertyManager**.

> **Tip**
> *When you move the cursor on a mate in the **FeatureManager Design Tree**, the edges of the entities used in the mate will be highlighted in the drawing area. On selecting the mate from the **FeatureManager Design Tree**, the surfaces of the entities used in the selected mate will be highlighted in the drawing area.*

Replacing Mated Entities

As discussed, you can edit the mate entities by using the **Mate PropertyManager**. They can also be modified by using the **Mated Entities PropertyManager**. Expand the **Mates** node from the **FeatureManager Design Tree**, select any mate and right-click to invoke the shortcut menu. Choose the **Replace Mate Entities** option from it; the **Mated Entities PropertyManager** will be displayed, as shown in Figure 13-21. Also, you will be prompted to select the entity to be replaced. Select the entity from the **Mate Entities** selection box. You can also expand the entity tree to edit an individual mate. On selecting a mate, its corresponding face will be highlighted in the drawing area and its name will be displayed in the **Replacement Mate Entity** selection box. Also, you will be prompted to select the entity to be replaced. Select the entity that will replace the previously selected entity. If the selected entity over-defines the mate or if the mating is not possible between the entities, the **SOLIDWORKS** message box will be displayed, informing about the possible cause of error. You can select the **Defer update** check box to update all the replaced mates after you exit the PropertyManager instead of solving it immediately. This will save some time, if many mates are to be replaced. The **Show all mates** check box is used to display all the mated entities. The **Flip Mate Alignment** button is used to flip the direction of the mate.

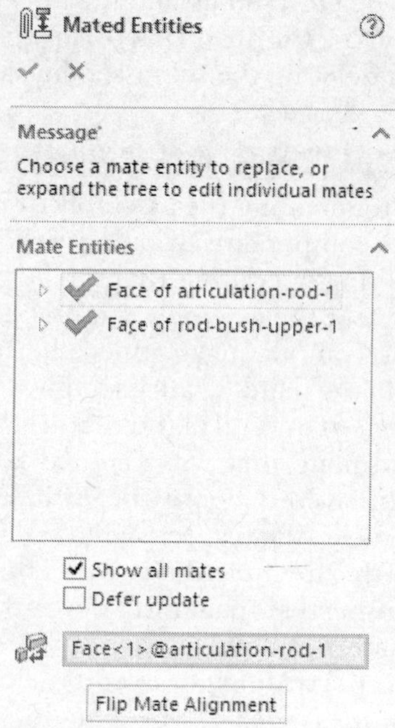

***Figure 13-21** The Mated Entities PropertyManager*

In SOLIDWORKS, on invoking the **Mated Entities PropertyManager**, a pop-up toolbar consisting of missing entities is displayed. You can use the options in this toolbar to cycle through the components.

EDITING COMPONENTS

CommandManager:	Assembly > Edit Component
Toolbar:	Assembly > Edit Component *(Customize to add)*

At some stage of your design cycle, you may need to edit the components after placing and mating them in the assembly document. This may include editing the features, sketches, and sketch planes. To edit the components, you first need to select the component and invoke the part modeling environment in the assembly document. To do so, select the component from the drawing area or from the **FeatureManager Design Tree** and choose the **Edit Component** button from the **Assembly CommandManager** or choose the **Edit Part** option from the pop-up toolbar. The part modeling environment will be invoked and the entire assembly, except the component to be edited, will become transparent. If not, choose the **Assembly Transparency** button in the **Features CommandManager**; a flyout will be invoked and the options in it can be used to set the transparency of the assembly. On choosing the **Opaque** option, all components of the assembly will be set to opaque. The **Maintain Transparency** option retains the default transparency settings of the individual components. If the **Force Transparency** option is chosen, all components of the assembly except the component being edited will be set as transparent.

Tip

*Select the **Mates** node from the **FeatureManager Design Tree** and right-click to invoke the shortcut menu. Choose the **Parent/Child** option from the shortcut menu; the **Parent/Child Relationships** dialog box will be displayed. You can display the child and parent relationships of any component placed in the assembly using the **Parent/Child Relationships** dialog box.*

The name of the component to be edited will be displayed in blue in the **FeatureManager Design Tree**. Left-click on the (▸) sign to expand the component node, select the feature to be edited and invoke the respective PropertyManager. If required, you can also add new features to the component. This type of editing is technically termed as Editing in the Context of Assembly. After editing the component, again choose the **Edit Component** button from the **Features CommandManager** to return to the assembly environment.

Tip

You can also modify the dimensions of an assembled component or those placed in the assembly by double-clicking on the desired feature in the graphics area of that component. All dimensions of that feature will be displayed in the graphics area. Invoke the ***Modify*** *dialog box by double-clicking on the dimension to be modified. Enter the new dimension in the* ***Modify*** *dialog box and press the ENTER key; the dimension will be modified, but the geometry of the feature will not be changed. You need to rebuild the assembly to reflect the modifications. To do so, choose the* ***Rebuild*** *button from the Menu Bar or use the CTRL+B keys.*

While editing the part in the assembly document, you can use the ***Instant3D*** *tool to edit the features dynamically.*

Note

To edit the components separately in their part documents, select the component, and then choose the ***Open Part*** *option from the pop-up toolbar; the part document of the selected component will be opened. You can edit the component individually in the part document. After editing, save the part, close the part document and return to the assembly document; the* ***SOLIDWORKS (Automatically dismissing in 10 seconds)*** *message box will be displayed, stating that the models contained within the assembly have changed. It will further prompt you to specify whether you would like to rebuild the assembly. Choose the* ***Yes*** *button from this message box.*

EDITING SUB-ASSEMBLIES

CommandManager:	Assembly > Edit Component	
Toolbar:	Assembly > Edit Component	*(Customize to add)*

To edit sub-assemblies, select them from the **FeatureManager Design Tree** and choose the **Edit Component** button from the **Assembly CommandManager**. You can add components to a sub-assembly, modify the mates, and replace the components while they are in the editing mode. After editing the sub-assembly, choose the **Edit Component** button again to exit the editing mode.

Note

To edit a component of the sub-assembly, select the component from the drawing area, invoke the pop-up toolbar, and choose the ***Edit Part*** *option; the part editing mode will be invoked in the assembly document.*

You need to expand the desired sub-assembly from the ***FeatureManager Design Tree*** *to select its components. All the components assembled in that sub-assembly will be displayed once the sub-assembly is expanded.*

DISSOLVING SUB-ASSEMBLIES

Dissolving the sub-assembly means the components of the selected sub-assembly will become the components of the next higher level sub-assembly. When you dissolve a sub-assembly, the sub-assembly will disappear from the **FeatureManager Design Tree** and the components of that sub-assembly will become the components of the next higher level sub-assembly. To dissolve a sub-assembly, select it from the **FeatureManager Design Tree**. Invoke the shortcut menu and choose the **Dissolve Subassembly** option from it; the sub-assembly will be removed from the **FeatureManager Design Tree** and its components will be displayed as the components of an assembly or a sub-assembly in the **FeatureManager Design Tree**.

REPLACING COMPONENTS

Sometimes in the assembly design cycle, you may need to replace a component of the assembly with some other component. To replace a component, select the component to be replaced, invoke the shortcut menu, expand the shortcut menu, if required, and then choose the **Replace Components** option; the **Replace PropertyManager** will be displayed. You can also invoke this PropertyManager by choosing the **Replace Components** button from the **Assembly CommandManager** after customizing it.

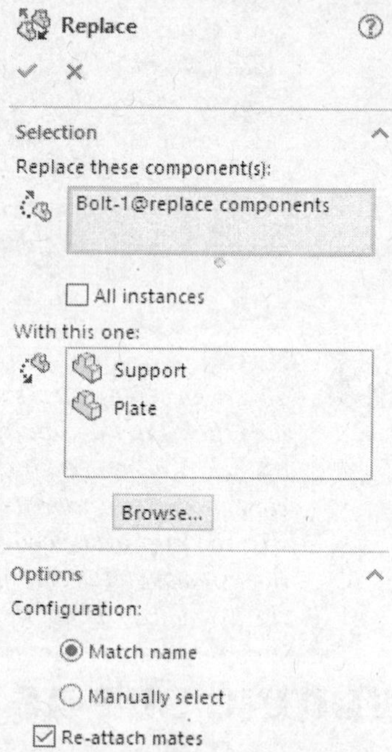

Figure 13-22 The ***Replace PropertyManager***

On invoking the **Replace PropertyManager**, you will be prompted to select the components to be replaced. Select the component; the name of the selected component will be displayed in the **Components to be Replaced** selection box. If any component is opened in another window, the name of that component will be displayed in the **Replacement Component** selection box in the **With this one** area, refer to Figure 13-22. If the replacement component is listed in the **Replacement Component** selection box, select it or choose the **Browse** button and select the part. Figure 13-23 shows the assembly in which the bolt has to be replaced by a pin.

The **All instances** check box available in the **Selection** rollout is used to replace all the instances of the selected component. The options in the **Configuration** area of the **Options** rollout are used to define the selection procedure of the configurations. You will learn more about configurations in the later chapters.

The **Re-attach mates** check box in the **Options** rollout is selected by default. On choosing the **OK** button, the component will be replaced and the mates will be displayed in the **Mated Entities PropertyManager**. Choose **OK** to accept the new mates. However, if the new mates are not re-attached automatically in the software, then on choosing the **OK** button from the **Replace PropertyManager**, following options will be displayed: the **What's Wrong** dialog box, the **Mated Entities PropertyManager**, preview of the replacement entity, and a pop-up toolbar will be displayed, refer to Figure 13-23. Choose the **Disable Preview** button from the **Mated Entities PropertyManager** to close the preview of the replacement entity. Select the entity from the **Mate Entities** selection box. Next, select appropriate feature in the replacement component so that the new mate is validated. If the selection of feature is correct, a green colored tick mark will appear.

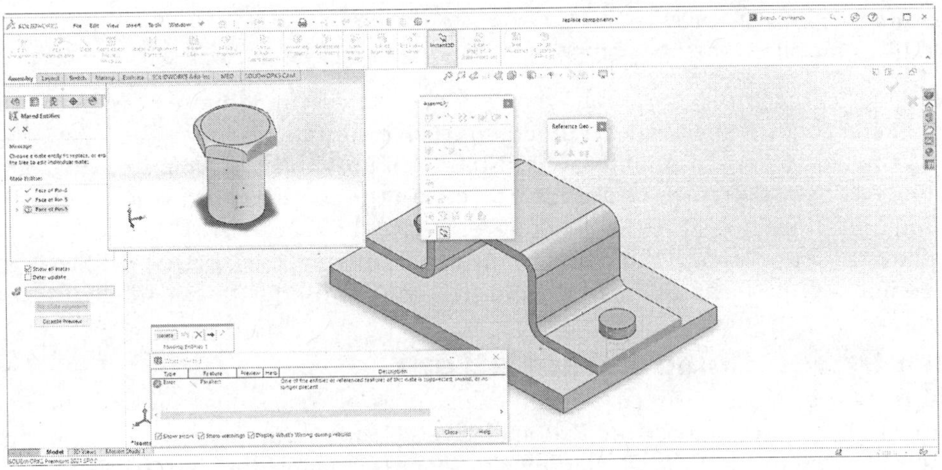

Figure 13-23 *The assembly in which the bolt has to be replaced by a pin*

Similarly, edit all the missing mates and choose the **OK** button. Figure 13-24 shows the isometric view of the assembly after the bolts are replaced by pins.

If the **Re-attach mates** check box is cleared, the **What's Wrong** dialog box will be displayed. However, the **Mated Entities PropertyManager** will not be displayed after you choose the **OK** button in the **Replace PropertyManager**. This dialog box displays the name of the mates that contain errors. You need to redefine the mates. To do so, expand the **Mates** node from the **FeatureManager Design Tree**. Select the mate that has an error symbol on the left; a pop-up toolbar will be displayed. Next, choose the **Edit Feature** button from the pop-up toolbar; the **Mate PropertyManager** of the corresponding mate will be displayed and you can edit the mate entities.

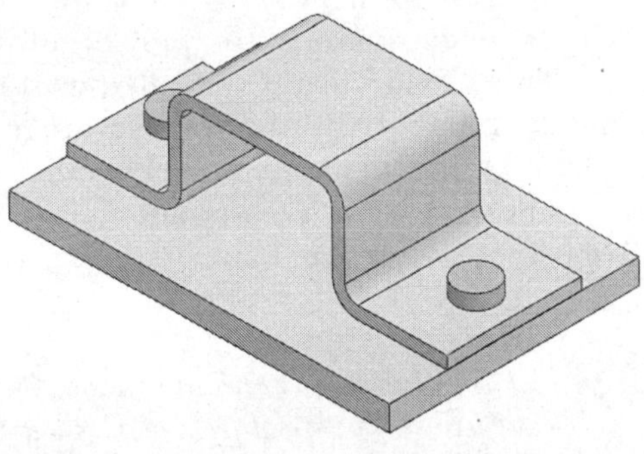

Figure 13-24 *Bolts replaced by pins in the assembly*

Tip

*The exclamation symbol displayed on the **Mates** option in the **FeatureManager Design Tree** indicates that the mates have errors in them. You can find out the possible cause of those errors. To do so, expand the **Mates** node. Next, right-click on the mate that has an exclamation mark; a shortcut menu will be displayed. Choose the **What's Wrong?** option; the **What's Wrong** dialog box will be displayed showing the possible cause of error.*

*If you choose the **MateXpert** option from the shortcut menu, the **MateXpert PropertyManager** will be displayed. The **Diagnose** button in this PropertyManager is used to display the entities that caused errors in the mate. Right-click on the mate and choose the **Edit Mates** option from the shortcut menu to edit the mate that has errors.*

CREATING PATTERNS OF COMPONENTS IN AN ASSEMBLY

CommandManager: Assembly > Linear Component Pattern flyout
SOLIDWORKS menus: Insert > Component Pattern

While working on a complex assembly, you may need to assemble more than one instance of the component about a specified arrangement. For example, consider the case of a flange coupling where you have to assemble eight instances of nuts and bolts to fasten the coupling. If you assemble eight instances of the nuts and bolts with the couplings individually, it will be very tedious and time-consuming process. Therefore, to save the time, SOLIDWORKS has provided various pattern tools to create the patterns of the components. SOLIDWORKS has different types of component patterns. Some of the most commonly used patterns are discussed next.

Pattern Driven Component Pattern

This tool is used to create pattern using the instances of the pattern created on a part. To create this type of pattern, choose the **Pattern Driven Component Pattern** tool from the **Linear Component Pattern** flyout in the **Assembly CommandManager**; the **Pattern Driven Property Manager** will be displayed, as shown in Figure 13-25.

Select the components to be patterned from the drawing area; the name of the selected components will be listed in the **Components to Pattern** selection box. Click in the **Driving feature or component** selection box in the **Driving Feature or Component** rollout; the **Driving feature or component** selection box will be highlighted. Select a pattern feature that will drive the component pattern; the preview of the resulting pattern will be displayed in the drawing area. This driving feature is called as seed feature. If the driving feature is created using the **Hole Wizard** tool, the resulting feature may not align with the existing hole feature, as shown in Figure 13-26. Choose the **Select Seed Position** button and select the new seed feature to align the resulting feature, as shown in Figure 13-27. Choose the **OK** button from the **Pattern Driven PropertyManager**; the pattern will be created, as shown in Figure 13-28.

Note

*The **Alignment method** is available in the **Driving Feature or Component** rollout when you select a hole wizard feature as the driving feature. The **Align to holes** and **Align to seed** radio buttons are available under **Alignment method**. The **Align to holes** radio button is used to align instances to the hole wizard feature. This is the default align method for new pattern features. The **Align to seed** radio button is used to align instances to the seed instance. This is the default alignment method for existing pattern features.*

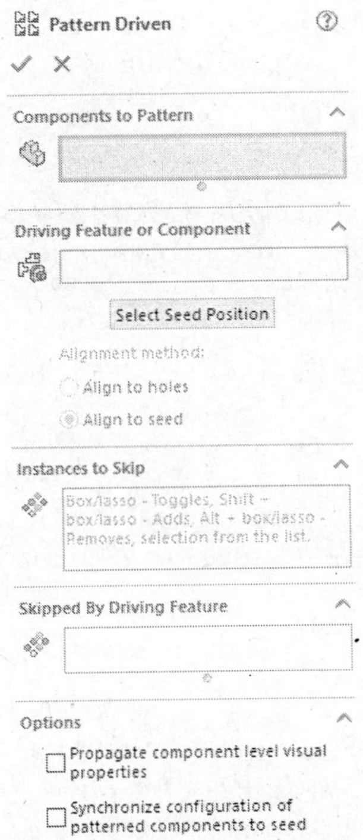

Figure 13-25 *The **Pattern Driven PropertyManager***

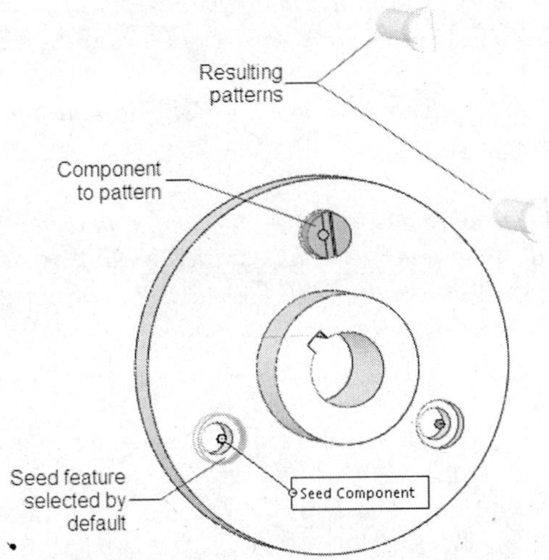

Figure 13-26 *The default seed feature selected and the resulting patterns*

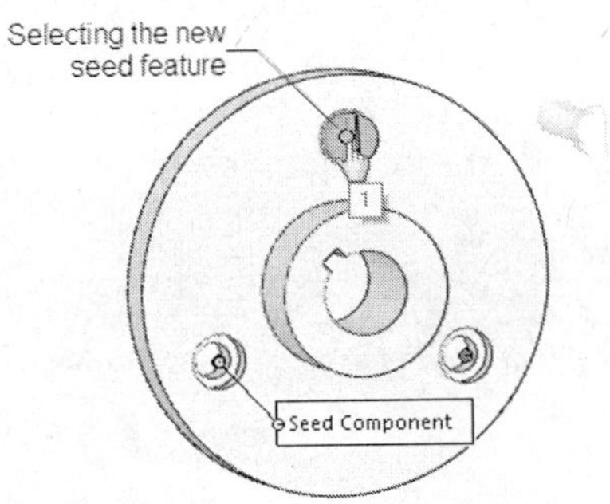

Figure 13-27 *The cursor selecting the new seed feature*

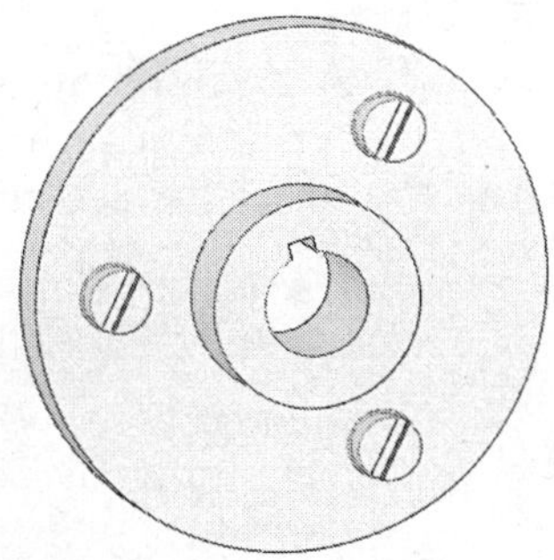

Figure 13-28 *Assembly after creating the Pattern Driven Component Pattern*

In order to skip some of the instances of the pattern created, select the derived pattern feature from the **FeatureManager Design Tree** and right-click. Choose the **Edit Feature** option from the shortcut menu; the corresponding PropertyManager will be displayed. Click once in the **Instances to Skip** selection box; the preview of the instances of the pattern will be displayed filled with magenta dots. Select a dot on the instance that you need to skip; the selected instances will disappear from the display and the color of the dot will change to white. To restore the instances again, select the corresponding white colored dot. After selecting the instances to skip, choose the **OK** button from the PropertyManager.

Note

1. The number of instances of the component pattern are automatically modified when you change the number of instances of the pattern feature that were used to derive the component pattern. This indicates the associative nature of the derived component pattern.

*2. You may have to choose the **Rebuild** button after editing the number of entities in the pattern feature.*

3. Remember that you need to modify the mates if the feature that was used to assemble the seed component is deleted while reducing the number of features in the pattern. This is because the original feature on which the mates were applied does not exist anymore and so there is an error in associating the elements to mate.

Tip

*To skip a pattern instance, expand the component pattern feature; all instances of the patterned component will be displayed. Select the instance to be skipped from the **FeatureManager Design Tree** and press the DELETE key; the **Confirm Delete** dialog box will be displayed. Choose the **Yes** button from it.*

*To restore the skipped pattern instance, select the derived pattern from the **FeatureManager Design Tree** and choose the **Edit Feature** option from the pop-up toolbar. Select the skipped instance from the **Instances to Skip** rollout and right-click. Choose the **Delete** option from the shortcut menu; the instance will be restored.*

Local Pattern

You can create the patterns of the components individually even if there is no existing pattern feature. This type of component pattern is known as local pattern. You can create two types of local patterns, the linear pattern and the circular pattern. Both the types of local patterns are discussed next.

Tip

If one instance of the component pattern is modified or edited, the other instances of the component will also be modified.

You can also create the component pattern of a component patterned feature.

Linear Pattern

To create the local linear pattern, choose the **Linear Component Pattern** button from the **Assembly CommandManager**; the **Linear Pattern PropertyManager** will be displayed. Select the direction reference and then the component to be patterned from the drawing area. You can specify the spacing or the number of instances independently using the **Spacing and instances** radio button.

You can also specify the spacing and the number of instances based on the selected reference geometry. To do so, select the **Up to reference** radio button; various options will be displayed. The **Reference Geometry** selection box is used to specify the reference geometry that controls the pattern. The **Reverse offset direction** button is used to reverse the direction in which the pattern is offset from the reference geometry. The **Offset distance** edit box is used to specify the distance of the last pattern instance from the reference geometry. The **Selected reference** radio button calculates the offset distance from the reference geometry to the selected seed feature geometry reference. The **Reference Geometry** selection box is used to specify the seed feature geometry from which the offset distance needs to be calculated. This option will be displayed only when you select the **Selected reference** radio button.

In SOLIDWORKS, you can rotate patterned instances about an axis. To do so, select the **Rotate instances** check box in the **Direction 1** rollout; various options are displayed. Select an axis for rotation using the **Axis of rotation** selection box and then define the angle between the instances using the **Angle** edit box. If the **Fixed axis of rotation** check box is cleared, the rotation axis for each instance of a component gets translated along direction 1 and the patterned instances start rotating about the axis of rotation. Other options in this PropertyManager are same as those discussed while creating a linear pattern of features, faces, and bodies in the earlier chapters.

Circular Pattern

To create a local circular pattern, choose the **Circular Component Pattern** button from the **Linear Component Pattern** flyout; the **Circular Pattern PropertyManager** will be displayed. Select the direction reference and then the component to be patterned from the drawing area. You can also include a second direction using the **Direction 2** option to make the spacing and the instance count symmetric to the first pattern direction. Other options in this PropertyManager are same as those discussed while creating the circular pattern of the features, faces, and bodies in the earlier chapters.

COPYING AND MIRRORING COMPONENTS

CommandManager: Assembly > Linear Component Pattern flyout > Mirror Components
SOLIDWORKS menus: Insert > Mirror Components

In the assembly mode of SOLIDWORKS, you can mirror a component and place a new instance in the assembly document. To mirror a component, choose the **Mirror Components** button from the **Linear Component Pattern** flyout; the **Mirror Components PropertyManager** will be displayed, as shown in Figure 13-29.

Select a planar face or plane that will act as a mirror plane, as shown in Figure 13-30. Next, select the components to be mirrored; the names of the components will be listed in the **Components to Mirror** area. Now, choose the **Next** button from the PropertyManager; the **Step:2 Set Orientation** and **Orient Components** rollouts will be displayed. The components selected to mirror will also be listed in the **Orient Components** rollout. Also, five buttons are available in the **Orient Components** area of the **Orient Components** rollout. These buttons allow you to reorient the view of the mirrored component in five different ways. Choose the **Create opposite hand version** button to create a new component which is the mirror of the selected component. Now, choose the **Next** button from the PropertyManager; the **Step:3 Opposite Hand** and **Opposite Hand Versions** rollouts will be displayed. Choose the **Create new files** radio button and then the **Next** button from the PropertyManager; the **Step:4 Import Features** and other rollouts will be displayed. Select the check box of the feature to import from the **Transfer** rollout. In SOLIDWORKS, you can also import material from the parent component to the new component by using the **Body Material and Part Material** check box. After specifying required parameters, choose the **OK** button.

Adding Custom Properties in Assembly or Sub-assembly

You can include custom properties in an opposite-hand mirror assembly or subassembly. On doing so, a link gets established between the mirrored assembly and the original assembly. Custom properties include global properties and configuration-specific properties.

To include custom properties in a mirrored assembly, open an assembly that has a custom property and choose the **Mirror Components** tool from the **CommandManager**. In Step 2, choose the **Create opposite hand version** button to move to the next step in the **PropertyManager**. In Step 4, import required features in the **Transfer** rollout and then select the required custom properties. If you select the **Break link to original part** check box in the **Link** rollout, the changes made in the original assembly will not be included in the mirrored assembly. Choose **OK** to create the mirrored component.

Figure 13-29 *The* ***Mirror Components PropertyManager***

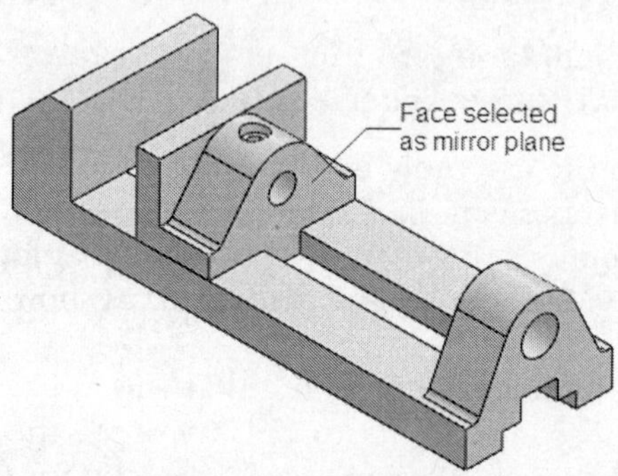

Figure 13-30 *Face selected as a mirror plane*

Figure 13-31 shows the mirrored component in one of the four possible orientations and the Figure 13-32 shows the opposite hand version of the component to be mirrored.

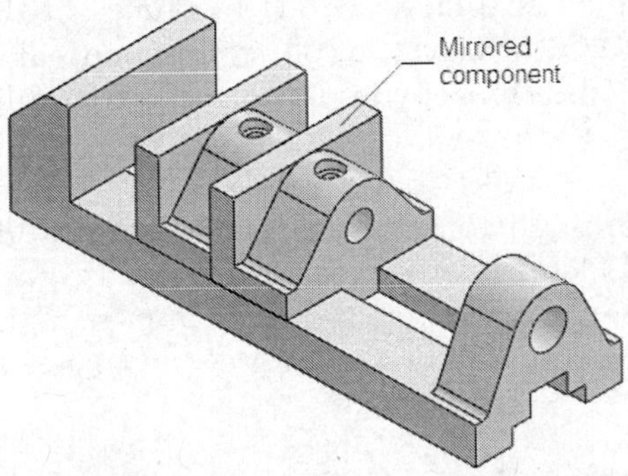

Figure 13-31 *Preview of the mirrored component*

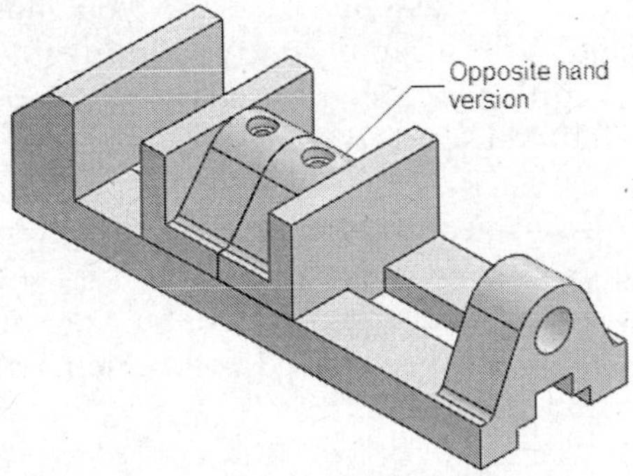

Figure 13-32 *Instance created by reorienting the component*

COPYING A COMPONENT ALONG WITH MATES

CommandManager: Assembly > Insert Components flyout > Copy with Mates
SOLIDWORKS menus: Insert > Component > Copy with Mates

In SOLIDWORKS, you can copy a component along with the mates. This will reduce the time in assembling the components that have similar mates. To copy a component that is already assembled, choose the **Copy with Mates** button from the **Insert Components** flyout; the **Copy with Mates PropertyManager** will be displayed, as shown in Figure 13-33. Also, you will be prompted to select the components to copy. Select the component from the drawing area; the name of the selected component will be listed in the **Components to Copy** selection box in the **Selected Components** rollout. Now, choose the **Next** button from the PropertyManager; the **Step 2: Mates** rollout will be displayed and the corresponding mates will be listed in the **Mates** rollout. Click once in the **New Entity To Mate To** selection box and select the face or the plane as the location for the new mates. Then, specify the new location for all the mates and choose the **OK** button in the **Copy with Mates PropertyManager**. If you need to copy more components, follow the same procedure. Select the **Repeat** check box, if you need to use the same reference for all the copied instances. Else, choose the **OK** button in the **Copy with Mates PropertyManager**. Figure 13-34 shows the component to be copied with the mates and Figure 13-35 shows the resultant copied components.

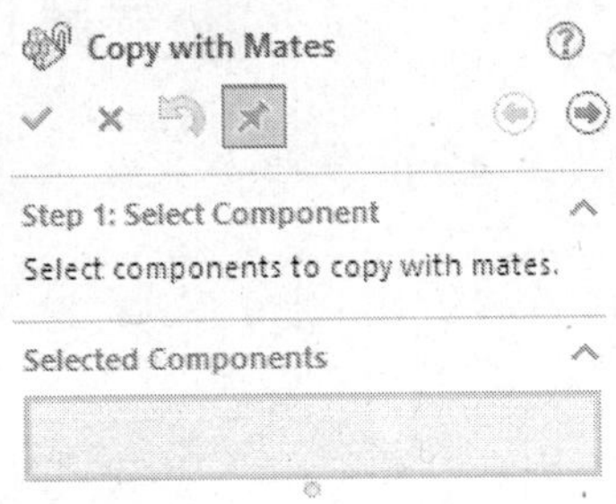

Figure 13-33 *The* ***Copy with Mates PropertyManager***

Note

While specifying the mates, it is not necessary to specify all the mates that are in the original component. You can specify few mates of the original component and add new mates later, if required.

COPYING MULTIPLE COMPONENTS

Sometimes in the assembly design, you may need to place various instances of different components in the assembly document. In SOLIDWORKS, you can copy components along with the mates applied between the selected components. Hence, you do not need to apply mates again in between selected components.

To do so, go to **FeatureManager Design Tree**, press the CTRL or SHIFT key and select the components to copy. Next, press and hold the CTRL key and drag the selected components and drop them in the graphics area; new instances of the components are created. Mates that exist between the selected components are retained between the new instances, refer to Figures 13-36 and 13-37.

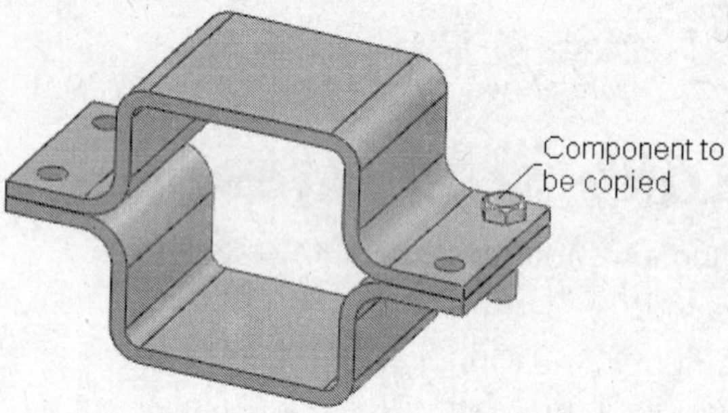

Figure 13-34 *Component to be copied*

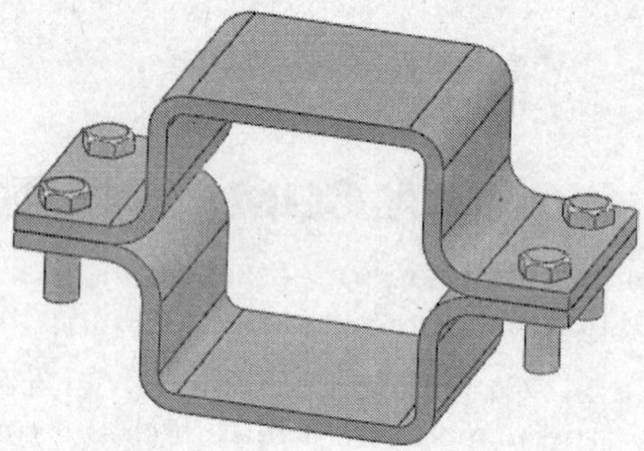

Figure 13-35 *Component copied with the mates*

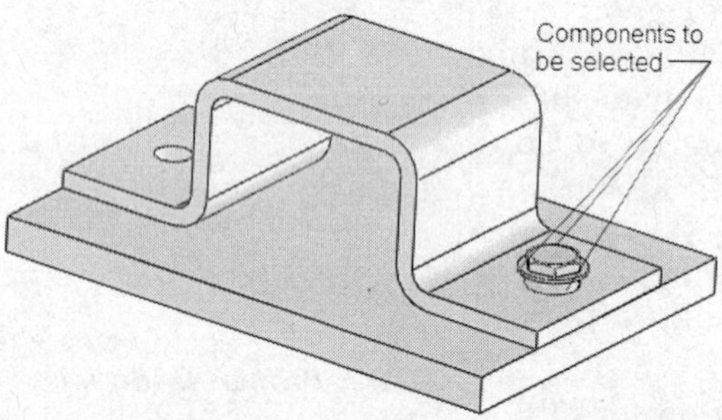

Figure 13-36 *Components to be selected*

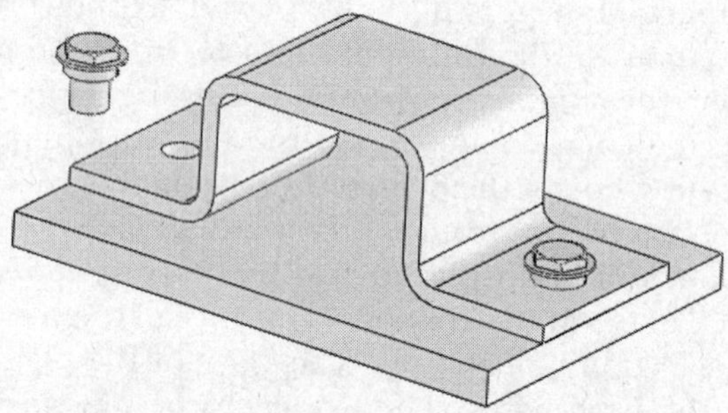

Figure 13-37 *Dragged components with mates applied*

MAGNETIC MATES

On working with large assembly models, such as plant layouts, it is very tedious and time consuming process to assemble a large number of parts. It takes lot of time to place such large number of components in an assembly by defining various mates between each component to get the desired assembly model. In SOLIDWORKS, assembly of such models can now be done within short intervals of time using the **Magnetic Mates** tool. Using various tools and options, you can publish a model as an asset in part or an assembly mode by defining ground plane and connection points on the model. Next, you will define a ground plane of the assembly so that when you insert an asset into the assembly, the ground plane of the asset will snap to the ground plane of the assembly and also the connection point of the asset will snap corresponding connection points of the other assets. After snapping corresponding connection points and ground plane, model gets placed and a **Magnetic** mate is automatically added between the components. The procedure and tools for defining magnetic mates are discussed next.

Publishing an Asset

You can now define connections points and ground plane on a model and then save it as an asset. When this asset is inserted in the assembly model it snaps to the relative connections points of the other assets and the ground plane of the assembly. To publish a model as an asset, invoke the **Asset Publisher** tool by choosing **Tools > Asset Publisher** from the SOLIDWORKS menus. After invoking the tool, the **Asset Publisher PropertyManager** will be displayed, as shown in Figure 13-38.

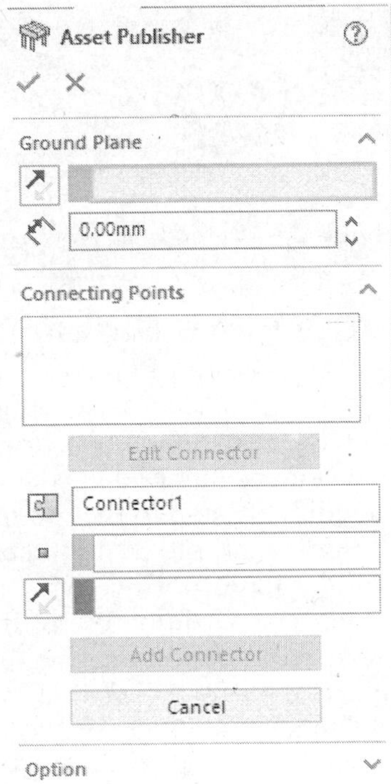

*Figure 13-38 The **Asset Publisher PropertyManager***

Select a face of the model to define as ground plane so that when it is inserted in the assembly, it snaps to the ground plane of the assembly. The name of the selected face will be listed in the **Ground Plane** selection box. You can reverse the alignment by using the **Reverse Direction** button provided on the left of the **Ground Plane** selection box. You can also define the offset distance for the selected face from the ground plane by using the **Ground Plane Distance** spinner provided below the selection box. As soon as you define the ground plane, the Connect point selection box in the **Connecting Points** rollout will be activated. Select a vertex, linear edge, or a circular edge to define as a connect point which will snap to the other assets while inserting in an assembly. The **Connect direction** selection box is used to select a face for defining the direction of alignment for connecting points. You can reverse the alignment direction by using the **Reverse Direction** button provided on the left of the **Connect direction** selection box. Use the **Connect Reference Name** edit box to define a name for the connecting point or use the default name displayed in this edit box. After assigning name and connecting point, click on the **Add Connector** button; the model will be displayed with connection point and direction of the connecting point, refer to Figure 13-39. Also, the name of the connection point will be displayed in the **Connect Reference Name** list box. Similarly, you can add more connection points to the model, refer to Figure 13-40. Choose the **OK** button; a **Published References** node will be added in the **FeatureManager Design Tree** with sub-nodes of ground plane and connection points added.

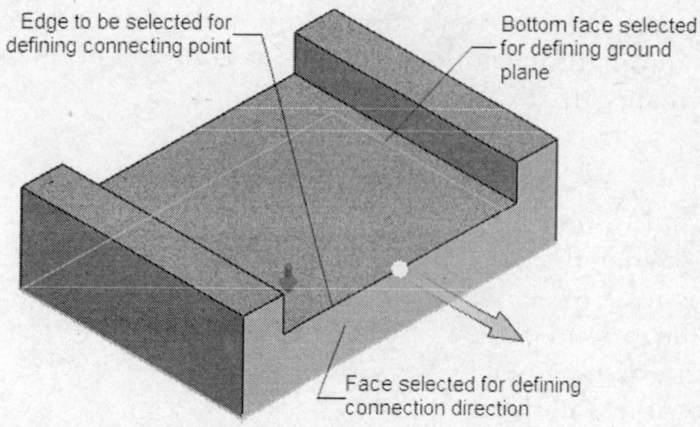

Figure 13-39 *Model with connection point and arrow specifying direction of connection point*

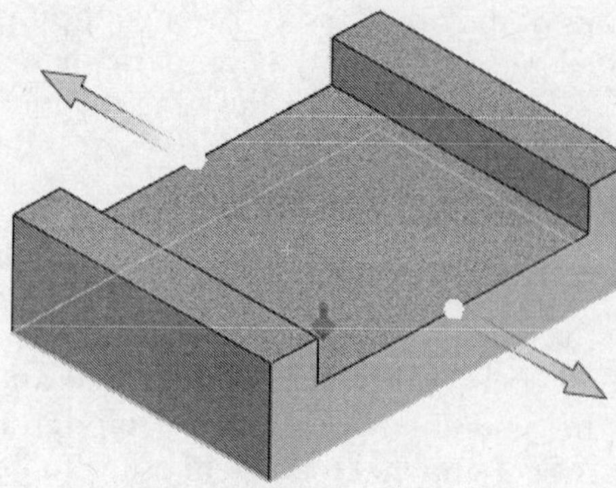

Figure 13-40 *Model after adding two connection points*

Defining the Ground Plane

The **Ground Plane** tool allows you define a plane or a planar surface of a model as the ground plane of the assembly. When you insert a model defined with connections points in the assembly, the ground plane of the model will snap to the ground plane of the assembly. To assign a ground plane in an assembly, invoke the **Ground Plane** tool by choosing **Insert > Reference Geometry > Ground Plane** from the SOLIDWORKS menus. After invoking the tool, the **Ground Plane PropertyManager** will be displayed. Select the face of the model to define as a ground plane, refer to Figure 13-41. You can also select a default assembly plane as a ground plane. The selected face or plane will be listed in the **Ground Plane** selection box. You can reverse the alignment of ground plane snapping by using the **Reverse Direction** button provided on the left of this selection box. Choose the **OK** button to close this PropertyManager; the **Ground Plane** node will be added to the **FeatureManager Design Tree**. In SOLIDWORKS, you can add as many ground planes as required. The names of the ground planes are listed under the **Ground Planes** folder in the **FeatureManager Design Tree**. To activate a ground plane, double-click on it or right-click on the ground plane name and choose the **Activate** option from the shortcut menu displayed; an arrow appears on the left of the selected ground plane in the **FeatureManager Design Tree**.

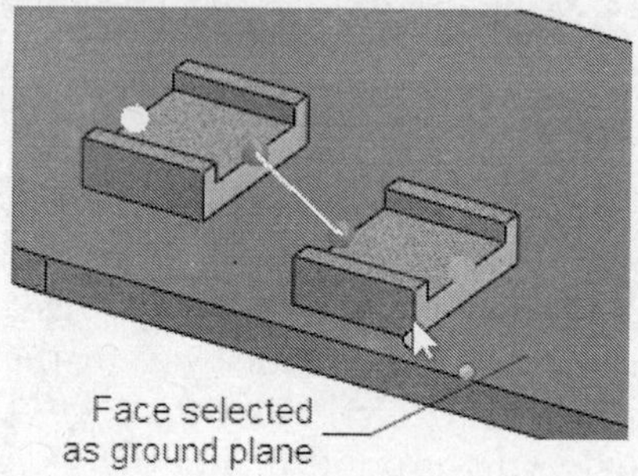

Figure 13-41 *Magnetic line attaching connection points of different assets*

Inserting the Published Asset

After saving the model as an asset, start a new assembly document and insert the model to be used as a ground plane. Then define the ground plane on the model by following the procedure discussed previously. Now, insert the published model in the assembly; the asset's ground plane will automatically snap the ground plane defined in the assembly and will get placed. Similarly, insert another asset into the assembly and then move the newly inserted asset close to the previous asset. You will notice that a yellow colored magnetic line appears joining the corresponding connections points of the two assets, refer to Figure 13-41. Click to place the newly inserted asset; it will automatically get placed and positioned with respect to the other asset and a Magnetic mate will be added in between them. Similarly, add as many as assets and complete the assembly with much reduced time as compared to the conventional assembly methods.

> **Tip**
> *In SOLIDWORKS, you can lock a magnetic mate applied to an asset in the assembly. When you place an asset by snapping connection points on another asset, the* ***Lock mate*** *button pop-ups in the graphics area. Choose this button to lock the magnetic mate applied. To unlock the magnetic mate, right-click on the magnetic mate in the* ***FeatureManager Design Tree*** *and choose the* ***Unlock Magnetic Mate*** *option from the shortcut menu displayed.*

SIMPLIFYING ASSEMBLIES USING THE VISIBILITY OPTIONS

When you assemble components in a large assembly or a small assembly, you may need to simplify the assembly using the visibility options. To simplify the assembly, you can hide the components or set their transparency at any stage of the design cycle. You can also suppress and unsuppress the components at any stage of the design cycle. Various methods of simplifying an assembly are discussed next.

Hiding Components

CommandManager:	Assembly > Hide/Show Components (*Customize to add*)
SOLIDWORKS menus:	Edit > Hide > Current Display State
Toolbar:	Assembly > Hide/Show Components (*Customize to add*)

In order to hide a component placed in the assembly, select the component from the drawing area or from the **FeatureManager Design Tree**. You can select more than one component to hide by using the CTRL key. Choose the **Hide Components** option from the pop-up toolbar; the display of the component will be turned off and its icon will turn transparent in the **FeatureManager Design Tree**. To display the hidden component, select the icon of the component from the **FeatureManager Design Tree** and choose **Show Components** from the pop-up toolbar; the hidden component will be displayed again in the drawing area. You can also choose the **Hide/Show Components** button from the **Assembly CommandManager** to turn on the display of the hidden components.

Hiding Faces Temporarily

In SOLIDWORKS, you can use the ALT key to simplify the selection of entities while applying mates, you can use the ALT key to temporarily hide faces of a component to select the obscured faces. To show the temporarily hidden face, use the SHIFT+ALT keys. You can also view all the temporary hidden faces in semi-transparent state using the CTRL+SHIFT+ALT keys.

Suppressing and Unsuppressing the Components

CommandManager:	Assembly > Change Suppression State	*(Customize to add)*
SOLIDWORKS menus:	Edit > Suppress/Unsuppress > This Configuration	
Toolbar:	Assembly > Change Suppression State	*(Customize to add)*

You can also suppress the components placed in the assembly to simplify the assembly representation. To do so, select a component from the drawing area or from the **FeatureManager Design Tree**, and then choose the **Suppress** option from the pop-up toolbar; the component will not be displayed in the assembly document and the icon of the suppressed component will be displayed in gray in the **FeatureManager Design Tree**. Alternatively, you can also select the component to be suppressed and choose the **Change Suppression State** button from the **Assembly CommandManager**; a flyout will be displayed. Choose the **Suppress** option to suppress the component in the assembly.

To unsuppress a suppressed component, select the component to be resolved from the **FeatureManager Design Tree**, and then choose the **Unsuppress** option from the pop-up toolbar.

You can also unsuppress a component using the **Change Suppression State** button from the **Assembly CommandManager**. To do so, select the component and choose the **Change Suppression State** button from the **Assembly CommandManager**; a flyout will be displayed. Choose the **Resolve** option from this flyout. The **Resolve** option is used to set the suppressed or the lightweight components to the resolve state.

Changing the Transparency Conditions

In SOLIDWORKS, you can change the transparency of the components or the selected faces to simplify the assembly. To change the transparency, select a component and then choose the **Change Transparency** option from the pop-up toolbar; the transparency of the selected component will be changed.

Changing the Display States

In assembly environment also, you can display different components in different display states as you did in the Part environment. To create different display states, invoke the **ConfigurationManager**, select the default display state in the **Display States** area, and right-click; a shortcut menu will be displayed. Choose the **Add Display State** option from the shortcut menu; a new display state will be added and it will become the active display state. Rename the newly added display state. Next, invoke the **FeatureManager Design Tree** and change the display state of the component. Invoke the **ConfigurationManager** again and double-click on the display state that is inactive to view the changes.

CHECKING INTERFERENCES IN AN ASSEMBLY

CommandManager:	Evaluate > Interference Detection
SOLIDWORKS menus:	Tools > Evaluate > Interference Detection
Toolbar:	Assembly > Interference Detection

After creating the assembly design, the first and the most essential step is to check the interference between the components of an assembly. If there is an interference, the components may not assemble properly after they come out from the machine shop or the tool room. Therefore, it is essential to check interference before sending the part and assembly files for detailing and drafting. To do so, choose the **Interference Detection** button from the **Evaluate CommandManager**; the **Interference Detection PropertyManager** will be displayed, as shown in Figure 13-42. By default the name of the current assembly will be displayed in the **Components to Check** selection box in the **Selected Components** rollout. You can also check interference between two or more than two components. To do so, first clear the current selection set and select the components from the assembly. Next, choose the **Calculate** button from the **Selected Components** rollout to check interference. If there is any interference between the components in the assembly, it will be displayed in the assembly and also the interfering components will be displayed in the **Results** rollout. Expand the names of the interfering components to view the cause of interference. You can select a component/interference from the **Results** rollout and choose the **Ignore** button to ignore that particular component/interference while calculating the interference.

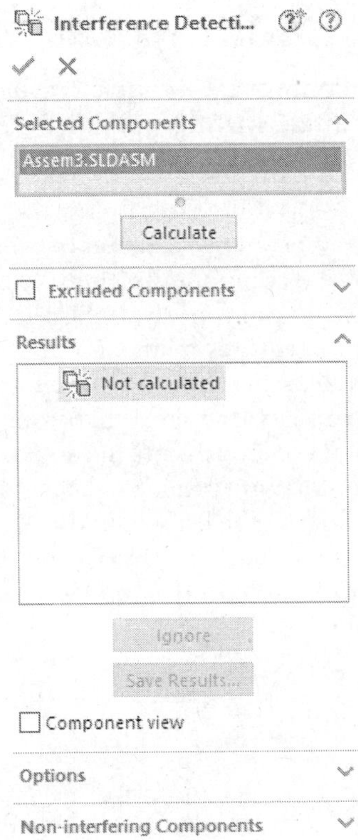

*Figure 13-42 Partial view of the **Interference Detection PropertyManager***

In SOLIDWORKS, you can exclude some of the components from the assembly while calculating the interference. To do so, expand the **Excluded Components** rollout by selecting the check box placed on the left in the title bar of this rollout. In this expanded rollout of the **FeatureManager Design Tree**, select the components to be excluded from the graphical area. Next, choose the **Calculate** button from the **Selected Components** rollout to check interference. The interface between the excluded components will not be detected. If you select the **Treat coincidence as interference** check box in the **Options** rollout, then the **Coincident** mates are also considered as interference. The **Show ignored interferences** check box is selected to display the interferences that you ignored by using the **Ignore** button in the **Results** rollout. If you select the **Treat subassemblies as components** check box, all the subassemblies in the current assembly will be treated as single component and any interference in the sub-assembly will be ignored. The **Include multibody part interferences** check box is selected to analyze the multibody parts for interference. If you select the **Make interfering parts transparent** check box, the interfering parts will be made transparent in the drawing window. The **Create fasteners folder** check box is selected to place the interfering fasteners in a separate folder in the **Results** rollout. The **Create matching cosmetic threads folder** check box is selected to place the cosmetic threaded components in a separate folder in the **Results** rollout. Select the **Ignore hidden bodies/components** check box to ignore the interferences between the hidden components.

The **Non-interfering Components** rollout is used to select the display option for the non-interfering parts. After analyzing the assembly, you can edit or modify the part.

CHECKING THE HOLE ALIGNMENT

CommandManager: Evaluate > Hole Alignment
SOLIDWORKS menus: Tools > Evaluate > Hole Alignment
Toolbar: Assembly > Hole Alignment

While assembling the components having hole features, it is recommended to apply concentric mates between the two holes. Sometimes based on the requirement or criticality of the components, their side walls may be given constraints. As a result, the hole features may not align properly. In SOLIDWORKS, you can find the deviation of the centerpoints of the two hole features by using the **Hole Alignment** tool. To check the hole alignment in an assembly, invoke the **Hole Alignment** tool from the **Evaluate CommandManager**; the **Hole Alignment PropertyManager** will be displayed, as shown in Figure 13-43. Specify the permissible deviation of the centerpoints in the **Hole center deviation** spinner and choose the **Calculate** button; the centerpoints that deviate more than the permissible limits will be listed with their deviation values in the list box in the **Results** rollout, refer to Figure 13-43. Figure 13-44 shows an assembly of two plates in the **Hidden Lines Visible** display state. Figure 13-45 shows the misalignment of the hole in the top view and Figure 13-46 shows the misalignment of the holes in the right side view.

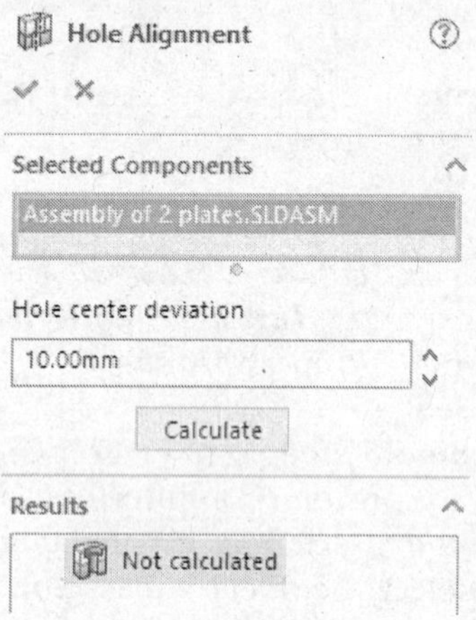

*Figure 13-43 The **Hole Alignment PropertyManager***

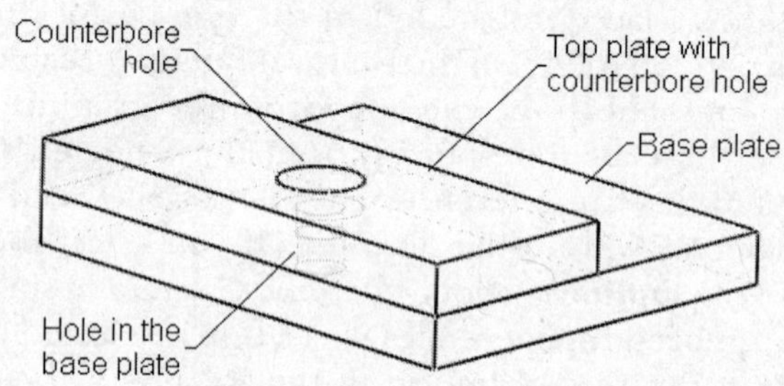

Figure 13-44 An assembly of two plates

Tip

*In SOLIDWORKS, you can check the clearance between the selected components or faces in an assembly. To do so, invoke the **Clearance Verification PropertyManager** by choosing the **Clearance Verification** button from the **Evaluate CommandManager**. Next, select the components or faces; the name of the selected components or faces will be displayed in the **Components to Check** selection box. Specify the clearance value in the **Minimum Acceptable Clearance** spinner and choose the **Calculate** button. If the clearance between the selected components or faces is less than or equal to the minimum acceptable clearance you specified, then the result is displayed in the **Results** rollout.*

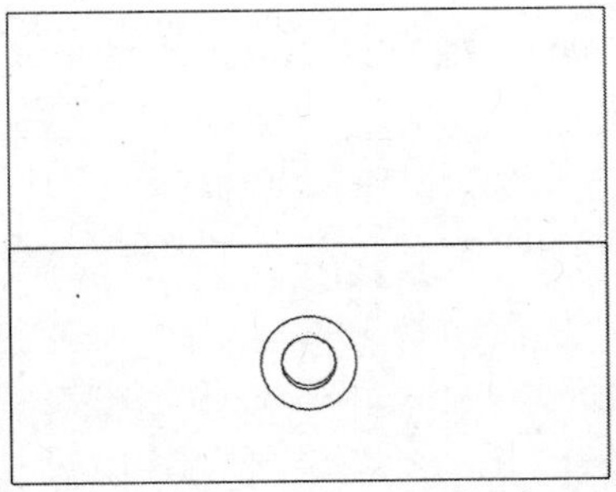

Figure 13-45 *Top view of the assembly*

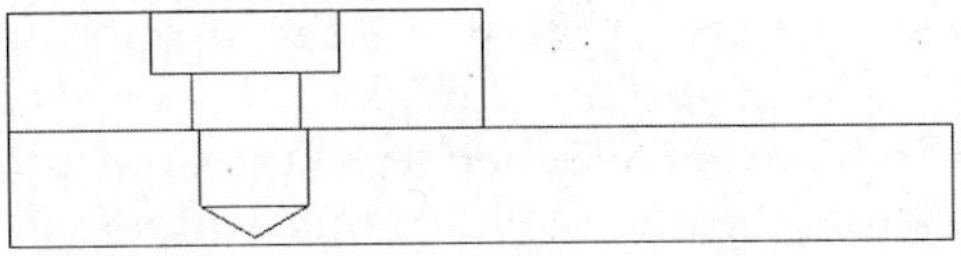

Figure 13-46 *Right side view of the assembly*

CREATING ASSEMBLIES FOR MECHANISM

As mentioned earlier, there are two types of assemblies. The first one is the fully defined assembly in which the relative movement of all the components is constrained. The second type of assembly is the one in which the components are not fully defined and some degrees of freedom are kept unconstrained. As a result, they can move in a certain direction with respect to the surroundings of the assembly. This flexibility in turn helps you to create mechanisms so that you can move the assembly to check the mechanisms that you have designed. Consider the case of a Bench Vice in which you are assembling the Vice Jaw with the Vice Body. For this assembly to work, the linear movement of the Vice Jaw should be free when placed on the Vice Body. Therefore, while creating this assembly for mechanism, you should not apply the mates for constraining the linear motion of the Vice Jaw with respect to the Vice Body. Figure 13-47 shows the degree of freedom that is required to be free to allow motion in assembly.

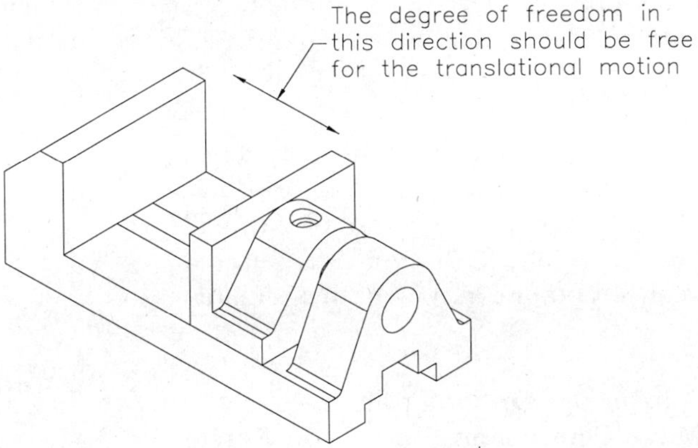

Figure 13-47 *Direction in which the degree of freedom should be free*

After creating the assembly for mechanism by defining minimum mates, invoke the **Move Component** tool. Select one of the faces of the component that you need to move and drag the cursor to move the assembly. The options available for analyzing the assembly while moving the assembly for mechanism design are discussed next.

Analyzing Collisions Using the Collision Detection Tool

In SOLIDWORKS, you can also analyze any collision between the components of the assembly while the assembly is in motion. Invoke the **Move Component PropertyManager** and then select the **Collision Detection** radio button from the **Options** rollout, as shown in Figure 13-48; the **Check between** area will be displayed. The options in this area are used to specify the components between which the collision will be detected. The options in the **Check between** area are discussed next.

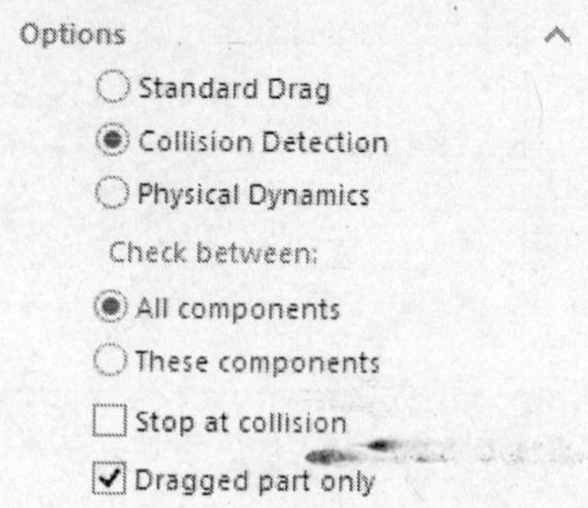

*Figure 13-48 The **Options** rollout in the **Move Component PropertyManager***

All components

This radio button is selected to check the collision between all the components of the assembly.

These components

The **These components** radio button is selected to check the collision between the selected components when the assembly is in motion. On selecting this radio button, the **Components for Collision Check** selection box and the **Resume Drag** button will be displayed in the **Options** rollout, as shown in Figure 13-49. The name of the components between which the collision is to be detected will be displayed in the **Components for Collision Check** selection box. After selecting the components, choose the **Resume Drag** button from the **Options** rollout and drag the cursor to move the assembly.

Stop at collision

The **Stop at collision** check box is selected to stop the motion of the assembly when one of the components collides with another component during the assembly motion.

Dragged part only

Select the **Dragged part only** check box if you need to detect the collision only between the components that you have selected to move. If this check box is cleared, the collision will be determined between the components that you have selected to move as well as between any other component that is mated with the selected component.

After setting the options in the **Options** rollout, drag the assembly using the **Move Component** tool or the **Rotate Component** tool. If a component of the assembly collides with another component while the assembly is in motion, the faces of the components that collide with each other will be displayed in a different color. If the **Stop at collision** check box is selected, the motion of the assembly will be stopped when one of the components collides with another component of the assembly.

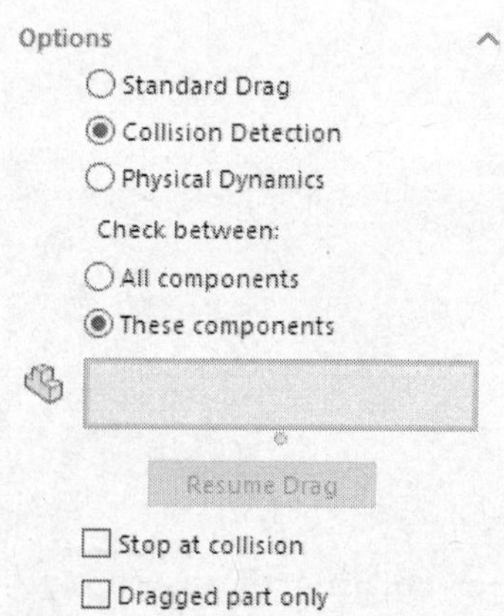

*Figure 13-49 The **Options** rollout with the **These components** radio button selected*

Consider the assembly shown in Figure 13-50. In this assembly, you need to move the slider in the given direction. To do so, invoke the **Move Component PropertyManager** and select the **Collision Detection** radio button in the **Options** rollout. Drag the slider to move it in the given direction. Figure 13-51 shows that the slider collides with the extrusion feature created in the vertical column of the base component. The faces of the components that collide will be highlighted. If the **Stop at collision** check box is selected, you cannot move the component further after it collides with one of the components of the assembly.

Once the collision is detected in the assembly, you can edit and modify the components that collide during the assembly motion.

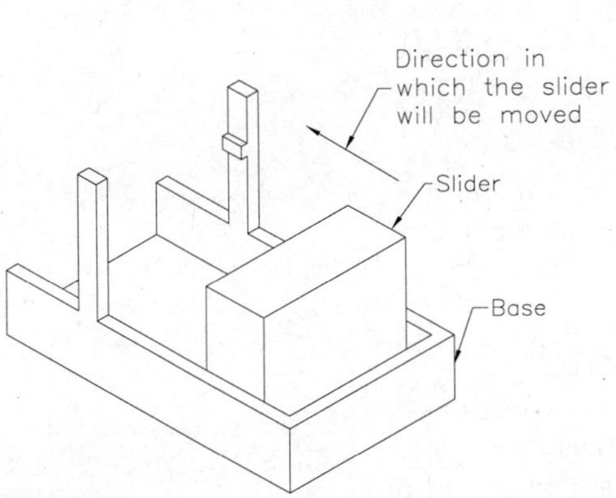

Figure 13-50 *Direction in which the slider will be moved inside the base*

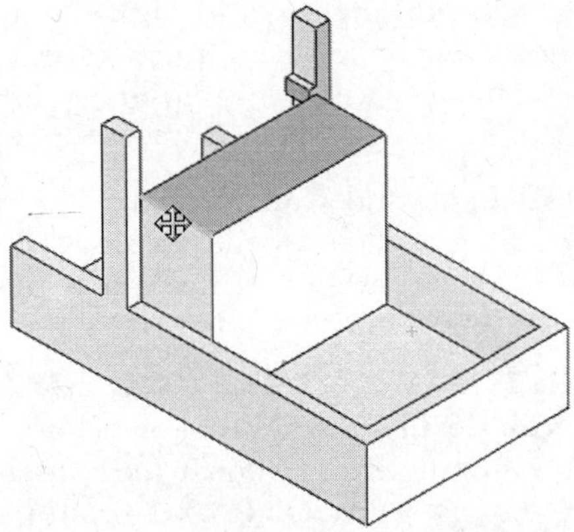

Figure 13-51 *The faces of the components highlighted in blue after the collision*

Tip

In SOLIDWORKS, you can move and place a component at a distance with respect to another component. To do so, expand the ***Dynamic Clearance*** *rollout in the* ***Move Component PropertyManager*** *and click on the* ***Components for Collision Check*** *edit box. Then, select the two components. Next, select the* ***Collision Detection*** *radio button from the* ***Options*** *rollout and then choose the* ***Stop at Specified Clearance*** *button in the* ***Dynamic Clearance*** *rollout. Enter the clearance distance and choose the* ***Resume Drag*** *button. Now, if you move one of the components, it will move and stop at the specified clearance.*

CREATING EXPLODED STATE OF AN ASSEMBLY

CommandManager: Assembly > Exploded View flyout > Exploded View
SOLIDWORKS menus: Insert > Exploded View
Toolbar: Assembly > Exploded View

In SOLIDWORKS, you can create exploded state of an assembly using the **Explode PropertyManager**. To invoke this PropertyManager, choose the **Exploded View** button from the **Assembly CommandManager**. Alternatively, invoke the **ConfigurationManager**, select the **Default** option from the **ConfigurationManager** and right-click. Choose the **New Exploded View** option from the shortcut menu; the **Explode PropertyManager** will be displayed, as shown in Figure 13-52.

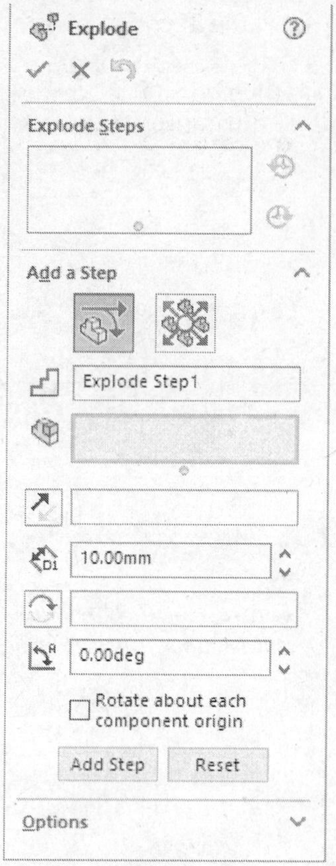

Figure 13-52 The Explode PropertyManager

The **Roll Back** and **Roll Forward** buttons available in the **Explode Steps** rollout of the **Explode PropertyManager** are used to roll back and roll forward the exploded steps.

Regular step (translate and rotate)

The **Explode PropertyManager** allows you to explode an assembly using the manipulator. In the **Explode PropertyManager**, the **Regular step (translate and rotate)** button is chosen by default. Select the component to be exploded; a triad will be displayed on the component and the name of the component will be displayed in the **Explode Step Components** selection box of the **Add a Step** rollout. Now, to explode the component along any of the axes of the triad, move the cursor over the arrowhead of that axis. When the cursor changes into a move cursor, press and hold the left mouse button and drag the cursor to explode the component. You can also set the exact numeric value of the explode distance. To do so, select the direction using the triad and set the value of the explosion distance in the **Explode Distance** spinner of the **Add a Step** rollout. The name of the direction axis will be displayed in the **Explode Direction** selection box. You can flip the direction of triad by choosing the **Reverse direction** button in the **Add a Step** rollout. As you move the component, the name of the **Add a Step** rollout gets changed to **Editing Explode Step 1**. Explode Step 1 is the default name of the first exploded step and this will change simultaneously with the next exploded steps. Next, choose the **Done** button from the **Editing Explode Step 1** rollout; the component will be moved. To align the component in any particular direction, right-click on the triad arrow. Next, choose the **Align with selection** option from the shortcut menu and select an edge; the manipulator arrows will reorient. Drag the triad arrows to move the component in that direction.

The **Rotate about each component origin** check box is used to rotate the component about its origin. The **Add Step** button is used to add the current step in **Existing explode steps** area of **Explode Steps** rollout. The **Reset** button is used to reset the values and selections.

If the **Auto-space components on drag** check box is selected in the **Options** rollout, the explosion will be displayed as **Chain 1** in the **Existing explode steps** area of the **Explode Steps** rollout. However, if the **Auto-space components on drag** check box is cleared, the explosion will be displayed as **Explode Step1**. You will learn more about the **Auto-space components on drag** check box later in this chapter. To edit the **Chain 1** or **Explode Step 1**, select it from the **Existing explode steps** area of the **Explode Steps** rollout. Now, you can edit the position of the selected component.

You can delete an explode step by selecting it and choosing the **Delete** option from the shortcut menu. After exploding a component, select another component to be exploded. Similarly, you can create as many explode steps as you want.

The options in the **Options** rollout, as shown in Figure 13-53, are used to specify the explode options. The **Auto-space components** check box is used to specify automatic spacing between the components after exploding them using the auto-explode method. The **Spacing** slider bar is used to adjust spacing between components in a chain. The **Select subassembly parts** check box is used to select the components of the sub-assembly for exploding. The **Show rotation rings** check box is used to show triad rings.

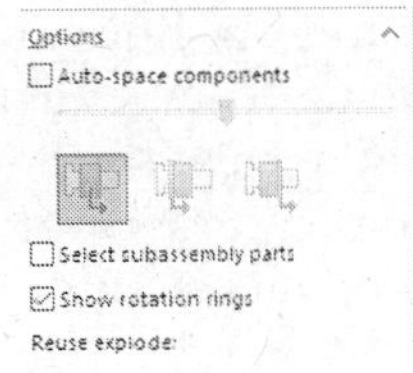

Figure 13-53** The **Options** rollout in the **Explode PropertyManager

You can also perform the auto-explosion by selecting all the components of an assembly. You can drag a window across the assembly to select all its components. To auto explode, select the **Auto-space components** check box in the **Options** rollout. Select the direction triad and drag it; the components will be exploded automatically.

The **From Subassembly** button is chosen to reuse the explode steps of a sub-assembly in the current assembly.

Figure 13-54 shows the assembly exploded using the auto-explode method. Figure 13-55 shows the systematic exploded state of an assembly.

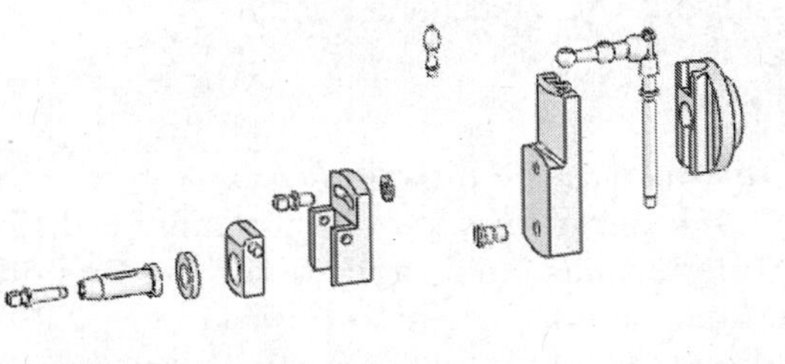

***Figure 13-54** Auto-explosion of an assembly*

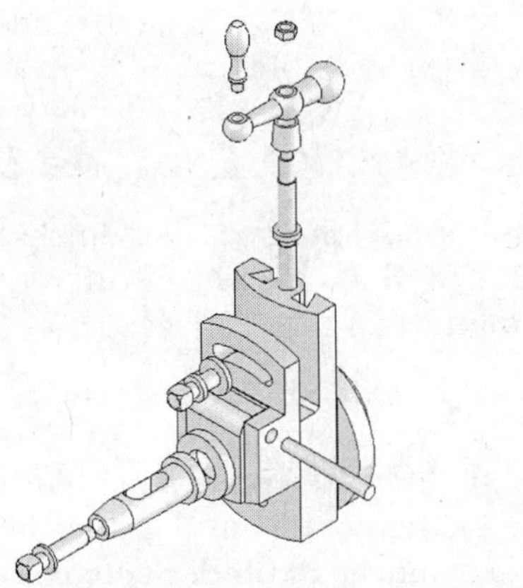

***Figure 13-55** The systematic exploded state of an assembly*

To collapse an exploded view, right-click in the graphics area and choose the **Collapse** option from the shortcut menu. To view the exploded view again, invoke the **ConfigurationManager**. Expand the **Default** option and double-click on the **ExplView1** option. Alternatively, invoke the shortcut menu by right-clicking on the name of the assembly in the **FeatureManager Design Tree** and then select the **Explode** option from it. To view the animation of the exploded view, invoke the **ConfigurationManager**, select the **ExplView1** option and right-click. Then, choose the **Animate explode** option; the exploded view will be animated and you can control its speed using the **Animation Controller** toolbar. To delete the exploded view, invoke the **ConfigurationManager**, select the **ExplView1** option and right-click. Choose the **Delete** option from the shortcut menu.

In SOLIDWORKS, you can create multiple exploded views of an assembly. After creating the initial exploded view of an assembly, invoke the **ConfigurationManager** and right-click on the **Default** configuration; a shortcut menu will be displayed. Next, choose the **New Exploded View** option from the shortcut menu; the **Explode PropertyManager** will be displayed. Create the exploded view and then exit the PropertyManager. On doing so, a new exploded view **ExplView 2** will be added to the **ConfigurationManager** under the **Default** configurations node. This added view will now become activated. Similarly, multiple exploded views of an assembly can be created.

Radial step

The **Radial step** button is used to explode components radially. To explode components radially, choose the **Radial step** button in the **Explode PropertyManager** and then select all the components to be exploded; the name of the selected components will be displayed in the **Explode Step Components** selection box of the **Add a Step** rollout. Also, a drag handle will be displayed in the drawing area. Now, select the drag handle and move the cursor in the drawing area. Alternatively, you can specify the explode distance in the **Explode Distance** spinner and choose the **Done** button in the **Editing Chain** rollout. Figure 13-56 shows the radial exploded state of an assembly.

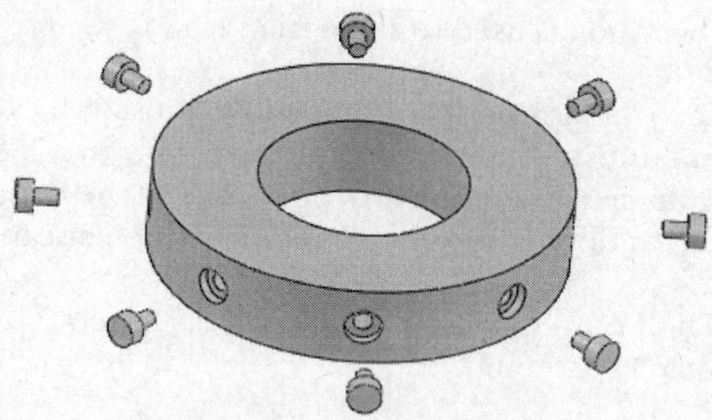

Figure 13-56 *Radial exploded state of an assembly*

Creating the Explode Line Sketch

CommandManager:	Assembly > Exploded View flyout > Explode Line Sketch
SOLIDWORKS menus:	Insert > Explode Line Sketch
Toolbar:	Assembly > Explode Line Sketch

The explode lines are the parametric axes that display the direction of explosion of the components in an exploded state. Figure 13-57 shows an exploded assembly with the explode lines. To create an explode line sketch, explode an assembly and choose the **Explode Line Sketch** tool from the **Assembly CommandManager**; the sketching environment will be invoked and the **Explode Sketch** toolbar will be displayed. Also, the **Route Line PropertyManager** will be displayed, as shown in Figure 13-58. Also, you will be prompted to select a cylindrical face, planar face, vertex, point, arc, or line entities. Select the cylindrical faces of the two components in succession to create an explode line between them. For example, in order to create an explode line between the Oval Fillister and the Vice Jaw, select the cylindrical face of the Oval Fillister that goes inside the Vice Jaw. Now, select the cylindrical hole of the Vice Jaw; the preview of the explode line will be displayed. Choose **OK** to create the explode line. The names of the selected faces will be displayed in the **Items To Connect** selection box in the **Route Line PropertyManager**. When you select an entity to create an explode line, an arrow will also be displayed with the line. You can use that arrow or select the **Reverse** check box from the **Options** rollout to reverse the direction of the explode line creation. Next, choose the **OK** button from the **Route Line PropertyManager** and exit the sketching environment.

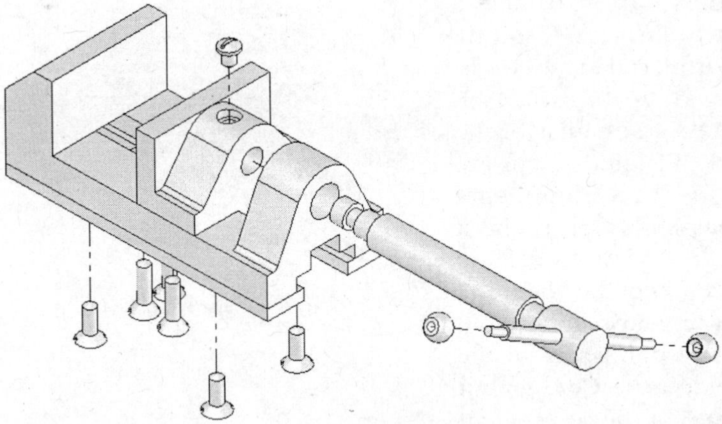

***Figure 13-57** Explode line sketch created on an exploded assembly*

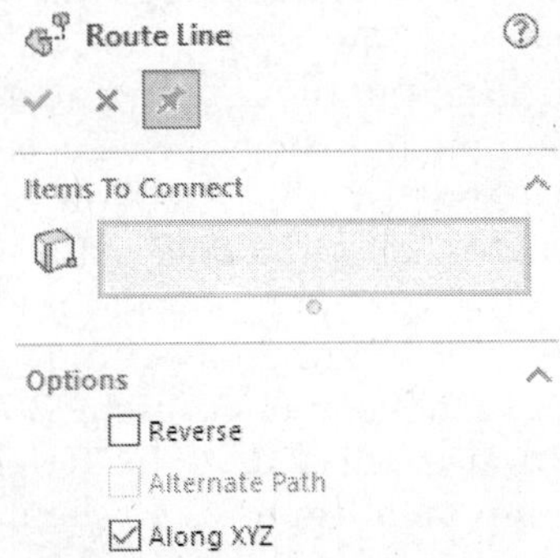

Figure 13-58** The **Route Line PropertyManager

Creating Smart Explode Lines

CommandManager: Assembly > Exploded View flyout > Insert/Edit Smart Explode Lines
Toolbar: Assembly > Insert/Edit Smart Explode Lines *(Customize to add)*

In SOLIDWORKS, you can automatically add route lines sketch to an assembly to display the direction of explosion of the components. Also, when you change any explode step, these route lines are updated automatically. To add an explode line sketch, choose the **Insert/Edit Smart Explode Lines** button from the **Assembly CommandManager**; the **Smart Explode Lines PropertyManager** will be displayed, as shown in Figure 13-59. A preview of the route lines will be displayed in the drawing area. Also, the names of the components which are associated to explode steps are displayed in the selection box in the **Components** rollout. Select the **Select the subassembly parts** check box to include components from subassembly. By default, the route line originates from the center of the bounding box of the component as the **Bounding box center** radio button is selected in the **Reference point** area of the **Component route line** rollout. Select the **Component origin** radio button to define origin of the component as reference for the route line. You can also select the **Selected point** radio button to define reference point by selecting a sketched line, arc, point, vertex, or circular edge of a component. Note that whenever you change the reference point option, the **Apply to all component instances** button appears below the selection box in the **Components** rollout to apply the current reference point settings to all the instances of the components selected. The explode steps associated with the selected components are displayed in the **Explode Steps** rollout. You can exclude any explode steps by clearing the respective check box of the explode step. Choose the **OK** button to close the PropertyManager; the explode lines will be added to the assembly. Now, if you change any explode step, the explode route lines will be updated automatically.

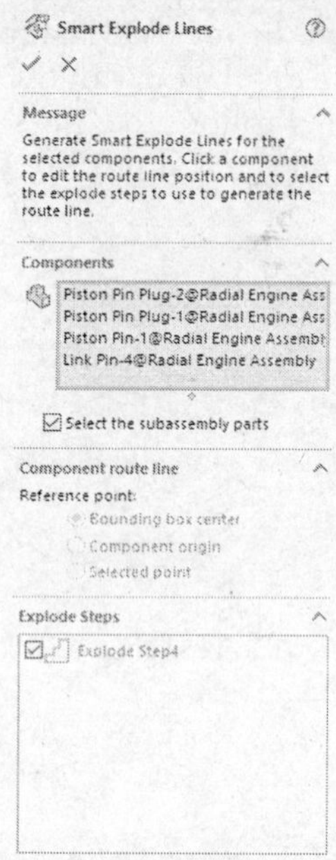

Figure 13-59** Partial view of the **Smart Explode Lines PropertyManager

Tip

*You will observe that the **Lightweight** option in the **Mode** drop-down list is provided in the **Open** dialog box. If this option is chosen before opening the assembly file, the assembly will be opened only with the lightweight components.*

*A lightweight component is the one in which the feature information is available in the part document and only the graphical representation of the component is displayed in the assembly document. Therefore, the assembly environment becomes light. An icon of a lightweight component is displayed as a feather attached to the component icon in the **FeatureManager Design Tree**.*

*To get the feature information of the lightweight component, you need to resolve the component to the normal state. To do so, select the component from the drawing area or from the **FeatureManager Design Tree** and right-click. Choose the **Set to Resolved** option from this shortcut menu. To set a resolved component to a lightweight component, select the component and right-click. Then, choose **Set to Lightweight** from the shortcut menu.*

TUTORIALS

Tutorial 1

In this tutorial, you will create the radial engine assembly shown in Figure 13-60. This assembly will be created in two parts: sub-assembly and main assembly. You will also create the exploded state of the assembly and then create the explode line sketch. The exploded state of the assembly is displayed in Figure 13-61. The views and dimensions of all the components of this assembly are displayed in Figures 13-62 through 13-65. **(Expected time: 3 hr)**

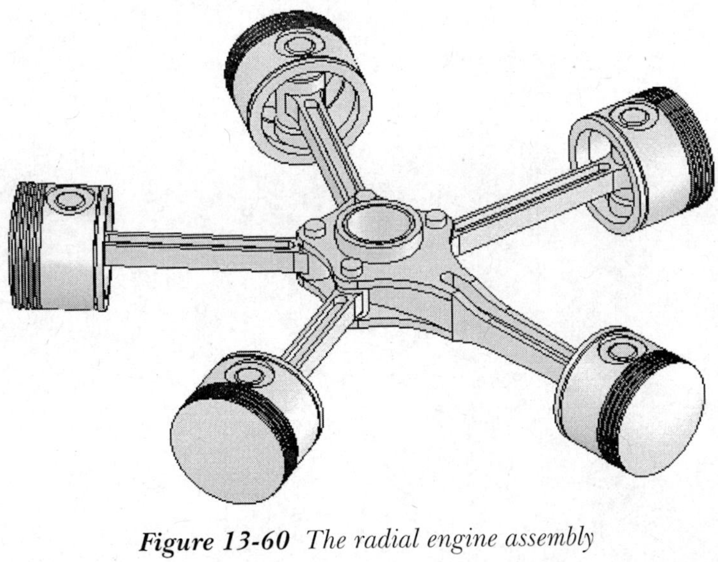

Figure 13-60 *The radial engine assembly*

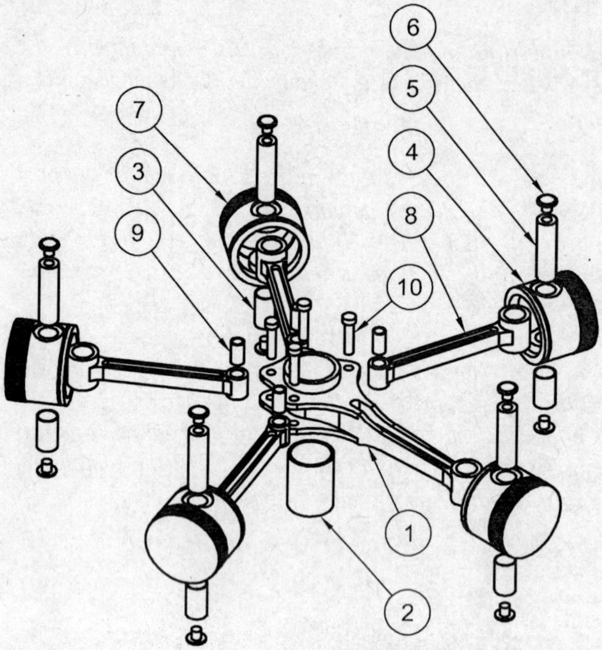

ITEM NO.	PART NO.	QTY.
1	Master Rod	1
2	Master Rod Bearing	1
3	Rod Bush Upper	5
4	Piston	5
5	Piston Pin	5
6	Piston Pin Plug	10
7	Piston Ring	20
8	Articulated Rod	4
9	Rod Bush Lower	4
10	Link Pin	4

Figure 13-61 *Exploded view of the assembly*

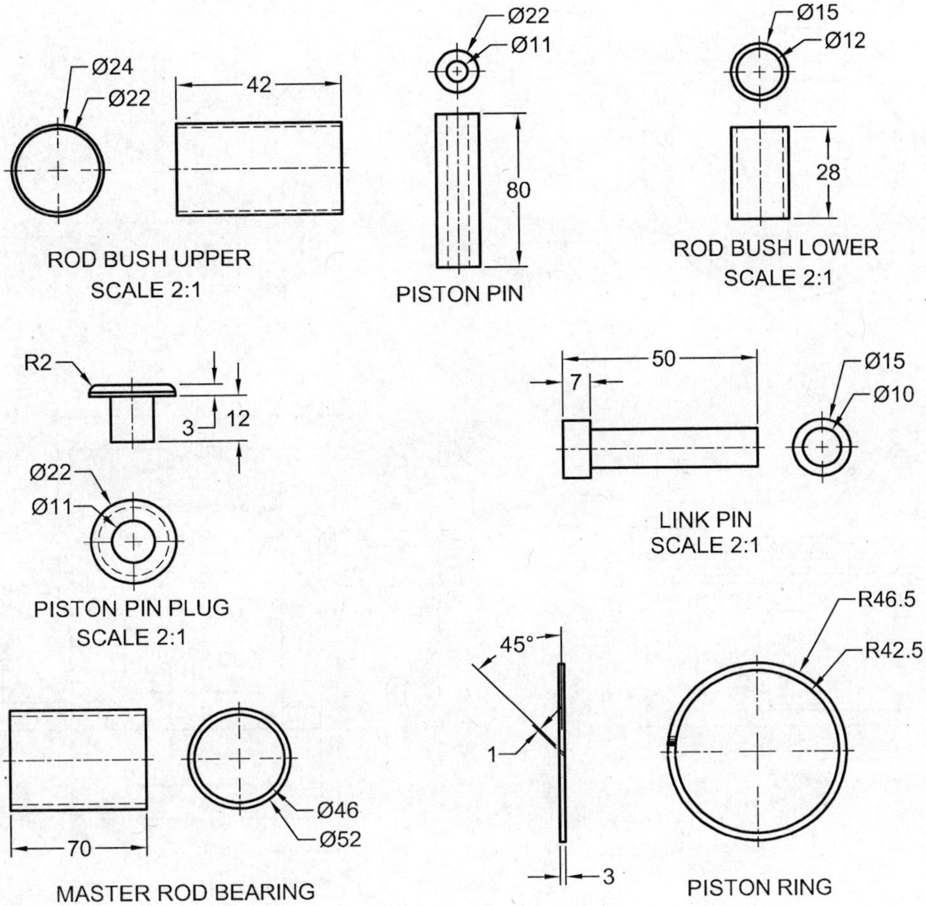

Figure 13-62 *Views and dimensions of other components*

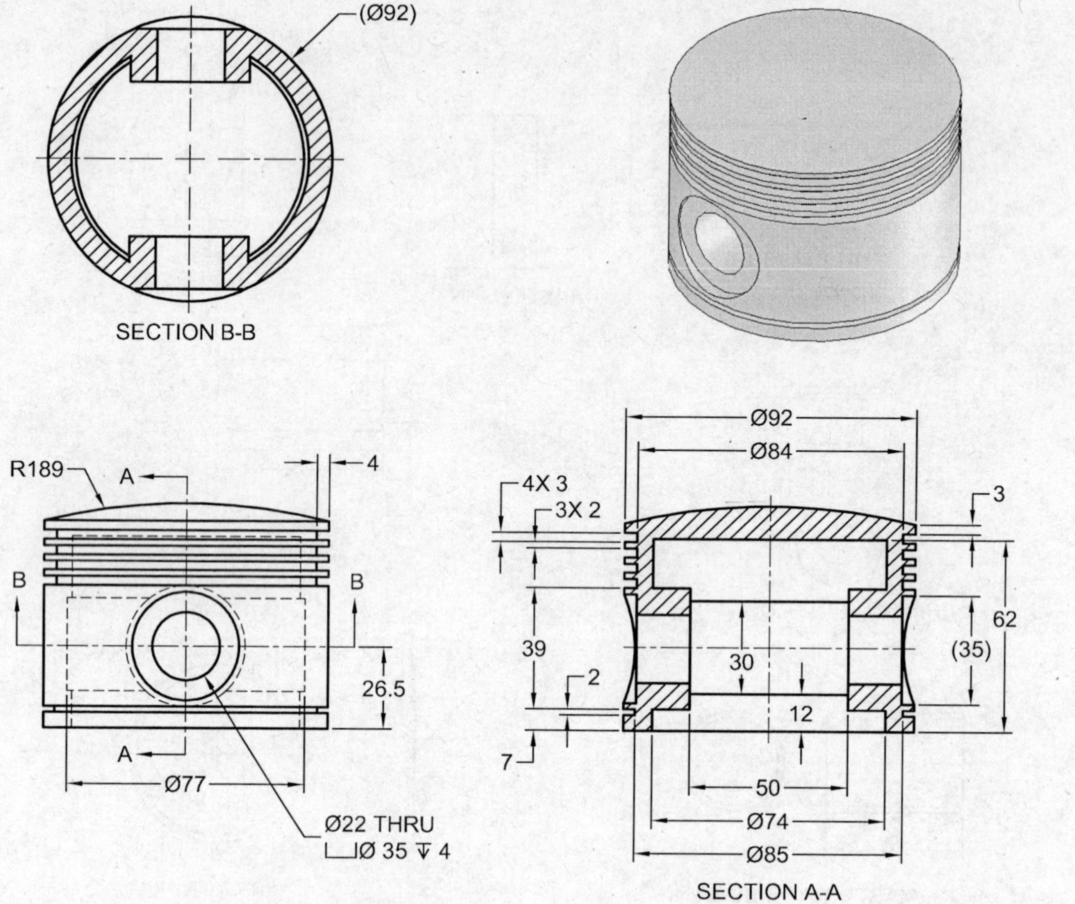

Figure 13-63 Views and dimensions of the Piston

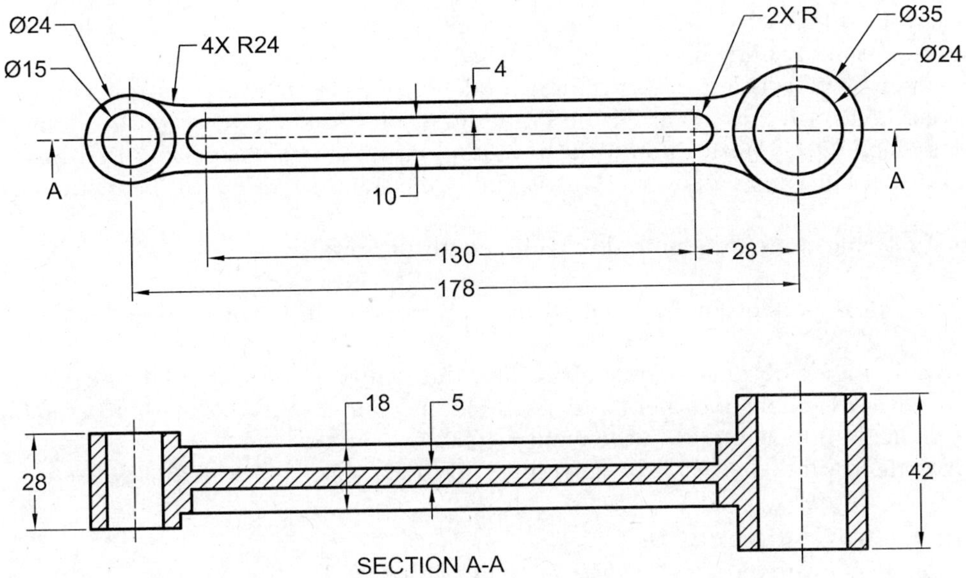

Figure 13-64 Views and dimensions of the Articulated Rod

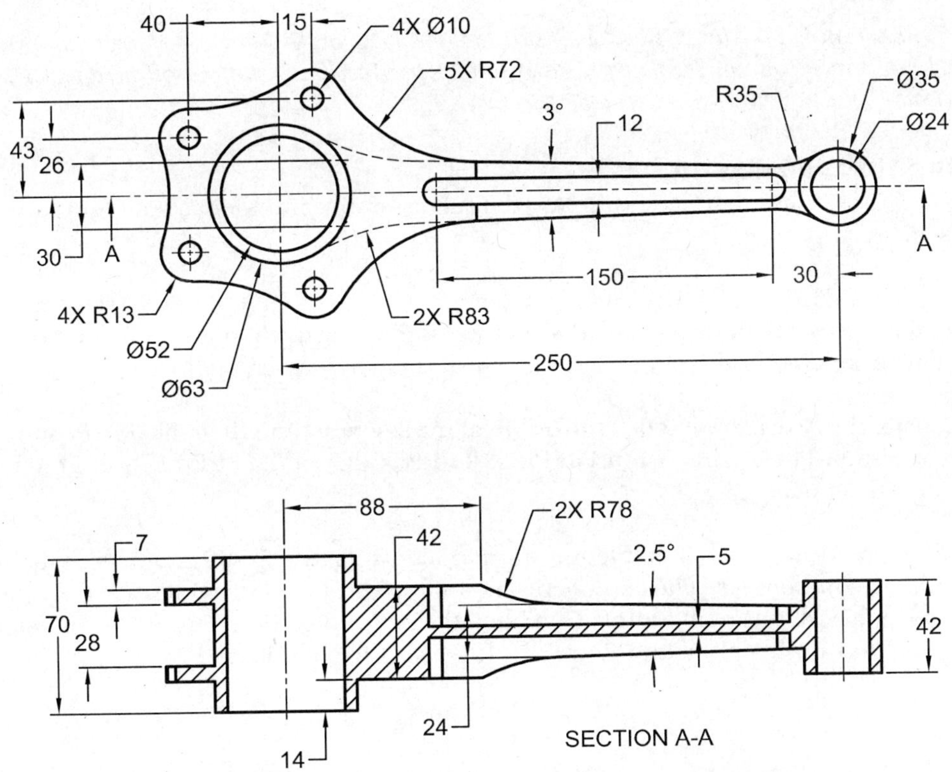

Figure 13-65 Views and dimensions of the Master Rod

You need to break this assembly in two steps because it is a large assembly. One will be the sub-assembly and the other will be the main assembly. First, you need to create the sub-assembly consisting of Articulated Rod, Piston, Piston Rings, Piston Pin, Rod Bush Upper, Rod Bush Lower, and Piston Pin Plug. Next, you need to create the main assembly by assembling the Master Rod with the Piston, Piston Rings, Piston Pin, Rod Bush Upper, and Piston Pin Plug. Finally, you will assemble the sub-assembly with the main assembly.

The following steps are required to complete this tutorial:

a. Create all components of the assembly in the **Part** mode and save them in the *Radial Engine Assembly* folder.
b. Start a new assembly document and assemble the components to complete the sub-assembly.
c. Start a new assembly document and assemble the components of the main assembly.
d. Assemble the sub-assembly in the main assembly.
e. Create the exploded view of the assembly and then create the explode line sketch.

Creating the Components

1. Create a folder with the name *Radial Engine Assembly* at the location *\Documents\SOLIDWORKS\c13*. Create all components in the individual part documents and save them in this folder.

Note

While creating the Master Rod, make sure that the holes on the Master Rod are created using the sketch-driven pattern. This is to ensure while assembling the Link Pin, you need to assemble the Link Pin using the sketch-driven pattern feature.

Creating the Sub-assembly

As discussed earlier, you first need to create the sub-assembly and then assemble it with the main assembly.

1. Start a new SOLIDWORKS assembly document and close the **Open** dialog box and **Begin Assembly PropertyManager**. Next, save the assembly with the name **Piston Articulated Rod Sub-assembly** in the same folder in which the parts are created.

2. First, place the Articulated Rod at the origin of the assembly and then the other components such as Piston, Piston Pin, Piston Pin Plug, Rod Bush Upper, and Rod Bush Lower in the assembly document.

3. Apply required mates to assemble these components. Figure 13-66 shows the sequence of assembling components. The exploded view and the explode line sketch are given only for your reference. The assembly after assembling the Articulated Rod, Piston, Piston Pin, Piston Pin Plug, Rod Bush Upper, and Rod Bush Lower is shown in Figure 13-67.

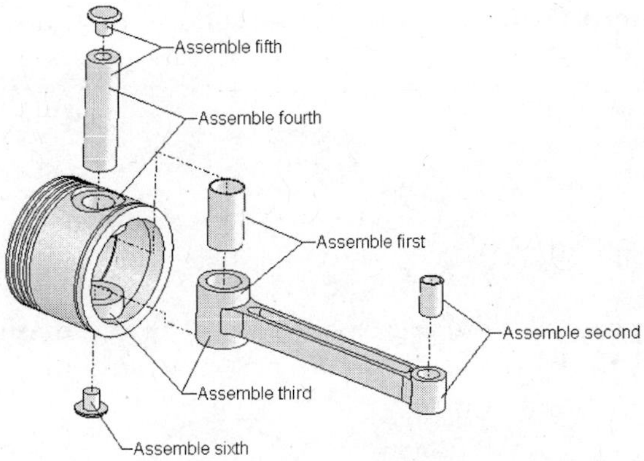

Figure 13-66 *Assembly of the Articulated Rod, Piston, Piston Pin, Piston Pin Plug, Rod Bush Upper, and Rod Bush Lower*

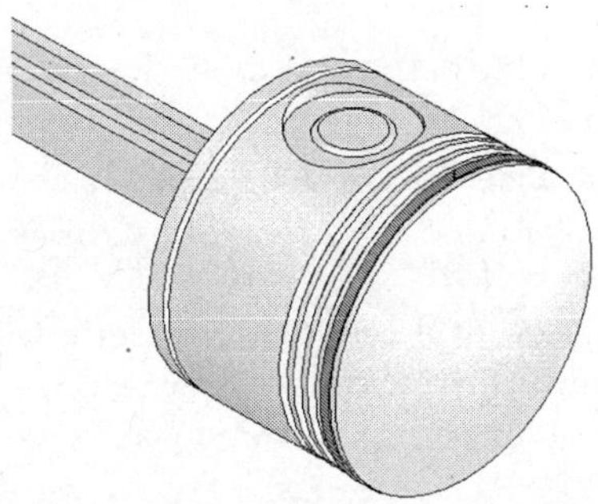

Figure 13-67 *First instance of the Piston Ring assembled with the Piston*

It is clear from the assembly that you need to assemble four instances of the Piston Ring. You will assemble only one instance of the Piston Ring at the uppermost groove of the ring and then create a local linear pattern.

4. Insert the Piston Ring in the assembly document and assemble the Piston Ring at the uppermost groove of the Piston using the assembly mates, refer to Figure 13-67. Next select the Piston Ring; a pop-up toolbar is displayed. Choose the **Appearances** button from the pop-up toolbar; a flyout is displayed. Choose the name of the component; the **Color PropertyManager** is displayed. Set the color using the option available in this PropertyManager.

   Next, you need to create the local linear pattern of the Piston Ring.

5. Choose the **Linear Component Pattern** button from the **Assembly CommandManager**; the **Linear Pattern PropertyManager** is displayed.

6. Select any one of the horizontal edges of the Articulated Rod to define the direction of pattern creation.

7. Click once in the **Components to Pattern** selection box and then select the Piston Ring from the drawing area; preview of the linear pattern with default settings is displayed in the drawing area.

8. Choose the **Reverse Direction** button to reverse the direction of the pattern creation if required.

9. Set 5 as the value in the **Spacing** spinner and **4** in the **Number of Instances** spinner.

10. Choose the **OK** button from the **Linear Pattern PropertyManager**; the sub-assembly after patterning the Piston Ring is shown in Figure 13-68.

11. Save and close the assembly document.

Creating the Main Assembly

Next, you need to create the main assembly and then assemble the sub-assembly with it.

1. Start a new SOLIDWORKS assembly document and close the **Open** dialog box and **Begin Assembly PropertyManager**. Now, save it with the name **Radial Engine assembly** in the same folder in which the parts are saved.

2. First, place the Master Rod at the origin of the assembly and then place the Piston, Piston Pin, Piston Pin Plug, Piston Ring, Rod Bush Upper, and Master Rod Bearing in the current assembly document.

3. Assemble all components of the main assembly using the assembly mates.

   The components after assembling them in the main assembly are displayed in Figure 13-69.

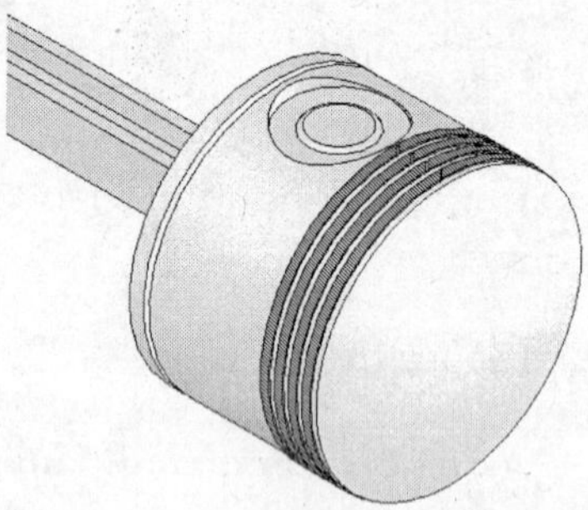

Figure 13-68 *Sub-assembly after patterning the Piston Ring*

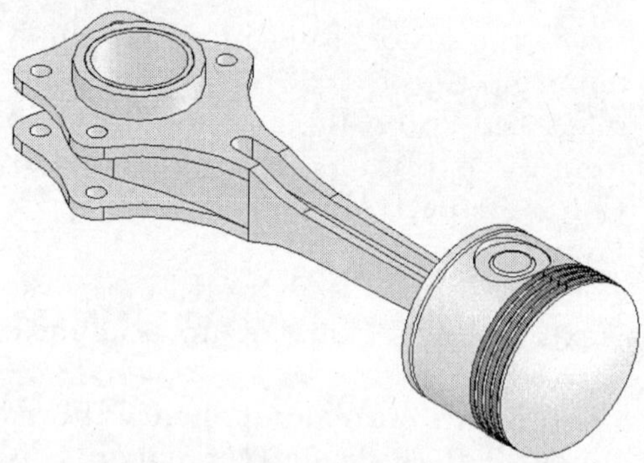

Figure 13-69 *Components assembled in the main assembly*

Assembling the Sub-assembly with the Main Assembly

Next, you need to place the sub-assembly in the main assembly and then assemble them together.

1. Choose the **Insert Components** button from the **Assembly CommandManager**; the **Insert Component PropertyManager** along with the **Open** dialog box is displayed.

2. If the sub-assembly document is not opened, browse the *Piston Articulated Rod Sub-assembly* file or else close the **Open** dialog box.

3. Select **SOLIDWORKS Assembly** (**.asm, *.sldasm*) from the **Files of type** drop-down list for refining the search.

4. Double-click on *Piston Articulated Rod Sub-assembly* and place the sub-assembly in the main assembly. Figure 13-70 shows the sub-assembly and the main assembly placed together.

5. Assemble the sub-assembly with the main assembly using the assembly mates. Refer to Figure 13-71 which shows the assembly structure that will help you in assembling the instances of the sub-assembly.

   Figure 13-72 shows all instances of the sub-assembly assembled with the main assembly.

Assembling the Link Pin

After assembling the sub-assembly with the main assembly, you need to assemble the Link Pin with the main assembly.

1. Place the Link Pin in the current assembly document. Next, assemble the Link Pin with the main assembly using the assembly mates. Figure 13-73 shows the first instance of the Link Pin assembled with the main assembly.

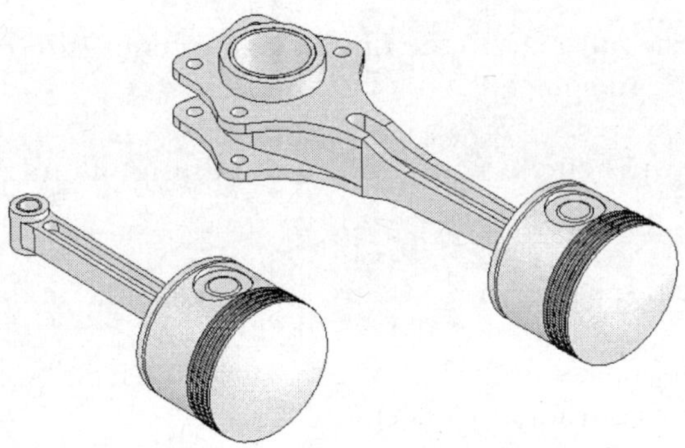

Figure 13-70 *Sub-assembly and the main assembly placed together*

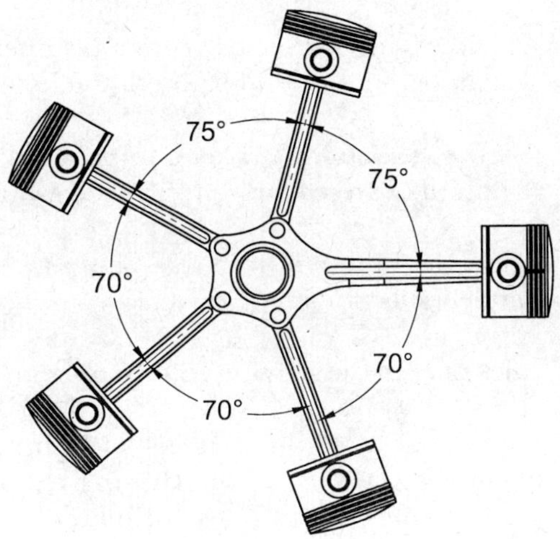

Figure 13-71 *Assembly structure*

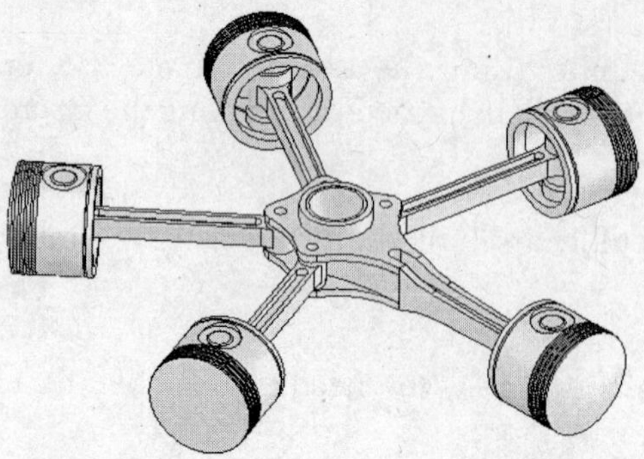

Figure 13-72 *The sub-assembly assembled with the main assembly*

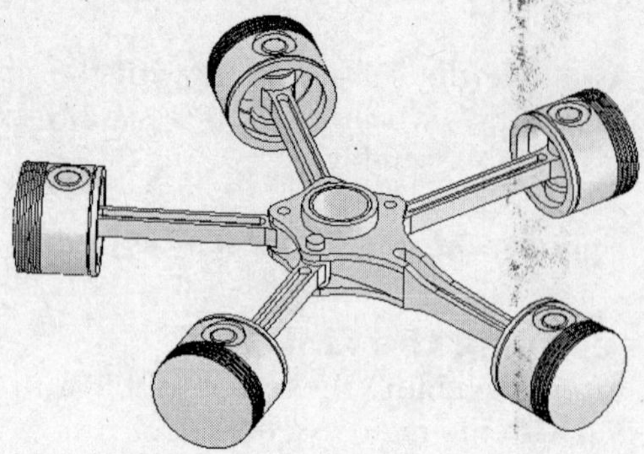

Figure 13-73 *The first instance of the Link Pin assembled with the main assembly*

As discussed earlier, the other instances of the Link Pin will be assembled using the sketch-driven pattern feature of the holes created on the left of the master rod.

2. Choose the **Pattern Driven Component Pattern** button from the **Linear Component Pattern** flyout; the **Pattern Driven PropertyManager** is displayed.

3. Select the Link Pin from the main assembly; its name is displayed in the **Components to Pattern** selection box.

4. Click once in the **Driving feature or component** selection box to activate the selection mode.

5. Select any one of the hole instances from the master rod; the name of the sketch pattern feature is displayed in the **Driving feature or component** selection box and a preview of the resulting pattern is also displayed.

6. If the instances are not placed properly, choose the **Select Seed Position** button and select the correct seed feature.

7. Choose the **OK** button from the **Pattern Driven PropertyManager**. Figure 13-74 shows the final assembly.

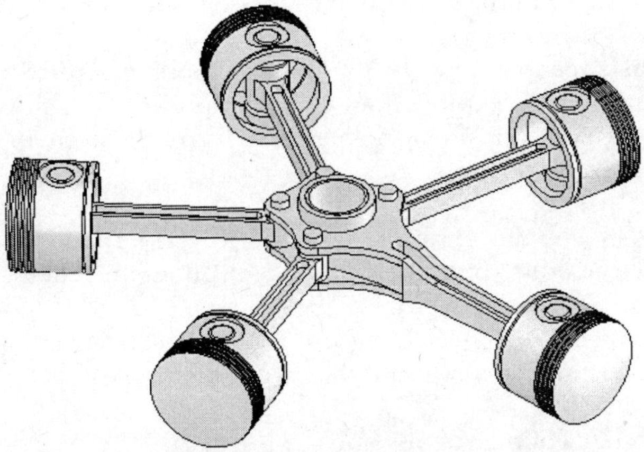

Figure 13-74 Final assembly

Exploding the Assembly

After creating the assembly, you need to explode it using the **Exploded View** tool. The current assembly contains a sub-assembly that needs to be exploded first to create the final exploded view. Therefore, you need to open the Piston Articulated Rod Sub-assembly.

1. Open the Piston Articulated Rod Sub-assembly document.

2. Choose the **Exploded View** button from the **Assembly CommandManager**; the **Explode PropertyManager** is displayed. 

3. Choose the **Regular step (translate and rotate)** button from the **Add a Step** rollout of the **Explode PropertyManager** if not selected by default.

4. Ensure that all check boxes are cleared.

5. Select the top face of the Piston Pin Plug; a triad is displayed.

6. Select the arrow of the triad that is normal to the selected face.

7. Set the **Explode Distance** spinner to **170** and then choose the **Add Step** button; the selected instance of the Piston Pin Plug is exploded and the component is removed from the selection set. Also, the sequence of explosion is displayed as **Explode Step1** in the **Existing explode steps** list box of the **Explode Steps** rollout.

8. If the piston pin plug is moved downward, choose the **Reverse Direction** button on the left of the **Explode Direction** selection box in the **Add a Step** rollout and then choose **Done**.

   Similarly, explode the another instance of Piston Pin Plug in the opposite direction.

9. Select the flat face of the Piston Pin in the drawing area; a triad is displayed.

10. Select the arrow of the triad that is normal to the selected face.

11. Set the **Explode Distance** spinner to **150**, and then choose the **Add Step** button; the selected instance of the Piston Pin is exploded and the component is removed from the selection set. Also, the sequence of explosion is displayed as **Explode Step3** in the **Existing explode steps** list box of the **Explode Steps** rollout.

12. If the Piston Pin is moved downward, choose the **Reverse Direction** button on the left of the **Explode Direction** edit box in the **Add a Step** rollout and then choose **Done**.

    When the triad is displayed on selecting the face, you can select an arrow to specify the direction and drag the arrow to relocate the component.

13. Explode all components of the sub-assembly.

14. Save the sub-assembly and then open the main assembly document; the **SOLIDWORKS** message box is displayed stating that the models in the assembly have changed and would you like to rebuild them. Choose **OK** to save the models and rebuild the sub-assembly.

15. Choose the **Exploded View** button from the **Assembly CommandManager**; the **Explode PropertyManager** is displayed. Ensure that all check boxes are cleared.

16. As discussed earlier, explode the components of the main assembly only.

    Next, you need to explode the parts of the remaining sub-assemblies.

17. Select all sub-assemblies from the drawing area and choose the **From Subassembly** button in the **Explode PropertyManager**; all sub-assemblies are exploded.

18. Choose **OK** to exit the **Explode PropertyManager**. The assembly after exploding the components is shown in Figure 13-75.

Creating the Explode Line Sketch

After exploding the assembly, you need to create the explode line sketch of the exploded state of the assembly.

1. Choose the **Explode Line Sketch** button from the **Assembly CommandManager**; the **Route Line PropertyManager** is displayed and you are prompted to select a cylindrical face, planar face, vertex, point, arc, or a line entity.

2. Select the cylindrical face of piston pin plug, refer to Figure 13-76, as the first selection; the name of the selected face is displayed in the **Items To Connect** selection box. Also, preview of the explode line sketch is displayed at the center of the selected face.

3. Refer to Figure 13-76 and select the other cylindrical faces to create the explode line sketch.

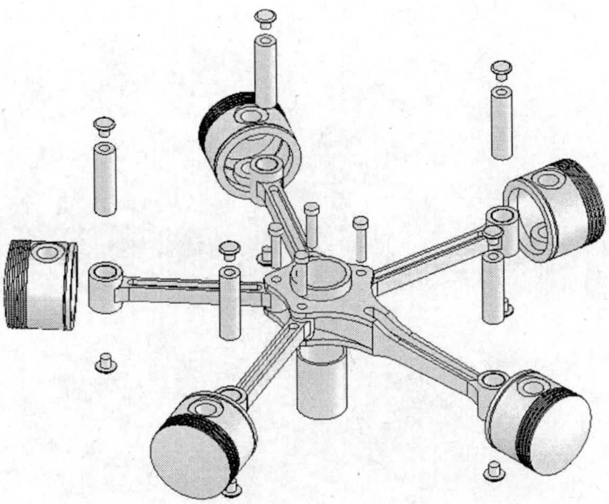

Figure 13-75 Final exploded assembly

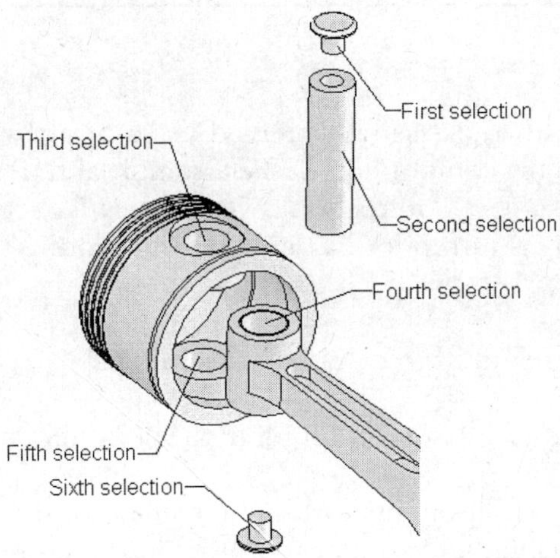

Figure 13-76 Faces to be selected to create the explode line sketch

4. Next, choose the **OK** button; an exploded line is created.

5. Similarly, create explode lines between the other parts of the exploded assembly. Figure 13-77 shows the assembly after creating the explode line sketch.

6. Invoke the **ConfigurationManager** and expand the **Default** node. Next, select **ExplView1** node and right-click; a shortcut menu is displayed.

7. Choose the **Animate collapse** option from the menu to view the animation of the exploded view.

8. Save and close the assembly document.

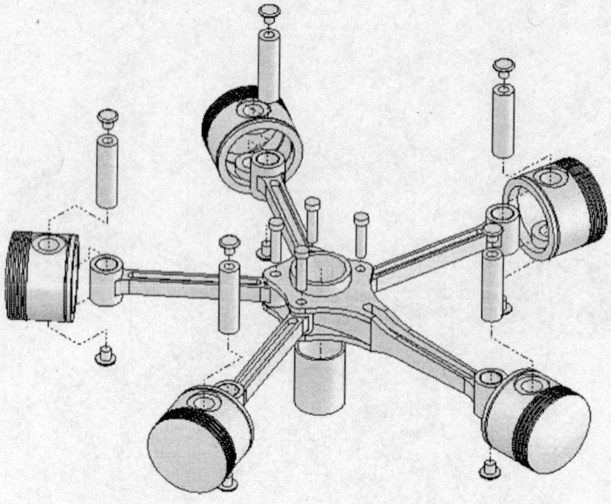

Figure 13-77 Explode line sketch created for the exploded state of the assembly

Tutorial 2

In this tutorial, you will modify the assembly created in Tutorial 1 (Bench Vice) of Chapter 12. You will modify the design of the components of the assembly and then suppress some mates that enable it to have a particular degree of freedom. Next, you will check the assembly for collision detection when the assembly is in motion. Then, you will modify the assembly and check the interference. **(Expected time: 1 hr)**

The following steps are required to complete this tutorial:

a. Copy and save the Bench Vice assembly folder in the *c13* directory and then open the Bench Vice assembly.
b. Modify the design of the components within the context of the assembly.
c. Suppress the mate to enable the Vice Jaw to move along the slide ways of the Vice Body.
d. Check the new assembly design for the collision detection when the assembly is in motion. Modify the design, if there is any collision between the components.
e. Check the interference in the modified assembly.

Opening the Bench Vice Assembly

The assembly created in Tutorial 1 of Chapter 12 is the Bench Vice assembly. You need to copy and save it in the current folder of Chapter 13.

1. Copy the folder in which the Bench Vice assembly is saved and paste it in the *c13* folder.

2. Start SOLIDWORKS, invoke the **Open** dialog box, and then browse to the Bench Vice assembly document. Double-click on it to open the assembly document.

Modifying the Design of the Components of the Bench Vice Assembly

You need to modify the components in the context of the assembly because of alteration in the design of some of the components.

Before you start modifying the components, it is recommended that you hide some of them. This will simplify the assembly and facilitate the selection of components while editing and modifying them.

1. Press and hold the CTRL key and select the Clamping Plate, Base Plate, four Set Screw 1, two Set Screw 2, Oval Fillister, Screw Bar, Bar Globes, and Jaw Screw from the **FeatureManager Design Tree**.

2. When you release the CTRL key, a pop-up toolbar is displayed. Choose the **Hide Components** option from the pop-up toolbar; the visibility of the selected components is turned off.

The design alteration includes creating a through slot on the right face of the Vice Jaw. To modify its design, you first need to enable the part editing environment.

3. Select the Vice Jaw from the assembly and choose the **Edit Component** button from the **Assembly CommandManager**; the part modeling environment is invoked.

4. Make sure that the Vice Body is transparent. If not, choose the **Assembly Transparency** button from the **Features CommandManager**; a flyout is displayed. Choose the **Force Transparency** option from the flyout. The Vice Body becomes transparent, as shown in Figure 13-78.

5. Select the right face of the Vice Jaw and invoke the sketching environment.

6. Create the sketch of the slot, as shown in Figure 13-79.

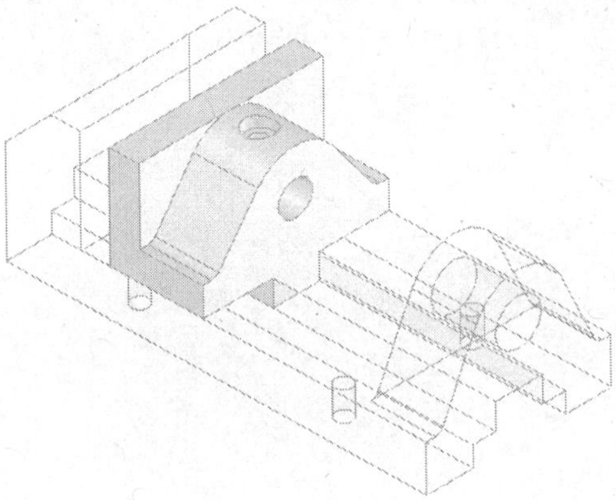

Figure 13-78 *Vice Jaw in the part edit mode in the assembly document*

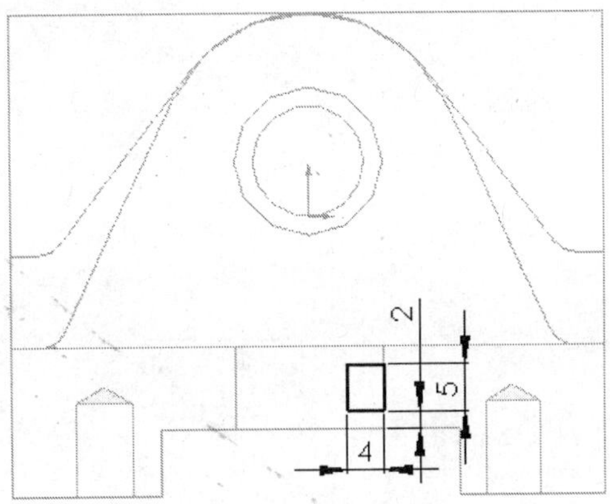

Figure 13-79 *Sketch of the slot*

7. Invoke the **Cut-Extrude PropertyManager**.

8. Create the cut feature using the **Through All** option and exit the **PropertyManager**.

9. Choose the **Edit Component** button to exit the part editing environment.

   Figure 13-80 shows the assembly after modifying the design of the Vice Jaw.

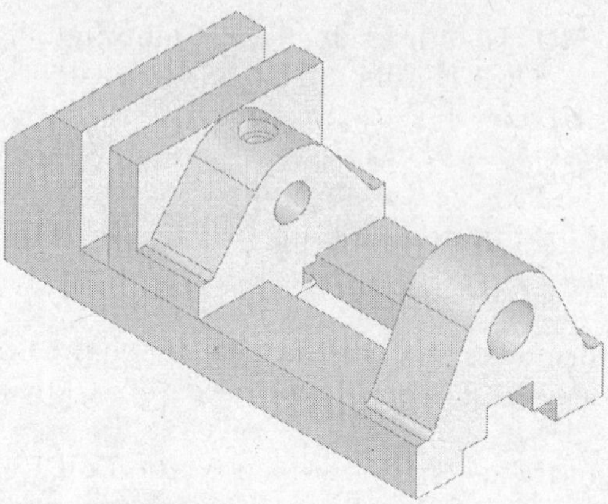

Figure 13-80 Modified Vice Jaw

10. Similarly, modify the design of the Vice Body by creating a blind extruded boss feature up to 60 mm depth on the right face of the Vice Body. Note that you need to reverse the direction of feature creation.

    The sketch of the extruded boss feature is shown in Figure 13-81. Figure 13-82 shows the assembly after exiting the part editing environment.

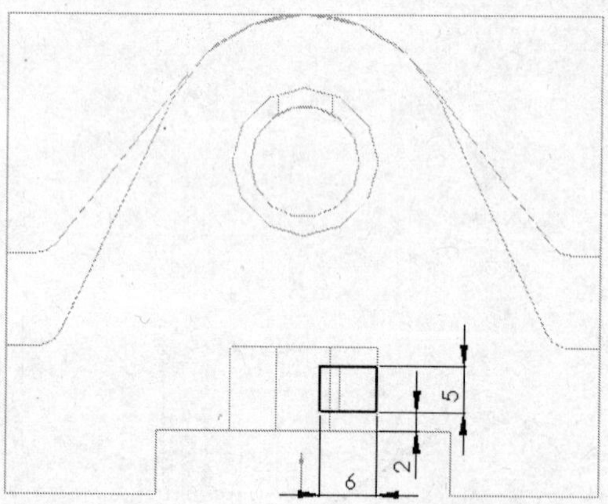

Figure 13-81 Sketch of the extruded boss feature

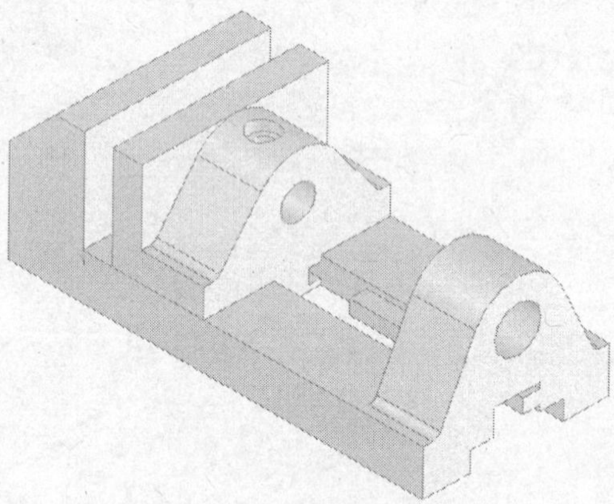

Figure 13-82 Modified assembly

11. Exit the **Edit Component** mode and choose the **Save** button from the Menu Bar; the **Save Modified Documents** dialog box is displayed. Choose **Save All** to save the referenced models also.

Suppressing the Mate Constraint to Move the Vice Jaw Freely

To analyze the movement of the Bench Vice assembly, you need to make the movement of the Vice Jaw free in the X direction. On doing so, the Vice Jaw will slide on the sideways of the Vice Body.

1. Expand the **Vice Jaw** node from the **FeatureManager Design Tree** and then expand the **Mates in Bench Vice** sub node. Next, select the **LimitDistance1** mate; the planar faces of the Vice Jaw and the Vice Body to which this mate is applied get highlighted and a pop-up toolbar is displayed.

2. Choose **Suppress** from the pop-up toolbar; the degree of freedom along the X direction becomes free.

3. Select a horizontal edge of the Vice Jaw and choose the **Move Component** button from the **Assembly CommandManager**; the **Move Component PropertyManager** is displayed. On dragging the cursor, you will observe that you can move the Vice Jaw in the X direction.

4. Drag the Vice Jaw back to its original position and choose the **OK** button from the **Move Component PropertyManager**.

Analyzing the Collision between the Components when the Assembly is in Motion

Next, you need to analyze the collision between the components of the assembly when the assembly is in motion.

1. Choose the **Move Component** button from the **Assembly CommandManager**. Next, select the **Collision Detection** radio button.

2. Select the Vice Jaw and drag the cursor to move in the direction shown in Figure 13-83.

   On moving the Vice Jaw in the specified direction, you will observe that the right face of the Vice Jaw and the newly created extrusion feature of the Vice Body are highlighted, refer to Figure 13-84. This indicates that the Vice Jaw has collided with the Vice Body. Leave the assembly at this location.

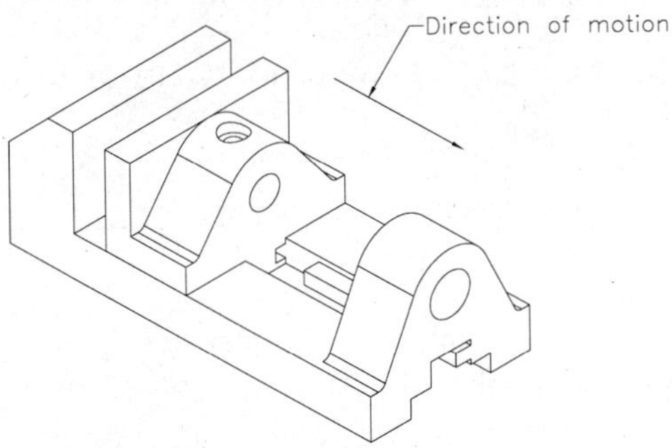

***Figure 13-83** Direction in which the Vice Jaw will move*

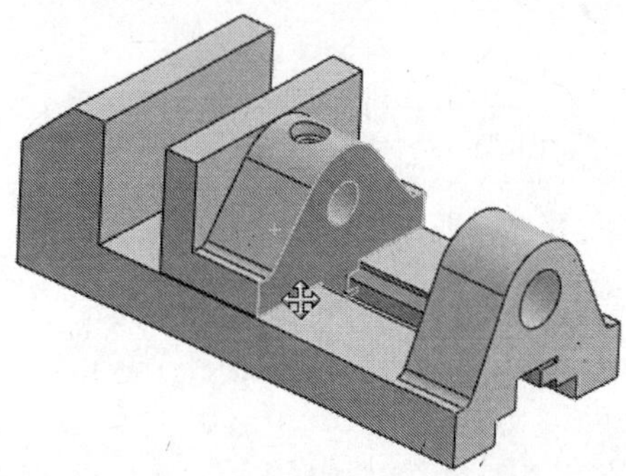

***Figure 13-84** Faces of the Vice Jaw and the Vice Body highlighted in different colors*

3. Choose the **OK** button from the **Move Component PropertyManager**.

   The collision has been detected in the assembly, and therefore you need to modify the design of one of the components. In this case, you will modify the dimensions of the extruded boss feature.

4. Double-click on the newly created extrusion feature of the Vice Body; the dimensions of the newly created feature are displayed.

5. Double-click on the dimension having the value **6**; the **Modify** dialog box is displayed. Set the value of the dimension to **4** and then press the ENTER key.

6. Press CTRL+B on the keyboard to rebuild the entire assembly.

7. Choose the **Interference Detection** button from the **Evaluate CommandManager**; the **Interference Detection PropertyManager** is displayed.

8. Choose the **Calculate** button. You will observe that **No Interferences** is displayed in the **Interference Results** selection box in the **Results** rollout of this PropertyManager.

9. Choose the **Cancel** button from the **Interference Detection PropertyManager**.

   Next, you need to show all the components of this assembly.

10. Press and hold the CTRL key, select the hidden components from the **FeatureManager Design Tree**, and then choose **Show Components** from the pop-up toolbar.

11. Expand the **Mates** node from the **FeatureManager Design Tree**. Select the **LimitDistance1** mate that is suppressed, and then choose **Unsuppress** from the pop-up toolbar.

12. Save the assembly document and all the referenced part documents.

Self-Evaluation Test

Answer the following questions and then compare them to those given at the end of this chapter:

1. The component patterns created individually without the use of any existing pattern feature are known as __________ patterns.

2. The component patterns created using an existing pattern feature are known as __________ patterns.

3. In a __________ component, the feature information is available in the part document and only the graphical representation of the component is displayed in the assembly document.

4. After selecting a component, choose the __________ option from the pop-up toolbar to change the transparency condition of the selected component.

5. You can create the explode line sketch by choosing the __________ button from the **Assembly CommandManager**.

6. You can create subassemblies in the assembly environment of SOLIDWORKS. (T/F)

7. You cannot create a sub-assembly of the components that are already placed in an assembly document. (T/F)

8. When you move the cursor on a mate in the **FeatureManager Design Tree**, the entities used in the mate are highlighted in a different color in the drawing area. (T/F)

9. You cannot edit the assembly mates. (T/F)

10. While in the part editing mode in the assembly document, you can use the **Move/Copy Features** tool to edit the features dynamically by using the editing handles. (T/F)

11. You can create multiple exploded views of an assembly in the assembly environment. (T/F)

Review Questions

Answer the following questions:

1. Which of the following options is used to open a component separately in the part document?

   (a) **Modify** (b) **Edit**
   (c) **Open Part** (d) None of these

2. Which of the following options is used to define whether a component collides with another component of an assembly or not?

   (a) **Collision Detection** (b) **Hole Alignment**
   (c) **Mass Properties** (d) None of these

3. Which of the following options needs to be selected in the **Open** dialog box to open an assembly with lightweight parts?

   (a) **Lightweight** (b) **Open Lightweight**
   (c) **Lightweight parts** (d) **Lightweight assembly**

4. Which of the following buttons in the **Assembly CommandManager** needs to be chosen to suppress a component?

   (a) **Change Suppression State** (b) **Suppress**
   (c) **Hide/Show Component** (d) **Move Component**

5. Which of the following buttons needs to be chosen from the **Assembly CommandManager** to create an exploded view?

   (a) **Exploded View** (b) **Assembly Exploder**
   (c) **Mate** (d) None of these

6. The exploded state of an assembly is created using the __________ **PropertyManager**.

7. The __________ option is used to create a local linear pattern.

8. To show a hidden component, select the icon of the component from the **FeatureManager Design Tree**, invoke the shortcut menu, and then choose the __________ option from it.

9. The __________ option is used to pattern the instances of the components using an existing pattern feature.

10. The __________ check box needs to be selected to stop the motion of the assembly when one of the components collides with another component while the assembly is in motion.

EXERCISE

Exercise 1

Create the assembly shown in Figure 13-85. Ensure that its back plate is fixed and the entire assembly can move in the Y direction with respect to the back plate. Keep the rotational degree of freedom of the screw rod free, so that it can also rotate on its axis. After creating the assembly, explode it and create the explode line sketch. The exploded view of the assembly with the explode line sketch is shown in Figure 13-86. The dimensions of the model are given in Figures 13-87 through 13-92. Assume the missing dimensions. **(Expected time: 4 hr)**

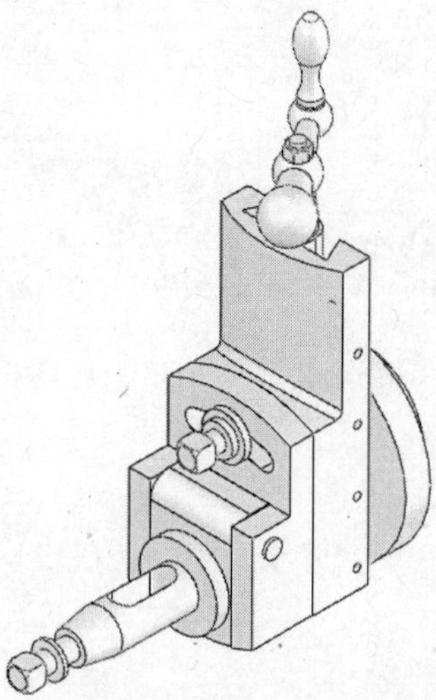

Figure 13-85 *Shaper tool holder assembly*

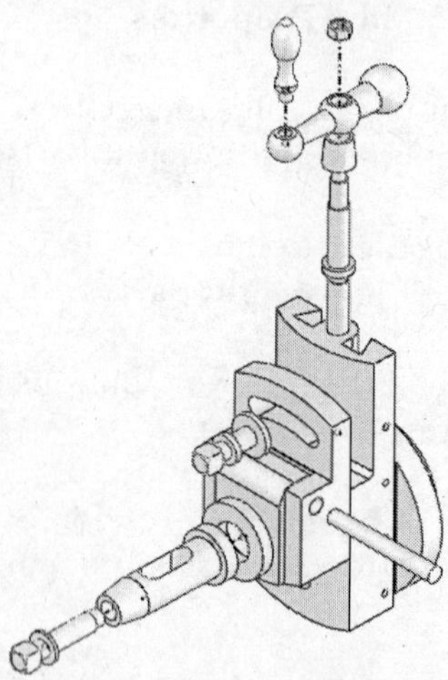

Figure 13-86 *Exploded view of the Shaper tool holder assembly with explode lines*

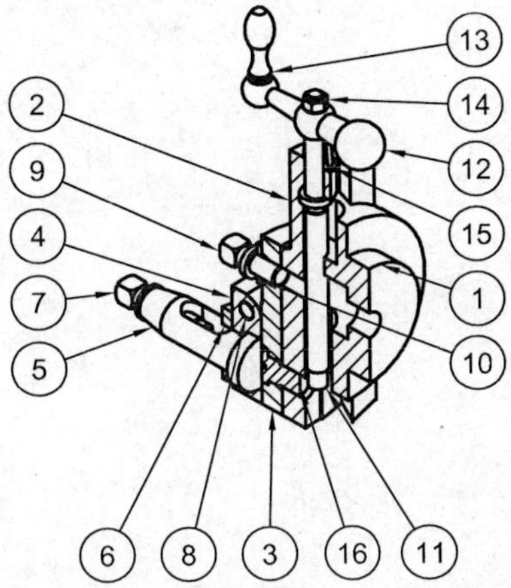

ITEM NO.	PART NO.	DESCRIPTION	QTY.
1	Back Plate		1
2	Vertical Slide		1
3	Swivel Plate		1
4	Drag Plate		1
5	Tool Holder		1
6	Washer		1
7	Tool Fixing Screw		1
8	Pivot Pin		1
9	Clamping Screw		1
10	Small Washer		1
11	Screw Bar		1
12	Handle Bar		1
13	Handle		1
14	Nut M10		1
15	Spacer Bush		1
16	Swivel Screw Pin		1

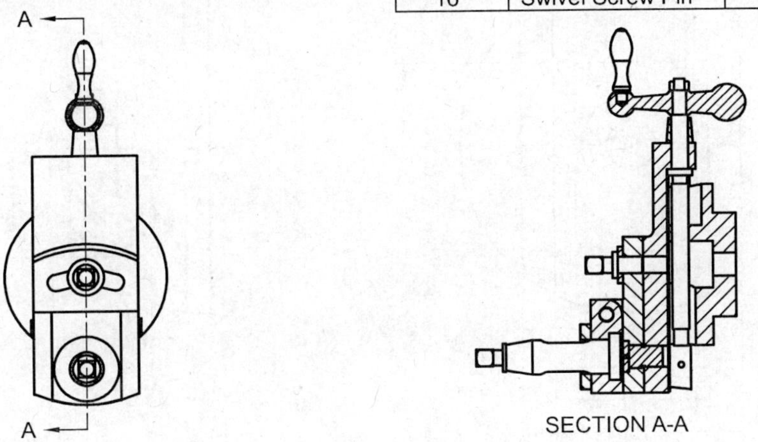

Figure 13-87 *Shaper tool holder assembly*

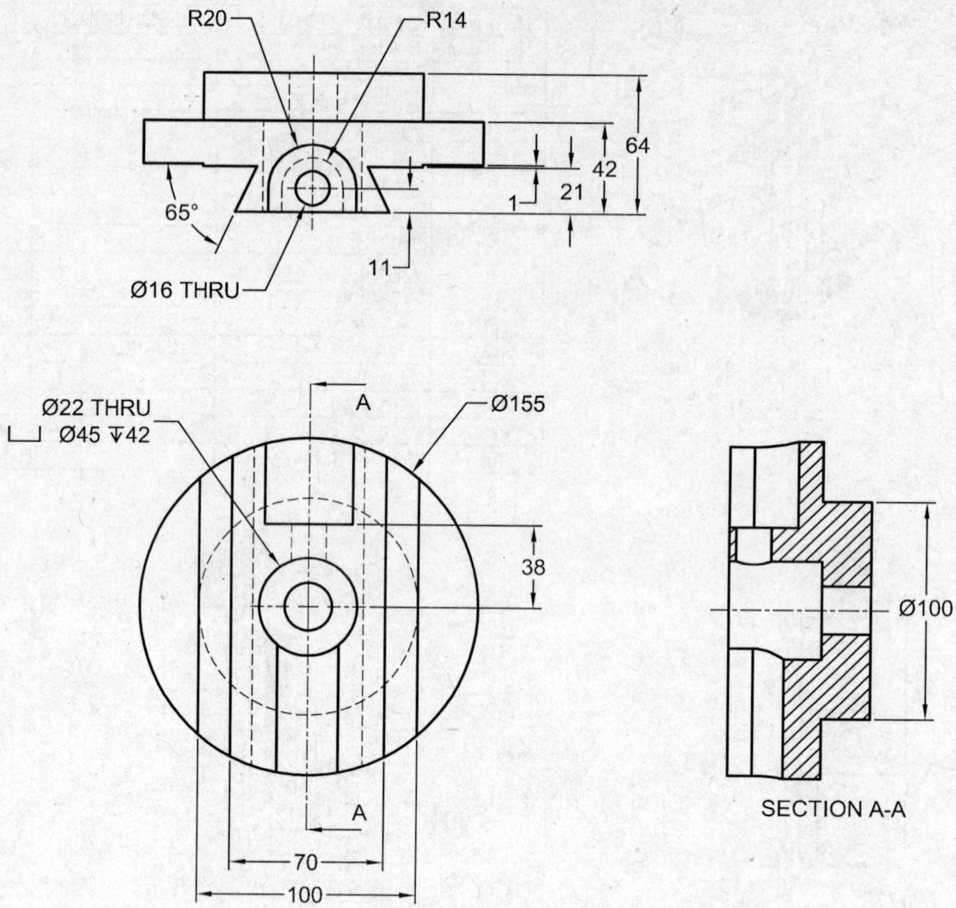

Figure 13-88 Views and dimensions of the Back Plate

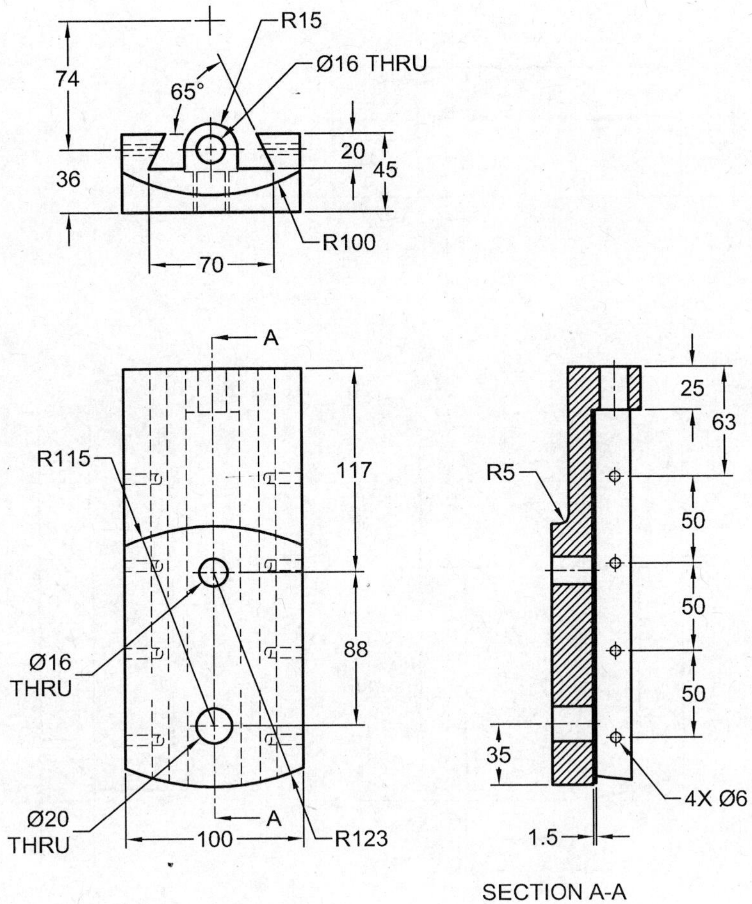

Figure 13-89 Views and dimensions of the Vertical Slide

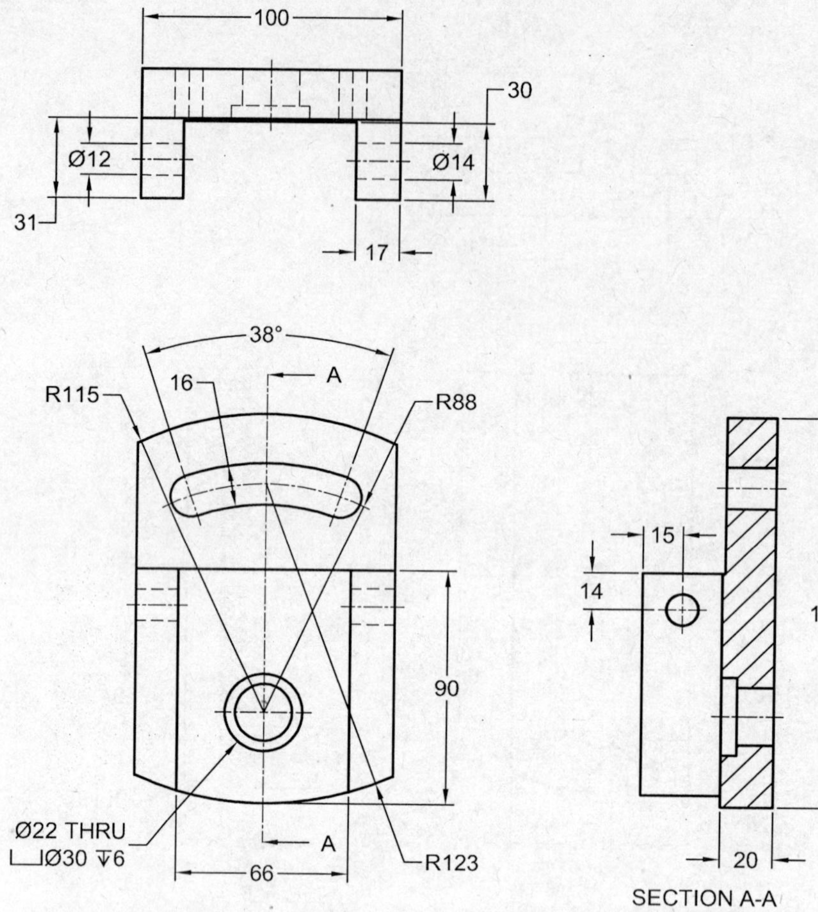

Figure 13-90 Views and dimensions of the Swivel Plate

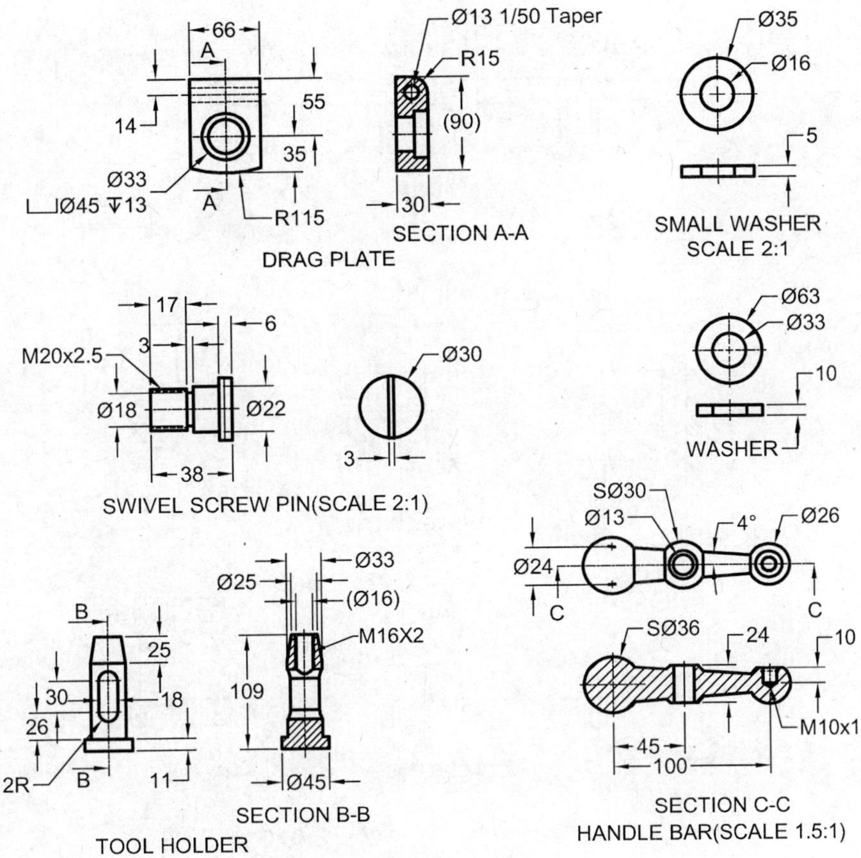

Figure 13-91 *Views and dimensions of other components*

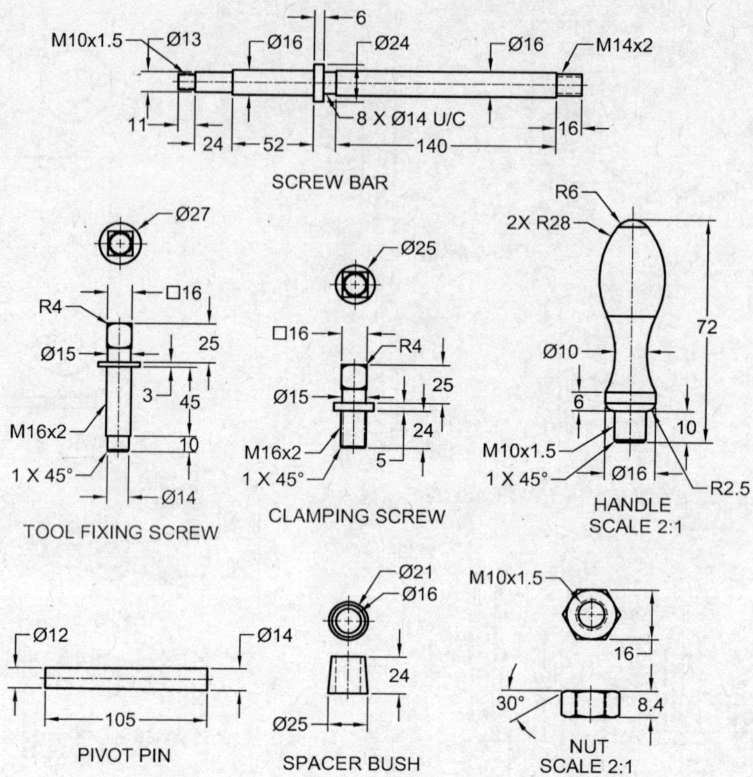

Figure 13-92 Views and dimensions of the components

Answers to Self-Evaluation Test

1. Local, **2.** Derived, **3.** Lightweight, **4. Change Transparency**, **5. Explode Line Sketch**, **6.** T, **7.** F, **8.** T, **9.** F, **10.** F, **11.** T

Chapter 14

Working with Drawing Views-I

Learning Objectives

After completing this chapter, you will be able to:

- *Generate different types of views*
- *Generate the view of an assembly in exploded state*
- *Work with interactive drafting*
- *Edit drawing views*
- *Change the scale of drawing views*
- *Delete drawing views*
- *Modify the hatch pattern of section views*

THE DRAWING MODE

After creating solid models or assemblies, you need to generate their two-dimensional (2D) drawing views. These views are the lifeline of all manufacturing systems because at the shop floor or the machine floor, the machinist needs 2D drawing for manufacturing. SOLIDWORKS provides a specialized environment known as the **Drawing** mode. This mode provides all the tools required to generate and modify drawing views and add dimensions and annotations to them. In other words, you can get final shop floor drawing using this mode.

You can also sketch 2D drawings in the **Drawing** mode of SOLIDWORKS using the sketching tools provided in this mode. In other words, there are two types of drafting methods available in SOLIDWORKS: Generative and Interactive. Generative drafting is a technique of generating the drawing views by using a solid model or an assembly. Interactive drafting is a technique of sketching the drawing views in the **Drawing** mode by using the sketching tools. In this chapter, you will learn about generating the drawing views of parts or assemblies.

One of the major advantages of working in SOLIDWORKS is that this software has bidirectional associative property. This property ensures that the modifications made in a model in the **Part** mode are reflected in the **Assembly** and **Drawing** modes, and vice versa.

STARTING A DRAWING DOCUMENT

To generate drawing views, you need to start a new drawing document. There are different methods to start a drawing document in SOLIDWORKS. The first method is to start a drawing document by using the **Welcome - SOLIDWORKS** dialog box, the second method is by using the **New SOLIDWORKS Document** dialog box, and the third method is by using the options available in the part or assembly document. All these methods are discussed next.

Starting a New Drawing Document Using the Welcome - SOLIDWORKS Dialog Box

To start a new drawing document for generating the drawing views, invoke the **Welcome - SOLIDWORKS Document** dialog box as shown in Figure 14-1. Next, choose the **Drawing** button; a new drawing document will open and the **Sheet Format/Size** dialog box will be displayed. Figure 14-2 shows the initial screen of the drawing document with the **Sheet Format/Size** dialog box. Double-click on a drawing template file in this dialog box; a new drawing document will be started. Also, the **Model View PropertyManager** will be invoked automatically. Its appearance will depend on whether any part or assembly document was opened or not when you started the new drawing document.

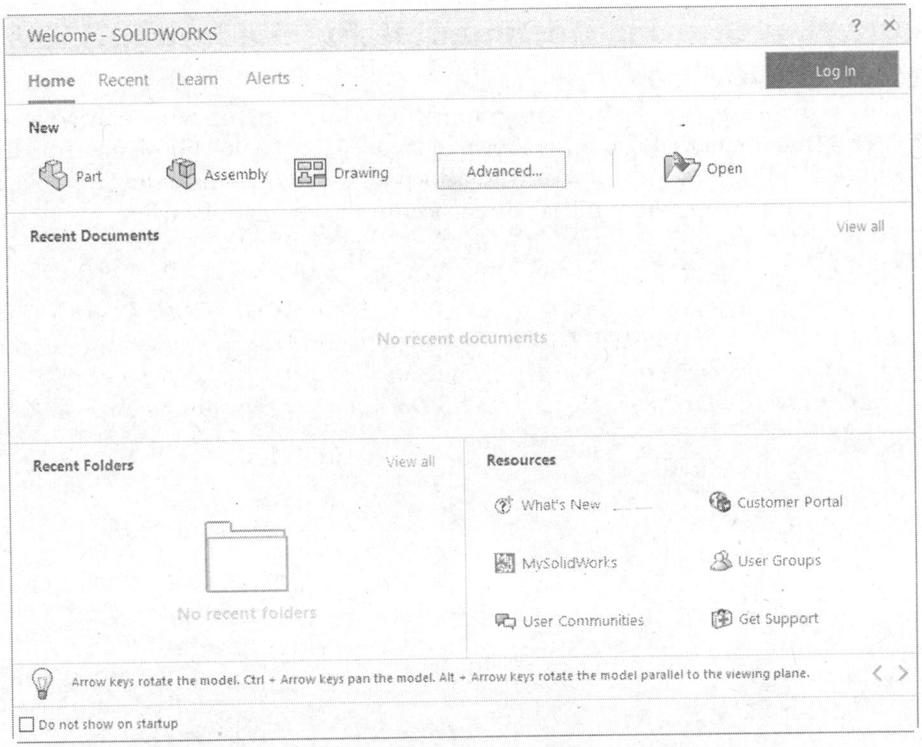

*Figure 14-1 The **Welcome - SOLIDWORKS** dialog box*

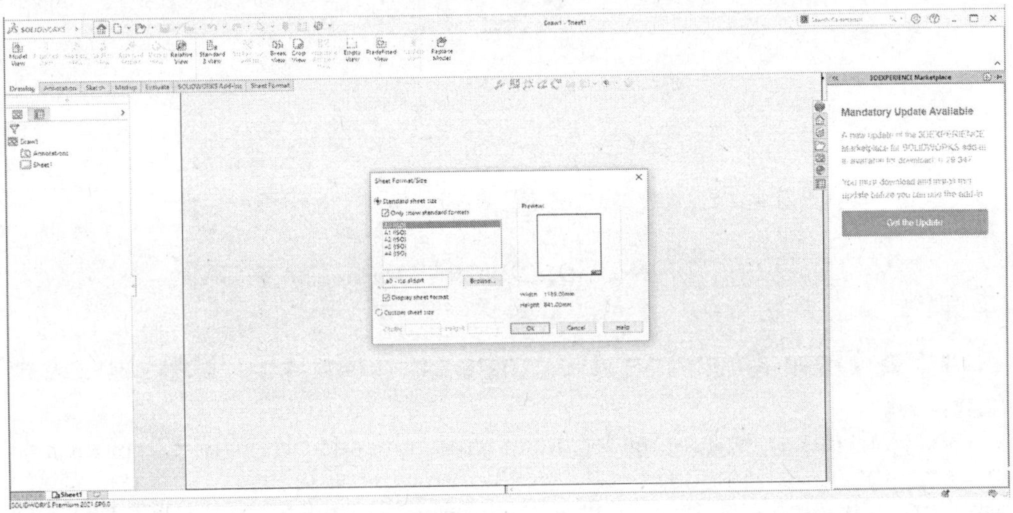

*Figure 14-2 Initial screen of the drawing document with the **Sheet Format/Size** dialog box*

Starting a New Drawing Document Using the New SOLIDWORKS Document Dialog Box

To start a new drawing document for generating the drawing views, invoke the **New SOLIDWORKS Document** dialog box, as shown in Figure 14-3. Next, choose the **Drawing** button and then choose the **OK** button; a new drawing document will open and the **Sheet Format/Size** dialog box will be displayed. Next, follow the procedure as discussed earlier.

> **Tip**
> *If you are in the practice of using advanced form of the **New SOLIDWORKS Document** dialog box, the **New SOLIDWORKS Document** dialog box will be displayed every time you choose the **Make Drawing from Part/Assembly** option. Select a drawing template from the **Templates** tab in the **New SOLIDWORKS Document** dialog box and choose **OK**.*

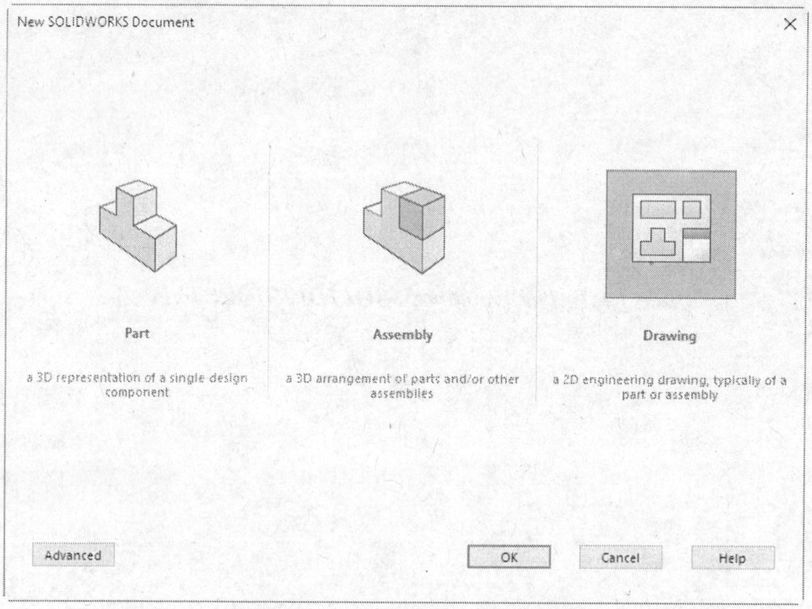

*Figure 14-3 The **New SOLIDWORKS Document** dialog box*

Starting a New Drawing Document from the Part/Assembly Document

This method of starting a new drawing document is recommended when the part or the assembly document for which you want to generate the drawing views is opened in another window. In this case, choose **New > Make Drawing from Part/Assembly** from the SOLIDWORKS menubar of the part or the assembly document; the **New SOLIDWORKS Document** dialog box will be displayed, if you are using it in the advanced mode. Select a drawing template and choose the **OK** button; a new drawing document will start and the **Sheet Format/Size** dialog box will be displayed. You can select the desired format and size of the sheet from this dialog box. On selecting the format and size, the new document will start with the set format and size and the **View Palette** task pane will be displayed on the right in the drawing window, refer to Figure 14-4.

The **View Palette** task pane displays the preview of all the views of the component in the part file that was used to start this drawing file. You can drag the required view from this task pane to the drawing sheet. As you drag a view to the drawing sheet, the **View Palette** task pane will be closed and the **Projected View PropertyManager** will be displayed for creating the projected views.

Note
*The **Projected View PropertyManager** will be displayed automatically only if the **Auto-start projected view** check box is selected in the **View Palette** task pane.*

Figure 14-4 *A new drawing document with the **View Palette** task pane*

Tip
*If you choose the **Cancel** button from the **Sheet Format/Size** dialog box, a blank custom sheet of size 431.80 mm x 279.40 mm will be inserted in the drawing document.*

TYPES OF VIEWS

You can generate different types of views in SOLIDWORKS. You first need to generate a standard view such as the top view or the front view, and then use it to derive the remaining views from the standard view. You can generate the following types of drawing views:

Model View

A model view is used to create the base view in the drawing sheet. You can generate orthogonal views such as the front, top, left, and so on as the model view. You can also generate an isometric, a trimetric, or a dimetric view as the model view.

Projected View

A projected view is generated by using an existing view as the parent view. It is generated by projecting the lines normal to the parent view or at an angle. The resulting view will be an orthographic view or an isometric view.

Section View

A section view is generated by chopping a part of an existing view using a section plane and then viewing the parent view from a direction normal to that plane. In SOLIDWORKS, the section plane is defined using one or more sketched line segments.

Aligned Section View

An aligned section view is used to section the features that are created at a certain angle to the main section planes. The aligned sections straighten these features by revolving them about an axis that is normal to the view plane. Remember that the axis about which the feature is straightened should lie on the cutting planes.

Removed Section View

A removed section view is used to show the sections of the model at selected locations in the drawing view.

Auxiliary View

An auxiliary view is generated by projecting the lines normal to the specified edge of an existing view.

Detail View

A detail view is used to display the details of a portion of an existing view. You can select a portion whose detailing has to be shown in the parent view. On doing so, the selected portion will be magnified and placed as a separate view. You can control the magnification of the detail view.

Break View

A break view is the one in which a portion of the drawing view is removed from the existing view keeping the ends of the drawing view intact. This type of view is used to display the components whose length to width ratio is very high. This means that either the length is very large as compared to the width or the width is very large as compared to the length. The broken view will break the view along the horizontal or vertical direction such that the drawing view fits the required area.

Broken-out Section View

A broken-out sectionview is used to remove a part of an existing view and display the area of a model or an assembly that lies behind the removed portion. This type of view is generated by using a closed sketch associated with the parent view.

Crop View

A crop view is used to crop an existing view enclosed in a closed sketch associated to that view. The portion of the view that lies inside the associated sketch is retained and the remaining portion is removed.

Alternate Position View

The alternate position view is used to create a view in which you can show two different positions of an assembly while it is in motion. The main position is displayed in the drawing view in continuous lines and the alternate position of the assembly is displayed in the same view in dashed lines (phantom lines).

GENERATING STANDARD DRAWING VIEWS

Generally, a standard view is the first view that is generated in the current drawing sheet. There are several methods used for generating the standard drawing views. All these methods are discussed next.

Generating Model Views

CommandManager:	Drawing> Model View
SOLIDWORKS menus:	Insert > Drawing View > Model
Toolbar:	Drawing > Model View

As mentioned earlier, the **Model View** tool is used to generate a base view in the drawing sheet. When you invoke the drawing environment of SOLIDWORKS, the **Model View PropertyManager** is displayed to generate the base view of the model in the drawing sheet. If it is not displayed by default, invoke the **Model View PropertyManager** by choosing the **Model View** button from the **Drawing CommandManager**.

If you start the new drawing document from the part or assembly document, the part or the assembly will automatically be selected and you can place the view by using the **View Palette** task pane. However, if you start the new drawing document by using the **New SOLIDWORKS Document** dialog box, the **Model View PropertyManager** will be displayed and you will be prompted to select a part or an assembly to generate the drawing view. If any part or assembly document is opened, it will be displayed in the selection box of the **Part/Assembly to Insert** rollout. You can preview the part or the assembly document by expanding the **Thumbnail Preview** rollout, as shown in Figure 14-5. Note that the **Start command when creating new drawing** check box is selected by default in the **Options** rollout. As a result, the **Model View PropertyManager** is invoked automatically when a new drawing file is started. If this check box is cleared, then you need to choose the **Model View** button to invoke this PropertyManager. Choose the **Next** button at the top of the PropertyManager to view the options related to generating the standard views, as shown in Figure 14-6.

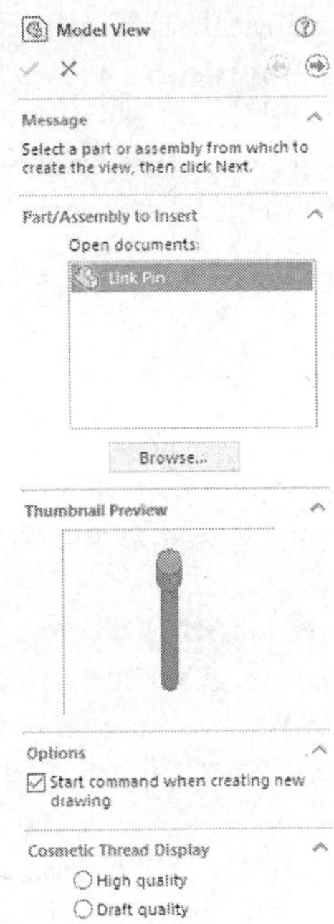

***Figure 14-5** Previewing the thumbnail view of the part*

If you need to generate drawing views for an unopened model, choose the **Browse** button from the **Part/ Assembly to Insert** rollout and use the **Open** dialog box to select the model; the **Model View PropertyManager** will automatically be modified and the options related to generating the standard views will be displayed.

The rollouts in this PropertyManager are discussed next.

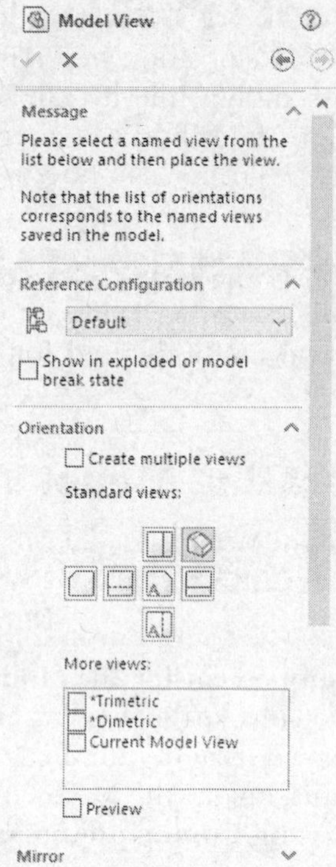

Figure 14-6 *Partial view of the* ***Model View PropertyManager*** *showing the standard view options*

Reference Configuration Rollout

If you have created multiple configurations of a part, then select the configuration for which you need to create the drawing views from the drop-down list in the **Reference Configuration** rollout. The procedure to create configurations is discussed in the later chapters.

Orientation Rollout

By default, single view is created for the selected model and it can be any one of the orthographic views, **Dimetric**, **Trimetric**, or the current view of the model. Select the **Preview** check box to preview the drawing view. To generate the multiple orthographic views, select the **Create multiple views** check box and then choose the required buttons from the **Standard views** area. You can also select additional orientations by selecting the required check box from the **More views** list box.

Note

You can change the orientation of the model view even after placing the view. To do so, click on the parent view; the ***Drawing View PropertyManager*** *will be displayed. Select the desired view from the* ***Orientation*** *rollout and then choose the* ***Close Dialog*** *button; the orientation of the view will be modified.*

Mirror Rollout

If you want to generate mirrored view of a component without actually creating the part, then, select the **Mirror view** check box from the **Mirror** rollout. The mirror view of the component is created. Select the required radio button to change the direction of mirror under this rollout.

Import options Rollout

If you have dimensioned the model by using the **DimXpert** tool in the part or the assembly mode, then on selecting the **Import annotations** check box and other required check boxes in this rollout, the dimensions will be generated automatically.

Options Rollout

On selecting the **Auto-start projected view** check box and placing the selected view, the **Projected View PropertyManager** will be displayed. Therefore, the projected view of the existing view can be generated. Note that this rollout will not be displayed if you generate the isometric view of the model.

Display State Rollout

If the selected component has multiple display states, then they will be listed in the **Display State** rollout. Select the display state in which you need to display the drawing view. Remember that the drawing view will be visible in the selected display state only if the drawing view is created in shaded model.

Display Style Rollout

The options in this rollout are used to specify the display styles for the model view. These display styles are similar to those available in the **View** toolbar to display the parts or the assemblies in the part document or the assembly document.

Scale Rollout

By default, the **Use sheet scale** radio button is selected in the **Scale** rollout. Therefore, when you select a template to start a new drawing sheet, a default scale is automatically defined to generate drawing views. To define a custom scale for the model view, select the **Use custom scale** radio button and then the scale factor from the drop-down list below this radio button.

Dimension Type Rollout

The radio buttons in this rollout are used to specify whether the model view will have true dimensions or projected dimensions. The true dimensions are the exact model dimensions that were specified while creating the model. The projected dimensions are the reduced dimensions that are used in case of the standard and custom orthographic views, whereas the true dimensions are used in case of isometric, dimetric, or trimetric view. Generally, the value of the projected dimension is about 81.6% of the value of true dimension.

Cosmetic Thread Display Rollout

If the model has cosmetic threads, then the visibility of the threads can be controlled by selecting the **High quality** or **Draft quality** radio button from this rollout.

After specifying all parameters, choose the **OK** button; the model view(s) will be generated.

Using the View Palette to Place the Drawing Views

In SOLIDWORKS, the **View Palette** is automatically displayed when you start a new drawing file from the part or the assembly document, as shown in Figure 14-7. You can also display the **View Palette** manually by invoking the task pane and then choosing the **View Palette** tab.

To place a view using the **View Palette**, select the preview of the view in the **View Palette** task pane and then drag it to the drawing sheet at the desired location; the **Projected View PropertyManager** will be invoked. Now, create the projected views from the view placed earlier.

You can choose the **Browse to select a part/assembly** button from the **View Palette** to browse and select a part or an assembly to generate the drawing views.

If you have dimensioned the model by using the **DimXpert** tool in the part or the assembly mode, then on selecting the **Import Annotations** check box and the other check boxes in the **Options** area, the dimensions will be generated automatically. The **Auto-start projected view** check box in the **Options** area is used to invoke the **Projected View** tool automatically to generate the projected view immediately after placing the model view.

Note

You can also select the quality of cosmetic thread to be displayed before selecting the model for projected, auxiliary and detail views in their respective PropertyManagers.

Generating the Three Standard Views

CommandManager: Drawing > Standard 3 View
SOLIDWORKS menus: Insert > Drawing View > Standard 3 View
Toolbar: Drawing > Standard 3 View

You can generate three default orthographic views of the specified part or the assembly by using the **Standard 3 View** tool. To create the standard views, choose the **Standard 3 View** tool from the **Drawing CommandManager**; the **Standard 3 View PropertyManager** will be displayed. If any part or assembly document is opened in the current session of SOLIDWORKS, it will be displayed in the list box in the **Part/Assembly to Insert** rollout, as shown in Figure 14-8.

You can select the document from this list box or choose the **Browse** button to select the part or the assembly document, if no documents are opened. As soon as you double-click on a document, three standard views will be generated based on the default scale of the current sheet. Figure 14-9 shows three standard views of a model generated in the third angle projection by using the **Standard 3 View** tool.

Figure 14-7 The ***View Palette***

Figure 14-8 The ***Standard 3 View PropertyManager***

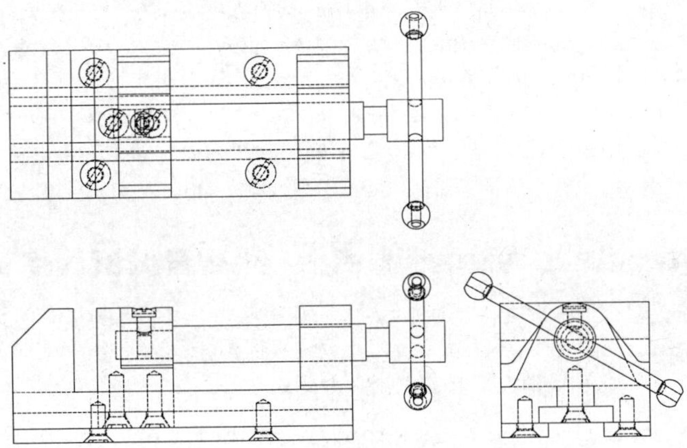

Figure 14-9 Three views generated using the ***Standard 3 View*** *tool*

Tip

The generation of drawing views depends on the default projection type of the current sheet. If the sheet is configured for the first angle projection, the drawing views will be generated accordingly.

*To change the projection type of the current sheet, right-click on **Sheet1** in the **Feature Manager Design Tree** and choose **Properties** from the shortcut menu; the **Sheet Properties** dialog box will be displayed. Set the required projection type by using the options in the **Type of projection** area.*

Note

*The name of the part document whose drawing views are generated is displayed in the **DWG. NO.** text box of the title block. The size of the sheet is also displayed at the lower right corner of the title block. Try changing the sheet format if these parameters are not displayed.*

*You will observe that the center marks are automatically created on generating the drawing views. If they are not generated automatically, you can set the option. To do so, invoke the **System Options - General** dialog box and choose the **Document Properties** tab; the **Drafting Standard** option will be chosen by default. Choose the **Detailing** option from the area available on the left of the dialog box. Select the **Center marks-holes -part** check box from the **Auto insert on view creation** area. You can also set the auto-insertion of centerlines, balloons, and so on using the options provided in this dialog box.*

Tip

*If the view generated using the **Standard 3 View** tool overlaps the title block, then you need to move this view. To do so, place the cursor over the view; the bounding box of the view will be displayed in dashed orange lines. At this point, click to select the view. Next, move the cursor to the boundary of the selected view; the cursor will be replaced by the move cursor. Press and hold the left mouse button and drag the cursor to move the view. Remember that on moving the parent view, all the views generated by using this tool will also be moved.*

Generating Standard Views Using the Relative View Tool

CommandManager:	Drawing > Relative View
SOLIDWORKS menus:	Insert > Drawing View > Relative To Model
Toolbar:	Drawing > Relative View

The **Relative View** tool is used to generate an orthographic view such that the orientation of the view is defined by selecting two reference planes or the planar faces of the model. This option is very useful if you need the orientation of the parent view other than the default orientations.

To create a relative view, open the part or the assembly document and invoke the drawing document by choosing **New > Make Drawing from Part/Assembly** from the Menu Bar. Invoke the **Relative View** tool and then switch back to the respective part or the assembly window. As the Part or the Assembly window is invoked, the **Relative View PropertyManager** will be displayed in it, as shown in Figure 14-10, and you will be prompted to select a planar face of the model.

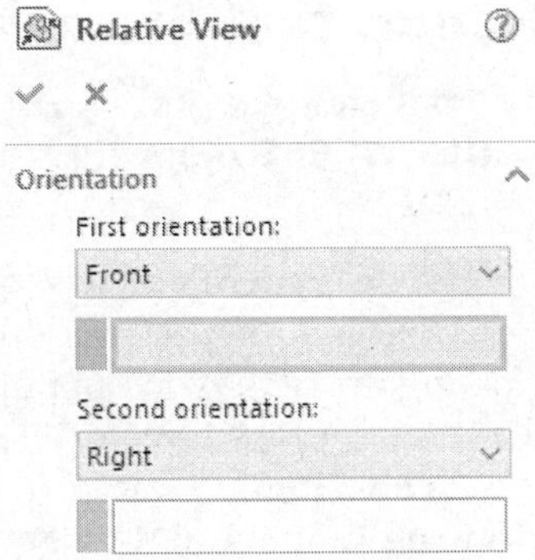

Figure 14-10 *The* ***Relative View PropertyManager***

Select the orientation for the first plane or the planar face from the drop-down list in the **First orientation** area. Then select the plane or the planar face of the model to be oriented in that direction. For example, if you select the **Top** option from this drop-down list and then select a planar face, the selected face will be displayed in the top view.

Select the orientation for the second reference from the drop-down list and then select a plane or a planar face. Next, choose **OK** from the **Relative View PropertyManager**; you will return to the drawing document. Place the view at the required location. Figure 14-11 shows the faces of the model selected to generate a standard view and Figure 14-12 shows the resultant view.

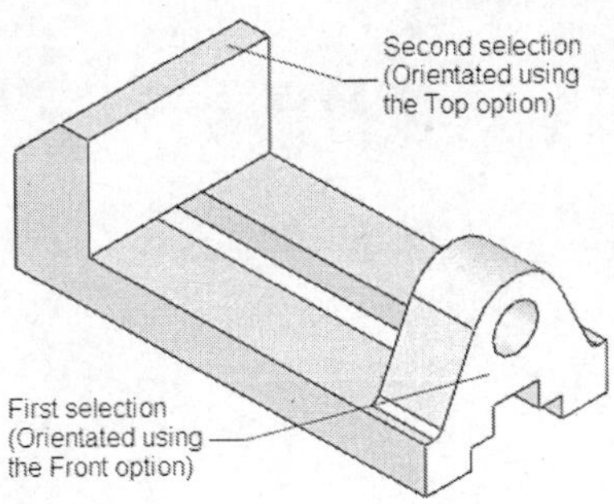

Figure 14-11 *The selected faces*

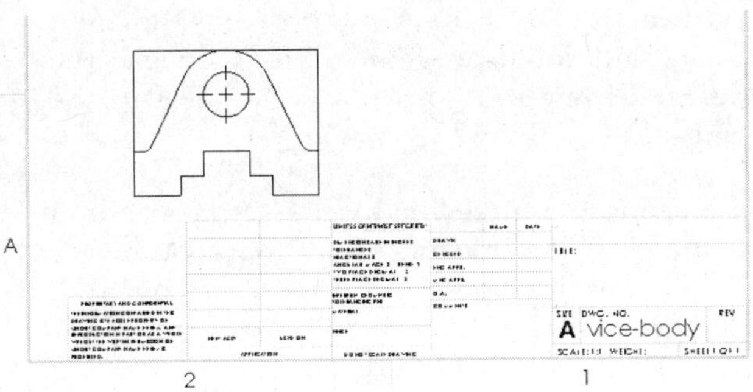

Figure 14-12 *Resultant view*

Generating Standard Views Using the Predefined View Tool

CommandManager: Drawing> Predefined View
SOLIDWORKS menus: Insert > Drawing View > Predefined
Toolbar: Drawing > Predefined View

The **Predefined View** tool is used to create empty views with the predefined orientation. After creating the views, you can populate them by inserting the component. To create the predefined views, invoke the **Predefined View** tool from the customized **Drawing CommandManager**; an empty view will be attached to the cursor. Specify a point in the drawing document to place the predefined view; a rectangle defining the boundary of the view will be placed in the drawing document and the **Drawing View PropertyManager** will be displayed, as shown in Figure 14-13.

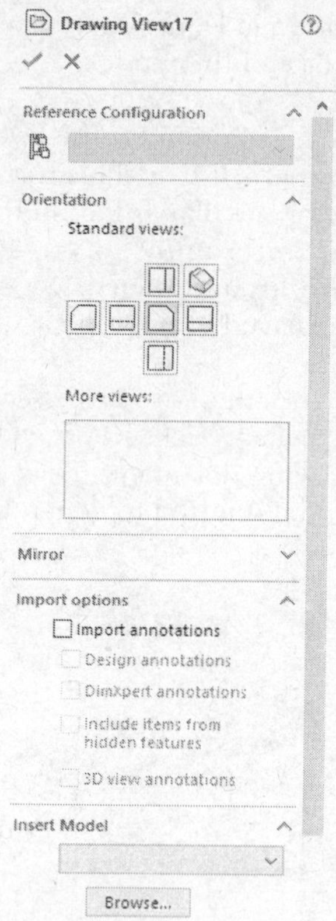

Figure 14-13 Partial view of the ***Drawing View PropertyManager***

Select the view orientation from the **Standard views** area in the **Orientation** rollout and choose the **OK** button from the **Drawing View PropertyManager**. To create additional predefined views, invoke the **Predefined View** tool and place the view in the drawing sheet.

After creating the predefined views, click once in a predefined view; the **Drawing View PropertyManager** will be displayed. Choose the **Browse** button from the **Insert Model** rollout in the **Drawing View PropertyManager** and insert the model; the drawing will be created, as soon as you choose the **OK** button from the PropertyManager.

If you need to align multiple predefined views, right-click inside a bounding box and choose **Alignment > Align Horizontal by Center/Align Vertical by Center**. Next, select the previous predefined view to align the corresponding view. Similarly, align the other predefined views by using this option.

Figure 14-14 shows the selected predefined views with the orientation in which the views are created. Figure 14-15 shows the drawing document after populating the drawing views.

Note

The views generated in the Drawing mode of SOLIDWORKS are automatically scaled on the basis of the size of the sheet. The views also get scaled automatically if the drawing contains more than one predefined view. A predefined view placed in the drawing document will be scaled with respect to the Custom Scale value, if specified. Otherwise, it will be scaled with the default scale factor of the drawing sheet. You can change the view scale by using the ***Sheet Properties*** *dialog box. You will learn more about scaling the views in the next chapter.*

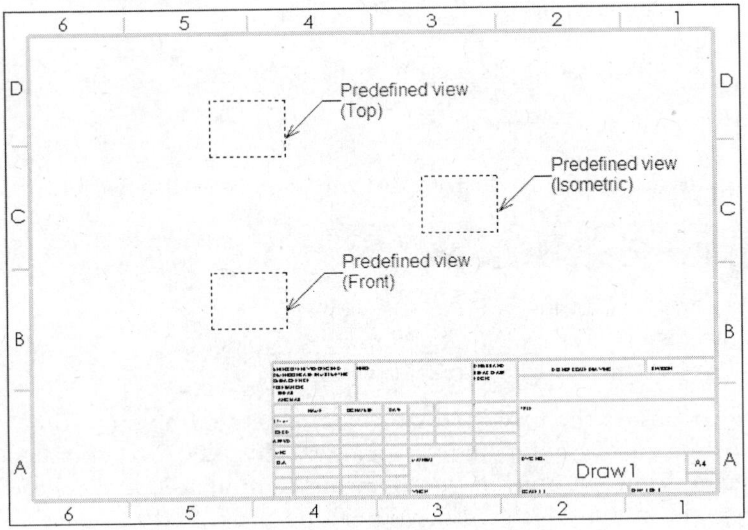

Figure 14-14 Various predefined views

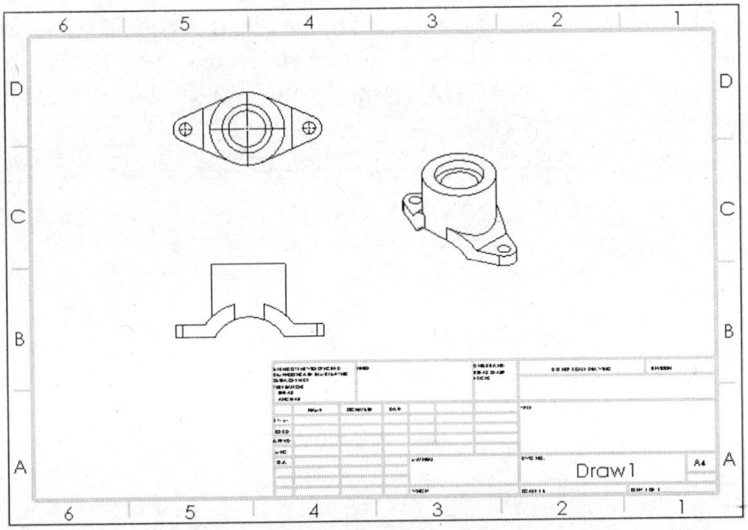

Figure 14-15 Views created after populating the predefined views

GENERATING DERIVED VIEWS

Views generated from a view that is already placed in the drawing document are known as derived views. These views include:

1. Projected view
2. Section view
3. Removed Section view
4. Aligned Section view
5. Broken-out Section view
6. Auxiliary view

7. Detail view
8. Crop view
9. Broken view
10. Alternate Position view

The methods of generating various derived drawing views are discussed next.

Generating Projected Views

CommandManager:	Drawing > Projected View
SOLIDWORKS menus:	Insert > Drawing View > Projected
Toolbar:	Drawing > Projected View

As mentioned earlier, the projected views are generated by projecting the normal lines from an existing view or at an angle from an existing view. To generate a projected view, choose the **Projected View** button from the **Drawing CommandManager**; the **Projected View PropertyManager** will be displayed. Also, you will be prompted to select a drawing view to project the normal lines. Select the parent view and move the cursor vertically to generate the top view or the bottom view, or move the cursor horizontally to generate the right or left view. If you move the cursor at an angle, a 3D view will be generated. Specify a point on the drawing sheet to place the view. To generate more than one projected view, choose the **Keep Visible** button to pin the **Projected View PropertyManager**. Figure 14-16 shows the front view generated from the top view.

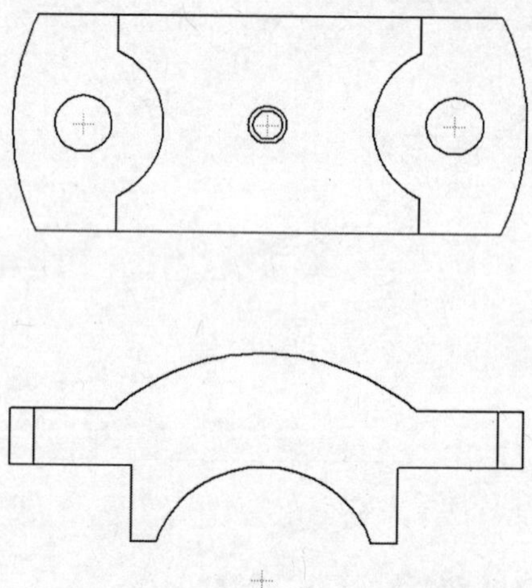

Figure 14-16 *Front view generated from the top view*

Tip

When you generate a projected drawing view, it is aligned to the parent view. To place the projected view that is not in alignment with the parent view, press and hold the CTRL key before placing it and then move the cursor to the desired location and place the view.

All standard and derived views such as projected views, section view, detailed view, and so on are linked to their parent view by a Parent-Child relationship. If you select the child view, the bounding box of the parent view will also be displayed.

*Select the child view, invoke the shortcut menu, and choose the **Jump to Parent View** option from it; the parent view will be selected automatically.*

Generating Section Views

CommandManager:	Drawing> Section View
SOLIDWORKS menus:	Insert > Drawing View > Section
Toolbar:	Drawing > Section View

As mentioned earlier, the section views are generated by chopping a portion of an existing view using a cutting plane (defined by the section lines) and then viewing the parent view from a direction normal to the cutting plane.

In SOLIDWORKS, you can use the **Section View** tool to create a full section view and a half section view, as shown in Figures 14-17 and 14-18, respectively. A full section view is defined using a single line segment, whereas a half section view is defined using two or more than two line segments. By using this tool, you can also create the auxiliary section view and aligned section views. The procedure for creating different types of section views by using the **Section View** tool is discussed next.

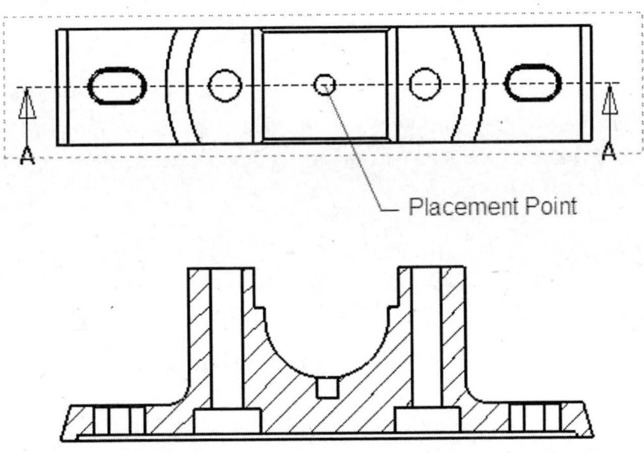

Figure 14-17 *Full section view*

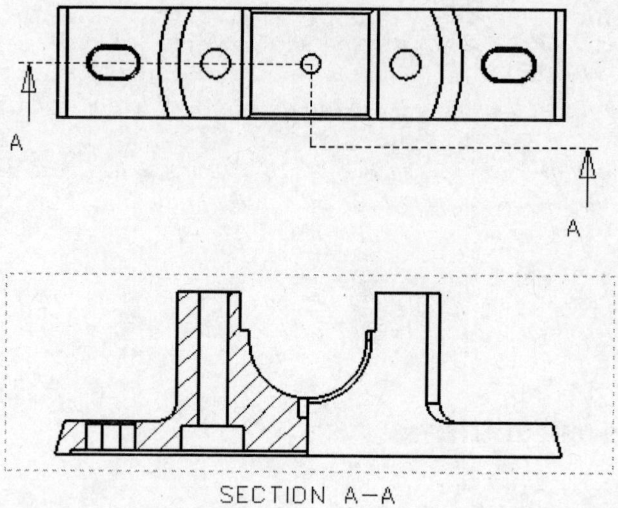

Figure 14-18 Half section view

Creating Horizontal/Vertical Full Section View

To create a full section view, activate the view in which you need to draw the section line. The view symbol will be displayed below the cursor and the bounding box of the view will also be displayed. Now, choose the **Section View** button from the **Drawing CommandManager**; the **Section View Assist PropertyManager** will be displayed, as shown in Figure 14-19. Choose the **Horizontal** button in the **Cutting Line** rollout of the **Section View Assist PropertyManager**. As you move the cursor in the drawing, the attached section line will also move. Now, you need to specify the placement point for the section line. Specify the placement point in the drawing view, refer to Figure 14-17; the **Section View** pop-up toolbar will be displayed in the drawing area. Also, the **Edit sketch** button will be enabled in the PropertyManager.

Note

*Note that if the **Auto-start section view** check box is selected in the **Cutting Line** rollout of the PropertyManager, then after specifying the placement point for the section line in the drawing area, the **Section View** pop-up toolbar will not be displayed and the preview of the section view will be attached with the cursor directly.*

By using the **Section View** pop-up toolbar and the **Edit Sketch** button, you can edit the section line. After editing the section line, choose the **OK** button from the pop-up toolbar; the section view will be attached to the cursor. Also, the options in the **Section View Assist PropertyManager** will be modified, as shown in Figure 14-20.

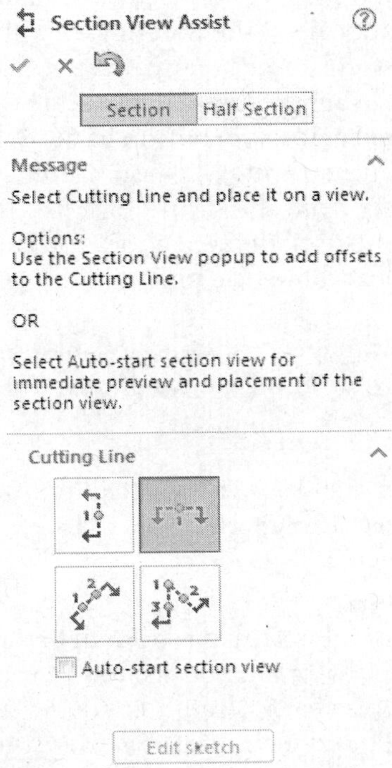

Figure 14-19 The ***Section View Assist PropertyManager*** *with the* ***Section*** *tab selected*

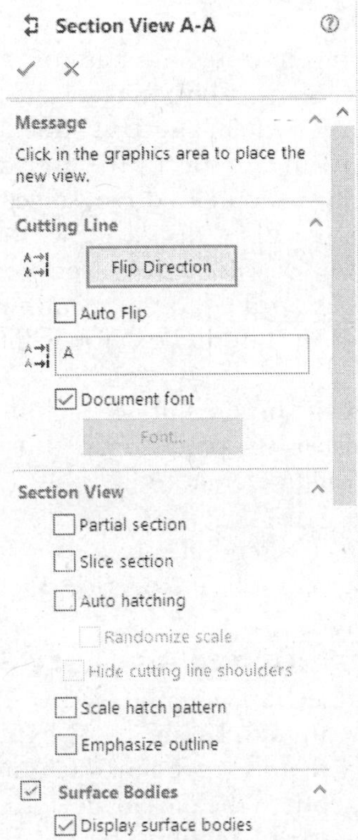

Figure 14-20 Partial view of the modified ***Section View Assist PropertyManager***

Some of the options in the modified PropertyManager are discussed next.

Flip Direction

The **Flip Direction** button is used to flip the direction of the section view.

Auto Flip

The **Auto Flip** check box is used to flip the direction of the section view automatically, based on the position of the cursor in the drawing area.

Document Font

By default, the **Document font** check box is selected in the **Cutting Line** rollout. As a result, the default font style is applied to the section view label. If you want to change the font style of the label, clear the **Document font** check box. On clearing this check box, the **Font** button below the **Document font** check box in the **Cutting Line** rollout of the PropertyManager will be activated. Choose the **Font** button; the **Choose Font** dialog box will be displayed. Select the required font, font style, space, specify the height, and then choose the **OK** button to apply the changes.

Scale Rollout

The options in this rollout are used to set the scale of the section view. By default, the **Use parent scale** radio button is selected. As a result, the scale of the parent view will be applied to the section view. The **Use sheet scale** radio button is used to apply the scale set for the sheet. You can also specify the user-defined scale by using the **Use custom scale** radio button in the **Scale** rollout. To do so, select the **Use custom scale** radio button in the **Scale** rollout; an edit box will be displayed with a down arrow at its right. Click on the down arrow; a drop-down list will be displayed. Select any scale set from the drop-down list; the selected scale will be applied to the section view. To apply the user-defined scale, you can enter the scale value in the edit box. You will learn more about scaling the model in the next chapter.

After modifying the default settings in the PropertyManager, click the left mouse button to specify the placement point for the horizontal section view in the drawing area; the horizontal section view will be generated.

Similarly, you can generate the vertical section view by choosing the **Vertical** button from the **Cutting Line** rollout of the **Section View Assist PropertyManager**.

Generating Aligned/Auxiliary Section Views

In the aligned section view, the sectioned portion revolves about an axis normal to the view such that it is straightened. Figure 14-21 explains the concept of an aligned section view of a model. You will notice that as the inclined feature sectioned in this view is straightened, the section view becomes longer than the parent view. To generate the aligned section view, activate the base view and then choose the **Section View** button from the **Drawing CommandManager**; the **Section View Assist PropertyManager** will be displayed. Choose the **Aligned** button from the **Cutting Line** rollout and specify three points to define the section lines; the **Section View** pop-up toolbar will be displayed. Choose the **OK** button from the **Section View** pop-up toolbar; the aligned section view will be generated and attached with the cursor. Place the view at an appropriate location in the drawing sheet. Note that the resulting view will be projected normal to the vertical line defined in the section lines. To toggle the alignment of the aligned section view choose the **Toggle Alignment** button from the **Section View** rollout. Therefore, the aligned section view similar to one shown in Figure 14-21, should be drawn by using default settings. Figure 14-22 shows the aligned section view in which the alignment is toggled normal to the inclined line. On the other hand, Figure 14-23 shows the view in which the alignment is set to default setting.

Tip

You can also create a section view and aligned section view from a crop view, a detail view, and an orthogonal exploded view.

Note

You can also create a sketch associated to a view. This sketch can be selected as the section plane for generating the section view. To create an associated sketch, activate the view and draw the sketch by using the ***Line*** *tool to define the section plane.*

While creating aligned section view of a model with rib feature, a message box appears prompting for excluding or including the rib feature from the section view. Choose the required option and continue the process.

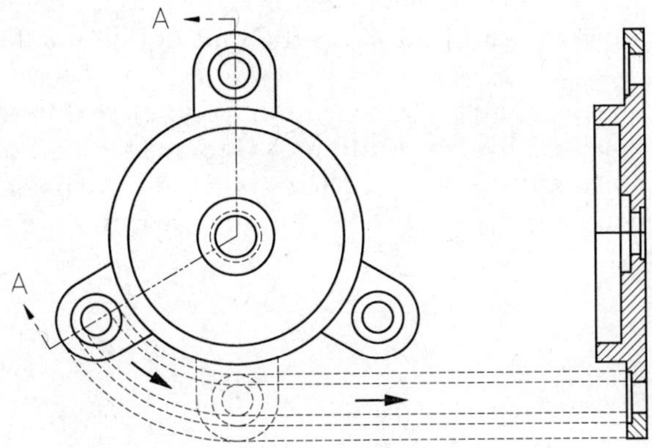

Figure 14-21 *Aligned section view*

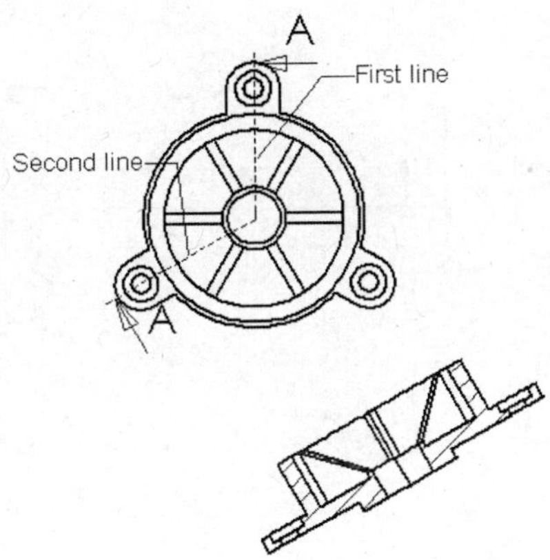

Figure 14-22 *Aligned section view when the alignment is toggled normal to the inclined line*

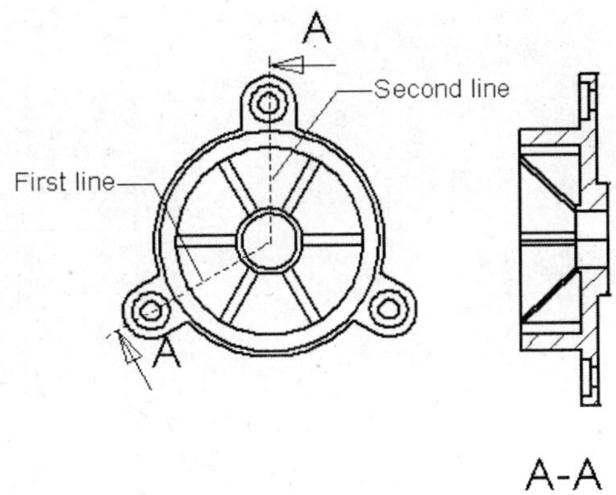

Figure 14-23 *Aligned section view when the alignment is set to default setting*

Similarly, you can create auxiliary section view by using the **Auxiliary** button from the **Cutting Line** rollout of the PropertyManager. You can also create the auxiliary section view by using the **Auxiliary View** tool available in the **Drawing CommandManager**. You will learn more about creating the auxiliary section views by using this tool later in this chapter.

Creating Half Section View

As discussed earlier, you can also generate a half section view by using the **Section View** tool. To do so, invoke the **Section View Assist PropertyManager** and choose the **Half Section** tab; the options used for creating the half section view will be displayed, refer to Figure 14-24. You can use the buttons available in the **Half Section** rollout to create different types of half section views. In this rollout, the **Topside Right** button is chosen by default. Choose the required button from the **Half Section** rollout of the PropertyManager; you will be prompted to specify the placement point for the section lines. Specify the placement point for the section lines, refer to Figure 14-25; the section view will be attached to the cursor and the modified **Section View PropertyManager** will be displayed. If the **Section View** dialog box is displayed then choose the **OK** button. The options in the modified **Section View PropertyManager** are same as those discussed while creating the full section view. Next, specify the placement point in the drawing area to place the section view. Figure 14-25 shows the topside right half section view generated.

In SOLIDWORKS, you can specify an arrow type for a section line different from the dimension arrow type. To do so, invoke the **System Options - General** dialog box and then choose the **Document Properties** tab. Next, expand the **Views** node and then select the **Section** option. Now, you can change the arrow type for the section line by using the **Style** drop-down list in the **Section/view size** area.

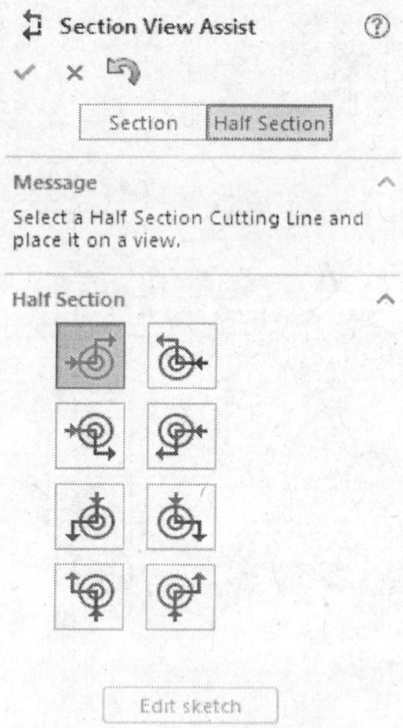

Figure 14-24 *The* ***Section View Assist PropertyManager*** *with* ***Half Section*** *tab chosen*

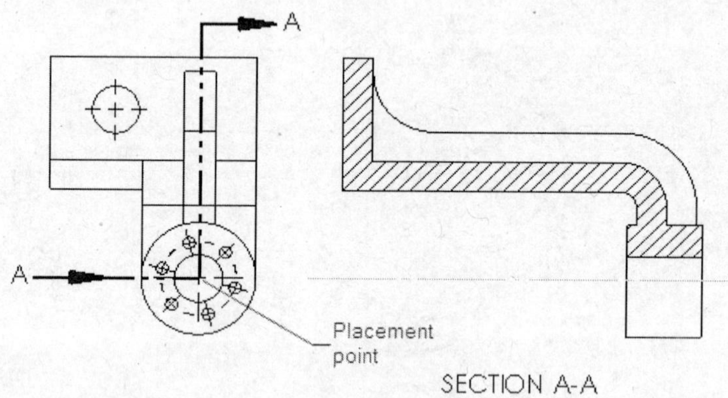

Figure 14-25 *Topside right half section view*

Note

The default hatch pattern in the section view depends on the material assigned to the model. You may need to increase the spacing of the hatch pattern, if it is required. You will learn more about editing the hatch pattern later in this chapter.

Tip

On creating a section view and moving the cursor to place the section view, you will observe that the view is aligned to the direction of arrows on the section line. To remove this alignment, press and hold the CTRL key and move the view to the desired location. Now, select a point in the drawing sheet to place the view.

Creating the Section View by Using Sketch Lines

In addition to creating full section views and half section views by using the predefined section plane, you can also create section views by using the sketch lines drawn with the help of the sketch tools. To do so, draw a line or a chain of lines to define the cutting plane by using the **Line** tool available in the **Sketch CommandManager**, refer to Figure 14-26. Next, select the drawn sketch and choose the **Section View** button from the **Drawing CommandManager**; the **Section View** dialog box is displayed. Choose the **OK** button from the dialog box; section view will be generated, defined by the sketch entities and attached to the cursor. Also, the **Section View PropertyManager** will be displayed. Next, specify the placement point to place the section view in the drawing sheet.

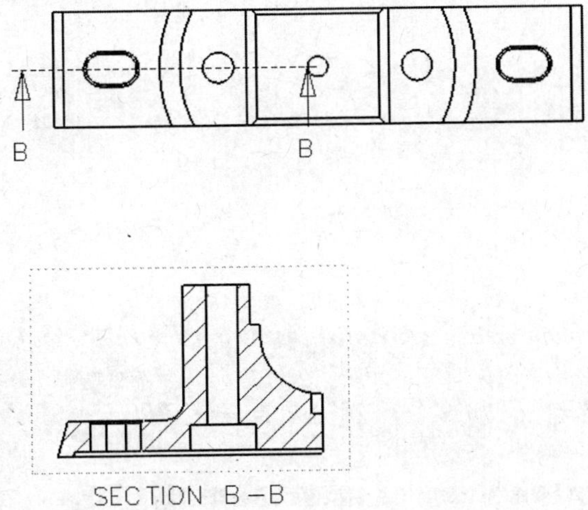

Figure 14-26 Section view created by using the sketch line

Creating the Slice View

A slice view is the one in which only the sectioned surface is displayed in the section view. To create a slice view, you first need to create the section view and then select the **Slice section** check box from the **Section View** rollout of the **Section View PropertyManager**. Figure 14-27 shows a slice view.

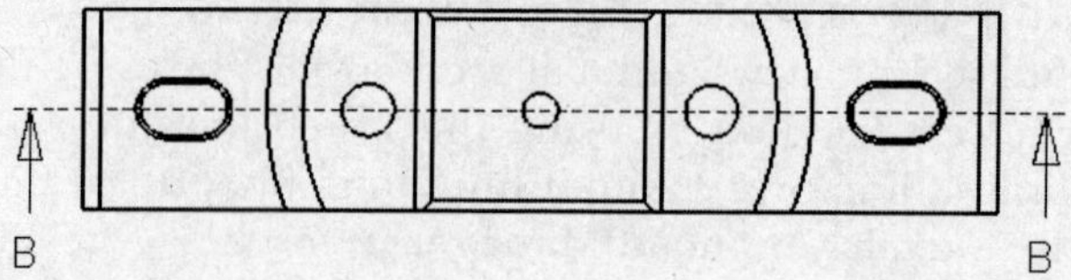

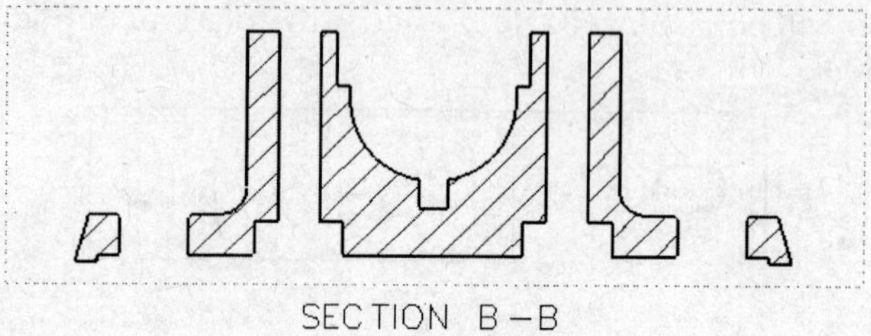

Figure 14-27 A slice view

Tip
Sometimes, the section view is generated upside down even if you have set the projection type to the third angle. In such cases, you need to flip the direction of the section line by choosing the ***Flip Direction*** *button from the* ***Section View PropertyManager****.*

Generating the Section View of an Assembly

According to the drawing standards, when you create the section view of an assembly, some components such as fasteners, shafts, keys, and so on should not be sectioned. You need to exclude such components from the section view of the assembly. You can do so by using the **Section View** dialog box that will be displayed while creating the section view of an assembly, as shown in Figure 14-28.

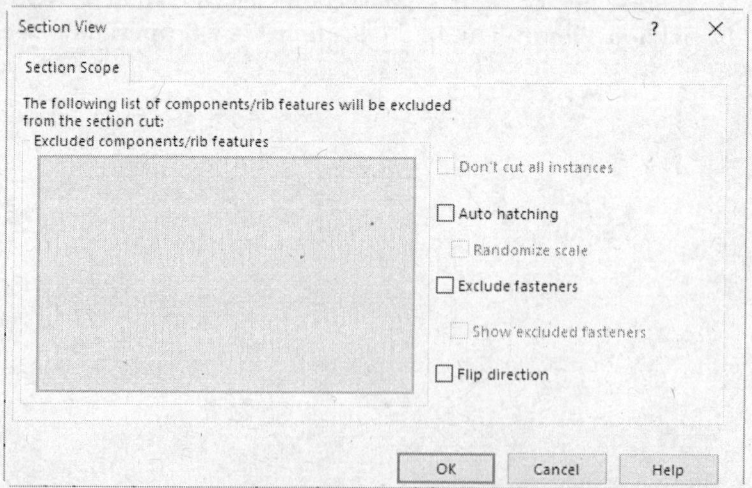

Figure 14-28 The ***Section View*** *dialog box*

This dialog box allows you to select the components that will be excluded from the section cut. You can also select the components from the parent view. But, if the components are not visible in the parent view, you can invoke the **FeatureManager Design Tree** and expand the parent drawing view. Next, expand the assembly Design Tree to display all components of the assembly. Select the components that are not required to be sectioned; the name of the selected component will be displayed in the **Excluded components/rib features** selection box.

The **Auto hatching** check box is used to define the hatch patterns automatically. You can even change them if required. The method of changing the hatch patterns is discussed later. SOLIDWORKS provides you with an option to exclude the fasteners that are inserted in the assembly using the **Toolbox** add-in. This add-in is used to insert standard fasteners to the assembly. To exclude the fasteners that are inserted using the **Toolbox** add-in, select the **Exclude fasteners** check box from the **Section View** dialog box, if it is not selected.

The **Flip direction** check box is used to flip the direction of viewing the section view.

In case, you have more than one instance of the component in the assembly and you need to exclude all instances of the component from the section view, select the component from the drawing sheet and also the name of the component from the **Exclude components/rib features** selection box. Select the **Don't cut all instances** check box from the **Section View** dialog box; all instances of the selected component will be excluded from the section view. Figure 14-29 shows an assembly section view with the fasteners excluded from the cut.

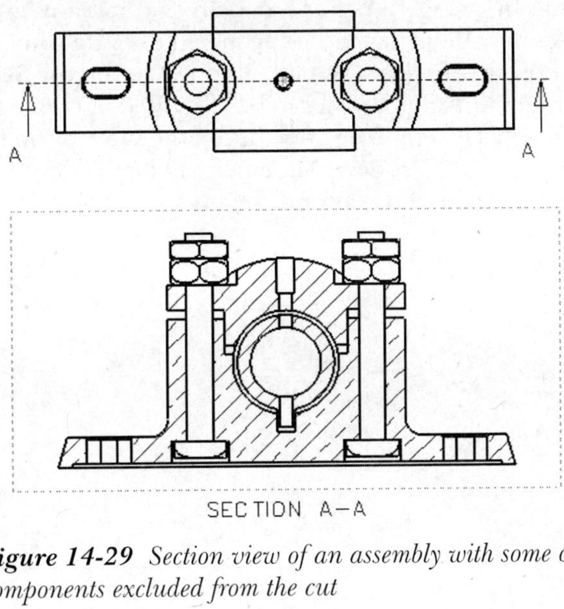

Figure 14-29 *Section view of an assembly with some of the components excluded from the cut*

Tip

To add or remove the components that are sectioned, right-click on the drawing view and choose ***Properties*** *from the shortcut menu; the* ***Drawing View Properties*** *dialog box will be displayed. Next, choose the* ***Section Scope*** *tab and add or remove the components.*

Generating Broken-out Section Views

CommandManager:	Drawing> Broken-out Section
SOLIDWORKS menus:	Insert > Drawing View > Broken-out Section
Toolbar:	Drawing > Broken-out Section

This tool is used to create a broken-out section view that is used to remove a part of an existing view and displays the area of the model or the assembly behind the removed portion. This view is generated using a closed sketch that is associated with the parent view. To create a broken-out section view, activate the view on which you need to create the broken-out section view. Choose the **Broken-out Section** button from the **Drawing CommandManager**; you will be prompted to create a closed sketch using the spline cursor. The cursor will be replaced by a spline cursor. Draw a closed sketch using the spline cursor; the **Broken-out Section PropertyManager** will be displayed, refer to Figure 14-30. If the **Section View** dialog box is displayed then choose the **OK** button. If you do not want a spline profile, select a closed profile before choosing the **Broken-out Section** button. Figure 14-31 shows an associated sketch created for generating a broken-out section view.

Enter the depth value in the **Depth** spinner and select the **Preview** check box to display the preview of the broken-out section view. You can also select an edge for depth reference in the same view or other views. The selection will be displayed in the **Depth Reference** selection box of the **Depth** rollout. Next, choose the **OK** button; the broken-out section view will be generated. Note that if you are generating the broken-out section view of an assembly then after creating the closed sketched profile by using the spline cursor, the **Section View** dialog box will be displayed. By using the **Section View** dialog box, you can exclude some of the components of the assembly that you do not want to be sectioned. To do so, when the **Section View** dialog box is displayed, select the components that are not to be sectioned to create the broken-out section view from the **FeatureManager Design Tree** and choose the **OK** button from the **Section View** dialog box; the **Broken-out Section PropertyManager** will be displayed, refer to Figure 14-30, and you will be prompted to specify the depth of the broken-out section.

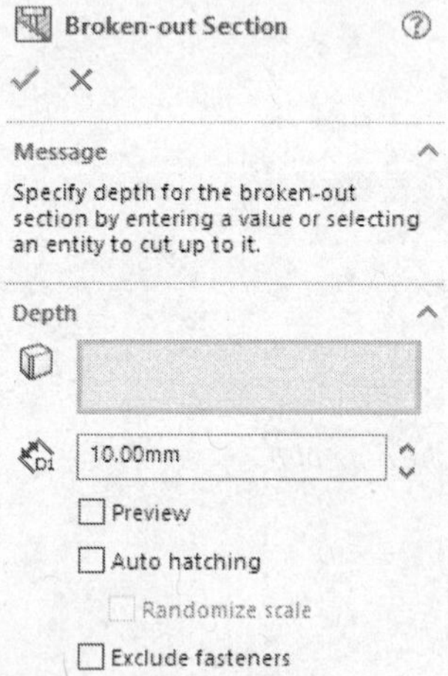

***Figure 14-30** The Broken-out Section PropertyManager*

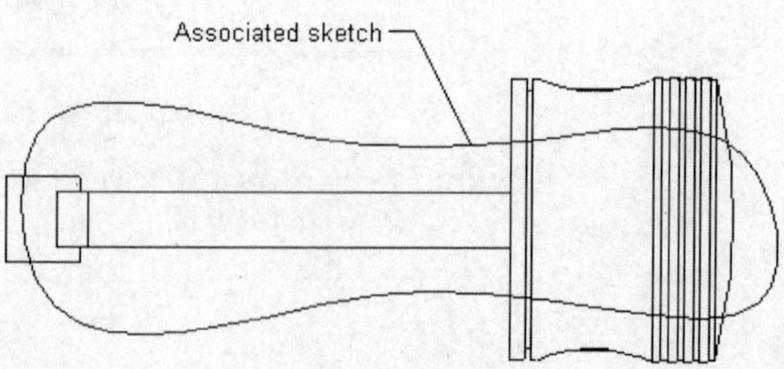

***Figure 14-31** Sketch for creating a broken-out section view*

The **Auto hatching** check box is available only for assemblies and is used to define the hatch pattern automatically to section the drawing view of the assembly. The **Exclude fasteners** check box, which will also be available only for assemblies, is used to exclude fasteners from getting sectioned in the broken-out section view. Figure 14-32 shows the preview of the broken-out section view of an assembly.

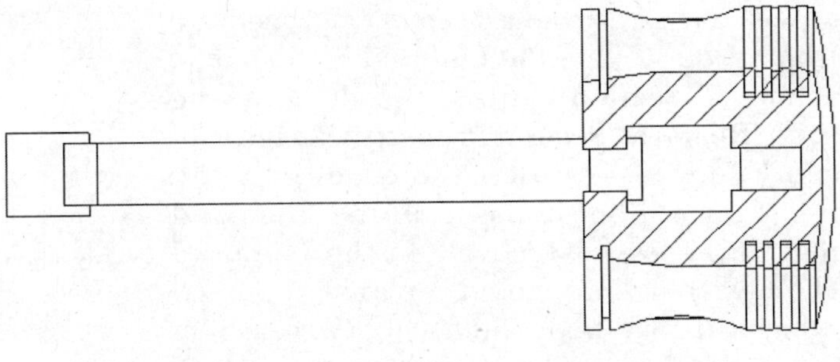

Figure 14-32 *Preview of the broken-out section view*

Set the value of the depth of the broken-out section in the **Depth** spinner; the preview of the section will be modified dynamically in the drawing view. After setting the value of the depth of the broken-out section, choose the **OK** button from the **Broken-out Section PropertyManager**. Figure 14-33 shows a broken-out section view with a different depth value.

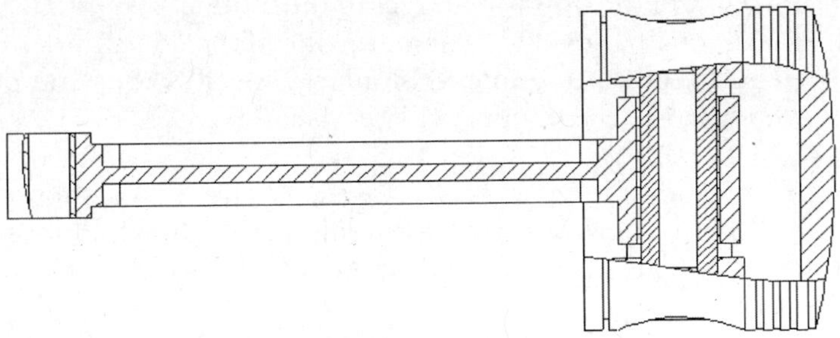

Figure 14-33 *Broken-out section view*

Generating Removed Section Views

CommandManager:	Drawing > Removed Section
SOLIDWORKS menus:	Insert > Drawing View > Removed Section
Toolbar:	Drawing > Removed Section

The **Removed Section** tool is used to create views of slices in a drawing view. To create a removed section view, activate the view on which you need to create the removed section view. Next, choose the **Removed Section** button from the **Drawing CommandManager**; the **Removed Section PropertyManager** will be displayed, refer to Figure 14-34. Select two edges from the drawing view. These edges will be displayed in the **Edge** and **Opposed Edge** selection boxes, respectively in the **Opposed Geometry** rollout. The edges must be opposed or partially opposed geometry between which the solid body will be cut. On selection of edges, the **Cutting Line Placement** rollout gets activated. In this rollout, you need specify the cutting line placement method. By default, the **Automatic** radio button is selected. As a result, the preview of the cutting line is displayed within the area between the opposing model edges. To place the cutting line, move the cursor at required place and press left mouse button. The **Manual** radio button is used for positioning the cutting line between two points that you select on each of the opposing edges of the model. To place the cutting line manually, hover the cursor on one of the edges and press the left mouse button to specify one end of the cutting line it. Similarly, specify other end of the cutting line on another edge. Next, click; the cutting line will be placed.

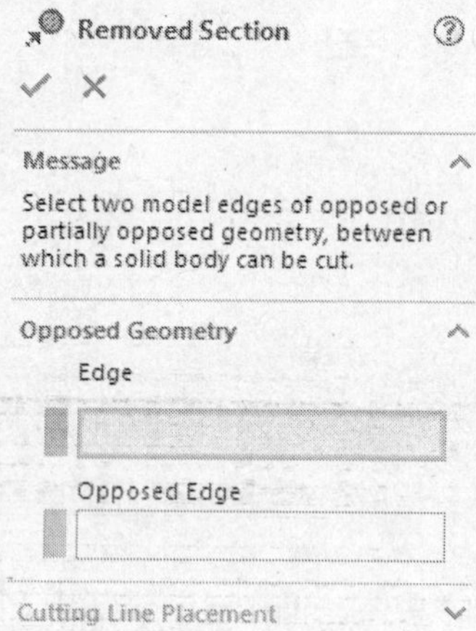

***Figure 14-34** The Removed Section PropertyManager*

Figure 14-35 shows front and side views of a washer. Figure 14-36 shows the bottom and removed section views of the washer considering the silhouette edges as opposing model edges. The removed section view will always be created perpendicular to the cutting line.

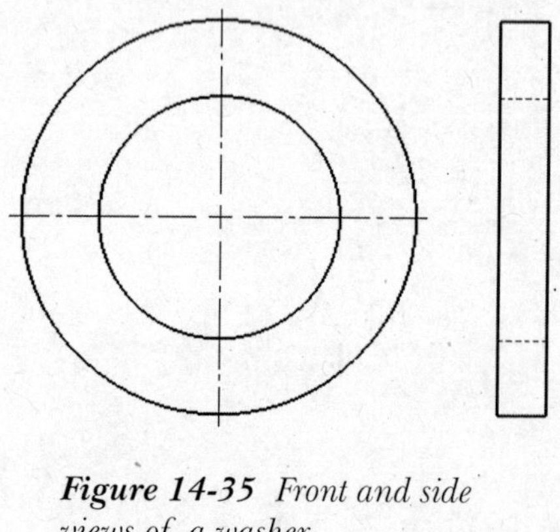

***Figure 14-35** Front and side views of a washer*

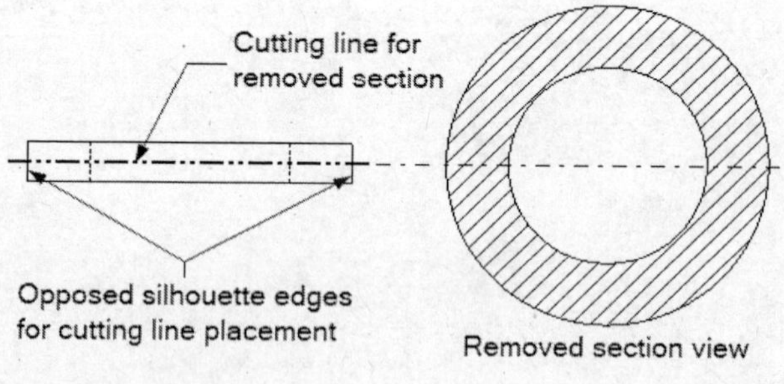

***Figure 14-36** The removed section view of washer*

Generating Auxiliary Views

CommandManager:	Drawing > Auxiliary View
SOLIDWORKS menus:	Insert > Drawing View > Auxiliary
Toolbar:	Drawing > Auxiliary View

An auxiliary view is a drawing view that is generated by projecting the lines normal to a specified edge of an existing view. SOLIDWORKS also allows you to create a line segment associated with the view that can be used to generate the auxiliary view. For this, the associated line segment needs to be created before invoking **Auxiliary View** tool. As discussed earlier, you can create the auxiliary view by using the **Section View** tool and the **Auxiliary View** tool.

To create an auxiliary view by using the **Auxiliary View** tool, choose the **Auxiliary View** button from the **Drawing CommandManager**; the **Auxiliary View PropertyManager** will be displayed and you will be prompted to select a reference edge to continue. Select the edge or the associated sketch; a view will be attached to the cursor and some additional options will be displayed in the **Auxiliary View PropertyManager**, as shown in Figure 14-37. Also, you will be prompted to specify the location to place the view. Specify the placement point to place the auxiliary view in the drawing sheet.

Select the check box in the **Arrow** rollout to display the arrow of the viewing direction in the drawing views. The name of the auxiliary view is specified in the **Label** edit box. You can flip the viewing direction for creating the auxiliary view by selecting the **Flip direction** check box. Figure 14-38 shows the reference edge to be selected to create the auxiliary view. If the selected component has multiple display state it will be listed in the **Display State** rollout. Select the display state for which you need the auxiliary view. While generating the auxiliary view of an assembly, the **Display Style** rollout will be displayed. This rollout allows you to select the display state whose auxiliary view will be generated.

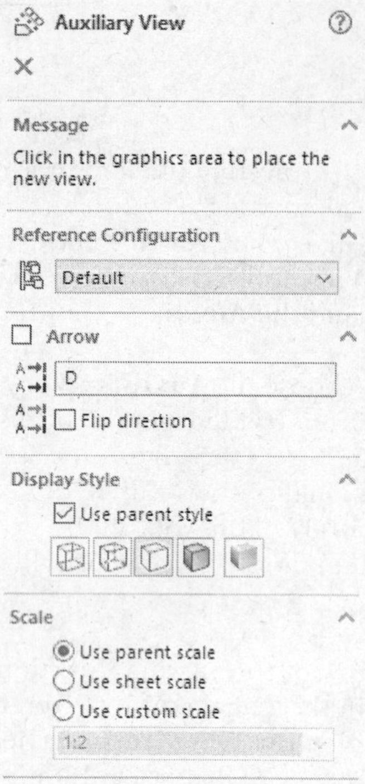

Figure 14-37** Partial view of the **Auxiliary View PropertyManager

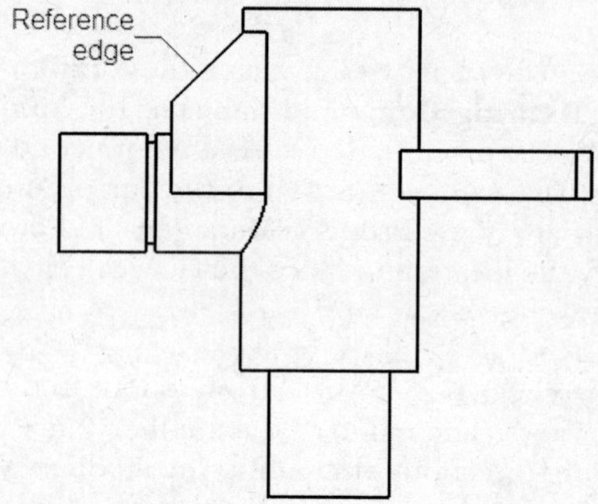

***Figure 14-38** Reference edge to be selected to create the auxiliary view*

Figure 14-39 shows the auxiliary view created with the default viewing direction. Figure 14-40 shows the auxiliary view created with the **Flip direction** check box selected.

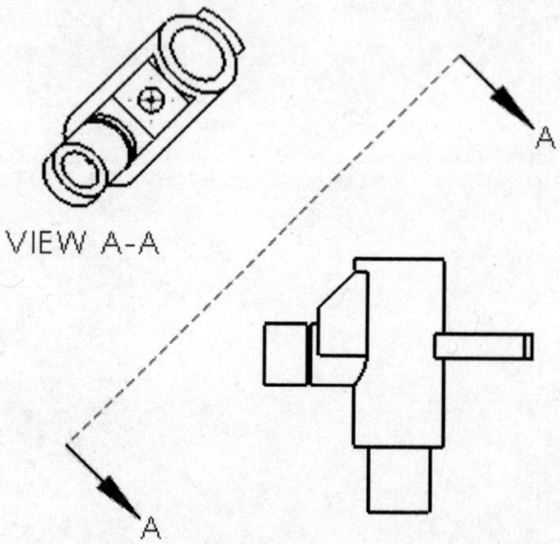

***Figure 14-39** Auxiliary view created with the **Flip direction** check box cleared*

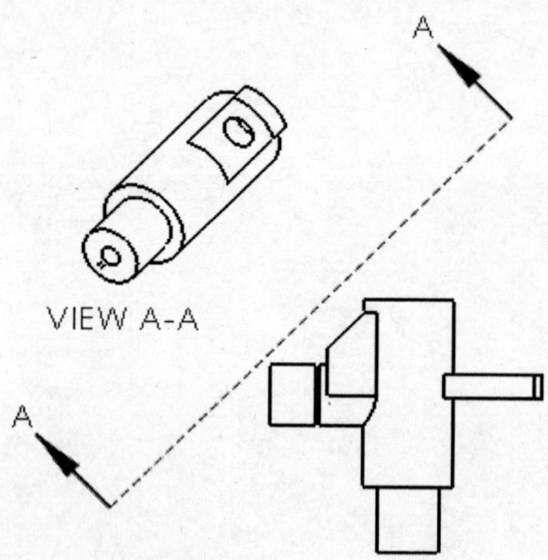

***Figure 14-40** Auxiliary view created with the **Flip direction** check box selected*

Generating Detail Views

CommandManager:	Drawing > Detail View
SOLIDWORKS menus:	Insert > Drawing View > Detail
Toolbar:	Drawing > Detail View

The detail view is used to display the details of a portion of an existing view. You can select the portion whose detailing needs to be shown in the parent view. The portion that is selected will be magnified and placed as a separate view. You can control the magnification of the detail view. To create a detail view, activate the view from which you will generate the detail view. Next, choose the **Detail View** button from the **Drawing CommandManager**; the **Detail View PropertyManager** will be displayed and you will be prompted to sketch a circle to continue the view creation and the cursor will be replaced by a circle cursor.

Create the circle on the portion of the view that is to be displayed in the detail view; the detail view will be attached to the cursor and the options will be displayed in the **Detail View PropertyManager**, as shown in Figure 14-41. Also, you will be prompted to select a location for the new view. Specify a point on the drawing sheet to place the view. To use a profile other than the circular profile, you need to create the profile in a view. Then, select the profile and invoke the **Detail View** tool. The rollouts in the **Detail View PropertyManager** are discussed next.

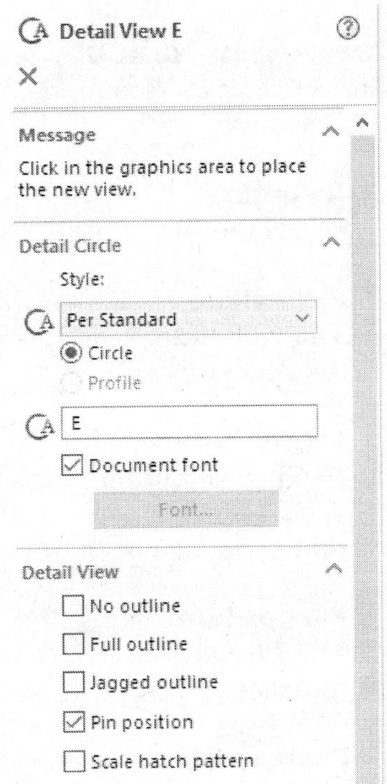

*Figure 14-41 Partial view of the **Detail View PropertyManager***

Detail Circle Rollout

This rollout is used to define the options to display the circle of the detail view. You can also apply the leader to the detail view using the options in the rollout. These options are discussed next.

Style

The **Style** drop-down list in the **Style** area is used to specify the style of a closed profile. By default, the **Circle** radio button is selected below the **Style** drop-down list. Therefore, the portion of the parent view that is shown in the detail view is highlighted in the circle. Select the **Profile** radio button, if you have already created a closed profile for defining the portion to be shown in the detail view. The options in the **Style** drop-down list are discussed next.

Per Standard: The **Per Standard** option is used to create the detail view as per the default standards.

Broken Circle: The **Broken Circle** option is used to display the area of the parent view to be displayed in the detailed view in a broken circle.

With Leader: The **With Leader** option is used to add the leader to the callout of the detail view.

No Leader: The **No Leader** option is used to remove the leader from the callout of the detail view.

Connected: This option is used to create a line that connects the detail view with the closed profile in the parent view.

Detail View Rollout

This rollout is used to set the parameters of the detail view. Various options in this rollout are discussed next.

No outline

The **No outline** check box is used to remove the outline of the closed profile in the detail view.

Full outline

The **Full outline** check box is used to display the complete outline of the closed profile in the detail view.

Jagged outline

The **Jagged outline** check box is used to display jagged outline of the closed profile in the detail view. The intensity of the jagged outline can be changed using the **Shape Intensity** slider provided below this check box.

Pin position

The **Pin position** check box is used to pin the position of the detail view. It is selected by default.

Scale hatch pattern

While creating a detail view of a section view, the **Scale hatch pattern** check box is used to scale the hatch pattern with respect to the scale factor of the detail view.

If you create a detail view with another detail view or a crop view as the parent view, the default scale factor of the resulting detail view will be twice the immediate parent view. Figure 14-42 shows the detail view generated by using the **Detail View** tool.

Tip

*1. To specify the default scale factor for the detail view, invoke the **System Options** dialog box and select the **Drawings** option from its left. Set the value of the scale factor of the detail view in the **Detail view scaling** edit box and choose the **OK** button; the detail view will be created with the scale factor defined in the **System Options** dialog box.*

2. In SOLIDWORKS, you can add a broken-out section view to a detail view, section view and on alternate position view. Figure 14-43 shows a view of a model with detail view added and also a broken-out section view added in the detail view.

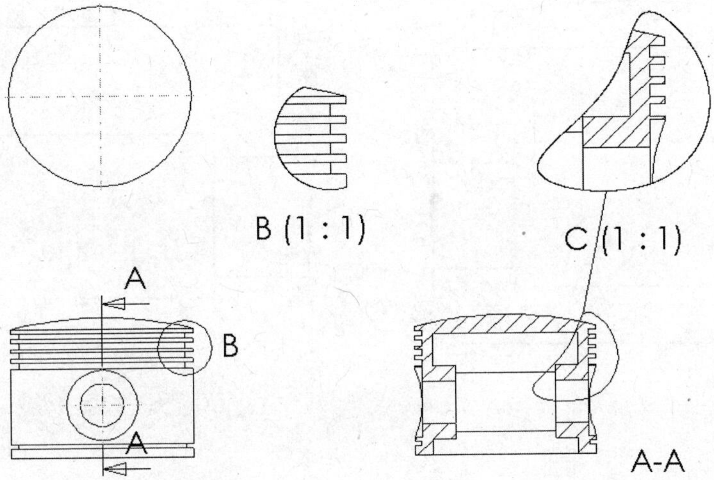

*Figure 14-42 Detail views generated by using the **Detail View** tool*

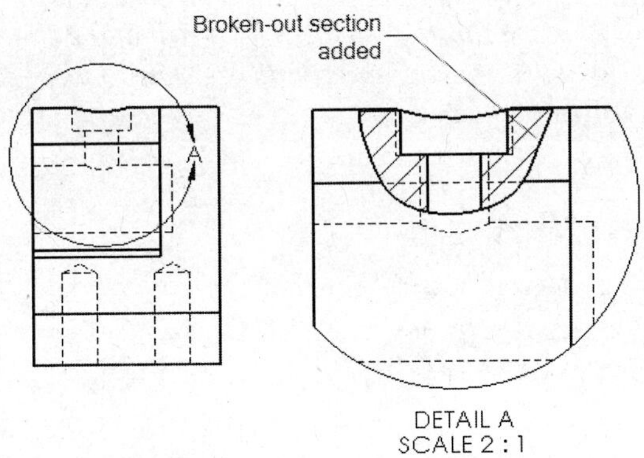

Figure 14-43 Broken-out section view added in the detail view

Generating Crop Views

CommandManager:	Drawing > Crop View
SOLIDWORKS menus:	Insert > Drawing View > Crop
Toolbar:	Drawing > Crop View

This tool is used to crop an existing view by using a closed sketch associated to it. The portion of the view that lies inside the associated sketch is retained and the remaining portion is removed. To crop a view, you first need to create a closed profile that defines the area of the view to be displayed. Select the closed profile and choose the **Crop View** button from the **Drawing CommandManager**; the area of the view outside the closed profile will not be displayed. Figure 14-44 shows the closed profile used to crop the view and Figure 14-45 shows the cropped view.

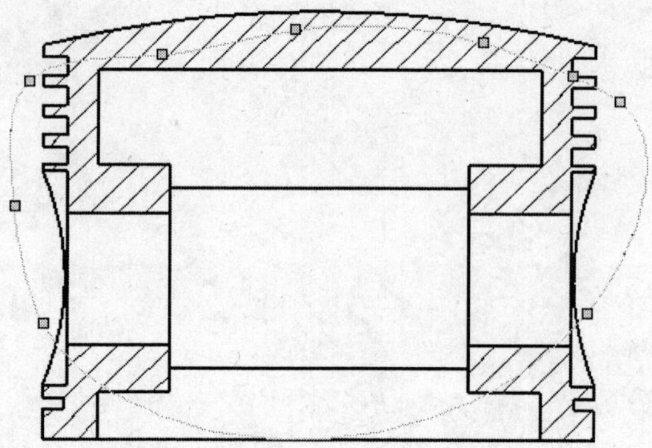

Figure 14-44 Closed profile to crop the view

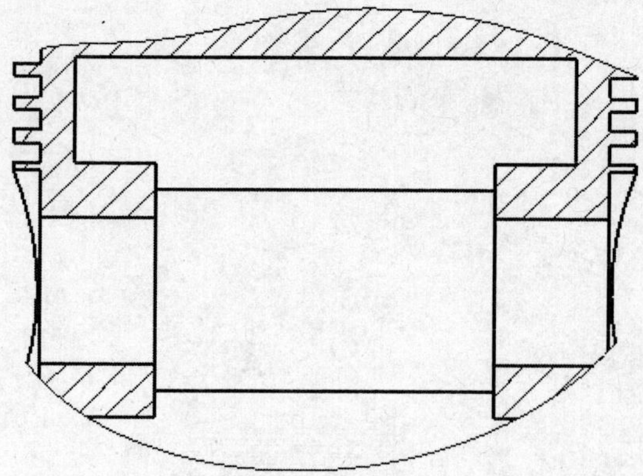

Figure 14-45 Resulting crop view

Tip

To remove the crop view, invoke the shortcut menu, and then choose ***Crop View > Remove Crop*** *from the shortcut menu.*

To edit the closed profile of the crop view, select the crop view and right-click. Next, choose ***Crop View > Edit Crop*** *from the shortcut menu. The sketch of the closed profile and the complete view will be displayed in the drawing sheet. Edit the closed profile and choose the* ***Exit Sketch*** *button from the Confirmation Corner.*

Generating Broken Views

CommandManager:	Drawing > Break View
SOLIDWORKS menus:	Insert > Drawing View > Break
Toolbar:	Drawing > Break View

A broken view is the one in which a portion of the drawing view is removed between the ends keeping the ends of the drawing view intact. This view is used to display the component whose length to width ratio is very high. This means that either the length is very large as compared to the width, or the width is very large as compared to the length. The **Break** tool will break the view along the horizontal or vertical direction such that the drawing view fits the required area. To create a broken view, choose the **Break View** button from the **Drawing CommandManager** and then select the view; the **Break View PropertyManager** will be displayed. Depending on the direction in which you need to break the view, choose the **Add vertical break line** or the **Add horizontal break line** button in the **Break View Settings** rollout of the PropertyManager; a break line will be displayed on the selected view. Place the first break line and then the second break line; the model will break up between the two break lines, as shown in Figure 14-46.

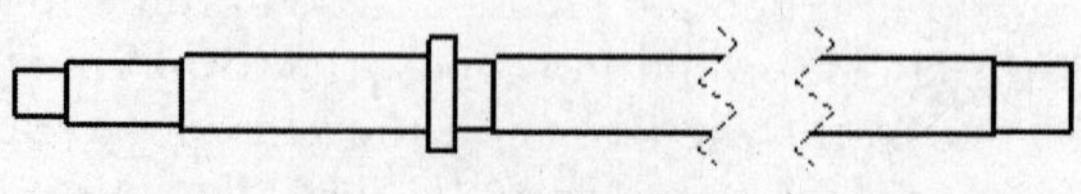

Figure 14-46 Break lines added to the view

Similarly, you can continue adding break lines to create multiple breaks in the drawing view, as shown in Figure 14-47. You can define the gap between the broken lines by using the **Gap size** spinner in the **Break View PropertyManager**. You can also modify the style of the break line by using the options in the **Break line style** area in the **Break View PropertyManager**. Figure 14-48 shows a view with the curved break lines.

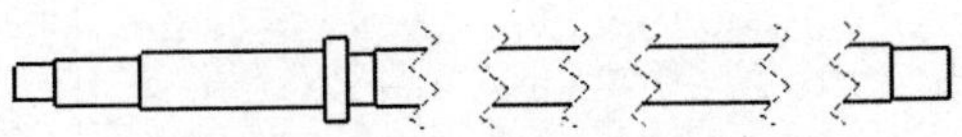

Figure 14-47 *Multiple break lines*

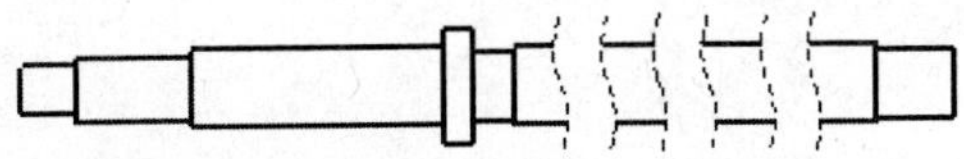

Figure 14-48 *Curved break lines*

You can also break an isometric view. The procedure of breaking an isometric view or any 3D view is the same as discussed earlier. Figure 14-49 shows a broken isometric view.

In SOLIDWORKS, you can lock the position of break lines. To do so, after placing two break lines, exit the **Break View PropertyManager**. Invoke the **Smart Dimension** tool from the **Sketch CommandManager** and dimension both the break lines with respect to an entity in the drawing view. Click anywhere in the drawing area; the dimension will disappear. Select the break lines to view the dimension that is used to lock them.

If you change the dimension of the model in the part document after locking the break lines, the gap between the break lines will not change. Remember that this dimension is not displayed when you print a drawing document.

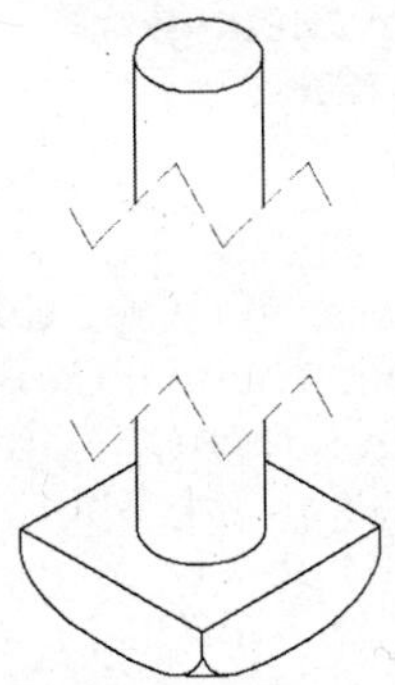

Figure 14-49 *A broken isometric view*

To unbreak a broken view, select the view, invoke the shortcut menu, and then choose the **Un-Break View** option from it.

Note

1. If the break lines are not locked, you can select and drag them to modify the gap between the broken views dynamically.

2. If you generate a projected view from a broken view, the resultant projected view will also be a broken view.

3. If you break the isometric view of a component placed horizontally, the two parts of the view will lose their alignment because of the break.

Tip

You can also change the style of the break line by selecting it and invoking the shortcut menu, which consists of various break line styles such as straight cut, curve cut, zig zag cut, small zig zag cut, and jagged cut.

*Select the view, invoke the shortcut menu, and then choose **Drawing Views > Break View** to break the view again.*

If you select the break lines and press the DELETE key, the broken view will be replaced by the parent view.

Generating Alternate Position Views

CommandManager:	Drawing > Alternate Position View
SOLIDWORKS menus:	Insert > Drawing View > Alternate Position
Toolbar:	Drawing > Alternate Position View

An alternate position view is used to create a view in which you can show two different positions of an assembly during the motion. The main position of the assembly is displayed with continuous lines in the drawing view, while the alternate position of the assembly is shown in the same view with the dashed (phantom) lines. To create an alternate position view, activate and select the view of the assembly drawing on which you need to create the alternate position view. Choose the **Alternate Position View** button from the **Drawing CommandManager**; the **Alternate Position PropertyManager** will be displayed, as shown in Figure 14-50.

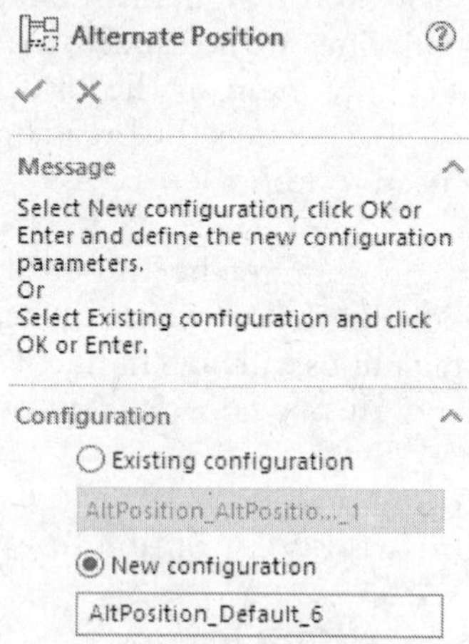

*Figure 14-50 The **Alternate Position PropertyManager***

The **Alternate Position PropertyManager** prompts you to select a new configuration. Select the required configuration from the **Existing configuration** drop-down list and then choose the **OK** button. The alternate position of the same view with dashed lines will be displayed. If you have not created any configurations, the **New configuration** radio button will be automatically selected to create new configuration. Enter the name of the new configuration in the edit box given below the **New configuration** radio button and choose the **OK** button from the **Alternate Position PropertyManager**.

The assembly document will open and the **Move Component PropertyManager** will be displayed in the assembly document. The **Move Component PropertyManager** will prompt you to move the desired components to the position that will be shown in the alternate view. Note that the component or components that you need to move should have that particular degree of freedom free. These components should not be fully defined in the assembly. Select and drag the cursor to move the components to the desired location. After defining the alternate position of the components, choose the **OK** button from the **Move Component PropertyManager**; you will return to the drawing document automatically. The alternate position of the components moved will be displayed in phantom lines in the drawing view, as shown in Figure 14-51.

You can also create the alternate position view of an isometric view or a 3D view. The procedure to create the alternate position view of a 3D view is the same as that discussed earlier. Figure 14-52 shows the alternate position view of an isometric view.

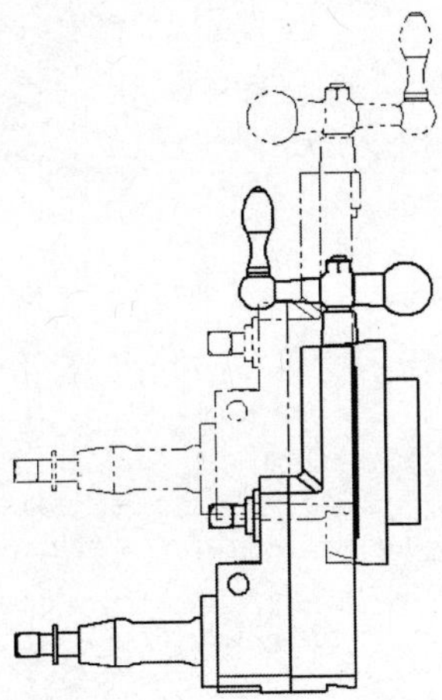

Figure 14-51 *Alternate position view*

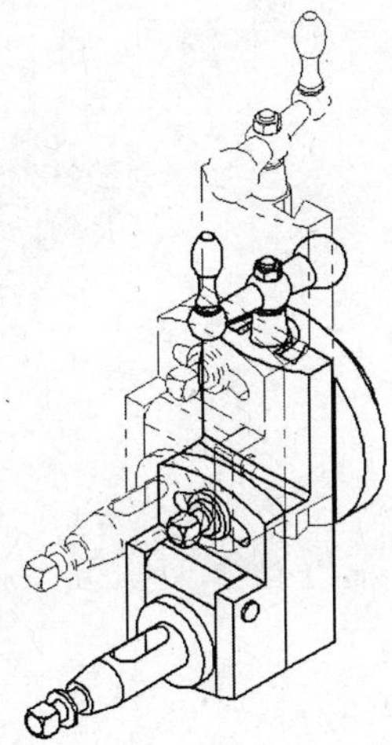

Figure 14-52 *Alternate view of an isometric view*

Note

On creating an alternate view of an assembly, a new configuration will be created inside the assembly document with the same name that is assigned to the configuration while creating the alternate position view. Open the assembly document and invoke the ***ConfigurationManager****; you will notice that a new configuration has been created along with the default configuration. The default configuration is selected in the* ***ConfigurationManager****. Therefore, the assembly is displayed with the components placed at default positions. To switch to the new configuration, select the new configuration from the* ***ConfigurationManager****, right-click and choose the* ***Show Configuration*** *option from the shortcut menu. You will notice that the assembly is displayed with the components moved to their new positions. If the* ***Show Configuration*** *option is not available in the shortcut menu, the assembly will retain its default configuration.*

Generating Drawing Views of the Exploded State of an Assembly

You can create the drawing views of the exploded state of an assembly. To do so, you need to have an exploded state defined in the assembly document. Generate the isometric view of the assembly on the drawing sheet. Select the view, invoke the shortcut menu, and then choose the **Properties** option from it; the **Drawing View Properties** dialog box will be displayed along with the **View Properties** tab chosen by default. Select the **Show in exploded or model break state** check box from the **Configuration information** area and then choose the **OK** button. Figure 14-53 shows the drawing view of the exploded state of an assembly with explode lines. If you have created multiple configurations for exploded views in the assembly document then you can generate the drawing views of multiple explode views of the assembly. To do so, select the required exploded view from the **Explode State** drop-down list under the **Show in exploded or model break state** check box of the **Configuration information** area in the **Drawing View Properties** dialog box.

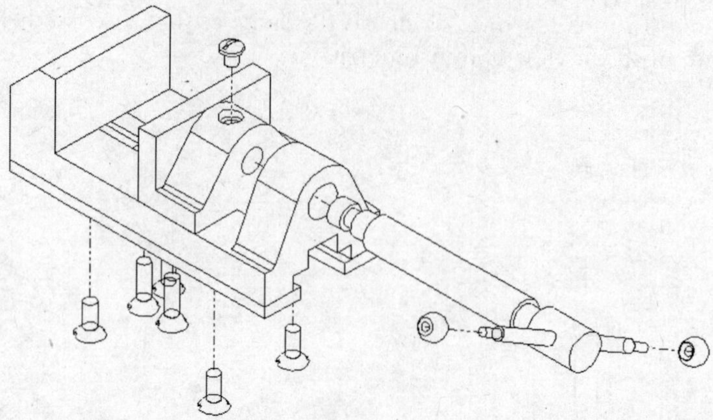

Figure 14-53 *Drawing view of the exploded state of an assembly with explode lines*

Tip

1. You can also create the drawing view of the exploded state of an assembly by using the ***Drawing View PropertyManager****. To do so, select a drawing to invoke the* ***Drawing View PropertyManager****, then select the* ***Show in exploded or model break state*** *check box in the* ***Reference Configuration*** *rollout.*

2. If an assembly in the assembly document is in the exploded state and you drag and drop the assembly to generate the drawing views, then all the views of the assembly will be generated in the exploded state.

To collapse the exploded state in the drawing view, select the view and invoke the ***Drawing View Properties*** *dialog box. Clear the* ***Show in exploded or model break state*** *check box in the* ***View Properties*** *tab of this dialog box.*

WORKING WITH INTERACTIVE DRAFTING IN SOLIDWORKS

As mentioned earlier, you can also sketch the 2D drawings in the drawing document of SOLIDWORKS. In technical terms, sketching 2D drawings is known as interactive drafting. Before starting the drawing, it is recommended that you insert an empty view. To create an empty view, choose **Insert > Drawing View > Empty** from the SOLIDWORKS menus; an empty view will be attached to the cursor. Select a point at the desired location to place an empty view. Now, select the empty view to activate and use the tools in the **Sketch CommandManager** to sketch the view. If you move the empty view by selecting and dragging it, the sketched entities will also move. This is because the sketch that you have drawn is associated to the empty view.

EDITING AND MODIFYING DRAWING VIEWS

In SOLIDWORKS, you can perform various kinds of editing operations and modifications on the drawing views. For example, you can change the orientation of the view or the view scale, or you can also delete the view. All these operations are discussed next.

Changing the View Orientation

You can change the orientation of the views generated by using the **Model View** option. To change the orientation, select the view; the **Drawing View PropertyManager** will be displayed in both the cases. Click on the view orientation that you want as the current one in the **Orientation** rollout; a message box displays warning about the position of the dependent views. Choose the **Yes** button to close the message box; the orientation of the selected view will be modified. Choose the **OK** button from the **Drawing View PropertyManager**.

All the derived views will also change their orientation, when you change the orientation of the parent view.

Changing the Scale of Drawing Views

In SOLIDWORKS, you can change the scale of the drawing views. To do so, select the drawing view and then select the **Use custom scale** radio button in the **Scale** rollout of the **Drawing View PropertyManager**. Select the new scale for the drawing view from the drop-down list available below this radio button. You can also change the scales of derived views. However, the scale of the parent view will not change even if you change the scale of a derived view. To display the scale of the drawing views, choose the **Options** button to invoke the **System Options - General** dialog box. Then, choose the **Document Properties** tab and expand the **Views** node and then click on the **Orthographic** sub node. Next, select the **Add view label on view creation** check box.

Deleting Drawing Views

You can delete unwanted views from the drawing sheet by using the **FeatureManager Design Tree** or directly from the drawing sheet. To do so, select the view to be deleted from the **FeatureManager Design Tree**. Next, invoke the shortcut menu and choose the **Delete** option from it; the **Confirm Delete** dialog box will be displayed. Choose the **Yes** button from this dialog box. You can also delete a view by selecting it directly from the drawing sheet and pressing the DELETE key; the **Confirm Delete** dialog box will be displayed. Choose the **Yes** button from this dialog box. On deleting a parent view, the projected views will not be deleted. However, if you delete a view that has a section, detail, or an auxiliary view generated, the name of the dependent views will also be displayed in the **Confirm Delete** dialog box. If you choose **Yes**, the dependent views will also be deleted.

Rotating Drawing Views

SOLIDWORKS allows you to rotate a drawing view in the 2D plane. To do so, select the view and choose the **Rotate View** button from the **View (Heads-Up)** toolbar; the **Rotate Drawing View** dialog box will be displayed, as shown in Figure 14-54. You can enter the value or the rotation angle in this dialog box or you can also dynamically rotate the drawing view by dragging the mouse. If you select the **Dependent views update to change in orientation** check box, the views dependent on the rotated view will also change their orientation.

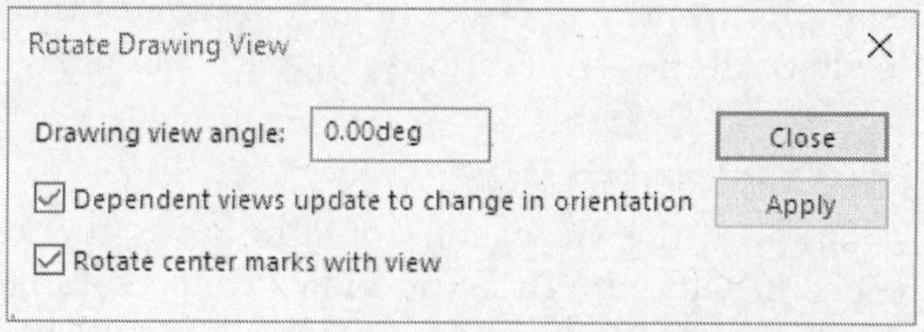

*Figure 14-54 The **Rotate Drawing View** dialog box*

Tip

You can also copy and paste a drawing view in the drawing sheet. To do so, select the view to copy and press CTRL+C on the keyboard. Now, click anywhere on the drawing sheet to select and press CTRL+V to paste the drawing view.

Manipulating the Drawing Views

SOLIDWORKS allows you to manipulate the drawing views dynamically. Select a view and invoke the **3D Drawing View** tool in the **View (Heads-Up)** toolbar; a pop-up toolbar will be displayed. Invoke a tool from the toolbar and manipulate the drawing view. After manipulating the view, choose the **Exit** button; the drawing will revert to the original view.

MODIFYING THE HATCH PATTERN IN SECTION VIEWS

As discussed earlier, when you generate a section view of an assembly or a component, a hatch pattern is applied to the component or components. The hatch pattern is based on the material assigned to the components in the part document. If you need to modify the default hatch pattern, select it from the section view; the **Area Hatch/Fill PropertyManager** will be displayed, as shown in Figure 14-55. The rollouts in this dialog box are discussed next.

Properties Rollout

The **Properties** rollout is used to define the type of hatch pattern and its properties. Some of the options in this area are not available by default. This is because, by default, the material-dependent hatch pattern is applied to the component. If you want to make the other options also available, clear the **Material crosshatch** check box. The options in this rollout are discussed next.

Hatch

The **Hatch** radio button is used to apply the standard hatch patterns to the section view. On selecting this radio button, some options available in the dialog box are activated.

Solid

The **Solid** radio button is used to apply the solid filled hatch pattern to the section view. By default, the black color is applied to the solid filled hatch pattern.

None

Select the **None** radio button, if you do not need to apply any hatch pattern in the section view.

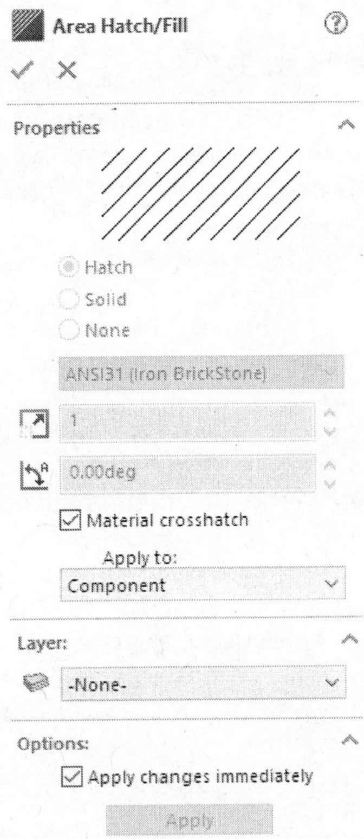

Figure 14-55 The ***Area Hatch/Fill PropertyManager***

Hatch Pattern

The **Hatch Pattern** drop-down list is used to define the style of the standard hatch pattern that you need to apply to the section view. The preview of the hatch pattern selected from this drop-down list is displayed in the **Preview** area of the **Area Hatch/Fill PropertyManager**.

Hatch Pattern Scale

The **Hatch Pattern Scale** spinner is used to specify the scale factor of the standard hatch pattern selected from the **Hatch Pattern** drop-down list. When you change the scale factor using this spinner, the preview displayed in the **Preview** area updates dynamically.

Hatch Pattern Angle

The **Hatch Pattern Angle** spinner is used to define the angle of the selected hatch pattern.

Material crosshatch

The **Material crosshatch** check box is selected to apply the hatch pattern based on the material assigned to the model. Clear this check box to change the type of the hatch pattern.

Apply to

The **Apply to** drop-down list is used to specify whether you need to apply this hatch pattern to the selected component, region, body, or to the entire view. Note that some of these options are available only while modifying the hatch pattern of an assembly section view.

Layer Rollout

In SOLIDWORKS, you can change layers of the hatch pattern. To change the layer of a hatch pattern, select a predefined layer from the **Layer** drop-down list in the rollout, preview of the hatch pattern will be modified dynamically.

Options Rollout

On selecting the **Apply changes immediately** check box in this rollout, the changes will be applied immediately to the view and the preview will be modified dynamically. If you clear this check box, you need to choose the **Apply** button after making the changes.

TUTORIALS

Tutorial 1

In this tutorial, you will generate the front view, top view, right view, aligned section view, detail view, and isometric view of the model created in Tutorial 2 of Chapter 8. Use the Standard A4 Landscape sheet format for generating these views. **(Expected time: 30 min)**

The following steps are required to complete this tutorial:

a. Copy the part document of Tutorial 2 of Chapter 8 in the folder of the current chapter.
b. Open the copied part document and start a new drawing document from within the part document.
c. Select the standard A4 landscape sheet format and generate the parent view.
d. Generate projected views using the **Projected View** tool.
e. Generate the aligned section view using the **Section View** tool.
f. Generate the detail view.
g. Save and close the drawing document.

Copying and Opening the Part Document

1. Create a folder with the name *c14* in the *SOLIDWORKS* directory and copy *c08_tut02.sldprt* from the location *\Documents\SOLIDWORKS\c08*.

2. Start SOLIDWORKS and open the part document that you copied in the *c14* folder.

Starting a New Drawing Document

As mentioned earlier in this chapter, you can start a new drawing document from the part document. This way, the model in the part document is automatically selected and you can generate its drawing views.

1. Choose **New > Make Drawing from Part/Assembly** from the Menu Bar; the **Sheet Format/Size** dialog box is displayed.

Note

*If you are using advanced form of the **New SOLIDWORKS Document** dialog box, the **New SOLIDWORKS Document** dialog box will be displayed every time you choose the **Make Drawing from Part/Assembly**. In the **New SOLIDWORKS Document** dialog box, select a drawing template from the **Templates** tab and choose **OK**. Remember that if you are not using advanced form of the **New SOLIDWORKS Document** dialog box, then a new drawing document will start directly and the **Sheet Format/Size** dialog box will be displayed.*

2. Clear the **Only show standard formats** check box and select the **A4 (ANSI) Landscape** sheet from the list box in this dialog box and choose the **OK** button; a new drawing document is started with the standard A4 sheet and the **View Palette** task pane is displayed automatically. By default, the model of Tutorial 2 of Chapter 8 is selected for generating the drawing views.

Generating the Parent View and the Projected Views

Before you proceed to generate the drawing views, you need to confirm whether the projection type for the current sheet is set to the third angle.

1. Click anywhere on the sheet to close the **View Palette** task pane. Select **Sheet1** from the **FeatureManager Design Tree** and then right-click to display the shortcut menu. Choose the **Properties** option from the shortcut menu; the **Sheet Properties** dialog box is displayed.

2. Select the **Third angle** radio button from the **Type of projection** area if not selected by default and then choose the **Apply Changes** button.

3. Choose the **View Palette** tab to view the **View Palette** task pane and make sure the **Auto-start projected view** check box is selected.

4. Select the **Front** view from the **View Palette** task pane and drag it to the middle left of the drawing sheet above the title block. Drop the view at this location to place the front view, refer to Figure 14-56. The **Projected View PropertyManager** is invoked automatically and preview of the projected view is attached to the cursor.

5. Next, move the cursor vertically upward from the front view; a preview of the top view is displayed. Specify a point to place the top view, refer to Figure 14-56. Preview of another projected view with the front view as the parent view is attached to the cursor.

6. Next, move the cursor horizontally toward right from the front view, a preview of the side view is displayed. Specify a point to place the side view, refer to Figure 14-56.

7. Move the cursor horizontally toward the right and then move it upward; a preview of the isometric view is displayed. Specify a point to place the isometric view. Next, choose the **OK** button in the PropertyManager.

   The current location of the isometric view of the model is such that it will interfere with the aligned section view that you need to place next. Therefore, you need to move the isometric view close to the top right corner of the drawing sheet.

8. Move the cursor over the isometric view; the bounding box of the view is displayed in orange.

9. Click to select the view; the border of the view is highlighted.

10. Move the cursor on one of the borderlines of the view; the cursor changes into a move cursor.

11. Press and hold the left mouse button and drag the view close to the upper right corner of the drawing sheet. The drawing sheet after generating and moving the isometric view is shown in Figure 14-56.

Tip

You can turn on/off the origins displayed in the drawing views by using the ***View (Heads-Up)*** *toolbar.*

The center marks are automatically created in the drawing views of the circular features in a model.

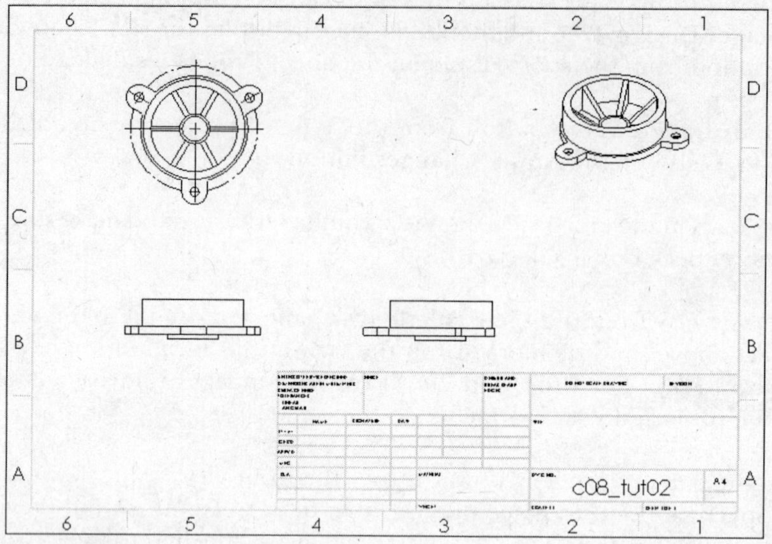

Figure 14-56 Drawing sheet after generating the front, top, right, and isometric views

Generating the Aligned Section View

Next, you need to generate the aligned section view on the top circular feature of the model. Before doing so, you need to activate the view from which you will generate the section view.

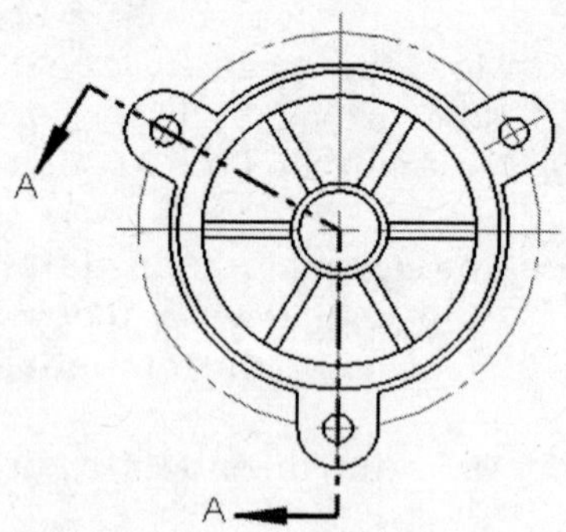

Figure 14-57 Sketch of planes created for the aligned section view

1. Click on the top view to activate it.

2. Invoke the **Drawing CommandManager** and choose the **Section View** button; the **Section View Assist PropertyManager** is displayed.

3. Choose the **Aligned** button in the **Cutting Line** rollout and create the cutting plane line, as shown in Figure 14-57; the **Section View** pop-up toolbar is displayed. Choose the **OK** button from the pop-up toolbar; the **SOLIDWORKS** information box is displayed with the message that the selected model has a rib feature that will vary the hatching of the section view. It also asks you whether to make an aligned section view or a foreshortened section view.

4. Choose the **Make aligned section view** option from the **SOLIDWORKS** information box; the aligned section view is attached to the cursor.

   The view generated is normal to the vertical line. If the direction of viewing the aligned section view is in opposite direction, you need to flip it after placing the view.

5. Move the cursor to the right of the top view and place the aligned section view; the **Section View PropertyManager** is displayed. If the direction of viewing is not the required one, select the **Flip Direction** button. Click anywhere on the sheet to exit the PropertyManager.

The sheet after generating the aligned section view is shown in Figure 14-58.

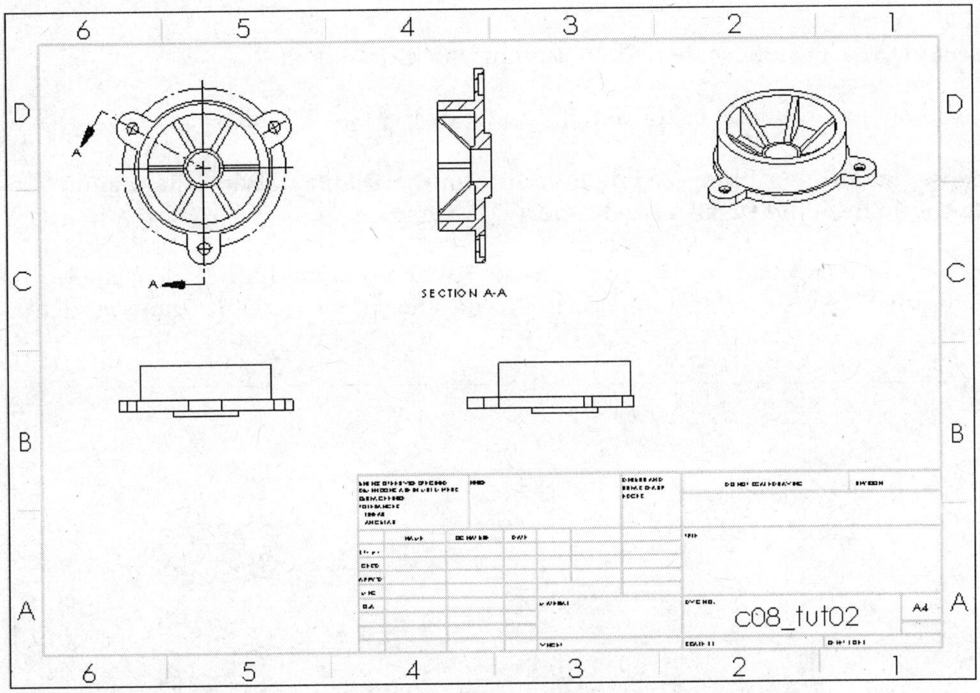

Figure 14-58 Sheet after generating the aligned section view

Modifying the Hatch Pattern of the Aligned Section View

The gap between the hatching lines in the aligned section view is large. Therefore, you need to modify the spacing.

1. Select the hatch pattern from one of the sections in the aligned section view; the **Area Hatch/Fill PropertyManager** is displayed.

2. Clear the **Material crosshatch** check box; the **Hatch Pattern**, **Hatch Pattern Scale**, and **Hatch Pattern Angle** options become available. Set the value **2** in the **Hatch Pattern Scale** spinner and exit the PropertyManager by choosing the **OK** button.

Generating the Detail View

Next, you need to generate the detail view of the right circular feature of the model. Before doing so, you need to activate the view from which you will derive the detail view.

1. Activate the top view and choose the **Detail View** button from the **Drawing CommandManager**; the **Detail View PropertyManager** is displayed and you are prompted to sketch a circle to continue viewing the creation. Also, the cursor is replaced by the circle cursor. 

2. Draw a small circle on the right circular feature of the model in the top view, refer to Figure 14-59. As you draw the circle, the detail view is attached to the cursor.

3. Place the view on the right side of the drawing sheet above the title block, refer to Figure 14-59.

4. Select the **Use custom scale** radio button in the **Scale** rollout.

5. Set the value of the scale factor of the detail view to **3:1**.

6. Choose the **Hidden Lines Visible** button from the **Display Style** rollout and choose the **OK** button from the **Detail View PropertyManager**.

   You may need to move the drawing view and its label so that the view does not overlap the title block. Figure 14-59 shows the final drawing sheet displayed after generating the detail view from the top view.

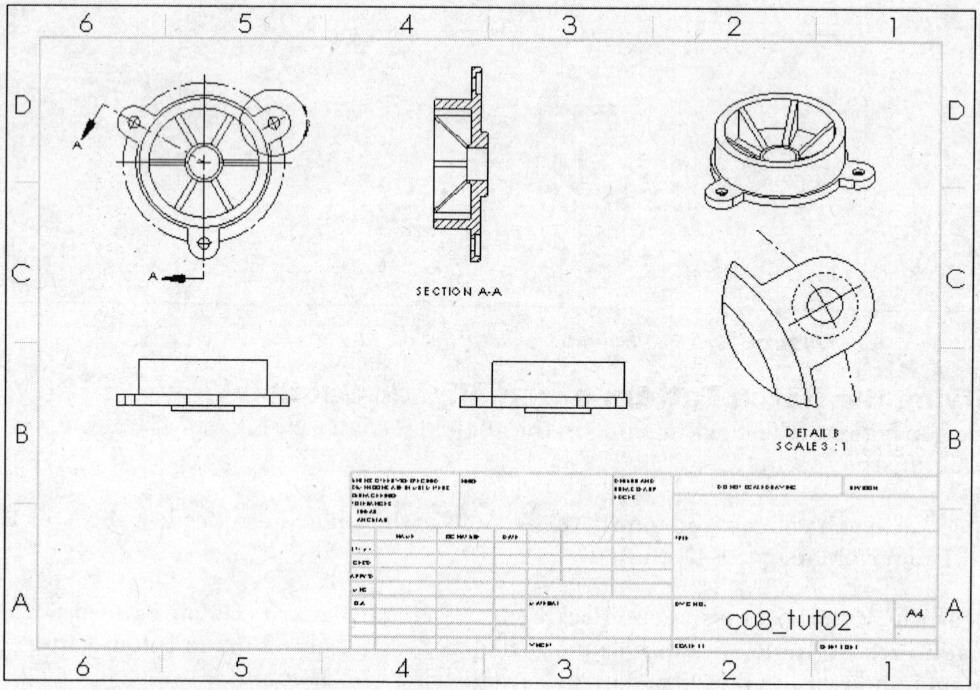

***Figure 14-59** The detail view derived from the top view*

Saving the Drawing

1. Choose the **Save** button from the Menu Bar and save the drawing file with the name *c14_tut01* at the following location:
   \Documents\SOLIDWORKS\c14

2. Choose **File > Close** to close this document. Also, close the part file of Tutorial 2 of Chapter 8.

Tutorial 2

In this tutorial, you will generate the drawing view of the Bench Vice assembly created in Chapter 12. You will generate the top view, sectioned front view, right view, and isometric view of the assembly in an exploded state. **(Expected time: 45 min)**

The following steps are required to complete this tutorial:

a. Copy the folder of the Bench Vice assembly from *c12* to the *c14* folder.
b. Create the exploded view of the Bench Vice assembly.
c. Start a new drawing document from the assembly document using A4 landscape sheet format and generate the top view.
d. Generate the section view using the **Section View** tool.
e. Generate the right view using the **Projected View** tool.
f. Generate the isometric view and change the state of the isometric view to the exploded state.
g. Save and close the drawing and assembly documents.

Copying the Folder of the Bench Vice Assembly

First, you need to copy the folder of the Bench Vice assembly to the *c14* folder.

1. Copy the folder of the Bench Vice assembly from *Documents\SOLIDWORKS\c12* to the *c14* folder.

Creating the Exploded View of the Assembly

Before proceeding further to generate the drawing views of the assembly, you need to create the exploded state of the assembly in the **Assembly** mode.

1. Open the Bench Vice assembly and create an exploded view of the assembly with explode lines as shown in Figure 14-60.

   Note that you must save an assembly in collapsed state only otherwise the subsequent views will be generated in exploded state.

2. Right-click on the assembly name in the **FeatureManager Design Tree** and choose **Collapse** to unexplode the assembly.

3. Save the assembly.

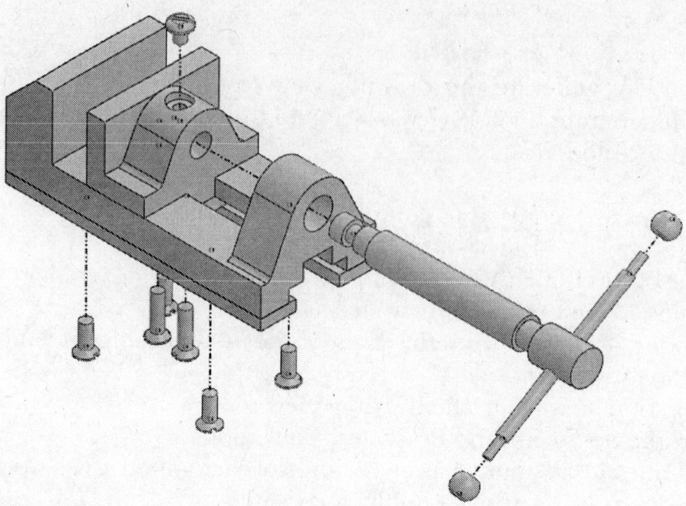

Figure 14-60 Exploded view of the assembly with explode lines

Starting a New Drawing Document from the Assembly Document

As mentioned earlier, you can also start a drawing document from the assembly document.

1. Choose **New > Make Drawing from Assembly** from the Menu Bar; the **Sheet Format/Size** dialog box is displayed. 

2. Select the **A4 (ANSI) Landscape** sheet and choose the **OK** button. Right-click on **Sheet1** and choose **Properties** from the shortcut menu. Set the current projection type to third angle using the **Sheet Properties** dialog box if not set by default.

Generating the Top View

1. Invoke the **Model View** tool and double-click on **Bench Vice** in the **Part/Assembly to Insert** rollout; the **Model View PropertyManager** gets modified.

2. Choose the **Top** button from the **Standard views** area in the **Orientation** rollout of the **Model View PropertyManager**.

3. Select the **Use custom scale** radio button from the **Scale** rollout.

4. Set the value of the scale factor to **1:2** and then select the **Preview** check box from the **Orientation** rollout; a preview of the top view of the assembly is displayed.

5. Make sure that the **Auto-start projected view** check box is cleared in the **Options** rollout.

6. Place the view close to the top left corner of the drawing sheet, refer to Figure 14-61. Click anywhere on the sheet to exit the PropertyManager.

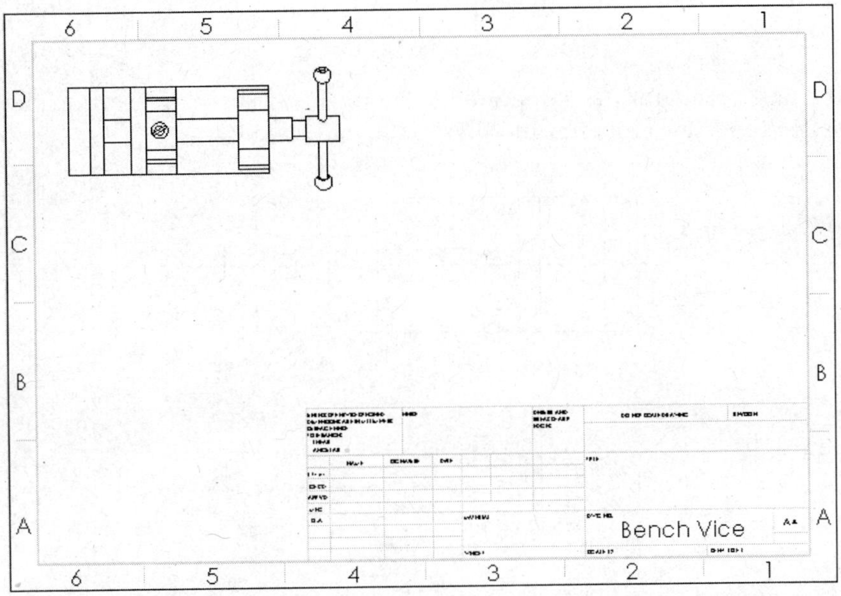

*Figure 14-61 Top view generated using the **Model View** tool*

Creating the Sectioned Front View

Next, you need to generate the sectioned front view that is derived from the top view.

1. Activate the top view and choose the **Section View** button from the **Drawing CommandManager**; the **Section View Assist PropertyManager** is displayed.

2. Choose the **Horizontal** button from the **Cutting Line** rollout of the **Section View Assist PropertyManager** and create the cutting plane line, refer to Figure 14-62; the **Section View** pop-up toolbar is displayed. Choose the **OK** button from the pop-up toolbar; the **Section View** dialog box is displayed.

   This dialog box is used to exclude components from the section cut.

3. Invoke the **FeatureManager Design Tree** and click on the ▸ sign located on the left of the **Drawing View1** to display the name of the assembly. Next, expand the assembly.

4. Select Screw Bar, Bar Globes, Jaw Screw, Oval Fillister, Set Screw1, and Set Screw2. Next, click on the **Section View** dialog box in the drawing area to activate it. Select one of the components displayed in the **Exclude components/rib features** selection box and then select the **Don't cut all instances** check box. Similarly, select all the components one by one from this selection box and then select the **Don't cut all instances** check box.

5. Next, select the **Auto hatching** check box and choose the **OK** button from the **Section View** dialog box; a preview of the section view gets attached to the cursor. Also, the **Section View PropertyManager** is displayed.

6. If the direction of viewing of the section view is not as required, flip the direction by selecting the **Flip Direction** button from the **Cutting Line** rollout.

7. Place the section view below the top view. Click anywhere on the sheet to exit the PropertyManager.

8. Modify the hatch scale for the components. Figure 14-62 shows the section view generated using the **Section View** tool after modifying the hatch scale.

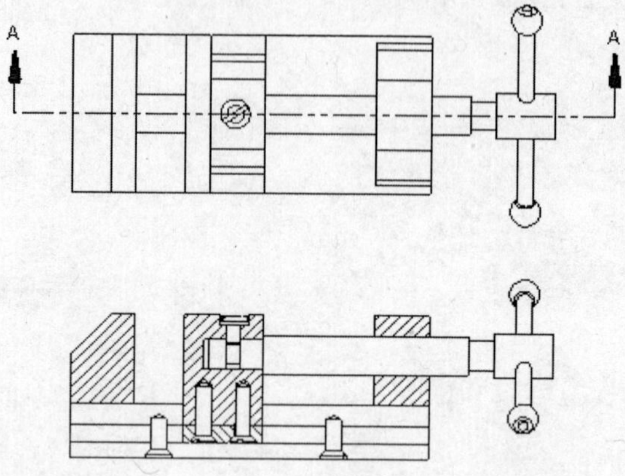

Figure 14-62 *Section view generated using the* ***Section View*** *tool*

Generating the Right Side View

The next view that you need to generate is the right side view derived from the sectioned front view and it will be generated using the **Projected View** tool.

1. Select the sectioned front view and invoke the **Projected View** tool; the **Projected View PropertyManager** is displayed and a projected view is attached to the cursor. 

2. Move the cursor to the right of the sectioned front view and place the view on the right of the sectioned front view. Next, exit the PropertyManager.

3. The sheet after generating the projected view is shown in Figure 14-63.

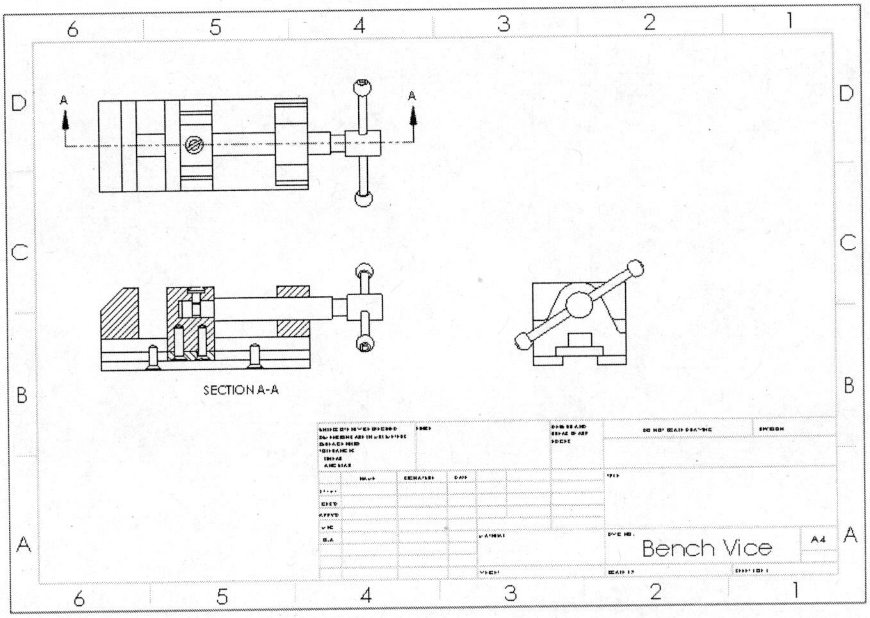

Figure 14-63 Right side view generated using the ***Projected View*** *tool*

Creating the Isometric View of the Assembly in the Exploded State

The last view to be generated is the isometric view of the assembly in the exploded state.

1. Invoke the **Model View** tool and generate the isometric view, and then place it close to the upper right corner of the drawing sheet.

2. Set the scale factor of the drawing view to **1:2**.

3. Right-click on the view to invoke the shortcut menu. Choose the **Properties** option from the shortcut menu; the **Drawing View Properties** dialog box is displayed.

4. Select the **Show in exploded or model break state** check box in the **View Properties** tab of the **Drawing View Properties** dialog box and choose the **OK** button.

5. Move the views to place them in the drawing sheet. Figure 14-64 shows the final drawing sheet after generating all the drawing views.

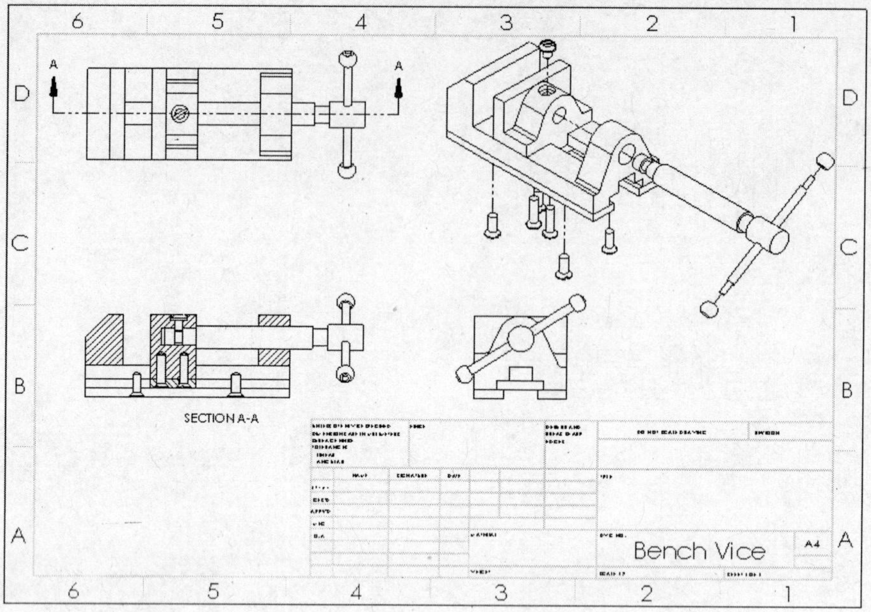

Figure 14-64 Drawing sheet after generating all views

Saving the Drawing

Next, you need to save the drawing file.

1. Choose the **Save** button from the Menu Bar and save the drawing document with the name *c14_tut02* at the following location:
   \Documents\SOLIDWORKS\c14

2. Close the drawing and assembly files.

Self-Evaluation Test

Answer the following questions and then compare them to those given at the end of this chapter:

1. In technical terms, creating a 2D drawing in the drawing document is known as __________.

2. Choose the __________ button from the Menu Bar to start a new drawing document from the part document.

3. The __________ check box available in the **Detail View** rollout of the **Detail View PropertyManager** is used to display the complete outline of the closed profile in the detail view.

4. Select the drawing view and then the __________ radio button from the **Scale** rollout to change the scale of the drawing views.

5. Select the view and choose the __________ button from the **View (Heads-Up)** toolbar to rotate a drawing view.

6. The **Standard sheet size** radio button is selected by default in the **Sheet Format/Size** dialog box. (T/F)

7. If you want to use an empty sheet without any margin lines or title block, then select the **Display sheet format** check box in the **Sheet Format/Size** dialog box. (T/F)

8. The **Relative View** tool is used to generate an orthographic view by defining its orientation using the reference planes or planar faces of the model. (T/F)

9. An auxiliary view is a drawing view that is generated by projecting the lines normal to the specified edge of an existing view. (T/F)

10. You cannot change the style of the break lines in a broken view. (T/F)

Review Questions

Answer the following questions:

1. Which of the following types of views is generated from a view that is already placed in the drawing sheet?

   (a) Child views (b) Derived views
   (c) Predefined views (d) Empty views

2. In which of the following shapes is the detail view boundary displayed by default?

   (a) Circle (b) Ellipse
   (c) Rectangle (d) None

3. Which of the following edit boxes is used to specify the name of the auxiliary view?

   (a) **Label** (b) **Arrow**
   (c) **Name** (d) **Detail view label**

4. Which of the following rollouts is used to select the view orientation in the **Model View PropertyManager**?

   (a) **Orientation** (b) **Define View**
   (c) **Specify View** (d) **Scale View**

5. Choose the __________ button from the **View Layout CommandManager** to create an alternate position view.

6. The __________ **PropertyManager** is used to modify the hatch pattern of a section view.

7. The __________ check box needs to be cleared to modify the scale of the hatch pattern.

8. A __________ view is a section view in which only the sectioned surface is displayed.

9. When you delete the views, the __________ dialog box is displayed to confirm the deletion.

10. Select a view and invoke the __________ tool in the **View (Heads-Up)** toolbar to manipulate the display style of the model in the drawing view.

EXERCISE

Exercise 1

Download *c14_exr01.zip* from *www.cadcim.com*. The complete path for downloading the files is as follows: Textbooks > CAD/CAM > SOLIDWORKS > SOLIDWORKS 2021 for Designers. In this exercise, you will generate the front view, section right view, isometric view, and the alternate position view on the isometric view. You need to scale the parent view to the scale factor of 1:3. The views that you need to generate are shown in Figure 14-65. **(Expected time: 30 min)**

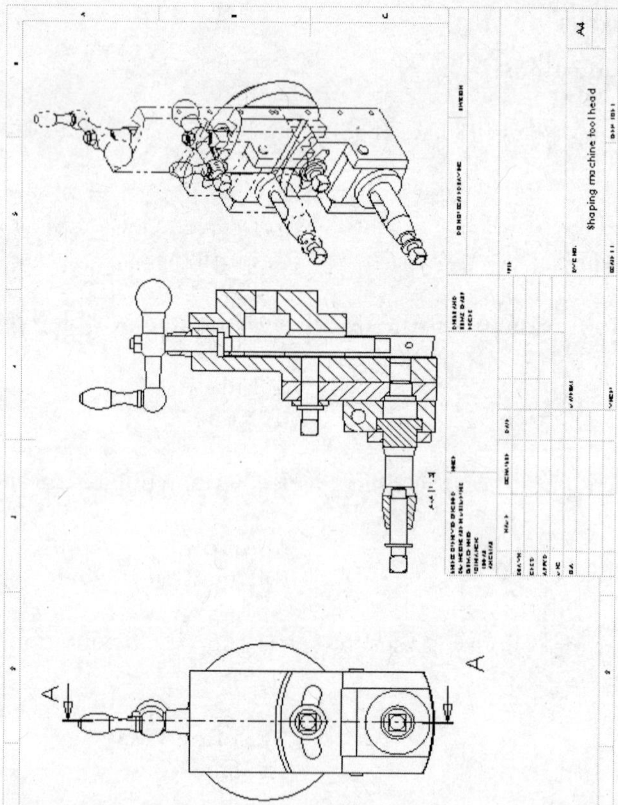

***Figure 14-65** Views to be generated for Exercise 1*

Answers to Self-Evaluation Test

1. Interactive drafting, **2. Make Drawing from Part/Assembly**, **3. Full outline**, **4. Use custom scale**, **5. Rotate View**, **6.** T, **7.** F, **8.** T, **9.** T, **10.** F

Chapter 15

Working with Drawing Views-II

Learning Objectives

After completing this chapter, you will be able to:
- *Add and edit annotations in drawing views*
- *Add reference dimensions and notes to drawing views*
- *Add surface finish and datum feature symbols to drawing views*
- *Add geometric tolerance and datum target symbols to drawing views*
- *Add center marks, callouts, and centerlines to drawing views*
- *Add cosmetic threads and multi-jog leader to drawing views*
- *Add dowel pin symbol to drawing views*
- *Add Bill of Material (BOM) to drawing sheet*
- *Add balloons to assembly drawing views*
- *Add new sheets in the drawing document*
- *Edit the sheet format*
- *Create a user-defined sheet format*
- *Create magnetic lines*

ADDING ANNOTATIONS TO DRAWING VIEWS

After generating drawing views, you need to generate dimensions and add annotations such as notes, surface finish symbols, geometric tolerance, and so on to them. Two types of annotations can be generated in the drawing views. The first type of annotations are generative annotations that are added while creating a part in the Part mode. For example, the dimensions that you add to the sketch and features of the part are generative annotations. The second type of annotations are added manually to the geometry of drawing views such as reference dimensions, notes, surface finish symbols, and so on. Both these types of annotations are discussed next.

Generating Annotations Using the Model Items Tool

CommandManager:	Annotation > Model Items
SOLIDWORKS menus:	Insert > Model Items
Toolbar:	Annotation > Model Items

The **Model Items** tool is used to generate the annotations that were added while creating the model in the Part mode. To generate annotations, choose the **Model Items** button from the **Annotation CommandManager**; the **Model Items PropertyManager** will be displayed, as shown in Figure 15-1. The options in this PropertyManager are discussed next.

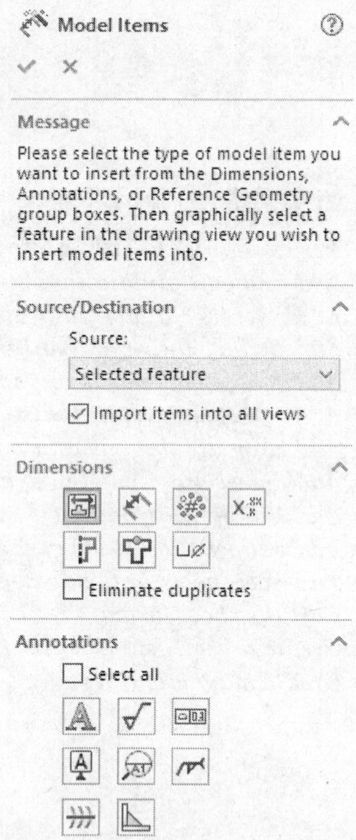

__Figure 15-1__ Partial view of the __Model Items PropertyManager__

Source/Destination Rollout

The **Source** drop-down list in the **Source/Destination** rollout defines the options from where the annotations are imported. The options in this drop-down list are discussed next.

Entire model

The **Entire model** option is selected to import the annotations from the entire model. After selecting this option, select a drawing view in which all the annotations of the model are to be imported. In case of assemblies, the annotations from all the components of the assembly are imported even if a single component of the assembly is selected.

Selected component

The **Selected component** option will be available only when you generate the drawing views of an assembly. This option is selected to import annotations only from the selected component.

Selected feature

The **Selected feature** option is selected to import the annotations only from the selected feature or features of a model.

Only assembly

The **Only assembly** option will be available only when you generate the drawing views of an assembly. This option is selected to import the annotations that are applied to the assembly in the Assembly mode such as the offset distance and so on.

Import items into all views

This check box is selected to import the dimensions to all the drawing views available on the sheet. This check box is selected by default. If this check box is cleared, the **Destination view(s)** selection box will be displayed in this rollout. Use this selection box to select the drawing views in which the dimensions will be placed.

Dimensions Rollout

This rollout is used to select the type of dimensions, pattern annotations, tolerances, and the hole annotations that you need to generate in the drawing views. You can choose the button of the required annotation type. You can also choose all the buttons in this rollout. The **Eliminate duplicates** check box is selected to remove duplicate instances of annotations.

Annotations Rollout

The options in the **Annotations** rollout are used to select the annotations that are to be generated in the drawing views. Use the buttons in this rollout to generate the cosmetic threads, datums, datum targets, dimensions, geometric tolerances, notes, surface finish, and weld symbols. You can also select the **Select all** check box to select all options.

Reference Geometry Rollout

The **Reference Geometry** rollout is used to generate the reference geometries that were used for creating the part. You can generate axes, curves, planes, surfaces, center of mass, and so on through this rollout. Choose a button to specify the type of reference geometry that you need to generate in the drawing views. You can also select the **Select all** check box to select all buttons.

Options Rollout

The options in this rollout are discussed next.

Include items from hidden features

This check box is selected to display the annotation that belongs to a hidden feature of the model. By default, this check box is cleared. It is recommended to keep this check box cleared as it helps in eliminating the display of the unwanted annotations.

Use dimension placement in sketch

Select this check box to place the dimension at the exact location where it was placed in the sketch while creating the part.

Layer Rollout

This rollout allows you to select the layers in which the dimensions will be placed.

After setting all the parameters in the **Model Items PropertyManager**, choose the **OK** button to display the annotations.

Tip

*1. When the **Model Items PropertyManager** is displayed, you can toggle the display of an annotation by right-clicking on it.*

2. The annotations mostly overlap each other when they are generated. Therefore, you may need to move the annotations after generating them. To move an annotation, move the cursor on the annotation; the annotation will be highlighted in orange color. Press and hold the left mouse button and drag the cursor to place the annotation at the desired location. Release the left mouse button when the cursor is placed at the desired location.

3. The dimensions that are generated while generating the annotations are the same as the those used to create the model. These dimensions are linked to the model because of the bidirectional associativity in SOLIDWORKS.

*4. Double-click on the dimension to modify it; the **Modify** dialog box will be displayed. Modify the value of the dimension in this dialog box and rebuild the drawing views using the **Rebuild** button; the dimension will change in the drawing as well as in the original model. If the model is used in an assembly, the changes will also reflect in the assembly.*

Adding Reference Annotations

In SOLIDWORKS, you can add reference annotations to the drawing views. These include reference dimensions, notes, surface finish symbols, datum feature symbols, geometric tolerance, and so on. The methods of adding reference annotations are discussed next.

Adding Reference Dimensions

CommandManager:	Annotation > Smart Dimension
SOLIDWORKS menus:	Tools > Dimensions > Smart
Toolbar:	Annotation > Smart Dimension

You can use the **Smart Dimension** tool to add reference dimensions to the drawing views in the **Drawing** mode of SOLIDWORKS. On invoking the **Smart Dimension** tool, the **Dimension PropertyManager** will be displayed, as shown in Figure 15-2. By default, the **Smart dimensioning** button is chosen in the **Dimension Assist Tools** rollout of this PropertyManager. Therefore, you can create dimensions in the drawing views as discussed in the earlier chapters.

If you choose the **DimXpert** button in the **Dimension Assist Tools** rollout, the **Dimension PropertyManager** will be modified, as shown in Figure 15-3. Specify the datum by selecting an option in the **Datum** rollout. Next, specify the dimensioning scheme and dimensioning pattern scheme in the corresponding rollouts. Then, select an entity to create dimension. Choose **OK** to exit the PropertyManager.

The **Rapid dimensioning** check box is selected by default in the **Dimension Assist Tools** rollout. Therefore, when you select an entity, the rapid dimension manipulator will be displayed. Move the cursor over the manipulator to place the dimension in any one of the quadrants.

You can also create the dimensions automatically. To do so, choose the **Autodimension** tab in the **Dimension PropertyManager**, specify the parameters, and then choose **OK.**

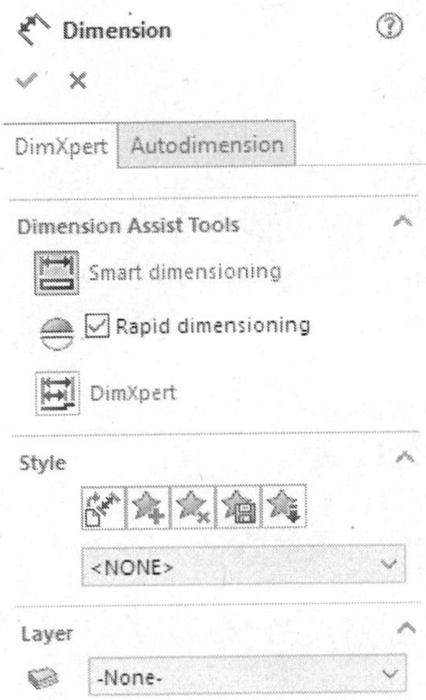

Figure 15-2 *The* **Dimension PropertyManager**

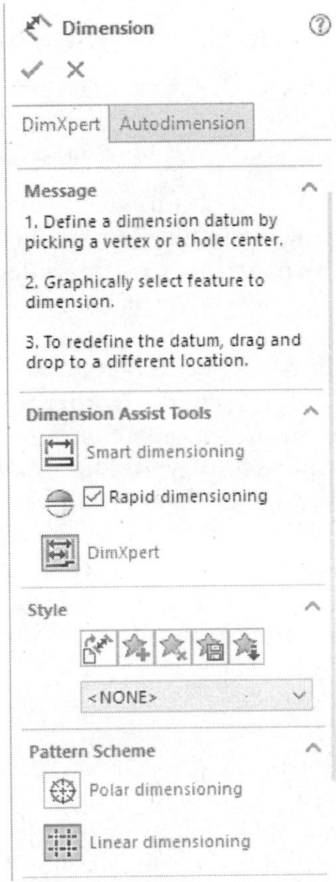

Figure 15-3 *Partial view of the* **Dimension PropertyManager** *displayed on choosing the* **DimXpert** *button*

Adding Chamfer Dimensions

CommandManager:	Annotation > Smart Dimension flyout > Chamfer Dimension
SOLIDWORKS menus:	Tools > Dimensions > Chamfer
Toolbar:	Annotation > Smart Dimension flyout > Chamfer Dimension

The **Chamfer Dimension** tool is used to add the dimension to the chamfers in the drawing view. To add a chamfer dimension, choose **Smart Dimension > Chamfer Dimension** from the **Annotation CommandManager**; the cursor will be replaced by the chamfer dimension cursor. Now, select the inclined chamfered edge and then select a horizontal or a vertical edge; the chamfer dimension will be attached to the cursor. Select a placement point on the sheet to place the dimension. Figure 15-4 shows a chamfer dimension added using the **Chamfer Dimension** tool.

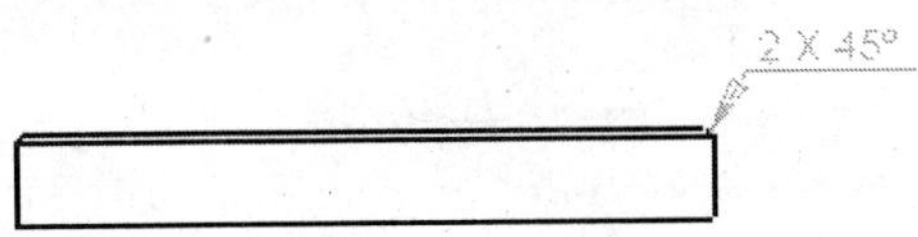

Figure 15-4 *Chamfer dimension added using the* **Chamfer Dimension** *tool*

Adding Notes to the Drawing Views

CommandManager:	Annotation > Note
SOLIDWORKS menus:	Insert > Annotations > Note
Toolbar:	Annotation > Note

In SOLIDWORKS, you can add notes to the drawing views in the Drawing mode. To do so, choose the **Note** button from the **Annotation CommandManager**; the **Note PropertyManager** will be displayed, as shown in Figure 15-5.

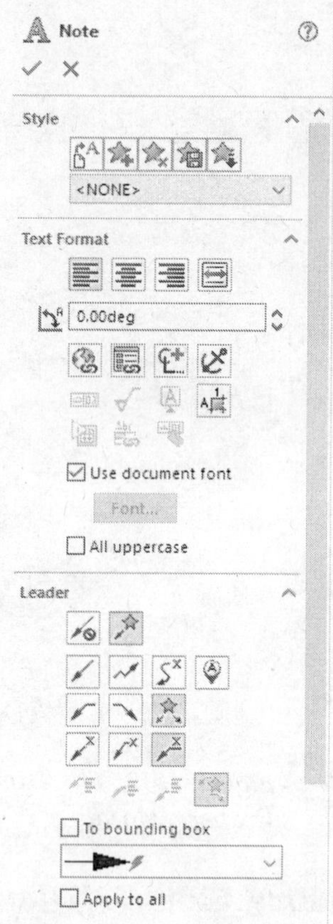

*Figure 15-5 Partial view of the **Note PropertyManager***

On invoking the **Note PropertyManager**, a shape defined using the **Style** drop-down list in the **Border** rollout will be attached to the cursor. If you move the cursor close to an edge in the drawing view, a leader will be displayed. This is because the **Auto Leader** button is chosen in the **Leader** rollout. You can also place a multi-jog leader line. After selecting an edge, place the endpoint of the leader at the desired location; the **Formatting** toolbar and the **Text** edit box will be displayed in the drawing area. Enter the text in the edit box. Next, choose **OK** from the **Note PropertyManager**. The rollouts in the **Note PropertyManager** are discussed next.

Style Rollout

You can save a note as a favorite using the options in the **Style** rollout. The options available in this rollout are the same as those discussed in Chapter 4.

Text Format Rollout

The **Text Format** rollout is used to set the format of the text such as font, size, justification, and rotation of the text. You can also add symbols and hyperlinks to the text using the options available in this rollout.

Leader Rollout

The options in the **Leader** rollout are used to define the style of arrows and leaders that are displayed in the notes.

Leader Style Rollout

The options in this rollout are used to define the style and thickness of the leader. By default, the **Use document display** check box is selected. So, the leader will be displayed with the default style and thickness. On clearing this check box, the **Leader Style** and **Leader Thickness** drop-down lists will be enabled. Using these drop-down lists, you can specify different styles and thickness for the leader.

Border Rollout

The options in the **Border** rollout are used to define the border in which the note text will be displayed. You can assign various types of borders from the **Style** drop-down list. The **Size** drop-down list available in this rollout is used to define the size of the border in which the text will be placed.

Wordwrap Rollout

The option in the **Wordwrap** rollout is used to define the wordwrap width of a paragraph.

Parameters Rollout

The **Parameters** rollout is used to specify the X and Y coordinate values of the note center.

Layer Rollout

This rollout is used to assign existing layer or create new layer to the notes.

Note

In SOLIDWORKS, you can create a linear pattern and a circular pattern of notes by using the ***Linear Note Pattern*** *and* ***Circular Note Pattern*** *tools, respectively. The procedure to create the pattern of notes is similar to that of creating sketch pattern, as discussed in Chapter 3.*

Adding Surface Finish Symbols to the Drawing Views

CommandManager:	Annotation > Surface Finish
SOLIDWORKS menus:	Insert > Annotations > Surface Finish Symbol
Toolbar:	Annotation > Surface Finish

You can add the surface finish symbols to the edges or the faces in the drawing views using the **Surface Finish** tool. To do so, choose the **Surface Finish** button from the **Annotation CommandManager**; the **Surface Finish PropertyManager** will be displayed, as shown in Figure 15-6. Also, a surface finish symbol will be attached to the cursor. The rollouts in the **Surface Finish PropertyManager** are discussed next.

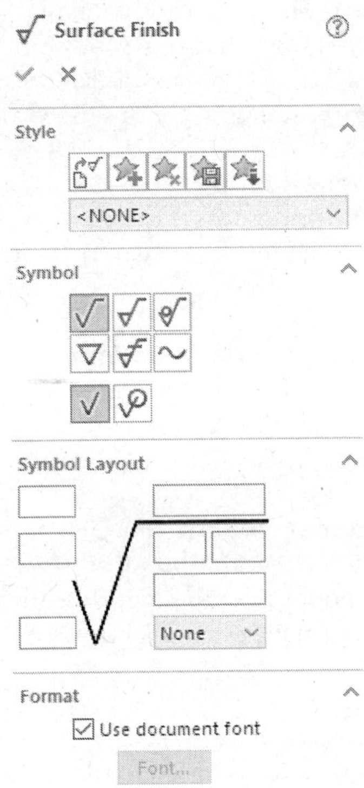

Figure 15-6 *Partial view of the* ***Surface Finish PropertyManager***

Style Rollout

The options in this rollout are the same as those discussed in Chapter 4. You can use the options in the **Style** rollout to save the surface finish as a favorite.

Symbol Rollout

The **Symbol** rollout is used to define the type of surface finish symbol that you need to add to the drawing views. There are many types of surface finish symbols in this rollout such as **Basic**, **Machining Required**, **Machining Prohibited**, **JIS Basic**, **JIS Machining Required**, **JIS Machining Prohibited**, and so on.

Symbol Layout Rollout

The options in the **Symbol Layout** rollout are used to define the parameters of the surface finish symbol.

Format Rollout

The options in the **Format** rollout are used to define the font size and the orientation of the surface finish symbol.

Angle Rollout

The options in the **Angle** rollout are used to define the angle of the surface finish symbol. You can enter the angle value in the spinner provided in this rollout or choose the buttons available below the spinner.

The other options in the **Surface Finish PropertyManager** are the same as those discussed while adding notes.

Adding a Datum Feature Symbol to the Drawing Views

CommandManager:	Annotation > Datum Feature
SOLIDWORKS menus:	Insert > Annotations > Datum Feature Symbol
Toolbar:	Annotation > Datum Feature

The **Datum Feature** tool is used to add a datum feature symbol to an entity in the drawing view. The datum feature symbols are used as datum references while adding the geometric tolerances in the drawing view. To add the datum feature symbol, choose the **Datum Feature** button from the **Annotation CommandManager**; the **Datum Feature PropertyManager** will be displayed, as shown in Figure 15-7. Also, a datum feature symbol with the default parameters will be attached to the cursor. The options in the **Datum Feature PropertyManager** are discussed next.

Figure 15-7 Partial view of the Datum Feature PropertyManager

Style Rollout

The options in this rollout are the same as those discussed in Chapter 4. You can use the options in the **Style** rollout to save a datum feature symbol as a favorite.

Label Settings Rollout

The **Label Settings** rollout is used to define the label to be used in the datum feature symbol. You can use alphabets or numeric characters as labels.

Leader Rollout

The **Use document style** check box is selected in this rollout to use the datum feature style that is defined in the document to display the datum feature symbol.

Square

If you clear the **Use document style** check box, the **Square** button below it becomes available. This button is used to place the text of the datum feature inside a square. By default, the text of the datum feature is placed using this option. You can use the buttons below the **Square** button to set the type of datum feature such as filled triangle, filled triangle with shoulder, empty triangle, and empty triangle with shoulder.

Round (GB)

On clearing the **Use document style** check box, the **Round (GB)** button becomes available. This button is used to place the text of the datum feature inside a circle. To do so, you first need to clear the **Use document style** check box and then choose the **Round (GB)** button. On choosing this button, additional buttons will be displayed below it. These buttons are used to set the style of the datum feature.

Text Rollout

This rollout is used to enter text or insert symbols along with the datum feature. To enter the text, left-click in the **Text** edit box and type the text. To add symbols, choose the **More** button located at the lower part of this rollout; the **Symbol Library** dialog box will be displayed. Select the required symbol from this dialog box and choose **OK**; the preview of the selected symbol will also be attached with the preview of datum feature.

Leader Style Rollout

The options in this rollout are used to define the style and thickness of the leader. By default, the **Use document display** check box is selected. As a result, the leader will be displayed with the default style and thickness. On clearing this check box, the **Leader Style** and **Leader Thickness** drop-down lists will be enabled. You can specify different styles and thickness for the leader by using these drop-down lists.

Frame Style Rollout

The options in this rollout are used to define the style and thickness of the frame. By default, the **Use document display** check box is selected. As a result, the frame will be displayed with the default style and thickness. On clearing this check box, the **Frame Style** and **Frame Thickness** drop-down lists will be enabled. You can specify different styles and thickness for the frame by using these drop-down lists.

Layer Rollout

This rollout is used to assign existing layers or create new layers for the datum features.

After defining all parameters of the datum feature symbol, specify a point on an existing entity in the drawing sheet. Next, move the cursor to define the length and the placement of the datum feature symbol. As soon as you place one datum feature symbol, another datum feature symbol will be attached to the cursor. Therefore, you can place as many datum feature symbols as you want using the **Datum Feature PropertyManager**. As you place multiple datum feature symbols, the sequence of the names of the datum feature symbols automatically follows the order based on the labels.

Adding a Geometric Tolerance to the Drawing Views

CommandManager:	Annotation > Geometric Tolerance
SOLIDWORKS menus:	Insert > Annotations > Geometric Tolerance
Toolbar:	Annotation > Geometric Tolerance

In a shop floor drawing, you need to provide various other parameters along with the dimensions and dimensional tolerance. These parameters can be geometric condition, surface profile, material condition, and so on. All these parameters are defined using the **Geometric Tolerance** tool. To add the geometric tolerance to the drawing views, choose the

Geometric Tolerance button from the **Annotation CommandManager**; the **Properties** dialog box will be displayed, as shown in Figure 15-8. Also, a geometric tolerance symbol will be attached to the cursor.

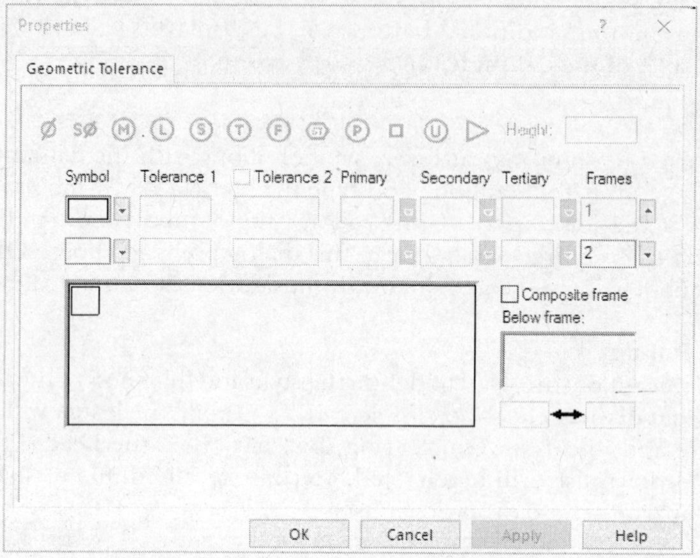

*Figure 15-8 The **Properties** dialog box used to apply the geometric tolerance*

Both the rows in this dialog box are separate frames. You can add additional frames using the **Frames** spinner provided at the right of the **Tertiary** edit box. The parameters that can be added to these frames are geometric condition symbols, diameter symbol, value of tolerance, material condition, and datum references. The options in the **Properties** dialog box are used to add the geometric tolerance to the drawing views and are discussed next.

Symbol

The **Symbol** drop-down list is used to define the geometric condition symbol. When you choose the down arrow button on the right of this drop-down list, the **Symbols** flyout will be displayed, as shown in Figure 15-9. This flyout is used to define the geometric condition symbols in the geometric tolerance. You can select the standard of the geometric condition symbol from this flyout. As soon as you select a symbol, the flyout will be closed and the selected symbol will be displayed in the **Symbol** edit box. Also, a preview of the geometric tolerance will be displayed in the preview area.

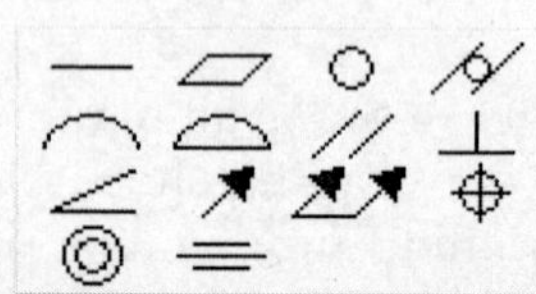

*Figure 15-9 The **Symbols** flyout used to define the geometric condition symbols*

Tolerance 1

The **Tolerance 1** edit box is used to specify the tolerance value with respect to the geometric condition defined using the **Symbols** flyout. You can use the buttons available above the rows of frames to add the symbols such as diameter, spherical diameter, material conditions, and so on.

Tolerance 2
The use of the **Tolerance 2** edit box is the same as that of **Tolerance 1** edit box. This edit box is used to define the second geometric tolerance, if required.

Primary
The **Primary** edit box is used to specify the characters to define the datum reference added to the entities in the drawing view using the **Datum Feature** tool.

Similarly, you can define the secondary and tertiary datum references.

Frames
The **Frames** spinner is used to increase the number of frames for applying more complex geometric tolerances.

Projected tolerance
The **Projected tolerance** button is available above the rows of frames. This button is chosen to define the height of the projected tolerance. When you choose this button, the **Height** edit box will be enabled and you can specify the projected tolerance zone height in this edit box.

Composite frame
The **Composite frame** check box is selected to use a composite frame to add the tolerance. If you select this check box, the tolerance frame will be converted into a composite frame and the preview will be modified accordingly.

Between Two Points
The **Between Two Points** edit boxes are used to apply the geometric tolerance between two points or entities. To apply the geometric tolerance, specify the reference in the **Between Two Points** edit boxes.

After specifying the tolerance in the **Properties** dialog box, move the cursor near the entity; the tolerance will be displayed with a leader. Now place the tolerance. Figure 15-10 shows a drawing after adding annotations to some of the entities in the drawing view.

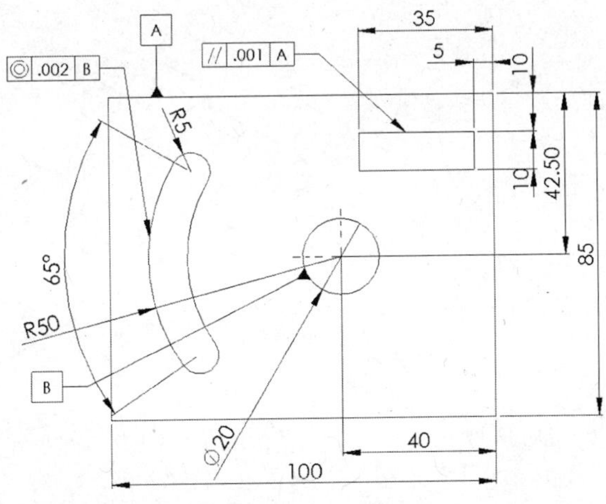

Figure 15-10 A drawing after adding some annotations

Adding Datum Target Symbols to the Drawing Views

CommandManager:	Annotation > Datum Target
SOLIDWORKS menus:	Insert > Annotations > Datum Target
Toolbar:	Annotation > Datum Target

The **Datum Target** tool is used to add the datum targets to the entities in the drawing view. A datum target may be used to establish a datum by specifying a point, a line or an area on a part. This is sometimes significant while creating a datum on part, which is too large or irregular in shape. To add the datum targets, choose the **Datum Target** button from the **Annotation CommandManager**; the cursor will be replaced by the datum target cursor and the **Datum Target PropertyManager** will be displayed, as shown in Figure 15-11. Select a face, an edge, or a line of the model from the view on which you need to add the datum target and then place the datum target.

The **Datum Target PropertyManager** is used to define the properties of the datum target symbol. Set the parameters of the datum target symbol in the **Settings** rollout of this PropertyManager. You can set the target shape as a point, a circle, or a rectangle. You can also define the width of the target area, if the shape of the target area is selected as a circle or a rectangle. If the shape of the selected target is a rectangle, you need to define its width and height. You can apply the datum references to the datum target symbol by using the **First Reference**, **Second Reference**, and **Third Reference** edit boxes. Figure 15-12 shows the datum target symbols added to the entities in the drawing view.

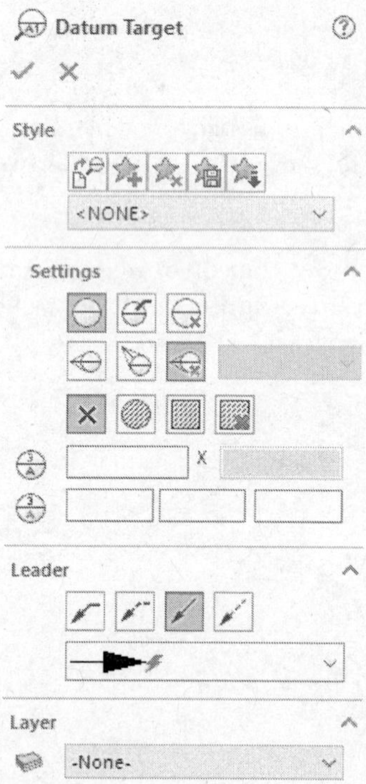

*Figure 15-11 The **Datum Target PropertyManager***

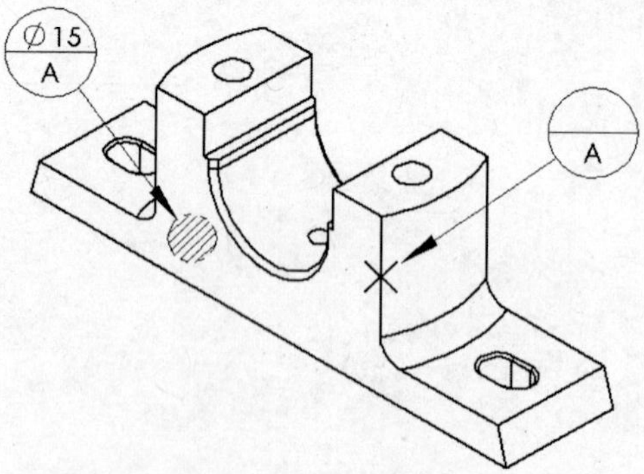

Figure 15-12 Datum target symbols added to the model

Adding Center Marks to the Drawing Views

CommandManager:	Annotation > Center Mark
SOLIDWORKS menus:	Insert > Annotations > Center Mark
Toolbar:	Annotation > Center Mark

The **Center Mark** tool is used to add center marks to the circular entities. As discussed earlier, center marks are generated automatically when you generate the dimensions for the model. But if the center marks are not generated while generating the drawing view, or if you have sketched a view, you can use this tool to add the center marks to the drawing views. To add the center marks to the drawing views, choose the **Center Mark** button from the **Annotation CommandManager**; the **Center Mark PropertyManager** will be displayed, as shown in Figure 15-13. Also, the cursor will be replaced by the center mark cursor and you will be prompted to select a circular edge, a slot edge, or an arc for the center mark insertion.

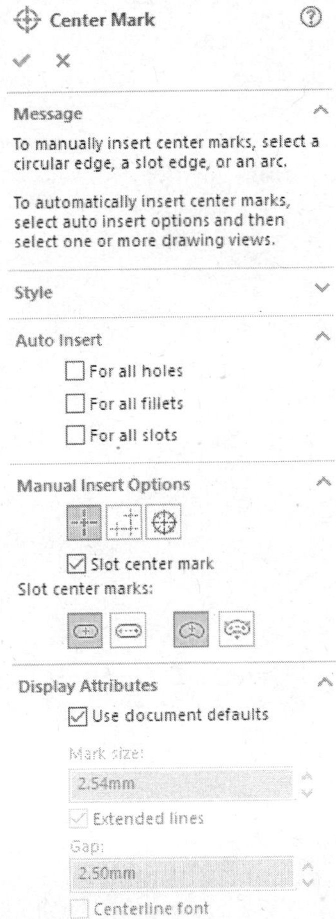

Figure 15-13 Partial view of the Center Mark PropertyManager

You can add center marks to holes, fillets, and slots in the selected views by selecting the respective check boxes from the **Auto Insert** rollout of the PropertyManager.

By default, the **Single Center Mark** button is chosen in the **Manual Insert Options** rollout of the **Center Mark PropertyManager**. Select the circular edge or the arc to add the center mark. On selecting an arc which represents a hole that is part of a linear or a circular pattern, the **Propagate** button will be displayed near the center mark. If you choose this button, the center marks will be added to all remaining instances of the pattern, as shown in Figure 15-14.

The center marks can also be applied in linear and circular patterns using the **Linear Center Mark** and **Circular Center Mark** buttons, respectively. When you add the center marks in the linear pattern format, the **Connection lines** check box is selected by default in the **Manual Insert Options** rollout. As a result, the center marks will be connected using the centerlines, as shown in Figure 15-15.

You can add the center mark in the circular pattern format by using the **Circular Center Mark** button. When you choose this button, the **Circular lines**, **Radial lines**, and **Base center mark** check boxes will be displayed. The **Circular lines** check box is used to create a circular line passing through the centers of the circles arranged in a circular pattern. The **Radial lines** check box is used to display the radial lines from the center of the pattern to the center of each instance. The **Base center mark** check box is used to display the center mark at the center of a base circle of the pattern. Figures 15-16 and 15-17 show the center marks created with the **Base center mark** check box cleared and selected respectively. Figure 15-18 shows the center marks created with the **Radial lines** check box selected. You will observe that in all these figures, the **Circular lines** check box is selected.

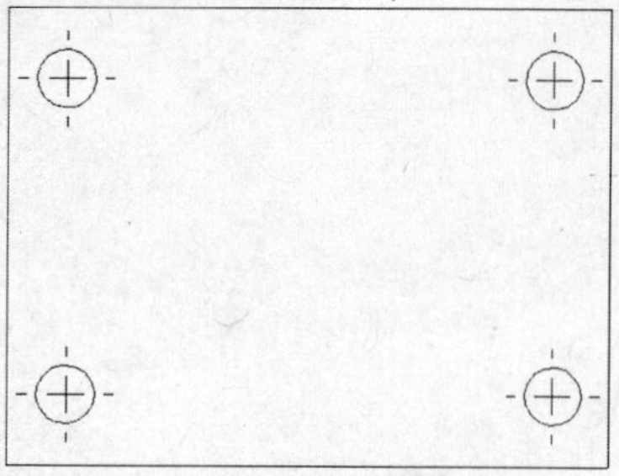

***Figure 15-14** Center marks added using the **Single Center Mark** option*

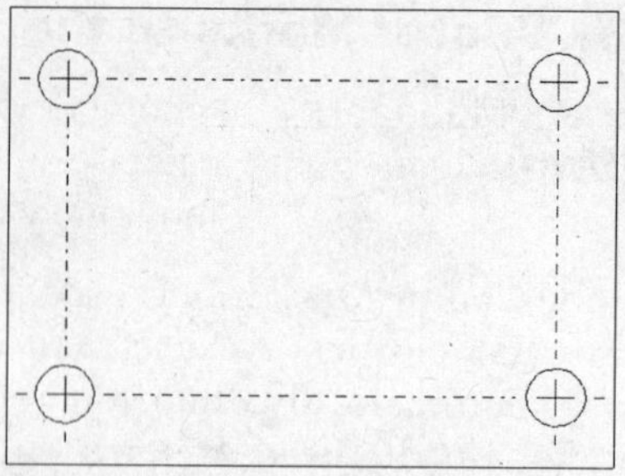

***Figure 15-15** Center marks added using the **Linear Center Mark** option*

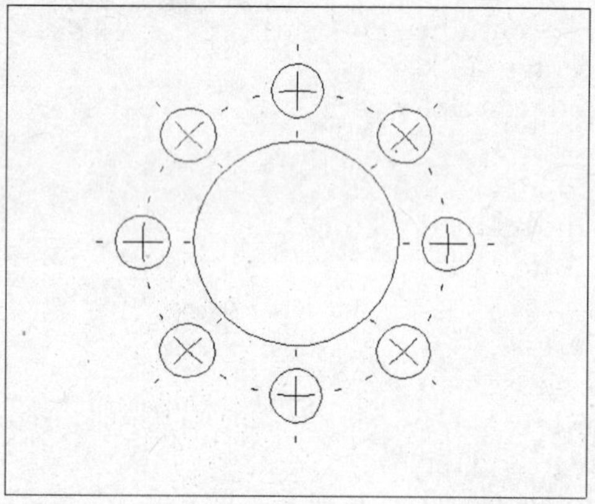

***Figure 15-16** Center marks created with the **Base center mark** check box cleared*

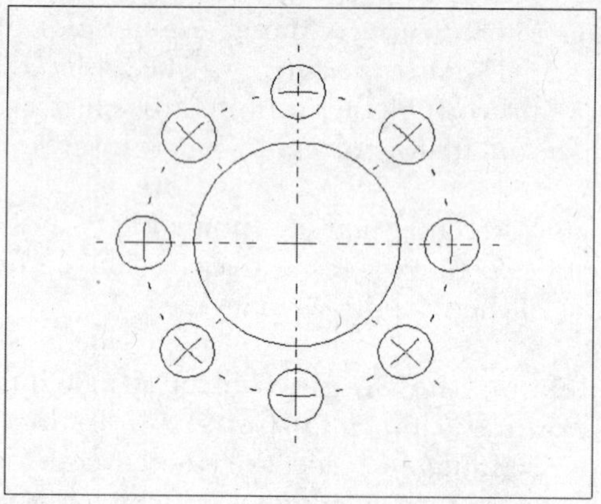

***Figure 15-17** Center marks created with the **Base center mark** check box selected*

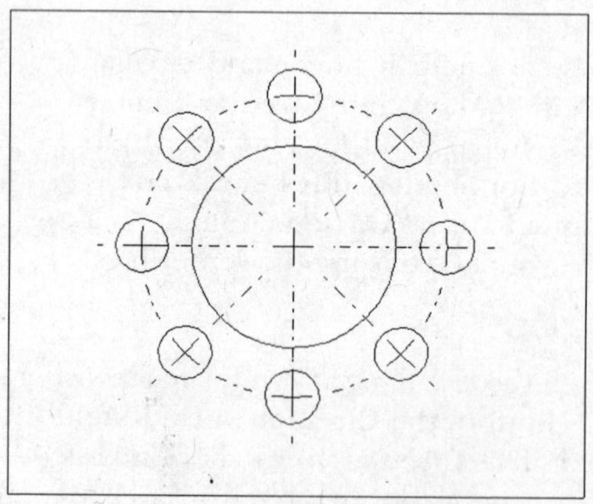

***Figure 15-18** Center marks created with the **Radial lines** check box selected*

You can also add center marks to the slots by choosing the respective buttons from the **Slot center marks** area of the **Manual Insert Options** rollout. By default, the **Slot Centers** button is chosen in this area of the **Manual Insert Options** rollout. Choose the semi-circular edge of the slot to add the center mark into the center of the straight slot. If you select the **Slot Ends** button, the center marks will be added to the slot ends of the straight slot. Similarly, you can also add center marks to the arc slots by choosing the respective buttons from this area.

The **Display Attributes** rollout available in the **Center Mark PropertyManager** is used to define the size of the center mark and the extended lines. The **Angle** rollout is used to rotate the center mark at an angle.

Adding Centerlines to the Drawing Views

CommandManager:	Annotation > Centerline
SOLIDWORKS menus:	Insert > Annotations > Centerline
Toolbar:	Annotation > Centerline

The **Centerline** tool is used to add the centerlines to the views by selecting two edges/sketch segments or a single cylindrical/conical face. To add a centerline, choose the **Centerline** button from the **Annotation CommandManager**; the **Centerline PropertyManager** will be invoked and you will be prompted to select two edges/sketch segments or a single cylindrical/conical face. Select the entity or entities from the view to add the centerline. Figure 15-19 shows the centerlines added to the drawing views by using the **Centerline** tool.

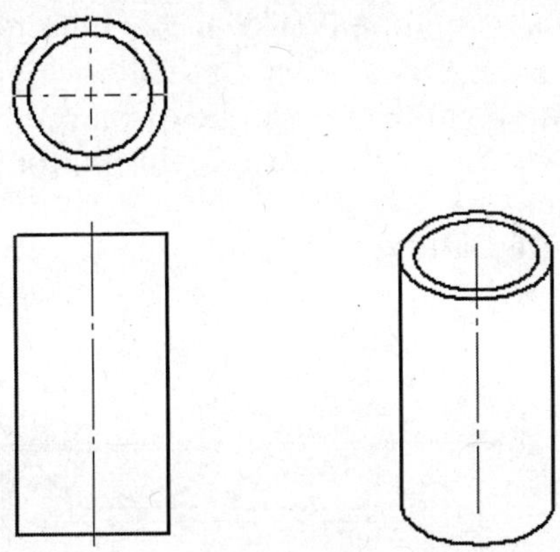

Figure 15-19 *Centerlines added to the front and isometric views using the **Centerline** tool*

Tip

1. To display the hidden lines in a drawing view, select the view and then choose the ***Hidden Lines Visible*** *button from the* ***Display Style*** *flyout in the* ***View (Heads-Up)*** *toolbar.*

2. You can also set the option for the automatic creation of a centerline while generating the drawing views. To do so, choose ***Options*** *from the Menu Bar to invoke the* ***System Options - General*** *dialog box and choose the* ***Document Properties*** *tab. Next, select* ***Detailing*** *and select the* ***Centerlines*** *check box from the* ***Auto insert on view creation*** *area and choose* ***OK*** *button to close the dialog box.*

3. You can also right-click on a view and choose ***Annotations > Center Mark/Centerline*** *to add the centerlines.*

Adding a Hole Callout to the Drawing Views

CommandManager:	Annotation > Hole Callout
SOLIDWORKS menus:	Insert > Annotations > Hole Callout
Toolbar:	Annotation > Hole Callout

The **Hole Callout** tool is generally used to generate hole callouts for the holes that are created in the **Part** mode using the **Simple Hole**, **Hole Wizard**, **Advanced Hole** or **Extruded Cut** tool. You can also generate callouts for slots created in the Part mode. To generate a hole callout, choose the **Hole Callout** button from the **Annotation CommandManager**; the cursor will be replaced by a hole callout cursor. Select a hole from the drawing view; a hole callout will be attached to the cursor. Pick a point on the drawing sheet; the hole callout will be placed and the **Dimension PropertyManager** will be displayed. You can also reverse the hole callout order for an advanced hole. Choose the **Close Dialog** button to close this PropertyManager. Similarly, you can create a callout for the slot. Figure 15-20 shows a drawing view with hole callouts generated using the **Hole Callout** tool.

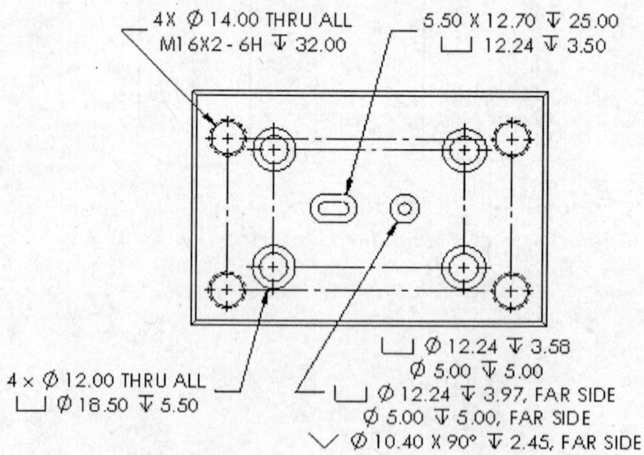

Figure 15-20 *Hole callouts generated using the* ***Hole Callout*** *tool*

Adding Cosmetic Threads to the Drawing Views

CommandManager:	Annotation > Cosmetic Thread (*Customize to add*)
SOLIDWORKS menus:	Insert > Annotations > Cosmetic Thread
Toolbar:	Annotation > Cosmetic Thread (*Customize to add*)

The **Cosmetic Thread** tool is used to add the cosmetic threads that will display the thread conventions in the drawing views. If the cosmetic thread is already added in the model then there is no need to add it in the drawing view, it will be displayed automatically in the drawing view. But if you have not added the cosmetic thread in the part model, you can add it in the drawing view. To do so, choose the **Cosmetic Thread** button from the customized **Annotation CommandManager**; the **Cosmetic Thread PropertyManager** will be displayed, as shown in Figure 15-21. The rollouts in the **Cosmetic Thread PropertyManager** are discussed next.

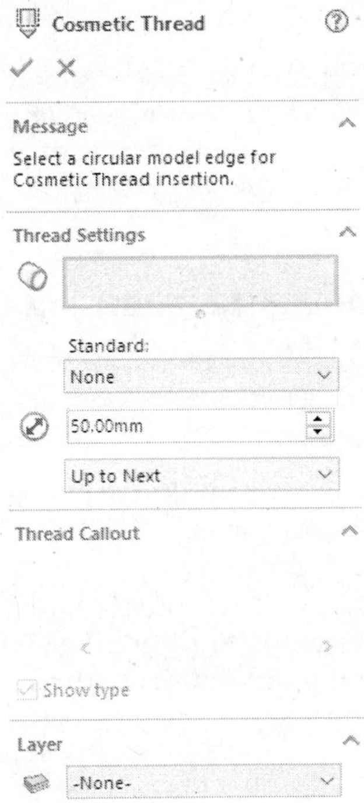

Figure 15-21 The ***Cosmetic Thread PropertyManager***

Thread Settings Rollout

The options in the **Thread Settings** rollout are used to define various parameters of the cosmetic thread. On invoking the **Cosmetic Thread** tool, you will be prompted to select the edges for adding the threads and set the parameters for threads. Select the required circular edge on which you need to add a cosmetic thread; the name of the selected edge will be displayed in the **Circular Edges** selection box. Specify the end condition and set the minor diameter of the thread. It will be displayed in both the current view and the projected view. Note that the thread will be displayed in the projected view only if the hidden lines are displayed in that view.

Thread Callout Rollout

The edit box in this rollout is used to specify the text to be used in the thread callout for the cosmetic thread. Note that the edit box in this rollout will be available only when the **None** option is selected in the **Standard** drop-down list in the **Thread Settings** rollout.

Layer Rollout

This rollout is used to assign existing layers to the hole callouts or create new layers as per the requirement.

After setting all the parameters, choose **OK** from the **Cosmetic Thread PropertyManager**. On adding a cosmetic thread to a generated drawing view, the thread convention will be displayed in all the drawing views. Figure 15-22 shows the cosmetic thread added to drawing views.

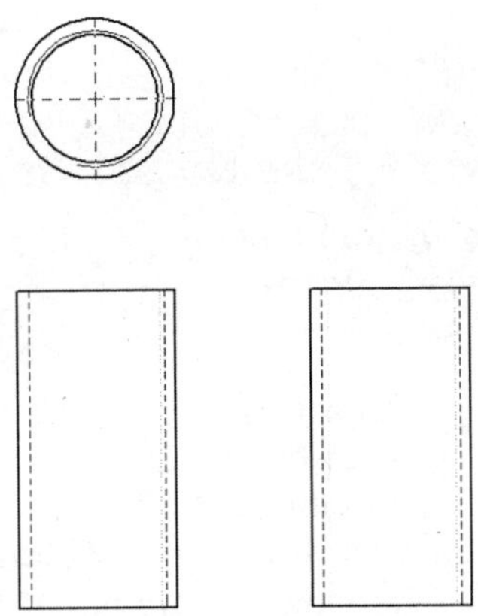

Figure 15-22 Cosmetic threads added to drawing views

Note

The thread conventions added to the drawing views can be deleted only from the part document. You cannot delete the thread conventions from the drawing document. To do so, expand the ***Hole*** *or* ***Cut*** *feature in the* ***FeatureManager Design Tree****. Now, select the thread convention and delete it.*

Tip

If you add cosmetic threads to the drawing views, you can also view them in the part document because of the bidirectional associativity. You can use any display mode to view the cosmetic threads in the model.

Adding the Multi-jog Leader to the Drawing Views

CommandManager:	Annotation > Multi-jog Leader (*Customize to add*)
SOLIDWORKS menus:	Insert > Annotations > Multi-jog Leader
Toolbar:	Annotation > Multi-jog Leader (*Customize to add*)

You can add a multi-jog leader line to the drawing views by using the **Multi-jog Leader** tool. A multi-jog leader is a leader in which you can add multiple jog lines with arrowheads at both the ends. To add a multi-jog leader line, choose the **Multi-jog Leader** button from the **Annotation CommandManager**; the cursor will be replaced by the multi-jog line cursor. Select a point on the sheet or on an entity from where you need to start the leader. Now, specify the points on the drawing sheet to mark the location of the jogs and then select the second entity where the end of the leader will be placed; a multi-jog leader will be created. You can also double-click anywhere on the sheet to specify the second end of the multi-jog leader. Figure 15-23 shows a multi-jog leader added to the drawing view. Note that in this figure, the text and the hyphen is added separately.

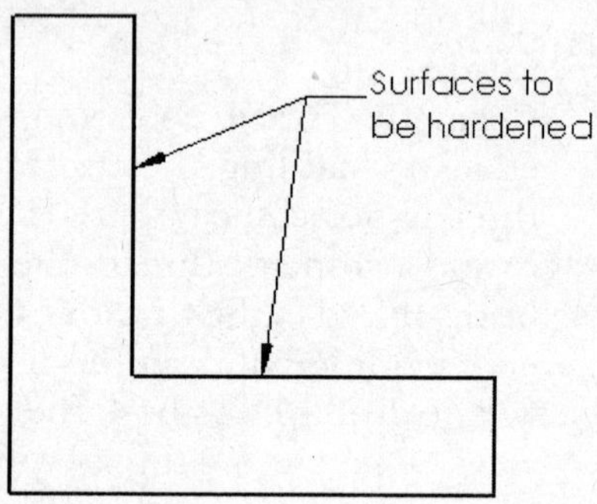

Figure 15-23 *Multi-jog leader added to the drawing view*

Adding the Dowel Pin Symbols to the Drawing Views

CommandManager:	Annotation > Dowel Pin Symbol (*Customize to add*)
SOLIDWORKS menus:	Insert > Annotations > Dowel Pin Symbol
Toolbar:	Annotation > Dowel Pin Symbol (*Customize to add*)

The **Dowel Pin Symbol** tool is used to add the dowel pin symbol to the holes in the drawing views. It is also used to confirm the size of the selected hole. To create a dowel pin symbol, select a hole or a circular edge from the drawing view and choose the **Dowel Pin Symbol** button from the **Annotation CommandManager**; the dowel pin symbol will be created and the **Dowel Pin Symbol PropertyManager** will be displayed. You can flip the direction of the dowel pin symbol by using the **Flip symbol** check box in the **Display Attributes** rollout.

Aligning the Dimensions

In a drawing view, you can apply some of the dimensions of a part by using the **Smart Dimension** tool while others can be applied by using the **Model Items** tool. While doing so, the dimensions may overlap. In SOLIDWORKS, you can align the applied dimensions easily. To align the dimensions, press and hold the CTRL key and select all dimensions. After selecting all dimensions, release the CTRL key and do not move the cursor; the **Dimension Palette rollover** button will be displayed. Move the cursor over this button; the Dimension Palette will be displayed, as shown in Figure 15-24.

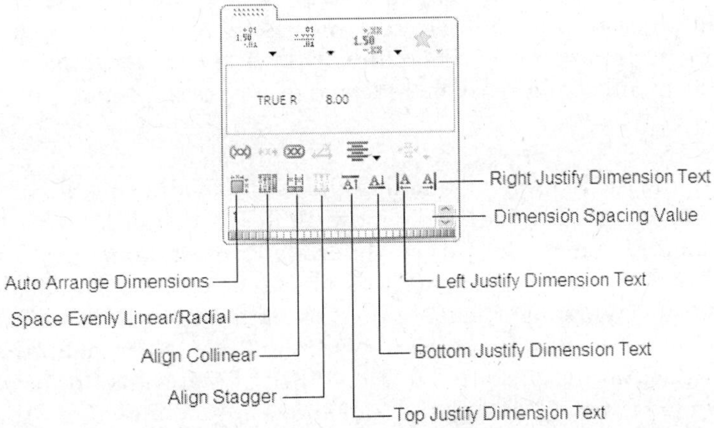

Figure 15-24 *The Dimension Palette*

Depending upon the dimensions chosen, the buttons to align them will be enabled in the Dimension Palette. Choose any one of the four dimension buttons available on the left to align the dimensions.

There are four buttons available on the right to justify the dimension text. On choosing any one of the four justification buttons, you can justify the dimension text to top, bottom, left, or right.

While dimensioning an entity by using the **Rapid dimensioning** option of the **Smart Dimension** tool, the dimension will be placed at a predefined space from the selected entity. To view this default spacing, choose the **Options** button from the Menu Bar; the **System Options - General** dialog box will be displayed. Choose the **Document Properties** tab and then select the **Dimensions** node; the corresponding options will be displayed on the right. The default spacing is displayed in the **Offset distances** area. To change the scale factor of this default spacing, set a value in the **Dimension Spacing Value** spinner or scroll the spinner in the Dimension Palette. For example, if you enter 0.5, the spacing distance will be reduced to half and if you enter 2, the spacing distance will be doubled.

Editing Annotations

You can edit the annotations added to drawing views by selecting them or by double-clicking on them. As a result, their respective PropertyManagers or dialog boxes will be displayed. You can edit the parameters of the selected annotation using these edit boxes.

ADDING THE BILL OF MATERIALS (BOM) TO A DRAWING

CommandManager: Annotation > Tables > Bill of Materials
SOLIDWORKS menus: Insert > Tables > Bill of Materials
Toolbar: Annotation > Tables > Bill of Materials

The Bill of Materials (BOM) is a table that displays the list of components used in an assembly or a part. This table can also be used to provide information related to the number of components in an assembly or a part, their names, quantity, or any other information required to assemble the components. Remember that the sequence of parts in the BOM depends on the sequence in which they were inserted in the assembly document. The BOM, placed in the drawing document, is parametric. Therefore, if you add or delete a part from the assembly in the assembly document, changes will be reflected in the corresponding BOM in the drawing document.

To insert a BOM in the drawing file containing the assembly drawing views, select any one of the views from the drawing document and choose **Tables > Bill of Materials** button from the **Annotation CommandManager**; the **Bill of Materials PropertyManager** will be displayed, as shown in Figure 15-25. Specify the required parameters. After setting all parameters in the **Bill of Materials PropertyManager**, choose the **OK** button; the BOM will be attached to the cursor. Specify a point on the drawing sheet to place the BOM. Next, select the anchor point of the BOM added to the drawing sheet; the modified **Bill of Materials PropertyManager** will be displayed, as shown in Figure 15-26. Figure 15-27 shows a BOM added to a drawing sheet. The rollouts in the modified **Bill of Materials PropertyManager** are discussed next.

Table Template Rollout

The **Table Template** rollout is used to define the template to be used in the BOM. By default, the **bom-standard** template is chosen. If you choose the **Open table template for Bill of Materials** button from this rollout, the **Open** dialog box will be displayed. You can choose any default template available in SOLIDWORKS by using this dialog box.

Table Position Rollout

You can specify the stationary position of the BOM using the **Table Position** rollout. If the **Attach to anchor point** check box is selected in this rollout, the table will be automatically attached to the anchor point of the drawing sheet. But if the **Attach to anchor point** check box is cleared, the table will be attached to the cursor only after choosing the **OK** button from the **Bill of Materials PropertyManager**. Next, you need to specify a point in the drawing sheet to place the table. The procedure to define the anchor point is discussed later in this chapter.

BOM Type Rollout

The **BOM Type** rollout is used to specify the different levels of an assembly. The options in this rollout are discussed next.

Top-level only

The **Top-level only** radio button is used to list only the parts and the subassemblies in BOM. The parts of the subassemblies are not listed in the BOM.

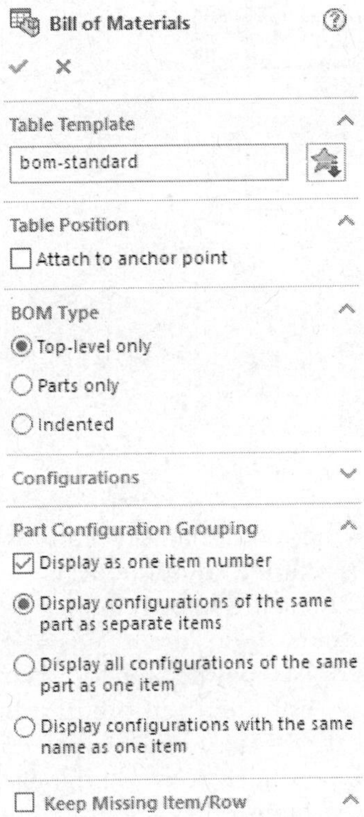

Figure 15-25 Partial view of the ***Bill of Materials PropertyManager***

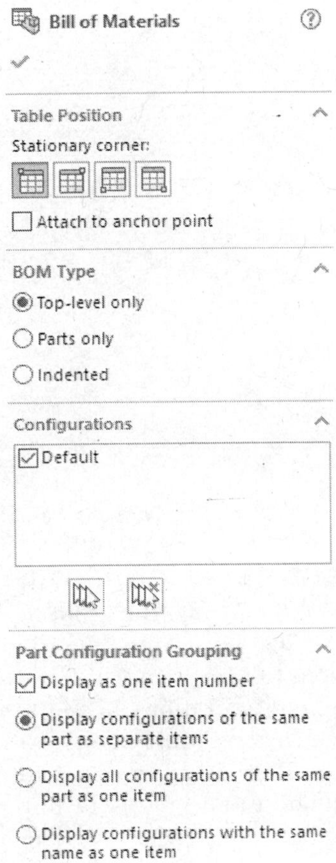

Figure 15-26 Partial view of the modified ***Bill of Materials PropertyManager***

Parts only

If you select the **Parts only** radio button then instead of subassemblies, the components of the subassemblies will be listed as individual components in the BOM.

Indented

The **Indented** radio button is selected to list the components along with their subassemblies. The components of the subassemblies are listed as indented below their respective subassemblies and are not listed with their respective item numbers.

Configurations Rollout

The **Configurations** rollout is used to specify the configuration for creating the BOM. By default, the **Default** configuration is selected.

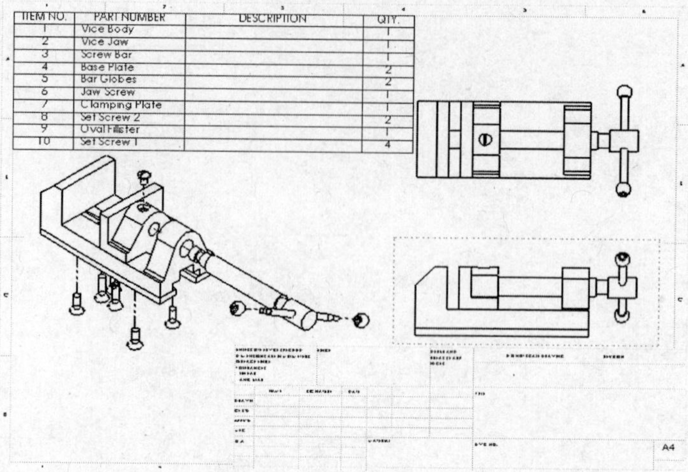

Figure 15-27 BOM added to a drawing sheet

Part Configuration Grouping Rollout

This rollout is used to set the grouping options for a part having more than one configuration. Selecting the **Display as one item number** check box ensures that if a component has multiple configurations, all of them will be listed in the BOM with the same item number. Selecting the **Display configurations of the same part as separate items** radio button ensures that if a component has multiple configurations, they will be listed as separate items in the BOM. Selecting the **Display all configurations of the same part as one item** radio button ensures that all configurations of a part will be listed as one item in the BOM. Similarly, selecting the **Display configurations with the same name as one item** radio button ensures that if the multiple components have configurations with the same name, they will be listed as a single item in the BOM.

Keep Missing Item/Row Rollout

After creating an assembly, if any part file is deleted from the folder in which the part files and assembly are saved then those parts will not be displayed in the assembly, and not listed in the BOM. However, if you select the check box on the left of the **Keep Missing Item/Row** rollout then those parts will be listed in the BOM. If you select the **Strikeout** check box in this rollout, the names of those parts in the BOM will be struck out.

Item Numbers Rollout

You can specify a numeric value from where the sequence of the components will start in a BOM. Enter this value in the **Start at** edit box of this rollout. Additionally, you can specify the increment for the numeric value in the BOM using the **Increment** edit box. If you select the **Do not change item numbers** check box in this rollout, the **Start at** edit box will get disabled. Therefore, after selecting this check box, you will not be able to change the numeric value of the first component of the BOM.

Border Rollout

This rollout is used to set the border lines of the bill of material table. You can specify the thickness of the borders by using the **Box Border** and **Grid Border** options in the drop-down list. You can also set the borders of the BOM table similar to the sheet layer by selecting the **Use document settings** check box in the rollout.

After setting all the parameters in the **Bill of Materials PropertyManager**, choose the **OK** button; a BOM will be attached to the cursor. Specify a point on the drawing sheet to place the BOM.

Setting Anchor Point for the BOM

In SOLIDWORKS, you can also set the anchor point for the BOM. To do so, expand the **Sheet Format1** node in the **FeatureManager Design Tree**. Next, right-click on the **Bill of Materials Anchor1** option; a shortcut menu will be displayed. Choose the **Set Anchor** option from it; the drawing sheet will be displayed in the edit sheet format. If you move the cursor on any intersection, an orange colored point will be displayed. This point defines the anchor point for the BOM. Specify a position in the drawing sheet where you need to anchor the BOM; the anchor point will be specified and the drawing sheet will be displayed in the normal mode. Note that you can specify the anchor point after placing the BOM in the drawing sheet.

LINKING BILL OF MATERIALS

In SOLIDWORKS, you can add Bill of Materials both in the Part as well as in the Assembly environment. To do so, open the part or assembly files and then choose **Insert > Tables > Bill of Materials** from the SOLIDWORKS menus; the BOM will be added to the part or assembly. Now, if you add BOM in the drawing view by choosing the **Bill of Materials** button, the **Bill of Materials PropertyManager** will be displayed with different options as compared to those discussed earlier. In this case, the **BOM options** rollout will have two options. To add a new BOM as discussed earlier, select the **Create new table** radio button and choose the **OK** button. To copy the BOM created in part or assembly, select the **Copy existing table** radio button. If you need to link it with the copied BOM then select the **Linked** check box and choose the **OK** button.

Tip

*To exclude an item from BOM, move the cursor over the BOM and expand it by choosing the side arrows. Next, right-click on a component in the assembly structure and then choose the **Exclude from BOM** option. To include that component again, right-click on it in the **FeatureManager Design Tree** and choose the **Include in BOM** option.*

ADDING BALLOONS TO THE DRAWING VIEWS

CommandManager:	Annotation > Balloon
SOLIDWORKS menus:	Insert > Annotations > Balloon
Toolbar:	Annotation > Balloon

After adding the BOM, you need to add the balloons to the components in the drawing views. Figure 15-28 shows the drawing sheet in which the balloons have been added to the assembly drawing. The balloons can be added manually using the **Balloon** tool.

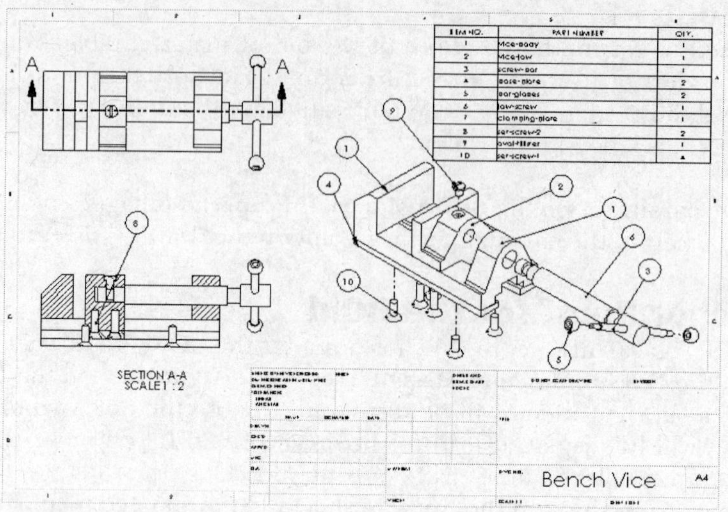

Figure 15-28 Balloons added to the assembly drawing view

The numbering of balloons depends on the sequence of the parts in the BOM. The method of adding balloons to the components in the drawing views is discussed next.

To add the balloons to a drawing view, choose the **Balloon** button from the **Annotation CommandManager**; the **Balloon PropertyManager** will be displayed, as shown in Figure 15-29.

On invoking the **Balloon PropertyManager**, you will be prompted to select one or more locations to place the balloons. Set the properties of the balloon using the options in the **Settings** rollout. Select the components from the assembly drawing view to add the balloons. If you select the face of a component, the balloon will have a filled circle at the attachment point. However, if you select an edge of the component, the balloon will have a closed filled arrow. In SOLIDWORKS, you can also specify the quantity of the parts in the assembly. To do so, you need to select the check box in the **Quantity** rollout; this rollout will expand. Specify the type of placement and the denotation required. To override the quantity value, select the **Override value** check box and enter a new value in the **Quantity value** edit box. After adding the balloons to all components, choose the **OK** button from the **Balloon PropertyManager**.

Adding Balloons Using the AutoBalloon Tool

CommandManager:	Annotation > Auto Balloon
SOLIDWORKS menus:	Insert > Annotations > Auto Balloon
Toolbar:	Annotation > Auto Balloon

The **Auto Balloon** tool is used to add the balloons automatically. To do so, select the drawing view in which you need to add the balloons and choose the **Auto Balloon** button from the **Annotation CommandManager**; the balloons will be added to the selected drawing view with default settings and the **Auto Balloon PropertyManager** will be displayed, as shown in Figure 15-30. The rollouts in the **Auto Balloon PropertyManager** are discussed next.

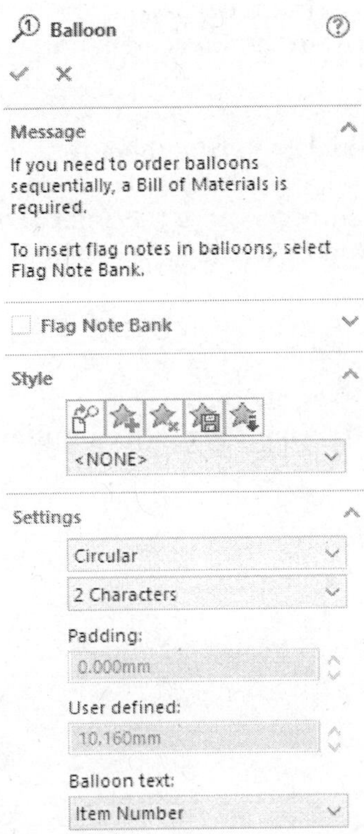

Figure 15-29 *Partial View of the* ***Balloon Property Manager***

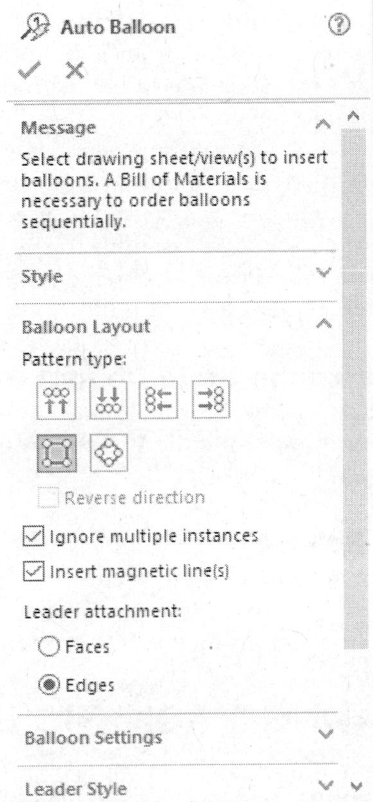

Figure 15-30 *Partial view of the* ***Auto Balloon PropertyManager***

Balloon Layout Rollout

The options in the **Balloon Layout** rollout are used to set the layout of the balloons when they are placed automatically. By default, the **Layout Balloons to Square** button is chosen in the **Balloon Layout** rollout, therefore the balloons are placed in a square form. You can also arrange the balloons in various other alignments such as circular, top, bottom, left, and right. To do so, choose the corresponding buttons in this rollout. The **Ignore multiple instances** check box is selected by default. As a result, multiple instances of the balloons are not created. In this rollout, the **Insert magnetic line(s)** check box is also selected by default. As a result, all the balloons are automatically aligned with each other with the help of the magnetic lines.

Balloon Settings Rollout

The **Balloon Settings** rollout is used to set the style, size, and type of the text in the balloons.

Item Numbers Rollout

The **Item Numbers** rollout is used to specify the sequence of balloons in the drawing view. Note that this rollout will be available in the PropertyManager only if the BOM of the assembly is available in the drawing sheet. You can specify the sequence of balloons and BOM such that it follows the assembly order as displayed in the **FeatureManager Design Tree**. To do so, choose the **Follow assembly order** button from the **Item Numbers** rollout of the PropertyManager. You can also specify the order of balloons and the BOM in a sequence that starts from the value specified in the **Start at** edit box with the increment specified in the **Increment** edit box of the PropertyManager.

The **Start at** edit box of this rollout is used to specify the initial or start number for the balloon and **Increment** edit box is used to specify the incremental value between two balloons. You can also select a part of an assembly as the first item of the order by choosing the **Select First Item** button from the PropertyManager. Note that this button will be available only after choosing the **Order sequentially** button.

Leader/Frame Style Rollout

The options in the **Leader/Frame Style** rollout are used to specify the style and thickness for the leader/frame using the **Leader/Frame Style** and **Leader/Frame Thickness** drop-down lists, respectively.

Layer Rollout

The options in this rollout are used to assign layers to the balloons.

After setting all parameters, choose **OK** from the **Auto Balloon PropertyManager**.

CREATING MAGNETIC LINES

CommandManager:	Annotation > Magnetic Line
SOLIDWORKS menus:	Insert > Annotations > Magnetic Line

In SOLIDWORKS, you can create magnetic lines to align the balloons in the drawing environment by using the **Magnetic Line** tool. To create a magnetic line, choose the **Magnetic Line** button from the **Annotation CommandManager**; the **Magnetic Line PropertyManager** will be displayed and you will be prompted to specify the start point of the magnetic line. Click to specify the start point of the magnetic line; a rubber band magnetic line will be attached with the cursor. Next, specify the end point of the magnetic line by clicking the left mouse button. You can also specify the length and angle of the magnetic line by entering the length and angle values in the respective edit boxes of the **Magnetic Line PropertyManager**. After creating the magnetic lines, exit from the PropertyManager.

Now, you can align balloons to the magnetic lines. To do so, drag the balloons towards the magnetic line and release the left mouse button when the balloons snaps to magnetic line and the magnetic symbol displayed below the cursor. Figure 15-31 shows the non-aligned balloons and Figure 15-32 shows the balloons aligned to the magnetic line.

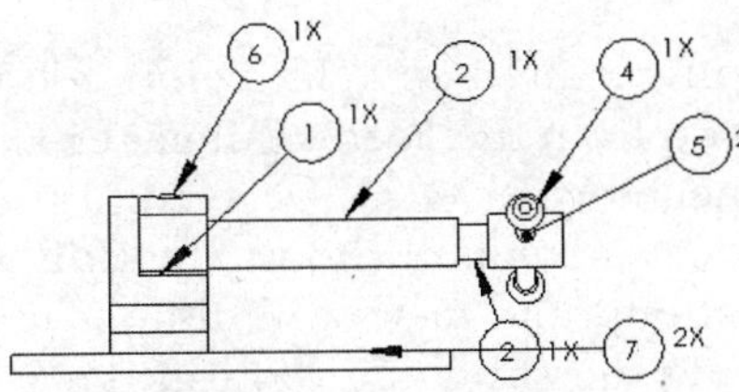

Figure 15-31 Non-aligned balloons

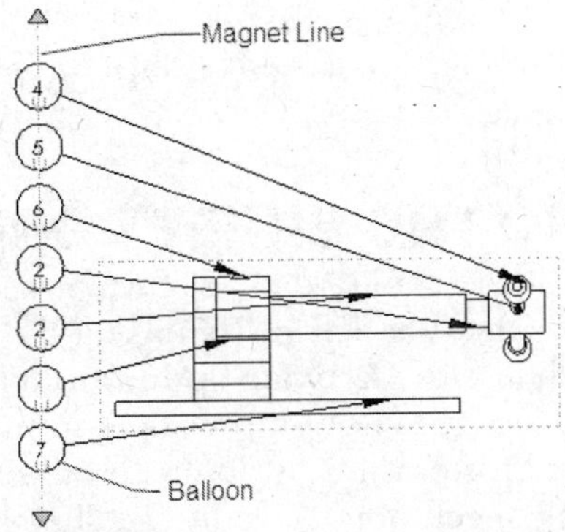

Figure 15-32 Balloons aligned to magnetic line

ADDING NEW SHEETS TO THE DRAWING DOCUMENT

You can also add new sheets to a drawing document. A multisheet drawing document can be used to generate the drawing views of all the components and the drawing views of the assembly in the same document. You can switch between the sheets easily to refer to the drawing views of different parts of an assembly within the same document, without opening separate drawing documents. To add a sheet to the drawing document, choose the **Add Sheet** tab above the status bar; a new sheet will be added to it. Figure 15-33 shows a drawing document with three new drawing sheets added. To add a sheet to the drawing document, you can also select **Sheet1** from the **FeatureManager Design Tree** and right-click to display a shortcut menu. Next, select the **Add Sheet** option from the shortcut menu displayed to add a sheet to the drawing document.

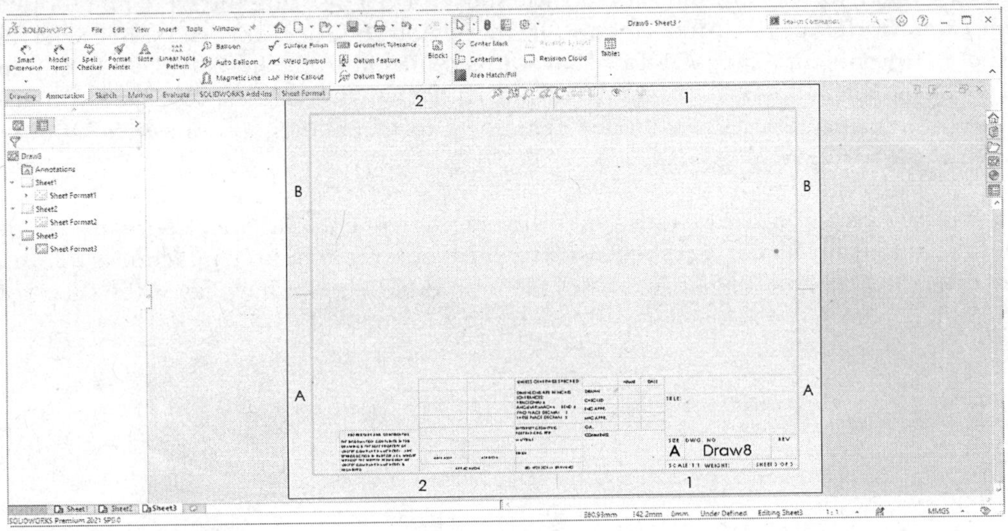

Figure 15-33 Drawing sheets added to the drawing document

To activate a drawing sheet, select it by choosing the corresponding tab above the status bar. To change the properties of a sheet, select it, invoke the shortcut menu, and choose the **Properties** option from it.

EDITING THE SHEET FORMAT

You can edit the standard sheet format according to your requirement. But before editing a sheet ensure that it is active. To make a sheet active, select it from the **FeatureManager Design Tree** and choose the **Activate** option from the shortcut menu displayed. Now, to edit the sheet format, again right-click on the sheet to invoke the shortcut menu and choose the **Edit Sheet Format** option from it. On doing so, all entities, annotations, and views will disappear from the drawing sheet. You can edit the sheet format by using the sketching tools in the **Sketch CommandManager**. After editing the sheet format, select the active sheet again and invoke the shortcut menu. Choose the **Edit Sheet** option from the shortcut menu to switch back to the edit sheet environment.

CREATING USER-DEFINED SHEET FORMATS

In SOLIDWORKS, you can also create a user-defined sheet format. To do so, when you start a new drawing document, select the **Custom sheet size** radio button from the **Sheet Format/Size** dialog box. On the basis of your design requirements, set the size of the sheet in the **Width** and **Height** edit boxes in this dialog box and choose **OK**; the new customized drawing sheet will be displayed. Select **Sheet1** from the **FeatureManager Design tree** and invoke the shortcut menu. Choose the **Edit Sheet Format** option; the edit sheet format environment will be invoked. Note that the **Edit Sheet Format** option will be available in the shortcut menu only when the selected sheet is activated. You can create or modify the sheet format by using the sketching tools in the **Sketch CommandManager**. After creating or modifying the sheet format, switch back to the edit sheet environment. Choose **File > Save Sheet Format** from the SOLIDWORKS menus; the **Save Sheet Format** dialog box will be displayed. Browse to the location where you need to save the sheet format. Specify the name of the sheet format and choose the **Save** button from the **Save Sheet Format** dialog box.

To use the saved sheet format, start a new drawing document; the **Sheet Format/Size** dialog box will be displayed. Now, select the **Standard sheet size** radio button and choose the **Browse** button from the dialog box. Next, browse to the location where you have saved the sheet format and open it. Figure 15-34 shows a user-defined sheet format.

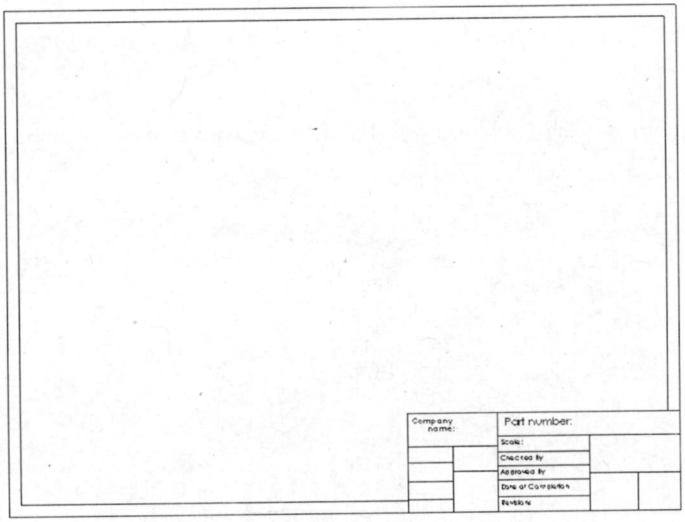

Figure 15-34 A user-defined sheet format

TUTORIALS

Tutorial 1

In this tutorial, first you will open the drawing created in Tutorial 1 of Chapter 14 and then generate dimensions and add annotations to it. Next, you will change the display of the front and right views to make hidden lines visible. Finally, you will change the display of the isometric view to the shaded mode. **(Expected time: 45 min)**

The following steps are required to complete this tutorial:

a. Copy the part document from Chapter 8 (*c08_tut02.sldprt*) and the drawing document from Chapter 14 (*c14_tut01.slddrw*) to the folder of the current chapter.
b. Configure the font settings and generate the dimensions using the **Model Items** tool.
c. Arrange the dimensions and delete the unwanted ones.
d. Add the datum symbol and geometric tolerance to the drawing views.
e. Change the model display state of the drawing views.

Copying the Documents in the Folder of the Current Chapter

Before proceeding, you need to copy the model and the drawing document in the folder of the current chapter.

1. Create a folder with the name *c15* in the *SOLIDWORKS* folder. Next, copy *c08_tut02.sldprt* and *c14_tut01.slddrw* from *\Documents\SOLIDWORKS\c08* and *\Documents\SOLIDWORKS\c14*, respectively and paste them in the *c15* folder.

Opening the Drawing Document

Next, you need to open the drawing document in the SOLIDWORKS window.

1. Invoke the **Open** dialog box and open the *c14_tut01.slddrw* document from the folder of the current chapter.

The drawing document in which you need to add the dimensions is displayed in the drawing area, as shown in Figure 15-35.

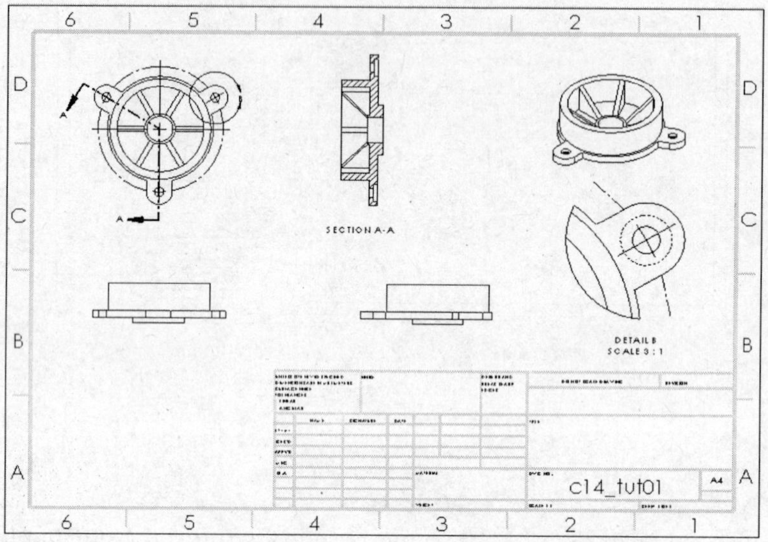

***Figure 15-35** Drawing views generated in Chapter 14*

Applying the Document Settings

Before generating the model dimensions, you need to configure the document settings. These settings will allow the dimensions and other annotations in the current sheet to be viewed properly.

1. Invoke the **System Options - General** dialog box by choosing the **Options** button from the Menu Bar.

2. Next, choose the **Document Properties** tab from the **System Options - General** dialog box to invoke the **Document Properties - Drafting Standard** dialog box and then choose **Annotations > Notes** from the area on the left in the dialog box.

3. Choose the **Font** button from the **Text** area of the dialog box; the **Choose Font** dialog box is invoked.

4. Select the **Points** radio button from the **Height** area and set the value of the font size as **9** from the list box.

5. Choose the **OK** button from the **Choose Font** dialog box.

6. Choose the **Dimensions** option from the area on the left in the dialog box; the related options are displayed on the right.

7. Set the values of height, width, and length of the arrows as **1**, **3**, and **6**, respectively using their respective edit boxes in the **Arrows** area.

8. Now, choose **Views > Section** from the left in the dialog box; the related options are displayed on the right. Set the values of height, width, and length of the section arrows as **2**, **4**, and **8** using their respective edit boxes in the **Section/view size** area.

9. Choose the **OK** button from the **Document Properties - Section** dialog box.

Generating the Dimensions

Next, you need to generate dimensions using the **Model Items** tool. As discussed earlier if you do not select any view on generating the dimensions using the **Model Items** tool, all the dimensions will be displayed in all the views. Sometimes, the dimensions may overlap each other. Therefore, select the view in which you need to generate the dimension and then invoke the **Model Items** tool.

1. Select the top view and choose the **Model Items** button from the **Annotation CommandManager**; the **Model Items PropertyManager** is displayed and the name of the selected view is displayed in the **Place annotations in these views** selection box under the **Source/Destination** rollout.

2. Select the **Entire model** option from the **Source** drop-down list and choose the **OK** button from the **Model Items PropertyManager**; the dimensions of the model which can be displayed in the selected view are generated.

   Note that the generated dimensions are scattered arbitrarily on the drawing sheet. Therefore, you need to arrange the dimensions by moving them to the required locations.

3. Select all the dimensions by dragging a window around them; the **Dimension Palette** button is displayed.

4. Move the cursor over this button; the **Dimension Palette** is displayed.

5. Choose the **Auto Arrange Dimensions** button from this palette; the dimensions are arranged at equal distance.

6. Select the dimensions one by one and drag them to the desired location. You can reverse the direction of arrowheads by clicking on the control point that is displayed on them. Any radial dimension attached to the counterbore hole in the top view needs to be deleted because you will add a hole callout to this counterbore hole later.

7. Select the radial dimension and press the DELETE key to delete the dimension. Similarly, delete the diameter dimension value 20. The drawing view after arranging the dimensions and deleting the diameter dimension is shown in Figure 15-36.

Note

In Figure 15-36, the display of hidden lines is turned on. To hide them, first select the top view from the drawing area and then choose the ***Hidden Lines Removed*** *button from the* ***Display Style*** *rollout of the* ***Drawing View PropertyManager****.*

8. Select the aligned section view and generate the dimensions using the **Model Items** tool. After placing the dimensions, move them to appropriate places, as shown Figure 15-37. You may need to change the arrowheads to closed filled arrowheads if they are not closed filled already.

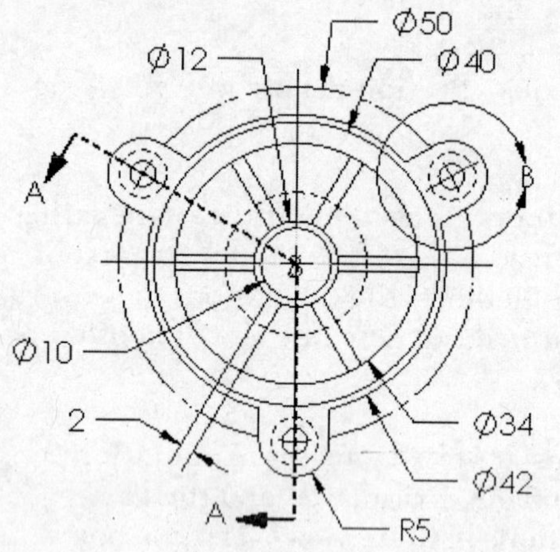

Figure 15-36 *Top view after generating and arranging the dimensions*

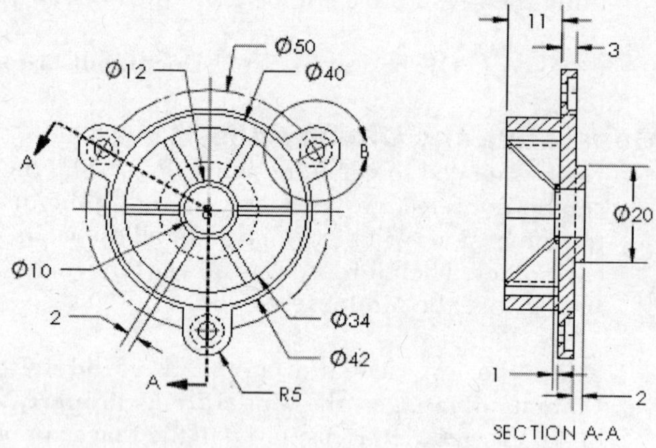

Figure 15-37 *Partial view of the sheet after generating and arranging the dimensions in the aligned section view*

9. Choose the **Hole Callout** button from the **Annotation CommandManager** and select the outer circle of one of the counterbore features in the top view; the hole callout is attached to the cursor. Pick a point on the drawing sheet to place the hole callout, as shown in Figure 15-38.

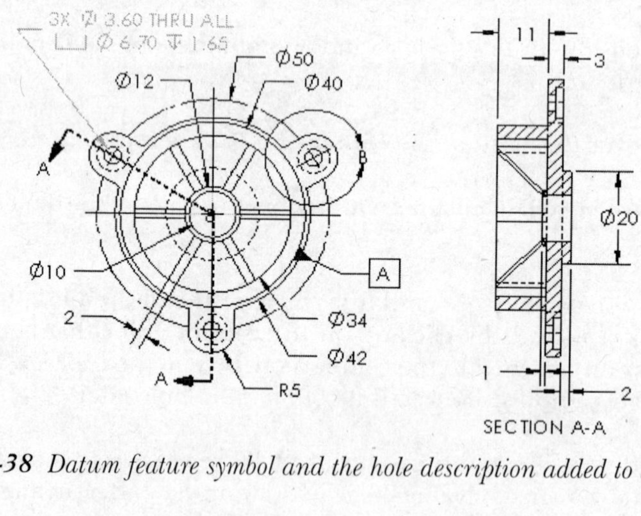

Figure 15-38 *Datum feature symbol and the hole description added to the top view*

Adding the Datum Feature Symbol to the Drawing Views

After generating the dimensions, you need to add the datum feature symbol to the drawing view. The datum feature symbols are used as datum reference for adding the geometric tolerance to the drawing views.

1. Select the edge of the outer cylindrical feature from the top view and then choose the **Datum Feature** button from the **Annotation CommandManager**; the **Datum Feature PropertyManager** is displayed and a datum callout is attached to the cursor.

2. Place the datum symbol at an appropriate location, refer to Figure 15-38.

3. Choose the **OK** button from the **Datum Feature PropertyManager**.

Adding the Geometric Tolerance to the Drawing Views

After defining the datum feature symbol, you need to add the geometric tolerance to the drawing view.

1. Select the circular edge that has a diameter of 12 mm from the top view and choose the **Geometric Tolerance** button from the **Annotation CommandManager**; the **Properties** dialog box is displayed. This dialog box is used to specify the parameters of the geometric tolerance.

2. Select the down arrow in the **Symbol** drop-down list in the first row; the **Symbols** flyout is displayed.

3. Choose the **Concentricity** option from this flyout and then enter **0.002** in the **Tolerance 1** edit box.

4. Enter **A** in the **Primary** edit box to define the primary datum reference.

5. Choose the **OK** button from the **Properties** dialog box; the geometric tolerance is attached to the selected circular edge. You may need to move the geometric tolerance if it overlaps the dimensions. Figure 15-39 shows the drawing view after adding and rearranging the geometric tolerance.

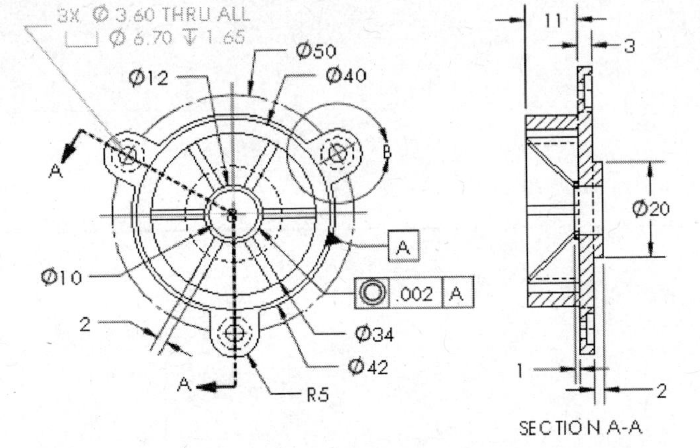

Figure 15-39 Geometric tolerance added and arranged in the drawing view

Changing the View Display Options

After adding all annotations to the drawing views, you need to change the display setting of the drawing views.

1. Press and hold the CTRL key, select the front view and then the right-side view from the drawing sheet.

2. Choose the **Hidden Lines Visible** button from the **View (Heads-Up)** toolbar; the hidden lines are displayed in the selected drawing views. You can also choose this button from the **Display Style** rollout of the **Multiple Views PropertyManager** that is displayed when you select the front and right-side views.

3. Now, select the isometric view from the drawing sheet.

4. Choose the **Shaded With Edges** button from the **View (Heads-Up)** toolbar or the **Drawing View PropertyManager**. Figure 15-40 shows the final drawing sheet after changing the display view settings.

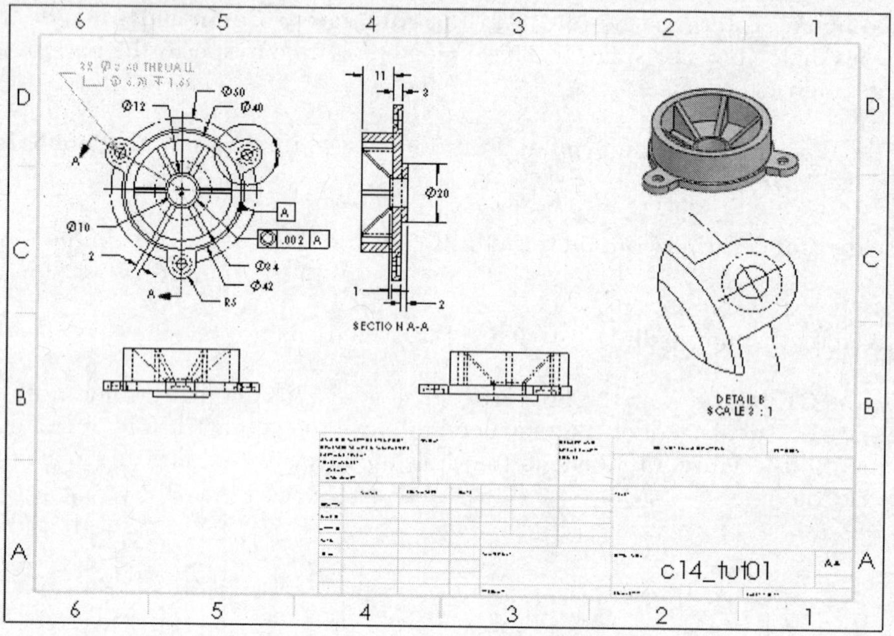

Figure 15-40 *Final drawing sheet*

5. Save and close the drawing document.

Tutorial 2

In this tutorial, you will generate the Bill of Materials (BOM) of the Bench Vice assembly and then add balloons to the isometric view in the exploded state. **(Expected time: 45 min)**

The following steps are required to complete this tutorial:

a. Copy the Bench Vice folder, which contains parts, assembly, and the drawing document, from Chapter 14 to the folder of the current chapter.
b. Delete the views that are not required in the drawing sheet.
c. Move the views and arrange them in the drawing sheet.
d. Set the anchor on the drawing sheet where the BOM will be attached.
e. Generate the BOM.
f. Add balloons to the isometric view.

Copying the Bench Vice Assembly Folder to the Current Folder

Before proceeding, you need to copy the model and the drawing document in the folder of the current chapter.

1. Copy the *Bench Vice* folder from the *\Documents\SOLIDWORKS\c14* folder to the folder of the current chapter.

Opening the Drawing Document

After copying the folder, you need to open the drawing document in the SOLIDWORKS window.

1. Open the *c14_tut02.slddrw* document.

The drawing document in which you need to generate the BOM and balloons is displayed in Figure 15-41.

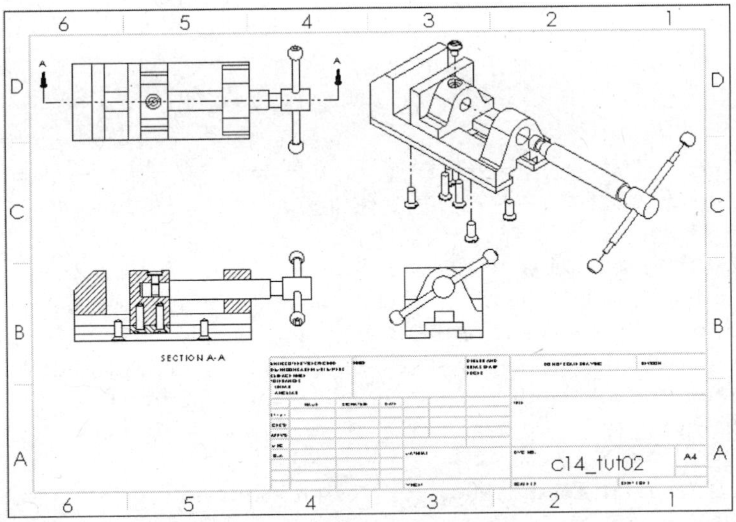

Figure 15-41 *Drawing views*

Deleting the Unwanted View

You need to delete the right view because it is not required in this tutorial.

1. Select the right-side view and press the DELETE key; the **Confirm Delete** dialog box is displayed.

2. Choose the **Yes** button from this dialog box; the view is deleted from the current drawing sheet.

Moving the Isometric View

You need to move the exploded isometric view because the BOM will be generated and placed at the top right corner of the drawing sheet.

1. Select the isometric view; the border of the view is highlighted.

2. Move the cursor to the border; the cursor is replaced by the move cursor.

3. Select the border and drag the cursor to move the drawing view and then place it at the required location, as shown in Figure 15-42.

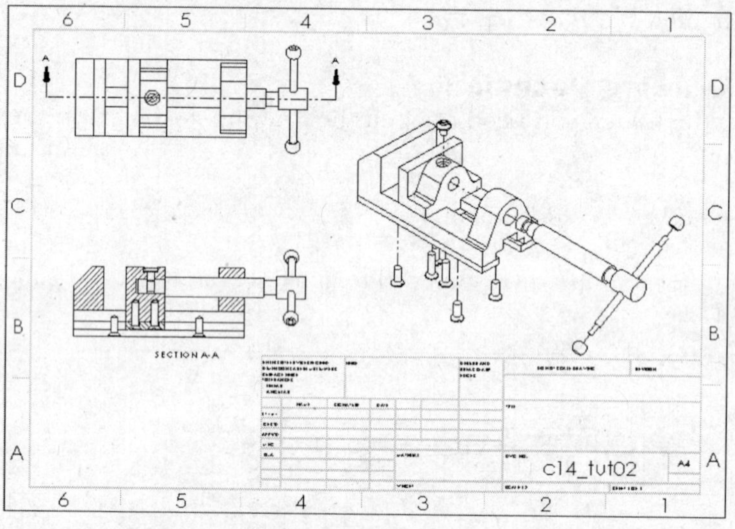

***Figure 15-42** Drawing sheet after deleting and moving the drawing views*

Setting the Anchor for the BOM

Before generating the BOM, you need to set its anchor. The anchor is a point on the drawing sheet to which one of the corners of the BOM coincides. By default, the anchor is defined at the top left corner of the drawing sheet. But in this tutorial, you need to add the BOM at the top right corner of the drawing sheet. Therefore, you need to set the anchor before generating the BOM.

1. Expand **Sheet1** from the **FeatureManager Design Tree** and then expand **Sheet Format1**.

2. Select the **Bill of Materials Anchor1** option, right-click on it to invoke a shortcut menu and then choose the **Set Anchor** option from it; the drawing views disappear from the sheet.

3. Specify the anchor point on the inner top right corner of the drawing sheet; a point is placed at the selected location.

After you specify the anchor point, the drawing views are displayed automatically in the sheet because the sheet editing environment is invoked automatically.

Generating the BOM

Next, you need to generate the BOM. As discussed earlier, the BOM generated in SOLIDWORKS is parametric. If a component is deleted or added in the assembly, the change is reflected automatically in the BOM. But before generating the BOM, you need to set its text parameters.

1. Invoke the **System Options - General** dialog box by choosing the **Options** button from the Menu Bar.

2. Next, choose the **Document Properties** tab in the **System Options - General** dialog box to invoke the **Document Properties - Drafting Standard** dialog box and then choose **Annotations > Notes** from the area on the left.

3. Choose the **Font** button from the **Text** area of the dialog box; the **Choose Font** dialog box is invoked. Select the **Points** radio button from the **Height** area and set the value of the font size to **9** from the list box.

4. Choose the **OK** button from the **Choose Font** dialog box. Similarly, change the text height of balloons to **14** and close the dialog box.

5. Select the isometric view and choose **Tables > Bill of Materials** from the **Annotation CommandManager**; the **Bill of Materials PropertyManager** is displayed.

6. Select the **Attach to anchor point** check box in the **Table Position** rollout.

7. Choose the **OK** button from the **Bill of Materials PropertyManager**; the BOM is generated. If the BOM is displayed outside the drawing sheet, move the cursor over the BOM; an anchor symbol is displayed. Click on the symbol; the **Bill of Materials PropertyManager** is displayed. Select an appropriate position for placing the BOM from the **Table Position** rollout and then choose the **Close Dialog** button; you will notice that the **Description** column is also displayed in the BOM. But this column is not required, so you need to delete it.

8. Move the cursor over the **Description** heading and right-click to display a shortcut menu. Choose **Delete > Column** from the shortcut menu; the column is deleted. The drawing sheet after generating the BOM and deleting the **Description** column is displayed, as shown in Figure 15-43.

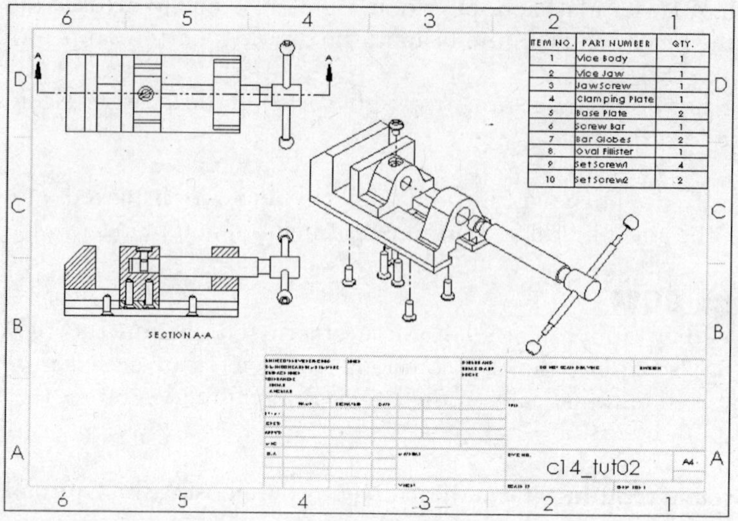

Figure 15-43 Drawing sheet after generating the BOM

Adding Balloons to the Components

After generating the BOM, you need to add balloons to the components. Before proceeding, make sure that you have changed the font height of balloons to **14**, as discussed in the previous section.

1. Select the isometric view and choose the **Auto Balloon** button from the **Annotation CommandManager**; the balloons are automatically added to all the components in the isometric view and the **Auto Balloon PropertyManager** is also displayed.

The multiple instances of any component are ignored because the **Ignore multiple instances** check box is already selected in the **Balloon Layout** rollout. Also, make sure that the **Insert magnetic line(s)** check box is cleared.

2. Select **1 Character** from the **Size** drop-down list in the **Balloon Settings** rollout. Next, choose **OK** to close this PropertyManager.

The balloons are added to all the components. You will notice that the balloons are not properly arranged on the sheet and are placed arbitrarily. Therefore, you need to drag each balloon manually to place it properly.

3. Move the cursor over any one of the balloons and when it is highlighted, drag it to place it at another location, refer to Figure 15-44.

4. Similarly, drag and place the remaining balloons at proper locations. The final drawing sheet after adding and rearranging balloons is shown in Figure 15-44.

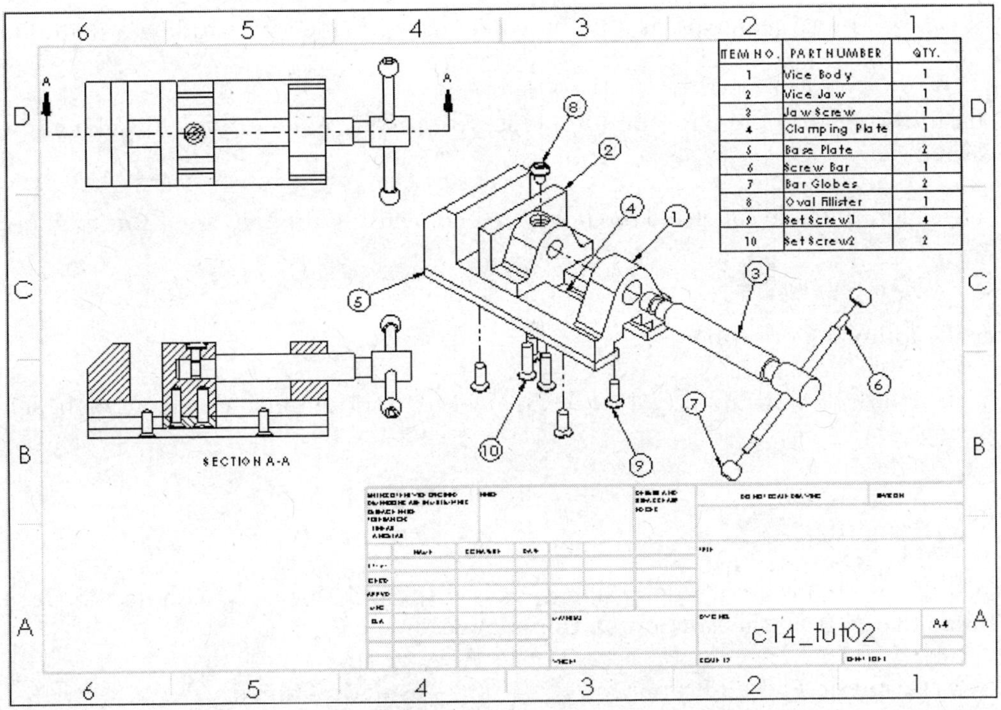

Figure 15-44 Final drawing sheet after adding balloons

5. Save and close the drawing document.

Self-Evaluation Test

Answer the following questions and then compare them to those given at the end of this chapter:

1. The __________ tool is used to add balloons manually to the components of the assembly in the drawing view.

2. The __________ spinner is used to define the major diameter of the thread.

3. The __________ rollout in the **Bill of Materials PropertyManager** is used to specify the template needed to create the BOM.

4. The __________ tool is used to create a hole callout.

5. In SOLIDWORKS, you cannot add annotations while creating the parts. (T/F)

6. You can add the surface finish symbols to the drawing views. (T/F)

7. The **Projected tolerance zone** area is used to define the quality of the projected tolerance. (T/F)

8. You can set the target shape as a point, circle, or rectangle while adding a datum target. (T/F)

9. You can also set the option for the automatic creation of the centerline while generating the drawing views. (T/F)

10. You can add the hole callout to the holes created by using the **Extruded Cut** tool. (T/F)

Review Questions

Answer the following questions:

1. Which of the following PropertyManagers is invoked to add automatic balloons to the selected drawing view?

   (a) **AutoBalloon** (b) **Balloon**
   (c) **Properties** (d) **Center Mark**

2. Which of the following PropertyManagers is displayed when you choose the **Cosmetic Thread** button from the **Annotation CommandManager**?

   (a) **Cosmetic Thread Properties** (b) **Cosmetic Thread**
   (c) **Cosmetic Thread Convention** (d) None of the above

3. Which of the following PropertyManagers is used to add center marks to the drawing views?

   (a) **Add Center Mark** (b) **Create Center Mark**
   (c) **Center Mark** (d) **Cosmetic Thread**

4. Which of the following rollouts in the **Cosmetic Thread PropertyManager** is used to define the depth of the cosmetic thread?

   (a) **Thread Settings** (b) **Thread Depth**
   (c) **Cosmetic Thread** (d) None of the above

5. Which of the following PropertyManagers is used to add balloons to the drawing views?

   (a) **Add Balloons** (b) **Balloon Properties**
   (c) **Balloons** (d) None of these

6. The __________ tool is used to add cosmetic threads to display the thread conventions in the drawing views.

7. The __________ tool is used to add reference dimensions to drawing views.

8. You can change the model display setting from hidden lines removed to hidden lines visible, wireframe, or shaded using the options available in the __________ toolbar.

9. While generating the views, select the __________ check box in the **Auto insert on view creation** area to automatically create the centerlines.

10. The __________ tool is used to create centerlines in the views.

EXERCISE

Exercise 1

Generate the isometric view of the exploded view of the assembly created in Tutorial 1 of Chapter 13 on the standard A4 sheet format. The scale of the view will be 1:5. After generating the view, generate the BOM and add balloons to the assembly view, as shown in Figure 15-45.

(Expected time: 30 min)

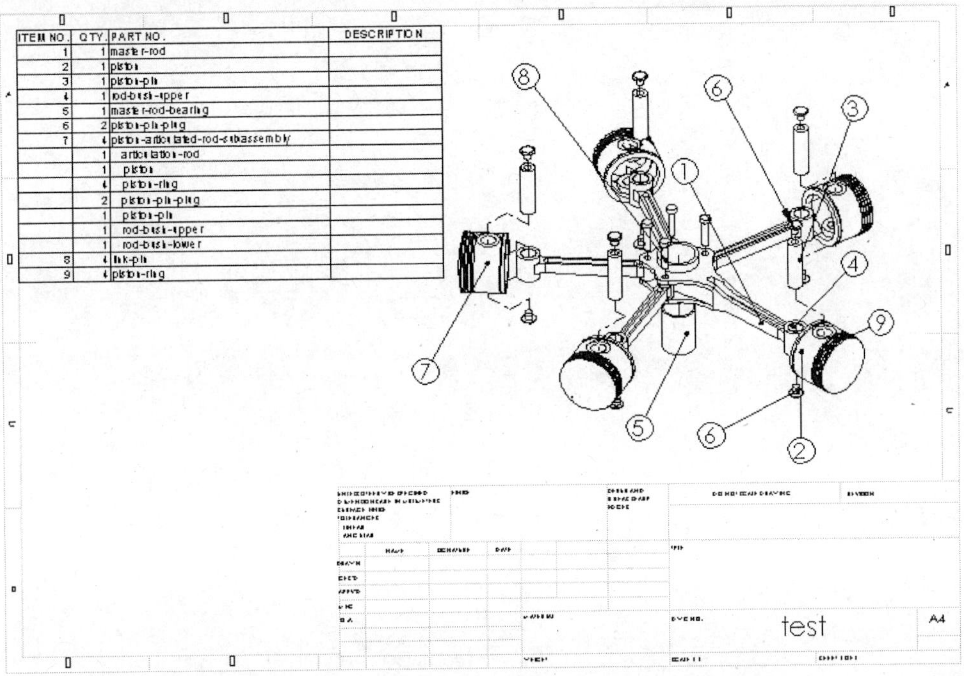

Figure 15-45 Drawing view for Exercise 1

Answers to Self-Evaluation Test

1. Balloon, **2.** Major Diameter, **3.** Table Template, **4.** Hole Callout, **5.** F, **6.** T, **7.** F, **8.** T, **9.** T, **10.** T

Chapter 16

Surface Modeling

Learning Objectives

After completing this chapter, you will be able to:

- *Create Extruded, Revolved, and Swept surfaces*
- *Create Lofted, Planar, and Boundary surfaces*
- *Create Fill and Radiated surfaces*
- *Extend, trim, and untrim surfaces*
- *Offset, fillet, and knit surfaces*
- *Create a Mid-surface*
- *Delete holes*
- *Replace and delete faces*
- *Move and copy surfaces*
- *Thicken a surface body*
- *Create a thickened surface cut*
- *Create a surface cut*

SURFACE MODELING

Surface modeling is a technique of creating planar or non-planar geometry of zero thickness. This zero thickness geometry is known as surface. Surfaces are generally used to create models of complex shapes. You can easily convert surface models into solid models. You can also extract a surface from a solid model using the surface modeling tools. This chapter deals with the surface modeling tools in SOLIDWORKS. Using these tools, you can create complex shapes as surfaces and then convert them into solid models, if required.

Most of the real world components are created using solid modeling. But sometimes, you may need to create some complex features that can only be created by surface manipulation. Surface manipulation is done by using surface modeling tools. After creating the required complex surface, you can convert it into a solid model. The reasons to convert a surface model into a solid model are that a surface is a zero-thickness geometry and it has no mass and mass properties. But, while designing real world models, you may need mass and mass properties. The other reason is that you can generate a section view only if the model is a solid.

In SOLIDWORKS, surface modeling is done in the **Part** mode and the tools used for surface modeling are available in the **Surfaces CommandManager**. The **Surfaces CommandManager** will not be available by default. Therefore, you need to right-click on any one of the **CommandManager** tabs and then choose the **Tabs > Surfaces** option from the shortcut menu. The surface modeling tools can also be invoked by choosing **Insert > Surface** from the SOLIDWORKS menus. You will notice that some of the tools available in the **Surfaces CommandManager**, such as extrude, revolve, sweep, and loft are similar to those discussed in the solid modeling.

The tools in the **Surfaces CommandManager** and the other advanced surface modeling tools are discussed next.

Creating an Extruded Surface

CommandManager:	Surfaces > Extruded Surface
SOLIDWORKS menus:	Insert > Surface > Extrude
Toolbar:	Surfaces > Extruded Surface

In SOLIDWORKS, the **Extruded Surface** tool is used to extrude a closed or an open sketch for creating an extruded surface. To create an extruded surface, create a sketch in the sketching environment and then choose the **Extruded Surface** button from the **Surfaces CommandManager**; the **Surface-Extrude PropertyManager** will be displayed, as shown in Figure 16-1. Also, the preview of the extruded surface with the default values will be displayed in the drawing area. To define feature termination, select the required option from the **End Condition** drop-down list in the PropertyManager. The feature termination options are available in the **Direction 1** and **Direction 2** rollouts. The other options in this PropertyManager are the same as those discussed in part modeling. You can also define the extrusion depth dynamically by dragging the handle displayed in the

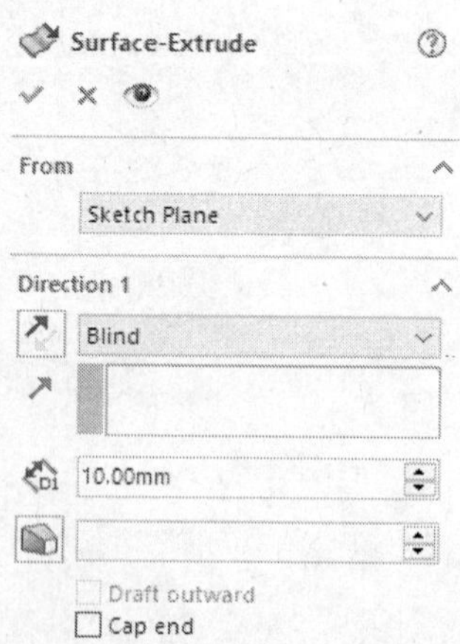

***Figure 16-1** Partial view of the Surface-Extrude PropertyManager*

drawing area. In SOLIDWORKS, you can extrude a 2D face such that all its edges are extruded and it results into an extruded surface. To extrude a 2D face, choose the **Extruded Surface** tool without drawing a sketch. Next, press the ALT key and select the surface; all edges of the selected 2D surface will be extruded. You can also select the surface of a solid model. If you do so, the edges of the model will be extruded as surfaces.

Figure 16-2 shows a closed sketch and Figure 16-3 shows the surface created by extruding the closed sketch. Figure 16-4 shows an open sketch and Figure 16-5 shows the surface created by extruding that open sketch.

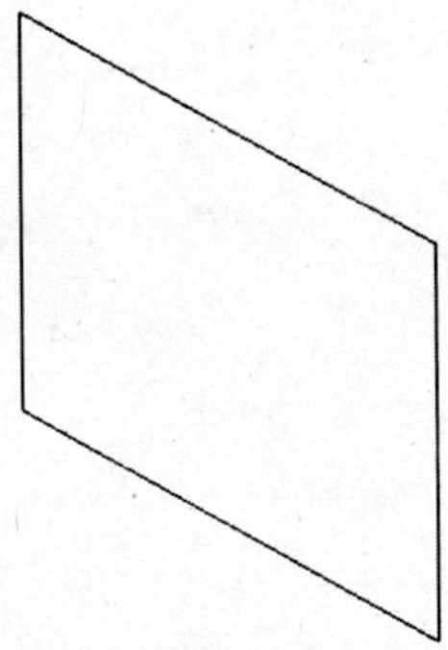

Figure 16-2 *A closed sketch*

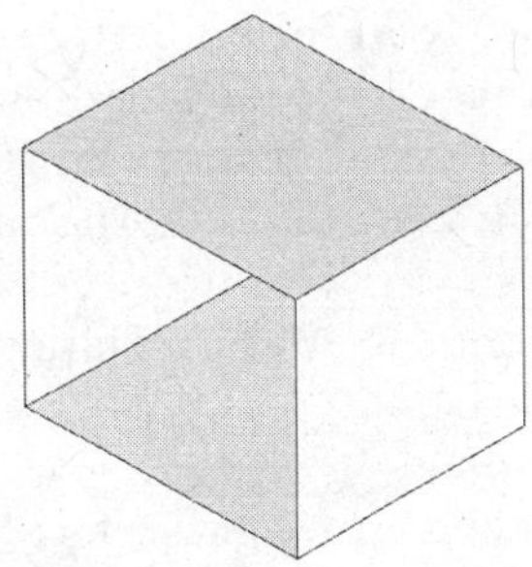

Figure 16-3 *Surface created by extruding the closed sketch*

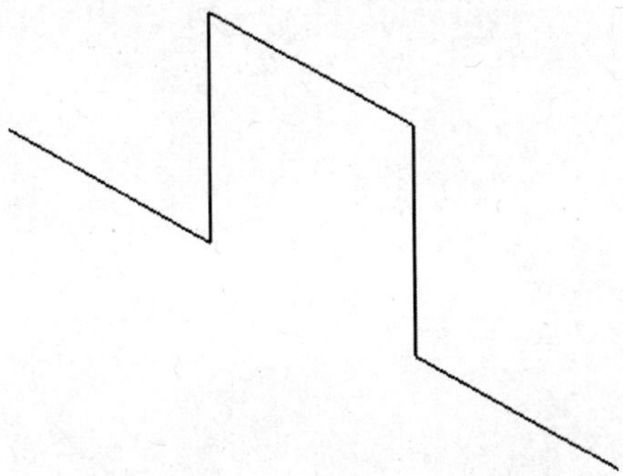

Figure 16-4 *An open sketch*

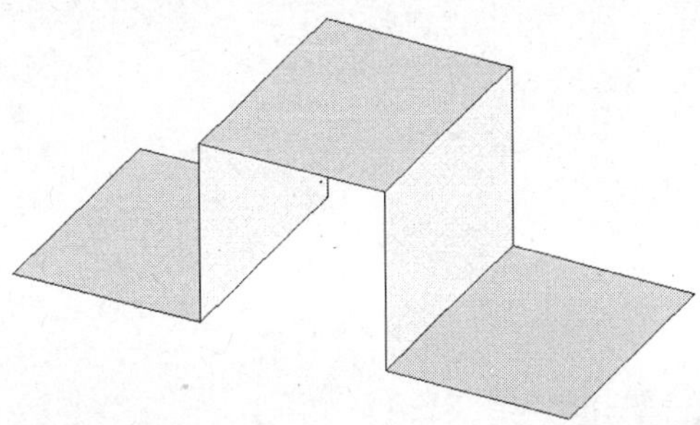

Figure 16-5 *Surface created by extruding the open sketch*

Creating a Revolved Surface

CommandManager:	Surfaces > Revolved Surface
SOLIDWORKS menus:	Insert > Surface > Revolve
Toolbar:	Surfaces > Revolved Surface

You can also create a surface by revolving a closed or an open sketch along a centerline. Revolving a sketch along a centerline to create a revolved surface is similar to revolving a sketch along a centerline to create a solid feature. To create a revolved surface, first create a sketch and a centerline in the sketching environment. Next, choose the **Revolved Surface** button from the **Surfaces CommandManager**; the **Surface-Revolve PropertyManager** will be displayed, as shown in Figure 16-6. Also, preview of the revolved surface with the drag handle will be displayed in the drawing area. The feature termination options and other options in this PropertyManager are similar to those discussed while creating a solid revolved feature.

Figure 16-6 *The* ***Surface-Revolve PropertyManager***

Figure 16-7 shows an open sketch for creating a revolved surface. Figure 16-8 shows the revolved surface created by revolving the sketch through an angle of 270 degrees.

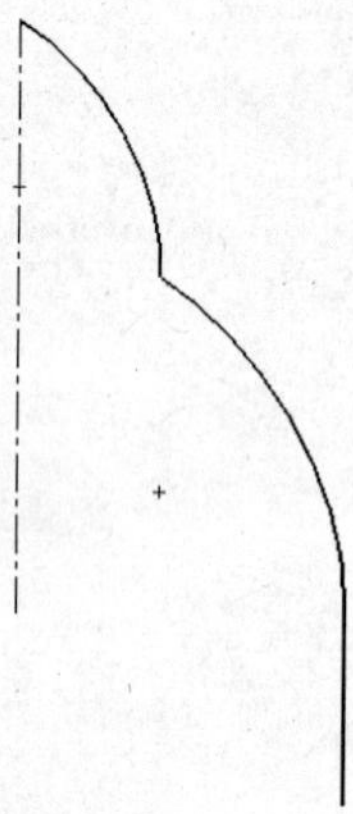

Figure 16-7 *Sketch for creating a revolved surface*

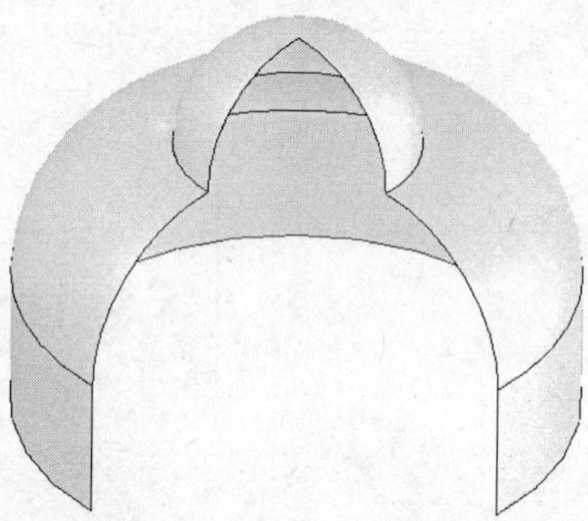

Figure 16-8 *Surface created by revolving the sketch through an angle of 270 degrees*

Creating a Swept Surface

CommandManager:	Surfaces > Swept Surface
SOLIDWORKS menus:	Insert > Surface > Sweep
Toolbar:	Surfaces > Swept Surface

You can also create a swept surface by sweeping a closed or an open profile along a closed or an open path. To create a sketch profile, first draw a closed or an open sketch as a sweep profile and another sketch as a sweep path in the sketching environment. Next, choose the **Swept Surface** button from the **Surfaces CommandManager**; the **Surface-Sweep PropertyManager** will be displayed, as shown in Figure 16-9. Also, you will be prompted to select a sweep profile. Select a closed sketch or an open sketch as the profile of the sweep feature; you will be prompted to select the sweep path. Select a closed or an open sketch as the sweep path. On doing so, the preview of the sweep feature will be displayed in the drawing area.

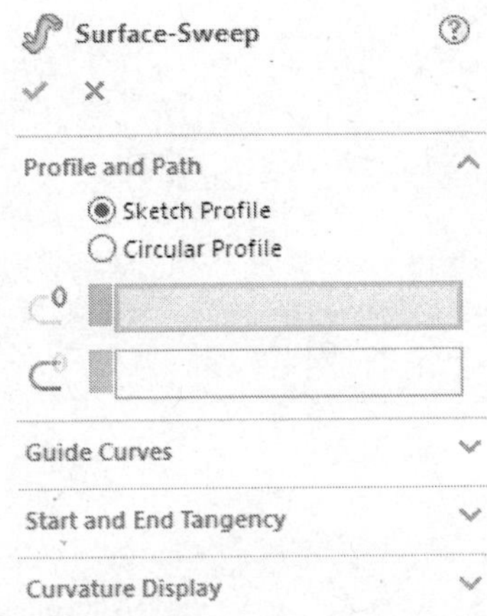

Figure 16-9** The **Surface-Sweep PropertyManager

To create a circular swept surface using the **Circular Profile** option, you need to draw only a closed or an open sketch for sweep path in the sketching environment.

All other options used to create a swept surface are similar to those discussed while creating the solid sweep feature.

You can also select guide curves while creating the sweep surface.

Figures 16-10 through 16-19 illustrate various ways to create a sweep feature. Figure 16-10 shows an open profile and an open path and Figure 16-11 shows the resultant sweep surface. Figure 16-12 shows a closed profile and an open path and Figure 16-13 shows the resultant sweep surface. Figure 16-14 shows an open profile and a closed path and Figure 16-15 shows the resultant sweep surface. Figure 16-16 shows a closed path for circular sweep and Figure 16-17 shows the resultant sweep surface. Figure 16-18 shows a profile, a path, and three guide curves and Figure 16-19 shows the resultant sweep surface.

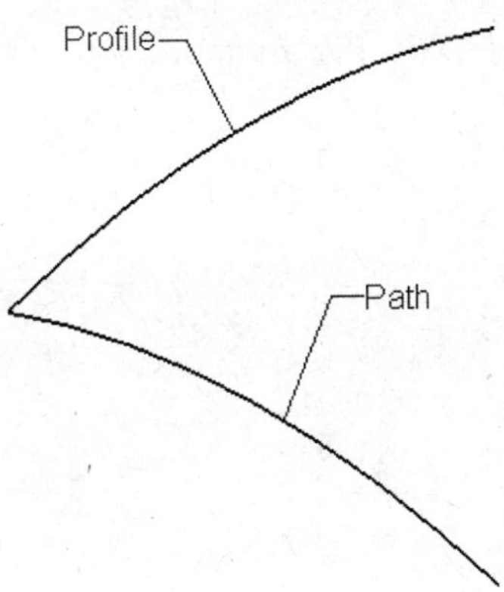

***Figure 16-10** An open profile and an open path*

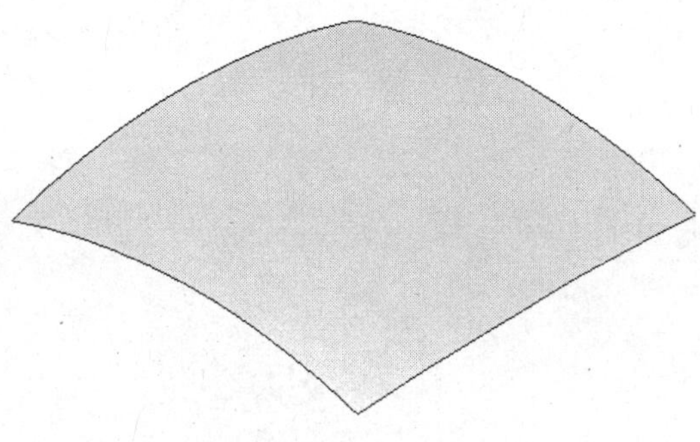

***Figure 16-11** Resultant sweep surface*

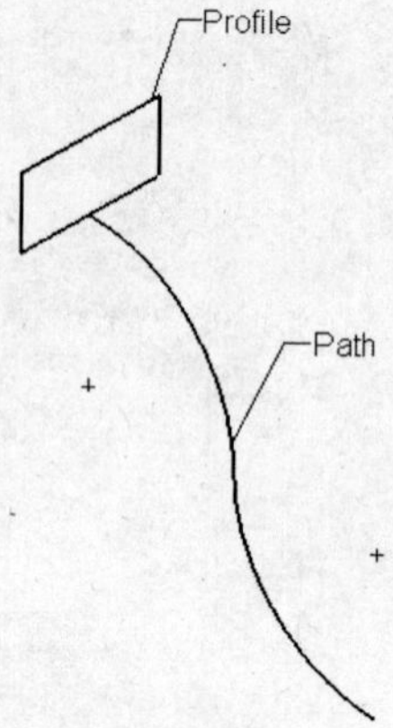

Figure 16-12 A closed profile and an open path

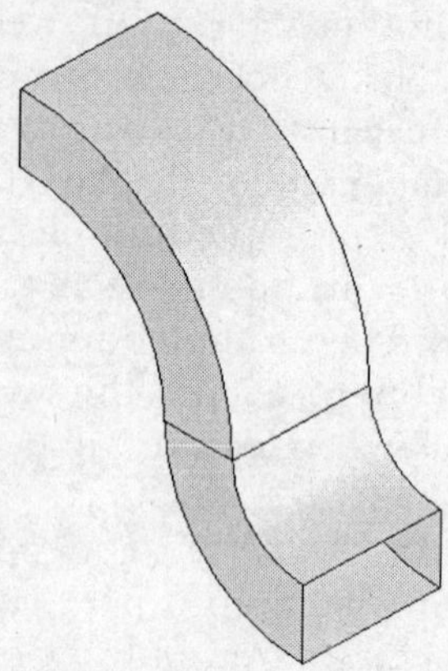

Figure 16-13 Resultant sweep surface

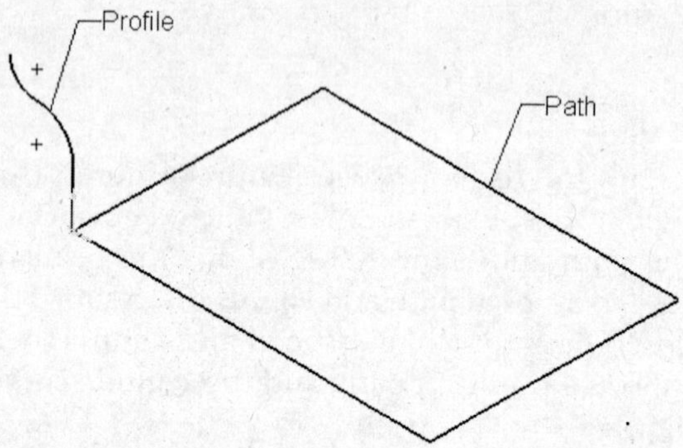

Figure 16-14 An open profile and a closed path

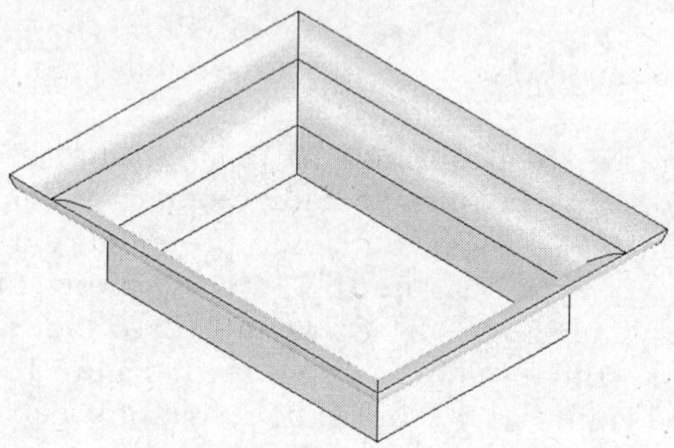

Figure 16-15 Resultant sweep surface

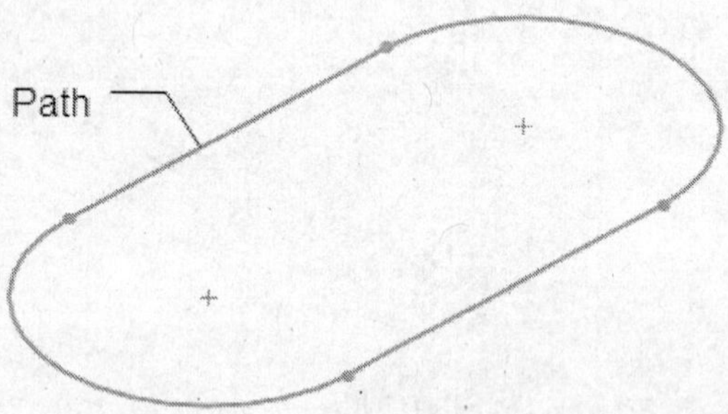

Figure 16-16 A closed path for circular sweep

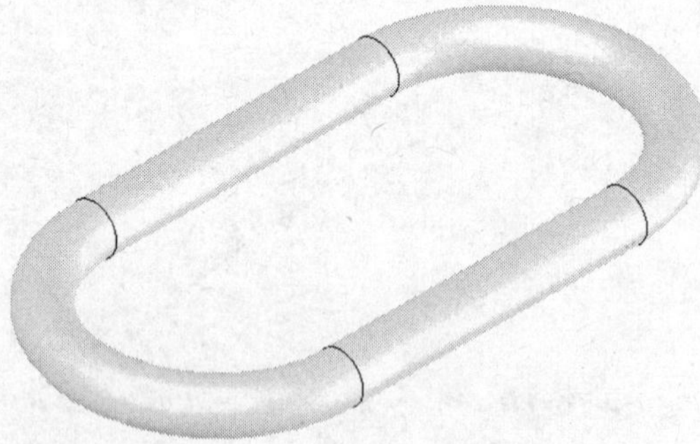

Figure 16-17 Resultant sweep surface

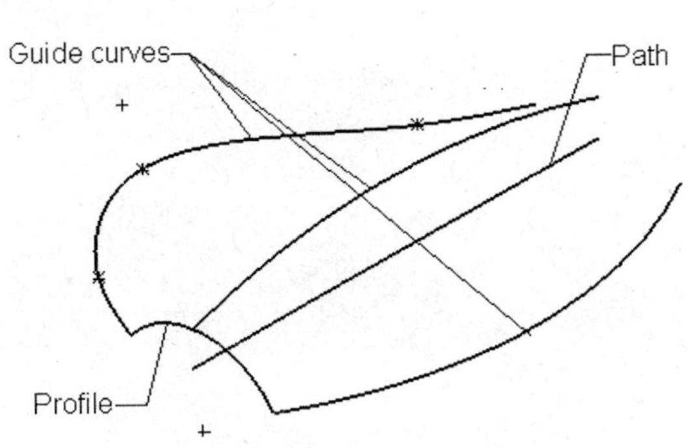

Figure 16-18 Profile, path, and guide curves

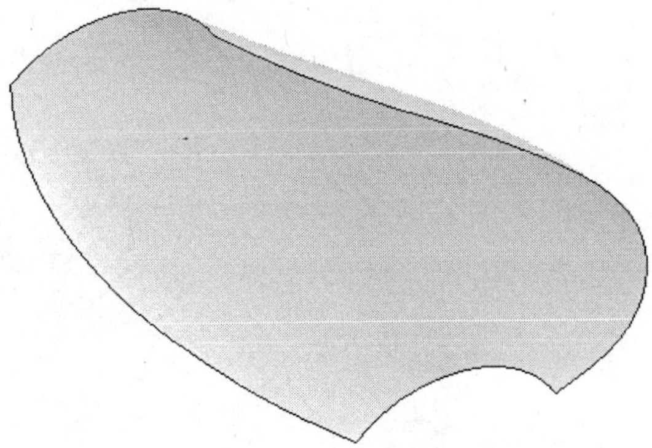

Figure 16-19 Resultant sweep feature

Creating a Lofted Surface

CommandManager:	Surfaces > Lofted Surface
SOLIDWORKS menus:	Insert > Surface > Loft
Toolbar:	Surfaces > Lofted Surface

In SOLIDWORKS, you can also create a surface by lofting two or more sections. To create a lofted surface, choose the **Lofted Surface** button from the **Surfaces CommandManager**; the **Surface-Loft PropertyManager** will be displayed, as shown in Figure 16-20, and you will be prompted to select at least two profiles. Select the profiles to be lofted. All the options for creating a lofted surface are similar to those discussed while creating a solid lofted feature.

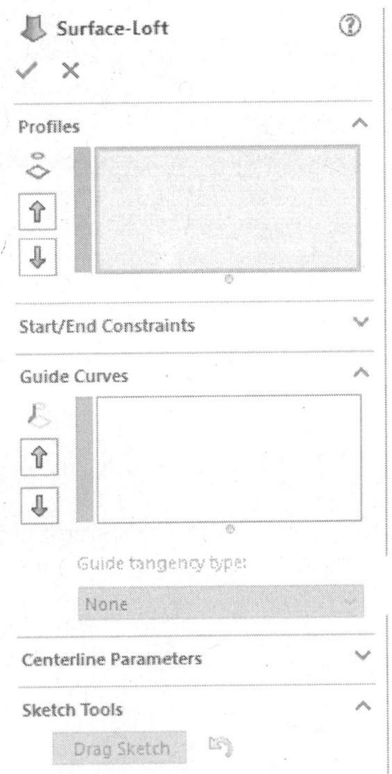

*Figure 16-20 Partial view of the **Surface-Loft PropertyManager***

Note that if you want to create a lofted surface with open section, all the sections to be lofted must be opened. Similarly, if you want to create a closed lofted surface, all the sections must be closed. This means that in a lofted surface, the combination of closed and opened sections is not possible. Figure 16-21 shows the two open sections to be lofted and Figure 16-22 shows the resultant lofted surface.

Figure 16-23 shows two closed sections to be lofted and Figure 16-24 shows the resultant lofted surface. Figure 16-25 shows two sections and a centerline and Figure 16-26 shows the resultant lofted surface.

Figure 16-27 shows two sections and guide curves and Figure 16-28 shows the resultant lofted surface.

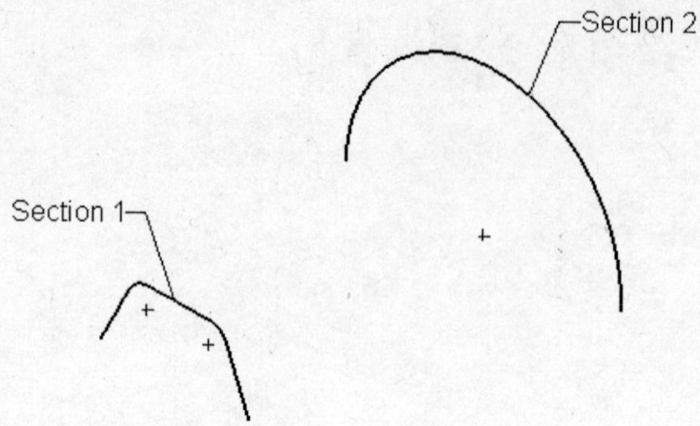

Figure 16-21 Open sections

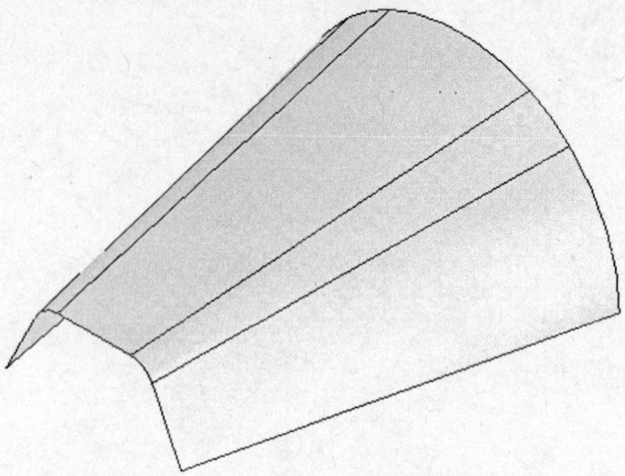

Figure 16-22 Resultant lofted surface

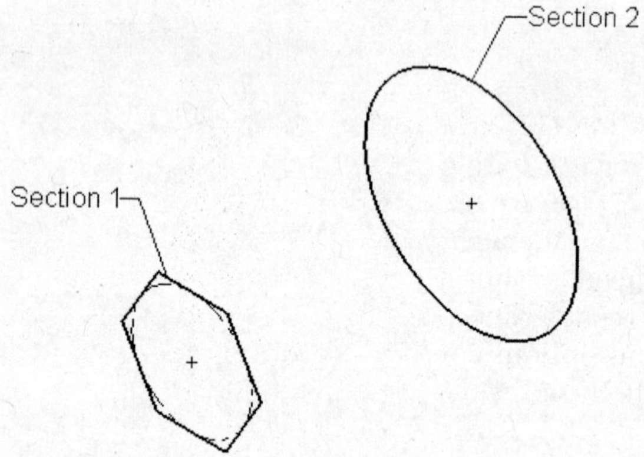

Figure 16-23 Closed sections

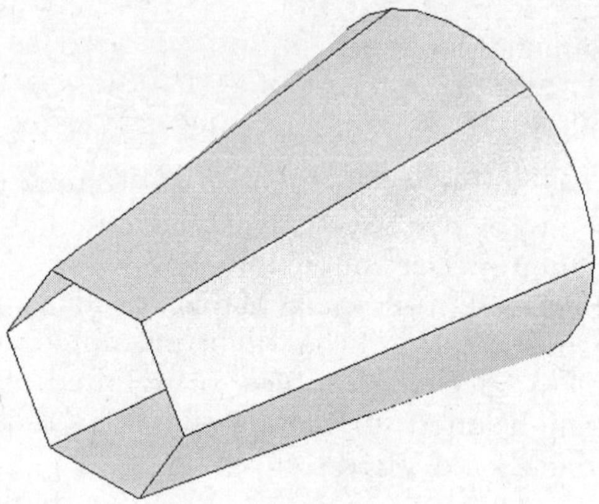

Figure 16-24 Resultant lofted surface

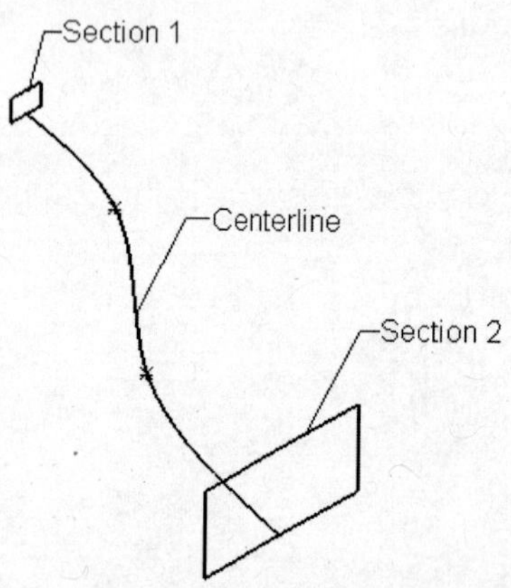

Figure 16-25 Sections and centerline

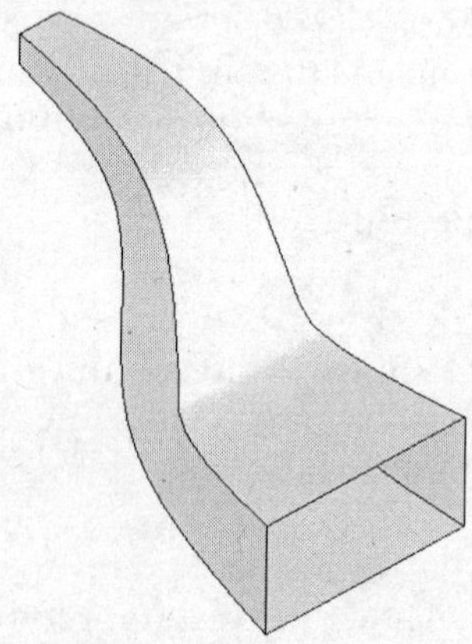

Figure 16-26 Resultant lofted surface

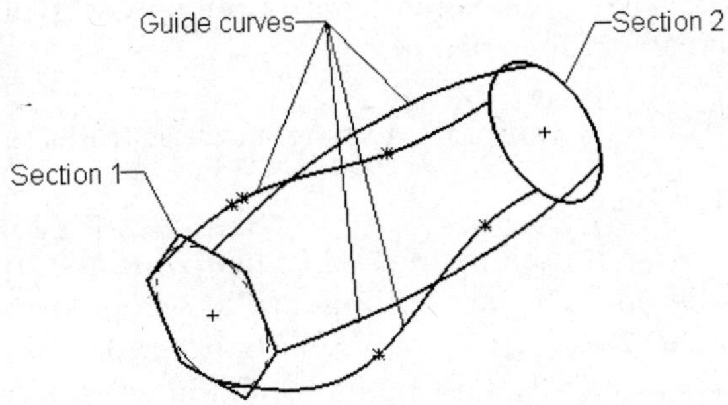

Figure 16-27 Sections and guide curves

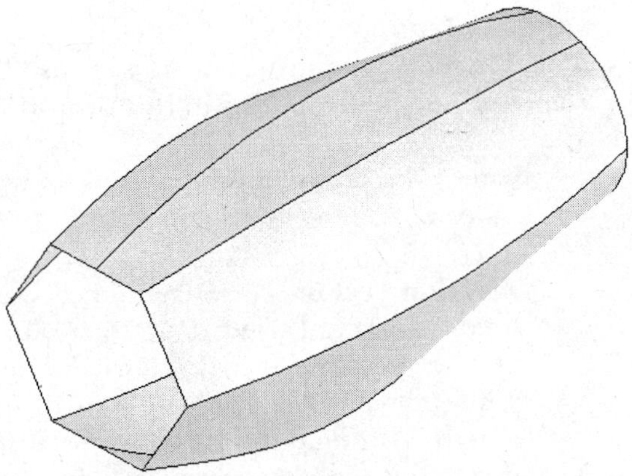

Figure 16-28 Resultant lofted surface

Creating a Boundary Surface

CommandManager:	Surfaces > Boundary Surface
SOLIDWORKS menus:	Insert > Surface > Boundary Surface
Toolbar:	Surfaces > Boundary Surface

The **Boundary Surface** tool is used to create complex models with high accuracy as well as high surface quality, while maintaining the curvature continuity. To create a boundary surface, choose the **Boundary Surface** button from the **Surfaces CommandManager**; the **Boundary-Surface PropertyManager** will be displayed, as shown in Figure 16-29 and you will be prompted to select the profiles for the boundary surface. Select the curves from the drawing area; the selected curves will be displayed in the **Direction 1** rollout of the PropertyManager and the preview will be displayed in the drawing area. To select the curves for the **Direction 2** rollout, click in the **Curves** selection box of the **Direction 2** rollout and then select the curves from the drawing area; the selected curves will be displayed in the **Curves** selection box. The other options in this PropertyManager are discussed next.

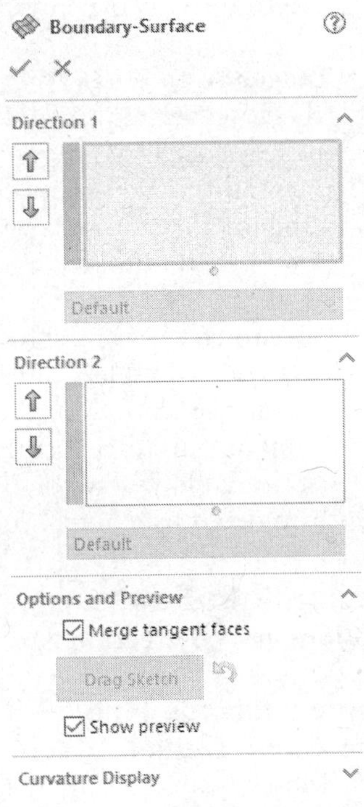

*Figure 16-29 The **Boundary-Surface PropertyManager***

Direction 1 Rollout

The **Direction 1** rollout is used to control the tangency and curvature continuity of curves in direction 1. The boundary surface is created based on the order of curves selected from the drawing area. You can change the order of curves in the **Curves** selection box by choosing the **Move Up** and **Move Down** buttons. The options that affect curves in the direction 1 are discussed next.

Tangent Type

The **Tangent Type** drop-down list is used to display options that control the tangency of the curvature. The options in this drop-down list are discussed next.

None: The **None** option is used to apply zero curvature or no tangency constraint to curves.

Direction Vector: The **Direction Vector** option is used to apply tangency constraint to curves. When you select the **Direction Vector** option from the **Tangent Type** drop-down list, the **Alignment** drop-down list and the **Direction Vector** selection box will be displayed below the **Tangent Type** drop-down list. Select the required alignment option from the **Alignment** drop-down list and then select the direction based on the selected curves. You can also specify the draft angle and tangent length for curves in the **Draft angle** and **Tangent Length** spinners, respectively.

Default: The **Default** option will be available in the **Tangent Type** drop-down list, only when at least three curves are selected in one direction.

Normal To Profile: The **Normal To Profile** option is used to apply the tangency constraint normal to the selected curves. You can also set the draft angle and tangent length for curves using this option.

Tangency To Face: This option will be available in the **Tangent Type** drop-down list only when you select the edges of existing surfaces as boundary curve. Select this option to make the surface tangent to the existing surface at the selected boundary curve. Select the required alignment option from the **Alignment** drop-down list available below the **Tangent Type** drop-down list. The options in the **Alignment** drop-down list control the flow of the boundary surface.

Curvature To Face: This option will be available in the **Tangent Type** drop-down list only when you select the edges of existing surfaces as boundary curve. This option makes the surface smoother and curvature continuous to the existing surface at the selected boundary curve. Select the required alignment option from the **Alignment** drop-down list available below the **Tangent Type** drop-down list. The options in the **Alignment** drop-down list control the flow of the boundary surface.

Direction 2 Rollout

The options in the **Direction 2** rollout are the same as those discussed in the **Direction 1** rollout.

Curve Influence Type

The **Curve Influence Type** drop-down list will be displayed in the **Direction 1** and **Direction 2** rollouts only when you select a curve for the second direction. The options available in this drop-down list are discussed next.

Global: The **Global** option is selected by default in this drop-down list. This option is used to extend the curve influence up to the entire boundary feature.

To Next Curve: The **To Next Curve** option is used to extend the curve influence up to the next curve only.

To Next Sharp: The **To Next Sharp** option is used to extend the curve influence up to the next sharp only. Sharp is a hard corner of the sketch entity. This option is applicable between two sketch entities that do not have a tangency and curvature relation with each other.

To Next Edge: The **To Next Edge** option is used to extend the curve influence up to the next edge only.

Linear: The **Linear** option is used to extend the curve influence linearly up to the entire boundary feature.

Note

While selecting curves from the drawing area, select a point on the curve such that it follows the required path of the boundary feature. The selected points on the curves act as connectors of the boundary feature. You can also flip the boundary feature connectors. To do so, right-click in the drawing area; a shortcut menu will be displayed. Choose the ***Flip Connectors*** *option from the shortcut menu to flip the direction of connectors.*

Options and Preview Rollout

You can merge the tangent faces of a boundary feature by selecting the **Merge tangent faces** check box available in this rollout. To separate the tangent faces of the boundary feature, you need to clear this check box. If you have selected the curves that lie in two different directions, then you can trim the surfaces up to the curve(s) by selecting the **Trim by direction 1** and **Trim by direction 2** check boxes. The **Close surface** check box is selected to create a closed surface. Note that the angle between the start and end sections should be more than 180 degrees to create the closed surface and also there should be at least three sections. To view the preview of the boundary feature, select the **Show preview** check box available in this rollout.

Curvature Display Rollout

The **Curvature Display** rollout is used to display the mesh preview, zebra stripes, and curvature combs of the boundary feature. The **Mesh preview** and **Curvature combs** check boxes are selected by default in the **Curvature Display** rollout of the **Boundary-Surface PropertyManager**. The **Mesh preview** check box allows you to toggle the mesh preview of the boundary surface. You can increase or decrease the number of lines of the mesh by using the **Mesh density** spinner available below the **Mesh preview** check box in this rollout. By selecting the **Zebra stripes** check box, you can visually determine the type of boundary existing between surfaces such as contact, tangency, and curvature continuous. Using the **Zebra stripes** check box, you can also identify wrinkles or defects in surfaces. On selecting the **Curvature combs** check box, you can visualize the continuity of the curve and also get a better idea of the quality of the surfaces that will be generated. It also helps you to magnify discontinuities in a curve. The **Direction 1** and **Direction 2** check boxes, available below the **Curvature combs** check box in this rollout, are used to toggle the display of curvature combs along the direction 1 and direction 2. You can also adjust the scale and density of curvature combs by using the **Curvature Comb Scale** and **Curvature Comb Density** spinners, respectively.

Figure 16-30 shows three curves for creating a boundary surface in direction 1 and Figure 16-31 shows the resultant boundary surface. Figure 16-32 shows six curves for creating a boundary surface in direction 1 and direction 2 and Figure 16-33 shows the resultant boundary surface.

Figure 16-34 shows the direction 2 curves extended beyond the direction 1 curves and Figure 16-35 shows the resultant preview of the boundary surface without trimming the direction 2 curves. Figure 16-36 shows the resultant preview of the boundary surface after trimming the direction 2 curves by using the direction 1 curves.

Figure 16-37 shows two sketches for creating a boundary surface in direction 1 and Figure 16-38 shows the resultant boundary surface with merge tangent faces. Figure 16-39 shows the resultant boundary surface without merge tangent faces.

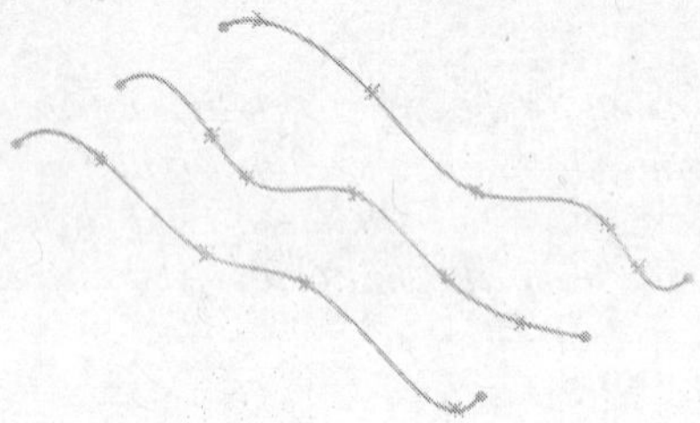

Figure 16-30 *Three curves for creating a boundary surface in direction 1*

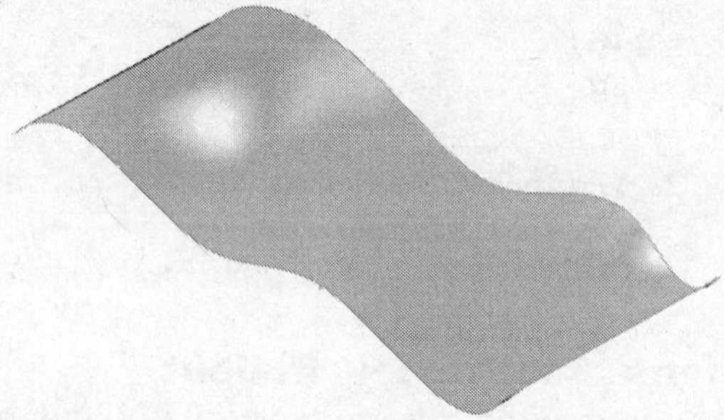

Figure 16-31 *Resultant boundary surface*

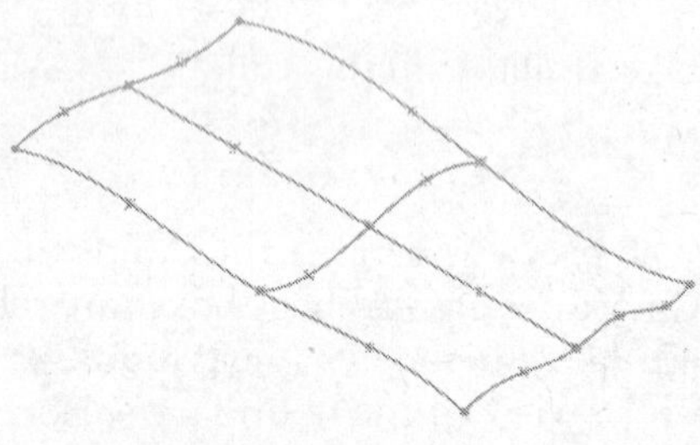

Figure 16-32 *Curves for creating a boundary surface in direction 1 and direction 2*

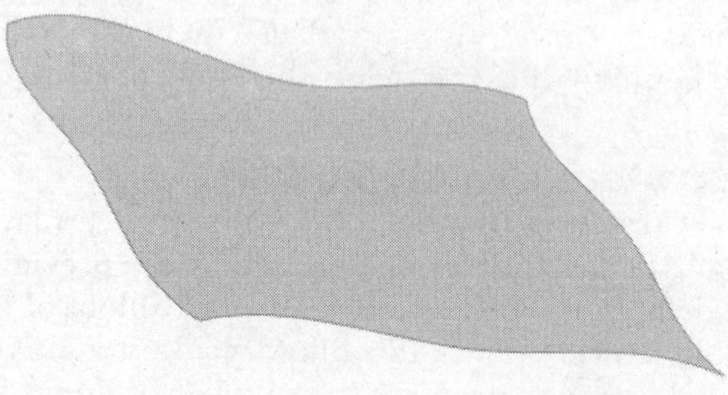

Figure 16-33 *The resultant boundary surface*

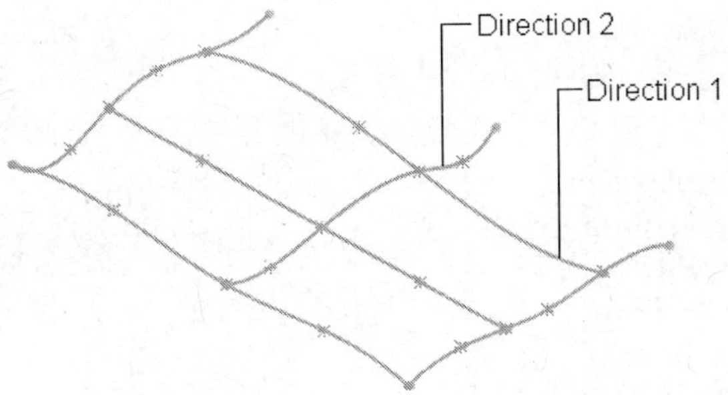

Figure 16-34 *The direction 2 curves extended beyond the direction 1 curves*

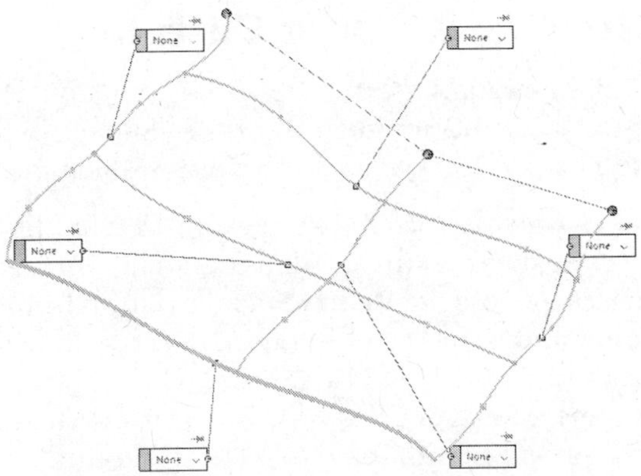

Figure 16-35 *Preview of the boundary surface without trimming the direction 2 curves*

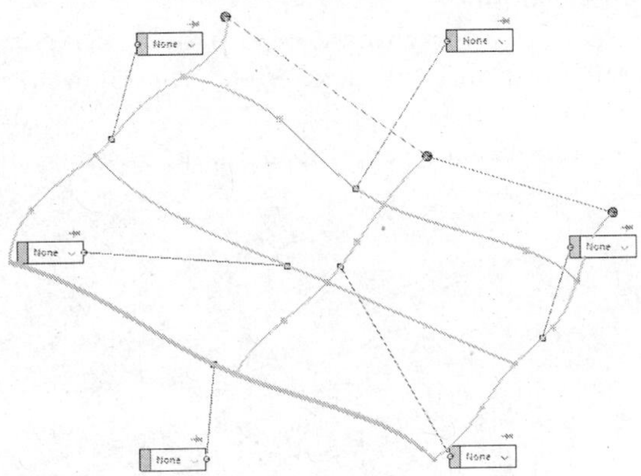

Figure 16-36 *Preview of the boundary surface after trimming the direction 2 curves by using the direction 1 curves*

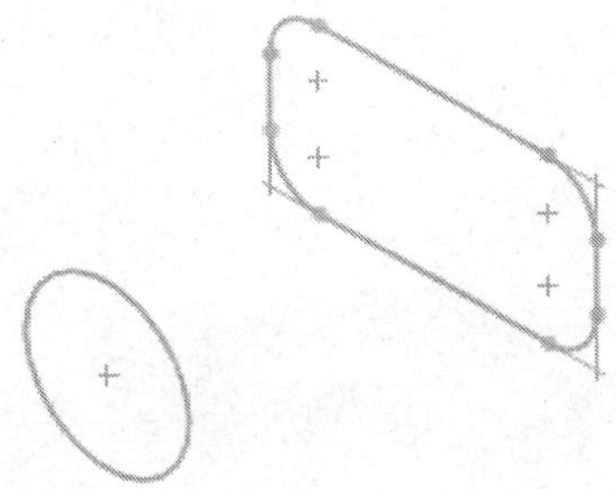

Figure 16-37 *The sketches for creating a boundary surface*

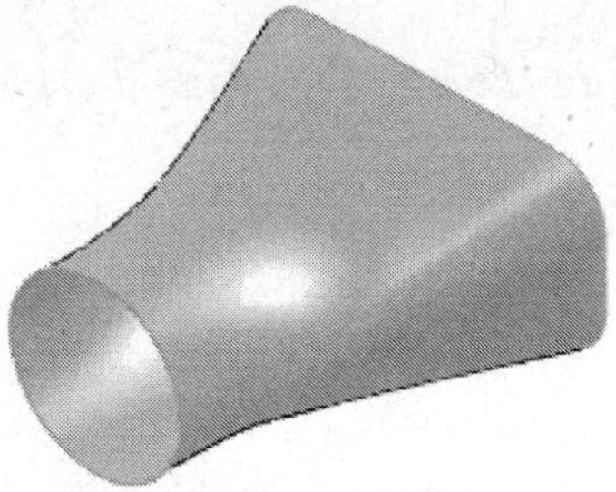

Figure 16-38 *The boundary surface with merge tangent faces*

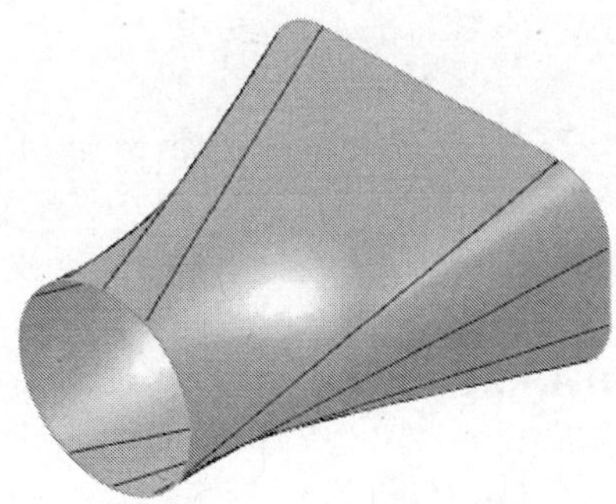

Figure 16-39 *The boundary surface without merge tangent faces*

Creating a Planar Surface

CommandManager:	Surfaces > Planar Surface
SOLIDWORKS menus:	Insert > Surface > Planar
Toolbar:	Surfaces > Planar Surface

A planar surface is generally used to fill gaps between surfaces using a planar patch. To create a planar surface, choose the **Planar Surface** button from the **Surfaces CommandManager** or choose **Insert > Surface > Planar** from the SOLIDWORKS menus; the **Planar Surface PropertyManager** will be displayed, as shown in Figure 16-40, and you will be prompted to select the bounding entities such as a sketch, an edge, or a curve.

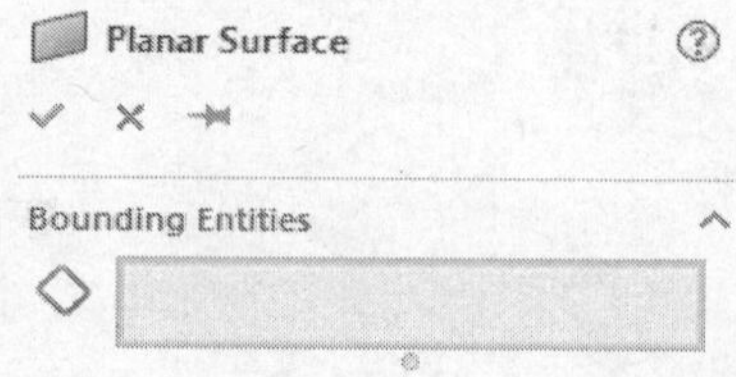

Figure 16-40** The **Planar Surface PropertyManager

Select the bounding entities; the names of the bounding entities will be displayed in the **Bounding Entities** rollout. Next, choose the **OK** button from the **Planar Surface PropertyManager**; a planar surface will be created using the selected entities. Note that the bounding entities should be coplanar.

Figure 16-41 shows the bounding entities to be selected for creating a planar surface and Figure 16-42 shows the resultant planar surface.

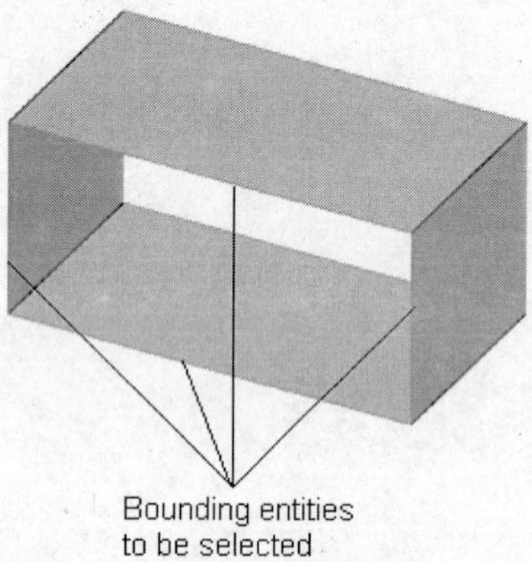

***Figure 16-41** Bounding entities to be selected*

***Figure 16-42** The resultant planar surface*

Creating a Fill Surface

CommandManager:	Surfaces > Filled Surface
SOLIDWORKS menus:	Insert > Surface > Fill
Toolbar:	Surfaces > Filled Surface

The **Filled Surface** tool is used to create a surface patch along N number of sides. The sides to be selected for creating a filled surface can be the edges of the existing model, 2D or 3D sketch entities, or 2D or 3D curves. The difference between a planar surface and a fill surface is that you cannot create a planar surface using 3D curves or edges. For example, the 3D edge created in Figure 16-43 cannot be used to create a planar surface. But, you can fill this gap by selecting the 3D edge and creating a fill surface.

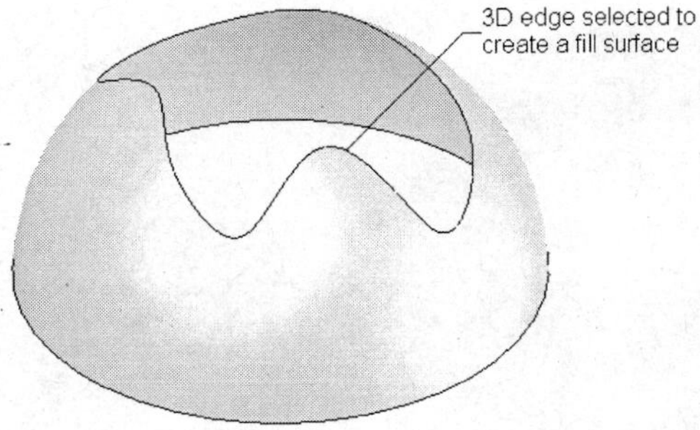

Figure 16-43 *Entity selected for creating a fill surface*

To create a fill surface, choose the **Filled Surface** button from the **Surfaces CommandManager**; the **Fill Surface PropertyManager** will be displayed, as shown in Figure 16-44, and you will be prompted to select bounding entities and set the required options. Select the entities that will define the boundary; the selected entities will be displayed in different color, and callouts will be attached to them. On selecting the last entity that will close the current selection chain, the preview of the fill surface along with the mesh will be displayed in the drawing area. Now, choose the **OK** the button from the **Fill Surface PropertyManager**. Figure 16-45 shows preview of the fill surface along with the mesh and Figure 16-46 shows the resultant fill surface.

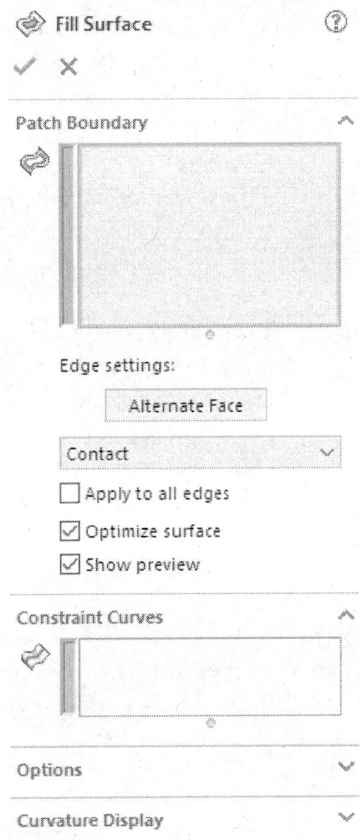

Figure 16-44 *The* ***Fill Surface PropertyManager***

Note
The surface model used in this example is created by trimming a surface. You will learn about trimming the surfaces later in this chapter.

The other options in the **Fill Surface PropertyManager** are discussed next.

Edge settings

The options in the **Edge settings** area are used to define various parameters to specify references with respect to the selected edges, type of curvature, and so on. These options are discussed next.

Alternate Face

The **Alternate Face** button in the **Edge settings** area is used to specify the face reference to be included while creating a fill surface for controlling the curvature of the fill surface. This option is only used when you are creating a fill surface on a solid body.

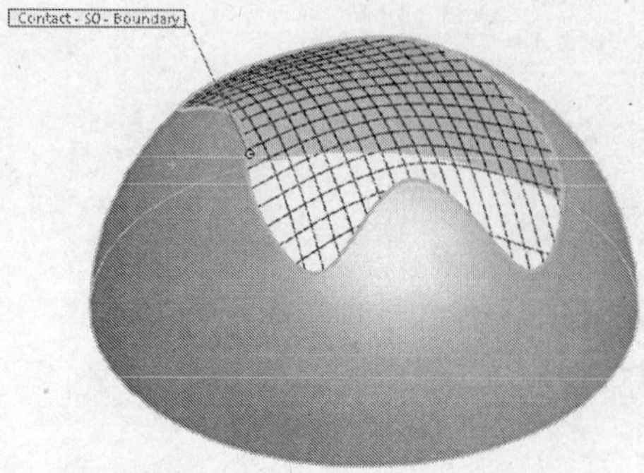

Figure 16-45 Preview of the fill surface along with the mesh

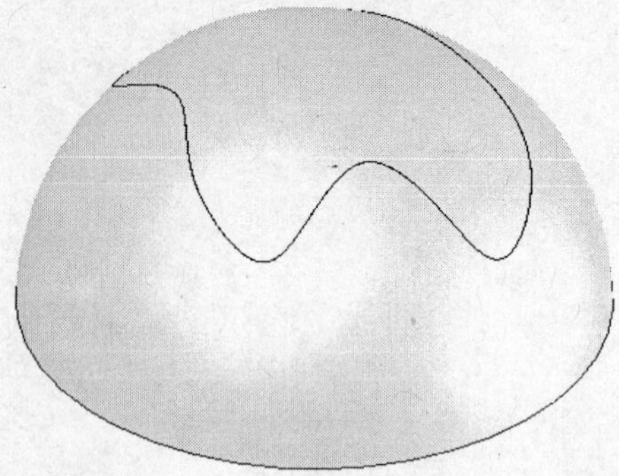

Figure 16-46 Resultant fill surface

Curvature Control

The **Curvature Control** drop-down list is used to define the type of curvature that you need to apply on the fill surface. There are different types of curvatures in this drop-down list that are discussed next.

Contact

The **Contact** option is selected by default and is used to create a patch using the fill surface option within the selected patch boundary.

Tangent

The **Tangent** option is selected to create a patch such that the resulting patch maintains tangency with the selected edges. On selecting this option for creating a patch, the **Reverse Surface** button is also displayed, if there is a possibility of creating a patch in the other direction. Choose this button to reverse the direction of the surface created.

Curvature

The **Curvature** option is selected to create a patch such that the resulting patch maintains curvature continuity with the selected edge.

Figure 16-47 shows the circular edge selected as the patch boundary. Figure 16-48 shows the fill surface created with the **Contact** option selected in the **Curvature Control** drop-down list. Figure 16-49 shows the fill surface created with the **Tangent** option selected in the **Curvature Control** drop-down list.

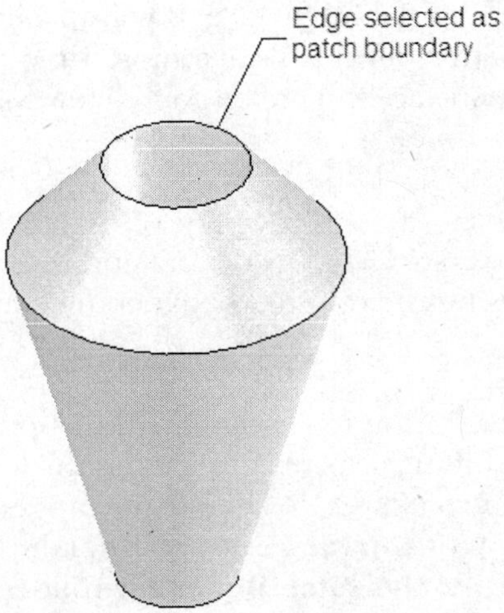

Figure 16-47 Edge selected as the patch boundary

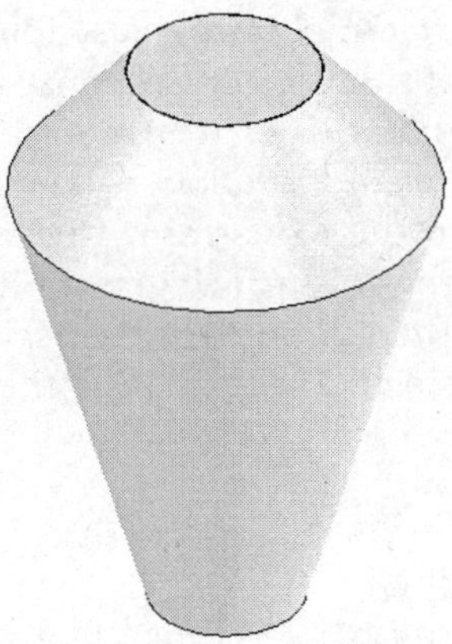

Figure 16-48 Fill surface created using the **Contact** option

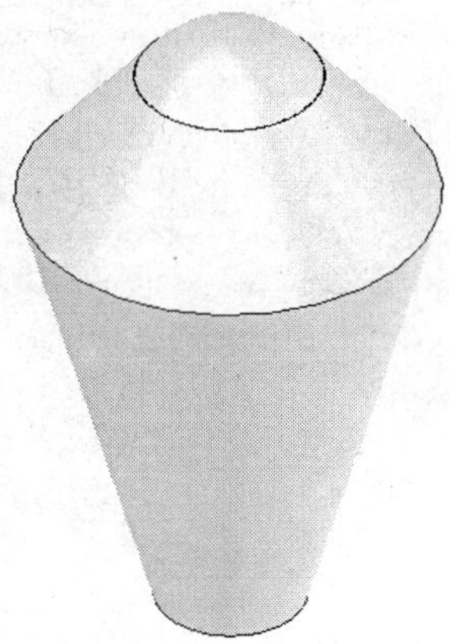

Figure 16-49 Fill surface created using the **Tangent** option

Apply to all edges

This option is used to apply curvature settings to all edges. If this check box is not selected, the current curvature setting will only be applied to the edge of the boundary that is selected in the **Patch Boundaries** selection box.

Optimize surface

The **Optimize surface** check box is selected to create a simple patch of a surface along the selected patch boundary. This check box is selected by default. Therefore, if you create a surface patch, the time taken to create a surface will be less and the model will be rebuilt faster. When you clear this check box, the **Resolution Control** rollout will be displayed, as shown in Figure 16-50. The slider available in this rollout is

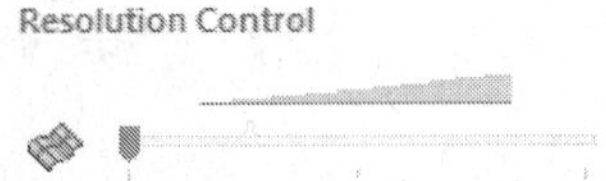

Figure 16-50 The **Resolution Control** rollout

used to specify the resolution of the fill surface. If you specify higher resolution, the quality of the fill surface will be better but it will take more time in rebuilding. In case of lower resolution, the quality of the surface will not be good. However, in such a case, the rebuilding of the model will take lesser time.

Show preview

The **Show preview** check box is selected by default and is used to display the preview of the fill surface that is created using the selected patch boundary.

Reverse Surface

Choose the **Reverse Surface** button to change the direction of filling the surface. You can reverse the direction of the fill surface only when it has the tangency or curvature continuity with the existing surface to be patched. To change the tangency or curvature continuity of a fill surface, select the **Tangent** or **Curvature** option from the **Curvature Control** drop-down list in the **Edge settings** area of the **Patch Boundary** rollout.

Constraint Curves

The **Constraint Curves** rollout is used to define constraint curves while creating a fill surface. To create a fill surface using constraint curves, invoke the **Fill Surface PropertyManager** and then select the patch boundary. Now, click once in the **Constraint Curves** selection box of the **Constraint Curves** rollout to invoke the selection mode and then select the constraint curves. Note that the constraint curves to be selected can be sketched entities, an edge, or a curve. The selected constraint curve will be displayed in a different color and a callout will be attached to it. Also, the name of the selected entity will be displayed in the **Constraint Curves** selection box. When you select the constraint curves, the preview of the fill surface gets modified. After specifying all constraint curves, choose the **OK** button from the **Fill Surface PropertyManager**. Figure 16-51 shows the sketch and the constraint curves selected for patching the boundary. Figure 16-52 shows the resultant fill surface.

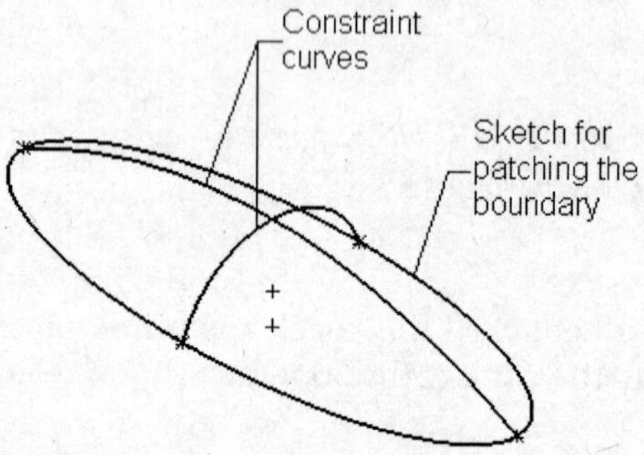

Figure 16-51 *Sketch and constraint curves to be selected*

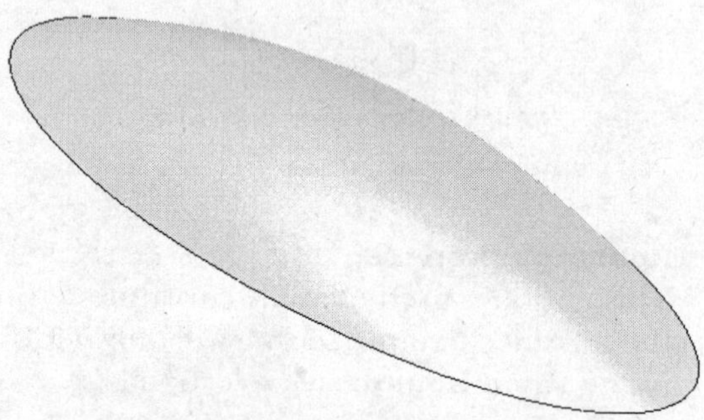

Figure 16-52 *Resultant fill surface*

Creating a Radiated Surface

CommandManager:	Surfaces > Radiate Surface *(Customize to Add)*
SOLIDWORKS menus:	Insert > Surface > Radiate
Toolbar:	Surfaces > Radiate Surface *(Customize to Add)*

In SOLIDWORKS, you can also create a surface by radiating a surface along an edge or a split line. The radiated surface is always created parallel to the plane or the face selected as the radiate direction reference. This type of surface is generally used in mold design as parting surface for extracting the core and cavity. To create a radiated surface, choose the **Radiate Surface** button from the **Surfaces CommandManager**; the **Radiate Surface PropertyManager** will be displayed, as shown in Figure 16-53.

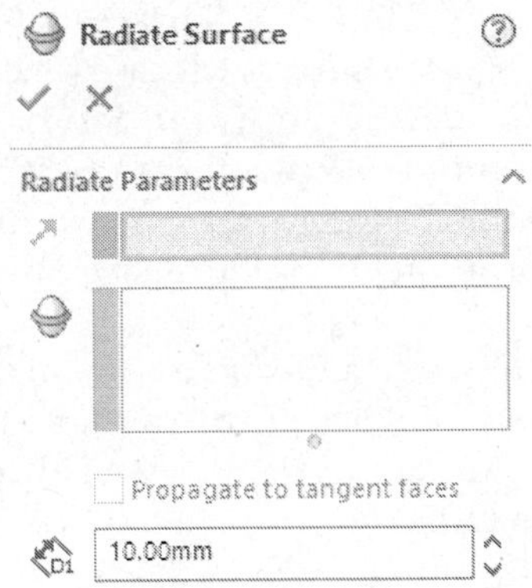

Figure 16-53 The ***Radiate Surface PropertyManager***

You will observe that the **Radiate Direction Reference** selection box is activated by default in this PropertyManager. Therefore, first you need to select a plane or a planar face parallel to which the surface will be radiated. The selected reference will be highlighted in a different color and an arrow symbol normal to the selected face will be displayed. On selecting a face, the **Edges To Radiate** selection box will be activated. Now, select the edges along which the surface will be radiated; the names of the selected edges will be displayed in the **Edges To Radiate** selection box. Note that the arrows will be displayed in the drawing area, showing the direction in which the surface will be radiated. Now, set the value of the distance of the surface to be radiated in the **Radiate Distance** spinner. The **Propagate to tangent faces** check box is used to radiate surfaces along all the edges that are tangent to the selected edge. After setting all parameters, choose the **OK** button from the **Radiate Surface PropertyManager**.

Figure 16-54 shows the radiate direction reference and the edges to be selected. Figure 16-55 shows the resultant radiated surface with the **Propagate to tangent faces** check box selected.

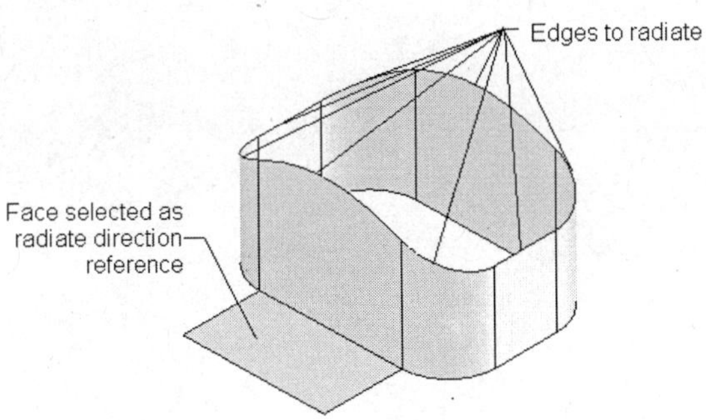

Figure 16-54 *Reference and the edges to be selected*

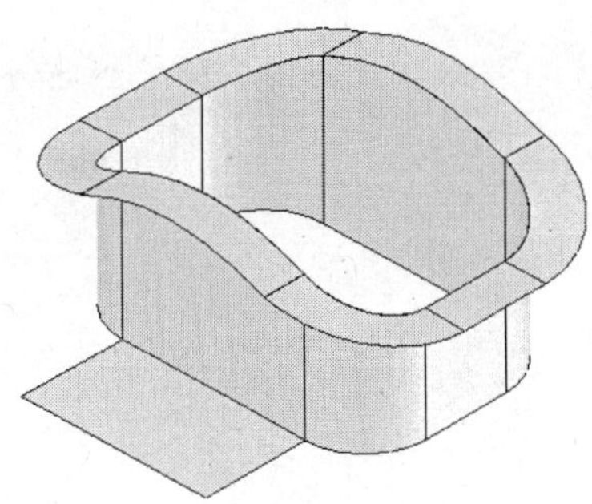

Figure 16-55 *The radiated surface created with the* ***Propagate to tangent faces*** *check box selected*

Offsetting Surfaces

CommandManager:	Surfaces > Offset Surface
SOLIDWORKS menus:	Insert > Surface > Offset
Toolbar:	Surfaces > Offset Surface

The **Offset Surface** tool is used to offset a selected surface or surfaces to a given distance. To offset a surface, choose the **Offset Surface** tool from the **Surfaces CommandManager**; the **Offset Surface PropertyManager** will be displayed, as shown in Figure 16-56, and you will be prompted to select a face or a surface to offset.

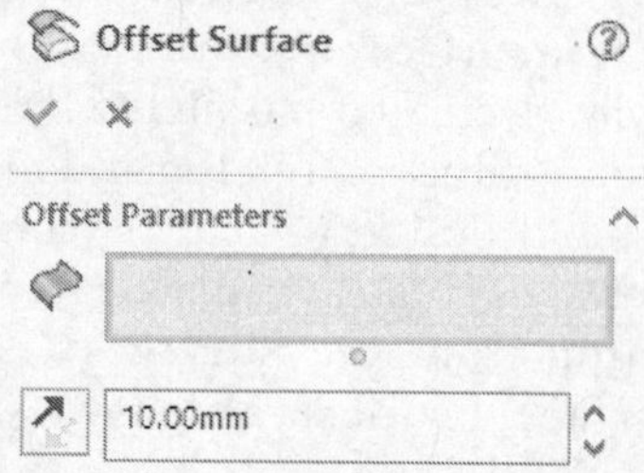

Figure 16-56** The **Offset Surface PropertyManager

Now, select the face or the surface that you need to offset; the selected face or the surface will be highlighted in a different color and its name will be displayed in the **Surface or Faces to Offset** selection box. Also, preview of the offset surface with the default value will be displayed in the drawing area. Set the value of the offset distance using the **Offset Distance** spinner. You can flip the direction of the surface creation using the **Flip Offset Direction** button available on the left of the **Offset Distance** spinner. After setting all parameters, choose the **OK** button from the **Offset Surface PropertyManager**. Figure 16-57 shows the surface selected to offset and Figure 16-58 shows the resultant offset surface. If the **Offset Surface** tool fails to create offset, the **Offset Surface PropertyManager** lists and highlights the failing faces in the **Offset Parameters** area. Right-click on any of the failing faces then choose **Remove All Failing Faces** to remove all failing face from the short-cut menu.

Tip

*If you want to extract a surface from a solid body or a surface body, invoke the **Offset Surface PropertyManager** and select the surfaces to be extracted. Next, enter **0** in the **Offset Distance** spinner; the **Offset Surface PropertyManager** turns to **Copy Surface PropertyManager**. Choose the **OK** button from the **Copy Surface PropertyManager**.*

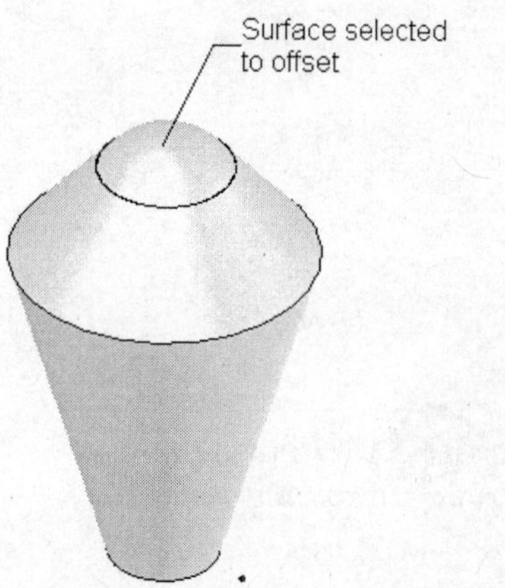

***Figure 16-57** Surface selected to offset*

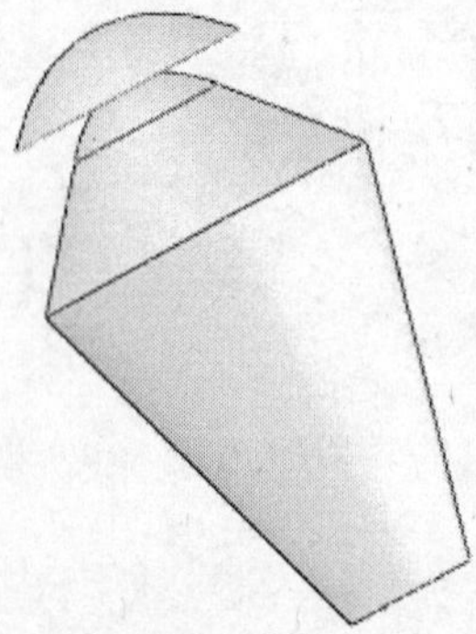

***Figure 16-58** Resultant offset surface*

Trimming Surfaces

CommandManager:	Surfaces > Trim Surface
SOLIDWORKS menus:	Insert > Surface > Trim
Toolbar:	Surfaces > Trim Surface

The **Trim Surface** tool is used to trim surfaces using an entity as the trim tool. A surface, a sketched entity, or an edge can be used as a trim tool. To trim a surface, choose the **Trim Surface** button from the **Surfaces CommandManager**; the **Trim Surface PropertyManager** will be displayed, as shown in Figure 16-59, and you will be prompted to select pieces to keep or remove.

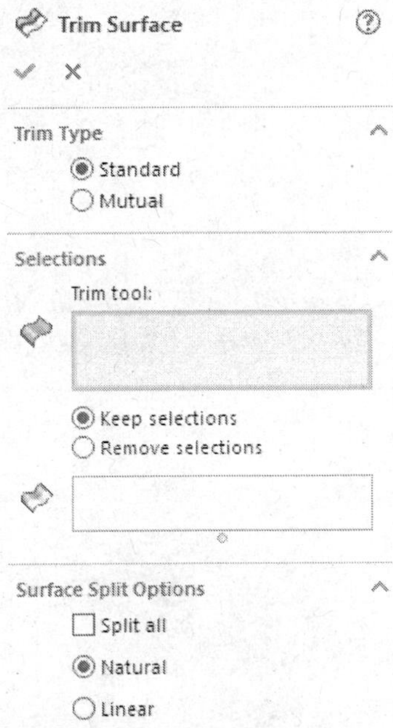

*Figure 16-59 The **Trim Surface** PropertyManager*

There are two methods of trimming a surface, namely Standard trim and Mutual trim. The **Standard** radio button is selected by default in the **Trim Type** rollout of the PropertyManager. Therefore, while using the first method, if you select the trimming surface using the cursor, this surface will act as a trim tool. You can select a surface, a plane, a sketch, or an edge as a trimming surface. On doing so, the selected entity will be highlighted in a different color and the name of the trimming surface will be displayed in the **Trim tool** display area. By default, the **Keep selections** radio button is selected in the **Selections** rollout. Also, the selection mode in the **Pieces to Keep** selection box will be activated and you will be prompted to select pieces to keep. Also, the cursor will be replaced by the surface body cursor when you move it on the surface. Move the cursor on the surface being trimmed; the pieces of the surface on which you place the cursor will be displayed in a different color. Select the piece or pieces of the surface to keep; the selected pieces will be displayed in different color and their names will be displayed in the **Pieces to Keep** selection box. Next, choose the **OK** button from the **Trim Surface PropertyManager**. If you select the **Remove selections** radio button, the **Pieces to Keep** selection box will change into **Pieces to Remove** selection box. As a result, the selected surfaces will be removed.

Figure 16-60 shows the trimming surface and the piece to keep after trimming. Figure 16-61 shows the resultant trimmed surface. Figure 16-62 shows the sketch selected as a trimming entity and Figure 16-63 shows the resultant trimmed surface.

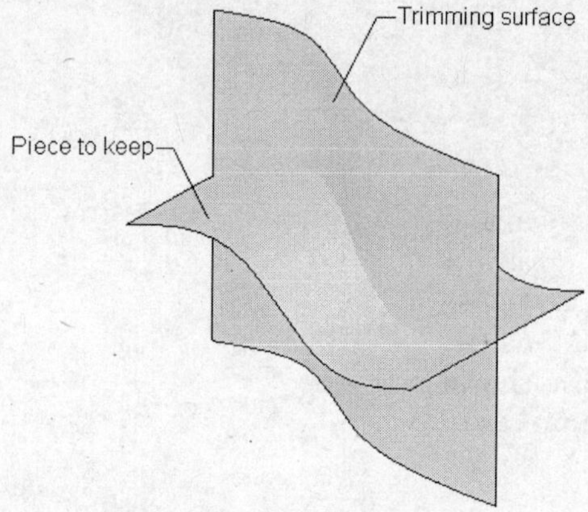

Figure 16-60 Trimming surface and the piece to keep after trimming the surface

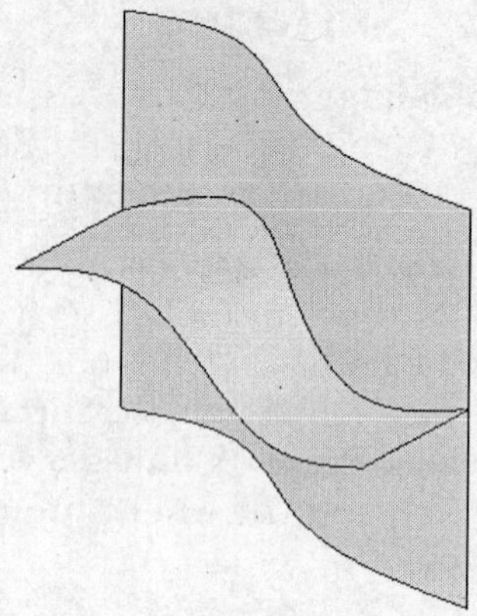

Figure 16-61 Resultant trimmed surface

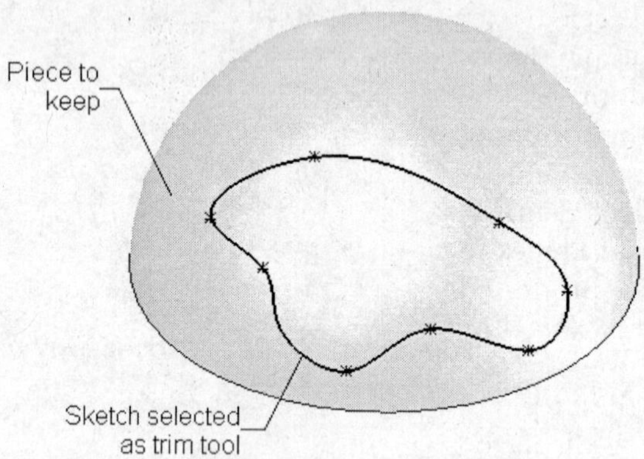

Figure 16-62 Sketch selected as a trimming entity

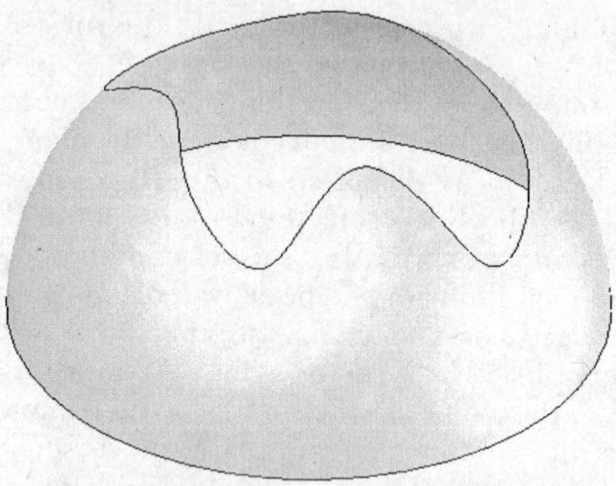

Figure 16-63 Resultant trimmed surface

The other method of trimming a surface is known as the Mutual trim method. In this method, you need to select two surfaces as the trimming surfaces. To trim these surfaces, invoke the **Trim Surface PropertyManager** and then choose the **Mutual** radio button from the **Trim Type** rollout; you will be prompted to select the surfaces to trim, followed by the pieces to keep. First, select the trimming surfaces and then select the pieces to keep, refer to Figure 16-64. After setting all parameters, choose the **OK** button from the **Trim Surface PropertyManager**. Figure 16-65 shows the resultant trimmed surface.

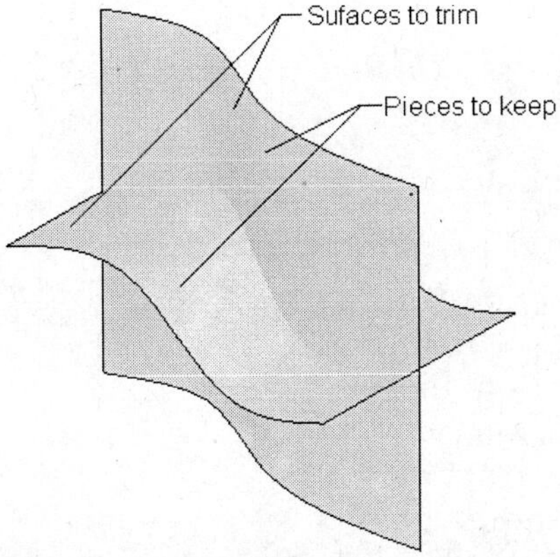

Figure 16-64 Surfaces to trim and pieces to keep

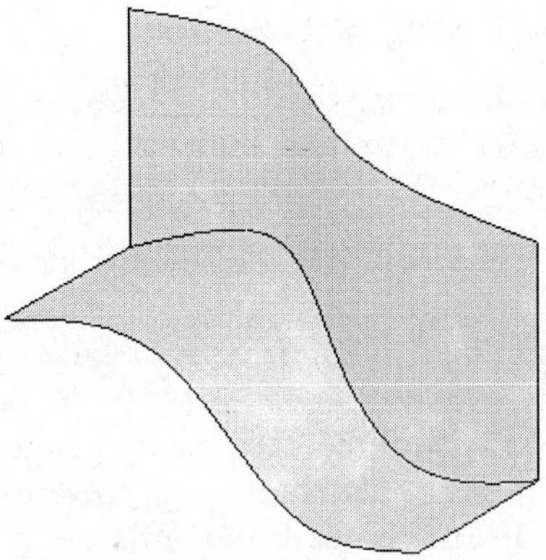

Figure 16-65 Resultant trimmed surface

If you select the **Split all** check box in the **Surface Split Options** rollout then all possible splits in the target surface are displayed. By default, the **Natural** radio button is selected in the **Surface Split Options** rollout. As a result, the endpoint of the split line will be extended tangentially to the boundary of target surface. If you select the **Linear** radio button from the **Surface Split Options** rollout then the endpoint of the split line will be extended linearly to the boundary of the target surface. Figure 16-66 shows the trimming of surface when the **Natural** radio button is selected and Figure 16-67 shows the trimming of surface when the **Linear** radio button is selected.

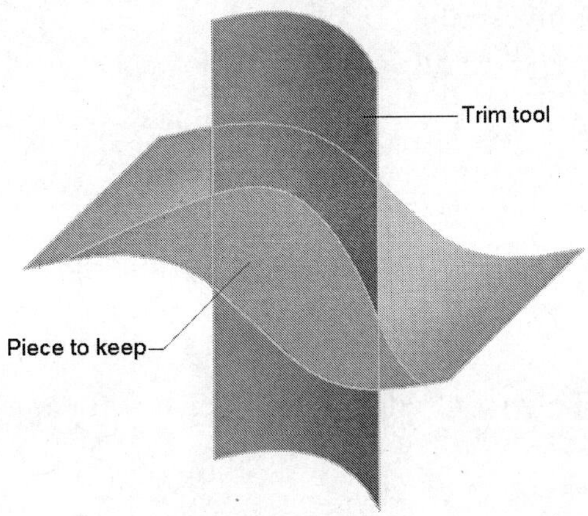

*Figure 16-66 Piece to keep when the **Natural** radio button is selected*

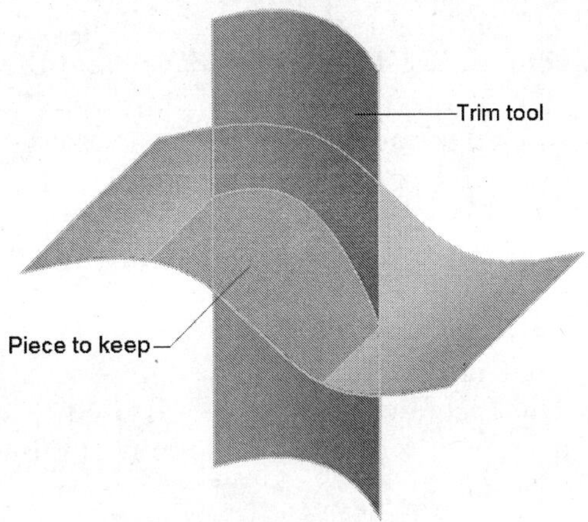

*Figure 16-67 Piece to keep when the **Linear** radio button is selected*

Untrimming Surfaces

CommandManager:	Surfaces > Untrim Surface
SOLIDWORKS menus:	Insert > Surface > Untrim
Toolbar:	Surfaces > Untrim Surface

The **Untrim Surface** tool is used to create a surface patch by extending the existing surfaces. Using this tool, you can fill the trimmed portion of a surface with a surface patch. To untrim a surface, choose **Insert > Surface > Untrim** from the SOLIDWORKS menus. Alternatively, choose the **Untrim Surface** button from the **Surfaces CommandManager**; the **Untrim Surface PropertyManager** will be displayed, as shown in Figure 16-68 and you will be prompted to select the surface bodies or edges of a surface. Select the surface bodies to be untrimmed.

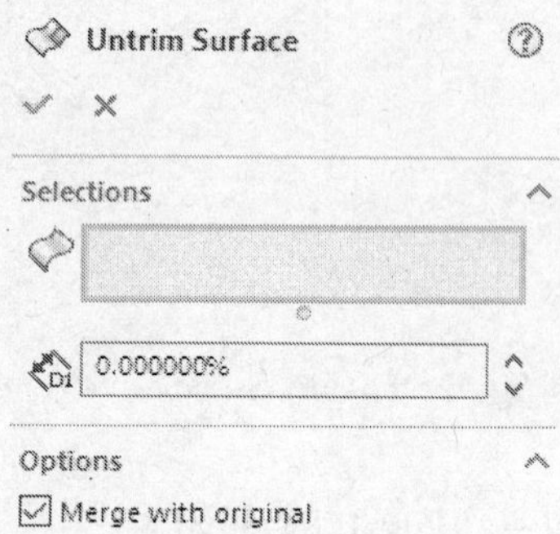

Figure 16-68 The Untrim Surface PropertyManager

In SOLIDWORKS, there are two methods to untrim surfaces. In the first method, you need to select the face that you want to untrim and in the second method, you need to select the edges of the trimmed portion of the surface. Both these methods are discussed next.

Untrimming Surfaces by Selecting Faces

In this method, you will untrim the surface by selecting the face or faces of the surface to be untrimmed. To do so, invoke the **Untrim Surface PropertyManager** and then select the face of the surface that needs to be untrimmed; the preview of the untrimmed surface with the default settings will be displayed in the drawing area. As soon as you select the face or faces of the surface to untrim, the **Options** rollout will be displayed with different options, as shown in Figure 16-69. These options are discussed next.

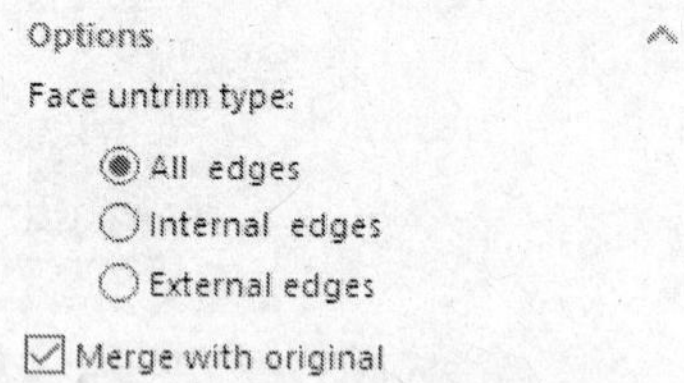

*Figure 16-69 The **Options** rollout*

Face untrim type

The **Face untrim type** area is used to specify the type of edges along which you want to untrim the surface. The options in this area are discussed next.

All edges

The **All edges** radio button is selected by default. As a result, all internal and external edges of the selected surface are extended to be untrimmed. Figure 16-70 shows the surface selected and Figure 16-71 shows the resultant untrimmed surface with the **All edges** radio button selected.

Internal edges

Select the **Internal edges** radio button to patch only the internal edges of a selected surface. Figure 16-70 shows the surface selected for untrimming and Figure 16-72 shows the resultant untrimmed surface with the **Internal edges** radio button selected.

External edges

Select the **External edges** radio button to patch only the external edges of a selected surface. Figure 16-70 shows the surface selected for untrimming and Figure 16-73 shows the resultant untrimmed surface with the **External edges** radio button selected.

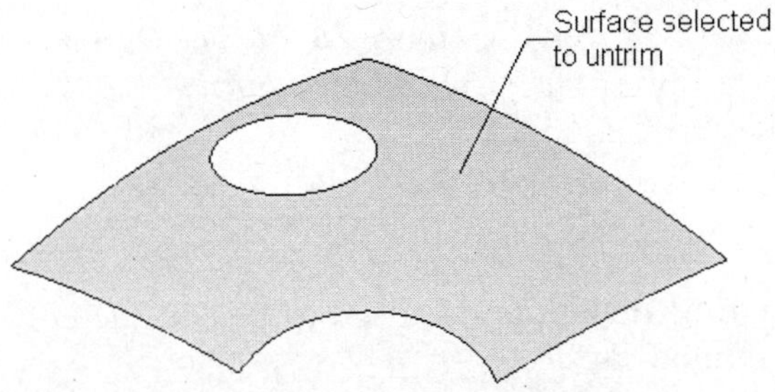

Figure 16-70 Surface selected to be untrimmed

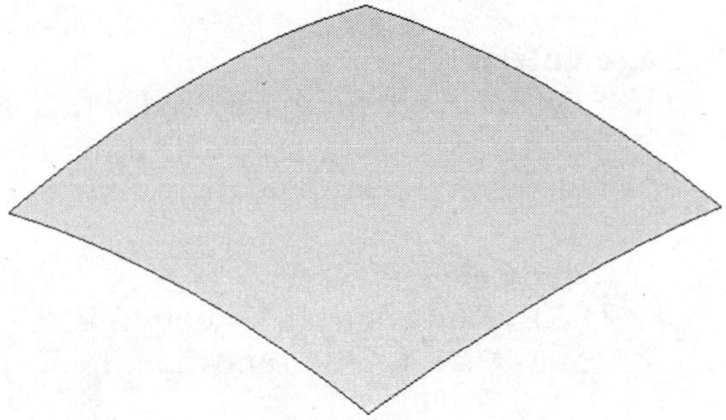

*Figure 16-71 Resultant untrimmed surface with the **All edges** radio button selected*

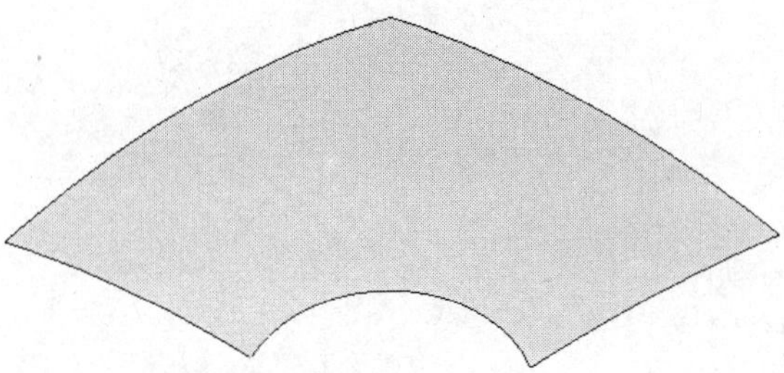

*Figure 16-72 Resultant untrimmed surface with the **Internal edges** radio button selected*

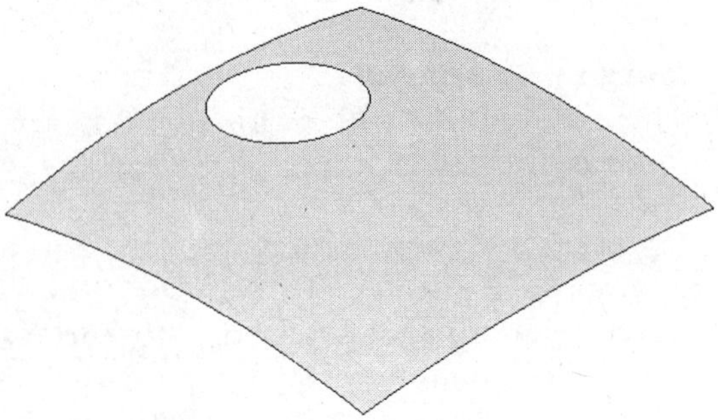

*Figure 16-73 Resultant untrimmed surface with the **External edges** radio button selected*

Merge with original

The **Merge with original** check box is used to merge the untrimmed surface created with the original surface. This check box is selected by default in the **Options** rollout. If you clear this check box, the resultant untrimmed surface will be a separate surface body.

You can also specify the percentage of distance up to which you need to extend the surface depending on the type of edges selected from the **Face untrim type** area of the **Options** rollout. The **Distance** spinner is used to define the percentage of distance for extending the surface. A preview of the surface extension is displayed in the drawing area.

Untrimming Surfaces by Selecting Edges

You can also patch a trimmed surface using the **Untrim Surface** tool by selecting the edges of the trimmed portion of the surface. To do so, invoke the **Untrim Surface PropertyManager** and then select the edge of the surface along which you want to patch the trimmed surface; the preview of the patched surface will be displayed in the drawing area. As soon as you select the edge of the surface to patch the trimmed surface, the **Options** rollout will be displayed with different options, as shown in Figure 16-74. These options are discussed next.

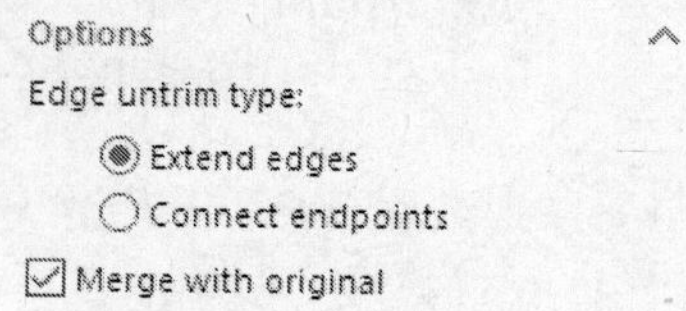

*Figure 16-74 The **Options** rollout with different options*

Edge untrim type

The **Edge untrim type** area is used to specify the options for patching the trimmed surface by using the selected edges. The options in this area are discussed next.

Extend edges

The **Extend edges** radio button is selected by default and is used to extend the edge to create a corner for untrimming the trimmed surface.

Connect endpoints

The **Connect endpoints** radio button is selected to patch the trimmed surface by joining the endpoints of the selected edge.

Merge with original

The use of **Merge with original** check box is the same as discussed earlier.

Figure 16-75 shows the edge to be selected to untrim a surface. Figure 16-76 shows an untrimmed surface created with the **Extend edges** radio button selected. Figure 16-77 shows the untrimmed surface created with the **Connect endpoints** radio button selected.

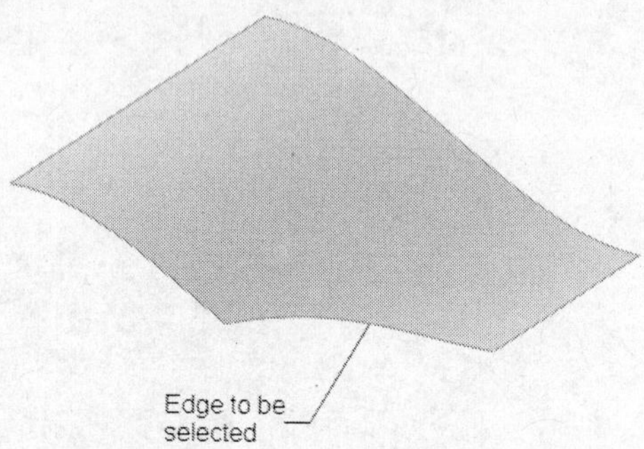

Figure 16-75 Edge to be selected to untrim the surface

*Figure 16-76 Untrimmed surface created by selecting the **Extend edges** radio button*

*Figure 16-77 Untrimmed surface created by selecting the **Connect endpoints** radio button*

Extending Surfaces

CommandManager:	Surfaces > Extend Surface
SOLIDWORKS menus:	Insert > Surface > Extend
Toolbar:	Surfaces > Extend Surface

The **Extend Surface** tool is used to extend a surface along a selected edge or a selected face. To extend a surface, choose the **Extend Surface** button from the **Surfaces CommandManager**; the **Extend Surface PropertyManager** will be displayed, refer to Figure 16-78. Also, you will be prompted to select a face or edge(s) and set the properties to extend. There are two methods to extend a surface and these are discussed next.

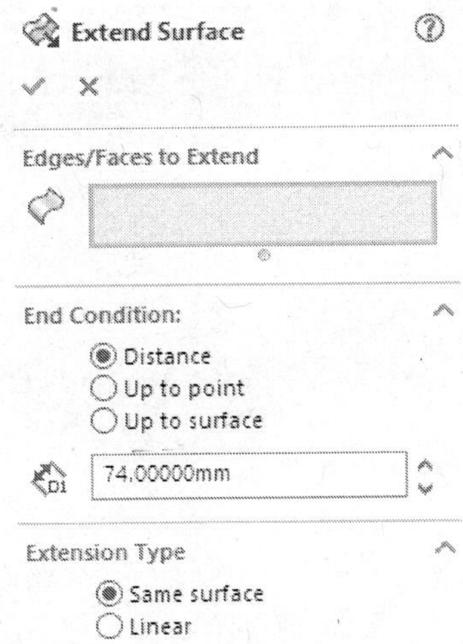

Figure 16-78 The ***Extend Surface PropertyManager***

Extending a Surface Using the Same surface Option

You can extend a surface by using the **Same surface** radio button in the **Extension Type** rollout of the **Extend Surface PropertyManager**. Select this radio button to extend a surface by maintaining its curvature. After selecting this radio button, you need to select the edge or face that you need to extend. Note that when you select the face to extend the surface, the surface extends equally in all directions. You can extend a surface dynamically using the drag handle or set the extending distance in the **Distance** spinner available in the **End Condition** rollout. You can also use other feature termination options available in the **End Condition** rollout. By default, the **Distance** radio button is selected in the **End Condition** rollout. If you want to extend the surface up to a particular point or vertex, select the **Up to point** radio button from the **End Condition** rollout and then select the required point or vertex from the drawing area. If you want to extend the surface up to a particular surface, select the **Up to surface** radio button and then select the required surface from the drawing area. After setting all parameters, choose the **OK** button from the **Extend Surface PropertyManager**.

Figure 16-79 shows the edge selected to extend the surface. Figure 16-80 shows preview of the surface being extended by selecting the edge with the **Same surface** radio button selected. Figure 16-81 shows the face selected to extend the surface. Figure 16-82 shows preview of the surface being extended by selecting the face with the **Same surface** radio button selected.

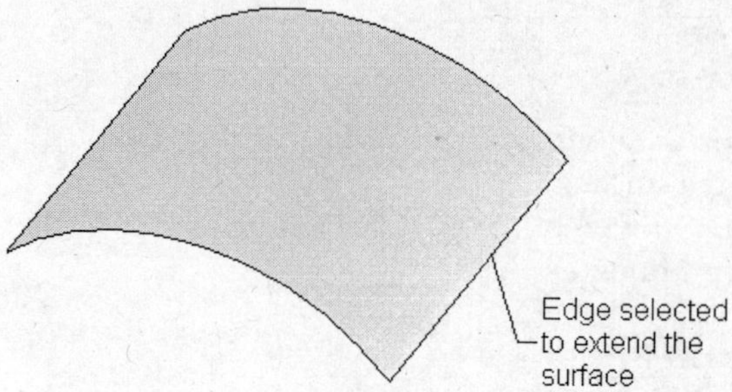

Figure 16-79 *Edge selected to extend the surface*

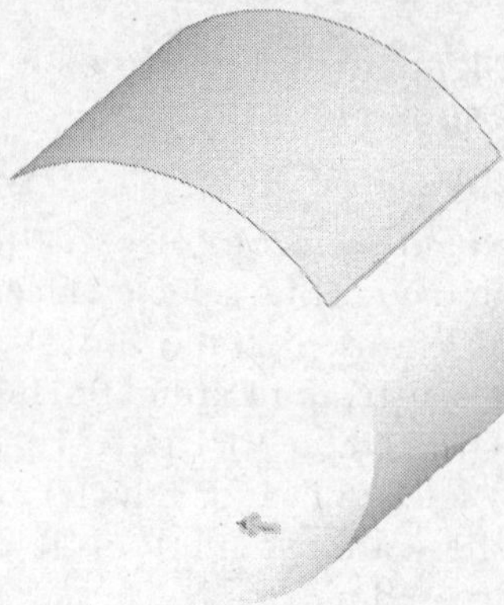

Figure 16-80 *Preview of the extended surface with the **Same surface** radio button selected*

Note

If any edge of the selected surface is merged with another surface, the surface will not extend along that edge.

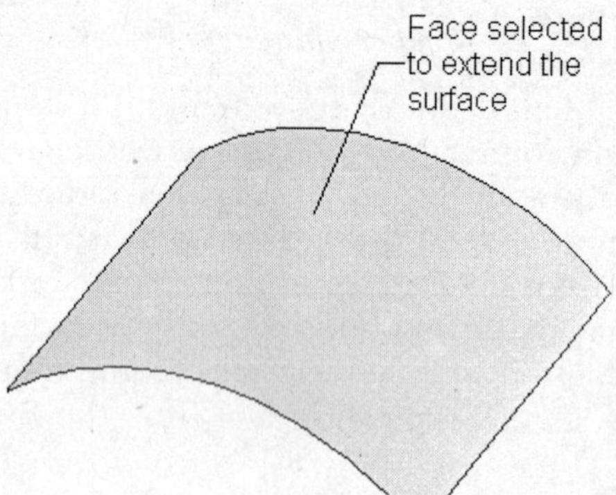

Figure 16-81 *Face selected to extend the surface*

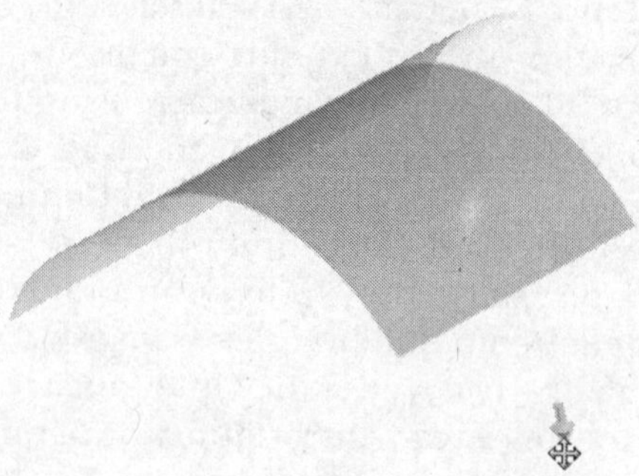

Figure 16-82 *Preview of the extended surface with the **Same surface** radio button selected*

Extending a Surface Using the Linear Option

You can extend a surface in the linear direction up to an existing surface by maintaining tangency. To do so, invoke the **Extend Surface PropertyManager** and then select the **Linear** radio button from the **Extension Type** rollout. Next, select the face or the edge along which you need to extend the surface and then specify the feature termination using the **End Condition** rollout. After setting all parameters, choose the **OK** button.

Figure 16-83 shows the edge selected to extend the surface and Figure 16-84 shows preview of the surface being extended with the **Linear** radio button selected. Figure 16-85 shows the face selected to extend the surface and Figure 16-86 shows preview of the surface being extended with the **Linear** radio button selected.

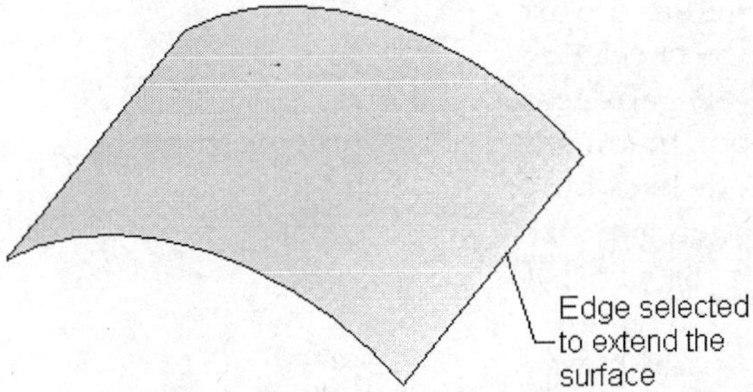

Figure 16-83 Edge selected to extend the surface

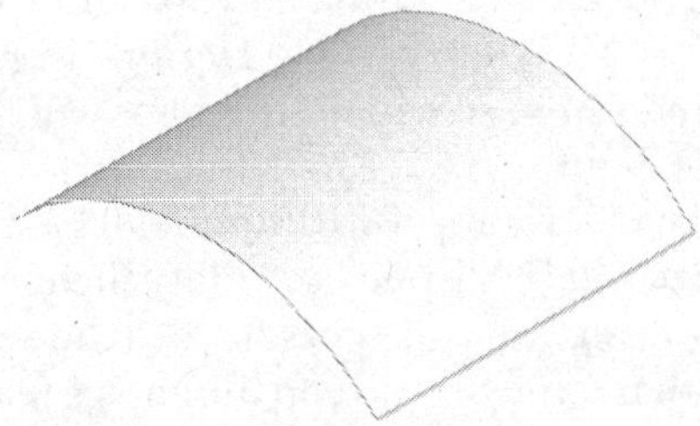

Figure 16-84 Preview of the extended surface with the **Linear** radio button selected

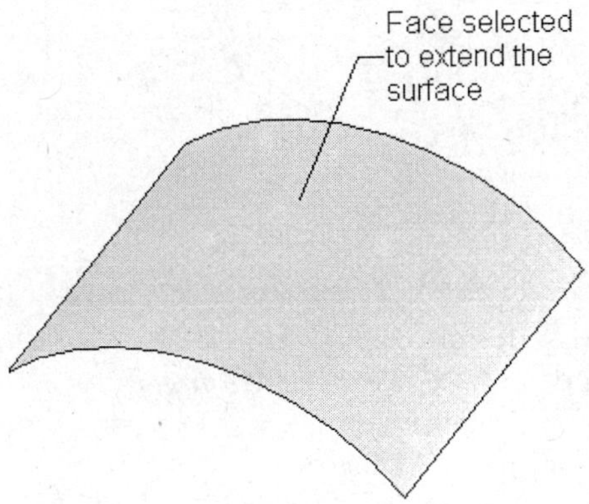

Figure 16-85 Face selected to extend the surface

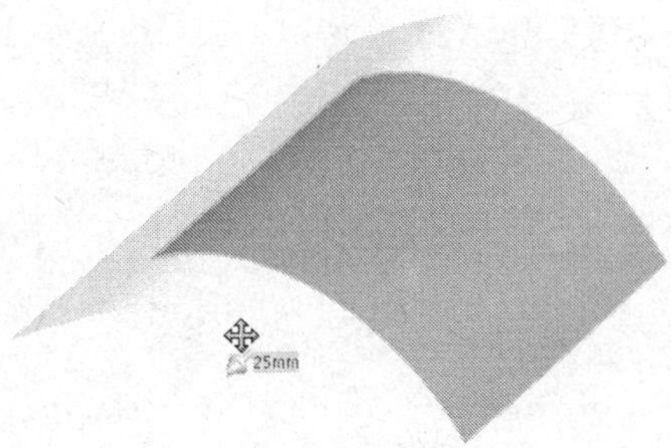

Figure 16-86 Preview of the extended surface with the **Linear** radio button selected

Knitting Surfaces

CommandManager:	Surfaces > Knit Surface
SOLIDWORKS menus:	Insert > Surface > Knit
Toolbar:	Surfaces > Knit Surface

The **Knit Surface** tool is used to knit multiple surfaces together to create a single surface. You can also knit a surface with the faces of a solid body. The surfaces to be knitted together must be in contact with each other. This means that you cannot knit disjointed surfaces or faces. The **Knit Surface** tool is widely used for extracting core and cavity while designing a mold.

To knit surfaces, choose the **Knit Surface** button from the **Surfaces CommandManager**; the **Knit Surface PropertyManager** will be displayed, refer to Figure 16-87. Select the surfaces to be knitted together; the names of surfaces will be displayed in the **Surfaces and Faces to Knit** selection box of the **Selections** rollout. Specify the knitting tolerance in the **Knitting tolerance** spinner. If the size of a gap is lower than the tolerance specified then the gap will be knitted and closed. Specify a tolerance if you want to display the gaps, which are within that range. Depending on the knitting tolerance and range specified, the gaps will be listed in the list box, refer to Figure 16-87. Move the cursor near the check box in the list box; a tooltip with the message **Knit all gaps less than gap size** will be displayed. Select the check box to knit all gaps. Now, if you move the cursor near the selected check box, a tooltip with the message **Keep all gaps greater than gap size** will be displayed. Clear the check box to retain the gaps, if needed. Select the **Create solid** check box to convert the knitted entities to solid. Select the **Merge entities** check box to merge all knitted surfaces. After specifying all parameters, choose the **OK** button from the **Knit Surface PropertyManager**; a knitted surface will be created.

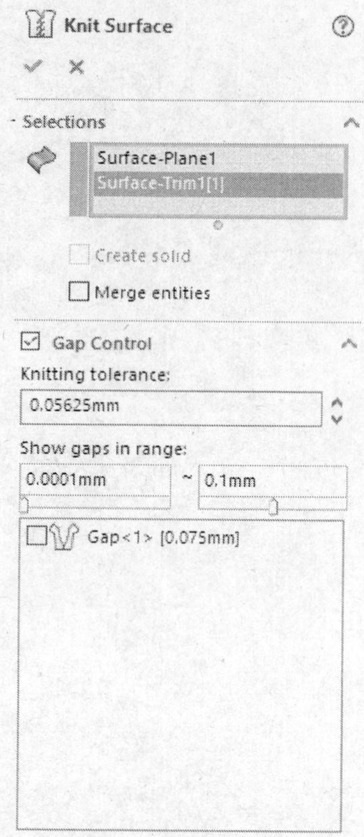

*Figure 16-87 The **Knit Surface PropertyManager***

Filleting Surfaces

CommandManager:	Surfaces > Fillet
SOLIDWORKS menus:	Insert > Surface > Fillet/Round
Toolbar:	Surfaces > Fillet

You can add fillets on sharp edges of surfaces by using the **Fillet** tool. The procedure of filleting the surfaces is the same as filleting solid models discussed earlier. But there are some exceptions. These exceptions are discussed next.

1. While applying the face fillet to a surface, you need to define the direction in which the fillet needs to be added.

2. You cannot use the **Keep features** option while filleting a surface.

3. You cannot select a surface using the **FeatureManager Design Tree** while filleting all the edges in a surface.

While applying face fillet, by default the **Trim and attach** radio button is selected in the **Trim surfaces** area of the **Fillet Options** rollout. As a result, the filleted faces will be trimmed and knit into a single surface. Select the **Don't trim or attach** radio button if you want to create the fillet as a new surface and not as a single trimmed and knitted surface.

Note

You can only fillet the edge of surface that is created at the intersection of two surfaces. Make sure that if an edge is created using two surfaces, then you need to knit them before filleting.

Creating a Mid-Surface

CommandManager:	Surfaces > Mid-Surface	*(Customize to add)*
SOLIDWORKS menus:	Insert > Surface > Mid Surface	
Toolbar:	Surfaces > Mid-Surface	*(Customize to add)*

The **Mid-Surface** tool is used to create a surface between the two parallel faces of a solid model. You can define the placement of a surface in terms of percentage value with respect to the face selected first. Note that the faces to be selected to create a mid-surface should be two parallel faces or two concentric curved faces. To create a mid surface, choose the **Mid-Surface** button from the **Surfaces CommandManager**; the **MidSurface1 PropertyManager** will be displayed, as shown in Figure 16-88. Also, you will be prompted to either select the face pairs manually or use the **Find Face Pairs** button to automatically recognize the face pairs. Next, select the faces between which you need to create the mid-surface. On doing so, both the selected faces will be highlighted in different colors. Also, the names of the selected faces will be displayed in the **Face pairs** display area. By default, the mid-surface is placed in the middle of the selected faces. You can also define the percentage distance for the placement of the mid-surface using the **Position** spinner that is available in the **Selections** rollout of the PropertyManager. The position of the mid-surface is defined from the first selected surface. After setting all the parameters, choose the **OK** button from the **MidSurface1 PropertyManager**.

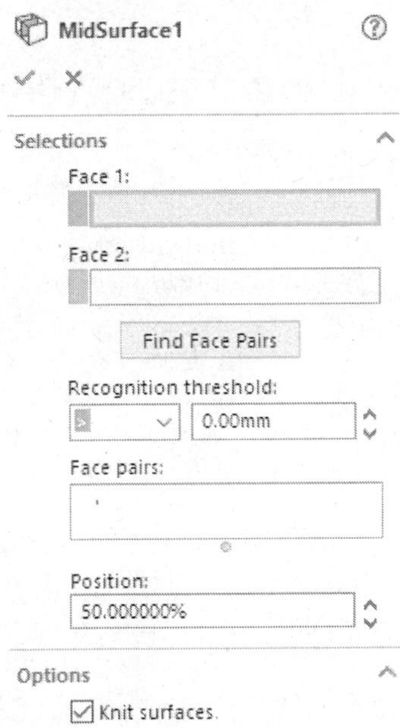

Figure 16-88** The **MidSurface1 PropertyManager

Figure 16-89 shows the offset faces to be selected and Figure 16-90 shows the mid-surface created in the middle of the selected faces.

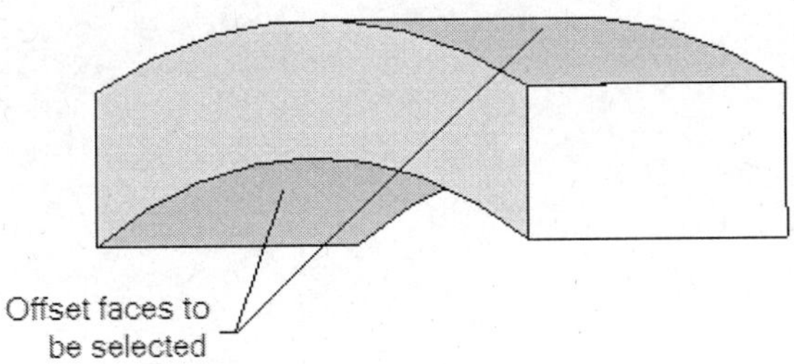

***Figure 16-89** Offset faces to be selected*

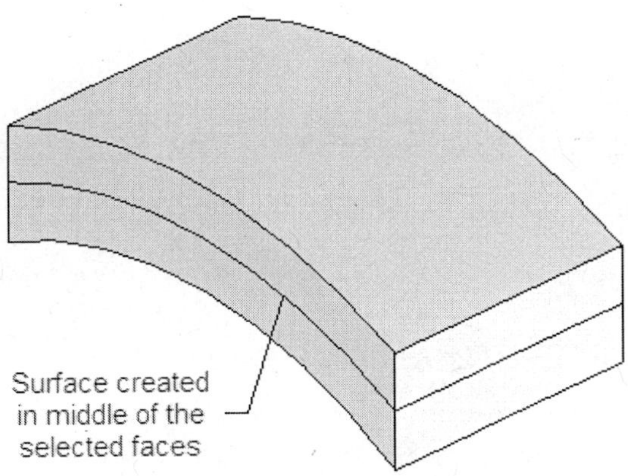

***Figure 16-90** Resultant mid-surface*

The **Find Face Pairs** button is used to find the faces that are adjacent to the selected face. The options in the **Recognition threshold** area are used to filter the faces depending on the wall thickness of the face searched using the **Find Face Pairs** option. Using the **Threshold Operator** drop-down list in the **Recognition threshold** area, you can set the mathematical operators such as >, <, =, and so on. Using the **Threshold Thickness** spinner, you can specify the threshold thickness.

Deleting Holes from Surfaces

CommandManager:	Surfaces > Delete Hole
SOLIDWORKS menus:	Insert > Surface > Delete Hole

The **Delete Hole** tool is used to delete holes from a surface or any closed contours that cut surface. To do so, select an edge from the drawing area and choose the **Delete Hole** tool from the **CommandManager**; the **Delete Hole PropertyManager** will be displayed, as shown in Figure 16-91; the empty area of the selected edge will be patched and the tangency and curvature with the surrounding surfaces will be maintained.

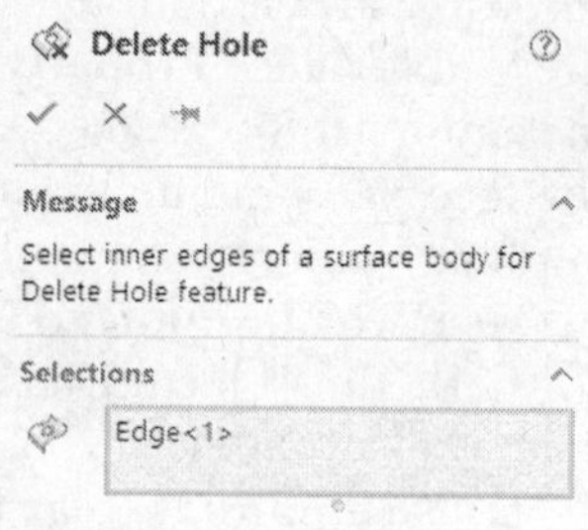

***Figure 16-91** The Delete Hole PropertyManager*

You can also select more edges to delete the hole; the name of selected edge/s will be displayed in the **Selected Edges to remove** selection box in the **Selections** rollout. Choose the **OK** button from this PropertyManager; you will notice that the **DeleteHole** node is added in the **FeatureManager Design Tree**.

Figure 16-92 shows the edge of the closed contour to be selected. Figure 16-93 shows the hole deleted using the **Delete Hole** tool.

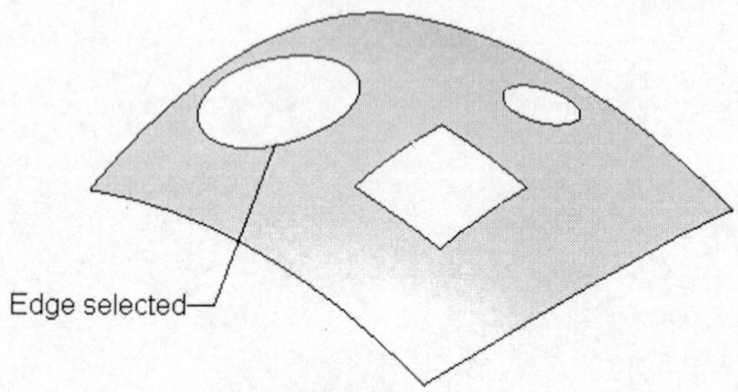

***Figure 16-92** Edge selected*

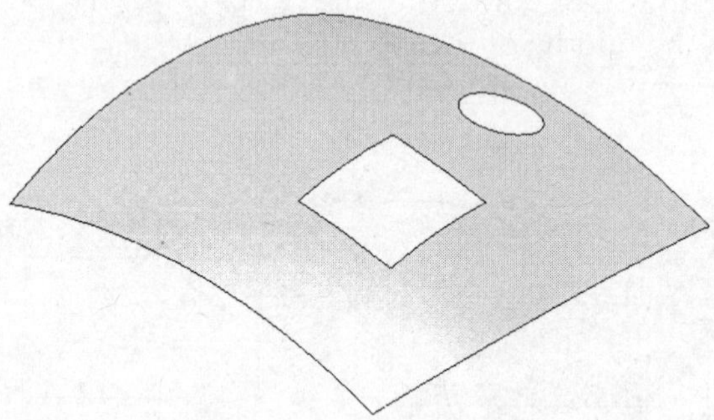

***Figure 16-93** Resultant surface*

Replacing Faces

CommandManager:	Surfaces > Replace Face
SOLIDWORKS menus:	Insert > Face > Replace
Toolbar:	Surfaces > Replace Face

In SOLIDWORKS, you can replace the selected faces of a solid body with one or more surfaces. When you replace the selected faces with another surface or surfaces, the resultant solid body retains the shape of the replaced surface by adding or subtracting material from the solid body. To replace a surface, choose the **Replace Face** button from the **Surfaces CommandManager**; the **Replace Face1 PropertyManager** will be displayed, as shown in Figure 16-94.

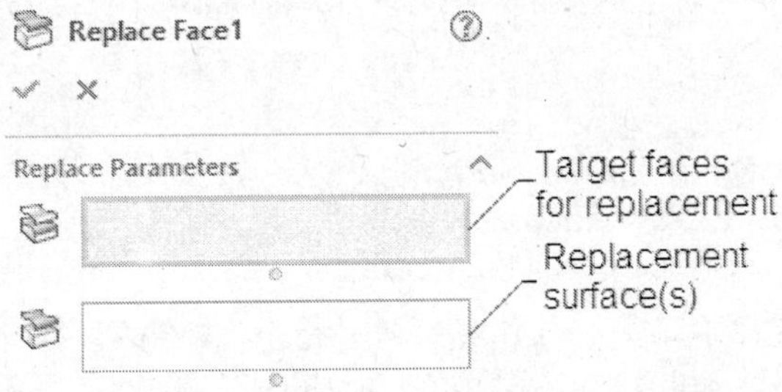

Figure 16-94 *The* ***Replace Face1 PropertyManager***

Select the face to be replaced; the name of the selected face will be displayed in the **Target faces for replacement** selection box. Next, click once in the **Replacement surface(s)** selection box to invoke the selection mode. Now, select the replacement surface; the name of the replacement surface will be displayed in the **Replacement surface(s)** selection box. Choose the **OK** button from the **Replace Face1 PropertyManager**; the selected face of the solid body will be replaced.

Figure 16-95 shows the target face to be replaced and the replacement surface. Figure 16-96 shows the resultant replaced face. Figure 16-97 shows the solid body after hiding the surface body. To hide the surface body, select the surface body and then invoke the shortcut menu. Then, choose the **Hide** option from the shortcut menu.

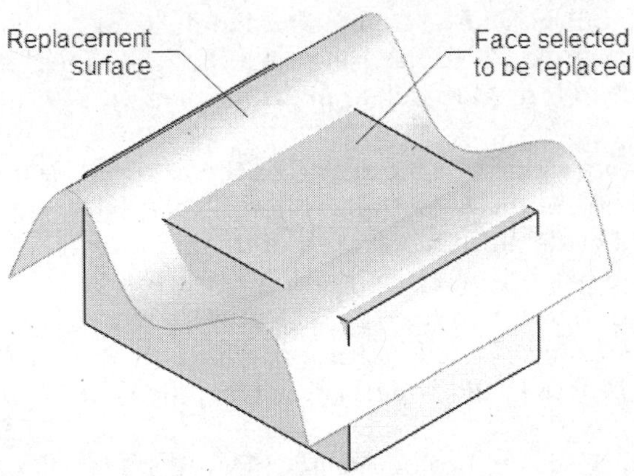

Figure 16-95 *The target face and the replacement surface*

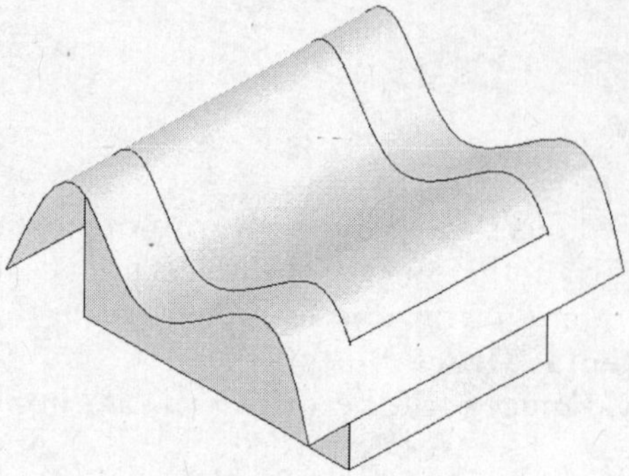

Figure 16-96 Resultant replaced face

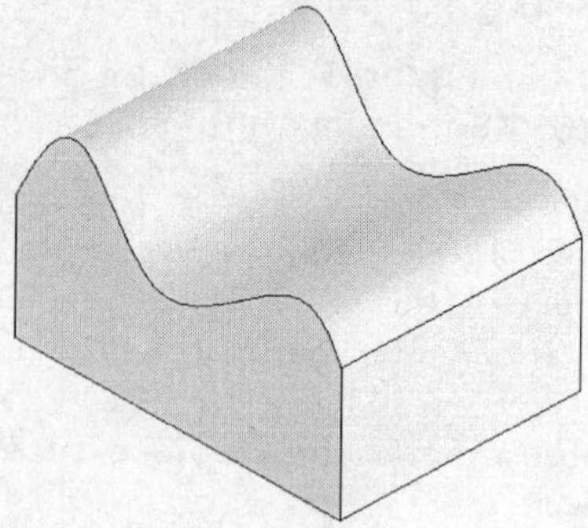

Figure 16-97 Model after hiding the surface

Deleting Faces

CommandManager:	Surfaces > Delete Face
SOLIDWORKS menus:	Insert > Face > Delete
Toolbar:	Surfaces > Delete Face

The **Delete Face** tool is used to delete the faces of the selected surface or the solid body. When you delete a face of a solid body, the solid body is converted into a surface body. If you patch the deleted face, the solid body will not be converted into a surface body. To delete a face, choose the **Delete Face** button from the **Surfaces CommandManager**; the **Delete Face PropertyManager** will be displayed, as shown in Figure 16-98.

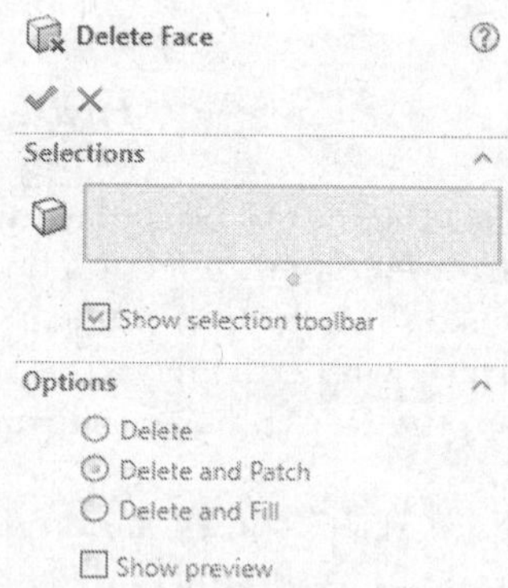

Figure 16-98** The **Delete Face PropertyManager

The **Delete** radio button in the **Options** rollout of the **Delete Face PropertyManager** is used to delete the faces of a solid body without patching and trimming it. In this case, the solid body is converted into a surface body. The **Delete and Patch** radio button is selected by default. It is used to delete the faces of a solid or a surface body by patching and trimming it. The **Show preview** check box will be invoked only when the **Delete and Patch** radio button is selected. And it is used to display the preview of the model in the drawing area. The **Delete and Fill** radio button is used to delete multiple faces and generate a single face.

Select the face or faces to be deleted; the name of the selected face will be displayed in the **Faces to delete** selection box of the **Selections** rollout. Next, select the **Delete and Patch** radio button, if it is not selected by default; the preview of the model will be displayed in the drawing area. If the preview of the patch is not displayed, it confirms that the selected face cannot be deleted and patched. In this case, you need to select the **Delete** radio button from the **Options** rollout so that the face gets only deleted, but not patched. After setting all parameters, choose the **OK** button from the **Delete Face PropertyManager**; the resulting model will be displayed.

Figure 16-99 shows the face selected to be deleted. Figure 16-100 shows the face deleted with the **Delete and Patch** radio button selected. Figure 16-101 shows the face deleted with the

Delete radio button selected. Figure 16-102 shows multiple faces to be selected to generate a single face. Figure 16-103 shows a single face generated using the **Delete and Fill** radio button.

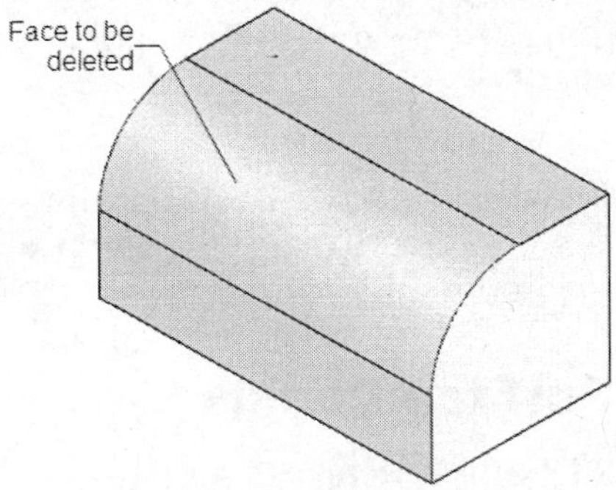

Figure 16-99 *Face to be deleted*

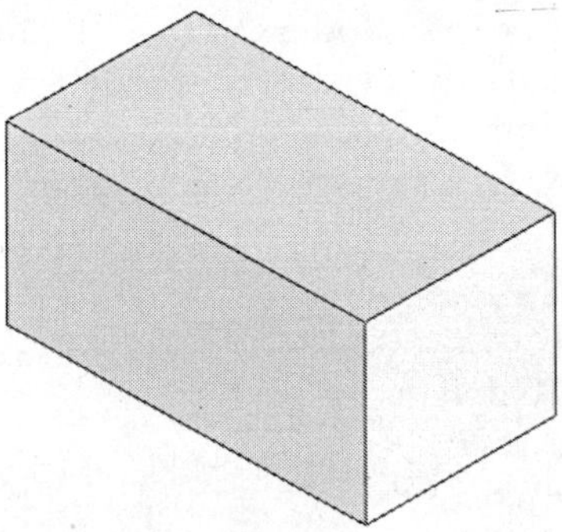

Figure 16-100 *Face deleted with the* ***Delete and Patch*** *radio button selected*

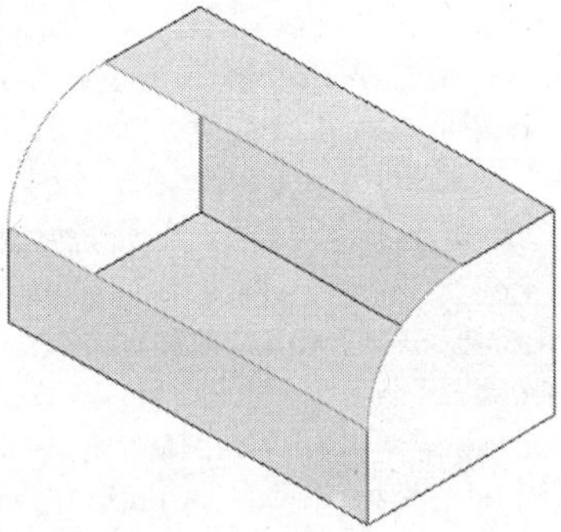

Figure 16-101 *Face deleted with the* ***Delete*** *radio button selected*

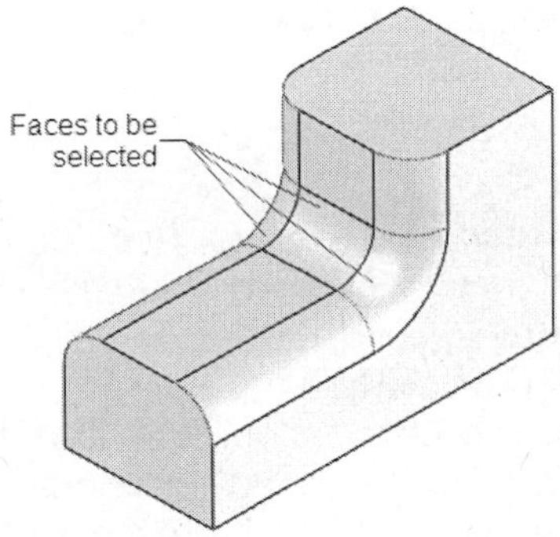

Figure 16-102 *Faces to be selected to generate a single face*

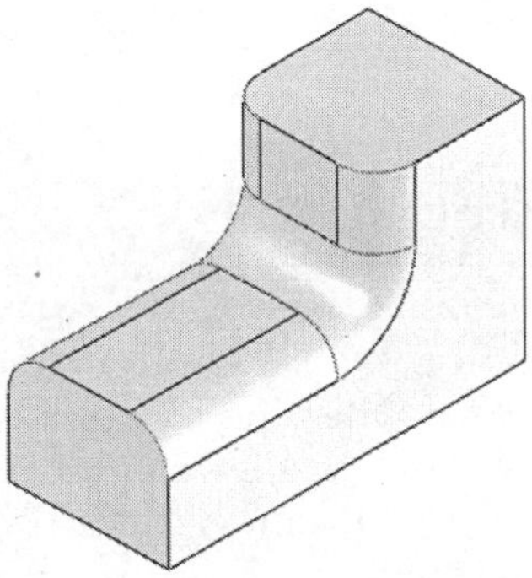

Figure 16-103 *Face deleted with the* ***Delete and Fill*** *radio button selected*

Note

You can also delete surface bodies using the ***Delete/Keep Body PropertyManager****. The procedure of deleting surface bodies is the same as deleting solid bodies discussed earlier.*

Moving and Copying Surfaces

You can move and copy the surfaces using the **Move/Copy Bodies** tool. The methods of moving and copying surface bodies using the **Move/Copy Bodies** tool are the same as those discussed for moving and copying solid bodies.

Mirroring Surface Bodies

You can mirror the surface bodies using the **Mirror** tool. The procedure of mirroring surface bodies is the same as that discussed in the solid bodies.

Adding Thickness to Surface Bodies

CommandManager:	Surfaces > Thicken
SOLIDWORKS menus:	Insert > Boss/Base > Thicken

In SOLIDWORKS, you can also add thickness to the surface bodies. There are two methods of adding thickness to surface bodies. In the first method, you need to add wall thickness to the surface body. In the second method, you need to solidify the closed, stitched surface body to create a solid body. These two methods are discussed next.

Adding Thickness to a Surface Body

To add thickness to a surface body, choose the **Thicken** tool from the **Surfaces CommandManager** or choose **Insert > Boss/Base > Thicken** from the SOLIDWORKS menus; the **Thicken PropertyManager** will be displayed, as shown in Figure 16-104. Also, you will be prompted to select the surface to thicken. Select the surface; preview of the thickened body with default values will be displayed in the drawing area. Using the buttons in the **Thickness** area of this PropertyManager, you can specify the side on which you want to thicken the surface. You can specify the direction of thickness by selecting any linear sketch entity, sketch point, reference plane, reference axis, or linear edge in the drawing area. The selected entity will get displayed in the **Direction of Thicken** box. You can also specify the wall thickness by using the **Thickness** spinner available in the **Thicken Parameters** rollout. Select the **Merge result** check box if you want to merge existing solid body from the drawing area with the thickened surface. This check box will only be available if a surface and a solid is present in the drawing area. After setting all the parameters, choose the **OK** button from the **Thicken PropertyManager**; thickness will be added to the surface body. Figure 16-105 shows surface body to be thickened and Figure 16-106 shows the model after adding thickness to surface body.

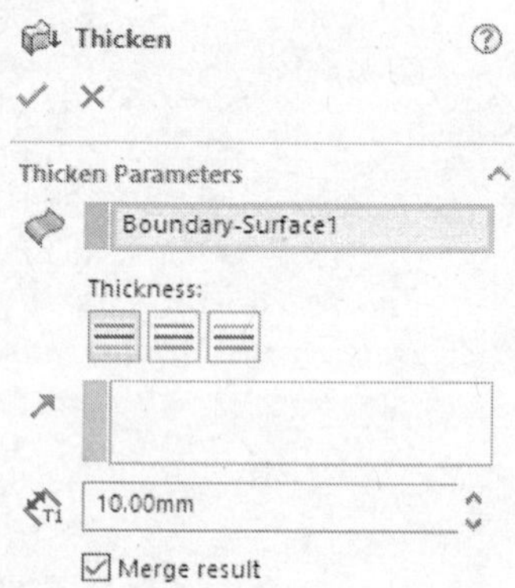

Figure 16-104 The Thicken PropertyManager

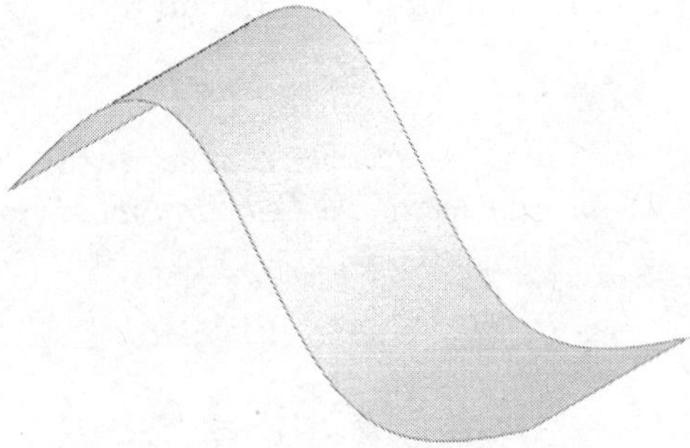

Figure 16-105 Surface to be thickened

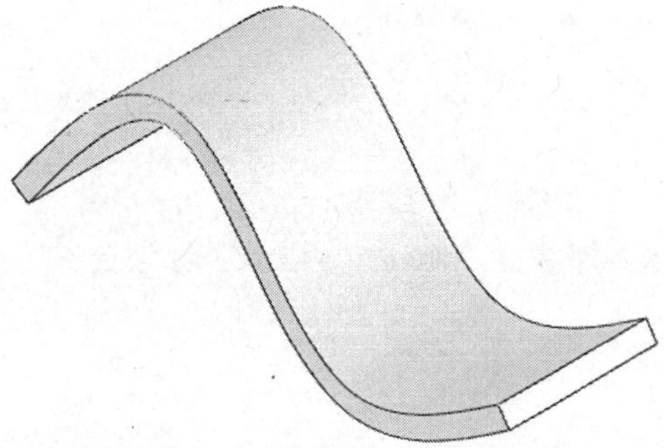

Figure 16-106 Model after thickening the surface

Solidifying a Closed Surface Body

To solidify a closed surface body, the surface body needs to be free from any type of gap and all surfaces should be stitched together using the **Knit** tool. To solidify the surface body, invoke the **Thicken PropertyManager** and then select a closed surface body; the **Create solid from enclosed volume** check box will be displayed. Select this check box; the **Thickness** area and the **Thickness** spinner will be disabled. Next, choose the **OK** button from the **Thicken PropertyManager**; a solid volume will be created from the closed surface.

> **Tip**
> *If the surface model to be thickened consists of multiple joined surface bodies, you first need to knit the surfaces together and then add thickness to them.*

Creating a Thicken Surface Cut

CommandManager:	Surfaces > Thickened Cut
SOLIDWORKS menus:	Insert > Cut > Thicken

*Figure 16-107 The **Cut-Thicken PropertyManager***

In SOLIDWORKS, you can cut a solid body by thickening a surface. To do so, create a solid body and a surface intersecting each other and then choose the **Thickened Cut** button from the **Surfaces CommandManager**; the **Cut-Thicken PropertyManager** will be displayed, as shown in Figure 16-107. Also, you will be prompted to select the surface to be thickened. Select the surface that you want to use as the cutting tool and then specify the parameters for defining the side in which you want to add thickness and thickness of cut. On doing so, a preview will be displayed in the drawing area. Now, choose the **OK** button from the **Cut-Thicken PropertyManager**. If the thicken cut results in the creation of multiple bodies, the **Bodies to Keep** dialog box will be displayed. Using this dialog box, you can define the bodies that you need to keep.

Figure 16-108 shows the surface selected for creating the thicken cut. Figure 16-109 shows the resultant thicken surface cut. You can specify direction of thicken same as **Thicken** tool.

> **Tip**
> *If you create a thicken surface cut or a surface cut on multiple solid bodies, the* ***Feature Scope*** *rollout will be displayed with different options and you can specify the bodies on which you need to add this feature.*

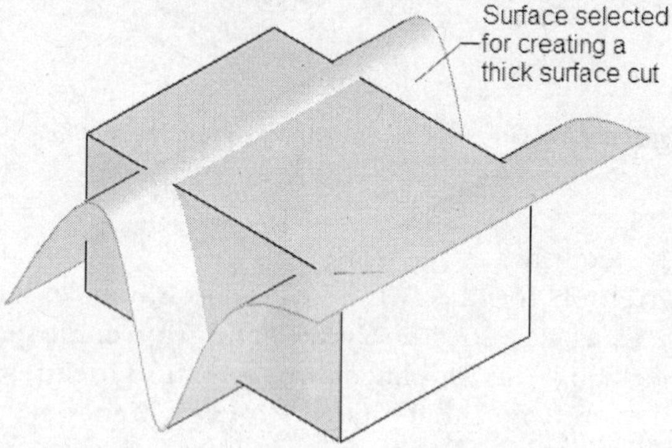

Figure 16-108 *Surface to be selected*

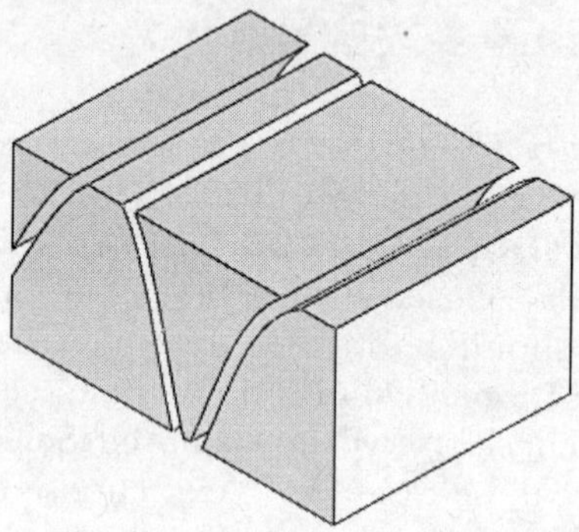

Figure 16-109 *Resultant thicken surface cut*

Creating a Surface Cut

CommandManager:	Surfaces > Cut With Surface
SOLIDWORKS menus:	Insert > Cut > With Surface

In SOLIDWORKS, you can also cut a solid body by using a surface. To create this type of surface cut, choose the **Cut With Surface** button from the **Surfaces CommandManager**; the **SurfaceCut PropertyManager** will be displayed with the **Surface Cut Parameters** rollout. But, if there are multiple bodies, then on choosing the **Cut With Surface** button, the modified **SurfaceCut PropertyManager** will be displayed, as shown in Figure 16-110.

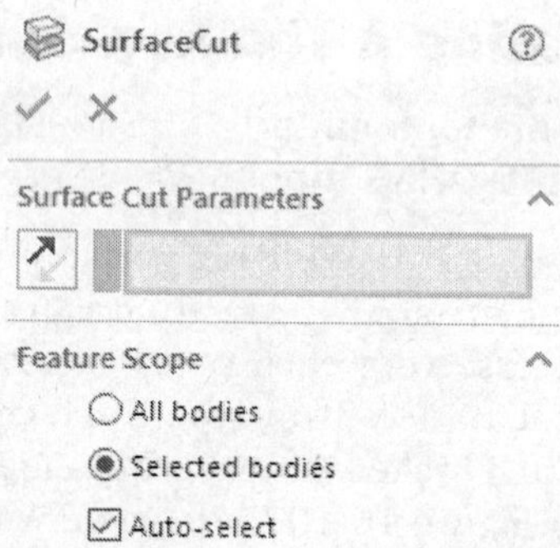

Figure 16-110 *The modified* ***SurfaceCut PropertyManager***

On invoking this PropertyManager, you will also be prompted to select the cutting surface. Select the cutting surface; the name of the selected surface will be displayed in the **Selected surface for cut** selection box in the **Surface Cut Parameters** rollout. Also, an arrow will be displayed in the drawing area, indicating the direction of removal of the material. Using the **Flip Cut** button, available on the left of the **Selected surface for cut** selection box or the arrow displayed in the drawing area, you can flip the direction of material removal. Choose the **OK** button from the **SurfaceCut PropertyManager**; the surface cut will be created. Figure 16-111 shows the surface to be selected to create a surface cut. Figure 16-112 shows the resultant surface cut after hiding the surface body.

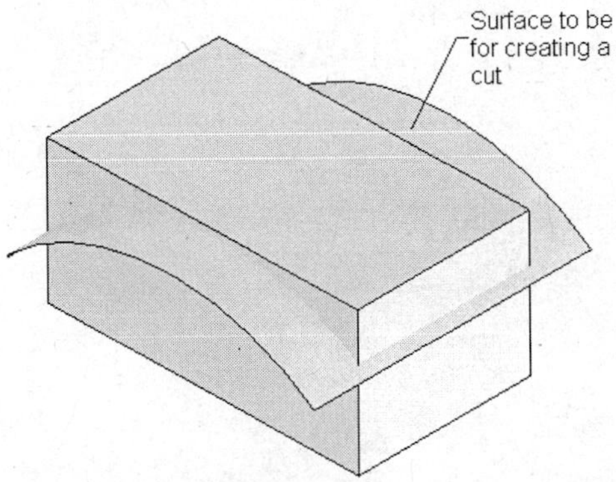

Figure 16-111 *Surface to be selected to create a surface cut*

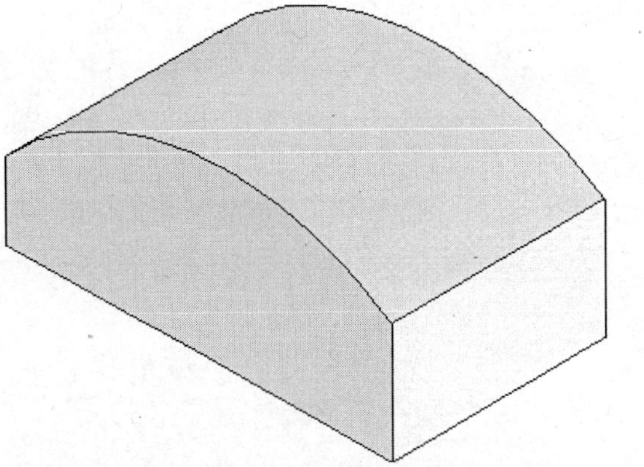

Figure 16-112 *Resultant surface cut after hiding the surface body*

In Figure 16-113, an example is shown in which a surface cuts a solid in several parts. In such cases, once you select a cut surface and choose **OK** from the **SurfaceCut** Property Manager; the **Bodies to Keep** dialog box will be displayed refer to Figure 16-114. The options in the dialog box are discussed next. By default, the **All bodies** radio button under the **Bodies** area is selected and used to create a surface cut by keeping all bodies in selected direction. The **Selected bodies** radio button is used to retain the selected bodies, refer to Figure 16-115.

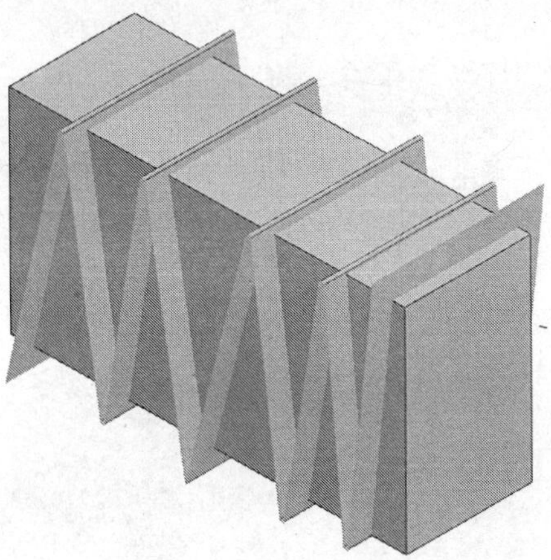

Figure 16-113 *Surface cutting solid in several parts*

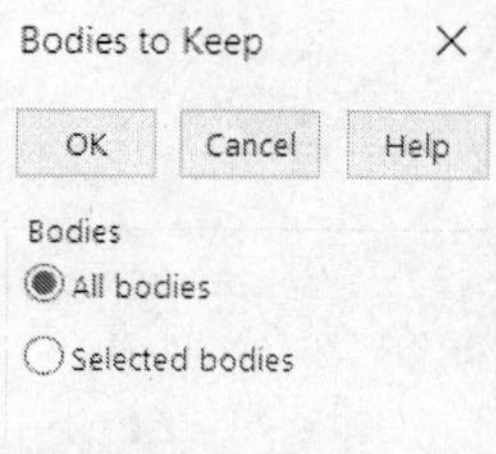

Figure 16-114 *The* ***Bodies to Keep*** *dialog box with the* ***All bodies*** *radio button selected*

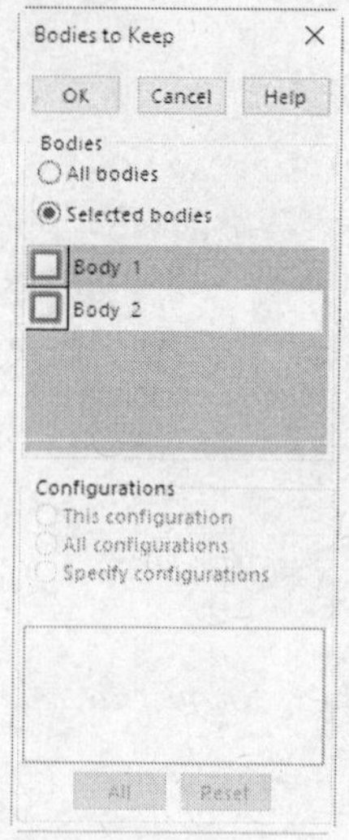

Figure 16-115 *The* ***Bodies to Keep*** *dialog box with the* ***Selected bodies*** *radio button selected*

Figure 16-116 shows the resultant surface cut after selecting **Body 1**, **Body 3** and **Body 5** bodies from the **Bodies** area.

Figure 16-116 *The resultant surface*

TUTORIALS

Tutorial 1

In this tutorial, you will create the model shown in Figure 16-117. You will create the model using the surface modeling tools available in the **Surfaces CommandManager** and then add wall thickness to the surface model. The views and dimensions of the model are shown in Figure 16-118.

(Expected time: 1hr)

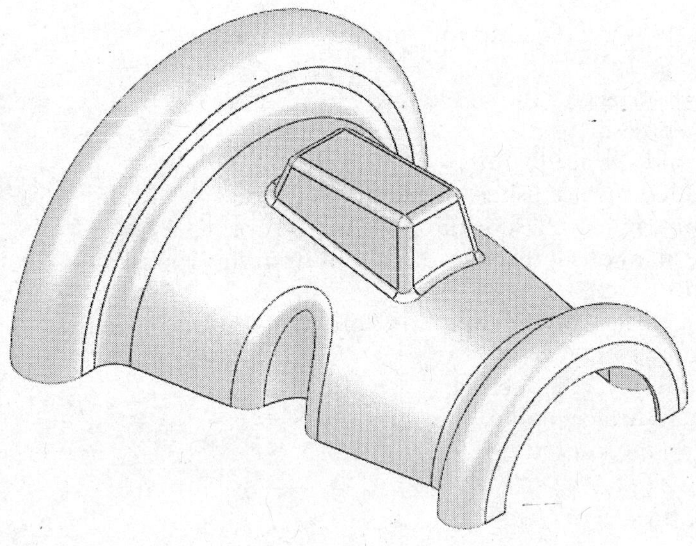

Figure 16-117 Model for Tutorial 1

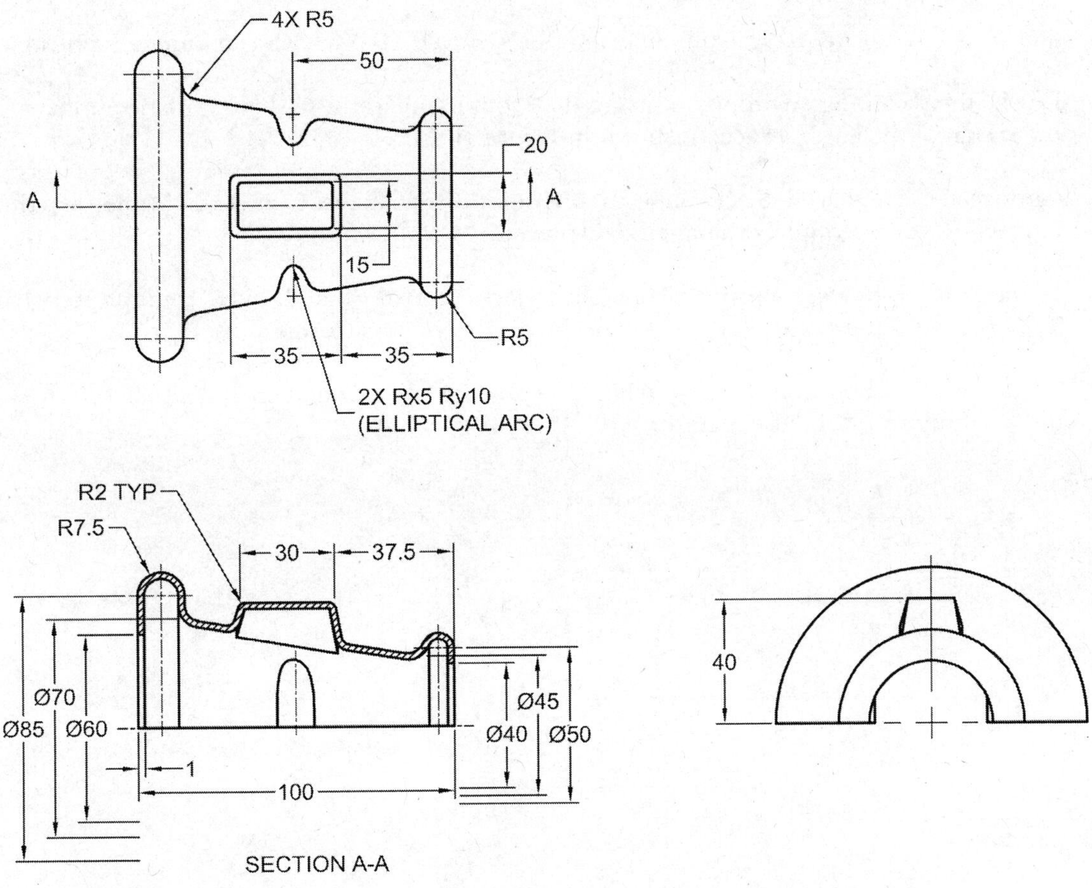

Figure 16-118 Views and dimensions of the model for Tutorial 1

The following steps are required to complete this tutorial:

a. Create the base surface of the model by revolving the sketch using the **Mid Plane** option through 180 degrees.
b. Create the second surface feature.
c. Trim the extruded surface using the trim tool.
d. Add fillet to the trimmed base surface.
e. Create a plane at an offset distance of 40 mm from the Top plane.
f. Create a lofted surface.
g. Create a planar surface on the top of the lofted feature and trim the base feature using the lofted feature.
h. Trim and knit all surfaces together.
i. Add fillets to the surface model.
j. Add thickness to the knitted surface.

Creating the Base Surface

To create this model, first you need to create the base surface. The base surface will be created by revolving the sketch created on the Front plane.

1. Start SOLIDWORKS part document using the **New SOLIDWORKS Document** dialog box.

2. Invoke the sketching environment using the Front plane as the sketching plane and create the sketch of the base surface, as shown in Figure 16-119.

3. Choose the **Revolved Surface** button from the **Surfaces CommandManager**; the **Surface-Revolve PropertyManager** is displayed.

4. In the **Surface-Revolve PropertyManager**, select the **Mid Plane** option from the **Revolve Type** drop-down list and set the value of the **Angle** spinner to **180**.

5. Choose the **OK** button from the **Surface-Revolve PropertyManager**. Figure 16-120 shows the resulting revolved base feature.

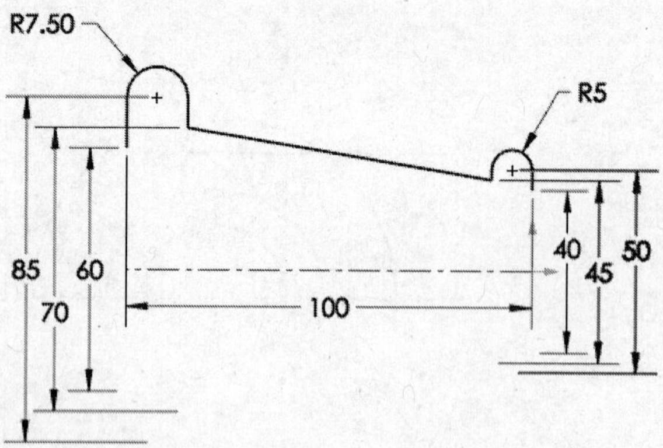

Figure 16-119 *Sketch of the base surface*

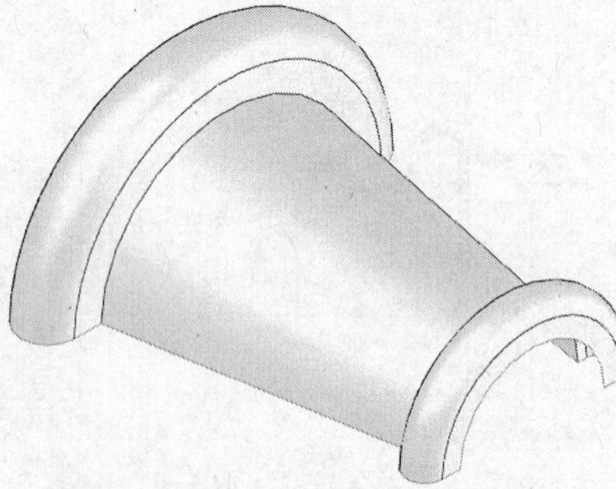

Figure 16-120 *Revolved base surface*

Creating the Second Surface Feature

The second surface feature is an extruded surface. This surface will be created by extruding a sketch created on the Top plane.

1. Select the Top plane as the sketching plane and invoke the sketching environment.

2. Create the sketch of the second surface feature, as shown in Figure 16-121. Note that you may have to apply the Horizontal or Vertical relation between the points of the ellipse to constrain them.

3. Next, choose the **Extruded Surface** button from the **Surfaces CommandManager**; the **Surface-Extrude PropertyManager** is displayed.

4. Set **40** in the **Depth** spinner and choose the **OK** button from the **Surface-Extrude PropertyManager**.

The surface created after extruding the sketch is shown in Figure 16-122.

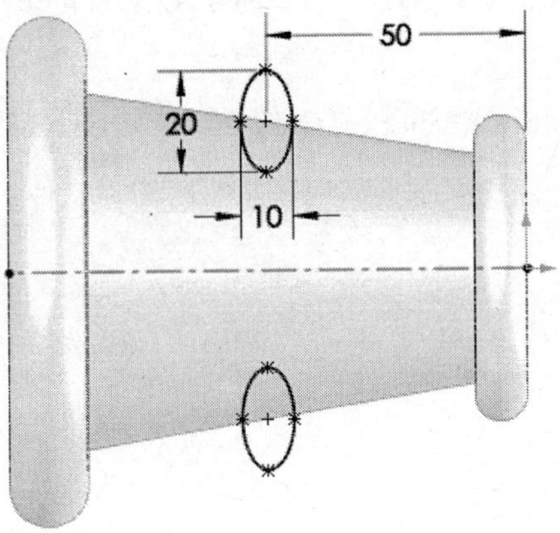

Figure 16-121 Sketch of the second surface feature

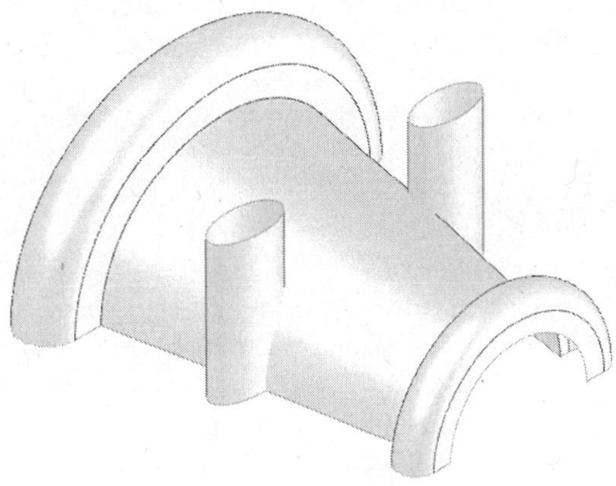

Figure 16-122 Extruded surface

Trimming the Base Surface Using the Extruded Surface

Next, you need to trim the unwanted portions of the base surface by using the extruded surface.

1. Choose the **Trim Surface** button from the **Surfaces CommandManager**; the **Trim Surface PropertyManager** is displayed.

2. Select the **Mutual** radio button from the **Trim Type** rollout and then select the surfaces, refer to Figure 16-123.

3. Next, click in the **Pieces to Keep** selection box to invoke the selection mode. Next, select the pieces to be kept, refer to Figure 16-123.

4. Choose the **OK** button from the **Trim Surface PropertyManager**. The model after trimming the base surface is displayed in Figure 16-124.

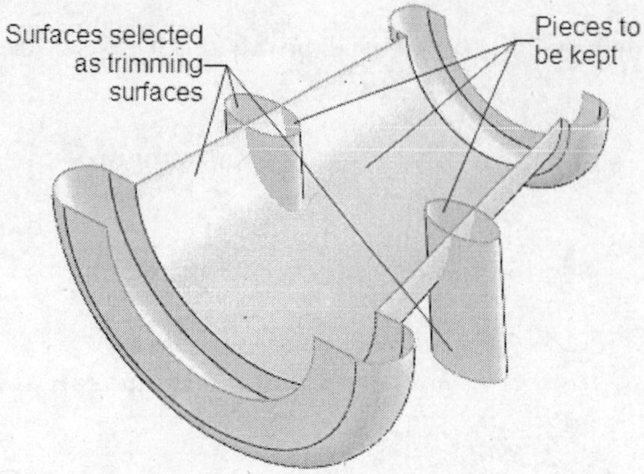

Figure 16-123 Surfaces selected for trimming

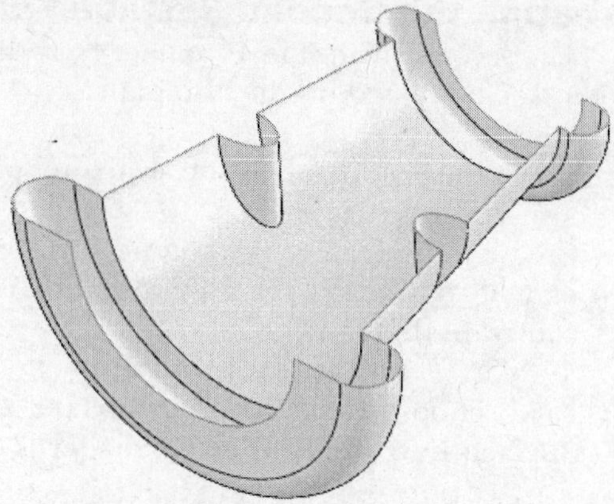

Figure 16-124 Model after trimming the base surface

Filleting the Edges of the Trimmed Surface

Next, you need to fillet the edges created at the intersection of the base surface with the extruded surfaces.

1. Choose the **Fillet** button from the **Surfaces CommandManager**; the **Fillet PropertyManager** is displayed.

2. Select the edges to fillet, as shown in Figure 16-125.

3. Set **5** in the **Radius** spinner and then choose the **OK** button from the **Fillet PropertyManager**. Figure 16-126 shows the model after adding fillet.

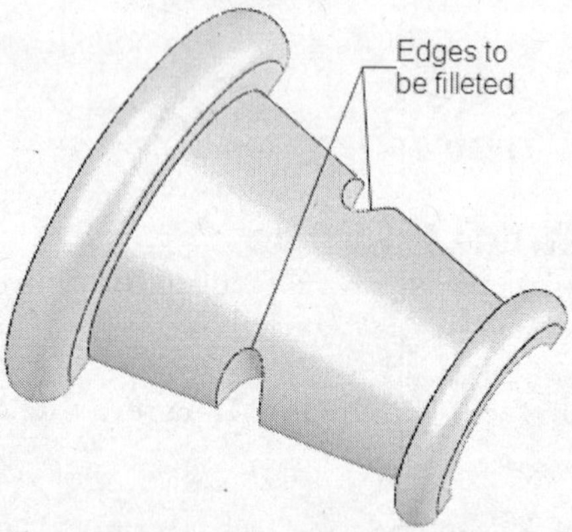

Figure 16-125 Edges to be filleted

Figure 16-126 Resultant fillet feature

Creating the Lofted Surface

Next, you need to create a lofted surface. The lofted surface will be created between two curves. The first curve is to be created on the Top plane and projected on the surface. The next curve is to be created on an offset plane.

1. Create a plane at an offset distance of 40 mm from the Top plane and then invoke the sketching environment using the top plane as the sketching plane.

2. Create the sketch, as shown in Figure 16-127, and exit the sketching environment.

   Next, you need to project this sketch on the base surface.

3. Choose **Curves > Project Curve** from the **Surfaces CommandManager**; the **Projected Curve PropertyManager** is invoked.

4. Select the **Sketch on faces** radio button from the **Projection type** area.

5. Next, select the sketch. When you select the sketch, the **Projection Faces** selection box gets activated.

6. Select the middle portion of the base surface. Choose the **OK** button from the **Projected Curve PropertyManager**.

   Next, you need to create second curve for creating the loft surface.

7. Invoke the sketching environment with the newly created plane as the sketching plane and then create the sketch, as shown in Figure 16-128. Then, exit the sketching environment. Figure 16-129 shows the model after creating the sketch and the projected curve.

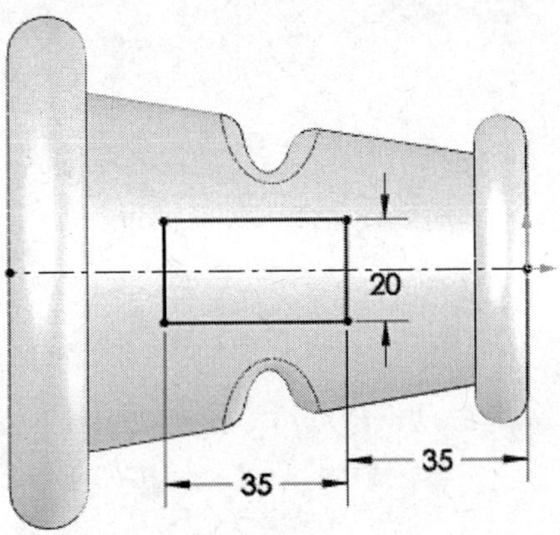

Figure 16-127 *Sketch to create the projected curve*

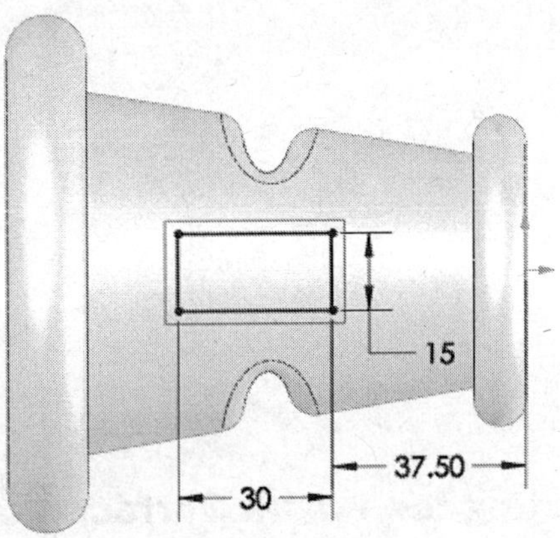

Figure 16-128 *Second sketch for the loft surface*

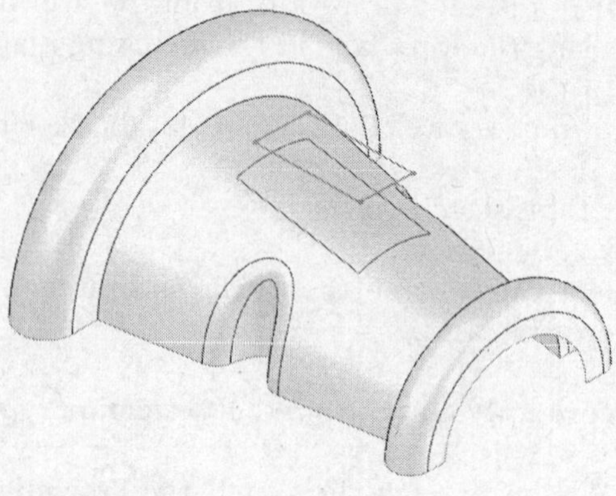

Figure 16-129 Model after creating the sketch and the projected curve

8. Choose the **Lofted Surface** button from the **Surfaces CommandManager**; the **Surface-Loft PropertyManager** is displayed.

9. Select the loft section, as shown in Figure 16-130, and choose the **OK** button from the **Surface-Loft PropertyManager**. Figure 16-131 shows the model after creating the lofted surface.

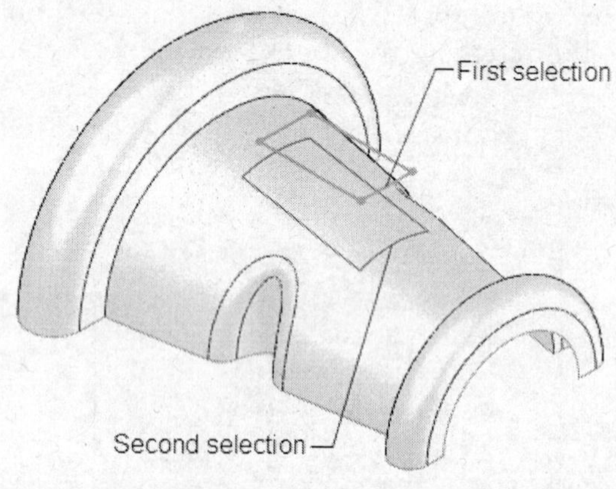

Figure 16-130 Section selected for the lofted surface

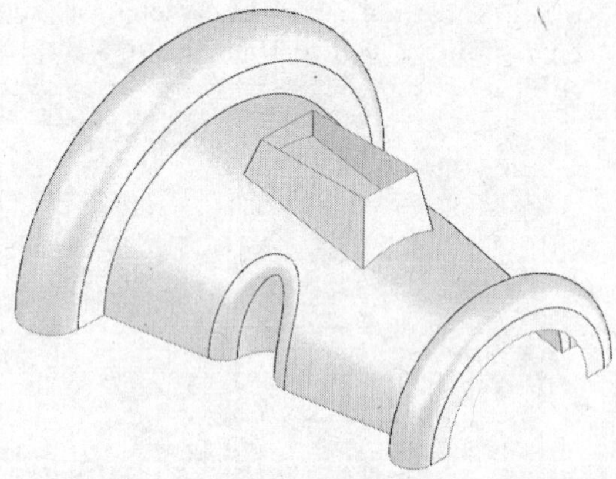

Figure 16-131 Resultant lofted surface

Creating the Planar Surface

Next, you need to create the planar surface by using the top edges of the lofted surface.

1. Choose the **Planar Surface** button from the **Surfaces CommandManager**; the **Planar Surface PropertyManager** is displayed.

2. Select the edges, as shown in Figure 16-132, to create the planar surface; the names of the selected edges are displayed in the **Bounding Entities** selection box of the **Planar Surface PropertyManager**.

3. Choose the **OK** button from the **Planar Surface PropertyManager**; the planar surface is created. Figure 16-133 shows the resultant planar surface.

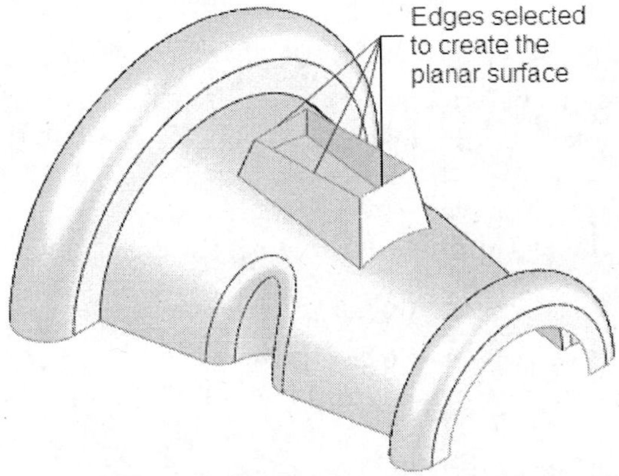

Figure 16-132 Edges selected to create the planar surface

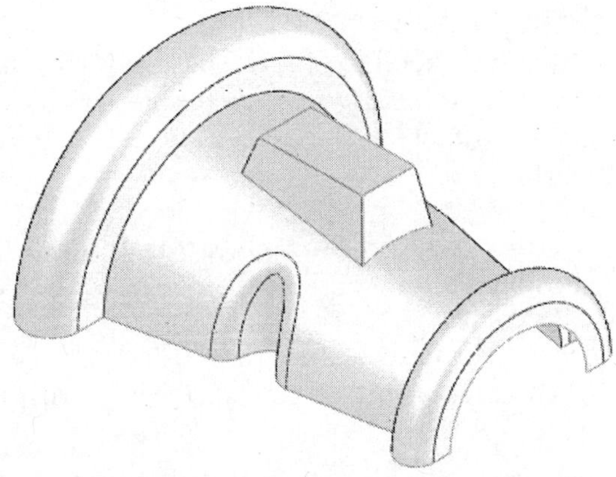

Figure 16-133 Resultant planar surface

Trimming the Base Surface Using the Lofted Surface

Next, you need to trim the base surface by using the lofted surface.

1. Choose the **Trim Surface** button from the **Surfaces CommandManager** to invoke the **Trim Surface PropertyManager**.

2. Select the **Standard** radio button from the **Trim Type** rollout. Next, select the lofted surface as the trimming tool and then select the base surface as the piece to be retained.

3. Choose the **OK** button from the **Trim Surface PropertyManager**.

Figure 16-134 shows the model after the base feature has been trimmed by using the lofted surface.

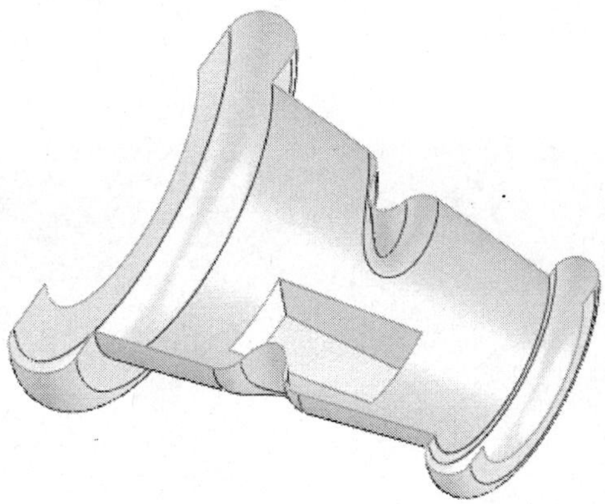

Figure 16-134 Model after trimming the base surface

Knitting All Surfaces

Next, you need to knit the base surface, the lofted surface, and the planar surface together by using the **Knit Surface** tool to create fillets on the edges. Note that, if you want to add wall thickness to the surface model created using multiple surfaces, you need to knit all the surfaces first.

1. Choose the **Knit Surface** button from the **Surfaces CommandManager**; the **Knit Surface PropertyManager** is invoked.

2. Select the base surface, the lofted surface, and the planar surface from the drawing area; the names of the selected surfaces are displayed in the **Surfaces and Faces to Knit** selection box.

3. Next, choose the **OK** button from the **Knit Surface PropertyManager**; the selected surfaces are knitted.

4. Add required fillets to the model. For dimensions of the fillets, refer to Figure 16-118. Final surface model after adding the fillets is shown in Figure 16-135.

Adding Thickness to the Surface Model

Next, you need to add thickness to the surface model.

1. Choose the **Thicken** button from the **Surfaces CommandManager** to invoke the **Thicken PropertyManager**.

2. Select the surface model and then set **1** in the **Thickness** spinner. Next, choose the **Thicken Side 1** button to add thickness in the other direction.

3. Choose the **OK** button from the **Thicken PropertyManager**.

Figure 16-136 shows the rotated view of the final model after thickening the surface.

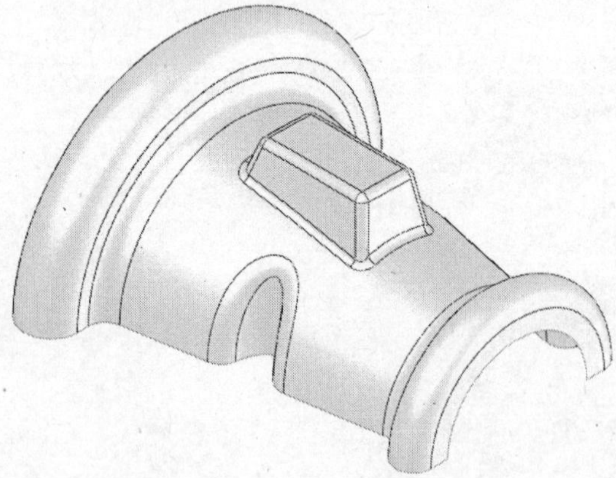

Figure 16-135 Final surface model

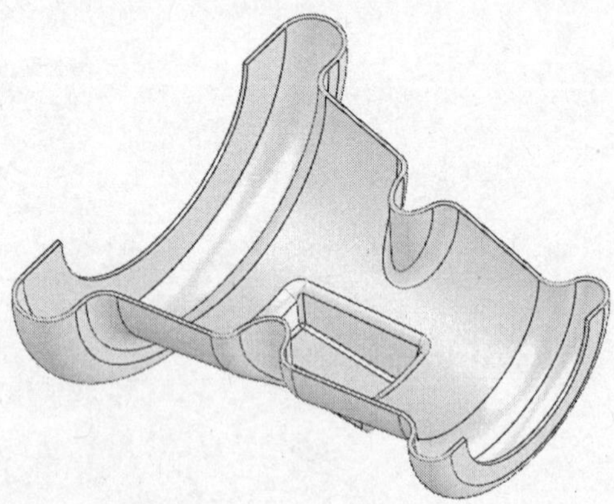

Figure 16-136 Rotated view of the final model after thickening the surface

Saving the Model

1. Choose the **Save** button from the Menu Bar and save the drawing with the name *c16_tut01* at the following location and close the file.

   \Documents\SOLIDWORKS\c16

Tutorial 2

In this tutorial, you will create the cover of a hair dryer, as shown in Figure 16-137. First, you will create the model by using surfaces and then thicken it. The views and dimensions of the model are shown in Figure 16-138. **(Expected time: 1.5 hr)**

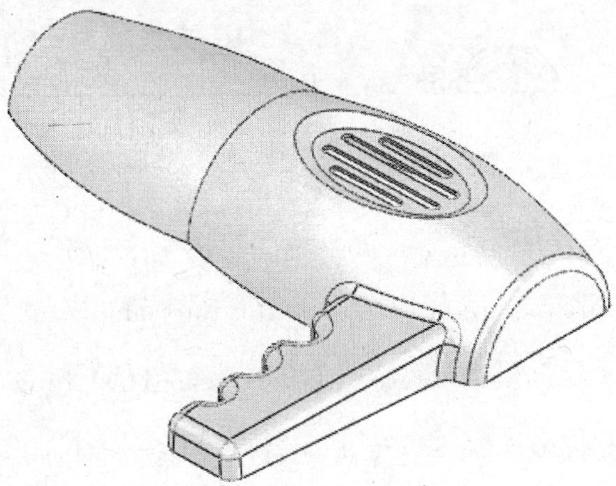

Figure 16-137 *Cover of hair dryer*

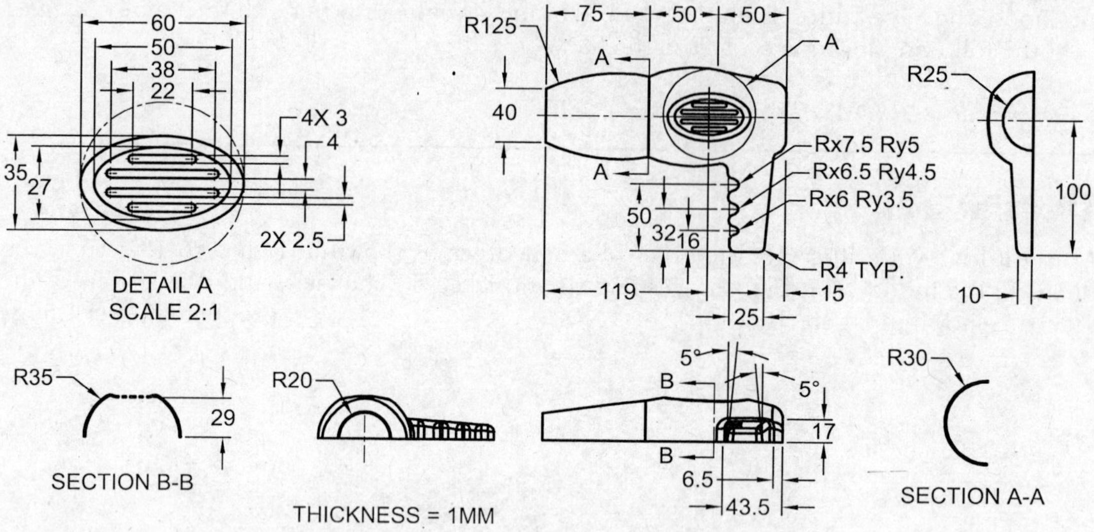

Figure 16-138 Views and dimensions of the model for Tutorial 2

The following steps are required to complete this tutorial:

a. First, create the base surface. The base surface is created by lofting the open sections along the guide curves.
b. Create a planar surface to close the right face of the base surface.
c. Create the basic structure of the handle of the hair dryer cover by creating a lofted surface between two open sections.
d. Trim the unwanted portion of the lofted surface that is used to create the handle.
e. Create a planar surface to close the front face of the handle.
f. Extrude the elliptical sketches to create the grips of the handle and then trim the unwanted surfaces.
g. Create a dip on the top surface of the hair dryer.
h. Trim the surface to create air vents.
i. Knit all surfaces together and add fillets to the model.
j. Thicken the surface.

Creating the Base Surface

To create the hair dryer cover, you first need to create the base surface of the model. The base surface will be created by lofting semicircular sections along the guide curves. These sections will be created on different planes. Therefore, you first need to create three planes at an offset distance from the Right plane.

1. Start SOLIDWORKS part document using the **New SOLIDWORKS Document** dialog box.

2. Create three planes at an offset distance from the Right plane, as shown in Figure 16-139. For the offset distance of planes, refer to Figure 16-138.

3. Create sections and guide curves to create a lofted surface, as shown in Figure 16-139. For dimensions, refer to Figure 16-138.

4. Invoke the **Lofted Surface** tool and create a lofted surface, as shown in Figure 16-140.

5. Invoke the sketching environment by selecting **Plane3** as the sketching plane.

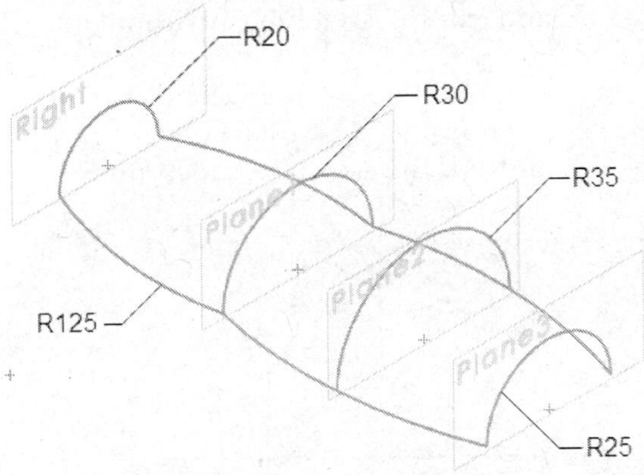

Figure 16-139 *Sections and guide curves to create a lofted surface*

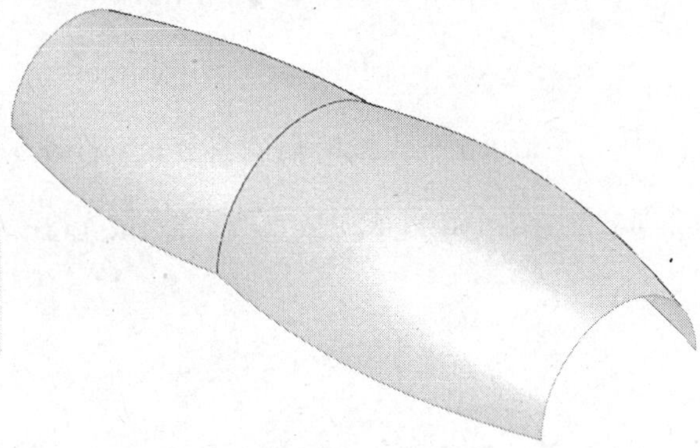

Figure 16-140 *Resultant lofted surface*

6. Create a closed sketch to create a planar surface, as shown in Figure 16-141.

7. Invoke the **Planar Surface PropertyManager** and then select the closed sketch from the drawing area. Next, choose the **OK** button from the **Planar Surface PropertyManager**; the planar surface is created, as shown in Figure 16-142.

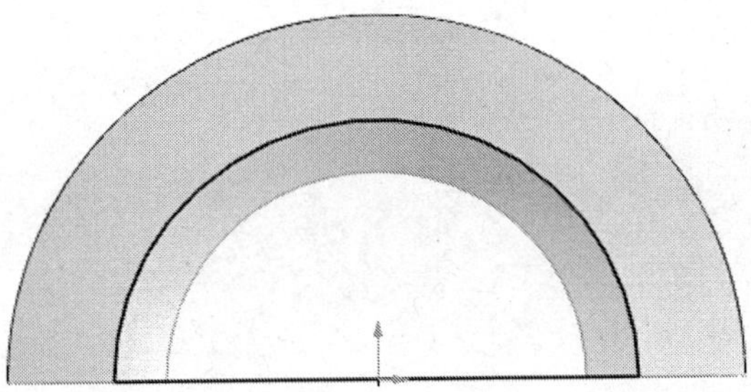

Figure 16-141 *Sketch for creating the planar surface*

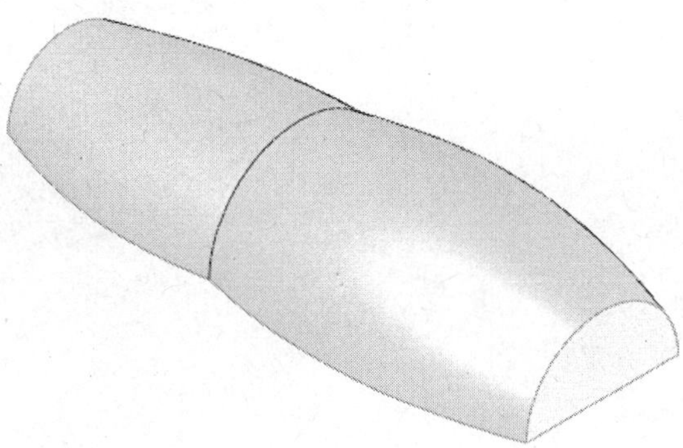

Figure 16-142 *Resultant planar surface*

Creating the Base Surface for the Handle

Next, you need to create the base surface for the handle. The base surface for the handle will be created by lofting two open sections. The first section for the lofted surface will be created on a plane at an offset distance from the Front plane and the second section will be created on the Front plane. Therefore, you first need to create a plane at an offset distance from the Front plane.

1. Create a plane at an offset distance of **100** mm from the Front plane.
2. Invoke the sketching environment using the newly created plane as the sketching plane.
3. Create an open sketch, as shown in Figure 16-143, and exit the sketching environment.
4. Next, invoke the sketching environment by using the Front plane as the sketching plane.
5. Create an open sketch, as shown in Figure 16-144, and exit the sketching environment.
6. Create the lofted surface by using the **Lofted Surface** tool, as shown in Figure 16-145.

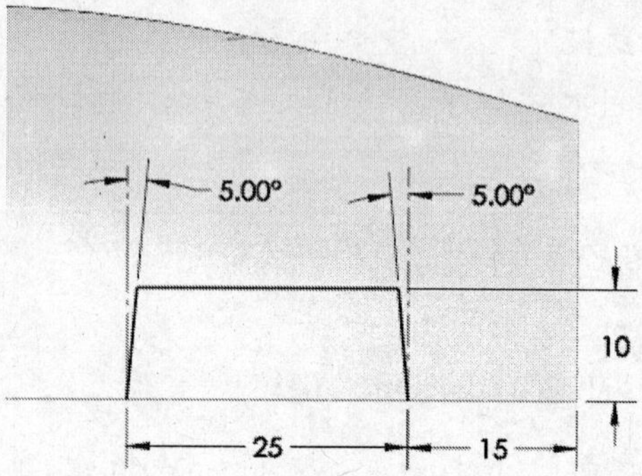

***Figure 16-143** Sketch of the first section for creating the lofted surface of the handle*

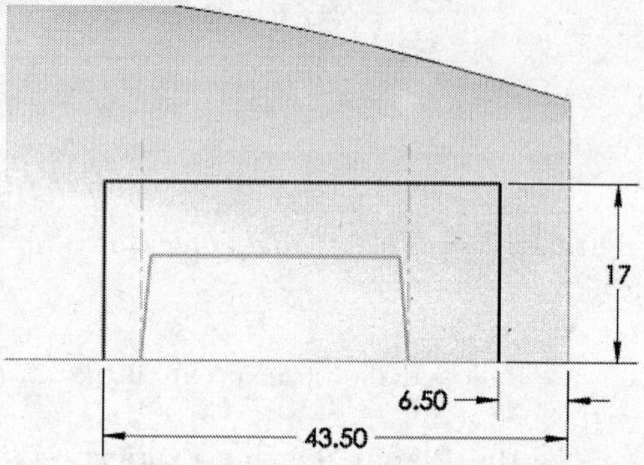

***Figure 16-144** Sketch of the second section for creating the lofted surface of the handle*

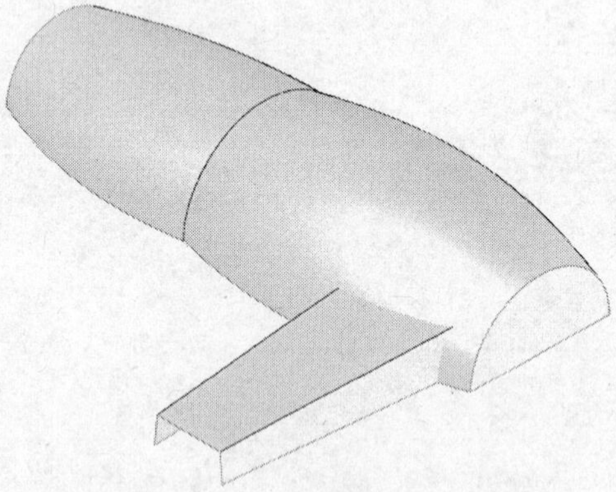

***Figure 16-145** Resultant lofted surface*

Trimming the Unwanted Portion from the Lofted Surface of the Handle

If you rotate the model after creating the lofted surface for the handle, you will observe that a portion of the lofted surface needs to be trimmed. The method for trimming the unwanted portion of the lofted surface is discussed next.

1. Invoke the **Trim Surface PropertyManager** and then select the **Mutual** radio button from the **Trim Type** rollout.

2. Select the trimming surfaces and the pieces to be kept, as shown in Figure 16-146. Next, choose the **OK** button from the **Trim Surface PropertyManager**. Figure 16-147 shows the resultant trimmed surface.

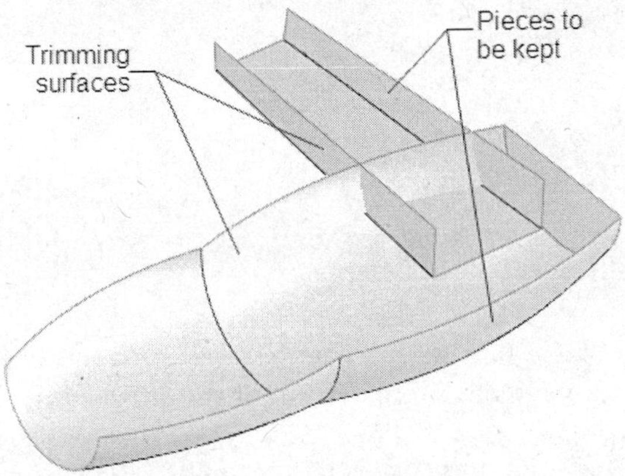

Figure 16-146 *Trimming surfaces and pieces to be kept*

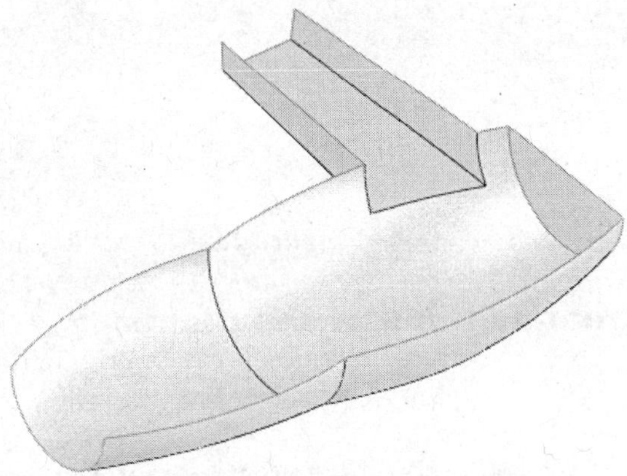

Figure 16-147 *Resultant trimmed surface*

Creating the Planar Surface

Next, you need to create a planar surface to close the front face of the handle.

1. Select the plane created at an offset distance from the Front plane and invoke the sketching environment.

2. Create a closed sketch to create the planar surface and then exit the sketching environment.

3. Choose the **Planar Surface** button from the **Surfaces CommandManager**; the **Planar Surface PropertyManager** is displayed. Next, select the closed sketch from the drawing area; the name of the selected sketch is displayed in the **Bounding Entities** selection box of the **Planar Surface PropertyManager**. Also, preview of the planar surface is displayed in the drawing area. Next, choose the **OK** button from the PropertyManager.

The model after creating the planar surface is shown in Figure 16-148.

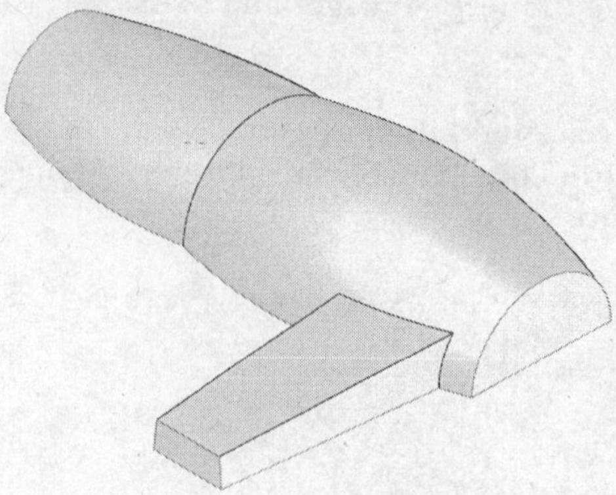

Figure 16-148 Model after creating the planar surface

Creating Grips on the Handle

Next, you need to create grips on the handle of the hair dryer. The grip will be created by extruding the elliptical surface and then trimming unwanted portion of the surfaces.

1. Invoke the sketching environment using the Top plane as the sketching plane.

2. Create a sketch for extruding the surface, as shown in Figure 16-149.

3. Invoke the **Surface-Extrude PropertyManager** and extrude the sketch up to a depth of **25** mm. The extruded surface is displayed, as shown in Figure 16-150.

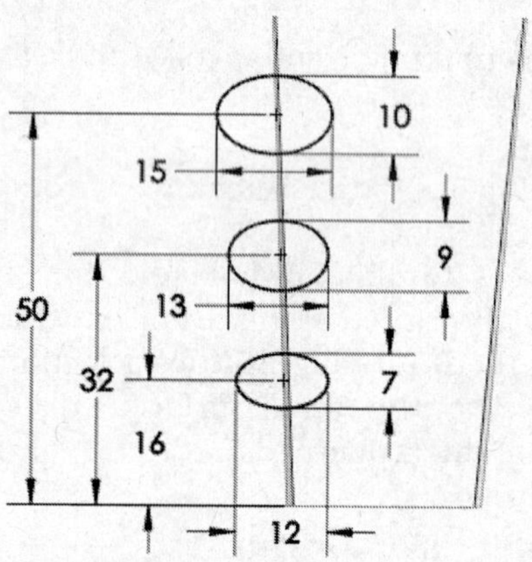

Figure 16-149 Sketch created for extruding the surface

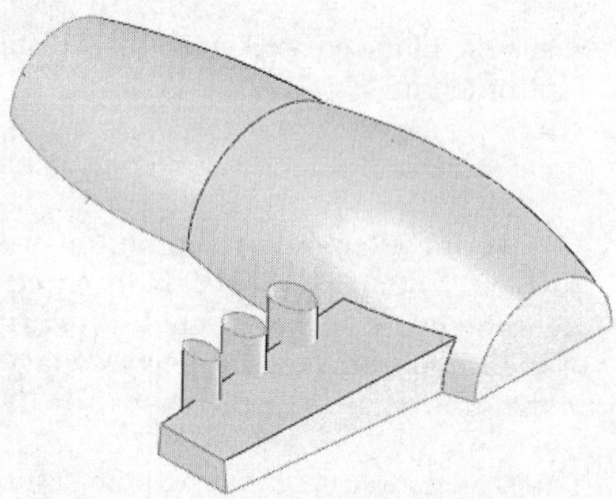

Figure 16-150 Resultant extruded surface

Next, you need to trim the handle and unwanted portions of the extruded surface to achieve desired shape of the grips.

4. Invoke the **Trim Surface PropertyManager** and then select the **Mutual** radio button from the **Trim Type** rollout.

5. Select the trimming surfaces and the pieces to be kept, as shown in Figure 16-151.

6. Choose the **OK** button from the **Trim Surface PropertyManager**; the surface is trimmed. Figure 16-152 shows the resultant trimmed surface.

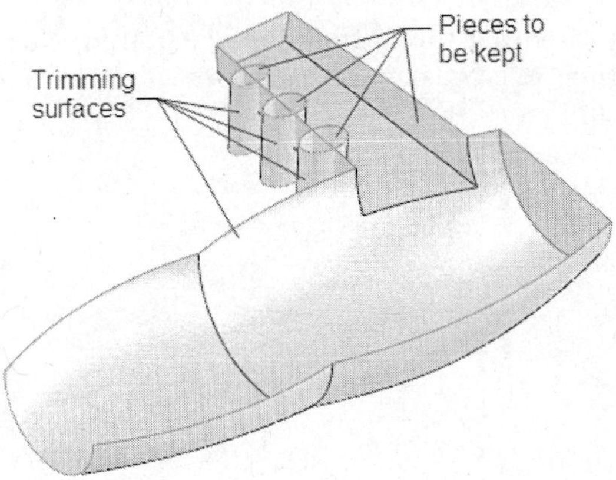

Figure 16-151 *Trimming surfaces and the pieces to be kept*

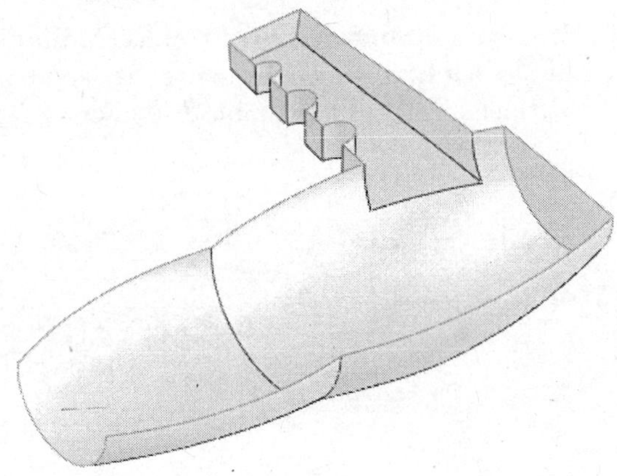

Figure 16-152 *Resultant trimmed surface*

Creating a Dip on the Upper Surface of the Base Surface

Next, you need to create a dip on the base surface. To do so, you need to use various tools for offsetting planes, creating lofted surface, trimming unwanted surfaces, and creating a planar surface.

1. Invoke the sketching environment using the Top plane as the sketching plane.

2. Create a sketch, as shown in Figure 16-153, and then exit the sketching environment.

3. Next, choose **Curves > Project Curve** from the **Surfaces CommandManager** and project the newly created sketch on the base surface. The model after projecting the sketch is displayed, as shown in Figure 16-154.

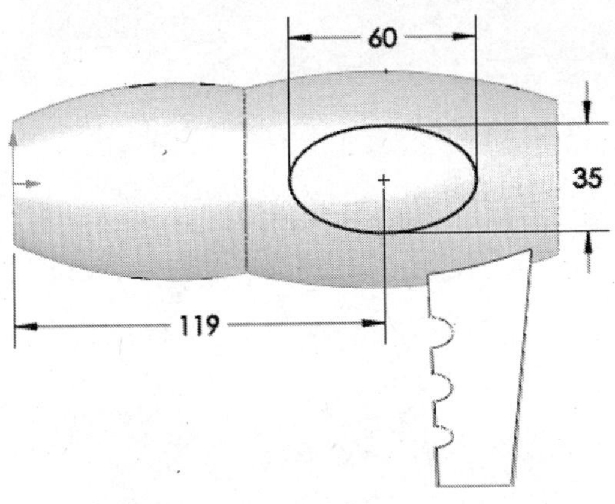

Figure 16-153 *Sketch created*

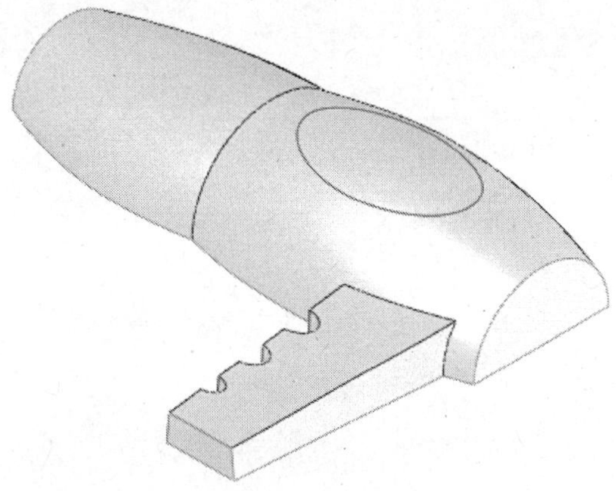

Figure 16-154 *Resultant projected curve*

4. Create a plane at an offset distance of **29** mm from the Top plane in an upward direction.

5. Next, invoke the sketching environment by using the newly created plane as the sketching plane and create a sketch, as shown in Figure 16-155. Next, exit the sketching environment.

6. Invoke the **Surface-Loft PropertyManager** by choosing the **Lofted Surface** button. Next, create a lofted surface by using the sketch and the projected curve created earlier. The lofted surface after hiding the base surface is shown in Figure 16-156.

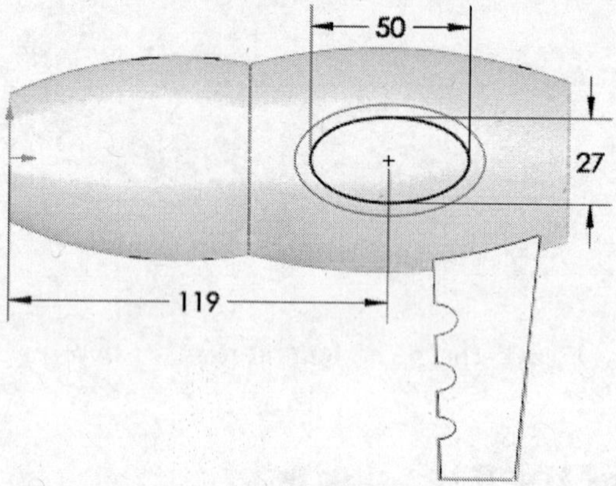

Figure 16-155 *Sketch to be created*

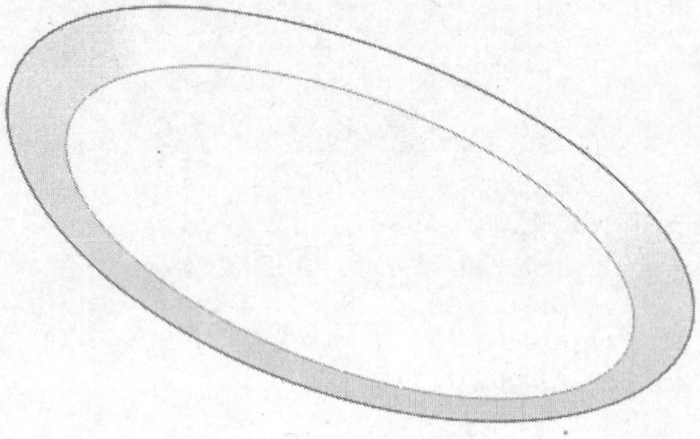

Figure 16-156 *Lofted surface*

7. Expand the **Surface Bodies** folder in the **FeatureManager Design Tree**. Next, select the surface and right-click on it to invoke the shortcut menu. Next, choose **Hide/Show** from the shortcut menu; the view of the selected surface gets modified.

8. Invoke the **Trim Surface** tool and trim the base surface using the newly created lofted surface. The model after trimming the surface is shown in Figure 16-157. Next, create the planar surface by using the **Planar Surface** tool, as shown in Figure 16-158.

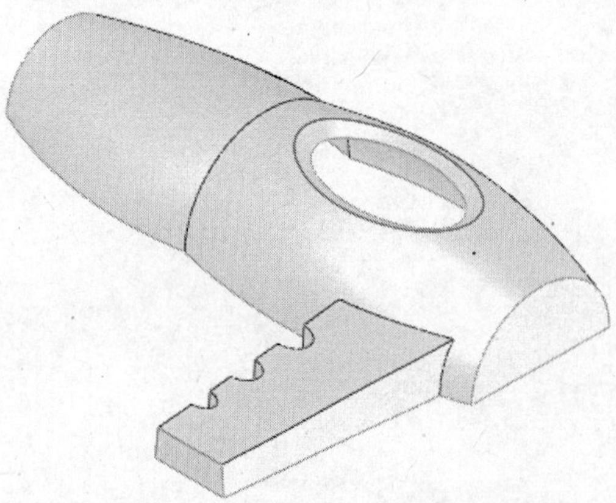

Figure 16-157 *Model after trimming the surface*

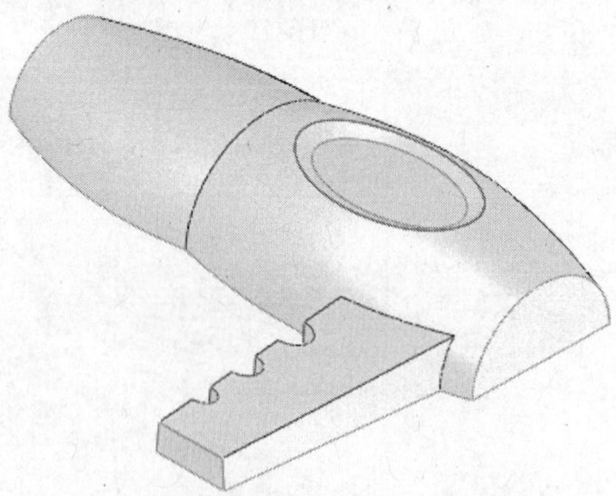

Figure 16-158 *Planar surface*

Creating Air Vents

Next, you need to create air vents on the newly created planar surface. Air vents are created by drawing the sketch of air vents on the planar surface and then trimming the planer surface.

1. Select the newly created planar surface as the sketching plane and then invoke the sketching environment.

2. Create the sketch of air vents. For dimensions, refer to Figure 16-138.

3. Invoke the **Trim Surface** tool by choosing the **Trim Surface** button from the **Surfaces CommandManager**. Then, select the pieces to be kept or removed from the planar surface.

   The surface model after creating air vents is shown in Figure 16-159.

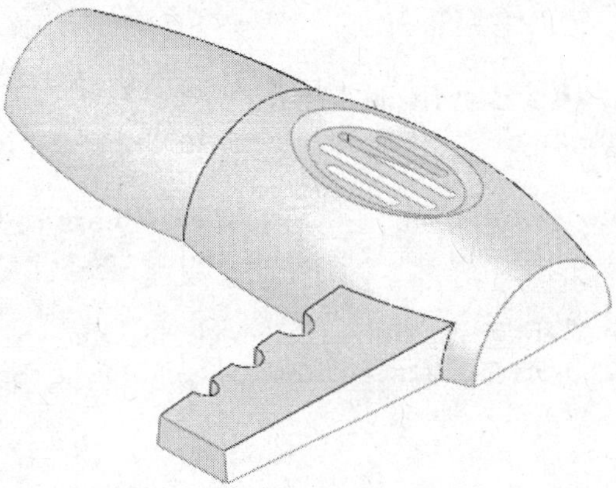

Figure 16-159 *Surface model after trimming the planar surface*

Knitting all Surfaces

After creating all the surfaces, you need to knit all the surfaces together and then add fillets to surfaces and thicken the model.

1. Choose the **Knit Surface** button from the **Surfaces CommandManager**; the **Knit Surface PropertyManager** is displayed and you are prompted to select the surfaces to be knit.

2. Expand the **Surface Bodies** folder in the design area of the **FeatureManager Design Tree** and then select all surface bodies from it.

3. Next, choose the **OK** button from the **Knit Surface PropertyManager**. If the surfaces do not knit properly then adjust the gaps using the list box provided at the bottom of the **Knit Surface PropertyManager**.

4. Add required fillets to the surface model. The model after adding fillets is displayed in Figure 16-160.

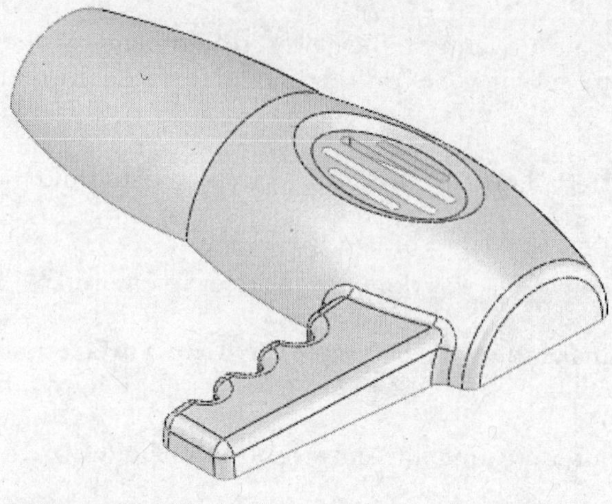

Figure 16-160 Surface model after adding fillets

Adding Thickness to the Surface Model

After creating the entire model, you need to add thickness to the surface model.

1. Choose the **Thicken** button from the **Surfaces CommandManager**; the **Thicken PropertyManager** is invoked and you are prompted to select the surface to thicken.

2. Set the value as **1** in the **Thickness** spinner then choose the **Thicken Side 2** button. Next, select the surface model from the drawing area; preview of the thickened model is displayed in the drawing area.

3. Next, choose the **OK** button from the **Thicken PropertyManager**; the final model is displayed, as shown in Figure 16-161.

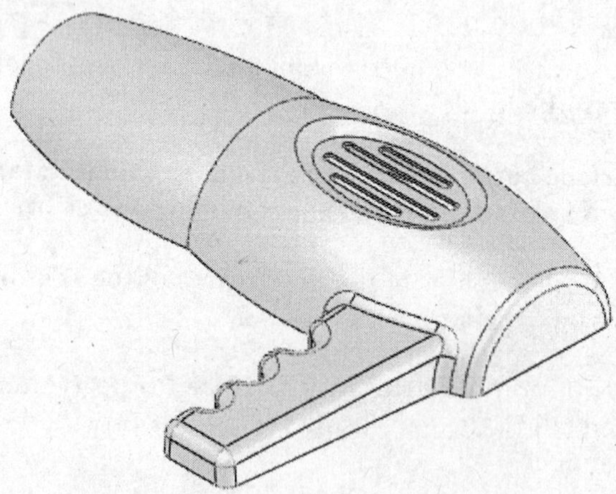

Figure 16-161 Final model

Saving the Model

1. Choose the **Save** button from the Menu Bar and save the drawing with the name *c16_tut02* at the following location and close the file.

   \Documents\SOLIDWORKS\c16

Self-Evaluation Test

Answer the following questions and then compare them to those given at the end of this chapter:

1. In SOLIDWORKS, the __________ tool is used to extrude a closed or an open sketch.
2. The __________ **PropertyManager** is used to create a revolved surface.
3. The __________ tool is used to create a surface patch by extending existing surfaces.
4. The __________ tool is used to offset a surface or surfaces up to a given distance.
5. The __________ **PropertyManager** is used to create a lofted surface.
6. You cannot patch the deleted faces of a solid model using the **Delete Face** tool. (T/F)
7. Using the **Knit Surface** tool, you can knit multiple surfaces together to create a single surface. (T/F)
8. You cannot create a filled surface by selecting a 3D sketch as a patch boundary. (T/F)
9. The **Curvature Control** drop-down list is used to define curvature type for creating a fill surface. (T/F)
10. The **SurfaceCut PropertyManager** is used to create a surface cut. (T/F)

Review Questions

Answer the following questions:

1. Which of the following PropertyManagers is used to create a fillet surface?

   (a) **Fill Surface** (b) **Surface Fill**
   (c) **Fillet** (d) None of these

2. Which of the following buttons in the **Surfaces CommandManager** is used to invoke the **Replace Face1 PropertyManager**?

   (a) **Face Replace** (b) **Replace Face**
   (c) **Offset Surface** (d) **Fillet Surface**

3. Which of the following rollouts is used to define constraint curves while creating a fill surface?

(a) **Define Constraint Curves** (b) **Constraint Curves**
(c) **Patch Boundaries** (d) None of these

4. Which of the following PropertyManagers is used to create a surface by radiating a surface along an edge or a split line?

(a) **Surface Fill** (b) **Surface-Sweep**
(c) **Radiate Surface** (d) **Thicken**

5. The __________ **PropertyManager** is used to add thickness to a surface body.

6. To extend a surface linearly, invoke the **Extend Surface PropertyManager** and select the __________ radio button from the **Extension Type** rollout.

7. The __________ check box is used to solidify a closed surface model.

8. The __________ tool is used to delete the faces of a surface or a solid body.

9. The **Mid-Surface** tool is used to create a surface between the two parallel faces of a solid model. (T/F)

10. At least two sections are required to create a closed boundary surface. (T/F)

EXERCISES

Exercise 1

In this exercise, create the model shown in Figure 16-162 by using surfaces. After creating and knitting all surfaces, add thickness to the model. The views and dimensions of the model are shown in the same figure. For better visualization,some fillets are hidden. **(Expected time: 1hr)**

Hint:
In this model, first you need to knit the surfaces and then fillet the edges of the resultant knit surface.

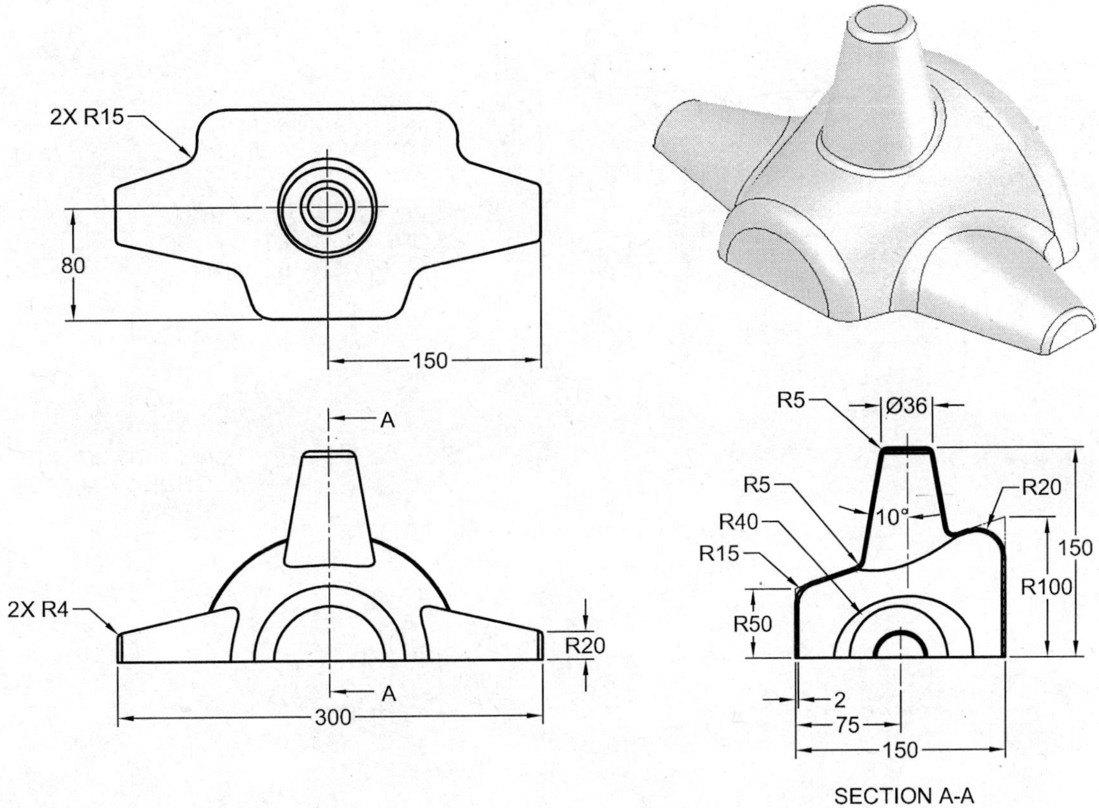

Figure 16-162 Views and dimensions of the model for Exercise 1

Exercise 2

In this exercise, create the model of binoculars shown in Figure 16-163 by using surfaces. First, create a closed surface model, knit all the surfaces together, and then solidify it. The views and dimensions of the model are shown in Figure 16-164. **(Expected time: 1hr)**

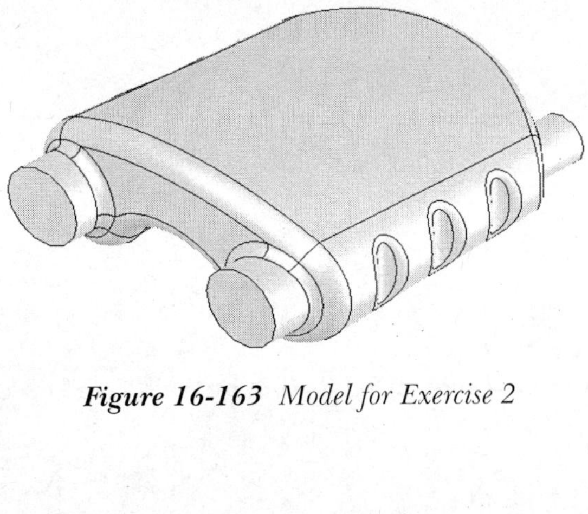

Figure 16-163 Model for Exercise 2

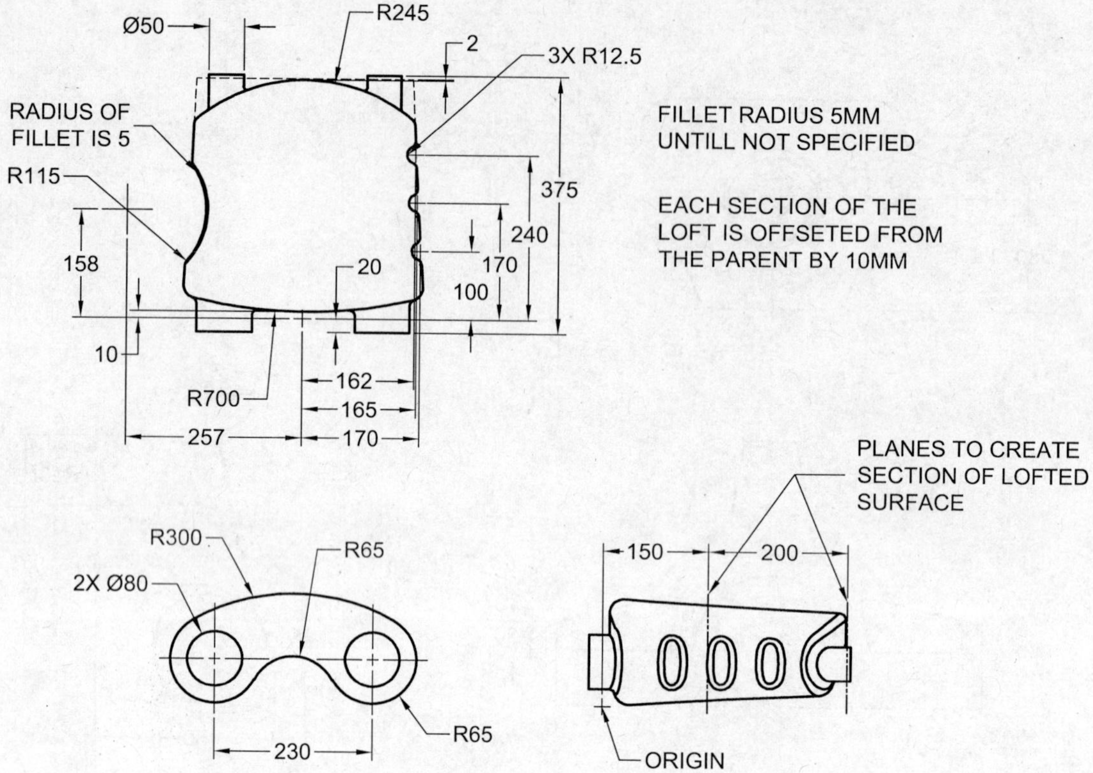

Figure 16-164 *Views and dimensions of the model for Exercise 2*

Answer to Self-Evaluation Test

1. **Extruded Surface**, **2.** **Surface-Revolve**, **3.** **Untrim Surface**, **4.** **Offset Surface**, **5.** **Surface-Loft**, **6.** F, **7.** T, **8.** F, **9.** T, **10.** T

Chapter 17

Working with Blocks

Learning Objectives

After completing this chapter, you will be able to:

- *Use tools in the Blocks toolbar*
- *Save a sketch as a block in the Design Library*
- *Create mechanisms by using blocks*
- *Create parts from blocks*

INTRODUCTION TO BLOCKS

A block is a set of entities grouped together as a single entity. The blocks are used to create complex mechanisms using sketches and check their functioning before developing them into a complex 3D model. You can create a block from a single entity or from a combination of multiple sketched entities. To create a block, first you need to draw an object and then convert it into a block by using the tools available in the **Blocks** toolbar. Tools available in this toolbar are also used to perform other operations such as edit, save, explode, rebuild, and so on. You can convert a block into a part in the Layout environment. In this chapter, you will learn to create a part and an assembly from the blocks.

Blocks Toolbar

The **Blocks** toolbar, as shown in Figure 17-1, is used to control the sketched entities of the blocks. You can perform different operations related to blocks such as create, edit, insert, save, and so on by using the **Blocks** toolbar. The tools in this toolbar are discussed next.

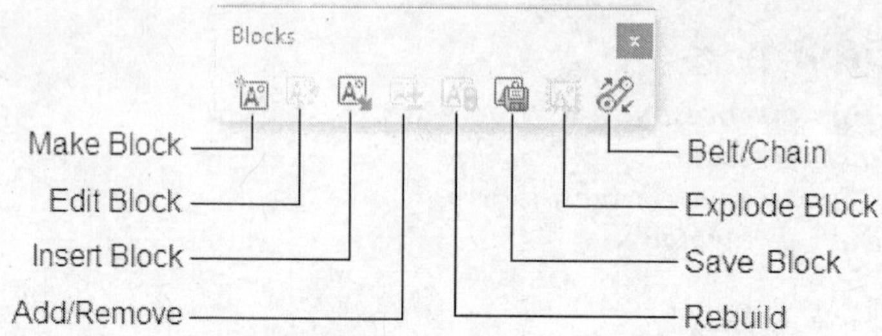

*Figure 17-1 The **Blocks** toolbar*

Make Block

The **Make Block** tool is used to convert the sketch entities into a block. Using this tool, you can make each entity of a sketch as a separate block that can be moved with respect to one another. In such a case, there will be a motion between the sketched entities. This tool will be available only when you invoke the Sketching environment. To create a block, select an entity from the sketch. Next, choose the **Make Block** button from the **Blocks** toolbar or choose **Tools > Blocks > Make** from the SOLIDWORKS menus; the **Make Block PropertyManager** will be displayed, as shown in Figure 17-2, and the name of the selected entity will be displayed in the selection box of the **Block Entities** rollout. The **Insertion Point** rollout of the **Make Block PropertyManager** is used to specify the location of the insertion point of the resulting block. When you insert a block later in a sketch, the cursor will snap the block at the specified insertion point. To specify the insertion point, expand the **Insertion Point** rollout; a manipulator will be displayed in the drawing area. Drag the manipulator and place it at the location where the insertion point is to be specified. When you move the manipulator to specify the insertion point in the drawing area, it will snap to the sketched entity and relations will be added between the insertion point and the sketched entity. Finally, choose the **OK** button; the sketched entity will be converted into a block. Similarly, convert other entities of the sketch into blocks.

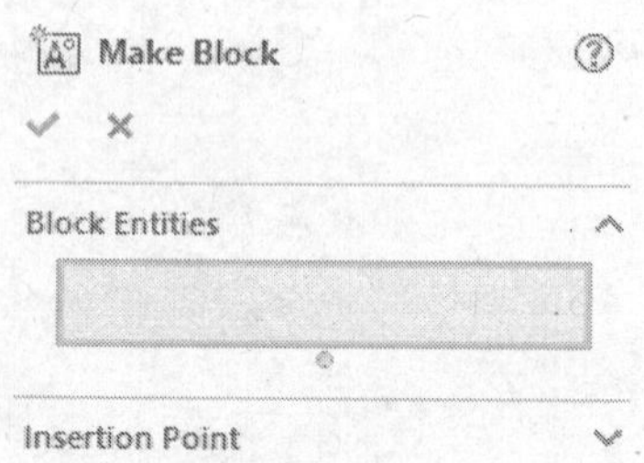

Figure 17-2** The **Make Block PropertyManager

Note

Although you can convert all entities of a sketch into a block, it is recommended to create each entity of the sketch as a separate block; else, there will be no motion between the sketched entities.

Save Block

The **Save Block** tool is used to save the current sketch as a block. In this case, the motion between the sketched entities will be frozen. To save a sketch as a block, draw a sketch and then save it by choosing the **Save Block** button from the **Blocks** toolbar. Alternatively, choose **Tools > Blocks > Save** from the SOLIDWORKS menus; the sketch will be saved as a block. The file extension of a block file is *.Sldblk* .

Insert Block

The **Insert Block** tool is used to insert the blocks into an active sketch. To insert a block after exiting from an active sketch, choose the **Insert Block** button from the **Blocks** toolbar; the **Edit Sketch PropertyManager** will be displayed, as shown in Figure 17-3. Also, you will be prompted to select a sketching plane or an existing sketch. Select the sketching plane from the drawing area or from the **FeatureManager Design Tree**; the **Insert Block PropertyManager** will be displayed, as shown in Figure 17-4. Note that if you are in the sketching environment, the **Insert Block PropertyManager** will be displayed directly. The options available in this PropertyManager are discussed next.

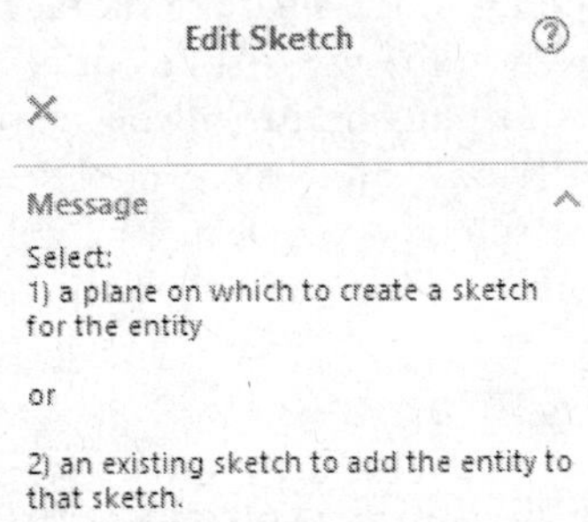

*Figure 17-3 The **Edit Sketch PropertyManager***

Blocks to Insert

The existing blocks of an active sketch are listed in the **Block List** selection box of the **Blocks to Insert** rollout. You can insert multiple copies of the existing blocks into an active sketch. To do so, select a block from the **Block List** selection box in the **Blocks to Insert** rollout; the selected block will be attached to the cursor. Next, click in the drawing area to insert it into the current sketch. Note that the block will still be attached to the cursor, which implies that you can insert multiple copies of that block by clicking repeatedly in the drawing area. You can also browse to the blocks by choosing the **Browse** button from the **Blocks to Insert** rollout. When you insert a block by browsing it from its location, the **Link to file** check box gets activated. Select this check box to link the block file to all the blocks that you have to place. The changes made in the original block will get reflected in all the blocks placed. Choose the **OK** button from the **Insert Block PropertyManager** to exit from it.

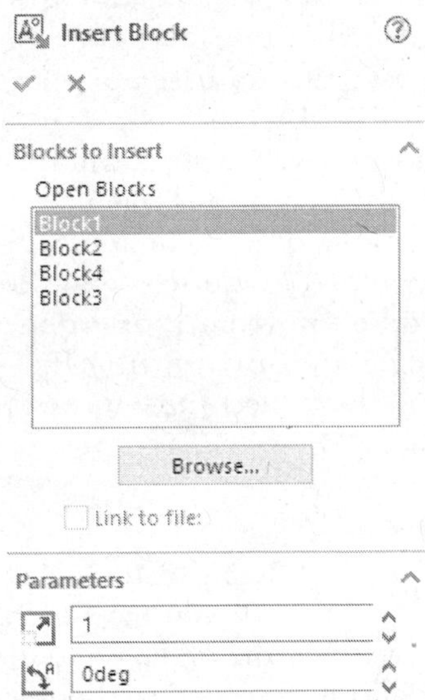

*Figure 17-4 The **Insert Block PropertyManager***

Parameters

In this rollout, the **Block Scale** and **Block Rotation** spinners are available. By default, 1 is displayed as the scale value in the **Block Scale** spinner. It indicates that the current scale factor of the entity is 1. You can change the scale value of the block by using this spinner or by entering the scale value using the keyboard. The **Block Rotation** spinner is used to rotate the block by an angle or adjust the orientation of the block. The default angle value in the **Block Rotation** spinner is 0. You can change the default rotational angle value by using this spinner.

Edit Block

The **Edit Block** tool is used to add, remove, or modify the block entities, as well as change the existing relations and dimensions of the block entities. This tool is enabled in the **Blocks** toolbar only when you select a block from the drawing area. To edit a block, first ensure that the Sketching environment is activated. Then, click on the ▸ sign available on the left of **Sketch** in the **FeatureManager Design Tree** to expand the node and display the blocks, if they are not already displayed. Next, select the required block from the design tree and right-click; a shortcut menu will be displayed. Choose the **Edit Block** option from the shortcut menu. Alternatively, you can choose the **Edit Block** button from the **Blocks** toolbar. Now, you can edit the selected block as per your requirement. Once the changes are made, click on the block confirmation corner on the top right corner of the drawing area to exit from it.

Add/Remove

The **Add/Remove** tool is used to add or remove the sketch entities from a block. To add the sketch entities to a block by using the **Add/Remove** tool, select the required block from the drawing area or from the **FeatureManager Design Tree** and right-click; a shortcut menu will be displayed. Next, choose the **Edit Block** option from the shortcut menu; the **Add/Remove** button will be enabled in the **Blocks** toolbar. Choose the **Add/Remove** button to add or remove the sketched entities from the block; the **Add/Remove Entities PropertyManager** will be displayed, as shown in Figure 17-5. The names of the entities of the selected block will be displayed in the selection box of the **Block Entities** rollout. Select the required sketched entities from the drawing area to add them to the block. Note that the selected sketch entities will also be added to the selection box of the **Block Entities** rollout. Choose the **OK** button from the **Add/Remove Entities PropertyManager**; the selected sketch entities will be added to the block. To remove an entity from the selected block, invoke the **Add/Remove Entities PropertyManager** and then select the entity from the selection box of the **Block Entities** rollout. Next, press the DELETE key.

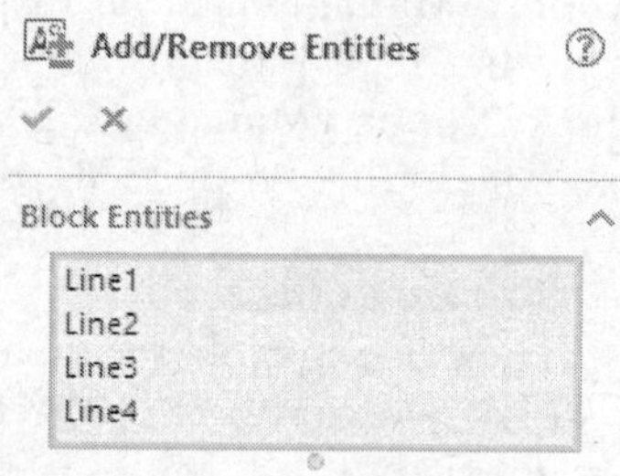

***Figure 17-5** The Add/Remove Entities PropertyManager*

Rebuild

The **Rebuild** tool enables you to refresh or update the parent sketches after editing a block. If you have edited the position of a block by using the **Edit Block** tool, you will notice that the block no longer maintains relations with the other entities. To re-establish the relations, you need to choose the **Rebuild** button from the **Blocks** toolbar. Alternatively, choose **Tools > Blocks > Rebuild** from the SOLIDWORKS menus to re-establish or update the sketched entities.

Explode Block

The **Explode Block** tool is used to explode a selected block and dissolve it into the sketch entity. To explode a block, select the block from the **FeatureManager Design Tree**; the **Explode Block** button will be enabled in the **Blocks** toolbar. Choose the **Explode Block** button from the **Blocks** toolbar or choose **Tools > Blocks > Explode** from the SOLIDWORKS menus; the selected block will dissolve into the sketch. After dissolving a block, you can again turn it into a block by using the **Make Block** button, but a new name will be assigned to it.

Belt/Chain

The **Belt/Chain** tool is used to insert a belt between pulleys. This tool helps you to create the mechanisms such as multiple gear sets, cable and belt pulleys, chain sprocket system, and so on. A belt automatically creates the link motion of the pulleys based on their diameters. To add a belt/chain between pulleys, create sketches of the two or more pulleys in the drawing area and then convert them into separate blocks. The sketch of a pulley should be a circle or an arc only. Choose the **Belt/Chain** button from the **Blocks** toolbar or choose **Tools > Sketch Entities > Belt/Chain** from the SOLIDWORKS menus; the **Belt/Chain PropertyManager** will be displayed, as shown in Figure 17-6, and you will be prompted to select a circle or an arc to define the belt members around which the belt will pass. The options available in this PropertyManager are discussed next.

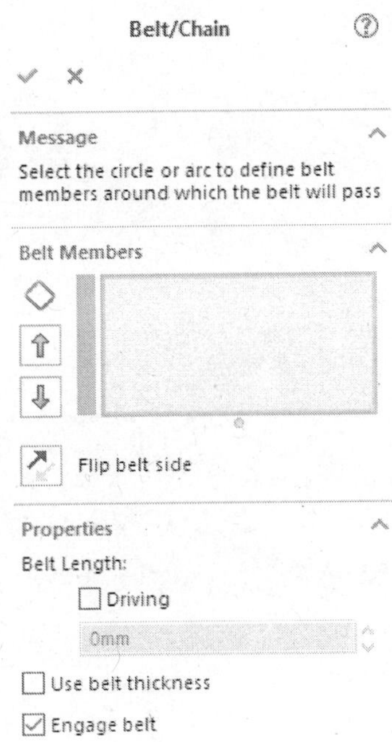

*Figure 17-6 The **Belt/Chain PropertyManager***

Belt Members

The **Belt Members** rollout is used to display the name of the blocks that are selected to define belt members. Select the circular blocks from the drawing area to define the belt members. The selected blocks will be displayed in the **Pulley components** selection box of this rollout and the preview of the belt/chain mechanism will be displayed in the drawing area. You can also remove a selected block from the **Pulley components** selection box. To do so, select a block from the **Pulley components** selection box and invoke the shortcut menu. Next, choose the **Delete** option from the shortcut menu; the selected block will be removed from the selection box. Figure 17-7 shows the preview of the belt/chain mechanism after selecting the belt members.

The **Move Up** and **Move Down** buttons available on the left of the **Belt Members** rollout are used to change the order of the belt members. To move a particular block up in the selection area, select it and then choose the **Move Up** button. Similarly, the **Move Down** button is used to move the selected belt member down in the order. Using these buttons, you can arrange the sequence of the belt members in the selection area of the **Belt Members** rollout. You can also flip the side of the selected belt member on which the belt is placed, by choosing the **Flip belt side** button available in this rollout. Alternatively, you can flip the side of the belt member by clicking on the arrow of the belt member from the drawing area. Figure 17-8 shows the belt member whose side has to be flipped and Figure 17-9 shows the belt member after flipping the side.

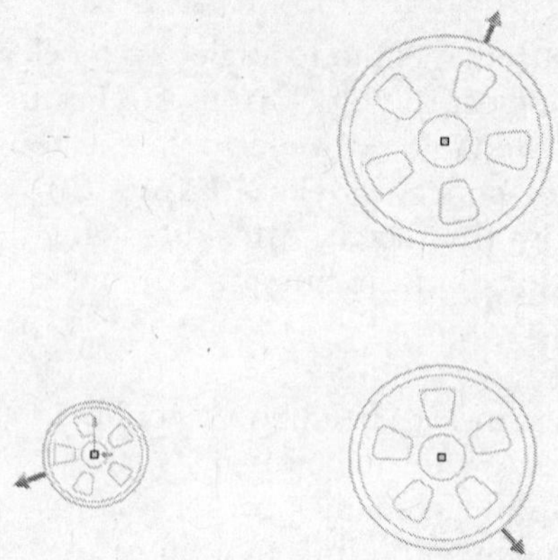

Figure 17-7 *Preview of the belt/chain mechanism*

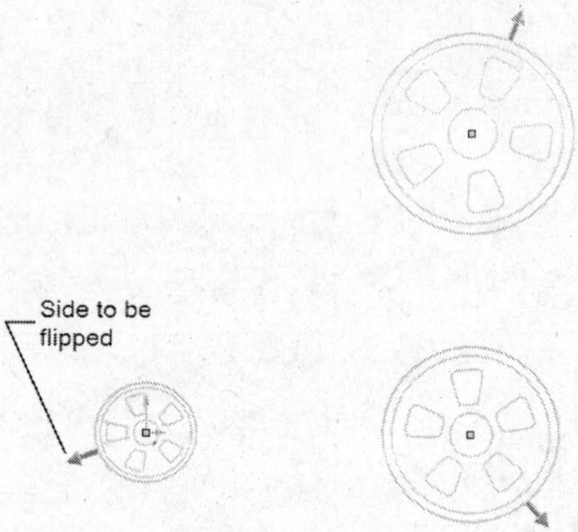

Figure 17-8 *The block entity before flipping the side*

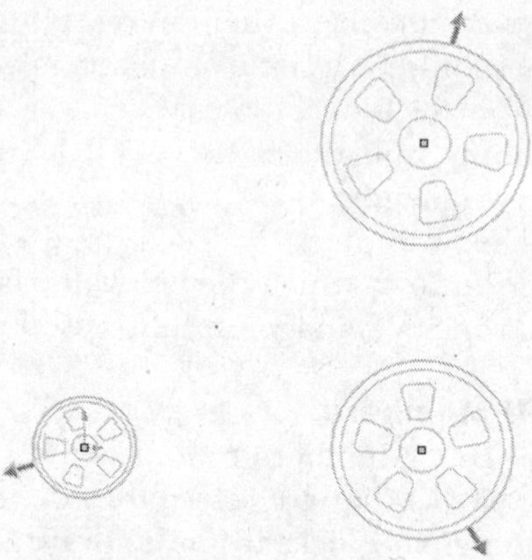

Figure 17-9 *The block entity after flipping the side*

Properties

By default, the **Driving** check box is clear in this rollout, and therefore, the driving length of the belt will be calculated automatically. Select the **Driving** check box to define the length of the belt as per your requirement; the length spinner will be activated. You can specify the driving length of the belt by using this spinner. To specify the thickness of the belt, select the **Use belt thickness** check box; the **Belt thickness** spinner will be displayed. You can specify the thickness of the belt in this spinner. The **Engage belt** check box is used to engage or disengage the belt mechanism. By default, this check box is selected and is used to engage the belt mechanism. To disengage the belt mechanism, clear this check box. Figure 17-10 shows the mechanism without specifying the belt thickness and Figure 17-11 shows the same mechanism after specifying the belt thickness.

Tip

If you draw spoke lines in the pulley, you can easily visualize the rotation of the pulley.

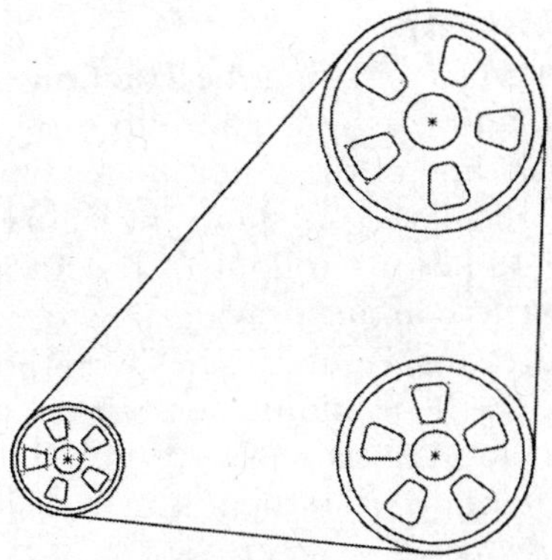

Figure 17-10 Mechanism without specifying the belt thickness

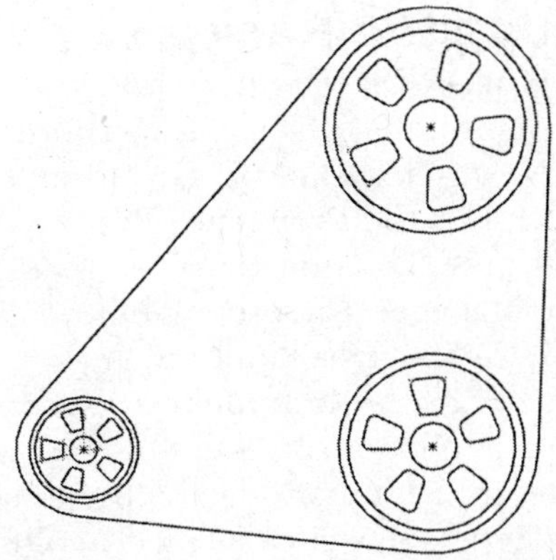

Figure 17-11 Mechanism after specifying the belt thickness

SAVING A SKETCH AS A BLOCK IN THE DESIGN LIBRARY

In SOLIDWORKS, you can directly save a sketch as a block in the **Design Library**. To do so, select the sketch from the **FeatureManager Design Tree** and then choose the **Design Library** tab from the task pane; the **Design Library** task pane will be invoked. Next, choose the **Add to Library** button from the **Design Library** task pane; the **Add to Library PropertyManager** will be displayed, as shown in Figure 17-12, and the name of the selected sketch will be displayed in the selection box available in the **Items to Add** rollout of the PropertyManager. Enter the file name in the **File name** edit box in the **Save To** rollout of the PropertyManager. Next, select the folder in which you want to save this file from the **Design Library folder** area. You can also create a new folder in the **Design Library folder** area by choosing the **Create New Folder** button from the **Design Library** task pane. The **Options** rollout in the **Add to Library PropertyManager** is used to view the file type or the extension of the file. Select the file type **SOLIDWORKS Blocks (*.sldblk)** from the **File type** drop-down list, if it is not selected. The **Enter Description** edit box in this rollout is used to enter the description of the block. This description will be displayed as a tooltip. After setting all the required parameters in the rollout, choose the **OK** button from the **Add to Library PropertyManager** to exit.

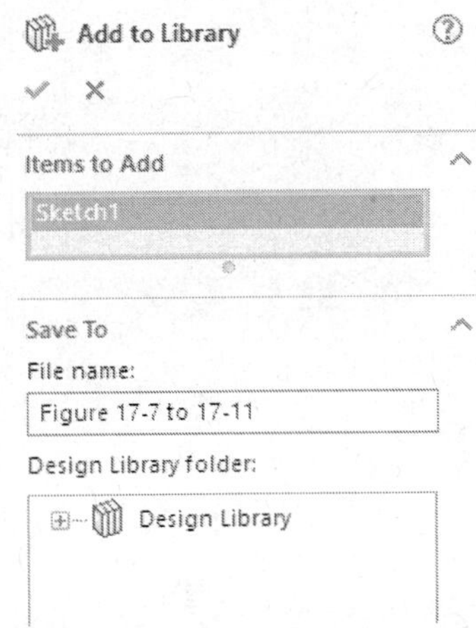

Figure 17-12 Partial view of the Add to Library PropertyManager

CREATING MECHANISMS BY USING BLOCKS

In SOLIDWORKS, you can create simple mechanisms by adding a suitable relation between the blocks. For example, the **Traction** relation is used to create mechanisms such as gear trains, rack and pinion, and so on. Similarly, you can create the cam and follower mechanism using the **Make Path** relation. The procedures to create these mechanisms are discussed next.

Creating the Rack and Pinion Mechanism

In SOLIDWORKS, you can create a rack and pinion mechanism by using the **Traction** relation. To do so, create two sketches, as shown in Figure 17-13, and convert them into two separate blocks. Next, select the circular block and then the vertical line of the other block by pressing the CTRL key; the **Properties PropertyManager** will be displayed, as shown in Figure 17-14. Note that the **Traction** button is available in the **Add Relations** rollout of the **Properties PropertyManager**. Choose this button and then click anywhere in the drawing area to exit from this PropertyManager. Similarly, apply other suitable constraints. Figure 17-15 shows the blocks before applying the **Traction** relation and Figure 17-16 shows the resultant blocks after applying the **Traction** relation. To check the linkage between these blocks, click on the vertical line of the block and drag it up or down in the drawing area. You will notice that the linear translation of one part results in a circular motion of the other part and vice-versa.

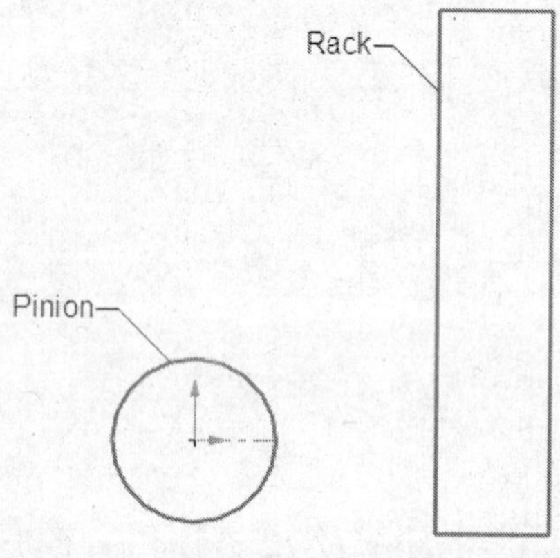

Figure 17-13 Sketches to create blocks

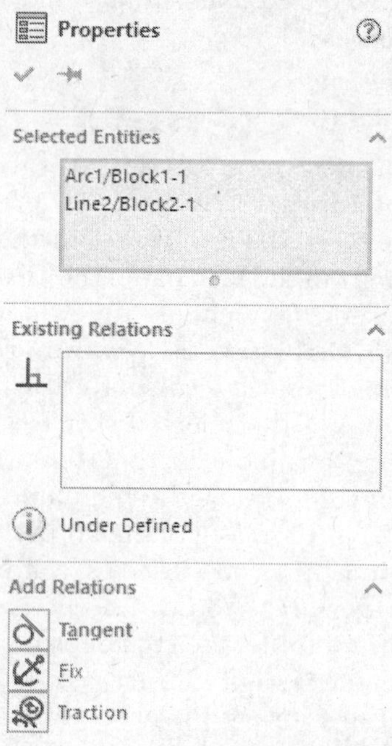

*Figure 17-14 The **Properties PropertyManager***

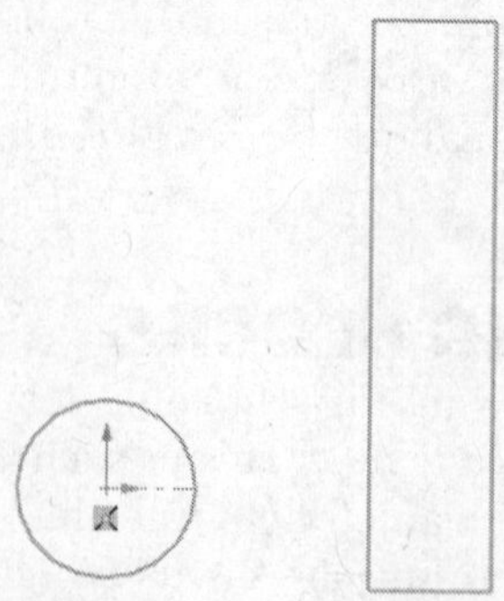

*Figure 17-15 The blocks before applying the **Traction** relation*

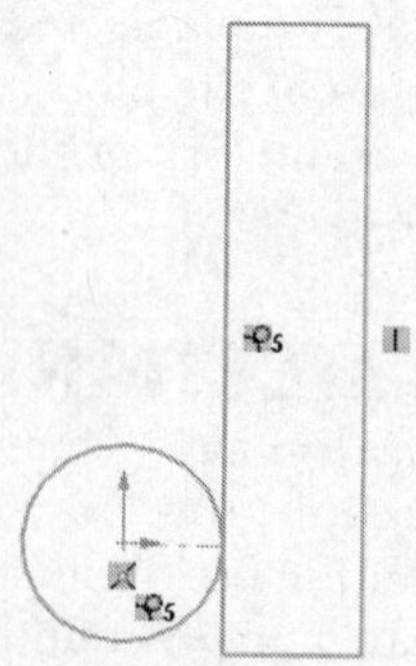

*Figure 17-16 The resultant blocks after applying the **Traction** relation*

Creating the Cam and Follower Mechanism

A cam is a rotating machine element which gives reciprocating or oscillating motion to another element known as follower. In SOLIDWORKS, you can create a cam and follower mechanism between two blocks by using the **Make Path** tool. To create a cam and follower mechanism, first you need to convert a cam profile into a single path by using the **Make Path** tool and then apply tangent relation between the cam and follower profiles. Note that the sketched entities of the cam profile to be converted as path should coincide with each other and form a single chain. The procedure to create a cam and follower mechanism is given below.

Create two sketches that represent a cam and a follower, as shown in Figure 17-17. Next, you need to convert the cam profile into a single path by using the **Make Path** tool. To do so, select the lower arc of the cam, as shown in Figure 17-18, and then choose **Tools > Sketch Tools > Make Path** from the SOLIDWORKS menus; the **Path Properties PropertyManager** will be displayed, as shown in Figure 17-19. In this PropertyManager, the selection box of the **Existing Relations** rollout displays the relations between the sketched entities that make up the path and the sketched entities with which the path interacts. Choose the **Edit Path** button from the **Definition** rollout of this PropertyManager; the **Path PropertyManager** will be displayed, as shown in Figure 17-20, and you will be prompted to select the entities that are coincident end to end and form a single chain. Note that the selected arc of the cam will be displayed in the **Selected Entities** rollout of the **Path PropertyManager**. Now, select the remaining sketched entities of the cam that have a tangent relation with each other from the drawing area to make a path. Choose the **OK** button to exit from the PropertyManager and then convert the sketches of cam and follower into separate blocks. Next, apply the relations, as shown in Figure 17-21. Figure 17-22 shows the cam and follower mechanism after applying the relations. To check the motion between the cam and the follower, click on the cam and drag it clockwise in the drawing area.

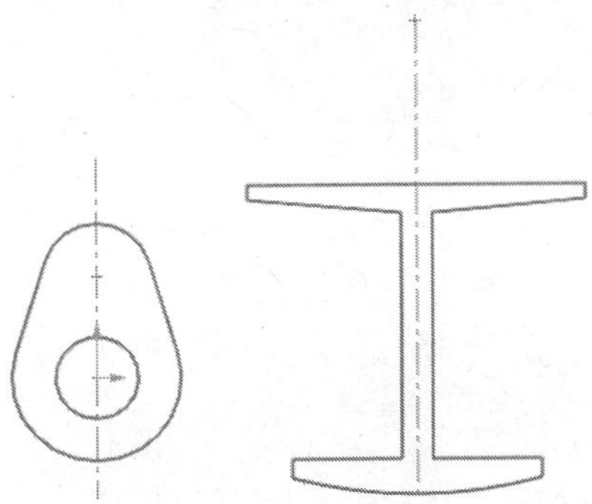

Figure 17-17 *Sketches of cam and follower*

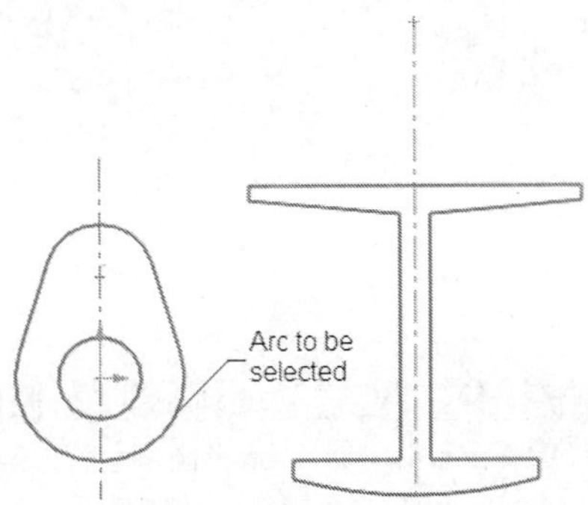

Figure 17-18 *The arc of the cam to be selected*

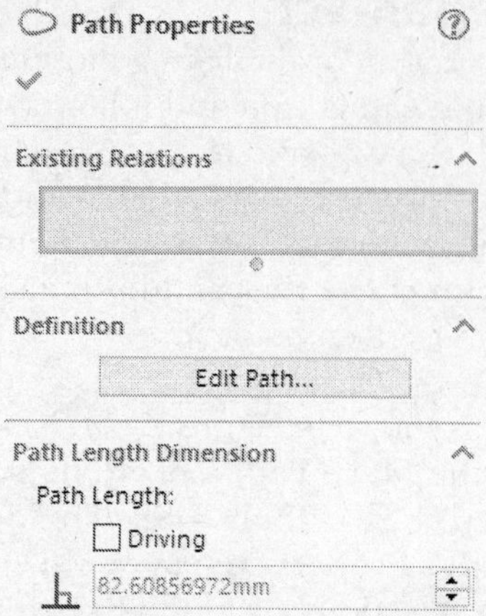

Figure 17-19 The ***Path Properties PropertyManager***

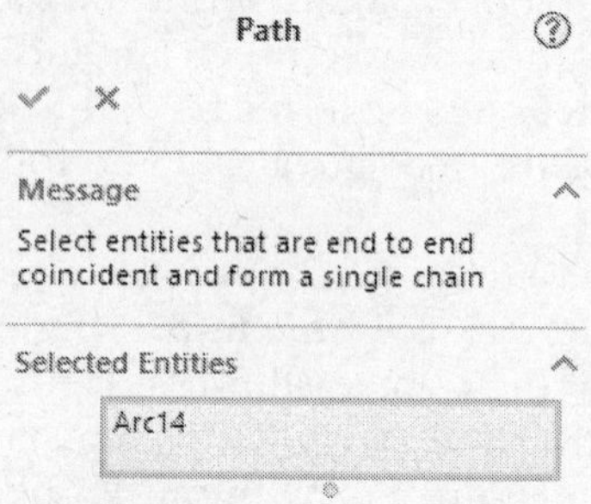

Figure 17-20 The ***Path PropertyManager***

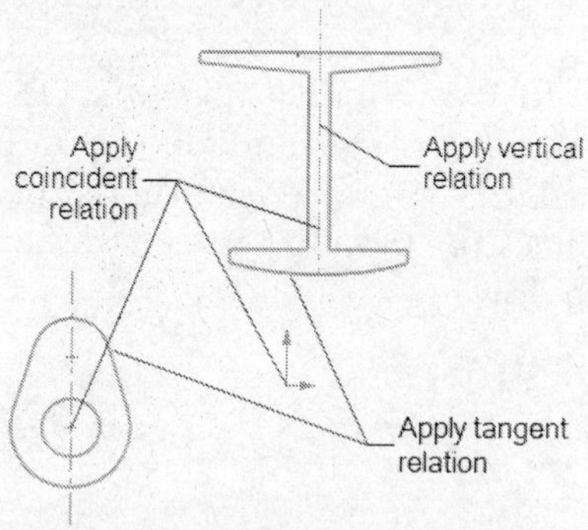

Figure 17-21 *Entities to be selected for adding relations*

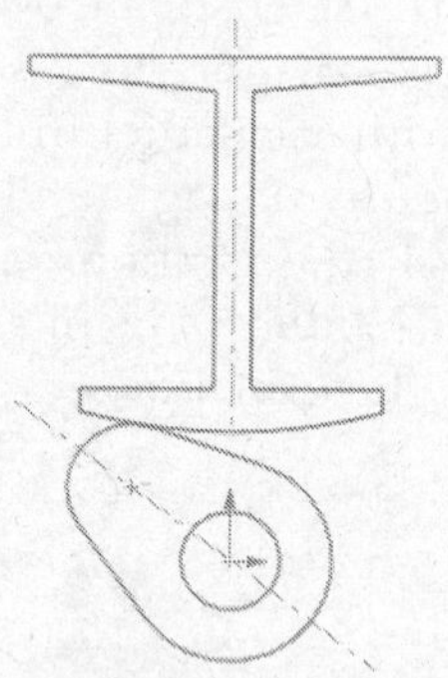

Figure 17-22 *Cam and follower after applying the relation*

APPLYING MOTION TO BLOCKS

In SOLIDWORKS, you can animate the mechanism created using blocks by applying motion to it. To do so, you need to create all the entities of the mechanism individually and then save them as separate blocks. Next, start a new SOLIDWORKS Assembly document by choosing the **Assembly** button from the **New SOLIDWORKS Document** dialog box; a new assembly session will be started and the **Begin Assembly PropertyManager** along with the **Open** dialog box will be invoked. Close the **Open** dialog box and then Choose the **Create Layout** button from the **Begin Assembly PropertyManager**; the Layout environment will be invoked. Insert all the blocks one by one in the drawing area by choosing the **Insert Block** button from the **Blocks** toolbar and apply the required relations between the blocks of the mechanism. After applying the required relation, choose the **Layout** button from the **Layout CommandManager** to exit from it. To add a motor, choose the **Motion Study 1** tab available at the lower left corner of the drawing area. Next, expand the **Expand MotionManager** rollout by clicking on the arrow at the lower-right corner of the drawing area if it is not expanded. In this MotionManager, the **Animation** option is selected by default in the Type of Study drop-down list. Choose the **Motor** button from the **MotionManager** toolbar; the **Motor PropertyManager** will be displayed. Select the required motor from the **Motor Type** rollout and then specify the location of the motor in the **Motor Location** selection box of the **Component/Direction** rollout. After specifying all the required parameters, choose the **OK** button from the **Motor PropertyManager** to exit. To calculate the motion, choose the **Calculate** button from the **MotionManager** toolbar. Now, you can view the motion of the mechanism by choosing the **Play** button from the **MotionManager** toolbar.

To understand the process of applying motion to the blocks, consider the example of pulleys. In this example, in order to create a driver driven mechanism between three pulleys having diameters 10, 20, and 30, as well as to animate it, you need to draw three circles of diameters 10, 20, and 30 respectively in separate sketching environments and save them as block files. Make sure that you draw a centerline inside the circles to view the motion clearly. Next, open the Layout environment by choosing the **Create Layout** button from the **Begin Assembly PropertyManager**. Now, insert the circles which are saved as blocks, one by one into the drawing area by choosing the **Insert Block** button from the **Blocks** toolbar, as shown in Figure 17-23. Next, select the bigger and medium sized circles from the drawing area by pressing the CTRL key; the **Properties PropertyManager** will be displayed. Choose the **Traction** button from the **Add Relations** rollout of the PropertyManager to apply the **Traction** relation. Similarly, select the bigger and smaller circles from the drawing area and apply the **Traction** relation on them. Figure 17-24 shows the circles after applying the **Traction** relation on them. Finally, choose the **Layout** button from the **Layout CommandManager** to exit.

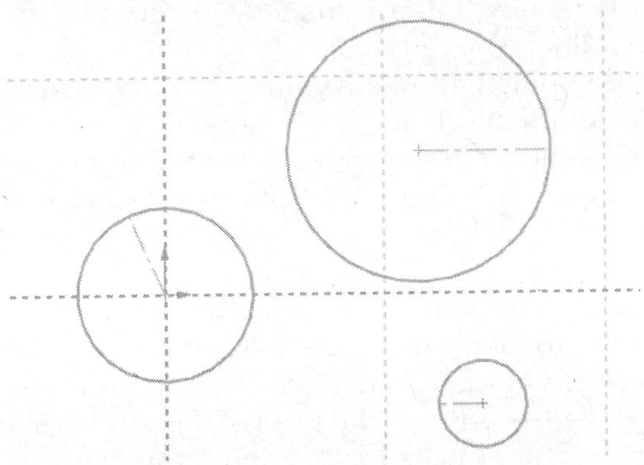

Figure 17-23 *Circles inserted in the drawing area*

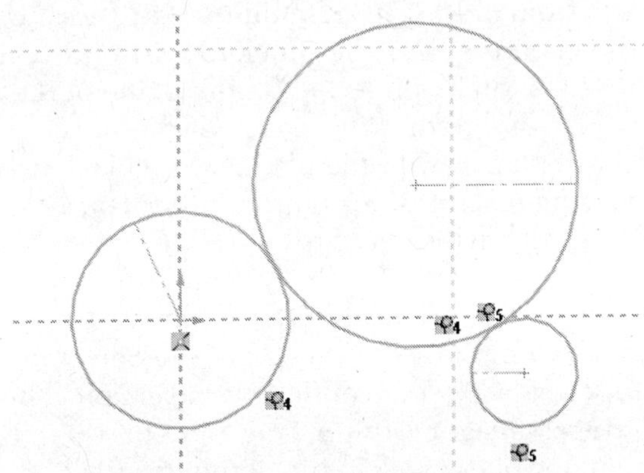

Figure 17-24 *Circles after applying the **Traction** relation*

Now, to animate these circles, choose the **Motion Study 1** tab, the **MotionManager** will be displayed. In the **MotionManager**, the **Animation** option is selected by default in the **Type of Study** drop-down list. Choose the **Motor** button from the **MotionManager** toolbar; the **Motor PropertyManager** will be displayed. By default, the **Rotary Motor** button is chosen in the **Motor Type** rollout of the PropertyManager. Now, you need to select the direction and location of the motor. Select any one of the circles to specify the location and direction of the motor from the drawing area. Choose the **OK** button from the PropertyManager to exit. To calculate the motion, choose the **Calculate** button from the **MotionManager** toolbar. Next, choose the **Play** button to view the motion between the three circles after applying the **Traction** relation.

Note

You can also create the sketches of the mechanism and convert them into separate blocks in the Layout environment itself.

CREATING PARTS FROM BLOCKS

As discussed earlier, you can create parts from the blocks. To create a part from a block, choose the **Make Part from Block** button from the **Layout CommandManager**; the **Make Part From Block PropertyManager** will be displayed, as shown in Figure 17-25. The options in this PropertyManager are discussed next.

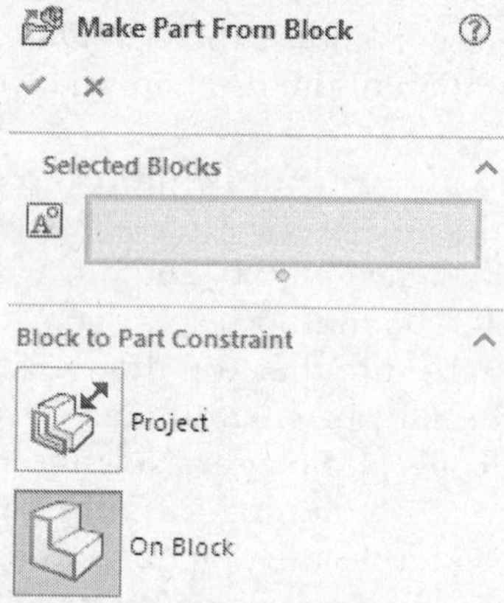

Figure 17-25 The Make Part From Block PropertyManager

Selected Blocks

This rollout lists the blocks that will be selected for creating parts from the drawing area. Select a block from the drawing area; the selected block will be displayed in the selection box of **Selected Blocks** rollout. You can select more than one block from the drawing area.

Block to Part Constraint

In this rollout, there are two buttons: **Project** and **On Block**. These buttons are used to create parts from blocks. By default, the **On Block** button is chosen in this rollout. On choosing the **Project** button from the **Block to Part Constraint** rollout, you can create a part from the block. This part will be projected on the plane of the block in the Layout environment. You can drag this part in the drawing area, normal to the plane of the block and it will not be constrained to be coplanar with the plane of the block in the layout environment, but the part created by choosing the **On Block** button will be constrained to be coplanar with the plane of the block in the layout environment.

Select a block from the drawing area of the Layout environment; the selected block will be displayed in the selection box of the **Selected Blocks** rollout. Choose the **OK** button from the PropertyManager to confirm the selection. The selected block will be displayed as a part in the **FeatureManager Design Tree**. The part name will be the same as the block name. Note that the name of the part in the design tree will be covered by a square bracket, indicating that it is a virtual component. The virtual components are saved internally in the assembly file in which they are created. You can save these components into external files later on. Next, right-click on the part name or virtual component in the design tree; a shortcut menu will be displayed. Choose the **Open Part** button from the shortcut menu; the selected part will open in the **Part** environment. Now, you can convert it into a solid feature using the tools available in the **Features CommandManager**. Next, open the layout environment again by choosing **Window > name of the layout assembly** from the SOLIDWORKS menus.

TUTORIALS

Tutorial 1

In this tutorial, you will create a reciprocating mechanism by assembling different blocks, as shown in Figure 17-26. You will also convert the blocks of the reciprocating mechanism into parts. The final assembly of the mechanism after converting blocks into parts is shown in Figure 17-27. Figures 17-28 through 17-30 show different views of the parts of the mechanism with the required dimensions. **(Expected time: 45 min)**

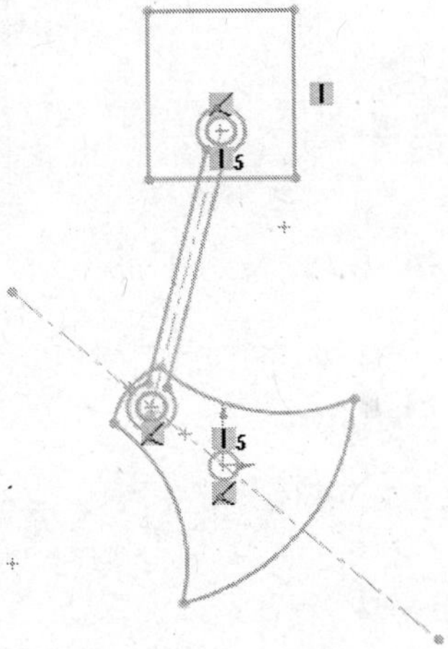

Figure 17-26 *Reciprocating mechanism created by assembling the blocks*

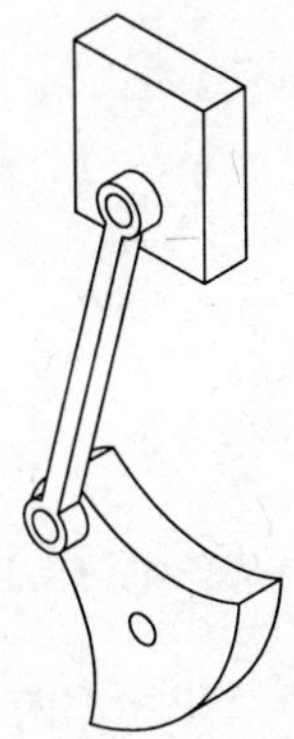

Figure 17-27 *Reciprocating mechanism after converting the blocks into parts*

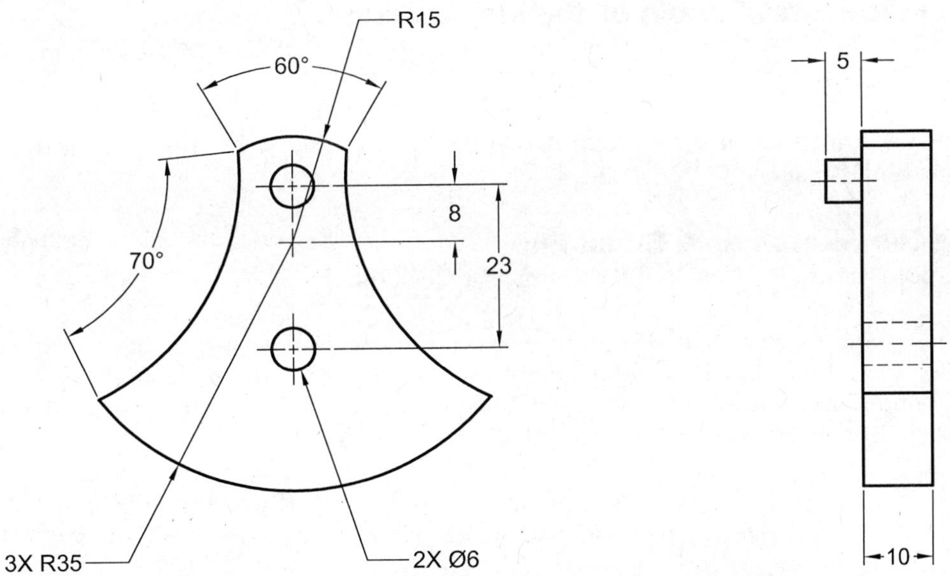

Figure 17-28 *The front and right views of the crank*

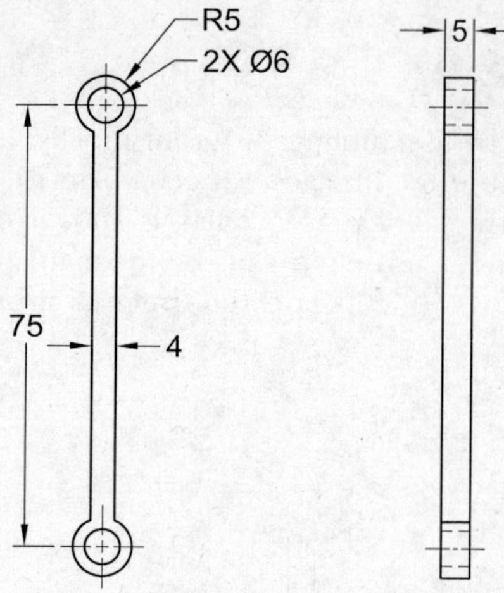

Figure 17-29 The front and side views of the piston rod

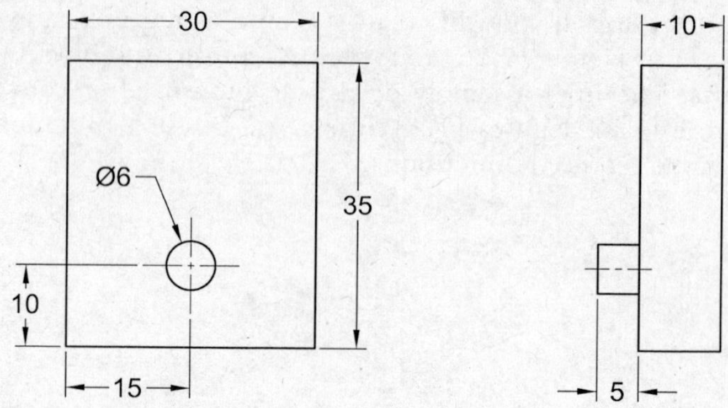

Figure 17-30 The front and side views of the piston tank

The following steps are required to complete this tutorial:

a. Create the sketches of the mechanism by using the sketch tools.
b. Save sketches as different block files.
c. Insert blocks into the Layout environment.
d. Apply relations between blocks.
e. Convert blocks into parts.
f. Save and close the document.

Creating the First Sketch of the Mechanism

1. Start a new SOLIDWORKS part document using the **New SOLIDWORKS Document** dialog box and invoke the sketching environment.

2. Draw the front view of the crank, refer to Figure 17-28, by using the tools in the **Sketch CommandManager**.

Saving the Sketch as a Block File

You need to save the sketch of the crank as a block file.

1. Choose the **Save Sketch as Block** button from the **Blocks** toolbar; the **Save As** dialog box is displayed. Enter **Crank** as the name of the sketch in the **File name** edit box. Browse to the required location and then choose the **Save** button to exit from it. Alternatively, choose **Tools > Blocks > Save** from the SOLIDWORKS menus to save the sketch as a block file.

2. Close the current sketching environment by choosing **File > Close** from the SOLIDWORKS menus; the **SOLIDWORKS** message window is displayed. Choose the **Don't Save** button from it.

Creating the other Sketches of the Mechanism and Saving them as Block Files

You need to create other sketches of the mechanism in different sketching environments and then save them as separate block files.

1. Start a new SOLIDWORKS part document by using the **New SOLIDWORKS Document** dialog box and invoke the sketching environment.

2. Draw the sketch of the front view of the piston rod, refer to Figure 17-29.

3. Select the sketch and save it as a block file by choosing the **Save Sketch as Block** button from the **Blocks** toolbar. Enter **Piston_rod** in the **File name** edit box of the **Save As** dialog box and then choose the **Save** button.

4. Similarly, draw the sketch of the piston tank, refer to Figure 17-30, and then save the sketch as a separate block file with the name **Piston_tank**.

Inserting Blocks in the Layout Environment

You need to insert blocks in the layout environment and then apply the required relation between them.

1. Start a new SOLIDWORKS Assembly environment by using the **New SOLIDWORKS Document** dialog box. Close the **Open** dialog box and then choose the **Create Layout** button from the **Begin Assembly PropertyManager**; the layout environment is invoked.

2. Choose the **Insert Block** button from the **Blocks** toolbar; the **Insert Block PropertyManager** is displayed.

3. Choose the **Browse** button from the **Blocks to Insert** rollout of the **Insert Block PropertyManager**; the **Open** dialog box is displayed.

4. Select **Crank** from the **Open** dialog box and then choose the **Open** button; the selected block is attached to the cursor.

5. Click anywhere in the drawing area to place the block and then right-click to display the shortcut menu. Choose **OK** from the shortcut menu.

6. Similarly, insert the **Piston_rod** and **Piston_tank** blocks in this layout environment. To change the current view orientation normal to the screen, choose the **View Orientation** button from the **View (Heads-Up)** toolbar; a flyout is displayed. Choose the **Normal To** button from the flyout. Figure 17-31 shows the blocks inserted in the layout environment.

Applying Relations to the Blocks

You need to apply relations to the blocks to assemble them and to view the motion of the mechanism.

1. Press and hold the CTRL key, and then select the center of the lower circle of the **Crank** and the origin, as shown in Figure 17-32; the **Properties PropertyManager** is displayed.
2. Choose the **Coincident** button from the **Add Relations** rollout of the **Properties PropertyManager**; the Coincident relation is applied between the selected points. Click anywhere in the drawing area to exit the **Properties PropertyManager**.

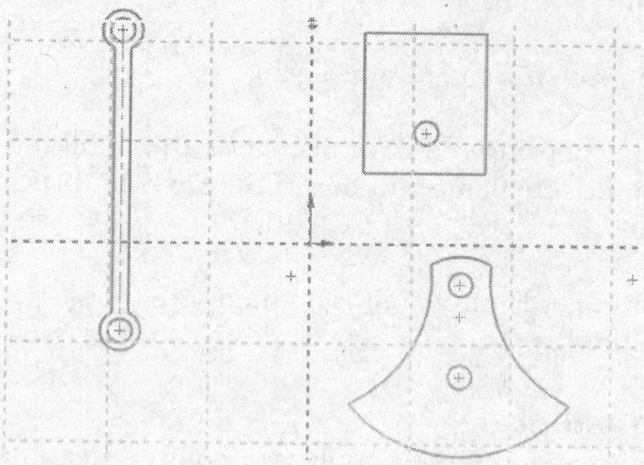

Figure 17-31 *Blocks after they are inserted in the layout environment*

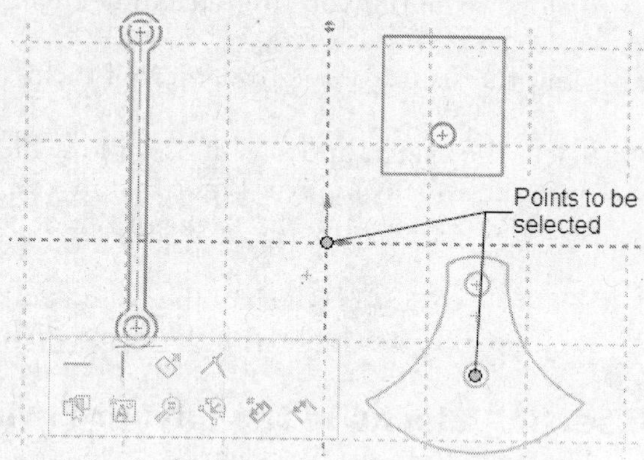

Figure 17-32 *Points to be selected to apply the relation*

3. Next, apply the relations, as shown in Figure 17-33. Figure 17-34 shows the blocks after applying the required relations. Now, the blocks act as a reciprocating mechanism.

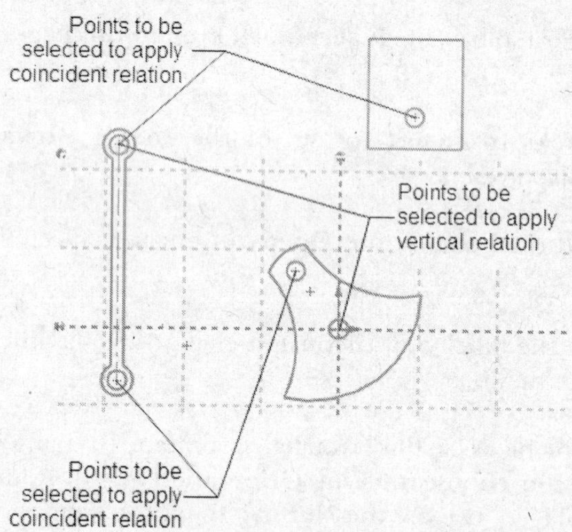

Figure 17-33 *Points selected to apply the relations*

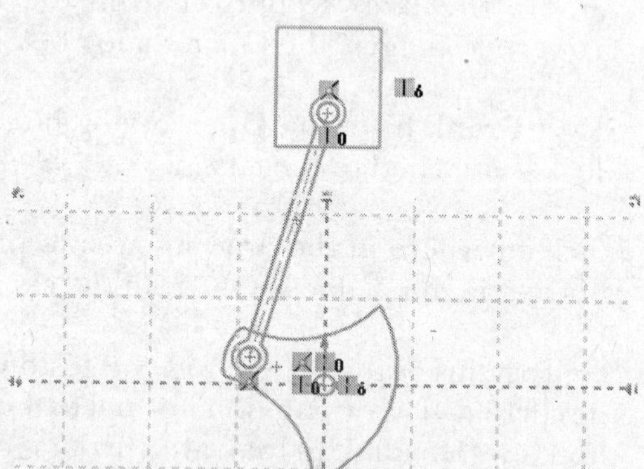

Figure 17-34 *Blocks after applying the required relations*

4. To view the motion of the mechanism, press and hold the left mouse button on the point, as shown in Figure 17-35, and then rotate the cursor in the clockwise direction.

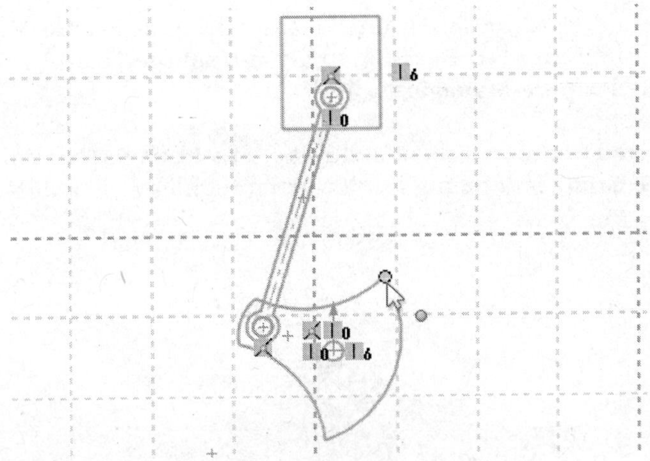

Figure 17-35 Point selected to view the motion of the mechanism

Converting Blocks into Parts

Now, you need to convert the blocks into parts to create a 3D mechanism.

1. Choose the **Make Part from Block** button from the **Layout CommandManager**; the **Make Part From Block PropertyManager** is displayed.

2. Select all the blocks from the drawing area; the names of the selected blocks are displayed in the **Selected Blocks** rollout of the PropertyManager. Make sure that the **On Block** button is chosen in the **Block to Part Constraint** rollout of **Make Part From Block PropertyManager**. Choose the **OK** button; all the blocks are displayed as parts in the **FeatureManager Design Tree** with the part symbol on their left.

3. Choose the **Rebuild** button from the Menu Bar to update the change.

4. Select the **Crank** block from the **FeatureManager Design Tree**; a pop-up toolbar is displayed. Choose the **Edit Part** button from the pop-up toolbar; the Part environment is invoked. Choose the **Features** tab from the **CommandManager**.

5. Next, choose the **Extruded Boss/Base** button from the **Feature CommandManager**; the **Extrude PropertyManager** is displayed and you are prompted to select a sketching plane or an existing sketch. Select the sketch of the crank from the drawing area or from the **FeatureManager Design Tree**; its preview is displayed in the drawing area.

6. In the **Direction 1** rollout of the PropertyManager, the **Blind** option is selected by default in the **End Condition** drop-down list. Enter **10** mm in the **Depth** spinner of the **Direction 1** rollout and choose the **Reverse Direction** button to flip the direction of the extrusion. Make sure the **Thin Feature** rollout is not activated. Choose the **OK** button to exit the PropertyManager.

Next, you need to extrude the upper hole of the **Crank**, refer to Figure 17-28.

7. Select the sketch of the previously extruded feature from the **FeatureManager Design Tree** and then choose the **Extruded Boss/Base** button from the **Features CommandManager**; the **Boss-Extrude PropertyManager** is displayed.

8. Expand the **Selected Contours** rollout in this PropertyManager. Move the cursor toward the upper hole of the **Cran**k and then select it when it highlights in a different color, as shown in Figure 17-36.

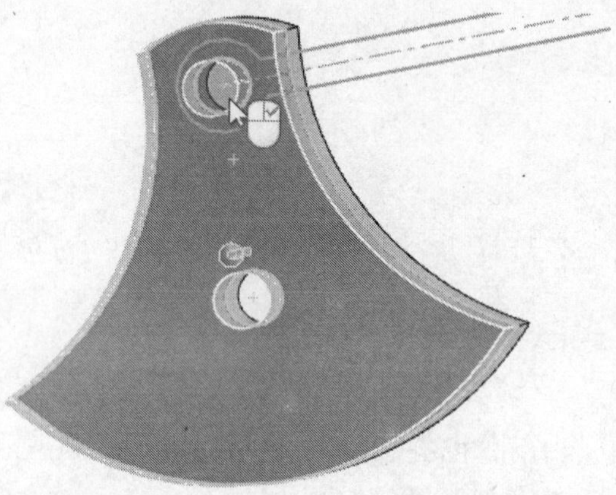

Figure 17-36 Hole of the crank to be selected

9. Enter **5** mm in the **Depth** spinner of the **Direction 1** rollout. Expand the **Direction 2** rollout and enter **10** mm in the **Depth** spinner. Choose the **OK** button to exit from it; the crank feature is displayed in the drawing area.

10. Click on the confirmation corner in the upper right of the drawing area. If the rebuild icon is available on the left of the **Crank** in the design tree. Choose the **Rebuild** button from the Menu Bar to rebuild the part.

11. Select the **Piston_rod** block from the **FeatureManager Design Tree**; a pop-up toolbar is displayed.

12. Choose the **Edit Part** button from the pop-up toolbar to invoke the Part environment. Choose the **Features** tab, if it is not already invoked.

13. Invoke the **Extrude PropertyManager**, select the sketch of the **Piston_rod** from the drawing area or from the **FeatureManager Design Tree** and enter **5** mm in the **Depth** spinner in the **Direction 1** rollout of the PropertyManager. Choose the **OK** button to exit from it.

14. Next, click on the confirmation corner in the upper right of the drawing area and then choose the **Rebuild** button from the Menu Bar.

15. Similarly, select the **Piston_tank** block from the **FeatureManager Design Tree** and invoke the Part environment.

16. Invoke the **Extrude PropertyManager** and select the sketch of the piston tank from the drawing area or from the **FeatureManager Design Tree**; its preview is displayed.

17. Enter **10** mm in the **Depth** spinner of the **Direction 1** rollout.

18. Choose the **Reverse Direction** button from the **Direction 1** rollout of the PropertyManager and then choose **OK**.

Next, you need to create the shaft for the **Piston_tank**, refer to Figure 17-30.

19. Select the sketch of the **Piston_tank** from the **FeatureManager Design Tree** and then invoke the **Extrude PropertyManager**.

20. Expand the **Selected Contours** rollout of the PropertyManager and move the cursor toward the hole of the **Piston_tank**. Next, select it by using the left mouse button when it is highlighted in a different color.

21. Enter **5** mm in the **Depth** spinner of the **Direction 1** rollout. Next, expand the **Direction 2** rollout and enter **10** mm in the **Depth** spinner of this rollout. Now, choose **OK** from this PropertyManager and then exit by clicking on the confirmation corner available at the upper right of the drawing area.

22. Choose the **Rebuild** button from the Menu Bar to rebuild the part. Next, choose the **Visibility Off** button from the **View (Heads-Up)** toolbar; a flyout is displayed. Choose the **View Sketches** option to hide the sketches. Figure 17-37 shows the mechanism after hiding the sketches of the parts.

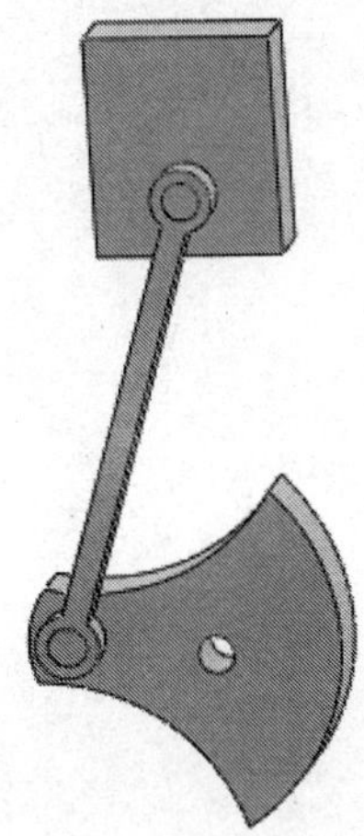

Figure 17-37 Reciprocating mechanism after hiding the sketches

Saving the Model

You can see that the name of the components in the **FeatureManager Design Tree** is enclosed in parenthesis. This indicates that these are virtual components and will be saved internally, if you choose the **Save** button. So, first you need to make them regular components and save externally.

1. Right-click on the **Crank** block and choose the **Save Part (in External File)** option from the shortcut menu displayed; the **Save As** dialog box will be displayed.

2. Choose the **Specify Path** button and browse to the location.

3. Similarly, save other components.

4. Choose the **Save** button from the Menu Bar and save the mechanism with the name *c17_tut01* at the location given below:
\Documents\SOLIDWORKS\c17

5. Close the document by choosing **File > Close** from the SOLIDWORKS menus.

Tutorial 2

In this tutorial, you will convert 2D blocks into parts in the Layout environment and then assemble them to create a mechanism, as shown in Figure 17-38. Also, you will animate the mechanism by applying the rotary motor. Figures 17-39 through 17-42 show different views of the parts of the mechanism with required dimensions. **(Expected time: 45 min)**

Figure 17-38 Mechanism created by assembling the parts

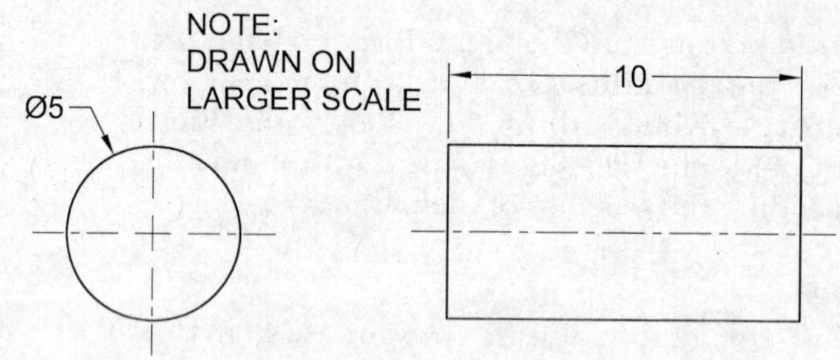

Figure 17-39 The front and side views of the Shaft

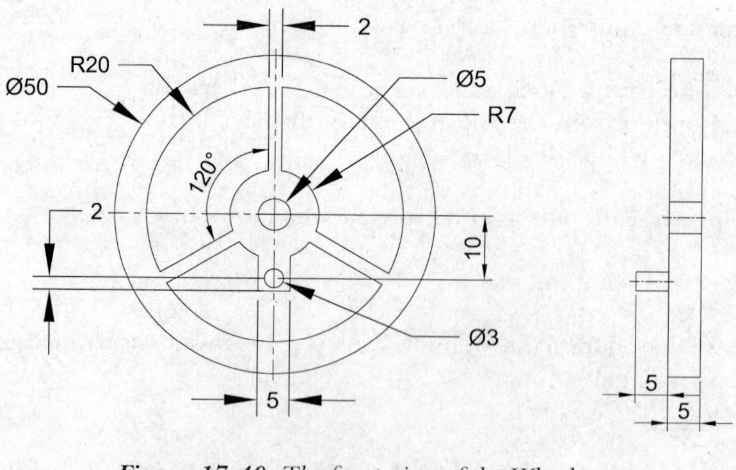

Figure 17-40 The front view of the Wheel

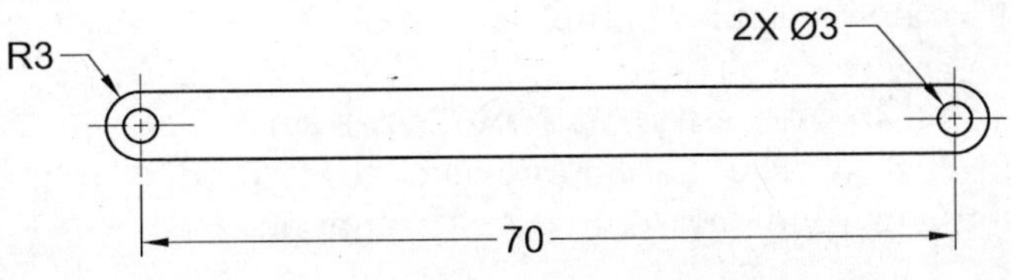

Figure 17-41 The front view of the Connecting rod

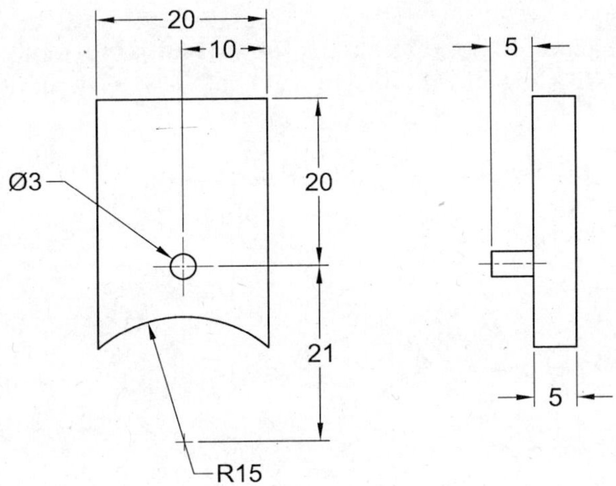

Figure 17-42 The front and side views of the Slider

The following steps are required to complete this tutorial:

a. Create the sketches of the mechanism by using the sketch tools and save them as different block files.
b. Insert blocks into the layout environment.
c. Convert blocks into parts.
d. Assemble parts.
e. Animate the mechanism by applying the rotary motor.
f. Save the mechanism and then close the document.

Creating the Sketches of the Mechanism and Saving them as Block Files

1. Start a new SOLIDWORKS part document by using the **New SOLIDWORKS Document** dialog box and invoke the sketching environment.

2. Draw the sketch of the front view of the Shaft by using the tools in the **Sketch CommandManager**. For dimensions of the shaft, refer to Figure 17-39. Save the sketch of the Shaft as a block file in the *c17* folder by choosing the **Save Block** button in the **Blocks** toolbar.

3. Similarly, create the sketches of the Wheel, Connecting rod, and Slider in a separate sketching environment. For dimensions of the sketches, refer to Figures 17-40 through 17-42. Save all the sketches as separate block files in the *c17* folder.

Inserting all Blocks in the Layout Environment

After you have saved all sketches as separate block files, you need to place these blocks one by one in the layout environment to convert them into parts.

1. Start a new Assembly document by choosing the **Assembly** button from the **New SOLIDWORKS Document** dialog box. Close the **Open** dialog box and then choose the **Create Layout** button from the **Begin Assembly PropertyManager**; the layout environment is invoked.

2. Choose the **View Orientation** button from the **View (Heads-Up)** toolbar; a flyout is displayed. Choose the **Normal To** button from the flyout to change the orientation of the plane normal to the screen.

3. Choose the **Insert Block** button from the **Blocks** toolbar and insert the Shaft, Wheel, Connecting rod, and Slider in the layout environment, as shown in Figure 17-43.

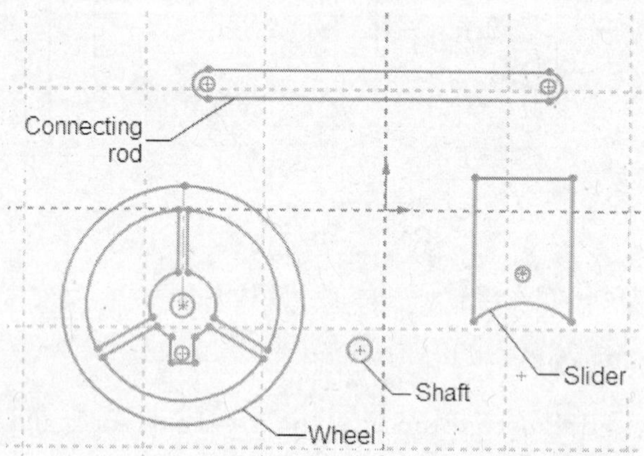

Figure 17-43 *The blocks inserted in the Layout environment*

Converting Blocks into Parts

Now, you need to convert all the blocks into parts to create a 3D mechanism.

1. Choose the **Make Part from Block** button from the **Layout CommandManager**; the **Make Part From Block PropertyManager** is displayed.

2. Select all the blocks from the drawing area or from the **FeatureManager Design Tree**; the names of the selected blocks are displayed in the **Selected Blocks** selection box. Choose the **OK** button from the PropertyManager; all blocks are displayed with the part symbol on the left in the **FeatureManager Design Tree**.

3. Choose the **Rebuild** button from the Menu Bar to update the change.

4. Select **Shaft** from the **FeatureManager Design Tree** and right-click; a pop-up toolbar is displayed. Choose the **Edit Part** button from this toolbar; the Part environment is invoked.

5. Choose the **Features** tab from the CommandManager.

6. Choose the **Extruded Boss/Base** button from the **Features CommandManager**; the **Extrude PropertyManager** is displayed and you are prompted to select the sketch.

7. Select the sketch of the **Shaft** from the drawing area; the preview of the shaft is displayed.

8. Enter **10** mm in the **Depth** spinner of the **Direction 1** rollout and then choose the **Reverse Direction** button. Next, choose the **OK** button to exit from the PropertyManager.

9. Click on the confirmation corner available in the upper right corner of the screen.

10. Similarly, select the Wheel from the **FeatureManager Design Tree** and right-click; a pop-up toolbar is displayed. Invoke the Part environment by choosing the **Edit Part** button from the pop-up toolbar.

11. Invoke the **Extrude PropertyManager** by choosing the **Extruded Boss/Base** button from the **Feature CommandManager**.

12. Select the sketch of Wheel from the drawing area or from the **FeatureManager Design Tree**; its preview is displayed. Enter **5** mm in the **Depth** spinner and choose the **Reverse Direction** button in the **Direction 1** rollout of the PropertyManager. Choose the **OK** button.

13. Click on the ▸ sign available on the left of the **Boss-Extrude** feature of the Wheel in the **FeatureManager Design Tree**; the sketch of the extrude feature is displayed.

14. Select the sketch of the extrude feature from the **FeatureManager Design Tree** and invoke the **Boss-Extrude PropertyManager**.

15. Expand the **Selected Contours** rollout in the PropertyManager. Zoom the wheel feature and select the area of the Wheel to be extruded, as shown in Figure 17-44.

Figure 17-44 *The area selected to be extruded*

16. Enter **10** mm in the **Depth** spinner of the **Direction 1** rollout and extrude it by using the **Mid Plane** option. Click on the confirmation corner to exit from it.

17. Select the Connecting rod from the **FeatureManager Design Tree** and right-click; a pop-up toolbar is displayed. Invoke the Part environment by choosing the **Edit Part** button from the pop-up toolbar.

18. Invoke the **Extrude PropertyManager** and select the sketch of the Connecting rod from the design tree. Enter **5** mm in the **Depth** spinner of the **Direction 1** rollout and then choose the **OK** button to from the **Boss-Extrude PropertyManager**. Next, click on the confirmation corner.

19. Select the Slider from the **FeatureManager Design Tree** and invoke the Part environment by choosing the **Edit Part** button from the pop-up toolbar displayed.

20. Invoke the **Extrude PropertyManager** and select the sketch of the slider from the drawing area; its preview is displayed.

21. Enter **5** mm in the **Depth** spinner of the **Direction 1** rollout and choose the **Reverse Direction** button in the PropertyManager. Next, choose the **OK** button to exit.

22. Click on the ▸ sign available on the left of the **Boss-Extrude** feature of the slider in the design tree; the sketch of the extrude feature is displayed.

23. Select the sketch of the extrude feature from the design tree and invoke the **Boss-Extrude PropertyManager**. Next, expand the **Selected Contours** rollout and select the area enclosed by the hole of diameter 3 mm in the Slider; its preview is displayed.

24. Enter **10** mm in the **Depth** spinner of the **Direction 1** rollout and extrude it using the **Mid Plane** option. Finally, choose the **OK** button to exit from the PropertyManager.

25. Click on the confirmation corner to exit from the Part environment. Figure 17-45 shows the blocks after they have been converted into parts.

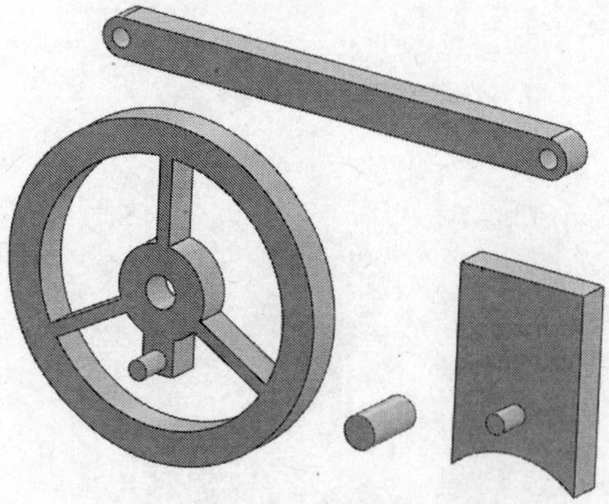

***Figure 17-45** Blocks after being converted into parts*

Assembling the Parts

Once all parts have been created, you need to assemble them in the Assembly environment using the mate relations.

1. Choose the **Assembly** tab from the **CommandManager**; the **Assembly CommandManager** is displayed.

   First, you need to assemble the Wheel with the Shaft. Therefore, you need to fix the Shaft.

2. Select the Shaft from the drawing area and right-click; a shortcut menu is displayed. Choose the **Fix** option from the shortcut menu; the Shaft gets fixed. Now, you cannot move or rotate it.

3. Invoke the **Mate PropertyManager** and apply the **Concentric** mate between the innermost circular face of the Wheel and the Shaft, refer to Figure 17-46. Choose the **Add/Finish Mate** button from the **Mate** pop-up toolbar.

4. Apply the **Concentric** mate between the left-most inner circular face of the **Connecting rod** and the cylindrical face of the handle on the Wheel, refer to Figure 17-46. Choose the **Add/Finish Mate** button from the **Mate** pop-up toolbar.

5. Similarly, apply the **Concentric** mate between the cylindrical face of the handle on the Slider and the other circular face of the Connecting rod, refer to Figure 17-46. Choose the **Add/Finish Mate** button from the **Mate** pop-up toolbar.

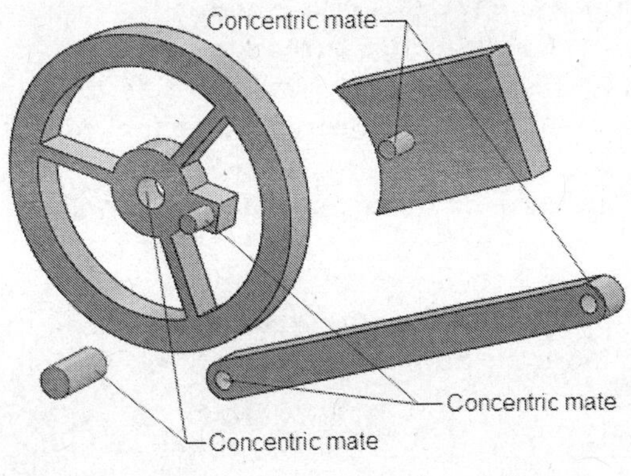

Figure 17-46 *Parts faces selected to apply the mates*

6. Next, apply the **Coincident** mate between the horizontal planes of the Shaft and the Slider, refer to Figure 17-47. Next, exit from the **Mate PropertyManager**. Figure 17-48 shows the final assembly of the mechanism.

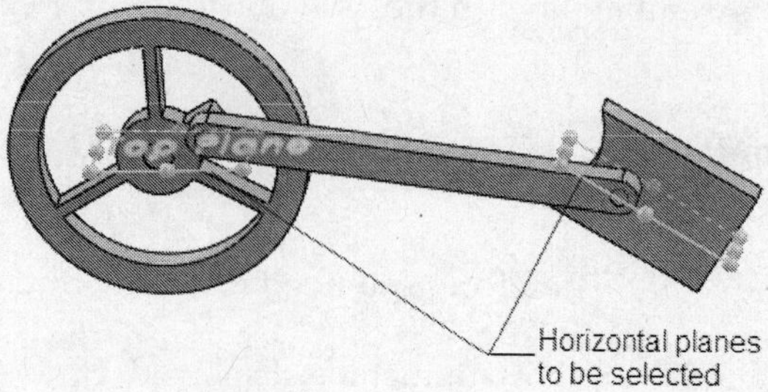

Figure 17-47 The planes to be selected

Figure 17-48 The final mechanism

Applying Motion to the Mechanism

Next, you need to apply motion to the mechanism to check its working.

1. Choose the **Motion Study 1** tab available at the lower left corner of the drawing area; the **MotionManager** is displayed.

2. Choose the **Motor** button from the **MotionManager** toolbar; the **Motor PropertyManager** is displayed.

3. The **Rotary Motor** is selected by default in this PropertyManager. Select the front face of the Wheel as reference for specifying the direction of rotation; the selected face is displayed in the **Motor Direction** selection box of the **Component / Direction** rollout of the PropertyManager. You can flip the direction of the rotation of the motor, if required, by choosing the **Reverse Direction** button from the **Component / Direction** rollout.

4. Choose the **OK** button from the **Motor PropertyManager** to exit.

5. Choose the **Calculate** button from the **MotionManager** toolbar to calculate the motion of the mechanism.

6. Choose the **Play** button from the **MotionManager** toolbar to view the motion of the mechanism and then choose the **Stop** button to stop the motion of the mechanism.

7. Finally, choose the **Rebuild** button from the Menu Bar.

Saving the Model

1. Choose the **Save** button from the Menu Bar; the **Save Modified Documents** dialog box is displayed.

2. Ensure that all the check boxes in the file name column are selected. Next, choose the **Save All** button; the **Save As** dialog box is displayed.

3. Browse to the location, enter **c17_tut02** as the file name and choose the **Save** button; the **SOLIDWORKS** message box is displayed.

4. Choose the **OK** button from this message box; the **Save As** dialog box is displayed again.

5. Select the **Save externally (specify paths)** radio button and choose the **OK** button; the assembly is saved.

6. Close the document by choosing **File > Close** from the SOLIDWORKS menus.

Self-Evaluation Test

Answer the following questions and then compare them to those given at the end of this chapter:

1. In SOLIDWORKS, the __________ button in the **Blocks** toolbar is used to make each entity of a sketch as a separate block.

2. The __________ check box in the **Belt/Chain PropertyManager** is selected to specify the thickness of the belt.

3. Choose the ________ button in the **Definition** rollout of the **Path Properties PropertyManager** to invoke the **Path PropertyManager**.

4. The __________ button in the **Blocks** toolbar is used to edit a block.

5. The __________ button in the **Belt Members** rollout of the **Belt/Chain PropertyManager** is used to flip the side of a selected belt member.

6. The **Traction** relation is used to create a driver-driven mechanism. (T/F)

7. In SOLIDWORKS, you can save a sketch directly as a block in the **Design Library**. (T/F)

8. In SOLIDWORKS, you cannot animate a mechanism created out of blocks by applying motor to it. (T/F)

9. You cannot change the order of the belt members that are selected in the selection area of the **Belt Members** rollout. (T/F)

10. The **Insert Block** tool is used to insert the blocks into an active sketch. (T/F)

Review Questions

Answer the following questions:

1. Which of the following buttons in the **Blocks** toolbar is used to add or remove the sketch entities?

   (a) **Edit Block** (b) **Make Block**
   (c) **Add/Remove** (d) **Explode Block**

2. Which of the following tools is used to make each entity of a sketch as a separate block?

   (a) **Save Blocks** (b) **Make Block**
   (c) **Edit Block** (d) **Add/Remove**

3. Which of the following tools is used to dissolve a block into a sketched entity?

   (a) **Belt/Chain** (b) **Rebuild**
   (c) **Add/Remove** (d) **Explode Block**

4. The __________ tool helps you to create a path of sketched entities that are coincident end to end and form a single chain.

5. The __________ button in the **Make Part From Block PropertyManager** is used to create a part that is constrained to be coplanar with the plane of the block in the Layout environment.

6. The __________ button is used to invoke the **Make Part From Block PropertyManager**.

7. While inserting a block in an active sketch, you can change its scale value by using the __________ spinner.

8. To refresh or update the sketches, choose the __________ button from the **Blocks** toolbar.

9. To create a part from the block, you need to invoke the __________ **PropertyManager**.

10. The **Belt/Chain** tool is used to insert a belt between__________.

EXERCISE

Exercise 1

Create a mechanism by assembling the blocks, as shown in Figure 17-49, and then convert the blocks of the mechanism into parts. Figure 17-50 shows the mechanism after converting blocks into parts. Figures 17-51 through 17-54 show different views of parts of the mechanism with required dimensions.

(Expected time: 45 min)

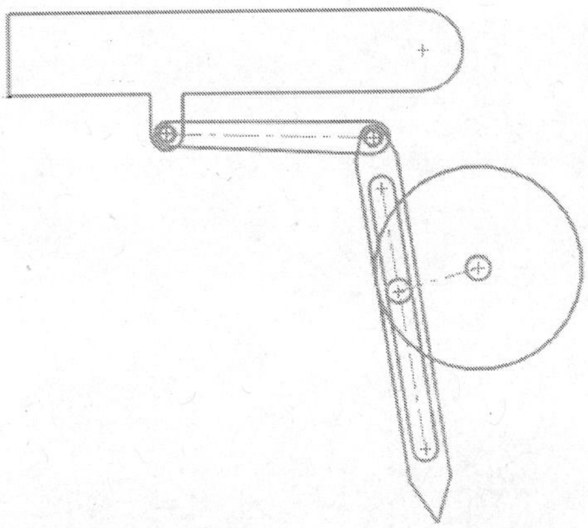

Figure 17-49 Mechanism created by assembling the blocks

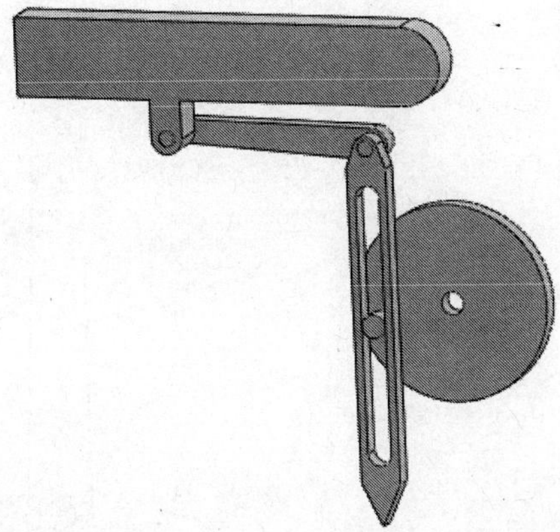

Figure 17-50 Mechanism after converting the blocks into parts

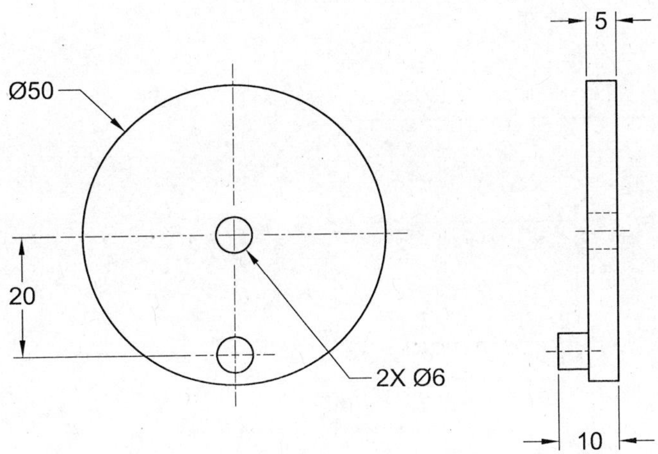

Figure 17-51 The front and side views of the Wheel

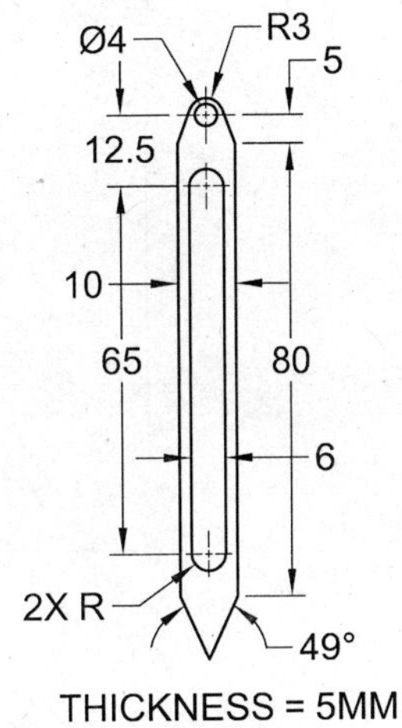

Figure 17-52 The front view of the Connecting rod1

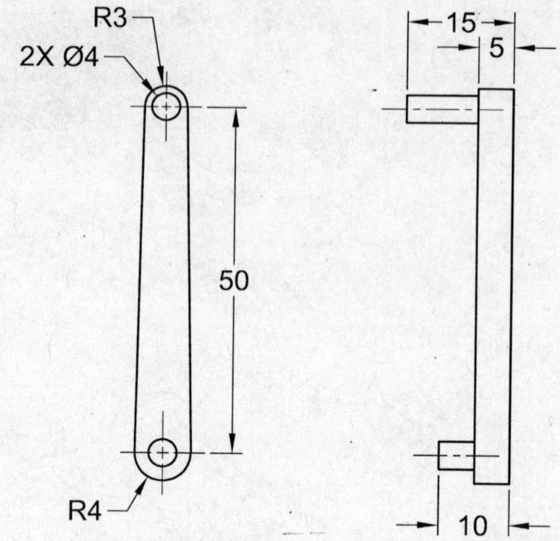

Figure 17-53 The front and side views of the Connecting rod2

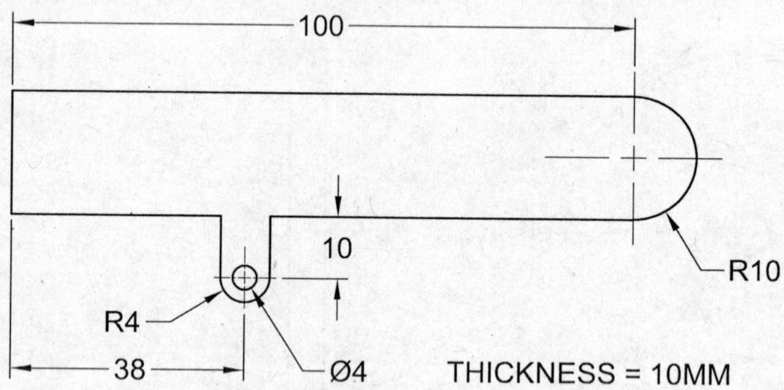

Figure 17-54 The top view of the Ram

Answers to Self-Evaluation Test

1. **Make Block**, **2.** **Use belt thickness**, **3.** **Edit Path**, **4.** **Edit Block**, **5.** **Flip belt side**, **6.** T, **7.** T, **8.** F, **9.** F, **10.** T

Chapter 18

Sheet Metal Design

Learning Objectives

After completing this chapter, you will be able to:

- *Create base, edge, and miter flanges*
- *Understand the FeatureManager Design Tree of a sheet metal component*
- *Create tabs, closed corners, and hems*
- *Create sketched, lofted, and jogged bends*
- *Break corners of sheet metal components*
- *Create cuts on the flat faces of sheet metal components*
- *Create the flat pattern of sheet metal components*
- *Create swept flange along a sheet metal component or sketch*
- *Create sheet metal components from a flat sheet and a flat part*
- *Create sheet metal component by designing it as a part*
- *Design sheet metal part from a shelled solid model*
- *Create cuts in sheet metal component across the bends*
- *Create cylindrical and conical sheet metal components*
- *Generate the drawing views of the flat pattern of the sheet metal components*
- *Create new forming tools*
- *Edit forming tools*

SHEET METAL DESIGN

In SOLIDWORKS, you can design the sheet metal components using various tools available for manipulating the sheet metal components in the **Part** mode. Generally, the solid models of the sheet metal components are created to generate the flat pattern of the sheet, study the design of the dies and punches, and study the process plan for designing the tools needed for manufacturing the sheet metal components. In a tool room or a machine shop, the most important thing that you need before designing the press tool, bending tool or any other tool for creating a sheet metal component is the flat pattern layout of a component. Figure 18-1 shows the model of a sheet metal component and Figure 18-2 shows its flat pattern layout. A flat pattern layout displays the flattened view of the sheet metal component, refer to Figure 18-2.

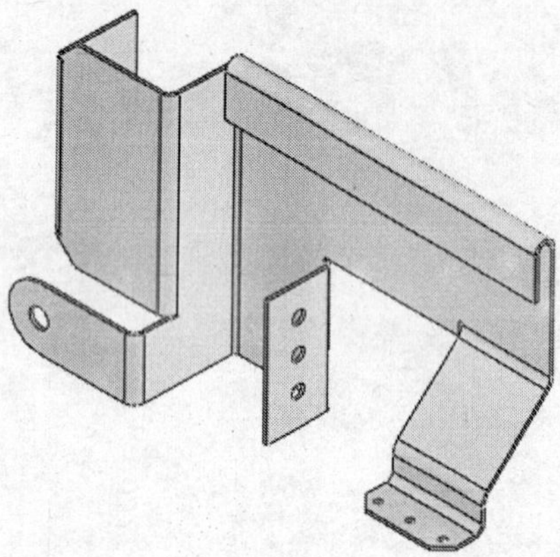

Figure 18-1 *Solid model of a sheet metal component*

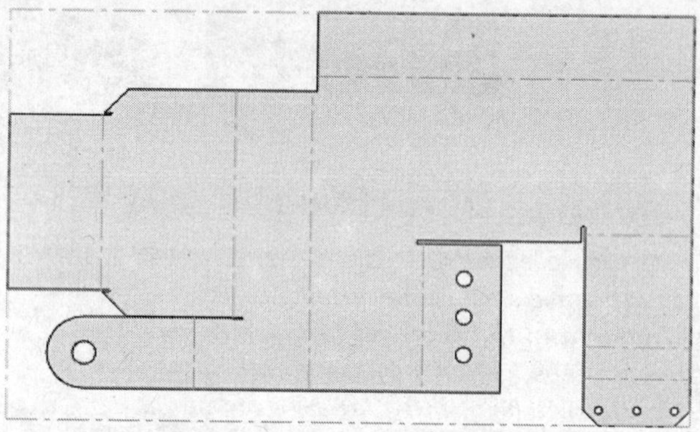

Figure 18-2 *Flat pattern layout of the sheet metal component*

As discussed earlier, the sheet metal components can also be created in the **Part** mode of SOLIDWORKS. To create a sheet metal component, start a new SOLIDWORKS document in the **Part** mode and then invoke the **Sheet Metal CommandManager**. If this CommandManager is not available by default, invoke it by right-clicking on the tab of a CommandManager and choosing **Sheet Metal** from the shortcut menu. All tools that are used to design a sheet metal component are available in this CommandManager. You can also invoke these tools from the **Sheet Metal** toolbar. The methods to create sheet metal components are discussed in this chapter.

DESIGNING THE SHEET METAL COMPONENTS BY CREATING THE BASE FLANGE

The most widely used method of designing a sheet metal component is by first creating the base flange. In this method, first you will create the base flange and then add the sheet metal feature on the base flange to obtain the required sheet metal component. In this method, all the parameters related to the sheet metal such as the bending radius, the bend allowance, and the relief are defined while creating the base flange. Various tools used to create the sheet metal components are discussed next.

Creating the Base Flange

CommandManager: Sheet Metal > Base Flange/Tab
SOLIDWORKS menus: Insert > Sheet Metal > Base Flange
Toolbar: Sheet Metal > Base Flange/Tab

To create a sheet metal component, you first need to create a base feature or a base sheet. This base sheet is known as the base flange. You can create a base flange from a closed sketch or an open sketch. To create a base flange, draw the sketch of the base flange and then choose the **Base Flange/Tab** button from the **Sheet Metal CommandManager**; the **Base Flange PropertyManager** will be displayed. Also, preview of the base flange will be displayed with the default values. Figure 18-3 shows the **Base Flange PropertyManager** for an open sketch. The rollouts in the **Base Flange PropertyManager** are discussed next.

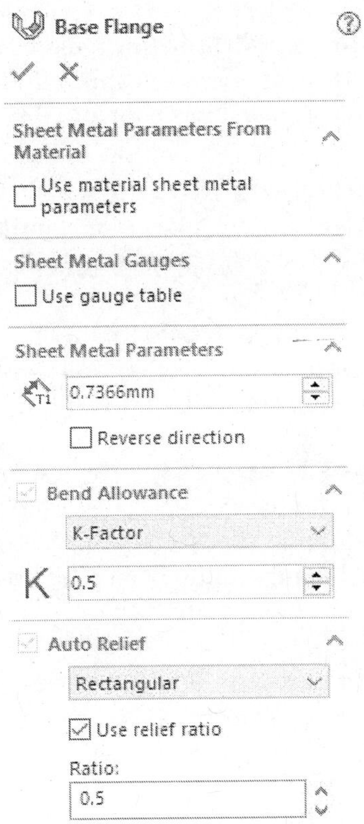

Figure 18-3 Partial view of the ***Base Flange PropertyManager***

Note

The parameters that you define in the ***Base Flange PropertyManager*** *are used as the default parameters throughout the current document. However, you can modify these values using the PropertyManagers of other tools.*

Sheet Metal Parameters From Material Rollout

The options in this rollout are discussed next.

Use material sheet metal parameters Check Box

This check box is used to link the custom material parameters with the sheet metal parameters. The procedure to create a custom material is discussed next.

To create a custom material, right-click on **Material** in the **FeatureManager Design Tree** and select the **Edit Material** option from the shortcut menu; the **Material** dialog box will be displayed. Next, right-click on the **Custom Materials** node and select **New Category** option; the **New Category** node will be added in **Custom Materials** node. Click anywhere in the **Material** dialog box to avoid renaming. Now, right-click on the **New Category** option and select the **New Material** option from the shortcut menu; the options related to newly added material will be enabled in the tabs on the right. Define the custom material properties in each tab. Options in the **Sheet Metal** tab are available for custom materials only. Choose the **Sheet Metal** tab and select the **Thickness Range** radio button. Click the **Add** button twice to add two rows in the table and set the values in each row, as shown in Figure 18-4.

	From	<	Thickness	<=	To	Unit	Bend Allowance	Value
1	0	<	Thickness	<=	3	millimete	K-Factor	0.375
2	3	<	Thickness	<=	6	millimete	K-Factor	0.4

Figure 18-4 *Values to set in the table*

In the table, the thickness range defined must be continuous without any gap in the range. For example, you cannot define one range from 0 to 3 and next range from 4 to 6 because the range between 3 and 4 is not covered. Click **Apply** and then **Close**.

Direction 1 Rollout

This rollout is displayed only if the sketch of the base flange is open. The options in this rollout are used to define the feature termination in the first direction.

Direction 2 Rollout

The options in the **Direction 2** rollout are used to define the feature termination in the second direction. This rollout is displayed only if the sketch for the base flange is open.

Sheet Metal Gauges Rollout

This rollout enables you to use the gauge table to create the sheet metal parts. Select the **Use gauge table** check box; the **Select Table** drop-down list will be displayed. Select any of the default gauge tables from this drop-down list. You can also choose the **Browse** button and select a user-defined gauge table.

Sheet Metal Parameters Rollout

The options in the **Sheet Metal Parameters** rollout are used to define the thickness and the bend radius of the sheet. These options are discussed next.

Thickness

The **Thickness** spinner in the **Sheet Metal Parameters** rollout is used to define the thickness of the sheet.

Reverse direction

The **Reverse direction** check box is used to flip the direction of material addition while adding the thickness to the base flange.

Bend Radius

The **Bend Radius** spinner is used to specify the bend radius of the base flange. If the sketch of the base flange is closed, the **Bend Radius** spinner will not be available in the **Sheet Metal Parameters** rollout.

Bend Allowance Rollout

The options in the **Bend Allowance Type** drop-down list of this rollout are used to specify the bend allowance for all bends in a sheet metal component. These options are discussed next.

Bend Table

The **Bend Table** option is selected to specify the bending allowance by using the bend tables. On selecting this option, the **Bend Table** drop-down list will be displayed below the **Bend Allowance Type** drop-down list. In SOLIDWORKS, various bend tables are provided to calculate the bending radius. The **BASE BEND TABLE** option is selected by default in the **Bend Table** drop-down list. The other bend tables available in this list are **BEND_CALCULATION**, **KFACTOR BASE BEND TABLE**, **METRIC BASE BEND TABLE**, and **SAMPLE**. Choose the **Browse** button available below this drop-down list to browse the location of the folder, if you have saved a user-defined bending table file that is created in Microsoft Excel. The default location of the bend tables is *C:\Program Files\SOLIDWORKS Corp\SOLIDWORKS\ lang\ english\Sheetmetal Bend Tables.*

K-Factor

K-Factor is defined as the ratio of the distance between the inner bend of the sheet and the neutral axis of the sheet to the thickness of the sheet. On selecting the **K-Factor** option, the **K-Factor** spinner will be displayed. Specify the K-Factor value in this spinner. If you are using **Gauge Table** from the **Sheet Metal Gauges** rollout then the **K-Factor** spinner will not be displayed.

Bend Allowance

Bend allowance is defined as the arc length of the bend measured along the neutral axis of the sheet metal. On selecting the **Bend Allowance** option, the **Bend Allowance** spinner will be displayed. You can specify the bend allowance value in this spinner.

Bend Deduction

The bend deduction, sometimes called the bend compensation, describes how much the outside of the sheet has been stretched. Therefore, the bend deduction equals the difference between the sum of flange lengths and the total flat length. The flange length is the distance measured from the edge of the part to the apex of the bend. The **Bend Deduction** option is used to define the bend deduction. When you select this option, the **Bend Deduction** spinner will be displayed. Specify the bend deduction value in this spinner.

Bend Calculation

The **Bend Calculation** option is used to calculate the bending allowance by using the bend tables. On selecting this option, the **Bend Table** drop-down list will be displayed. The options in the **Bend Table** drop-down list are same as those discussed earlier.

Auto Relief Rollout

The **Auto Relief** rollout is used to define the relief in the sheet metal component. The reliefs are provided in the sheet metal components to avoid tearing of the sheet while bending. The options in this rollout are discussed next. You will learn about the types of reliefs in detail later in this chapter.

Auto Relief Type

The **Auto Relief Type** drop-down list is used to define the type of relief that you need to specify to the base flange. The types of reliefs available in this drop-down list are **Rectangular**, **Tear**, and **Obround**. If you select the **Rectangular** or **Obround** type of relief, the **Relief Ratio** spinner will be displayed. You can use this spinner to define the relief ratio.

Figure 18-5 shows an open sketch with a single sketched entity. Figure 18-6 shows the resulting base flange. Figure 18-7 shows the open sketch with multiple sketched entities. Figure 18-8 shows the resulting base flange with the bending radius applied automatically to the edges. Figure 18-9 shows a closed sketch and Figure 18-10 shows the resulting base flange.

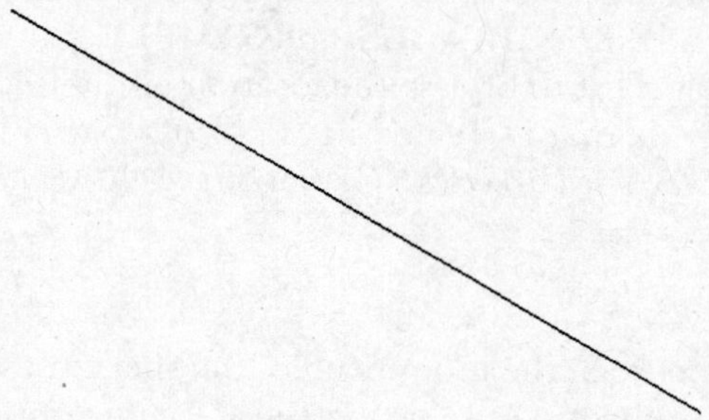

Figure 18-5 *Open sketch with a single entity*

Figure 18-6 *Resulting base flange*

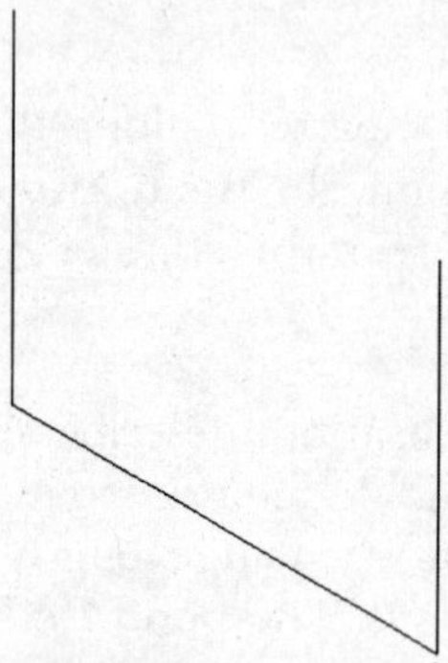

Figure 18-7 *Open sketch with multiple entities*

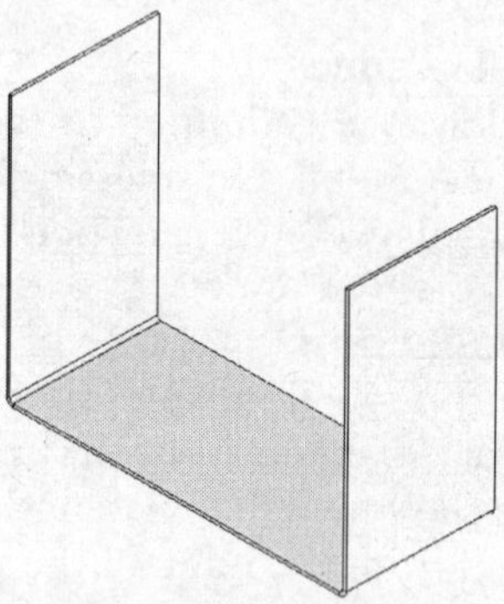

Figure 18-8 *Resulting base flange*

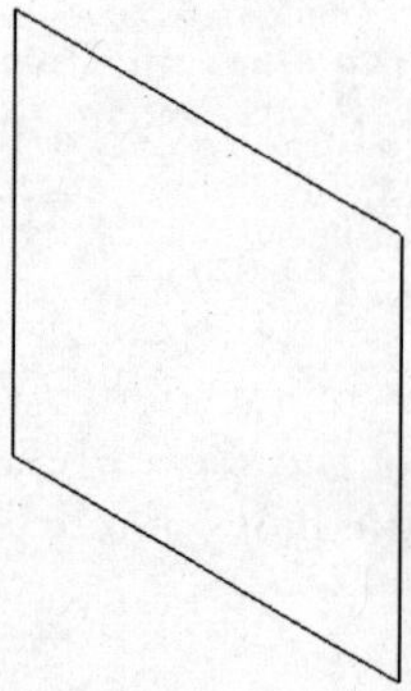

Figure 18-9 *Closed sketch*

Figure 18-10 *Resulting base flange*

Understanding the FeatureManager Design Tree of a Sheet Metal Component

After creating the base flange, you will notice that some nodes are displayed in the **FeatureManager Design Tree**, as shown in Figure 18-11. The nodes are discussed next.

Cut list(1)

In SOLIDWORKS, you can create multiple sheet metal parts in a single sheet metal component. You can also create a combination of sheet metal parts and weldments in a sheet metal component. Whenever you create sheet metal parts for a sheet metal component, they are listed in the **Cut list** node. The **Cut list** node is similar to the **Solid Bodies** node in the **Part** environment. The number that is displayed next to this node shows the number of multiple bodies in the component.

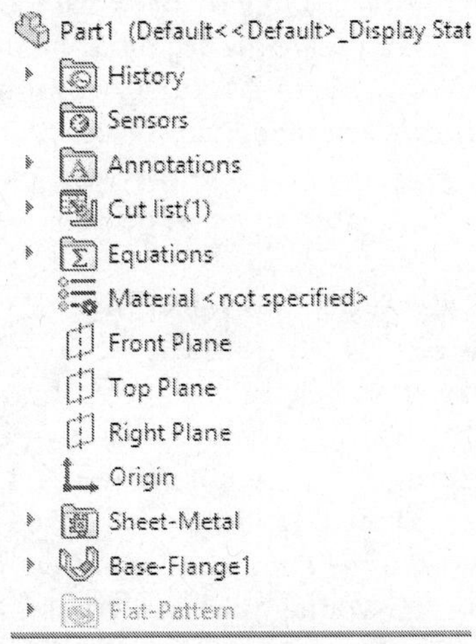

***Figure 18-11** Various nodes displayed in the **FeatureManager Design Tree** after creating the base flange*

Sheet-Metal Node

The **Sheet-Metal** node contains all information about the sheet metal parameters such as bend, bend allowance, and auto relief that are specified while creating the base flange. The values assigned to these parameters are automatically applied to all other sheet metal features that will be added to the base flange. At any stage of the design, you can edit these parameters. To edit the sheet metal parameters, select **Sheet-Metal** in the **FeatureManager Design Tree**; a pop-up toolbar will be displayed. Choose **Edit Feature** from the pop-up toolbar; the **Sheet-Metal PropertyManager** will be displayed. You can modify the default sheet metal parameters using this PropertyManager.

Base-Flange1 Node

The **Base-Flange1** node is displayed after creating the base flange. You can change the thickness of the sheet by editing this feature. You can also edit the sketch of the base flange using this feature.

Flat-Pattern Node

The **Flat-Pattern** node is also displayed after creating the base flange. This feature is used to create the flat pattern of the bent sheet metal component. By default, this feature is suppressed. You will learn more about the flat patterns later in this chapter.

Creating the Edge Flange

CommandManager:	Sheet Metal > Edge Flange
SOLIDWORKS menus:	Insert > Sheet Metal > Edge Flange
Toolbar:	Sheet Metal > Edge Flange

Edge flange is a bent sheet metal wall created at an angle on the edge of an existing base flange or an existing flange. To create an edge flange, choose the **Edge Flange** button from the **Sheet Metal CommandManager**; the **Edge-Flange PropertyManager** will be displayed, as shown in Figure 18-12, and you will be prompted to select the linear edge of a planar face to create the edge flange.

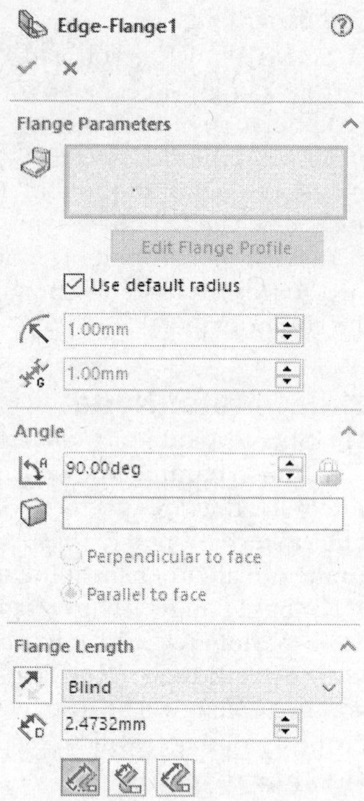

Figure 18-12 Partial view of ***Edge-Flange PropertyManager***

Next, you need to select the edge along which the flange will be created, refer to Figure 18-13. As soon as you select the edge, preview of the edge flange with the drag handle will be displayed in the drawing area, as shown in Figure 18-14. The length of the resulting flange will change dynamically as you move the cursor. Next, you need to specify the parameters of the edge flange in the **Edge-Flange PropertyManager**. The rollouts in the **Edge-Flange PropertyManager** are discussed next.

Flange Parameters Rollout

The options in the **Flange Parameters** rollout are used to define the edge reference to be used for creating the edge flange, the bending radius, and the profile of the edge flange. These options are discussed next.

Edge

The **Edge** selection box is used to select the edges to create the edge flange.

Edit Flange Profile

The **Edit Flange Profile** button is chosen to edit the profile of the edge flange. By default, the edge flange is created along the entire length of the selected edge. To edit the profile of the edge flange, choose the **Edit Flange Profile** button; the **Profile Sketch** dialog box will be displayed informing you that the sketch is valid. Also, the sketching environment will be invoked in the background. Edit the sketch of the profile of the edge flange using the sketching tools.

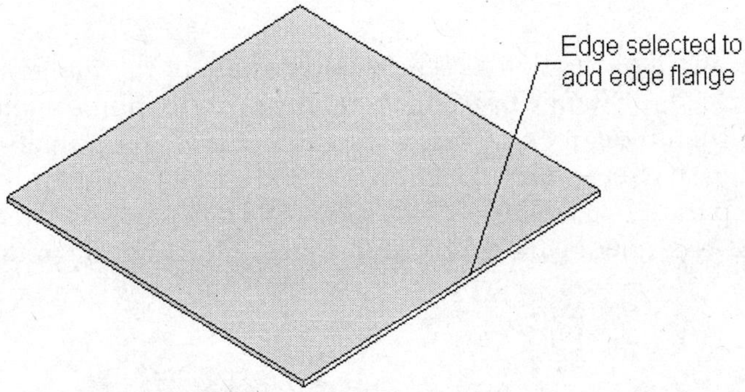

Figure 18-13 Edge selected to add the edge flange

Figure 18-14 Preview of the edge flange with the drag handle

You will also notice that while editing the sketch of the edge flange, the **Profile Sketch** dialog box informs you whether the sketch is valid for creating the edge flange or not. If the status of the sketch is shown valid in the **Profile Sketch** dialog box, the preview of the flange will be displayed in the drawing area. After editing the profile, choose the **Finish** button from the **Profile Sketch** dialog box; the flange will be created and the **Edge-Flange PropertyManager** will be automatically closed. Note that if you want to modify the other parameters of the flange, choose the **Back** button from the **Profile Sketch** dialog box. Figure 18-15 shows the edge flange created along the entire length of the selected edge. Figure 18-16 shows the edited sketch of the edge flange and Figure 18-17 shows the resulting edge flange.

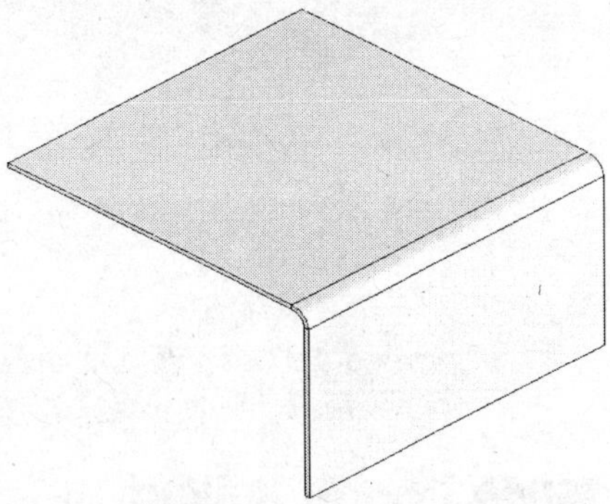

Figure 18-15 Edge flange created along the entire length of the edge

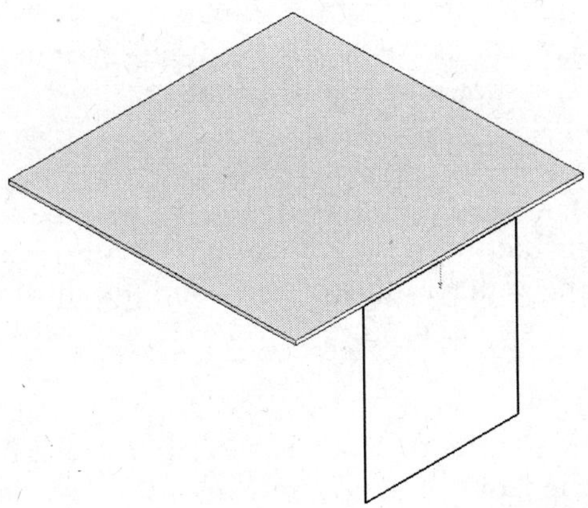

Figure 18-16 Edited sketch of the edge flange

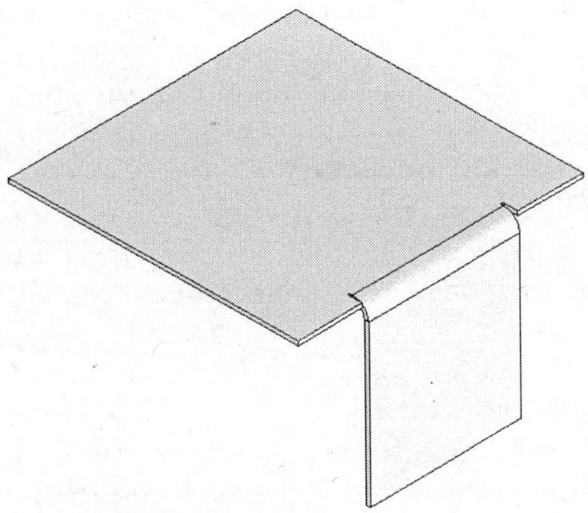

Figure 18-17 Resulting edge flange

Angle Rollout

The **Angle** rollout is used to define the angle of the flange. The default angle of the flange is 90 degrees. You can define any other angle of the flange by using the **Flange Angle** spinner. The angle of the edge flange can be greater than 0 degree and less than 180 degrees. You can also select a face for directional reference using the **Select face** selection box and specify whether the resulting flange will be perpendicular or parallel to it. Figure 18-18 shows an edge flange created at an angle of 45 degrees. Figure 18-19 shows an edge flange created at an angle of 135 degrees.

***Figure 18-18** Edge flange created at an angle of 45 degrees*

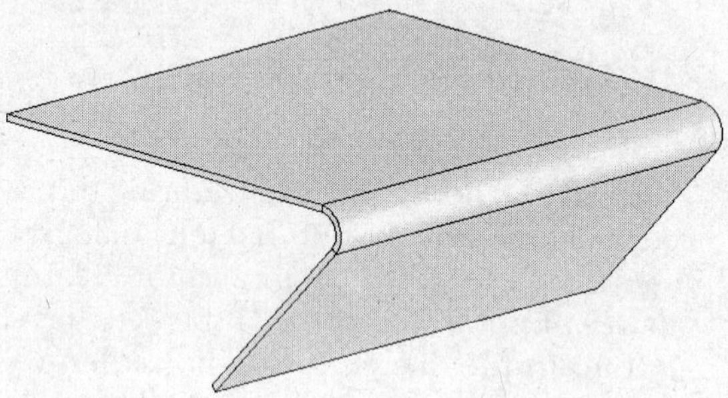

***Figure 18-19** Edge flange created at an angle of 135 degrees*

Flange Length Rollout

The **Flange Length** rollout is used to define the length of the flange. In other words, the options for feature termination are available in this rollout. These options are the same as discussed earlier. The other three options provided in this rollout are discussed next.

Outer Virtual Sharp

The **Outer Virtual Sharp** button is used to define the length of the flange from the outer virtual sharp. The outer virtual sharp is an imaginary vertex created by extending the tangent lines virtually from the outer radius of the bend, as shown in Figure 18-20.

Inner Virtual Sharp

The **Inner Virtual Sharp** button is chosen by default and is used to define the length of the flange from the inner virtual sharp. The inner virtual sharp is an imaginary vertex created by extending the tangent lines virtually from the inner radius of the bend, as shown in Figure 18-20.

Tangent Bend

The **Tangent Bend** button is used to define the length of the flange from the imaginary line. This line is created by extending the tangent line from the outer radius of the bend and parallel to the end edge of the flange to be created, refer to Figure 18-21. This button will be available only for the flange to be created whose bend radius is greater than 90 degree.

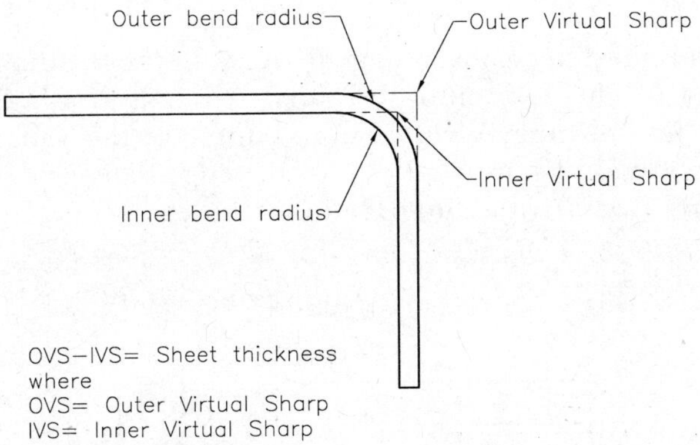

Figure 18-20 Outer Virtual Sharp and Inner Virtual Sharp

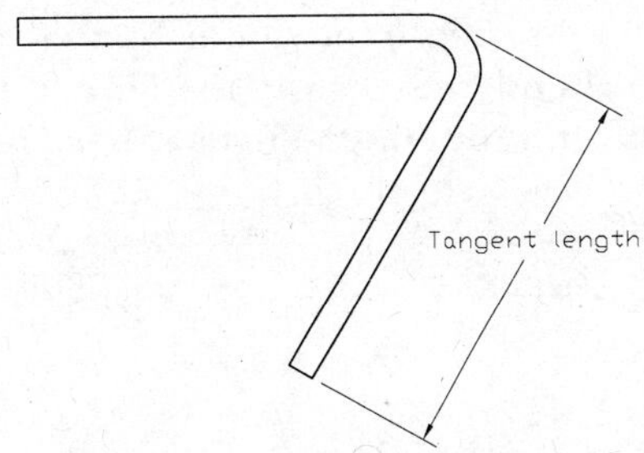

Figure 18-21 Tangent length of Tangent Bend in base flange

Flange Position Rollout

The **Flange Position** rollout is used to define the position of the flange on an edge. The options in this rollout are discussed next.

Material Inside

The **Material Inside** button is used to create the edge flange in such a way that the material of the flange after the bend lies inside the maximum limit of the sheet. Figure 18-22 shows the edge flange created with the **Material Inside** button chosen.

Material Outside

The **Material Outside** button is chosen by default and the edge flange is created such that the material of the flange after the bend lies outside the maximum limit of the sheet. Figure 18-23 shows the edge flange created with the **Material Outside** button chosen.

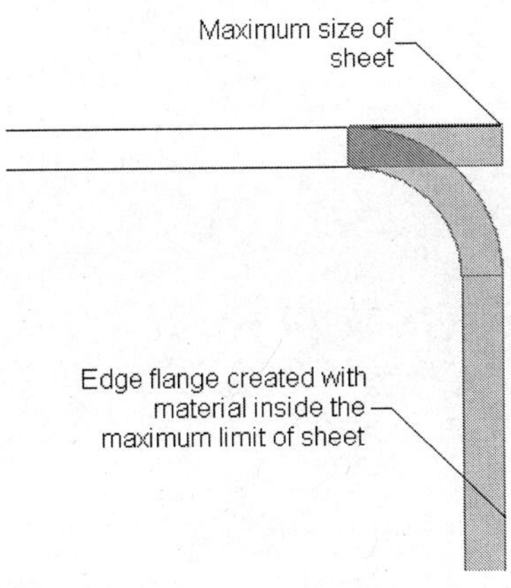

Figure 18-22 Edge flange created with the ***Material Inside*** *button chosen*

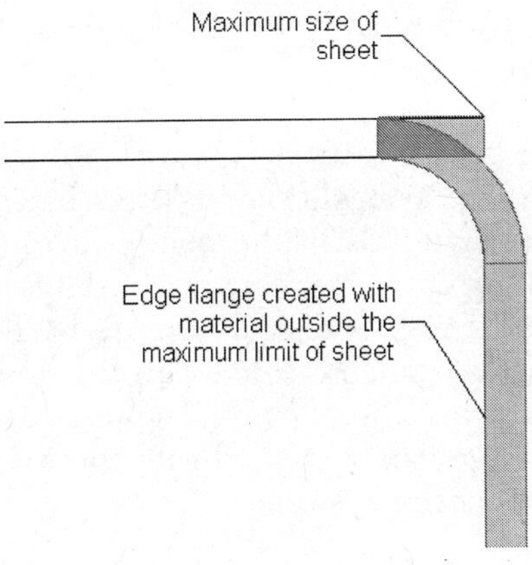

Figure 18-23 Edge flange created with the ***Material Outside*** *button chosen*

Bend Outside

The **Bend Outside** button is used to create an edge flange such that the bending of the sheet starts from the point that is beyond the maximum limit of the sheet, as shown in Figure 18-24.

Bend from Virtual Sharp

The **Bend from Virtual Sharp** button is used to create an edge flange with the bending of the sheet starting from the virtual sharp. The position of the flange depends on whether you choose the **Outer Virtual Sharp** button, **Inner Virtual Sharp** button, or the **Tangent Bend** button from the **Flange Length** rollout. Figure 18-25 shows the edge flange created with the **Inner Virtual Sharp** and **Bend from Virtual Sharp** buttons chosen.

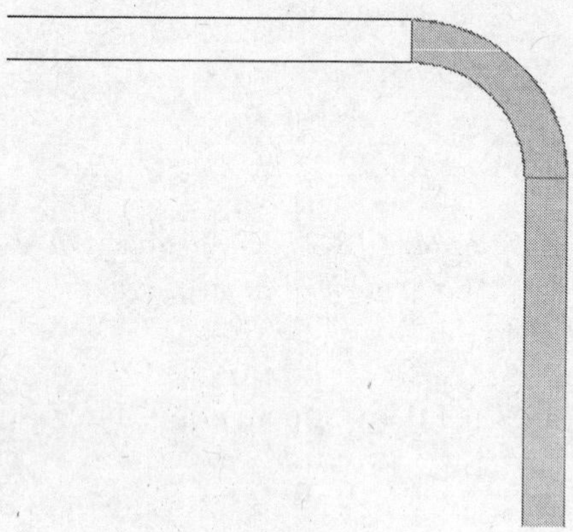

Figure 18-24 Edge flange created with the ***Bend Outside*** *button chosen*

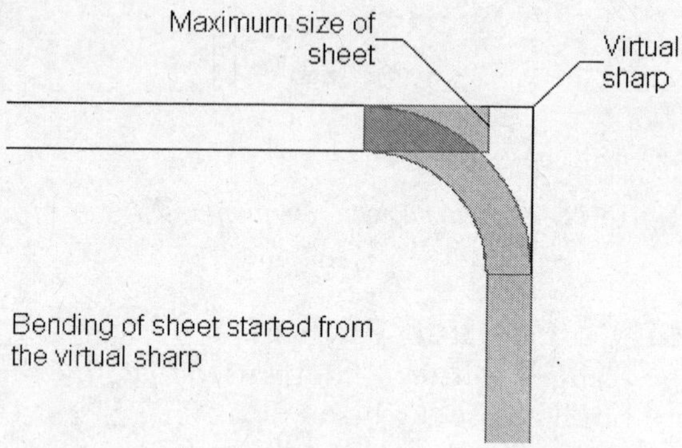

Figure 18-25 Edge flange created with the ***Bend from Virtual Sharp*** *button chosen*

Tangent to Bend

The **Tangent to Bend** button is used to create the edge flange in such a way that the material of the flange after bending lies tangent to the maximum limit of the sheet, refer to Figure 18-26. Note that this option is not valid for the bend angle less than 90 degree.

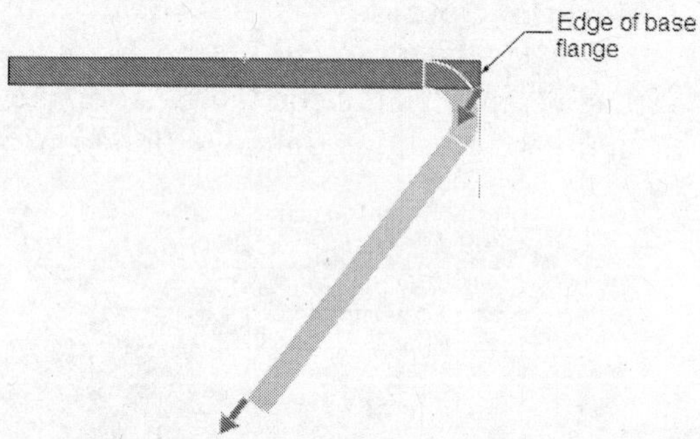

Figure 18-26 Edge flange created with the ***Tangent to Bend*** *button chosen*

Trim side bends

Select the **Trim side bends** check box to trim extra materials in the bends surrounding the current edge flange. By default, this check box is not selected. Figure 18-27 shows the edge flange created with the **Trim side bends** check box cleared. Figure 18-28 shows the edge flange created with the **Trim side bends** check box selected.

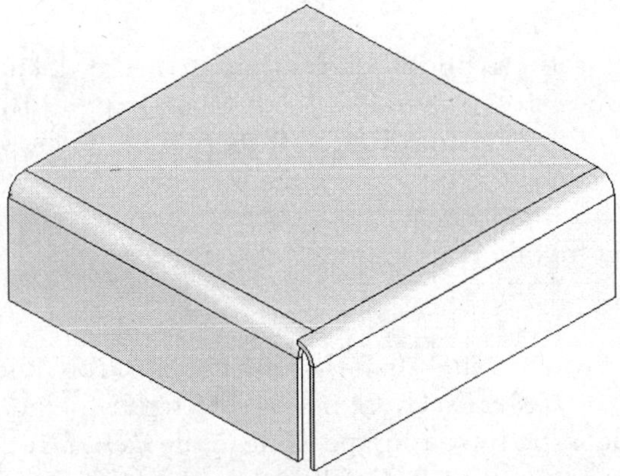

Figure 18-27 Edge flange created with the ***Trim side bends*** *check box cleared*

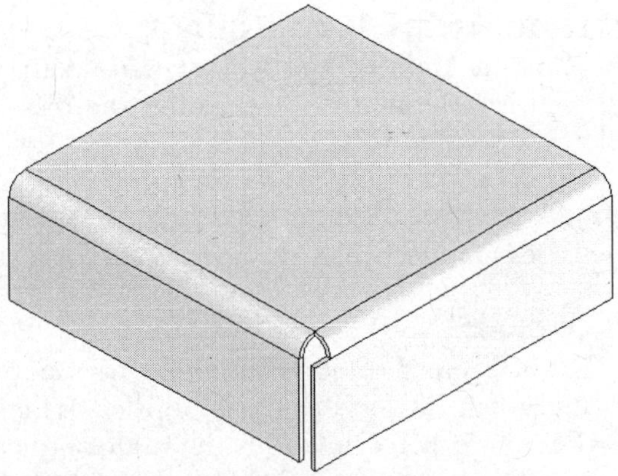

Figure 18-28 Edge flange created with the ***Trim side bends*** *check box selected*

Offset

The **Offset** check box is available only when you create an edge flange using the **Material Inside**, **Material Outside**, **Bend Outside**, or **Tangent to Bend** option. This check box is used to create an edge flange at an offset distance from the selected edge reference. On selecting the **Offset** check box, the **Offset End Condition** drop-down list and the **Offset Distance** spinner will be displayed. Specify the offset distance using this spinner. Figure 18-29 shows the edge flange created with the **Offset** check box cleared. Figure 18-30 shows the edge flange created with the **Offset** check box selected and the offset distance specified in the **Offset Distance** spinner.

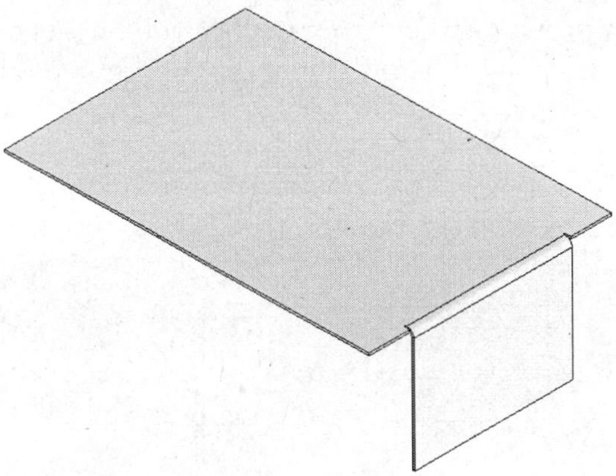

Figure 18-29 Edge flange created with the ***Offset*** *check box cleared*

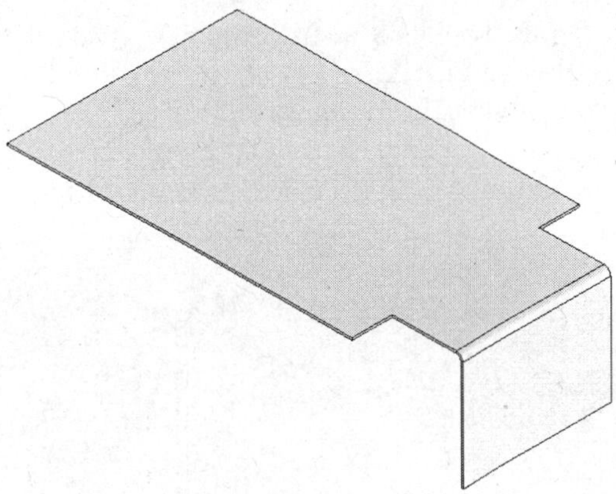

Figure 18-30 Edge flange created with the ***Offset*** *check box selected*

Custom Bend Allowance Rollout

The **Custom Bend Allowance** rollout is used to define the bend allowance other than the default bend allowance that you defined while creating the base flange. To apply the custom bend allowance, expand this rollout by selecting the **Custom Bend Allowance** check box. Then use the options in this rollout to define the bend allowance for the current bend as discussed earlier.

Custom Relief Type Rollout

The **Custom Relief Type** rollout is used to define the type of relief other than the default one that was defined while creating the base flange. To apply the custom relief, expand this rollout by selecting the check box in the title bar of the **Custom Relief Type** rollout, as shown in Figure 18-31.

The types of reliefs that can be defined for a sheet metal component are discussed next.

Obround

The **Obround** option is used to provide the obround relief such that the edges of the relief merging with the sheet are rounded. The **Use relief ratio** check box is selected by default. Therefore, you can modify the value of the relief ratio by setting the value in the **Relief Ratio** spinner. If you clear the **Use relief ratio** check box, the **Relief Width** and **Relief Depth** spinners will be displayed, as shown in Figure 18-32. You can modify the relief width and relief depth individually by using these two spinners.

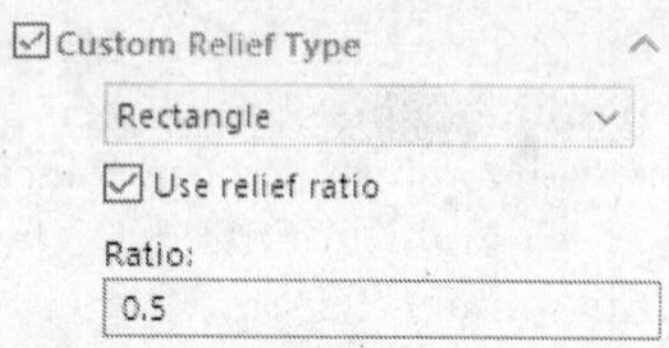

*Figure 18-31 The **Custom Relief Type** rollout*

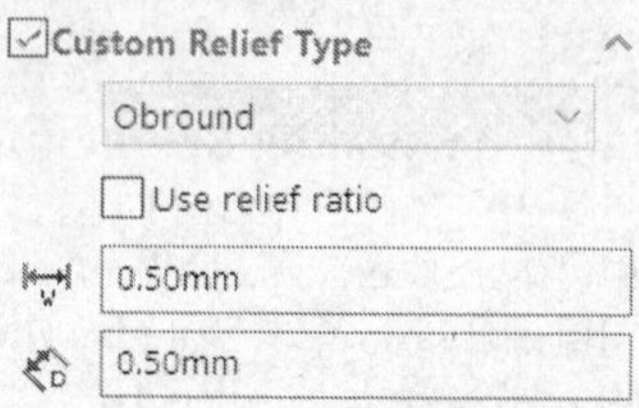

*Figure 18-32 The **Relief Width** and **Relief Depth** spinners displayed in the **Custom Relief Type** rollout*

Figure 18-33 shows the edge flange created by providing the obround relief with the default relief ratio. Figure 18-34 shows the edge flange created by providing obround relief after modifying the relief ratio.

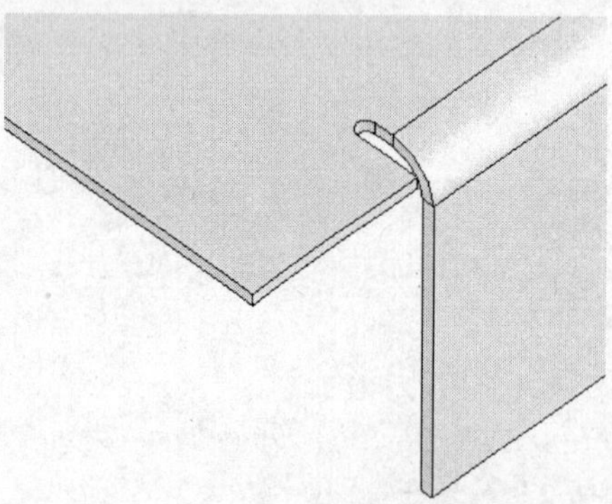

Figure 18-33 Edge flange created with the default relief ratio

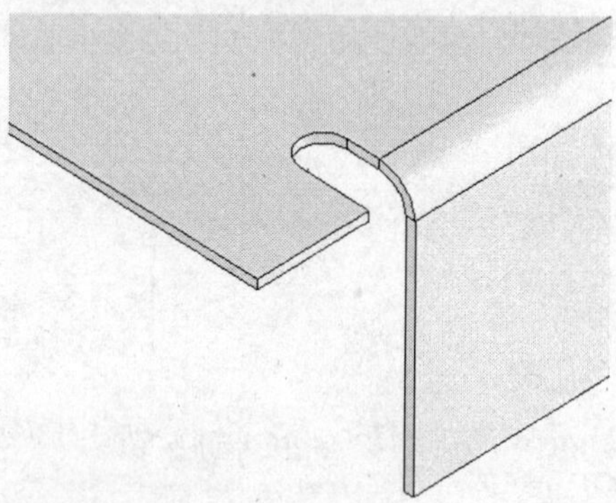

Figure 18-34 Edge flange created after modifying the relief ratio

Rectangle

The **Rectangle** option is selected by default in this rollout. This option is used to provide the rectangular relief to the sheet metal components. The options for defining the rectangular relief are the same as discussed in the previous paragraph. Figure 18-35 shows an edge flange created by providing the rectangular relief with the default relief ratio. Figure 18-36 shows an edge flange created by providing rectangular relief after modifying the relief ratio.

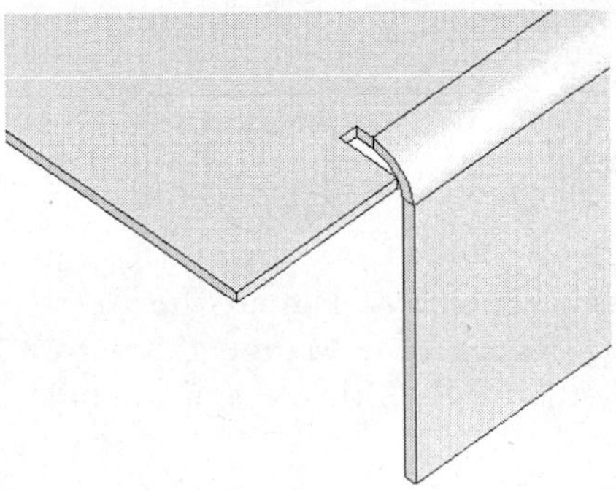

Figure 18-35 Edge flange created by providing the rectangular relief with default relief ratio

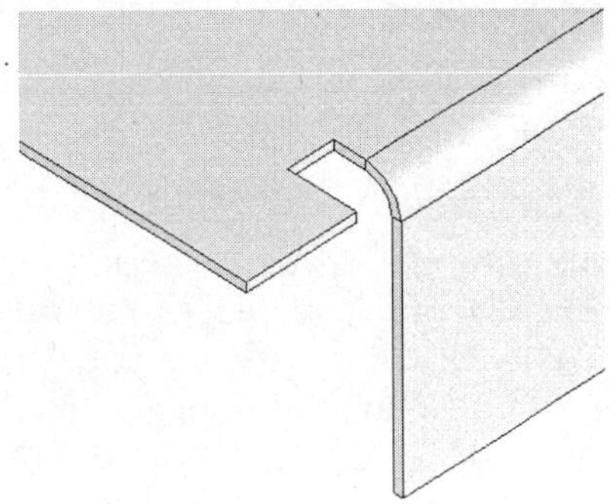

Figure 18-36 Edge flange created by providing rectangular relief after modifying the relief ratio

Tear

You can provide the tear relief to an edge flange by using the **Tear** option. The tear relief will tear the sheet in order to accommodate the bending of the sheet. When you select the **Tear** option from the **Relief Type** drop-down list, all the other options are replaced by the **Rip** and **Extend** buttons, as shown in Figure 18-37.

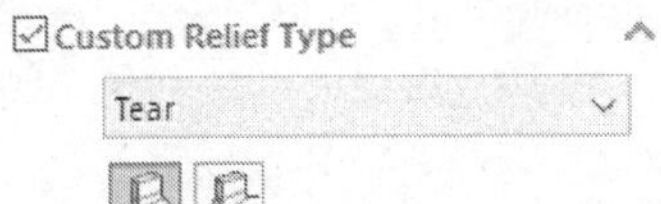

*Figure 18-37 The **Custom Relief Type** rollout with the **Tear** option selected from the **Relief Type** drop-down list*

The **Rip** button is chosen by default. This option rips or tears the sheet to accommodate the bending of the sheet, as shown in Figure 18-38. When the **Extend** button is chosen, the outer faces of the bend will be extended to the outer faces of the sheet on which you create the edge flange, as shown in Figure 18-39.

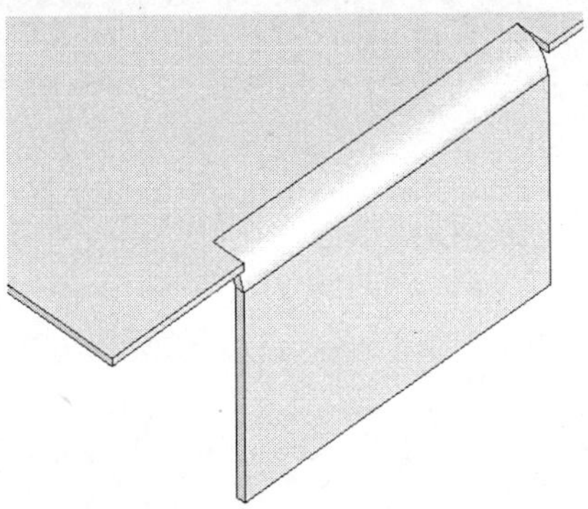

*Figure 18-38 Tear relief with the **Rip** button chosen*

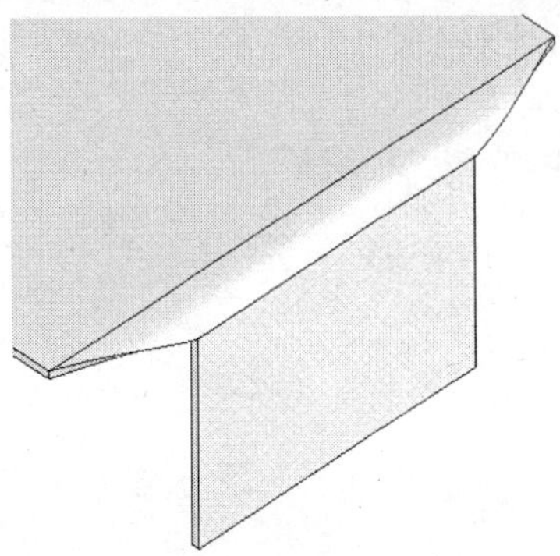

*Figure 18-39 Tear relief with the **Extend** button chosen*

Tip

You can edit the sketch of an edge flange after creating it. To do so, select the edge flange feature from the ***FeatureManager Design Tree*** *and invoke the pop-up toolbar. Next, choose* ***Edit Sketch*** *from it; the sketching environment will be invoked. Now, edit the sketch and exit the sketching environment.*

Creating Tabs

CommandManager:	Sheet Metal > Base Flange/Tab
SOLIDWORKS menus:	Insert > Sheet Metal > Base Flange
Toolbar:	Sheet Metal > Base Flange/Tab

A tab feature is created by adding material to the walls of the sheet metal component. To create a tab, select the face to be used as the sketching plane and create the sketch of the tab. Remember that the sketch must be closed. Now, choose the **Base Flange/Tab** button from the **Sheet Metal CommandManager**; a tab will be created and the thickness of the tab will be automatically adjusted according to the thickness of the sheet.

In SOLIDWORKS, you can also create a new tab and add it as a separate body. To do so, clear the **Merge result** check box in the **Sheet Metal Parameters** rollout. When a new tab is created by clearing the **Merge result** check box, you will notice that a new sub-node, **Sheet-Metal2**, is added to the **Sheet-Metal** node in the **FeatureManager Design Tree** and the name of the new tab is added in the feature tree. Also, the name of the new tab will be listed under the **Cut list** node. Figure 18-40 shows the sketch for creating a tab and Figure 18-41 shows the resulting tab.

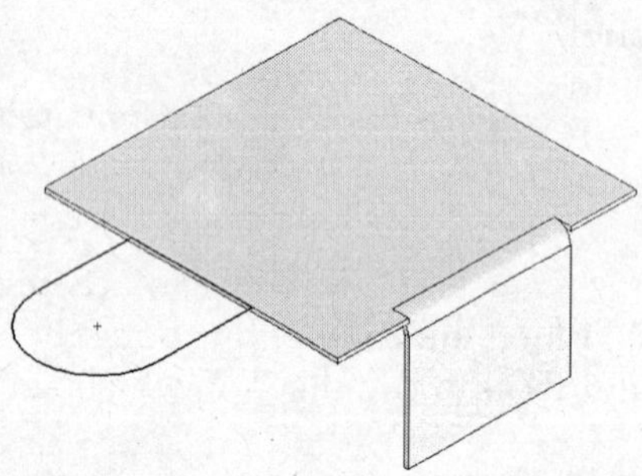

Figure 18-40 *Sketch for creating a tab*

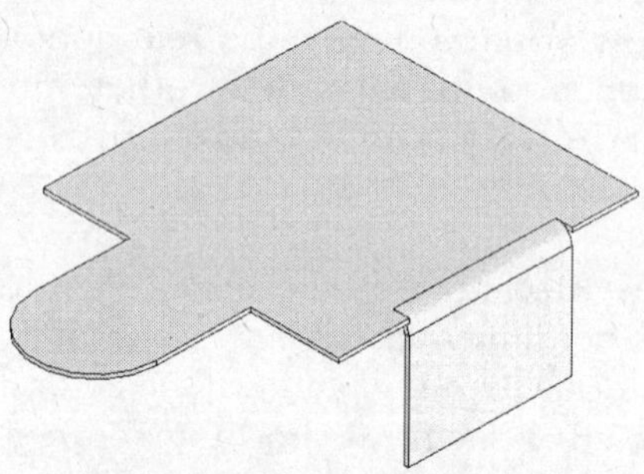

Figure 18-41 *Resulting tab*

Note

As the thickness of the tab feature is automatically adjusted according to the thickness of the sheet. So, you cannot edit it individually. However, you can edit its sketch.

Creating a Tab and Slot

CommandManager:	Sheet Metal > Tab and Slot
SOLIDWORKS menus:	Insert > Sheet Metal > Tab and Slot
Toolbar:	Sheet Metal > Tab and Slot *(Customize to add)*

The **Tab and Slot** tool is used to create tabs and slots (holes) respectively on the bodies to be interlocked. This feature helps in minimizing the use of welding fixtures. This tool can be used on parts other than sheet metal parts. To create a tab and slot feature, choose the **Tab and Slot** tool from the **Sheet Metal CommandManager**; the **Tab and Slot PropertyManager** will be displayed. Partial view of the PropertyManager is shown in Figure 18-42. The rollouts in the **Tab and Slot PropertyManager** are discussed next.

Selection Rollout

The options in the **Selection** rollout are used to define the edge and face to be used for creating the tab and slot feature. These options are discussed next.

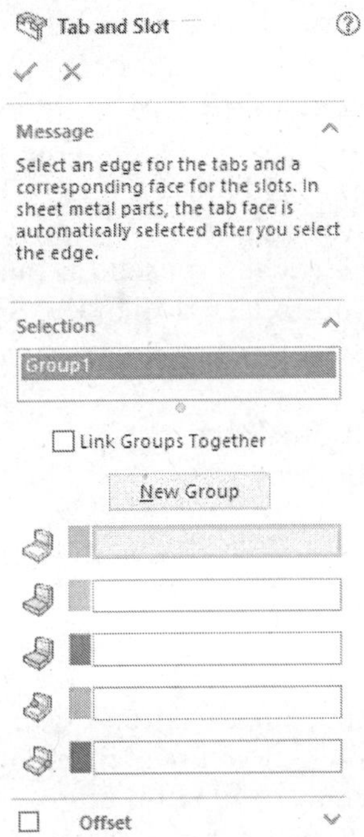

Figure 18-42 Partial view of the Tab and Slot PropertyManager

Group List

The **Group List** selection box is used to define groups of edges and faces for creating tab and slot feature. The **New Group** button provided below is used to add a new group to the **Group List** selection box. The **Link Groups Together** check box is used to link groups of tab and slot features together so that all parameters apply uniformly to the features. If you edit a parameter for a linked group, all tabs and slot features in the group get updated accordingly. To link groups, select entities in the **Group List** selection box and then select the **Link Groups Together** check box.

Tab Edge

The **Tab Edge** selection box is used to select an edge for adding tabs. In case of a sheet metal part, the tab face is automatically defined as soon as you select an edge for adding tabs. You can also select nonlinear edges when creating a tab and slot feature.

Slot Face

The **Slot Face** selection box is used to select a face for creating slots in the part. Note that the direction of the slot face must be normal to the tab face selected.

Tab Face

The **Tab Face** selection box is used to select a face to create the tab. Note that, the tab face selected should be shared with the edge selected for tab creation. This selection box is also available for non-sheet metal parts.

Start Reference Point

The **Start Reference Point** selection box is used to define start point on the edge for tab creation. By default, the endpoint of the selected edge is defined as the Start Reference Point. You can also select any sketched point or a vertex as the start point.

End Reference Point

The **End Reference Point** selection box is used to define end point on the edge for tab creation. By default, the endpoint of the selected edge is defined as the End Reference Point. You can also select any sketched point or a vertex as the end point.

Offset Rollout

The options in the **Offset** rollout are used to define offset values for the positioning of tabs from the start and end points defined earlier. To set the offset values, select the check box provided on the left of the **Offset** rollout; the **Start Offset** and **End Offset** edit boxes get enabled. Define the start offset value in the **Start Offset** edit box and similarly end offset value in the **End Offset** edit box.

Spacing Rollout

The options in the **Spacing** rollout are used to define numbers of the tabs to be created and the spacing between them. If you select the **Equal Spacing** radio button then the **Number of Instances** spinner will be available in this rollout. Therefore, the number of instances defined will be equally spaced on the selected edge. On the other hand, if the **Spacing Length** radio button is selected then the **Spacing** spinner will be available. In this case, the number of tabs will depend upon the spacing defined between the tabs.

Tabs Rollout

The options in the **Tabs** rollout are used to define various parameters of the profile of a tab. You can define the length of the tab using the **Tab Length** spinner available in this rollout. You can define the thickness of the tab using the **Tab Thickness** spinner available. Note that this spinner is only available for non-sheet metal parts. The end condition of the tab can be defined using the various options available in the **Tab Height** drop-down list. By default, the **Up To Surface** option is selected in this drop-down list. You can also select the **Blind** and **Offset From Surface** options from this drop-down list. In the **Edges Type** area, there are three buttons available for defining the shape of the edge of the tab. By default the **Sharp Edge** button is selected. You can also choose the **Fillet Edge** or **Chamfer Edge** button for rounded or bevelled edge respectively. When you select the **Fillet Edge** or **Chamfer Edge** button then a spinner will be available for defining the fillet or chamfer values for the edges.

Slot Rollout

The options in this rollout are used to define the parameters for slot size and corners.

No Through Cut

Generally, slots are created as through all cuts unless the cuts are impractical. If you do not want a through all cut, select the **No Through Cut** check box in the **Slot** rollout. In case, the through cut is impractical for the model, such as model with a single body, the **No Through Cut** check box will not be available.

Slot Length Offset
This spinner is used to set the slot length offset value.

Slot Width Offset
This spinner is used to set the slot width offset value.

Equal Offset
Select the **Equal Offset** check box to set equal values for the **Slot Length Offset** and **Slot Width Offset** spinners. The **Slot Width Offset** spinner will be disabled when this check box is selected.

Corner Type
In the **Corner Type** area, there are four buttons: **Slot Sharp Corner**, **Slot Fillet Corner**, **Slot Chamfer Corner**, and **Slot Circular Corner**. These buttons are used to define the corner shape of the slot.

After defining all the parameters, choose the **OK** button from the **Tab and Slot PropertyManager** to create the tab and slot feature. Figures 18-43 and 18-44 show a sheet metal part indicating entities to be selected and the tab and slot feature created.

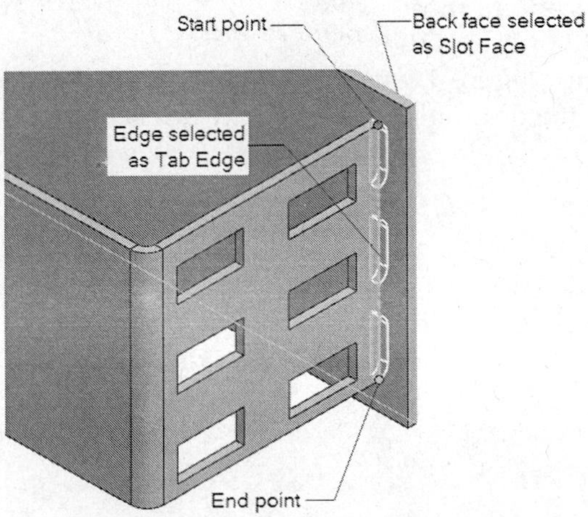

Figure 18-43 *Entities to be selected for Tab and Slot feature*

Figure 18-44 *The Tab and Slot feature created*

Creating the Sketched Bend

CommandManager:	Sheet Metal > Sketched Bend
SOLIDWORKS menus:	Insert > Sheet Metal > Sketched Bend
Toolbar:	Sheet Metal > Sketched Bend

The **Sketched Bend** tool is used to create a bend by using a sketch as the bending line. To create a sketched bend, select the face of the sheet on which you need to create a bend line and invoke the sketching environment. Draw a line to define the bend line by using the **Line** tool. Now, choose the **Sketched Bend** button from the **Sheet Metal CommandManager**; the **Sketched Bend PropertyManager** will be displayed, as shown in Figure 18-45. Also, you will be prompted to specify the planar face to be fixed while creating the bend. Select the side of the sheet that will be fixed when you create the bend; a black sphere will be displayed on the selected point and the **Reverse Direction** arrow will also be displayed to reverse the direction of the bend creation. You will notice that the **Bend Centerline** button is chosen by default in the **Bend position** area. Therefore, the sheet is bent equally on both sides of the bend line. The other options in the **Sketched Bend PropertyManager** are the same as those discussed earlier. After setting all parameters, choose the **OK** button from the **Sketched Bend PropertyManager**. Figure 18-46 shows the sketch to be used as the bending line and the side of the face to be fixed while bending. Figure 18-47 shows the resulting bend.

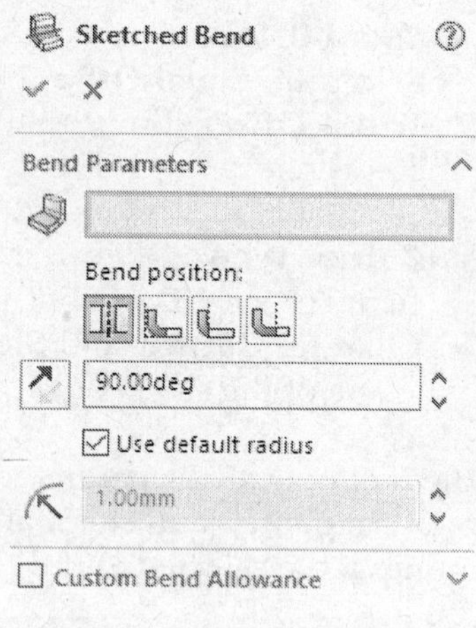

Figure 18-45** The **Sketched Bend PropertyManager

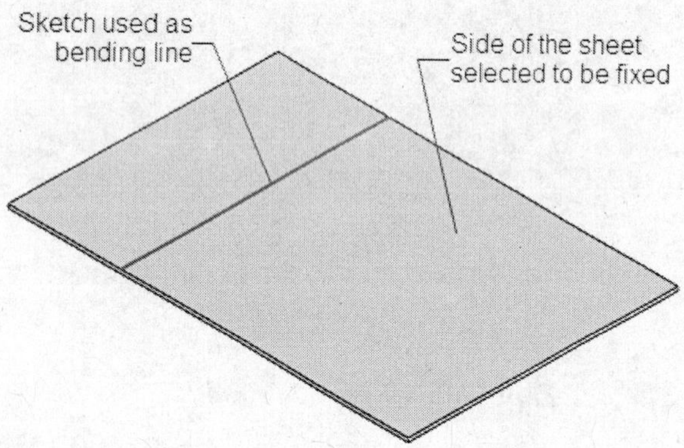

***Figure 18-46** The face to be fixed and the bending line*

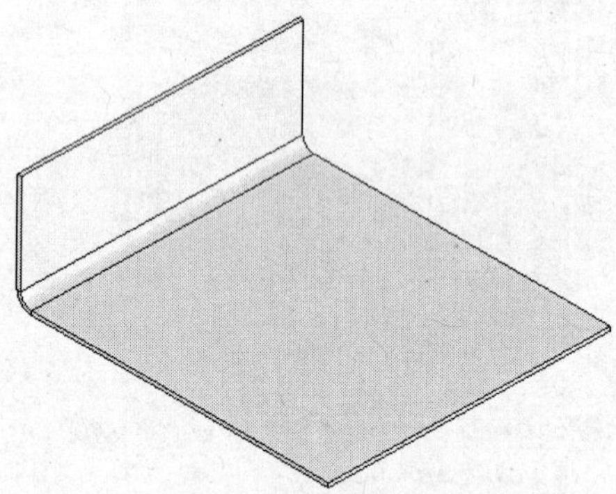

***Figure 18-47** Resulting sketched bend*

Note

You can also create more than one sketch line for creating multiple bends by using a single sketch bend feature. But make sure that the bend sketches do not intersect each other. Figure 18-48 shows the sheet and two bend lines and Figure 18-49 shows the resulting bends.

Figure 18-48 *Two bend lines*

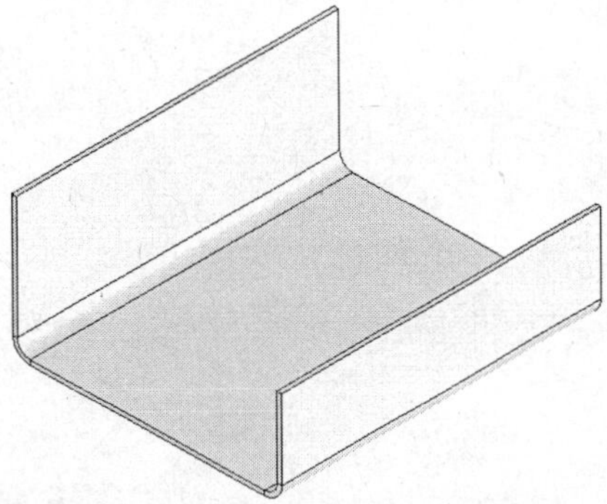

Figure 18-49 *Resulting sketched bend*

Creating the Miter Flange

CommandManager:	Sheet Metal > Miter Flange
SOLIDWORKS menus:	Insert > Sheet Metal > Miter Flange
Toolbar:	Sheet Metal > Miter Flange

The **Miter Flange** tool is used to create a series of flanges along the edges of a sheet metal component. The profile of the miter flange is defined by the sketch created on a sketching plane normal to the direction of extrusion of the flange. To create a miter flange, select the sketching plane and invoke the sketching environment. Create a sketch for the miter flange and then choose the **Miter Flange** button from the **Sheet Metal CommandManager**; the **Miter Flange PropertyManager** will be displayed, as shown in Figure 18-50.

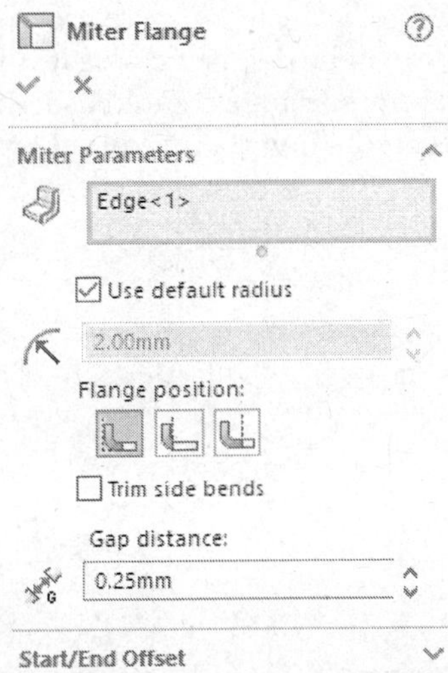

Figure 18-50 *Partial view of the* ***Miter Flange PropertyManager***

The preview of the flange with the default settings will be displayed in the drawing area and you will be prompted to select the linear edge(s) to attach the miter flange. Figure 18-51 shows the sketch for creating the miter flange and Figure 18-52 shows preview of the miter flange. You can select other continuous edges, if required, as shown in Figure 18-53. After selecting the edges, choose the **OK** button from the **Miter Flange PropertyManager**; the miter flange will be created, as shown in Figure 18-54.

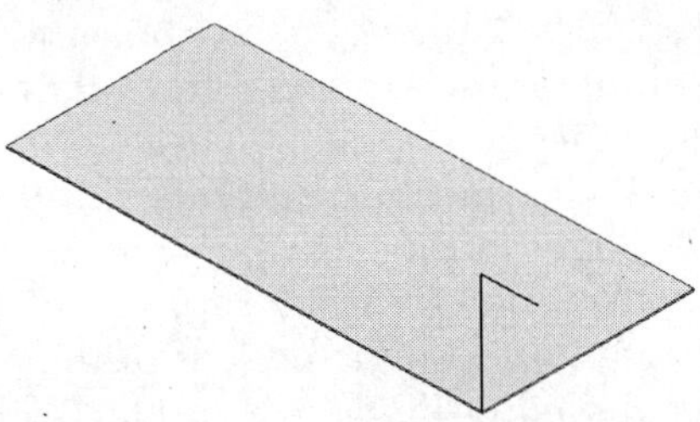

Figure 18-51 *Sketch for creating the miter flange*

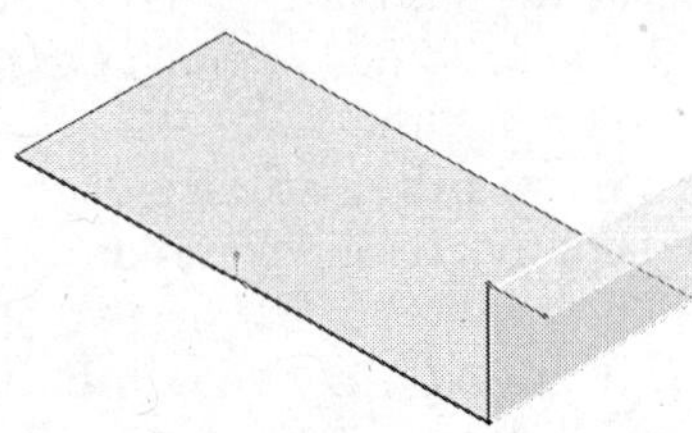

Figure 18-52 *Preview of the miter flange*

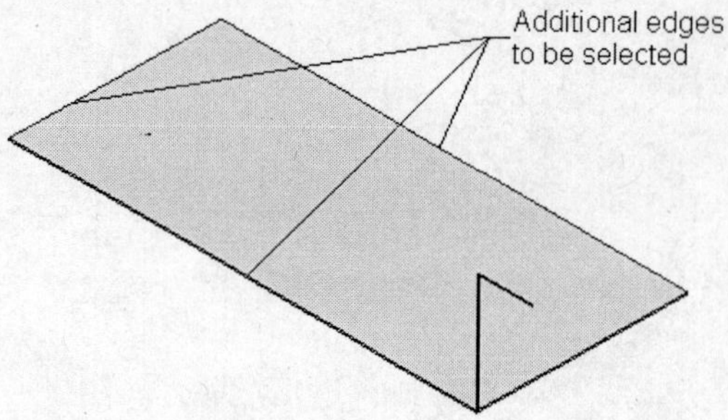

Figure 18-53 Sketch and the additional edges to be selected

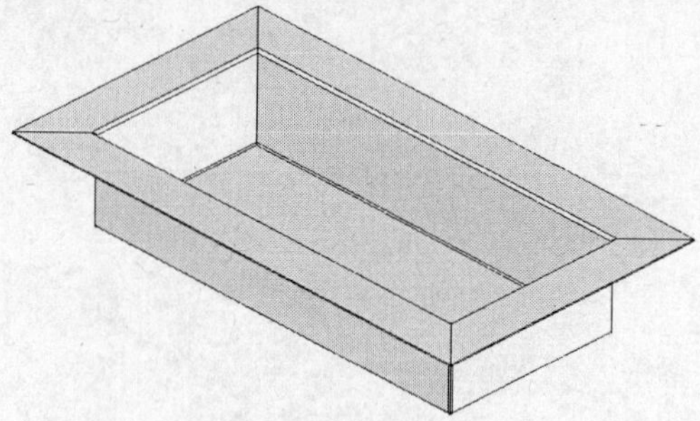

Figure 18-54 Resulting miter flange

The **Gap distance** area in the **Miter Flange PropertyManager** is discussed next.

Gap distance Area

The spinner in this area is used to define the rip distance between two consecutive flanges. Set the value in the **Rip Gap** spinner to modify the distance value of the rip. While creating a miter flange, if the feature creation is aborted due to default rip distance, the **Rebuild Errors** message box will be displayed and it will prompt you to enter a larger distance value. Figure 18-55 shows the miter flange created using the default distance value and Figure 18-56 shows the miter flange created using the modified rip distance.

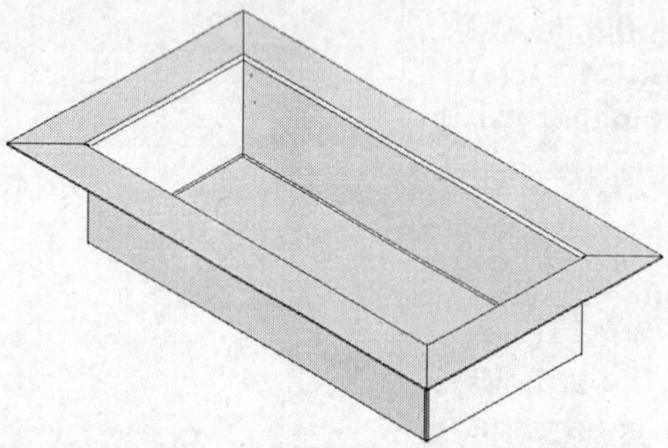

Figure 18-55 Miter flange with the default rip distance

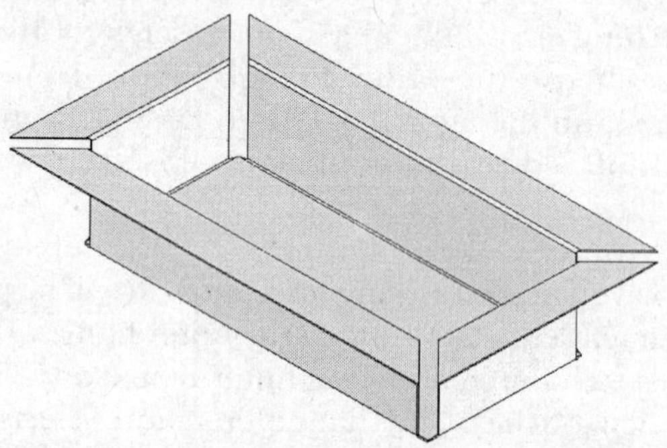

Figure 18-56 Miter flange with the modified rip distance

Start/End Offset Rollout

You can specify the start and end offset distances of the miter flange by using the options in the **Start/End Offset** rollout. The **Start Offset Distance** spinner is used to specify the offset distance from the start face of the miter flange. The **End Offset Distance** spinner is used to specify the offset distance from the end face of the miter flange. If the start and end offset distances are applied to the miter flange created on the continuous edges of the base flange, the start offset distance will be applied to the first edge and the end offset distance will be applied to the edge selected last. Figure 18-57 shows the miter flange created on a single edge with the start and end offsets. Figure 18-58 shows the offsets applied to the miter flange created by selecting all the edges of the base flange.

Figure 18-57 *Miter flange created at an offset distance on a single edge*

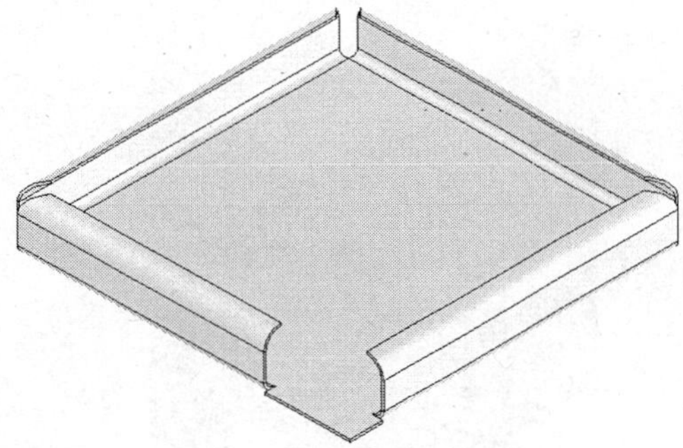

Figure 18-58 *Miter flange created at an offset distance on all edges*

Tip

While creating a miter flange, if an edge is tangent to the selected edge, then symbol will be displayed. Click on this symbol; the edges that are tangent to the selected edge will be selected automatically.

Creating Closed Corners

CommandManager:	Sheet Metal > Corners flyout > Closed Corner
SOLIDWORKS menus:	Insert > Sheet Metal > Closed Corner
Toolbar:	Sheet Metal > Corners flyout > Closed Corner

When you create walls using the **Edge Flange** tool, there may be a gap between the corners due to relief. You can close this gap and create a closed corner. To do so, choose the **Closed Corner** button from the **Corners** flyout of the **Sheet Metal CommandManager**; the **Closed Corner PropertyManager** will be displayed, as shown in Figure 18-59, and you will be prompted to select the planar corner face(s) to be extended for creating a closed corner. Select the face or the edge that you need to extend, as shown in Figure 18-60; the selected face will be highlighted. Note that both the flanges must be normal to each other for creating the closed corners. After selecting the faces, select the type of corner that you need to create by choosing the buttons in the **Corner type** area of the **Faces to Extend** rollout; the preview of the closed corner will be displayed in the drawing area. Choose the **OK** button from the **Closed Corner PropertyManager**. If the **Coplanar faces** check box is selected, then the faces that are on the same plane as that of the selected face will also be selected, as shown in Figures 18-60 and 18-61. Clear the **Open bend region** check box if you want to close the gap created by the slant face that has more bend radius, as shown in Figure 18-62. Select this check box if you want to create the model with a closed corner, as shown in Figure 18-63.

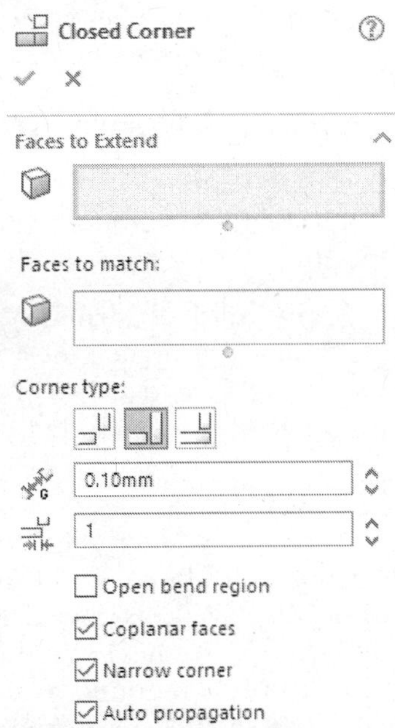

Figure 18-59 *The* ***Closed Corner PropertyManager***

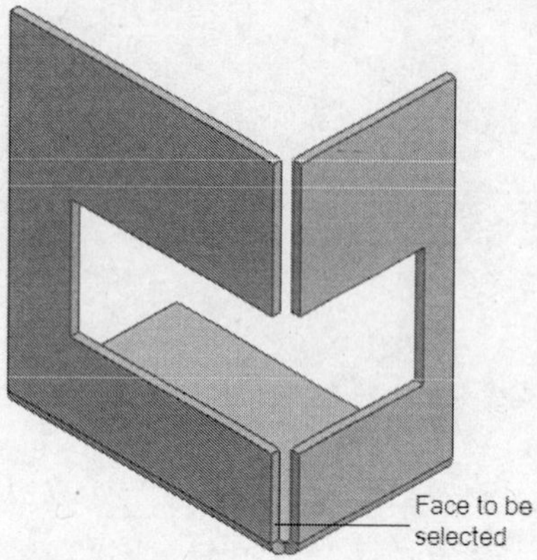

Figure 18-60 *Face selected to create a closed corner*

Figure 18-61 *Closed corner created with the* ***Coplanar faces*** *check box selected*

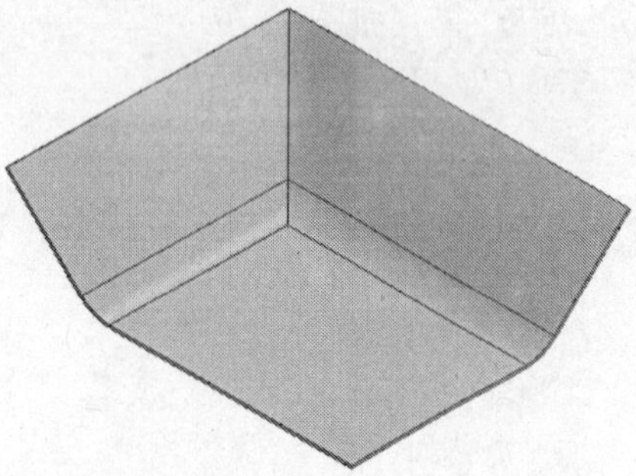

Figure 18-62 *Closed corner created with the* ***Open bend region*** *check box cleared*

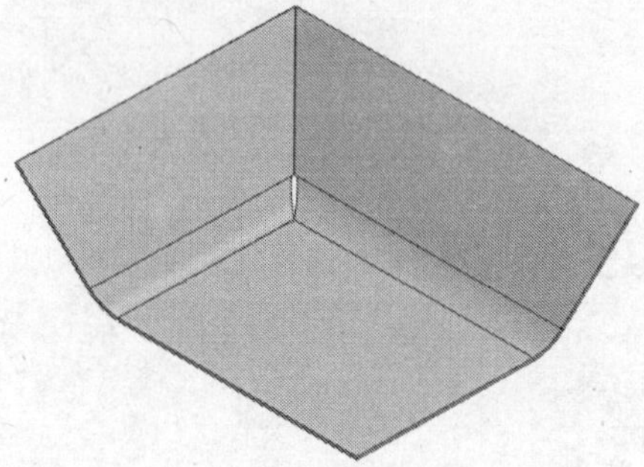

Figure 18-63 *Closed corner created with the* ***Open bend region*** *check box selected*

Creating Welded Corners

CommandManager:	Sheet Metal > Corners flyout > Welded Corner
SOLIDWORKS menus:	Insert > Sheet Metal > Welded Corner
Toolbar:	Sheet Metal > Corners flyout > Welded Corner

The **Welded Corner** tool allows you to create a weld bead along the corners of a folded sheet metal part. You can create a weld bead between miter flanges, edge flanges, and closed corners. The welded corners are supressed in flattened state.

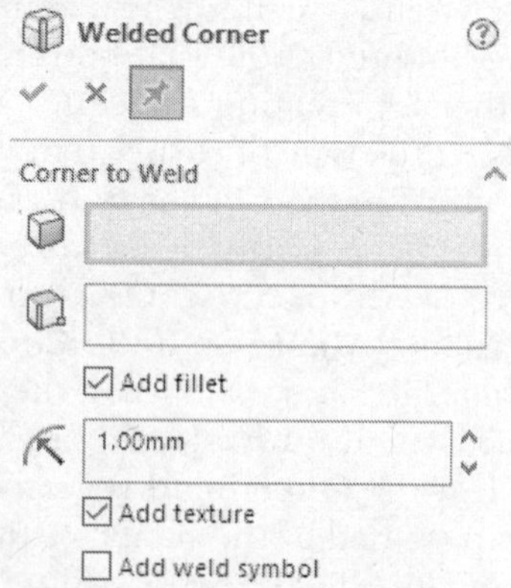

Figure 18-64 *The* ***Welded Corner PropertyManager***

To create a welded corner, choose the **Welded Corner** tool from the CommandManager; the **Welded Corner PropertyManager** will be displayed, as shown in Figure 18-64. Next, select the side face of the sheet metal corner to be welded, as shown in Figure 18-65. If required, you can select a vertex and edge, or a face to specify the termination point, as shown in Figures 18-66. So, you can specify the radius of the fillet when the **Add fillet** check box is selected and choose the **OK** button from the **Welded Corner PropertyManager**.

While using this feature, the options except the **Welded Corner** option in the **Corners** drop-down list will disappear. Therefore, it is recommended to use this tool at the end.

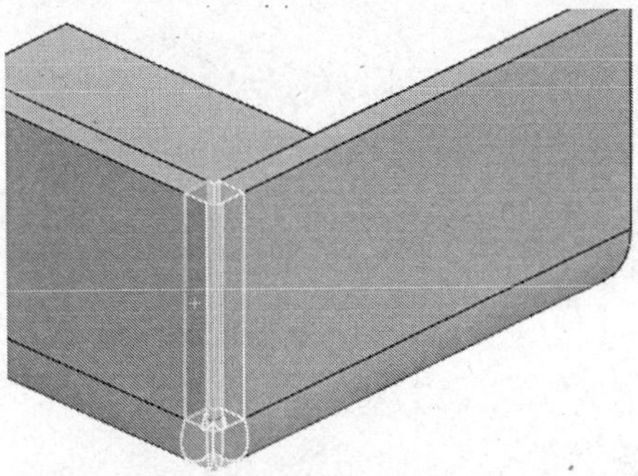

Figure 18-65 Face selected to create a welded corner

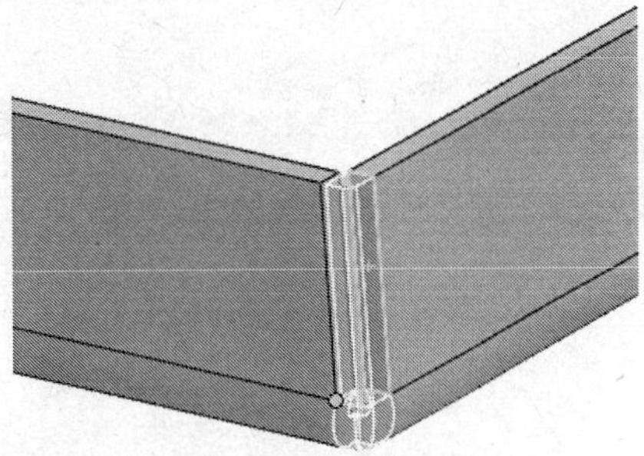

Figure 18-66 Vertex is selected as a termination point

Breaking the Corners

CommandManager:	Sheet Metal > Corners flyout > Break-Corner/Corner-Trim
SOLIDWORKS menus:	Insert > Sheet Metal > Break-Corner
Toolbar:	Sheet Metal > Corners flyout > Break-Corner/Corner-Trim

In SOLIDWORKS, you are provided with an option to break the edges of the sheet metal components to create chamfer or fillet. The edges of the sheet metal components are chamfered or filleted using the **Break-Corner/Corner-Trim** tool. To break a corner, choose the **Break-Corner/Corner-Trim** tool from the **Corners** flyout; the **Break Corner PropertyManager** will be displayed, as shown in Figure 18-67. Also, you will be prompted to select corner edge(s) or flange face(s). Select the faces or the edges that you need to break; the preview of the corner break is displayed in the drawing area with the default settings. As the **Chamfer** button is chosen by default in the **Break Corner Options** rollout, the corner break created by default is a chamfer. You can set the value of the chamfer by using the **Distance** spinner. If you need to create a corner break as fillet, choose the **Fillet** button from the **Break Corner Options** rollout; the **Distance** spinner will be replaced by the **Radius** spinner. After setting all parameters, choose the **OK** button from the **Break Corner PropertyManager**. Figures 18-68 and 18-69 show the sheet metal component before and after adding the chamfers and fillets using the **Break Corner PropertyManager**.

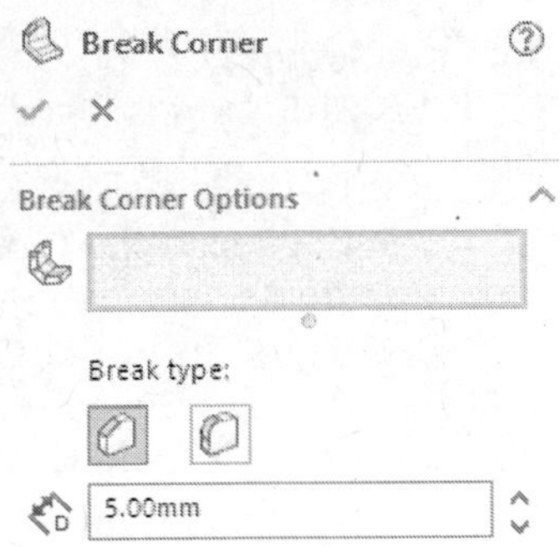

Figure 18-67** The **Break Corner PropertyManager

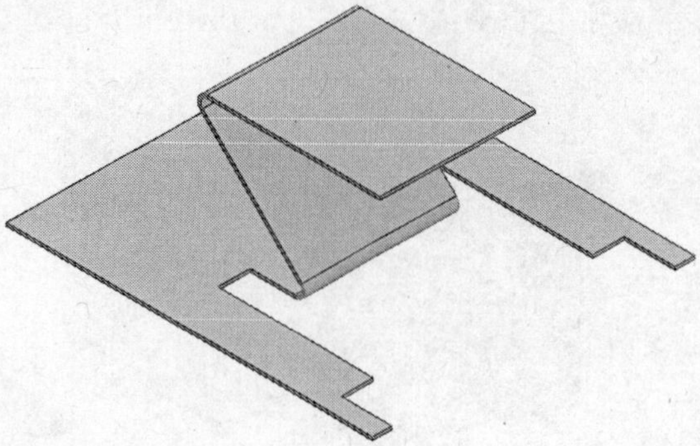

Figure 18-68 *Sheet metal component before adding chamfers and fillets*

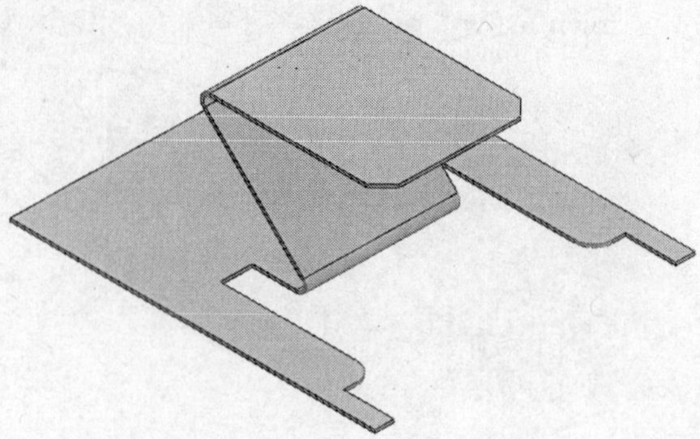

Figure 18-69 *Sheet metal component after adding chamfers and fillets*

Note

If you invoke the ***Corner*** *tool after creating a flat pattern of the sheet metal component, some more options will be displayed in the* ***Break Corner PropertyManager****. These options are discussed later in this chapter.*

Creating Corner Relief

CommandManager:	Sheet Metal > Corners flyout > Corner Relief
SOLIDWORKS menus:	Insert > Sheet Metal > Corner Relief
Toolbar:	Sheet Metal > Corners flyout > Corner Relief

The **Corner Relief** tool is used to modify sheet metal corners so that they can be bended or welded easily in the manufacturing process. To create a corner relief, choose the **Corner Relief** tool from the CommandManager; the **Corner Relief** PropertyManager will be displayed. Also, the sheet metal part will be automatically selected and displayed in the **Scope** rollout. Select the **2 Bend Corner** or **3 Bend Corner** radio button from the **Corner Type** rollout based on the corner on which the relief need to be applied. Once the part/body and type of corner is selected, choose the **Collect all corners** button from the **Corners** rollout to automatically select all the corners of the body; the selected corners will be highlighted with orange colored dots. The **Define Corner** rollout displays the faces that define a selected corner. You can also select a new corner by selecting the **New Corner** button and then selecting two adjacent bend faces from the drawing window. In the **Relief Options** rollout, you can select a relief type such as **Rectangular**, **Circular**, **Tear**, **Obround**, **Constant Width**, **Full Round**, or **Suitcase**. The **Suitcase** option can be used to close a 3 bend corner with a spherical shape. Figure 18-70 shows the rectangular corner relief using the **2 Bend Corner** radio button. Figure 18-71 shows the rectangular corner relief using the **3 Bend Corner** radio button.

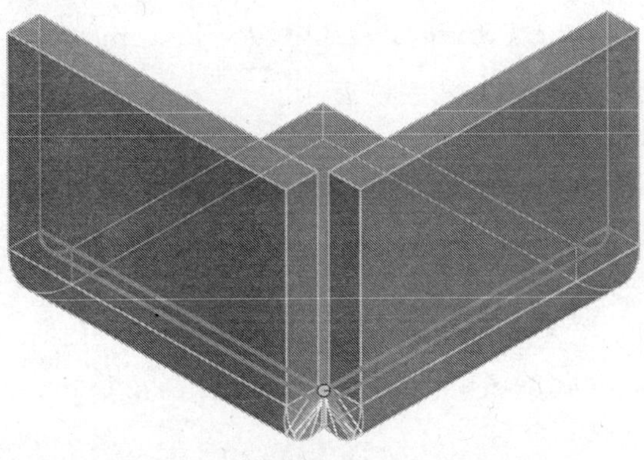

Figure 18-70 *A rectangular corner relief using the* ***2 Bend Corner*** *radio button*

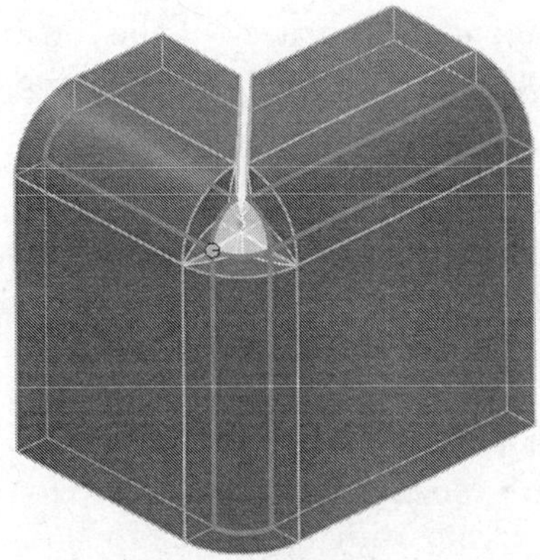

Figure 18-71 *A rectangular corner relief using the* ***3 Bend Corner*** *radio button*

Creating Hems

CommandManager:	Sheet Metal > Hem
SOLIDWORKS menus:	Insert > Sheet Metal > Hem
Toolbar:	Sheet Metal > Hem

Hems are generally used to bend a small area of sheet in order to eliminate the sharp edges in a sheet metal component. Hems are also used to connect two walls by interlocking their edges. To create a hem, choose the **Hem** button from the **Sheet Metal CommandManager**; the **Hem PropertyManager** will be displayed, as shown in Figure 18-72. Also, you will be prompted to select an edge on a planar face to create a hem feature. Select the edge on a planar face; the preview of the hem with the default settings will be displayed in the drawing area. The rollouts in the **Hem PropertyManager** are discussed next.

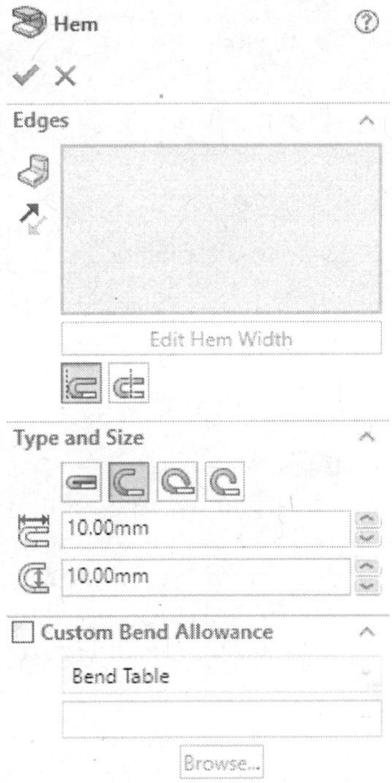

Figure 18-72 *Partial view of the* ***Hem PropertyManager***

Edges Rollout

The options in the **Edges** rollout are used to specify the edges on which hem will be created. When you select the edges, the names of the edges will be listed in the **Edges** selection box and the preview of the hem will be displayed. The **Reverse Direction** button in this rollout is used to reverse the direction of the hem. You can choose the **Edit Hem Width** button below the **Edges** selection box to change the width of the hem on the selected edge. Choose this button; the **Profile Sketch** dialog box will be displayed with the message informing that the sketch created is valid. Also, the sketching environment will be invoked. Now, edit the sketch to make a hem of a particular width and then place it at a particular position. The edited sketch should contain only one segment and also it should be constrained to the selected edge. If the edited sketch contains more segments then a message will be displayed in the **Profile Sketch** dialog box, informing that the sketch is invalid.

By default, the **Material Inside** button is chosen in the **Edges** rollout. So, the hem is created such that the material of the hem after the bend lies inside the maximum limit of sheet. If you choose the **Bend Outside** button, the hem will be created with the bend starting from the maximum limit of the sheet.

Type and Size Rollout

The **Type and Size** rollout is used to define the type and size of the hem. The types of hem that you can create using options in this rollout are discussed next.

Closed Hem

The closed hem is a hem that has no gap between the inner face of the hem and the face adjacent to the edge on which the hem is created. To create a closed hem, choose the **Closed** button and set the length of the closed hem by using the **Length** spinner. If you select more than one edge to create the hem, the **Miter Gap** rollout will be displayed. You can specify the miter gap in this rollout. Figure 18-73 shows the edge selected to create a closed hem and Figure 18-74 shows the resulting closed hem.

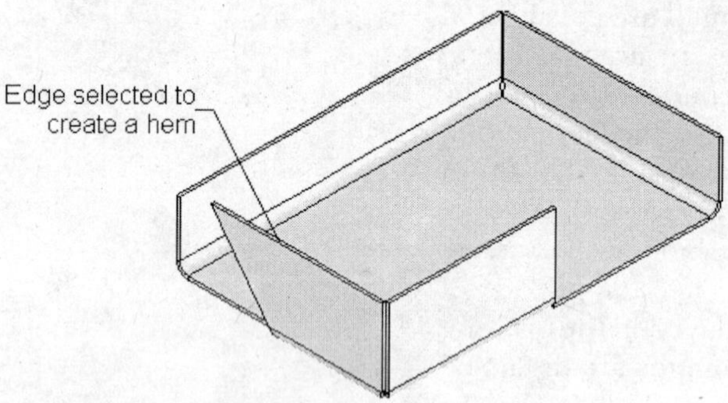

Figure 18-73 Edge selected to create a closed hem

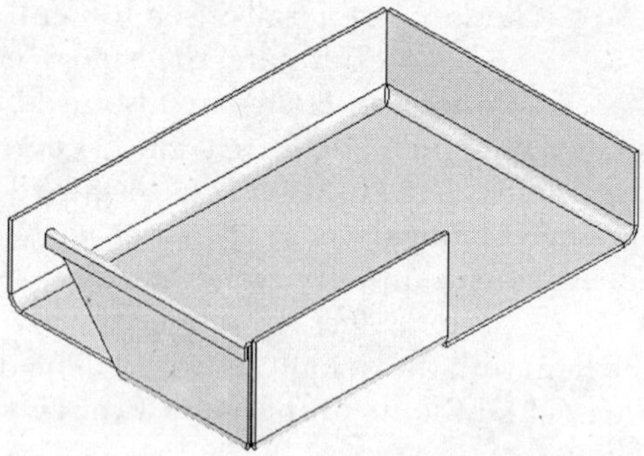

Figure 18-74 Resulting closed hem

Open Hem

The open hem is a hem with a gap between the inner face of the hem and the face adjacent to the edge on which the hem is created. To create an open hem, choose the **Open** button; the **Length** and **Gap Distance** spinners will be displayed. You can specify the value of the length and the gap distance in these spinners. Figure 18-75 shows the edge selected to create an open hem and Figure 18-76 shows the resulting open hem.

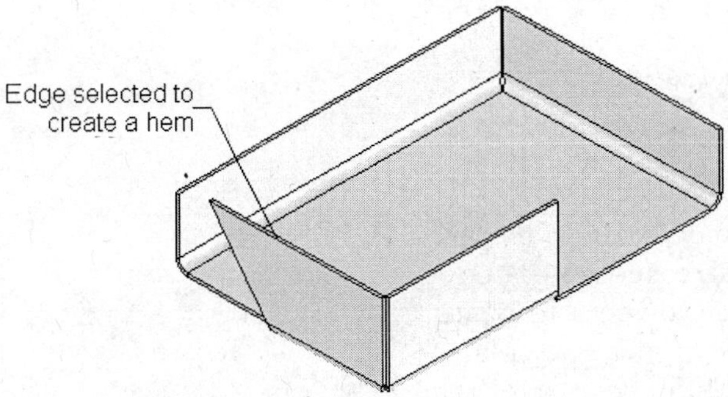

Figure 18-75 *Edge selected to create an open hem*

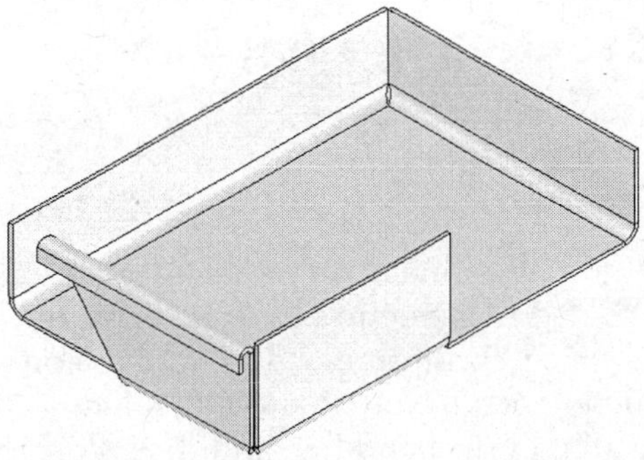

Figure 18-76 *Resulting open hem*

Tear Drop Hem

By default, the **Tear Drop** button is chosen when you invoke the **Hem PropertyManager**. As a result, a tear drop shaped hem will be created on the selected edge. Set the angle and the radius of the tear drop in the **Angle** and **Radius** spinners, respectively. Figure 18-77 shows a tear drop hem created on a sheet metal component.

Rolled Hem

The **Rolled** button is used to create the rolled shaped hem. When you choose this button, the **Angle** and **Radius** spinners are displayed where you can set the angle and radius values, respectively.

Figure 18-78 shows the rolled hem created on a sheet metal component.

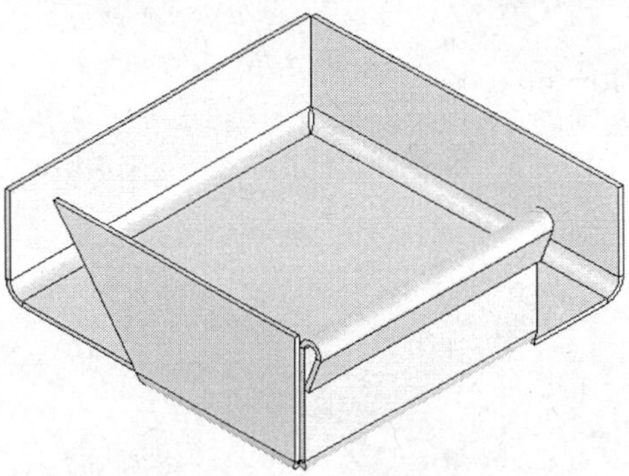

Figure 18-77 *Tear drop hem*

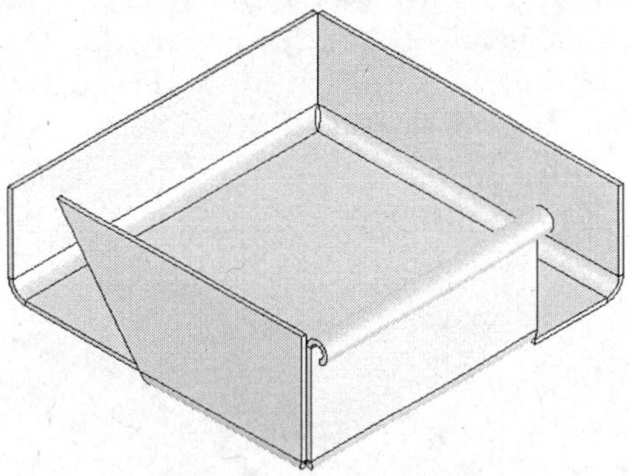

Figure 18-78 *Rolled hem*

Creating the Jog Bend

CommandManager:	Sheet Metal > Jog
SOLIDWORKS menus:	Insert > Sheet Metal > Jog
Toolbar:	Sheet Metal > Jog

You can create two bends in a sheet metal component by using a bend line. The bend line is sketched on the face of the sheet metal component on which you need to create the jog bend. Note that the first bend will be on the same plane as that of the bend line and the second bend will be at an offset distance. Note that the sketch of the bend line must lie inside or on the face of the sheet metal. After creating the bend line, choose the **Jog** button from the **Sheet Metal CommandManager**; the **Jog PropertyManager** will be displayed, as shown in Figure 18-79, and you will be prompted to select the planar face to be fixed for creating the bend. Select the side of the face to be fixed; the preview of the jog bend with the default values will be displayed in the drawing area. Figures 18-80 and 18-82 show the bend line and the faces to be fixed. Figures 18-81 and 18-83 show their respective jog bends. The rollouts in the **Jog PropertyManager** are discussed next.

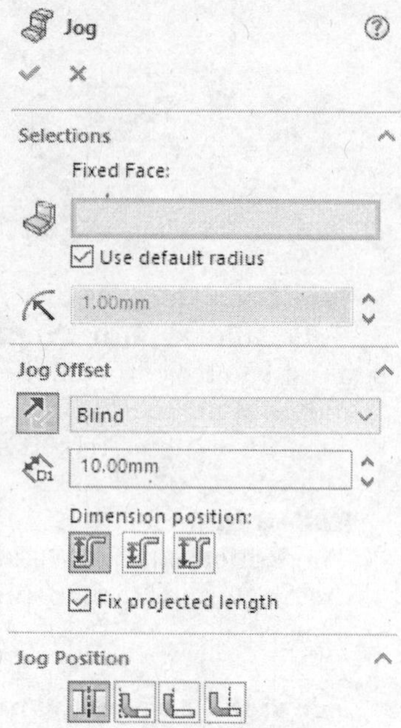

*Figure 18-79 Partial view of the **Jog PropertyManager***

Selections Rollout

The options in the **Selections** rollout are used to define the face to be fixed while bending and to define the radius of the bend. The name of the selected face that needs to be fixed while bending will be displayed in the **Fixed Face** selection box. By default, the **Use default radius** check box will be selected. If you need to define the bending radius other than the default radius, clear this check box and set the value of the radius in the **Bend Radius** spinner.

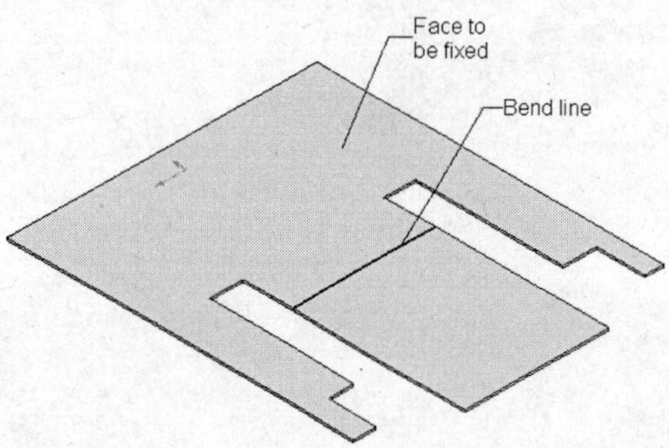

***Figure 18-80** Bend line and face to be fixed*

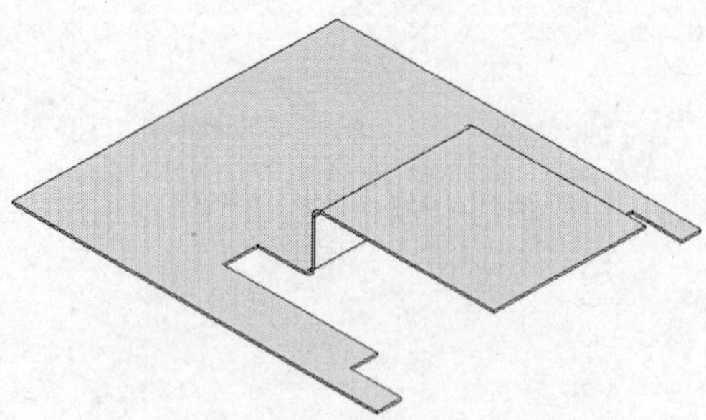

***Figure 18-81** Resulting jog bend*

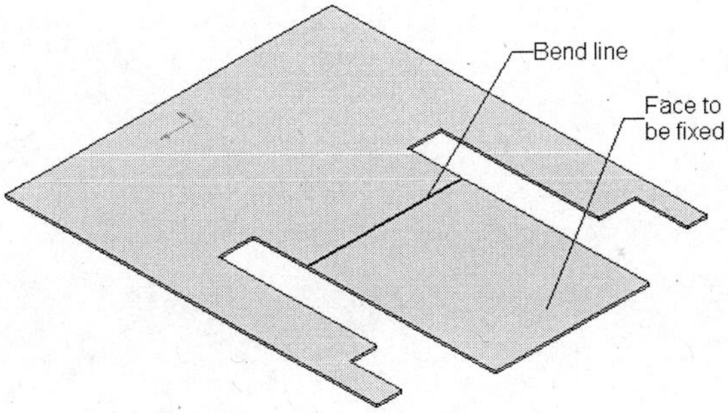

Figure 18-82 Bend line and face to be fixed

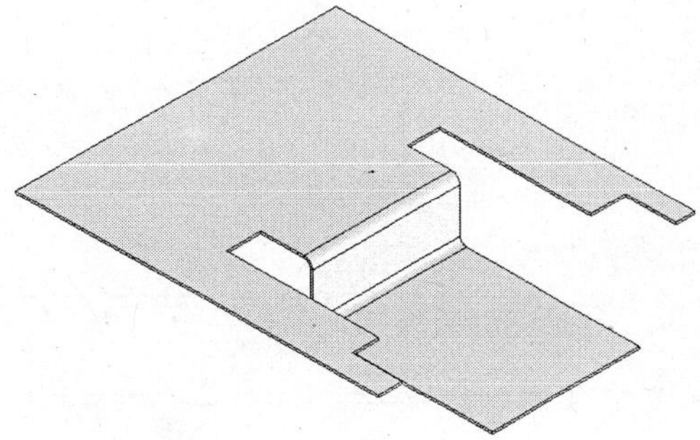

Figure 18-83 Resulting job bend

Jog Offset Rollout

The **Jog Offset** rollout is used to define various parameters of the jog. You can define the feature termination option for the jog by using this rollout. You can also create a jog with zero blind depth. The options in this rollout are discussed next.

Dimension position Area

The **Dimension position** area of the **Jog Offset** rollout is used to define the position from where the dimension of the jog offset will be calculated. The buttons in this area are used to specify the offset by calculating the inside offset, outside offset, and overall dimension, refer to Figure 18-84.

Fix projected length

The **Fix projected length** check box is selected by default and is used to maintain the length of the bent sheet equal to the projected length of the original sheet after adding a jog bend. If you clear this check box, the overall length of the sheet will be maintained equal to the original sheet even after adding the jog bend. Figure 18-85 shows the bend line that will be used to create a jog bend. Figure 18-86 shows the preview of the jog bend created with the **Fix projected length** check box selected. Figure 18-87 shows the preview of the jog bend created with the **Fix projected length** check box cleared.

Jog Position Rollout

The **Jog Position** rollout is used to define the position of bending. The options in this rollout are similar to those discussed earlier.

Jog Angle Rollout

The **Jog Angle** rollout is used to define the angle of the jog bend. The default value of the jog angle is 90 degree. You can set the value of the angle at which you need to create the jog bend in the **Jog Angle** spinner. Figure 18-88 shows the jog bend created at an angle of 135 degree.

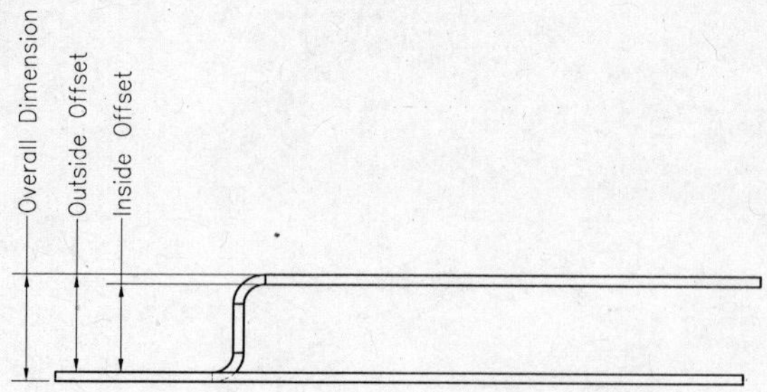

Figure 18-84 Inside offset, outside offset, and overall dimension

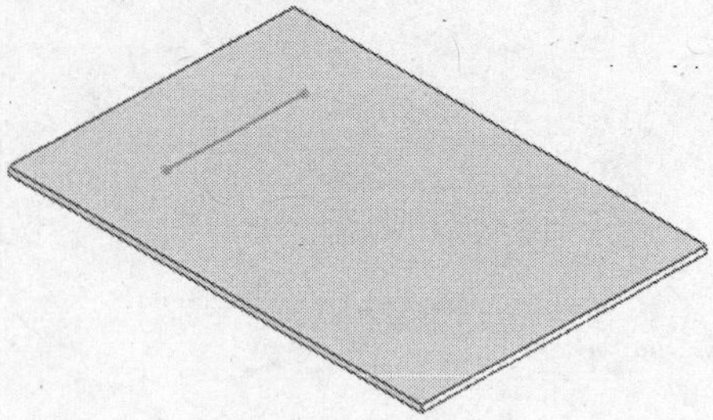

Figure 18-85 Bend line used to create the jog bend

Figure 18-86 *Jog bend created with the* ***Fixed projected length*** *check box selected*

Figure 18-87 *Jog bend created with the* ***Fixed projected length*** *check box cleared*

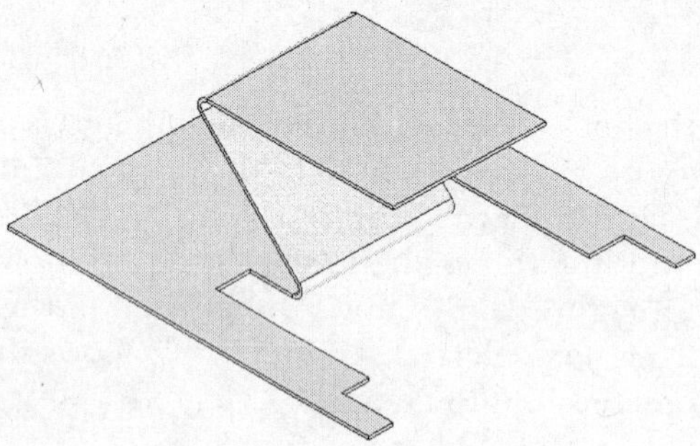

Figure 18-88 Jog bend created at an angle of 135 degrees

Creating the Swept Flange

CommandManager:	Sheet Metal > Swept Flange
SOLIDWORKS menus:	Insert > Sheet Metal > Swept Flange
Toolbar:	Sheet Metal > Swept Flange *(Customize to add)*

The **Swept Flange** tool is used to create a series of flanges along a sketched path or edges of a sheet metal component. The profile of the swept flange is defined by the sketch created on a sketching plane normal to the direction of extrusion of the flange. To create a swept flange, select the sketching plane and invoke the sketching environment. Next, create a sketch for the swept flange and then choose the **Swept Flange** button from the **Sheet Metal CommandManager**; the **Swept Flange PropertyManager** will be displayed, as shown in Figure 18-89. Also, you will be prompted to select the linear edge(s) to attach the swept flange profile. Select the profile created from the drawing area; the **Path** selection box gets activated. Select the edges of the model as the path for swept flange. Note that the sketch created will define the profile of the flange and the edge selected will define the path for creating the swept flange. You can also select the chain of edges one by one to create a swept flange. The other options in this PropertyManager are similar to those discussed earlier. Figure 18-90 shows the sheet metal component with profile and path to be selected and Figure 18-91 shows the component after creating the swept flange.

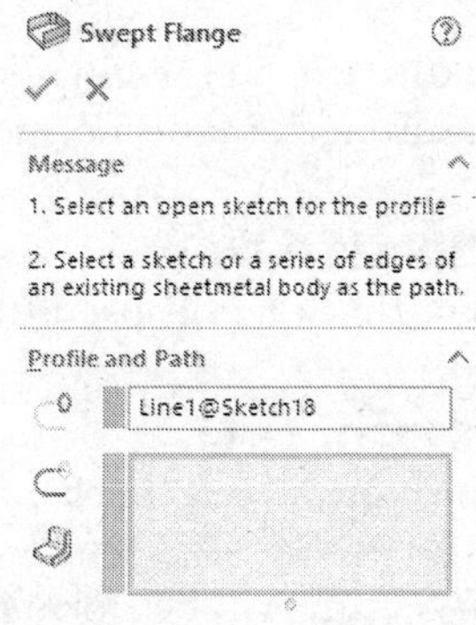

***Figure 18-89** The Swept Flange PropertyManager*

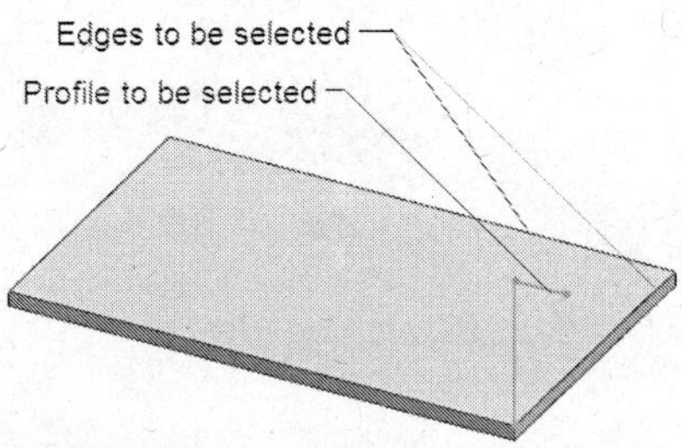

***Figure 18-90** Sketch for creating the swept flange*

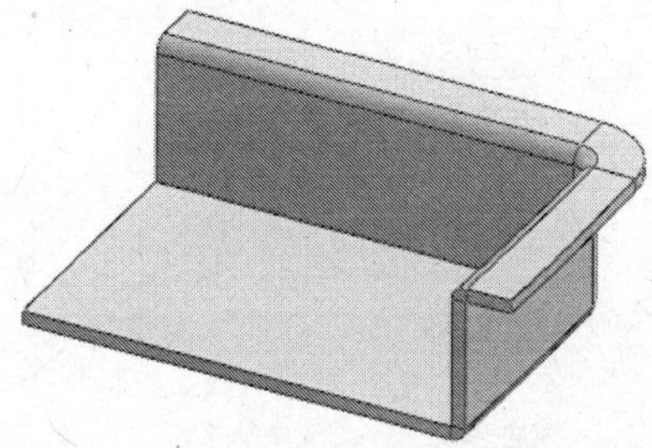

***Figure 18-91** Resulting swept flange*

Creating Cuts on the Planar Faces of the Sheet Metal Components

CommandManager:	Sheet Metal > Extruded Cut
SOLIDWORKS menus:	Insert > Cut > Extrude
Toolbar:	Sheet Metal > Extruded Cut

Creating cuts in the sheet metal components is similar to creating cuts in the solid models. To create cuts on the planar faces of the sheet metal components, select a face or a plane as the sketching plane and invoke the sketching environment. Draw a sketch for creating the cut feature and choose the **Extruded Cut** button from the **Sheet Metal CommandManager**; the **Cut-Extrude PropertyManager** will be displayed. Set the options for feature termination in the **Cut-Extrude PropertyManager**. You will observe that some additional options are displayed in the **Direction 1** rollout of the **Cut-Extrude PropertyManager**. These additional options are discussed next.

Link to thickness

The **Link to thickness** check box is used to set the value of the feature termination according to the thickness of the sheet and it is cleared by default. On selecting this check box, the cut feature will be terminated at the blind distance equal to the sheet thickness, irrespective of the feature termination option selected.

Flip side to cut

This check box is used to reverse the side of the sheet metal part to cut.

Normal cut

The **Normal cut** check box is selected by default and is used for the bent sheet metal components. If the profile of the cut feature is on a different plane and this check box is selected, the resulting cut feature will be normal to the sheet metal component. However, if you clear this check box, the resulting cut feature will be created normal to the sketching plane. Figure 18-92 shows the side view of a sheet metal component in which a cut feature is created with the **Normal cut** check box selected and a cut feature created with the **Normal cut** check box cleared.

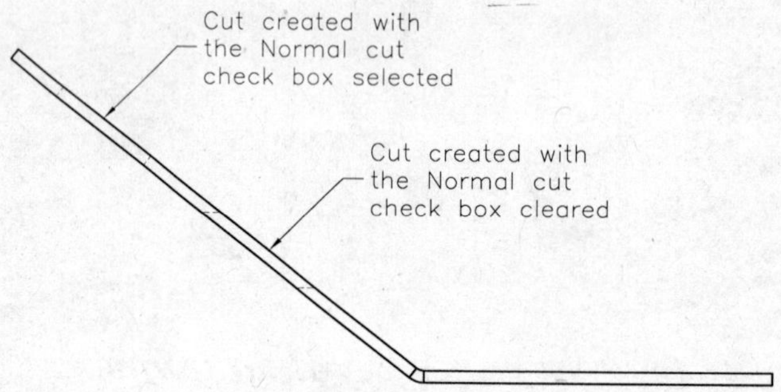

Figure 18-92 *Cut created with the* ***Normal cut*** *check box selected and cleared*

Creating Lofted Bends

CommandManager:	Sheet Metal > Lofted-Bend
SOLIDWORKS menus:	Insert > Sheet Metal > Lofted Bends
Toolbar:	Sheet Metal > Lofted-Bend

Lofted-Bend

The lofted bends are created by defining a transition of sheet between two open sections placed apart at some offset distance. To create the lofted bends, you have to create the open sections. Note that in SOLIDWORKS, you can also create the lofted bends between two non-planar sketches. You can create sections with or without vertices. To create lofted bends, choose the **Lofted-Bend** button from the **Sheet Metal CommandManager**; the **Lofted Bends PropertyManager** will be displayed and you will be prompted to select two profiles. Select two profiles to create the lofted bends; the preview of the lofted bend will be displayed in the drawing area. Set the thickness of the sheet using the **Thickness** spinner and choose the **OK** button from the **Lofted Bends PropertyManager**. Figure 18-93 shows the open sections that you need to select for creating a lofted bend. Figure 18-94 shows the resulting lofted bend.

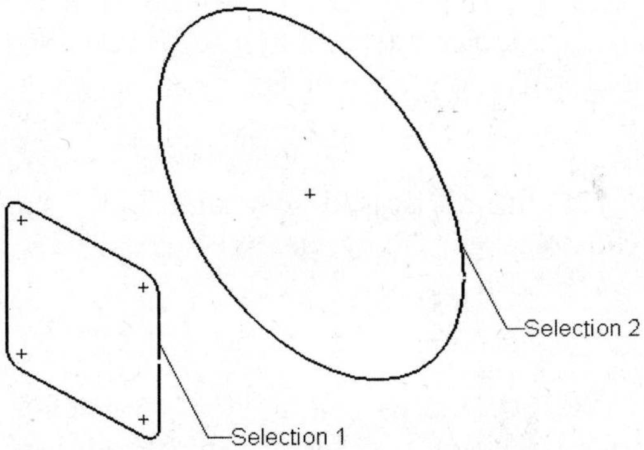

Figure 18-93 Sections for creating lofted bend

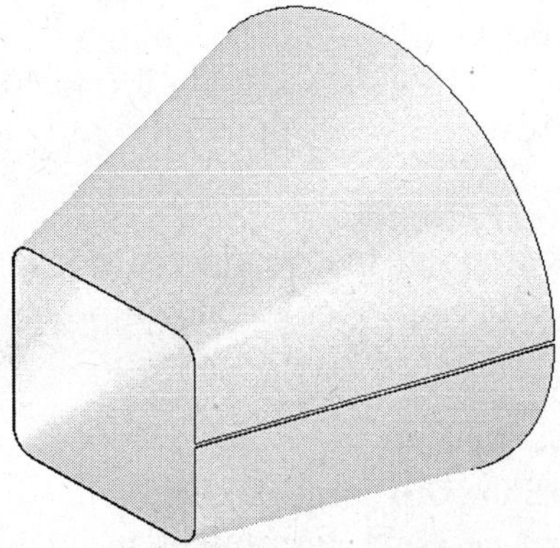

Figure 18-94 Resulting lofted bend

Creating a Flat Pattern View of the Sheet Metal Components

CommandManager:	Sheet Metal > Flatten
Toolbar:	Sheet Metal > Flatten

The flat pattern view of a sheet metal component is extensively used in the tool room or the machine shop to define the size of the raw sheet, and also the shape of the sheet that you need before bending. It is also used for process planning to start the manufacturing of the tool that will create the sheet metal component. Before creating the flat pattern, you can set the option for the flat pattern. To set the options for the flat pattern, expand the **Flat-Pattern** node and then select the **Flat-Pattern1** feature from the **FeatureManager Design Tree** and invoke the pop-up toolbar. Next, choose the **Edit Feature** option from this toolbar; the **Flat-Pattern PropertyManager** will be invoked, as shown in Figure 18-95. The rollouts in the **Flat-Pattern PropertyManager** are discussed next.

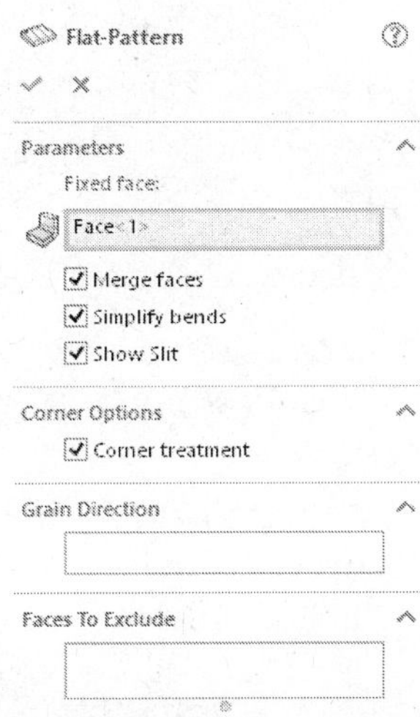

Figure 18-95** The **Flat-Pattern PropertyManager

Parameters Rollout

The options in the **Parameters** rollout are used to define various parameters to create the flat pattern of the sheet metal component. The options in this rollout are discussed next.

Fixed Face

The **Fixed Face** display area is used to specify the face that will be fixed while opening the sheet to create the flat pattern. Select a face; the face will be highlighted in different color and its name will be displayed in the **Fixed Face** selection box. You can select any face from the drawing area that needs to be fixed while creating the flat pattern.

Merge faces

The **Merge faces** check box is used to merge the flat faces and the bending faces while creating the flat pattern. This check box is selected by default. If you clear this check box, the flat faces and bend faces will not be merged. Figure 18-96 shows the flat pattern of a sheet metal component created with the **Merge faces** check box selected. Figure 18-97 shows the flat pattern of a sheet metal component created with the **Merge faces** check box cleared.

Simplify bends

The **Simplify bends** check box is selected by default and is used to straighten the curved edges of the sheet metal component in the flat pattern. If you clear this check box, the curved edge will not be straightened in the flat pattern.

Show Slit

The **Show Slit** check box is selected to show slits that are added for some corner relief feature. When you create a rectangular or circular corner relief that is smaller than the bend area, a slit is added so that the part can still be bent. Selecting the **Show Slit** check box will make the slit to be displayed in the flat pattern.

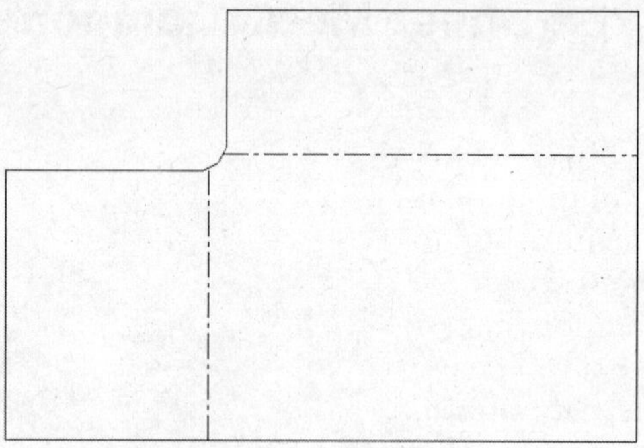

Figure 18-96 *Flat pattern created using the* ***Merge faces*** *check box selected*

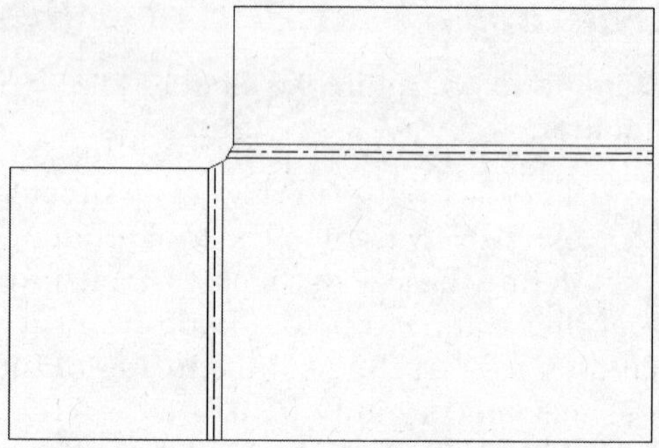

Figure 18-97 *Flat pattern created using the* ***Merge faces*** *check box cleared*

Corner Options

The **Corner Options** rollout is used to set the option to dress up the corners of the flattened sheet metal component. The option available in this rollout is discussed next.

Corner treatment

The **Corner treatment** check box is selected by default and is used to automatically apply the corner treatment to the flattened sheet. This option removes or adds the material at the corners of the sheet. If you clear this check box, the corner treatment is not applied to the flattened sheet. Figure 18-98 shows the flat pattern of a sheet metal component with the **Corner treatment** check box selected. Figure 18-99 shows the flat pattern of a sheet metal component with the **Corner treatment** check box cleared.

Grain Direction

In SOLIDWORKS, you can select the grain direction of the bounding box sketch for creating sheet metal. The bounding box sketch is an imaginary construction line sketch showing minimum area required to manufacture the sheet metal component. With grain direction you can select the edge which might not require any machining in manufacturing process.

Faces To Exclude

In SOLIDWORKS, you can exclude faces that are intersecting with the bends of the sheet metal components from the flat pattern by using the **Faces To Exclude** selection box of the **Flat-Pattern PropertyManager**. To do so, click on the **Please select face(s) to exclude** selection box to activate it and then select the faces that you want to exclude from the flat pattern. Figure 18-100 shows the edges of the sheet metal component selected to be excluded and the edge selected to be kept fixed and Figure 18-101 shows the sheet metal component after generating flat pattern.

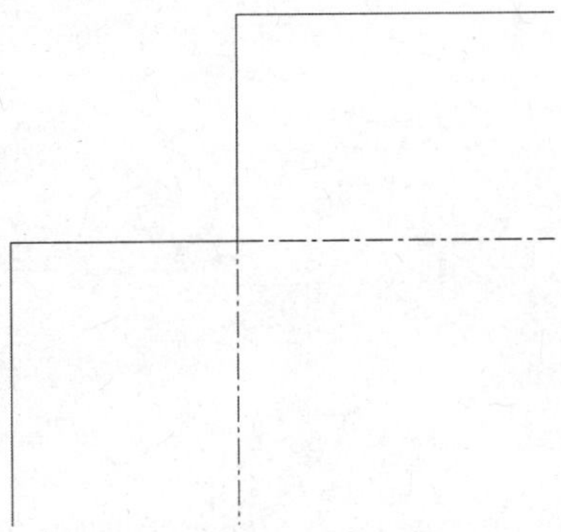

Figure 18-98 Flat pattern with the ***Corner Treatment*** *check box selected*

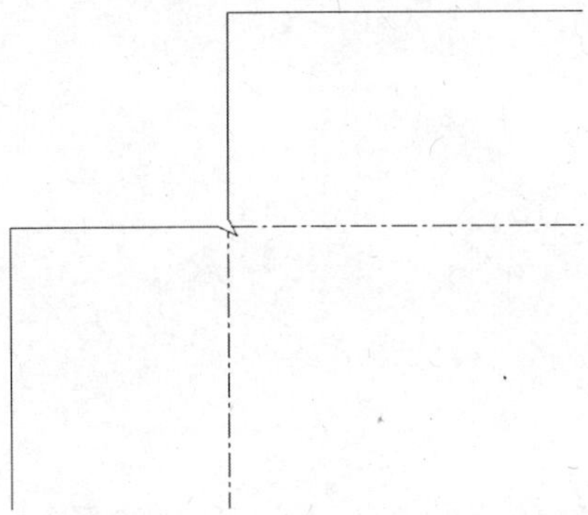

Figure 18-99 Flat pattern with the ***Corner Treatment*** *check box cleared*

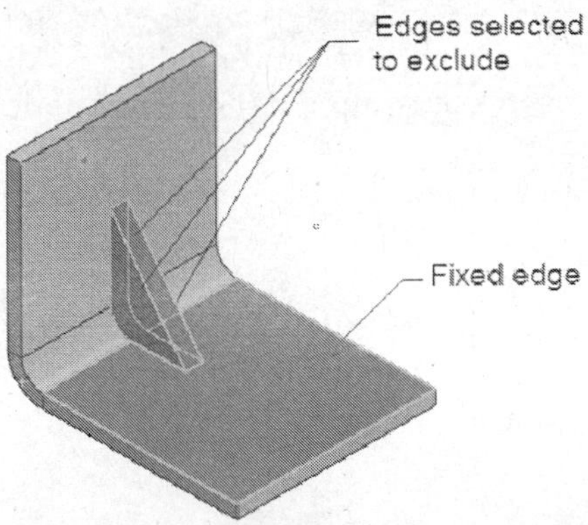

Figure 18-100 Faces selected for applying flat-pattern

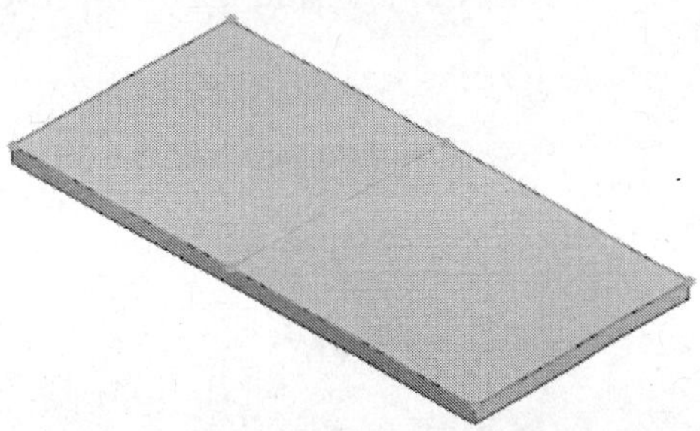

Figure 18-101 Sheet metal component after generating flat-pattern

After setting all the options, choose the **OK** button from the **Flat-Pattern PropertyManager**. Now, to flatten the sheet metal component, choose the **Flatten** button from the **Sheet Metal** toolbar. You can also select the **Flat-Pattern1** feature from the **FeatureManager Design Tree** and invoke the pop-up toolbar. Next, choose the **Unsuppress** option from this toolbar to flatten the sheet metal component. The sheet metal component is flattened by selecting the base flange as the face to be fixed. When there are multiple parts, you can also choose the **Flatten** option by expanding the **Cut list** node and right-clicking on the name of the part to be flattened. In SOLIDWORKS, a bounding box is displayed around the flattened component.

CREATING SHEET METAL COMPONENTS FROM A FLAT SHEET

In SOLIDWORKS, you can create a sheet metal component by first creating the flat sheet and then adding bends to it to get the required shape of the component. Consider an example of the sheet metal component shown in Figure 18-102. The flat pattern of this component is shown in Figure 18-103.

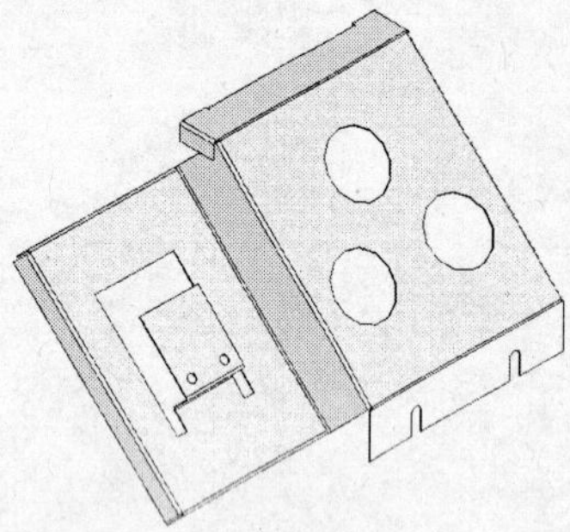

Figure 18-102 *Sheet metal component*

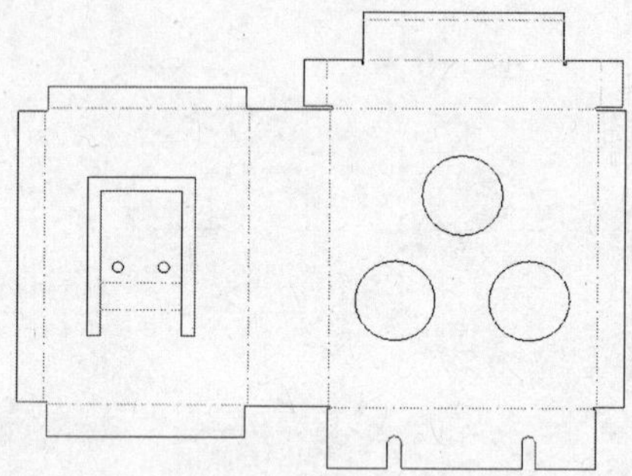

Figure 18-103 *Flat pattern of the sheet metal component*

To create this component from a flat sheet, you first need to create the base flange similar to the flat pattern by invoking the **Base Flange/Tab** tool, as shown in Figure 18-104. Next, create the bend lines in a single sketch, as shown in Figure 18-105. Now, choose the **Sketched Bend** tool to bend the sheet metal component along the sketch created as the bending lines, as shown in Figure 18-106. You can also add other sheet metal features to complete the component.

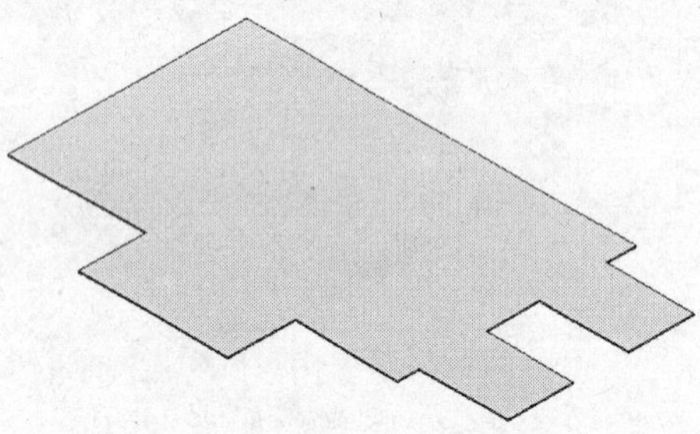

Figure 18-104 *Base flange*

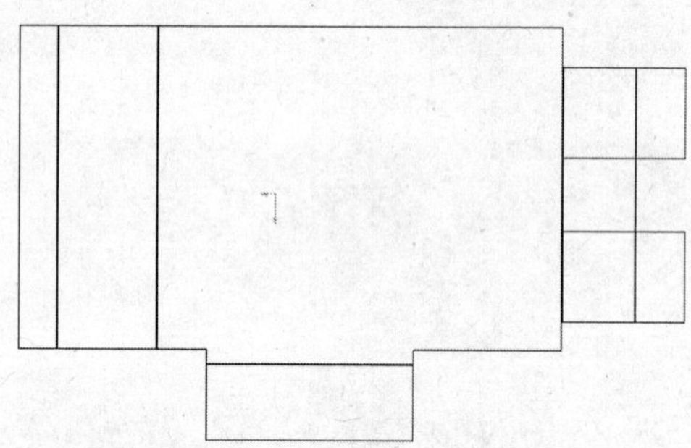

Figure 18-105 *Bend lines*

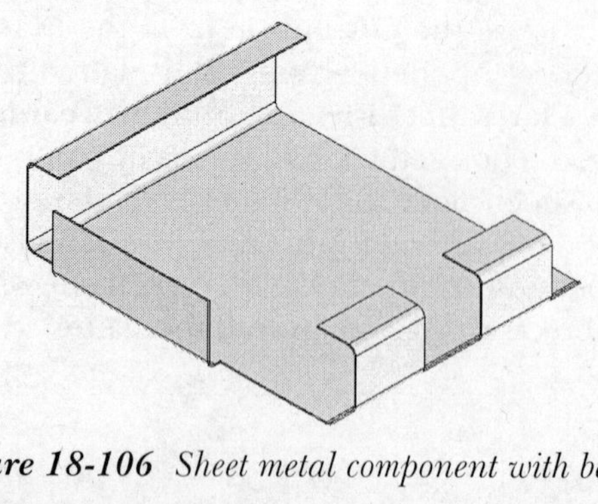

Figure 18-106 *Sheet metal component with bend*

CREATING A SHEET METAL COMPONENT FROM A FLAT PART

You can create a sheet metal component by creating the flat state of the sheet as a solid part in the **Part** mode and then converting the solid part into sheet metal. To create a sheet metal component by using this method, create a closed sketch that will define the flat state of the sheet. Extrude the sketch using the blind depth equal to the thickness of the flat sheet using the **Extruded Boss/Base** tool. Next, convert the flat part into a sheet metal component in flattened state. The procedure to convert a flat part into a sheet metal component is discussed next.

Converting a Part or a Flat Part into Sheet Metal by Adding Bends

CommandManager:	Sheet Metal > Insert Bends
SOLIDWORKS menus:	Insert > Sheet Metal > Bends
Toolbar:	Sheet Metal > Insert Bends

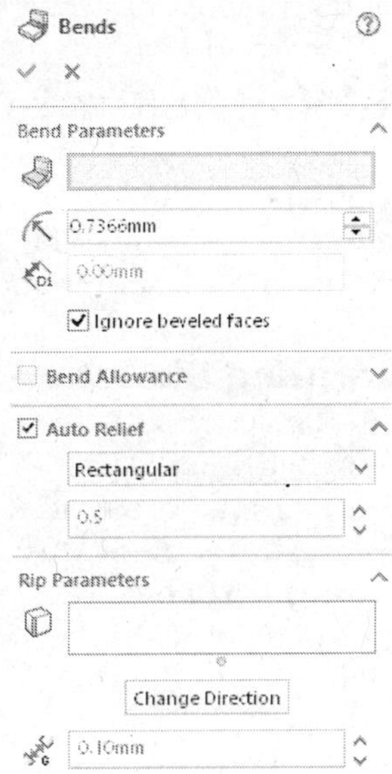

Figure 18-107 *The* ***Bends PropertyManager***

To convert a part into a sheet metal component, you need to add bends to the part. The bends are added to the part using the **Insert Bends** tool. To do so, create a solid part and choose the **Insert Bends** button from the **Sheet Metal CommandManager**; the **Bends PropertyManager** will be displayed and you will be prompted to select the fixed face or edge and set the bend parameters. The **Bends PropertyManager** is shown in Figure 18-107.

Select the top face of the flat part, as shown in Figure 18-108; the selected face will be highlighted in different color and the name of the face will be displayed in the **Fixed Face or Edge** selection box. Set the parameters of the bend allowance and the relief in the **Bend Allowance** and **Auto Relief** rollouts, respectively. After specifying all these parameters, choose the **OK** button from the **Bends PropertyManager**; the **SOLIDWORKS** message box will be displayed, as shown in Figure 18-109. It will inform you that no bends were found. Choose the **OK** button from the **SOLIDWORKS** message box.

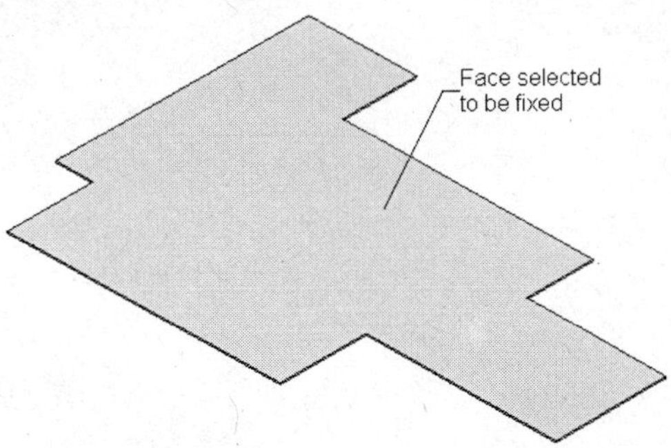

Figure 18-108 *Face selected to be fixed*

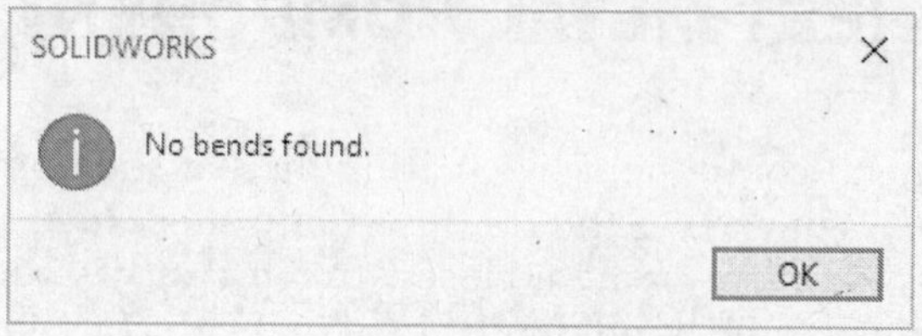

Figure 18-109 The ***SOLIDWORKS*** *message box*

After choosing the **OK** button from the **SOLIDWORKS** message box, you will notice that some new nodes are added to the **FeatureManager Design Tree**. The usage of these nodes is discussed later in this chapter. Note that although no bends are added to the flat part, you can observe that the flat part is converted into a sheet metal part. Now, you can add all features of a sheet metal component to this part.

Adding Bends to the Flattened Sheet Metal Component

After converting the solid part into a sheet metal component, you can add bends to the sheet metal component. There are two methods to add bends to the flattened sheet metal components that are extracted from a flat part. The first method of creating sketched bends has been discussed earlier in this chapter and the second method is discussed next.

Creating Sketched Bends Using the Process Bends Method

The Process Bends method is used to create sketched bends in the sheet metal components extracted from a part. These bends are also called Flat Bends. All bends created using the bending lines are placed in the **Process-Bends1** node in the **FeatureManager Design Tree**. To create the bends using this method, expand the **Process-Bends1** node and select the **Flat-Sketch1** node. Next, choose the **Edit Sketch** option from the pop-up toolbar; the sketching environment will be invoked. Create the sketch of the bending lines and exit the sketching environment; the sheet metal component will be bent along the bend lines. If you expand the **Process-Bends1** node again, you will observe that all bend features that you have added using the process bends are displayed. Figure 18-110 shows the sketches that will be used as bend lines to create bends. Figure 18-111 shows the resulting sheet metal component.

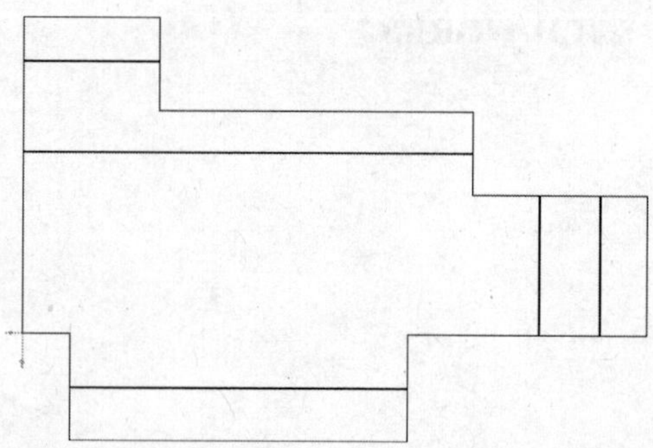

Figure 18-110 *Bend lines*

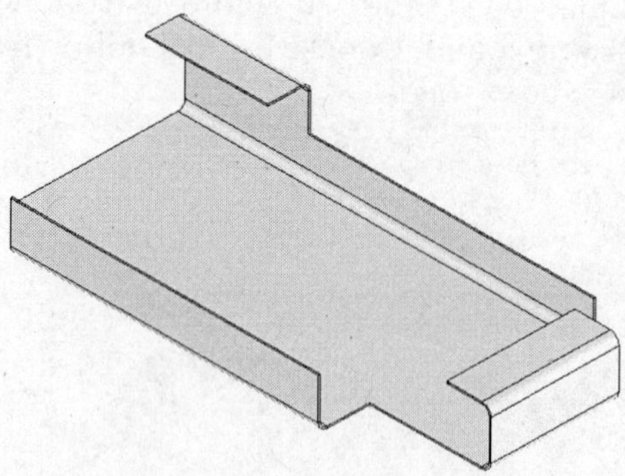

Figure 18-111 *Resulting bends*

> **Tip**
> *If you need to edit the radius of the bends individually, expand the **Process-Bends1** node in the **FeatureManager Design Tree**. Select the bend that you need to modify and invoke the pop-up toolbar. Next, choose the **Edit Feature** option from this toolbar; the **FlatBend PropertyManager** will be displayed which can be used to edit the parameters of the bend.*

Unbending the Sheet Metal Part Using the No Bends Tool

CommandManager: Sheet Metal > No Bends
Toolbar: Sheet Metal > No Bends

The **No Bends** tool is used to straighten the bends in the sheet metal component that are created from a solid part and roll it back to the stage when it did not have any bends. Choose the **No Bends** button from the **Sheet Metal** toolbar; the **FeatureManager Design Tree** roll backs to the stage where no bends were added. It is a toggle tool. You can also roll back a sheet metal component by moving the rollback bar up above the **Flatten-Bends1** feature in the **FeatureManager Design Tree**.

After invoking the **No Bends** tool, if you add an extruded feature to the part such that the depth of the extruded feature is equal to the sheet thickness, it will automatically convert into a flange when you resume the sheet metal part. Consider the model shown in Figure 18-112. This figure shows an extruded feature added to an unbent sheet metal part. Now, if you choose the **No Bends** button from the **Sheet Metal** toolbar, the flange with the default settings for bending and relief will be created, as shown in Figure 18-113. If you want to specify custom bending and relief, expand the **Flatten-Bends1** node in the **FeatureManager Design Tree** and select **SharpBend1**. Next, invoke the pop-up toolbar and choose the **Edit Feature** option from it. You can define the custom parameters of bend radius, bend allowance, and relief by using the **SharpBend PropertyManager**.

> **Tip**
> *Remember that if the original sketch of the sheet metal part had multiple lines at an angle to each other such as the L or U sections, they will not unbent.*

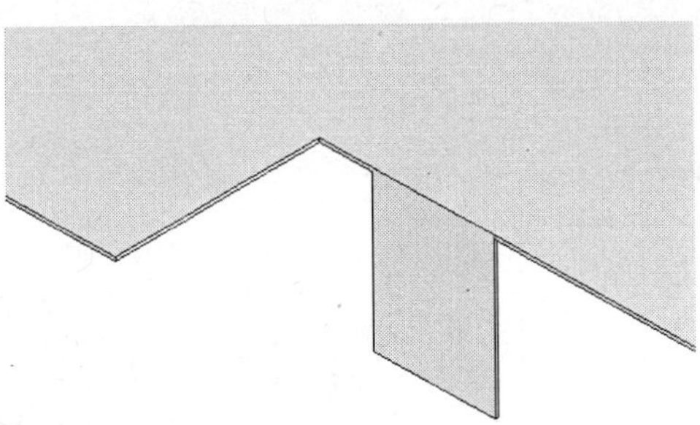

Figure 18-112 *Model with an extruded feature*

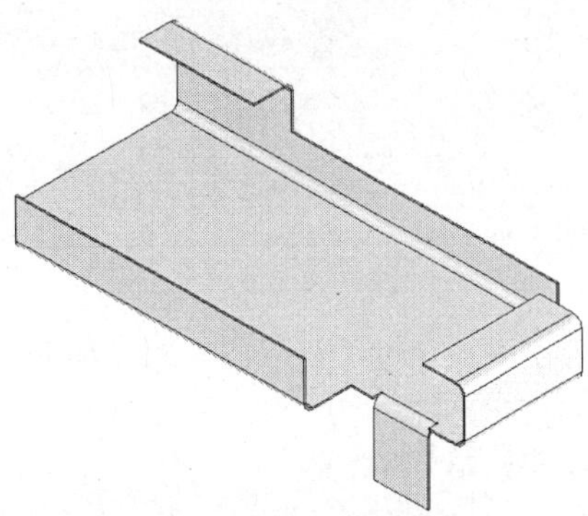

Figure 18-113 *Flange with the default settings for bending and relief*

CREATING A SHEET METAL COMPONENT BY DESIGNING IT AS A PART

SOLIDWORKS provides you with an option to first design the entire part in the **Part** mode and then convert it into a sheet metal component. Consider the example of a sheet metal component shown in Figure 18-114. To create this component, create the design of the sheet metal component by using the part modeling tools, as shown in Figure 18-115.

After designing it as a part, invoke the **Insert Bends** tool from the **Sheet Metal** toolbar; the **Bends PropertyManager** will be displayed. Select the face that will be fixed and specify the sheet metal parameters. Choose the **OK** button from the **Bends PropertyManager**; the part file will be converted into a sheet metal part. If some reliefs are added to the sheet metal component, the **SOLIDWORKS** message box will be displayed and you will be informed that auto relief cuts were made for one or more bends. Choose the **OK** button from this message box; the sheet metal component will be created. Figure 18-116 shows the flat pattern of the sheet metal component shown in Figure 18-114.

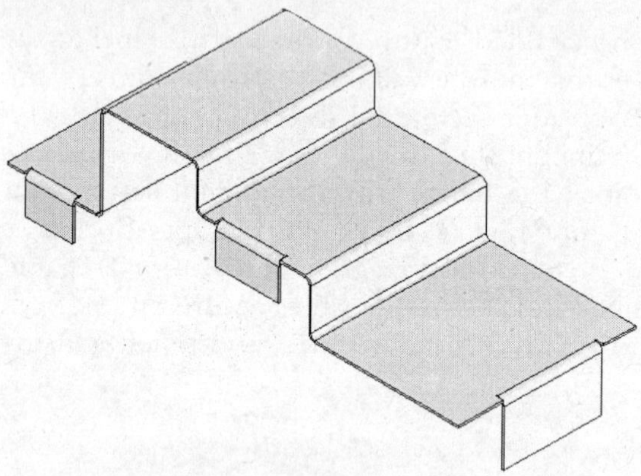

Figure 18-114 A sheet metal component

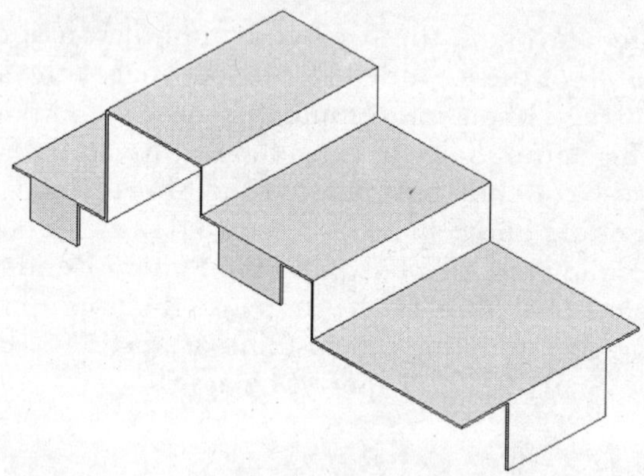

Figure 18-115 Component designed as a part

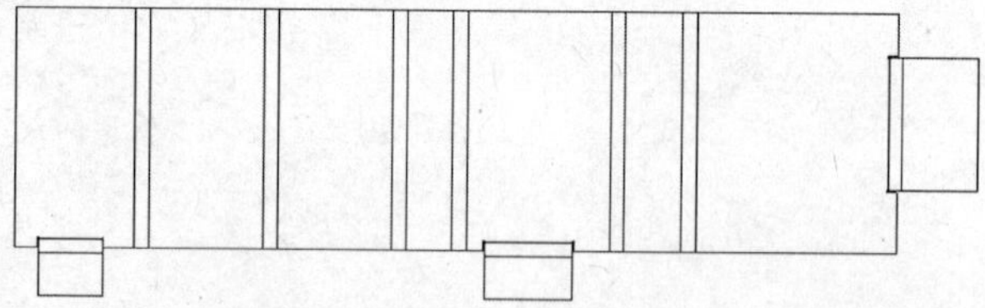

Figure 18-116 Flat pattern of the desired sheet metal component

Types of Bends

Now, you need to learn about various types of bends that are added to sheet metal components while creating them by converting a part. The types of bends that are added to the sheet metal components during this conversion are discussed next.

Sharp Bends

If you create a part with sharp edges and convert it into a sheet metal component, the bends added to the sheet metal component are recognized as sharp bends. The sharp bends are placed in the **Flatten-Bends1** feature in the **FeatureManager Design Tree**. Figure 18-117 shows a part created with sharp edges. Figure 18-118 shows the part converted into the sheet metal component.

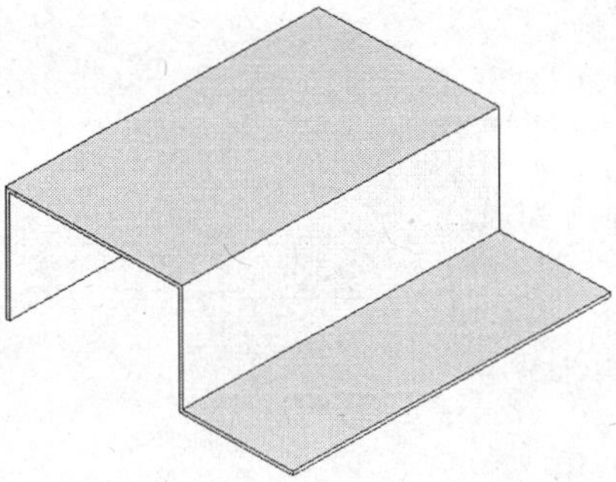

Figure 18-117 *Part created with sharp edges*

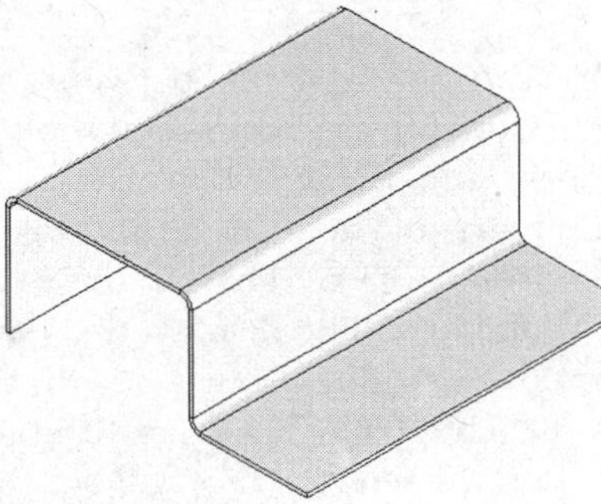

Figure 18-118 *Part converted into the sheet metal component*

Round Bends

If you have applied fillets to the sketch of a model such that their radius is equal to bend radius and convert the model into a sheet metal component, the fillets added to the model will be recognized as round bends. The round bends are placed in the **Flatten-Bends1** feature in the **FeatureManager Design Tree**. Figure 18-119 shows a part created with round edges. Figure 18-120 shows the part converted into the sheet metal component.

Flat Bends

The flat bends are the bends that are created by bending the flattened sheet. The flat bends are placed in the **Process-Bends1** feature in the **FeatureManager Design Tree**. The procedure to create these types of bends has been discussed earlier.

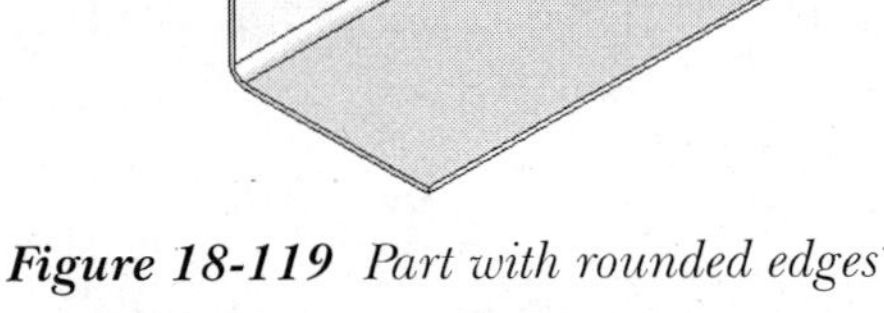

Figure 18-119 *Part with rounded edges*

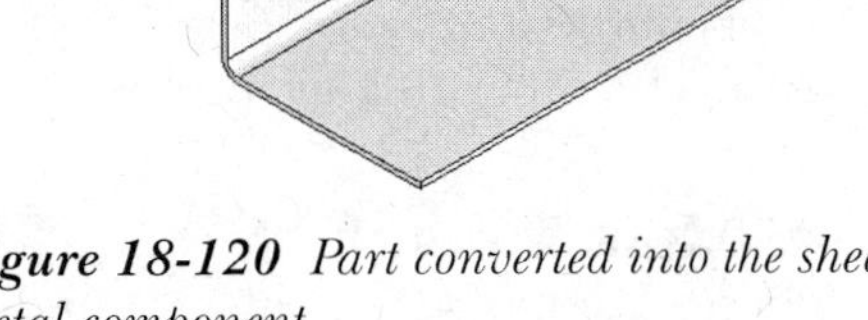

Figure 18-120 *Part converted into the sheet metal component*

CONVERTING A SOLID BODY INTO A SHEET METAL PART

CommandManager:	Sheet Metal > Convert to Sheet Metal
SOLIDWORKS menus:	Insert > Sheet Metal > Convert To Sheet Metal
Toolbar:	Sheet Metal > Convert to Sheet Metal

Convert to Sheet Metal

You can convert a solid body into a sheet metal part using the **Convert to Sheet Metal** tool. To do so, create a solid body in the **Part** mode and then choose the **Convert to Sheet Metal** button from the **Sheet Metal CommandManager**; the **Convert To Sheet Metal PropertyManager** will be displayed, as shown in Figure 18-121. Next, select the face of the solid body that will remain fixed while opening the sheet to create the flat pattern, as shown in Figure 18-122; the selected face will be highlighted in a different color and its name will be displayed in the **Select a fixed entity** selection box in the **Sheet Metal Parameters** rollout. Set the sheet thickness and the radius of the bend using the **Sheet thickness** and **Default radius for bends** spinners. You can flip the direction of the sheet metal thickness by selecting the **Reverse thickness** check box in this rollout. You can also use the custom material parameters by selecting the **Use material sheet metal parameters** check box in the **Sheet Metal Parameters From Material** rollout. Select the **Use gauge table** check box; the **Select Table** drop-down list will be displayed. Select any of the default gauge tables from this drop-down list. You can also choose the **Browse** button and select a user-defined gauge table.

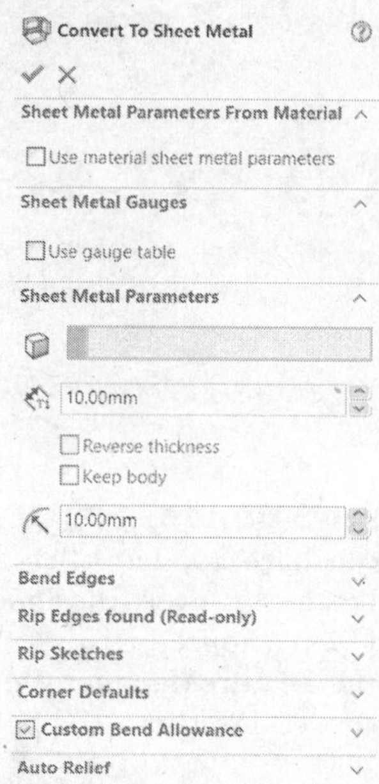

*Figure 18-121 The **Convert To Sheet Metal PropertyManager***

Next, select the edges that are on the selected face, as shown in Figure 18-123; the name of the selected edges will be displayed in the **Select edges/faces that represent bends** selection box of the **Bend Edges** rollout. You can change the bend radius of the edges individually by entering the values in the attached callouts. Note that the rip edges corresponding to the bend edges are selected automatically and their names will be displayed in the **Automatically found rip edges (un-editable)** selection box of the **Rip Edges found (Read-only)** rollout. After setting the required parameters, choose the **OK** button from the **Convert To Sheet Metal PropertyManager**; the solid body will be converted into a sheet metal component. If the **Keep body** check box is selected in the **Sheet Metal Parameters** rollout, then the model will be retained and a new sheet metal component will be created. Figure 18-124 shows the solid body to be converted into a sheet metal component and Figure 18-125 shows the flat pattern of the resulting sheet metal component. The other rollouts in this PropertyManager are discussed next.

Rip Sketches Rollout

This rollout is used to define the required rips. The **Select a sketch to add a rip** selection box in this rollout is used to select a sketch from the drawing area to define the required rip. To do so, you first need to create a sketch of the rip in the sketching environment. Alternatively, You can specify the gap between the rips by using the **Default gap for all rips** spinner in the **Corner Defaults** rollout.

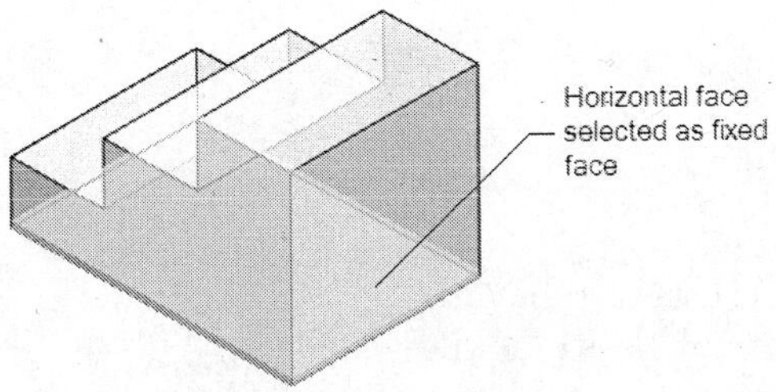

Figure 18-122 The face selected to be fixed

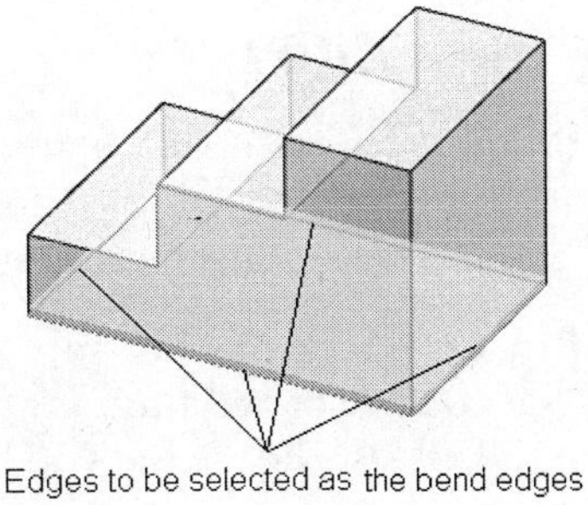

Figure 18-123 Edges selected

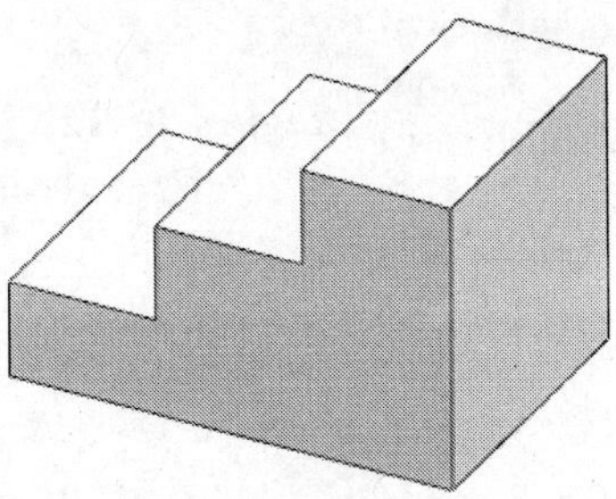

Figure 18-124 The solid part to be converted into a sheet metal component

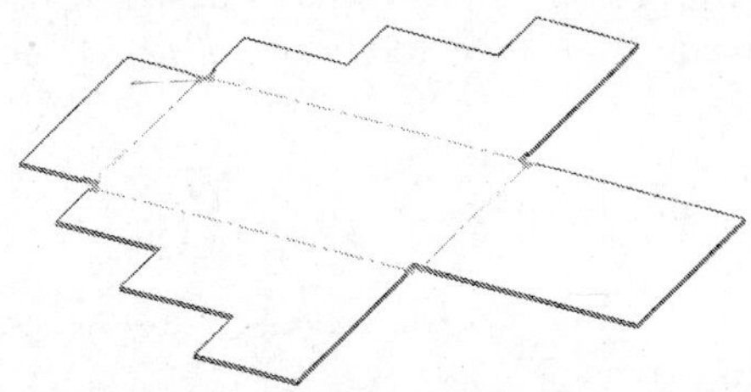

Figure 18-125 The flat pattern of the sheet metal component

Auto Relief Rollout

The options in the **Auto Relief** rollout of this PropertyManager are same as discussed earlier in the **Base Flange PropertyManager**.

After setting all parameters, choose the **OK** button; the selected solid part will be converted into a sheet metal part. Note that if there are multiple bodies in the solid part, then you need to convert each body into sheet metal part separately.

DESIGNING A SHEET METAL PART FROM A SOLID SHELLED MODEL

In SOLIDWORKS you can design a sheet metal part as a solid model and then shell the model. Remember that while shelling the model, you need to remove at least one face. After shelling the model, you need to rip the edges of the thin solid model. The ripping is done in order to cut the sheet so that it can be opened easily while creating the flat pattern. The procedure to rip the edges of a solid part is discussed next.

Ripping the Edges

CommandManager:	Sheet Metal > Rip
SOLIDWORKS menus:	Insert > Sheet Metal > Rip
Toolbar:	Sheet Metal > Rip

The **Rip** tool is used to add a gap between the edges of a shelled solid part before converting it into a sheet metal component. To rip the edges, choose the **Rip** button from the **Sheet Metal CommandManager**; the **Rip PropertyManager** will be displayed, as shown in Figure 18-126. Also, you will be prompted to set the rip gap and select the edge(s) to rip. Select the internal edges or external edges that you need to rip; direction arrows will be displayed on the selected edge and the name of the selected edge will be displayed in the **Edges to Rip** selection box. The two arrows displayed on the selected edge indicate that the ripping will be done on both sides of the selected edge. Use the **Change Direction** button to toggle between the two directions. The **Rip Gap** spinner is used to set the value of the rip gap.

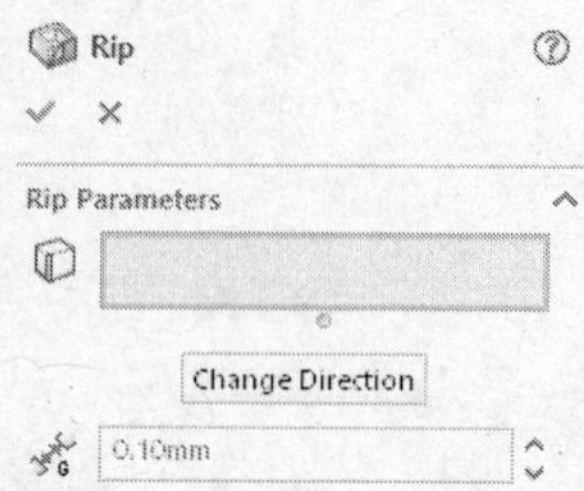

***Figure 18-126** The Rip PropertyManager*

Figure 18-127 shows the edge selected to create rip in both directions. Figure 18-128 shows the resulting rip.

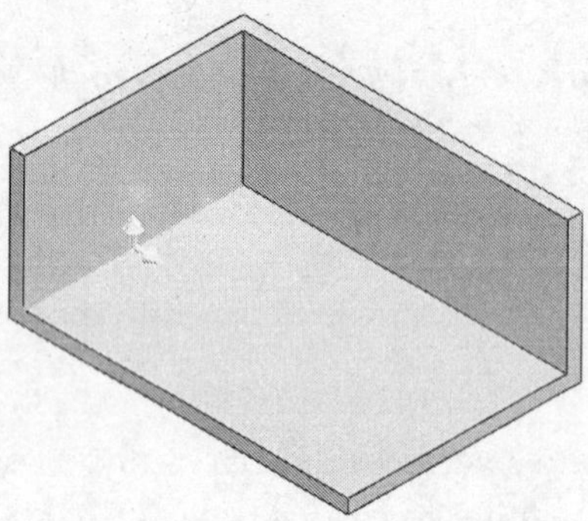

***Figure 18-127** Edge selected to create the rip*

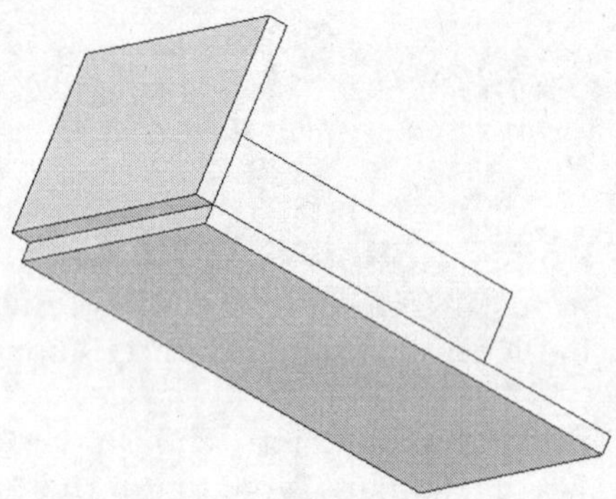

***Figure 18-128** Resulting rip*

After ripping the edges, choose the **Insert Bends** button to invoke the **Bends PropertyManager**. Next, select the fixed face, set the sheet metal parameters and then choose the **OK** button. Figure 18-129 shows the shelled solid model and Figure 18-130 shows the model after ripping and converting it into a sheet metal component. Figure 18-131 shows the flat pattern of the sheet metal component.

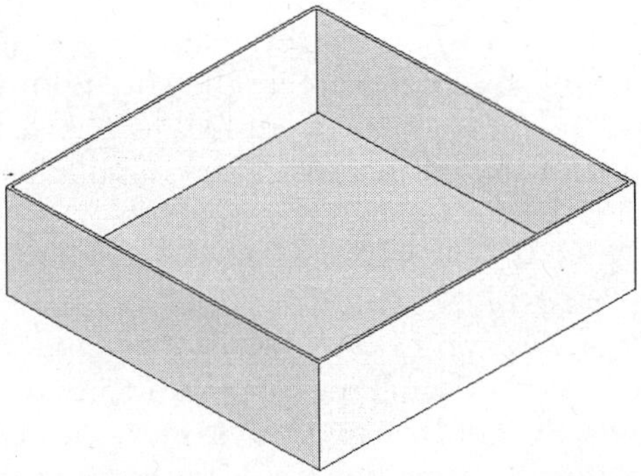

Figure 18-129 Shelled solid model

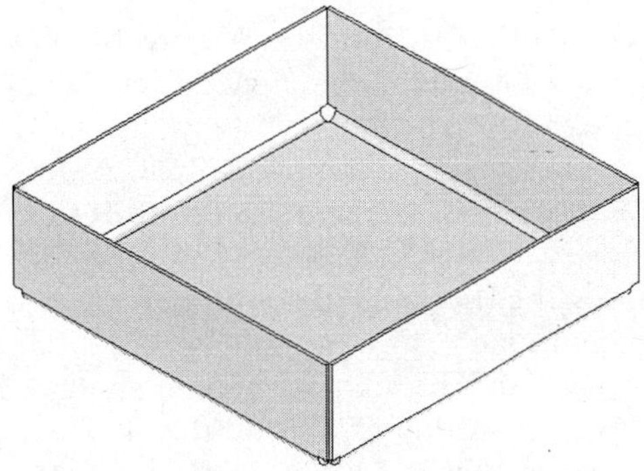

Figure 18-130 Model after ripping and then converting into a sheet metal component

Tip
*You can also rip the edges by using the **Rip Parameters** rollout available in the **Bends PropertyManager**.*

CREATING CUTS IN SHEET METAL COMPONENTS ACROSS THE BENDS

In this section, you will learn to create cuts across the bends, as shown in Figure 18-132. The methods of creating cuts across the bends are different for the sheet metal components created from the base flange and the sheet metal component created by converting a solid part. The methods for creating cuts for both types of sheet metal components are discussed next.

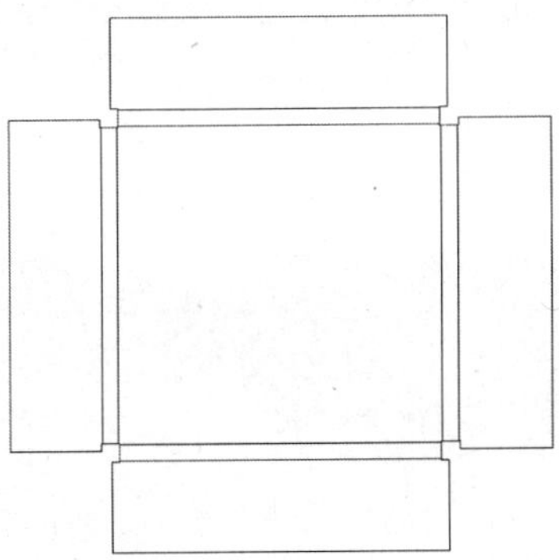

Figure 18-131 Flat pattern of the sheet metal component

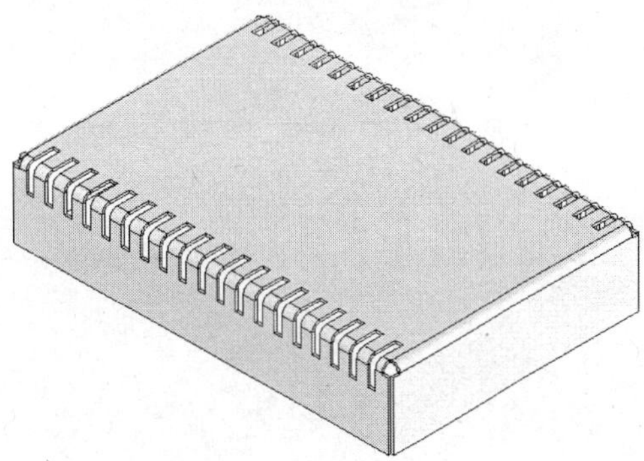

Figure 18-132 A sheet metal component with cuts across the bends

Creating Cuts in a Sheet Metal Component Created from a Solid Model

You can create cuts in a sheet metal component that was created from a solid model. To do so, create a solid model and then convert it into a sheet metal component by invoking the **Insert**

Bends tool. Next, from the **FeatureManager Design Tree**, roll back the features just above the **Process-Bends** node. Now, select the face on which you need to create the cut and invoke the sketching environment. Create the sketch and extrude it to create a cut feature. Make sure that the cut is across the bend. Now, create a pattern of the cut feature. Next, right-click on the **LPattern** node and choose the **Roll to End** option; the cut will be created across the bends.

Consider the sheet metal component shown in Figure 18-133. Create flat pattern of the sheet metal component, as shown in Figure 18-134 by following the procedure discussed above. Select the top face of the flattened sheet metal component as the sketching plane and invoke the sketching environment. Create the sketch and extrude the cut by using the **Link to thickness** option from the **Cut-Extrude PropertyManager**. After creating the cut, choose the **Linear Pattern** tool to create a linear pattern of the cut feature. The flattened sheet metal component after creating and patterning the cut feature is shown in Figure 18-135. Next, right-click on the **LPattern** node and choose the **Roll to End** option to display the sheet metal component with cuts across the bends, as shown in Figure 18-136.

Note

*If you choose the **Flatten** button from the **Sheet Metal** toolbar and create cuts on a flattened sheet, the cuts will not be displayed on the unflattened sheet metal component.*

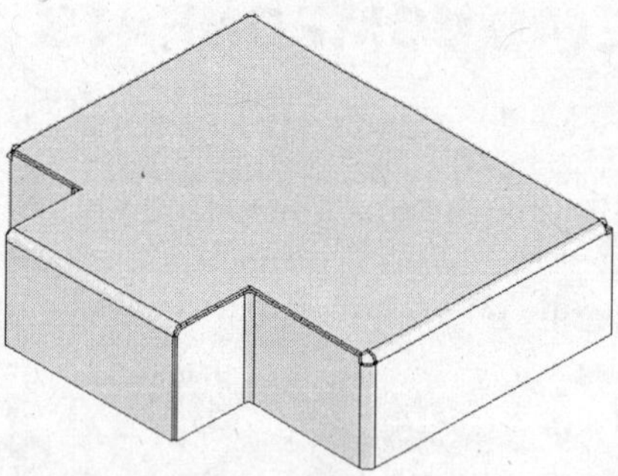

Figure 18-133 *Sheet metal component*

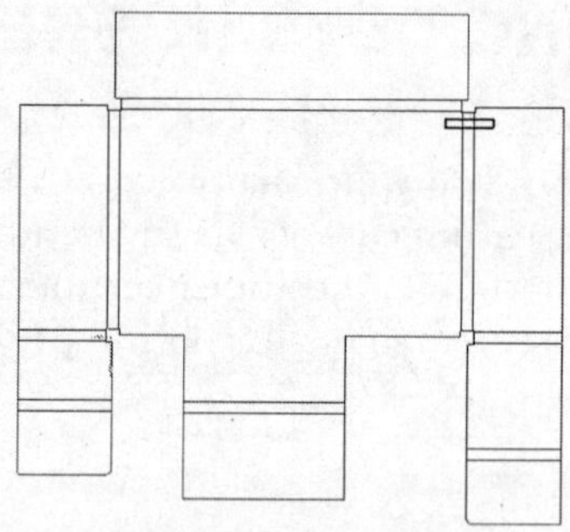

Figure 18-134 *Flat pattern of the sheet metal component*

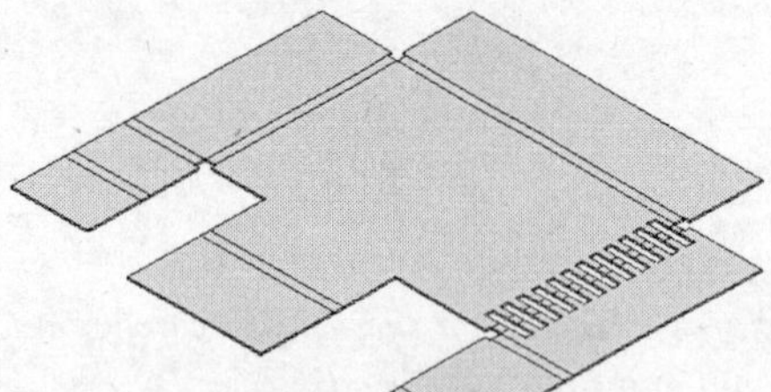

Figure 18-135 *Flattened sheet after creating and patterning the cuts*

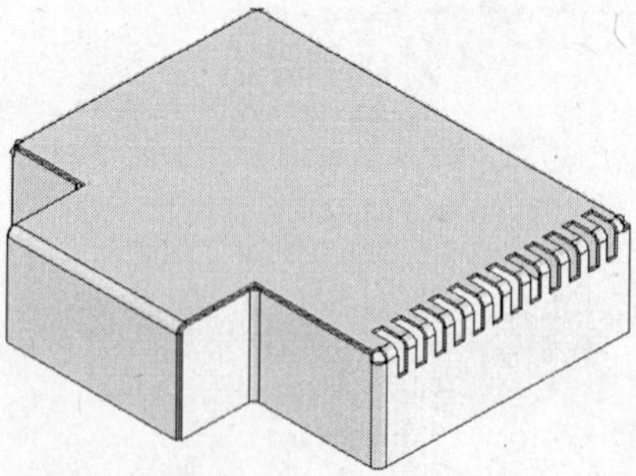

Figure 18-136 *Final sheet metal component*

Creating Cuts in a Sheet Metal Component Created Using the Base Flange

A sheet metal component designed by using a base flange does not include the **Flatten-Bends1** and the **Process-Bends1** features. Therefore, for creating cuts in such a sheet metal component, you first need to unfold the sheet using the **Unfold** tool and then create the cut feature. After creating the feature, you need to fold the sheet again using the **Fold** tool. Consider the example of the sheet metal component displayed in Figure 18-137. For creating cuts in this sheet metal component, you first need to unfold the sheet. The method of unfolding the sheet is discussed next.

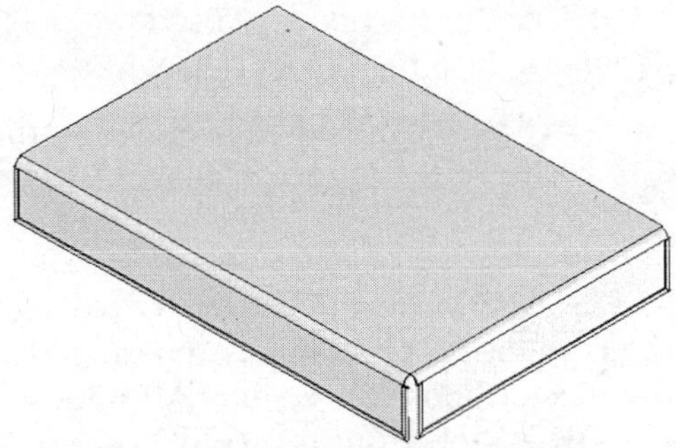

Figure 18-137 A sheet metal component

Unfolding the Sheet

CommandManager:	Sheet Metal > Unfold
SOLIDWORKS menus:	Insert > Sheet Metal > Unfold
Toolbar:	Sheet Metal > Unfold

To unfold a sheet, invoke the **Unfold** tool from the **Sheet Metal CommandManager**; the **Unfold PropertyManager** will be displayed, as shown in Figure 18-138. Also, you will be prompted to select a face to be fixed and the bends to be unfolded.

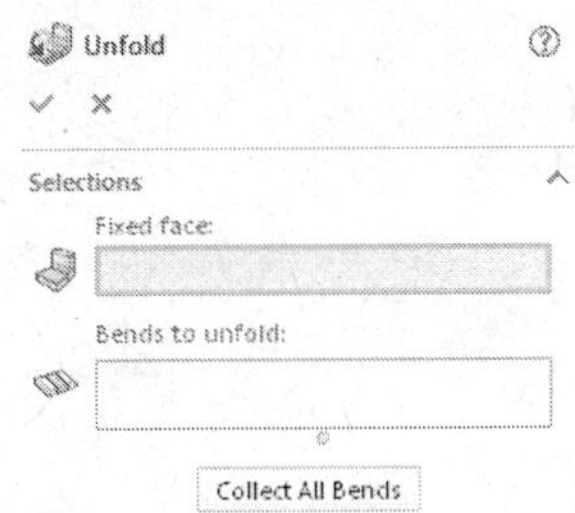

*Figure 18-138 The **Unfold PropertyManager***

Select the face that you need to fix and the bends that you need to unfold. To unfold all bends, choose the **Collect All Bends** button in the **Selections** rollout and choose the **OK** button from the **Unfold PropertyManager**. You will notice that the sheet metal component is unfolded. Figure 18-139 shows the unfolded sheet. After unfolding the sheet, create the required cut feature. The unfolded sheet after creating the cut feature is shown in Figure 18-140. Fold the sheet again after creating the cut feature by using the **Fold** tool. The method of folding the sheet is discussed next.

Figure 18-139 The unfolded sheet

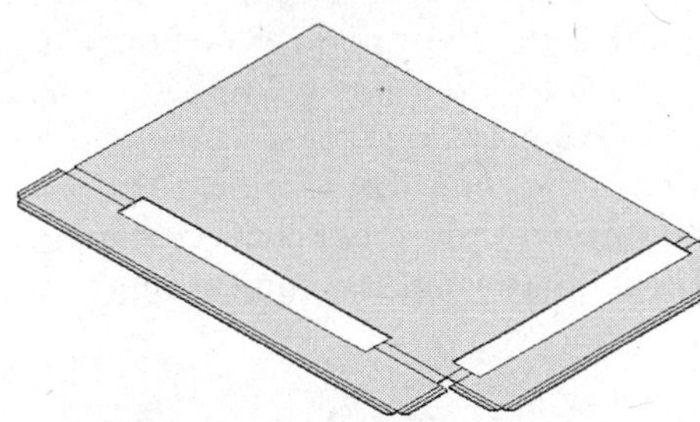

Figure 18-140 The unfolded sheet after creating the cut feature

Folding the Sheet

CommandManager:	Sheet Metal > Fold
SOLIDWORKS menus:	Insert > Sheet Metal > Fold
Toolbar:	Sheet Metal > Fold

Fold To fold an unfolded sheet, choose the **Fold** button from the **Sheet Metal CommandManager**; the **Fold PropertyManager** will be displayed, as shown in Figure 18-141. Also, you will be prompted to select a face to be fixed and the bends to be folded.

The face of the sheet that was fixed while unfolding the sheet is selected by default while invoking the **Fold PropertyManager**. You can also select any other face that you need to fix while folding the sheet. Choose the **Collect All Bends** button to select all bends to be folded and then choose the **OK** button from the **Fold PropertyManager**. Figure 18-142 shows the final sheet metal component after folding it using the **Fold** tool.

Note

If you create edge flanges throughout the length of edges of the base flange, SOLIDWORKS may not fold the component back.

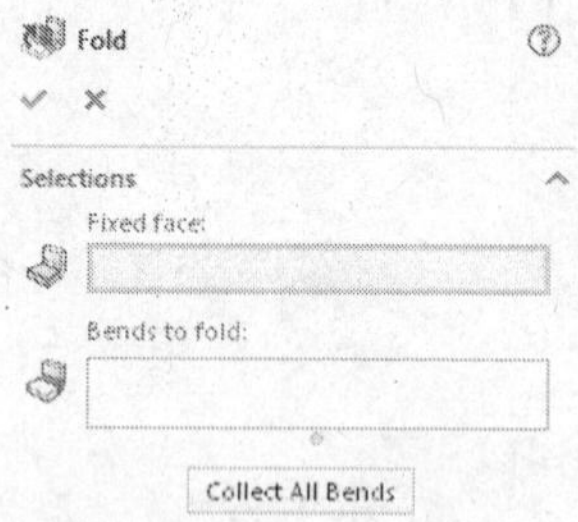

***Figure 18-141** The **Fold** PropertyManager*

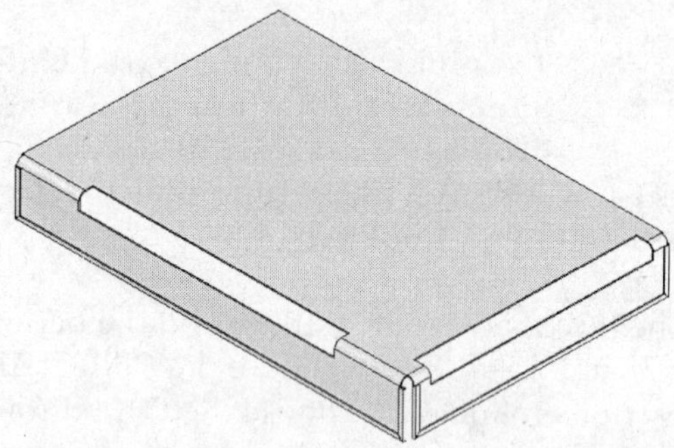

***Figure 18-142** Sheet metal component after folding*

Creating Cylindrical and Conical Sheet Metal Components

SOLIDWORKS also allows you to create cylindrical and conical sheet metal components. For creating a cylindrical or conical sheet metal component, you need to make sure that there is some gap to unfold the sheet. Create a conical or cylindrical solid model part and then invoke the **Bends PropertyManager** to convert the part into a sheet metal component. Now, select a linear edge of the conical or cylindrical part that is to be fixed, refer to Figure 18-143. Choose the **OK** button from the **Bends PropertyManager**. Next, choose the **Flatten** button. Figure 18-144 shows the flat pattern of the conical sheet metal component.

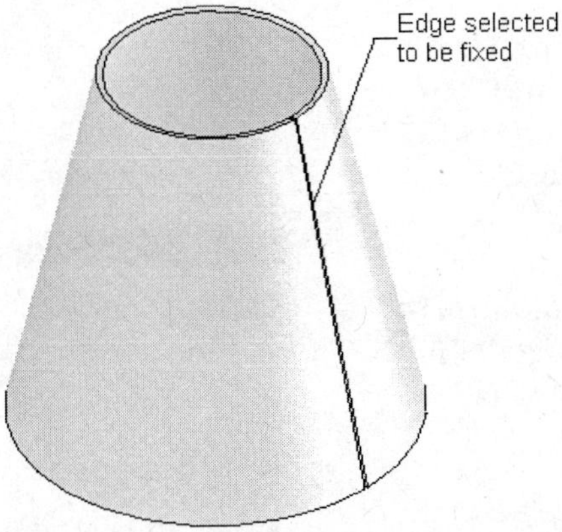

Figure 18-143 Edge selected to be fixed

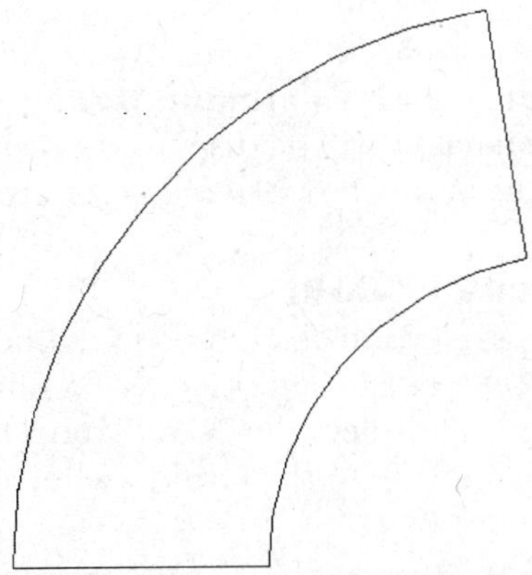

Figure 18-144 Flat pattern of the conical sheet metal component

Note

*1. If you create a cylindrical or conical sheet metal component by lofted-bend, you can directly use the **Flat Pattern** option to create the flat pattern.*

*2. In SOLIDWORKS, you can mirror the edge flanges and miter flanges by using the **Mirror** tool. Similarly, you can create the linear pattern of edge flanges and tabs by using the **Linear Pattern** tool.*

Creating Normal Cuts

CommandManager:	Sheet Metal > Normal Cut
SOLIDWORKS menus:	Insert > Sheet Metal > Normal Cut
Toolbar:	Sheet Metal > Normal Cut (Customize to add)

In SOLIDWORKS, using the **Normal Cut** tool, all the non-normal side walls of a cut feature in a sheet metal part can be made normal. Although the **Normal cut** option available in the **Extrude Cut** tool also allows you to create normal cuts, but this option is limited to the cuts created using the **Extrude Cut** tool. However, the **Normal Cut** tool applies the normal cut feature to all cut features. Note that the normal cut is created in the direction of thickness of the sheet metal part. Figures 18-145 and 18-146 show a lofted cut in a sheet metal before and after using the **Normal Cut** tool.

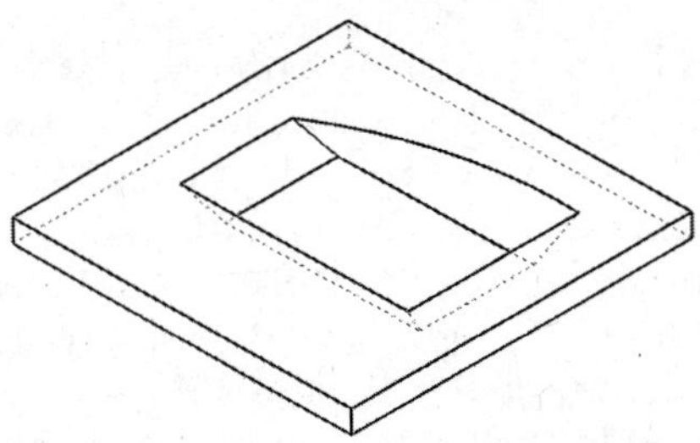

*Figure 18-145 Lofted cut before using **Normal Cut** tool*

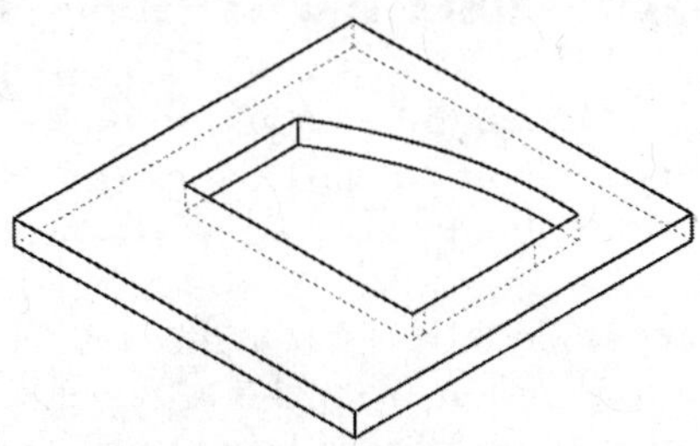

*Figure 18-146 Lofted cut after using **Normal Cut** tool*

To create a normal cut feature, invoke the **Normal Cut** tool from the **Sheet Metal CommandManager**; the **Normal Cut PropertyManager** will be displayed, as shown in Figure 18-147. The options in this PropertyManager are discussed next.

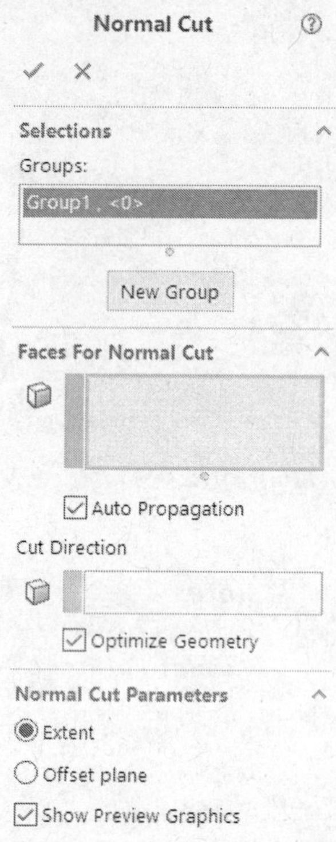

Figure 18-147 The Normal Cut PropertyManager

Selections Rollout

The **Groups** selection box is used to define groups of non-normal faces of a cut feature. Select faces of a non-normal cut to define in a group, then select the **New Group** button provided below to add a new group to the **Groups** selection box.

Faces For Normal Cut Rollout

The options in the **Faces For Normal Cut** rollout are used to define faces and direction of the normal cut. Select the faces of the non-normal cut in the **Face** selection box; the names of the selected faces will be displayed in the selection box. If the **Auto-Propagation** check box is selected then on selecting a face of the given cut, all the connected faces of the cut will be automatically selected. By default, the direction of the cut is normal to the top or bottom face of the sheet metal part. The **Edge/Curve/Face** selection box is used to define direction of the cut feature. To produce smoother cuts, select the **Optimize Geometry** check box.

Normal Cut Parameters Rollout

The options in the **Normal Cut Parameters** rollout are used to define the extent of the boundaries of the cut feature. Select the **Extent** radio button to cut maximum amount of material from the intersection of the profiles on the top and bottom of the part. You can also modify the position of the profiles by selecting the **Offset plane** radio button. When you select the **Offset plane** radio button, you are prompted to select a face as top plane reference. An edit box is also provided in which you can enter a value for modifying the position of the profile curves. Select the **Show Preview Graphics** check box to view the preview of the cut feature.

After defining all the parameters, choose the **OK** button to create the normal cut feature.

INSERTING FORMING TOOLS

In SOLIDWORKS, you can insert different types of forming tools such as **embosses, extruded flanges, lances, louvers**, and so on in a sheet metal component. To do so, choose the **Design Library** tab from the task pane available on the right of the graphic area; the **Design Library** task pane will be displayed. Next, expand the **Design Library** node in the task pane. If this node is not available in the task pane, you need to customize to add it. To add the **Design Library** node in the task pane, invoke the **System Options** dialog box and choose the **File Locations** option from the left in the dialog box. Next, select the **Design Library** option from the **Show folders for** drop-down list and then specify the path for the design library *C:\ProgramData\Solidworks\SOLIDWORKS 2021\Design Library* by choosing the **Add** button. Next, exit the dialog box by choosing the **OK** button. The **Design Library** node will be displayed in the **Design Library** task pane.

On expanding the **Design Library** node, different categories of tools will be displayed as sub-nodes. Select the **forming tools** sub-node and right-click. Next, choose **Forming Tools Folder** from the shortcut menu displayed, if it is not chosen by default. On doing so, the **SOLIDWORKS** message box will be displayed. Next, choose the **Yes** button from the message box. The tools in the selected folder and its sub-folders will act as forming tools. Next, expand the **forming tools** sub-node and select the required forming tool folder from it; the forming tools available in the selected folder will be displayed at the bottom of the task pane.

Next, select and drag the required forming tool from the bottom side of the **Design Library** task pane and place it on the required face of the sheet metal component; the **Form Tool Feature PropertyManager** will be displayed, as shown in Figure 18-148. Also, a preview of the forming tool will be displayed in the drawing area. You can also flip the direction of forming tool by choosing the **Flip Tool** button from the PropertyManager. The **Replace Tool** button in this PropertyManager is used to replace the inserted forming tool with some other tool. This button gets active only after inserting 1st form tool in the component.

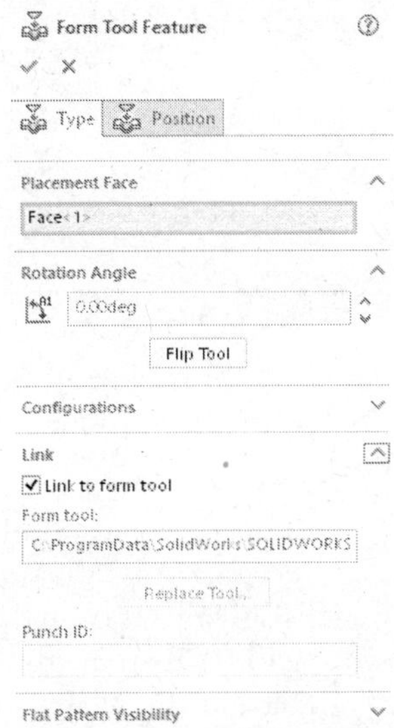

Figure 18-148** The **Form Tool Feature PropertyManager

To position the inserted forming tool, you can apply dimensions to it. To do so, choose the **Position** tab from the PropertyManager; the PropertyManager changes to **Position PropertyManager**. Figure 18-149 shows preview of forming tools being placed on the surface of a sheet metal component and Figure 18-150 shows the resultant sheet metal component.

The **Link to form tool** check box in the **Link** rollout of the PropertyManager is selected to apply links between the applied form tool and the parent one. In this case, if any modification is made in the parent form tool, the same will be reflected in the applied form tool.

Note

*In SOLIDWORKS, you can edit the form tools available in **Design Library** by double-clicking on the required form tool in the **Design Library Task Pane**. The forming tool will be opened in the new graphics window where you can modify it as per your requirement. After editing the forming tool, you need to save it.*

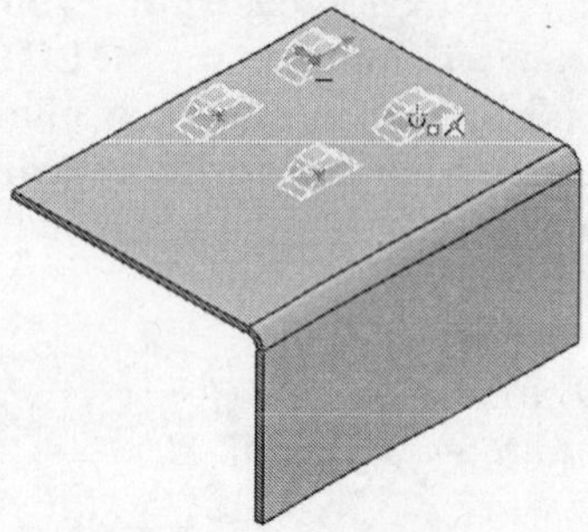

Figure 18-149 *Preview of sheet metal while placing forming tools at different places*

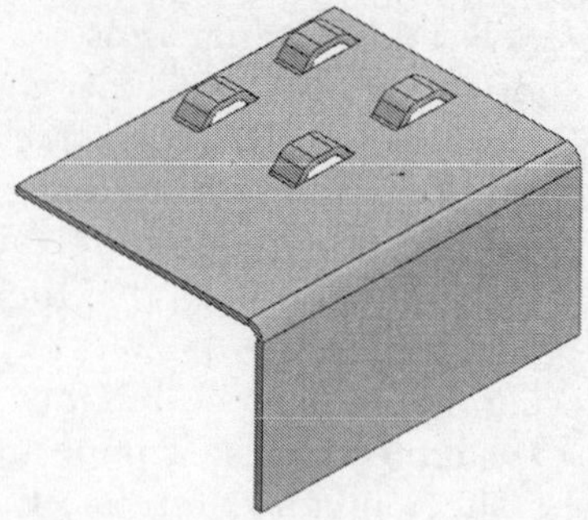

Figure 18-150 *Resultant sheet metal component*

CREATING FORMING TOOLS

CommandManager:	Sheet Metal > Forming Tool
SOLIDWORKS menus:	Insert > Sheet Metal > Forming Tool
Toolbar:	Sheet Metal > Forming Tool

Forming Tool

The **Forming Tool** is used to create forming tools. To do so, first create a form tool component by using the modeling tools of SOLIDWORKS and then choose the **Forming Tool** button from the **Sheet Metal CommandManager**; the **Form Tool PropertyManager** will be displayed. Also, you will be prompted to specify the stopping face. Select the face of the tool as the face to be stopped when it is applied to the target part. As soon as you specify the stopping face, the **Faces to Remove** selection area will be activated and you will be prompted to specify the faces to be removed. Select the faces to be removed from the target part. If you do not want to remove any face from the target part after inserting the form tool, do not select any face to be removed. Figure 18-151 shows the stopping face selected. Note that, in this figure the other faces selected as the faces to be removed except the inclined face of the component. Figure 18-152 shows the sheet metal component after inserting the form tool, shown in Figure 18-151.

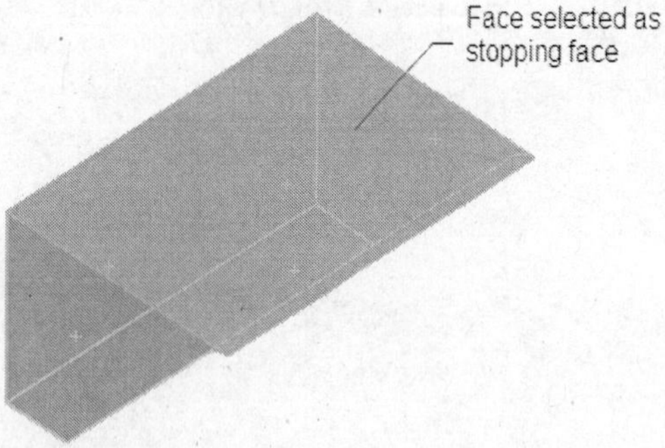

Figure 18-151 *Faces to be selected for applying the form tool*

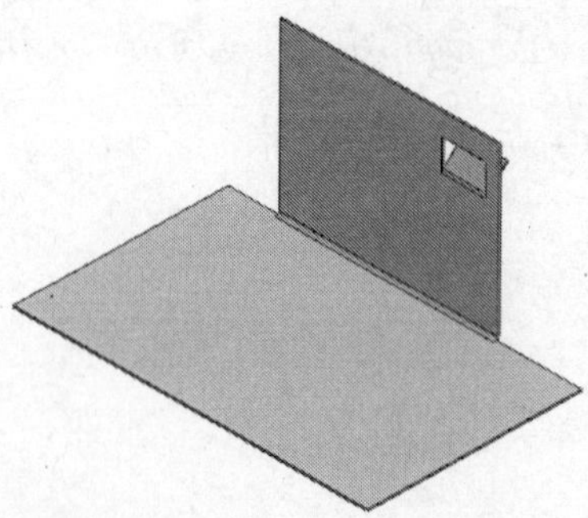

Figure 18-152 *Resultant sheet metal component after applying the form tool*

GENERATING THE DRAWING VIEW OF THE FLAT PATTERN OF THE SHEET METAL COMPONENTS

After creating a sheet metal component, the next step is to generate the drawing view of the flat pattern of the sheet metal component. Choose the **Make Drawing from Part/Assembly** button from the **New** flyout of the Menu Bar. To generate the drawing view of the flat pattern, select the **Flat Pattern** check box in the **More views** area of the **Orientation** rollout in the **Model View PropertyManager** and place the drawing view on the sheet. Figure 18-153 shows a sheet metal component and Figure 18-154 shows the resulting flat pattern view. Figure 18-155 shows the drawing view of the flat pattern of the sheet metal component.

In SOLIDWORKS, you can display bounding box of the flat pattern after creating the drawing view of the flat pattern. To do so, right-click on the view and choose the **Properties** option; the **Drawing View Properties** dialog box will be displayed. Select the **Display bounding box** check box from the **View properties** tab and choose the **OK** button.

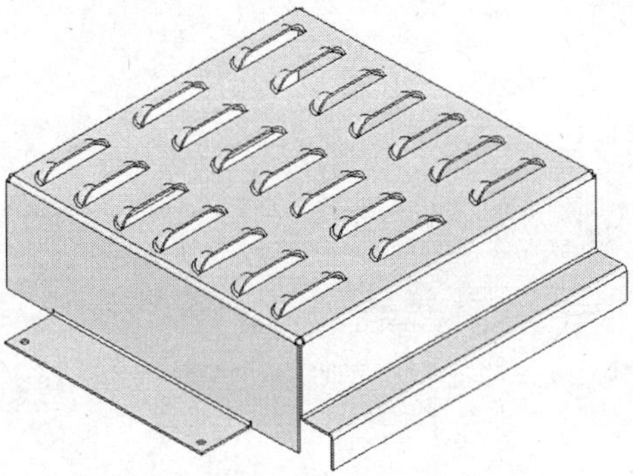

Figure 18-153 *Sheet metal component*

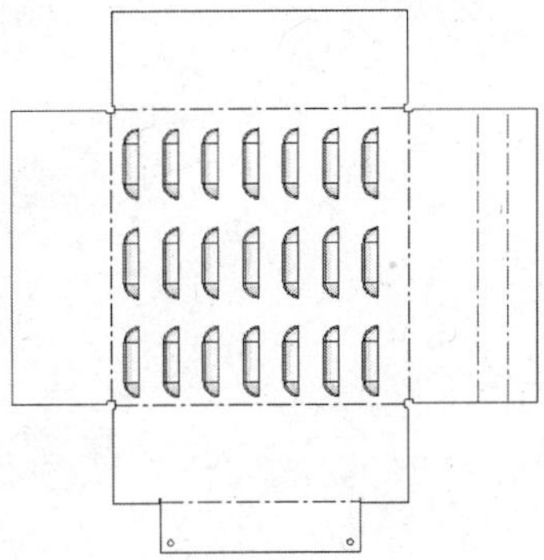

Figure 18-154 *Flat pattern*

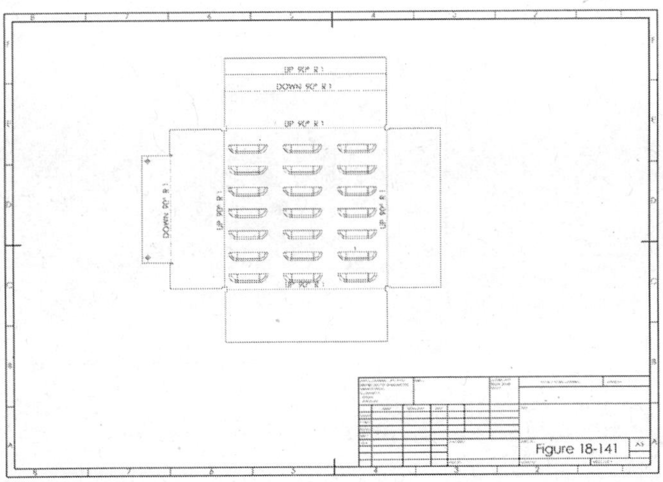

Figure 18-155 *Drawing view of the flat pattern*

TUTORIALS

Tutorial 1

In this tutorial, you will create the sheet metal component shown in Figure 18-156. Flat pattern of the sheet metal component and its views and dimensions are shown in Figures 18-157 and 18-158, respectively. You will first create the base flange and then the other features. After creating the model, you will create its flat pattern. **(Expected time: 45 min)**

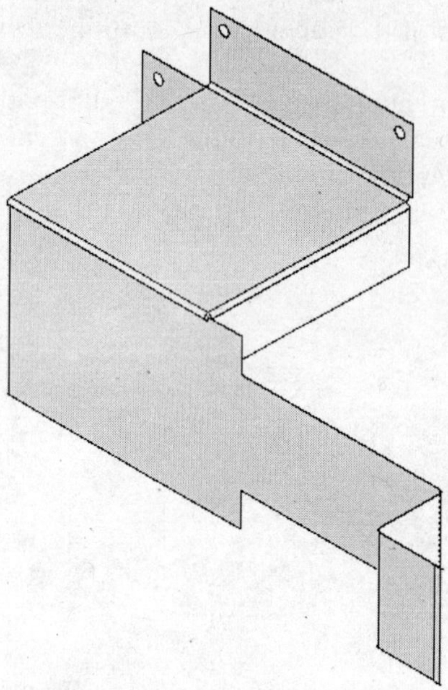

Figure 18-156 *Sheet metal component*

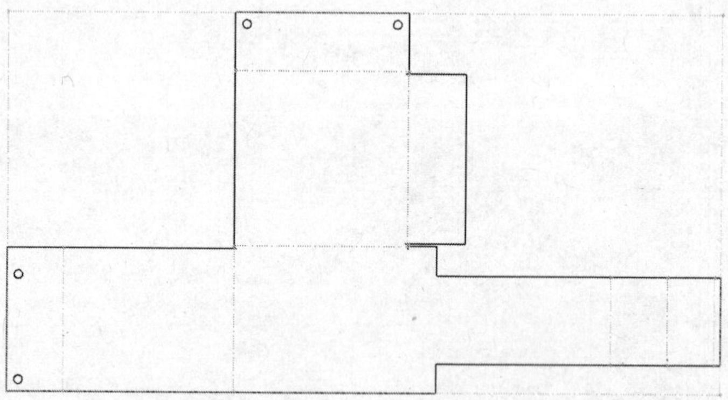

Figure 18-157 *Flat pattern of the sheet metal component*

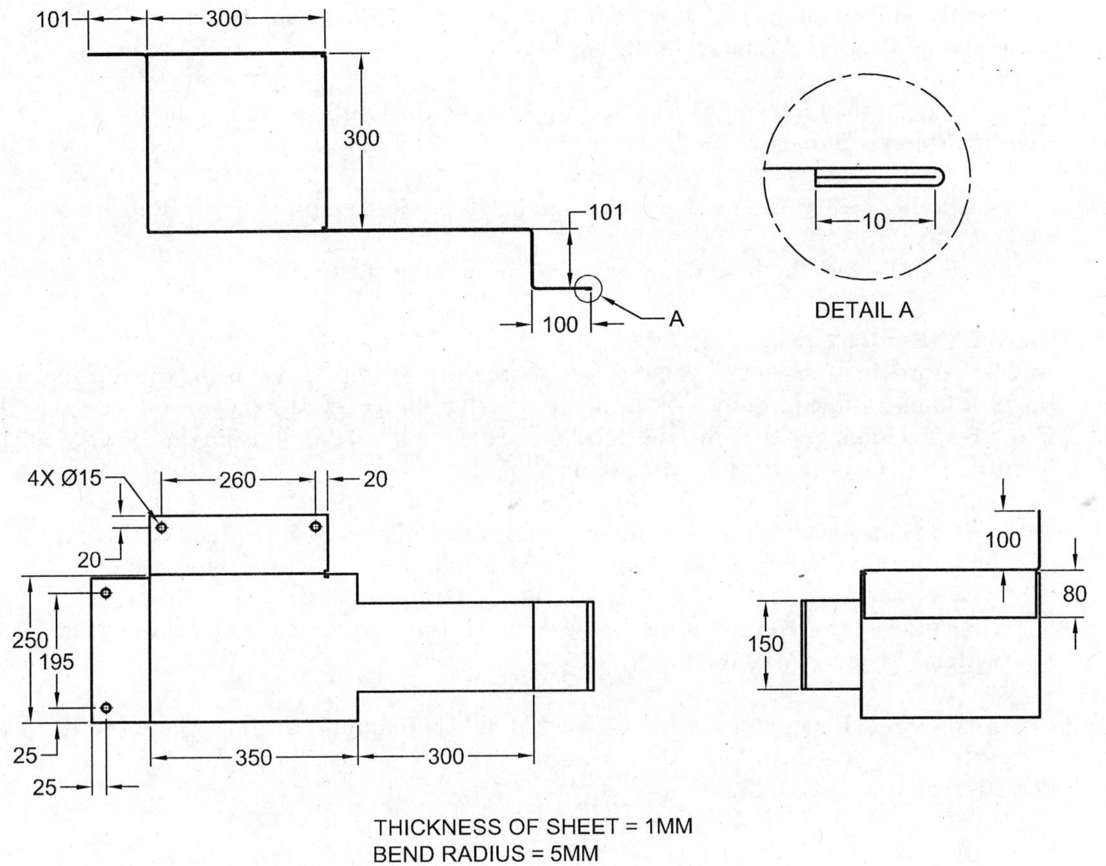

Figure 18-158 Drawing views and dimensions for Tutorial 1

The following steps are required to complete this tutorial:

a. Create the base flange of the sheet metal component.
b. Add other required flanges to the sheet metal component.
c. Create the tab feature.
d. Add a hem to the right most flange.
e. Create the flat pattern of the sheet metal component.
f. Save the model.

Creating the Base Flange

For creating this sheet metal component, you first need to create the base flange. The base flange will be created by using a rectangular sketch drawn on the Front Plane.

1. Start a new SOLIDWORKS document in the **Part** mode.

2. Invoke the sketching environment using the **Front Plane** as the sketching plane.

3. Create a rectangle of 350x250 mm as the sketch of the base flange, refer to Figure 18-158.

4. Choose the **Base Flange/Tab** tool from the **Sheet Metal CommandManager**; the **Base Flange PropertyManager** is displayed.

5. Set the value of the following parameters and choose the **OK** button from the **Base Flange PropertyManager**.

   Thickness: **1** K-Factor: **1** Auto Relief Type: **Rectangular** Ratio: **0.5**

   Figure 18-159 shows the base flange created on the Front Plane.

Creating the First Edge Flange

After creating the base flange, you need to create the first edge flange using the top edge of the base flange as the reference. You will observe that the **Sheet-Metal1** feature is displayed in the **FeatureManager Design Tree**. Modify the default bend radius using the **Sheet-Metal1** feature before creating the first edge flange.

1. Select the **Sheet-Metal** node from the **FeatureManager Design Tree** to invoke the pop-up toolbar. Next, choose the **Edit Feature** option from the pop-up toolbar.

2. Set the value in the **Bend Radius** spinner to **5** and choose the **OK** button from the **Sheet-Metal PropertyManager**.

3. Choose the **Edge Flange** tool from the **Sheet Metal CommandManager**; the **Edge-Flange1 PropertyManager** is displayed. Also, you are prompted to select the linear edge of a planar face to create the edge flange.

4. Select the edge of the base flange, as shown in Figure 18-160.

5. In the **Flange Length** rollout, set the value in the **Length** spinner to **300**. Choose the **Material Outside** button from the **Flange Position** rollout. Make sure that the flange is being created in the backward direction.

   Next, you need to edit the profile of the edge flange.

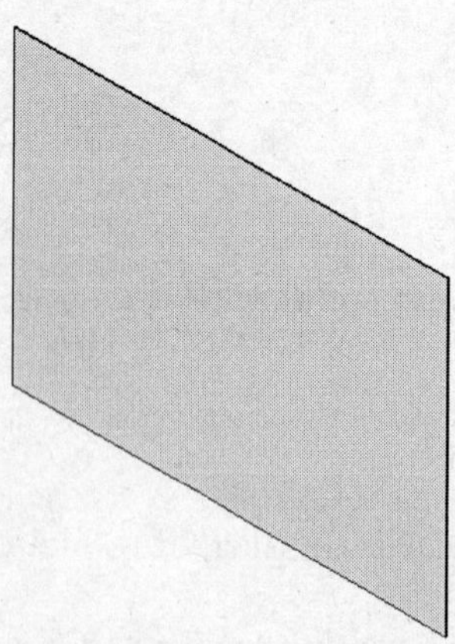

Figure 18-159 *Base flange*

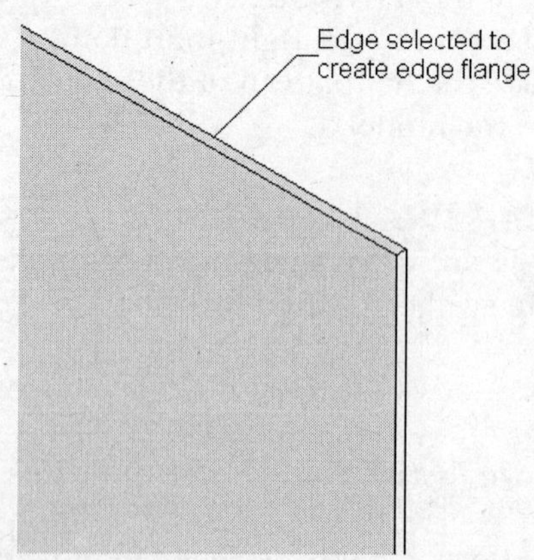

Figure 18-160 *Edge selected to create edge flange*

6. Choose the **Edit Flange Profile** button from the **Flange Parameters** rollout. As soon as you choose this button, the sketching environment is invoked and the **Profile Sketch** dialog box is displayed.

7. Edit the sketch, refer to Figure 18-161. Choose the **Finish** button from the **Profile Sketch** dialog box. The model after creating the first flange is as shown in Figure 18-162.

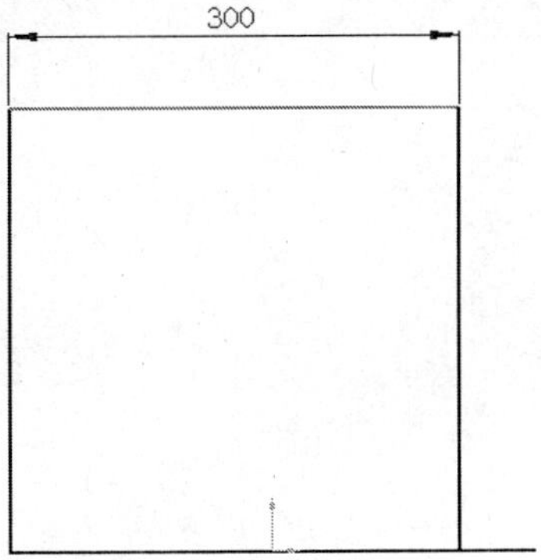

Figure 18-161 Modified sketch of the edge flange

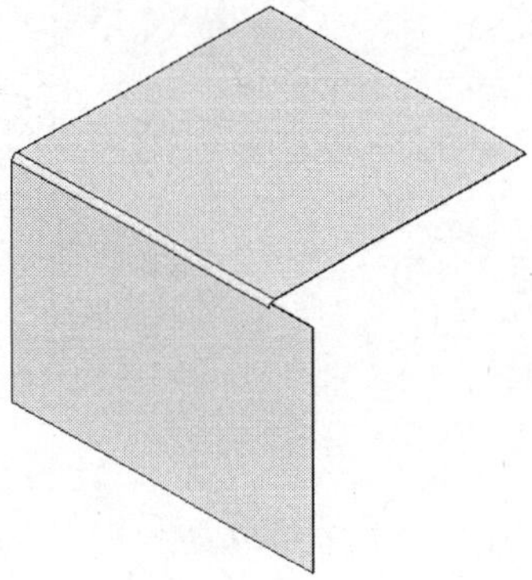

Figure 18-162 Model after creating the edge flange

Creating the Second Edge Flange

Next, you need to create the second edge flange with the holes.

1. Choose the **Edge Flange** tool from the **Sheet Metal CommandManager** to invoke the **Edge-Flange PropertyManager**.

2. Select the edge, as shown in Figure 18-163; a preview of the edge flange is displayed.

3. Set the value in the **Length** spinner to **100** and choose the **OK** button from the **Edge-Flange PropertyManager**.

4. Next, create two circular holes of diameter **15** mm each, refer to Figure 18-164.

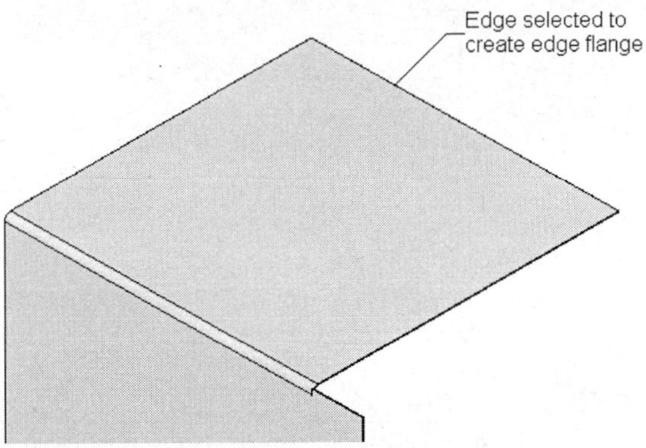

Figure 18-163 Edge selected to create the edge flange

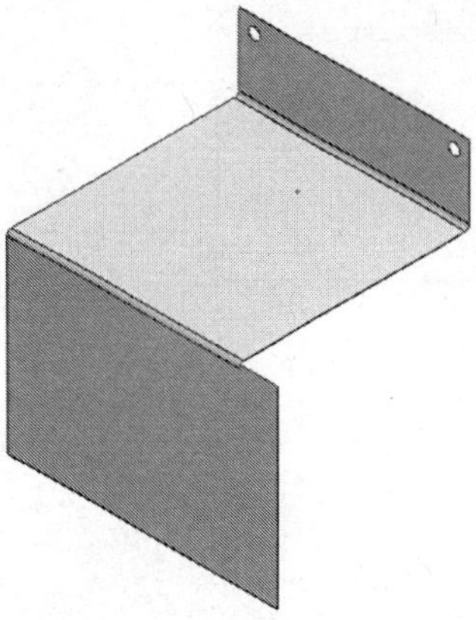

Figure 18-164 Model after creating the second edge flange

5. Similarly, create the edge flanges on the left side of the sheet metal component.

6. Edit the sketch of the edge flanges and draw the sketch for the holes. Refer to Figure 18-158 for dimensions. Edge-flanges with the holes are shown in Figure 18-165.

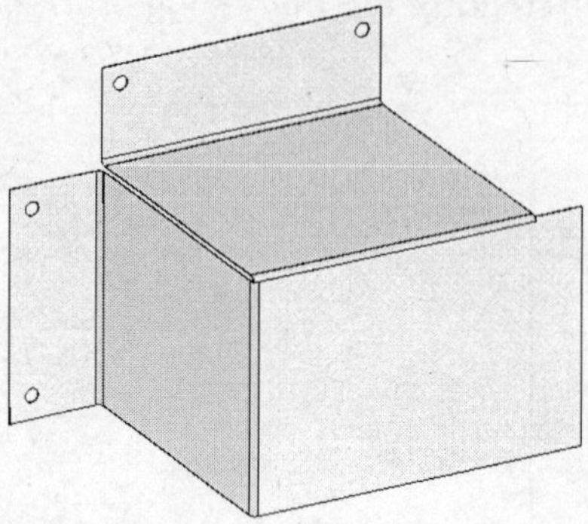

Figure 18-165 Model after creating edge flanges and holes on the left of the model

Creating the Tab and Flange Features

Next, you need to add a tab feature to the sheet metal component. A tab feature is used to add material to the base flange or any other flange feature.

1. Select the front face of the base flange as the sketching plane and invoke the sketching environment.

2. Draw the sketch of the tab feature, as shown in Figure 18-166.

3. Choose the **Base-Flange/Tab** tool from the **Sheet Metal CommandManager**; the **Base Flange PropertyManager** is displayed. Select the **Merge result** check box if it is not selected by default, and choose the **OK** button; the tab feature is created, as shown in Figure 18-167.

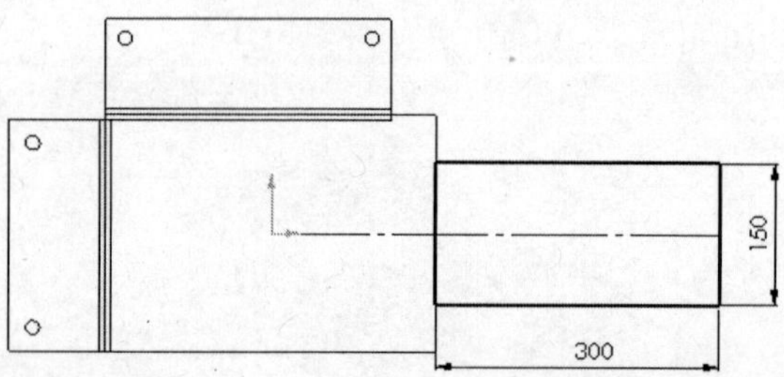

Figure 18-166 Sketch of the tab feature

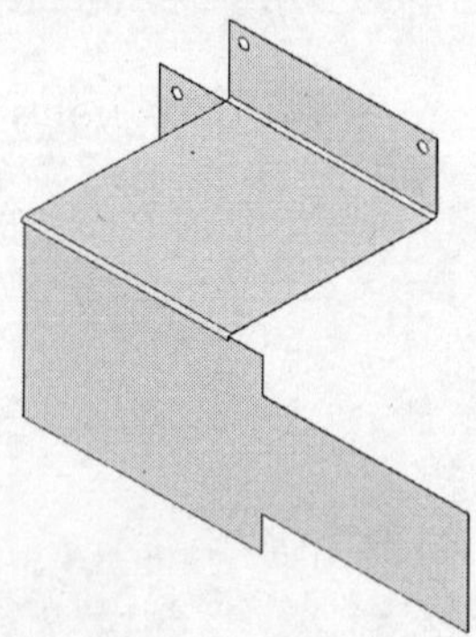

Figure 18-167 Model after creating the tab feature

4. Create three more edge flanges, one of length 100 mm, one of length 101 mm, and one of length 80 mm, refer to Figure 18-158. The model after creating all edge flanges is shown in Figure 18-168.

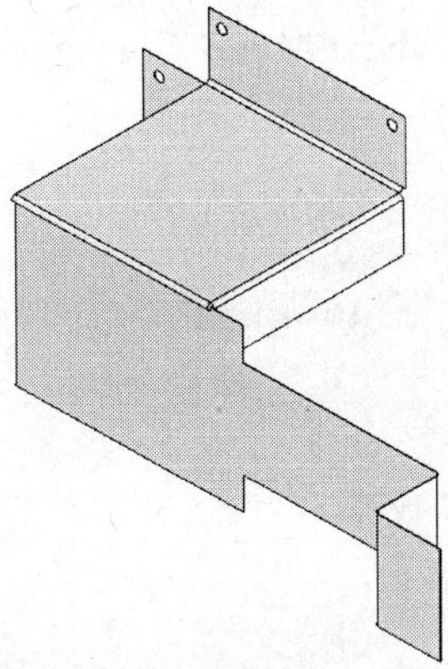

Figure 18-168 Model after creating all edge flanges

Creating the Hem Feature

After creating the other sheet metal features, you need to create the hem on the right most edge flange.

1. Choose the **Hem** tool from the **Sheet Metal CommandManager**; the **Hem PropertyManager** is displayed.
2. Choose the **Bend Outside** button from the **Edges** rollout and the **Closed** button from the **Type and Size** rollout. Next, set the value in the **Length** spinner to **10**.
3. Select the edge to create the hem, as shown in Figure 18-169; the hem is created, as shown in Figure 18-170.

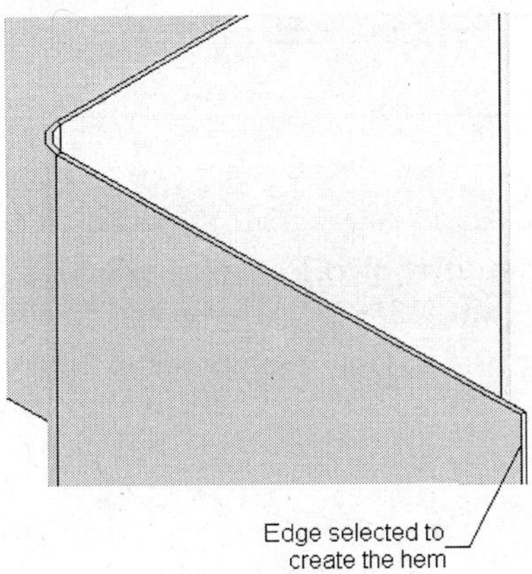

Figure 18-169 Edge selected to create the hem

Figure 18-170 Resultant hem

Creating the Flat Pattern

After creating the sheet metal component, you need to create its flat pattern.

1. Choose the **Flatten** tool from the **Sheet Metal CommandManager** to create the flat pattern of the sheet metal component.

2. Orient the flattened model parallel to the screen.

The flattened sheet metal component is displayed in Figure 18-171.

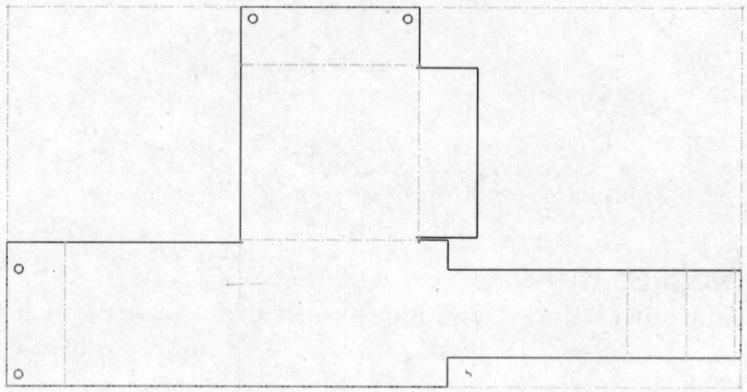

Figure 18-171 *Flattened sheet metal component*

Saving the Model

Next, you need to save the model.

1. Choose the **Save** button from the Menu Bar and save the drawing with the name *c18_tut01* at the location given below and then close the file.

\Documents\SOLIDWORKS\c18

Tutorial 2

In this tutorial, you will create the sheet metal component shown in Figure 18-172. The flat pattern of the sheet metal component is displayed in Figure 18-173. After creating the model, you need to generate its drawing views, as shown in Figure 18-174. The drawing views and the dimensions of the model are displayed in Figure 18-175. **(Expected time: 1 hr)**

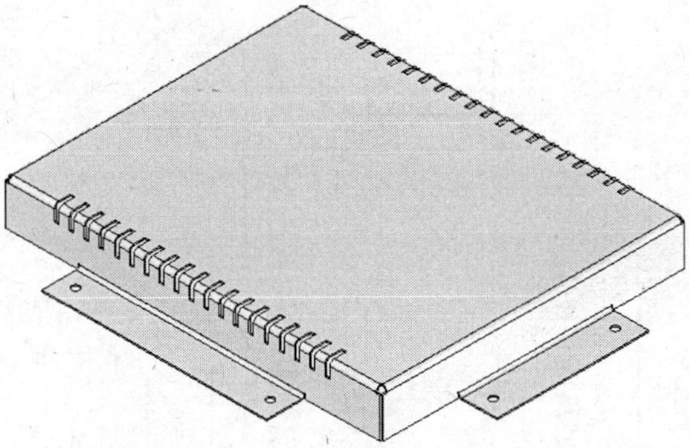

Figure 18-172 Sheet metal component

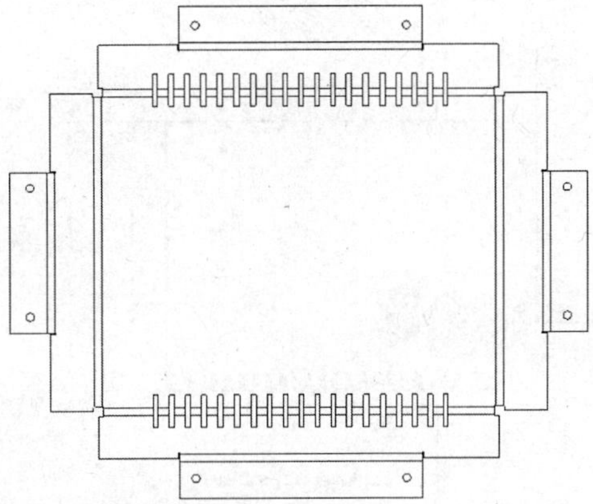

Figure 18-173 Flattened sheet metal component

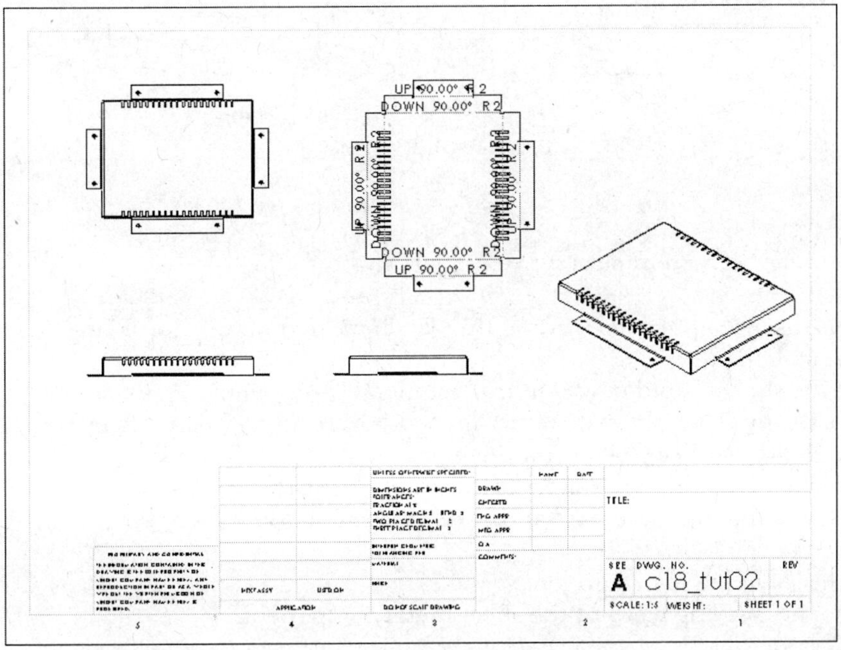

Figure 18-174 Drawing views of the model

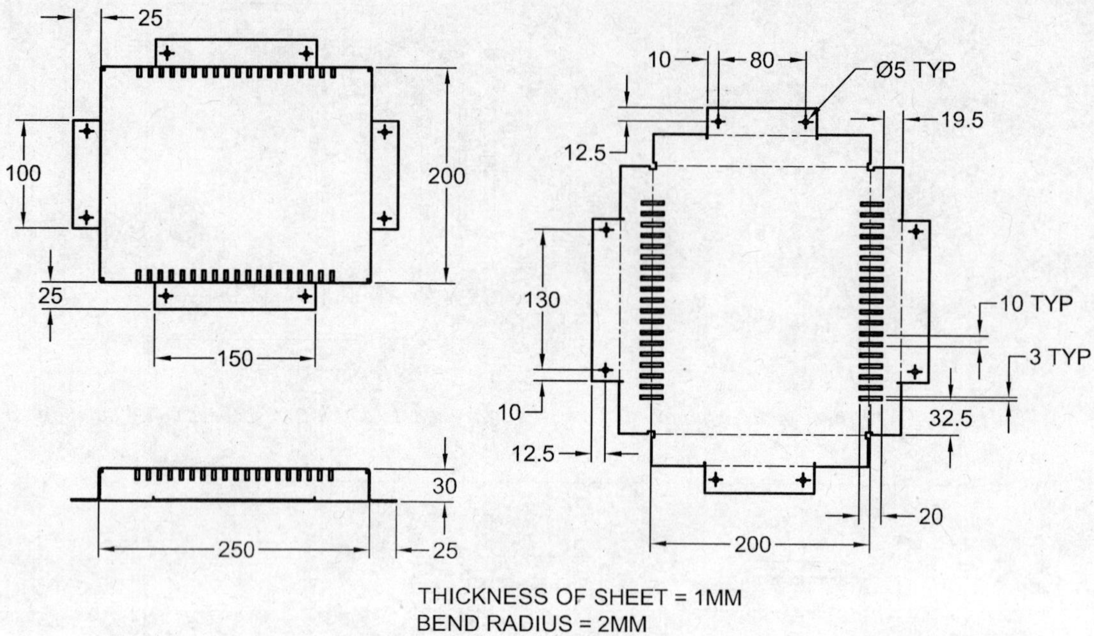

Figure 18-175 *Views and dimensions for Tutorial 2*

The following steps are required to complete this tutorial:

a. Create the base feature by extruding the sketch created on the Top Plane.
b. Shell the base feature.
c. Convert the shelled solid model into sheet metal component.
d. Roll back the model to the state where no bends were added to the sheet metal component.
e. Add flanges to the sheet metal component.
f. Create the flat pattern of the sheet metal component.
g. Create slots using the cut feature and pattern them on the sides of the flattened sheet metal component.
h. Refold the sheet metal component.
i. Generate the drawing views of the sheet metal component.
j. Save the model.

Creating the Base Feature

You will create this model by converting a shelled part into a sheet metal component. Therefore, you first need to create the base feature of the model by extruding the sketch created on the Top Plane.

1. Start a new SOLIDWORKS document in the **Part** mode.

2. Invoke the sketching environment by selecting the Top Plane as the sketching plane.

3. Draw the sketch of the base feature that consists of a rectangle of **250x200**.

4. Extrude the sketch upto a distance of **30** mm; the base feature of the model is displayed, as shown in Figure 18-176.

Shelling the Base Feature

Next, you need to add the shell feature to the model by removing the bottom face of the base feature.

1. Rotate the model so that its bottom face is clearly visible.

2. Invoke the **Shell** tool and select the bottom face of the base feature as the face to remove.

3. Set the value in the **Thickness** spinner to **1** and choose the **OK** button from the **Shell PropertyManager**; the shell feature is created, as shown in Figure 18-177.

> **Tip**
> *You can also convert a solid model into a sheet metal component by using the **Convert to Sheet Metal** tool.*

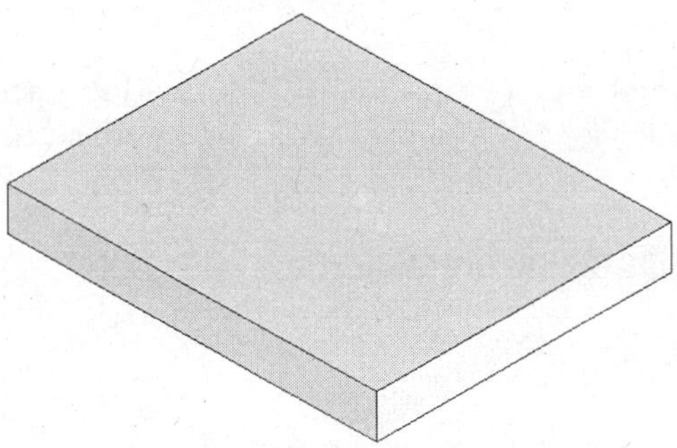

Figure 18-176 *Base feature*

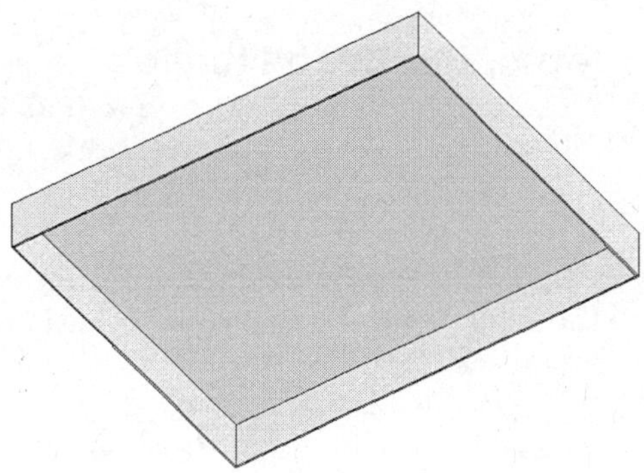

Figure 18-177 *Model after shelling*

Converting the Shelled Model into Sheet Metal Component

After creating the base feature and shelling the model, you need to convert it into a sheet metal component using the **Insert Bends** tool.

1. Choose the **Insert Bends** tool from the **Sheet Metal CommandManager** to invoke the **Bends PropertyManager**. Insert Bends

2. Select the top face of the model to fix.

3. Click once in the **Edges to Rip** selection box in the **Rip Parameters** rollout to activate the selection mode.

4. Select all the inner vertical edges of the base feature as the edges to rip.

5. Set the value **2** in the **Bend Radius** spinner.

6. Choose the **OK** button from the **Bends PropertyManager**; the **SOLIDWORKS** message box is displayed which informs you that the Auto relief cuts were made for one or more bends. Choose the **OK** button from this message box.

The model after converting the solid shelled model into the sheet metal component is shown in Figure 18-178.

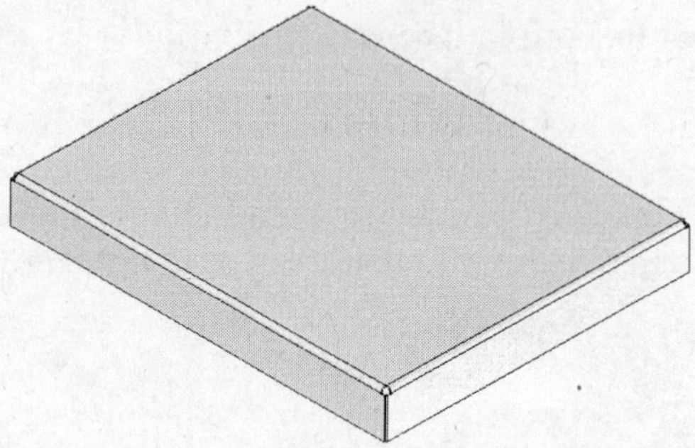

Figure 18-178 *Solid shelled model after converting into sheet metal component*

Creating the Edge Flanges

Next, you need to add the edge flanges to the sheet metal component. Before adding the edge flanges, you need to roll back the model to the stage when there were no bends in the sheet metal component.

1. Choose the **No Bends** button from the **Sheet Metal CommandManager** to roll back the model to the stage where it had no bends. Note that the four walls of the model are not unbent.

2. Now, select the bottom face of one of the four walls of the model as the sketching plane and invoke the sketching environment.

3. Draw the sketch of the flanges, as shown in Figure 18-179.

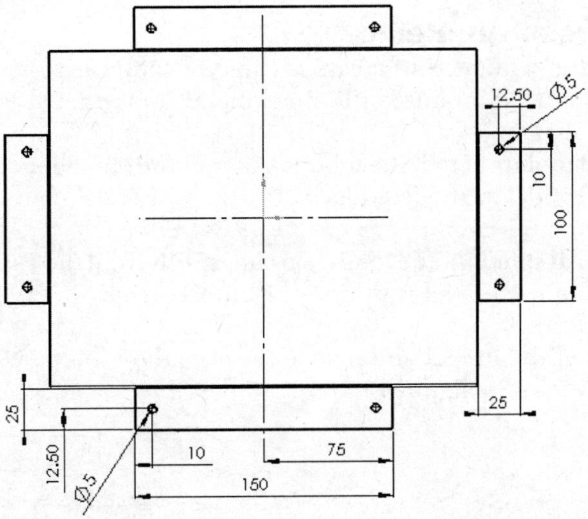

Figure 18-179 *Sketch of the flanges*

4. Invoke the **Boss-Extrude PropertyManager**. Select the **Link to thickness** check box and choose the **Reverse Direction** button. Make sure that the **Merge result** check box is selected in the **Direction 1** rollout.

5. Choose the **OK** button from the **Boss-Extrude PropertyManager**. Figure 18-180 shows the model after extruding the flanges.

   Now, you need to roll the model back to the bending stage.

6. Again, choose the **No Bends** tool from the **Sheet Metal CommandManager** to roll the model to the bending stage.

   Figure 18-181 shows the model after having been rolled back to the bending stage.

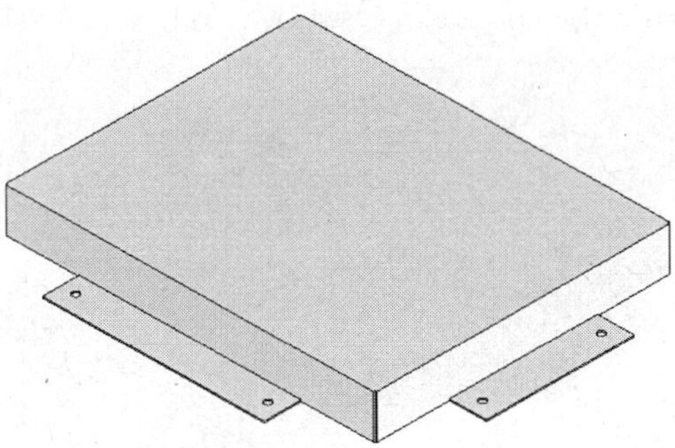

Figure 18-180 *Model after extruding the flanges*

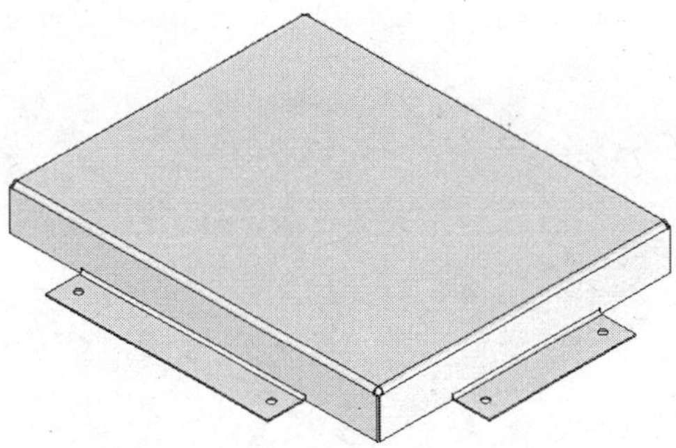

Figure 18-181 *Model rolled back to the bending stage*

Creating Cuts across the Bends

The next feature that you need to create is the cut feature across the bends. For creating this feature, you first need to unfold the sheet metal component.

1. Choose the **Unfold** tool from the **Sheet Metal CommandManager** and select the top face of the model as the fixed face.

2. Choose the **Collect All Bends** button and then choose **OK** from the **Unfold PropertyManager**. The unfolded view of the model is shown in Figure 18-182.

3. Select the top face of the model and invoke the sketching plane. Next, draw the sketch of the cut feature, as shown in Figure 18-183.

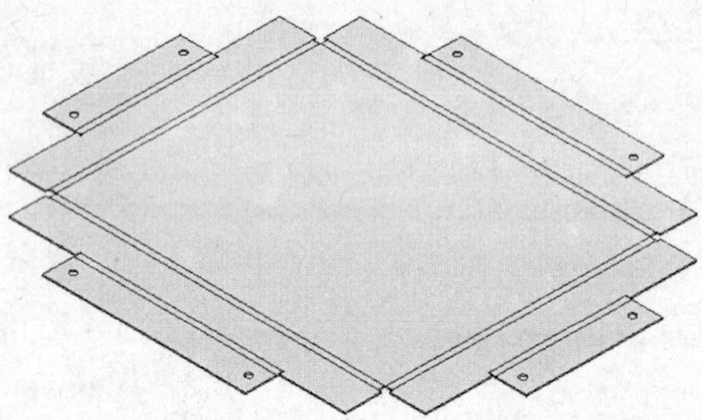

Figure 18-182 *Unfolded view of the model*

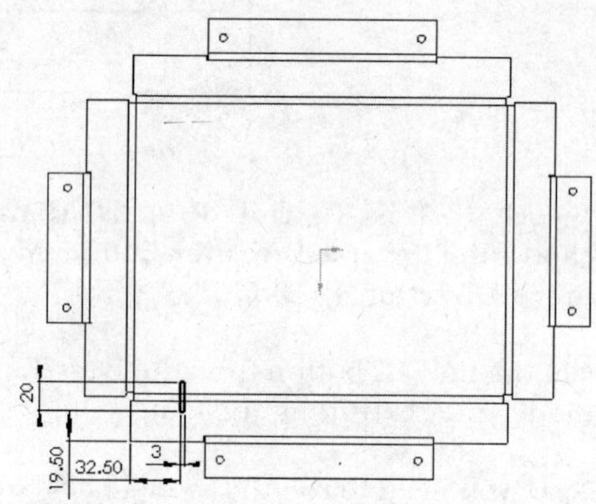

Figure 18-183 *Sketch of the cut feature*

4. Invoke the **Cut-Extrude PropertyManager** and create the cut feature. The model after adding the cut feature is shown in Figure 18-184.

5. Pattern the cut feature. The model after patterning the cut feature is shown in Figure 18-185.

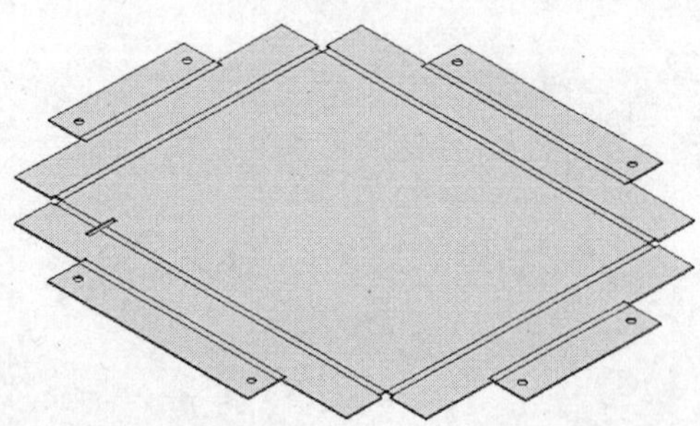

Figure 18-184 *Model after adding the cut feature*

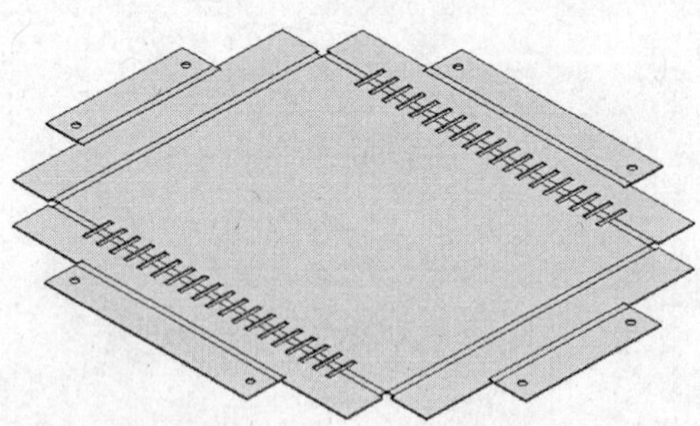

Figure 18-185 *Model after patterning the cut feature*

Refolding the Sheet Metal Part

After creating the sheet metal component, you need to refold the sheet.

1. Choose the **Fold** button from the **Sheet Metal CommandManager**; the **Fold PropertyManager** is displayed and the top face is selected by default.

2. Choose the **Collect All Bends** button and then choose **OK**. The sheet metal component after refolding is shown in Figure 18-186.

3. Save the model with the name *c18_tut02* at the following location:

   \Documents\SOLIDWORKS\c18

Note
You can also create flat pattern of the sheet metal component as a new configuration. The procedure to add configurations is discussed in the next chapter.

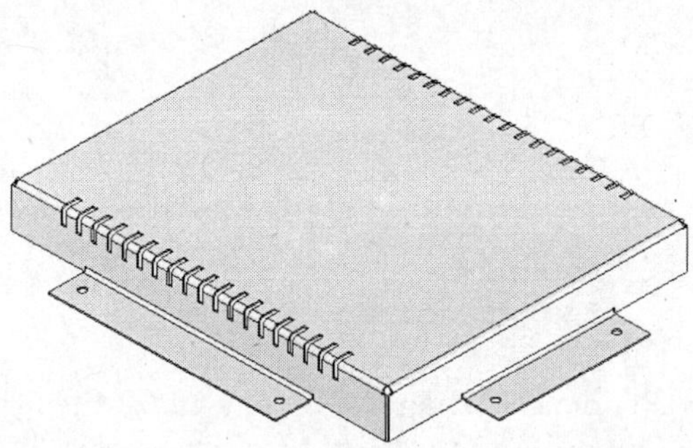

Figure 18-186 *Sheet metal component after refolding*

Generating the Drawing Views of the Sheet Metal Component

You will generate the drawing views of the sheet metal component on an A4 size drawing sheet with third angle projection.

1. Choose **New > Make Drawing from Part/Assembly** from the Menu Bar; the **Sheet Format/Size** dialog box is displayed.

2. Select the **A4 (ANSI) Landscape** option from the list box in the **Sheet Format/Size** dialog box and then choose **OK**.

3. If the default projection type is in the first angle, change it to the third angle using the **Sheet Properties** dialog box.

4. Generate the three default standard views of the model by dragging it from the **View Palette** task pane. Figure 18-187 shows the drawing sheet after generating the three standard views.

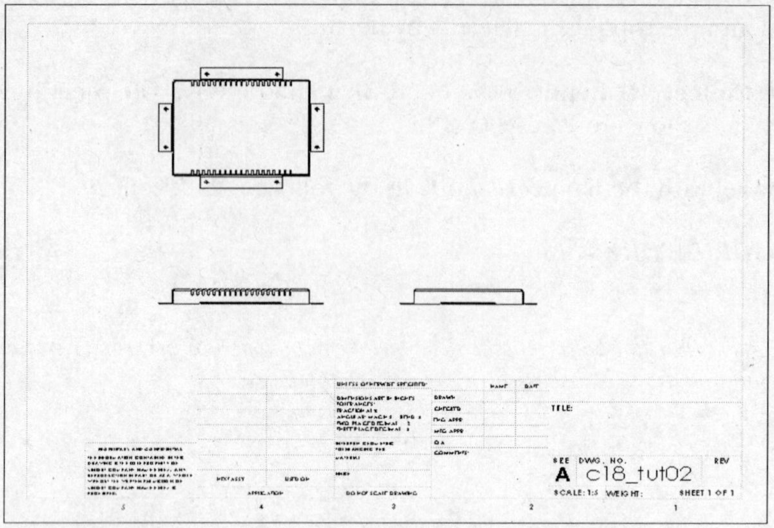

Figure 18-187 Drawing sheet after generating the three standard views

After generating the three standard views, you need to generate the drawing view of the flat pattern.

5. Invoke the **Model View PropertyManager**; the *c18_tut02* file is selected by default and its name is displayed in the **Open documents** list box. Choose the **Next** button from the **Model View PropertyManager**.

6. Select the **Flat pattern** check box in the **More views** list box of the **Orientation** rollout. Make sure that the **DEFAULTSM-FLAT-PATTERN** option is selected in the drop-down list of the **Reference Configuration** rollout of the PropertyManager.

7. Move the cursor to the top-right corner of the drawing sheet and left-click to place the flat pattern of the drawing view. Next, choose the **OK** button from the PropertyManager.

   Figure 18-188 shows the drawing sheet after generating the drawing view of the flat pattern.

   Next, you need to generate the isometric view.

8. Generate an isometric view and place the view close to the right corner of the drawing sheet. Change the scale of the isometric view to 1:4.

   The drawing sheet after generating all drawing views is displayed in Figure 18-189.

Saving the Model

Next, you need to save the model after generating the drawing views.

1. Choose the **Save** button from the **Menu Bar** and save the file with the name *c18_tut02* at the following location:

   \Documents\SOLIDWORKS\c18

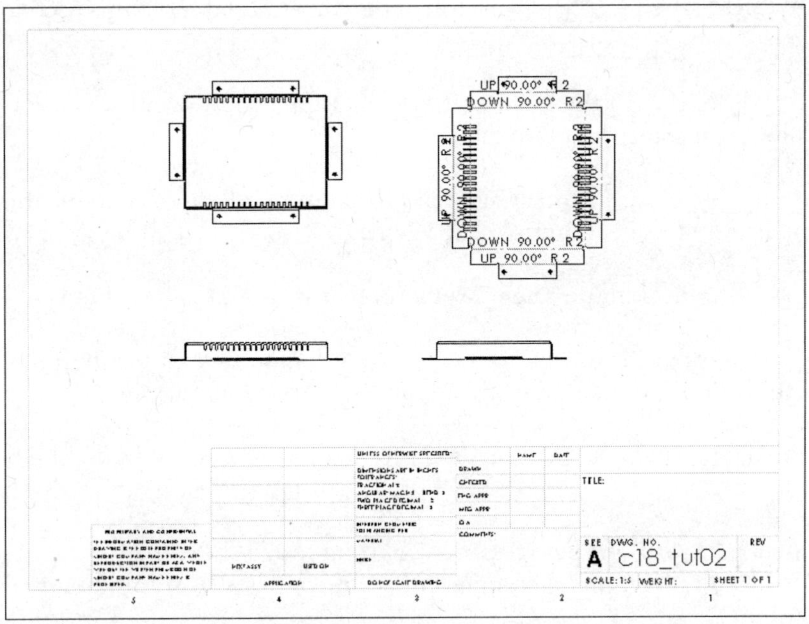

Figure 18-188 Drawing sheet after generating the flat pattern view

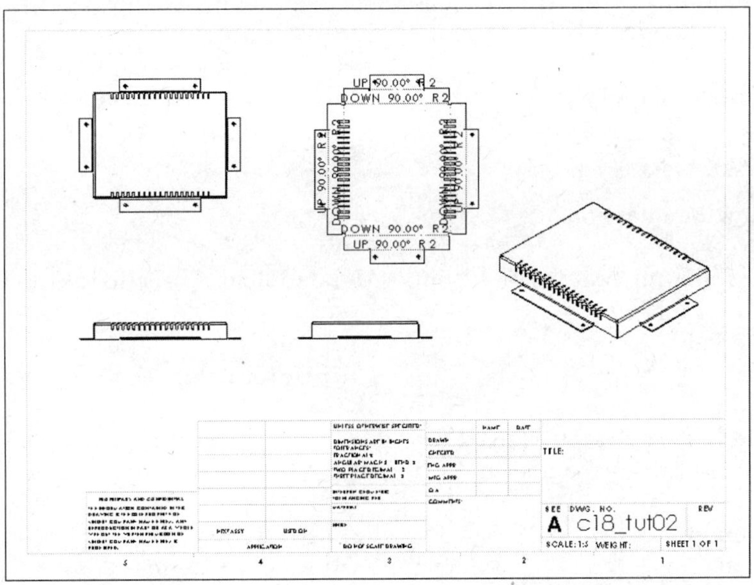

Figure 18-189 Final drawing sheet

Self-Evaluation Test

Answer the following questions and then compare them to those given at the end of this chapter:

1. In SOLIDWORKS, the __________ button in the **Sheet Metal** toolbar is used to create a base flange.

2. The __________ option in the **Bend Allowance Type** drop-down list is used to specify the bending allowance using the bend tables.

3. Select the __________ check box in the **View Orientation** rollout to generate the drawing view of the flat pattern of a sheet metal component.

4. The __________ button in the **Sheet Metal** toolbar is used to create hems.

5. The __________ rollout is used to define the bend allowance other than the default bend allowance that you have defined while creating the base flange.

6. To create the flat pattern of a sheet metal component, you need to choose the **Flatten** button. (T/F)

7. If you create a part with sharp edges and convert it into a sheet metal component, then the bends added to the sheet metal component are recognized as round bends. (T/F)

8. To create a closed corner, choose the **Closed Corner** button from the **Features** toolbar. (T/F)

9. The **Rip Gap** spinner in the **Rip Parameters** rollout is used to define the rip distance between two consecutive flanges. (T/F)

10. The **Sketched Bend** tool is used to create a bend by using a sketch as the bending line. (T/F)

Review Questions

Answer the following questions:

1. Which of the following buttons in the **Sheet Metal** toolbar is used to fold an unfolded sheet?

   (a) **Flattened** (b) **Fold**
   (c) **Bends** (d) **Unfold**

2. Which of the following tools is used to roll back the sheet metal component to the stage when it did not have any bends?

   (a) **Flattened** (b) **No Bends**
   (c) **Unfold** (d) **Remove Bends**

3. Which of the following tools is used to unfold a sheet metal component?

   (a) **Unfold** (b) **Flattened**
   (c) **No Bends** (d) None of these

4. Which of the following tools is used to draw the bending lines?

   (a) **Centerline** (b) **Arc**
   (c) **Spline** (d) **Line**

5. The __________ option in the **Bend Allowance Type** drop-down list is used to define the K-Factor.

6. The __________ tool is used to create a series of flanges along the edges of a sheet metal component.

7. The __________ check box is used to set the value of the feature termination according to the thickness of the sheet.

8. While creating a miter flange, the distance value of the rip is modified using the __________ spinner.

9. Choose the __________ button from the **Sheet Metal** toolbar to create lofted bends.

10. Lofted bends are created between__________.

EXERCISE

Exercise 1

In this exercise, you will create the sheet metal component shown in Figure 18-190. The flat pattern of this model is shown in Figure 18-191. To create this model, first create the base flange. Then, you need to create a miter flange to complete the sheet metal component. The default bend radius is 2 mm, K-Factor is 0.5, and Rectangular Relief ratio is 0.5. Thickness of the sheet is 1 mm. Rip gap for miter flange is 2 mm. Views and dimensions for this model are shown in Figure 18-192. **(Expected time: 20 min)**

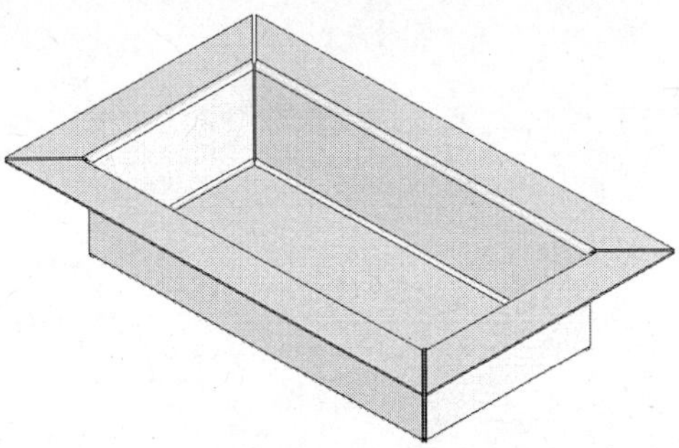

Figure 18-190 *Sheet metal component*

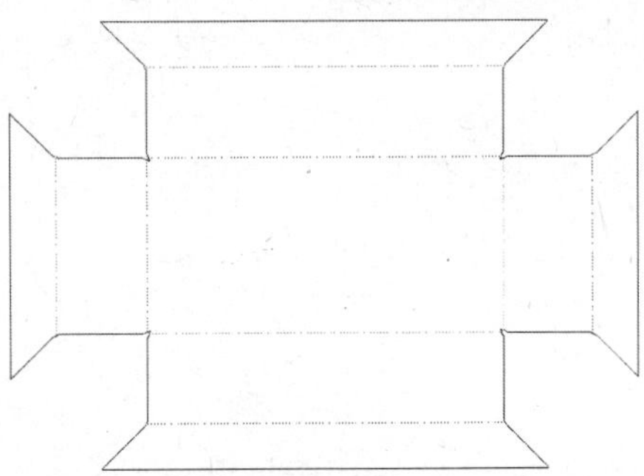

Figure 18-191 *Flat pattern of the sheet metal component*

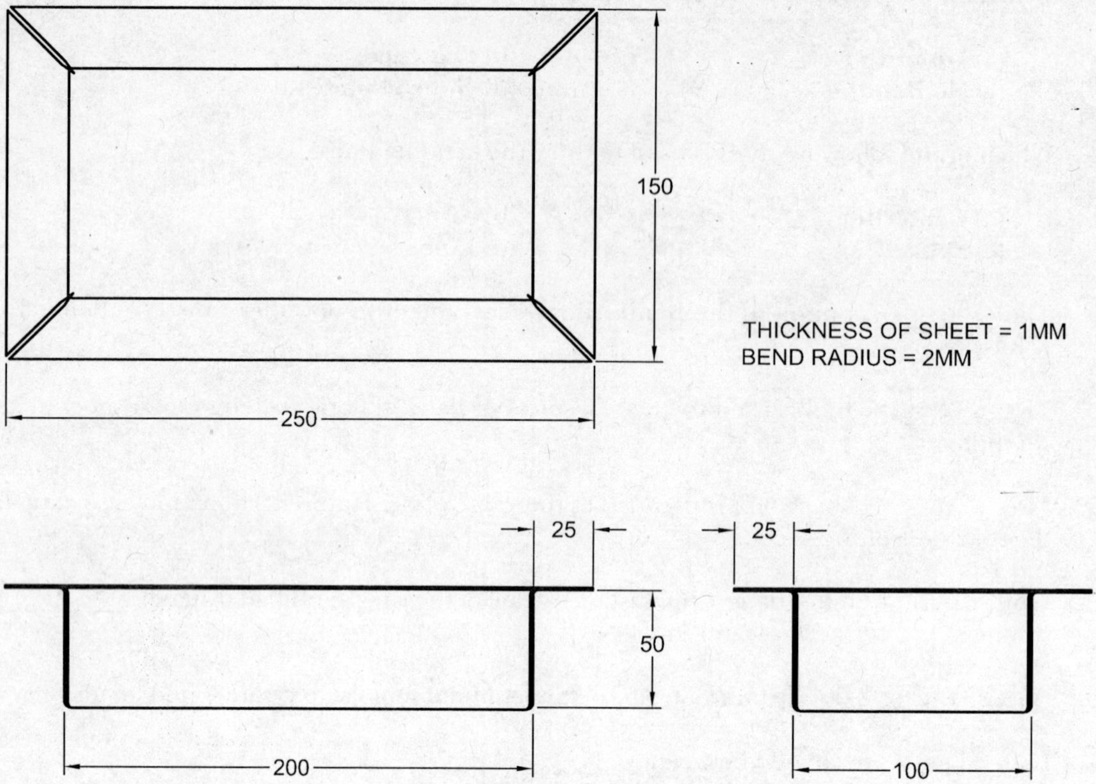

Figure 18-192 Views and dimensions of the sheet metal component for Exercise 1

Answers to Self-Evaluation Test

1. Base Flange/Tab, 2. Bend Table, 3. Flat Pattern, 4. Hem, 5. Custom Bend Allowance, 6. T, **7.** F, **8.** F, **9.** T, **10.** T

Chapter 19

Equations, Configurations, and Library Features

Learning Objectives

After completing this chapter, you will be able to:

- *Work with equations*
- *Add global variables*
- *Suppress and unsuppress features*
- *Add equations*
- *Work with configurations*
- *Create configurations by using design tables*
- *Change the suppression state of components using the design table*
- *Change the visibility of components using the design table*
- *Edit and delete design tables*
- *Create library features*

In this chapter, you will learn some of the advanced tools that are used to increase the productivity in the **Part**, **Drawing**, and **Assembly** modes of SOLIDWORKS. These tools are used to create equations in part modeling, configurations, and library features. The tools and the procedure to create the equations and configurations are discussed next.

WORKING WITH EQUATIONS

SOLIDWORKS menus:	Tools > Equations
Toolbar:	Tools > Equations

Equations are mathematical relations between the dimensions of a sketch or a feature. In an equation, the names of dimensions are used as variables. To add equations to a sketching environment or a part modeling environment, choose the **Equations** button from the **Tools** toolbar; the **Equations, Global Variables, and Dimensions** dialog box will be displayed, as shown in Figure 19-1.

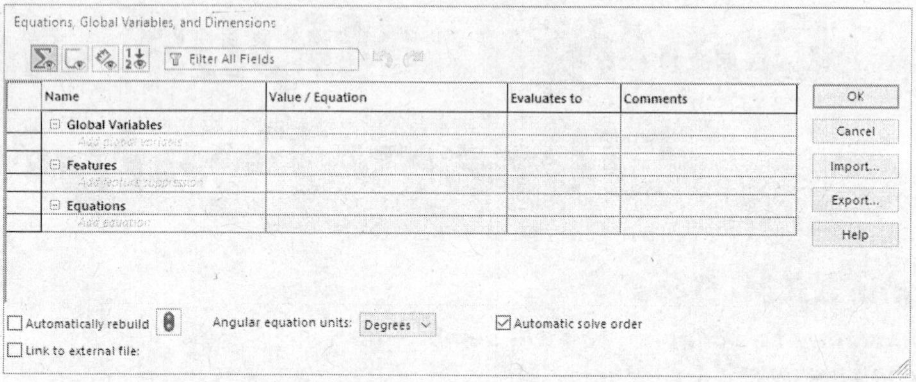

Figure 19-1 The ***Equations, Global Variables, and Dimensions*** *dialog box*

The options in this dialog box are used to add equations, suppress and unsuppress features, and apply global variables to the design. These options are discussed next.

Equation View

If the **Equation View** button is chosen in the **Equations, Global Variables, and Dimensions** dialog box, all global variables, equations for the features, and the dimensions applied to the active part will be displayed in the dialog box.

Sketch Equation View

If the **Sketch Equation View** button is chosen in the **Equations, Global Variables, and Dimensions** dialog box, all global variables and equations applied to the active sketch will be displayed. Also, this button allows you to add, delete, or edit sketch equations.

Dimension View

If the **Dimension View** button is chosen in the dialog box, all global variables, equations for the features, and dimensions of the part will be displayed in it. Note that, on choosing this button, all the dimensions of the active part will be displayed, even if the equations are not applied in it.

Ordered View

If the **Ordered View** button is chosen, all equations and global variables are displayed in the order in which they are solved because the **Automatic solve order** check box is selected by default in the dialog box. To change this order, you need to clear the check box. You will learn more about changing the order of the equations and global variables later in this chapter. Also, if an equation of the active part is suppressed, it will be displayed in the dialog box, so that you can unsuppress it. To do so, right-click on the suppressed equation; a shortcut menu will be displayed. Next, choose the **Enable Equation** option from the shortcut menu.

Rebuild

The **Rebuild** button is used to refresh or update the sketches, models, or assemblies after editing the equations. If you have edited the equations in the **Equations, Global Variables, and Dimensions** dialog box, you will notice that the changes will not be updated automatically. To generate the changes, choose the **Rebuild** button. You can choose this button any time to update the equations and re-generate the sketches, models, assemblies, and drawings with the modified equations.

Automatically rebuild

The **Automatically rebuild** check box is used to rebuild the model automatically when you make changes in it.

Angular equation units

The options in the **Angular equation units** drop-down list are used to change the angular units to radians or degrees. By default, the **Degrees** option is selected in this drop-down list.

Automatic solve order

This check box is selected by default. As a result, SOLIDWORKS automatically identifies the dependencies of the equations. As the equations in the **Value / Equation** column are dependent on the independent equations in the **Name** column, the equations in the **Name** column get solved automatically before the equations in the **Value / Equation** column. Therefore, the global variables, equations for the dimensions, and the features added in the part or assembly get arranged automatically in an order to get solved. To change the default order of the equations, you need to clear the **Automatic solve order** check box. Once the check box is cleared, you can select the required row of the equations to be reordered and then drag it to the required position.

Filter All Fields

The **Filter All Fields** search box is used to search the required equations, dimensions, features, and global variables in the dialog box. To search an entity, enter its name in this search box; the required entity will be displayed in the dialog box.

Configuration

The **Configuration** drop-down list is only displayed when you are working over a part with multiple configurations and is used to display all the configurations. By using this drop-down list, you can select the required configuration and apply the equations and global variables to its dimensions.

Link to external file

The **Link to external file** check box is used to create link between an external text file containing equations and global variables and the active part. You can also export the applied equations and global variables of the active part to a text file by using this check box.

Adding Global Variables

In SOLIDWORKS, you can add global variables by using the **Equations, Global Variables, and Dimensions** dialog box. To do so, invoke the dialog box and choose the **Equation View** button, if it is not chosen by default. Next, click on the empty cell of the **Global Variables** node under the **Name** column and specify a name for the global variable in it, refer to Figure 19-2. Next, click on the cell corresponding to this cell in the **Value / Equation** column; a shortcut menu will be displayed. Also, the name specified for the global variable in the previous cell will be displayed in quotation marks.

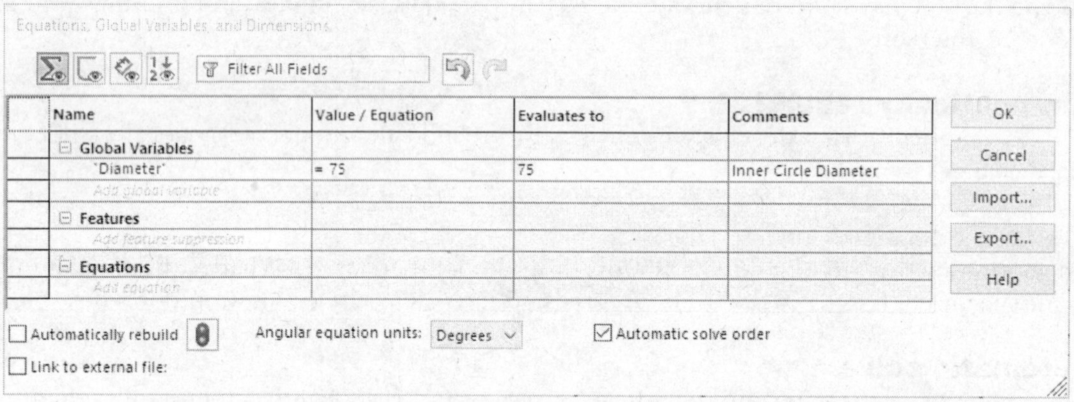

Figure 19-2 The global variable added in the ***Equations, Global Variables, and Dimensions*** *dialog box*

Now, you can specify the value for the global variable by using the options available in the shortcut menu or by directly entering the desired value in the edit box . You can also select the dimensions from the drawing area as the value of the global variable. You can perform various mathematical operations using symbols such as plus (+), minus (-) and so on, while specifying the values for the equation and global variable in the respective cell. You can also add a comment to the added global variable in its respective cell under the **Comments** column.

After adding the global variable, you can use it to relate all the equations of the component with each other. Consider a case of the part whose sketch is shown in Figure 19-3. Invoke the **Equations, Global Variables, and Dimensions** dialog box and add a global variable with the name **length** by following the procedure discussed earlier, refer to Figure 19-4. Next, click on the corresponding empty cell in the **Value / Equation** column and then specify the value of the global variable as **200**. Now, add a comment to the global variable added in its respective cell under the **Comments** column, refer to Figure 19-4.

Next, add one more global variable as **width** in the dialog box and click on the corresponding empty cell in the **Value / Equation** column; a shortcut menu will be displayed. Next, choose **Global Variable > length(200)** from the shortcut menu; the "**length**" global variable is highlighted in the **Value / Equation** column, and a green colored check mark is also displayed. Now, press the minus (-) key and enter **50** in this cell. Next, select the check mark; the **width** global variable is added to the dialog box. You can also add a comment to the added global variable in its respective cell under the **Comments** column, refer to Figure 19-4.

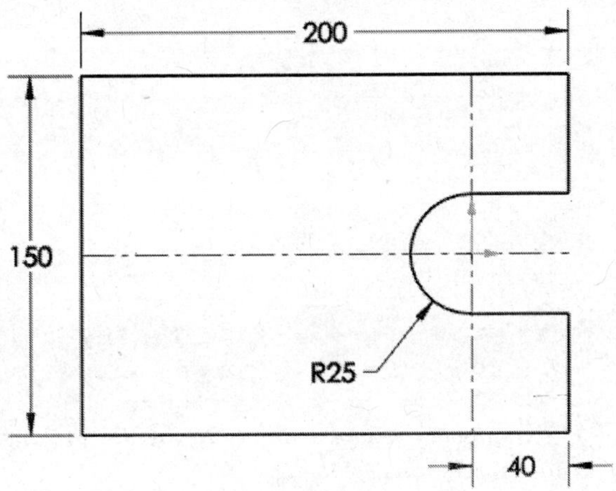

Figure 19-3 *Sketch of a part*

After adding global variables, you need to add equations to relate them with each other by using the added global variables. To do so, click on the empty cell of the **Equations** node under the **Name** column and select the dimension with the value **200** from the drawing area; its name is displayed in the selected cell. Also, a shortcut menu is displayed in the corresponding cell of the **Value / Equation** column. Next, choose **Global Variable > length(200)** from the shortcut menu; the **"length"** global variable is now highlighted in the **Value / Equation** column, and a green colored check mark is also displayed. Select this check mark; the equation will be added to the dialog box, refer to Figure 19-4.

To add second equation, click on the empty cell of the **Equations** node under the **Name** column and select the dimension with the value **40** from the drawing area; its name is displayed in the selected cell. Also, a shortcut menu is displayed in the corresponding cell of the **Value / Equation** column. Next, choose **Global Variable > length(200)** from the shortcut menu; the **"length"** global variable is highlighted in the **Value / Equation** column, and a green colored check mark is also displayed. Now, press the forward slash (/) key and enter **5** in this cell, refer to Figure 19-4. Now, select the check mark; the equation is added to the dialog box. Similarly, add equations to the other dimensions of the sketch, refer to Figure 19-4. Note that, after adding all the equations to the sketch, if you change the value of the **length** global variable from **200** to **100** in the **Value / Equation** column, all the dimensions will get changed proportionally.

In SOLIDWORKS, you can create the equations in different dimension units like inches, centimeters, millimeters. The dimension can also be used in all these units together. You can also create a length variable in the equations by adding relations to different dimensional values of different unit systems. SOLIDWORKS will automatically solve the relations of the dimensions and display the final value of the dimensions.

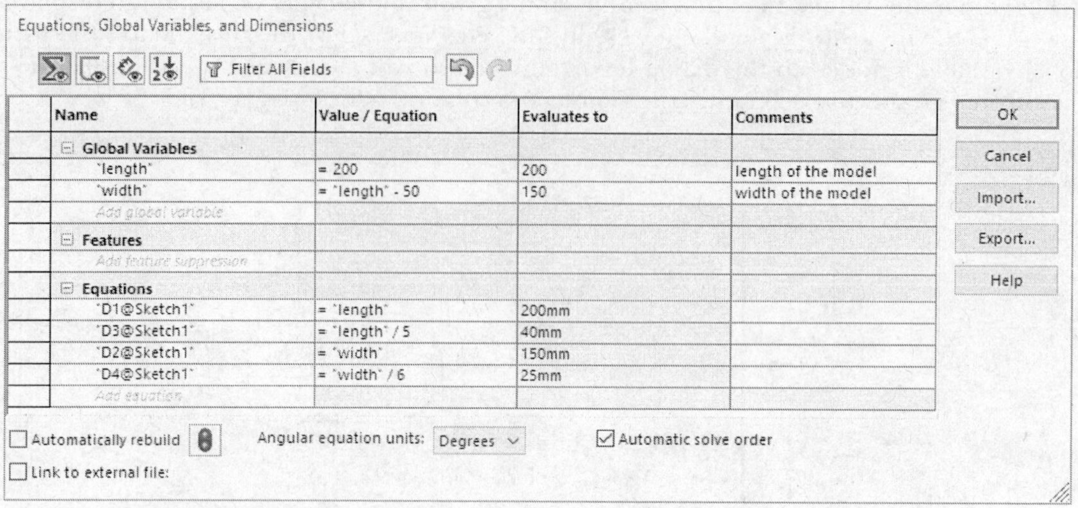

Figure 19-4 The global variables added to the ***Equations, Global Variables, and Dimensions*** *dialog box*

Suppressing and Unsuppressing Features

You can also suppress and unsuppress the features of a part or assembly. To do so, invoke the **Equations, Global Variables, and Dimensions** dialog box and click on the empty cell of the **Features** node under the **Name** column. Next, select the feature to be suppressed/unsuppressed from the **FeatureManager Design Tree**; the name of the feature will be displayed in the selected cell. Also, a shortcut menu will be displayed under the **Value / Equation** column. Next, choose **Global Variable > suppress** / **unsuppress** from the shortcut menu; the applied option will be highlighted in the corresponding cell with a green colored check mark. Click on the green colored check mark; the feature gets suppressed/unsuppressed, refer to Figure 19-5. Alternatively, you can use numeric value **0** and **1** to unsuppress and suppress a feature, respectively. To do so, enter the value in the desired cell of the **Value / Equation** column. You can also change an existing option. To do so, click in the corresponding cell and delete the applied option. Next, apply the desired option.

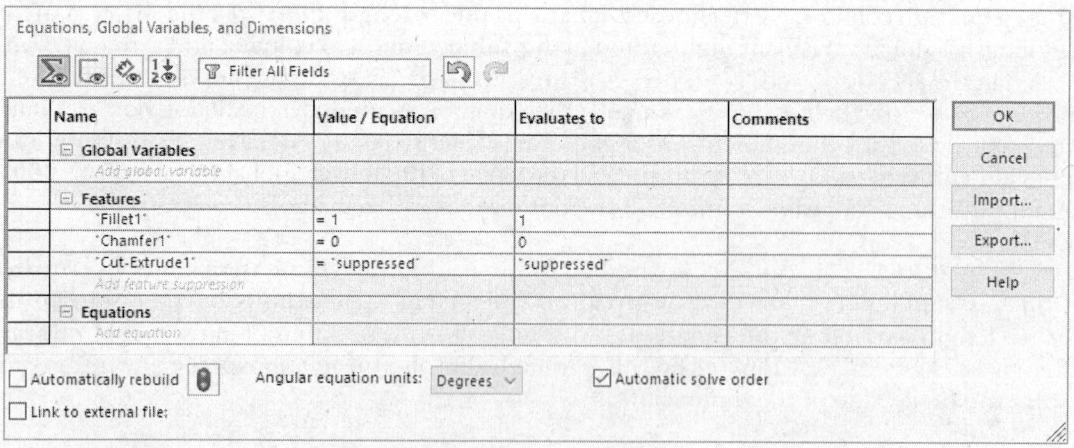

Figure 19-5 Suppressing and unsuppressing features in the ***Equations, Global Variables, and Dimensions*** *dialog box*

Adding Equations

You can also add equations to a sketch or a feature. To do so, create a sketch and apply dimensions to it. Next, choose **Tools > Equations** from the SOLIDWORKS menus; the **Equations, Global Variables, and Dimensions** dialog box will be displayed. If you add equations in the **Part** mode, then you need to show their feature dimensions. To show the feature dimensions in the drawing area, invoke the shortcut menu by right clicking on the **Annotations** node in the **FeatureManager Design Tree** and select the **Show Feature Dimensions** option. Next, select a dimension from the drawing area. This dimension is called the driven dimension and it will have to equate with other dimensions. The other dimension that the driven dimension will equate with is known as driving dimension. If you modify the driving dimension, the driven dimensions will also be modified accordingly. To select an equation as a driven equation, click on the empty cell of the **Equations** node under the **Name** column and select any dimension from the drawing area; its name will be displayed as a variable in the corresponding cell in the dialog box. Next, select the driving dimension from the drawing area; its name will be displayed in the **Value / Equation** column with a green colored check mark. Now, add the required mathematical relations and select the check mark; an equation will be added. Also, the solution of the equation will be displayed in the **Evaluates to** column of the dialog box. You can also add different names, comments and so on to all the equations in the **Comments** column. Next, choose the **OK** button to exit the dialog box. You may also need to rebuild the model after adding the equations if the **Automatically rebuild** check box is not selected by default.

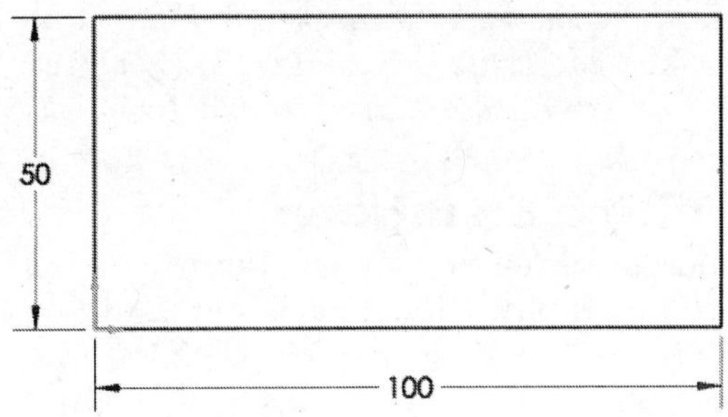

Figure 19-6 Sketch of the rectangle with dimensions

If you want to draw a rectangle, as shown in Figure 19-6, whose width automatically reduces to half of its length when the length is modified, you need to apply equations. To do so, invoke the **Equations, Global Variables, and Dimensions** dialog box and then click on the empty cell of the **Equations** node under the **Name** column. Select the dimension with the value **50** from the drawing area; the name of the dimension gets displayed in the corresponding cell of the **Name** column in the dialog box. Also, a shortcut menu is displayed in the corresponding cell of the **Value/Equation** column. Next, select the dimension with the value **100** from the drawing area. Press the asterisk (*) key and enter **0.5** in the corresponding cell of the **Value / Equation** column, as shown in Figure 19-7. Next, click on the green colored check mark. The value after solving the equation will be displayed in the **Evaluates to** column of the dialog box. Next, choose the **OK** button from this dialog box; the sketch will be regenerated and the dimension value of the width of the rectangle will be modified based on the equation applied to it. Also, the equation symbol will be added to the width of the rectangle.

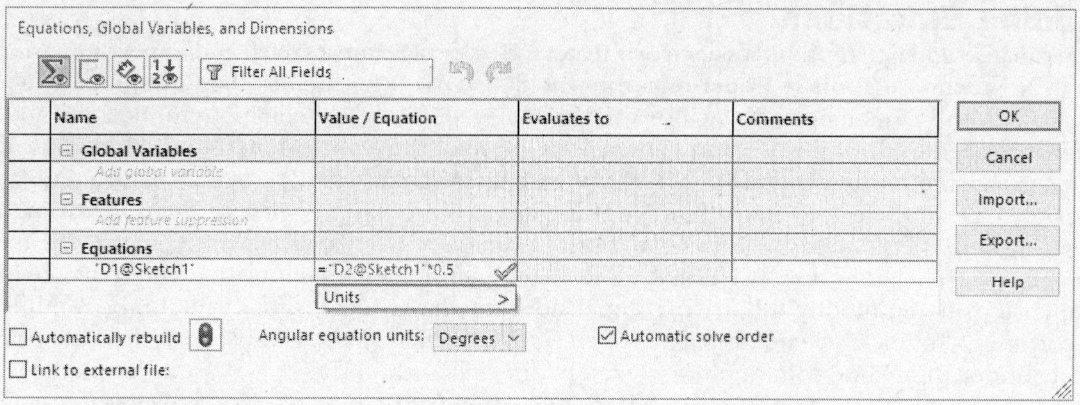

*Figure 19-7 The **Equations, Global Variables, and Dimensions** dialog box after adding the equation*

On adding the equations in the part or in the sketch, the **Equations** folder is automatically created in the **FeatureManager Design Tree**, as shown in Figure 19-8. You will learn more about this folder later in this chapter.

Note

*You can also invoke the **Equations, Global Variables, and Dimensions** dialog box from the **FeatureManager Design Tree**. To do so, right-click on the **Equations** folder in the **FeatureManager Design Tree** and select **Manage Equations**.*

Editing Equations

You can edit the equations added to a design by using the **Equations, Global Variables, and Dimensions** dialog box. To do so, invoke the dialog box and click in the cell with equations to be edited in the **Value / Equation** column; the cell will become editable and you can now edit the equation. Once the editing is done, click on the green colored check mark displayed in the cell; the changes made will be reflected in the model in the drawing area. Make sure that the **Automatically rebuild** check box is selected in the dialog box to automatically rebuild the applied equation.

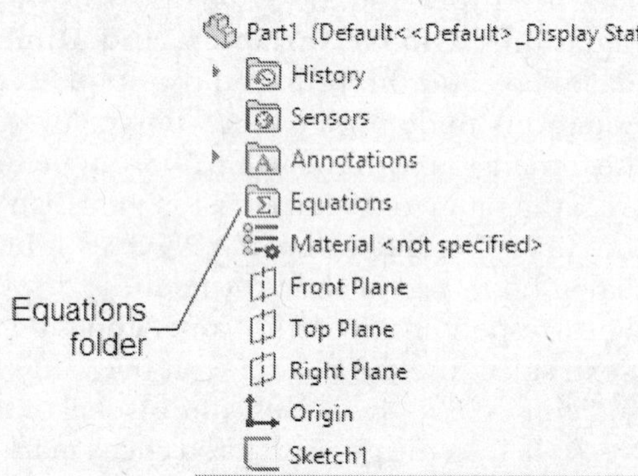

*Figure 19-8 The **Equations** folder created in the **FeatureManager Design Tree***

Tip

*You can also edit the equations from the drawing area. To do so, double-click on the dimension that has equations; the **Modify** dialog box will be displayed with the equations applied in it. Now, you can modify the equations as per your requirement.*

Deleting/Disabling Equations

You can delete an unwanted equation from the **Equations, Global Variables, and Dimensions** dialog box. To do so, invoke the dialog box and right-click on the equation to be deleted; a shortcut menu will be displayed. Select the **Delete Equation** option from the shortcut menu. Similarly, you can also disable an equation by choosing the **Disable Equation** option from the shortcut menu displayed.

Exporting/Importing Equations

In SOLIDWORKS, you can export the equations created for one entity and share them with other entities. To do so, choose the **Export** button from the **Equations, Global Variables, and Dimensions** dialog box and save equations in a text file. Next, open another model and import the equations text file into it by choosing the **Import** button. However, it is recommended to change the name of the dimension in the **Primary Value** rollout in the **Dimension PropertyManager** by selecting the dimension. Similar to exporting the equation, you can also import an equation by using the **Import** button.

WORKING WITH CONFIGURATIONS

In SOLIDWORKS, you can create multiple instances of a part or an assembly with ease. For example, if you need to create a bolt and nut of different dimensions, you do not need to create the parts of different dimensions, instead you can create multiple configurations. There are two methods of creating configurations: manually and by using the design table. The method of creating configurations manually is discussed next and the second method will be discussed later in this chapter.

Creating Configurations Manually

You can create the configurations manually and can specify their properties. Then, you can modify the model or the assembly to create variations in the new configuration. Consider the machine bed shown in Figure 19-9. You need to create two types of designs for the same machine bed. In the first design, you need to have a circular pocket on the top face of the machine bed, whereas in the second design, the circular pocket is to be removed from the top face of the machine bed.

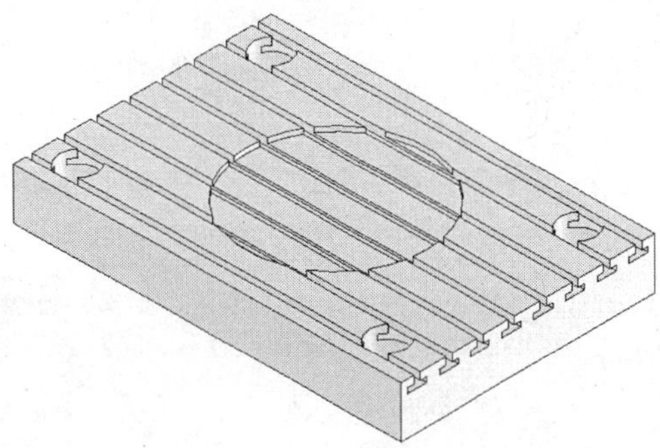

Figure 19-9 Model of a machine bed

To create configurations manually, you need to invoke the **ConfigurationManager**. To do so, choose the **ConfigurationManager** button next to the **PropertyManager** button below the **CommandManager**. You will observe that the model of the machine bed shown in Figure 19-9 is saved as the **Default** configuration and becomes active. The active configuration is shown with a green check mark.

To create a new configuration, select the name of the part in the **ConfigurationManager** and right-click to invoke the shortcut menu. Choose the **Add Configuration** option from the shortcut menu, as shown in Figure 19-10. On choosing this option from the shortcut menu, the **Add Configuration PropertyManager** will be displayed, as shown in Figure 19-11. In the **Configuration Properties** rollout, you can specify the name of the configuration in the **Configuration name** edit box.

The description of the configuration can be specified in the **Description** edit box. Select the **Use in bill of materials** check box to display the information in the BOM that is provided in this rollout. You can use the **Comment** edit box to specify the comment about the configuration.

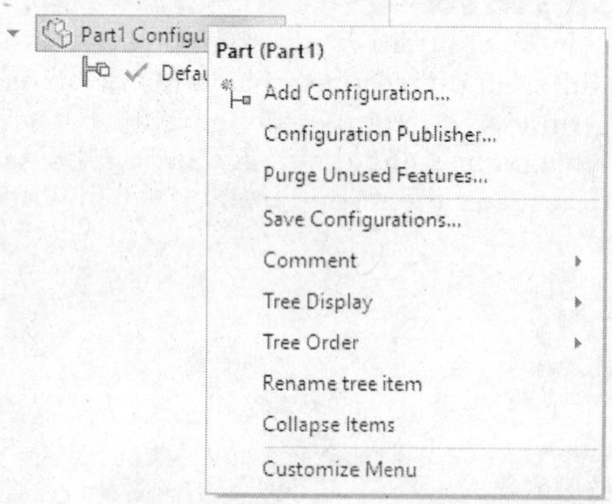

*Figure 19-10 Choosing the **Add Configuration** option from the shortcut menu*

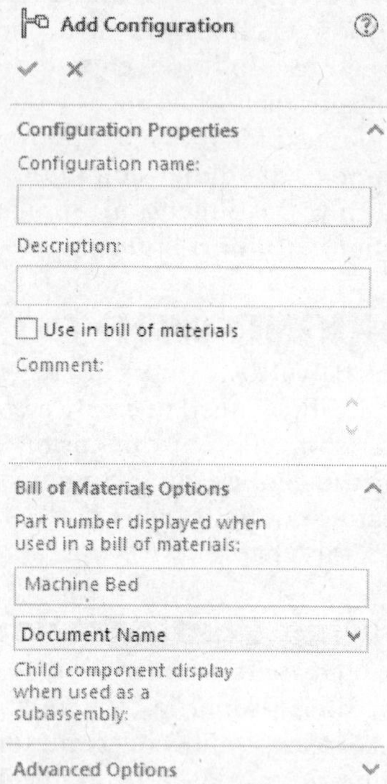

*Figure 19-11 The **Add Configuration PropertyManager***

The drop-down list in the **Bill of Materials Options** rollout is used to specify the name of the part that has to be displayed in BOM when the drawing views are generated with the selected configuration.

On expanding the **Advanced Options** rollout, you will observe that the **Suppress new features and mates** check box is selected by default. Therefore, the new features and mates added in some other configuration of the same part will be automatically suppressed in this configuration. Select the **Use configuration specific color** check box to specify a color for the newly created configuration. On selecting this check box, the **Color** button will be enabled. Invoke the **Color** dialog box by choosing this button and specify the color for the configuration.

After adding all the information in the **Add Configuration PropertyManager**, choose the **OK** button; the new configuration will be created and will activate automatically. The node of the new configuration will be displayed with a green color check mark in the **ConfigurationManager**. Figure 19-12 shows the name of the new configuration displayed in the **ConfigurationManager**.

After creating the configuration, edit the features of the model that are required to be displayed in the newly created configuration. The design requirement for the machine bed is that the circular recess needs to be removed in the second configuration of the machine bed. Therefore, you need to suppress the cut feature that is used to create the circular recess in the machine bed. To do so, invoke the **FeatureManager Design Tree** and suppress the cut feature. Now, if you want to switch back to the **Default** configuration, select the **Default** configuration from the **ConfigurationManager** and invoke the shortcut menu. Choose the **Show Configuration** option; the **Default** configuration will be displayed and you will observe that the circular recess is not suppressed in this configuration. Alternatively, double-click on the **Default** configuration in the **ConfigurationManager** to switch back to it. On the other hand, when you invoke the newly created configuration, you will observe that the circular recess is not displayed in the machine bed. Figure 19-13 shows the machine bed with the **Default** configuration and Figure 19-14 shows the machine bed with the modified design configuration.

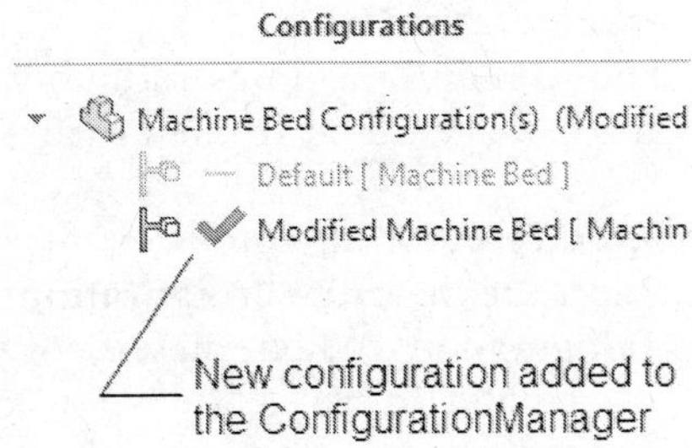

Figure 19-12** New configuration displayed in the **ConfigurationManager

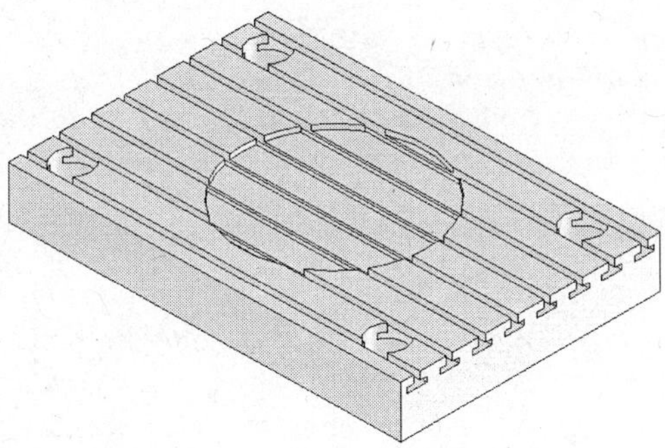

***Figure 19-13** Machine bed with the **Default** configuration*

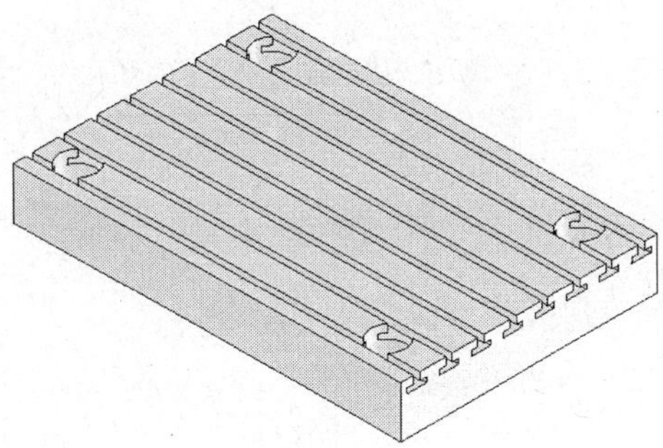

***Figure 19-14** Machine bed with the modified design configuration*

Editing the Features of a Part with Multiple Configurations

When you edit the features of a part with multiple configurations, the **Configurations** rollout will be displayed in the PropertyManager of the feature to be edited, as shown in Figure 19-15. You can specify the configuration that you need to modify using the options in this rollout. These options are discussed next.

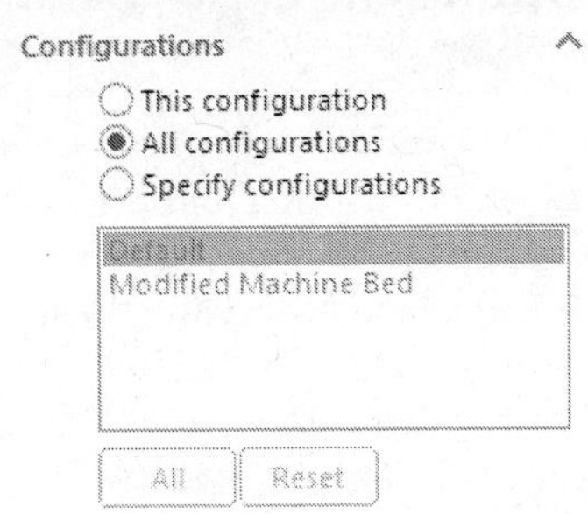

***Figure 19-15** The **Configurations** rollout*

This configuration

If you select the **This configuration** radio button, the modification made in the feature will be applied only to the current configuration. The same feature will not be modified in the remaining configurations.

All configurations

The **All configurations** radio button is selected by default. As a result, modification made in a feature will be applied to all the configurations of the current part document.

Specify configurations

Select the **Specify configurations** radio button to apply modification only to the selected configurations. When you select this radio button, configurations in the part document will be listed in the list box. The current configuration is selected by default. Select the configuration in which you want to apply the modification. On choosing this radio button, the **All** and **Reset** buttons get activated. The **All** button is used to select all the configurations displayed in the list box and the **Reset** button is used to reset the listed configurations in the list box.

> **Tip**
>
> *1. When you place a component with multiple configurations in an assembly document, the name of the current configuration will be displayed along with the name of the part in the* ***FeatureManager Design Tree****.*
>
> *2. To change the configuration of the components placed in an assembly document, select a component and invoke the shortcut menu. Choose the* ***Component Properties*** *option from the shortcut menu; the* ***Component Properties*** *dialog box will be displayed. Select the required configuration from the* ***Referenced configuration*** *area and choose the* ***OK*** *button. Alternatively, you can select the desired configuration from the drop-down list displayed above the shortcut menu. After selecting the desired configuration, select the green check mark displayed on the right of the configurations drop-down list.*
>
> *3. You can also change the configurations of a part in each drawing view independently. To do so, select and right-click on the drawing view and choose the* ***Properties*** *option from the shortcut menu; the* ***Drawing View Properties*** *dialog box will be displayed. In this dialog box, you can change the configuration by selecting different options from the* ***Use named configuration*** *drop-down list.*

Creating Configurations by Using Design Tables

SOLIDWORKS menus:	Insert > Tables > Design Table
Toolbar:	Tools > Design Table

Sometimes you may need to create a part that is used repeatedly in your design work. Each instance of that part may have the same geometry but different dimensions. You can create a part having different configurations by modifying dimensions manually. However, it is recommended to create these types of configurations using the **Design Table** tool. To do so, choose the **Design Table** button from the **Tools** toolbar or choose **Insert > Tables > Design Table** from the SOLIDWORKS menus; the **Design Table PropertyManager** will be displayed, as shown in Figure 19-16.

The rollouts in the **Design Table PropertyManager** are discussed next.

Source Rollout

The **Source** rollout is used to specify the type and the source for inserting the design table in the part or assembly document. The options in this rollout are discussed next.

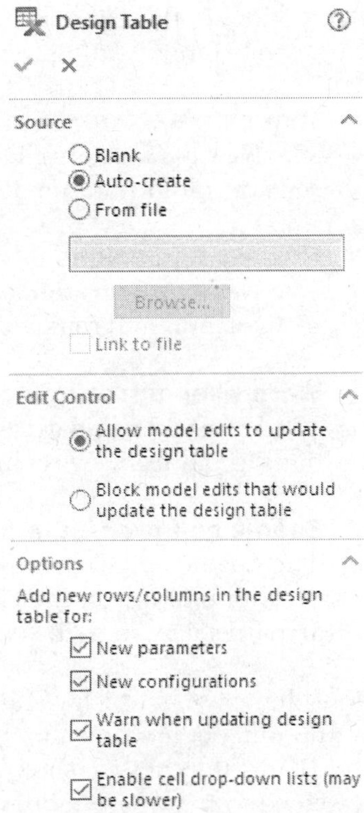

*Figure 19-16 The **Design Table PropertyManager***

Blank

The **Blank** radio button is used to insert a blank design table. You need to manually enter the parameters in a blank design table.

Auto-create

The **Auto-create** radio button is selected by default when you invoke the **Design Table PropertyManager**. On selecting this radio button, you can insert a new design table in the part or the assembly document. It will also load all the parameters and their associated values in the design table.

From file

Select the **From file** radio button if you need to insert an existing design table. The design tables are created as Microsoft Excel files. To retrieve a saved design table, select this radio button and choose the **Browse** button provided in this rollout; the **Open** dialog box will be displayed. Browse and open the file that you need to insert as design table; the name and the path of the selected file will be displayed in the display box provided below the radio button. The **Link to file** check box will be available only when you select the **From file** radio button. On selecting this check box, any change made in the Microsoft Excel file will reflect in the part model or the assembly, and vice versa.

Edit Control Rollout

The **Edit Control** rollout is used to specify the settings of bidirectional control on the design table. The options available in this rollout are discussed next.

Allow model edits to update the design table

The **Allow model edits to update the design table** radio button is selected by default and is used to add a bidirectional relation between the model and the design table. If you select this radio button, the changes made in the model will be updated in the design table automatically.

Block model edits that would update the design table

The **Block model edits that would update the design table** radio button is used to block the editing of the parameters of the model that tend to update the design table.

Options Rollout

The options in the **Options** rollout are used to add rows or columns to the design table and to warn you before updating the design table. The options in this rollout are discussed next.

New parameters

The **New parameters** check box is selected by default and is used to automatically add new rows or columns in the design table when new parameters are added to the model.

New configurations

The **New configurations** check box is selected by default and is used to automatically add new columns and rows in the design table when a new configuration is added to the model.

Warn when updating design table

The **Warn when updating design table** check box is selected by default. As a result, a warning message appears every time the design table updates.

Enable cell drop-down lists

The **Enable cell drop-down lists** check box is selected by default. As a result, a drop-down list with multiple entries is created in the each cell. When you enable drop-down lists, an arrow displays in each cell.

Consider a case in which you need to create a washer of 100 mm outer diameter, 50 mm inner diameter, and 10 mm thickness, as shown in Figure 19-17. Also, you need to create five more washers with different dimensions. As the geometry of the washers is same and only the dimensions are different, it is recommended to create a single part document of the washer and then create different configurations of the washer using the design table.

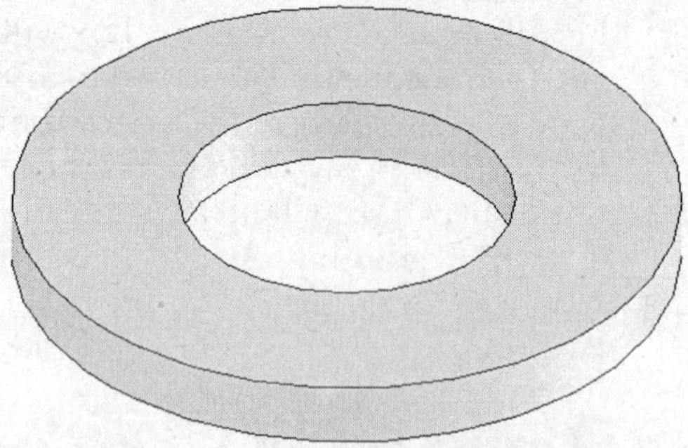

Figure 19-17 *Washer created using the given dimensions*

After creating the part model, invoke the **Design Table PropertyManager**. Select the **Auto-create** radio button and choose the **OK** button from the **Design Table PropertyManager**; the design table will be created with the default settings and the tools in the toolbars of SOLIDWORKS window will be replaced by the Microsoft Excel tools. Also, the **Creating design table** dialog box will be displayed, overlapped by the **Dimensions** dialog box. Figure 19-18 shows the SOLIDWORKS window after you have chosen the **OK** button from the **Design Table PropertyManager**.

Next, press and hold the CTRL key and select all the dimensions displayed in the **Dimensions** dialog box. Choose the **OK** button; the name of the selected dimensions with the dimensional values of the **Default** configuration will be displayed in Microsoft Excel sheet in the drawing area, refer to Figure 19-19. Next, you need to specify the name of the second instance to be created for the model and enter dimensions for that instance in the excel sheet. Similarly, specify the names and dimensions of other instances, refer to Figure 20.

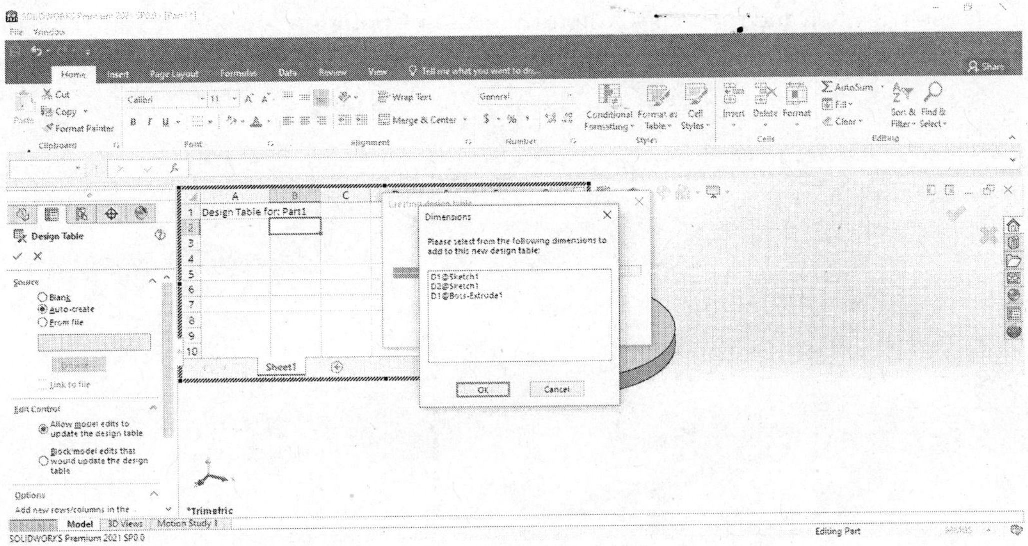

Figure 19-18 SOLIDWORKS window displayed while creating the design table

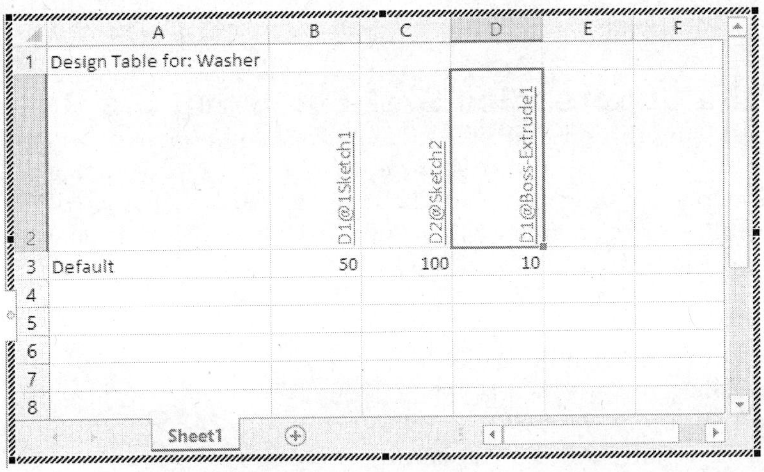

Figure 19-19 Microsoft Excel sheet after adding features to the design table

After specifying the configurations and dimensions in the Microsoft Excel sheet, click anywhere in the drawing area; the **SOLIDWORKS** message box will be displayed with the names of the configurations generated by the design table. Choose the **OK** button to close it.

Now, you can observe that different configurations are created in the **ConfigurationManager** and the **Default [Washer]** configuration is activated, as shown in Figure 19-21. The Microsoft Excel icon displayed before the **Design Table** node in the **ConfigurationManager** confirms that the configuration is generated by using the design table. If you need to view any other configuration, select the configuration and right-click. Choose the **Show Configuration** option from the shortcut menu. Alternatively, you can double-click on the configuration in the **ConfigurationManager**.

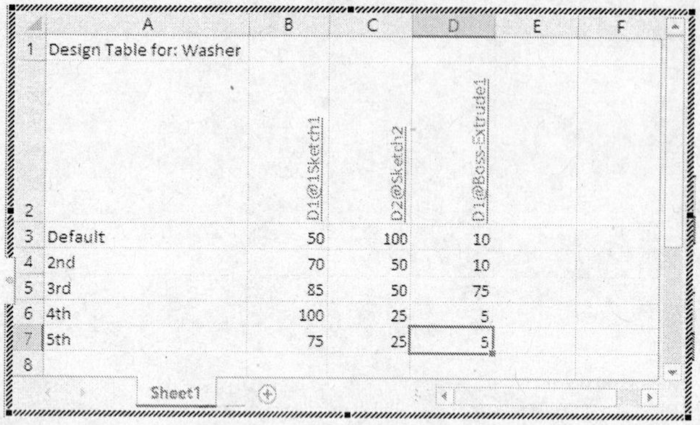

Figure 19-20 Microsoft Excel sheet after specifying the name of the new instances and adding dimensions to those instances

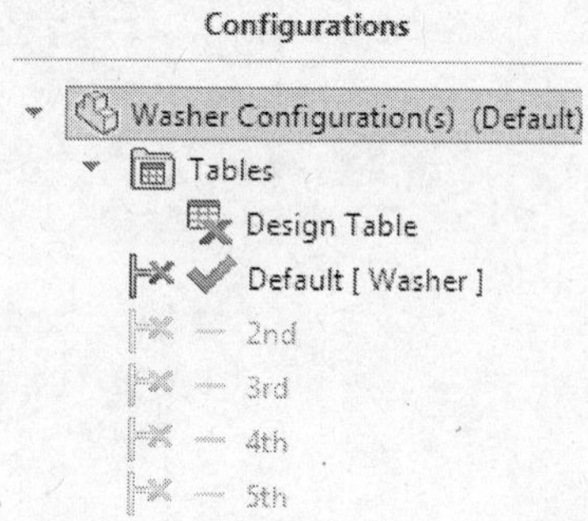

Figure 19-21 *The* ***Configuration Manager*** *with different configurations*

Note

You can create only one design table in a part or an assembly document.

Changing the Suppression State by Using the Design Table

You can change the suppression state of the features of a component by using the design table. This method is of great use in the design department because you can generate different configurations of a part showing the feature to be created after each stage of the manufacturing process. Assume that you are provided with the finished billet stock and you need to manufacture the plate shown in Figure 19-22.

To manufacture the plate from the billet, you first need to perform the pocket milling operation to remove the material from inside the plate. Next, you need to drill the holes inside the pocket as well as on the top face of the plate. After performing all operations, you need to chamfer the top edges of the plate.

To represent all these stages, you need to create different configurations displaying each of these stages of the manufacturing process using the design table. You can also create these configurations manually but that will be a time-consuming process.

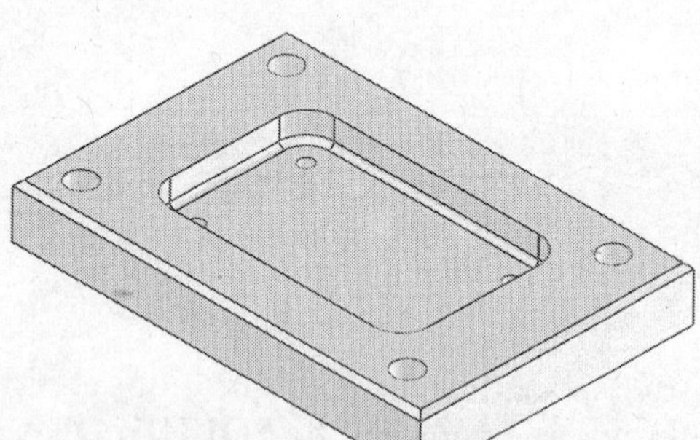

Figure 19-22 *Finished plate*

Before creating these types of configurations, you need to change the names of the feature in the **FeatureManager Design Tree**. To change the name of a feature, select the feature and again left-click on it; the name of the feature will be displayed in a text box. Enter a new name for the feature. Remember changing the names of the features is done to avoid confusion and is not mandatory. Save the model and then invoke the **Design Table PropertyManager**. In the PropertyManager, select the **Auto-create** radio button, and then choose the **OK** button; the **Dimensions** dialog box will be displayed. Without selecting any dimension from the **Dimensions** dialog box, choose the **OK** button; an excel sheet is displayed only with the name of the design table. Next, double-click on all the features displayed in the **FeatureManager Design Tree**. You will notice that the names of the features will be displayed in the top row and their respective suppression states will be displayed under the names of the features in Microsoft Excel, refer to Figure 19-23.

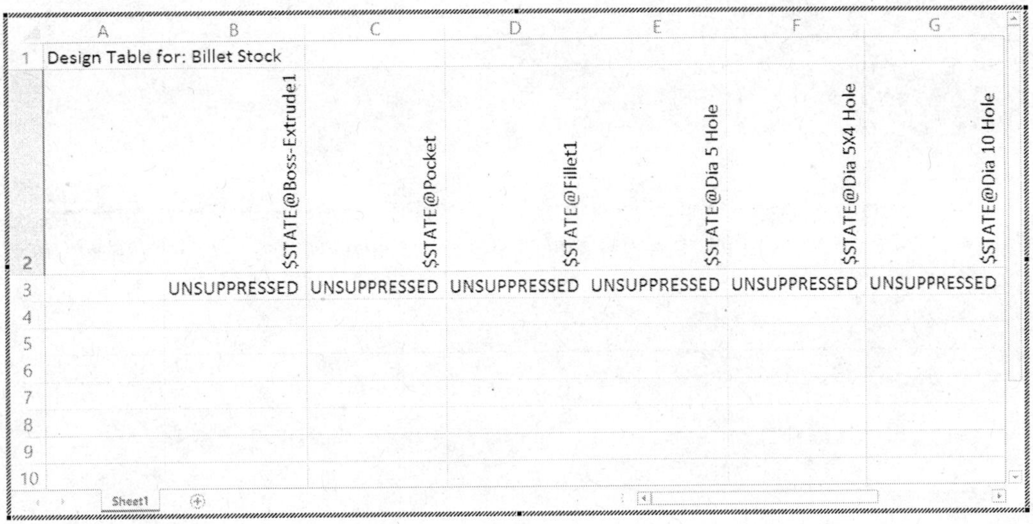

Figure 19-23 *Microsoft Excel sheet after adding features to the design table*

Note that all the features are displayed as unsuppressed. Enter **Finished Plate** as the name of the configuration in the **A3** cell. Enter **Billet Stock** as the name of the second configuration in the **A4** cell. Now, specify the suppression state as suppressed in all the features in the design table except the base feature. Instead of specifying the complete spelling of suppress and unsuppress, you can enter **S** for suppressed state and **U** for unsuppressed state. Next, enter **Pocket Milling** as the name of the third configuration in the **A5** cell and suppress all the features except the base feature, pocket, and fillet features. Similarly, create other configurations. Figure 19-24 shows the design table after specifying all the configurations and their respective suppression states.

Next, click anywhere in the drawing area and choose the **OK** button from the **SOLIDWORKS** message box displayed to return to the part modeling environment. Figures 19-25 through 19-29 show different configurations of the plate created by changing the suppression state of the feature by using the design table.

	A	B	C	D	E	F	G	H	I	J	K
1	Design Table for: Billet Stock										
2		$STATE@Boss-Extrude1	$STATE@Pocket	$STATE@Fillet1	$STATE@Dia 5 Hole	$STATE@Dia 5X4 Hole	$STATE@Dia 10 Hole	$STATE@Dia 10X4 Hole	$STATE@Chamfer1		
3	Finished Table	U	U	U	U	U	U	U	U		
4	Billet Stock	U	S	S	S	S	S	S	S		
5	Pocket Milling	U	U	U	S	S	S	S	S		
6	Dia 5 Holes	U	U	U	U	U	S	S	S		
7	Dia 10 Holes	U	U	U	U	U	U	U	S		
8	Chamfer	U	U	U	U	U	U	U	U		
9											

Sheet1

***Figure 19-24** Design table after specifying all configurations and their respective suppression states*

***Figure 19-25** Plate shown in the **Billet Stock** configuration*

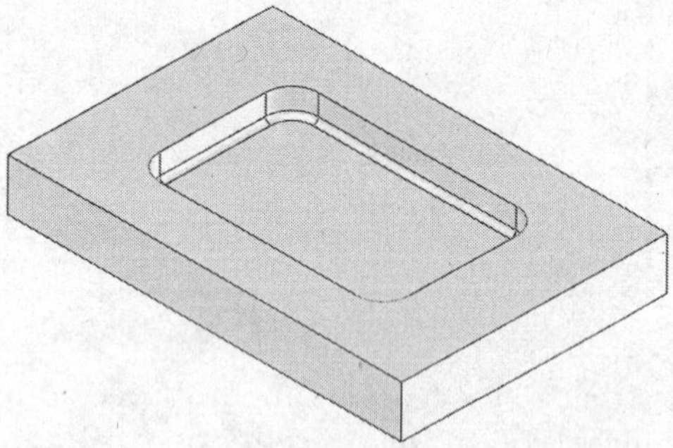

***Figure 19-26** Plate shown in the **Pocket Milling** configuration*

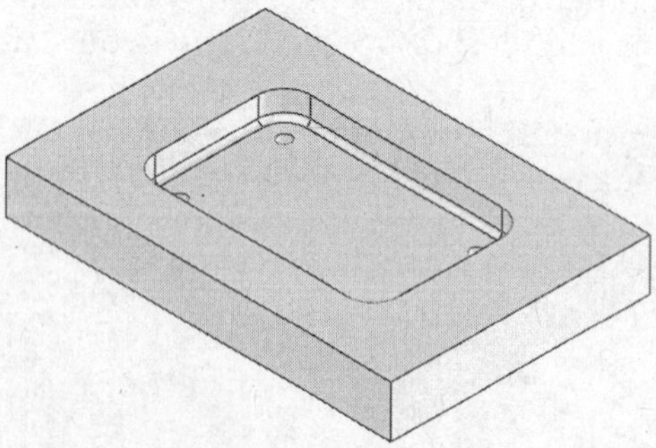

***Figure 19-27** Plate shown in the **Dia 5 Holes** configuration*

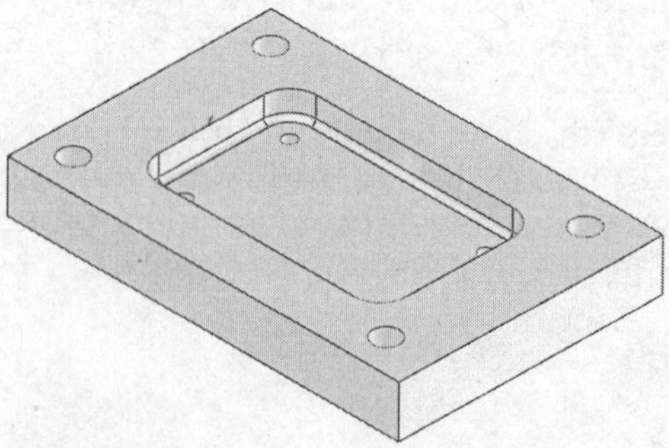

***Figure 19-28** Plate shown in the **Dia 10 Holes** configuration*

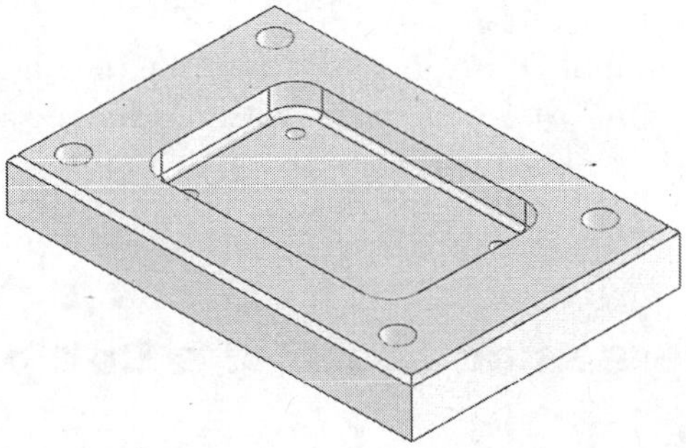

*Figure 19-29 Plate shown in the **Chamfer** configuration*

Editing the Design Table

You can also edit a design table created in the part or the assembly document. To do so, expand the **Tables** node, and then right-click on the **Design Table** icon from the **ConfigurationManager** to invoke the shortcut menu. Choose the **Edit Table** option from the shortcut menu; the **Add Rows and Columns** dialog box will be displayed. If some configurations or parameters are added to the model after creating the design table, those configurations and parameters will be listed in the **Configurations** and **Parameters** areas of the **Add Rows and Columns** dialog box. You can select the parameters or the configurations displayed in this dialog box to be included in the design table and then choose the **OK** button from this dialog box; the part modeling environment will be replaced by the Microsoft Excel application environment and the Microsoft Excel sheet will be displayed in the drawing area. Edit the sheet and then click anywhere in the drawing area to return to the part modeling environment of SOLIDWORKS.

You can also edit the properties of the design table by invoking the **Design Table PropertyManager**. To do so, select the **Design Table** icon from the **ConfigurationManager** and invoke the shortcut menu. Choose the **Edit Feature** option from the shortcut menu; the **Design Table PropertyManager** will be displayed and now you can edit the properties of the design table.

Tip

*1. You can also edit the design table in a separate Microsoft Excel window. To do so, right-click on the **Design Table** icon from the **ConfigurationManager** to invoke the shortcut menu. Choose the **Edit Table in New Window** option from the shortcut menu; a separate Microsoft Excel window will be invoked. After editing the design table, close the excel file; the design table will be updated in SOLIDWORKS.*

*2. You can also save the design table created in the part or the assembly document. To do so, right-click on the design table icon from the **ConfigurationManager** and invoke the shortcut menu. Choose the **Save Table** option from the shortcut menu; the Microsoft Excel sheet will be displayed. If you have updated the model after creating the design table, the **Add Rows and Columns** dialog box will be displayed. Choose the **OK** button in this dialog box; the **Save As** dialog box will be displayed. Enter the file name and select the required location to save the design table.*

Deleting the Design Table

You can also delete the design table if it is not required in a part or assembly document. To do so, select the **Design Table** icon from the **ConfigurationManager** and press the DELETE key; the **Confirm Delete** message box will be displayed. Next, choose the required option from the message box. Note that even if you delete the design table, the configurations created by using it will not be deleted.

Changing the Suppression State of a Component without Invoking the Design Table

In the previous section, you learned to change the suppression state of various features of a component using the design table. However, you can also change the suppression state of a feature without invoking the design table.

To change the suppression state of the features, select them from the **FeatureManager Design Tree** and invoke the shortcut menu. Choose the **Configure Feature** option from the shortcut menu; the **Modify Configurations** window will be displayed with the names of selected features displayed in the columns, as shown in Figure 19-30.

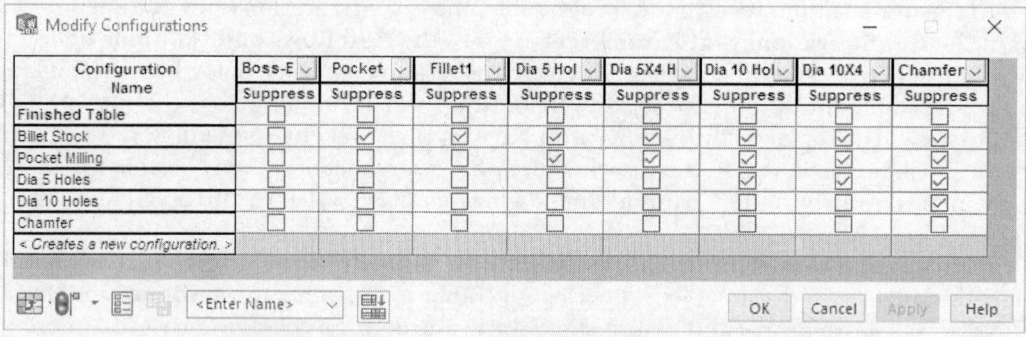

***Figure 19-30** The **Modify Configurations** window*

Click once in the ***<Creates a new configuration.>*** cell, enter a name for the new configuration, and click once in any of the cells; a new row with check boxes will be created for the new configuration. Create some more configurations. Next, to suppress a particular feature in a configuration, select the check box of the corresponding feature, as shown in Figure 19-31. You can also change the dimensions of a feature. Note that the dimensions of a feature refer to the dimensions entered in the PropertyManager while creating the feature and not the dimensions of the sketch. To change the dimensions of a feature, click on the down-arrow in the title bar of a column; a flyout will be displayed with a name. Select the check box next to the name; the dimension will be listed in the **Modify Configurations** window, as shown in Figure 19-32. If needed, you can change the dimensions of the feature in this window. Choose the **OK** button; the configurations will be created and displayed in the **ConfigurationManager**.

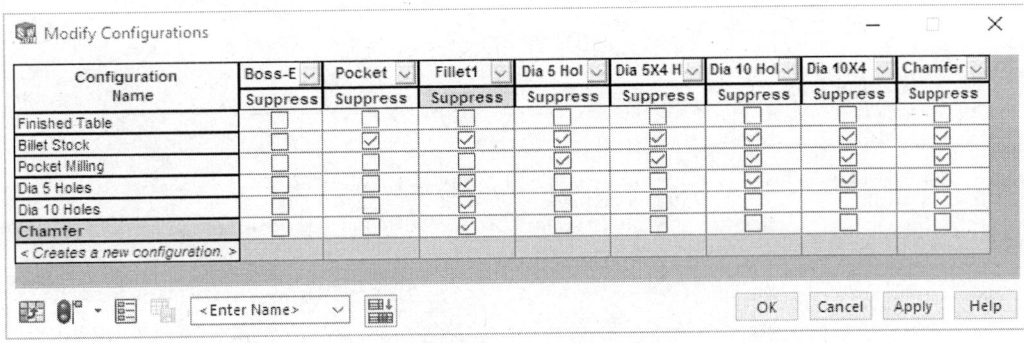

*Figure 19-31 The **Modify Configurations** window after specifying the features to be suppressed in various configurations*

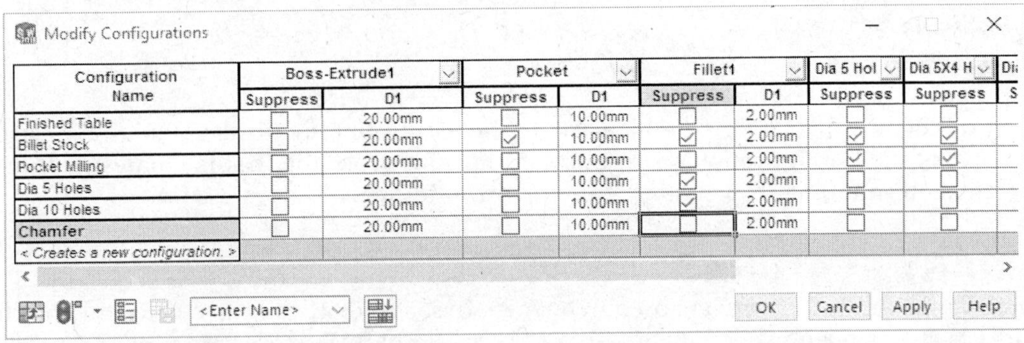

*Figure 19-32 The **Modify Configurations** window after adding dimensions to features*

To change the name of a configuration or to delete a configuration, select the configuration and right-click to invoke the shortcut menu. Choose the corresponding option from the shortcut menu to change the name or to delete the configuration.

To edit a configuration, select the features or a feature and invoke the **Modify Configurations** window. Select or clear the check boxes to modify the configuration and choose **OK**.

Changing the Visibility of Components in Different Configurations of an Assembly

In the **Assembly** mode, you can also change the visibility of components in different configurations. To do so, invoke the **ConfigurationManager**, and then right-click in the **Display States** area; a shortcut menu will be displayed. Choose the **Add Display State** option from the shortcut menu; a new display state will be added. Similarly, you can add as many display states as required. The **Display States** area after adding more display states is shown in Figure 19-33. To change the color, texture, and display state, double-click on a display state and make it active. Next, invoke the **FeatureManager Design Tree** and click on the arrow symbol to display the display pane. Now, change the color, display state, or transparency of a part in the assembly. Similarly, make other display states active and change the corresponding color or transparency. Figure 19-34 shows the display pane with color, transparency, and display mode changed for different parts of an assembly.

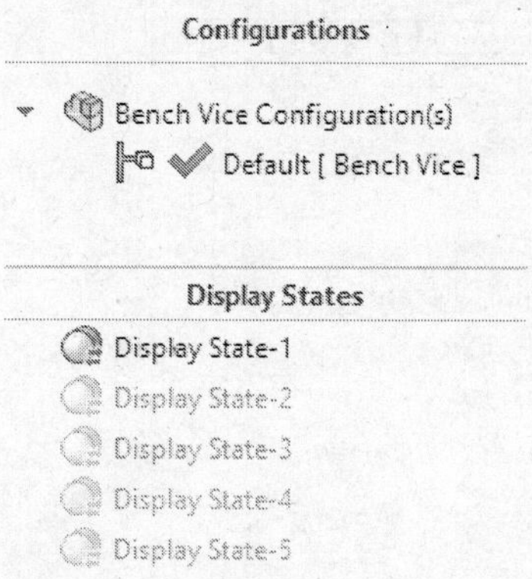

Figure 19-33 The display states created

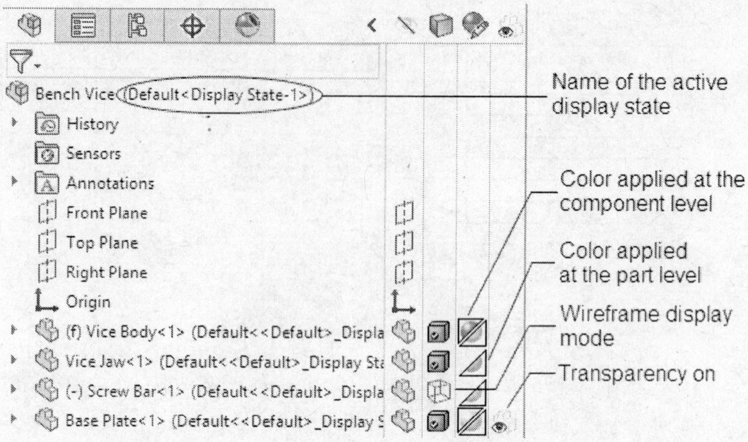

***Figure 19-34** The **FeatureManager Design Tree** with the display pane*

To view different display states, double-click on the corresponding display state in the **Display States** area of the **ConfigurationManager**. Alternatively, invoke the **Display States** toolbar and select the corresponding display state from the drop-down list.

LIBRARY FEATURES

In most designs, some features are used frequently. In such a case, you can create and save those features as library features so that you can use them in a part whenever required. This reduces the time to create the same part or feature repeatedly. In this section, you will learn how to create the library feature, place them in a part, edit them, and dissolve them.

Creating a Library Feature

A library feature is created by saving an existing feature with different file extension. To save a feature as a library feature, you first need to create a base feature and then the feature or features to be added as the library feature. Next, you need to select the features to be added as the library features and then save them with *.sldlfp* file extension.

Consider a case in which you need to save an extruded feature and a fillet feature as a library feature. In this case, first you need to create a base feature. Next, create an extruded feature and add fillets to this feature. After creating the model, select the name of the model from the **FeatureManager Design Tree** and choose the **Add to Library** option from the **Design Library** task pane; the **Add to Library PropertyManager** will be displayed, as shown in Figure 19-35. Also, you will notice that the name of the model is displayed by default in the selection box in the **Items to Add** rollout. Clear the current selection and select the features to be added as the library feature from the **FeatureManager Design Tree**. The extruded feature and fillet feature of the model, as shown in Figure 19-36, are selected as library features.

Specify the name for the library feature in the **File name** edit box of the **Save To** rollout. Then, select the location to save the library feature by expanding the nodes in the **Design Library folder** list box.

Select the **Lib Feat Part (*.sldlfp)** option from the **File type** drop-down list in the **Options** rollout, if it is not selected by default. If you want to give a brief description about the feature, specify it in the **Description** edit box in the **Options** rollout.

Figure 19-35 The Add to Library PropertyManager

Choose **OK** after setting all parameters; the features will be saved as the library features. The features that are selected to be saved as library features will have an **L** symbol displayed on their icons, and the library symbol will be displayed with the name of the part document in the **FeatureManager Design Tree**, as shown in Figure 19-37.

Invoke the **Design Library** task pane and browse to the location where you have saved the library feature to view it.

Note

If the library feature is placed with respect to an entity in a feature in which it has been created, then you need to specify the reference while placing the library feature.

Placing Library Features in a Part

After creating and saving the library features, you can place them in a part document. To place a library feature, invoke the **Design Library** task pane by choosing the **Design Library** tab and browse to the location where you have saved the library feature. Then, drag the feature and drop it on one of the faces of the model; the preview of corresponding library feature will be displayed, as shown in Figure 19-38. If you need to change the placement plane for the library feature, clear the existing placement plane displayed in the **Placement Plane** rollout of the **Library Feature PropertyManager** and select a new placement plane. If the selected library feature has more than one configuration, it will be displayed in the **Configuration** rollout.

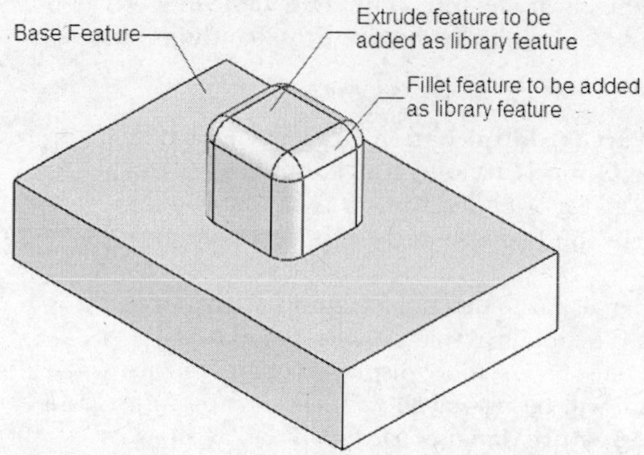

Figure 19-36 *The features to be added as library features*

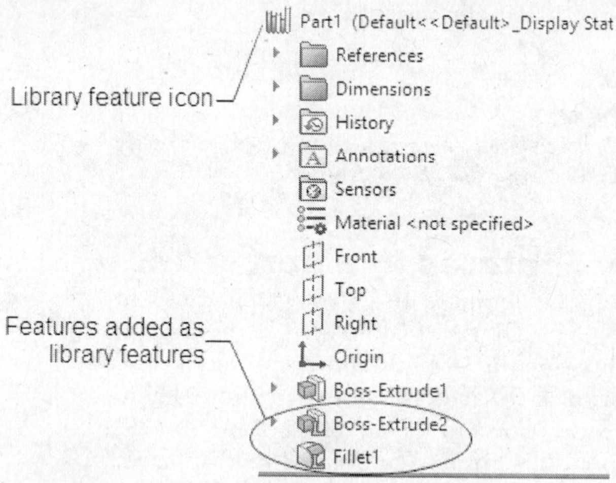

Figure 19-37 *Library icon and the **L** symbol displayed on the feature icons*

On selecting a library feature created with references, the preview of the feature will be displayed in a window. Also, you will be prompted to specify references. If you click in the preview window, the **View (Heads-Up)** toolbar will be displayed and you can view the feature by using the tools in this toolbar. Specify the references in the drawing area; the preview window will disappear and the location of the feature with respect to the selected references will be displayed in the **Locating Dimensions** area of the **Library Feature PropertyManager**.

If the selected library feature does not have any references, the **Location** rollout will be displayed. Choose the **Edit Sketch** button from this rollout and specify the location of the feature.

If you want to modify the existing dimensions of the library feature, select the **Override dimension values** check box in the **Size Dimensions** rollout and modify the values. The modified feature will be displayed with the name **Custom configuration** in the **Configuration** rollout.

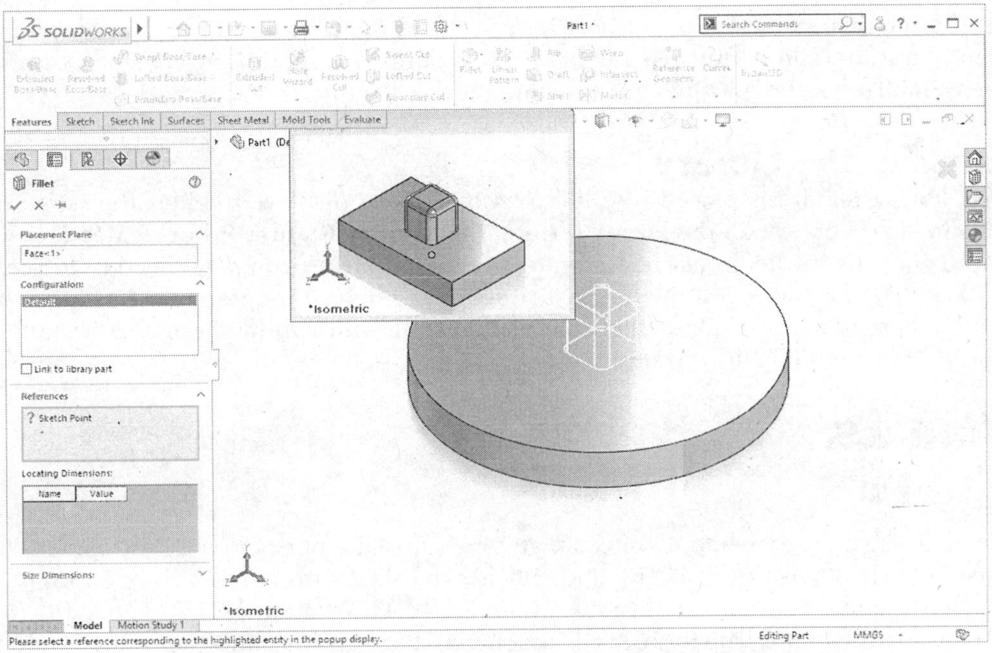

Figure 19-38 The preview of the liberary feature placed on the part

If you select the **Link to library part** check box in the **Configuration** rollout, the references of the library feature will be saved in the part. Therefore, if you modify the library feature, the modification will be reflected in the model. Figure 19-39 shows the library feature placed on the top face of the model.

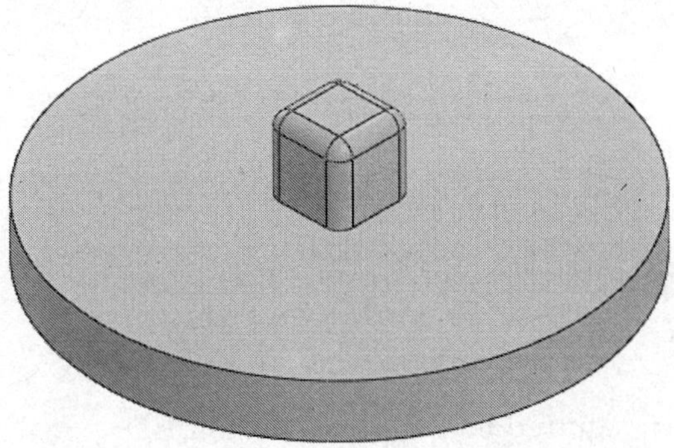

Figure 19-39 Library feature placed on the top face of the model

Editing the Library Features

You can edit or change the features included in the library feature part document. To remove a library feature from the library, select that library feature from the **Design Library** task pane. Now, invoke the shortcut menu and choose the **Delete** option from it. If you need to edit the library feature, select the feature from the **Design Library** task pane. Next, invoke the shortcut menu and then, choose the **Open** option from it; the part document of the library feature will open. Edit the feature and save it. If you have selected the **Link to library part** check box in the **Configuration** rollout while placing the library feature, the modification made in the library feature will reflect in the document in which the library feature is placed.

Dissolving the Library Features

When a library feature is placed, the library icon will be displayed before the name of the feature. So, if you try to edit the library feature, the **Library Feature PropertyManager** will be displayed. To convert the library feature into a separate part feature, you need to dissolve the library feature. To do so, select the library feature from the **Feature Manager Design Tree** and invoke the shortcut menu. Choose the **Dissolve Library Feature** option from the shortcut menu; the library feature will be dissolved into individual features.

TUTORIALS

Tutorial 1

In this tutorial, you will open the sketch created in Tutorial 3 of Chapter 2, add dimensions to the sketch, as shown in Figure 19-40, and extrude the sketch up to a depth of **50** mm. Then, you will add equations to the dimensions of the sketch. The dimension **150** will be the driving dimension. While adding equations, you can change the vertical dimensions **20** and **40** to **25** and **50**, respectively, for the convenience of calculation.

(Expected time: 30 min)

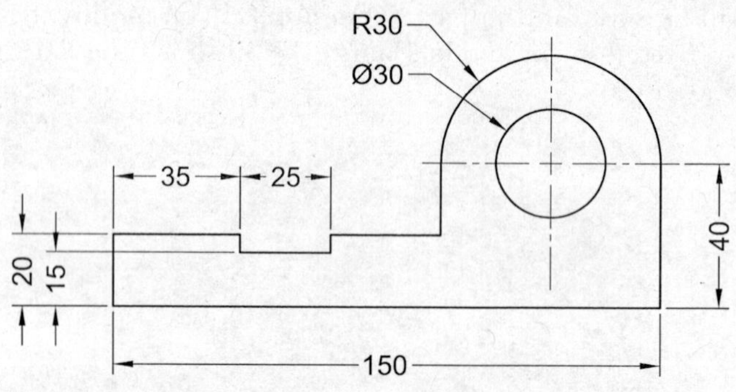

Figure 19-40 *Sketch for Tutorial 1*

The following steps are required to complete this tutorial:

a. Start SOLIDWORKS and Open Tutorial 3 of Chapter 2.
b. Extrude the sketch to a depth of **50** mm.
c. Edit dimensions and add equations using the **Equations** tool.
d. Save the model.

Opening Tutorial 3 of Chapter 2 and Creating an Extrude Feature

1. Start SOLIDWORKS and open Tutorial 3 of Chapter 2.

2. Add relations and dimensions to fully define the sketch, refer to Figure 19-40.

3. Extrude the sketch up to a depth of **50** mm.

4. Choose the **Save As** button and save the model with the name *c19_tut01*.

Adding Equations to the Dimensions in the Sketch

For this model, you will keep the horizontal dimension 150 as the driving dimension and other dimensions as the driven dimensions. Also, you will change the vertical dimensions to **25** mm and **50** mm to ease the calculation.

1. Invoke the sketching environment to edit the sketch of the base feature, double-click on the vertical dimensions in succession, and change the dimension values from **20** to **25** and **40** to **50**.

2. Choose the **Equations** button from the **Tools** toolbar; the **Equations, Global Variables, and Dimensions** dialog box is displayed.

3. Click on the empty cell of the **Global Variables** node under the **Name** column and enter **Length** as the name for the global variable, refer to Figure 19-41. Next, click on the corresponding empty cell in the **Value / Equation** column and select the dimension with value **150** from the drawing area. Now, add a comment to the global variable added in the respective cell under the **Comments** column.

4. Now, click on the empty cell of the **Equations** node under the **Name** column.

5. Select the radius value **30** from the drawing area; the name of the selected dimension is displayed in the selected cell.

6. Next, select the horizontal dimension value **150** from the drawing area; the name of the selected dimension is displayed in the **Value / Equation** column with a green colored check mark.

7. Press the forward slash (/) key and enter **5**; the equation will become **"D2@Sketch1" = "D1@Sketch1" / 5**, where **D2@Sketch1** = 30 and **D1@Sketch1** = 150. The names of the dimensions can be different as they are based on the sequence in which the dimensions are applied to the sketch.

8. Next, click on the corresponding cell in the **Comments** column; the value **30** mm is displayed in the **Evaluates to** column and a new empty cell under the **Equations** node will be displayed. Next, you need to enter **Radius** in the corresponding cell in the **Comments** column.

   Note that you can also use global variables while adding equations.

9. Similarly, click on the empty cell of the **Equations** node under the **Name** column and select the diameter value **30** from the drawing area; the name of the selected dimension is displayed in the **Name** column.

10. Select the horizontal dimension value **150** from the drawing area; the name of the selected dimension is displayed in the **Value / Equation** column with a green colored check mark.

11. Press the forward slash (/) key and enter **5**; the equation becomes **"D3@Sketch1" = "D1@Sketch1" / 5**, where **D3@Sketch1** = 30 and **D1@Sketch1** = 150.

12. Next, click on the corresponding cell of the **Comments** column; the value **30** mm is displayed in the **Evaluates to** column. Next, you need to enter **Diameter** in the corresponding cell of the **Comments** column.

13. Similarly, add equations to all dimensions given below.

Dimension to be selected	Equation to be added	Comment
Vertical dimension 25	150/6	Height
50	150/3	Hole location
35	150/30*7	Slot location
Horizontal dimension 25	150/6	Slot
15	150/10	Slot depth

14. Resize the **Equations, Global Variables, and Dimensions** dialog box, if required. The dialog box after adding all the equations is shown in Figure 19-41.

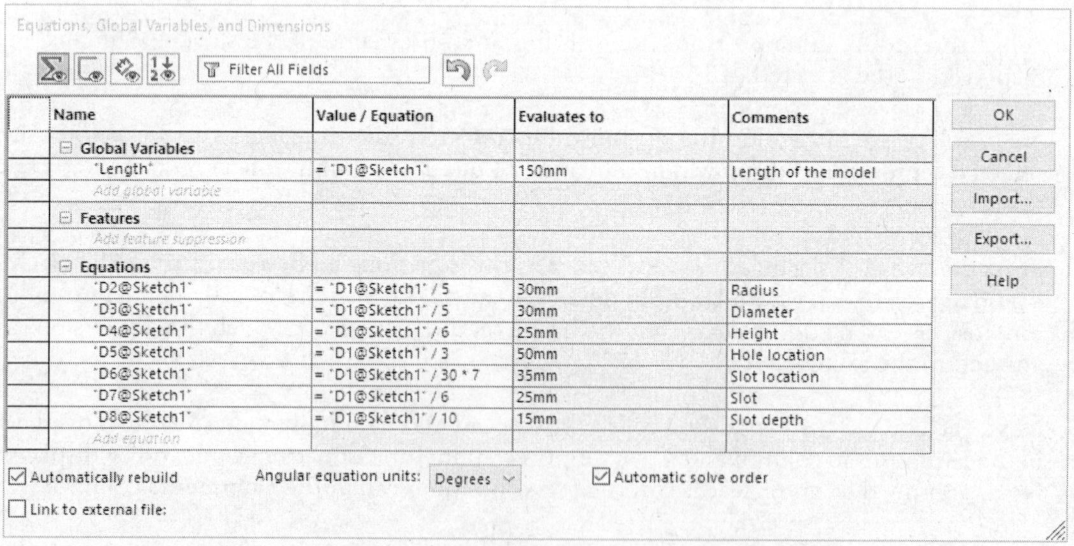

*Figure 19-41 The **Equations, Global Variables, and Dimensions** dialog box after adding all equations*

15. Choose the **OK** button from the dialog box; the dimensions are displayed in the sketch environment with the equation symbol ($\sum$). Also, the **Equations** folder is added to the **FeatureManager Design Tree**. Next, exit the sketch environment.

Adding Equation to the Extrude Feature

Next, you need to add equation to the extrude feature such that the equation is controlled by the horizontal dimension value **150**.

1. Right-click on the **Equations** folder in the **FeatureManager Design Tree**; a shortcut menu is displayed. Choose the **Manage Equations** option from it; the **Equations, Global Variables, and Dimensions** dialog box is displayed.

2. Click on the model in the drawing area; the dimensions of the sketch and the feature are displayed.

3. Next, click on the empty cell of the **Equations** node under the **Name** column and select the dimension value **50** which is the dimension of the extrude feature.

4. Select the horizontal dimension value **150** in the drawing area. Next, press the forward slash (/) and enter **3** in the cell corresponding to this dimension value in the **Equations** node, refer to Figure 19-42.

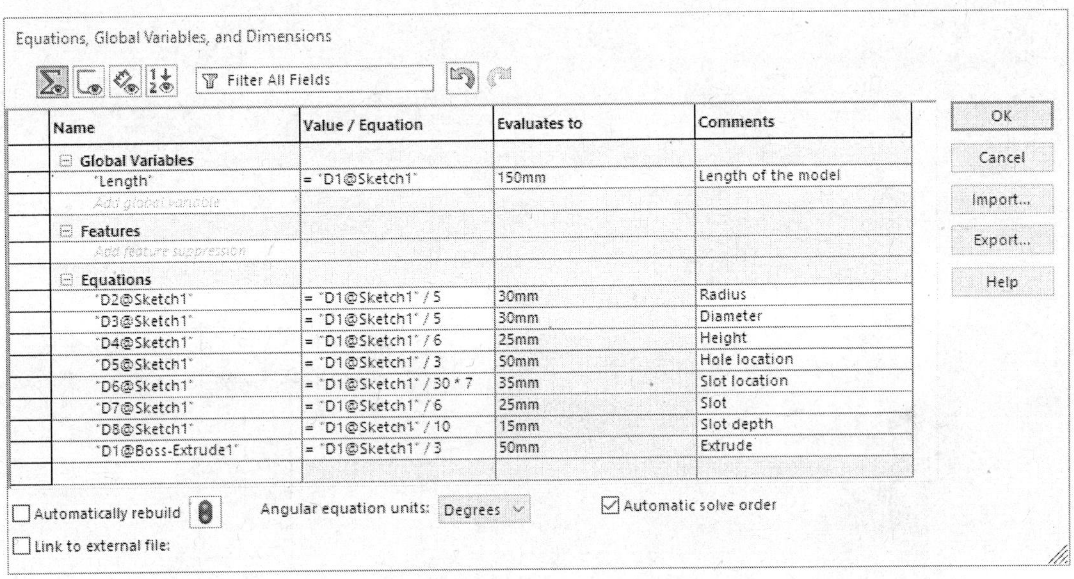

Figure 19-42 The ***Equations, Global Variables, and Dimensions*** *dialog box after adding equations to extrude feature*

5. Click and enter **Extrude** in the corresponding cell of the **Comments** column.

6. Choose the **OK** button to exit the dialog box.

Changing the Dimensions of the Model

1. Double-click on the model; all dimensions of the model are displayed.
2. Double-click on the dimensional value **150** and enter **300** in the text box.
3. Rebuild the model; all the dimensions of the model are modified.

Note

For convenience, all dimensions are in round figures. However, you can add any mathematical relation to a feature/dimension, but make sure that it does not override the design intent of the model.

4. Save and close the document by choosing **File > Close** from the SOLIDWORKS menus.

Tutorial 2

In this tutorial, you will create the Socket Head Screw shown in Figure 19-43. Assume the base diameter of the screw **d** as **30** mm. Add equations to the model, as shown in Figure 19-44. Then, create different configurations by changing the base diameter to **20** mm, **50** mm, **40** mm, and **5** mm and the other related parameters with respect to the relations given in Figure 19-44.

(Expected time: 30 min)

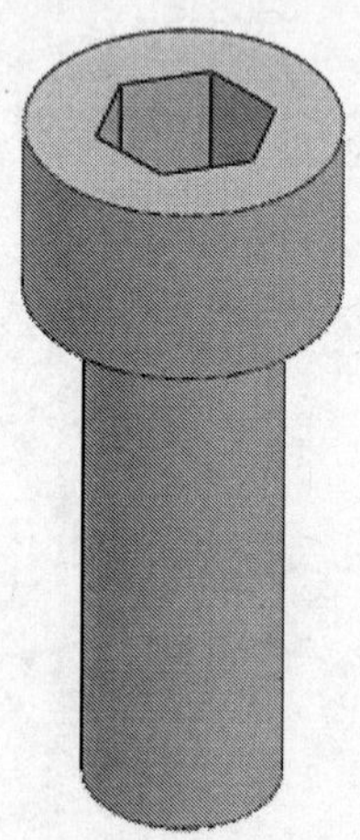

Figure 19-43 *Socket Head Screw*

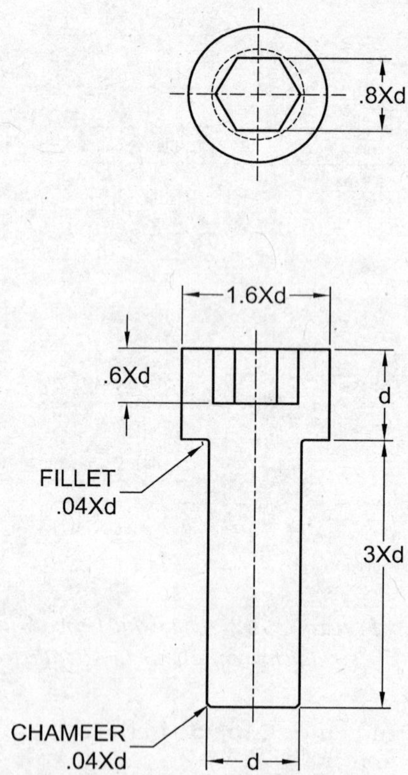

Figure 19-44 *Parameters of the Socket Head Screw*

The following steps are required to complete this tutorial:

a. Create the socket head screw using the **Revolved Boss/Base** and **Extruded Cut** tools.
b. Create different configurations using the design table.
c. Save the model.

Creating the Socket Head Screw

1. Start a new SOLIDWORKS document and draw the sketch of the base feature. The base feature is created by revolving the sketch about **360** degrees. Do not create fillet and chamfer.

2. Dimension the sketch based on the relations given in Figure 19-44. While placing the dimensions, you need to change the name of the dimensions in the **Primary Value** rollout of the **Dimension PropertyManager**. Refer to Figure 19-45 for the names of dimensions.

3. Create the base feature using the **Revolved Boss/Base** tool.

4. Draw a hexagon on the top face of the base feature and dimension it. Change the name of the dimension, as shown in Figure 19-45.

5. Create the hexagonal cut on the base feature using the **Extruded Cut** tool.

6. Add fillets and chamfers to the model.

7. Save the model with the name *c19_tut02* in the folder created for Chapter 19.

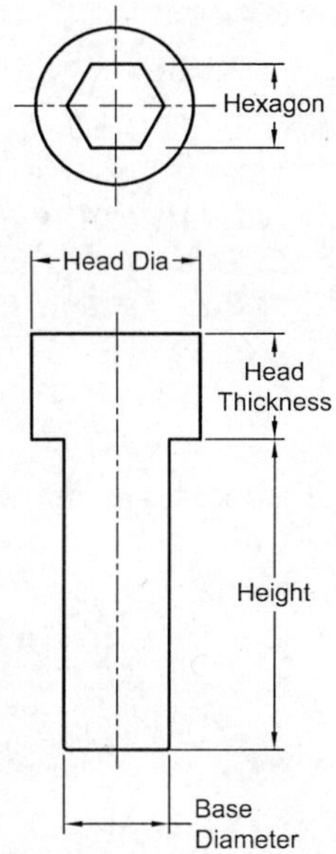

Figure 19-45 *The names of dimensions*

Creating Configurations Using the Design Table

Next, you need to create the Socket Head Screw of the same geometry with different dimensions using the **Design Table**.

1. Choose **Insert > Tables > Design Table** from the SOLIDWORKS menus; the **Design Table PropertyManager** is displayed.

2. Select the **Auto-create** radio button from the **Source** rollout. Make sure that the **Allow model edits to update the design table** radio button and all other check boxes in the **Design Table PropertyManager** are selected.

3. Choose the **OK** button from the **Design Table PropertyManager**; the **Dimensions** dialog box is displayed.

4. Next, press and hold the CTRL key and select the names of all the dimensions, except the **D1@Revolve1**, **D1@Fillet1**, and **D1@Chamfer1**, from the list box in the **Dimensions** dialog box. These names correspond to the revolve, fillet, and chamfer features respectively.

5. Choose **OK** from the **Dimensions** dialog box; the design table with default dimensions is displayed, as shown in Figure 19-46.

6. Enter **20x60**, **50x150**, **40x120**, and **5x15** as the names of the new instances in the **A4**, **A5**, **A6**, and **A7** cells, respectively.

Note

*If you click in the drawing area, the design table will disappear. To display it again, invoke the **ConfigurationManager**, right-click on the **Design Table** node, and then choose the **Edit Table** option from the shortcut menu.*

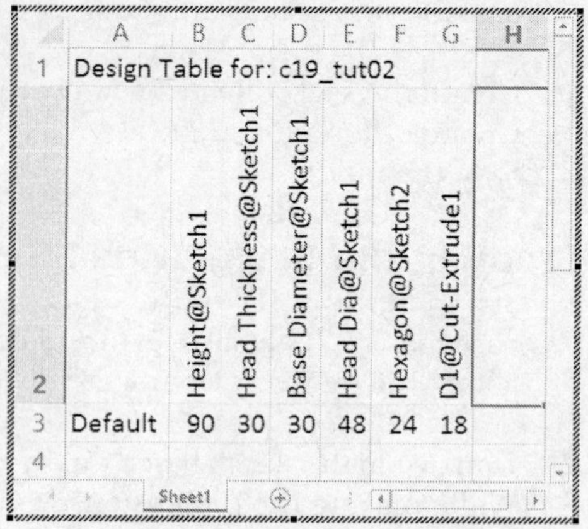

	A	B	C	D	E	F	G	H
1	Design Table for: c19_tut02							
2		Height@Sketch1	Head Thickness@Sketch1	Base Diameter@Sketch1	Head Dia@Sketch1	Hexagon@Sketch2	D1@Cut-Extrude1	
3	Default	90	30	30	48	24	18	
4								

Figure 19-46 The design table with the default dimensions

7. In the **A3** cell, change the **Default** name to **30x90**.

8. Enter the dimensions for the new instances with respect to the equations shown in Figure 19-44. The Excel sheet after adding the dimensions is shown in Figure 19-47.

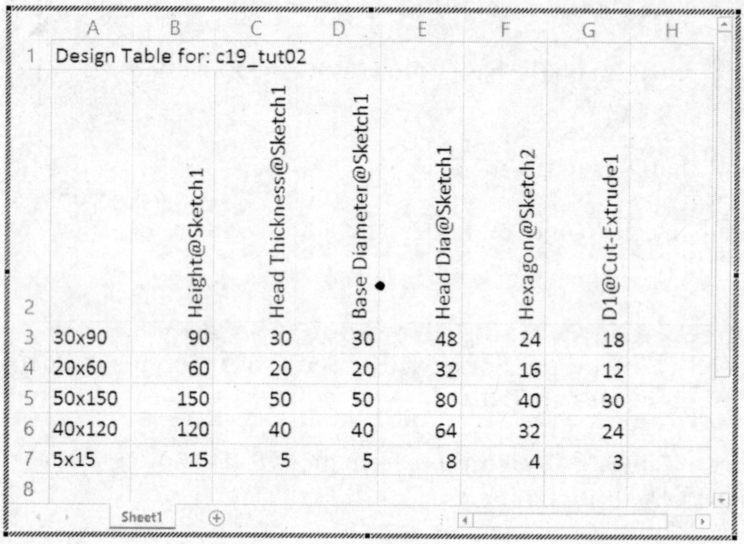

	A	B	C	D	E	F	G	H
1	Design Table for: c19_tut02							
2		Height@Sketch1	Head Thickness@Sketch1	Base Diameter@Sketch1	Head Dia@Sketch1	Hexagon@Sketch2	D1@Cut-Extrude1	
3	30x90	90	30	30	48	24	18	
4	20x60	60	20	20	32	16	12	
5	50x150	150	50	50	80	40	30	
6	40x120	120	40	40	64	32	24	
7	5x15	15	5	5	8	4	3	
8								

***Figure 19-47** The new instances and their dimensions*

9. Click anywhere in the drawing area; the **SOLIDWORKS** message box with the names of the configurations created is displayed.

10. Choose **OK** in the message box.

11. Add equations to the fillet and chamfer dimensions using the **Equations** dialog box, as specified in Figure 19-44.

12. Invoke the **ConfigurationManager**; the configurations created are listed in it. Double-click on a configuration to make it active.

13. Save and close the document by choosing **File > Close** from the SOLIDWORKS menus.

Self-Evaluation Test

Answer the following questions and then compare them to those given at the end of this chapter:

1. Which of the following PropertyManagers is used to create a design table?

   (a) **Design Table** (b) **Create Design Table**
   (c) **Physical Dynamics** (d) None of these

2. The __________ radio button is selected by default in the **Source** rollout when you invoke the **Design Table PropertyManager**.

3. Choose the __________ option from the shortcut menu to dissolve a library feature.

4. The features to be added as library features are saved with the __________ file extension.

5. You can add mathematical relations between model dimensions or sketch dimensions by using the **Equations** tool. (T/F)

6. You can edit the equations added to a design by using the **Equations, Global Variables, and Dimensions** dialog box. (T/F)

7. You can suppress the equations that are not required at a particular stage. (T/F)

8. Configurations help you create multiple instances of a part or an assembly within a single SOLIDWORKS document. (T/F)

9. You can change the suppression state of the features of a component using the design table. (T/F)

10. You cannot suppress the feature of a configuration without using the design table. (T/F)

Review Questions

Answer the following questions:

1. Which of the following should be invoked to change the color, texture, and display state of a configuration?

   (a) Display pane in the **FeatureManager**
   (b) Display pane in the **PropertyManager**
   (c) Display pane in the **ConfigurationManager**
   (d) None of these

2. If you try to edit a library feature, the **Library Feature PropertyManager** will be displayed. (T/F)

3. You can place the library feature only in an empty SOLIDWORKS part document after including the base feature into the library feature. (T/F)

4. You can preview a configuration in the **ConfigurationManager** even if it has not been opened and saved once. (T/F)

5. You can create only one design table in a part or assembly document. (T/F)

6. You need to suppress an equation to modify the corresponding driven dimension. (T/F)

7. You can invoke the **Equations, Global Variables, and Dimensions** dialog box by using the **Equations** node in the **FeatureManager Design Tree**. (T/F)

8. If library feature is placed with respect to an entity in the feature in which it has been created, then you need to specify reference while placing the library feature. (T/F)

9. You can also change the visibility of components in different configurations. (T/F)

10. You can drag and drop a specific configuration from the **ConfigurationManager** to an assembly or a drawing document. (T/F)

EXERCISES

Exercise 1

Create the model shown in Figure 19-48. The dimensions of the model are shown in Figure 19-49. Extrude the sketch up to a depth of **20** mm. Then, add equations to the dimensions of the sketch and the feature. The dimension **80** will be the driving dimension. While adding equations, it is suggested to change the dimensions **30** and **15** to **40** and **20**, respectively, for the convenience of calculation. **(Expected time: 30 min)**

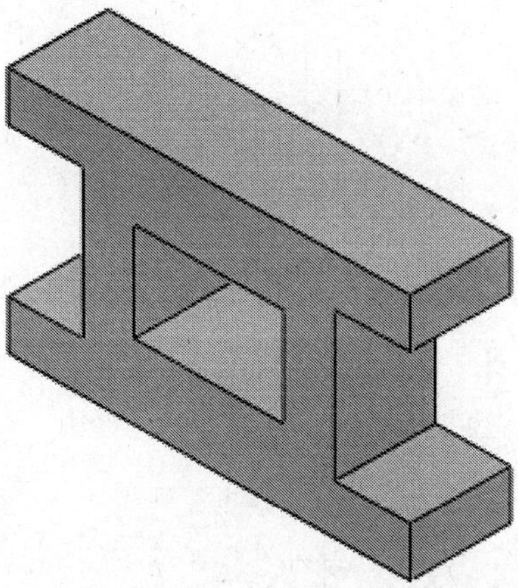

Figure 19-48 *Solid model for Exercise 1*

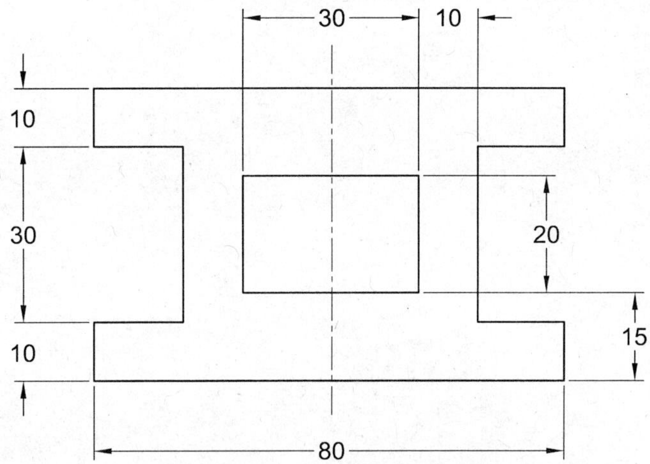

Figure 19-49 *Dimensions of the model*

Exercise 2

Draw the sketch of the model shown in Figure 19-50. The sketch to be drawn is shown in Figure 19-51. Extrude the sketch up to a depth of **20** mm. Then, add equations to the dimensions of the sketch and the feature. **(Expected time: 30 min)**

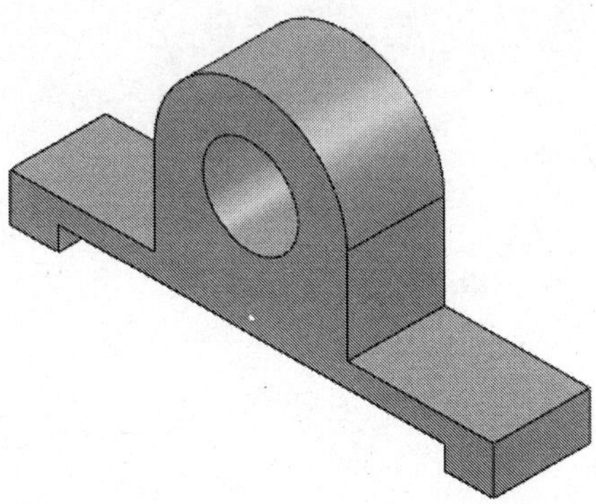

Figure 19-50 *Solid model for Exercise 2*

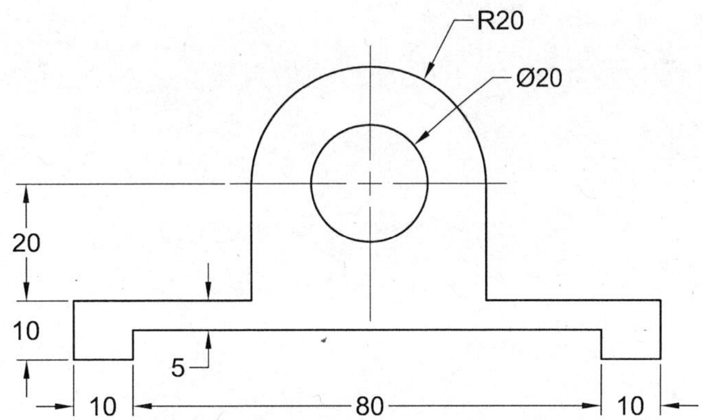

Figure 19-51 *Sketch for Exercise 2*

Exercise 3

Create the Cheese Head Screw shown in Figure 19-52. Assume the base diameter of the screw, **d** as **25** mm. Create the model by using the relations shown in Figure 19-53. Then, create different configurations by changing the base diameter to **20** mm, **15** mm, **12** mm, and **6** mm. Create other related parameters with respect to the relations given in Figure 19-53.

(Expected time: 30 min)

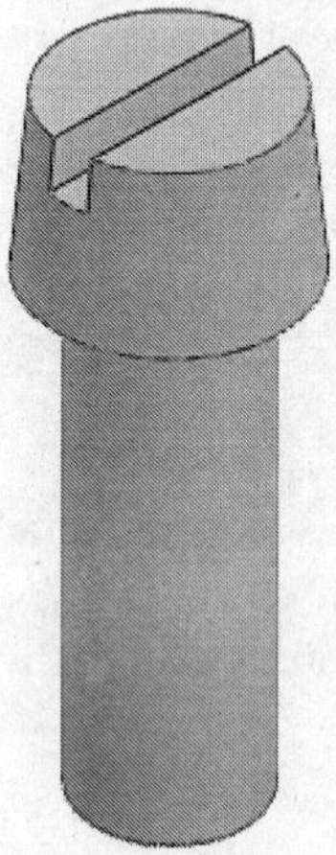

***Figure 19-52** The Cheese Head Screw*

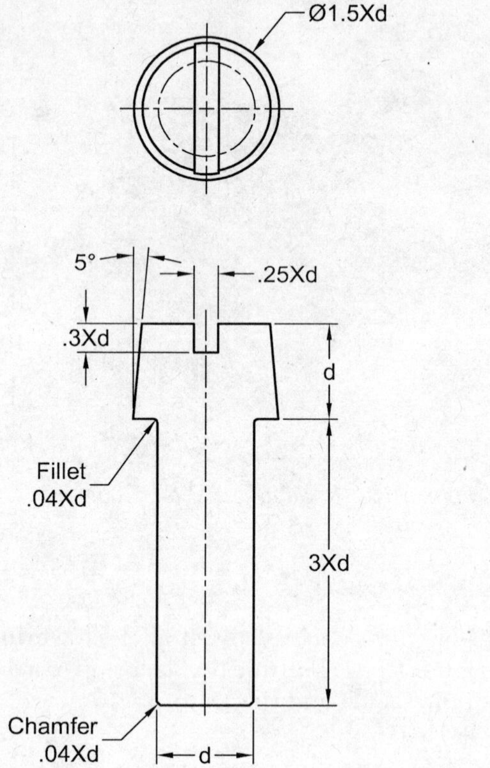

***Figure 19-53** Parameters of the Cheese Head Screw*

Answers to Self-Evaluation Test

1. a, **2. Auto-create, 3. Dissolve Library Feature, 4.** *.sldlfp*, **5.** T, **6.** T, **7.** T, **8.** T, **9.** T, **10.** F

Chapter 20

Motion Study

Learning Objectives

After completing this chapter, you will be able to:

- *Understand the concept of motion study*
- *Understand the interface of motion study*
- *Create various types of motions in assembly*
- *Modify properties of motion study setup*

INTRODUCTION TO MOTION STUDY

Motion study is used to simulate the motion of the assembly components. In SOLIDWORKS, you can use the **MotionManager**, a time-line based interface, for defining the simulation of motion of an assembly. Note that the properties of the assembly being simulated will remain intact. The two types of motion studies are: Basic Motion and Animation.

Basic Motion

In the Basic Motion study, the motion between various components of an assembly can be defined by physical conditions such as motor, spring, gravity, and contact. To specify the physical conditions, you can use the tools such as **Motor**, **Spring**, **Gravity**, and **Contact**, available in the **MotionManager**.

Animation

In the Animation study, the motion between various components of an assembly is defined by assembly mates, free hand drag, and triad (for positioning). Also, you can use the key frames to animate a model.

SIMULATING THE MOTION OF AN ASSEMBLY

In SOLIDWORKS, you can simulate the motion of an assembly by using the **MotionManager**. To invoke the **MotionManager**, click on the **Motion Study 1** tab available below the graphics area, refer to Figure 20-1; the **MotionManager** will be displayed, as shown in Figure 20-1. Before you start simulating the assembly, it is important to understand the components of **MotionManager**. These components are discussed next.

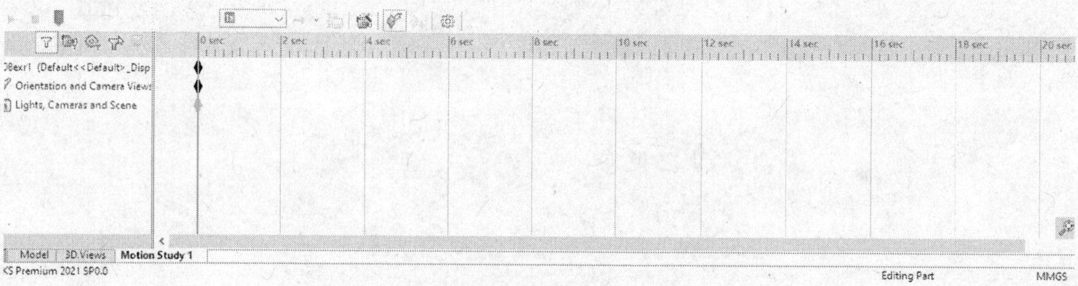

***Figure 20-1** The MotionManager*

Timeline

The Timeline is used to specify the duration for the motion. The time taken for a complete motion will be highlighted in yellow color on the timeline. You can view the movement of the components at a specific time by clicking on the corresponding position in the timeline.

Timebar

This is a vertical gray line which is used to represent the current position of the components on the time scale, while in motion.

Keypoint

Keypoints are used to represent the start and end of the changing phase of the components in the motion. The space elapsed between two key points is called key frame.

MotionManager Design Tree

The **MotionManager Design Tree** controls various settings related to the camera, components of assembly, orientation of the model, mates applied on the components, and so on. The settings of **MotionManager Design Tree** will be discussed later in this chapter.

Toolbar

The toolbar in the **MotionManager** consists of various tools and options to perform the motion study of an assembly, refer to Figure 20-2. These tools and options are discussed next.

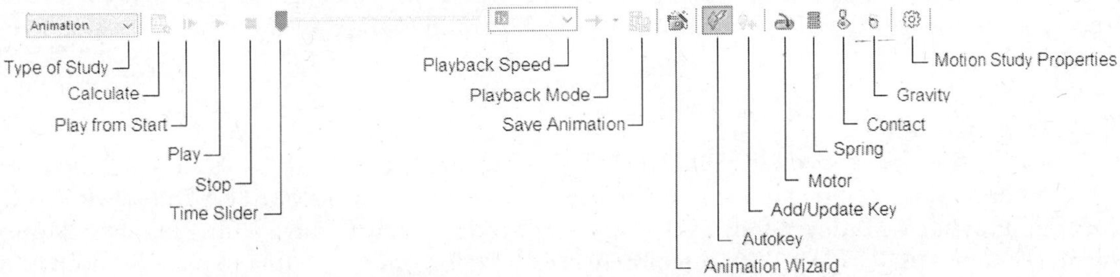

Figure 20-2 The toolbar in the ***MotionManager***

Type of Study

The options in this drop-down list are used to specify the type of study that you want to perform. There are three options available in this drop-down list: **Animation**, **Basic Motion** and **Motion Analysis**. By default, the **Motion Analysis** option will not be available in the **Type of Study** drop-down list. To make it available, select **Solidworks Motion** from **Solidworks Add-ins CommandManager**.

Calculate

This button is used to generate simulation of an assembly under some specified conditions. Note that every time you change the parameters related to an assembly motion study, you need to choose the **Calculate** button to simulate the assembly according to the new parameters.

Play from Start

This button is used to start the animation of current asssembly from the beginning.

Play

This button is used to play simulation from the last position in the timeline. Note that when you modify the parameters during the simulation and choose the **Play** button, the changes will not be reflected in the simulation. To play the simulation with the modified parameters, you need to choose the **Calculate** button.

Stop

This button is used to pause a simulation at a specific position.

Time Slider

This slider is used to jump to a specific point of time in the animation. To do so, click at the location in the slider. Alternatively, you can drag the dragger in the time slider to a specific location.

Playback Speed

This drop-down list is used to specify the speed multiplier. The speed multiplier is the factor by which you increase or decrease the playback speed of animation. You can select an option from the predefined list or you can enter the desired multiplier number followed by x.

Playback Mode

The options available in the **Playback Mode** drop-down list are used to define the direction of animation. There are three options available in this drop-down list: **Playback Mode: Normal**, **Playback Mode: Loop**, and **Playback Mode: Reciprocate**. The **Playback Mode: Normal** option is used to play the animation in one direction only. Note that to play the animation again, you need to choose the **Play** button. The **Playback Mode: Loop** option is used to play the animation in a closed loop. Note that after completing the path, the animation will start again from the initial position automatically. The **Playback Mode: Reciprocate** option is used to play the animation in reciprocating manner. After completing the path, the animation will start again in the reverse direction.

Save Animation

This button is used to save the current animation. To do so, choose the **Save Animation** button from the **MotionManager** toolbar; the **Save Animation to File** dialog box will be displayed, as shown in Figure 20-3. After specifying the options in the dialog box, choose the **Save** button; the **Video Compression** dialog box will be displayed, as shown in Figure 20-4. The options available in the **Video Compression** dialog box are used to specify the type of compressor, Compression Quality, and number of Key Frames. After specifying the required parameters, choose the **OK** button from the dialog box; the **SOLIDWORKS** message box will be displayed as shown in Figure 20-5. In the dialog box, choose the **Yes** button to recalculate the results; the file will be saved with the calculated results.

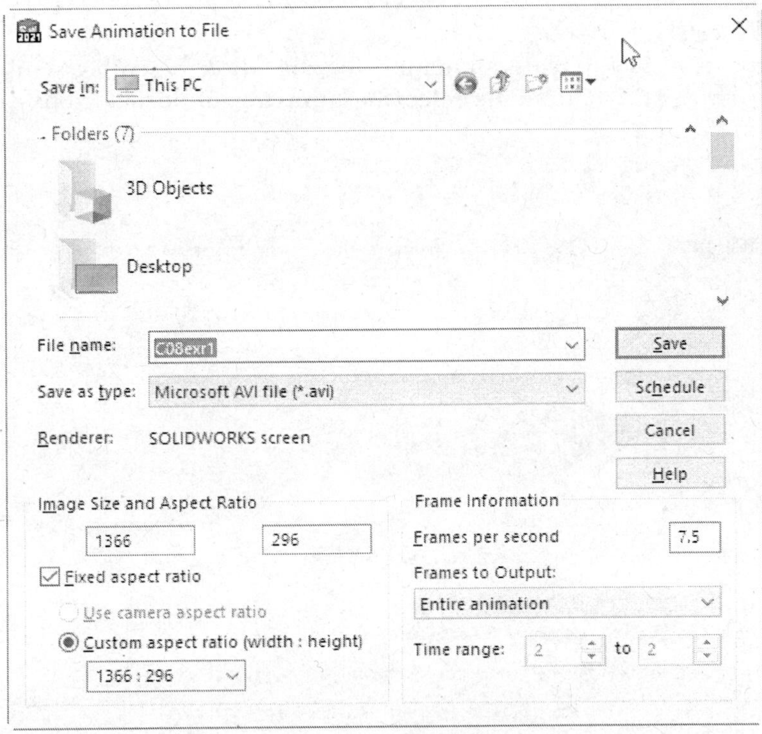

Figure 20-3 The ***Save Animation to File*** *dialog box*

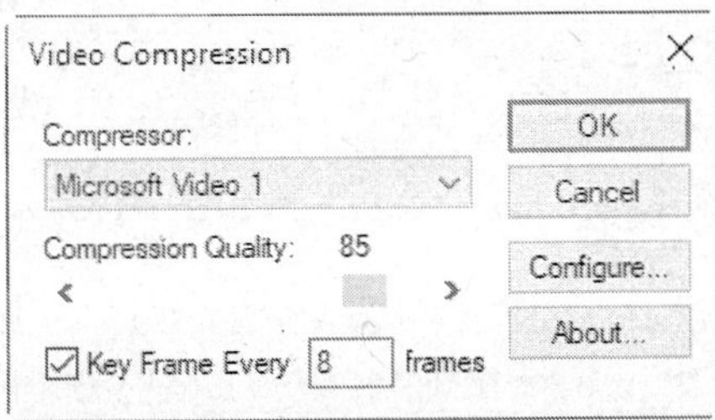

Figure 20-4 The ***Video Compression*** *dialog box*

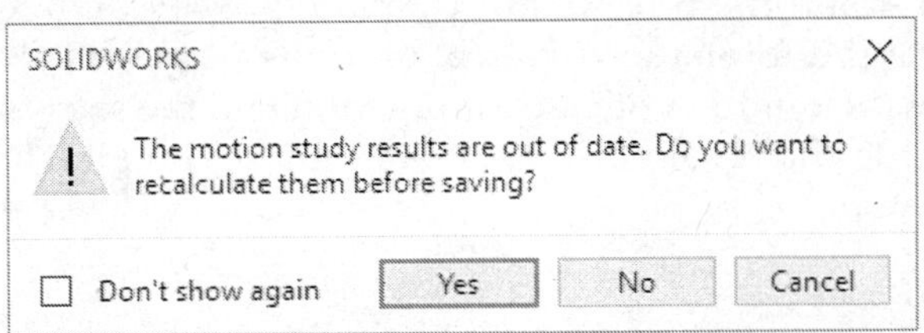

Figure 20-5 The ***SOLIDWORKS*** *message box*

Animation Wizard

This button is used to create animation for the whole assembly setup. To create an animation, choose this button; the **Select an Animation Type** dialog box will be displayed, as shown in Figure 20-6.

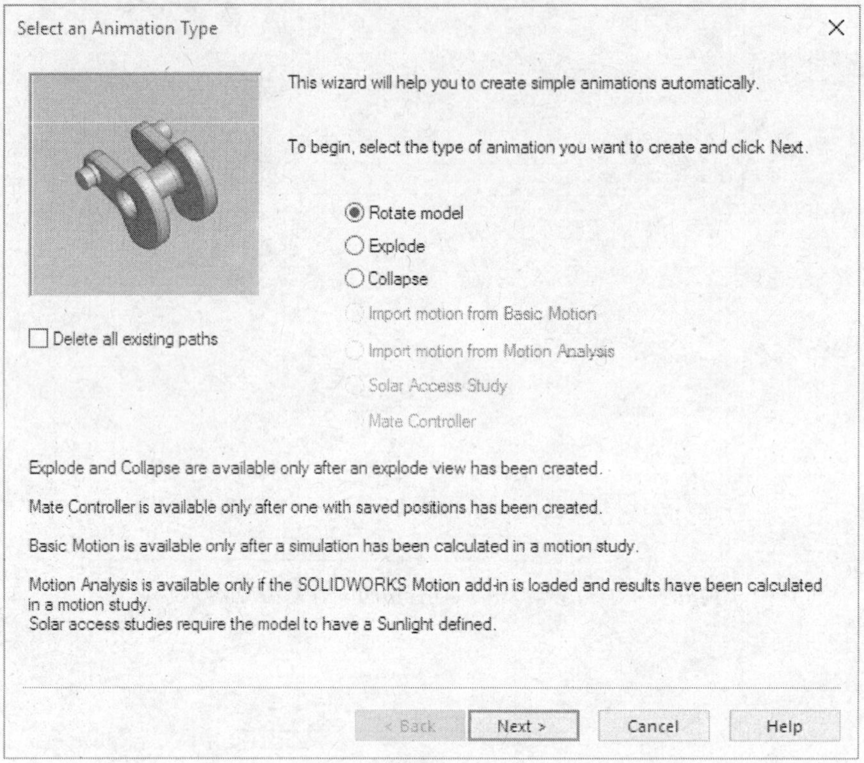

***Figure 20-6** The **Select an Animation Type** dialog box*

Using the radio buttons available in the **Select an Animation Type** dialog box, an assembly can be rotated, exploded, collapsed, and so on. You can select the required radio button from the dialog box. By default, the **Rotate model** radio button is selected in the dialog box. Therefore, when you choose the **Next** button, the **Select an Axis of Rotation** page of the dialog box will be displayed, as shown in Figure 20-7. In the dialog box, you can specify the axis of rotation, the number of rotations, and the direction of rotation. Specify the required parameters and choose the **Next** button; the **Animation Control Options** page will be displayed, as shown in Figure 20-8. You can set the duration of entire animation and the start time of the animation in this page. After specifying the required parameters, choose the **Finish** button; the animation will be applied to the setup.

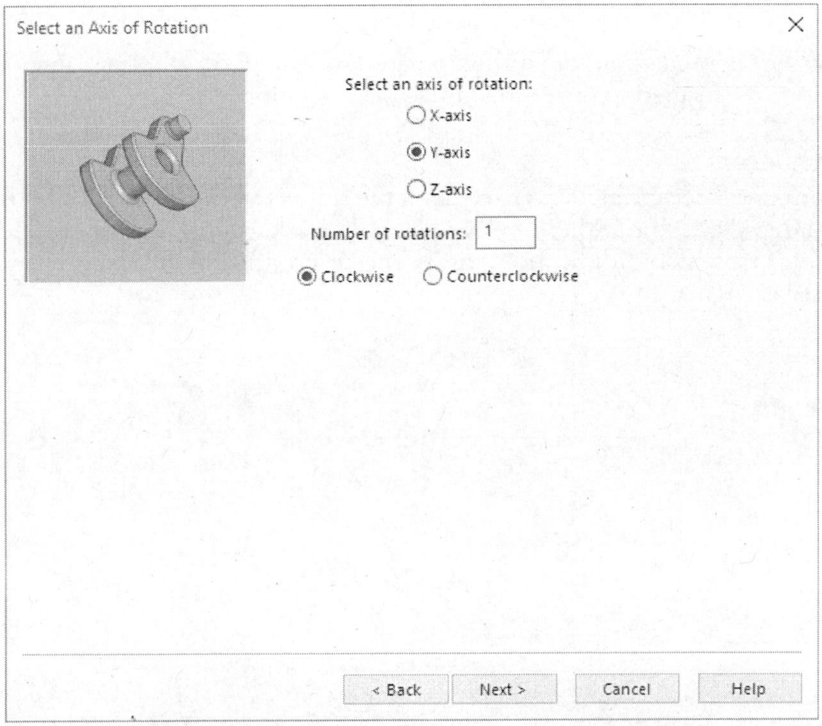

Figure 20-7 *The* ***Select an Axis of Rotation*** *page*

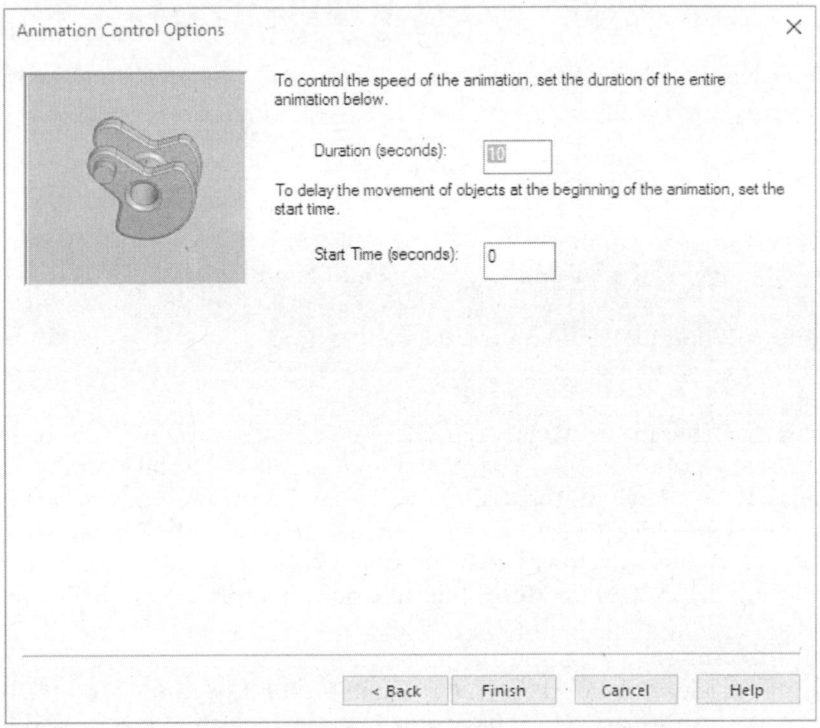

Figure 20-8 *The* ***Animation Control Options*** *page*

Autokey

This button is used to automatically create key points on the time line, based on the operations performed in order to animate the assembly.

Add/Update Key

This button will be activated after selecting the respective part. You can choose this button to add a new keypoint to the time line or update a keypoint that was created earlier. To add a keypoint, right-click on the time line at the desired location; a shortcut menu will be displayed, refer to Figure 20-9.

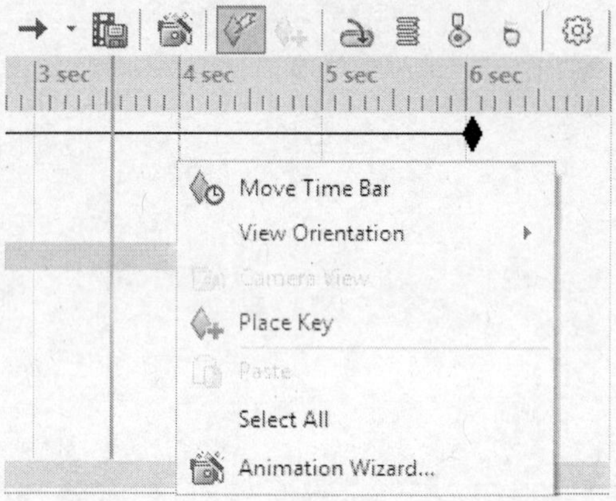

Figure 20-9 *Shortcut menu for placing key points*

Choose the **Place Key** option from the shortcut menu; the key point will be placed at the desired location.

Motor

This button is used to add rotary or linear motor to a component to set up a motion between different components of an assembly. On choosing this button; the **Motor PropertyManager** will be displayed, as shown in Figure 20-10.

The options in this PropertyManager are discussed next.

Motor Type

The buttons available in the **Motor Type** rollout are used to specify the type of motor to be applied. There are three buttons available in this rollout: **Rotary Motor**, **Linear Motor (Actuator),** and **Path Mate Motor**. Using the **Rotary Motor** button, you can apply a rotary motor that helps the object to get rotated along its axis. Using the **Linear Motor (Actuator)** button, you can create an actuator that helps an object to get translated along the linear direction. Using the **Path Mate Motor** button, you can apply a motion along a path.

Component/Direction

There are three selection boxes in this rollout: **Motor Location**, **Motor Direction**, and **Component to Move Relative to**. The **Motor Location** selection box is used to specify the body on which you are applying the motor. The **Motor Direction** selection box is used to specify the direction in which the motor will rotate or move the selected object. The **Component to Move Relative to** selection box is used to specify the object relative to which the component will move.

Motion

The options available in this rollout are used to specify the speed of the motor. The options available in the **Function** drop-down list of this rollout are discussed next.

Figure 20-10 The Motor PropertyManager

Constant Speed

Using this option, you can specify a constant speed (in RPM) for the motor. On selecting this option, the **Speed** edit box below the **Function** drop-down list will be displayed. In the **Speed** spinner box, you can specify the speed of the motion.

Distance

Using this option, you can specify the displacement being covered by the motor. You can also specify the starting time of the motor and the total time in which the displacement will be covered.

Oscillating

Using this option, you can specify the motion of motor as oscillating. On selecting this option, the edit boxes for specifying displacement, frequency, and phase shift become available. You can specify the desired values in these edit boxes.

Segments

Using this option, you can specify the rotational speed of motor into various segments. On selecting this option, the **Function Builder** dialog box will be displayed with the **Segments** button chosen, refer to Figure 20-11. Using the options in this dialog box, you can set variable speed for the motor.

Data Points

Using this option, you can specify data points for the motor speed. Based on these data points, speed of the motor is calculated with respect to time. On selecting the **Data Points** option, the **Function Builder** dialog box will be displayed with the **Data Points** button chosen, refer to Figure 20-12.

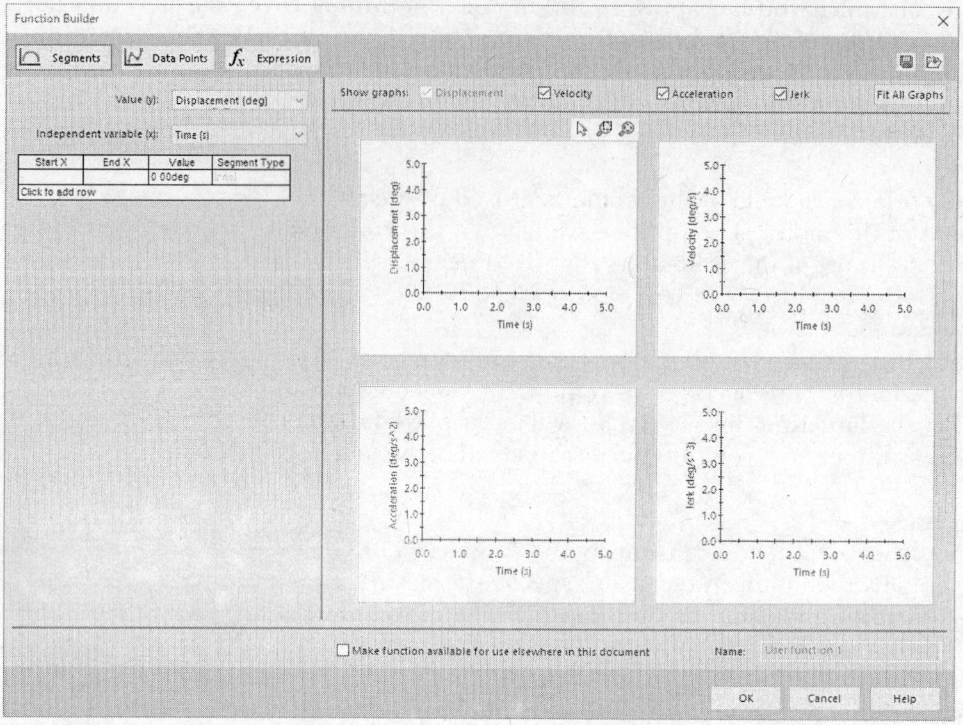

*Figure 20-11 The **Function Builder** dialog box with the **Segments** button chosen*

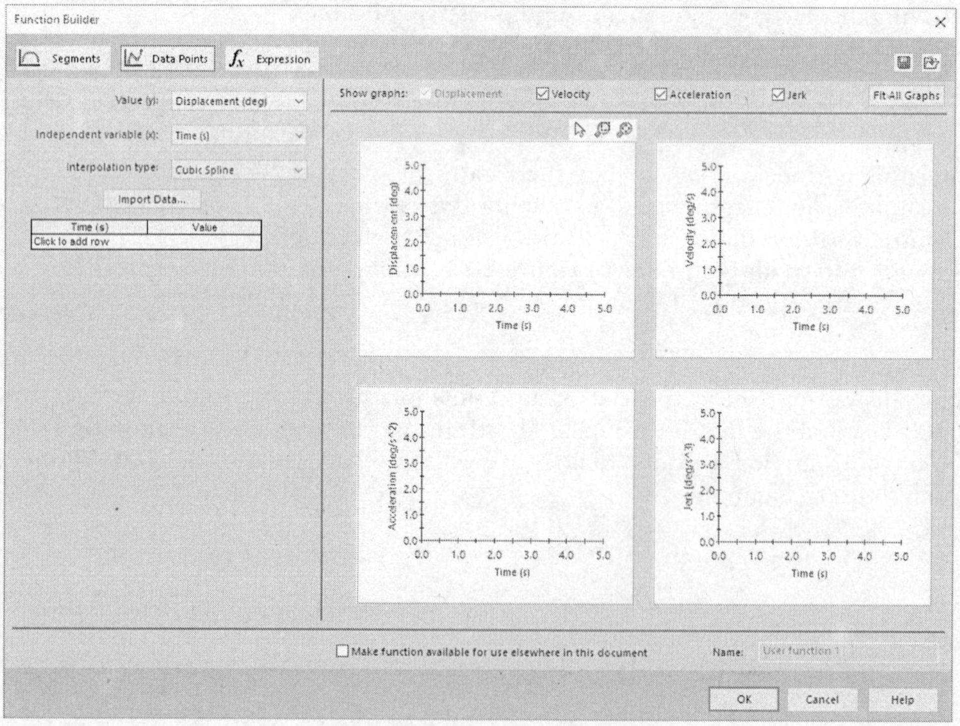

*Figure 20-12 The **Function Builder** dialog box with the **Data Points** button chosen*

Expression: Using this option, you can create a mathematical function for specifying the motor speed. On selecting this option, the **Function Builder** dialog box will be displayed with the **Expression** button chosen, refer to Figure 20-13.

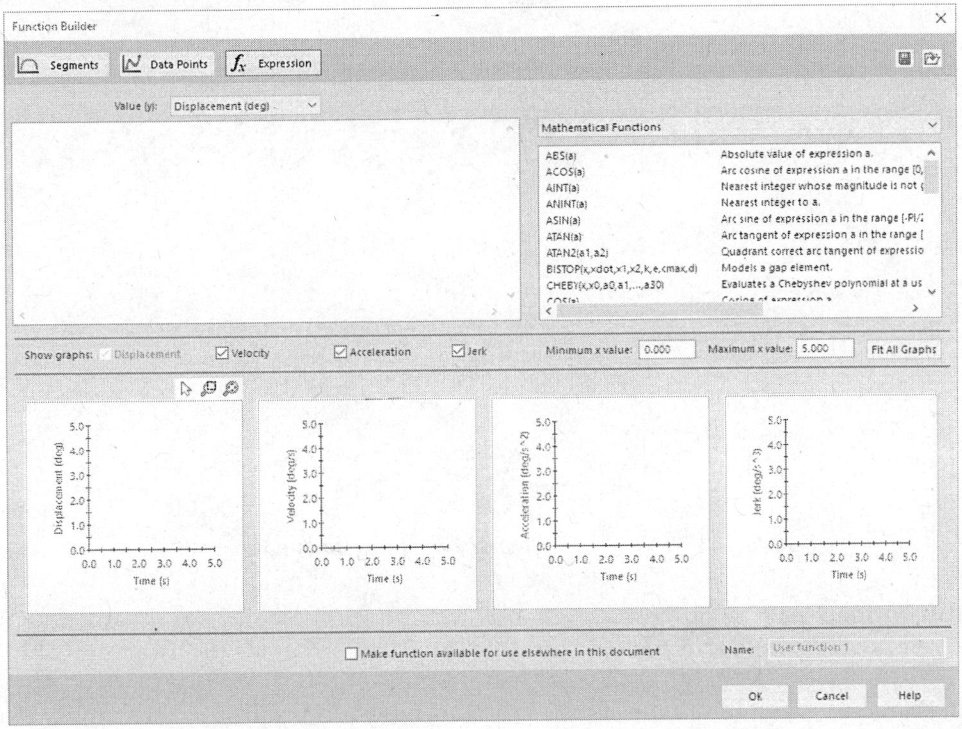

*Figure 20-13 The **Function Builder** dialog box with the **Expression** button chosen*

Load Function from File: Using this option, you can use a SOLIDWORKS function file to load mathematical function. Based on that function, the speed of the motor with respect to time will be calculated. On selecting this option, the **Open** dialog box will be displayed. Using the options in this dialog box, you can load function from a file.

Delete Functions: Using this option, you can delete a motion function of the motor. On selecting this option, the **Delete Motion Functions** dialog box will be displayed, refer to Figure 20-14. Using the options in this dialog box, you can delete the selected functions.

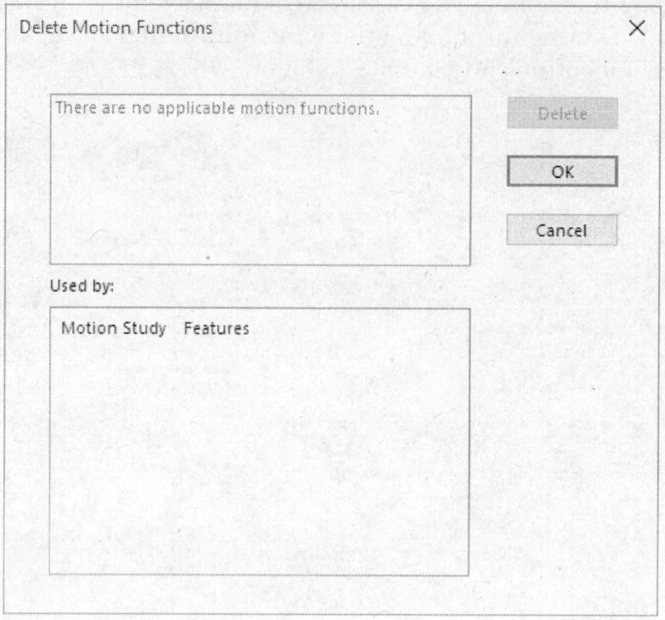

Figure 20-14 The **Delete Motion Functions** dialog box

More Options

The option in this rollout is used to specify load-bearing faces for the assembly component.

After specifying the desired options, choose the **OK** button from the PropertyManager to add the motor.

Spring

This button is used to add a torsional or linear spring to the assembly. On choosing this button, the **Spring PropertyManager** will be displayed, as shown in Figure 20-15. The options in this PropertyManager are discussed next.

Spring Type

There are two buttons available in this rollout: **Linear Spring** and **Torsional Spring**. The **Linear Spring** button is used to create a linear spring. Similarly, the **Torsional Spring** button is used to create a torsional spring.

Spring Parameters

The options in this rollout are used to specify parameters of the spring. The **Spring Endpoints** selection box in this rollout is used to specify the end points of the spring. The options in the **Exponent of Spring Force Expression** drop-down list are used to specify the exponential value. The **Spring Constant** spinner is used to specify the value of spring constant (k). The **Free Length** spinner is used to specify the free length of the spring. This edit box is available for linear spring. In case of a torsional spring, the **Free Angle** spinner will be displayed. Select the **Update to model changes** check box to update the model while changing the parameters. If you are using the torsional spring, you can also specify the base component by using the **Base Component** selection box.

Damper

The options in this rollout are used to specify the parameters related to dampers. The **Exponent of Damper Force Expression** is used to specify the exponential value for the damper force expression. The **Damping Constant** spinner box is used to specify the value of damping constant.

Display

The options in this rollout are used to specify the display style of the spring model. The **Coil Diameter** spinner box in this rollout is used to specify the diameter of the coil of spring. The **Number of Coils** spinner box is used to specify the number of coils displayed in the spring model. The **Wire Diameter** spinner box in this rollout is used to specify the diameter of the wire used for spring.

Load Bearing Faces

The option in this rollout is used to specify the faces/edges for bearing/load that can be used in simulation.

After specifying all parameters, choose the **OK** button from the PropertyManager to create the spring motion.

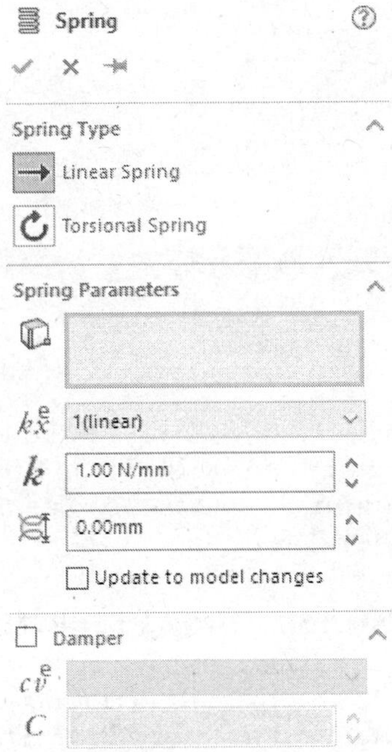

*Figure 20-15 Partial view of the **Spring PropertyManager***

Contact

This button is used to add a contact in the motion study so that the assembly components do not penetrate into each other. To add a contact in the assembly, choose the **Contact** button from the **MotionManager** toolbar; the **Contact PropertyManager** will be displayed, refer to Figure 20-16.

Now, select the components between which you want to add the contact; the selected components will be added to the **Components** selection box in the **Selections** rollout. Next, choose the **OK** button from the PropertyManager; the contact will be created.

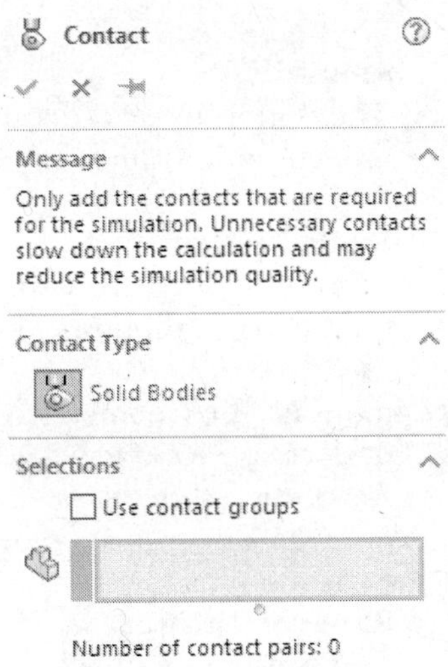

*Figure 20-16 The **Contact PropertyManager***

Gravity

This button is used to add gravity to the motion study. On choosing this button, the **Gravity PropertyManager** will be displayed, as shown in Figure 20-17.

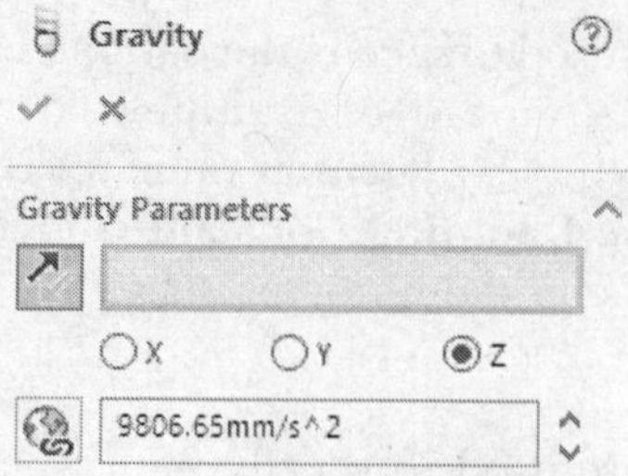

*Figure 20-17 The **Gravity PropertyManager***

Select the **X**, **Y**, or **Z** radio button to specify the direction of gravity. You can also select an entity of the model in the **Direction Reference** selection box to specify the direction vector for gravity. To specify the value of gravity, click on the **Numeric gravity value** edit box and enter the desired value.

Motion Study Properties

This button is used to specify the properties of the motion study being performed. To specify the properties, choose the **Motion Study Properties** button; the **Motion Study Properties PropertyManager** will be displayed, as shown in Figure 20-18.

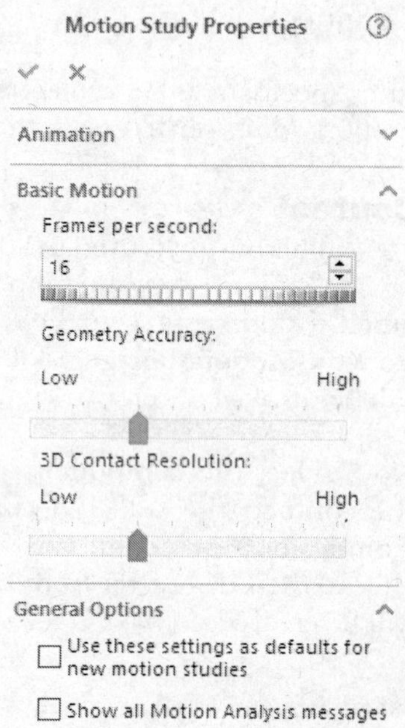

*Figure 20-18 The **Motion Study Properties PropertyManager***

The options in the PropertyManager are discussed next.

Animation

The option in this rollout is used to specify the quality of animation in frames per second.

Basic Motion

The options in this rollout are used to specify the parameters for the basic motion. The **Frames per second** spinner is used to set the number of frames per second for the basic motion. The **Geometry Accuracy** slider is used to increase or decrease accuracy of geometrical mesh. The **3D Contact Resolution** slider is used to increase or decrease the quality of contact between two or more meshing components.

General Options

The options in this rollout are used to specify general settings for the animation. There are two check boxes available in this rollout. The **Use these settings as defaults for new motion studies** check box is used to set the current settings for all the new motion studies. The **Show all Motion Analysis messages** check box is used to display all the messages related to computation of motion study.

TUTORIALS

Tutorial 1

In this tutorial, first you will open the assembly file created in Tutorial 1 of Chapter 12, refer to Figure 20-19 and then you will do motion study of the assembly. **(Expected time: 30 min)**

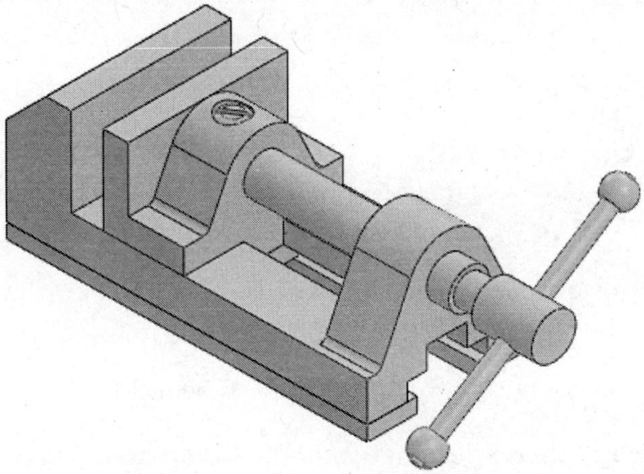

Figure 20-19 *Assembly model for motion study*

The following steps are required to complete this tutorial:

a. Copy the Bench Vice folder from Chapter 12 to the folder of the current chapter.
b. Open the Bench Vice assembly document from the Bench Vice folder.
c. Add motor in the assembly.
d. Simulate motion of the assembly.

Copying the Documents in the Folder of the Current Chapter

Before proceeding further, you need to create the folder of the current chapter and then copy the model and the drawing document in the folder created.

1. Create a folder with the name *c20* in the *SOLIDWORKS* folder. Next, copy the *Bench Vice* folder from *\Documents\SOLIDWORKS\c12* and paste it in the *c20* folder.

Opening the Assembly Document

Next, you need to open the assembly document in the SOLIDWORKS window.

1. Invoke the **Open** dialog box and open the *Bench Vice.SLDASM* document from it; the assembly document for which you want to perform the motion analysis is displayed in the assembly window.

2. Click on the **Motion Study 1** tab displayed at the bottom; the **MotionManager** interface is displayed, as shown in Figure 20-20.

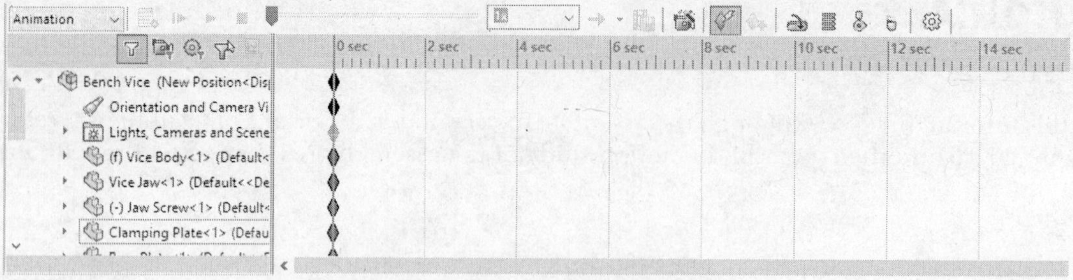

Figure 20-20 The ***MotionManager*** *interface*

Adding Motor to the Assembly

Before performing the motion analysis, you need to add motion between the components by adding a motor.

1. Choose the **Motor** button from the **MotionManager** toolbar; the **Motor PropertyManager** is displayed, as shown in Figure 20-21.

2. Choose the **Rotary Motor** button from the **Motor Type** rollout, if it is not chosen by default.

3. Click in the **Motor Location** selection box of the **Component/Direction** rollout and select the cylindrical face of the Jaw Screw, refer to Figure 20-22. The name of the selected face is displayed in the **Motor Direction** selection box.

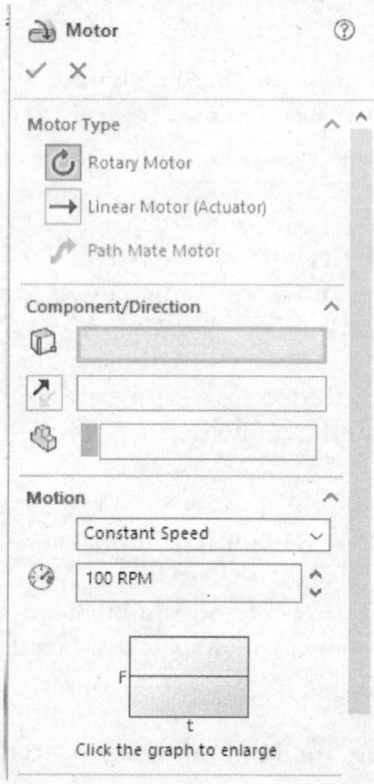

Figure 20-21 Partial view of the ***Motor PropertyManager***

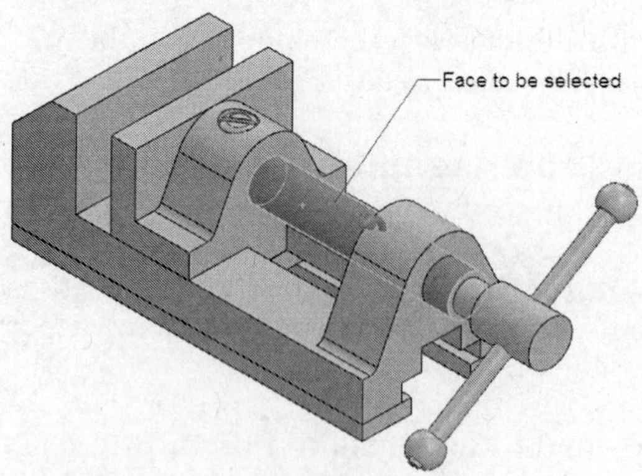

Figure 20-22 The face to be selected

4. Make sure that the **Constant Speed** option is selected in the **Function** drop-down list of the **Motion** rollout. Set the value **150** in the **Speed** spinner of the **Motion** rollout.

5. Choose the **OK** button in the **Motor PropertyManager** to add the motor.

Simulating the Motion Study

1. Choose the **Calculate** button from the **MotionManager** toolbar; the motion of the assembly components is displayed in the assembly window.

2. Choose the **Stop** button from the **MotionManager** toolbar to stop the animation and then to increase the play time of animation, select the key point of first row and drag it to the desired time point, refer to Figures 20-23 and 20-24.

3. Choose the **Calculate** button again to play the animation till the specified time point.

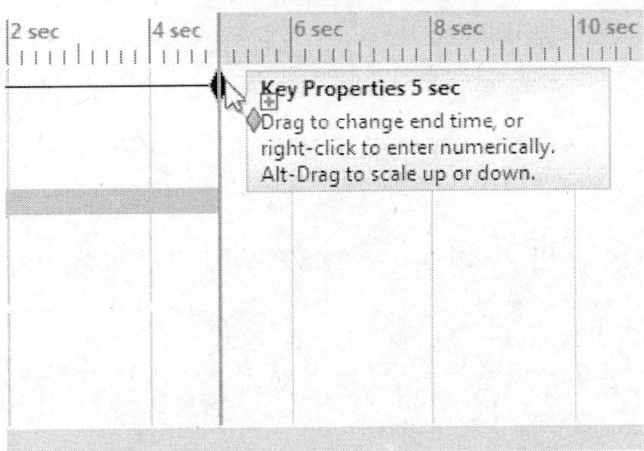

Figure 20-23 *Timeline before moving the key point*

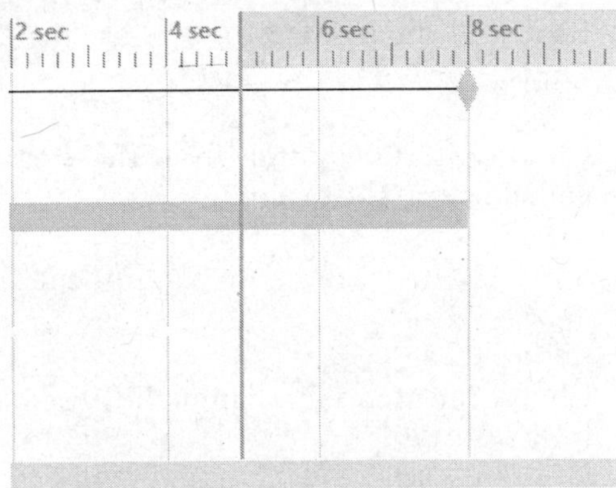

Figure 20-24 *Timeline after moving the key point*

Tip

*The motion of the assembly can be made continuous by selecting the **Playback Mode: Loop** option from the **MotionManager** toolbar. On selecting this option, the motion will start from the beginning after one cycle of motion has ended.*

Tutorial 2

In this tutorial, you will study the motion of a cam spring assembly. The assembly files for this tutorial can be downloaded from *www.cadcim.com*. **(Expected time: 30 min)**

The following steps are required to complete this tutorial:

a. Download the assembly files from *www.cadcim.com*.
b. Assemble the downloaded components.
c. Apply rotary motor to the cam.
d. Simulate the motion of the assembly.

Downloading the Cam Spring Tutorial Files

Before starting the tutorial, you need to download the tutorial file. After downloading the file, extract it to the desired location.

1. Download the *c20_sw_2021_tut.zip* file from *www.cadcim.com*. The path of the files is as follows:

   Textbooks > CAD/CAM > SOLIDWORKS > SOLIDWORKS 2021 for Designers > Tutorial files

Assembling the Components

After extracting the file, you need to assemble the components in the Assembly environment.

1. Start a new SOLIDWORKS assembly document; the **Begin Assembly PropertyManager** along with the **Open** dialog box is displayed.

2. Browse to the Pin part and choose the **Open** button from the dialog box; the model of the Pin is attached to the cursor.

3. Choose the **OK** button from the **Begin Assembly PropertyManager**; the Pin is placed coincident to the origin.

4. Similarly, insert the Cam component and place it at an arbitrary location in the graphics area.

5. Choose the **Mate** button from the **Assembly CommandManager**; the **Mate PropertyManager** is displayed.

6. Select the cylindrical face of the Pin and inner circular face of the Cam; the concentric mate is applied between the cylindrical faces of the Pin and Cam. Also, a pop-up toolbar is displayed.

7. Choose the **Add/Finish Mate** button from the pop-up toolbar; you are prompted to select other references to apply a mate.

8. Choose the **Distance** button from the **Standard Mates** rollout of the PropertyManager; the **Distance** edit box is activated.

9. Specify the value of distance as **4** in the edit box and press ENTER. Next, select the planar faces of the Pin and Cam, refer to Figure 20-25; the distance mate is applied between the planar faces. Also, a pop-up toolbar is displayed.

10. Choose the **Add/Finish Mate** button from the pop-up toolbar; the mate is applied.

11. Follow the above steps and assemble the other components of the assembly. Figure 20-26 shows the assembly after assembling all the components.

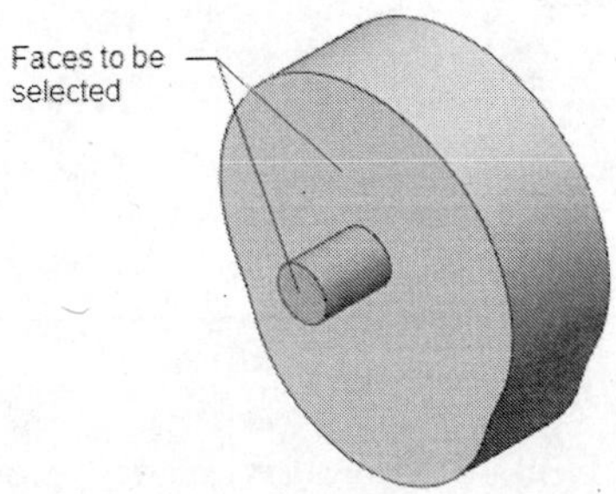

Figure 20-25 Faces to be selected

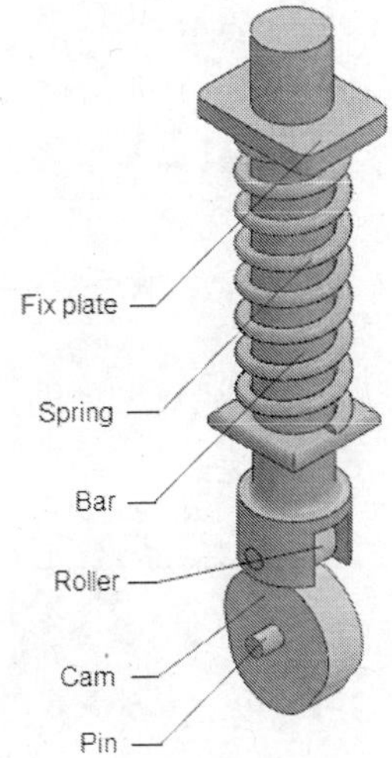

Figure 20-26 Assembly for performing motion study

Adding Motor to the Assembly

Before performing the motion analysis, you need to add motion between the components by adding motor.

1. Click on the **Motion Study 1** tab displayed at the bottom left of the window; the **MotionManager** interface is displayed.

2. Choose the **Motor** button from the **MotionManager** toolbar; the **Motor PropertyManager** is displayed.

3. Select the round face of the cam; a motor is applied. Also, the direction of rotation is indicated by a red arrow, refer to Figure 20-27.

4. Accept the other default settings and choose the **OK** button from the PropertyManager; the rotational motion is added to the component.

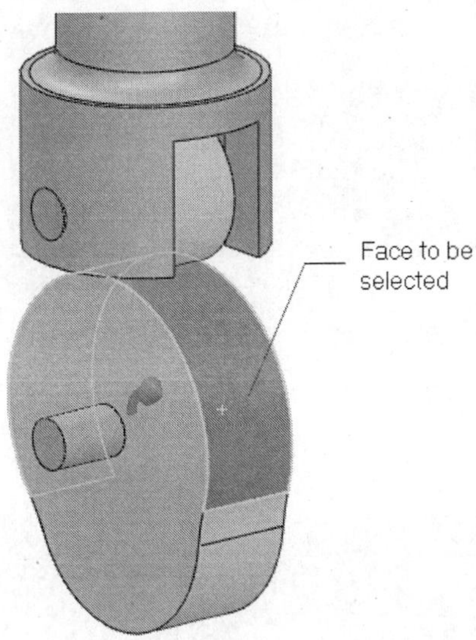

Figure 20-27 Face to be selected for specifying direction of rotation

Simulating the Motion Study

1. Choose the **Calculate** button from the **MotionManager** toolbar; the motion of assembly components is displayed in the assembly window.

   You can increase or decrease the play time of motion, as discussed in Tutorial 1 of this chapter.

   Figure 20-28 shows the annotated time line for the motion study.

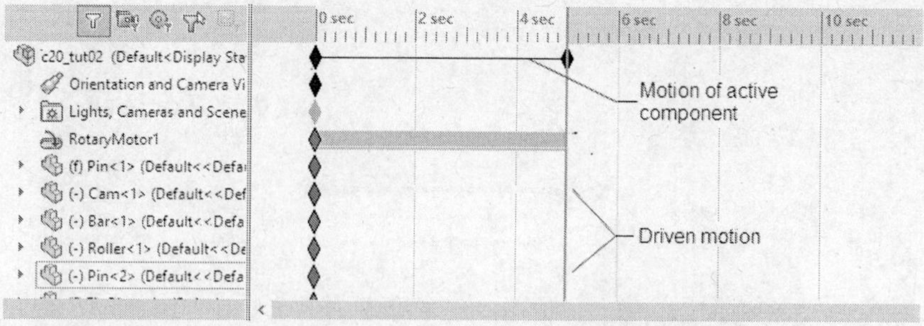

Figure 20-28 Annotated time line for the motion study

Self-Evaluation Test

Answer the following questions and then compare them to those given at the end of this chapter:

1. The **Animation** and _____________ options are available in the **Type of Study** drop-down list.

2. The Timeline is used to display the position of components at a specific point of time. (T/F)

3. The Time Bar is used to display the scale of time. (T/F)

4. The **Calculate** button is used to calculate the force applied on the component. (T/F)

5. Using the **Motor** button, you can provide the linear motion to the assembly. (T/F)

Review Questions

Answer the following questions:

1. Which of the following is used to represent the current position of components on the time scale?

   (a) Timeline (b) Timebar
   (c) Time slider (d) None of the these

2. Which of the following rollouts in the **Motor PropertyManager** is used to specify the motion type of the motor?

   (a) **Component/Direction** (b) **Motion**
   (c) **More Options** (d) None of the these

3. The __________ tool is used to add actuator to the motion study.

4. You can save the animation clip of current motion study by using the __________ tool.

5. The options in the __________ drop-down list are used to increase or decrease the playback speed of motion study.

EXERCISES

Exercise 1

Simulate the motion of Blower assembly created in Exercise 2 of Chapter 12, refer to Figure 20-29. **(Expected time: 30 min)**

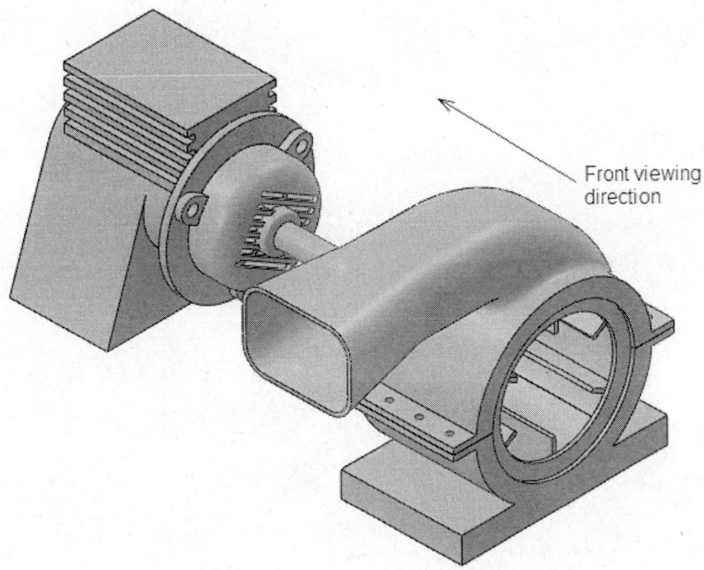

Figure 20-29 *Blower assembly*

Exercise 2

Simulate the motion of Pipe Vice assembly created in Tutorial 2 of Chapter 12, refer to Figure 20-30. **(Expected time: 30 min)**

Figure 20-30 *Pipe Vice assembly*

Answers to Self-Evaluation Test

1. **Basic Motion, 2.** F, **3.** F, **4.** F, **5.** T

Chapter 21

Introduction to Mold Design

Learning Objectives

After completing this chapter, you will be able to:

- *Understand basic concepts of mold design*
- *Design split molds*
- *Design mold with complex core and cavity*
- *Analyze draft angles*
- *Scale models for mold design*

INTRODUCTION TO MOLD DESIGN

In this chapter, you will learn about the tools that you can use to design molds for a cast or plastic molded component. Generally, the complete mold designing consists of designing of mold base, gates and runners, ejection mechanism, and core and cavity. But in the mold design using SOLIDWORKS, you will only learn about designing of core and cavity which means extraction of core and cavity from a part created. You will also learn about creating inserts for extracting the core and cavity of complex parts. Figure 21-1 shows a soap case created in the **Part** mode of SOLIDWORKS. Figure 21-2 shows the core for manufacturing this part and Figure 21-3 shows the respective cavity.

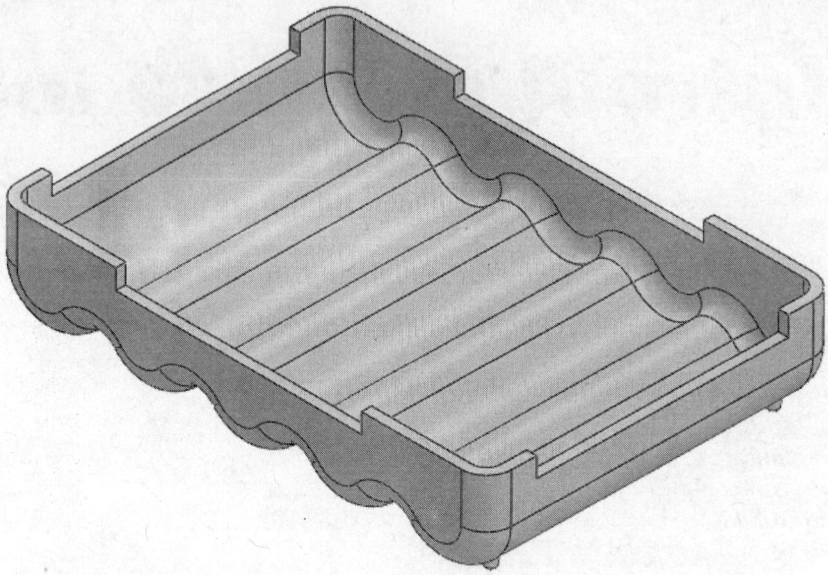

Figure 21-1 *Soap case created in the part mode of SOLIDWORKS*

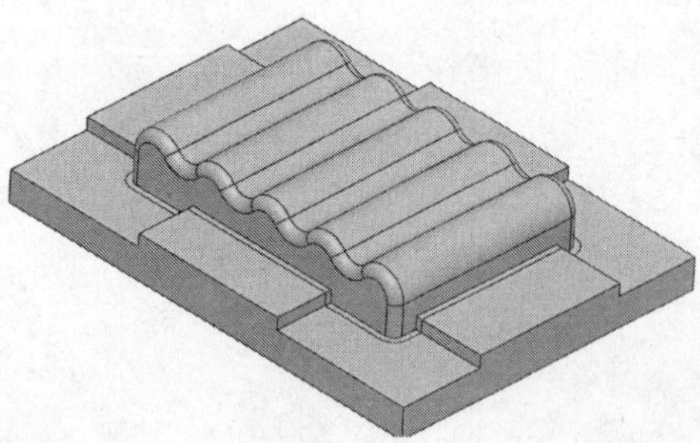

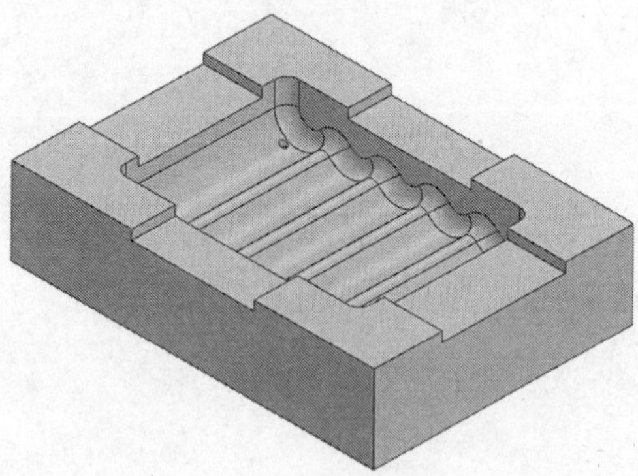

Figure 21-2 *Core of the mold for manufacturing* ***Figure 21-3*** *Cavity of the mold for manufacturing*

Before you learn about mold design, it is necessary that you first learn about some of the major terms and definitions related to mold design.

MOLD ASSEMBLY

Mold assembly is an assembly created by assembling a number of parts such as top plate, back plate, core back plate, cavity back plate, ejector mechanism, guide bushes, guide pillars, fasteners, cooling mechanism, and so on. The complete mold is designed by considering the part to be molded and the design depends on the complexity of the part. Some of the elements mentioned above are discussed next.

Cavity

The cavity is the female part of the mold and remains hollow from inside. The molten metal or the molten plastic is poured into it so that it can take the shape of the cavity to create the component.

Core

The core is the male part of the mold and it defines the area where the molten metal should not reach. The core generally helps in defining the holes, pockets, and other cut out features of a part while molding.

Parting Line

Parting line is a line from where the molds split and open in their respective directions. Figure 21-4 shows an assembly of core and cavity with the parting line. Figure 21-5 shows the exploded view of the core and cavity assembly with the component that will be created using this combination of core and cavity.

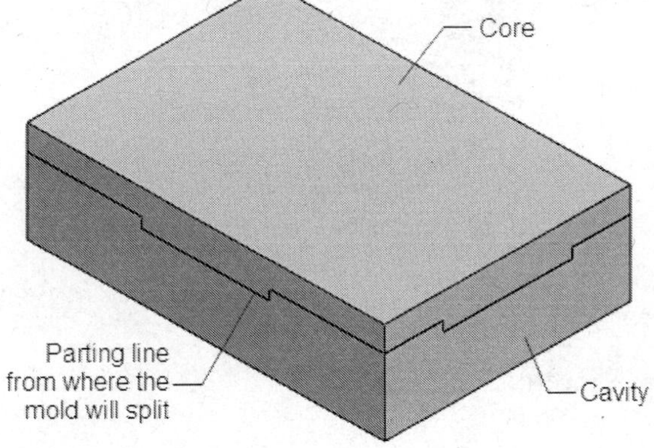

Figure 21-4 *Assembly of core and cavity with the parting line*

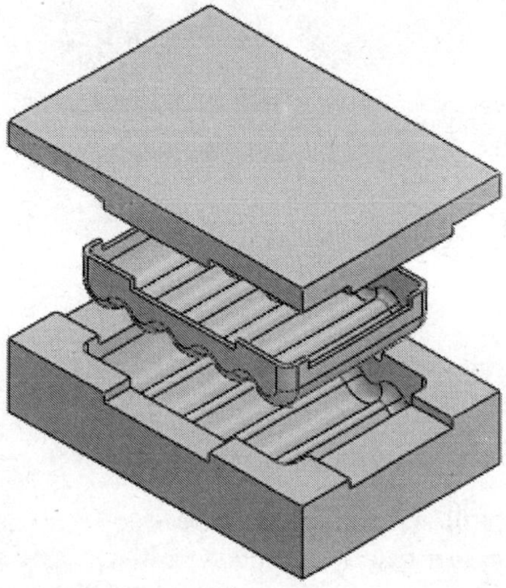

Figure 21-5 *Exploded view of the core and cavity assembly*

Scale factor

Scale factor is defined as the amount by which the molded or cast component shrinks depending on the type of material and the shape of the mold. The scale factor is defined in terms of percentage.

Draft Angle

In the molded or cast component, the draft angles are of great importance. It is very important to add draft angle to the core and cavity because if the faces of the core and cavity do not have any draft angle, then you cannot take out the molded or cast component from the mold. Therefore, it is very important that you should add the required draft angles to the component in the Part mode so that the same draft is also added in the core and cavity.

MOLD DESIGNING USING SOLIDWORKS

In SOLIDWORKS, there are two methods of designing the mold. The first method is generally used to design the split molds and the second method is generally used to design the molds that have core and cavity. Both the methods of designing the core and cavity are discussed next.

Designing a Split Mold

In technical terms, a simple mold consisting of two cavities is called a split mold. For designing this type of mold, you first need to create the part for which you want to design the mold. Figure 21-6 shows a part whose mold is to be designed. Next, you need to create the mold base which is generally an extruded cube or cuboid. Figure 21-7 shows the mold base. The over all dimensions of the mold base are greater than the part. The dimensions of the mold base depend on the size of the part, injection pressure of the molten metal, temperature of the molten metal, and so on.

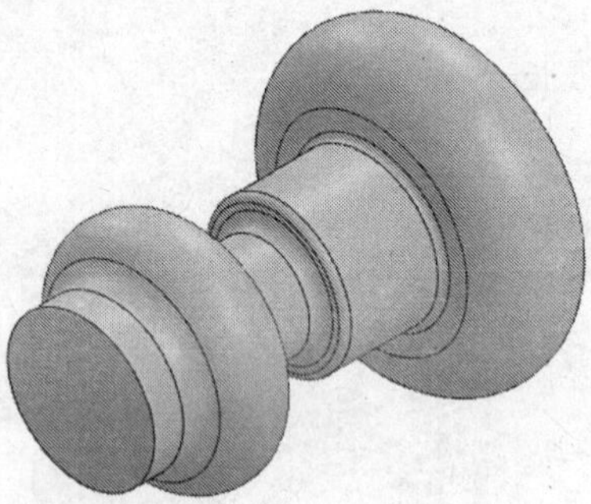

Figure 21-6 *Part whose mold is to be designed*

Figure 21-7 *Mold base*

The following steps are required to create a split mold:

1. Creating an interim assembly
2. Creating the cavity in the Mold base
3. Creating the derived component

Creating the Interim Assembly

After creating the part and the mold base, you need to create an interim assembly in which you will assemble the part with the mold base. Create a new assembly file and save it. Now, place the mold base in the assembly file. Select the mold base from the **FeatureManager Design Tree** and choose the **Change Transparency** option from the shortcut menu displayed on right-clicking;

a transparent mold base will be displayed. Now, place the part in the assembly and assemble it using the assembly mates such that the part is placed in the middle of the mold base. Figure 21-8 shows the part placed in the middle of the mold base.

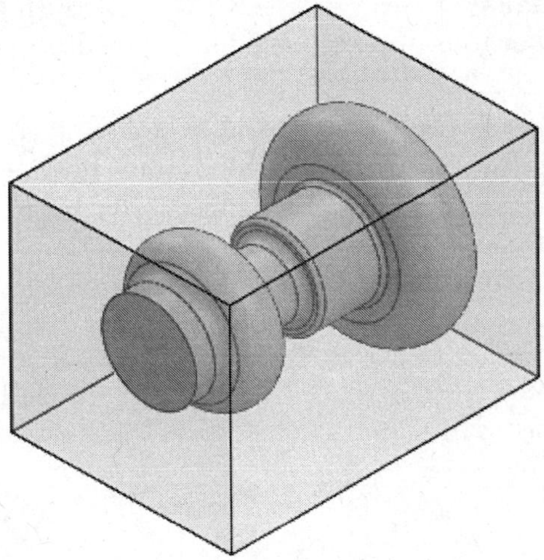

Figure 21-8 Part placed and assembled in the middle of the mold base

Creating the Cavity

CommandManager:	Mold Tools > Cavity *(Customize to add)*
SOLIDWORKS menus:	Insert > Molds > Cavity
Toolbar:	Mold Tools > Cavity *(Customize to add)*

After assembling the part with the mold base, you need to create the cavity in the mold base. The cavity is created using the **Cavity** tool. To create a cavity, select the mold base and choose the **Edit Component** button from the **Assembly CommandManager**; the Part modeling environment will be invoked for the mold base part. Now, choose the **Cavity** button from the **Mold Tools** toolbar. If the **Mold Tools** toolbar is not available, choose **View > Toolbars > Mold Tools** from the SOLIDWORKS menus to display this toolbar. When you invoke the **Cavity** tool, the **Cavity PropertyManager** will be displayed, as shown in Figure 21-9. After invoking the **Cavity** tool, select the part from the **FeatureManager Design Tree**. The name of the selected part is displayed in the **Design Component Parts** selection box. After selecting the component, you need to define scale factor for mold cavity. The scale factor is defined to create a cavity larger than the part. This is done because after solidification, the resultant component shrinks. Since the **Uniform scaling** check box is selected in the **Scale Parameters** rollout, the cavity will be scaled uniformly. Using the **Scaling %** spinner, set the value of the scale factor. If you need to apply a nonuniform scaling to the cavity, then clear the **Uniform scaling** check box. The **X**, **Y**, and **Z** spinners are displayed to specify the different scale factors in all the axes.

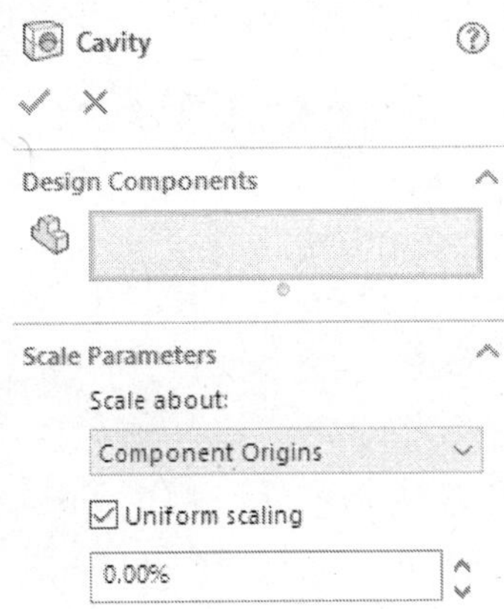

Figure 21-9 The ***Cavity PropertyManager***

The options available in the **Scale about** drop-down list in the **Scale Parameters** rollout are used to define the origin about which you need to scale the cavity. After setting all the parameters, choose the **OK** button from the **Cavity PropertyManager**. You will observe that a **Cavity1** feature is displayed in the **FeatureManager Design Tree**. Choose the **Edit Component** button from the **Assembly CommandManager** to return to the assembly environment.

Creating the Derived Component

After creating the cavity in the mold base, you need to create the derived component of the mold base that will be used to create the cavity. To create the derived component, select the mold base from the **FeatureManager Design Tree** and choose **File > Derive Component Part** from the SOLIDWORKS menus; the **Insert Part PropertyManager** is displayed. Choose the **OK** button to insert the part at the origin; a new part file will be created that contains the mold base with the cavity created inside the mold base. Since the mold base is displayed shaded, therefore, you first need to change the model display to Wireframe. The derived component after changing the model display state is shown in Figure 21-10.

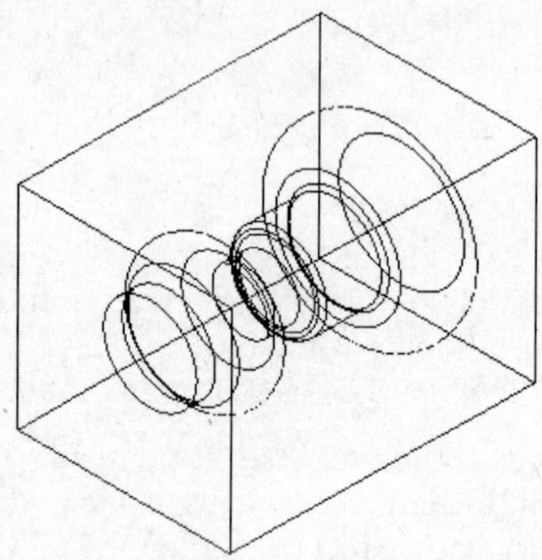

Figure 21-10 *Derived part with the model display set to Wireframe*

Select the front face of the derived component and invoke the sketching environment. Create a single line sketch, as shown in Figure 21-11.

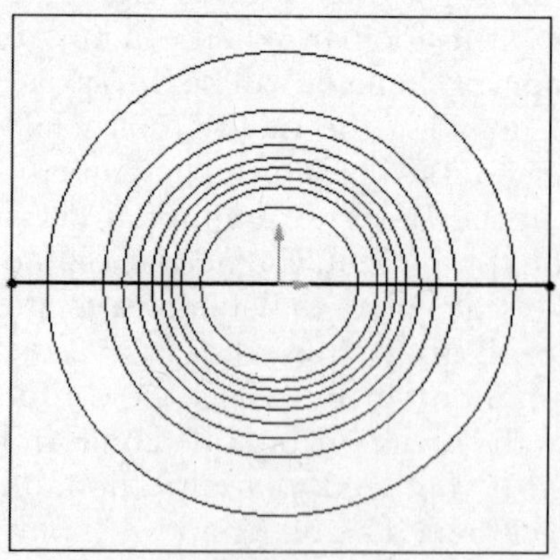

Figure 21-11 *Sketch for creating the cut feature*

Save the derived part and choose **Insert > Molds > Split** from the SOLIDWORKS menus; the **Split PropertyManager** will be displayed, as shown in Figure 21-12. The earlier drawn sketch will be automatically selected in the **Trimming Surfaces** selection box in the **Trim Tools** rollout. Choose the **Cut Part** button to split the mold base. This creates the top and bottom plates of the split mold. Choose the **Auto-assign Names** button and uncheck the first file in the **Resulting Bodies** rollout. Also, make sure that the **Consume cut bodies** check box is selected. Choose the **OK** button and the resulting mold bottom plate will be displayed, as shown in Figure 21-13.

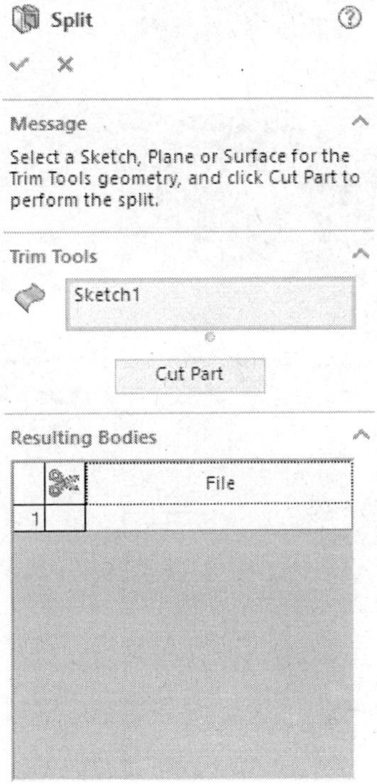

Figure 21-12** Partial view of the **Split PropertyManager

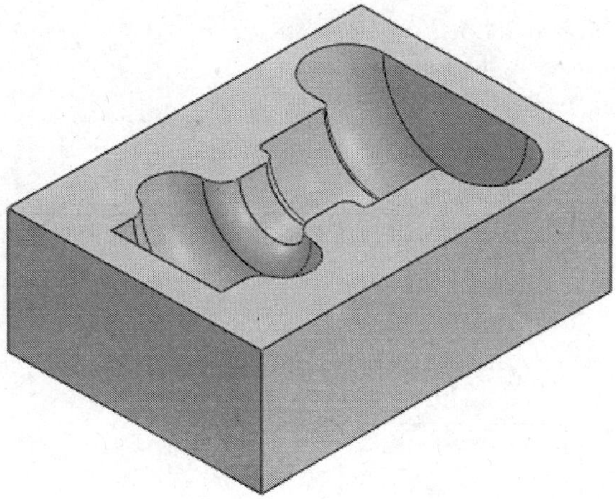

***Figure 21-13** Mold bottom plate*

Tip
*To see the mold top plate, you can select it from the **Split PropertyManager**. Click the **Split** feature from the **FeatureManager Design Tree** and choose **Edit Feature**. Uncheck the body you want to be displayed from the **Resulting Bodies** rollout and choose the **OK** button.*

Note
To create the gates, runners, and other features, you can use the standard modeling tools.

Designing a Mold with Core and Cavity

The second type is the one that has core and cavity. To create such a mold, you need to create the part in the **Part** mode. Make sure that you add the required draft angle while creating the part so that the component gets easily extracted from the mold. You also need to make sure that the required scaling is added to the model so that the same scale factor is also reflected in the core and cavity. Consider an example of the Carburetor Cover shown in Figure 21-14. Figure 21-15 shows the other side of the model. Figure 21-16 shows the views and dimensions of the Carburetor Cover. This type of component requires a mold with core and cavity. The method of designing such a mold is discussed next.

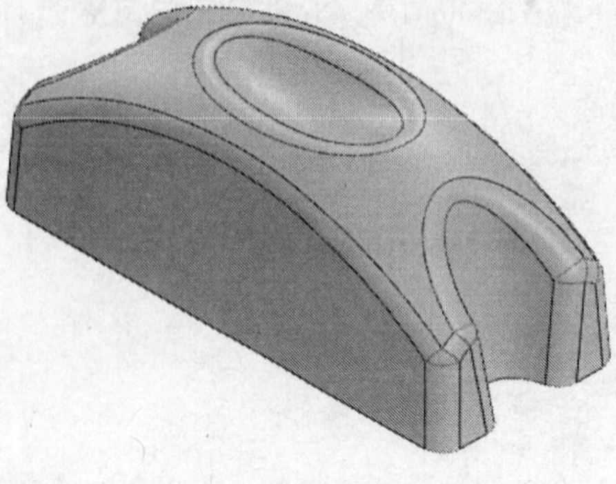

Figure 21-14 *Model of the Carburetor Cover*

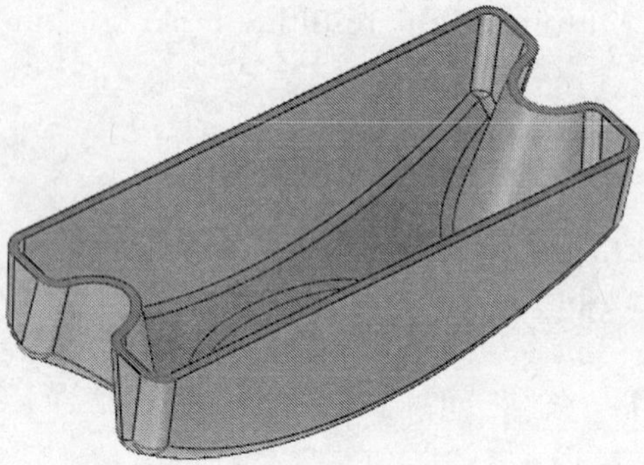

Figure 21-15 *Rotated view to display the other side of the Carburetor Cover*

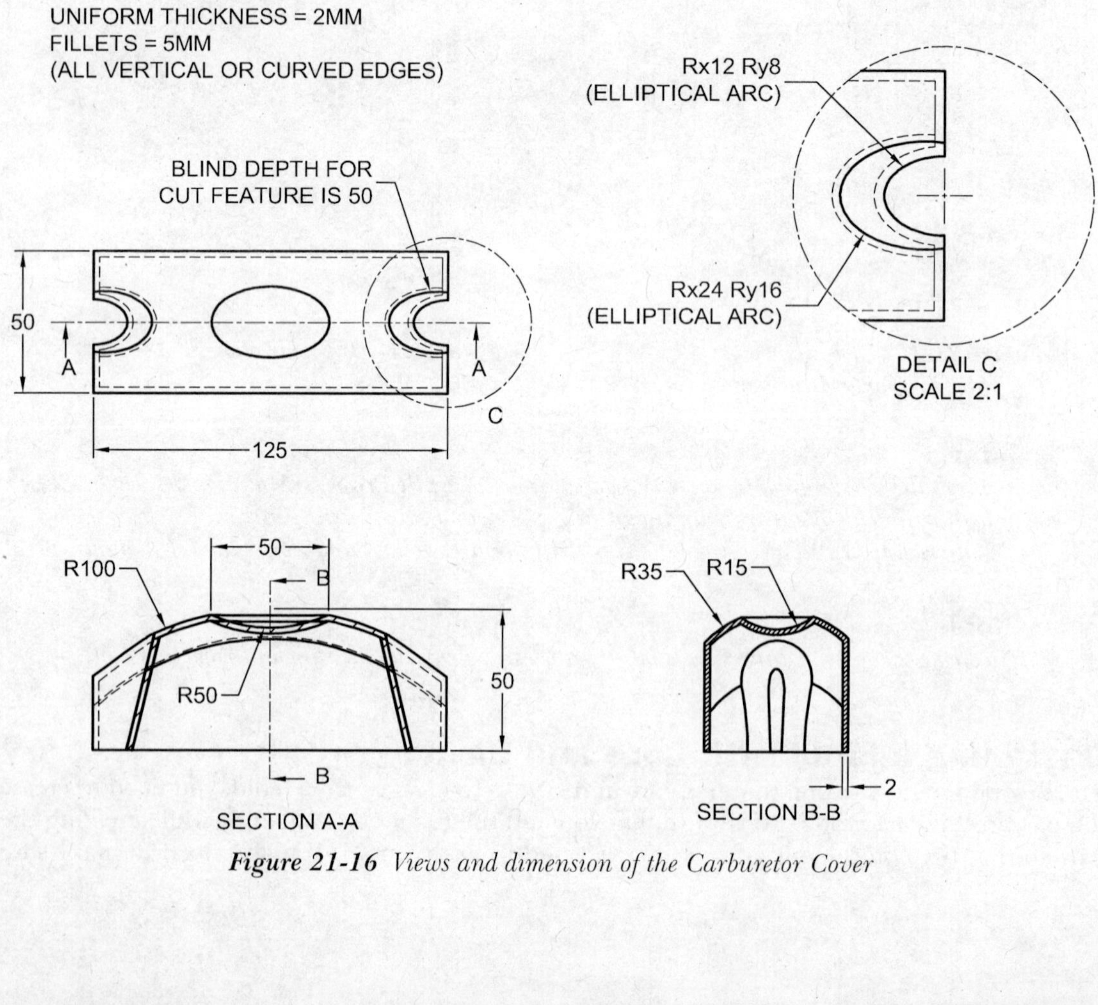

Figure 21-16 *Views and dimension of the Carburetor Cover*

Analyzing the Draft Angles

CommandManager:	Mold Tools > Draft Analysis
Toolbar:	Mold Tools > Draft Analysis

Before generating the core and cavity, you need to analyze and apply drafts to the model. The **Draft Analysis** tool is used to analyze the draft angles of the model. Choose the **Draft Analysis** button from the **Mold Tools** toolbar; the **Draft Analysis PropertyManager** will be displayed, as shown in Figure 21-17. First you need to select a plane, face, or an edge that will define the direction of the pull. The name of the selected entity is displayed in the **Direction of Pull** selection box. The default draft angle value is displayed in the **Draft Angle** spinner. You can modify the value of the draft angle in the spinner. Choose the **Top Plane** as the direction of pull. The faces of the model will be displayed in different colors specifying the status of drafted faces; the faces displayed in green color indicate that they have a positive draft. The faces displayed in yellow indicate that they require a draft angle. The faces displayed in red indicate that they have a negative draft angle.

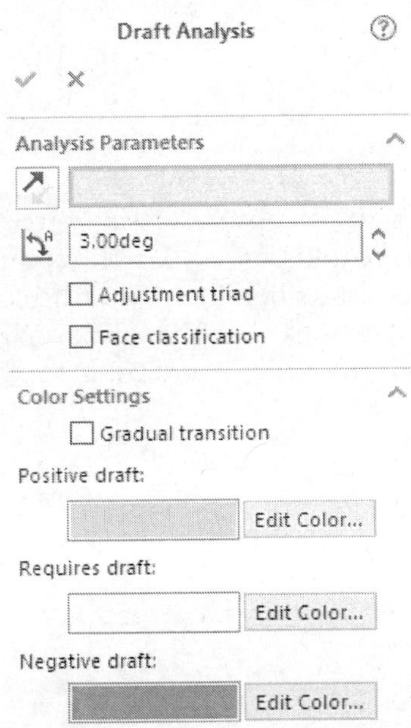

*Figure 21-17 The **Draft Analysis PropertyManager***

Choose the **OK** button from the **Draft Analysis PropertyManager** and add the draft to the faces that were displayed in yellow. The other options available in the **Draft Analysis PropertyManager** are discussed next.

Adjustment triad

The **Adjustment triad** check box is selected to display the triad in graphical area. You can adjust the direction of pull with the help of the rings of the triad. As you change the direction of pull, the model will be updated automatically.

Face classification

The **Face classification** check box available in the **Analysis Parameters** rollout is used to refine the draft analysis depending on the type of draft. When you select this check box, the **Show/Hide** buttons are provided with the **Positive draft**, **Requires draft**, **Negative draft**, **Straddle faces** areas. Using this **Show/Hide** button, you can display the type of faces that need to be analyzed.

Find steep faces

The **Find steep faces** check box is selected to analyze the positive steep faces and the negative steep faces. This check box is only available if you select the **Face classification** check box.

Gradual transition

The **Gradual transition** check box is selected to display color variations specifying the draft angles on the model. This displays the range of angles starting from the positive draft through negative draft depending on the value of the angle specified in the **Draft Angle** spinner.

Scaling the Model

CommandManager:	Mold Tools > Scale
SOLIDWORKS menus:	Insert > Molds > Scale
Toolbar:	Mold Tools > Scale

After creating the model and draft angle analysis, you need to scale the model so that the resultant core and cavity are created bigger than the component that will be manufactured using that core and cavity. As discussed earlier, the size of the core and the cavity is always bigger than the resultant component because the component will shrink after solidification. For scaling the model, choose the **Scale** button from the **Mold Tools** toolbar; the **Scale PropertyManager** is displayed, as shown in Figure 21-18.

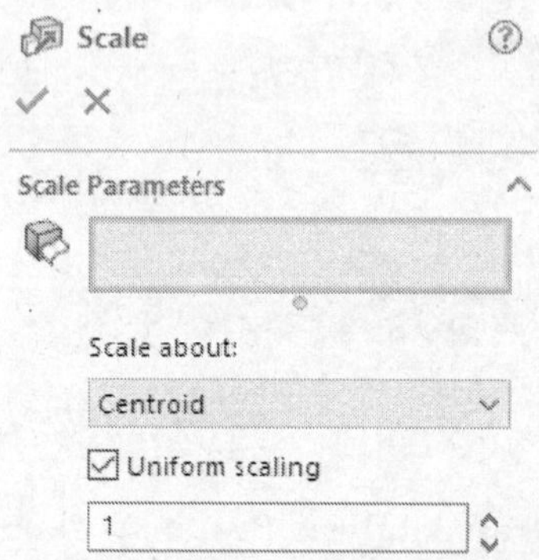

Figure 21-18** The **Scale PropertyManager

Using the options available in the **Scale About** drop-down list, you can specify the option about which you need to scale the model. Using the **Scale Factor** spinner, you can specify the scale factor for scaling the model.

The **Uniform scaling** check box is selected by default so the model gets uniformly scaled. If you clear this check box, then the **X Scale Factor**, **Y Scale Factor**, and **Z Scale Factor** spinners will become available to specify the scale factor individually along all the three directions.

Note

If you have more than one solid or surface body, then you need to select the bodies that are to be scaled using the ***Scale PropertyManager****.*

Creating the Interim Assembly to Generate the Core and Cavity

After creating, analyzing, and scaling the part, you need to create an interim assembly in which you will place the component and then extract the core and cavity. Create a new SOLIDWORKS document in the Assembly mode and then place the component in the assembly coincident to the assembly origin. The component placed coincident to the assembly origin is displayed in Figure 21-19. Save the assembly file.

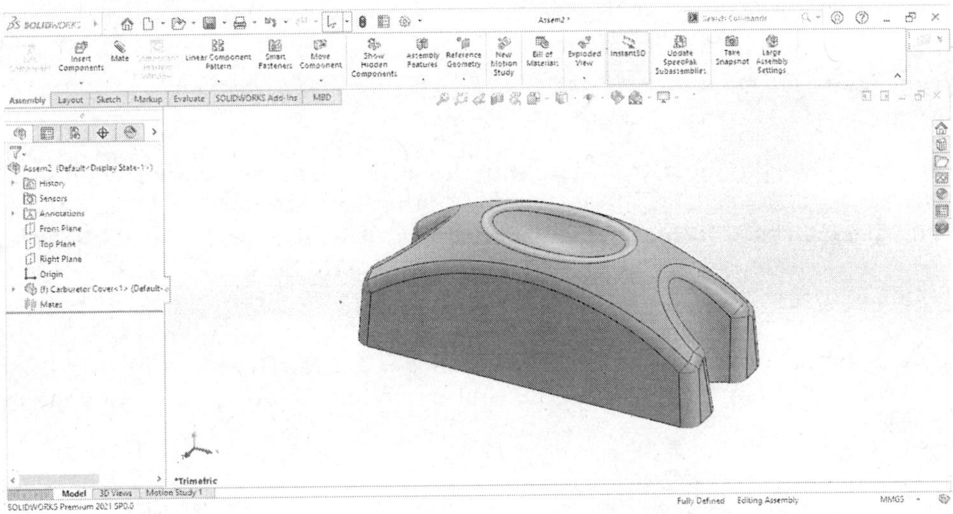

Figure 21-19 *Carburetor Cover placed coincident to the assembly origin*

Extracting the Core

After placing the component in the assembly, you need to create a new part document in which you will extract the core and cavity. The extraction of the core and cavity is a top-down assembly design approach. Therefore, you will create a new part document in the assembly file. Choose **Insert > Component > New Part** from the SOLIDWORKS menus. You will be prompted to select the face or plane on which the new part is to be positioned. Select **Front Plane**; the sketching environment is invoked and the Carburetor Cover is displayed transparent. Right-click the new part node added in the **FeatureManager Design Tree** and rename the part as Core. Exit the sketching environment.

Now, you need to create a radiated surface that will be used as the parting surface for extracting the core. Invoke the **Radiate Surface** tool from the **Mold Tools CommandManager** and select the **Top Plane** as the **Radiate Direction Reference**. Now, select the outer edge of the base as the **Edges to Radiate**. Select the **Propagate to tangent faces** check box. Figure 21-20 shows the radiate direction and the edges to be radiated. Set the value of the **Radiate Distance** spinner to **40 mm** and choose **OK**. Figure 21-21 shows the resultant radiated surface.

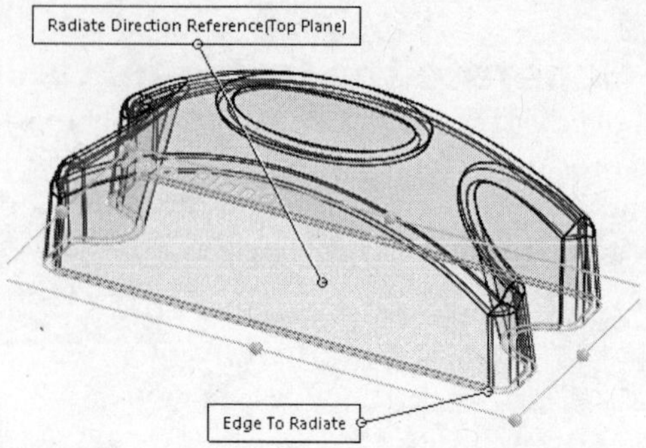

Figure 21-20 Radiate direction and the edges to radiate

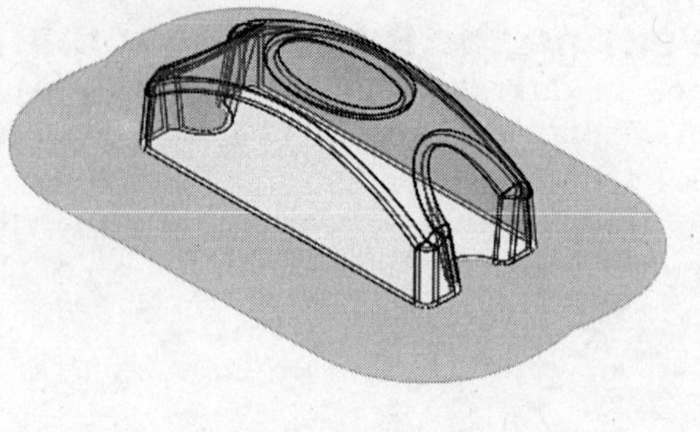

Figure 21-21 Resultant radiated surface

Next, you need to knit the radiated surface with the seed surface for creating a knit surface that will be used to generate the core. To do so, invoke the **Knit Surface** tool. Select the radiated surface and seed surface in the **Surfaces and Faces to Knit** and the **Seed Faces** selection boxes respectively, refer to Figure 21-22. Choose the **OK** button from the **Knit Surface PropertyManager**.

Select the Carburetor Cover from the **FeatureManager Design Tree** and invoke the shortcut menu. Choose **Hide Components** from the shortcut menu. Figure 21-23 shows the resultant knitted surface.

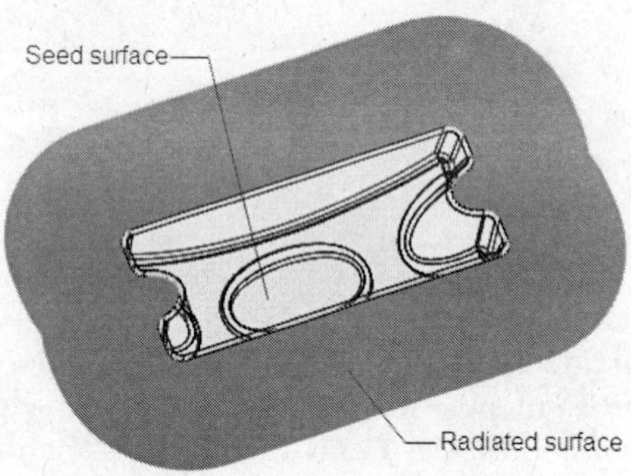

Figure 21-22 Radiated surface and the seed surface

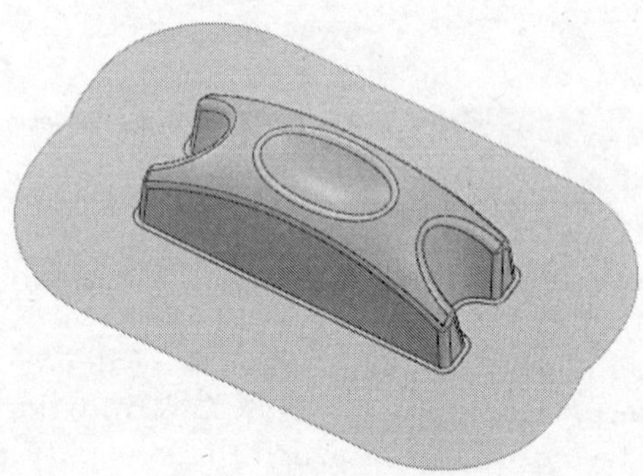

Figure 21-23 Resultant knit surface

Now, create a new plane at some offset distance below the radiated surface. Select the newly created plane as the sketching plane and invoke the sketching environment. Create the sketch of the core base and extrude it using the **Up To Surface** option with the knitted surface as reference. Hide the knitted surface. Figure 21-24 shows the final core.

Choose the **Edit Component** button from the assembly toolbar to return to the assembly environment.

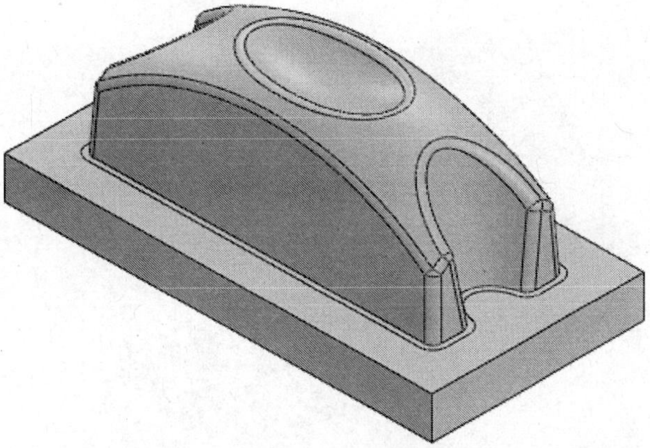

Figure 21-24 Final Core

Extracting the Cavity

In this section you need to generate the Cavity in the mold. Before proceeding further, hide the Core and then unhide the Carburetor Cover. Now, create a new SOLIDWORKS part in the assembly file; choose **Insert > Component > New Part** from the SOLIDWORKS menus. You will be prompted to select the face or the plane on which the new part is to be positioned. Select **Front Plane**; the sketching environment is invoked and the Carburetor Cover is displayed as transparent. Right-click on the new part node added in **FeatureManager Design Tree** and rename the part as Cavity. Exit the sketching environment. As discussed earlier, create a radiated surface. Next, you need to create a knit surface. Invoke the **Knit Surface PropertyManager** and select the radiated surface and the seed surface, refer to Figure 21-25. Choose the **OK** button from the **Knit Surface PropertyManager**. Figure 21-26 shows the resultant knit surface.

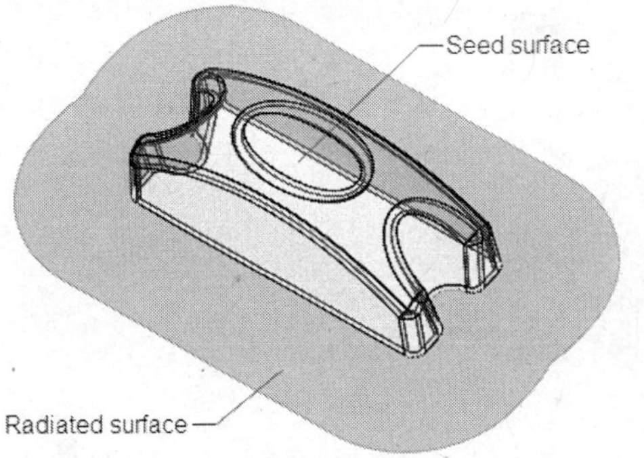

Figure 21-25 Radiated surface and the seed surface

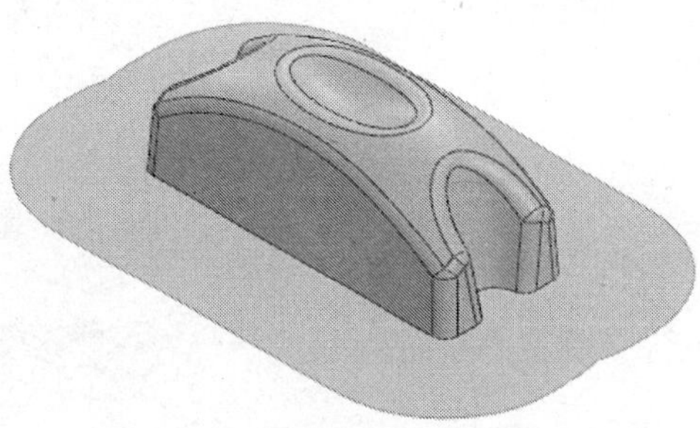

Figure 21-26 Resultant knit surface

Now, create a new plane offsetted vertically upward from the radiated surface. Remember that the offset distance should be more than the total height of the carburetor cover. Select this plane as the sketching plane and create the sketch for the cavity base and extrude it using the **Up To Surface** option. Now, hide the surface body. The final cavity is shown in Figure 21-27.

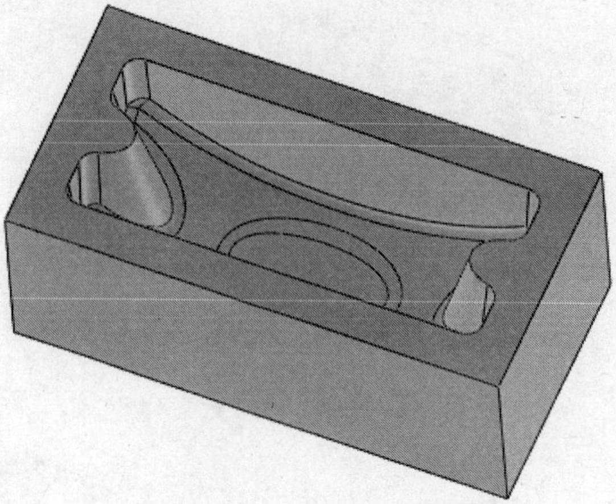

Figure 21-27 Final cavity

Now, unhide all other components and create the exploded view using the **Exploded View** tool, as shown in Figure 21-28.

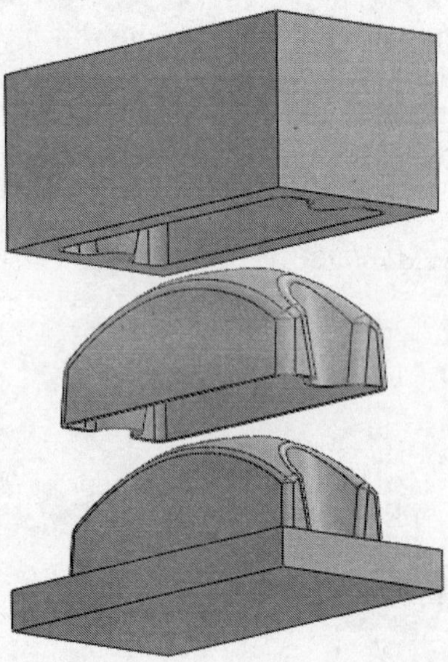

Figure 21-28 Exploded view of the final assembly

Save the assembly. The separate part documents of the Core and Cavity are also created. You can use these part documents for further use such as tool path generation or for performing some analysis. You also need to use the standard modeling tools to create the gates, runners, and so on.

Note

Sometimes, you may need to place some inserts in the mold to restrict the flow of metal in the mold. While designing a mold in SOLIDWORKS, you need to create the inserts using the top-down assembly approach.

TUTORIALS

Tutorial 1

In this tutorial, you will extract the core and cavity of a plastic cover shown in Figure 21-29. The resultant core is displayed in Figure 21-30 and the cavity is displayed in Figure 21-31. Figure 21-32 shows the exploded view of the assembly of the Mold Base. Figure 21-33 shows the views and dimensions of the plastic cover. Figure 21-34 shows the dimensions of the core plate. The dimensions of the cavity plate are displayed in Figure 21-35. **(Expected time: 1.5 hr)**

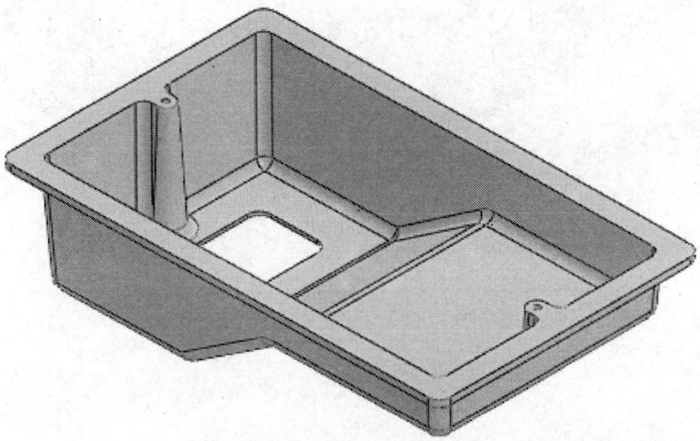

Figure 21-29 *Plastic cover*

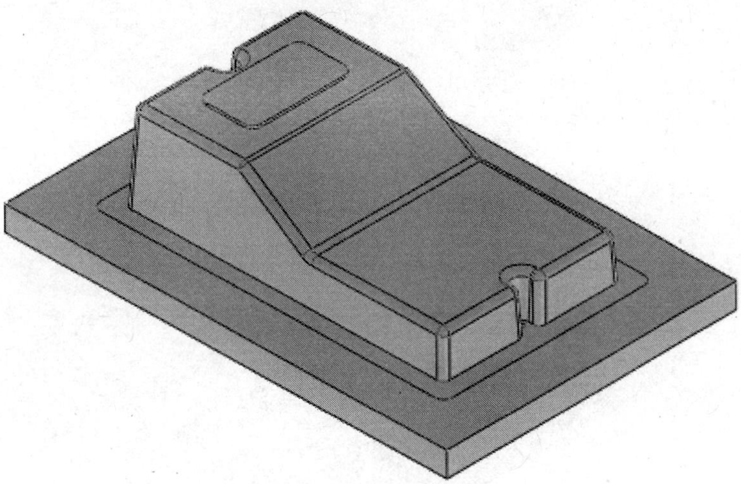

Figure 21-30 *Core of the Plastic Cover*

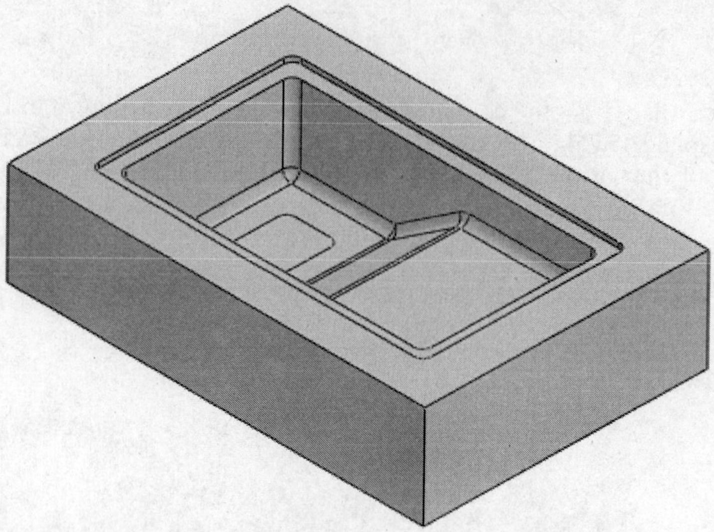

***Figure 21-31** Cavity of the Plastic Cover*

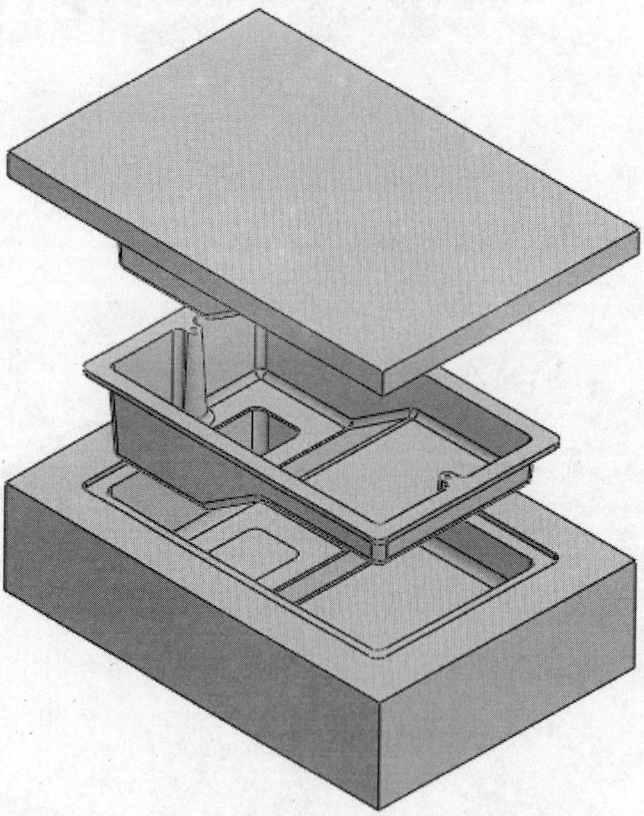

***Figure 21-32** Exploded view of the Mold Base assembly*

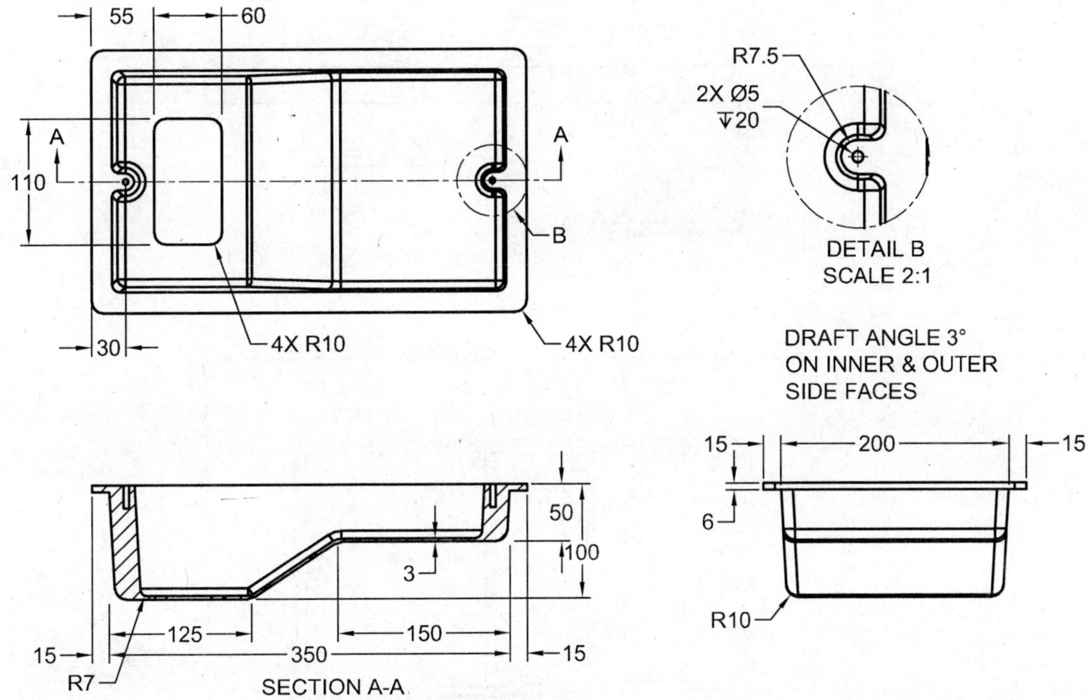

Figure 21-33 Views and dimensions of the plastic cover

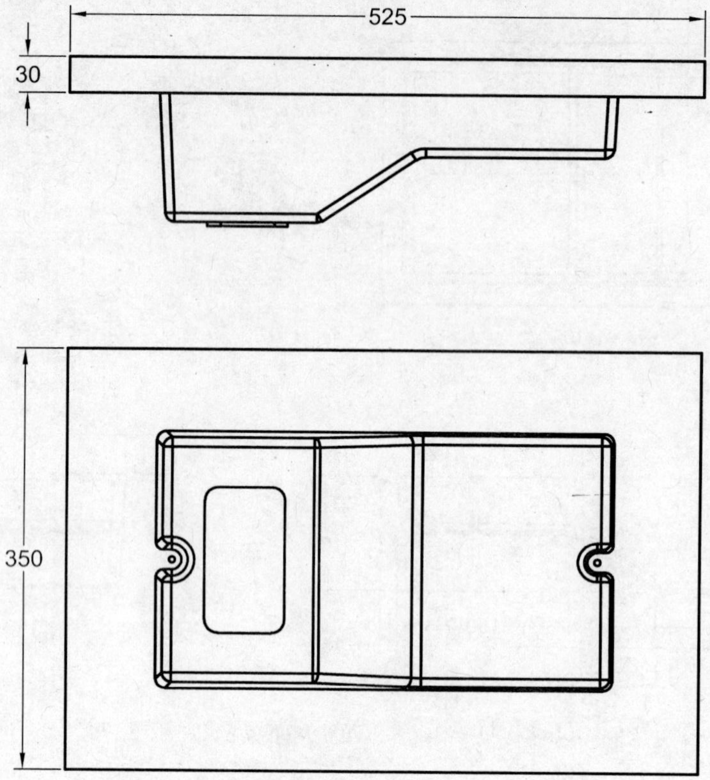

Figure 21-34 Dimensions of the core plate

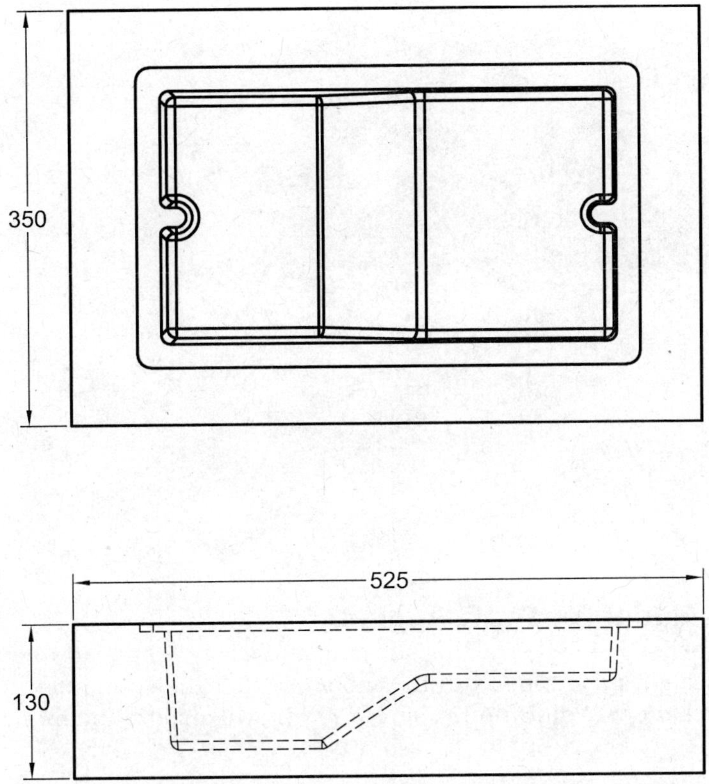

Figure 21-35 Dimensions of the cavity plate

The following steps are required to complete this tutorial:

a. Start a new SOLIDWORKS document and then create the model of the plastic cover.
b. Analyze the model for draft angles using the Draft analysis.
c. Scale the model.
d. Create the shut off surfaces.
e. Start a new SOLIDWORKS document in the Assembly mode and place the plastic cover in the assembly document.
f. Use the top-down approach to extract the core and cavity of the Plastic Cover.
g. Explode the assembly.

Creating the Plastic Cover

First, you need to create the plastic cover in the Part mode of SOLIDWORKS.

1. Start a new SOLIDWORKS document in the Part mode.

2. Using the standard modeling tools, create the model of the plastic cover. For dimensions, refer to Figure 21-33.

3. Save the model. Figure 21-36 shows the final model created using the standard modeling tools.

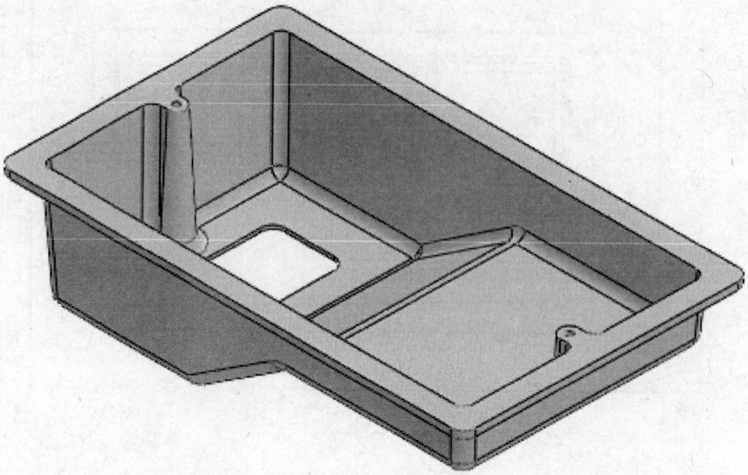

Figure 21-36 Final model of the Plastic Cover

Analyzing the Model for Draft Angles

As discussed earlier, before extracting the core and cavity, you need to make sure that the required draft angles are applied to the model so that the component is easily removed from the model after solidification. Therefore, you will analyze the model using the **Draft Analysis** tool.

1. Choose the **Draft Analysis** button from the **Mold Tools** toolbar; the **Draft Analysis PropertyManager** is displayed.

   First, you need to select the direction of pull along which the mold will be pulled out.

2. Select the top face of the plastic cover to define the direction of pull. Choose the **Reverse Direction** button available on the left of the **Direction of Pull** selection box.

   You will notice that the faces having positive draft and negative draft are displayed in green and red color respectively. Also, some small faces are displayed in yellow color, suggesting that the draft angle is required on these faces. Since these faces are very small in height as compared to the other faces of the part, therefore the draft angle is not required on them. You will also notice that the hole placed on one of the top faces of the part also displays its inner faces in yellow color. But you do not need to add draft to the inner faces of these holes because these holes will not be included in the core. These type of holes are drilled in the final molded part.

   If any face other than the faces having minor thickness are displayed in yellow, then you need to add required draft angle on those faces.

3. Choose the **OK** button from the **Draft Analysis PropertyManager**.

Scaling the Model and Creating Shut-Off Surfaces

After analyzing the model for draft angles, you need to scale the model. As discussed earlier, the scaling of the model is done in order to create the core and cavity larger than the component to be manufactured as the component shrinks after solidification. The scale factor always depends on the material to be used for molding or casting and also on the type of mold.

1. Choose the **Scale** button from the **Mold Tools** toolbar to invoke the **Scale PropertyManager**. 

2. Set the value of the scale factor in the **Scale Factor** spinner to 1.1.

3. Choose the **OK** button from the **Scale PropertyManager**.

4. Invoke the **Planar Surface** tool and select the edges, as shown in Figure 21-37. Next, create the shutoff surface and then close the **Planar Surface PropertyManager**. Model after creating the shutoff surface using the **Planar Surface** tool is shown in Figure 21-38.

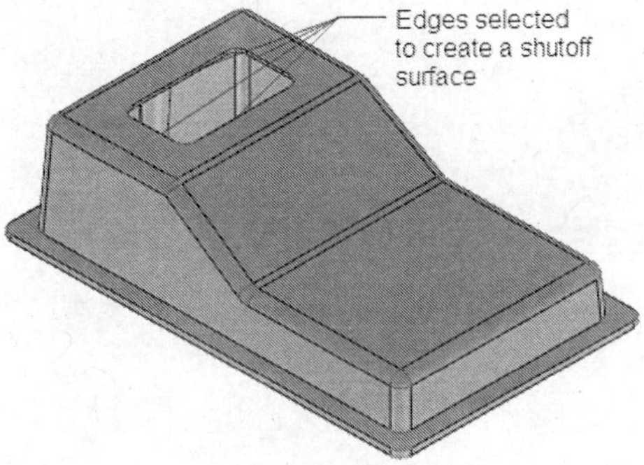

Figure 21-37 Edges selected to create a shutoff surface

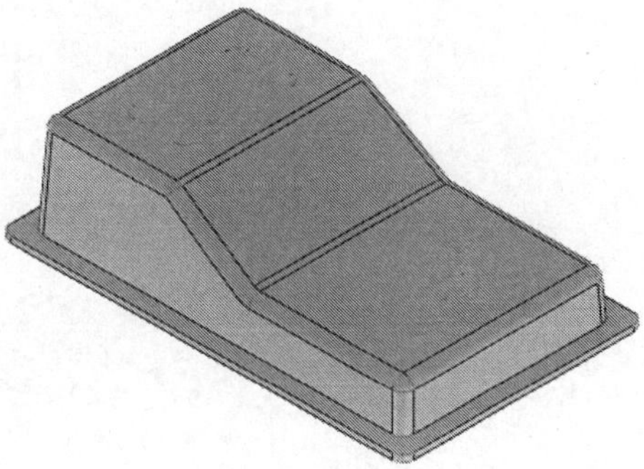

Figure 21-38 Model after creating the shutoff surface

5. Using the **Planar Surface** tool, create the shutoff surfaces on the edges of the holes created on one of the top faces of the model.

6. Save the model.

Creating the Interim Assembly

After finalizing the model, you need to create an interim assembly. Using this interim assembly and the top-down approach, you will extract the core and cavity of the model. To create the interim assembly, you first need to start a new SOLIDWORKS assembly document.

1. Start a new SOLIDWORKS assembly document.

2. Place the Plastic Cover coincident to the assembly origin.

3. Save the assembly file with the name Mold Base.

Extracting the Cavity

After creating the interim assembly, you need to extract the cavity. For extracting the cavity, you will use the top-down approach of the assembly.

1. Choose **Insert > Component > New Part** from the SOLIDWORKS menus.

2. Select the **Front plane** from the **FeatureManager Design Tree** to place the new component.

   As you place the component, the plastic cover is displayed transparent and the sketching environment in invoked. Right-click on the new part node added to the **FeatureManager Design Tree** and rename the part as Cavity.

3. Exit the sketching environment.

4. Using the **Radiate Surface** tool, create a radiated surface with a radiate distance of 10 mm, refer to Figure 21-39.

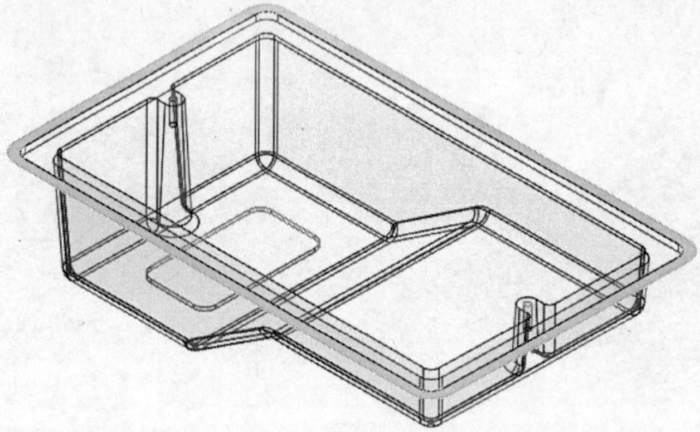

Figure 21-39 *The cover after creating the radiated surface*

Remember that if you have created shutoff surfaces in the model, there will be no seed surface. You need to select all the other faces of the model and the radiated surface as the surface to knit. To knit the radiated surface with the outer faces of the Plastic cover, you need to select all the outer faces of the model and the radiated surface.

5. Select the outer faces of the model and the radiated surface. Also, select the shut off surfaces created on the bottom face of the Plastic cover. Next, invoke the **Knit Surface** tool.

6. Choose the **OK** button from the **Knit Surface PropertyManager**.

7. Select the Plastic Cover from the **FeatureManager Design Tree** and invoke the shortcut menu. Choose the **Hide Components** option from the shortcut menu. The resultant surface body is displayed in Figure 21-40.

   Next, you need to create a plane at an offset distance from the radiated surface and then create the sketch of the cavity on the newly created plane. Then, extrude the sketch of the cavity up to the knitted surface.

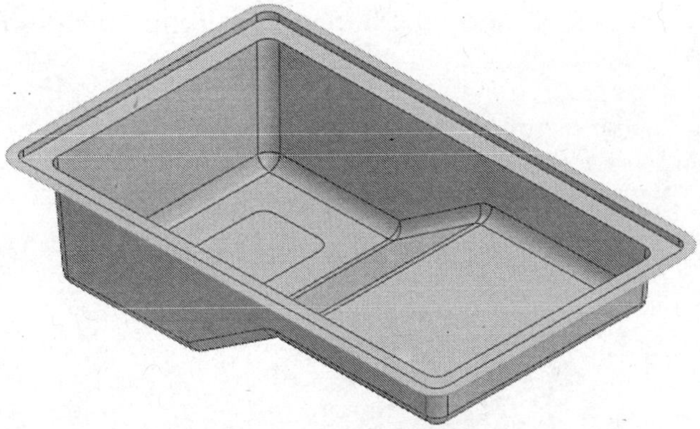

Figure 21-40 Resultant knitted surface after hiding the plastic cover

8. Create a new plane vertically downward at an offset distance of 130 mm from the radiated surface.

9. Create the sketch on the newly created plane for creating the solid cavity with help of the **Convert Entities** tool, as shown in Figure 21-41.

10. Now, using the **Up To Surface** option, extrude the sketch up to the knitted surface.

11. Hide the knit surface.

The resultant cavity is displayed in Figure 21-42.

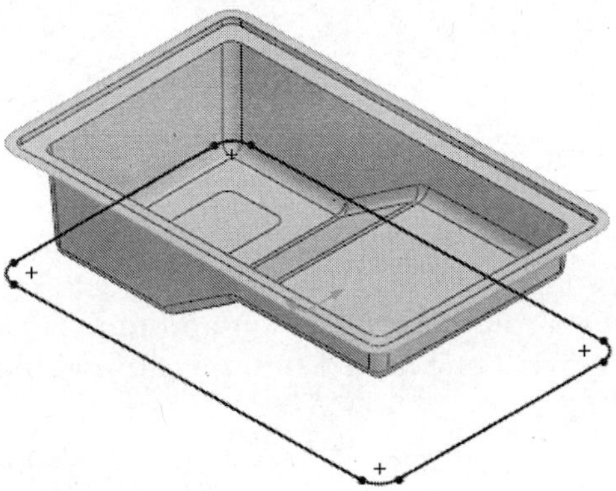

Figure 21-41 Sketch for the cavity

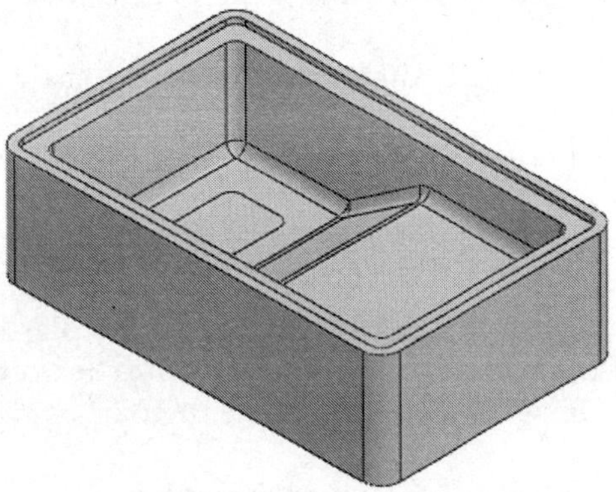

Figure 21-42 Resultant cavity

Next, you need to create the cavity plate. This plate will be created by extruding a rectangular sketch upto a distance of 130 mm.

12. Select the bottom face of the cavity as the sketching plane and invoke the sketching environment.

13. Create a rectangular sketch of dimension 525 × 350.

14. Extrude the sketch upto a distance of 130 mm by selecting the desired contour from the **Selected Contours** rollout.

15. Save the assembly. While saving the assembly the **Save As** message box is displayed. Select the desired option to save the files externally or internally.

Figure 21-43 shows the final cavity plate.

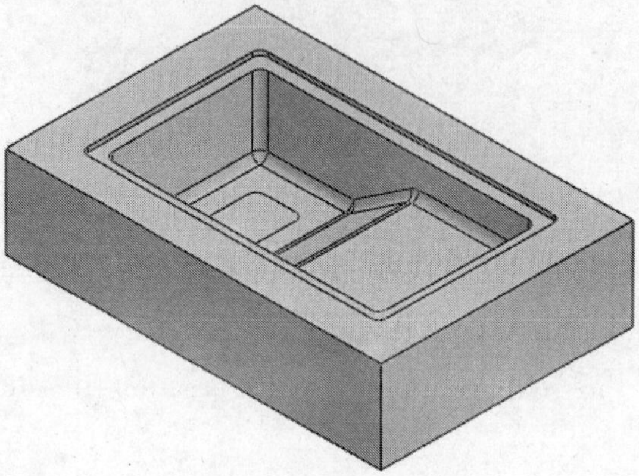

Figure 21-43 *Final cavity plate*

Extracting the Core

Next, you need to extract the core from the plastic cover. The core will also be extracted using the top-down approach of the assembly. Before proceeding further, you need to hide the cavity and unhide the plastic cover.

1. Hide the cavity and unhide the plastic cover.

2. Choose **Insert > Component > New Part** from the SOLIDWORKS menus.

3. Select the **Front plane** from the **FeatureManager Design Tree** to place the new component.

   As you place the component, the plastic cover is displayed transparent and the sketching environment is invoked. Right-click on the new part node added to the **FeatureManager Design Tree** and rename the part as Core.

4. Exit the sketching environment.

5. Create a radiated surface as created earlier.

6. Now, knit all the internal surfaces of the plastic cover with the radiated surface.

7. Hide the plastic cover.

   The resultant extracted surface is displayed in Figure 21-44.

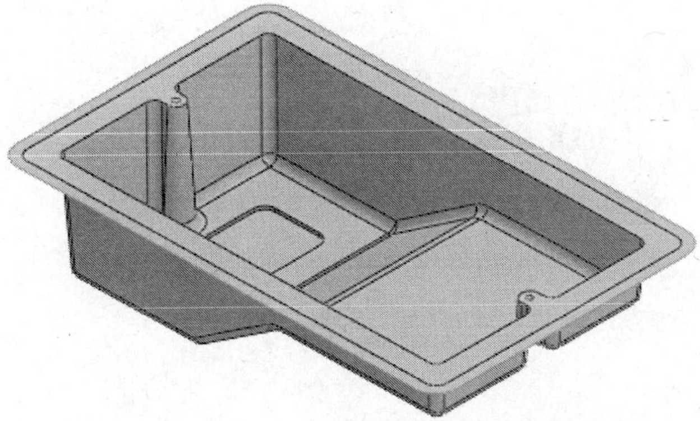

Figure 21-44 Resultant extracted surface

8. Now, create a plane at an offset distance of 30 mm from the top face of the extracted surface.

9. Select the newly created plane as the sketching plane and create the sketch of the Core using the **Convert Entities** tool, as shown in Figure 21-45.

10. Extrude the sketch up to the knitted surface and hide the knitted surface. Figure 21-46 shows the resultant core extracted from the plastic cover.

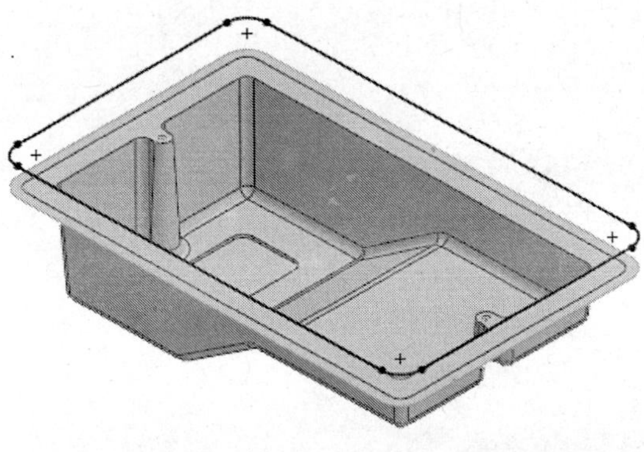

Figure 21-45 Sketch for creating the Core

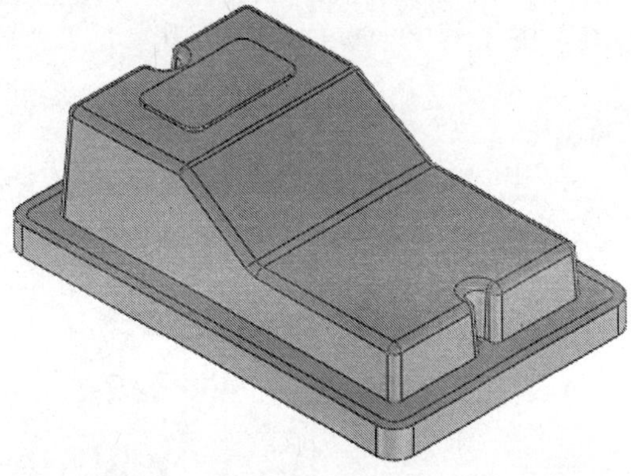

Figure 21-46 Resultant Core

11. Now, create the core plate by extruding the sketch created on the top face of the Core.

12. Save the assembly.

The final Core is displayed in Figure 21-47.

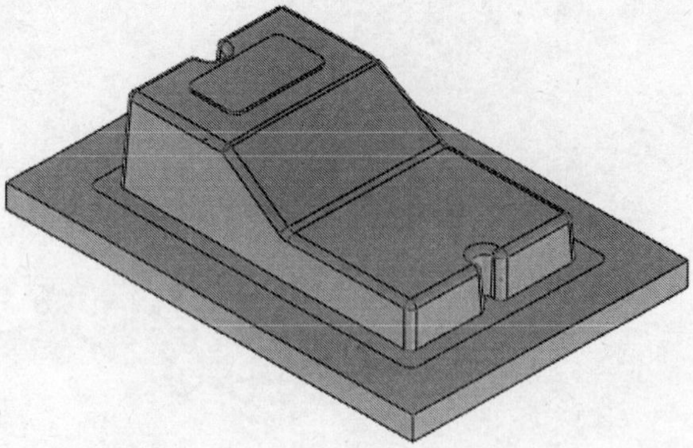

Figure 21-47 Rotated view of the core

Creating the Exploded View of the Assembly

After extracting the core and cavity of the plastic cover, you need to create exploded view of the Mold base assembly. For creating the exploded view of the Mold base assembly, first you need to unhide the Cavity and the Plastic Cover.

1. Unhide the Cavity and the Plastic Cover.

2. Using the **Exploded View** tool in **Assembly CommandManager**, explode the Mold Base assembly, refer to Figure 21-48.

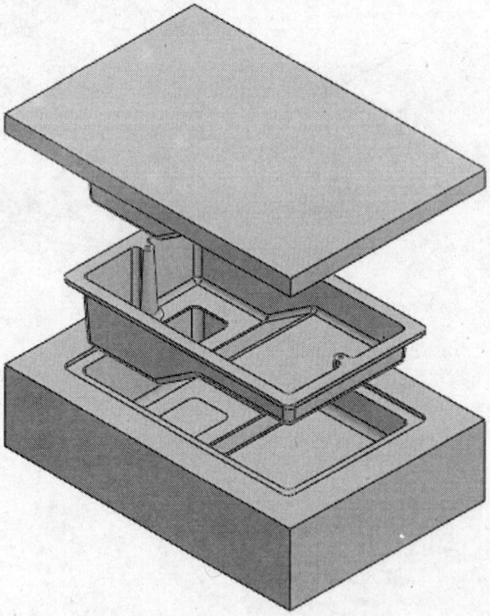

Figure 21-48 Exploded view of the Mold base assembly

3. Save the assembly.

Tutorial 2

In this tutorial, you will extract the core and cavity of the cover shown in Figure 21-49. The other side of the cover is displayed in Figure 21-50. The core of the cover is displayed in Figure 21-51 and the cavity in Figure 21-52. The first Insert to be inserted in the mold is displayed in Figure 21-53. The second insert is also the same as displayed in Figure 21-53. Figure 21-54 shows the exploded view of the Mold base assembly. Figure 21-55 shows the views and dimensions of the cover. Figure 21-56 shows the views and dimensions of the core. Figure 21-57 shows the views and dimensions of the cavity. Figure 21-58 shows the views and dimensions of the insert. After creating the Mold base assembly, you will also create the exploded view of the assembly.

(Expected time: 2 hr)

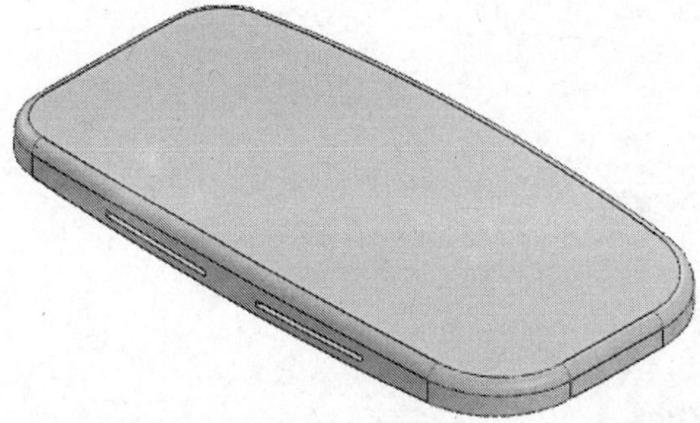

Figure 21-49 *Isometric view of the cover*

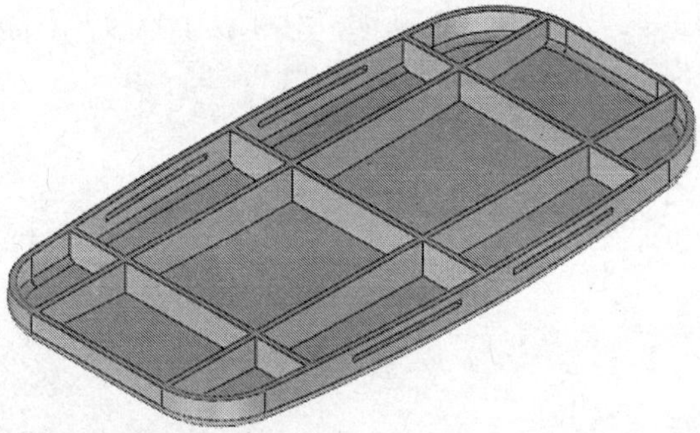

Figure 21-50 *Rotated view of the cover*

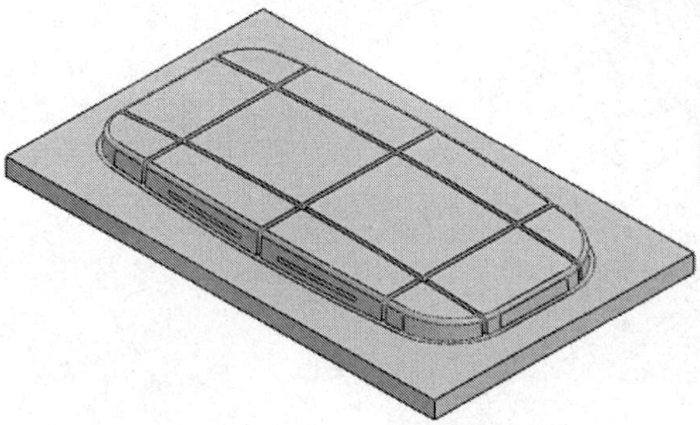

Figure 21-51 *Isometric view of the Core Plate*

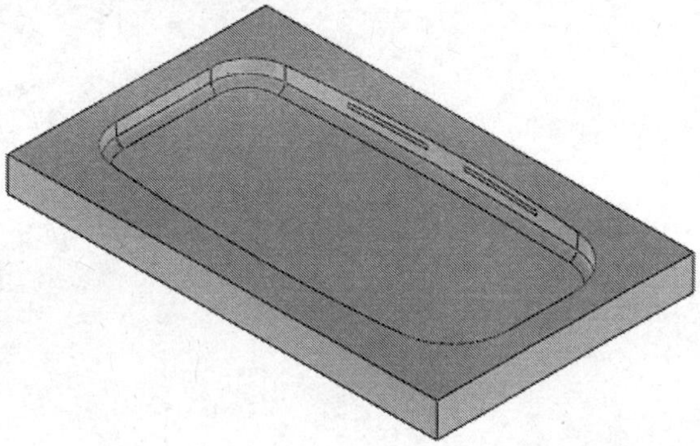

Figure 21-52 *Isometric view of the Cavity Plate*

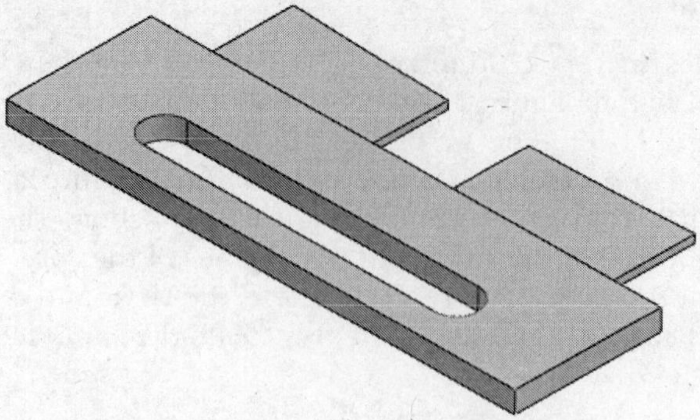

Figure 21-53 *Isometric view of the Insert*

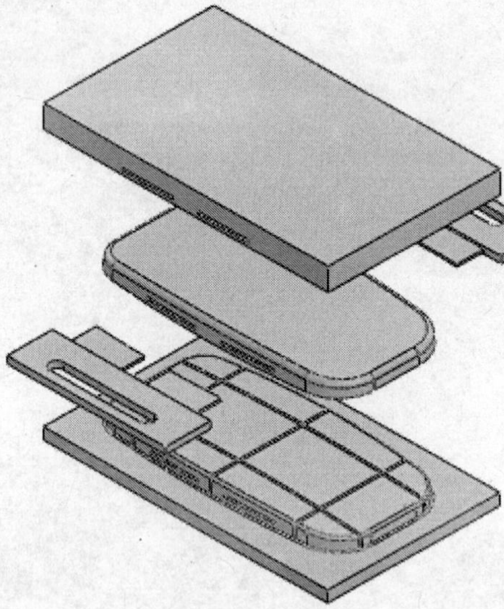

Figure 21-54 *Exploded view of the Mold Base assembly*

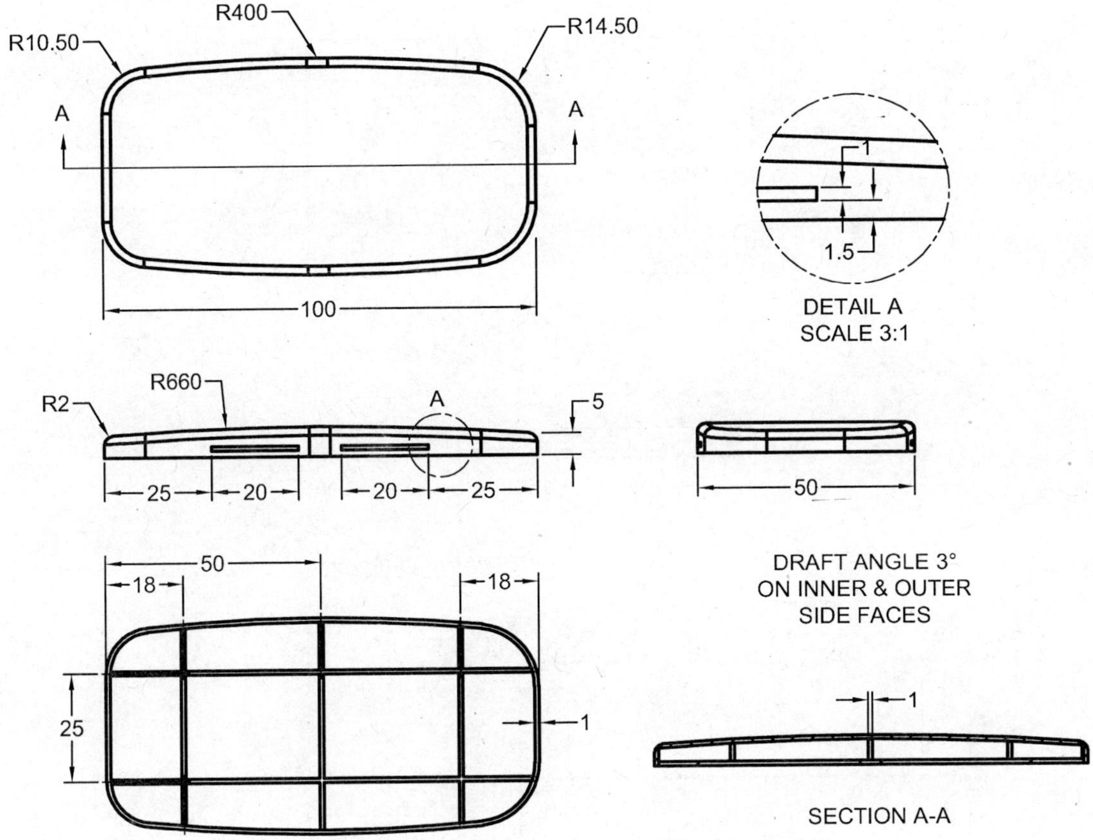

Figure 21-55 *Views and dimensions of the cover*

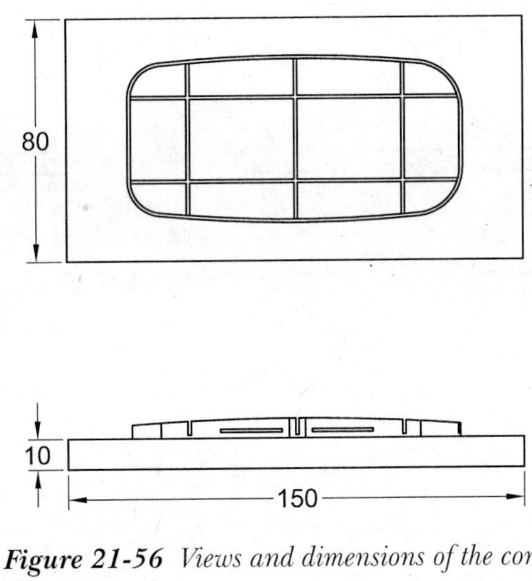

Figure 21-56 *Views and dimensions of the core*

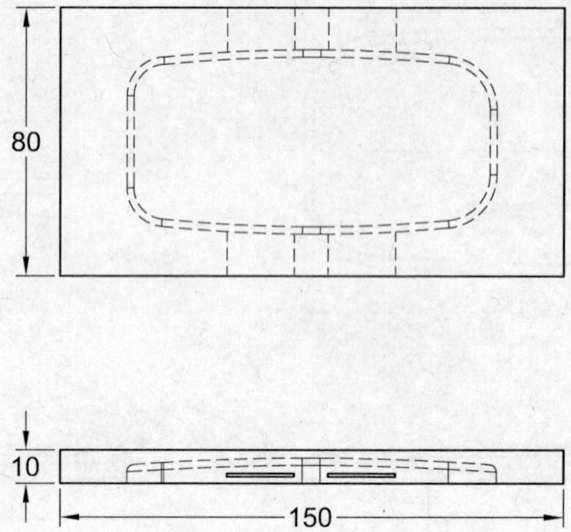

Figure 21-57 Views and dimensions of the cavity

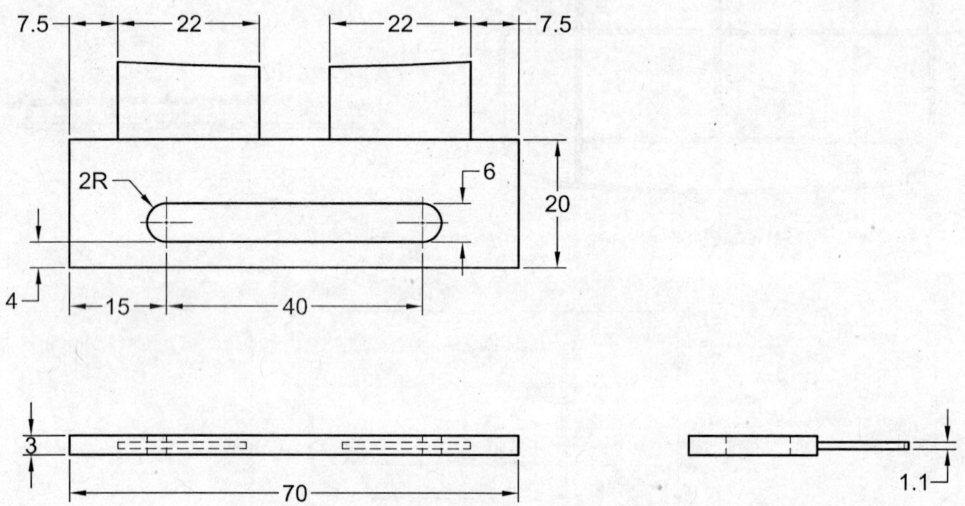

Figure 21-58 Views and dimensions of the insert

The following steps are required to complete this tutorial:

a. Start a new SOLIDWORKS document and using the standard modeling tools, create the model of the cover.
b. Analyze the model for the draft angles.
c. Scale the model.
d. Create the shutoff surfaces.
e. Create the interim assembly.
f. Extract the core.
g. Extract the cavity.
h. Create the slots in the cavity for the insertion of inserts.
i. Using the top-down approach, create the inserts.
j. Create the exploded view of the assembly.

Creating the Cover Part

First, you need to create the model of the cover. For creating the model, start a new SOLIDWORKS document in the Part mode.

1. Start a new SOLIDWORKS document in the Part mode.

2. Using the standard modeling tools, create the model of the cover. The completed model of the cover is displayed in Figure 21-59.

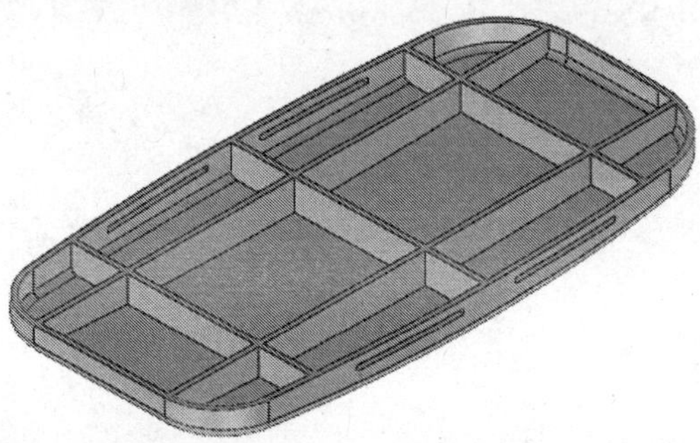

Figure 21-59 *Model of the cover*

Analyzing the Draft Angles

After creating the model, you need to analyze the model for draft angles using the **Draft Analysis** tool.

1. Invoke the **Draft Analysis** tool from the **Mold Tools** toolbar to display the **Draft Analysis PropertyManager**. Using this tool, analyze the draft angles in the model. If some faces of the model are displayed in yellow, then you need to add the draft angles to those faces.

Note

If some part of the middle portion of the curved face is displayed in yellow, you can ignore that.

Scaling the Model

After analyzing the model for draft angles and adding the drafts as required, you need to scale the model.

1. Invoke the **Scale PropertyManager**.
2. Set the value of the scale factor in the **Scale Factor** spinner to 1.1 and choose the **OK** button to scale the model.

Creating the Shutoff Surfaces

After scaling the model, you need to create the shutoff surfaces.

1. Using the **Filled Surface** tool, shut the openings on the outer front face and on the inner front face.
2. Shut the openings on the outer back face and on the inner back face using the **Filled Surface** tool.

Creating the Interim Assembly

After creating and saving the part model, you need to create an interim assembly. In this interim assembly, you will extract the core and cavity using the top-down approach.

1. Start a new SOLIDWORKS assembly document.
2. Save the assembly with the name Mold Base.
3. Place the Cover part coincident to the assembly origin.

Extracting the Core

For extracting the core, first you need to place a new part in the assembly document using the top-down approach.

1. Choose **Insert > Component > New Part** from the SOLIDWORKS menus.
2. Select the **Front plane** from the **FeatureManager Design Tree** to place the new component.

   As you place the component, the cover is displayed transparent and the sketching environment is invoked.

3. Right-click on the new part node added in the **FeatureManager Design Tree** and rename the part as Core using the option from the shortcut menu.
4. Exit the sketching environment.
5. Using the **Radiate Surface** tool, create the radiated surface using the outer edges of the bottom face of the cover.

6. Using the **Knit Surface** tool, knit all the inner surfaces of the cover with the radiated surface to create a single knitted surface.

7. Hide the cover and create a new offset plane vertically downward at a distance from the radiated surface.

8. Select the newly created plane as the sketching plane and invoke the sketching environment.

9. Create the sketch of the core and extrude it up to the knitted surface.

10. Select the bottom face of the core and invoke the sketching environment.

11. Create the sketch of the core plate and extrude it upto the required depth.

12. Return to the assembly environment and save the assembly.

    The final core is shown in Figure 21-60.

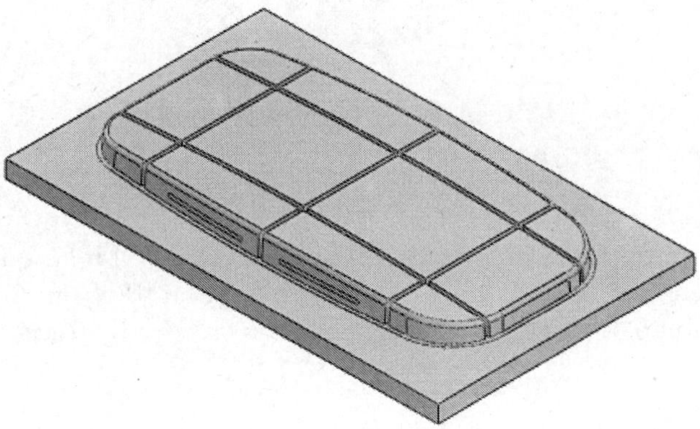

Figure 21-60 *Final core*

Extracting the Cavity

After extracting the core, you need to the extract the cavity. The cavity will also be extracted using the same procedure that was used to extract the core. For this, you first need to create a new component in the assembly.

1. Choose **Insert > Component > New Part** from the SOLIDWORKS menus.

2. Select the **Front plane** from the **FeatureManager Design Tree** to place the new component.

   As you place the component, the cover is displayed transparent and the sketching environment is invoked. Right-click on the new part node added in the **FeatureManager Design Tree** and rename the part as Core.

3. Exit the sketching environment.

4. Create the radiated surface and knit the radiated surface with the outer surfaces of the part.

5. Create a plane vertically upward at an offset distance of 10 mm from the radiated surface.

6. Select the newly created plane and invoke the sketching environment.

7. Create the sketch of the cavity and then extrude the sketch up to the knitted surface.

8. Add the remaining features to create the final cavity plate, refer to Figure 21-61.

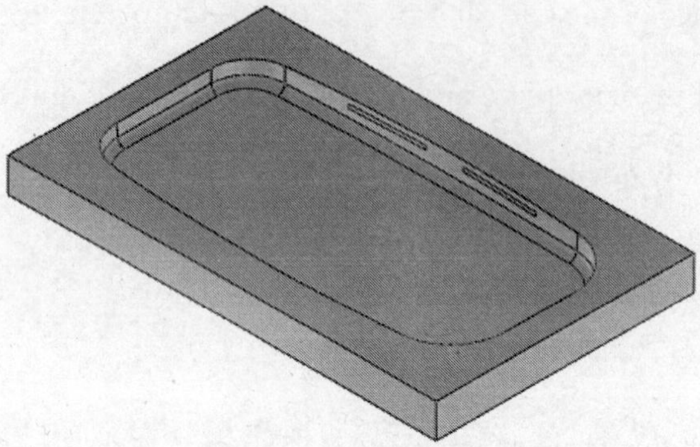

Figure 21-61 *Cavity plate displayed after hiding the cover*

Next, you need to create the slots in the cavity plate that will be used to place the inserts. The slots will be created by extruding a sketch created on the front face of the cavity plate using the cut option. The sketch of the slots will be created by using the **Convert Entities** tool on the edges of the slots of the cover.

9. Select the front face of the cavity plate as the sketching plane and invoke the sketching environment.

10. Choose the **Convert Entities** tool and select the edges of two slots displayed on the front face of the cover.

11. Invoke the **Cut-Extrude PropertyManager** and extrude the sketch using the **Through All** option.

12. Return to the assembly environment and save the assembly.

The final cavity after creating the slots is displayed in Figure 21-62.

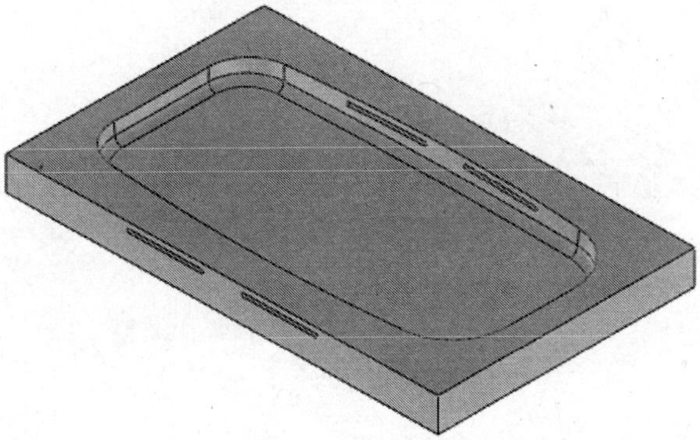

Figure 21-62 Cavity after creating the slots

Creating the Insert

After extracting the core and cavity, you need to create the insert that will be used to restrict the flow of molten material in the portion where the insert is placed. This in turn will create the slot in the molded plastic component. The insert will also be created as a separate part using the top-down approach.

1. Choose **Insert > Component > New Part** from the SOLIDWORKS menus.

2. Select the **Front plane** from the **FeatureManager Design Tree** to place the new component.

   Right-click on the new part node added in **FeatureManager Design Tree** and rename the part as Insert1.

3. Exit the sketching environment.

4. Select the front face of the cavity plate as the sketching plane and invoke the sketching environment.

5. Using the **Convert Entities** tool, select the edges of the slots placed on the front face of the cavity plate.

6. Extrude the sketch of each slot using contour selection up to the inner front curved face of the cover. Figure 21-63 shows the assembly with the preview of base feature being extruded using contour selection.

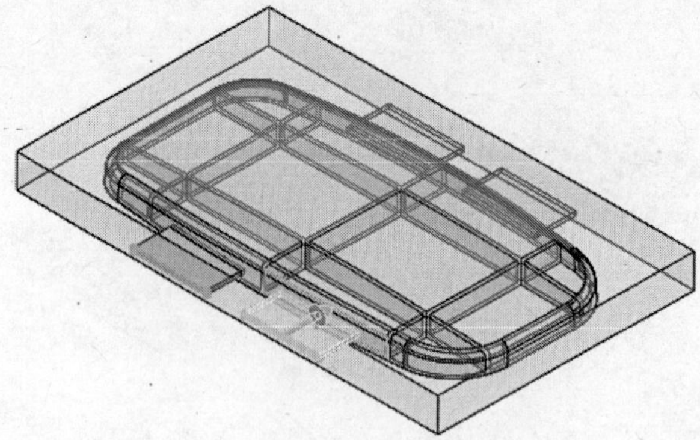

Figure 21-63 *Base feature of Insert1*

7. Using the standard modeling tools, create the back plate of the insert.

   Figure 21-64 shows the assembly after creating Insert1.

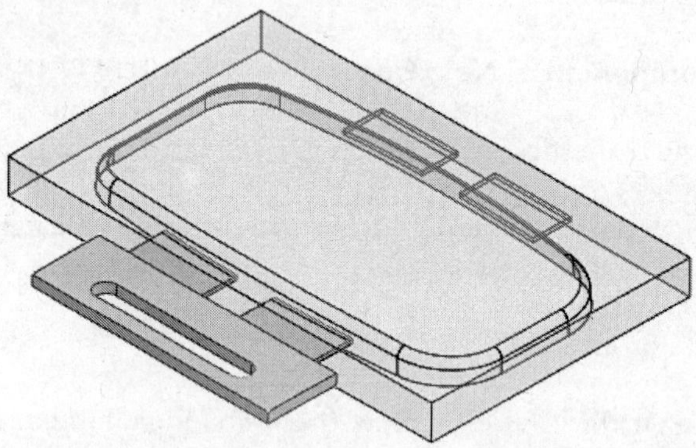

Figure 21-64 *Assembly after completing the insert*

Similarly, create another insert. The final Mold base assembly is shown in Figure 21-65.

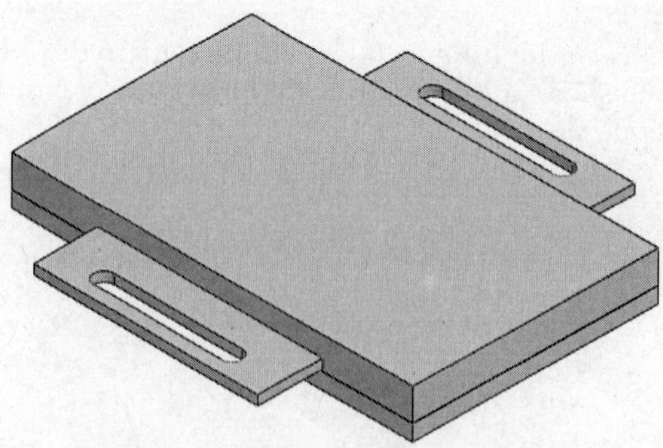

Figure 21-65 *Final Mold Base assembly*

Next, you need to create the exploded view of the assembly, refer to Figure 21-66.

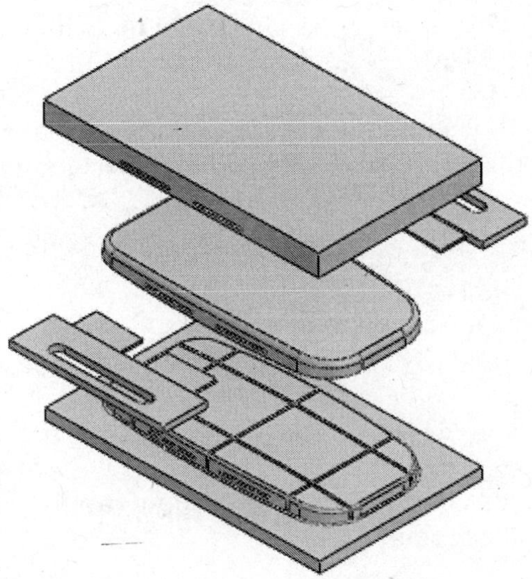

Figure 21-66 Exploded view of the Mold Base assembly

Self-Evaluation Test

Answer the following questions and then compare them to those given at the end of this chapter:

1. The _________ is the female part of the mold, it is hollow from inside and the molten metal or plastic is poured into it so that it can take the shape of the cavity to create the component.

2. The __________ is the male part of the mold and it defines the area where the molten metal should not reach.

3. The cavity is created using the _________ tool.

4. The options available in the _________ drop-down list provided in the **Scale Parameters** area of the **Cavity PropertyManager** are used to define the origin about which you need to scale the cavity.

5. For creating the derived components, you need to choose the _________ from the **File** menu in SOLIDWORKS menus.

6. If the **Mold Tools** toolbar is not available by default, then choose **View > Toolbars >Mold Tools** from the menu bar to display this toolbar. (T/F)

7. To invoke the **Scale PropertyManager,** you need to choose the **Scale** tool from the **Mold Tools** toolbar. (T/F)

8. The **Uniform scaling** check box is not selected by default and the model is uniformly scaled. (T/F)

9. You need to select the **Find steep faces** check box to analyze the positive steep faces and the negative steep faces. (T/F)

10. You can analyze the draft angle by choosing the **Calculate** button from the **Analysis Parameters** rollout in the **Draft Analysis PropertyManager**. (T/F)

Review Questions

Answer the following questions:

1. The __________ tool is used to analyze the draft angles of the model.

2. For scaling the model, you need to invoke the __________ tool.

3. Using the options available in the __________ drop-down list, you can specify the direction along which you can scale the model.

4. The __________ **PropertyManager** is used to analyze the draft angles.

5. The __________ check box is selected to display color variations specifying the draft angles on the model in the **Draft Analysis PropertyManager**.

6. The **Gradual transition** check box available in the **Color Settings** rollout of the **Draft Analysis PropertyManager** is used to display color variations specifying the draft angles on the model. (T/F)

7. Using the **Scale Factor** spinner, you can specify the scale factor for scaling the model. (T/F)

8. The **Face classification** check box available in the **Analysis Parameters** rollout is used to refine the draft analysis depending on the type of draft. (T/F)

9. Using the **Scale About** drop-down list, you can specify the entity about which the model will be scaled. (T/F)

10. The **Find steep faces check box** is selected to analyze the positive steep faces and the negative steep faces. (T/F)

EXERCISE

Exercise 1

In this exercise, you will extract the core and cavity of the model created in Tutorial 2 of Chapter 7, refer to Figure 21-67 and Figure 21-68. Before proceeding further, you need to modify the model by deleting the lip created as an extruded feature and then add required draft angles to the model. **(Expected time: 2 hr)**

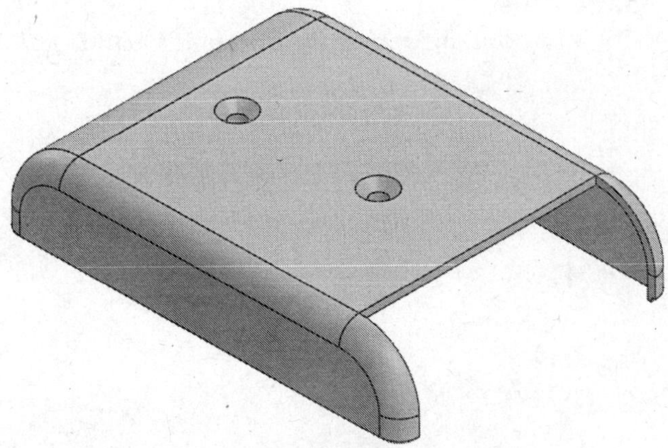

Figure 21-67 Model for creating mold with core and cavity

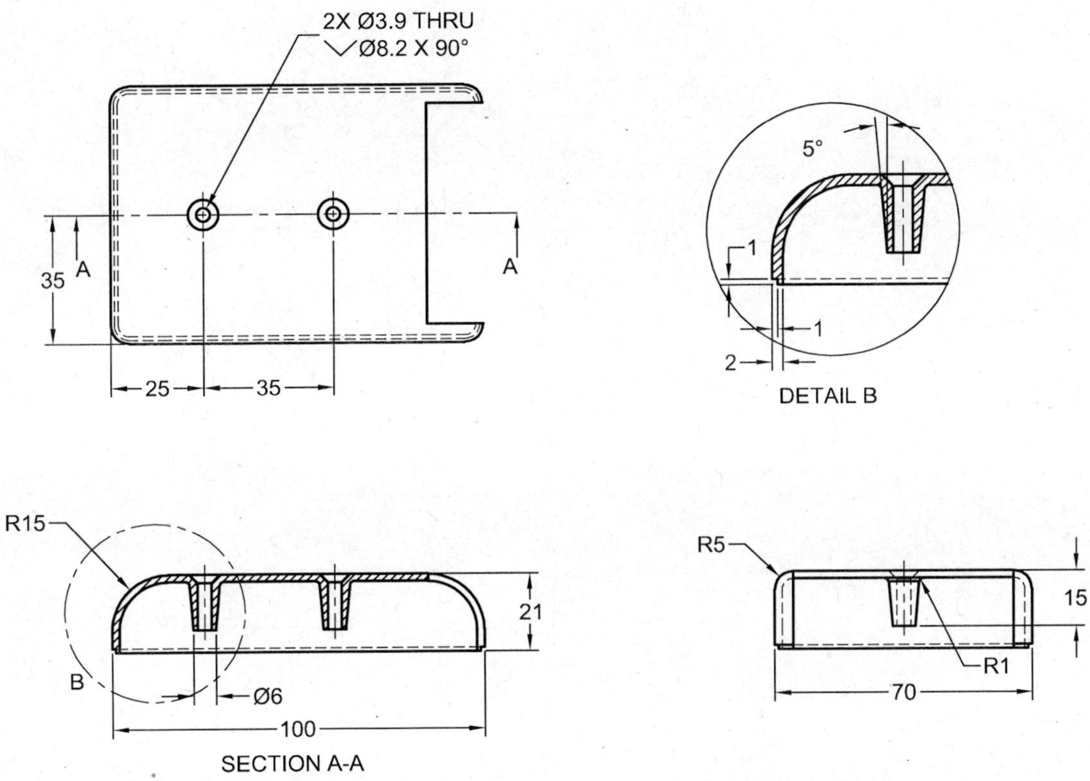

Figure 21-68 Top view, front section view, and right side view with dimensions

Answers to Self-Evaluation Test

1. cavity, **2.** core, **3. Cavity**, **4. About**, **5. Derive Component Part**, **6.** T, **7.** T, **8.** F, **9.** T, **10.** T

SOLIDWORKS Certification Exam

In the current challenging world, the competition in CAD industry has been increasing day by day. Companies today want to hire proficient designers so that they are productive from the day one. Therefore, many of the software developer companies have introduced certification programs to assess the technical knowledge of the designers and then certify them. As one of the most widely used MCAD packages in the industry, SOLIDWORKS is an excellent example of how certification can help you to standout in the crowd of engineers. SOLIDWORKS has so far issued 4,16,922 certifications and the figure is expected to become bigger in the future, indicating the importance of certification at student and industrial level.

Types of Certification

In SOLIDWORKS, the certification is provided in three major categories. These categories are:

1) Associate Level
2) Professional Level
3) Expert Level

The following certifications are also provided in SOLIDWORKS:
CSWPA-Drawing Tools
CSWPA-Mold Making
CSWPA-Sheet Metal
CSWPA-Surfacing
CSWPA-Weldments
And many more.

Certified SOLIDWORKS Associate (CSWA) – Mechanical Design

This certification is for the users having basic level of understanding of the software. The exam length is 3 hours and minimum passing grade is 70%. There is a 14 day waiting period between every attempt of CSWA exam.

All candidates get electronic certificates and personal listing on the CSWA directory when they pass the exam.

Certified SOLIDWORKS Professional (CSWP) - Mechanical Design

This certification is intended for advanced level users. The exam length is 3 hours 20 minutes. There is a 14 day waiting period between every attempt of CSWA exam.

All candidates get electronic certificates and personal listing on the CSWP directory when they pass the exam.

There are three segments in this exam, which are as follows:
Segment 1: This segment has 70 minutes duration and 70 points are required to pass this segment.

Segment 2: This segment has 50 minutes duration and 77 points are required to pass this segment.

Segment 3: This segment has 80 minutes duration and 77 points are required to pass this segment.

Note
The range of tools covered in this exam is more than CSWP exam.

Certified SOLIDWORKS Expert (CSWE) - Mechanical Design

This certification is an expert level exam. The exam length is 4 hour and minimum passing grade is 80%. There is a 90 day waiting period between every attempt of CSWE exam.

All candidates get electronic certificates, business card logo and personal listing on the CSWE directory when they pass the exam.

This exam has some prerequisites, which are as follows:
(a) Successfully passed the CSWP exam.
(b) Successfully passed at least four of the CSWP advanced topic exams (Sheet Metal, Weldments, Surfacing, Mold Tools, and Drawing Tools).

TUTORIALS

To perform the tutorials, you need to download the zipped file named as *c19_SW_input* from the **Input Files** section of the CADCIM website. The complete path for downloading the file is:

Textbooks > CAD/CAM > SOLIDWORKS > SOLIDWORKS 2021 for Designers > Input Files

Tutorial 1

In this tutorial, download the file and open it in SOLIDWORKS, as shown in Figure 1. Next, you need to change the value of A and B parameters in the sketch, refer to Figure 2. Next, move the hole in the part 30 mm in X-direction, as shown in Figure 3.

Details of the part are given next:
Material: Brass
Density: 8500 kg / m^3
Part Units: MM
Decimal Places: 2

Origin: Default
A = R10
B = Φ18

What is the Center of mass of the part?

Enter Coordinates:

X: ----------

Y: ----------

Z: ----------

(Expected time: 10 min)

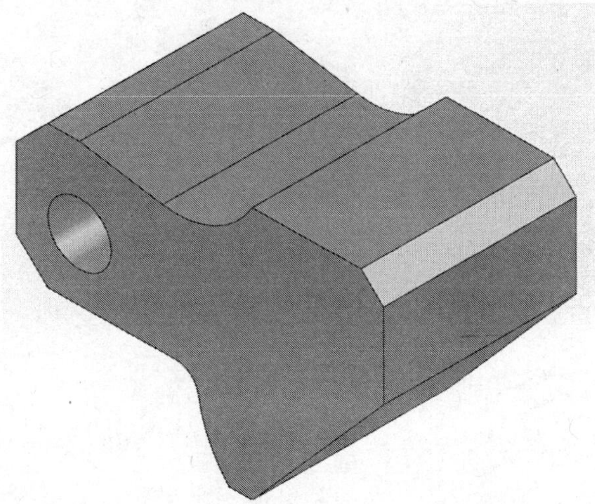

Figure 1 *The isometric view of the model*

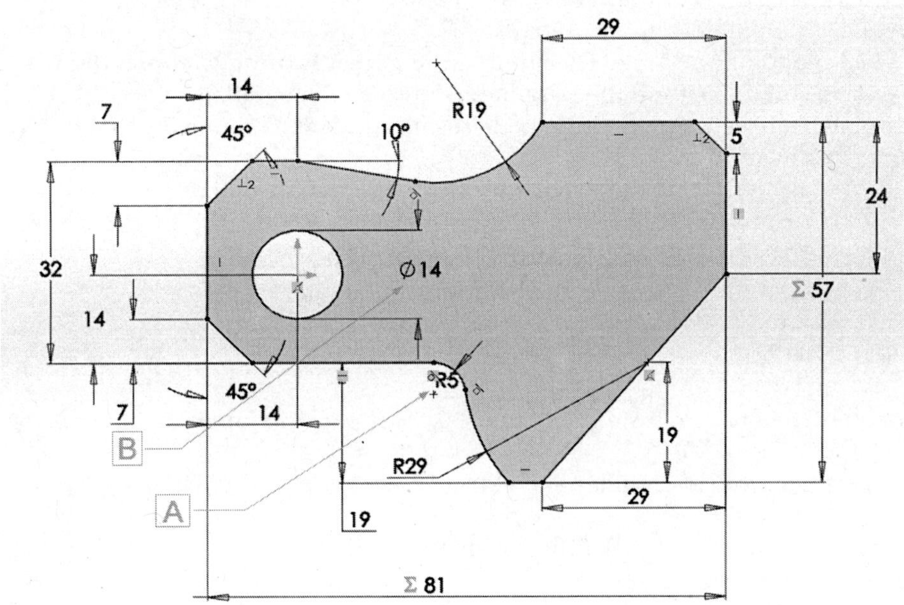

Figure 2 *The A and B parameters in the sketch of the model*

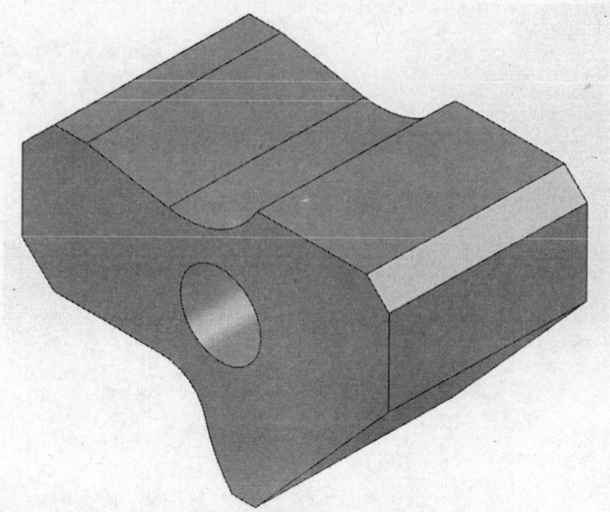

Figure 3 The model after changing parameters and hole position

The following steps are required to complete this tutorial:

a. Start **SOLIDWORKS 2021** and open the model.
b. Edit A and B parameters in the sketch.
c. Move the hole using the **Move Face** tool in the **Direct Editing CommandManager**.
d. Set the precision to measure the parameters upto 2 decimal places.
e. Measure the Center of Mass of the model using the **Mass Properties** tool in the **Evaluate CommandManager**.
f. Save the file using the **SAVE AS** tool and then close the document.

Starting SOLIDWORKS 2021 and Opening the Model

First, you need to start SOLIDWORKS and open a model.

1. Start SOLIDWORKS 2021.

2. Choose the **Open** button from the Menu Bar to display the **Open** dialog box.

3. Browse to the downloaded folder and extract the *CSW_tut_01.zip* file.

4. Select the *CSW_tut_01.SLDPRT* file from the *CSW_tut_01* folder and then choose the **Open** button. The model gets opened in the part environment, as shown in Figure 4.

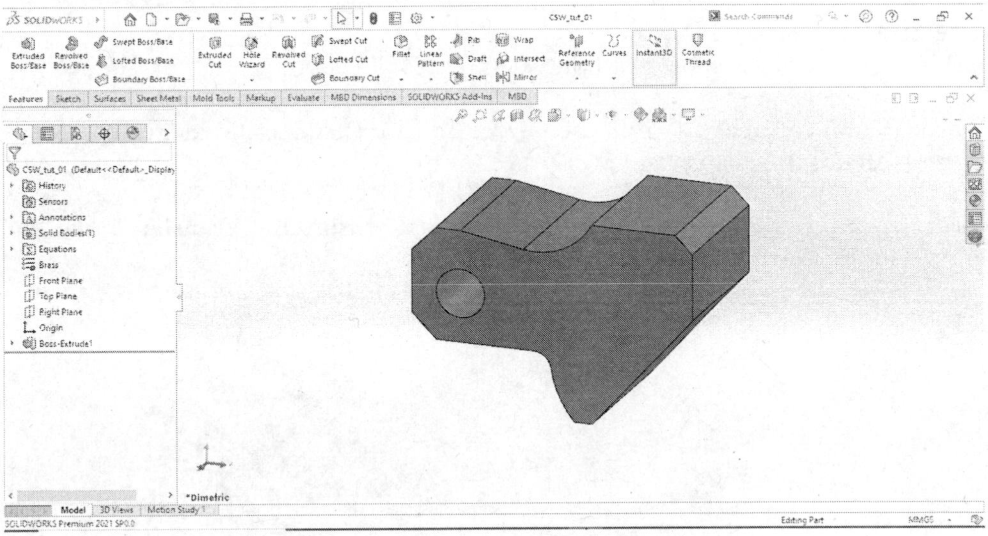

Figure 4 The model in the part environment

Editing the Sketch

In this section, you will change the value of A and B parameters provided in the question.

1. Select **Boss-Extrude1** from the **FeatureManager Design Tree**; a pop-up toolbar is displayed.

2. Choose **Edit Sketch** from the pop-up toolbar; the sketching environment is displayed. Change A and B parameters as provided in the question. Exit the sketching environment. The modified model is shown in Figure 5.

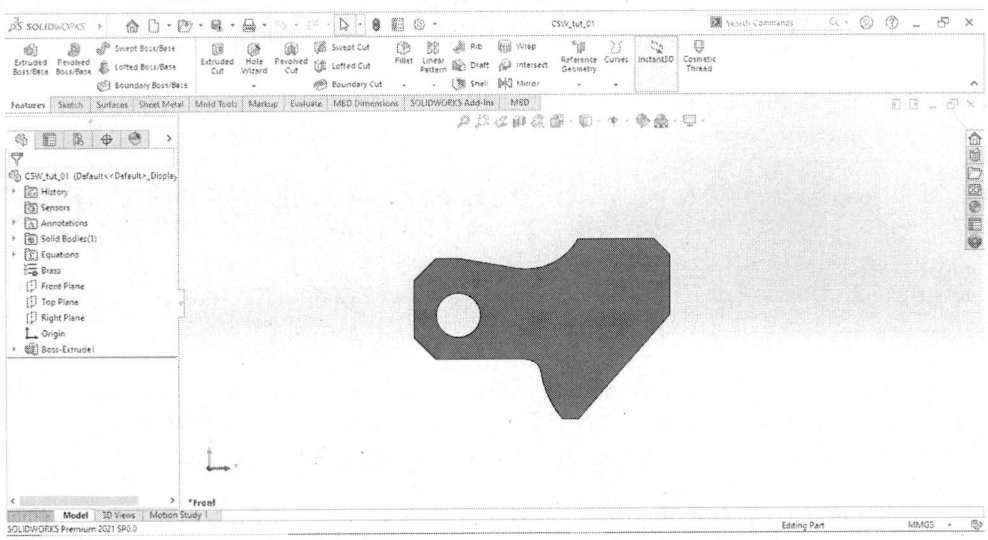

Figure 5 The modified model

Moving the Hole

In this section, you will move the hole 30 mm in X direction.

1. Choose the **Move Face** tool from the **Direct Editing CommandManager**; the **Move Face PropertyManager** is displayed.

2. Select the face of the hole, refer to Figure 6. Also, ensure the **Translate** radio button is selected in the **Move Face** rollout.

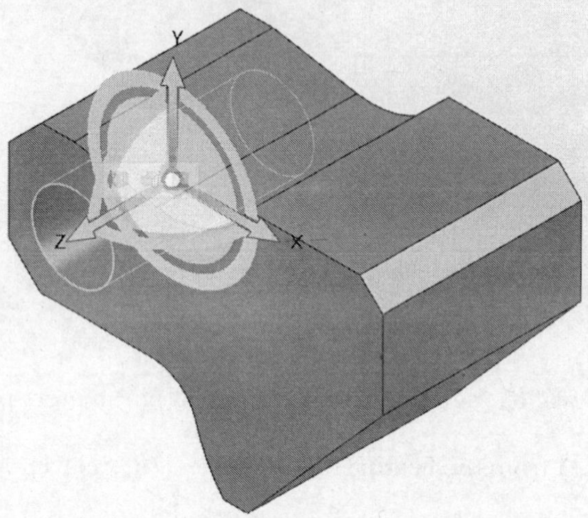

Figure 6 *The face selected in the model*

3. Select the X direction arrowhead and specify **30 mm** in the **Delta X** edit box.

4. Choose the **OK** button to close the **Move Face PropertyManager**.

Measuring the Center of Mass

In this section, you need to measure the center of mass of the model.

Before measuring the center of mass of the model, ensure that 2 decimal places precision is selected.

1. Select the **Edit Document Units** option from the **Unit system** in the status bar; the **Document Properties - Units** dialog box gets displayed.

2. Click the **Units** option in the dialog box and ensure that the **MMGS** radio button is selected in the **Unit system** area. Next, select **.12** from the **Length** row in the **Basic Units** area and also select **.12** from the **Length** row in the **Mass/Section Properties** area.

3. Choose **OK** button to close the dialog box.

4. Select the **Mass Properties** tool from the **Evaluate CommandManager**; the **Mass Properties** dialog box with the center of mass value is displayed, refer to Figure 7.

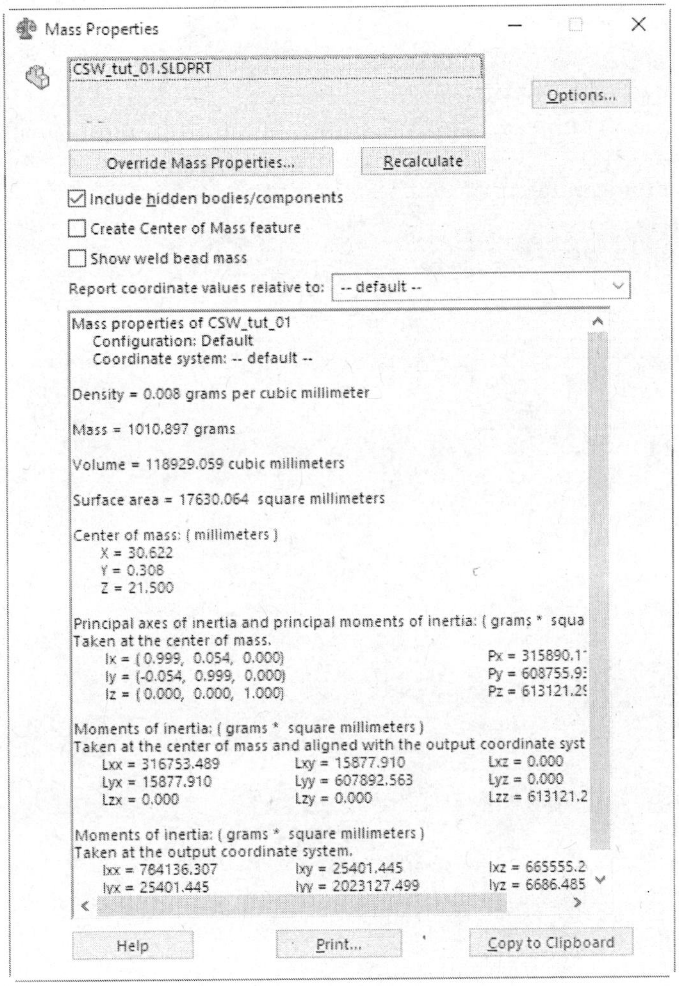

Figure 7 *The* ***Mass Properties*** *dialog box*

Center of mass of the model
x = **28.89**, y = **0.26**, and z = **21.50**

Saving the Model

Next, you need to save the file.

1. Choose the **Save As** button to save the file; the **Save As** dialog box is displayed. Specify the path to save the file and then choose the **Save** button.

Tutorial 2

In this tutorial, you need to download the file and open *CSW_tut_02.SLDASM* in SOLIDWORKS, as shown in Figure 8. Now, you need to assemble the components, refer to Figures 9 to 11.

Details of the part are given next:
Material: Titanium
Density: 4600 kg / m^3
Part Units: MM
Decimal Places: 2

Origin: Default

What is the Center of mass of the part?
Enter Coordinates:
X: ----------
Y: ----------
Z: ----------

(Expected time: 10 min)

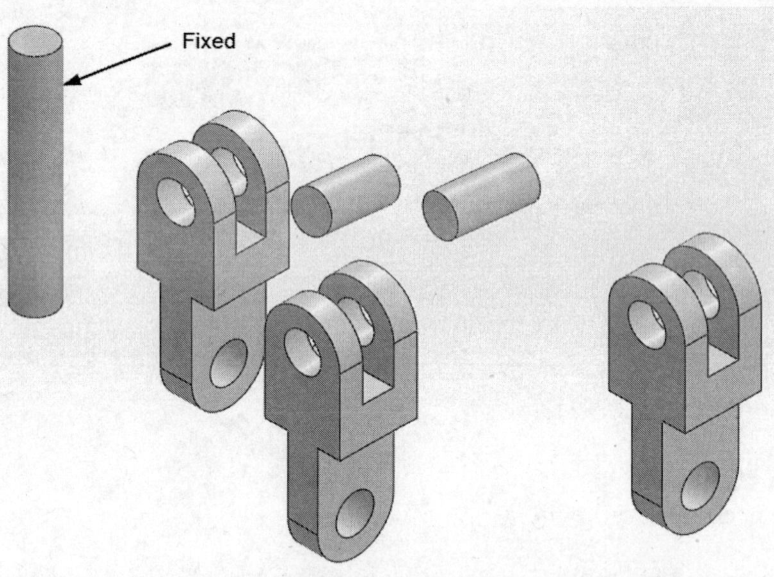

Figure 8 *The parts needed to assemble*

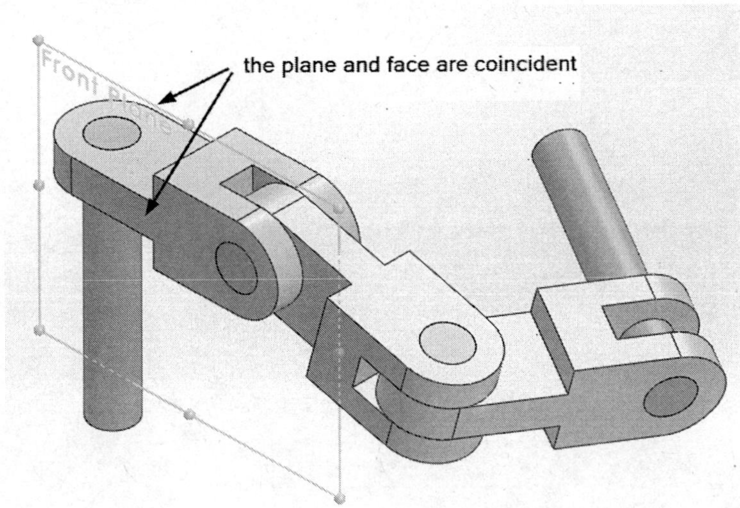

Figure 9 *The final assembly of parts*

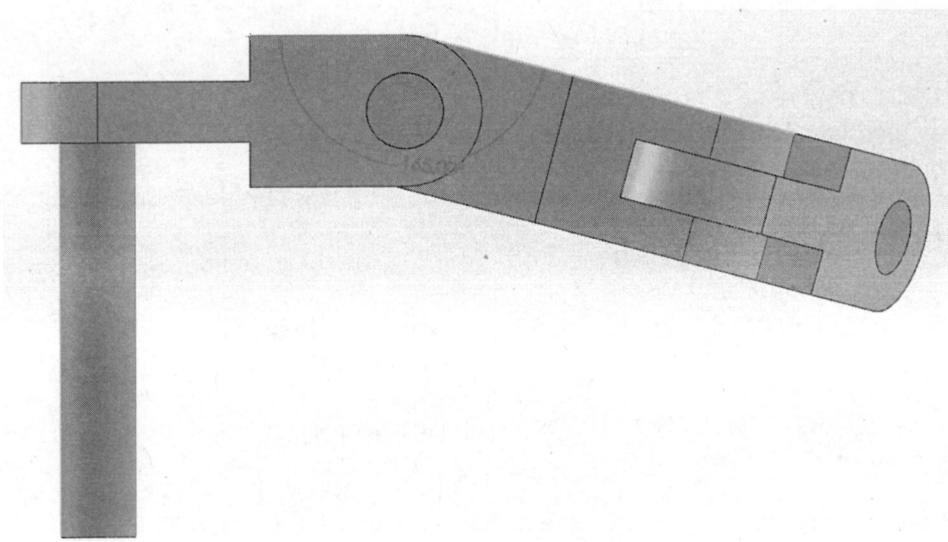

Figure 10 *The arrangement of parts*

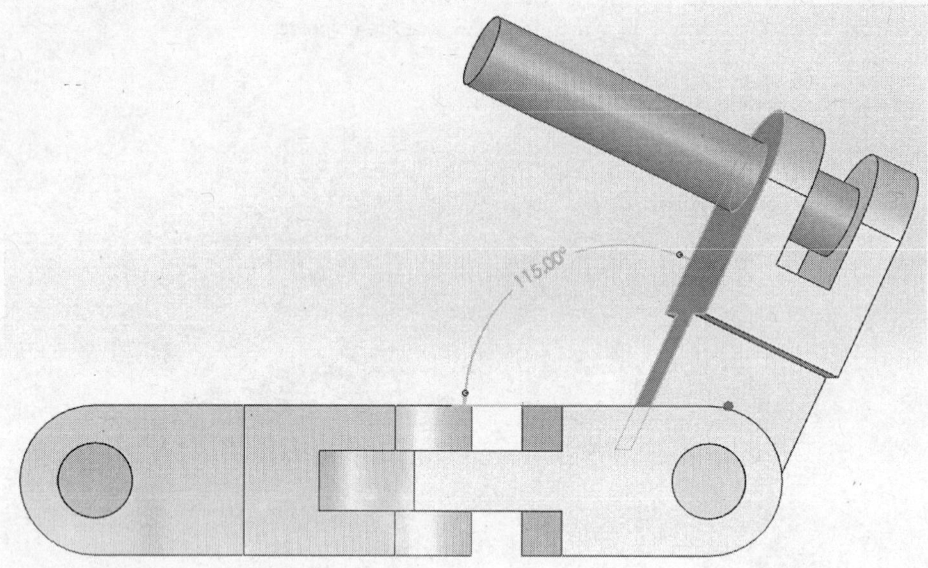

Figure 11 *The arrangement of parts*

The following steps are required to complete this tutorial:

a. Start **SOLIDWORKS 2021** and open the assembly file.
b. Apply the Mate constraint between the parts.
c. Copy the part and apply constraints between parts.
d. Measure the Center of Mass of the assembly by using the **Mass Properties** tool in the **Evaluate CommandManager**.
e. Save the file using the **SAVE AS** tool and then close the document.

Starting SOLIDWORKS 2021 and Opening the Model

First, you need to start SOLIDWORKS and open the model.

1. Double-click on the SOLIDWORKS 2021 shortcut icon on the desktop of your computer to start SOLIDWORKS.

2. Choose the **Open** button from the Menu Bar to display the **Open** dialog box.

3. Browse to the downloaded folder and extract the *CSW_tut_02.zip* file.

4. Select the *CSW_tut_02.SLDPRT* file from the *CSW_tut_02* folder and then choose the **Open** button. The model gets opened in the assembly environment, as shown in Figure 12.

Figure 12 The arrangement of parts in assembly environment

Applying Constraints

In this section, you will apply constraints between the parts.

1. Choose the **Mate** tool from the **Assembly CommandManager**; the **Mate PropertyManager** gets displayed.

2. Now apply the Concentric and Coincident constraints between the parts. The arrangement of parts after applying the constraints is shown in Figure 13.

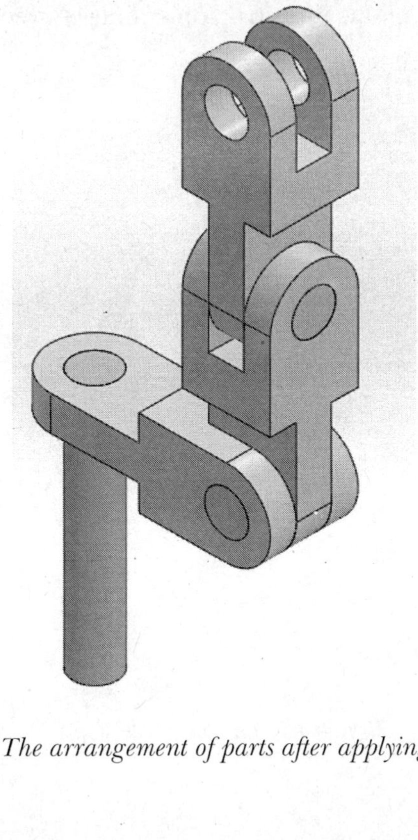

Figure 13 The arrangement of parts after applying constraints

3. Now, apply the angle constraint between parts, refer to Figures 10 and 11 for angle dimension.

4. Now apply the Concentric and Coincident constraints between parts. The arrangement of parts after applying the constraints is shown in Figure 14.

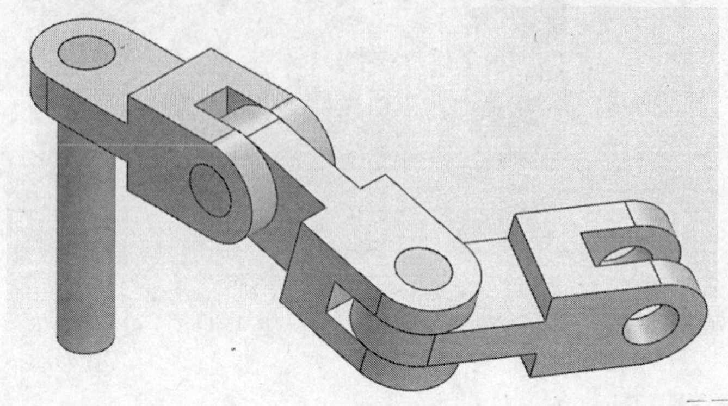

Figure 14 The arrangement of parts after applying constraints

Copying the Parts and Applying Constraints

In this section, you will copy the parts.

1. Hold the CTRL key and drag the part to be copied, refer to Figure 15.

2. Now apply the Coincident and Concentric constraints between the parts by using the **Mate** tool, refer to Figure 9.

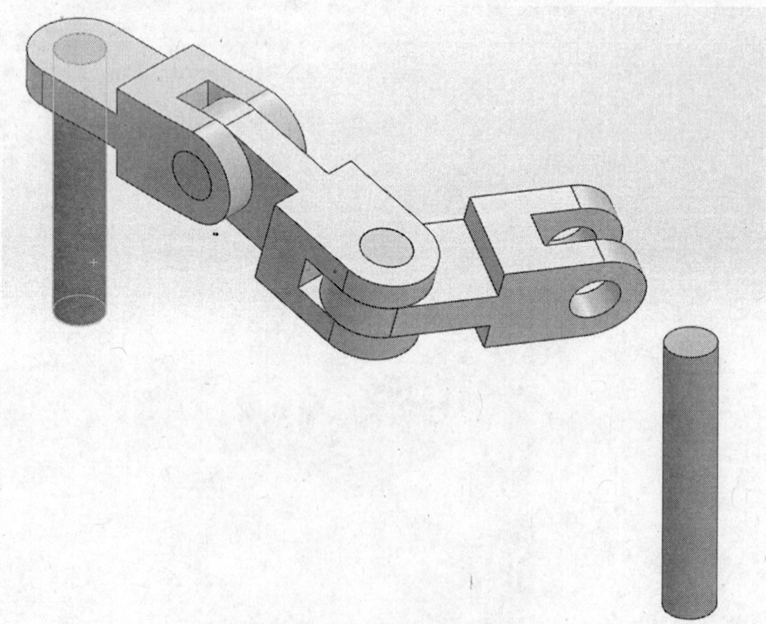

Figure 15 The part to be copied

Measuring the Center of Mass

In this section, you will measure the center of mass of the model.

Before measuring the center of mass of the model, ensure that 2 decimal places precision is selected.

1. Select the **Edit Document Units** option from the **Unit System** in the status bar; the **Document Properties - Units** dialog box gets displayed.

2. Click the **Units** option in the dialog box and ensure that the **MMGS** radio button is selected in the **Unit system** area. Next, select **.12** from the **Length** row in the **Basic Units** area and also select **.12** from the **Length** row in the **Mass/Section Properties** area.

3. Choose the **OK** button to close the dialog box.

4. Select the **Mass Properties** tool from the **Evaluate CommandManager**; the **Mass Properties** dialog box is displayed with the center of mass value in this dialog box, refer to Figure 16.

Center of mass of the model
x = **269.68**, y = **-62.98**, and z = **-48.07**

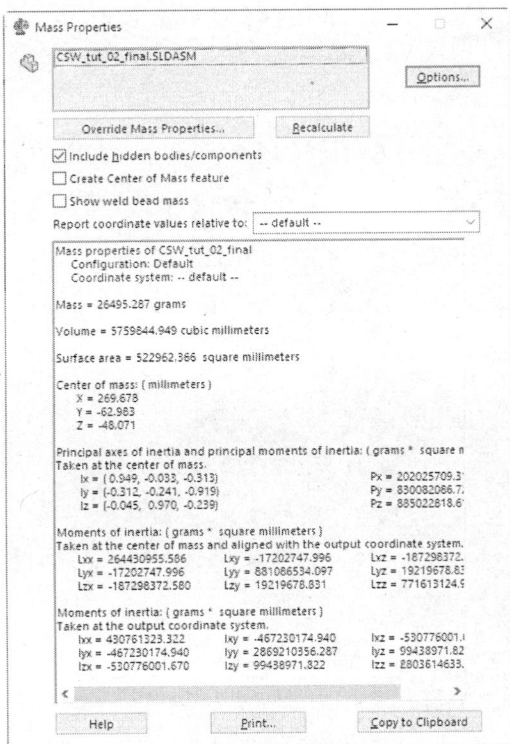

Figure 16 The **Mass Properties** dialog box

Saving the Model

Next, you need to save the file.

1. Choose the **Save As** button to save the file; the **Save As** dialog box is displayed. Specify the path to save the file and then choose the **Save** button.

Tutorial 3

In this tutorial, you need to download the file and open *CSW_tut_03.SLDPRT* in SOLIDWORKS, as shown in Figure 17. Next, apply fillets to the model, refer to Figure 18. Figure 19 shows the detailed D view of the model.

Details of the model are given next:
Material: 6061 alloy
Density: 2700 kg / m^3
Part Units: MM
Decimal Places: 2
Origin: Default
A = 2
B = 0.5
C = 6.5
What is the mass of the model?

(Expected time: 15 min)

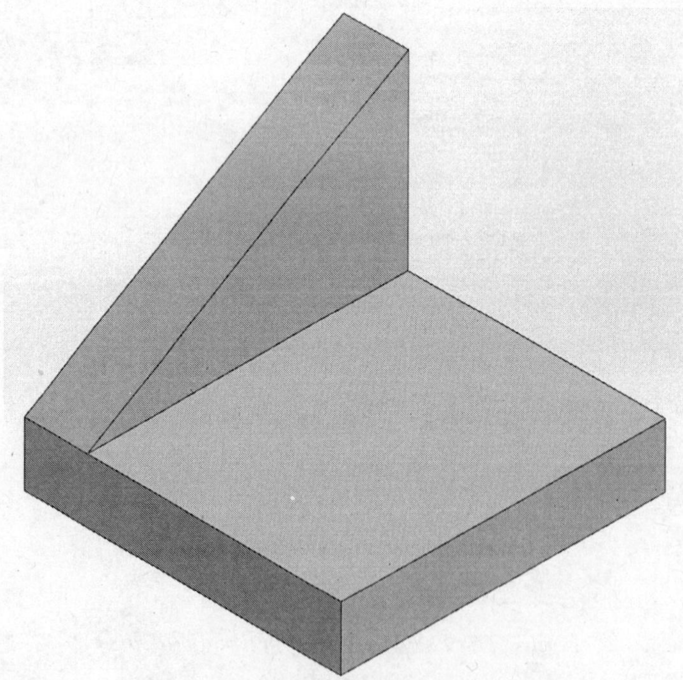

Figure 17 The isometric view of the model

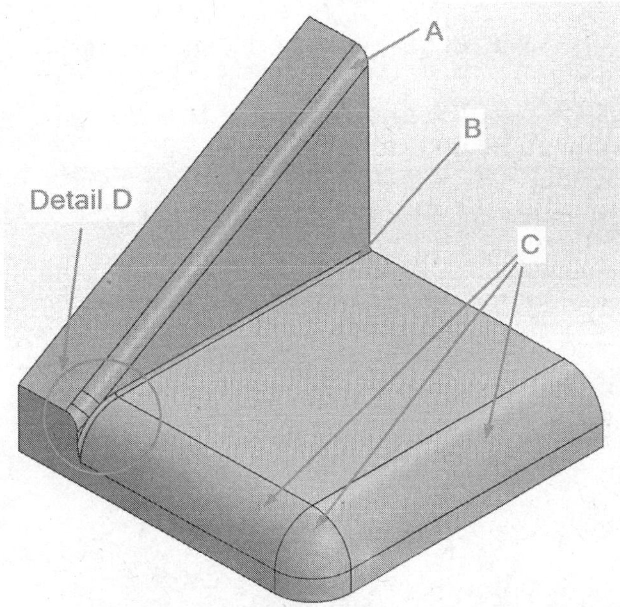

Figure 18 *The A, B and C parameters in the model*

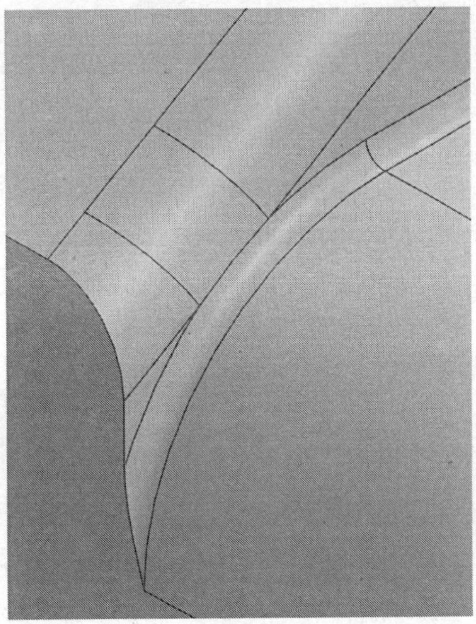

Figure 19 *The Detail D view of the model*

The following steps are required to complete this tutorial:

a. Start **SOLIDWORKS 2021** and open the part file.
b. Change the unit to **MMGS**.
c. Set measuring precision upto 2 decimal places.

d. Apply fillets to the model.
e. Save the file using the **SAVE AS** tool and then close the document.

Starting SOLIDWORKS 2021 and Opening the Model

First, you need to start SOLIDWORKS and open a model.

1. Double-click on the **SOLIDWORKS 2021** shortcut icon on the desktop of your computer to start SOLIDWORKS.

2. Choose the **Open** button from the Menu Bar to display the **Open** dialog box.

3. Browse the downloaded folder and extract the *CSW_tut_03.zip* file.

4. Select the *CSW_tut_03.SLDPRT* file from the *CSW_tut_03* folder and then choose the **Open** button; the model gets opened in the assembly environment, as shown in Figure 20.

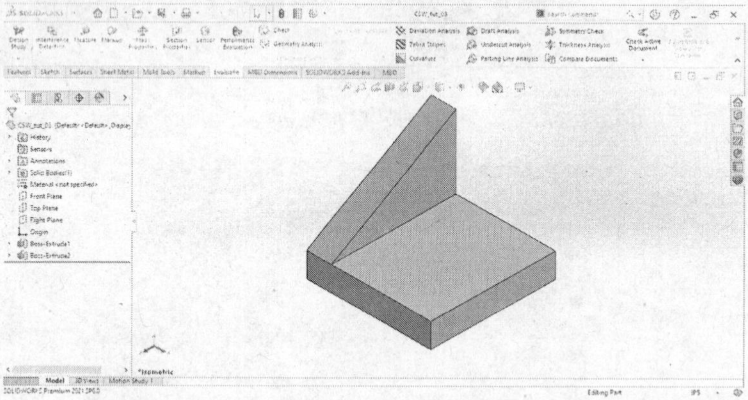

Figure 20 The model in the part environment

Changing Dimension Unit

In this section, you will need to change the dimesion unit and its precision.

1. Select the **Edit Document Units** option from the Unit system in the status bar; the **Document Properties - Units** dialog box gets displayed.

2. Click the **Units** option in the dialog box and select the **MMGS** radio button in the **Unit system** area. Next, select **.12** from the **Length** row in the **Basic Units** area and also select **.12** from the **Length** row in the **Mass/Section Properties** area.

3. Choose the **OK** button to close the dialog box.

Applying Fillets

In this section, you will apply fillets to the model.

1. Choose the **Fillet** tool from the **Features CommandManager**; the **Fillet PropertyManager** gets displayed.

2. Set the value to **2 mm** in the **Radius** spinner.

3. Select the edge, as shown in Figure 21; the selected edge is displayed in the **Edges, Faces, Features and Loops** selection box. Choose the **OK** button to close the **Fillet PropertyManager**. Figure 22 shows the model with fillet.

   Similarly, apply another fillet of radius **0.5 mm** to the model , refer to Figure 23.

4. Apply next fillet of radius **6.5 mm** by using the **Face Fillet** option, refer to Figure 24.

   You will notice the fillet arrangement achieved is not as shown in Figure 19. Here the sequence of fillet creation plays a major role.

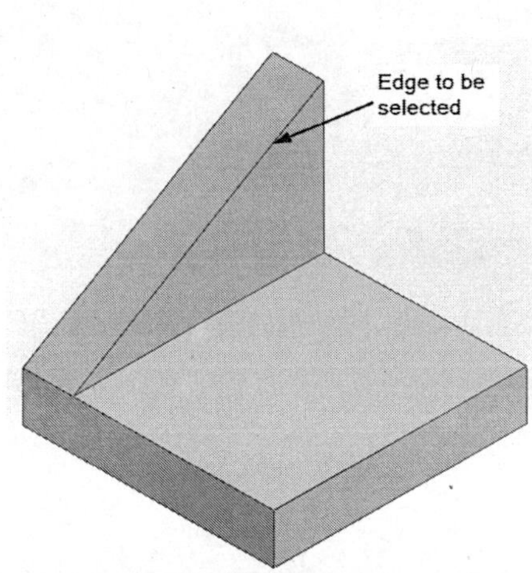

Figure 21 *The edge to be selected for adding fillet*

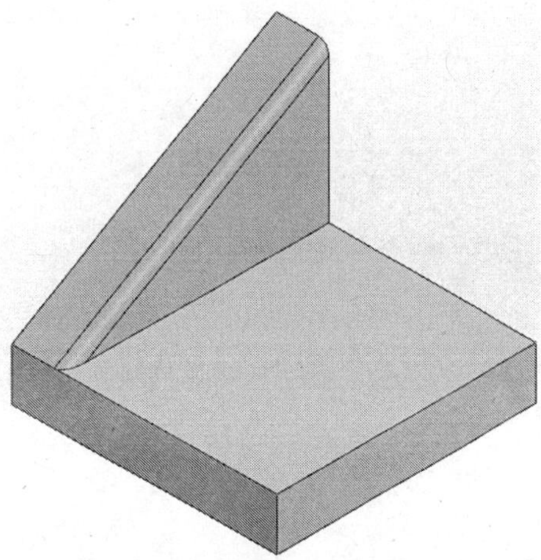

Figure 22 *The model after adding fillet*

To achieve the desired result, you need to first delete some fillets and then reapply some.

5. Delete fillets, refer to Figure 25. Now, apply fillet to the model, refer to Figure 26. Similary, apply next fillet to the other edge of the model, refer to Figures 27 and 28. Here, you will notice that you get the desired model.

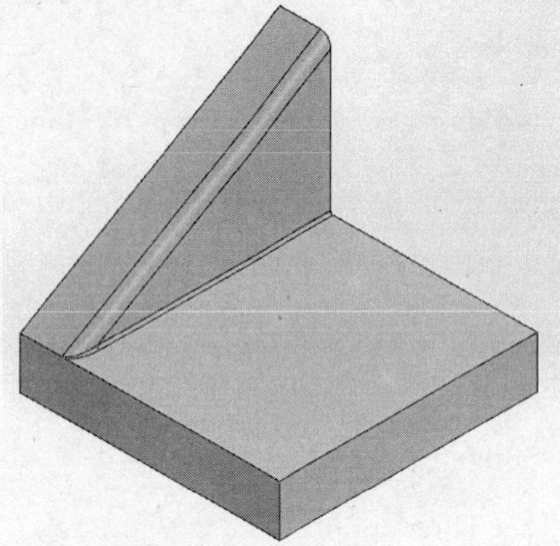

***Figure 23** The model after adding fillet*

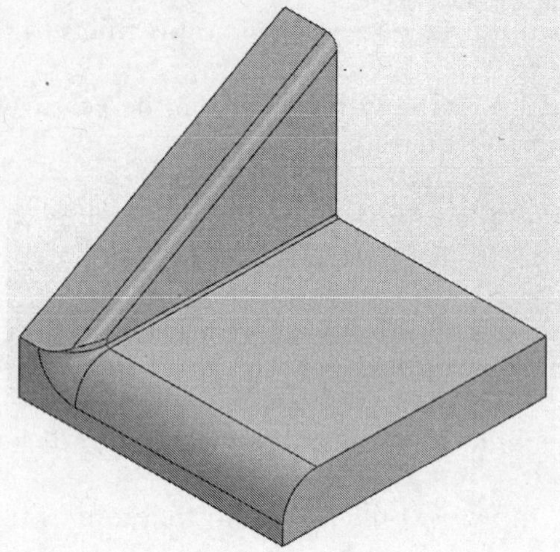

***Figure 24** The model after adding fillet*

***Figure 25** The model after removing the fillet*

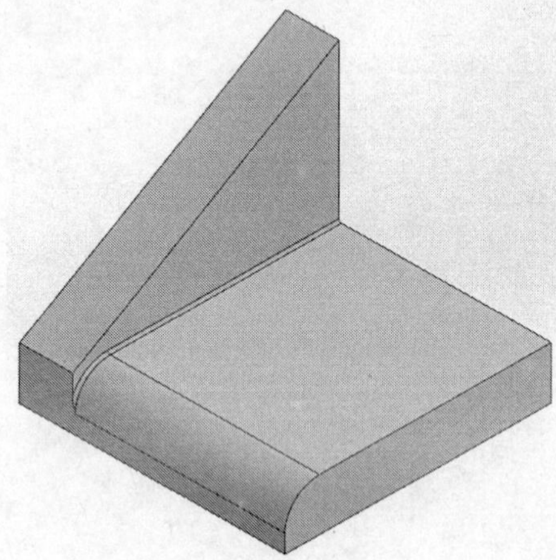

***Figure 26** The model after applying the fillet*

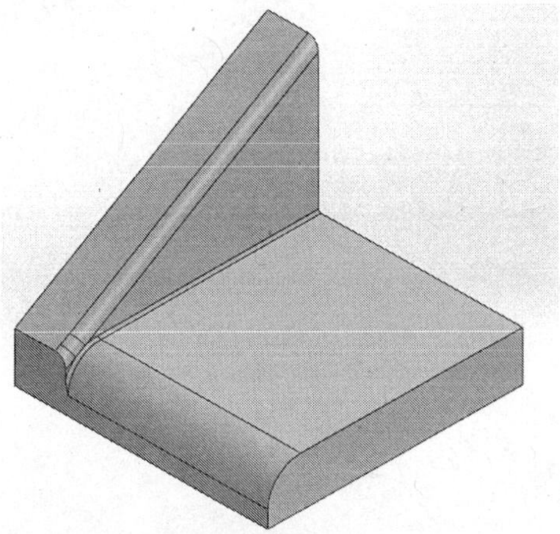

Figure 27 The model after applying the fillet

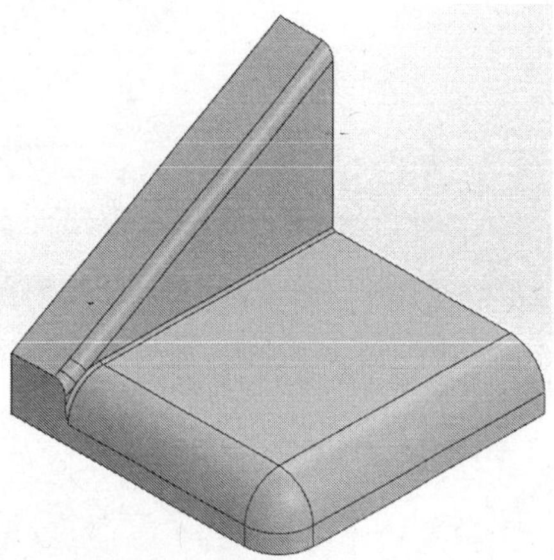

Figure 28 The model after applying the remaining fillet

Measuring the Mass of the Model

In this section, you will need to measure mass of the model.

1. Before measuring the mass of the model, ensure that desired material is applied to the model.

2. Right click on **Material <not specified>** from the **Feature Manager Design Tree**; a shortcut menu is displayed. Choose the **Edit Material** option from the shortcut menu; the **Material** dialog box is displayed.

3. Expand the **SOLIDWORKS Materials** node in the **Material** dialog box and select the **Aluminium Alloys** node. Expand the **Aluminium Alloys** node and select **6061 alloy**. Choose the **Apply** button to apply the material and then choose the **Close** button to close the dialog box.

4. Select the **Mass Properties** tool from the **Evaluate CommandManager**; the **Mass Properties** dialog box with the mass value is displayed, refer to Figure 29.

Mass of the model is **85.30** grams.

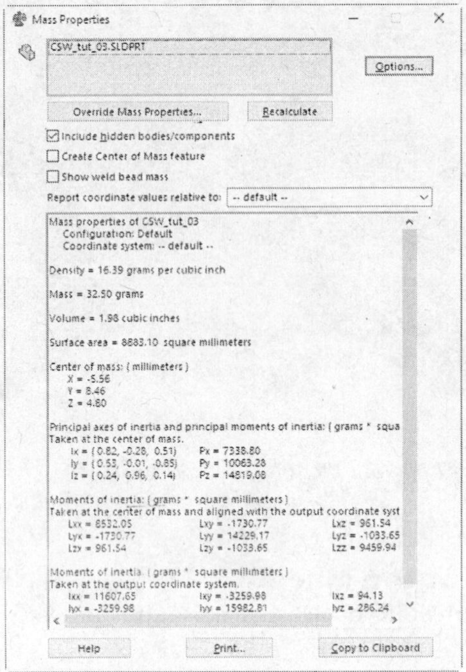

*Figure 29 The **Mass Properties** dialog box*

Saving the Model

Next, you need to save the file.

1. Choose the **Save As** button to save the file; the **Save As** dialog box is displayed. Specify the path to save the file and then choose the **Save** button.

EXERCISES

To perform the exercises, you need to download the zipped file named as *c19_SW_input* from the **Input Files** section of the CADCIM website. The complete path for downloading the file is:

Textbooks > CAD/CAM > SolidWorks > SOLIDWORKS 2021 for Designers > Input Files

Exercise 1

Create a spring based on the sketch provided in Figure 30. The 3D model of the spring shown in Figure 31.

Details of the Spring model are given next:
Material: 6061 alloy
Density: 2700 kg /m3

Mass: grams
Decimal Places: 3
Part Units: MM

A = 45.000
B = 45.000 radius
C = 50.000
D = 3.000 diameter
E = 25.000 diameter

Number of coils: 10

What is the overall mass of the part?

(Expected time: 10 min)

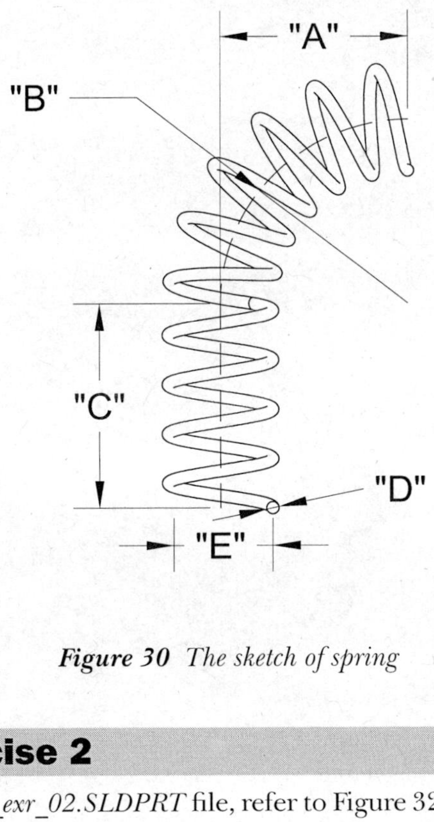

Figure 30 *The sketch of spring*

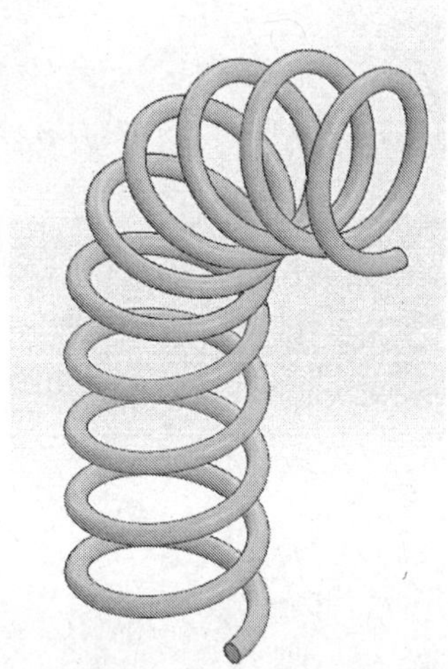

Figure 31 *The 3d model of spring*

Exercise 2

Open *csw_exr_02.SLDPRT* file, refer to Figure 32. Add a hole of 80 mm diameter passing through the model, refer Figure 33 and 34. Before adding the hole, create its configuration with the name *add_hole*.

Details of the model are given next:
Material: AISI 1020
Density: 7900 kg / m3

Mass: grams
Decimal Places: 2
Part Units: MM

What is the overall mass of the *add_hole* configuration part?

(Expected time: 10 min)

Figure 32 *The 3D cylindrical model*

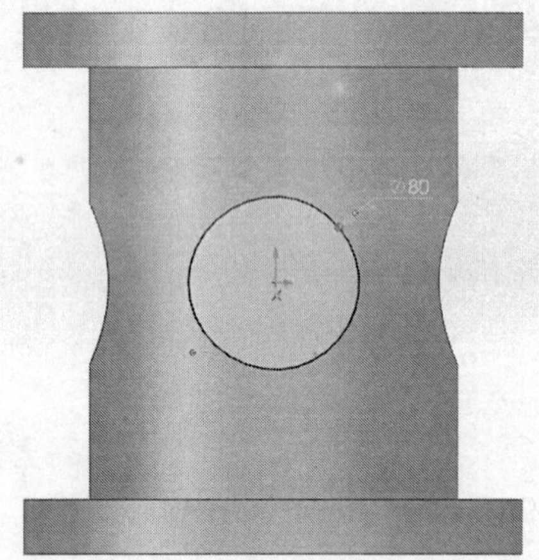

Figure 33 *The dimension of hole*

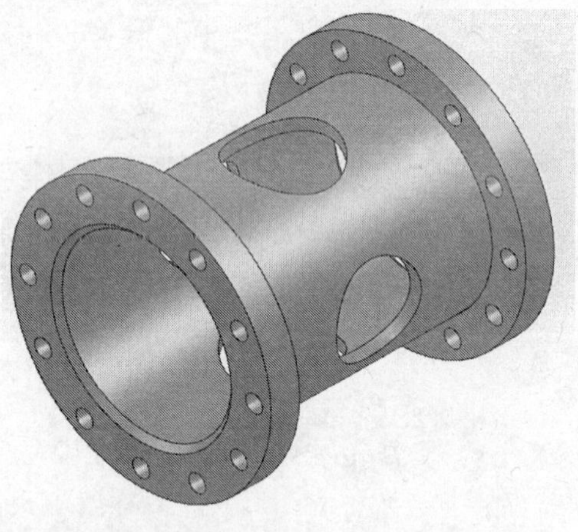

Figure 34 *The 3D cylindrical model after adding hole*

Index

D

E

F

R

S

T

U

V

W

Z

Other Titles of Interest - BPB/TICKOO Serires

Publication by BPB/TICKOO SERIES

The following is the list of some of the publications by BPB/TICKOO.

AutoCAD Textbooks

- AutoCAD 2022 for Engineers and Designers - Basic and Intermediate
- AutoCAD 2021 for Engineers and Designers - Basic and Intermediate
- AutoCAD 2021(3D and Advanced) for Engineers and Designers
- AutoCAD 2020 for Engineers and Designers - Basic and Intermediate
- AutoCAD 2019: A Problem-Solving Approach, Basic and Intermediate
- AutoCAD 2020 Workbook

Autodesk Inventor Textbooks

- Autodesk Inventor Professional 2022 for Engineers and Designers
- Autodesk Inventor Professional 2021 for Designers
- Inventor 2020 Workbook

AutoCAD MEP Textbooks

- AutoCAD MEP 2020 for Engineers and Designers
- AutoCAD MEP 2018 for Designers

AutoCAD Plant 3D Textbooks

- AutoCAD Plant 3D 2021 for Designers
- AutoCAD Plant 3D 2020 for Designers
- AutoCAD Plant 3D 2018 for Designers

Autodesk Fusion 360 Textbook

Autodesk Fusion 360: A Tutorial Approach
Autodesk Fusion 360: A Learner's Guide

Solid Edge Textbooks

- Solid Edge 2019 for Engineers and Designers
- Solid Edge 2020 for Designers
- Solid Edge ST 10 for Designers

NX Textbooks

- Siemens NX 2021 for Engineers and Designers
- Siemens NX 2020 for Engineers and Designers
- Siemens NX 2019 for Engineers and Designers
- Siemens NX 12.0 for Designers
- Seimens NX 2019 Workbook

NX Mold Textbook

- Mold Design Using NX 11.0: A Tutorial Approach

NX Nastran Textbook
- NX Nastran 9.0 for Designers

SOLIDWORKS Textbooks
- SOLIDWORKS 2020 for Designers
- SOLIDWORKS 2019 for Designers
- Learning SOLIDWORKS 2019: A Project Based Approach
- SOLIDWORKS 2020: A Tutorial Approach

SOLIDWORKS Simulation Textbooks
- SOLIDWORKS Simulation 2018: A Tutorial Approach
- SOLIDWORKS Simulation 2016: A Tutorial Approach

CATIA Textbooks
- CATIA V5-6R2020 for Designers, 18th Edition
- CATIA V5-6R2019 for Designers, 17th Edition

Creo Parametric Textbooks
- Creo Parametric 7.0 for Designers
- Creo Parametric 6.0 for Designers
- Creo Parametric 6.0 Workbook

ANSYS Textbooks
- ANSYS Workbench 2019 R2: A Tutorial Approach
- ANSYS Workbench 14.0: A Tutorial Approach

Creo Direct Textbook
- Creo Direct 2.0 and Beyond for Designers

Autodesk Alias Textbooks
- Learning Autodesk Alias Design 2016
- Learning Autodesk Alias Design 2015

AutoCAD LT Textbooks
- AutoCAD LT 2022 for Engineers and Designers
- AutoCAD LT 2020 for Engineers and Designers
- AutoCAD LT 2017 for Designers

EdgeCAM Textbooks
- EdgeCAM 11.0 for Manufacturers
- EdgeCAM 10.0 for Manufacturers

Autodesk Revit MEP Textbooks
- Exploring Autodesk Revit 2021 for MEP
- Exploring Autodesk Revit 2019 for MEP

AutoCAD Civil 3D Textbooks
- Exploring AutoCAD Civil 3D 2020 for Engineers and Designers
- Exploring AutoCAD Civil 3D 2019 for Engineers and Designers
- Exploring AutoCAD Civil 3D 2018

AutoCAD Map 3D Textbooks
- Exploring AutoCAD Map 3D 2018
- Exploring AutoCAD Map 3D 2017

RISA-3D Textbook
- Exploring RISA-3D 14.0

Autodesk Navisworks Textbooks
- Exploring Autodesk Navisworks 2021
- Exploring Autodesk Navisworks 2020
- Exploring Autodesk Navisworks 2019
- Exploring Autodesk Navisworks 2017

AutoCAD Raster Design Textbooks
- Exploring AutoCAD Raster Design 2017
- Exploring AutoCAD Raster Design 2016

Bentley STAAD.Pro Textbooks
- Exploring Bentley STAAD.Pro (CONNECT) Edition, V22
- Exploring Bentley STAAD.Pro (CONNECT) Edition
- Exploring Bentley STAAD.Pro V8i (SELECTseries 6)

Autodesk 3ds Max Design Textbooks
- Autodesk 3ds Max Design 2015: A Tutorial Approach, 15th Edition
- Autodesk 3ds Max Design 2014: A Tutorial Approach

Autodesk 3ds Max Textbooks
- Autodesk 3ds Max 2021: A Comprehensive Guide
- Autodesk 3ds Max 2020: A Comprehensive Guide
- Autodesk 3ds Max 2019: A Comprehensive Guide
- Autodesk 3ds Max 2019 for Beginners: A Tutorial Approach

Autodesk Maya Textbooks
- Autodesk Maya 2020: A Comprehensive Guide
- Autodesk Maya 2019: A Comprehensive Guide
- Character Animation: A Tutorial Approach

Pixologic ZBrush Textbooks
- Pixologic ZBrush 2020: A Comprehensive Guide
- Pixologic ZBrush 2018: A Comprehensive Guide
- Pixologic ZBrush 4R8: A Comprehensive Guide, 4th Edition

MAXON CINEMA 4D Textbooks
- MAXON CINEMA 4D R20 Studio: A Tutorial Approach
- MAXON CINEMA 4D R19 Studio: A Tutorial Approach
- MAXON CINEMA 4D R18 Studio: A Tutorial Approach

Oracle Primavera Textbooks
- Exploring Oracle Primavera P6 Professional 18
- Exploring Oracle Primavera P6 v8.4